Dígalo en español

Dígalo en inglés, pero . . .

Diga exactamente lo que Vd. intenta

Esto es justamente lo que este nuevo diccionario bilingüe hace posible. Cuando busca una palabra en español o en inglés, encuentra sus equivalentes inscritos y *además* signos clasificantes de significación, a fin de que escoja la palabra que dé a entender lo más exactamente lo que Vd. intenta. Se incluye bajo la palabra clave las frases y modismos . . . así que pueda emplear el idioma *como lo emplean los nativos.* La guía fonética es de la forma internacional oficialmente aceptada para que pronuncie *palabras según el uso de los nativos.*

Para manifestar el idioma *actual,* el redactor consultó escritores y parlantes de español de todas partes, a fin que este diccionario sea tan exacto por español como por inglés. Diez años de rebusca y compilación le trae el NEW WORLD DICCIONARIO ESPANOL/INGLES Y INGLES/ESPANOL, con 70,000 términos, más que ningún otro diccionario provechioso de su tipo. Es corriente y compacto . . . de ayuda estimable tanto por el viajero como por el estudiante.

The New World
SPANISH-ENGLISH
and
ENGLISH-SPANISH
Dictionary

PREPARED UNDER THE SUPERVISION OF
MARIO A. PEI
Professor of Romance Philology, Columbia University

SALVATORE RAMONDINO
EDITOR

A SIGNET BOOK
NEW AMERICAN LIBRARY
A DIVISION OF PENGUIN BOOKS USA INC.

Published by arrangement with Andrew and Philip Morehead. The hardcover edition was published simultaneously in Canada by Nelson, Foster & Scott Ltd.

SIGNET TRADEMARK REG. U.S. PAT. OFF. AND FOREIGN COUNTRIES
REGISTERED TRADEMARK—MARCA REGISTRADA
HECHO EN DRESDEN, TN

SIGNET, SIGNET CLASSIC, MENTOR, ONYX, PLUME, MERIDIAN and NAL BOOKS are published by New American Library, a division of Penguin Books USA Inc., 1633 Broadway, New York, New York 10019

First Signet Printing, May, 1969

21 22 23 24 25 26 27 28 29

PRINTED IN THE UNITED STATES OF AMERICA

Prepared and edited by
THE NATIONAL LEXICOGRAPHIC BOARD
Albert H. Morehead, *Chairman*
Waldemar von Zedtwitz, *President*
Loy C. Morehead, *Vice-President*
Salvatore Ramondino, *Vice-President*
Philip D. Morehead, *Secretary*

Staff of
The New World SPANISH-ENGLISH and ENGLISH-SPANISH Dictionary
Salvatore Ramondino, Editor
Albert H. Morehead, *General Editor*
Waldemar von Zedtwitz, *General Editor*
Mario A. Pei, *Supervisory Editor*
Jay H. Borcelo-Molins, *Consulting Editor*
Pedro Sutton, *Consulting Editor*

José Donday Hernandez
Felipe Silva
George Obligado
Luis Rojas Martz
José L. Martin
Roberto Silva
Jules J. Selles
Robert A. Wasserman
Ana M. Auchterlonie
Helenia Foix Baker
Charles A. Hughes
Joseph A. Cassanova
Elisabeth Krasnitski
Beverly Bowers
Marta Celorio
Camelia C. Yanes

CONTENTS

ÍNDICE GENERAL

FOREWORD

American bilingual lexicography is gradually pulling itself away from its traditional dependence upon Britain. While it is still fairly common practice for American publishing houses to reprint British works when dealing with the old cultural languages, with or without revision and adaptation to American use, Americans are beginning, particularly for those new languages whose study has become widespread within the last half-century (notably Spanish and Russian), to strike out for themselves and offer works that reflect not merely present colloquial usage in both English and foreign language, but also the specific usage of the United States and of that foreign-language area with which they are in closest contact.

The present work has been under way for the better part of ten years. It embodies the most recent methodological findings of linguistic science, combined with the highest utilitarian principles. It contains an estimated 70,000 entries, more than any comparable dictionary. There is a built-in principle of selective labeling of meanings that removes all doubt as to which one of various possible Spanish equivalents best fits the meaning of an English word in a given context. Full pronunciation, in International Phonetic Alphabet transcription, is given for all words in both languages. Prefixes and suffixes are fully defined in the text. Idiomatic phrases and expressions are likewise included in the text, and listed under the key word with their exact and usable equivalents on the same level of diction. The typography is designed to help, not to hinder, the reader. A separate condensation of grammar and irregularities does not always overcome the stumbling block of inflectional forms that deviate from the normal pattern. Hence the reader will welcome the appearance of irregular forms in the text itself, providing immediate guidance in their recognition and use.

Completeness in lexicography is only an ideal. Even if it were possible to attain, it would disappear within days or even hours, since innovations are continually being made in all living languages. More desirable and attainable are the qualities of selectivity, adequacy, and accuracy. These have been the constant preoccupation of the Editorial Board. In what measure they have been achieved will, in the final analysis, be determined solely by the reader and user. This volume is offered in the hope that the verdict may be favorable.

Mario A. Pei

PREFACIO

La lexicografía bilingüe norteamericana se está apartando gradualmente de su tradicional dependencia de Inglaterra. Todavía es práctica bastante común, respecto a las lenguas de enseñanza tradicional (francés, alemán, latín, italiano), que las casas editoras norteamericanas reproduzcan las obras inglesas, muchas veces con poca revisión y adaptación al uso norteamericano. Se nota la tendencia, sin embargo, particularmente respecto a los idiomas cuyo estudio se ha difundido en los últimos cincuenta años (especialmente el español y el ruso) a actuar por cuenta propia y ofrecer obras que reflejen, no meramente el uso de expresiones familiares y modismos que estén rigurosamente al día, tanto en inglés como en el idioma extranjero, sino también el que se le da en los Estados Unidos y en el área de la lengua extranjera con la que estemos en más estrecho contacto.

La presente obra es el resultado de una labor que ha tomado cerca de diez años. Abarca los más recientes descubrimientos de la ciencia lingüística en lo que atañe a la metodología, junto con los más altos principios utilitarios. Contiene aproximadamente 70.000 voces, más que las que aparecen en cualquier otro diccionario semejante. Cuenta con un sistema de clasificación selectiva de los significados, que elimina toda duda respecto a cual de los distintos equivalentes en el idioma español es el que mejor se ajusta al significado de la palabra inglesa en un contexto dado. Para todas las palabras, en ambos idiomas, se ofrece su pronunciación en la transcripción del Alfabeto Fonético Internacional. Los prefijos y sufijos aparecen perfectamente definidos en el texto. Asimismo, se incluyen frases idiomáticas y modismos clasificados bajo la palabra más importante con sus equivalentes exactos en el mismo nivel idiomático. Desde el punto de vista tipográfico la obra se ha diseñado con el propósito de simplificarle la tarea al lector y evitarle dificultades. Las inflexiones que se apartan del patrón normal constituyen un obstáculo que no siempre se puede superar mediante una condensación separada de reglas gramáticales e irregularidades; por lo tanto, el lector recibirá con agrado la presencia de tales formas en el texto mismo, de manera que pueda tener una guía inmediata para reconocerlas y usarlas.

Un diccionario que abarque todos los vocablos de un idioma es nada más que un ideal. Aunque fuera posible alcanzarlo, sería efímero debido a la constante evolución a que están sujetas las lenguas vivas. Más deseable y asequible es la calidad de la selección, que ésta sea adecuada y precisa. Esto ha sido la preocupación constante del Consejo Editorial. Pero, en el análisis final, será el lector el que determinará en que medida se ha logrado. Este volumen se ofrece con la esperanza de que el veredicto sea favorable.

Mario A. Pei

INTRODUCTION

THE NEW WORLD SPANISH-ENGLISH AND ENGLISH-SPANISH DICTIONARY has been designed to fill a long-standing need: the need for a modern, up-to-date, practical dictionary of current usage.

In the treatment of Spanish words, virtually all existing bilingual dictionaries have relied on the highly conservative lexicons of the Spanish language. They do little more than translate, literally, the definitions of each Spanish word as given in the standard Spanish dictionaries, without giving the user of the bilingual dictionary any indication of the relative importance or usefulness of the various senses with their English equivalents.

In an effort to improve on this method, and in order to convey the living substance of the Spanish language to the English-speaking user, the editors of this dictionary have consulted representative writers and speakers of Spanish in all areas. The Spanish-speaking user, for his part, will find exact, usable, and current equivalents in English of the elements of his own language.

All the most important and useful words in both languages, and *only* the most important and useful, have been selected for inclusion. Common prefixes, suffixes, and combining elements are included, with equivalents, if they exist, or with an explanation in the opposite language of the meaning and use of the element, or both. The most distinctive and frequently used idiomatic and colloquial expressions have been rendered in the opposite language by usable equivalents on the same level of usage and as far as possible conveying the same flavor. Slang and colloquial terms are included when important and in common usage and are defined by standard terms unless an exact equivalent at the same level of usage exists. Classical Spanish and English terms are covered. All words used in definitions in one section of the dictionary appear as entries in the other section.

Throughout this dictionary the emphasis is on usage in the Western Hemisphere. American English usage and spellings are preferred; British and dialectal forms and meanings are included only if they are widely known in America, and pronunciation follows best usage in regions where there is no marked peculiarity in speech and in normal conversation rather than in formal speech.

Similarly, Americanisms in Spanish—i.e., words and phrases customary in Latin America and in Spanish-speaking sections of the U.S. Southwest and Far West—receive special attention, and the standards of pronunciation, spelling, and usage prevailing in the Spanish-speaking countries of the New World are given prominence.

Currency and practicality are the qualities that students and travelers alike demand in a foreign-language dictionary and these they will be sure to find here.

In this dictionary, each main entry is composed of two or more of the following elements, explained here in the order in which they may be expected to appear.

1. The *main* entry is printed in boldface type and may be a simple or compound word or a phrase. Variant spellings commonly used are also in boldface type.

2. The *pronunciation* follows the entry word in parentheses. All entries are pronounced, with the exception of compound words or phrases whose elements are pronounced as main entries elsewhere in the dictionary. If a variant spelling is pronounced the same as the main entry, only one pronunciation is given; if the variant spelling and the main entry have different pronunciations, each is pronounced separately. Symbols used in the pronunciations are explained on page 543.

3. *Parts of speech.* All words, simple or compound, are identified as to part of speech; phrases are not so identified. If a word is used as more than one part of speech, each part of speech is defined separately. Part-of-speech labels are combined only in cases in which the entry word and the word or words used to define it are the same in more than one part of speech.

4. *Inflected forms* of irregular verbs, irregular plurals of nouns, and irregular comparative forms of adjectives are given in boldface type within brackets. Regular inflections are shown only when a word has both irregular and regular forms that are commonly used. In some cases inflected forms of irregular

verbs are not given, but another verb is referred to as a model. Pronunciation of inflected forms is given unless the form is listed as a main entry.

5. *Definitions.* Each distinct meaning of a word is separately numbered and defined. Numbers are used only to separate distinct meanings, or denotations, of a word. Within each numbered definition there may be two or more words or phrases used to define the word in that meaning. These are separated by semicolons, indicating that they differ only in *connotation*—that is, in nuance of meaning—but have in general the same *denotation.* A word may also be defined by reference to a main entry that is a synonym.

6. *Labels,* in italics, furnish information of a special sort concerning the word being defined. They may indicate its currency of usage (*archaic, historical,* etc.), standard of usage (*colloq., slang, offensive,* etc.), special geographical area of usage (*Amer., Brit., W.I.,* etc.), or special field of usage (*law, medicine, math.,* etc.). A list of labels, together with the abbreviations used in this dictionary, is found on page xiv.

7. In the *English-Spanish section,* each distinct sense of an English word is identified by a *label* in parentheses. This label (the "contextual gist" label) is a concise identification of the specific sense in which the word is being rendered by the Spanish equivalent. This contextual gist label may be supplemented or replaced by a special field label (see 6, above).

8. *Qualifying word or phrase.* A definition may be complemented by a word or phrase to clarify its meaning. If the word or phrase can be used with the definition to form a semantic unit, it is printed in roman type in parentheses; if it cannot, it is printed in italic type in parentheses.

9. *Subsidiary entries* appear in boldface type following the last defined part of speech. They may be:

a. *inflected forms* of main entry words that have senses that differ from those of the principal form;

b. *variant forms,* including common variant spellings, and synonymous forms based on the same or related stems;

c. *derivatives,* i.e., words formed on the same stem as the main entry, but with distinctive form and meaning. Derivatives are pronounced only when the elements used to form them are not separately listed in this dictionary;

d. *idiomatic phrases,* i.e., phrases formed of the principal word, whether that word is a main entry or a subsidiary entry, plus one or more other elements (usually adverbs or object nouns).

INTRODUCCIÓN

EL DICCIONARIO NEW WORLD DE INGLÉS-ESPAÑOL Y ESPAÑOL-INGLÉS tiene el propósito de llenar una necesidad existente desde hace mucho tiempo: la necesidad de un diccionario moderno, práctico, que contenga palabras de uso corriente y actual.

En cuanto al idioma español, todos los diccionarios bilingües existentes han tomado como fuente los léxicos castellanos más conservadores. Hacen poco más que traducir literalmente cada palabra. No dan al que consulta el diccionario ninguna indicación de la relativa importancia o utilidad que ofrece el conocimiento de las varias acepciones de una palabra con su equivalente en inglés.

Con el objeto de mejorar este método y el de transmitir la substancia viva de la lengua española a la persona de habla inglesa que utiliza esta obra, los redactores de este diccionario han consultado a escritores y nacionales de todas las regiones de habla española, representativos de las mismas. A su vez, la persona de habla española encontrará traducciones fieles, de uso práctico y frecuente, que corresponden a los elementos de su propio idioma.

Las palabras más importantes y útiles de ambas lenguas, y *sólo* las más importantes y útiles, han sido seleccionadas para su inclusión. Se incluyen, igualmente, los prefijos comunes, sufijos y elementos que se usan para formar palabras. Siempre que sea posible, se da un equivalente exacto en el otro idioma. En caso contrario, se ofrece una explicación sobre su significado y uso. En ocasiones figuran ambas cosas. Las expresiones idiomáticas y familiares más características y más frecuentes se han traducido de modo que revelan un uso similar en ambas lenguas y un mismo sabor idiomático, de ser posible. Los vulgarismos y giros familiares se incluyen cuando son importantes y de uso común, con su correspondiente explicación, a menos que exista una traducción exacta de la expresión. Los vocablos clásicos de ambos idiomas aparecen en esta obra. Todas las palabras que se emplean en una definición aparecen como vocablos en la otra sección.

En este diccionario se da mayor énfasis al uso del idioma en el Hemisferio Occidental. La ortografía y el uso de inglés de los Estados Unidos tienen carácter preferente al de Inglaterra. Las expresiones británicas y los regionalismos se incluyen sólo cuando son ampliamente conocidos en los Estados Unidos. La pronunciación que se ofrece es la del mejor uso en las regiones donde no hay marcadas peculiaridades de pronunciación, y refleja una dicción conversacional más que clásica.

De igual modo, los americanismos de la lengua española—es decir, palabras y frases de uso común en Hispanoamérica y en regiones de habla española del Suroeste y Oeste de los Estados Unidos—reciben una atención especial, dándosele una mayor importancia a la pronunciación, ortografía y uso del idioma en los países de habla española del Nuevo Mundo. Tanto el estudiante como el viajero buscan en un diccionario bilingüe las palabras de uso corriente y práctico. Esto hallarán aquí con toda seguridad.

En este diccionario, cada artículo o palabra se compone de dos o más de los siguientes elementos, que se explican a continuación en el orden en que aparacen.

1. Cada *artículo* figura en negrilla y puede ser una palabra simple, una palabra compuesta o una frase. Las variantes ortográficas de uso frecuente se dan también en negrilla.

2. La *pronunciación* sigue, entre paréntesis, a cada artículo. Se exceptúan aquellas palabras compuestas o frases cuyos elementos componentes y su correspondiente pronunciación aparezcan como artículo principal en el lugar que les corresponde. Si la variante ortográfica se pronuncia de igual modo, se indica la pronunciación una sola vez; sì cambia la pronunciación se ofrecen ambas. Los símbolos fonéticos se explican en la página 543.

3. *Partes de la oración.* El oficio que desempeña en la oración cada palabra, simple o compuesta, aparece indicado. No así en el caso de frases. Si una palabra desempeña diversos oficios, se define cada uno separadamente, a menos que la definición sea idéntica, en cuyo caso aparecen combinados los oficios en un mismo rótulo.

4. *Accidentes gramaticales.* Terminaciones irregulares de los verbos, plurales irregulares de los nombres y adjetivos comparativos irregulares aparecen en negrilla dentro de corchetes. Las inflexiones regulares aparecen sólo cuando una palabra se usa comúnmente en ambas formas, regular e irregular. En algunos casos, las terminaciones irregulares de un verbo no se dan, sino que se refiere el mismo a otro verbo que se toma como modelo. La pronunciación de estas variantes se da siempre, a menos que la misma aparezca como artículo principal en el lugar que le corresponde.

5. *Definiciones.* Los distintos significados de cada palabra se numeran y definen separadamente. Se usan los números

solamente para separar los distintos significados o denotaciones de una palabra. En cada definición numerada puede haber dos o más palabras o frases, separadas por punto y coma, que se emplean para definir el artículo con ese significado. Esto indica que difieren solamente en la *connotación*—esto es, matices del significado—pero que tienen en general la misma *denotación*. También puede definirse una palabra refiriéndola a un sinónimo ya definido.

6. *Rótulos*. Palabras en bastardilla, dentro de paréntesis, ofrecen información especial relacionada con el vocablo definido. Pueden indicar frecuencia del uso (*arcaico, histórico,* etc.), clase de uso (*familiar, vulgar, ofensivo,* etc.), uso regional (*Estados Unidos, Inglaterra, Antillas,* etc.) o ámbito especial del uso (*derecho, medicina, matemáticas,* etc.). Una lista de estos rótulos, con las abreviaturas usadas en este diccionario, aparece en la página xiv.

7. En el texto inglés-español, cada variación del sentido de una palabra inglesa tiene su *rótulo* en paréntesis. Este rótulo ("esencia del contexto") muestra precisamente el sentido especial de su equivalente en español. Este rótulo puede tener adición o ser sustituido por el rótulo de una área especial (véase supra, 6).

8. *Palabra o frase explicativa*. Puede complementarse una definición con una palabra o frase que aclare su significado. Si la aclaración forma una unidad semántica con la definición, aparece aquélla entre paréntesis, con letra de tipo romano; en caso contrario aparece en bastardilla.

9. Los *artículos secundarios* figuran en negrilla después de la última definición del artículo principal en el oficio que desempeña como parte de la oración. Estos artículos pueden ser:

a. *accidentes* de palabras variables en su flexión, cuyo significado difiere del principal después del cambio;
b. *variantes*, incluyendo las ortográficas, y sinónimos que se basan en la misma raíz;
c. *derivados*, esto es, palabras que tienen la misma raíz que el artículo principal, pero distinta forma y significado. Su pronunciación aparece sólo en el caso de que sus componentes no figuren en otra parte de este diccionario;
d. *expresiones idiomáticas*, esto es, frases que se forman de la palabra principal, ya sea artículo principal o secundario, con la adición de uno o más elementos (generalmente adverbios o complementos).

LABELS AND ABBREVIATIONS USED IN THE DICTIONARY

LOS RÓTULOS Y ABREVIATURAS USADOS EN EL DICCIONARIO

abbr., abr.	abbreviation	abreviatura
acc.	accusative	acusativo
act.	active	activo
A.D.	Anno Domini	año de Cristo
adj.	adjective, adjectival	adjetivo, adjetival
adv.	adverb, adverbial	adverbio, adverbial
aero.	aeronautics	aeronáutica
agri.	agriculture	agricultura
alg.	algebra	álgebra
alt.	alternate	alternativo
A.M.	ante meridiem	antemeridiano, por la mañana
Amer.	American	americano
anat.	anatomy	anatomía
archaeol.	archaeology	arqueología
archaic	archaic	arcaico
archit.	architecture	arquitectura
Arg.	Argentina	Argentina
arith.	arithmetic	aritmética
armor	armor	armadura
art.	article	artículo
astrol.	astrology	astrología
astron.	astronomy	astronomía
attrib.	attributive	atributivo
aug.	augmentative	aumentativo
auto.	automotive	automóviles
aux.	auxiliary	auxiliar
baseball	baseball	béisbol
B.C.	before Christ	antes de Jesucristo
Bib.	Bible, biblical	Biblia, bíblico
biol.	biology	biología
bot.	botany	botánica
Brit.	British	británico
C.A.	Central America	América Central, Centroamérica
cap.	capital, capitalized	mayúscula
cards	cards	naipes
carpentry	carpentry	carpintería
ceramics	ceramics	cerámica
chem.	chemistry	química
colloq.	colloquial	familiar
comb. form	combining form	forma de composición
comm.	commerce, commercial	comercio, comercial
comp.	comparative	comparativo
compound	compound	compuesto
cond.	conditional	condicional
conj.	conjunction	conjunción

contr.	contraction	contracción
Cuba	Cuba	Cuba
dat.	dative	dativo
decl.	declined, declension	declinado, declinación
def.	definite	definido
defect.	defective	defectivo
dem.	demonstrative	demonstrativo
dent.	dentistry	odontología
derog.	derogatory	despectivo
dial.	dialect, dialectal	dialecto, dialectal
dim.	diminutive	diminutivo
dir.	direct	directo
drama	drama	drama
dynamics	dynamics	dinámica
eccles.	ecclesiastical	eclesiástico
econ.	economics	economía
educ.	education	educación
EE.UU.	United States (of America)	Estados Unidos (de América)
electricity	electricity	electricidad
electronics	electronics	electrónica
embryol.	embryology	embriología
Eng.	English	inglés
engin.	engineering	ingeniería
entom.	entomology	entomología
esp.	especially	especialmente
etc.	et cetera	etcétera
ethnol.	ethnology	etnología
exc.	except	excepto
fem., f.	feminine	femenino
fig.	figurative	figurativo
finance	finance	finanzas
financial	financial	financiero
1st	first	primero
fol.	followed	seguido
freq.	frequentative	frecuentativo
fut.	future	futuro
games	games	juegos
gen.	genitive	genitivo
geog.	geography	geografía
geol.	geology	geología
geom.	geometry	geometría
ger.	gerund	gerundio
gram.	grammar, grammatical	gramática, gramático
heraldry	heraldry	heráldica
hist.	history, historical	historia, histórico
hortic.	horticulture	horticultura
hunting	hunting	caza, montería
ichthy.	ichthyology	ictiología
impers.	impersonal	impersonal
impf.	imperfect	imperfecto
impve.	imperative	imperativo
ind.	indicative	indicativo
indecl.	indeclinable	indeclinable
indef.	indefinite	indefinido
indir.	indirect	indirecto
inf.	infinitive	infinitivo
infl.	inflection	inflexión

interj.	interjection	interjección
interrog., interr.	interrogative	interrogativo
intr.	intransitive	intransitivo
ironic	ironic	irónico
irreg.	irregular	irregular
journalism	journalism	periodismo
law	law	derecho
l.c.	lower case	minúscula
lexic.	lexicography	lexicografía
ling.	linguistics	lingüística
lit.	literal, literally	literal, literalmente
marca registrada	trade name	marca registrada
masc., m.	masculine	masculino
masonry	masonry	albañilería
math., matem.	mathematics	matemática
mech.	mechanics	mecánica
med.	medicine	medicina
metall.	metallurgy	metalurgia
meteorol.	meteorology	meteorología
Mex.	Mexico	México
mfg.	manufacturing	fabricación
mil.	military	militar
mineralogy	mineralogy	mineralogía
mining	mining	minería
motion pictures	motion pictures	cine
music	music	música
myth.	mythology	mitología
n.	noun	nombre, sustantivo
naut.	nautical	náutico
nav.	navigation	navegación
naval	naval	marino, naval militar
neg.	negative	negativo
neut.	neuter	neutro
n.f.	feminine noun	nombre o sustantivo femenino
n.m.	masculine noun	nombre o sustantivo masculino
nom.	nominative	nominativo
numeral	numeral	cifra
obj.	object, objective	objeto, objetivo
obs.	obsolete	desusado
obstetrics	obstetrics	obstetricia
offensive	offensive	despectivo, denostador
optics	optics	óptica
ornith.	ornithology	ornitología
Orth.Ch.	Orthodox Church	iglesia ortodoxa
orthography	orthography	ortografía
p.	participle	participio
p.adj.	participial adjective	adjetivo participial
painting	painting	pintura
paleontol.	paleontology	paleontología
particle	particle	partícula
pass., pasivo	passive	pasivo
pathol., patol.	pathology	patología
perf.	perfect	perfecto
pers.	person, personal	persona, personal
pert.	pertaining	perteneciente
pharm.	pharmacology	farmacología

philol.	philology	filología
philos.	philosophy	filosofía
phonet.	phonetics	fonética
photog.	photography	fotografía
physics	physics	física
physiol.	physiology	fisiología
pl.	plural	plural
plupf.	pluperfect	pluscuamperfecto
P.M.	post meridiem	por la tarde, post-meridiano
poet., poét.	poetic	poético
polit.	politics, political	política, político
poss., pos.	possessive	posesivo
p.p.	past participle	participio pasivo
prefix, prefijo	prefix	prefijo
prep.	preposition	preposición
pres.	present	presente
pret.	preterit	pretérito
print.	printing	imprenta
pron.	pronoun	pronombre
pros.	prosody	prosodia
prov.	provincial	provincial
pr.p., p.pr.	present participle	participio presente o activo
Prot.	Protestant	protestante, evangélico
psychoanal.	psychoanalysis	psicoanálisis
psychol.	psychology	psicología
p.t., pret.	past tense	pretérito
publishing	publishing	publicación
quím.	chemistry	química
R.C.Ch.	Roman Catholic Church	iglesia católica romana
refl.	reflexive	reflexivo
reg.	regular	regular
rel.	relative	relativo
relig.	religion	religión
rhet.	rhetoric	retórica
R.R.	railroads, railroading, railways	ferroviario
sc.	science	ciencia
sculp.	sculpture	escultura
2nd	second	segundo
seismol.	seismology	sismología
sing.	singular	singular
slang	slang	vulgarismo, jerga
So.Amer.	South America	Sudamérica
sports	sports	deporte, deportivo
St., Ste.	Saint	san, santo, santa
subj.	subject	sujeto
subjve.	subjunctive	subjuntivo
suffix, sufijo	suffix	sufijo
superl.	superlative	superlativo
surg.	surgery	cirugía
surv.	surveying	agrimensura
technol.	technology	tecnología
teleg.	telegraphy	telegrafía
theat.	theater, theatrical	teatro, teatral
theol.	theology	teología
3rd	third	tercero

T.N.	trade name	marca registrada
topog.	topography	topografía
trig.	trigonometry	trigonometría
TV	television	televisión
typog.	typography	tipografía
U.S.	United States (of America)	Estados Unidos (de América)
usu.	usually	usualmente
v.	verb	verbo
v.a.	active or transitive verb	verbo activo
var.	variant	variante
vet.med.	veterinary medicine	veterinaria
v.i.	intransitive verb	verbo intransitivo o neutro
v.n.	neuter or intransitive verb	verbo neutro
voc.	vocative	vocativo
v.r.	reflexive verb	verbo reflexivo
vs.	versus	contra
v.t.	transitive verb	verbo transitivo o activo
vulg.	vulgar, vulgarism	vulgar, vulgarismo
W.I.	West Indies	Antillas
zool.	zoology	zoología
=	equals	equivalente a

The New World
SPANISH-ENGLISH and ENGLISH-SPANISH
Dictionary

SPANISH-ENGLISH SECTION

(*Parte Española-Inglesa*)

A

A, a (a) *n.f.* first letter of the Spanish alphabet.

a (a) *prep.* **1,** to; toward. **2,** at; in; on; upon. **3,** by; near. **4,** of; for. **5,** with. **6,** against; next to. **7,** according to. **8,** used before the direct object when it denotes a person or the name of a place: *Vimos a Juan ayer,* We saw John yesterday. *Visitamos a Londres el año pasado,* We visited London last year.

a- (a) *prefix* **1,** *var. of* **ab-**: *aversión,* aversion. **2,** *var. of* **ad-**: *ascribir,* ascribe. **3,** not; without: *asimetría,* asymmetry; *acatólico,* acatholic.

ab- (aβ) *prefix* ab-. **1,** off: *absolver,* absolve; away; from: *abjurar,* abjure. *Also* **a-** *before* m, p, v: *aversión,* aversion; *often* **abs-** *before* c, t: *abstracto,* abstract. **2,** origin: *aborígenes,* aborigines.

abacería (a·βa·θe'ri·a; –se'ri·a) *n.f.* grocery. —**abacero** (–'θe·ro; –'se·ro) *n.m.* grocer.

ábaco ('a·βa·ko) *n.m.* abacus.

abad (a'βað) *n.m.* abbot. —**abadesa** (-'ðe·sa) *n.f.* abbess. —**abadía** (-'ði·a) *n.f.* abbey.

abajo (a'βa·xo) *adv.* **1,** down; below. **2,** downstairs. —*interj.* down with . . . . ! —**boca abajo,** face down; upside down. —**hasta abajo,** all the way down; to the bottom. —**para** *or* **hacia abajo,** down; downwards. —**por abajo,** under; below; underneath.

abalanzar (a·βa·lan'θar; –'sar) *v.t.* [*pres.subjve.* **abalance** (–'lan·θe; –se); *pret.* **abalancé** (–'θe; –'se)] **1,** to balance; weigh. **2,** to hurl. —**abalanzarse,** *v.r.* **1,** to rush headlong. **2,** *Amer.* to pounce; spring.

abalear (a·βa·le'ar) *v.t., Amer.* to riddle with bullets; rain bullets on.

abalorio (a·βa'lo·rjo) *n.m.* **1,** bead; glass bead. **2,** ornament made of beads; trinket.

abanderado (a·βan·de'ra·ðo) *n.m.* standard-bearer.

abanderar (a·βan·de'rar) *v.t.* to register (a ship) under a flag.

abanderizar (a·βan·de·ri'θar; –'sar) *v.t.* [*pres.subjve.* **abanderice** (–'ri·θe; –se); *pret.* **abandericé** (–'θe; –'se)] to cause to take sides; split into factions. —**abanderizarse,** *v.r.* to take sides.

abandonado (a·βan·do'na·ðo) *adj.* **1,** abandoned; forsaken. **2,** careless; slovenly.

abandonar (a·βan·do'nar) *v.t.* to abandon. —*v.i., chess* to resign. —**abandonarse,** *v.r.* **1,** to give oneself up (to); abandon oneself (to). **2,** to become careless or slovenly.

abandono (a·βan'do·no) *n.m.* **1,** abandon. **2,** carelessness; slovenliness. **3,** abandonment; forsaken condition.

abanico (a·βa'ni·ko) *n.m.* fan. —**abanicar** (–ni'kar) *v.t.* [*pres. subjve.* **abanique** (–'ni·ke); *pret.* **abaniqué** (–'ke)] to fan.

abaratar (a·βa·ra'tar) *v.t.* to cheapen. —**abaratarse,** *v.r.* to fall in price; become cheap or cheaper.

abarcar (a·βar'kar) *v.t.* [*pres. subjve.* **abarque** (–'βar·ke); *pret.* **abarqué** (–'ke)] to encompass; embrace; take in.

abarrancar (a·βa·rran'kar) *v.t.* [*infl.:* **embarrancar**] to run into a ditch. —*v.i.* to run aground. —**abarrancarse,** *v.r.* **1,** to run into a ditch. **2,** to run aground. **3,** to get into a jam.

abarrotar (a·βa·rro'tar) *v.t.* **1,** to stuff; cram. **2,** *Amer.* to glut; flood (the market).

abarrotes (a·βa'rro·tes) *n.m.pl., Amer.* groceries. —**abarrotero,** *n.m., Amer.* grocer. —**tienda de abarrotes,** *Amer.* grocery.

abastecer (a·βas·te'θer; –'ser) *v.t.* [*pres.ind.* **abastezco** (a·βas'teθ·ko; –'tes·ko); *pres.subjve.* **abastezca** (–ka)] to supply. —**abastecedor,** *adj.* supplying. —*n.m.* supplier.

abastecimiento (a·βas·te·θi·'mjen·to; –si'mjen·to) *n.m.* **1,** supply; supplying. **2,** *pl.* supplies.

abasto (a'βas·to) *n.m.* **1,** supply. **2,** *pl.* supplies; provisions. —**dar abasto,** to supply enough; give enough.

abatanar (a·βa·ta'nar) *v.t.* to full (cloth).

abate (a'βa·te) *n.m.* abbé.

abatir (a·βa'tir) *v.t.* **1,** to bring down; fell. **2,** to discourage; dishearten. —*v.i.* to diminish; abate. —**abatirse,** *v.r.* to lose spirit; become depressed or discouraged. —**abatido,** *adj.* dejected; crestfallen. —**abatimiento,** *n.m.* depression; dejection.

abdicar (aβ·ði'kar) *v.t.* & *i.* [*pres. subjve.* **abdique** (-'ði·ke); *pret.* **abdiqué** (-'ke)] to abdicate. —**abdicación,** *n.f.* abdication.

abdomen (aβ'ðo·men) *n.m.* abdomen. —**abdominal** (–mi'nal) *adj.* abdominal.

abecé (a·βe'θe; -'se) *n.m.* **1,** alphabet; abc's. **2,** rudiments (*pl.*).

abecedario (a·βe·θe'ða·rjo; a·βe·se–) *n.m.* **1,** alphabet. **2,** spelling primer.

abedul (a·βe'ðul) *n.m.* birch.

abeja (a'βe·xa) *n.f.* bee. —**abeja maestra** *or* **reina,** queen bee. —**abeja obrera,** worker bee.

abejarrón (a·βe·xa'rron) *also,* **abejorro** (–'xo·rro) *n.m.* bumblebee.

abejera (a·βe'xe·ra) *n.f.* apiary.

abejero (a·βe'xe·ro) *n.m.* beekeeper. —*adj.* bee (*attrib.*).

abejón (a·βe'xon) *n.m.* **1,** drone. **2,** bumblebee.

aberración (a·βe·rra'θjon; –'sjon) *n.f.* **1,** aberration; mental disturbance. **2,** *optics; astron.* aberration; deviation.

aberrugado (a·βe·rru'ɣa·ðo) *adj.* = **averrugado.**

abertura (a·βer'tu·ra) *n.f.* opening; aperture.

abeto (a'βe·to) *n.m.* fir. —**abeto rojo,** spruce.

abierto (a'βjer·to) *v., p.p. of* **abrir.** —*adj.* **1,** open. **2,** frank; sincere.

abigarrado (a·βi·ɣa'rra·ðo) *adj.* motley; variegated; speckled.

-abilidad (a·βi·li'ðað) *suffix* -ability; *forming nouns from adjectives ending in* **-able:** *probabilidad,* probability.

abismado (a·βis'ma·ðo) *adj.* **1,** dejected. **2,** absorbed; engrossed. **3,** *Amer.* astonished; flabbergasted.

abismarse (a·βis'mar·se) *v.r.* **1,** to grieve deeply. **2,** to be absorbed or engrossed.

abismo (a'βis·mo) *n.m.* abyss; chasm. —**abismal** (–'mal) *adj.* abysmal.

abjurar (aβ·xu'rar) *v.t.* to abjure; renounce. —**abjuración,** *n.f.* abjuration; renunciation. —**abjurar de,** to abjure; renounce.

ablandar (a·βlan'dar) *v.t.* to soften. —**ablandarse,** *v.r.* to relent. —**ablandador,** *n.m.* softener. —**ablandamiento,** *n.m.* softening.

ablativo (a·βla'ti·βo) *n.m.* ablative case.

-able ('a·βle) *suffix* -able; *forming adjectives expressing* ability; capability: *favorable,* favorable.

abnegar (aβ·ne'ɣar) *v.t.* [*infl.:* **negar**] to abnegate; renounce. —**abnegarse,** *v.r.* to devote *or* dedicate oneself. —**abnegación,** *n.f.* abnegation; renunciation.

abobamiento (a·βo·βa'mjen·to) *n.m.* **1,** silliness; stupidity. **2,** stupefaction; shock.

abobarse (a·βo'βar·se) *v.r.* to become silly. —**abobado,** *adj.* silly-looking; stupid-looking.

abocar (a·βo'kar) *v.t.* [*pres.subjve.* **aboque;** *pret.* **aboqué**] **1,** to face; come to grips with. **2,** to seize with the mouth. **3,** to pour; decant. —**abocarse,** *v.r.* to meet; come together; come face to face.

abochornar (a·βo·tʃor'nar) *v.t.* to make blush; to shame; to embarrass. —**abochornado,** *adj.* embarrassed.

abofetear (a·βo·fe·te'ar) *v.t.* **1,** to slap in the face. **2,** to insult.

abogado (a·βo'ɣa·ðo) *n.m.* lawyer; attorney. —**abogacía** (–'θi·a; –'si·a) *n.f.* legal profession.

abogar (a·βo'ɣar) *v.i.* [*pres. subjve.* **abogue** (a'βo·ɣe); *pret.* **abogué** (-'ɣe)] **1,** to plead. **2,** to intercede. —**abogar contra,** to argue against; oppose. —**abogar por,** to advocate; support.

abolengo (a·βo'len·go) *n.m.* ancestry; heritage.

abolición (a·βo·li'θjon; –'sjon) *n.f.* abolition; abolishment. —**abolicionismo,** *n.m.* abolitionism. —**abolicionista,** *adj.* & *n.m.* & *f.* abolitionist.

abolir (a·βo'lir) *v.t.,* defective (*used only in tenses with terminations beginning with* i) to abolish.

abolsarse (a·βol'sar·se) *v.r.* to bag; become baggy. —**abolsado,** *adj.* baggy; puffed.

abollar (a·βo'ʎar; –'jar) *v.t.* to dent. —**abolladura,** *n.f.* dent.

abollonar (a·βo·ʎo'nar; -jo'nar) *v.t.* to emboss. —**abollonadura,** *n.f.* embossing; embossment.

abombar (a·βom'bar) *v.t.* **1,** to cause to bulge or swell; make convex. **2,** *Amer., colloq.* to cause to smell bad; stink up. —**abombarse,** *v.r., Amer., colloq.* to smell bad; smell spoiled or rotten.

abominable (a·βo·mi'na·βle) *adj.* abominable. —**abominación,** *n.f.* abomination.

abominar (a·βo·mi'nar) *v.t.* to abominate; condemn. —**abominar de,** to detest; abhor. —**abominar contra,** to rail at *or* against.

abonar (a·βo'nar) *v.t.* **1,** to credit. **2,** to fertilize. **3,** to pay. —**abonarse,** *v.r.* to subscribe. —**abonado,** *n.m.* subscriber. —**abonador,** *n.m.* guarantor.

abonaré (a·βo·na're) *n.m.* promissory note; I.O.U.

abono (a'βo·no) *n.m.* **1,** subscription. **2,** fertilizer; manure. **3,** surety. **4,** *comm.* credit; receipt. **5,** season ticket. **6,** commutation ticket. **7,** contribution. **8,** payment.

aboque (a'βo·ke) *v., pres.subjve. of* **abocar.**

aboqué (a·βo'ke) *v., 1st pers.sing. pret. of* **abocar.**

abordar (a·βor'ðar) *v.t.* **1,** to board (a ship). **2,** to approach; accost. **3,** to bring up; broach. —**abordaje,** *n.m., naut.* boarding.

aborígenes (a·βo'ri·xe·nes) *n.m. & f.pl.* natives; aborigines. —**aborigen** (–'ri·xen) *adj.* aboriginal. —*n.m. & f.sing.* aborigine.

aborrascarse (a·βo·rras'kar·se) *v.r.* [*infl.:* **tocar**] to become stormy.

aborrecer (a·βo·rre'θer; –'ser) *v.t.* [*pres.ind.* **aborrezco** (–'rreθ·ko; –'rres·ko); *pres.subjve.* **aborrezca** (–ka)] to abhor. —**aborrecible,** *adj.* abhorrent. —**aborrecimiento,** *n.m.* abhorrence.

abortar (a·βor'tar) *v.t. & i.* to abort. —*v.i.* to miscarry. —**abortivo** (–'ti·βo) *adj.* abortive.

aborto (a'βor·to) *n.m.* **1,** abortion. **2,** miscarriage.

abotagar (a·βo·ta'ɣar) *v.t.* [*pres. subjve.* **abotague** (–'ta·ɣe); *pret.* **abotagué** (–'ɣe)] to bloat; cause to be or feel bloated. —**abotagarse,** *v.r.* to be or feel bloated. —**abotagamiento,** *n.m.* bloated feeling.

abotonar (a·βo·to'nar) *v.t.* to button.

abovedar (a·βo·βe'ðar) *v.t.* to vault; to arch. —**abovedado,** *adj.* vaulted.

abra ('a·βra) *n.f.* **1,** gorge. **2,** cove.

abracadabra (a·βra·ka'ða·βra) *n.m.* abracadabra.

abracadabrante (a·βra·ka·ða·'βran·te) *adj.* **1,** riotous; boisterous. **2,** puzzling.

abrasar (a·βra'sar) *v.t.* to burn. —**abrasarse,** *v.r.* to get burned; to feel too much heat. —**abrasador,** *adj.* extremely hot.

abrasión (a·βra'sjon) *n.f.* abrasion.

abrasivo (a·βra'si·βo) *adj. & n.m.* abrasive.

abrazadera (a·βra·θa'ðe·ra; a·βra·sa–) *n.f.* clamp; cleat.

abrazar (a·βra'θar; –'sar) *v.t.* [*pres.subjve.* **abrace** (a'βra·θe; –se); *pret.* **abracé** (–'θe; –'se)] **1,** to embrace; clasp; hug. **2,** to include; comprise. **3,** to take up; follow; adopt.

abrazo (a'βra·θo; –so) *n.m.* embrace; hug.

abrelatas (a·βre'la·tas) *n.m.sing. & pl.* can opener.

abrevadero (a·βre·βa'ðe·ro) *n.m.* watering place for cattle; trough.

abrevar (a·βre'βar) *v.t.* **1,** to water (cattle). **2,** to soak; drench.

abreviar (a·βre'βjar) *v.t.* to shorten; abridge; abbreviate. —**abreviación,** *n.f.* shortening; abridgement. —**abreviadamente,** *n.f.* briefly; summarily.

abreviatura (a·βre·βja'tu·ra) *n.f.* abbreviation.

abridor (a·βri'ðor) *n.m.* opener. —*adj.* opening.

abrigar (a·βri'ɣar) *v.t. & i.* [*pres. subjve.* **abrigue** (a'βri·ɣe); *pret.* **abrigué** (–'ɣe)] **1,** to shelter. **2,** to protect from cold; keep (one) warm. **3,** to harbor; cherish; hold. —**abrigarse,** *v.r.* to keep warm; cover oneself.

abrigo (a'βri·ɣo) *n.m.* **1,** overcoat; wrap. **2,** shelter; protection. **3,** *naut.* harbor; haven. —**al abrigo de,** sheltered or protected from *or* by; in the lee of. —**de abrigo,** warm; that keeps warm.

abril (a'βril) *n.m.* April.

abrillantar (a·βri·ʎan'tar; -jan·'tar) *v.t.* to brighten.

abrir (a'βrir) *v.t.* [*p.p.* **abierto**] **1,** to open. **2,** to whet (the appetite). —**abrirse,** *v.r.* **1,** to open. **2,** to open up; come out of one's shell. —**abrir paso,** to clear the way.

abrochar (a·βro'tʃar) *v.t.* to hook; fasten; button.
abrogar (a·βro'ɣar) *v.t.* [*pres. subjve.* **abrogue** (a'βro·ɣe); *pret.* **abrogué** (-'ɣe)] to abrogate. —**abrogación,** *n.f.* abrogation.
abrojo (a'βro·xo) *n.m.* thistle.
abrumar (a·βru'mar) *v.t.* to overwhelm. —**abrumarse,** *v.r.* to become hazy or foggy. —**abrumador,** *adj.* overwhelming; crushing; oppressive.
abrupto (a'βrup·to) *adj.* rugged; steep; abrupt.
abrutado (a·βru'ta·ðo) *adj.* brutish.
abs- (aβs) *prefix, var. of* **ab-** *before* c, t: *abstracto,* abstract; *abscisa,* abscissa.
absceso (aβs'θe·so; aβ'se·so) *n.m.* abscess; small tumor; boil.
abscisa (aβs'θi·sa; aβ'si·sa) *n.f.* abscissa.
absentismo (aβ·sen'tis·mo) *n.m.* absenteeism. —**absentista,** *n.m. & f.* absentee owner.
ábside ('aβ·si·ðe) *n.m.* apse.
absintio (aβ'sin·tjo) *n.m.* absinthe.
absolución (aβ·so·lu'θjon; -'sjon) *n.f.* **1,** absolution. **2,** acquittal.
absoluto (aβ·so'lu·to) *adj.* absolute; complete. —**absolutismo,** *n.m.* absolutism. —**en absoluto, 1,** not at all. **2,** absolutely.
absolutorio (aβ·so·lu'to·rjo) *adj.* acquitting; absolving.
absolver (aβ·sol'βer) *v.t.* [*pres. ind.* **absuelvo;** *pres.subjve.* **absuelva;** *p.p.* **absuelto**] to absolve; acquit.
absorbencia (aβ·sor'βen·θja; -sja) *n.f.* **1,** absorption. **2,** absorbency.
absorbente (aβ·sor'βen·te) *adj.* **1,** absorbing. **2,** absorptive. —*adj. & n.m.* absorbent.
absorber (aβ·sor'βer) *v.t.* to absorb.
absorción (aβ·sor'θjon; -'sjon) *n.f.* absorption.
absorto (aβ'sor·to) *adj.* absorbed; engrossed.
abstemio (aβs'te·mjo) *adj.* abstemious.
abstención (aβs·ten'θjon; -'sjon) *n.f.* abstention.
abstenerse (aβs·te'ner·se) *v.r.* [*infl.:* **tener**] to abstain.
abstinencia (aβs·ti'nen·θja; -sja) *n.f.* abstinence. —**abstinente,** *adj.* abstinent; abstentious. —*n.m. & f.* abstainer.
abstracción (aβs·trak'θjon; -'sjon) *n.f.* **1,** abstraction. **2,** preoccupation.
abstracto (aβs'trak·to) *adj. & n.m.* abstract.
abstraer (aβs·tra'er) *v.t.* [*infl.:* **traer**] to abstract. —**abstraerse,** *v.r.* to become absorbed or abstracted.
abstraído (aβs·tra'i·ðo) *adj.* **1,** absentminded. **2,** aloof.
abstruso (aβs'tru·so) *adj.* abstruse.
absuelto (aβ'swel·to) *v., p.p. of* **absolver.**
absuelva (aβ'swel·βa) *v., pres. subjve. of* **absolver.**
absuelvo (aβ'swel·βo) *v., pres. ind. of* **absolver.**
absurdo (aβ'sur·ðo) *adj.* absurd. —*n.m.* [*also,* **absurdidad,** *n.f.*] absurdity.
abuelo (a'βwe·lo) *n.m.* grandfather; *pl.* grandparents; forefathers. —**abuela,** *n.f.* grandmother.
abultar (a·βul'tar) *v.i.* **1,** to bulge. **2,** to bulk large. —*v.t.* **1,** to cause to bulge; make bulky. **2,** to exaggerate; magnify. —**abultado,** *adj.* bulky.
abundamiento (a·βun·da'mjen·to) *n.m., in* **a mayor abundamiento,** furthermore; and what is more . . .
abundancia (a·βun'dan·θja; -sja) *n.f.* abundance; plenty. —**abundante,** *adj.* abundant; plentiful.
abundar (a·βun'dar) *v.i.* to abound.
aburguesarse (a·βur·ɣe'sar·se) *v.r.* to acquire bourgeois attitudes.
aburrir (a·βu'rrir) *v.t.* to bore. —**aburrirse,** *v.r.* to be bored.—**aburrido,** *adj.* wearying; boring. —**aburrimiento,** *n.m.* tediousness; boredom.
abusador (a·βu·sa'ðor) *adj.* bullying. —*n.m.* bully.
abusar (a·βu'sar) *v.i., usu.fol. by* **de, 1,** to abuse. **2,** to use in excess; overindulge in. **3,** to take advantage of.
abusivo (a·βu'si·βo) *adj.* **1,** abusive. **2,** *Amer.* bullying. —*n.m., Amer.* bully.
abuso (a'βu·so) *n.m.* abuse.
abyecto (aβ'jek·to) *adj.* abject; vile. —**abyección** (-jek'θjon; -'sjon) *n.f.* abjectness; servility.
ac- (ak) *prefix, var. of* **ad-** *before*

c: *acceder,* accede. *In some words, reduced to* **a-**: *aceptar,* accept.
acá (a'ka) *adv.* here; over here. —**por acá,** through here; this way.
acabado (a·ka'βa·ðo) *adj.* **1,** finished; complete. **2,** faultless. **3,** emaciated. —*n.m.* **1,** finish; polish. **2,** finishing touch.
acaballadero (a·ka·βa·ʎa'ðe·ro; -ja'ðe·ro) *n.m.* stud farm.
acabar (a·ka'βar) *v.t.* & *i.* to finish; end. —**acabar con,** to finish; finish off *or* with; make an end of. —**acabar de,** to have just: *Acaba de salir,* He has just gone out. —**acabar por,** to end up by *or* in; end by doing; do finally.
acabóse (a·ka'βo·se) *n.m., colloq.* the end; the limit; the last straw.
acacia (a'ka·θja; –sja) *n.f.* acacia.
academia (a·ka'ðe·mja) *n.f.* **1,** private school. **2,** academy.
académico (a·ka'ðe·mi·ko) *adj.* academic. —*n.m.* **1,** academician. **2,** professor; teacher.
acaecer (a·ka·e'θer; –'ser) *v.impers.* [*pres.subjve.* **acaezca** (–'eθ·ka; –'es·ka)] to happen; come to pass. —**acaecimiento,** *n.m.* event.
acalambrarse (a·ka·lam'brar·se) *v.r.* to have cramps; become cramped.
acalenturarse (a·ka·len·tu'rar·se) *v.r.* to become feverish.
acalorado (a·ka·lo'ra·ðo) *adj.* **1,** heated; hot. **2,** angry; excited.
acalorar (a·ka·lo'rar) *v.t.* **1,** to warm; cause to feel warm or hot. **2,** to inflame; excite. —**acaloramiento,** *also,* **acaloro** (–'lo·ro) *n.m.* heat; ardor.
acallar (a·ka'ʎar; –'jar) *v.t.* **1,** to quiet; silence. **2,** to assuage.
acampar (a·kam'par) *v.i.* to encamp; camp.
acanalar (a·ka·na'lar) *v.t.* to flute; groove.
acantilado (a·kan·ti'la·ðo) *n.m.* cliff. —*adj.* steep.
acanto (a'kan·to) *n.m.* acanthus.
acantonar (a·kan·to'nar) *v.t.* to quarter (troops). —**acantonamiento,** *n.m.* cantonment.
acaparar (a·ka·pa'rar) *v.t.* to monopolize; hoard; corner. —**acaparador,** *n.m.* monopolizer; hoarder. —**acaparamiento,** *n.m.* hoarding.
acaracolado (a·ka·ra·ko'la·ðo) *adj.* spiral.
acaramelado (a·ka·ra·me'la·ðo) *adj.* **1,** sugary; sugared. **2,** *colloq.* mawkish; sentimental.
acaramelar (a·ka·ra·me'lar) *v.t.* **1,** to caramelize. **2,** to sugar-coat. —**acaramelarse,** *v.r.* **1,** to caramelize. **2,** *fig., colloq.* to become sweet; put on sweetness.
acariciar (a·ka·ri'θjar; –'sjar) *v.t.* to caress. —**acariciador,** *adj.* caressing.
ácaro ('a·ka·ro) *n.m.* mite.
acarrear (a·ka·rre'ar) *v.t.* **1,** to cart; transport. **2,** to cause; bring on. —**acarreador,** *n.m.* carrier. —*adj.* transporting; used for transport. —**acarreo** (–'rre·o) *also,* **acarramiento,** *n.m.* cartage.
acaso (a'ka·so) *adv.* perhaps; maybe. —*n.m.* chance; eventuality. —**al acaso,** aimlessly. —**por si acaso,** just in case.
acatar (a·ka'tar) *v.t.* to comply with; respect; obey. —**acatamiento,** *also,* **acato** (a'ka·to) *n.m.* compliance; respect. —**darse acato de,** to realize; take account of.
acatarrarse (a·ka·ta'rrar·se) *v.r.* to catch cold.
acaudalar (a·kau·ða'lar) *v.t.* **1,** to acquire; to accumulate. **2,** to hoard (wealth). —**acaudalado,** *adj.* wealthy.
acaudillar (a·kau·ði'ʎar; –'jar) *v.t.* to command; to lead; to head. —**acaudillamiento,** *n.m.* lead; command.
acceder (ak·θe'ðer; ak·se–) *v.i.* to accede; agree; acquiesce.
accesible (ak·θe'si·βle; ak·se–) *adj.* accessible. —**accesibilidad,** *n.f.* accessibility.
accesión (ak·θe'sjon; ak·se-) *n.f.* accession.
acceso (ak'θe·so; ak'se–) *n.m.* access.
accesorio (ak·θe'so·rjo; ak·se–) *adj.* & *n.m.* accessory. —**accesoria,** *n.f.* outbuilding.
accidentado (ak·θi·ðen'ta·ðo; ak·si–) *adj.* rough; uneven. —*n.m.* accident casualty.
accidente (ak·θi'ðen·te; ak·si–) *n.m.* accident. —**accidental,** *adj.* accidental. —**accidentarse,** *v.r.* to suffer an accident.
acción (ak'θjon; -'sjon) *n.f.* **1,** action; act. **2,** *finance* share. **3,** lawsuit. —**accionar,** *v.i.* to gesticulate. —*v.t.* to drive; to operate. —**accionista,** *n.m.* stockholder. —**acción de gracias,** thanksgiving.

-áceas ('a·θe·as; 'a·se·as) *suffix, fem. form of* **-áceos.** *See* **-áceo.**
acebo (a'θe·βo; a'se–) *n.m.* holly.
acece (a'θe·θe; a'se·se) *v., pres. subjve. of* **acezar.**
acecé (a·θe'θe; a·se'se) *v., 1st pers.sing. pret. of* **acezar.**
acechar (a·θe'tʃar; a·se–) *v.t.* to watch; keep an eye on. —*v.i.* to lie in wait; lurk. —**acecho** (a'θe·tʃo; a'se–) *n.m., also,* **acechanza,** *n.f.* watch; watching.
acedera (a·θe'ðe·ra; a·se–) *n.f.* sorrel. —**acedera menor,** oxalis.
acedía (a·θe'ði·a; a·se–) *n.f.* heartburn.
acedo (a'θe·ðo; a'se–) *adj.* sour; acid.
aceitar (a·θei'tar; a·sei–) *v.t.* to oil; lubricate. —**aceitado,** *n.m.* oiling; lubrication.
aceite (a'θei·te; a'sei–) *n.m.* oil. —**aceitoso,** *adj.* oily.
aceitera (a·θei'te·ra; a·sei–) *n.f.* **1,** oil can. **2,** oil cup.
aceitillo (a·θei'ti·ʎo; a·sei'ti·jo) *n.m.* satinwood.
aceituna (a·θei'tu·na; a·sei–) *n.f.* olive. —**aceitunado,** *adj.* olive-colored. —**aceituno,** *n.m.* olive tree.
acelerar (a·θe·le'rar; a·se–) *v.t. & i.* to accelerate. —**aceleración,** *n.f.* acceleration. —**aceleradamente,** *adv.* hastily. —**acelerador,** *n.m.* accelerator —*adj.* accelerating.
acelga (a'θel·ɣa; a'sel–) *n.f.* chard.
acémila (a'θe·mi·la; a'se–) *n.f.* pack mule.
acemita (a·θe'mi·ta; a·se–) *n.f.* bran bread.
acendrado (a·θen'dra·ðo; a·sen–) *adj.* pure; concentrated.
acento (a'θen·to; a'sen–) *n.m.* accent.
acentuar (a·θen'twar; a·sen–) *v.t.* [*infl.:* **continuar**] **1,** to accent. **2,** to accentuate; emphasize. —**acentuación,** *n.f.* accentuation.
-áceo ('a·θe·o; –se·o) *suffix* -aceous. **1,** *forming adjectives and nouns expressing* quality; relationship: *cetáceo,* cetaceous. **2,** *bot.; zool., in pl.* **-áceos, -áceas,** -aceae; -acea, *used to form names of families, orders and classes: crustáceos,* crustacea; *gramináceas,* graminaceae.
acepción (a·θep'θjon; a·sep'sjon) *n.f., gram.* meaning; acceptation.
acepillar (a·θe·pi'ʎar, a·se·pi'jar) *v.t.* = **cepillar.**
aceptar (a·θep'tar; a·sep–) *v.t.* **1,** to accept. **2,** *comm.* to honor. —**aceptabilidad,** *n.f.* acceptability. —**aceptable,** *adj.* acceptable. —**aceptación,** *n.f.* acceptance.
acequia (a'θe·kja; a'se–) *n.f.* ditch, esp. irrigation ditch.
acera (a'θe·ra; a'se–) *n.f.* sidewalk.
acerar (a·θe'rar; a·se–) *v.t.* **1,** to edge with steel. **2,** to pave. **3,** *fig.* to strengthen. —**acerarse,** *v.r.* to take courage. —**acerado,** *adj.* steely.
acerbo (a'θer·βo; a'ser–) *adj.* tart; bitter. —**acerbidad,** *n.f.* acerbity; bitterness.
acerca de (a'θer·ka·ðe; a'ser–) about; concerning; with regard to.
acercamiento (a·θer·ka'mjen·to; a·ser–) *n.m.* **1,** approach. **2,** rapprochement.
acercar (a·θer'kar; a·ser–) *v.t.* [*pres.subjve.* **acerque** (a'θer·ke; –'ser·ke); *pret.* **acerqué** (–'ke)] to bring near; draw up. —**acercarse,** *v.r.* to come near; approach.
acero (a'θe·ro; –'se·ro) *n.m.* steel. —**aceros,** *n.m.pl.* temper; mettle. —**acero al carbono,** carbon steel. —**acero de herramientas,** tool steel. —**acero inoxidable,** stainless steel. —**acero de aleación,** alloy steel.
acerolo (a·θe'ro·lo; a·se–) *n.m.* hawthorn. —**acerola,** *n.f.* hawthorn berry.
acérrimo (a'θe·rri·mo; a'se–) *adj., superl. of* **acre.**
acerro (a'θe·rro; a'se–) *n.m.* **1,** heap. **2,** *law* common property.
acertado (a·θer'ta·ðo; a·ser–) *adj.* right; apt; well-considered.
acertar (a·θer'tar; a·ser–) *v.t. & i.* [*pres.ind.* **acierto;** *pres.subjve.* **acierte**] to hit; hit upon; guess correctly. —**acertar a, 1,** to succeed in. **2,** to happen to.
acertijo (a·θer'ti·xo; a·ser–) *n.m.* riddle.
acetanilida (a·θe·ta·ni'li·ða; a·se–) *n.f.* acetanilide.
acetato (a·θe'ta·to; a·se–) *n.m.* acetate.
acético (a'θe·ti·ko; a'se–) *adj.* acetic.
acetileno (a·θe·ti'le·no; a·se–) *n.m.* acetylene.
acetona (a·θe'to·na; a·se–) *n.f.* acetone.

acezar (a·θe'θar; a·se'sar) *v.i.* [*pres.subjve.* **acece**; *pret.* **acecé**] to pant; gasp.
-acia ('a·θja; -sja) *suffix* -acy; *forming nouns expressing* quality; condition: *aristocracia,* aristocracy.
aciago (a'θja·ɣo; a'sja–) *adj.* fateful; disastrous.
aciano (a'θja·no; a'sja-) *n.m.* cornflower.
acíbar (a'θi·βar; a'si–) *n.m.* **1,** = **áloe. 2,** *fig.* bitterness.
acicalar (a·θi·ka'lar; a·si·) *v.t.* to adorn; to embellish. —**acicalarse,** *v.r.* to dress up. —**acicalamiento,** *n.m.* embellishment.
acicate (a·θi'ka·te; a·si–) *n.m.* **1,** spur. **2,** incentive. —**acicatear,** *v.t., Amer.* to spur; prod.
-acidad (a·θi'ðað; a·si-) *suffix* -acity; *forming nouns denoting* quality; tendency: *pugnacidad,* pugnacity.
ácido ('a·θi·ðo; 'a·si-) *adj. & n.m.* acid. —**acidez,** *n.f.* acidity.
acierte (a'θjer·te; –'sjer·te) *v., pres.subjve. of* **acertar.**
acierto (a'θjer·to; –'sjer·to) *n.m.* **1,** dexterity; ability. **2,** success. **3,** appropriateness.
acierto (a'θjer·to; –'sjer·to) *v., pres.ind. of* **acertar.**
acimut (a·θi'mut; a·si-) *n.m.* [*pl.* **acimuts** (–'muts)] azimuth.
-ación (a'θjon; -'sjon) *suffix* -ation; *forming verbal nouns expressing* action; result of action: *abdicación,* abdication.
aclamar (a·kla'mar) *v.t.* to acclaim. —**aclamación,** *n.f.* acclamation.
aclarar (a·kla'rar) *v.t.* **1,** to clear. **2,** to explain. **3,** to thin. **4,** to rinse. —*v.i.* to become clear. —**aclaración,** *n.f.* explanation. —**aclarador,** *also,* **aclaratorio,** *adj.* explanatory.
aclimatar (a·kli·ma'tar) *v.t.* to acclimate; acclimatize. —**aclimatación,** *n.f.* acclimation; acclimatization.
acné (ak'ne) *n.f.* acne.
-aco (a·ko) *suffix* -ac; *forming adjectives expressing* **1,** characteristic of: *elegíaco,* elegiac. **2,** relating to; of: *cardíaco,* cardiac. **3,** affected by; possessed by: *maníaco,* maniac. **4,** nationality: *austríaco,* Austrian. **5,** derog. sense, in some nouns: *libraco,* poor or cheap book.
acobardar (a·ko·βar'ðar) *v.t.* to intimidate. —**acobardarse,** *v.r.* to become frightened; to turn tail.
acodado (a·ko'ða·ðo) *adj.* elbow-shaped; bent in the form of an elbow.
acodarse (a·ko'ðar·se) *v.r.* to rest the elbow; to lean.
acodillar (a·ko·ði'ʎar; -'jar) *v.t.* to bend in the form of an elbow.
acogedor (a·ko·xe'ðor) *adj.* **1,** sheltering. **2,** kind; hospitable.
acoger (a·ko'xer) *v.t.* [*pres.ind.* **acojo** (a'ko·xo); *pres.subjve.* **acoja** (–xa)] **1,** to receive; greet. **2,** to harbor; shelter. —**acogerse,** *v.r.* to take refuge.
acogida (a·ko'xi·ða) *n.f.* reception; greeting; welcome. *Also,* **acogimiento** (–'mjen·to) *n.m.*
acogotar (a·ko·ɣo'tar) *v.t.* **1,** to kill with a blow in the nape. **2,** *colloq.* to strangle. **3,** *colloq.* to grab by the nape of the neck.
acolchar (a·kol'tʃar) *v.t.* **1,** to quilt. **2,** to pad; put padding in.
acólito (a'ko·li·to) *also,* **acolitado** (-'ta·ðo) *n.m.* altar boy; acolyte.
acombar (a·kom'bar) *v.t.* = **combar.**
acomedirse (a·ko·me'ðir·se) *v.r., Amer.* [*infl.:* **medir**] to volunteer.
acometer (a·ko·me'ter) *v.t.* **1,** to attack. **2,** to undertake. —**acometedor,** *adj.* enterprising. —**acometividad** (-ti·βi'ðað) *n.f.* aggressiveness.
acometida (a·ko·me'ti·ða) *n.f., also,* **acometimiento,** *n.m.* **1,** attack. **2,** service connection (of wires, pipes, etc.).
acomodar (a·ko·mo'ðar) *v.t.* **1,** to accommodate. **2,** to place; put; locate. **3,** to arrange. **4,** to lodge. **5,** to usher. —**acomodarse,** *v.r.* **1,** to make oneself comfortable. **2,** to adapt oneself. —**acomodable,** *adj.* adaptable. —**acomodamiento,** *n.m., also,* **acomodación,** *n.f.* accommodation. —**acomodadizo,** *also,* **acomodaticio,** *adj.* accommodating. —**acomodado,** *adj.* well-to-do. —**acomodador,** *n.m.* theater usher.
acomodo (a·ko'mo·ðo) *n.m.* **1,** job; position. **2,** convenience. **3,** accommodations (*pl.*). **4,** space; room (to contain something). **5,** solution; arrangement.
acompañamiento (a·kom·pa·ɲa'mjen·to) *n.m.* **1,** accompani-

ment. **2,** retinue. **3,** *theat.* extras (*pl.*).

acompañar (a·kom·pa'ɲar) *v.t.* **1,** to accompany. **2,** to keep (someone) company; be company for. **3,** to go well with; agree with. **—acompañador,** *n.m.* accompanist. **—acompañante,** *n.m.* [*fem.* **-ta**] companion; escort.

acompasado (a·kom·pa'sa·ðo) *adj.* **1,** rhythmic; regular. **2,** deliberate; measured.

acomplejado (a·kom·ple'xa·ðo) *adj.* having a mental complex.

aconchar (a·kon'tʃar) *v.t.* **1,** to cup, as the hands. **2,** to shelter. **—aconcharse,** *v.r., So.Amer.* to form a deposit; settle.

acondicionar (a·kon·di·θjo'nar; –sjo'nar) *v.t.* **1,** to condition. **2,** to arrange. **—acondicionamiento,** *n.m.* conditioning. **—aire acondicionado,** air conditioning. **—con aire acondicionado,** air conditioned.

acongojar (a·kon·go'xar) *v.t.* to afflict; grieve.

acónito (a'ko·ni·to) *n.m.* aconite.

aconsejar (a·kon·se'xar) *v.t.* to advise; to counsel. **—aconsejable,** *also,* **aconsejado,** *adj.* advisable. **—aconsejador,** *n.m.* = **consejero.**

acontecer (a·kon·te'θer; –'ser) *v.impers.* [*pres.subjve.* **acontezca** (–'teθ·ka; –'tes·ka)] to happen. **—acontecimiento,** *n.m.* happening; event.

acopiar (a·ko'pjar) *v.t.* to gather; store; amass. **—acopio** (a'ko·pjo) *n.m.* amassing; gathering; collection.

acoplar (a·ko'plar) *v.t.* **1,** to couple; to hitch; to join. **2,** to reconcile. **—acoplarse a,** to join; join with; hitch onto. **—acoplado,** *n.m.* coupled vehicle; trailer. **—acoplamiento,** *n.m., also,* **acopladura,** *n.f.* coupling.

acoquinar (a·ko·ki'nar) *v.t., colloq.* = **amedrentar.**

acoralado (a·ko·ra'la·ðo) *adj.* coral (*color*).

acorazar (a·ko·ra'θar; –'sar) *v.t.* [*pres.subjve.* **acorace** (–'ra·θe; –se); *pret.* **acoracé** (–'θe; –'se)] to armor; cover with armor. **—acorazado,** *adj.* armored; ironclad. **—***n.m.* battleship.

acorazonado (a·ko·ra·θo'na·ðo; –so'na·ðo) *adj.* heartshaped.

acordar (a·kor'ðar) *v.t.* [*pres.ind.* **acuerdo;** *pres.subjve.* **acuerde**] **1,** to resolve. **2,** to agree upon; settle upon. **3,** to recall; remind. **—acordarse,** *v.r.* to remember. **—si mal no me acuerdo,** if my memory serves me.

acorde (a'kor·ðe) *n.m., music* chord. **—***adj. & adv.* agreed; in accord.

acordeón (a·kor·ðe'on) *n.m.* accordion. **—acordeonista,** *n.m. & f.* accordionist.

acordonar (a·kor·ðo'nar) *v.t.* **1,** to lace (shoes). **2,** to mill (coins). **3,** to put a cordon around.

acornear (a·kor·ne'ar) *v.t.* to gore; pierce with a horn. *Also,* **cornear.**

acorralar (a·ko·rra'lar) *v.t.* **1,** to corral (animals). **2,** to corner (an opponent).

acorrucarse (a·ko·rru'kar·se) *v.r.* = **acurrucarse.**

acortar (a·kor'tar) *v.t.* to shorten. **—acortarse,** *v.r.* to draw back; be bashful. **—acortar la marcha,** to slow down.

acosar (a·ko'sar) *v.t.* to pursue relentlessly; to harass. **—acosador,** *n.m.* pursuer. **—acosamiento,** *n.m.* relentless persecution.

acostar (a·kos'tar) *v.t.* [*pres.ind.* **acuesto;** *pres.subjve.* **acueste**] **1,** to put to bed. **2,** to lay flat. **—acostarse,** *v.r.* to go to bed; lie down.

acostumbrar (a·kos·tum'brar) *v.t.* to accustom. **—***v.i., fol. by inf.* to be in the habit of; to be used to. **—acostumbrado,** *adj.* accustomed.

acotación (a·ko·ta'θjon; -'sjon) *n.f.* **1,** elevation mark. **2,** marginal note; annotation.

acotar (a·ko'tar) *v.t.* **1,** to mark off. **2,** to annotate.

acotillo (a·ko'ti·ʎo; –jo) *n.m.* sledgehammer.

acre ('a·kre) *adj.* acrid; bitter. **—***n.m.* acre.

acrecencia (a·kre'θen·θja; –'sen·sja) *n.f.* accretion; accrual; increase.

acrecentar (a·kre·θen'tar; -sen·'tar) [*pres.ind.* **acreciento** (-'θjen·to; -'sjen·to); *pres.subjve.* **acreciente** (-te)] *v.t.* to increase. **—acrecentamiento,** *n.m.* increase.

acrecer (a·kre'θer; –'ser) *v.t.* [*infl.:* **crecer**] = **acrecentar.**

acreción (a·kre'θjon; –'sjon) *n.f.* accretion.

acreditar (a·kre·ði'tar) *v.t.* to accredit. —**acreditarse,** *v.r.* to acquire reputation. —**acreditado,** *adj.* accredited; reputable.
acreedor (a·kre·e'ðor) *n.m.* creditor. —*adj.* deserving. —**acreedor hipotecario,** mortgagee.
acribillar (a·kri·βi'ʎar; –'jar) *v.t.* to riddle. —**acribillado a balazos,** riddled with bullets.
acrílico (a'kri·li·ko) *adj.* acrylic.
acriminar (a·kri·mi'nar) *v.t.* to accuse; incriminate. —**acriminación,** *n.f.* accusation; incrimination.
acrimonia (a·kri'mo·nja) *n.f.* acrimony. —**acrimonioso,** *adj.* acrimonious.
acriollarse (a·krjo'ʎar·se; –'jar·se) *v.r., Amer.* to adopt Latin American customs.
acrisolar (a·kri·so'lar) *v.t.* to purify; refine. —**acrisolado,** *adj.* pure; spotless.
acritud (a·kri'tuð) *n.f.* acridity; acridness.
acro- (a·kro) *prefix* acro-; top; tip; edge: *acrópolis,* acropolis; *acrobacia,* acrobatics.
acróbata (a'kro·βa·ta) *n.m.* & *f.* acrobat. —**acrobacia** (–'βa·θja; –sja) *n.f.* acrobatics. —**acrobático** (-'βa·ti·ko) *adj.* acrobatic. —**acrobatismo** (-'tis·mo) *n.m.* acrobatics.
acta ('ak·ta) *n.f.* **1,** record of proceedings. **2,** official certificate. —**acta notarial,** affidavit.
actínico (ak'ti·ni·ko) *adj.* actinic.
actinio (ak'ti·njo) *n.m.* actinium.
actinón (ak·ti'non) *n.m.* actinon.
actitud (ak·ti'tuð) *n.f.* attitude.
activar (ak·ti'βar) *v.t.* to activate. —**activación,** *n.f.* activation; promotion. —**activador,** *n.m.* activator.
actividad (ak·ti·βi'ðað) *n.f.* **1,** activity. **2,** activeness.
activo (ak'ti·βo) *adj.* **1,** active. **2,** *gram.* transitive. —*n.m.* assets (*pl.*).
acto ('ak·to) *n.m.* **1,** act. **2,** *theat.* act. **3,** public ceremony. **4,** law. —**acto seguido,** immediately afterwards. —**en el acto,** at once.
actor (ak'tor) *n.m.* **1,** actor. **2,** *law* [*fem.* **actora**] plaintiff. —**actriz** (–'triθ; –'tris) *n.f.* actress.
actuación (ak·twa'θjon; –'sjon) *n.f.* **1,** actuation. **2,** conduct; behavior. **3,** performance; acting of a role. **4,** legal proceedings.
actual (ak'twal) *adj.* actual; present. —**actualidad,** *n.f.* present time. —**actualmente,** *adv.* at present.
actualizar (ak·twa·li'θar; –'sar) *v.t.* [*pres.subjve.* **actualice** (–'li·θe; –se); *pret.* **actualicé** (–'θe; –'se)] to bring up to date.
actuar (ak'twar) *v.t.* & *i.* [*pres.ind.* **actúo** (–'tu·o); *pres.subjve.* **actúe** (-'tu·e)] to act. —*v.t.* to actuate.
actuario (ak'twa·rjo) *n.m.* **1,** actuary. **2,** court recorder. —**actuarial** (–'rjal) *adj.* actuarial.
acuarela (a·kwa're·la) *n.f.* water color. —**acuarelista,** *n.m.* & *f.* water-color painter.
acuario (a'kwa·rjo) *n.m.* **1,** aquarium. **2,** *cap., astron.* Aquarius.
acuartelar (a·kwar·te'lar) *v.t.* to quarter; to billet. —**acuartelamiento,** *n.m.* quartering; billeting.
acuático (a'kwa·ti·ko) *adj.* aquatic.
acuatinta (a·kwa'tin·ta) *n.f.* aquatint.
acucia (a'ku·θja; –sja) *n.f.* **1,** zeal; diligence. **2,** keen desire. **3,** acuteness (of pain).
acuciar (a·ku'θjar; –'sjar) *v.t.* **1,** to urge. **2,** to desire greatly; be eager for. —**acuciamiento,** *n.m.* urging.
acucioso (a·ku'θjo·so; –'sjo·so) *adj.* greatly desirous; eager.
acuclillarse (a·ku·kli'ʎar·se; –'jar·se) *v.r.* to squat.
acuchillar (a·ku·tʃi'ʎar; –'jar) *v.t.* to knife; to stab to death; to cut. —**acuchillarse,** *v.r.* to fight with knives.
acudir (a·ku'ðir) *v.i.* **1,** to betake oneself. **2,** to respond (to a call); come to one's aid. **3,** to resort; have recourse.
acueducto (a·kwe'ðuk·to) *n.m.* aqueduct.
ácueo ('a·kwe·o) *adj.* aqueous.
acuerde (a'kwer·ðe) *v., pres.subjve. of* **acordar.**
acuerdo (a'kwer·ðo) *v., pres.ind. of* **acordar.** —*n.m.* **1,** agreement. **2,** resolution. —**de acuerdo,** in accord; in agreement. —**de común acuerdo,** with one accord. —**hacerle acuerdo a uno,** to remind one; bring to one's mind.
acueste (a'kwes·te) *v., pres.subjve. of* **acostar.**
acuesto (a'kwes·to) *v., pres.ind. of* **acostar.**

acullá (a·ku'ʎa; –'ja) *adv.* there; over there.
acumen (a'ku·men) *n.m.* acumen.
acumular (a·ku·mu'lar) *v.t.* to accumulate; to amass. —**acumulación,** *n.f.* accumulation. —**acumulador,** *n.m.* storage battery. —*adj.* accumulative.
acunar (a·ku'nar) *v.t.* to cradle.
acuñación (a·ku·ɲa'θjon; –'sjon) *n.f.* **1,** coinage. **2,** wedging. **3,** die stamping.
acuñar (a·ku'ɲar) *v.t.* **1,** to coin; mint. **2,** to wedge. **3,** to die-stamp.
acuoso (a'kwo·so) *adj.* watery; aqueous. —**acuosidad,** *n.f.* wateriness.
acurrucarse (a·ku·rru'kar·se) *also,* **acorrucarse** (a·ko–) *v.r.* [*infl.:* **tocar**] **1,** to huddle; huddle up. **2,** to crouch.
acusar (a·ku'sar) *v.t.* **1,** to accuse. **2,** to indict. **3,** to acknowledge (receipt). **4,** *cards* to declare; meld. —**acusación,** *n.f.* accusation; indictment. —**acusado,** *n.m.* accused; defendant. —*adj.* well attested. —**acusador,** *n.m.* accuser; prosecutor. —*adj.* accusing.
acusativo (a·ku·sa'ti·βo) *adj.* & *n.m., gram.* accusative.
acuse (a'ku·se) *n.m.* **1,** acknowledgment (*of receipt*). **2,** winning card.
acusón (a·ku'son) *n.m., colloq.* tattletale. *Also, Amer.,* **acusete** (–'se·te).
acústica (a'kus·ti·ka) *n.f.* acoustics (*pl.*). —**acústico,** *adj.* acoustic.
achacar (a·tʃa'kar) *v.t.* [*pres. subjve.* **achaque** (–'tʃa·ke); *pret.* **achaqué** (–'ke)] to impute.
achacoso (a·tʃa'ko·so) *adj.* sickly; ailing.
achaflanar (a·tʃa·fla'nar) *v.t.* to bevel; chamfer.
achampañado (a·tʃam·pa'ɲa·ðo) *adj.* champagne-like.
achantarse (a·tʃan'tar·se) *v.r., colloq.* to cringe; cower.
achaparrado (a·tʃa·pa'rra·ðo) *adj.* squat; stubby.
achaque (a'tʃa·ke) *n.m.* **1,** chronic ailment. **2,** pretext; excuse. **3,** *usu.pl.* matters; affairs.
achatar (a·tʃa'tar) *v.t.* to flatten.
achicar (a·tʃi'kar) *v.t.* [*pres. subjve.* **achique** (a'tʃi·ke); *pret.* **achiqué** (–'ke)] **1,** to diminish; shorten. **2,** *naut.* to bail out. —**achicarse,** *v.r.* to humble oneself; efface oneself. —**achicador,** *n.m.* bailing scoop.
achicoria (a·tʃi'ko·rja) *n.f.* chicory.
achicharrar (a·tʃi·tʃa'rrar) *v.t.* **1,** to scorch. **2,** to overcook. **3,** *colloq.* to bedevil.
achinado (a·tʃi'na·ðo) *adj., Amer.* having Mongoloid features.
achispar (a·tʃis'par) *v.t., colloq.* to make tipsy. —**achispado,** *adj., colloq.* tipsy.
-acho ('a·tʃo) *suffix, forming nouns and adjectives with derog. sense: hombracho,* husky big fellow; *ricacho,* vulgar rich person.
achocolatado (a·tʃo·ko·la'ta·ðo) *adj.* chocolate-colored.
-achuelo (a'tʃwe·lo) *fem.* **-achuela** (-la) *suffix, forming diminutives: riachuelo,* rivulet.
achulado (a·tʃu'la·ðo) *adj., colloq.* rough; rowdy.
ad- (að) *prefix* ad-; *denoting* direction toward; tendency; addition: *adherirse,* adhere.
-ada ('a·ða) *suffix, forming nouns expressing* **1,** action; result of action: *emboscada,* ambuscade. **2,** group; ensemble; structure: *empalizada,* palisade. **3,** names of some drinks: *limonada,* lemonade. **4,** period of time: *otoñada,* autumn time. **5,** amount held or contained: *brazada,* armful; *cucharada,* spoonful.
adagio (a'ða·xjo) *n.m.* **1,** adage. **2,** *music* adagio.
adalid (a·ða'lið) *n.m.* chieftain; leader.
adamado (a·ða'ma·ðo) *adj.* **1,** womanish; feminine. **2,** garish.
adamascado (a·ða·mas'ka·ðo) *adj.* damask.
adaptar (a·ðap'tar) *v.t.* to adapt; to fit; to accustom. —**adaptable,** *adj.* adaptable. —**adaptación,** *n.f.* adaptation. —**adaptador,** *n.m.* adapter.
adarga (a'ðar·ɣa) *n.f.* leather shield.
adarme (a'ðar·me) *n.m.* speck; bit.
adecentar (a·ðe·θen'tar; –sen'tar) *v.t.* to make decent (in appearance).
adecuado (a·ðe'kwa·ðo) *adj.* **1,** adequate. **2,** appropriate; apt.
adefesio (a·ðe'fe·sjo) *n.m., colloq.* **1,** *usu.pl.* nonsense (*sing.*); ab-

surdity (*sing.*). **2,** ridiculous attire. **3,** ludicrous spectacle; sight.

adelantado (a·ðe·lan'ta·ðo) *adj.* **1,** advanced; precocious. **2,** fast, as a clock. —**por adelantado,** in advance.

adelantar (a·ðe·lan'tar) *v.t. & i.* **1,** to advance. **2,** to gain. **3,** to accelerate. **4,** to anticipate. —**adelantarse,** *v.r.* to move ahead; gain the lead. —**adelantamiento,** *n.m.* advancement.

adelante (a·ðe'lan·te) *adv.* ahead; forward. —*interj.* **1,** forward! **2,** come in! **3,** go on!; go ahead! —**de aquí en adelante,** henceforth; hereafter. —**más adelante, 1,** later. **2,** further on; further ahead.

adelanto (a·ðe'lan·to) *n.m.* **1,** progress. **2,** *comm.* advance payment. **3,** advancement (*of a time schedule, clock, etc.*).

adelfa (a'ðel·fa) *n.f.* oleander.

adelgazar (a·ðel·ɣa'θar; –'sar) *v.t.* [*pres.subjve.* **adelgace** (–'ɣa·θe; -se); *pret.* **adelgacé** (-'θe; -'se)] to make thin; to taper; to slenderize. —*v.i.* to grow slender; become thin.

ademán (a·ðe'man) *n.m.* **1,** gesture. **2,** attitude. —**ademanes,** *n.m.pl.* manners. —**hacer ademán de,** to make as if to.

además (a·ðe'mas) *adv.* furthermore; besides. —**además de,** besides; in addition to.

adenoide (a·ðe'noi·ðe) *n.f.* adenoid. —**adenoideo** (-'ðe·o) *adj.* adenoidal.

adentrarse (a·ðen'trar·se) *v.r.* **1,** to enter; penetrate. **2,** to trespass; encroach.

adentro (a'ðen·tro) *adv.* inside; within.

adepto (a'ðep·to) *adj.* **1,** adept. **2,** initiated. —*n.m.* follower; adherent.

aderezamiento (a·ðe·re·θa·'mjen·to; -sa'mjen·to) *n.m.* **1,** embellishment. **2,** seasoning. **3,** starch, gum, etc. used for stiffening.

aderezar (a·ðe·re'θar; -'sar) *v.t.* [*pres.subjve.* **aderece** (–'re·θe; –se); *pret.* **aderecé** (-'θe; -'se)] **1,** to embellish. **2,** to season; prepare (food). **3,** to clean; repair. **4,** to patch up; gloss over.

aderezo (a·ðe're·θo; -so) *n.m.* **1,** dressing. **2,** seasoning. **3,** size (*for stiffening*). **4,** embellishment. **5,** set of jewels.

-adero (a'ðe·ro) *suffix, var. of* **-dero:** *invernadero,* greenhouse; *pagadero,* payable.

adestrar (a·ðes'trar) *v.t.* [*infl.:* **acertar**] = **adiestrar.**

adeudar (a·ðeu'ðar) *v.t.* **1,** to owe. **2,** *comm.* to debit; to charge.

adherir (a·ðe'rir) *v.t.* [*pres.ind.* **adhiero** (a'ðje·ro); *pres.subjve.* **adhiera** (–ra)] to stick; to make adhere. —**adherirse,** *v.r.* **1,** to adhere. **2,** *fol. by* **a,** to embrace (a point of view). —**adherencia,** *n.f.* adherence. —**adherente,** *n.m.* follower; adherent. —*adj.* adhering.

adhesión (a·ðe'sjon) *n.m.* **1,** adhesion. **2,** cohesion. —**adhesivo** (–'si·βo) *adj. & n.m.* adhesive.

adición (a·ði'θjon; -'sjon) *n.f.* addition. —**adicional,** *adj.* additional. —**adicionar,** *v.t.* to add to; to augment.

adicto (a'ðik·to) *adj.* addicted. *n.m.* **1,** addict. **2,** follower. **3,** habitué.

adiestrar (a·ðjes'trar) *also,* **adestrar,** *v.t.* to train; to instruct; to drill. —**adiestrador,** *n.m.* trainer; instructor. —**adiestramiento,** *n.m.* training.

adinerado (a·ði·ne'ra·ðo) *adj.* wealthy.

adiós (a'ðjos) *interj.* goodbye; farewell. —*n.m.* farewell; adieux (*pl.*).

adiposo (a·ði'po·so) *adj.* **1,** adipose. **2,** fat; obese. —**adiposis,** *n.f.* obesity.

aditamento (a·ði·ta'men·to) *n.m.* attachment; addition; accessory.

aditicio (a·ði'ti·θjo; -sjo) *adj.* added; additional.

aditivo (a·ði'ti·βo) *adj. & n.m.* additive.

adivinar (a·ði·βi'nar) *v.t.* **1,** to predict. **2,** to guess; divine. **3,** to solve (a riddle). —**adivinación,** *n.f.* prediction; divination. —**adivinanza,** *n.f.* riddle. —**adivino** (–'βi·no), **adivinador,** *n.m.* forecaster; soothsayer; fortuneteller.

-adizo (a'ði·θo; -so) *suffix, var. of* **-izo:** *voladizo,* projecting.

adjetivo (að·xe'ti·βo) *adj. & n.m.* adjective. —**adjetival,** *adj.* adjectival.

adjudicar (að·xu·ði'kar) *v.t.* [*pres.subjve.* **adjudique** (-'ði·ke); *pret.* **adjudiqué** (–'ke)] to adjudicate; award. —**adjudicación,** *n.f.* adjudication; judgment.

adjuntar (aðxun'tar) *v.t., Amer.* to enclose; to include.
adjunto (að'xun·to) *adj.* **1,** attached. **2,** adjunct. **3,** enclosed (*in a communication*). —*n.m.* **1,** attachment; addition. **2,** adjunct. **3,** *law* appurtenance.
adminículo (að·mi'ni·ku·lo) *n.m.* accessory item.
administración (að·mi·nis·tra·'θjon; –'sjon) *n.f.* **1,** administration. **2,** manager's office. —**por administración,** by *or* under the management *or* the government; officially.
administrar (að·mi·nis'trar) *v.t.* to administer. —**administrador,** *n.m.* administrator. —**administradora,** *n.f.* administratrix. —**administrativo,** *adj.* administrative.
admiración (að·mi·ra'θjon; –'sjon) *n.f.* **1,** admiration; wonder. **2,** [*also,* **punto de admiración**] exclamation point.
admirar (að·mi'rar) *v.t.* to admire. —**admirarse,** *v.r.* to wonder; to be amazed. —**admirable,** *adj.* admirable. —**admirador,** *n.m.* admirer. —**admirativo,** *adj.* admiring.
admisible (að·mi'si·βle) *adj.* admissible.
admisión (að·mi'sjon) *n.f.* admission.
admitir (að·mi'tir) *v.t.* **1,** to admit. **2,** to permit.
admonición (að·mo·ni'θjon; –'sjon) *n.f.* = **amonestación.**
-ado ('a·ðo) *suffix, forming adjectives and nouns* **1,** *equivalent to a past participle: aislado,* isolated. **2,** likeness; shape: *almendrado,* almond-shaped. **3,** office; dignity: *profesorado,* professorship. **4,** place: *consulado,* consulate. **5,** period of time: *reinado,* reign.
adobar (a·ðo'βar) *v.t.* to dress; to prepare (food). —**adobado,** *adj.* dressed; prepared. —*n.m.* pickled meat. —**adobo** (a'ðo·βo) *n.m.* dressing for cooking or pickling.
adobe (a'ðo·βe) *n.m.* adobe.
adoctrinar (a·ðok·tri'nar) *v.t.* indoctrinate. —**adoctrinamiento,** *n.m.* indoctrination.
adolecer (a·ðo·le'θer; –'ser) *v.i.* [*pres.ind.* **adolezco** (-'leθ·ko; -'les·ko); *pres.subjve.* **adolezca** (–ka)] to become ill. —**adolecer de,** to suffer from; be afflicted with.
adolescencia (a·ðo·les'θen·θja; –le'sen·sja) *n.f.* adolescence.
—**adolescente,** *adj.* & *n.m.* & *f.* adolescent.
adolorido (a·ðo·lo'ri·ðo) *also,* **adolorado** (-'ra·ðo) *adj.* = **dolorido.**
adonde (a'ðon·de) *adv.* where; to which place; whither.
adondequiera (a·ðon·de'kje·ra) *adv.* anywhere; wherever; whithersoever.
adopción (a·ðop'θjon; -'sjon) *n.f.* adoption.
adoptar (a·ðop'tar) *v.t.* to adopt. —**adoptable,** *adj.* adoptable. —**adoptador,** *n.m.* adopter.
adoptivo (a·ðop'ti·βo) *adj.* adoptive.
adoquín (a·ðo'kin) *n.m.* cobblestone. —**adoquinado,** *adj.* paved with cobblestones; cobbled.
-ador (a'ðor), *fem.* **-adora** (a'ðo·ra) *suffix, var. of* **-dor**: *creador,* creator; *encantador,* enchanting.
adorar (a·ðo'rar) *v.t.* to adore. —**adorable,** *adj.* adorable. —**adoración,** *n.f.* adoration.
adormecer (a·ðor·me'θer; -'ser) *v.i.* [*pres.ind.* **adormezco** (–'meθ·ko; –'mes·ko); *pres.subjve.* **adormezca** (–'ka)] to lull; make drowsy; put to sleep. —**adormecerse,** *v.r.* to become sleepy; grow numb. —**adormecimiento,** *n.m.* drowsiness; sleepiness; numbness.
adormidera (a·ðor·mi'ðe·ra) *n.f.* poppy.
adormilarse (a·ðor·mi'lar·se) *v.r.* to drowse; doze.
adornar (a·ðor'nar) *v.t.* to adorn. —**adorno** (a'ðor·no) *n.m.* adornment.
adosar (a·ðo'sar) *v.t.* to lean (something) against (another); place (something) close to or up against (another).
adquirir (að·ki'rir) *v.t.* [*pres.ind.* **adquiero** (–'kje·ro); *pres.subjve.* **adquiera** (–'kje·ra)] to acquire.
adquisición (að·ki·si'θjon; –'sjon) *n.f.* acquisition. —**adquisitivo** (–'ti·βo) *adj.* of or pert. to acquisition; serving to acquire. —**poder adquisitivo,** purchasing power.
adrede (a'ðre·ðe) *adv.* purposely; intentionally.
adrenalina (a·ðre·na'li·na) *n.f.* adrenalin.
adscribir (aðs·kri'βir) *v.t.* [*p.p.* **adscrito** (–to) *also,* **adscripto**

(–'krip·to)] 1, to ascribe; to attribute. 2, to allot; to assign.
adscripción (aðs·krip'θjon; –'sjon) *n.f.* 1, ascription; attribution. 2, allotment; assignment.
aduana (a'ðwa·na) *n.f.* custom house. —**aduanal, aduanero,** *adj.* of or pert. to customs. —**aduanero,** *n.m.* customs officer.
aducir (a·ðu'θir; -'sir) *v.t.* [*pres. ind.* **aduzco**; *pres.subjve.* **aduzca**; *pret.* **aduje** (a'ðu·xe)] to adduce.
adueñarse (a·ðwe'ɲar·se) *v.r., fol. by* **de,** to seize; take possession of.
adular (a·ðu'lar) *v.t.* to flatter. —**adulación,** *n.f.* flattery. —**adulador,** *n.m.* flatterer.
adularia (a·ðu'la·rja) *n.f.* moonstone.
adulón (a·ðu'lon) *n.m.* [*fem.* **–ona**] gross flatterer.
adulterar (a·ðul·te'rar) *v.t.* to adulterate. —**adulterante,** *adj.* & *n.m.* & *f.* adulterant. —**adulteración,** *n.f.* adulteration.
adulterino (a·ðul·te'ri·no) *adj.* adulterous.
adulterio (a·ðul'te·rjo) *n.m* adultery.
adúltero (a'ðul·te·ro) *adj.* adulterous. —*n.m.* adulterer. —**adúltera,** *n.f.* adulteress.
adulto (a'ðul·to) *adj.* & *n.m.* adult.
-adura (a'ðu·ra) *suffix, forming verbal nouns expressing* action; result of action; means: *quemadura,* burn; *añadidura,* addition; *desembocadura,* opening; outlet.
adusto (a'ðus·to) *adj.* grim; forbidding. —**adustez,** *n.f.* grimness.
aduzca (a'ðuθ·ka; -'ðus·ka) *v., pres.subjve. of* **aducir.**
aduzco (a'ðuθ·ko; –'ðus·ko) *v., 1st pers.sing. pres.ind. of* **aducir.**
advenedizo (að·βe·ne'ði·θo; -so) *adj.* & *n.m.* 1, alien. 2, immigrant. 3, upstart; parvenu.
advenimiento (að·βe·ni'mjen·to) *n.m.* 1, advent; arrival. 2, accession.
adventicio (að·βen'ti·θjo; -sjo) *adj.* extraneous.
adverbio (að'βer·βjo) *n.m.* adverb. —**adverbial,** *adj.* adverbial.
adversario (að·βer'sa·rjo) *n.m.* adversary; foe; opponent.
adverso (að'βer·so) *adj.* adverse. —**adversidad,** *n.f.* adversity.
advertir (að·βer'tir) *v.t.* [*pres. ind.* **advierto** (–'βjer·to); *pres. subjve.* **advierta** (–ta); *pret.* **advertí** -βer'ti), **advirtió** (-βir'tjo)] 1, to notice. 2, to warn; advise. —**advertencia,** *n.f.* admonition; warning. —**advertidamente,** *adv.* knowingly. —**advertido,** *adj.* alert; capable.
Adviento (að'βjen·to) *n.m.* Advent.
adyacente (að·ja'θen·te; –'sen·te) *adj.* adjacent.
aeración (a·e·ra'θjon; -'sjon) *n.f.* aeration.
aéreo (a'e·re·o) *adj.* 1, aerial; airborne. 2, aeronautic. 3, *fig.* fantastic.
aero- (a·e·ro) *also,* **aer-** (a·er), **aeri-** (a·e·ri) *prefix* aero-; aeri-: *aerodinámica,* aerodynamics; *aeriforme,* aeriform.
aerodinámica (a·e·ro·ði'na·mi·ka) *n.f.* aerodynamics (*pl.*) —**aerodinámico,** *adj.* aerodynamic. —**de forma aerodinámica,** streamlined.
aeródromo (a·e'ro·ðro·mo) *n.m.* airdrome.
aerograma (a·e·ro'ɣra·ma) *n.m.* = **radiograma.**
aerolínea (a·e·ro'li·ne·a) *n.f.* airline.
aerolito (a·e·ro'li·to) *n.m.* meteorite.
aeromoza (a·e·ro'mo·θa; –sa) *n.f., Amer.* airline stewardess.
aeronauta (a·e·ro'nau·ta) *n.m.* & *f.* aeronaut. —**aeronáutica** (–'nau·ti·ka) *n.f.* aeronautics. —**aeronáutico,** *adj.* aeronautic; aeronautical.
aeronave (a·e·ro'na·βe) *n.f.* airship.
aeroplano (a·e·ro'pla·no) *n.m.* airplane.
aeropostal (a·e·ro·pos'tal) *adj.* of or by air mail.
aeropuerto (a·e·ro'pwer·to) *n.m.* airport.
aerostación (a·e·ros·ta'θjon; –'sjon) *n.f.* ballooning; balloon navigation.
aerostática (a·e·ros'ta·ti·ka) *n.f.* aerostatics. —**aerostático,** *adj.* aerostatic.
aeróstato (a·e'ros·ta·to) *n.m.* aerostat.
aerovía (a·e·ro'βi·a) *n.f.* airway.
afable (a'fa·βle) *adj.* affable; agreeable. —**afabilidad,** *n.f.* affability; geniality.
afamado (a·fa'ma·ðo) *adj.* renowned; famous.

afán (a'fan) *n.m.* 1, eagerness; zeal. 2, toil.
afanar (a·fa'nar) *v.t.* to trouble; bother. —**afanarse,** *v.r.* 1, to strive; toil. 2, to be perturbed.
afanoso (a·fa'no·so) *adj.* 1, laborious; painful. 2, eager. 3, perturbed; anxious.
afear (a·fe'ar) *v.t.* to deface; to make ugly.
afección (a·fek'θjon; -'sjon) *n.f.* affection.
afectar (a·fek'tar) *v.t.* to affect. —**afectarse,** *v.r.* to feel; to be moved. —**afectación,** *n.f.* affectation. —**afectado,** *adj.* affected.
afectivo (a·fek'ti·βo) *adj.* 1, affective. 2, sensitive. —**afectividad,** *n.f.* sensitivity; sensibility.
afecto (a'fek·to) *n.m.* affection. —*adj.* fond.
afectuoso (a·fek'two·so) *adj.* affectionate. —**afectuosidad,** *n.f.* affectionateness.
afeitar (a·fei'tar) *v.t.* 1, to shave. 2, to smooth. —**afeitada,** *n.f., Amer.* shave.
afeite (a'fei·te) *n.m., usu.pl.* cosmetics; make-up.
afelio (a'fe·ljo) *n.m.* aphelion.
afelpado (a·fel'pa·ðo) *adj.* velvety; plushy.
afeminado (a·fe·mi'na·ðo) *adj.* effeminate. —*n.m.* effeminate man. —**afeminación,** *n.f.;* **afeminamiento,** *n.m.* effeminacy. —**afeminar,** *v.t.* to make effeminate.
aferramiento (a·fe·rra'mjen·to) *n.m.* 1, grasping. 2, obstinacy.
aferrar (a·fe'rrar) *v.t.* & *i.* 1, to grip; hold. 2, to moor; anchor. —**aferrarse,** *v.r.* to cling; hold fast.
afestonado (a·fes·to'na·ðo) *adj.* festooned.
afianzamiento (a·fjan·θa'mjen·to; -sa'mjen·to) *n.m.* 1, security. 2, support.
afianzar (a·fjan'θar; -'sar) *v.t.* [*pres.subjve.* **afiance** (–'fjan·θe; –se); *pret.* **afiancé** (–'θe; –'se)] 1, to make fast; secure. 2, to give security for; guarantee. 3, to place firmly; set in place. 4, to support; uphold; strengthen.
afición (a·fi'θjon; –'sjon) *n.f.* 1, fondness; inclination. 2, avocation; hobby.
aficionado (a·fi·θjo'na·ðo; -sjo·'na·ðo) *n.m.* [*fem.* **-da**] amateur; devotee; fan. —**aficionado a,** fond of; addicted to.
aficionar (a·fi·θjo'nar) *v.t.* to attract. —**aficionarse a,** 1, to take an interest in; become a fan of. 2, to become fond of.
afiche (a'fi·tʃe) *n.m.* 1, *Amer.* notice; poster; bill. 2, *motion pictures* publicity still.
afiebrarse (a·fje'βrar·se) *v.r., Amer.* to become feverish; have fever.
afijo (a'fi·xo) *n.m.* affix. —*adj.* affixed.
afilar (a·fi'lar) *v.t.* to sharpen. —**afilado,** *adj.* sharp; keen. —**afilador,** *n.m.* grinder (person); sharpener (tool).
afiliar (a·fi'ljar) *v.t.* to affiliate. —**afiliarse a,** to affiliate with. —**afiliación,** *n.f.* affiliation.
afín (a'fin) *adj.* similar; related. —*n.m.* & *f.* relative by marriage.
afinación (a·fi·na'θjon; -'sjon) *n.f.* 1, perfection; refinement. 2, tuning.
afinado (a·fi'na·ðo) *adj.* 1, refined. 2, well-tuned; in tune.
afinar (a·fi'nar) *v.t.* 1, to perfect; refine. 2, to tune. 3, to sharpen; make more acute. —*v.i.* to play *or* sing in tune. —**afinador,** *n.m.* piano tuner.
afincarse (a·fin'kar·se) *v.r.* [*infl.:* **tocar**] to get a foothold.
afinidad (a·fi·ni'ðað) *n.f.* 1, affinity. 2, relationship by marriage.
afirmado (a·fir'ma·ðo) *n.m.* roadbed.
afirmar (a·fir'mar) *v.t.* 1, to affirm; declare. 2, to strengthen; prop up. 3, to set or place firmly. —**afirmarse,** *v.r.* to steady oneself. —**afirmación,** *n.f.* affirmation; assertion. —**afirmativo,** *adj.* & *n.m.* affirmative. —**afirmativa,** *n.f.* affirmation; consent.
aflicción (a·flik'θjon; –'sjon) *n.f.* affliction. —**aflictivo** (–'ti·βo) *adj.* afflicting; distressing.
afligir (a·fli'xir) *v.t.* [*pres.ind.* **aflijo** (–'fli·xo); *pres.subjve.* **aflija** (–xa); *p.p.* **aflicto** (–'flik·to)] to afflict. —**afligirse,** *v.r.* to grieve.
aflojar (a·flo'xar) *v.t.* 1, to loosen; slacken. 2, *colloq.* to hand over; loosen up with, as money. 3, *colloq.* to let go with; strike with. —*v.i.* to abate. —**aflojamiento,** *n.m.* loosening; slackening.
aflorar (a·flo'rar) *v.i.* to come to the surface; appear; crop up.

afluir (a'fluir) *v.i.* [*pres.ind.* **afluyo** (–'flu·jo); *pres.subjve.* **afluya** (–ja)] **1,** to come together. **2,** to flow (into). —**afluencia,** *n.f.* affluence. —**afluente,** *adj.* affluent. —*n.m.* tributary.
afónico (a'fo·ni·ko) *adj.* hoarse; speechless.
aforador (a·fo·ra'ðor) *n.m.* **1,** appraiser. **2,** gauger.
aforar (a·fo'rar) *v.t.* **1,** to appraise. **2,** to measure; to gauge.
aforismo (a·fo'ris·mo) *n.m.* aphorism. —**aforístico,** *adj.* aphoristic.
aforo (a'fo·ro) *n.m.* **1,** appraisal. **2,** gauging. **3,** seating capacity.
afortunado (a·for·tu'na·ðo) *adj.* fortunate; lucky.
afrancesar (a·fran·θe'sar; –se'sar) *v.t.* to Gallicize; to Frenchify.
afrecho (a'fre·tʃo) *n.m.* bran.
afrenta (a'fren·ta) *n.f.* affront. —**afrentar,** *v.t.* to affront. —**afrentoso,** *adj.* insulting.
africano (a·fri'ka·no) *adj.* & *n.m.* African.
afrodisiaco (a·fro·ði'si·a·ko) *adj.* & *n.m.* aphrodisiac.
afrontar (a·fron'tar) *v.t.* **1,** to confront; put face to face. **2,** to face; be situated opposite. **3,** to face up to; brave.
aftoso (af'to·so) *adj., in* **fiebre aftosa,** hoof-and-mouth disease.
afuera (a'fwe·ra) *adv.* **1,** out; outside. **2,** away. —*interj.* one side! make way! —**afueras,** *n.f.pl.* outskirts.
agachada (a·ɣa'tʃa·ða) *n.f.* **1,** trick; stratagem. **2,** ducking of the head or body.
agachadiza (a·ɣa·tʃa'ði·θa; -sa) *n.f.* snipe.
agachar (a·ɣa'tʃar) *v.t.* to bow down; bend. —**agacharse,** *v.r.* **1,** to bend down; crouch; stoop. **2,** *fig.* to bow one's head; submit.
agalla (a'ɣa·ʎa; –ja) *n.f.* **1,** *bot.* gallnut. **2,** *ichthy.* gill. **3,** *vet.med.* windgall. **4,** *pl., colloq.* tonsils. —**tener agallas,** *colloq.* **1,** to have guts. **2,** *Amer.* to be greedy.
agangrenarse (a·ɣan·gre'nar·se) *v.r.* = **gangrenarse.**
ágape ('a·ɣa·pe) *n.m.* banquet.
agarrada (a·ɣa'rra·ða) *n.f., colloq.* wrangle; hassle.
agarradera (a·ɣa·rra'ðe·ra) *n.f., also,* **agarradero** (–ro) *n.m.* handle; holder.
agarrado (a·ɣa'rra·ðo) *adj., colloq.* stingy.
agarrar (a·ɣa'rrar) *v.t.* **1,** to grasp; seize. **2,** to catch, as an illness. —*v.i.* **1,** to take root. **2,** to take; take hold. —**agarrarse,** *v.r.* **1,** to hold on; catch hold. **2,** to fight; wrangle. —**agarrarse de,** to resort to; use as a pretext or excuse.
agarrón (a·ɣa'rron) *n.m., Amer., colloq.* **1,** tug; yank. **2,** = **agarrada.**
agarrotar (a·ɣa·rro'tar) *v.t.* **1,** to strangle. **2,** to bind tightly with ropes. —**agarrotarse,** *v.r.* **1,** *mech.* to seize, as a bearing. **2,** to stiffen, as a muscle.
agasajar (a·ɣa·sa'xar) *v.t.* to entertain; regale. —**agasajador,** *adj.* obliging; attentive.
agasajo (a·ɣa'sa·xo) *n.m.* **1,** regalement. **2,** party favor; treat.
ágata ('a·ɣa·ta) *n.f.* agate.
agazaparse (a·ɣa·θa'par·se; a·ɣa·sa–) *v.r.* to crouch.
agencia (a'xen·θja; –sja) *n.f.* agency. —**agencia de colocaciones,** employment agency.
agenciar (a·xen'θjar; –'sjar) *v.t.* to promote; to manage to bring about. —**agenciarse,** *v.r., colloq.* to manage; to get along.
agenda (a'xen·da) *n.f.* **1,** agenda. **2,** memorandum.
agente (a'xen·te) *n.m.* agent. —**agente de policía,** policeman. —**agente** *or* **corredor de aduana,** customs broker.
agigantar (a·xi·ɣan'tar) *v.t.* to exaggerate; build up; magnify. —**agigantado,** *adj.* enormous. —**a pasos agigantados,** by leaps and bounds.
ágil ('a·xil) *adj.* agile. —**agilidad,** *n.f.* agility.
agio ('a·xjo) *n.m.* speculation. —**agiotaje** (–'ta·xe) *n.m.* illicit speculation. —**agiotista** (–'tis·ta) *n.m.* & *f.* speculator.
agitador (a·xi·ta'ðor) *adj.* agitating. —*n.m.* **1,** agitator. **2,** stirring rod.
agitanado (a·xi·ta'na·ðo) *adj.* gypsylike.
agitar (a·xi'tar) *v.t.* to agitate; to shake; to stir. —**agitarse,** *v.r.* to become excited; to become disturbed. —**agitación,** *n.f.* agitation; excitement.
aglomerar (a·ɣlo·me'rar) *v.t.* to agglomerate. —**aglomeración,** *n.f*

agglomeration. —**aglomerante,** *n.m.* = **aglutinante.**

aglutinar (a·ɣlu·ti'nar) *v.t.* to agglutinate; to bind together. —**aglutinación,** *n.f.* agglutination. —**aglutinante,** *adj.* & *n.m.* agglutinant.

agnosticismo (aɣ·nos·ti'θis·mo; –'sis·mo) *n.m.* agnosticism. —**agnóstico** (–'nos·ti·ko) *adj.* & *n.m.* agnostic.

agobiar (a·ɣo'βjar) *v.t.* to overwhelm; to weigh down. —**agobiante,** *adj.* exhausting. —**agobio** (a'ɣo·βjo) *n.m.* burden; anguish.

agolpar (a·ɣol'par) *v.t.* to crowd; jam. —**agolparse,** *v.r.* to rush; rush together.

agonía (a·ɣo'ni·a) *n.f.* agony.

agónico (a'ɣo·ni·ko) *adj.* **1,** of death; death (*attrib.*). **2,** agonizing.

agonizar (a·ɣo·ni'θar; –'sar) *v.i.* [*pres.subjve.* **agonice** (–'ni·θe; –se); *pret.* **agonicé** (–'θe; –'se)] **1,** to agonize; suffer. **2,** to be dying. —**agonizante,** *adj.* dying. —*n.m.* & *f.* dying person.

agorero (a·ɣo're·ro) *adj.* **1,** ill-omened. **2,** foreboding; foretelling. —*n.m.* augur; soothsayer.

agostar (a·ɣos'tar) *v.t.* to wither; to parch. —**agostarse,** *v.r.* to wither away; to fade away.

agosto (a'ɣos·to) *n.m.* August. —**hacer su agosto,** to make a fortune; strike it rich.

agotar (a·ɣo'tar) *v.t.* to exhaust; to drain. —**agotador,** *adj.* exhausting. —**agotamiento,** *n.m.* exhaustion.

agraciar (a·ɣra'θjar; –'sjar) *v.t.* to favor; to reward. —**agraciado,** *adj.* favored; charming.

agradable (a·ɣra'ða·βle) *adj.* pleasant; agreeable.

agradar (a·ɣra'ðar) *v.t.* to please. —*v.i.* to be pleasing. —**agradarse de,** to be pleased at.

agradecer (a·ɣra·ðe'θer; –'ser) *v.t.* [*pres.ind.* **agradezco** (–'ðeθ·ko; -'ðes·ko); *pres.subjve.* **agradezca** (-ka)] **1,** to show gratitude to (someone); to thank (someone). **2,** to be thankful for (something). —**agradecido,** *adj.* grateful. —**agradecimiento,** *n.m.* gratitude.

agrado (a'gra·ðo) *n.m.* liking; pleasure. —**de mi agrado,** to my liking.

agrandar (a·ɣran'dar) *v.t.* to enlarge. —**agrandamiento,** *n.m.* enlargement.

agrario (a'ɣra·rjo) *adj.* agrarian.

agravar (a·ɣra'βar) *v.t.* to aggravate; to make worse. —**agravador,** *adj.* aggravating. —**agravamiento,** *n.m., also,* **agravación,** *n.f.* aggravation.

agraviar (a·ɣra'βjar) *v.t.* to wrong; offend. —**agraviarse,** *v.r.* to take offense. —**agraviarse de,** to be offended with (someone). —**agraviarse por,** to take offense at (something). —**agraviante,** *adj.* offending; offensive.

agravio (a'ɣra·βjo) *n.m.* insult; offense; affront. —**agravioso,** *adj.* offensive; insulting.

agredir (a·ɣre'ðir) *v.t., defective (used only in tenses with terminations beginning with* i) to assault; attack.

agregado (a·ɣre'ɣa·ðo) *n.m.* **1,** aggregate. **2,** supernumerary. **3,** attaché; assistant. **4,** addition; something added or attached.

agregar (a·ɣre'ɣar) *v.t.* to add; to annex. —**agregarse,** *v.r.* to join; to attach oneself. —**agregación,** *n.f.* aggregation.

agremiar (a·ɣre'mjar) *v.t.* to unionize. —**agremiarse,** *v.r.* to join a union. —**agremiación,** *n.f.* unionization.

agresión (a·ɣre'sjon) *n.f.* aggression.

agresivo (a·ɣre'si·βo) *adj.* aggressive. —**agresividad,** *n.f.* aggressiveness.

agresor (a·ɣre'sor) *n.m.* aggressor. —*adj.* aggressive.

agreste (a'ɣres·te) *adj.* rustic; uncouth.

agriar (a'ɣrjar) *v.t.* to sour. —**agriarse,** *v.r.* to turn sour.

agrícola (a'ɣri·ko·la) *adj.* agricultural.

agricultor (a·ɣri·kul'tor) *n.m.* agriculturist; farmer.

agricultura (a·ɣri·kul'tu·ra) *n.f.* agriculture.

agridulce (a·ɣri'ðul·θe; -se) *adj.* & *n.m.* bittersweet.

agrietarse (a·ɣrje'tar·se) *v.r.* to crack; to become filled with cracks.

agrimensura (a·ɣri·men'su·ra) *n.f.* land surveying. —**agrimensor,** *n.m.* surveyor.

agrio ('a·ɣrjo) *adj.* **1,** sour; acid. **2,** *fig.* rude; rough; harsh.

agronomía (a·ɣro·no'mi·a) *n.f.* agronomy. —**agrónomo** (a'ɣro·no·mo) *n.m.* agronomist.
agropecuario (a·ɣro·pe'kwa·rjo) *adj.* pertaining to agriculture and cattle-raising.
agrumar (a·ɣru'mar) *v.t.* to curdle; clot.
agrupar (a·ɣru'par) *v.t.* to group. —**agruparse,** *v.r.* to form a group; gather. —**agrupación,** *n.f.* grouping; group; cluster.
agrura (a'ɣru·ra) *n.f.* sourness; sour taste.
agua ('a·ɣwa) *n.f.* **1,** water. **2,** rain. **3,** luster of precious stones. **4,** slope (of a roof). —**agua bendita,** holy water. —**agua de coco,** coconut milk. —**agua de Seltz,** soda water. —**agua dulce,** fresh water. —**agua fuerte,** nitric acid. —**agua oxigenada,** hydrogen peroxide. —**agua salobre** *or* **salada,** salt water. —**aguas jurisdiccionales,** territorial waters. —**ahogarse en poca agua,** to worry unnecessarily. —**estar con el agua al cuello,** to be in deep water. —**estar entre dos aguas,** to be on the fence. —**hacer agua,** to leak. —**¡hombre al agua!,** man overboard!
aguacate (a·ɣwa'ka·te) *n.m.* avocado; alligator pear.
aguacero (a·ɣwa'θe·ro; –'se·ro) *n.m.* downpour.
aguachento (a·ɣwa'tʃen·to) *adj., Amer.* = **aguado.**
aguada (a'ɣwa·ða) *n.f.* waterhole; source of water, esp. for men and livestock.
aguadero (a·ɣwa'ðe·ro) *n.m.* waterhole; drinking place, as for wild animals.
aguadija (a·ɣwa'ði·xa) *n.f.* water, as in a blister, sore, etc.
aguado (a'ɣwa·ðo) *adj.* **1,** mushy; bland. **2,** watery; thin.
aguador (a·ɣwa'ðor) *n.m.* water carrier.
aguafiestas (a·ɣwa'fjes·tas) *n.m. & f.sing. & pl., colloq.* killjoy; wet blanket.
aguafuerte (a·ɣwa'fwer·te) *n.f.* **1,** [*also,* **agua fuerte**] nitric acid. **2,** etching. —**grabar al aguafuerte,** to etch.
aguamala (a·ɣwa'ma·la) *n.f.* = **medusa.**
aguamarina (a·ɣwa·ma'ri·na) *n.f.* aquamarine.
aguamiel (a·ɣwa'mjel) *n.m.* mead.
aguantar (a·ɣwan'tar) *v.t.* **1,** to bear; to endure; to tolerate. **2,** to hold on to. **3,** to hold back; contain; restrain. —*v.i.* to hold out. —**aguantarse,** *v.r.* to restrain oneself.
aguante (a'ɣwan·te) *n.m.* endurance; fortitude.
aguar (a'ɣwar) *v.t.* **1,** to dilute with water. **2,** *colloq.,* to spoil (a party). —**aguarse,** *v.r.* **1,** to become diluted. **2,** to become filled with water.
aguardar (a·ɣwar'ðar) *v.t.* to await; to wait for. —*v.i.* to wait.
aguardentoso (a·ɣwar·ðen'to·so) *adj.* hoarse; raucous.
aguardiente (a·ɣwar'ðjen·te) *n.m.* raw brandy. —**aguardiente de caña,** raw rum.
aguarrás (a·ɣwa'rras) *n.m.* turpentine.
aguazal (a·ɣwa'θal; –'sal) *n.m.* large puddle; pool.
aguce (a'ɣu·θe; –se) *v., pres. subjve. of* **aguzar.**
agucé (a·ɣu'θe; –'se) *v., 1st pers. sing. pret. of* **aguzar.**
agudeza (a·ɣu'ðe·θa; –sa) *n.f.* **1,** sharpness. **2,** *fig.* witticism.
agudo (a'ɣu·ðo) *adj.* **1,** sharp; acute. **2,** high-pitched. **3,** *gram.* accented on the last syllable.
agüero (a'ɣwe·ro) *n.m.* **1,** augury; omen. **2,** *Amer.* augur; soothsayer.
aguerrido (a·ɣe'rri·ðo) *adj.* **1,** combat-hardened. **2,** brave; valiant.
aguijada (a·ɣi'xa·ða) *n.f.* goad.
aguijar (a·ɣi'xar) *v.t.* to goad.
aguijón (a·ɣi'xon) *n.m.* **1,** goad. **2,** sting. —**aguijonear** (–ne'ar) *v.t.* to prick; goad.
águila ('a·ɣi·la) *n.f.* eagle.
aguileño (a·ɣi'le·ɲo) *adj.* aquiline.
aguilera (a·ɣi'le·ra) *n.f.* eagle's nest; eyrie.
aguilón (a·ɣi'lon) *n.m.* **1,** boom of a crane. **2,** peak of a roof or gable. **3,** large eagle.
aguilucho (a·ɣi'lu·tʃo) *n.m.* eaglet.
aguinaldo (a·ɣi'nal·do) *n.m.* Christmas or New Year gift.
aguja (a'ɣu·xa) *n.f.* **1,** needle. **2,** hand (of a clock); pointer. **3,** compass. **4,** steeple; spire. **5,** *R.R., usu. pl.* switch (*sing.*). **6,** firing pin. **7,** sailfish. —**agujazo,** *n.m.* pinprick.
agujero (a·ɣu'xe·ro) *n.m.* hole.

—**agujerear**, *v.t.* to make holes in; perforate.
aguzar (a·ɣu'θar; –'sar) *v.t.* [*pres. subjve.* **aguce**; *pret.* **agucé**] to sharpen.
¡ah! (a) *interj.* ah!
ahí (a'i) *adv.* there. —**de ahí**, thence. —**de ahí que**, hence; therefore. —**por ahí**, around there; thereabouts.
ahijar (a·i'xar) *v.t.* to adopt; father. —*v.i.* to breed; sprout. —**ahijado**, *n.m.* godchild; protégé.
ahinco (a'in·ko) *n.m.* eagerness; insistence.
ahitar (ai'tar) *v.t.* to satiate. —**ahito** (a'i·to) *n.m.* indigestion. —*adj.* gorged.
ahogar (a·o'ɣar) *v.t.* [*pres.subjve.* **ahogue** (a'o·ɣe); *pret.* **ahogué** (–'ɣe)] to drown; to smother; to throttle. —**ahogarse**, *v.r.* **1**, to drown. **2**, to feel suffocated.
ahogo (a'o·ɣo) *n.m.* **1**, suffocation. **2**, *fig.* oppression.
ahondar (a·on'dar) *v.t.* **1**, to deepen. **2**, to delve into.
ahora (a'o·ra) *adv.* **1**, now. **2**, just now; a little while ago. **3**, soon. —**ahora bien**, now and then. —**ahora mismo**, right now; at once. —**ahora que**, nevertheless. —**por ahora**, for the time being.
ahorcar (a·or'kar) *v.t.* [*pres.subjve.* **ahorque** (a'or·ke); *pret.* **ahorqué** (–'ke)] to hang (a person). —**ahorcadura**, *n.f.* hanging.
ahorita (a·o'ri·ta) *adv., colloq.* **1**, just now; a little while ago. **2**, right away; soon.
ahorquillar (a·or·ki'ʎar; –'jar) *v.t. & i.* to fork. —**ahorquillarse**, *v.r.* to be *or* become forked. —**ahorquillado**, *adj.* forked.
ahorrar (a·o'rrar) *v.t. & i.* to save; economize. —**ahorrador**, *adj.* thrifty. —**ahorrativo** (–'ti·βo) *adj.* frugal; stingy.
ahorro (a'o·rro) *n.m.* **1**, thrift. **2**, saving. **3**, *pl.* savings.
ahuecar (a·we'kar) *v.t.* [*pres. subjve.* **ahueque** (–'we·ke); *pret.* **ahuequé** (–'ke)] **1**, to make hollow; hollow out. **2**, to deepen; make throaty, as the voice. **3**, to cup, as the hands.
ahumar (a·u'mar) *v.t.* to smoke; to cure with smoke. —*v.i.* to give off smoke. —**ahumarse**, *v.r.* **1**, to become smoky (in taste *or* appearance). **2**, *colloq.* to get drunk. —**ahumado**, *adj.* smoked.
ahuyentar (au·jen'tar) *v.t.* **1**, to frighten away. **2**, to banish *or* dismiss (a thought, grief, etc.). **3**, to overcome (an emotion). —**ahuyentarse**, *v.r.* to flee; take flight.
-aina ('ai·na) *suffix, colloq., forming nouns of various meanings: azotaina,* spanking; *chanfaina,* a kind of stew.
airar (ai'rar) *v.t.* to make angry. —**airarse**, *v.r.* to become angry. —**airado**, *adj.* angry.
aire ('ai·re) *n.m.* **1**, air. **2**, wind; breeze. **3**, song. **4**, aspect. —**al aire libre**, outdoors. —**azotar el aire**, to work in vain. —**tener** *or* **darse un aire a otro**, to look like someone else. —**palabras al aire**, idle talk.
aire acondicionado air conditioning.
aireado (ai·re'a·ðo) *adj.* airy.
airear (ai·re'ar) *v.t.* to air; ventilate. —**airearse**, *v.r.* **1**, to take the air. **2**, to catch cold. —**aireación**, *n.f.* ventilation.
airón (ai'ron) *n.m.* egret.
airoso (ai'ro·so) *adj.* **1**, graceful. **2**, successful. —**salir airoso**, to come through with flying colors; to win.
aislacionismo (ais·la·θjo'nis·mo; –sjo'nis·mo) *n.m.* isolationism. —**aislacionista**, *n.m. & f.* isolationist.
aislado (ais'la·ðo) *adj.* **1**, isolated. **2**, insulated.
aislador (ais·la'ðor) *n.m.* insulator. —*adj.* **1**, isolating. **2**, insulating.
aislamiento (ais·la'mjen·to) *n.m.* **1**, isolation, **2**, insulation.
aislar (ais'lar) *v.t.* [*pres.ind.* **aíslo** (a'is·lo); *pres.subjve.* **aísle** (-le)] **1**, to isolate. **2**, to insulate. —**aislarse**, *v.r.* to seclude oneself; keep to oneself.
¡ajá! (a'xa) *interj.* aha!
ajar (a'xar) *v.t.* **1**, to muss; rumple. **2**, to fade; wilt; wither. **3**, to wear out by use.
-aje ('a·xe) *suffix,* -age; -ing; *forming nouns expressing* **1**, action: *pillaje,* pillage. **2**, action and result: *embalaje,* wrapping. **3**, place: *hospedaje,* boarding house. **4**, fee charged for a service: *almacenaje,* storage. **5**, group; ensemble: *follaje,* foliage. **6**, state; condition: *aprendizaje,* apprenticeship.
ajedrea (a·xe'ðre·a) *n.f., bot.* savory.

ajedrez (a·xe'ðreθ; -'ðres) *n.m.* chess. —**ajedrecista** (–'θis·ta; –'sis·ta) *n.m.* & *f.* chess player. —**ajedrezado,** *adj.* checkered; checked.
ajenjo (a'xen·xo) *n.m.* absinthe.
ajeno (a'xe·no) *adj.* **1,** of or belonging to another; another's. **2,** extraneous; foreign; alien. **3,** other; different. —**estar ajeno de,** to be unaware of.
ajetrearse (a·xe·tre'ar·se) *v.r.* to busy oneself; to hustle about. —**ajetreo** (–'tre·o) *n.m.* bustle; agitation.
ají (a'xi) *n.m.* **1,** chili; red pepper. **2,** sweet pepper.
ajiaco (a'xja·ko) *n.m., Amer.* a stew of meat and local vegetables.
ajo ('a·xo) *n.m.* garlic. —**echar ajos,** *colloq.* to talk obscenely. —**revolver el ajo,** *colloq.* to stir up a row.
-ajo ('a·xo) *suffix, forming nouns, usu. with derog. meaning: lagunajo,* puddle; *espantajo,* scarecrow.
ajonjolí (a·xon·xo'li) *n.m.* sesame.
ajorca (a'xor·ka) *n.f.* bangle.
ajuar (a'xwar) *n.m.* **1,** furnishings, esp. for the home. **2,** trousseau. **3,** layette.
ajustador (a·xus·ta'ðor) *n.m.* **1,** corselet. **2,** *Amer.* brassiere. **3,** *mech.* assembler; fitter.
ajustar (a·xus'tar) *v.t.* **1,** to adjust. **2,** to fit; fit together. **3,** to settle. **4,** to tighten. —*v.i.* to fit. —**ajustarse,** *v.r.* to conform; comply. —**ajustado,** *adj.* close-fitting; tight.
ajuste (a'xus·te) *n.m.* **1,** agreement. **2,** adjustment. **3,** fit. **4,** arrangement.
ajusticiar (a·xus·ti'θjar; –'sjar) *v.t.* to execute; to put to death.
al (al) *contr. of* **a** + **el.**
al- (al) *prefix: in words of Arabic origin, representing the Arabic definite article: Alcorán,* (the) Koran.
-al (al) *suffix* **1,** -al; *forming adjectives expressing* relation; connection: *arbitral,* arbitral; *esferoidal,* spheroidal. **2,** *forming nouns expressing* place where something abounds: *cerezal,* cherry orchard; *peñascal,* rocky ground.
ala ('a·la) *n.f.* **1,** wing. **2,** brim (of a hat). **3,** *mil.* flank. **4,** propeller blade. **5,** *pl., fig.* airs; swagger (*sing*). —**ahuecar el ala,** *colloq.* to beat it.
Alá (a'la) *n.m.* Allah.
alabar (a·la'βar) *v.t.* to praise; glorify. —**alabarse,** *v.r.* to praise oneself; brag. —**alabanza,** *n.f.* praise.
alabarda (a·la'βar·ða) *n.f.* halberd. —**alabardero,** *n.m.* halberdier.
alabastro (a·la'βas·tro) *n.m.* alabaster. —**alabastrino,** *adj.* of or like alabaster.
alacena (a·la'θe·na; –'se·na) *n.f.* cupboard.
alacrán (a·la'kran) *n.m.* scorpion.
alacridad (a·la·kri'ðað) *n.f.* alacrity.
alada (a'la·ða) *n.f.* beat *or* flutter of wings.
alado (a'la·ðo) *adj.* winged.
alamar (a·la'mar) *n.m.* frog (*ornamental fastening*).
alambicar (a·lam·bi'kar) *v.t.* [*pres.subjve.* **alambique** (–'bi·ke); *pret.* **alambiqué** (–'ke)] **1,** to distill. **2,** to overrefine; complicate.
alambique (a·lam'bi·ke) *n.m.* still.
alambrada (a·lam'bra·ða) *n.f., mil.* wire entanglement.
alambrado (a·lam'bra·ðo) *n.m.* **1,** wire fence. **2,** wiring; wires (*pl.*). —*adj.* fenced with wire.
alambre (a'lam·bre) *n.m.* wire. —**alambrera** (–'bre·ra) *n.f.* wire screen; wire cover.
alameda (a·la'me·ða) *n.f.* **1,** mall. **2,** tree-lined walk. **3,** poplar grove.
álamo ('a·la·mo) *n.m.* poplar. —**álamo temblón,** aspen.
alano (a'la·no) *n.m.* mastiff.
alarde (a'lar·ðe) *n.m.* **1,** ostentation; display. **2,** *mil.* review; show of force. —**hacer alarde,** *also,* **alardear,** *v.i.* to show off; boast.
alargar (a·lar'ɣar) *v.t.* [*pres. subjve.* **alargue** (a'lar·ɣe); *pret.* **alargué** (–'ɣe)] to lengthen; to prolong. —**alargarse,** *v.r.* to become longer; to last longer. —**alargamiento,** *n.m.* lengthening.
alarido (a·la'ri·ðo) *n.m.* howl; yell.
alarma (a'lar·ma) *n.f.* alarm. —**alarmar,** *v.t.* to alarm. —**alarmarse,** *v.r.* to be alarmed; to take alarm. —**alarmista,** *n.m.* & *f.* alarmist.
alazán (a·la'θan; –'san) *adj.* sorrel; reddish-brown. —*n.m.* sorrel (*horse*).
alba ('al·βa) *n.f.* dawn.
albacea (al·βa'θe·a; –'se·a) *n.m.* executor. —*n.f.* executrix. —**albaceazgo,** *n.m.* executorship.

albacora (al·βa'ko·ra) *n.f.* albacore.
albahaca (al·βa'a·ka) *n.f.* sweet basil.
albañal (al·βa'ɲal) *n.m.* sewer.
albañil (al·βa'ɲil) *n.m.* bricklayer; mason. —**albañilería,** *n.f.* masonry.
albarda (al'βar·ða) *n.f.* packsaddle.
albardilla (al·βar'ði·ʎa; -ja) *n.f.* 1, small packsaddle. 2, *archit.* cope; coping.
albaricoque (al·βa·ri'ko·ke) *n.m.* apricot. —**albaricoquero** (–'ke·ro) *n.m.* apricot tree.
albatros (al'βa·tros) *n.m.* albatross.
albayalde (al·βa'jal·de) *n.m.* white lead.
albedrío (al·βe'ðri·o) *n.m.* will; free will.
albéitar (al'βei·tar) *n.m.* veterinarian.
alberca (al'βer·ka) *n.f.* cistern.
albérchigo (al'βer·tʃi·ɣo) *n.m.* 1, clingstone (peach). 2, tree producing this fruit.
albergar (al·βer'ɣar) *v.t.* [*pres. subjve.* **albergue** (–'βer·ɣe); *pret.* **albergué** (-'ɣe)] to harbor; shelter.
albergue (al'βer·ɣe) *n.m.* 1, shelter; lodging; inn. 2, lair.
albino (al'βi·no) *adj.* & *n.m.* albino. —**albinismo** (–'nis·mo) *n.m.* albinism.
albo ('al·βo) *adj. poet.* white.
albóndiga (al'βon·di·ɣa) *n.f.* meatball; fishball.
albondigón (al·βon·di'ɣon) *n.m.* hamburger.
albor (al'βor) *n.m.* 1, *usu.pl.* beginning. 2, dawn. 3, *poet.* whiteness.
alborada (al·βo'ra·ða) *n.f.* 1, dawn. 2, morning song. 3, reveille.
alborear (al·βo·re'ar) *v.i.* to dawn.
albornoz (al·βor'noθ; –'nos) *n.m.* 1, burnoose. 2, terry cloth. 3, bathrobe (*of terry cloth*).
alborotar (al·βo·ro'tar) *v.t.* to excite; to arouse; to agitate. —*v.i.* to make noise; to cause a disturbance; to riot. —**alborotarse,** *v.r.* 1, to get excited. 2, to riot. 3, (*of the sea*) to become rough. —**alborotadizo,** *adj.* excitable; restless. —**alborotado,** *adj.* rash; rough (*of the sea*).
alboroto (al·βo'ro·to) *n.m.* disturbance; tumult; riot.
alborozo (al·βo'ro·θo; –so) *n.m.* joy; exultation. —**alborozar,** *v.t.* [*pres.subjve.* **alboroce** (–'ro·θe; –se); *pret.* **alborocé** (–'θe; –'se)] to cheer; fill with joy.
albricias (al'βri·θjas; –sjas) *n.f. pl.* & *interj.* congratulations.
album ('al·βum) *n.m.* album.
albumen (al'βu·men) *n.m.* albumen.
albúmina (al'βu·mi·na) *n.f.* albumin.
albur (al'βur) *n.m.* chance; risk. —**correr un albur,** to take a chance.
alca ('al·ka) *n.f.* auk.
alcachofa (al·ka'tʃo·fa) *n.f.* artichoke. *Also,* **alcacil** (–'θil; –'sil) *n.m.*
alcahueta (al·ka'we·ta) *n.f.* 1, bawd; procuress. 2, *fem. of* alcahuete.
alcahuete (al·ka'we·te) *n.m.* 1, procurer; pander. 2, *colloq.* go-between. 3, *colloq.* meddler. 4, *colloq.* gossip.
alcahuetear (al·ka·we·te'ar) *v.t.* 1, to procure. 2, to pander to. —*v.i.* 1, to pander. 2, *colloq.* to act as go-between.
alcahuetería (al·ka·we·te'ri·a) *n.f.* 1, pandering; procuring. 2, chicanery. 3, malicious gossip.
alcaide (al'kai·ðe) *n.m.* warden.
alcalde (al'kal·de) *n.m.* 1, mayor. 2, justice of the peace.
alcaldesa (al·kal'de·sa) *n.f.* 1, mayor's wife. 2, mayoress.
alcaldía (al·kal'di·a) *n.f.* 1, mayoralty. 2, mayor's office. 3, city hall.
álcali ('al·ka·li) *n.m.* alkali. —**alcalinidad,** *n.f.* alkalinity. —**alcalino,** *adj.* alkaline.
alcalizar (al·ka·li'θar; –'sar) *v.t.* [*pres.subjve.* **alcalice** (–'li·θe; –se); *pret.* **alcalicé** (–'θe; –'se)] to alkalize. —**alcalización,** *n.f.* alkalization.
alcaloide (al·ka'loi·ðe) *n.m.* alkaloid.
alcance (al'kan·θe; –se) *n.m.* 1, reach; scope; range (*of a gun*). 2, *comm.* balance due. 3, *usu.pl.* capacity; capability. 4, import; significance. 5, latest news. —**al alcance de,** within reach of. —**dar alcance a,** to overtake.
alcancía (al·kan'θi·a; –'si·a) *n.f.* 1, child's bank; piggy bank. 2, *Amer.* poorbox.
alcanfor (al·kan'for) *n.m.* camphor. —**alcanforado,** *adj.* camphorated. —**alcanforero,** *n.m.* camphor tree.

alcantarilla (al·kan·ta'ri·ʎa; –ja) *n.f.* 1, culvert. 2, sewer. —**alcantarillado,** *n.m.* sewerage; sewer system.
alcanzado (al·kan'θa·ðo; -'sa·ðo) *adj.* needy; in financial straits.
alcanzar (al·kan'θar; –'sar) *v.t.* [*pres.subjve.* **alcance** (–'kan·θe; –se); *pret.* **alcancé** (–'θe; –'se)] 1, to overtake. 2, to reach. 3, to attain. 4, to manage; succeed in doing. 5, to reach for; get. —*v.i.* 1, to reach. 2, to be sufficient.
alcaparra (al·ka'pa·rra) *n.f.* 1, caper bush. 2, caper.
alcaravea (al·ka·ra'βe·a) *n.f.* caraway.
alcatraz (al·ka'traθ; –'tras) *n.m.* pelican.
alcaudón (al·kau'ðon) *n.m.* shrike.
alcayata (al·ka'ja·ta) *n.f.* hook; spike.
alcázar (al'ka·θar; –sar) *n.m.* 1, royal palace; castle. 2, *naut.* quarterdeck. 3, fortress.
alce ('al·θe; –se) *n.m.* 1, moose; elk. 2, *cards* raise. 3, *cards* cut.
alce ('al·θe; –se) *v., pres.subjve. of* **alzar.**
alcé (al'θe; –'se) *v., 1st pers.sing. pret. of* **alzar.**
alcista (al'θis·ta; –'sis·ta) *n.m.* & *f., finance* bull. —*adj.* bullish.
alcoba (al'ko·βa) *n.f.* 1, bedroom. 2, alcove.
alcohol (al'kol) *n.m.* alcohol. —**alcohólico,** *adj.* & *n.m.* alcoholic. —**alcoholismo,** *n.m.* alcoholism.
Alcorán (al·ko'ran) *n.m.* (the) Koran.
alcornoque (al·kor'no·ke) *n.m.* 1, cork tree. 2, blockhead.
alcurnia (al'kur·nja) *n.f.* lineage; ancestry.
alcuza (al'ku·θa; –sa) *n.f.* oil can.
aldaba (al'da·βa) *n.f.* 1, door knocker. 2, hasp. —**aldabilla,** *n.f.* latch.
aldea (al'de·a) *n.f.* village; hamlet. —**aldeano,** *n.m.* villager. —*adj.* & *n.m.* rustic; hick.
aldehido (al·de'i·ðo) *n.m.* aldehyde.
aldehuela (al·de'we·la) *n.f.* tiny village; hamlet.
alderredor (al·de·rre'ðor) *adv.* = **alrededor.**
alear (a·le'ar) *v.t.* to alloy. —**aleación,** *n.f.* alloy.
aleccionar (a·lek·θjo'nar; -sjo·'nar) *v.t.* to brief; coach; instruct.
aledaño (a·le'ða·ɲo) *adj.* bordering; outlying. —*n.m., usu.pl.* 1, environs; outskirts. 2, limits.
alegación (a·le·ɣa'θjon; –'sjon) *n.f.* allegation.
alegar (a·le'ɣar) *v.t.* [*pres.subjve.* **alegue** (–'le·ɣe); *pret.* **alegué** (–'ɣe)] 1, to allege. 2, to invoke; cite. 3, to argue; plead. —*v.i., Amer.* to quarrel; dispute.
alegato (a·le'ɣa·to) *n.m.* 1, *law* brief; plea. 2, argument; reasoning. 3, *Amer.* dispute; quarrel.
alegoría (a·le·ɣo'ri·a) *n.f.* allegory. —**alegórico** (–'ɣo·ri·ko) *adj.* allegoric.
alegrar (a·le'ɣrar) *v.t.* 1, to gladden; to enliven. 2, *fig.* to brighten. —**alegrarse,** *v.r.* 1, to rejoice; to be glad. 2, *colloq.* to get tipsy.
alegre (a'le·ɣre) *adj.* 1, gay. 2, *colloq.* tipsy.
alegría (a·le'ɣri·a) *n.f.* gaiety; cheer.
alegro (a'le·ɣro) *n.m.* & *adj. music* allegro.
alegrón (a·le'ɣron) *n.m., colloq.* thrill.
alejamiento (a·le·xa'mjen·to) *n.m.* 1, drawing apart. 2, *fig.* estrangement.
alejar (a·le'xar) *v.t.* 1, to separate; estrange. 2, to put further apart. —**alejarse,** *v.r.* to draw away.
alelar (a·le'lar) *v.t.* to daze. —**alelado,** *adj.* dazed; aghast.
alelí (a·le'li) *n.m.* = **alhelí.**
aleluya (a·le'lu·ja) *n.f.* & *interj.* hallelujah; alleluia. —**aleluyas,** *n.f.pl.* doggerel (*sing.*)
alemán (a·le'man) *adj.* & *n.m.* German.
alentado (a·len'ta·ðo) *adj.* 1, courageous; spirited. 2, hardy; resistant. 3, presumptuous.
alentar (a·len'tar) *v.t.* [*pres.ind.* **aliento** (a'ljen·to); *pres.subjve.* **aliente** (–te)] to encourage; to cheer. —**alentada,** *n.f.* long breath. —**alentador,** *adj.* encouraging; cheering.
alerce (a'ler·θe; –se) *n.m.* larch.
alergia (a'ler·xja) *n.f.* allergy. —**alergeno** (–'xe·no) *n.m.* allergen. —**alérgico** (–xi·ko) *adj.* allergic.
alero (a'le·ro) *n.m.* eaves (*pl.*).
alerón (a·le'ron) *n.m.* aileron.
alerta (a'ler·ta) *adv.* on the alert.

—*interj.* look out!; watch out! —*n.m.* alarm; alert. —**alertar,** *v.t.* to alert.
alerto (a'ler·to) *adj.* alert.
alesna (a'les·na) *n.f.* awl.
aleta (a'le·ta) *n.f.* **1,** small wing. **2,** fin. **3,** blade (of a propeller or blower). —**aletazo,** *n.m.* flap (with a wing).
aletargado (a·le·tar'ɣa·ðo) *adj.* lethargic. —**aletargarse,** *v.r.* to become lethargic.
aletear (a·le·te'ar) *v.i.* to flutter. —**aleteo** (–'te·o) *n.m.* fluttering.
aleve (a'le·βe) *adj.* = **alevoso.**
alevosía (a·le·βo'si·a) *n.f.* perfidy; treachery. —**alevoso,** *adj.* treacherous; perfidious.
alfa ('al·fa) *n.f.* alpha.
alfabetizar (al·fa·βe·ti'θar; -'sar) *v.t.* [*pres.subjve.* **alfabetice** (–'ti·θe; –se); *pret.* **alfabeticé** (–'θe; –'se)] to alphabetize.
alfabeto (al·fa'βe·to) *n.m.* alphabet. —**alfabético** (–'βe·ti·ko) *adj.* alphabetical.
alfajor (al·fa'xor) *n.m.* a name given to various types of pastry, usu. with a cream or honey filling.
alfalfa (al'fal·fa) *n.f.* alfalfa. —**alfalfar,** *n.m.* alfalfa field.
alfanje (al'fan·xe) *n.m.* cutlass.
alfarda (al'far·ða) *n.f.* joist; light beam.
alfarería (al·fa·re'ri·a) *n.f.* **1,** pottery. **2,** potter's shop. —**alfarero,** *n.m.* potter.
alfeñicarse (al·fe·ɲi'kar·se) *v.r.* [*infl.:* **tocar**] **1,** to become thin. **2,** to be or become squeamish.
alfeñique (al·fe'ɲi·ke) *n.m.* **1,** sugar paste. **2,** thin, gaunt person. **3,** squeamishness.
alférez (al'fe·reθ; –res) *n.m.* **1,** *naval* ensign. **2,** *mil.* second lieutenant. —**alférez de navío,** naval lieutenant (j.g.).
alfil (al'fil) *n.m., chess* bishop.
alfiler (al·fi'ler) *n.m.* **1,** common pin. **2,** brooch. —**alfileres,** *n.m.pl.* pin money. —**de veinticinco alfileres; con todos sus alfileres,** *colloq.* in one's best bib and tucker.
alfilerazo (al·fi·le'ra·θo; –so) *n.m.* pinprick.
alfiletero (al·fi·le'te·ro) *n.m.* pincushion.
alfombra (al'fom·bra) *n.f.* carpet; rug. —**alfombrado,** *n.m.* carpeting. —**alfombrar,** *v.t.* to carpet.
alfombrilla (al·fom'bri·ʎa; –ja) *n.f.* **1,** small rug; mat. **2,** German measles.
alfóncigo (al'fon·θi·ɣo; -si·ɣo) *n.m.* pistachio.
alforfón (al·for'fon) *n.m.* buckwheat.
alforja (al'for·xa) *n.f.* **1,** *usu.pl.* saddlebag. **2,** knapsack. **3,** provisions for a journey. —**pasarse a la otra alforja,** *Amer.* to overstep one's bounds.
alforza (al'for·θa; –sa) *n.f.* hem; tuck. —**alforzar,** *v.t.* [*infl.:* **rezar**] to tuck.
alga ('al·ɣa) *n.f.* alga; seaweed.
algarabía (al·ɣa·ra'βi·a) *n.f.* **1,** jargon; gibberish. **2,** *colloq.* uproar.
algarroba (al·ɣa'rro·βa) *n.f.* carob bean; St.-John's-bread.
algarrobo (al·ɣa'rro·βo) *n.m., also,* **algarrobera** (–'βe·ra) *n.f.* carob tree.
algazara (al·ɣa'θa·ra; –'sa·ra) *n.f.* din; uproar.
álgebra ('al·xe·βra) *n.f.* algebra. —**algebraico** (–'βrai·ko) *adj.* algebraic.
algo ('al·ɣo) *indef.pron.* something. —*adv.* somewhat; rather. —**algo es algo,** every little bit counts. —**algo por el estilo,** something of the sort.
algodón (al·ɣo'ðon) *n.m.* **1,** cotton. **2,** cotton plant. —**algodonal,** *n.m.* cotton plantation. —**algodonar,** *v.t.* to stuff with cotton. —**algodonoso,** *adj.* cottony. —**algodón en rama,** raw cotton.
algodonero (al·ɣo·ðo'ne·ro) *adj.* of or pert. to cotton. —*n.m.* **1,** cotton plant. **2,** cotton trader.
alguacil (al·ɣwa'θil; –'sil) *n.m.* bailiff; constable.
alguien ('al·ɣjen) *indef. pron.* someone; anyone.
algún (al'ɣun) *adj.* = **alguno** *before a masc. noun.*
alguno (al'ɣu·no) *adj.* some; any; —*pron.* someone; something. —**alguna que otra vez,** once in a while. —**alguno que otro,** a few.
alhaja (a'la·xa) *n.f.* **1,** jewel; gem. **2,** *colloq., ironic* sly one; fine one. —**alhajar,** *v.t.* to bejewel.
alharaca (a·la'ra·ka) *n.f., usu.pl.* fuss; ado; ballyhoo. —**alharaquiento** (-'kjen·to) fussy; overdemonstrative.
alhelí *also,* **alelí** (a·le'li) *n.m.* gillyflower.

alheña (a'le·ɲa) *n.f.* henna. —**alheñar,** *v.t.* to henna.
alianza (a'ljan·θa; –sa) *n.f.* alliance.
aliarse (a'ljar·se) *v.r.* [*infl.:* **enviar**] to ally (oneself); become allied. —**aliado,** *adj.* allied. —*n.m.* ally.
alias ('a·ljas) *n.m.* alias.
alicaído (a·li·ka'i·ðo) *adj., colloq.* crestfallen; downhearted.
alicates (a·li'ka·tes) *n.m.pl.* pliers.
aliciente (a·li'θjen·te; –'sjen·te) *n.m.* incentive; inducement.
-alidad (a·li'ðað) *suffix* -ality; *forming nouns denoting* quality; condition: *racionalidad,* rationality.
alienable (a·lje'na·βle) *adj.* alienable.
alienación (a·lje·na'θjon; -'sjon) *n.f., law; med.* alienation.
alienista (a·lje'nis·ta) *n.m.* & *f.* alienist.
aliento (a'ljen·to) *n.m.* 1, breath. 2, encouragement. 3, courage.
aligerar (a·li·xe'rar) *v.t.* 1, to lighten. 2, to ease; to mitigate. —*v.i., colloq.* to hurry; to hasten. —**aligerar el paso,** to hurry.
alijar (a·li'xar) *v.t.* 1, to unload; lighten. 2, to gin (cotton). —**alijadora,** *n.f.* cotton gin.
alijo (a'li·xo) *n.m.* 1, smuggling. 2, contraband.
alimaña (a·li'ma·ɲa) *n.f.* animal pest; varmint.
alimentar (a·li·men'tar) *v.t.* 1, to feed; to nourish. 2, *fig.* to foster; to encourage. —**alimentarse,** *v.r.* to feed oneself. —**alimentación,** *n.f.* feeding; nourishment.
alimenticio (a·li·men'ti·θjo; –sjo) *adj.* 1, nourishing; nutritious. 2, alimentary.
alimento (a·li'men·to) *n.m.* 1, nourishment; food. 2, *pl.* allowance (*sing.*); pension (*sing.*); alimony (*sing.*).
alindar (a·lin'dar) *v.t.* 1, to mark off; limit. 2, to adorn; beautify.
alinear (a·li·ne'ar) *v.t.* to align. —**alinearse,** *v.r.* to line up; fall into line. —**alineación,** *n.f., also,* **alineamiento,** *n.m.* alignment.
aliñar (a·li'ɲar) *v.t.* 1, to dress *or* season (food). 2, to adorn. —**aliño** (a'li·ɲo) *n.m.* seasoning; dressing.
alisar (a·li'sar) *v.t.* to smooth.
alisios (a'li·sjos) *n.m.pl.* trade winds.
aliso (a'li·so) *n.m., bot.* alder.
alistamiento (a·lis·ta'mjen·to) *n.m.* 1, listing. 2, enlistment; recruitment.
alistar (a·lis'tar) *v.t.* 1, to make ready; prepare. 2, to list; enter in a list. —**alistarse,** *v.r.* to enlist.
aliteración (a·li·te·ra'θjon; -'sjon) *n.f.* alliteration. —**aliterado** (-'ra·ðo) *adj.* alliterative.
aliviar (a·li'βjar) *v.t.* to relieve; mitigate. —**aliviarse,** *v.r.* to be soothed or relieved. —**alivio** (a'li·βjo) *n.m.* relief.
aljaba (al'xa·βa) *n.f.* quiver (*for arrows*).
aljibe (al'xi·βe) *n.m.* 1, cistern. 2, *naut.* water tender.
alma ('al·ma) *n.f.* 1, soul. 2, core. 3, web (*of a beam*). 4, *fig.* spirit; heart. 5, bore (*of a gun*). —**alma de Dios,** simple soul. —**caérsele el alma a los pies,** to be deeply disappointed. —**volverle a uno el alma al cuerpo,** to recover, as from fear.
almacén (al·ma'θen; –'sen) *n.m.* 1, warehouse. 2, wholesale store. 3, department store. 4, *Amer.* general store. —**almacén de víveres,** grocery.
almacenar (al·ma·θe'nar; -se·'nar) *v.t.* to store. —**almacenaje,** *n.m.* storage.
almacenero (al·ma·θe'ne·ro; -se·'ne·ro) *n.m., So. Amer.* storekeeper.
almacenista (al·ma·θe'nis·ta; –se'nis·ta) *n.m.* & *f.* 1, wholesale merchant. 2, *Amer.* salesman in a wholesale store. 3, *Amer.* storekeeper.
almácigo (al'ma·θi·ɣo; –si·ɣo) *n.m.* mastic tree. —**almáciga,** *n.f.* mastic.
almadía (al·ma'ði·a) *n.f.* raft.
almagre (al'ma·ɣre) *n.m.* red ocher.
almanaque (al·ma'na·ke) *n.m.* almanac; calendar.
almeja (al'me·xa) *n.f.* clam.
almena (al'me·na) *n.f.* battlement.
almenado (al·me'na·ðo) *adj.* crenelated; embattled. —*n.m.* [*also,* **almenaje**] battlements (*pl.*).
almendra (al'men·dra) *n.f.* almond. —**almendro,** *n.m.* almond tree.
almendrado (al·men'dra·ðo) *adj.* almond-shaped. —*n.m.* macaroon.

almiar (al'mjar) *n.m.* haystack; hayrick.
almíbar (al'mi·βar) *n.m.* sugar syrup.
almibarar (al·mi·βa'rar) *v.t.* to candy; sugar-coat.
almidón (al·mi'ðon) *n.m.* starch. —**almidonar,** *v.t.* to starch.
almidonado (al·mi·ðo'na·ðo) *adj.* **1,** starched. **2,** *fig.* stiff; dressed with affectation.
alminar (al·mi'nar) *n.m.* minaret.
almirante (al·mi'ran·te) *n.m.* admiral. —**almiranta,** *n.f.* vice-admiral's ship. —**almirantazgo,** *n.m.* admiralty.
almizcle (al'miθ·kle; –'mis·kle) *n.m.* musk. —**almizcleño,** *adj.* musky.
almizclero (al·miθ'kle·ro; al·mis–) *n.m.* musk deer. —*adj.* **1,** musky. **2,** musk (*attrib.*). —**almizclera,** *n.f.* [*also,* **rata almizclera**] muskrat.
almohada (al·mo'a·ða) *n.f.* pillow.
almohadilla (al·mo·a'ði·ʎa; –ja) *n.f.* **1,** small pillow. **2,** cushion. **3,** pad.
almohadón (al·mo·a'ðon) *n.m.* cushion.
almohaza (al·mo'a·θa; –sa) *n.f.* currycomb. —**almohazador,** *n.m.* groom. —**almohazar,** *v.t.* to curry.
almoneda (al·mo'ne·ða) *n.f.* **1,** public auction. **2,** clearance sale. —**almonedear,** *v.t.* to auction.
almorranas (al·mo'rra·nas) *n.f.pl.* hemorrhoids; piles.
almorzar (al·mor'θar; –'sar) *v.i.* [*pres.ind.* **almuerzo** (–'mwer·θo; –so); *pres.subjve.* **almuerce** (–θe; –se); *pret.* **almorcé** (–'θe; –'se)] to lunch. —*v.t.* to eat for lunch.
almuédano (al'mwe·ða·no) *n.m.* muezzin. *Also,* **almuecín** (–'θin; –'sin).
almuerzo (al'mwer·θo; –so) *n.m.* lunch.
alo- (a·lo) *prefix* allo-; divergency; alternative: *alopatía,* allopathy.
alocar (a·lo'kar) *v.t.* [*pres.subjve.* **aloque** (a'lo·ke); *pret.* **aloqué** (–'ke)] to drive mad. —**alocado,** *adj.* reckless; wild.
alocución (a·lo·ku'θjon; –'sjon) *n.f.* brief speech; talk.
áloe ('a·lo·e) *n.m.* **1,** aloe. **2,** aloes.
aloja (a'lo·xa) *n.f.* mead.
alojamiento (a·lo·xa'mjen·to) *n.m.* **1,** lodging. **2,** *mil.* quarters.
alojar (a·lo'xar) *v.t.* **1,** to lodge. **2,** to station (troops). —**alojarse,** *v.r.* to take lodgings.
alón (a'lon) *n.m.* plucked wing of a bird.
alondra (a'lon·dra) *n.f., ornith.* lark.
alopatía (a·lo·pa'ti·a) *n.f.* allopathy. —**alopático** (–'pa·ti·ko) *adj.* allopathic.
alotropía (a·lo·tro'pi·a) *n.f.* allotropy. —**alotrópico** (-'tro·pi·ko) *adj.* allotropic. —**alótropo** (a'lo·tro·po) *n.m.* allotrope.
alpaca (al'pa·ka) *n.f.* alpaca.
alpargata (al·par'ɣa·ta) *n.f.* a sandal with hemp sole.
alpinismo (al·pi'nis·mo) *n.m.* alpinism; mountain-climbing. —**alpinista,** *n.m.* & *f.* alpinist; mountain-climber.
alpino (al'pi·no) *adj.* alpine. *Also,* **alpestre** (al'pes·tre).
alpiste (al'pis·te) *n.m.* canary seed. —**dejar a uno alpiste,** to disappoint; to leave out (of plans, etc.).
alquería (al·ke'ri·a) *n.f.* farmhouse.
alquilar (al·ki'lar) *v.t.* to let; to rent; to hire.
alquiler (al·ki'ler) *n.m.* **1,** rent. **2,** leasing. —**de alquiler,** for rent *or* hire.
alquimia (al'ki·mja) *n.f.* alchemy. —**alquimista** (–'mis·ta) *n.m.* alchemist.
alquitrán (al·ki'tran) *n.m.* tar; coal tar. —**alquitranar,** *v.t.* to tar.
alrededor (al·re·ðe'ðor) *adv.* around. —**alrededores,** *n.m.pl.* environs. —**alrededor de,** around, about.
alta ('al·ta) *n.f.* **1,** discharge, esp. from a hospital. **2,** enrollment. —**dar de alta,** to discharge, esp. from a hospital. —**darse de alta,** to join (an organization).
altamente (al·ta'men·te) *adv.* highly.
altanería (al·ta·ne'ri·a) *n.f.* haughtiness; arrogance. —**altanero** (-'ne·ro) haughty; arrogant.
altar (al'tar) *n.m.* altar.
altavoz (al·ta'βoθ; –'βos) *n.m.* loudspeaker.
altea (al'te·a) *n.f.* marsh mallow.
alteración (al·te·ra'θjon; -'sjon) *n.f.* **1,** alteration; change. **2,** disturbance; agitation.
alterar (al·te'rar) *v.t.* **1,** to alter. **2,** to disturb; upset. —**alterarse,**

v.r. to become upset; become irritated.
altercar (al·ter'kar) *v.i.* [*pres. subjve.* **alterque** (-'ter·ke); *pret.* **alterqué** (-'ke)] to wrangle; altercate. —**altercado,** *n.m., also,* **altercación,** *n.f.* wrangle; altercation.
alternador (al·ter·na'ðor) *n.m.* alternator.
alternar (al·ter'nar) *v.t.* & *i.* to alternate. —**alternarse,** *v.r.* to take turns. —**alternar con, 1,** to associate with. **2,** to compete with.
alternativa (al·ter·na'ti·βa) *n.f.* **1,** alternative. **2,** *sports* initiation of a bullfighter. **3,** *pl.,colloq.* ups and downs. —**alternativo,** *adj.* alternate.
alterno (al'ter·no) *adj.* **1,** alternate. **2,** alternating.
alteza (al'te·θa; –sa) *n.f.* Highness.
alti- (al·ti) *prefix* alti-; high; height: *altímetro,* altimeter.
altibajos (al·ti'βa·xos) *n.m.pl.* ups and downs.
altillo (al'ti·ʎo; –jo) *n.m.* **1,** hillock. **2,** *So.Amer.* attic.
altímetro (al'ti·me·tro) *n.m.,* altimeter.
altiplano (al·ti'pla·no) *n.m., also,* **altiplanicie** (–'ni·θje; –sje) *n.f.* high plateau.
altísimo (al'ti·si·mo) *adj., superl. of* **alto.** —*n.m., cap.* Most High; God.
altisonante (al·ti·so'nan·te) *adj.* high-sounding; highflown. —**altisonancia,** *n.f.* highflown language.
altísono (al'ti·so·no) *adj.* high-sounding.
altitud (al·ti'tuð) *n.f.* altitude.
altivo (al'ti·βo) *adj.* haughty; proud. —**altivez** (–'βeθ; –'βes) *n.f.* haughtiness; pride.
alto ('al·to) *adj.* **1,** high; tall. **2,** loud. —*n.m.* **1,** height. **2,** *pl., Amer.* top floor. **3,** *Amer.* pile; bunch. —*adj.* & *n.m., music* alto. —*adv.* **1,** high. **2,** loud; loudly. —**altas horas,** late hours. —**pasar por alto,** to overlook.
alto ('al·to) *n.m.* halt. —*interj.* halt! —**hacer alto,** to stop; halt.
alto- (al·to) *prefix* alto-; high; height: *alto-cúmulo,* alto-cumulus.
altoparlante (al·to·par'lan·te) *n.m., Amer.* loudspeaker.
altozano (al·to'θa·no; –'sa·no) *n.m.* **1,** hillock. **2,** elevation; high place.
altruismo (al·tru'is·mo) *n.m.* altruism. —**altruísta,** *n.m.* & *f.* altruist. —*adj.* altruistic.
altura (al'tu·ra) *n.f.* **1,** height. **2,** *often pl.* stage; point; level. **3,** latitude. —**estar a la altura de,** to measure up to; be equal to.
alucinar (a·lu·θi'nar; –si'nar) *v.t.* **1,** to delude. **2,** to fascinate. —**alucinarse,** *v.r.* to delude oneself. —**alucinación,** *n.f.* hallucination.
alud (a'luð) *n.m.* avalanche.
aludir (a·lu'ðir) *v.i.* to allude.
alumbramiento (a·lum·bra·'mjen·to) *n.m.* **1,** childbirth. **2,** lightning.
alumbrar (a·lum'brar) *v.t.* **1,** to light. **2,** *fig.* to enlighten. —*v.i.* to give birth. —**alumbrarse,** *v.r.* **1,** to light one's way. **2,** *slang* to get tipsy. —**alumbrado,** *adj.* lighted; lit. —*n.m.* lighting system.
alumbre (a'lum·bre) *n.m.* alum.
alúmina (a'lu·mi·na) *n.f.* alumina.
aluminio (a·lu'mi·njo) *n.m.* aluminum.
alumna (a'lum·na) *n.f.* pupil.
alumnado (a·lum'na·ðo) *n.m.* **1,** student body. **2,** boarding school.
alumno (a'lum·no) *n.m.* pupil.
alusión (a·lu'sjon) *n.f.* allusion. —**alusivo** (–'si·βo) *adj.* allusive.
aluvión (a·lu'βjon) *n.m.* **1,** alluvium. **2,** freshet. —**aluvial,** *adj.* alluvial.
alvéolo (al'βe·o·lo) *n.m.* alveolus. —**alveolar,** *adj.* alveolar.
alza ('al·θa; –sa) *n.f.* **1,** rise. **2,** rear sight (*of a firearm*). **3,** *print.* overlay. —**jugar al alza,** to buy on margin.
alzada (al'θa·ða; al'sa–) *n.f.* **1,** height (of a horse). **2,** *law* appeal. **3,** *archit.* front elevation.
alzado (al'θa·ðo; al'sa-) *adj.* **1,** insurgent. **2,** *Amer.* haughty; proud. **3,** *Amer.* in heat; in rut. **4,** *Amer.* gone wild, as an animal.
alzamiento (al·θa'mjen·to) *n.m.* **1,** rise in prices. **2,** overbid. **3,** rebellion.
alzar (al'θar; –'sar) *v.t.* [*pres. subjve.* **alce;** *pret.* **alcé**] **1,** to raise; lift. **2,** to erect. **3,** to elevate (the Host). **4,** to cut (cards). —**alzarse,** *v.r.* **1,** to rise in revolt. **2,** to make a fraudulent bankruptcy. **3,** to abscond. —**alzar el codo,** to drink heavily. —**alzar el vuelo,** to take to flight.

allá (a'ʎa; a'ja) *adv.* **1,** there; yonder; far away. **2,** long ago. —**allá él (ella; Vd.),** that's his (her, your) concern. —**allá voy,** I'm coming. —**el más allá,** the beyond. —**más allá,** farther.

-alla ('a·ʎa; –ja) *suffix, forming collective nouns: vitualla,* victuals; *canalla,* populace.

allanamiento (a·ʎa·na'mjen·to; a·ja–) *n.m.* **1,** razing; leveling. **2,** acquiescence. **3,** incursion; irruption. —**allanamiento de morada,** housebreaking.

allanar (a·ʎa'nar; a·ja–) *v.t.* **1,** to raze; to level. **2,** to overcome (a difficulty). —**allanarse,** *v.r.* to acquiesce. —**allanar el camino,** to pave the way.

allegado (a·ʎe'ɣa·ðo; a·je–) *adj.* close; near. —*n.m.* **1,** close friend *or* relative. **2,** follower; devotee. —**allegarse,** *v.r.* to become close or intimate.

allende (a'ʎen·de; a'jen–) *adv.* beyond. —**allende los mares,** overseas; abroad.

allí (a'ʎi; -'ji) *adv.* there; right there. —**por allí,** that way; through there.

ama ('a·ma) *n.f.* **1,** mistress (of a household). **2,** owner; landlady. —**ama de leche** (*or* **de cría** *or* **de teta**) wet nurse. —**ama de llaves,** housekeeper. —**ama seca,** governess; nanny.

amable (a'ma·βle) *adj.* amiable; kind; good. —**amabilidad,** *n.f.* amiability; kindness; goodness.

amachado (a·ma'tʃa·ðo) *adj.* **1,** manly; virile. **2,** (*of a woman*) mannish.

amachetear (a·ma·tʃe·te'ar) *v.t.* = **machetear.**

amado (a'ma·ðo) *adj. & n.m.* beloved.

amaestrar (a·ma·es'trar) *v.t.* **1,** to train. **2,** to tame; to break (a horse). —**amaestrado,** *adj.* trained.

amagar (a·ma'ɣar) *v.t. & i.* **1,** to feint. **2,** to threaten. **3,** to feign.

amago (a'ma·ɣo) *n.m.* **1,** feint. **2,** indication; sign. **3,** threat.

amainar (a·mai'nar) *v.i.* to subside. —*v.t.* to take in; lower (sails).

amalgama (a·mal'ɣa·ma) *n.f.* amalgam. —**amalgamación,** *n.f.* amalgamation. —**amalgamar,** *v.t.* to amalgamate.

amamantar (a·ma·man'tar) *v.t.* to suckle.

amanecer (a·ma·ne'θer; –'ser) *v.i.* [*pres.ind.* **amanezco** (–'neθ·ko; –'nes·ko) *pres.subjve.* **amanezca** (-ka)] **1,** to dawn. **2,** to arrive or appear at dawn. —*n.m.* dawn.

amanecida (a·ma·ne'θi·ða; -'si·ða) *n.f.* daybreak; dawn.

amanerarse (a·ma·ne'rar·se) *v.r.* to adopt mannerisms *or* affectations. —**amanerado,** *adj.* affected; artificial. —**amaneramiento,** *n.m.* affectation; mannerism.

amansar (a·man'sar) *v.t.* to tame.

amante (a'man·te) *n.m.* lover. —*n.f.* mistress. —*adj.* loving.

amanuense (a·ma'nwen·se) *n.m. & f.* amanuensis.

amañado (a·ma'ɲa·ðo) *adj.* **1,** clever; cunning. **2,** contrived; spurious. **3,** inured; habituated.

amañarse (a·ma'ɲar·se) *v.r.* **1,** to contrive. **2,** to become inured or habituated.

amaño (a'ma·ɲo) *n.m.* **1,** cleverness; cunning. **2,** *pl.* tools; instruments. **3,** *often pl.* machinations; intrigue.

amapola (a·ma'po·la) *n.f.* poppy.

amar (a'mar) *v.t. & i.* to love. —**amarse,** *v.r.* to love each other; be in love.

amaranto (a·ma'ran·to) *n.m.* amaranth.

amargar (a·mar'ɣar) *v.t.* [*pres. subjve.* **amargue** (–'mar·ɣe); *pret.* **amargué** (–'ɣe)] to make bitter. —**amargarse,** *v.r.* to become bitter. —**amargado,** *adj.* embittered.

amargo (a'mar·ɣo) *adj.* bitter. —*n.m.* bitterness. —**amargos,** *n.m. pl.* bitters.

amargor (a·mar'ɣor) *n.m.* **1,** bitterness. **2,** sorrow. *Also,* **amargura** (–'ɣu·ra) *n.f.*

amarilis (a·ma'ri·lis) *n.f.* amaryllis.

amarillear (a·ma·ri·ʎe'ar; -je·'ar) *v.t.* to color yellow. —*v.i.* to yellow; become yellow.

amarillo (a·ma'ri·ʎo; –jo) *adj.* yellow. —**amarillento,** *adj.* yellowish.

amarra (a'ma·rra) *n.f.* **1,** tie; fastening. **2,** *naut.* hawser; cable; *pl.* moorings.

amarradero (a·ma·rra'ðe·ro) *n.m.* **1,** hitching post. **2,** *naut.* mooring; dock; berth.

amarrar (a·ma'rrar) *v.t.* **1,** to

fasten; tie; bind. 2, *also intr.* to moor.
amarre (a'ma·rre) *n.m.* 1, fastening; binding. 2, mooring. 3, moorage.
amarrete (a·ma'rre·te) *adj., Amer.* tight; stingy. —*n.m.* tightwad.
amartillar (a·mar·ti'ʎar; –'jar) *v.t.* 1, to hammer. 2, to cock (a gun).
amasar (a·ma'sar) *v.t.* 1, to knead. 2, to amass. 3, to concoct.
amasijo (a·ma'si·xo) *n.m.* 1, dough. 2, kneading. 3, mess; hodgepodge. 4, plot; intrigue.
amatista (a·ma'tis·ta) *n.f.* amethyst.
amatorio (a·ma'to·rjo) *adj.* amatory.
amazacotado (a·ma·θa·ko'ta·ðo; a·ma·sa-) *adj.* 1, thick; heavy; lumpy. 2, clumsy (*as of style*); heavy-handed.
amazona (a·ma'θo·na; –'so·na) *n.f.* 1, amazon. 2, horsewoman; equestrienne; 3, woman's riding habit.
ambages (am'ba·xes) *n.m.pl.* circumlocution (*sing.*); ambiguity (*sing.*). —**sin ambages,** to the point.
ámbar ('am·bar) *n.m.* amber. —**ambarino,** *adj.* amber. —**ámbar gris,** ambergris.
ambas ('am·bas) *adj., fem. of* **ambos.**
ambi- (am·bi) *prefix* ambi-. 1, both; on both sides: *ambivalente,* ambivalent. 2, around: *ambiente;* ambient.
ambición (am·bi'θjon; -'sjon) *n.f.* ambition. —**ambicionar,** *v.t.* to covet; aspire to. —**ambicioso** (–'θjo·so; –'sjo·so) *adj.* ambitious; greedy.
ambidextro (am·bi'ðeks·tro) *adj.* ambidextrous.
ambiente (am'bjen·te) *n.m.* atmosphere; surroundings; environment. —*adj.* [*also,* **ambiental**] surrounding; environmental.
ambiguo (am'bi·ɣwo) *adj.* ambiguous. —**ambigüedad** (–ɣwe'ðað) *n.f.* ambiguity.
ámbito ('am·bi·to) *n.m.* ambit; limits (*pl.*); confines (*pl.*).
ambivalente (am·bi·βa'len·te) *adj.* ambivalent. —**ambivalencia,** *n.f.* ambivalence.
amblar (am'blar) *v.i.* to pace; amble (*as a horse*).
ambo ('am·bo) *n.m., in lotto,* a pair of numbers.
ambos ('am·bos) *adj.m.pl.* [*fem.* **ambas**] both.
ambrosía (am·bro'si·a) *n.f.* 1, ambrosia. 2, *bot.* ragweed.
ambulancia (am·bu'lan·θja; –sja) *n.f.* 1, ambulance. 2, *mil.* field hospital.
ambular (am·bu'lar) *v.i.* to wander. —**ambulante,** *adj.* roving. —**vendedor ambulante,** peddler.
ameba (a'me·βa) *n.f.* ameba. *Also,* **amiba.**
amedrentar (a·me·ðren'tar) *v.t.* to intimidate; to frighten. —**amedrentarse,** *v.r.* to become frightened.
amén (a'men) *n.m., adv. & interj.* amen. —**amén de,** besides.
-amen ('a·men) *suffix, forming nouns with collective meaning: certamen,* contest; *velamen,* rigging.
amenaza (a·me'na·θa; –sa) *n.f.* threat; menace.
amenazar (a·me·na'θar; –'sar) *v.t. & i.* [*pres.subjve.* **amenace** (–'na·θe; –se); *pret.* **amenacé** (–'θe; –'se)] to threaten. —**amenazante, amenazador,** *adj.* threatening; impending.
amenguar (a·men'gwar) *v.t.* to diminish; lessen.
ameno (a'me·no) *adj.* pleasing; agreeable. —**amenidad,** *n.f.* amenity. —**amenizar** (–ni'θar; –'sar) *v.t.* [*pres.subjve.* **amenice** (–'ni·θe; –se) *pret.* **amenicé** (–'θe; –'se)] to make pleasant.
amento (a'men·to) *n.m.* ament; catkin.
americana (a·me·ri'ka·na) *n.f.* man's jacket.
americanizar (a·me·ri·ka·ni·'θar –'sar) *v.t.* [*infl.:* **realizar**] to Americanize. —**americanización,** *n.f.* Americanization.
americano (a·me·ri'ka·no) *adj.* American. —*n.m.* 1, American. 2, Latin-American. —**americanismo,** *n.m.* Americanism. —**americanista,** *n.m. & f.* student of American languages and cultures.
americio (a·me'ri·θjo; –sjo) *n.m.* americium. *Also,* **américo** (a'me·ri·ko).
amerizar (a·me·ri'θar; –'sar) *v.t.* [*pres.subjve.* **americe** (–'ri·θe; –se); *pret.* **americé** (–'θe; –'se)] to land (an aircraft) on the water.
ametralladora (a·me·tra·ʎa·'ðo·ra; -ja'ðo·ra) *n.f.* machine gun.

—**ametrallador** (-'ðor) *n.m.* machine gunner. —**ametrallar** (–'ʎar; –'jar) *v.t.* to machine-gun.
amianto (a'mjan·to) *n.m.* asbestos.
amiba (a'mi·βa) *n.f.* = **ameba.**
-**amiento** (a'mjen·to) *suffix, form of* -**miento**: *atrincheramiento,* entrenchment.
amigdala (a'miɣ·ða·la) *n.f.* tonsil. —**amigdalitis,** *n.f.* tonsillitis.
amigo (a'mi·ɣo) *n.m.* friend; boy friend. —*adj.* friendly. —**amiga,** *n.f.* friend; girl friend. **amigable,** *adj.* friendly. —**amigote** (–'ɣo·te) *n.m.* pal; chum. —**pie de amigo,** prop; support. —**ser amigo de,** to be fond of; take to; be inclined to.
amilanar (a·mi·la'nar) *v.t.* to cow. —**amilanarse,** *v.r.* to be cowed; funk it.
amillarar (a·mi·ʎa'rar; –ja'rar) *v.t.* to assess. —**amillaramiento,** *n.m.* assessment.
aminorar (a·mi·no'rar) *v.t.* to diminish; to lessen.
amir (a'mir) *n.m.* emir.
amistad (a·mis'tað) *n.f.* **1,** friendship. **2,** friend. —**trabar amistad,** to strike up a friendship.
amistar (a·mis·'tar) *v.t.* to reconcile; restore to friendship. —*v.i.* [*also,* **amistarse,** *v.r.*] to be reconciled; resume friendly relations.
amistoso (a·mis'to·so) *adj.* friendly; amicable.
amnesia (am'ne·sja) *n.f.* amnesia. —**amnésico** (–si·ko) *adj.* & *n.m.* amnesic.
amnistía (am·nis'ti·a) *n.f.* amnesty. —**amnistiar** (–'tjar) *v.t.* to grant amnesty; to pardon.
amo ('a·mo) *n.m.* **1,** master. **2,** head of a family *or* household. **3,** owner; landlord.
amoblar (a·mo'βlar) *v.t.* [*infl.:* **poblar**] = **amueblar.**
amodorrarse (a·mo·ðo'rrar·se) *v.r.* to become drowsy. —**amodorrar,** *v.t.* to make drowsy. —**amodorrado,** *adj.* drowsy; sleepy.
amohinar (a·mo·i'nar) *v.t.* to annoy; discomfit.
amolar (a·mo'lar) *v.t.* [*pres.ind.* **amuelo;** *pres.subjve.* **amuele**] **1,** to grind; sharpen. **2,** *colloq.* to bother; annoy. —**amoladera,** *n.f.* grinder; grindstone. —**amolador,** *n.m.* grinder; one who grinds or sharpens. —*adj., colloq.* bothersome; annoying. —**amoladura,** *n.f.* grinding; sharpening. —**amoladuras,** *n.f.pl.* grit (*sing.*).
amoldar (a·mol'dar) *v.t.* to mold; fashion. -**amoldarse,** *v.r.* to adapt *or* adjust oneself.
amonestar (a·mo·nes'tar) *v.t.* to admonish. -**amonestación,** *n.f.* admonition. —**correr las amonestaciones,** to publish marriage banns.
amoníaco (a·mo'ni·a·ko) *n.m.* ammonia.
amonio (a'mo·njo) *n.m.* ammonium.
amoniuro (a·mo'nju·ro) *n.m.* ammoniate.
amontonar (a·mon·to'nar) *v.t.* to heap; to accumulate. —**amontonarse,** *v.r.* to crowd together. —**amontonamiento,** *n.m.* accumulation; gathering.
amor (a'mor) *n.m.* love. —**amores,** *n.m.pl.* love affair. —**amor patrio,** patriotism. —**amor propio,** pride; self-esteem.
amoral (a·mo'ral) *adj.* amoral. —**amoralidad,** *n.f.* amorality.
amoratado (a·mo·ra'ta·ðo) *adj.* livid; black and blue.
amoratarse (a·mo·ra'tar·se) *v.r.* **1,** to turn blue or purple, as with cold. **2,** to become black and blue, as from a blow.
amorcillo (a·mor'θi·ʎo; –'si·jo) *n.m.* **1,** flirtation. **2,** cupid figure.
amordazar (a·mor·ða'θar; -'sar) *v.t.* [*pres.subjve.* **amordace** (-'ða·θe; –se); *pret.* **amordacé** (–'θe; –'se)] to gag; muzzle.
amorfo (a'mor·fo) *adj.* amorphous; vague; shapeless.
amorío (a·mo'ri·o) *n.m., colloq.* flirtation; infatuation; love affair.
amoroso (a·mo'ro·so) *adj.* amorous.
amorrar (a·mo'rrar) *v.i.* [*also,* **amorrarse,** *v.r.*] *colloq.* to sulk.
amortajar (a·mor·ta'xar) *v.t.* to enshroud.
amortiguador (a·mor·ti·gwa·'ðor) *adj.* cushioning; softening; muffling. —*n.m.* **1,** shock absorber. **2,** muffler.
amortiguar (a·mor·ti'gwar) *v.t.* **1,** to deaden; cushion; soften. **2,** to muffle. **3,** to dim (lights). —**amortiguamiento,** *n.m., also,* **amortiguación,** *n.f.* cushioning; softening.
amortizar (a·mor·ti'θar; –'sar) *v.t.* [*pres.subjve.* **amortice** (–'ti·θe; –se); *pret.* **amorticé** (–'θe; –'se)]

amortize; to redeem. —**amortiza-n**, *n.f.* amortization.
oscarse (a·mos'kar·se) *v.r.* *fl.:* **tocar**] **1**, to be or become noyed. **2**, *Amer.* to blush; be barrassed.
ostazar (a·mos·ta'θar; –'sar) ., *colloq.* [*infl.:* **amenazar**] to irate; annoy.
otinado (a·mo·ti'na·ðo) *adj.* itinous; rebellious. —*n.m.* mutier; rebel.
otinar (a·mo·ti'nar) *v.t.* to ine to mutiny *or* riot. —**amoti-rse**, *v.r.* to mutiny; to rebel; to t. —**amotinamiento**, *n.m.* muy; riot.
parar (am·pa'rar) *v.t.* to prot; to shelter; to help. —**ampa-se**, *v.r.* to find protection. —**am-ro** (am'pa·ro) *n.m.* shelter; protion.
perímetro (am·pe'ri·me·tro) *n.* ammeter.
perio (am'pe·rjo) *n.m.* ampere.
amperaje (–'ra·xe) *n.m.* ampere.
pliar (am'pljar) *v.t.* to amplify; broaden; to extend; to enlarge. **ampliación**, *n.f.* extension; engement.
plificar (am·pli·fi'kar) *v.t.* *es.subjve.* **amplifique** (–'fi·ke); *et.* **amplifiqué** (–'ke)] to amplify. **amplificación**, *n.f.* amplification. **amplificador**, *n.m.* amplifier. *adj.* amplifying.
plio ('am·pljo) *adj.* **1**, broad. ample. **3**, generous; openhanded. broadminded.
plitud (am·pli'tuð) *n.f.* **1**, eadth. **2**, amplitude.
polla (am'po·ʎa; -ja) *n.f.* **1**, ster. **2**, decanter; cruet. —**am-llar**, *v.t.* to blister. —**ampollarse**, . to become blistered.
polleta (am·po'ʎe·ta; –'je·ta) . **1**, ampoule. **2**, hourglass. **3**, all vial.
puloso (am·pu'lo·so) *adj.* mbastic; wordy.
putar (am·pu'tar) *v.t.* to ampue. —**amputación**, *n.f.* amputation.
uchachado (a·mu·tʃa'tʃa·ðo) *.* childish.
ueblar (a·mwe'βlar) *v.t.* to nish.
uele (a'mwe·le) *v.*, *pres.subjve.* **amolar.**
uelo (a'mwe·lo) *v.*, *pres.ind.* **amolar.**

amulatado (a·mu·la'ta·ðo) *adj.* like a mulatto; having mulatto features.
amuleto (a·mu'le·to) *n.m.* amulet.
amura (a'mu·ra) *n.f.*, *naut.* **1**, tack of a sail. **2**, grommet. **3**, forepart of a ship; bow.
amurallar (a·mu·ra'ʎar; –'jar) *v.t.* to wall; surround with a wall.
amurrarse (a·mu'rrar·se) *v.r.*, *Amer.* to become glum or downcast.
an- (an) *prefix* **1**, not; without; *var. of* **a-** *before a vowel: anarquía,* anarchy. **2**, *var. of* **ana-** *before a vowel: ánodo,* anode.
-án (an) *suffix, forming nouns expressing* characteristic; relation: *holgazán,* lazy; *patán,* peasant.
ana ('a·na) *n.f.* ell (*measure*).
ana- (a·na) *prefix* ana-. **1**, up: *anatema,* anathema. **2**, back; against: *anagrama,* anagram; *anacronismo,* anachronism. **3**, again: *anabaptista,* Anabaptist. **4**, thorough: *análisis,* analysis. **5**, in accordance: *analogía,* analogy.
anabolismo (a·na·βo'lis·mo) *n.m.* anabolism. —**anabólico** (–'βo·li·ko) *adj.* anabolic.
anacardo (a·na'kar·ðo) *n.m.* cashew.
anaconda (a·na'kon·da) *n.f.* anaconda.
anacoreta (a·na·ko're·ta) *n.m.* & *f.* hermit.
anacronismo (a·na·kro'nis·mo) *n.m.* anachronism. —**anacrónico** (–'kro·ni·ko) *adj.* anachronistic.
ánade ('a·na·ðe) *n.m.* **1**, duck. **2**, any ducklike bird.
anadear (a·na·ðe'ar) *v.i.* to waddle. —**anadeo** (-'ðe·o) *n.m.* waddle.
anadeja (a·na'ðe·xa) *n.f.* duckling. **Also**, **anadino** (-'ði·no) *n.m.* [*fem.* **-na**].
anaerobio (a·na·e'ro·βjo) *adj.* anaerobic. —*n.m.* anaerobe.
anafe (a'na·fe) *n.m.* brazier.
anagrama (a·na'ɣra·ma) *n.m.* anagram.
anal (a'nal) *adj.* anal.
anales (a'na·les) *n.m.pl.* annals.
analfabeto (a·nal·fa'βe·to) *adj.* & *n.m.* illiterate. —**analfabetismo**, *n.m.* illiteracy.
analgesia (a·nal'xe·sja) *n.f.* analgesia. —**analgésico** (–si·ko) *adj.* & *n.m.* analgesic.

análisis (a'na·li·sis) *n.m. or f.* **1,** analysis. **2,** *gram.* parsing.
analista (a·na'lis·ta) *n.m. & f.* **1,** analyst. **2,** annalist.
analítico (a·na'li·ti·ko) *adj.* analytic; analytical.
analizar (a·na·li'θar; –'sar) *v.t.* [*pres.subjve.* **analice** (–'li·θe; –se); *pret.* **analicé** (-'θe; -'se)] **1,** to analyze. **2,** *gram.* to parse.
analogía (a·na·lo'xi·a) *n.f.* analogy. —**analógico** (–'lo·xi·ko) *adj.* analogical. —**análogo** (a'na·lo·ɣo) *adj.* analagous.
anamorfosis (a·na·mor'fo·sis) *n.f.sing. & pl.* anamorphosis.
ananás (a·na'nas) *also,* **ananá,** *n.f.* pineapple.
anapesto (a·na'pes·to) *n.m.* anapest. —**anapéstico,** *adj.* anapestic.
anaquel (a·na'kel) *n.m.* shelf.
anaranjado (a·na·ran'xa·ðo) *adj.* orange-colored. —*n.m.* orange color.
anarquía (a·nar'ki·a) *n.f.* anarchy. —**anárquico** (a'nar·ki·ko) *adj.* anarchic; anarchical.
anarquismo (a·nar'kis·mo) *n.m.* anarchism. —**anarquista,** *n.m. & f.* anarchist. —*adj.* anarchistic.
anatema (a·na'te·ma) *n.f.* anathema. —**anatematizar** (–ti'θar; –'sar) *v.t.* [*pres.subjve.* **anatematice** (–'ti·θe; –se); *pret.* **anatematicé** (–'θe; –'se)] to anathematize.
anatomía (a·na·to'mi·a) *n.f.* **1,** anatomy. **2,** dissection. —**anatómico** (–'to·mi·ko) *adj.* anatomical. —**anatomista,** *n.m. & f.* anatomist.
anatomizar (a·na·to·mi'θar; –'sar) *v.t.* [*pres.subjve.* **anatomice** (–'mi·θe; –se); *pret.* **anatomicé** (–'θe; –'se)] to anatomize; dissect.
anca ('an·ka) *n.f.* **1,** buttock; rump. **2,** haunch; croup. —**ancas de rana,** frogs' legs.
ancestral (an·θes'tral; an·ses–) *adj.* ancestral.
-ancia ('an·θja; -sja) *suffix* -ance; -ancy; *forming nouns from adjectives ending in* **-ante:** *vigilancia,* vigilance.
anciano (an'θja·no; an'sja-) *adj.* aged; old. —*n.m.* old man. —**anciana,** *n.f.* old woman. —**ancianidad,** *n.f.* old age.
ancla ('an·kla) *n.f.* anchor.
ancladero (an·kla'ðe·ro) *n.m.* anchorage; anchoring place.
anclaje (an'kla·xe) *n.m.* **1,** anchoring. **2,** anchorage; anchor place. **3,** fee paid for anchorage
anclar (an'klar) *v.i.* **1,** to anch cast anchor. **2,** to ride at anch
anclote (an'klo·te) *n.m.* ked kedge anchor.
áncora ('an·ko·ra) *n.f.* = **ancl**
ancho ('an·tʃo) *adj.* **1,** wi broad. **2,** ample; spacious. —*n* width; breadth. —**a sus anchas,** one's ease; at one's leisure.
anchoa (an'tʃo·a) *n.f.* ancho *Also,* **anchova** (–βa).
anchura (an'tʃu·ra) *n.f.* **1,** wid breadth. **2,** looseness; freed —**anchuroso,** *adj.* wide; spacious
andadas (an'da·ðas) *n.f.pl.* tra (*of animals*). —**andada,** *n.f.si* *Amer.* long walk; ramble. —**vol a las andadas,** to go back to o old tricks; fall back into old hab
andaderas (an·da'ðe·ras) *n.f.* child's walker.
andado (an'da·ðo) *adj.* well-tr den; well-worn.
andador (an·da'ðor) *n.m.* **1,** mover. **2,** walker (for a child invalid). —**andadores,** *n.m.pl.* le ing strings.
andadura (an·da'ðu·ra) *n.f.* pacing. **2,** gait. **3,** amble; walk.
¡ándale! ('an·da·le) *interj., Am* get on!; move!
andamio (an'da·mjo) *n.m.* w platform; scaffold. —**andami** *n.m., also,* **andamiada,** *n.f.* sc folding.
andanada (an·da'na·ða) *n.f.* *naut.* broadside. **2,** grandstand. *colloq.* tirade.
andante (an'dan·te) *adv. & n.* *music* andante. —*adj.* walki —**caballero andante,** knight erra
andanza (an'dan·θa; –sa) *n.f.* happening; occurrence. **2,** fortu luck.
andar (an'dar) *v.i.* [*pret.* **andu** **1,** to walk. **2,** to move; go. **3,** get along; fare. **4,** to function; r **5,** to go about. **6,** *fol. by* **con** *or* to indulge in; engage in. **7,** to pa elapse (*of time*). **8,** to be (*in specified state or activity*): *an en pecado,* to be (*or* live) in s **9,** to continue; keep on. —*v.t.* go *or* walk (a certain way *or* d tance). —*n.m.* walk; gait; pa —**andarse,** *v.r.* **1,** to pass; ela (*of time*). **2,** to go on; contin **3,** to go off; go away. **4,** to

about. —¡**andando**!, *interj.* get on!; go on! —**andando el tiempo**, in the course of time. —**a todo andar**, at full speed.
andariego (an·da'rje·ɣo) *adj.* restless; roving.
andarivel (an·da·ri'βel) *n.m.* **1**, ferry cable. **2**, *colloq.* contraption; makeshift.
andas ('an·das) *n.f.pl.* **1**, stretcher (*sing.*); litter (*sing.*). **2**, bier, esp. one with carrying poles. **3**, portable platform used in processions. —**en andas**, in triumph.
andén (an'den) *n.m.* **1**, station platform. **2**, walk; footwalk.
andino (an'di·no) *adj.* Andean.
andrajo (an'dra·xo) *n.m.* **1**, rag; tatter. **2**, *fig.* despicable person. —**andrajoso**, *adj.* ragged; in tatters.
andro- (an·dro) *prefix* andro-. **1**, man; male: *andrógino*, androgynous. **2**, *bot.* stamen: *androceo*, androecium.
-andro ('an·dro) *suffix* -androus; male: *monandro*, monandrous.
andullo (an'du·ʎo; –jo) *n.m.* **1**, plug tobacco. **2**, rolled tobacco leaf. **3**, *Amer.* any large leaf used as a wrapper.
andurrial (an·du'rrjal) *n.m.*, *usu. pl.* **1**, byway; lonely road. **2**, out-of-the-way place.
anduve (an'du·βe) *v.*, *pret. of* **andar**.
aneblar (a·ne'βlar) *v.t.* [*pres.ind.* **anieblo**; *pres.subjve.* **anieble**] to cloud; becloud. —**aneblarse**, *v.r.* to cloud over; become cloudy.
anécdota (a'nek·ðo·ta) *n.f.* anecdote.
anegar (a·ne'ɣar) *v.t.* [*pres. subjve.* **anegue** (a'ne·ɣe); *pret.* **anegué** (–'ɣe)] **1**, to flood. **2**, to drown. —**anegación**, *n.f.*, *also*, **anegamiento**, *n.m.* flooding. —**anegadizo**, *adj.* subject to frequent flooding.
anejo (a'ne·xo) *adj.* annexed; attached.
anemia (a'ne·mja) *n.f.* anemia. —**anémico** (–mi·ko) *adj.* & *n.m.* anemic.
anemómetro (a·ne'mo·me·tro) *n.m.* anemometer.
anémona (a'ne·mo·na) *also*, **anémone**, *n.f.* anemone.
-áneo ('a·ne·o) *suffix* -an; -aneous; -ary; *forming adjectives expressing* relation; connection: *mediterráneo*, Mediterranean; *instantáneo*, instantaneous; *contemporáneo*, contemporary.
aneroide (a·ne'roi·ðe) *adj.* aneroid. —*n.m.* aneroid barometer.
anestesia (a·nes'te·sja) *n.f.* anesthesia. —**anestesiar** (–'sjar) *v.t.* to anesthetize. —**anestésico** (–'te·si·ko) *n.m.* & *adj.* anesthetic. —**anestesista** (–te'sis·ta) *n.m.* & *f.* anesthetist.
aneurisma (a·neu'ris·ma) *n.m. or f.* aneurysm.
anexar (a·nek'sar) *v.t.* to annex. —**anexión** (-'sjon) *n.f.* annexation.
anexo (a'nek·so) *adj.* annexed; attached. —*n.m.* annex.
anfi- (an·fi) *prefix* amphi-. **1**, around: *anfiteatro*, amphitheater. **2**, at both sides or ends: *anfipróstilo*, amphiprostyle. **3**, of both kinds: *anfibología*, amphibology; *anfibio*, amphibious.
anfibio (an'fi·βjo) *adj.* amphibious. —*n.m.* amphibian.
anfiteatro (an·fi·te'a·tro) *n.m.* amphitheater.
anfitrión (an·fi'trjon) *n.m.* host. —**anfitriona** (–'trjo·na) *n.f.* hostess.
ánfora ('an·fo·ra) *n.f.* amphora.
angarillas (an·ga'ri·ʎas; –jas) *n.f.pl.* **1**, handbarrow (*sing.*). **2**, panniers. **3**, cruets; cruet stand. **4**, stretcher (*sing.*)
angel ('an·xel) *n.m.* angel.
angelical (an·xe·li'kal) *adj.* angelic; angelical. *Also*, **angélico** (an'xe·li·ko).
angina (an'xi·na) *n.f.* angina. —**angina de pecho**, angina pectoris.
anglicanismo (an·gli·ka'nis·mo) *n.m.* Anglicanism. —**anglicano** (–'ka·no) *adj.* & *n.m.* Anglican.
anglicismo (an·gli'θis·mo; –'sis·mo) *n.m.* Anglicism.
anglicización (an·gli·θi·θa'θjon; –si·sa'sjon) *n.f.* Anglicization.
anglo ('an·glo) *adj.* Anglian. —*n.m.* Angle.
anglo- (an·glo) *prefix* Anglo-; English; England: *angloamericano*, Anglo-American; *anglófobo*, Anglophobe.
angloamericano (an·glo·a·me·ri'ka·no) *adj.* & *n.m.* Anglo-American.
anglófilo (an'glo·fi·lo) *adj.* & *n.m.* Anglophile.
anglófobo (an'glo·fo·βo) *n.m.* Anglophobe.

anglosajón (an·glo·sa'xon) *adj. & n.m.* Anglo-Saxon.
angostar (an·gos'tar) *v.t.* to narrow; make narrow.
angosto (an'gos·to) *adj.* narrow. —**angostura,** *n.f.* narrowness.
anguila (an'gi·la) *n.f.* **1,** eel. **2,** *pl., naut.* ways.
angula (an'gu·la) *n.f.* young eel.
angular (an·gu'lar) *adj.* angular. —**piedra angular,** cornerstone.
ángulo ('an·gu·lo) *n.m.* angle; corner.
anguloso (an·gu'lo·so) *adj.* angular; sharp.
angurria (an'gu·rrja) *n.f., Amer.* greed; hoggishness; gluttony. —**angurriento,** *adj., Amer., colloq.* greedy; grasping; hoggish.
angustia (an'gus·tja) *n.f.* anguish; affliction; distress. —**angustiar,** *v.t.* to distress; anguish. —**angustiarse,** *v.r.* to torment oneself. —**angustioso,** *adj.* painful; anguished.
anhelar (a·ne'lar) *v.t.* to crave; to long for. —**anhelo** (a'ne·lo) *n.m.* yearning; longing; eagerness. —**anheloso,** *adj.* anxious; eager.
anidar (a·ni'ðar) *v.i.* **1,** to nest. **2,** to nestle. —*v.t.* to nestle; shelter.
anieble (a'nje·βle) *v., pres.subjve. of* **aneblar.**
anieblo (a'nje·βlo) *v., pres.ind. of* **aneblar.**
anilina (a·ni'li·na) *n.f.* aniline.
anilla (a'ni·ʎa; –ja) *n.f.* **1,** ring; hoop. **2,** curtain ring. **3,** ring fastener.
anillo (a'ni·ʎo; –jo) *n.m.* ring.
ánima ('a·ni·ma) *n.f.* **1,** soul; spirit. **2,** *usu.pl.* souls in purgatory.
animación (a·ni·ma'θjon; –'sjon) *n.f.* animation; liveliness.
animado (a·ni'ma·ðo) *adj.* **1,** animate. **2,** animated; lively.
animador (a·ni·ma'ðor) *adj.* animating; enlivening. —*n.m.* master of ceremonies.
animadversión (a·ni·mað·βer·'sjon) *n.f.* animadversion.
animal (a·ni'mal) *n.m. & adj.* animal. —**animalada,** *n.f., colloq.* stupidity. —**animalidad,** *n.f.* animality. —**animalote,** *n.m.* large animal.
animar (a·ni'mar) *v.t.* **1,** to encourage. **2,** to enliven. **3,** to revive. —**animarse,** *v.r.* to be encouraged; to take heart.
anímico (a'ni·mi·ko) *adj.* psychic; spiritual.
animismo (a·ni'mis·mo) *n.m.* animism. —**animista,** *adj.* animistic —*n.m. & f.* animist.
ánimo ('a·ni·mo) *n.m.* spirit; courage. —**¡ánimo!** *interj.* cheer up —**animoso,** *adj.* spirited.
animosidad (a·ni·mo·si'ðað) *n.* animosity.
aniñado (a·ni'ɲa·ðo) *adj.* childish.
anión (a·ni'on) *n.m.* anion.
aniquilar (a·ni·ki'lar) *v.t.* to annihilate. —**aniquilarse,** *v.r.* to be destroyed; to be ruined. —**aniquilación,** *n.f., also,* **aniquilamiento** *n.m.* annihilation.
anís (a'nis) *n.m.* **1,** anise. **2,** aniseed. **3,** anisette.
anisado (a·ni'sa·ðo) *adj.* anise flavored. —*n.m.* [*also,* **anisete** (–'se·te)] anisette.
aniversario (a·ni·βer'sa·rjo) *adj. & n.m.* anniversary.
ano ('a·no) *n.m.* anus.
-ano ('a·no) *suffix* **1,** -an; *forming adjectives and nouns expressing* relation; connection: *americano* American. **2,** *chem.* -ane; denoting saturated hydrocarbons: *metano* methane.
anoche (a'no·tʃe) *adv.* last night
anochecer (a·no·tʃe'θer; –'ser) *v.i.* [*pres.ind.* **anochezco** (–'tʃeθ·ko –'tʃes·ko); *pres.subjve.* **anochezca** (–θka; –ska)] **1,** to grow dark **2,** to be *or* arrive at nightfall. —*n.m.* nightfall. —**anochecida,** *n.f* dusk; nightfall.
anodino (a·no'ði·no) *adj. & n.m.* anodyne. —*adj., colloq.* insignificant; insipid.
ánodo ('a·no·ðo) *n.m.* anode.
anofeles (a·no'fe·les) *n.m. sing. & pl.* anopheles.
anomalía (a·no·ma'li·a) *n.f.* anomaly. —**anómalo** (a'no·ma·lo) *adj.* anomalous; extraordinary.
anón (a'non) *n.m., also,* **anona,** *n.f.* custard apple (*tree and fruit*).
anonadar (a·no·na'ðar) *v.t.* to overwhelm. —**anonadarse,** *v.r.* to be completely discouraged.
anonimato (a·no·ni'ma·to) *n.m* anonymity.
anónimo (a'no·ni·mo) *adj.* anonymous. —*n.m.* **1,** anonymous letter. **2,** anonymity. —**sociedad anónima,** corporation.
anormal (a·nor'mal) *adj.* abnor-

nal. —*n.m.* & *f.* abnormal person. —**anormalidad,** *n.f.* abnormality.
notación (a·no·ta'θjon; –'sjon) *ı.f.* **1,** annotation; written comment. **2,** score. **3,** note.
notador (a·no·ta'ðor) *n.m.* **1,** annotator; commentator. **2,** scorer.
notar (a·no'tar) *v.t.* **1,** to make notes on; to comment on. **2,** to score.
nquilosarse (an·ki·lo'sar·se) *v.r.* **1,** to become stiff in the joints. **2,** to grow creaky with age.
nsar ('an·sar) *n.m.* wild goose.
nsarino (an·sa'ri·no) *n.m.* gosling.
nsia ('an·sja) *n.f.* **1,** anxiety. **2,** yearning. **3,** *pl.* nausea. —**ansiar,** *v.t.* to desire earnestly; to long for. —**ansiedad,** *n.f.* anxiety. —**ansioso,** *adj.* anxious.
nta ('an·ta) *n.f.* elk; moose.
ntagónico (an·ta'ɣo·ni·ko) *adj.* antagonistic.
ntagonista (an·ta·ɣo'nis·ta) *n.m.* & *f.* antagonist. —**antagonismo,** *n.m.* antagonism.
ntagonizar (an·ta·ɣo·ni'θar; –'sar) *v.t.* [*infl.:* **agonizar**] to antagonize.
ntaño (an'ta·ɲo) *adv.* formerly; in olden times. —**de antaño,** of old; of yore.
ntártico (an'tar·ti·ko) *adj.* antarctic.
nte ('an·te) *n.m.* elk.
nte ('an·te) *prep.* **1,** in the presence of; before. **2,** in comparison with. **3,** over; above; in preference to.
nte- (an·te) *prefix* ante-. **1,** before; prior to: *antecedente,* antecedent. 2, in front of: *antecámara,* antechamber.
-nte ('an·te) *suffix* **1,** -ant; -ing; forming *adjectives equivalent to participles: desafiante,* defiant. **2,** forming *nouns denoting* activity; occupation: *ayudante,* adjutant.
nteanoche (an·te·a'no·tʃe) *adv.* night before last.
nteayer (an·te·a'jer) *adv.* day before yesterday.
ntebrazo (an·te'βra·θo; –so) *n.m.* forearm.
ntecámara (an·te'ka·ma·ra) *n.f.* anteroom; lobby.
ntecedente (an·te·θe'ðen·te; –se'ðen·te) *adj.* & *n.m.* antecedent. —**antecedentes,** *n.m.pl.* **1,** forefathers. **2,** past history; record (*sing.*).
anteceder (an·te·θe'ðer; -se'ðer) *v.t.* to precede.
antecesor (an·te·θe'sor; –se'sor) *n.m.* **1,** predecessor. **2,** ancestor.
antedata (an·te'ða·ta) *n.f.* antedate. —**antedatar,** *v.t.* to antedate.
antedicho (an·te'ði·tʃo) *adj.* aforesaid.
antelación (an·te·la'θjon; -'sjon) *n.f.* anticipation. —**con antelación,** in advance; beforehand.
antemano (an·te'ma·no) *adv., usu.* **de antemano,** previously; beforehand.
antemeridiano (an·te·me·ri'ðja·no) *adj.* in the forenoon; A.M.
antena (an'te·na) *n.f.* antenna.
antenoche (an·te'no·tʃe) *adv.* = **anteanoche.**
anteojera (an·te·o'xe·ra) *n.f.* **1,** spectacle case. **2,** *usu.pl.* blinkers.
anteojo (an·te'o·xo) *n.m.* **1,** spyglass; telescope. **2,** sight (*of instruments*). **3,** eyeglass. —**anteojos,** *n.m.pl.* **1,** binoculars. **2,** spectacles.
antepasado (an·te·pa'sa·ðo) *n.m., usu.pl.* ancestor. —*adj.* previous to the last; before the last.
antepecho (an·te'pe·tʃo) *n.m.* **1,** parapet. **2,** railing. **3,** sill.
anteponer (an·te·po'ner) *v.t.* [*infl.:* **poner**] **1,** to put before. **2,** to prefer. —**anteponerse,** *v.r.* to push oneself ahead. —**anteponerse a,** to overcome.
anteproyecto (an·te·pro'jek·to) *n.m.* preliminary design or draft.
antepuesto (an·te'pwes·to) *v., p.p. of* **anteponer.** —*adj.* aforementioned.
antera (an'te·ra) *n.f.* anther.
anterior (an·te'rjor) *adj.* preceding; former; anterior. —**anterioridad,** *n.f.* priority. —**con anterioridad,** previously.
antes ('an·tes) *adv.* **1,** formerly. **2,** rather; better; preferably. —*conj., fol. by* **de, que** *or* **de que,** before. —*adj.* previous; preceding. —**cuanto antes,** as soon as possible.
antesala (an·te'sa·la) *n.f.* anteroom; sitting room.
anti- (an·ti) *prefix* anti-. **1,** against; opposed: *anticlerical,* anticlerical. **2,** false; rival: *antipapa,* antipope. **3,** located opposite; against; *antípoda,* antipode. **4,** *med.* preventive; curative: *antitoxina,* antitoxin; *antídoto,*

antidote. *Before vowels sometimes* **ant-**: *antártico,* Antarctic.
antiácido (an'tja·θi·ðo; -si·ðo) *adj.* & *n.m.* antacid.
antiaéreo (an·tja'e·re·o) *adj.* antiaircraft.
antialcalino (an·tjal·ka'li·no) *n.m.* antalkali.
antiamericano (an·tja·me·ri·'ka·no) *adj.* un-American.
antibiótico (an·ti'βjo·ti·ko) *adj.* & *n.m.* antibiotic.
anticipación (an·ti·θi·pa'θjon; –si·pa'sjon) *n.f.* **1,** anticipation. **2,** advance. —**con anticipación,** in advance.
anticipar (an·ti·θi'par; –si'par) *v.t.* **1,** to advance (a date). **2,** to advance (money). **3,** to forestall. **4,** to anticipate; act ahead of. —**anticiparse,** *v.r.* to act or occur early or prematurely. —**anticiparse a, 1,** to anticipate; act ahead of. **2,** to hurry to; be in a rush to. —**anticipadamente,** *adv.* beforehand. —**anticipante,** *adj.* anticipatory. —**por anticipado,** in advance.
anticipo (an·ti'θi·po; –'si·po) *n.m.* **1,** anticipation. **2,** advance; advance payment.
anticlerical (an·ti·kle·ri'kal) *adj.* anticlerical.
anticlímax (an·ti'kli·maks) *n.m.* anticlimax.
anticonstitucional *adj.* unconstitutional.
anticristiano (an·ti·kris'tja·no) *adj.* unchristian.
Anticristo (an·ti'kris·to) *n.m.* Antichrist.
anticuar (an·ti'kwar) *v.t.* to outdate. —**anticuarse,** *v.r.* to become outdated. —**anticuado,** *adj.* outdated; antiquated; obsolete.
anticuario (an·ti'kwa·rjo) *adj.* antiquarian. —*n.m.* **1,** antiquary; antiquarian. **2,** antique dealer *or* collector.
anticuerpo (an·ti'kwer·po) *n.m.* antibody.
antidemocrático (an·ti·ðe·mo'kra·ti·ko) *adj.* undemocratic.
antídoto (an'ti·ðo·to) *n.m.* antidote.
antieconómico (an·tje·ko'no·mi·ko) *adj.* uneconomical; wasteful.
antier (an'tjer) *adv.* = **anteayer.**
antifaz (an·ti'faθ; –'fas) *n.m.* mask.
antífona (an'ti·fo·na) *n.f.* **1,** antiphon. **2,** anthem.
antigás (an·ti'ɣas) *adj.* protecting against gas. —**máscara antigás,** gas mask.
antigualla (an·ti'ɣwa·ʎa; –ja) *n.f.* **1,** old story; old hat. **2,** antique relic; museum piece.
antigüedad (an·ti·ɣwe'ðað) *n.f.* **1,** antiquity. **2,** seniority. **3,** *pl.* antics. **4,** *pl.* antiques.
antiguo (an'ti·ɣwo) *adj.* ancient; old. —**antiguamente,** *adv.* formerly; long ago.
antihigiénico (an·ti·i'xje·ni·ko) *adj.* unhygienic; unsanitary.
antílope (an'ti·lo·pe) *n.m.* antelope.
antimonio (an·ti'mo·njo) *n.m.* antimony.
antipapa (an·ti'pa·pa) *n.m.* antipope.
antiparras (an·ti'pa·rras) *n.f.pl.* *colloq.* = **anteojos.**
antipatía (an·ti·pa'ti·a) *n.f.* antipathy; dislike. —**antipático** (–'pa·ti·ko) *adj.* antipathetic; disagreeable.
antipatriótico (an·ti·pa'trjo·ti·ko) *adj.* unpatriotic.
antípoda (an'ti·po·ða) *n.m.* antipode. —*adj. m.* & *f.* antipodal.
antiprohibicionista (an·ti·pro·i·βi·θjo'nis·ta; -sjo'nis·ta) *adj.* & *n.m.* & *f.* (one) opposed to prohibition; wet.
antiquísimo (an·ti'ki·si·mo) *adj.* *superl. of* **antiguo.**
antisemita (an·ti·se'mi·ta) *n.m.* & *f.* anti-Semite. —**antisemítico,** *adj.* anti-Semitic. —**antisemitismo,** *n.m.* anti-Semitism.
antisepsia (an·ti'sep·sja) *n.f.* antisepsis. —**antiséptico** (–ti·ko) *adj.* & *n.m.* antiseptic.
antisocial (an·ti·so'θjal; –'sjal) *adj.* antisocial.
antitanque (an·ti'tan·ke) *adj.* anti-tank.
antítesis (an'ti·te·sis) *n.f.* antithesis. —**antitético** (–'te·ti·ko) *adj.* antithetical; opposing.
antitoxina (an·ti·to'ksi·na) *n.f.* antitoxin. —**antitóxico** (–'tok·si·ko) *adj.* antitoxic.
anto- (an·to) *prefix* antho-; flower: *antología,* anthology.
-anto ('an·to) *suffix* -anthous; flower: *monanto,* monanthous.
antojo (an'to·xo) *n.m.* whim. —**antojadizo,** *adj.* capricious. —**an-**

:ojarse, *v.r., impers.* to come to one's whim *or* fancy.
ntología (an·to·lo'xi·a) *n.f.* anhology.
ntónimo (an'to·ni·mo) *n.m.* anonym. —*adj.* antonymous; oppoite.
ntorcha (an'tor·tʃa) *n.f.* torch.
ntracita (an·tra'θi·ta; –'si·ta) *n.f.* anthracite.
ntrax ('an·traks) *n.m.* anthrax.
ntro ('an·tro) *n.m.* den; lair.
ntropo- (an·tro·po) *prefix* anhropo-; man: *antropología,* anhropology.
ntropófago (an·tro'po·fa·ɣo) *n.m.* cannibal. —*adj.* cannibalistic.
ntropoide (an·tro'poi·ðe) *adj. & n.m. & f.* anthropoid. *Also,* **anropideo** (-'ðe·o) *adj. & n.m.*
ntropología (an·tro·po·lo'xi·a) *n.f.* anthropology. —**antropológico** (–'lo·xi·ko) *adj.* anthropological. —**antropólogo** (–'po·lo·ɣo) *n.m.* anthropologist.
nual (a'nwal) *adj.* annual; yearly. —**anualidad,** *n.f.* annuity; yearly ent.
nuario (a'nwa·rjo) *n.m.* yearbook.
nublar (a·nu'βlar) *v.t.* to cloud up; to darken. —**anublarse,** *v.r.* **1,** to become cloudy. **2,** *fig.* to wither away.
nudar (a·nu'ðar) *v.t.* **1,** to knot; fasten with a knot. **2,** to tie in; reate.
nular (a·nu'lar) *adj.* circular. —**dedo anular,** ring finger.
nular (a·nu'lar) *v.t.* **1,** to nullify; void; annul. **2,** to incapacitate; render powerless. —**anulación,** *n.f.;* **anulamiento,** *n.m.* annulment.
nunciante (a·nun'θjan·te; 'sjan·te) *n.m. & f., also,* **anunciador,** *n.m.* **1,** announcer. **2,** adverlser. —*adj.* **1,** announcing. **2,** advertising.
nunciar (a·nun'θjar; –'sjar) *v.t.* **1,** to announce. **2,** to advertise. —**anunciación,** *n.f.* annunciation.
nuncio (a'nun·θjo; –sjo) *n.m.* **1,** advertisement. **2,** notice; announcement. **3,** poster; sign.
nverso (an'βer·so) *adj. & n.m.* obverse.
nza ('an·θa; –sa) *suffix, var. of* **ancia:** *templanza,* temperance.
nzuelo (an'θwe·lo; an'swe–) *n.m.* **1,** fishhook. **2,** *fig.* lure; enticement.
ña ('a·ɲa) *suffix, forming nouns of various meanings: hazaña,* feat; *montaña,* mountain.
añadir (a·ɲa'ðir) *v.t.* to add. —**añadidura,** *n.f.* increment; addition.
añagaza (a·ɲa'ɣa·θa; –sa) *n.f.* trick; chicanery.
añejo (a'ɲe·xo) *adj.* aged, as wine. —**añejarse,** *v.r.* to age, as wine.
añicos (a'ɲi·kos) *n.m.pl.* fragments. —**hacer añicos,** to break into small bits.
añil (a'ɲil) *n.m.* indigo; anil.
año ('a·ɲo) *n.m.* year. —**año bisiesto,** leap year. —**año económico,** fiscal year. —**año en curso,** current year. —**entrado en años,** well along in years. —**tener . . . años,** to be . . . years old.
añojo (a'ɲo·xo) *n.m.* yearling.
añorar (a·ɲo'rar) *v.t.* to recall with nostalgia; yearn for. —**añoranza,** *n.f.* nostalgia; yearning.
añoso (a'ɲo·so) *adj.* aged; old.
aojar (a·o'xar) *v.t.* **1,** to jinx; hoodoo; give the evil eye. **2,** to eye; ogle. —**aojo** (a'o·xo) *n.m.* evil eye; jinx; hoodoo.
aorta (a'or·ta) *n.f.* aorta.
aovado (a·o'βa·ðo) *adj.* eggshaped.
apabullar (a·pa·βu'ʎar; –'jar) *v.t., colloq.* **1,** to crush. **2,** to squelch.
apacentar (a·pa·θen'tar; -sen·'tar) *v.t.* [*pres.ind.* **apaciento** ('–θjen·to; –'sjen·to); *pres.subjve.* **apaciente**] to graze; pasture. —**apacentadero,** *n.m.* pasture.
apacibilidad (a·pa·θi·βi·li'ðað; a·pa·si–) *n.f.* **1,** peacefulness. **2,** peaceableness.
apacible (a·pa'θi·βle; –'si·βle) *adj.* **1,** peaceful; quiet. **2,** peaceable.
apaciguar (a·pa·θi'ɣwar; -si·'ɣwar) *v.t.* to appease; pacify. —**apaciguarse,** *v.r.* to calm down. —**apaciguador,** *adj.* calming; pacifying. —*n.m.* appeaser. —**apaciguamiento,** *n.m.* calming down; appeasement
apache (a'pa·tʃe) *n.m.* **1,** Apache. **2,** *slang* thug.
apachurrar (a·pa·tʃu'rrar) *v.t., Amer., colloq.* = **despachurrar.**
apadrinar (a·pa·ðri'nar) *v.t.* **1,** to sponsor; favor. **2,** to second (*in a duel*). **3,** to act as best man *or* godfather to.
apagado (a·pa'ɣa·ðo) *adj.* **1,** dull

(*of colors*). 2, extinct (*of a volcano*). 3, *fig.* unassuming; self-effacing.
apagar (a·pa'ɣar) *v.t.* [*pres. subjve.* **apague** (a'pa·ɣe); *pret.* **apagué** (–'ɣe)] 1, to extinguish; quench. 2, to put out; turn off. 3, to deaden; muffle; mute. 4, to dull *or* soften (colors). 5, to slake (lime). —**apagarse**, *v.r.* to go out; die out; go off.
apagón (a·pa'ɣon) *n.m.* blackout.
apalabrar (a·pa·la'βrar) *v.t.* to confer on; discuss. —**apalabrarse**, *v.r.* to agree; reach an agreement.
apalear (a·pa·le'ar) *v.t.* 1, to beat; cudgel. 2, to thresh.
apandillarse (a·pan·di'ʎar·se; –'jar·se) *v.r.* to band together.
apañar (a·pa'ɲar) *v.t.* 1, to grasp; seize. 2, to dress; deck out. 3, to cloak; conceal. 4, to abet. 5, *colloq.* to steal; filch. —**apañarse**, *v.r.*, *colloq.* to contrive; scheme.
aparador (a·pa·ra'ðor) *n.m.* sideboard; cupboard.
aparato (a·pa'ra·to) *n.m.* 1, apparatus. 2, machine. 3, device; gadget. 4, show; ostentation.
aparatoso (a·pa·ra'to·so) *adj.* 1, showy. 2, exaggerated.
aparcería (a·par·θe'ri·a; –se'ri·a) *n.f.* 1, partnership. 2, sharecropping.
aparcero (a·par'θe·ro; –'se·ro) *n.m.* 1, partner; associate. 2, sharecropper.
aparear (a·pa·re'ar) *v.t.* to couple; to match. —**aparearse**, *v.r.* to be paired; to form a pair. —**apareamiento**, *n.m.* coupling; matching.
aparecer (a·pa·re'θer; –'ser) *v.i.* [*pres.ind.* **aparezco** (–'reθ·ko; –'res·ko); *pres.subjve.* **aparezca**] to appear. —**aparecerse**, *v.r.* to show up. —**aparecido**, *n.m.* ghost.
aparejar (a·pa·re'xar) *v.t.* 1, to prepare. 2, to rig. 3, to harness. 4, *Amer.* to pair. 5, *painting* to prime; to size. —**aparejarse**, *v.r.* to equip oneself; get ready.
aparejo (a·pa're·xo) *n.m.* 1 preparation. 2, harness; rigging; tackle. 3, sizing; priming. 4, gear; equipment.
aparentar (a·pa·ren'tar) *v.t.* to feign; to pretend. —**aparenta treinta años**, he (she) seems to be about thirty.
aparente (a·pa'ren·te) *adj.* 1, apparent. 2, feigned. 3, suitable. conspicuous.
aparición (a·pa·ri'θjon; –'sjon) *n.f.* 1, appearance. 2, apparition.
apariencia (a·pa'rjen·θja; –sja) *n.f.* appearance.
aparragarse (a·pa·rra'ɣar·se) *v.r.*, *Amer.* 1, to nestle. 2, to flatte oneself; crouch.
apartadero (a·par·ta'ðe·ro) *n.m* *R.R.* siding.
apartadizo (a·par·ta'ði·θo; –so) *adj.* unsociable. —*n.m.* 1, screene off room. 2, recluse.
apartado (a·par'ta·ðo) *adj.* di tant; secluded. —*n.m.* post offi box.
apartamiento (a·par·ta'mjen·to *also*, **apartamento** (–'men·to) *n.n* 1, apartment. 2, retiring place.
apartar (a·par'tar) *v.t.* 1, separate; set aside. 2, to push asid push away. —**apartarse**, *v.r.* 1, withdraw. 2, to stand aside.
aparte (a'par·te) *adj.* 1, apar aside. 2, elsewhere. —*n.m.* 1, *theo* aside. 2, new paragraph. 3, side r mark.
apartidar (a·par·ti'ðar) *v.t.* to back; support; side with. 2, win the support of. —**apartidars** *v.r.* to side; take sides.
apasionamiento (a·pa·sjo·n 'mjen·to) *n.m.* 1, passion. 2, v hemence.
apasionar (a·pa·sjo'nar) *v.t.* 1, inspire passion in; impassion. 2, captivate. —**apasionarse**, *v.r.* become impassioned. —**apasionad** *adj.* passionate; impassione —**apasionante**, *adj.* captivatin gripping.
apatía (a·pa'ti·a) *n.f.* apath —**apático** (a'pa·ti·ko) *adj.* ap thetic.
apear (a·pe'ar) *v.t.* to help to d mount. —**apearse**, *v.r.* to get dov or off; dismount; alight. —**apear del burro**, to admit one's err **apearse por la cola** (*or* **las orejas** to go off at a tangent.
apechugar (a·pe·tʃu'ɣar) [*pres.subjve.* **apechugue** (–'tʃu·ɣ *pret.* **apechugué** (–'ɣe)] to pu with the chest; breast one's w —*v.t.*, *Amer.* to grab off; snat —**apechugar con**, to do *or* be reluctantly; resign oneself to.
apedrear (a·pe·ðre'ar) *v.t.* stone.

apego (a'pe·ɣo) *n.m.* attachment. —**apegarse** (–'ɣar·se) *v.t.* to become attached.

apelar (a·pe'lar) *v.i.* **1,** *law* to appeal. **2,** to relate; refer; have reference. —**apelación,** *n.f., law* appeal.

apelativo (a·pe·la'ti·βo) *adj.* & *n.m.* appellative. —*n.m.* name; appellation.

apelmazar (a·pel·ma'θar; '–sar) *v.t.* [*pres.subjve.* **apelmace** (–'ma·θe; –se); *pret.* **apelmacé** (–'θe; –'se)] **1,** to thicken; make lumpy. **2,** to tighten; compress.

apelotonar (a·pe·lo·to'nar) *v.t.* to gather; mass together. —**apelotonarse,** *v.r.* to cluster.

apellidar (a·pe·ʎi'ðar; -ji'ðar) *v.t.* to name; call by a name. —**apellidarse,** *v.r.* to have for a surname.

apellido (a·pe'ʎi·ðo; -'ji·ðo) *n.m.* **1,** surname; family name. **2,** nickname.

apenar (a·pe'nar) *v.t.* to grieve; cause pain. —**apenarse,** *v.r.* to grieve.

apenas (a'pe·nas) *adv.* **1,** scarcely; hardly. **2,** with difficulty. —*conj.* as soon as.

apendectomía (a·pen·dek·to·'mi·a) *n.f.* appendectomy.

apéndice (a'pen·di·θe; -se) *n.m.* **1,** appendix. **2,** appendage.

apendicitis (a·pen·di'θi·tis; –'si·tis) *n.f.* appendicitis.

aperar (a·pe'rar) *v.t.* **1,** to construct *or* repair (wagons, farm equipment, etc.). **2,** *Amer.* to harness. —**aperador,** *n.m.* wheelwright.

apercibimiento (a·per·θi·βi·'mjen·to; a·per·si-) *n.m.* **1,** preparation. **2,** warning. **3,** perception.

apercibir (a·per·θi'βir; –si'βir) *v.t.* **1,** to prepare. **2,** to warn. **3,** to perceive. —**apercibirse,** *v.r.* to get ready.

apergaminado (a·per·ɣa·mi·'na·ðo) *adj.* like parchment; dried up; yellowed.

aperitivo (a·pe·ri'ti·βo) *n.m.* appetizer; aperitif.

aperlado (a·per'la·ðo) *adj.* pearly.

apero (a'pe·ro) *n.m., usu.pl.* **1,** farm implements. **2,** set of tools. **3,** *Amer.* harness; riding gear.

apertura (a·per'tu·ra) *n.f.* **1,** aperture; opening. **2,** beginning.

apesadumbrar (a·pe·sa·ðum·'brar) *v.t.* to distress. —**apesadumbrarse,** *v.r.* to grieve. —**apesadumbrado,** *adj.* grieved; distressed.

apestar (a·pes'tar) *v.i.* & *t.* **1,** to stink; smell. **2,** *colloq.* to pester. —**apestarse,** *v.r.* to suffer a plague or blight. —**apestoso** (–'to·so) *adj.* stinking.

apetecer (a·pe·te'θer; –'ser) *v.t.* [*pres.ind.* **apetezco** (–'teθ·ko; –'tes·ko); *pres.subjve.* **apetezca**] to crave; desire. —**apetecible,** *adj.* desirable.

apetencia (a·pe'ten·θja; –sja) *n.f.* appetite; desire.

apetito (a·pe'ti·to) *n.m.* appetite. —**apetitoso,** *adj.* appetizing; tasty; savory. —**abrir el apetito,** to whet the appetite.

apiadarse (a·pja'ðar·se) *v.r. fol. by* **de,** to have pity on.

ápice ('a·pi·θe; –se) *n.m.* **1,** apex. **2,** iota; jot. **3,** crux.

apícola (a'pi·ko·la) *adj.* of or pert. to beekeeping.

apicultura (a·pi·kul'tu·ra) *n.f.* beekeeping. —**apicultor** (–'tor) *n.m.* beekeeper.

apilar (a·pi'lar) *v.t.* to pile up.

apiñar (a·pi'ɲar) *v.t.* to jam; squeeze; press. —**apiñarse,** *v.r.* to crowd together; crowd up. —**apiñamiento,** *n.m.* crowd; press; jam.

apio ('a·pjo) *n.m.* celery.

apisonar (a·pi·so'nar) *v.t.* to tamp; to ram down.

aplacar (a·pla'kar) *v.t.* [*pres. subjve.* **aplaque** (a'pla·ke); *pret.* **aplaqué** (–'ke)] to placate; to calm down. —**aplacarse,** *v.r.* to subside. —**aplacamiento,** *n.m.* placation.

aplanar (a·pla'nar) *v.t.* to flatten; to level. —**aplanarse,** *v.r.* to become discouraged. —**aplanadora** (-'ðo·ra) *n.f.* steam roller.

aplastar (a·plas'tar) *v.t.* to flatten; to crush. —**aplastarse,** *v.r.* to become flat. —**aplastante,** *adj.* crushing; *fig.* dumfounding.

aplaudir (a·plau'ðir) *v.t.* to applaud. —**aplauso** (a'plau·so) *n.m.* applause.

aplazamiento (a·pla·θa'mjen·to; a·pla·sa–) *n.m.* **1,** postponement. **2,** adjournment.

aplazar (a·pla'θar; –'sar) *v.t.* [*pres.subjve.* **aplace** (a'pla·θe; –se); *pret.* **aplacé** (–'θe; –'se)] **1,** to postpone. **2,** to adjourn. **3,** *Amer.* to fail (a student); hold back from promotion.

aplicable (a·pli'ka·βle) *adj.* applicable. —**aplicabilidad,** *n.f.* applicability.
aplicación (a·pli·ka'θjon; -'sjon) *n.f.* **1,** application. **2,** devotion to study.
aplicado (a·pli'ka·ðo) *adj.* **1,** applied. **2,** studious.
aplicar (a·pli'kar) *v.t.* [*pres.subjve.* **aplique** (a'pli·ke); *pret.* **apliqué** (–'ke)] **1,** to apply. **2,** to assign; place. **3,** to attribute; impute. **4,** *law* to adjudge. —**aplicarse,** *v.r.* **1,** to apply; be applicable. **2,** to apply oneself; devote oneself.
aplomar (a·plo'mar) *v.t.* to plumb; make plumb. —**aplomarse,** *v.r.* to collapse.
aplomo (a'plo·mo) *n.m.* aplomb; poise. —**aplomado,** *adj.* poised.
apo- (a·po) *prefix* apo-; off; from; away: *apogeo,* apogee; *apotema,* apothem.
Apocalipsis (a·po·ka'lip·sis) *n.m.* Apocalypse. —**apocalíptico** (–'lip·ti·ko) *adj.* apocalyptic.
apocar (a·po'kar) *v.t.* [*pres.subjve.* **apoque** (a'po·ke); *pret.* **apoqué** (–'ke)] **1,** to restrict; limit. **2,** to reduce; make smaller. **3,** to belittle. —**apocarse,** *v.r.* **1,** to humble oneself. **2,** to wilt; cringe. —**apocado,** *adj.* diffident; shy. —**apocamiento,** *n.m.* diffidence; shyness.
apócrifo (a'po·kri·fo) *adj.* apocryphal. —**libros apócrifos,** Apocrypha.
apodar (a·po'ðar) *v.t.* to nickname.
apoderar (a·po·ðe'rar) *v.t.* to grant power of attorney to. —**apoderarse,** *v.r., fol. by* **de,** to seize; take possession of. —**apoderado,** *n.m.* proxy; holder of power of attorney.
apodo (a'po·ðo) *n.m.* nickname.
apogeo (a·po'xe·o) *n.m.* **1,** *astron.* apogee. **2,** *fig.* height (of fame, power, etc.).
apolillarse (a·po·li'ʎar·se; –'jar·se) *v.r.* to become motheaten. —**apolillado,** *adj.* motheaten.
apolítico (a·po'li·ti·ko) *adj.* nonpolitical.
apología (a·po·lo'xi·a) *n.f.* **1,** apology. **2,** defense. **3,** eulogy. —**apologético** (–'xe·ti·ko) *adj.* apologetic. —**apologista** (–'xis·ta) *n.m. & f.* apologist.
apologizar (a·po·lo·xi'θar; –'sar) *v.t.* [*infl.:* **realizar**] to defend. —*v.*[…] to apologize; make a formal de[…]fense.
apoltronarse (a·pol·tro'nar·se[…] *v.r.* **1,** to become lazy. **2,** to sprawl[…] lounge.
apoplejía (a·po·ple'xi·a) *n.f.* apo[…]plexy. —**apoplético** (–'ple·ti·ko[…] *adj.* apoplectic.
aporrear (a·po·rre'ar) *v.t.* t[…] beat; cudgel. —**aporreo** (–'rre·o[…] *n.m.* beating.
aportar (a·por'tar) *v.t.* to con[…]tribute (one's share). —*v.i.* t[…] make port; arrive. —**aportació**[…] *n.f., also,* **aporte** (a'por·te) *n.m*[…] contribution.
aportillar (a·por·ti'ʎar; –'jar[…] *v.t.* **1,** to open a hole in; breach[…] **2,** to break up; break apart.
aposento (a·po'sen·to) *n.m.* room[…] —**aposentar,** *v.t.* to lodge.
aposición (a·po·si'θjon; -'sjon[…] *n.f.* apposition.
apostar (a·pos'tar) *v.t.* [*pres.ind*[…] **apuesto** (a'pwes·to) *pres.subjve*[…] **apueste**] **1,** to bet. **2,** to station[…] —**apostarse,** *v.r.* to station onesel[…] —**apostadero,** *n.m.* military post[…] naval station.
apostatar (a·pos·ta'tar) *v.i.* t[…] apostatize. —**apostasía** (–'si·a) *n.*[…] apostasy. —**apóstata** (a'pos·ta·ta[…] *n.m. & f.* apostate.
apostilla (a·pos'ti·ʎa; –ja) *n.*[…] marginal note. —**apostillar,** *v.t.* t[…] make marginal notes in or on.
apóstol (a'pos·tol) *n.m.* apostle[…] —**apostolado,** *n.m.* apostolate[…] —**apostólico** (–'to·li·ko) *adj.* apos[…]tolic.
apostrofar (a·pos·tro'far) *v.t.* **1**[…] *rhet.* to apostrophize. **2,** to insult.
apóstrofe (a'pos·tro·fe) *n.m.* o[…] *f.* **1,** *rhet.* apostrophe. **2,** *usu.masc*[…] invective; insult.
apóstrofo (a'pos·tro·fo) *n.m.* *gram.* apostrophe (').
apostura (a·pos'tu·ra) *n.f.* **1**[…] handsomeness; grace; neatness. **2**[…] look; aspect.
apoteosis (a·po·te'o·sis) *n.*[…] apotheosis. —**apoteósico** (–'o·si[…] ko) *adj.* glorifying; glorious.
apoyar (a·po'jar) *v.t.* **1,** to lean[…] rest. **2,** to support. **3,** to favor[…] sponsor. **4,** to base (an argument[…] opinion, etc.). —**apoyarse,** *v.r.* **1**[…] to lean; rest. **2,** to base oneself.
apoyo (a'po·jo) *n.m.* **1,** prop; sup[…]port. **2,** patronage; protection.

apreciable (a·pre'θja·βle; -'sja·βle) *adj.* 1, valuable. 2, estimable.
apreciar (a·pre'θjar; -'sjar) *v.t.* 1, to esteem. 2, to appraise; to estimate. —**apreciación,** *n.f.* estimate; judgment.
aprecio (a'pre·θjo; -sjo) *n.m.* 1, esteem. 2, appraisal.
aprehender (a·pre·en'der; a·pren'der) *v.t.* to apprehend. —**aprehensión** (-'sjon) *n.f.* apprehension. —**aprehensivo** (-'si·βo) *adj.* apprehensive. —**aprehensor** (-'sor) *n.m.* one who arrests; arresting officer.
apremiar (a·pre'mjar) *v.t.* to urge; to compel. —**apremiante,** *adj.* urgent; pressing.
apremio (a'pre·mjo) *n.m.* 1, compulsion. 2, judicial order.
aprender (a·pren'der) *v.t.* & *i.* to learn. —**aprender de memoria,** to learn by heart.
aprendiz (a·pren'diθ; -'dis) *n.m.* & *f.* apprentice. —**aprendizaje,** *n.m.* apprenticeship.
aprensión (a·pren'sjon) *n.f.* fear; scruple. —**aprensivo** (-'si·βo) *adj.* apprehensive.
apresar (a·pre'sar) *v.t.* to seize.
aprestar (a·pres'tar) *v.t.* 1, to prepare. 2, to size (cloth).
apresto (a'pres·to) *n.m.* 1, preparation. 2, size (*for cloth*).
apresurar (a·pre·su'rar) *v.t.* to hasten. —**apresurarse,** *v.r.* to make haste. —**apresurado,** *adj.* hasty. —**apresuramiento,** *n.m.* haste; hastiness.
apretado (a·pre'ta·ðo) *adj.* 1, tight. 2, risky; allowing little margin. 3, difficult. 4, urgent.
apretar (a·pre'tar) *v.t.* [*pres.ind.* **aprieto** (a'prje·to); *pres.subjve.* **apriete**] 1, to tighten; to squeeze; to clench. 2, *fig.* to press; to harass. —*v.i.* to worsen; to pinch. —**apretar el paso,** to hurry.
apretazón (a·pre·ta'θon; -'son) *n.m., Amer.* congestion; jam.
apretón (a·pre'ton) *n.m.* squeeze; sudden pressure. —**apretón de manos,** handshake; handclasp.
apretujar (a·pre·tu'xar) *v.t., colloq.* to squeeze or press tight.
apretura (a·pre'tu·ra) *n.f.* 1, crush; press. 2, = **aprieto.**
aprieto (a'prje·to) *n.m.* 1, predicament; tight spot. 2, = **apretura.**
aprisa (a'pri·sa) *adv.* swiftly.
aprisco (a'pris·ko) *n.m.* fold; sheepfold.
aprisionar (a·pri·sjo'nar) *v.t.* 1, to imprison; confine. 2, to seize; hold.
aprobar (a·pro'βar) *v.t.* [*pres. ind.* **apruebo** (a'prwe·βo); *pres. subjve.* **apruebe**] 1, to approve. 2, to pass; give a passing mark to. —**aprobación,** *n.f.* approval. —**aprobado,** *n.m.* passing mark. —**aprobatorio,** *adj.* approving.
aprontar (a·pron'tar) *v.t.* 1, to ready; make ready with. 2, to prompt; prepare (a person). —**apronte** (a'pron·te) *n.m.,* sports workout.
apropiar (a·pro'pjar) *v.t.* 1, to adapt. 2, to take possession of. —**apropiarse,** *v.r., usu.fol. by* **de,** to appropriate. —**apropiación,** *n.f.* appropriation. —**apropiado,** *adj.* appropriate.
apropincuarse (a·pro·pin'kwar·se) *v.r., colloq.* = **acercarse.**
aprovechable (a·pro·βe'tʃa·βle) *adj.* 1, usable. 2, available.
aprovechado (a·pro·βe'tʃa·ðo) *adj.* 1, industrious; studious. 2, self-seeking.
aprovechamiento (a·pro·βe·tʃa'mjen·to) *n.m.* 1, utilization; use; exploitation. 2, profit; advantage. 3, improvement; progress.
aprovechar (a·pro·βe'tʃar) *v.t.* 1, to make use of. 2, to aid; to avail. —*v.i.* to make progress. —**aprovecharse,** *v.r., usu.fol. by* **de,** to take advantage (of); to benefit (from).
aprovisionar (a·pro·βi·sjo'nar) *v.t.* to supply; provide.
aproximación (a·pro·ksi·ma'θjon; -'sjon) *n.f.* 1, approximation. 2, consolation prize.
aproximado (a·pro·ksi'ma·ðo) *adj.* approximate; close. —**aproximadamente,** *adv.* approximately; nearly.
aproximar (a·pro·ksi'mar) *v.t.* 1, to approach. 2, to estimate. —**aproximarse,** *v.r.* to draw near; approach. —**aproximarse a,** to approximate; be almost or close to.
apto ('ap·to) *adj.* apt. —**aptitud,** *n.f.* aptitude.
apuesta (a'pwes·ta) *n.f.* bet; wager.
apuesto (a'pwes·to) *adj.* handsome; elegant.
apuntación (a·pun·ta'θjon; -'sjon)

n.f. 1, annotation. 2, memorandum. 3, musical notation. —**apuntador,** *n.m.* prompter.
apuntalar (a·pun·ta'lar) *v.t.* 1, to prop up; shore. 2, to give support to; help.
apuntar (a·pun'tar) *v.t.* 1, to aim; to point. 2, to make a note of. 3, to prompt. 4, *cards* to bet; to stake. —*v.i.* to begin to show or appear.
apunte (a'pun·te) *n.m.* 1, annotation; memorandum. 2, examination mark. 3, stake.
apuñalar (a·pu·ɲa'lar) *v.t.* to stab.
apurado (a·pu'ra·ðo) *adj.* 1, needy. 2, pressed; hurried. 3, drained. 4, risky; perilous.
apurar (a·pu'rar) *v.t.* 1, to press; hurry. 2, to drain. —**apurarse,** *v.r.* 1, to worry; be concerned. 2, *Amer.* to hurry; make haste.
apuro (a'pu·ro) *n.m.* 1, predicament. 2, need; distress. 3, *Amer.* haste.
aquejar (a·ke'xar) *v.t.* to ail; pain.
aquel (a'kel) *dem.adj.masc.* [*fem.* **aquella** (a'ke·ʎa; –ja); *pl.* **aquellos** (–ʎos; –jos), **aquellas** (–ʎas; –jas)] 1, that; *pl.* those. 2, former.
aquél (a'kel) *dem.pron.masc.* [*fem.* **aquélla** (a'ke·ʎa; –ja); *pl.* **aquéllos** (–ʎos; –jos), **aquéllas** (–ʎas; –jas)] 1, that; that one; *pl.* those. 2, the former.
aquello (a'ke·ʎo; -jo) *dem.pron. neut.* that; that matter.
aquende (a'ken·de) *adv.* hither.
aquerenciarse (a·ke·ren'θjar·se; –'sjar·se) *v.r.* to become fond.
aquí (a'ki) *adv.* here; hither. —**de aquí en adelante,** henceforth. —**de aquí que,** hence; consequently. —**hasta aquí,** hitherto. —**por aquí,** this way.
aquiescencia (a·kjes'θen·θja; –kje'sen·sja) *n.f.* acquiescence.
aquietar (a·kje'tar) *v.t.* to quiet; to calm. —**aquietarse,** *v.r.* to calm down.
aquilatar (a·ki·la'tar) *v.t.* 1, to assay. 2, to judge; to evaluate.
aquilino (a·ki'li·no) *adj., poet.* = **aguileño.**
aquilón (a·ki'lon) *n.m.* 1, north. 2, north wind.
ar- (ar) *prefix, var. of* **ad-** *before* r: *arrestar,* arrest.
-ar (ar) *suffix* 1, -ar; *forming adjectives expressing* relation; connection: *familiar,* familiar; *capsular,* capsular. 2, *forming nouns expressing* place where something abounds: *yesar,* gypsum pit; *malvar,* field of mallows.
ara ('a·ra) *n.f.* 1, altar, *esp.* sacrificial altar. 2, communion table.
árabe ('a·ra·βe) *adj.* & *n.m.* & *f.* Arabian; Arab. —*adj.* & *n.m.* Arabic (*language*).
arabesco (a·ra'βes·ko) *n.m.* arabesque.
arábico (a'ra·βi·ko) *adj.* Arabic, Arabian.
arábigo (a'ra·βi·ɣo) *adj.* Arabic; Arabian. —*n.m.* Arabic (*language*)
arable (a'ra·βle) *adj.* arable.
arácnido (a'rak·ni·ðo) *n.m., zool.* arachnid.
arado (a'ra·ðo) *n.m.* plow.
arameo (a·ra'me·o) *adj.* & *n.m.* Aramaic.
arancel (a·ran'θel; –'sel) *n.m.* tariff. —**derechos arancelarios,** customs duties.
arándano (a'ran·da·no) *n.m.* bilberry; whortleberry. —**arándano agrio,** cranberry.
arandela (a·ran'de·la) *n.f.* 1, *mech.* washer. 2, drip bowl of a candlestick.
araña (a'ra·ɲa) *n.f.* 1, spider. 2, chandelier. —**tela de araña,** spider web.
arañar (a·ra'ɲar) *v.t.* to scratch. —**arañazo,** *also,* **arañón, araño** (a'ra·ɲo) *n.m.* scratch.
arar (a'rar) *v.t.* to plow.
arbitrar (ar·βi'trar) *v.t.* & *i.* 1, to arbitrate. 2, to referee; umpire. 3, to contrive. —**arbitrador,** *n.m.* arbitrator. —**arbitraje,** *n.m.* arbitration.
arbitrario (ar·βi'tra·rjo) *adj.* arbitrary. —**arbitrariedad,** *n.f.* arbitrariness.
arbitrio (ar'βi·trjo) *n.m.* 1, free will. 2, judgment. 3, tax, esp. municipal.
árbitro ('ar·βi·tro) *n.m.* 1, arbiter; judge. 2, referee; umpire. 3, arbitrator.
árbol ('ar·βol) *n.m.* 1, tree. 2, *mech.* arbor; shaft. 3, *naut.* mast.
arbolado (ar·βo'la·ðo) *adj.* wooded; grown with trees. —*n.m.* wooded area; wood.
arboladura (ar·βo·la'ðu·ra) *n.f., naut.* masts and spars.
arboleda (ar·βo'le·ða) *n.f.* grove; wood.

arbóreo (ar'βo·re·o) *adj.* arboreal.
arbusto (ar'βus·to) *n.m.* shrub.
arca ('ar·ka) *n.f.* 1, chest; coffer. 2, strongbox; vault. 3, ark. —**arca de agua,** water tower.
-arca ('ar·ka) *suffix* -arch; ruler; chief: *monarca,* monarch; *tetrarca,* tetrarch.
arcabuz (ar·ka'βuθ; –'βus) *n.m.* [*pl.* –**buces**] harquebus.
arcada (ar'ka·ða) *n.f.* 1, arcade. 2, retching.
arcaico (ar'kai·ko) *adj.* archaic. —**arcaísmo** (–ka'is·mo) *n.m.* archaism.
arcángel (ar'kan·xel) *n.m.* archangel.
arcano (ar'ka·no) *adj.* hidden; secret. —*n.m.* secret.
arce ('ar·θe; –se) *n.m.* maple tree.
arcediano (ar·θe'ðja·no; ar·se–) *n.m.* archdeacon.
arcilla (ar'θi·ʎa; –'si·ja) *n.f.* clay. —**arcilloso,** *adj.* clayey.
arcipreste (ar·θi'pres·te; ar·si–) *n.m.* archpriest.
arco ('ar·ko) *n.m.* 1, bow. 2, arc. 3, arch. 4, hoop. —**arco iris,** rainbow.
archi- (ar·tʃi) *also,* **arqui-**; **arz-**; *prefix* arch-; archi-; arche-; first; chief: *archiduque,* archduke; *arquitecto,* architect; *arzobispo,* archbishop.
archidiácono (ar·tʃi'ðja·ko·no) *n.m.* = **arcediano.**
archidiócesis (ar·tʃi'ðjo·θe·sis; –se·sis) *n.f.* archdiocese.
archiduque (ar·tʃi'ðu·ke) *n.m.* archduke. —**archiducado,** *n.m.* archduchy. —**archiducal,** *adj.* archducal. —**archiduquesa,** *n.f.* archduchess.
archipiélago (ar·tʃi'pje·la·ɣo) *n.m.* archipelago.
archivador (ar·tʃi·βa'ðor) *n.m.* filing cabinet or case.
archivo (ar'tʃi·βo) *n.m.* file; archives (*pl.*). —**archivar,** *v.t.* to file. —**archivero,** *n.m.* archivist.
ardentísimo (ar·ðen'ti·si·mo) *adj., superl. of* **ardiente.**
arder (ar'ðer) *v.i.* 1, to burn; blaze. 2, to rage. 3, to yearn. 4, *Amer.* to itch; chafe.
ardid (ar'ðið) *n.m.* stratagem.
ardiente (ar'ðjen·te) *adj.* ardent.
ardilla (ar'ði·ʎa; –ja) *n.f.* squirrel.
ardimiento (ar·ði'mjen·to) *n.m.* courage; daring.
ardite (ar'ði·te) *n.m.* an ancient Spanish coin of little value. —**no valer un ardite,** not to be worth a tinker's dam.
-ardo ('ar·ðo) *suffix, forming nouns and adjectives, usu. with derog. meaning: bastardo,* bastard.
ardor (ar'ðor) *n.m.* 1, ardor; heat. 2, courage; valor. —**ardoroso,** *adj.* fiery.
arduo ('ar·ðwo) *adj.* arduous. —**arduidad,** *n.f.* arduousness.
área ('a·re·a) *n.f.* 1, area; region. 2, are.
arena (a're·na) *n.f.* 1, sand. 2, arena. —**arena movediza,** quicksand.
arenal (a·re'nal) *n.m.* 1, sandy terrain; desert. 2, quicksand.
arenga (a'ren·ga) *n.f.* harangue.
arengar (a·ren'gar) *v.t. & i.* [*pres. subjve.* **arengue** (a'ren·ge); *pret.* **arengué** (–'ge)] to harangue.
arenisca (a·re'nis·ka) *n.f.* sandstone.
arenoso (a·re'no·so) *also,* **arenisco** (–'ni·sko) *adj.* sandy.
arenque (a'ren·ke) *n.m.* herring.
arete (a're·te) *n.m.* earring.
argamasa (ar·ɣa'ma·sa) *n.f.* mortar. —**argamasar,** *v.t.* 1, to mix (mortar). 2, to join with mortar.
argentar (ar·xen'tar) *v.t.* to silver; to trim with silver.
argentino (ar·xen'ti·no) *adj.* 1, [*also, poet.,* **argentado** (–'ta·ðo), **argénteo** (–'xen·te·o)] silvery. 2, Argentine; Argentinian. —*n.m.* Argentine.
argentoso (ar·xen'to·so) *adj.* mixed with silver.
argirol (ar·xi'rol) *n.m.* argyrol.
argo ('ar·ɣo) *n.m.* argon. *Also,* **argón.**
argolla (ar'ɣo·ʎa; –ja) *n.f.* 1, metal ring or band. 2, *Amer.* engagement *or* wedding band.
argón (ar'ɣon) *n.m.* argon.
argot (ar'ɣo) *n.m.* [*pl.* **argots** (ar·'ɣo)] argot; jargon.
argucia (ar'ɣu·θja; –sja) *n.f.* sophistry.
argüir (ar'ɣwir) *v.t. & i.* [*infl.:* **huir**] to argue.
argumentar (ar·ɣu·men'tar) *v.t.* to deduce; to infer. —*v.i.* to argue. —**argumentación,** *n.f.* argument; argumentation. —**argumentador,** *adj.* argumentative. —*n.m.* arguer. —**argumentativo,** *adj.* argumentative.

argumento (ar·ɣu'men·to) *n.m.* 1, argument. 2, plot (*of a play, novel, etc.*).
aria ('a·rja) *n.f.* aria.
-aria ('a·rja) *suffix, forming feminine nouns expressing* relation; connection: *funeraria,* funeral home.
árido ('a·ri·ðo) *adj.* arid. —**aridez,** *n.f.* aridity.
Aries ('a·rjes) *n.m.* Aries.
ariete (a'rje·te) *n.m.* battering ram. —**ariete hidráulico,** hydraulic ram.
ario ('a·rjo) *adj.* & *n.m.* Aryan.
-ario ('a·rjo) *suffix* -ary; -arian; -arious; -arium; *forming adjectives and nouns expressing* relation; connection: *voluntario,* voluntary; *autoritario,* authoritarian; *temerario,* temerarious; *acuario,* aquarium.
arisco (a'ris·ko) *adj.* untamed; rough.
arista (a'ris·ta) *n.f.* 1, awn. 2, edge; ridge; rib.
aristocracia (a·ris·to'kra·θja; –sja) *n.f.* aristocracy. —**aristócrata** (–'to·kra·ta) *n.m.* & *f.* aristocrat. —**aristocrático** (–'kra·ti·ko) *adj.* aristocratic.
aritmética (a·rit'me·ti·ka) *n.f.* arithmetic. —**aritmético,** *adj.* arithmetical. —*n.m.* arithmetician.
arlequín (ar·le'kin) *n.m.* harlequin. —**arlequinada,** *n.f.* buffoonery; harlequinade.
arma ('ar·ma) *n.f.* weapon. —**armas,** *n.f.pl.* 1, arms. 2, military profession. 3, coat of arms. **alzarse en armas,** to rebel. **-arma blanca,** steel weapon. —**de armas tomar,** easily aroused; ready to fight. —**maestro de armas,** fencing master. —**pasar por las armas,** to execute. —**rendir las armas,** to surrender. —**sobre las armas,** under arms.
armada (ar'ma·ða) *n.f.* navy; fleet.
armadía (ar·ma'ði·a) *n.f.* raft.
armadillo (ar·ma'ði·ʎo; -jo) *n.m.* armadillo.
armado (ar'ma·ðo) *adj.* 1, armed. 2, reinforced. —*n.m.* assembly; mounting.
armador (ar·ma'ðor) *n.m.* 1, assembler; rigger. 2, *naut.* outfitter.
armadura (ar·ma'ðu·ra) *n.f.* 1, armor. 2, armature; framework. 3, *electricity* armature.
armamento (ar·ma'men·to) *n.m.* 1, armament. 2, *naut.* fitting out.
armar (ar'mar) *v.t.* 1, to arm. 2, to load (a weapon). 3, *carpentry* to assemble. 4, *mech.* to mount; to rig up. 5, *naut.* to equip; to fit out. 6, *colloq.* to start (a noisy action). —**armarse,** *v.r.* 1, to arm; arm oneself. 2, *Amer., colloq.* to strike it rich. —**armar caballero,** to knight.
armario (ar'ma·rjo) *n.m.* wardrobe; cabinet.
armatoste (ar·ma'tos·te) *n.m.* clumsy person or thing; hulk.
armazón (ar·ma'θon; –'son) *n.f.* framework; frame. —*n.m.* skeleton.
armella (ar'me·ʎa; –ja) *n.f.* screw-eye.
armería (ar·me'ri·a) *n.f.* 1, armory. 2, gunsmith's trade *or* shop. 3, arms collection; arms museum.
armero (ar'me·ro) *n.m.* 1, gunsmith. 2, keeper of arms. 3, rifle rack.
armiño (ar'mi·ɲo) *n.m.* ermine.
armisticio (ar·mis'ti·θjo; –sjo) *n.m.* armistice.
armonía (ar·mo'ni·a) *n.f.* 1, harmony. 2, harmoniousness. 3, harmonics (*pl.*).
armónica (ar'mo·ni·ka) *n.f.* harmonica.
armónico (ar'mo·ni·ko) *adj.* & *n.m.* harmonic.
armonioso (ar·mo'njo·so) *adj.* harmonious.
armonizar (ar·mo·ni'θar; –'sar) *v.t.* & *i.* [*pres.subjve.* **armonice** (–'ni·θe; –se); *pret.* **armonicé** (–'θe; –'se)] to harmonize.
arnés (ar'nes) *n.m.* coat of mail —**arneses,** *n.m.pl.* harness (*sing.*)
árnica ('ar·ni·ka) *n.f.* arnica.
aro ('a·ro) *n.m.* 1, hoop; large ring 2, croquet wicket. **-aro de émbolo,** piston ring. **-entrar por el aro,** to be forced to submit.
aroma (a'ro·ma) *n.m.* aroma
aromático (a·ro'ma·ti·ko) *adj* aromatic. —**sales aromáticas,** smelling salts.
aromatizar (a·ro·ma·ti'θar; –'sar) *v.t.* [*pres.subjve.* **aromatice** (–'ti·θe –se); *pret.* **aromaticé** (–'θe; –'se)] to perfume. —**aromatizador,** *n.m* atomizer.
arpa ('ar·pa) *n.f.* harp.
arpeo (ar'pe·o) *n.* grapple; grappling iron.
arpía (ar'pi·a) *n.f.* harpy; shrew.
arpillera (ar·pi'ʎe·ra; –'je·ra) *n.f.* = **harpillera.**

arpista (ar'pis·ta) *n.m.* & *f.* harpist.
arpón (ar'pon) *n.m.* harpoon. —**arponear** (–ne'ar) *also,* **arponar** (–'nar) *v.t.* to harpoon.
arponero (ar·po'ne·ro) *n.m.* 1, harpooner. 2, harpoon maker.
arque- (ar·ke) *prefix* arche-; *var. of* **archi-**: *arquetipo,* archetype.
arqueada (ar·ke'a·ða) *n.f.* retch; retching.
arquear (ar·ke'ar) *v.t.* to arch; bend; bow. —*v.i.* to retch.
arqueo (ar'ke·o) *n.m.* 1, arching; bending. 2, inventory, esp. of cash.
arqueo- (ar·ke·o) *prefix* archeo-; ancient: *arqueología,* archæology.
arqueología (ar·ke·o·lo'xi·a) *n.f.* archaeology. —**arqueológico** (–'lo·xi·ko) *adj.* archaeological. —**arqueólogo** (–'o·lo·ɣo) *n.m.* archaeologist.
arquero (ar'ke·ro) *n.m.* 1, archer. 2, bow maker. 3, *sports* goalkeeper.
arquetipo (ar·ke'ti·po) *n.m.* archetype.
arqui- (ar·ki) *prefix, var. of* **archi-**: *arquitecto,* architect.
-arquía (ar'ki·a) *suffix* -archy; rule; dignity: *jerarquía,* hierarchy.
arquidiócesis (ar·ki-) *n.f.* = **archidiócesis.**
arquitectura (ar·ki·tek'tu·ra) *n.f.* architecture. —**arquitecto** (–'tek·to) *n.m.* architect. —**arquitectónico** (–'to·ni·ko) *adj.* architectural.
arrabal (a·rra'βal) *n.m.* 1, suburb; *pl.* outskirts. 2, poor quarter; slum. 3, *Amer.* slum dwelling; tenement.
arrabalero (a·rra·βa'le·ro) *adj.* 1, suburban; of the outskirts. 2, slum (*attrib.*). 3, ill-bred. —*n.m.* 1, slum dweller. 2, roughneck; rowdy.
arracimar (a·rra·θi'mar; –si'mar) *v.t.* to cluster; bunch. —**arracimarse,** *v.r.* to form in a cluster. —**arracimado,** *adj.* clustered; bunched.
arraigar (a·rrai'ɣar) *v.i.* [*pres. subjve.* **arraigue** (a'rrai·ɣe); *pret.* **arraigué** (–'ɣe)] to take root. —**arraigarse,** *v.r.* to settle; become established. —**arraigado,** *adj.* deep-rooted.
arraigo (a'rrai·ɣo) *n.m.* 1, settling; taking root. 2, property; real estate.
arrancada (a·rran'ka·ða) *n.f.* 1, start; takeoff. 2, spurt; burst of speed.
arrancado (a·rran'ka·ðo) *adj., slang* broke; penniless.
arrancar (a·rran'kar) *v.t.* [*pres. subjve.* **arranque** (a'rran·ke); *pret.* **arranqué** (–'ke)] 1, to uproot. 2, to pull out. 3, to tear off or away. 4, to force out; eject; heave (a sigh). —*v.i.* to start; take off. —**arrancar de,** to spring from; stem from.
arranchar (a·rran'tʃar) *v.t., Amer.* to snatch; grab. —*v.i., Amer., colloq.* to live (with someone); cohabit.
arranque (a'rran·ke) *n.m.* 1, start; starting. 2, outburst. 3, sudden impulse; fit. 4, *mech.* starter.
arras ('a·rras) *n.f.pl.* traditional gift of thirteen coins given by the bridegroom to the bride.
arrasar (a·rra'sar) *v.t.* 1, to raze; level. 2, to fill; cause to brim over. —*v.i.* [*also,* **arrasarse,** *v.r.*] to clear up, as the sky.
arrastrar (a·rras'trar) *v.t.* to drag; haul. —*v.i.* to play trumps. —**arrastrarse,** *v.r.* 1, to crawl. 2, *fig.* to cringe; fawn. —**arrastrado,** *adj.* miserable. —*n.m.* knave; miscreant.
arrastre (a'rras·tre) *n.m.* 1, drayage; haulage. 2, dragging; hauling. 3, *Amer.* drag; pull. 4, *cards* trump lead.
arrayán (a·rra'jan) *n.m.* myrtle.
¡arre! ('a·rre) *interj.* gee up!; giddap!
arrear (a·rre'ar) *v.t.* 1, to drive (animals). 2, to deal (a blow, insult, etc.). 3, *Amer.* to rustle (livestock).
arrebatar (a·rre·βa'tar) *v.t.* 1, to snatch. 2, to captivate. —**arrebatarse,** *v.r.* to be carried away emotionally. —**arrebatado,** *adj.* rash; violent; *slang* crazy. —**arrebatador,** *adj.* captivating; stirring.
arrebato (a·rre'βa·to) *n.m.* 1, paroxysm; rage. 2, rapture.
arrebol (a·rre'βol) *n.m.* 1, red or rosy tinge. 2, rouge. —**arreboles,** *n.m.pl.* [*also,* **arrebolada,** *n.f.sing.*] red clouds. —**arrebolarse,** *v.r.* to redden; turn red.
arrebujar (a·rre·βu'xar) *v.t.* to cover up; bundle up; muffle.
arreciar (a·rre'θjar; –'sjar) *v.i.* to rage; to become more intense.

arrecife (a·rre'θi·fe; –'si·fe) *n.m.* reef.
arredrarse (a·rre'ðrar·se) *v.r.* to shrink; draw back, as in fright.
arreglar (a·rre'ɣlar) *v.t.* **1,** to arrange. **2,** to settle; adjust. **3,** to repair; fix. **4,** to tidy; put in order. —**arreglarse,** *v.r.* **1,** to conform. **2,** to agree; reach an agreement. —**arreglárselas,** *colloq.* to get along; manage.
arreglo (a'rre·ɣlo) *n.m.* **1,** settlement; compromise. **2,** arrangement; order. **3,** putting in order; tidying. **4,** repair. —**con arreglo a,** in accordance with; according to.
arrellanarse (a·rre·ʎa'nar·se; –ja'nar·se) *v.r.* to lounge; loll; sprawl.
arremangar (a·rre·man'gar) *v.t.* [*infl.:* **llegar**] to roll *or* tuck up (one's sleeves, trousers, skirts, etc.)
arremeter (a·rre·me'ter) *v.i.* to attack. —**arremetida,** *n.f.* attack.
arremolinarse (a·rre·mo·li'nar·se) *v.r.* to spin; whirl; eddy.
arrendador (a·rren·da'ðor) *n.m.* **1,** lessor. **2,** tenant.
arrendajo (a·rren'da·xo) *n.m.* jay bird.
arrendamiento (a·rren·da·'mjen·to) *n.m.* **1,** rent; lease. **2,** rental.
arrendar (a·rren'dar) *v.t.* [*pres. ind.* **arriendo;** *pres.subjve.* **arriende**] **1,** to rent. **2,** to lease.
arrendatario (a·rren·da'ta·rjo) *adj.* **1,** renting. **2,** leasing. —*n.m.* **1,** tenant. **2,** lessee.
arreos (a'rre·os) *n.m.pl.* harness (*sing.*). —*adv.* uninterruptedly.
arrepentirse (a·rre·pen'tir·se) *v.r.* [*pres.ind.* **arrepiento** (–'pjen·to); *pres.subjve.* **arrepienta;** *pret.* **arrepentí** (-pen'ti); **arrepintió** (-pin·'tjo)] to repent. —**arrepentido,** *adj.* repentant. —**arrepentimiento,** *n.m.* repentance.
arrestar (a·rres'tar) *v.t.* to arrest.
arresto (a'rres·to) *n.m.* arrest.
arriar (a'rrjar) *v.t.,* [*infl.:* **variar**] to lower. —**arriar las velas,** to take in sail. —**arriar la bandera,** to strike the colors. —**arriar un cabo,** to pay out a rope.
arriba (a'rri·βa) *adv.* **1,** above; up; on high. **2,** upstairs. —**arriba de,** upwards of (*in expressions of quantity*). —**boca arriba,** face up; right side up. —**de arriba abajo,** from head to foot; from top to bottom. —**hasta arriba,** all the way up; to the top. —**para** *or* **hacia arriba,** up; upwards.
arribar (a·rri'βar) *v.i.* to arrive. —**arribo** (a'rri·βo) *n.m.,* *also,* **arribada,** *n.f.* arrival.
arriende (a'rrjen·de) *v.,* *pres. subjve. of* **arrendar.**
arriendo (a'rrjen·do) *n.m.* = **arrendamiento.** —*v.,* *pres.ind. of* **arrendar.**
arriero (a'rrje·ro) *n.m.* muleteer; teamster.
arriesgado (a·rrjes'ɣa·do) *adj.* **1,** risky. **2,** reckless.
arriesgar (a·rrjes'ɣar) *v.t.* [*pres. subjve.* **arriesgue** (a'rrjes·ɣe); *pret.* **arriesgué** (–'ɣe)] to risk. —**arriesgarse,** *v.r., colloq.* to take a chance.
arrimar (a·rri'mar) *v.t.* to bring close; to place near. —**arrimarse,** *v.r.* to draw near. —**arrimarse a, 1,** to get close to. **2,** to seek the protection of.
arrinconado (a·rrin·ko'na·ðo) *adj.* **1,** shelved; put aside; neglected. **2,** secluded; remote. **3,** cornered.
arrinconar (a·rrin·ko'nar) *v.t.* **1,** to place in a corner. **2,** to corner. **3,** to shelve; put aside. —**arrinconarse,** *v.r.* to seclude oneself.
arriscarse (a·rris'kar·se) *v.r.* [*pres.subjve.* **arrisque** (a'rris·ke); *pret.* **arrisqué** (–'ke)] to become angry; to flare up. —**arriscado,** *adj.* conceited.
arroba (a'rro·βa) *n.f.* **1,** a Spanish unit of weight of about 25 pounds. **2,** a Spanish liquid measure varying by region and the weight of the liquid.
arrobar (a·rro'βar) *v.t.* to entrance. —**arrobo** (a'rro·βo) *also,* **arrobamiento,** *n.m.* ecstasy.
arrocero (a·rro'θe·ro; –'se·ro) *n.m.* rice grower. —*adj.* of or pert. to rice.
arrodillarse (a·rro·ði'ʎar·se; –'jar·se) *v.r.* to kneel.
arrogancia (a·rro'ɣan·θja; –sja) *n.f.* **1,** arrogance. **2,** gallantry.
arrogante (a·rro'ɣan·te) *adj.* **1,** arrogant. **2,** gallant.
arrogarse (a·rro'ɣar·se) *v.r.* [*pres.subjve.* **arrogue** (a'rro·ɣe); *pret.* **arrogué** (–'ɣe)] to arrogate to oneself; usurp. —**arrogación,** *n.f.* arrogation.
arrojadizo (a·rro·xa'ði·θo; -so)

adj. for throwing or hurling, as a weapon.
ırrojado (a·rro'xa·ðo) *adj.* reckless; bold. —**arrojo** (a'rro·xo) *n.m.* boldness; recklessness.
ırrojar (a·rro'xar) *v.t.* **1,** to throw. **2,** to cast out. **3,** to shed; to give off. **4,** to show (balance *or* numerical result). —**arrojarse,** *v.r.* to rush; to throw oneself. —*v.i.* to vomit.
ırrollar (a·rro'ʎar; –'jar) *v.t.* **1,** to overwhelm. **2,** to run over. **3,** to sweep away.
ırropar (a·rro'par) *v.t.* to clothe; to cover. —**arroparse,** *v.r.* to clothe *or* cover oneself.
ırrostrar (a·rros'trar) *v.t.* to brave; to face.
ırroyo (a'rro·jo) *n.m.* **1,** brook. **2,** gutter.
ırroz (a'rroθ; a'rros) *n.m.* rice. —**arrozal,** *n.m.* rice field.
ırruga (a'rru·ɣa) *n.f.* wrinkle.
ırrugar (a·rru'ɣar) *v.t.* [*pres. subjve.* **arrugue** (a'rru·ɣe); *pret.* **arrugué** (–'ɣe)] to wrinkle. —**arrugar la frente** *or* **el entrecejo,** to frown.
ırruinar (a·rrwi'nar) *v.t.* to ruin. —**arruinador,** *adj.* ruinous.
ırrullar (a·rru'ʎar; –'jar) *v.t.* **1,** to coo to. **2,** to whisper or murmur to; say sweet nothings to. **3,** to lull.
ırrullo (a'rru·ʎo; –jo) *n.m.* **1,** coo; cooing. **2,** whisper; murmur. **3,** lullaby.
ırrumaco (a·rru'ma·ko) *n.m., usu.pl., colloq.* show of affection.
ırrumar (a·rru'mar) *v.t.* to stow (cargo). —**arrumarse,** *v.r., naut.* to become overcast. —**arrumaje,** *n.m.* stowage.
ırrumbar (a·rrum'bar) *v.t.* to put aside; shelve.
ırsenal (ar·se'nal) *n.m.* **1,** shipyard. **2,** arsenal. **3,** *fig.* store; storehouse.
arsénico (ar'se·ni·ko) *n.m.* arsenic. —**arsenical,** *adj.* arsenical.
arte ('ar·te) *n.m. or f.* art. —**artes y oficios,** arts and crafts. —**bellas artes,** fine arts. —**no tener arte ni parte en,** to have nothing to do with.
artefacto (ar·te'fak·to) *n.m.* **1,** artifact. **2,** device; gadget.
artejo (ar'te·xo) *n.m.* joint; segment.
arteria (ar'te·rja) *n.f.* artery. —**arterial** (–'rjal) *adj.* arterial.
artería (ar·te'ri·a) *n.f.* trickery; chicanery.
arteriosclerosis (ar·te·rjos·kle·'ro·sis) *n.f.* arteriosclerosis.
artero (ar'te·ro) *adj.* sly; underhanded; artful.
artesa (ar'te·sa) *n.f.* trough; kneading trough.
artesanía (ar·te·sa'ni·a) *n.f.* **1,** craftsmanship. **2,** = **artesanado.**
artesano (ar·te'sa·no) *n.m.* artisan; craftsman. —**artesanado,** *n.m.* artisans or craftsmen collectively.
artesiano (ar·te'sja·no) *adj.* artesian.
ártico ('ar·ti·ko) *adj.* arctic. —*n.m., cap.* Arctic Ocean.
articulación (ar·ti·ku·la'θjon; –'sjon) *n.f.* **1,** joint. **2,** articulation.
articulado (ar·ti·ku'la·ðo) *adj.* **1,** articulated; jointed. **2,** articulate.
articular (ar·ti·ku'lar) *v.t.* to articulate.
articulista (ar·ti·ku'lis·ta) *n.m. & f.* feature writer; columnist.
artículo (ar'ti·ku·lo) *n.m.* article. —**artículo de comercio,** commodity. —**artículo de fondo,** editorial. —**artículo de primera necesidad,** basic commodity.
artífice (ar'ti·fi·θe; -se) *n.m. & f.* **1,** artist; craftsman (*or* craftswoman). **2,** artificer.
artificial (ar·ti·fi'θjal; –'sjal) *adj.* artificial. —**artificialidad,** *n.f.* artificiality.
artificio (ar·ti'fi·θjo; –sjo) *n.m.* **1,** skill; craftsmanship. **2,** artifice; device. —**artificioso,** *adj.* artful; contrived.
artilugio (ar·ti'lu·xjo) *n.m.* low trick.
artillado (ar·ti'ʎa·ðo; -'ja·ðo) *n.m.* complement of guns; artillery.
artillar (ar·ti'ʎar; –'jar) *v.t.* to arm with guns or artillery.
artillería (ar·ti·ʎe'ri·a; ar·ti·je–) *n.f.* **1,** artillery. **2,** gunnery. —**artillería de campaña,** field artillery.
artillero (ar·ti'ʎe·ro; –'je·ro) *n.m.* **1,** gunner. **2,** artilleryman.
artimaña (ar·ti'ma·ɲa) *n.f.* trap; snare; trick.
artista (ar'tis·ta) *n.m. & f.* artist. —**artístico,** *adj.* artistic.
artritis (ar'tri·tis) *n.f.* arthritis. —**artrítico,** *adj.* arthritic.
artrópodo (ar'tro·po·ðo) *n.m.* arthropod.

arveja (ar'βe·xa) *n.f.* **1,** vetch. **2,** *Amer.* pea.
arz- (arθ; ars) *prefix, var. of* **archi-**: *arzobispo,* archbishop.
arzobispo (ar·θo'βis·po; ar·so–) *n.m.* archbishop. **—arzobispado,** *n.m.* archbishopric. **—arzobispal,** *adj.* archiepiscopal.
as (as) *n.m.* ace.
asa ('a·sa) *n.f.* handle.
-asa ('a·sa) *suffix* -ase; *forming nouns denoting* enzymes: *diastasa,* diastase.
asado (a'sa·ðo) *n.m.* roast. **—*adj.*** roasted. **—asador,** *n.m.* spit; roaster.
asaetear (a·sa·e·te'ar) *v.t.* **1,** to shoot with an arrow; rain arrows upon. **2,** to harass; importune.
asafétida (a·sa'fe·ti·ða) *n.f.* asafetida.
asalariado (a·sa·la'rja·ðo) *adj.* salaried; paid. **—*n.m.*** paid worker; salaried employee.
asaltar (a·sal'tar) *v.t.* to assault. **—asaltador, asaltante,** *n.m.* assailant. **—*adj.*** assailing.
asalto (a'sal·to) *n.m.* **1,** assault. **2,** *fencing* bout. **3,** *boxing* round. **4,** *Amer.* surprise party. **—por asalto,** by storm.
asamblea (a·sam'ble·a) *n.f.* assembly. **—asambleísta** (–'is·ta) *n.m. & f.* assemblyman *or* assemblywoman.
asar (a'sar) *v.t.* to roast. **—asarse,** *v.r.* to feel extremely hot.
asaz (a'saθ; a'sas) *adv.* very; extremely; exceedingly.
asbesto (as'βes·to) *n.m.* asbestos.
ascalonia (as·ka'lo·nja) *n.f.* shallot. *Also,* **escalonia** (es–).
ascendencia (as·θen'den·θja; a·sen'den·sja) *n.f.* **1,** ancestry. **2,** ascendancy; influence. **—ascendente,** *adj.* ascending; rising; ascendant.
ascender (as·θen'der; a·sen–) *v.t.* [*pres.ind.* **asciendo** (as'θjen·do; a'sjen·do); *pres.subjve.* **ascienda** (–da)] to promote; advance in grade or rank. **—*v.i.* 1,** to ascend; climb. **2,** to be promoted or advanced. **—ascender a,** to come to; amount to.
ascendiente (as·θen'djen·te; a·sen–) *n.m. & f.* ancestor. **—*n.m.*** ascendancy; influence. **—*adj.* = ascendente.**
ascensión (as·θen'sjon; a·sen–) *n.f.* **1,** ascent; ascension. **2,** elevation; exaltation. **3,** *cap.,* rel Ascension. **—ascensionista,** *n.m. f.* balloonist.
ascenso (as'θen·so; a'sen–) *n.* **1,** promotion; rise. **2,** career st or grade.
ascensor (as·θen'sor; a·sen–) *n.* elevator.
asceta (as'θe·ta; a'se–) *n.m. &* ascetic.
ascético (as'θe·ti·ko; a'se-) *a* ascetic. **—ascetismo,** *n.m.* asce cism.
asco ('as·ko) *n.m.* repugnanc **—estar hecho un asco,** to be dirt to be slovenly.
ascua ('as·kwa) *n.f.* ember. **—est en** *or* **sobre ascuas,** *colloq.* to on pins and needles.
asear (a·se'ar) *v.t.* to clean; tid **—aseado,** *adj.* clean; tidy.
asechar (a·se'tʃar) *v.t.* to a bush; waylay. **—asechanza,** *n* trap; snare.
asediar (a·se'ðjar) *v.t.* to besieg **—asedio** (a'se·ðjo) *n.m.* siege.
asegurar (a·se·ɣu'rar) *v.t.* **1,** secure; make fast. **2,** to assure. to insure.
asemejar (a·se·me'xar) *v.t.* **1,** make alike. **2,** to liken; compa **—*v.i.*** [*also,* **asemejarse,** *v.r.*] to alike; have a likeness or rese blance.
asenso (a'sen·so) *n.m.* **1,** asse **2,** credence; belief.
asentada (a·sen'ta·ða) *n.f.* s ting. **—de una asentada,** at o sitting.
asentaderas (a·sen·ta'ðe·ra *n.f.pl., colloq.* buttocks.
asentado (a·sen'ta·ðo) *adj.* seated; situated. **2,** stable; perm nent. **3,** tranquil.
asentar (a·sen'tar) *v.t.* [*pres.in* **asiento;** *pres.subjve.* **asiente**] **1,** put; set; place. **2,** to flatten; tam **3,** to affirm; assert. **4,** to go w with; agree with. **5,** to consolida **6,** to note down; record. **7,** to liver; deal (a blow). **8,** *slang* to (someone) down. **—*v.i.* 1,** to be coming. **2,** to agree; go w **—asentarse,** *v.r.* **1,** to settle; beco settled. **2,** to become firm. **3,** lie heavy, as food.
asentir (a·sen'tir) *v.i.* [*infl.:* se **tir**] to assent. **—asentimiento,** *n.* assent.

seo (a'se·o) *n.m.* cleanliness; neatness.
sepsia (a'sep·sja) *n.f.* asepsis. —**aséptico** (a'sep·ti·ko) *adj.* aseptic.
sequible (a·se'ki·βle) *adj.* **1,** attainable. **2,** obtainable. **3,** (*of persons*) approachable.
serción (a·ser'θjon; -'sjon) *n.f.* assertion.
serrar (a·se'rrar) *v.t.* [*pres.ind.* **asierro** (a'sje·rro); *pres.subjve.* **asierre**] to saw. —**aserradero,** *n.m.* sawmill. —**aserrado,** *adj.* serrated. —**aserrador,** *n.m.* sawyer. —**aserradura,** *n.f.* cut; *pl.* sawdust (*sing.*).
serrín (a·se'rrin) *n.m.* sawdust.
serruchar (a·se·rru'tʃar) *v.t., Amer.* to saw, esp. with a handsaw.
serto (a'ser·to) *n.m.* assertion. —**asertivo** (–'ti·βo) *adj.* assertive.
sesinar (a·se·si'nar) *v.t.* to assassinate. —**asesinato,** *n.m.* assassination.
sesino (a·se'si·no) *n.m.* assassin. —*adj.* murderous.
sesor (a·se'sor) *n.m.* adviser; consultant.
sesorar (a·se·so'rar) *v.t.* to advise. —**asesorarse,** *v.r.* to take advice; seek counsel.
sestar (a·ses'tar) *v.t.* **1,** to aim; direct. **2,** to deal (a blow). **3,** to hurl; fire (a shot).
severar (a·se·βe'rar) *v.t.* to affirm; assert. —**aseveración,** *n.f.* positive statement; assertion. —**aseveradamente,** *adv.* positively.
severativo (a·se·βe·ra'ti·βo) *adj.* **1,** assertive; affirmative. **2,** *gram.* declarative.
sexual (a·sek'swal) *adj.* asexual.
sfalto (as'fal·to) *n.m.* asphalt. —**asfaltar,** *v.t.* to pave with asphalt.
sfixia (as'fik·sja) *n.f.* asphyxia; suffocation. —**asfixiar,** *v.t.* to asphyxiate.
sfódelo (as'fo·ðe·lo) *n.m.* asphodel.
asga ('as·ɣa) *v., pres.subjve. of* **asir.**
asgo ('as·ɣo) *v., 1st pers.sing. pres.ind. of* **asir.**
así (a'si) *adv.* so; thus. —*conj.* though; although. —**así así,** so-so. —**así como, 1,** just as. **2,** as well as. **3,** as soon as. —**así . . . . . como,** both . . . . . and; not only . . . . . but also. —**así como así; así que así,** anyway; anyhow —**así no más,** *Amer., colloq.* so-so. —**así que, 1,** so that. **2,** as soon as. —**así sea,** would that it be (*or* were) so. —**así y todo,** nevertheless.
asiático (a'sja·ti·ko) *adj. & n.m.* Asiatic. —**lujo asiático,** Oriental splendor.
asidero (a·si'ðe·ro) *n.m.* **1,** grip; handle. **2,** pretext.
asiduo (a'si·ðwo) *adj.* assiduous. —*n.m.* habitué. —**asiduidad,** *n.f.* assiduity.
asienta (a'sjen·ta) *v.* **1,** *pres. subjve. of* **asentir. 2,** *pres.ind. 3rd pers.sing. of* **asentar.**
asiente (a'sjen·te) *v., pres.subjve. of* **asentar.**
asiento (a'sjen·to) *n.m.* **1,** seat. **2,** sediment. **3,** *comm.* entry. **4,** settling (*of a building*). **5,** *fig.* good judgment; stability. —*v.* **1,** *pres.ind. of* **asentar. 2,** *pres.ind. of* **asentir.**
asignación (a·siɣ·na'θjon; -'sjon) *n.f.* **1,** assignment. **2,** salary; allowance.
asignar (a·siɣ'nar) *v.t.* to assign.
asignatario (a·siɣ·na'ta·rjo) *n.m., law, Amer.* trustee; legatee.
asignatura (a·siɣ·na'tu·ra) *n.f.* academic subject.
asilado (a·si'la·ðo) *n.m.* **1,** inmate (*of an asylum, home, etc.*). **2,** refugee.
asilar (a·si'lar) *v.t.* **1,** to shelter; give asylum to. **2,** to place in a home or asylum.
asilo (a'si·lo) *n.m.* asylum; refuge.
asimetría (a·si·me'tri·a) *n.f.* asymmetry. —**asimétrico** (–'me·tri·ko) *adj.* asymmetrical.
asimilar (a·si·mi'lar) *v.t. & i.* to assimilate. —**asimilarse,** *v.r.* to be or become alike. —**asimilación,** *n.f.* assimilation.
asimismo (a·si'mis·mo) *adv.* likewise; also; exactly.
asir (a'sir) *v.t.* [*pres.ind.* **asgo;** *pres.subjve.* **asga**] to grasp; seize. —**asirse,** *v.r.* to take hold. —**asirse a,** to catch at; hold on to. —**asirse de,** to seize (as an opportunity); take advantage of.
asirio (a'si·rjo) *adj. & n.m.* Assyrian.
-asis (a·sis) *suffix* -asis; *forming nouns denoting* diseases: *elefantíasis,* elephantiasis.
asistencia (a·sis'ten·θja; –sja) *n.f.* **1,** assistance; aid. **2,** attendance. **3,** *pl.* subsistence (*sing.*); support (*sing.*).

asistenta (a·sis'ten·ta) *n.f.* 1, female assistant. 2, day maid.
asistente (a·sis'ten·te) *n.m.* 1, assistant; helper; *mil.* orderly. 2, attendant.
asistir (a·sis'tir) *v.t.* 1, to assist; aid. 2, to attend; stand by. 3, to serve; minister to. —*v.i.* 1, to be present. 2, *cards* to follow suit.
asma ('as·ma) *n.f.* asthma. —**asmático** (–'ma·ti·ko) *adj.* & *n.m.* asthmatic.
-asmo ('as·mo) *suffix* -asm; *forming nouns denoting* action; tendency; quality: *orgasmo,* orgasm; *entusiasmo,* enthusiasm; *pleonasmo,* pleonasm.
asnada (as'na·ða) *n.f.* asininity.
asnería (as·ne'ri·a) *n.f.* 1, drove of asses. 2, asininity.
asno ('as·no) *n.m.* ass; donkey. —**asnal,** *adj.* asinine; of or pert. to asses.
asociación (a·so·θja'θjon; -sja·'sjon) *n.f.* 1, association. 2, partnership.
asociado (a·so'θja·ðo; -'sja·ðo) *adj.* 1, associated. 2, associate. —*n.m.* member; associate.
asociar (a·so'θjar; –'sjar) *v.t.* 1, to associate. 2, to attach; join. 3, to take into membership *or* partnership. —**asociarse,** *v.r.* 1, to associate; consort. 2, to associate oneself; become a member *or* partner. 3, to form a partnership *or* association. —**asociarse a** *or* **con,** to join.
asolar (a·so'lar) *v.t.* 1, [*pres.ind.* **asuelo;** *pres.subjve* **asuele**] to raze; devastate. 2, [*regularly inflected*] to burn up; parch (vegetation). —**asolador,** *adj.* devastating. —**asolamiento,** *n.m.* devastation.
asoleada (a·so·le'a·ða) *n.f., Amer.* 1, sunning; sunbath. 2, sunstroke.
asolear (a·so·le'ar) *v.t.* to sun. —**asoleado,** *adj.* sunny.
asomar (a·so'mar) *v.t.* to show; to allow to be seen. —*v.i.* to begin to appear. —**asomarse,** *v.r.* to lean out.
asombrar (a·som'brar) *v.t.* to amaze. —**asombrarse,** *v.r.* to be amazed.
asombro (a'som·bro) *n.m.* amazement. —**asombroso,** *adj.* amazing.
asomo (a'so·mo) *n.m.* sign; indication. —**ni por asomo,** not by a long shot; by no means.
asonancia (a·so'nan·θja; –sja) *n.f.* assonance. —**asonante,** *adj.* assonant.
aspa ('as·pa) *n.f.* 1, X-shaped cross. 2, arm of a windmill.
aspaventero (as·pa·βen'te·ro) *adj.* excitable; fussy. —*n.m.* demonstrative person; ham actor; ham.
aspaviento (as·pa'βjen·to) *n.m.* fuss.
aspecto (as'pek·to) *n.m.* aspect; countenance; appearance.
asperilla (as·pe'ri·ʎa; -ja) *n.f.* woodruff.
áspero ('as·pe·ro) *adj.* 1, rough; harsh. 2, *fig.* sharp; sour. 3, severe. —**aspereza,** *n.f.* roughness; harshness.
aspersión (as·per'sjon) *n.f.* sprinkling; aspersion.
áspid ('as·pið) *n.f.* asp.
aspiración (as·pi·ra'θjon; –'sjon) *n.f.* 1, inhalation. 2, aspiration. 3, suction.
aspirar (as·pi'rar) *v.t.* & *i.* 1, to inhale. 2, to aspirate. 3, to aspire; covet. —**aspiradora,** *n.f., also,* **aspirador,** *n.m.* vacuum cleaner. —**aspirante,** *n.m.* & *f.* aspirant; candidate. —**bomba aspirante,** vacuum pump.
aspirina (as·pi'ri·na) *n.f.* aspirin.
asquear (as·ke'ar) *v.t.* to consider with disgust. —*v.i.* to feel nauseated.
asqueroso (as·ke'ro·so) *adj.* 1, filthy. 2, loathsome; disgusting. 3, easily disgusted; squeamish. 4, nauseated. —**asquerosidad,** *n.f.* filth; filthiness.
asta ('as·ta) *n.f.* 1, shaft; handle. 2, lance; pike; spear. 3, flagpole. 4, antler; horn. —**a media asta,** at half mast.
-asta ('as·ta) *suffix* -ast; *forming nouns of agency corresponding to nouns ending in* **-asmo**: *entusiasta,* enthusiast.
astacio (as'ta·θjo; -sjo) *n.m.* astatine.
aster ('as·ter) *n.f.* aster.
asterisco (as·te'ris·ko) *n.m.* asterisk.
asteroide (as·te'roi·ðe) *n.m.* asteroid.
astigmático (as·tiɣ'ma·ti·ko) *adj.* astigmatic.
astigmatismo (as·tiɣ·ma'tis·mo) *n.m.* astigmatism.
astil (as'til) *n.m.* 1, shaft (*of an*

arrow or feather). **2,** beam (*of a balance*).
astilla (as'ti·ʎa; –ja) *n.f.* splinter. —**astillar,** *v.t.* to splinter.
astillero (as·ti'ʎe·ro; –'je·ro) *n.m.* shipyard.
-astra ('as·tra) *suffix, fem. of* **-astro.**
astral (as'tral) *adj.* astral.
-astre ('as·tre) *suffix* = **-astro.**
astringir (as·trin'xir) *v.t.* [*pres. ind.* **astrinjo** (as'trin·xo); *pres. subjve.* **astrinja** (–xa)] to astringe. —**astringencia,** *n.f.* astringency. —**astringente,** *adj. & n.m.* astringent.
astro ('as·tro) *n.m.* **1,** heavenly body; star. **2,** *fig.* male star.
astro- (as·tro) *prefix* astro-; star: *astrología,* astrology.
-astro ('as·tro) *also,* **-astra, -astre,** *suffix, forming nouns with dim. or derog. meaning: oleastro,* oleaster; *hijastro,* stepson; *madrastra,* stepmother; *poetastro,* poetaster; *pillastre,* scoundrel.
astofísica (as·tro'fi·si·ka) *n.f.* astrophysics. —**astrofísico,** *adj.* astrophysical.
astrología (as·tro·lo'xi·a) *n.f.* astrology. —**astrológico** (-'lo·xi·ko) *adj.* astrological. —**astrólogo** (as'tro·lo·ɣo) *n.m.* astrologer.
astronauta (as·tro'nau·ta) *n.m. & f.* astronaut. —**astronáutica** (–'nau·ti·ka) *n.f.* astronautics.
astronave (as·tro'na·βe) *n.f.* spaceship; spacecraft.
astronomía (as·tro·no'mi·a) *n.f.* astronomy. —**astronómico** (–'no·mi·ko) *adj.* astronomical. —**astrónomo** (as'tro·no·mo) *n.m.* astronomer.
astucia (as'tu·θja; –sja) *n.f.* **1,** astuteness. **2,** ruse.
astuto (as'tu·to) *adj.* astute; sly.
asuele (a'swe·le) *v., pres.subjve. of* **asolar.**
asuelo (a'swe·lo) *v., pres.ind. of* **asolar.**
asueto (a'swe·to) *n.m.* vacation; holiday.
asumir (a·su'mir) *v.t.* to assume; to take upon oneself.
asunción (a·sun'θjon; –'sjon) *n.f.* **1,** assumption. **2,** elevation (to a high office). **3,** *cap., R.C.Ch.* Assumption.
asunto (a'sun·to) *n.m.* subject matter; affair; business.
asustar (a·sus'tar) *v.t.* to frighten. —**asustarse,** *v.r.* to be frightened. —**asustadizo,** *adj.* easily frightened.
atabal (a·ta'βal) *n.m.* kettledrum.
atacar (a·ta'kar) *v.t.* [*pres. subjve.* **ataque** (a'ta·ke); *pret.* **ataqué** (–'ke)] to attack.
atadero (a·ta'ðe·ro) *n.m.* **1,** place *or* means of attachment. **2,** hitching post.
atado (a'ta·ðo) *n.m.* bundle.
atadura (a·ta'ðu·ra) *n.f.* **1,** tying; fastening. **2,** rope; cord. **3,** knot. **4,** *fig.* bond; tie.
atajar (a·ta'xar) *v.t.* **1,** to intercept. **2,** to restrain. —*v.i.* to take a short cut.
atajo (a'ta·xo) *n.m.* short cut.
atalaya (a·ta'la·ja) *n.f.* watchtower.
atañer (a·ta'ɲer) *v.t.* [*infl.:* **tañer**] to concern.
ataque (a'ta·ke) *n.m.* attack.
atar (a'tar) *v.t.* to tie. —**atarse,** *v.r., fig.* to tie oneself in knots; to be confused. —**atar cabos,** to put two and two together.
atarantar (a·ta·ran'tar) *v.t.* to confuse, bewilder. —**atarantado,** *adj., colloq.* restless; nervous; impulsive.
atardecer (a·tar·ðe'θer; –'ser) *n.m.* late afternoon; dusk.
atarear (a·ta·re'ar) *v.t.* to assign work to. —**atarearse,** *v.r.* to be busy; busy oneself. —**atareado,** *adj.* busy.
-atario (a'ta·rjo) *suffix* -er; -atory; -atary; *forming adjectives and nouns expressing* agency, relation; connection: *arrendatario,* renter; *mandatario,* mandatory; *signatario,* signatory.
atarugar (a·ta·ru'ɣar) *v.t.* [*pres. subjve.* **atarugue** (–'ru·ɣe); *pret.* **atarugué** (–'ɣe)] to wedge; to stuff; to plug. —**atarugarse,** *v.r.* **1,** to choke. **2,** to stumble (in speaking). —**atarugamiento,** *n.m.* stuffing; choking.
atascadero (a·tas·ka'ðe·ro) *n.m.* **1,** mudhole. **2,** obstruction.
atascar (a·tas'kar) *v.t.* [*pres.subjve.* **atasque** (a'tas·ke); *pret.* **atasqué** (–'ke)] **1,** to clog; choke. **2,** to plug; stop up. **3,** to obstruct; impede. —**atascarse,** *v.r.* to bog down.
atasco (a'tas·ko) *n.m.* **1,** obstacle; impediment. **2,** clog; jam; obstruction.
ataúd (a·ta'uð) *n.m.* coffin.
ataviar (a·ta'βjar) *v.t.* to deck

out. —**ataviarse,** *v.r.* to dress up.
atávico (a'ta·βi·ko) *adj.* atavistic.
atavío (a·ta'βi·o) *n.m.* dress; attire. —**atavíos,** *n.m.pl.* finery.
atavismo (a·ta'βis·mo) *n.m.* atavism.
ataxia (a'tak·sja) *n.f.* ataxia. —**ataxia locomotriz,** locomotor ataxia.
-ate ('a·te) *suffix, forming nouns expressing* **1,** action; result: *disparate,* blunder. **2,** quality; condition: *botarate,* madcap.
atece (a'te·θe; -se) *v., pres.subjve. of* **atezar.**
atecé (a·te'θe; -'se) *v., 1st pers. sing. pret. of* **atezar.**
ateísmo (a·te'is·mo) *n.m.* atheism. —**ateísta,** *n.m. & f.* atheist. —*adj.* [*also,* **ateístico**] atheistic.
atemorizar (a·te·mo·ri'θar; -'sar) *v.t.* [*pres.subjve.* **atemorice** (-'ri·θe; -se); *pret.* **atemoricé** (-'θe; -'se)] to intimidate. —**atemorizarse,** *v.r.* to become frightened.
atención (a·ten'θjon; -'sjon) *n.f.* **1,** attention. **2,** *usu.pl.* courtesy. —**¡atención!** *interj.* attention! look out! —**en atención a,** in view of; considering.
atender (a·ten'der) *v.t. & i.* [*pres. ind.* **atiendo;** *pres.subjve.* **atienda**] **1,** to pay attention (to); attend (to). **2,** to assist; take care (of). **3,** to show courtesy (to).
ateneo (a·te'ne·o) *n.m.* club, esp. literary or artistic.
atenerse (a·te'ner·se) *v.t.* [*infl.:* **tener**] *usu.fol.by* **a,** to abide (by); go (by); rely (on).
atenio (a'te·njo) *n.m.* athenium.
atenta (a'ten·ta) *n.f.* favor (*letter*).
atentado (a·ten'ta·ðo) *n.m.* **1,** attempt; attack. **2,** abuse of authority. **3,** crime; offense, esp. against authority.
atentar (a·ten'tar) *v.t.* [*pres.ind.* **atiento;** *pres.subjve.* **atiente**] to attempt, as a crime. —**atentar a** *or* **contra,** to make an attempt on.
atento (a'ten·to) *adj.* **1,** attentive. **2,** courteous. —**atento a,** in view of; considering.
atenuación (a·te·nwa'θjon; -'sjon) *n.f.* **1,** attenuation. **2,** extenuation.
atenuar (a·te'nwar) *v.t.* [*infl.:* **continuar**] **1,** to attenuate. **2,** to extenuate. —**atenuante,** *adj.* extenuating. —*n.m.* extenuating circumstance.
ateo (a'te·o) *n.m.* atheist. —*adj.* atheistic.
aterciopelado (a·ter·θjo·pe'la·ðo; a·ter·sjo–) *adj.* velvety.
aterirse (a·te'rir·se) *v.r., defective* (*used only in tenses with terminations beginning with* i) to become numb or stiff with cold.
aterrador (a·te·rra'ðor) *adj.* terrifying; appalling.
aterrar (a·te'rrar) *v.* [*pres.ind.* **atierro;** *pres.subjve.* **atierre**] —*v.t.* to pull down, demolish. —*v.i.* = **aterrizar.** - **aterrarse,** *v.r., naut.* to stand inshore *This verb is regular in the following senses:* —*v.t.* to terrify. —**aterrarse,** *v.r.* to be appalled.
aterrizar (a·te·rri'θar; -'sar) *v.i., aero.* [*pres.subjve.* **aterrice** (-'ri·θe; -se); *pret.* **aterricé** (-'θe; -'se)] to land. —**aterrizaje,** *n.m.* landing. —**pista de aterrizaje,** landing strip.
aterrorizar (a·te·rro·ri'θar; -'sar) *v.t.* [*pres.subjve.* **aterrorice** (-'ri·θe; -se); *pret.* **aterroricé** (-'θe; -'se)] to terrify. —**aterrorizarse,** *v.r.* to become terrified.
atesorar (a·te·so'rar) *v.t.* **1,** to hoard; to treasure. **2,** to possess (good qualities).
atestar (a'tes·tar) *v.t.* **1,** [*pres. ind.* **atiesto** *pres.subjve.* **atieste**] to cram; fill up, jam **2,** [*regularly inflected*] to attest. —**atestación,** *n.f.* attestation
atestiguar (a·tes·ti'ɣwar) *v.t.* to witness; attest to. —**atestiguación,** *n.f., also,* **atestiguamiento,** *n.m.* testimony; deposition.
atezado (a·te'θa·ðo; -'sa·ðo) *adj.* **1,** tan; tanned; swarthy. **2,** smooth; silken, as the skin.
atezar (a·te'θar; -'sar) *v.t.* [*pres. subjve.* **atece;** *pret.* **atecé**] **1,** to tan; darken. **2,** to make smooth.
atiborrar (a·ti·βo'rrar) *v.t.* **1,** to stuff; cram. **2,** to gorge; glut.
atice (a'ti·θe; -se) *v., pres.subjve. of* **atizar.**
aticé (a·ti'θe; -'se) *v., 1st pers. sing. pret. of* **atizar.**
ático ('a·ti·ko) *n.m.* attic. —*adj.* **1,** Attic. **2,** elegant; classic.
-ático ('a·ti·ko) *suffix* -atic; *forming adjectives expressing* connection; relation: *fanático,* fanatic; *acuático,* aquatic.

atienda (a'tjen·da) *v., pres. subjve. of* **atender.**
atiendo (a'tjen·do) *v., pres.ind. of* **atender.**
atiente (a'tjen·te) *v., pres.subjve. of* **atentar.**
atiento (a'tjen·to) *v., pres.ind. of* **atentar.**
atierre (a'tje·rre) *v., pres.subjve. of* **aterrar.**
atierro (a'tje·rro) *v., pres.ind. of* **aterrar.**
atiesar (a·tje'sar) *v.t.* **1,** to stiffen. **2,** to tense.
atieste (a'tjes·te) *v., pres.subjve. of* **atestar.**
atiesto (a'tjes·to) *v., pres.ind. of* **atestar.**
atigrado (a·ti'ɣra·ðo) *adj.* spotted.
atildado (a·til'da·ðo) *adj.* neat; fastidious; nice.
atinadamente (a·ti·na·ða'men·te) *adv.* **1,** wisely. **2,** pertinently.
atinar (a·ti'nar) *v.i.* to guess correctly; *slang* to hit the mark. **—atinar a,** to succeed in.
atisbar (a·tis'βar) *v.t.* to watch; spy on. **—atisbo** (a'tis·βo) *n.m.* glimpse. **—al atisbo,** on the watch.
-ativo (a'ti·βo) *suffix* -ative; *forming adjectives expressing* **1,** tendency; disposition: *ahorrativo,* frugal. **2,** relation; connection: *demostrativo,* demonstrative.
¡atiza! (a'ti·θa; –sa) *interj.* my goodness!
atizar (a·ti'θar; –'sar) *v.t.* [*pres. subjve.* **atice;** *pret.* **aticé**] **1,** to stir up; poke (a fire). **2,** *fig.* to rouse. **3,** *colloq.* to deal (a blow, kick, etc.) **—atizador,** *n.m.* poker; fire iron.
atlántico (a'tlan·ti·ko) *adj.* Atlantic. *—n.m., cap.* Atlantic Ocean.
atlas ('at·las) *n.m.* atlas.
atleta (at'le·ta) *n.m. & f.* athlete. **—atlético,** *adj.* athletic. **—atletismo,** *n.m.* athletics.
atmósfera (at'mos·fe·ra) *n.f.* atmosphere. **-atmosférico** (–'fe·ri·ko) *adj.* atmospheric.
-ato ('a·to) *suffix* **1,** -ate; -ship; *forming nouns expressing* office; dignity: *cardenalato,* cardinalate; *generalato,* generalship. **2,** *forming nouns denoting the young of animals: ballenato,* young whale.
atolón (a·to'lon) *n.m.* atoll.
atolondrado (a·to·lon'dra·ðo) *adj.* giddy; harebrained. **—atolondramiento,** *n.m.* giddiness.
atolondrar (a·to·lon'drar) *v.t.* to bewilder. **—atolondrarse,** *v.r.* to become confused or bewildered.
atolladero (a·to·ʎa'ðe·ro; a·to·ja–) *n.m.* **1,** mudhole. **2,** *colloq.* impasse.
atollarse (a·to'ʎar·se; –'jar·se) *v.r.* to get stuck; bog down.
atómico (a'to·mi·ko) *adj.* atomic.
atomizar (a·to·mi'θar; –'sar) *v.t.* [*infl.:* **realizar**] to spray; atomize. **-atomización,** *n.f.* spray. **—atomizador,** *n.m.* atomizer.
átomo ('a·to·mo) *n.m.* atom.
atonal (a·to'nal) *adj.* atonal. **—atonalidad,** *n.f.* atonality.
atónito (a'to·ni·to) *adj.* astonished.
atontar (a·ton'tar) *v.t.* to stun. **—atontarse,** *v.r.* **1,** to become stupid. **2,** to be stunned. **—atontadamente,** *adv.* foolishly. **—atontado,** *adj.* stunned; groggy.
atorar (a·to'rar) *v.t.* to choke; plug; clog. **—atorarse,** *v.r.* to choke; become plugged or clogged.
-atorio (a'to·rjo) *suffix* -atory; *forming* **1,** *adjectives denoting* relation, connection: *declaratorio,* declaratory. **2,** *nouns denoting* place: *lavatorio,* lavatory.
atormentar (a·tor·men'tar) *v.t.* to torment; torture. **—atormentarse,** *v.r.* to distress oneself. **—atormentador,** *n.m.* tormentor. *—adj.* tormenting.
atornillar (a·tor·ni'ʎar; –'jar) *v.t.* to screw. **—atornillador,** *n.m.* screwdriver.
atorrante (a·to'rran·te) *n.m., Amer.* tramp; bum.
atosigar (a·to·si'ɣar) *v.t.* [*pres. subjve.* **atosigue** (–'si·ɣe); *pret.* **atosigué** (–'ɣe)] **1,** to poison. **2,** to harry; press.
atrabiliario (a·tra·βi'lja·rjo) *adj.* ill-humored.
atracadero (a·tra·ka'ðe·ro) *n.m.* dock; landing.
atracar (a·tra'kar) *v.t.* [*pres. subjve.* **atraque;** *pret.* **atraqué**] **1,** to gorge. **2,** to hold up; rob. **3,** to swindle. **4,** *colloq.* to place *or* hold against. *—v.i.* to dock; berth. **—atracarse,** *v.r.* to gorge; stuff oneself. **—atracarse a,** *colloq.* to get close to; hug.
atracción (a·trak'θjon; –'sjon) *n.f.* **1,** attraction. **2,** amusement.

atraco (a'tra·ko) *n.m.* holdup; swindle.
atracón (a·tra'kon) *n.m.* overeating; gorging. —**darse un atracón,** to gorge oneself.
atractivo (a·trak'ti·βo) *adj.* attractive. —*n.m.* 1, attraction. 2, attractiveness.
atraer (a·tra'er) *v.t.* [*infl.*: **traer**] to attract.
atragantarse (a·tra·ɣan'tar·se) *v.r.* to choke; gag.
atrancar (a·tran'kar) *v.t.* [*infl.*: **trancar**] = **trancar.** —**trancarse,** *v.r.,* *Amer.* to be stubborn or opinionated.
atrapar (a·tra'par) *v.t.* to catch; to trap.
atraque (a'tra·ke) *v., pres.subjve. of* **atracar.**
atraqué (a·tra'ke) *v., 1st pers. sing. pret. of* **atracar.**
atrás (a'tras) *adv.* back; behind; ago. —**¡atrás!** *interj.* back!
atrasado (a·tra'sa·ðo) *adj.* 1, late. 2, in arrears. 3, backward. 4, slow, as a clock. —**número atrasado,** back number.
atrasar (a·tra'sar) *v.t.* 1, to retard. 2, to set back (hands of a clock). —**atrasarse,** *v.r.* 1, to lag behind; be late. 2, to be slow, as a clock.
atraso (a'tra·so) *n.m.* 1, tardiness. 2, delay; lag. 3, backwardness. 4, *pl.* arrears.
atravesado (a·tra·βe'sa·ðo) *adj.* 1, crosswise. 2, somewhat crosseyed. 3, crossbred; hybrid; mongrel. 4, ill-natured.
atravesar (a·tra·βe'sar) *v.t.* [*pres.ind.* **atravieso** (–'βje·so); *pres.subjve.* **atraviese**] 1, to cross. 2, to pierce. 3, to lay across. —**atravesarse,** *v.r.* to interfere; get in the way.
atrayente (a·tra'jen·te) *adj.* attractive.
atreverse (a·tre'βer·se) *v.r.* to venture; dare. —**atrevido,** *adj.* bold; impudent. —**atrevimiento,** *n.m.* audacity; impudence.
atribución (a·tri·βu'θjon; –'sjon) *n.f.* 1, attribution. 2, *usu.pl.* prerogatives; powers.
atribuir (a·tri·βu'ir) *v.t.* [*infl.*: **contribuir**] to attribute.
atribular (a·tri·βu'lar) *v.t.* to pain; grieve. —**atribularse,** *v.r.* to suffer pain or grief.
atributo (a·tri'βu·to) *n.m.* attribute. —**atributivo,** *adj.* attributive.
atril (a'tril) *n.m.* 1, lectern. 2, music stand.
atrincherar (a·trin·tʃe'rar) *v.t.* to entrench. —**atrincherarse,** *v.r.* to entrench oneself; take cover, as in trenches. —**atrincheramiento,** *n.m.* entrenchment.
atrio ('a·trjo) *n.m.* entrance hall; inner court; atrium.
atrocidad (a·tro·θi'ðað; -si·'ðað) *n.f.* 1, atrocity. 2, *colloq.* enormity. —**¡qué atrocidad!,** how terrible!
atrofia (a'tro·fja) *n.f.* atrophy. —**atrofiarse** *v.r.* to atrophy.
atronar (a·tro'nar) *v.t.* [*infl.*: **tronar**] 1, to deafen. 2, to discomfit; rattle. —**atronado,** *adj.* reckless; harebrained; scatterbrained. —**atronador,** *adj.* deafening; thunderous.
atropellar (a·tro·pe'ʎar; –'jar) *v.t.* 1, to run over; trample. 2, *fig.* to ride roughshod over. —**atropellarse,** *v.r.* to stumble over oneself in haste. —**atropellado,** *adj.* precipitate.
atropello (a·tro'pe·ʎo; –jo) *n.m.* 1, trampling; a running or being run over. 2, *fig.* abuse; outrage. *Also,* **atropellamiento.**
atropina (a·tro'pi·na) *n.f.* atropine.
atroz (a'troθ; a'tros) *adj.* atrocious; outrageous.
atún (a'tun) *n.m.* tuna.
aturdido (a·tur'ði·ðo) *adj.* scatterbrained.
aturdir (a·tur'ðir) *v.t.* to stun; bewilder. —**aturdirse,** *v.r.* to be stunned or bewildered. —**aturdimiento,** *n.m.* bewilderment.
aturullar (a·tu·ru'ʎar; –'jar) *also,* **aturrullar** (a·tu·rru–) *v.t.* to confuse; flurry; fluster. —**aturullamiento,** *n.m.* confusion; flurry; fluster.
audacia (au'ða·θja; -sja) *n.f.* audacity.
audaz (au'ðaθ; -'ðas) *adj.* audacious.
audible (au'ði·βle) *adj.* audible.
audición (au·ði'θjon; -'sjon) *n.f.* 1, audition. 2, radio performance. 3, musical program; recital.
audiencia (au'ðjen·θja; –sja) *n.f.* 1, audience; hearing. 2, *law* district

court. 3, court building. —**dar audiencia**, to grant a hearing.

audifono (au'ði·fo·no) *n.m.* 1, hearing aid; audiphone. 2, = **auricular**.

audio- (au·ðjo) *also*, **audi-** (au ði) *prefix* audio-; audi-; hearing: *audiómetro*, audiometer; *audífono*, audiphone.

auditivo (au·ði'ti·βo) *adj.* auditory.

auditor (au·ði'tor) *n.m.* 1, law judge advocate. 2, *Amer.* auditor.

auditorio (au·ði'to·rjo) *n.m.* audience.

auge ('au·xe) *n.m.* 1, culmination. 2, *colloq.* increment.

augur (au'ɣur) *n.m.* augur.

augurar (au·ɣu'rar) *v.t.* to augur. —**augurio** (–'ɣu·rjo) *n.m.* augury.

augusto (au'ɣus·to) *adj.* august.

aula ('au·la) *n.f.* 1, classroom. 2, lecture hall. 3, *poet.* palace.

aulaga (au'la·ɣa) *n.f.* furze.

aullar (a·u'ʎar; –'jar) *v.i.* [*pres. ind.* **aúllo** (a'u·ʎo; –jo); *pres. subjve.* **aúlle** (–je)] to howl.

aullido (au'ʎi·ðo; -'ji·ðo) *n.m.* howl.

aumentación (au·men·ta'θjon; –'sjon) *n.f.* 1, augmentation; increase. 2, *rhet.* climax.

aumentar (au·men'tar) *v.t.* to augment; increase. —**aumentativo**, *n.m.* & *adj.*, *gram.* augmentative.

aumento (au'men·to) *n.m.* 1, augmentation; increase. 2, enlargement. 3, promotion. 4, *gram.* augment.

aun *also*, **aún** (a'un) *adv.* 1, yet; still. 2, even. 3, further.

aunque (a'un·ke; 'aun·ke) *conj.* although.

aura ('au·ra) *n.f.* 1, aura. 2, *poet.* breeze; breath. 3, popular acclaim. 4, *ornith.* turkey buzzard.

áureo ('au·re·o) *adj.* *of* gold; golden.

aureola (au·re'o·la) *also*, **auréola** (au're–) *n.f.* halo.

aureomicina (au·re·o·mi'θi·na; –'si·na) *n.f.* aureomycin.

aurícula (au'ri·ku·la) *n.f.* auricle (*of the heart*).

auricular (au·ri·ku'lar) *adj.*, *anat.* auricular. —*n.m.* telephone receiver; headphone.

aurífero (au'ri·fe·ro) *adj.* auriferous.

auriga (au'ri·ɣa) *n.m.* charioteer.

aurora (au'ro·ra) *n.f.* dawn; aurora. —**aurora austral**, aurora australis. —**aurora boreal**, aurora borealis.

auscultar (aus·kul'tar) *v.t.* to auscultate. —**auscultación**, *n.f.* auscultation.

ausencia (au'sen·θja; –sja) *n.f.* absence.

ausentar (au·sen'tar) *v.t.* to drive away; cause to depart. —**ausentarse**, *v.r.* to absent oneself; leave.

ausente (au'sen·te) *adj.* 1, absent. 2, missing. —*n.m.* & *f.* 1, absentee. 2, missing person. —**ausentismo** *n.m.* absenteeism.

auspicio (aus'pi·θjo; –sjo) *n.m.* 1, omen. 2, patronage. —**auspicios**, *n.m.pl.* auspices. —**auspiciar**, *v.t.*, *Amer.* to sponsor. —**auspicioso**, *adj.*, *Amer.* auspicious.

austero (aus'te·ro) *adj.* austere. —**austeridad**, *n.f.* austerity.

austral (aus'tral) *adj.* southern; austral.

austro ('aus·tro) *n.m.* 1, south wind. 2, south.

autarquía (au·tar'ki·a) *n.f.* 1, autarchy. 2, autarky.

autárquico (au'tar·ki·ko) *adj.* 1, autarchic; autarchical. 2, autarkic; autarkical.

autenticar (au·ten·ti'kar) *v.t.* [*pres.subjve.* **autentique** (–'ti·ke); *pret.* **autentiqué** (–'ke)] to authenticate. —**autenticación**, *n.f.* authentication.

auténtico (au'ten·ti·ko) *adj.* authentic. —**autenticidad** (–θi'ðað; –si'ðað) *n.f.* authenticity.

auto ('au·to) *n.m.* 1, writ; judicial act. 2, *colloq.* auto; automobile.

auto- (au·to) *prefix* auto-; self: *autobiografía* autobiography.

autobiografía (au·to·βjo·ɣra'fi·a) *n.f.* autobiography. —**autobiográfico** (–'ɣra·fi·ko) *adj.* autobiographical.

autobús (au·to'βus) *n.m.* omnibus; bus.

autocargador (au·to·kar·ɣa'ðor) *adj.* self-loading.

autocracia (au·to'kra·θja; –sja) *n.f.* autocracy. —**autócrata** (–'to·kra·ta) *n.m.* & *f.* autocrat. —**autocrático** (–'kra·ti·ko) *adj.* autocratic.

autocrítica (au·to'kri·ti·ka) *n.f.* self-criticism.

autóctono (au'tok·to·no) *adj.* native; aboriginal.
autodestrucción *n.f.* self-destruction.
autodeterminación *n.f.* self-determination.
autodidacto (au·to·ði'ðak·to) *adj.* self-educated; self-taught.
autodisciplina *n.f.* self-discipline.
autogiro (au·to'xi·ro) *n.m.* autogiro.
autógrafo (au'to·ɣra·fo) *n.m.* autograph.
autómata (au'to·ma·ta) *n.m.* automaton.
automático (au·to'ma·ti·ko) *adj.* automatic.
automatizar (au·to·ma·ti'θar; –'sar) *v.t.* [*pres.subjve.* **automatice** (–'ti·θe; –se); *pret.* **automaticé** (–'θe; –'se)] to automate. —**automatización,** *n.f.* automation.
automotor (au·to·mo'tor) *adj.* **1,** automotive. **2,** self-propelled. —*n.m.* railway motor coach.
automotriz (au·to·mo'triθ; –'tris) *adj.fem.* [*pl.* **–trices** (–'tri·θes; –ses)] self-propelled.
automóvil (au·to'mo·βil) *adj.* & *n.m.* automobile. —**automovilismo,** *n.m.* motoring. —**automovilista,** *n.m.* & *f.* motoring devotee; motorist. —**automovilístico,** *adj.* automobile (*attrib.*)
autonomía (au·to·no'mi·a) *n.f.* autonomy. —**autónomo** (au'to·no·mo) *adj.* autonomous.
autonómico (au·to'no·mi·ko) *adj.* autonomic.
autopista (au·to'pis·ta) *n.f.* turnpike; parkway.
autopropulsado (au·to·pro·pul'sa·ðo) *adj.* self-propelled.
autopsia (au'top·sja) *n.f.* autopsy.
autor (au'tor) *n.* author. —**autora** (–ra) *n.f.* authoress.
autoridad (au·to·ri'ðað) *n.f.* authority.
autoritario (au·to·ri'ta·rjo) *adj.* authoritative. —*adj.* & *n.m.* authoritarian.
autorizado (au·to·ri'θa·ðo; -'sa·ðo) *adj.* **1,** authorized. **2,** authoritative.
autorizar (au·to·ri'θar; –'sar) *v.t.* [*pres.subjve.* **autorice** (–'ri·θe; –se); *pret.* **autoricé** (–'θe; –'se)] to authorize. —**autorización,** *n.f.* authorization.
autorretrato (au·to·rre'tra·to) *n.m.* self-portrait.
autorriel (au·to'rrjel) *n.m.* = **autovía.**
autoservicio *n.m.* self-service.
autosugestión *n.f.* autosuggestion.
autovía (au·to'βi·a) *n.m. or f.* railway motor coach.
autumnal (au·tum'nal) *adj.* autumnal.
auxiliar (au·ksi'ljar) *v.t.* to aid; assist. —*adj.* auxiliary. —*n.m.* & *f.* aid; assistant; auxiliary.
auxilio (au'ksi·ljo) *n.m.* assistance. —**¡auxilio!,** *interj.* help! —**prestar auxilio,** to aid.
aval (a'βal) *n.m.* **1,** endorsement; countersignature. **2,** affidavit. —**avalar,** *v.t.* to vouch for, esp. by an affidavit.
avalancha (a·βa'lan·tʃa) *n.f.* avalanche.
avalorar (a·βa·lo'rar) *v.t.* to evaluate.
avaluar (a·βa'lwar) *v.t.* = **valuar.** —**avaluación,** *n.f., also,* **avalúo** (–'lu·o) *n.m.* = **valuación.**
avanzar (a·βan'θar; –'sar) *v.t.* & *i.* [*pres.subjve.* **avance** (a'βan·θe; –se); *pret.* **avancé** (–'θe; –'se)] to advance. —**avance,** *n.m.* advance. —**avanzada,** *n.f.* vanguard; outpost.
avaricia (a·βa'ri·θja; –sja) *n.f.* avarice. —**avaricioso,** *adj.* avaricious.
avariento (a·βa'rjen·to) *adj.* avaricious; miserly. —*n.m.* miser. *Also,* **avaro** (a'βa·ro) *adj.* & *n.m.*
avasallar (a·βa·sa'ʎar; –'jar) *v.t.* to subject; enslave. —**avasallarse,** *v.r.* **1,** to submit. **2,** to become a vassal.
ave ('a·βe) *n.f.* bird. —**ave de corral,** domestic *or* barnyard fowl. —**ave de paso,** bird of passage. —**ave de rapiña,** bird of prey.
avecinarse (a·βe·θi'nar·se; a·βe·si–) *v.r.* to approach.
avecindarse (a·βe·θin'dar·se; a·βe·sin–) *v.r.* to settle; take up residence.
avechucho (a·βe'tʃu·tʃo) *n.m.* **1,** ugly bird. **2,** *colloq.* queer duck; odd bird.
avefría (a·βe'fri·a) *n.f.* plover.
avejentarse (a·βe·xen'tar·se) *v.r.* to age prematurely.
avellana (a·βe'ʎa·na; –'ja·na) *n.f.* filbert; hazelnut. —**avellanar,**

n.m. *also,* **avellanedo,** *n.m.,* **avellaneda,** *n.f.* hazel grove. —**avellano,** *n.m.* hazel.
avellanar (a·βe·ʎa'nar; –ja'nar) *v.t.* to countersink. —**avellanador,** *n.m.* countersink (*tool*).
avemaría (a·βe·ma'ri·a) *n.f.* Hail Mary. —**¡Ave María!,** *interj.* Good Heavens!
avena (a'βe·na) *n.f.* oats.
avenencia (a·βe'nen·θja; –sja) *n.f.* agreement; understanding.
avenida (a·βe'ni·ða) *n.f.* **1,** avenue. **2,** flood; flash flood.
avenir (a·βe'nir) *v.t.* [*infl.:* **venir**] to reconcile. —**avenirse,** *v.r.* to agree; to compromise.
aventadura (a·βen·ta'ðu·ra) *n.f., vet.med.* windgall.
aventajar (a·βen·ta'xar) *v.t.* **1,** to give preference or advantage to. **2,** to surpass; excel - **aventajarse,** *v.r.* **1,** to gain preference or advantage. **2,** to excel. —**aventajado,** *adj.* outstanding.
aventar (a·βen'tar) *v.t.* [*pres.ind.* **aviento;** *pres.subjve* **aviente**] **1,** to winnow. **2,** *colloq.* to throw out; eject (a person). **3,** *Amer. colloq.* to throw; hurl. —**aventarse,** *v.r.* **1,** to swell. **2,** *colloq.* to escape. —**aventamiento,** *n.m.* winnowing. —**aventón** (–'ton) *n.m., Amer., colloq.* shove; push.
aventura (a·βen'tu·ra) *n.f.* **1,** adventure. **2,** venture. —**aventurado,** *adj.* venturesome; risky. —**aventurar,** *v.t.* to venture. —**aventurarse,** *v.r.* to risk oneself; *colloq.* to take a chance. —**aventurero,** *n.m.* adventurer. —**aventurera,** *n.f.* adventuress.
avergonzar (a·βer·ɣon'θar; –'sar) *v.t.* [*pres.ind.* **avergüenzo** (–'ɣwen·θo; –so); *pres.subjve.* **avergüence;** *pret.* **avergoncé** (–'θe; -'se)] to shame. —**avergonzarse,** *v.r.* to be ashamed.
avería (a·βe'ri·a) *n.f.* **1,** damage. **2,** defect; imperfection. —**averiar,** *v.t.* [*infl.:* **enviar**] to damage. —**averiarse,** *v.r.* to suffer damage.
averiguación (a·βe·ri·ɣwa'θjon; –'sjon) *n.f.* **1,** ascertainment. **2,** inquiry; investigation.
averiguar (a·βe·ri'ɣwar) *v.t.* [*pres.subjve.* **averigüe** (–'ri·ɣwe); *pret.* **averigüé** (–'ɣwe)] to ascertain.
averno (a'βer·no) *n.m.* hell; Hades.
averrugarse (a·βe·rru'ɣar·se) *v.r.* [*infl.:* **jugar**] to become warty. —**averrugado,** *adj.* warty.
aversión (a·βer'sjon) *n.f.* aversion.
avestruz (a·βes'truθ; –'trus) *n.f.* ostrich.
avetoro (a·βe'to·ro) *n.m.* bittern. *Also,* **ave toro.**
avezado (a·βe'θa·ðo; -'sa·ðo) *adj.* **1,** inured; accustomed. **2,** experienced; well versed.
avi- (a·βi) *prefix* avi-; bird: *avicultura,* aviculture.
aviación (a·βja'θjon; –'sjon) *n.f.* **1,** aviation **2,** air force.
aviador (a·βja'ðor) *n.m.* aviator. —**aviatriz** (–'triθ; –'tris) [*pl.* **-trices** (–'tri θes; –ses)] *also,* **aviadora,** *n.f.* aviatrix.
aviar (a'βjar) *v.t.* [*infl.:* **enviar**] **1,** to get ready; prepare **2,** *colloq.* to equip; fit out - **aviado,** *adj., colloq.* in a quandary in a tight spot.
avidez (a·βi ðeθ -'ðes) *n.f.* avidity. —**ávido** ('a·βi·ðo) *adj.* avid.
aviente (a'βjen·te) *v., pres.subjve. of* **aventar.**
aviento (a'bjen·to) *v., pres.ind. of* **aventar.**
avieso (a'βje·so) *adj.* perverse; evil-minded.
avillanar (a·βi·ʎa'nar; –ja'nar) *v.t.* to debase - **avillanarse,** *v.r.* to degenerate. - **avillanado** *adj.* vile.
avinagrado (a·βi·na'ɣra·ðo) *adj.* **1,** sour; vinegary. **2,** *colloq.* bad-tempered.
avión (a'βjon) *n.m.* airplane. —**avión de caza** pursuit plane. —**avión de propulsión** (*or* **reacción**) **a chorro,** jet plane.
avíos (a'βi·os) *n.m.pl.* equipment (*sing.*).
avisar (a·βi'sar) *v.t.* to inform; to announce; to advise. —**avisado,** *adj.* judicious.
aviso (a'βi·so) *n.m.* **1,** warning. **2,** notice; advertisement. **3,** sign; poster. —**sobre aviso,** on notice; alerted.
avispa (a'βis·pa) *n.f.* **1,** wasp. **2,** clever person. —**avispado,** *adj.* clever; sharp. —**avispar,** *v.t.* to stir up; rouse.
avispero (a·βis'pe·ro) *n.m.* **1,** wasp's nest. **2,** swarm of wasps. **3,** *colloq.* hornet's nest; touchy matter.
avispón (a·βis'pon) *n.m.* hornet.

avistar (a·βis'tar) *v.t.* to sight; catch sight of. —**avistarse,** *v.r.* to have an interview.

avivar (a·βi'βar) *v.t.* to enliven; to inflame.

avizor (a·βi'θor; –'sor) *adj.* watchful. —*n.m.* watcher. —**avizorar,** *v.t.* to watch.

-avo ('a·βo) *suffix* -th; *forming ordinal numerals: dozavo,* twelfth.

axial (a'ksjal) *adj.* axial.

axila (a'ksi·la) *n.f.* armpit.

axioma (a'ksjo·ma) *n.m.* axiom. —**axiomático** (–'ma·ti·ko) *adj.* axiomatic.

axis ('ak·sis) *n.m.sing. & pl., anat.* axis.

¡ay! (ai) *interj.* alas!; ouch! —**¡ay de mí!,** woe is me!

aya ('a·ja) *n.f.* governess.

ayer (a'jer) *adv.* & *n.m.* yesterday.

ayo ('a·jo) *n.m.* tutor; preceptor.

ayuda (a'ju·ða) *n.m.* help. —**ayuda de cámara,** valet.

ayudante (a·ju'ðan·te) *n.m.* **1,** helper. **2,** *mil.* aide; adjutant.

ayudar (a·ju'ðar) *v.t. & i.* to help.

ayunar (a·ju'nar) *v.i.* to fast. —**ayunador,** *n.m.* one who fasts.

ayuno (a'ju·no) *adj.* fasting. —*n.m.* fast; fasting. —**en ayunas,** on an empty stomach. —**en ayunas de; ayuno de,** abysmally ignorant of. —**quedarse en ayunas,** *colloq.* to miss the point.

ayuntamiento (a·jun·ta'mjen·to) *n.m.* **1,** municipal government. **2,** city hall. **3,** union; coupling.

-az ('aθ; 'as) *suffix* -acious; *forming adjectives denoting* tendency; disposition: *locuaz,* loquacious.

-aza ('a·θa; –sa) *suffix, forming feminine nouns with collective or derog. meaning: linaza,* linseed; *cachaza,* phlegm.

azabache (a·θa'βa·tʃe; a·sa–) *n.m.* **1,** jet (*mineral*). **2,** jet-black color. —**azabachado,** *adj.* jet; of or like jet; jet-black.

azada (a'θa·ða; a'sa-) *n.f.* hoe. —**azadón,** *n.m.* large curved hoe. —**azadonar,** *v.t. & i.* to hoe.

azafata (a·θa'fa·ta; a·sa–) *n.f.* **1,** lady in waiting. **2,** hostess; stewardess.

azafate (a·θa'fa·te; a·sa–) *n.m.* tray; server.

azafrán (a·θa'fran; a·sa-) *n.m.* saffron.

azagaya (a·θa'ɣa·ja; a·sa–) *n.f.* javelin.

azahar (a·θa'ar; a·sa–) *n.m.* citrus blossom.

azalea (a·θa'le·a; a·sa–) *n.f.* azalea.

azar (a'θar; a'sar) *n.m.* hazard; chance. —**al azar,** at random.

azaroso (a·θa'ro·so; a·sa-) *adj.* **1,** hazardous. **2,** unfortunate.

-azgo ('aθ·ɣo; 'as-) *suffix* -ty; ship; *forming nouns expressing* **1,** office; dignity: *almirantazgo,* admiralty. **2,** function: *padrinazgo,* godfathership; sponsorship. **3,** state; condition: *noviazgo,* courtship. **4,** action; result: *hallazgo,* find.

azimut (a·θi'mut; a·si–) *n.m.* = **acimut.**

ázimo ('a·θi·mo; 'a·si–) *adj.* unleavened.

-azo ('a·θo; –so) *suffix* **1,** *forming augmentative nouns and adjectives, often derog.: animalazo,* big beast. **2,** blow; stroke: *latigazo,* a stroke with a whip.

ázoe ('a·θo·e; -so·e) *n.m.* nitrogen. —**azoado,** *adj.* = **nitrogenado.** —**azoato,** *n.m.* = **nitrato.**

azogue (a'θo·ɣe; a'so–) *n.m.* mercury. —**azogar,** *v.t.* [*pres.subjve.* **azogue;** *pret.* **azogué** (–'ɣe)] to coat with mercury; to silver (a mirror). —**ser un azogue,** *colloq.* to be restless.

azoico (a'θoi·ko; a'soi–) *adj.* **1,** *chem.* = **nítrico. 2,** *geol.* azoic.

-azón (a'θon; a'son) *suffix, forming nouns of augmentative and derog. meaning: ligazón,* ligament; *cargazón,* burden; heaviness.

azor (a'θor; a'sor) *n.m.* goshawk.

azorar (a·θo'rar; a·so-) *v.t.* **1,** to confound; abash. **2,** to excite; rouse.

azotar (a·θo'tar; a·so–) *v.t.* to beat; lash; whip. —**azotaina** (–'tai·na) *n.f., colloq.* spanking; whipping. —**azotazo** (–'ta·θo; –so) *n.m.* blow with a whip or rod; spank.

azote (a'θo·te; a'so–) *n.m.* **1,** whip; rod; scourge. **2,** whipping; beating.

azotea (a·θo'te·a; a·so–) *n.f.* flat roof.

azteca (aθ'te·ka; as–) *adj.* & *n.m.* & *f.* Aztec.

azúcar (a'θu·kar; a'su-) *n.m. or f.* sugar. —**azucarado,** *adj.* sugary. —**azucarar,** *v.t.* to sweeten. —**azucararse,** *v.r., Amer.* to crystallize. —**azucarera,** *n.f.* sugar bowl. —**azucarero,** *adj.* pert. to sugar. —*n.m.*

sugar producer. —**azúcar blanca,** refined sugar. —**azúcar cande,** rock candy. —**azúcar negra, morena** *or* **prieta,** brown sugar.
azucena (a·θu'θe·na; a·su'se–) *n.f.* white lily.
azuela (a'θwe·la; a'swe–) *n.f.* adz.
azufre (a'θu·fre; a'su–) *n.m.* sulfur. —**azufrado,** *adj.* sulfured; sulfurated; sulfurous. —*n.m.* sulfuring. —**azufrar,** *v.t.* to sulfur; sulfurate. —**azufrera,** *n.f.* sulfur mine.
azul (a'θul; –'sul) *adj.* & *n.m.* blue. —**azulado,** *adj.* bluish; blue.
azular (a·θu'lar; a·su–) *v.t.* to blue; color or dye blue. —**azularse,** *v.r.* to turn blue.
azulejo (a·θu'le·xo; a·su–) *n.m.* glazed tile. —**azulejar,** *v.t.* to tile.
azulino (a·θu'li·no; a·su–) *adj.* bluish.
azur (a'θur; a'sur) *adj.* & *n.m.* azure.
azuzar (a·θu'θar; –su'sar) *v.t.* [*pres.subjve.* **azuce** (a'θu·θe; –'su·se); *pret.* **azucé** (–'θe; –'se)] **1,** to sick; set (dogs) on. **2,** *fig.* to incite.

B

B, b (be) *n.f.* 2nd letter of the Spanish alphabet.
baba ('ba·βa) *n.f.* drivel; slaver; slime. —**babaza,** *n.f.* slime.
babear (ba·βe'ar) *v.i.* to drivel; slaver; drool. —**babeo** (–'βe·o) *n.m.* driveling; drooling.
babel (ba'βel) *n.m. or f.* **1,** babel; bedlam; confusion. **2,** *cap.* Babel.
babero (ba'βe·ro) *n.m.* bib.
Babia ('ba·βja) *n.f.* a mountain district of León. —**estar en Babia,** *colloq.* to be absentminded; to be forgetful.
babilonia (ba·βi'lo·nja) *n.f.* **1,** babel; confusion. **2,** *cap.* Babylonia; Babylon. —**babilonio,** *adj.* & *n.m.* Babylonian.
babilónico (ba·βi'lo·ni·ko) *adj.* **1,** Babylonian. **2,** sumptuous; magnificent.
babor (ba'βor) *n.m., naut.* port; larboard.
babosa (ba'βo·sa) *n.f., zool.* slug.
babosear (ba·βo·se'ar) *v.t.* to drivel; to slaver.
baboso (ba'βo·so) *adj.* driveling.
babucha (ba'βu·tʃa) *n.f.* slipper.
babuino (ba'βwi·no) *n.m.* baboon.
baca ('ba·ka) *n.f.* top of a bus, stagecoach, etc., covered with canvas or leather, used for passengers or baggage; also, the cover itself.
bacalao (ba·ka'la·o) *also,* **bacallao** (–'ʎa·o; –'ja·o) *n.m.* **1,** codfish. **2,** *colloq.* skinny person.
bacanal (ba·ka'nal) *n.f.* bacchanal. —*adj.* bacchanalian. —**bacanales,** *n.f.pl.* bacchanalia.
bacará (ba·ka'ra) *n.m.* baccarat.
baceta (ba'θe·ta; –'se·ta) *n.f., cards* widow.
bacía (ba'θi·a; –'si·a) *n.f.* metal basin; shaving dish.
bacilo (ba'θi·lo; –'si·lo) *n.m.* bacillus.
bacín (ba'θin; –'sin) *n.m.* chamber pot. *Also,* **bacineta, bacinica, bacinilla.**
bacteria (bak'te·rja) *n.f.* bacterium. —**bacterias,** *n.f.pl.* bacteria. —**bacteriano** (–'rja·no), *also,* **bacterial** (–'rjal), **bactérico** (–'te·ri·ko) *adj.* bacterial.
bacteriología (bak·te·rjo·lo'xi·a) *n.f.* bacteriology. —**bacteriológico** (–'lo·xi·ko) *adj.* bacteriological. —**bacteriólogo** (–'rjo·lo·ɣo) *n.m.* bacteriologist.
báculo ('ba·ku·lo) *n.m.* **1,** stick; staff. **2,** *fig.* support; aid.
bache ('ba·tʃe) *n.m.* rut; pothole.
bachiller (ba·tʃi'ʎer; –'jer) *n.m.* **1,** recipient of a college degree; bachelor. **2,** prattler; chatterbox. —**bachillerato,** *n.m.* baccalaureate.
bada ('ba·ða) *n.f.* = **rinoceronte.**
badajada (ba·ða'xa·ða) *n.f.* **1,** stroke of a bell. **2,** foolish talk; nonsense.
badajo (ba'ða·xo) *n.m.* **1,** clapper of a bell. **2,** *colloq.* prattler.
badán (ba'ðan) *n.m.* trunk of a plant or animal.
badana (ba'ða·na) *n.f.* dressed sheepskin. —**zurrarle a uno la badana,** *colloq.* to tan someone's hide; give a dressing-down.

badén (ba'ðen) *n.m.* natural drainage ditch; gully.
badulaque (ba·ðu'la·ke) *n.m.* fool; sap.
bagaje (ba'ɣa·xe) *n.m.* **1,** beast of burden. **2,** *mil.* baggage.
bagasa (ba'ɣa·sa) *n.f.* prostitute; baggage.
bagatela (ba·ɣa'te·la) *n.f.* bagatelle; trifle.
bagazo (ba'ɣa·θo; –so) *n.m.* bagasse.
bagre ('ba·ɣre) *n.m., Amer.* a kind of catfish.
bagual (ba'ɣwal) *adj., Amer.* wild; untamed.
¡bah! (ba) *interj.* bah!
bahía (ba'i·a) *n.f.* bay; harbor.
bahuno (ba'u·no) *also,* **bajuno** (–'xu·no) *adj.* depraved; vile.
bailar (bai'lar) *v.i.* & *t.* **1,** to dance. **2,** to spin. —**bailador** (–'ðor) *n.m.* dancer. —**bailarín** (–'rin) *n.m.* [*fem.* **-ina**] dancer.
baile ('bai·le) *n.m.* dance; ball; ballet.
bailía (bai'li·a) *n.f.* bailiwick.
bailotear (bai·lo·te'ar) *v.i.* to hop about, as in dancing. —**bailoteo** (–'te·o) *n.m.* dancing; hopping.
baja ('ba·xa) *n.f.* **1,** fall (in price); diminution. **2,** *mil.* casualty. —**dar de baja,** *mil.* to report as missing, or as a casualty. —**darse de baja,** to resign.
bajá (ba'xa) *n.m.* pasha.
bajada (ba'xa·da) *n.f.* slope; descent.
bajamar (ba·xa'mar) *n.f.* low tide.
bajamente (ba·xa'men·te) *adv.* basely; meanly.
bajar (ba'xar) *v.i.* to descend; to alight. —*v.t.* to lower; to reduce. —**bajarse,** *v.r.* **1,** to descend; to alight. **2,** to grovel.
bajareque (ba·xa're·ke) *n.m., Cuba* hovel; shack.
bajel (ba'xel) *n.m.* boat; vessel.
bajero (ba'xe·ro) *adj.* lower; under; placed or used below or under.
bajete (ba'xe·te) *n.m.* short person; shorty.
bajeza (ba'xe·θa; –sa) *n.f.* baseness; meanness.
bajío (ba'xi·o) *n.m.* **1,** shoal; sand bank. **2,** *Amer.* lowland.
bajista (ba'xis·ta) *n.m., finance* bear.
bajo ('ba·xo) *adj.* **1,** short; low. **2,** soft; not loud. **3,** *music* bass. **4,** shallow. **5,** base; mean; vulgar. —*n.m.* **1,** deep place. **2,** shoal. **3,** *music* bass. —*prep.* beneath; under. —*adv.* **1,** below. **2,** softly.
bajón (ba'xon) *n.m.* **1,** bassoon. **2,** bassoonist. —**bajonista,** *n.m.* & *f.* bassoonist.
bajorrelieve (ba·xo·rre'lje·βe) *n.m.* bas-relief.
bala ('ba·la) *n.f.* **1,** bullet; shot. **2,** bale.
balada (ba'la·ða) *n.f.* ballad.
baladí (ba·la'ði) *adj.* trivial; worthless.
baladrar (ba·la'ðrar) *v.i.* to shout; to cry. –**baladro** (–'la·ðro) *n.m.* shout; howl.
baladronear (ba·la·ðro·ne'ar) *v.i.* & *t.* **1,** to boast. **2,** to bluff; to bully. —**baladrón,** *n.m.* boaster; bully. –**baladronada,** *n.f.* boast; bluff.
bálago ('ba·la·ɣo) *n.m.* **1,** grain stalk; straw. **2,** [*also,* **balaguero** (–'ɣe·ro)] haystack.
balance (ba'lan·θe; –se) *n.m.* **1,** oscillation. **2,** equilibrium. **3,** *comm.* balance; balance sheet. **4,** *naut.; aero.* roll.
balancear (ba·lan·θe'ar; –se'ar) *v.i.* **1,** to roll; sway. **2,** to waver. **3,** to teeter; seesaw. —*v.t.* to balance. –**balanceo** (–'θe·o; –'se·o) *n.m.* balancing; wavering.
balancín (ba·lan'θin; –'sin) *n.m.* **1,** crossbeam; balance beam. **2,** outrigger (*of a canoe*). **3,** seesaw. **4,** whiffletree. **5,** balancing pole.
balandra (ba'lan·dra) *n.f.* sloop. —**balandro,** *n.m.* small sloop; fishing boat.
balandrán (ba·lan'dran) *n.m.* cassock.
bálano ('ba·la·no) *also,* **balano** (–'la·no) *n.m., anat.* glans.
balanza (ba'lan·θa; –sa) *n.f.* scale; balance. —**balanza de comercio,** balance of trade.
balar (ba'lar) *v.i.* to bleat.
balasto (ba'las·to) *n.m., R.R.* ballast.
balaustre (ba'laus·tre) *n.m.* baluster. —**balaustrada,** *n.f.* balustrade.
balazo (ba'la·θo; –so) *n.m.* **1,** shot. **2,** bullet wound.
balboa (bal'βo·a) *n.m.* monetary unit of Panama equivalent to one U.S. dollar; balboa.
balbucear (bal·βu·θe'ar; –se'ar) *v.i.* to babble; prattle. —**balbucencia,** *n.f.* babbling; prattling.

—**balbuceo** (-'θe·o; -'se·o) *n.m.* babble; prattle.
balbucir (bal·βu'θir; -'sir) *v.i., defective (used only in tenses with terminations beginning with* i) = **balbucear.**
balcánico (bal'ka·ni·ko) *adj.* Balkan. —**los Balcanes,** the Balkans.
balcón (bal'kon) *n.m.* **1,** balcony. **2,** railing.
baldaquín (bal·da'kin) *n.m.* canopy.
baldar (bal'dar) *v.t.* to cripple.
balde ('bal·de) *n.m.* bucket; pail. —**de balde,** *adv.* gratis; free. —**en balde,** in vain.
baldear (bal·de'ar) *v.i.* to flush or drench with pails of water.
baldío (bal'di·o) *adj.* untilled; uncultivated.
baldón (bal'don) *n.m.* **1,** affront; insult. **2,** blot; stain; stigma. —**baldonar,** *v.t.* to insult; to affront.
baldosa (bal'do·sa) *n.f.* **1,** flat paving stone. **2,** floor tile. —**baldosado** (-'sa·ðo) *n.m.* tile pavement; tile flooring. —**baldosar** (-'sar) *v.t.* to tile; pave with tile.
baleo (ba'le·o) *n.m.* round rug *or* mat.
balido (ba'li·ðo) *n.m.* bleat; bleating.
balín (ba'lin) *n.m.* small bore bullet; pellet. —**balines,** *n.m.pl.* buckshot.
balística (ba'lis·ti·ka) *n.f.* ballistics. —**balístico,** *adj.* ballistic.
baliza (ba'li·θa; -sa) *n.f.* signal buoy.
balneario (bal·ne'a·rjo) *n.m.* spa; watering place. —*adj.* of or for baths or bathing.
balompié (ba·lom'pje) *n.m.* football; soccer.
balón (ba'lon) *n.m.* **1,** large ball; balloon. **2,** football. **3,** bale.
baloncesto (ba·lon'θes·to; -'ses·to) *n.m.* basketball.
balota (ba'lo·ta) *n.f.* ballot. —**balotar,** *v.i.* to ballot; to vote.
balsa ('bal·sa) *n.f.* **1,** raft; barge. **2,** pond; pool. **3,** *bot.* balsa. —**balsear,** *v.t.* to cross on raft or ferry.
balsámico (bal'sa·mi·ko) *adj.* **1,** balmy; fragrant. **2,** soothing; healing.
bálsamo ('bal·sa·mo) *n.m.* balsam; balm.
báltico ('bal·ti·ko) *adj.* Baltic. —*n.m., cap.* Baltic.
baluarte (ba'lwar·te) *n.m.* bastion; bulwark.
ballena (ba'ʎe·na; ba'je–) *n.f.* **1,** whale. **2,** whalebone; corset stay. **3,** baleen. —**ballenato,** *n.m.* young whale. —**ballenero,** *n.m.* whaler. —*adj.* of or pert. to whaling.
ballesta (ba'ʎes·ta; –'jes·ta) *n.f.* **1,** crossbow. **2,** carriage spring; auto spring.
ballet (ba'le) *n.m.* [*pl.* **ballets** (ba·'le)] ballet.
ballueca (ba'ʎwe·ka; –'jwe·ka) *n.f.* wild oats.
bambalina (bam·ba'li·na) *n.f., theat.* flies (*pl.*).
bambolear (bam·bo·le'ar) *v.i., also,* **bambolearse,** *v.r.* to reel; to stagger; to sway. —**bamboleo** (–'le·o) *n.m.* reeling; staggering.
bambú (bam'bu) *n.m.* [*pl.* **-búes**] bamboo.
banal (ba'nal) *adj.* banal; trivial. —**banalidad,** *n.f.* banality.
banana (ba'na·na) *n.f.* banana. —**bananal,** *n.m.* banana plantation. —**bananero,** *adj.* of or pert. to bananas. —*n.m.* banana tree.
banano (ba'na·no) *n.m.* **1,** banana. **2,** banana tree.
banasta (ba'nas·ta) *n.f.* large basket.
banca ('ban·ka) *n.f.* **1,** bench. **2,** banking. **3,** bank (*in games*). —**bancario** (–'ka·rjo) *adj.* of or pert. to banking.
bancarrota (ban·ka'rro·ta) *n.f.* bankruptcy. —**hacer bancarrota,** to go into bankruptcy.
banco ('ban·ko) *n.m.* **1,** bench; seat **2,** bank. **3,** shoal; sandbar. **4,** *geol.* stratum **5,** school of fish.
banda ('ban·da) *n.f.* **1,** sash; ribbon; scarf. **2,** band; gang. **3,** edge; border. **4,** *music* band.
bandada (ban'da·ða) *n.f.* **1,** covey; flock of birds. **2,** *colloq.* flock of people.
bandazo (ban'da·θo; –so) *n.m., chiefly naut.* lurch; roll.
bandeado (ban·de'a·ðo) *adj.* striped.
bandeja (ban'de·xa) *n.f.* tray.
bandera (ban'de·ra) *n.f.* banner; flag; standard.
bandería (ban·de'ri·a) *n.f.* band; faction.
banderilla (ban·de'ri·ʎa; –ja) *n.f.* banderilla. —**banderillero,** *n.m.* banderillero.
banderín (ban·de'rin) *n.m.* signal

flag. —**banderín de enganche,** recruiting post.
banderola (ban·de'ro·la) *n.f.* 1, streamer; pennant. 2, signal flag.
bandido (ban'di·ðo) *n.m.* bandit; outlaw. —**bandidaje** (–'ða·xe) *n.m.* banditry.
bando ('ban·do) *n.m.* 1, decree; edict. 2, faction; party.
bandola (ban'do·la) *n.f.* mandolin.
bandolera (ban·do'le·ra) *n.f.* 1, bandoleer. 2, female bandit. —**bandolerismo,** *n.m.* brigandage. —**bandolero,** *n.m.* brigand; highwayman.
bandurria (ban'du·rrja) *n.f.* a twelve-stringed instrument of the lute family; bandurria.
baniano (ba'nja·no) *n.m.* banyan.
banjo ('ban·xo) *n.m.* banjo. —**banjoísta,** *n.m.* & *f.* banjoist.
banquero (ban'ke·ro) *n.m.* 1, banker. 2, dealer.
banqueta (ban'ke·ta) *n.f.* 1, footstool; stool. 2, *Mex.* sidewalk.
banquete (ban'ke·te) *n.m.* banquet; feast. —**banquetear,** *v.t.* & *i.* to banquet.
banquillo (ban'ki·ʎo; –jo) *n.m.* small stool.
bañadera (ba·ɲa'ðe·ra) *n.f., Amer.* bathtub.
bañador (ba·ɲa'ðor) *n.m.* swim suit.
bañar (ba'ɲar) *v.t.* 1, to bathe; to wash. 2, to dip. 3, to coat. —**bañarse,** *v.r.* to bathe.
bañera (ba'ɲe·ra) *n.f.* bathtub.
bañista (ba'ɲis·ta) *n.m.* & *f.* bather.
baño ('ba·ɲo) *n.m.* 1, bath; bathing. 2, bathroom. 3, covering; coating. —**baño de María,** double boiler.
baptista (bap'tis·ta) *adj.* & *n.m.* & *f.* = **bautista.**
baptisterio (bap·tis'te·rjo) *n.m.* baptistery.
baquelita *also,* **bakelita** (ba·ke'li·ta) *n.f.* bakelite.
baqueta (ba'ke·ta) *n.f.* 1, ramrod. 2, drumstick. 3, gantlet. —**correr baquetas; pasar por baquetas,** to run the gantlet. —**tratar a (la) baqueta,** to treat with scorn.
baquetear (ba·ke·te'ar) *v.t.* 1, to beat; to put through the gantlet. 2, to annoy. —**baqueteado,** *adj.* inured; accustomed.
baquiano (ba'kja·no) *n.m.* guide. —*adj.* experienced; skillful.
bar (bar) *n.m.* bar; taproom.
baraja (ba'ra·xa) *n.f.* pack of cards.
barajar (ba·ra'xar) *v.t.* 1, to shuffle (cards). 2, to mix. —*v.i.* to quarrel.
barajón (ba·ra'xon) *n.m.* snowshoe.
baranda (ba'ran·da) *n.f.* railing; rail.
barandal (ba·ran'dal) *n.m.* 1, railing. 2, banister.
barandilla (ba·ran'di·ʎa; –ja) *n.f.* 1, railing. 2, balustrade.
barata (ba'ra·ta) *n.f.* 1, barter. 2, *Amer.* bargain sale. —**baratear,** *v.t.* to sell cheaply.
baratería (ba·ra·te'ri·a) *n.f., law* 1, fraud. 2, barratry.
baratijas (ba·ra'ti·xas) *n.f.pl.* trinkets; novelties.
baratillo (ba·ra'ti·ʎo; –jo) *n.m.* 1, secondhand goods. 2, secondhand shop; bargain counter. 3, bargain sale.
barato (ba'ra·to) *adj.* cheap; low-priced. —*n.m.* bargain sale. —*adv.* cheaply.
baraúnda *also,* **barahunda** (ba·ra'un·da) *n.f.* noise; tumult; turmoil.
barba ('bar·βa) *n.f.* 1, chin. 2, beard. 3, *pl.* fine roots; fibers. 4, wattle (*of birds*). —**barbado,** *adj.* bearded; barbed.
barbacoa (bar·βa'ko·a) *n.f., Amer.* barbecue.
barbárico (bar'βa·ri·ko) *adj.* barbaric.
barbaridad (bar·βa·ri'ðað) *n.f.* 1, barbarity; brutality. 2, rashness; rudeness. 3, enormity.
barbarie (bar'βa·rje) *n.f.* savagery; brutality; incivility.
bárbaro ('bar·βa·ro) *adj.* 1, barbarous; savage; crude. 2, *colloq.* huge. —*n.m.* barbarian. —**barbarismo,** *n.m.* barbarism.
barbechar (bar·βe'tʃar) *v.t.* to fallow. —**barbechera** (–'tʃe·ra) *n.f.* fallowing; fallowing season. —**barbecho** (–'βe·tʃo) *n.m.* fallow.
barbería (bar·βe'ri·a) *n.f.* barber shop. —**barbero** (–'βe·ro) *n.m.* barber. —**barberil** (-'ril) *adj.* tonsorial.
barbilla (bar'βi·ʎa; –ja) *n.f.* point of the chin.
barbiturato (bar·βi·tu'ra·to) *n.m.* barbiturate. —**barbitúrico** (–'tu·ri·ko) *adj.* barbituric.
barbotar (bar·βo'tar) *also,* **bar-**

botear (–te'ar) *v.t. & i.* to mutter; mumble. —**barboteo** (–'te·o) *n.m.* muttering; mumbling.
barbudo (bar'βu·ðo) *adj.* long-bearded.
barbulla (bar'βu·ʎa; –ja) *n.f., colloq.* hullaballoo. —**barbullar** (–'ʎar; –'jar) *v.i.* to prattle; chatter noisily. —**barbullón** (–'ʎon; –'jon) *adj.* loudmouthed. —*n.m.* [*fem.* **-ona**] loudmouth.
barca ('bar·ka) *n.f.* small boat; launch. —**barcaza** (–'ka·θa; –sa) *n.f.* barge; lighter.
barcarola (bar·ka'ro·la) *n.f.* barcarole.
barcia ('bar·θja; –sja) *n.f.* chaff.
barcino (bar'θi·no; –'si·no) *adj.* (*of animals*) white with brown or reddish spots.
barco ('bar·ko) *n.m.* boat; ship.
bardo ('bar·ðo) *n.m.* bard.
bari- (ba·ri) *prefix* bari-; heavy: *barítono,* baritone.
bario ('ba·rjo) *n.m.* barium.
barítono (ba'ri·to·no) *adj. & n.m.* baritone.
barlovento (bar·lo'βen·to) *n.m., naut.* windward.
barniz (bar'niθ; –'nis) *n.m.* **1,** varnish. **2,** gloss; glaze. **3,** face paint. **4,** printer's ink.
barnizar (bar·ni'θar; –'sar) *v.t.* [*pres.subjve.* **barnice** (–'ni·θe; –se); *pret.* **barnicé** (-'θe; -'se)] **1,** to varnish. **2,** to glaze. **3,** to shine; to polish.
baro- (ba·ro) *prefix* baro-; pressure: *barómetro,* barometer.
barómetro (ba'ro·me·tro) *n.m.* barometer. —**barométrico,** *adj.* barometric.
barón (ba'ron) *n.m.* baron. —**baronesa,** *n.f.* baroness. —**baronía,** *n.f.* barony.
barquero (bar'ke·ro) *n.m.* boatman.
barqueta (bar'ke·ta) *n.f.* small boat.
barquichuelo (bar·ki'tʃwe·lo) *n.m.* small boat.
barquilla (bar'ki·ʎa; –ja) *n.f.* **1,** small boat. **2,** *naut.* log. **3,** wafer mold. **4,** *aero.* control car; gondola.
barquillero (bar·ki'ʎe·ro; -'je·ro) *n.m.* **1,** wafer mold. **2,** waffle iron.
barquillo (bar'ki·ʎo; -jo) *n.m.* **1,** wafer. **2,** wafer cone. **3,** waffle.
barquín (bar'kin) *n.m.* bellows.
barquinazo (bar·ki'na·θo; –so) *n.m.* jolting, swaying or upset of a boat or vehicle.
barra ('ba·rra) *n.f.* **1,** bar; rod; beam; lever. **2,** sandbar. **3,** ingot.
barrabás (ba·rra'βas) *n.m.* fiend; devil. —**barrabasada,** *n.f.* fiendishness; fiendish act.
barraca (ba'rra·ka) *n.f.* **1,** barrack; cabin. **2,** *Amer.* warehouse. —**barracón,** *n.m.* large barrack or cabin.
barracuda (ba·rra'ku·ða) *n.f.* barracuda.
barrado (ba'rra·ðo) *adj.* (*of cloth*) ribbed; corded.
barranca (ba'rran·ka) *n.f.* ravine; gorge; cleft.
barranco (ba'rran·ko) *n.m.* **1,** cliff; precipice. **2,** *fig.* obstacle; difficulty. **3,** = **barranca.**
barrancoso (ba·rran'ko·so) *adj.* **1,** uneven; rough. **2,** steep; precipitous.
barrar (ba'rrar) *v.t.* to daub; to smear.
barredera (ba·rre'ðe·ra) *n.f.* sweeper (*person or tool*).
barredura (ba·rre'ðu·ra) *n.f.* sweeping. —**barreduras,** *n.f.pl.* sweepings.
barreminas (ba·rre'mi·nas) *n.m. sing. & pl.* mine sweeper.
barrena (ba'rre·na) *n.f.* **1,** borer; drill; auger. **2,** *aero.* tailspin.
barrenar (ba·rre'nar) *v.t.* **1,** to drill; to bore. **2,** to scuttle (a ship). **3,** *fig.* to foil; thwart. **4,** to infringe; violate.
barrendero (ba·rren'de·ro) *n.m.* [*fem.* **-ra**] sweeper.
barreno (ba'rre·no) *n.m.* **1,** large drill or borer. **2,** drilled or bored hole. **3,** blast hole.
barreño (ba'rre·ɲo) *n.m.* earthen pan; dishpan. *Also,* **barreña,** *n.f.*
barrer (ba'rrer) *v.t.* to sweep.
barrera (ba'rre·ra) *n.f.* barrier; barricade; fence.
barreta (ba'rre·ta) *n.f.* **1,** small bar. **2,** shoe lining.
barriada (ba'rrja·ða) *n.f.* = **barrio.**
barrica (ba'rri·ka) *n.f.* cask.
barricada (ba·rri'ka·ða) *n.f.* barricade.
barrido (ba'rri·ðo) *n.m.* sweep; sweeping.
barriga (ba'rri·ɣa) *n.f.* belly; bulge. —**barrigón** (–'ɣon), **barrigudo** (–'ɣu·ðo) *adj.* pot-bellied.

barril (ba'rril) *n.m.* barrel; cask. —**barrilero,** *n.m.* cooper.
barrilete (ba·rri'le·te) *n.m.* **1,** keg. **2,** clamp.
barrilla (ba'rri·ʎa; -ja) *n.f.* **1,** saltwort. **2,** soda ash.
barrillo (ba'rri·ʎo; –jo) *n.m.* pimple.
barrio ('ba·rrjo) *n.m.* **1,** ward; precinct; district; quarter. **2,** suburb. —**barrio bajo,** slum. —**el otro barrio,** *colloq.* the other world.
barrizal (ba·rri'θal; –'sal) *n.m.* mire; mud pit.
barro ('ba·rro) *n.m.* **1,** clay; mud; mire. **2,** earthenware. **3,** pimple. —**barro cocido,** terra cotta.
barroco (ba'rro·ko) *adj.* & *n.m.* baroque.
barroso (ba'rro·so) *adj.* **1,** muddy. **2,** pimply.
barrote (ba'rro·te) *n.m.* **1,** iron bar; rod. **2,** brace.
barrumbada (ba·rrum'ba·ða) *n.f.* **1,** boastfulness. **2,** extravagance.
barruntar (ba·rrun'tar) *v.t.* **1,** to foresee. **2,** to conjecture.
barrunto (ba'rrun·to) *n.m.* **1,** foreboding. **2,** conjecture.
bartola (bar'to·la) *n.f.,* *in* **a la bartola,** *colloq.* in a carefree way; carelessly.
bártulos ('bar·tu·los) *n.m.pl.* **1,** belongings; tools. **2,** business. —**liar los bártulos,** *colloq.* to pack up. —**preparar los bártulos,** *colloq.* to get set.
baruca (ba'ru·ka) *n.f., colloq.* artifice; trickery.
barullo (ba'ru·ʎo; –jo) *n.m.* tumult; confusion.
barzón (bar'θon; -'son) *n.m.* **1,** idle stroll; wandering. **2,** ring of a yoke.
basa ('ba·sa) *n.f.* **1,** pedestal; base. **2,** foundation; basis.
basal (ba'sal) *adj.* basal; basic.
basalto (ba'sal·to) *n.m.* basalt.
basar (ba'sar) *v.t.* **1,** to base; to found. **2,** to support; to secure. —**basarse en,** to rely on.
basca ('bas·ka) *n.f.* nausea; queasiness.
báscula ('bas·ku·la) *n.f.* platform scale.
base ('ba·se) *n.f.* **1,** base. **2,** basis. **3,** foot. —**básico** ('ba·si·ko) *adj.* basic.
basílica (ba'si·li·ka) *n.f.* basilica.
basilisco (ba·si'lis·ko) *n.m.* basilisk.
basquear (bas·ke'ar) *v.i.* to be nauseated.
básquetbol ('bas·ket·βol) *n.m.* basketball.
basta ('bas·ta) *n.f.* basting; basting stitch.
¡basta! ('bas·ta) *interj.* enough!
bastante (bas'tan·te) *adj.* sufficient; enough. —*adv.* **1,** enough. **2,** rather.
bastar (bas'tar) *v.i.* to suffice; to be enough.
bastardear (bas·tar·ðe'ar) *v.t.* & *i.* to degenerate; to bastardize.
bastardía (bas·tar'ði·a) *n.f.* **1,** bastardy. **2,** meanness; depravity.
bastardillo (bas·tar'ði·ʎo; -jo) *adj., print.* italic. —**bastardillas,** *n.f. pl.* italics.
bastardo (bas'tar·ðo) *n.m.* & *adj.* bastard.
baste ('bas·te) *n.m.* **1,** basting. **2,** saddle pad. —**bastear,** *v.t.* to baste; to tack.
bastidor (bas·ti'ðor) *n.m.* **1,** frame. **2,** window sash. **3,** stretcher for hand embroidery. **4,** *paint.* canvas stretcher. **5,** *theat.* wing. —**entre bastidores,** behind the scenes.
bastilla (bas'ti·ʎa; –ja) *n.f.* hem. —**bastillar,** *v.t.* to hem.
bastimento (bas·ti'men·to) *n.m.* **1,** provisions; supplies. **2,** vessel; ship.
bastión (bast'tjon) *n.m.* bastion; bulwark. —**bastionado,** *adj.* fortified.
basto ('bas·to) *adj.* coarse; rude. —*n.m.* **1,** packsaddle. **2,** *cards* club (*in the Spanish deck*). **3,** basting; basting stitch.
bastón (bas'ton) *n.m.* cane; stick; staff. —**bastonada,** *n.f., also,* **bastonazo,** *n.m.* blow with a cane or stick. —**bastón de mando,** baton; staff of office.
bastoncillo (bas·ton'θi·ʎo; -'si·jo) *n.m.* **1,** small cane or stick. **2,** narrow trimming lace.
bastonera (bas·to'ne·ra) *n.f.* cane stand; umbrella stand.
basura (ba'su·ra) *n.f.* sweepings (*pl.*); trash; refuse.
basurero (ba·su're·ro) *n.m.* **1,** garbage collector; street cleaner. **2,** trash can. **3,** garbage dump; refuse heap.
bata ('ba·ta) *n.f.* robe; housecoat; bathrobe.
batacazo (ba·ta'ka·θo; –so) *n.m.* thud.

batahola (ba·ta'o·la) *n.f., colloq.* bustle; clatter.
batalla (ba'ta·ʎa; –ja) *n.f.* battle; combat; struggle. —**batallador** (–'ðor) *n.m.* warrior; combatant. —*adj.* battling; fighting. —**batallar,** *v.i.* to fight; to struggle.
batallón (ba·ta'ʎon; -'jon) *n.m.* battalion.
batán (ba'tan) *n.m.* fulling mill. —**batanar,** *v.t.* to full (cloth). —**batanero,** *n.m.* fuller.
batanear (ba·ta·ne'ar) *v.t., colloq.* to beat; to thrash.
bataola (ba·ta'o·la) *n.f.* = **batahola.**
batata (ba'ta·ta) *n.f.* sweet potato.
batayola (ba·ta'jo·la) *n.f., naut.* rail.
bate ('ba·te) *n.m.* baseball bat.
batea (ba'te·a) *n.f.* **1,** tray; trough. **2,** *Amer.* washtub. **3,** flat-bottomed boat; punt. **4,** *R.R.* flatcar.
batear (ba·te'ar) *v.t. & i., baseball* to bat. —**bateador** (–'ðor) *n.m.* batter.
bateo (ba'te·o) *n.m., baseball* batting.
batería (ba·te'ri·a) *n.f.* **1,** *electricity; mil.; baseball* battery. **2,** kitchenware. **3,** *music* percussion section; drums. **4,** *theat.* footlights (*pl.*).
batey (ba'tei) *n.m., Cuba* sugar mill.
bati- (ba·ti) *prefix* bathy-; deep: *batiscafo,* bathyscaphe.
batida (ba'ti·ða) *n.f.* **1,** beating (for game). **2,** search; reconnoitering.
batido (ba'ti·ðo) *adj.* beaten, as a path. —*n.m.* **1,** batter. **2,** beaten whites or yolks of eggs.
batidor (ba·ti'ðor) *adj.* beating. —*n.m.* **1,** beater (*person or tool*). **2,** scout.
batiente (ba'tjen·te) *n.m.* **1,** jamb; doorpost. **2,** leaf of a double door.
batín (ba'tin) *n.m.* smoking jacket.
batintín (ba·tin'tin) *n.m.* gong.
batir (ba'tir) *v.t.* **1,** to beat; to strike; to pound. **2,** to raze; to demolish. **3,** to mix; to stir. **4,** to defeat. **5,** to reconnoiter. **6,** to strike (camp). —**batirse,** *v.r.* to fight.
batiscafio (ba·tis'ka·fjo) *n.m.* bathyscaphe.
batisfera (ba·tis'fe·ra) *n.f.* bathysphere.
batista (ba'tis·ta) *n.f.* batiste.
bato- (ba·to) *prefix* batho-; depth: *batómetro,* bathometer.
baturrillo (ba·tu'rri·ʎo; –jo) *n.m.* hodgepodge; medley.
batuta (ba'tu·ta) *n.f.* baton.
baúl (ba'ul) *n.m.* trunk.
bauprés (bau'pres) *n.m.* bowsprit.
bautismo (bau'tis·mo) *n.m.* baptism; christening. —**bautismal** *adj.* baptismal.
bautista (bau'tis·ta) *n.m.* baptizer. —*adj.* & *n.m.* & *f.* Baptist.
bautisterio (bau·tis'te·rjo) *n.m.* baptistery.
bautizar (bau·ti'θar; –'sar) *v.t.* [*pres.subjve.* **bautice** (–'ti·θe; –se); *pret.* **bauticé** (–'θe; –'se)] to baptize; christen.
bautizo (bau'ti·θo; –so) *n.m.* christening.
bauxita (bau'ksi·ta) *n.f.* bauxite.
baya ('ba·ja) *n.f.* berry.
bayeta (ba'je·ta) *n.f.* **1,** baize. **2,** mop; swab.
bayetón (ba·je'ton) *n.m.* **1,** shaggy wool cloth, used for coats. **2,** *Amer.* a kind of long poncho.
bayo ('ba·jo) *adj.* bay. —*n.m.* bay (*horse*).
bayoneta (ba·jo'ne·ta) *n.f.* bayonet. —**bayonetazo,** *n.m.* bayonet thrust or wound.
baza ('ba·θa; –sa) *n.f. cards* trick. —**no dejar meter baza,** *colloq.* to monopolize the conversation. —**meter baza,** *colloq.* to butt in.
bazar (ba'θar; –'sar) *n.m.* bazaar; market.
bazo ('ba·θo; –so) *n.m.* spleen. —*adj.* yellowish-brown.
bazofia (ba'θo·fja; ba'so-) *n.f.* offal; refuse.
bazucar (ba·θu'kar; ba·su–) [*pres. subjve.* **bazuque** (–'θu·ke; –'su·ke); *pret.* bazuqué (–'ke)] *also,* **bazuquear** (–ke'ar) *v.t.* to stir; to shake (liquids). —**bazuqueo** (–'ke·o) *n.m.* stirring; shaking.
beata (be'a·ta) *adj.* & *n., fem. of* **beato.** —*n.f.* lay sister.
beatificar (be·a·ti·fi'kar) *v.t.* [*pres.subjve.* **beatifique** (–'fi·ke); *pret.* **beatifiqué** (–'ke)] to beatify. —**beatificación,** *n.f.* beatification.
beatífico (be·a'ti·fi·ko) *adj.* beatific.
beatísimo (be·a'ti·si·mo) *adj.* most holy.
beatitud (be·a·ti'tuð) *n.f.* **1** beati-

tude. 2, *cap., R.C.Ch.* a title of the Pope.
beato (be'a·to) *adj.* 1, blessed; beatified. 2, pious; devout. 3, prudish; bigoted. —*n.m.* 1, devout person. 2, prude; bigot. —**beatón,** *n.m.* [*fem.* **-ona**] bigot; hypocrite.
bebé (be'βe) *n.m.* baby.
bebedero (be·βe'ðe·ro) *n.m.* drinking trough.
bebedizo (be·βe'ði·θo; –so) *n.m.* potion; philter.
beber (be'βer) *v.t.* & *i.* to drink. —*n.m.* drink; drinking. —**bebedor** (–'ðor) *n.m.* tippler; drunkard. —**bebible,** *adj., colloq.* barely drinkable. —**bebida** (–'βi·ða) *n.f.* drink; beverage. —**bebido** (–ðo) *adj.* tipsy.
beca ('be·ka) *n.f.* scholarship; fellowship. —**becario** (–'ka·rjo) *also, Amer.* **becado** (–'ka·ðo) *n.m.* holder of a scholarship; fellow.
becerra (be'θe·rra; be'se–) *n.f.* 1, yearling calf. 2, *bot.* snapdragon.
becerril (be·θe'rril; be·se–) *adj.* of or pert. to a calf.
becerro (be'θe·rro; be'se–) *n.m.* 1, yearling calf. 2, calfskin.
becuadro (be'kwa·ðro) *n.m., music* natural sign.
bedel (be'ðel) *n.m.* beadle. —**bedelía** (–'li·a) *n.f.* beadleship.
beduino (be'ðwi·no) *adj.* & *n.m.* Bedouin. —*n.m.* barbarian.
befa ('be·fa) *n.f.* derision; scoff. —**befar,** *v.t.* to scoff at; mock.
befo ('be·fo) *adj.* 1, thick-lipped. 2, knock-kneed. —*n.m.* 1, lip (*of some animals*). 2, a long-tailed monkey.
begonia (be'ɣo·nja) *n.f.* begonia.
behaviorismo (be·a·βjo'ris·mo) *n.m.* behaviorism. —**behaviorista,** *adj.* & *n.m.* & *f.* behaviorist. —*adj.* behavioristic.
behemot (be·e'mot) *n.m., Bib.* behemoth.
béisbol ('beis·bol) *n.m.* baseball. —**beisbolero, beisbolista,** *n.m.* baseball player.
bejín (be'xin) *n.m., bot.* puffball.
bejuco (be'xu·ko) *n.m.* rattan; reed. —**bejucal,** *n.m.* an area where reeds grow.
beldad (bel'dað) *n.f.* 1, beauty. 2, beautiful woman.
Belén (be'len) *n.m.* 1, Bethlehem. 2, *l.c.* crèche.
beleño (be'le·ɲo) *n.m.* henbane.
belfo ('bel·fo) *adj.* thick-lipped. —*n.m.* lip (*of some animals*).
belga ('bel·ɣa) *adj.* & *n.m.* & *f.* Belgian.
belicismo (be·li'θis·mo; –'sis·mo) *n.m.* militarism. —**belicista,** *adj.* militaristic.
bélico ('be·li·ko) *adj.* 1, of or pert. to war. 2, warlike; martial. —**belicosidad** (–si'ðað) *n.f.* bellicosity. —**belicoso** (–'ko·so) *adj.* bellicose.
beligerancia (be·li·ɣe'ran·θja; –sja) *n.f.* belligerence; belligerency. —**beligerante,** *adj.* & *n.m.* & *f.* belligerent.
bellaco (be'ʎa·ko; be'ja–) *adj.* cunning; vile. —*n.m.* villain; rogue. —**bellacada** ('ka·ða) *n.f.* villainous act. —**bellaquear** (-ke'ar) *v.i.* to cheat; to play roguish tricks. —**bellaquería** (–ke'ri·a) *n.f.* roguery; cunning; vile act or expression.
belladona (be·ʎa'ðo·na; be·ja–) *n.f.* belladonna.
belleza (be'ʎe·θa; –'je·sa) *n.f.* 1, beauty. 2, beautiful woman.
bello ('be·ʎo; –jo) *adj.* fair; beautiful.
bellota (be'ʎo·ta; be'jo–) *n.f.* acorn.
bemol (be'mol) *adj.* & *n.m., music* flat. —**tener bemoles,** *colloq.* to be very difficult; to be hard to take.
bencedrina (ben·θe'ðri·na; ben·se–) *n.f.* benzedrine.
benceno (ben'θe·no; –'se·no) *n.m.* benzene.
bencina (ben'θi·na; –'si·na) *n.f.* benzine.
bendecir (ben·de'θir; –'sir) *v.t.* [*infl:* **decir;** *impve.* **bendice** (–'di·θe; –se); *fut.* **bendeciré;** *p.p.* **bendecido, bendito**] to bless. —**bendición,** *n.f.* blessing; benediction. —**bendito,** *adj.* blessed. —*n.m.* simple soul.
benedictino (be·ne·ðik'ti·no) *adj.* & *n.m.* Benedictine.
benefactor (be·ne·fak'tor) *n.m.* benefactor.
beneficencia (be·ne·fi'θen·θja; –'sen·sja) *n.f.* beneficence; welfare.
beneficiado (be·ne·fi'θja·ðo; -'sja·ðo) *n.m.* 1, person benefited or receiving benefits. 2, *eccles.* beneficiary.
beneficiar (be·ne·fi'θjar; –'sjar) *v.t.* 1, to benefit. 2, to improve. 3, to cultivate (land). 4, to exploit (natural resources). 5, to work (a mine). 6, to process (ores). 7,

Amer. to slaughter (cattle). —*v.i.* [*also,* **beneficiarse,** *v.r.*] to profit; gain; benefit.
beneficiario (be·ne·fi'θja·rjo; –'sja·rjo) *n.m.* beneficiary.
beneficio (be·ne'fi·θjo; -sjo) *n.m.* **1,** benefit; utility; profit. **2,** *eccles.* benefice. —**beneficioso,** *adj.* beneficial; profitable.
benéfico (be'ne·fi·ko) *adj.* beneficial; beneficent; benevolent.
benemérito (be·ne'me·ri·to) *adj.* worthy; deserving.
beneplácito (be·ne'pla·θi·to; -si·to) *n.m.* approval; sanction.
benevolencia (be·ne·βo'len·θja; –sja) *n.f.* benevolence.
benévolo (be'ne·βo·lo) *adj.* benevolent.
bengala (ben'ga·la) *n.f.* flare; signal flare.
benigno (be'niɣ·no) *adj.* benign; gentle; mild. —**benignidad** (-ni·ðað) *n.f.* kindness; mildness.
benjuí (ben'xwi) *n.m.* benzoin.
benzoato (ben·θo'a·to; ben·so–) *n.m.* benzoate. —**benzoico** (-'θoi·ko; –'soi·ko) *adj.* benzoic. —**benzol** (–'θol; –'sol) *n.m.* benzol.
beodo (be'o·ðo) *adj.* drunk. —*n.m.* drunkard. —**beodez** (-'ðeθ; -'ðes) *n.f.* drunkenness.
berbiquí (ber·βi'ki) *n.m.* drill brace.
bereber (be·re'βer) *also,* **berberí** (ber·βe'ri) *adj* & *n.m.* & *f.* Berber.
berenjena (be·ren'xe·na) *n.f.* eggplant.
berenjenal (be·ren·xe'nal) *n.m.* **1,** eggplant patch. **2,** *colloq.* mess; predicament.
bergante (ber'ɣan·te) *n.m.* rascal.
bergantín (ber·ɣan'tin) *n.m.* brigantine.
beriberi (be·ri'βe·ri) *n.m.* beriberi.
berilio (be'ri·ljo) *n.m.* beryllium.
berilo (be'ri·lo) *n.m.* beryl.
berkelio (ber'ke·ljo) *n.m.* berkelium.
berlina (ber'li·na) *n.f.* closed carriage; coupé.
bermejo (ber'me·xo) *adj.* bright red; vermillion. —**bermejizo** (-'xi·θo; –so) *adj.* reddish. —**bermejón** (–'xon) *adj.* reddish. —**bermellón** (–'ʎon; –'jon) *n.m.* vermillion.
berrear (be·rre'ar) *v.i.* to bellow; scream. —**berrido** (-'rri·ðo) *n.m.* bellow; scream.
berrinche (be'rrin·tʃe) *n.m., colloq.* rage; tantrum.
berro ('be·rro) *n.m.* watercress. —**berrizal** (–rri'θal; –'sal) *n.m.* watercress bed.
berza ('ber·θa; –sa) *n.f.* cabbage. —**berzal** (–'θal; –'sal) *n.m.* cabbage patch.
besar (be'sar) *v.t.* to kiss.
beso ('be·so) *n.m.* kiss.
bestia ('bes·tja) *n.f.* beast. —*n.m.* & *f.* dunce; dimwit. —*adj.* stupid. —**bestia de carga,** beast of burden.
bestial (bes'tjal) *adj.* bestial; brutish. —**bestialidad,** *n.f.* bestiality; brutishness.
besucar (be·su'kar) *v.t.* *colloq.* [*pres.subjve.* **besuque** (-'su·ke); *pret.* **besuqué** (-'ke)] = **besuquear.**
besucón (be·su'kon) *adj.* *colloq.* much given to kissing. —*n.m. colloq.* [*fem.* **–ona**] a person much given to kissing.
besugo (be'su·ɣo) *n.m.* sea bream.
besuquear (be·su·ke'ar) *v.t. colloq.* to kiss repeatedly or excessively. —**besuqueo** (–'ke·o) *n.m., colloq.* repeated kissing.
beta ('be·ta) *n.f.* **1,** piece of string or thread; tape. **2,** beta.
betarraga (be·ta'rra·ɣa) *also,* **betarrata** (-'rra·ta) *n.f.* beet.
betel (be'tel) *n.m.* betel.
betún (be'tun) *n.m.* **1,** pitch; bitumen. **2,** shoe polish.
betunar (be·tu'nar) *v.t.* **1,** to pitch; tar. **2,** to polish (shoes). **3,** to blacken.
bezo ('be·θo; –so) *n.m.* **1,** blubber lip. **2,** proud flesh.
bi- (bi) *prefix* bi-. **1,** two: *biáxico,* biaxial. **2,** doubly: *bilingüe,* bilingual. **3,** every other: *bienal,* biennial. **4,** twice: *bisemanal,* twice weekly.
biberón (bi·βe'ron) *n.m.* nursing bottle.
Biblia ('bi·βlja) *n.f.* Bible. —**bíblico** ('bi·βli·ko) *adj.* Biblical.
biblio- (bi·βljo) *prefix* biblio-; book: *bibliografía,* bibliography.
bibliófilo (bi'βljo·fi·lo) *n.m.* bibliophile.
bibliografía (bi·βljo·ɣra'fi·a) *n.f.* bibliography. —**bibliográfico** (–'ɣra·fi·ko) *adj.* bibliographical.
bibliomanía (bi·βljo·ma'ni·a) *n.f.* bibliomania. —**biblíomano** (bi·'βljo·ma·no) *n.m.* bibliomaniac.
biblioteca (bi·βljo'te·ka) *n.f.* **1,** li-

brary. **2,** bookcase. —**bibliotecario,** *n.m.* librarian.
bicameral (bi·ka·me'ral) *adj.* bicameral.
bicarbonato (bi·kar·βo'na·to) *n.m.* bicarbonate.
bicentenario (bi·θen·te'na·rjo; bi·sen-) *adj.* & *n.m.* bicentennial.
bíceps ('bi·θeps; –seps) *n.m.* biceps.
bicicleta (bi·θi'kle·ta; bi·si–) *n.f.* bicycle.
biciclo (bi'θi·klo; bi'si–) *n.m.* early form of bicycle with large front wheel; velocipede.
bicimoto (bi·θi'mo·to; bi·si–) *n.f.* motorbike.
bicloruro (bi·klo'ru·ro) *n.m.* bichloride.
bicoca (bi'ko·ka) *n.f.* trifle; bagatelle.
bicolor (bi·ko'lor) *adj.* bicolor; bicolored.
bicornio (bi'kor·njo) *n.m.* two-cornered hat.
bicúspide (bi'kus·pi·ðe) *adj.* bicuspid.
bichero (bi'tʃe·ro) *n.m.* boat hook.
bicho ('bi·tʃo) *n.m.* **1,** insect; vermin. **2,** *colloq.* despicable person. —**bicharraco** (–tʃa'rra·ko) *n.m., colloq.* repulsive animal or person.
biela ('bje·la) *n.f.* connecting rod.
bieldo ('bjel·do) *n.m., also,* **bielda,** *n.f.* **1,** pitchfork. **2,** winnowing fork. **3,** wooden rake.
bien (bjen) *adv.* **1,** well; properly; right. **2,** all right; fine. **3,** much; very; fully. **4,** indeed. **5,** willingly; readily. —**ahora bien,** now then. —**bien que,** although. —**más bien,** rather; somewhat. —**por bien,** willingly. —**si bien,** while; though. —*n.m.* good; welfare; benefit; sake. —**bienes,** *n.m.pl.* wealth. —**bienes muebles,** chattels. —**bienes raíces** *or* **inmuebles,** real estate.
bienal (bje'nal) *adj.* biennial.
bienamado (bjen·a'ma·ðo) *adj.* dearly beloved.
bienandante (bjen·an'dan·te) *adj.* happy; prosperous. —**bienandanza,** *n.f.* happiness; prosperity.
bienaventurado (bjen·a·βen·tu'ra·ðo) *adj.* blessed.
bienaventuranza (bjen·a·βen·tu'ran·θa; –sa) *n.f.* bliss; beatitude; *cap., usu.pl.* Beatitudes.
bienestar (bjen·es'tar) *n.m.* well-being; welfare.
bienfortunado (bjen·for·tu'na·ðo) *adj.* fortunate; lucky.
bienhablado (bjen·a'βla·ðo) *adj.* well-spoken.
bienhadado (bjen·a'ða·ðo) *adj.* fortunate; lucky.
bienhechor (bjen·e'tʃor) *n.m.* benefactor.
bienintencionado (bjen·in·ten·θjo'na·ðo; -sjo'na·ðo) *adj.* well-meaning.
bienio ('bje·njo) *n.m.* biennium.
bienmesabe (bjen·me'sa·βe) *n.m.* meringue batter.
bienoliente (bjen·o'ljen·te) *adj.* pleasant-smelling; fragrant.
bienquerencia (bjen·ke'ren·θja; –sja) *n.f.* **1,** affection. **2,** good will.
bienquerer (bjen·ke'rer) *v.t.* [*infl.:* **querer**] **1,** to be fond of. **2,** to wish (someone) well.
bienqueriente (bjen·ke'rjen·te) *adj.* **1,** affectionate; fond. **2,** well-adjusted.
bienquistar (bjen·kis'tar) *v.t.* to reconcile.
bienquisto (bjen'kis·to) *adj.* respected; esteemed.
bienvenida (bjen·βe'ni·ða) *n.f.* welcome. —**bienvenido,** *adj.* welcome. —**dar la bienvenida a,** to welcome.
bifocal (bi·fo'kal) *adj.* bifocal.
biftec (bif'tek) *also,* **bistec** (bis'tek), **bisté** (–'te) *n.m.* beefsteak.
bifurcación (bi·fur·ka'θjon; -'sjon) *n.f.* **1,** bifurcation. **2,** fork (*of a road*). **3,** junction.
bifurcarse (bi·fur'kar·se) *v.r.* [*pres.subjve.* **bifurque** (–'fur·ke) *pret.* **bifurqué** (–'ke)]; to bifurcate; to fork; to branch off. - **bifurcado,** *adj.* bifurcate(d); forked; branched.
bigamia (bi'ɣa·mja) *n.f.* bigamy.
bígamo ('bi·ɣa·mo) *adj.* bigamous. —*n.m.* [*fem.* –**ma**] bigamist.
bigardo (bi'ɣar·ðo) *adj.* dissolute; licentious. - **bigardía** (–'ði·a) *n.f.* dissoluteness; licentiousness.
bigornia (bi'ɣor·nja) *n.f.* anvil.
bigote (bi'ɣo·te) *n.m.* mustache. —**bigotudo** (–'tu·ðo) *adj.* heavy-mustached.
bigotera (bi·ɣo'te·ra) *n.f.* bow compass.
bilateral (bi·la·te'ral) *adj.* bilateral.
-bilidad (bi·li'ðað) *suffix* -bility; *forming nouns from adjectives ending in* **-ble:** *responsabilidad,* responsibility.

bilingüe (bi'lin·gwe) *adj.* bilingual. —**bilingüismo** (-'guis·mo) *n.m.* bilingualism.
bilis ('bi·lis) *n.f.* bile; gall. —**bilioso,** (-'ljo·so) *adj.* bilious. —**biliosidad,** *n.f.* biliousness.
billar (bi'ʎar; -'jar) *n.m.* **1,** billiards. **2,** billiard table.
billete (bi'ʎe·te; bi'je-) *n.m.* **1,** ticket. **2,** bill; note; banknote. —**medio billete,** half-fare; half-price ticket.
billetera (bi·ʎe'te·ra; bi·je-) *n.f., Amer.* wallet; billfold.
billón (bi'ʎon; -'jon) *n.m.* a million million; *U.S.* trillion; *Brit.* billion. —**billonario,** *n.m.* billionaire. —**billonésimo,** *n.m.* & *adj.* million millionth; *U.S.* trillionth; *Brit.* billionth.
bimensual (bi·men'swal) *adj.* twice monthly; semimonthly.
bimestral (bi·mes'tral) *adj.* bimonthly.
bimestre (bi'mes·tre) *adj.* bimonthly. —*n.m.* **1,** a period of two months. **2,** bimonthly payment.
bin- (bin) *prefix, var. of* **bi-**: *binocular,* binocular.
binar (bi'nar) *v.t.* to plow the ground for the second time. —**binador** (-'ðor) *n.m.* weeder; hoe.
binario (bi'na·rjo) *adj.* binary.
binocular (bi·no·ku'lar) *adj.* binocular. —**binóculo** (-'no·ku·lo) *n.m.* binoculars (*pl.*).
binomio (bi'no·mjo) *n.m.* binomial. —**binómico** (-'no·mi·ko) *adj.* binomial.
binza ('bin·θa; -sa) *n.f.* thin membrane.
bio- (bi·o) *prefix* bio-; life: *bioquímica,* biochemistry.
biografía (bjo·ɣra'fi·a) *n.f.* biography. —**biográfico** (-'ɣra·fi·ko) *adj.* biographical. —**biógrafo** ('bjo·ɣra·fo) *n.m.* biographer.
biología (bjo·lo'xi·a) *n.f.* biology. —**biológico** (-'lo·xi·ko) *adj.* biological. —**biólogo** ('bjo·lo·ɣo) *n.m.* biologist.
biombo ('bjom·bo) *n.m.* folding screen.
biopsia (bi'op·sja) *n.f.* biopsy.
bioquímica (bi·o'ki·mi·ka) *n.f.* biochemistry. —**bioquímico,** *adj.* biochemical. —*n.m.* biochemist.
-biosis ('bjo·sis) *suffix* -biosis; way of life: *simbiosis,* symbiosis.
bióxido (bi'ok·si·ðo) *n.m.* dioxide.
bípede ('bi·pe·ðe) *adj.* biped. —**bípedo** (-ðo) *adj.* & *n.m.* biped.
biplano (bi'pla·no) *n.m.* biplane.
birimbao (bi·rim'ba·o) *n.m.* jew's-harp.
birlar (bir'lar) *v.t., colloq.* **1,** to snatch away; to rob; to swindle. **2,** to fell with one blow or shot. —**birlador,** *n.m.* swindler.
birlocha (bir'lo·tʃa) *n.f.* paper kite.
birlocho (bir'lo·tʃo) *n.m.* buggy; surrey.
birreta (bi'rre·ta) *n.f.* biretta.
birrete (bi'rre·te) *n.m.* **1,** biretta. **2,** academic cap; mortarboard.
birretina (bi·rre'ti·na) *n.f.* grenadier's cap; hussar's cap; busby.
bis (bis) *adv.* twice; repeated. —*interj.* encore!
bis- (bis) *prefix, var. of* **bi-** *before a vowel: bisabuelo,* great-grandfather; *bisojo,* crosseyed. *Also, in some words,* **biz-**: *biznieto,* great-grandson; *bizcocho,* biscuit.
bisabuelo (bis·a'βwe·lo) *n.m.* great-grandfather. —**bisabuela,** *n.f.* great-grandmother.
bisagra (bi'sa·ɣra) *n.f.* hinge.
bisbisar (bis·βi'sar) *v.i.* & *t., colloq.* to mumble; to mutter. —**bisbiseo** (-'se·o) *n.m., colloq.* mumbling; muttering.
bisecar (bi·se'kar) *v.t.* to bisect. —**bisección** (-sek'θjon; -'sjon) *n.f.* bisection.
bisector (bi·sek'tor) *adj.* [*fem.* **-triz**] bisecting. —**bisectriz** [*pl.* **-trices**] *n.f.* bisector; bisectrix.
bisel (bi'sel) *n.m.* bevel. —**biselado,** *adj.* beveled. —*n.m.* beveling. —**biselar,** *v.t.* to bevel.
bisemanal (bi·se·ma'nal) *adj.* twice weekly.
bisiesto (bi'sjes·to) *adj.* bissextile. —**año bisiesto,** leap year.
bisílabo (bi'si·la·βo) *adj.* disyllabic. —*n.m.* disyllable.
bismuto (bis'mu·to) *n.m.* bismuth.
bisnieto (bis'nje·to) *also,* **biznieto,** *n.m.* great-grandson. —**bisnieta, biznieta,** *n.f.* great-granddaughter.
bisojo (bi'so·xo) *adj.* squint-eyed. —*n.m.* squinter.
bisonte (bi'son·te) *n.m.* bison.
bisoño (bi'so·ɲo) *adj.* inexperienced. —*n.m.* novice; rookie.
bistec (bis'tek) *also,* **bisté** (-'te) *n.m.* beefsteak.
bisturí (bis·tu'ri) *n.m.* scalpel.

bisulco (bi'sul·ko) *adj.* cloven-hoofed.
bitácora (bi'ta·ko·ra) *n.f., naut.* binnacle.
bitoque (bi'to·ke) *n.m.* **1,** bung; stopper. **2,** *Amer.* syringe tip. **3,** *Amer.* faucet; tap.
bituminoso (bi·tu·mi'no·so) *adj.* bituminous.
bivalente (bi·βa'len·te) *adj.* bivalent. —**bivalencia,** *n.f.* bivalence.
bivalvo (bi'βal·βo) *adj.* & *n.m.* bivalve.
biz- (biθ; bis) *prefix, var. of* **bis-.**
bizantino (bi·θan'ti·no; bi·san–) *adj.* & *n.m.* Byzantine.
bizarro (bi'θa·rro; bi'sa–) *adj.* brave; gallant. —**bizarría,** *n.f.* gallantry; courage.
bizcar (biθ'kar; bis–) *v.t.* [*pres.subjve.* **bizque** ('biθ·ke; 'bis–); *pret.* **bizqué** (–'ke)] to wink (the eye). —*v.i.* to squint.
bizco ('biθ·ko; 'bis–) *adj.* cross-eyed; squint-eyed.
bizcocho (biθ'ko·tʃo; bis–) *n.m.* biscuit; cookie; cake. —**bizcochuelo** (–'tʃwe·lo) *n.m.* small biscuit.
bizma ('biθ·ma; 'bis–) *n.f.* poultice. —**bizmar,** *v.t.* to poultice.
blanca ('blan·ka) *n.f.,* *in* **estar sin blanca,** *also,* **no tener blanca,** *colloq.* to be penniless; be flat broke.
blancazo (blan'ka·θo; –so) *adj., colloq.* whitish.
blanco ('blan·ko) *adj.* **1,** white. **2,** blank. **3,** fair; light-complexioned. —*n.m.* **1,** white person. **2,** white color. **3,** target. **4,** blank. —**blancor** (–'kor) *n.m.,* **blancura** (–'ku·ra) *n.f.* whiteness. —**blancuzco** (–'kuθ·ko; –'kus·ko) *adj.* whitish.
blandeador (blan·de·a'ðor) *adj.* **1,** softening. **2,** persuading.
blandear (blan·de'ar) *v.t.* **1,** to soften. **2,** to brandish. **3,** to persuade.
blandir (blan'dir) *v.t.* to brandish; to swing; to flourish.
blando ('blan·do) *adj.* **1,** bland; soft; pliant. **2,** weak; delicate.
blandura (blan'du·ra) *n.f.* **1,** softness; gentleness. **2,** blandishment; flattery.
blanquear (blan·ke'ar) *v.t.* **1,** to whiten; to bleach. **2,** to clean. **3,** to whitewash. **4,** to blanch. —*v.i.* to blanch; to pale.
blanquecer (blan·ke'θer; –'ser) *v.t.* [*pres.ind.* **blanquezco** (–'keθ·ko; –'kes·ko); *pres.subjve.* **blanquezca** (–ka)] **1,** to whiten; to bleach. **2,** to blanch.
blanquecino (blan·ke'θi·no; -'si·no) *adj.* whitish.
blanqueo (blan'ke·o) *n.m.* whitening; bleaching.
blanquillo (blan'ki·ʎo; –jo) *adj.* whitish. —*n.m., Mex.* egg.
blasfemar (blas·fe'mar) *v.i.* to blaspheme; to curse. —**blasfemador, blasfemante,** *n.m.* blasphemer. —*adj.* blaspheming; blasphemous. —**blasfemia** (–'fe·mja) *n.f.* blasphemy. —**blasfemo** (–'fe·mo) *adj.* blasphemous. —*n.m.* blasphemer.
blasón (bla'son) *n.m.* **1,** blazon; coat of arms. **2,** blazonry; heraldry. **3,** honor; glory.
blasonar (bla·so'nar) *v.t.* to blazon. —*v.i.* to boast. —**blasonador** (–na'ðor) *adj.* boasting. —**blasonería** (–ne'ri·a) *n.f.* boasting.
-ble (βle) *suffix* -ble; *var. of* **-able, -ible:** *soluble* soluble
bledo ('ble·ðo) *n.m.* wild amaranth. —**no importarle un bledo,** *colloq.* not to care at all. —**no valer un bledo,** *colloq.* to be worthless.
blindado (blin'da·ðo) *adj.* armored; protected - **blindaje** (-'da·xe) *n.m.* armor; armor plate; shield. —**blindar** (–'dar) *v.t.* to armor; to shield.
bloc (blok) *n.m.* **1,** bloc. **2,** notebook.
blondo ('blon·do) *adj.* blond.
bloque ('blo·ke) *n.m.* block.
bloquear (blo·ke'ar) *v.t.* to block; to blockade. —**bloqueo** (–'ke·o) *n.m.* blockade.
blusa ('blu·sa) *n.f.* blouse.
boa ('bo·a) *n.f.* boa.
boato (bo'a·to) *n.m.* pomp; ostentation.
bobada (bo'βa·ða) *n.f.* = **bobería.**
bobalicón (bo·βa·li'kon) *n.m.* & *adj.* = **bobo.**
bobear (bo·βe'ar) *v.i.* to talk or act foolishly.
bobería (bo·βe'ri·a) *n.f.* foolishness; nonsense.
bobina (bo'βi·na) *n.f.* bobbin; spool; reel; coil.
bobo ('bo·βo) *adj.* foolish; silly. —*n.m.* fool; simpleton; booby.
boca ('bo·ka) *n.f.* mouth; opening; orifice; entrance. - **boca abajo,** face downward. —**boca arriba,** face upward. —**a pedir de boca,** according to one's wish. —**no decir esta boca es mía,** not to utter a word.

bocacalle (bo·ka'ka·ʎe; –je) *n.f.* street intersection.
bocacaz (bo·ka'kaθ; –'kas) *n.m.* spillway; sluice.
bocací (bo·ka'θi; –'si) *n.m.* buckram.
bocadillo (bo·ka'ði·ʎo; –jo) *n.m.* 1, morsel; tidbit. 2, sandwich.
bocado (bo'ka·ðo) *n.m.* 1, mouthful. 2, morsel. 3, bite. 4, bridle bit.
bocallave (bo·ka'ʎa·βe; -'ja·βe) *n.f.* keyhole.
bocamanga (bo·ka'man·ga) *n.f.* cuff (*of a sleeve*).
bocanada (bo·ka'na·ða) *n.f.* 1, mouthful. 2, puff (*of smoke*).
bocaza (bo'ka·θa; –sa) *n.f.* big mouth. —*n.m. & f., colloq.* blabbermouth.
boceto (bo'θe·to; bo'se–) *n.m.* sketch; outline; drawing.
bocina (bo'θi·na; bo'si–) *n.f.* horn; trumpet; megaphone. —**bocinar,** *v.i.* to blow a horn.
bocio ('bo·θjo; –sjo) *n.m.* goiter.
bocoy (bo'koi) *n.m.* hogshead.
bocha ('bo·tʃa) *n.f.* bowling ball. —**bochas,** *n.f.pl.* the game of bowls.
boche ('bo·tʃe) *n.m.* 1, = **bochas.** 2, *Venez.; W.I.* slight; rebuff. —**dar boche a,** to slight; to rebuff.
bochinche (bo'tʃin·tʃe) *n.m.* tumult; uproar. —**bochinchero,** *n.m.* rowdy person.
bochista (bo'tʃis·ta) *n.m. & f.* bowler.
bochorno (bo'tʃor·no) *n.m.* 1, hot breeze. 2, embarrassment; shame.
bochornoso (bo·tʃor'no·so) *adj.* 1, embarrassing. 2, sultry.
boda ('bo·ða) *n.f.* wedding; nuptials.
bodega (bo'ðe·ɣa) *n.f.* 1, wine cellar. 2, storeroom; warehouse. 3, ship's hold. 4, *Amer.* grocery.
bodegón (bo·ðe'ɣon) *n.m.* 1, cheap restaurant. 2, *paint.* still life.
bodeguero (bo·ðe'ɣe·ro) *n.m.* 1, owner or keeper of a wine cellar. 2, *Amer.* grocer.
bodoque (bo'ðo·ke) *n.m.* 1, lump; bump; bulge. 2, bundle; package. 3, lummox; lug. 4, *Amer.* bump or swelling on the head or body.
bóer ('bo·er) *adj. & n.m. & f.* Boer.
bofes ('bo·fes) *n.m.pl.* lungs (*of an animal*). —**echar los bofes,** to work very hard; to slave.
bofetada (bo·fe'ta·ða) *n.f.* slap in the face.
bofetón (bo·fe'ton) *n.m.* hard slap; buffet.
bofo ('bo·fo) *adj.* = **fofo.**
boga ('bo·ɣa) *n.f.* vogue; fashion. —**estar en** *or* **de boga,** to be fashionable.
bogar (bo'ɣar) *v.i.* [*pres.subjve.* **bogue** ('bo·ɣe); *pret.* **bogué** (–'ɣe)] 1, to row. 2, to sail.
bohardilla (bo·ar'ði·ʎa; -ja) *n.f.* = **buhardilla.**
bohemio (bo'e·mjo) *adj. & n.m.* Bohemian; bohemian.
bohío (bo'i·o) *n.m., Amer.* rustic dwelling; shack; hut.
boicot (boi'kot) *n.m.* boycott. —**boicotear** (–te'ar) *v.t.* to boycott; to picket. —**boicoteo** (–'te·o) *n.m.* boycotting.
boina ('boi·na) *n.f.* beret; flat round cap.
boj (box) *n.m., bot.* box; boxwood.
bola ('bo·la) *n.f.* 1, ball; sphere. 2, *Amer.* bowling. 3, *colloq.* lie; hoax. 4, *Amer., colloq.* brawl. 5, *cards* slam.
bolchevique (bol·tʃe'βi·ke) *adj. & n.m. & f.* Bolshevik; Bolshevist. —**bolchevismo** (–'βis·mo), **bolcheviquismo** (–βi'kis·mo) *n.m.* Bolshevism.
boleadoras (bo·le·a'ðo·ras) *n.f. pl., Arg.* a lariat with balls attached, used by gauchos; bolas.
bolear (bo·le'ar) *v.i.* 1, to bowl. 2, to throw balls. 3, *Arg.* to throw bolas. —*v.t.* 1, to blackball. 2, to confuse. 3, to deceive. 4, *Mex.* to shine (shoes).
boleo (bo'le·o) *n.m.* 1, bowling. 2, bowling green.
bolera (bo'le·ra) *n.f.* bowling alley.
bolero (bo'le·ro) *n.m.* bolero (*dance; jacket*).
boleta (bo'le·ta) *n.f.* 1, admission ticket; pass. 2, pay slip. 3, *Amer.* ballot. —**boletería** (–te'ri·a) *n.f., Amer.* box office.
boletín (bo·le'tin) *n.m.* 1, bulletin. 2, pay slip. 3, admission ticket.
boleto (bo'le·to) *n.m., Amer.* ticket.
boliche (bo'li·tʃe) *n.m.* 1, small bowling ball. 2, bowling. 3, bowling alley. 4, small dragnet. 5, *colloq.* gambling house.
bólido ('bo·li·ðo) *n.m.* shooting star; meteor.
bolígrafo (bo'li·ɣra·fo) *n.m.* ballpoint pen.

bolita (bo'li·ta) *n.f.* small ball; marble.
bolívar (bo'li·βar) *n.m.* monetary unit of Venezuela; bolivar.
boliviano (bo·li'βja·no) *adj.* & *n.m.* Bolivian. —*n.m.* monetary unit of Bolivia; boliviano.
bolo ('bo·lo) *n.m.* **1,** ninepin; tenpin. **2,** dunce; dull person. **3,** bolo knife. **4,** *cards* slam. —**bolos,** *n.m. pl.* bowls; bowling.
boloña (bo'lo·ɲa) *n.f.* bologna.
bolsa ('bol·sa) *n.f.* **1,** purse; bag; pouch. **2,** stock exchange. **3,** *anat.* bursa.
bolsear (bol·se'ar) *v.t., Amer.* to pick the pocket of.
bolsillo (bol'si·ʎo; –jo) *n.m.* **1,** pocket. **2,** small purse; pocketbook.
bolsín (bol'sin) *n.m., finance* curb exchange.
bolsista (bol'sis·ta) *n.m.* stockbroker.
bolso ('bol·so) *n.m.* change purse; money bag.
bollo ('bo·ʎo; –jo) *n.m.* **1,** small loaf; roll; muffin; brioche. **2,** dent; bump. **3,** *Amer.* loaf of bread. **4,** *Amer.* tamale. **5,** *Amer., colloq.* trouble; perplexity.
bomba ('bom·ba) *n.f.* **1,** pump. **2,** fire engine. **3,** bomb; bombshell.
bombacho (bom'ba·tʃo) *adj.* loose-fitting (*of breeches*). —**bombachas,** *n.f.pl., Amer.* knickers.
bombardear (bom·bar·ðe'ar) *v.t.* to bombard; to bomb. —**bombardeo** (–'ðe·o) *n.m.* bombardment. —**bombardero** (–'ðe·ro) *n.m.* bomber; bombardier.
bombástico (bom'bas·ti·ko) *adj.* bombastic.
bombazo (bom'ba·θo; –so) *n.m.* **1,** bomb burst. **2,** bomb damage.
bombear (bom·be'ar) *v.t.* **1,** to pump. **2,** to bomb.
bombeo (bom'be·o) *n.m.* **1,** bombing. **2,** *Amer.* pumping. **3,** bulge; swelling.
bombero (bom'be·ro) *n.m.* fireman.
bombilla (bom'bi·ʎa; –ja) *n.f.* also, *Amer.,* **bombita,** *n.f.,* **bombillo,** *n.m.* light bulb.
bombo ('bom·bo) *n.m.* **1,** bass drum. **2,** revolving drum. **3,** barge; lighter. **4,** ballyhoo. —*adj.* **1,** lukewarm. **2,** slightly spoiled (*of food*). **3,** astonished. —**darse bombo,** to put on airs.
bombón (bom'bon) *n.m.* **1,** bonbon; sweet; candy. **2,** handsome man or woman. —**bombonera** (-'ne·ra) *n.f* candy dish or box.
bombona (bom'bo·na) *n.f.* carboy.
bonachón (bo·na'tʃon) *adj., colloq.* kind; good-natured.
bonancible (bo·nan'θi·βle; -'si·βle) *adj.* calm; fair (*of weather*).
bonanza (bo'nan·θa; –sa) *n.f.* **1,** bonanza. **2,** fair weather.
bondad (bon'dað) *n.f.* goodness; kindness. —**bondadoso,** *adj.* kind; good.
bonete (bo'ne·te) *n.m.* bonnet; cap.
bongó (bon'go) *n.m.* bongo drum.
boniato (bo'nja·to) *n.m.* = **buniato.**
bonificación (bo·ni·fi·ka'θjon; –'sjon) *n.f.* **1,** bonus. **2,** allowance; discount. **3,** improvement.
bonísimo (bo'ni·si·mo) *adj., superl. of* **bueno.**
bonitamente (bo·ni·ta'men·te) *adv.* **1,** prettily; neatly. **2,** slowly; gradually.
bonito (bo'ni·to) *adj.* pretty; neat. —*n.m., ichthy.* bonito.
bono ('bo·no) *n.m.* **1,** bond. **2,** certificate; voucher. **3,** bonus.
boñiga (bo'ɲi·ɣa) *n.f.* cow dung; manure.
boquear (bo·ke'ar) *v.i.* **1,** to gape. **2,** to gasp. **3,** to expire; to be dying.
boquerón (bo·ke'ron) *n.m.* **1,** wide opening. **2,** fresh anchovy.
boquete (bo'ke·te) *n.m.* gap; narrow opening.
boquiabierto (bo·ki·a'βjer·to) *adj.* open-mouthed; astonished.
boquilla (bo'ki·ʎa; –ja) *n.f.* **1,** small opening. **2,** mouthpiece. **3,** nozzle. **4,** cigarette tip or holder.
borato (bo'ra·to) *n.m.* borate. —**boratado** (–'ta·ðo) *adj.* borated.
bórax ('bo·raks) *n.m.* borax.
borbollar (bor·bo'ʎar; –'jar) *also,* **borbollear** (–ʎe'ar; –je'ar) *v.i.* to bubble out; to boil up; to gush out.
borbollón (bor·βo'ʎon; -'jon) *n.m.* spurt; bubbling; boiling; gushing of water. —**a borbollones,** impetuously; precipitately.
Borbón (bor'βon) *n.m., hist.* Bourbon.
borbor (bor'βor) *n.m.* bubbling.
borbotar (bor·βo'tar) *v.i.* to gush out; to boil over.
borbotón (bor·βo'ton) *n.m.* = **borbollón.**

borcegui (bor·θe'ɣi; bor·se–) *n.m.* 1, buskin. 2, half boot.
borda ('bor·ða) *n.f.* 1, cottage; hut. 2, *naut.* gunwale.
bordada (bor'ða·ða) *n.f., naut.* tack; tacking. —**dar bordadas,** to tack back and forth.
bordar (bor'ðar) *v.t.* to embroider. —**bordado,** *adj.* embroidered. —*n.m.* embroidery. —**bordador** (-'ðor) *n.m.* embroiderer. —**bordadura** (–'ðu·ra) *n.f.* embroidery.
borde ('bor·ðe) *n.m.* 1, border; edge; brim. 2, hem; fringe. 3, *naut.* board.
bordear (bor·ðe'ar) *v.t.* 1, to border; to trim. 2, to skirt. —*v.i., naut.* to tack. —**bordeo** (–'ðe·o) *n.m., naut.* tacking.
bordo ('bor·ðo) *n.m., naut.* 1, board; side of a ship. 2, tack. —**a bordo,** on board; aboard.
bordón (bor'ðon) *n.m.* 1, staff; support. 2, *music* refrain; burden. 3, *music* bass string.
boreal (bo·re'al) *adj.* boreal; northern.
borgoña (bor'ɣo·ɲa) *n.m.* Burgundy (*wine*).
bórico ('bo·ri·ko) *adj.* boric. —**ácido bórico,** boric acid.
borinqueño (bo·rin'ke·ɲo) *also,* **boricua** (bo'ri·kwa) *adj.* & *n.m.* Puerto Rican. —**Borinquen** (bo·'rin·ken) *n.f.* Puerto Rico.
borla ('bor·la) *n.f.* 1, tassel. 2, doctor's cap. 3, doctor's degree. —**tomar la borla,** to take a doctor's degree.
borne ('bor·ne) *n.m.* 1, tip of a lance or spear. 2, *electricity* terminal.
bornear (bor·ne'ar) *v.t.* to twist; to turn; to bend. —**bornearse,** *v.r.* to warp; to bulge. —**borneo** (–'ne·o) *n.m.* turning; winding; swinging about.
boro ('bo·ro) *n.m.* boron.
borona (bo'ro·na) *n.f.* 1, millet. 2, Indian cornbread.
borra ('bo·rra) *n.f.* 1, yearling ewe. 2, cotton *or* wool waste. 3, *colloq.* trash; rubbish. 4, *colloq.* idle talk. 5, borax.
borracho (bo'rra·tʃo) *adj.* drunk. —**borrachera** (–'tʃe·ra) *n.f.* drunkenness; revelry. —**borrachez** (–'tʃeθ; –'tʃes) *n.f.* intoxication. —**borrachín** (–'tʃin) *n.m., colloq.* drunkard. —*adj., colloq.* tipsy. —**borrachón** (–'tʃon) *n.m.* drunkard.
borrador (bo·rra'ðor) *n.m.* 1, rough draft; sketch. 2, *Amer.* eraser. —**libro borrador,** blotter.
borradura (bo·rra'ðu·ra) *n.f.* erasure.
borrajear (bo·rra·xe'ar) *v.t.* & *i.* 1, to scribble. 2, to doodle.
borrar (bo'rrar) *v.t.* to erase; to blot; to blur; to obliterate.
borrasca (bo'rras·ka) *n.f.* 1, storm; squall. 2, *colloq.* spree; orgy. —**borrascoso** *adj.* stormy.
borregada (bo·rre'ɣa·ða) *n.f.* 1, flock of sheep. 2, *colloq.* silly action; foolishness.
borrego (bo'rre·ɣo) *n.m.* 1, yearling lamb. 2, *colloq.* dunce.
borrica (bo'rri·ka) *n.f.* 1, she-ass. 2, *colloq.* stupid woman.
borricada (bo·rri'ka·ða) *n.f.* 1, drove of asses. 2, foolish action.
borrico (bo'rri·ko) *n.m.* 1, donkey; ass. 2, sawhorse. 3, *colloq.* simpleton. —**borricón** (–'kon) *n.m., colloq.* plodder.
borrón (bo'rron) *n.m.* blotch; blot; blur. —**borronear** (–ne'ar) *v.t.* to blotch; to scribble; to sketch.
borroso (bo'rro·so) *adj.* blurred; blurry.
borrumbada (bo·rrum'ba·ða) *n.f.* = **barrumbada.**
boruca (bo'ru·ka) *n.f., colloq.* noise; racket.
borujo (bo'ru·xo) *n.m.* small lump. —**borujón** (–'xon) *n.m.* lump; bump.
boscaje (bos'ka·xe) *n.m.* 1, wood; thicket. 2, *paint.* woodland scene.
bosque ('bos·ke) *n.m.* forest; woods.
bosquejo (bos'ke·xo) *n.m.* sketch; outline. —**bosquejar** (–'xar) *v.t.* to sketch; to outline.
bosta ('bos·ta) *n.f.* manure; dung.
bostezar (bos·te'θar; –'sar) *v.i.* [*pres.subjve* **bostece** (–'te·θe; –se); *pret.* **bostecé** (–'θe; –'se)] to yawn; to gape. —**bostezo** (–'te·θo; –so) *n.m.* yawn; gape.
bota ('bo·ta) *n.f.* 1, boot. 2, wineskin. 3, butt; cask. 4, a liquid measure equal to 516 liters or 125 gallons.
botadura (bo·ta'ðu·ra) *n.f.* launching; christening (*of a ship*).
botalón (bo·ta'lon) *n.m., naut.* boom.
botánica (bo'ta·ni·ka) *n.f.* botany.

—**botánico,** *adj.* botanical. —*n.m.* botanist. —**botanista,** *n.m.* & *f.* botanist.

botar (bo'tar) *v.t.* **1,** to cast; to hurl. **2,** to throw away. **3,** to launch; to christen (a ship). **4,** *Amer.* to squander. **5,** *Amer.* to dismiss. —*v.i.* to bounce; to jump.

botarate (bo·ta'ra·te) *n.m., colloq.* **1,** madcap. **2,** *Amer.* spendthrift.

botarel (bo·ta'rel) *n.m.* buttress; brace.

botavara (bo·ta'βa·ra) *n.f., naut.* boom; gaff.

bote ('bo·te) *n.m.* **1,** boat. **2,** thrust with a weapon. **3,** bounce; jump; prance. **4,** jar; can; pot.

botella (bo'te·ʎa; –ja) *n.f.* bottle; flask.

botellero (bo·te'ʎe·ro; –'je·ro) *n.m.* **1,** bottlemaker. **2,** bottle rack.

botellón (bo·te'ʎon; -'jon) *n.m.* **1,** large bottle. **2,** *Mex.* demijohn.

botica (bo'ti·ka) *n.f.* **1,** drugstore. **2,** medicine. —**boticario** (–'ka·rjo) *n.m.* druggist; apothecary.

botija (bo'ti·xa) *n.f.* **1,** earthen jug. **2,** *Amer., colloq.* belly. **3,** *Amer., colloq.* fat person.

botijo (bo'ti·xo) *n.m.* **1,** earthen jar with a spout and handle. **2,** *colloq.* fat person.

botín (bo'tin) *n.m.* **1,** boot. **2,** buskin; high shoe. **3,** booty; plunder. —**botinero,** *n.m.* shoemaker; bootmaker.

botiquín (bo·ti'kin) *n.m.* **1,** medicine chest. **2,** first-aid kit.

boto ('bo·to) *adj.* **1,** blunt. **2,** dull-witted.

botón (bo'ton) *n.m.* **1,** button. **2,** bud. **3,** knob. **4,** push button. —**botonadura** (–na'ðu·ra) *n.f.* set of buttons. —**botón de oro,** buttercup.

botones (bo'to·nes) *n.m. sing.* & *pl.* bellboy; bellhop.

botulismo (bo·tu'lis·mo) *n.m.* botulism.

bóveda ('bo·βe·ða) *n.f.* **1,** arch; vault; arched roof. **2,** cavern; crypt.

bovino (bo'βi·no) *adj.* & *n.m.* bovine.

boxear (bok·se'ar) *v.i.* to box. —**boxeador** (–'ðor) *n.m.* boxer. —**boxeo** (–'se·o) *n.m.* boxing.

bóxer ('bok·ser) *n.m.* boxer (*dog*).

boya ('bo·ja) *n.f.* **1,** buoy. **2,** net float. —**boyante.** *adj.* buoyant. —**boyar,** *v.i.* to float.

boyada (bo'ja·ða) *n.f.* drove of oxen. —**boyera** (–'je·ra) *n.f.* cattle shed. —**boyero** (–ro) *n.m.* cowherd; ox driver.

bozal (bo'θal; –'sal) *adj.* **1,** *colloq.* inexperienced; green. **2,** stupid. **3,** wild; untamed. —*n.m.* **1,** muzzle. **2,** *Amer.* boor; coarse person.

bozo ('bo·θo; –so) *n.m.* **1,** fuzz or down on the cheeks or upper lip. **2,** part of the mouth around the lips.

braceaje (bra·θe'a·xe; bra·se–) *n.m.* **1,** coinage. **2,** brewing.

bracear (bra·θe'ar; –se'ar) *v.i.* **1,** to swing the arms. **2,** to swim the crawl. **3,** to struggle. **4,** to brace. —*v.t.* to brew.

bracero (bra'θe·ro; –'se·ro) *adj.* (*of a weapon*) thrown with the hand. —*n.m.* **1,** day laborer. **2,** one who offers his arm, esp. to a lady. —**de bracero,** arm in arm.

bracete (bra'θe·te; –'se·te) *n.m., in* **de bracete,** arm in arm.

braco ('bra·ko) *adj.* pug-nosed. —*n.m.* pointer (*dog*).

braga ('bra·ɣa) *n.f.* diaper. —**bragas,** *n.f.pl.* **1,** breeches. **2,** panties. —**bragadura** (–ɣa'ðu·ra) *n.f.* crotch. —**braguero** (–'ɣe·ro) *n.m., med.* truss; brace. —**bragueta** (–'ɣe·ta) *n.f.* fly (*of trousers*).

brahmán (bra'man) *also,* **brahmín** (–'min) *n.m.* Brahman. —**brahmanismo,** *n.m.* Brahmanism.

Braille (breil) *n.m.* Braille.

brama ('bra·ma) *n.f.* rut; mating season.

bramar (bra'mar) *v.i.* to roar; to bellow; to blare. —**bramador** (–'ðor) *adj.* bellowing. —*n.m.* bellower; roarer. —**bramante,** *adj.* bellowing. —**bramido** (–'mi·ðo) *n.m.* bellow.

brancada (bran'ka·ða) *n.f.* dragnet.

branquia ('bran·kja) *n.f., ichthy.* gill. —**branquial** (–'kjal) *adj.* branchial.

braqui- (bra·ki) *prefix* brachy-; short: *braquicéfalo,* brachycephalous.

braquial (bra'kjal) *adj.* brachial.

brasa ('bra·sa) *n.f.* red-hot coal. —**asar a la brasa,** to braise.

brasero (bra'se·ro) *n.m.* **1,** brazier. **2,** *Mex.* hearth.

bravamente (bra·βa'men·te) *adv.* **1,** bravely. **2,** cruelly. **3,** very well.

bravata (bra'βa·ta) *n.f.* brag; boast; bravado.
bravear (bra·βe'ar) *v.i.* to bluster; boast.
bravío (bra'βi·o) *adj.* wild; savage.
bravo ('bra·βo) *adj.* **1,** brave; fearless. **2,** wild; fierce. **3,** excellent; elegant. **4,** ill-tempered; angry. *—interj.* bravo!; well done!
bravucón (bra·βu'kon) *adj.* boastful. **—bravuconería** (-ne'ri·a) *n.f.* bravado.
bravura (bra'βu·ra) *n.f.* **1,** courage; boldness; bravery. **2,** fierceness. **3,** bravado.
braza ('bra·θa; –sa) *n.f.* fathom.
brazada (bra'θa·ða; –'sa·ða) *n.f.* **1,** armful. **2,** stroke or pull with the arms.
brazado (bra'θa·ðo; -'sa·ðo) *n.m.* armful.
brazal (bra'θal; –'sal) *n.m.* **1,** armband. **2,** irrigation ditch.
brazalete (bra·θa'le·te; bra·sa–) *n.m.* bracelet.
brazo ('bra·θo; –so) *n.m.* **1,** arm. **2,** foreleg of an animal. **3,** branch; division. **4,** *fig.* strength; power. **—brazos,** *n.m.pl.* manual laborers; hands. **—de** *or* **del brazo,** arm in arm. **—no dar su brazo a torcer,** to persevere; stick to one's guns.
brea ('bre·a) *n.f.* **1,** pitch; tar. **2,** sackcloth; canvas.
brear (bre'ar) *v.t., colloq.* to annoy; to molest.
brebaje (bre'βa·xe) *n.m.* **1,** badtasting potion. **2,** *naut.* grog.
brécol ('bre·kol) *n.m.* broccoli.
brecha ('bre·tʃa) *n.f.* breach; gap.
brega ('bre·ɣa) *n.f.* **1,** strife; struggle. **2,** trick; practical joke.
bregar (bre'ɣar) *v.i.* [*pres.subjve.* **bregue** ('bre·ɣe); *pret.* **bregué** (–'ɣe)] **1,** to fight; to struggle. **2,** to work hard; to contend; to strive.
brema ('bre·ma) *n.f., ichthy.* bream.
bren (bren) *n.m.* bran.
breña ('bre·ɲa) *also,* **breñal, breñar,** *n.m.* craggy ground covered with brambles. **—breñoso,** *adj.* craggy; brambly.
bresca ('bres·ka) *n.f.* honeycomb.
Bretaña (bre'ta·ɲa) *n.f.* Britain; Britannia.
brete ('bre·te) *n.m.* **1,** fetters (*pl.*); shackles (*pl.*). **2,** perplexity; quandary.
bretón (bre'ton) *adj.* & *n.m.* Breton.
bretones (bre'to·nes) *n.m.pl.* Brussels sprouts.
breve ('bre·βe) *adj.* brief; short. *—n.f., music* breve. **—en breve, 1,** in short. **2,** soon; shortly.
brevedad (bre·βe'ðað) *n.f.* brevity; shortness.
brevete (bre'βe·te) *n.m.* memorandum.
brevi- (bre·βi) *prefix* brevi-; brief; short: *brevipenne,* brevipennate.
breviario (bre'βja·rjo) *n.m.* breviary.
brezal (bre'θal; –'sal) *n.m.* heath. **—brezo** ('bre·θo; –so) *n.m.* heather; heath (*shrub*); brier.
bribón (bri'βon) *adj.* rascally. *—n.m.* rascal. **—bribonada,** *also,* **bribonería,** *n.f.* knavery; rascality.
bric-a-brac (brik·a'βrak) *n.m.* bric-a-brac.
bricho ('bri·tʃo) *n.m.* spangle.
brida ('bri·ða) *n.f.* **1,** bridle; rein. **2,** curb; check. **—a toda brida,** posthaste.
bridge (bridʒ; britʃ) *n.m.* bridge (*card game*).
brigada (bri'ɣa·ða) *n.f.* brigade. *—n.m.* staff sergeant. **—general de brigada,** brigadier general; brigadier.
brigadier (bri·ɣa'ðjer) *n.m.* **1,** brigadier; brigadier general. **2,** rear admiral.
brillante (bri'ʎan·te; bri'jan–) *adj.* brilliant; shining; sparkling. *—n.m.* diamond. **—brillantez** (–'teθ; –'tes) *n.f.* brilliance; splendor. **—brillar** (bri'ʎar; –'jar) *v.i.* to shine; to gleam. **—brillo** ('bri·ʎo; –jo) *n.m.* sparkle; glitter; shine.
brincar (brin'kar) *v.i.* & *t.* [*pres. subjve.* **brinque** ('brin·ke); *pret.* **brinqué** (–'ke)] to jump; to hop; to bounce. **—brinco** ('brin·ko) *n.m.* jump; leap; hop; bounce.
brindar (brin'dar) *v.i.* to drink a toast. *—v.t.* to offer; to invite. **—brindis** ('brin·dis) *n.m.* toast (*to a person's health*).
brío ('bri·o) *n.m.* vigor; liveliness. **—brioso** (bri'o·so) *adj.* vigorous; lively.
brioche ('brjo·tʃe) *n.m.* brioche.
briqueta (bri'ke·ta) *n.f.* briquette.
brisa ('bri·sa) *n.f.* breeze.
británico (bri'ta·ni·ko) *adj.* Brit-

ish; Britannic. —**britano** (–'ta·no) *adj.* British. —*n.m.* Briton.
brizna ('briθ·na; 'bris–) *n.f.* **1,** fragment; chip. **2,** string; filament.
broca ('bro·ka) *n.f.* **1,** reel; bobbin. **2,** drill bit. **3,** shoemaker's tack.
brocado (bro'ka·ðo) *adj.* brocaded. —*n.m.* brocade.
brocal (bro'kal) *n.m.* **1,** edge of a well. **2,** metal rim.
bróculi ('bro·ku·li) *n.m.* broccoli.
brocha ('bro·tʃa) *n.f.* **1,** paint brush. **2,** shaving brush. —**de brocha gorda,** crude; amateurish. —**pintor de brocha gorda,** housepainter.
brochada (bro'tʃa·ða) *n.f.* brush stroke.
brochadura (bro·tʃa'ðu·ra) *n.f.* set of hook-and-eye fasteners.
brochazo (bro'tʃa·θo; –so) *n.m.* brush stroke.
broche ('bro·tʃe) *n.m.* **1,** brooch. **2,** clasp; fastener.
brocheta (bro'tʃe·ta) *n.f.* skewer.
broma ('bro·ma) *n.f.* **1,** joke; jest; gaiety. **2,** *Amer.* disappointment; contretemps. —**broma pesada,** crude practical joke.
bromear (bro·me'ar) *v.i., also,* **bromearse,** *v.r.* to joke; to have fun. —**bromista,** *n.m.* & *f.* joker.
bromo ('bro·mo) *n.m.* bromine. —**bromuro** (–'mu·ro) *n.m.* bromide.
bronca ('bron·ka) *n.m.* quarrel; heated dispute.
bronce ('bron·θe; –se) *n.m.* bronze.
broncear (bron·θe'ar; –se'ar) *v.t.* to bronze; to braze. —**broncearse,** *v.r.* to become tanned. —**bronceado,** *adj.* bronzed; tanned; sunburned.
broncíneo (bron'θi·ne·o; –'si·ne·o) *adj.* of bronze; bronzelike.
bronco ('bron·ko) *adj.* **1,** coarse; rough. **2,** brittle. **3,** hoarse; harsh. **4,** wild; untamed.
broncoscopio (bron·kos'ko·pjo) *n.m.* bronchoscope.
bronquedad (bron·ke'ðað) *n.f.* roughness; harshness; hoarseness.
bronquio ('bron·kjo) *n.m.* bronchus. —**bronquial** (–'kjal) *adj.* bronchial. —**bronquitis** (–'ki·tis) *n.f.* bronchitis.
brontosauro (bron·to'sau·ro) *n.m.* brontosaurus.
broquel (bro'kel) *n.m.* shield; buckler.
broqueta (bro'ke·ta) *n.f.* = **brocheta.**
brotar (bro'tar) *v.i.* **1,** to bud. **2,** to come out; to gush; to flow. —*v.t.* to grow; to produce. —**brotadura** (–'ðu·ra) *n.f.* budding. —**brotador** (–'ðor) *adj.* budding. —**brote** ('bro·te) *n.m.* bud; budding; sprouting.
broza ('bro·θa; –sa) *n.f.* **1,** brushwood. **2,** trash; rubbish. **3,** *fig.* nonsense.
bruces ('bru·θes; –ses) *n.m.pl.* lips. —**a** *or* **de bruces,** face downward.
bruja ('bru·xa) *n.f.* witch; sorceress; hag. —**brujería** (–xe'ri·a) *n.f.* witchcraft. —**brujo,** *n.m.* wizard; sorcerer. —**estar brujo,** *Amer.* to be penniless.
brujear (bru·xe'ar) *v.i.* to practice witchcraft.
brújula ('bru·xu·la) *n.f.* **1,** compass; magnetic needle. **2,** gunsight.
bruma ('bru·ma) *n.f.* mist; fog; haze. —**brumal,** *adj.* foggy; hazy. —**brumoso,** *adj.* foggy; misty.
bruno ('bru·no) *adj.* dark brown.
bruñir (bru'ɲir) *v.t.* [*pret.* **bruñí** (–'ɲi), **bruñó** (–'ɲo); *ger.* **bruñendo** (–'ɲen·do)] to burnish; polish. —**bruñido** (–'ɲi·ðo) *adj.* burnished. —**bruñidor** (–'ðor) *adj.* burnishing; polishing. —*n.m.* polisher.
brusco ('brus·ko) *adj.* brusque; rough; blunt. —**bruscamente,** *adv.* brusquely; abruptly. —**brusquedad** (–ke'ðað) *n.f.* brusqueness.
brutal (bru'tal) *adj.* brutal; savage. —**brutalidad,** *n.f.* brutality; savageness.
bruteza (bru'te·θa; –sa) *n.f.* brutality; stupidity.
bruto ('bru·to) *adj.* **1,** brutish; gross; stupid. **2,** raw; unfinished. —*n.m.* brute. —**diamante en bruto,** uncut diamond. —**peso bruto,** gross weight.
bruza ('bru·θa; –sa) *n.f.* hard scrubbing brush.
bu (bu) *interj.* boo! —*n.m., colloq.* bogy; bugaboo.
buba ('bu·βa) *n.f.* pustule; swollen gland.
bubia ('bu·βja) *n.f.* gannet.
bubón (bu'βon) *n.m.* tumor; bubo. —**bubónico** (–'βo·ni·ko) *adj.* bubonic. —**peste bubónica,** bubonic plague.
bucal (bu'kal) *adj.* of or pert. to the mouth; oral.

bucanero (bu·ka'ne·ro) *n.m.* buccaneer.
bucarán (bu·ka'ran) *n.m.* buckram.
búcaro ('bu·ka·ro) *n.m.* vase.
buccino (buk'θi·no; –'si·no) *n.m., zool.* whelk.
buce ('bu·θe; -se) *v., pres.subjve. of* **buzar.**
bucear (bu·θe'ar; bu·se–) *v.i.* to dive. —**buceo** (–'θe·o; –'se·o) *n.m.* diving.
bucle ('bu·kle) *n.m.* curl; lock of hair.
bucólico (bu'ko·li·ko) *adj.* bucolic. —**bucólica,** *n.f.* bucolic.
buche ('bu·tʃe) *n.m.* **1,** crop (*of a bird*). **2,** stomach. **3,** mouthful (*of fluid*). —**buchada** (–'tʃa·ða) *n.f.* mouthful. —**buchón** (–'tʃon) *adj.* bulging; bellied.
Buda ('bu·ða) *n.m.* Buddha. —**budismo,** *n.m.* Buddhism. —**budista,** *adj.* & *n.m.* & *f.* Buddhist.
budín (bu'ðin) *n.m.* pudding. —**budinera** (–'ne·ra) *n.f.* pudding mold.
buen (bwen) *adj.* = **bueno** *before a masc. noun.*
buenaventura (bwe·na·βen'tu·ra) *n.f.* **1,** good luck. **2,** fortune; fortunetelling.
bueno ('bwe·no) *adj.* **1,** good; kind; virtuous. **2,** useful; fit. **3,** great; strong. **4,** healthy. **5,** tasty. —*adv.* **1,** very well. **2,** enough. —**de buenas a primeras,** suddenly. —**por las buenas,** willingly.
buey (bwei) *n.m.* ox; steer; bull; bullock.
bufa ('bu·fa) *n.f.* buffoonery. —**bufo,** *adj.* comic. —**ópera bufa,** comic opera.
búfalo ('bu·fa·lo) *n.m.* buffalo.
bufanda (bu'fan·da) *n.f.* muffler; scarf.
bufar (bu'far) *v.i.* to snort; to puff angrily.
bufete (bu'fe·te) *n.m.* **1,** desk. **2,** lawyer's office.
buffet *also,* **bufet** (bu'fe) *n.m.* buffet; informal meal.
bufido (bu'fi·ðo) *n.m.* snort; bellow.
bufón (bu'fon) *adj.* comical. —*n.m.* jester; buffoon. —**bufonada** (-'na·ða) *also,* **bufonería** (-ne'ri·a) *n.f.* buffoonery.
bufonearse (bu·fo·ne'ar·se) *v.r.* to jest; clown.
bugalla (bu'ɣa·ʎa; –ja) *n.f.* gallnut.
buganvilla (bu·ɣan'βi·ʎa; –ja) *n.f.* bougainvillaea.
buhardilla (bu·ar'ði·ʎa; –ja) *n.f.* **1,** garret. **2,** dormer; dormer window. **3,** skylight. *Also,* **buharda** (-ða).
buho ('bu·o) *n.m.* owl.
buhonero (bu·o'ne·ro) *n.m.* peddler. —**buhonería** (–ne'ri·a) *n.f.* peddling.
buitre ('bwi·tre) *n.m.* vulture.
buitrero (bwi'tre·ro) *adj.* vulturine; vulturous.
buje ('bu·xe) *n.m.* axle box; shaft pillow.
bujería (bu·xe'ri·a) *n.f.* trinket.
bujía (bu'xi·a) *n.f.* **1,** candle. **2,** candle power. **3,** spark plug.
bula ('bu·la) *n.f., R.C.Ch.* bull; edict.
bulbo ('bul·βo) *n.m.* bulb. —**bulbar,** *adj., pathol.* bulbous. —**bulboso,** *adj.* bulbous.
bulevar (bu·le'βar) *n.m.* boulevard.
bulto ('bul·to) *n.m.* **1,** bulk; lump. **2,** bundle; package. **3,** shadowy object. —**escurrir** *or* **pasar el bulto,** to pass the buck.
bulla ('bu·ʎa; –ja) *n.f.* noise; clatter; bustle.
bullanguero (bu·ʎan'ge·ro; bu·jan-) *adj.* loud; vulgar.
bullicio (bu'ʎi·θjo; –'ji·sjo) *n.m.* noise; tumult. —**bullicioso,** *adj.* noisy.
bullir (bu'ʎir; –'jir) *v.i.* [*pret.* **bullí** (-'ʎi; -'ji), **bulló** (-'ʎo; -'jo); *ger.* **bullendo** (–'ʎen·do; –'jen·do)] **1,** to boil; bubble. **2,** to budge; move; stir. **3,** to bustle; fidget. **4,** to swarm; teem. —*v.t.* to stir; budge.
bumerang (bu·me'rang) *n.m.* [*pl.* **–rangs**] boomerang.
-bundo ('βun·do) *suffix, forming adjectives expressing* tendency; beginning of an action: *vagabundo,* wandering; *moribundo,* moribund.
buniato (bu'nja·to) *n.m.* sweet potato.
buñuelo (bu'ɲwe·lo) *n.m.* cruller; fritter. —**buñolero** (bu·ɲo'le·ro) *n.m.* one who makes or sells fritters.
buque ('bu·ke) *n.m.* ship; steamer. —**buque cisterna; buque tanque,** tanker. —**buque mercante,** mer-

chant vessel. —**buque velero,** sailing vessel.
buqué (bu'ke) *n.m.* bouquet (*of wine or flowers*).
burato (bu'ra·to) *n.m.* crêpe; crêpe de Chine.
burbuja (bur'βu·xa) *n.f.* bubble; blob. —**burbujear** (–xe'ar) *v.i.* to bubble; to burble. —**burbujeo** (-'xe·o) *n.m.* bubbling; burbling.
burdel (bur'ðel) *n.m.* brothel.
burdo ('bur·ðo) *adj.* coarse; vulgar.
bureo (bu're·o) *n.m.* amusement; diversion.
burgués (bur'ɣes) *adj.* bourgeois; middle-class. —*n.m.* bourgeois; middle-class person. —**burguesía** (–ɣe'si·a) *n.f.* bourgeoisie.
buriel (bu'rjel) *adj.* dark red.
buril (bu'ril) *n.m.* **1,** burin. **2,** *dent.* explorer; burr.
burla ('bur·la) *n.f.* **1,** mockery; scoff. **2,** trick; joke.
burladero (bur·la'ðe·ro) *n.m.* **1,** safety door or screen in a bull ring. **2,** safety island.
burlador (bur·la'ðor) *adj.* joking; jesting. —*n.m.* **1,** practical joker; jester. **2,** seducer.
burlar (bur'lar) *v.t., fol. by* **de, 1,** to mock; to scoff at. **2,** to deceive. —**burlarse,** *v.r.* to jest; to jibe; to ridicule.
burlería (bur·le'ri·a) *n.f.* **1,** trick; deception. **2,** tall tale; yarn. **3,** banter; ridicule.
burlesco (bur'les·ko) *adj.* comical; burlesque.
burlete (bur'le·te) *n.m.* weather strip.
burlón (bur'lon) *adj.* mocking. —*n.m.* mocker; scoffer.
buró (bu'ro) *n.m.* desk; writing desk.
burocracia (bu·ro'kra·θja; –sja) *n.f.* bureaucracy. —**burócrata** (bu·'ro·kra·ta) *n.m.* & *f.* bureaucrat. —**burocrático** (–'kra·ti·ko) *adj.* bureaucratic.
burra ('bu·rra) *n.f.* **1,** she-ass. **2,** ignorant woman.
burrada (bu'rra·ða) *n.f.* **1,** drove of asses. **2,** stupid word or deed.
burro ('bu·rro) *n.m.* **1,** ass; donkey; burro. **2,** sawhorse. **3,** ignorant man.
bursátil (bur'sa·til) *adj.* of or pert. to the stock exchange or stock market.
bursitis (bur'si·tis) *n.f.* bursitis.
busardo (bu'sar·ðo) *n.m.* buzzard.
busca ('bus·ka) *n.f.* search; hunt. —**buscas,** *n.f.pl., Amer.* perquisites.
buscador (bus·ka'ðor) *adj.* searching. —*n.m.* searcher.
buscapié (bus·ka'pje) *n.m.* [*pl.* **–piés**] hint; clue; lead.
buscapleitos (bus·ka'plei·tos) *n.m. & f. sing. & pl., Amer.* **1,** quarrelsome person; troublemaker. **2,** *colloq.* ambulance chaser.
buscar (bus'kar) *v.t.* [*pres.subjve.* **busque** ('bus·ke); *pret.* **busqué** (–'ke)] to search; to seek; to hunt.
buscarruidos (bus·ka'rrwi·ðos) *n.m. & f. sing. & pl.* quarrelsome person; troublemaker.
buscavidas (bus·ka'βi·ðas) *n.m. & f. sing. & pl., colloq.* **1,** busybody. **2,** hustler; go-getter.
buscón (bus'kon) *n.m.* **1,** searcher. **2,** swindler; pilferer. —**buscona,** *n.f.* prostitute.
búsqueda ('bus·ke·ða) *n.f.* search; hunt.
busto ('bus·to) *n.m.* bust.
butaca (bu'ta·ka) *n.f.* **1,** armchair. **2,** orchestra seat. —**butacón** (–'kon) *n.m.* large armchair.
butano (bu'ta·no) *n.m.* butane.
butifarra (bu·ti'fa·rra) *n.f.* sausage. —**butifarrero,** *adj.* maker or seller of sausages.
butilo (bu'ti·lo) *n.m.* butyl. —**butileno** (-'le·no) *n.m.* butylene.
buz (buθ; bus) *n.m.* ceremonial kiss.
buzar (bu'θar; -'sar) *v.i.* [*pres. subjve.* **buce**] *geol.; mining* to dip. —**buzamiento,** *n.m.* dip.
buzo ('bu·θo; –so) *n.m.* diver.
buzón (bu'θon; -'son) *n.m.* mailbox.

C

C, c (θe; se) *n.f.* 3rd letter of the Spanish alphabet.
cabal (ka'βal) *adj.* exact; perfect; faultless. —**estar en sus cabales,** to be in one's right mind. —**por sus cabales,** exactly; perfectly.

cábala ('ka·βa·la) *n.f.* 1, intrigue; scheme. 2, cabal. —**cabalista,** *n.m.* cabalist. —**cabalístico,** *adj.* cabalistic.
cabalgadura (ka·βal·ɣa'ðu·ra) *n.f.* 1, riding animal; mount. 2, beast of burden.
cabalgar (ka·βal'ɣar) *v.i.* [*pres. subjve.* **cabalgue** (-'βal·ɣe); *pret.* **cabalgué** (-'ɣe)] 1, to ride horseback. 2, to parade on horseback. —*v.t.* to cover (a mare). —**cabalgador,** *n.m.* rider; horseman.
cabalgata (ka·βal'ɣa·ta) *n.f.* cavalcade.
caballa (ka'βa·ʎa; -ja) *n.f.* horse mackerel.
caballada (ka·βa'ʎa·ða; -'ja·ða) *n.f.* 1, herd of horses. 2, *Amer.* stupidity.
caballar (ka·βa'ʎar; -'jar) *adj.* equine.
caballear (ka·βa·ʎe'ar; -je'ar) *v.i., colloq.* to ride horseback often; to be fond of riding.
caballejo (ka·βa'ʎe·xo; -'je·xo) *n.m.* poor horse; nag.
caballeresco (ka·βa·ʎe'res·ko; ka·βa·je-) *adj.* chivalrous.
caballerete (ka·βa·ʎe're·te; -je·'re·te) *n.m., colloq.* dude; dandy.
caballería (ka·βa·ʎe'ri·a; -je·'ri·a) *n.f.* 1, horse; mule; mount. 2, cavalry. 3, knighthood; chivalry. 4, chivalrous deed. 5, knightly privilege. 6, order of knights. 7, *Amer.* a land measure of about 33 acres. —**caballería andante,** knight-errantry.
caballeriza (ka·βa·ʎe'ri·θa; -je·'ri·sa) *n.f.* 1, stable. 2, staff of grooms.
caballerizo (ka·βa·ʎe'ri·θo; -je·'ri·so) *n.m.* chief groom.
caballero (ka·βa'ʎe·ro; -'je·ro) *n.m.* 1, gentleman. 2, nobleman. 3, knight. —*adj.* riding; on horseback. —**caballero andante,** knight-errant.
caballeroso (ka·βa·ʎe'ro·so; -je·'ro·so) *adj.* gentlemanly; genteel. —**caballerosidad,** *n.f.* gentlemanliness.
caballerote (ka·βa·ʎe'ro·te; -je·'ro·te) *n.m., colloq.* gross, unpolished man.
caballete (ka·βa'ʎe·te; -'je·te) *n.m.* 1, *archit.* ridge of a roof. 2, sawhorse; trestle. 3, *painting* easel. 4, *anat.* bridge of the nose. 5, *print.* gallows of a press.
caballista (ka·βa'ʎis·ta; -'jis·ta) *n.m.* riding performer; circus rider.
caballito (ka·βa'ʎi·to; -'ji·to) *n.m.* 1, *dim. of* **caballo.** 2, *Mex.* diaper. 3, *pl.* merry-go-round. 4, hobbyhorse. —**caballito del diablo,** dragonfly. —**caballito de mar,** sea horse.
caballo (ka'βa·ʎo; -jo) *n.m.* 1, horse. 2, *chess* knight. —**a caballo,** on horseback. —**caballo de fuerza,** horsepower. —**caballo marino,** sea horse.
caballón (ka·βa'ʎon; -'jon) *n.m.* 1, ridge (*in plowed soil*). 2, dike.
cabaña (ka'βa·ɲa) *n.f.* 1, cabin; hut. 2, drove of mules.
cabaret (ka·βa'ret; -'re) *n.m.* cabaret; night club.
cabecear (ka·βe·θe'ar; -se'ar) *v.i.* 1, to nod the head; to nod in assent; to bob the head. 2, *naut.* to pitch; to lurch.
cabeceo (ka·βe'θe·o; -'se·o) *n.m.* 1, nodding of the head. 2, *naut.* pitching; lurching.
cabecera (ka·βe'θe·ra; -'se·ra) *n.f.* 1, beginning; head; heading. 2, headboard. 3, bolster. 4, capital of a province or district. 5, *print.* headpiece; vignette. 6, *journalism* headline. 7, foot (*of a bridge*). —**cabecera de puente,** bridgehead.
cabecero (ka·βe'θe·ro; -'se·ro) *n.m.* foreman of a mining crew.
cabecilla (ka·βe'θi·ʎa; -'si·ja) *n.f., dim. of* **cabeza.** —*n.m.* ringleader.
cabellera (ka·βe'ʎe·ra; -'je·ra) *n.f.* 1, long hair; head of hair. 2, *astron.* comet's tail.
cabello (ka'βe·ʎo; -jo) *n.m.* hair of the head. —**cabello de ángel,** 1, fine noodles; 2, cotton candy. 3, corn silk. —**en cabellos,** bareheaded.
cabelludo (ka·βe'ʎu·ðo; -'ju·ðo) *adj.* 1, hairy. 2, *bot.* fibrous.
caber (ka'βer) [*pres.ind.* **quepo;** *pres.subjve.* **quepa;** *fut.* **cabré;** *pret.* **cupe**] *v.i.* 1, to be admissible. 2, to fit; to be contained. 3, *impers.* to befall (*as luck*). —*v.t.* to contain; to include. —**no cabe duda,** there is no doubt. —**no cabe más,** that's the end. —**no caber en el pellejo; no caber en sí,** to be conceited.
cabestrillo (ka·βes'tri·ʎo; -jo) *n.m.* 1, sling; support for the arm. 2, *carpentry* strap; diagonal tie. 3, *naut.* rope; cord.
cabestro (ka'βes·tro) *n.m.* 1, hal-

ter. 2, leading ox. —**traer del cabestro,** to lead by the nose.
cabeza (ka'βe·θa; -sa) *n.f.* 1, head. 2, chief; leader. 3, mind; brains. 4, origin; source. —**cabezas,** *n.f.pl.* bow and stern of a ship. —**cabeza de puente,** bridgehead.
cabezada (ka·βe'θa·ða; -'sa·ða) *n.f.* 1, a nod of the head, as in dozing. 2, *naut.* pitching of a ship. 3, = **cabezazo.** 4, headgear (*for a horse*).
cabezal (ka·βe'θal; -'sal) *n.m.* 1, pillow. 2, *med.* compress.
cabezalero (ka·βe·θa'le·ro; ka·βe·sa-) *n.m.* executor. —**cabezalera,** *n.f.* executrix
cabezazo (ka·βe'θa·θo; -'sa·so) *n.m.* a blow with the head.
cabezón (ka·βe'θon; -'son) *adj.* 1, big-headed 2, stubborn.
cabezota (ka·βe'θo·ta; -'so·ta) *n.f., colloq.* stubborn person.
cabezudo (ka·βe'θu·ðo; -'su·ðo) *adj.* obstinate; stubborn. —*n.m.* mullet.
cabida (ka'βi·ða) *n.f.* space; room.
cabildear (ka·βil·de'ar) *v.i.* to lobby. —**cabildeo** (-'de·o) *n.m.* lobbying. —**cabildero** (-'de·ro) *n.m.* lobbyist.
cabildo (ka'βil·do) *n.m.* 1, cathedral chapter. 2, chapter meeting. 3, town council. 4, town hall.
cabilla (ka'βi·ʎa; -ja) *n.f., naut.* dowel.
cabillo (ka'βi·ʎo; -jo) *n.m.* 1, *bot.* stem; stalk. 2, end of a cord.
cabina (ka'βi·na) *n.f.* 1, cabin. 2, cab; driver's compartment. —**cabina telefónica,** telephone booth; call booth.
cabio ('ka·βjo) *n.m.* 1, joist. 2, lintel.
cabizbajo (ka·βiθ'βa·xo; ka·βis-) *adj.* sad; melancholy.
cable ('ka·βle) *n.m.* cable.
cablegrafiar (ka·βle·ɣra'fjar) *v.t. & i.* [*infl.:* **fotografiar**] to cable. —**cablegráfico** (-'ɣra·fi·ko) *adj.* of or by cable.
cablegrama (ka·βle'ɣra·ma) *n.m.* cablegram.
cabo ('ka·βo) *n.m.* 1, end; extremity; tip. 2, *geog.* cape. 3, *naut.* chief; commander. 4, *naut.* rope; line. 5, *mil.* corporal. —**cabos,** *n.m.pl.* 1, mane of a horse. 2, accessories of apparel. —**al cabo,** at last. —**dar cabo a,** to finish. —**de cabo a cabo,** *also,* **de cabo a rabo,** from head to tail.
cabotaje (ka·βo'ta·xe) *n.m.* coastwise trade.
cabra ('ka·βra) *n.f.* goat. —**cabras,** *n.f.pl* small white clouds. —**cabrero** (-'βre·ro), **cabrerizo** (-'ri·θo; -'ri·so) *n.m.* goatherd.
cabré (ka'βre) *v., fut. of* **caber.**
cabrería (ka·βre'ri·a) *n.f.* 1, herd of goats 2, goat stable.
cabrestante (ka·βres'tan·te) *n.m.* capstan.
cabria ('ka·βrja) *n.f.* crane; windlass; hoist
cabrilla (ka'βri·ʎa; -ja) *n.f.* 1, sawhorse 2, *ichthy.* grouper. —**cabrillas** *n.f.pl.* 1, whitecaps. 2, *cap., astron* Pleiades.
cabrio ('ka·βrjo) *n.m.* joist; rafter.
cabrío (ka'βri·o) *adj.* of or pert. to goats goatlike
cabriola (ka'βrjo·la) *n.f.* caper; leap; somersault. —**cabriolar** (-'lar), **cabriolear** (-le'ar) *v.i.* to cut capers; to prance
cabriolé (ka·βrjo'le) *n.m.* 1, cabriolet 2, sleeveless cloak.
cabrita (ka'βri·ta) *n.f.* she-kid.
cabritilla (ka·βri'ti·ʎa; -ja) *n.f.* kidskin, goatskin.
cabritillo (ka·βri'ti·ʎo; -jo) *n.m.* 1, kid; young goat. 2, kidskin.
cabrito (ka'βri·to) *n.m.* kid.
cabrón (ka'βron) *n.m.* 1, buck; he-goat 2, *colloq.* cuckold.
cabronada (ka·βro'na·ða) *n.f., vulg.* affront indignity.
cacahual (ka·ka'wal) *n.m.* cacao plantation
cacahuete (ka·ka'we·te) *n.m.* peanut. *Also.* **cacahuate** (-'wa·te); **cacahué** (-'we), **cacahuey** (-'wei).
cacalote (ka·ka'lo·te) *n.m., Mex.* raven.
cacao (ka'ka·o) *n.m.* 1, cacao. 2, cocoa; chocolate. —**manteca de cacao,** cocoa butter.
cacaotal (ka·ka·o'tal) *n.m.* = **cacahual.**
cacareador (ka·ka·re·a'ðor) *adj.* 1, cackling; crowing. 2, *colloq.* bragging; boasting.
cacarear (ka·ka·re'ar) *v.i.* 1, to cackle (*as a hen*); to crow (*as a cock*). 2, *colloq.* to brag; to boast.
cacareo (ka·ka're·o) *n.m.* 1, crowing; cackling. 2, brag; boast.
cacatúa (ka·ka'tu·a) *n.f.* cockatoo.

cace ('ka·θe; -se) *v., pres.subjve. of* **cazar.**
cacé (ka'θe; -'se) *v., 1st pers. sing. pret. of* **cazar.**
cacera (ka'θe·ra; -'se·ra) *n.f.* canal; conduit.
cacería (ka·θe'ri·a; ka·se-) *n.f.* **1,** hunt. **2,** hunting party. **3,** bag.
cacerina (ka·θe'ri·na; ka·se-) *n.f.* cartridge pouch.
cacerola (ka·θe'ro·la; ka·se-) *n.f.* casserole; saucepan.
cacique (ka'θi·ke; -'si·ke) *n.m.* **1,** chief. **2,** political boss. **—caciquismo** (-'kis·mo) *n.m.* political bossism.
caco ('ka·ko) *n.m.* **1,** pickpocket; thief. **2,** *colloq.* coward.
cacofonía (ka·ko·fo'ni·a) *n.f.* cacophony. **—cacofónico** (-'fo·ni·ko) *adj.* cacophonous.
cacto ('kak·to) *n.m.* cactus.
cacumen (ka'ku·men) *n.m.* **1,** top; height. **2,** acumen; insight.
cachalote (ka·tʃa'lo·te) *n.m.* sperm whale; cachalot.
cachano (ka'tʃa·no) *n.m., colloq.* the devil.
cachar (ka'tʃar) *v.t.* **1,** to break in pieces. **2,** to split lengthwise.
cacharro (ka'tʃa·rro) *n.m.* **1,** coarse earthen pot. **2,** worthless thing. **3,** *pl.* crockery. **—tener cuatro cacharros,** to have nothing.
cachaza (ka'tʃa·θa; -sa) *n.f.* slowness; tardiness. **—cachazudo,** *adj.* slow.
cachear (ka·tʃe'ar) *v.t.* to frisk (a person) for hidden weapons. **—cacheo** (-'tʃe·o) *n.m.* frisking.
cachemir (ka·tʃe'mir) *n.m., also,* **cachemira** (-'mi·ra) *n.f.* = **casimir.**
cachete (ka'tʃe·te) *n.m.* **1,** slap; cuff. **2,** chubby cheek.
cachiporra (ka·tʃi'po·rra) *n.f.* club; cudgel. **—cachiporrazo,** *n.m.* blow with a club.
cachivache (ka·tʃi'βa·tʃe) *n.m.* **1,** *derog.* junk; trash. **2,** *colloq.* good-for-nothing. **3,** *pl.* odds and ends; truck. **4,** *pl.* pots and pans.
cacho ('ka·tʃo) *n.m.* **1,** slice; piece. **2,** *Amer.* horn.
cachondo (ka'tʃon·do) *adj.* **1,** in heat; in rut. **2,** *colloq.* passionate; sexy.
cachorro (ka'tʃo·rro) *n.m.* **1,** puppy; cub. **2,** pocket pistol.
cachucha (ka'tʃu·tʃa) *n.f.* **1,** rowboat. **2,** a kind of cap. **3,** an Andalusian dance.
cachuela (ka'tʃwe·la) *n.f.* **1,** pork fricassee. **2,** fricassee of rabbit's innards.
cada ('ka·ða) *adj.* each; every. **—cada cual,** everyone. **—cada uno,** each one. **—cada vez,** every time. **—cada vez más,** (*fol. by comp.*) more and more.
cadalso (ka'ðal·so) *n.m.* **1,** platform; stage; stand. **2,** scaffold; gallows.
cadáver (ka'ða·βer) *n.f.* cadaver; corpse. **—cadavérico** (-'βe·ri·ko) *adj.* cadaverous.
cadena (ka'ðe·na) *n.f.* **1,** chain; bond. **2,** *archit.* buttress. **3,** [*also,* **cadena perpetua**] life imprisonment. **4,** *radio; TV* hookup.
cadencia (ka'ðen·θja; -sja) *n.f.* **1,** cadence; rhythm. **2,** *music* cadenza. **—cadencioso,** *adj.* rhythmical.
cadente (ka'ðen·te) *adj.* decaying; declining.
cadera (ka'ðe·ra) *n.f.* hip.
cadete (ka'ðe·te) *n.m., mil.* cadet.
cadmio ('kað·mjo) *n.m.* cadmium.
caducar (ka·ðu'kar) *v.i.* [*pres. subjve.* **caduque** (-'ðu·ke); *pret.* **caduqué** (-'ke)] **1,** to be decrepit, senile or superannuated. **2,** to be out of date. **3,** *comm.; law* to lapse; to expire.
caduceo (ka·ðu'θe·o; -'se·o) *n.m.* caduceus.
caducidad (ka·ðu·θi'ðað; -si·'ðað) *n.f.* **1,** transitoriness. **2,** *comm.; law* expiration.
caduco (ka'ðu·ko) *adj.* **1,** senile; decrepit. **2,** transitory.
caduquez (ka·ðu'keθ; -'kes) *n.f.* **1,** senility; decrepitude. **2,** *comm.; law* state of lapse or expiration.
caer (ka'er) *v.i.* [*pres.ind.* **caigo;** *pres.subjve.* **caiga;** *pret.* **caí, cayó**] to fall; to drop; to tumble down. **—caer bien, 1,** to fit. **2,** to be suitable; to be becoming. **3,** to please; to impress favorably. **—caer enfermo,** to fall sick. **—caer en gracia a,** to please; to impress favorably. **—caer en la cuenta,** to catch on. **—dejar caer,** to drop.
café (ka'fe) *n.m.* **1,** coffee. **2,** coffee tree. **3,** coffeehouse; café.
cafeína (ka·fe'i·na) *n.f.* caffeine.
cafetal (ka·fe'tal) *n.m.* coffee plantation.
cafetera (ka·fe'te·ra) *n.f.* coffee pot.
cafetería (ka·fe·te'ri·a) *n.f., Amer.* **1,** coffee seller's shop. **2,** cafeteria.

cafetero (ka·fe'te·ro) *n.m.* 1, coffee grower. 2, coffee seller. —*adj.* of or pert. to coffee.
cafeto (ka'fe·to) *n.m.* coffee tree.
cagar (ka'ɣar) *v.* [*pres.subjve.* **cague** ('ka·ɣe); *pret.* **cagué** (-'ɣe)] —*v.i.* to defecate. —*v.t.* to soil. —**cagada** (-'ɣa·ða) *n.f.* excrement. —**cagadero,** *n.m.* latrine.
caí (ka'i) *v., 1st pers.sing. pret. of* **caer.**
caída (ka'i·ða) *n.f.* 1, fall; tumble; downfall. 2, *geol.* dip. —**caídas,** *n.f.pl.* coarse wool. —**a la caída de la tarde,** at dusk. —**a la caída del sol,** at sunset.
caído (ka'i·ðo) *v., p.p. of* **caer.** —*adj.* languid; downfallen. —**caídos,** *n.m.pl.* arrears of taxes.
caiga ('kai·ɣa) *v., pres.subjve. of* **caer.**
caigo ('kai·ɣo) *v., 1st pers.sing. pres.ind. of* **caer.**
caimán (kai'man) *n.m.* alligator.
caimiento (ka·i'mjen·to) *n.m.* 1, fall; drop; decline. 2, languor; torpor.
caja ('ka·xa) *n.f.* 1, box; case; chest. 2, safe; strongbox. 3, coffin. 4, cashier's office, desk or window. 5, cabinet (*of a radio, TV set, etc.*). 6, *print.* case. 7, body (*of a car, carriage or wagon*). 8, denture; set of false teeth; plate. 9, hollow; socket. 10, *bot.* capsule. 11, stairwell; shaftway. —**caja de ahorros,** savings bank. —**caja de caudales,** safe; vault. —**caja de menores,** petty cash. —**caja de seguridad,** safe-deposit box. —**caja de sorpresa,** jack-in-the-box. —**caja registradora,** cash register. —**en caja,** 1, on hand. 2, in good health; in good spirits. —**libro de caja,** cash book.
cajero (ka'xe·ro) *n.m.* 1, boxmaker. 2, cashier. 3, treasurer.
cajeta (ka'xe·ta) *n.f.* little box.
cajetilla (ka·xe'ti·ʎa; -ja) *n.f.* 1, little box. 2, pack (*of cigarettes or snuff*).
cajista (ka'xis·ta) *n.m., print.* compositor.
cajón (ka'xon) *n.m.* 1, box; case; chest. 2, *Amer.* coffin. 3, locker. 4, caisson. —**ser de cajón,** to go without saying.
cajonería (ka·xo·ne'ri·a) *n.f.* set of drawers.
cal (kal) *n.f.* lime. —**cal hidráulica,** cement; hydraulic lime. —**cal muerta** *or* **apagada,** slaked lime. —**cal viva,** quicklime.
cala ('ka·la) *n.f.* 1, inlet. 2, *naut.* bilge. 3, calla lily. 4, suppository. 5, probe.
calabaza (ka·la'βa·θa; -sa) *n.f.* pumpkin. gourd; calabash. —**dar calabazas,** *colloq.* 1, to jilt. 2, [*also,* **calabacear** (-θe'ar; -se'ar) *v.t.*] to flunk; fail.
calabozo (ka·la'βo·θo; -so) *n.m.* 1, dungeon. 2, jail; calaboose. 3, jail cell.
calada (ka'la·ða) *n.f.* 1, soak; soaking. 2, dive; plunge; swoop.
calado (ka'la·ðo) *n.m.* 1, openwork; fretwork. 2, *naut.* draft. —*adj.* soaked; wet. —**calados,** *n.m. pl.* lace.
calafatear (ka·la·fa·te'ar) *v.t.* to calk.
calamar (ka·la'mar) *n.m.* squid.
calambre (ka'lam·bre) *n.m.* cramp; crick.
calamidad (ka·la·mi'ðað) *n.f.* misfortune; calamity. —**calamitoso** (-'to·so) *adj.* calamitous.
calamina (ka·la'mi·na) *n.f.* calamine.
calandria (ka'lan·drja) *n.f.* 1, *ornith.* lark. 2, rolling press. —*n.m. & f.* malingerer.
calar (ka'lar) *v.t.* 1, to soak through; to permeate. 2, to make openwork or fretwork in. 3, to wedge. 4, *naut.* to submerge (tackle). 5, *naut.* to draw (a specified depth of water). 6, to lower (a draw bridge). 7, to fix (a bayonet). 8, *colloq.* to size up. —**calarse,** *v.r.* to be soaked. —**calarse el sombrero,** to pull one's hat down on one's head.
calavera (ka·la'βe·ra) *n.f.* skull. —*n.m. & f., colloq.* madcap. —**calaverear,** *v.i.* to act foolishly. —**calaverada,** *n.f.* tomfoolery.
calcañal (kal·ka'ɲal) *n.m.* heel; heelbone. *Also,* **calcañar** (-'ɲar).
calcar (kal'kar) *v.t.* [*pres.subjve.* **calque;** *pret.* **calqué**] 1, to trace; to copy. 2, to imitate; to ape.
calcáreo (kal'ka·re·o) *adj.* calcareous.
calce ('kal·θe; -se) *n.m.* 1, wedge. 2, tire of a wheel. 3, wheel shoe.
calce ('kal·θe; -se) *v., pres.subjve. of* **calzar.**
calcé (kal'θe; -'se) *v., 1st pers. sing. pret. of* **calzar.**
calceta (kal'θe·ta; -'se·ta) *n.f.*

hose; stocking. —**calcetería** (-te·'ri·a) *n.f.* hosiery. —**calcetero** (-'te·ro) *n.m.* hosier. —**calcetín** (-'tin) *n.m.* half hose; sock. —**hacer calceta,** to knit.
calcificar (kal·θi·fi'kar; kal·si-) *v.t.* [*pres.subjve.* **calcifique** (-'fi·ke); *pret.* **calcifiqué** (-'ke)] to calcify. —**calcificación,** *n.f.* calcification.
calcinar (kal·θi'nar; -si'nar) *v.t.* & *i.* to calcine. —**calcina** (-'θi·na; -'si·na) *n.f.* mortar.
calcio ('kal·θjo; -sjo) *n.m.* calcium.
calco ('kal·ko) *n.m.* tracing; drawing.
calcomanía (kal·ko·ma'ni·a) *n.f.* decalcomania.
calculador (kal·ku·la'ðor) *adj.* calculating. —**calculadora,** *n.f.* computer; calculator.
calcular (kal·ku'lar) *v.t.* & *i.* to calculate; to compute; to estimate. —**calculable,** *adj.* calculable. —**calculista,** *n.m.* schemer.
cálculo ('kal·ku·lo) *n.m.* **1,** calculation; computation. **2,** *math.; med.* calculus.
caldear (kal·de'ar) *v.t.* **1,** to warm; to heat. **2,** to weld (iron). —**calda** ('kal·da) *n.f.* warming; heating. —**caldas,** *n.f.pl.* hot mineral baths.
caldera (kal'de·ra) *n.f.* **1,** caldron; boiler. **2,** *mining* well sump. —**caldera de vapor,** steam boiler.
calderero (kal·de're·ro) *n.m.* brazier; coppersmith; boilermaker.
caldero (kal'de·ro) *n.m.* kettle.
calderón (kal·de'ron) *n.m.* **1,** large kettle. **2,** *print.* paragraph sign (¶). **3,** *music* hold; fermata (𝄐).
caldo ('kal·do) *n.m.* **1,** broth; bouillon; sauce. **2,** *Mex.* juice of sugar cane. **3,** *Mex.* salad dressing. —**caldos,** *n.m.pl.* juices or liquids extracted from fruits. —**caldo de cultivo,** *biol.* culture.
calefacción (ka·le·fak'θjon; -'sjon) *n.f.* heating; heat.
calefactor (ka·le·fak'tor) *adj.* heating. —*n.m.* **1,** heater. **2,** heating element.
calendario (ka·len'da·rjo) *n.m.* almanac; calendar.
caléndula (ka'len·du·la) *n.f.* calendula.
calentar (ka·len'tar) [*pres.ind.* **caliento**; *pres.subjve.* **caliente**] *v.t.* to warm; to heat. —**calentarse,** *v.r.* **1,** to become warm. **2,** to become angry. **3,** to be in heat. —**calentador,** *n.m.* heater; warmer. —*adj.* heating; warming. —**calentar a uno las orejas,** to scold someone. —**calentarse la cabeza** *or* **los sesos,** to rack one's brains.
calentura (ka·len'tu·ra) *n.f.* fever. —**calenturiento,** *adj.* feverish.
calera (ka'le·ra) *n.f.* lime kiln; lime pit.
calesa (ka'le·sa) *n.f.* chaise. —**calesín** (-'sin) *n.m.* light chaise.
caleta (ka'le·ta) *n.f.* inlet; cove.
caletre (ka'le·tre) *n.m., colloq.* judgment; good sense.
calibrar (ka·li'βrar) *v.t.* to calibrate; gauge; graduate. —**calibración,** *n.f.* calibration. —**calibrador,** *n.m.* caliper; micrometer.
calibre (ka'li·βre) *n.m.* **1,** caliber. **2,** capacity.
calicanto (ka·li'kan·to) *n.m.* stone masonry.
calicó (ka·li'ko) *n.m.* [*pl.* **calicós** (-'kos)] calico.
calidad (ka·li'ðað) *n.f.* quality; condition; character; rank. —**calidades,** *n.f.pl.* **1,** conditions. **2,** personal qualifications. **3,** *cards* rules. —**en calidad de,** in the capacity of.
cálido ('ka·li·ðo) *adj.* **1,** warm; hot. **2,** piquant; spicy.
calidoscopio (ka·li·ðos'ko·pjo) *n.m.* kaleidoscope. —**calidoscópico** (-'ko·pi·ko) *adj.* kaleidoscopic.
calientapiés (ka·ljen·ta'pjes) *n.m.sing.* & *pl.* foot warmer.
caliente (ka'ljen·te) *adj.* **1,** warm; hot; scalding. **2,** *Amer., colloq.* ardent; hot. —**en caliente,** piping hot.
caliente *v., pres.subjve. of* **calentar.**
caliento (ka'ljen·to) *v., pres.ind. of* **calentar.**
califa (ka'li·fa) *n.m.* caliph. —**califato,** *n.m.* caliphate.
calificar (ka·li·fi'kar) *v.t.* & *i.* [*pres.subjve.* **califique** (-'fi·ke); *pret.* **califiqué** (-'ke)] to qualify. —**calificable,** *adj.* qualifiable. —**calificación,** *n.f.* qualification; judgment. —**calificado,** *adj.* qualified; competent. —**calificador,** *n.m.* qualifier; censor. —**calificativo,** *adj., gram.* qualifying. —*n.m.* appellation.
californio (ka·li'for·njo) *n.m.* californium.
caligrafía (ka·li·ɣra'fi·a) *n.f.* calligraphy. —**caligráfico** (-'ɣra·

fi·ko) *adj.* calligraphic. —**calígrafo** (-'li-ɣra·fo) *n.m.* calligrapher.
calina (ka'li·na) *n.f.* haze; mist.
calistenia (ka·lis'te·nja) *n.f.* calisthenics. —**calisténico** (-'te·ni·ko) *adj.* calisthenic.
cáliz ('ka·liθ; -lis) *n.m.* **1,** chalice. **2,** *bot.* calyx. **3,** *poet.* cup; vase.
calizo (ka'li·θo; -so) *adj.* limy; of lime or limestone. —**piedra caliza,** limestone.
calma ('kal·ma) *n.f.* **1,** *naut.* calm; calm weather. **2,** calmness; composure. **3,** cessation (*of pain*).
calmar (kal'mar) *v.t.* to calm; to quiet; to compose; to pacify. —*v.i.* to fall calm. —**calmado,** *adj.* quiet; calm; pacified. —**calmante,** *adj.* soothing; sedative. —*n.m.* narcotic; sedative. —**calmoso** *adj.* calm.
calmo ('kal·mo) *adj.* **1,** empty of vegetation; treeless; barren. **2,** uncultivated; unfilled. **3,** calm; quiet.
caló (ka'lo) *n.m.* cant; gypsy slang.
calofriarse (ka·lo·fri'ar·se) *also,* **calosfriarse** (ka·los-) *v.r.* to shiver with cold; to have a chill. —**calofriado, calosfriado,** *adj.* = **escalofriado.** —**calofrío, calosfrío,** *n.m.* = **escalofrío.**
calor (ka'lor) *n.m.* **1,** heat; glow; warmth. **2,** excitement; animation; vivacity. —**coger calor; entrar en calor,** to warm oneself. —**hacer calor,** to be warm *or* hot (*of the weather*).
caloría (ka·lo'ri·a) *n.f.* calorie. —**calórico** (-'lo·ri·ko) *adj.* caloric.
calorífero (ka·lo'ri·fe·ro) *n.m.* stove; heater; furnace; radiator. —*adj.* heating; producing heat.
caloso (ka'lo·so) *adj.* porous (*of paper*).
calque ('kal·ke) *v., pres.subjve. of* **calcar.**
calqué (kal'ke) *v., 1st pers.sing. pret. of* **calcar.**
calumnia (ka'lum·nja) *n.f.* calumny; slander. —**calumnioso,** *adj.* calumnious; slanderous.
calumniar (ka·lum'njar) *v.t.* to calumniate; to slander. —**calumniador,** *n.m.* calumniator; slanderer.
caluroso (ka·lu'ro·so) *adj.* warm; hot.
calva ('kal·βa) *n.f.* **1,** bald spot. **2,** clearing.
calvario (kal'βa·rjo) *n.m.* **1,** calvary. **2,** *colloq.* debt; tally; score.
calvez (kal'βeθ; -'βes) *n.f.* baldness. *Also,* **calvicie** (-'βi·θje; -'βi·sje) *n.f.*
calvo ('kal·βo) *adj.* **1,** bald. **2,** barren; treeless.
calza ('kal·θa; -sa) *n.f.* **1,** wedge. **2,** *Amer.* gold inlay or filling. **3,** *pl.* breeches; trousers. **4,** *pl., colloq.* hose; stockings —**calza de arena,** sandbag —**en calzas prietas,** in difficulties
calzada (kal'θa·ða; -'sa·ða) *n.f.* causeway, paved highway.
calzado (kal'θa·ðo; -'sa·ðo) *adj.* **1,** shod (*usu. said of certain friars*). **2,** (*of animals*) having feet of a different color. **3,** (*of birds*) having feathers down to the feet. —*n.m.* footwear.
calzador (kal·θa'ðor; -sa'ðor) *n.m.* shoehorn.
calzar (kal'θar; -'sar) *v.t.* [*pres. subjve.* **calce,** *pret.* **calcé**] **1,** to put on (shoes, spurs, gloves, etc.). **2,** to provide shoes for. **3,** to wear *or* take (a certain size). **4,** to wedge; put a wedge under. **5,** *Amer.* to fill (a tooth).
calzo ('kal·θo; -so) *n.m.* **1,** wedge. **2,** wheel shoe. **3,** wooden skid.
calzón (kal'θon; -'son) *n.m.* **1,** *usu.pl.* breeches; trousers. **2,** safety rope used by roofers and housepainters. **3,** ombre.
calzoncillos (kal·θon'θi·ʎos; -son'si·jos) *n.m.pl.* drawers; underdrawers.
callado (ka'ʎa·ðo; -'ja·ðo) *adj.* **1,** quiet; silent. **2,** secret; stealthy. —**callada,** *n.f., naut.* lull. —**de callada; a las calladas,** privately; on the quiet.
callar (ka'ʎar; -'jar) *v.t.* to silence. —*v.i.* **1,** to be silent. **2,** *poet.* to abate; to fall into a lull. —**¡calla!; ¡calle!,** you don't say! —**callarse el pico,** *colloq.* to hold one's tongue; to shut up.
calle ('ka·ʎe; -je) *n.f.* **1,** street. **2,** *colloq.* liberty. —*interj.* make way! —**calle abajo** down the street. —**calle arriba,** up the street. —**hacer** *or* **abrir calle,** to make way. —**dejar en la calle,** leave penniless.
calleja (ka'ʎe·xa; -'je·xa) *n.f.* alley; lane.
callejear (ka·ʎe·xe'ar; ka·je-) *v.i.* to walk the streets; to gad about. —**callejero** (-'xe·ro) *n.m.* loiterer; gadabout.
callejón (ka·ʎe'xon; ka·je-) *n.m.*

lane; alley. —**callejón sin salida,** blind alley.
allejuela (ka·ʎe'xwe·la; ka·je-) *n.f.* 1, alley; lane. 2, *colloq.* subterfuge; shift.
allista (ka'ʎis·ta; -'jis·ta) *n.m.* & *f.* chiropodist.
allo ('ka·ʎo; -jo) *n.m.* corn; callus. —**callos,** *n.m.pl.* tripe (*sing.*).
alloso (ka'ʎo·so; ka'jo-) *adj.* callous. —**callosidad,** *n.f.* callosity.
ama ('ka·ma) *n.f.* 1, bed; couch; bedstead. 2, straw bedding (*for animals*). 3, *geol.* layer; stratum. —**hacer cama,** to be confined to bed. —**hacer la cama a uno,** to work against someone behind his back.
amada (ka'ma·ða) *n.f.* 1, litter of animals. 2, bed; layer. 3, *colloq.* band of thieves.
amafeo (ka·ma'fe·o) *n.m.* cameo.
amaleón (ka·ma·le'on) *n.m.* 1, *zool.* chameleon. 2, *colloq.* self-serving person; one who changes his mind to suit his interests.
ámara ('ka·ma·ra) *n.f.* 1, hall; parlor. 2, chamber. 3, either house of a bicameral legislature. 4, chamber of a firearm. 5, inner tube. 6, camera. 7, *naut.* cabin. —**cámaras,** *n.f.pl.* diarrhea. —**moza de cámara,** chambermaid.
amarada (ka·ma'ra·ða) *n.m.* 1, comrade; partner. 2, *colloq.* chum; buddy. —*n.f.* company or reunion of friends. —**camaradería,** *n.f.* camaraderie.
amaranchón (ka·ma·ran'tʃon) *n.m.* garret; attic.
amarera (ka·ma're·ra) *n.f.* 1, chambermaid; housekeeper. 2, waitress. 3, lady in waiting. 4, stewardess.
amarero (ka·ma're·ro) *n.m.* 1, waiter. 2, steward. 3, chamberlain.
camarilla (ka·ma'ri·ʎa; -ja) *n.f.* 1, inner circle; clique. 2, political machine.
camarín (ka·ma'rin) *n.m.* 1, small room. 2, dressing room; boudoir. 3, *eccles.* niche behind an altar where images are kept.
camarlengo (ka·mar'len·go) *n.m.* chamberlain.
camarón (ka·ma'ron) *n.m.* shrimp. *Also,* **cámaro** ('ka·ma·ro).
camarote (ka·ma'ro·te) *n.m.* stateroom; cabin; berth.
cambalachear (kam·ba·la·tʃe·'ar) *v.t.* & *i.* to barter. —**cambalache** (-'la·tʃe) *n.m.* barter. —**cambalachero,** *adj.* bartering; of or by barter. —*n.m.* barterer.
cambiadiscos (kam·bja'ðis·kos) *n.m.sing.* & *pl.* record changer.
cambiador (kam·bja'ðor) *adj.* exchanging; bartering. —*n.m.* 1, changer; exchanger. 2, *Amer.* switch; switchman.
cambiante (kam'bjan·te) *adj.* changing; altering. —*n.m., usu.pl.* iridescence. —*n.m.* & *f.* money changer.
cambiar (kam'bjar) *v.t.* & *i.* to change; to exchange; to barter.
cambiavía (kam·bja'βi·a) *n.m., Amer., R.R.* 1, switch. 2, switchman.
cambio ('kam·bjo) *n.m.* 1, barter; exchange. 2, *comm.* premium; rate. 3, exchange value of currency. 4, public or private bank. 5, gearshift. —**en cambio,** on the other hand. —**letra de cambio,** bill of exchange. —**libre cambio,** free trade.
cambista (kam'bis·ta) *n.m.* banker; money broker; *Amer.* switchman.
cambray (kam'brai) *n.m.* cambric.
camelia (ka'me·lja) *n.f.* camellia.
camello (ka'me·ʎo; -jo) *n.m.* 1, camel. 2, *naut.* caisson. —**camellero** (-'ʎe·ro; -'je·ro) *n.m.* camel driver.
camerino (ka·me'ri·no) *n.m.* dressing room.
camilla (ka'mi·ʎa; -ja) *n.f.* 1, small bed; cot. 2, stretcher. —**camillero** (-'ʎe·ro; -'je·ro) *n.m.* stretcher-bearer.
caminar (ka·mi'nar) *v.i.* & *t.* to go; to travel; to walk; to march. —**caminata** (-'na·ta) *n.f., colloq.* long walk; jaunt; promenade.
camino (ka'mi·no) *n.m.* 1, way; course. 2, road; highway. 3, passage; trip; journey. —**camino real,** highroad; highway. —**camino vecinal,** country road. —**de camino,** on the way. —**ponerse en camino,** to set out.
camión (ka'mjon) *n.m.* 1, truck; wagon; lorry. 2, *W.I.* bus. —**camionaje,** *n.m.* truck transport; truckage. —**camionero,** *n.m.* truck driver.
camioneta (ka·mjo'ne·ta) *n.f.* 1, small truck. 2, *Amer.* station wagon. 3, *W.I.* small bus.
camisa (ka'mi·sa) *n.f.* shirt; chemise. —**camisa de fuerza,** strait jacket. —**en mangas de camisa,** in shirt sleeves. —**meterse en camisa**

de once varas, to bite off more than one can chew. —**no tener camisa,** to be destitute.
camisería (ka·mi·se'ri·a) *n.f.* haberdashery. —**camisero** (-'se·ro) *n.m.* shirtmaker; haberdasher.
camiseta (ka·mi'se·ta) *n.f.* undershirt.
camisilla (ka·mi'si·ʎa; -ja) *n.f.* 1, small shirt. 2, *W.I.* undershirt.
camisola (ka·mi'so·la) *n.f.* ruffled shirt.
camisolín (ka·mi·so'lin) *n.m.* shirtfront; dickey.
camisón (ka·mi'son) *n.m.* 1, long shirt. 2, nightshirt. 3, nightgown; nightdress.
camita (ka'mi·ta) *n.f.* small bed; cot; couch.
camita (ka'mi·ta) *adj.* & *n.m.* & *f.* Hamite. —**camítico** (-'mi·ti·ko) *adj.* Hamitic.
camomila (ka·mo'mi·la) *n.f.* camomile.
camón (ka'mon) *n.m.* large bed.
camorra (ka'mo·rra) *n.f.* 1, quarrel; row. 2, Camorra. —**armar camorra,** to quarrel; to raise a row. —**buscar camorra,** to look for trouble.
camorrista (ka·mo'rris·ta) *n.m.* & *f.* 1, noisy, quarrelsome person. 2, member of the Camorra.
campamento (kam·pa'men·to) *n.m.* encampment; camp.
campana (kam'pa·na) *n.f.* 1, bell; any bell-shaped object. 2, *fig.* parish; church. —**campana de buzo,** diving bell. —**campana de rebato,** alarm bell. —**picar la campana,** *naut.* to sound the bell.
campanada (kam·pa'na·ða) *n.f.* 1, peal of a bell. 2, *fig.* scandal; sensation. —**dar una campanada,** to cause scandal.
campanario (kam·pa'na·rjo) *n.m.* belfry; bell tower; campanile.
campanear (kam·pa·ne'ar) *v.t.* to ring; to ring repeatedly. —*v.i.* to reverberate; to chime. —**campaneo** (-'ne·o) *n.m.* bell ringing; chime.
campanero (kam·pa'ne·ro) *n.m.* 1, bell ringer. 2, bell founder.
campanilla (kam·pa'ni·ʎa; -ja) *n.f., dim.* 1, small bell; hand bell. 2, *anat.* uvula. 3, *bot.* bellflower. —**campanillazo,** *n.m.* loud ringing.
campanudo (kam·pa'nu·ðo) *adj.* bell-shaped.
campaña (kam'pa·ɲa) *n.f.* 1, campaign. 2, *naut.* cruise.
campañol (kam·pa'ɲol) *n.m.* field mouse.
campar (kam'par) *v.i.* 1, to camp; to encamp. 2, to excel in ability or talent.
campear (kam·pe'ar) *v.i.* 1, to be in the field; to pasture. 2, to grow green (*of fields*). 3, to excel; to be eminent.
campechano (kam·pe'tʃa·no) *adj., colloq.* jovial; hearty.
campeón (kam·pe'on) *n.m.* champion; defender. —**campeonato,** *n.m.* championship.
campero (kam'pe·ro) *adj.* exposed to the outdoors; unsheltered. —*n.m.* field guard
campesino (kam·pe'si·no) *n.m.* 1, rustic; country dweller. 2, farmer; peasant —*adj.* [*also,* **campestre** (-'pes·tre)] rural; pastoral.
campiña (kam'pi·ɲa) *n.f.* open country fields (*pl.*).
campo ('kam·po) *n.m.* 1, country; field. 2, camp 3, athletic field. —**a campo raso,** outdoors. —**campo de veraneo,** summer camp.
camposanto (kam·po'san·to) *n.m.* cemetery.
camuflar (ka·mu'flar) *v.t.* to camouflage —**camuflaje** (-'fla·xe) *n.m.* camouflage.
can (kan) *n.m.* 1, dog. 2, trigger. 3, *astron.* Dog Star.
cana ('ka·na) *n.f.* gray hair. —**echar una cana al aire,** *colloq.* to go on a spree – **peinar canas,** to be old; to be grayhaired.
canal (ka'nal) *n.m.* 1, channel; canal; duct. 2, inlet; strait. 3, *TV* channel. —*n.f.* 1, natural underground waterway. 2, long, narrow valley. 3, *anat.* duct. 4, roof gutter; gutter tile. 5, pipe; conduit. 6, dressed animal carcass. —**canalón** *n.m.* large gutter; spout.
canalizar (ka·na·li'θar; -'sar) *v.t.* [*infl.:* **realizar**] to canalize; to channel; to pipe —**canalización,** *n.f.* canalization; piping.
canalla (ka'na·ʎa; -ja) *n.f.* mob; rabble. —*n.m.* scoundrel.
canallesco (ka·na'ʎes·ko; -'jes·ko) *adj.* 1, of the rabble; low; vulgar. 2, mean; scoundrelly.
canana (ka'na·na) *n.f.* cartridge belt. —**cananas,** *n.f.pl., Amer.* handcuffs.
canapé (ka·na'pe) *n.m.* 1, couch; sofa. 2, canapé.

canario (ka'na·rjo) *n.m.* canary. —*interj.* great Scott!
canasta (ka'nas·ta) *n.f.* 1, basket. 2, crate. 3, canasta (*card game*).
canastero (ka·nas'te·ro) *n.m.* 1, basketmaker. 2, canasta player.
canasto (ka'nas·to) *also*, **canastro,** *n.m.* large basket; hamper. —**¡canastos!** confound it!
cancán (kan'kan) *n.m.* cancan.
cancela (kan'θe·la; -'se·la) *n.f.* grating; grille.
cancelar (kan·θe'lar; kan·se-) *v.t.* to cancel. —**cancelación,** *n.f.* cancellation; obliteration.
cáncer ('kan·θer; -ser) *n.m.* 1, cancer. 2, *cap., astron.* Cancer. —**canceroso,** *adj.* cancerous.
cancerarse (kan·θe'rar·se; kan·se-) *v.r.* to become cancerous.
canciller (kan·θi'ʎer; -si'jer) *n.m.* chancellor.
cancillería (kan·θi·ʎe'ri·a; kan·si·je-) *n.f.* 1, chancellery. 2, chancellorship. 3, chancery.
canción (kan'θjon; -'sjon) *n.f.* song; lyric poem; ballad. —**cancionero,** *n.m.* song book. —**cancionista,** *n.m.* & *f.* singer *or* composer.
cancha ('kan·tʃa) *n.f.* 1, *sports* field; court; ground; (golf) links. 2, cockpit. 3, *Amer.* race track. —*interj.* make way!
candar (kan'dar) *v.t.* to lock; to shut. —**candado** (-'da·ðo) *n.m.* padlock.
candela (kan'de·la) *n.f.* 1, candle. 2, *colloq.* light; flame; fire. —**estar con la candela en la mano,** *colloq.* to be dying. —**arrimar candela,** *colloq.* to spank; to beat.
candelabro (kan·de'la·βro) *n.m.* candelabrum.
candelaria (kan·de'la·rja) *n.f.* mullein.
candelero (kan·de'le·ro) *n.m.* candlestick. —**candeleros,** *n.m.pl., naut.* stanchions. —**estar en el candelero,** *colloq.* to be in the limelight.
candelilla (kan·de'li·ʎa; -ja) *n.f.* 1, *surg.* catheter. 2, *bot.* catkin. 3, *Amer.* will-o'-the-wisp.
candente (kan'den·te) *adj.* incandescent; white hot. —**candencia,** *n.f.* incandescence.
candidato (kan·di'ða·to) *n.m.* candidate. —**candidatura** (-'tu·ra) *n.f.* candidacy.
candidez (kan·di'ðeθ; -'ðes) *n.f.* 1, candor; simplicity; frankness. 2, whiteness.
cándido ('kan·di·ðo) *adj.* 1, candid; simple; frank. 2, white.
candileja (kan·di'le·xa) *n.f.* small oil lamp. —**candilejas,** *n.f.pl., theat.* footlights.
candor (kan'dor) *n.m.* 1, candor; frankness. 2, innocence.
candoroso (kan·do'ro·so) *adj.* 1, candid; frank. 2, innocent.
canela (ka'ne·la) *n.f.* 1, cinnamon. 2, *colloq.* an exquisite thing. —**canelo,** *n.m.* cinnamon tree.
canelón (ka·ne'lon) *n.m.* 1, gargoyle. 2, roof gutter. —**canelones,** *n.m.pl.* ends of a cat-o'-nine-tails.
cangreja (kan'gre·xa) *n.f.* fore-and-aft sail. —**cangreja de popa,** spanker.
cangrejo (kan'gre·xo) *n.m.* 1, crab; crawfish. 2, *cap., astron.* Cancer. —**cangrejo bayoneta** *or* **de las Molucas** horseshoe crab.
cangrena (kan'gre·na) *n.f.* = gangrena. —**cangrenarse,** *v.r.* = gangrenarse. —**cangrenoso,** *adj.* = gangrenoso.
canguro (kan'gu·ro) *n.m.* kangaroo.
caníbal (ka'ni·βal) *n.m.* cannibal. —*adj.* cannibalistic. —**canibalismo,** *n.m.* cannibalism.
canica (ka'ni·ka) *n.f.* 1, game of marbles. 2, marble.
canicie (ka'ni·θje; -sje) *n.f.* whiteness of the hair.
canícula (ka'ni·ku·la) *n.f.* 1, dog days. 2, *cap., astron.* Dog Star.
canilla (ka'ni·ʎa; -ja) *n.f.* 1, long bone. 2, petcock. 3, faucet. 4, spool; reel. 5, rib *or* stripe (*in cloth*). 6, *slang* slender leg.
canillita (ka·ni'ʎi·ta; -'ji·ta) *n.m., Amer.* newsboy.
canino (ka'ni·no) *adj.* canine. —*n.m.* canine tooth.
canjear (kan·xe'ar) *v.t.* to exchange. —**canje** ('kan·xe) *n.m.* exchange. —**canjeable,** *adj.* exchangeable.
cano ('ka·no) *adj.* gray; grayhaired.
canoa (ka'no·a) *n.f.* 1, canoe. 2, launch. 3, *Amer.* trough. 4, *Amer.* water ditch or trench. —**canoero,** *n.m.* canoeist.
canódromo (ka'no·ðro·mo) *n.m.* dog track.
canon ('ka·non) *n.m.* canon. —**canones,** *n.m.pl.* canon law. —**canónico** (-'no·ni·ko) *adj.* canonical.

canonicato (ka·no·ni'ka·to) *n.m.* = **canonjía.**
canonicidad (ka·no·ni·θi'ðað; -si'ðað) *n.f.* canonicity.
canónigo (ka'no·ni·ɣo) *n.m.* canon (*churchman*).
canonista (ka·no'nis·ta) *n.m.* canonist.
canonizar (ka·no·ni'θar; -'sar) *v.t.* [*pres.subjve.* **canonice** (-'ni·θe; -se); *pret.* **canonicé** (-'θe; -'se)] to canonize. —**canonización,** *n.f.* canonization.
canonjía (ka·non'xi·a) *n.m.* **1,** canonry. **2,** *colloq.* sinecure.
canoro (ka'no·ro) *adj.* melodious; musical. —**ave canora,** songbird.
canoso (ka'no·so) *adj.* gray; gray-haired.
canotié (ka·no'tje) *n.m.* straw hat with a flat crown; sailor.
cansado (kan'sa·ðo) *adj.* **1,** tired. **2,** boring; tedious; tiresome. —*n.m., colloq.* bore; tiresome person.
cansancio (kan'san·θjo; -sjo) *n.m.* fatigue; weariness.
cansar (kan'sar) *v.t.* **1,** to tire; to fatigue. **2,** to exhaust (land). —**cansarse,** *v.r.* to tire; to become weary.
cantable (kan'ta·βle) *adj.* singable.
cantalupo (kan·ta'lu·po) *n.m.* cantaloupe.
cantante (kan'tan·te) *n.m.* & *f.* singer.
cantar (kan'tar) *v.t.* & *i.* **1,** to sing. **2,** *colloq.* to squeal; to confess. **3,** *poet.* to compose; to recite. —*n.m.* song; singing.
cántara ('kan·ta·ra) *n.f.* **1,** liquid measure equal to 16.13 liters, or about 16 quarts. **2,** = **cántaro.**
cantarín (kan·ta'rin) *n.m., colloq.* songster; singer.
cántaro ('kan·ta·ro) *n.m.* pitcher; jug. —**llover a cántaros,** to rain cats and dogs.
cantata (kan'ta·ta) *n.f.* cantata.
cantatriz (kan·ta'triθ; -'tris) *n.f.* singer.
cantazo (kan'ta·θo; -so) *n.m.* **1,** blow; cuff. **2,** bump; knock.
cantera (kan'te·ra) *n.f.* **1,** quarry. **2,** *Amer.* block of stone. **3,** *fig.* talents; genius. —**cantería** (-te'ri·a) *n.f.* stonecutting. —**cantero** (-'te·ro) *n.m.* stonecutter.
cantidad (kan·ti'ðað) *n.f.* quantity.
cantilena (kan·ti'le·na) *n.f.* song; ballad. —**la misma cantilena,** the same old song *or* story.
cantimplora (kan·tim'plo·ra) *n.f.* **1,** canteen. **2,** siphon. **3,** water cooler. **4,** flask; decanter. **5,** *Amer.* powder flask. **6,** *Amer.* mumps.
cantina (kan'ti·na) *n.f.* **1,** mess hall. **2,** wine shop. **3,** canteen. **4,** *Amer.* barroom; tavern; saloon.
cantinela (kan·ti'ne·la) *n.f.* = **cantilena.**
cantinero (kan·ti'ne·ro) *n.m.* bartender; tavernkeeper.
canto ('kan·to) *n.m.* **1,** song; singing. **2,** epic poem. **3,** canto. **4,** *W.I.* small piece; bit. **5,** edge; end. —**al canto de,** by the side of. —**al canto del gallo,** *colloq.* at daybreak.
cantón (kan'ton) *n.m.* **1,** canton; region. **2,** corner; edge.
cantonar (kan·to'nar) *v.t.* = **acantonar.**
cantonera (kan·to'ne·ra) *n.f.* **1,** corner plate; angle iron. **2,** *vulg.* streetwalker.
cantonero (kan·to'ne·ro) *n.m.* loafer; idler. —*adj.* loafing; idle.
cantor (kan'tor) *n.m.* **1,** singer. **2,** *colloq.* minstrel.
canturía (kan·tu'ri·a) *n.f.* **1,** vocal music. **2,** vocal exercise. **3,** singsong. **4,** singability; ease of singing *or* playing.
canturrear (kan·tu·rre'ar) *also,* **canturriar** (-tu'rrjar) *v.t.* & *i.* to hum; to sing softly. —**canturreo** (-'rre·o) *n.m.* hum; humming.
cánula ('ka·nu·la) *n.f., med.* **1,** cannula. **2,** hypodermic needle.
caña ('ka·ɲa) *n.f.* **1,** cane; reed. **2,** *Amer., colloq.* walking stick. **3,** *naut.* helm. **4,** *Amer., colloq.* bluff; boast. —**caña de pescar,** fishing rod.
cañada (ka'ɲa·ða) *n.f.* glen; dell.
cañal (ka'ɲal) *n.m.* **1,** = **cañaveral.** **2,** fishing channel. **3,** weir (*for fishing*).
cañamazo (ka·ɲa'ma·θo; -so) *n.m.* canvas for embroidery.
cañamelar (ka·ɲa·me'lar) *n.m.* sugar cane plantation.
cañamiel (ka·ɲa'mjel) *n.f.* sugar cane.
cáñamo ('ka·ɲa·mo) *n.m.* hemp.
cañaveral (ka·ɲa·βe'ral) *n.m.* canebrake; cane field.
cañería (ka·ɲe'ri·a) *n.f.* **1,** conduit; pipeline. **2,** sewer pipe. **3,**

water *or* gas main. 4, *music* organ pipes.

caño ('ka·ɲo) *n.m.* 1, spout; faucet. 2, pipe; tube. 3, common sewer. 4, *music* organ pipe. 5, *naut.* channel. 6, *Amer.* gully; ravine.

cañón (ka'ɲon) *n.m.* 1, cannon. 2, pipe; tube. 3, barrel of a gun. 4, *mech.* socket. 5, canyon. —**cañón de chimenea,** chimney flue.

cañonear (ka·ɲo·ne'ar) *v.t.* to bombard; to cannonade. —**cañonazo,** *n.m.* cannon shot. —**cañoneo,** *n.m.* bombardment.

cañonería (ka·ɲo·ne'ri·a) *n.f.* 1, cannonry; cannons collectively. 2, organ pipes collectively.

cañonero (ka·ɲo'ne·ro) *n.m.* [*also,* **lancha cañonera**] gunboat.

cañuto (ka'ɲu·to) *n.m.* small tube; small pipe.

caoba (ka'o·βa) *n.f.* mahogany tree; mahogany wood.

caobo (ka'o·βo) *n.m.* mahogany tree.

caos ('ka·os) *n.m.* chaos. —**caótico** (-'o·ti·ko) *adj.* chaotic.

capa ('ka·pa) *n.f.* 1, cape; cloak; mantle. 2, covering; coating. 3, layer; stratum.

capacidad (ka·pa·θi'ðað; -si'ðað) *n.f.* 1, capacity. 2, ability; talent.

capacitar (ka·pa·θi'tar; -si'tar) *v.t.* 1, to enable; to prepare. 2, to empower; to authorize.

capacho (ka'pa·tʃo) *n.m.* 1, large basket; hamper. 2, *ornith.* barn owl.

capar (ka'par) *v.t.* 1, to castrate. 2, *vulg.* to curtail.

caparazón (ka·pa·ra'θon; -'son) *n.m.* 1, caparison. 2, horse blanket. 3, feedbag. 4, shell of insects or crustaceans.

capataz (ka·pa'taθ; -'tas) *n.m.* overseer; superintendent; foreman.

capaz (ka'paθ; -'pas) *adj.* 1, capable; competent. 2, spacious; roomy.

capcioso (kap'θjo·so; -'sjo·so) *adj.* captious; insidious. —**capciosidad,** *n.f.* captiousness.

capear (ka·pe'ar) *v.t.* 1, to challenge (a bull) with a cape. 2, to dodge; to wait out. —*v.i.* 1, *naut.* to lay to. 2, *colloq.* to lie low. —**capeador,** *n.m.* bullfighter who challenges a bull with a cape. —**capeo** (-'pe·o) *n.m.* challenging of a bull with a cape.

capellán (ka·pe'ʎan; -'jan) *n.m.* chaplain.

caperuza (ka·pe'ru·θa; -sa) *n.f.* 1, hood; cowl. 2, cap or covering, esp. cone-shaped.

capilar (ka·pi'lar) *adj.* & *n.m.* capillary. —**capilaridad,** *n.f.* capillarity.

capilla (ka'pi·ʎa; -ja) *n.f.* 1, chapel. 2, hood; cowl. 3, *print.* proof sheet. 4, death house. —**capilla ardiente,** funeral chapel. —**estar en capilla,** to await execution; *fig.* to be on pins and needles.

capillo (ka'pi·ʎo; -jo) *n.m.* 1, child's cap. 2, baptismal cap. 3, christening fee.

capirotazo (ka·pi·ro'ta·θo; -so) *n.m.* fillip.

capirote (ka·pi'ro·te) *n.m.* 1, hood. 2, cone-shaped cap. 3, fillip. —**tonto de capirote** nincompoop.

capitación (ka·pi·ta'θjon; -'sjon) *n.f.* poll tax.

capital (ka·pi'tal) *adj.* capital. —*n.m.* 1, capital; assets (*pl.*). 2, asset. —*n.f.* capital (*city*).

capitalismo (ka·pi·ta'lis·mo) *n.m.* capitalism. —**capitalista,** *n.m.* & *f.* capitalist. —*adj.* capitalistic.

capitalizar (ka·pi·ta·li'θar; -'sar) *v.t.* [*pres.subjve.* **capitalice** (-'li·θe; -se); *pret.* **capitalicé** (-'θe; -'se)] 1, *comm.* to capitalize. 2, to compound (interest). —**capitalización,** *n.f.* capitalization.

capitán (ka·pi'tan) *n.m.* captain.

capitana (ka·pi'ta·na) *n.f.* 1, flagship. 2, captain's wife.

capitanear (ka·pi·ta·ne'ar) *v.t.* to command; to head; to lead.

capitanía (ka·pi·ta'ni·a) *n.f.* captainship; captaincy. —**Capitanía General,** Captaincy General; *l.c.* captain-generalcy.

capitel (ka·pi'tel) *n.m., archit.* capital.

capitolio (ka·pi'to·ljo) *n.m.* capitol.

capitulado (ka·pi·tu'la·ðo) *n.m.* capitulation; contract.

capitular (ka·pi·tu'lar) *v.i.* 1, to conclude an agreement. 2, to draw articles of a contract. 3, *mil.* to capitulate. —*v.t.* to impeach. —*adj.,* *eccles.* capitular; capitulary. —**capitulación,** *n.f.* capitulation; agreement. —**capitulaciones,** *n.f.pl.* marriage contract.

capítulo (ka'pi·tu·lo) *n.m.* 1, chapter; division. 2, *law* charge; count. —**capítulos matrimoniales,** articles of marriage. —**llamar a capítulo,** to call to account; to bring to book.

capó (ka'po) *n.m.* = **capot.**
capolar (ka·po'lar) *v.t.* to mince; chop. —**capolado,** *n.m.* hash; minced meat.
capón (ka'pon) *n.m.* capon. —*adj.* castrated; gelded.
caporal (ka·po'ral) *n.m.* **1,** boss; chief. **2,** cattle boss.
capot (ka'pot) *n.m.* hood (*of an engine*).
capota (ka'po·ta) *n.f.* **1,** automobile top; convertible top. **2,** *aero.* cowling. **3,** = **capot.**
capotar (ka·po'tar) *v.i.* to turn or flip over.
capote (ka'po·te) *n.m.* **1,** bullfighter's cape. **2,** *mil.* close-fitting cloak with sleeves. **3,** *Amer.* beating; thrashing. —**capote de monte,** poncho. —**dar capote,** to win all the tricks, in certain card games. —**para mi capote,** (I said) to myself.
capotear (ka·po·te'ar) *v.t.* **1,** = **capear. 2,** to evade; to shirk. **3,** to bamboozle.
capotera (ka·po'te·ra) *n.f., Amer.* clothes rack; clothes tree.
Capricornio (ka·pri'kor·njo) *n.m.* Capricorn.
capricho (ka'pri·tʃo) *n.m.* **1,** caprice; whim. **2,** desire; yen. **3,** *music* capriccio; caprice. —**caprichoso,** *adj.* capricious; whimsical; willful. —**caprichudo,** *adj.* obstinate; stubborn.
caprino (ka'pri·no) *adj.* = **cabrío.**
cápsula ('kap·su·la) *n.f.* **1,** bottle cap. **2,** cartridge. **3,** capsule. —**capsular,** *adj.* capsule; capsular. —*v.t.* to cap (a bottle).
captar (kap'tar) *v.t.* **1,** to catch; to grasp. **2,** to capture; to attract; to win. **3,** to impound.
capturar (kap·tu'rar) *v.t.* to capture. —**captura** (-'tu·ra) *n.f.* capture.
capucha (ka'pu·tʃa) *n.f.* **1,** cowl; hood (*of a cloak*). **2,** *print.* circumflex accent.
capuchina (ka·pu'tʃi·na) *n.f.* nasturtium.
capuchino (ka·pu'tʃi·no) *adj.* & *n.m., eccles.* Capuchin. —*n.m., zool.* capuchin monkey.
capuchón (ka·pu'tʃon) *n.m.* **1,** hooded cloak. **2,** short domino.
capullo (ka'pu·ʎo; -jo) *n.m.* **1,** cocoon. **2,** flower bud.
capuz (ka'puθ; -'pus) *n.m.* **1,** cowl. **2,** hooded cloak.
caqui ('ka·ki) *adj.* & *n.m.* khaki. —*n.m., bot.* persimmon.
cara ('ka·ra) *n.f.* **1,** face; countenance. **2,** expression. **3,** façade; front. **4,** surface. **5,** heads (*of a coin*). **6,** side (*of a phonograph record*). —**cara a cara,** face to face. —**de cara,** opposite; facing. —**echar en cara; dar en cara,** to reproach (with). —**hacer cara a,** to face; to confront. —**tener mala cara, 1,** to look ill. **2,** to make a bad appearance.
carabao (ka·ra'βa·o) *n.m.* water buffalo; carabao.
carabela (ka·ra'βe·la) *n.f.* caravel.
carabina (ka·ra'βi·na) *n.f.* carbine. —**carabinazo,** *n.m.* carbine shot.
carabinero (ka·ra·βi'ne·ro) *n.m.* **1,** carabineer. **2,** customs guard.
caracol (ka·ra'kol) *n.m.* **1,** snail; snail shell. **2,** sea shell. **3,** *anat.* cochlea. **4,** *archit.* spiral. —**escalera de caracol,** winding stairway.
caracolear (ka·ra·ko·le'ar) *v.i.* to caper; prance. —**caracoleo** (-'le·o) *n.m.* caper; prancing.
carácter (ka'rak·ter) *n.m.* [*pl.* **caracteres** (-'te·res)] **1,** character. **2,** mark; letter. **3,** *pl., print.* type; type faces.
característica (ka·rak·te'ris·ti·ka) *n.f.* **1,** characteristic; trait. **2,** character actress.
característico (ka·rak·te'ris·ti·ko) *adj.* characteristic; typical. —*n.m.* character actor.
caracterizado (ka·rak·te·ri'θa·ðo; -'sa·ðo) *adj.* characterized; distinguished.
caracterizar (ka·rak·te·ri'θar; -'sar) *v.t.* [*pres.subjve.* **caracterice** (-'ri·θe; -se); *pret.* **caractericé** (-'θe; -'se)] **1,** to characterize. **2,** *theat.* to play (a role). —**caracterización,** *n.f.* characterization.
caracul (ka·ra'kul) *n.m.* caracul.
carado (ka'ra·ðo) *adj., used only in:* **bien carado; biencarado,** kind-faced; pleasant; **mal carado; malcarado,** grim-faced; frowning.
caramba (ka'ram·ba) *interj. of surprise or annoyance* gracious! darn it!
carámbano (ka'ram·ba·no) *n.m.* icicle.
carambola (ka·ram'bo·la) *n.f.* **1,** carom. **2,** *colloq.* trick; indirection. —**por carambola,** by chance.

carambolear (ka·ram·bo·le'ar) *v.t.* to carom.
caramelo (ka·ra'me·lo) *n.m.* **1,** caramel. **2,** candy; sugar drop. **—caramelizar** (-li'θar; -li'sar) *v.t.* [*infl.*: **realizar**] = acaramelar.
caramente (ka·ra'men·te) *adv.* **1,** dearly. **2,** expensively.
caramillo (ka·ra'mi·ʎo; -jo) *n.m.* **1,** small flute. **2,** *colloq.* deceit; trick. **—armar un caramillo,** *colloq.* to raise a rumpus.
carapacho (ka·ra'pa·tʃo) *n.m.* shell; carapace.
carátula (ka'ra·tu·la) *n.f.* **1,** mask. **2,** *Amer.* title page.
caravana (ka·ra'βa·na) *n.f.* caravan.
carbohidrato (kar·βo·i'ðra·to) *n.m.* carbohydrate.
carbólico (kar'βo·li·ko) *n.m.* carbolic.
carbón (kar'βon) *n.m.* **1,** coal. **2,** carbon filament, electrode, etc. **—carbón de leña; carbón vegetal,** charcoal. **—carbón de piedra; carbón mineral,** coal. **—echar carbón,** *colloq.* to stir things up; to inflame someone.
carbonado (kar·βo'na·ðo) *n.m.* black diamond.
carbonar (kar·βo'nar) *v.t.* to make into charcoal.
carbonatar (kar·βo·na'tar) *v.t.* to carbonate.
carbonato (kar·βo'na·to) *n.m.* **1,** carbonate. **2,** [*also,* **carbonato de soda**] washing soda. **3,** *erroneous* = **bicarbonato.** *—adj.* carbonated.
carboncillo (kar·βon'θi·ʎo; -'si·jo) *n.m.* **1,** small coal. **2,** charcoal pencil.
carbonear (kar·βo·ne'ar) *v.t.* to char; to make into charcoal. **—carboneo** (-'ne·o) *n.m.* carbonization; charcoal burning.
carbonera (kar·βo'ne·ra) *n.f.* **1,** wood used for burning into charcoal. **2,** coal cellar; coal bin. **3,** a woman who sells coal; charcoal dealer; charcoal maker.
carbonería (kar·βo·ne'ri·a) *n.f.* coal yard; coal shed.
carbonero (kar·βo'ne·ro) *n.m.* charcoal dealer; charcoal maker; coal man. *—adj.* pert. to coal or charcoal.
carbónico (kar'βo·ni·ko) *adj.* carbonic.
carbonífero (kar·βo'ni·fe·ro) *adj.* carboniferous.
carbonizar (kar·βo·ni'θar; -'sar) *v.t.* [*pres.subjve.* **carbonice** (-'ni·θe; -se); *pret.* **carbonicé** (-'θe; -'se)] to carbonize; to char. **—carbonización,** *n.f.* carbonization.
carbono (kar'βo·no) *n.m., chem.* carbon. **—carbonoso,** *adj.* carbonaceous.
carborundo (kar·βo'run·do) *n.m.* carborundum.
carbunclo (kar'βun·klo) *n.m.* **1,** = **carbunco. 2,** = **carbúnculo.**
carbunco (kar'βun·ko) *n.m., pathol.* carbuncle.
carbúnculo (kar'βun·ku·lo) *n.m., jewelry* carbuncle.
carburador (kar·βu·ra'ðor) *n.m.* carburetor.
carburante (kar·βu'ran·te) *n.m.* gas or liquid fuel.
carburo (kar'βu·ro) *n.m.* carbide.
carca ('kar·ka) *n.f., Amer.* grime.
carcaj (kar'kax) *also,* **carcax** (-'kaks) *n.m., also,* **carcaza** (-'ka·θa; -sa) *n.f.* quiver.
carcajada (kar·ka'xa·ða) *n.f.* loud laughter; guffaw.
cárcava ('kar·ka·βa) *n.f.* **1,** gully; ditch. **2,** grave.
cárcel ('kar·θel; -sel) *n.f.* **1,** jail. **2,** groove of a sluice gate. **—carcelario,** *adj.* of or pert. to a jail or prison. **—carcelero,** *n.m.* jailer; warden.
carcinoma (kar·θi'no·ma; kar·si-) *n.f.* carcinoma.
carcoma (kar'ko·ma) *n.f.* **1,** *entom.* wood borer. **2,** dry rot. **3,** anxiety. **4,** wasting; waste. **5,** wastrel.
carcomer (kar·ko'mer) *v.t.* to gnaw; to rot; to erode. **—carcomerse,** *v.r.* to become worm-eaten; to decay.
carda ('kar·ða) *n.f.* **1,** carding. **2,** card (*for carding*).
cardar (kar'ðar) *v.t.* to card (fibers); to tease (hair).
cardelina (kar·ðe'li·na) *n.f.* goldfinch; linnet.
cardenal (kar·ðe'nal) *n.m., eccles.; ornith.* cardinal. **—cardenalato,** *n.m.* cardinalate.
cardencha (kar'ðen·tʃa) *n.f.* **1,** *bot.* teasel. **2,** card (*for carding*).
cárdeno ('kar·ðe·no) *adj.* livid; purple.
cardi- (kar·ði) *prefix, var. of* **cardio-** *before vowels: cardialgia,* cardialgia.
cardíaco (kar'ði·a·ko) *adj.* & *n.m.* cardiac.

cardialgia (kar·ði'al·xja) *n.f.* cardialgia; heartburn.
cardinal (kar·ði'nal) *adj.* cardinal; principal; fundamental.
cardio- (kar·ðjo) *prefix* cardio-; heart: *cardiograma,* cardiogram.
cardiología (kar·ði·o·lo'xi·a) *n.f.* cardiology. —**cardológico** (-'lo·xi·ko) *adj.* cardiological. —**cardiólogo** (-'o·lo·ɣo) *n.m.* cardiologist.
carditis (kar'ði·tis) *n.f.* carditis.
cardo ('kar·ðo) *n.m.* thistle.
cardumen (kar'ðu·men) *also,* **cardume** (-me) *n.m.* school of fish.
carear (ka·re'ar) *v.t.* **1,** to confront. **2,** to bring face to face. **3,** to compare. —**carearse,** *v.r.* to assemble; to meet face to face.
carecer (ka·re'θer; -'ser) *v.i.* [*pres. ind.* **carezco** (-'reθ·ko; -'res·ko); *pres.subjve.* **carezca** (-'reθ·ka; -'res·ka)] to be in need. —**carecer de,** to lack; be in need of.
carencia (ka'ren·θja; -sja) *n.f.* lack; want; need.
careo (ka're·o) *n.m.* **1,** meeting; confrontation. **2,** comparison.
carero (ka're·ro) *adj., colloq.* expensive; overpriced.
carestía (ka·res'ti·a) *n.f.* **1,** scarcity; lack. **2,** high prices.
careta (ka're·ta) *n.f.* **1,** mask. **2,** wire mask (*esp. as used in fencing and beekeeping*).
carey (ka'rei) *n.m.* **1,** a kind of marine turtle. **2,** tortoise shell.
carga ('kar·ɣa) *n.f.* **1,** load; burden; charge. **2,** freight; cargo. **3,** charge (*of gunpowder*).
cargadero (kar·ɣa'ðe·ro) *n.m.* loading station *or* platform.
cargado (kar'ɣa·ðo) *adj.* **1,** loaded. **2,** thick; strong (*of drinks*). **3,** cloudy; overcast. **4,** sultry. —**cargado de espaldas,** stoop-shouldered.
cargador (kar·ɣa'ðor) *n.m.* **1,** loader; stevedore. **2,** porter. **3,** battery charger.
cargamento (kar·ɣa'men·to) *n.m.* cargo.
cargar (kar'ɣar) *v.t.* & *i.* [*pres. subjve.* **cargue** ('kar·ɣe); *pret.* **cargué** (-'ɣe)] **1,** to load; to charge. **2,** to burden. **3,** to entrust. **4,** *colloq.* to weary; to annoy. **5,** *Amer.* to carry; to lug. —**cargarse,** *v.r.* to lean; to sway. —**cargar con,** to assume; to take on oneself. —**cargar con el muerto,** to get the blame (unjustly). —**cargarse de,** to have in plenty.
cargazón (kar·ɣa'θon; -'son) *n.f.* **1,** cargo. **2,** feeling of heaviness (*in the head, stomach, etc.*). **3,** sultriness. **4,** *Amer., colloq.* bother; nuisance.
cargo ('kar·ɣo) *n.m.* **1,** act of loading; weight; burden. **2,** charge. **3,** position; job. —**cargo de conciencia,** remorse. —**hacerse cargo de, 1,** to realize. **2,** to take over; to take charge of.
carguero (kar'ɣe·ro) *adj.* of burden; load-carrying; freight-carrying. —*n.m., Amer.* beast of burden.
cari ('ka·ri) *n.m.* curry.
cariarse (ka'rjar·se) *v.r.* to become carious; to decay. —**cariado,** *adj.* carious; decayed.
caribe (ka'ri·βe) *adj.* Caribbean. —*adj.* & *n.m.* Carib. —*n.m.* savage.
caricatura (ka·ri·ka'tu·ra) *n.f.* caricature; cartoon. —**caricaturesco,** *adj.* in caricature.
caricaturista (ka·ri·ka·tu'ris·ta) *n.m.* & *f.* caricaturist; cartoonist.
caricaturizar (ka·ri·ka·tu·ri·'θar; -'sar) *v.t.* [*infl.:* **realizar**] to caricature. *Also,* **caricaturar.**
caricia (ka'ri·θja; -sja) *n.f.* caress; petting.
caridad (ka·ri'ðað) *n.f.* **1,** charity. **2,** alms.
caries ('ka·rjes) *n.f.pl.* caries.
carillón (ka·ri'ʎon; -'jon) *n.m.* carillon.
cariño (ka'ri·ɲo) *n.m.* **1,** affection; love. **2,** *colloq.* gift. —**cariños,** *n.m.pl.* affectionate regards. —**cariñoso,** *adj.* affectionate; loving; endearing.
caritativo (ka·ri·ta'ti·βo) *adj.* charitable.
cariz (ka'riθ; -'ris) *n.m.* appearance; look; aspect.
carlinga (kar'lin·ga) *n.f.* cockpit.
carmen ('kar·men) *n.m., in Granada,* a country house; a garden.
carmenar (kar·me'nar) *v.t.* **1,** to disentangle; to unravel. **2,** *colloq.* to pull (someone's hair). **3,** *fig.* to swindle.
carmesí (kar·me'si) *adj.* crimson. —*n.m.* cochineal powder.
carmín (kar'min) *adj.* & *n.m.* carmine.
carnal (kar'nal) *adj.* **1,** carnal. **2,** fleshy; sensual. —**carnalidad,** *n.f.* carnality; lustfulness.
carnaval (kar·na'βal) *n.m.* carni-

val; mardigras. —**carnavalesco,** *adj.* like a carnival; of or pert. to a carnival.
carne ('kar·ne) *n.f.* meat; flesh. —**carne de gallina,** goose pimples. —**en carnes,** nude. —**ser de carne y hueso,** to be human.
carnero (kar'ne·ro) *n.m.* **1,** sheep; ram. **2,** mutton **3,** *Amer.* namby-pamby; milquetoast.
carnicería (kar·ni·θe'ri·a; -se'ri·a) *n.f.* **1,** butcher store; meat market. **2,** *So. Amer.* slaughterhouse. **3,** slaughter.
carnicero (kar·ni'θe·ro; -'se·ro) *n.m.* butcher. —*adj.* **1,** carnivorous. **2,** *fig.* bloodthirsty.
carnívoro (kar'ni·βo·ro) *adj.* carnivorous. —*n.m.* carnivore.
carnoso (kar'no·so) *adj.* fleshy; meaty. —**carnosidad** *n.f.* fleshiness.
caro ('ka·ro) *adj.* **1,** dear. **2,** expensive; costly. —*adv.* at a high price; expensively. —**cara mitad,** better half.
carona (ka'ro·na) *n.f.* saddle pad.
carótida (ka'ro·ti·ða) *n.f. & adj.* carotid.
carozo (ka'ro·θo; -so) *n.m.* **1,** corncob. **2,** core (*of a fruit*).
carpa ('kar·pa) *n.f.* **1,** *ichthy.* carp. **2,** *Amer.* tent.
carpelo (kar'pe·lo) *n.m.* carpel.
carpeta (kar'pe·ta) *n.f.* **1,** table cover. **2,** portfolio. **3,** letter file. **4,** *Amer.* school desk. **5,** writing pad.
carpintería (kar·pin·te'ri·a) *n.f.* **1,** carpentry. **2,** carpenter's shop.
carpintero (kar·pin'te·ro) *n.m.* carpenter. —**pájaro carpintero,** woodpecker.
-carpio (kar·pjo) *suffix* -carp; fruit: *endocarpio,* endocarp.
carpo- (kar·po) *prefix* carpo-; fruit: *carpología,* carpology.
carraspear (ka·rras·pe'ar) *v.i.* to hawk; to clear the throat. —**carraspeo** (-'pe·o) *n.m.* hawking; clearing the throat. —**carraspera,** *n.f., colloq.* hoarseness; sore throat.
carrera (ka'rre·ra) *n.f.* **1,** race. **2,** run; dash. **3,** route; course; run. **4,** career; profession. **5,** *mech.* stroke; travel. **6,** row; line. **7,** run (*as in a stocking*), **8,** *baseball* run; score. —**de carrera; a la carrera,** hastily.
carreta (ka'rre·ta) *n.f.* narrow cart; wagon.
carretada (ka·rre'ta·ða) *n.f.* cartload. —**a carretadas,** in great quantity; in heaps.
carretaje (ka·rre'ta·xe) *n.m.* cartage.
carrete (ka'rre·te) *n.m.* spool; reel.
carretear (ka·rre·te'ar) *v.t.* to cart; to convey. —*v.i.* to drive a cart.
carretera (ka·rre'te·ra) *n.f.* highway.
carretero (ka·rre'te·ro) *n.m.* wagoner; carter.
carretilla (ka·rre'ti·ʎa; -ja) *n.f.* wheelbarrow, hand cart.
carretón (ka·rre'ton) *n.m.* **1,** cart. **2,** go-cart.
carril (ka'rril) *n.m.* **1,** cartway; narrow road. **2,** *R.R.* rail.
carrillo (ka'rri·ʎo; -jo) *n.m.* cheek; jowl
carriola (ka'rrjo·la) *n.f.* **1,** cariole. **2,** carryall. **3,** trundle bed; truckle bed.
carro ('ka·rro) *n.m.* **1,** car; railway car; streetcar **2,** cart: wagon. **3,** *Amer.* automobile **4,** chariot. **5,** carriage (*of a typewriter, printing press, etc.*). **6,** *cap., astron.* Dipper.
carrocería (ka·rro·θe'ri·a; -se·'ri·a) *n.f.* **1,** carriage shop. **2,** body (*of a vehicle*).
carromato (ka·rro'ma·to) *n.m.* a long, narrow covered cart with two wheels.
carroña (ka'rro·ɲa) *n.f.* carrion; carcass.
carroza (ka'rro·θa; -sa) *n.f.* **1,** carriage of state. **2,** *Amer.* hearse; funeral car. **3,** [*also,* **carroza alegórica**] parade float.
carruaje (ka'rrwa·xe) *n.m.* carriage; coach; vehicle.
carrusel (ka·rru'sel) *n.m., Amer.* merry-go-round.
carta ('kar·ta) *n.f.* **1,** letter. **2,** playing card. **3,** charter. **4,** chart; map. **5,** bill of fare; menu. —**carta blanca,** carte blanche.
cartabón (kar·ta'βon) *n.m.* **1,** *carpentry* square. **2,** *drawing* triangle. **3,** size stick.
Carta Magna ('kar·ta'mag·na) *n.f.* Magna Charta
cartapacio (kar·ta'pa·θjo; -sjo) *n.m.* **1,** notebook. **2,** portfolio; briefcase.
cartearse (kar·te'ar·se) *v.r.* to correspond.
cartel (kar'tel) *n.m.* **1,** poster; placard. **2,** *theat.* show bill. **3,** *comm.* cartel.
cartela (kar'te·la) *n.f.* **1,** tag; slip; small card. **2,** part of a wall

tablet bearing the inscription. 3, bracket; support. 4, *archit.* console.
cartelera (kar·te'le·ra) *n.f.* billboard. —**cartelero,** *n.m.* billposter.
cartelón (kar·te'lon) *n.m.* large poster.
cárter ('kar·ter) *n.m., mech.* housing; case.
cartera (kar'te·ra) *n.f.* 1, portfolio. 2, desk pad. 3, wallet. 4, letter file. 5, *Amer.* handbag; purse.
carterista (kar·te'ris·ta) *n.m.* pickpocket.
cartero (kar'te·ro) *n.m.* postman; mailman.
cartílago (kar'ti·la·ɣo) *n.m.* cartilage. —**cartilaginoso** (-xi'no·so) *adj.* [*also, zool.,* **cartilagíneo** (-'xi·ne·o)] cartilaginous.
cartilla (kar'ti·ʎa; -ja) *n.f.* 1, primer. 2, passbook. 3, short treatise. —**cartilla de racionamiento,** ration book. —**no saber la cartilla,** to be ignorant. —**leer la cartilla a,** to reprimand; to call down.
cartografía (kar·to·ɣra'fi·a) *n.f.* cartography. —**cartógrafo** (-'to·ɣra·fo) *n.m.* cartographer. —**cartográfico** (-'ɣra·fi·ko) *adj.* cartographic.
cartón (kar'ton) *n.m.* 1, pasteboard; cardboard. 2, carton; cardboard box. —**cartón piedra,** papier-maché.
cartonero (kar·to'ne·ro) *n.m.* vendor of pasteboard or cardboard.
cartucho (kar'tu·tʃo) *n.m.* cartridge. —**cartuchera** (-'tʃe·ra) *n.f.* cartridge belt.
cartulina (kar·tu'li·na) *n.f.* fine, stiff pasteboard or cardboard.
casa ('ka·sa) *n.f.* 1, house; dwelling. 2, home; household. 3, *chess* square. 4, *comm.* firm. —**echar la casa por la ventana,** *colloq.* to blow the works. —**poner casa,** to set up house.
casaca (ka'sa·ka) *n.f.* coat; dress coat. —**cambiar de casaca,** *colloq.* to become a turncoat.
casadero (ka·sa'ðe·ro) *adj.* marriageable.
casado (ka'sa·ðo) *adj.* wed; married. —**recién casado,** *adj.* & *n.m.* newlywed.
casamentero (ka·sa·men'te·ro) *n.m.* matchmaker. —*adj.* matchmaking.
casamiento (ka·sa'mjen·to) *n.m.* marriage; wedding.
casar (ka'sar) *v.i.* to marry; to wed. —**casarse,** *v.r.* to marry; be or get married. —*v.t.* 1, to marry; to mate; to unite in marriage. 2, *fig.* to match; to harmonize (colors). 3, to blend (paint). —**casarse con,** to marry; to get married to. —**no casarse con nadie,** *colloq.* to get tied up with nobody.
cascabel (kas·ka'βel) *n.f.* jingle bell; tinkle. —**serpiente de cascabel** [*also, W.I.,* **cascabela** (-'βe·la) *n.f.*] rattlesnake.
cascabillo (kas·ka'βi·ʎo; -jo) *n.m.* chaff; husk; hull.
cascada (kas'ka·ða) *n.f.* cascade; waterfall.
cascado (kas'ka·ðo) *adj.* broken; burst.
cascajo (kas'ka·xo) *n.m.* 1, gravel. 2, *colloq.* rubbish. —**estar hecho un cascajo,** *colloq.* to be a wreck.
cascanueces (kas·ka'nwe·θes; -ses) *n.m.sing.* & *pl.* nutcracker.
cascar (kas'kar) *v.t.* [*pres.subjve.* **casque;** *pret.* **casqué**] 1, to crack; to break; to burst. 2, *Amer., colloq.* to beat; to wallop. —**cascarse, cascárselas,** *Amer., colloq.* to beat it.
cáscara ('kas·ka·ra) *n.f.* shell; husk; rind. —**ser de la cáscara amarga,** *colloq.* to be wild; *derog.* to be extremist.
cascarón (kas·ka'ron) *n.m.* shell; eggshell.
cascarrabias (kas·ka'rra·βjas) *n.m.sing.* & *pl., colloq.* grouch; crab.
cascarudo (kas·ka'ru·ðo) *adj.* thick-shelled; hard-shelled.
casco ('kas·ko) *n.m.* 1, skull; cranium. 2, helmet. 3, cask. 4, hoof (*of a horse, mule, etc.*). 5, *naut.* hull. 6, *colloq.* talent. —**caliente de cascos,** hot-headed. —**ligero** *or* **alegre de cascos,** frivolous. —**romperse los cascos,** to rack one's brains.
caseína (ka·se'i·na) *n.f.* casein.
casera (ka'se·ra) *n.f.* 1, landlady. 2, *Amer.* = **parroquiana.**
casería (ka·se'ri·o) *n.m.* 1, country house. 2, hamlet; village.
casero (ka'se·ro) *n.m.* 1, landlord; caretaker. 2, *Amer.* = **parroquiano.** —*adj.* 1, of the home; domestic. 2, homely; homespun. 3, *colloq.* home-loving; retiring.
caserón (ka·se'ron) *n.m.* large house.
caseta (ka'se·ta) *n.f.* small house;

cottage. —**caseta de baños,** locker; bathhouse.
casi ('ka·si) *adv.* almost; nearly.
casia ('ka·sja) *n.f.* cassia.
casilla (ka'si·ʎa; -ja) *n.f.* **1,** hut; booth. **2,** square (*on a sheet of paper; in checkers*). **3,** *Amer.* mail box (*at a residence*). **4,** ticket office. **5,** pigeonhole; cubbyhole. —**sacar de sus casillas,** *colloq.* to drive crazy. —**salirse de sus casillas,** *colloq.* to go crazy; to forget oneself.
casillero (ka·si'ʎe·ro; -'je·ro) *n.m.* **1,** filing cabinet. **2,** desk with pigeonholes.
casimir (ka·si'mir) *n.m.* cashmere.
casino (ka'si·no) *n.m.* **1,** casino. **2,** club; clubhouse.
caso ('ka·so) *n.m.* **1,** case. **2,** event; chance; occurrence. —**dado caso que,** supposing that. —**en caso (de) que,** in case that; if. —**en todo caso,** in any case; in any event. —**en tal caso,** in such an event. —**hablar al caso; ir al caso,** to get to the point. —**hacer caso a** *or* **de,** to pay attention to. —**hacer caso omiso de; no hacer caso de,** to pass over. —**caso fortuito,** mischance.
casón (ka'son) *n.m.* large house.
casorio (ka'so·rjo) *n.m., colloq.* ill-considered marriage; mismatch.
caspa ('kas·pa) *n.f.* dandruff. —**casposo,** *adj.* full of dandruff.
caspera (kas'pe·ra) *n.f.* comb for removing dandruff; fine-toothed comb.
¡cáspita! ('kas·pi·ta) *interj.* **1,** great! **2,** confound it!
casque ('kas·ke) *v., pres.subjve. of* **cascar.**
casqué (kas'ke) *v., 1st pers.sing. pret. of* **cascar.**
casquete (kas'ke·te) *n.m.* **1,** helmet. **2,** skullcap.
casquivano (kas·ki'βa·no) *adj.* frivolous.
casta ('kas·ta) *n.f.* **1,** caste; race. **2,** generation. **3,** pedigree; kind; breed.
castaña (kas'ta·ɲa) *n.f.* chestnut. —**dar a uno para castaña,** to play a trick on someone.
castañal (kas·ta'ɲal) *n.m.* chestnut grove. *Also,* **castañar** (-'ɲar).
castañeo (kas·ta'ɲe·o) *n.m.* the sound of castanets. *Also,* **castañeteado** (-te'a·ðo).
castañero (kas·ta'ɲe·ro) *n.m.* chestnut dealer.
castañeta (kas·ta'ɲe·ta) *n.f.* **1,** castanet. **2,** snapping of the fingers.
castañetear (kas·ta·ɲe·te'ar) *v.i.* **1,** to rattle castanets. **2,** to chatter (*of the teeth*). **3,** to shudder; to shiver. **4,** to crackle.
castañeteo (kas·ta·ɲe'te·o) *n.m.* **1,** the sound of castanets. **2,** chattering (*of the teeth*).
castaño (kas'ta·ɲo) *n.m.* chestnut tree, wood *or* color. —*adj.* chestnut. —**pasar de castaño oscuro,** *colloq.* to be unbearable *or* too much.
castañuela (kas·ta'ɲwe·la) *n.f.* castanet.
castellano (kas·te'ʎa·no; -'ja·no) *adj.* & *n.m.* Castilian; Spanish.
castidad (kas·ti'ðað) *n.f.* chastity; virginity.
castigar (kas·ti'ɣar) *v.t.* [*pres. subjve.* **castigue** (-'ti·ɣe) *pret.* **castigué** (-'ɣe)] to chastise; to castigate; to punish.
castigo (kas'ti·ɣo) *n.m.* punishment; chastisement; castigation.
castillo (kas'ti·ʎo; -jo) *n.m.* castle; fortress. —**castillo de proa,** forecastle. —**hacer castillos en el aire,** to build castles in Spain.
castizo (kas'ti·θo; -so) *adj.* **1,** *of* noble descent. **2,** pure (*of language*).
casto ('kas·to) *adj.* pure; chaste.
castor (kas'tor) *n.m.* **1,** beaver. **2,** *cap., astron.* Castor. **3,** [*also,* **aceite de castor**] castor oil. **4,** beaver hat.
castrado (kas'tra·ðo) *adj.* castrated. —*n.m.* eunuch.
castrar (kas'trar) *v.t.* to castrate; to geld. —**castración,** *n.f.* castration; gelding.
casual (ka'swal) *adj.* casual; fortuitous.
casualidad (ka·swa·li'ðað) *n.f.* **1,** chance; hazard. **2,** coincidence. —**por casualidad,** by chance.
casucha (ka'su·tʃa) *n.f.* hut; shack; hovel. *Also,* **casuca** (-ka).
casuista (ka·su'is·ta) *n.m.* & *f.* casuist. —*adj.* [*also,* **casuístico** (-'is·ti·ko)] casuistic. —**casuística** (-'is·ti·ka) *n.f.* casuistry.
casulla (ka'su·ʎa; -ja) *n.f.* chasuble.
cata ('ka·ta) *n.f.* **1,** tasting; sampling. **2,** taste; sample.
cata- (ka·ta) *prefix* cata-; *forming nouns and adjectives denoting* **1,** against: *catapulta,* catapult. **2,** down; downward: *catabolismo,* catabolism. **3,** completely; away: *cataclismo,* cataclysm.
catabolismo (ka·ta·βo'lis·mo)

n.m. catabolism. —**catabólico** (-'βo·li·ko) *adj.* catabolic.
cataclismo (ka·ta'klis·mo) *n.m.* cataclysm; deluge.
catacumbas (ka·ta'kum·bas) *n.f. pl.* catacombs.
catadura (ka·ta'ðu·ra) *n.f.* **1,** tasting; sampling. **2,** *colloq.* countenance.
catafalco (ka·ta'fal·ko) *n.m.* catafalque.
catalán (ka·ta'lan) *adj.* & *n.m.* Catalan; Catalonian.
catalejo (ka·ta'le·xo) *n.m.* spyglass.
catalepsia (ka·ta'lep·sja) *n.f.* catalepsy. —**cataléptico** (-'lep·ti·ko) *adj.* & *n.m.* cataleptic.
catálisis (ka'ta·li·sis) *n.m.* catalysis. —**catalítico** (-'li·ti·ko) *adj.* catalytic. —**catalizador** (-li·θa'ðor; -sa'ðor) *n.m.* catalyst.
catalogar (ka·ta·lo'ɣar) *v.t.* [*pres. subjve* **catalogue** (-'lo·ɣe); *pret.* **catalogué** (-'ɣe)] to catalogue; to list.
catálogo (ka'ta·lo·ɣo) *n.m.* catalogue; table; list.
catalpa (ka'tal·pa) *n.f.* catalpa.
cataplasma (ka·ta'plas·ma) *n.f.* **1,** poultice; mustard plaster. **2,** *fig., colloq.* nuisance; bore.
catapulta (ka·ta'pul·ta) *n.f.* catapult.
catar (ka'tar) *v.t.* to taste; to sample.
catarata (ka·ta'ra·ta) *n.f.* **1,** cataract; cascade. **2,** *med.* cataract.
catarro (ka'ta·rro) *n.m.* **1,** catarrh. **2,** cold, esp. a head cold. —**catarral,** *adj.* catarrhal. —**catarroso,** *adj.* suffering from or subject to colds.
catarsis (ka'tar·sis) *n.f.* catharsis. —**catártico** (-ti·ko) *adj.* & *n.m.* cathartic.
catástrofe (ka'tas·tro·fe) *n.f.* catastrophe. —**catastrófico** (-'tro·fi·ko) *adj.* catastrophic.
catavinos (ka·ta'βi·nos) *n.m. sing. & pl.* **1,** winetaster. **2,** *colloq.* drunkard; tippler.
catear (ka·te'ar) *v.t.* **1,** *colloq.* to flunk. **2,** *So. Amer.* to prospect. **3,** *Mex.* to break into; to search (a house).
catecismo (ka·te'θis·mo; -'sis·mo) *n.m.* catechism.
catecúmeno (ka·te'ku·me·no) *n.m.* catechumen.
cátedra ('ka·te·ðra) *n.f.* **1,** professorship. **2,** lecture room. **3,** *eccles.* cathedra. —**Cátedra del Espíritu Santo,** *n.f.* pulpit.
catedral (ka·te'ðral) *n.f.* & *adj.* cathedral.
catedrático (ka·te'ðra·ti·ko) *n.m.* professor.
categoría (ka·te·ɣo'ri·a) *n.f.* category; rank; class. —**categórico** (-'ɣo·ri·ko) *adj.* categorical.
catequista (ka·te'kis·ta) *n.m.* & *f.* catechist. —**catequístico,** *adj.* catechetical.
catequizador (ka·te·ki·θa'ðor; -sa'ðor) *n.m.* persuader.
catequizante (ka·te·ki'θan·te; -'san·te) *adj.* catechizing. —*n.m.* & *f.* catechist.
catequizar (ka·te·ki'θar; -'sar) *v.t.* [*pres.subjve* **catequice** (-'ki·θe; -se); *pret.* **catequicé** (-'θe; -'se)] **1,** to catechize **2,** *fig.* to induce; to persuade. **catequización,** *n.f.* catechizing.
catéter (ka'te·ter) *n.m.* catheter.
cateto (ka'te·to) *n.m., geom.* leg. —*adj.* & *n.m* rustic.
catión (ka'tjon) *n.m.* cation.
cátodo ('ka·to·ðo) *n.m.* cathode.
catolicismo (ka·to·li'θis·mo; -'sis·mo) *n.m* Catholicism.
católico (ka'to·li·ko) *adj.* **1,** Catholic. **2,** universal. —*n.m.* Catholic. —**catolicidad** (-θi'ðað; -si'ðað) *n.f.* catholicity.
catorce (ka'tor·θe; -se) *adj.* fourteen; fourteenth (*in dates*).
catorzavo (ka·tor'θa·βo; -'sa·βo) *adj.* & *n.m.* fourteenth.
catre ('ka·tre) *n.m.* cot. —**catre de tijera,** field cot.
catrecillo (ka·tre'θi·ʎo; -'si·jo) *n.m.* canvas stool.
catrín (ka'trin) *n.m.* fop; dandy. —*adj.* foppish; dandified.
caucásico (kau'ka·si·ko) *adj.* Caucasian.
cauce ('kau·θe; -se) *n.m.* river bed.
caución (kau'θjon; -'sjon) *n.f.* **1,** security; pledge; bond. **2,** warning; foresight.
caucho ('kau·tʃo) *n.m.* rubber.
caudal (kau'ðal) *n.m.* **1,** volume (*of fluids*). **2,** wealth; property; fortune. —*adj.* **1,** [*also,* **caudaloso**] containing water. **2,** *zool.* caudal.
caudillaje (kau·ði'ʎa·xe; -'ja·xe) *n.m.* **1,** military leadership. **2,** *Amer.* political bossism.
caudillo (kau'ði·ʎo; -jo) *n.m.* **1,**

leader; commander. 2, *Amer.* political boss.
causa ('kau·sa) *n.f.* 1, cause. 2, lawsuit. —**a causa de,** on account of.
causador (kau·sa'ðor) *adj.* causing. —*n.m.* one who causes; agent.
causal (kau'sal) *adj., gram.* causal. —*n.f.* ground; reason; motive.
causalidad (kau·sa·li'ðað) *n.f.* causality.
causar (kau'sar) *v.t.* to cause; produce.
cáustico ('kaus·ti·ko) *adj.* & *n.m.* caustic.
cautela (kau'te·la) *n.f.* 1, caution; prudence. 2, craftiness. —**cauteloso,** *adj.* cautious; wary.
cautelar (kau·te'lar) *v.t.* to prevent. —*v.i.* to proceed prudently; to take necessary precautions.
cauterizar (kau·te·ri'θar; -'sar) *v.t.* [*pres.subjve.* **cauterice** (-'ri·θe; -se); *pret.* **cautericé** (-'θe; -'se)] to cauterize. —**cauterización,** *n.f.* cauterization. —**cauterizador,** *n.m.* cauterizer. —**cauterizante,** *adj.* cauterizing.
cautivar (kau·ti'βar) *v.t.* to captivate; to charm.
cautiverio (kau·ti'βe·rjo) *n.m.* captivity; confinement. *Also,* **cautividad** (-βi'ðað) *n.f.*
cautivo (kau'ti·βo) *adj.* & *n.m.* captive.
cauto ('kau·to) *adj.* cautious.
cavado (ka'βa·ðo) *adj.* hollowed; excavated.
cavador (ka·βa'ðor) *n.m.* digger; sandhog.
cavadura (ka·βa'ðu·ra) *n.f.* digging.
cavar (ka'βar) *v.t.* to dig; to excavate. —*v.i.* to penetrate far; to dig.
caverna (ka'βer·na) *n.f.* cavern; cave. —**cavernoso,** *adj.* cavernous.
cavernícola (ka·βer'ni·ko·la) *adj.* cave-dwelling. —*n.m.* & *f.* cave man; cave woman.
caviar (ka'βjar) *also,* **cavial** (-'βjal) *n.m.* caviar.
cavidad (ka·βi'ðað) *n.f.* cavity.
cavilar (ka·βi'lar) *v.i.* to muse; ruminate.
cayado (ka'ja·ðo) *n.m. also,* **cayada** (-ða) *n.f.* 1, shepherd's crook. 2, walking stick. 3, *eccles.* crozier.
cayo ('ka·jo) *n.m.* island reef; key.
cayó (ka'jo) *v., 3rd pers.sing. pret. of* **caer.**
caz (kaθ; kas) *n.m.* 1, canal; ditch. 2, channel of a stream. 3, millrace.
caza ('ka·θa; -sa) *n.f.* 1, chase; hunt; hunting. 2, pursuit. —*n.m., aero.* pursuit plane. —**dar caza (a un empleo),** to pursue (a job).
cazabe (ka'θa·βe; -'sa·βe) *n.m.* cassava.
cazador (ka·θa'ðor; ka·sa-) *n.m.* hunter. —*adj.* hunting. —**cazadores,** *n.m.pl.* light infantry.
cazaperros (ka·θa·pe'rros; ka·sa-) *n.m.sing.* & *pl.* dogcatcher.
cazar (ka'θar; -'sar) *v.t.* [*pres. subjve.* **cace;** *pret.* **cacé**] to chase; to hunt. —**cazar moscas,** *colloq.* to dawdle.
cazatorpedero (ka·θa·tor·pe·'ðe·ro; ka·sa-) *n.m.* destroyer.
cazo ('ka·θo; -so) *n.m.* dipper; ladle.
cazón (ka'θon; -'son) *n.m.* dogfish.
cazuela (ka'θwe·la; ka'swe-) *n.f.* 1, stewpan. 2, theater gallery.
cea ('θe·a; 'se·a) *n.f.* = **cía.**
ceba ('θe·βa; 'se-) *n.f.* fattening (*of animals*).
cebada (θe'βa·ða; se-) *n.f.* barley.
cebadero (θe·βa'ðe·ro; se-) *n.m.* 1, feeding place (*for animals*). 2, breeder of hawks. 3, barley dealer.
cebado (θe'βa·ðo; se-) *adj.* fattened; fed.
cebar (θe'βar; se-) *v.t.* 1, to feed; to fatten (animals). 2, to encourage (a passion). 3, to bait (a fishhook). 4, to prime (arms). 5, *fig.* to penetrate. —**cebarse,** *v.r.* to rage.
cebellina (θe·βe'ʎi·na; se·βe'ji-) *n.f.* sable.
cebo ('θe·βo; 'se-) *n.m.* 1, fodder. 2, primer; priming (*of firearms*). 3, incentive; lure.
cebolla (θe'βo·ʎa; se'βo·ja) *n.f.* onion. —**cebollar,** *n.m.* onion patch.
cebollina (θe·βo'ʎi·na; se·βo'ji-) *n.f.* chive. *Also,* **cebollino,** *n.m.*
cebón (θe'βon; se-) *n.m.* fattened hog. —*adj.* fattened (*of animals*).
cebra ('θe·βra; 'se-) *n.f.* zebra. —**cebrado,** *adj.* having zebra-like stripes.
cebú (θe'βu; se-) *n.m.* zebu.
ceca ('θe·ka; 'se-) *n.f., in:* **de ceca en meca; de la ceca a la meca,** to and fro.
cecear (θe·θe'ar; se·se-) *v.i.* 1, to

lisp. 2, (θe·θe'ar) to pronounce z and c as θ before e or i.

ceceo (θe'θe·o; se'se-) *n.m.* 1, lisping. 2, pronunciation as (θ) of z and of c before e or i. —**ceceoso,** *n.m.* lisper. —*adj.* lisping.

cecina (θe'θi·na; se'si-) *n.f.* dried beef; jerked beef.

cecografía (θe·ko·ɣra'fi·a; se-) *n.f.* Braille. —**cecográfico** (-'ɣra·fi·ko) *adj.* of or in Braille. —**cecógrafo** (-'ko·ɣra·fo) *n.m.* Braille writer.

cedazo (θe'ða·θo; se'ða·so) *n.m.* sieve.

cedente (θe'ðen·te; se-) *adj.* granting; transferring. —*n.m.* grantor; transferrer.

ceder (θe'ðer; se-) *v.t.* 1, to yield; cede; grant. 2, to convey; transfer. —*v.i.* 1, to yield; give in; give way. 2, to diminish; abate. —**ceder el paso,** to make way; step aside.

cedilla (θe'ði·ʎa; se'ði·ja) *n.f.* cedilla.

cedro ('θe·ðro; 'se-) *n.m.* cedar.

cédula ('θe·ðu·la; 'se-) *n.f.* 1, certificate; permit. 2, government order; decree. —**cédula de vecindad; cédula personal,** identification papers.

cefálico (θe'fa·li·ko; se-) *adj.* cephalic.

cefalópodo (θe·fa'lo·po·ðo; se-) *adj.* & *n.m.* cephalopod.

céfiro ('θe·fi·ro; 'se-) *n.m.* zephyr.

cegajoso (θe·ɣa'xo·so; se-) *adj.* bleary-eyed.

cegar (θe'ɣar; se-) *v.i.* [*pres.ind.* **ciego;** *pres.subjve.* **ciegue;** *pret.* **cegué** (-'ɣe)] to grow blind; to become blind. —*v.t.* 1, to blind. 2, to block; to close up (an opening).

cegato (θe'ɣa·to; se-) *adj.* dimsighted; shortsighted. *Also,* **cegatón.**

ceguedad (θe·ɣe'ðað; se-) *n.f.* 1, blindness. 2, *fig.* ignorance.

ceguera (θe'ɣe·ra; se-) *n.f.* total blindness.

ceiba ('θei·βa; 'sei-) *n.f.* a tropical tree. —**algodón de ceiba,** kapok.

ceja ('θe·xa; 'se-) *n.f.* 1, eyebrow. 2, edge (*of clothes, books, etc.*). —**hasta las cejas,** to the utmost. —**quemarse las cejas,** to burn the midnight oil. —**tener entre ceja y ceja,** 1, *fol. by inf.* to have a yearning for (doing something). 2, to have a strong dislike for (a person).

cejar (θe'xar; se-) *v.i.* 1, to go back; to step back. 2, to desist; to give in; to yield.

celada (θe'la·ða; se-) *n.f.* 1, helmet. 2, ambush. 3, artful trick.

celador (θe·la'ðor; se-) *n.m.* watcher; caretaker. —*adj.* vigilant.

celaje (θe'la·xe; se-) *n.m.* 1, skylight. 2, *usu.pl.* sky with many-hued clouds.

celar (θe'lar; se-) *v.t.* 1, to watch over; to keep an eye on. 2, to conceal; to cover; to hide.

celda ('θel·da; 'sel-) *n.f.* cell.

celdilla (θel'di·ʎa; sel'di·ja) *n.f.* cell.

celebérrimo (θe·le'βe·rri·mo; se-) *adj., superl. of* **célebre.**

celebración (θe·le·βra'θjon; se·le·βra'sjon) *n.f.* celebration.

celebrante (θe·le'βran·te; se-) *n.m.* celebrant. —*adj.* celebrating.

celebrar (θe·le'βrar; se-) *v.t.* 1, to celebrate. 2, to praise; to honor. 3, to hold (a conference, meeting, etc.). 4, to rejoice.

célebre ('θe·le·βre; 'se-) *adj.* 1, celebrated; famous; known. 2, *colloq.* gay; funny.

celebridad (θe·le·βri'ðað; se-) *n.f.* 1, celebrity; fame. 2, celebration; pageant.

celeridad (θe·le·ri'ðað; se-) *n.f.* celerity; speed.

celerímetro (θe·le'ri·me·tro; se-) *n.m.* speedometer.

celeste (θe'les·te; se-) *adj.* 1, skyblue. 2, celestial.

celestial (θe·les'tjal; se-) *adj.* celestial.

celestina (θe·les'ti·na; se-) *n.m.* 1, *mineralogy* celestine; celestite. 2, procuress.

célibe ('θe·li·βe; 'se-) *adj.* & *n.m.* celibate; bachelor. —**celibato** (-'βa·to) *n.m.* celibacy; bachelorhood.

celo ('θe·lo; 'se-) *n.m.* 1, zeal; ardor. 2, envy. 3, heat; rut (*of animals*). —**celos,** *n.m.pl.* 1, jealousy. 2, suspicions. —**dar celos a,** to make jealous. —**tener celos,** to be jealous.

celofana (θe·lo'fa·na; se-) *n.f.* cellophane. *Also,* **celofán** (-'fan) *n.m.*

celosía (θe·lo'si·a; se-) *n.f.* 1, lattice. 2, Venetian blind. 3, jalousie.

celoso (θe'lo·so; se-) *adj.* 1, zealous. 2, jealous. 3, suspicious.

celta ('θel·ta; 'sel-) *n.m.* & *f.* Celt. —*adj.* Celtic. —*n.m.* Celtic (*language*).

céltico ('θel·ti·ko; 'sel-) *adj.* Celtic.
célula ('θe·lu·la; 'se-) *n.f., bot.; zool.* cell. —**celular,** *adj.* cellular.
celuloide (θe·lu'loi·ðe; se-) *n.m.* celluloid.
celulosa (θe·lu'lo·sa; se-) *n.f.* cellulose.
celuloso (θe·lu'lo·so; se-) *adj.* cellulous.
cellisca (θe'ʎis·ka; se'jis-) *n.f.* sleet. —**cellisquear** (-ke'ar) *v.i.* to sleet.
cementar (θe·men'tar; se-) *v.t.* **1,** to cement. **2,** *mining* to precipitate.
cementerio (θe·men'te·rjo; se-) *n.m.* cemetery; graveyard.
cemento (θe'men·to; se-) *n.m.* cement.
cena ('θe·na; 'se-) *n.f.* supper; evening meal.
cenadero (θe·na'ðe·ro; se-) *n.m.* **1,** supper room. **2,** summerhouse.
cenador (θe·na'ðor; se-) *n.m.* arbor; summerhouse.
cenagal (θe·na'ɣal; se-) *n.m.* bog.
cenagoso (θe·na'ɣo·so; se-) *adj.* marshy.
cenar (θe'nar; se-) *v.t.* to eat (something) for supper; to sup on. —*v.i.* to sup; to have supper.
cenceño (θen'θe·ɲo; sen'se-) *adj.* lean; thin.
cencerrada (θen·θe'rra·ða; sen·se-) *n.f.* tin-pan serenade.
cencerrear (θen·θe·rre'ar; sen·se-) *v.i.* **1,** to tinkle, as a cowbell. **2,** to jangle; clank.
cencerro (θen'θe·rro; sen'se-) *n.m.* cowbell.
cendal (θen'dal; sen-) *n.m.* gauze.
cenefa (θe'ne·fa; se-) *n.f.* border; edging; trim.
cenicero (θe·ni'θe·ro; se·ni'se-) *n.m.* **1,** ash tray. **2,** ash pit; ash bin.
Cenicienta (θe·ni'θjen·ta; se·ni·'sjen-) *n.f.* Cinderella.
ceniciento (θe·ni'θjen·to; se·ni·'sjen-) *adj.* ashen; ash-colored.
cénit ('θe·nit; 'se-) *n.m.* zenith.
ceniza (θe'ni·θa; se'ni-sa) *n.f.* ash; ashes. —**cenizas,** *n.f.pl.* remains (*of a dead person*). —**huir de la ceniza, caer en las brasas,** to go from the frying pan into the fire.
cenizo (θe'ni·θo; se'ni·so) *adj.* ashen; ash-colored. —*n.m., colloq.* jinx.
ceno- (θe·no; se-) *prefix* **1,** ceno-; coeno-; common: *cenobita,* cenobite; coenobite. **2,** ceno-; new; recent: *cenozoico,* Cenozoic.
-ceno ('θe·no; 'se-) *suffix* -cene; recent; new: *mioceno,* Miocene.
cenotafio (θe·no'ta·fjo; se-) *n.m.* cenotaph.
censo ('θen·so; 'sen-) *n.m.* **1,** census. **2,** *law* rent. **3,** *fig.* burden; charge. —**censor** (-'sor) *n.m.* censor. —**censorio** (-'so·rjo) *adj.* censorial.
censura (θen'su·ra; sen-) *n.f.* **1,** censorship. **2,** office of censor. **3,** censure; critical review.
censurable (θen·su'ra·βle; sen-) *adj.* censurable.
censurador (θen·su·ra'ðor; sen-) *adj.* censorious. —*n.m.* censurer.
censurar (θen·su'rar; sen-) *v.t.* **1,** to censure. **2,** to review; to judge.
cent- (θent; sent) *prefix, var. of* **centi-** *before vowels: centenario,* centennial.
centauro (θen'tau·ro; sen-) *n.m.* centaur.
centavo (θen'ta·βo; sen-) *adj.* hundredth. —*n.m.* **1,** hundredth part. **2,** *U.S.* cent.
centella (θen'te·ʎa; sen'te·ja) *n.f.* flash; spark.
centellar (θen·te'ʎar; sen·te'jar) *also,* **centellear** (-ʎe'ar; -je'ar) *v.i.* to flash; sparkle. —**centelleo** (-'ʎe·o; -'je·o) *n.m.* flash; sparkle.
centena (θen'te·na; sen-) *n.f.* hundred; quantity of a hundred.
centenada (θen·te'na·ða; sen-) *n.f.* quantity of about a hundred. —**a centenadas,** by hundreds.
centenar (θen·te'nar; sen-) *n.m.* hundred; quantity of a hundred. —**a centenares,** by hundreds.
centenario (θen·te'na·rjo; sen-) *n.m. & adj.* centenary; centenarian; centennial.
centeno (θen'te·no; sen-) *adj.* hundredth. —*n.m.* rye.
centésimo (θen'te·si·mo; sen-) *adj. & n.m.* hundredth; centesimal.
centi- (θen·ti; sen-) *prefix* centi-; hundred; hundredth: *centígrado,* centigrade; *centímetro,* centimeter.
centiárea (θen·ti'a·re·a; sen-) *n.f.* centiare.
centigrado (θen'ti·ɣra·ðo; sen-) *adj.* centigrade.
centigramo (θen·ti'ɣra·mo; sen-) *n.m.* centigram.
centilitro (θen·ti'li·tro; sen-) *n.m.* centiliter.

centímetro (θen'ti·me·tro; sen-) *n.m.* centimeter.
céntimo ('θen·ti·mo; 'sen-) *adj.* & *n.m.* hundredth. —*n.m.* cent; centime; hundredth part of various monetary units.
centinela (θen·ti'ne·la; sen-) *n.m.* & *f.* sentry; guard. —**estar de centinela; hacer de centinela,** to be on guard duty; to keep watch.
centón (θen'ton; sen-) *n.m.* crazy quilt.
central (θen'tral; sen-) *adj.* central. —*n.f.* **1,** main office; headquarters. **2,** powerhouse. —**central telefónica,** telephone exchange.
centralizar (θen·tra·li'θar; sen·tra·li'sar) *v.t.* [*pres.subjve.* **centralice** (-'li·θe; -'li·se); *pret.* **centralicé** (-'θe; -'se)] to centralize. —**centralización,** *n.f.* centralization.
centrar (θen'trar; sen-) *v.t.* to center. —**centrarse,** *v.r.* to center; be centered.
centri- (θen·tri; sen-) *prefix, var. of* **centro-**: *centrífugo,* centrifugal.
céntrico ('θen·tri·ko; 'sen-) *adj.* central.
centrífugo (θen'tri·fu·ɣo; sen-) *adj.* centrifugal. —**centrífuga,** *n.f.* centrifuge.
centrípeto (θen'tri·pe·to; sen-) *adj.* centripetal.
centro ('θen·tro; 'sen-) *n.m.* **1,** center; middle. **2,** hub; nucleus. **3,** headquarters; club. **4,** midtown.
centro- (θen·tro; sen-) *prefix* centro-; center; central: *centrosoma,* centrosome; *centrobárico,* centrobaric.
centroamericano *adj.* & *n.m.* Central American.
centuplicar (θen·tu·pli'kar; sen-) *v.t.* & *v.i.* [*pres.subjve.* **centuplique** (-'pli·ke); *pret.* **centupliqué** (-'ke)] to centuple.
céntuplo ('θen·tu·plo; 'sen-) *n.m.* hundredfold. —*adj.* centuple.
centuria (θen'tu·rja; sen-) *n.f.* century.
centurio (θen'tu·rjo; sen-) *n.m.* centurium.
centurión (θen·tu'rjon; sen-) *n.m.* centurion.
ceñido (θe'ɲi·ðo; se-) *adj.* **1,** moderate. **2,** tight; close-fitting.
ceñidor (θe·ɲi'ðor; se-) *n.m.* **1,** belt; sash. **2,** girdle.
ceñidura (θe·ɲi'ðu·ra; se-) *n.f.* **1,** act of girding. **2,** *fig.* contraction; reduction.
ceñir (θe'ɲir; se-) *v.t.* [*pres.ind.* **ciño;** *pres.subjve.* **ciña;** *pret.* **ceñí** (-'ɲi), **ciñó**] **1,** to gird; to girdle. **2,** to surround. **3,** *fig.* to reduce; to contract. —**ceñirse,** *v.r.* to limit oneself.
ceño ('θe·ɲo; 'se-) *n.m.* **1,** frown; scowl. **2,** countenance. **3,** brow. —**ceñudo,** *adj.* frowning.
cepa ('θe·pa; 'se-) *n.f.* **1,** stump; stub (*of a tree*). **2,** origin; stock (*of a family*).
cepilladura (θe·pi·ʎa'ðu·ra; se·pi·ja-) *n.f.* planing. —**cepilladuras,** *n.f.pl.* shavings.
cepillar (θe·pi'ʎar; se·pi'jar) *v.t.* **1,** to brush. **2,** to plane.
cepillo (θe'pi·ʎo; se'pi·jo) *n.m.* **1,** brush. **2,** plane. **3,** alms box.
cepo ('θe·po; 'se-) *n.m.* **1,** branch (*of a tree*). **2,** trap; snare (*for animals*). **3,** stocks (*instrument of punishment*). —**¡cepos quedos!,** *colloq.* cut it out!; enough!
cera ('θe·ra; 'se-) *n.f.* wax.
cerámico (θe'ra·mi·ko; se-) *adj.* ceramic; of or pert. to ceramics. —**cerámica,** *n.f.* ceramics.
cerbatana (θer·βa'ta·na; ser-) *n.f.* blowgun; popgun; peashooter.
cerca ('θer·ka; 'ser-) *n.f.* enclosure; fence. —**cercas** *n.m.pl.* foreground (*of paintings*). —*adv.* near; close. —**cerca de,** near, about. —**de cerca,** close by. —**en cerca,** roundabout.
cercado (θer'ka·ðo; ser-) *adj.* enclosed; fenced in. —*n.m.* enclosure; fence.
cercador (θer·ka'ðor; ser-) *n.m.* **1,** enclosure. **2,** repoussé chisel. —*adj.* enclosing.
cercanía (θer·ka'ni·a; ser-) *n.f.* proximity. —**cercanías,** *n.f.pl.* surroundings; vicinity.
cercano (θer'ka·no; ser-) *adj.* near; neighboring.
cercar (θer'kar; ser-) *v.t.* [*pres. subjve.* **cerque;** *pret.* **cerqué**] **1,** to fence; to enclose; to encircle. **2,** *mil.* to besiege.
cercenadura (θer·θe·na'ðu·ra; ser·se-) *n.f.* clipping. —**cercenaduras,** *n.f.pl.* cuttings.
cercenar (θer·θe'nar; ser·se-) *v.t.* **1,** to pare; to clip off. **2,** to curtail; to reduce.
cerceta (θer'θe·ta; ser'se-) *n.f.* widgeon.
cerciorar (θer·θjo'rar; ser·sjo-) *v.t.* to assure; to affirm. —**cercio-**

rarse, *v.r.* to ascertain; to make sure.

cerco ('θer·ko; 'ser-) *n.m.* 1, hoop; ring; rim. 2, border; edge. 3, siege. 4, frame (*of a door*).

cerda ('θer·ða; 'ser-) *n.f.* 1, bristle; horsehair. 2, sow.

cerdear (θer·ðe'ar; ser-) *v.i.* 1, to totter; to stumble in the forelegs. 2, to rasp; to scrape roughly.

cerdo ('θer·ðo; 'ser-) *n.m.* hog; pig.

cerdoso (θer'ðo·so; ser-) *adj.* bristly.

cerdudo (θer'ðu·ðo; ser-) *adj.* 1, bristly. 2, hairy; hirsute.

cereal (θe·re'al; se-) *adj.* & *n.m.* cereal.

cerebelo (θe·re'βe·lo; se-) *n.m.* cerebellum.

cerebro (θe're·βro; se-) *n.m.* 1, cerebrum. 2, brain. 3, *fig.* brains; talent; skill. —**cerebral** (-'βral) *adj.* cerebral.

cerebro- (θe're·βro-; se-) *prefix* cerebro-; brain; mind: *cerebroespinal,* cerebrospinal.

ceremonia (θe·re'mo·nja; se-) *n.f.* ceremony.

ceremonial (θe·re·mo'njal; se-) *adj.* ceremonial. —*n.m.* book of ceremonies. —**ceremonioso** (-'njo·so) *adj.* ceremonious.

cerero (θe're·ro; se-) *n.m.* candlemaker.

cereza (θe're·θa; se're·sa) *n.f.* cherry. —**cerezo,** *n.m.* cherry tree. —**cerezal,** *n.m.* cherry orchard.

cerguillo (θer'ɣi·ʎo; ser'ɣi·jo) *n.m.* 1, small circle; small hoop. 2, seam; welt (*of a shoe*).

cerilla (θe'ri·ʎa; se'ri·ja) *n.f.* 1, wax match; *colloq.* match. 2, cerumen; earwax. 3, wax taper.

cerillo (θe'ri·ʎo; se'ri·jo) *n.m., Amer.* wax match; match.

cerio ('θe·rjo; 'se-) *n.m.* cerium.

cernada (θer'na·ða; ser-) *n.f.* 1, cinder. 2, glue size; priming.

cernedor (θer·ne'ðor; ser-) *n.m.* sifter.

cerner (θer'ner; ser-) *v.t.* [*pres.ind.* **cierno;** *pres.subjve.* **cierna**] 1, to sift; to bolt. 2, *fig.* to refine. —*v.i.* 1, to blossom; to bud. 2, *fig.* to drizzle. —**cernerse,** *v.r.* 1, to hover. 2, to be imminent; to impend; to threaten.

cernido (θer'ni·ðo; ser-) *adj.* sifted. —*n.m.* sifting.

cernir (θer'nir; ser-) *v.t.* & *i.* = cerner.

cero ('θe·ro; 'se-) *n.m.* zero; naught. —**ser un cero a la izquierda,** to be of no account.

ceroso (θe'ro·so; se-) *adj.* waxen; waxy.

cerque ('θer·ke; 'ser-) *v., pres. subjve. of* **cercar.**

cerqué (θer'ke; ser-) *v., 1st pers. sing. pret. of* **cercar.**

cerquita (θer'ki·ta; ser-) *n.f.* enclosure; fence. —*adv.* at a small distance. —**aquí cerquita,** just by.

cerradera (θe·rra'ðe·ra; se-) *n.f.* lock; clasp. —**echar la cerradera,** to turn a deaf ear.

cerradero (θe·rra'ðe·ro; se-) *adj.* of or pert. to a lock, or a thing or place that is locked. —*n.m.* 1, lock; bolt; clasp. 2, catch (*of a lock*). 3, purse strings.

cerradizo (θe·rra'ði·θo; se·rra·'ði·so) *adj.* that may be locked.

cerrado (θe'rra·ðo; se-) *adj.* 1, closed. 2, secretive; concealed. 3, reserved. 4, *anat.* ductless. —*n.m.* fence; enclosure.

cerrador (θe·rra'ðor; se-) *n.m.* 1, locker; lock. 2, shutter.

cerradura (θe·rra'ðu·ra; se-) *n.f.* 1, closure. 2, lock. —**cerradura de golpe** *or* **muelle,** spring lock.

cerraja (θe'rra·xa; se-) *n.f.* lock.

cerrajería (θe·rra·xe'ri·a; se-) *n.f.* 1, locksmith's trade; locksmith's store. 2, light ironwork.

cerrajero (θe·rra'xe·ro; se-) *n.m.* locksmith.

cerrar (θe'rrar; se-) *v.t.* [*pres.ind.* **cierro;** *pres.subjve.* **cierre**] 1, to lock; to close; to fasten. 2, to clench (the fist). 3, to fence in; to enclose. 4, to be stubborn in; to persist in. —**cerrarse,** *v.r.* 1, to remain firm in an opinion. 2, to grow cloudy. 3, to be shut up. 4, to heal.

cerrazón (θe·rra'θon; se·rra'son) *n.m.* gathering storm clouds; blackening of the sky.

cerrero (θe'rre·ro; se-) *adj.* untamed (*of animals*); rude; rough (*of persons*).

cerril (θe'rril; se-) *adj.* 1, wild; untamed. 2, rude; boorish.

cerrillar (θe·rri'ʎar; se·rri'jar) *v.t.* to knurl.

cerrión (θe'rrjon; se-) *n.m.* icicle.

cerro ('θe·rro; 'se-) *n.m.* 1, hill. 2, neck (*of animals*); backbone. —**por**

los cerros de Ubeda, *colloq.* off the track.
cerrojo (θe'rro·xo; se-) *n.m.* bolt; latch.
certamen (θer'ta·men; ser-) *n.m.* contest.
certero (θer'te·ro; ser-) *adj.* well-aimed; sharp.
certeza (θer'te·θa; ser'te·sa) *n.f.* certainty, assurance.
certidumbre (θer·ti'ðum·bre; ser-) *n.f.* = **certeza.**
certificación (θer·ti·fi·ka'θjon; ser·ti·fi·ka'sjon) *n.f.* **1,** certificate. **2,** certification.
certificado (θer·ti·fi'ka·ðo; ser-) *n.m.* **1,** certification. **2,** certificate; affidavit. —*adj.* **1,** certified. **2,** registered (*mail*).
certificar (θer·ti·fi'kar; ser-) *v.t.* [*pres.subjve* **certifique** (-'fi·ke); *pret.* **certifiqué** (-'ke)] **1,** to certify. **2,** to register (*mail*).
certísimo (θer'ti·si·mo; ser-) *adj., superl. of* **cierto.**
certitud (θer·ti'tuð; ser-) *n.f.* = **certeza.**
cerúleo (θe'ru·le·o; se-) *adj.* cerulean.
cerumen (θe'ru·men; se-) *n.m.* cerumen; earwax.
cerval (θer'βal; ser-) *adj.* = **cervino.**
cervato (θer'βa·to; ser-) *n.m.* fawn.
cervecería (θer·βe·θe'ri·a; ser·βe·se-) *n.f.* **1,** brewery. **2,** *colloq.* saloon; tavern.
cervecero (θer·βe'θe·ro; ser·βe·'se-) *n.m.* **1,** brewer. **2,** beer dealer. —*adj.* pert. to beer.
cerveza (θer'βe·θa; ser'βe·sa) *n.f.* beer.
cervical (θer·βi'kal; ser-) *adj.* cervical.
cervino (θer'βi·no; ser-) *adj.* deer-like; cervine.
cerviz (θer'βiθ; ser'βis) *n.f.* **1,** cervix. **2,** nape.
cesación (θe·sa'θjon; se·sa'sjon) *n.f.* cessation; suspension. *Also,* **cesamiento** (-'mjen·to) *n.m.*
cesante (θe'san·te; se-) *n.m.* **1,** dismissed employee. **2,** unemployed person.
cesantía (θe·san'ti·a; se-) *n.f.* **1,** unemployment. **2,** unemployment compensation. **3,** dismissal.
cesar (θe'sar; se-) *v.i.* to cease; to stop; to discontinue.
cesáreo (θe'sa·re·o; se-) *adj.* imperial; Caesarean. —**operación cesárea,** Caesarean operation.
cese ('θe·se; 'se·se) *n.m.* cessation; stoppage, esp of wages or pension.
cesio ('θe·sjo, 'se-) *n.m.* cesium.
cesión (θe'sjon, se-) *n.f.* **1,** cession. **2,** transfer conveyance. —**cesionario,** *n.m.* grantee. —**cesionista** *n.m.* & *f.* grantor.
césped ('θes·peð; 'ses-) *n.m.* lawn; turf, grass.
cesta ('θes·ta; 'ses-) *n.f.* basket.
cestería (θes·te'ri·a; ses-) *n.f.* basketwork. basketry; wickerwork.
cesto ('θes·to; 'ses-) *n.m.* **1,** basket. **2,** hamper.
cesura (θe'su·ra; se-) *n.f.* caesura.
cetáceo (θe'ta·θe·o; se'ta·se·o) *adj.* cetaceous. —*n.m.* cetacean.
cetona (θe'to·na, se-) *n.f.* ketone.
cetrería (θe·tre'ri·a; se-) *n.f.* falconry; hawking.
cetrino (θe'tri·no; se-) *adj.* **1,** lemon-colored. **2,** *fig.* melancholic; gloomy.
cetro ('θe·tro; 'se-) *n.m.* **1,** scepter. **2,** *fig.* reign; throne (*of a king*). **3,** perch; roost.
cía ('θi·a; 'si-) *n.f.* **1,** hipbone. **2,** *naut.* sternway.
-cia (θja, sja) *suffix* -cy; *forming nouns denoting* **1,** qualities; abstract entities: *conveniencia,* expediency; *democracia,* democracy. **2,** arts; professions: *nigromancia,* necromancy.
cianógeno (θja'no·xe·no; sja-) *n.m.* cyanogen.
cianosis (θja'no·sis; sja-) *n.f.* cyanosis.
cianuro (θja'nu·ro; sja-) *n.m.* cyanide.
ciática ('θja·ti·ka; 'sja-) *n.f.* sciatica.
cicatero (θi·ka'te·ro; si-) *adj.* miserly; stingy. —*n.m.* miser.
cicatriz (θi·ka'triθ; si·ka'tris) *n.f.* scar.
cicatrizar (θi·ka·tri'θar; si·ka·tri'sar) v.t. [*pres.subjve.* **cicatrice** (-'tri·θe; -se) *pret.* **cicatricé** (-'θe; -'se)] to heal.
cícero ('θi·θe·ro; 'si·se-) *n.m., typog.* pica.
cicerone (θi·θe'ro·ne; si·se-) *n.m.* guide; cicerone.
cíclico ('θi·kli·ko; 'si-) *adj.* cyclical.
ciclismo (θi'klis·mo; si-) *n.m.* cycling.

ciclista (θiˈklis·ta; si-) *n.m. & f.* cyclist.

ciclo (ˈθi·klo; ˈsi-) *n.m.* cycle.

ciclo- (θi·klo; si-) *prefix* cyclo-; circle; circular: *ciclorama,* cyclorama.

cicloide (θiˈkloi·ðe; si-) *n.f.* cycloid. —**cicloidal** *also,* **cicloideo** (-ˈðe·o) *adj.* cycloid; cycloidal.

ciclón (θiˈklon; si-) *n.m.* hurricane; cyclone.

ciclonal (θi·kloˈnal; si-) *adj.* cyclonic. *Also,* **ciclónico** (-ˈklo·ni·ko).

Ciclope (ˈθi·klo·pe; ˈsi-) *also,* **Ciclope** (-ˈklo·pe) *n.m.* Cyclops. —**ciclópeo** (-ˈklo·pe·o) *adj.* Cyclopean.

ciclorama (θi·kloˈra·ma; si-) *n.m.* cyclorama.

ciclotrón (θi·kloˈtron; si-) *n.m.* cyclotron.

-cico (ˈθi·ko; ˈsi-), *fem.* **-cica** (-ka) *suffix, var. of* **-ico;** *forming diminutives: corazoncico,* little heart; *mujercica,* little woman; young woman.

cicuta (θiˈku·ta; si-) *n.f.* hemlock (*herb; poison*).

cid (θið. sið) *n.m.* hero; chief. —**el Cid Campeador,** Rodrigo Díaz de Vivar, Spain's national hero.

-cida (ˈθi·ða; ˈsi-) *suffix* **1,** -cide; *forming nouns denoting* killer; agent that kills *insecticida* insecticide. **2,** -cidal; *forming adjectives denoting* relation to killing: *homicida,* homicidal.

-cidio (ˈθi·ðjo; ˈsi-) *suffix* -cide; *forming nouns denoting* act of killing: *homicidio,* homicide.

cidra (ˈθi·ðra; ˈsi-) *n.f.* citron.

cidro (ˈθi·ðro; ˈsi-) *n.m.* **1,** citron tree. **2,** citrus.

cidronela (θi·ðroˈne·la; si-) *n.f.* balm.

ciego (ˈθje·ɣo; ˈsje-) *adj.* **1,** blind. **2,** closed; blocked. **3,** without exit.

ciego (ˈθje·ɣo; ˈsje-) *v., pres.ind. of* **cegar.**

ciegue (ˈθje·ɣe; ˈsje-) *v., pres. subjve. of* **cegar.**

cielito (θjeˈli·to; sje-) *n.m.* **1,** a So. Amer. dance. **2,** sweetheart.

cielo (ˈθje·lo; ˈsje-) *n.m.* **1,** sky; firmament; heaven. **2,** God; the supreme power. **3,** glory; Paradise; felicity. **4,** roof (*of the mouth*). **5,** canopy. —**cielo raso,** ceiling; flat ceiling. —**cielo de mi vida,** my dear; my darling. —**¡cielo santo!; ¡cielos santos!** good heavens! —**dormir a cielo raso,** to sleep outdoors.

ciempiés (θjemˈpjes, sjem-) *n.m. sing. & pl* centipede.

cien (θjen. sjen) *adj.* hundred.

ciénaga (ˈθje·na·ɣa; ˈsje-) *n.f.* marsh.

ciencia (ˈθjen·θja; ˈsjen·sja) *n.f.* **1,** science **2,** knowledge. —**a ciencia cierta,** knowingly.

cienmilésimo *adj. & n.m.* hundred-thousandth.

cienmillonésimo *adj. & n.m.* hundred-millionth.

cieno (ˈθje·no; ˈsje-) *n.m.* mud; slime.

científico (θjenˈti·fi·ko; sjen-) *adj.* scientific —*n.m* scientist.

ciento (ˈθjen·to ˈsjen-) *adj. & n.m.* hundred —**por ciento,** percent.

cierna (ˈθjer·na, ˈsjer-) *v., pres. subjve. of* **cerner.**

cierne (ˈθjer·ne; ˈsjer-) *n.m.* blossoming, flowering —**en cierne, 1,** in an early stage **2,** in the offing. **3,** hanging, pending.

cierno (ˈθjer·no; ˈsjer-) *v., pres. ind. of* **cerner.**

cierre (ˈθje·rre; ˈsje-) *n.m.* **1,** closing; locking **2,** snap; clasp. **3,** plug (*of a valve*); lock. —**cierre de seguridad** safety lock. —**cierre relámpago; cierre de corredera,** zipper.

cierre *v., pres.subjve. of* **cerrar.**

cierro (ˈθje·rro; ˈsje-) *n.m., So. Amer.* enclosure.

cierro (ˈθje·rro; ˈsje-) *v., pres.ind. of* **cerrar.**

cierto (ˈθjer·to; ˈsjer-) *adj.* certain; sure; doubtless —*adv.* surely.

cierva (ˈθjer·βa; ˈsjer-) *n.f.* doe. —**ciervo,** *n.m* deer.

cifra (ˈθi·fra; ˈsi-) *n.f.* **1,** cipher; number. **2,** cipher, code. **3,** sum. —**en cifra,** briefly, in short.

cifrar (θiˈfrar; si-) *v.t.* **1,** to cipher. **2,** *fig.* to abridge - **cifrador,** *n.m.* cipherer. —*adj.* ciphering. —**cifrar la esperanza en,** pin one's hopes on.

cigarra (θiˈɣa·rra; si-) *n.f.* cicada; locust.

cigarrera (θi·ɣaˈrre·ra; si-) *n.f.* **1,** cigarette maker. **2,** cigar box. **3,** cigar case.

cigarrería (θi·ɣa·rreˈri·a; si-) *n.f., Amer.* cigar store.

cigarrero (θi·ɣaˈrre·ro; si-) *n.m.* cigar maker, cigar seller.

cigarrillo (θi·ɣaˈrri·ʎo; si·ɣa·ˈrri·jo) *n.m.* cigarette.

cigarro (θi'ɣa·rro; si-) *n.m.* **1,** cigarette. **2,** cigar.
cigoñal (θi·ɣo'ɲal; si-) *n.m.* = **cigüeñal.**
cigoto (θi'ɣo·to; si-) zygote.
cigüeña (θi'ɣwe·ɲa; si-) *n.f.* **1,** stork. **2,** *mech.* crank.
cigüeñal (θi·ɣwe'ɲal; si-) *n.m.* crankshaft.
ciliado (θi'lja·ðo; si-) *adj.* ciliate; ciliated.
ciliar (θi'ljar; si-) *adj.* ciliary.
cilindrar (θi·lin'drar; si-) *v.t.* to roll. **—cilindro** (-'lin·dro) *n.m.* cylinder; roller. **—cilindrado,** *adj.* rolled. **—cilíndrico** (-'lin·dri·ko) *adj.* cylindrical.
cilio ('θi·ljo; 'si-) *n.m.* cilium. **—cilios,** *n.m.pl.* cilia.
-cillo ('θi·ʎo; 'si·jo), *fem.* **-cilla** (-ʎa; -ja) *suffix, var. of* **-illo;** *forming diminutives: dolorcillo,* slight pain; *piedrecilla,* little stone.
cima ('θi·ma; 'si-) *n.f.* summit; peak; apex.
cimarrón (θi·ma'rron; si-) *adj., Amer.* wild; untamed.
címbalo ('θim·ba·lo; 'sim-) *n.m.* cymbal. **—cimbalero,** *n.m., also,* **cimbalista,** *n.m.* & *f.* cymbalist.
cimbrar (θim'brar; sim-) *also,* **cimbrear** (-bre'ar) *v.t.* to brandish (a rod). **—cimbrarse,** *v.r.* to bend; to sway.
cimbreo (θim'bre·o; sim-) *n.m.* bending; swaying.
cimentación (θi·men·ta'θjon; si·men·ta'sjon) *n.f.* foundation.
cimentar (θi·men'tar; si-) *v.t.* [*pres.ind.* **cimiento** (-'mjen·to); *pres.subjve.* **cimiente** (-'mjen·te)] **1,** to lay the foundation of. **2,** to refine (metals). **3,** *fig.* to establish (principles); to found. **—cimentación,** *n.f.* foundation; laying of a foundation.
cimiento (θi'mjen·to; si-) *n.m.* foundation; basis. **—abrir los cimientos,** to break ground.
cimitarra (θi·mi'ta·rra; si-) *n.f.* scimitar.
cinabrio (θi'na·βrjo; si-) *n.m.* cinnabar.
cinc (θink; sink) *n.m.* zinc.
cincel (θin'θel; sin'sel) *n.m.* chisel.
cincelar (θin·θe'lar; sin·se-) *v.t.* to chisel; to engrave; to carve. **—cincelador,** *n.m.* engraver; stonecutter. **—cinceladura,** *n.f.* carving; chasing. **—cincelado,** *adj.* chiselled; carved. **—*n.m.*** carving; engraving.
cinco ('θin·ko; 'sin-) *adj.* & *n.m.* five.
cincuenta (θin'kwen·ta; sin-) *adj.* & *n.m.* fifty.
cincuentavo (θin·kwen'ta·βo; sin-) *adj.* & *n.m.* fiftieth.
cincuentena (θin·kwen'te·na; sin-) *n.f.* a quantity of fifty.
cincuentón (θin·kwen'ton; sin-) *adj.* & *n.m.* quinquagenarian.
cincha ('θin·tʃa; 'sin-) *n.f.* cinch.
cinchar (θin'tʃar; sin-) *v.t.* **1,** to cinch. **2,** to bind, as with bands or hoops.
cincho ('θin·tʃo; 'sin-) *n.m.* **1,** belt; girdle. **2,** iron hoop on a barrel.
cinema (θi'ne·ma; si-) *also, colloq.* **cine** ('θi·ne; 'si-) *n.m.* **1,** motion pictures; movies. **2,** motion-picture theater.
cinematografía (θi·ne·ma·to·ɣra'fi·a; si-) *n.f.* cinematography; film production. **—cinematográfico** (-'ɣra·fi·ko) *adj.* cinematographic; cinematic. **—cinematógrafo** (-'to·ɣra·fo) *n.m.* cinematograph.
cinético (θi'ne·ti·ko; si-) *adj.* kinetic. **—cinética,** *n.f.* kinetics.
cíngaro ('θin·ga·ro; 'sin-) *adj.* & *n.m.* gypsy.
cíngulo ('θin·gu·lo; 'sin-) *n.m.* cingulum.
cínico ('θi·ni·ko; 'si-) *adj.* cynical. **—*n.m.*** cynic.
cinismo (θi'nis·mo; si-) *n.m.* cynicism.
cinosura (θi·no'su·ra; si-) *n.f.* cynosure.
cinta ('θin·ta; 'sin-) *n.f.* **1,** ribbon; band; tape. **2,** film. **3,** *naut.* wale. **—cinta adhesiva,** friction tape. **—cinta métrica,** tape measure. **—cinta magnetofónica,** recording tape.
cintillo (θin'ti·ʎo; sin'ti·jo) *n.m.* **1,** hatband. **2,** headband; snood.
cinto ('θin·to; 'sin-) *n.m.* belt; girdle.
cintura (θin'tu·ra; sin-) *n.f.* waist; waistline. **—cinturilla,** *n.f., Amer.* small girdle. **—meter en cintura,** to bring to heel.
cinturón (θin·tu'ron; sin-) *n.m.* belt.
ciña ('θi·ɲa; 'si-) *v., pres.subjve. of* **ceñir.**
ciño ('θi·ɲo; 'si-) *v., pres.ind. of* **ceñir.**
ciñó (θi'ɲo; si-) *v., 3rd pers.sing. pret. of* **ceñir.**

-ción (θjon; sjon) *suffix* -tion; *forming verbal nouns expressing* action; result of action: *concepción,* conception.
-cioso ('θjo·so; 'sjo·so) *suffix* -tious; *forming adjectives corresponding to nouns ending in* **-cia** *or* **-ción**; *tendencioso,* tendentious; *sedicioso,* seditious.
cipayo (θi'pa·jo; si-) *n.m.* sepoy.
ciprés (θi'pres; si-) *n.m.* cypress tree. —**cipresal,** *n.m.* cypress grove.
circo ('θir·ko; 'sir-) *n.m.* circus.
circón (θir'kon; sir-) *n.m.* zircon.
circonio (θir'ko·njo; sir-) *n.m.* zirconium.
circuir (θir·ku'ir; sir-) *v.t.* [*pres. ind.* **circuyo** (-'ku·jo); *pres.subjve.* **circuya** (-'ku·ja); *pret.* **circuí** (-ku'i), **circuyó** (-ku'jo)] to surround; to encircle.
circuito (θir'kwi·to; sir-) *n.m.* circuit.
circulación (θir·ku·la'θjon; sir·ku·la'sjon) *n.f.* **1,** circulation. **2,** traffic.
circular (θir·ku'lar; sir-) *v.t.* & *i.* to circulate. —*adj.* circular. —*n.f.* circular; circular letter.
circulatorio (θir·ku·la'to·rjo; sir-) *adj.* circulatory.
círculo ('θir·ku·lo; 'sir-) *n.m.* **1,** circle. **2,** club.
circum- (θir·kum; sir-) *also,* **circun-** (-kun) *prefix* circum-; around: *circumpolar,* circumpolar; *circunnavegar,* circumnavigate.
circuncidar (θir·kun·θi'ðar; sir·kun·si-) *v.t.* to circumcise. —**circuncisión** (-'sjon) *n.f.* circumcision. —**circunciso** (-'θi·so; -'si·so) *adj.* circumcised.
circundar (θir·kun'dar; sir-) *v.t.* to circle; to surround.
circunferencia (θir·kun·fe'ren·θja; sir·kun·fe'ren·sja) *n.f.* circumference.
circunflejo (θir·kun'fle·xo; sir-) *adj.* circumflex.
circunlocución (θir·kun·lo·ku·'θjon; sir·kun·lo·ku'sjon) *n.f.* circumlocution. *Also,* **circunloquio** (-'lo·kjo) *n.m.*
circunnavegar (θir·kun·na·βe·'ɣar; sir-) *v.t.* [*infl.:* **navegar**] to circumnavigate. —**circunnavegación,** *n.f.* circumnavigation.
circunscribir (θir·kuns·kri'βir; sir-) *v.t.* [*p.p.* **circunscrito** (-'kri·to) *also,* **circunscripto** (-pto)] **1,** to circumscribe. **2,** to limit; to restrict. —**circunscripción** (-krip·'θjon; -'sjon) *n.f.* circumscription.
circunspección (θir·kuns·pek·'θjon; sir·kuns·pek'sjon) *n.f.* circumspection. —**circunspecto** (-'pek·to) *adj.* circumspect.
circunstancia (θir·kuns'tan·θja; sir·kuns'tan·sja) *n.f.* circumstance.
circunstanciado (θir·kuns·tan·'θja·ðo; sir·kuns·tan'sja·ðo) *adj.* detailed; minute.
circunstancial (θir·kuns·tan·'θjal; sir·kuns·tan'sjal) *adj.* circumstantial.
circunstante (θir·kuns'tan·te; sir-) *adj.* **1,** surrounding. **2,** present. —**circunstantes** *n.m.pl.* bystanders.
circunvalar (θir·kun·βa'lar; sir-) *v.t.* to circle surround.
circunvecino (θir·kun·βe'θi·no; sir·kun·βe'si·no) *adj.* adjacent; surrounding.
cirila (θi'ri·la; si-) *n.f., bot.* titi.
cirílico (θi'ri·li·ko; si-) *adj.* & *n.m.* Cyrillic.
cirio ('θi·rjo; 'si-) *n.m., eccles.* wax candle.
cirro ('θi·rro; 'si-) *n.m.* cirrus.
cirrosis (θi'rro·sis; si-) *n.f.* cirrhosis.
ciruela (θi'rwe·la; si-) *n.f.* plum; prune. —**ciruelo,** *n.m.* plum tree.
cirugía (θi·ru'xi·a; si-) *n.f.* surgery.
cirujano (θi·ru'xa·no; si-) *n.m.* surgeon.
cisma ('θis·ma; 'sis-) *n.m.* schism. —**cismático** (-'ma·ti·ko) *adj.* schismatic.
cisne ('θis·ne; 'sis-) *n.m.* swan.
cisterna (θis'ter·na; sis-) *n.f.* cistern.
cístico ('θis·ti·ko; 'sis-) *adj.* cystic.
cistitis (θis'ti·tis; sis-) *n.f.* cystitis.
cistología (θis·to·lo'xi·a; sis-) *n.f.* cystology.
cistoscopio (θis·tos'ko·pjo; sis-) *n.m.* cystoscope.
cita ('θi·ta; 'si-) *n.f.* **1,** appointment; engagement. **2,** quotation.
citable (θi'ta·βle; si-) *adj.* quotable.
citación (θi·ta'θjon; si·ta'sjon) *n.f.* **1,** citation. **2,** *law* summons.
citado (θi'ta·ðo; si-) *adj.* abovementioned.
citar (θi'tar; si-) *v.t.* **1,** to make an appointment with. **2,** to cite; to quote. **3,** *law* to summon. **4,** *bullfighting* to incite.
cítara ('θi·ta·ra; 'si-) *n.f.* cithara; zither.

cito- (θi·to; si-) *prefix* cyto-; cell: *citología,* cytology.
-cito ('θi·to; 'si·to) *suffix* **1,** [*fem.* **-cita** (-ta)] *var. of* **-ito**; *forming diminutives: cochecito,* small coach; *jovencita,* young girl. **2,** -cyte; cell: *trombocito,* thrombocyte.
citología (θi·to·lo'xi·a; si-) *n.f.* cytology. —**citológico** (-'lo·xi·ko) *adj.* cytological. —**citólogo** (-'to·lo·ɣo) *n.m.* cytologist.
citoplasma (θi·to'plas·ma; si-) *n.m.* cytoplasm.
citrato (θi'tra·to; si-) *n.m.* citrate.
cítrico ('θi·tri·ko; 'si-) *adj.* citric; citrous.
ciudad (θju'ðað; sju-) *n.f.* city.
ciudadano (θju·ða'ða·no; sju-) *adj.* pert. to a city; civic. —*n.m.* citizen. —**ciudadanía** (-'ni·a) *n.f.* citizenship.
ciudadela (θju·ða'ðe·la; sju-) *n.f.* citadel.
civeta (θi'βe·ta; si-) *n.f.* civet cat. —**civeto,** *n.m.* civet.
cívico ('θi·βi·ko; 'si-) *adj.* civic.
civil (θi'βil; si-) *adj.* civil. —**civilidad,** *n.f.* civility.
civilizar (θi·βi·li'θar; si·βi·li'sar) *v.t.* [*pres.subjve.* **civilice** (-'li·θe; -se); *pret.* **civilicé** (-'θe; -'se)] to civilize. —**civilización,** *n.f.* civilization.
cizaña (θi'θa·ɲa; si'sa-) *n.f.* **1,** *bot.* darnel; rye grass. **2,** *fig.* discord.
clamar (kla'mar) *v.i.* to clamor. —*v.t.* to clamor for; to cry out for.
clamor (kla'mor) *n.m.* clamor; uproar. —**clamoroso,** *adj.* clamorous; uproarious.
clamorear (kla·mo·re'ar) *v.t.* & *i.* to clamor. —*v.i.* to toll; knell.
clamoreo (kla·mo're·o) *n.m.* **1,** clamor. **2,** toll; tolling.
clan (klan) *n.m.* clan.
clandestino (klan·des'ti·no) *adj.* clandestine; underhanded. —**clandestinidad,** *n.f.* clandestineness; underhandedness.
claque ('kla·ke) *n.f.* claque.
clara ('kla·ra) *n.f.* white (*of an egg*).
claraboya (kla·ra'βo·ja) *n.f.* skylight; transom.
clarear (kla·re'ar) *v.t.* to give light to. —*v.i.* to dawn; to grow light. —**clarearse,** *v.r.* **1,** to be transparent. **2,** *colloq.* to give oneself away.
clarecer (kla·re'θer; -'ser) *v.i.* [*pres.subjve.* **clarezca** (-'reθ·ka; -'res·ka)] to dawn.
clarete (kla're·te) *n.m.* claret.
claridad (kla·ri'ðað) *n.f.* **1,** clarity; clearness. **2,** brightness. —**claridades,** *n.f.pl.* plain truth.
claridoso (kla·ri'ðo·so) *adj., Amer.* outspoken; blunt.
clarificar (kla·ri·fi'kar) *v.t.* [*pres. subjve.* **clarifique** (-'fi·ke); *pret.* **clarifiqué** (-'ke)] **1,** to brighten. **2,** to clarify. —**clarificación,** *n.f.* clarification.
clarín (kla'rin) *n.m.* bugle; clarion. —**clarinero,** *n.m.* bugler.
clarinete (kla·ri'ne·te) *n.m.* **1,** clarinet. **2,** clarinet player.
clarión (kla'rjon) *n.m.* chalk; chalk crayon.
clarividencia (kla·ri·βi'ðen·θja; -sja) *n.f.* clairvoyance. —**clarividente,** *adj.* & *n.m.* & *f.* clairvoyant.
claro ('kla·ro) *adj.* **1,** clear; transparent. **2,** bright; serene (*of weather*). **3,** light (*of colors*). **4,** thin (*of liquids, hair, etc.*). **5,** weak (*of tea*). **6,** evident; indisputable. **7,** *fig.* shrewd; smart. —*n.m.* **1,** skylight. **2,** interval; pause. **3,** break; gap. —*adv.* clearly; of course; indeed. —**a las claras,** openly. —**de claro en claro,** evidently.
clase ('kla·se) *n.f.* **1,** class; category; rank. **2,** class of students; classroom. **3,** kind; sort.
clásico ('kla·si·ko) *adj.* **1,** classic; classical. **2,** *colloq.* customary. —*n.m.* classic. —**clasicismo** (-'θis·mo; -'sis·mo) *n.m.* classicism. —**clasicista,** *n.m.* & *f.* classicist.
clasificar (kla·si·fi'kar) *v.t.* [*pres. subjve.* **clasifique** (-'fi·ke); *pret.* **clasifiqué** (-'ke)] to classify; to arrange. —**clasificación,** *n.f.* classification.
claustro ('klaus·tro) *n.m.* **1,** cloister. **2,** *educ.* faculty.
claustrofobia (klaus·tro'fo·βja) *n.f.* claustrophobia.
cláusula ('klau·su·la) *n.f.* **1,** *gram.* clause; sentence. **2,** *law* clause; stipulation.
clausura (klau'su·ra) *n.f.* **1,** confinement. **2,** adjournment. **3,** closure. **4,** restricted area in a convent or monastery.
clausurar (klau·su'rar) *v.t.* **1,** to close, as by official order. **2,** to seal off.
clava ('kla·βa) *n.f.* bat; club; cudgel.

clavado (kla'βa·ðo) *adj.* 1, studded with nails. 2, exact; just right.
clavar (kla'βar) *v.t.* 1, to nail; to stick (*as a bayonet*). 2, to prick (*in horseshoeing*). 3, *colloq.* to swindle.
clave ('kla·βe) *n.f.* 1, key; code. 2, *music* clef. —**clave de do,** tenor *or* C clef. —**clave de fa,** bass *or* F clef. —**clave de sol,** treble *or* G clef.
clavel (kla'βel) *n.m.* carnation.
clavetear (kla·βe·te'ar) *v.t.* 1, to stud; trim with nails, tacks, etc. 2, to tip with metal.
clavicordio (kla·βi'kor·ðjo) *n.m.* harpsichord.
clavícula (kla'βi·ku·la) *n.f.* clavicle.
clavija (kla'βi·xa) *n.f.* 1, pin; peg. 2, *music* peg (*of a stringed instrument*). 3, *electricity* plug; jack. —**apretar las clavijas a,** *colloq.* to put the screws on.
clavijero (kla·βi'xe·ro) *n.m.* 1, *music* pegbox (*of a stringed instrument*). 2, hat and coat rack.
clavillo (kla'βi·ʎo; -jo) *n.m.* 1, clove (*spice*). 2, [*also,* **clavito**] brad; tack.
clavo ('kla·βo) *n.m.* 1, nail; spike. 2, clove (*spice*). 3, corn (*on the foot*). 4, *slang* disappointment; failure. —**dar en el clavo,** to hit the mark. —**agarrarse de un clavo ardiendo,** *colloq.* to grasp at a straw.
clemátide (kle'ma·ti·ðe) *n.f.* clematis.
clemencia (kle'men·θja; -sja) *n.f.* clemency. —**clemente,** *adj.* clement.
clepsidra (klep'si·ðra) *n.f.* hourglass.
cleptomanía (klep·to·ma'ni·a) *n.f.* kleptomania. —**cleptomaníaco,** *n.m.* & *adj.* kleptomaniac. *Also,* **cleptómano** (-'to·ma·no).
clerecía (kle·re'θi·a; -'si·a) *n.f.* clergy.
clerical (kle·ri'kal) *adj.* 1, of or pert. to the clergy; clerical. 2, favoring or supporting the interests of the clergy.
clericato (kle·ri'ka·to) *n.m.* office or dignity of a clergyman.
clericatura (kle·ri·ka'tu·ra) *n.f.* clergy.
clérigo ('kle·ri·ɣo) *n.m.* clergyman; cleric.
clero ('kle·ro) *n.m.* clergy.
cliente ('kljen·te) *n.m.* & *f.* client; customer.
clientela (kljen'te·la) *n.f.* clientele; customers.
clima ('kli·ma) *n.m.* 1, climate. 2, climatic zone. 3, region; clime. 4, *Amer., colloq.* weather.
climatérico (kli·ma'te·ri·ko) *adj.* climacteric.
climático (kli'ma·ti·ko) *adj.* climatic.
clímax ('kli·maks) *n.m.* climax.
clínico ('kli·ni·ko) *adj.* clinical. —**clínica,** *n.f.* clinic.
clíper ('kli·per) *n.m.* clipper; clipper ship.
clisar (kli'sar) *v.t.* to stereotype. —**clisé** (-'se) *n.m.* stereotype.
clítoris ('kli·to·ris) *n.m.* clitoris.
cloaca (klo'a·ka) *n.f.* 1, sewer. 2, *zool.* large intestine.
clocar (klo'kar) *v.i.* [*pres.subjve.* **cloque** ('klo·ke); *pret.* **cloqué** (-'ke)] to cluck.
cloque ('klo·ke) *n.m.* harpoon.
cloquear (klo·ke'ar) *v.i.* to cluck; to cackle. —**cloqueo** (-'ke·o) *n.m.* cluck; cackle.
clorato (klo'ra·to) *n.m.* chlorate.
cloro ('klo·ro) *n.m.* chlorine.
clorofila (klo·ro'fi·la) *n.f.* chlorophyll. —**clorofílico** (-'fi·li·ko) *adj.* of or pert. to chlorophyll.
cloroformizar (klo·ro·for·mi'θar; -'sar) *v.t.* [*pres.subjve.* **cloroformice** (-'mi·θe; -'mi·se); *pret.* **cloroformicé** (-'θe; -'se)] to chloroform.
cloroformo (klo·ro'for·mo) *n.m.* chloroform.
cloruro (klo'ru·ro) *n.m.* chloride.
club (kluβ) *n.m.* [*pl.* **clubs**] club.
co- (ko) *prefix, var. of* **com-**. 1, association: *coautor,* coauthor; 2, joint action: *cooperación,* cooperation. 3, *math.* complement of: *coseno,* cosine.
coacción (ko·ak'θjon; -'sjon) *n.f.* compulsion; coercion.
coadyuvar (ko·að·ju'βar) *v.t.* to contribute; to aid.
coagular (ko·a·ɣu'lar) *v.t.* to coagulate; to curdle. —**coagulación,** *n.f.* coagulation; curdling.
coágulo (ko'a·ɣu·lo) *n.m.* 1, clot. 2, curd.
coalición (ko·a·li'θjon; -'sjon) *n.f.* coalition.
coartada (ko·ar'ta·ða) *n.f.* alibi.
coartar (ko·ar'tar) *v.t.* to limit; to restrict.
coaxial (ko·ak'sjal) *adj.* coaxial.

coba ('ko·βa) *n.f.* flattery; cajolery.
cobalto (ko'βal·to) *n.m.* cobalt.
cobarde (ko'βar·ðe) *n.m.* & *f.* coward. —*adj.* cowardly. —**cobardía**, *n.f.* cowardice.
cobertera (ko·βer'te·ra) *n.f.* **1**, pot lid; cover. **2**, procuress.
cobertizo (ko·βer'ti·θo; -so) *n.m.* shed.
cobertor (ko·βer'tor) *n.m.* bedspread.
cobija (ko'βi·xa) *n.f.* **1**, overlapping roof tile. **2**, *Amer.* blanket. **3**, *Amer.* poncho. **4**, *pl.*, *Amer.* bedclothes.
cobijar (ko·βi'xar) *v.t.* to cover; to protect; to shelter. —**cobijadura**, *also*, **cobijo** (-'βi·xo) *n.f.* *covering.* —**cobijamiento**, *n.m.* lodging.
cobra ('ko·βra) *n.f.* cobra.
cobrable (ko'βra·βle) *adj.* collectible. *Also*, **cobradero** (-'ðe·ro).
cobrador (ko·βra'ðor) *n.m.* **1**, collector. **2**, *R.R.* conductor.
cobranza (ko'βran·θa; -sa) *n.f.* **1**, collection. **2**, retrieving (*of game*).
cobrar (ko'βrar) *v.t.* **1**, to collect. **2**, to acquire; to win (fame, etc.). **3**, to retrieve (game). **4**, to pull in (a rope). **5**, to charge (a certain price). —*v.i.* to get hit; get a beating; be punished. —**cobrarse**, *v.r.* to recover; come to. —**cobrar ánimo**, to take courage. —**cobrar afición**, to take a liking. —**cobrar odio**, to take a dislike.
cobre ('ko·βre) *n.m.* **1**, copper. **2**, brass cooking utensils. —**cobres**, *n.m.pl.*, *music* brass instruments. —**batir el cobre**, *colloq.* to bustle.
cobrizo (ko'βri·θo; -so) *adj.* **1**, of or containing copper. **2**, copper-colored.
cobro ('ko·βro) *n.m.* collection.
coca ('ko·ka) *n.f.* **1**, *bot.* coca. **2**, *colloq.* [*also*, **coco**] head; brains. **3**, *Amer.* eggshell. **4**, *Amer.* rind. —**de coca**, *Amer.* **1**, free; gratis. **2**, in vain.
cocaína (ko·ka'i·na) *n.f.* cocaine.
cóccix ('kok·θiks; -siks) *n.m.sing.* & *pl.* coccyx.
cocear (ko·θe'ar; ko·se-) *v.i.* to kick. —**coceadura**, *n.f.*, *also*, **coceamiento**, *n.m.* kicking.
cocedor (ko·θe'ðor; ko·se-) *n.m.* baking oven.
cocer (ko'θer; -'ser) *v.t.* & *i.* [*pres. ind.* **cuezo**; *pres.subjve.* **cueza**] to boil; to cook; to bake. —**cocerse**, *v.r.* to suffer intense pain.
coces ('ko·θes; -ses) *n.f.*, *pl. of* **coz.**
cocido (ko'θi·ðo; ko'si-) *n.m.* Spanish stew. —*adj.* boiled; cooked; baked.
cociente (ko'θjen·te; ko'sjen-) *n.m.* = **cuociente.**
cocimiento (ko·θi'mjen·to; ko·si-) *n.m.* **1**, cooking; boiling; baking. **2**, brew of medicinal herbs.
cocina (ko'θi·na; ko'si-) *n.f.* **1**, kitchen. **2**, stove. **3**, cookery; cuisine.
cocinar (ko·θi'nar; ko·si-) *v.i.* & *t.* **1**, to cook. **2**, *Amer.* to bake.
cocinero (ko·θi'ne·ro; ko·si-) *n.m.* cook; chef.
coco ('ko·ko) *n.m.* **1**, coconut. **2**, [*also*, **cocotero** (-'te·ro)] coconut tree. **3**, coccus. **4**, bugbear; bugaboo. **5**, *colloq.* head; brains. **6**, *Amer.* derby hat. **7**, *Amer.* blow on the head. **8**, *colloq.* face; grimace. —**hacer cocos a**, *colloq.* to make eyes at; flirt with.
cocodrilo (ko·ko'ðri·lo) *n.m.* crocodile.
cocotal (ko·ko'tal) *n.m.* coconut grove; coconut plantation.
coctel (kok'tel) *n.m.* cocktail. —**coctelera** (-'le·ra) *n.f.* cocktail shaker.
coche ('ko·tʃe) *n.m.* **1**, coach; carriage. **2**, railway car. **3**, car; automobile. —**coche de San Francisco**, Shank's mare.
cochecillo (ko·tʃe'θi·ʎo; -'si·jo) *n.m.* baby carriage; perambulator.
cochera (ko'tʃe·ra) *n.f.* **1**, garage; carriage house. **2**, *R.R.* depot.
cochería (ko·tʃe'ri·a) *n.f.*, *So. Amer.* car rental agency; livery.
cochero (ko'tʃe·ro) *n.m.* **1**, coachman. **2**, cab driver. —*adj.* easily cooked.
cochevira (ko·tʃe'βi·ra) *n.f.* lard.
cochina (ko'tʃi·na) *n.f.* sow.
cochinería (ko·tʃi·ne'ri·a) *n.f.*, *colloq.* dirtiness; filthiness.
cochinilla (ko·tʃi'ni·ʎa; -ja) *n.f.* **1**, wood louse. **2**, cochineal (*insect & dye*).
cochino (ko'tʃi·no) *n.m.* pig. —*adj.* *colloq.* sloppy; filthy.
coda ('ko·ða) *n.f.* **1**, *music* coda. **2**, *carpentry* wedge.
codal (ko'ðal) *n.m.* **1**, vineshoot. **2**, *archit.* buttress. **3**, frame (*of a saw*). **4**, shore; prop. —*adj.* bent; elbowed.
codazo (ko'ða·θo; -so) *n.m.* nudge with the elbow.

codear (ko·ðe'ar) *v.i.* to elbow; to jostle. —**codearse,** *v.r.* to mingle; to hobnob.
codeína (ko·ðe'i·na) *n.f.* codeine.
codelincuente (ko·ðe·lin'kwen·te) *n.m.* & *f.* accomplice. —*adj.* jointly responsible; in complicity. —**codelincuencia** *n.f.* complicity.
codemandado (ko·ðe·man'da·ðo) *n.m* person sued jointly with another; co-respondent.
codeso (ko'ðe·so) *n.m.* laburnum.
códice('ko·ði·θe; -se) *n.m.* codex.
codicia (ko'ði·θja; -sja) *n.f.* covetousness; greed.
codiciar (ko·ði'θjar; -'sjar) *v.t.* to covet.
codicilo (ko·ði'θi·lo; -'si·lo) *n.m.* codicil.
codicioso (ko·ði'θjo·so; -'sjo·so) *adj.* greedy; covetous.
codificar (ko·ði·fi'kar) *v.t.* [*pres. subjve.* **codifique** (-'fi·ke); *pret.* **codifiqué** (-'ke)] to codify. —**codificación,** *n.f.* codification.
código ('ko·ði·ɣo) *n.m.* code. —**código penal,** criminal law; penal code.
codillo (ko'ði·ʎo; -jo) *n.m.* 1, bend; angle. 2, elbow. 3, *naut.* stirrup.
codo ('ko·ðo) *n.m.* 1, *anat.* elbow. 2, *mech.* angle; elbow; —**hablar por los codos,** *colloq.* to chatter. —**empinar el codo,** *colloq.* to drink too much.
codorniz (ko·ðor'niθ; -'nis) *n.f.* quail.
coeducación (ko·e·ðu·ka'θjon; -'sjon) *n.f.* coeducation. —**coeducativo** (-'ti·βo) *adj.* coeducational.
coeficiente (ko·e·fi'θjen·te; -'sjen·te) *n.m.* & *adj.* coefficient.
coercer (ko·er'θer; -'ser) *v.t.* [*pres.ind.* **coerzo** (-'er·θo; -so); *pres.subjve.* **coerza** (-θa; -sa)] to coerce. —**coerción,** *n.f.* coercion.
coercible (ko·er'θi·βle; -'si·βle) *adj.* 1, coercible. 2, compressible.
coetáneo (ko·e'ta·ne·o) *adj.* contemporary.
coevo (ko'e·βo) *adj.* coeval.
coexistir (ko·ek·sis'tir) *v.i.* to coexist. —**coexistencia,** *n.f.* coexistence.
cofia ('ko·fja) *n.f.* 1, *coif.* 2, hairnet.
cofín (ko'fin) *n.m.* small basket.
cofrade (ko'fra·ðe) *n.m.* & *f.* brother *or* sister (*of a confraternity*).
cofradía (ko·fra'ði·a) *n.f.* confraternity; brotherhood.
cofre ('ko·fre) *n.m.* trunk; coffer.
cogedero (ko·xe'ðe·ro) *adj.* ready for gathering —*n.m.* handle.
coger (ko'xer) *v.t.* [*pres.ind.* **cojo;** *pres.subjve* **coja**] 1, to pick; to get; to collect 2, to catch; to seize; to arrest. 3, to occupy, to take up (space). —*v.i.* to fit; to have room.
cogida (ko'xi·ða) *n.f.* 1, fruit harvest. 2, catch (*in fishing*).
cogido (ko'xi·ðo) *n.m.* fold; pleat.
cognado (koɣ'na·ðo) *adj.* & *n.m.* cognate
cognomen (koɣ'no·men) *n.m.* cognomen (*Roman family name*).
cognomento (koɣ·no'men·to) *n.m.* cognomen appellation.
cogollo (ko'ɣo·ʎo; -jo) *n.m.* 1, heart (*of vegetables*). 2, shoot (*of plants*).
cogote (ko'ɣo·te) *n.m.* nape.
cogulla (ko'ɣu·ʎa; -ja) *n.f.* cowl.
cohabitar (ko·a·βi'tar) *v.i.* to cohabit. —**cohabitación,** *n.f.* cohabitation.
cohechar (ko·e'tʃar) *v.t.* to bribe.
cohecho (ko'e·tʃo) *n.m.* 1, bribe. 2, bribery.
coheredero (ko·e·re'ðe·ro) *n.m.* coheir.
coherencia (ko·e'ren·θja; -sja) *n.f.* 1, coherence 2, *physics* cohesion.
coherente (ko·e'ren·te) *adj.* 1, coherent. 2, *physics* cohesive.
cohesión (ko·e'sjon) *n.f.* cohesion.
cohesivo (ko·e'si·βo) *adj.* cohesive.
cohete (ko'e·te) *n.m.* rocket.
cohibir (ko·i'βir) *v.t.* to restrain. —**cohibición,** *n.f.* restraint.
cohombro (ko'om·bro) *n.m.* cucumber.
cohorte (ko'or·te) *n.f.* cohort.
coima ('koi·ma) *n.f., Amer.* graft; bribe; bribery. —**coimear,** *v.i.* & *t., Amer.* to graft.
coincidencia (ko·in·θi'ðen·θja; -si'ðen·sja) *n.f.* coincidence. —**coincidente,** *adj.* coincident; coincidental.
coincidir (ko·in·θi'ðir; -si'ðir) *v.i.* to coincide.
coito ('koi·to) *n.m.* coitus; coition.
coja ('ko·xa) *v., pres.subjve. of* **coger.**
cojear (ko·xe'ar) *v.i.* 1, to limp. 2, to wobble (*as a table, chair, etc.*).

cojera (ko'xe·ra) *n.f.* limp; lameness.
cojín (ko'xin) *n.m.* 1, cushion. 2, saddle pad.
cojinete (ko·xi'ne·te) *n.m.* ball bearing.
cojo ('ko·xo) *adj.* 1, (*of persons*) lame; crippled. 2, (*of a table*) wobbly. —*n.m.* cripple. —**no ser cojo ni manco,** to be clever.
cojo ('ko·xo) *v., 1st pers.sing.pres. ind. of* **coger.**
cok (kok) *n.m.* coke.
col (kol) *n.f.* cabbage; cole; kale. —**col de Bruselas,** Brussels sprouts.
cola ('ko·la) *n.f.* 1, tail. 2, train (*of a gown*). 3, hind part. 4, queue; line. 5, tail end; last place. 6, glue. —**hacer cola,** to stand in line; queue up. —**tener** *or* **traer cola,** to have serious consequences.
colaborar (ko·la·βo'rar) *v.i.* to collaborate. —**colaboración,** *n.f.* collaboration. —**colaboracionista,** *adj.* & *n.m.* & *f.* collaborationist. —**colaborador,** *n.m.* collaborator.
colación (ko·la'θjon; -'sjon) *n.f.* 1, collation. 2, *educ.* conferring (*of a degree, honor, etc.*). —**sacar** *or* **traer a colación,** to bring up; to adduce.
colada (ko'la·ða) *n.f.* 1, laundry; drenching; soaking (*of clothes*). 2, tap (*of a furnace*).
coladera (ko·la'ðe·ra) *n.f.* 1, strainer; colander. 2, *Mex.* drain; sewer.
colado (ko'la·ðo) *adj.* cast (*of iron*).
colador (ko·la'ðor) *n.m.* strainer. *Also,* **coladero** (-'ðe·ro).
coladura (ko·la'ðu·ra) *n.f.* filtration.
colapso (ko'lap·so) *n.m.* collapse.
colar (ko'lar) *v.t.* & *i.* 1, [*pres.ind.* **cuelo;** *pres.subjve.* **cuele**)] to strain; filter. 2, to sneak in; slip in. 3, to foist. —**colarse,** *v.r.* to sneak in or out; slip by. —**estar colado por,** *colloq.* to be madly in love with.
colateral (ko·la·te'ral) *adj.* collateral.
colcha ('kol·tʃa) *n.f.* quilt; bedspread; counterpane. —**colchadura,** *n.f.* quilting. —**colchar,** *v.t.* to quilt.
colchón (kol'tʃon) *n.m.* mattress. —**colchón de muelles,** spring mattress. —**colchón neumático,** air mattress.
colchoneta (kol·tʃo'ne·ta) *n.f.* 1, light mattress. 2, mat (*for gymnastics*).
colear (ko·le'ar) *v.i.* 1, to wag the tail. 2, *Amer., colloq.* to move ridiculously (*in walking*). —**todavía colea,** *colloq.* it is not finished yet.
colección (ko·lek'θjon; -'sjon) *n.f.* collection. —**coleccionar,** *v.t.* to collect. —**coleccionista,** *n.m.* & *f.* collector; one who collects as a hobby.
colecta (ko'lek·ta) *n.f.* 1, *liturgy* collect. 2, money collected, esp. for charity.
colectar (ko·lek'tar) *v.t.* to collect.
colectividad (ko·lek·ti·βi'ðað) *n.f.* collectivity; community.
colectivo (ko·lek'ti·βo) *adj.* collective. —*n.m., Arg.* bus; public conveyance. —**colectivismo,** *n.m.* collectivism.
colector (ko·lek'tor) *n.m.* collector.
colega (ko'le·ɣa) *n.m.* & *f.* colleague.
colegiado (ko·le'xja·ðo) *adj.* collegiate.
colegial (ko·le'xjal) *adj.* collegiate. —*n.m.* & *f.* collegian.
colegiatura (ko·le·xja'tu·ra) *n.f.* fellowship; scholarship.
colegio (ko'le·xjo) *n.m.* 1, college; school. 2, professional association.
colegir (ko·le'xir) *v.t.* [*pres.ind.* **colijo;** *pres.subjve.* **colija;** *pret.* **colegí, coligió**] 1, to gather. 2, to infer.
cólera ('ko·le·ra) *n.f.* anger; wrath. —*n.m.* [*also,* **cólera morbo**] cholera. —**montar en cólera,** to blow up; to hit the ceiling.
colérico (ko'le·ri·ko) *adj.* 1, irritable; choleric. 2, of, pertaining to or suffering from cholera.
coleta (ko'le·ta) *n.f.* ponytail; queue. —**cortarse la coleta,** to quit, esp. bullfighting.
coleto (ko'le·to) *n.m.* 1, jacket. 2, *colloq.* oneself; one's body. —**decir para su coleto,** to say to oneself. —**echarse (algo) al coleto,** to gulp down; polish off; toss off.
colgadero (kol·ɣa'ðe·ro) *n.m.* hanger. —*adj.* made to be hung up.
colgadizo (kol·ɣa'ði·θo; -so) *n.m.* lean-to.
colgadura (kol·ɣa'ðu·ra) *n.f.* hangings; tapestry; drapery.
colgante (kol'ɣan·te) *adj.* hanging. —*n.m.* earring. —**puente colgante,** suspension bridge.
colgar (kol'ɣar) *v.t.* [*pres.ind.*

cuelgo; *pres.subjve.* **cuelgue**; *pret.* **colgué** (-'ɣe)] **1,** to hang; to suspend. **2,** to adorn (*with hangings*). **3,** *colloq.* to flunk. **4,** *colloq.* to hang; to kill by hanging. **5,** to impute; to attribute. —*v.i.* to hang.

colibrí (ko·li'βri) *n.m.* hummingbird.

cólico ('ko·li·ko) *adj.* & *n.m.* colic.

coliflor (ko·li'flor) *n.f.* cauliflower.

coligarse (ko·li'ɣar·se) *v.r.* [*infl.:* **ligar**] to band together; join forces.

coligió (ko·li'xjo) *v., 3rd pers.sing. pret. of* **colegir.**

colija (ko'li·xa) *v., pres.subjve. of* **colegir.**

colijo (ko'li·xo) *v., 1st pers.sing. pres.ind. of* **colegir.**

colilla (ko'li·ʎa; -ja) *n.f.* stub; butt.

colina (ko'li·na) *n.f.* hill.

colinabo (ko·li'na·βo) *n.m.* kohlrabi.

colindar (ko·lin'dar) *v.i.* to abut; border. —**colindante,** *adj.* contiguous; adjacent.

coliseo (ko·li'se·o) *n.m.* **1,** theatre; playhouse. **2,** coliseum.

colisión (ko·li'sjon) *n.f.* collision; clash.

colitis (ko'li·tis) *n.f.* colitis.

colmado (kol'ma·ðo) *adj.* full; chock-full; overflowing. —*n.m.* **1,** specialty restaurant, usu. a sea food house. **2,** food store.

colmar (kol'mar) *v.t.* **1,** to fill to the brim; to heap up. **2,** to fulfill. **3,** to overwhelm.

colmena (kol'me·na) *n.f.* beehive.

colmenar (kol·me'nar) *n.m.* apiary.

colmenilla (kol·me'ni·ʎa; -ja) *n.f.* **1,** *dim. of* **colmena. 2,** morel.

colmillo (kol'mi·ʎo; -jo) *n.m.* **1,** *anat.* eyetooth; canine tooth. **2,** *zool.* fang; tusk.

colmo ('kol·mo) *n.m.* **1,** heap; mound. **2,** overflow. **3,** summit; top. —*adj.* heaping full; overflowing. —**a colmo,** abundantly. —**para colmo de,** *colloq.* to top off. —**esto es el colmo,** *colloq.* this is the limit.

colocación (ko·lo·ka'θjon; -'sjon) *n.f.* **1,** place; position. **2,** employment; job. **3,** placement.

colocar (ko·lo'kar) *v.* [*pres.subjve.* **coloque**; *pret.* **coloqué**] —*v.t.* **1,** to arrange; to set. **2,** to place; to put in place. **3,** *comm.* to invest. —*v.i.* to be placed; to find employment.

colodión (ko·lo'ðjon) *n.m.* collodion.

coloide (ko'loi·ðe) *n.m.* colloid. —**coloideo** (-'ðe·o) *adj.* colloidal.

colon ('ko·lon) *n.m.* **1,** *anat.* colon. **2,** *gram.* clause, esp. main clause.

colón (ko'lon) *n.m.* monetary unit of El Salvador; colón.

colonia (ko'lo·nja) *n.f.* **1,** colony. **2,** cologne; eau de cologne. —**colonial,** *adj.* colonial. —**colonialismo,** *n.m.* colonialism.

colonizar (ko·lo·ni'θar; -'sar) *v.t.* [*pres.subjve.* **colonice** (-'ni·θe; -se); *pret.* **colonicé** (-'θe; -'se)] to colonize. —**colonización,** *n.f.* colonization.

colono (ko'lo·no) *n.m.* **1,** colonist; settler; colonial. **2,** tenant farmer.

coloque (ko'lo·ke) *v., pres.subjve. of* **colocar.**

coloqué (ko·lo'ke) *v., 1st pers. sing.pret. of* **colocar.**

coloquio (ko'lo·kjo) *n.m.* colloquy; conversation.

color (ko'lor) *n.m.* **1,** color. **2,** rouge. **3,** *fig.* character. —**dar color a,** *colloq.* to exaggerate. —**ponerse de mil colores,** *colloq.* to blush; to turn a dozen colors. —**perder el color,** *colloq.* to become pale; to pale. —**so color de,** under pretext of.

colorado (ko·lo'ra·ðo) *adj.* **1,** red; reddish. **2,** *fig.* embarrassed. **3,** off-color; risqué. —**ponerse colorado,** to blush.

colorante (ko·lo'ran·te) *adj.* & *n.m.* coloring.

colorar (ko·lo'rar) *v.t.* to dye; to color; to stain. —*v.i.* to blush. —**coloración,** *n.f.* coloration.

colorear (ko·lo·re'ar) *v.t.* to make plausible; to palliate. —*v.i.* to redden.

colorete (ko·lo're·te) *n.m.* rouge.

colorido (ko·lo'ri·ðo) *n.m.* coloring.

colosal (ko·lo'sal) *adj.* colossal; huge.

coloso (ko'lo·so) *n.m.* colossus.

columbio (ko'lum·bjo) *n.m.* columbium.

columbrar (ko·lum'brar) *v.t.* **1,** to espy; to perceive. **2,** to infer; to guess.

columna (ko'lum·na) *n.f.* column. —**columnario,** *adj.* columnar.

columnata (ko·lum'na·ta) *n.f.* colonnade.

columnista (ko·lum'nis·ta) *n.m.* & *f.* columnist.
columpiar (ko·lum'pjar) *v.t.* to swing; to sway.
columpio (ko'lum·pjo) *n.m.* **1,** swing. **2,** [*also,* **columpio de tabla**] seesaw.
colusión (ko·lu'sjon) *n.f.* collusion.
colusorio (ko·lu'so·rjo) *adj.* collusive.
colza ('kol·θa; -sa) *n.f., bot.* rape.
collado (ko'ʎa·ðo; ko'ja-) *n.m.* hill.
collar (ko'ʎar; -'jar) *n.m.* **1,** collar. **2,** necklace.
collera (ko'ʎe·ra; -'je·ra) *n.f.* collar.
com- (kom) *prefix* com-; with; jointly; entirely. *The form* **com-** *is used before* b *and* p: *combinar,* combine; *componer,* compose. *The form* **co-** *is used before vowels and before* h, l, m, r (*with doubling of* r) *and* y: *coalición,* coalition; *cohabitar,* cohabit; *colateral,* collateral; *comarca,* province; *corresponder,* correspond; *coyuntura,* conjuncture. *The form* **con-** *is used before* c, d, f, g, j, ll, n, q, s, t, v.
coma ('ko·ma) *n.f.* comma. —*n.m.* coma. —**punto y coma,** semicolon.
comadre (ko'ma·ðre) *n.f.* **1,** midwife. **2,** gossip. **3,** *colloq.* go-between. **4,** (the relationship of) godmother.
comadrear (ko·ma·ðre'ar) *v.i.* to gossip; to tattle.
comadreja (ko·ma'ðre·xa) *n.f.* weasel.
comadrona (ko·ma'ðro·na) *n.f.* midwife.
comandar (ko·man'dar) *v.t.* to command. —**comandante,** *n.m.* commandant; commander; major.
comandita (ko·man'di·ta) *n.f.* silent partnership.
comando (ko'man·do) *n.m.* **1,** command. **2,** control.
comarca (ko'mar·ka) *n.f.* county; district. —**comarcano,** *adj.* neighboring; bordering.
comatoso (ko·ma'to·so) *adj.* comatose.
comba ('kom·ba) *n.f.* **1,** bend; bulge; warp. **2,** jump rope. —**hacer combas,** *colloq.* to sway.
combar (kom'bar) *v.t.* to bend; to warp.
combate (kom'ba·te) *n.m.* combat; battle.
combatiente (kom·ba'tjen·te) *adj.* & *n.m.* & *f.* combatant.
combatir (kom·ba'tir) *v.i.* to combat; to fight. —*v.t.* to attack; to beat.
combinación (kom·bi·na'θjon; -'sjon) *n.f.* **1,** combination. **2,** *chem.* compound.
combinar (kom·bi'nar) *v.t.* to combine; to blend; to compound.
combo ('kom·bo) *adj.* bent; crooked; warped.
combustible (kom·bus'ti·βle) *adj.* combustible. —*n.m.* fuel.
combustión (kom·bus'tjon) *n.f.* combustion.
comedero (ko·me'ðe·ro) *n.m.* feeding place (*for animals*).
comedia (ko'me·ðja) *n.f.* comedy; play; farce. —**hacer la comedia (de),** to pretend; to make believe.
comedianta (ko·me'ðjan·ta) *n.f.* actress; comedienne.
comediante (ko·me'ðjan·te) *n.m.* comedian; player.
comedido (ko·me'ði·ðo) *adj.* **1,** moderate. **2,** civil; polite.
comedirse (ko·me'ðir·se) *v.r.* [*infl.:* **medir**] **1,** to refrain; to be moderate. **2,** *Amer.* to volunteer.
comedón (ko·me'ðon) *n.m.* blackhead.
comedor (ko·me'ðor) *adj.* eating much. —*n.m.* **1,** dining room. **2,** heavy eater.
comelón (ko·me'lon) *adj.* & *n.m., Amer.* = **comilón.**
comendador (ko·men·da'ðor) *n.m.* **1,** knight commander. **2,** prefect of certain religious orders.
comensal (ko·men'sal) *n.m.* & *f.* **1,** retainer; dependent. **2,** guest.
comentador (ko·men·ta'ðor) *n.m.* commentator.
comentar (ko·men'tar) *v.t.* to comment on. —*v.i.* to comment.
comentario (ko·men'ta·rjo) *n.m.* commentary; comment.
comentarista (ko·men·ta'ris·ta) *n.m.* & *f.* commentator.
comento (ko'men·to) *n.m.* comment; commentary.
comenzar (ko·men'θar; -'sar) *v.t.* & *v.i.* [*pres.ind.* **comienzo;** *pres. subjve.* **comience;** *pret.* **comencé** (-'θe; -'se)] to commence; to begin.
comer (ko'mer) *v.t.* **1,** to eat. **2,** to consume; to corrode. **3,** *chess; checkers* to take. **4,** to fade. **5,** to expend; to waste. —**comerse con los ojos,** *colloq.* to gaze at. —**tener qué**

comer, to have an income. —**dar de comer,** *colloq.* to feed. —**comerse los codos,** *colloq.* **1,** to be starved. **2,** to retract.
comerciable (ko·mer'θja·βle; -'sja·βle) *adj.* **1,** salable; marketable. **2,** sociable.
comercial (ko·mer'θjal; -'sjal) *adj.* commercial. —**comercializar,** *v.t.* [*infl.:* **realizar**] to commercialize.
comerciante (ko·mer'θjan·te; -'sjan·te) *n.m.* merchant; trader; dealer.
comerciar (ko·mer'θjar; -'sjar) *v.i.* to trade; to deal.
comercio (ko'mer·θjo; -sjo) *n.m.* commerce; trade; business. —**comercio exterior,** foreign trade. —**comercio interior,** domestic trade.
comestible (ko·mes'ti·βle) *adj.* eatable; edible. —**comestibles,** *n.m. pl.* provisions.
cometa (ko'me·ta) *n.m.* comet. —*n.f.* kite.
cometer (ko·me'ter) *v.t.* **1,** to commit. **2,** to perpetrate.
cometido (ko·me'ti·ðo) *n.m.* **1,** commitment; duty; task. **2,** purpose.
comezón (ko·me'θon; -'son) *n.f.* **1,** itching. **2,** *fig.* desire.
cómico ('ko·mi·ko) *adj.* comic; comical. —*n.m.* **1,** comedian. **2,** player; actor.
comida (ko'mi·ða) *n.f.* **1,** food; eating. **2,** dinner.
comience (ko'mjen·θe; -se) *v., pres.subjve. of* **comenzar.**
comienzo (ko'mjen·θo; -so) *v., pres.ind. of* **comenzar.** —*n.m.* origin; beginning.
comilitona (ko·mi·li'to·na) *n.f., colloq.* hearty meal; feast. *Also,* **comilona** (-'lo·na).
comilón (ko·mi'lon) *n.m.* glutton. —*adj.* gluttonous.
comillas (ko'mi·ʎas; -jas) *n.f.pl.* quotation marks.
comisaría (ko·mi·sa'ri·a) *n.f.* **1,** police station. **2,** commissioner's office. **3,** commissary.
comisario (ko·mi'sa·rjo) *n.m.* **1,** commissioner. **2,** trustee. **3,** chief of police; police official. —**comisariado,** *n.m.* commissariat.
comisión (ko·mi'sjon) *n.f.* **1,** commission. **2,** committee. **3,** assignment.
comisionado (ko·mi·sjo'na·ðo) *adj.* commissioned. —*n.m.* **1,** commissioner. **2,** agent. **3,** trustee.
comisionar (ko·mi·sjo'nar) *v.t.* to commission; to appoint.
comisorio (ko·mi'so·rjo) *adj., law* binding; compulsory.
comistrajo (ko·mis'tra·xo) *n.m.* strange concoction of food; mess; slop.
comité (ko·mi'te) *n.m.* committee.
comitiva (ko·mi'ti·βa) *n.f.* retinue.
como ('ko·mo) *adv.* & *conj.* **1,** how. **2,** as (*in comparisons*). **3,** why. **4,** like; as. **5,** if.—**¿cómo?** what is it? —**¿cómo no?** why not? —**como quiera que sea,** however.
cómoda ('ko·mo·ða) *n.f.* chest of drawers; bureau.
comodidad (ko·mo·ði'ðað) *n.f.* comfort; convenience.
comodín (ko·mo'ðin) *n.m., cards* joker.
cómodo ('ko·mo·ðo) *adj.* **1,** comfortable. **2,** convenient. **3,** comfort-loving; self-indulgent.
comodoro (ko·mo'ðo·ro) *n.m.* commodore.
compacto (kom'pak·to) *adj.* compact.
compadecer (kom·pa·ðe'θer; -'ser) *v.t. also, refl.,* **compadecerse** [*infl.:* **padecer**] *fol. by* **de,** to pity; to condole.
compadrar (kom·pa'ðrar) *v.i.* to get along; to be on good terms.
compadrazgo (kom·pa'ðraθ·ɣo; -'ðras·ɣo) *n.m.* **1,** relation of a godfather to the parents of a child. **2,** *derog.* tight circle; clique.
compadre (kom'pa·ðre) *n.m.* **1,** godfather. **2,** *colloq.* crony.
compañerismo (kom·pa·ɲe'ris·mo) *n.m.* fellowship; companionship.
compañero (kom·pa'ɲe·ro) *n.m.* companion; friend; mate. —**compañero de habitación** *or* **cuarto,** roommate.
compañía (kom·pa'ɲi·a) *n.f.* **1,** company; society. **2,** companionship.
comparar (kom·pa'rar) *v.t.* to compare. —**comparable,** *adj.* comparable. —**comparación,** *n.f.* comparison. —**comparado,** *adj.* comparative. —**comparativo,** *adj.* comparative. —*n.m., gram.* comparative.
comparecencia (kom·pa·re'θen·

θja; -'sen·sja) *n.f., law* appearance.
comparecer (kom·pa·re'θer; -'ser) *v.i.* [*infl.:* **parecer**] 1, to appear; to turn up. 2, *law* to appear (in court).
comparendo (kom·pa'ren·do) *n.m., law* 1, summons. 2, *Amer.* = **comparecencia.**
comparsa (kom'par·sa) *n.m. & f., theat.* extra; supernumerary. —*n.f.* extras collectively; chorus.
compartimiento (kom·par·ti·'mjen·to) *n.m.* division; compartment; department.
compartir (kom·par'tir) *v.t.* to divide; to share.
compás (kom'pas) *n.m.* 1, compass. 2, calipers. 3, *music* measure; time; beat. —**llevar el compás,** to beat *or* keep time. —**fuera de compás,** offbeat.
compasar (kom·pa'sar) *v.t.* to measure (*with a rule and compass*).
compasible (kom·pa'si·βle) *adj.* compassionate; lamentable.
compasión (kom·pa'sjon) *n.f.* compassion; pity.
compasivo (kom·pa'si·βo) *adj.* compassionate; humane.
compatible (kom·pa'ti·βle) *adj.* compatible. —**compatibilidad,** *n.f.* compatibility.
compatriota (kom·pa'trjo·ta) *n.m. & f.* compatriot; fellow citizen.
compeler (kom·pe'ler) *v.t.* [*p.p.* **compulso**] to compel; to force.
compendiar (kom·pen'djar) *v.t.* to abridge; to condense.
compendio (kom'pen·djo) *n.m.* compendium; summary.
compensación (kom·pen·sa'θjon; -'sjon) *n.f.* 1, compensation. 2, *comm.* clearing.
compensar (kom·pen'sar) *v.t.* 1, to compensate. 2, to compensate for; offset. —**compensatorio** (-'to·rjo) *also,* **compensativo** (-'ti·βo) *adj.* compensatory.
competencia (kom·pe'ten·θja; -sja) *n.f.* 1, competition; rivalry. 2, competence.
competente (kom·pe'ten·te) *adj.* competent; able; apt.
competer (kom·pe'ter) *v.i.* to be one's interest or concern; be incumbent on one.
competición (kom·pe·ti'θjon; -'sjon) *n.f.* contest; competition.
competidor (kom·pe·ti'ðor) *adj.* 1, competing. 2, competitive. —*n.m.* competitor; rival.
competir (kom·pe'tir) *v.i.* [*pres. ind.* **compito** (-'pi·to); *pres.subjve.* **compita** (-ta); *pret.* **competí** (-pe'ti), **compitió** (-pi'tjo); *ger.* **compitiendo** (-'tjen·do) to compete; contend; vie.
compilar (kom·pi'lar) *v.t.* to compile. —**compilación,** *n.f.* compilation.
compinche (kom'pin·tʃe) *n.m. & f., colloq.* chum; buddy.
complacencia (kom·pla'θen·θja; -'sen·sja) *n.f.* 1, complacency; indulgence. 2, pleasure; satisfaction.
complacer (kom·pla'θer; -'ser) *v.t.* [*pres.ind.* **complazco** (-'plaθ·ko; -'plas·ko); *pres.subjve.* **complazca** (-ka)] to please; to accommodate. —**complacerse,** *v.r.* 1, *fol. by* **de** *or* **con,** to be pleased. 2, *fol. by* **en,** to take pleasure in.
complaciente (kom·pla'θjen·te; -'sjen·te) *adj.* 1, complacent. 2, accommodating; obliging.
complejo (kom'ple·xo) *adj. & n.m.* complex. —**complejidad,** *n.f.* complexity.
complementar (kom·ple·men'tar) *v.t.* to complement.
complementario (kom·ple·men'ta·rjo) *adj.* complementary.
complemento (kom·ple'men·to) *n.m.* 1, complement. 2, *gram.* object.
completar (kom·ple'tar) *v.t.* to complete; to finish. —**completamiento,** *n.m.* completion.
completo (kom'ple·to) *adj.* 1, complete; finished. 2, full; full to capacity.
complexión (kom·plek'sjon) *n.f.* 1, complexion. 2, constitution; nature.
complicar (kom·pli'kar) *v.t.* [*pres. subjve.* **complique** (-'pli·ke); *pret.* **compliqué** (-'ke)] to complicate; to entangle. —**complicación,** *n.f.* complication.
cómplice ('kom·pli·θe; -se) *n.m. & f.* accomplice; accessory.
complicidad (kom·pli·θi'ðað; -si'ðað) *n.f.* complicity.
complot (kom'plot) *n.m.* [*pl.* **complots**] plot; scheme.
componenda (kom·po'nen·da) *n.f.* 1, arbitrary or unjust agreement or settlement. 2, *colloq.* bribe; fix. 3, *colloq.* excuse; blandishment.
componente (kom·po'nen·te) *n.m. & adj.* component.
componer (kom·po'ner) *v.t.* [*infl.:*

poner] 1, to compound. 2, to repair; to fix. 3, to put in order; to arrange. 4, to settle (differences); to reconcile. 5, to write (poetry). 6, to compose (music). 7, *print.* to compose. 8, to mix (drinks). 9, to amount to; to come to. —**componérselas,** to manage; to get through (a task).

comportar (kom·por'tar) *v.t.* 1, to endure; to bear. 2, *Amer.* to entail. —**comportarse,** *v.r.* to behave. —**comportamiento,** *n.m.* comportment; deportment.

composición (kom·po·si'θjon; -'sjon) *n.f.* 1, composition. 2, settlement; deal.

compositor (kom·po·si'tor) *adj.* composing. —*n.m.* composer.

compostura (kom·pos'tu·ra) *n.f.* 1, behavior; manners. 2, repair; repairing. 3, composure.

compota (kom'po·ta) *n.f.* compote. —**compotera** (-'te·ra) *n.f.* compote dish.

compra ('kom·pra) *n.f.* 1, purchase. 2, shopping; marketing. —**hacer compras; salir de compras,** to go shopping.

comprador (kom·pra'ðor) *n.m.* buyer; shopper.

comprar (kom'prar) *v.t.* to buy. —*v.i.* to shop.

comprender (kom·pren'der) *v.t.* 1, to comprehend; to understand. 2, to comprise; to include.

comprensible (kom·pren'si·βle) *adj.* comprehensible. —**comprensibilidad,** *n.f.* comprehensibility.

comprensión (kom·pren'sjon) *n.f.* 1, comprehension. 2, comprehensiveness.

comprensivo (kom·pren'si·βo) *adj.* 1, comprehensive. 2, understanding.

compresa (kom'pre·sa) *n.f.* compress.

compresión (kom·pre'sjon) *n.f.* compression.

compresor (kom·pre'sor) *adj.* compressing. —*n.m.* compressor.

compresora (kom·pre'so·ra) *n.f.* compressor.

comprimido (kom·pri'mi·ðo) *adj.* compressed. —*n.m.* tablet; pill.

comprimir (kom·pri'mir) *v.t.* 1, to compress. 2, to constrain.

comprobación (kom·pro·βa·'θjon; -'sjon) *n.f.* verification; check; checking.

comprobante (kom·pro'βan·te) *n.m.* receipt; voucher; check.

comprobar (kom·pro'βar) *v.t.* [*infl.:* **probar**] to verify; to check.

comprometer (kom·pro·me'ter) *v.t.* 1, to compromise. 2, to involve; to implicate. 3, to endanger. —**comprometerse,** *v.r.* 1, to commit oneself. 2, to be or become engaged.

comprometido (kom·pro·me'ti·ðo) *adj.* 1, engaged. 2, committed. 3, embarrassing.

compromisario (kom·pro·mi·'sa·rjo) *n.m.* arbitrator; umpire.

compromiso (kom·pro'mi·so) *n.m.* 1, compromise; settlement; deal. 2, appointment; engagement. 3, commitment. 4, embarrassment. 5, engagement (*prior to marriage*).

compuerta (kom'pwer·ta) *n.f.* 1, sluice; floodgate. 2, canal lock. 3, half door.

compuesto (kom'pwes·to) *v., p.p. of* **componer.** —*adj.* 1, composed; constituted. 2, repaired; fixed. 3, compound; composite. 4, calm; collected. —*n.m.* compound; composite.

compulsión (kom·pul'sjon) *n.f., law* compulsion.

compulsivo (kom·pul'si·βo) *adj.* compulsive.

compulso (kom'pul·so) *v., p.p. of* **compeler.**

compunción (kom·pun'θjon; -'sjon) *n.f.* compunction.

compungido (kom·pun'xi·ðo) *adj.* sorrowful; remorseful.

compungirse (kom·pun'xir·se) *v.r.* [*pres.ind.* **compunjo** (-'pun·xo); *pres.subjve.* **compunja** (-xa)] to feel compunction.

computar (kom·pu'tar) *v.t.* to compute; to calculate. —**computación,** *n.f.* computation; calculation.

cómputo ('kom·pu·to) *n.m.* computation; calculation.

comulgante (ko·mul'ɣan·te) *n.m. & f., eccles.* communicant.

comulgar (ko·mul'ɣar) *v.* [*pres. subjve.* **comulgue** (-'mul·ɣe); *pret.* **comulgué** (-'ɣe)] *v.t.* to be in agreement with; to believe in. —*v.i.* to receive Communion. —**comulgar ruedas de molino,** to take everything for granted; to believe everything.

común (ko'mun) *adj.* common; usual; general. —*n.m.* 1, community; public. 2, lavatory. —**por lo común,** in general.

comuna (ko'mu·na) *n.f.* commune.

comunal (ko·mu'nal) *adj.* common; communal. —*n.m.* community.
comunero (ko·mu'ne·ro) *n.m.* **1,** shareholder; co-owner. **2,** *hist.* a member of the old Castilian communities.
comunicación (ko·mu·ni·ka·'θjon; -'sjon) *n.f.* communication.
comunicado (ko·mu·ni'ka·ðo) *n.m.* communiqué.
comunicar (ko·mu·ni'kar) *v.t.* [*pres.subjve.* **comunique** (-'ni·ke); *pret.* **comuniqué** (-'ke)] **1,** to communicate; to transmit. **2,** to connect; to put in communication.
comunicativo (ko·mu·ni·ka'ti·βo) *adj.* communicative.
comunidad (ko·mu·ni'ðað) *n.f.* **1,** community. **2,** commonwealth. —**de comunidad,** jointly.
comunión (ko·mu'njon) *n.f.* **1,** communion. **2,** political party. **3,** *eccles.* congregation.
comunismo (ko·mu'nis·mo) *n.m.* communism. —**comunista,** *n.m.* & *f.* communist. —*adj.* communistic.
comunizar (ko·mu·ni'θar; -'sar) *v.t.* [*pres.subjve.* **comunice** (-'ni·θe; -se); *pret.* **comunicé** (-'θe; -'se)] to communize.
con (kon) *prep.* **1,** with: *salí con él,* I left with him. **2,** in spite of: *con todo esto,* in spite of all this. **3,** *fol. by inf.* by: *con pedirlo lo tendrás,* by asking for it, you will get it. —**con tal (de) que,** provided that. —**con que,** so that; whereupon. —**con todo,** nevertheless.
con- (kon) *prefix, var. of* **com-** *before* c, d, f, g, j, ll, n, q, s, t, v: *cóncavo,* concave; *condonar,* condone; *confiar,* confide; *congreso,* congress; *conjunto,* conjunct; *conllevar,* bear *or* suffer together; *connotar,* connote; *conquista,* conquest; *consentir,* consent; *contacto,* contact; *convertir,* convert.
conato (ko'na·to) *n.m.* endeavor; effort; attempt.
cóncavo ('kon·ka·βo) *adj.* concave; hollow. —**concavidad,** *n.f.* concavity; hollowness.
concebir (kon·θe'βir; -se'βir) *v.i.* & *v.t.* [*pres.ind.* **concibo;** *pres. subjve.* **conciba;** *pret.* **concebí** (-θe·'βi; -se'βi), **concibió**] to conceive. —**concebible,** *adj.* conceivable.
conceder (kon·θe'ðer; kon·se-) *v.t.* to concede; to grant.
concejal (kon·θe'xal; kon·se-) *n.m.* councilman; alderman.
concejo (kon'θe·xo; kon'se-) *n.m.* **1,** city council. **2,** town hall.
concentrar (kon·θen'trar; kon·sen-) *v.t.* to concentrate; to center. —**concentración,** *n.f.* concentration.
concéntrico (kon'θen·tri·ko; kon'sen-) *adj.* concentric. —**concentricidad** (-θi'ðað; -si'ðað) *n.f.* concentricity.
concepción (kon·θep'θjon; -sep·'sjon) *n.f.* conception.
concepto (kon'θep·to; -'sep·to) *n.m.* **1,** concept; idea. **2,** opinion; judgment. —**conceptual** (-'twal) *adj.* conceptual.
concernir (kon·θer'nir; kon·ser-) *v.i., used only in 3rd pers.* [*pres.ind.* **concierne;** *pres.subjve.* **concierna**] to concern; to appertain. —**concernirse,** *v.r., colloq.* to concern oneself; to be concerned.
concertar (kon·θer'tar; -ser'tar) *v.t.* [*pres.ind.* **concierto;** *pres.subjve.* **concierte**] to concert; to arrange. —**concertarse,** *v.r.* **1,** to agree. **2,** *Amer., colloq.* to hire out.
concertina (kon·θer'ti·na; kon·ser-) *n.f.* concertina.
concertino (kon·θer'ti·no; kon·ser-) *n.m.* first violin.
concesión (kon·θe'sjon; kon·se-) *n.f.* **1,** concession. **2,** grant.
concesionario (kon·θe·sjo'na·rjo; kon·se-) *n.m.* **1,** concessionaire. **2,** *law* grantee.
conciba (kon'θi·βa; kon'si-) *v., pres.subjve. of* **concebir.**
concibió (kon·θi'βjo; -si'βjo) *v., 3rd pers.sing. pret. of* **concebir.**
concibo (kon'θi·βo; -'si·βo) *v., pres.ind. of* **concebir.**
conciencia (kon'θjen·θja; -'sjen·sja) *n.f.* **1,** conscience. **2,** consciousness. —**a conciencia, 1,** conscientiously. **2,** on purpose.
concienzudo (kon·θjen'θu·ðo; -sjen'su·ðo) *adj.* conscientious; businesslike.
concierna (kon'θjer·na; -'sjer·na) *v., pres.subjve. of* **concernir.**
concierne (kon'θjer·ne; -'sjer·ne) *v., 3rd pers.sing.pres.ind. of* **concernir.**
concierte (kon'θjer·te; kon'sjer-) *v., pres.subjve. of* **concertar.**
concierto (kon'θjer·to; -'sjer·to) *v., pres.ind. of* **concertar.**
concierto *n.m.* **1,** *music* concert;

concerto. **2,** order; harmony. **3,** agreement; bargain.
conciliación (kon·θi·lja'θjon; -si·lja'sjon) *n.f.* **1,** conciliation. **2,** likeness; affinity. **3,** favor; protection.
conciliar (kon·θi'ljar; kon·si-) *v.t.* to conciliate; to reconcile. —**conciliarse,** *v.r.* to gain; to win.
conciliar *adj.* of or pert. to a council. —*n.m.* council member.
conciliatorio (kon·θi·lja'to·rjo; kon·si-) *adj.* conciliatory.
concilio (kon'θi·ljo; kon'si-) *n.m.* council.
concisión (kon·θi'sjon; kon·si-) *n.f.* brevity; conciseness.
conciso (kon'θi·so; kon'si-) *adj.* concise; short.
conciudadano (kon·θju·ða·ða·no; kon·sju-) *n.m.* fellow citizen.
cónclave ('kon·kla·βe) *also,* **conclave** (kon'kla-) *n.m.* conclave.
concluir (kon·klu'ir) *v.t.* [*pres.ind.* **concluyo** (-'klu·jo); *pres.subjve.* **concluya** (kon'klu·ja) [*p.p.* **concluído, concluso** (-'klu·so)] **1,** to conclude; to end; to finish. **2,** to infer. —**concluirse,** *v.r.* to come to an end; to conclude.
conclusión (kon·klu'sjon) *n.f.* **1,** conclusion; end. **2,** inference. —**conclusivo** (-'si·βo) *adj.* concluding; final; conclusive.
concluyente (kon·klu'jen·te) *adj.* conclusive; convincing.
concomerse (kon·ko'mer·se) *v.r., colloq.* **1,** to shrug the shoulders. **2,** to itch; twitch with an itch.
concomitancia (kon·ko·mi'tan·θja; -sja) *n.f.* concomitance. —**concomitante,** *adj.* concomitant.
concordancia (kon·kor'ðan·θja; -sja) *n.f.* **1,** concordance. **2,** *gram.* agreement; concord. **3,** *music* concord. **4,** *pl.* concordance; index of words and phrases. —**concordante,** *adj.* concordant.
concordar (kon·kor'ðar) *v.i.* [*pres.ind.* **concuerdo;** *pres.subjve.* **concuerde**] to accord; agree. —*v.t.* to harmonize; make agree.
concordia (kon'kor·ðja) *n.f.* **1,** concord; harmony. **2,** *law* agreement.
concreción (kon·kre'θjon; -'sjon) *n.f.* concretion.
concretar (kon·kre'tar) *v.t.* to define; to make concrete. —**concretarse a,** to limit oneself to.
concreto (kon'kre·to) *adj.* concrete; real. —*n.m.* **1,** concrete. **2,** concretion. —**en concreto,** in sum; in conclusion.
concubina (kon·ku'βi·na) *n.f.* concubine. —**concubinato,** *n.m.* concubinage.
concupiscencia (kon·ku·pis'θen·θja; -pi'sen·sja) *n.f.* concupiscence. —**concupiscente,** *adj.* concupiscent.
concuerde (kon'kwer·ðe) *v., pres. subjve. of* **concordar.**
concuerdo (kon'kwer·ðo) *v., pres. ind. of* **concordar.**
concurrencia (kon·ku'rren·θja; -sja) *n.f.* **1,** concurrence. **2,** attendance; gathering.
concurrente (kon·ku'rren·te) *n.m.* & *f., usu.pl.* one present at a gathering, spectacle, etc. —*adj.* concurrent.
concurrir (kon·ku'rrir) *v.i.* **1,** to concur; to agree. **2,** to attend; to be present. **3,** to compete. **4,** to frequent.
concurso (kon'kur·so) *n.m.* **1,** gathering; attendance; crowd. **2,** contest; competition.
concusión (kon·ku'sjon) *n.f.* **1,** concussion. **2,** *law* extortion.
concusionario (kon·ku·sjo'na·rjo) *adj.* extortionate. —*n.m.* extortioner.
concha ('kon·tʃa) *n.f.* **1,** shell; seashell. **2,** oyster. **3,** *theat.* prompter's shell. **4,** *Amer., colloq.* impudence.
conchabarse (kon·tʃa'βar·se) *v.r., colloq.* to conspire; to plot.
conchudo (kon'tʃu·ðo) *adj.* **1,** shell-like. **2,** *colloq.* crafty; sly. **3,** *Amer., colloq.* impudent.
conde ('kon·de) *n.m.* earl; count. —**condado** (-'da·ðo) *n.m.* earldom; county.
condecorar (kon·de·ko'rar) *v.t.* to decorate; confer a decoration upon. —**condecoración,** *n.f.* decoration; honor; medal.
condena (kon'de·na) *n.f.* term of imprisonment; sentence.
condenación (kon·de·na'θjon; -'sjon) *n.f.* **1,** condemnation. **2,** *theol.* damnation.
condenar (kon·de'nar) *v.t.* **1,** to condemn. **2,** to damn. **3,** to convict. **4,** to sentence.
condensar (kon·den'sar) *v.t.* to condense. —**condensación,** *n.f.* condensation. —**condensador,** *n.m.* condenser.
condesa (kon'de·sa) *n.f.* countess.
condescendencia (kon·des·θen·

'den·θja; -de·sen'den·sja) *n.f.* 1, condescension. 2, indulgence; leniency.
condescender (kon·des·θen'der; -de·sen'der) *v.i.* [*infl.:* **descender**] to condescend; to be complacent.
condescendiente (kon·des·θen·'djen·te; kon·de·sen-) *adj.* 1, condescending. 2, indulgent; lenient.
condición (kon·di'θjon; -'sjon) *n.f.* 1, condition; quality. 2, quality; rank. 3, stipulation. —**a condición de que**, on condition that.
condicional (kon·di·θjo'nal; -sjo·'nal) *adj.* conditional.
condicionar (kon·di·θjo'nar; -sjo'nar) *v.t.* = **acondicionar.** —*v.i.* to impose conditions.
condigno (kon'diɣ·no) *adj.* condign.
condimentar (kon·di·men'tar) *v.t.* to dress; to season.
condimento (kon·di'men·to) *n.m.* seasoning; condiment.
condiscípulo (kon·dis'θi·pu·lo; -di'si·pu·lo) *n.m.* fellow student.
condolencia (kon·do'len·θja; -sja) *n.f.* condolence; sympathy.
condolerse (kon·do'ler·se) *v.r.* [*infl.:* **doler**] to condole; feel sorry. —**condolerse de**, to feel sorry for; sympathize with.
condominio (kon·do'mi·njo) *n.m.* condominium.
condonar (kon·do'nar) *v.t.* to pardon; condone. —**condonación**, *n.f.* pardon; condonement.
cóndor ('kon·dor) *n.m.* condor.
conducción (kon·duk'θjon; -'sjon) *n.f.* 1, conduction. 2, conveyance. 3, transportation. 4, driving; drive. 5, wage *or* price agreement.
conducente (kon·du'θen·te; 'sen·te) *adj.* conducive.
conducir (kon·du'θir; -'sir) *v.* [*pres.ind.* **conduzco**; *pres.subjve.* **conduzca**; *pret.* **conduje**] —*v.t.* 1, to convey; to transport. 2, to conduct; to direct; to lead. 3, to drive (a vehicle). —*v.i.* to conduce; to be conducive. —**conducirse**, *v.r.* to conduct oneself; to behave.
conducta (kon'duk·ta) *n.f.* behavior.
conductible (kon·duk'ti·βle) *adj.* conductible. —**conductibilidad**, *n.f.* conductibility.
conductivo (kon·duk'ti·βo) *adj.* conductive. —**conductividad**, *n.f.* conductivity.
conducto (kon'duk·to) *n.m.* 1, conduit; tube; pipe. 2, drain; sewer. 3, channel; route. 4, intermediary; go-between. 5, *anat.* duct; canal. —**por conducto de**, through.
conductor (kon·duk'tor) *adj.* conducting. —*n.m.* conductor; driver.
conduje (kon'du·xe) *v., pret. of* **conducir.**
conduzca (kon'duθ·ka; -'dus·ka) *v., pres.subjve. of* **conducir.**
conduzco (kon'duθ·ko; -'dus·ko) *v., 1st pers.sing.pres.ind. of* **conducir.**
conectar (ko·nek'tar) *v.t.* & *i.* to connect.
conectivo (ko·nek'ti·βo) *adj.* connective.
conejera (ko·ne'xe·ra) *n.f.* rabbit hutch; burrow; warren.
conejillo (ko·ne'xi·ʎo; -jo) *n.m., dim. of* **conejo.** —**conejillo de Indias**, guinea pig.
conejo (ko'ne·xo) *n.m.* rabbit. —**conejo de Noruega**, lemming.
conexión (ko·nek'sjon) *n.f.* connection.
confección (kon·fek'θjon; -'sjon) *n.f.* confection.
confeccionar (kon·fek·θjo'nar; -sjo'nar) *v.t.* to prepare; to make.
confederar (kon·fe·ðe'rar) *v.t.* to confederate. —**confederación**, *n.f.* confederation; confederacy. —**confederado**, *adj.* & *n.m.* confederate.
conferencia (kon·fe'ren·θja; -sja) *n.f.* 1, conference; meeting. 2, lecture. —**conferenciante**, *n.m.* & *f.* lecturer.
conferenciar (kon·fe·ren'θjar; -'sjar) *v.i.* to confer; to hold a conference.
conferir (kon·fe'rir) *v.t.* [*pres.ind.* **confiero**; *pres.subjve.* **confiera**; *pret.* **conferí, confirió**; *ger.* **confiriendo**] to confer; to bestow.
confesar (kon·fe'sar) *v.t.* [*pres.ind.* **confieso**; *pres.subjve.* **confiese**; *p.p.* **confesado, confeso** (-'fe·so)] to confess; to avow. —**confesarse**, *v.r.* to confess; to make confession.
confesión (kon·fe'sjon) *n.f.* confession.
confesionario (kon·fe·sjo'na·rjo) *n.m.* 1, confessional; book of confession. 2, confessional box.
confeso (kon'fe·so) *adj., law* confessed. —*n.m.* lay brother.
confesonario (kon·fe·so'na·rjo) *n.m.* confessional box.

confesor (kon·fe'sor) *n.m.* confessor.
confeti (kon'fe·ti) *n.m.* confetti.
confiado (kon'fja·ðo) *adj.* 1, confident; self-confident. 2, trusting; credulous.
confianza (kon'fjan·θa; -sa) *n.f.* 1, confidence; trust; reliance. 2, familiarity; camaraderie. —**de confianza**, trusted; reliable. —**en confianza**, 1, confidentially. 2, without formality.
confianzudo (kon·fjan'θu·ðo; -'su·ðo) *adj., colloq.* 1, overfamiliar; presumptuous. 2, *Amer.* meddlesome.
confiar (kon'fjar) *v.i.* [*infl.:* **enviar**] 1, to hope. 2, to have trust (in). —*v.t.* to confide; to entrust.
confidencia (kon·fi'ðen·θja; -sja) *n.f.* confidence; secret. —**confidencial**, *adj.* confidential.
confidente (kon·fi'ðen·te) *n.m.* 1, confidant. 2, love seat. —*n.f.* confidante.
confiera (kon'fje·ra) *v., pres. subjve. of* **conferir**.
confiero (kon'fje·ro) *v., pres.ind. of* **conferir**.
confiese (kon'fje·se) *v., pres.subjve. of* **confesar**.
confieso (kon'fje·so) *v., pres.ind. of* **confesar**.
configurar (kon·fi·ɣu'rar) *v.t.* to outline; to shape; to give configuration to. —**configuración**, *n.f.* configuration.
confín (kon'fin) *n.m.* limit; boundary.
confinamiento (kon·fi·na'mjen·to) *n.m.* 1, confinement. 2, exile. 3, restriction under surveillance.
confinar (kon·fi'nar) *v.t.* 1, to confine. 2, to exile; to banish. —*v.i.* to border. —**confinar con**, to border on.
confines (kon'fi·nes) *n.m.pl.* confines; limits.
confiriendo (kon·fi'rjen·do) *v., ger. of* **conferir**.
confirió (kon·fi'rjo) *v., 3rd pers. sing.pret. of* **conferir**.
confirmar (kon·fir'mar) *v.t.* to confirm. —**confirmación**, *n.f.* confirmation. —**confirmatorio**, *adj.* confirmatory.
confiscar (kon·fis'kar) *v.t.* [*pres. subjve.* **confisque** (-'fis·ke); *pret.* **confisqué** (-'ke)] to confiscate. —**confiscación**, *n.f.* confiscation.
confitar (kon·fi'tar) *v.t.* to candy; glaze.
confite (kon'fi·te) *n.m.* candy; sweetmeat.
confitería (kon·fi·te'ri·a) *n.f.* candy shop; confectionery. —**confitero** (-'te·ro) *n.m.* confectioner.
confitura (kon·fi'tu·ra) *n.f.* confection; preserve.
conflagración (kon·fla·ɣra·'θjon; -'sjon) *n.f.* conflagration.
conflicto (kon'flik·to) *n.m.* conflict.
confluencia (kon·flu'en·θja; -sja) *n.f.* confluence.
confluente (kon·flu'en·te) *adj.* confluent. —*n.m.* confluence.
confluir (kon·flu'ir) *v.i.* [*infl.:* **huir**] 1, to join; converge (*of roads or rivers*). 2, to gather (*of crowds*).
conformar (kon·for'mar) *v.t.* & *i.* to conform; to adjust; to fit. —**conformarse**, *v.r.* 1, to conform; to comply. 2, *Amer.* to resign oneself; to acquiesce. —**conformación**, *n.f.* conformation.
conforme (kon'for·me) *adj.* 1, conformable; suited; in accordance. 2, compliant; conforming. 3, resigned. —**conforme a** *or* **con**, according to; in accordance with.
conformidad (kon·for·mi'ðað) *n.f.* 1, agreement. 2, conformity. —**de conformidad con**, in accordance with; according to.
conformista (kon·for'mis·ta) *n.m.* & *f.* conformist.
confortable (kon·for'ta·βle) *adj.* 1, comforting. 2, comfortable.
confortación (kon·for·ta'θjon; -'sjon) *n.f.* consolation; comfort.
confortante (kon·for'tan·te) *adj.* comforting. —*n.m.* & *f.* comforter.
confortar (kon·for'tar) *v.t.* & *i.* to comfort.
conforte (kon'for·te) *n.m.* = **confortación**.
confraternidad (kon·fra·ter·ni'ðað) *n.f.* fellowship; confraternity.
confrontación (kon·fron·ta'θjon; -'sjon) *n.f.* confrontation.
confrontar (kon·fron'tar) *v.t.* 1, to confront; to bring face to face. 2, to compare. —*v.i.* to border. —**confrontarse con**, to face; to confront.
confundir (kon·fun'dir) *v.t.* to confuse; to confound. —**confundirse**, *v.r.* to be bewildered; to be abashed.

confusión (kon·fu'sjon) *n.f.* confusion.
confuso (kon'fu·so) *adj.* confused; perplexed.
confutar (kon·fu'tar) *v.t.* to confute. —**confutación,** *n.f.* confutation.
congelar (kon·xe'lar) *v.t.* to congeal; to freeze. —**congelación,** *n.f.* freezing. —**congelador,** *n.m.* freezer.
congenial (kon·xe'njal) *adj.* congenial. —**congeniar,** *v.i.* to get along; be congenial.
congénito (kon'xe·ni·to) *adj.* congenital.
congestión (kon·xes'tjon) *n.f.* congestion. —**congestionar** (-'nar) *v.t.* to congest, as with blood; cause congestion in.
conglomerar (kon·glo·me'rar) *v.t.* to conglomerate. —**conglomeración,** *n.f.* conglomeration.
congoja (kon'go·xa) *n.f.* anguish; grief.
congoleño (kon·go'le·ɲo) *adj.* & *n.m.* Congolese. *Also,* **congolés.**
congraciar (kon·gra'θjar; -'sjar) *v.t.* to ingratiate. —**congraciador,** *adj.* ingratiating. —**congraciamiento,** *n.m.* ingratiation.
congratular (kon·gra·tu'lar) *v.t.* to congratulate. —**congratulación,** *n.f.* congratulation.
congregación (kon·gre·ɣa'θjon; -'sjon) *n.f.* congregation. —**congregacionalista,** *adj.* congregational.
congregar (kon·gre'ɣar) *v.t.* [*pres.subjve.* **congregue** (-'gre·ɣe); *pret.* **congregué** (-'ɣe)] to assemble; to bring together. —**congregarse,** *v.r.* to congregate; to assemble; to meet.
congresista (kon·gre'sis·ta) *n.m.* & *f.* member of Congress.
congreso (kon'gre·so) *n.m.* **1,** congress; assembly. **2,** convention.
congrio ('kon·grjo) *n.m.* eel.
congruencia (kon'grwen·θja; -sja) *n.f.* **1,** congruence. **2,** congruity. **3,** congruousness.
congruente (kon'grwen·te) *adj.* **1,** congruent. **2,** congruous.
congruo ('kon·grwo) *adj.* congruous. —**congruidad,** *n.f.* congruousness; congruity.
cónico ('ko·ni·ko) *adj.* conical; conic.
conífero (ko'ni·fe·ro) *adj.* coniferous. —**conífera,** *n.f.* conifer.
conjetura (kon·xe'tu·ra) *n.f.* conjecture. —**conjetural,** *adj.* conjectural. —**conjeturar,** *v.t.* & *i.* to conjecture.
conjugar (kon·xu'ɣar) *v.t.* [*pres. subjve.* **conjugue** (-'xu·ɣe); *pret.* **conjugué** (-'ɣe)] to conjugate. —**conjugación,** *n.f.* conjugation.
conjunción (kon·xun'θjon; -'sjon) *n.f.* conjunction.
conjuntivitis (kon·xun·ti'βi·tis) *n.f.* conjunctivitis.
conjuntivo (kon·xun'ti·βo) *adj.* conjunctive.
conjunto (kon'xun·to) *n.m.* **1,** mass; whole; entirety. **2,** *music* ensemble. —*adj.* joined; related.
conjuración (kon·xu·ra'θjon; -'sjon) *n.f.* conspiracy; plot. *Also,* **conjura** (kon'xu·ra).
conjurado (kon·xu'ra·ðo) *n.m.* conspirator.
conjurar (kon·xu'rar) *v.t.* **1,** to entreat. **2,** to exorcise. **3,** to plot; to scheme. —*v.i.* to conspire.
conjuro (kon'xu·ro) *n.m.* **1,** spell; incantation. **2,** entreaty; plea.
conmemorar (kon·me·mo'rar; ko·me-) *v.t.* to commemorate. —**conmemoración,** *n.f.* commemoration.
conmemorativo (kon·me·mo·ra'ti·βo) *adj.* commemorative.
conmensurable (kon·men·su·'ra·βle) *adj.* commensurable. —**conmensurado** (-'ra·ðo) *adj.* commensurate.
conmigo (kon'mi·ɣo) with me; with myself.
conminar (kon·mi'nar) *v.t.* to threaten, esp. with punishment; denounce. —**conminación,** *n.f.* threat, esp. of punishment; denunciation. —**conminatorio,** *adj.* threatening; denunciatory.
conmiseración (kon·mi·se·ra·'θjon; ko·mi·se·ra'sjon) *n.f.* commiseration; pity.
conmoción (kon·mo'θjon; -'sjon) *n.f.* commotion; excitement.
conmover (kon·mo'βer; ko·mo-) *v.t.* [*infl.:* **mover**] **1,** to disturb; to stir up; to rouse. **2,** to move; to affect emotionally. —**conmovedor** (-βe'ðor) *adj.* moving; touching.
conmutación (kon·mu·ta'θjon; ko·mu·ta'sjon) *n.f.* commutation.
conmutador (kon·mu·ta'ðor; ko·mu-) *adj.* commutating. —*n.m.* electric switch. —**cuadro conmutador,** switchboard.
conmutar (kon·mu'tar; ko·mu-)

v.t. **1,** to commute; to change. **2,** to barter; to exchange.
connatural (kon·na·tu'ral) *adj.* inborn; inherent. **—connaturalización,** *n.f.* acclimation. **—connaturalizarse,** *v.r.* [*infl.:* **naturalizar**] to become acclimated *or* accustomed.
connivencia (kon·ni'βen·θja; -sja) *n.f.* connivance.
connotar (kon·no'tar) *v.t.* to connote. **—connotación,** *n.f.* connotation. **—connotado,** *adj., Amer.* outstanding.
cono ('ko-no) *n.m.* cone.
conocedor (ko·no·θe'ðor; -se'ðor) *adj.* expert; skilled. *—n.m.* connoisseur; critic.
conocer (ko·no'θer; -'ser) *v.t.* [*pres.ind.* **conozco** (-'noθ·ko; -'nos·ko); *pres.subjve.* **conozca** (-ka)] **1,** to know; to be *or* become acquainted with. **2,** to perceive; to distinguish. **3,** *law* to try (a case). **—dar a conocer,** to make known.
conocido (ko·no'θi·ðo; -'si·ðo) *adj.* well-known. *—n.m.* acquaintance.
conocimiento (ko·no·θi'mjen·to; ko·no·si-) *n.m.* **1,** knowledge; skill. **2,** understanding. **3,** consciousness. **4,** *Amer.* baggage check. **—conocimiento de embarque,** bill of lading.
conopeo (ko·no'pe·o) *n.m., eccles.* canopy.
conque ('kon·ke) *adv. & conj.* so then; now then. *—n.m., colloq.* condition; stipulation.
conquista (kon'kis·ta) *n.f.* conquest.
conquistar (kon·kis'tar) *v.t.* to conquer; to vanquish. **—conquistador,** *n.m.* conqueror.
consabido (kon·sa'βi·ðo) *adj.* aforementioned.
consagrar (kon·sa'ɣrar) *v.t.* **1,** to consecrate. **2,** to dedicate; to devote. **3,** to sanction. **—consagración,** *n.f.* consecration.
consanguíneo (kon·san'gi·ne·o) *adj.* consanguineous; kindred. **—consanguinidad** (-ni'ðað) *n.f.* consanguinity.
consciente (kons'θjen·te; kon·'sjen·te) *adj. & n.m.* conscious. **—consciencia,** *n.f.* consciousness.
conscripción (kons·krip'θjon; -'sjon) *n.f.* conscription.
conscripto (kons'krip·to) *n.m.* conscript.
consecución (kon·se·ku'θjon; -'sjon) *n.f.* attainment; acquisition.
consecuencia (kon·se'kwen·θja; -sja) *n.f.* **1,** consequence; outcome. **2,** consistency; accordance. **—en consecuencia,** accordingly. **—por consecuencia,** therefore; consequently.
consecuente (kon·se'kwen·te) *adj.* consequent.
consecutivo (kon·se·ku'ti·βo) *adj.* consecutive.
conseguir (kon·se'ɣir) *v.t.* [*infl.:* **seguir**] **1,** to attain; to achieve. **2,** to get; to obtain. **3,** *colloq.* to find; to locate.
conseja (kon'se·xa) *n.f.* saga; fairy tale.
consejero (kon·se'xe·ro) *n.m.* **1,** counselor; adviser. **2,** councilor; board member.
consejo (kon'se·xo) *n.m.* **1,** counsel; advice. **2,** council; board. **—consejo de guerra, 1,** council of war. **2,** court-martial.
consenso (kon'sen·so) *n.m.* consensus.
consentido (kon·sen'ti·ðo) *adj.* **1,** pampered; spoiled. **2,** complaisant; indulgent.
consentimiento (kon·sen·ti·'mjen·to) *n.m.* consent.
consentir (kon·sen'tir) *v.* [*infl.:* **sentir**] *—v.t.* **1,** to permit; to allow. **2,** to consent to; to agree to. **3,** to spoil; to pamper. *—v.i.* to weaken; to become loose. **—consentirse,** *v.r.* to crack; to give way.
conserje (kon'ser·xe) *n.m.* janitor; concierge; porter. **—conserjería,** *n.f.* porter's desk.
conserva (kon'ser·βa) *n.f.* conserve; preserve. **—conservas alimenticias,** canned goods. **—en conserva,** canned.
conservación (kon·ser·βa'θjon; -'sjon) *n.f.* **1,** conservation. **2,** preservation.
conservador (kon·ser·βa'ðor) *adj. & n.m.* **1,** conservative. **2,** preservative. *—n.m.* preserver; keeper; guardian.
conservar (kon·ser'βar) *v.t.* to conserve; to keep. **—conservarse,** *v.r.* to take care of oneself; to keep fit.
conservatorio (kon·ser·βa'to·rjo) *n.m.* conservatory.
considerable (kon·si·ðe'ra·βle) *adj.* considerable.
consideración (kon·si·ðe·ra·'θjon; -'sjon) *n.f.* consideration.
considerado (kon·si·ðe'ra·ðo)

adj. **1,** considered. **2,** considerate.
considerar (kon·si·de'rar) *v.t.* to consider.
consigna (kon'siɣ·na) *n.f.* **1,** *mil.* password. **2,** *R.R.* checkroom.
consignar (kon·siɣ'nar) *v.t.* **1,** to assign. **2,** to consign. **3,** to point out; indicate. **—consignación,** *n.f.* consignment. **—consignador,** *n.m.* consignor. **—consignatario,** *n.m.* consignee.
consigo (kon'si·ɣo) with you; with him; with her; with them; with himself; with herself; with oneself; with yourself; with yourselves; with themselves.
consiguiente (kon·si'ɣjen·te) *adj.* consequent; consequential. **—por consiguiente,** therefore; consequently.
consistente (kon·sis'ten·te) *adj.* consistent. **—consistencia,** *n.f.* consistency.
consistir (kon·sis'tir) *v.i.* to consist. **—consistir en,** to consist of *or* in.
consocio (kon'so·θjo; -sjo) *n.m.* partner; associate.
consola (kon'so·la) *n.f.* console; console table.
consolar (kon·so'lar) *v.t.* [*pres. ind.* **consuelo;** *pres.subjve.* **consuele**] to console; comfort. **—consolación,** *n.f.* consolation; comfort.
consolidar (kon·so·li'ðar) *v.t.* to consolidate. **—consolidación,** *n.f.* consolidation.
consomé *also,* **consommé** (kon·so·'me) *n.m.* consommé.
consonancia (kon·so'nan·θja; -sja) *n.f.* **1,** consonance. **2,** harmony; accord. **3,** rhyme.
consonante (kon·so'nan·te) *adj.* consonant; rhyming. **—***n.m.* rhyme. **—***n.f.* consonant.
consonar (kon·so'nar) *v.i.* [*infl.:* **sonar**] to harmonize; to rhyme.
consorte (kon'sor·te) *n.m.* & *f.* consort. **—consortes,** *n.m.* & *f.pl.,* *law* colitigants.
conspicuo (kons'pi·kwo) *adj.* conspicuous.
conspirar (kons·pi'rar) *v.i.* to conspire; to plot. **—conspiración,** *n.f.* conspiracy. **—conspirador,** *n.m.* conspirator.
constancia (kons'tan·θja; -sja) *n.f.* **1,** constancy. **2,** certainty; proof.
constante (kons'tan·te) *adj.* constant; firm. **—***n.f.* constant.
constar (kons'tar) *v.i.* **1,** to be clear; to be evident. **2,** to consist (in *or* of). **—hacer constar,** to state.
constatar (kons·ta'tar) *v.t.* to prove; establish. **—constatación,** *n.f.* proof.
constelación (kons·te·la'θjon; -'sjon) *n.f.* constellation.
consternar (kons·ter'nar) *v.t.* to consternate; to upset. **—consternación,** *n.f.* consternation.
constipación (kons·ti·pa'θjon; -'sjon) *n.f.* **1,** cold. **2,** constipation.
constipado (kons·ti'pa·ðo) *adj.* **1,** suffering from a cold. **2,** constipated. **—***n.m.* cold.
constipar (kons·ti'par) *v.t.* **1,** to constrict; to stop up. **2,** to constipate. **—constiparse,** *v.r.* to catch cold.
constitución (kons·ti·tu'θjon; -'sjon) *n.f.* constitution. **—constitucional,** *adj.* constitutional. **—***n.m.* & *f.* constitutionalist.
constituir (kons·ti·tu'ir) *v.t.* [*pres.ind.* **constituyo** (-'tu·jo); *pres.subjve.* **constituya** (-ja); *pret.* **constituí** (-tu'i); **constituyó** (-'jo)] to constitute.
constituyente (kons·ti·tu'jen·te) *adj.* & *n.m.* constituent; component. *Also,* **constitutivo** (-'ti·βo).
constreñimiento (kons·tre·ɲi·'mjen·to) *n.m.* constraint; compulsion.
constreñir (kons·tre'ɲir) *v.t.* [*pres.ind.* **constriño** (-'tri·ɲo); *pres. subjve.* **constriña** (-ɲa); *pret.* **constreñí** (-tre'ɲi), **constriñó** (-tri'ɲo)] to constrain; to compel.
constricción (kons·trik'θjon; -'sjon) *n.f.* constriction.
constrictor (kons·trik'tor) *adj.* constricting; constrictive. **—***n.m., anat.* constrictor.
construcción (kons·truk'θjon; -'sjon) *n.f.* **1,** construction; fabrication. **2,** edifice; structure. **3,** *gram.* construction.
constructivo (kons·truk'ti·βo) *adj.* constructive.
constructor (kons·truk'tor) *adj.* building; constructing. **—***n.m.* builder; constructor.
construir (kons·tru'ir) *v.t.* [*pres. ind.* **construyo** (-'tru·jo) *pres. subjve.* **construya** (-'tru·ja); *pret.* **construí** (-tru'i), **construyó** (-tru·'jo)] **1,** to form; to build; to construct. **2,** to construe.

consuele (kon'swe·le) *v., pres. subjve. of* consolar.
consuelo (kon'swe·lo) *v., pres.ind. of* consolar.
consuelo *n.m.* consolation; relief; comfort.
consuetudinario (kon·swe·tu·ði'na·rjo) *adj.* habitual; customary.
cónsul ('kon·sul) *n.m.* consul.
consulado (kon·su'la·ðo) *n.m.* consulate; consulship.
consulta (kon'sul·ta) *n.f.* **1,** consultation; conference. **2,** (professional) opinion.
consultación (kon·sul·ta'θjon; -'sjon) *n.f.* consultation; conference.
consultante (kon·sul'tan·te) *adj.* & *n.m.* & *f.* = **consultor.**
consultar (kon·sul'tar) *v.t.* **1,** to consult. **2,** to ask advice on; to discuss. —*v.i.* to consult; to confer. —**consultar con la almohada,** *colloq.* to sleep on a problem.
consultivo (kon·sul'ti·βo) *adj.* consultative; advisory.
consultor (kon·sul'tor) *adj.* consulting. —*n.m.* **1,** consultant. **2,** counsel; counselor.
consultorio (kon·sul'to·rjo) *n.m.* doctor's office.
consumado (kon·su'ma·ðo) *adj.* finished; accomplished; consummate. —*n.m.* consommé.
consumar (kon·su'mar) *v.t.* to consummate; to finish. —**consumación,** *n.f.* consummation.
consumido (kon·su'mi·ðo) *adj.* emaciated; spent.
consumidor (kon·su·mi'ðor) *adj.* consuming. —*n.m.* **1,** consumer. **2,** restaurant customer; diner; drinker.
consumir (kon·su'mir) *v.t.* [*p.p.* **consumido, consunto** (-'sun·to)] **1,** to consume. **2,** to eat; to corrode. —**consumirse,** *v.r.* to waste away; to languish.
consumo (kon'su·mo) *n.m.* consumption (*of food, goods, etc.*).
consunción (kon·sun'θjon; -'sjon) *n.f., med.* consumption.
contabilidad (kon·ta·βi·li'ðað) *n.f.* bookkeeping; accounting.
contable (kon'ta·βle) *n.m.* accountant; bookkeeper. —*adj.* countable.
contacto (kon'tak·to) *n.m.* contact; touch.
contado (kon'ta·ðo) *adj.* rare; scarce. —**contados,** *adj.pl.* few; a few. —**al contado,** cash. —**de contado,** at once.
contador (kon·ta'ðor) *n.m.* **1,** accountant. **2,** *law* auditor. **3,** controller. **4,** meter; counter. **5,** cash register. **6,** *naut.* purser.
contaduría (kon·ta·ðu'ri·a) *n.f.* **1,** accountancy. **2,** cashier's or accountant's office. **3,** *theat.* box office.
contagiar (kon·ta'xjar) *v.t.* **1,** to infect. **2,** to communicate (disease, ideas, etc.).
contagio (kon'ta·xjo) *n.m.* contagion. —**contagioso** (-'xjo·so) *adj.* contagious.
contaminar (kon·ta·mi'nar) *v.t.* to contaminate. —**contaminación,** *n.f.* contamination.
contante (kon'tan·te) *adj.* (*of money*) ready. —**dinero contante y sonante,** ready cash.
contar (kon'tar) *v.t.* & *i.* [*pres.ind.* **cuento;** *pres. subjve.* **cuente**] to count. —*v.t.* to tell; relate. —**a contar desde,** starting from *or* with. —**contar con, 1,** to count on. **2,** to reckon with. —**contar hacer (una cosa)** to count on doing; expect to do.
contemplar (kon·tem'plar) *v.t.* & *i.* to contemplate. —**contemplación,** *n.f.* contemplation. —**contemplativo,** *adj.* contemplative.
contemporáneo (kon·tem·po·'ra·ne·o) *adj.* contemporaneous; contemporary.
contemporizar (kon·tem·po·ri·'θar; -'sar) *v.i.* [*infl.:* **temporizar**] to temporize.
contención (kon·ten'θjon; -'sjon) *n.f.* **1,** contention. **2,** *law* litigation; suit.
contencioso (kon·ten'θjo·so; -'sjo·so) *adj.* **1,** quarrelsome. **2,** *law* litigious; contentious.
contender (kon·ten'der) *v.i.* [*infl.:* **tender**] to contend; to dispute.
contener (kon·te'ner) *v.t.* [*infl.:* **tener**] to contain. —**contenerse,** *v.r.* to keep one's temper; to refrain.
contenido (kon·te'ni·ðo) *n.m.* contents; content.
contenta (kon'ten·ta) *n.f.* **1,** present; gift. **2,** *comm.* endorsement.
contentadizo (kon·ten·ta'ði·θo; -so) *adj.* [*also,* **bien contentadizo**] easy to please. —**mal contentadizo,** hard to please.

contentamiento (kon·ten·ta·'mjen·to) *n.m.* contentment.
contentar (kon·ten'tar) *v.t.* **1,** to please; to content. **2,** *comm.* to endorse. **3,** *W.I.* = **reconciliar.** —**contentarse,** *v.r.* to be satisfied.
contento (kon'ten·to) *adj.* glad; happy; pleased. —*n.m.* joy; mirth.
conteo (kon'te·o) *n.m.* countdown.
contera (kon'te·ra) *n.f.* **1,** tip (*of a cane, umbrella, etc.*). **2,** refrain (*of a song or poem*).
contérmino (kon'ter·mi·no) *adj.* contiguous.
contertulio (kon·ter'tu·ljo) *n.m.* **1,** party guest. **2,** fellow member. *Also,* **contertuliano** (-'lja·no).
contesta (kon'tes·ta) *n.f., Amer.* **1,** answer. **2,** chat.
contestar (kon·tes'tar) *v.t.* & *i.* to answer; to reply. —**contestación,** *n.f.* answer; reply.
contexto (kon'teks·to) *n.m.* context.
contextura (kon·teks'tu·ra) *n.f.* texture; composition.
contienda (kon'tjen·da) *n.f.* contest; dispute.
contigo (kon'ti·ɣo) with you; with thee; with yourself; with thyself.
contigüidad (kon·ti·ɣwi'ðað) *n.f.* contiguity; proximity.
contiguo (kon'ti·ɣwo) *adj.* contiguous.
continencia (kon·ti'nen·θja; -sja) *n.f.* continence.
continente (kon·ti'nen·te) *adj.* continent; moderate. —*n.m.* **1,** container. **2,** *geog.* continent. **3,** countenance; mien. —**continental,** *adj.* continental.
contingencia (kon·tin'xen·θja; -sja) *n.f.* contingency.
contingente (kon·tin'xen·te) *adj.* & *n.m.* contingent.
continuación (kon·ti·nwa'θjon; -'sjon) *n.f.* **1,** continuation. **2,** continuance. —**a continuación,** following; next.
continuamente (kon·ti·nwa·'men·te) *adv.* continuously. *Also,* **continuadamente** (-nwa·ða'men·te).
continuar (kon·ti'nwar) *v.t.* [*pres. ind.* **continúo** (-'nu·o); *pres.subjve.* **continúe** (-'nu·e)] to continue; pursue. —*v.i.* **1,** [*also,* **continuarse,** *v.r.*] to continue; last; go on; keep on; keep up. **2,** to stay; remain. —**continuar con,** to adjoin. —**continuarse con,** to join; connect with.
continuidad (kon·ti·nwi'ðað) *n.f.* continuity. —**solución de continuidad,** break in continuity.
continuo (kon'ti·nwo) *adj.* **1,** continuous; continual. **2,** persistent. —*n.m.* continuum. —*adv.* [*also,* **de continuo**] continuously.
contonearse (kon·to·ne'ar·se) *v.r.* **1,** to strut; to swagger. **2,** to waddle. —**contoneo** (-'ne·o) *n.m.* strut; swagger; waddle.
contorcerse (kon·tor'θer·se; -'ser·se) *v.r.* [*infl.:* **torcer**] to be contorted; to twist.
contornar (kon·tor'nar) *v.t.* **1,** to go around. **2,** to trace; to outline. *Also,* **contornear** (-ne'ar).
contorno (kon'tor·no) *n.m.* **1,** contour; outline. **2,** *usu.pl.* environs; vicinity. —**en contorno,** around.
contorsión (kon·tor'sjon) *n.f.* contortion.
contorsionista (kon·tor·sjo'nis·ta) *n.m.* & *f.* contortionist.
contra ('kon·tra) *prep.* **1,** against; opposite; in opposition to. **2,** facing. —*n.m.* opposite opinion; con. —*n.f.* difficulty; obstacle. —**el pro y el contra,** the pros and cons. —**llevar la contra a,** *colloq.* to disagree with.
contra- (kon·tra) *prefix* contra-; against; opposite: *contravenir,* contravene.
contraalmirante (kon·tra·al·mi'ran·te; -tral·mi'ran·te) *n.m.* rear admiral.
contraatacar (kon·tra·a·ta'kar; -tra·ta'kar) *v.t.* & *i.* [*infl.:* **atacar**] to counterattack.
contraataque (kon·tra·a'ta·ke; -tra'ta·ke) *n.m.* counterattack.
contrabalancear (kon·tra·βa·lan·θe'ar; -se'ar) *v.t.* to counterbalance.
contrabandear (kon·tra·βan·de'ar) *v.t.* to smuggle. —**contrabandista,** *adj.* smuggling. —*n.m.* & *f.* smuggler.
contrabando (kon·tra'βan·do) *n.m.* **1,** contraband. **2,** smuggling.
contrabajo (kon·tra'βa·xo) *n.m.* bass; double bass.
contracarril (kon·tra·ka'rril) *n.m.* guard rail.
contracción (kon·trak'θjon; -'sjon) *n.f.* contraction.
contractual (kon·trak'twal) *adj.* contractual.

contradanza (kon·tra'ðan·θa; -sa) *n.f.* country dance; square dance.
contradecir (kon·tra·ðe'θir; -'sir) *v.t.* [*infl.:* **decir**] to contradict.
contradicción (kon·tra·ðik'θjon; -'sjon) *n.f.* contradiction.
contradictorio (kon·tra·ðik'to·rjo) *adj.* contradictory.
contraer (kon·tra'er) *v.t.* & *i.* [*infl.:* **traer**; *p.p.* **contraído** (-tra·'i·ðo), **contracto** (-'trak·to)] **1,** to contract. **2,** to shrink.
contraespionaje (kon·tra·es·pjo'na·xe) *n.m.* counterespionage.
contrafuerte (kon·tra'fwer·te) *n.m.* **1,** stiffener (*for a shoe*). **2,** girth; strap (*for a saddle*). **3,** *archit.* buttress.
contragolpe (kon·tra'ɣol·pe) *n.m.* **1,** backlash. **2,** *mech.* back or reverse stroke.
contrahacer (kon·tra·a'θer; -tra·'ser) *v.t.* [*infl.:* **hacer**] **1,** to counterfeit; to falsify. **2,** to mimic; to ape.
contrahecho (kon·tra'e·tʃo) *v.*, *p.p. of* **contrahacer.** —*adj.* **1,** counterfeit. **2,** humpbacked. **3,** malformed. —*n.m.* humpback; hunchback.
contralor (kon·tra'lor) *n.m.*, *Amer.* comptroller; auditor.
contralto (kon'tral·to) *n.m.* & *f.* contralto.
contramaestre (kon·tra·ma'es·tre) *n.m.* **1,** foreman. **2,** *naut.* boatswain; petty officer.
contramandar (kon·tra·man·'dar) *v.t.* to countermand. —**contramandato** (-'da·to) *n.m.* countermand.
contramarca (kon·tra'mar·ka) *n.f.* countermark. —**contramarcar,** *v.t.* [*infl.:* **marcar**] to countermark.
contranatural (kon·tra·na·tu·'ral) *adj.* unnatural; abnormal.
contraofensiva (kon·tra·o·fen·'si·βa) *n.f.* counteroffensive.
contraorden (kon·tra'or·ðen) *n.f.* countermand.
contraparte (kon·tra'par·te) *n.f.* counterpart; complement.
contrapartida (kon·tra·par'ti·ða) *n.f.*, *comm.* corrective entry.
contrapelo (kon·tra'pe·lo) *n.m.*, *in* **a contrapelo,** against the grain.
contrapesar (kon·tra·pe'sar) *v.t.* to counterbalance. —**contrapeso** (-'pe·so) *n.m.* counterpoise; counterbalance.
contraproducente (kon·tra·pro·ðu'θen·te; -'sen·te) *adj.* self-defeating; counter to one's purposes.
contrapunto (kon·tra'pun·to) *n.m.* counterpoint.
contrariar (kon·tra'rjar) *v.t.* [*pres.ind.* **contrarío** (-'ri·o); *pres. subjve.* **contraríe** (-'ri·e)] **1,** to contradict; to oppose. **2,** to vex; to annoy.
contrariedad (kon·tra·rje'ðað) *n.f.* **1,** contrariness; contradiction; opposition. **2,** vexation; annoyance.
contrario (kon'tra·rjo) *adj.* contrary; opposite. —*n.m.* **1,** opponent; competitor. **2,** obstacle. —**al contrario; por el contrario; por lo contrario,** on the contrary. —**llevar la contraria a,** *colloq.* to be against; to disagree with.
contrarreferencia (kon·tra·rre·fe'ren·θja; -sja) *n.f.* cross reference.
contrarrestar (kon·tra·rres'tar) *v.t.* **1,** to resist. **2,** to offset; to counteract. **3,** to hit back; to return (a ball).
contrarrevolución (kon·tra·rre·βo·lu'θjon; -'sjon) *n.f.* counterrevolution. —**contrarrevolucionario,** *adj.* & *n.m.* counterrevolutionary.
contraseña (kon·tra'se·ɲa) *n.f.* **1,** countersign. **2,** baggage check. **3,** check; ticket stub. **4,** *mil.* countersign. —**contraseña de salida,** door pass; theater check.
contrastar (kon·tras'tar) *v.t.* **1,** to contrast; to compare. **2,** to check (weights and measures). **3,** to assay. —*v.i.* to contrast.
contraste (kon'tras·te) *n.m.* **1,** contrast. **2,** assay. —*adj.* contrasting.
contrata (kon'tra·ta) *n.f.* contract; agreement.
contratar (kon·tra'tar) *v.t.* **1,** to contract for. **2,** to engage; to hire.
contratiempo (kon·tra'tjem·po) *n.m.* mishap; accident.
contratista (kon·tra'tis·ta) *n.m.* & *f.* contractor.
contrato (kon'tra·to) *n.m.* contract; covenant; agreement.
contravención (kon·tra·βen·'θjon; -'sjon) *n.f.* contravention; infraction; violation.
contraveneno (kon·tra·βe'ne·no) *n.m.* antidote.
contravenir (kon·tra·βe'nir) *v.t.* [*infl.:* **venir**] to contravene; to infringe; to violate.

contraventana (kon·tra·βen'ta·na) *n.f.* window shutter.
contravidriera (kon·tra·βi'ðrje·ra) *n.f.* storm window.
contribución (kon·tri·βu'θjon; -'sjon) *n.f.* **1,** contribution. **2,** tax.
contribuidor (kon·tri·βu·i'ðor) *adj.* **1,** contributing; contributory. **2,** taxpaying. —*n.m.* **1,** contributor. **2,** taxpayer.
contribuir (kon·tri·βu'ir) *v.t.* [*pres.ind.* **contribuyo** (-'βu·jo); *pres.subjve.* **contribuya** (-'βu·ja); *pret.* **contribuí** (-βu'i), **contribuyó** (-βu'jo)] **1,** to contribute. **2,** to pay (taxes).
contribuyente (kon·tri·βu'jen·te) *adj.* & *n.m.* & *f.* = **contribuidor.**
contrición (kon·tri'θjon; -'sjon) *n.f.* contrition.
contrincante (kon·trin'kan·te) *n.m.* & *f.* **1,** contestant; competitor. **2,** opponent; rival.
contrito (kon'tri·to) *adj.* contrite.
control (kon'trol) *n.m.* **1,** control. **2,** checkpoint.
controlador (kon·tro·la'ðor) *n.m.*, *Amer.* = **contralor.**
controlar (kon·tro'lar) *v.t.* **1,** to control; check. **2,** to monitor. **3,** *Amer.* to audit.
controversia (kon·tro'βer·sja) *n.f.* controversy. —**controversial,** *adj.* controversial.
controvertir (kon·tro·βer'tir) *v.t.* [*infl.:* **advertir**] to controvert. —**controvertible,** *adj.* controvertible.
contumacia (kon·tu'ma·θja; -sja) *n.f.* **1,** contumacy. **2,** *law* contempt.
contumaz (kon·tu'maθ; -'mas) *adj.* **1,** contumacious. **2,** *law* guilty of contempt.
contumelia (kon·tu'me·lja) *n.f.* contumely. —**contumelioso,** *adj.* contumelious.
contusión (kon·tu'sjon) *n.f.* contusion.
convalecer (kon·βa·le'θer; -'ser) *v.i.* [*pres.ind.* **convalezco** (-'leθ·ko); *pres.subjve.* **convalezca** (-ka)] to convalesce. —**convalecencia,** *n.f.* convalescence. —**convaleciente,** *adj.* & *n.m.* & *f.* convalescent.
convalidar (kon·βa·li'ðar) *v.t.* to confirm.
convecino (kon·βe'θi·no; -'si·no) *adj.* near; neighboring. —*n.m.* neighbor.
convencer (kon·βen'θer; -'ser) *v.t.* [*infl.:* **vencer**] to convince. —**convencimiento** (-θi'mjen·to; -si'mjen·to) *n.m.* conviction; convincing.
convención (kon·βen'θjon; -'sjon) *n.f.* **1,** convention; assembly. **2,** agreement. —**convencional,** *adj.* conventional. —**convencionalismo,** *n.m.* conventionality.
conveniencia (kon·βe'njen·θja; -sja) *n.f.* **1,** conformity; congruity; propriety. **2,** advantage; comfort; convenience. **3,** agreement.
conveniente (kon·βe'njen·te) *adj.* **1,** convenient; advantageous. **2,** fit; suitable; proper.
convenio (kon'βe·njo) *n.m.* covenant; compact.
convenir (kon·βe'nir) *v.i.*, *also, refl.*, **convenirse** [*infl.:* **venir**] **1,** to agree; to come to an agreement. **2,** to gather; to assemble; to convene. **3,** to fit; to be suitable.
convento (kon'βen·to) *n.m.* convent.
converger (kon·βer'xer) *v.i.* to converge. —**convergencia,** *n.f.* convergence. —**convergente,** *adj.* convergent.
conversar (kon·βer'sar) *v.i.* to converse. —**conversación,** *n.f.* conversation.
conversión (kon·βer'sjon) *n.f.* conversion.
convertir (kon·βer'tir) *v.t.* [*infl.:* **advertir**] to convert. —**convertible,** *adj.* convertible.
convexo (kon'βek·so) *adj.* convex. —**convexidad,** *n.f.* convexity.
convicción (kon·βik'θjon; -'sjon) *n.f.* conviction.
convicto (kon'βik·to) *adj.* convicted. —*n.m.* convict.
convidado (kon·βi'ða·ðo) *n.m.* guest.
convidar (kon·βi'ðar) *v.t.* **1,** to invite. **2,** to treat. —**convidarse,** *v.r.* to offer one's services.
convincente (kon·βin'θen·te; -'sen·te) *adj.* convincing.
convite (kon'βi·te) *n.m.* **1,** invitation. **2,** dinner party; banquet. —**convite a escote,** Dutch treat.
convival (kon·βi'βal) *adj.* convivial.
convocar (kon·βo'kar) *v.t.* [*pres. subjve.* **convoque** (-'βo·ke); *pret.* **convoqué** (-'ke)] to convoke; to call (a meeting). —**convocación,** *n.f.* convocation.
convocatoria (kon·βo·ka'to·rja)

n.f. letter of convocation; summons.
convoy (kon'βoi) *n.m.* **1,** convoy. **2,** *Amer.* train. **3,** *colloq.* retinue.
convoyar (kon·βo'jar) *v.t.* to convoy; to escort.
convulsión (kon·βul'sjon) *n.f.* convulsion. —**convulsivo** (-'si·βo) *adj.* convulsive. —**tos convulsiva,** whooping cough.
convulsionar (kon·βul·sjo'nar) *v.t.* to convulse.
conyugal (kon·ju'ɣal) *adj.* conjugal.
cónyuge ('kon·ju·xe) *n.m.* & *f.* spouse. —**cónyuges,** *n.m.pl.* married couple.
coñac (ko'ɲak) *n.m.* cognac.
cooperar (ko·o·pe'rar) *v.i.* to coöperate. —**cooperación,** *n.f.* coöperation. —**cooperativo,** *adj.* coöperative. —**cooperativa,** *n.f.* coöperative.
coordenado (ko·or·ðe'na·ðo) *adj., math.* coördinate. —**coordenada,** *n.f., math.* coördinate.
coordinar (ko·or·ði'nar) *v.t.* to coördinate. —**coordinación,** *n.f.* coördination. —**coordinado,** *adj.* coördinated; coördinate.
copa ('ko·pa) *n.f.* **1,** goblet; cup. **2,** treetop. **3,** crown (*of a hat*). **4,** *cards* heart (*in the French deck*); goblet (*in the Spanish deck*).
copar (ko'par) *v.t.* **1,** *mil.* to capture by surprise. **2,** to sweep (a game, election, etc.). **3,** to cover (a bet) completely.
coparticipación (ko·par·ti·θi·pa'θjon; -si·pa'sjon) *n.f.* joint partnership. —**copartícipe** (-'ti·θi·pe; -si·pe) *n.m.* & *f.* joint partner.
copec *also,* **copeck** (ko'pek) *n.m.* [*pl.* **copecs,** *also,* **copecks** (ko'peks)] kopeck.
copete (ko'pe·te) *n.m.* **1,** tuft. **2,** crest. —**de alto copete,** of noble lineage; high class.
copiar (ko'pjar) *v.t.* to copy. —**copia** ('ko·pja) *n.f.* copy.
copioso (ko'pjo·so) *adj.* copious; abundant.
copista (ko'pis·ta) *n.m.* & *f.* copyist.
copla ('ko·pla) *n.f.* **1,** couplet. **2,** popular song; ballad. —**coplas de ciego,** doggerel.
copo ('ko·po) *n.m.* **1,** tuft. **2,** ball (*of cotton, wool, etc.*). **3,** snowflake. **4,** coup; sweep.
copra ('ko·pra) *n.f.* copra.
copto ('kop·to) *adj.* Coptic. —*n.m.* **1,** Copt. **2,** Coptic (*language*). —**cóptico** ('kop·ti·ko) *adj.* Coptic.
cópula ('ko·pu·la) *n.f.* **1,** bond; tie. **2,** copula. **3,** copulation. **4,** = **cúpula.**
copular (ko·pu'lar) *v.i.* [*also, refl.,* **copularse**] to copulate. —**copulación,** *n.f.* copulation. —**copulativo,** *adj.* copulative.
coque ('ko·ke) *n.m.* coke.
coqueta (ko'ke·ta) *n.f.* **1,** coquette; flirt. **2,** dressing table. —*adj.* coquettish.
coquetear (ko·ke·te'ar) *v.i.* to flirt; act coquettishly. —**coquetería,** *n.f., also* **coqueteo** (-'te·o) *n.m.* flirtation; coquetry.
coquetón (ko·ke'ton) *adj.* [*fem.* **-ona**] flirtatious; coquettish.
coquina (ko'ki·na) *n.f., zool.* cockle; cockleshell.
coraje (ko'ra·xe) *n.m.* **1,** courage; spirit. **2,** anger.
coral (ko'ral) *adj., music* choral. —*n.m.* **1,** coral. **2,** *music* chorale. **3,** glee club, chorus. —*n.f., zool.* coral snake. —**corales,** *n.m.pl.* coral beads. —**ser más fino que el coral,** to be very shrewd.
coralino (ko·ra'li·no) *adj.* coral; of or resembling coral.
Corán (ko'ran) *n.m.* Koran.
coraza (ko'ra·θa; -sa) *n.f.* **1,** armor; armor plate. **2,** *sports* guard; protector. **3,** shell (*of a crustacean*).
corazón (ko·ra'θon; -'son) *n.m.* **1,** heart. **2,** *fig.* love; affection. **3,** *fig.* courage. —**de corazón,** heartily. —**hacer de tripas corazón,** to pluck up; to take heart.
corazonada (ko·ra·θo'na·ða; -so'na·ða) *n.f.* hunch; presentiment.
corbata (kor·'βa·ta) *n.f.* tie; cravat. —**corbata de lazo,** bow tie.
corbeta (kor'βe·ta) *n.f.* corvette.
corcel (kor'θel; -'sel) *n.m.* battle mount; charger.
corcova (kor'ko·βa) *n.f.* hump; hunch. —**corcovado,** *adj.* hunchbacked. —*n.m.* hunchback.
corcovo (kor'ko·βo) *n.m.* **1,** buck; leap, as of a horse. **2,** *colloq.* bend; curve. —**corcovear,** *v.i.* to buck; leap.
corchea (kor'tʃe·a) *n.f., music* quaver; eighth note.
corchete (kor'tʃe·te) *n.m.* hook and eye; hook (*of a hook and eye*).

—**corcheta,** *n.f.* eye (*of a hook and eye*).
corcho ('kor·tʃo) *n.m.* 1, cork. 2, stopper; cork. —**corchoso,** *adj.* corklike; corky.
cordaje (kor'ða·xe) *n.m.* 1, cordage. 2, *naut.* rigging.
cordal (kor'ðal) *n.m.* wisdom tooth.
cordel (kor'ðel) *n.m.* cord; string.
cordelería (kor·ðe·le'ri·a) *n.f.* = cordaje.
cordero (kor'ðe·ro) *n.m.* lamb.
cordial (kor'ðjal) *adj.* & *n.m.* cordial. —**cordialidad,** *n.f.* cordiality.
cordillera (kor·ði'ʎe·ra; -'je·ra) *n.f.* mountain range; cordillera.
cordobán (kor·ðo'βan) *n.m.* cordovan (*leather*).
cordón (kor'ðon) *n.m.* 1, cord; braid. 2, *mil.* line; cordon. 3, shoelace.
cordoncillo (kor·ðon'θi·ʎo; -'si·jo) *n.m.* 1, knurl; milling (*on coins*). 2, piping; braid.
cordura (kor'ðu·ra) *n.m.* prudence.
corear (ko·re'ar) *v.t.* to chorus; sing or recite in chorus.
corégono (ko're·ɣo·no) *n.m.* whitefish.
coreografía (ko·re·o·ɣra'fi·a) *n.f.* choreography. —**coreógrafo,** (-'o·ɣra·fo) choreographer.
corista (ko'ris·ta) *n.m.* & *f.* chorus singer; chorister. —*n.f.* chorus girl.
cornada (kor'na·ða) *n.f.* goring; thrust with a horn.
córnea ('kor·ne·a) *n.f.* cornea.
cornear (kor·ne'ar) *v.t.* = **acornear.**
corneja (kor'ne·xa) *n.f.* crow.
cornejo (kor'ne·xo) *n.m.* dogwood.
corneta (kor'ne·ta) *n.f.* 1, cornet. 2, bugle. —*n.m.* 1, cornetist. 2, bugler. —**corneta acústica,** ear trumpet. —**corneta de monte,** hunting horn.
cornezuelo (kor·ne'θwe·lo; -'swe·lo) *n.m., bot.; pharm.* ergot.
cornisa (kor'ni·sa) *n.f.* cornice.
cornuda (kor'nu·ða) *n.f., ichthy.* hammerhead. *Also,* **cornudilla** (-'ði·ʎa; -ja).
cornudo (kor'nu·ðo) *adj.* 1, horned; antlered. 2, cuckold; cuckolded. —*n.m.* cuckold.
coro ('ko·ro) *n.m.* choir; chorus.
corola (ko'ro·la) *n.f., bot.* corolla.
corolario (ko·ro'la·rjo) *n.m.* corollary.
corona (ko'ro·na) *n.f.* 1, crown. 2, wreath. 3, name of various coins.
coronal (ko·ro'nal) *adj.* coronal.
coronar (ko·ro'nar) *v.t.* to crown. —**coronación,** *n.f.* coronation.
coronel (ko·ro'nel) *n.m.* colonel. —**coronelía,** *n.f.* colonelcy.
coronilla (ko·ro'ni·ʎa; -ja) *n.f.* 1, small crown. 2, crown of the head. —**estar hasta la coronilla (de),** *colloq.* to be fed up (with).
corpachón (kor·pa'tʃon) *n.m., colloq.* large body; carcass. *Also,* **corpanchón** (-pan'tʃon).
corpiño (kor'pi·ɲo) *n.m.* bodice.
corporación (kor·po·ra'θjon; -'sjon) *n.f.* corporation; association; society.
corporal (kor·po'ral) *adj.* corporal.
corpóreo (kor'po·re·o) *adj.* corporeal.
corpulento (kor·pu'len·to) *adj.* corpulent. —**corpulencia,** *n.f.* corpulence.
corpúsculo (kor'pus·ku·lo) *n.m.* corpuscle.
corral (ko'rral) *n.m.* 1, corral. 2, barnyard.
corralón (ko·rra'lon) *n.m., Amer.* vacant lot; sandlot.
correa (ko'rre·a) *n.f.* strap; belt. —**tener correa,** to be good-natured.
corrección (ko·rrek'θjon; -'sjon) *n.f.* 1, correction. 2, correctness. 3, proofreading. —**correccional,** *adj.* corrective; correctional. —*n.m.* house of correction.
correctivo (ko·rrek'ti·βo) *adj.* & *n.m.* corrective.
correcto (ko'rrek·to) *adj.* correct; exact.
corrector (ko·rrek'tor) *adj.* corrective. —*n.m.* 1, corrector. 2, proofreader.
corredera (ko·rre'ðe·ra) *n.f.* 1, *mech.* track; rail; tongue. 2, race course. —**de corredera,** sliding.
corredizo (ko·rre'ði·θo; -so) *adj.* sliding; slipping. —**nudo corredizo,** slip knot; hangman's knot.
corredor (ko·rre'ðor) *n.m.* 1, runner; racer. 2, corridor. 3, *comm.* broker. 4, *mil.* scout. —*adj.* running; speeding.
corregidor (ko·rre·xi'ðor) *n.m.* former Spanish magistrate; corregidor.
corregir (ko·rre'xir) *v.t.* [*pres.ind.* **corrijo;** *pres.subjve.* **corrija;** *pret.*

corregí (-'xi), corrigió] 1, to correct. 2, to reprove. 3, to proofread.
correlación (ko·rre·la'θjon; -'sjon) *n.f.* correlation. —**correlacionar** (-'nar) *v.t.* to correlate. —**correlativo** (-'ti·βo) *adj.* & *n.m.* correlative.
correligionario (ko·rre·li·xjo·'na·rjo) *adj.* of the same religious or political beliefs. —*n.m.* coreligionist; fellow believer.
correo (ko'rre·o) *n.m.* 1, mail; mail service. 2, postman. 3, post office. —**echar al correo,** to mail.
correón (ko·rre'on) *n.m.* large strap.
correoso (ko·rre'o·so) *adj.* gristly; sinewy.
correr (ko'rrer) *v.t.* 1, to run. 2, to race (a car, horse, etc.). 3, to draw (a curtain). 4, to embarrass. —*v.i.* 1, to run. 2, to flow. —**a todo correr,** at full speed. —**correr el albur,** to take the chance. —**correr el cerrojo,** to lock; to turn the key. —**correr de cuenta de uno,** to be on one's account. —**correrla,** *colloq.* to carouse.
correría (ko·rre'ri·a) *n.f.* 1, raid; foray. 2, tour; trip; circuit; *pl.* travels.
correspondencia (ko·rres·pon·'den·θja; -sja) *n.f.* 1, correspondence. 2, mail. 3, communication; contact. —**correspondencia urgente,** special delivery.
corresponder (ko·rres·pon'der) *v.t.* 1, to return; to reciprocate. 2, to belong to; to concern. —*v.i.* to correspond; to communicate. —**corresponderse,** *v.r.* 1, to correspond. 2, to agree.
correspondiente (ko·rres·pon·'djen·te) *adj.* correspondent; corresponding. —*n.m.* & *f.* correspondent.
corresponsal (ko·rres·pon'sal) *n.m.* & *f.* correspondent.
corretaje (ko·rre'ta·xe) *n.m.* commission; brokerage.
corretear (ko·rre·te'ar) *v.i.* 1, to romp; run about. 2, to roam; roam the streets.
corrida (ko'rri·ða) *n.f.* 1, race. 2, course; travel. 3, bullfight. —**de corrida,** fast; without stopping.
corrido (ko'rri·ðo) *adj.* 1, over the weight *or* measure. 2, experienced; worldly-wise. 3, ashamed; abashed. 4, elapsed; past (*of time*). 5, flowing; fluent. 6, uninterrupted; unbroken. —**de corrido** = **de corrida.**
corriente (ko'rrjen·te) *adj.* 1, current; present. 2, running; flowing. 3, standard; common. —*n.f.* 1, current; flow; stream. 2, *electricity* current. —*adv.* all right. —**estar al corriente,** to be up-to-date; to be well-informed. —**seguir la corriente,** to follow the crowd.
corrigió (ko·rri'xjo) *v., 3rd pers. sing. pret. of* **corregir.**
corrija (ko'rri·xa) *v., pres.subjve. of* **corregir.**
corrijo (ko'rri·xo) *v., pres.ind. of* **corregir.**
corrillo (ko'rri·ʎo; -jo) *n.m.* a group chatting intimately, apart from the main body; huddle.
corro ('ko·rro) *n.m.* group of people; circle.
corroborar (ko·rro·βo'rar) *v.t.* to corroborate. —**corroboración,** *n.f.* corroboration. —**corroborativo,** *adj.* corroborative.
corroer (ko·rro'er) *v.t.* [*infl.:* **roer**] to corrode. —**corrosión** (-'sjon) *n.f.* corrosion. —**corrosivo** (-'si·βo) *adj.* corrosive.
corromper (ko·rrom'per) *v.t.* [*infl.:* **romper**; *p.p.* **corrompido, corrupto** (-'rup·to)] 1, to corrupt; to bribe. 2, to rot; to spoil. —**corromperse,** *v.r.* 1, to rot; to spoil. 2, to become corrupted.
corrupción (ko·rrup'θjon; -'sjon) *n.f.* 1, corruption; corruptness. 2, stench; stink.
corruptible (ko·rrup'ti·βle) *adj.* corruptible.
corsario (kor'sa·rjo) *n.m.* 1, privateer; corsair. 2, pirate ship. 3, pirate. —*adj.* privateering.
corsé (kor'se) *n.m.* corset.
corsear (kor·se'ar) *v.i.* to privateer.
corso ('kor·so) *n.m.* 1, *hist.* privateering; cruise of a privateer. 2, *So. Amer.* festive parade. —**ir** *or* **salir a corso,** to privateer; go privateering.
cortabolsas (kor·ta'βol·sas) *n.m.* & *f. sing.* & *pl., colloq.* pickpocket.
cortacircuito (kor·ta·θir'kwi·to; -sir'kwi·to) *n.m., Amer.* shortcircuit. —**cortacircuitos,** *n.m. sing.* & *pl.* circuit breaker; fuse.
cortada (kor'ta·ða) *n.f., Amer.* cut; slash.
cortador (kor·ta'ðor) *adj.* cutting.

—*n.m.* 1, cutter. 2, butcher. 3, slicing machine.
cortadura (kor·ta'ðu·ra) *n.f.* cut; slash.
cortalápiz (kor·ta'la·piθ; -pis) *n.m.sing.* & *pl.* pencil sharpener. *Also,* **cortalápices** (-'la·pi·θes; -ses).
cortante (kor'tan·te) *adj.* cutting; sharp. —*n.m.* butcher; meat cutter.
cortapapel (kor·ta·pa'pel) *n.m.* paper cutter; paper knife; letter opener. *Also,* **cortapapeles,** *n.m. sing.* & *pl.*
cortaplumas (kor·ta'plu·mas) *n.m.sing.* & *pl.* penknife.
cortar (kor'tar) *v.t.* 1, to cut; to cut out; to cut off; to disjoin. 2, to intersect. —**cortarse,** *v.r.* 1, to become confused; to be embarrassed. 2, to be speechless. 3, to sour; curdle. 4, to chap (*of the skin*). 5, to run (*of paint, varnish, etc.*).
corte ('kor·te) *n.m.* 1, cut; cutting. 2, cutting edge. 3, material (*for a garment*). 4, fit; cut (*of a garment*). —*n.f.* 1, court; yard. 2, *Amer.* court of justice. —**hacer la corte a,** to court; to woo. —**darse corte,** *Amer.* to put on airs.
cortedad (kor·te'ðað) *n.f.* 1, shortness. 2, bashfulness; shyness.
cortejar (kor·te'xar) *v.t.* to court; to woo.
cortejo (kor'te·xo) *n.m.* 1, courtship. 2, cortege. 3, entourage.
cortés (kor'tes) *adj.* courteous; gracious.
Cortes ('kor·tes) *n.f.pl.* the Spanish Parliament.
cortesano (kor·te'sa·no) *adj.* courtly; courteous. —*n.m.* courtier. —**cortesana,** *n.f.* courtesan.
cortesía (kor·te'si·a) *n.f.* 1, courtesy. 2, gift. 3, expression of respect. 4, bow; curtsy.
corteza (kor'te·θa; -sa) *n.f.* 1, bark; crust; skin; rind; peel. 2, rusticity. 3, *anat.; bot.* cortex.
cortical (kor·ti'kal) *adj.* cortical.
cortijo (kor'ti·xo) *n.m.* farmhouse; farm.
cortina (kor'ti·na) *n.f.* curtain; drape; screen.
cortisona (kor·ti'so·na) *n.f.* cortisone.
corto ('kor·to) *adj.* 1, short. 2, bashful. —**a la corta o a la larga,** sooner or later. —**corto de vista,** shortsighted.
corva ('kor·βa) *n.f.* back of the knee; ham.
corvadura (kor·βa'ðu·ra) *n.f.* bend; curvature.
corveta (kor'βe·ta) *n.* prance; rearing, as of a horse. —**corvetear,** *v.i.* to prance; rear.
corvo ('kor·βo) *adj.* hooked; arched; curved.
corzo ('kor·θo; -so) *n.m.* roe deer.
cosa ('ko·sa) *n.f.* thing; matter. —**a cosa hecha,** on purpose. —**como si tal cosa,** *colloq.* as if nothing had happened. —**cosa de,** 1, a matter of. 2, about; approximately. —**cosa de otro jueves,** *colloq.* something unusual. —**cosas de,** doings of; pranks of. —**poquita cosa,** *colloq.* puny; feeble person.
cosaco (ko'sa·ko) *adj.* & *n.m.* Cossack.
cosecante (ko·se'kan·te) *n.f.* cosecant.
cosecha (ko'se·tʃa) *n.f.* crop; harvest. —**de su propia cosecha,** out of one's own imagination.
cosechar (ko·se'tʃar) *v.t.* & *i.* to reap; harvest.
coseno (ko'se·no) *n.m.* cosine.
coser (ko'ser) *v.t.* to sew. —**coser a puñaladas,** to stab to death. —**coser y cantar,** *colloq.* in a jiffy. —**ser coser y cantar,** to be a cinch.
cosmético (kos'me·ti·ko) *n.m.* & *adj.* cosmetic.
cósmico ('kos·mi·ko) *adj.* cosmic.
cosmo- (kos·mo) *prefix* cosmo-; cosmos: *cosmografía,* cosmography.
cosmogonía (kos·mo·ɣo'ni·a) *n.f.* cosmogony.
cosmografía (kos·mo·ɣra'fi·a) *n.f.* cosmography.
cosmología (kos·mo·lo'xi·a) *n.f.* cosmology.
cosmopolita (kos·mo·po'li·ta) *adj.* cosmopolitan. —*n.m.* & *f.* cosmopolitan; cosmopolite.
cosmos ('kos·mos) *n.m.* cosmos.
cosquillas (kos'ki·ʎas; -jas) *n.f. pl.* 1, tickles; tickling. 2, ticklishness. —**hacer cosquillas a,** to tickle. —**tener cosquillas,** to be ticklish.
cosquillear (kos·ki·ʎe'ar; -je'ar) *v.t.* (*of things*) to tickle. *Also,* **cosquillar** (-'ʎar; -'jar).
cosquilleo (kos·ki'ʎe·o; -'je·o) *n.m.* tickle; tickling.
cosquilloso (kos·ki'ʎo·so; -'jo·so) *adj.* ticklish.
costa ('kos·ta) *n.f.* 1, coast; shore.

2, cost; expense. —**a costa de,** at the expense of. —**a toda costa,** at all costs; at any price.
costado (kos'ta·ðo) *n.m.* **1,** side. **2,** *mil.* flank. —**costados,** *n.m.pl.* lineage; ancestors.
costal (kos'tal) *n.m.* sack; bag.
costanera (kos·ta'ne·ra) *n.f.* slope. —**costaneras,** *n.f.pl.* rafters.
costanero (kos·ta'ne·ro) *adj.* **1,** coastal. **2,** sloping.
costar (kos'tar) *v.t. & i.* [*pres.ind.* **cuesto;** *pres.subjve.* **cueste**] to cost. —**cueste lo que cueste,** cost what it may.
coste ('kos·te) *also,* **costo** (-to) *n.m.* cost; expense.
costear (kos·te'ar) *v.t.* to defray. —*v.i.* to navigate along the coast.
costero (kos'te·ro) *adj.* coastal.
costilla (kos'ti·ʎa; -ja) *n.f.* **1,** rib. **2,** *colloq.* wife; better half.
costoso (kos'to·so) *adj.* expensive; dear; costly.
costra ('kos·tra) *n.f.* crust; scale; scab. —**costroso,** *adj.* crusty; scaly; scabby.
costumbre (kos'tum·bre) *n.f.* custom; habit. —**de costumbre,** usual; usually. —**tener por costumbre,** to be used to; to be in the habit of.
costura (kos'tu·ra) *n.f.* **1,** sewing. **2,** seam. —**alta costura,** high fashion. —**sentar las costuras (a uno),** to call (someone) up on the carpet.
costurera (kos·tu're·ra) *n.f.* seamstress; dressmaker.
costurero (kos·tu're·ro) *n.m.* **1,** sewing table. **2,** sewing box. **3,** sewing room.
costurón (kos·tu'ron) *n.m.* **1,** large stitch or stitching. **2,** patch. **3,** prominent scar.
cota ('ko·ta) *n.f.* **1,** [*also,* **cota de malla**] coat of mail. **2,** *topog.* elevation; number on a map indicating elevation.
cotangente (ko·tan'xen·te) *n.f.* cotangent.
cotarro (ko'ta·rro) *n.m.* lodging for beggars. —**armar un cotarro,** *colloq.* to stir up a row.
cotejar (ko·te'xar) *v.t.* to compare; collate. —**cotejo** (-'te·xo) *n.m.* comparison; collation.
cotidiano (ko·ti'ðja·no) *adj.* **1,** daily. **2,** everyday.
cotiledón (ko·ti·le'ðon) *n.m.* cotyledon.
cotillón (ko·ti'ʎon; -'jon) *n.m.* cotillion.
cotización (ko·ti·θa'θjon; -sa·'sjon) *n.f.* **1,** price quotation. **2,** current price. **3,** dues; quota; assessment.
cotizar (ko·ti'θar; -'sar) *v.t.* [*pres.subjve.* **cotice** (-'ti·θe; -se); *pret.* **coticé** (-'θe; -'se)] **1,** to quote (prices). **2,** to prorate. —*v.i* to pay *or* collect dues.
coto ('ko·to) *n.m.* **1,** enclosure of a pasture. **2,** preserve. **3,** limit; boundary.
cotorra (ko'to·rra) *n.f.* **1,** parrot. **2,** magpie. **3,** *colloq.* chatterbox. —**cotorrear** (-rre'ar) *v.i., colloq.* to chatter. —**cotorreo** (-'rre·o) *n.m., colloq.* chatter; chattering.
covacha (ko'βa·tʃa) *n.f.* **1,** small cave. **2,** *Amer.* cubbyhole. **3,** *Amer.* hut; shanty.
coyote (ko'jo·te) *n.m.* coyote.
coyuntura (ko·jun'tu·ra) *n.f.* **1,** juncture. **2,** *anat.* joint; articulation. **3,** opportunity.
coz (koθ; kos) *n.f.* **1,** kick. **2,** recoil (*of a gun*).
craal (kra'al) *n.m.* kraal.
-cracia ('kra·θja; -sja) *suffix* -cracy; *forming nouns denoting* **1,** rule: *autocracia,* autocracy. **2,** ruling class: *aristocracia,* aristocracy. **3,** form of government: *democracia,* democracy.
cráneo ('kra·ne·o) *n.m.* cranium; skull. —**craneal,** *adj.* cranial.
crápula ('kra·pu·la) *n.f.* **1,** drunkenness. **2,** lewdness.
crapuloso (kra·pu'lo·so) *adj.* **1,** drunk. **2,** lewd.
crasitud (kra·si'tuð) *n.f.* **1,** obesity; corpulence. **2,** fattiness; greasiness. **3,** crassness; grossness.
craso ('kra·so) *adj.* **1,** fat; thick; coarse. **2,** fatty; greasy. **3,** crass; gross.
-crata (kra·ta) *suffix* -crat; *forming nouns denoting persons, corresponding to nouns ending in* **-cracia:** *autócrata,* autocrat; *aristócrata,* aristocrat; *demócrata,* democrat.
cráter ('kra·ter) *n.m.* crater.
-crático ('kra·ti·ko) *suffix* -cratic; *forming adjectives from nouns ending in* **-crata** *or* **-cracia:** *autocrático,* autocratic; *aristocrático,* aristocratic; *democrático,* democratic.
crear (kre'ar) *v.t.* to create. —**creación,** *n.f.* creation. —**creador,** *adj.* creative. —*n.m.* creator.

crecer (kre'θer; -'ser) *v.i.* [*pres.ind.* **crezco**; *pres.subjve.* **crezca**] to grow; to increase. —**crecerse,** *v.r.* to swell with pride.
crecida (kre'θi·ða; -'si·ða) *n.f.* freshet.
crecido (kre'θi·ðo; -'si·ðo) *adj.* **1,** large; grown. **2,** swollen.
creciente (kre'θjen·te; kre'sjen-) *adj.* **1,** growing; increasing. **2,** crescent. —*n.m. heraldry* crescent; half moon. —*n.f.* **1,** high tide; flood tide. **2,** freshet. **3,** crescent (*of the moon*). **4,** sourdough.
crecimiento (kre·θi'mjen·to; kre·si-) *n.m.* growth; increase.
credenciales (kre·ðen'θja·les; -'sja·les) *n.f.pl.* credentials.
credibilidad (kre·ði·βi·li'ðað) *n.f.* credibility.
crédito ('kre·ði·to) *n.m.* credit.
credo ('kre·ðo) *n.m.* creed; credo. —**más viejo que el credo,** very ancient. —**no saber el credo,** to be very ignorant.
crédulo ('kre·ðu·lo) *adj.* credulous. —**credulidad** (-li'ðað) *n.f.* credulity.
creencia (kre'en·θja; -sja) *n.f.* belief.
creer (kre'er) *v.t.* & *i.* [*pret.* **creí** (kre'i), **creyó**; *ger.* **creyendo**] to believe; to think. —**¡ya lo creo!** *colloq.* I should say so!
creíble (kre'i·βle) *adj.* credible.
crema ('kre·ma) *n.f.* **1,** cream. **2,** *gram.* dieresis.
cremallera (kre·ma'ʎe·ra; -'je·ra) *n.f.* **1,** *mech.* rack; toothed bar. **2,** zipper.
crematorio (kre·ma'to·rjo) *n.m.* crematory.
cremera (kre'me·ra) *n.f.* creamer.
crémor ('kre·mor) *n.m.* cream of tartar. *Also,* **crémor tártaro.**
creosota (kre·o'so·ta) *n.f.* creosote.
crepé (kre'pe) *n.m.* crêpe.
crepitación (kre·pi·ta'θjon; -'sjon) *n.f.* **1,** crackling; snapping. **2,** rattle (*of the breath*).
crepitar (kre·pi'tar) *v.i.* to crackle; snap.
crepúsculo (kre'pus·ku·lo) *n.m.* twilight. —**crepuscular,** *adj.* of or at twilight.
cresa ('kre·sa) *n.f.* maggot.
crescendo (kres'θen·do; kre'sen-) *adj., adv.* & *n.m.* crescendo.
crespo ('kres·po) *adj.* curly; curled. —*n.m., Amer.* curl.
crespón (kres'pon) *n.m.* crêpe.
cresta ('kres·ta) *n.f.* **1,** crest. **2,** comb (*of birds*). —**cresta de gallo,** cockscomb.
creta ('kre·ta) *n.f.* limestone; chalk.
cretino (kre'ti·no) *n.m.* cretin. —**cretinismo,** *n.m.* cretinism.
cretona (kre'to·na) *n.f.* cretonne.
creyendo (kre'jen·do) *v., ger. of* **creer.**
creyente (kre'jen·te) *adj.* believing. —*n.m.* & *f.* believer.
creyó (kre'jo) *v., 3rd pers.sing. pret. of* **creer.**
creyón (kre'jon) *n.m.* **1,** crayon. **2,** charcoal pencil.
crezca ('kreθ·ka; 'kres-) *v., pres. subjve. of* **crecer.**
crezco ('kreθ·ko; 'kres-) *v., 1st. pers.sing. pres.ind. of* **crecer.**
cría ('kri·a) *n.f.* **1,** breeding; raising. **2,** brood; offspring. **3,** litter.
criadero (kri·a'ðe·ro) *n.m.* **1,** breeding place. **2,** nursery. **3,** fish hatchery. —*adj.* fruitful; prolific.
criado (kri'a·ðo) *n.m.* servant. —*adj.* bred; raised.
criador (kri·a'ðor) *adj.* **1,** creative. **2,** fruitful. **3,** nurturing. —*n.m.* raiser; breeder. —**criadora,** *n.f.* wet nurse.
criandera (kri·an'de·ra) *n.f., Amer.* wet nurse.
crianza (kri'an·θa; -sa) *n.f.* breeding; raising. —**hermano de crianza,** foster brother.
criar (kri'ar) *v.t.* [*pres.ind.* **crío** ('kri·o); *pres.subjve.* **críe** (-e)] **1,** to raise; rear. **2,** to breed. —**criarse,** *v.r.* **1,** to grow. **2,** to grow up; be raised.
criatura (kri·a'tu·ra) *n.f.* **1,** creature. **2,** baby.
criba ('kri·βa) *n.f.* sieve.
cribar (kri'βar) *v.t.* to sift.
crimen ('kri·men) *n.m.* crime.
criminal (kri·mi'nal) *adj.* & *n.m.* & *f.* criminal. —**criminalidad,** *n.f.* criminality.
criminalista (kri·mi·na'lis·ta) *n.m.* & *f.* criminologist.
criminología (kri·mi·no·lo'xi·a) *n.f.* criminology.
crin (krin) *n.f.* **1,** mane, esp. of horses. **2,** horsehair.
crinolina (kri·no'li·na) *n.f.* crinoline.
criollo ('krjo·ʎo; -jo) *adj.* & *n.m.* **1,** native. **2,** creole.
cripta ('krip·ta) *n.f.* crypt.

cripto- (krip·to) *prefix* crypto-; hidden: *criptograma,* cryptogram.
criptografía (krip·to·ɣra'fi·a) *n.f.* cryptography. —**criptográfico** (-'ɣra·fi·ko) *adj.* cryptographic.
criptógrafo (krip'to·ɣra·fo) *n.m.* **1,** cryptographer. **2,** cryptograph (*device*).
criptograma (krip·to'ɣra·ma) *n.m.* cryptograph (*message*); cryptogram.
criptón (krip'ton) *n.m.* krypton.
crisálida (kri'sa·li·ða) *n.f.* chrysalis.
crisantemo (kri·san'te·mo) *n.m.* chrysanthemum. *Also,* **crisantema,** *n.f.*
crisis ('kri·sis) *n.f.* crisis.
crisol (kri'sol) *n.m.* crucible; melting pot.
crispar (kris'par) *v.t.* to contract; cause to twitch, as the muscles. —**crisparse,** *v.r.* to contract; twitch. —**crispamiento,** *n.m.* twitching; contraction.
cristal (kris'tal) *n.m.* **1,** crystal. **2,** glass. **3,** pane of glass.
cristalera (kris·ta'le·ra) *n.f.* **1,** sideboard; china closet. **2,** glass door.
cristalería (kris·ta·le'ri·a) *n.f.* glassware.
cristalino (kris·ta'li·no) *adj.* crystalline; transparent. —*n.m., anat.* crystalline lens.
cristalizar (kris·ta·li'θar; -'sar) *v.t.* [*infl.:* **realizar**] to crystallize. —**cristalización,** *n.f.* crystallization.
cristianar (kris·tja'nar) *v.t., colloq.* to christen.
cristiandad (kris·tjan'dað) *n.f.* Christendom.
cristianismo (kris·tja'nis·mo) *n.m.* **1,** Christianity; Christendom. **2,** christening.
cristiano (kris'tja·no) *adj.* & *n.m.* Christian.
Cristo ('kris·to) *n.m.* Christ.
criterio (kri'te·rjo) *n.m.* **1,** criterion. **2,** judgment.
crítica ('kri·ti·ka) *n.f.* **1,** criticism. **2,** censure.
criticar (kri·ti'kar) *v.t.* [*pres. subjve.* **critique** (-'ti·ke); *pret.* **critiqué** (-'ke)] **1,** to criticize; to judge. **2,** to censure.
crítico ('kri·ti·ko) *adj.* critical. —*n.m.* critic. —*adj.* & *n.m., Amer.* = **criticón.**
criticón (kri·ti'kon) *adj., colloq.* critical; carping; faultfinding. —*n.m., colloq.* [*fem.* **-ona**] critic; faultfinder.
croar (kro'ar) *v.i.* to croak.
croata (kro'a·ta) *n.m.* & *f.* Croat; Croatian. —*adj.* Croatian.
croché (kro'tʃe) *n.m.* crochet.
crom- (krom) *prefix, var. of* **cromo-** *before a vowel or* h: *cromidrosis,* chromidrosis.
cromado (kro'ma·ðo) *adj.* & *n.m.* chrome.
cromático (kro'ma·ti·ko) *adj.* chromatic.
cromato- (kro·ma·to) *prefix* chromato-. **1,** color: *cromatología,* chromatology. **2,** chromatin: *cromatólisis,* chromatolysis.
cromi- (kro·mi) *prefix, var. of* **cromo-**: *cromífero,* chromiferous.
cromo ('kro·mo) *n.m.* chromium.
cromo- (kro·mo-) *prefix* chromo-. **1,** color: *cromolitografía,* chromolithography. **2,** *chem.* chromium: *cromo-arseniato,* chromo-arsenate.
-cromo (kro·mo) *suffix* -chrome. **1,** color: *polícromo,* polychrome. **2,** *chem.* chromium: *mercurocromo,* mercurochrome.
cromosoma (kro·mo'so·ma) *n.m.* chromosome.
crónica ('kro·ni·ka) *n.f.* chronicle.
crónico ('kro·ni·ko) *adj.* chronic; long-standing.
cronista (kro'nis·ta) *n.m.* & *f.* **1,** chronicler. **2,** feature writer. —**cronista de radio,** newscaster.
crono- (kro·no-) *prefix* chrono-; time: *cronología,* chronology.
cronología (kro·no·lo'xi·a) *n.f.* chronology. —**cronológico** (-'lo·xi·ko) *adj.* chronological.
cronómetro (kro'no·met·ro) *n.m.* **1,** chronometer. **2,** stopwatch. **3,** *So.Amer.* watch.
croqueta (kro'ke·ta) *n.f.* croquette.
croquis ('kro·kis) *n.m. sing.* & *pl.* rough sketch.
cruce ('kru·θe; -se) *n.m.* **1,** cross; crossing. **2,** crossroads; intersection.
crucero (kru'θe·ro; -'se·ro) *n.m.* **1,** cross-bearer. **2,** crossing; intersection. **3,** cruise. **4,** cruiser. **5,** crossbeam. **6,** *archit.* transept.
crucial (kru'θjal; -'sjal) *adj.* crucial.
crucificar (kru·θi·fi'kar; kru·si-) *v.t.* [*infl.:* **picar**] to crucify.
crucifijo (kru·θi'fi·xo; kru·si-) *n.m.* crucifix.

crucifixión (kru·θi·fik'sjon; kru·si-) *n.f.* crucifixion.
crucigrama (kru·θi'ɣra·ma; kru·si-) *n.m.* crossword puzzle.
crudelísimo (kru·ðe'li·si·mo) *adj., superl. of* cruel.
crudeza (kru'ðe·θa; -sa) *n.f.* 1, rawness. 2, crudeness; crudity. 3, roughness; harshness.
crudo ('kru·ðo) *adj.* 1, raw. 2, crude. 3, rough; harsh. —**agua cruda**, hard water. —**estar crudo**, *Amer.* to have a hangover.
cruel (krwel) *adj.* cruel. —**crueldad**, *n.f.* cruelty.
cruento (kru'en·to) *adj.* bloody.
crujido (kru'xi·ðo) *n.m.* 1, creak; crack; crackle. 2, gnashing (*of the teeth*).
crujir (kru'xir) *v.i.* 1, to creak; crack; crackle. 2, to make a gnashing sound, as the teeth.
crupié (kru'pje) *n.m.* croupier.
crustáceo (krus'ta·θe·o; -se·o) *adj.* & *n.m.* crustacean.
cruz (kruθ; krus) *n.f.* 1, cross. 2, reverse side of a coin; tails (*pl.*). 3, withers (*pl.*). 4, *math.* plus sign. —**cruz gamada** (ga'ma·ða) swastika. —**cruz y raya**, *colloq.* that's enough. —**en cruz**, crosswise. —**hacer la cruz a**, to be through with; wash one's hands of.
cruzada (kru'θa·ða; -'sa·ða) *n.f.* crusade.
cruzado (kru'θa·ðo; -'sa·ðo) *adj.* 1, crossed. 2, double-breasted. —*n.m.* crusader.
cruzamiento (kru·θa'mjen·to; kru·sa-) *n.m.* crossing.
cruzar (kru'θar; -'sar) *v.t.* [*pres. subjve.* **cruce** ('kru·θe; -se); *pret.* **crucé** (-'θe; 'se)] 1, to cross. 2, *naut.* to cruise.
cuaderno (kwa'ðer·no) *n.m.* notebook.
cuadr- (kwaðr) *prefix, var. of* **cuadri-**: *cuadrángulo,* quadrangle.
cuadra ('kwa·ðra) *n.f.* 1, stable. 2, hospital ward. 3, quarter (of a mile). 4, *naut.* quarter. 5, *Amer.* city block.
cuadrado (kwa'ðra·ðo) *adj.* & *n.m.* 1, square. 2, quadrate. —*adj.* perfect; complete. —*n.m.* 1, ruler (*for drawing lines*). 2, clock; design in hose. 3, *print.* quad; quadrat.
cuadragésimo (kwa·ðra'xe·si·mo) *adj.* fortieth. —**Quadragésima**, *n.f.* Lent; Quadragesima.
cuadrangular (kwa·ðran·gu'lar) *adj.* quadrangular. —*n.m., baseball* home run.
cuadrángulo (kwa'ðran·gu·lo) *adj.* quadrangular. —*n.m.* quadrangle.
cuadrante (kwa'ðran·te) *n.m.* 1, dial. 2, *math.* quadrant.
cuardar (kwa'ðrar) *v.t.* 1, to square. 2, to arrange in squares. 3, *Amer.* to set aright. —*v.i.* to fit; to suit. —**cuadrarse**, *v.r.* to stand at attention.
cuadrático (kwa'ðra·ti·ko) *adj.* quadratic. —**cuadrática**, *n.f.* quadratic equation.
cuadratín (kwa·ðra'tin) *n.m., print.* = **cuadrado.**
cuadri- (kwa·ðri) *prefix* quadri; four: *cuadrinomio,* quadrinomial.
cuadricular (kwa·ðri·ku'lar) *v.t.* to divide into squares; rule squares in or on. —**papel cuadriculado**, graph paper.
cuadrienio (kwa·ðri'e·njo) *n.m.* quadrennium. —**cuadrienal** (-'nal) *adj.* quadrennial.
cuadrilátero (kwa·ðri'la·te·ro) *adj.* & *n.m.* quadrilateral.
cuadrilla (kwa'ðri·ʎa; -ja) *n.f.* 1, group; gang. 2, quadrille. 3, *bullfighting* team.
cuadringentésimo (kwa·ðrin·xen'te·si·mo) *adj.* & *n.m.* four-hundredth.
cuadro ('kwa·ðro) *n.m.* 1, square. 2, picture; painting. 3, *mil.* cadre. 4, frame; support. 5, chart; table; schedule. 6, *theat.* scene; tableau. —*adj.* square. —**cuadro de distribución**, switchboard; control panel.
cuadrúpedo (kwa'ðru·pe·ðo) *adj.* & *n.m.* quadruped.
cuádruple ('kwa·ðru·ple) *adj.* quadruple. —**cuádruplo**, *adj.* & *n.m.* quadruple.
cuadrúpleto (kwa'ðru·ple·to) *n.m.* quadruplet.
cuadruplicar (kwa·ðru·pli'kar) *v.t.* [*infl.:* **duplicar**] 1, to quadruple. 2, to quadruplicate. —**cuadruplicarse**, *v.r.* to quadruple. —**cuadruplicado**, *adj.* & *n.m.* quadruplicate.
cuajada (kwa'xa·ða) *n.f.* curd.
cuajado (kwa'xa·ðo) *n.m.* 1, curd. 2, mincemeat.
cuajar (kwa'xar) *v.t.* 1, to coagulate; to curdle. 2, to adorn to excess. —*v.i.* 1, to take shape; to jell. 2, to be pleasing. —**cuajarse**, *v.r.* 1,

to coagulate; to curdle. 2, to fill up; to be covered all over.
cuajo ('kwa·jo) *n.m.* 1, curd. 2, rennet. 3, clot. —**de cuajo,** by the roots.
cuákero ('kwa·ke·ro) *also, Amer.* **cuakero** (-'ke·ro) *adj.* & *n.m.* = **cuáquero, cuaquero.** —**cuakerismo,** *n.m.* = **cuaquerismo.**
cual (kwal) *rel.* & *indef. adj.* & *pron.* which. —*adv.* as; like. —**¿cuál?** *interr. adj.* & *pron.* which? what? —**cada cual,** each one. —**por lo cual,** for which reason. —**tal cual,** as is. —**tal .... cual,** like .... like. —**un tal por cual,** *colloq.* a good-for-nothing.
cualesquiera (kwa·les'kje·ra), **cualesquier** (-'kjer), *indef.adj.* & *pron., pl. of* **cualquiera, cualquier.**
cualidad (kwa·li'ðað) *n.f.* quality; property; characteristic.
cualitativo (kwa·li·ta'ti·βo) *adj.* qualitative.
cualquier (kwal'kjer) *indef.adj.* & *pron.* = **cualquiera** *before a noun.*
cualquiera (kwal'kje·ra) *indef.adj.* & *pron.* anyone; whichever; any.
cuan (kwan) *adv., contr. of* **cuanto,** how; as. *Used only before adjs.* & *advs.*
cuando ('kwan·do) *adv.* & *conj.* when. —*prep.* during. —**aún cuando,** even though; although. —**cuando más,** at the most. —**cuando menos,** at least. —**cuando no,** if not; otherwise. —**¿de cuándo acá?** since when? —**de cuando en cuando; de vez en cuando,** from time to time; once in a while.
cuantía (kwan'ti·a) *n.f.* 1, quantity. 2, personal worth; esteem. 3, *law* degree (*specifying a criminal charge*).
cuántico ('kwan·ti·ko) *adj.* quantum. —**unidad cuántica,** quantum.
cuantioso (kwan'tjo·so) *adj.* 1, plentiful. 2, large; substantial.
cuantitativo (kwan·ti·ta'ti·βo) *adj.* quantitative.
cuanto ('kwan·to) *rel.adj.* & *pron.* as much as; as many as; all that. —*n.m.* [*pl.* **cuanta** (-ta)] quantam. —**¿cuánto?** *interr.adj.* & *pron.* how much? *pl.* how many? —**cuanto antes,** as soon as possible. —**en cuanto,** as soon as. —**en cuanto a,** as for. —**unos cuantos,** a few.
cuáquero ('kwa·ke·ro) *also, Amer.* **cuaquero** (-'ke·ro) *adj.* & *n.m.* Quaker. —**cuaquerismo,** *n.m.* Quakerism.
cuarenta (kwa'ren·ta) *n.m.* & *adj.* forty.
cuarentavo (kwa·ren'ta·βo) *adj.* & *n.m.* fortieth.
cuarentena (kwa·ren'te·na) *n.f.* 1, quarantine. 2, a quantity of forty.
cuarentón (kwa·ren'ton) *n.m.* a man in his forties.
cuaresma (kwa'res·ma) *n.f.* Lent.
cuarta ('kwar·ta) *n.f.* 1, quarter; one fourth. 2, *Amer.* span (*of the hand*). 3, *Amer.* additional horses, etc., needed to perform a task. 4, *Amer.* horsewhip. 5, *music* fourth.
cuartear (kwar·te'ar) *v.t.* 1, to quarter. 2, to raise (a bid, price, etc.) by a quarter. 3, to zigzag along or over. 4, *Amer.* to whip. 5, to make a fourth in, as a card game. —*v.i., Amer.* to back down; compromise. —**cuartearse,** *v.r.* to crack; split, as a wall or ceiling.
cuartel (kwar'tel) *n.m.* 1, quarter. 2, *mil.* barracks. —**cuartelada,** *n.f.* military uprising. —**cuartel general,** *mil.* headquarters.
cuarterón (kwar·te'ron) *n.m.* 1, quarter. 2, quarter of a pound. 3, door or window panel. 4, [*fem.* **-ona**] quarter-breed; quadroon.
cuarteto (kwar'te·to) *n.m.* 1, quartet. 2, quatrain.
cuartilla (kwar'ti·ʎa; -ja) *n.f.* 1, quarter sheet (*of paper*). 2, a dry measure equal to about 1½ pecks. 3, a liquid measure equal to about 4 quarts. 4, quarter of an arroba.
cuartillo (kwar'ti·ʎo; -jo) *n.m.* 1, a dry measure equal to about ¼ peck. 2, a liquid measure equal to about a pint. 3, quarter of a real.
cuarto ('kwar·to) *n.m.* 1, room; bedroom. 2, quarter; fourth. —*adj.* fourth. —**de tres al cuarto,** insignificant; of little *or* no importance. —**echar su cuarto a espadas,** *colloq.* to butt into conversation. —**estar sin un cuarto; no tener un cuarto,** *colloq.* to be penniless; to be broke.
cuarzo ('kwar·θo; -so) *n.m.* quartz.
cuasi- (kwa·si) *prefix* quasi-; almost: *cuasicontrato,* quasicontract.
cuaternario (kwa·ter'na·rjo) *adj.* & *n.m.* quaternary.
cuaterno (kwa'ter·no) *adj.* quaternary.
cuatrero (kwa'tre·ro) *n.m.* horse thief; cattle thief.
cuatrillón (kwa·tri'ʎon; -'jon)

n.m. a billion quadrillion; *U.S.* septillion; *Brit.* quadrillion.
cuatro ('kwa·tro) *adj.* & *n.m.* four.
cuatrocientos (kwa·tro'θjen·tos; -'sjen·tos) *adj.* & *n.m. pl.* [*fem.* **–tas**] four hundred.
cuba ('ku·βa) *n.f.* **1,** cask; vat. **2,** *colloq.* tubby; fat person. **3,** *colloq.* tippler; drunkard.
cubeta (ku'βe·ta) *n.f.* shallow pan or tray.
cubicar (ku·βi'kar) *v.t.* [*pres. subjve.* **cubique** (-'βi·ke); *pret.* **cubiqué** (-'ke)] **1,** to determine the volume of. **2,** *math.* to cube; raise to the third power.
cúbico ('ku·βi·ko) *adj.* cubic.
cubiculo (ku'βi·ku·lo) *n.m.* cubicle; cubbyhole.
cubierta (ku'βjer·ta) *n.f.* **1,** cover; bedspread. **2,** *naut.* deck. **3,** *auto.; aero.* cowling.
cubierto (ku'βjer·to) *v., p.p. of* **cubrir.** —*n.m.* **1,** tableware; silver. **2,** place setting. **3,** course; meal.
cubismo (ku'βis·mo) *n.m.* cubism. —**cubista,** *adj.* & *n.m.* & *f.* cubist.
cúbito ('ku·βi·to) *n.m.* ulna.
cubo ('ku·βo) *n.m.* **1,** cube. **2,** bucket. **3,** hub.
cubrecama (ku·βre'ka·ma) *n.f.* bedspread; counterpane.
cubretablero (ku·βre·ta'βle·ro) *n.m., auto.* cowl.
cubrir (ku'βrir) *v.t.* [*p.p.* **cubierto**] **1,** to cover. **2,** to hide; to cloak. **3,** to protect. —**cubrirse,** *v.r.* **1,** to put on one's hat. **2,** to insure oneself.
cucaracha (ku·ka'ra·tʃa) *n.f.* cockroach.
cuclillas (ku'kli·ʎas; -jas) *n.f.pl., in* **en cuclillas,** squatting.
cuclillo (ku'kli·ʎo; -jo) *n.m.* cuckoo.
cuco ('ku·ko) *adj.* **1,** shrewd; crafty. **2,** *colloq.* dainty; neat. —*n.m.* **1,** cuckoo. **2,** a kind of caterpillar. **3,** a card game. **4,** *colloq.* cardsharp; gambler.
cucurucho (ku·ku'ru·tʃo) *n.m.* **1,** paper cone. **2,** *Amer.* mountain cap; peak. **3,** *Amer.* = **capirote.**
cuchara (ku'tʃa·ra) *n.f.* spoon; tablespoon. —**cucharada,** *n.f.* spoonful. —**cucharadita,** *n.f.* teaspoonful. —**cucharita,** *n.f.* teaspoon.
cucharear (ku·tʃa·re'ar) *v.t.* to spoon; ladle.
cucharón (ku·tʃa'ron) *n.m.* large spoon; ladle.
cuchichear (ku·tʃi·tʃe'ar) *v.t.* & *i.* to whisper. —**cuchicheo** (-'tʃe·o) *n.m.* whisper; whispering.
cuchilla (ku'tʃi·ʎa; -ja) *n.f.* **1,** large knife; cleaver. **2,** *Amer.* jackknife. **3,** blade; runner. —**cuchillada,** *n.f.* slash; cut; knife wound.
cuchillería (ku·tʃi·ʎe'ri·a; -je·'ri·a) *n.f.* **1,** cutlery. **2,** cutlery shop.
cuchillero (ku·tʃi'ʎe·ro; -'je·ro) *n.m.* **1,** cutler. **2,** clamp; cleat.
cuchillo (ku'tʃi·ʎo; -jo) *n.m.* knife.
cuchitril (ku·tʃi'tril) *n.m.* hovel.
cuele ('kwe·le) *v., pres.subjve. of* **colar.**
cuelgo ('kwel·ɣo) *v., pres.ind. of* **colgar.**
cuelgue ('kwel·ɣe) *v., pres.subjve. of* **colgar.**
cuelo ('kwe·lo) *v., pres.ind. of* **colar.**
cuello ('kwe·ʎo; -jo) *n.m.* **1,** neck. **2,** collar (*of a shirt, dress, etc.*).
cuenca ('kwen·ka) *n.f.* **1,** wooden bowl. **2,** socket of the eye. **3,** river basin; valley.
cuenco ('kwen·ko) *n.m.* **1,** earthen bowl. **2,** cavity; hollow; depression.
cuenta ('kwen·ta) *n.f.* **1,** count; calculation. **2,** bill. **3,** account. **4,** bead. —**caer en la cuenta,** to get the point. —**dar cuenta,** to report. —**darse cuenta de,** to realize. —**tener en cuenta,** to take into account.
cuentagotas (kwen·ta'ɣo·tas) *n.m. sing.* & *pl.* dropper.
cuentapasos (kwen·ta'pa·sos) *n.m.sing.* & *pl.* pedometer.
cuente ('kwen·te) *v., pres.subjve. of* **contar.**
cuentista (kwen'tis·ta) *n.m.* & *f.* **1,** storyteller. **2,** writer of stories or tales. **3,** *colloq.* fibber; liar.
cuento ('kwen·to) *n.m.* story; tale. —**sin cuento,** countless.
cuento ('kwen·to) *v., pres.ind. of* **contar.**
cuentón (kwen'ton) *n.m., colloq.* **1,** gossip. **2,** fibber; storyteller.
cuerda ('kwer·ða) *n.f.* **1,** cord; rope; string. **2,** winding (*of a spring mechanism*). **3,** watch spring. **4,** *anat.* cord; tendon. **5,** *geom.* chord. **6,** cord (*cubic measure*). —**aflojar la cuerda,** to ease up. —**apretar la cuerda,** to tighten up. —**bajo cuerda,** underhandedly. —**dar cuerda a, 1,** to wind. **2,** *fig.* to encourage.

cuerdo ('kwer·ðo) *adj.* 1, wise; prudent. 2, rational; sane.
cuerear (kwe·re'ar) *v.t., Amer.* to whip; flog. —**cuereada,** *n.f., Amer.* whipping; flogging.
cuerno ('kwer·no) *n.m.* horn. —*interj.* [*also,* **cuernos**] nuts!; hell!
cuero ('kwe·ro) *n.m.* hide; skin; leather. —**en cueros,** nude.
cuerpear (kwer·pe'ar) *v.i., Amer.* to dodge; evade one's responsibility. —**cuerpeada,** *n.f., Amer.* evasion; dodge.
cuerpo ('kwer·po) *n.m.* 1, body. 2, build; figure. 3, substance. 4, *mil.* corps. —**a cuerpo descubierto,** unprotected. —**cuerpo a cuerpo,** hand to hand. —**hacer** *or* **irse del cuerpo,** to move the bowels. —**sacar el cuerpo,** to dodge.
cuervo ('kwer·βo) *n.m.* crow; raven.
cuesta ('kwes·ta) *n.f.* hill; slope. —**cuesta abajo,** downhill. —**cuesta arriba,** uphill.
cueste ('kwes·te) *v., pres.subjve. of* **costar.**
cuestión (kwes'tjon) *n.f.* 1, question; dispute. 2, affair; matter.
cuestionar (kwes·tjo'nar) *v.t.* to dispute; debate. —**cuestionable,** *adj.* debatable; doubtful.
cuestionario (kwes·tjo'na·rjo) *n.m.* questionnaire.
cuesto ('kwes·to) *v., pres.ind. of* **costar.**
cueva ('kwe·βa) *n.f.* 1, cave. 2, cellar.
cueza ('kwe·θa; -sa) *v., pres.subjve. of* **cocer.**
cuezo ('kwe·θo; -so) *v., 1st pers. sing.pres.ind. of* **cocer.**
cuguar (ku'ɣwar) *n.m.* cougar.
cuico ('kwi·ko) *n.m., Amer.* 1, outlander; foreigner. 2, policeman; cop. 3, halfbreed. 4, tubby; dumpy person.
cuidado (kwi'ða·ðo) *n.m.* care; attention. —*interj.* look out! —**al cuidado de,** in care of. —**cuidado con,** beware of. —**tener cuidado,** to be careful; to take care.
cuidadoso (kwi·ða'ðo·so) *adj.* 1, careful; attentive. 2, concerned; anxious.
cuidar (kui'ðar) *v.t.* to look after; to take care of. —**cuidar de,** to take care of.
cuita ('kwi·ta) *n.f.* grief; misfortune.
cuitado (kwi'ta·ðo) *adj.* 1, grieved; afflicted. 2, timid; shy.
cuja ('ku·xa) *n.f.* bedstead.
culata (ku'la·ta) *n.f.* 1, butt (*of a gun*). 2, breech (*of a cannon*).
culatazo (ku·la'ta·θo; -so) *n.m.* 1, recoil. 2, a blow with the butt of a gun.
culebra (ku'le·βra) *n.f.* 1, snake. 2, *colloq.* cunning woman. —**culebra de cascabel,** rattlesnake.
culebrear (ku·le·βre'ar) *v.i.* to wriggle; zigzag; snake. —**culebreo** (-'βre·o) *n.m.* wriggling.
culinario (ku·li'na·rjo) *adj.* culinary.
culminar (kul·mi'nar) *v.i.* to culminate. —**culminación,** *n.f.* culmination; climax.
-culo (ku·lo), *fem.* **-cula,** *suffix* -cule; *forming diminutives of nouns and adjectives: minúsculo,* minuscule; *molécula,* molecule.
culombio (ku'lom·bjo) *n.m.* coulomb.
culpa ('kul·pa) *n.f.* guilt; blame; fault. —**echar la culpa a,** to blame.
culpable (kul'pa·βle) *adj.* culpable; guilty. —*n.m.* & *f.* culprit. —**culpabilidad,** *n.f.* culpability.
culpar (kul'par) *v.t.* to blame; to accuse.
cultivador (kul·ti·βa'ðor) *adj.* cultivating; growing; farming. —*n.m.* cultivator; grower; farmer. —**cultivadora,** *n.f.* cultivator (*machine*).
cultivar (kul·ti'βar) *v.t.* 1, to cultivate. 2, *bacteriology* to culture. —**cultivación,** *n.f.* cultivation.
cultivo (kul'ti·βo) *n.m.* 1, cultivation; farming. 2, *bacteriology* culture.
culto ('kul·to) *n.m.* 1, worship. 2, cult. —*adj.* cultured; learned.
cultura (kul'tu·ra) *n.f.* culture. —**cultural,** *adj.* cultural.
cumbre ('kum·bre) *n.f.* summit. —*adj.* top; greatest.
cúmplase ('kum·pla·se) *n.m.* 1, approval. 2, decree. 3, *Amer.* countersign (*of a decree*).
cumpleaños (kum·ple'a·ɲos) *n.m. sing.* & *pl.* birthday.
cumplido (kum'pli·ðo) *adj.* 1, complete; perfect. 2, fulfilled. 3, due. 4, dutiful; correct. —*n.m.* courtesy; compliment.
cumplimiento (kum·pli'mjen·to) *n.m.* 1, fulfillment. 2, compliance. 3, courtesy; compliment.

cumplir (kum'plir) *v.t.* to fulfill; to accomplish. —*v.i.* to be quits. —**cumplir .... años,** to be .... years old. —**cumplir con,** to fulfill.
cúmulo ('ku·mu·lo) *n.m.* **1,** heap; pile; accumulation. **2,** cumulus.
cuna ('ku·na) *n.f.* **1,** cradle. **2,** origin; ancestry.
cuneiforme (ku·ne·i'for·me) *adj.* & *n.m.* cuneiform.
cuneta (ku'ne·ta) *n.f.* gutter (*of a road*).
cuña ('ku·ɲa) *n.f.* **1,** wedge. **2,** *Amer., colloq.* influence; pull.
cuñado (ku'ɲa·ðo) *n.m.* brother-in-law. —**cuñada,** *n.f.* sister-in-law.
cuociente (kwo'θjen·te; -'sjen·te) *n.m.* quotient.
cuota ('kwo·ta) *n.f.* quota.
cuotidiano (kwo·ti'ðja·no) *adj.* = **cotidiano.**
cupe ('ku·pe) *v., pret. of* **caber.**
cupé (ku'pe) *n.m.* coupé.
cupón (ku'pon) *n.m.* coupon.
cúpula ('ku·pu·la) *n.f.* dome; cupola.
cura ('ku·ra) *n.f.* cure; treatment. —*n.m.* priest; curate. —**no tener cura,** *colloq.* to be hopeless. —**ponerse en cura,** to undergo treatment.
curable (ku'ra·βle) *adj.* curable.
curación (ku·ra'θjon; -'sjon) *n.f.* healing; cure.
curador (ku·ra'ðor) *n.m.* **1,** caretaker; curator. **2,** *law* guardian. **3,** healer. —*adj.* curing; healing.
cúralotodo (ku·ra·lo'to·ðo) *n.m.* **1,** cure-all. **2,** quack.
curandero (ku·ran'de·ro) *n.m.* **1,** healer. **2,** witch doctor. **3,** quack. —**curanderismo** (-'ris·mo) *n.m., also,* **curandería** (-'ri·a) *n.f.* quackery.
curar (ku'rar) *v.t.* to treat; to cure. —**curarse,** *v.r.* **1,** to undergo treatment. **2,** to recover. **3,** *Amer. colloq.* to get drunk. —**curarse de,** to get over; to recover from.
curativo (ku·ra'ti·βo) *adj.* curative. —**curativa,** *n.f.* curative; remedy; treatment.
curato (ku'ra·to) *n.m.* **1,** curacy. **2,** parish.
cúrcuma ('kur·ku·ma) *n.f.* turmeric.
curie (ku'ri) *n.m., physics* curie.
curio ('ku·rjo) *n.m.* curium.
curiosear (ku·rjo·se'ar) *v.i.* to snoop; pry. —**curioseo** (-'se·o) *n.m.* snooping; prying.
curioso (ku'rjo·so) *adj.* curious. —**curiosidad,** *n.f.* curiosity.
curro ('ku·rro) *adj., colloq.* gaudy; flashy. —*n.m., colloq.* fop; dandy.
curruca (ku'rru·ka) *n.f.* warbler.
currutaco (ku·rru'ta·ko) *adj., colloq.* affected or garish in dress. —*n.m., colloq.* loud dresser; sport.
cursi ('kur·si) *adj.* showy; gaudy; pretentious. —**cursilería** (-le'ri·a) *n.f.* pretentiousness; gaudiness.
cursivo (kur'si·βo) *adj.* cursive.
curso ('kur·so) *n.m.* **1,** course; direction. **2,** school year. **3,** course of study.
curtido (kur'ti·ðo) *n.m.* **1,** tanning. **2,** tanbark.
curtidor (kur·ti'ðor) *n.m.* tanner.
curtiduría (kur·ti·ðu'ri·a) *n.f.* tannery.
curtiembre (kur'tjem·bre) *n.f., Amer.* **1,** = **curtiduría. 2,** tanning.
curtir (kur'tir) *v.t.* **1,** to tan. **2,** to harden; to inure. —**estar curtido en,** to be skilled in.
curva ('kur·βa) *n.f.* curve; bend.
curvar (kur'βar) *v.t.* **1,** to curve. **2,** to bend; warp.
curvatura (kur·βa'tu·ra) *n.f.* curvature.
curvo ('kur·βo) *adj.* curved; bent.
cuscurro (kus'ku·rro) *n.m.* crouton.
cúspide ('kus·pi·ðe) *n.f.* **1,** summit; peak. **2,** cusp. **3,** cuspid.
custodia (kus'to·ðja) *n.f.* **1,** custody. **2,** guard; escort.
custodiar (kus·to'ðjar) *v.t.* to guard; keep; have custody of.
custodio (kus'to·ðjo) *n.m.* guard; custodian.
cúter ('ku·ter) *n.m., naut.* cutter.
cutí (ku'ti) *n.m.* **1,** ticking. **2,** crash (*cloth*).
cutícula (ku'ti·ku·la) *n.f.* cuticle.
cutis ('ku·tis) *n.m.* skin; complexion.
cuy (kwi) *n.m., So. Amer.* guinea pig.
cuyo ('ku·jo) *poss.adj.* whose; of whom; of which. —*n.m., colloq.* lover; beau.
czar (θar; sar) *n.m.* = **zar.**
czarevitz (θa·re'βits; sa-) *n.m.* = **zarevitz.**
czarina (θa'ri·na; sa-) *n.f.* = **zarina.**

CH

Ch, ch (tʃe) *n.f.* 4th letter of the Spanish alphabet.
cha (tʃa) *n.m.* shah.
chabacano (tʃa·βa'ka·no) *adj.* awkward; crude; tasteless; vulgar. —**chabacanería,** *n.f.* vulgarity; inane act or expression.
chacal (tʃa'kal) *n.m.* jackal.
chacarero (tʃa·ka're·ro) *n.m. & adj., Amer.* farmhand.
chacó (tʃa'ko) *n.m.* shako.
chacota (tʃa'ko·ta) *n.f.* **1,** frolic. **2,** derision.
chacotear (tʃa·ko·te'ar) *v.i.* to banter; jest. —**chacotero** (-'te·ro) *adj.* waggish. —*n.m.* wag.
chacra ('tʃa·kra) *n.f., Amer.* small ranch or farm.
cháchara ('tʃa·tʃa·ra) *n.f.* chatter; prattle. —**chacharear,** *v.i.* to chatter.
chafar (tʃa'far) *v.t.* **1,** to flatten; level. **2,** to muss; rumple (clothing). —**chafadura,** *n.f.* leveling; flattening.
chafarrinar (tʃa·fa·rri'nar) *v.t.* to blot; taint.
chaflán (tʃa'flan) *n.m.* bevel; chamfer. —**chaflanar** (-'nar) *v.t.* = **achaflanar.**
chagra ('tʃa·ɣra) *n.f., Amer.* = **chacra.** —*adj. & n.m. & f., Amer.* peasant; rustic.
chal (tʃal) *n.m.* shawl.
chalado (tʃa'la·ðo) *adj. colloq.* **1,** eccentric; odd. **2,** madly in love; smitten.
chalán (tʃa'lan) *n.m.* **1,** huckster. **2,** horse dealer. **3,** *Amer.* broncobuster.
chalana (tʃa'la·na) *n.f.* barge; lighter.
chalanear (tʃa·la·ne'ar) *v.t.* **1,** to trade astutely. **2,** to deal in horses.
chaleco (tʃa'le·ko) *n.m.* vest.
chalet (tʃa'let) *n.m.* chalet.
chalina (tʃa'li·na) *n.f.* scarf; *Amer.* necktie.
chalote (tʃa'lo·te) *n.m.* shallot.
chalupa (tʃa'lu·pa) *n.f.* **1,** sloop. **2,** *Amer.* canoe.
chamaco (tʃa'ma·ko) *n.m., Mex.* boy.
chamán (tʃa'man) *n.m.* shaman. —**chamanismo,** *n.m.* shamanism.
chamarasca (tʃa·ma'ras·ka) *n.f.* **1,** brushwood. **2,** brushwood fire.
chamarra (tʃa'ma·rra) *n.f.* a coarsely woven jacket.
chamarreta (tʃa·ma'rre·ta) *n.f.* **1,** loose jacket. **2,** *Amer.* poncho.
chambelán (tʃam·be'lan) *n.m.* chamberlain.
chambón (tʃam'bon) *adj.* clumsy; bungling. —*n.m.* blunderer; bungler. —**chambonada,** *n.f.* blunder; botch.
chambra ('tʃam·bra) *n.f.* woman's jacket.
chamicera (tʃa·mi'θe·ra; -'se·ra) *n.f.* burned-out woodland.
chamorro (tʃa'mo·rro) *adj.* shorn.
champaña (tʃam'pa·ɲa) *n.m.* champagne.
champú (tʃam'pu) *n.m.* shampoo.
champurrar (tʃam·pu'rrar) *v.t.* to mix (drinks).
chamuscar (tʃa·mus'kar) *v.t.* [*pres.subjve.* **chamusque** (-'mus·ke); *pret.* **chamusqué** (-'ke)] to singe; scorch; sear.
chamusquina (tʃa·mus'ki·na) *n.f.* **1,** scorching; singeing. **2,** quarreling; wrangling. —**oler a chamusquina,** *colloq.* to smell fishy.
chancear (tʃan·θe'ar; se'ar) *v.i.* to jest; fool. —**chancearse con,** to tease; banter.
chancero (tʃan'θe·ro; -'se·ro) *adj.* playful; jesting.
chancla ('tʃan·kla) *n.f.* **1,** slipper. **2,** worn-out shoe. —**chancleta,** *n.f.* slipper. —**chanclo,** *n.m.* overshoe.
chancro ('tʃan·kro) *n.m.* chancre.
chancho ('tʃan·tʃo) *adj., colloq.* dirty. —*n.m., colloq.* hog; pig.
chanchullo (tʃan'tʃu·ʎo; -jo) *n.m., colloq.* trickery; collusion.
chanfaina (tʃan'fai·na) *n.f.* **1,** kind of stew; olio. **2,** hodgepodge; mixup.
changador (tʃan·ga'ðor) *n.m., Amer.* porter; handyman.
chango ('tʃan·go) *n.m., Amer., colloq.* **1,** pest. **2,** whimsical person; wag. —*adj., Amer., colloq.* **1,** cumbersome; tiresome. **2,** whimsical; waggish.
chantaje (tʃan'ta·xe) *n.m.* blackmail. —**chantajear,** *v.t.* to black-

mail. —**chantajista**, *n.m. & f.* blackmailer.
chantar (tʃan'tar) *vt.* **1,** to put on; stick on; jam on. **2,** to tell (something) straight to someone's face. —**chantarse,** *v.r., cards* to stand pat.
chanza ('tʃan·θa; -sa) *n.f.* joke; jest.
chapa ('tʃa·pa) *n.f.* **1,** metal plate; foil. **2,** veneer. **3,** = **chapeta. 4,** *colloq.* good sense; prudence. **5,** *Amer.* lock. —**chapas,** *n.f.pl.* a coin-tossing game.
chapalear (tʃa·pa·le'ar) *v.i.* to splash in the water; paddle.
chapaleteo (tʃa·pa·le'te·o) *n.m.* lapping or splashing of water.
chapapote (tʃa·pa'po·te) *n.m., Amer.* asphalt.
chapar (tʃa'par) *v.t.* to plate; to coat. —**chapado a la antigua,** old-fashioned.
chaparrear (tʃa·pa·rre'ar) *v.i.* to rain heavily. —**chaparrón,** *n.m.* downpour.
chaparreras (tʃa·pa'rre·ras) *n.f. pl., Amer.* cowboy chaps; riding chaps.
chaparro (tʃa'pa·rro) *n.m.* **1,** evergreen oak. **2,** *Amer.* chubby, short person.
chapear (tʃa·pe'ar) *v.t.* **1,** to inlay with metal. **2,** *Cuba* to clear (brush) with a machete.
chapeo (tʃa'pe·o) *n.m., colloq.* hat.
chapeta (tʃa'pe·ta) *n.f.* rosy cheek.
chapitel (tʃa·pi'tel) *n.m.* **1,** *archit.* capital. **2,** spire.
chapotear (tʃa·po·te'ar) *v.t.* to moisten (*with a sponge or cloth*). —*v.i.* = **chapalear.**
chapoteo (tʃa·po'te·o) *n.m.* **1,** moistening; sponging. **2,** splashing.
chapucear (tʃa·pu·θe'ar; -se'ar) *v.t.* to bungle; work clumsily.
chapucería (tʃa·pu·θe'ri·a; -se'ri·a) *n.f.* bungle; botch.
chapucero (tʃa·pu·'θe·ro; -'se·ro) *adj.* clumsy; sloppy. —*n.m.* bungler.
chapulín (tʃa·pu'lin) *n.m., Amer.* grasshopper; locust.
chapurrear (tʃa·pu·rre'ar) *v.t. & i.* to jabber. *Also,* **chapurrar.**
chapuz (tʃa'puθ; -'pus) *n.m.* **1,** ducking. **2,** bungle; botch.
chapuza (tʃa'pu·θa; -sa) *n.f.* bungle; botch.
chapuzar (tʃa·pu'θar; -'sar) *v.t.* [*pres.subjve.* **chapuce** (-'pu·θe; se); *pret.* **chapucé** (-'θe; -'se)] to duck; immerse. —*v.i.* to duck; dive.
chapuzón (tʃa·pu'θon; -'son) *n.m.* dip; ducking.
chaqué (tʃa'ke) *n.m.* cutaway; morning coat.
chaqueta (tʃa'ke·ta) *n.f.* jacket. —**chaquetón,** *n.m.* coat.
chaquete (tʃa'ke·te) *n.m.* backgammon.
charada (tʃa'ra·ða) *n.f.* charade.
charamusca (tʃa·ra'mus·ka) *n.f., Mex.* candy twist. —**charamuscas,** *n.f.pl., Amer.* firewood.
charanga (tʃa'ran·ga) *n.f.* **1,** fanfare. **2,** brass band.
charca ('tʃar·ka) *n.f.* pond. —**charco** (-ko) *n.m.* puddle.
charla ('tʃar·la) *n.f.* conversation; chat.
charlar (tʃar'lar) *v.i.* to chatter; prate.
charlatán (tʃar·la'tan) *n.m.* **1,** charlatan. **2,** prattler. —*adj.* talkative; garrulous.
charlatanería (tʃar·la·ta·ne·'ri·a) *n.f.* **1,** charlatanism. **2,** garrulity.
charnela (tʃar'ne·la) *n.f.* hinge; joint; *mech.* knuckle.
charol (tʃa'rol) *n.m.* **1,** patent leather. **2,** varnish. —**charolar** (-'lar) *v.t.* to varnish; to polish.
charpa ('tʃar·pa) *n.f.* **1,** holster. **2,** *surg.* sling.
charqui ('tʃar·ki) *n.m., Amer.* jerked beef.
charrada (tʃa'rra·ða) *n.f.* **1,** rustic speech or action. **2,** gaudiness.
charrán (tʃa'rran) *adj.* roguish. —*n.m.* rogue; knave.
charrería (tʃa·rre'ri·a) *n.f.* gaudiness; tawdriness.
charretera (tʃa·rre'te·ra) *n.f.* epaulet.
charro ('tʃa·rro) *adj.* **1,** rustic. **2,** gaudy. —*n.m., Mex.* horseman.
chascar (tʃas'kar) *v.t.* [*pres. subjve.* **chasque** ('tʃas·ke); *pret.* **chasqué** (-'ke)] **1,** to click (the tongue). **2,** to chew noisily; munch. —*v.i.* to crack; snap.
chascarillo (tʃas·ka'ri·ʎo; -jo) *n.m.* joke; anecdote.
chasco ('tʃas·ko) *n.m.* **1,** joke; prank. **2,** disappointment. —**llevarse un chasco,** to be disappointed.
chasis ('tʃa·sis) *n.m. sing. & pl.* chassis.

chasquear (tʃas·ke'ar) *v.t.* **1,** to trick; dupe. **2,** to disappoint; disillusion. **3,** to crack (a whip).
chasqui ('tʃas·ki) *n.m., Amer.* messenger.
chasquido (tʃas'ki·ðo) *n.m.* crack (*of a whip*); cracking sound; snap (*of the fingers*).
chata ('tʃa·ta) *n.f.* **1,** bedpan. **2,** *Amer.* barge; scow. **3,** *Amer.* flat car.
chatarra (tʃa'ta·rra) *n.f.* scrap iron.
chato ('tʃa·to) *adj.* **1,** flat; flattened; blunt. **2,** flat-nosed. —*n.m., colloq.* wine glass.
chauvinismo (tʃau·βi'nis·mo) *n.m.* chauvinism. —**chauvinista,** *n.m. & f.* chauvinist. —*adj.* chauvinistic.
chaval (tʃa'βal) *n.m., colloq.* boy; kid.
chaveta *also,* **chabeta** (tʃa'βe·ta) *n.f.* **1,** forelock. **2,** pin; cotter pin. **3,** wedge. —**perder la chaveta,** to go out of one's mind.
che (tʃe) *interj., Amer.* hey!; ho! —*n.m., colloq.* fellow; guy.
checo ('tʃe·ko) *adj. & n.m.* Czech.
checoslovaco (tʃe·kos·lo'βa·ko) *also,* **checoeslovaco** (-es·lo'βa·ko) *adj. & n.m.* Czechoslovak; Czechoslovakian.
chelín (tʃe'lin) *n.m.* shilling.
chepa ('tʃe·pa) *n.f.* hump; hunch.
cheque ('tʃe·ke) *n.m.* check; bank draft. —**talonario de cheques,** checkbook.
cherna ('tʃer·na) *n.f.* sea bass.
cheslón (tʃes'lon) *n.m.* chaise longue.
cheviot (tʃe'βjot) *n.m.* [*pl.* **cheviots** (-'βjots)] cheviot.
chica ('tʃi·ka) *n.f.* **1,** little girl. **2,** girl servant.
chicle ('tʃi·kle) *n.m.* chicle; chewing gum.
chico ('tʃi·ko) *adj.* **1,** small. **2,** young. —*n.m.* little boy.
chicoria (tʃi'ko·rja) *n.f.* = **achicoria.**
chicote (tʃi'ko·te) *n.m.* **1,** sturdy youngster. **2,** *naut.* end of a rope or cable. **3,** *colloq.* cigar; cigar butt. **4,** *Amer.* whip.
chicotear (tʃi·ko·te'ar) *v.t. Amer.* **1,** to whip; flog. **2,** to kill. —*v.i., Amer.* to quarrel.
chicoteo (tʃi·ko'te·o) *n.m., Amer.* **1,** whipping; flogging. **2,** killing. **3,** quarreling.
chicuelo (tʃi'kwe·lo) *adj., n.m.* child; boy.
chicha ('tʃi·tʃa) *n.f., Amer.* corn liquor.
chícharo ('tʃi·tʃa·ro) *n.m.* **1,** pea. **2,** *Amer.* poor cigar. **3,** *Amer.* apprentice.
chicharra (tʃi'tʃa·rra) *n.f.* **1,** cicada. **2,** rattler. **3,** *colloq.* chatterbox.
chicharrón (tʃi·tʃa'rron) *n.m.* **1,** crisply fried pork rind. **2,** burnt piece of meat.
chichear (tʃi·tʃe'ar) *v.t. & i.* to hiss. —**chicheo** (-'tʃe·o) *n.m.* hissing.
chichón (tʃi'tʃon) *n.m.* bump or lump on the head. —*adj., Amer.* joking; jesting. —**chichona,** *adj. fem., Amer.* bosomy.
chifla ('tʃi·fla) *n.f.* whistle; hoot.
chiflado (tʃi'fla·ðo) *adj., colloq.* daffy; nutty.
chifladura (tʃi·fla'ðu·ra) *n.f.* **1,** whistling. **2,** hissing. **3,** mania; fad.
chiflar (tʃi'flar) *v.t.* to hiss; ridicule. —*v.i.* to whistle.
chifle ('tʃi·fle) *n.m.* whistle.
chiflido (tʃi'fli·ðo) *n.m.* sound of a whistle.
chiflón (tʃi'flon) *n.m., Amer.* draft (*of air*).
chile ('tʃi·le) *n.m.* **1,** chili. **2,** red pepper.
chilindrina (tʃi·lin'dri·na) *n.f., colloq.* bagatelle.
chilla ('tʃi·ʎa; -ja) *n.f.* clapboard.
chillar (tʃi'ʎar; -'jar) *v.i.* **1,** to shriek; scream; screech. **2,** to creak; squeak. **3,** *Amer.* to balk; protest. —**chillido** (-'ʎi·ðo; -'ji·ðo) *n.m.* shriek; scream.
chillón (tʃi'ʎon; -'jon) *adj.* **1,** shrieking. **2,** shrill. **3,** gaudy. **4,** *Amer.* whining. —*n.m.* screamer; shrieker.
chimenea (tʃi·me'ne·a) *n.f.* **1,** chimney; smokestack. **2,** fireplace.
chimpancé (tʃim·pan'θe; -'se) *n.m.* chimpanzee.
china ('tʃi·na) *n.f.* **1,** pebble. **2,** porcelain; chinaware. **3,** *Amer.* maid; servant. **4,** *W.I.* orange.
chinapo (tʃi'na·po) *n.m., Mex.* obsidian.
chinche ('tʃin·tʃe) *n.f.* **1,** bedbug. **2,** thumbtack. —*n.m. & f.* boring person. —**chincharrero** (-tʃa'rre·ro) *n.m.* place infested with bugs.

chinchilla (tʃin'tʃi·ʎa; -ja) *n.f.* chinchilla.
chinchorrería (tʃin·tʃo·rre'ri·a) *n.f.* malicious gossip; false report.
chinchorro (tʃin'tʃo·rro) *n.m.* small rowboat.
chinela (tʃi'ne·la) *n.f.* slipper.
chinero (tʃi'ne·ro) *n.m.* **1,** china closet. **2,** cupboard.
chinesco (tʃi'nes·ko) *adj.* Chinese.
chinito (tʃi'ni·to) *n.m., Amer.* [*fem.* **-ta**] darling; dear.
chino ('tʃi·no) *adj. & n.m.* Chinese.
chiquear (tʃi·ke'ar) *v.t., Cuba; Mex.* to fondle.
chiquero (tʃi'ke·ro) *n.m.* **1,** pigsty. **2,** *colloq.* messy place.
chiquitico (tʃi·ki'ti·ko) *adj.* tiny; wee. *Also,* **chiquirritico** (-rri'ti·ko).
chiquito (tʃi'ki·to) *adj.* small; tiny. —*n.m.* little boy; tot. —**chiquita,** *n.f.* little girl.
chirigota (tʃi·ri'ɣo·ta) *n.f.* joke; jest.
chirimbolo (tʃi·rim'bo·lo) *n.m.* utensil; *pl.* pots and pans; trappings.
chirimía (tʃi·ri'mi·a) *n.f.* hornpipe.
chiripa (tʃi'ri·pa) *n.f.* **1,** *billiards* fluke. **2,** stroke of good luck.
chirivía (tʃi·ri'βi·a) *n.f.* parsnip.
chirona (tʃi'ro·na) *n.f., colloq.* jail.
chirriar (tʃi'rrjar) *v.i.* **1,** to hiss; sizzle. **2,** to squeak; chirp. **3,** *colloq.* to sing off key.
chirrido (tʃi'rri·ðo) *n.m.* **1,** chirping. **2,** shrill sound.
chisguete (tʃis'ɣe·te) *n.m., colloq.* spurt; squirt.
chisme ('tʃis·me) *n.m.* gossip; mischievous tattle. —**chismear** (-'ar) *v.i.* to gossip; tattle. —**chismero,** *also,* **chismoso,** *adj.* gossiping. —*n.m.* gossip.
chismografía (tʃis·mo·ɣra'fi·a) *n.f., colloq.* gossip.
chispa ('tʃis·pa) *n.f.* **1,** spark. **2,** sparkle. **3,** small particle; bit. **4,** small amount; drop. **5,** wit; acumen. **6,** *colloq.* tipsiness. **7,** *Amer.* false rumor.
chispazo (tʃis'pa·θo; -so) *n.m.* **1,** spark. **2,** burn caused by a spark.
chispeante (tʃis·pe'an·te) *adj.* witty; brilliant.
chispear (tʃis·pe'ar) *v.i.* to sparkle; scintillate.
chispo ('tʃis·po) *adj., colloq.* tipsy. —*n.m., colloq.* nip; small drink.
chisporrotear (tʃis·po·rro·te'ar) *v.i.* **1,** to sizzle; sputter. **2,** to throw off sparks.
chisporroteo (tʃis·po·rro'te·o) *n.m.* **1,** sizzling. **2,** sparkling.
chistar (tʃis'tar) *v.i.* to mumble; mutter.
chiste ('tʃis·te) *n.m.* joke; witty sally. —**chistoso,** *adj.* humorous; witty.
chistera (tʃis'te·ra) *n.f.* **1,** top hat. **2,** fish basket; creel.
¡chito! ('tʃi·to) *interj., colloq.* silence!; hist! *Also,* **chitón** (-'ton).
chiva ('tʃi·βa) *n.f.* **1,** female goat. **2,** *Amer.* goatee. —**chivo,** *n.m.* male goat.
chocante (tʃo'kan·te) *adj.* **1,** surprising; shocking. **2,** funny; amusing. **3,** *Amer.* impertinent; annoying.
chocar (tʃo'kar) *v.* [*pres.subjve.* **choque;** *pret.* **choqué**] —*v.i.* **1,** to collide; clash. **2,** to be surprising; be shocking.
chocarrear (tʃo·ka·rre'ar) *v.i.* to joke; clown. —**chocarrería,** *n.f.* buffoonery; vulgarity. —**chocarrero,** *adj.* clownish; buffoonish. —*n.m.* buffoon; wiseacre.
choclo ('tʃo·klo) *n.m.* **1,** clog; sabot. **2,** *Amer.* ear of corn.
chocolate (tʃo·ko'la·te) *n.m.* chocolate.
chocha ('tʃo·tʃa) *n.f.* woodcock.
chochear (tʃo·tʃe'ar) *v.i.* to dote; act senilely.
chochera (tʃo'tʃe·ra) *n.f.* dotage; senility. *Also,* **chochez** (-'tʃeθ; -'tʃes) *n.f.*
chocho ('tʃo·tʃo) *adj.* doting.
chofer (tʃo'fer) *also,* **chófer** ('tʃo·fer) *n.m.* chauffeur.
chofeta (tʃo'fe·ta) *n.f.* chafing dish.
cholo ('tʃo·lo) *n.m., Amer.* **1,** halfbreed. **2,** Indian.
cholla ('tʃo·ʎa; -ja) *n.f., colloq.* **1,** skull; head. **2,** brains; talent.
chopo ('tʃo·po) *n.m.* black poplar.
choque ('tʃo·ke) *n.m.* **1,** shock; clash; collision. **2,** skirmish; conflict. **3,** dispute.
choque ('tʃo·ke) *v., pres.subjve. of* **chocar.**
choqué (tʃo'ke) *v., 1st pers. sing.pret. of* **chocar.**

choquezuela (tʃo·ke'θwe·la; -'swe·la) *n.f.* kneecap.
chorizo (tʃo'ri·θo; -so) *n.m.* sausage.
chorlito (tʃor'li·to) *n.m.* curlew; gray plover. —**cabeza de chorlito,** addle-brained person.
chorrear (tʃo·rre'ar) *v.i.* to drip; spout; gush. —**chorreo** (-'rre·o) *n.m.* dripping; spouting.
chorrera (tʃo'rre·ra) *n.f.* **1,** spout. **2,** *colloq.* gush; spate. **3,** rapids. **4,** trace left by trickling.
chorro ('tʃo·rro) *n.m.* **1,** gush; spurt. **2,** stream.
chotacabras (tʃo·ta'ka·βras) *n.m.sing. & pl.* nighthawk.
chotear (tʃo·te'ar) *v.i., Amer.* to mock; jeer; banter. —**chotearse de,** *colloq.* to tease; pull the leg of.
choza ('tʃo·θa; -sa) *n.f.* hut; hovel; shanty.
chubasco (tʃu'βas·ko) *n.m.* squall.
chúcaro ('tʃu·ka·ro) *adj., Amer.* **1,** untamed. **2,** *fig.* diffident.
chucruta (tʃu'kru·ta) *n.f.* sauerkraut.
chuchería (tʃu·tʃe'ri·a) *n.f.* trifle; trinket.
chucho ('tʃu·tʃo) *n.m., colloq.* dog.
chueco ('tʃwe·ko) *adj., Amer.* **1,** crooked; lopsided. **2,** bowlegged; knockkneed.
chufar (tʃu'far) *v.i.* to mock; scorn.
chufeta (tʃu'fe·ta) *n.f.* **1,** jest; joke. **2,** chafing dish.
chufleta (tʃu'fle·ta) *n.f.* **1,** taunt; jeer. **2,** jest; joke.
chuleta (tʃu'le·ta) *n.f.* cutlet; chop.
chulo ('tʃu·lo) *adj.* **1,** roguish. **2,** *Amer.* handsome; graceful. —*n.m.* **1,** dandy. **2,** clownish person. **3,** pimp. **4,** bullfighter's assistant.
chumacera (tʃu·ma'θe·ra; -'se·ra) *n.f.* **1,** *naut.* rowlock. **2,** *mech.* bearing; journal bearing.
chumbera (tʃum'be·ra) *n.f.* prickly pear cactus. —**higo chumbo** ('tʃum·bo) prickly pear.
chunga ('tʃun·ga) *n.f.* banter; jest.
chupada (tʃu'pa·ða) *n.f.* **1,** suck; sucking. **2,** sip; nip. **3,** *Amer.* puff; draw (*on a cigar or cigarette*).
chupado (tʃu'pa·ðo) *adj. colloq.* gaunt; emaciated; shriveled.
chupador (tʃu·pa'ðor) *adj.* sucking; absorbent. —*n.m.* **1,** sucker. **2,** teething ring.
chupaflor (tʃu·pa'flor) *n.m. Amer.* hummingbird. *Also,* **chuparrosa** (-'rro·sa).
chupar (tʃu'par) *v.t. & i.* to suck; draw; sip; absorb. —**chuparse,** *v.r.* to shrivel up.
chupete (tʃu'pe·te) *n.m.* **1,** nipple of a feeding bottle. **2,** teething ring. **3,** *Amer.* pacifier. **4,** *Amer.* lollipop. —**de chupete,** *colloq.* splendid; great.
chupón (tʃu'pon) *n.m.* **1,** *bot.* sucker. **2,** *mech.* plunger. **3,** *colloq.* swindler.
churrasco (tʃu'rras·ko) *n.m., Amer.* roasted meat; barbecue. —**churrasquear** (-ke'ar) *v.t.* to roast; barbecue.
churre ('tʃu·rre) *n.m.* oozing grease; sweaty, greasy thing. —**churriento** (-'rrjen·to) *adj.* greasy.
churrigueresco (tʃu·rri·ɣe'res·ko) *adj.* **1,** tawdry. **2,** rococo; in the style of Churriguera, 18th-century Spanish architect. —**churriguerismo,** *n.m., archit.* the style of Churriguera.
churro ('tʃu·rro) *n.m.* a fritter or cruller of oblong shape.
churruscar (tʃu·rrus'kar) [*infl.:* **chamuscar**] *v.t.* to frizzle; make crisp, as by frying.
chuscada (tʃus'ka·ða) *n.f.* drollery; jest.
chusco ('tʃus·ko) *adj.* droll; amusing. —**perro chusco,** *Amer.* mongrel dog.
chusma ('tʃus·ma) *n.f.* rabble; mob.
chuzo ('tʃu·θo; -so) *n.m.* pike; lance.

D

D, d (de) *n.f.* 5th letter of the Spanish alphabet.
dable ('da·βle) *adj.* feasible; easy.
daca ('da·ka) *contr. of* **da acá,** give (it) here. —**andar al daca y toma,** *colloq.* to be at cross purposes.
dáctilo ('dak·ti·lo) *n.m.* **1,** *pros.*

dactyl. 2, *zool.* finger; toe. —**dactilado**, *adj.* finger-shaped. —**dactílico** (-ˈti·li·ko) *adj.* dactylic.
dactilografía (dak·ti·lo·ɣraˈfi·a) *n.f.* typewriting. —**dactilógrafo** (-ˈlo·ɣra·fo) *n.m.* typist.
-dad (ˈdað) *suffix* -ty; -ness; -hood; *forming abstract and collective nouns: vecindad,* vicinity; neighborhood; *maldad,* wickedness.
dádiva (ˈda·ði·βa) *n.f.* gift; grant. —**dadivoso**, *adj.* generous; munificent.
dado (ˈda·ðo) *n.m.* 1, die; (*pl.*) dice. 2, bushing; pivot collar. —*v., p.p. of* **dar**.
dador (ðaˈðor) *adj.* giving. —*n.m.* donor.
daga (ˈda·ɣa) *n.f.* dagger.
daguerrotipo (da·ɣe·rroˈti·po) *n.m.* daguerreotype.
dalia (ˈda·lja) *n.f.* dahlia.
daltonismo (dal·toˈnis·mo) *n.m.* color blindness; Daltonism. —**daltoniano** (-toˈnja·no) *n.m.* color-blind person. —*adj.* color-blind.
dallar (daˈʎar; -ˈjar) *v.t.* to mow.
dalle (ˈda·ʎe; -je) *n.m.* scythe; sickle.
dálmata (ˈdal·ma·ta) *adj.* & *n.m.* & *f.* Dalmatian.
dama (ˈda·ma) *n.f.* lady. —**juego de damas**, checkers.
damajuana (da·maˈxwa·na) *n.f.* demijohn.
damasco (daˈmas·ko) *n.m.* 1, (fabric) damask. 2, (fruit) damson plum; apricot.
damisela (da·miˈse·la) *n.f.* damsel.
damnificar (dam·ni·fiˈkar) *v.t.* [*pres.subjve.* **damnifique** (-ˈfi·ke); *pret.* **damnifiqué** (-ˈke)] to injure; damage. —**damnificador**, *adj.* damaging. —*n.m.* injurer.
dance (ˈdan·θe; -se) *v., pres.subjve. of* **danzar**.
dancé (danˈθe; -ˈse) *v., pret. of* **danzar**.
danés (daˈnes) *adj.* Danish. —*n.m.* 1, Dane. 2, Danish language.
danta (ˈdan·ta) *n.f.* tapir.
danza (ˈdan·θa; -sa) *n.f.* dance; ball.
danzante (danˈθante; -ˈsan·te) *n.m.* 1, dancer. 2, *slang* hustler.
danzar (danˈθar; -ˈsar) *v.t.* [*pres. subjve.* **dance**; *pret.* **dancé**] to dance.
danzarín (dan·θaˈrin; -saˈrin) *n.m.* 1, dancer. 2, *slang* meddler.
danzón (danˈθon; -ˈson) *n.m.* a Cuban dance.
dañado (daˈɲa·ðo) *adj.* 1, spoiled; injured. 2, wicked; damned.
dañar (daˈɲar) *v.t.* to damage; hurt; spoil.
dañino (daˈɲi·no) *adj.* harmful; noxious.
daño (ˈda·ɲo) *n.m.* 1, damage. 2, prejudice. 3, loss. 4, nuisance.
dañoso (daˈɲo·so) *adj.* = **dañino**.
dar (dar) *v.t.* [*pres.ind.* **doy**; *pres. subjve.* **dé**; *pret.* **dí**] 1, to give. 2, to supply; deliver. 3, to grant; concede; yield. 4, to emit. 5, to cause. 6, *theat.* to present. 7, to deal (cards). 8, to strike (the hour). —*v.i.* 1, to forecast. 2, to look out (on). 3, to strike blows (on); give a beating (to). —**darse**, *v.r.* 1, to surrender. 2, to happen. —**dar con**, to find. —**dar de sí**, to stretch; give. —**dar en**, to hit upon; to succeed in striking (a mark). —**dar por sentado**, to assume. —**dárselas de**, to boast of. —**darse por**, 1, to think oneself (to be something). 2, *fol. by inf.* to take a notion to.
dardo (ˈdar·ðo) *n.m.* 1, dart. 2, *fig.* sarcasm.
dares y tomares (ˈda·res·i·to·ˈma·res) *colloq.* 1, give and take. 2, quarrel; dispute.
dársena (ˈdar·se·na) *n.f.* harbor; dockyard.
data (ˈda·ta) *n.f.* 1, date. 2, *comm.* item of a bill.
datar (daˈtar) *v.t.* 1, to date. 2, *comm.* to credit. —*v.i.* to date; date back (to).
dátil (ˈda·til) *n.m.* date (*fruit*).
dativo (daˈti·βo) *adj.* & *n.m.* dative.
dato (ˈda·to) *n.m.* datum; fact.
de (de) *prep., denoting* 1, (derivation) of; from; by. 2, (possession) of; belonging to. 3, (cause) from; because of. 4, (character; material) of; made of; with. 5, (time; measurement) of. 6, (agency) by. 7, (subject) about; concerning. 8, (comparison) than: *mas de diez metros,* more than ten meters. 9, (origin) from; of. 10, *in adverbial phrases of manner* in; on; with: *caer de rodillas,* to fall on one's knees. 11, *fol. by inf., equivalent to a conditional clause: de correr yo . . . . . ,* if I were to run . . . . .
dé (de) *v., pres.subjve. of* **dar**.
de- (de) *prefix* de-; 1, down: *degradar,* degrade. 2, negation: *demérito,* demerit. 3, privation: *de-*

foliación, defoliation. **4,** intensification: *demostrar,* demonstrate; prove.
deán (de'an) *n.m., eccles.* dean.
debajo (de'βa·xo) *adv.* under; underneath; below.
debate (de'βa·te) *n.m.* debate; discussion; contest; quarrel.
debatir (de·βa'tir) *v.t.* **1,** to argue; debate. **2,** to battle; fight. **—debatirse,** *v.r.* to struggle helplessly; founder. **—debatible,** *adj.* arguable.
debe ('de·βe) *n., bookkeeping* debit; debit side of a ledger.
debelar (de·βe'lar) *v.t.* to subdue; conquer. **—debelación,** *n.f.* conquest.
deber (de'βer) *n.m.* duty; obligation; debt. *—v.t.* to owe; *—aux.v.* to be obliged (to); to have the duty (to); ought (to); must.
debido (de'βi·ðo) *adj.* due; just; exact; proper. **—debidamente,** *adv.* justly; duly; properly.
débil ('de·βil) *adj.* weak; feeble; debilitated. **—debilidad,** *n.f.* debility; weakness.
debilitar (de·βi·li'tar) *v.t.* to debilitate; to weaken. **—debilitación,** *n.f.* debilitation.
débito ('de·βi·to) *n.m.* **1,** debt. **2,** *comm.* debit.
debutar (de·βu'tar) *v.t.* **1,** to begin. **2,** to make one's debut. **—debutante,** *adj.* beginning. *—n.m.* & *f.* beginner; novice; debutant.
deca- (de·ka) *prefix* deca-; ten: *decámetro,* decameter.
década ('de·ka·ða) *n.f.* decade.
decadente (de·ka'ðen·te) *adj.* & *n.m.* & *f.* decadent. **—decadencia,** *n.f.* decadence.
decaedro (de·ka'e·ðro) *n.m.* decahedron.
decaer (de·ka'er) *v.i.* [*infl.:* **caer**] to decay; decline; fade.
decágono (de'ka·ɣo·no) *n.m.* decagon.
decagramo (de·ka'ɣra·mo) *n.m.* decagram.
decaimiento (de·ka·i'mjen·to) *n.m.* **1,** decay; decline. **2,** weakness.
decalcomanía (de·kal·ko·ma'ni·a) *n.f.* decalcomania.
decalitro (de·ka'li·tro) *n.m.* decaliter.
decálogo (de'ka·lo·ɣo) *n.m.* decalogue.
decámetro (de'ka·me·tro) *n.m.* decameter.
decampar (de·kam'par) *v.i.* to decamp.
decano (de'ka·no) *n.m.* dean; senior member. **—decanato,** *n.m.* deanship.
decantar (de·kan'tar) *v.t.* **1,** to decant; pour. **2,** to exaggerate; exalt.
decapitar (de·ka·pi'tar) *v.t.* to decapitate. **—decapitación,** *n.f.* decapitation.
decárea (de'ka·re·a) *n.f.* decare.
decasílabo (de·ka'si·la·βo) *adj.* decasyllabic. *—n.m.* decasyllable.
decastéreo (de·ka'ste·re·o) *n.m.* decastere.
decatlon (de'ka·tlon) *n.m.* decathlon.
decena (de'θe·na; -'se·na) *n.f.* a quantity of ten.
decenal (de·θe'nal; -se'nal) *adj.* decennial.
decencia (de'θen·θja; -'sen·sja) *n.f.* decency; propriety. **—decente,** *adj.* decent; decorous.
decenio (de'θe·njo; -'se·njo) *n.m.* **1,** decade. **2,** decennial.
deceno (de'θe·no; -'se·no) *adj.* & *n.m.* tenth.
decentar (de·θen'tar; de·sen-) *v.t.* [*pres.ind.* **deciento** (-'θjen·to; -'sjen·to); *pres.subjve.* **deciente** (-te)] **1,** to use for the first time. **2,** to begin eroding, consuming, damaging (something). **3,** to injure.
decepción (de·θep'θjon; -sep'sjon) *n.f.* deception; illusion. **—decepcionar** (-'nar) *v.t.* to disappoint; disillusion.
deci- (de·θi; de·si) *prefix* deci-. **1,** ten: *decimal,* decimal. **2,** one-tenth: *decímetro,* decimeter.
decibel (de·θi'βel; de·si-) *n.m.* decibel. *Also,* **decibelio** (-'βe·ljo).
decidir (de·θi'ðir; de·si-) *v.t.* to decide; resolve. **—decidido,** *adj.* decided; determined.
deciduo (de'θi·ðwo; -'si·ðwo) *adj.* deciduous.
decigramo (de·θi'ɣra·mo; de·si-) *n.m.* decigram.
decilitro (de·θi'li·tro; de·si-) *n.m.* deciliter.
decillón (de·θi'ʎon; de·si'jon) *n.m.* an octillion decillion; *Brit.* decillion.
décima ('de·θi·ma; 'de·si-) *n.f.* **1,** tenth; tenth part. **2,** = **diezmo.**
decimal (de·θi'mal; de·si-) *adj.* decimal.

decimetro (de'θi·me·tro; de'si-) *n.m.* decimeter.
décimo ('de·θi·mo; 'de·si-) *adj.* & *n.m.* tenth.
décimoctavo (de·θi·mok'ta·βo; de·si-) *adj.* & *n.m.* eighteenth.
décimocuarto (de·θi·mo'kwar·to; de·si-) *adj.* & *n.m.* fourteenth.
décimonono (de·θi·mo'no·no; de·si-) *adj.* & *n.m.* nineteenth.
décimoquinto (de·θi·mo'kin·to; de·si-) *adj.* & *n.m.* fifteenth.
decimoséptimo (de·θi·mo'sep·ti·mo; de·si-) *adj.* & *n.m.* seventeenth.
décimosexto (de·θi·mo'seks·to; de·si-) *adj.* & *n.m.* sixteenth.
décimotercero (de·θi·mo·ter'θe·ro; de·si·mo·ter'se·ro) *adj.* & *n.m.* thirteenth.
decimotercio (de·θi·mo'ter·θjo; de·si·mo'ter·sjo) *adj.* & *n.m.* thirteenth.
decir (de'θir; -'sir) *v.t.* [*pres.ind.* **digo**; *pres.subjve.* **diga**; *fut.* **diré**; *pret.* **dije**; *ger.* **diciendo**; *p.p.* **dicho**] **1,** to say; speak. **2,** to call; name. **3,** to assert; declare. **4,** to denote. —*n.m.* saying. —**decir de repente,** to improvise. —**es decir,** that is to say. —**querer decir,** to mean.
decisión (de·θi'sjon; de·si-) *n.f.* **1,** decision. **2,** judgment; verdict. —**decisivo,** *adj.* decisive.
declamar (de·kla'mar) *v.i.* to declaim; harangue. —**declamación,** *n.f.* declamation. —**declamador,** *n.m.* orator; declaimer. —*adj.* declaiming. —**declamatorio,** *adj.* declamatory.
declarar (de·kla'rar) *v.t.* **1,** to declare; state. **2,** to decide. —*v.i.* to testify. —**declaración,** *n.f.* declaration; testimony. —**declarante,** *adj.* declaring. —*n.m.* & *f., law* witness.
declinación (de·kli·na'θjon; -'sjon) *n.f.* **1,** *gram.* declension. **2,** slope. **3,** decay.
declinar (de·kli'nar) *v.i.* **1,** to decline; decay. **2,** to bend down. **3,** to diminish; abate. —*v.t.* **1,** to decline; reject. **2,** *gram.* to decline.
declive (de'kli·βe) *n.m.* declivity; descent. —**declividad,** *n.f.* declivity.
decocción (de·kok'θjon; -'sjon) *n.f.* decoction.
decoloración (de·ko·lo·ra'θjon; -'sjon) *n.f.* discoloration.
decomisar (de·ko·mi'sar) *v.t.* to confiscate; to seize. —**decomiso** (-'mi·so) *n.m.* confiscation; seizure.
decoración (de·ko·ra'θjon; -'sjon) *n.f.* **1,** decoration. **2,** stage scenery. **3,** commitment to memory.
decorado (de·ko'ra·ðo) *n.m.* **1,** decoration. **2,** something memorized.
decorar (de·ko'rar) *v.t.* **1,** to decorate; adorn. **2,** to memorize. **3,** to recite. —**decorador,** *n.m.* decorator. —**decorativo,** *adj.* decorative.
decoro (de'ko·ro) *n.m.* decorum; honor; respect; honesty. —**decoroso,** *adj.* decorous; decent.
decrecer (de·kre'θer; -'ser) *v.i.* [*infl.:* **crecer**] to decrease. —**decreciente,** *adj.* decreasing. —**decremento,** *n.m.* decrement; decrease.
decrepitar (de·kre·pi'tar) *v.i.* to pop with the heat; crackle.
decrépito (de'kre·pi·to) *adj.* decrepit; broken down. —**decrepitud,** *n.f.* old age.
decretar (de·kre'tar) *v.t.* to decree; resolve. —**decreto** (-'kre·to) *n.m.* decree; decision.
decuplicar (de·ku·pli'kar) *v.t.* [*infl.:* **duplicar**] to multiply by ten; increase tenfold. *Also,* **decuplar.**
décuplo ('de·ku·plo) *adj.* tenfold.
dechado (de'tʃa·ðo) *n.m.* model; pattern; sample.
dedal (de'ðal) *n.m.* thimble.
dedicar (de·ði'kar) *v.t.* [*pres. subjve.* **dedique** (-'ði·ke); *pret.* **dediqué** (-'ke)] to dedicate; devote; consecrate. —**dedicación,** *n.f.* dedication; inscription. —**dedicatoria** (-'to·rja) *n.f.* dedication. —**dedicatorio,** *adj.* dedicatory.
dedillo (de'ði·ʎo; -jo) *n.m.,* *in* **saber al dedillo,** to have at one's fingertips.
dedo ('de·do) *n.m.* **1,** finger. **2,** toe. —**a dos dedos de,** *colloq.* within an ace of. —**dedo anular** *or* **médico,** ring finger. —**dedo auricular** *or* **meñique,** little finger. —**dedo cordial** *or* **del corazón,** *also,* **dedo mayor** *or* **de en medio,** middle finger. —**dedo índice** *or* **mostrador** *or* **saludador,** index finger; forefinger. —**dedo pulgar,** *also,* **dedo gordo, 1,** thumb. **2,** big toe.
deducción (de·ðuk'θjon; -'sjon) *n.f.* **1,** deduction. **2,** inference.
deducible (de·ðu'θi·βle; -'si·βle) *adj.* **1,** deducible. **2,** deductible.
deducir (de·ðu'θir; -'sir) *v.t.* [*infl.:* **conducir**] **1,** to deduce; infer. **2,** to deduct.

deductivo (de·ðuk'ti·βo) *adj.* deductive.
defalcar (de·fal'kar) *v.t.* = **desfalcar.**
defecación (de·fe·ka'θjon; -'sjon) *n.f.* **1,** defecation. **2,** excrement.
defecar (de·fe'kar) *v.t.* [*pres. subjve.* **defeque**; *pret.* **defequé**] **1,** to purify. **2,** to defecate.
defección (de·fek'θjon; -'sjon) *n.f.* defection.
defecto (de'fek·to) *n.m.* defect; fault; imperfection. —**defectible** *also,* **defectivo, defectuoso** (-'two·so) *adj.* defective; lacking; faulty.
defender (de·fen'der) *v.t.* [*pres. ind.* **defiendo**; *pres.subjve.* **defienda**] **1,** to defend; protect. **2,** to justify. **3,** to maintain. **4,** to resist. —**defendible,** *adj.* defensible.
defensa (de'fen·sa) *n.f.* **1,** defense; protection. **2,** justification. **3,** *Amer.* automobile bumper. —**defensiva,** *n.f.* defensive. —**defensivo,** *adj.* defensive. —*n.m.* defense; safeguard. —**defensor,** *adj.* defending. —*n.m.* defender; defense attorney.
defeque (de'fe·ke) *v., pres.subjve. of* **defecar.**
defequé (de·fe'ke) *v., pret. of* **defecar.**
deferir (de·fe'rir) *v.i.* [*pres.ind.* **defiero** (-'fje·ro); *pres.subjve.* **defiera** (-ra)] to defer; submit; yield. —**deferencia,** *n.f.* deference. —**deferente,** *adj.* deferential.
deficiencia (de·fi'θjen·θja; -'sjen·sja) *n.f.* deficiency. —**deficiente,** *adj.* deficient; defective.
déficit ('de·fi·θit; -sit) *n.m.* deficit.
defienda (de'fjen·da) *v., pres. subjve. of* **defender.**
defiendo (de'fjen·do) *v., pres.ind. of* **defender.**
definible (de·fi'ni·βle) *adj.* definable.
definido (de·fi'ni·ðo) *adj.* definite; defined.
definir (de·fi'nir) *v.t.* **1,** to define. **2,** to determine. —**definición,** *n.f.* definition. —**definidor,** *adj.* defining. —*n.m.* definer.
definitivo (de·fi·ni'ti·βo) *adj.* **1,** definitive. **2,** conclusive.
deflagrar (de·fla'ɣrar) *v.i.* to burn rapidly. —**deflagración,** *n.f.* conflagration.
deflector (de·flek'tor) *n.m.* deflector.
deflexión (de·flek'θjon; -'sjon) *n.f.* deflection.
defoliación (de·fo·lja'θjon; -'sjon) *n.f.* defoliation.
deformar (de·for'mar) *v.t.* to deform. —**deformación,** *n.f.* deformation.
deforme (de'for·me) *adj.* deformed; misshapen.
deformidad (de·for·mi'ðað) *n.f.* **1,** deformity. **2,** unsightliness. **3,** *fig.* crime; depravity.
defraudar (de·frau'ðar) *v.t.* **1,** to defraud. **2,** to frustrate. **3,** to disappoint. —**defraudación,** *n.f.* defrauding; cheating. —**defraudador,** *adj.* defrauding. —*n.m.* defrauder.
defuera (de'fwe·ra) *adv.* externally; on the outside.
defunción (de·fun'θjon; -'sjon) *n.f.* death; demise.
degenerar (de·xe·ne'rar) *v.i.* to degenerate. —**degeneración,** *n.f.* degeneration. —**degenerado,** *adj.* degenerate.
deglutir (de·ɣlu'tir) *v.t.* & *i.* to swallow. —**deglución,** *n.f.* swallowing.
degolladero (de·ɣo·ʎa'ðe·ro; -ja'ðe·ro) *n.m.* **1,** throat; windpipe. **2,** slaughterhouse. **3,** scaffold.
degollar (de·ɣo'ʎar; -'jar) *v.t.* [*pres.ind.* **degüello**; *pres.subjve.* **degüelle**] **1,** to behead. **2,** to cut (a dress) low in the neck. —**degollación,** *n.f.* decapitation. —**degollado,** *n.m.* décolletage.
degradación (de·ɣra·ða'θjon; -'sjon) *n.f.* **1,** degradation; debasement. **2,** *painting* blending; gradation.
degradar (de·ɣra'ðar) *v.t.* to degrade; to debase.
degüelle (de'ɣwe·ʎe; je) *v., pres. subjve. of* **degollar.**
degüello (de'ɣwe·ʎo; -jo) *v., pres. ind. of* **degollar.** —*n.m.* slaughter; massacre.
degustación (de·ɣus·ta'θjon; -'sjon) *n.f.* tasting.
dehesa (de'e·sa) *n.f.* pasture; meadow.
deidad (de·i'ðað) *n.f.* deity.
deificar (de·i·fi'kar) *v.t.* [*pres. subjve.* **deifique** (-'fi·ke); *pret.* **deifiqué** (-'ke)] to deify. —**deificación,** *n.f.* deification.
deísmo (de'is·mo) *n.m.* deism. —**deísta,** *adj.* deistic. —*n.m.* & *f.* deist.
dejación (de·xa'θjon; -'sjon) *n.f.*

1, abandonment. 2, negligence. 3, *law* assignment.
dejado (de'xa·ðo) *adj.* 1, negligent; slovenly. 2, *fig.* dejected. —**dejadez,** *n.f.* negligence; slovenliness.
dejar (de'xar) *v.t.* 1, to leave; relinquish. 2, to cease. 3, to omit. 4, to entrust. 5, to permit. 6, to fail; forsake. 7, to bequeath. —*v.i.* to stop; cease. —**dejar plantado,** *slang* to leave in the lurch. —**dejarse de cuentos,** to ignore trivialities.
dejo ('de·xo) *n.m.* 1, end. 2, aftereffect. 3, carelessness.
del (del) *contr. of* **de** + **el.**
delación (de·la'θjon; -'sjon) *n.f.* denunciation; accusation.
delantal (de-lan'tal) *n.m.* apron.
delante (de'lan·te) *adv.* in front; before; ahead; in the presence (of).
delantera (de·lan'te·ra) *n.f.* 1, front; forefront. 2, advantage; lead. —**delantero,** *adj.* foremost; first.
delatar (de·la'tar) *v.t.* 1, to inform against; denounce. 2, to betray; give away.
delator (de·la'tor) *adj.* denouncing; —*n.m.* informer; denouncer.
deleble (de'le·βle) *adj.* erasable.
delectación (de·lek·ta'θjon; -'sjon) *n.f.* delight; pleasure.
delegación *n.f.* 1, delegation. 2, group of delegates.
delegar (de·le'ɣar) *v.t.* [*pres. subjve.* **delegue** (-'le·ɣe); *pret.* **delegué** (-'ɣe)] to delegate. —**delegado,** *adj.* delegated. —*n.m.* delegate.
deleitar (de·lei'tar) *v.t.* to delight; please. —**deleitación,** *n.f.* enjoyment. —**deleitante,** *adj.* pleasing.
deleite (de'lei·te) *n.m.* delight; gratification. —**deleitoso,** *also,* **deleitable,** *adj.* delightful; delectable.
deletéreo (de·le'te·re·o) *adj.* deleterious.
deletrear (de·le·tre'ar) *v.i.* 1, to spell. 2, to decipher; interpret. —**deletreo** (-'tre·o) *n.m.* spelling.
deleznable (de·leθ'na·βle; de·les-) *adj.* 1, slippery. 2, brittle; fragile. 3, perishable.
delfín (del'fin) *n.m.* 1, dolphin. 2, dauphin.
delgadez (del·ɣa'ðeθ; -'ðes) *n.f.* 1, thinness; fineness; slenderness. 2, acuteness.
delgado (del'ɣa·ðo) *adj.* 1, thin; delicate; gaunt. 2, acute; ingenious.
deliberar (de·li·βe'rar) *v.t.* & *i.* to deliberate; consider carefully. —**deliberación,** *n.f.* deliberation. —**deliberadamente,** *adv.* deliberately; resolutely. —**deliberativo,** *adj.* deliberating; deliberative.
delicadez (de·li·ka'ðeθ; -'ðes) n.f. 1, delicacy; frailty. 2, sensitiveness.
delicadeza (de·li·ka'ðe·θa; -sa) *n.f.* 1, considerateness. 2, daintiness; refinement; delicacy.
delicado (de·li'ka·ðo) *adj.* 1, delicate; frail. 2, exquisite. 3, considerate; tactful. 4, palatable; tasty. 5, sensitive.
delicia (de'li·θja; -sja) *n.f.* delight. —**delicioso,** *adj.* delicious; delightful.
delictuoso (de·lik'two·so) *adj.* unlawful; criminal. *Also,* **delictivo** (-'ti·βo).
delicuescente (de·li·kwes'θen·te; -kwe'sen·te) *adj.* deliquescent. —**delicuescencia,** *n.f.* deliquescence.
delincuente (de·lin'kwen·te) *adj.* & *n.m.* & *f.* delinquent. —**delincuencia,** *n.f.* delinquency.
delinear (de·li·ne'ar) *v.t.* to delineate; sketch; describe; draft. —**delineación,** *n.f.* delineation. —**delineante,** *n.m.* draftsman.
delinquir (de·lin'kir) *v.i.* [*pres. ind.* **delinco** (-'lin·ko); *pres.subjve.* **delinca** (-ka)] to transgress. —**delinquimiento,** *n.m.* transgression.
delirar (de·li'rar) *v.i.* to be delirious; rave. —**delirante,** *adj.* delirious.
delirio (de'li·rjo) *n.m.* 1, delirium. 2, *fig.* nonsense.
delito (de'li·to) *n.m.* crime; transgression.
delta ('del·ta) *n.f.* delta.
deludir (de·lu'ðir) *v.t.* to delude; deceive.
delusorio (de·lu'so·rjo) *also,* **delusivo** (-'si·βo) *adj.* delusive.
demacrar (de·ma'krar) *v.t.* to emaciate. —**demacración,** *n.f.* emaciation. —**demacrado,** *adj.* emaciated.
demagogia (de·ma'ɣo·xja) *n.f.* demagoguery. —**demagógico** (-'ɣo·xi·ko) *adj.* demagogic. —**demagogo** (-'ɣo·ɣo) *adj.* demagogic. —*n.m.* demagogue.
demanda (de'man·da) *n.f.* 1, demand; petition. 2, question; inquiry. 3, endeavor; quest. 4, *law* claim; lawsuit. 5, *comm.* order.
demandar (de·man'dar) *v.t.* 1, to demand; ask; claim. 2, *law* to sue; file a suit against. —**demandado,**

n.m. defendant; accused. —**demandador,** *adj.* demanding. —*n.m., law* claimant; plaintiff. —**demandante,** *adj.* demanding. —*n.m.* & *f.* plaintiff.
demarcar (de·mar'kar) *v.t.* [*pres. subjve.* **demarque** (-'mar·ke); *pret.* **demarqué** (-'ke)] to survey; fix the boundaries of. —**demarcación,** *n.f.* demarcation.
demás (de'mas) *adj.* other. —*adv.* besides; moreover. —**lo demás,** the rest. —**los** *or* **las demás,** the others. —**por demás, 1,** too much; to excess. **2,** in vain. —**por lo demás,** as for the rest.
demasía (de·ma'si·a) *n.f.* **1,** excess; surplus. **2,** insolence; boldness.
demasiado (de·ma'sja·ðo) *adj.* too much; excessive. —*adv.* excessively; too.
demencia (de'men·θja; -sja) *n.f.* dementia; insanity. —**dementar** (-'tar) *v.t.* to drive mad. —**demente** (-'men·te) *adj.* demented. —*n.m.* & *f.* insane person.
demérito (de'me·ri·to) *n.m.* demerit.
democracia (de·mo'kra·θja; -sja) *n.f.* democracy. —**demócrata** (-'mo·kra·ta) *adj.* democratic. —*n.m.* & *f.* democrat. —**democrático** (-'kra·ti·ko) *adj.* democratic.
democratizar (de·mo·kra·ti'θar; -'sar) *v.t.* [*pres.subjve.* **democratice** (-'ti·θe; -se); *pret.* **democraticé** (-'θe; -'se) to democratize. —**democratización,** *n.f.* democratization.
demografía (de·mo·ɣra'fi·a) *n.f.* demography. —**demográfico** (-'ɣra·fi·ko) *adj.* demographic. —**demógrafo** (-'mo·ɣra·fo) *n.m.* demographer.
demoler (de·mo'ler) *v.t.* [*infl.:* **moler**] to demolish. —**demolición,** *n.f.* demolition.
demonio (de'mo·njo) *n.m.* demon; devil. —**demoníaco** (-'ni·a·ko) *adj.* demoniacal.
demontre (de'mon·tre) *n.m., colloq.* devil. —*interj.* damn!; the devil!
demora (de'mo·ra) *n.f.* delay.
demorar (de·mo'rar) *v.t.* to delay; hinder; detain. —**demorarse,** *v.r.* to linger; tarry.
demostrar (de·mos'trar) *v.t.* [*infl.:* **mostrar**] to demonstrate; show; prove. —**demostrable,** *adj.* demonstrable. —**demostración,** *n.f.* demonstration. —**demostrativo,** *adj.* demonstrative.
demudar (de·mu'ðar) *v.t.* **1,** to alter; change. **2,** to disguise. —**demudarse,** *v.r.* **1,** to become disturbed. **2,** (of the face) to change color suddenly. —**demudación,** *n.f.* alteration; change.
dendro- (den·dro) *prefix* dendro-; tree; *dendrografía,* dendrography.
-dendro ('den·dro) *suffix* -dendron; tree: *rododendro,* rhododendron.
denegar (de·ne'ɣar) *v.t.* [*infl.:* **negar**] to deny; refuse. —**denegación,** *n.f.* denial; refusal.
dengue ('den·ge) *n.m.* **1,** coyness; affectation. **2,** *med.* dengue. —**dengoso** (-'go·so) *adj.* fastidious.
denigrar (de·ni'ɣrar) *v.t.* to defame; insult; revile. —**denigración,** *n.f.* defamation.
denodado (de·no'ða·ðo) *adj.* intrepid; bold.
denominar (de·no·mi'nar) *v.t.* to denominate; name. —**denominación,** *n.f.* denomination. —**denominador,** *adj.* denominating. —*n.m.* denominator. —**denominativo,** *adj.* denominative.
denostar (de·nos'tar) *v.t.* [*pres. ind.* **denuesto**; *pres.subjve.* **denueste**] to affront; outrage; abuse.
denotar (de·no'tar) *v.t.* to denote; indicate; express. —**denotación,** *n.f.* denotation; indication.
densidad (den·si'ðað) *n.f.* **1,** density; thickness. **2,** *physics* specific gravity.
denso ('den·so) *adj.* dense; thick; compact.
dentado (den'ta·ðo) *adj.* toothed; serrated; cogged.
dentadura (den·ta'ðu·ra) *n.f.* **1,** teeth collectively. **2,** set of teeth; denture.
dental (den'tal) *also,* **dentario** (-'ta·rjo) *adj.* dental.
dentar (den'tar) *v.t.* [*pres.ind.* **diento**; *pres.subjve.* **diente**] **1,** to provide with teeth or prongs. **2,** to indent. —*v.i.* to teethe.
dentellada (den·te'ʎa·ða; -'ja·ða) *n.f.* **1,** biting; bite. **2,** tooth mark.
dentellado (den·te'ʎa·ðo; -'ja·ðo) *adj.* **1,** toothed; serrated. **2,** bitten.
dentellar (den·te'ʎar; -'jar) *v.i.* (*of the teeth*) to chatter.
dentellear (den·te·ʎe'ar; -je'ar) *v.t.* to nibble.

denti- (den·ti) *also,* **dent-** (dent), **dento-** (den·to) *prefix* denti-; tooth: *dentífrico,* dentifrice.

dentición (den·ti'θjon; -'sjon) *n.f.* dentition.

dentífrico (den'ti·fri·ko) *n.m.* dentifrice. —**pasta dentífrica,** toothpaste.

dentina (den'ti·na) *n.f.* dentin.

dentista (den'tis·ta) *n.m.* & *f.* dentist.

dentro ('den·tro) *adv.* inside; within. —**hacia dentro,** toward the center or interior. —**dentro de poco,** soon.

denudar (de·nu'ðar) *v.t.* to denude. —**denudación,** *n.f.* denudation.

denuedo (de'nwe·ðo) *n.m.* intrepidity; bravery.

denueste (de'nwes·te) *v., pres. subjve. of* **denostar.**

denuesto (de'nwes·to) *v., pres.ind. of* **denostar.** —*n.m.* affront; outrage; abuse.

denuncia (de'nun·θja; -sja) *n.f.* 1, denunciation; accusation. 2, announcement. 3, miner's claim.

denunciar (de·nun'θjar; -'sjar) *v.t.* 1, to denounce; accuse. 2, to advise; give notice. 3, to predict. 4, to register (a mining claim). —**denunciante,** *n.m.* & *f.* denouncer; informer. —**denuncio** (-'nun·θjo; -sjo) *n.m.* establishment of a mining claim.

denutrición (de·nu·tri'θjon; -'sjon) *n.f.* malnutrition.

deparar (de·pa'rar) *v.t.* to offer; present; furnish.

departamento (de·par·ta'men·to) *n.m.* 1, department. 2, *R.R.* compartment. 3, *Arg.* apartment; room. —**departamental,** *adj.* departmental.

departir (de·par'tir) *v.i.* to talk; chat.

depauperación (de·pau·pe·ra·'θjon; -'sjon) *n.f.* 1, impoverishment. 2, weakening; debilitation. 3, exhaustion; depletion.

depauperar (de·pau·pe'rar) *v.t.* 1, to impoverish; pauperize. 2, to weaken; debilitate. 3, to exhaust; deplete.

dependencia (de·pen'den·θja; -sja) *n.f.* 1, dependency. 2, branch office. 3, staff of employees.

depender (de·pen'der) *v.i.* to depend. —**depender de,** to depend on or upon; be dependent on or upon; rely on or upon.

dependiente (de·pen'djen·te) *adj.* dependent. —*n.m.* & *f.* 1, dependent. 2, salesclerk.

depilar (de·pi'lar) *v.t.* to depilate. —**depilación,** *n.f.* depilation. —**depilatorio,** *adj.* depilatory.

deplorar (de·plo'rar) *v.t.* to deplore; regret. —**deplorable,** *adj.* deplorable.

deponente (de·po'nen·te) *n.m.* & *f.* 1, deposer. 2, *law* deponent.

deponer (de·po'ner) *v.t.* [*infl.:* **poner**] 1, to depose; remove. 2, *law* to testify. —*v.i.* to defecate.

deportar (de·por'tar) *v.t.* to deport. —**deportación,** *n.f.* deportation.

deporte (de'por·te) *n.m.* sport; recreation. —**deportista,** *n.m.* sportsman. —*n.f.* sportswoman. —**deportivo,** *adj.* sporting; sport (*attrib.*).

deposición (de·po·si'θjon; -'sjon) *n.f.* 1, deposition; written testimony. 2, dismissal or removal from office. 3, bowel movement.

depositar (de·po·si'tar) *v.t.* 1, to deposit. 2, to entrust. 3, to enclose. —**depositarse,** *v.r.* to settle (*of sediment*). —**depositario,** *adj.* depository. —*n.m.* receiver; trustee.

depositaría (de·po·si·ta'ri·a) *n.f.* 1, depository. 2, public treasury. 3, receivership; trust.

depósito (de'po·si·to) *n.m.* 1, deposit. 2, depository. 3, storehouse; warehouse. 4, sediment.

depravar (de·pra'βar) *v.t.* to deprave; pervert. —**depravación,** *n.f.* depravity. —**depravado,** *adj.* depraved; perverted.

deprecar (de·pre'kar) *v.t.* [*pres. subjve.* **depreque** (-'pre·ke); *pret.* **deprequé** (-'ke)] to entreat; implore. —**deprecación,** *n.f.* entreaty; prayer.

depreciar (de·pre'θjar; -'sjar) *v.t.* to depreciate; devaluate. —**depreciación,** *n.f.* depreciation.

depredar (de·pre'ðar) *v.t.* to rob; pillage; plunder. —**depredación,** *n.f.* depredation; embezzlement.

depresión (de·pre'sjon) *n.f.* 1, depression; dip. 2, *econ.* depression; decline. 3, dejection. 4, *meteorol.* low. —**depresivo** (-'si·βo) *adj.* depressive. —**depresor** (-'sor) *n.m.* depressor.

deprimir (de·pri'mir) *v.t.* to depress. —**deprimente,** *adj.* depressing; depressive.

depurar (de·pu'rar) *v.t.* to purify. —**depuración,** *n.f.* purification. —**depurativo,** *adj.* purifying. —*n.m.* purifier.
derecha (de're·tʃa) *n.f.* 1, right; right side; right hand. 2, *polit.* right; right wing.
derechista (de·re'tʃis·ta) *adj.* & *n.m.* & *f.* rightist.
derecho (de're·tʃo) *adj.* 1, right. 2, straight; direct. 3, upright; vertical. 4, just; lawful. —*adv.* straight; directly. —*n.m.* 1, right. 2, justice; law. 3, tax; duty.
deriva (de'ri·βa) *n.f.* drift; drifting. —**ir a la deriva,** to drift.
derivar (de·ri'βar) *v.t.* 1, to derive; trace. 2, to lead; turn (one's attention). —*v.i.* 1, to derive; be derived. 2, to come (from); emanate (from). —**derivación,** *n.f.* derivation. —**derivado,** *adj.* & *n.m.* derivative. —**derivativo,** *adj.* derivative.
derm- (derm) *prefix, var. of* **dermo-** *before vowels: dermalgia,* dermalgia.
dermat- (der·mat) *prefix, var. of* **dermato-** *before vowels: dermatemia,* dermathemia.
dermatitis (der·ma'ti·tis) *n.f.* dermatitis.
dermato- (der·ma·to) *prefix* dermato-; skin: *dermatología,* dermatology.
dermatología (der·ma·to·lo'xi·a) *n.f.* dermatology. —**dermatológico** (-'lo·xi·ko) *adj.* dermatological. —**dermatólogo** (-'to·lo·ɣo) *n.m.* dermatologist.
dermis ('der·mis) *n.f.* dermis.
dermo- (der·mo) *prefix* dermo-; skin: *dermoblasto,* dermoblast.
-dermo ('der·mo) *suffix* -derm; skin: *paquidermo,* pachyderm.
-dero ('ðe·ro), *fem.* **-dera** (-ra) *suffix* 1, *forming nouns* (*usu.masc.*) *denoting* place: *abrevadero,* watering place. 2, *forming nouns* (*usu. fem.*) *denoting* instrument: *regadera,* watering pot. 3, *forming adjectives expressing* ability; capability: *pagadero,* payable; *hacedero,* feasible.
derogación (de·ro·ɣa'θjon; -'sjon) *n.f.* 1, derogation. 2, annulment; repeal.
derogar (de·ro'ɣar) *v.t.* [*pres. subjve.* **derogue** (-'ro·ɣe); *pret.* **derogué** (-'ɣe)] 1, to derogate. 2, to annul; repeal.
derrabar (de·rra'βar) *v.t.* to cut or clip the tail of; dock.
derrama (de'rra·ma) *n.f.* tax assessment.
derramar (de·rra'mar) *v.t.* to spill; scatter. —**derramarse,** *v.r.* to overflow; leak. —**derramamiento,** *n.m.* spilling.
derrame (de'rra·me) *n.m.* 1, leakage; spillage; overflow. 2, declivity. 3, discharge; hemorrhage.
derredor (de·rre'ðor) *n.m.* circumference; contour; circuit.
derrelicción (de·rre·lik'θjon; -'sjon) *n.f.* dereliction; abandonment.
derrelicto (de·rre'lik·to) *v., p.p. of* **derrelinquir.** —*adj.* abandoned; derelict. —*n.m., naut.* derelict.
derrelinquir (de·rre·lin'kir) *v.t.* [*pres.ind.* **derrelinco** (-'lin·ko); *pres.subjve.* **derrelinca** (-ka); *p.p.* **derrelicto** (-'lik·to)] to forsake; abandon.
derrengar (de·rren'gar) *v.t.* [*pres. subjve.* **derrengue** (-'rren·ge); *pret.* **derrengué** (-'ge)] 1, to sprain the hip or spine of; cripple. 2, *fig.* to overburden; overwhelm.
derretimiento (de·rre·ti'mjen·to) *n.m.* 1, melting. 2, *fig.* consuming love.
derretir (de·rre'tir) *v.t.* [*pres.ind.* **derrito** (-'rri·to) *pres.subjve.* **derrita** (-ta)] 1, to melt; smelt. 2, *fig.* to waste; exhaust.
derribar (de·rri'βar) *v.t.* 1, to demolish; tear down; fell. 2, to overthrow; depose. —**derribo** (-'rri·βo) *n.m.* demolition; ruin.
derrocar (de·rro'kar) *v.t.* [*infl.:* **tocar**] throw down; overthrow. —**derrocadero,** *n.m.* precipice. —**derrocamiento,** *n.m.* headlong fall; overthrow.
derrochar (de·rro'tʃar) *v.t.* to waste; dissipate. —**derrochador,** *adj.* wasteful. —*n.m.* spendthrift. —**derroche** (-'rro·tʃe) *n.m.* squandering; waste.
derrota (de'rro·ta) *n.f.* 1, defeat. 2, road; path. 3, *naut.* ship's course.
derrotar (de·rro'tar) *v.t.* 1, to defeat; rout. 2, to squander; destroy.
derrotero (de·rro'te·ro) *n.m.* 1, road; path. 2, *naut.* ship's course; route.
derrotismo (de·rro'tis·mo) *n.m.* defeatism. —**derrotista,** *adj.* & *n.m.* & *f.* defeatist.
derrubiar (de·rru'βjar) *v.t.* to

erode; waste away. —**derrubio** (-'rru·βjo) *n.m.* erosion.
derruir (de·rru'ir) *v.t.* [*infl.:* **destruir**] to raze; destroy.
derrumbadero (de·rrum·ba'ðe·ro) *n.m.* precipice.
derrumbar (de·rrum'bar) *v.t.* to throw down. —**derrumbarse,** *v.r.* to crumble.
derrumbe (de'rrum·be) *n.m.* **1,** landslide; collapse. **2,** precipice.
derviche (der'βi·tʃe) *n.m.* dervish.
des- (des) *prefix* dis-; di-. **1,** negation: *desconfiar,* distrust. **2,** opposition: *descrédito,* discredit. **3,** apart; asunder; in different directions: *desunir,* disjoin: *deshechar,* reject; *desplazar,* displace.
desabarrancar (des·a·βa·rran·'kar) *v.t.* [*infl.:* **embarrancar**] to pull out of a ditch; extricate.
desabastecer (des·a·βas·te'θer; -'ser) *v.t.* [*infl.:* **abastecer**] to cut off supplies from.
desabollar (des·a·βo'ʎar; -'jar) *v.t.* to remove the dents from.
desabono (des·a'βo·no) *n.m.* **1,** injury; prejudice. **2,** cancellation of a subscription. —**desabonarse** *v.r.* to cancel one's subscription.
desabotonar (des·a·βo·to'nar) *v.t.* to unbutton. —*v.i., fig.* to blossom.
desabrido (de·sa'βri·ðo) *adj.* **1,** tasteless. **2,** sour. **3,** peevish. **4,** unseasonable, as weather.
desabrigar (des·a·βri'ɣar) *v.t.* [*infl.:* **abrigar**] **1,** to deprive of shelter. **2,** to strip of warm or protective clothing.
desabrigo (des·a'βri·ɣo) *n.m.* **1,** unsheltered state or condition; exposure. **2,** lack of warm or protective clothing.
desabrir (de·sa'βrir) *v.t.* **1,** to taint, as food. **2,** to vex.
desabrochar (des·a·βro'tʃar) *v.t.* **1,** to unbutton; unfasten. **2,** to burst open. —**desabrocharse,** *v.r., fig.* to confide; unburden oneself.
desacalorarse (des·a·ka·lo'rar·se) *v.r.* to cool off.
desacatar (des·a·ka'tar) *v.t.* to treat disrespectfully.
desacato (des·a'ka·to) *n.m.* **1,** disrespect; irreverence. **2,** *law* contempt of court.
desacerbar (des·a·θer'βar; -ser·'βar) *v.t.* to mitigate; temper.
desacertar (des·a·θer'tar; -ser'tar) *v.i.* [*infl.:* **acertar**] to err; miss one's aim. —**desacierto** (-'θjer·to; -'sjer·to) *n.m.* blunder; error.
desacomodado (des·a·ko·mo·'ða·ðo) *adj.* **1,** uncomfortable. **2,** unemployed.
desacomodar (des·a·ko·mo'ðar) *v.t.* **1,** to inconvenience. **2,** to dismiss. **3,** to disarrange.
desacomodo (des·a·ko'mo·ðo) *n.m.* **1,** inconvenience. **2,** dismissal.
desacompasado (des·a·kom·pa·'sa·ðo) *adj., Amer.* = **descompasado,** def. 1.
desacoplar (des·a·ko'plar) *v.t.* to uncouple; disconnect.
desacordar (des·a·kor'ðar) *v.t.* [*infl.:* **acordar**] to put out of tune. —**desacordarse,** *v.r.* to be forgetful.
desacorde (des·a'kor·ðe) *adj.* discordant.
desacostumbrado (des·a·kos·tum'bra·ðo) *adj.* unusual; unaccustomed.
desacostumbrar (des·a·kos·tum'brar) *v.t.* to break of a habit.
desacotar (des·a·ko'tar) *v.t.* **1,** to lay open (a grazing ground). **2,** to remove (a restriction). —**desacoto** *n.m.* removal of a restriction.
desacreditado (des·a·kre·ði'ta·ðo) *adj.* **1,** discredited. **2,** disreputable; in disrepute.
desacreditar (des·a·kre·ði'tar) *v.t.* to discredit; disparage.
desacuerdo (des·a'kwer·ðo) *n.m.* **1,** discordance; disagreement. **2,** inaccuracy. **3,** forgetfulness.
desadvertido (des·að·βer'ti·ðo) *adj.* **1,** inadvertent. **2,** unnoticed.
desadvertir (des·að·βer'tir) *v.t.* [*infl.:* **advertir**] to overlook; pay no heed (to).
desafección (des·a·fek'θjon; -'sjon) *n.f.* disaffection.
desafecto (des·a'fek·to) *adj.* opposed; alienated. —*n.m.* ill will; lack of affection. —**desafectado,** *adj.* unaffected.
desaferrar (des·a·fe'rrar) *v.t.* **1,** to loosen; detach. **2,** to persuade.
desafiar (des·a·fi'ar) *v.t.* [*infl.:* **fiar**] to defy; dare; challenge. —**desafiador,** *adj.* challenging. —*n.m.* challenger; duelist.
desaficionar (des·a·fi·θjo'nar; -sjo'nar) *v.t.* to disaffect; disincline.
desafinar (des·a·fi'nar) *v.i.* **1,** *music* to be discordant. **2,** *fig.* to speak irrelevantly. —**desafinado,** *adj.* dissonant; out of tune.

desafio (des·a'fio) *n.m.* challenge; duel.
desaforar (des·a·fo'rar) *v.t.* to encroach on the rights of. —**desaforarse,** *v.r.* to be disorderly. —**desaforado,** *adj.* disorderly; impudent. —**desafuero** (-'fwe·ro) *n.m.* violation; outrage; abuse.
desafortunado (des·a·for·tu·'na·do) *adj.* unfortunate.
desagradar (des·a·ɣra'ðar) *v.t.* to displease. —**desagrado** (-'ɣra·ðo) *n.m.* displeasure. —**desagradable,** *adj.* disagreeable.
desagradecer (des·a·ɣra·ðe'θer; -'ser) *v.t.* [*infl.:* **agradecer**] to be ungrateful. —**desagradecido,** *adj.* ungrateful. —*n.m.* ingrate. —**desagradecimiento,** *n.m.* ingratitude.
desagraviar (des·a·ɣra'βjar) *v.t.* to make amends to; atone to. —**desagravio** (-'ɣra·βjo) *n.m.* vindication; amends (*pl.*).
desagregar (des·a·ɣre'ɣar) *v.t.* [*infl.:* **agregar**] to separate; disjoin. —**desagregación,** *n.f.* separation.
desaguar (des·a'ɣwar) *v.t.* to drain; empty. —*v.i.* to flow into the sea. —**desaguadero,** *n.m.* drain. —**desagüe** (-'a·ɣwe) *n.m.* drainage; sluice.
desaguisado (des·a·ɣi'sa·ðo) *adj.* unjust; unfair. —*n.m.* outrage; wrong.
desahogado (des·a·o'ɣa·ðo) *adj.* **1,** well-to-do; comfortable. **2,** unencumbered. **3,** petulant; impudent.
desahogar (des·a·o'ɣar) *v.t.* [*infl.:* **ahogar**] to relieve; alleviate. —**desahogarse,** *v.r.* **1,** to recover from distress, fatigue or grief. **2,** to vent one's feeling.
desahogo (des·a'o·ɣo) *n.m.* relief. —**vivir con desahogo,** to live comfortably.
desahuciar (des·au'θjar; -'sjar) *v.t.* **1,** to give up (a patient) as hopeless. **2,** to evict; dispossess. —**desahucio** (-'au·θjo; -sjo) *n.m.* eviction.
desahumar (des·a·u'mar) *v.t.* to clear of smoke. —**desahumado,** *adj.* vapid; flat, as champagne.
desairar (des·ai'rar) *v.t.* **1,** to slight; snub (a person). **2,** to disdain (a thing). —**desaire** (-'ai·re) *n.m.* slight; rebuff.
desajustar (des·a·xus'tar) *v.t.* to disarrange; put out of adjustment. —**desajustarse,** *v.r.* **1,** to be or become out of adjustment. **2,** to break an agreement. **3,** to disagree; be incompatible.
desalar (de·sa'lar) *v.t.* to desalt.
desalarse (de·sa'lar·se) *v.r.* **1,** to hasten. **2,** *fig.* to be eager. —**desalado,** *adj.* eager; anxious.
desalentar (des·a·len'tar) *v.t.* [*infl.:* **alentar**] to discourage. —**desalentador,** *adj.* discouraging. —**desaliento** (-'ljen·to) *n.m.* dismay; discouragement.
desalinear (des·a·li·ne'ar) *v.t.* to put out of alignment. —**desalineado,** *adj.* out of alignment.
desaliñar (des·a·li'ɲar) *v.t.* to ruffle; disarrange. —**desaliño** (-'li·ɲo) *n.m.* slovenliness; disarray; neglect.
desalivar (de·sa·li'βar) *v.i.* to salivate.
desalmar (des·al'mar) *v.t.* to weaken; deplete. —**desalmarse,** *v.r.* **1,** to be eager. **2,** to lose strength or spirit. —**desalmado,** *adj.* heartless; cruel; inhuman.
desalojar (des·a·lo'xar) *v.t.* to dislodge; dispossess; evict. —*v.i.* to move out. —**desalojamiento,** *n.m.* dislodgment.
desalquilar (des·al·ki'lar) *v.t.* to discontinue the lease or rental of. —**desalquilado,** *adj.* vacant; untenanted.
desalumbramiento (des·a·lum·bra'mjen·to) *n.m.* **1,** blindness. **2,** lack of knowledge *or* judgment.
desamarrar (des·a·ma'rrar) *v.t.* **1,** to untie; unfasten. **2,** *naut.* to cast off; unmoor.
desamistarse (des·a·mis'tar·se) *v.r.* to quarrel; have a falling out.
desamor (des·a'mor) *n.m.* **1,** coldness; indifference. **2,** dislike; enmity. —**desamorar,** *v.t.* to alienate. —**desamorado,** *adj.* coldhearted.
desamparar (des·am·pa'rar) *v.t.* to abandon; forsake. —**desamparo** (-'pa·ro) *n.m.* abandonment; helplessness; dereliction.
desamueblar (des·a·mwe'βlar) *v.t.* to strip of furniture; dismantle. —**desamueblado** *also,* **desamoblado** (-mo'βla·ðo) *adj.* unfurnished.
desandar (des·an'dar) *v.t.* [*infl.:* **andar**] to retrace one's steps. —**desandadura,** *n.f.* turning back.
desangrar (de·san'grar) *v.t.* **1,** to bleed copiously. **2,** to drain. **3,** to impoverish. —**desangrarse,** *v.r.* to lose blood.
desanimar (des·a·ni'mar) *v.t.* to

dishearten; discourage. —**desánimo** (-'a·ni·mo) *n.m.* discouragement.
desanudar (des·a·nu'ðar) *also,* **desañudar** (-ɲu'ðar) *v.t.* to untie; disentangle.
desaparecer (des·a·pa·re'θer; -'ser) *v.i.* [*infl.:* **aparecer**] to disappear. —**desaparición,** *n.f.* disappearance.
desaparejar (des·a·pa·re'xar) *v.t.* to unhitch; unrig.
desapasionarse (des·a·pa·sjo·'nar·se) *v.r.* to be or become indifferent. —**desapasionado,** *adj.* dispassionate; disinterested. —**desapasionamiento,** *n.m.* dispassion; disinterest.
desapegarse (des·a·pe'ɣar·se) *v.r.* [*infl.:* **pegar**] to detach *or* dissociate oneself. —**desapego** (-'pe·ɣo) *n.m.* disinterest.
desapercibido (des·a·per·θi'βi·ðo; -si'βi·ðo) *adj.* **1,** unprepared; unprovided. **2,** unnoticed. —**desapercibimiento,** *n.m.* unpreparedness.
desaplicado (des·a·pli'ka·ðo) *adj.* indolent; negligent. —**desaplicación,** *n.f.* indolence; negligence.
desapoderar (des·a·po·ðe'rar) *v.t.* **1,** to dispossess. **2,** *law* to invalidate.
desapreciar (des·a·pre'θjar; -'sjar) *v.t.* to disparage; underestimate. —**desaprecio** (-'pre·θjo; -sjo) *n.m.* underestimation; disparagement.
desaprender (des·a·pren'der) *v.t.* to unlearn.
desaprobar (des·a·pro'βar) *v.t.* [*infl.:* **aprobar**] to disapprove; censure; reprove. —**desaprobación,** *n.f.* disapproval; censure; reproof.
desaprovechado (des·a·pro·βe·'tʃa·ðo) *adj.* **1,** unused; unexploited. **2,** unproductive. **3,** indolent.
desaprovechar (des·a·pro·βe·'tʃar) *v.t.* to waste; misspend; misuse.
desapuntalar (des·a·pun·ta'lar) *v.t.* to remove the props or supports of.
desarmar (des·ar'mar) *v.t.* **1,** to disarm. **2,** to dismount; dismantle. **3,** *fig.* to calm; pacify. —**desarmado,** *adj.* unarmed; defenseless. —**desarme** (-'ar·me) *n.m.* disarmament.
desarraigar (des·a·rrai'ɣar) *v.t.* [*infl.:* **arraigar**] **1,** to uproot; eradicate. **2,** to expel; banish.
desarraigo (des·a'rrai·ɣo) *n.m.* **1,** eradication. **2,** expulsion; banishment.
desarrapado *adj.* = **desharrapado.**
desarreglar (des·a·rre'ɣlar) *v.t.* to disarrange; discompose; upset. —**desarreglado,** *adj.* immoderate; extravagant. —**desarreglo** (-'rre·ɣlo) *n.m.* disorder; confusion.
desarrollar (des·a·rro'ʎar; -'jar) *v.t.* **1,** to develop; expand; improve. **2,** to explain; propound. —**desarrollarse,** *v.r.* **1,** to grow; become. **2,** to happen; befall. —**desarrollo** (-'rro·ʎo; -jo) *n.m.* development; course.
desarropar (des·a·rro'par) *v.t.* to uncover; remove a garment from.
desarrugar (des·a·rru'ɣar) *v.t.* [*infl.:* **arrugar**] to unwrinkle.
desarticular (des·ar·ti·ku'lar) *v.t.* **1,** to disjoint; dislocate. **2,** to break up; break apart.
desaseado (des·a·se'a·ðo) *adj.* unclean; slovenly. —**desaseo** (-'se·o) *n.m.* uncleanliness; slovenliness.
desasir (des·a'sir) *v.t.* [*infl.:* **asir**] to loosen. —**desasirse,** *v.r.* **1,** to disengage oneself. **2,** to rid oneself (of).
desasosegar (des·a·so·se'ɣar) *v.t.* [*infl.:* **sosegar**] to disturb; make uneasy. —**desasosiego** (-'sje·ɣo) *n.m.* uneasiness.
desastrado (des·as'tra·ðo) *adj.* **1,** unfortunate; unlucky. **2,** shabby; seedy.
desastre (de'sas·tre) *n.m.* disaster. —**desastroso,** *adj.* disastrous.
desatar (des·a'tar) *v.t.* to untie; loose. —**desatarse,** *v.r.* **1,** to talk volubly; burst out talking. **2,** to lose all restraint. **3,** to loosen up. **4,** to break loose; break out.
desatascar (des·a·tas'kar) *v.t.* [*infl.:* **atascar**] **1,** to unclog. **2,** to extricate.
desataviar (des·a·ta'βjar) *v.t.* [*infl.:* **enviar**] **1,** to strip of ornaments. **2,** to disarray. —**desatavío** (-'βi·o) *n.m.* slovenliness; disarray.
desatención (des·a·ten'θjon; -'sjon) *n.f.* **1,** inattention. **2,** discourtesy.
desatender (des·a·ten'der) *v.t.* [*infl.:* **atender**] to neglect; disregard.
desatento (des·a'ten·to) *adj.* **1,** inattentive. **2,** discourteous.
desatinar (des·a·ti'nar) *v.i.* **1,** to act or talk foolishly. **2,** to blunder. —*v.t.* to confuse; bewilder. —**desatinarse,** *v.r.* to rave; lose one's bearings. —**desatinado,** *adj.* foolish; ex-

travagant. —**desatino** (-'ti·no) *n.m.* blunder; error; extravagance.
lesatracar (des·a·tra'kar) *v.t.* [*infl.:* **atracar**] *naut.* to cast off.
lesatrancar (des·a·tran'kar) *v.t.* [*infl.:* **trancar**] **1,** to unbar; unbolt. **2,** to unclog.
lesautorizar (des·au·to·ri'θar; -'sar) *v.t.* [*infl.:* **autorizar**] **1,** to deprive of authority. **2,** to disallow; deny approval of.
lesavenencia (des·a·βe'nen·θja; -sja) *n.f.* disagreement; discord.
lesavenirse (des·a·βe'nir·se) *v.r.* [*infl.:* **venir**] to disagree; quarrel.
lesayunar (des·a·ju'nar) *v.i.* [*also, refl.* **desayunarse**] to eat breakfast. —*v.t.* to have (something) for breakfast; breakfast on (something).
lesayuno (des·a'ju·no) *n.m.* breakfast.
desazón (de·sa'θon; -'son) *n.m.* **1,** uneasiness. **2,** displeasure. **3,** insipidity.
lesazonar (de·sa·θo'nar; -so'nar) *v.t.* **1,** to render insipid. **2,** to annoy; to disgust. —**desazonarse,** *v.r.* **1,** to become restless. **2,** to become indisposed.
lesbancar (des·βan'kar) *v.t.* [*pres. subjve.* **desbanque** (-'βan·ke); *pret.* **desbanqué** (-'ke)] **1,** *in gambling* to break the bank. **2,** to supplant (in affection).
lesbandarse (des·βan'dar·se) *v.r.* **1,** to disband; disperse. **2,** *mil.* to desert. —**desbandada,** *n.f.* disbandment. —**a la desbandada,** in disorder; helter-skelter.
lesbarajustar (des·βa·ra·xus·'tar) *v.t.* to disarrange. —**desbarajuste** (-'xus·te) *n.m.* disorder; confusion.
lesbaratar (des·ba·ra'tar) *v.t.* **1,** to destroy; ruin. **2,** to upset; disturb. **3,** to disperse. —**desbaratamiento,** *n.m.* breakage; destruction. *Also,* **desbarate** (-'ra·te).
lesbastar (des·βas'tar) *v.t.* **1,** to plane; smooth. **2,** to give social polish.
lesbocado (des·βo'ka·ðo) *adj.* **1,** runaway, as a horse. **2,** unrestrained; uninhibited. **3,** foul-mouthed.
lesbocarse (des·βo'kar·se) *v.r.* [*pres.subjve.* **desboque** (-'βo·ke); *pret.* **desboqué** (-'ke)] **1,** (of horses) to run away. **2,** to burst forth (in feeling, speech, etc.).
lesbordar (des·βor'ðar) *v.i.* to overflow. —**desbordarse,** *v.r.* **1,** to overflow. **2,** to lose one's restraint; be carried away. —**desbordamiento,** *n.m.* overflow.
desbrozar (des·βro'θar; -'sar) *v.t.* [*pres.subjve.* **desbroce** (-'bro·θe; -se); *pret.* **desbrocé** (-'θe; -'se)] to clear of brush. —**desbroce** (-'bro·θe; -se) *n.m.* clearing of brush. *Also,* **desbrozo** (-θo; -so).
descabal (des·ka'βal) *adj.* imperfect; incomplete. —**descabalar,** *v.t.* to break up; impair the unity or completeness of.
descabellar (des·ka·βe'ʎar; -'jar) *v.t.* to kill (an animal). —**descabellado,** *adj.* absurd; harebrained.
descabezar (des·ka·βe'θar; -'sar) *v.t.* [*pres.subjve.* **descabece** (-'βe·θe; -se); *pret.* **descabecé** (-'θe; -'se)] to behead; lop off the head or top of. —**descabezarse,** *v.r.* to rack one's brain. —**descabezado,** *adj.* reckless; harebrained.
descaecer (des·ka·e'θer; -'ser) *v.i.* [*infl.:* **acaecer**] to decline; decay; decrease.
descaecimiento (des·ka·e·θi·'mjen·to; -si'mjen·to) *n.m.,* **1,** weakness; debility. **2,** despondency; dejection.
descalabrar (des·ka·la'βrar) *v.t.* **1,** to wound on the head. **2,** *fig.* to hurt; offend. —**descalabrarse,** *v.r.* to suffer a head wound. —**descalabradura,** *n.f.* head wound or scar. —**descalabro** (-'la·βro) *n.m.* misfortune; loss.
descalificar (des·ka·li·fi'kar) *v.t.* [*infl.:* **calificar**] to disqualify. —**descalificación,** *n.f.* disqualification.
descalzar (des·kal'θar; -'sar) *v.t.* [*infl.:* **calzar**] **1,** to bare the feet of. **2,** *mech.* to remove a brake or impediment from. —**descalzarse,** *v.r.* to remove one's shoes. —**descalzarse los guantes,** to remove one's gloves.
descalzo (des'kal·θo; -so) *adj.* barefooted.
descaminar (des·ka·mi'nar) *v.t.* to mislead; lead astray.
descamisado (des·ka·mi'sa·ðo) *adj.* **1,** shirtless. **2,** destitute. —*n.m., colloq.* ragamuffin.
descansar (des·kan'sar) *v.i.* to rest; relax. —*v.t.* **1,** to rest; lean. **2,** to relieve. —**descansadero,** *n.m.* resting place.

descanso (des'kan·so) *n.m.* **1,** rest; relief. **2,** stair landing.
descantear (des·kan·te'ar) *v.t.* to smooth the edges of.
descantillar (des·kan·ti'ʎar; -'jar) *v.t.* to chip off. *Also,* **descantonar** (-to'nar).
descararse (des·ka'rar·se) *v.r.* to behave impudently. —**descarado,** *adj.* impudent; brazen; shameless. —**descaro** (-'ka·ro) *n.m.* effrontery; impudence.
descarga (des'kar·ɣa) *n.f.* discharge; unloading.
descargador (des·kar·ɣa'ðor) *n.m.* unloader; longshoreman.
descargar (des·kar'ɣar) *v.t.* [*infl.:* **cargar**] **1,** to discharge; unload. **2,** to empty. **3,** to fire (a weapon). **4,** to acquit; exonerate. **5,** *electricity* to discharge. **6,** *comm.* to discharge (a debt). **7,** to deal; strike (a blow). **8,** *fig.* to ease; unburden. —*v.i.* to burst, as clouds.
descargo (des'kar·ɣo) *n.m.* **1,** [*also,* **descargue** (-ɣe)] unloading; discharge. **2,** exoneration; acquittal. **3,** *comm.* discharge (*of a debt*).
descarnar (des·kar'nar) *v.t.* **1,** to remove the flesh from. **2,** to corrode; eat away. —**descarnarse,** *v.r.* to lose flesh; become emaciated. —**descarnado,** *adj.* emaciated; fleshless.
descaro (des'ka·ro) *n.m.* effrontery; impudence.
descarriar (des·ka'rrjar) *v.t.* to mislead; lead astray. —**descarriarse,** *v.r.* to go astray.
descarrilar (des·ka·rri'lar) *v.i.* to derail; run off the rails; be derailed. —**descarrilamiento,** *n.m.* derailment.
descarrío (des·ka'rri·o) *n.m.* straying; a going astray; waywardness.
descartar (des·kar'tar) *v.t.* to discard; put aside; dismiss.
descarte (des'kar·te) *n.m.* **1,** discarding; discard. **2,** subterfuge; evasion.
descasar (des·ka'sar) *v.t.* **1,** to separate (a married couple). **2,** to annul the marriage of. **3,** to disturb or change the arrangement of. —**descasamiento,** *n.m.* divorce; annulment.
descascarar (des·kas·ka'rar) *v.t.* to shell; peel.
descastar (des·kas'tar) *v.t.* to exterminate.
descender (des·θen'der; de·sen'der) *v.i.* [*pres.ind.* **desciende** (-'θjen·do; -'sjen·do); *pres.subjve.* **descienda** (-da)] **1,** to descend; go down. **2,** to come (from); be derived (from). —*v.t.* to let down; lower. —**descendencia,** *n.f.* descent; lineage. —**descendiente,** *adj.* [*also* **descendente**] descending. —*n.m.* descendant. —**descenso** (des'θen·so; de'sen-) *n.m.* descent; lowering; degradation.
descentralizar (des·θen·tra·li'θar; de·sen·tra·li'sar) *v.t.* [*infl.* **centralizar**] to decentralize. —**descentralización** *n.f.* decentralization.
descentrar (des·θen'trar; de·sen-) *v.t.* to make eccentric; to put off center.
desceñir (des·θe'ɲir; de·se-) *v.t.* [*infl.:* **ceñir**] to ungird; take off (a belt, girdle, etc.).
descifrar (des·θi'frar; de·si'frar) *v.t.* **1,** to decipher; decode. **2,** to interpret. **3,** *fig.* to unravel. —**descifrable,** *adj.* decipherable.
descifre (des'θi·fre; de'si·fre) *n.m.* decoding; deciphering; decipherment.
descoagular (des·ko·a·ɣu'lar) *v.t.* to dissolve (a clot).
descobijar (des·ko·βi'xar) *v.t.* to uncover; unwrap.
descocarse (des·ko'kar·se) *v.r.* *colloq.* [*pres.subjve.* **descoque;** *pret.* **descoqué**] to be impudent. —**descoco** (-'ko·ko) *n.m.* impudence; impertinence.
descocer (des·ko'θer; -'ser) *v.t.* [*infl.:* **cocer**] to digest.
descogollar (des·ko·ɣo'ʎar; -'jar) *v.t.* **1,** to prune (a tree) of shoots. **2,** to remove the heart (of vegetables).
descolgar (des·kol'ɣar) *v.t.* [*infl.* **colgar**] **1,** to take down; unhook. **2,** to remove the draperies, hangings, etc. from. —**descolgarse,** *v.r.* **1,** to descend gently; slip down. **2,** to appear unexpectedly. —**descolgar con,** to come out with; blurt out.
descolorar (des·ko·lo'rar) *also* **descolorir** (-'rir) *v.t.* to discolor. —**descoloramiento, descolorimiento,** *n.m.* discoloration.
descollar (des·ko'ʎar; -'jar) *v.i.* [*infl.:* **acollar**] to stand out; excel.
descombrar (des·kom'brar) *v.t.* to disencumber. —**descombro** (-'kom·bro) *n.m.* disencumbrance.

lescomedido (des·ko·me'ði·ðo) *adj.* 1, immoderate; excessive. 2, rude; insolent. —**descomedimiento,** *n.m.* rudeness.

lescomodidad (des·ko·mo·ði'ðað) *n.f.* = **incomodidad.**

lescompaginar (des·kom·pa·xi'nar) *v.t.* 1, to disorganize; mix up. 2, to confuse; fluster.

lescompasado (des·kom·pa'sa·ðo) *adj.* 1, [*also, Amer.,* **desacompasado**] irregular; offbeat. 2, extravagant; immoderate.

lescompletar (des·kom·ple'tar) *v.t.* to make incomplete; to break up (a set).

lescomponer (des·kom·po'ner) *v.t.* [*infl.:* **poner**] 1, to upset; disturb. 2, to put out of order. 3, to decompose. 4, *optics* to disperse.

lescomposición (des·kom·po·si·'θjon; -'sjon) *n.f.* 1, discomposure. 2, disarrangement. 3, decomposition.

lescompostura (des·kom·pos·'tu·ra) *n.f.* 1, disorder; disarrangement. 2, impudence; disrespect. 3, untidiness; uncleanliness.

lescompuesto (des·kom'pwes·to) *adj.* 1, out of order. 2, insolent; brazen; indecent. —*v., p.p. of* **descomponer.**

lescomulgado (des·ko·mul'ɣa·ðo) *adj.* 1, excommunicated. 2, wicked; perverse.

lescomulgar (des·ko·mul'ɣar) *v.t.* [*infl.:* **comulgar**] to excommunicate.

lescomunal (des·ko·mu'nal) *adj.* 1, enormous. 2, monstrous.

lesconcertar (des·kon·θer'tar; -ser'tar) *v.t.* [*infl.:* **concertar**] to disconcert; disturb; confound. —**desconcierto** (-'θjer·to; -'sjer·to) *n.m.* disagreement; disorder.

lesconchar (des·kon'tʃar) *v.t.* to scrape off; peel off; chip off. —**desconchadura,** *n.f.* peeling; scaling.

lesconectar (des·ko·nek'tar) *v.t.* to disconnect.

lesconfiar (des·kon'fjar) *v.i.* to distrust. —**desconfiado,** *adj.* distrustful. —**desconfianza,** *n.f.* distrust.

lesconformar (des·kon·for'mar) *v.i.* to disagree; dissent. —**disconforme** (-'for·me) *adj.* disagreeing; discordant. —**desconformidad,** *n.f.* disagreement; nonconformity.

lescongelar (des·kon·xe'lar) *v.t.* to melt; thaw; defrost. —**descongelador,** *n.m.* defroster.

descongestionar (des·kon·xes·tjo'nar) *v.t.* to relieve congestion in.

descongojar (des·kon·go'xar) *v.t.* to comfort; solace.

desconocer (des·ko·no'θer; -'ser) *v.t.* [*infl.:* **conocer**] 1, to fail to recognize. 2, to disown; disavow. 3, to be ignorant of. 4, to pretend not to know. 5, to ignore; to overlook.

desconocido (des·ko·no'θi·ðo; -'si·ðo) *adj.* 1, unknown. 2, unrecognizable. —*n.m.* stranger.

desconocimiento (des·ko·no·θi'mjen·to; -si'mjen·to) *n.m.* 1, disregard. 2, ignorance. 3, oversight; failure to notice.

desconsiderado (des·kon·si·ðe·'ra·ðo) *adj.* 1, inconsiderate. 2, thoughtless; rash; ill-considered.

desconsolar (des·kon·so'lar) *v.t.* [*infl.:* **consolar**] to grieve; sadden; afflict. —**desconsolarse,** *v.r.* to lose heart. —**desconsolado,** *adj.* disconsolate; sad. —**desconsuelo** (-'swe·lo) *n.m.* sadness; affliction; distress.

descontar (des·kon'tar) *v.t.* [*infl.:* **contar**] to discount; deduct.

descontentadizo (des·kon·ten·ta'ði·θo; -so) *adj.* 1, hard to please. 2, easily displeased.

descontentar (des·kon·ten'tar) *v.t.* to displease; dissatisfy. —**descontento** (-'ten·to) *adj.* discontented; displeased. —*n.m.* discontent; dissatisfaction.

descontinuar (des·kon·ti'nwar) *v.t.* [*infl.:* **continuar**] to discontinue. —**descontinuación,** *n.f.* discontinuation; discontinuance. —**descontinuo** (-'ti·nwo) *adj.* discontinuous.

descontrol (des·kon'trol) *n.m.* decontrol. —**descontrolar,** *v.t.* to decontrol.

desconveniencia (des·kon·βe·'njen·θja; -sja) *n.f.* 1, inconvenience. 2, disadvantage.

desconveniente (des·kon·βe·'njen·te) *adj.* 1, inconvenient. 2, unsuitable.

desconvenir (des·kon·βe'nir) *v.i.* [*infl.:* **venir**] 1, to disagree. 2, to be mismatched or unsuited.

descoque (des'ko·ke) *v., pres. subjve. of* **descocar.**

descoqué (des·ko'ke) *v., pret. of* **descocar.**

descorazonar (des·ko·ra·θo'nar; -so'nar) *v.t.* **1,** to tear out the heart of. **2,** to dishearten; discourage. —**descorazonamiento,** *n.f.* dejection; discouragement.
descorchar (des·kor'tʃar) *v.t.* **1,** to uncork. **2,** to strip of bark. **3,** to break into.
descortés (des·kor'tes) *adj.* discourteous; ill-bred. —**descortesía,** *n.f.* discourtesy.
descortezar (des·kor·te'θar; -'sar) *v.t.* [*pres.subjve.* **descortece** (-'te·θe; -se); *pret.* **descortecé** (-'θe; -'se)] **1,** to remove the bark, crust, shell, etc. of. **2,** *colloq.* to refine; give social polish to.
descoser (des·ko'ser) *v.t.* to rip out (sewing); unstitch. —**descoserse,** *v.r.* to blab; let out a secret.
descosido (des·ko'si·ðo) *n.m.* rip; tear. —*adj.* **1,** indiscreet. **2,** wild; disorderly.
descostrar (des·kos'trar) *v.t.* to remove the crust or scale from.
descotar (des·ko'tar) *v.t.* to cut (a dress) low in the neck. —**descotado,** *adj.* décolleté. —**descote** (-'ko·te) *n.m.* décolletage.
descoyuntamiento (des·ko·jun·ta'mjen·to) *n.m.* **1,** dislocation. **2,** fatigue.
descoyuntar (des·ko·jun'tar) *v.t.* **1,** to dislocate; disjoint. **2,** *fig.* to annoy.
descrédito (des'kre·ði·to) *n.m.* discredit.
descreer (des·kre'er) *v.t.* [*infl.:* **creer**] **1,** to disbelieve. **2,** to discredit; deny credit to.
descreído (des·kre'i·ðo) *adj.* unbelieving. —*n.m.* unbeliever. —**descreimiento,** *n.m.* unbelief.
describir (des·kri'βir) *v.t.* [*infl.:* **escribir;** *p.p.* **descrito** (-'kri·to), **descripto** (-'krip·to)] to describe; delineate. —**descripción,** *n.f.* description; design; delineation. —**descriptivo,** *adj.* descriptive.
descuajar (des·kwa'xar) *v.t.* **1,** to liquefy; dissolve. **2,** to root out. **3,** *fig.* to dishearten.
descuajaringarse (des·kwa·xa·rin'gar·se) *v.r., colloq.* [*infl.:* **llegar**] to collapse, as with fatigue; fall apart.
descuartizar (des·kwar·ti'θar; -'sar) *v.t.* [*pres.subjve.* **descuartice** (-'ti·θe; -se); *pret.* **descuarticé** (-'θe; -'se)] **1,** to carve. **2,** to quarter. **3,** to tear or cut into pieces.
descubrir (des·ku'βrir) *v.t.* [*infl.:* **cubrir**] to discover; reveal; uncover. —**descubierto,** *adj.* discovered; uncovered; exposed. —**descubridor,** *n.m.* discoverer; *mil.* scout. —**descubrimiento,** *n.m.* discovery.
descuelle (des'kwe·ʎe; -je) *v., pres.subjve. of* **descollar.**
descuello (des'kwe·ʎo; -jo) *v., pres.ind. of* **descollar.**
descuento (des'kwen·to) *n.m.* discount; rebate. —*v., pres.ind. of* **descontar.**
descuidar (des·kui'ðar) *v.t.* **1,** to neglect; overlook. **2,** to distract. —*v.i.* to lack diligence; be careless. —**descuidarse,** *v.r.* **1,** to be careless. **2,** to be unwary. —**descuidado,** *adj.* negligent; careless; slovenly. —**descuido** (-'kwi·ðo) *n.m.* carelessness; neglect.
descuidero (des·kwi'ðe·ro) *n.m.* pickpocket.
desde ('des·ðe) *prep.* from; since; after. —**desde luego, 1,** of course. **2,** at once. —**desde que,** ever since; since. —**desde ya,** *colloq.* right now; forthwith.
desdecir (des·ðe'θir; -'sir) *v.i.* [*infl.:* **decir**] *fol. by* **de 1,** to degenerate; decline (*from an earlier condition*). **2,** to detract (from). **3,** to be out of harmony (with). —**desdecirse,** *v.r.* to retract.
desdén (des'ðen) *n.m.* disdain; scorn; contempt. —**al desdén,** contemptuously; with affected neglect.
desdentado (des·ðen'ta·ðo) *adj.* toothless.
desdeñar (des·ðe'ɲar) *v.t.* to disdain; scorn. —**desdeñable,** *adj.* contemptible.
desdeñoso (des·ðe'ɲo·so) *adj.* disdainful.
desdicha (des'ði·tʃa) *n.f.* misfortune; misery. —**desdichado,** *adj.* unfortunate; wretched. —*n.m.* wretch.
desdoblar (des·ðo'βlar) *v.t.* to spread open; unfold.
desdorar (des·ðo'rar) *v.t.* **1,** to tarnish. **2,** to dishonor; sully.
desdoro (des'ðo·ro) *n.m.* **1,** tarnish; blemish. **2,** dishonor.
desear (de·se'ar) *v.t.* to desire; want; wish; crave. —**deseable,** *adj.* desirable.
desecar (de·se'kar) *v.t.* [*infl.:* **secar**] **1,** to desiccate; dry. **2,** to drain

—**desecación,** *n.f.* desiccation. —**desecante,** *adj.* & *n.m.* desiccant.
desechar (des·e'tʃar) *v.t.* to reject; exclude; cast aside.
desecho (des'e·tʃo) *n.m.* **1,** remainder; residue. **2,** rubbish; debris. **3,** reject. **4,** *fig.* contempt.
desedificar (des·e·ði·fi'kar) *v.t.* [*infl.:* **edificar**] to set a bad example for; demoralize.
desellar (de·se'ʎar; -'jar) *v.t.* to unseal.
desembalar (des·em·ba'lar) *v.t.* to unpack. —**desembalaje,** *n.m.* unpacking.
desembarazar (des·em·ba·ra'θar; -'sar) *v.t.* [*infl.:* **embarazar**] to disembarrass; disencumber; clear. —**desembarazo** (-'ra·θo; -so) *n.m.* ease; freedom.
desembarcadero (des·em·bar·ka'ðe·ro) *n.m.* wharf; dock; pier.
desembarcar (des·em·bar'kar) *v.t.* [*infl.:* **embarcar**] to unload. —*v.i.* to disembark; debark.
desembarco (des·em'bar·ko) *n.m.* unloading; debarkation (*of passengers*).
desembargar (des·em·bar'ɣar) *v.t.* [*infl.:* **embargar**] **1,** to lift the embargo on. **2,** to free from a hindrance or encumbrance. —**desembargo** (-'bar·ɣo) *n.m.* lifting of an embargo or encumbrance.
desembarque (des·em'bar·ke) *n.m.* unloading; debarkation (*of cargo*).
desembarrancar (des·em·ba·rran'kar) *v.t. & i.* [*infl.:* **embarrancar**] to float, as a grounded ship.
desembocar (des·em·bo'kar) *v.i.* [*infl.:* **embocar**] **1,** to flow out; empty, as a stream. **2,** to end, as a street. —**desembocadero** (-ka·'ðe·ro) *n.m., also,* **desembocadura** (-ka'ðu·ra) *n.f.* mouth (*of a river or canal*); outlet; exit.
desembolsar (des·em·bol'sar) *v.t.* to disburse; pay out. —**desembolso** (-'bol·so) *n.m.* disbursement; expenditure.
desembotar (des·em·bo'tar) *v.t.* to sharpen (wits).
desembragar (des·em·bra'ɣar) *v.t.* [*infl.:* **embragar**] *mech.* to disengage (gears); disconnect (a shaft).
desembriagar (des·em·brja'ɣar) *v.t.* [*infl.:* **embriagar**] to sober up.
desemejar (de·se·me'xar) *v.i.* to be dissimilar. —*v.t.* to deform; disguise. —**desemejante,** *adj.* dissimilar. —**desemejanza,** *n.f.* dissimilarity.
desempacar (des·em·pa'kar) *v.t.* [*infl.:* **empacar**] to unpack. —**desempacarse,** *v.r.* to become calm; calm down.
desempachar (des·em·pa'tʃar) *v.t.* to relieve of indigestion (by disgorging). —**desempacharse,** *v.r.* to cast off one's timidity or inhibition.
desempacho (des·em'pa·tʃo) *n.m.* **1,** ease; nonchalance. **2,** boldness.
desempatar (des·em·pa'tar) *v.t.* **1,** to make unequal. **2,** to break a tie in (a score, a vote, etc.).
desempeñar (des·em·pe'ɲar) *v.t.* **1,** to recover; redeem. **2,** to free from obligation. **3,** to perform (a duty or job); to act (a role).
desempeño (des·em'pe·ɲo) *n.m.* **1,** recovery; redemption. **2,** discharge; freedom from obligation. **3,** fulfillment; performance.
desempleado (des·em·ple'a·ðo) *adj.* unemployed.
desempleo (des·em'ple·o) *n.m.* unemployment.
desempolvar (des·em·pol'βar) *also,* **desempolvorar** (-βo'rar) *v.t.* **1,** to dust; remove the dust from. **2,** *fig.* to dust off; resurrect.
desencadenar (des·en·ka·ðe'nar) *v.t.* **1,** to unchain; free. **2,** *fig.* to unleash; let forth. —**desencadenarse,** *v.r.* **1,** to break loose. **2,** to lose one's self-control.
desencajar (des·en·ka'xar) *v.t.* to disjoint; disconnect. —**desencajarse,** *v.r.* **1,** to get out of gear. **2,** to be contorted (*with emotion or pain, as the face*).
desencallar (des·en·ka'ʎar; -'jar) *v.t.* to refloat (a grounded ship).
desencantar (des·en·kan'tar) *v.t.* to disenchant; disillusion. —**desencanto** (-'kan·to) *also,* **desencantamiento,** *n.m.* disenchantment.
desencarcelar (des·en·kar·θe·'lar; -se'lar) *v.t.* to set free; release from prison.
desencarnar (des·en·kar'nar) *v.t.* to disembody. —**desencarnarse,** *v.r.* to die.
desencoger (des·en·ko'xer) *v.t.* [*infl.:* **coger**] to unfold; straighten out. —**desencogerse,** *v.r.* to grow bold.
desenconar (des·en·ko'nar) *v.t.* **1,** to relieve (an inflammation or irri-

tation). 2, to appease (anger, passion, etc.). —**desencono** (-'ko·no) *n.m.* mitigation; appeasement.

desencordar (des·en·kor'ðar) *v.t.* [*infl.:* **acordar**] to unstring, esp. a musical instrument.

desencordelar (des·en·kor·ðe·'lar) *v.t.* to unstring; untie.

desenchufar (des·en·tʃu'far) *v.t.* to disconnect.

desenfadar (des·en·fa'ðar) *v.t.* to appease; calm. —**desenfadarse,** *v.r.* to calm down. —**desenfadaderas** (-ða'ðe·ras) *n.f.pl., colloq.* means of escaping difficulties; resourcefulness (*sing.*).

desenfado (des·en'fa·ðo) *n.m.* 1, ease; calmness. 2, presumptuousness; boldness.

desenfrenar (des·en·fre'nar) *v.t.* to unbridle. —**desenfrenarse,** *v.r.* to give vent to one's feelings. —**desenfrenado,** *adj.* unbridled; reckless; licentious. —**desenfreno** (-'fre·no) *n.m.* unruliness; wantonness; licentiousness.

desenganchar (des·en·gan'tʃar) *v.t.* 1, to unhook; unfasten. 2, to unhitch; unharness. 3, *R.R.* to uncouple.

desengañar (des·en·ga'ɲar) *v.t.* 1, to undeceive. 2, to disillusion; disappoint. —**desengaño** (-'ga·ɲo) *n.m.* disillusionment; disappointment.

desengranar (des·en·gra'nar) *v.t.* to put out of gear; disengage. —**desengrane** (-'gra·ne) *n.m.* disengagement (*of gears*).

desenlazar (des·en·la'θar; -'sar) *v.t.* [*infl.:* **enlazar**] 1, to unlace; untie. 2, to unravel, as the plot of a play, novel, etc. —**desenlace** (-'la·θe; -se) *n.m.* outcome; dénouement.

desenmarañar (des·en·ma·ra'ɲar) *v.t.* to disentangle; unravel.

desenmascarar (des·en·mas·ka·'rar) *v.t.* to unmask; expose.

desenredar (des·en·re'ðar) *v.t.* 1, to disentangle; unravel. 2, to set in order. 3, to clear up; resolve. —**desenredarse,** *v.r.* to extricate oneself; get clear.

desenredo (des·en're·ðo) *n.m.* 1, disentanglement. 2, dénouement.

desenrollar (des·en·ro'ʎar; -'jar) *v.t.* to unroll; unwind.

desenroscar (des·en·ros'kar) *v.t.* [*infl.:* **enroscar**] to untwist; unscrew.

desensartar (des·en·sar'tar) *v.t.* to unstring; unthread.

desensillar (des·en·si'ʎar; -'jar) *v.t.* to unsaddle.

desentenderse (des·en·ten'der·se) *v.r.* [*infl.:* **entender**] *fol. by* **de,** 1, to pretend not to understand. 2, to ignore. 3, to wash one's hands of. —**desentendido,** *adj.* unmindful; heedless.

desenterrar (des·en·te'rrar) *v.t.* [*infl.:* **enterrar**] 1, to disinter; exhume. 2, to dig up; unearth. 3, *fig.* to recall to memory. —**desenterramiento,** *n.m.* disinterment.

desentonar (des·en·to'nar) *v.t.* to belittle; humble. —*v.i.* 1, to be incongruous. 2, *music* to be out of tune. —**desentonarse,** *v.r.* to speak or behave with impropriety.

desentono (de·sen'to·no) *n.m.* 1, discord; harsh tone. 2, impropriety of speech or behavior.

desentrañar (des·en·tra'ɲar) *v.t.* 1, to eviscerate. 2, *fig.* to delve into. —**desentrañarse,** *v.r.* 1, to give one's all, esp. to a loved one. 2, *fol. by* **de** to give up; forsake.

desenvainar (des·en·βai'nar) *v.t.* to draw; draw out; unsheathe.

desenvoltura (de·sen·βol'tu·ra) *n.f.* 1, ease; poise. 2, boldness; impudence.

desenvolver (des·en·βol'βer) *v.t.* [*infl.:* **envolver**] 1, to unwrap; unfold. 2, *fig.* to develop; evolve.

desenvuelto (de·sen'βwel·to) *adj.* 1, free; easy. 2, forward; impudent.

deseo (de'se·o) *n.m.* desire; wish; longing. —**deseoso,** *adj.* desirous.

desequilibrar (des·e·ki·li'βrar) *v.t.* to unbalance. —**desequilibrado,** *adj.* unbalanced; foolish. —*n.m.* mental imbalance.

desequilibrio (des·e·ki'li·βrjo) *n.m.* imbalance.

deserción (de·ser'θjon; -'sjon) *n.f.* desertion.

desertar (de·ser'tar) *v.t.* to desert; abandon. —**desertor,** *n.m.* deserter.

deservir (de·ser'βir) *v.t.* [*infl.:* **servir**] to do a disservice to; fail. —**deservicio** (-'βi·θjo; -sjo) *n.m.* disservice.

deseslabonar (des·es·la·βo'nar) *v.t.* to unlink. —**deseslabonarse,** *v.r.* to withdraw; stand aloof.

desesperación (des·es·pe·ra·'θjon; -'sjon) *n.f.* despair; desperation; hopelessness.

desesperado (des·es·pe'ra·ðo) *adj.* **1,** desperate; hopeless. **2,** impatient.
desesperanza (des·es·pe'ran·θa; -sa) *n.f.* despair. —**desesperanzado,** *adj.* despairing. —**desesperanzar,** *v.t.* [*infl.:* **lanzar**] to discourage; deprive of hope.
desesperar (des·es·pe'rar) *v.i.* to despair. —*v.t.* to exasperate; annoy. —**desesperarse,** *v.r.* to be or become impatient; to be annoyed.
desestimación (des·es·ti·ma·'θjon; -'sjon) *n.f.* **1,** low regard; contempt. **2,** rejection; denial, esp. of a plea or application. *Also,* **desestima** (-'ti·ma).
desestimar (des·es·ti'mar) *v.t.* **1,** to hold in low esteem; undervalue. **2,** to reject; deny; refuse, esp. a plea or application.
desfachatez (des·fa·tʃa'teθ; -'tes) *n.f.* impudence; shamelessness. —**desfachatado** (-'ta·ðo) *adj.* impudent; shameless.
desfalcar (des·fal'kar) *v.t.* [*pres. subjve.* **desfalque** (-'fal·ke); *pret.* **desfalqué** (-'ke)] to embezzle. —**desfalco** (-'fal·ko) *n.m.* embezzlement; defalcation. —**desfalcador,** *n.m.* embezzler.
desfallecer (des·fa·ʎe'θer; -je·'ser) *v.i.* [*infl.:* **fallecer**] to faint; languish. —*v.t.* to debilitate. —**desfallecimiento,** *n.m.* faintness; weakness; languor.
desfavorable (des·fa·βo'ra·βle) *adj.* unfavorable.
desfavorecer (des·fa·βo·re'θer; -'ser) *v.t.* [*infl.:* **favorecer**] to disfavor.
desfigurar (des·fi·ɣu'rar) *v.t.* **1,** to disfigure. **2,** to misrepresent; distort. —**desfiguración,** *n.f.* disfigurement. *Also,* **desfiguramiento,** *n.m.*
desfiladero (des·fi·la'ðe·ro) *n.m.* defile.
desfilar (des·fi'lar) *v.i.* **1,** to file; march in file. **2,** to parade. —**desfile** (-'fi·le) *n.m.* parade.
desflorar (des·flo'rar) *v.t.* to deflower. —**desfloración,** *n.f.* defloration. *Also,* **desfloramiento,** *n.m.*
desfogar (des·fo'ɣar) *v.t.* [*pres. subjve.* **desfogue** (-'fo·ɣe); *pret.* **desfogué** (-'ɣe)] **1,** to give vent to. **2,** to slake (lime). —**desfogarse,** *v.r.* to vent one's feelings.
desfondar (des·fon'dar) *v.t.* **1,** to break or remove the bottom of. **2,** *naut.* to pierce or sheer off the hull of (a ship).
desgaire (des'ɣai·re) *n.m.* graceless manner; untidiness.
desgajar (des·ɣa'xar) *v.t.* to tear; rend. —**desgajarse,** *v.r.* to fall off; break off.
desgana (des'ɣa·na) *n.f.* **1,** lack of appetite. **2,** indifference; boredom.
desganar (des·ɣa'nar) *v.t.* to dissuade. —**desganarse,** *v.r.* **1,** to lose one's appetite. 2, to be bored.
desgarbo (des'ɣar·βo) *n.m.* clumsiness. —**desgarbado** (-'βa·ðo) *adj.* clumsy; ungainly.
desgarrado (des·ɣa'rra·ðo) *adj.* **1,** torn. **2,** dissolute; wicked.
desgarradura (des·ɣa·rra'ðu·ra) *n.f.* rip; rent; tear.
desgarrar (des·ɣa'rrar) *v.t.* to rend; tear. —*v.i., Amer.* to hawk; clear the throat. —**desgarrador,** *adj.* heartrending.
desgarro (des'ɣa·rro) *n.m.* **1,** laceration; tear. **2,** *fig.* boldness; impudence. —**desgarrón,** *n.m.* large tear.
desgastar (des·ɣas'tar) *v.t.* to wear away; consume. —**desgaste** (-'ɣas·te) *n.m.* wear and tear.
desglosar (des·ɣlo'sar) *v.t.* to separate the parts or divisions of; to arrange under respective headings.
desgracia (des'ɣra·θja; -sja) *n.f.* **1,** misfortune; mishap; affliction. **2,** disgrace; dishonor. —**desgraciado,** *adj.* unfortunate; unhappy. —*n.m.* wretch. —**desgraciadamente,** *adv.* unfortunately.
desgranar (des·ɣra'nar) *v.t.* to thresh (grain); to shell (peas).
desgreñar (des·ɣre'ɲar) *v.t.* to dishevel.
desguarnecer (des·ɣwar·ne'θer; -'ser) *v.t.* [*infl.:* **guarnecer**] **1,** to strip of ornaments or trimmings. **2,** to unharness. **3,** to dismantle; strip down. **4,** to unman (a garrison). **5,** to remove fortifications from.
desguazar (des·ɣwa'θar; -'sar) *v.t.* [*infl.:* **deslizar**] **1,** to hew. **2,** *naut.* to dismantle (a ship).
deshabitar (des·a·βi'tar) *v.t.* **1,** to vacate; move out of. **2,** to depopulate. —**deshabitado,** *adj.* uninhabited; vacant.
deshacer (des·a'θer; -'ser) *v.t.* [*infl.:* **hacer**] **1,** to undo; destroy. **2,** to take apart; dissolve. —**desha-**

cerse, *v.r.* **1,** to melt; vanish. **2,** to waste away. —**deshacerse de,** to get rid of.
desharrapado *also,* **desarrapado** (des·a·rra'pa·ðo) *adj.* ragged; shabby; grubby.
deshebillar (des·e·βi'ʎar; -'jar) *v.t.* to unbuckle.
deshecha (des'e·tʃa) *n.f.* feint; sham.
deshecho (des'e·tʃo) *adj.* **1,** undone; destroyed. **2,** melted. **3,** shattered.
deshelar (des·e'lar) *v.t.* [*infl.:* **helar**] to thaw; melt.
desherbar (des·er'βar) *v.t.* [*pres. ind.* **deshierbo** (-'jer·βo); *pres.subjve.* **deshierbe** (-βe)] **1,** to weed. **2,** to pull out (weeds).
desheredar (des·e·re'ðar) *v.t.* to disinherit. —**desheredación,** *n.f., also,* **desheredamiento,** *n.m.* disinheritance.
deshidratar (des·i·ðra'tar) *v.t.* to dehydrate. —**deshidratación,** *n.f.* dehydration.
deshielo (des'je·lo) *n.m.* thaw.
deshierba (des'jer·βa) *n.f.* weeding.
deshilachar (des·i·la'tʃar) *v.t.* to ravel; fray.
deshilar (des·i'lar) *v.t.* **1,** to ravel. **2,** *sewing* to draw threads from.
deshilvanar (des·il·βa'nar) *v.t., sewing* to unbaste; untack.—**deshilvanado,** *adj.* disconnected; incoherent.
deshojar (de·so'xar) *v.t.* to strip of leaves or petals.
deshollejar (de·so·ʎe'xar; -je'xar) *v.t.* to pare; peel; husk.
deshollinar (des·o·ʎi'nar; -ji·'nar) *v.t.* **1,** to sweep (a chimney) **2,** to remove soot from.
deshonestidad (des·o·nes·ti'ðað) *n.f.* **1,** dishonesty. **2,** immodesty.
deshonesto (des·o'nes·to) *adj.* **1,** dishonest. **2,** immodest.
deshonor (des·o'nor) *n.m.* dishonor.
deshonrar (des·on'rar) *v.t.* **1,** to dishonor. **2,** to defame. **3,** to seduce. —**deshonra** (-'on·ra) *n.f.* dishonor. —**deshonroso,** *adj.* dishonorable.
deshora (des'o·ra) *n.f.* inopportune time. —**a deshora,** untimely.
deshuesar (des·we'sar) *v.t.* = **desosar.**
deshuese (des'we·se) *v., pres.subjve. of* **desosar.**
deshueso (des'we·so) *v., pres.ind. of* **desosar.**
desidia (de'si·ðja) *n.f.* laziness; idleness. —**desidioso,** *adj.* lazy; idle; listless.
desierto (de'sjer·to) *adj.* deserted. —*n.m.* desert; wilderness.
designar (de·siɣ'nar) *v.t.* to designate. —**designación,** *n.f.* designation; appointment.
designio (de'siɣ·njo) *n.m.* design; purpose.
desigualar (des·i·ɣwa'lar) *v.t.* to make dissimilar, unequal *or* uneven. —**desigual,** *adj.* dissimilar; unequal; uneven. —**desigualdad,** *n.f.* dissimilarity; inequality; unevenness.
desilusionar (des·i·lu·sjo'nar) *v.t.* to disillusion. —**desilusión** (-'sjon) *n.f.* disillusionment.
desimantar (des·i·man'tar) *v.t.* to demagnetize.
desinclinar (des·in·kli'nar) *v.t.* to disincline. —**desinclinarse,** *v.r.* to disincline; be disinclined; be unwilling.
desinencia (de·si'nen·θja; -sja) *n.f., gram.* word ending.
desinfección (des·in·fek'θjon; -'sjon) *n.f.* disinfection.
desinfectar (des·in·fek'tar) *v.t.* to disinfect. —**desinfectante,** *adj.* & *n.m.* disinfectant.
desinflar (des·in'flar) *v.t.* to deflate. —**desinflación,** *n.f.* deflation.
desintegrar (des·in·te'ɣrar) *v.t.* to disintegrate. —**desintegración,** *n.f.* disintegration.
desinterés (des·in·te'res) *n.m.* disinterestedness. —**desinteresado,** *adj.* disinterested; impartial.
desinteresarse (des·in·te·re'sar·se) *v.r., fol. by* **de,** to lose interest (in).
desistimiento (de·sis·ti'mjen·to) *n.m.* **1,** desistance. **2,** *law* waiving; waiver. *Also,* **desistencia** (-'ten·θja; -sja) *n.f.*
desistir (de·sis'tir) *v.i.* **1,** to desist. **2,** *law* to waive.
desjarretar (des·xa·rre'tar) *v.t.* to hamstring.
deslavar (des·la'βar) *v.t.* **1,** to wash superficially. **2,** to weaken; fade. —**deslavado,** *adj.* impudent; barefaced.
desleal (des·le'al) *adj.* disloyal. —**deslealtad,** *n.f.* disloyalty.
desleimiento (des·le'mjen·to) *n.m.* **1,** dissolving. **2,** dilution. *Also,* **desleidura,** *n.f.*
desleir (des·le'ir) *v.t.* [*infl.:* **reír**]

1, to dissolve. **2,** to dilute. **3,** *fig.* to expatiate on; be prolix about.
deslenguado (des·len'gwa·ðo) *adj.* talkative; foul-mouthed.
deslice (des'li·θe; -se) *v., pres. subjve. of* **deslizar.**
deslicé (des·li'θe; -'se) *v., pret. of* **deslizar.**
desligar (des·li'ɣar) *v.t.* [*infl.:* **ligar**] **1,** to untie; loosen. **2,** to disentangle. **3,** to release from an obligation.
deslindar (des·lin'dar) *v.t.* **1,** to demarcate. **2,** to define. —**deslinde** (-'lin·de) *n.m.* demarcation.
desliz (des'liθ; -'lis) *n.m.* **1,** slip; slide. **2,** error; false step.
deslizamiento (des·li·θa'mjen·to; -sa'mjen·to) *n.m.* **1,** = **desliz.** **2,** landslide.
deslizar (des·li'θar; -'sar) *v.t.* [*pres.subjve.* **deslice;** *pret.* **deslicé**] to let slide; let slip. —**deslizarse,** *v.r.* to slip away; shirk. —**deslizadero,** *n.m.* slippery place. —**deslizadizo,** *adj.* slippery. —**deslizador,** *n.m.* scooter; glider.
deslucir (des·lu'θir; -'sir) *v.t.* [*infl.:* **lucir**] to mar; tarnish; discredit. —**deslucido,** *adj.* tarnished; dull. —**quedar** *or* **salir deslucido,** to be disappointing.
deslumbrar (des·lum'brar) *v.t.* to dazzle; daze. —**deslumbrante,** *also,* **deslumbrador,** *adj.* dazzling.
deslustrar (des·lus'trar) *v.t.* **1,** to tarnish. **2,** to sully (a reputation). —**deslustre** (-'lus·tre) *n.m.* stain; tarnish.
desmadejar (des·ma·ðe'xar) *v.t.* to weaken; enervate.
desmalezar (des·ma·le'θar; -'sar) *v.t., Amer.* [*infl.:* **empezar**] to weed; grub; clear (the earth).
desmán (des'man) *n.m.* **1,** misconduct; abuse. **2,** disaster; misfortune.
desmantelar (des·man·te'lar) *v.t.* to dismantle. —**desmantelamiento,** *n.m.* dismantling; dismantlement.
desmaña (des'ma·ɲa) *n.f.* clumsiness; awkwardness. —**desmañado,** *adj.* clumsy; awkward. —*n.m.* dub; duffer.
desmayar (des·ma'jar) *v.t.* to dismay; discourage. —*v.i.* to be dispirited *or* discouraged. —**desmayarse,** *v.r.* to faint.
desmayo (des'ma·jo) *n.m.* **1,** faint; loss of strength. **2,** discouragement; dismay.
desmedirse (des·me'ðir·se) *v.r.* to lose self-control; to exceed the bounds of propriety. —**desmedido,** *adj.* immoderate; extravagant.
desmedrar (des·me'ðrar) *v.t.* to impair. —*v.i.* to deteriorate. —**desmedro** (-'me·ðro) *n.m.* detriment.
desmejorar (des·me·xo'rar) *v.t.* to impair; make worse.
desmelenar (des·me·le'nar) *v.t.* to dishevel.
desmembrar (des·mem'brar) *v.t.* [*pres.ind.* **desmiembro** (-'mjem·bro); *pres.subjve.* **desmiembre** (-bre)] **1,** to dismember. **2,** to separate. —**desmembrarse,** *v.r.* to disintegrate. —**desmembramiento,** *n.m.* dismemberment.
desmentir (des·men'tir) *v.t.* [*infl.:* **mentir**] **1,** to belie. **2,** to disprove. **3,** to dissemble.
desmenuzar (des·me·nu'θar; -'sar) *v.t.* [*pres.subjve.* **desmenuce** (-'nu·θe; -se); *pret.* **desmenucé** (-'θe; -'se)] **1,** to chip; crumble; mince; shred. **2,** to examine minutely.
desmerecer (des·me·re'θer; -'ser) *v.t.* [*infl.:* **merecer**] to be or become unworthy of. —*v.i.* **1,** to deteriorate. **2,** to compare unfavorably (with something else). —**desmerecedor,** *adj.* unworthy; underserving. —**desmerecimiento,** *n.m.* unworthiness.
desmesurar (des·me·su'rar) *v.t.* to exaggerate; overstate. —**desmesurarse,** *v.r.* to speak or act unbecomingly. —**desmesurado,** *adj.* immoderate.
desmigajar (des·mi·ɣa'xar) *v.t.* to crumble.
desmigar (des·mi'ɣar) *v.t.* [*pres. subjve.* **desmigue** (-'mi·ɣe); *pret.* **desmigué** (-'ɣe)] to crumble (bread).
desmilitarizar (des·mi·li·ta·ri·'θar; -'sar) *v.t.* [*infl.:* **militarizar**] to demilitarize. —**desmilitarización,** *n.f.* demilitarization.
desmochar (des·mo'tʃar) *v.t.* **1,** to cut off; lop. **2,** to mutilate.
desmolado (des·mo'la·ðo) *adj.* toothless; without molars.
desmontar (des·mon'tar) *v.t.* **1,** to dismount. **2,** to dismantle. **3,** to cut down (a forest); to clear *or* level (ground). —*v.i.* to dismount; alight.
desmoralizar (des·mo·ra·li'θar;

-'sar) *v.t.* [*infl.:* **moralizar**] to demoralize; corrupt. —**desmoralización,** *n.f.* demoralization; depravity.
desmoronar (des·mo·ro'nar) *v.t.* to crumble; to abrade.
desmotar (des·mo'tar) *v.t.* to gin (cotton). —**desmotadora,** *n.f.* cotton gin.
desmovilizar (des·mo·βi·li'θar; -'sar) *v.t.* [*infl.:* **movilizar**] to demobilize. —**desmovilización,** *n.f.* demobilization.
desnatar (des·na'tar) *v.t.* **1,** to skim (milk). **2,** *fig.* to remove the best part of.
desnaturalizar (des·na·tu·ra·li·'θar; -'sar) *v.t.* [*infl.:* **naturalizar**] **1,** to denaturalize; deprive of citizenship. **2,** to denature. **3,** *fig.* to pervert.
desnivel (des·ni'βel) *n.m.* **1,** unevenness. **2,** gradient.
desnivelar (des·ni·βe'lar) *v.t.* **1,** to make uneven. **2,** to make unlevel.
desnucar (des·nu'kar) *v.t.* [*pres. subjve.* **desnuque** (-'nu·ke); *pret.* **desnuqué** (-'ke)] to break the neck of.
desnudar (des·nu'ðar) *v.t.* **1,** to undress. **2,** to denude. —**desnudez** (-'ðeθ; -'ðes) *n.f.* nudity; nakedness.
desnudo (des'nu·ðo) *adj.* **1,** naked; nude. **2,** *fig.* patent; evident.
desnutrición (des·nu·tri'θjon; -'sjon) *n.f.* malnutrition.
desobedecer (des·o·βe·ðe'θer; -'ser) *v.t.* [*infl.:* **obedecer**] to disobey. —**desobediencia,** *n.f.* disobedience. —**desobediente,** *adj.* disobedient.
desobligar (des·o·βli'ɣar) *v.t.* [*infl.:* **obligar**] **1,** to disoblige; offend. **2,** to free of an obligation.
desocupado (des·o·ku'pa·ðo) *adj.* **1,** empty; vacant. **2,** idle; unemployed.
desocupar (des·o·ku'par) *v.t.* to vacate; empty.
desodorante (des·o·ðo'ran·te) *n.m. & adj.* deodorant.
desodorizar (des·o·ðo·ri'θar; -'sar) *v.t.* [*infl.:* **realizar**] to deodorize. —**desodorización,** *n.f.* deodorization.
desoír (des·o'ir) *v.t.* [*infl.:* **oír**] to be deaf to; not to hear *or* heed.
desolación (de·so·la'θjon; -'sjon) *n.f.* **1,** desolation; ruin. **2,** affliction; anguish.
desolar (de·so'lar) *v.t.* [*pres.ind.* **desuelo;** *pres.subjve.* **desuele**] to desolate. —**desolarse,** *v.r.* to be forlorn. —**desolado,** *adj.* desolate.
desollar (des·o'ʎar; -'jar) *v.t.* [*pres.ind.* **desuello;** *pres.subjve.* **desuelle**] **1,** to flay; skin. **2,** to fleece; swindle. —**desolladura,** *n.f.* flaying.
desorbitado (des·or·βi'ta·ðo) *adj.* **1,** out of orbit. **2,** *Amer.* popeyed; wide-eyed. **3,** *Amer.* unhinged; crazy.
desorden (des'or·ðen) *n.m.* disorder; confusion.
desordenar (des·or·ðe'nar) *v.t.* to disorder; disarrange; upset; confuse. —**desordenado,** *adj.* disordered; disorderly.
desorganizar (des·or·ɣa·ni'θar; -'sar) *v.t.* [*infl.:* **organizar**] to disorganize. —**desorganización,** *n.f.* disorganization.
desorientar (des·o·rjen'tar) *v.t.* to disorient; confuse. —**desorientación,** disorientation.
desosar (des·o'sar) *v.t.* [*pres.ind.* **deshueso;** *pres.subjve.* **deshuese**] to bone; remove the bone from.
desovar (des·o'βar) *v.t.* to spawn. —**desove** (-'o·βe) *n.m.* spawning.
despabilado (des·pa·βi'la·ðo) *adj.* alert; lively. *Also,* **espabilado.**
despabilar (des·pa·βi'lar) *v.t.* **1,** to snuff (a candle). **2,** to trim (a wick). **3,** *fig.* to perk; rouse.
despacio (des'pa·θjo; -sjo) *adv.* slowly. —**despacioso,** *adj.* slow; deliberate.
despachar (des·pa'tʃar) *v.t.* **1,** to dispatch. **2,** to wait on (a customer). —**despachador,** *n.m.* dispatcher.
despacho (des'pa·tʃo) *n.m.* **1,** dispatch; shipment. **2,** office; study. **3,** official communication.
despachurrar (des·pa·tʃu'rrar) *v.t., colloq.* to squash; crush; mangle.
despampanarse (des·pam·pa·'nar·se) *v.r.* to be convulsed (*as with laughter, weeping, etc.*).
desparejar (des·pa·re'xar) *v.t.* **1,** to make uneven. **2,** to break up (a pair).
desparpajar (des·par·pa'xar) *v.t.* **1,** to disarrange; upset. **2,** *Amer.* to scatter; disperse. —*v.i.* [*also,* **desparpajarse,** *v.r.*] *colloq.* to rant; rave.
desparpajo (des·par'pa·xo) *n.m., colloq.* **1,** poise; ease. **2,** boldness; presumptuousness. **3,** witticism.
desparramar (des·pa·rra'mar)

v.t. **1,** to spread; scatter; spill. **2,** to squander. —**desparramo** (-'rra·mo) *n.m., Amer.* scattering; spreading.
despatillar (des·pa·ti'ʎar; -'jar) *v.t.* **1,** to groove (wood). **2,** *colloq.* to shave off (whiskers).
despavorido (des·pa·βo'ri·ðo) *adj.* terrified.
despectivo (des·pek'ti·βo) *adj.* derogatory; disparaging.
despecho (des'pe·tʃo) *n.m.* spite; rancor. —**a despecho de,** in spite of; despite.
despedazar (des·pe·ða'θar; -'sar) *v.t.* [*pres.subjve.* **despedace** (-'ða·θe; -se); *pret.* **despedacé** (-'θe; -'se)] to tear to pieces.
despedida (des·pe'ði·ða) *n.f.* **1,** farewell; parting. **2,** discharge; dismissal.
despedir (des·pe'ðir) *v.t.* [*infl.:* **pedir**] **1,** to dismiss; discharge. **2,** to emit. **3,** to bid farewell. —**despedirse,** *v.r.* to take one's leave; say goodbye.
despegar (des·pe'ɣar) *v.t.* [*infl.:* **pegar**] **1,** to detach. **2,** to unglue; unstick. —*v.i., aero.* to take off. —**despegado,** *adj.* curt. —**despego** (-'pe·ɣo) *n.m.* = **desapego.**
despeinar (des·pei'nar) *v.t.* to dishevel.
despegue (des'pe·ɣe) *n.m., aero.* take-off.
despejado (des·pe'xa·ðo) *adj.* **1,** bright; clear. **2,** unobstructed. **3,** clever.
despejar (des·pe'xar) *v.t.* to clear; remove obstacles from. —**despejarse,** *v.r.* to clear up (as weather); become bright.
despejo (des'pe·xo) *n.m.* **1,** clearing; removal of obstacles. **2,** cleverness.
despeluzar (des·pe·lu'θar; -'sar) *v.t.* [*infl.:* **azuzar**] **1,** to muss; dishevel. **2,** to make (the hair) stand on end. **3,** *Amer.* to clear out; clean out; strip bare. *Also,* **despeluznar** (-luθ'nar; -lus'nar).
despeluznante (des·pe·luθ'nan·te; -lus'nan·te) *adj.* = **espeluznante.**
despellejar (des·pe·ʎe'xar; -je·'xar) *v.t.* to skin; flay.
despensa (des'pen·sa) *n.f.* pantry; larder. —**despensero,** *n.m.* steward.
despeñar (des·pe'ɲar) *v.t.* to precipitate; cast down. —**despeñadero,** *n.m.* precipice.
despepitar (des·pe·pi'tar) *v.t.* to remove the seeds from. —**despepitarse por,** to yearn for.
desperdiciar (des·per·ði'θjar; -'sjar) *v.t.* to waste; misuse. —**desperdicio** (-'ði·θjo; -sjo) *n.m.* waste. —**desperdicios,** *n.m.pl.* garbage (*sing.*); offal (*sing.*).
desperezarse (des·pe·re'θar·se; -'sar·se) *v.r.* [*infl.:* **rezar**] to stretch; stretch one's legs. *Also,* **esperezarse.**
desperfecto (des·per'fek·to) *n.m.* damage; defect; flaw.
despertar (des·per'tar) *v.t.* [*pres. ind.* **despierto** (-'pjer·to); *pres. subjve.* **despierte** (-te)] **1,** to awake; rouse. **2,** to arouse; stimulate. —**despertador,** *adj.* awakening; arousing. —*n.m.* alarm clock.
despiadado (des·pja'ða·ðo) *adj.* merciless; cruel.
despicar (des·pi'kar) *v.t.* [*infl.:* **picar**] to satisfy; appease.
despida (des'pi·ða) *v., pres.subjve. of* **despedir.**
despido (des'pi·ðo) *n.m.* dismissal; dispatch. —*v., pres.ind. of* **despedir.**
despierto (des'pjer·to) *adj.* **1,** awake. **2,** alert.
despilfarrar (des·pil·fa'rrar) *v.t.* to squander; waste. —**despilfarro** (-'fa·rro) *n.m.* waste; prodigality.
despintarse (des·pin'tar·se) *v.r.* to fade. —**no despintársele a uno,** to remember (someone or something) well.
despique (des'pi·ke) *n.m.* revenge.
despistar (des·pis'tar) *v.t.* to throw off the scent; mislead.
desplacer (des·pla'θer; -'ser) *v.t.* [*infl.:* **placer**] to displease. —*n.m.* displeasure.
desplantar (des·plan'tar) *v.t.* **1,** to uproot. **2,** to move or sway from an upright position; throw off balance. —**desplantador,** *n.m.* garden trowel.
desplante (des'plan·te) *n.m.* barefaced act or attitude.
desplazar (des·pla'θar; -'sar) *v.t.* [*infl.:* **aplazar**] to displace. —**desplazamiento,** *n.m., naut.* displacement.
desplegar (des·ple'ɣar) *v.t.* [*infl.:* **plegar**] **1,** to unfold; unfurl. **2,** *mil.* to deploy. **3,** to explain; show.
despliegue (des'plje·ɣe) *n.m.* **1,** unfolding; unfurling. **2,** *mil.* deployment.
desplomar (des·plo'mar) *v.t.* to put out of plumb. —**desplomarse,**

v.r. to slump; collapse; tumble down. —**desplome** (-ˈplo·me) *n.m.* collapse.

desplumar (des·pluˈmar) *v.t.* **1,** to pluck (fowl). **2,** *colloq.* to fleece; to rob.

despoblar (des·poˈβlar) *v.t.* to depopulate. —**despoblado,** *n.m.* desert; uninhabited place.

despojar (des·poˈxar) *v.t.* to despoil; divest; denude.

despojo (desˈpo·xo) *n.m.* **1,** spoils (*pl.*); booty; plunder. **2,** scrap; offal. **3,** despoilment; divestment. —**despojos,** *n.m.pl.* **1,** debris; rubble. **2,** leavings; leftovers. **3,** mortal remains. **4,** flotsam.

desportillar (des·por·tiˈʎar; -ˈjar) *v.t.* to chip; nick. —**desportilladura,** *n.f.* chip; fragment.

desposar (des·poˈsar) *v.t.* to marry; wed. —**desposado,** *adj.* & *n.m.* newly wed.

desposeer (des·po·seˈer) *v.t.* **1,** to deprive. **2,** to dispossess. —**desposeimiento,** *n.m.* dispossession.

desposorio (des·poˈso·rjo) *n.m.* **1,** betrothal; engagement. **2,** wedding.

déspota (ˈdes·po·ta) *n.m.* despot. —**despótico** (-ˈpo·ti·ko) *adj.* despotic. —**despotismo,** *n.m.* despotism.

despotricar (des·po·triˈkar) *v.i.* [*pres.subjve.* **despotrique** (-ˈtri·ke); *pret.* **despotriqué** (-ˈke)] to rant; rave.

despreciar (des·preˈθjar; -ˈsjar) *v.t.* to disdain; scorn; despise. —**despreciable,** *adj.* despicable; contemptible. —**desprecio** (-ˈpre·θjo; -sjo) *n.m.* disdain; contempt.

desprender (des·prenˈder) *v.t.* to loosen; unfasten; detach. —**desprenderse,** *v.r.* to be inferred *or* inferable.

desprendido (des·prenˈdi·ðo) *adj.* **1,** loose; detached. **2,** *fig.* generous.

desprendimiento (des·pren·diˈmjen·to) *n.m.* **1,** separation; detaching. **2,** detachment; indifference. **3,** generosity.

despreocuparse (des·pre·o·kuˈpar·se) *v.r., fol. by* de, to ignore. —**despreocupación,** *n.f.* carelessness; indifference. —**despreocupado,** *adj.* careless; indifferent.

desprestigiar (des·pres·tiˈxjar) *v.t.* **1,** to discredit. **2,** to sully (a reputation). —**desprestigio** (-ˈti·xjo) *n.m.* discredit.

desprevenido (des·pre·βeˈni·ðo) *adj.* unprepared.

desproporción (des·pro·porˈθjon; -ˈsjon) *n.f.* disproportion. —**desproporcionado,** *adj.* disproportionate. —**desproporcionar,** *v.t.* to make disproportionate.

desproveer (des·pro·βeˈer) *v.t.* [*p.p.* **desproveído** (-βeˈi·ðo), **desprovisto** (-ˈβis·to)] to deprive of provisions. —**desprovisto,** *adj.* deprived; lacking; devoid.

después (desˈpwes) *adv.* after; afterwards; then; later.

despuntar (des·punˈtar) *v.t.* **1,** to blunt. **2,** to crop. —*v.i.* **1,** to sprout. **2,** to excel. —**despuntar el alba,** to dawn.

desquiciar (des·kiˈθjar; -ˈsjar) *v.t.* **1,** to unhinge. **2,** *fig.* to madden; enrage.

desquitarse (des·kiˈtar·se) *v.r.* **1,** to recoup; recover. **2,** to retaliate; get even.

desquite (desˈki·te) *n.m.* **1,** retaliation; compensation. **2,** (in sports) return match.

desrazonable des·ra·θoˈna·βle; des·ra·so-) *adj.* unreasonable.

desrizar (des·riˈθar; -ˈsar) *v.t.* [*infl.:* **rizar**] to uncurl.

destacar (des·taˈkar) *v.t.* [*infl.:* **atacar**] **1,** to detach. **2,** to emphasize. —**destacarse,** *v.r.* to excel; stand out. —**destacamento,** *n.m.*, *mil.* detachment; outpost.

destajar (des·taˈxar) *v.t.* **1,** to do (work) by the piece. **2,** to contract for (work) by the piece.

destajero (des·taˈxe·ro) *n.m.* pieceworker. *Also,* **destajista,** *n.m.* & *f.*

destajo (desˈta·xo) *n.m.* **1,** job; contract. **2,** piecework. —**a destajo,** **1,** on contract. **2,** by the piece; on piecework. **3,** *fig.* eagerly; tirelessly.

destapar (des·taˈpar) *v.t.* to uncover; remove the lid from.

destaponar (des·ta·poˈnar) *v.t.* to uncork.

destartalado (des·tar·taˈla·ðo) *adj.* ramshackle; falling apart.

destejer (des·teˈxer) *v.t.* **1,** to unweave; unknit. **2,** to upset; disturb.

destellar (des·teˈʎar; -ˈjar) *v.t.* to sparkle; flash. —**destello** (-ˈte·ʎo; -jo) *n.m.* sparkle; gleam.

destemplanza (des·temˈplan·θa; -sa) *n.f.* **1,** intemperance. **2,** indis-

position; distemper. 3, irregularity of the pulse.
destemplar (des·tem'plar) *v.t.* 1, to distemper. 2, to make discordant. 3, to jar; jangle. —**destemplarse,** *v.r.* 1, to become indisposed. 2, to behave intemperately.
destemple (des'tem·ple) *n.m.* 1, dissonance. 2, disorder. 3, indisposition.
desteñir (des·te'ɲir) *v.t.* [*infl.:* **teñir**] to discolor; fade.
desternillarse (des·ter·ni'ʎar·se; -'jar·se) *v.r.* to split one's sides, as with laughter.
desterrar (des·te'rrar) *v.t.* [*pres. ind.* **destierro** (-'tje·rro); *pres. subjve.* **destierre** (-re)] 1, to exile; banish. 2, to remove earth from, as roots.
destetar (des·te'tar) *v.t.* to wean. —**destete** (-'te·te) *n.m.* weaning.
destiempo (des'tjem·po) *in* **a destiempo,** untimely; inopportunely.
destierro (des'tje·rro) *n.m.* exile; banishment.
destilar (des·ti'lar) *v.t.* 1, to distil. 2, to filter. —*v.i.* to trickle. —**destilación,** *n.f.* distillation. —**destiladera,** *n.f.* still. —**destilería,** *n.f.* distillery. *Also,* **destilatorio,** *n.m.*
destinar (des·ti'nar) *v.t.* 1, to destine. 2, to designate; assign. —**destinación,** *n.f.* destination.
destinatario (des·ti·na'ta·rjo) *n.m.* addressee; consignee.
destino (des'ti·no) *n.m.* 1, destiny. 2, destination. 3, purpose. 4, assignment; post; job.
destitución (des·ti·tu'θjon; -'sjon) *n.f.* 1, destitution. 2, dismissal (*from a job*).
destituir (des·ti·tu'ir) *v.t.* [*infl.:* **huir**] 1, to deprive. 2, to dismiss (*from a job*). —**destituído,** *adj.* destitute.
destocar (des·to'kar) *v.t.* [*infl.:* **tocar**] 1, to remove the headgear of. 2, to undo the hair of.
destorcer (des·tor'θer; -'ser) *v.t.* [*infl.:* **torcer**] to untwist.
destornillar (des·tor·ni'ʎar; -'jar) *v.t.* to unscrew. —**destornillarse,** *v.r.* to act foolishly; become unhinged. —**destornillador,** *n.m.* screwdriver.
destral (des'tral) *n.m.* small axe; hatchet.
destrenzar (des·tren'θar; -'sar) *v.t.* [*infl.:* **trenzar**] to unbraid.
destreza (des'tre·θa; -sa) *n.f.* dexterity.
destripar (des·tri'par) *v.t.* 1, to disembowel. 2, to crush; mash.
destrísimo (des'tri·si·mo) *adj., superl. of* **diestro.**
destrizar (des·tri'θar; -'sar) *v.t.* [*infl.:* **trizar**] to break to bits; shatter. —**destrizarse,** *v.r.* to go to pieces.
destronar (des·tro'nar) *v.t.* to dethrone. —**destronamiento,** *n.m.* dethronement.
destroncar (des·tron'kar) *v.t.* [*pres.subjve.* **destronque** (-'tron·ke); *pret.* **destronqué** (-'ke)] 1, to truncate; lop. 2, to interrupt; cut short. 3, to behead; decapitate. —**destroncarse,** *v.r.* to come apart.
destrozar (des·tro'θar; -'sar) *v.t.* [*pres.subjve.* **destroce** (-'tro·θe; -se); *pret.* **destrocé** (-'θe; -'se)] to destroy; shatter. —**destrozo** ('tro·θo; -so) *n.m.* destruction; havoc.
destrucción (des·truk'θjon; -'sjon) *n.f.* destruction. —**destructivo** (-'ti·βo) *adj.* destructive.
destructible (des·truk'ti·βle) *adj.* destructible.
destructor (des·truk'tor) *adj.* destructive. —*n.m.* 1, destroyer. 2, *naval* destroyer.
destruíble (des·tru'i·βle) *adj.* destructible.
destruidor (des·tru·i'ðor) *adj.* destructive. —*n.m.* destroyer.
destruir (des·tru'ir) *v.t.* [*infl.:* **construir**] to destroy.
destusar (des·tu'sar) *v.t., Amer.* to husk (corn).
desuele (de'swe·le) *v., pres.subjve. of* **desolar.**
desuelo (de'swe·lo) *v., pres.ind. of* **desolar.**
desuelle (des'we·ʎe; -je) *v., pres. subjve. of* **desollar.**
desuello (des'we·ʎo; -jo) *v., pres. ind. of* **desollar.**
desuncir (des·un'θir; -'sir) *v.t.* [*infl.:* **uncir**] to unyoke.
desunión (des·u'njon) *n.f.* disunion; disunity.
desunir (des·u'nir) *v.t.* 1, to disunite; divide; separate. 2, to set against one another. 3, to detach; disengage. —**desunirse,** *v.r.* to disintegrate; fall apart.
desusar (des·u'sar) *v.t.* to stop using; disuse. —**desusado,** *adj.* out of use; obsolete. —**desuso** (-'u·so) *n.m.* disuse.

desvaído (des·βa'i·ðo) *adj.* **1,** lanky; gangling. **2,** dull; faded.
desvainar (des·βai'nar) *v.t.* to shell (peas, beans, etc.).
desvalido (des·βa'li·ðo) *adj.* helpless; destitute.
desvalijar (des·βa·li'xar) *adj.* **1,** to rifle (a bag). **2,** to rob; fleece. —**desvalijamiento,** *n.m.* robbery; fleecing.
desvalorizar (des·βa·lo·ri'θar; -'sar) *v.t.* [*infl.:* **realizar**] to devaluate; devalue. *Also,* **desvalorar** (-'rar). —**desvalorización,** *n.f.* devaluation.
desván (des'βan) *n.m.* attic; loft.
desvanecer (des·βa·ne'θer; -'ser) *v.t.* [*pres.ind.* **desvanezco** (-'neθ·ko; -'nes·ko); *pres.subjve.* **desvanezca** (-ka)] to banish; dispel. —**desvanecerse,** *v.r.* **1,** to vanish; disappear. **2,** to evaporate; dissipate. **3,** to faint.
desvanecimiento (des·βa·ne·θi'mjen·to; -si'mjen·to) *n.m.* **1,** disappearance. **2,** evaporation; dissipation. **3,** faint; swoon.
desvarar (des·βa'rar) *v.t.* **1,** to slip; slide. **2,** *naut.* to set afloat (a grounded ship).
desvariado (des·βa'rja·ðo) *adj.* **1,** delirious; raving. **2,** dreamy; vague. **3,** nonsensical; incoherent.
desvariar (des·βa'rjar) *v.i.* [*infl.:* **variar**] to rave; rant.
desvarío (des·βa'ri·o) *n.m.* **1,** raving; delirium. **2,** madness; absurdity. **3,** monstrosity.
desvedar (des·βe'ðar) *v.t.* to remove a prohibition or restriction from.
desvelar (des·βe'lar) *v.t.* to keep awake. —**desvelarse,** *v.r.* **1,** to lose sleep; be wakeful. **2,** to concern oneself.
desvelo (des'βe·lo) *n.m.* **1,** wakefulness. **2,** care; concern.
desvencijar (des·βen·θi'xar; -si·'xar) *v.t.* to pull apart; loosen; wear out. —**desvencijarse,** *v.r.* to fall apart; wear out.
desventaja (des·βen'ta·xa) *n.f.* disadvantage. —**desventajoso,** *adj.* disadvantageous.
desventura (des·βen'tu·ra) *n.f.* misfortune. —**desventurado,** *adj.* unfortunate; wretched.
desvergonzarse (des·βer·ɣon·'θar·se; -'sar·se) *v.r.* [*infl.:* **avergonzar**] to speak or act shamelessly. —**desvergonzado,** *adj.* shameless.
desvergüenza (des·βer'ɣwen·θa; -sa) *n.f.* shamelessness; impudence.
desvestir (des·βes'tir) *v.t.* [*infl.:* **vestir**] to undress; denude.
desviar (des·βi'ar) *v.t.* [*infl.:* **enviar**] to deviate; deflect; divert. —**desviarse,** *v.r.* **1,** to turn aside; swerve. **2,** to stray. **3,** *aero.* to yaw. —**desviación,** *n.f.* deviation; deflection.
desvío (des'βi·o) *n.m.* **1,** = **desviación. 2,** detour. **3,** indifference. **4,** aversion; dislike. **5,** *aero.* yaw.
desvirgar (des·βir'ɣar) *v.t., colloq.* [*infl.:* **llegar**] to deflower.
desvirtuar (des·βir'twar) *v.t.* [*infl.:* **continuar**] to detract from; diminish or destroy the value of. —**desvirtuarse,** *v.r.* to spoil; lose strength, flavor, etc.
desvivirse (des·βi'βir·se) *v.r.* **1,** to long; yearn. **2,** to be eager; strive.
desvolvedor (des·βol·βe'ðor) *n.m.* wrench.
desvolver (des·βol'βer) *v.t.* [*infl.:* **volver**] **1,** to change the shape of. **2,** to turn up (the soil). **3,** to unscrew; unbolt.
desyerbar (des·jer'βar) *v.t.* = **desherbar.** —**desyerba** (-'jer·βa) *n.f.* = **deshierba.**
detallar (de·ta'ʎar; -'jar) *v.t.* **1,** to detail; enumerate. **2,** to retail. —**detallista,** *n.m.* & *f.* retailer.
detalle (de'ta·ʎe; -je) *n.m.* **1,** detail. **2,** retail.
detectar (de·tek'tar) *v.t., radio* to detect. —**detección,** *n.f., radio* detection.
detective (de·tek'ti·βe) *n.m.* detective. *Also,* **detectivo** (-βo).
detector (de·tek'tor) *n.m.* detector.
detención (de·ten'θjon; -'sjon) *n.f.* **1,** detention; arrest. **2,** stop; halt. **3,** delay. **4,** thoroughness; meticulousness. *Also,* **detenimiento** (de·te·ni'mjen·to)) *n.m.*
detener (de·te'ner) *v.t.* [*infl.:* **tener**] **1,** to detain. **2,** to stop; arrest. —**detenerse,** *v.r.* **1,** to linger. **2,** to pause.
detenido (de·te'ni·ðo) *adj.* **1,** niggardly. **2,** thorough; meticulous.
detentar (de·ten'tar) *v.t., law* to retain unlawfully. —**detentación,** *n.f., law* unlawful retention of property.

detergente (de·ter'xen·te) *adj.* & *n.m.* detergent.
deteriorar (de·te·rjo'rar) *v.t.* to deteriorate. —**deterioro** (de·te'rjo·ro) *n.m.* deterioration. *Also,* **deterioración,** *n.f.*
determinado (de·ter·mi'na·ðo) *adj.* **1,** determined; resolved. **2,** specified. **3,** definite; specific.
determinar (de·ter·mi'nar) *v.t.* **1,** to determine; decide. **2,** to specify; define. —**determinación,** *n.f.* determination.
detestar (de·tes'tar) *v.t.* to detest. —**detestable,** *adj.* detestable. —**detestación,** *n.f.* detestation.
detonar (de·to'nar) *v.t.* to detonate. —**detonación,** *n.f.* detonation. —**detonador,** *n.m.* detonator.
detracción (de·trak'θjon; -'sjon) *n.f.* detraction.
detractar (de·trak'tar) *v.t.* to detract; defame. —**detractor,** *n.m.* detractor; defamer.
detraer (de·tra'er) *v.t.* [*infl.:* **traer**] **1,** to detract; remove. **2,** = **detractar.**
detrás (de'tras) *adv.* behind; after. —**detrás de,** behind; in back of.
detrimento (de·tri'men·to) *n.m.* detriment.
detritus (de'tri·tus) *n.m.* detritus.
deuda ('deu·ða) *n.f.* debt; indebtedness.
deudo ('deu·ðo) *n.m.* kinsman.
deudor (deu'ðor) *adj.* indebted. —*n.m.* debtor.
deuter- (deu·ter) *prefix, var. of* **deutero-** *before vowels: deuteragonista,* deuteragonist.
deuterio (deu'te·rjo) *n.m.* deuterium.
deuterión (deu·te'rjon) *n.m.* deuteron.
deutero- (deu·te·ro) *prefix* deutero-; second; later: *Deuteronomio,* Deuteronomy.
deuto- (deu·to) *prefix* deuto-; second; later: *deutoplasma,* deutoplasm.
devaluación (de·βa·lwa'θjon; -'sjon) *n.f.* devaluation.
devanar (de·βa'nar) *v.t.* to reel; wind, as yarn. —**devanadera,** *n.f.* reel; spool; bobbin. —**devanarse los sesos,** to cudgel one's brains. —**devanarse de risa,** *Amer.* to be convulsed with laughter.
devanear (de·βa·ne'ar) *v.i.* **1,** to rave; be delirious. **2,** to daydream. **3,** to flirt.
devaneo (de·βa'ne·o) *n.m.* **1,** frenzy; derangement. **2,** idle pursuit. **3,** flirtation.
devastar (de·βas'tar) *v.t.* to devastate. —**devastación,** *n.f.* devastation. —**devastador,** *adj.* devastating.
devengar (de·βen'gar) *v.t.* [*infl.:* **vengar**] to earn.
devoción (de·βo'θjon; -'sjon) *n.f.* devotion. —**devocionario,** *n.m.* prayer book.
devolución (de·βo·lu'θjon; -'sjon) *n.f.* return; restitution.
devolutivo (de·βo·lu'ti·βo) *adj.* **1,** returnable. **2,** *law* restorable.
devolver (de·βol'βer) *v.t.* [*infl.:* **volver**] to return; restore; repay.
devorar (de·βo'rar) *v.t.* to devour. —**devorador,** *adj.* voracious.
devoto (de'βo·to) *adj.* **1,** devout; pious. **2,** devoted; strongly attached. **3,** devotional. —*n.m.* **1,** devotee. **2,** object of devotion.
devuelto (de'βwel·to) *v., p.p. of* **devolver.**
dextro- (deks·tro) *prefix* dextro-; right; turning to the right: *dextrógiro,* dextrogyrate.
dextrosa (deks'tro·sa) *n.f.* dextrose.
deyección (de·jek'θjon; -'sjon) *n.f.* **1,** volcanic debris. **2,** defecation; feces.
di (di) *v., impve. of* **decir.**
dí (di) *v., 1st pers.sing.pret. of* **dar.**
di- (di) *prefix* **1,** dis-; opposition: *disentir,* dissent. **2,** origin: *dimanar,* to spring. **3,** dis-; diffusion; extension: *difusión,* diffusion; *disolución,* dissolution. **4,** di-; two; twofold; double; *digrafo,* digraph; *dicloruro,* dichloride; *dicromático,* dichromatic. **5,** *var. of* **dia-** *before vowels: dieléctrico,* dielectric.
día ('di·a) *n.m.* day; daylight. —**al día,** per day. —**al otro día,** the next day. —**buenos días,** good morning. —**dar los días, 1,** to greet someone. **2,** to give birthday greetings. —**de día,** by day; during the day. —**de hoy en ocho días,** a week from today. —**día diado,** appointed day. —**día natural,** from sunup to sundown. —**día quebrado,** half-holiday. —**en el mejor día,** some fine day. —**es de día,** it is daylight *or* daytime. —**estar al día,** to be up to date. —**hoy día,** nowadays. —**ser del día,** to be in style. —**tener días, 1,** to be old. **2,** to

be moody. **—vivir al día**, to spend all one earns.
dia- (di·a) *prefix* dia-. **1,** separation: *diacrítico*, diacritical. **2,** opposition: *diamagnético*, diamagnetic. **3,** through; across: *diagonal*, diagonal.
diabetes (dja'βe·tes) *n.f.* diabetes. **—diabético** (-'βe·ti·ko) *adj.* diabetic.
diablo ('dja·βlo) *n.m.* devil. **—diablura**, *n.f.* deviltry; mischievousness. **—diabólico** (-'βo·li·ko) *adj.* diabolical; devilish.
diaconisa (dja·ko'ni·sa) *n.f.* deaconess.
diácono ('dja·ko·no) *n.m.* deacon.
diacrítico (dja'kri·ti·ko) *adj.* **1,** *gram.* diacritical. **2,** *med.* diagnostic.
diadema (dja'ðe·ma) *n.f.* diadem.
diáfano ('dja·fa·no) *adj.* diaphanous. **—diafanidad**, *n.f.* transparency.
diafragma (dja'fraɣ·ma) *n.m.* diaphragm.
diagnosis (djaɣ'no·sis) *n.m. sing.* & *pl.* diagnosis. **—diagnóstico** (-'nos·ti·ko) *adj.* diagnostic. **—*n.m.*** diagnosis.
diagnosticar (djaɣ·nos·ti'kar) *v.t.* [*pres.subjve.* **diagnostique** (-'ti·ke); *pret.* **diagnostiqué** (-'ke)] to diagnose.
diagonal (dja·ɣo'nal) *adj.* & *n.m.* diagonal.
diagrama (dja'ɣra·ma) *n.m.* diagram. **—diagramático** (-'ma·ti·ko) *adj.* diagrammatic.
dial (di'al) *n.m.* **1,** *radio* selector; dial. **2,** telephone dial.
dialéctica (dja'lek·ti·ka) *n.f.* logic; dialectics (*pl.*). **—dialéctico**, *adj.* logical; dialectical. **—*n.m.*** dialectician.
dialecto (dja'lek·to) *n.m.* dialect. **—dialectal**, *adj.* dialectal.
diálogo ('dja·lo·ɣo) *n.m.* dialogue.
diamante (dja'man·te) *n.m.* diamond.
diámetro (di'a·me·tro) *n.m.* diameter. **—diametral** (dja·me'tral) *adj.* diametrical.
diana ('dja·na) *n.f.* **1,** *mil.* reveille. **2,** target; bull's eye.
diantre ('djan·tre) *n.m.*, *slang* deuce; devil. *Also*, **dianche** (-tʃe).
diapasón (dja·pa'son) *n.m.* **1,** diapason. **2,** tuning fork.
diario ('dja·rjo) *adj.* daily. **—*n.m.*** **1,** diary; journal. **2,** daily newspaper. **—diariamente**, *adv.* daily. **—a diario**, daily. **—diario de navegación**, log book.
diarrea (dja'rre·a) *n.f.* diarrhea. **—diarreico** (-'rrei·ko) *adj.* diarrhetic.
Diáspora ('djas·po·ra) *n.f.* Diaspora.
diástole ('djas·to·le) *n.m.* diastole. **—diastólico** (-'to·li·ko) *adj.* diastolic.
diatermia (dja'ter·mja) *n.f.* diathermy. **—diatérmico**, *also*, **diatérmano**, *adj.* diathermic.
diatomea (dja·to'me·a) *n.f.*, *bot.* diatom.
diatónico (dja'to·ni·ko) *adj.*, *music* diatonic.
diatriba (dja'tri·βa) *n.f.* diatribe.
dibujar (di·βu'xar) *v.t.* to draw; sketch; depict. **—dibujarse**, *v.r.* to appear; stand out. **—dibujante**, *n.m.* draftsman; designer.
dibujo (di'βu·xo) *n.m.* **1,** drawing. **2,** pattern; design.
dicción (dik'θjon; -'sjon) *n.f.* diction; phraseology.
diccionario (dik·θjo'na·rjo; dik·sjo-) *n.m.* dictionary. **—diccionarista**, *n.m.* & *f.* lexicographer.
diciembre (di'θjem·bre; di'sjem-) *n.m.* December.
diciendo (di'θjen·do; -'sjen·do) *v.*, *ger. of* **decir.**
dicotomía (di·ko·to'mi·a) *n.f.* dichotomy.
dictado (dik'ta·ðo) *n.m.* **1,** dictation. **2,** rank; title. **—dictados**, *n.m.pl.* dictates; maxims.
dictador (dik·ta'ðor) *n.m.* dictator. **—dictadura**, *n.f.* dictatorship. **—dictatorial**, *also* **dictatorio**, *adj.* dictatorial.
dictáfono (dik'ta·fo·no) *n.m.* Dictaphone (*marca registrada*).
dictamen (dik'ta·men) *n.m.* dictum; pronouncement. **—dictaminar** (-mi'nar) *v.i.* to pass judgment.
dictar (dik'tar) *v.t.* to dictate.
dicha ('di·tʃa) *n.f.* joy; good fortune. **—dichoso**, *adj.* fortunate; joyous.
dicharacho (di·tʃa'ra·tʃo) *n.m.*, *colloq.* **1,** wisecrack. **2,** vulgar expression.
dicho ('di·tʃo) *v.*, *p.p. of* **decir.** **—*adj.*** said; aforesaid. **—*n.m.*** **1,** saying; proverb. **2,** witticism. **—dicho y hecho**, no sooner said than done.

didáctica (di'ðak·ti·ka) *n.f.* didactics. —**didáctico,** *adj.* didactic.
didimio (di'ði·mjo) *n.m.* didymium.
diecinueve (dje·θi'nwe·βe; dje·si-) *adj.* & *n.m.* nineteen. —**diecinueveavo,** *adj* & *n.m.* nineteenth.
dieciocho (dje'θjo·tʃo; dje'sjo-) *adj.* & *n.m.* eighteen. —**dieciochavo,** *adj.* & *n.m.* eighteenth. *Also,* **dieciocheno.**
dieciseis (dje·θi'seis; dje·si-) *adj.* & *n.m.* sixteen. —**dieciseisavo,** *adj.* & *n.m.* sixteenth. *Also,* **dieciseiseno.**
diecisiete (dje·θi'sje·te; dje·si-) *adj.* & *n.m.* seventeen. —**diecisieteavo,** *adj.* & *n.m.* seventeenth.
diedro (di'e·ðro) *adj.* dihedral.
dieléctrico (di·e'lek·tri·ko) *adj.* & *n.m.* dielectric.
diente ('djen·te) *n.m.* **1,** tooth. **2,** cog. **3,** tine; prong. **4,** clove, as of garlic. —**diente de león,** dandelion. —**diente de leche; diente mamón,** baby tooth; milk tooth. —**diente de perro, 1,** sculptor's two-pointed chisel. **2,** *archit.* dogtooth. **3,** *bot.* dogtooth violet. —**pelar el diente,** *colloq.* to smile affectedly. —**tener buen diente,** *colloq.* to be a hearty eater.
diente ('djen·te) *v., pres.subjve. of* **dentar.**
diento ('djen·to) *v., pres.ind. of* **dentar.**
diéresis ('dje·re·sis) *n.f.* dieresis.
diestra ('djes·tra) *n.f.* right hand. —**a diestra y siniestra,** every which way.
diestro ('djes·tro) *adj.* **1,** skillful; dexterous. **2,** propitious; favorable. —*n.m., sports* expert; deft hand.
dieta ('dje·ta) *n.f.* **1,** diet (*regimen*). **2,** diet (*legislative body*). **3,** = **honorarios.**
dietética (dje'te·ti·ka) *n.f.* dietetics. —**dietético,** *adj.* dietetic; dietary.
diez (djeθ; djes) *adj.* & *n.m.* ten.
diezmar (djeθ'mar; djes-) *v.t.* **1,** to decimate. **2,** to pay a tithe of.
diezmilésimo (djeθ·mi'le·si·mo; djes-) *adj.* & *n.m.* ten-thousandth.
diezmo ('djeθ·mo; 'djes-) *n.m.* tithe; tenth part.
difamar (di·fa'mar) *v.t.* to defame. —**difamación,** *n.f.* defamation. —**difamatorio,** *adj.* defamatory.
diferencia (di·fe'ren·θja; -sja) *n.f.* difference.
diferencial (di·fe·ren'θjal; -'sjal) *adj.* & *n.m.* differential.
diferenciar (di·fe·ren'θjar; -'sjar) *v.t.* to differentiate. —**diferenciarse,** *v.r.* to differ; be distinguished. —**diferenciación,** *n.f.* differentiation.
diferente (di·fe'ren·te) *adj.* different.
diferir (di·fe'rir) *v.t.* [*pres.ind.* **difiero;** *pres.subjve.* **difiera**] to defer; delay. —*v.i.* to differ; have a different opinion.
difícil (di'fi·θil; -sil) *adj.* difficult.
dificultad (di·fi·kul'tað) *n.f.* difficulty. —**dificultar,** *v.t.* to make difficult; impede. —**dificultoso,** *adj.* difficult; laborious.
difidencia (di·fi'ðen·θja; -sja) *n.f.* distrust. —**difidente,** *adj.* distrustful.
difiera (di'fje·ra) *v., pres.subjve. of* **diferir.**
difiero (di'fje·ro) *v., pres.ind. of* **diferir.**
difracción (di·frak'θjon; -'sjon) *n.f.* diffraction. —**difractar** (-'tar) *v.t.* to diffract.
difteria (dif'te·rja) *n.f.* diphtheria.
difundir (di·fun'dir) *v.t.* to diffuse; spread; broadcast.
difunto (di'fun·to) *n.m.* corpse. —*adj.* defunct; dead.
difusión (di·fu'sjon) *n.f.* diffusion; broadcasting. —**difusor** (-'sor) *adj.* diffusive; broadcasting.
difuso (di'fu·so) *adj.* **1,** diffuse. **2,** verbose.
diga ('di·ɣa) *v., pres.subjve. of* **decir.**
digerir (di·xe'rir) *v.t.* [*pres.ind.* **digiero** (-'xje·ro); *pres.subjve.* **digiera** (-ra)] to digest. —**digerible,** *adj.* digestible.
digestión (di·xes'tjon) *n.f.* digestion. —**digestible,** *adj.* digestible. —**digestivo,** *adj.* digestive.
digesto (di'xes·to) *n.m., law* digest.
digital (di·xi'tal) *adj.* digital. —*n.m.* digitalis.
dígito ('di·xi·to) *n.m.* digit. —*adj.* [*also,* **digital**] digital.
dignarse (diɣ'nar·se) *v.r.* to deign; condescend.
dignatario (diɣ·na'ta·rjo) *n.m.* dignitary.
dignidad (diɣ·ni'ðað) *n.f.* dignity; rank.
dignificar (diɣ·ni·fi'kar) *v.t.* [*pres.subjve.* **dignifique** (-'fi·ke); *pret.* **dignifiqué** (-'ke)] to dignify.

digno (ˈdiɣ·no) *adj.* **1,** worthy; deserving. **2,** fitting; appropriate.
digo (ˈdi·ɣo) *v., 1st pers.sing. pres. ind. of* **decir.**
digresión (di·ɣreˈsjon) *n.f.* digression. **—digresivo,** *adj.* digressive.
dije (ˈdi·xe) *n.m.* **1,** bauble; charm. **2,** *colloq.* jewel (*person*).
dije (ˈdi·xe) *v., pret. of* **decir.**
dilación (di·laˈθjon; -ˈsjon) *n.f.* delay.
dilapidación (di·la·pi·ðaˈθjon; -ˈsjon) *n.f.* **1,** dilapidation. **2,** squandering.
dilapidar (di·la·piˈðar) *v.t.* **1,** to dilapidate. **2,** to squander.
dilatar (di·laˈtar) *v.t.* **1,** to dilate. **2,** to retard; defer. **—dilatarse,** *v.r.* **1,** to expatiate. **2,** *Amer.* to be late. **—dilatación,** *n.f.* dilation; dilatation. **—dilatoria** (-ˈto·rja) *n.f.* delay. **—dilatorio** (-ˈto·rjo) *adj.* dilatory.
dilección (di·lekˈθjon; -ˈsjon) *n.f.* love; affection. **—dilecto** (-ˈlek·to) *adj.* beloved.
dilema (diˈle·ma) *n.m.* dilemma.
diletante (di·leˈtan·te) *n.m.* dilettante.
diligencia (di·liˈxen·θja; -sja) *n.f.* **1,** diligence; industry. **2,** stagecoach. **3,** errand. **—diligente,** *adj.* diligent; active.
diligenciar (di·li·xenˈθjar; -ˈsjar) *v.t.* to set about (something); apply oneself to (something).
dilucidar (di·lu·θiˈðar; -siˈðar) *v.t.* to elucidate. **—dilucidación,** *n.f.* elucidation.
diluir (di·luˈir) *v.t.* [*infl.:* **huir**] to dilute. **—dilución,** *n.f.* dilution. **—diluente,** *adj.* diluting; dissolving.
diluvio (diˈlu·βjo) *n.m.* deluge; flood. **—diluvial,** *also,* **diluviano,** *adj.* diluvial.
dimanar (di·maˈnar) *v.i.* to emanate; proceed; stem. **—dimanación,** *n.f.* emanation; origin.
dimensión (di·menˈsjon) *n.f.* dimension. **—dimensional,** *adj.* dimensional.
dimes y diretes (ˈdi·mes·i·ðiˈre·tes) *colloq.* quibbling; bickering. **—andar en dimes y diretes,** to quibble; argue.
diminución (di·mi·nuˈθjon; -ˈsjon) *n.f.* diminution; contraction. **—diminutivo,** *adj.* & *n.m.* diminutive.
diminuendo (di·miˈnwen·do) *adj., adv.* & *n.m., music* diminuendo.
diminuto (di·miˈnu·to) *adj.* diminutive; minute.
dimitir (di·miˈtir) *v.t.* to resign; relinquish. **—dimisión,** *n.f.* resignation.
dina (ˈdi·na) *n.f.* dyne.
dina- (di·na) *prefix* dyna-; force; power: *dinatrón,* dynatron.
dinamarqués (di·na·marˈkes) *adj.* Danish. **—*n.m.*** **1,** Dane. **2,** Danish language.
dinámica (diˈna·mi·ka) *n.f.* dynamics. **—dinámico,** *adj.* dynamic. **—dinamismo,** *n.m.* dynamism.
dinamita (di·naˈmi·ta) *n.f.* dynamite. **—dinamitar,** *v.t.* to dynamite.
dínamo (ˈdi·na·mo) *n.f.* [*also, Amer., n.m.*] dynamo.
dinamo- (di·na·mo) *prefix* dynamo-; power: *dinamómetro,* dynamometer.
dinamómetro (di·naˈmo·me·tro) *n.m.* dynamometer.
dinastía (di·nasˈti·a) *n.f.* dynasty. **—dinasta** (-ˈnas·ta) *n.m.* dynast. **—dinástico** (-ˈnas·ti·ko) *adj.* dynastic.
din-dán (dinˈdan) *n.m.* ding-dong
dinero (diˈne·ro) *n.m.* money; coin; currency. **—dineral,** *n.m.* a large sum of money.
-dino (ˈdi·no) *suffix* -dyne; power: *superheterodino,* superheterodyne.
dinosauro (di·noˈsau·ro) *n.m* dinosaur.
dintel (dinˈtel) *n.m.* **1,** lintel. **2** doorway.
diócesis (ˈdjo·θe·sis; -se·sis) *n.f* diocese. **—diocesano** (-θeˈsa·no -seˈsa·no) *adj.* diocesan.
diodo (ˈdi·o·ðo) *n.m.* diode.
diorama (djoˈra·ma) *n.m.* diorama. **—diorámico,** *adj.* dioramic
dios (djos) *n.m.* god; *cap.* God **—a la buena de Dios,** *colloq.* **1** without malice; guilelessly. **2,** a random; haphazardly.
diosa (ˈdjo·sa) *n.f.* goddess.
dióspiro (ˈdjos·pi·ro) *n.m.* persimmon.
dióxido (diˈok·si·ðo) *n.m.* dioxide
diploma (diˈplo·ma) *n.m.* diploma.
diplomático (di·ploˈma·ti·ko) *adj* diplomatic. **—*n.m.*** diplomat. **—diplomacia** (-ˈma·θja; -sja) *n.f.* diplomacy.
dipsomanía (dip·so·maˈni·a) *n.f* dipsomania. **—dipsómano** (-ˈso ma·no) *also,* **dipsomaníaco** (-maˈni·a·ko) *adj.* & *n.m.* dipsomaniac

diptongo (dip'ton·go) *n.m.* diphthong.
diputar (di·pu'tar) *v.t.* to depute; commission; delegate. —**diputación,** *n.f.* deputation. —**diputado,** *n.m.* deputy; representative; delegate.
dique ('di·ke) *n.m.* **1,** dike; dam. **2,** [*also,* **dique seco** *or* **de carena**] dry dock. —**dique flotante,** floating dry dock.
diré (di're) *v., fut. of* **decir.**
dirección (di·rek'θjon; -'sjon) *n.f.* **1,** direction; course; aim. **2,** management. **3,** command; advice. **4,** address. **5,** director's office. —**direccional,** *adj.* directional.
directiva (di·rek'ti·βa) *n.f.* **1,** directive. **2,** [*also,* **junta directiva**] board of governors; board of directors.
directivo (di·rek'ti·βo) *adj.* directive; directing. —*adj.* & *n.m.* executive.
directo (di'rek·to) *adj.* direct; straight.
director (di·rek'tor) *adj.* directing. —*n.m.* **1,** director; manager. **2,** editor. **3,** *music* conductor.
directorio (di·rek'to·rjo) *n.m.* **1,** directorate. **2,** *cap., hist.* Directory.
dirigible (di·ri'xi·βle) *adj.* & *n.m.* dirigible.
dirigir (di·ri'xir) *v.t.* [*pres.ind.* **dirijo** (-'ri·xo); *pres.subjve.* **dirija** (-xa)] **1,** to direct; guide; steer. **2,** to govern; manage; lead. **3,** *music* to conduct. —**dirigirse a, 1,** to address (someone). **2,** to betake oneself. —**dirigente,** *n.m.* leader (usu. one of a group of leaders).
dirimir (di·ri'mir) *v.t.* to settle; adjust.
dis- (dis) *prefix* dis-. **1,** negation: *dispar,* dissimilar. **2,** opposition; reversal: *discordancia,* discordancy. **3,** apart; asunder; in different directions: *disparar,* to shoot. **4,** *med.* dys-; difficulty; illness: *dispepsia,* dyspepsia.
discernir (dis·θer'nir; di·ser-) *v.t.* [*pres.ind.* **discierno** (dis'θjer·no; di'sjer-); *pres.subjve.* **discierna** (-na)] to discern. —**discernimiento,** *n.m.* discernment.
disciplina (dis·θi'pli·na; di·si-) *n.f.* **1,** discipline. **2,** whip; scourge.
disciplinado (dis·θi·pli'na·ðo; di·si-) *adj.* **1,** disciplined. **2,** variegated (*of flowers*).
disciplinar (dis·θi·pli'nar; di·si-) *v.t.* **1,** to discipline. **2,** to scourge.
disciplinario (dis·θi·pli'na·rjo; di·si-) *adj.* disciplinary.
discípulo (dis'θi·pu·lo; di'si-) *n.m.* disciple; pupil.
disco ('dis·ko) *n.m.* **1,** disk. **2,** phonograph record. **3,** telephone dial.
díscolo ('dis·ko·lo) *adj.* unruly; disobedient.
disconformidad (dis·kon·for·mi'ðað) *n.f.* = **desconformidad.**
discontinuar (dis·kon·ti'nwar) *v.t.* [*infl.:* **continuar**] to discontinue. —**discontinuación,** *n.f.* discontinuation; discontinuance.
discontinuo (dis·kon'ti·nwo) *adj.* discontinuous. —**discontinuidad,** *n.f.* discontinuity.
disconvenir (dis·kon·βe'nir) *v.i.* = **desconvenir.**
discordancia (dis·kor'ðan·θja; -sja) *n.f.* discord; disagreement. —**discordante,** *adj.* discordant.
discordar (dis·kor'ðar) *v.i.* **1,** to disagree. **2,** to be out of tune. —**discorde** (-'kor·ðe) *adj.* discordant. —**discordia** (-'kor·ðja) *n.f.* discord.
discoteca (dis·ko'te·ka) *n.f.* **1,** record library. **2,** record cabinet.
discreción (dis·kre'θjon; -'sjon) *n.f.* discretion. —**discrecional,** *adj.* discretionary; optional.
discrepancia (dis·kre'pan·θja; -sja) *n.f.* discrepancy. —**discrepante,** *adj.* disagreeing. —**discrepar,** *v.i.* to differ; disagree.
discreto (dis'kre·to) *adj.* **1,** discreet. **2,** discrete.
discriminar (dis·kri·mi'nar) *v.t.* to discriminate. —**discriminación,** *n.f.* discrimination.
disculpar (dis·kul'par) *v.t.* to exculpate; excuse. —**disculpa** (-'kul·pa) *n.f.* excuse; apology. —**disculpable,** *adj.* excusable.
discurrir (dis·ku'rrir) *v.i.* **1,** to ramble. **2,** to flow, as a river. **3,** to reason; reflect. **4,** to discourse. —*v.t.* **1,** to invent; scheme. **2,** to deduce; infer.
discurso (dis'kur·so) *n.m.* **1,** speech; discourse. **2,** course (*of time*).
discusión (dis·ku'sjon) *n.f.* discussion.
discutir (dis·ku'tir) *v.t.* & *i.* to discuss; argue. —**discutible,** *adj.* disputable.
disecar (di·se'kar) *v.t.* [*pres.subjve.* **diseque** (-'se·ke); *pret.* **disequé**

(-ke)] to dissect. —**disección,** *n.f.* dissection. —**disector,** *n.m.* dissector.
diseminar (di·se·mi'nar) *v.t.* to disseminate. —**diseminación,** *n.f.* dissemination.
disentería (di·sen·te'ri·a) *n.f.* dysentery.
disentir (di·sen'tir) *v.i.* [*infl.:* **sentir**] to dissent. —**disención,** *n.f.* dissension. —**disentimiento,** *n.m.* dissent; dissension.
diseñar (di·se'ɲar) v.t. to design; draw. —**diseñador,** *n.m.* designer.
diseño (di'se·ɲo) *n.m.* **1,** drawing. **2,** design; pattern.
disertar (di·ser'tar) *v.i. to* discourse. —**disertación,** *n.f.* dissertation. —**disertante,** *n.m.* speaker; lecturer.
disfavor (dis·fa'βor) *n.m.* disfavor.
disformar (dis·for'mar) *v.t.* = **deformar.** —**disforme** (-'for·me) *adj.* = **deforme.** —**disformidad,** *n.f.* = **deformidad.**
disfraz (dis'fraθ; -'fras) *n.m.* disguise. —**baile de disfraces,** costume ball.
disfrazar (dis·fra'θar; -'sar) *v.t.* [*pres.subjve.* **disfrace** (-'fra·θe; -se); *pret.* **disfracé** (-'θe; -'se)] to disguise; conceal.
disfrutar (dis·fru'tar) *v.t.* [*also v.i., fol. by* **de**] to enjoy; have the benefit of; make use of. —**disfrute** (-'fru·te) *n.m.* enjoyment; benefit; use.
disgustar (dis·ɣus'tar) *v.t.* to displease; annoy. —**disgustarse,** *v.r.* to disagree; quarrel. —**disgusto** (-'ɣus·to) *n.m.* displeasure; annoyance.
disidir (di·si'ðir) *v.i.* to dissent. —**disidencia,** *n.f.* dissidence. —**disidente,** *adj.* dissident.
disílabo (di'si·la·βo) *adj.* disyllabic. —*n.m.* disyllable.
disimetría (di·si·me'tri·a) *n.f.* dissymmetry. —**disimétrico** (-'me·tri·ko) *adj.* dissymmetrical.
disímil (di'si·mil) *adj.* dissimilar. —**disimilitud,** *n.f.* dissimilarity.
disimilar (di·si·mi'lar) *adj.* dissimilar. —*v.t.* to dissimilate. —**disimilación,** *n.f.* dissimilation.
disimular (di·si·mu'lar) *v.t.* **1,** to dissimulate; dissemble. **2,** to overlook; tolerate. —**disimulación,** *n.f.* dissimulation; hypocrisy. —**disimulado,** *adj.* sly; underhanded.
disimulo (di·si'mu·lo) *n.m.* **1,** dissimulation; deceit. **2,** tolerance.
disipar (di·si'par) *v.t.* to dissipate; scatter. —**disipación,** *n.f.* dissipation. —**disipado,** *adj.* dissipated; dissolute.
dislate (dis'la·te) *n.m.* nonsense.
dislocar (dis·lo'kar) *v.t.* [*pres. subjve.* **disloque** (-'lo·ke); *pret.* **disloqué** (-'ke)] to dislocate. —**dislocación,** *n.f.* dislocation.
disminuir (dis·mi·nu'ir) *v.t.* [*infl.:* **huir**] to diminish. —**disminución,** *n.f.* diminution.
disociar (di·so'θjar; -'sjar) *v.t.* to dissociate. —**disociación,** *n.f.* dissociation.
disolución (di·so·lu'θjon; -'sjon) *n.f.* **1,** dissolution. **2,** dissoluteness; licentiousness.
disoluto (di·so'lu·to) *adj.* dissolute.
disolver (di·sol'βer) *v.t.* [*infl.:* **absolver**] to dissolve. —**disolvente,** *adj.* & *n.m.* dissolvent; solvent.
disonar (di·so'nar) *v.i.* [*infl.:* **sonar**] to be dissonant. —**disonancia,** *n.f.* dissonance. —**disonante** *also,* **dísono** ('di·so·no) *adj.* dissonant.
dispar (dis'par) *adj.* unlike; unequal.
disparar (dis·pa'rar) *v.t.* to shoot; fire; discharge. —**disparada,** *n.f. Amer.* flight; hurried start. —**disparador,** *n.m.* trigger.
disparate (dis·pa'ra·te) *n.m.* **1** absurdity; nonsense. **2,** blunder —**disparatado,** *adj.* absurd; foolish —**disparatar,** *v.i.* to talk nonsense
disparejo (dis·pa're·xo) *adj.* **1** unlike. **2,** uneven.
disparidad (dis·pa·ri'ðað) *n.f* disparity.
disparo (dis'pa·ro) *n.m.* shooting discharge; shot.
dispendio (dis'pen·djo) *n.m.* expense, esp. an unusual or excessive one. —**dispendioso,** *adj.* expensive
dispensar (dis·pen'sar) *v.t.* **1,** to dispense. **2,** to excuse; absolve —**dispensa** (-'pen·sa) *also,* **dispensación,** *n.f.* dispensation. —**dispensable,** *adj.* dispensable.
dispensario (dis·pen'sa·rjo) *n.m* dispensary.
dispepsia (dis'pep·sja) *n.f.* dyspepsia. —**dispéptico,** (-'pep·ti·ko) *adj.* dyspeptic.
dispersar (dis·per'sar) *v.t.* to disperse; rout. —**dispersión,** *n.f.* dis

persion. —**disperso** (-'per·so) *adj.* dispersed.
displicente (dis·pli'θen·te; -'sen·te) *adj.* **1,** unpleasant. **2,** indifferent; aloof. —**displicencia,** *n.f.* indifference; aloofness.
disponer (dis·po'ner) *v.t.* & *i.* [*infl.:* **poner**] to dispose; arrange. —**disponerse,** *v.r.* **1,** to prepare oneself; dispose oneself. **2,** to line up; align oneself. —**disponer de, 1,** to have available; have at one's disposal. **2,** to make use of; put to use.
disponible (dis·po'ni·βle) *adj.* **1,** disposable. **2,** available.
disposición (dis·po·si'θjon; -'sjon) *n.f.* **1,** disposition; arrangement. **2,** disposal. **3,** aptitude; predisposition. **4,** state of health. **5,** decree; order.
dispositivo (dis·po·si'ti·βo) *n.m.* device; apparatus.
disprosio (dis'pro·sjo) *n.m.* dysprosium.
dispuesto (dis'pwes·to) *v., p.p. of* **disponer.** —*adj.* **1,** disposed; ready. **2,** apt.
disputa (dis'pu·ta) *n.f.* **1,** dispute. **2,** disputation; debate. —**sin disputa,** indisputably; beyond dispute.
disputar (dis·pu'tar) *v.t.* & *i.* to dispute. —**disputable,** *adj.* disputable. —**disputador,** *n.m.* disputant. —*adj.* disputatious.
disquisición (dis·ki·si'θjon; -'sjon) *n.f.* disquisition.
disruptivo (dis·rup'ti·βo) *adj., electricity* disruptive.
distancia (dis'tan·θja; -sja) *n.f.* distance. —**distanciar,** *v.t.* to place at a distance; separate. —**distanciarse,** *v.r.* to be aloof; be distant.
distante (dis'tan·te) *adj.* distant.
distar (dis'tar) *v.i.* to be distant (from).
distender (dis·ten'der) *v.t.* [*infl.:* **tender**] to distend. —**distensión,** *n.f.* distention.
distinguir (dis·tin'gir) *v.t.* [*infl.:* **extinguir**] to distinguish. —**distinguirse,** *v.r.* **1,** to excel. **2,** to differ; be different. —**distinción,** *n.f.* distinction. —**distinguible,** *adj.* distinguishable. —**distinguido,** *adj.* distinguished.
distinto (dis'tin·to) *adj.* distinct; different. —**distintivo,** *adj.* distinctive. —*n.m.* distinguishing mark or feature.
distorsión (dis·tor'sjon) *n.f.* distortion. —**distorsionar,** *v.t.* to distort.
distracción (dis·trak'θjon; -'sjon) *n.f.* **1,** distraction. **2,** amusement; pastime.
distraer (dis·tra'er) *v.t.* [*infl.:* **traer**] **1,** to distract; divert. **2,** to amuse; beguile. —**distraído,** *adj.* distracted; absent-minded.
distribuir (dis·tri·βu'ir) *v.t.* [*infl.:* **contribuir**] to distribute; allot. —**distribución,** *n.f.* distribution. —**distribuidor,** *adj.* distributing. —*n.m.* distributor.
distributivo (dis·tri·βu'ti·βo) *adj.* & *n.m.* distributive. —**distributor** (-'tor) *n.m.* distributor.
distrito (dis'tri·to) *n.m.* district.
disturbar (dis·tur'βar) *v.t.* to disturb. —**disturbio** (-'tur·βjo) *n.m.* disturbance.
disuadir (di·swa'ðir) *v.t.* to dissuade. —**disuasión,** *n.f.* dissuasion. —**disuasivo,** *adj.* dissuasive.
disuelto (di'swel·to) *adj.* dissolved. —*v., p.p. of* **disolver.**
disyunción (dis·jun'θjon; -'sjon) *n.f.* disjunction. —**disyuntivo** (-'ti·βo) *adj.* disjunctive.
dita ('di·ta) *n.f.* surety; bond.
diuresis (di·u're·sis) *n.f.* diuresis. —**diurético** (-'re·ti·ko) *adj.* & *n.m.* diuretic.
diurno ('djur·no) *adj.* diurnal.
diva ('di·βa) *n.f.* **1,** diva. **2,** *poet.* goddess.
divagar (di·βa'ɣar) *v.i.* [*infl.:* **vagar**] to digress; roam. —**divagación,** *n.f.* digression.
divalente (di·βa'len·te) *adj.* = **bivalente.**
diván (di'βan) *n.m.* divan.
divergir (di·βer'xir) *v.i.* [*infl.:* **dirigir**] to diverge. —**divergencia,** *n.f.* divergence. —**divergente,** *adj.* divergent.
diversificar (di·βer·si·fi'kar) *v.t.* [*pres.subjve.* **diversifique** (-'fi·ke); *pret.* **diversifiqué** (-'ke)] to diversify. —**diversificación,** *n.f.* diversification.
diversión (di·βer'sjon) *n.f.* **1,** diversion. **2,** amusement.
diverso (di'βer·so) *adj.* diverse. —**diversidad,** *n.f.* diversity.
divertir (di·βer'tir) *v.t.* [*infl.:* **advertir**] **1,** to turn aside; divert. **2,** to amuse. —**divertirse,** *v.r.* to enjoy oneself; have a good time. —**divertido,** *adj.* diverting; amusing.

dividendo (di·βi'ðen·do) *n.m.* dividend.

dividir (di·βi'ðir) *v.t.* **1,** to divide. **2,** to separate.

divieso (di'βje·so) *n.m.* boil (*sore*).

divinidad (di·βi·ni'ðað) *n.f.* **1,** divinity; deity. **2,** *cap.* God. **3,** *colloq.* a beautiful woman; an exquisite object; a charming expression.

divinizar (di·βi·ni'θar; -'sar) *v.t.* [*pres.subjve.* **divinice** (-'ni·θe; -se); *pret.* **diviniсé** (-'θe; -'se)] to deify.

divino (di'βi·no) *adj.* divine.

divisa (di'βi·sa) *n.f.* **1,** badge; emblem; motto. **2,** currency (esp. foreign).

divisar (di·βi'sar) *v.t.* to glimpse; espy.

divisible (di·βi'si·βle) *adj.* divisible. —**divisibilidad,** *n.f.* divisibility.

división (di·βi'sjon) *n.f.* division. —**divisional,** *adj.* divisional.

divisivo (di·βi'si·βo) *adj.* divisive.

divisor (di·βi'sor) *adj.* dividing. —*n.m.* divisor.

divisorio (di·βi'so·rjo) *adj.* dividing. —**línea divisoria,** divide.

divorciar (di·βor'θjar; -'sjar) *v.t.* to divorce. —**divorciarse,** *v.r.* to be divorced; get a divorce. —**divorciado,** *n.m.* divorcé. —**divorciada,** *n.f.* divorcée.

divorcio (di'βor·θjo; -sjo) *n.m.* divorce.

divulgar (di·βul'ɣar) *v.t.* [*pres. subjve.* **divulgue** (-'βul·ɣe); *pret.* **divulgué** (-'ɣe)] to divulge; spread abroad. —**divulgación,** *n.f.* divulgence.

-dizo ('ði·θo; -so) *fem.* **-diza** (-θa; -sa) *suffix, var. of* **-izo**: *olvidadizo,* forgetful.

do (do) **n.m.,** *music* do; C.

dobladillo (do·βla'ði·ʎo; -jo) *n.m.* hem.

doblado (do'βla·ðo) *adj.* **1,** stocky; hefty. **2,** double-dealing; two-faced. **3,** uneven, as ground.

doblar (do'βlar) *v.t.* **1,** to bend; fold. **2,** to double. **3,** to toll (a bell). **4,** to turn, as a corner. **5,** *motion pictures* to dub. —**doblarse,** *v.r.* to bend; stoop.

doble ('do·βle) *adj.* **1,** double; twofold. **2,** two-faced. —*adv.* double; doubly. —*n.m.* **1,** double. **2,** fold. **3,** hem. **4,** toll (*of a bell*).

doblegar (do·βle'ɣar) *v.t.* [*pres. subjve.* **doblegue** (-'βle·ɣe); *pret.* **doblegué** (-'ɣe)] **1,** to bend; fold. **2,** to cause to yield; sway. —**doblegarse,** *v.r.* to bend; yield. —**doblegable,** *adj.* pliable; flexible.

doblez (do'βleθ; -'βles) *n.m.* **1,** fold. **2,** hem. **3,** trouser cuff. **4,** [*also fem.*] duplicity.

doce ('do·θe; -se) *adj.* & *n.m.* twelve.

docena (do'θe·na; -'se·na) *n.f.* dozen. —**docena del fraile,** baker's dozen.

doceno (do'θe·no; -'se·no) *adj.* twelfth.

docente (do'θen·te; do'sen-) *adj.* **1,** educational. **2,** teaching.

dócil ('do·θil; -sil) *adj.* docile; obedient. —**docilidad,** *n.f.* docility.

doctor (dok'tor) *n.m.* doctor. —**doctorado,** *n.m.* doctorate. —**doctorar,** *v.t.* to confer a doctor's degree on.

doctrina (dok'tri·na) *n.f.* doctrine. —**doctrinal,** *adj.* doctrinal. —**doctrinario,** *adj.* & *n.m.* doctrinaire.

documentar (do·ku·men'tar) *v.t.* **1,** to document. **2,** to inform; brief. —**documentación,** *n.f.* documentation.

documento (do·ku'men·to) *n.m.* document. —**documental,** *adj.* & *n.m.* documentary; documental.

dodo ('do·ðo) *also,* **dodó** (do'ðo) *n.m.* dodo.

dogal (do'ɣal) *n.m.* **1,** halter. **2,** dog collar. **3,** hangman's noose.

dogma ('doɣ·ma) *n.m.* dogma. —**dogmático** (-'ma·ti·ko) *adj.* dogmatic. —**dogmatismo** (-'tis·mo) *n.m.* dogmatism.

dólar ('do·lar) *n.m.* dollar.

dolencia (do'len·θja; -sja) *n.f.* ailment; disease.

doler (do'ler) *v.i.* [*pres.ind.* **duelo;** *pres.subjve.* **duela**] to pain; hurt. —**dolerse,** *v.r., usu. fol. by* **de, 1,** to regret. **2,** to sympathize (with). **3,** to complain (of).

doliente (do'ljen·te) *adj.* **1,** suffering; sick. **2,** sorrowful. —*n.m.* & *f.* **1,** sufferer. **2,** mourner.

dolo ('do·lo) *n.m.* fraud; deceit. —**doloso,** *adj.* fraudulent; deceitful.

dolor (do'lor) *n.m.* **1,** pain. **2,** affliction. **3,** grief; sorrow.

dolorido (do·lo'ri·ðo) *adj.* pained; in pain.

doloroso (do·lo'ro·so) *adj.* painful.

doma ('do·ma) *n.f.* breaking; taming (*as of animals*).

domar (do'mar) *v.t.* to tame; subdue. —**domador,** *n.m.* tamer.
domeñar (do·me'ɲar) *v.t.* to tame; subdue; dominate.
domesticar (do·mes·ti'kar) *v.t.* [*pres.subjve.* **domestique** (-'ti·ke); *pret.* **domestiqué** (-'ke)] to domesticate.
doméstico (do'mes·ti·ko) *adj.* & *n.m.* domestic. —**domesticidad** (-θi·'ðað; -si'ðað) *n.f.* domesticity.
domiciliar (do·mi·θi'ljar; -si'ljar) *v.t.* to house; lodge. —**domiciliarse,** *v.r.* **1,** to take up residence. **2,** to reside.
domicilio (do·mi'θi·ljo; -'si·ljo) *n.m.* domicile; residence.
dominante (do·mi'nan·te) *adj.* **1,** dominant. **2,** domineering.
dominar (do·mi'nar) *v.t.* to dominate; master; control. —*v.i.* to stand out; be conspicuous. —**dominación,** *n.f.* domination; dominance.
dómine ('do·mi·ne) *n.m.* schoolmaster; pedant.
domingo (do'min·go) *n.m.* Sunday. —**dominical,** (-mi·ni'kal) *adj.* dominical; Sunday (*attrib.*).
dominicano (do·mi·ni'ka·no) *adj.* & *n.m.* Dominican.
domínico (do·mi'ni·ko) *adj.* & *n.m.* Dominican (*of the order of St. Dominic*).
dominio (do'mi·njo) *n.m.* **1,** dominion. **2,** domination. **3,** domain. **4,** *law* fee; ownership.
dominó (do·mi'no) *also,* **dómino** ('do·mi·no) *n.m.* **1,** domino. **2,** dominoes.
domo ('do·mo) *n.m.* dome; cupola.
don (don) *n.m.* **1,** gift; talent. **2,** *cap.,* title of respect; Don.
donador (do·na'ðor) *n.m.* donor; giver.
donaire (do'nai·re) *n.m.* **1,** grace; elegance. **2,** wit; witticism.
donairoso (do·nai'ro·so) *adj.* **1,** graceful; elegant. **2,** witty; clever.
donar (do'nar) *v.t.* to donate; give; bestow. —**donación,** *n.f., also,* **donativo,** *n.m.* donation. —**donante,** *adj.* donating. —*n.m.* & *f.* donor.
donatario (do·na'ta·rjo) *n.m.* grantee; donee.
doncella (don'θe·ʎa; -'se·ja) *n.f.* maiden; maid. —**doncellez,** *n.f.* maidenhood.
donde ('don·de) *rel.adv.* where. —*prep., colloq.* at, in *or* to the house or place of business of. —**a donde,** where; whither. —**de donde,** from where; whence. —**por donde,** whereby. —**dónde,** *interrog.* & *exclamatory adv.* where? where!
dondequiera (don·de'kje·ra) *indef.* & *rel. adv.* anywhere; everywhere; wherever.
dondiego (don'dje·ɣo) *n.m.* morning-glory. *Also,* **dondiego de día.**
donoso (do'no·so) *adj.* graceful; charming. —**donosura,** *n.f.* grace; charm.
doña ('do·ɲa) *n.f.* **1,** duenna. **2,** *cap.* title of respect; Doña.
doquier (do'kjer) *also,* **doquiera** (-'kje·ra) *adv.* = **dondequiera.**
-dor ('ðor) *suffix* **1,** *forming nouns expressing* agency; instrument: *vendedor,* salesman; *batidor,* beater. **2,** *forming adjectives expressing* tendency: *encantador,* enchanting.
dorado (do'ra·ðo) *adj.* gilded; golden. —*n.m.* **1,** gilt; gilding. **2,** *ichthy.* dory.
dorar (do'rar) *v.t.* **1,** to gild. **2,** to palliate. **3,** *cookery* to brown.
dórico ('do·ri·ko) *adj.* Doric.
dormilón (dor·mi'lon) *n.m.* sleepyhead.
dormir (dor'mir) *v.i.* [*pres.ind.* **duermo;** *pres.subjve.* **duerma;** *pret.* **dormí, durmió;** *ger.* **durmiendo**] to sleep. —**dormirse,** *v.r.* to fall asleep. —**dormir a pierna suelta,** *colloq.* to sleep soundly.
dormitar (dor·mi'tar) *v.i.* to nap; doze.
dormitorio (dor·mi'to·rjo) *n.m.* **1,** dormitory. **2,** bedroom.
dorso ('dor·so) *n.m.* back. —**dorsal,** *adj.* dorsal.
dos (dos) *adj.* & *n.m.* two.
doscientos (dos'θjen·tos; do·'sjen·tos) *adj.* & *n.m.pl.* [*fem.* **-tas**] two hundred. —*adj.* two hundredth.
dosel (do'sel) *n.m.* canopy (*usu. over an altar, throne, statue, etc.*).
dosificar (do·si·fi'kar) *v.t.* [*pres. subjve.* **dosifique** (-'fi·ke); *pret.* **dosifiqué** (-'ke)] *v.t.* to dose; measure out (medicine) in doses. —**dosificación,** *n.f.* dosage.
dosis ('do·sis) *n.f.* dose; dosage.
dotación (do·ta'θjon; -'sjon) *n.f.* **1,** endowment. **2,** equipment. **3,** staff; crew.
dotal (do'tal) *adj.* of or pert. to endowment: *póliza dotal,* endowment policy.
dotar (do'tar) *v.t.* **1,** to endow.

2, to equip; provide. —**dote** ('do·te) *n.m.* & *f.* dower; dowry. —**dotes,** *n.f.pl.* talents; natural gifts.
doxología (dok·so·lo'xi·a) *n.f.* doxology.
doy (doi) *v., 1st pers.sing. pres.ind. of* **dar.**
dozavo (do'θa·βo; -'sa·βo) *adj.* & *n.m.* twelfth.
dracma ('drak·ma) *n.f.* **1,** drachma. **2,** dram.
draga ('dra·ɣa) *n.f.* dredge.
dragado (dra'ɣa·ðo) *n.m.* **1,** dredging. **2,** dragging; drag.
dragaminas (dra·ɣa'mi·nas) *n.m.sing.* & *pl.* mine sweeper.
dragar (dra'ɣar) *v.t.* [*pres.subjve.* **drague** ('dra·ɣe); *pret.* **dragué** (-'ɣe)] to dredge; drag.
dragón (dra'ɣon) *n.m.* **1,** dragon. **2,** dragoon.
drama ('dra·ma) *n.m.* drama. —**dramática** (-'ma·ti·ka) *n.f.* dramatics. —**dramático,** *adj.* dramatic. —**dramaturgo** (-'tur·ɣo) *n.m.* dramatist; playwright.
dramatizar (dra·ma·ti'θar; -'sar) *v.t.* [*pres.subjve.* **dramatice** (-'ti·θe; -se); *pret.* **dramaticé** (-'θe; -'se)] to dramatize. —**dramatización,** *n.f.* dramatization.
drástico ('dras·ti·ko) *adj.* drastic.
drenaje (dre'na·xe) *n.m.* drainage.
drenar (dre'nar) *v.t.* to drain. —**drenaje,** *n.m.* drainage.
dríada ('dri·a·ða) *also,* **dríade** (-ðe) *n.f.* dryad.
driblar (dri'βlar) *v.t.* & *i., sports* to dribble. —**dribling** ('dri·βlin) *n.m.* dribble; dribbling.
dril (dril) *n.m.* **1,** drill (*cloth*). **2,** *zool.* mandrill.
driza ('dri·θa; -sa) *n.f.* halyard.
droga ('dro·ɣa) *n.f.* drug.
droguería (dro·ɣe'ri·a) *n.f.* **1,** drugstore. **2,** drug trade. **3,** hardware store.
droguista (dro'ɣis·ta) *n.m.* **1,** [*also,* **droguero** (-'ɣe·ro)] druggist. **2,** *Amer.,* impostor; cheat.
dromedario (dro·me'ða·rjo) *n.m.* dromedary.
druida ('drui·ða) *n.m.* druid.
dual (du'al) *adj.* dual. —**dualidad,** *n.f.* duality. —**dualismo,** *n.m.* dualism. —**dualístico,** *adj.* dualistic.
ducado (du'ka·ðo) *n.m.* **1,** duchy; dukedom. **2,** ducat.
ducal (du'kal) *adj.* ducal.
ducentésimo (du·θen'te·si·mo; du·sen-) *adj.* & *n.m.* two-hundredth.
dúctil ('duk·til) *adj.* ductile. —**ductilidad,** *n.f.* ductility.
ducha ('du·tʃa) *n.f.* **1,** shower bath. **2,** douche.
duchar (du'tʃar) *v.t.* **1,** to douche. **2,** to give a shower bath to.
ducho ('du·tʃo) *adj.* skillful.
duda ('du·ða) *n.f.* doubt.
dudar (du'ðar) *v.t.* & *i.* to doubt. —**dudar de,** to distrust.
dudoso (du'ðo·so) *adj.* doubtful; dubious.
duela ('dwe·la) *v., pres.subjve. of* **doler.**
duelo ('dwe·lo) *v., pres.ind. of* **doler.**
duelo ('dwe·lo) *n.m.* **1,** duel. **2,** sorrow; affliction; bereavement. **3,** mourning. **4,** group of mourners. —**duelista,** *n.m.* duelist.
duende ('dwen·de) *n.m.* goblin; fairy.
dueña ('dwe·ɲa) *n.f.* **1,** owner; mistress. **2,** duenna.
dueño ('due·ɲo) *n.m.* owner; master; landlord.
duerma ('dwer·ma) *v., pres. subjve. of* **dormir.**
duermo ('dwer·mo) *v., pres.ind. of* **dormir.**
dueto (du'e·to) *n.m.* duo; duet.
dulce ('dul·θe; -se) *adj.* **1,** sweet. **2,** gentle; mild. **3,** fresh, as water. —*n.m.* **1,** candy; sweetmeat. **2,** preserves. —**dulcería,** *n.f.* candy shop.
dulcero (dul'θe·ro; -'se·ro) *adj., colloq.* fond of sweets; having a sweet tooth. —*n.m.* **1,** confectioner. **2,** candy dish.
dulcificar (dul·θi·fi'kar; dul·si-) *v.t.* [*pres.subjve.* **dulcifique** (-'fi·ke); *pret.* **dulcifiqué** (-'ke)] to sweeten. —**dulcificante,** *adj.* sweetening. —*n.m.* sweetener.
dulzura (dul'θu·ra; -'su·ra) *n.m.* **1,** sweetness. **2,** gentleness; mildness. **3,** pleasantness. *Also,* **dulzor** (-'θor; -'sor) *n.m.*
duna ('du·na) *n.f.* dune.
dúo ('du·o) *n.m.* duet; duo.
duo- (du·o) *prefix* duo-; two: *duodecimal,* duodecimal.
duodecimal (du·o·ðe·θi'mal; si·'mal) *adj.* duodecimal.
duodécimo (du·o'de·θi·mo; -si·mo) *adj.* & *n.m.* twelfth.
duodeno (dwo'ðe·no) *adj.* twelfth. —*n.m., anat.* duodenum. —**duodenal,** *adj.* duodenal.

duplicar (du·pli'kar) *v.t.* [*pres. subjve.* **duplique** (-'pli·ke); *pret.* **dupliqué** (-'ke)] **1,** to duplicate. **2,** to repeat. **3,** to double. —**duplicación,** *n.f.* duplication; doubling. —**duplicado,** *n.m.* & *adj.* duplicate. —**duplicador,** *adj.* duplicating. —*n.m.* duplicator.

duplicidad (du·pli·θi'ðað; -si·'ðað) *n.f.* duplicity.

duplo ('du·plo) *adj.* & *n.m.* double; duplex.

duque ('du·ke) *n.m.* duke. —**duquesa,** *n.f.* duchess.

dura ('du·ra) *n.f., colloq.* durability.

-dura ('ðu·ra) *suffix, forming nouns denoting* **1,** action; result: *bordadura,* embroidery. **2,** collectivity: *brochadura,* set of hooks and eyes.

durable (du'ra·βle) *adj.* durable. —**durabilidad,** *n.f.* durability.

duración (du·ra'θjon; -'sjon) *n.f.* duration.

duradero (du·ra'ðe·ro) *adj.* durable.

duramadre (du·ra'ma·ðre) *n.f.* dura mater. *Also,* **duramáter** (-'ma·ter).

durante (du'ran·te) *prep.* during.

durar (du'rar) *v.i.* to last; endure.

durazno (du'raθ·no; du'ras-) *n.m.* **1,** peach. **2,** [*also,* **duraznero**] peach tree.

dureza (du're·θa; -sa) *n.f.* **1,** hardness. **2,** harshness; cruelty. **3,** obstinacy.

durmiendo (dur'mjen·do) *v., ger. of* **dormir.** —*adj.* sleeping; dormant.

durmiente (dur'mjen·te) *v., pr.p. or* **dormir.** —*adj.* sleeping; dormant. —*n.m.* **1,** *archit.* girder; crossbeam. **2,** *Amer.* railroad tie; sleeper.

durmió (dur'mjo) *v., 3rd pers. sing.pret. of* **dormir.**

duro ('du·ro) *adj.* **1,** hard; solid. **2,** harsh; oppressive; cruel. **3,** stingy. **4,** obstinate. **5,** hard-boiled (*of eggs; also fig. sense*). —*adv.* hard. —*n.m.* a Spanish coin worth 5 pesetas; duro. —**a duras penas, 1,** with great difficulty. **2,** hardly; scarcely. —**duro de corazón,** *also,* **de corazón duro,** hardhearted. —**duro de oído, 1,** hard of hearing. **2,** tone deaf. —**duro de oreja,** hard of hearing. —**ser duro para (con),** to be hard on. —**tomar las duras con las maduras,** *colloq.* to take the good with the bad.

E

E, e (e) *n.f.* 6th letter of the Spanish alphabet.

e (e) *conj.* and. *Used in place of* **y** *before words beginning with* i *or with* hi *when not followed by* e.

e- (e) *prefix, var. of* **ex-**: *emerger,* emerge; *evasión,* evasion.

¡ea! ('e·a) *interj.* heigh!; heigh-ho!; ho!; now!; well!; there now! *Also, Amer.,* **¡epa!**

-ear (e'ar) *suffix, forming verbs from nouns or adjectives: telefonear,* to telephone; *blanquear,* to whiten.

ebanista (e·βa'nis·ta) *n.m.* cabinetmaker.

ebanistería (e·βa·nis·te'ri·a) *n.f.* **1,** cabinetwork. **2,** cabinetmaker's shop. **3,** cabinetmaking.

ébano ('e·βa·no) *n.m.* ebony.

ebrio ('e·βrjo) *adj.* inebriated; intoxicated; drunk. —**ebriedad,** *n.f.* inebriety; intoxication; drunkenness.

ebullición (e·βu·ʎi'θjon; e·βu·ji'sjon) *also,* **ebulición** (e·βu·li-) *n.f.* ebullition; boiling.

-ececico (e·θe'θi·ko; e·se'si·ko), *fem.* **-ececica** (-ka); **-ececillo** (e·θe·'θi·ʎo; e·se'si·jo), *fem.* **-ececilla** (-ʎa; -ja); **-ececito** (e·θe'θi·to; e·se'si·to), *fem.* **-ececita** (-ta); **-ecezuelo** (e·θe'θwe·lo; e·se'swe·lo), *fem.* **-ecezuela** (-la) *suffixes, forming diminutives: piececico, piececillo, etc.* little foot.

-ecer (e'θer; e'ser) *suffix* -esce; *forming verbs of inceptive or inchoative sense: convalecer,* convalesce.

-ecico (e'θi·ko; e'si·ko) *fem.* **-ecica** (-ka) *suffix, forming diminutives: puentecico,* small bridge.

-ecillo (e'θi·ʎo; e'si·jo) *fem.* **-ecilla** (-ʎa; -ja) *suffix, forming* *diminutives: geniecillo,* little genie.

-ecito (e'θi·to; e'si·to) *fem.* **-ecita** (-ta) *suffix, forming diminutives: hombrecito,* little man.

ecléctico (e'klek·ti·ko) *adj.* & *n.m.* eclectic.

eclesiástico (e·kle'sjas·ti·ko) *adj.* ecclesiastical. —*n.m.* priest; clergyman; ecclesiastic.

eclipse (e'klip·se) *n.m.* eclipse. —**eclipsar,** *v.t.* to eclipse. —**eclipsarse,** *v.r.* to vanish; disappear.

eclíptico (e'klip·ti·ko) *adj.* ecliptic. —**eclíptica,** *n.f.* ecliptic.

écloga ('ek·lo·ɣa) *n.f.* eclogue.

eco ('e·ko) *n.m.* echo.

ecología (e·ko·lo'xi·a) *n.f.* ecology. —**ecológico** (-'lo·xi·ko) *adj.* ecological. —**ecólogo** (e'ko·lo·ɣo) *n.m.* ecologist.

economía (e·ko·no'mi·a) *n.f.* **1,** economy. **2,** economics. —**economías,** *n.f.pl.* savings. —**economista,** *n.m.* & *f.* economist.

económico (e·ko'no·mi·ko) *adj.* **1,** economic. **2,** economical; thrifty.

economizar (e·ko·no·mi'θar; -'sar) *v.t.* & *i.* [*pres.subjve.* **economice** ('mi·θe; -se); *pret.* **economicé** (-'θe; -'se)] to economize; save.

ecónomo (e'ko·no·mo) *n.m.* **1,** curator. **2,** trustee. **3,** *Amer.* economist.

ecto- (ek·to) *prefix* ecto-; outer; external: *ectodermo,* ectoderm.

-ectomía (ek·to'mi·a) *suffix* -ectomy; excision; surgical removal: *apendectomía,* appendectomy.

ectoplasma (ek·to'plas·ma) *n.m.* ectoplasm.

ecuable (e'kwa·βle) *adj.* equable.

ecuación (e·kwa'θjon; -'sjon) *n.f.* equation.

ecuador (e·kwa'ðor) *n.m.* equator.

ecuánime (e'kwa·ni·me) *adj.* **1,** even-tempered; calm. **2,** fair; impartial. —**ecuanimidad,** *n.f.* equanimity.

ecuatorial (e·kwa·to'rjal) *adj.* equatorial.

ecuestre (e'kwes·tre) *adj.* equestrian.

ecuménico (e·ku'me·ni·ko) *adj.* ecumenical.

eczema (ek'θe·ma; ek'se-) *n.f.* eczema.

echadillo (e·tʃa'ði·ʎo; -jo) *n.m.* foundling.

echar (e'tʃar) *v.t.* **1,** to cast; throw; hurl. **2,** to pour; pour out. **3,** to turn *or* cast away. **4,** to eject; throw out. **5,** to put *or* throw in *or* on. **6,** to lay *or* set down. **7,** to deal out; distribute. **8,** to turn. **9,** to impute; ascribe. **10,** to move. **11,** to tell (fortunes). **12,** to discharge; dismiss. **13,** to sprout; put forth; grow. **14,** to emit; exude. **15,** to infer; gather; guess. **16,** to utter; pronounce. —*v.i.* **1,** to lean; tend; pull; turn (*in a certain direction*). **2,** to sprout. —**echarse,** *v.r.* **1,** to lie down. **2,** to throw *or* hurl oneself; plunge. **3,** to sit, as a hen. **4,** to devote oneself. —**echar a,** *fol. by inf.* to start. —**echar a perder,** to spoil. —**echar a pique,** to sink (a ship). —**echar de menos,** to miss. —**echar de ver,** to notice. —**echar el guante a,** to grab; arrest. —**echar en saco roto,** to disregard. —**echar mano a,** to grab. —**echarse a (reír, llorar,** *etc.*), to burst out (laughing, crying, etc.). —**echársela** (*or* **echárselas**) **de,** to boast of; boast of being.

echazón (e·tʃa'θon; -'son) *n.f.* jettison; jetsam.

edad (e'ðað) *n.f.* age. —**edad media,** Middle Ages. —**mayor de edad,** of age. —**menor de edad,** underage.

-edad (e'ðað) *suffix, var. of* **-dad** *in trisyllabic nouns: brevedad,* brevity; *suciedad,* dirtiness.

-edal (e'ðal) *suffix, forming nouns expressing* place where something abounds: *bojedal,* growth of boxwood.

edecán (e·ðe'kan) *n.f.* aide-de-camp; aide.

Edén (e'ðen) *n.m.* Eden; paradise.

-edero (e'ðe·ro), *fem.* **-edera** (-ra) *suffix, var. of* **-dero**: *comedero,* feeding trough; *raedera,* scraper: *valedero,* valid.

edición (e·ði'θjon; -'sjon) *n.f.* **1,** edition; issue. **2,** publication.

edicto (e'ðik·to) *n.m.* edict.

edificación (e·ði·fi·ka'θjon; -'sjon) *n.f.* **1,** edification. **2,** building; erection.

edificar (e·ði·fi'kar) *v.t.* & *i.* [*pres. subjve.* **edifique** (-'fi·ke); *pret.* **edifiqué** (-'ke)] **1,** to edify. **2,** to build; erect. —**edificador,** *adj.* edifying. —*n.m.* builder.

edificio (e·ði'fi·θjo; -sjo) *n.m.* edifice; building.

editar (e·ði'tar) *v.t.* to publish.

editor (e·ði'tor) *n.m.* **1,** publisher;

editor. **2,** *colloq.* plagiarist. —*adj.* publishing; editing.
editorial (e·ði·to'rjal) *adj.* & *n.m.* editorial.
-edizo (e'ði·θo; -so), *fem.* **-ediza** (-θa; -sa) *suffix, var. of* **-izo**: *acogedizo,* easy to gather; *advenedizo,* strange.
-edo ('e·ðo), *fem.* **-eda** (-ða) *suffix, forming collective nouns: robledo,* oak grove; *alameda,* poplar grove.
-edor (e'ðor), *fem.* **-edora** (e'ðo·ra) *suffix, var. of* **-dor**: *vendedor,* seller; *tenedor,* holder; fork; *bebedor,* given to drink.
edredón (e·ðre'ðon) *n.m.* **1,** eider down. **2,** comforter.
-édrico ('e·ðri·ko) *suffix* -hedral; *forming adjectives corresponding to nouns ending in* **-edro**: *poliédrico,* polyhedral.
-edro ('e·ðro) *suffix* -hedron; *forming nouns denoting geometrical solid figures with a specified number of faces: poliedro,* polyhedron.
educación (e·ðu·ka'θjon; -'sjon) *n.f.* education; training; breeding.
educar (e·ðu'kar) *v.t.* [*pres.subjve.* **eduque** (-'ðu·ke); *pret.* **eduqué** (-'ke)] to educate; train. —**educador,** *n.* educator. —*adj.* educating. —**educativo,** *adj.* educational.
-edura (e'ðu·ra) *suffix, var. of* **-dura**: *barredura,* sweeping.
efectivamente (e·fek·ti·βa·'men·te) *adv.* **1,** effectively. **2,** really.
efectivo (e·fek'ti·βo) *adj.* **1,** effective. **2,** true; certain; actual. —*n.m.* cash.
efecto (e'fek·to) *n.m.* **1,** effect. **2,** impression. —**efectos,** *n.m.pl.* **1,** assets. **2,** merchandise; chattels; goods. **3,** drafts. —**efectos a pagar,** bills receivable.
efectuar (e·fek'twar) *v.t.* [*pres. ind.* **efectúo** (-'tu·o); *pres.subjve.* **efectúe** (-'tu·e)] to effect; effectuate; carry out; accomplish. —**efectuación,** *n.f.* accomplishment.
efemérides (e·fe'me·ri·ðes) *n.f. pl.* diary (*sing.*).
efervescencia (e·fer·βes'θen·θja; -βe'sen·sja) *n.f.* **1,** effervescence. **2,** ardor; ebullience. —**efervescente,** *adj.* effervescent.
eficaz (e·fi'kaθ; -'kas) *adj.* effective. —**eficacia,** *n.f.* efficacy.
eficiente (e·fi'θjen·te; -'sjen·te) *adj.* efficient. —**eficiencia,** *n.f.* efficiency.
efigie (e'fi·xje) *n.f.* effigy.
efímero (e'fi·me·ro) *adj.* ephemeral.
eflorescencia (e·flo·res'θen·θja; -re'sen·sja) *n.f.* efflorescence. —**eflorescente,** *adj.* efflorescent.
efluvio (e'flu·βjo) *n.m.* efluvium.
efusión (e·fu'sjon) *n.f.* effusion. —**efusivo,** *adj.* effusive.
égida ('e·ɣi·ða) *also,* **egida** (e'ɣi-) *n.f.* aegis; egis.
egipcio (e'xip·θjo; -sjo) *adj.* & *n.m.* Egyptian.
eglantina (e·ɣlan'ti·na) *n.f.* sweetbrier; eglantine.
égloga ('e·ɣlo·ɣa) *also* **écloga** ('e·klo-) *n.f.* eclogue.
ego ('e·ɣo) *n.m.* ego.
egoísmo (e·ɣo'is·mo) *n.m.* selfishness; egoism. —**egoísta,** *adj.* selfish; egoistic. —*n.m.* & *f.* egoist.
egolatría (e·ɣo·la'tri·a) *n.f.* self-worship.
egotismo (e·ɣo'tis·mo) *n.m.* egotism. —**egotista,** *n.m.* & *f.* egotist. —*adj.* egotistic.
egregio (e'ɣre·xjo) *adj.* illustrious; excellent.
egresar (e·ɣre'sar) *v.t., Amer.* to graduate (*from school*).
egreso (e'ɣre·so) *n.m.* **1,** expense; debit. **2,** *Amer.* graduation.
¡eh! (e) *interj.* eh!; here!; hey!
eider (e'i·ðer) *n.m.* eider; eider duck.
einsteinio (ain'stai·njo) *n.m.* einsteinium.
eje ('e·xe) *n.m.* **1,** axis. **2,** axle. **3,** shaft; spindle; arbor. **4,** *fig.* crucial point; crux.
ejecutar (e·xe·ku'tar) *v.t.* **1,** to execute; perform; carry out. **2,** *law* to attach; seize. **3,** to put to death. —**ejecución,** *n.f.* execution.
ejecutivo (e·xe·ku'ti·βo) *adj.* & *n.m.* executive.
ejecutor (e·xe·ku'tor) *adj.* executive. —*n.m.* **1,** executor. **2,** executive. —**ejecutor de la justicia,** executioner.
ejecutora (e·xe·ku'to·ra) *n.f.* **1,** executrix. **2,** executive.
ejecutorio (e·xe·ku'to·rjo) *adj., law* executory; effective; in force.
¡ejem! (e'xem) *interj.* hem!; ahem!
ejemplar (e·xem'plar) *adj.* exemplary. —*n.m.* **1,** pattern; model. **2,** example. **3,** prototype; sample.

4, copy (*of a book*). —**sin ejemplar**, exceptional.
ejemplificar (e·xem·pli·fi'kar) *v.t.* [*pres.subjve.* **ejemplifique** (-'fi·ke); *pret.* **ejemplifiqué** (-'ke)] to exemplify. —**ejemplificación**, *n.f.* exemplification.
ejemplo (e'xem·plo) *n.m.* 1, example. 2, pattern; exemplar. —**por ejemplo**, for example.
ejercer (e·xer'θer; -'ser) *v.t.* [*pres. ind.* **ejerzo** (-'xer·θo; -so); *pres. subjve.* **ejerza** (-θa; -sa)] 1, to practice; exercise; perform. 2, to exert.
ejercicio (e·xer'θi·θjo; -'si·sjo) *n.m.* 1, exercise. 2, practice. 3, profession; task. 4, military drill. 5, fiscal year.
ejercitar (e·xer·θi'tar; -si'tar) *v.t.* 1, to exercise. 2, to train; drill.
ejército (e'xer·θi·to; -si·to) *n.m.* army.
ejido (e'xi·ðo) *n.m.* public land; common.
-ejo ('e·xo) *suffix, forming nouns and adjectives, usu. with derog. meaning: caballejo,* nag; *medianejo,* fair to middling.
el (el) *def.art. masc.sing.* the. —*dem. pron. masc.sing.* that; the one (that).
él *pers.pron. masc.sing.* 1, *subj. of a verb* he; it. 2, *obj. of a prep.* him; it.
elaboración (e·la·βo·ra'θjon; -'sjon) *n.f.* 1, elaboration. 2, manufacture.
elaborado (e·la·βo'ra·ðo) *adj.* 1, elaborate. 2, manufactured.
elaborar (e·la·βo'rar) *v.t.* 1, to elaborate. 2, to manufacture.
elación (e·la'θjon; -'sjon) *n.f.* 1, haughtiness; pride. 2, elevation; grandeur. 3, magnanimity. 4, ornateness of style.
elástico (e'las·ti·ko) *adj.* & *n.m.* elastic. —**elásticos**, *n.m.pl.* suspenders. —**elasticidad** (-θi'ðað; -si·'ðað) *n.f.* elasticity; resiliency.
elección (e·lek'θjon; -'sjon) *n.f.* 1, election. 2, choice; selection.
electo (e'lek·to) *adj.* & *n.m.* elect; chosen. —**electivo**, *adj.* elective.
elector (e·lek'tor) *adj.* electing. —*n.m.* elector. —**electorado**, *n.m.* electorate. —**electoral**, *adj.* electoral.
electricidad (e·lek·tri·θi'ðað; -si'ðað) *n.f.* electricity.
electricista (e·lek·tri'θis·ta· -'sis·ta) *n.m.* electrician.
eléctrico (e'lek·tri·ko) *adj.* electric; electrical.
electrificar (e·lek·tri·fi'kar) *v.t.* [*pres.subjve.* **electrifique** (-'fi·ke); *pret.* **electrifiqué** (-'ke)] to electrify; provide with electricity. —**electrificación**, *n.f.* electrification.
electrizar (e·lek·tri'θar; -'sar) *v.t.* [*pres.subjve.* **electrice** (-'tri·θe; -se); *pret.* **electricé** (-'θe; -'se)] to electrify; stimulate. —**electrización**, *n.f.* electrification; stimulation.
electro (e'lek·tro) *n.m.* 1, amber. 2, electrum.
electro- (e·lek·tro) *prefix* electro-; electricity: *electrocardiograma,* electrocardiogram.
electrocutar (e·lek·tro·ku'tar) *v.t.* to electrocute. —**electrocución**, *n.f.* electrocution. —**electrocutor**, *n.m.* electrocutionist.
electrodo (e·lek'tro·ðo) *n.m.* electrode.
electrolizar (e·lek·tro·li'θar; -'sar) *v.t.* [*pres.subjve.* **electrolice** (-'li·θe; -se); *pret.* **electrolicé** (-'θe; -'se)] to electrolyze. —**electrólisis** (-'tro·li·sis) *n.f.* electrolysis. —**electrolítico** (-'li·ti·ko) *adj.* electrolytic. —**electrólito** (-'tro·li·to) *n.m.* electrolyte.
electromagnético (e·lek·tro·maɣ'ne·ti·ko) *adj.* electromagnetic. —**electromagnetismo** (-'tis·mo) *n.m.* electromagnetism.
electromotriz (e·lek·tro·mo'triθ; -'tris) *adj.* electromotive.
electrón (e·lek'tron) *n.m.* electron. —**electrónico**, *adj.* electronic. —**electrónica**, *n.f.* electronics.
electrostática (e·lek·tros'ta·ti·ka) *n.f.* electrostatics. —**electrostático**, *adj.* electrostatic.
electrotipo (e·lek·tro'ti·po) *n.m.* electrotype.
elefancía (e·le·fan'θi·a; -'si·a) *n.f.* elephantiasis.
elefante (e·le'fan·te) *n.m.* & *f.* elephant. —**elefantino**, *adj.* elephantine.
elefantiasis (e·le·fan'tja·sis) *n.f.* elephantiasis.
elegante (e·le'ɣan·te) *adj.* elegant. —**elegancia**, *n.f.* elegance.
elegía (e·le'xi·a) *n.f.* elegy. —**elegíaco**, *adj.* elegiac.
elegible (e·le'xi·βle) *adj.* eligible. —**elegibilidad**, *n.f.* elegibility.
elegir (e·le'xir) *v.t.* [*pres.ind.* **elijo**; *pres.subjve.* **elija**; *pret.* **elegí, eligió**]

1, to elect; choose. 2, to name; nominate. —**elegido**, *adj.* elect.

elemental (e·le·men'tal) *adj.* 1, elementary. 2, elemental.

elemento (e·le'men·to) *n.m.* element.

elenco (e'len·ko) *n.m.* 1, catalogue; list; index. 2, *theat.* cast.

elevación (e·le·βa'θjon; -'sjon) *n.f.* elevation.

elevado (e·le'βa·ðo) *adj.* elevated.

elevador (e·le'βa'ðor) *n.m.* elevator; hoist; lift.

elevar (e·le'βar) *v.t.* 1, to raise; elevate. 2, to exalt. —**elevarse**, *v.r.* to rise; soar; ascend.

elfo ('el·fo) *n.m.* elf.

elidir (e·li'ðir) *v.t.* to elide.

eligió (e·li'xjo) *v., 3rd pers.sing. pret. of* **elegir**.

elija (e'li·xa) *v., pres.subjve. of* **elegir**.

elijo (e'li·xo) *v., pres.ind. of* **elegir**.

eliminar (e·li·mi'nar) *v.t.* to eliminate. —**eliminación**, *n.f.* elimination.

elipse (e'lip·se) *n.f.* ellipse.

elipsis (e'lip·sis) *n.f.sing. & pl.* ellipsis.

elíptico (e'lip·ti·ko) *adj.* elliptical.

elisión (e·li'sjon) *n.f.* elision.

elixir (e'lik·sir) *also*, **elixir** (-'sir) *n.m.* elixir.

elocución (e·lo·ku'θjon; -'sjon) *n.f.* elocution.

elocuente (e·lo'kwen·te) *adj.* eloquent. —**elocuencia**, *n.f.* eloquence.

elogiar (e·lo'xjar) *v.t.* to praise; eulogize. —**elogio** (e'lo·xjo) *n.m.* eulogy; praise.

elote (e'lo·te) *n.m., Amer.* ear of corn.

elucidar (e·lu·θi'ðar; -si'ðar) *v.t.* to elucidate. —**elucidación**, *n.f.* elucidation.

eludir (e·lu'ðir) *v.t.* to elude. —**eludible**, *adj.* avoidable.

ella ('e·ʎa; 'e·ja) *pers.pron.fem. sing.* 1, *subj. of a verb* she; it. 2, *obj. of a prep.* her; it.

ellas ('e·ʎas; 'e·jas) *pers.pron., pl. of* **ella**.

ello ('e·ʎo; -jo) *pers. & dem.pron. neut.sing.* it; that.

ellos ('e·ʎos; 'e·jos) *pers.pron., pl. of* **él**.

em- (em) *prefix* em-; *var. of* **en-** *before* b, p: *embalsamar*, embalm; *empobrecer*, impoverish.

emaciación (e·ma·θja'θjon; -sja·'sjon) *n.f.* emaciation.

emanar (e·ma'nar) *v.i.* to emanate. —**emanación**, *n.f.* emanation.

emancipar (e·man·θi'par; -si'par) *v.t.* to emancipate. —**emancipación**, *n.f.* emancipation. —**emancipador**, *adj.* emancipating. —*n.m.* emancipator.

emasculación (e·mas·ku·la'θjon; -'sjon) *n.f.* emasculation.

embajada (em·ba'xa·ða) *n.f.* 1, embassy. 2, errand. —**embajador**, *n.m.* ambassador.

embalar (em·ba'lar) *v.t.* to pack; bale. —*v.i.* to exert full force *or* speed. —**embalador**, *n.m.* packer. —**embalaje**, *n.m.* packing.

embaldosar (em·bal·do'sar) *v.t.* to tile; pave with tile. —**embaldosado**, *n.m.* tiling; tile floor *or* flooring.

embalsamar (em·bal·sa'mar) *v.t.* 1, to embalm. 2, to perfume. —**embalsamador**, *n.m.* embalmer. —**embalsamamiento**, *n.m.* embalming; embalment.

embarazada (em·ba·ra'θa·ða; -'sa·ða) *adj., fem.* pregnant.

embarazar (em·ba·ra'θar; -'sar) *v.t.* [*pres.subjve.* **embarace** (-'ra·θe; -se); *pret.* **embaracé** (-'θe; -'se)] 1, to embarrass. 2, *colloq.* to make pregnant. 3, to encumber.

embarazo (em·ba'ra·θo; -so) *n.m.* 1, encumbrance. 2, embarrassment. 3, pregnancy.

embarazoso (em·ba·ra'θo·so; -'so·so) *adj.* 1, cumbersome. 2, embarrassing.

embarcación (em·bar·ka'θjon; -'sjon) *n.f.* 1, vessel; boat; ship. 2, embarkation (*of passengers*).

embarcadero (em·bar·ka'ðe·ro) *n.m.* 1, pier; wharf. 2, *R.R.* platform.

embarcar (em·bar'kar) *v.t.* [*pres. subjve.* **embarque** (-'bar·ke); *pret.* **embarqué** (-'ke)] to ship. —**embarcarse**, *v.r.* to embark. —**embarcador**, *n.m.* shipper.

embarco (em'bar·ko) *n.m.* embarkation (*of passengers*).

embargar (em·bar'ɣar) *v.t.* [*pres. subjve.* **embargue** (-'bar·ɣe); *pret.* **embargué** (-'ɣe)] 1, to embargo. 2, *law* to attach; seize. 3, to impede; restrain. 4, to seize; clutch.

embargo (em'bar·ɣo) *n.m.* 1, embargo. 2, *law* seizure; attachment.

—**sin embargo,** nevertheless; however.
embarque (em'bar·ke) *n.m.* **1,** embarkation (*of cargo*). **2,** shipment.
embarradura (em·ba·rra'ðu·ra) *n.f.* smear; smearing.
embarrancar (em·ba·rran'kar) *v.i.* [*pres.subjve.* **embarranque** (-'rran·ke); *pret.* **embarranqué** (-'ke)] **1,** to run aground. **2,** to run into a ditch.
embarrar (em·ba'rrar) *v.t.* **1,** to bemire; make muddy; soil. **2,** *Amer.* to botch up; mess up. —**embarrarlas,** *Amer., colloq.* to foul things up.
embarullar (em·ba·ru'ʎar; -'jar) *v.t., colloq.* to botch; mess up.
embastar (em·bas'tar) *v.t.* to baste; tack. —**embaste** (-'bas·te) *n.m.* basting.
embate (em'ba·te) *n.m.* **1,** pounding; banging. **2,** sudden attack.
embaucar (em·bau'kar) *v.t.* [*pres. subjve.* **embauque** (-'bau·ke); **embauqué** (-'ke)] to swindle; dupe. —**embaucador,** *n.m.* swindler; deceiver. —*adj.* tricky.
embebecer (em·be·βe'θer; -'ser) *v.t.* [*infl.:* **crecer**] **1,** to amuse; entertain. **2,** to charm; fascinate. —**embebecido,** *adj.* amazed; rapt. —**embebecimiento,** *n.m.* fascination; rapture.
embeber (em·be'βer) *v.t.* **1,** to drink; absorb. **2,** to soak; saturate. **3,** to insert. **4,** to shrink; shorten; compress. —*v.i.* to shrink. —**embeberse,** *v.r.* **1,** to be delighted. **2,** to be absorbed *or* engrossed. **3,** *fig.* to immerse oneself; delve.
embelecar (em·be·le'kar) *v.t.* [*pres.subjve.* **embeleque** (-'le·ke); *pret.* **embelequé** (-'ke)] **1,** to deceive; trick. **2,** *Amer., colloq.* to give (someone) a line; string (someone) along.
embeleco (em·be'le·ko) *n.m.* **1,** deceit; trickery. **2,** *Amer., colloq.* humbug; bunk.
embelesar (em·be·le'sar) *v.t.* to charm; fascinate. —**embeleso** (-'le·so) *n.m.* charm; fascination.
embellecer (em·be·ʎe'θer; -je'ser) *v.t.* [*pres.ind.* **embellezco** (-'ʎeθ·ko; -'jes·ko); *pres.subjve.* **embellezca** (-ka)] to adorn; embellish. —**embellecimiento,** *n.m.* embellishment.
embestida (em·bes'ti·ða) *n.f.* assault; onset.
embestir (em·bes'tir) *v.t.* [*pres. ind.* **embisto** (-'bis·to); *pres.subjve.* **embista** (-'bis·ta); *pret.* **embestí, embistió** (-bis'tjo)] to assail; attack.
emblandecer (em·blan·de'θer; -'ser) *v.t.* [*pres.ind.* **emblandezco** (-'deθ·ko; -'des·ko); *pres.subjve.* **emblandezca** (-ka)] to soften; mollify.
emblanquecer (em·blan·ke'θer; -'ser) *v.t.* = **blanquecer.**
emblema (em'ble·ma) *n.m.* emblem; badge. —**emblemático** (-'ma·ti·ko) *adj.* emblematic.
embobar (em·bo'βar) *v.t.* **1,** to amuse. **2,** to fascinate.
embocadura (em·bo·ka'ðu·ra) *n.f.* **1,** entrance; opening. **2,** river mouth. **3,** *music* mouthpiece. **4,** taste, as of wine.
embolada (em·bo'la·ða) *n.f.* piston stroke.
embolado (em·bo'la·ðo) *n.m.* **1,** a bull with tipped horns. **2,** *fig.* ineffectual person. **3,** *theat.* bit part. **4,** *colloq.* trick; deception.
embolar (em·bo'lar) *v.t.* **1,** to tip (a bull's horns) with wooden balls. **2,** to black (shoes).
embolia (em'bo·lja) *n.f.* embolism. *Also,* **embolismo** (-'lis·mo).
émbolo ('em·bo·lo) *n.m.* **1,** piston; plunger. **2,** *pathol.* embolus.
embolsar (em·bol'sar) *v.t.* to pocket; put in one's pocket *or* purse.
embonar (em·bo'nar) *v.t.* to improve; make satisfactory.
emborrachar (em·bo·rra'tʃar) *v.t.* to intoxicate; make drunk. —**emborracharse,** *v.r.* to become intoxicated; get drunk.
emborrascar (em·bo·rras'kar) *v.t., colloq.* [*infl.:* **rascar**] to anger. —**emborrascarse,** *v.r.* to become stormy, as weather.
emborronar (em·bo·rro'nar) *v.t.* **1,** to blur; blot. **2,** to scribble.
emboscar (em·bos'kar) *v.t.* [*pres. subjve.* **embosque** (-'bos·ke); *pret.* **embosqué** (-'ke)] to place in ambush. —**emboscarse,** *v.r.* **1,** to lie in ambush. **2,** *colloq.* to shirk. —**emboscada,** *n.f.* ambuscade; ambush.
embotar (em·bo'tar) *v.t.* to blunt; make dull.
embotellar (em·bo·te'ʎar; -'jar) *v.t.* to bottle; bottle up.
embozar (em·bo'θar; -'sar) *v.t.*

[*pres. subjve.* **emboce** (-'bo·θe; -se); *pret.* **embocé** (-'θe; -'se)] **1,** to muffle (the face). **2,** to cloak; conceal. **3,** to muzzle. —**embozarse,** *v.r.* to muffle one's face.

embragar (em·bra'ɣar) *v.t.* [*pres. subjve.* **embrague** (-'bra·ɣe); *pret.* **embragué** (-'ɣe)] to engage (a clutch, driveshaft, etc.).

embrague (em'bra·ɣe) *n.m.* **1,** clutch; coupling. **2,** engaging (of a clutch, driveshaft, etc.).

embravecer (em·bra·βe'θer; -'ser) *v.t.* [*pres.ind.* **embravezco** (-'βeθ·ko; 'βes·ko); *pres.subjve.* **embravezca** (-ka)] to enrage; irritate. —*v.i., bot.* to become strong. —**embravecerse,** *v.r.* **1,** to become enraged. **2,** to swell, as waves.

embrear (em·bre'ar) *v.t.* to coat with pitch.

embriagar (em·brja'ɣar) *v.t.* [*pres.subjve.* **embriague** (-'brja·ɣe); *pret.* **embriagué** (-'ɣe)] to intoxicate; inebriate. —**embriagado,** *adj.* intoxicated; drunk. —**embriaguez** (-'ɣeθ; -'ɣes) *n.f.* intoxication; drunkenness.

embriología (em·brjo·lo'xi·a) *n.f.* embryology. —**embriólogo** (em'brjo·lo·ɣo) *n.m.* embryologist.

embrión (em·bri'on) *n.m.* embryo. —**embrionario,** *adj.* embryonic.

embrollador (em·bro·ʎa'ðor; -ja'ðor) *adj.* **1,** embroiling. **2,** troublesome. —*n.m.* **1,** muddler. **2,** troublemaker.

embrollar (em·bro'ʎar; -'jar) *v.t.* to entangle; embroil.

embrollo (em'bro·ʎo; -jo) *n.m.* tangle; muddle. *Also,* **embrolla,** *n.f., colloq.*

embromar (em·bro'mar) *v.t.* **1,** to tease; joke with. **2,** *Amer.* to bore; annoy. **3,** *Amer.* to detain; delay.

embrujar (em·bru'xar) *v.t.* to bewitch; charm. —**embrujo** (-'bru·xo) *n.m.* charm; bewitchment.

embrutecer (em·bru·te'θer; -'ser) *v.t.* [*infl.:* **crecer**] to stupefy; make brutish or dull.

embudo (em'bu·ðo) *n.m.* **1,** funnel. **2,** *fig.* trick. —**ley del embudo,** *colloq.* unfairly applied law.

embuste (em'bus·te) *n.m.* **1,** fib; lie. **2,** trick; fraud. —**embustes,** *n.m.pl.* baubles; trinkets. —**embustero,** *n.m.* fibber; liar.

embutido (em·bu'ti·ðo) *adj.* inlaid. —*n.m.* **1,** inlaid work. **2,** salami; sausage. **3,** *Amer.* lace.

embutir (em·bu'tir) *v.t.* **1,** to inlay; insert. **2,** to stuff; cram. **3,** *colloq.* to gobble; gulp down.

emergencia (e·mer'xen·θja; -sja) *n.f.* **1,** emergence. **2,** emergency. —**emergente,** *adj.* emergent.

emerger (e·mer'xer) *v.i.* to emerge.

emérito (e'me·ri·to) *adj.* emeritus.

emético (e'me·ti·ko) *n.m.* & *adj.* emetic.

-emia ('e·mja) *suffix* -emia; *forming nouns denoting* condition or disease of the blood: *anemia,* anemia.

emigración (e·mi·ɣra'θjon; -'sjon) *n.f.* **1,** emigration. **2,** migration.

emigrar (e·mi'ɣrar) *v.i.* **1,** to emigrate. **2,** to migrate. —**emigrante,** *adj.* & *n.m.* & *f.* emigrant.

eminencia (e·mi'nen·θja; -sja) *n.f.* **1,** height; hill. **2,** eminence.

eminente (e·mi'nen·te) *adj.* **1,** eminent. **2,** lofty; high.

emir (e'mir) *n.m.* emir.

emisario (e·mi'sa·rjo) *n.m.* emissary.

emisión (e·mi'sjon) *n.f.* **1,** emission. **2,** *radio; TV* broadcast. **3,** *finance* issue (of paper money, bonds, etc.).

emisor (e·mi'sor) *adj.* **1,** emitting. **2,** *radio; TV* broadcasting. —*n.m.* transmitter. —**emisora,** *n.f.* broadcasting station.

emitir (e·mi'tir) *v.t.* **1,** to emit. **2,** to issue, as bonds. **3,** to utter. **4,** *radio; TV* to broadcast.

emoción (e·mo'θjon; -'sjon) *n.f.* emotion. —**emocional,** *adj.* emotional.

emocionar (e·mo·θjo'nar; e·mo·sjo-) *v.t.* to move; touch; thrill. —**emocionante,** *adj.* moving; touching; thrilling.

emoliente (e·mo'ljen·te) *n.m.* & *adj.* emollient.

emolumento (e·mo·lu'men·to) *n.m.* emolument.

emotivo (e·mo'ti·βo) *adj.* emotive; emotional.

empacar (em·pa'kar) *v.t.* & *i.* [*pres.subjve.* **empaque** (-'pa·ke); *pret.* **empaqué** (-'ke)] to pack; package. —**empacado,** *n.m.* packing; packaging. —**empacador,** *n.m.* packer.

empachar (em·pa'tʃar) *v.t.* **1,** to cause indigestion. **2,** to gorge; glut.

—**empacharse, 1,** to get indigestion. **2,** to become embarrassed.

empacho (em'pa·tʃo) *n.m.* **1,** scruple; restraint. **2,** gorge; bellyful. **3,** indigestion.

empadronar (em·pa·ðro'nar) *v.t.* to take a census of; register. —**empadronamiento,** *n.m.* census.

empalagar (em·pa·la'ɣar) *v.t.* [*pres.subjve.* **empalague** (-'la·ɣe); *pret.* **empalagué** (-'ɣe)] **1,** to cloy. **2,** to weary; bore.

empalago (em·pa'la·ɣo) *n.m.* **1,** surfeit. **2,** bore.

empalagoso (em·pa·la'ɣo·so) *adj.* **1,** cloying. **2,** oversweet. **3,** overrich; overornate. **4,** boring.

empalar (em·pa'lar) *v.t.* to impale.

empalizar (em·pa·li'θar; -'sar) *v.t.* [*infl.:* **realizar**] to fence; palisade. —**empalizada,** *n.f.* palisade; fence.

empalmar (em·pal'mar) *v.t.* to join; splice; couple. —*v.i.* (of trains, conveyances, etc.) to make connection.

empalme (em'pal·me) *n.m.* **1,** joint; splice. **2,** *R.R.* junction.

empanada (em·pa'na·ða) *n.f.* meat pie.

empanar (em·pa'nar) *v.t.* to bread.

empañar (em·pa'ɲar) *v.t.* **1,** to swaddle. **2,** to darken; tarnish.

empañetar (em·pa·ɲe'tar) *v.t.* to plaster.

empapar (em·pa'par) *v.t.* to soak; saturate. —**empaparse,** *v.r.* to steep oneself; delve.

empapelado (em·pa·pe'la·ðo) *n.m.* **1,** wallpaper. **2,** paperhanging.

empapelador (em·pa·pe·la'ðor) *n.m.* paperhanger.

empapelar (em·pa·pe'lar) *v.t.* to paper.

empaque (em'pa·ke) *n.m.* **1,** packing. **2,** *fig.* presence; bearing.

empaquetadura (em·pa·ke·ta·'ðu·ra) *n.f.* **1,** packing. **2,** gasket.

empaquetar (em·pa·ke'tar) *v.t.* to pack.

emparedado (em·pa·re'ða·ðo) *n.m.* **1,** recluse. **2,** sandwich.

emparedar (em·pa·re'ðar) *v.t.* to confine; wall in.

emparejar (em·pa·re'xar) *v.t.* **1,** to pair; match. **2,** to level; make even. **3,** to close (a door, window, etc.) without locking. —**emparejar con, 1,** to come abreast of; catch up with. **2,** to be even with; be on a level with.

emparentar (em·pa·ren'tar) *v.i.* [*pres.ind.* **empariento** (-'rjen·to); *pres.subjve.* **empariente** (-te)] to be or become related by marriage.

emparrado (em·pa'rra·ðo) *n.m.* arbor; bower.

empastar (em·pas'tar) *v.t.* **1,** *dent.* to fill (a tooth). **2,** to paste. **3,** to bind (a book) in a stiff cover. **4,** *paint.* to impaste.

empaste (em'pas·te) *n.m.* **1,** *dent.* filling. **2,** stiff binding. **3,** *paint.* impasto.

empatar (em·pa'tar) *v.t.* **1,** to tie (a vote, score, etc.). **2,** *Amer.* to couple; splice.

empate (em'pa·te) *n.m.* **1,** tie; tie score. **2,** *Amer.* joint; splice.

empatía (em·pa'ti·a) *n.f.* empathy.

empecé (em·pe'θe; -'se) *v., 1st pers.sing. pret. of* **empezar.**

empecinarse (em·pe·θi'nar·se; em·pe·si-) *v.r., Amer.* to be stubborn; persist. —**empecinado,** *adj., Amer.* stubborn; persistent.

empedernir (em·pe·ðer'nir) *v.t.* [*defective: used only in tenses with terminations beginning with* i] to harden. —**empedernido,** *adj.* hardhearted.

empedrar (em·pe'ðrar) *v.t.* to pave with stones. —**empedrado,** *n.m.* stone pavement. —*adj.* dotted with clouds, as the sky.

empegado (em·pe'ɣa·ðo) *n.m.* tarpaulin.

empeine (em'pei·ne) *n.m.* **1,** *anat.* groin. **2,** *anat.* instep. **3,** *pathol.* tetter; ringworm. **4,** cotton blossom.

empellar (em·pe'ʎar; -'jar) *v.t.* [*pres.ind.* **empiello** (-'pje·ʎo; -jo); *pres.subjve.* **empielle** (-ʎe; -je)] to push; jostle.

empellón (em·pe'ʎon; -'jon) *n.m.* push; shove. —**a empellones,** rudely.

empeñar (em·pe'ɲar) *v.t.* **1,** to pawn; pledge. **2,** to compel; oblige. —**empeñarse,** *v.r.* **1,** to bind oneself. **2,** to persist. **3,** to intercede.

empeño (em'pe·ɲo) *n.m.* **1,** pledge; pawn. **2,** longing; desire. **3,** determination. **4,** boldness. —**casa de empeños,** pawnshop. —**con empeño,** eagerly; persistently.

empeorar (em·pe·o'rar) *v.t.* & *i.* to worsen.

empequeñecer (em·pe·ke·ɲe'θer;

-'ser) *v.t.* [*pres.ind.* **empequeñezco** (-'ɲe·θko; -'ɲes·ko); *pres.subjve.* **empequeñezca** (-ka)] **1,** to diminish; make smaller. **2,** to belittle.
emperador (em·pe·ra'ðor) *n.m.* emperor.
emperatriz (em·pe·ra'triθ; -'tris) *n.f.* empress.
emperifollar (em·pe·ri·fo'ʎar; -'jar) *v.t.* to adorn; dress up.
empero (em'pe·ro) *conj.* yet; however; notwithstanding.
emperrarse (em·pe'rrar·se) *v.r.* to be or become stubborn.
empezar (em·pe'θar; -'sar) *v.t.* [*pres.ind.* **empiezo** (-'pje·θo; -so); *pres.subjve.* **empiece** (-θe; -se); *pret.* **empecé**] to begin; commence.
empicotar (em·pi·ko'tar) *v.t.* to pillory; punish in a pillory.
empinado (em·pi'na·ðo) *adj.* **1,** high. **2,** steep. **3,** *fig.* conceited.
empinar (em·pi'nar) *v.t.* to raise. **—empinarse,** *v.r.* **1,** to rear up, as a horse. **2,** to stand on tiptoe. **3,** to tower. **4,** *aero.* to zoom. **—empinar el codo,** *colloq.* to drink heavily; bend the elbow.
empiojado (em·pjo'xa·ðo) *adj.* lousy.
empírico (em'pi·ri·ko) *adj.* empirical. *—n.m.* quack; charlatan.
empirismo (em·pi'ris·mo) *n.m.* **1,** empiricism. **2,** quackery.
empizarrar (em·pi·θa'rrar; -sa·'rrar) *v.t.* to slate; cover with slate.
emplastar (em·plas'tar) *v.t.* **1,** to plaster. **2,** to daub; smear.
emplasto (em'plas·to) *n.m.* **1,** plaster; poultice. **2,** unsatisfactory settlement; poor bargain. **3,** *colloq.* weakling; sickly or puny person.
emplazamiento *n.m.* **1,** summoning; summons. **2,** emplacement; location.
emplazar (em·pla'θar; -'sar) *v.t.* [*pres.subjve.* **emplace** (-'pla·θe; -se); *pret.* **emplacé** (-'θe; -'se)] **1,** to summon. **2,** to place; locate.
empleado (em·ple'a·ðo) *adj.* employed. *—n.m.* employee.
emplear (em·ple'ar) *v.t.* **1,** to employ; engage. **2,** to spend; invest. **3,** to use.
empleo (em'ple·o) *n.m.* **1,** employ; employment. **2,** business; profession. **3,** investment. **4,** use.
emplomar (em·plo'mar) *v.t.* **1,** to lead; fill *or* line with lead. **2,** *Amer.* to fill (a tooth).
emplumar (em·plu'mar) *v.t.* to feather.
empobrecer (em·po·βre'θer; -'ser) *v.t.* [*pres.ind.* **empobrezco** (-'βreθ·ko; -'βres·ko); *pres.subjve.* **empobrezca** (-ka)] to impoverish. **—empobrecerse,** *v.r.* **1,** to become poor. **2,** to languish; fade away. **—empobrecimiento,** *n.m.* impoverishment.
empolvar (em·pol'βar) *v.t.* **1,** to powder. **2,** to cover with dust or powder.
empollar (em·po'ʎar; -'jar) *v.t.* & *i.* to hatch.
empollón (em·po'ʎon; -'jon) *n.m.*, *colloq.* bookworm; grind.
emponzoñar (em·pon·θo'ɲar; -so'ɲar) *v.t.* **1,** to poison. **2,** to taint; corrupt. **—emponzoñador,** *n.m.* poisoner. *—adj.* poisoning; poisonous. **—emponzoñamiento,** *n.m.* poisoning.
emporio (em'po·rjo) *n.m.* emporium.
empotrar (em·po'trar) *v.t.* **1,** to imbed, as in a wall. **2,** *carpentry* to mortise. **3,** *naut.* to fasten (cannon).
emprendedor (em·pren·de'ðor) *adj.* enterprising.
emprender (em·pren'der) *v.t.* **1,** to undertake. **2,** to begin. **—emprenderla con,** to squabble with.
empreñar (em·pre'ɲar) *v.t.* to impregnate; make pregnant.
empresa (em'pre·sa) *n.f.* **1,** enterprise; undertaking. **2,** design; purpose. **3,** *theat.* management.
empresario (em·pre'sa·rjo) *n.m.* **1,** entrepreneur. **2,** *theat.* impresario.
empréstito (em'pres·ti·to) *n.m.* corporation *or* government loan.
empujar (em·pu'xar) *v.t.* to push; propel.
empuje (em'pu·xe) *n.m.* **1,** push; impulse. **2,** *fig.* energy; enterprise. **3,** *mech.* thrust.
empujón (em·pu'xon) *n.m.* push; shove. **—a empujones, 1,** violently; rudely. **2,** by fits and starts.
empulgueras (em·pul'ɣe·ras) *n.f.pl.* thumbscrew (*instrument of torture*).
empuñadura (em·pu·ɲa'ðu·ra) *n.f.* **1,** hilt (*of a sword*). **2,** beginning (*of a story*). **3,** *Amer.* handle (*of an umbrella or cane*).
empuñar (em·pu'ɲar) *v.t.* to clutch; grasp.

emular (e·mu'lar) *v.t.* to emulate. —**emulación,** *n.f.* emulation.

émulo ('e·mu·lo) *adj.* emulous. —*n.m.* competitor; rival.

emulsión (e·mul'sjon) *n.f.* emulsion. —**emulsionar,** *v.t.* to emulsify. —**emulsionamiento,** *n.m.* emulsification. —**emulsor** (-'sor) *n.m.* emulsifier.

en (en) *prep.* **1,** in; into. **2,** at. **3,** on; upon. **4,** *fol. by ger., colloq.* on; upon.

en- (en) *prefix* **1,** in; into: *encerrar,* enclose; *encierro,* enclosure. **2,** *forming verbs from nouns and adjectives: endiosar,* deify; *engordar,* fatten. **3,** in (*esp. in words of Greek origin*): *endémico,* endemic.

-ena ('e·na) *suffix* **1,** *forming fem. collective numeral nouns: docena,* dozen; *cuarentena,* a quantity of forty. **2,** *fem. of* **-eno.**

enagua (e'na·ɣwa) *n.f., usu. pl.* petticoat.

enajenación (en·a·xe·na'θjon; -'sjon) *n.f.* **1,** alienation. **2,** absentmindedness. **3,** rapture. —**enajenación mental,** mental derangement. *Also,* **enajenamiento,** *n.m.*

enajenar (en·a·xe'nar) *v.t.* **1,** to alienate. **2,** to transport; enrapture. —**enajenarse,** *v.r.* **1,** to become estranged. **2,** to be carried away.

enaltecer (en·al·te'θer; -'ser) *v.t.* [*pres.ind.* **enaltezco** (-'teθ·ko; -'tes·ko); *pres.subjve.* **enaltezca** (-ka)] to praise; extol; exalt. —**enaltecimiento,** *n.m.* praise; exaltation.

enamorado (en·a·mo'ra·ðo) *adj.* in love; enamored; smitten. —*n.m.* lover; sweetheart.

enamorar (en·a·mo'rar) *v.t.* **1,** to enamor. **2,** to court; woo. —**enamorarse,** *v.r., fol. by* **de,** to fall in love (with). —**enamoramiento,** *n.m.* love; being in love.

enano (e'na·no) *adj.* dwarfish; dwarf (*attrib.*) —*n.m.* dwarf.

enarbolar (en·ar·βo'lar) *v.t.* to hoist; hang (a flag). —**enarbolarse,** *v.r.* = **encabritarse.**

enarcar (en·ar'kar) *v.t.* [*pres. subjve.* **enarque** (-'ar·ke); *pret.* **enarqué** (-'ke)] **1,** to arch. **2,** to hoop (a barrel).

enardecer (en·ar·ðe'θer; -'ser) *v.t.* [*pres.ind.* **enardezco** (-'ðeθ·ko; -'ðes·ko); *pres.subjve.* **enardezca** (-ka)] to fire with passion; arouse; excite. —**enardecerse,** *v.r.* to be aroused *or* inflamed.

enarenar (en·a·re'nar) *v.t.* to sand; cover with sand *or* gravel.

encabezamiento (en·ka·βe·θa·'mjen·to; -sa'mjen·to) *n.m.* **1,** = **empadronamiento. 2,** tax; tax rate. **3,** heading (*of a document*). **4,** salutation (*of a letter*).

encabezar (en·ka·βe'θar; -'sar) *v.t.* [*infl.:* **rezar**] **1,** = **empadronar. 2,** to give a heading *or* title to. **3,** to head; lead. **4,** *carpentry* to join. *Also,* **encabezonar** (-θo'nar; -so·'nar).

encabritarse (en·ka·βri'tar·se) *v.r.* **1,** to rise on the hind legs; rear. **2,** to pitch with an upward motion. **3,** *fig.* to become aroused *or* excited.

encadenamiento (en·ka·ðe·na·'mjen·to) *n.m.* **1,** connection; linkage. **2,** concatenation. *Also,* **encadenación** (-'θjon; -'sjon) *n.f.*

encadenar (en·ka·ðe'nar) *v.t.* **1,** to chain; shackle. **2,** to subjugate; enslave. **3,** to connect; link together. **4,** to captivate.

encajar (en·ka'xar) *v.t.* **1,** to encase; insert. **2,** to fit closely, as a lid. **3,** *carpentry* to join. **4,** *fig.* to toss in, as a remark. **5,** to deal *or* land (a blow). **6,** to palm off; foist. —*v.i.* to fit; be fitting. —**encajarse,** *v.r.* **1,** to intrude. **2,** to squeeze oneself in. **3,** to jam; become stuck.

encaje (en'ka·xe) *n.m.* **1,** fitting; fit. **2,** socket; groove. **3,** *carpentry* join. **4,** lace. **5,** inlaid work; mosaic.

encajonar (en·ka·xo'nar) *v.t.* to pack; box; crate. —**encajonarse,** *v.r.* to narrow; become narrow. —**encajonado,** *adj.* narrow; boxed-in.

encallar (en·ka'ʎar; -'jar) *v.i., naut. & fig.* to run aground.

encamarse (en·ka'mar·se) *v.r., colloq.* to take to one's bed. —**encamado,** *adj., colloq.* bedridden.

encaminar (en·ka·mi'nar) *v.t.* **1,** to guide; direct; show the way. **2,** to send (something) on its way. —**encaminarse,** *v.r.* **1,** to betake oneself. **2,** to start out.

encamotarse (en·ka·mo'tar·se) *v.r., Amer.* to become infatuated.

encandilar (en·kan·di'lar) *v.t.* to blind; dazzle. —**encandilarse,** *v.r.* to light up; be set aglow.

encanecer (en·ka·ne'θer; -'ser) *v.i.* [*pres.ind.* **encanezco** (-'neθ·ko;

-ˈnes·ko); *pres.subjve.* **encanezca** (-ka)] to become grayhaired.
encanijarse (en·ka·niˈxar·se) *v.r.* to become sickly; become thin or emaciated.
encantador (en·kan·taˈðor) *adj.* delightful; charming; enchanting. —*n.m.* enchanter; charmer; sorcerer.
encantamiento (en·kan·ta·ˈmjen·to) *n.m.* **1,** enchantment. **2,** incantation.
encantar (en·kanˈtar) *v.t.* to enchant; charm. —**encantado,** *adj.* charmed; enchanted.
encanto (enˈkan·to) *n.m.* **1,** enchantment; spell. **2,** delight.
encapotado (en·ka·poˈta·ðo) **1,** overcast. **2,** frowning; grim.
encapotadura (en·ka·po·taˈðu·ra) *n.f.* **1,** overcast. **2,** frown; grim expression. *Also,* **encapotamiento** (-ˈmjen·to) *n.m.*
encapotar (en·ka·poˈtar) *v.t.* to cloak; muffle. —**encapotarse,** *v.r.* **1,** to become cloudy; darken; become overcast. **2,** to frown; lower.
encapricharse (en·ka·priˈtʃar·se) *v.r.* **1,** to become stubborn. **2,** *colloq.* to become infatuated.
encapuchar (en·ka·puˈtʃar) *v.t.* to cover with a hood.
encaramar (en·ka·raˈmar) *v.t.* **1,** to lift; raise; elevate. **2,** *fig.* to extol. —**encaramarse,** *v.r.* to scramble up; climb.
encarar (en·kaˈrar) *v.t.* to aim; point. —**encararse a** *or* **con,** to confront; come face to face with.
encarcelar (en·kar·θeˈlar; -seˈlar) *v.t.* **1,** to incarcerate; imprison. **2,** *archit.* to imbed in mortar. **3,** *carpentry* to clamp. —**encarcelación,** *n.f.,* *also,* **encarcelamiento,** *n.m.* incarceration; imprisonment.
encarecer (en·ka·reˈθer; -ˈser) *v.t.* [*infl.:* **crecer**] **1,** to increase the price of. **2,** to praise; extol. —*v.i.* to increase in price.
encarecidamente (en·ka·re·θi·ðaˈmen·te; -si·ðaˈmen·te) *adv.* **1,** exceedingly; highly. **2,** ardently; earnestly.
encarecimiento (en·ka·re·θi·ˈmjen·to; -siˈmjen·to) *n.m.* **1,** increase; rise (*in price*). **2,** enhancement; exaggeration. —**con encarecimiento,** ardently; earnestly.
encargado (en·karˈɣa·ðo) *n.m.* **1,** agent. **2,** person in charge; foreman; supervisor, etc. —**encargado de negocios,** chargé d'affaires.
encargar (en·karˈɣar) *v.t.* [*infl.:* **cargar**] **1,** to commend; entrust. **2,** to recommend; counsel. **3,** to order; commission; assign.
encargo (enˈkar·ɣo) *n.m.* **1,** charge; trust. **2,** recommendation; counsel. **3,** order; commission; assignment. **4,** errand.
encariñarse (en·ka·riˈɲar·se) *v.r.,* *fol. by* **con,** to grow fond (of); become attached (to). —**encariñado,** *adj.* fond; attached. —**encariñamiento,** *n.m.* fondness; attachment.
encarnar (en·karˈnar) *v.t.* **1,** to incarnate; embody. **2,** to bury in the flesh, as a weapon; imbed. —*v.i.* to become incarnate. —**encarnarse,** *v.r.* **1,** to become incarnate. **2,** to blend; fuse. **3,** to become ingrown, as a nail. —**encarnación,** *n.f.* incarnation; embodiment.
encarnizado (en·kar·niˈθa·ðo; -ˈsa·ðo) *adj.* **1,** irate; furious. **2,** bloody.
encarnizar (en·kar·niˈθar; -ˈsar) *v.t.* [*pres.subjve.* **encarnice** (-ˈni·θe; -se); *pret.* **encarnicé** (-ˈθe; -ˈse)] to provoke; move to fury. —**encarnizarse,** *v.r.* **1,** to be glutted with flesh. **2,** = **ensañarse. 3,** to fight a bloody battle.
encaro (enˈka·ro) *n.m.* **1,** stare. **2,** blunderbuss. **3,** stock (*of a rifle*).
encarrilar (en·ka·rriˈlar) *v.t.* **1,** to put on the right track; set aright. **2,** to put (a train) back on the track.
encasillar (en·ka·siˈʎar; -ˈjar) *v.t.* **1,** to pigeonhole. **2,** to sort; catalog. —**encasillado,** *n.m.* set of pigeonholes.
encauchar (en·kauˈtʃar) *v.t.* to treat with rubber; rubberize.
encauzar (en·kauˈθar; -ˈsar) *v.t.* [*pres.subjve.* **encauce** (-ˈkau·θe; -se); *pret.* **encaucé** (-ˈθe; -ˈse)] to channel; direct.
encefalitis (en·θe·faˈli·tis; en·se-) *n.f.* encephalitis.
encefalo- (en·θe·fa·lo; en·se-) *prefix* encephalo-; brain: *encefalograma,* encephalogram.
encelar (en·θeˈlar; en·se-) *v.t.* to make jealous. —**encelarse,** *v.r.* to become jealous.
encender (en·θenˈder; en·sen-) *v.t.* [*pres.ind.* **enciendo;** *pres.subjve.* **encienda**] **1,** to kindle; light. **2,** *fig.*

to inflame. —**encenderse,** *v.r.* to blush. —**encendedor,** *n.m.* cigarette lighter.
encendido (en·θen'di·ðo; en·sen-) *adj.* **1,** inflamed. **2,** blushing. —*n.m., mech.* ignition.
encerado (en·θe'ra·ðo; en·se-) *adj.* waxed. —*n.m.* **1,** coat of wax; polish. **2,** oilcloth. **3,** blackboard.
encerar (en·θe'rar; en·se-) *v.t.* to wax; polish.
encerrar (en·θe'rrar; en·se-) *v.t.* [*pres.ind.* **encierro**; *pres.subjve.* **encierre**] **1,** to lock up; confine. **2,** to include; embrace; comprise. —**encerrarse,** *v.r.* to live in seclusion.
encía (en'θi·a; -'si·a) *n.f., anat.* gum.
-encia ('en·θja; -sja) *suffix* -ence; -ency; *forming nouns corresponding to adjectives ending in* **-ente** *or* **-ento**: *urgencia,* urgency; *violencia,* violence.
encíclico (en'θi·kli·ko; en'si-) *adj.* encyclical. —**encíclica,** *n.f.* encyclical.
enciclopedia (en·θi·klo'pe·ðja; en·si) *n.f.* encyclopedia. —**enciclopédico** (-'pe·ði·ko) *adj.* encyclopedic. —**enciclopedista,** *n.m.* & *f.* encyclopedist.
encienda (en'θjen·da; -'sjen·da) *v., pres.subjve. of* **encender.**
enciendo (en'θjen·do; en'sjen-) *v., pres.ind. of* **encender.**
encierre (en'θje·rre; en'sje-) *v., pres. subjve. of* **encerrar.**
encierro (en'θje·rro; en'sje-) *n.m.* **1,** locking up; confinement. **2,** lockup. **3,** enclosure. —*v., pres.ind. of* **encerrar.**
encima (en'θi·ma; en'si-) *adv.* **1,** over; above. **2,** besides; over and above. —**encima de,** on; upon. —**por encima,** superficially. —**por encima de,** in spite of.
encina (en'θi·na; -'si·na) *n.f.* evergreen oak.
encinta (en'θin·ta; en'sin-) *adj. fem.* pregnant.
encintado (en·θin'ta·ðo; en·sin-) *n.m.* curb (*of a sidewalk*).
encintar (en·θin'tar; en·sin-) *v.t.* **1,** trim with ribbon. **2,** to put a curb on (a sidewalk).
enclaustrar (en'klaus'trar) *v.t.* to cloister; seclude.
enclavado (en·kla'βa·ðo) *adj.* hemmed in. —*n.m.* enclave.
enclavar (en·kla'βar) *v.t.* **1,** to nail down. **2,** to pierce through. **3,** *colloq.* to deceive.
enclave (en'kla·βe) *n.m.* enclave.
enclavijar (en·kla·βi'xar) *v.t.* **1,** to join; pin. **2,** to peg; put pegs on.
enclenque (en'klen·ke) *adj.* weak; feeble; sickly. —*n.m.* & *f.* weak or sickly person.
encocorar (en·ko·ko'rar) *v.t., colloq.* to annoy.
encoger (en·ko'xer) *v.t.* [*pres.ind.* **encojo** (-'ko·xo); *pres.subjve.* **encoja** (-xa)] **1,** to contract; shorten; shrink. **2,** *fig.* to abash; humble. —**encogerse,** *v.r.* **1,** to shrink; contract. **2,** to be abashed; humble oneself. —**encogerse de hombros,** to shrug one's shoulders.
encogido (en·ko'xi·ðo) *adj.* timid; shy.
encogimiento (en·ko·xi'mjen·to) *n.m.* **1,** contraction; shrinkage. **2,** pusillanimity. **3,** bashfulness; awkwardness.
encolar (en·ko'lar) *v.t.* to glue.
encolerizar (en·ko·le·ri'θar; -'sar) *v.t.* [*pres.subjve.* **encolerice** (-'ri·θe; -se); *pret.* **encolericé** (-'θe; -'se)] to anger; irritate. —**encolerizarse,** *v.r.* to become angry.
encomendable (en·ko·men'da·βle) *adj.* commendable.
encomendar (en·ko·men'dar) *v.t.* [*pres.ind.* **encomiendo** (-'mjen·do); *pres.subjve.* **encomiende** (-de)] to commend; entrust. —**encomendarse,** *v.r.* to send one's compliments. —**encomendamiento,** *n.m.* commission; charge.
encomiar (en·ko'mjar) *v.t.* to eulogize; praise; extol.
encomienda (en·ko'mjen·da) *n.f.* **1,** commission; charge. **2,** complimentary message. **3,** *hist.* estate granted by the Spanish kings. **4,** *colloq.* errand. —**encomiendas,** *n.f. pl.* compliments; respects. —**encomienda postal,** *Amer.* parcel-post package.
encomio (en'ko·mjo) *n.m.* praise; eulogy; encomium.
enconamiento (en·ko·na'mjen·to) *n.m.* **1,** inflammation; festering. **2,** = **encono.**
enconar (en·ko'nar) *v.t.* **1,** to infect. **2,** to inflame; provoke. —**enconarse,** *v.r.* **1,** to fester. **2,** *fig.* to rankle.
encono (en'ko·no) *n.m.* malevolence; rancor.
enconoso (en·ko'no·so) *adj.* **1,**

hurtful; prejudicial; malevolent. **2,** resentful; rancorous.
encontrado (en·kon'tra·ðo) *adj.* **1,** opposite; in front; facing. **2,** hostile; opposed; contrary.
encontrar (en·kon'trar) *v.t.* & *i.* [*pres.ind.* **encuentro**; *pres.subjve.* **encuentre**] **1,** to meet; encounter. **2,** to find; come upon. —**encontrarse,** *v.r.* **1,** to meet; come together. **2,** to be; find oneself. **3,** to feel; feel oneself to be. **4,** *fig.* to clash; conflict.
encontrón (en·kon'tron) *n.m.* bump; collision; jolt. *Also,* **encontronazo** (-'na·θo; -so).
encopetado (en·ko·pe'ta·ðo) *adj.* presumptuous; haughty; high-hat.
encopetar (en·ko·pe'tar) *v.t.* to dress (the hair) high on the head. —**encopetarse,** *v.r.* to become conceited.
encordar (en·kor'ðar) v.t. **1,** [*infl.:* **acordar**] to provide with strings. **2,** to string; tie or bind with string.
encordelar (en·kor·ðe'lar) *v.t.* to string; tie or bind with string.
encorvada (en·kor'βa·ða) *n.f.* **1,** stoop; stooping. **2,** buck; bucking (*of an animal*).
encorvadura (en·kor·βa'ðu·ra) *n.f.* **1,** bending. **2,** crookedness; curvature. *Also,* **encorvamiento,** *n.m.*
encorvar (en·kor'βar) *v.t.* to bend; curve. —**encorvarse,** *v.r.* **1,** to bend; stoop. **2,** to be biased.
encrespar (en·kres'par) *v.t.* **1,** to curl; frizzle. **2,** to make (the hair) stand on end. **3,** to ruffle (feathers). —**encresparse,** *v.r.* **1,** to become rough, as the sea. **2,** *fig.* to bristle. **3,** to curl; become curly.
encristalar (en·kris·ta'lar) *v.t.* to glass; glaze; furnish with glass.
encrucijada (en·kru·θi'xa·ða; en·kru·si-) *n.f.* **1,** intersection; crossroads. **2,** ambush. **3,** opportunity to harm someone.
encuadernador (en·kwa·ðer·na·'ðor) *n.m.* **1,** binder (*for papers*). **2,** bookbinder.
encuadernar (en·kwa·ðer'nar) *v.t.* to bind (books). —**encuadernación,** *n.f.* binding.
encuadrar (en·kwa'ðrar) *v.t.* **1,** to frame. **2,** to fit in; insert. **3,** to encompass; comprise. **4,** *Amer.* to summarize.
encubridor (en·ku·βri'ðor) *n.m.* **1,** concealer. **2,** procurer; bawd. —*adj.* concealing.
encubrimiento (en·ku·βri'mjen·to) *n.m.* **1,** concealment. **2,** *law* being an accessory after the fact.
encubrir (en·ku'βrir) *v.t.* [*infl.:* **cubrir**] to hide; conceal.
encuentre (en'kwen·tre) *v., pres. subjve. of* **encontrar.**
encuentro (en'kwen·tro) *v., pres. ind. of* **encontrar.** —*n.m.* **1,** encounter; sudden meeting. **2,** clash; collision. **3,** bout; match. **4,** find; finding. —**salirle al encuentro a** *or* **de, 1,** to go to meet. **2,** to oppose. **3,** to anticipate.
encuerar (en·kwe'rar) *v.t.* to strip (of clothes or money). —**encuerado,** *adj., Amer.* naked; ragged.
encuesta (en'kwes·ta) *n.f.* inquiry; inquest.
encumbrar (en·kum'brar) *v.t.* to raise; elevate. —**encumbrarse,** *v.r.* **1,** to rise; be raised. **2,** to become pretentious; put on airs. —**encumbrado,** *adj.* high; lofty. —**encumbramiento,** *n.m.* elevation; height.
encurtir (en·kur'tir) *v.t.* to pickle. —**encurtidos,** *n.m.pl.* pickled vegetables.
enchapado (en·tʃa'pa·ðo) *n.m.* **1,** veneer. **2,** overlay; plating.
enchapar (en·tʃa'par) *v.t.* **1,** to veneer. **2,** to overlay; cover with sheets or plates.
encharcar (en·tʃar'kar) *v.t.* [*infl.:* **tocar**] to inundate; flood.
enchilada (en·tʃi'la·ða) *n.f., Amer.* enchilada.
enchufar (en·tʃu'far) *v.t.* **1,** to connect; plug in. **2,** to place in office through political favor.
enchufe (en'tʃu·fe) *n.m.* **1,** *electricity* plug; socket. **2,** pipe joint. **3,** *fig.* office obtained through political favor.
ende ('en·de) *in* **por ende,** consequently; therefore.
endeble (en'de·βle) *adj.* **1,** feeble; frail. **2,** flimsy.
endeblez (en·de'βleθ; -'βles) *n.f.* **1,** feebleness. **2,** flimsiness.
endecha (en'de·tʃa) *n.f.* dirge; lament.
endémico (en'de·mi·ko) *adj.* endemic.
endemoniado (en·de·mo'nja·ðo) *adj.* devilish; perverse.
endemoniar (en·de·mo'njar) *v.t., colloq.* to irritate; enrage.
endentar (en·den'tar) *v.t.* [*infl.:*

dentar] 1, to mesh; engage. 2, to put or form teeth in, as a saw, gearwheel, etc.
enderezador (en·de·re·θa'ðor; -sa'ðor) *adj.* managing well. —*n.m.* 1, good manager. 2, [*also,* **enderezador de entuertos**] troubleshooter.
enderezamiento (en·de·re·θa·'mjen·to; -sa'mjen·to) *n.m.* 1, straightening. 2, guiding; directing. 3, setting right.
enderezar (en·de·re'θar; -'sar) *v.t.* [*pres.subjve.* **enderece** (-'re·θe; -se); *pret.* **enderecé** (-'θe; -'se)] 1, to straighten; unbend. 2, to rectify; set right. 3, to manage well. 4, to address. 5, to guide; direct.
endeudarse (en·deu'ðar·se) *v.r.* to go into debt.
endiablado (en·dja'βla·ðo) *adj.* devilish; perverse.
endiablar (en·dja'βlar) *v.t.* 1, to enrage. 2, *fig.* to corrupt; pervert. —**endiablarse,** *v.r.* to become furious.
endibia (en'di·βja) *n.f.* endive; chicory.
endiosar (en·djo'sar) *v.t.* to deify. —**endiosarse,** *v.r.* to put on airs; be haughty. —**endiosamiento,** *n.m.* deification.
endo- (en·do) *prefix* endo-: internal; within: *endocrino,* endocrine.
endocrino (en·do'kri·no) *adj.* & *n.m.* endocrine.
endomingarse (en·do·min'gar·se) *v.r.* [*infl.:* **pagar**] to dress up in one's Sunday best.
endorsar (en·dor'sar) *v.t.* = **endosar.** —**endorso** (-'dor·so) *n.m.* = **endoso.**
endosar (en·do'sar) *v.t.* 1, to endorse. 2, to foist; palm off. 3, to give; deal (a blow, insult, etc.). —**endosante,** *n.m.* endorser. —**endosatario,** *n.m.* endorsee. —**endoso** (-'do·so) *n.m.* endorsement.
endrino (en'dri·no) *n.m.,* 1, sloe tree. 2, sloe. —*adj.* sloe-colored; blue-black. —**endrina,** *n.f.* sloe.
endulzar (en·dul'θar; -'sar) *v.t.* [*pres.subjve.* **endulce** (-'dul·θe; -se); *pret.* **endulcé** (-'θe; -'se)] 1, to sweeten. 2, to soothe; soften. —**endulzadura,** *n.f.* sweetening.
endurar (en·du'rar) *v.t.* 1, to endure; bear. 2, to put off; delay. 3, to save; economize.
endurecer (en·du·re'θer; -'ser) *v.t.* [*pres.ind.* **endurezco** (-'reθ·ko; -'res·ko); *pres.subjve.* **endurezca** (-ka)] to harden; stiffen. —**endurecimiento,** *n.m.* hardening; stiffening.
enebro (e'ne·βro) *n.m.* juniper tree. —**enebrina,** *n.f.* juniper berry.
eneldo (e'nel·do) *n.m.* dill.
enema (e'ne·ma) *n.f.* enema.
enemigo (e·ne'mi·ɣo) *n.m.* enemy; foe. —*adj.* 1, inimical; hostile. 2, averse.
enésimo (e'ne·si·mo) *adj.* *n*th.
enemistad (e·ne·mis'tað) *n.f.* enmity; hostility.
enemistar (e·ne·mis'tar) *v.t.* to alienate; estrange. —**enemistarse con,** to fall out with.
energía (en·er'xi·a) *n.f.* energy; power.
enérgico (e'ner·xi·ko) *adj.* energetic; vigorous.
energúmeno (e·ner'ɣu·me·no) *n.m.* 1, violent person. 2, madcap.
enero (e'ne·ro) *n.m.* January.
enervar (e·ner'βar) *v.t.* to enervate. —**enervarse,** *v.r.* to weaken. —**enervación,** *n.f.* enervation.
enfadar (en·fa'ðar) *v.t.* to vex; annoy. —**enfadarse,** *v.r.* 1, to become annoyed. 2, to fret. —**enfadadizo,** *adj.* irritable; peevish.
enfado (en'fa·ðo) *n.m.* annoyance; vexation. —**enfadoso,** *adj.* annoying; vexatious.
enfangar (en·fan'gar) *v.t.* [*pres. subjve.* **enfangue** (-'fan·ge); *pret.* **enfangué** (-'ge)] to muddy. —**enfangarse,** *v.r.* 1, to sink in the mud. 2, to become muddy.
enfardar (en·far'ðar) *v.t.* to bale; pack; bundle. *Also,* **enfardelar** (-ðe'lar).
énfasis ('en·fa·sis) *n.m. or f.* emphasis. —**enfático** (en'fa·ti·ko) *adj.* emphatic.
enfermar (en·fer'mar) *v.i.* [*also, refl.,* **enfermarse**] to fall ill. —*v.t.* 1, to make sick. 2, *fig.* to weaken; enervate.
enfermedad (en·fer·me'ðað) *n.f.* sickness; illness.
enfermizo (en·fer'mi·θo; -so) *adj.* 1, sickly; infirm. 2, unwholesome; unhealthful.
enfermo (en'fer·mo) *adj.* sick; ill. —*n.m.* patient. —**enfermería,** *n.f.* infirmary. —**enfermero,** *n.m.* [*fem.* **-era**] nurse.
enfilar (en·fi'lar) *v.t.* 1, to align; line up. 2, to thread; string. 3, *mil.* to enfilade. 4, to bear *or* head

toward. —**enfilada,** *n.f., mil.* enfilade.
enflaquecer (en·fla·ke'θer; -'ser) *v.t. & i.* [*pres.ind.* **enflaquezco** (-'keθ·ko; -'kes·ko); *pres.subjve.* **enflaquezca** (-ka)] to weaken. —**enflaquecerse,** *v.r.* to weaken; be discouraged.
enfocar (en·fo'kar) *v.t.* [*pres. subjve.* **enfoque** (-'fo·ke); *pret.* **enfoqué** (-'ke)] to focus; focus on; bring into focus.
enfoque (en'fo·ke) *n.m.* **1,** focus; focussing. **2,** approach (*to a matter*).
enfrascamiento (en·fras·ka·'mjen·to) *n.m.* **1,** involvement. **2,** distraction; absent-mindedness.
enfrascar (en·fras'kar) *v.t.* [*infl.:* **tocar**] to bottle; put in a flask *or* jar. —**enfrascarse,** *v.r.* to be absorbed *or* engrossed.
enfrenar (en·fre'nar) *v.t.* **1,** to restrain; bridle. **2,** to brake; put the brake on.
enfrentar (en·fren'tar) *v.t.* **1,** to confront; put face to face. **2,** to face; be situated opposite. —**enfrentarse a** *or* **con, 1,** to face. **2,** to oppose.
enfrente (en'fren·te) *adv.* opposite; facing. —**enfrente de,** opposite; in front of.
enfriamiento (en·fri·a'mjen·to) *n.m.* **1,** cooling; refrigeration. **2,** cold; chill.
enfriar (en·fri'ar) *v.t.* [*pres.ind.* **enfrío** (-'fri·o); *pres.subjve.* **enfríe** (-'fri·e)] to cool; chill. —**enfriarse,** *v.r.* **1,** to cool. **2,** to grow cold. **3,** to catch cold.
enfundar (en·fun'dar) *v.t.* to sheathe; put in a case, sack, etc.
enfurecer (en·fu·re'θer; -'ser) *v.t.* [*pres.ind.* **enfurezco** (-'reθ·ko; -'res·ko); *pres.subjve.* **enfurezca** (-ka)] to enrage; infuriate. —**enfurecerse,** *v.r.* to rage; become infuriated. —**enfurecimiento,** *n.m.* fury.
enfurruñarse (en·fu·rru'ɲar·se) *v.r., colloq.* to show annoyance; scowl.
enfurtir (en·fur'tir) *v.t.* **1,** to full (cloth). **2,** to tighten; frizzle (the hair).
engalanar (en·ga·la'nar) *v.t.* **1,** to deck out; adorn. **2,** *naut.* to dress (a ship).
enganchar (en·gan'tʃar) *v.t.* **1,** to hook; hang on a hook. **2,** to hitch. **3,** to connect; link; couple. **4,** *colloq.* to ensnare. **5,** *colloq.* to decoy into military service. —**engancharse,** *v.r.* **1,** to enlist. **2,** to engage; become hooked. **3,** to get caught on a hook.
enganche (en'gan·tʃe) *n.m.* **1,** enlistment. **2,** hooking. **3,** *R.R.* coupling; coupler. *Also,* **enganchamiento.**
engañar (en·ga'ɲar) *v.t.* **1,** to deceive; beguile; fool. **2,** to wile away (time). —**engañarse,** *v.r.* **1,** to be deceived. **2,** to be mistaken. —**engañador,** *adj.* deceiving. —*n.m.* deceiver; cheat.
engañifa (en·ga'ɲi·fa) *n.f., colloq.* deception; inveiglement.
engaño (en'ga·ɲo) *n.m.* **1,** fraud; deceit. **2,** misunderstanding; mistake. **3,** lure; hoax. —**engañoso,** *adj.* false; deceitful; misleading.
engarzar (en·gar'θar; -'sar) *v.t.* [*pres.subjve.* **engarce** (-'gar·θe; -se); *pret.* **engarcé** (-'θe; -'se)] **1,** to string, esp. jewels. **2,** = **engastar. 3,** *Amer.* to link; connect; couple. —**engarce** (-'gar·θe; -se) *n.m.* = **engaste.**
engastar (en·gas'tar) *v.t.* to chase; set; mount, esp. jewels. —**engaste** (-'gas·te) *n.m.* setting; mounting, esp. of jewels.
engatusar (en·ga·tu'sar) *v.t., colloq.* to inveigle; coax. —**engatusador,** *adj., colloq.* coaxing. —*n.m.* coaxer.
engendrar (en·xen'drar) *v.t.* **1,** to engender; beget. **2,** to create; produce.
engendro (en'xen·dro) *n.m.* **1,** fetus. **2,** shapeless offspring; monster. **3,** abortive scheme; botch.
englobar (en·glo'βar) *v.t.* to include; comprise.
engolfarse (en·gol'far·se) *v.r.* **1,** to go deeply (into); delve. **2,** to become absorbed or engrossed.
engomar (en·go'mar) *v.t.* to gum.
engordar (en·gor'ðar) *v.t. & i.* to fatten.
engoznar (en·goθ'nar; en·gos-) *v.t.* to hinge.
engranaje (en·gra'na·xe) *n.m.* gearing; gear; gears.
engranar (en·gra'nar) *v.t.* to gear; interlock. —*v.i.* to engage, as gears.
engrandecer (en·gran·de'θer; -'ser) *v.t.* [*pres.ind.* **engrandezco** (-'deθ·ko; -'des·ko); *pres.subjve.* **engrandezca** (-ka)] **1,** to augment; aggrandize. **2,** to exalt; magnify.

engrandecimiento (en·gran·de·θi'mjen·to; -si'mjen·to) *n.m.* **1,** increase; aggrandizement. **2,** magnification.
engrane (en'gra·ne) *n.m.* **1,** mesh; meshing (*of gears*). **2,** = **engranaje.**
engrapador (en·gra·pa'ðor) *n.m.* stapler.
engrapar (en·gra'par) *v.t.* **1,** to cramp with irons. **2,** to staple.
engrasar (en·gra'sar) *v.t.* **1,** to oil; grease; lubricate. **2,** to stain with grease. —**engrasador,** *n.m.* oiler; lubricator. —**engrase** (-'gra·se) *n.m.* greasing; lubrication.
engreído (en·gre'i·ðo) *adj.* **1,** vain; conceited; spoiled. **2,** infatuated.
engreír (en·gre'ir) *v.t.* [*infl.:* **reír**] **1,** to make vain or conceited; spoil, esp. a child. **2,** to infatuate. —**engreírse,** *v.r.* to become vain or conceited. —**engreimiento,** *n.m.* vanity; conceit; presumption.
enguantar (en·gwan'tar) *v.t.* to glove.
engrudo (en'gru·ðo) *n.m.* paste.
enguirnaldar (en·gir·nal'dar) *v.t.* **1,** to wreathe; garland. **2,** to trim; adorn.
engullir (en·gu'ʎir; -'jir) *v.t.* to gulp; devour.
enhebrar (en·e'βrar) *v.t.* to string; thread.
enhiesto (en'jes·to) *adj.* erect; upright.
enhilar (en·i'lar) *v.t.* to thread; string.
enhorabuena (en·o·ra'βwe·na) *n.f.* congratulation. —*adv.* well and good. —**estar de enhorabuena,** to be glad; be content.
enhuerar (en·we'rar) *v.t.* to addle.
enigma (e'niɣ·ma) *n.m.* enigma. —**enigmático** (-'ma·ti·ko) *adj.* enigmatic.
enjabonar (en·xa·βo'nar) *v.t.* **1,** to soap; lather. **2,** *colloq.* to softsoap. **3,** *colloq.* to reprimand.
enjaezar (en·xa·e'θar; -'sar) *v.t.* [*infl.:* **rezar**] to harness.
enjalbegar (en·xal·βe'ɣar) *v.t.* [*infl.:* **llegar**] **1,** to whitewash. **2,** to daub; smear (the face).
enjambre (en'xam·bre) *n.m.* **1,** swarm of bees. **2,** crowd; multitude. —**enjambrar,** *v.i.* to swarm.
enjaular (en·xau'lar) *v.t.* **1,** to cage. **2,** *colloq.* to jail.
enjoyar (en·xo'jar) *v.t.* to gem; bejewel.
enjuagadientes (en·xwa·ɣa·'ðjen·tes) *n.m. sing. & pl.* mouthwash.
enjuagar (en·xwa'ɣar) *v.t.* [*pres. subjve.* **enjuague** (-'xwa·ɣe); *pret.* **enjuagué** (-'ɣe)] to rinse.
enjuague (en'xwa·ɣe) *n.m.* rinse.
enjugar (en·xu'ɣar) *v.t.* **1,** to dry; wipe. **2,** to cancel; wipe out (a debt or deficit). —**enjugarse,** *v.r.* to become thin; take off weight.
enjuiciar (en·xwi'θjar; -'sjar) *v.t.* to judge; pass judgment on.
enjundia (en'xun·dja) *n.f.* **1,** nub; gist. **2,** vigor; vim.
enjuto (en'xu·to) *adj.* lean; gaunt.
enlace (en'la·θe; -se) *n.m.* **1,** connection. **2,** liaison; link. **3,** interlocking. **4,** marriage.
enladrillado (en·la·ðri'ʎa·ðo; -'ja·ðo) *n.m.* **1,** brick pavement. **2,** brickwork.
enladrillar (en·la·ðri'ʎar; -'jar) *v.t.* to pave with brick. —**enladrillador,** *n.m.* bricklayer.
enlatar (en·la'tar) *v.t.* to can.
enlazar (en·la'θar; -'sar) *v.t.* [*pres.subjve.* **enlace** (-'la·θe; -se); *pret.* **enlacé** (-'θe; -'se)] **1,** to tie; bind. **2,** to link; connect. **3,** to lasso. —**enlazarse,** *v.r.* **1,** to be joined. **2,** to interlock. **3,** to be joined in marriage. **4,** to become related by marriage.
enlistonado (en·lis·to'na·ðo) *n.m.* furring; lathing.
enlodar (en·lo'ðar) *v.t.* **1,** to muddy; bemire. **2,** to sully; besmirch.
enloquecer (en·lo·ke'θer; -'ser) *v.t.* [*pres.ind.* **enloquezco** (-'keθ·ko; -'kes·ko); *pres. subjve.* **enloquezca** (-ka)] to make insane; drive crazy. —*v.i.* [*also, refl.,* **enloquecerse**] **1,** to become insane; be driven crazy. **2,** *hortic.* to become barren. —**enloquecedor,** *adj.* maddening. —**enloquecimiento,** *n.m.* madness; insanity.
enlosar (en·lo'sar) *v.t.* to tile. —**enlosado,** *n.m.* tilework; tile floor.
enlutar (en·lu'tar) *v.t.* **1,** to put in mourning. **2,** to dress or drape with mourning. **3,** *fig.* to sadden.
enllantar (en·ʎan'tar; en·jan-) *v.t.* to shoe (a wheel).
enmaderar (en·ma·ðe'rar) *v.t.* to timber; construct or cover with timber. —**enmaderamiento,** *n.m.* timberwork; woodwork.

enmarañar (en·ma·ra'ɲar) *v.t.* to tangle; entangle; confuse; mix up. —**enmarañamiento,** *n.m.* tangle; entanglement.

enmascarar (en·mas·ka'rar) *v.t.* to mask. —**enmascararse,** *v.r.* to masquerade; disguise oneself.

enmelar (en·me'lar) *v.t.* [*pres.ind.* **enmielo** (-'mje·lo); *pres.subjve.* **enmiele** (-le)] **1,** to cover or smear with or as with honey. **2,** *fig.* to sweeten; sugar-coat.

enmendar (en·men'dar) *v.t.* [*pres. ind.* **enmiendo** (-'mjen·do); *pres. subjve.* **enmiende** (-de)] **1,** to amend; emend. **2,** to make amends for. —**enmendarse,** *v.r.* to mend one's ways.

enmienda (en'mjen·da) *n.f.* **1,** correction; emendation. **2,** amendment. **3,** amends (*pl.*).

enmohecer (en·mo·e'θer; -'ser) *v.t.* [*pres.ind.* **enmohezco** (-'eθ·ko; -'es·ko); *pres.subjve.* **enmohezca** (-ka)] **1,** to mildew; mold. **2,** to rust.

enmohecido (en·mo·e'θi·ðo; -'si·ðo) *adj.* **1,** mildewed; moldy; musty. **2,** rusty; rusted.

enmohecimiento (en·mo·e·θi·'mjen·to; -si'mjen·to) *n.m.* **1,** mustiness; moldiness. **2,** rustiness; rust.

enmollecer (en·mo·ʎe'θer; -je·'ser) *v.t.* [*pres.ind.* **enmollezco** (-'ʎeθ·ko; -'jes·ko); *pres.subjve.* **enmollezca** (-ka)] to soften; mollify.

enmudecer (en·mu·ðe'θer; -'ser) *v.t.* [*pres.ind.* **enmudezco** (-'ðeθ·ko; -'ðes·ko); *pres.subjve.* **enmudezca** (-ka)] to silence. —*v.i.* to be *or* become silent.

ennegrecer (en·ne·ɣre'θer; -'ser) *v.t.* [*pres.ind.* **ennegrezco** (-'ɣreθ·ko; -'ɣres·ko); *pres.subjve.* **ennegrezca** (-ka)] to obscure; darken; blacken. —**ennegrecimiento,** *n.m.* blackening; darkening.

ennoblecer (en·no·βle'θer; -'ser) *v.t.* [*pres.ind.* **ennoblezco** (-'βleθ·ko; -'βles·ko); *pres.subjve.* **ennoblezca** (-ka)] **1,** to ennoble. **2,** to adorn; embellish. —**ennoblecedor,** *adj.* ennobling. —**ennoblecimiento,** *n.m.* ennoblement.

-eno ('e·no) *suffix* **1,** -th; *forming ordinal numerals: noveno,* ninth. **2,** *forming adjectives denoting* quality; relation; tendency: *terreno,* terrestrial; *moreno,* dark brown. **3,** -ene; *forming the names of certain hydrocarbons: etileno,* ethylene.

enojadizo (e·no·xa'ði·θo; -so) *adj.* cross; irritable.

enojar (e·no'xar) *v.t.* to annoy; irritate. —**enojado,** *adj.* annoyed; peevish.

enojo (e'no·xo) *n.m.* annoyance; bother; trouble. —**enojoso,** *adj.* annoying; bothersome; troublesome.

enorgullecer (e·nor·ɣu·ʎe'θer; -je'ser) *v.t.* [*pres.ind.* **enorgullezco** (-'ʎeθ·ko; -'jes·ko); *pres.subjve.* **enorgullezca** (-ka)] to make proud. —**enorgullecerse,** *v.r.* to be proud. —**enorgullecido,** *adj.* haughty; arrogant; extremely proud.

enorme (e'nor·me) *adj.* **1,** huge; enormous. **2,** horrible; wicked.

enormidad (e·nor·mi'ðað) *n.f.* **1,** enormousness. **2,** enormity.

enrabiar (en·ra'βjar) *v.t.* to enrage; anger.

enramada (en·ra'ma·ða) *n.f.* bower; arbor.

enramar (en·ra'mar) *v.t.* to decorate with branches. —*v.i.* to branch (*of trees*).

enranciar (en·ran'θjar; -'sjar) *v.t.* to make rancid; spoil. —**enranciarse,** *v.r.* to become rancid; spoil.

enrarecer (en·ra·re'θer; -'ser) *v.t.* [*pres.ind.* **enrarezco** (-'reθ·ko; -'res·ko); *pres.subjve.* **enrarezca** (-ka)] to thin; rarefy. —**enrarecerse,** *v.r.* **1,** to become rare or scarce. **2,** to become stuffy, as the air in a room.

enredadera (en·re·ða'ðe·ra) *n.f.* climbing plant; vine. —*adj.fem.* climbing (*of plants*).

enredador (en·re·ða'ðor) *adj.* **1,** mischievous. **2,** gossipy. —*n.m.* **1,** mischief-maker. **2,** busybody; gossip.

enredar (en·re'ðar) *v.t.* **1,** to entangle; confuse. **2,** to intertwine. **3,** to embroil. —*v.i.* **1,** to fiddle; trifle. **2,** to be frisky; romp.

enredo (en're·ðo) *n.m.* **1,** tangle; entanglement. **2,** mischief. **3,** fib; mischievous lie. **4,** plot (*of a play*). —**enredos,** *n.m.pl.* belongings.

enredoso (en·re'ðo·so) *adj.* tangled; complex; intricate.

enrejado (en·re'xa·ðo) *n.m.* **1,** trellis; lattice. **2,** grillwork; grating.

enrejar (en·re'xar) *v.t.* to provide with grillwork or latticework.

enrevesado (en·re·βe'sa·ðo) *adj.* = **revesado.**

enrielar (en·rje'lar) *v.t., Amer.* = **encarrilar.**

enriquecer (en·ri·ke'θer; -'ser) *v.t.* [*pres.ind.* **enriquezco** (-'keθ·ko; -'kes·ko); *pres.subjve.* **enriquezca** (-ka)] to enrich. —**enriquecerse,** *v.r.* to become rich. —**enriquecimiento,** *n.m.* enrichment.

enrocar (en·ro'kar) *v.t. & i.* [*infl.:* **tocar**] *chess* to castle.

enrojecer (en·ro·xe'θer; -'ser) *v.t.* [*pres.ind.* **enrojezco** (-'xeθ·ko; 'xes·ko); *pres.subjve.* **enrojezca** (-ka)] **1,** to redden; **2,** to make red-hot. **3,** to cause to blush. —**enrojecerse,** *v.r.* **1,** to blush. **2,** to turn red.

enrojecido (en·ro·xe'θi·ðo; -'si·ðo) *adj.* **1,** reddened. **2,** red-hot. **3,** blushing.

enrolar (en·ro'lar) *v.t.* to enlist. —**enrolamiento,** *n.m.* enlistment.

enrollar (en·ro'ʎar; -'jar) *v.t.* to wind; coil; roll up.

enronquecer (en·ron·ke'θer; -'ser) *v.t.* [*infl.:* **crecer**] to make hoarse. —**enronquecerse,** *v.r.* to become hoarse. —**enronquecimiento,** *n.m.* hoarseness.

enroscar (en·ros'kar) *v.t.* [*pres. subjve.* **enrosque** (-'ros·ke); *pret.* **enrosqué** (-'ke)] **1,** to twist; twine. **2,** to screw in.

ensacar (en·sa'kar) *v.t.* [*infl.:* **sacar**] to bag; put in a bag or sack.

ensalada (en·sa'la·ða) *n.f.* **1,** salad. **2,** *fig.* medley; hodgepodge. —**ensaladera,** *n.f.* salad bowl.

ensalmo (en'sal·mo) *n.m.* spell; incantation. —**por ensalmo,** miraculously.

ensalzar (en·sal'θar; -'sar) *v.t.* [*pres.subjve.* **ensalce** (-'sal·θe; -se); *pret.* **ensalcé** (-'θe; -'se)] to exalt; extol. —**ensalzarse,** *v.r.* to vaunt oneself. —**ensalzamiento,** *n.m.* exaltation.

ensamblar (en·sam'blar) *v.t.* to join; assemble; dovetail; *carpentry* to mortise. —**ensamblador,** *n.m.* joiner. —**ensambladura,** *n.f.* mortise; joint; dovetail.

ensanchar (en·san'tʃar) *v.t.* to stretch; extend; expand; enlarge; widen. —**ensanchador,** *n.m.* stretcher; expander. —**ensanchamiento,** *n.m.* extension; enlargement.

ensanche (en'san·tʃe) *n.m.* **1,** extension; enlargement; widening. **2,** *sewing* turn-in of a seam. **3,** undeveloped land on the outskirts of a city.

ensangrentar (en·san·gren'tar) *v.t.* [*pres.ind.* **ensangriento** (-'grjen·to); *pres.subjve.* **ensangriente** (-te)] to bloody; stain with blood.

ensartar (en·sar'tar) *v.t.* **1,** to string (beads). **2,** to thread (a needle). **3,** to link. —*v.i.* to talk rigmarole.

ensayar (en·sa'jar) *v.t.* **1,** to try; essay. **2,** to rehearse; practice. **3,** to test; assay. —**ensayarse,** *v.r.* to practice.

ensayo (en'sa·jo) *n.m.* **1,** test; assay. **2,** experiment; trial. **3,** practice; rehearsal. **4,** essay. —**ensayista,** *n.m. & f.* essayist.

-ense ('en·se) *suffix, forming nouns and adjectives denoting* origin; relation: *londinense,* Londoner; of London.

enseguida (en·se'ɣi·ða) *adv.* = **en seguida.**

ensenada (en·se'na·ða) *n.f.* inlet; cove.

enseña (en'se·ɲa) *n.f.* ensign; colors (*pl.*).

enseñanza (en·se'ɲan·θa; -sa) *n.f.* **1,** doctrine. **2,** teaching; instruction. **3,** education.

enseñar (en·se'ɲar) *v.t.* **1,** to train; teach. **2,** to show; point out.

enseres (en'se·res) *n.m.pl.* furnishings; tools; equipment (*sing.*).

ensilaje (en·si'la·xe) *n.m.* ensilage. —**ensilar,** *v.t.* to ensile.

ensillar (en·si'ʎar; -'jar) *v.t.* to saddle.

ensimismarse (en·si·mis'mar·se) *v.r.* to be engrossed; be abstracted. —**ensimismamiento,** *n.m.* absorption; engrossment.

ensoberbecer (en·so·βer·βe'θer; -'ser) *v.t.* [*infl.:* **crecer**] to excite pride in; make proud or haughty. —**ensoberbecerse,** *v.r.* **1,** to become proud or haughty. **2,** to become rough or choppy, as the sea. —**ensoberbecimiento,** *n.m.* pride; haughtiness.

ensombrecer (en·som·bre'θer; -'ser) *v.t.* [*pres.ind.* **ensombrezco** (-'breθ·ko; -'bres·ko); *pres.subjve.* **ensombrezca** (-ka)] **1,** to darken; cloud. **2,** *fig.* to overshadow.

ensopar (en·so'par) *v.t.* to soak; steep.

ensordecer (en·sor·ðe'θer; -'ser) *v.t.* [*pres.ind.* **ensordezco** (-'ðeθ·ko; -'ðes·ko); *pres.subjve.* **ensordezca** (-ka)] to deafen. —*v.i.* to become deaf. —**ensordecedor,** *adj.* deafening. —**ensordecimiento,** *n.m.* deafness.

ensortijar (en·sor·ti'xar) *v.t.* to curl; kink. —**ensortijado,** *adj., colloq.* bejeweled.

ensuciar (en·su'θjar; -'sjar) *v.t.* to soil; dirty. —**ensuciarse,** *v.r.* **1,** to soil oneself. **2,** *colloq.* to be dishonest or corrupt.

ensueño (en'swe·ɲo) *n.m.* **1,** illusion; fantasy. **2,** dream.

entablar (en·ta'βlar) *v.t.* **1,** to cover with boards; board up. **2,** to start (a negotiation). **3,** *law* to bring (an action). —**entablarse,** *v.r.* to settle, as the wind.

entablillar (en·ta·βli'ʎar; -'jar) *v.t., surg.* to splint.

entallar (en·ta'ʎar; -'jar) *v.t.* **1,** to notch. **2,** to carve; engrave. **3,** to tailor; cut close to the figure. —*v.t.* & *i.* to fit, as a garment.

entapizar (en·ta·pi'θar; -'sar) *v.t.* to hang or adorn with tapestry.

entarimar (en·ta·ri'mar) *v.t.* to floor; provide with flooring. —**entarimado,** *n.m.* hardwood floor.

ente ('en·te) *n.m.* being; entity.

-ente ('en·te) *suffix* **1,** -ent; -ing; *forming adjectives equivalent to participles: descendente,* descending. **2,** *forming nouns of agency: asistente,* assistant.

enteco (en'te·ko) *adj.* sickly; emaciated. *Also,* **entecado** (-'ka·ðo).

entendedor (en·ten·de'ðor) *n.m.* perceptive or understanding person.

entender (en·ten'der) *v.t.* & *i.* [*pres.ind.* **entiendo** (-'tjen·do); *pres.subjve.* **entienda** (-da)] **1,** to understand; comprehend. **2,** to suppose; guess. **3,** to conclude; infer. **4,** *fol. by* **de** *or* **en,** to be familiar with; be good at. **5,** *fol. by* **en** *or* **de,** to be in charge of; have authority or responsibility in. —**entenderse,** *v.r.* **1,** to be understood. **2,** to be meant. **3,** to know what one is about. **4,** to agree. **5,** to understand each other. **6,** to have an understanding. **7,** *fol. by* **con,** to deal with; have dealings with. —*n.m.* understanding; opinion.

entendido (en·ten'di·ðo) *adj.* **1,** experienced; able. **2,** well-informed. —**darse por entendido,** to take a hint; take notice.

entendimiento (en·ten·di'mjen·to) *n.m.* **1,** understanding. **2,** mind; intellect.

enterado (en·te'ra·ðo) *adj.* **1,** informed; aware. **2,** *Amer.* conceited; arrogant. —*n.m.* acknowledgment (by signing) that one has read and understood a document.

enteramente (en·te·ra'men·te) *adv.* completely; fully.

enterar (en·te'rar) *v.t.* to inform. —**enterarse de,** to find out; become aware of.

entereza (en·te're·θa; -sa) *n.f.* **1,** integrity. **2,** entirety. **3,** firmness; fortitude.

enterizo (en·te'ri·θo; -so) *adj.* of one piece.

enternecer (en·ter·ne'θer; -'ser) *v.t.* [*pres. ind.* **enternezco** (-'neθ·ko; -'nes·ko); *pres.subjve.* **enternezca** (-ka)] **1,** to soften; make tender. **2,** to move to compassion. —**enternecedor,** *adj.* touching.

entero (en'te·ro) *adj.* **1,** entire; whole. **2,** sound; perfect. **3,** upright; honest. **4,** constant; firm. —*n.m.* **1,** *math.* integer. **2,** *Amer.* payment.

entero- (en·te·ro) *prefix* entero-; intestine: *enterocolitis,* enterocolitis.

enterrador (en·te·rra'ðor) *n.m.* gravedigger.

enterramiento (en·te·rra'mjen·to) *n.m.* **1,** burial; interment. **2,** grave; tomb.

enterrar (en·te'rrar) *v.t.* [*pres.ind.* **entierro** (-'tje·rro); *pres.subjve.* **entierre** (-rre)] to bury; inter.

entibar (en·ti'βar) *v.i.* = **estribar.** —*v.t.* to prop; shore up. —**entibo** (-'ti·βo) *n.m.* prop; shoring.

entibiar (en·ti'βjar) *v.t.* **1,** to make lukewarm. **2,** to cool down (temper, passions, etc.).

entidad (en·ti'ðað) *n.f.* **1,** entity. **2,** value; importance. **3,** business establishment. **4,** group; body.

entierro (en'tje·rro) *n.m.* **1,** burial; interment. **2,** funeral. **3,** grave; tomb. **4,** buried treasure.

entintar (en·tin'tar) *v.t.* to ink; spread ink on; stain with ink.

ento- (en·to) *prefix* ento-; within; inner: *entofita,* entophyte.

-ento ('en·to) *suffix, forming adjectives denoting* manner; tendency: *violento,* violent; *amarillento,* yellowish.

entoldar (en·tol'dar) *v.t.* **1,** to cover with a hood or awning. **2,** to cover (walls) with tapestries, cloth, etc. —**entoldarse,** *v.r.* to become overcast.

entomo- (en·to·mo) *prefix* entomo-; insect: *entomología,* entomology.

entomología (en·to·mo·lo'xi·a) *n.f.* entomology. —**entomológico** (-'lo·xi·ko) *adj.* entomological. —**entomólogo** (-'mo·lo·ɣo) *n.m.* entomologist.

entonación (en·to·na'θjon; -'sjon) *n.f.* **1,** intonation. **2,** modulation (*of the voice*). **3,** *fig.* pride; presumption.

entonado (en·to'na·ðo) *adj.* arrogant; haughty.

entonar (en·to'nar) *v.t.* **1,** to modulate (the voice). **2,** to intone. **3,** *painting* to harmonize (colors). **4,** *med.* to tone up. **5,** to make flexible; limber.

entonces (en'ton·θes; -ses) *adv.* **1,** then; at that time. **2,** well then; now then; so then. —**en aquel entonces,** at that time.

entono (en'to·no) *n.m.* **1,** intonation. **2,** arrogance; haughtiness.

entontecer (en·ton·te'θer; -'ser) *v.t.* [*pres.ind.* **entontezco** (-'teθ·ko; -'tes·ko); *pres.subjve.* **entontezca** (-ka)] to stupefy; make foolish.

entornar (en·tor'nar) *v.t.* **1,** to half-open; set ajar. **2,** to half-close (the eyes).

entorpecer (en·tor·pe'θer; -'ser) *v.t.* [*pres.ind.* **entorpezco** (-'peθ·ko; -'pes·ko); *pres.subjve.* **entorpezca** (-ka)] to obstruct; hamper.

entorpecimiento (en·tor·pe·θi·'mjen·to; -si'mjen·to) *n.m.* **1,** delay; obstruction. **2,** stupidity.

entrada (en'tra·ða) *n.f.* **1,** entrance; door; gate. **2,** entry; admission; admittance. **3,** ticket of admission. **4,** total of admissions *or* receipts; gate. **5,** beginning. **6,** *cards* trump hand. **7,** main dish; entrée. **8,** earnings; income. **9,** *comm.* receipts; gross. **10,** ledger entry.

entrambos (en'tram·bos) *adj.* & *pron.masc.pl.* [*fem.* **entrambas**] both.

entrampar (en·tram'par) *v.t.* **1,** to trap; entrap. **2,** to trick. **3,** *colloq.* to entangle. **4,** *colloq.* to burden with debt. —**entrampamiento;** *n.m.* entrapment; ensnarement.

entramparse (en·tram'par·se) *v.r., colloq.* to fall into debt; become encumbered with debts.

entrante (en'tran·te) *adj.* **1,** entering. **2,** coming; next. —*n.m.* recessed part.

entraña (en'tra·ɲa) *n.f., usu.pl.* **1,** *anat.* entrail. **2,** core; center. **3,** *fig.* heart; soul.

entrañable (en·tra'ɲa·βle) *adj.* **1,** most affectionate. **2,** deep; profound.

entrañar (en·tra'ɲar) *v.t.* to contain; carry within; involve. —**entrañarse,** *v.r.* to become closely attached.

entrar (en'trar) *v.i.* **1,** to enter; go in; come in. **2,** to flow in. **3,** to join; become a member *or* part. **4,** to begin; enter (upon). —*v.t.* **1,** to introduce; put in. **2,** to invade; enter in force. **3,** to exercise influence in *or* on. **4,** *comm.* to enter (*in a ledger*). —**entrarse,** *v.r.* to enter; gain entry.

entre ('en·tre) *prep.* among; between. —**entre tanto,** in the meantime. —**entre manos,** in hand.

entre- (en·tre) *prefix* **1,** inter-; between; among: *entrelazar,* interlace. **2,** *limiting the force of verbs and adjectives: entreabrir,* to half-open; *entrecano,* graying (*of hair*).

entreabrir (en·tre·a'βrir) *v.t.* [*infl.:* **abrir**] to half-open; set ajar. —**entreabierto,** *adj.* ajar.

entreacto (en·tre'ak·to) *n.m.* intermission.

entrecano (en·tre'ka·no) *adj.* grayish; graying (*of the hair*).

entrecasa (en·tre'ka·sa) *n.f., in* **de** *or* **para entrecasa,** to be worn in the house.

entrecejo (en·tre'θe·xo; -'se·xo) *n.m.* **1,** space between the eyebrows. **2,** *fig.* frown.

entrecoro (en·tre'ko·ro) *n.m.* chancel.

entrecortado (en·tre·kor'ta·ðo) *adj.* broken; interrupted; halting.

entredicho (en·tre'ði·tʃo) *n.m.* **1,** injunction; prohibition. **2,** interdict.

entrega (en'tre·ɣa) *n.f.* **1,** delivery; conveyance. **2,** surrender; submission. **3,** installment, as of a novel.

entregar (en·tre'ɣar) *v.t.* [*pres. subjve.* **entregue** (-'tre·ɣe); *pret.* **entregué** (-'ɣe)] to give up; deliver. —**entregarse,** *v.r.* to surrender; submit.

entrelazar (en·tre·la'θar; -'sar) *v.t.* [*infl.:* **lazar**] to interlace; interweave.

entremedias (en·tre'me·ðjas) *adv.* **1,** in the meantime. **2,** in between; amidst.

entremés (en·tre'mes) *n.m., theat.* interlude; farce. —**entremeses,** *n.m. pl.* hors d'oeuvres.

entremeter (en·tre·me'ter) *v.t.* to insert; place between. —**entremeterse,** *v.r.* to intrude; meddle.

entremetido (en·tre·me'ti·ðo) *adj.* meddlesome; intrusive; officious. —*n.m.* **1,** meddler; intruder. **2,** go-between.

entremetimiento (en·tre·me·ti·'mjen·to) *n.m.* intrusion; meddling.

entremezclar (en·tre·meθ'klar; -mes'klar) *v.t.* to intermingle.

entrenar (en·tre'nar) *v.t.* to train. —**entrenador,** *adj.* training. —*n.m.* trainer; coach. —**entrenamiento,** *n.m.* training.

entrepierna (en·tre'pjer·na) *n.f., usu.pl.* **1,** inner surface of the thigh. **2,** crotch (*of trousers*).

entreponer (en·tre·po'ner) *v.t.* [*infl.:* **poner**] to interpose.

entresacar (en·tre·sa'kar) *v.t.* [*infl.:* **sacar**] **1,** to pick out; cull. **2,** to thin out; trim.

entresuelo (en·tre'swe·lo) *n.m.* mezzanine.

entretanto (en·tre'tan·to) *adv.* & *n.m.* meanwhile; meantime.

entretejer (en·tre·te'xer) *v.t.* to interweave; intertwine.

entretela (en·tre'te·la) *n.f.* **1,** interlining. **2,** buckram. —**entretelas,** *n.f.pl., colloq.* innermost being; bowels.

entretener (en·tre·te'ner) *v.t.* [*infl.:* **tener**] **1,** to amuse; entertain. **2,** to trifle with. **3,** to delay; postpone. **4,** to detain. —**entretenido,** *adj.* entertaining; pleasant.

entretenimiento (en·tre·ten·i·'mjen·to) *n.m.* **1,** sport; amusement; entertainment. **2,** delay.

entretiempo (en·tre'tjem·po) *n.m.* middle season; spring *or* fall. —**abrigo de entretiempo,** spring coat.

entrever (en·tre'βer) *v.t.* [*infl.:* **ver**] **1,** to glimpse. **2,** to guess; divine.

entreverar (en·tre·βe'rar) *v.t.* to intermix; intermingle.

entrevista (en·tre'βis·ta) *n.f.* interview. —**entrevistar** (-'tar) *v.t.* to interview. —**entrevistarse,** *v.r.* to be interviewed.

entristecer (en·tris·te'θer; -'ser) *v.t.* [*pres.ind.* **entristezco** (-'teθ·ko; -'tes·ko); *pres.subjve.* **entristezca** (-ka)] to grieve; sadden. —**entristecerse,** *v.r.* to grieve; grow sad. —**entristecimiento,** *n.m.* sadness.

entrometer (en·tro·me'ter) *v.t.* = **entremeter.** —**entrometido,** *adj.* & *n.m.* = **entremetido.** —**entrometimiento,** *n.m.* = **entremetimiento.**

entronar (en·tro'nar) *v.t.* = **entronizar.**

entronizar (en·tro·ni'θar; -'sar) *v.t.* [*pres.subjve.* **entronice** (-'ni·θe; -se); *pret.* **entronicé** (-'θe; -'se)] to enthrone. —**entronización,** *n.f.* enthronement.

entruchar (en·tru'tʃar) *v.t.* to lure; decoy. —**entruchón** (-'tʃon) *n.m.* decoy.

entuerto (en'twer·to) *n.m.* injustice; wrong. —**entuertos,** *n.m.pl.* afterpains.

entumecer (en·tu·me'θer; -'ser) *v.t.* [*pres.ind.* **entumezco** (-'meθ·ko; -'mes·ko); *pres.subjve.* **entumezca** (-ka)] to benumb. —**entumecerse,** *v.r.* to become numb. —**entumecimiento,** *n.m.* numbness.

enturbiar (en·tur'βjar) *v.t.* **1,** to muddy. **2,** *fig.* to confuse; obscure. **3,** to upset; disarrange.

entusiasmar (en·tu·sjas'mar) *v.t.* to enrapture; transport. —**entusiasmarse,** *v.r.* to become enthusiastic; be enraptured. —**entusiasmado,** *adj.* enthusiastic.

entusiasmo (en·tu'sjas·mo) *n.m.* enthusiasm.

entusiasta (en·tu'sjas·ta) *n.m.* enthusiast; fan. —*adj.* enthusiastic.

entusiástico (en·tu'sjas·ti·ko) *adj.* enthusiastic.

enumerar (e·nu·me'rar) *v.t.* to enumerate. —**enumeración,** *n.f.* enumeration.

enunciar (e·nun'θjar; -'sjar) *v.t.* to enunciate. —**enunciación,** *n.f.* [*also,* **enunciado,** *n.m.*] enunciation.

envainar (en·βai'nar) *v.t.* to sheathe (a sword).

envalentonar (en·βa·len·to'nar) *v.t.* to encourage; make bold. —**envalentonarse,** *v.r.* **1,** to become bold *or* courageous. **2,** to brag.

envanecer (en·βa·ne'θer; -'ser) *v.t.* [*pres.ind.* **envanezco** (-'neθ·ko; -'nes·ko); *pres.subjve.* **envanezca** (-ka)] to make vain. —**envanecerse,** *v.r.* to become vain. —**envanecimiento,** *n.m.* conceit.

envasar (en·βa'sar) *v.t.* **1,** to bottle; put into a barrel, cask, sack, or other container. **2,** *fig.* to drink to

excess. **3,** *fig.* to thrust into the body, as a sword.
envase (en'βa·se) *n.m.* **1,** bottling. **2,** cask, barrel, or other container for liquids. **3,** packing.
envejecer (en·βe·xe'θer; -'ser) *v.t.* [*pres.ind.* **envejezco** (-'xeθ·ko; -'xes·ko); *pres.subjve.* **envejezca** (-ka)] **1,** to make old. **2,** to make look old. —*v.i.* **1,** to grow old. **2,** to become inveterate. —**envejecerse,** *v.r.* **1,** to become old. **2,** to go out of use.
envejecido (en·βe·xe'θi·ðo; -'si·ðo) *adj.* **1,** grown old. **2,** old-looking. **3,** inveterate. **4,** old-fashioned.
envenenar (en·βe·ne'nar) *v.t.* to poison; envenom. —**envenenador,** *adj.* poisonous. —*n.m.* poisoner.
envergadura (en·βer·ɣa'ðu·ra) *n.f.* **1,** wing span. **2,** *naut.* breadth (*of sails*). **3,** *fig.* compass; scope.
enviar (en·βi'ar) *v.t.* [*pres.ind.* **envío** (-'βi·o); *pres.subjve.* **envíe** (-'βi·e)] *v.t.* **1,** to send. **2,** to transmit; forward; convey. —**enviado,** *n.m.* envoy.
enviciar (en·βi'θjar; -'sjar) *v.t.* to corrupt; vitiate. —**enviciarse,** *v.r.* to acquire bad habits.
envidia (en'βi·ðja) *n.f.* envy; jealousy.
envidiable (en·βi'ðja·βle) *adj.* enviable; desirable.
envidiar (en·βi'ðjar) *v.t.* to envy; be jealous of.
envidioso (en·βi'ðjo·so) *adj.* **1,** envious; jealous. **2,** invidious.
envilecer (en·βi·le'θer; -'ser) *v.t.* [*pres.ind.* **envilezco** (-'leθ·ko; -'les·ko); *pres.subjve.* **envilezca** (-ka)] to vilify; debase; degrade. —**envilecimiento,** *n.m.* vilification; debasement; degradation.
envío (en'βi·o) *n.m.* **1,** remittance. **2,** consignment; shipment.
envite (en'βi·te) *n.m., cards* bet; stake.
enviudar (en·βju'ðar) *v.i.* to become a widower *or* widow.
envoltorio (en·βol'to·rjo) *n.m.* **1,** bundle; package. **2,** covering; wrapping.
envoltura (en·βol'tu·ra) *n.f.* **1,** swaddling clothes. **2,** covering; wrapper; envelope.
envolvedor (en·βol·βe'ðor) *n.m.* **1,** cover; wrapping. **2,** wrapping clerk.
envolver (en·βol'βer) *v.t.* [*infl.:* **volver**] **1,** to wrap up. **2,** to diaper (a baby). **3,** to encircle; surround. **4,** to imply; involve. —**envolverse,** *v.r.* **1,** to be involved *or* implicated. **2,** to be mixed with a crowd. **3,** to bundle up.
envolvimiento (en·βol·βi'mjen·to) *n.m.* **1,** envelopment. **2,** involvement. **3,** encirclement.
envuelto (en'βwel·to) *v., p.p. of* **envolver.**
enyesar (en·je'sar) *v.t.* **1,** to plaster. **2,** to chalk. **3,** to whitewash. —**enyesado,** *n.m., also,* **enyesadura,** *n.f.* plaster; plastering; plasterwork.
enyugar (en·ju'ɣar) *v.t.* [*pres.subjve.* **enyugue** (-'ju·ɣe); *pret.* **enyugué** (-'ɣe)] to yoke.
enzima (en'θi·ma; -'si·ma) *n.f.* enzyme.
enzunchar (en·θun'tʃar; en·sun-) *v.t.* to hoop; bind with hoops or bands.
-eño ('e·ɲo) *suffix, forming adjectives denoting* **1,** origin: *madrileño,* of Madrid. **2,** quality; relation: *aguileño,* aquiline.
eo- (e·o) *prefix* eo-; early; primitive: *eolítico,* eolithic.
-eo *suffix* **1,** (e·o) *forming adjectives denoting* quality; condition: *arbóreo,* arboreal; *acotiledóneo,* acotyledonous. **2,** ('e·o) *forming nouns of action from verbs ending in* **-ear**: *bailoteo,* prancing.
ep- (ep) *prefix, var. of* **epi-**: *epónimo,* eponymous.
¡epa! ('e·pa) *interj., Amer.* = **¡ea!**
eperlano (e·per'la·no) *n.m., ichthy.* smelt.
epi- (e·pi) *prefix* epi-; on; upon; over; among. *epicentro,* epicenter; *epidemia,* epidemic.
épica ('e·pi·ka) *n.f.* epic poetry. —**épico,** *adj.* epic.
epicúreo (e·pi'ku·re·o) *n.m.* epicure. —*adj.* epicurean.
epidemia (e·pi'ðe·mja) *n.f.* epidemic. —**epidémico** (-'ðe·mi·ko) *adj.* epidemic.
epidermis (e·pi'ðer·mis) *n.f.* epidermis.
Epifanía (e·pi·fa'ni·a) *n.f.* Epiphany.
epiglotis (e·pi'ɣlo·tis) *n.f.* epiglottis.
epigrama (e·pi'ɣra·ma) *n.m.* **1,** epigram. **2,** inscription. —**epigramático** (-'ma·ti·ko) *adj.* epigrammatic. —**epigramista** (-'mis·ta) *also,* **epigramatista** (-ma'tis·ta) *n.m.* epigrammatist.

epigramatario (e·pi·ɣra·ma'ta·rjo) *adj.* epigrammatic. —*n.m.* **1,** collection of epigrams. **2,** = epigramista.
epilepsia (e·pi'lep·sja) *n.f.* epilepsy. —**epiléptico** (-'lep·ti·ko) *adj.* & *n.m.* epileptic.
epilogar (e·pi·lo'ɣar) *v.t.* [*pres. subjve.* **epilogue** (-'lo·ɣe); *pret.* **epilogué** (-'ɣe)] to sum up; recapitulate.
epílogo (e'pi·lo·ɣo) *n.m.* **1,** epilogue. **2,** recapitulation.
episcopado (e·pis·ko'pa·ðo) *n.m.* **1,** episcopacy; bishopric. **2,** episcopate.
episcopal (e·pis·ko'pal) *adj.* episcopal; *cap.* Episcopal. —**episcopalista,** *also,* **episcopaliano** (-pa'lja·no) *adj.* Episcopal. —*n.m.* Episcopalian.
episodio (e·pi'so·ðjo) *n.m.* episode. —**episódico** (-'so·ði·ko) *adj.* episodic.
epístola (e'pis·to·la) *n.f.* epistle.
epistolar (e·pis·to'lar) *adj.* epistolary.
epistolario (e·pis·to'la·rjo) *n.m.* **1,** book or collection of letters. **2,** *eccles.* epistolary.
epitafio (e·pi'ta·fjo) *n.m.* epitaph.
epíteto (e'pi·te·to) *n.m.* epithet.
epítome (e'pi·to·me) *n.m.* epitome. —**epitomar** (-'mar) *v.t.* to epitomize.
época ('e·po·ka) *n.f.* **1,** epoch; age; era. **2,** time.
epopeya (e·po'pe·ja) *n.f.* epic.
equi- (e·ki) *prefix* equi-; equal: *equivalente,* equivalent.
equidad (e·ki'ðað) *n.f.* equity; fairness; justice.
equidistante (e·ki·ðis'tan·te) *adj.* equidistant.
equilátero (e·ki'la·te·ro) *adj.* equilateral.
equilibrar (e·ki·li'βrar) *v.t.* **1,** to equilibrate; balance. **2,** to counterbalance.
equilibrio (e·ki'li·βrjo) *n.m.* equilibrium; counterbalance. —**equilibrista** (-'βris·ta) equilibrist; aerialist.
equinoccio (e·ki'nok·θjo; -sjo) *n.m.* equinox. —**equinoccial** (-'θjal; -'sjal) *adj.* equinoctial.
equipaje (e·ki'pa·xe) *n.m.* **1,** luggage; baggage. **2,** equipment.
equipar (e·ki'par) *v.t.* to equip; furnish.
equipo (e'ki·po) *n.m.* **1,** equipping; fitting out. **2,** equipment. **3,** team; crew.
equitación (e·ki·ta'θjon; -'sjon) *n.f.* **1,** riding. **2,** horsemanship.
equitativo (e·ki·ta'ti·βo) *adj.* equitable; fair; just.
equivalente (e·ki·βa'len·te) *adj.* equal; tantamount; equivalent. —*n.m.* equivalent. —**equivalencia,** *n.f.* equivalence.
equivaler (e·ki·βa'ler) *v.i.* [*infl.:* **valer**] to be equal; be equivalent.
equivocar (e·ki·βo'kar) *v.t.* [*pres. subjve.* **equivoque** (-'βo·ke); *pret.* **equivoqué** (-ke)] to mistake; confuse. —**equivocarse,** *v.r.* **1,** to be mistaken. **2,** to make a mistake. —**equivocación,** *n.f.* error; mistake; blunder. —**equivocado,** *adj.* mistaken; wrong.
equívoco (e'ki·βo·ko) *adj.* equivocal. —*n.m.* **1,** equivocation. **2,** misinterpretation.
era ('e·ra) *n.f.* **1,** age; era; time. **2,** threshing floor.
era ('e·ra) *v., impf. of* **ser.**
erario (e'ra·rjo) *n.m.* public treasury.
erbio ('er·βjo) *n.m.* erbium.
erección (e·rek'θjon; -'sjon) *n.f.* erection.
eremita (e·re'mi·ta) *n.m.* hermit.
eres ('e·res) *v., 2nd pers.sing. pres. ind. of* **ser.**
erg ('erɣ) *n.m.* erg; unit of energy. *Also,* **ergio** ('er·xjo).
ergotina (er·ɣo'ti·na) *n.f.* ergotin.
ergotismo (er·ɣo'tis·mo) *n.m.* **1,** *plant pathol.* ergot. **2,** *pathol.* ergotism.
erguir (er'ɣir) *v.t.* [*pres.ind.* **irgo,** *also,* **yergo;** *pres.subjve.* **irga,** *also* **yerga;** *pret.* **erguí, irguió;** *ger.* **irguiendo**] to put up straight; erect. —**erguirse,** *v.r.* **1,** to straighten; take an erect pose. **2,** to stiffen; take a proud stand.
-ería (e'ri·a) *suffix* -ery; *forming nouns denoting* **1,** collectivity: *ferretería,* hardware. **2,** quality; condition: *tontería,* foolishness. **3,** place where something is made or sold: *cervecería,* brewery; *mercería,* haberdashery.
erial (e'rjal) *n.m.* wasteland.
eriazo (e'rja·θo; -so) *adj.* uncultivated; untilled.
erigir (e·ri'xir) *v.t.* [*pres.ind.* **erijo** (e'ri·xo) *pres.subjve.* **erija** (-xa)]

1, to establish; found; erect. **2,** to raise; elevate (*to a position or situation*).

erisipela (e·ri·si'pe·la) *n.f.* erysipelas.

erizado (e·ri'θa·ðo; -'sa·ðo) *adj.* **1,** covered with bristles; bristly. **2,** bristling.

erizar (e·ri'θar; -'sar) *v.t.* [*pres. subjve.* **erice** (e'ri·θe; -se) *pret.* **ericé** (-'θe; -'se)] **1,** to set on end, as the hair. **2,** to surround with difficulties; make bristle with difficulties. —**erizarse,** *v.r.* **1,** to bristle; stand on end. **2,** to become upset; become rattled.

erizo (e'ri·θo; -so) *n.m.* **1,** hedgehog; porcupine. **2,** *fig.* irascible person. **3,** *bot.* bur. —**erizo de mar,** sea urchin.

ermita (er'mi·ta) *n.f.* hermitage. —**ermitaño,** *n.m.* hermit.

-erna ('er·na) *suffix* -ern; *forming nouns with several meanings: linterna,* lantern; *caverna,* cavern.

-erno ('er·no) *suffix* -ern; *forming adjectives: moderno,* modern.

-ero ('e·ro), *fem.* **-era** ('e·ra) *suffix* **1,** *forming nouns denoting* agency; function: *aduanero,* customs officer; *carretero,* cartwright. **2,** *forming names of trees: melocotonero,* peach tree. **3,** *forming nouns denoting* place: *abejera,* apiary. **4,** *forming adjectives denoting* relation; tendency; quality: *algodonero,* pert. to cotton; *parlero,* talkative; *verdadero,* true.

erogar (e·ro'ɣar) *v.t.* [*infl.:* **derogar**] **1,** to divide; apportion (an estate, money, etc.). **2,** *Amer.* to bring about; cause.

-erón (e'ron) *suffix, forming augmentatives, usu. with derog. sense: caserón,* old crumbling house.

erosión (e·ro'sjon) *n.f.* erosion. —**erosivo** (-'si·βo) *adj.* erosive.

erótico (e'ro·ti·ko) *adj.* erotic. —**eroticismo** (-'θis·mo; -'sis·mo) *n.m.* eroticism. —**erotismo** (-'tis·mo) *n.m.* erotism.

errabundo (e·rra'βun·do) *adj.* wandering.

erradicar (e·rra·ði'kar) *v.t.* [*infl.:* **radicar**] to eradicate. —**erradicación,** *n.f.* eradication. —**erradicador,** *n.m.* eradicator.

errado (e'rra·ðo) *adj.* mistaken; erroneous.

errante (e'rran·te) *adj.* errant; wandering; roving.

errar (e'rrar) *v.* [*pres.ind.* **yerro;** *pres.subjve.* **yerre**] —*v.t.* **1,** to miss (a target). **2,** to mistake; choose erroneously. —*v.i.* **1,** to err. **2,** to roam; wander. —**errarse,** *v.r.* to be mistaken.

errata (e'rra·ta) *n.f.* erratum; misprint. —**fe de erratas,** list of errata.

errático (e'rra·ti·ko) *adj.* wandering; vagrant.

erróneo (e'rro·ne·o) *adj.* erroneous.

error (e'rror) *n.m.* error; mistake.

erso ('er·so) *adj.* & *n.m.* Erse.

eructación (e·ruk·ta'θjon; -'sjon) *n.f.* = **eructo.**

eructar (e·ruk'tar) *also,* **erutar** (e·ru'tar) *v.i.* to belch; eruct. —**eructo** (e'ruk·to) *also,* **eruto** (e'ru·to) *n.m.* belch; belching; eructation.

erudito (e·ru'ði·to) *adj.* erudite. —*n.m.* scholar; pundit. —**erudición,** *n.f.* erudition.

erumpir (e·rum'pir) *v.i.* to erupt.

erupción (e·rup'θjon; -'sjon) *n.f.* eruption. —**eruptivo,** *adj.* eruptive.

es (es) *v., 3rd pers.sing. pres.ind. of* **ser.**

-es (es) *suffix* **1,** *forming the 2nd pers.sing. pres.ind. of verbs of the 2nd and 3rd conjugations: temes,* you are afraid; *partes,* you break. **2,** *forming the plural of nouns and adjectives ending in a consonant, or* y, *or an accented vowel other than* e: *árbol, árboles; ley, leyes; rubí, rubíes;* but *café, cafés.*

-és ('es), *fem.* **-esa** ('e·sa) *suffix, forming nouns and adjectives denoting* origin; nationality; language; relation: *francés,* French; Frenchman; *cortés,* courteous.

esa ('e·sa) *dem.adj.* [*pl.* **esas**] *fem. of* **ese.**

ésa ('e·sa) *dem.pron.* [*pl.* **ésas**] *fem. of* **ése.**

-esa ('e·sa) *suffix* **1,** -ess; *forming feminine nouns of* dignity, profession, etc.: *abadesa,* abbess; *princesa,* princess. **2,** *fem. of* **-és:** *francesa,* Frenchwoman.

esbelto (es'βel·to) *adj.* svelte; lithe. —**esbeltez,** *n.f.* elegance of figure; litheness.

esbirro (es'βi·rro) *n.m.* **1,** bailiff. **2,** *colloq.* hired ruffian.

esbozar (es·βo'θar; -'sar) *v.t.* [*pres.subjve.* **esboce** (-'βo·θe; -se); *pret.* **esbocé** (-'θe; -'se)] to sketch.

—**esbozo** (-'βo·θo; -so) *n.m.* sketch; rough draft.
escabechar (es·ka·βe'tʃar) *v.t.* 1, to pickle. 2, *fig.* to dye (gray hair). 3, *colloq.* to stab to death; cut to ribbons. 4, *colloq.* to flunk.
escabeche (es·ka'βe·tʃe) *n.m.* 1, pickled fish; pickled food of any kind. 2, pickling solution.
escabel (es·ka'βel) *n.m.* stool; footstool.
escabiosis (es·ka'βjo·sis) *n.f.* scabies.
escabrosidad (es·ka·βro·si'ðað) *n.f.* 1, cragginess; ruggedness. 2, asperity; severity.
escabroso (es·ka'βro·so) *adj.* 1, craggy; rugged (*of terrain*). 2, difficult; touchy. 3, risqué.
escabullirse (es·ka·βu'ʎir·se; -'jir·se) *v.r.* to slip away; escape. —**escabullimiento,** *n.m.* evasion.
escafandra (es·ka'fan·dra) *n.m.* diving suit.
escala (es'ka·la) *n.f.* 1, ladder. 2, *music* scale. 3, proportion; scale. 4, measuring scale. 5, scale (*of values*). 6, port of call. 7, stop (*in an itinerary*).
escalador (es·ka·la'ðor) *n.m.* 1, climber. 2, burglar; housebreaker.
escalafón (es·ka·la'fon) *n.m.* 1, roll; roster. 2, rank; echelon.
escalar (es·ka'lar) *v.t.* 1, to climb; scale. 2, to enter surreptitiously. 3, to measure according to a scale.
escaldar (es·kal'dar) *v.t.* 1, to scald; burn. 2, to make red-hot. —**escaldarse,** *v.r.* to be vexed; become annoyed. —**escaldadura,** *n.f.* scald; scalding.
escalera (es·ka'le·ra) *n.f.* 1, staircase; stairs (*pl.*). 2, ladder. 3, *poker* straight. —**en escalera,** in sequence.
escalfar (es·kal'far) *v.t.* to poach (eggs). —**escalfador,** *n.m.* chafing dish.
escalinata (es·ka·li'na·ta) *n.f.* front step; front stoop.
escalo (es'ka·lo) *n.m.* 1, housebreaking. 2, climbing; scaling.
escalofrío (es·ka·lo'fri·o) *n.m.* chill; shiver. —**escalofriado,** *adj.* chilled.
escalón (es·ka'lon) *n.m.* 1, step (*of a stair*). 2, stepping stone. 3, echelon.
escalonar (es·ka·lo'nar) *v.t.* 1, to arrange in steps or echelons. 2, to terrace.
escaloña (es·ka'lo·ɲa) *n.f.* = **ascalonia.**
escalpar (es·kal'par) *v.t.* to scalp.
escalpelo (es·kal'pe·lo) *n.m.* scalpel.
escama (es'ka·ma) *n.f.* 1, scale (*of fish, reptiles, etc.*); flake. 2, *fig.* distrust; suspicion.
escamar (es·ka'mar) *v.t.* 1, to scale (a fish). 2, to ornament with a scaly design. 3, *colloq.* to arouse suspicion in. —**escamarse,** *v.r.* to become cagy. —**escamoso,** *adj.* scaly; flaky.
escamotear (es·ka·mo·te'ar) *also,* **escamotar** (-'tar) *v.t.* 1, to palm. 2, to filch. 3, to make disappear.
escamoteo (es·ka·mo'te·o) *n.m.* 1, sleight-of-hand. 2, filching; theft.
escampar (es·kam'par) *v.t.* to clear; unclutter. —*v.i.* 1, to stop raining; clear up. 2, *Amer.* to seek shelter from the rain.
escandalizar (es·kan·da·li'θar; -'sar) *v.t.* [*pres.subjve.* **escandalice** (-'li·θe; -se); *pret.* **escandalicé** (-'θe; -'se)] to scandalize.
escándalo (es'kan·da·lo) *n.m.* 1, scandal. 2, licentiousness. 3, commotion.
escandaloso (es·kan·da'lo·so) *adj.* 1, scandalous; scandalizing. 2, noisy; boisterous.
escandinavo (es·kan·di'na·βo) *adj.* & *n.m.* Scandinavian.
escandio (es'kan·djo) *n.m.* scandium.
escandir (es·kan'dir) *v.t.* to scan (verse). —**escansión** (-'sjon) *n.f.* scansion.
escantillón (es·kan·ti'ʎon; -'jon) *n.m.* templet; pattern. —**escantillar** (-'ʎar; -'jar) *v.t.* to gauge; measure off.
escapada (es·ka'pa·ða) *n.f.* 1, escape; fleeing. 2, escapade.
escapar (es·ka'par) *v.i.* [*also, refl.,* **escaparse**] to escape; flee.
escaparate (es·ka·pa'ra·te) *n.m.* 1, glass cabinet. 2, show window.
escapatoria (es·ka·pa'to·rja) *n.f.* 1, escape; flight. 2, way out (*of trouble, difficulties, etc.*); loophole. 3, *colloq.* evasion; subterfuge.
escape (es'ka·pe) *n.m.* 1, escape; flight. 2, escapement. 3, *mech.* exhaust. —**a escape,** at full speed.
escapismo (es·ka'pis·mo) *n.m.* escapism. —**escapista,** *adj.* & *n.m.* & *f.* escapist.
escápula (es'ka·pu·la) *n.f.* scap-

ula. —**escapular,** *adj.* scapular. —**escapulario,** *n.m.* scapular.
escaque (es'ka·ke) *n.m.* check; square.
escara (es'ka·ra) *n.f., med.* slough.
escarabajo (es·ka·ra'βa·xo) *n.m.* **1,** scarab. **2,** stumpy person. —**escarabajos,** *n.m.pl.* scribble (*sing.*).
escaramuza (es·ka·ra'mu·θa; -sa) *n.f.* skirmish.
escaramuzar (es·ka·ra·mu'θar; -'sar) *v.i.* [*pres.subjve.* **escaramuce** (-'mu·θe; -se); *pret.* **escaramucé** (-'θe; -'se)] to skirmish. *Also,* **escaramucear** (-θe'ar; -se'ar).
escarbadientes (es·kar·βa'ðjen·tes) *n.m.* = **mondadientes.**
escarbar (es·kar'βar) *v.t.* **1,** to scrape; scratch (*as fowls*). **2,** to stir; poke. **3,** to dig into; delve into. **4,** to pick (the teeth).
escarcha (es'kar·tʃa) *n.f.* frost; hoarfrost.
escarchado (es·kar'tʃa·ðo) *adj.* frosted. —*n.m.* **1,** gold or silver embroidery. **2,** cake icing; frosting.
escarchar (es·kar'tʃar) *v.t.* & *i.* to freeze; frost. —*v.t.* to frost (a cake).
escarcho (es'kar·tʃo) *n.m., ichthy.* roach.
escarda (es'kar·ða) *n.* **1,** weeding; weeding time. **2,** weeding hoe; spud.
escardar (es·kar'ðar) *v.t* & *i.* **1,** to weed. **2,** to cull; weed out.
escariar (es·ka'rjar) *v.t.* to ream. —**escariador,** *n.m.* reamer.
escarlata (es·kar'la·ta) *adj.* & *n.f.* scarlet. —*n.f.* = **escarlatina.**
escarlatina (es·kar·la'ti·na) *n.f.* scarlet fever.
escarmentar (es·kar·men'tar) *v.t.* [*pres.ind.* **escarmiento** (-'mjen·to); *pres.subjve.* **escarmiente** (-te)] to punish severely; teach a lesson. —*v.i.* to profit from experience; learn one's lesson.
escarmiento (es·kar'mjen·to) *n.m.* **1,** warning; lesson. **2,** chastisement.
escarnecer (es·kar·ne'θer; -'ser) *v.t.* **1,** to mock; jeer at. **2,** to besmirch. —**escarnio** (es'kar·njo) *n.f.* contempt; scoff.
escarola (es·ka'ro·la) *n.f.* escarole.
escarpa (es'kar·pa) *n.f.* scarp; escarpment. *Also,* **escarpadura.**
escarpado (es·kar'pa·ðo) *adj.* steep; craggy.
escarpelo (es·kar'pe·lo) *n.m.* **1,** rasp. **2,** = **escalpelo.**
escarpia (es'kar·pja) *n.f.* **1,** hook; meat hook. **2,** spike.
escasamente (es·ka·sa'men·te) *adv.* **1,** sparingly; scantily. **2,** scarcely; barely; just.
escasear (es·ka·se'ar) *v.t.* to skimp; be sparing with. —*v.i.* to be scarce; be in short supply.
escasez (es·ka'seθ; -'ses) *n.f.* **1,** scarcity; lack; want. **2,** poverty; indigence. **3,** stinginess.
escaso (es'ka·so) *adj.* **1,** small; limited. **2,** sparing; niggardly. **3,** scarce; scanty. **4,** scant.
escatimar (es·ka·ti'mar) *v.t.* to scrimp; give sparingly of.
escena (es'θe·na; e'se·na) *n.f.* **1,** scene. **2,** *theat.* stage. —**poner en escena,** to stage (a play).
escenario (es·θe'na·rjo; e·se-) *n.m.* **1,** *theat.* stage. **2,** setting; background; scenery. **3,** site; scene.
-escencia (es'θen·θja; e'sen·sja) *suffix* -escence; *forming nouns corresponding to adjectives ending in* **-escente**: *adolescencia,* adolescence.
escénico (es'θe·ni·ko; e'se-) *adj.* of or pert. to the stage.
escenificar (es·θe·ni·fi'kar; e·se-) *v.t.* [*pres.subjve.* **escenifique** (-'fi·ke); *pret.* **escenifiqué** (-'ke)] **1,** to stage; portray. **2,** to dramatize; adapt for the stage.
-escente (es'θen·te; e'sen·te) *suffix* -escent; *forming adjectives and nouns with inceptive or inchoative meaning: adolescente,* adolescent.
escéptico (es'θep·ti·ko; e'sep-) *adj.* skeptical. —*n.m.* skeptic. —**escepticismo** (-'θis·mo; -'sis·mo) *n.m.* skepticism.
esclarecer (es·kla·re'θer; -'ser) *v.* [*pres.ind.* **esclarezco** (-'reθ·ko; -'res·ko); *pres.subjve.* **esclarezca** (-ka)] —*v.t.* **1,** to illuminate; lighten. **2,** to give renown; make known. **3,** to elucidate. **4,** to enlighten (the mind). —*v.i.* to dawn
esclarecido (es·kla·re'θi·ðo; -'si·ðo) *adj.* illustrious; prominent.
esclarecimiento (es·kla·re·θi·'mjen·to; -si'mjen·to) *n.m.* **1,** elucidation; clarification. **2,** dawning **3,** enlightenment.
esclavitud (es·kla·βi'tuð) *n.f* slavery; enslavement.
esclavizar (es·kla·βi'θar; -'sar *v.t.* [*pres.subjve.* **esclavice** (-'βi·θe -se); *pret.* **esclavicé** (-'θe; -'se) **1,** to enslave. **2,** to hold in submission; make dependent. —**esclavización,** *n.f.* enslavement; enthrallment.

esclavo (es'kla·βo) *adj.* enslaved. —*n.m.* slave.
esclavón (es·kla'βon) *also,* **esclavonio** (-'βo·njo) *adj.* & *n.m.* = **eslavo.**
esclero- (es·kle·ro) *prefix* sclero-; hard: *esclerodermia,* scleroderma.
esclerosis (es·kle'ro·sis) *n.f.* sclerosis.
esclerótico (es·kle'ro·ti·ko) *adj.* sclerotic.
esclusa (es'klu·sa) *n.f.* **1,** canal lock. **2,** sluice; floodgate.
-esco ('es·ko) *suffix* -esque; having the form or manner of; like: *pintoresco,* picturesque.
escoba (es'ko·βa) *n.f.* broom. —**escobar,** *v.t.* to sweep.
escobilla (es·ko'βi·ʎa; -ja) *n.f.* brush (*implement*). —**escobillar,** *v.t.* to brush.
escocer (es·ko'θer; -'ser) *v.i.* [*infl.:* **cocer**] *also,* **escocerse,** *v.r.* to smart. —**escocedura,** *n.f., also,* **escocimiento,** *n.m.* = **escozor.**
escocés (es·ko'θes; -'ses) *adj.* Scotch; Scottish. —*n.m.* Scot; Scotsman.
escofina (es·ko'fi·na) *n.f.* rasp; file. —**escofinar,** *v.t.* to rasp; file.
escoger (es·ko'xer) *v.t.* [*infl.:* **coger**] to select; choose. —**escogido,** *adj.* choice; select.
escogidamente (es·ko·xi·ða·'men·te) *adv.* **1,** selectively; carefully. **2,** with excellence; completely.
escolar (es·ko'lar) *adj.* scholastic; school (*attrib.*) —*n.m.* student. —**escolástico** (-'las·ti·ko) *adj.* & *n.m.* scholastic.
escoltar (es·kol'tar) *v.t.* to escort. —**escolta** (-'kol·ta) *n.f.* escort.
escollera (es·ko'ʎe·ra; -'je·ra) *n.f.* jetty; breakwater.
escollo (es'ko·ʎo; -jo) *n.m.* **1,** hidden rock or reef. **2,** *fig.* difficulty; obstacle. **3,** *fig.* danger; risk.
escombro (es'kom·bro) *n.m.* **1,** rubble; debris. **2,** mackerel.
esconder (es·kon'der) *v.t.* to conceal; hide. —**a escondidas,** covertly.
escondite (es·kon'di·te) *n.m.* hiding place; hide-out; cache. *Also,* **escondrijo** (-'dri·xo). —**jugar al escondite,** to play hide-and-seek.
escopeta (es·ko'pe·ta) *n.f.* shotgun.
escopetazo (es·ko·pe'ta·θo; -so) *n.m.* **1,** gunshot. **2,** gunshot wound. **3,** *fig.* sudden shock; surprise.
escoplo (es'ko·plo) *n.m.* chisel; gouge. —**escopladura,** *n.f.* notch; groove.
escopolamina (es·ko·po·la'mi·na) *n.f.* scopolamine.
escora (es'ko·ra) *n.f.* **1,** prop; shore. **2,** *naut.* list; heel.
escorar (es·ko'rar) *v.t.* to prop; shore. —*v.i., naut.* to list; heel.
escorbuto (es·kor'βu·to) *n.m.* scurvy. —**escorbútico,** *adj.* scorbutic.
escoria (es'ko·rja) *n.f.* **1,** dross; slag. **2,** refuse; trash. —**escorial,** *n.m.* slag heap.
escorpión (es·kor'pjon) *n.m.* **1,** scorpion. **2,** *cap.,* Scorpio.
escota (es'ko·ta) *n.f., naut.* sheet; rope fastened to a sail.
escotado (es·ko'ta·ðo) *adj.* décolleté. —*n.m.* [*also,* **escotadura,** *n.f.*] décolletage.
escotar (es·ko'tar) *v.t.* **1,** to cut or trim to measurement. **2,** to cut (a bodice) low in the neck. **3,** to pay one's share of.
escote (es'ko·te) *n.m.* **1,** décolletage. **2,** share (*of a joint expense*).
escotilla (es·ko'ti·ʎa; -ja) *n.f., naut.* hatchway. —**escotillón,** *n.m.* trapdoor.
escozor (es·ko'θor; -'sor) *n.m.* smart; smarting.
escriba (es'kri·βa) *n.m., Bib.* scribe.
escribano (es·kri'βa·no) *n.m.* notary; scrivener. —**escribanía,** *n.f.* office or employment of a notary or scrivener. —**escribano del agua,** whirligig beetle.
escribiente (es·kri'βjen·te) *n.m.* & *f.* clerk; scribe.
escribir (es·kri'βir) *v.t.* [*p.p.* **escrito**] to write. —**escribirse,** *v.r.* to carry on correspondence; correspond. —**escribir a máquina,** to type. —**máquina de escribir,** typewriter.
escrito (es'kri·to) *v., p.p. of* **escribir.** —*n.m.* **1,** writing; manuscript. **2,** literary composition. **3,** report; paper. **4,** *law* writ; brief. —**por escrito,** in writing.
escritor (es·kri'tor) *n.m.* writer; author.
escritorio (es·kri'to·rjo) *n.m.* **1,** desk. **2,** study. **3,** business office.
escritura (es·kri'tu·ra) *n.f.* **1,** penmanship; handwriting. **2,** writing. **3,** *law* instrument. **4,** *cap.* Scripture.
escrófula (es'kro·fu·la) *n.f.* scro-

fula. —**escrofuloso**, *adj.* scrofulous.
escroto (es'kro·to) *n.m.* scrotum.
escrupulizar (es·kru·pu·li'θar; -'sar) *v.i.* [*infl.:* **realizar**] to scruple; have or feel scruples; stickle.
escrúpulo (es'kru·pu·lo) *n.m.* **1,** scruple. **2,** [*also,* **escrupulosidad,** *n.f.*] scrupulousness; conscientiousness. **3,** *pharm.* scruple. —**escrupuloso,** *adj.* scrupulous.
escrutar (es·kru'tar) *v.t.* **1,** to scrutinize. **2,** to count (votes) officially. —**escrutador,** *adj.* searching; scrutinizing. —*n.m.* examiner; inspector; teller (*of votes*).
escrutinio (es·kru'ti·njo) *n.m.* **1,** scrutiny. **2,** official count (*of election returns*).
escuadra (es'kwa·ðra) *n.f.* **1,** L-shaped or T-shaped square. **2,** *mil.* squad. **3,** fleet. —**escuadrilla,** *n.f.* squadron. —**escuadrón,** *n.m.* squadron (*of cavalry*).
escuálido (es'kwa·li·ðo) *adj.* **1,** squalid. **2,** thin; emaciated. —**escualidez** (-li'ðeθ; -'ðes) squalor; wretchedness.
escucha (es'ku·tʃa) *n.f.* **1,** [*also, Amer.,* *n.m.*] advanced sentry; scout. **2,** listening post. **3,** listening. **4,** monitor; listener. **5,** monitoring; monitoring post. —**estar a la escucha,** to monitor; listen.
escuchar (es·ku'tʃar) *v.i.* to listen. —*v.t.* to listen to. —**escucharse,** *v.r.* to be fond of one's own voice; speak with affectation.
escudar (es·ku'ðar) *v.t.* to shield.
escudero (es·ku'ðe·ro) *n.m.* **1,** squire; shield-bearer. **2,** henchman. **3,** = **hidalgo. 4,** shieldmaker.
escudete (es·ku'ðe·te) *n.m., sewing* gusset.
escudilla (es·ku'ði·ʎa; -ja) *n.f.* bowl; soup bowl.
escudo (es'ku·ðo) *n.m.* **1,** shield. **2,** coat of arms. **3,** escudo (*coin*).
escudriñar (es·ku·ðri'ɲar) *v.t.* to scrutinize. —**escudriñador,** *adj.* searching; scrutinizing. —**escudriñamiento,** *n.m.* scrutiny.
escuela (es'kwe·la) *n.f.* **1,** school. **2,** schooling.
escuelante (es·kwe'lan·te) *n.m., Amer.* schoolboy. —*n.f., Amer.* schoolgirl.
escueto (es'kwe·to) *adj.* **1,** free; unencumbered. **2,** bare; raw (*of facts*).
esculcar (es·kul'kar) *v.t.* **1,** to delve into; search. **2,** *Amer.* to frisk; search (a person).
esculpir (es·kul'pir) *v.t.* **1,** to sculpture. **2,** to engrave; carve. —**esculpidor,** *n.m.* engraver.
escultura (es·kul'tu·ra) *n.f.* sculpture. —**escultural,** *adj.* sculptural. —**escultor,** *n.m.* sculptor.
escullirse (es·ku'ʎir·se; -'jir·se) *v.r.* = **escabullirse.**
escuna (es'ku·na) *n.f., naut.* schooner.
escupidera (es·ku·pi'ðe·ra) *n.f.* **1,** spitoon; cuspidor. **2,** *Amer.* chamber pot. **3,** *Amer.* bedpan.
escupidero (es·ku·pi'ðe·ro) *n.m.* disgraceful situation or position.
escupir (es·ku'pir) *v.t.* & *i.* **1,** to spit; expectorate. **2,** to spew.
escupo (es'ku·po) *n.m.* spittle; expectoration.
escurridizo (es·ku·rri'ði·θo; -so) *adj.* **1,** slippery. **2,** *fig.* elusive.
escurrido (es·ku'rri·ðo) *adj.* narrow-hipped.
escurrimiento (es·ku·rri'mjen·to) *n.m.* **1,** dripping. **2,** *fig.* sneaking away.
escurrir (es·ku'rrir) *v.t.* & *i.* to drain. —**escurrirse,** *v.r.* to escape; slip away.
esdrújulo (es'ðru·xu·lo) *adj.* accented on the antepenultimate syllable. —*n.m.* a word so accented.
ese ('e·se) *dem.adj.m.sing.* that.
ése ('e·se) *dem.pron.m.sing.* that; that one.
esencia (e'sen·θja; -sja) *n.f.* essence. —**esencial,** *adj.* essential. —**quinta esencia,** quintessence.
esfera (es'fe·ra) *n.f.* **1,** sphere. **2,** dial (*of a watch or clock*). —**esférico,** *adj.* spherical.
esfero- (es·fe·ro) *prefix* sphero-; sphere: *esferómetro,* spherometer.
esferoide (es·fe'roi·ðe) *n.m.* spheroid. —**esferoidal,** *adj.* spheroidal.
esfinge (es'fin·xe) *n.f., also sometimes masc.* sphinx.
esforzado (es·for'θa·ðo; -'sa·ðo) *adj.* spirited; enterprising; daring.
esforzar (es·for'θar; -'sar) *v.t.* [*infl.:* **forzar**] **1,** to invigorate; strengthen. **2,** to encourage; give confidence. —*v.i.* to take courage. —**esforzarse,** *v.r.* to exert oneself.
esfuerzo (es'fwer·θo; -so) *n.m.* **1,** effort. **2,** spirit; daring. **3,** *engin.* stress.
esfumar (es·fu'mar) *v.t., painting*

to tone down. —**esfumarse**, *v.r.* to vanish; dissipate.
esgrima (es'ɣri·ma) *n.f.* fencing; swordplay.
esgrimir (es·ɣri'mir) *v.t.* to wield; brandish. —**esgrimidor**, *n.m.*, fencer; swordsman.
-ésimo ('e·si·mo) *suffix, forming ordinal numerals above the 20th: centésimo,* hundredth.
eslabón (es·la'βon) *n.m.* **1,** link (*of a chain*). **2,** steel for striking fire with a flint. **3,** *fig.* tie; bond. —**eslabonar**, *v.t.* to link.
eslavo (es'la·βo) *adj.* & *n.m.* Slav; Slavic.
eslovaco (es·lo'βa·ko) *adj.* & *n.m.* Slovak.
esloveno (es·lo'βe·no) *adj.* & *n.m.* Slovene.
esmaltar (es·mal'tar) *v.t.* **1,** to enamel. **2,** *fig.* to adorn; embellish.
esmalte (es'mal·te) *n.m.* **1,** enamel. **2,** *fig.* polish; shine.
esmaque (es'ma·ke) *n.m.* fishing smack.
esmerado (es·me'ra·ðo) *adj.* **1,** carefully done. **2,** careful; exacting.
esmeralda (es·me'ral·da) *n.f.* emerald. —**esmeraldino**, *adj.* emerald (*of color*).
esmerar (es·me'rar) *v.t.* to brighten; polish. —**esmerarse**, *v.r.* **1,** to do one's best; take pains. **2,** to strive for excellence.
esmerejón (es·me·re'xon) *n.m., ornith.* merlin.
esmeril (es·me'ril) *n.m.* emery. —**esmerilar**, *v.t.* to burnish.
esmero (es'me·ro) *n.m.* meticulousness.
esmoladera (es·mo·la'ðe·ra) *n.f.* whetstone.
esmoquin (es'mo·kin) *n.m.* [*pl.* **esmoquins**] tuxedo.
esnob (es'nob) *n.m.* & *f.* [*pl.* **esnobs** (es'nobs)] snob. —**esnobismo**, *n.m.* snobbism.
esnórquel (es'nor·kel) *n.m.* snorkel.
eso ('e·so) *dem.pron.neut.* that. —**eso de**, that matter of. —**eso es**, that's right. —**eso mismo**, the very thing; exactly. —**por eso**, for that reason; on that account.
eso- (e·so) *prefix* eso-; into; internal; hidden: *esotérico,* esoteric.
esófago (e'so·fa·ɣo) *n.m.* esophagus.
esos ('e·sos) *dem.adj., pl. of* ese.
ésos ('e·sos) *dem.pron., pl. of* ése.
esotérico (e·so'te·ri·ko) *adj.* esoteric.
espabilar (es·pa·βi'lar) *v.t.* = **despabilar**.
espacial (es·pa'θjal; -'sjal) *adj.* **1,** spatial. **2,** space (*attrib.*).
espaciar (es·pa'θjar; -'sjar) *v.t.* **1,** to space. **2,** to disperse; diffuse. —**espaciarse**, *v.r.* **1,** to expatiate. **2,** to enjoy oneself; relax.
espacio (es'pa·θjo; -sjo) *n.m.* space.
espacioso (es·pa'θjo·so; -'sjo·so) *adj.* **1,** spacious. **2,** slow; deliberate. —**espaciosidad**, *n.f.* spaciousness.
espada (es'pa·ða) *n.f.* **1,** sword. **2,** *often masc.* swordsman. **3,** *cards* spade. —**pez espada**, swordfish.
espadachín (es·pa·ða'tʃin) *n.m.* **1,** skillful swordsman. **2,** bully.
espadilla (es·pa'ði·ʎa; -ja) *n.f.* **1,** scull (*oar*). **2,** *cards* ace of spades. **3,** large hairpin.
espahí (es·pa'i) *n.m.* spahi.
espalda (es'pal·da) *n.f., also pl.,* **espaldas**, **1,** *anat.* back. **2,** rear; back. —**a espaldas**, treacherously; behind one's back. —**de espaldas**, on one's back. —**irse de espaldas**, to fall backwards.
espaldar (es·pal'dar) *n.m.* **1,** back. **2,** back (*of a chair*). **3,** dorsal section, as of armor, a turtle shell, etc. **4,** trellis. **5,** *pl.* hangings; tapestry.
espaldarazo (es·pal·da'ra·θo; -so) *n.m.* **1,** slap *or* pat on the back. **2,** dubbing (*of a knight*).
espaldera (es·pal'de·ra) *n.f.* trellis.
espaldudo (es·pal'du·ðo) *adj.* broad-shouldered.
espantada (es·pan'ta·ða) *n.f.* **1,** bolting (*of an animal*); stampede. **2,** *colloq.* sudden fright; cold feet.
espantadizo (es·pan·ta'ði·θo; -so) *adj.* scary; timid.
espantajo (es·pan'ta·xo) *n.m.* **1,** scary thing. **2,** scarecrow.
espantapájaros (es·pan·ta'pa·xa·ros) *n.m. sing.* & *pl.* scarecrow.
espantar (es·pan'tar) *v.t.* **1,** to frighten; terrify. **2,** to drive; chase away (*usu. animals*). —**espantarse**, *v.r.* to be astonished; be astounded.
espanto (es'pan·to) *n.m.* **1,** dread; terror. **2,** shock; astonishment. **3,** *pathol.* shock. **4,** *Amer.* ghost; apparition. **5,** *colloq.* horror.
espantoso (es·pan'to·so) *adj.* **1,**

dreadful; terrifying. **2,** shocking; astonishing.
español, (es·pa'ɲol) *adj.* Spanish, —*n.m.* **1,** Spanish language. **2,** Spaniard.
esparadrapo (es·pa·ra'ðra·po) *n.m.* adhesive tape.
esparcir (es·par'θir; -'sir) *v.t.* [*pres.ind.* **esparzo** (-'par·θo; -so); *pres.subjve.* **esparza** (-θa; -sa)] **1,** to scatter. **2,** to amuse; divert.
espárrago (es'pa·rra·ɣo) *n.m.* asparagus.
espartano (es·par'ta·no) *adj.* & *n.m.* Spartan.
esparto (es'par·to) *n.m.* esparto; esparto grass.
espasmo (es'pas·mo) *n.m.* spasm. —**espasmódico** (-'mo·ði·ko) *adj.* spasmodic.
espástico (es'pas·ti·ko) *adj.* & *n.m.* spastic.
espato (es'pa·to) *n.m., mineralogy* spar.
espátula (es'pa·tu·la) *n.f.* **1,** spatula. **2,** *painting* palette knife. **3,** *ornith.* spoonbill.
espavorido (es·pa·βo'ri·ðo) *adj.* = **despavorido.**
especia (es'pe·θja; -sja) *n.f.* spice.
especial (es·pe'θjal; -'sjal) *adj.* special. —**en especial,** specially; in particular.
especialidad (es·pe·θja·li'ðað; -sja·li'ðað) *n.f.* specialty.
especialista (es·pe·θja'lis·ta; -sja'lis·ta) *n.m.* & *f.* specialist.
especializar (es·pe·θja·li'θar; -sja·li'sar) *v.i.* [*pres.subjve.* **especialice** (-'li·θe; -se); *pret.* **especialicé** (-'θe; -'se)] to specialize. —**especialización,** *n.f.* specialization.
especiar (es·pe'θjar; -'sjar) *v.t.* to spice; season.
especie (es'pe·θje; -sje) *n.f.* **1,** species; kind. **2,** image; mental picture. —**en especie,** in kind.
especificar (es·pe·θi·fi'kar; es·pe·si-) *v.t.* [*pres.subjve.* **especifique** (-'fi·ke); *pret.* **especifiqué** (-'ke)] to specify. —**especificación,** *n.f.* specification.
específico (es·pe'θi·fi·ko; es·pe'si-) *adj.* & *n.m.* specific. —*n.m.* proprietary medicine.
espécimen (es'pe·θi·men; -si·men) *n.m.* specimen.
especiosidad (es·pe·θjo·si'ðað; -sjo·si'ðað). *n.f.* **1,** attractiveness; neatness. **2,** speciousness.
especioso (es·pe'θjo·so; -'sjo·so) *adj.* **1,** attractive; neat. **2,** specious.
espectáculo (es·pek'ta·ku·lo) *n.m.* spectacle; show. —**espectacular,** *adj.* spectacular.
espectador (es·pek·ta'ðor) *n.m.* spectator.
espectro (es'pek·tro) *n.m.* **1,** specter. **2,** spectrum. —**espectral,** *adj.* spectral.
espectroscopio (es·pek·tros'ko·pjo) *n.m.* spectroscope. —**espectroscópico** (-'ko·pi·ko) *adj.* spectroscopic.
especular (es·pe·ku'lar) *v.t.* **1,** to inspect; view. **2,** to speculate on; ponder. —*v.i.* to speculate. —**especulación,** *n.f.* speculation. —**especulador,** *n.m.* speculator. —**especulativo,** *adj.* speculative.
espejismo (es·pe'xis·mo) *n.m.* mirage.
espejo (es'pe·xo) *n.m.* mirror.
espejuelos (es·pe'xwe·los) *n.m.pl.* **1,** spectacles; eyeglasses. **2,** eyeglass lenses.
espelta (es'pel·ta) *n.f., bot.* spelt.
espeluznar (es·pe·luθ'nar; lus·'nar) *v.t.* to horrify; frighten; raise the hair of. —**espeluznante,** *adj.* frightful; hairraising.
espera (es'pe·ra) *n.f.* **1,** wait; waiting. **2,** respite. **3,** expectation. —**en espera,** waiting; expecting. —**en espera de,** waiting for. —**sala de espera,** waiting room.
esperanza (es·pe'ran·θa; -sa) *n.f.* hope; hopefulness. —**esperanzado,** *adj.* hopeful. —**esperanzar,** *v.t.* [*infl.:* **lanzar**] to encourage.
esperar (es·pe'rar) *v.t.* **1,** to hope for. **2,** to expect. **3,** to wait for; await. —*v.i.* **1,** to hope. **2,** to wait. —**esperarse,** *v.r.* to wait.
esperezarse (es·pe·re'θar·se; -'sar·se) *v.r.* = **desperezarse.**
esperma (es'per·ma) *n.f.* **1,** sperm. **2,** *also masc.* semen.
espermato- (es·per'ma·to) *prefix* spermato-; sperm; seed: *espermatogénesis,* spermatogenesis.
esperpento (es·per'pen·to) *n.m.* **1,** *colloq.* eyesore. **2,** absurdity; nonsense.
espesar (es·pe'sar) *v.t.* **1,** to thicken; make dense. **2,** to weave tighter.
espeso (es'pe·so) *adj.* **1,** thick; dense. **2,** *fig.* dirty; slovenly. **3,** *Amer., colloq.* boorish; loutish.
espesor (es·pe'sor) *n.m.* **1,** thickness. **2,** denseness; density.

espesura (es·pe'su·ra) *n.f.* 1, denseness; thickness. 2, thicket. 3, filth; dirt.
espetar (es·pe'tar) *v.t.* 1, to spit; skewer. 2, *colloq.* to surprise (someone) with, as a blow, piece of news, etc.
espetera (es·pe'te·ra) *n.f.* scullery.
espetón (es·pe'ton) *n.m.* 1, poker. 2, skewer. 3, large pin. 4, poke; jab.
espía (es'pi·a) *n.m.* & *f.* spy. —*n.f.*, *naut.* warp.
espiar (es·pi'ar) *v.t.* & *i.* [*pres. ind.* **espío** (-'pi·o); *pres.subjve.* **espíe** (-'pi·e)] to spy. —*v.i.*, *naut.* to warp a ship.
espicanardo (es·pi·ka'nar·ðo) *n.m.* spikenard; nard.
espiga (es'pi·ɣa) *n.f.* 1, spike *or* ear of grain. 2, *carpentry* tenon; dowel; pin; peg. 3, *mech.* tongue; shank. 4, brad. 5, *naut.* masthead.
espigado (es·pi'ɣa·ðo) *adj.* 1, ripe; eared. 2, *fig.* tall; grown.
espigadora (es·pi·ɣa'ðo·ra) *n.f.* gleaner. *Also,* **espigadera** (-'ðe·ra).
espigar (es·pi'ɣar) *v.t.* [*pres. subjve.* **espigue** (-'pi·ɣe); *pret.* **espigué** (-'ɣe)] 1, to glean. 2, *carpentry* to tenon. —*v.i.* to ear, as grain. —**espigarse,** *v.r.* to grow tall.
espina (es'pi·na) *n.f.* 1, thorn. 2, spine; backbone. 3, fishbone. 4, splinter. —**dar mala espina,** *colloq.* to cause suspicion. —**sacarse la espina,** *colloq.* to get even.
espinaca (es·pi'na·ka) *n.f.* spinach.
espinal (es·pi'nal) *adj.* spinal; dorsal.
espinazo (es·pi'na·θo; -so) *n.m.* spine; backbone.
espineta (es·pi'ne·ta) *n.f.* spinet.
espinilla (es·pi'ni·ʎa; -ja) *n.f.* 1, shinbone. 2, blackhead.
espino (es'pi·no) *n.m.* hawthorn.
espinoso (es·pi'no·so) *adj.* 1, spiny; thorny. 2, *fig.* difficult; thorny; prickly.
espión (es·pi'on) *n.m.* spy.
espionaje (es·pi·o'na·xe) *n.m.* espionage.
espira (es'pi·ra) *n.f.* 1, coil; spiral; spire. 2, turn (*of a spiral*).
espiral (es·pi'ral) *adj.* spiral. —*n.f.* spiral. —*n.m.* hairspring of a watch.
espirar (es·pi'rar) *v.t.* & *i.* to exhale; expire. —**espiración,** *n.f.* exhalation; expiration.
espiritismo (es·pi·ri'tis·mo) *n.m.* spiritualism. —**espiritista,** *n.m.* & *f.* spiritualist. —*adj.* spiritualistic.
espíritu (es'pi·ri·tu) *n.m.* spirit. —**espiritual** (-'twal) *adj.* spiritual. —**espirituoso** (-'two·so) *adj.* spirituous.
espiro- (es·pi·ro) *prefix* spiro-. 1, breath; respiration: *espirómetro,* spirometer. 2, spiral: *espiroqueta,* spirochete.
espita (es'pi·ta) *n.f.* 1, tap; spigot. 2, *colloq.* tippler; drunkard.
esplendidez (es·plen·di'ðeθ; -'ðes) *n.f.* 1, splendor; magnificence. 2, liberality; largess.
espléndido (es'plen·di·ðo) *adj.* 1, splendid; magnificent. 2, liberal; munificent.
esplendor (es·plen'dor) *n.m.* splendor. —**esplendoroso,** *adj.* splendorous.
espliego (es'plje·ɣo) *n.m., bot.* lavender.
esplín (es'plin) *n.m.* spleen.
espolear (es·po·le'ar) *v.t.* to spur.
espoleta (es·po'le·ta) *n.f.* 1, fuse (*of a bomb or grenade*). 2, wishbone.
espolón (es·po'lon) *n.m.* 1, cock's spur. 2, fetlock. 3, beak; ram (*of a warship*). 4, cutwater. 5, mountain ridge *or* spur. 6, breakwater; jetty. 7, *archit.* buttress.
espolvorear (es·pol·βo·re'ar) *v.t.* to dust; sprinkle with or as with dust.
esponja (es'pon·xa) *n.f.* 1, sponge. 2, *colloq.* sponger. —**esponjoso,** *adj.* spongy.
esponjar (es·pon'xar) *v.t.* 1, to make spongy. 2, *Amer., colloq.* to sponge on. —**esponjarse,** *v.r.* 1, to swell; puff up (with pride). 2, to glow (with health).
espontáneo (es·pon'ta·ne·o) *adj.* spontaneous. —**espontaneidad,** *n.f.* spontaneity.
espora (es'po·ra) *n.f.* spore.
esporádico (es·po'ra·ði·ko) *adj.* sporadic.
esporo- (es·po·ro) *prefix* sporo-; spore: *esporocarpio,* sporocarp.
esposa (es'po·sa) *n.f.* wife; spouse. —**esposas,** *n.f.pl.* handcuffs; fetters. —**esposar,** *v.t.* to shackle.
esposo (es'po·so) *n.m.* husband; spouse.
espuela (es'pwe·la) *n.f.* 1, spur. 2, *fig.* incitement; stimulus. —**espuela de caballero,** larkspur.

espuerta (es'pwer·ta) *n.f.* basket.
espulgar (es·pul'ɣar) *v.t.* [*pres. subjve.* **espulgue** (-'pul·ɣe); *pret.* **espulgué** (-'ɣe)] **1,** to delouse. **2,** *fig.* to examine closely.
espuma (es'pu·ma) *n.f.* foam; scum; lather. —**espuma de mar,** meerschaum.
espumar (es·pu'mar) *v.t.* to skim. —*v.i.* **1,** to froth; foam. **2,** to sparkle, as wine. **3,** *fig.* to grow up. —**espumadera,** *n.f.* skimmer.
espumarajo (es·pu·ma'ra·xo) *n.m.* drivel; foam (*from the mouth*).
espumilla (es·pu'mi·ʎa; -ja) *n.f.* voile.
espumoso (es·pu'mo·so) *adj.* **1,** frothy; foamy. **2,** sparkling (*of wine*).
espurio (es'pu·rjo) *also,* **espúreo** (-'pu·re·o) *adj.* **1,** bastard; illegitimate. **2,** spurious; false.
esputar (es·pu'tar) *v.t.* to expectorate.
esputo (es'pu·to) *n.m.* **1,** spit; saliva. **2,** sputum.
esquela (es'ke·la) *n.m.* **1,** note. **2,** announcement card, esp. an obituary notice.
esqueleto (es·ke'le·to) *n.m.* **1,** skeleton. **2,** framework. —**esquelético** (-'le·ti·ko) *adj.* thin; skinny.
esquema (es'ke·ma) *n.m.* **1,** outline; sketch. **2,** plan; scheme. —**esquemático** (-'ma·ti·ko) *adj.* schematic.
esquí (es'ki) *n.m.* **1,** ski. **2,** skiing.
esquiar (es·ki'ar) *v.i.* [*pres.ind.* **esquío** (-'ki·o); *pres.subjve.* **esquíe** (-'ki·e)] to ski. —**esquiador,** *n.m.* skier.
esquiciar (es·ki'θjar; -'sjar) *v.t.* to sketch. —**esquicio** (-'ki·θjo; -sjo) *n.m.* sketch.
esquife (es'ki·fe) *n.m.* **1,** skiff. **2,** *archit.* barrel vault.
esquiismo (es·ki'is·mo) *n.m.* skiing.
esquila (es'ki·la) *n.f.* **1,** hand bell. **2,** cowbell. **3,** shearing.
esquilar (es·ki'lar) *v.t.* **1,** to shear; crop; clip. **2,** *fig.* to fleece; swindle.
esquileo (es·ki'le·o) *n.m.* **1,** shearing. **2,** shearing season.
esquimal (es·ki'mal) *adj.* & *n.m.* & *f.* Eskimo.
esquina (es'ki·na) *n.f.* corner.
esquinazo (es·ki'na·θo; -so) *n.m., colloq.* corner. —**dar esquinazo a uno,** *colloq.* to shake off someone.
esquirol (es·ki'rol) *n.m.* strikebreaker; scab.
esquisto (es'kis·to) *n.m.* schist; slate.
esquivar (es·ki'βar) *v.t.* to avoid; elude; shun. —**esquivarse,** *v.r.* to withdraw; be reserved; be coy.
esquivo (es'ki·βo) *adj.* **1,** elusive; evasive. **2,** reserved; coy.
esquizo- (es·ki·θo; -so) *prefix* schizo-; split; division; cleavage: *esquizofrenia,* schizophrenia.
esquizofrenia (es·ki·θo'fre·nja; es·ki·so-) *n.f.* schizophrenia. —**esquizofrénico** (-'fre·ni·ko) *adj.* & *n.m.* schizophrenic; schizoid.
esta ('es·ta) *dem.adj., fem of* **este.**
ésta ('es·ta) *dem.pron., fem. of* **éste.**
estabilizar (es·ta·βi·li'θar; -'sar) *v.t.* [*pres.subjve.* **estabilice** (-'li·θe; -se); *pret.* **estabilicé** (-'θe; -'se)] to stabilize. —**estabilización,** *n.f.* stabilization. —**estabilizador,** *n.m.* stabilizer. —*adj.* stabilizing.
estable (es'ta·βle) *adj.* stable. —**estabilidad,** *n.f.* stability.
establecer (es·ta·βle'θer; -'ser) *v.t.* [*pres.ind.* **establezco** (-'βleθ·ko; -'βles·ko); *pres.subjve.* **establezca** (-ka)] **1,** to establish. **2,** to fix; settle. **3,** to decree.
establecimiento (es·ta·βle·θi·'mjen·to; -si'mjen·to) *n.m.* **1,** establishment. **2,** settlement. **3,** law; statute.
establo (es'ta·βlo) *n.m.* stable; barn.
estaca (es'ta·ka) *n.f.* **1,** stake; pale. **2,** cudgel; stick. —**estacada,** *n.f.* paling; fence. —**estacazo,** *n.m.* blow with a stick.
estacar (es·ta'kar) *v.t.* [*pres. subjve.* **estaque** (-'ta·ke); *pret.* **estaqué** (-'ke)] **1,** to stake (an animal); tie to a stake. **2,** to stake out; mark with stakes. —**estacarse,** *v.r.* to stand straight; stand stiff.
estación (es·ta'θjon; -'sjon) *n.f.* **1,** station. **2,** season. **3,** stop; stay. **4,** *eccles.* devotional church visit. —**estacional,** *adj.* seasonal.
estacionamiento (es·ta·θjo·na·'mjen·to; -sjo·na'mjen·to) *n.m.* **1,** placement; stationing. **2,** parking.
estacionar (es·ta·θjo'nar; -sjo'nar) *v.t.* **1,** to place; station. **2,** to park. —**estacionarse,** *v.r.* **1,** to stand; be or remain stationary. **2,** to park; be parked.

estacionario (es·ta·θjo'na·rjo; -sjo'na·rjo) *adj.* stationary.
estada (es'ta·ða) *n.f.* stay; sojourn.
estadía (es·ta'ði·a) *n.f.* **1,** *comm; naut.* demurrage. **2,** *Amer.* stay; sojourn.
estadio (es'ta·ðjo) *n.m.* stadium.
estadista (es·ta'ðis·ta) *n.m.* statesman.
estadística (es·ta'ðis·ti·ka) *n.f.* statistics. —**estadístico,** *adj.* statistical. —*n.m.* statistician.
estado (es'ta·ðo) *n.m.* **1,** state. **2,** condition. **3,** estate; class; rank. **4,** status. **5,** account; statement. —**estado mayor,** *mil.* staff.
estadounidense (es·ta·ðo·u·ni·'ðen·se) *adj.* American; of or pert. to the United States.
estafa (es'ta·fa) *n.f.* swindle; fraud.
estafar (es·ta'far) *v.t.* to swindle; defraud. —**estafador,** *n.m.* swindler.
estafeta (es·ta'fe·ta) *n.f.* **1,** mail. **2,** diplomatic courier. **3,** [*also,* **estafeta de correos**] post office.
estalactita (es·ta·lak'ti·ta) *n.f.* stalactite.
estalagmita (es·ta·laɣ'mi·ta) *n.f.* stalagmite.
estallar (es·ta'ʎar; '-jar) *v.i.* to explode; burst.
estallido (es·ta'ʎi·ðo; -'ji·ðo) *n.m.* **1,** burst; explosion; report (*of a firearm*). **2,** crack; snap.
estambre (es'tam·bre) *n.m.* **1,** worsted; woolen yarn. **2,** *bot.* stamen.
estameña (es·ta'me·ɲa) *n.f.* serge.
estampa (es'tam·pa) *n.f.* **1,** print. **2,** engraving. **3,** *fig.* stamp; kind; sort. **4,** image; portrait. **5,** printing; press.
estampado (es·tam'pa·ðo) *n.m.* **1,** cotton print. **2,** stamping. **3,** cloth printing.
estampar (es·tam'par) *v.t.* **1,** to stamp; print. **2,** to plant (a kiss). **3,** to impress (on the mind).
estampía (es·tam'pi·a) *in* **de estampía,** in a rush; precipitously.
estampida (es·tam'pi·ða) *n.f.* **1,** stampede. **2,** = **estampido.**
estampido (es·tam'pi·ðo) *n.m.* crash; explosion; report (*of a firearm*).
estampilla (es·tam'pi·ʎa; -ja) *n.f.* **1,** signet; seal. **2,** rubber stamp. **3,** *Amer.* postage *or* tax stamp.
estancación (es·tan·ka'θjon; -'sjon) *n.f.* stagnation. *Also,* **estancamiento,** *n.m.*
estancar (es·tan'kar) *v.t.* [*pres. subjve.* **estanque** (-'tan·ke); *pret.* **estanqué** (-'ke)] **1,** to stanch; stop; check. **2,** to suspend. **3,** *comm.* to monopolize. **4,** to restrict the sale of. —**estancarse,** *v.r.* to be or become stagnant.
estancia (es'tan·θja; -sja) *n.f.* **1,** sojourn; stay. **2,** *Amer.* ranch. **3,** sitting room; any large room. **4,** stanza. —**estanciero,** *n.m., Amer.* rancher; ranchman.
estanco (es'tan·ko) *adj.* watertight. —*n.m.* **1,** government monopoly. **2,** monopoly store, esp. tobacco store. **3,** file; archive. **4,** *Amer.* liquor store.
estándar (es'tan·dar) *n.m., Amer.* standard; norm.
estandardizar (es·tan·dar·ði·'θar; -'sar) *v.t., Amer.* [*infl.:* **realizar**] to standardize. *Also,* **estandarizar** (-ri'θar; -'sar). —**estandardización,** *n.f. Amer.* standardization.
estandarte (es·tan'dar·te) *n.m.* standard.
estanque (es'tan·ke) *n.m.* reservoir; basin; pond.
estanquillo (es·tan'ki·ʎo; -jo) *n.m.* **1,** tobacco store. **2,** *Amer.* small store. **3,** *Amer.* liquor store; tavern.
estante (es'tan·te) *adj.* fixed; permanent. —*n.m.* **1,** shelf. **2,** book rack; bookcase. **3,** support; post. —**estantería,** *n.f.* set of shelves; shelving.
estantío (es·tan'ti·o) *adj.* **1,** still; stagnant. **2,** slow; torpid.
estañar (es·ta'ɲar) *v.t.* **1,** to tin. **2,** to solder.
estaño (es'ta·ɲo) *n.m.* tin.
estaquilla (es·ta'ki·ʎa; -ja) *n.f.* **1,** peg; pin. **2,** brad. **3,** long nail; spike.
estar (es'tar) *v.i.* [*pres.ind.* **estoy, estás** (es'tas), **está** (es'ta); *pres. subjve.* **esté**; *pret.* **estuve**] **1,** to be (*in a certain place or condition*). **2,** to remain; stay. —*aux.v., used with the gerund to form the progressive tenses: estoy escribiendo,* I am writing. —**estarse,** *v.r.* **1,** to remain; stay. **2,** to be stopped or delayed. —**está bien,** fine; (it's) all right. —**¿a cuántos** *or* **a cómo estamos?** what is today's date? **estamos a diez,** today is the tenth.

—**estar a (cierto precio),** to cost (a certain amount). —**estar a dos velas,** *colloq.* **1,** to know nothing. **2,** to be broke. —**estar al caer,** *colloq.* **1,** to be about to happen. **2,** to be about to strike (*of the hour*). —**estar a la que salta,** *colloq.* to be ready to make the most of something. —**estar a matar,** to be bitter enemies. —**estar a oscuras,** *colloq.* to know nothing. —**estar bien,** to be well. —**estar bien con,** *colloq.* to be on good terms with. —**estar con,** *colloq.* to be with; be on the side of; favor. —**estar con** *or* **en ánimo de,** to be in the mood of; like; feel like. —**estar** *or* **estarse de más,** *colloq.* **1,** to be idle. **2,** to be unnecessary. —**estar en,** *colloq.* **1,** to understand. **2,** to cost. —**estar en lo cierto,** to be sure. —**estar en todo,** *colloq.* **1,** to have a finger in everything. **2,** to take good care. —**estar mal, 1,** to be bad. **2,** to be ill. —**estar mal con,** to be on bad terms with. —**estar** *or* **estarse mano sobre mano,** *colloq.* **1,** to do nothing; be idle. **2,** to stand by idly. —**estar para,** to be ready *or* about to. —**estar por,** *colloq.* **1,** to favor; be in favor of; be for *or* with. **2,** *fol. by inf.* to remain to be; have yet to be. —**estar que bota; estar que estalla; estar que echa chispas,** to be in a rage. —**¿está Vd.?** *colloq.* do you understand? do you follow me? —**estar sobre sí,** to control oneself. —**estar sobre uno** *or* **algo,** to watch cautiously.

estarcir (es·tar'θir; -'sir) *v.t.* to stencil. —**estarcido,** *n.m.* stencil.

estas ('es·tas) *dem.adj., fem.pl. of* **este.**

éstas ('es·tas) *dem.pron., fem.pl. of* **éste.**

estatal (es·ta'tal) *adj.* state (*attrib.*).

estático (es'ta·ti·ko) *adj.* static. —**estática,** *n.f.* statics.

estatidad (es·ta·ti'ðað) *n.f.* statehood.

estato- (es·ta·to) *prefix* stato-; stable; stability: *estatocisto,* statocyst.

estator (es·ta'tor) *n.m.* stator.

estatua (es'ta·twa) *n.f.* statue. —**estatuaria,** *n.f.* statuary. —**estatuilla,** *also,* **estatuita,** *n.f.* statuette.

estatuir (es·ta·tu'ir) *v.t.* [*infl.:* **constituir**] **1,** to enact; ordain. **2,** to demonstrate; prove.

estatura (es·ta'tu·ra) *n.f.* stature; height.

estatuto (es·ta'tu·to) *n.m.* statute; law; ordinance. —**estatutario,** *adj.* statutory.

estay (es'tai) *n.m.* [*pl.* **estayes**] *naut.* stay.

este ('es·te) *n.m.* **1,** east. **2,** east wind.

este ('es·te) *dem.adj.masc.* [*fem.* **esta;** *pl.* **estos, estas**] **1,** this; *pl.* these. **2,** latter.

éste ('es·te) *dem.pron.masc.* [*fem.* **ésta;** *pl.* **éstos, éstas**] **1,** this; this one; *pl.* these. **2,** the latter.

esté (es'te) *v., pres.subjve. of* **estar.**

esteatita (es·te·a'ti·ta) *n.f.* soapstone.

estela (es'te·la) *n.f.* trail; wake.

estelar (es·te'lar) *adj.* stellar.

estenografía (es·te·no·ɣra'fi·a) *n.f.* stenography. —**estenográfico** (-'ɣra·fi·ko) *adj.* stenographic. —**estenógrafo** (-'no·ɣra·fo) *n.m.* stenographer.

estentóreo (es·ten'to·re·o) *adj.* stentorian.

estepa (es'te·pa) *n.f.* steppe.

éster ('es·ter) *n.m.* ester.

estera (es'te·ra) *n.f.* **1,** door mat. **2,** rug made of hemp, rope or fiber. —**esterado,** *adj.* matted; covered with a mat. —*n.m.* matting.

estercolar (es·ter·ko'lar) *v.t.* [*infl.:* **colar**] to manure; fertilize. —*n.m.* dunghill. —**estercoladura,** *n.f., also* **estercolamiento,** *n.m.* manuring; fertilizing.

estercolero (es·ter·ko'le·ro) *n.m.* **1,** manure collector. **2,** dunghill; manure pile.

estéreo (es'te·re·o) *n.m.* **1,** stere. **2,** stereo.

estereo- (es·te·re·o) *prefix* stereo-; solid; firm; three-dimensional: *estereoscopio,* stereoscope.

estereofónico (es·te·re·o'fo·ni·ko) *adj.* stereophonic.

estereoscopio (es·te·re·os'ko·pjo) *n.m.* stereoscope. —**estereoscópico** (-'ko·pi·ko) *adj.* stereoscopic. —**estereoscopia** (-'ko·pja) *n.f.* stereoscopy.

estereotipo (es·te·re·o'ti·po) *n.m.* stereotype. —**estereotipar,** *v.t.* to stereotype. —**estereotipia** (-'ti·pja) *n.f.* stereotypy. —**estereotípico** (-'ti·pi·ko) *adj.* stereotype.

estéril (es'te·ril) *adj.* sterile; bar-

ren; unproductive. —**esterilidad,** *n.f.* sterility; barrenness.
esterilizar (es·te·ri·li'θar; -'sar) *v.t.* [*pres.subjve.* **esterilice** (-'li·θe; -se); *pret.* **esterilicé** (-'θe; -'se)] to sterilize. —**esterilización,** *n.f.* sterilization. —**esterilizador,** *adj.* sterilizing. —*n.m.* sterilizer.
esterilla (es·te'ri·ʎa; -ja) *n.f.* small mat.
esterlina (es·ter'li·na) *adj.fem.* sterling. —**libra esterlina,** pound sterling.
esternón (es·ter'non) *n.m.* sternum.
estero (es'te·ro) *n.m.* **1,** inlet; creek. **2,** tideland. **3,** salt marsh.
estertor (es·ter'tor) *n.m.* **1,** death rattle. **2,** rattle in the throat. **3,** noisy breathing; panting. —**estertoroso,** *adj.* stertorous.
-estesia (es'te·sja) *suffix* -esthesia; feeling: *anestesia,* anesthesia.
esteta (es'te·ta) *n.m.* & *f.* esthete.
estética (es'te·ti·ka) *n.f.* esthetics. —**estético,** *adj.* esthetic.
estetoscopio (es·te·tos'ko·pjo) *n.m.* stethoscope.
estiaje (es'tja·xe) *n.m.* low water.
estibar (es·ti'βar) *v.t.* **1,** to compress; bale. **2,** *naut.* to stow. —**estibador,** *n.m.* longshoreman.
estibio (es'ti·βjo) *n.m.* antimony.
estiércol (es'tjer·kol) *n.m.* **1,** dung; manure. **2,** *fig.* filth.
estigio (es'ti·xjo) *adj.* Stygian.
estigma (es'tiɣ·ma) *n.m.* stigma.
estigmatizar (es·tiɣ·ma·ti'θar; -'sar) *v.t.* [*pres.subjve.* **estigmatice** (-'ti·θe; -se); *pret.* **estigmaticé** (-'θe; -'se)] to stigmatize; brand.
estilete (es·ti'le·te) *n.m.* **1,** stiletto. **2,** *surg.* probe.
estilista (es·ti'lis·ta) *n.m.* & *f.* stylist.
estilístico (es·ti'lis·ti·ko) *adj.* stylistic. —**estilística,** *n.f.* stylistics.
estilizar (es·ti·li'θar; -'sar) *v.t.* [*infl.:* **realizar**] to stylize.
estilo (es'ti·lo) *n.m.* **1,** stylus. **2,** style. **3,** fashion; use; custom. **4,** kind; class; sort.
estilográfica (es·ti·lo'ɣra·fi·ka) *n.f.* fountain pen.
estima (es'ti·ma) *n.f.* **1,** esteem; respect. **2,** *naut.* dead reckoning.
estimable (es·ti'ma·βle) *adj.* **1,** estimable; worthy. **2,** computable.
estimación (es·ti·ma'θjon; -'sjon) *n.f.* **1,** esteem; regard. **2,** appraisal.
estimar (es·ti'mar) *v.t.* **1,** to esteem; regard. **2,** to estimate; appraise.
estimulante (es·ti·mu'lan·te) *adj.* stimulating. —*n.m.* stimulant.
estimular (es·ti·mu'lar) *v.t.* **1,** to stimulate. **2,** to encourage.
estímulo (es'ti·mu·lo) *n.m.* **1,** stimulus. **2,** stimulation.
estío (es'ti·o) *n.m.* summer.
estipendio (es·ti'pen·djo) *n.m.* stipend.
estíptico (es'tip·ti·ko) *adj.* & *n.m.* styptic. —*adj.* **1,** constipated. **2,** stingy; miserly.
estipular (es·ti·pu'lar) *v.t.* to stipulate. —**estipulación,** *n.f.* stipulation.
estirado (es·ti'ra·ðo) *adj.* **1,** stretched; expanded. **2,** *fig.* haughty; stiff. **3,** drawn (*of metals*). —*n.m.* **1,** stretching. **2,** drawing.
estirar (es·ti'rar) *v.t.* **1,** to draw; pull. **2,** to stretch; extend. **3,** to draw (metals). —**estirarse,** *v.r.* **1,** to stretch. **2,** to grow haughty.
estirena (es·ti're·na) *n.f.* styrene.
estirón (es·ti'ron) *n.m.* **1,** strong pull; stretch. **2,** haul; hauling. **3,** *colloq.* rapid growth.
estirpe (es'tir·pe) *n.f.* ancestry; stock; pedigree.
estival (es·ti'βal) *adj.* summer (*attrib.*).
esto ('es·to) *dem.pron.neut.* this. —**en esto,** at this moment. —**por esto,** hereby.
estocada (es·to'ka·ða) *n.f.* **1,** stab; thrust; lunge. **2,** stab wound.
estofa (es'to·fa) *n.f.* **1,** quilted cloth, usu. of silk. **2,** *fig.* quality.
estofado (es·to'fa·ðo) *adj.* **1,** quilted. **2,** stewed. —*n.m.* stew.
estofar (es·to'far) *v.t.* **1,** to quilt. **2,** to stew.
estoico (es'toi·ko) *adj.* stoic; stoical. —*n.m.* stoic. —**estoicismo** (-'θis·mo; -'sis·mo) *n.m.* stoicism.
estola (es'to·la) *n.f.* stole.
estólido (es'to·li·ðo) *adj.* stupid; foolish. —**estolidez,** *n.f.* stupidity.
estolón (es·to'lon) *n.m., bot.; zool.* runner.
estomacal (es·to·ma'kal) *adj.* stomachic.
estomagar (es·to·ma'ɣar) *v.t.* [*pres.subjve.* **estomague** (-'ma·ɣe); *pret.* **estomagué** (-'ɣe)] to upset the stomach of. —**estomagársele a uno,** to annoy; upset; disgust (someone). —**estomagado,** *adj.* annoying; upsetting; disgusting.

estómago (es'to·ma·ɣo) *n.m.* **1,** stomach. **2,** *slang, fig.* nerve; insouciance.

estomato- (es·to·ma·to) *also,* **estomat-** (-mat) *prefix* stomato-; mouth: *estomatología,* stomatology.

estopa (es'to·pa) *n.f.* **1,** tow. **2,** oakum. **3,** burlap.

estoque (es'to·ke) *n.m.* **1,** rapier. **2,** sword cane. **3,** *bot.* gladiolus. —**estoquear,** *v.t.* to pierce with a rapier.

estorbar (es·tor'βar) *v.t.* to hinder; obstruct. —**estorbo** (es'tor·βo) *n.m.* hindrance; obstacle.

estornino (es·tor'ni·no) *n.m.* starling.

estornudar (es·tor·nu'ðar) *v.i.* to sneeze. —**estornudo** (-'nu·ðo) *n.m.* sneeze.

estos ('es·tos) *dem.adj., pl. of* **este.**

éstos ('es·tos) *dem.pron., pl. of* **éste.**

estotro (es'to·tro) *dem.adj. & pron.* [*fem.* **estotra**] *archaic, contr. of* **este otro** (*or* **esta otra**), this other.

estoy (es'toi) *v., 1st pers.sing. pres. ind. of* **estar.**

estrabismo (es·tra'βis·mo) *n.m.* strabismus.

estrada (es'tra·ða) *n.f.* lane; road. —**batir la estrada,** *mil.* to reconnoiter.

estrado (es'tra·ðo) *n.m.* **1,** dais. **2,** drawing room.

estrafalario (es·tra·fa'la·rjo) *adj., colloq.* **1,** extravagant; fantastic. **2,** slovenly; slatternly. —*n.m., colloq.* eccentric.

estragar (es·tra'ɣar) *v.t.* [*pres. subjve.* **estrague** (-'tra·ɣe); *pret.* **estragué** (-'ɣe)] **1,** to deprave; corrupt. **2,** to ravage; ruin.

estrago (es'tra·ɣo) *n.m.* **1,** ravage; ruin; havoc. **2,** wickedness; depravity.

estragón (es·tra'ɣon) *n.m.* tarragon.

estrambótico (es·tram'bo·ti·ko) *adj.* eccentric; extravagant.

estrangular (es·tran·gu'lar) *v.t.* **1,** to strangle; choke. **2,** *med.* to strangulate. **3,** *mech.* to throttle; choke. —**estrangulación,** *n.f.* strangulation; choking.

estraperlo (es·tra'per·lo) *n.m.* black market. —**estraperlista,** *n.m. & f.* black marketeer.

estratagema (es·tra·ta'xe·ma) *n.f.* **1,** stratagem. **2,** deception trick. **3,** craftiness.

estrategia (es·tra'te·xja) *n.f.* **1,** strategy. **2,** *fig.* craftiness. —**estratega** (-'te·ɣa) *also,* **estratego** (-'te·ɣo) *n.m.* strategist. —**estratégico** (-'te·xi·ko) *adj.* strategic. —*n.m.* strategist.

estrati- (es·tra·ti) *prefix* strati-; stratum: *estratificación,* stratification.

estratificar (es·tra·ti·fi'kar) *v.t* [*infl.:* **tocar**] to stratify. —**estratificación,** *n.f.* stratification.

estrato (es'tra·to) *n.m.* **1,** stratum; layer; bed. **2,** *meteorol.* stratus.

estrato- (es·tra·to) *prefix* strato-; stratum; layer: *estratosfera,* stratosphere.

estratosfera (es·tra·tos'fe·ra) *n.f.* stratosphere.

-estre ('es·tre) *suffix, forming adjectives denoting* relation; connection: *campestre,* of the country; rural.

estrechar (es·tre'tʃar) *v.t.* **1,** to narrow. **2,** to tighten. **3,** to constrain; compel. —**estrecharse,** *v.r.* **1,** to narrow; become narrow. **2,** to tighten; become tight. **3,** to restrict one's expenses. **4,** to become more intimate; become friendlier. —**estrechar la mano,** to shake hands.

estrechez (es·tre'tʃeθ; -'tʃes) *n.f.* **1,** narrowness. **2,** tightness; snugness. **3,** intimacy; closeness. **4,** stinginess. **5,** trouble; tight spot. **6,** want; poverty.

estrecho (es'tre·tʃo) *adj.* **1,** narrow. **2,** tight; snug. **3,** close; intimate. **4,** strict; rigorous. **5,** stingy. —*n.m.* strait.

estrechura (es·tre'tʃu·ra) *n.f.* **1,** narrowness. **2,** want; poverty.

estregar (es·tre'ɣar) *v.t.* [*pres. ind.* **estriego**; *pres.subjve.* **estriegue**; *pret.* **estregué** (-'ɣe)] to rub; scrub; scour. —**estregamiento,** *n.m.* rubbing; scrubbing; scouring.

estrella (es'tre·ʎa; -ja) *n.f.* star. —**estrella fugaz,** shooting star. —**poner por las estrellas,** to praise to the skies.

estrellado (es·tre'ʎa·ðo; 'ja·ðo) *adj.* **1,** starry. **2,** *colloq.* smashed; cracked up. **3,** (*of eggs*) sunny side up.

estrellamar (es·tre·ʎa'mar; -ja·'mar) *n.f.* [*also,* **estrella de mar**] starfish.

estrellar (es·tre'ʎar; -'jar) *v.t.*

1, to star; mark or sprinkle with stars. **2,** *colloq.* to smash; dash to pieces. **3,** to fry (eggs) sunny side up. —**estrellarse,** *v.r.* **1,** to become starry. **2,** to smash up; crash. **3,** to fail; come to naught.
estrellón (es·tre'ʎon; -'jon) *n.m.* **1,** big star. **2,** *Amer.* smashup; crackup. —**pegarse un estrellón,** *Amer., colloq.* to smash up; crash.
estremecer (es·tre·me'θer; -'ser) *v.t.* [*pres.ind.* **estremezco** (-'meθ·ko; -'mes·ko); *pres.subjve.* **estremezca** (-ka)] **1,** to shake; make tremble. **2,** to frighten; upset. —**estremecerse,** *v.r.* to tremble; shudder. —**estremecimiento,** *n.m.* shudder; tremor.
estrenar (es·tre'nar) *v.t.* **1,** to use for the first time. **2,** to open (a play, movie, etc.). —**estrenarse,** *v.r.* to make one's debut.
estreno (es'tre·no) *n.m.* **1,** opening; premiere. **2,** debut.
estreñir (es·tre'ɲir) *v.t.* [*infl.*. **constreñir**] to constipate. —**estreñido,** *adj.* constipated. —**estreñimiento,** *n.m.* constipation.
estrenuo (es'tre·nwo) *adj.* strenuous; vigorous. —**estrenuidad,** *n.f.* strenuousness; vigor.
estrépito (es'tre·pi·to) *n.m.* din; noise. —**estrepitoso,** *adj.* noisy; loud.
estreptococo (es·trep·to'ko·ko) *n.m.* streptococcus.
estreptomicina (es·trep·to·mi·'θi·na; -'si·na) *n.f.* streptomycin.
estría (es'tri·a) *n.f.* groove; flute. —**estriado,** *adj.* striate; fluted. —**estriar,** *v.t.* to striate; flute.
estribación (es·tri·βa'θjon; -'sjon) *n.f.* foothill.
estribar (es·tri'βar) *v.i.* **1,** to rest; be supported. **2,** to be based.
estribillo (es·tri'βi·ʎo; -jo) *n.m.* refrain.
estribo (es'tri·βo) *n.m.* **1,** stirrup. **2,** abutment; buttress. **3,** running board; footboard. **4,** spur (*of a mountain range*). —**perder los estribos,** to lose one's head.
estribor (es·tri'βor) *n.m.* starboard.
estricnina (es·trik'ni·na) *n.f.* strychnine.
estricto (es'trik·to) *adj.* strict. —**estrictez,** *n.f., Amer.* strictness.
estridente (es·tri'ðen·te) *adj.* strident. —**estridencia,** *n.f.* stridency.
estriego (es'trje·ɣo) *v., pres.ind. of* **estregar.**
estriegue (es'trje·ɣe) *v., pres. subjve. of* **estregar.**
estrobo (es'tro·βo) *n.m., naut.* grommet.
estroboscopio (es·tro·βos'ko·pjo) *n.m.* stroboscope.
estrofa (es'tro·fa) *n.f.* stanza.
estroncio (es'tron·θjo; -sjo) *n.m.* strontium.
estropajo (es·tro'pa·xo) *n.m.* **1,** scrubbing pad; scrub cloth. **2,** rag.
estropear (es·tro·pe'ar) *v.t.* **1,** to cripple; damage. **2,** to spoil.
estropeo (es·tro'pe·o) *n.m.* **1,** wear and tear. **2,** damage.
estructura (es·truk'tu·ra) *n.f.* structure. —**estructural,** *adj.* structural.
estruendo (es'trwen·do) *n.m.* **1,** thunderous noise. **2,** commotion; fracas. **3,** fanfare. —**estruendoso,** *adj.* thunderous.
estrujar (es·tru'xar) *v.t.* to squeeze. —**estrujadura,** *n.f., also,* **estrujamiento,** *n.m.* squeezing; squeeze.
estrujón (es·tru'xon) *n.m.* crush; squeeze.
estuario (es'twa·rjo) *n.m.* estuary.
estuco (es'tu·ko) *n.m.* stucco. —**estucado,** *n.m.* stuccowork. —**estucar** (-'kar) *v.t.* [*infl.:* **tocar**] to stucco.
estuche (es'tu·tʃe) *n.m.* **1,** case; box; jewel box. **2,** *colloq.* man of many skills.
estudiante (es·tu'ðjan·te) *n.m.* & *f.* student. —**estudiantado** (-'ta·ðo) *n.m.* student body; students collectively.
estudiar (es·tu'ðjar) *v.t.* to study.
estudio (es'tu·ðjo) *n.m.* **1,** study. **2,** studio.
estudioso (es·tu'ðjo·so) *adj.* studious.
estufa (es'tu·fa) *n.f.* stove; heater.
estupefacto (es·tu·pe'fak·to) *adj.* stupefied. —**estupefacción,** *n.f.* stupefaction.
estupendo (es·tu'pen·do) *adj.* stupendous.
estúpido (es'tu·pi·ðo) *adj.* stupid. —**estupidez,** *n.f.* stupidity.
estupor (es·tu'por) *n.m.* **1,** stupor. **2,** stupefaction; amazement.
estuprar (es·tu'prar) *v.t.* to rape; violate. —**estuprador,** *n.m.* rapist. —**estupro** (-'tu·pro) *n.m.* rape, esp. statutory rape.

esturión (es·tu'rjon) *n.m.* sturgeon.
estuve (es'tu·βe) *v., pret. of* **estar.**
-eta ('e·ta) *suffix* **1,** -et; *forming fem. diminutive nouns: trompeta,* trumpet; *isleta,* islet. **2,** *fem. of* **-ete.**
etano (e'ta·no) *n.m.* ethane.
etapa (e'ta·pa) *n.f.* **1,** *mil.* field ration. **2,** stage; step; phase.
etcétera (et'θe·te·ra; et'se-) *n.f.* et cetera.
-ete ('e·te) *suffix* **1,** -et; -ish; *forming adjectives denoting* lesser or inferior quality or degree: *clarete,* claret; *agrete;* sourish. **2,** *forming masc. diminutive nouns and adjectives, often with derog. sense: mozalbete,* lad; *pobrete,* wretch; wretched.
éter ('e·ter) *n.m.* ether.
etéreo (e'te·reo) *adj.* ethereal.
eternal (e·ter'nal) *adj.* = **eterno.**
eternamente (e·ter·na'men·te) *adv.* **1,** eternally; forever. **2,** evermore.
eterno (e'ter·no) *adj.* eternal. —**eternidad,** *n.f.* eternity.
ética ('e·ti·ka) *n.f.* ethics. —**ético,** *adj.* ethical; ethic.
etileno (e·ti'le·no) *n.m.* ethylene.
etilo (e'ti·lo) *n.m.* ethyl.
etimología (e·ti·mo·lo'xi·a) *n.f.* etymology. —**etimológico** (-'lo·xi·ko) *adj.* etymological. —**etimologista,** *also,* **etimólogo** (-'mo·lo·ɣo) *n.m.* etymologist.
etiología (e·tjo·lo'xi·a) *n.f.* etiology.
etíope (e'ti·o·pe) *also,* **etiope** (e'tjo·pe) *adj.* & *n.m.* & *f.* Ethiopian. —**etiópico** (e'tjo·pi·ko) *adj.* Ethiopian.
etiqueta (e·ti'ke·ta) *n.f.* **1,** etiquette. **2,** formality. **3,** label; tag. —**de etiqueta, 1,** formal. **2,** formally.
étnico ('et·ni·ko) *adj.* ethnic.
etno- (et·no) *prefix* ethno-; people; race: *etnografía,* ethnography.
etnología (et·no·lo'xi·a) *n.f.* ethnology. —**etnológico** (-'lo·xi·ko) *adj.* ethnological. —**etnólogo** (-'no·lo·ɣo) *n.m.* ethnologist.
eu- (eu) *prefix* eu-; well; good; *eufónico,* euphonic.
eucalipto (eu·ka'lip·to) *n.m.* eucalyptus.
Eucaristía (eu·ka·ris'ti·a) *n.f.* Eucharist. —**eucarístico** (-'ris·ti·ko) *adj.* Eucharistic.
eufemismo (eu·fe'mis·mo) *n.m.* euphemism. —**eufemístico,** *adj.* euphemistic.
eufonía (eu·fo'ni·a) *n.f.* euphony. —**eufónico** (-'fo·ni·ko) *adj.* euphonic; euphonious.
euforia (eu'fo·rja) *n.f.* euphoria. —**eufórico** (-'fo·ri·ko) *adj.* euphoric.
eugenesia (eu·xe'ne·sja) *n.f.* eugenics. —**eugenésico** (-'ne·si·ko) *adj.* eugenic.
eunuco (eu'nu·ko) *n.m.* eunuch.
eurásico (eu'ra·si·ko) *adj.* & *n.m.* Eurasian.
europeo (eu·ro'pe·o) *adj.* & *n.m.* European.
europio (eu'ro·pjo) *n.m.* europium.
eutanasia (eu·ta'na·sja) *n.f.* euthanasia.
evacuar (e·βa'kwar) *v.t.* & *i.* [*infl.:* **vacuar**] to evacuate —*v.t.* to discharge; fulfill. —**evacuación,** *n.f.* evacuation.
evadir (e·βa'ðir) *v.t.* to escape; evade. —**evadirse,** *v.r.* to escape; get away; flee.
evaluar (e·βa'lwar) *v.t.* [*infl.:* **valuar**] to evaluate. —**evaluación,** *n.f.* evaluation.
evanescente (e·βa·nes'θen·te; -ne'sen·te) *adj.* evanescent. —**evanescencia,** *n.f.* evanescence.
evangélico (e·βan'xe·li·ko) *adj.* **1,** evangelical. **2,** *also n.m.* Protestant.
evangelio (e·βan'xe·ljo) *n.m.* gospel; evangel. —**evangelismo** (-'lis·mo) *n.m.* evangelism. —**evangelista,** *n.m.* & *f.* evangelist.
evangelizar (e·βan·xe·li'θar; -'sar) *v.t.* [*infl.:* **realizar**] to evangelize.
evaporar (e·βa·po'rar) *v.t.* to evaporate. —**evaporarse,** *v.r.* to vanish; evaporate. —**evaporación,** *n.f.* evaporation.
evaporizar (e·βa·po·ri'θar; -'sar) *v.t.* & *i.* = **vaporizar.** —**evaporización,** *n.f.* = **vaporización.**
evasión (e·βa'sjon) *n.f.* **1,** escape; flight. **2,** = **evasiva.**
evasiva (e·βa'si·βa) *n.f.* evasion; quibble. —**evasivo,** *adj.* evasive.
evasor (e·βa'sor) *adj.* evading; evasive. —*n.m.* evader; dodger.
evento (e'βen·to) *n.m.* event. —**eventual** (-'twal) *adj.* eventual. —**eventualidad,** *n.f.* eventuality.
evicción (e·βik'θjon; -'sjon) *n.f.* eviction.
evidencia (e·βi'ðen·θja; -sja) *n.f.*

1, manifestness; obviousness. 2, *Amer.* evidence; proof. —**evidenciar,** *v.t.* to evince; evidence. —**evidente,** *adj.* evident.
eviscerar (e·βis·θe'rar; e·βi·se-) *v.t.* to eviscerate. —**evisceración,** *n.f.* evisceration.
evitar (e·βi'tar) *v.t.* **1,** to prevent. **2,** to avoid.
evocar (e·βo'kar) *v.t.* [*infl.:* **convocar**] to evoke. —**evocación,** *n.f.* evocation. —**evocador,** *adj.* evocative.
evolución (e·βo·lu'θjon; -'sjon) *n.f.* **1,** evolution; development. **2,** maneuver (*of troops or ships*).
evolucionar (e·βo·lu·θjo'nar; -sjo'nar) *v.i.* **1,** to evolve; develop. **2,** to engage in maneuvers; maneuver (*of ships or troops*). **3,** to become different; change (*in attitude or conduct*).
evolucionismo (e·βo·lu·θjo'nis·mo; -sjo'nis·mo) *n.m.* evolutionism. —**evolucionista,** *adj.* evolutionary. —*n.m.* & *f.* evolutionist.
evolutivo (e·βo·lu'ti·βo) *adj.* evolutionary.
ex- (eks; *also sometimes* es *before* c, q, p, t) *prefix* ex-: **1,** beyond; forth: *extender,* to extend. **2,** out; out of; off: *expulsar,* to expel. **3,** formerly: *expresidente,* ex-president.
exacción (ek·sak'θjon; -'sjon) *n.f.* **1,** exaction. **2,** impost; tax.
exacerbar (ek·sa·θer'βar; -ser·'βar) *v.t.* to exacerbate. —**exacerbación,** *n.f.* exacerbation.
exactitud (ek·sak·ti'tuð) *n.f.* **1,** precision; accuracy. **2,** exactitude. **3,** punctuality.
exacto (ek'sak·to) *adj.* **1,** exact; precise; accurate. **2,** punctual.
exagerar (ek·sa·xe'rar) *v.t.* to exaggerate. —**exageración,** *n.f.* exaggeration.
exaltado (ek·sal'ta·ðo) *adj.* **1,** excitable; hotheaded. **2,** exaggerated; extreme.
exaltar (ek·sal'tar) *v.t.* to exalt. —**exaltarse,** *v.r.* to be gripped by emotion; become elated. —**exaltación,** *n.f.* exaltation.
examen (ek'sa·men) *n.m.* examination.
examinar (ek·sa·mi'nar) *v.t.* to examine. —**examinarse,** *v.r.* to take an examination. —**examinador,** *n.m.* examiner.
exangüe (ek'san·gwe) *adj.* **1,** deprived of blood; bloodless. **2,** exhausted; spent. **3,** lifeless; dead.
exánime (ek'sa·ni·me) *adj.* **1,** unconscious. **2,** dead; lifeless. **3,** spiritless; dismayed.
exasperar (ek·sas·pe'rar) *v.t.* to exasperate. —**exasperación,** *n.f.* exasperation.
excarcelar (eks·kar·θe'lar; -se'lar) *v.t.* to release from prison.
excavar (eks·ka'βar) *v.t.* to excavate. —**excavación,** *n.f.* excavation. —**excavador,** *adj.* excavating. —*n.m.* excavator (*person*). —**excavadora,** *n.f.* excavator (*machine*).
excedente (eks·θe'ðen·te; ek·se-) *adj.* excessive. —*adj.* & *n.m.* surplus; excess.
exceder (eks·θe'ðer; ek·se'ðer) *v.t.* to exceed; surpass. —*v.i.* [*also, refl.,* **excederse**] to overstep oneself.
excelencia (eks·θe'len·θja; ek·se'len·sja) *n.f.* **1,** excellence; superiority. **2,** *cap.* Excellency. —**por excelencia,** par excellence.
excelente (eks·θe'len·te; ek·se-) *adj.* excellent. —**excelentísimo,** *adj.* most excellent.
excéntrico (eks'θen·tri·ko; ek·'sen-) *adj.* eccentric. —**excéntrica,** *n.f.* [*also,* **excéntrico,** *n.m.*] *mech.* eccentric. —**excentricidad** (-θi·'ðað; -si'ðað) *n.f.* eccentricity.
excepción (eks·θep'θjon; ek·sep·'sjon) *n.f.* exception. —**excepcional,** *adj.* exceptional.
excepto (eks'θep·to; ek'sep·to) *adv.* except; excepting.
exceptuar (eks·θep'twar; ek·sep-) *v.t.* [*pres.ind.* **exceptúo** (-'tu·o); *pres.subjve.* **exceptúe** (-'tu·e)] **1,** to except. **2,** to exempt.
excerta (eks'θer·ta; ek'ser-) *n.f.* excerpt; extract. *Also,* **excerpta** (-pta).
exceso (eks'θe·so; ek'se-) *n.m.* excess. —**excesivo** (-'si·βo) *adj.* excessive.
excisión (eks·θi'sjon; ek·si-) *n.f.* excision.
excitable (eks·θi'ta·βle; ek·si-) *adj.* excitable. —**excitabilidad,** *n.f.* excitability.
excitación (eks·θi·ta'θjon; ek·si·ta'sjon) *n.f.* **1,** excitation. **2,** excitement.
excitado (eks·θi'ta·ðo; ek·si-) *adj.* excited; agitated.
excitante (eks·θi'tan·te; ek·si-) *adj.* exciting. —*n.m.* **1,** *electricity* exciter. **2,** stimulant.

excitar (eks·θi'tar; ek·si-) *v.t.* **1,** to excite. **2,** *electricity* to energize. —**excitarse,** *v.r.* to become excited.
exclamar (eks·kla'mar) *v.i.* to exclaim. —**exclamación,** *n.f.* exclamation. —**exclamatorio,** *also,* **exclamativo,** *adj.* exclamatory.
excluir (eks·klu'ir) *v.t.* [*infl.:* **concluir**] to exclude.
exclusión (eks·klu'sjon) *n.f.* exclusion.
exclusiva (eks·klu'si·βa) *n.f.* **1,** exclusion; denial of access. **2,** special privilege.
exclusive (eks·klu'si·βe) *adv.* exclusively. —*prep.* [*also,* **exclusive de**] not including; exclusive of.
exclusivo (eks·klu'si·βo) *adj.* exclusive. —**exclusivamente,** *adv.* exclusively. —**exclusividad,** *n.f.* exclusiveness.
excluso (eks'klu·so) *v., p.p. of* **excluir.**
excomulgado (eks·ko·mul'ɣa·ðo) *adj.* excommunicated. —*n.m., colloq.* miscreant.
excomulgar (eks·ko·mul'ɣar) *v.t.* [*infl.:* **comulgar**] **1,** to excommunicate. **2,** *colloq.* to ostracize.
excomunión (eks·ko·mu'njon) *n.f.* excommunication.
excoriar (eks·ko'rjar) *v.t.* **1,** to scrape off (the skin). **2,** *fig.* to excoriate; flay. —**excoriación,** *n.f.* excoriation.
excrecencia (eks·kre'θen·θja; -'sen·sja) *n.f.* excrescence. —**excrecente,** *adj.* excrescent.
excreción (eks·kre'θjon; -'sjon) *n.f.* excretion.
excremento (eks·kre'men·to) *n.m.* excrement.
excrescencia (eks·kres'θen·θja; -kre'sen·sja) *n.f.* = **excrecencia.**
excretar (eks·kre'tar) *v.i.* to excrete wastes.
exculpar (eks·kul'par) *v.t.* to exculpate. —**exculpación,** *n.f.* exculpation.
excursión (eks·kur'sjon) *n.f.* excursion; tour. —**excursionista,** *n.m.* & *f.* excursionist.
excusa (eks'ku·sa) *n.f.* **1,** excuse. **2,** *law* demurrer. —**a excusas,** cunningly; by subterfuge.
excusable (eks·ku'sa·βle) *adj.* excusable.
excusado (eks·ku'sa·ðo) *adj.* **1,** exempted; privileged. **2,** needless; unnecessary. **3,** reserved; private. —*n.m.* toilet; water closet.
excusar (eks·ku'sar) *v.t.* **1,** to excuse. **2,** to exempt. **3,** to eschew; avoid. **4,** *fol. by inf.* to excuse oneself from; refrain from. —**excusarse de,** to decline to.
execrar (ek·se'krar) *v.t.* to execrate. —**execrable,** *adj.* execrable. —**execración,** *n.f.* execration.
exégesis (ek'se·xe·sis) *n.f.sing.* & *pl.* exegesis. —**exégeta** (-ta) *n.m.* & *f.* exegete. —**exegético** (-'xe·ti·ko) *adj.* exegetic; exegetical.
exención (ek·sen'θjon; -'sjon) *n.f.* exemption.
exentar (ek·sen'tar) *v.t.* = **eximir.**
exento (ek'sen·to) *adj.* exempt; free; clear.
exequias (ek'se·kjas) *n.f.pl.* funeral rites.
exhalación (ek·sa·la'θjon; -'sjon) *n.f.* **1,** exhalation. **2,** shooting star. **3,** flash; lightning.
exhalar (ek·sa'lar) *v.t.* to exhale. —**exhalarse,** *v.r.* = **desalarse.**
exhausto (ek'saus·to) *adj.* exhausted.
exhibición (ek·si·βi'θjon; -'sjon) *n.f.* exhibition. —**exhibicionismo,** *n.m.* exhibitionism. —**exhibicionista,** *n.m.* & *f.* exhibitionist.
exhibir (ek·si'βir) *v.t.* to exhibit; display.
exhortar (ek·sor'tar) *v.t.* to exhort. —**exhortación,** *n.f.* exhortation. —**exhortatorio,** *adj.* hortatory; exhortatory.
exhumar (ek·su'mar) *v.t.* to exhume. —**exhumación,** *n.f.* exhumation.
exigir (ek·si'xir) *v.t.* [*pres.ind.* **exijo** (-'si·xo); *pres.subjve.* **exija** (-xa)] to demand; require; exact. —**exigencia,** *n.f.* exigency; demand. —**exigente,** *adj.* exigent; demanding; exacting.
exiguo (ek'si·ɣwo) *adj.* exiguous; sparse; meager. —**exigüidad** (-ɣwi·'dad) *n.f.* exiguousness; meagerness.
exilio (ek'si·ljo) *n.m.* exile; banishment. —**exiliar** [*also, Amer.,* **exilar** (-'lar)] *v.t.* to exile.
eximio (ek'si·mjo) *adj.* most excellent.
eximir (ek·si'mir) *v.t.* to exempt.
existencia (ek·sis'ten·θja; -sja) *n.f.* existence. —**existencias,** *n.f.pl., comm.* supply (*sing.*); stock (*sing.*).
existencial (ek·sis·ten'θjal; -'sjal) *adj.* existential. —**existencialismo,** *n.m.* existentialism. —**existencia-**

lista, *adj.* & *n.m.* & *f.* existentialist.
xistente (ek·sis'ten·te) *adj.* **1,** existent; extant. **2,** *comm.* on hand.
xistir (ek·sis'tir) *v.i.* to exist.
xito ('ek·si·to) *n.m.* **1,** end; termination. **2,** success.
xitoso (ek·si'to·so) *adj., Amer.* successful.
xo- (ek·so) *prefix* exo-; outside; out; external: *exógeno,* exogenous.
xodo ('ek·so·ðo) *n.m.* exodus.
xonerar (ek·so·ne'rar) *v.t.* to exonerate. —**exoneración,** *n.f.* exoneration.
xorbitante (ek·sor·βi'tan·te) *adj.* exorbitant. —**exorbitancia,** *n.f.* exorbitance.
xorcizar (ek·sor·θi'θar; -si'sar) *v.t.* [*pres.subjve.* **exorcice** (-'θi·θe; -'si·se); *pret.* **exorcicé** (-'θe; -'se)] to exorcize. —**exorcismo** (-'θis·mo; -'sis·mo) *n.m.* exorcism.
xotérico (ek·so'te·ri·ko) *adj.* exoteric.
xótico (ek'so·ti·ko) *adj.* exotic. —**exotismo,** *n.m.* exoticism.
xpandir (eks·pan'dir) *v.t., Amer.* to expand.
xpansible (eks·pan'si·βle) *adj.* expansible.
xpansión (eks·pan'sjon) *n.f.* **1,** expansion. **2,** expansiveness. **3,** recreation; amusement.
xpansionarse (eks·pan·sjo'nar·se) *v.r.* **1,** to be or become expansive. **2,** to rest *or* relax, esp. by a change of activity.
xpansivo (eks·pan'si·βo) *adj.* **1,** expansive. **2,** expansile.
xpatriar (eks·pa'trjar) *v.t.* to exile; expatriate. —**expatriarse,** *v.r.* to expatriate oneself; leave one's country. —**expatriación,** *n.f.* expatriation. —**expatriado,** *adj.* & *n.m.* expatriate.
xpectación (eks·pek·ta'θjon; -'sjon) *n.f.* expectation.
xpectante (eks·pek'tan·te) *adj.* expectant.
xpectativa (eks·pek·ta'ti·βa) *n.f.* **1,** expectation. **2,** expectancy.
xpectorar (eks·pek·to'rar) *v.t.* to expectorate. —**expectoración,** *n.f.* expectoration. —**expectorante,** *adj.* & *n.m.* expectorant.
xpedición (eks·pe·ði'θjon; -'sjon) *n.f.* **1,** expedition. **2,** forwarding; sending; dispatch. —**expedicionario,** *adj.* expeditionary.
xpediente (eks·pe'ðjen·te) *n.m.* **1,** expedient. **2,** dossier; record. **3,** *comm.* procedure. **4,** *law* proceedings (*pl.*). **5,** expeditiousness; dispatch.
expedienteo (eks·pe·ðjen'te·o) *n.m.* red tape.
expedir (eks·pe'ðir) *v.t.* [*infl.:* **pedir**] **1,** to expedite. **2,** to dispatch; send; forward. **3,** to issue (a decree, order, etc.).
expeditar (eks·pe·ði'tar) *v.t., Amer.* to expedite.
expeditivo (eks·pe·ði'ti·βo) *adj.* expeditious.
expedito (eks·pe'ði·to) *adj.* **1,** clear; unobstructed. **2,** ready.
expeler (eks·pe'ler) *v.t.* to expel; eject. —**expelente,** *adj.* & *n.m.* & *f.* expellant.
expender (eks·pen'der) *v.t.* **1,** to expend; spend. **2,** to sell at retail.
expendio (eks'pen·djo) *n.m.* expenditure; expense.
expensas (eks'pen·sas) *n.f.pl.* expenses. —**a expensas de,** at the expense of.
experiencia (eks·pe'rjen·θja; -sja) *n.f.* **1,** experience. **2,** experiment; trial.
experimentar (eks·pe·ri·men'tar) *v.t.* **1,** to experiment with; test. **2,** to experience. —**experimentación,** *n.f.* experimentation. —**experimentado,** *adj.* experienced.
experimento (eks·pe·ri'men·to) *n.m.* experiment. —**experimental,** *adj.* experimental.
experto (eks'per·to) *adj.* & *n.m.* expert.
expiar (eks·pi'ar) *v.t.* to expiate; atone for. —**expiación,** *n.f.* expiation; atonement.
expirar (eks·pi'rar) *v.i.* to expire. —**expiración,** *n.f.* expiration.
explanada (eks·pla'na·ða) *n.f.* esplanade.
explayarse (eks·pla'jar·se) *v.r.* **1,** to expatiate. **2,** to find solace; unburden oneself.
expletivo (eks·ple'ti·βo) *adj.* expletive.
explicable (eks·pli'ka·βle) *adj.* explicable.
explicación (eks·pli·ka'θjon; -'sjon) *n.f.* explanation.
explicar (eks·pli'kar) *v.t.* [*pres. subjve.* **explique** (-'pli·ke); *pret.* **expliqué** (-'ke)] to explain. —**explicarse,** *v.r.* to make oneself understood. —**explicarse una cosa,** to understand something.

explicativo (eks·pli·ka'ti·βo) *adj.* explanatory; expository.
explícito (eks'pli·θi·to; -si·to) *adj.* explicit.
explorador (eks·plo·ra'ðor) *adj.* exploring. —*n.m.* **1,** explorer. **2,** *cap.* Boy Scout.
explorar (eks·plo'rar) *v.t.* **1,** to explore. **2,** to scout; reconnoiter. —**exploración,** *n.f.* exploration. —**exploratorio,** *adj.* exploratory.
explosión (eks·plo'sjon) *n.f.* explosion. —**explosivo** (-'si·βo) *adj.* & *n.m.* explosive.
explotación (eks·plo·ta'θjon; -'sjon) *n.f.* **1,** exploitation; development. **2,** plant; works. **3,** working; operation.
explotar (eks·plo'tar) *v.t.* **1,** to exploit; develop. **2,** to work; run; operate. —*v.i.* to explode.
exponente (eks·po'nen·te) *adj.* indicating; typifying. —*n.m.* exponent.
exponer (eks·po'ner) *v.t.* [*infl.:* **poner**] **1,** to expose; exhibit. **2,** to endanger; risk. **3,** to reveal; disclose. **4,** to expound. —**exponerse,** *v.r.* to hazard; venture; risk.
exportar (eks·por'tar) *v.t.* to export. —**exportación,** *n.f.* exportation; export. —**exportador,** *adj.* exporting. —*n.m.* exporter.
exposición (eks·po·si'θjon; -'sjon) *n.f.* **1,** exposition. **2,** exposure. **3,** exhibit; exhibition; fair.
expositivo (eks·po·si'ti·βo) *adj.* expository.
expósito (eks'po·si·to) *adj.* abandoned. —*n.m.* foundling.
expositor (eks·po·si'tor) *n.m.* **1,** exponent; expositor. **2,** commentator. **3,** exhibitor. —*adj.* expository.
expresamente (eks·pre·sa'men·te) *adv.* **1,** expressly. **2,** clearly; decisively.
expresar (eks·pre'sar) *v.t.* to express; manifest.
expresión (eks·pre'sjon) *n.f.* expression.
expresivo (eks·pre'si·βo) *adj.* **1,** expressive. **2,** affectionate.
expreso (eks'pre·so) *adj.* **1,** expressed; evident. **2,** express; special. **3,** clear; decisive. —*adv.* = **expresamente.** —*n.m.* **1,** *Amer.* special delivery. **2,** express agency. **3,** express train.
exprimir (eks·pri'mir) *v.t.* **1,** to squeeze; extract. **2,** to wring. —**exprimidor,** *n.m.,* *also,* **exprimider**[a] *n.f.* juice extractor; wringer.
expropiar (eks·pro'pjar) *v.t.* [to] expropiate. —**expropiación,** *n.f.* ex[pro]propiation.
expuesto (eks'pwes·to) *v.,* *p.p.* *[of]* **exponer.** —*adj.* **1,** exposed. **2,** di[s]played. **3,** liable. **4,** at risk; [in] danger.
expugnar (eks·puɣ'nar) *v.t.* t[o] storm; take by storm. —**expug[]nación,** *n.f.* storming; taking b[y] storm.
expulsar (eks·pul'sar) *v.t.* to expe[l]; eject. —**expulsión** (-'sjon) *n.f.* ex[]pulsion; ejection. —**expulsivo** (-'si[·]βo) *adj.* & *n.m.* expellant. —**expul[]sor,** *n.m.* ejector (*of a firearm*).
expurgar (eks·pur'ɣar) *v.t.* [*infl.:* **purgar**] to expurgate. —**expurg[o]** (-'pur·ɣo) *n.m.,* *also,* **expurga[]ción,** *n.f.* expurgation.
exquisito (eks·ki'si·to) *adj.* ex[]quisite. —**exquisitez,** *n.f.* exquisite[]ness.
extasiar (eks·ta'sjar) *v.t.* to de[]light. —**extasiarse,** *v.r.* to be de[]lighted; be enraptured.
éxtasis ('eks·ta·sis) *n.m.* ecstas[y]. —**extático** (-'ta·ti·ko) *adj.* ecstati[c].
extemporáneo (eks·tem·po'ra[]ne·o) *adj.* **1,** untimely; inoppo[r]tune. **2,** curt; abrupt.
extender (eks·ten'der) *v.t.* [*infl.:* **tender**] **1,** to extend; spread; stretch. **2,** to draw up (a document). —**ex[]tenderse,** *v.r.* **1,** to extend; sprea[d]; stretch out. **2,** to expatiate.
extendido (eks·ten'di·ðo) *adj.* [1,] extended; stretched out. **2,** spaciou[s]; roomy. **3,** general; widespread.
extensible (eks·ten'si·βle) *ad[j.]* extensible.
extensión (eks·ten'sjon) *n.f.* [1,] extension. **2,** extent. **3,** expanse. [4,] *geom.* space; dimension.
extensivo (eks·ten'si·βo) *adj.* e[x]tensive; ample.
extenso (eks'ten·so) *adj.* **1,** e[x]tended. **2,** extensive.
extenuación (eks·te·nwa'θjo[n]; -'sjon) *n.f.* **1,** extenuation. **2,** em[a]ciation; exhaustion; enervation.
extenuado (eks·te'nwa·ðo) *a[dj.]* **1,** extenuated. **2,** emaciated; e[x]hausted; enervated.
extenuar (eks·te'nwar) *v.t.* [*pr[es.]* *ind.* **extenúo** (-'nu·o); *pres.subj[v.]* **extenúe** (-'nu·e)] to weaken; ene[r]vate.
exterior (eks·te'rjor) *adj.* & *n.[m.]*

exterior; outside. —*adj.* foreign; external. —*n.m.* outward appearance.

xterioridad (eks·te·rjo·ri'ðað) *n.f.* **1,** exterior thing. **2,** demeanor; outward appearance.

xteriorizar (eks·te·rjo·ri'θar; -'sar) *v.t.* [*pres.subjve.* **exteriorice** (-'ri·θe; -se); *pret.* **exterioricé** (-'θe; -'se)] to make manifest; reveal.

xterminar (eks·ter·mi'nar) *v.t.* to exterminate. —**exterminador,** *adj.* exterminating. —*n.m.* exterminator.

xterminio (eks·ter'mi·njo) *n.m.* extermination.

xterno (eks'ter·no) *adj.* **1,** external. **2,** outward. —*n.m.* day pupil.

xtinción (eks·tin'θjon; -'sjon) *n.f.* extinction; extinguishment.

xtinguir (eks·tin'gir) *v.t.* [*infl.:* **distinguir**] to extinguish.

xtinto (eks'tin·to) *adj.* **1,** extinguished. **2,** extinct.

xtintor (eks·tin'tor) *n.m.* fire extinguisher.

xtirpar (eks·tir'par) *v.t.* to extirpate. —**extirpación,** *n.f.* extirpation.

xtorsión (eks·tor'sjon) *n.f.* extortion. —**extorsionar,** *v.t.* to extort.

xtra ('eks·tra) *prep.* without; besides; outside of. —*adj., colloq.* extra; extraordinary; remarkable. —*n.m.* extra.

xtra- (eks·tra) *prefix* extra-; beyond; outside: *extralegal,* extralegal.

xtracción (eks·trak'θjon; -'sjon) *n.f.* extraction.

xtractar (eks·trak'tar) *v.t.* to abstract; abridge.

xtracto (eks'trak·to) *n.m.* **1,** extract. **2,** summary; abstract. **3,** number drawn in a lottery.

xtractor (eks·trak'tor) *adj.* extracting. —*n.m.* extractor.

xtradición (eks·tra·ði'θjon; -'sjon) *n.f.* extradition.

xtraer (eks·tra'er) *v.t.* [*infl.:* **traer**] to extract.

xtranjero (eks·tran'xe·ro) *adj.* foreign; alien. —*n.m.* alien; foreigner. —**en el extranjero; al extranjero,** abroad.

xtrañar (eks·tra'ɲar) *v.t.* **1,** to banish; exile. **2,** to wonder at; be amazed at. **3,** *Amer.* to miss; feel the lack of.

extrañeza (eks·tra'ɲe·θa; -sa) *n.f.* **1,** oddity; strangeness. **2,** wonderment; amazement.

extraño (eks'tra·ɲo) *adj.* **1,** strange. **2,** extraneous; foreign.

extraordinario (eks·tra·or·ði·'na·rjo) *adj.* extraordinary.

extraterritorial (eks·tra·te·rri·to'rjal) *adj.* extraterritorial.

extravagante (eks·tra·βa'ɣan·te) *adj.* extravagant. —**extravagancia,** *n.f.* extravagance.

extravelocidad (eks·tra·βe·lo·θi'ðað; -si'ðað) *n.f.* excessive speed; speeding.

extraversión (eks·tra·βer'sjon) *n.f., psychol.* extroversion.

extraviado (eks·tra'βja·ðo) *adj.* **1,** stray; wandering. **2,** strayed; mislaid. **3,** of unsound mind.

extraviar (eks·tra'βjar) *v.t.* **1,** to lead astray. **2,** to mislay; misplace. —**extraviarse,** *v.r.* **1,** to go astray; lose one's way. **2,** to err; deviate.

extravío (eks·tra'βi·o) *n.m.* **1,** deviation. **2,** going astray; straying. **3,** misplacement. **4,** aberration; irregularity.

extremado (eks·tre'ma·ðo) *adj.* extreme; excessive.

extremar (eks·tre'mar) *v.t.* to carry to extreme. —**extremarse,** *v.r.* to take special pains.

extremidad (eks·tre·mi'ðað) *n.f.* **1,** end; extremity. **2,** brink; border.

extremista (eks·tre'mis·ta) *n.m.* & *f.* extremist.

extremo (eks'tre·mo) *adj.* extreme. —*n.m.* **1,** end; extremity. **2,** extreme; utmost. —**en** *or* **por extremo,** extremely.

extremoso (eks·tre'mo·so) *adj.* extreme; vehement. —**extremosidad,** *n.f.* extremeness; vehemence.

extrínseco (eks'trin·se·ko) *adj.* extrinsic.

extroversión (eks·tro·βer'sjon) *n.f.* extroversion.

extrovertido (eks·tro·βer'ti·ðo) *adj.* extroverted. —*n.m.* extrovert.

extrusión (eks·tru'sjon) *n.f.* extrusion (*of plastics, metals, etc.*).

exuberancia (ek·su·βe'ran·θja; -sja) *n.f.* exuberance. —**exuberante,** *adj.* exuberant.

exudar (ek·su'ðar) *v.i.* to exude. —**exudación,** *n.f.* exudation.

exultar (ek·sul'tar) *v.i.* to exult. —**exultación,** *n.f.* exultation.

eyacular (e·ja·ku'lar) *v.t.* to ejacu-

late. —**eyaculación**, *n.f.* ejaculation.
eyector (e·jek'tor) *n.m.* ejector (*of a firearm*).
-ez ('eθ; 'es) *suffix, forming abstract nouns from adjectives: vejez,* senility; *niñez,* boyhood; *avidez,* greediness.
-eza ('e·θa; 'e·sa) *suffix, forming abstract nouns from adjectives: alteza,* Highness; *aspereza,* roughness.
-ezno ('eθ·no; 'es-) *suffix, forming diminutives: lobezno,* wolf cub.
-ezuelo (e'θwe·lo; e'swe-) *fem.* **-ezuela** (-la) *suffix, forming diminutives: reyezuelo,* kinglet.

F

F, f ('e·fe) *n.f.* 7th letter of the spanish alphabet.
fa (fa) *n.m., music* fa; F.
fábrica ('fa·βri·ka) *n.f.* **1,** factory; plant; mill. **2,** fabric.
fabricar (fa·βri'kar) *v.t.* [*pres. subjve.* **fabrique** (-'βri·ke); *pret.* **fabriqué** (-ke)] to manufacture; build; fabricate. —**fabricación**, *n.f.* manufacture; fabrication. —**fabricante**, *n.m.* manufacturer; builder. —**fabril** (fa'βril) *adj.* manufacturing.
fábula ('fa·βu·la) *n.f.* fable. —**fabulista**, *n.m.* & *f.* fabulist. —**fabuloso**, *adj.* fabulous.
facción (fak'θjon; -'sjon) *n.f.* faction; opposing group.
facciones (fak'θjo·nes; -'sjo·nes) *n.f.pl.* facial features.
faccioso (fak'θjo·so; -'sjo·so) *adj.* **1,** partisan. **2,** rebellious; factious. —*n.m.* rebel.
faces ('fa·θes; -ses) *n.f., pl. of* **faz.**
faceta (fa'θe·ta; -'se·ta) *n.f.* facet.
facial (fa'θjal; -'sjal) *adj.* facial.
-faciente (fa'θjen·te; -'sjen·te) *suffix* -facient; making; tending to make: *estupefaciente,* stupefacient.
fácil ('fa·θil; -sil) *adj.* easy; facile. —**facilidad**, *n.f.* ease; facility.
facilitación (fa·θi·li·ta'θjon; fa·si·li·ta'sjon) *n.f.* **1,** facilitation. **2,** supplying; supply.
facilitar (fa·θi·li'tar; fa·si-) *v.t.* **1,** to facilitate. **2,** to supply; furnish.
facineroso (fa·θi·ne'ro·so; fa·si-) *adj.* wicked; rascally. —*n.m.* rascal; criminal.
facsímile (fak'si·mi·le) *n.m.* facsimile. *Also,* **facsímil** (-mil).
factible (fak'ti·βle) *adj.* feasible. —**factibilidad**, *n.f.* feasibility.
facticio (fak'ti·θjo; -sjo) *adj.* factitious.
factor (fak'tor) *n.m.* **1,** factor; element. **2,** *R.R.*, baggagemaster. **3,** *comm.* commission merchant; factor. —**factoraje**, *n.m., comm.* factoring. —**factorial**, *adj.* factorial.
factoría (fak·to'ri·a) *n.f.* **1,** trading post. **2,** *W.I.* factory. **3,** *comm.* factoring. **4,** *comm.* office of factor.
factorizar (fak·to·ri'θar; -'sar) *v.t., Amer., math.* [*pres.subjve.* **factorice** (-'ri·θe; -se); *pret.* **factoricé** (-'θe; -'se)] to factor.
factura (fak'tu·ra) *n.f.* invoice.
facturar (fak·tu'rar) *v.t.* **1,** to invoice; bill. **2,** *R.R.* to check (baggage). —**facturación**, *n.f.* invoicing; billing.
facultad (fa·kul'tað) *n.f.* **1,** faculty; capacity. **2,** authority; authorization. **3,** *educ.* faculty.
facultar (fa·kul'tar) *v.t.* to authorize; empower.
facultativo (fa·kul·ta'ti·βo) *n.m.* physician; surgeon. —*adj.* **1,** facultative. **2,** optional.
facundia (fa'kun·dja) *n.f.* eloquence. —**facundo** (-do) *adj.* eloquent.
facha ('fa·tʃa) *n.f., colloq.* **1,** appearance. **2,** ludicrous person.
fachada (fa'tʃa·ða) *n.f.* **1,** façade. **2,** title page. **3,** appearance; build. —**hacer fachada a,** to front on.
fachenda (fa'tʃen·da) *n.f.* airs (*pl.*); pretentiousness. —**fachendoso**, *adj.* pretentious.
faena (fa'e·na) *n.f.* task.
faetón (fa·e'ton) *n.m.* phaeton.
-fagia ('fa·xja) *suffix* -phagy; -phagia; eating: *antropofagia,* anthropophagy.
fago– (fa·ɣo) *prefix* phago–; eating: *fagocito,* phagocyte.
-fago (fa·ɣo) *suffix* **1,** -phagous; *forming adjectives:* eating; devouring; *antropófago,* anthropophagous. **2,** -phage; *forming nouns*

eater; devourer: *xilófago,* xylophage.

fagocito (fa·ɣo'θi·to; -'si·to) *n.m.* phagocyte.

fagot (fa'got) *n.m.* **1,** bassoon. **2,** bassoonist. —**fagotista,** *n.m.* & *f.* bassoonist.

Fahrenheit (fa·ren'xait; -'xeit) *n.m.* Fahrenheit.

faisán (fai'san) *n.m.* pheasant.

faja ('fa·xa) *n.f.* **1,** girdle. **2,** band; strip.

fajar (fa'xar) *v.t.* **1,** to girdle. **2,** to swaddle. **3,** to bandage. **4,** *Amer., colloq.* to beat; maul. —**fajarse,** *v.r.* **1,** *Amer., colloq.* to fight; brawl. **2,** to put on a girdle.

falacia (fa'la·θja; -sja) *n.f.* **1,** deceit. **2,** fallacy.

falange (fa'lan·xe) *n.f.* **1,** phalanx. **2,** *cap.* Falange. —**Falangista,** *n.m.* & *f.* Falangist.

falaz (fa'laθ; -'las) *adj.* **1,** deceitful. **2,** fallacious.

falda ('fal·da) *n.f.* **1,** skirt. **2,** flap; fold. **3,** foothill. **4,** *chiefly W.I.* lap. —**faldas,** *n.f.pl., colloq.* women; females.

faldear (fal·de'ar) *v.t.* to skirt (a hill).

faldero (fal'de·ro) *adj.* skirt (*attrib.*); lap (*attrib.*).

faldilla (fal'di·ʎa; -ja) *n.f.* flap (*of a garment*).

faldón (fal'don) *n.m.* **1,** flowing skirt. **2,** coattail; shirttail. **3,** gable.

falible (fa'li·βle) *adj.* fallible. —**falibilidad,** *n.f.* fallibility.

falo ('fa·lo) *n.m.* phallus. —**fálico,** *adj.* phallic.

falsario (fal'sa·rjo) *n.m.* faker; deceiver.

falsear (fal·se'ar) *v.t.* to falsify; misrepresent. —*v.i.* to weaken.

falsedad (fal·se'ðað) *n.f.* falsity; falsehood.

falsete (fal'se·te) *n.m.* **1,** falsetto. **2,** plug; bung.

falsía (fal'si·a) *n.f.* falsity; duplicity.

falsificar (fal·si·fi'kar) *v.t.* [*pres. subjve.* **falsifique** (-'fi·ke); *pret.* **falsifiqué** (-'ke)] to counterfeit; forge; falsify. —**falsificación,** *n.f.* forgery; falsification. —**falsificador,** *n.m.* forger; counterfeiter.

falso ('fal·so) *adj.* **1,** false. **2,** forged; counterfeit. —*n.m., sewing* facing; padding. —**en falso, 1,** false(ly). **2,** mistaken(ly). **3,** improper(ly).

falta ('fal·ta) *n.f.* **1,** lack; want. **2,** fault; mistake. **3,** *colloq.* defect; flaw. **4,** misbehavior; misdemeanor. —**hacer falta,** to be wanting; be lacking; be needed. —**sin falta,** without fail.

faltar (fal'tar) *v.i.* **1,** to be lacking; be wanting; be needed. **2,** to fail; be derelict. **3,** to be absent. **4,** to offend. —**faltar a su palabra,** to break one's word. —**¡no faltaba más!,** the idea!; what nonsense!

falto ('fal·to) *adj.* **1,** *fol. by* **de,** lacking; wanting. **2,** mean; base; low. **3,** *Amer.* stupid; cloddish.

faltriquera (fal·tri'ke·ra) *n.f.* **1,** purse. **2,** pocket.

falúa (fa'lu·a) *n.f., naut.* tender.

falla ('fa·ʎa; -ja) *n.f.* **1,** defect; flaw. **2,** *Amer.* fault; mistake. **3,** *geol.* fault.

fallada (fa'ʎa·ða; 'ja·ða) *n.f. cards* act of trumping; ruff.

fallar (fa'ʎar; -'jar) *v.i.* **1,** to fail. **2,** to miss. —*v.t.* & *i., law* to render judgment (on); pass sentence (on). —*v.t., cards* to trump.

fallecer (fa·ʎe'θer; -je'ser) *v.i.* [*pres.ind.* **fallezco** (-'ʎeθ·ko; -'jes·ko); *pres.subjve.* **fallezca** (-ka)] to die; die out. —**fallecido,** *adj.* late; dead. —**fallecimiento,** *n.m.* death.

fallido (fa'ʎi·ðo; -'ji·ðo) *adj.* **1,** frustrated; unsuccessful. **2,** bankrupt.

fallo ('fa·ʎo; -jo) *n.m.* **1,** decision; judgment. **2,** *law* verdict; sentence. —**estar fallo,** *cards* to be unable to follow suit.

fama ('fa·ma) *n.f.* fame; reputation. —**correr fama,** to be rumored.

famélico (fa'me·li·ko) *adj.* famished.

familia (fa'mi·lja) *n.f.* family.

familiar (fa·mi'ljar) *adj.* **1,** familial; domestic. **2,** familiar. —*n.m.* **1,** relative. **2,** house servant. **3,** familiar. —**familiaridad,** *n.f.* familiarity.

familiarizar (fa·mi·lja·ri'θar; -'sar) *v.t.* [*pres.subjve.* **familiarice** (-'ri·θe; -se); *pret.* **familiaricé** (-'θe; -'se)] to familiarize.

-fana ('fa·na) *suffix* -phane; resembling: *cimofana,* cymophane.

famoso (fa'mo·so) *adj.* famous.

fanático (fa'na·ti·ko) *adj.* fanatic; fanatical. —*n.m.* fanatic. —**fanatismo,** *n.m.* fanaticism.

fandango (fan'dan·go) *n.m.* **1,** fandango. **2,** *colloq.* hullabaloo.

fanega (fa'ne·ɣa) *n.f.* Spanish grain measure (*about 1.5 bushels*). —**fanega de tierra**, Spanish land measure (*about 1.6 acres*).
fanfarria (fan'fa·rrja) *n.f.* ostentation; fanfare.
fanfarrón (fan·fa'rron) *n.m.* braggart. —*adj.* boastful. —**fanfarronada** (fan·fa·rro'na·da) *n.f.* boast. —**fanfarronear** (-ne'ar) *v.i.* to boast; brag.
fango ('fan·go) *n.m.* mud; mire. —**fangal**, *n.m.* bog. —**fangoso**, *adj.* muddy.
fantasía (fan·ta'si·a) *n.f.* fantasy. —**de fantasía**, imitation (*of jewelry*).
fantasma (fan'tas·ma) *n.m.* phantom; ghost.
fantasmagoría (fan·tas·ma'ɣo·rja) *n.f.* phantasmagoria. —**fantasmagórico** (-'ɣo·ri·ko) *adj.* phantasmagoric.
fantástico (fan'tas·ti·ko) *adj.* **1,** fantastic. **2,** *colloq.* swell; great.
fantoche (fan'to·tʃe) *n.m.* puppet.
fañoso (fa'ɲo·so) *adj., Amer.* nasal; twangy.
faquir (fa'kir) *n.m.* fakir.
faradio (fa'ra·ðjo) *n.m.* farad. *Also,* **farad** (fa'rað).
faralá (fa·ra'la) *n.m.* frill.
farallón (fa·ra'ʎon; -'jon) *n.m.* cliff; palisade.
faramalla (fa·ra'ma·ʎa; -ja) *n.f., colloq.* show; affectation; frill.
farándula (fa'ran·du·la) *n.f.* **1,** theatrical troupe. **2,** bohemian life.
Faraón (fa·ra'on) *n.m.* **1,** Pharaoh. **2,** *l.c.* faro.
fardo ('far·ðo) *n.m.* bale; bundle. —**pasar el fardo**, *Amer., colloq.* to pass the buck.
farfolla (far'fo·ʎa; -ja) *n.f.* claptrap; nonsense.
farfulla (far'fu·ʎa; -ja) *n.f., colloq.* **1,** sputtering; stumbling. **2,** mumbling. **3,** [*also,* **farfolla**] idle talk; nonsense.
farfullar (far·fu'ʎar; -'jar) *v.t. & i., colloq.* **1,** to sputter; stumble (over). **2,** to mumble.
farináceo (fa·ri'na·θe·o; -se·o) *adj.* farinaceous.
faringe (fa'rin·xe) *n.f.* pharynx. —**faríngeo** (-xe·o), pharyngeal. —**faringitis**, *n.f.* pharyngitis.
fariseo (fa·ri'se·o) *n.m.* pharisee. —**farisaico** (-'sai·ko) *adj.* pharisaic.
farmacéutico (far·ma'θeu·ti·ko; -'seu·ti·ko) *n.m.* pharmacist; druggist. —*adj.* pharmaceutical.
farmacia (far'ma·θja; -sja) *n.f.* pharmacy.
farmacología (far·ma·ko·lo'xi·a) *n.f.* pharmacology. —**farmacológico**, (-'lo·xi·ko) *adj.* pharmacological. —**farmacólogo** (-'ko·lo·go) *n.m.* pharmacologist.
farmacopea (far·ma·ko'pe·a) *n.f.* pharmacopeia.
faro ('fa·ro) *n.m.* **1,** lighthouse. **2,** beacon. **3,** floodlight. **4,** headlight. **5,** faro.
farol (fa'rol) *n.m.* **1,** lantern; headlight; street lamp. **2,** *fig.* bluff (esp. in games). **3,** *colloq.* = **fanfarrón.** —**farolear** (-le'ar) *v.i., colloq.* to boast; swagger.
farola (fa'ro·la) *n.f.* **1,** large street lamp. **2,** lighthouse.
farolero (fa·ro'le·ro) *n.m.* **1,** lamplighter. **2,** *colloq.* braggart. —*adj.* boastful.
farra ('fa·rra) *n.f., Amer.* spree.
farruco (fa'rru·ko) *adj.* **1,** bold; daring. **2,** *colloq.* impudent; saucy. —*n.m., Amer., colloq.* Galician or Asturian immigrant.
farsa ('far·sa) *n.f.* farce. —**farsante**, *adj.* & *n.m.* & *f.* fake.
fascículo (fas'θi·ku·lo; fa'si-) *n.m.* fascicle.
fascinar (fas·θi'nar; fa·si-) *v.t.* to fascinate. —**fascinación**, *n.f.* fascination.
fascismo (fas'θis·mo; fa'sis-) *n.m.* fascism. —**fascista**, *n.m.* & *f.* fascist. —*adj.* fascistic.
fase ('fa·se) *n.f.* phase.
-fasia ('fa·sja) *suffix* -phasia; speech disorder: *afasia,* aphasia.
fastidiar (fas·ti'ðjar) *v.t.* **1,** to bother; bore. **2,** to disrupt; upset. —**fastidio** (-'ti·ðjo) *n.m.* boredom; nuisance. —**fastidioso**, *adj.* boring.
fastuoso (fas'two·so) *adj.* ostentatious.
fatal (fa'tal) *adj.* **1,** fatal. **2,** fateful.
fatalidad (fa·ta·li'ðað) *n.f.* **1,** fate; destiny. **2,** calamity; misfortune. **3,** fatality.
fatalismo (fa·ta'lis·mo) *n.m.* fatalism. —**fatalista**, *n.m.* & *f.* fatalist. —*adj.* fatalistic.
fatídico (fa'ti·ði·ko) *adj.* fateful.
fatiga (fa'ti·ɣa) *n.f.* **1,** fatigue. **2,** hardship; bother. —**fatigoso**, *adj.* tiring; tiresome.
fatigar (fa·ti'ɣar) *v.t.* [*pres.*

subjve. **fatigue** (-'ti·ɣe); *pret.* **fatigué** (-'ɣe)] to tire; fatigue.
fatuo ('fa·two) *adj.* fatuous. —**fatuidad,** *n.f.* fatuity.
fauna ('fau·na) *n.f.* fauna.
fauno ('fau·no) *n.m.* faun.
fausto ('faus·to) *n.m.* pomp; splendor. —*adj.* fortunate.
favor (fa'βor) *n.m.* favor. —**a favor de, 1,** in behalf of. **2,** in favor of. —**favor de,** *fol. by inf., Amer.* please. —**por favor,** please; if you please.
favorable (fa·βo'ra·βle) *adj.* favorable.
favorecer (fa·βo·re'θer; -'ser) *v.t.* [*pres.ind.* **favorezco** (-'reθ·ko; -'res·ko); *pres.subjve.* **favorezca** (-ka)] to favor. —**favorecedor,** *adj.* favoring; becoming.
favorito (fa·βo'ri·to) *n.m. & adj.* favorite. —**favoritismo,** *n.m.* favoritism.
faz (faθ; fas) *n.f.* [*pl.* **faces**] face.
fe (fe) *n.f.* **1,** faith. **2,** testimony. —**dar fe, 1,** *fol. by* **de,** to attest. **2,** *fol. by* **a,** to believe; credit.
fealdad (fe·al'dað) *n.f.* ugliness.
febrero (fe'βre·ro) *n.m.* February.
febri- (fe·βri) *prefix* febri-; fever: *febrífugo,* febrifuge.
febril (fe'βril) *adj.* feverish.
fecal (fe'kal) *adj.* fecal.
fécula ('fe·ku·la) *n.f.* starch.
fecundo (fe'kun·do) *adj.* fecund. —**fecundar,** *v.t.* to fecundate. —**fecundación,** *n.f.* fecundation. —**fecundidad,** *n.f.* fecundity.
fecha ('fe·tʃa) *n.f.* date; day. —**fechar,** *v.t.* to date. —**para estas fechas,** by this time (*in the future*). —**por estas fechas,** at this time (*in the past*).
fechoría (fe·tʃo'ri·a) *n.f.* misdeed; atrocity.
federal (fe·ðe'ral) *adj.* federal. —**federalismo,** *n.m.* federalism. —**federalista,** *n.m. & f.* federalist.
federar (fe·ðe'rar) *v.t.* to federate. —**federación,** *n.f.* federation.
fehaciente (fe·a'θjen·te; -'sjen·te) *adj.* authentic; genuine.
feldespato (fel·des'pa·to) *n.m.* feldspar.
felicidad (fe·li·θi'ðað; -si'ðað) *n.f.* happiness; good fortune. —**¡felicidades!** congratulations!
felicitar (fe·li·θi'tar; -si'tar) *v.t.* to congratulate. —**felicitación,** *n.f.* congratulation.
feligrés (fe·li'ɣres) *n.m.* parishioner.
feligresía (fe·li·ɣre'si·a) *n.f.* **1,** parish. **2,** parishioners collectively.
felino (fe'li·no) *adj. & n.m.* feline.
feliz (fe'liθ; -'lis) *adj.* happy. —**Felices Pascuas** *or* **Navidades,** Merry Christmas.
felón (fe'lon) *n.m.* felon; criminal. —*adj.* criminal. —**felonía,** *n.f.* misdeed.
felpa ('fel·pa) *n.f.* plush.
felpilla (fel'pi·ʎa; -ja) *n.f.* chenille.
felpudo (fel'pu·ðo) *adj.* plushy. —*n.m.* mat; plush mat.
femenil (fe·me'nil) *adj.* womanly; womanish.
femenino (fe·me'ni·no) *adj.* feminine.
fementido (fe·men'ti·ðo) *adj.* false; unfaithful.
femineidad (fe·mi·nei'ðað) *also,* **feminidad** (-ni'ðað) *n.f.* femininity.
feminismo (fe·mi'nis·mo) *n.m.* feminism. —**feminista,** *n.m. & f.* feminist.
fémur ('fe·mur) *n.m.* femur. —**femoral** (-mo'ral) *adj.* femoral.
fen- (fen) *prefix, chem.* phen-; derived from or compounded with benzene: *fenacetina,* phenacetin.
fenecido (fe·ne'θi·ðo; -'si·ðo) *adj.* dead; deceased.
fenicio (fe'ni·θjo; -sjo) *adj. & n.m.* Phoenician.
fénico ('fe·ni·ko) *adj.* carbolic.
fénix ('fe·niks) *n.m.* phoenix.
feno- (fe·no) *prefix, var. of* **fen-**.
fenobárbito (fe·no'βar·βi·to) *n.m.* phenobarbital.
fenol (fe'nol) *n.m.* phenol.
fenómeno (fe'no·me·no) *n.m.* phenomenon. —**fenomenal,** *adj.* phenomenal.
feo ('fe·o) *adj.* ugly; unbecoming. —*n.m.* snub; slight. —**dar feo a,** to insult. —**sexo feo,** the male sex.
feracidad (fe·ra·θi'ðað; -si'ðað) *n.f.* fertility.
feraz (fe'raθ; -'ras) *adj.* fruitful; fertile.
féretro ('fe·re·tro) *n.m.* coffin.
feria ('fe·rja) *n.f.* fair.
feriante (fe'rjan·te) *n.m. & f.* peddler; hawker, esp. at fairs.
fermentar (fer·men'tar) *v.t. & i.* to ferment. —**fermentación,** *n.f.* fermentation. —**fermento** (-'men·to) *n.m.* ferment.
fermio ('fer·mjo) *n.m.* fermium.

-fero (fe·ro) *suffix* -ferous; containing; yielding; producing: *conífero,* coniferous.
feroz (fe'roθ; -'ros) *adj.* ferocious. —**ferocidad** (-θi'ðað; -si'ðað) *n.f.* ferocity.
férreo ('fe·rre·o) *adj.* **1,** ferrous; iron (*attrib.*). **2,** *fig.* stern; inflexible. —**vía férrea,** railroad.
ferretería (fe·rre·te'ri·a) *n.f.* **1,** hardware store. **2,** hardware. —**ferretero** (-'te·ro) *n.m.* hardware merchant.
ferri- (fe·rri) *prefix* ferri-; iron: *ferrífero,* ferriferous.
ferro- (fe·rro) *prefix* ferro-; iron: *ferrocromo,* ferrochromium.
ferrocarril (fe·rro·ka'rril) *n.m.* railroad. —**ferrocarrilero,** *n.m., Amer.* = **ferroviario.**
ferroso (fe'rro·so) *adj.* ferrous.
ferrotipo (fe·rro'ti·po) *n.m.* tintype; ferrotype.
ferroviario (fe·rro'βja·rjo) *adj.* railroad (*attrib.*) —*n.m.* railroad employee.
ferruginoso (fe·rru·xi'no·so) *adj.* containing iron; ferruginous.
fértil ('fer·til) *adj.* fertile. —**fertilidad,** *n.f.* fertility.
fertilizar (fer·ti·li'θar; -'sar) *v.t.* [*pres.subjve.* **fertilice** (-'li·θe; -se); *pret.* **fertilicé** (-'θe; -'se)] to fertilize. —**fertilización,** *n.f.* fertilization. —**fertilizante,** *n.m.* fertilizer. —*adj.* [*also,* **fertilizador**] fertilizing.
férula ('fe·ru·la) *n.f.* **1,** ferule. **2,** *fig.* rule; authority. **3,** *surg.* splint.
férvido ('fer·βi·ðo) *adj.* fervid.
ferviente (fer'βjen·te) *adj.* fervent. *Also,* **fervoroso** (-βo'ro·so).
fervor (fer'βor) *n.m.* fervor.
festear (fes·te'ar) *v.i., colloq.* to pay court; keep company. —**festeo** (-'te·o) *n.m., colloq.* courtship.
festejar (fes·te'xar) *v.t.* **1,** to entertain; fête. **2,** to celebrate; honor. **3,** to woo.
festejo (fes'te·xo) *n.m.* **1,** *usu.pl.* celebration; festivities. **2,** courtship.
festín (fes'tin) *n.m.* banquet; feast.
festinar (fes·ti'nar) *v.t., Amer.* to hasten; rush. —**festinado,** *adj.* precipitous; premature.
festival (fes·ti'βal) *n.m.* festival.
festivo (fes'ti·βo) *adj.* **1,** festive. **2,** humorous. —**festividad,** *n.f.* festivity.
festón (fes'ton) *n.m.* **1,** wreath; garland. **2,** edging.
festonear (fes·to·ne'ar) *v.t.* to wreathe; festoon. *Also,* **festonar.**
fetal (fe'tal) *adj.* fetal.
fetiche (fe'ti·tʃe) *n.m.* fetish; idol. —**fetichismo,** *n.m.* fetishism. —**fetichista,** *n.m.* & *f.* fetishist. —*adj.* fetishistic.
fétido ('fe·ti·ðo) *adj.* fetid. —**fetidez,** *n.f.* fetidness.
feto ('fe·to) *n.m.* fetus.
feudal (feu'ðal) *adj.* feudal. —**feudalismo,** *n.m.* feudalism.
feudo ('feu·ðo) *n.m.* fief. —**feudo franco,** freehold.
fez (feθ; fes) *n.m.* fez.
fiado (fi'a·ðo) *adj.* on credit. —**al fiado,** on credit. —**dar fiado,** to give credit.
fiador (fi·a'ðor) *n.m.* **1,** guarantor. **2,** bondsman. **3,** fastener; clasp. **4,** safety catch. **5,** tumbler (*of a lock*).
fiambre ('fjam·bre) *n.m.* **1,** cold cuts. **2,** *fig.* stale news. **3,** *slang* corpse. —*adj.* served cold, as food. —**fiambrera,** *n.f.* lunch basket.
fianza ('fjan·θa; -sa) *n.f.* **1,** bail. **2,** surety; guarantee.
fiar (fi'ar) *v.t.* [*infl.:* **enviar**] **1,** to guarantee. **2,** to sell on credit. —**fiarse,** *v.r. fol. by* **de,** to trust. —**de fiar,** trustworthy.
fiasco ('fjas·ko) *n.m.* fiasco.
fibra ('fi·βra) *n.f.* **1,** fiber. **2,** *fig.* energy; firmness. —**fibroso,** *adj.* fibrous.
-ficación (fi·ka'θjon; -'sjon) *suffix* -fication; *forming nouns from verbs ending in* **-ficar:** *glorificación,* glorification.
-ficar (fi'kar) *suffix,* -fy; make: *purificar,* purify.
ficción (fik'θjon; -'sjon) *n.f.* fiction.
-fico (fi·ko) *suffix* -fic; causing; producing: *terrorífico,* terrific.
ficticio (fik'ti·θjo; -sjo) *adj.* fictitious.
ficha ('fi·tʃa) *n.f.* **1,** chip; token; counter. **2,** domino piece. **3,** card file; record. **4,** index card. **5,** *colloq.* character. **6,** dossier. —**fichar,** *v.t.* to tag; peg (*a person*). —*v.t.* & *i.* to move (*in dominoes*).
fichero (fi'tʃe·ro) *n.m.* **1,** file. **2,** filing cabinet.
fidedigno (fi·ðe'ðiɣ·no) *adj.* reliable.
fidelidad (fi·ðe·li'ðað) *n.f.* loyalty; fidelity.
fideo (fi'ðe·o) *n.m.* **1,** *usu.pl.* vermicelli; spaghetti. **2,** *colloq.* very thin person.

fiduciario (fi·ðu'θja·rjo; -'sja·rjo) *adj.* & *n.m.* fiduciary.
fiebre ('fje·βre) *n.f.* fever. —**limpiarse de fiebre,** to rid oneself of fever.
fiel (fjel) *adj.* faithful; true. —*n.m.* **1,** needle of a balance. **2,** inspector (*of weights and measures*).
fieltro ('fjel·tro) *n.m.* felt.
fiera ('fje·ra) *n.f.* **1,** wild beast. **2,** fiend.
fiero ('fje·ro) *adj.* **1,** wild; fierce. **2,** rude; rough. **3,** cruel. **4,** huge. —**fieros,** *n.m.pl.* boasts; threats. —**fiereza,** *n.f.* ferocity; cruelty.
fierro ('fje·rro) *n.m., Amer.* = **hierro.**
fiesta ('fjes·ta) *n.f.* **1,** festival; fiesta. **2,** party; entertainment. **3,** holy day; holiday. —**estar de fiesta,** to revel. —**hacer fiestas a,** to fawn on.
fiestero (fjes'te·ro) *adj.* fond of merrymaking. —*n.m.* merrymaker; reveler.
figón (fi'ɣon) *n.m.* cheap or unpretentious restaurant; joint.
figura (fi'ɣu·ra) *n.f.* **1,** figure; shape. **2,** mien; countenance. **3,** character; personage. **4,** design; pattern. **5,** figure of speech. **6,** face card.
figuración (fi·ɣu·ra'θjon; -'sjon) *n.f.* **1,** figuration. **2,** *Amer.* role; participation.
figurado (fi·ɣu'ra·ðo) *adj.* figurative.
figurar (fi·ɣu'rar) *v.t.* **1,** to shape; form. **2,** to portray; represent. **3,** to feign. —*v.i.* to figure; take part. —**figurarse,** *v.r.* to imagine; picture.
figurativo (fi·ɣu·ra'ti·βo) *adj.* figurative.
figurín (fi·ɣu'rin) *n.m.* **1,** fashion plate. **2,** pattern book. **3,** *colloq.* dandy.
figurón (fi·ɣu'ron) *n.m.* figurehead.
fijación (fi·xa'θjon; -'sjon) *n.f.* **1,** fixation. **2,** setting; fixing.
fijado (fi'xa·ðo) *n.m., photog.* fixing; fixation.
fijar (fi'xar) *v.t.* to fix; set. —**fijarse,** *v.r.* to notice; pay attention.
fijeza (fi'xe·θa; -sa) *n.f.* **1,** fixity. **2,** firmness.
fijo ('fi·xo) *adj.* **1,** fixed; set; agreed upon. **2,** firm; secure. **3,** stationary. **4,** fast (*of colors*). —**de fijo,** surely; undoubtedly.
fil- (fil) *prefix, var. of* **filo-,** *used before vowels: filantropía,* philanthropy.
fila ('fi·la) *n.f.* **1,** file; row; line. **2,** *mil.* rank.
-fila ('fi·la) *suffix* -phyl; leaf: *clorofila,* chlorophyl.
filacteria (fi·lak'te·rja) *n.f.* phylactery.
filamento (fi·la'men·to) *n.m.* filament.
filantropía (fi·lan·tro'pi·a) *n.f.* philanthropy. —**filantrópico** (-'tro·pi·ko) *adj.* philanthropic. —**filántropo** (-'lan·tro·po) *n.* philanthropist.
filarmónico (fi·lar'mo·ni·ko) *adj.* philharmonic. —*n.m.* music lover.
filatelia (fi·la'te·lja) *n.f.* philately. —**filatélico** (-'te·li·ko) *adj.* philatelic. —**filatelista,** *n.m.* & *f.* philatelist.
filete (fi'le·te) *n.m.* **1,** fillet; filet. **2,** hem. **3,** screw thread. —**filete de solomillo,** filet mignon.
-filia ('fi·lja) *suffix* -philism; -philia; *forming nouns from adjectives ending in* **-filo**: *bibliofilia,* bibliophilism; *cromatofilia,* chromatophilia.
filiación (fi·lja'θjon; -'sjon) *n.f.* **1,** affiliation. **2,** personal description. **3,** filial relationship; descent.
filial (fi'ljal) *adj.* filial.
filibustero (fi·li·βus'te·ro) *n.m.* freebooter.
filigrana (fi·li'ɣra·na) *n.f.* **1,** filigree. **2,** watermark. **3,** finely wrought object; jewel.
filipino (fi·li'pi·no) *adj.* & *n.m.* Philippine.
filisteo (fi·lis'te·o) *adj.* & *n.m.* Philistine. —*n.m.* tall, burly man.
film (film) *also,* **filme** ('fil·me) *n.m.* film.
filmar (fil'mar) *v.t.* to film; photograph. —**filmación,** *n.f.* filming.
filo ('fi·lo) *n.m.* **1,** edge; sharp edge. **2,** dividing line. **3,** *biol.* phylum. —**de filo,** *Amer.* directly; resolutely. —**por filo,** precisely.
filo- (fi·lo) *prefix* **1,** philo–; liking; loving: *filologia,* philology. **2,** phyll-; phyllo-; leaf: *filoma,* phyllome; *filoxera,* phylloxera.
-filo (fi·lo) *suffix* **1,** -phile; liking; loving: *bibliófilo,* bibliophile. **2,** -phyllous; having a specified number or kind of leaves: *clorófilo,* chlorophyllous.
filología (fi·lo·lo'xi·a) *n.f.* philology. —**filológico** (-'lo·xi·ko) *adj.* philological. —**filólogo** (-'lo·lo·ɣo) *n.m.* philologist.

filón (fi'lon) *n.m.* **1,** lode. **2,** *fig.* gold mine.
filoso (fi'lo·so) *adj. Amer.* sharp.
filosofar (fi·lo·so'far) *v.i.* to philosophize.
filosofía (fi·lo·so'fi·a) *n.f.* philosophy. —**filosófico** (-'so·fi·ko) *adj.* philosophical. —**filósofo** (-'lo·so·fo) *n.m.* philosopher.
filtrar (fil'trar) *v.t.* & *i.* to filter; filtrate. —**filtrarse,** *v.r.* **1,** to filter or seep through. **2,** to be wasted away, as a fortune, money, etc. —**filtración,** *n.f.* filtration; seepage. —**filtrado,** *n.m.* filtrate.
filtro ('fil·tro) *n.m.* **1,** filter. **2,** love potion; philter.
fílum ('fi·lum) *n.m., biol.* phylum.
fin (fin) *n.m.* end. —**a fin de,** in order to. —**a fin de que,** in order that. —**al fin; al fin y al cabo,** in the end; after all. —**en fin; por fin,** finally; at last.
finado (fi'na·ðo) *n.m.* deceased.
final (fi'nal) *adj.* final. —*n.m.* end; finish. —**finalista,** *n.m.* & *f.* finalist.
finalidad (fi·na·li'ðað) *n.f.* purpose; end.
finalizar (fi·na·li'θar; -'sar) *v.t.* & *i.* [*pres.subjve.* **finalice** (-'li·θe; -se); *pret.* **finalicé** (-'θe; -'se)] to finish; end.
financiar (fi·nan'θjar; -'sjar) *v.t.* to finance.
financiero (fi·nan'θje·ro; -'sje·ro) *adj.* financial. —*n.m.* financier.
finanzas (fi'nan·θas; -sas) *n.f.pl.* **1,** finances. **2,** finance (*sing.*).
finca ('fin·ka) *n.f.* **1,** estate; property. **2,** *Amer.* farm; ranch.
finés (fi'nes) *adj.* & *n.m.* = **finlandés.**
fineza (fi'ne·θa; -sa) *n.f.* **1,** delicacy; graciousness. **2,** fineness. **3,** kind word or gesture. **4,** small gift; favor. **5,** *cards, Amer.* finesse.
fingir (fin'xir) *v.t.* [*pres.ind.* **finjo** ('fin·xo); *pres.subjve.* **finja** (-xa)] to feign; pretend. —**fingido,** *adj.* feigned; false. —**fingimiento,** *n.m.* feigning; deceit.
finiquitar (fi·ni·ki'tar) *v.t.* **1,** to close out (an account). **2,** to bring to an end; conclude. —**finiquito** (-'ki·to) *n.m.* closing out; settlement (*of an account*).
finito (fi'ni·to) *adj.* finite.
finlandés (fin·lan'des) *adj.* Finnish. —*n.m.* **1,** Finn. **2,** Finnish language.
fino ('fi·no) *adj.* **1,** fine. **2,** courteous; urbane. **3,** subtle.
finta ('fin·ta) *n.f.* feint.
finura (fi'nu·ra) *n.f.* **1,** daintiness. **2,** courtesy; urbanity. **3,** finesse; subtlety.
fiordo ('fjor·ðo) [*pl.* **fiordos**] *also,* **fiord** (fjorð) [*pl.* **fiores** ('fjo·res)] *n.m.* fiord.
firma ('fir·ma) *n.f.* **1,** signature. **2,** firm.
firmamento (fir·ma'men·to) *n.m.* firmament.
firmar (fir'mar) *v.t.* to sign; affix one's signature to. —**firmante,** *adj.* & *n.m.* & *f.* signatory.
firme ('fir·me) *adj.* firm. —*adv.* firmly. —*n.m., engin.* **1,** firm soil (*for foundations*). **2,** roadbed. —**de firme,** firmly; steadily. —**en firme,** *comm.* firm, as an offer. —**¡firmes!** *mil.* attention!
firmeza (fir'me·θa; -sa) *n.f.* firmness.
firulete (fi·ru'le·te) *n.m., Amer., colloq.* frill; fanciness.
fiscal (fis'kal) *adj.* **1,** fiscal. **2,** governmental; of the public treasury. —*n.m.* **1,** auditor of public moneys. **2,** public prosecutor; district attorney.
fiscalizar (fis·ka·li'θar; -'sar) *v.t.* [*pres.subjve.* **fiscalice** (-'li·θe; -se); *pret.* **fiscalicé** (-'θe; -'se)] **1,** to control; audit. **2,** *fig.* to criticize.
fisco ('fis·ko) *n.m.* public treasury.
fisgón (fis'ɣon) *adj.* prying; snoopy. —*n.m.* prier; snoop.
fisgonear (fis·ɣo·ne'ar) *v.i.* to pry; snoop. —**fisgoneo** (-'ne·o) *n.m.* prying; snooping.
física ('fi·si·ka) *n.f.* physics.
físico ('fi·si·ko) *adj.* physical. —*n.m.* **1,** physicist. **2,** physique. **3,** appearance. **4,** *archaic* physician.
fisio- (fi·sjo) *prefix* physio-; nature; natural: *fisiología,* physiology.
fisiología (fi·sjo·lo'xi·a) *n.f.* physiology. —**fisiológico** (-'lo·xi·ko) *adj.* physiological. —**fisiólogo** (-'sjo·lo·ɣo) *n.m.* physiologist.
fisión (fi'sjon) *n.f.* fission. —**fisionable,** *adj.* fissionable. —**fisionar,** *v.t.* to split.
fisioterapia (fi·sjo·te'ra·pja) *n.f.* physiotherapy. —**fisioterapeuta** (-'peu·ta) *n.m.* & *f.* physiotherapist.
fisonomía (fi·so·no'mi·a) *n.f.* physiognomy. —**fisonómico** (-'no·mi·ko) *adj.* physiognomic.
fístula ('fis·tu·la) *n.f.* fistula.

fisura (fi'su·ra) *n.f.* fissure.
fito- (fi·to) *prefix* phyto-; plant; vegetable: *fitogénesis,* phytogenesis.
-fito (fi·to) *suffix* -phyte; *forming nouns denoting* a plant, having a specified habitat or nature: *saprófito,* saprophyte.
fláccido ('flak·θi·ðo; 'flak·si-) *adj.* flaccid. —**flaccidez,** *n.f.* flaccidity.
flaco ('fla·ko) *adj.* **1,** thin; lean; skinny. **2,** weak. —*n.m.* weakness; weak point. —**flacura,** *n.f.* thinness; leanness; scrawniness.
flagelar (fla·xe'lar) *v.t.* to flagellate; whip. —**flagelación,** *n.f.* flagellation. —**flagelante,** *n.m.* & *f.* flagellant.
flagelo (fla'xe·lo) *n.m.* **1,** whip; lash. **2,** scourge.
flagrante (fla'ɣran·te) *adj.* flagrant. —**flagrancia,** *n.f.* flagrancy.
flama ('fla·ma) *n.f.* **1,** flame. **2,** firelight.
flamante (fla'man·te) *adj.* **1,** resplendent. **2,** brand new.
flamear (fla·me'ar) *v.i.* to flame; shine.
flamenco (fla'men·ko) *adj.* **1,** Flemish. **2,** gypsylike. **3,** roguish; bold. —*n.m.* **1,** flamingo. **2,** Fleming. **3,** Flemish (*language*).
flan (flan) *n.m.* custard.
flanco ('flan·ko) *n.m.* flank; side. —**flanquear** (-ke'ar) *v.t.* to flank.
flaquear (fla·ke'ar) *v.i.* to weaken.
flaqueza (fla'ke·θa; -sa) *n.f.* **1,** = **flacura. 2,** weakness. **3,** *fig.* misstep.
flato ('fla·to) *n.m.* **1,** a breaking wind. **2,** *Amer., colloq.* hangover.
flatulento (fla·tu'len·to) *adj.* flatulent. —**flatulencia,** *n.f.* flatulence.
flauta ('flau·ta) *n.f.* flute. —**flautista,** *n.m.* & *f.* flutist.
flautín (flau'tin) *n.m.* piccolo.
flebitis (fle'βi·tis) *n.f.* phlebitis.
flebo- (fle·βo) *prefix* phlebo-; vein; *flebotomía,* phlebotomy.
fleco ('fle·ko) *n.m.* **1,** fringe; flounce. **2,** jagged or threadbare edge.
flecha ('fle·tʃa) *n.f.* arrow.
flechar (fle'tʃar) *v.t.* **1,** to fit an arrow to (a bow). **2,** to pierce with an arrow. **3,** *fig.* to inspire love in.
flechazo (fle'tʃa·θo; -so) *n.m.* **1,** stroke of an arrow. **2,** bowshot. **3,** arrow wound. **4,** *fig.* sudden love.
flechero (fle'tʃe·ro) *n.m.* **1,** bowman. **2,** arrowmaker.
fleje ('fle·xe) *n.m.* iron hoop; steel strap.
flema ('fle·ma) *n.f.* phlegm. —**flemático,** (-'ma·ti·ko) *adj.* phlegmatic.
fleo ('fle·o) *n.m.* timothy; timothy grass.
flequillo (fle'ki·ʎo; -jo) *n.m.* bang (*or* bangs) of hair.
fletamento (fle·ta'men·to) *n.m.* **1,** charter or chartering of a vessel. **2,** charter party.
fletar (fle'tar) *v.t.* **1,** to charter (a vessel). **2,** *Amer.* to hire (a conveyance). **3,** *Amer., colloq.* to give (a blow, slap, etc.). —**fletarse,** *v.r., Amer. colloq.* to clear out; get out.
flete ('fle·te) *n.m.* **1,** freight charges. **2,** freight. **3,** *Amer.* hire; rental (*of a conveyance*).
flexible (flek'si·βle) *adj.* flexible. —**flexibilidad,** *n.f.* flexibility.
flexión (flek'sjon) *n.f.* **1,** bending; bend. **2,** *gram.* flexion; inflection. —**flexionar** (-'nar) *v.t.* to bend; flex.
flirtear (flir·te'ar) *v.i.* to flirt. —**flirteador,** *adj.* flirtatious. —*n.m.* flirt. —**flirteo** (-'te·o) *n.m.* flirtation.
flojear (flo·xe'ar) *v.i.* **1,** to idle; be lazy. **2,** to flag; weaken.
flojedad (flo·xe'ðað) *n.f.* **1,** looseness; slack. **2,** [*also, colloq.* **flojera** (-'xe·ra)] laziness; indolence.
flojel (flo'xel) *n.m.* **1,** nap (*of cloth*). **2,** soft feathers; down. —**pato de flojel,** eider duck.
flojo ('flo·xo) *adj.* **1,** loose; slack. **2,** feeble; lacking force. **3,** lazy; indolent. **4,** incompetent; poor.
flor (flor) *n.f.* **1,** flower. **2,** *fig.* compliment; flattery. —**a flor de agua,** afloat; at water level. —**a flor de labios,** on the tip of one's tongue. —**echar flores a,** *colloq.* to flatter; butter up. —**flor de lis, 1,** amaryllis. **2,** fleur-de-lis. —**flor de muerto,** marigold. —**flor de un día,** *colloq.* flash in the pan. —**flor y nata,** elite; cream. —**juegos florales,** poetry contest.
flora ('flo·ra) *n.f.* flora.
floración (flo·ra'θjon; -'sjon) *n.f.* flowering.
floral (flo'ral) *adj.* floral.
florear (flo·re'ar) *v.t.* to adorn with flowers. —*v.i.* **1,** to flit; gad about. **2,** *colloq.* to compliment; flatter. **3,** *Amer.* = **florecer.**
florecer (flo·re'θer; -'ser) *v.i.* [*pres.ind.* **florezco** (-'reθ·ko; -'res·ko); *pres.subjve.* **florezca** (-ka)] **1,**

to flower; blossom. 2, to flourish; prosper. —**florecerse**, *v.r.* to become moldy. —**floreciente**, *adj.* flourishing; prospering.
florecimiento (flo·re·θi'mjen·to; -si'mjen·to) *n.m.* 1, flowering; blossoming. 2, flourishing.
floreo (flo're·o) *n.m.* 1, flourish; brandishing (*of a sword*). 2, *colloq.* idle talk; nonsense. 3, floweriness (*in speech or writing*).
florero (flo're·ro) *adj.*, *fig.* flowery. —*n.m.* flower vase. —**florería**, *n.f.*, *Amer.* flower shop.
florescencia (flo·res'θen·θja; -re'sen·sja) *n.f.* florescence.
floresta (flo'res·ta) *n.f.* forest; wood.
florete (flo're·te) *n.m.* fencing foil. —**floretista**, *n.m.* swordsman.
flori- (flo·ri) *prefix* flori-; flower: *floricultor*, floriculturist.
floricultura (flo·ri·kul'tu·ra) *n.f.* floriculture. —**floricultor** (-'tor) *n.m.* floriculturist.
florido (flo'ri·ðo) *adj.* flowery. —**floridez** (-'ðeθ; -'ðes) floweriness.
florín (flo'rin) *n.m.* florin.
florista (flo'ris·ta) *n.m.* & *f.* florist. —**floristería**, *n.f.* flower shop.
-floro (flo·ro) *suffix* -florous; bearing a specified kind or number of flower: *unífloro*, uniflorous.
flota ('flo·ta) *n.f.* fleet.
flotación (flo·ta'θjon; -'sjon) *n.f.* flotation; floating. —**línea de flotación**, waterline (*of a ship*).
flotar (flo'tar) *v.i.* to float. —**flotador**, *n.m.* float.
flote ('flo·te) *n.m.* = **flotación**. —**a flote**, afloat.
flotilla (flo'ti·ʎa; -ja) *n.f.* flotilla.
flox (floks) *n.m.* phlox.
fluctuar (fluk'twar) *v.i.* [*infl.:* **continuar**] *to* fluctuate. —**fluctuación**, *n.f.* fluctuation.
fluidez (flu·i'ðeθ; -'ðes) *n.f.* 1, fluidity. 2, fluency.
flúido ('flu·i·ðo) *adj.* 1, fluid. 2, fluent. —*n.m.* 1, fluid. 2, electric current.
fluir (flu'ir) *v.i.* [*infl.:* **huir**] to flow.
flujo ('flu·xo) *n.m.* 1, flow; flux. 2, rising tide. 3, *med.* discharge; secretion. 4, menstruation.
flúor ('flu·or) *n.m.* fluorine.
fluorescencia (flu·o·res'θen·θja; -re'sen·sja) *n.f.* fluorescence. —**fluorescente**, *adj.* fluorescent.
fluorización (flu·o·ri·θa'θjon; -sa'sjon) *n.f.* fluoridation.
fluoroscopio (flu·o·ros'ko·pjo) *n.m.* fluoroscope. —**fluoroscopia** (-pja) *n.f.* fluoroscopy. —**fluoroscópico** (-'ko·pi·ko) *adj.* fluoroscopic.
fluoruro (flu·o'ru·ro) *n.m.* fluoride.
fluvial (flu'βjal) *adj.* fluvial.
flux (fluks) *n.m.* 1, *cards* flush. 2, *Amer.* suit of clothes. —**hacer flux**, *colloq.* to go broke. —**tener flux**, *Amer.*, *colloq.* to be lucky.
¡fo! (fo) *interj.* pew!; ¡phew!
fobia ('fo·βja) *n.f.* phobia.
-fobia ('fo·βja) *suffix* -phobia; dread; fear; hatred: *claustrofobia*, claustrophobia.
-fobo (fo·βo) *suffix* -phobe; fearing; hating: *anglófobo*, Anglophobe.
foca ('fo·ka) *n.f.*, *zool.* seal.
foco ('fo·ko) *n.m.* 1, focus; center. 2, street lamp. 3, *Amer.* light bulb. 4, lamp globe. —**focal**, *adj.* focal.
fofo ('fo·fo) *adj.* flabby; spongy.
fogata (fo'ɣa·ta) *n.f.* bonfire; campfire.
fogón (fo'ɣon) *n.m.* hearth; stove.
fogonazo (fo·ɣo'na·θo; -so) *n.m.* flash.
fogonero (fo·ɣo'ne·ro) *n.m.* stoker.
fogoso (fo'ɣo·so) *adj.* 1, impetuous; fiery; spirited. 2, ardent; lustful. —**fogosidad**, *n.f.* impetuosity; fieriness; spirit.
folio ('fo·ljo) *n.m.* folio.
folklore (fol'klo·re) *n.m.* folklore. —**folklórico**, *adj.* folkloristic.
follaje (fo'ʎa·xe; -'ja·xe) *n.m.* foliage.
folletín (fo·ʎe'tin; -je'tin) *n.m.* newspaper serial; regular newspaper feature; column. —**folletinista**, *n.m.* & *f.* columnist.
folleto (fo'ʎe·to; -'je·to) *n.m.* pamphlet; booklet.
fomentar (fo·men'tar) *v.t.* to foment; foster; promote.
fomento (fo'men·to) *n.m.* 1, fostering; promotion. 2, fomentation. 3, poultice.
fonda ('fon·da) *n.f.* 1, inn. 2, modest restaurant.
fondear (fon·de'ar) *v.t.*, *naut.* to sound. —*v.i.* to cast anchor. —**fondeadero**, *n.m.* anchorage.
fondillos (fon'di·ʎos; -jos) *n.m. pl.* 1, seat of the pants. 2, buttocks.

fondista (fon'dis·ta) *n.m.* & *f.* innkeeper.
fondo ('fon·do) *n.m.* **1,** bottom. **2,** depth. **3,** background. **4,** fund. **5,** essence; pith. **6,** end (*of a street*). **7,** back; rear (*of a house, room, etc.*). —**a fondo,** thoroughly. —**en el fondo, 1,** at heart. **2,** in essence. —**tener buen fondo,** to be good-natured.
fonducho (fon'du·tʃo) *n.m.* cheap restaurant; joint.
fonética (fo'ne·ti·ka) *n.f.* phonetics. —**fonético,** *adj.* phonetic.
-fonía (fo'ni·a) *suffix* -phony; -phonia; voice; sound: *telefonía,* telephony.
fónico ('fo·ni·ko) *adj.* phonic. —**fónica,** *n.f.* phonics.
fono- (fo·no) *prefix* phono-; sound; voice: *fonógrafo,* phonograph.
-fono (fo·no) *suffix* -phone; producing or connected with sound, voice, etc.: *teléfono,* telephone.
fonocaptor (fo·no·kap'tor) *n.m.* pickup (*as of a phonograph*).
fonógrafo (fo'no·ɣra·fo) *n.m.* phonograph. —**fonográfico** (-'ɣra·fi·ko) *adj.* phonographic.
fontanería (fon·ta·ne'ri·a) *n.f.* plumbing. —**fontanero** (-'ne·ro) *n.m.* plumber.
foque ('fo·ke) *n.m., naut.* jib.
forajido (fo·ra'xi·ðo) *adj.* & *n.m.* outlaw; bandit.
foráneo (fo'ra·ne·o) *adj.* foreign.
forastero (fo·ras'te·ro) *n.m.* stranger; foreigner. —*adj.* strange; foreign.
forcé (for'θe; -'se) *v., 1st pers. sing.pret. of* **forzar.**
forcejear (for·θe·xe'ar; for·se-) *also,* **forcejar** (-'xar) *v.i.* to struggle; strive.
fórceps ('for·θeps; -seps) *n.m.* forceps.
forense (fo'ren·se) *adj.* forensic. —**médico forense,** coroner.
forestal (fo·res'tal) *adj.* forest (*attrib.*).
forja ('for·xa) *n.f.* **1,** forge; smithy. **2,** forging.
forjador (for·xa'ðor) *n.m.* **1,** forger of metals; smith. **2,** storyteller; fibber.
forjar (for'xar) *v.t.* **1,** to forge. **2,** *fig.* to fabricate; concoct. —**forjado,** *adj.* forged; wrought. —**forjadura,** *n.f.* forging.
forma ('for·ma) *n.f.* **1,** form; shape. **2,** manner; method. **3,** pattern; mold. **4,** format. —**formas,** *n.f.pl.* curves (*of a female figure*).
formación (for·ma'θjon; -'sjon) *n.f.* **1,** formation; shape. **2,** upbringing; training.
formal (for'mal) *adj.* **1,** formal. **2,** serious-minded; reliable.
formaldehido (for·mal·de'i·ðo) *n.m.* formaldehyde.
formalidad (for·ma·li'ðað) *n.f.* **1,** formality. **2,** seriousness; reliability.
formalismo (for·ma'lis·mo) *n.m.* **1,** formalism. **2,** formality; red tape. —**formalista,** *adj.* formalistic. —*n.m.* & *f.* formalist.
formalizar (for·ma·li'θar; -'sar) *v.t.* [*pres.subjve.* **formalice** (-'li·θe; -se); *pret.* **formalicé** (-'θe; -'se)] to formalize. —**formalizarse,** *v.r., colloq.* to become earnest.
formar (for'mar) *v.t.* **1,** to form; constitute. **2,** to shape.
formativo (for·ma'ti·βo) *adj.* formative.
formato (for'ma·to) *n.m.* format.
-forme ('for·me) *suffix* -form; -shaped; in the form of: *cuneiforme,* cuneiform.
formidable (for·mi'ða·βle) *adj.* **1,** formidable. **2,** *colloq.* tremendous.
formol (for'mol) *n.m.* formaldehyde.
formón (for'mon) *n.m.* chisel.
fórmula ('for·mu·la) *n.f.* **1,** formula. **2,** prescription. —**por fórmula,** as a matter of form.
formular (for·mu'lar) *v.t.* to formulate. —**formulación,** *n.f.* formulation.
formulario (for·mu'la·rjo) *adj.* formal; purely formal. —*n.m.* blank; blank form.
formulismo (for·mu'lis·mo) *n.m.* formality; red tape.
fornicar (for·ni'kar) *v.i.* [*pres. subjve.* **fornique** (-'ni·ke); *pret.* **forniqué** (-'ke)] to fornicate. —**fornicación,** *n.f.* fornication.
fornido (for'ni·ðo) *adj.* husky; robust.
foro ('fo·ro) *n.m.* **1,** forum. **2,** bar; legal profession. **3,** *theat.* back (*of the stage scenery*).
-foro (fo·ro) *suffix* -phore; bearer: *electróforo,* electrophore.
forraje (fo'rra·xe) *n.m.* forage; fodder. —**forrajear,** *v.t.* & *i.* to forage.
forrar (fo'rrar) *v.t.* **1,** to line; put

a lining in. **2,** to put a cover on.
forro ('fo rro) *n.m.* **1,** lining. **2,** cover.
fortalecer (for·ta·le'θer; -'ser) *v.t.* [*pres.ind.* **fortalezco** (-'leθ·ko; -'les·ko); *pres.subjve.* **fortalezca** (-ka)] to strengthen; fortify. —**fortalecimiento,** *n.m.* strengthening; fortification.
fortaleza (for·ta'le·θa; -sa) *n.f.* **1,** strength; vigor. **2,** fortitude. **3,** fortress.
fortificar (for·ti·fi'kar) *v.t.* [*pres. subjve.* **fortifique** (-'fi·ke); *pret.* **fortifiqué** (-'ke)] to fortify. —**fortificación,** *n.f.* fortification.
fortín (for'tin) *n.m.* small fort.
fortísimo (for'ti·si·mo) *adj.* & *adv.* **1,** *superl.* *of* **fuerte. 2,** *music* fortissimo.
fortuito (for'twi·to) *adj.* fortuitous.
fortuna (for'tu·na) *n.f.* **1,** fortune; chance. **2,** fate; luck. **3,** success; good fortune. **4,** wealth.
forzado (for'θa·ðo; -'sa·ðo) *adj.* forced. —*n.m.* convict at hard labor.
forzar (for'θar; -'sar) *v.t.* [*pres. ind.* **fuerzo;** *pres.subjve.* **fuerce;** *pret.* **forcé**] **1,** to force. **2,** to ravish; rape.
forzosamente (for·θo·sa'men·te; for·so-) *adv.* **1,** by force; forcibly. **2,** forcefully. **3,** necessarily; perforce.
forzoso (for'θo·so; -'so·so) *adj.* inevitable; necessary; compulsory. —**hacer la forzosa a,** *colloq.* to put pressure on; coerce.
forzudo (for'θu·ðo; -'su·ðo) *adj.* strong; robust.
fosa ('fo·sa) *n.f.* **1,** grave. **2,** pit; cavity. —**fosas nasales,** nostrils.
fosca ('fos·ka) *n.f.* haze; mist.
fosco ('fos·ko) *adj.* **1,** dark. **2,** irritable; cross.
fosfato (fos'fa·to) *n.m.* phosphate.
fosforecer (fos·fo·re'θer; -'ser) *v.i.* [*pres.ind.* **fosforezco** (-'reθ·ko; -'res·ko); *pres.subjve.* **fosforezca** (-ka)] **1,** to be phosphorescent. **2,** to shine in the dark. *Also,* **fosforescer** (-res'θer; -re'ser).
fosforescencia (fos·fo·res'θen·θja; -re'sen·sja) *n.f.* phosphorescence. —**fosforescente,** *adj.* phosphorescent.
fósforo ('fos·fo·ro) *n.m.* **1,** phosphorus. **2,** match.
fósil ('fo·sil) *adj.* & *n.m.* fossil.
fosilizar (fo·si·li'θar; -'sar) *v.t.* [*pres.subjve.* **fosilice** (-'li·θe; -se); *pret.* **fosilicé** (-'θe; -'se)] to fossilize.
foso ('fo·so) *n.m.* **1,** pit. **2,** moat.
foto ('fo·to) *n.f.* photo.
foto- (fo·to) *prefix* photo-; light; photography: *fotoeléctrico,* photoelectric.
fotocopia (fo·to'ko·pja) *n.f.* photocopy.
fotoeléctrico (fo·to·e'lek·tri·ko) *adj.* photoelectric.
fotogénico (fo·to'xe·ni·ko) *adj.* photogenic.
fotograbado (fo·to·ɣra'βa·ðo) *n.m.* **1,** photoengraving. **2,** photogravure.
fotograbar (fo·to·ɣra'βar) *v.t.* to photoengrave.
fotografía (fo·to·ɣra'fi·a) *n.f.* **1,** photography. **2,** photograph. **3,** photographic studio. —**fotográfico** (-'ɣra·fi·ko) *adj.* photographic. —**fotógrafo** (fo'to·ɣra·fo) *n.m.* photographer.
fotografiar (fo·to·ɣra'fjar) *v.t.* & *i.* [*pres.ind.* **fotografío** (-'fi·o); *pres.subjve.* **fotografíe** (-'fi·e)] to photograph.
fotómetro (fo'to·me·tro) *n.m.* photometer.
fotón (fo'ton) *n.m.* photon.
fotosfera (fo·tos'fe·ra) *n.f.* photosphere.
fotosíntesis (fo·to'sin·te·sis) *n.f.* photosynthesis.
fotóstato (fo'tos·ta·to) *also,* **fotostato** (-'ta·to) *n.m.* photostat. —**fotostatar** (-'tar) *v.t.* & *i.* to photostat. —**fotostático** (-'ta·ti·ko) *adj.* photostatic.
frac (frak) *n.m.* [*pl.* **fracs** (fraks) *also,* **fraques** ('fra·kes)] full dress; tails.
fracaso (fra'ka·so) *n.m.* failure. —**fracasar,** *v.i.* to fail; come to naught.
fracción (frak'θjon; -'sjon) *n.f.* fraction. —**fraccionario,** *adj.* fractional.
fraccionar (frak·θjo'nar; -sjo·'nar) *v.t.* to split; divide into parts or fractions. —**destilación fraccionada,** fractional distillation.
fractura (frak'tu·ra) *n.f.* fracture. —**fracturar,** *v.t.* to fracture.
fragante (fra'ɣan·te) *adj.* **1,** fragrant. **2,** = **flagrante.** —**fragancia,** *n.f.* fragrance.
fragata (fra'ɣa·ta) *n.f.* frigate.

frágil ('fra·xil) *adj.* fragile. —**fragilidad,** *n.f.* fragility.
fragmentar (fraɣ·men'tar) *v.t.* to fragment. —**fragmentación,** *n.f.* fragmentation.
fragmento (fraɣ'men·to) *n.m.* fragment. —**fragmentario,** *adj.* fragmentary.
fragor (fra'ɣor) *n.m.* din; clamor. —**fragoroso,** *adj.* deafening; thunderous.
fragoso (fra'ɣo·so) *adj.* **1,** rough; bumpy. **2,** = **fragoroso.** —**fragosidad,** *n.f.* roughness; bumpiness.
fragua ('fra·ɣwa) *n.f.* forge.
fraguar (fra'ɣwar) *v.t.* **1,** to forge (metals). **2,** to concoct; contrive; devise. —*v.i.* to set, as plaster, cement, etc.
fraile ('frai·le) *n.m.* friar.
frambesia (fram'be·sja) *n.f.* yaws.
frambuesa (fram'bwe·sa) *n.f.* raspberry. —**frambueso,** *n.m.* raspberry bush.
francachela (fran·ka'tʃe·la) *n.f., colloq.* **1,** banquet. **2,** revel.
francés (fran'θes; -'ses) *adj.* French. —*n.m.* **1,** Frenchman. **2,** French language. —**francesa** (-'θe·sa; -'se·sa) *n.f.* Frenchwoman.
francio ('fran·θjo; -sjo) *n.m.* francium.
francmasón (frank·ma'son) *n.m.* Freemason. —**francmasonería,** *n.f.* Freemasonry. —**francmasónico** (-'so·ni·ko) *adj.* Freemasonic.
franco ('fran·ko) *adj.* **1,** frank. **2,** free; open; clear. **3,** generous; liberal. **4,** exempt; privileged. —*n.m.* franc. —**franco a bordo,** *also,* **franco bordo,** free on board. —**franco de porte,** postpaid.
franco- (fran·ko) *prefix* Franco-; French: *francoamericano,* Franco-American.
francote (fran'ko·te) *adj., colloq.* candid; frank.
francotirador (fran·ko·ti·ra·'ðor) *n.m.* sniper.
franela (fra'ne·la) *n.f.* flannel.
franja ('fran·xa) *n.f.* **1,** fringe; border. **2,** stripe; band; strip.
franquear (fran·ke'ar) *v.t.* **1,** to free; exempt. **2,** to get over *or* across. **3,** to clear; open. **4,** to expedite; open the way to. **5,** to pay postage on. —**franquearse,** *v.r.* to unbosom oneself.
franqueo (fran'ke·o) *n.m.* postage.
franqueza (fran'ke θa; -sa) *n.f.* **1,** frankness. **2,** freedom; exemption. **3,** generosity.
franquicia (fran'ki·θja; -sja) *n.f.* franchise; exemption. —**franquicia postal,** franking privilege.
frasco ('fras·ko) *n.m.* flask; vial.
frase ('fra·se) *n.f.* **1,** phrase. **2,** sentence. **3,** phrasing. —**frasear** (fra·se'ar) *v.t.* to phrase.
fraseología (fra·se·o·lo'xi·a) *n.f.* **1,** phraseology. **2,** verbosity.
fraternal (fra·ter'nal) *adj.* fraternal; brotherly. —**fraternidad,** *n.f.* fraternity; brotherhood.
fraternizar (fra·ter·ni'θar; -'sar) *v.i.* [*pres.subjve.* **fraternice** (-'ni·θe; -se); *pret.* **fraternicé** (-'θe; -'se)] to fraternize. —**fraternización,** *n.f.* fraternization.
fraterno (fra'ter·no) *adj.* = **fraternal.**
fratricida (fra·tri'θi·ða; -'si·ða) *adj.* fratricidal. —*n.m.* & *f.* fratricide (*agent*). —**fratricidio** (-'θi·ðjo; -'si·ðjo) *n.m.* fratricide (*act*).
fraude ('frau·ðe) *n.m.* fraud.
fraudulento (frau·ðu'len·to) *adj.* fraudulent. —**fraudulencia,** *n.f.* fraudulence.
fray (frai) *n.m., contr. of* **fraile** *used before a name;* Fra.
frazada (fra'θa·ða; -'sa·ða) *n.f.* blanket.
frecuencia (fre'kwen·θja; -sja) *n.f.* frequency. —**frecuente,** *adj.* frequent.
frecuentar (fre·kwen'tar) *v.t.* to frequent. —**frecuentación,** *n.f.* frequentation. —**frecuentativo** (-'ti·βo) *adj.* frequentative.
fregar (fre'ɣar) *v.t.* [*pres.ind.* **friego**; *pres.subjve.* **friegue**; *pret.* **fregué** (-'ɣe)] **1,** to scrub; scour. **2,** to wash (dishes). **3,** *Amer., colloq.* to pester; annoy. —**fregadero,** *n.m.* sink.
freír (fre'ir) *v.t.* [*pres.ind.* **frío**; *pres.subjve.* **fría**; *pret.* **freí, frió**; *ger.* **friendo**; *p.p.* **frito,** *also,* **freído**] to fry.
fréjol ('fre·xol) *n.m.* = **frijol.**
frenar (fre'nar) *v.t.* **1,** to brake. **2,** to bridle; restrain.
frenesí (fre·ne'si) *n.m.* frenzy. —**frenético** (-'ne·ti·ko) *adj.* frantic; mad; furious.
frenillo (fre'ni·ʎo; -jo) *n.m., anat.* frenum.
freno ('fre·no) *n.m.* **1,** brake. **2,** bridle; bit. **3,** restraint.
frenología (fre·no·lo'xi·a) *n.f.*

phrenology. —**frenológico** (-'lo·xi·ko) *adj.* phrenological. —**frenólogo** (-'no·lo·ɣo) *n.m.* phrenologist.
frente ('fren·te) *n.m.* front. —*n.f.* forehead. —*adv.* = **enfrente.** —**al frente,** in front; out front. —**de frente, 1,** facing forward; abreast. **2,** resolutely; directly. —**en frente,** opposite; across. —**frente a,** in front of. —**frente a frente,** face to face. —**hacer frente a,** to face; confront.
fresa ('fre·sa) *n.f.* **1,** strawberry. **2,** drill; bit. **3,** milling cutter. **4,** *dent.* burr.
fresar (fre'sar) *v.t.* **1,** to mill (metals). **2,** to ream. —**fresadora,** *n.f.* milling machine.
fresca ('fres·ka) *n.f.* **1,** fresh air; cool (*of the morning or evening*). **2,** *colloq.* wisecrack.
fresco ('fres·ko) *adj.* fresh; cool. —*n.m.* **1,** coolness; freshness. **2,** fresco. **3,** *colloq.* impudent person. **4,** *Amer.* = **refresco.**
frescor (fres'kor) *n.m.* **1,** freshness; coolness. **2,** *painting* vivid tone; glowing quality.
frescura (fres'ku·ra) *n.f.* **1,** freshness; coolness. **2,** impudence; boldness.
fresno ('fres·no) *n.m.* ash (*tree and wood*).
freza ('fre·θa; -sa) *n.f.* **1,** spawn. **2,** spawning. **3,** spawning season. —**frezar,** *v.i.* [*infl.:* **rezar**] to spawn.
fría ('fri·a) *v., pres.subjve. of* **freír.**
frialdad (fri·al'dað) *n.f.* **1,** coldness; coolness. **2,** frigidity.
fricasé (fri·ka'se) *n.m.* fricassee.
fricción (frik'θjon; -'sjon) *n.f.* **1,** friction. **2,** rubbing. —**friccional,** *adj.* frictional. —**friccionar,** *v.t.* to rub.
friega ('frje·ɣa) *n.f.* **1,** *colloq.* rubdown. **2,** *slang* nuisance; bother.
friego ('frje·ɣo) *v., pres.ind. of* **fregar.**
friegue ('frje·ɣe) *v., pres.subjve. of* **fregar.**
friendo (fri'en·do) *v., ger. of* **freír.**
frígido ('fri·xi·ðo) *adj.* frigid. —**frigidez,** *n.f.* frigidity.
frigorífico (fri·ɣo'ri·fi·ko) *adj.* refrigerating. —*n.m.* cold storage plant.
frijol (fri'xol) *also,* **fríjol** ('fri·xol) *n.m.* bean; kidney bean.
frío ('fri·o) *adj.* cold; cool. —*n.m.* cold; chill. —**friolento,** *adj.* sensitive to cold.
frío ('fri·o) *v., pres.ind. of* **freír.**
frió (fri'o) *v., 3rd pers.sing. pret. of* **freír.**
friolera (fri·o'le·ra) *n.f.* trifle; something trivial.
frisa ('fri·sa) *n.f.* **1,** frieze (*cloth*). **2,** *P.R.* blanket.
friso ('fri·so) *n.m.* **1,** frieze. **2,** baseboard. **3,** dado.
fritada (fri'ta·ða) *n.f.* **1,** fry. **2,** fritter.
frito ('fri·to) *v., p.p. of* **freír.** —*n.m.* **1,** fry. **2,** fritter.
fritura (fri'tu·ra) *n.f.* = **fritada.**
frivolité (fri·βo·li'te) *n.m.* tatting.
frívolo ('fri·βo·lo) *adj.* frivolous. —**frivolidad,** *n.f.* frivolousness.
fronda ('fron·da) *n.f.* frond.
frondoso (fron'do·so) *adj.* luxuriant. —**frondosidad,** *n.f.* luxuriant growth.
frontal (fron'tal) *adj.* frontal.
frontera (fron'te·ra) *n.f.* **1,** frontier; border. **2,** = **frontispicio.** —**fronterizo,** *adj.* frontier.
frontispicio (fron·tis'pi·θjo; -sjo) *n.m.* **1,** frontispiece. **2,** façade. *Also,* **frontis** ('fron·tis) *n.m.sing. & pl.*
frontón (fron'ton) *n.m.* **1,** jai alai wall *or* court. **2,** escarpment; scarp. **3,** *archit.* frontispiece. **4,** [*also,* **juego de frontón**] handball.
frotar (fro'tar) *v.t.* to rub.
frotis ('fro·tis) *n.m., bacteriol.* smear.
fructífero (fruk'ti·fe·ro) *adj.* = **fructuoso.**
fructificar (fruk·ti·fi'kar) *v.i.* [*pres.subjve.* **fructifique** (-'fi·ke); *pret.* **fructifiqué** (-'ke)] to bear fruit; fructify. —**fructificación,** *n.f.* fructification.
fructuoso (fruk'two·so) *adj.* bearing fruit; fruitful.
frugal (fru'ɣal) *adj.* frugal. —**frugalidad,** *n.f.* frugality.
fruición (fru·i'θjon; -'sjon) *n.f.* enjoyment; gratification.
frunce ('frun·θe; -se) *n.m.* pleat; shirr.
fruncir (frun'θir; -'sir) *v.t.* [*pres. ind.* **frunzo** ('frun·θo; -so); *pres. subjve.* **frunza** (-θa; -sa)] **1,** to wrinkle (the brow, nose, etc.). **2,** to pucker. **3,** *sewing* to gather; shirr. —**fruncirse,** *v.r.* to frown.
fruslería (frus·le'ri·a) *n.f.* bauble.
frustrar (frus'trar) *v.t.* to frustrate. —**frustración,** *n.f.* frustration.
fruta ('fru·ta) *n.f.* fruit (*edible*).

—**frutal** (fru'tal) *adj.* fruit-bearing. —**frutar,** *v.i.* to yield fruit.
fruta bomba *Cuba* papaya.
frutero (fru'te·ro) *adj.* fruit (*attrib.*). —*n.m.* **1,** fruit bowl. **2,** fruit seller; fruiterer. —**frutería,** *n.f.* fruit shop.
fruto ('fru·to) *n.m.* **1,** fruit (*yield of a plant*). **2,** *fig.* result; consequence. **3,** *fig.* benefit; profit.
fucsia ('fuk·sja) *n.f.* fuchsia.
¡fuche! ('fu·tʃe) *interj., Amer.* ugh!; pew!; phew! *Also,* **¡fucha!** (-tʃa).
fue (fwe) *v., 3rd pers.sing. pret. of* **ir** *and* **ser.**
fuego ('fwe·ɣo) *n.m.* **1,** fire. **2,** light (*for a fire*). **3,** itchy rash; skin eruption. —**fuego fatuo,** will-o'-the-wisp. —**fuegos artificiales,** fireworks. —**hacer fuego,** to fire; shoot. —**pegar fuego,** to set fire.
fuelle ('fwe·ʎe; -je) *n.m.* bellows.
fuente ('fwen·te) *n.f.* **1,** fountain. **2,** spring; fountainhead. **3,** platter. **4,** *fig.* source.
fuer (fwer) *n.m., contr. of* **fuero,** *in* **a fuer de,** by reason of; by way of.
fuera ('fwe·ra) *adv.* out; outside; without. —*interj.* out!; get out! —**fuera de,** outside of. —**por fuera,** on the outside.
fuera ('fwe·ra) *v., impf.subjve. of* **ir** *and* **ser.**
fuerce ('fwer·θe; -se) *v., pres. subjve. of* **forzar.**
fuere ('fwe·re) *v., fut.subjve. of* **ir** *and* **ser.**
fuero ('fwe·ro) *n.m.* **1,** jurisdiction; authority. **2,** statute. **3,** exemption; privilege. **4,** *fig.* arrogance. —**fuero interno,** conscience.
fueron ('fwe·ron) *v., 3rd pers.pl. pret. of* **ir** *and* **ser.**
fuerte ('fwer·te) *adj.* **1,** strong. **2,** loud. —*adv.* **1,** hard; vigorously. **2,** loud. —*n.m.* **1,** fort. **2,** forte.
fuerza ('fwer·θa; -sa) *n.f.* **1,** strength. **2,** force; power. —**fuerzas,** *n.f.pl., mil.* forces. —**a fuerza de,** by dint of. —**fuerza mayor,** act of God. —**por fuerza,** necessarily.
fuerzo ('fwer·θo; -so) *v., pres.ind. of* **forzar.**
fuese ('fwe·se) *v., impf.subjve. of* **ir** *and* **ser.**
fuete ('fwe·te) *n.m., Amer.* = **látigo.** —**fuetazo,** *n.m., Amer.* = **latigazo.**
fuga ('fu·ɣa) *n.f.* **1,** flight; escape. **2,** *music* fugue.
fugarse (fu'ɣar·se) *v.r.* [*pres. subjve.* **fugue** ('fu·ɣe); *pret.* **fugué** (-'ɣe)] to flee; escape.
fugaz (fu'ɣaθ; -'ɣas) *adj.* fleeting.
fugitivo (fu·ɣi'ti·βo) *adj.* & *n.m.* fugitive.
-fugo (fu·ɣo) *suffix* -fuge; expelling: *centrífugo,* centrifuge.
fui (fwi) *v., 1st pers.sing. pret. of* **ir** *and* **ser.**
fulano (fu'la·no) *n.m.* so-and-so. —**fulano de tal,** John Doe. —**fulano, zutano y mengano,** Tom, Dick and Harry.
fular (fu'lar) *n.m.* foulard.
fulcro ('ful·kro) *n.m.* fulcrum.
fulgente (ful'xen·te) *adj.* fulgent. —**fulgencia,** *n.f.* effulgence.
fulgir (ful'xir) *v.i.* = **fulgurar.**
fulgor (ful'ɣor) *n.m.* brilliance; effulgence.
fulgurar (ful·ɣu'rar) *v.i.* to shine: gleam. —**fulguroso,** *adj.* bright: shining.
fúlica ('fu·li·ka) *n.f., ornith.* coot.
fulján (ful'xan) *n.m., poker* full house.
fulminante (ful·mi'nan·te) *adj.* **1,** sudden; violent. **2,** instantly fatal. —*n.m.* **1,** percussion cap. **2,** fulminate.
fulminar (ful·mi'nar) *v.t.* **1,** to strike, as with lightning. **2,** to hurl, as insults, threats, etc. **3,** to fulminate against. —**fulminación,** *n.f.* fulmination.
fullería (fu·ʎe'ri·a; fu·je-) *n.f.* **1,** cheating at games. **2,** trickery.
fullero (fu'ʎe·ro; -'je·ro) *adj.* **1,** cheating. **2,** tricky. **3,** mischievous. —*n.m.* **1,** cheat. **2,** trickster.
fumada (fu'ma·ða) *n.f.* **1,** puff *or* draw (*in smoking*). **2,** *Amer.* act of smoking; smoke.
fumadero (fu·ma'ðe·ro) *n.m.* smoking room.
fumar (fu'mar) *v.t.* to smoke. —*v.i.* to smoke; fume. —**fumarse (algo),** to squander (something). —**fumarse (una persona)** *Amer., colloq.* to fix; take care of (someone). —**fumarse la clase,** to cut class.
fumarada (fu·ma'ra·ða) *n.f.* **1,** puff (*of smoke*). **2,** pipeful.
fumigar (fu·mi'ɣar) *v.t.* [*pres. subjve.* **fumigue** (-'mi·ɣe); *pret.* **fumigué** (-'ɣe)] to fumigate. —**fu-**

migación, *n.f.* fumigation. —**fumigador**, *n.m.* fumigator.
función (fun'θjon; -'sjon) *n.f.* **1,** function. **2,** *theat.* performance. —**funcional**, *adj.* functional.
funcionar (fun·θjo'nar; -sjo'nar) *v.i.* to function; perform. —**funcionamiento**, *n.m.* performance.
funcionario (fun·θjo'na·rjo; fun·sjo-) *n.m.* functionary; public official; civil servant.
funda ('fun·da) *n.f.* **1,** covering; wrapper. **2,** pillow slip.
fundamento (fun·da'men·to) *n.m.* **1,** basis. **2,** = **cimiento.** —**fundamental**, *adj.* fundamental. —**fundamentar**, *v.t.* lay the foundation of.
fundar (fun'dar) *v.t.* **1,** to found. **2,** to base; rest. —**fundación**, *n.f.* foundation. —**fundadamente**, *adv.* with good reason. —**fundador**, *n.* founder.
fundente (fun'den·te) *n.m., chem.; metall.* flux.
fundible (fun'di·βle) *adj.* fusible.
fundición (fun·di'θjon; -'sjon) *n.f.* **1,** foundry. **2,** founding; casting. **3,** fusion; melting. **4,** *print.* font.
fundidor (fun·di'ðor) *n.m.* founder; foundryman.
fundillos (fun'di·ʎos; -jos) *n.m.pl.* = **fondillos.**
fundir (fun'dir) *v.t.* **1,** to fuse; melt. **2,** to cast; found. —**fundirse**, *v.r.* **1,** to fuse; merge. **2,** *Amer., colloq.* to fail; flop.
fúnebre ('fu·ne·βre) *adj.* funereal; gloomy. —**honras** *or* **pompas fúnebres**, funeral services.
funeral (fu·ne'ral) *n.m., often pl.* funeral. —*adj.* funeral.
funeraria (fu·ne'ra·rja) *n.f.* funeral parlor.
funerario (fu·ne'ra·rjo) *adj.* funeral (*attrib.*). —*n.m.* funeral director.
funesto (fu'nes·to) *adj.* **1,** baneful; fatal. **2,** regrettable; unfortunate.
fungicida (fun·xi'θi·ða; -'si·ða) *n.m.* fungicide. —*adj.* fungicidal.
fungo ('fun·go) *n.m.,* fungus. —**fungoso**, *adj.* fungous; spongy.
funicular (fu·ni·ku'lar) *adj.* & *n.m.* funicular.
furgón (fur'ɣon) *n.m.,* **1,** freight car. **2,** caboose. **3,** covered wagon.
furia ('fu·rja) *n.f.* fury.
furibundo (fu·ri'βun·do) *adj.* furious; maddened.
furioso (fu'rjo·so) *adj.* furious.
furor (fu'ror) *n.m.* rage; furor. —**hacer furor**, *colloq.* to be the rage.
furtivo (fur'ti·βo) *adj.* furtive.
furúnculo (fu'run·ku·lo) *n.m.* furuncle; boil.
fuselaje (fu·se'la·xe) *n.m.* fuselage.
fusible (fu'si·βle) *adj.* fusible. —*n.m., electricity* fuse. —**fusibilidad**, *n.f.* fusibility.
fusil (fu'sil) *n.m.* gun; rifle. —**fusilar**, *v.t.* to shoot; kill by shooting. —**fusilamiento**, *n.m.* shooting; execution by shooting.
fusilería (fu·si·le'ri·a) *n.f.* **1,** rifles collectively. **2,** body of fusiliers or riflemen.
fusilero (fu·si'le·ro) *n.m.* fusilier; rifleman.
fusión (fu'sjon) *n.f.* **1,** fusion. **2,** merger. —**fusionar**, *v.t.* to fuse; merge.
fusta ('fus·ta) *n.f.* **1,** horsewhip. **2,** switch; rod.
fustán (fus'tan) *n.m.* **1,** fustian. **2,** *Amer.* woman's slip.
fuste ('fus·te) *n.m.* **1,** shaft. **2,** *fig.* substance; sinew.
fustigar (fus·ti'gar) *v.t.* [*pres. subjve.* **fustigue** (-'ti·ɣe); *pret.* **fustigué** (-'ɣe)] to lash. —**fustigación**, *n.f.* lashing.
fútbol ('fut·βol) *n.m.* soccer; football. —**futbolista**, *n.m.* football player; soccer player.
fútil ('fu·til) *adj.* futile. —**futilidad**, *n.f.* futility.
futuro (fu'tu·ro) *adj.* & *n.m.* future. —**futurismo**, *n.m.* futurism. —**futurista**, *adj.* futuristic.

G

G, g (xe) *n.f.* 8th letter of the Spanish alphabet.
gabacho (ga'βa·tʃo) *adj.* & *n.m.* Pyrenean. —*adj., derog.* French. —*n.m.* **1,** *derog.* Frenchman. **2,** Gallicized Spanish.
gaban (ga'βan) *n.m.* **1,** overcoat. **2,** *W.I.* jacket.

gabardina (ga·βar'ði·na) *n.f.* **1,** gabardine. **2,** mackintosh.
gabarra (ga'βa·rra) *n.f.* lighter; barge.
gabinete (ga·βi'ne·te) *n.m.* **1,** cabinet. **2,** study; office.
gablete (ga'βle·te) *n.m.* gable.
gacela (ga'θe·la; ga'se-) *n.f.* gazelle.
gaceta (ga'θe·ta; ga'se-) *n.f.* gazette.
gacetilla (ga·θe'ti·ʎa; ga·se'ti·ja) *n.f.* **1,** short news item. **2,** gossip column. **3,** *colloq.* newsmonger; gossip. **—gacetillero,** *n.m.* newsmonger; gossip columnist.
gacha ('ga·tʃa) *n.f., often pl.* mush; pap; gruel.
gacho ('ga·tʃo) *adj.* turned downward; drooping. **—a gachas,** bending low; stooping; on all fours.
gadolinio (ga·ðo'li·njo) *n.m.* gadolinium.
gaélico (ga'e·li·ko) *adj.* & *n.m.* Gaelic.
gafa ('ga·fa) *n.f.* = **grapa. —gafas,** *n.f.pl.* spectacles.
gafe ('ga·fe) *n.m.* & *f., colloq.* jinx.
gago ('ga·ɣo) *n.m., Amer., colloq.* = **tartamudo. —gaguear** (ga·ɣe'ar) *v.i.* = **tartamudear. —gagueo** (ga·'ɣe·o) *n.m.* = **tartamudez.**
gaita ('gai·ta) *n.f.* **1,** bagpipe. **2,** *colloq.* bother; nuisance. **—gaitero,** *n.m.* piper.
gajes ('ga·xes) *n.m.pl.* wages. **—gajes del oficio,** occupational hazards *or* drawbacks.
gajo ('ga·xo) *n.m.* **1,** torn or fallen branch. **2,** segment (*of an orange, tangerine, etc.*).
gala ('ga·la) *n.f.* **1,** finery; gala. **2,** grace; pleasing manner. **3,** pride and joy. **—de gala,** gala; festal. **—hacer gala de,** to make a display of; boast of.
galáctico (ga'lak·ti·ko) *adj.* galactic.
galán (ga'lan) *adj.* [*also,* **galano** (ga'la·no)] **1,** spruce; dapper. **2,** elegant; handsome. **—***n.m.* **1,** leading man. **2,** suitor. **3,** handsome man; gallant.
galante (ga'lan·te) *adj.* gallant; courtly; attentive.
galantear (ga·lan·te'ar) *v.t.* **1,** to flatter; compliment (a woman). **2,** to court; woo.
galanteo (ga·lan'te·o) *n.m.* **1,** flattery; gallantry. **2,** courtship; wooing.
galantería (ga·lan·te'ri·a) *n.f.* **1,** compliment; flattery; gallantry. **2,** courtesy; attention.
galápago (ga'la·pa·ɣo) *n.m.* turtle; terrapin.
garlardón (ga·lar'ðon) *n.m.* reward; prize; award. **—galardonar,** *v.t.* to reward.
galaxia (ga'lak·sja) *n.f.* galaxy.
galena (ga'le·na) *n.f.* galena.
galeno (ga'le·no) *n.m., colloq.* physician.
galeón (ga·le'on) *n.m.* galleon.
galeote (ga·le'o·te) *n.m.* galley slave.
galera (ga'le·ra) *n.f.* **1,** galley (*ship*). **2,** van; wagon. **3,** *print.* galley. **4,** *Amer.* top hat; silk hat.
galerada (ga·le'ra·ða) *n.f.* **1,** *print.* galley. **2,** *print.* galley proof. **3,** wagonload.
galería (ga·le'ri·a) *n.f.* **1,** gallery. **2,** *theat.* balcony.
galés (ga'les) *adj.* Welsh. **—***n.m.* **1,** Welshman. **2,** Welsh language.
galga ('gal·ɣa) *n.f.* **1,** female greyhound. **2,** wheel brake; skid. **3,** rash; mange.
galgo ('gal·ɣo) *n.m.* greyhound.
galicismo (ga·li'θis·mo; -'sis·mo) *n.m.* Gallicism.
galillo (ga'li·ʎo; -jo) *n.m.* uvula.
galio ('ga·ljo) *n.m.* gallium.
galo ('ga·lo) *adj.* Gallic. **—***n.m.* Gaul.
galo- (ga·lo) *prefix* Gallo-; French: *galófilo.* Gallophile.
galocha (ga'lo·tʃa) *n.f.* galosh; overshoe.
galón (ga'lon) *n.m.* **1,** gallon. **2,** chevron; stripe. **3,** braid; trimming.
galope (ga'lo·pe) *n.m.* gallop. **—galopar** (-'par) *also,* **galopear** (-pe'ar) *v.i.* to gallop. **—galopante,** *adj.* galloping. **—a galope tendido,** at full speed.
galvánico (gal'βa·ni·ko) *adj.* galvanic. **—galvanismo,** *n.m.* galvanism.
galvanizar (gal·βa·ni'θar; -'sar) *v.t.* [*pres.subjve.* **galvanice** (-'ni·θe; -se); *pret.* **galvanicé** (-'θe; -'se)] to galvanize. **—galvanización,** *n.f.* galvanization.
galvano- (gal·βa·no) *prefix* galvano-; electricity: *galvanómetro,* galvanometer.
galvanómetro (gal·βa'no·me·tro) *n.m.* galvanometer.

gallardete (ga·ʎar'ðe·te; ga·jar-) *n.m.* pennant.
gallardo (ga'ʎar·ðo; ga'jar-) *adj.* gallant. —**gallardía,** *n.f.* gallantry.
gallear (ga·ʎe'ar; ga·je-) *v.i., colloq.* to bluster.
gallego (ga'ʎe·ɣo; ga'je-) *adj.* & *n.m.* Galician.
galleta (ga'ʎe·ta; ga'je-) *n.f.* **1,** cracker; biscuit. **2,** *colloq.* slap in the face.
gallina (ga'ʎi·na; ga'ji-) *n.f.* hen; chicken. —*n.m. or f., colloq.* coward; chickenhearted person.
gallinazo (ga·ʎi'na·θo; -ji'na·so) *n.m.* turkey buzzard.
gallinero (ga·ʎi'ne·ro; ga·ji-) *n.m.* **1,** poultry yard; chicken coop. **2,** poulterer. **3,** *colloq.* peanut gallery.
gallo ('ga·ʎo; -jo) *n.m.* **1,** rooster; cock. **2,** *colloq.* bully. **3,** *colloq.* cracking of the voice. **4,** *ichthy.* dory. —*adj., Amer.* cocky; brave. —**gallo de pelea,** gamecock. —**misa del gallo,** midnight Mass at Christmas. —**patas de gallo,** crow's-feet.
gama ('ga·ma) *n.f.* **1,** gamut. **2,** doe. **3,** = **gamma.**
gambito (gam'bi·to) *n.m.* gambit.
-gamia ('ɣa·mja) *suffix* -gamy; *forming nouns denoting* marriage; union: *bigamia,* bigamy.
gamma ('ga·ma) *n.f.* gamma. —**rayos gamma,** gamma rays.
gamarra (ga'ma·rra) *n.f.* martingale (*piece of harness*).
gamo ('ga·mo) *n.m.* male fallow deer.
gamo- (ga·mo) *prefix, biol.* gamo-; joined; united: *gamopétalo,* gamopetalous.
-gamo (ɣa·mo) *suffix* -gamous; *forming adjectives* denoting marriage; union: *monógamo,* monogamous.
gamón (ga'mon) *n.m.* asphodel.
gamuza (ga'mu·θa; -sa) *n.f.* chamois.
gana ('ga·na) *n.f.* desire; inclination. —**de buena gana,** with pleasure; willingly. —**de mala gana,** unwillingly. —**no me da la gana,** *colloq.* I don't feel like it.
ganado (ga'na·ðo) *n.m.* livestock, esp. cattle. —**ganadería,** *n.f.* animal husbandry; cattle raising. —**ganadero,** *n.m.* rancher.
ganancia (ga'nan·θja; -sja) *n.f.* gain; profit; advantage. —**ganancia líquida,** net profit.
ganar (ga'nar) *v.t.* **1,** to gain. **2,** to win. **3,** to earn. —**ganador,** *adj.* winning. —*n.m.* winner.
gancho ('gan·tʃo) *n.m.* **1,** hook. **2,** *Amer.* hairpin. **3,** *Amer.* coat hanger. **4,** *colloq.* charm; allure. —**echar el gancho a,** to trap; hook (someone).
gandul (gan'dul) *n.m.* loafer; ne'er-do-well.
ganga ('gan·ga) *n.f.* **1,** gangue. **2,** *colloq.* bargain; good buy. **3,** *colloq.* cinch; snap.
ganglio ('gan·gljo) *n.m.* ganglion.
gangoso (gan'go·so) *adj.* twangy; nasal. —**gangosidad,** *n.f.* twanginess; twang.
gangrena (gan'gre·na) *n.f.* gangrene. —**gangrenarse,** *v.r.* to become gangrenous. —**gangrenoso,** *adj.* gangrenous.
gangster ('gang·ster) *n.m.* gangster.
ganguear (gan·ge'ar) *v.i.* to snuffle; talk through the nose. —**gangueo** (-'ge·o) *n.m.* snuffle; snuffling.
ganoso (ga'no·so) *adj.* **1,** desirous. **2,** *Amer.* spirited (*of a horse*).
ganso ('gan·so) *n.m.* **1,** goose; gander. **2,** *colloq.* oaf; lout.
ganzúa (gan'θu·a; -'su·a) *n.f.* picklock.
gañido (ga'ɲi·ðo) *n.m.* **1,** yelp; yelping. **2,** croak; croaking.
gañir (ga'ɲir) *v.i.* [*infl.:* **bruñir**] **1,** to yelp. **2,** to croak (*of birds*). **3,** to gasp; pant; wheeze.
garabato (ga·ra'βa·to) *n.m.* **1,** scrawl; doodle. **2,** grapnel; hook. —**garabatear,** *v.i.* to scrawl; doodle.
garaje *also,* **garage** (ga'ra·xe) *n.m.* garage.
garante (ga'ran·te) *n.m.* guarantor.
garantía (ga·ran'ti·a) *n.f.* guarantee.
garantizar (ga·ran·ti'θar; -'sar) *v.t.* [*pres.subjve.* **garantice** (-'ti·θe; -se); *pret.* **garanticé** (-'θe; -'se)] to guarantee.
garañon (ga·ra'ɲon) *n.m.* **1,** stud jackass *or* camel. **2,** *Amer.* stud horse; stallion.
garapiña (ga·ra'pi·ɲa) *n.f.* sugar coating; glaze. —**garapiñado,** *adj.* sugar-coated; glacé. —*n.m.* = **garapiña.** —**garapiñar,** *v.t.* to coat with sugar; glaze.
garbanzo (gar'βan·θo; -so) *n.m.* chick pea.

garbo ('gar·βo) *n.m.* grace; gallantry. —**garboso,** *adj.* graceful; gallant.
gardenia (gar'ðe·nja) *n.f.* gardenia.
garete (ga're·te) *n.m.,* *in* **al garete,** adrift.
garfa ('gar·fa) *n.f.* claw.
garfio ('gar·fjo) *n.m.* gaff; hook.
gargajo (gar'ɣa·xo) *n.m.* phlegm.
garganta (gar'ɣan·ta) *n.f.* **1,** throat. **2,** ravine. **3,** singing voice.
gárgara ('gar·ɣa·ra) *n.f.* gargle. —**hacer gárgaras,** to gargle.
gargarismo (gar·ɣa'ris·mo) *n.m.* gargle; gargling.
gargarizar (gar·ɣa·ri'θar; -'sar) *v.i.* [*pres.subjve.* **gargarice** (-'ri·θe; -se); *pret.* **gargaricé** (-'θe; -'se)] to gargle.
gárgola ('gar·ɣo·la) *n.f.* gargoyle.
garita (ga'ri·ta) *n.f.* sentry box; gatekeeper's box.
garito (ga'ri·to) *n.m.* gambling den.
garra ('ga·rra) *n.f.* claw.
garrafa (ga'rra·fa) *n.f.* carafe; decanter. —**garrafón,** *n.m.* demijohn.
garrafal (ga·rra'fal) *adj.* outrageous; monstrous.
garrapata (ga·rra'pa·ta) *n.f.* tick.
garrapato (ga·rra'pa·to) *n.m.* scribble; scrawl. —**garrapatear** (-te'ar) *v.i.* to scribble; scrawl.
garrocha (ga'rro·tʃa) *n.f.* **1,** goad. **2,** pole for vaulting. —**salto de garrocha,** pole vault.
garrote (ga'rro·te) *n.m.* **1,** cudgel. **2,** garrote. —**garrotazo,** *n.m.* blow with a cudgel.
garrotero (ga·rro'te·ro) *adj., Amer.* stingy. —*n.m.* *Amer.* **1,** brakeman. **2,** loan shark.
garrucha (ga'rru·tʃa) *n.f.* pulley.
gárrulo ('ga·rru·lo) *adj.* garrulous. —**garrulidad,** *n.f.* garrulity.
garúa (ga'ru·a) *n.f., naut.* & *Amer.* drizzle.
garza ('gar·θa; -sa) *n.f.* heron.
garzo ('gar·θo; -so) *adj.* blue; bluish.
garzón (gar'θon; -'son) *n.m.* boy; lad.
gas (gas) *n.m.* gas. —**gas hilarante,** laughing gas. —**gas lacrimógeno,** tear gas.
gasa ('ga·sa) *n.f.* **1,** gauze. **2,** chiffon.
gaseoso (ga·se'o·so) *adj.* **1,** gaseous. **2,** gassy. —**gaseosa,** *n.f.* soda water; soda.
gasfitero (gas·fi'te·ro) *n.m., Amer.* plumber; gas fitter.
gasista (ga'sis·ta) *n.m.* gas fitter.
gasolina (ga·so'li·na) *n.f.* gasoline.
gasolinera (ga·so·li'ne·ra) *n.f.* **1,** motorboat. **2,** filling station.
gasómetro (ga'so·me·tro) *n.m.* **1,** gas meter. **2,** gas tank.
gastar (gas'tar) *v.t.* **1,** to spend. **2,** to wear out. **3,** to use up; exhaust. **4,** to use or wear habitually. —**gastarse,** *v.r.* **1,** to burn oneself out. **2,** to wear out. —**gastador,** *n.m.* spendthrift. —**gastar una broma,** to play a joke. —**gastarlas,** to carry on.
gasto ('gas·to) *n.m.* **1,** expenditure; expense. **2,** use; consumption.
gástrico ('gas·tri·ko) *adj.* gastric.
gastritis (gas'tri·tis) *n.f.* gastritis.
gastro- (gas·tro) *prefix* gastro-; stomach: *gastrónomo,* gastronome.
gastronomía (gas·tro·no'mi·a) *n.f.* gastronomy. —**gastronómico** (-'no·mi·ko) *adj.* gastronomic. —**gastrónomo** (-'tro·no·mo) *n.m.* gourmet.
gata ('ga·ta) *n.f.* female cat. —**a gatas,** on all fours.
gatear (ga·te'ar) *v.i.* **1,** to climb; clamber. **2,** to go on all fours. —*v.t., colloq.* to claw.
gatillo (ga'ti·ʎo; -jo) *n.m.* **1,** trigger. **2,** hammer (*of a firearm*). **3,** *dent.* extractor. **4,** kitten. **5,** *colloq.* petty thief.
gato ('ga·to) *n.m.* **1,** cat. **2,** *mech.* jack. —**gatuno,** *adj.* feline; catlike. —**cuatro gatos,** a handful of people. **dar gato por liebre,** to foist something off. —**gato montés,** wildcat. —**hay gato encerrado,** I smell a rat.
gatuperio (ga·tu'pe·rjo) *n.m.* **1,** hodgepodge. **2,** *colloq.* intrigue; hanky-panky.
gaucho ('gau·tʃo) *n.m.* gaucho.
gaulteria (gaul'te·rja) *n.f.* wintergreen.
gaveta (ga'βe·ta) *n.f.* drawer.
gavetero (ga·βe'te·ro) *n.m., Amer.* dresser; chest of drawers.
gavia ('ga·βja) *n.f.* topsail.
gavilán (ga·βi'lan) *n.m.* **1,** sparrow hawk. **2,** *Amer.* ingrown toenail.
gavilla (ga'βi·ʎa; -ja) *n.f.* **1,** sheaf (*of grain, hay, etc.*). **2,** gang; mob.
gaviota (ga'βjo·ta) *n.f.* sea gull.
gavota (ga'βo·ta) *n.f.* gavotte.
gaza ('ga·θa; -sa) *n.f.* loop; noose.

gazmoño (gaθ'mo·ɲo; gas-) *adj.* prudish. —*n.m.* prude. —**gazmoñería,** *n.f.* prudishness.
gaznate (gaθ'na·te; gas-) *n.m.* **1,** gullet. **2,** a kind of fritter.
gazpacho (gaθ'pa·tʃo; gas-) *n.m.* a cold soup of various vegetables.
geiser ('xei·ser; 'gei-) *n.m.* geyser.
geisha ('xei·ʃa; -'gei-) *n.f.* geisha.
gelatina (xe·la'ti·na) *n.f.* gelatin. —**gelatinoso,** *adj.* gelatinous.
gélido ('xe·li·ðo) *adj., poet.* gelid.
gema ('xe·ma) *n.f.* gem.
gemelo (xe'me·lo) *adj.* twin. —*n.m.* **1,** twin. **2,** cuff link. —**gemelos,** *n.m.pl.* binoculars.
gemido (xe'mi·ðo) *n.m.* moan; howl.
geminar (xe·mi'nar) *v.t.* to geminate. —**geminación,** *n.f.* gemination. —**geminado,** *adj.* & *n.m.* geminate.
Géminis ('xe·mi·nis) *n.m.* Gemini.
gemir (xe'mir) *v.i.* [*pres.ind.* **gimo;** *pres.subjve.* **gima;** *pret.* **gemí, gimió;** *ger.* **gimiendo**] to moan; howl.
gen (xen) *n.m.* gene. *Also,* **gene.**
-gena (xe·na) *suffix* -genous; *forming adjectives meaning* born; produced: *indígena,* indigenous.
genciana (xen'θja·na; xen'sja-) *n.f.* gentian.
gendarme (xen'dar·me) *n.m.* gendarm.
gene ('xe·ne) *n.m.* = **gen.**
gene- (xe·ne) *prefix* gene-; ancestry; generation: *genealogía,* genealogy.
genealogía (xe·ne·a·lo'xi·a) *n.f.* genealogy. —**genealógico** (-'lo·xi·ko) *adj.* genealogical. —**genealogista,** *n.m.* & *f.* genealogist.
generación (xe·ne·ra'θjon; -'sjon) *n.f.* generation.
generador (xe·ne·ra'ðor) *adj.* generating. —*n.m.* generator.
general (xe·ne'ral) *adj.* & *n.m.* general. —**generales,** *n.f.pl.* personal data. —**en** *or* **por lo general,** generally; usually.
generalato (xe·ne·ra'la·to) *n.m.* generalship.
generalidad (xe·ne·ra·li'ðað) *n.f.* **1,** majority; greater part. **2,** generality.
generalísimo (xe·ne·ra'li·si·mo) *n.m.* generalissimo.
generalizar (xe·ne·ra·li'θar; -'sar) *v.t.* [*pres.subjve.* **generalice** (-'li·θe; -se); *pret.* **generalicé** (-'θe; -'se)] to generalize. —**generalizarse,** *v.r.* to become general; spread. —**generalización,** *n.f.* generalization.
generar (xe·ne'rar) *v.t.* to generate.
generativo (xe·ne·ra'ti·βo) *adj.* generative.
genérico (xe'ne·ri·ko) *adj.* generic.
género ('xe·ne·ro) *n.m.* **1,** genus. **2,** manner. **3,** genre. **4,** textile. **5,** gender. —**género chico,** one-act play. —**género humano,** mankind.
generoso (xe·ne'ro·so) *adj.* generous. —**generosidad,** *n.f.* generosity.
genésico (xe'ne·si·ko) *adj.* genetic.
génesis ('xe·ne·sis) *n.f.* origin; genesis. —*n.m., cap.* Genesis.
genética (xe'ne·ti·ka) *n.f.* genetics. —**genético,** *adj.* genetic.
-genia ('xe·nja) *suffix* -geny; *forming nouns denoting* origin: *ontogenia,* ontogeny.
genial ('xe·njal) *adj.* endowed with genius; brilliant.
genialidad (xe·nja·li'ðað) *n.f.* **1,** genius. **2,** *colloq.* whim; fancy.
-génico ('xe·ni·ko) *suffix* -genic; *forming adjectives corresponding to nouns ending in* **-geno** *or* **-genia:** *fotogénico,* photogenic.
genio ('xe·njo) *n.m.* **1,** genius; brilliance. **2,** temperament; temper. **3,** genie.
genital (xe·ni'tal) *adj.* genital. —**genitales,** *n.m.pl.* genitals.
genitivo (xe·ni'ti·βo) *adj.* & *n.m.* genitive.
genito- (xe·ni·to) *prefix* genito-; of or related to the genital system: *genitourinario,* genito-urinary.
-genito ('xe·ni·to) *suffix* begotten; born: *primogénito,* firstborn.
-geno (xe·no) *suffix* **1,** -genous; *forming adjectives meaning* born; produced: *nitrógeno,* nitrogenous. **2,** -gen; *forming nouns denoting: in chemistry,* something that produces: *halógeno,* halogen; *in biology,* something produced: *exógeno,* exogen.
genocidio (xe·no'θi·ðjo; -'si·ðjo) *n.m.* genocide. —**genocida** (-'θi·ða; -'si·ða) *adj.* genocidal.
gente ('xen·te) *n.f.* **1,** people; folk. **2,** *colloq.* family. —**don de gentes,** social graces. —**gente baja,** rabble. —**gente bien,** the well-to-do. —**gente de bien,** honest folk. —**gente de mar,** seafaring folk. —**gente de medio pelo,** *derog.* lower classes. —**gente gorda** *or* **de**

peso, *colloq.* big shots; brass. —**gente menuda,** children.
gentil (xen'til) *adj.* gentle; kind; gracious. —*n.m.* gentile.
gentileza (xen·ti'le·θa; -sa) *n.f.* **1,** politeness. **2,** gracious gesture. **3,** gentility.
gentilhombre (xen·ti'lom·bre) *n.m.* nobleman; gentleman.
gentilicio (xen·ti'li·θjo; -sjo) *adj.* & *n.m., gram.* gentile.
gentío (xen'ti·o) *n.m.* throng.
gentuza (xen'tu·θa; -sa) *n.f.* rabble.
genuflexión (xe·nu·flek'sjon) *n.f.* genuflection.
genuino (xe'nwi·no) *adj.* genuine.
geo- (xe·o) *prefix* geo-; earth: *geocéntrico,* geocentric.
geocéntrico (xe·o'θen·tri·ko; -'sen·tri·ko) *adj.* geocentric.
geodesia (xe·o'ðe·sja) *n.f.* geodesy. —**geodésico** (-'ðe·si·ko) *adj.* geodetic.
geografía (xe·o·ɣra'fi·a) *n.f.* geography. —**geográfico** (-'ɣra·fi·ko) *adj.* geographic. —**geógrafo** (xe'o·ɣra·fo) *n.m.* geographer.
geología (xe·o·lo'xi·a) *n.f.* geology. —**geológico** (-'lo·xi·ko) *adj.* geological. —**geólogo** (xe'o·lo·ɣo) *n.m.* geologist.
geometría (xe·o·me'tri·a) *n.f.* geometry. —**geómetra** (xe'o·me·tra) *n.m.* geometrician. —**geométrico** (-'me·tri·ko) *adj.* geometric. —**geometría del espacio,** solid geometry.
geopolítica (xe·o·po'li·ti·ka) *n.f.* geopolitics.
geranio (xe'ra·njo) *n.m.* geranium.
gerencia (xe'ren·θja; -sja) *n.f.* **1,** management. **2,** manager's office.
gerente (xe'ren·te) *n.m.* manager.
geriatría (xe·rja'tria) *n.f.* geriatrics. —**geriátrico** (-'rja·tri·ko) *adj.* geriatric.
germanía (xer·ma'ni·a) *n.f.* thieves' slang; cant; argot.
germánico (xer'ma·ni·ko) *adj.* Germanic.
germanio (xer'ma·njo) *n.m.* germanium.
germano (xer'ma·no) *adj.* = **alemán.**
germen ('xer·men) *n.m.* **1,** germ. **2,** origin; source.
germicida (xer·mi'θi·ða; -'si·ða) *n.m.* germicide. —*adj.* germicidal.
germinal (xer·mi'nal) *adj.* germinal.
germinar (xer·mi'nar) *v.i.* to germinate. —**germinación,** *n.f.* germination.
gerundio (xe'run·djo) *n.m.* gerund.
gesta ('xes·ta) *n.f.* feat.
gestación (xes·ta'θjon; -'sjon) *n.f.* gestation.
gesticular (xes·ti·ku'lar) *v.i.* to gesticulate. —**gesticulación,** *n.f.* gesticulation.
gestión (xes'tjon) *n.f.* **1,** effort. **2,** step; measure. **3,** démarche. **4,** management.
gesto ('xes·to) *n.m.* **1,** gesture; expression. **2,** appearance. —**estar de buen gesto,** to be agreeable. —**hacer gestos, 1,** to gesture. **2,** to signal. —**poner gesto,** *colloq.* to show anger.
gestor (xes'tor) *adj.* contriving; endeavoring. —*n.m.* agent.
ghetto ('ge·to) *n.m.* ghetto.
gibón (xi'βon) *n.m.* gibbon.
giga ('xi·ɣa) *n.f.* gigue.
gigante (xi'ɣan·te) *n.m.* giant. —*adj.* gigantic. —**giganta,** *n.f.* giantess. —**gigantesco,** *adj.* gigantic.
gigote (xi'ɣo·te) *n.m.* minced-meat stew.
gima ('xi·ma) *v., pres.subjve. of* **gemir.**
gimiendo (xi'mjen·do) *v., ger. of* **gemir.**
gimió (xi'mjo) *v., 3rd pers.sing. pret. of* **gemir.**
gimnasia (xim'na·sja) *also,* **gimnástica** (-'nas·ti·ka) *n.f.* gymnastics (*pl.*). —**gimnasta** (-'nas·ta) *n.m.* & *f.* gymnast. —**gimnástico,** *adj.* gymnastic.
gimnasio (xim'na·sjo) *n.m.* gymnasium.
gimo ('xi·mo) *v., pres.ind. of* **gemir.**
gimotear (xi·mo·te'ar) *v.i., colloq.* to whine. —**gimoteo** (-'te·o) *n.m., colloq.* whining.
gin- (xin) *prefix* gyn-; woman; female: *ginandro,* gynandrous.
gine- (xi·ne) *prefix* gyne-, *var. of* **gin-:** *gineolatría,* gyneolatry.
ginebra (xi'ne·βra) *n.f.* **1,** gin. **2,** confusion; bedlam.
gineco- (xi·ne·ko) *prefix* gyneco-; woman: *ginecología,* gynecology.
ginecología (xi·ne·ko·lo'xi·a) *n.f.* gynecology. —**ginecológico** (-'lo·xi·ko) *adj.* gynecological. —**gine-**

cólogo (-'ko·lo·ɣo) *n.m.* gynecologist.
gingivitis (xin·xi'βi·tis) *n.f.* gingivitis.
-ginia ('xi·nja) *prefix* -gyny; *forming nouns from adjectives ending in* **-gino**: *androginia*, androgyny.
gino- (xi·no) *prefix* gyno-; *var. of* **gin-**: *ginóforo*, gynophore.
-gino (xi·no) *suffix* -gynous; female: *andrógino*, androgynous.
gira ('xi·ra) *n.f.* outing; picnic.
girar (xi'rar) *v.i.* **1,** to turn; gyrate. **2,** *comm.* to draw (a check, draft, etc.). **3,** *mech.* to spin. **—girar contra** *or* **a cargo de,** *comm.* to draw on.
girasol (xi·ra'sol) *n.m.* sunflower.
giratorio (xi·ra'to·rjo) *adj.* gyrating; revolving.
giro ('xi·ro) *n.m.* **1,** gyration; rotation. **2,** trend. **3,** *comm.* draft; note; money order. **4,** *comm.* gross; turnover (*of business*). **5,** turn of phrase; figure of speech.
giro- (xi·ro) *prefix* gyro-; ring; circle; spiral; gyration: *giróscopo*, gyroscope.
giroscopio (xi·ros'ko·pjo) *also,* **giróscopo** (xi'ros·ko·po) *n.m.* gyroscope.
gitanería (xi·ta·ne'ri·a) *n.f.* **1,** flattery; cajolery. **2,** gypsies collectively. **3,** *slang* dirty trick.
gitano (xi'ta·no) *adj.* & *n.m.* gypsy. **—gitanesco,** *adj.* gypsy.
glacial (gla'θjal; -'sjal) *adj.* glacial.
glaciar (gla'θjar; -'sjar) *n.m.* glacier.
gladiador (gla·ðja'ðor) *n.m.* gladiator.
gladiolo (gla'ðjo·lo) *n.m.* gladiolus. *Also, Amer.,* **gladiola,** *n.f.*
glándula ('glan·du·la) *n.f.* gland. **—glandular,** *adj.* glandular.
glaucoma (glau'ko·ma) *n.m.* glaucoma.
glaseado (gla·se'a·ðo) *adj.* glossy.
glicerina (gli·θe'ri·na; gli·se-) *n.f.* glycerin.
globo ('glo·βo) *n.m.* **1,** globe. **2,** balloon.
glóbulo ('glo·βu·lo) *n.m.* globule; corpuscle. **—globular,** *adj.* globular.
gloria ('glo·rja) *n.f.* **1,** glory. **2,** heaven; paradise. **3,** blessing. **—estar en sus glorias,** *colloq.* to be in seventh heaven. **—saber a gloria,** *colloq.* to taste heavenly.
gloriarse (glo'rjar·se) *v.r.* to glory.
glorieta (glo'rje·ta) *n.f.* **1,** summerhouse; bower. **2,** small city park. **3,** traffic circle.
glorificar (glo·ri·fi'kar) *v.t.* [*pres.subjve.* **glorifique** (-'fi·ke); *pret.* **glorifiqué** (-'ke)] to glorify. **—glorificación,** *n.f.* glorification.
glorioso (glo'rjo·so) *adj.* **1,** glorious. **2,** blessed.
glosa ('glo·sa) *n.f.* gloss; comment. **—glosar,** *v.t.* to gloss; comment on.
glosario (glo'sa·rjo) *n.m.* glossary.
-glota (glo·ta) *suffix-* glot; tongue; language: *políglota*, polyglot.
glotis ('glo·tis) *n.f.* glottis.
glotón (glo'ton) *n.m.* **1,** glutton. **2,** *zool.* glutton; wolverine. **—***adj.* gluttonous. **—glotonería,** *n.f.* gluttony.
glucinio (glu'θi·njo; -'si·njo) *n.m.* glucinium.
glucosa (glu'ko-sa) *n.f.* glucose.
gluglú (glu'ɣlu) *n.m.* **1,** gurgle; gurgling. **2,** gobble (*of a turkey*).
gluglutear (glu·ɣlu·te'ar) *v.i.* **1,** to gurgle. **2,** to gobble, as a turkey.
gluten ('glu·ten) *n.m.* gluten. **—glutinoso** (-ti'no·so) *adj.* glutinous.
gnomo ('gno·mo; 'no·mo) *n.m.* gnome.
gnóstico ('gnos·ti·ko; 'nos-) *adj.* & *n.m.* gnostic. **—gnosticismo** (-'θis·mo; -'sis·mo) *n.m.* gnosticism.
gobernación (go·βer·na'θjon; -'sjon) *n.f.* government. **—Ministerio de la Gobernación,** Department of the Interior.
gobernador (go·βer·na'ðor) *n.m.* governor.
gobernadora (go·βer·na'ðo·ra) *n.f.* **1,** lady governor. **2,** governor's wife.
gobernar (go·βer'nar) *v.t.* [*pres. ind.* **gobierno** (-'βjer·no); *pres. subjve.* **gobierne** (-ne)] **1,** to govern; rule. **2,** to control; steer. **—gobernante,** *adj.* governing; ruling. **—***n.m.* ruler.
gobierno (go'βjer·no) *n.m.* **1,** government; administration. **2,** governorship. **3,** governor's offices; the building housing them. **4,** control; steering. **5,** helm; rudder. **—para su gobierno,** for your information and guidance. **—servir de gobierno,** to serve as guide. **—sin gobierno,** adrift.
gobio ('go·βjo) *n.m., ichthy.* gudgeon.

goce ('go·θe; -se) *n.m.* enjoyment.
goce ('go·θe; -se) *v., pres.subjve. of* **gozar.**
gocé (go'θe; -'se) *v., 1st pers.sing. pret. of* **gozar.**
godo ('go·ðo) *n.m.* Goth. —*adj.* Gothic.
gofio ('go·fjo) *n.m.* roasted corn meal.
gol (gol) *n.m.* goal.
goleta (go'le·ta) *n.f.* schooner.
golf (golf) *n.m.* golf.
golfa ('gol·fa) *n.f.* moll; tramp.
golfo ('gol·fo) *n.m.* **1,** gulf. **2,** ragamuffin. **3,** faro.
golilla (go'li·ʎa;-ja) *n.f.* ruff; lace collar.
golondrina (go·lon'dri·na) *n.f.* swallow.
golondrino (go·lon'dri·no) *n.m.* swelling in the armpit.
golosina (go·lo'si·na) *n.f.* **1,** delicacy; tidbit. **2,** sweet tooth.
goloso (go'lo·so) *adj.* sweet-toothed.
golpe ('gol·pe) *n.m.* **1,** blow; stroke. **2,** bump; bruise. **3,** knock (*at a door*). **4,** attack; fit. **5,** disappointment; blow. —**caer** *or* **caerse de golpe,** *colloq.* to collapse. —**de golpe,** suddenly. —**de golpe y porrazo,** *colloq.* **1,** in a rush. **2,** unexpectedly. —**de un golpe,** all at once. —**golpe de gente,** crowd; throng. —**golpe de mar,** tidal wave. —**golpe seco,** sharp blow. —**golpe de vista,** glance. —**no dar golpe,** *colloq.* not to hit a lick.
golpear (gol·pe'ar) *v.t.* **1,** to beat; strike. **2,** to knock. **3,** to bruise; bump.
golpetear (gol·pe·te'ar) *v.t. & i.* to knock; pound; rattle. —**golpeteo** (-'te·o) *n.m.* knocking; pounding; rattling.
gollería (go·ʎe'ri·a; go·je-) *n.f.* **1,** delicacy; dainty. **2,** extra; superfluity.
goma ('go·ma) *n.f.* **1,** gum. **2,** rubber. **3,** mucilage. **4,** rubber band. **5,** tire. —**gomas,** *n.f.pl., Amer.* galoshes; overshoes. —**goma de mascar,** chewing gum. —**goma hinchable,** bubble gum.
gomoso (go'mo·so) *adj.* gummy. —*n.m.* dandy; fop.
gonado (go'na·ðo) *n.m.* gonad.
góndola ('gon·do·la) *n.f.* gondola. —**gondolero,** *n.m.* gondolier.
gong (gong) *n.m.* [*pl.* **gongs**] gong.
-gonía (ɣo'ni·a) *suffix* -gony; genesis; origin: *cosmogonía,* cosmogony.
gono- (go·no) *prefix* gono-; related or pertaining to sex or the organs of reproduction: *gonorrea,* gonorrhea.
-gono (ɣo·no) *suffix* -gon; *forming nouns denoting geometrical plane figures with a specified number of sides or angles: polígono,* polygon.
gonorrea (go·no'rre·a) *n.f.* gonorrhea.
gordiflón (gor·ði'flon) *also,* **gordinflón** (gor·ðin-) *adj., colloq.* fat; obese; chubby. —*n.m., colloq.* chubby person.
gordo ('gor·ðo) *adj.* **1,** fat; stout; plump. **2,** fatty; greasy. —*n.m.* **1,** fat; grease. **2,** fat person. —**gordura,** *n.f.* stoutness. —**algo gordo,** something important. —**armar la gorda,** *colloq.* **1,** to have a fight. **2,** to create a furor. —**hacer la vista gorda,** to close one's eyes; pretend not to notice.
gordolobo (gor·ðo'lo·βo) *n.m.* mullein.
gorgojo (gor'ɣo·xo) *n.m.* weevil; grub.
gorgorito (gor·ɣo'ri·to) *n.m.* **1,** warble; trill. **2,** inarticulate sound; gurgle.
gorgoteo (gor·ɣo'te·o) *n.m.* gurgle; gurgling.
gorila (go'ri·la) *n.m.* gorilla.
gorjear (gor·xe'ar) *v.i.* **1,** to warble; trill. **2,** to gurgle. —**gorjeador,** *adj.* warbling. —*n.m.* warbler.
gorjeo (gor'xe·o) *n.m.* **1,** warble; warbling. **2,** gurgle; gurgling.
gorra ('go·rra) *n.f.* cap. —*n.m., colloq.* sponger. —**pegar la gorra; ir** *or* **andar de gorra,** *colloq.* to sponge.
gorrear (go·rre'ar) *v.t. & i., colloq.* to sponge; grub; beg.
gorrino (go'rri·no) *n.m.* hog; pig. —*adj.* hoggish; piggish.
gorrión (go'rrjon) *n.m.* sparrow.
gorro ('go·rro) *n.m.* cap; bonnet.
gorrón (go'rron) *n.m.* **1,** sponger. **2,** pebble. **3,** *mech.* spindle.
gota ('go·ta) *n.f.* **1,** drop. **2,** *pathol.* gout. —**gota a gota,** drop by drop. —**gotas amargas,** bitters. —**sudar la gota gorda,** *colloq.* to sweat blood.
gotear (go·te'ar) *v.i.* to drip; leak. —**goteo** (-'te·o) *n.m.* dripping; leaking.
gotera (go'te·ra) *n.f.* leak; drip.

gotero (go'te·ro) *n.m., Amer.* = **cuentagotas.**
gótico ('go·ti·ko) *adj.* & *n.m.* Gothic. —**niño gótico,** coxcomb.
gourmet (gur'me) *n.m.* & *f.* [*pl.* **gourmets** (-'mes)] gourmet.
gozar (go'θar; -'sar) *v.t.* [*pres. subjve.* **goce;** *pret.* **gocé**] *often fol. by* **de, 1,** to enjoy; have the benefit of. **2,** to enjoy; derive pleasure from. —*v.i.* to have enjoyment *or* pleasure. —**gozarse,** *v.r., often fol. by* **de, en** *or* **con, 1,** to rejoice. **2,** to enjoy oneself. —**gozar mucho,** *Amer., colloq.* to have a good time.
gozne ('goθ·ne; 'gos-) *n.m.* hinge.
gozo ('go·θo; -so) *n.m.* joy. —**gozoso,** *adj.* joyful; gleeful. —**el gozo en el pozo,** all hope is gone. —**no caber de gozo,** to be beside oneself with joy.
gozque ('goθ·ke; 'gos-) *n.m.* small barking dog. *Also,* **gozquejo** (-'ke·jo).
grabación (gra·βa'θjon; -'sjon) *n.f.* **1,** engraving. **2,** recording.
grabado (gra'βa·ðo) *n.m.* **1,** engraving; print. **2,** illustration. —*adj.* **1,** engraved. **2,** drawn; pictured. **3,** graven.
grabador (gra·βa'ðor) *n.m.* engraver. —*adj.* recording.
grabadora (gra·βa'ðo·ra) *n.f., also,* **grabadora de cinta,** tape recorder.
grabar (gra'βar) *v.t.* **1,** to engrave. **2,** to record (on a disc, etc.).
gracejo (gra'θe·xo; -'se·xo) *n.m.* **1,** wit; grace. **2,** *Amer.* buffoon. —**gracejar** (-'xar) *v.i.* to be witty. —**gracejada** (-'xa·ða) *n.f., Amer.* buffoonery.
gracia ('gra·θja; -sja) *n.f.* **1,** grace. **2,** charm. **3,** favor. **4,** (*as a polite formula*) name of a person. **5,** joke. —**gracias,** *n.f.pl.* thanks. —**caer en gracia,** to find favor; be favorably received. —**hacer gracia,** to be funny *or* amusing. —**no estar para gracias,** to be in no mood for jokes. —**¡tiene gracia!** isn't it funny!
gracioso (gra'θjo·so; -'sjo·so) *adj.* **1,** funny; witty. **2,** gracious; charming.
grada ('gra·ða) *n.f.* **1,** step (*in front of a building or an altar*). **2,** *often pl.* bleachers. **3,** harrow. —**gradar,** *v.t.* to harrow.
gradación (gra·ða'θjon; -'sjon) *n.f.* gradation.
gradería (gra·ðe'ri·a) *n.f.* **1,** series of steps. **2,** stands (*in an arena*). **3,** bleachers. —**gradería cubierta,** grandstand.
grado ('gra·ðo) *n.m.* **1,** degree. **2,** grade. **3,** rank. —**de buen grado,** with pleasure. —**de mal grado,** unwillingly.
-grado (ɣra·ðo) *suffix* -grade; *forming adjectives denoting* **1,** walking; movement: *digitígrado,* digitigrade. **2,** gradation: *centígrado,* centigrade.
graduación (gra·ðwa'θjon; -'sjon) *n.f.* **1,** graduation; measurement. **2,** *mil.* rank. **3,** proof (*of alcohol*). **4,** *Amer.* school *or* college graduation.
graduado (gra'ðwa·ðo) *adj.* **1,** graduated. **2,** graded. **3,** *mil.* brevet. —*adj.* & *n.m.* graduate. —**probeta graduada,** *chem.* graduate.
gradual (gra'ðwal) *adj.* gradual.
graduar (gra'ðwar) *v.t.* [*infl.:* **continuar**] **1,** to grade. **2,** to graduate. **3,** to adjust. —**graduarse,** *v.r.* to graduate.
-grafía (ɣra'fi·a) *suffix* -graphy; *forming nouns denoting:* **1,** descriptive sciences and studies: *geografía,* geography; *biografía,* biography. **2,** pictorial and representational arts: *fotografía,* photography; *coreografía,* choreography. **3,** the use of instruments for writing, drawing, recording, etc.: *telegrafía,* telegraphy. **4,** writing; representation in writing: *ortografía,* orthography. **5,** -graph; writing; drawing; recording; representation: *monografía,* monograph; *fotografía,* photograph.
gráfico ('gra·fi·ko) *adj.* graphic —*n.m.* diagram. —**gráfica,** *n.f.* graph.
-gráfico ('ɣra·fi·ko) *suffix* -graphic; *forming adjectives corresponding to nouns ending in* **-grafía:** *telegráfico,* telegraphic.
grafito (gra'fi·to) *n.m.* graphite.
grafo- (gra·fo) *prefix* grapho-; writing; drawing: *grafología,* graphology.
-grafo (ɣra·fo) *suffix forming nouns denoting* **1,** -graph; an instrument for writing, drawing, recording, etc.: *telégrafo,* telegraph; *fonógrafo,* phonograph. **2,** -grapher; -graphist; a person engaged in an art, science, study or craft of writing, drawing, recording, etc.: *bió-*

grafo, biographer; *coreógrafo,* choreographer; *calígrafo,* calligrapher.

gragea (gra'xe·a) *n.f.* **1,** sugar plum. **2,** sugar-coated pill.

grajo ('gra·xo) *n.m., ornith.* rook.

grama ('gra·ma) *n.f.* grass.

-grama (ɣra·ma) *suffix* -gram; *forming nouns denoting* something written, drawn or recorded: *telegrama,* telegram; *diagrama,* diagram.

gramática (gra'ma·ti·ka) *n.f.* grammar. —**gramatical,** *adj.* grammatical. —**gramático,** *adj.* grammatical. —*n.m.* grammarian. —**gramática parda,** shrewdness.

gramo ('gra·mo) *n.m.* gram.

-gramo ('ɣra·mo) *suffix* -gram; metric units of weight: *kilogramo,* kilogram.

gramófono (gra'mo·fo·no) *n.m.* phonograph.

grampa ('gram·pa) *n.f.* = **grapa.**

gran (gran) *adj., contr. of* **grande** *before a sing. noun.*

grana ('gra·na) *n.f.* **1,** ripening season. **2,** cochineal. **3,** scarlet dye or color. **4,** scarlet cloth.

granada (gra'na·ða) *n.f.* **1,** grenade. **2,** pomegranate. —**granadero,** *n.m.* grenadier.

granadina (gra·na'ði·na) *n.f.* grenadine.

granado (gra'na·ðo) *n.m.* pomegranate tree. —*adj.* **1,** mature; expert. **2,** choice; select.

granar (gra'nar) *v.i.* **1,** to ripen. **2,** *fig.* to become real.

granate (gra'na·te) *n.m.* garnet.

grande ('gran·de) *adj.* **1,** large. **2,** great; grand. —*n.m.* grandee. —**a lo grande,** in high style.

grandeza (gran'de·θa; -sa) *n.f.* **1,** greatness; grandeur. **2,** rank of a grandee. **3,** grandees collectively.

grandilocuente (gran·di·lo·'kwen·te) *adj* grandiloquent. —**grandilocuencia,** *n.f.* grandiloquence.

grandioso (gran'djo·so) *adj.* grandiose. —**grandiosidad,** *n.f.* grandeur; grandiosity.

granel (gra'nel) *n.m., in* **a granel, 1,** *comm.* in bulk; in odd lots. **2,** in abundance.

granero (gra'ne·ro) *n.m.* **1,** granary; barn. **2,** grain-producing district.

granito (gra'ni·to) *n.m.* **1,** granite. **2,** small grain. **3,** pimple.

granizar (gra·ni'θar; -'sar) *v.impers.* [*pres.subjve.* **granice** (-'ni·θe; -se)] to hail.

granizo (gra'ni·θo; -so) *n.m.* hail; hailstones (*pl*). —**granizada,** *n.f.* hailstorm. —**granizado,** *n.m.* snow cone.

granja ('gran·xa) *n.f.* farm; grange. —**granjero,** *n.m.* farmer.

granjear (gran·xe'ar) *v.t.* to win (friendship, favor, etc.).

grano ('gra·no) *n.m.* **1,** grain. **2,** boil; pimple. —**al grano,** to the point.

granuja (gra'nu·xa) *n.m.* rogue; rascal. —**granujada,** *n.f.* roguery; rascality.

granujoso (gra·nu'xo·so) *adj.* pimpled; pimply.

granular (gra·nu'lar) *v.t.* to granulate. —*adj.* granular. —**granulación,** *n.f.* granulation.

gránulo ('gra·nu·lo) *n.m.* granule.

grapa ('gra·pa) *n.f.* clamp; staple.

grasa ('gra·sa) *n.f.* grease; fat. —**grasiento,** *also,* **grasoso,** *adj.* greasy. —**graso,** *adj.* fatty.

grata ('gra·ta) *n.f., Amer.* = **atenta.**

gratificación (gra·ti·fi·ka'θjon; -'sjon) *n.f.* **1,** gratification. **2,** bonus; perquisite. **3,** expense allowance.

gratificar (gra·ti·fi'kar) *v.t.* [*pres.subjve.* **gratifique** (-'fi·ke); *pret.* **gratifiqué** (-'ke)] **1,** to gratify. **2,** to reward; tip.

gratis ('gra·tis) *adv.* gratis; free.

gratitud (gra·ti'tuð) *n.f.* gratitude.

grato ('gra·to) *adj.* pleasant; pleasing.

gratuito (gra'twi·to) *adj.* **1,** free; free of charge. **2,** gratuitous.

grava ('gra·βa) *n.f.* gravel.

gravamen (gra'βa·men) *n.m.* **1,** burden; obligation. **2,** *law* lien; mortgage.

gravar (gra'βar) *v.t.* **1,** to burden. **2,** *law* to encumber. **3,** to tax (a property).

grave ('gra·βe) *adj.* **1,** grave. **2,** *music* bass. **3,** accented on the penultimate syllable. —**gravedad,** *n.f.* gravity.

grávida ('gra·βi·ða) *adj.fem.* pregnant.

gravidez (gra·βi'ðeθ; -'ðes) *n.f.* pregnancy.

gravitar (gra·βi'tar) *v.i.* to gravitate. —**gravitación,** *n.f.* gravitation.

gravoso (gra'βo·so) *adj.* burdensome.

graznar (graθ'nar; gras-) *v.i.* to croak; caw.

graznido (graθ'ni·ðo; gras-) *n.m.* croak; caw.

greca ('gre·ka) *n.f.* **1,** fret; fretwork. **2,** *Amer.* coffee maker; coffee pot.

greco- (gre·ko) *prefix* Greco-; Greek: *grecorromano,* Greco-Roman.

grecorromano (gre·ko·rro'ma·no) *adj.* Greco-Roman.

greda ('gre·ða) *n.f.* fuller's earth.

gregario (gre'ɣa·rjo) *adj.* gregarious. —**gregarismo** (-'ris·mo) *n.m.* gregariousness.

gremio ('gre·mjo) *n.m.* **1,** guild; trade union. **2,** social *or* occupational group. —**gremial,** *adj.* of or pert. to a guild or trade union.

greña ('gre·ɲa) *n.f.* matted lock of hair. —**greñudo,** *adj.* matted.

grey (grei) *n.f.* congregation; flock.

grial (grjal) *n.m.* grail.

griego ('grje·ɣo) *adj.* & *n.m.* Greek; Grecian.

grieta ('grje·ta) *n.f.* **1,** crevice. **2,** cleft; crack.

grifo ('gri·fo) *n.m.* **1,** griffin. **2,** faucet; spigot. —*adj.* kinky; tangled.

grilla ('gri·ʎa; -ja) *n.f.* grid.

grillete (gri'ʎe·te; -'je·te) *n.m.* shackle.

grillo ('gri·ʎo; -jo) *n.m., entom.* cricket. —**grillos,** *n.m.pl.* shackles.

grima ('gri·ma) *n.f.* disgust.

gringo ('grin·go) *n.m., slang* gringo.

gripe ('gri·pe) *n.f.* grippe. —**gripal,** *adj.* of or like the grippe.

gris (gris) *adj.* & *n.m.* gray. —**grisáceo,** *adj.* grayish.

gritar (gri'tar) *v.i.* to shout; cry.

griterío (gri·te'ri·o) *n.m.* shouting; outcry; howl. *Also,* **gritería,** *n.f.*

grito ('gri·to) *n.m.* shout; cry. —**a grito pelado,** at the top of one's lungs.

gritón (gri'ton) *adj.* vociferous.

gro (gro) *n.m.* grosgrain.

grosella (gro'se·ʎa; -ja) *n.f.* red currant. —**grosella blanca** *or* **silvestre,** gooseberry.

grosero (gro'se·ro) *adj.* coarse; uncouth. —**grosería,** *n.f.* coarseness; vulgarity.

grosor (gro'sor) *n.m.* thickness.

grotesco (gro'tes·ko) *adj.* grotesque.

grúa ('gru·a) *n.f., mech.* crane.

gruesa ('grwe·sa) *n.f.* gross.

grueso ('grwe·so) *adj.* **1,** thick. **2,** stout. —*n.m.* **1,** thickness. **2,** greater part; bulk.

grulla ('gru·ʎa; -ja) *n.f. ornith.* crane.

grumete (gru'me·te) *n.m.* cabin boy.

grumo ('gru·mo) *n.m.* clot. —**grumo de la leche,** curd.

gruñido (gru'ɲi·ðo) *n.m.* grunt; growl.

gruñir (gru'ɲir) *v.i.* [*3rd pers.sing. pret.* **gruñó** (-'ɲo); *ger.* **gruñendo**] to grunt; growl; grumble. —**gruñón,** *adj., colloq.* grumpy; grouchy. —*n.m., colloq.* grouch; griper.

grupa ('gru·pa) *n.f.* croup; rump. —**grupera,** *n.f.* pillion. —**volver grupas,** to turn tail.

grupo ('gru·po) *n.m.* group.

gruta ('gru·ta) *n.f.* grotto.

guaca ('gwa·ka) *n.f., Amer.* Indian burial ground.

guacal (gwa'kal) *n.m., Amer.* wooden crate.

guacamayo (gwa·ka'ma·jo) *n.m.* macaw.

guacamole (gwa·ka'mo·le) *n.m.,* **1,** *Amer.* avocado salad. **2,** *Mex.* avocado.

guacho ('gua·tʃo) *n.m.* **1,** young bird, chick. **2,** young animal. —*adj.* & *n.m., Amer.* orphan; foundling. —*adj., Amer.* odd; unmatched; without pair.

guadaña (gwa'ða·ɲa) *n.f.* scythe.

guadañada (gwa·ða'ɲa·ða) *n.f.* swath.

guagua ('gwa·gwa) *n.f.* **1,** *W.I.* omnibus; bus. **2,** *So.Amer.* baby. —**de guagua,** free.

guaje ('gwa·xe) *n.m., Amer.* **1,** a kind of gourd or calabash. **2,** trinket; bauble. **3,** fool; simpleton. **4,** knave; rogue. —*adj., Amer.* **1,** foolish; simple. **2,** knavish; roguish.

guajiro (gwa'xi·ro) *n.m.* & *adj. Amer.* rustic.

guajolote (gwa·xo'lo·te) *n.m., Mex.* turkey.

guanaco (gwa'na·ko) *n.m.* guanaco.

guanajo (gwa'na·xo) *n.m., Amer.* turkey.

guano ('gwa·no) *n.m.* guano.

guante ('gwan·te) *n.m.* glove. —**arrojar el guante,** to challenge. —**echar el guante a,** to seize; nab.

guantelete (gwan·te'le·te) *n.m.* gauntlet.

guapo ('gwa·po) *adj.* **1,** handsome. **2,** *Amer., colloq.* brave. —*n.m.* **1,** dandy. **2,** bully. —**guapear,** *v.i., Amer.* to bluster. —**guapería,** *n.f., Amer.* bluster

guarache (gwa'ra·tʃe) *n.m., Mex.* **1,** leather sandal. **2,** tire patch.

guarapo (gwa'ra·po) *n.m.* sugarcane juice, esp. fermented.

guarda ('gwar·ða) *n.m. & f.* guard; custodian. —*n.f.* **1,** custody. **2,** ward (*of a lock*). **3,** flyleaf. **4,** *mech.* guard; shield.

guardabarreras (gwar·ða·βa·'rre·ras) *n.m. & f.sing. & pl.* gatekeeper.

guardabarro (gwar·ða'βa·rro) *n.m., usu.pl.* fender; mudguard.

guardabosque (gwar·ða'βos·ke) *n.m.* game warden.

guardabrisa (gwar·ða'βri·sa) *n.m.* = **parabrisa.**

guardacostas (gwar·ða'kos·tas) *n.m.sing & pl.* coast guard cutter.

guardafango (gwar·ða'fan·go) *n.m.* fender (*of an automobile*).

guardafrenos (gwar·ða'fre·nos) *n.m.sing. & pl.* brakeman.

guardafuegos (gwar·ða'fwe·ɣos) *n.m.sing. & pl.* fender (*of a fireplace*).

guardagujas (gwar·ða'ɣu·xas) *n.m.sing. & pl., R.R.* switchman.

guardalmacén (gwar·ðal·ma·'θen; -'sen) *n.m.* **1,** keeper of supplies or stores; storekeeper. **2,** warehouseman. *Also,* **guardaalmacén** (gwar·ða·al-).

guardameta (gwar·ða'me·ta) *n.m.* goalkeeper; goalie.

guardapelo (gwar·ða'pe·lo) *n.m.* locket.

guardapolvo (gwar·ða'pol·βo) *n.m.* **1,** dust cover. **2,** duster; light coat.

guardar (gwar'ðar) *v.t.* **1,** to hold; keep. **2,** to save; store. **3,** to watch over; protect. —**guardarse,** *v.r.* to take care; be wary. —**guardarse de,** to guard against; avoid.

guardarropa (gwar·ða'rro·pa) *n.m.* **1,** cloakroom. **2,** wardrobe; clothes closet. —*n.m. & f.* cloakroom attendant; *theat.* property man. —**guardarropía,** *n.f., theat.* property room.

guardavía (gwar·ða'vi·a) *n.m., R.R.* lineman; section hand.

guardería (gwar·ðe'ri·a) *n.f.* **1,** occupation of a guard or keeper. **2,** [*also,* **guardería infantil**] nursery; day nursery; nursery school.

guardia ('gwar·ðja) *n.f.* **1,** guard. **2,** *naut.* watch. **3,** protection; guarding. —*n.m.* policeman. —**guardia marina,** *n.m.* midshipman.

guardián (gwar'ðjan) *n.m.* **1,** guardian; custodian. **2,** keeper.

guarecer (gwa·re'θer; -'ser) *v.t.* [*pres.ind.* **guarezco** (-'reθ·ko; -'res·ko); *pres.subjve.* **guarezca** (-ka)] to shelter.

guarida (gwa'ri·ða) *n.f.* den; lair.

guarismo (gwa'ris·mo) *n.m.* digit; figure; number.

guarnecer (gwar·ne'θer; -'ser) *v.t.* [*pres.ind.* **guarnezco** (-'neθ·ko; -'nes·ko); *pres.subjve.* **guarnezca** (-ka)] **1,** to adorn; bedeck. **2,** to provide; equip. **3,** to garrison.

guarnición (gwar·ni'θjon; -'sjon) *n.f.* **1,** adornment; trim. **2,** guard (*of a sword*). **3,** garrison. **4,** setting or mounting for a jewel. **5,** *pl.* harness; trappings; gear. **6,** *pl.* fittings; fixtures.

guasa ('gwa·sa) *n.f.* **1,** jest. **2,** insipidity.

guasca ('gwas·ka) *n.f., Amer.* **1,** leather thong. **2,** rope. **3,** whip.

guaso ('gwa·so) *adj. & n.m., Amer.* rustic; yokel. —*n.m.* gaucho.

guasón (gwa'son) *adj., colloq.* waggish; humorous. —*n.m., colloq.* joker; wag.

guata ('gwa·ta) *n.f.* **1,** padding; quilt. **2,** *Amer.* belly.

guau (gwau) *interj. & n.m.* bowwow.

guayaba (gwa'ja·βa) *n.f.* guava. —**guayabo,** *n.m.* guava tree.

gubernamental (gu·βer·na·men'tal) *adj.* governmental.

gubernativo (gu·βer·na'ti·βo) *adj.* governmental.

gubia ('gu·βja) *n.f.* gouge (*tool*).
guedeja (ge'ðe·xa) *n.f.* long lock of hair. —**guedejas**, *n.f.pl.* mane (*sing.*).
güero ('gwe·ro) *adj., Amer.* blond. *Also,* **huero.**
guerra ('ge·rra) *n.m.* war. —**guerrera**, *n.f.* soldier's jacket. —**guerrero**, *adj.* martial; warlike. —*n.m.* warrior. —**dar guerra**, *colloq.* to be a nuisance.
guerrear (ge·rre'ar) *v.i.* to wage war.
guerrilla (ge'rri·ʎa; -ja) *n.f.* **1,** guerrilla band. **2,** *mil.* open formation. —**guerrillear**, *v.i.* to wage guerrilla warfare. —**guerrillero**, *n.m.* guerrilla fighter; guerrilla.
guía ('gi·a) *n.m.* & *f.* guide. —*n.f.* **1,** guidebook. **2,** sign; signpost. **3,** *mech.* rule; guide. **4,** *bot.* young shoot. **5,** directory. **6,** norm; guiding principle.
guiar (gi'ar) *v.t.* & *i.* [*pres.ind.* **guío** ('gi·o); *pres.subjve.* **guíe** ('gi·e)] **1,** to guide; lead. **2,** to steer.
guijarro (gi'xa·rro) *n.m.* pebble.
guijo ('gi·xo) *n.m.* gravel.
guillotina (gi·ʎo'ti·na; gi·jo-) *n.f.* guillotine. —**guillotinar**, *v.t.* to guillotine. —**ventana de guillotina,** sash window.
guinda ('gin·da) *n.f.* **1,** wild cherry. **2,** *colloq.* easy job; cinch.
guindar (gin'dar) *v.t.* **1,** to hoist. **2,** *colloq.* to hang; hang up. **3,** *colloq.* to win; gain (*esp. by beating out someone else*). **4,** *slang* to steal; filch.
guindo ('gin·do) *n.m.* wild cherry tree.
guinea (gi'ne·a) *n.f.* **1,** guinea. **2,** guinea hen.
guineo (gi'ne·o) *n.m., Amer.* banana.
guinga ('gin·ga) *n.f.* gingham.
guiñada (gi'ɲa·ða) *n.f.* **1,** wink. **2,** *naut.* yaw.
guiñapo (gi'ɲa·po) *n.m.* **1,** rag. **2,** ragged person; ragpicker. **3,** *colloq.* a nobody. —**dejar hecho un guiñapo; poner como un guiñapo,** **1,** to beat to a pulp. **2,** *fig.* to dress down; crush.
guiñar (gi'ɲar) *v.t.* to wink. —*v.i., naut.* to yaw. —**guiño** ('gi·ɲo) *n.m.* wink.
guión (gi'on) *n.m.* **1,** standard; pennant. **2,** leader. **3,** outline; guide. **4,** hyphen; dash. **5,** *theat.* script.
güira ('gwi·ra) *n.f.* **1,** calabash tree. **2,** gourd used as a container. —**güiro**, *n.m.* bottle gourd (*musical instrument*).
guirnalda (gir'nal·da) *n.f.* garland.
guisa ('gi·sa) *n.f.* manner. —**a guisa de,** in the manner of; like; as.
guisado (gi'sa·ðo) *n.m.* stew.
guisante (gi'san·te) *n.m.* pea. —**guisante de olor,** sweet pea.
guisar (gi'sar) *v.t.* to cook; stew.
guiso ('gi·so) *n.m.* **1,** stew. **2,** *fig., colloq.* mess; disorder. —**guisote** (-'so·te) *n.m.* slop.
guitarra (gi'ta·rra) *n.f.* guitar. —**guitarrista**, *n.m.* & *f.* guitarist.
gula ('gu·la) *n.f.* gluttony.
gurrumino (gu·rru'mi·no) *adj.* **1,** mean; despicable. **2,** uxorious; henpecked. —*n.m.* henpecked husband. —**gurrumina**, *n.f., colloq.* uxoriousness.
gusaniento (gu·sa'njen·to) *adj.* wormy.
gusanillo (gu·sa'ni·ʎo; -jo) *n.m.* **1,** small worm. **2,** *mech.* gimlet; auger bit. **3,** *mech.* small spring.
gusano (gu'sa·no) *n.m.* **1,** worm. **2,** any wormlike creature, as a maggot, caterpillar, etc. —**gusanoso**, *adj.* wormy.
gusarapo (gu·sa'ra·po) *n.m.* water-breeding larva.
gustar (gus'tar) *v.t.* **1,** to taste. **2,** to try; test —*v.i.* to please; be pleasing; be liked: *Me gustan los dulces,* I like candy; *Me gusta ir al teatro,* I like to go to the theater. —**gustar de,** to like (to); take pleasure in.
gustativo (gus·ta'ti·βo) *adj.* gustatory.
gustazo (gus'ta·θo; -so) *n.m.* **1,** great pleasure. **2,** fiendish delight.
gusto ('gus·to) *n.m.* **1,** taste. **2,** liking. **3,** pleasure. **4,** caprice; whim. —**a gusto, 1,** at will. **2,** to one's taste or liking. **3,** at ease; in comfort. —**con (mucho) gusto,** with (great) pleasure. —**tener gusto en,** to be pleased to. —**tomar gusto a,** to take a liking to.
gustoso (gus'to·so) *adj.* **1,** tasty. **2,** willing; content. **3,** enjoyable.
gutapercha (gu·ta'per·tʃa) *n.f.* gutta-percha.
gutural (gu·tu'ral) *adj.* guttural

H

H, h ('a·tʃe) *n.f.* 9th letter of the Spanish alphabet.

ha (a) **1,** *v., 3rd pers.sing. pres.ind. of* **haber. 2,** *contr. of* **hace** *in expressions of time elapsed: dos años ha,* two years ago.

¡ha! (a) *interj.* ha!

haba ('ha·βa) *n.f.* **1,** broad bean; horse bean. **2,** *Amer.* Lima bean.

habanera (a·βa'ne·ra) *n.f.* a Cuban dance; the music and rhythm of this dance.

habano (a'βa·no) *n.m.* havana cigar.

haber (a'βer) *v.t.* [*pres.ind.* **he, has, ha, hemos** or **habemos, habéis, han**; *pres.subjve.* **haya**; *fut.* **habré**; *pret.* **hube**] **1,** *archaic* to have; own; possess. **2,** *archaic* to catch; lay hold of: *la maestra lee cuantos libros puede haber,* the teacher reads all the books she can lay hold of. —*v.i., used only in 3rd pers.* to be; exist; *no había piano en la casa,* there was no piano in the house. —*aux.v., used with p.p. to form compound tenses: el año ha terminado,* the year has ended; *he dado el sombrero a mi hermano,* I have given the hat to my brother. —*n.m.* **1,** *bookkeeping* credit; credit side of a ledger. **2,** wage; wages. —**haberes,** *n.m.pl.* assets. —**haber de, 1,** to have to: *he de salir temprano,* I have to leave early. **2,** to be to: *hemos de comer a las seis,* we are to dine at six o'clock. —**haber que,** to be necessary: *hubo que matarlo,* it was necessary to kill him. —**habérselas con,** to face; deal with. —**no hay de qué,** you're welcome; don't mention it.

habichuela (a·βi'tʃwe·la) *n.f.* kidney bean. —**habichuela verde,** string bean.

hábil ('a·βil) *adj.* skillful; clever; capable. —**día hábil** *or* **laborable,** work day.

habilidad (a·βi·li'ðað) *n.f.* talent; skill; ability.

habilidoso (a·βi·li'ðo·so) *adj.* skillful; able.

habilitar (a·βi·li'tar) *v.t.* **1,** to habilitate. **2,** to qualify; enable.

habitable (a·βi'ta·βle) *adj.* habitable.

habitación (a·βi·ta'θjon; -'sjon) *n.f.* **1,** room. **2,** habitation; dwelling. **3,** habitat.

habitante (a·βi'tan·te) *n.m.* & *f.* inhabitant.

habitar (a·βi'tar) *v.t.* to inhabit; live in; dwell in.

hábito ('a·βi·to) *n.m.* habit.

habitat ('a·βi·tat) *n.m.* habitat.

habitual (a·βi'twal) *adj.* customary; habitual.

habituar (a·βi'twar) *v.t.* to accustom; habituate. —**habituarse,** *v.r.* to become accustomed; accustom oneself.

habitué (a·βi·tu'e) *n.m.* habitué.

habla ('a·βla) *n.f.* speech; tongue; language. —**al habla,** in verbal contact; (*in answering the telephone*) speaking. —**de habla española,** Spanish-speaking.

hablador (a·βla'ðor) *adj.* talkative. —*n.m.* chatterbox.

habladuría (a·βla·ðu'ri·a) *n.f.* gossip; rumor.

hablar (a'βlar) *v.t.* **1,** to speak. **2,** to utter. —*v.i.* **1,** to speak. **2,** to talk. —**hablarse,** *v.r.* **1,** to be on speaking terms. **2,** *colloq.* to go steady. —**bien hablado,** well-spoken. —**hablar a chorros,** to speak fast.—**hablar a gritos,** to shout. —**hablar por hablar,** to talk idly. —**hablar por los codos,** to talk too much. —**mal hablado,** ill-tongued.

hablilla (a'βli·ʎa; -ja) *n.f.* = **habladuría.**

habré (a'βre) *v., fut. of* **haber.**

hacedero (a·θe'ðe·ro; a·se-) *adj.* feasible.

hacedor (a·θe'ðor; a·se-) *n.m.* maker.

hacendado (a·θen'da·ðo; a·sen-) *adj.* landed; owning land. —*n.m.* **1,** landholder. **2,** *Amer.* cattle rancher.

hacendoso (a·θen'do·so; a·sen-) *adj.* industrious; diligent.

hacer (a'θer; a'ser) *v.t.* [*pres.ind.* **hago, haces;** *pres.subjve.* **haga;** *impve.* **haz;** *fut.* **haré;** *pret.* **hice, hizo;** *p.p.* **hecho.**] **1,** to do. **2,** to make. **3,** to prepare. **4,** to produce. **5,** to cause; bring about. —*v.i.* **1,** to matter. **2,** to be pertinent. —*v. impers.* **1,** *in expressions of weather: hace buen tiempo,* it is good weather; *hace calor,* it is warm; *hace frío,* it is cold; *hace mal tiempo,* it is bad weather; *hace viento,* it is windy. **2,** *in expressions of time: ¿Cuánto hace?* How long ago? *Hace poco,* A short time ago. *¿Cuánto hace que Vd. me espera?* How long have you been waiting for me? *¿Cuánto tiempo hace que salieron?* How long ago did they leave? How long has it been since they left? *Hace tiempo que salieron,* They left a long time ago. *Hace tiempo me gustaba bailar,* A long time ago I was fond of dancing. —**hacerse,** *v.r.* **1,** to become. **2,** to pretend to be. **3,** to move; move over, **4,** to accustom oneself. —**hacer alarde,** to boast. —**hacer caso,** to mind; pay attention. —**hacer daño,** to hurt; harm. —**hacer falta,** to be lacking; be missing. —**hacer hacer una cosa,** to have something done: *Hicimos construir una casa,* We had a house built. —**hacerle a uno hacer algo,** to have someone do something. *Le hicimos venir ayer,* We had him come yesterday. —**hacer la maleta,** to pack one's suitcase. —**hacer un viaje,** to take a trip. —**hacer vida de artista,** to lead an artist's life. —**hacerse rogar,** to want to be coaxed. —**no le hace,** *colloq.* never mind; it makes no difference.

haces ('a·θes; 'a·ses) *n.m. or f., pl. of* **haz.**

hacia ('a·θja; 'a·sja) *prep.* **1,** toward. **2,** near; about: *hacia las ocho,* about eight o'clock. —**hacia acá,** this way. —**hacia adelante,** forward. —**hacia atrás,** backwards.

hacienda (a'θjen·da; a'sjen-) *n.f.* **1,** estate. **2,** large ranch. **3,** *Amer.* cattle. —**Ministerio de Hacienda,** Ministry of Finance *or* Economics; *U.S.* Department of the Treasury.

hacinar (a·θi'nar; a·si-) *v.t.* **1,** to stack; heap. **2,** to overcrowd.

hacha ('a·tʃa) *n.f.* ax; hatchet. —**hachazo,** *n.m.* blow of an ax or hatchet.

hachear (a·tʃe'ar) *v.t.* to chop; hew.

hada ('a·ða) *n.f.* fairy.

hado ('a·ðo) *n.m.* destiny; fate.

hafnio ('af·njo) *n.m.* hafnium.

haga ('a·ɣa) *v., pres.subjve. of* **hacer.**

hago ('a·ɣo) *v., 1st pers.sing. pres. ind. of* **hacer.**

¡hala! ('a·la) *also,* **¡hale!** ('a·le) *interj.* get going!; pull!

halagar (a·la'ɣar) *v.t.* [*infl.:* **pagar**] **1,** to flatter. **2,** to please; delight.

halago (a'la·ɣo) *n.m.* flattery.

halagüeño (a·la'ɣwe·ɲo) *adj.* **1,** attractive; delightful. **2,** flattering.

halar (a'lar) *v.t.* to pull; tug; haul.

halcón (al'kon) *n.m.* falcon. —**halconería,** *n.f.* falconry. —**halconero,** *n.m.* falconer.

halibut (a·li'βut) *n.m.* halibut.

hálito ('a·li·to) *n.m.* **1,** breath. **2,** *poet.* breeze.

halitosis (a·li'to·sis) *n.f.* halitosis.

halo ('a·lo) *n.m.* halo.

halo- (a·lo) *prefix* halo-; salt: *halógeno,* halogen.

halógeno (a'lo·xe·no) *adj.* & *n.m.* halogen.

hallar (a'ʎar; -'jar) *v.t.* to find; come upon. —**hallarse,** *v.r.* **1,** to be (in a certain place or condition). **2,** to feel (well or ill).

hallazgo (a'ʎaθ·ɣo; -'jas·ɣo) *n.m.* discovery; find; findings (*pl.*).

hamaca (a'ma·ka) *n.f.* hammock. —**hamacar,** *v.t., Amer.* [*infl.:* **tocar**] to swing; rock.

hamamelis (a·ma'me·lis) *n.m.* witch hazel.

hambre ('am·bre) *n.f.* hunger.

hambrear (am·bre'ar) *v.t.* & *i.* to starve.

hambriento (am'brjen·to) *adj.* hungry; starved.

hambruna (am'bru·na) *n.f., Amer.* famine.

hamburguesa (am·bur'ɣe·sa) *n.f., Amer.* hamburger.

hampa ('am·pa) *n.f.* underworld.

hámster ('ams·ter) *n.m.* & *f.* [*pl.* **hámsters**] hamster.

han (an) *v., 3rd. pers.pl. pres.ind. of* **haber.**

handicap ('an·di·kap) *n.m.* handicap.

hangar (an'gar) *n.m.* hangar.

haplo- (a·plo) *prefix* haplo-; simple; single: *haplología,* haplology.

haragán (a·ra'ɣan) *n.m.* loafer; lazy person. —*adj.* lazy; indolent.

haraganear (a·ra·ɣa·ne'ar) *v.i.* **1,** to be lazy. **2,** to idle; loaf.

harakiri (a·ra'ki·ri) *n.m.* harakiri.

harapo (a'ra·po) *n.m.* rag. —**harapiento,** *also,* **haraposo,** *adj.* tattered; ragged.

haré (a're) *v., fut. of* **hacer.**

harén (a'ren) *also,* **harem** (a'rem) *n.m.* harem.
harina (a'ri·na) *n.f.* **1,** flour. **2,** meal; grounds (*pl.*); *Amer.* coffee grounds. —**harina de otro costal,** *colloq.* a horse of a different color.
harinoso (a·ri'no·so) *adj.* mealy.
harmonía (ar·mo'ni·a) *n.f.* = **armonía.**
harnero (ar'ne·ro) *n.m.* sifter; sieve.
harpa ('ar·pa) *n.f.* = **arpa.**
harpía (ar'pi·a) *n.f.* = **arpía.**
harpillera (ar·pi'ʎe·ra; -'je·ra) *n.f.* burlap.
hartar (ar'tar) *v.t.* **1,** to satiate. **2,** to glut. **3,** *fig.* to bother. —**hartarse,** *v.r.* **1,** to overeat. **2,** *colloq.* to be fed up.
harto ('ar·to) *adj.* **1,** satiated; full. **2,** *colloq.* fed up. —*adv.* enough.
has (as) *v., 2nd pers.sing. pres.ind. of* **haber.**
hasta ('as·ta) *prep.* until; as far as; up to. —*conj.* also; even. —**hasta ahora, 1,** heretofore. **2,** *colloq.* = **hasta luego.** —**hasta luego,** see you later; so long.
hastiar (as'tjar) *v.t.* [*infl.:* **enviar**] **1,** to surfeit. **2,** to bore. **3,** to disgust; sicken.
hastío (as'ti·o) *n.m.* **1,** excess; surfeit. **2,** boredom. **3,** disgust.
hato ('a·to) *n.m.* **1,** herd; flock. **2,** heap; lot. **3,** gang; band. —**liar el hato** *or* **el petate,** to get ready to go; pack.
haxix ('a·ʃiʃ) *n.m.* hashish.
hay (ai) *adverbial expression* (*formed from* **ha** + *archaic* **y,** there) there is; there are: *hay mucho que ver en esta ciudad,* there is much to see in this city. —**hay para,** *fol. by a noun* **1,** there is enough: *hay comida para todos,* there is enough food for everybody. **2,** there is something: *hay para todos los gustos,* there is something for every taste. *Fol. by inf.* it makes you want to: *Hay para reírse,* It makes you want to laugh. *Hay para matarlo,* It makes you want to kill him. —**hay que,** it is necessary. —**no hay de qué,** You're welcome; don't mention it. —**no hay remedio,** it can't be helped. —**¿qué hay?** what's the matter? —**¿qué hay de nuevo?** what's new?
haya ('a·ja) *n.f.* beech tree. —**hayuco** (a'ju·ko) *n.m.* beechnut.
haya ('a·ja) *v., pres.subjve. of* **haber.**
haz (aθ; as) *n.m.* [*pl.* **haces**] **1,** bundle; fagot; sheaf. **2,** beam, as of light. —*n.m. or f.* face; surface.
haz (aθ; as) *v., impve.sing. of* **hacer.**
hazaña (a'θa·ɲa; a'sa-) *n.f.* deed; feat.
hazmerreír (aθ·me·rre'ir; as-) *n.m.* laughingstock.
he (e) *interj.* behold; *usu.fol. by* **aquí** *or* **allí** *or by a pronoun: he aquí,* here you have; here is; here are. *Heme aquí,* Here I am. *Helos allí,* There they are. *He aquí que llegó,* Lo and behold, he has arrived.
he (e) *v., 1st.pers.sing. pres.ind. of* **haber.**
hebilla (e'βi·ʎa; -ja) *n.f.* buckle; clasp.
hebra ('e·βra) *n.f.* **1,** thread. **2,** fiber. **3,** *mining* vein. **4,** grain (*of wood*). —**de una hebra,** *Amer.* all at once.
hebreo (e'βre·o) *adj.* & *n.m.* Hebrew.
hebraico (e'βrai·ko) *adj.* Hebrew; Hebraic.
hebroso (e'βro·so) *adj.* fibrous; stringy.
hecatombe (e·ka'tom·be) *n.f.* hecatomb.
heces ('e·θes; 'e·ses) *n.f.pl.* **1,** feces. **2,** dregs. **3,** *fig.* scum; riffraff.
hectárea (ek'ta·re·a) *n.f.* hectare.
hecto- (ek·to) *prefix* hecto-; hundred: *hectogramo,* hectogram.
hectogramo (ek·to'ɣra·mo) *n.m.* hectogram.
hectolitro (ek·to'li·tro) *n.m.* hectoliter.
hectómetro (ek'to·me·tro) *n.m.* hectometer.
hechicero (e·tʃi'θe·ro; -'se·ro) *adj.* bewitching. —*n.m.* sorcerer. —**hechicera,** *n.f.* witch. —**hechicería,** *n.f.* witchcraft; sorcery.
hechizar (e·tʃi'θar; -'sar) *v.t.* [*pres.subjve.* **hechice** (-'tʃi·θe; -se); *pret.* **hechicé** (-'θe; -'se)] to bewitch.
hechizo (e'tʃi·θo; -so) *n.m.* enchantment; spell.
hecho ('e·tʃo) *v., p.p. of* **hacer.** —*adj.* **1,** made. **2,** ready-made. **3,** done. **4,** ripe. —*n.m.* **1,** fact. **2,** act; deed. **3,** event. —**bien hecho. 1,** well done. **2,** right. —**hecho y de-**

recho, perfect. —**mal hecho, 1,** badly done. **2,** wrong.
hechura (e'tʃu·ra) *n.f.* **1,** creation; handiwork. **2,** form; cut; shape. **3,** image; likeness. **4,** workmanship. —**hechuras,** *n.f.pl.* cost of making.
heder (e'ðer) *v.i.* [*pres.ind.* **hiedo;** *pres.subjve.* **hieda**] to stink.
hediondo (e'ðjon·do) *adj.* stinking; fetid. —**hediondez,** *n.f.* fetidness.
hedonismo (e·ðo'nis·mo) *n.m.* hedonism. —**hedonista,** *n.m.* & *f.* hedonist. —*adj.* hedonistic.
hedor (e'ðor) *n.m.* stench; stink.
hegemonía (e·xe·mo'ni·a) *n.f.* hegemony.
helada (e'la·ða) *n.f.* frost.
heladera (e·la'ðe·ra) *n.f.* **1,** [*also,* **heladora**] ice cream freezer. **2,** *Amer.* refrigerator.
heladería (e·la·ðe'ri·a) *n.f., Amer.* ice cream parlor.
helado (e'la·ðo) *adj.* frozen. —*n.m.* ice cream.
helar (e'lar) *v.t.* [*pres.ind.* **hielo;** *pres.subjve.* **hiele**] **1,** to freeze; congeal. **2,** *fig.* to shock; stupefy.
helecho (e'le·tʃo) *n.m.* fern.
helénico (e'le·ni·ko) *adj.* Hellenic; Greek.
hélice ('e·li·θe; -se) *n.f.* **1,** helix. **2,** propeller.
helico- (e·li·ko) *prefix* helico-; spiral; helix: *helicóptero,* helicopter.
helicóptero (e·li'kop·te·ro) *n.m.* helicopter.
helio ('e·ljo) *n.m.* helium.
helio- (e·ljo) *prefix* helio-; sun: *heliógrafo,* heliograph.
heliocéntrico (e·ljo'θen·tri·ko; -'sen·tri·ko) *adj.* heliocentric.
heliógrafo (e'ljo·ɣra·fo) *n.m.* heliograph.
heliotropo (e·ljo'tro·po) *n.m.* heliotrope.
hema- (e·ma) *also,* **hemo-** (e·mo) *prefix* hema-; hemo-; blood: *hemacroma,* hemachrome; *hemorragia,* hemorrhage.
hemato- (e·ma·to) *also,* **hemat-** (e·mat) *before vowels; prefix* hemato-; hemat-; blood: *hematólisis,* hematolysis; *hematémesis,* hematemesis.
hembra ('em·bra) *n.f.* **1,** female. **2,** *sewing* eye of a hook. **3,** *mech.* nut of a screw.
hembrilla (em'bri·ʎa; -ja) *n.f.* grommet; eyelet.
hemi- (e·mi) *prefix* hemi-; half: *hemiciclo,* hemycicle.
hemiplejía (e·mi·ple'xi·a) *n.f.* hemiplegia. —**hemipléjico** (-'ple·xi·ko) *adj.* & *n.m.* hemiplegic.
hemisferio (e·mis'fe·rjo) *n.m.* hemisphere. —**hemisférico** (-'fe·ri·ko) *adj.* hemispheric; hemispherical.
hemo- (e·mo) *prefix, var. of* **hema-.**
hemofilia (e·mo'fi·lja) *n.f.* hemophilia. —**hemofílico** (-'fi·li·ko) *adj.* hemophilic. —*n.m.* hemophiliac.
hemoglobina (e·mo·ɣlo'βi·na) *n.f.* hemoglobin.
hemorragia (e·mo'rra·xja) *n.f.* hemorrhage.
hemorroides (e·mo'rroi·ðes) *n.f. pl.* hemorrhoids.
hemos ('e·mos) *v. 1st pers.pl. pres. ind. of* **haber.**
henal (e'nal) *n.m.* = **henil.**
henar (e'nar) *n.m.* hayfield.
henchir (en'tʃir) *v.t.* [*pres.ind.* **hincho;** *pres.subjve.* **hincha;** *pret.* **henchí, hinchió**] to fill up; stuff; heap.
hender (en'der) *v.t.* [*pres.ind.* **hiendo;** *pres.subjve.* **hienda**] to crack; split.
hendidura (en·di'ðu·ra) *also,* **hendedura** (en·de-) *n.f.* crack; fissure.
henequén (e·ne'ken) *n.m.* **1,** sisal plant. **2,** sisal fiber.
henil (e'nil) *n.m.* hayloft.
heno ('e·no) *n.m.* hay.
heñir (e'ɲir) *v.t.* [*infl.:* **teñir**] to knead.
hepática (e'pa·ti·ka) *n.f.* hepatica.
hepático (e'pa·ti·ko) *adj.* hepatic.
hepatitis (e·pa'ti·tis) *n.f.* hepatitis.
hepta- (ep·ta) *prefix* hepta-; seven: *heptágono,* heptagon.
heptágono (ep'ta·ɣo·no) *n.m.* heptagon. —**heptagonal,** *adj.* heptagonal.
heraldo (e'ral·do) *n.m.* herald. —**heráldico,** *adj.* heraldic. —**heráldica,** *n.f.* heraldry.
herbáceo (er'βa·θe·o; -se·o) *adj.* herbaceous.
herbaje (er'βa·xe) *n.m.* herbage; grass.
herbario (er'βa·rjo) *adj.* herbal. —*n.m.* **1,** herbarium. **2,** herbal.
herbazal (er·βa'θal; -'sal) *n.m.* field of grass.
herbívoro (er'βi·βo·ro) *adj.* herbivorous.

herboso (er'βo·so) *adj.* grassy.
hercúleo (er'ku·le·o) *adj.* Herculean.
heredad (e·re'ðað) *n.f.* country estate.
heredar (e·re'ðar) *v.t.* to inherit. —**heredable,** *adj.* heritable.
heredera (e·re'ðe·ra) *n.f.* heiress.
heredero (e·re'ðe·ro) *n.m.* heir; inheritor. —**heredero forzoso,** heir apparent. —**presunto heredero,** heir presumptive.
hereditario (e·re·ði'ta·rjo) *adj.* hereditary.
hereje (e're·xe) *n.m.* & *f.* heretic. —**herejía,** *n.f.* heresy.
herencia (e'ren·θja; -sja) *n.f.* **1,** estate. **2,** heritage. **3,** heredity.
herético (e're·ti·ko) *adj.* heretical.
herida (e'ri·ða) *n.f.* wound.
herir (e'rir) *v.t.* [*pres.ind.* **hiero;** *pres. subjve.* **hiera;** *pret.* **herí** (e'ri), **hirió;** *ger.* **hiriendo**] to wound; hurt.
hermafrodita (er·ma·fro'ði·ta) *n.m.* & *f.* hermaphrodite. —*adj.* hermaphroditic.
hermana (er'ma·na) *n.f.* sister.
hermanar (er·ma'nar) *v.t.* & *i.* to match; harmonize; conform.
hermanastro (er·ma'nas·tro) *n.m.* stepbrother. —**hermanastra,** *n.f.* stepsister.
hermandad (er·man'dað) *n.f.* **1,** brotherhood; fraternity. **2,** sisterhood; sorority.
hermano (er'ma·no) *n.m.* brother. —**hermanos,** *n.m.pl.* brothers; brothers and sisters. —**hermano de leche** *or* **de crianza,** foster brother. —**hermano político,** brother-in-law.
hermético (er'me·ti·ko) *adj.* hermetic; airtight.
hermosear (er·mo·se'ar) *v.t.* to beautify.
hermoso (er'mo·so) *adj.* beautiful; handsome; lovely. —**hermosura,** *n.f.* beauty; handsomeness.
hernia ('er·nja) *n.f.* hernia.
héroe ('e·ro·e) *n.m.* hero.
heroico (e'roi·ko) *adj.* heroic.
heroína (e·ro'i·na) *n.f.* **1,** heroine. **2,** heroin.
heroísmo (e·ro'is·mo) *n.m.* heroism.
herpetología (er·pe·to·lo'xi·a) *n.f.* herpetology. —**herpetólogo** (-'to·lo·ɣo) *n.m.* herpetologist.
herrador (e·rra'ðor) *n.m.* blacksmith.
herradura (e·rra'ðu·ra) *n.f.* horseshoe.
herraje (e'rra·xe) *n.m.* **1,** ironwork; iron fittings. **2,** horseshoe and nails.
herramienta (e·rra'mjen·ta) *n.f.* tool; implement.
herrar (e'rrar) *v.t.* [*pres.ind.* **hierro;** *pres.subjve.* **hierre**] **1,** to shoe (a horse). **2,** to brand (cattle).
herrería (e·rre'ri·a) *n.f.* **1,** blacksmithing. **2,** blacksmith's shop.
herrero (e'rre·ro) *n.m.* blacksmith.
herrumbre (e'rrum·bre) *n.f.* **1,** rust. **2,** iron taste.
hervidero (er·βi'ðe·ro) *n.m.* **1,** bubbling (*of boiling liquids*). **2,** bubbling spring. **3,** swarm; mass; throng.
hervir (er'βir) *v.t.* & *i.* [*pres.ind.* **hiervo;** *pres.subjve.* **hierva;** *pret.* **herví** (-'βi), **hirvió;** *ger.* **hirviendo**] to boil.
hervor (er'βor) *n.m.* **1,** boiling. **2,** boiling point. **3,** *fig.* restlessness; fervor.
hesitar (e·si'tar) *v.i., rare* to hesitate. —**hesitación,** *n.f., rare* hesitation.
hetero- (e·te·ro) *prefix* hetero-; other; different: *heterosexual,* heterosexual.
heterodoxo (e·te·ro'ðok·so) *adj.* heterodox. —**heterodoxia** (-'ðok·sja) *n.f.* heterodoxy.
heterogéneo (e·te·ro'xe·ne·o) *adj.* heterogeneous.
hexa- (ek·sa) *prefix* hexa-; six: *hexágono,* hexagon.
hexágono (ek'sa·ɣo·no) *n.m.* hexagon. —**hexagonal,** *adj.* hexagonal.
hez (eθ; es) *n.f.* [*pl.* **heces**] scum.
hiato (i'a·to) *n.m.* hiatus.
hibernal (i·βer'nal) *adj.* hibernal.
hibernar (i·βer'nar) *v.i.* to hibernate. —**hibernación,** *n.f.* hibernation.
hibisco (i'βis·ko) *n.m.* hibiscus.
híbrido ('i·βri·ðo) *adj.* & *n.m.* hybrid; mongrel. —**hibridismo,** *n.m.* hybridism.
hice ('i·θe; 'i·se) *v., 1st pers.sing. pret. of* **hacer.**
hidalgo (i'ðal·ɣo) *n.m.* Spanish nobleman. —*adj.* noble.
hidalguía (i·ðal'ɣi·a) *n.f.* nobility.
hidratar (i·ðra'tar) *v.t.* to hydrate. —**hidratación,** n.m. hydration.

hidrato (i'ðra·to) *n.m.* hydrate.
hidráulico (i'ðrau·li·ko) *adj.* hydraulic. —**hidráulica,** *n.f.* hydraulics.
hidro- (i·ðro) *prefix* hydro-. **1,** water: *hidroeléctrico,* hydroelectric. **2,** *chem.* hydrogen: *hidrocarbono,* hydrocarbon.
hidroavión (i·ðro·a'βjon) *n.m.* hydroplane; seaplane.
hidrocarburo (i·ðro·kar'βu·ro) *n.m.* hydrocarbon.
hidrodinámico (i·ðro·ði'na·mi·ko) *adj.* hydrodynamic. —**hidrodinámica,** *n.f.* hydrodynamics.
hidroeléctrico (i·ðro·e'lek·tri·ko) *adj.* hydroelectric, —**hidroeléctrica,** *n.f.* hydroelectrics.
hidrófilo (i'ðro·fi·lo) *adj.* absorbent.
hidrofobia (i·ðro'fo·βja) *n.f.* hydrophobia. —**hidrófobo** (i'ðro·fo·βo) *adj.* hydrophobic. —*n.m.* hydrophobe.
hidrogenar (i·ðro·ɣe'nar) *v.t.* to hydrogenate. —**hidrogenación,** *n.f.* hydrogenation.
hidrógeno (i'ðro·xe·no) *n.m.* hydrogen.
hidrómetro (i'ðro·me·tro) *n.m.* hydrometer.
hidromiel (i·ðro'mjel) *n.m.* mead. *Also,* **hidromel** (-'mel).
hidropesía (i·ðro·pe'si·a) *n.f.* dropsy.
hidrópico (i'ðro·pi·ko) *adj.* **1,** dropsical. **2,** extremely thirsty. **3,** insatiable.
hidroplano (i·ðro'pla·no) *n.m.* = **hidroavión.**
hieda ('je·ða) *v., pres.subjve. of* **heder.**
hiedo ('je·ðo) *v., pres.ind. of* **heder.**
hiedra ('je·ðra) *n.f.* ivy.
hiel (jel) *n.f.* **1,** gall; bile. **2,** *fig.* bitterness.
hiele ('je·le) *v., pres.subjve. of* **helar.**
hielo ('je·lo) *n.m.* ice.
hielo ('je·lo) *v., pres.ind. of* **helar.**
hiena ('je·na) *n.f.* hyena.
hienda ('jen·da) *v., pres.subjve. of* **hender.**
hiendo ('jen·do) *v., pres.ind. of* **hender.**
hiera ('je·ra) *v., pres.subjve. of* **herir.**
hierba ('jer·βa) *n.f.* **1,** grass; weed. **2,** herb. —**mala hierba,** *colloq.* **1,** wayward person. **2,** ill-bred person.
hierbabuena (jer·βa'βwe·na) *n.f.* mint.
hierba mora ('mo·ra) nightshade.
hiero ('je·ro) *v., pres.ind. of* **herir.**
hierre ('je·rre) *v., pres.subjve. of* **herrar.**
hierro ('je·rro) *n.m.* iron. —**hierro colado** *or* **fundido,** cast iron. —**hierro dulce,** wrought iron.
hierro ('je·rro) *v., pres.ind. of* **herrar.**
hierva ('jer·βa) *v., pres.subjve. of* **hervir.**
hiervo ('jer·βo) *v., pres.ind. of* **hervir.**
hígado ('i·ɣa·ðo) *n.m.* liver.
higiene (i'xje·ne) *n.f.* hygiene. —**higiene pública,** public health.
higiénico (i'xje·ni·ko) *adj.* hygienic; sanitary.
higienista (i·xje'nis·ta) *n.m.* & *f.* hygienist.
higo ('i·ɣo) *n.m.* fig. —**higo chumbo; higo de tuna,** prickly pear. —**no doy un higo por,** I don't give a rap for. —**no se me da un higo,** I don't care a rap.
higrómetro (i'ɣro·me·tro) *n.m.* hygrometer. —**higrométrico** (-'me·tri·ko) *adj.* hygrometric.
higuera (i'ɣe·ra) *n.f.* fig tree. —**higuera chumba; higuera de tuna,** prickly pear cactus. —**higuera india,** banyan.
hija ('i·xa) *n.f.* daughter.
hijastro (i'xas·tro) *n.m.* stepchild; stepson. —**hijastra,** *n.m.* stepdaughter.
hijo ('i·xo) *n.m.* **1,** son; child. **2,** junior; Jr. —**hijo de leche** *or* **de crianza,** foster child. —**hijo político,** son-in-law.
hila ('i·la) *n.f.* **1,** row; line. **2,** *usu. pl.* dressing for a wound.
hilacha (i'la·tʃa) *n.f.* shred. —**hilachas,** *n.f.pl.* lint. —**hilachos,** *n.m. pl., Amer.* tatters.
hilada (i'la·ða) *n.f.* **1,** course (*of masonry*). **2,** = **hilera.**
hilado (i'la·ðo) *n.m.* **1,** spinning. **2,** yarn.
hilandera (i·lan'de·ra) *n.f.* spinner.
hilandería (i·lan·de'ri·a) *n.f.* **1,** spinning. **2,** spinning mill.
hilar (i'lar) *v.t.* & *i.* to spin.
hilarante (i·la'ran·te) *adj.* hilarious.
hilaridad (i·la·ri'ðað) *n.f.* hilarity.

hilaza (i'la·θa; -sa) *n.f.* coarse thread.
hilera (i'le·ra) *n.f.* row; line.
hilo ('i·lo) *n.m.* **1,** thread; fine yarn. **2,** string. **3,** wire. **4,** linen. —**a hilo,** without interruption. —**al hilo, 1,** along the weave. **2,** = **al filo.** —**hilo bramante,** twine. —**hilo de Escocia,** lisle. —**hilo de medianoche** (*or* **mediodía**), midnight (*or* noon) sharp.
hilván (il'βan) *n.m., sewing* basting; tacking.
hilvanar (il·βa'nar) *v.t.* **1,** *sewing* to baste; tack. **2,** *fig.* to do hastily; patch.
himen ('i·men) *n.m.* hymen.
himeneo (i·me'ne·o) *n.m.* marriage; hymen.
himno ('im·no) *n.m.* hymn. —**himnario,** *n.m.* hymnal.
hincapié (in·ka'pje) *n.m., in* **hacer hincapié en,** to emphasize.
hincar (in'kar) *v.t.* [*pres.subjve.* **hinque;** *pret.* **hinqué**] to thrust in; drive in. —**hincarse,** *v.r.* to kneel. —**hincar el diente,** to bite.
hincha ('in·tʃa) *n.m.* & *f., colloq.* **1,** grudge; ill will. **2,** *sports* fan; rooter.
hincha ('in·tʃa) *v., pres.subjve. of* **henchir.**
hinchar (in'tʃar) *v.t.* to swell; inflate. —**hincharse,** *v.t.* **1,** to swell. **2,** to become conceited; put on airs.
hinchazón (in·tʃa'θon; -'son) *n.m.* **1,** swelling. **2,** *fig.* conceit; vanity. **3,** *fig., colloq.* bellyful.
hinchió (in'tʃjo) *v., 3rd pers.sing. pret. of* **henchir.**
hincho ('in·tʃo) *v., pres.ind. of* **henchir.**
hindú (in'du) *adj.* & *n.m.* & *f.* Hindu. —**hinduísmo,** *n.m.* Hinduism.
hinojo (i'no·xo) *n.m.* **1,** fennel. **2,** knee; *only in* **de hinojos,** kneeling.
hinque ('in·ke) *v., pres.subjve. of* **hincar.**
hinqué (in'ke) *v., 1st.pers.sing. pret. of* **hincar.**
hiña ('i·ɲa) *v., pres.subjve. of* **heñir.**
hiñendo (i'ɲen·do) *v., ger. of* **heñir.**
hiño ('i·ɲo) *v., pres.ind. of* **heñir.**
hiñó (i'ɲo) *v., 3rd pers.sing. pret. of* **heñir.**
hipar (i'par) *v.i.* **1,** to hiccup. **2,** to pant. —**hipar por,** to yearn for; crave.
hiper- (i·per) *prefix* hyper-; over; above; beyond: *hipersensitivo,* hypersensitive.
hipérbola (i'per·βo·la) *n.f.* hyperbola. —**hiperbólico** (-'βo·li·ko) *adj.* hyperbolic.
hipérbole (i'per·βo·le) *n.f.* hyperbole.
hipertrofia (i·per'tro·fja) *n.f.* hypetrophy. —**hipertrofiarse** (-'fjar·se) *v.r.* to hypertrophy.
hípico ('i·pi·ko) *adj.* horse (*attrib.*); equestrian.
hipido (i'pi·ðo) *n.m.* hiccups (*pl.*).
hipnosis (ip'no·sis) *n.f.* hypnosis. —**hipnótico** (-'no·ti·ko) *adj.* hypnotic. —**hipnotismo** (-'tis·mo) *n.m.* hypnotism.
hipnotizar (ip·no·ti'θar; -'sar) *v.t.* [*pres.subjve.* **hipnotice** (-'ti·θe; -se); *pret.* **hipnoticé** (-'θe; -'se)] to hypnotize. —**hipnotizador,** *n.m.* hypnotist.
hipo ('i·po) *n.m.* **1,** hiccup. **2,** panting. —**tener hipo de** *or* **por,** to yearn for; crave.
hipo- (i·po) *prefix* **1,** hippo-; horse: *hipódromo,* hippodrome. **2,** hypo-; beneath; below; under: *hipodérmico,* hypodermic; *hipotaxis,* hypotaxis; *hipoplasia,* hypoplasia. **3,** *chem.* hypo-; least degree of oxidation: *hiposulfuro,* hyposulfite.
hipocondría (i·po·kon'dri·a) *n.f.* hypochondria. —**hipocondríaco,** *adj.* & *n.m.* hypochondriac.
hipocresía (i·po·kre'si·a) *n.f.* hypocrisy; insincerity.
hipócrita (i'po·kri·ta) *n.m.* & *f.* hypocrite. —*adj.* hypocritical.
hipodérmico (i·po'ðer·mi·ko) *adj.* & *n.m.* hypodermic.
hipódromo (i'po·ðro·mo) *n.m.* hippodrome; race track.
hipopótamo (i·po'po·ta·mo) *n.m.* hippopotamus.
hiposo (i'po·so) *adj.* suffering from hiccups.
hipoteca (i·po'te·ka) *n.f.* mortgage. —**hipotecario,** *adj.* mortgage (*attrib.*)
hipotecar (i·po·te'kar) *v.t.* [*infl.:* **tocar**] to mortgage.
hipotenusa (i·po·te'nu·sa) *n.f.* hypotenuse.
hipótesis (i'po·te·sis) *n.f.* hypothesis. —**hipotético** (-'te·ti·ko) *adj.* hypothetical.
hiriendo (i'rjen·do) *v., ger. of* **herir.**

hiriente (i'rjen·te) *v., pr.p. of* **herir.** —*adj.* cutting; hurtful.
hirió (i'rjo) *v., 3rd pers.sing. pret. of* **herir.**
hirsuto (ir'su·to) *adj.* hirsute.
hirviendo (ir'βjen·do) *v., ger. of* **hervir.**
hirvió (ir'βjo) *v., 3rd pers.sing. pret. of* **hervir.**
hisopo (i'so·po) *n.m.* hyssop.
hispánico (is'pa·ni·ko) *adj.* Hispanic.
hispano (is'pa·no) *adj.* **1,** Hispanic; Spanish. **2,** Spanish-American. —*n.m.* **1,** Spaniard. **2,** Spanish-American.
hispanoamericano (is·pa·no·a·me·ri'ka·no) *adj. & n.m.* Spanish-American.
histamina (is·ta'mi·na) *n.f.* histamine.
histerectomía (is·te·rek·to'mi·a) *n.f.* hysterectomy.
histeria (is'te·rja) *n.f.* **1,** hysteria. **2,** hysterics (*pl.*). *Also,* **histerismo,** *n.m.*
histérico (is'te·ri·ko) *adj.* hysterical. —*n.m.* hysteric.
histero- (is·te·ro) *prefix* hystero-. **1,** womb; uterus: *histerotomía,* hysterotomy. **2,** hysteria: *histerógeno,* hysterogenic.
histo- (is·to) *prefix* histo-; tissue: *histología,* hystology.
histología (is·to·lo'xi·a) *n.f.* histology. —**histológico** (-'lo·xi·ko) *adj.* histological. —**histólogo** (-'to·lo·ɣo) *n.m.* histologist.
historia (is'to·rja) *n.f.* **1,** history. **2,** story. **3,** fable; tale. —**historias,** *n.f.pl.* idle talk; palaver.
historiado (is·to'rja·ðo) *adj.* **1,** ornate; elaborate. **2,** *colloq.* storytelling; full of stories.
historiador (is·to·rja'ðor) *n.m.* historian.
historial (is·to'rjal) *n.* case history; record.
historiar (is·to'rjar) *v.t.* to write the history *or* story of.
histórico (is'to·ri·ko) *adj.* historical; historic. —**historicidad** (-θi·'ðað; -si'ðað) *n.f.* historicity.
historieta (is·to'rje·ta) *n.f.* **1,** short story. **2,** *pl.* comics; comic strips.
histriónico (is'trjo·ni·ko) *adj.* histrionic. —**histrionismo,** *n.m.* histrionics (*pl.*).
hito ('i·to) *adj.* fixed; firm. —*n.m.* landmark; guidepost; milestone. —**dar en el hito,** to hit the mark. —**mirar de hito en hito,** to fix with one's gaze.
hizo ('i·θo; -so) *v. 3rd pers.sing. pret. of* **hacer.**
hoce ('o·θe; 'o·se) *v., pres. subjve. of* **hozar.**
hocé (o'θe; o'se) *v., 1st pers.sing. pret. of* **hozar.**
hoces ('o·θes; 'o·ses) *n.f., pl. of* **hoz.**
hocicar (o·θi'kar; o·si-) *v.t.* [*pres. subjve.* **hocique** (o'θi·ke; o'si·ke); *pret.* **hociqué** (-'ke)] **1,** to root. **2,** to nuzzle. —*v.i., colloq.* to run smack up against a difficulty.
hocico (o'θi·ko; o'si-) *n.m.* **1,** snout. **2,** *slang* mug; kisser. **3,** *colloq.* pout; sulk. —**darse de hocicos, 1,** to fall flat on one's face. **2,** = **hocicar,** *v.i.*
hockey ('xo·ki) *n.m.* hockey.
hogaño (o'ɣa·ɲo) *adv.* nowadays.
hogar (o'ɣar) *n.m.* **1,** hearth; fireplace. **2,** home.
hogareño (o·ɣa're·ɲo) *adj.* **1,** homeloving. **2,** homey; cosy. **3,** of the home or family.
hoguera (o'ɣe·ra) *n.f.* blaze; bonfire.
hoja ('o·xa) *n.f.* **1,** leaf. **2,** sheet (*of paper or metal*). **3,** veneer. **4,** blade. **5,** pane; panel. —**hoja de lata,** tin plate. —**hoja suelta,** leaflet.
hojalata (o·xa'la·ta) *n.f.* tin plate.
hojalatería (o·xa·la·te'ri·a) *n.f.* **1,** tinware. **2,** tin shop. —**hojalatero** (-'te·ro) *n.m.* tinsmith.
hojaldre (o'xal·dre) *n.m. or f.* puff paste.
hojarasca (o·xa'ras·ka) *n.f.* **1,** dead leaves. **2,** excessive foliage. **3,** *fig.* rubbish.
hojear (o·xe'ar) *v.t.* to leaf through (a book). —*v.i.* to flake; scale off.
hojuela (o'xwe·la) *n.f.* **1,** pancake. **2,** gold or silver foil, used esp. in embroidery. **3,** tin foil or other metal foil.
¡hola! ('o·la) *interj.* hello! hi!
holanda (o'lan·da) *n.f.* Dutch linen.
holandés (o·lan'des) *adj.* Dutch. —*n.m.* **1,** Dutchman. **2,** Dutch language.
holgado (ol'ɣa·ðo) *adj.* **1,** loose; wide; roomy. **2,** comfortable; well-off. **3,** idle; at one's ease.
holganza (ol'ɣan·θa; -sa) *n.f.* **1,** leisure. **2,** idleness. **3,** recreation.

holgar (ol'ɣar) *v.i.* [*pres.ind.* **huelgo;** *pres.subjve.* **huelgue;** *pret.* **holgué]** **1,** to rest. **2,** to be idle. —**holgarse,** *v.r.* **1,** to be glad. **2,** to amuse oneself.
holgazán (ol·ɣa'θan; -'san) *n.m.* loafer; idler. —*adj.* lazy; indolent. —**holgazanear,** *v.i.* to idle; loiter. —**holgazanería,** *n.f.* idleness.
holgorio (ol'ɣo·rjo; xol-) *n.m., colloq.* revel; frolic. *Also,* **jolgorio.**
holgué (ol'ɣe) *v., 1st pers.sing.pret. of* **holgar.**
holgura (ol'ɣu·ra) *n.f.* **1,** comfort; ease. **2,** roominess; looseness.
holmio ('ol·mjo) *n.m.* holmium.
holo- (o·lo) *prefix* holo-; entire; whole: *holocausto,* holocaust.
holocausto (o·lo'kaus·to) *n.m.* holocaust.
hológrafo (o'lo·ɣra·fo) *adj.* & *n.m.* = **ológrafo.**
hollar (o'ʎar; -'jar) *v.t.* [*pres.ind.* **huello;** *pres.subjve.* **huelle]** to tread upon; step on.
hollejo (o'ʎe·xo; o'je-) *n.m.* thin skin *or* peel of certain fruits and vegetables.
hollín (o'ʎin; o'jin) *n.m.* soot. —**holliniento,** *adj.* sooty.
hombrada (om'bra·ða) *n.f.* manly deed; act of valor.
hombre ('om·bre) *n.m.* **1,** man. **2,** mankind. **3,** *colloq.* husband. —**hombre al agua,** man overboard. —**hombre de bien,** man of honor or integrity.
hombría (om'bri·a) *n.f.* manliness; courage. —**hombría de bien,** honesty; integrity.
hombro ('om·bro) *n.m.* shoulder. —**arrimar el hombro,** to lend a hand. —**echarse al hombro,** to shoulder; take responsibility for. —**encogerse de hombros,** to shrug one's shoulders. —**mirar por encima del hombro,** to shrug off; ignore.
hombruno (om'bru·no) *adj., colloq., derog.* mannish.
homenaje (o·me'na·xe) *n.m.* homage.
homeo- (o·me·o) *prefix* homeo-; similar; like: *homeopatía,* homeopathy.
homeopatía (o·me·o·pa'ti·a) *n.f.* homeopathy. —**homeópata** (-'o·pa·ta) *n.m.* homeopath. —**homeopático** (-'pa·ti·ko) *adj.* homeopathic.
homicida (o·mi'θi·ða; -'si·ða) *n.m.* murderer. —*n.f.* murderess. —*adj.* murderous; homicidal.
homicidio (o·mi'θi·ðjo; -'si·ðjo) *n.m.* homicide; murder.
homilético (o·mi'le·ti·ko) *adj.* homiletic. —**homilética,** *n.f.* homiletics (*pl.*).
homilía (o·mi'li·a) *n.f.* homily.
homo- (o·mo) *prefix* homo-; same: *homogéneo,* homogeneous.
homófono (o'mo·fo·no) *adj.* homophonous; homophonic. —*n.m.* homophone. —**homofonía** (-'ni·a) *n.f.* homophony.
homogéneo (o·mo'xe·ne·o) *adj.* homogeneous. —**homogeneidad,** (-ne·i'ðað) *n.f.* homogeneity.
homogenizar (o·mo·xe·ni'θar; -'sar) *v.t.* [*pres.subjve.* **homogenice** (-'ni·θe; -se); *pret.* **homogenicé** (-'θe; -'se)] to homogenize. —**homogenización,** *n.f.* homogenization.
homólogo (o'mo·lo·ɣo) *adj.* homologous. —**homología** (-'xi·a) *n.f.* homology.
homónimo (o'mo·ni·mo) *adj.* homonymous. —*n.m.* **1,** homonym. **2,** namesake.
homosexual (o·mo·sek'swal) *adj.* & *n.m.* & *f.* homosexual. —**homosexualidad,** *n.f.* homosexuality.
honda ('on·da) *n.f.* sling; slingshot.
hondo ('on·do) *adj.* deep. —*n.m.* bottom; depth.
hondonada (on·do'na·ða) *n.f.* hollow; dale.
hondura (on'du·ra) *n.f.* depth. —**meterse en honduras,** *colloq.* to get in over one's depth.
honesto (o'nes·to) *adj.* honest; upright; decent. —**honestidad,** *n.f.* honesty; uprightness.
hongo ('on·go) *n.m.* **1,** mushroom. **2,** fungus. **3,** derby hat.
honor (o'nor) *n.m.* honor. —**de honor,** honorary.
honorable (o·no'ra·βle) *adj.* honorable.
honorario (o·no'ra·rjo) *adj.* honorary. —**honorarios,** *n.m.pl.* fee (*sing.*); honorarium (*sing.*).
honorífico (o·no'ri·fi·ko) *adj.* **1,** honorary. **2,** honorific. —**mención honorífica,** honorable mention.
honra ('on·ra) *n.f.* **1,** honor. **2,** reputation. **3,** reverence. —**tener a mucha honra,** to be proud of.
honradez (on·ra'ðeθ; -'ðes) *n.f.* honesty.

honrado (on'ra·ðo) *adj.* 1, honest. 2, honored.
honrar (on'rar) *v.t.* to honor. —**honrarse,** *v.r.* 1, to be honored. 2, to take pleasure.
honroso (on'ro·so) *adj.* 1, honorable. 2, honoring; conferring honor.
hopo ('o·po; 'xo·po) *n.m.* 1, bushy tail. 2, tuft of hair.
hora ('o·ra) *n.f.* 1, hour. 2, time. —*adv., colloq.* = **ahora.** —**a buena hora,** 1, on time; punctually. 2, in time; opportunely. 3, *ironic* in good time. —**a estas horas,** at this time. —**a última hora,** at the last moment. —**dar hora,** to set the time. —**dar la hora,** to strike the hour. —**de última hora,** latest; up to date. —**no ver la hora de,** to be eager to. —**¿qué hora es?** what time is it?
horadar (o·ra'ðar) *v.t.* to perforate; pierce; drill.
horario (o'ra·rjo) *n.m.* 1, timetable; schedule. 2, hour hand. —*adj.* hourly.
horca ('or·ka) *n.f.* 1, gallows. 2, pitchfork. 3, forked prop. 4, string (*of garlic or onions*). 5, yoke (*for animals*).
horcajadas (or·ka'xa·ðas) *n.f.pl., in* **a horcajadas,** astride; astraddle.
horcón (or'kon) *n.m.* 1, pitchfork. 2, forked prop. 3, *Amer.* roof support.
horda ('or·ða) *n.f.* horde.
horizontal (o·ri·θon'tal; -son'tal) *adj. & n.m.* horizontal.
horizonte (o·ri'θon·te; -'son·te) *n.m.* horizon.
horma ('or·ma) *n.f.* 1, mold. 2, hatter's block. 3, shoemaker's last. —**hallar la horma de su zapato,** *colloq.* 1, to find just what one has been looking for. 2, to meet one's match.
hormiga (or'mi·ɣa) *n.f.* ant. —**hormiga blanca,** termite.
hormigón (or·mi'ɣon) *n.m.* concrete. —**hormigón armado,** reinforced concrete.
hormiguear (or·mi·ɣe'ar) *v.i.* 1, to crawl like ants. 2, to itch. —**hormigueo** (-'ɣe·o) *n.m.* itching.
hormiguero (or·mi'ɣe·ro) *n.m.* anthill; ant nest. —**oso hormiguero,** anteater.
hormona (or'mo·na) *n.f.* hormone.
hornada (or'na·ða) *n.f.* quantity baked at one time; batch.
hornear (or·ne'ar) *v.i.* to bake.
hornero (or'ne·ro) *n.m.* baker.
hornilla (or'ni·ʎa; -ja) *n.f.* 1, kitchen grate *or* stove. 2, pigeonhole.
hornillo (or'ni·ʎo; -jo) *n.m.* 1, portable stove; small stove. 2, kitchen stove.
horno ('or·no) *n.m.* 1, oven. 2, kiln. 3, furnace.
horología (o·ro·lo'xi·a) *n.f.* horology. —**horólogo** (o'ro·lo·ɣo) *n.m.* horologist.
horóscopo (o'ros·ko·po) *n.m.* horoscope.
horqueta (or'ke·ta) *n.f.* 1, fork (*of a tree*). 2, forked stick. 3, anything forked or bifurcated.
horquilla (or'ki·ʎa; -ja) *n.f.* 1, forked stick. 2, fork (*of a tree*). 3, pitchfork. 4, hairpin.
horrendo (o'rren·do) *adj.* horrible; horrendous.
horrible (o'rri·βle) *adj.* horrible.
horripilar (o·rri·pi'lar) *v.t.* to horrify; cause revulsion in.
horror (o'rror) *n.m.* horror. —**horroroso,** *adj.* horrid; horrible.
horrorizar (o·rro·ri'θar; -'sar) *v.t.* [*pres.subjve.* **horrorice** (-'ri·θe; -se); *pret.* **horroricé** (-'θe; -'se)] to horrify; shock.
hortaliza (or·ta'li·θa; -sa) *n.f.* garden vegetable.
hortelano (or·te'la·no) *n.m.* 1, gardener who tends a vegetable garden. 2, *ornith.* ortolan.
hortensia (or'ten·sja) *n.f.* hydrangea.
hortícola (or'ti·ko·la) *adj.* horticultural.
horticultura (or·ti·kul'tu·ra) *n.f.* horticulture. —**horticultor,** *n.m.* horticulturist.
hosanna (o'sa·na) *interj. & n.m.* hosanna.
hosco ('os·ko) *adj.* 1, dark-colored. 2, sullen; glum.
hospedaje (os·pe'ða·xe) *n.m.* lodging.
hospedar (os·pe'ðar) *v.t.* to lodge; provide lodging for. —**hospedarse,** *v.r.* to lodge; stay.
hospedería (os·pe·ðe'ri·a) *n.f.* hostel; inn.
hospedero (os·pe'ðe·ro) *n.m.* innkeeper; host.
hospicio (os'pi·θjo; -sjo) *n.m.* 1, poorhouse. 2, orphanage. 3, asylum.
hospital (os·pi'tal) *n.m.* hospital.
hospitalario (os·pi·ta'la·rjo) *adj.* hospitable.

hospitalidad (os·pi·ta·li'ðað) *n.f.* hospitality.
hospitalizar (os·pi·ta·li'θar; -'sar) [*pres.subjve.* **hospitalice** (-'li·θe; -se); *pret.* **hospitalicé** (-'θe; -'se)] to hospitalize. —**hospitalización,** *n.f.* hospitalization.
hosquedad (os·ke'ðað) *n.f.* glumness; sullenness.
hostelero (os·te'le·ro) *n.m.* innkeeper; host.
hostería (os·te'ri·a) *n.f.* inn; hostel.
hostia ('os·tja) *n.f., eccles.* Host.
hostigar (os·ti'γar) *v.t.* [*pres. subjve.* **hostigue** (-'ti·γe) *pret.* **hostigué** (-'γe)] **1,** to harass. **2,** *Amer.* to sicken; cloy.
hostil (os'til) *adj.* hostile. —**hostilidad,** *n.f.* hostility.
hostilizar (os·ti·li'θar; -'sar) *v.t.* [*pres.subjve.* **hostilice** (-'li·θe; -se); *pret.* **hostilicé** (-'θe; -'se)] to harry; harass.
hotel (o'tel) *n.m.* hotel. —**hotelero,** *n.m.* hotel manager. —*adj.* hotel (*attrib.*).
hoy (oi) *adv.* **1,** today. **2,** at the present time. —**de hoy en adelante,** from now on. —**hoy día,** *also,* **hoy en día,** nowadays. —**hoy por hoy,** at the present time.
hoya ('o·ja) *n.f.* **1,** dale; hollow. **2,** grave. **3,** *Amer.* river basin. **4,** hole or dip in a river bed or sea bottom.
hoyo ('o·jo) *n.m.* **1,** hole; pit. **2,** grave.
hoyuelo (o'jwe·lo) *n.m.* **1,** dimple. **2,** small hole.
hoz (oθ; os) *n.f.* [*pl.* **hoces**] **1,** sickle. **2,** ravine.
hozar (o'θar; -'sar) *v.t.* [*pres. subjve.* **hoce;** *pret.* **hocé**] to root; root up.
huaca ('wa·ka) *n.f.* = **guaca.**
huacal (wa'kal) *n.m.* = **guacal.**
huarache (wa'ra·tʃe) *n.m., Mex.* = **guarache.**
huasca ('was·ka) *n.f., Amer.* = **guasca.**
huaso ('wa·so) *adj.* & *n.m., Amer.* = **guaso.**
hube ('u·βe) *v., pret. of* **haber.**
hucha ('u·tʃa) *n.f.* **1,** = **alcancía. 2,** nest egg.
hueco ('we·ko) *adj.* **1,** hollow. **2,** *fig.* shallow. —*n.m.* **1,** hole. **2,** gap. **3,** *colloq.* place; opening.
huela ('we·la) *v., pres.subjve. of* **oler.**
huelga ('wel·γa) *n.f.* labor strike. —**huelguista,** (-'γis·ta) *n.m.* & *f.* striker.
huelgue ('wel·γe) *v., pres.subjve. of* **holgar.**
huelgo ('wel·γo) *v., pres.ind. of* **holgar.**
huelo ('we·lo) *v., pres.ind. of* **oler.**
huella ('we·ʎa; -ja) *n.f.* **1,** footprint. **2,** track; trail. **3,** trace; sign. —**huellas dactilares,** fingerprints.
huelle ('we·ʎe; -je) *v., pres.subjve. of* **hollar.**
huello ('we·ʎo; -jo) *v., pres.ind. of* **hollar.**
huérfano ('wer·fa·no) *adj.* & *n.m.* orphan.
huero ('we·ro) *adj.* **1,** empty; vain. **2,** *Amer.* = **güero. 3,** rotten (*of an egg*).
huerta ('wer·ta) *n.f.* large vegetable patch.
huerto ('wer·to) *n.m.* **1,** orchard. **2,** vegetable garden; garden patch.
hueso ('we·so) *n.m.* **1,** bone. **2,** stone; pit (*of fruits*). **3,** *fig.* drudgery. **4,** *Amer.* dross. —**la sin hueso,** *colloq.* the tongue. —**estar en los huesos,** *colloq.* to be nothing but skin and bones.
huésped ('wes·peð) *n.m.* **1,** [*fem.* **huéspeda**] guest. **2,** *biol.* host; host organism. —**casa de huéspedes,** boarding house.
hueste ('wes·te) *n.f.* **1,** host; army. **2,** body of followers *or* partisans.
huesudo (we'su·ðo) *adj.* bony.
huevera (we'βe·ra) *n.f.* **1,** ovary of birds. **2,** egg cup.
huevero (we'βe·ro) *n.m.* **1,** egg dealer. **2,** egg server.
huevo ('we·βo) *n.m.* egg.
huída (u'i·ða) *n.f.* escape; flight.
huir (u'ir) *v.i.* [*pres.ind.* **huyo;** *pres.subjve.* **huya;** *pret.* **huí** (u'i), **huyó;** *ger.* **huyendo**] **1,** to flee; escape. —*v.t.* to avoid; shun.
hule ('u·le) *n.m.* oilcloth.
hulla ('u·ʎa; -ja) *n.f.* soft coal.
humanar (u·ma'nar) *v.t.* = **humanizar.**
humanidad (u·ma·ni'ðað) *n.f.* **1,** humanity. **2,** humaneness. **3,** *colloq.* corpulence.
humanismo (u·ma'nis·mo) *n.m.* humanism. —**humanista,** *n.m.* & *f.* humanist. —*adj.* humanistic.
humanitario (u·ma·ni'ta·rjo) *adj.* humanitarian.
humanizar (u·ma·ni'θar; -'sar) *v.t.* [*pres.subjve.* **humanice** (-'ni·θe; -se); *pret.* **humanicé** (-'θe; -'se)] to

humanize. —**humanizarse,** *v.r.* to become more humane; soften.
humano (u'ma·no) *adj.* **1,** human. **2,** humane. —*n.m.* human.
humareda (u·ma're·ða) *n.f.* cloud of smoke.
humear (u·me'ar) *v.i.* to smoke; fume.
humedad (u·me'ðað) *n.f.* humidity; dampness; moisture.
humedecer (u·me·ðe'θer; -'ser) *v.t.* [*pres.ind.* **humedezco** (-'ðeθ·ko; -'ðes·ko); *pres.subjve.* **humedezca** (-ka)] to moisten; dampen.
húmedo ('u·me·ðo) *adj.* humid; moist; damp.
húmero ('u·me·ro) *n.m.* humerus.
humidificar (u·mi·ði·fi'kar) *v.t.* [*infl.:* **picar**] to humidify. —**humidificación,** *n.f.* humidification.
humildad (u·mil'dað) *n.f.* **1,** humility. **2,** humbleness. **3,** meekness.
humilde (u'mil·de) *adj.* **1,** humble. **2,** meek.
humillar (u·mi'ʎar; -'jar) *v.t.* **1,** to humiliate. **2,** to humble. —**humillarse,** *v.r.* to humble oneself. —**humillación,** *n.f.* humiliation.
humillos (u'mi·ʎos; -jos) *n.m.pl.* airs; conceit.
humita (u'mi·ta) *n.f., So.Amer.* a kind of tamale.
humo ('u·mo) *n.m.* **1,** smoke. **2,** vapor; fume. —**humos,** *n.m.pl.* airs; conceit.
humor (u'mor) *n.m.* **1,** humor. **2,** disposition; mood.
humorada (u·mo'ra·ða) *n.f.* drollery; humorous sally.
humorado (u·mo'ra·ðo) *adj., in* **bien humorado,** good-humored; **mal humorado,** ill-humored.
humorismo (u·mo'ris·mo) *n.m.* humor; humorous style; humorous literature. —**humorista,** *n.m.* & *f.* humorist. —**humorístico,** *adj.* humorous; humoristic.
humoso (u'mo·so) *adj.* smoky.
humus ('u·mus) *n.m.* humus.
hundir (un'dir) *v.t.* **1,** to sink. **2,** to plunge. **3,** to crush; overwhelm. **4,** to destroy; ruin.
hundirse (un'dir·se) *v.r.* **1,** to sink. **2,** to cave in; collapse. **3,** *colloq.* to melt away; vanish.
huracán (u·ra'kan) *n.m.* hurricane.
huraño (u'ra·ɲo) *adj.* shy; retiring. —**hurañía** (-'ɲi·a) *also,* **hurañez** (-'ɲeθ; -'ɲes) *n.f.* shyness; diffidence.
hurgar (ur'ɣar) *v.t.* [*pres.subjve.* **hurgue** ('ur·ɣe); *pret.* **hurgué** (-'ɣe)] **1,** to stir; poke. **2,** to search; rummage through.
hurgón (ur'ɣon) *n.m.* poker (*for a fire*).
hurgonear (ur·ɣo·ne'ar) *v.t.* to stir; poke. —*v.i., colloq.* to meddle; stir up trouble.
hurón (u'ron) *n.m.* **1,** *zool.* ferret. **2,** *colloq.* busybody; snoop. —**huronear,** *v.i., colloq.* to pry; snoop.
¡hurra! ('u·rra) *interj.* hurrah!
hurraca (u'rra·ka) *n.f.* = **urraca.**
hurtadillas (ur·ta'ði·ʎas; -jas) *n.f.pl., in* **a hurtadillas,** furtively.
hurtar (ur'tar) *v.t.* **1,** to steal; filch. **2,** to shortweight, shortchange, etc. —**hurtarse,** *v.r.* to withdraw; hide; steal away.
hurto ('ur·to) *n.m.* **1,** theft; filching. **2,** stolen article. —**a hurto,** furtively.
húsar ('u·sar) *n.m.* hussar. —**sombrero de húsar,** busby.
husmear (us·me'ar) *v.t.* **1,** to sniff; smell. **2,** *colloq.* to pry into; snoop into. —*v.i.* to smell; reek.
husmeo (us'me·o) *n.m.* **1,** sniffing; smelling. **2,** *colloq.* prying; snooping.
huso ('u·so) *n.m.* **1,** spindle. **2,** bobbin.
¡huy! (ui) *interj.* wow!; ouch!
huya ('u·ja) *v., pres.subjve. of* **huir.**
huyendo (u'jen·do) *v., ger. of* **huir.**
huyo ('u·jo) *v., pres.ind. of* **huir.**
huyó (u'jo) *v., 3rd pers.sing. pret. of* **huir.**

I

I, i (i) *n.f.* 10th letter of the Spanish alphabet.
i- (i) *prefix, var. of* **in-** *before l: ilegal,* illegal.
-ia (ja) *suffix* -y; -ia. **1,** *forming abstract and collective nouns: falacia,* fallacy; *milicia,* militia. **2,** *forming names of diseases: atrofia,*

atrophy; *difteria,* diphtheria. **3,** *forming names of countries:* .*Francia,* France; *Austria,* Austria. **4,** *forming names of plants: gardenia,* gardenia.

-ía ('i·a) *suffix* -y; *forming nouns denoting* **1,** sciences: *astronomía,* astronomy. **2,** office; rank; dignity; jurisdiction: *alcaldía,* mayoralty; *abadía,* abbacy. **3,** quality; condition: *alevosía,* treachery; *bastardía,* bastardy. **4,** collectivity: *feligresía,* parishioners. **5,** place: *sacristía,* sacristy. **6,** geographical names: *Turquía,* Turkey; *Lombardía,* Lombardy.

-ial ('jal) *suffix* -ial; *forming adjectives expressing* relation; connection: *ministerial,* ministerial.

-íasis ('i·a·sis) *suffix* -iasis; disease: *elefantíasis,* elephantiasis.

-iatría (ja'tri·a) *suffix* -iatry; -iatrics; science *or* treatment of disease: *psiquiatría,* psychiatry; *pediatría,* pediatrics.

iba ('i·βa) *v., impf. of* **ir.**

ibérico (i'βe·ri·ko) *adj.* Iberian.

ibero (i'βe·ro) *n.m.* & *adj.* Iberian. —**iberoamericano,** *n.m.* & *adj.* Latin-American.

íbice ('i·βi·θe; -se) *n.m.* ibex.

-ibilidad (i·βi·li'ðað) *suffix* -ibility; *forming nouns from adjectives ending in* **-ible**: *audibilidad,* audibility.

ibis ('i·βis) *n.m.* ibis.

-ible ('i·βle) *suffix* -ible: *forming adjectives expressing* ability; capability: *legible,* legible.

-ica *suffix* **1,** (i·ka) -ics; *forming nouns denoting* science; study; craft: *física,* physics; *gramática,* grammar; *gimnástica,* gymnastics. **2,** ('i·ka) *colloq., forming diminutives: casica,* little house.

-ical (i'kal) *suffix* -ic; -ical; *forming adjectives denoting* quality; relation: *angelical,* angelic; angelical.

ice ('i·θe; -se) *v., pres.subjve. of* **izar.**

icé (i'θe; -'se) *v., 1st pers.sing. pret. of* **izar.**

iceberg ('ais·βerɣ) *n.m.* iceberg.

-icia ('i·θja; 'i·sja) *suffix* -ice; *forming fem. abstract nouns denoting* quality; condition: *justicia,* justice; *avaricia,* avarice.

-icio ('i·θjo; 'i·sjo) *suffix* **1,** -ice; *forming masc. abstract nouns denoting* quality; condition: *servicio,* service. **2,** -itious; *forming adjectives denoting* tendency; relation: *alimenticio,* nutritious; *ficticio,* fictitious.

-ición (i'θjon; i'sjon) *suffix* -ition; *forming verbal nouns expressing* action; result of action: *aparición,* apparition.

-icioso (i'θjo·so; i'sjo-) *suffix* -icious; -itious; *forming adjectives denoting* quality; relation: *pernicioso,* pernicious; *supersticioso,* superstitious.

-ico (i·ko) *suffix* **1,** -ic; *forming adjectives denoting* quality; relation: *poético,* poetic. **2,** -ic; *chem., indicating presence of an element in a compound at a higher valence: nítrico,* nitric. **3,** -ician; *forming nouns denoting* practitioner: *matemático,* mathematician. **4,** ('i·ko) *forming diminutives: pajarico, colloq.,* small bird.

icono (i'ko·no) *n.m.* icon. *Also,* **icón** (i'kon).

iconoclasta (i·ko·no'klas·ta) *n.m.* & *f.* iconoclast. —*adj.* iconoclastic.

ictericia (ik·te'ri·θja; -sja) *n.f.* jaundice. —**ictérico** (-'te·ri·ko) *adj.* jaundiced.

ictio- (ik·tjo) *prefix* ichthyo-; fish: *ictiosauro,* ichthyosaur.

ictiología (ik·tjo·lo'xi·a) *n.f.* ichthyology. —**ictiológico** (-'lo·xi·ko) *adj.* ichthyological. —**ictiólogo** (ik·'tjo·lo·ɣo) ichthyologist.

-ichuelo (i'tʃwe·lo), *fem.* **-ichuela,** *suffix, forming diminutives: barquichuelo,* small boat.

id (ið) *v., 2nd pers.pl. impve. of* **ir.**

ida ('i·ða) *n.f.* departure; going. —**ida y vuelta,** round trip. —**idas y venidas,** comings and goings.

-idad (i'ðað) *suffix* -ity; *forming nouns denoting* condition; quality: *actividad,* activity; *benignidad,* benignity.

idea (i'ðe·a) *n.f.* idea.

ideación (i·ðe·a'θjon; -'sjon) *n.f.* ideation.

ideal (i·ðe'al) *adj.* & *n.m.* ideal. —**idealismo,** *n.m.* idealism. —**idealista,** *n.m.* idealist. —*adj.* idealistic.

idealizar (i·ðe·a·li'θar; -'sar) *v.t.* [*pres.subjve.* **idealice** (-'li·θe; -se) *pret.* **idealicé** (-'θe; -'se)] to idealize. —**idealización,** *n.f.* idealization.

idear (i·ðe'ar) *v.t.* **1,** to form an idea of; ideate. **2,** to devise; plan.

ideático (i·ðe'a·ti·ko) *adj., Amer.* crazy; touched.

idem ('i·ðem) *pron.* idem; the same; ditto.
idéntico (i'ðen ti·ko) *adj.* identical.
identidad (i·ðen·ti'ðað) *n.f.* identity.
identificar (i·ðen·ti·fi'kar) *v.t.* [*pres.subjve.* **identifique** (-'fi·ke); *pret.* **identifiqué** (-'ke)] to identify. —**identificación,** *n.f.* identification.
ideo- (i·ðe·o) *prefix* ideo-; idea: *ideología,* ideology.
ideología (i·ðe·o·lo'xi·a) *n.f.* ideology. —**ideológico** (-'lo·xi·ko) *adj.* ideological.
-idero (i'ðe·ro) *suffix, var. of* **-dero:** *mentidero,* gathering place for gossip; *venidero,* forthcoming.
idilio (i'ði·ljo) *n.m.* idyl. —**idílico** (i'ði·li·ko) *adj.* idyllic.
idio- (i·ðjo) *prefix* idio-; peculiar; personal: *idiosincrasia,* idiosyncrasy.
idioma (i'ðjo·ma) *n.m.* language; idiom.
idiomático (i·ðjo'ma·ti·ko) *adj.* idiomatic.
idiosincrasia (i·ðjo·sin'kra·sja) *n.f.* idiosyncrasy. —**idiosincrásico** (-'kra·si·ko) *adj.* idiosyncratic.
idiota (i'ðjo·ta) *n.m.* & *f.* idiot. —*adj.* idiotic. —**idiotez,** *n.f.* idiocy.
idiotismo (i·ðjo'tis·mo) *n.* **1,** ignorance; lack of learning. **2,** idiocy. **3,** = **modismo.**
idiotizar (i·ðjo·ti'θar; -'sar) *v.t.* [*pres.subjve.* **idiotice** (-'ti·θe; -se); *pret.* **idioticé** (-'θe; -'se)] to stultify; stupefy.
-idizo (i'ði·θo; -so) *suffix, var. of* **-izo:** *huidizo,* evasive.
ido ('i·ðo) *adj., colloq.* **1,** absent-minded. **2,** *Amer.* drunk.
ido ('i·ðo) *v., p.p. of* **ir.**
-ido *suffix* **1,** ('i·ðo) *forming adjectives equivalent to a past participle: partido,* broken. **2,** ('i·ðo) *forming nouns expressing* sound; outcry: *quejido,* whine; *aullido,* howl. **3,** (i·ðo) *forming adjectives denoting* quality; relation: *tórrido,* torrid; *flúido,* fluid. **4,** (i·ðo) *zool.* member of a family or group: *arácnido,* arachnid.
idólatra (i'ðo·la·tra) *adj.* idolatrous. —*n.m.* & *f.* idolater.
idolatrar (i·ðo·la'trar) *v.t.* to idolize; worship.
idolatría (i·ðo·la'tri·a) *n.f.* idolatry.
ídolo ('i·ðo·lo) *n.m.* idol.
idóneo (i'ðo·ne·o) *adj.* competent; qualified. —**idoneidad** (-nei'ðað) *n.f.* competence; capacity.
-idor (i'ðor), *fem.* **-idora** (i'ðo·ra) *suffix, var. of* **-dor:** *curtidor,* tanner; *decidor,* witty.
-idura (i'ðu·ra) *suffix, var. of* **-dura:** *añadidura,* addition.
idus ('i·ðus) *n.m.pl.* ides.
-iento ('jen·to) *suffix, var. of* **-ento:** *harapiento,* ragged.
iglesia (i'ɣle·sja) *n.f.* church.
iglú (i'ɣlu) *n.m.* igloo.
ígneo ('iɣ·ne·o) *adj.* igneous.
ignición (iɣ·ni'θjon; -'sjon) *n.f.* ignition. —**ignito** (-'ni·to) *adj.* ignited.
ignoble (ig'no·βle) *adj., Amer.* = **innoble.**
ignominia (iɣ·no'mi·nja) *n.f.* ignominy. —**ignominioso,** *adj.* ignominious.
ignorado (iɣ·no'ra·ðo) *adj.* unknown.
ignorante (iɣ·no'ran·te) *adj.* ignorant. —*n.m.* & *f.* ignoramus. —**ignorancia,** *n.f.* ignorance.
ignorar (iɣ·no'rar) *v.t.* **1,** to be ignorant of. **2,** to ignore.
ignoto (iɣ'no·to) *adj.* unknown.
igual (i'ɣwal) *adj.* **1,** equal. **2,** even; level. **3,** equable. —*n.m.* equal. —*adv.* in like manner. —**al igual,** equally. —**al igual que,** as well as; the same as. —**es igual,** *colloq.* it's all the same.
igualación (i·ɣwa·la'θjon; -'sjon) *n.f.* **1,** equalization. **2,** agreement; stipulation.
igualar (i·ɣwa'lar) *v.t.* **1,** to make equal; equalize. **2,** to equal. **3,** to even; level. **4,** to equate. —*v.i.* to be equal. —**igualarse,** *v.t.* to compare oneself; put oneself on a par.
igualdad (i·ɣwal'dað) *n.f.* **1,** equality. **2,** evenness; uniformity.
igualmente (i·ɣwal'men·te) *adv.* **1,** equally. **2,** likewise.
iguana (i'ɣwa·na) *n.f.* iguana.
-iguar (i'ɣwar) *suffix, forming verbs from nouns and adjectives: apaciguar,* pacify; *atestiguar,* testify.
ijada (i'xa·ða) *n.f.* flank; side. *Also,* **ijar** (i'xar) *n.m.*
-ijo ('i·xo) *suffix* **1,** *forming diminutives: atadijo,* small bundle. **2,** *forming nouns expressing* action; result of action; *revoltijo,* mess.
-il (il) *suffix* -il; -ile; *forming adjec-*

tives expressing relation; tendency: *civil,* civil; *frágil,* fragile.
ilación (i·la'θjon; -'sjon) *n.f.* **1,** inference. **2,** logical sequence; connection.
ilegal (i·le'ɣal) *adj.* illegal; unlawful. —**ilegalidad,** *n.f.* illegality.
ilegible (i·le'xi·βle) *adj.* illegible.
ilegítimo (i·le'xi·ti·mo) *adj.* illegitimate. —**ilegitimidad,** *n.f.* illegitimacy.
ileso (i'le·so) *adj.* unhurt; uninjured.
iletrado (i·le'tra·ðo) *adj.* = **iliterato.**
ilíaco (i'li·a·ko) *also,* **iliaco** (i'lja·ko) *adj.* iliac.
iliberal (i·li·βe'ral) *adj.* illiberal. —**iliberalidad,** *n.f.* illiberality.
ilícito (i'li·θi·to; -si·to) *adj.* illicit; unlawful.
-ilidad (i·li'ðað) *suffix* -ility; *forming nouns from adjectives ending in* **-il**: *civilidad,* civility.
ilimitable (i·li·mi'ta·βle) *adj.* illimitable.
ilimitado (i·li·mi'ta·ðo) *adj.* unlimited; boundless.
ilinio (i'li·njo) *n.m.* illinium.
iliterato (i·li·te'ra·to) *adj.* & *n.m.* illiterate.
ilógico (i'lo·xi·ko) *adj.* illogical.
iluminar (i·lu·mi'nar) *v.t.* **1,** to illuminate; light. **2,** to enlighten. —**iluminación,** *n.f.* illumination; lighting.
ilusión (i·lu'sjon) *n.f.* **1,** illusion. **2,** false hope.
ilusionar (i·lu·sjo'nar) *v.t., Amer.* **1,** to give false hopes to. **2,** to delude (by sleight). —**ilusionarse,** *v.r.* **1,** to become hopeful. **2,** to build up high hopes; be overconfident.
ilusivo (i·lu'si·βo) *adj.* illusive.
iluso (i'lu·so) *adj.* deluded; deceived. —*n.m.* dreamer.
ilusorio (i·lu'so·rjo) *adj.* illusory.
ilustración (i·lus·tra'θjon; -'sjon) *n.f.* **1,** illustration. **2,** culture; learning.
ilustrado (i·lus'tra·ðo) *adj.* **1,** illustrated. **2,** learned; cultured.
ilustrador (i·lus·tra'ðor) *n.m.* illustrator.
ilustrar (i·lus'trar) *v.t.* **1,** to illustrate. **2,** to enlighten. —**ilustrativo,** *adj.* illustrative.
ilustre (i'lus·tre) *adj.* illustrious; distinguished.
-illo ('i·ʎo; 'i·jo), *fem.* **-illa,** *suffix, forming diminutives: chiquillo,* small child.
im- (im) *prefix, var. of* **in-** *before* b *and* p: *imberbe,* beardless; *imposible,* impossible.
imagen (i'ma·xen) *n.f.* **1,** image. **2,** statue.
imaginar (i·ma·xi'nar) *v.t.* to imagine. —**imaginable,** *adj.* imaginable. —**imaginación,** *n.f.* imagination. —**imaginario,** *adj.* imaginary. —**imaginativo,** *adj.* imaginative.
imán (i'man) *n.m.* **1,** magnet. **2,** attraction.
imantación (i·man·ta'θjon; -'sjon) *also* **imanación** (i·ma·na·'θjon; -'sjon) *n.f.* magnetization.
imantar (i·man'tar) *also,* **imanar** (i·ma'nar) *v.t.* to magnetize.
imbécil (im'be·θil; -sil) *n.m.* & *f.* imbecile. —*adj.* imbecilic. —**imbecilidad,** *n.f.* imbecility.
imberbe (im'ber·βe) *adj.* beardless.
imborrable (im·bo'rra·βle) *adj.* indelible.
imbuir (im·bu'ir) *v.t.* [*pres.ind.* **imbuyo** (-'bu·jo); *pres.subjve.* **imbuya** (-ja); *pret.* **imbuí, imbuyó** (-'jo); *ger.* **imbuyendo** (-'jen·do)] to imbue. —**imbuimiento,** *n.m.* imbuement.
imitar (i·mi'tar) *v.t.* to imitate. —**imitable,** *adj.* imitable. —**imitación,** *n.f.* imitation. —**imitado,** *adj.* [*also,* **de imitación**] imitation. —**imitador,** *n.m.* imitator. —**imitativo,** *adj.* imitative.
-imo (i·mo) *suffix* -th; *forming ordinal numerals: décimo,* tenth.
impacientar (im·pa·θjen'tar; -sjen'tar) *v.t.* **1,** to make impatient. **2,** to vex; irritate. —**impacientarse,** *v.r.* to lose patience.
impaciente (im·pa'θjen·te; -'sjen·te) *adj.* impatient. —**impaciencia,** *n.f.* impatience.
impactado (im·pak'ta·ðo) *adj., dent.* impacted.
impacto (im'pak·to) *n.m.* impact.
impagable (im·pa'ɣa·βle) *adj.* **1,** unpayable. **2,** *Amer., colloq.* invaluable; priceless.
impago (im'pa·ɣo) *adj., Amer., colloq.* unpaid.
impalpable (im·pal'pa·βle) *adj.* impalpable.— **impalpabilidad,** *n.f.* impalpability.
impar (im'par) *adj.* **1,** unequal. **2,** unmatched. **3,** matchless; without equal. —**número impar,** odd number.
imparcial (im·par'θjal; -'sjal)

adj. impartial. —**imparcialidad,** *n.f.* impartiality.
impartir (im·par'tir) *v.t.* to impart.
impasable (im·pa'sa·βle) *adj.* **1,** impassable. **2,** *Amer., colloq.* unbearable; that cannot be swallowed.
impasible (im·pa'si·βle) *adj.* impassive. —**impasibilidad,** *n.f.* impassiveness.
impávido (im'pa·βi·ðo) *adj.* dauntless. —**impavidez,** *n.f.* dauntlessness.
impecable (im·pe'ka·βle) *adj.* impeccable. —**impecabilidad,** *n.f.* impeccability.
impedimenta (im·pe·ði'men·ta) *n.f.* impedimenta (*pl.*).
impedimento (im·pe·ði'men·to) *n.m.* impediment.
impedir (im·pe'ðir) *v.t.* [*infl.:* **pedir**] to prevent; impede. —**impedido,** *adj.* disabled; crippled.
impeditivo (im·pe·ði'ti·βo) *adj.* preventive; deterrent.
impeler (im·pe'ler) *v.t.* to impel.
impenetrable (im·pe·ne'tra·βle) *adj.* impenetrable. —**impenetrabilidad,** *n.f.* impenetrability.
impenitente (im·pe·ni'ten·te) *adj.* impenitent. —**impenitencia,** *n.f.* impenitence.
impensado (im·pen'sa·ðo) *adj.* unexpected; unforeseen. —**impensadamente,** *adv.* inadvertently; thoughtlessly.
imperar (im·pe'rar) *v.i.* to reign; hold sway.
imperativo (im·pe·ra'ti·βo) *adj.* & *n.m.* imperative.
imperceptible (im·per·θep'ti·βle; im·per·sep-) *adj.* imperceptible. —**imperceptibilidad,** *n.f.* imperceptibility.
imperdible (im·per'ði·βle) *n.m.* safety pin.
imperdonable (im·per·ðo'na·βle) *adj.* unpardonable; unforgivable.
imperecedero (im·pe·re·θe'ðe·ro; -se'ðe·ro) *adj.* everlasting; imperishable.
imperfección (im·per·fek'θjon; -'sjon) *n.f.* imperfection.
imperfecto (im·per'fek·to) *adj.* & *n.m.* imperfect.
imperial (im·pe'rjal) *adj.* imperial. —*n.f.* top (of a bus, carriage, etc.).
imperialismo (im·pe·rja'lis·mo) *n.m.* imperialism. —**imperialista,** *n.m.* & *f.* imperialist. —*adj.* imperialistic.
impericia (im·pe'ri·θja; -sja) *n.f.* unskillfulness.
imperio (im'pe·rjo) *n.m.* **1,** empire. **2,** rule; command. **3,** *fig.* haughtiness; pride. **4,** *fig.* imperiousness.
imperioso (im·pe'rjo·so) *adj.* **1,** imperious; domineering. **2,** urgent. —**imperiosidad,** *n.f.* imperiousness.
imperito (im·pe'ri·to) *adj.* unskilled; inexperienced.
impermeable (im·per·me'a·βle) *adj.* waterproof; impermeable; impervious. —*n.m.* raincoat. —**impermeabilidad,** *n.f.* impermeability; imperviousness.
impermeabilizar (im·per·me·a·βi·li'θar; -'sar) *v.t.* [*pres.subjve.* **impermeabilice** (-'li·θe; -se); *pret.* **impermeabilicé** (-'θe; -'se)] to waterproof. —**impermeabilización,** *n.f.* waterproofing.
impermutable (im·per·mu'ta·βle) *adj.* **1,** unchangeable. **2,** unexchangeable.
impersonal (im·per·so'nal) *adj.* impersonal.
impersuasible (im·per·swa'si·βle) *adj.* unpersuadable.
impertérrito (im·per'te·rri·to) *adj.* unruffled; undaunted.
impertinente (im·per·ti'nen·te) *adj.* **1,** impertinent; saucy. **2,** irrelevant. —**impertinentes,** *n.m.pl.* lorgnette (*sing.*). —**impertinencia,** *n.f.* impertinence; sauciness.
imperturbable (im·per·tur'βa·βle) *adj.* imperturbable. —**imperturbabilidad,** *n.f.* imperturbability. —**imperturbado,** *adj.* unperturbed; undisturbed.
impetrar (im·pe'trar) *v.t.* to entreat; beseech.
ímpetu ('im·pe·tu) *n.m.* **1,** impetus **2,** impulse. **3,** attack; fit.
impetuoso (im·pe'two·so) *adj.* **1** impetuous. **2,** violent. —**impetuosidad,** *n.f.* impetuosity.
impida (im'pi·ða) *v., pres.subjve* *of* **impedir.**
impidió (im·pi'ðjo) *v., 3rd pers* *sing. pret. of* **impedir.**
impido (im'pi·ðo) *v., pres.ind. o* **impedir.**
impiedad (im·pje'ðað) *n.f.* im piety; impiousness.
impío (im'pi·o) *adj.* impious; i religious.
implacable (im·pla'ka·βle) *ad*

implacable; relentless. —**implacabilidad,** *n.f.* implacability.
implantar (im·plan'tar) *v.t.* **1,** to implant; instill; inculcate. **2,** to introduce; establish.
implicación (im·pli·ka'θjon; -'sjon) *n.f.* **1,** implication. **2,** contradiction.
implicar (im·pli'kar) *v.t.* [*pres. subjve.* **implique** (-'pli·ke); *pret.* **impliqué** (-'ke)] **1,** to implicate; involve. **2,** to imply. —*v.i.* to imply contradiction (*usu. with adverbs of negation*).
implícito (im'pli·θi·to; -si·to) *adj.* implicit; implied.
implorar (im·plo'rar) *v.t.* to implore; entreat. —**imploración,** *n.f.* entreaty.
implume (im'plu·me) *adj.* unfledged; without feathers.
impolítico (im·po'li·ti·ko) *adj.* **1,** impolite. **2,** impolitic. —**impolítica,** *n.f.* discourtesy; impoliteness.
impoluto (im·po'lu·to) *adj.* unpolluted; pure.
imponderable (im·pon·de'ra·βle) *adj.* **1,** imponderable. **2,** beyond praise.
imponente (im·po'nen·te) *adj.* imposing.
imponer (im·po'ner) *v.t.* [*infl.:* **poner**] **1,** to impose. **2,** to acquaint; inform. —**imponerse,** *v.t.* to dominate; prevail.
imponible (im·po'ni·βle) *adj.* taxable; dutiable.
impopular (im·po·pu'lar) *adj.* unpopular. —**impopularidad,** *n.f.* unpopularity.
importante (im·por'tan·te) *adj.* important. —**importancia,** *n.f.* importance.
importar (im·por'tar) *v.t.* **1,** to import. **2,** to cost; cause expenditure of. —*v.i.* to matter. —**importación,** *n.f.* importation; import. —**importador,** *adj.* importing. —*n.m.* importer. —**no importa,** no matter; never mind. —**¿qué importa?** what does it matter?
importe (im'por·te) *n.m.* **1,** *comm.* amount. **2,** cost; price; value.
importunar (im·por·tu'nar) *v.t.* to importune. —**importunación,** *n.f.* annoying insistence.
importuno (im·por'tu·no) *adj.* **1,** inopportune. **2,** importunate; annoying. —**importunidad,** *n.f.* importunity.
imposibilitar (im·po·si·βi·li·'tar) *v.t.* **1,** to make impossible. **2,** to disable; incapacitate.
imposible (im·po'si·βle) *adj.* impossible. —**imposibilidad,** *n.f.* impossibility.
imposición (im·po·si'θjon; -'sjon) *n.f.* imposition.
impostergable (im·pos·ter'ɣa·βle) *adj.* that cannot be postponed.
impostor (im·pos'tor) *n.m.* impostor.
impostura (im·pos'tu·ra) *n.f.* **1,** imputation. **2,** imposture.
impotente (im·po'ten·te) *adj.* impotent. —**impotencia,** *n.f.* impotence.
impracticable (im·prak·ti'ka·βle) *adj.* impracticable. —**impracticabilidad,** *n.f.* impracticability.
impráctico (im'prak·ti·ko) *adj.* impractical.
imprecar ((im·pre'kar) *v.t.* [*pres. subjve.* **impreque** (-'pre·ke); *pret.* **imprequé** (-'ke)] to imprecate. —**imprecación,** *n.f.* imprecation.
impreciso (im·pre'θi·so; -'si·so) *adj.* not precise; vague; indefinite. —**imprecisión,** *n.f.* absence of precision; indefiniteness.
impregnar (im·preɣ'nar) *v.t.* to impregnate; saturate. —**impregnable,** *adj.* impregnable; saturable. —**impregnación,** *n.f.* impregnation; saturation.
impremeditado (im·pre·me·ði·'ta·ðo) *adj.* unpremeditated.
imprenta (im'pren·ta) *n.f.* **1,** printing. **2,** printing shop or office. **3,** print; character. **4,** publication. —**pie de imprenta,** publisher's mark; imprint.
imprescindible (im·pres·θin'di·βle; -pre·sin'di·βle) *adj.* essential; indispensable.
imprescriptible (im·pres·krip·'ti·βle) *adj.* inadvisable; not recommendable.
impresentable (im·pre·sen'ta·βle) *adj.* unpresentable.
impresión (im·pre'sjon) *n.f.* **1,** impression. **2,** impress; stamp. **3,** edition. **4,** print. **5,** printing. —**impresión digital,** fingerprint.
impresionante (im·pre·sjo'nan·te) *adj.* impressive.
impresionar (im·pre·sjo'nar) *v.t.* to impress. —**impresionable,** adj. impressionable.
impresionismo (im·pre·sjo'nis·

mo) *n.m.* impressionism. —**impresionista,** *n.m.* & *f.* impressionist. —*adj.* impressionistic.

impreso (im'pre·so) *v., p.p. of* **imprimir.** —*adj.* **1,** printed. **2,** stamped. —*n.m.* **1,** print; copy. **2,** booklet; pamphlet; handbill. —**impresos,** *n.m.pl.* printed matter.

impresor (im·pre'sor) *n.m.* printer.

imprevisible (im·pre·βi'si·βle) *adj.* unforeseeable.

imprevisión (im·pre·βi'sjon) *n.f.* improvidence; lack of foresight.

imprevisto (im·pre'βis·to) *adj.* unforeseen. —*n.m.* unforeseen thing *or* event. —**imprevistos,** *n.m. pl.* incidental *or* unforeseen expenses.

imprimir (im·pri'mir) *v.t.* [*p.p.* **impreso**] **1,** to print. **2,** to impress; imprint.

improbable (im·pro'βa·βle) *adj.* improbable. —**improbabilidad,** *n.f.* improbability.

ímprobo ('im·pro·βo) *adj.* **1,** dishonest. **2,** laborious; backbreaking. —**improbidad,** *n.f.* dishonesty; improbity.

improcedencia (im·pro·θe'ðen·θja; -se'ðen·sja) *n.* **1,** lack of legal sanction. **2,** untimeliness. **3,** inappropriateness.

improcedente (im·pro·θe'ðen·te; -se'ðen·te) *adj.* **1,** unlawful; unsanctioned. **2,** untimely; inopportune. **3,** inappropriate.

improductivo (im·pro·ðuk'ti·βo) *adj.* unproductive.

impronunciable (im·pro·nun·'θja·βle; -'sja·βle) *adj.* unpronounceable.

improperio (im·pro'pe·rjo) *n.m.* insult; abuse.

impropio (im'pro·pjo) *adj.* improper. —**impropiedad,** *n.f.* impropriety.

improrrogable (im·pro·rro'ɣa·βle) *adj.* that cannot be extended *or* postponed.

impróspero (im'pros·pe·ro) *adj.* unprosperous.

impróvido (im'pro·βi·ðo) *adj.* improvident. —**improvidencia,** *n.f.* improvidence.

improvisación (im·pro·βi·sa·'θjon; -'sjon) *n.f.* **1,** improvisation. **2,** sudden rise to fame or success. **3,** *music* impromptu.

improvisar (im·pro·βi'sar) *v.t.* to improvise. —**improvisado,** *adj.* improvised; impromptu.

improviso (im·pro'βi·so) *also,* **improvisto** (-'βis·to) *adj.* unforeseen. —**de improviso; a la improvista,** suddenly; unexpectedly.

imprudente (im·pru'ðen·te) *adj.* imprudent. —**imprudencia,** *n.f.* imprudence.

impúber (im'pu·βer) *also,* **impúbero** (-βe·ro) *adj.* below the age of puberty; immature.

impudente (im·pu'ðen·te) *adj.* impudent. —**impudencia,** *n.f.* impudence.

impúdico (im'pu·ði·ko) *adj.* immodest; brash. —**impudicia** (-'ði·θja; -sja) *n.f., also,* **impudor** (-'ðor) *n.m.* immodesty; brashness.

impuesto (im'pwes·to) *v., p.p. of* **imponer.** —*n.m.* tax; duty.

impugnar (im·puɣ'nar) *v.t.* to impugn. —**impugnable,** *adj.* impugnable. —**impugnación,** *n.f.* impugnment.

impulsar (im·pul'sar) *v.t.* **1,** to impel; urge. **2,** *mech.* to drive.

impulsión (im·pul'sjon) *n.f.* = **impulso.**

impulsivo (im·pul'si·βo) *adj.* impulsive. —**impulsividad,** *n.f.* impulsiveness.

impulso (im'pul·so) *n.m.* **1,** impulse. **2,** impetus.

impulsor (im·pul'sor) *n.m.* impeller. —*adj.* impelling.

impune (im'pu·ne) *adj.* unpunished.

impunidad (im·pu·ni'ðað) *n.f.* impunity.

impuro (im'pu·ro) *adj.* impure. **impureza,** *n.f.* impurity.

impuse (im'pu·se) *v., pret. of* **imponer.**

imputar (im·pu'tar) *v.t.* to impute. —**imputable,** *adj.* imputable. —**imputación,** *n.f.* imputation.

in- (in) *prefix* in-. **1,** not; without: *incauto,* incautious; *inarticulado,* inarticulate. **2,** in; into; within; toward: *innato,* inborn; *interior,* inland; *insinuar,* insinuate. **3,** *forming verbs denoting* existence, motion or direction inward: *incluir,* inclose; *inducir,* induce. *Sometimes is used as a mere intensive: inculpar,* beside *culpar,* to accuse; blame.

-ín ('in) *suffix, forming diminutives: chiquitín,* very small.

-ina ('i·na) *suffix* **1,** -in; -ine; *forming names of* chemical elements and compounds; minerals; pharmaceutical elements: *glicerina,* glyc-

erin; *calamina,* calamine. **2,** -ine; *forming abstract nouns: disciplina,* discipline. **3,** -ine; *forming feminine nouns: heroína,* heroine.
inabarcable (in·a·βar'ka·βle) *adj.* unencompassable.
inabordable (in·a·βor'ða·βle) *adj.* **1,** unapproachable. **2,** incapable of being boarded, as a ship, train, etc.
inacabado (in·a·ka'βa·ðo) *adj.* unfinished.
inacabable (in·a·ka'βa·βle) *adj.* endless; interminable.
inaccesible (in·ak·θe'si·βle; in·ak·se-) *adj.* inaccessible. —**inaccesibilidad,** *n.f.* inaccessibility.
inacción (in·ak'θjon; -'sjon) *n.f.* inaction.
inacentuado (in·a·θen'twa·ðo; in·a·sen-) *adj.* unaccented.
inaceptable (in·a·θep'ta·βle; in·a·sep-) *adj.* unacceptable.
inactivo (in·ak'ti·βo) *adj.* inactive. —**inactividad,** *n.f.* inactivity.
inadaptable (in·a·ðap'ta·βle) *adj.* unadaptable.
inadecuado (in·a·ðe'kwa·ðo) *adj.* **1,** inadequate. **2,** inappropriate.
inadmisible (in·að·mi'si·βle) *adj.* inadmissible. —**inadmisibilidad,** *n.f.* inadmissibility.
inadoptable (in·a·ðop'ta·βle) *adj.* unadoptable; impracticable.
inadulterado (in·a·ðul·te'ra·ðo) *adj.* unadulterated.
inadvertido (in·að·βer'ti·ðo) *adj.* **1,** inadvertent. **2,** unnoticed; unseen. —**inadvertencia,** *n.f.* inadvertency; oversight.
inafectado (in·a·fek'ta·ðo) *adj.* unaffected.
inagotable (in·a·ɣo'ta·βle) *adj.* inexhaustible.
inaguantable (in·a·ɣwan'ta·βle) *adj.* unbearable; unendurable.
inalámbrico (in·a'lam·bri·ko) *adj.* wireless.
inalcanzable (in·al·kan'θa·βle); -'sa·βle) *adj.* unattainable.
inalienable (in·a·lje'na·βle) *also,* **inajenable** (-xe'na·βle) *adj.* inalienable.
inalterable (in·al·te'ra·βle) *adj.* unalterable; unchangeable. —**inalterado** (-'ra·ðo) *adj.* unaltered; unchanged.
inamovible (in·a·mo'βi·βle) *adj.* immovable.
inane (i'na·ne) *adj.* inane. —**inanidad,** *n.f.* inanity.
inanición (i·na·ni'θjon; -'sjon) *n.f.* inanition; starvation.
inanimado (in·a·ni'ma·ðo) *adj.* inanimate.
inánime (i'na·ni·me) *adj.* **1,** = exánime. **2,** inanimate.
inanunciado (in·a·nun'θja·ðo; -'sja·ðo) *adj.* unannounced.
inapagable (in·a·pa'ɣa·βle) *adj.* inextinguishable; unquenchable.
inapelable (in·a·pe'la·βle) *adj.* **1,** unappealable. **2,** irremediable.
inapercibido (in·a·per·θi'βi·ðo; -si'βi·ðo) *adj.* unnoticed; unseen.
inapetente (in·a·pe'ten·te) *adj.* without appetite. —**inapetencia,** *n.f.* lack of appetite.
inaplazable (in·a·pla'θa·βle; -'sa·βle) *adj.* that cannot be postponed.
inaplicable (in·a·pli'ka·βle) *adj.* inapplicable. —**inaplicabilidad,** *n.f.* inapplicability.
inaplicado (in·a·pli'ka·ðo) *adj.* = **desaplicado.** —**inaplicación,** *n.f.* = **desaplicación.**
inapreciable (in·a·pre'θja·βle; -'sja·βle) *adj.* **1,** invaluable. **2,** inappreciable.
inaprovechable (in·a·pro·βe·'tʃa·βle) *adj.* unusable.
inapto (in'ap·to) *adj.* = **inepto.** —**inaptitud,** *n.f.* = **ineptitud.**
inarmónico (in·ar'mo·ni·ko) *adj.* inharmonious.
inarticulado (in·ar·ti·ku'la·ðo) *adj.* inarticulate.
inartístico (in·ar'tis·ti·ko) *adj.* inartistic.
inasequible (in·a·se'ki·βle) *adj.* **1,** unattainable. **2,** unapproachable.
inasimilable (in·a·si·mi'la·βle) *adj.* unassimilable.
inasistencia (in·a·sis'ten·θja; -sja) *n.f.* absence; unattendance.
inasociable (in·a·so'θja·βle; -'sja·βle) *adj.* that cannot be associated; unrelatable.
inastillable (in·as·ti'ʎa·βle; -'ja·βle) *adj.* splinterproof; shatterproof.
inatacable (in·a·ta'ka·βle) *adj.* unassailable.
inaudible (in·au'ði·βle) *adj.* inaudible.
inaudito (in·au'ði·to) *adj.* unheard-of.

inaugurar (in·au·ɣu'rar) *v.t.* to inaugurate. —**inauguración,** *n.f.* inauguration. —**inaugural,** *adj.* inaugural.
inaveriguable (in·a·βe·ri'ɣwa·βle) *adj.* unascertainable.
inca ('in·ka) *n.m.* & *adj.* Inca. —**incaico** (in'kai·ko) *adj.* Incan.
incalculable (in·kal·ku'la·βle) *adj.* incalculable.
incalificable (in·ka·li·fi'ka·βle) *adj.* **1,** unqualifiable. **2,** unspeakable.
incambiable (in·kam'bja·βle) *adj.* **1,** unchangeable. **2,** unexchangeable.
incandescente (in·kan·des'θen·te; -de'sen·te) *adj.* incandescent. —**incandescencia,** *n.f.* incandescence.
incansable (in·kan'sa·βle) *adj.* untiring; tireless.
incapaz (in·ka'paθ; -'pas) *adj.* incapable; unable. —*adj.* & *n.m.* & *f.* incompetent. —**incapacidad** (-θi·'ðað; -si'ðað) *n.f.* incapacity. —**incapacitar,** *v.t.* to incapacitate.
incasto (in'kas·to) *adj.* unchaste.
incautarse (in·kau'tar·se) *v.r.*, *fol. by* **de,** to attach (money, property, etc.). —**incautación,** *n.f.* attachment of property.
incauto (in'kau·to) *adj.* incautious; unwary.
incendiar (in·θen'djar; in·sen-) *v.t.* to set on fire. —**incendiarse,** *v.r.* to catch fire.
incendiario (in·θen'dja·rjo; in·sen-) *adj.* & *n.m.* incendiary.
incendio (in'θen·djo; in'sen-) *n.m.* conflagration; fire.
incensar (in·θen'sar; in·sen-) *v.t.* [*pres.ind.* **incienso;** *pres.subjve.* **inciense**] to flatter.
incensurable (in·θen·su'ra·βle; in·sen-) *adj.* uncensurable; unimpeachable.
incentivo (in·θen'ti·βo; in·sen-) *n.m.* incentive.
incertidumbre (in·θer·ti'ðum·bre; in·ser-) *n.f.* uncertainty.
incesante (in·θe'san·te; in·se-) *adj.* incessant; unceasing.
incesto (in'θes·to; in'ses-) *n.m.* incest. —**incestuoso** (-'two·so) *adj.* incestuous.
incidencia (in·θi'ðen·θja; -si·'ðen·sja) *n.f.* incidence.
incidental (in·θi·ðen'tal; in·si-) *adj.* incidental.
incidente (in·θi'ðen·te; in·si-) *adj.* & *n.m.* **1,** incidental. **2,** incident.
incidir (in·θi'ðir; in·si-) *v.i.*, *usu. fol. by* **en,** to fall into; fall upon.
inciense (in'θjen·se; in'sjen-) *v.*, *pres.subjve. of* **incensar.**
incienso (in'θjen·so; -'sjen·so) *n.m.* **1,** incense. **2,** *fig.* flattery.
incienso (in'θjen·so; -'sjen·so) *v.*, *pres.ind. of* **incensar.**
incierto (in'θjer·to; in'sjer-) *adj.* **1,** uncertain. **2,** untrue.
incinerar (in·θi·ne'rar; in·si-) *v.t.* to incinerate. —**incineración,** *n.f.* incineration. —**incinerador,** *adj.* incinerating. —*n.m.* incinerator.
incipiente (in·θi'pjen·te; in·si-) *adj.* incipient.
incircunciso (in·θir·kun'θi·so; -sir·kun'si·so) *adj.* uncircumcised.
incircunscrito (in·θir·kuns'kri·to; in·sir-) *adj.* uncircumscribed.
incisión (in·θi'sjon; in·si-) *n.f.* incision.
incisivo (in·θi'si·βo; in·si-) *adj.* incisive. —**incisivos,** *n.m.pl.* incisors.
inciso (in'θi·so; -'si·so) *adj.* concise; terse (*of style*). —*n.m.* **1,** clause; paragraph. **2,** comma.
incitar (in·θi'tar; in·si-) *v.t.* to incite. —**incitación,** *n.f.* incitement. —**incitante,** *adj.* inciting; appealing.
incivil (in·θi'βil; in·si-) *adj.* uncivil. —**incivilidad,** *n.f.* incivility.
incivilizado (in·θi·βi·li'θa·ðo; -si·βi·li'sa·ðo) *adj.* uncivilized.
inclasificable (in·kla·si·fi'ka·βle) *adj.* unclassifiable; nondescript.
inclasificado (in·kla·si·fi'ka·ðo) *adj.* unclassified.
inclemente (in·kle'men·te) *adj.* inclement. —**inclemencia,** *n.f.* inclemency.
inclinación (in·kli·na'θjon; -'sjon) *n.f.* **1,** inclination; bent. **2,** bow; curtsy. **3,** slant; tilt.
inclinado (in·kli'na·ðo) *adj.* inclined.
inclinar (in·kli'nar) *v.t.* & *i.* to incline. —*v.t.* **1,** to nod. **2,** to bend; bow; lean. —*v.r.* **1,** to be inclined; tend. **2,** to bow; curtsy. **3,** to slant; tilt.
ínclito ('in·kli·to) *adj.* illustrious; famed.
incluir (in·klu'ir) *v.t.* [*infl.:* **concluir**] **1,** to include. **2,** to enclose.
inclusa (in'klu·sa) *n.f.* foundling home.

inclusión (in·klu'sjon) *n.f.* **1,** inclusion. **2,** access; intimacy.
inclusive (in·klu'si·βe) *adv.* inclusively.
inclusivo (in·klu'si·βo) *adj.* inclusive. —**inclusivamente,** *adv.* inclusively.
incluso (in'klu·so) *adj.* enclosed; included. —*adv.* inclusively. —*prep.* including; inclusive of.
incoativo (in·ko·a'ti·βo) *adj.*, *gram.* inceptive; inchoative.
incobrable (in·ko'βra·βle) *adj.* uncollectible.
incógnito (in'koɣ·ni·to) *adj.* unknown; incognito. —**incógnita,** *n.f., math.* unknown; unknown quantity. —**de incógnito,** incognito.
incognoscible (in·koɣ·nos'θi·βle; -no'si·βle) *adj.* unknowable.
incoherente (in·ko·e'ren·te) *adj.* incoherent. —**incoherencia,** *n.f.* incoherence.
incoloro (in·ko'lo·ro) *adj.* colorless.
incólume (in'ko·lu·me) *adj.* unharmed; safe and sound.
incombustible (in·kom·bus'ti·βle) *adj.* incombustible.
incomible (in·ko'mi·βle) *adj.* inedible.
incomodar (in·ko·mo'ðar) *v.t.* to inconvenience; incommode.
incomodidad (in·ko·mo·ði'ðað) *n.f.* **1,** inconvenience. **2,** discomfort.
incómodo (in'ko·mo·ðo) *adj.* **1,** inconvenient. **2,** uncomfortable.
incomparable (in·kom·pa'ra·βle) *adj.* incomparable.
incompasivo (in·kom·pa'si·βo) *adj.* unmerciful; lacking compassion.
incompatible (in·kom·pa'ti·βle) *adj.* incompatible. —**incompatibilidad,** *n.f.* incompatibility.
incompetente (in·kom·pe'ten·te) *adj.* incompetent. —**incompetencia,** *n.f.* incompetence.
incompleto (in·kom'ple·to) *adj.* incomplete.
incomplexo (in·kom'plek·so) *also,* **incomplejo** (-'ple·xo) *adj.* **1,** unencumbered; free. **2,** uncomplicated; simple.
incomprensible (in·kom·pren·'si·βle) *adj.* incomprehensible.
incomprensión (in·kom·pren·'sjon) *n.f.* lack of understanding. —**incomprensivo,** *adj.* lacking understanding.
incompresible (in·kom·pre'si·βle) *adj.* incompressible.
incomunicable (in·ko·mu·ni·'ka·βle) *adj.* incommunicable.
incomunicado (in·ko·mu·ni'ka·ðo) *adj.* incommunicado; isolated.
incomunicar (in·ko·mu·ni'kar) *v.t.* [*infl.:* **comunicar**] to isolate; place incommunicado.
inconcebible (in·kon·θe'βi·βle; -se'βi·βle) *adj.* inconceivable.
inconciliable (in·kon·θi'lja·βle; -si'lja·βle) *adj.* irreconcilable.
inconcluso (in·kon'klu·so) *adj.* unfinished.
incondicional (in·kon·di·θjo·'nal; -sjo'nal) *adj.* unconditional.
inconducente (in·kon·du'θen·te; -'sen·te) *adj.* nonconducive.
inconexo (in·ko'nek·so) *adj.* **1,** unconnected. **2,** incoherent; disconnected.
inconfesable (in·kon·fe'sa·βle) *adj.* that cannot be confessed; too shameful for mention.
inconfeso (in·kon'fe·so) *adj.* **1,** unconfessed. **2,** unshriven.
inconfundible (in·kon·fun'di·βle) *adj.* unmistakable.
incongruente (in·kon'grwen·te) *adj.* incongruent; incongruous. —**incongruencia,** *n.f.* incongruence; incongruousness.
incongruo (in'kon·grwo) *adj.* incongruous. —**incongruidad** (-gwri·'ðað) *n.f.* incongruity; incongruousness.
inconmensurable (in·kon·men·su'ra·βle) *adj.* incommensurable. —**inconmensurabilidad,** *n.f.* incommensurability.
inconmovible (in·kon·mo·'βi·βle; in·ko·mo-) *adj.* unyielding; unpitying.
inconquistable (in·kon·kis'ta·βle) *adj.* unconquerable.
inconsciencia (in·kons'θjen·θja; -kon'sjen·sja) *n.f.* **1,** unconsciousness. **2,** unawareness.
inconsciente (in·kons'θjen·te; -kon'sjen·te) *adj.* **1,** unconscious. **2,** unaware. **3,** unconscionable. **4,** *colloq.* irresponsible.
inconsecuente (in·kon·se'kwen·te) *adj.* inconsequent; inconsistent.
inconsiderado (in·kon·si·ðe·'ra·ðo) *adj.* inconsiderate. —**inconsideración,** *n.f.* inconsiderateness.
inconsiguiente (in·kon·si'ɣjen·te) *adj.* inconsequent.

inconsistente (in·kon·sis'ten·te) *adj.* 1, lacking consistency; loose; thin. 2, inconsistent. —**inconsistencia,** *n.f.* inconsistency.
inconsolable (in·kon·so'la·βle) *adj.* inconsolable.
inconstante (in·kons'tan·te) *adj.* inconstant. —**inconstancia,** *n.f.* inconstancy.
inconstitucional (in·kons·ti·tu·θjo'nal; -sjo'nal) *adj.* unconstitutional.
incontable (in·kon'ta·βle) *adj.* countless; innumerable.
incontaminado (in·kon·ta·mi·'na·ðo) *adj.* uncontaminated.
incontestable (in·kon·tes'ta·βle) *adj.* unquestionable.
incontinente (in·kon·ti'nen·te) *adj.* incontinent. —**incontinencia,** *n.f.* incontinence.
incontinenti (in·kon·ti'nen·ti) *adv.* at once; immediately.
incontrovertible (in·kon·tro·βer'ti·βle) *adj.* incontrovertible. —**incontrovertibilidad,** *n.f.* incontrovertibility.
inconveniencia (in·kon·βe·'njen·θja; -sja) *n.f.* 1, inconvenience; hardship. 2, untimeliness. 3, indelicacy; impertinence.
inconveniente (in·kon·βe'njen·te) *adj.* 1, inconvenient; difficult. 2, unsuitable; unseemly. —*n.m.* 1, difficulty; hardship. 2, objection; impediment.
inconversable (in·kon·βer'sa·βle) *adj.* unsociable; uncommunicative.
incorporal (in·kor·po'ral) *adj.* 1, incorporeal. 2, insubstantial; unreal.
incorporar (in·kor·po'rar) *v.t.* 1, to incorporate. 2, to embody; include. —**incorporarse,** *v.r.* 1, to incorporate; form a group, society, etc. 2, to sit up; stand up; straighten up. —**incorporación,** *n.f.* incorporation.
incorpóreo (in·kor'po·re·o) *adj.* incorporeal.
incorrección (in·ko·rrek'θjon; '-sjon) *n.f.* 1, incorrectness. 2, impropriety.
incorrecto (in·ko'rrek·to) *adj.* incorrect.
incorregible (in·ko·rre'xi·βle) *adj.* incorrigible. —**incorregibilidad,** *n.f.* incorrigibility.
incorrupto (in·ko'rrup·to) *adj.* 1, incorrupt; uncorrupted. 2, chaste; pure. —**incorruptible,** *adj.* incorruptible. —**incorruptibilidad,** *n.f.* incorruptibility.
incredibilidad (in·kre·ði·βi·li·'ðað) *n.f.* incredibility.
incrédulo (in'kre·ðu·lo) *adj.* incredulous; unbelieving. —*n.m.* unbeliever. —**incredulidad,** *n.f.* incredulity.
increíble (in·kre'i·βle) *adj.* incredible.
incrementar (in·kre·men'tar) *v.t.* to increase.
incremento (in·kre'men·to) *n.m.* increment.
increpar (in·kre'par) *v.t.* to scold; reprimand.
incriminar (in·kri·mi'nar) *v.t.* to incriminate. —**incriminación,** *n.f.* incrimination.
incrustación (in·krus·ta'θjon; -'sjon) *n.f.* 1, incrustation. 2, scale; flaky deposit. 3, inlay; inlaying.
incrustar (in·krus'tar) *v.t.* 1, to inlay. 2, to incrust. 3, to imbed.
incubadora (in·ku·βa'ðo·ra) *n.f.* incubator.
incubar (in·ku'βar) *v.t.* & *i.* to incubate; hatch. —**incubación,** *n.f.* incubation; hatching.
íncubo ('in·ku·βo) *n.m.* incubus.
incuestionable (in·kwes·tjo'na·βle) *adj.* unquestionable.
inculcar (in·kul'kar) *v.t.* [*pres. subjve.* **inculque** (-'kul·ke); *pret.* **inculqué** (-'ke)] to inculcate. —**inculcación,** *n.f.* inculcation.
inculpar (in·kul'par) *v.t.* to inculpate. —**inculpación,** *n.f.* inculpation.
incultivable (in·kul·ti'βa·βle) *adj.* untillable; not arable.
inculto (in'kul·to) *adj.* 1, uncultured; unrefined. 2, uncultivated; untilled.
incultura (in·kul'tu·ra) *n.f.* lack of education; ignorance.
incumbencia (in·kum'ben·θja; -sja) *n.f.* charge; care; concern.
incumbir (in·kum'bir) *v.i.* 1, to pertain; apply. 2, to be incumbent (upon one).
incumplible (in·kum'pli·βle) *adj.* unenforceable.
incumplido (in·kum'pli·ðo) *adj.* 1, unfulfilled. 2, *colloq.* unreliable; untrustworthy.
incurable (in·ku'ra·βle) *adj.* incurable.
incuria (in'ku·rja) *n.f.* carelessness.

incurrir (in·ku'rrir) *v.i., fol. by* **en,** to fall *or* run (into sin, error, debt, etc.).
incursión (in·kur'sjon) *n.f.* incursion; inroad.
indagador (in·da·ɣa'ðor) *n.m.* investigator; inquirer. —*adj.* investigating; inquiring.
indagar (in·da'ɣar) *v.t.* [*pres. subjve.* **indague** (-'da·ɣe); *pret.* **indagué** (-'ɣe)] to investigate; inquire into. —**indagación,** *n.f.* investigation; inquiry; inquest. —**indagatoria** (-'to·rja) *n.f., law* unsworn statement taken from a suspect.
indebidamente (in·de·βi·ða·'men·te) *adv.* unduly; improperly.
indebido (in·de'βi·ðo) *adj.* undue; unwarranted; improper.
indecente (in·de'θen·te; -'sen·te) *adj.* indecent. —**indecencia,** *n.f.* indecency.
indecible (in·de'θi·βle; -'si·βle) *adj.* inexpressible; unutterable.
indecisión (in·de·θi'sjon; -si·'sjon) *n.f.* **1,** indecision. **2,** indecisiveness.
indeciso (in·de'θi·so; -'si·so) *adj.* **1,** undecided. **2,** indecisive.
indecoro (in·de'ko·ro) *n.m.* indecorum; indecorousness. —**indecoroso,** *adj.* indecorous; unbecoming.
indefectible (in·de·fek'ti·βle) *adj.* unfailing.
indefendible (in·de·fen'di·βle) *adj.* indefensible.
indefenso (in·de'fen·so) *adj.* defenseless.
indefinible (in·de·fi'ni·βle) *adj.* indefinable.
indefinido (in·de·fi'ni·ðo) *adj.* **1,** undefined. **2,** indefinite.
indeleble (in·de'le·βle) *adj.* indelible.
indeliberado (in·de·li·βe'ra·ðo) *adj.* unpremeditated; unconsidered.
indemne (in'dem·ne) *adj.* undamaged; unhurt; intact.
indemnidad (in·dem·ni'ðað) *n.f.* exemption from loss or liability; indemnity.
indemnización (in·dem·ni·θa·'θjon; -sa'sjon) *n.f.* **1,** indemnification. **2,** indemnity.
indemnizar (in·dem·ni'θar; -'sar) *v.t.* [*pres.subjve.* **indemnice** (-'ni·θe; -se); *pret.* **indemnicé** (-'θe; -'se)] to indemnify.
independencia (in·de·pen'den·θja; -sja) *n.f.* independence.
independiente (in·de·pen'djen·te) *adj.* independent.
independizar (in·de·pen·di'θar; -'sar) *v.t.* [*pres.subjve.* **independice** (-'di·θe; -se); *pret.* **independicé** (-'θe; -'se)] *Amer.* to grant independence to. —**independizarse,** *v.r.* to become independent.
indescifrable (in·des·θi'fra·βle; in·de·si-) *adj.* undecipherable.
indescriptible (in·des·krip'ti·βle) *adj.* indescribable.
indeseable (in·de·se'a·βle) *adj.* undesirable.
indestructible (in·des·truk'ti·βle) *adj.* indestructible.
indeterminado (in·de·ter·mi·'na·ðo) *adj.* **1,** indeterminate. **2,** irresolute. **3,** *gram.* indefinite. —**indeterminable,** *adj.* indeterminable.
indiada (in'dja·ða) *n.f., Amer.* **1,** group or multitude of Indians. **2,** Indian-like act or remark.
indiano (in'dja·no) *adj.* native of *or* resident in America. —*n.m.* nabob; one who returns rich from America.
indicación (in·di·ka'θjon; -'sjon) *n.f.* **1,** indication. **2,** suggestion.
indicado (in·di'ka·ðo) *adj.* **1,** indicated. **2,** appropriate.
indicador (in·di·ka'ðor) *n.m.* indicator; pointer; gauge. —*adj.* indicating.
indicar (in·di'kar) *v.t.* [*pres.subjve.* **indique;** *pret.* **indiqué**] **1,** to indicate; point out. **2,** to suggest.
indicativo (in·di·ka'ti·βo) *adj.* & *n.m.* indicative.
índice ('in·di·θe; -se) *n.m.* **1,** index. **2,** forefinger. **3,** hand; pointer (*of a clock, gauge, etc.*). **4,** rate (*of births, deaths, growth, etc.*).
indicio (in'di·θjo; -sjo) *n.m.* sign; clue; hint.
índico ('in·di·ko) *adj.* Indian (*of India*). —**Océano Índico,** Indian Ocean.
indiferente (in·di·fe'ren·te) *adj.* indifferent. —**indiferencia,** *n.f.* indifference.
indígena (in'di·xe·na) *adj.* indigenous; native. —*n.m.* & *f.* native.
indigente (in·di'xen·te) *adj.* indigent. —**indigencia,** *n.f.* indigence.
indigestarse (in·di·xes'tar·se) *v.r.* **1,** to cause indigestion. **2,** to have indigestion. **3,** *colloq.* (*usu. of per-*

sons) to be unbearable; be hard to take.
indigestible (in·di·xes'ti·βle) *adj.* indigestible.
indigestión (in·di·xes'tjon) *n.f.* indigestion.
indigesto (in·di'xes·to) *adj.* **1,** = **indigestible. 2,** undigested. **3,** stodgy; crude.
indignar (in·diɣ'nar) *v.t.* to anger; make indignant. —**indignación,** *n.f.* indignation. —**indignado,** *adj.* indignant.
indigno (in'diɣ·no) *adj.* **1,** unworthy. **2,** despicable; low. —**indignidad,** *n.f.* indignity.
índigo ('in·di·ɣo) *n.m.* indigo.
indio ('in·djo) *adj.* & *n.m.* Indian. —*n.m., chem.* indium.
indique (in'di·ke) *v., pres.subjve. of* **indicar.**
indiqué (in·di'ke) *v., 1st pers. sing. pret. of* **indicar.**
indirecta (in·di'rek·ta) *n.f.* **1,** innuendo; hint. **2,** *colloq.* dig; sarcasm.
indirecto (in·di'rek·to) *adj.* indirect.
indiscernible (in·dis·θer'ni·βle; in·di·ser-) *adj.* undiscernible.
indisciplina (in·dis·θi'pli·na; in·di·si-) *n.f.* lack of discipline.
indisciplinado (in·dis·θi·pli'na·ðo; in·di·si-) *adj.* undisciplined.
indisciplinarse (in·dis·θi·pli·'nar·se; in·di·si-) *v.r.* to rebel; defy discipline.
indiscreción (in·dis·kre'θjon; -'sjon) *n.f.* **1,** indiscreetness. **2,** indiscretion.
indiscreto (in·dis'kre·to) *adj.* indiscreet.
indiscutible (in·dis·ku'ti·βle) *adj.* indisputable; unquestionable.
indisoluble (in·di·so'lu·βle) *adj.* indissoluble. —**indisolubilidad,** *n.f.* indissolubility.
indispensable (in·dis·pen'sa·βle) *adj.* indispensable.
indisponer (in·dis·po'ner) *v.t.* [*infl.:* **poner**] **1,** to indispose; upset. **2,** to prejudice; turn (someone) against. —**indisponerse,** *v.r.* **1,** to become ill. **2,** to quarrel; fall out.
indisponible (in·dis·po'ni·βle) *adj.* unavailable.
indisposición (in·dis·po·si'θjon; -'sjon) *n.f.* indisposition.
indispuesto (in·dis'pwes·to) *v., p.p. of* **indisponer.** —*adj.* indisposed.
indisputable (in·dis·pu'ta·βle) *adj.* indisputable.
indistinguible (in·dis·tin'gi·βle) *adj.* indistinguishable.
indistinto (in·dis'tin·to) *adj.* **1,** indistinct. **2,** indiscriminate.
individual (in·di·βi'ðwal) *adj.* individual. —**individualidad,** *n.f.* individuality. —**individualismo,** *n.m.* individualism. —**individualista,** *adj.* individualistic. —*n.m.* & *f.* individualist.
individuo (in·di'βi·dwo) *n.m.* individual; person.
indivisible (in·di·βi'si·βle) *adj.* indivisible. —**indivisibilidad,** *n.f.* indivisibility.
indiviso (in·di'βi·so) *adj.* undivided.
indo- (in·do) *prefix* Indo-; Indian: *indoeuropeo,* Indo-European.
indócil (in'do·θil; -sil) *adj.* unruly; unmanageable. —**indocilidad,** *n.f.* unruliness.
indocto (in'dok·to) *adj.* uneducated; untutored.
indoeuropeo ('in·do·eu·ro'pe·o) *adj.* & *n.m.* Indo-European.
índole ('in·do·le) *n.f.* **1,** disposition; nature. **2,** kind; class.
indolente (in·do'len·te) *adj.* indolent. —**indolencia,** *n.f.* indolence.
indomable (in·do'ma·βle) *adj.* **1,** untamable. **2,** indomitable.
indomado (in·do'ma·ðo) *adj.* untamed; unsubdued.
indómito (in'do·mi·to) *adj.* **1,** untamed. **2,** indomitable.
indubitable (in·du·βi'ta·βle) *adj.* = **indudable.**
inducción (in·duk'θjon; -'sjon) *n.f.* **1,** inducement. **2,** *physics; logic* induction.
inducir (in·du'θir; -'sir) *v.t.* [*infl.:* **conducir**] to induce. —**inducimiento,** *n.m.* inducement.
inductivo (in·duk'ti·βo) *adj.* inductive.
indudable (in·du'ða·βle) *adj.* undoubted; indubitable.
indulgente (in·dul'xen·te) *adj.* indulgent. —**indulgencia,** *n.f.* indulgence.
indultar (in·dul'tar) *v.t.* to pardon; remit.
indulto (in'dul·to) *n.m.* pardon; remission.
indumentaria (in·du·men'ta·rja) *n.f.* apparel; dress.
indumento (in·du'men·to) *n.m.* garment.

induración (in·du·ra'θjon; -'sjon) *n.f.* hardening; induration; callosity.

industria (in'dus·trja) *n.f.* industry. —**industrial,** *adj.* industrial. —*n.m.* industrialist. —**de industria,** intentionally; on purpose.

industrialismo (in·dus·trja'lis·mo) *n.m.* industrialism. —**industrialista,** *n.m.* & *f., Amer.* industrialist.

industrializar (in·dus·trja·li'θar; -'sar) *v.t.* [*pres.subjve.* **industrialice** ('li·θe; -se); *pret.* **industrialicé** (-'θe; -'se)] to industrialize. —**industrialización,** *n.f.* industrialization.

industrioso (in·dus'trjo·so) *adj.* industrious.

induzca (in'duθ·ka; in'dus-) *v., pres.subjve. of* **inducir.**

induzco (in'duθ·ko; in'dus-) *v., 1st pers.sing.pres.ind. of* **inducir.**

inédito (in'e·ði·to) *adj.* unpublished.

ineducable (in·e·du'ka·βle) *adj.* uneducable. —**ineducación,** *n.f.* lack of education. —**ineducado,** *adj.* uneducated.

inefable (in·e'fa·βle) *adj.* ineffable. —**inefabilidad,** *n.f.* ineffability.

ineficaz (in·e·fi'kaθ; -'kas) *adj.* inefficacious; ineffective; ineffectual. —**ineficacia,** *n.f.* inefficacy; inefficiency.

ineficiente (in·e·fi'θjen·te; -'sjen·te) *adj.* inefficient. —**ineficiencia,** *n.f.* inefficiency.

inelegante (in·e·le'ɣan·te) *adj.* inelegant. —**inelegancia,** *n.f.* inelegance; inelegancy.

inelegible (in·e·le'xi·βle) *adj.* ineligible. —**inelegibilidad,** *n.f.* ineligibility.

ineluctable (in·e·luk'ta·βle) *adj.* ineluctable.

ineludible (in·e·lu'ði·βle) *adj.* unavoidable; inescapable.

-íneo ('i·ne·o) *suffix, forming adjectives denoting* condition; character; form: *sanguíneo,* sanguineous; *rectilíneo,* rectilinear.

inepto (in'ep·to) *adj.* inept. —**ineptitud,** *also* **inepcia** (in'ep·θja; -sja) *n.f.* ineptness; ineptitude.

inequívoco (in·e'ki·βo·ko) *adj.* unmistakable; unequivocal.

inercia (i'ner·θja; -sja) *n.f.* **1,** inertness. **2,** inertia.

inerme (in'er·me) *adj.* unarmed.

inerte (i'ner·te) *adj.* inert.

inescrupuloso (in·es·kru·pu'lo·so) *adj.* unscrupulous. —**inescrupulosidad,** *n.f.* unscrupulousness.

inescrutable (in·es·kru'ta·βle) *adj.* inscrutable. —**inescrutabilidad,** *n.f.* inscrutability.

inesperado (in·es·pe'ra·ðo) *adj.* unexpected.

inestable (in·es'ta·βle) *adj.* unstable. —**inestabilidad,** *n.f.* instability.

inestimable (in·es·ti'ma·βle) *adj.* inestimable.

inevitable (in·e·βi'ta·βle) *adj.* inevitable. —**inevitabilidad,** *n.f.* inevitability.

inexacto (in·ek'sak·to) *adj.* inexact; inaccurate. —**inexactitud,** *n.f.* inaccuracy; inexactness.

inexcusable (in·eks·ku'sa·βle) *adj.* inexcusable.

inexistente (in·ek·sis'ten·te) *adj.* nonexistent. —**inexistencia,** *n.f.* nonexistence.

inexorable (in·ek·so'ra·βle) *adj.* inexorable. —**inexorabilidad,** *n.f.* inexorableness; inexorability.

inexperiencia (in·eks·pe'rjen·θja; -sja) *n.f.* inexperience.

inexperto (in·eks'per·to) *adj.* inexperienced; unskillful.

inexpiable (in·eks·pi'a·βle) *adj.* inexpiable.

inexplicable (in·eks·pli'ka·βle) *adj.* inexplicable. —**inexplicado** (-'ka·ðo) *adj.* unexplained.

inexplorado (in·eks·plo'ra·ðo) *adj.* unexplored.

inexpresable (in·eks·pre'sa·βle) *adj.* inexpressible. —**inexpresado** (-'sa·ðo) *adj.* unexpressed.

inexpresivo (in·eks·pre'si·βo) *adj.* inexpressive.

inexpugnable (in·eks·puɣ'na·βle) *adj.* impregnable.

inextinguible (in·eks·tin'gi·βle) *adj.* inextinguishable.

inextirpable (in·eks·tir'pa·βle) *adj.* ineradicable.

inextricable (in·eks·tri'ka·βle) *adj.* inextricable.

infalible (in·fa'li·βle) *adj.* infallible. —**infalibilidad,** *n.f.* infallibility.

infamar (in·fa'mar) *v.t.* to defame.

infame (in'fa·me) *adj.* infamous. —*n.m.* & *f.* scoundrel; infamous person.

infamia (in'fa·mja) *n.f.* infamy.

infancia (in'fan·θja; -sja) *n.f.* infancy; childhood.
infando (in'fan·do) *adj.* unmentionable.
infanta (in'fan·ta) *n.f.* infanta.
infante (in'fan·te) *n.m.* **1,** infant. **2,** infante. **3,** infantryman.
infantería (in·fan·te'ri·a) *n.f.* infantry.
infanticida (in·fan·ti'θi·ða; -'si·ða) *n.m.* & *f.* infanticide (*agent*). —**infanticidio** (-'θi·ðjo; -'si·ðjo) *n.m.* infanticide (*act*).
infantil (in·fan'til) *adj.* infantile; childish.
infatigable (in·fa·ti'ɣa·βle) *adj.* indefatigable.
infatuación (in·fa·twa'θjon; -'sjon) *n.f.* **1,** vanity; conceit. **2,** infatuation.
infatuar (in·fa'twar) *v.t.* [*pres. ind.* **infatúo** (-'tu·o); *pres.subjve.* **infatúe** (-'tu·e)] **1,** to make vain or conceited. **2,** to infatuate. —**infatuarse,** *v.r.* **1,** to become vain or conceited. **2,** to become infatuated.
infausto (in'faus·to) *adj.* unfortunate; unlucky.
infección (in·fek'θjon; -'sjon) *n.f.* infection. —**infeccioso,** *adj.* infectious.
infectar (in·fek'tar) *v.t.* to infect. —**infectarse.** *v.r.* to become infected.
infecto (in'fek·to) *adj.* polluted; infected; corrupt.
infecundo (in·fe'kun·do) *adj.* infecund. —**infecundidad,** *n.f.* infecundity.
infelicidad (in·fe·li·θi'ðað; -si·'ðað) *n.f.* misfortune.
infeliz (in·fe'liθ; -'lis) *adj.* unhappy; unfortunate. —*n.m.* wretch.
inferior (in·fe'rjor) *adj.* **1,** inferior; subordinate. **2,** lower. —*n.m.* inferior. —**inferioridad,** *n.f.* inferiority.
inferir (in·fe'rir) *v.t.* [*infl.:* **diferir**] **1,** to infer. **2,** to imply. **3,** to inflict. —**inferencia,** *n.f.* inference.
infernal (in·fer'nal) *adj.* infernal.
infestar (in·fes'tar) *v.t.* to infest. —**infestación,** *n.f.* infestation.
inficionar (in·fi·θjo'nar; -sjo·'nar) *v.t.* **1,** to infect; contaminate. **2,** to corrupt.
infidelidad (in·fi·ðe·li'ðað) *n.f.* infidelity.
infiel (in'fjel) *adj.* unfaithful. —*adj.* & *n.m.* & *f.* infidel.
infierno (in'fjer·no) *n.m.* hell; inferno. —**en el quinto infierno,** *colloq.* far away.
infiltrar (in·fil'trar) *v.t.* to infiltrate. —**infiltración,** *n.f.* infiltration.
ínfimo ('in·fi·mo) *adj.* **1,** lowest. **2,** least.
infinidad (in·fi·ni'ðað) *n.f.* **1,** infinity. **2,** crowd; multitude.
infinitesimal (in·fi·ni·te·si'mal) *adj.* infinitesimal.
infinitivo (in·fi·ni'ti·βo) *adj.* & *n.m.* infinitive.
infinito (in·fi'ni·to) *adj.* infinite. —*n.m.* infinity. —*adv., colloq.* a great deal; much.
inflación (in·fla'θjon; -'sjon) *n.f.* inflation. —**inflacionista,** *adj.* inflationary.
inflamable (in·fla'ma·βle) *adj.* inflammable.
inflamación (in·fla·ma'θjon; -'sjon) *n.f.* inflammation.
inflamar (in·fla'mar) *v.t.* to inflame. —**inflamarse,** *v.r.* to become inflamed; become swollen.
inflamatorio (in·fla·ma'to·rjo) *adj.* inflammatory.
inflar (in'flar) *v.t.* to inflate. —**inflarse,** *v.r.* to puff up with pride; become elated.
inflexible (in·flek'si·βle) *adj.* inflexible. —**inflexibilidad,** *n.f.* inflexibility.
inflexión (in·flek'sjon) *n.f.* inflection.
infligir (in·fli'xir) *v.t.* [*pres.ind.* **inflijo** (-'fli·xo) *pres.subjve.* **inflija** (-xa)] to inflict.
influencia (in·flu'en·θja; -sja) *n.f.* influence.
influenza (in·flu'en·θa; -sa) *n.f.* influenza.
influir (in·flu'ir) *v.i.* [*infl.:* **fluir**] to have or exert influence. —**influir en,** to influence.
influjo (in'flu·xo) *n.m.* **1,** influence. **2,** influx.
influyente (in·flu'jen·te) *adj.* influential.
información (in·for·ma'θjon; -'sjon) *n.f.* **1,** information. **2,** *law* inquiry.
informal (in·for'mal) *adj.* **1,** informal. **2,** *colloq.* unreliable; untrustworthy. —**informalidad,** *n.f.* informality.
informante (in·for'man·te) *n.m.* & *f.* **1,** informant. **2,** informer.

informar (in·for'mar) *v.t.* **1,** to inform. **2,** *philos.* to give form to. —*v.i.* **1,** *law* to plead. **2,** to submit a report; report.

informativo (in·for·ma'ti·βo) *adj.* informative.

informe (in'for·me) *n.m.* **1,** report; account. **2,** *law* plea. —*adj.* shapeless; formless.

infortunio (in·for'tu·njo) *n.m.* misfortune.

infra- (in·fra) *prefix* infra-; below; under: *infrarrojo,* infrared.

infracción (in·frak'θjon; -'sjon) *n.f.* infraction; transgression. —**infractor** (-'tor) *n.m.* transgressor.

infrangible (in·fran'xi·βle) *adj.* infrangible.

infranqueable (in·fran·ke'a·βle) *adj.* insurmountable.

infrarrojo (in·fra'rro·xo) *adj.* infrared.

infrascrito (in·fras'kri·to) *n.m.* undersigned.

infrecuente (in·fre'kwen·te) *adj.* infrequent. —**infrecuencia,** *n.f.* infrequency.

infringir (in·frin'xir) *v.t.* [*pres. ind.* **infrinjo** (-'frin·xo); *pres.subjve.* **infrinja** (-xa)] to infringe; violate.

infructuoso (in·fruk'two·so) *adj.* fruitless; futile.

ínfulas ('in·fu·las) *n.f.pl.* conceit (*sing.*); airs.

infundado (in·fun'da·ðo) *adj.* groundless.

infundir (in·fun'dir) *v.t.* **1,** to infuse. **2,** to inspire; instill.

infusión (in·fu'sjon) *n.f.* infusion.

ingeniar (in·xe'njar) *v.t.* to contrive; invent. —**ingeniárselas,** to manage.

ingeniería (in·xe·nje'ri·a) *n.f.* engineering.

ingeniero (in·xe'nje·ro) *n.m.* engineer.

ingenio (in'xe·njo) *n.m.* **1,** ingenuity. **2,** talent. **3,** genius; talented person. **4,** engine; mechanical device. —**ingenio de azúcar, 1,** sugar refinery. **2,** sugar plantation.

ingenioso (in·xe'njo·so) *adj.* ingenious. —**ingeniosidad,** *n.f.* ingenuity.

ingénito (in'xe·ni·to) *adj.* inborn; innate.

ingenuo (in'xe·nwo) *adj.* ingenuous. —**ingenuidad,** *n.f.* ingenuousness.

ingerir (in·xe'rir) *v.t.* [*infl.:* **digerir**] to ingest. —**ingestión** (in·xes'tjon) *n.f.* ingestion.

ingle ('in·gle) *n.f.* groin.

inglés (in'gles) *adj.* English. —*n.m.* **1,** Englishman. **2,** English language. —**inglesa,** *n.f.* Englishwoman. —**a la inglesa,** in English fashion. —**ir a la inglesa,** *Amer.* to go Dutch.

inglesar (in·gle'sar) *v.t.* to Anglicize.

inglete (in'gle·te) *n.m.* miter; miter joint.

ingobernable (in·go·βer'na·βle) *adj.* ungovernable; uncontrollable.

ingramatical (in·gra·ma·ti'kal) *adj.* ungrammatical.

ingrato (in'gra·to) *adj.* **1,** ungrateful. **2,** thankless. **3,** disagreeable; unpleasant. —*n.m.* ingrate. —**ingratitud,** *n.f.* ingratitude.

ingrediente (in·gre'ðjen·te) *n.m.* ingredient.

ingresar (in·gre'sar) *v.t.* **1,** to enter; go in. **2,** to join; become a member.

ingreso (in'gre·so) *n.m.* **1,** entrance. **2,** *usu.pl.* income; revenue.

inhábil (in'a·βil) *adj.* inept; unskillful. —**día inhábil,** holiday. —**hora inhábil,** hour when an office is closed for business.

inhabilidad (in·a·βi·li'ðað) *n.f.* **1,** ineptitude. **2,** disability; impediment.

inhabilitar (in·a·βi·li'tar) *v.t.* to incapacitate. —**inhabilitación,** *n.f.* incapacitation.

inhabitable (in·a·βi'ta·βle) *adj.* uninhabitable. —**inhabitado** (-'ta·ðo) *adj.* uninhabited.

inhalador (in·a·la'ðor) *n.m.* **1,** inhalant. **2,** inhaler; inhalator.

inhalar (in·a'lar) *v.t.* & *i.* to inhale. —**inhalación,** *n.f.* inhalation.

inherente (in·e'ren·te) *adj.* inherent. —**inherencia,** *n.f.* inherence.

inhibir (in·i'βir) *v.t.* to inhibit. —**inhibirse,** *v.r. fol. by* **de** *or* **en,** to eschew; abstain from. —**inhibición,** *n.f.* inhibition.

inhospitalario (in·os·pi·ta'la·rjo) *adj.* inhospitable. *Also,* **inhóspito** (in'os·pi·to).

inhospitalidad (in·os·pi·ta·li·'ðað) *n.f.* inhospitability.

inhumano (in·u'ma·no) *adj.* **1,** inhuman. **2,** inhumane. —**inhumanidad,** *n.f.* inhumanity.

inhumar (in·u'mar) *v.t.* to bury; inter. —**inhumación**, *n.f.* burial; interment.
inicial (i·ni'θjal; -'sjal) *adj.* & *n.f.* initial.
iniciar (i·ni'θjar; -'sjar) *v.t.* to initiate. —**iniciarse**, *v.r.* to be initiated. —**iniciación**, *n.f.* initiation. —**iniciador**, *adj.* initiating. —*n.m.* initiator.
iniciativa (i·ni·θja'ti·βa; i·ni·sja-) *n.f.* initiative. —**iniciativo**, *adj.* initiating.
inicio (i'ni·θjo; -sjo) *n.m.* beginning; start.
inicuo (i'ni·kwo) *adj.* iniquitous.
inigualado (in·i·ɣwa'la·ðo) *adj.* unequaled.
inimaginable (in·i·ma·xi'na·βle) *adj.* unimaginable.
inimitable (in·i·mi'ta·βle) *adj.* inimitable.
ininteligible (in·in·te·li'xi·βle) *adj.* unintelligible.
ininterrumpido (in·in·te·rrum·'pi·ðo) *adj.* uninterrupted.
iniquidad (in·i·ki'ðað) *n.f.* iniquity.
injerir (in·xe'rir) *v.t.* [*infl.:* **herir**] to insert. —**injerirse**, *v.r.* to become involved.
injertar (in·xer'tar) *v.t.* to graft; implant.
injerto (in'xer·to) *n.m.* graft; implant.
injuria (in'xu·rja) *n.f.* **1,** affront; insult. **2,** injury; wrong.
injuriar (in·xu'rjar) *v.t.* **1,** to affront; insult. **2,** to wrong; injure.
injurioso (in·xu'rjo·so) *adj.* **1,** insulting; offensive. **2,** injurious; hurtful.
injusticia (in·xus'ti·θja; -sja) *n.f.* injustice.
injustificable (in·xus·ti·fi'ka·βle) *adj.* unjustifiable.
injustificado (in·xus·ti·fi'ka·ðo) *adj.* unjustified.
injusto (in'xus·to) *adj.* unjust; unfair.
inmaculado (in·ma·ku'la·ðo; i·ma-) *adj.* immaculate.
inmadurez (in·ma·ðu'reθ; -'res) *adj.* immaturity.
inmanejable (in·ma·ne'xa·βle; i·ma-) *adj.* unmanageable.
inmanente (in·ma'nen·te; i·ma-) *adj.* immanent. —**inmanencia**, *n.f.* immanence.
inmaterial (in·ma·te'rjal; i·ma-) *adj.* immaterial. —**inmaterialidad**, *n.f.* immateriality.
inmaturo (in·ma'tu·ro; i·ma-) *adj.* immature; unripe.
inmediación (in·me·ðja'θjon; -'sjon, *also,* i·me-) *n.f.* immediate vicinity; proximity. —**inmediaciones**, *n.f.pl.* environs.
inmediatamente (in·me·ðja·ta·'men·te) *adv.* immediately; at once.
inmediato (in·me'ðja·to; i·me-) *adj.* immediate. —**de inmediato**, immediately.
inmejorable (in·me·xo'ra·βle; i·me-) *adj.* most excellent; unsurpassable.
inmemorial (in·me·mo'rjal; i·me-) *adj.* immemorial.
inmenso (in'men·so; i'men-) *adj.* immense. —**inmensidad**, *n.f.* immensity.
inmensurable (in·men·su'ra·βle; i·men-) *adj.* immeasurable.
inmerecido (in·me·re'θi·do; -'si·ðo; *also,* i·me-) *adj.* undeserved; unmerited.
inmersión (in·mer'sjon; i·mer-) *n.f.* immersion.
inmigrar (in·mi'ɣrar; i·mi-) *v.i.* to immigrate. —**inmigración**, *n.f.* immigration. —**inmigrante**, *n.m.* & *f.* & *adj.* immigrant.
inminente (in·mi'nen·te; i·mi-) *adj.* imminent. —**inminencia**, *n.f.* imminence.
inmiscuir (in·mis·ku'ir; i·mis-) *v.t.* [*infl.:* **huir**] to mix; blend. —**inmiscuirse**, *v.r.* to meddle.
inmoderado (in·mo·ðe'ra·ðo; i·mo-) *adj.* immoderate. —**inmoderación**, *n.f.* immoderation.
inmodesto (in·mo'ðes·to; i·mo-) *adj.* immodest. —**inmodestia**, *n.f.* immodesty.
inmolar (in·mo'lar; i·mo-) *v.t.* to immolate. —**inmolación**, *n.f.* immolation.
inmoral (in·mo'ral; i·mo-) *adj.* immoral. —**inmoralidad**, *n.f.* immorality.
inmortal (in·mor'tal; i·mor-) *adj* & *n.m.* & *f.* immortal. —**inmortalidad**, *n.f.* immortality.
inmortalizar (in·mor·ta·li'θar -'sar, *also,* i·mor-) *v.t.* [*pres.subjve* **inmortalice** (-'li·θe; -se); *pret.* **inmortalicé** (-'θe; -'se)] to immortalize. —**inmortalización**, *n.f.* immortalization.

inmoto (in'mo·to; i'mo-) *adj.* unmoved.

inmovible (in·mo'βi·βle; i·mo-) *adj.* immovable.

inmóvil (in'mo·βil; i'mo-) *adj.* immobile; motionless. —**inmovilidad,** *n.f.* immobility.

inmovilizar (in·mo·βi·li'θar; -'sar, *also,* i·mo-) *v.t.* [*infl.:* **movilizar**] to immobilize. —**inmovilización,** *n.f.* immobilization.

inmueble (in'mwe·βle; i'mwe-) *adj., law* real (*of property*). —*n.m.* real property.

inmundicia (in·mun'di·θja; -sja, *also,* i·mun-) *n.f.* filth. —**inmundo** (in'mun·do; i'mun-) *adj.* filthy.

inmune (in'mu·ne; i'mu-) *adj.* immune. —**inmunidad,** *n.f.* immunity.

inmunizar (in·mu·ni'θar; -'sar; *also,* i·mu-) *v.t.* [*pres.subjve.* **inmunice** (-'ni·θe; -se); *pret.* **inmunicé** (-'θe; -'se)] to immunize —**inmunización,** *n.f.* immunization.

inmutable (in·mu'ta·βle; i·mu-) *adj.* immutable. —**inmutabilidad,** *n.f.* immutability.

inmutar (in·mu'tar; i·mu-) *v.t.* to alter; change. —**inmutarse,** *v.r.* to become ruffled; change countenance.

innato (in'na·to; i'na-) *adj.* innate; inborn.

innatural (in·na·tu'ral: i·na-) *adj.* unnatural.

innecesario (in·ne·θe'sa·rjo; -se'sa·rjo, *also,* i·ne-) *adj.* unnecessary.

innegable (in·ne'ɣa·βle; i·ne-) *adj.* undeniable.

innoble (in'no·βle; i'no-) *adj.* ignoble.

innocuo (in'no·kwo; i'no-) *adj.* innocuous; harmless.

innominado (in·no·mi'na·ðo; i·no-) *adj.* **1,** unnamed; nameless. **2,** *anat.* innominate.

innovar (in·no'βar; i·no-) *v.t.* to innovate. —**innovación,** *n.f.* innovation. —**innovador,** *adj.* innovating. —*n.m.* innovator.

innumerable (in·nu·me'ra·βle; i·nu-) *adj.* innumerable.

-ino ('i·no) *suffix* -ine; *forming adjectives and nouns meaning* like; made of; pertaining to: *opalino,* opaline; *sanguino,* sanguine; *canino,* canine.

inobservable (in·oβ·ser'βa·βle) *adj.* unobservable.

inobservancia (in·oβ·ser'βan·θja; -sja) *n.f.* noncompliance; nonobservance.

inocente (i·no'θen·te; -'sen·te) *adj.* & *n.m.* & *f.* innocent. —**inocencia,** *n.f.* innocence.

inocentón (i·no·θen'ton; -sen'ton) *n.m.* dupe; gull; simpleton.

inocuidad (i·no·kwi'ðað) *n.f.* innocuousness; harmlessness. —**inocuo** (i'no·kwo) *adj.* = **innocuo.**

inocular (i·no·ku'lar) *v.t.* to inoculate. —**inoculación,** *n.f.* inoculation.

inodoro (in·o'ðo·ro) *adj.* odorless. —*n.m.* **1,** deodorizer. **2,** *Amer.* water closet; toilet.

inofensivo (in·o·fen'si·βo) *adj.* inoffensive.

inolvidable (in·ol·βi'ða·βle) *adj.* unforgettable. —**inolvidado** (-'ða·ðo) *adj.* unforgotten.

inoperable (in·o·pe'ra·βle) *adj.* inoperable.

inoperante (in·o·pe'ran·te) *adj.* inoperative.

inopia (i'no·pja) *n.f.* **1,** poverty; indigence. **2,** *colloq.* blissful ignorance.

inopinado (in·o·pi'na·ðo) *adj.* unexpected.

inoportuno (in·o·por'tu·no) *adj.* inopportune. —**inoportunidad,** *n.f.* inopportuneness.

inorgánico (in·or'ɣa·ni·ko) *adj.* inorganic.

inorganizado (in·or·ɣa·ni'θa·ðo; -'sa·ðo) *adj.* unorganized.

inoxidable (in·ok·si'ða·βle) *adj.* stainless; rustproof.

inquietar (in·kje'tar) *v.t.* to disquiet; disturb; worry.

inquieto (in'kje·to) *adj.* **1,** uneasy; worried. **2,** restless.

inquietud (in·kje'tuð) *n.f.* **1,** restlessness. **2,** uneasiness; worry.

inquilino (in·ki'li·no) *n.m.* tenant.

inquina (in'ki·na) *n.f.* aversion; hatred.

inquirir (in·ki'rir) *v.t.* [*infl.:* **adquirir**] to inquire into; investigate.

inquisición (in·ki·si'θjon; -'sjon) *n.f.* inquisition. —**inquisidor,** *n.m.* inquisitor.

inquisitivo (in·ki·si'ti·βo) *adj.* inquisitive.

insabible (in·sa'βi·βle) *adj.* unknowable; unascertainable.

insaciable (in·sa'θja·βle; -'sja·βle) *adj.* insatiable. —**insaciabilidad,** *n.f.* insatiability.
insalubre (in·sa'lu·βre) *adj.* insalubrious; unhealthful; unsanitary.
insano (in'sa·no) *adj.* insane.
insatisfecho (in·sa·tis'fe·tʃo) *adj.* unsatisfied.
inscribir (ins·kri'βir) *v.t.* [*p.p.* **inscrito** (-'kri·to)] **1,** to inscribe. **2,** to register; enroll.
inscripción (ins·krip'θjon; -'sjon) *n.f.* **1,** inscription. **2,** registration; enrollment.
insecticida (in·sek·ti'θi·ða; -'si·ða) *n.m.* insecticide.
insecto (in'sek·to) *n.m.* insect.
inseguro (in·se'ɣu·ro) *adj.* **1,** insecure. **2,** uncertain. —**inseguridad,** *n.f.* insecurity.
insensato (in·sen'sa·to) *adj.* senseless; mad. —*n.m.* fool; madman. —**insensatez,** *n.f.* senselessness; madness.
insensible (in·sen'si·βle) *adj.* **1,** insensible. **2,** insensitive; unfeeling. —**insensibilidad,** *n.f.* insensibility.
inseparable (in·se·pa'ra·βle) *adj.* inseparable.
insepulto (in·se'pul·to) *adj.* unburied.
inserción (in·ser'θjon; -'sjon) *n.f.* **1,** insertion. **2,** insert.
insertar (in·ser'tar) *v.t.* [*p.p.* **insertado,** *also,* **inserto** (in'ser·to)] to insert.
inservible (in·ser'βi·βle) *adj.* useless.
insidia (in'si·ðja) *n.f.* **1,** snare; ambush. **2,** insidiousness. —**insidioso,** *adj.* insidious.
insigne (in'siɣ·ne) *adj.* renowned; famous.
insignia (in'siɣ·nja) *n.f.* **1,** insignia; badge; emblem. **2,** flag; pennant.
insignificante (in·siɣ·ni·fi·'kan·te) *adj.* insignificant. —**insignificancia,** *n.f.* insignificance.
insincero (in·sin'θe·ro; -'se·ro) *adj.* insincere. —**insinceridad,** *n.f.* insincerity.
insinuar (in·si'nwar) *v.t.* [*infl.:* **continuar**] to insinuate; hint. —**insinuación,** *n.f.* insinuation; hint.
insípido (in'si·pi·ðo) *adj.* insipid. —**insipidez,** *n.f.* insipidity.
insistir (in·sis'tir) *v.i.* to insist. —**insistencia,** *n.f.* insistence. —**insistente,** *adj.* insistent.
insociable (in·so'θja·βle; -'sja·βle) *adj.* unsociable.
insolación (in·so·la'θjon; -'sjon) *n.f.* sunstroke.
insolentar (in·so·len'tar) *v.t.* to make insolent. —**insolentarse,** *v.r.* to be or become insolent.
insolente (in·so'len·te) *adj.* insolent. —**insolencia,** *n.f.* insolence.
insolicitado (in·so·li·θi'ta·ðo; -si'ta·ðo) *adj.* unasked; unsolicited.
insólito (in'so·li·to) *adj.* **1,** uncommon; unusual. **2,** unaccustomed.
insoluble (in·so'lu·βle) *adj.* insoluble. —**insolubilidad,** *n.f.* insolubility.
insolvente (in·sol'βen·te) *adj.* insolvent. —**insolvencia,** *n.f.* insolvency.
insomnio (in'som·njo) *n.m.* insomnia. —**insomne** (in'som·ne) *adj.* sleepless.
insondable (in·son'da·βle) *adj.* unfathomable.
insonoro (in·so'no·ro) *adj.* **1,** soundless. **2,** dull-sounding. **3,** *phonet.* voiceless; unvoiced.
insoportable (in·so·por'ta·βle) *adj.* insupportable; unbearable.
insospechado (in·sos·pe'tʃa·ðo) adj. unsuspected.
insostenible (in·sos·te'ni·βle) *adj.* untenable.
inspección (ins·pek'θjon; -'sjon) *n.f.* inspection. —**inspeccionar,** *v.t.* to inspect. —**inspector** (-'tor) *n.m.* inspector.
inspirar (ins·pi'rar) *v.t.* **1,** to inhale. **2,** to inspire. —**inspirarse,** *v.r.* to become inspired. —**inspiración** *n.f.* inspiration.
instabilidad (ins·ta·βi·li'ðað) *n.f.* = **inestabilidad.**
instalar (ins·ta'lar) *v.t.* to install; set up. —**instalación,** *n.f.* installation.
instancia (ins'tan·θja; -sja) *n.f.* **1,** instance; urging. **2,** petition.
instantáneo (ins·tan'ta·ne·o) *adj.* **1,** instantaneous. **2,** instant (*attrib.*) —**instantánea,** *n.f.* snapshot.
instante (ins'tan·te) *n.m.* instant —**al instante, 1,** at once. **2,** instant (*attrib.*).
instar (ins'tar) *v.t.* to urge; beseech. —*v.i.* **1,** to insist. **2,** to be urgent.

instaurar (ins·tau'rar) *v.t.* to restore; renovate. —**instauración,** *n.f.* restoration; renovation.
instigar (ins·ti'ɣar) *v.t.* [*pres. subjve.* **instigue** (-'ti·ɣe); *pret.* **instigué** (-'ɣe)] to instigate. —**instigación,** *n.f.* instigation. —**instigador,** *n.m.* instigator.
instilar (ins·ti'lar) *v.t.* to instill. —**instilación,** *n.f.* instillation.
instinto (ins'tin·to) *n.m.* instinct. —**instintivo,** *adj.* instinctive.
institución (ins·ti·tu'θjon; -'sjon) *n.f.* institution. —**institucional,** *adj.* institutional.
instituir (ins·ti·tu'ir) *v.t.* [*infl.:* **constituir**] to institute.
instituto (ins·ti'tu·to) *n.m.* **1,** institute. **2,** constitution; statutes (*pl.*).
institutriz (ins·ti·tu'triθ; -'tris) *n.f.* governess.
instrucción (ins·truk'θjon; -'sjon) *n.f.* **1,** instruction. **2,** education; knowledge.
instructivo (ins·truk'ti·βo) *adj.* instructive.
instructor (ins·truk'tor) *n.m.* instructor.
instruir (ins·tru'ir) *v.t.* [*infl.:* **construir**] **1,** to instruct; train; educate. **2,** to apprise; inform. —**instruido,** *adj.* well-read; learned.
instrumento (ins·tru'men·to) *n.m.* instrument. —**instrumentación,** *n.f.* instrumentation. —**instrumental,** *adj.* instrumental. —**instrumentar,** *v.t.* to provide instrumentation for.
insubordinar (in·su·βor·ði'nar) *v.t.* to incite to insubordination. —**insubordinarse,** *v.r.* to rebel; commit insubordination. —**insubordinación,** *n.f.* insubordination. —**insubordinado,** *adj.* & *n.m.* insubordinate.
insubsanable (in·suβ·sa'na·βle) *adj.* irremediable; irreparable.
insubstancial (in·suβs·tan'θjal; -'sjal) *adj.* insubstantial.
insuficiente (in·su·fi'θjen·te; -'sjen·te) *adj.* insufficient. —**insuficiencia,** *n.f.* insufficiency.
insufrible (in·su'fri·βle) *adj.* insufferable; unbearable.
insula ('in·su·la) *n.f.* **1,** = **isla. 2,** *fig.* unimportant place, town, etc.
insular (in·su'lar) *adj.* insular. —**insularidad,** *n.f.* insularity.
insulina (in·su'li·na) *n.f.* insulin.
insulso (in'sul·so) *adj.* **1,** insipid; tasteless. **2,** dull; vapid.
insultada (in·sul'ta·ða) *n.f., Amer.* **1,** insult. **2,** act of insulting.
insultar (in·sul'tar) *v.t.* to insult. —**insulto** (-'sul·to) *n.m.* insult.
insumergible (in·su·mer'xi·βle) *adj.* unsinkable.
insuperable (in·su·pe'ra·βle) *adj.* **1,** insuperable. **2,** matchless; unsurpassable. —**insuperado** (-'ra·ðo) *adj.* unmatched; unsurpassed.
insurgente (in·sur'xen·te) *adj.* & *n.m.* & *f.* insurgent. —**insurgencia,** *n.f.* insurgence.
insurrección (in·su·rrek'θjon; -'sjon) *n.f.* insurrection. —**insurreccionarse,** *v.r.* to revolt.
insurrecto (in·su'rrek·to) *adj.* & *n.m.* insurgent. —*n.m.* insurrectionist.
insustancial (in·sus·tan'θjal; -'sjal) *adj.* = **insubstancial.**
intacto (in'tak·to) *adj.* intact.
intachable (in·ta'tʃa·βle) *adj.* irreproachable; faultless.
intangible (in·tan'xi·βle) *adj.* intangible. —**intangibilidad,** *n.f.* intangibility.
integral (in·te'ɣral) *adj.* & *n.f.* integral.
integrar (in·te'ɣrar) *v.t.* to integrate. —**integración,** *n.f.* integration.
integridad (in·te·ɣri'ðað) *n.f.* **1,** integrity. **2,** maidenhood; virginity. **3,** whole; entirety.
integro ('in·te·ɣro) *adj.* **1,** entire; whole; complete. **2,** honest; just; upright.
integumento (in·te·ɣu'men·to) *n.m.* integument.
intelecto (in·te'lek·to) *n.m.* intellect.
intelectual (in·te·lek'twal) *adj.* & *n.m.* & *f.* intellectual. —**intelectualidad,** *n.f.* intelligentsia (*pl.*).
inteligencia (in·te·li'xen·θja; -sja) *n.f.* intelligence. —**inteligente,** *adj.* intelligent.
inteligible (in·te·li'xi·βle) *adj.* intelligible. —**inteligibilidad,** *n.f.* intelligibility.
intemperante (in·tem·pe'ran·te) *adj.* intemperate. —**intemperancia,** *n.f.* intemperance.
intemperie (in·tem'pe·rje) *n.f.* raw weather. —**a la intemperie,** outdoors; exposed to the weather.
intempestivo (in·tem·pes'ti·βo) *adj.* **1,** untimely; ill-timed. **2,** unseasonable.

intención (in·ten'θjon; -'sjon) *n.f.* intention. —**intencional**; *adj.* intentional.
intencionado (in·ten·θjo'na·ðo; -sjo'na·ðo) *adj., usu.preceded by* **bien, mal, mejor** *or* **peor,** intended; meant.
intendencia (in·ten'den·θja; -sja) *n.f.* **1,** administration. **2,** mayor's *or* governor's office.
intendente (in·ten'den·te) *n.m.* **1,** administrator. **2,** *Amer.* governor of a province. **3,** *Amer.* = **alcalde.**
intensificar (in·ten·si·fi'kar) *v.t.* [*infl.:* **tocar**] to intensify. —**intensificación,** *n.f.* intensification.
intenso (in'ten·so) *adj.* intense. —**intensidad,** *n.f.* intensity. —**intensivo,** *adj.* intensive.
intentar (in·ten'tar) *v.t.* **1,** to try; attempt. **2,** to intend.
intento (in'ten·to) *n.m.* **1,** intent; purpose. **2,** attempt.
intentona (in·ten'to·na) *n.f., colloq.* try; attempt.
inter- (in·ter) *prefix,* inter-; between; during: *internacional,* international; *interregno,* interregnum.
interacción (in·ter·ak'θjon; '-sjon) *n.f.* interaction.
intercalar (in·ter·ka'lar) *v.t.* to intercalate. —**intercalación,** *n.f.* intercalation.
intercambio (in·ter'kam·bjo) *n.m.* interchange. —**intercambiar,** *v.t.* to interchange.
interceder (in·ter·θe'ðer; -se'ðer) *v.i.* to intercede.
interceptar (in·ter·θep'tar; -sep·'tar) *v.t.* to intercept. —**interceptación,** *also,* **intercepción** (-'θjon; -'sjon) *n.f.* interception. —**interceptor** (-'tor) *n.m.* interceptor.
intercesión (in·ter·θe'sjon; -se·'sjon) *n.f.* intercession. —**intercesor,** *n.m.* intercessor. —*adj.* interceding.
intercomunicarse (in·ter·ko·mu·ni'kar·se) *v.r.* [*infl.:* **comunicar**] to intercommunicate. —**intercomunicación,** *n.f.* intercommunication.
interdecir (in·ter·ðe'θir; -'sir) *v.t.* [*infl.:* **bendecir**] to interdict. —**interdicción** (-ðik'θjon; -'sjon) *n.f.* interdiction. —**interdicto** (-'ðik·to) *n.m.* interdict.
interdependiente (in·ter·ðe·pen'djen·te) *adj.* interdependent. —**interdependencia,** *n.f.* interdependence.
interés (in·te'res) *n.m.* interest. —**intereses creados,** vested interests.
interesado (in·te·re'sa·ðo) *adj.* **1,** interested. **2,** selfish; mercenary. —*n.m.* **1,** interested party. **2,** self-seeker.
interesante (in·te·re'san·te) *adj.* interesting.
interesar (in·te·re'sar) *v.i.* to be interesting. —*v.t.* **1,** to interest. **2,** to give an interest to. **3,** to involve. **4,** *med.* to affect (an organ). —**interesarse,** *v.r.* to be interested; take an interest.
interferir (in·ter·fe'rir) *v.i.* [*infl.:* **diferir**] to interfere. —**interferencia,** *n.f.* interference.
interin ('in·te·rin) *n.m.* interim; meantime. —**interino** (-'ri·no) *adj.* temporary; provisional.
interior (in·te'rjor) *adj.* interior; inner; internal. —*n.m.* interior; inside. —**interioridades,** *n.f.pl.* private matters.
interiorizar (in·te·rjo·ri'θar; -'sar) *v.t., Amer., colloq.* [*pres. subjve.* **interiorice** (-'ri·θe; -se), **interioricé** (-'θe; -'se)] to inform in detail; familiarize.
interjección (in·ter·xek'θjon; -'sjon) *n.f.* interjection.
interlinear (in·ter·li·ne'ar) *v.t.* to interline (a writing). —**interlineal,** *adj.* interlinear.
interlocución (in·ter·lo·ku'θjon; -'sjon) *n.f.* interlocution. **interlocutor,** *n.m.* interlocutor. —**interlocutorio,** *adj., law* interlocutory.
interludio (in·ter'lu·ðjo) *n.m.* interlude.
intermediar (in·ter·me'ðjar) *v.t.* = **mediar.**
intermediario (in·ter·me'ðja·rjo) *adj.* & *n.m.* intermediary.
intermedio (in·ter'me·ðjo) *adj.* intermediate. —*n.m.* **1,** interim. **2,** interlude. **3,** intermission. —**por intermedio de,** *Amer.* through the intervention of.
interminable (in·ter·mi'na·βle) *adj.* interminable; endless.
intermisión (in·ter·mi'sjon) *n.f.* intermission.
intermitente (in·ter·mi'ten·te) *adj.* intermittent. —**intermitencia,** *n.f.* intermittence.
internacional (in·ter·na·θjo'nal; -sjo'nal) *adj.* international. —**internacionalismo,** *n.m.* internationalism. —**internacionalista,** *n.m.* & *f.*

internationalist. —*adj.* internationalistic.

internado (in·ter'na·ðo) *n.m.* **1,** boarding school. **2,** boarding students collectively. **3,** boarding status. **4,** interneship.

internar (in·ter'nar) *v.t.* to intern. —*v.i.* [*also, refl.,* **internarse**] **1,** to penetrate; go in *or* through. **2,** to delve. —**internamiento,** *n.m.* internment.

interno (in'ter·no) *adj.* internal. —*n.m.* **1,** boarding school student. **2,** interne.

interpelar (in·ter·pe'lar) *v.t.* to question; interrogate.

interpolar (in·ter·po'lar) *v.t.* to interpolate. —**interpolación,** *n.f.* interpolation.

interponer (in·ter·po'ner) *v.t.* [*infl.:* **poner**] to interpose. —**interponerse,** *v.r.* **1,** to intercede; intervene. **2,** to come between. —**interposición** (-po·si'θjon; -'sjon) *n.f.* interposition.

interpretar (in·ter·pre'tar) *v.t.* to interpret. —**interpretación,** *n.f.* interpretation. —**interpretativo,** *adj.* interpretative.

intérprete (in'ter·pre·te) *n.m.* & *f.* interpreter.

interrogación (in·te·rro·ɣa·'θjon; -'sjon) *n.f.* **1,** interrogation; inquiry. **2,** question mark.

interrogar (in·te·rro'ɣar) *v.t.* [*pres.subjve.* **interrogue** (-'rro·ɣe); *pret.* **interrogué** (-'ɣe)] to interrogate; question. —**interrogador,** *n.m.* interrogator. —**interrogativo,** *adj.* interrogative.

interrogatorio (in·te·rro·ɣa'to·rjo) *n.m.* **1,** interrogatory. **2,** interrogation; questioning.

interrumpir (in·te·rrum'pir) *v.t.* to interrupt. —**interrupción** (-rrup·'θjon; -'sjon) *n.f.* interruption.

interruptor (in·te·rrup'tor) *adj.* interrupting; interruptive. —*n.m.* **1,** circuit breaker. **2,** light switch; electric switch.

intersecarse (in·ter·se'kar·se) *v.r.* to intersect.

intersección (in·ter·sek'θjon; -'sjon) *n.f.* intersection.

intersticio (in·ter'sti·θjo; -sjo) *n.m.* interstice.

intervalo (in·ter'βa·lo) *n.m.* interval.

intervención (in·ter·βen'θjon; -'sjon) *n.f.* **1,** intervention. **2,** auditing of accounts. **3,** *surg.* operation.

intervenir (in·ter·βe'nir) *v.i.* [*infl.:* **venir**] to intervene. —*v.t.* **1,** to intervene in. **2,** to audit. **3,** to place under official control *or* regulation.

interventor (in·ter·βen'tor) *n.m.* **1,** mediator; intervener. **2,** comptroller; auditor.

interviú (in·ter'βju) *n.f.* interview.

intestado (in·tes'ta·ðo) *adj.* & *n.m.* intestate.

intestino (in·tes'ti·no) *adj.* internal. —*n.m.* intestine. —**intestinal,** *adj.* intestinal.

intimar (in·ti'mar) *v.t.* to intimate; make known; announce. —*v.i.* [*also, refl.,* **intimarse**] **1,** to become intimate. **2,** to permeate; soak in. —**intimación,** *n.f.* intimation; announcement.

intimidar (in·ti·mi'ðar) *v.t.* to intimidate. —**intimidación,** *n.f.* intimidation.

íntimo ('in·ti·mo) *adj.* **1,** intimate. **2,** inner; inmost. —**intimidad,** *n.f.* intimacy.

intitular (in·ti·tu'lar) *v.t.* **1,** to entitle. **2,** to confer (*on someone or something*) the title of.

intocable (in·to'ka·βle) *adj.* untouchable.

intolerable (in·to·le'ra·βle) *adj.* intolerable. —**intolerabilidad,** *n.f.* intolerability.

intolerante (in·to·le'ran·te) *adj.* intolerant. —**intolerancia,** *n.f.* intolerance.

intoxicar (in·tok·si'kar) *v.t.* [*pres.subjve.* **intoxique** (-'si·ke); *pret.* **intoxiqué** (-'ke)] to poison; intoxicate. —**intoxicación,** *n.f.* poisoning; intoxication.

intra- (in·tra) *prefix* intra-; within: *intravenoso,* intravenous.

intraducible (in·tra·ðu'θi·βle; -'si·βle) *adj.* untranslatable.

intranquilidad (in·tran·ki·li·'ðað) *n.f.* **1,** restlessness. **2,** uneasiness.

intranquilo (in·tran'ki·lo) *adj.* **1,** restless. **2,** uneasy.

intransigente (in·tran·si'xen·te) *adj.* intransigent; uncompromising. —**intransigencia,** *n.f.* intransigence.

intransitable (in·tran·si'ta·βle) *adj.* impassable.

intransitivo (in·tran·si'ti·βo) *adj.* intransitive.

intratable (in·tra'ta·βle) *adj.* **1,** intractable. **2,** unsociable; uncom-

municative. —**intratabilidad,** *n.f.* intractability.
intravenoso (in·tra·βe'no·so) *adj.* intravenous.
intrépido (in'tre·pi·ðo) *adj.* intrepid; daring. —**intrepidez,** *n.f.* intrepidity; daring.
intriga (in'tri·ɣa) *n.f.* intrigue.
intrigante (in·tri'ɣan·te) *adj.* **1,** intriguing. **2,** plotting; scheming. —*n.m.* & *f.* intriguer; plotter; schemer.
intrigar (in·tri'ɣar) *v.t.* [*pres. subjve.* **intrigue** (-'tri·ɣe); *pret.* **intrigué** (-'ɣe)] to intrigue. —*v.i.* to plot; scheme.
intrincado (in·trin'ka·ðo) *adj.* intricate; involved. —**intrincación,** *n.f.* intricacy.
intrínseco (in'trin·se·ko) *adj.* intrinsic.
intro- (in·tro) *prefix* intro-: within; into; inward: *introducir,* introduce; *introvertido,* introvert.
introducción (in·tro·ðuk'θjon; -'sjon) *n.f.* introduction.
introducir (in·tro·ðu'θir; -'sir) *v.t.* [*infl.:* **conducir**] to introduce. —**introducirse,** *v.r.* to interfere; meddle.
intromisión (in·tro·mi'sjon) *n.f.* **1,** interposition. **2,** interference; meddling.
introspección (in·tros·pek'θjon; -'sjon) *n.f.* introspection. —**introspectivo** (-'ti·βo)) *adj.* introspective.
introvertido (in·tro·βer'ti·ðo) *adj.* introverted. —*n.m.* introvert. —**introversión,** (-'sjon) *n.f.* introversion.
intrusear (in·tru·se'ar) *v.i., Amer., colloq.* to intrude; poke in.
intrusión (in·tru'sjon) *n.f.* intrusion.
intruso (in'tru·so) *adj.* intrusive. —*n.m.* intruder.
intuición (in·twi'θjon; -'sjon) *n.f.* intuition.
intuir (in·tu'ir) *v.t.* [*infl.:* **huir**] to grasp intuitively; perceive by intuition.
intuitivo (in·twi'ti·βo) *adj.* intuitive.
inundar (i·nun'dar) *v.t.* to flood; inundate. —**inundación,** *n.f.* flooding; inundation.
inusitado (i·nu·si'ta·ðo) *adj.* **1,** unusual. **2,** unused; out of use.
inútil (in'u·til) *adj.* **1,** useless. **2,** incapacitated; noneffective. —*n.m.* & *f.* **1,** useless person; good-for-nothing. **2,** incapacitated person; noneffective.
inutilidad (in·u·ti·li'ðað) *n.f.* **1,** uselessness. **2,** incapacity.
inutilizar (in·u·ti·li'θar; -'sar) *v.t.* [*infl.:* **utilizar**] to render useless; disable.
invadir (in·βa'ðir) *v.t.* to invade.
invalidar (in·βa·li'ðar) *v.t.* to invalidate. —**invalidación,** *n.f.* invalidation.
invalidez (in·βa·li'ðeθ; -'ðes) *n.f.* **1,** invalidity. **2,** state of being an invalid.
inválido (in'βa·li·ðo) *adj.* **1,** invalid. **2,** null; void. —*n.m.* invalid.
invariable (in·βa'rja·βle) *adj.* invariable. —**invariabilidad,** *n.f.* invariability.
invasión (in·βa'sjon) *n.f.* invasion. —**invasor,** *adj.* invading. —*n.m.* invader.
invectiva (in·βek'ti·βa) *n.f.* invective.
invencible (in·βen'θi·βle; -'si·βle) *adj.* invincible. —**invencibilidad,** *n.f.* invincibility.
invención (in·βen'θjon; -'sjon) *n.f.* invention.
invendible (in·βen'di·βle) *adj.* unsaleable.
inventar (in·βen'tar) *v.t.* to invent.
inventario (in·βen'ta·rjo) *n.m.* inventory. —**inventariar,** *v.t.* to inventory.
inventivo (in·βen'ti·βo) *adj.* inventive. —**inventiva,** *n.f.* inventiveness; ingenuity.
invento (in'βen·to) *n.m.* invention.
inventor (in·βen'tor) *n.m.* inventor.
invernáculo (in·βer'na·ku·lo) *n.m.* greenhouse; hothouse.
invernadero (in·βer·na'ðe·ro) *n.m.* **1,** winter quarters. **2,** winter pasture. **3,** greenhouse; hothouse.
invernal (in·βer'nal) *adj.* winter (*attrib.*); wintry. —*n.m.* winter stable.
invernar (in·βer'nar) *v.i.* [*pres. ind.* **invierno**; *pres.subjve.* **invierne**] to winter; hibernate.
inverosímil (in·βe·ro'si·mil) *also,* **inverisímil** (in·βe·ri-) *adj.* unbelievable; improbable.
inversión (in·βer'sjon) *n.f.* **1,** inversion. **2,** investment. **3,** input.

inverso (in'βer·so) *adj.* inverse. —**a** *or* **por la inversa, 1,** on the contrary. **2,** in reverse order; upside-down.
invertebrado (in·βer·te'βra·ðo) *adj.* & *n.m.* invertebrate.
invertir (in·βer'tir) *v.t.* [*infl.:* **advertir**] **1,** to invert; reverse. **2,** to invest.
investidura (in·βes·ti'ðu·ra) *n.f.* **1,** investiture. **2,** installation (*in office*).
investigación (in·βes·ti·ɣa·'θjon; -'sjon) *n.f.* **1,** investigation; inquiry. **2,** research.
investigador (in·βes·ti·ɣa'ðor) *n.m.* **1,** investigator. **2,** researcher. —*adj.* investigating; investigative.
investigar (in·βes·ti'ɣar) *v.t. & i.* [*pres.subjve.* **investigue** (-'ti·ɣe); *pret.* **investigué** (-'ɣe)] to investigate.
investir (in·βes'tir) *v.t.* [*infl.:* **vestir**] to invest; vest.
inveterado (in·βe·te'ra·ðo) *adj.* inveterate.
invicto (in'βik·to) *adj.* undefeated; unvanquished.
invierne (in'βjer·ne) *v., pres.subjve. of* **invernar.**
invierno (in'βjer·no) *n.m.* winter.
invierno (in'βjer·no) *v., pres.ind. of* **invernar.**
invierta (in'βjer·ta) *v., pres. subjve. of* **invertir.**
invierto (in'βjer·to) *v., pres.ind. of* **invertir.**
inviolable (in·βjo'la·βle) *adj.* inviolable. —**inviolabilidad,** *n.f.* inviolability.
inviolado (in·βjo'la·ðo) *adj.* inviolate.
invirtiendo (in·βir'tjen·do) *v., ger. of* **invertir.**
invirtió (in·βir'tjo) *v., 3rd pers. sing. pret. of* **invertir.**
invisible (in·βi'si·βle) *adj.* invisible. —**invisibilidad,** *n.f.* invisibility.
invitación (in·βi·ta'θjon; -'sjon) *n.f.* **1,** invitation. **2,** *colloq.* treat.
invitado (in·βi'ta·ðo) *n.m.* invited guest.
invitar (in·βi'tar) *v.t.* **1,** to invite. **2,** to treat.
invocar (in·βo'kar) *v.t.* [*pres. subjve.* **invoque** (-'βo·ke); *pret.* **invoqué** (-'ke)] to invoke. —**invocación,** *n.f.* invocation.
involución (in·βo·lu'θjon; -'sjon) *n.f.* involution.
involucrar (in·βo·lu'krar) *v.t.* to involve; entail.
involuntario (in·βo·lun'ta·rjo) *adj.* involuntary.
invulnerable (in·βul·ne'ra·βle) *adj.* invulnerable. —**invulnerabilidad,** *n.f.* invulnerability.
inyección (in·jek'θjon; -'sjon) *n.f.* injection.
inyectado (in·jek'ta·ðo) *adj.* bloodshot.
inyectar (in·jek'tar) *v.t.* to inject. —**inyector** (-'tor) *n.m.* injector.
-io (jo) *suffix* -ium; *forming nouns used in scientific terminology: geranio,* geranium; *actinio,* actinium.
-io ('i·o) *suffix, forming adjectives denoting* **1,** intensity: *bravío,* fierce. **2,** -ish; related *or* pertaining to: *cabrío,* goatish; goat (*attrib.*). **3,** *forming collective nouns: griterío,* uproar; *gentío,* crowd.
ión (i'on) *n.m.* ion.
-ión ('jon) *suffix* -ion. **1,** *forming abstract nouns: opinión,* opinion; *fusión,* fusion. **2,** *forming concrete nouns denoting persons or things: centurión,* centurion; *legión,* legion.
ionio (i'o·njo) *n.m.* ionium.
ionosfera (i·o·nos'fe·ra) *n.f.* ionosphere.
-ioso ('jo·so) *suffix* -ious; *forming adjectives often corresponding to nouns ending in* **-ión**: *religioso,* religious; *ansioso,* anxious.
ipecacuana (i·pe·ka'kwa·na) *n.f.* ipecac.
ir (ir) *v.i.* [*pres.ind.* **voy, vas, va, vamos, vais, van;** *pres.subjve.* **vaya;** *impve.* **ve, vamos, id;** *impf.* **iba;** *pret.* **fui;** *ger.* **yendo;** *p.p.* **ido**] **1,** to go. **2,** to fit; suit; be becoming. **3,** to concern; affect. **4,** *expressing condition or progress* to be; do; get along: *El enfermo va bien,* the patient is doing well. *¿Cómo van los negocios?* How is business? **5,** *in expressions of time* to be; elapse: *Van tres años que no lo veo,* It has been three years since I saw him. —*aux.v.* **1,** *used with the gerund to form the progressive tenses: Va amaneciendo,* It is getting light. **2,** *used with the past participle to express the passive: Va vendido,* it is sold. **3,** *fol. by* **a** + *inf., expressing the immediate future: Voy a hablarle,* I am going to speak to him. *Van a cerrar,* they are about to close. —**irse,** *v.r.* **1,** to go; go away; leave.

2, to fail; give way; collapse. 3, to die; succumb. 4, to fade; fade away. —**ir a caballo**, to go on horseback. —**ir a pie**, to go on foot. —**ir en automóvil, tren, barco**, etc., to go by car, train, boat, etc. —**ir por, 1,** to be for; follow. **2,** to go after; pursue. **3,** to be at (*a certain state or stage*): *Voy por la mitad del libro,* I am at the middle of the book. —**irse a pique**, to sink. —**No me va ni me viene**, It makes no difference to me. —**¡qué va!**, nonsense!; you don't say! —**¿Quién va?**, Who's there?

ir- (ir) *prefix, var. of* **in-** *before* r: *irradiar,* irradiate; *irracional,* irrational.

ira ('i·ra) *n.f.* ire; wrath.

iracundo (i·ra'kun·do) *adj.* ireful; wrathful.

irascible (i·ras'θi·βle; i·ra'si·βle) *adj.* irascible. —**irascibilidad**, *n.f.* irascibility.

irga ('ir·ɣa) *v., pres.subjve. of* **erguir.**

irguiendo (ir'ɣjen·do) *v., ger. of* **erguir.**

irguió (ir'ɣjo) *v., 3rd pers.sing. pret. of* **erguir.**

iridio (i'ri·ðjo) *n.m.* iridium.

iridiscente (i·ri·ðis'θen·te; -ði·'sen·te) *adj.* iridescent. —**iridiscencia**, *n.f.* iridescence.

iris ('i·ris) *n.m.* **1,** iris. **2,** [*also,* **arco iris**] rainbow.

irisado (i·ri'sa·ðo) *adj.* iridescent.

irlandés (ir·lan'des) *adj.* Irish. —*n.m.* **1,** Irishman. **2,** Irish language.

ironía (i·ro'ni·a) *n.f.* irony. —**irónico** (i'ro·ni·ko) *adj.* ironic; ironical.

irracional (i·rra·θjo'nal; -sjo'nal) *adj.* irrational. —**irracionalidad**, *n.f.* irrationality.

irradiar (i·rra'ðjar) *v.t.* to irradiate. —**irradiación**, *n.f.* irradiation.

irrazonable (i·rra·θo'na·βle; -so'na·βle) *adj.* unreasonable.

irreal (i·rre'al) *adj.* unreal.

irrealidad (i·rre·a·li'ðað) *n.f.* unreality.

irrealizable (i·rre·a·li'θa·βle; -'sa·βle) *adj.* unrealizable.

irrebatible (i·rre·βa'ti·βle) *adj.* irrefutable.

irreconciliable (i'rre·kon·θi·'lja·βle; -si'lja·βle) *adj.* irreconcilable.

irreconocible (i·rre·ko·no'θi·βle; -'si·βle) *adj.* unrecognizable. —**irreconocido** (-'θi·ðo; -'si·ðo) *adj.* unrecognized.

irrecuperable (i·rre·ku·pe'ra·βle) *adj.* irrecoverable.

irrecusable (i·rre·ku'sa·βle) *adj.* unexceptionable; unimpeachable.

irreducible (i·rre·ðu'θi·βle; -'si·βle) *also,* **irreductible** (-ðuk'ti·βle) *adj.* irreducible.

irreemplazable (i·rre·em·pla·'θa·βle; -'sa·βle) *adj.* irreplaceable.

irreflexión (i·rre·flek'sjon) *n.f.* thoughtlessness. —**irreflexivo** (-'si·βo) *adj.* thoughtless.

irrefrenable (i·rre·fre'na·βle) *adj.* uncontrollable; unbridled.

irrefutable (i·rre·fu'ta·βle) *adj.* irrefutable.

irregular (i·rre·ɣu'lar) *adj.* irregular. —**irregularidad**, *n.f.* irregularity.

irreligioso (i·rre·li'xjo·so) *adj.* irreligious. —**irreligiosidad**, *n.f.* irreligiousness.

irremediable (i·rre·me'ðja·βle) *adj.* irremediable.

irreparable (i·rre·pa'ra·βle) *adj.* irreparable.

irreprensible (i·rre·pren'si·βle) *adj.* irreproachable; unimpeachable.

irreprimible (i·rre·pri'mi·βle) *adj.* irrepressible.

irreprochable (i·rre·pro'tʃa·βle) *adj.* irreproachable.

irresistible (i·rre·sis'ti·βle) *adj.* irresistible.

irresoluto (i·rre·so'lu·to) *adj.* irresolute. —**irresolución**, *n.f.* irresoluteness.

irrespetuoso (i·rres·pe'two·so) *adj.* disrespectful.

irresponsable (i·rres·pon'sa·βle) *adj.* irresponsible. —**irresponsabilidad**, *n.f.* irresponsibility.

irreverente (i·rre·βe'ren·te) *adj.* irreverent. —**irreverencia**, *n.f.* irreverence.

irrevocable (i·rre·βo'ka·βle) *n.f.* irrevocable. —**irrevocabilidad**, *n.f.* irrevocability.

irrigar (i·rri'ɣar) *v.t.* [*pres.subjve.* **irrigue** (-'rri·ɣe); *pret.* **irrigué** (-'ɣe)] to irrigate. —**irrigación**, *n.f.* irrigation.

irrisión (i·rri'sjon) *n.f.* **1,** derision; ridicule. **2,** laughable person or thing; object of ridicule.

irrisorio (i·rri'so·rjo) *adj.* **1** laughable. **2,** piddling; inconsequential.

irritable (i·rri'ta·βle) *adj.* irritable. —**irritabilidad,** *n.f.* irritability.
irritado (i·rri'ta·ðo) *adj.* **1,** irate. **2,** irritated.
irritar (i·rri'tar) *v.t.* to irritate. —**irritación,** *n.f.* irritation. —**irritante,** *adj.* irritating. —*n.m.* irritant.
irrompible (i·rrom'pi·βle) *adj.* unbreakable.
irrumpir (i·rrum'pir) *v.i.* to burst in.
irrupción (i·rrup'θjon; -'sjon) *n.f.* irruption.
-isa ('i·sa) *suffix* -ess; *forming feminine nouns from masculine nouns ending in vowels: poetisa,* poetess; *sacerdotisa,* priestess.
-isco ('is·ko) *suffix, forming adjectives meaning* having; pertaining or related to: *arenisco,* sandy.
isla ('is·la) *n.f.* island.
Islam (is'lam) *n.m.* Islam. —**islámico** (-'la·mi·ko) *adj.* Islamic. —**islamismo,** *n.m.* Mohammedanism. —**islamita,** *adj.* & *n.m.* & *f.* Mohammedan.
isleño (is'le·ɲo) *adj.* island (*attrib.*) —*n.m.* islander.
islote (is'lo·te) *n.m.* isle; islet.
ismo ('is·mo) *n.m.* ism.
-ismo ('is·mo) *suffix* -ism; *forming nouns denoting* doctrine; theory; practice; system; principle: *socialismo,* socialism.
iso- (i·so) *prefix* iso-; equal: *isoterma,* isotherm.
isométrico (i·so'me·tri·ko) *adj.* isometric.
isósceles (i'sos·θe·les; i'so·se·les) *adj.* isosceles.
isótopo (i'so·to·po) *n.m.* isotope.
israelí (is·ra·e'li) *adj.* & *n.m.* & *f.* Israeli. —**israelita** (-'li·ta) *adj.* & *n.m.* & *f.* Israelite.
-ista ('is·ta) *suffix* -ist; *forming nouns, sometimes used as adjectives denoting* one who practices, studies, believes, advocates: *pacifista,* pacifist; *socialista,* socialist.
-ística ('is·ti·ka) *suffix* -istics; *forming nouns from adjectives ending in* **-ista** *or* **-ístico** *denoting* practice or science of: *balística,* ballistics.
-ístico ('is·ti·ko) *suffix* -istic; -istical; *forming adjectives often corresponding to nouns ending in* **-ista:** *artístico,* artistic.
istmo ('ist·mo; 'is·mo) *n.m.* isthmus.
-ita ('i·ta) *suffix* -ite; *forming nouns denoting* **1,** origin; tribe: *israelita,* Israelite. **2,** follower; disciple: *carmelita,* Carmelite. **3,** rock; mineral: *dolomita,* dolomite. **4,** explosives: *dinamita,* dynamite; *cordita,* cordite. **5,** *fem. of* **-ito.**
italiano (i·ta'lja·no) *adj.* & *n.m.* Italian.
itálico (i'ta·li·ko) *adj.* Italic.
ítem ('i·tem) *adv.* moreover; also. —*n.m.* item.
iterar (i·te'rar) *v.t.* to iterate. —**iteración,** *n.f.* iteration.
iterbio (i'ter·βjo) *n.m.* ytterbium.
-ítico ('i·ti·ko) *suffix* -itic; -itical; *forming adjectives denoting* **1,** origin: *levítico,* Levitical. **2,** having to do with; like: *granítico,* granitic; *político,* political.
itinerario (i·ti·ne'ra·rjo) *adj.* & *n.m.* itinerary.
-itis ('i·tis) *suffix* -itis; inflammation: *bronquitis,* bronchitis.
-itivo (i'ti·βo) *suffix* -itive; *forming adjectives expressing* relation; tendency: *sensitivo,* sensitive.
-ito ('i·to) *suffix* **1,** -ite; *forming adjectives: contrito,* contrite; *erudito,* erudite. **2,** -ite; *forming names of* minerals: *grafito,* graphite. **3,** -ite; *forming names of* chemical compounds, esp. salts of acids with names ending in **-oso:** *sulfito,* sulfite. **4,** [*fem.* **-ita**] *forming diminutives: pajarito,* little bird; *estatuita,* statuette.
itrio ('i·trjo) *n.m.* yttrium.
-itud (i'tuð) *suffix* -tude; *forming nouns denoting* quality; condition: *longitud,* longitude; *esclavitud,* slavery; servitude.
-ivo ('i·βo) *suffix* -ive; *forming adjectives of quality from verbs and nouns, denoting* function; tendency; disposition: *nutritivo,* nutritive; *formativo,* formative.
-iza ('i·θa; 'i·sa) *suffix* **1,** *forming nouns expressing* place: *porqueriza,* pigpen; *caballeriza,* stable. **2,** *fem. of* **-izo.**
-ización (i·θa'θjon; i·sa'sjon) *suffix* -ization; *forming nouns from verbs ending in* **-izar:** *organización,* organization.
izar (i'θar; i'sar) *v.t.* [*pres.subjve.* **ice** ('i·θe; -se); *pret.* **icé** (-'θe; -'se)] to raise; hoist; haul up.
-izar (i'θar; i'sar) *suffix* -ize; *forming verbs from nouns and adjectives, expressing* **1,** *in transitive verbs* to make, render, treat, act upon in a particular way: *realizar,*

realize; *civilizar,* civilize. **2,** *in intransitive verbs* to act, function, practice in a particular way: *economizar,* economize; *cristalizar,* crystalize.

-izo ('i·θo; 'i·so) *fem.* **-iza,** *suffix, forming adjectives expressing* **1,** tendency; similarity: *enfermizo,* sickly; *pajizo,* straw-colored; pale. **2,** having; containing: *cobrizo,* copper-colored; cupric. **3,** tendency; capability: *arrojadizo,* easily thrown.

izquierda (iθ'kjer·ða; is-) *n.f.* left; left hand; left side.

izquierdista (iθ·kjer'ðis·ta; is-) *adj.* & *n.m.* & *f.* leftist.

izquierdo (iθ'kjer·ðo; is-) *adj.* **1,** left. **2,** = **zurdo.** —**levantarse por el lado izquierdo,** to get up on the wrong side of the bed.

J

J, j ('xo·ta) *n.f.* 11th letter of the Spanish alphabet.

¡ja! (xa) *interj.* ha!

jabalí (xa·βa'li) *n.m.* wild boar.

jabalina (xa·βa'li·na) *n.f.* **1,** javelin. **2,** *fem. of* **jabalí.**

jabón (xa'βon) *n.m.* **1,** soap. **2,** *Amer.* fear; scare. —**dar jabón,** *colloq.* to softsoap. —**dar un jabón,** *colloq.* to scold.

jabonadura (xa·βo·na'ðu·ra) *n.f.,* *also, Amer.* **jabonada** (-'na·ða) soaping; washing; lathering. —**jabonaduras,** *n.f.pl.* suds.

jabonar (xa·βo'nar) *v.t.* to soap; lather.

jabonera (xa·βo'ne·ra) *n.f.* **1,** soap dish. **2,** soapwort.

jabonoso (xa·βo'no·so) *adj.* soapy.

jaca ('xa·ka) *n.f.* small horse; cob.

jacal (xa'kal) *n.m., Mex.* shack; Indian hut.

jácara ('xa·ka·ra) *n.f.* **1,** lilt; merry ballad. **2,** group of merrymakers. **3,** merrymaking. **4,** *colloq.* bother; nuisance. **5,** *colloq.* fib; lie.

jacinto (xa'θin·to; -'sin·to) *n.m.* hyacinth.

jaco ('xa·ko) *n.m.* nag.

jactancia (xak'tan·θja; -sja) *n.f.* swagger; boasting. —**jactancioso,** *adj.* boastful.

jactarse (xak'tar·se) *v.r.* to boast; brag.

jaculatoria (xa·ku·la'to·rja) *n.f.* short prayer.

jade ('xa·ðe) *n.m., mineralogy* jade.

jadear (xa·ðe'ar) *v.i.* to pant; gasp for breath. —**jadeante,** *adj.* panting; out of breath. —**jadeo** (-'ðe·o) *n.m.* pant; panting.

jaez (xa'eθ; -'es) *n.m.* **1,** harness; trappings (*pl.*) **2,** sort; nature.

jaguar (xa'ɣwar) *n.m.* jaguar.

jai alai (xai·a'lai) *n.m.* jai alai.

jaiba ('xai·βa) *n.f., Amer.* crab.

jalar (xa'lar) *v.t., colloq.* **1,** = **halar. 2,** *W.I.* to woo.—**jalarse,** *v.r., Amer., colloq.* **1,** to get drunk. **2,** to get out; scram.

jalea (xa'le·a) *n.f.* jelly.

jalear (xa·le'ar) *v.t.* **1,** to urge; spur on; encourage loudly. **2,** *Amer., colloq.* to poke fun at.

jaleo (xa'le·o) *n.m.* **1,** boisterous encouragement; rooting. **2,** Andalusian dance. **3,** *colloq.* merrymaking. **4,** *colloq.* brawl; rumpus.

jaletina (xa·le'ti·na) *n.f.* fine, clear gelatine.

jalón (xa'lon) *n.m.* **1,** *surv.* pole; rod. **2,** landmark. **3,** *Amer., colloq.* swig; drink, esp. of liquor. **4,** *Amer.* jerk; pull; tug. **5,** *Amer.* distance; stretch.

jamás (xa'mas) *adv.* never. —**nunca jamás,** nevermore. —**por siempre jamás,** for evermore.

jamba ('xam·ba) *n.f.* jamb.

jamelgo (xa'mel·go) *n.m.* nag; hack; jade.

jamón (xa'mon) *n.m.* ham.

jamona (xa'mo·na) *n.f.* fat middle-aged woman.

japonés (xa·po'nes) *adj.* & *n.m.* Japanese.

jaque ('xa·ke) *n.m.* **1,** *chess* check. **2,** swashbuckler. —**jaquear,** *v.t., chess* to check. —**en jaque,** in check; at bay. —**jaque mate,** checkmate.

jaqueca (xa'ke·ka) *n.f.* migraine; headache.

jarabe (xa'ra·βe) *n.m.* **1,** syrup. **2,** sweet drink or infusion. **3,** *colloq.* sweet talk. **4,** a Mexican dance.

jarana (xa'ra·na) *n.f.* **1,** carousal; revel; romp. **2,** *colloq.* brawl; quarrel. **3,** *colloq.* trick; joke.—**jaranear,** *v.i.* to carouse; revel.

jardín (xar'ðin) *n.m.* garden. —**jardinera,** *n.f.* jardinière. —**jardinería,** *n.f.* gardening. —**jardinero,** *n.m.* gardener. —**jardín de infancia; jardín infantil,** kindergarten.
jarra ('xa·rra) *n.f.* pitcher; jug. —**de** *or* **en jarras,** akimbo.
jarro ('xa·rro) *n.m.* jug; mug.
jarrón (xa'rron) *n.m.* ornamental pot; vase; urn.
jaspe ('xas·pe) *n.m.* jasper. —**jaspeado,** *adj.* marbled; veined; mottled. —*n.m.* veins (*pl.*); streaks (*pl.*); mottle; streaking. —**jaspear,** *v.t.* to vein; streak; mottle.
jaula ('xau·la) *n.f.* **1,** cage. **2,** *colloq.* jail.
jauría (xau'ri·a) *n.f.* pack, as of hounds.
jazmín (xaθ'min; xas-) *n.m.* jasmine.
jazz (dʒas, *also,* xas) *n.m.* jazz.
jebe ('xe·βe) *n.m.* **1,** = **alumbre. 2,** *Amer.* rubber; raw rubber. **3,** *Amer.* elastic; rubber band.
jedive (xe'ði·βe) *n.m.* khedive.
jeep (dʒip) *n.m.* jeep.
jefatura (xe·fa'tu·ra) *n.f.* **1,** position of chief; chieftaincy; leadership. **2,** headquarters.
jefe ('xe·fe) *n.m.* chief; leader; head; boss. —**en jefe,** chief; principal; highest; head.
Jehová (xe·o'βa) *n.m.* Jehovah.
jején (xe'xen) *n.m., Amer.* gnat.
jengibre (xen'xi·βre) *n.m.* ginger.
jeque ('xe·ke) *n.m.* sheik.
jerarca (xe'rar·ka) *n.m.* hierarch. —**jerarquía** (-'ki·a) *n.f.* hierarchy. —**jerárquico** (xe'rar·ki·ko) *adj.* hierarchical.
jeremiada (xe·re'mja·ða) *n.f.* jeremiad.
jerez (xe'reθ; -'res) *n.m.* sherry.
jerga ('xer·ɣa) *n.f.* **1,** frieze; coarse cloth. **2,** jargon; cant; argot. **3,** = **jerigonza. 4,** = **jergón.**
jergón (xer'ɣon) *n.m.* **1,** pallet; straw mat. **2,** *colloq.* rags (*pl.*); shabby dress. **3,** *colloq.* lazy lummox.
jerigonza (xe·ri'ɣon·θa; -sa) *n.f., colloq.* **1,** lingo. **2,** gibberish; jabber; balderdash. **3,** rigmarole.
jeringa (xe'rin·ga) *n.f.* **1,** syringe. **2,** *colloq.* bother; nuisance.
jeringar (xe·rin'gar) *v.t.* [*pres. subjve.* **jeringue** (-'rin·ge); *pret.* **jeringué** (-'ge)] **1,** to squirt *or* inject with a syringe. **2,** *colloq.* to vex; annoy; bother.
jeroglífico (xe·roɣ'li·fi·ko) *adj.* & *n.m.* hieroglyphic.
jersey (xer'sei) *n.m.* jersey.
jesuita (xe'swi·ta) *adj.* & *n.m.* Jesuit.
jeta ('xe·ta) *n.f.* **1,** protruding lips. **2,** snout. **3,** *colloq.* mug; face. —**poner jeta,** to pout.
jíbaro ('xi·βa·ro) *adj., Amer.* rustic; uncivilized. —*n.m.* rustic; hick.
jibia ('xi·βja) *n.f.* cuttlefish.
jícara ('xi·ka·ra) *n.f.* mug; chocolate cup.
jifa ('xi·fa) *n.f.* offal.
¡ji, ji! (xi'xi) *interj.* te-hee!
jilguero (xil'ɣe·ro) *n.m.* linnet.
jineta (xi'ne·ta) *n.f., usu. in* **a la jineta,** with very short stirrups.
jinete (xi'ne·te) *n.m.* horseman.
jinetear (xi·ne·te'ar) *v.i.* to ride horseback for show; prance. —*v.t. Amer.* to break in; tame (a horse).
jingo ('xin·go) *n.m.* jingo. —**jingoísmo,** *n.m.* jingoism. —**jingoísta,** *adj.* & *n.m.* & *f.* jingoist.
jinrikisha (xin·ri'ki·ʃa) *n.m.* jinrikisha.
jira ('xi·ra) *n.f.* **1,** excursion; tour. **2,** outing; picnic.
jirafa (xi'ra·fa) *n.f.* giraffe.
jirón (xi'ron) *n.m.* **1,** strip of cloth. **2,** rag; tatter. **3,** *fig.* shred; bit.
jitomate (xi·to'ma·te) *n.m., Amer.* tomato.
jiu-jitsu (xju'xit·su) *n.m.* jujitsu.
jockey ('dʒo·ki) *n.m.* jockey.
jocoso (xo'ko·so) *adj.* jocose; jocular. —**jocosidad,** *n.f.* jocosity; jocularity.
jocundo (xo'kun·do) *adj.* jocund. —**jocundidad,** *n.f.* jocundity.
jofaina (xo'fai·na) *n.f.* washbasin.
jolgorio (xol'ɣo·rjo) *n.m.* = **holgorio.**
jónico ('xo·ni·ko) *adj.* Ionic.
jonrón (xon'ron) *n.m., baseball* home run.
jornada (xor'na·ða) *n.f.* **1,** journey. **2,** day's journey. **3,** day's work.
jornal (xor'nal) *n.m.* **1,** day's wages. **2,** day's work.
jornalero (xor·na'le·ro) *n.m.* laborer; day laborer.
joroba (xo'ro·βa) *n.f.* **1,** hump; humpback. **2,** *colloq.* bother; nuisance; importunity.
jorobado (xo·ro'βa·ðo) *adj.* **1,** humpbacked. **2,** *colloq.* in a fix. —*n.m.* hunchback; humpback.
jorobar (xo·ro'βar) *v.t., colloq.* to importune; bother; annoy.

jota ('xo·ta) *n.f.* **1,** the letter *j.* **2,** iota; jot. **3,** a Spanish dance.
joule (dʒul) *n.m.* = **julio.**
joven ('xo·βen) *adj.* young. —*n.m.* & *f.* youth; young person.
jovial (xo'βjal) *adj.* jovial. —**jovialidad,** *n.f.* joviality.
joya ('xo·ja) *n.f.* gem; jewel.
joyel (xo'jel) *n.m.* small jewel.
joyería (xo·je'ri·a) *n.f.* **1,** jewelry trade. **2,** jewelry shop. —**joyero** (-'je·ro) *n.m.* jeweler.
juanete (xwa'ne·te) *n.m.* **1,** bunion. **2,** *naut.* topgallant sail.
jubilación (xu·βi·la'θjon; -'sjon) *n.f.* **1,** retirement. **2,** pension.
jubilado (xu·βi'la·ðo) *adj.* retired. —*n.m.* pensioner.
jubilar (xu·βi'lar) *v.t.* to retire; pension.
jubileo (xu·βi'le·o) *n.m.* jubilee.
júbilo ('xu·βi·lo) *n.m.* jubilation; joy. —**jubiloso,** *adj.* jubilant.
jubón (xu'βon) *n.m.* **1,** doublet; jerkin. **2,** tight blouse; basque.
judaico (xu'ðai·ko) *adj.* Judaic. —**judaísmo,** (xu·ða'is·mo) *n.m.* Judaism.
judería (xu·ðe'ri·a) *n.f.* ghetto.
judía (xu'ði·a) *n.f.* **1,** Jewess. **2,** kidney bean.
judicatura (xu·ði·ka'tu·ra) *n.f.* **1,** judicature. **2,** judiciary.
judicial (xu·ði'θjal; -'sjal) *adj.* judicial; judiciary.
judío (xu'ði·o) *adj.* Jewish. —*n.m.* Jew.
judo ('xu·ðo) *n.m.* judo.
juego ('xwe·γo) *n.m.* **1,** game. **2,** gambling. **3,** play; move. **4,** matching set; set. **5,** works; movement; mechanism. **6,** *mech.* play. —*v., pres.ind. of* **jugar.** —**hacer juego (con),** to match; go (with). —**juego de palabras,** play on words; pun. —**juego limpio,** fair play. —**juego sucio,** foul play. —**juegos malabares,** juggling; jugglery.
juegue ('xwe·γe) *v., pres.subjve. of* **jugar.**
juerga ('xwer·γa) *n.f.* spree; revelry; carousal. —**juerguista** (-'γis·ta) *n.m.* & *f.* merrymaker; reveler.
jueves ('xwe·βes) *n.m.sing.* & *pl.* Thursday.
juez (xweθ; xwes) *n.m.* judge.
jugada (xu'γa·ða) *n.f.* **1,** play; move; stroke. **2,** *fig.* trick; prank.
jugador (xu·γa'ðor) *adj.* gambling. —*n.m.* **1,** player. **2,** gambler.
jugar (xu'γar) *v.i.* [*pres.ind.* **juego;** *pres.subjve.* **juegue;** *pret.* **jugué**] **1,** to play; engage in playing. **2,** to toy; trifle. **3,** to match; fit; suit. **4,** to gamble. **5,** *mech.* to have play. —*v.t.* **1,** to play; play at. **2,** to gamble; gamble away. **3,** to move; wield.
jugarreta (xu·γa'rre·ta) *n.f. colloq.* **1,** bad play; wrong move. **2,** mischief; misdeed.
juglar (xu'γlar) *n.m.* minstrel. —**juglaría,** *n.f.* minstrelsy.
jugo ('xu·γo) *n.m.* **1,** juice. **2,** *fig.* substance; meat; marrow. —**jugoso,** *adj.* juicy.
jugué (xu'γe) *v., 1st pers.sing. pret. of* **jugar.**
juguete (xu'γe·te) *n.m.* toy; plaything.
juguetear (xu·γe·te'ar) *v.i.* **1,** to toy; trifle. **2,** to frolic; romp.
juguetería (xu·γe·te'ri·a) *n.f.* toyshop.
juguetón (xu·γe'ton) *adj.* playful; frolicsome.
juicio ('xwi·θjo; -sjo) *n.m.* **1,** judgment. **2,** sense; wisdom. **3,** sanity. **4,** trial; lawsuit. —**juicioso,** *adj.* judicious; wise; sensible.
julepe (xu'le·pe) *n.m.* **1,** julep. **2,** *colloq.* scolding; reprimand. **3,** *Amer., colloq.* fear; fright. **4,** *Amer., colloq.* fuss; to-do.
julio ('xu·ljo) *n.m.* **1,** July. **2,** joule.
jumento (xu'men·to) *n.m.* ass; donkey.
junco ('xun·ko) *n.m.* **1,** *bot.* rush. **2,** junk (*ship*).
jungla ('xun·gla) *n.f.* jungle.
junio ('xu·njo) *n.m.* June.
junquillo (xun'ki·ʎo; -jo) *n.m.* **1,** *bot.* jonquil. **2,** rattan.
junta ('xun·ta) *n.f.* **1,** junta; assembly; board. **2,** meeting; gathering. **3,** joint; seam. **4,** junction.
juntar (xun'tar) *v.t.* **1,** to join; unite; place together. **2,** to collect; gather; amass. **3,** to close (a door or window) incompletely. **4,** to assemble; congregate. **5,** to pool. —**juntarse,** *v.r.* **1,** to meet; assemble. **2,** *fol. by* **a,** to get close to; hug. **3,** *fol. by* **con** *or* **a,** *to* associate with.
junto ('xun·to) *adj.* joined; united; placed together. —**juntos,** *adv.* together; jointly. —**junto a,** next to; beside. —**junto con,** together with.
juntura (xun'tu·ra) *n.f.* joint; juncture.

Júpiter ('xu·pi·ter) *n.m.* Jupiter; Jove.
jura ('xu·ra) *n.f.* oath; pledge.
jurado (xu'ra·ðo) *adj.* sworn. —*n.m.* **1,** jury. **2,** juror.
juramentar (xu·ra·men'tar) *v.t.* to swear in. —**juramentarse,** *v.r.* to take an oath.
juramento (xu·ra'men·to) *n.m.* oath.
jurar (xu'rar) *v.t.* **1,** to swear; vow. **2,** to be sworn into; take the oath of (a public office). —*v.i.* to curse; swear. —**jurársela a uno,** *colloq.* to have it in for someone.
jurel (xu'rel) *n.m., ichthy.* yellow jack.
jurídico (xu'ri·ði·ko) *adj.* juridical.
jurisconsulto (xu·ris·kon'sul·to) *n.m.* **1,** jurist. **2,** lawyer.
jurisdicción (xu·ris·ðik'θjon; -'sjon) *n.f.* jurisdiction. —**jurisdiccional,** *adj.* jurisdictional.
jurisperito (xu·ris·pe'ri·to) *n.m.* legal expert.
jurisprudencia (xu·ris·pru'ðen·θja; -sja) *n.f.* jurisprudence.
jurista (xu'ris·ta) *n.m.* jurist.
justa ('xus·ta) *n.f.* **1,** joust. **2,** contest.
justicia (xus'ti·θja; -sja) *n.f.* **1,** justice. **2,** police; law enforcement authority.
justiciero (xus·ti'θje·ro; -'sje·ro) *adj.* strictly fair; stern.
justificar (xus·ti·fi'kar) *v.t.* [*pres. subjve.* **justifique** (-'fi·ke); *pret.* **justifiqué** (-'ke)] to justify. —**justificable,** *adj.* justifiable. —**justificación,** *n.f.* justification.
justo ('xus·to) *adj.* **1,** just. **2,** correct; exact. **3,** = **apretado.** —*adv.* **1,** just; exactly. **2,** just right. **3,** tight.
juvenil (xu·βe'nil) *adj.* juvenile; youthful.
juventud (xu·βen'tuð) *n.f.* youth.
juzgado (xuθ'ɣa·ðo; jus-) *n.m.* tribunal; court of justice.
juzgar (juθ'ɣar; jus-) *v.t.* & *i.* [*pres.subjve.* **juzgue** ('xuθ·ɣe; 'xus-); *pret.* **juzgué** (-'ɣe)] to judge.

K

K, k (ka) *n.f.* 12th letter of the Spanish alphabet.
káiser ('kai·ser) *n.m.* Kaiser.
kajak (ka'xak) *n.m.* kayak.
kaki ('ka·ki) *adj.* & *n.m.* = **caqui.**
kaleidoscopio (ka·lei·ðos'ko·pjo) *n.m.* = **calidoscopio.**
kan (kan) *n.m.* khan. —**kanato** (-'na·to) *n.m.* khanate.
kanguro (kan'gu·ro) *n.m.* = **canguro.**
kapok (ka'pok) *n.m.* kapok.
kayak (ka'jak) *n.m.* = **kajak.**
kepis ('ke·pis) *n.m.sing.* & *pl.* kepi.
kerosina (ke·ro'si·na) *n.f., also, Amer.,* **kerosén** (-'sen), **kerosene** (-'se·ne) *n.m.* kerosene.
kilo ('ki·lo) *n.m.* = **kilogramo.**
kilo- (ki·lo) *prefix* kilo-; thousand: *kilogramo,* kilogram.
kilociclo (ki·lo'θi·klo; -'si·klo) *n.m.* kilocycle.
kilogramo (ki·lo'ɣra·mo) *n.m.* kilogram.
kilolitro (ki·lo'li·tro) *n.m.* kiloliter.
kilometraje (ki·lo·me'tra·xe) *n.m.* distance in kilometers.
kilométrico (ki·lo'me·tri·ko) *adj.* **1,** kilometric. **2,** *colloq.* lengthy.
kilómetro (ki'lo·me·tro) *n.m.* kilometer.
kilovatio (ki·lo'βa·tjo) *n.m.* kilowatt.
kimono (ki'mo·no) *n.m.* = **quimono.**
kindergarten (kin·der'ɣar·ten) *n.m.* kindergarten.
kinescopio (ki·nes'ko·pjo) *n.m.* kinescope.
kiosco *also,* **kiosko** ('kjos·ko) *n.m.* = **quiosco.**
kiwi ('ki·wi) *n.m.* kiwi.
klaxson ('klak·son) *n.m., Amer.* automobile horn.
knockout (no'kaut) *n.m.* knockout.
knut *also,* **knout** (nut) *n.m.* knout.
koala (ko'a·la) *n.m.* koala.
kopek (ko'pek) *n.m.* kopeck.
Kremlin ('krem·lin) *n.m.* Kremlin.
kulak (ku'lak) *n.m.* kulak.

L

L, l ('e·le) *n.f.* 13th letter of the Spanish alphabet.

la (la) *def.art. fem.sing.* the. —*pers. pron. fem.sing., used as dir. obj. of a verb* her; it; you. —*dem. pron. fem.sing.* that; the one (that).

la (la) *n.m., music* la; A.

laberinto (la·βe'rin·to) *n.m.* labyrinth. —**laberíntico,** *adj.* labyrinthine.

labia ('la·βja) *n.f., colloq.* glibness.

labial (la'βjal) *adj.* labial.

labihendido (la·βi·en'di·ðo) *adj.* harelipped.

labio ('la·βjo) *n.m.* lip. —**labio leporino,** harelip.

labor (la'βor) *n.f.* **1,** labor; work. **2,** embroidery; needlework. **3,** tillage; tilling.

laborar (la·βo'rar) *v.t.* = **labrar.** —*v.i.* to work; labor; strive. —**laborable,** *adj.* arable. —**día laborable,** workday; working day.

laboratorio (la·βo·ra'to·rjo) *n.m.* laboratory.

laborioso (la·βo'rjo·so) *adj.* **1,** laborious. **2,** industriousness. —**laboriosidad,** *n.f.* industriousness; industry.

laborista (la·βo'ris·ta) *n.m. & f.* Laborite. —**partido laborista,** Labor Party.

labrado (la'βra·ðo) *adj.* **1,** tilled; cultivated. **2,** wrought; worked. —*n.m.* **1,** working; carving; forging. **2,** tillage. **3,** *usu.pl.* cultivated land.

labrador (la·βra'ðor) *n.m.* **1,** farmer; peasant. **2,** farmhand.

labrantío (la·βran'ti·o) *n.m.* tillable land. —*adj.* tillable.

labranza (la'βran·θa; -sa) *n.f.* tillage; farming.

labrar (la'βrar) *v.t. & i.* **1,** to till. **2,** to work; carve; forge. **3,** to build.

labriego (la'βrje·ɣo) *n.m.* farmhand; peasant.

laburno (la'βur·no) *n.m.* laburnum.

laca ('la·ka) *n.f.* lac; lacquer; shellac.

lacayo (la'ka·jo) *n.m.* lackey.

lace ('la·θe; -se) *v., pres.subjve. of* **lazar.**

lacé (la'θe; -'se) *v., 1st pers.sing. pret. of* **lazar.**

lacear (la·θe'ar; la·se-) *v.t.* **1,** to adorn or tie with bows. **2,** *Amer.* to lasso.

lacerar (la·θe'rar; la·se-) *v.t.* to lacerate. —**laceración,** *n.f.* laceration.

lacio ('la·θjo; -sjo) *adj.* **1,** withered; shriveled. **2,** flaccid; limp; weak. **3,** straight; lank (*of hair*).

lacónico (la'ko·ni·ko) *adj.* laconic. —**laconismo** (-'nis·mo) *n.m.* brevity.

lacra ('la·kra) *n.f.* **1,** scar. **2,** blemish; defect. **3,** *Amer.* scab. **4,** *fig.* scum.

lacrar (la'krar) *v.t.* **1,** to impair the health of. **2,** to seal (*with sealing wax*).

lacre ('la·kre) *n.m.* sealing wax.

lacrimal (la·kri'mal) *adj.* lachrymal. —**lacrimoso** (-'mo·so) *adj.* lachrymose; tearful.

lacrimógeno (la·kri'mo·xe·no) *adj.* tear-producing. —**gas lacrimógeno,** tear gas.

lactar (lak'tar) *v.t. & i.* to suckle; nurse. —**lactación,** *also,* **lactancia,** *n.f.* lactation.

lácteo ('lak·te·o) *adj.* lacteal; milky.

láctico ('lak·ti·ko) *adj.* lactic.

lacto- (lak·to) *also,* **lacti-** (lak·ti) *prefix* lacto-; milk: *lactómetro,* lactometer; *lactífero,* lactiferous.

lactosa (lak'to·sa) *also,* **lactina** (-'ti·na) *n.f.* lactose.

ladeado (la·ðe'a·ðo) *adj.* **1,** tilted; lopsided. **2,** turned sideways.

ladear (la·ðe'ar) *v.t. & i.* to tilt; tip; lean. —*v.t.* to turn sideways. —*v.i.* to skirt around; go around the side.

ladeo (la'ðe·o) *n.m.* leaning; tilting; tilt.

ladera (la'ðe·ra) *n.f.* hillside; slope.

ladilla (la'ði·ʎa; -ja) *n.f.* crab louse.

ladino (la'ði·no) *adj.* sly; shifty.

lado ('la·ðo) *n.m.* **1,** side. **2,** direction. —**al lado,** alongside; next door. —**al lado de, 1,** next to; beside. **2,** on the side of. —**de lado,** sideways; tilted.

ladrar (la'ðrar) *v.i.* to bark. —**ladrido** (la'ðri·ðo) bark; barking.

ladrillo (la'ðri·ʎo; -jo) *n.m.* brick. —**ladrillado,** *n.m.* = **enladrillado.** —**ladrillar,** *n.m.* brickyard. —*v.t.* = **enladrillar.**
ladrón (la'ðron) *n.m.* thief. —*adj.* thieving; thievish.
ladronera (la·ðro'ne·ra) *n.f.* **1,** den of thieves. **2,** sluice gate.
lagaña (la'ɣa·ɲa) *n.f.* = **legaña.**
lagar (la'ɣar) *n.m.* **1,** wine press. **2,** winery.
lagartija (la·ɣar'ti·xa) *n.f.* a kind of small lizard.
lagarto (la'ɣar·to) *n.m.* **1,** lizard. **2,** *Mex.* alligator. **3,** *colloq.* sly person.
lago ('la·ɣo) *n.m.* lake.
lágrima ('la·ɣri·ma) *n.f.* tear; teardrop. —**lagrimal,** *adj.* lachrymal. —**lagrimar,** *v.i.* = **llorar.** —**lagrimoso,** *adj.* tearful; lachrymose.
lagrimear (la·ɣri·me'ar) *v.i.* to weep readily; be easily moved to tears.
laguna (la'ɣu·na) *n.f.* **1,** lagoon; pond. **2,** lacuna.
laicismo (lai'θis·mo; -'sis·mo) *n.m.* secularism.
laico ('lai·ko) *adj.* lay; laic.
laja ('la·xa) *n.f.* slab; flagstone.
lama ('la·ma) *n.f.* **1,** slime; ooze. **2,** = **lamé.**
lama ('la·ma) *n.m.* lama. —**lamaísmo,** *n.m.* Lamaism. —**lamaísta,** *adj.* & *n.m.* & *f.* Lamaist. —**lamasería** (-se'ri·a) *n.f.* lamasery.
lamé (la'me) *n.m., also,* **lama** ('la·ma) *n.f.* lamé.
lamedal (la·me'ðal) *n.m.* bog; quagmire.
lamedor (la·me'ðor) *adj.* **1,** licking. **2,** *fig.* & *colloq.* fawning; cajoling. —*n.m.* **1,** licker. **2,** syrup.
lamedura (la·me'ðu·ra) *n.f.* lick; licking.
lamentar (la·men'tar) *v.t.* & *i.* to lament. —**lamentable,** *adj.* lamentable. —**lamentación,** *n.f.* lamentation.
lamento (la'men·to) *n.m.* lament.
lamer (la'mer) *v.t.* to lick; lap against.
lámina ('la·mi·na) *n.f.* **1,** plate; sheet. **2,** illustration; picture. **3,** stamp; die.
laminar (la·mi'nar) *v.t.* **1,** to laminate. **2,** to roll (metal) into sheets. —*adj.* laminate. —**laminado,** *adj.* laminated. —*n.m.* [*also,* **laminación,** *n.f.*] lamination.
lampa ('lam·pa) *n.f., Amer.* shovel. —**lampear** (-pe'ar) *v.t., Amer.* to shovel.
lampacear (lam·pa·θe'ar; -se'ar) *v.t., naut.* to mop; swab. —**lampazo,** *n.m., naut.* mop; swab.
lámpara ('lam·pa·ra) *n.f.* lamp.
lamparón (lam·pa'ron) *n.m.* **1,** grease spot. **2,** scrofula.
lampiño (lam'pi·ɲo) *adj.* beardless; hairless.
lamprea (lam'pre·a) *n.f.* lamprey. —**lamprea glutinosa,** hagfish.
lana ('la·na) *n.f.* wool.
lanar (la'nar) *adj.* wool-producing; woolbearing. —**ganado lanar,** sheep.
lance ('lan·θe; -se) *n.m.* **1,** throw; cast. **2,** incident; episode; happening. **3,** situation; predicament. **4,** dispute; quarrel; fight. **5,** *Amer.* chance; risk. —**de lance,** bargain (*attrib.*); bought or sold at a bargain.
lance ('lan·θe; -se) *v., pres.subjve. of* **lanzar.**
lancé (lan'θe; -'se) *v., 1st pers. sing.pret. of* **lanzar.**
lancear (lan·θe'ar; lan·se-) *v.t.* to pierce; wound, as with a lance.
lancero (lan'θe·ro; -'se·ro) *n.m.* lancer.
lanceta (lan'θe·ta; -'se·ta) *n.f.* lancet; surgical knife. —**lancetada,** *n.f. also,* **lancetazo,** *n.m.* cut; lancing; incision.
lancha ('lan·tʃa) *n.f.* launch; boat.
lanchón (lan'tʃon) *n.m.* barge; scow.
langaruto (lan·ga'ru·to) *adj., colloq.* = **larguirucho.**
langosta (lan'gos·ta) *n.f.* **1,** lobster. **2,** locust. —**langostín** (-'tin) *also,* **langostino** (-'ti·no) *n.m.* crawfish.
languidecer (lan·gi·ðe'θer; -'ser) *v.i.* [*pres.ind.* **languidezco** (-'ðeθ·ko; -'ðes·ko); *pres.subjve.* **languidezca** (-ka)] to languish. —**languidecimiento,** *n.m.* languishment.
lánguido ('lan·gi·ðo) *adj.* languid. —**languidez,** *n.f.* languor; languidness.
lanilla (la'ni·ʎa; -ja) *n.f.* **1,** lightweight wool cloth. **2,** nap.
lanolina (la·no'li·na) *n.f.* lanolin.
lantano (lan'ta·no) *n.m.* lanthanum.
lanudo (la'nu·ðo) *adj.* woolly; fleecy. *Also,* **lanoso** (-'no·so).
lanza ('lan·θa; -sa) *n.f.* lance; spear.

lanzada (lan'θa·ða; -'sa·ða) *n.f.* **1,** thrust of a lance. **2,** wound from a lance or spear. *Also,* **lanzazo** (-'θa·θo; -'sa·so) *n.m.*
lanzadera (lan·θa'ðe·ra; lan·sa-) *n.f.* shuttle of a loom or sewing machine.
lanzamiento (lan·θa'mjen·to; lan·sa-) *n.m.* **1,** throwing; hurling. **2,** ejection; ousting. **3,** launching.
lanzar (lan'θar; -'sar) *v.t.* [*pres. subjve.* **lance;** *pret.* **lancé**] **1,** to hurl; throw. **2,** to eject. **3,** to launch.
lapa ('la·pa) *n.f.* **1,** *zool.* limpet. **2,** *Amer. colloq.* hanger-on; leech.
lapicero (la·pi'θe·ro; -'se·ro) *n.m., also, Amer.* **lapicera,** *n.f.* mechanical pencil.
lápida ('la·pi·ða) *n.f.* **1,** tombstone. **2,** stone tablet. **3,** stone slab.
lapidar (la·pi'ðar) *v.t.* **1,** to stone. **2,** *Amer.* to cut (gems).
lapidario (la·pi'ða·rjo) *adj.* & *n.m.* lapidary. —*adj.* concise; pithy.
lapislázuli (la·pis'la·θu·li; -su·li) *n.m.* lapis lazuli.
lápiz ('la·piθ; -pis) *n.m.* pencil. —**lápiz para los labios; lápiz de labios,** lipstick.
lapón (la'pon) *adj.* & *n.m.* Lapp.
lapso ('lap·so) *n.m.* lapse.
laquear (la·ke'ar) *v.t.* to lacquer; shellac.
lar (lar) *n.m.* **1,** hearth. **2,** *usu.pl.* home; family.
lardear (lar·ðe'ar) *also,* **lardar** (-'ðar) *v.t.* **1,** to lard. **2,** to baste.
lardo ('lar·ðo) *n.m.* lard.
largar (lar'ɣar) *v.t.* [*pres.subjve.* **largue** ('lar·ɣe); *pret.* **largué** (-'ɣe)] **1,** to let loose; let go. **2,** to unfurl. —**largarse,** *v.r., colloq.* to get out; leave.
largo ('lar·ɣo) *adj.* **1,** long. **2,** generous; liberal. **3,** abundant. —*n.m.* **1,** length. **2,** *music* largo. —*adj.* & *adv., music* largo. —*interj.* out! get out! —**a la larga, 1,** lengthwise. **2,** at length. **3,** in the long run. —**a lo largo, 1,** along; lengthwise. **2,** at length. **3,** in the distance.
largor (lar'ɣor) *n.m.* length.
largueza (lar'ɣe·θa; -sa) *n.f.* largess.
larguirucho (lar·ɣi'ru·tʃo) *adj., colloq.* lanky; gawky.
larguísimo (lar'ɣi·si·mo) *adj.* very long.
largura (lar'ɣu·ra) *n.f.* extent; length.
laringe (la'rin·xe) *n.f.* larynx —**laríngeo,** *adj.* laryngeal. —**laringitis,** *n.f.* laryngitis.
larva ('lar·βa) *n.f.* larva; grub —**larval,** *adj.* larval.
las (las) *def.art. fem.pl.* the. —*pers pron. fem.pl., used as dir.obj. of* *verb* them; you. —*dem.pron. fem pl.* those.
lascivo (las'θi·βo; la'si-) *adj.* lascivious. —**lascivia,** *n.f.* lasciviousness.
lasitud (la·si'tuð) *n.f.* lassitude.
lástima ('las·ti·ma) *n.f.* pity; compassion.
lastimadura (las·ti·ma'ðu·ra *n.f.* hurt; injury.
lastimar (las·ti'mar) *v.t.* to hurt injure.
lastimero (las·ti'me·ro) *ad* mournful.
lastimoso (las·ti'mo·so) *adj.* pitiful.
lastre ('las·tre) *n.m.* ballast; dea weight. —**lastrar,** *v.t.* to ballast.
lata ('la·ta) *n.f.* **1,** tin; tin plate; ti can. **2,** *colloq.* bore; nuisance.
latente (la'ten·te) *adj.* latent.
lateral (la·te'ral) *adj.* lateral.
látex ('la·teks) *n.m.* latex.
latido (la'ti·ðo) *n.m.* beat; throb.
latifundio (la·ti'fun·djo) *n.m* landed estate. —**latifundista,** *n.m* & *f.* large landowner.
látigo ('la·ti·ɣo) *n.m.* whip. —**latigazo,** *n.m.* lash; whiplash; crack c a whip.
latigudo (la·ti'ɣu·ðo) *adj., S Amer.* = **correoso.**
latín (la'tin) *n.m.* Latin; Lati language.
latinizar (la·ti·ni'θar; -'sar) *v.t.* *i.*[*pres.subjve.* **latinice** (-'ni·θe; -se *pret.* **latinicé** (-'θe; -'se)] to Latinize.
latino (la'ti·no) *adj.* & *n.m.* Lati —**vela latina,** lateen sail.
latinoamericano (la·ti·no·a me·ri'ka·no) *adj.* & *n.m.* Latin American.
latir (la'tir) *v.i.* to beat; throb.
latitud (la·ti'tuð) *n.f.* latitud —**latitudinal** (-ði'nal) *adj.* latitudinal.
lato ('la·to) *adj.* extended; broa
latón (la'ton) *n.m.* brass. —**latonería,** *n.f.* brass shop; brass work —**latonero,** *n.m.* brazier; bra dealer.
latoso (la'to·so) *adj., colloq.* annoying; boring.

-latra (la·tra) *suffix* -later; worshipper; worshipping: *idólatra,* idolater; *ególatra,* self-worshipping.
-latría (la'tri·a) *suffix* -latry; worship: *idolatría,* idolatry.
latrina (la'tri·na) *n.f.* = **letrina.**
latrocinio (la·tro'θi·njo; -'si·njo) *n.m.* larceny; theft.
laucha ('lau·tʃa) *n.f., Amer.* mouse. —*adj., Amer., colloq.* shifty; shrewd.
laúd (la'uð) *n.m.* **1,** lute. **2,** catboat.
laudable (lau'ða·βle) *adj.* laudable.
láudano ('lau·ða·no) *n.m.* laudanum.
laudatorio (lau·ða'to·rjo) *adj.* laudatory.
laureado (lau·re'a·ðo) *adj.* & *n.m.* laureate.
laurear (lau·re'ar) *v.t.* to honor.
laurel (lau'rel) *n.m.* **1,** laurel. **2,** honor; distinction.
lauréola (lau're·o·la) *n.f.* laurel wreath.
lauro ('lau·ro) *n.m.* honor; glory; praise.
lava ('la·βa) *n.f.* lava.
lavabo (la'βa·βo) *n.m.* **1,** washstand. **2,** lavatory.
lavadero (la·βa'ðe·ro) *n.m.* washing place; laundry shed.
lavado (la'βa·ðo) *n.m.* wash; washing.
lavadora (la·βa'ðo·ra) *n.f.* washer; washing machine.
lavamanos (la·βa'ma·nos) *n.m. sing.* & *pl.* washstand; washbowl.
lavanda (la'βan·da) *n.f.* lavender.
lavandera (la·βan'de·ra) *n.f.* laundress. —**lavandería,** *n.f.* laundry. —**lavandero,** *n.m.* launderer.
lavaplatos (la·βa'pla·tos) *n.m.* & *f. sing & pl.* dishwasher.
lavar (la'βar) *v.t.* **1,** to wash. **2,** *fig.* to wash away.
lavarropas (la·βa'rro·pas) *n.m. sing.* & *pl.* washing machine.
lavativa (la·βa'ti·βa) *n.f.* **1,** enema. **2,** syringe. **3,** *colloq.* nuisance; annoyance.
lavatorio (la·βa'to·rjo) *n.m.* **1,** wash; washing. **2,** washbowl. **3,** *Amer.* washroom; lavatory.
lavazas (la'βa·θas; -sas) *n.f.pl.* wash water.
laxante (lak'san·te) *also,* **laxativo** (-'ti·βo) *adj.* loosening; slackening. —*adj.* & *n.m.* laxative.
laxar (lak'sar) *v.t.* to loosen; slacken.
laxo ('lak·so) *adj.* lax. —**laxitud,** *n.f.* laxity; laxness.
lay (lai) *n.m., hist.* lay; ballad.
laya ('la·ja) *n.f.* **1,** sort; kind. **2,** garden spade. —**layar,** *v.t.* to spade; dig with a spade.
lazada (la'θa·ða; -'sa·ða) *n.f.* bow; bowknot.
lazar (la'θar: -'sar) *v.t.* [*pres. subjve.* **lace;** *pret.* **lacé**] to lasso; rope.
lazarillo (la·θa'ri·ʎo; la·sa'ri·jo) *n.m.* blindman's guide.
lázaro ('la·θa·ro; 'la·sa-) *n.m.* beggar.
lazo ('la·θo; -so) *n.m.* **1,** bow; loop. **2,** lasso. **3,** bond; tie. **4,** trap; snare.
le (le) *pers.pron.m.* & *f.sing.* **1,** *used as dir.obj. of a verb* him. **2,** *used as indir.obj. of a verb* to him; to her; to it; to you.
leal (le'al) *adj.* loyal. —**lealtad,** *n.f.* loyalty.
lebrato (le'βra·to) *n.m.* young hare.
lebrel (le'βrel) *n.m.* whippet.
lebrillo (le'βri·ʎo; -jo) *n.m.* earthenware tub.
lebrón (le'βron) *n.m.* **1,** large hare. **2,** *colloq.* coward.
lebruno (le'βru·no) *adj.* leporine.
lección (lek'θjon; -'sjon) *n.f.* lesson.
lector (lek'tor) *n.m.* **1,** reader. **2,** lecturer. —*adj.* fond of reading.
lectura (lek'tu·ra) *n.f.* reading.
lecha ('le·tʃa) *n.f., ichthy.* **1,** milt. **2,** milt sac.
lechada (le'tʃa·ða) *n.f.* **1,** thin grout. **2,** paper pulp. **3,** whitewash.
leche ('le·tʃe) *n.f.* milk. —**tener leche,** *Amer., colloq.* to be lucky; have luck.
lechera (le'tʃe·ra) *n.f.* **1,** milkmaid. **2,** milk can; milk pitcher. —*adj.fem.* milch.
lechería (le·tʃe'ri·a) *n.f.* dairy.
lechero (le'tʃe·ro) *n.m.* milkman. —*adj.* **1,** of milk; milk (*attrib.*). **2,** milch. **3,** *Amer., colloq.* lucky.
lechigada (le·tʃi'ɣa·ða) *n.f.* litter (*of animals*).
lecho ('le·tʃo) *n.m.* **1,** bed. **2,** straw bedding.
lechón (le'tʃon) *n.m.* **1,** suckling pig. **2,** *colloq.* babe in the woods.
lechosa (le'tʃo·sa) *n.f.* papaya.
lechoso (le'tʃo·so) *adj.* milky.
lechuga (le'tʃu·ɣa) *n.f.* lettuce.

lechuguilla (le·tʃu'ɣi·ʎa; -ja) *n.f.* **1,** wild lettuce. **2,** frill; frilled collar; ruff.
lechuza (le'tʃu·θa; -sa) *n.f.* owl.
leer (le'er) *v.t.* [*pret.* **leí, leyó;** *ger.* **leyendo**] to read.
legacía (le·ɣa'θi·a; -'si·a) *n.f.* legateship.
legación (le·ɣa'θjon; -'sjon) *n.f.* legation.
legado (le'ɣa·ðo) *n.m.* **1,** legate. **2,** legacy.
legajo (le'ɣa·xo) *n.m.* sheaf (*of papers or documents*).
legal (le'ɣal) *adj.* legal. —**legalidad,** *n.f.* legality.
legalizar (le·ɣa·li'θar; -'sar) *v.t.* [*pres.subjve.* **legalice** (-'li·θe; -se); *pret.* **legalicé** (-'θe; -'se)] to legalize.
légamo ('le·ɣa·mo) *n.m.* silt; mud. —**legamoso,** *adj.* silty; muddy.
legaña (le'ɣa·ɲa) *n.f.* eye secretion; rheum. —**legañoso,** *adj.* blear-eyed; bleary.
legar (le'ɣar) *v.t.* [*pres.subjve.* **legue;** *pret.* **legué**] **1,** to bequeath. **2,** to send as envoy.
legatario (le·ɣa'ta·rjo) *n.m.* legatee.
legendario (le·xen'da·rjo) *adj.* legendary.
legible (le'xi·βle) *adj.* legible. —**legibilidad,** *n.f.* legibility.
legión (le'xjon) *n.f.* legion. —**legionario,** *adj.* legionary. —*n.m.* legionnaire.
legislar (le·xis'lar) *v.t.* & *i.* to legislate. —**legislación,** *n.f.* legislation. —**legislador,** *n.m.* legislator. —**legislativo,** *adj.* legislative. —**legislatura,** *n.f.* legislature.
legista (le'xis·ta) *n.m.* & *f.* legal expert; student of the law.
legitimar (le·xi·ti'mar) *v.t.* to legitimize. —**legitimación,** *n.f.* legitimation.
legítimo (le'xi·ti·mo) *adj.* **1,** legitimate. **2,** genuine. —**legitimidad,** *n.f.* legitimacy.
lego ('le·ɣo) *adj.* **1,** laic; lay. **2,** uninformed; ignorant. —*n.m.* **1,** layman. **2,** lay brother.
legua ('le·ɣwa) *n.f.* league (*measure*).
legue ('le·ɣe) *v., pres.subjve. of* **legar.**
legué (le'ɣe) *v., 1st pers.sing. pret. of* **legar.**
leguleyo (le·ɣu'le·jo) *n.m.* dabbler at law; shyster.
legumbre (le'ɣum·bre) *n.f.* legume. **2,** vegetable (*edible* —**leguminoso** (le·ɣu·mi'no·so) *ad* leguminous.
leí (le'i) *v., pret. of* **leer.**
leíble (le'i·βle) *adj.* **1,** legible. readable.
leída (le'i·ða) *n.f.* reading.
leído (le'i·ðo) *v., p.p. of* **lee** —*adj.* well-read.
lejano (le'xa·no) *adj.* distant; r mote. —**lejanía,** *n.f.* distance; r moteness.
lejía (le'xi·a) *n.f.* lye.
lejos ('le·xos) *adv.* far; afar; f off. —**a lo lejos,** in the distance; f away. —**de lejos; desde lejos,** fro afar; from a distance.
lelo ('le·lo) *also, Amer.,* **lele** ('le·le *adj.* **1,** slow-witted; doltish. **2,** stup fied; aghast. —*n.m.* ninny; dolt.
lema ('le·ma) *n.m.* **1,** motto; sloga **2,** theme. **3,** caption.
lémur ('le·mur) *n.m.* lemur.
lencería (len·θe'ri·a; len·se-) *n.* **1,** dry goods. **2,** dry goods store.
lene ('le·ne) *adj.* soft; mild; gentl light.
lengua ('len·gwa) *n.f.* **1,** tongue. language.
lenguado (len'gwa·ðo) *n.m., ichth* sole; flounder.
lenguaje (len'gwa·xe) *n.m.* la guage; idiom; speech.
lenguaraz (len·gwa'raθ; -'ras *adj.* foulmouthed; loose-tongued.
lengüeta (len'gwe·ta) *n.f.* tongue (*of a shoe*). **2,** pin (*of buckle*). **3,** pointer (*of a scale*). *music* tongue; reed. **5,** epiglottis. *carpentry* tongue.
lengüetada (len·gwe'ta·ða) *n.* lick; lap. *Also,* **lengüetazo,** *n.m.*
lenidad (le·ni'ðað) *n.f.* leniency.
lenitivo (le·ni'ti·βo) *adj.* & *n.n* emollient. —*n.m., fig.* salve; baln relief.
lentamente (len·ta'men·te) *ad* slowly.
lente ('len·te) *n.m. or f.* len —**lentes,** *n.m.pl.* eyeglasses.
lenteja (len'te·xa) *n.f.* lentil.
lentejuela (len·te'xwe·la) *n.* spangle.
lenticular (len·ti·ku'lar) *adj.* le ticular.
lento ('len·to) *adj.* slow; sluggis tardy. —*adj.* & *adv., music* lent —**lentitud,** *n.f.* slowness; sluggis ness; tardiness.

leña ('le·ɲa) *n.f.* **1,** firewood; kindling. **2,** *colloq.* drubbing. **—leñador,** *n.m.* woodcutter; woodman. **—leñera,** *n.f.* woodshed.
leño ('le·ɲo) *n.m.* timber; heavy piece of wood. **—leñoso,** *adj.* woody; ligneous.
Leo ('le·o) *n.m., astron.* Leo.
león (le'on) *n.m.* lion. **—leona** (le'o·na) *n.f.* lioness.
leonado (le·o'na·ðo) *adj.* & *n.* tawny; yellowish brown.
leonera (le·o'ne·ra) *n.f.* **1,** lion's cage. **2,** *colloq.* untidy room. **3,** *colloq.* gambling den.
leonino (le·o'ni·no) *adj.* leonine.
leontina (le·on'ti·na) *n.f., Amer.* watch chain.
leopardo (le·o'par·ðo) *n.m.* leopard.
lépero ('le·pe·ro) *adj., Amer.* **1,** vulgar; coarse. **2,** *W.I.* shrewd; sly.
leporino (le·po'ri·no) *adj.* leporine. **—labio leporino,** harelip.
lepra ('le·pra) *n.f.* leprosy. **—leproso,** *adj.* leprous. **—***n.m.* leper.
lerdo ('ler·ðo) *adj.* **1,** slow; dull. **2,** clumsy.
les (les) *pers.pron.m.* & *f.pl.* **1,** *used as dir.obj. of a verb* them; you. **2,** *used as ind.obj. of a verb* to them; to you.
lesa ('le·sa) **majestad** lese majesty.
lesbiano (les'βja·no) *adj.* & *n.m.* Lesbian. *Also,* **lesbio** ('les·βjo).
lesión (le'sjon) *n.f.* lesion. **—lesionar,** *v.t.* to injure; wound.
lesna ('les·na) *n.f.* = **lezna.**
letal (le'tal) *adj.* lethal.
letanía (le·ta'ni·a) *n.f.* litany.
letargo (le'tar·ɣo) *n.m.* lethargy. **—letárgico** (-xi·ko) *adj.* lethargic.
letra ('le·tra) *n.f.* **1,** letter (*written character*). **2,** handwriting. **3,** words of a song; lyrics (*pl.*). **—al pie de la letra,** to the letter; literally.
letrado (le'tra·ðo) *adj.* learned; erudite. **—***n.m.* lawyer.
letrero (le'tre·ro) *n.m.* poster; sign.
letrina (le'tri·na) *n.f.* latrine; privy.
leucemia (leu'θe·mja; -'se·mja) *n.f.* leukemia.
leucocito (leu·ko'θi·to; -'si·to) *n.m.* leucocyte.
leudar (leu'ðar) *v.t.* to leaven. **—leudarse,** *v.r.* to ferment, as a leaven. **—leudo** ('leu·ðo) *adj.* leavened.
leva ('le·βa) *n.f.* **1,** departure (*from port*); weighing of anchor. **2,** levy (*of troops*). **3,** cam.
levadizo (le·βa'ði·θo; -so) *adj.* that can be raised. **—puente levadizo,** drawbridge; lift bridge.
levadura (le·βa'ðu·ra) *n.f.* yeast; leaven.
levantar (le·βan'tar) *v.t.* **1,** to raise; lift. **2,** to recruit. **3,** to erect. **4,** to clear (the table). **—levantarse,** *v.r.* to rise. **—levantado,** *adj.* elevated; high; sublime. **—levantamiento,** *n.m.* uprising.
levante (le'βan·te) *n.m.* East; Orient; Levant. **—levantino,** *adj.* & *n.m.* Levantine.
levar (le'βar) *v.t.* to weigh (anchor). **—levarse,** *v.r.* to set sail.
leve ('le·βe) *adj.* **1,** light; of little weight. **2,** slight; of little importance.
levedad (le·βe'ðað) *n.f.* **1,** levity. **2,** lightness; unimportance.
leviatán (le·βja'tan) *n.m.* leviathan.
levita (le'βi·ta) *n.m.* Levite. **—***n.f.* frock coat. **—levítico,** *adj.* Levitical.
levitación (le·βi·ta'θjon; -'sjon) *n.f.* levitation.
levo- (le·βo) *prefix* levo-; left: *levógiro,* levogyrate.
léxico ('lek·si·ko) *n.m.* [*also,* **lexicón** (-'kon)] lexicon. **—***adj.* lexical.
lexicografía (lek·si·ko·ɣra'fi·a) *n.f.* lexicography. **—lexicográfico** (-'ɣra·fi·ko) *adj.* lexicographic. **—lexicógrafo** (-'ko·ɣra·fo) *n.m.* lexicographer.
ley (lei) *n.f.* **1,** law. **2,** rule; norm. **3,** legal standard. **4,** loyalty; devotion. **5,** fineness (*of metals*). **—mala ley,** animosity; dislike.
leyenda (le'jen·da) *n.f.* legend.
leyendo (le'jen·do) *v., ger. of* **leer.**
leyó (le'jo) *v., 3rd pers.sing. pret. of* **leer.**
lezna ('leθ·na; les-) *n.f.* awl.
liar (li'ar) *v.t.* [*infl.:* **enviar**] **1,** to bind; tie; bundle. **2,** to embroil. **—liarse,** *v.r.* to become involved.
libar (li'βar) *v.t.* to sip; taste; savor. **—***v.i.* to make a libation. **—libación,** *n.f.* libation.
libelo (li'βe·lo) *n.m.* libel. **—libelista,** *n.m.* & *f.* libeler.
libélula (li'βe·lu·la) *n.f.* dragonfly.
liberación (li·βe·ra'θjon; -'sjon) *n.f.* **1,** liberation. **2,** *law* quittance.

liberal (li·βe'ral) *adj.* liberal. —**liberalismo,** *n.m.* liberalism.
liberalidad (li·βe·ra·li'ðað) *n.f.* liberality.
liberalizar li·βe·ra·li'θar; -'sar) *v.t.* [*pres.subjve.* **liberalice** (-'li·θe; -se); *pret.* **liberalicé** (-'θe; -'se)] to liberalize. —**liberalización,** *n.f.* liberalization.
liberar (li·βe'rar) *v.t.* to free; liberate; exempt.
libérrimo (li'βe·rri·mo) *adj., superl. of* **libre.**
libertad (li·βer'tað) *n.f.* liberty; freedom.
libertar (li·βer'tar) *v.t.* to liberate; free. —**libertador,** *n.m.* liberator. —*adj.* liberating.
libertino (li·βer'ti·no) *adj. & n.m.* libertine. —**libertinaje,** *n.m.* licentiousness.
liberto (li'βer·to) *n.m.* emancipated slave; freedman.
libídine (li'βi·ði·ne) *n.f.* lust; lewdness. —**libidinoso,** *adj.* libidinous.
libido (li'βi·ðo) *n.m.* libido.
libra ('li·βra) *n.f.* **1,** pound. **2,** *cap., astron.* Libra.
librado (li'βra·ðo) *n.m., comm.* drawee.
librador (li·βra'ðor) *n.m.* **1,** deliverer. **2,** *comm.* drawer (*of a draft or check*).
libramiento (li·βra'mjen·to) *n.m.* **1,** delivery; deliverance. **2,** *comm.* draft.
libranza (li'βran·θa; -sa) *n.f.* draft; bill of exchange. —**libranza postal,** money order.
librar (li'βrar) *v.t.* **1,** to free; deliver. **2,** to exempt. **3,** to issue; draw up. **4,** *comm.* to draw (a draft *or* check). **5,** to give (battle). —*v.i.* to deliver; give birth. —**librarse,** *v.r., fol. by* **de, 1,** to get out from; free oneself from. **2,** to avoid; keep away from. —**librarse de buena,** *colloq.* to have a close call. —**salir bien librado,** to get out (of something) well. —**salir mal librado,** to come out badly.
libre ('li·βre) *adj.* **1,** free. **2,** vacant; available. —*n.m., Mex.* taxi.
librea (li'βre·a) *n.f.* livery. —**de librea,** liveried.
librepensador (li·βre·pen·sa·'ðor) *n.m.* freethinker. —**libre pensamiento,** free thought.
librería (li·βre'ri·a) *n.f.* **1,** bookstore. **2,** bookshelf; bookcase.
librero (li'βre·ro) *n.m.* **1,** bookseller. **2,** *Amer.* bookcase.
libreta (li'βre·ta) *n.f.* notebook.
libreto (li'βre·to) *n.m.* libretto. —**libretista,** *n.m. & f.* librettist.
libro ('li·βro) *n.m.* book. —**libro borrador,** blotter. —**libro copiador,** *comm.* letter book. —**libro de actas,** minute book. —**libro de asiento** *or* **de cuentas,** account book. —**libro de caja,** cashbook. —**libro de memoria,** memorandum book. —**libro diario,** *comm.* journal. —**libro mayor,** ledger.
licencia (li'θen·θja; li'sen·sja) *n.f.* **1,** license. **2,** leave of absence. **3,** leave; furlough. **4,** *mil.* discharge. **5,** licentiousness.
licenciado (li·θen'θja·ðo; -sen·'sja·ðo) *n.m.* **1,** person licensed in a profession. **2,** *Amer.* lawyer. **3,** holder of a master's degree. **4,** discharged soldier.
licenciar (li·θen'θjar; -sen'sjar) *v.t.* **1,** to license. **2,** *mil.* to discharge. —**licenciarse,** *v.r.* to graduate; earn a master's degree. —**licenciatura,** *n.f.* master's degree.
licencioso (li·θen'θjo·so; li·sen·'sjo-) *adj.* licentious.
liceo (li'θe·o; -'se·o) *n.m.* **1,** lyceum. **2,** high school.
licitar (li·θi'tar; li·si-) *v.t.* to bid for. —**licitación,** *n.f.* bid; bidding. —**licitador,** *also,* **licitante,** *n.m.* bidder.
lícito ('li·θi·to; 'li·si-) *adj.* lawful; licit; permitted.
licor (li'kor) *n.m.* **1,** liquor. **2,** liqueur.
licuar (li'kwar) *v.t.* to liquefy. —**licuable,** *adj.* liquefiable. —**licuación,** *also,* **licuefacción** (li·kwe·fak'θjon; -'sjon) *n.f.* liquefaction.
lid (lið) *n.f.* struggle; fray.
líder ('li·ðer) *n.m.* leader.
lidia ('li·ðja) *n.f.* fight, esp. bullfight.
lidiar (li'ðjar) *v.i.* to fight; contend; struggle. —*v.t.* to fight, esp. a bull.
lie ('li·e) *v., pres.subjve. of* **liar.**
liebre ('lje·βre) *n.f.* hare.
lienzo ('ljen·θo; -so) *n.m.* **1,** linen or cotton cloth. **2,** canvas.
liga ('li·ɣa) *n.f.* **1,** league; alliance. **2,** garter. **3,** alloy. —**hacer ligas con,** to get along with.
ligado (li'ɣa·ðo) *adj. & adv., music* legato. —*n.m.* ligature.

ligadura (li·ɣa'ðu·ra) *n.f.* **1,** ligature. **2,** bond; tie.
ligamento (li·ɣa'men·to) *n.m.* ligament.
ligar (li'ɣar) *v.t.* [*pres.subjve.* **ligue;** *pret.* **ligué**] **1,** to bind; tie. **2,** to alloy. **3,** *Amer., colloq.* to get (something) by chance. —*v.i., cards* to draw matching cards; fill in. —**ligarse,** *v.r.* to ally; associate.
ligazón (li·ɣa'θon; -'son) *n.f.* union; bond.
ligereza (li·xe're·θa; -sa) *n.f.* **1,** lightness. **2,** swiftness. **3,** frivolity; levity.
ligero (li'xe·ro) *adj.* **1,** light; slight. **2,** swift; nimble; fast. **3,** fickle. —*adv., Amer.* fast. —**a la ligera,** recklessly. —**ligero de cascos,** lightheaded. —**ligero de lengua,** loose-tongued.
lignito (liɣ'ni·to) *n.m.* lignite.
ligue ('li·ɣe) *v., pres.subjve. of* **ligar.**
ligué (li'ɣe) *v., 1st pers.sing. pret. of* **ligar.**
lija ('li·xa) *n.f.* sandpaper. —**lijar,** *v.t.* to sandpaper.
lila ('li·la) *n.f.* lilac.
lima ('li·ma) *n.f.* **1,** lime. **2,** lime tree. **3,** file (*tool*).
limar (li'mar) *v.t.* to file; smooth. —**limar asperezas,** to smooth over differences.
limaza (li'ma·θa; -sa) *n.f.* snail; slug.
limbo ('lim·bo) *n.m.* **1,** limbo. **2,** edge; hem.
limero (li'me·ro) *n.m.* lime tree.
limitar (li·mi'tar) *v.t.* to limit; bound; restrict. —*v.i.* to border; abut. —**limitación,** *n.f.* limitation.
límite ('li·mi·te) *n.m.* limit; boundary; border.
limítrofe (li'mi·tro·fe) *adj.* bordering; contiguous.
limo ('li·mo) *n.m.* mud; slime.
limón (li'mon) *n.m.* **1,** lemon. **2,** lemon tree. —**limonada,** *n.f.* lemonade. —**limonero,** *n.m.* lemon tree.
limosna (li'mos·na) *n.f.* alms (*pl.*).
limosnero (li·mos'ne·ro) *adj.* charitable. —*n.m.* **1,** almoner. **2,** beggar.
limousine (li·mu'sin) *n.m.* limousine.
limpiabotas (lim·pja'βo·tas) *n.m.sing. & pl.* bootblack.
limpianieves (lim·pja'nje·βes) *n.m.sing. & pl.* snowplow.
limpiaparabrisas (lim·pja·pa·ra'βri·sas) *n.m.sing. & pl.* windshield wiper.
limpiar (lim'pjar) *v.t.* to clean; cleanse. —**limpiador,** *n.m.* cleaner; cleanser.
límpido ('lim·pi·ðo) *adj.* limpid. —**limpidez,** *n.f.* limpidity.
limpieza (lim'pje·θa; -sa) *n.f.* **1,** cleaning. **2,** cleanliness. **3,** *fig.* integrity; honesty.
limpio ('lim·pjo) *adj.* **1,** clean; neat. **2,** clear; pure. **3,** honest; upright.
linaje (li'na·xe) *n.m.* **1,** lineage. **2,** family; line.
linaza (li'na·θa; -sa) *n.f.* linseed; flaxseed.
lince ('lin·θe; -se) *n.m.* **1,** lynx. **2,** *colloq.* sharp person. —*adj.* sharp-eyed; shrewd.
linchar (lin'tʃar) *v.t.* to lynch. —**linchamiento,** *n.f.* lynching.
lindar (lin'dar) *v.i.* to border; adjoin. —**lindante,** *adj.* contiguous; bordering.
linde ('lin·de) *n.m. & f.* boundary; limit. —**lindero,** *n.m.* limit; boundary. —*adj.* contiguous; bordering.
lindo ('lin·do) *adj.* pretty; comely; handsome. —**lindeza,** *also,* **lindura,** *n.f.* prettiness; comeliness.
línea ('li·ne·a) *n.f.* line. —**lineal,** *adj.* lineal; linear. —**lineamento,** *n.m.* lineament.
linear (li·ne'ar) *v.t.* to line; draw lines on. —*adj.* linear.
linfa ('lin·fa) *n.f.* lymph. —**linfático** (-'fa·ti·ko) *adj.* lymphatic.
lingote (lin'go·te) *n.f.* ingot.
lingual (lin'gwal) *adj.* lingual.
lingüista (lin'gwis·ta) *n.m. & f.* linguist. —**lingüística,** *n.f.* linguistics. —**lingüístico,** *adj.* linguistic.
linimento (li·ni'men·to) *n.m.* liniment.
lino ('li·no) *n.m.* **1,** flax. **2,** linen.
linóleo (li'no·le·o) *n.m.* linoleum.
linón (li'non) *n.m.* lawn (*fabric*).
linotipia (li·no'ti·pja) *n.f.* linotype (*machine*). —**linotipista** (-ti·'pis·ta) *n.m. & f.* linotypist. —**linotipo** (-'ti·po) *n.m.* linotype (*plate*).
linterna (lin'ter·na) *n.f.* lantern; flashlight.
liño ('li·ɲo) *n.m.* row of trees or plants.
lío ('li·o) *n.m.* **1,** bundle; pack. **2,** *colloq.* mess; muddle. **3,** *colloq.* trouble; row. —*v., pres.ind. of* **liar.**

liquen ('li·ken) *n.m.* lichen.
liquidación (li·ki·ða'θjon; -'sjon) *n.f.* **1,** liquidation. **2,** *comm.* clearance; clearance sale.
liquidar (li·ki'ðar) *v.t.* **1,** to liquidate. **2,** *comm.* to close out. **3,** *comm.* to settle; close (an account). —**liquidable,** *adj., comm.* liquid; fluid (*of assets*).
líquido ('li·ki·ðo) *adj.* **1,** liquid; fluid. **2,** *comm.* net; clear. —*n.m.* **1,** liquid. **2,** *comm.* net; balance.
lira ('li·ra) *n.f.* **1,** lyre. **2,** lira.
lírico ('li·ri·ko) *adj.* lyric; lyrical. —*n.m.* lyricist. —**lírica,** *n.f.* lyric poetry. —**lirismo,** *n.m.* lyricism.
lirio ('li·rjo) *n.m.* lily.
lirón (li'ron) *n.m.* dormouse.
lisiar (li'sjar) *v.t.* to maim; cripple. —**lisiado,** *adj.* crippled; maimed. —*n.m.* cripple.
-lisis (li·sis) *suffix* -lysis; disintegration; destruction: *análisis,* analysis; *parálisis,* paralysis.
liso ('li·so) *adj.* **1,** smooth; even. **2,** simple; plain. **3,** *Amer., colloq.* impudent; fresh.
lisonja (li'son·xa) *n.f.* flattery; fawning. —**lisonjear,** *v.t.* to flatter; fawn on. —**lisonjero,** *adj.* flattering. —*n.m.* flatterer.
lista ('lis·ta) *n.f.* **1,** list; roll. **2,** strip; stripe. **3,** *law* docket. —**listado,** *adj.* striped.
listar (lis'tar) *v.t.* **1,** to list; enter in a list. **2,** *Amer.* to stripe; streak.
listo ('lis·to) *adj.* **1,** ready; prompt. **2,** clever; cunning.
listón (lis'ton) *n.m.* lath.
listonado (lis·to'na·ðo) *n.m.* lathing; lathwork.
lisura (li'su·ra) *n.f.* **1,** smoothness; evenness. **2,** *Amer.* impudence.
-lita ('li·ta) *suffix* -lite; *forming names of minerals: criolita,* cryolite.
litera (li'te·ra) *n.f.* **1,** litter (*portable bed*). **2,** berth.
literal (li·te'ral) *adj.* literal.
literario (li·te'ra·rjo) *adj.* literary.
literato (li·te'ra·to) *adj.* literate. —*n.m.* writer; *pl.* literati.
literatura (li·te·ra'tu·ra) *n.f.* literature.
-lítico ('li·ti·ko) *suffix* **1,** -lithic; *forming adjectives from nouns ending in* **-lito**: *monolítico,* monolithic. **2,** -lytic; *forming adjectives from nouns ending in* **-lisis**: *analítico,* analytic; *paralítico,* paralytic.
litigar (li·ti'ɣar) *v.t.* & *i.* [*pres. subjve.* **litigue** (-'ti·ɣe); *pret.* **litigué** (-'ɣe)] to litigate. —**litigación,** *n.f.* litigation. —**litigante,** *adj.* & *n.m.* & *f.* litigant. —**litigio** (li'ti·xjo) *n.m.* lawsuit; litigation.
litio ('li·tjo) *n.m.* lithium.
lito- (li·to) *prefix* litho-; stone: *litografía,* lithography.
-lito (li·to) *suffix* **1,** -lith; stone: *monolito,* monolith. **2,** -lyte; *forming nouns denoting* result or product of disintegration or destruction: *electrolito,* electrolyte.
litografía (li·to·ɣra'fi·a) *n.f.* **1,** lithography. **2,** lithograph. —**litográfico** (-'ɣra·fi·ko) *adj.* lithographic. —**litógrafo** (-'to·ɣra·fo) *n.m.* lithographer.
litografiar (li·to·ɣra'fjar) *v.t.* [*infl.:* **fotografiar**] to lithograph.
litoral (li·to'ral) *adj.* & *n.m.* littoral.
litorina (li·to'ri·na) *n.f., zool.* periwinkle.
litosfera (li·tos'fe·ra) *n.f.* lithosphere.
litro ('li·tro) *n.m.* **1,** liter. **2,** *W.I.* quart.
liturgia (li'tur·xja) *n.f.* liturgy. —**litúrgico** (-xi·ko) *adj.* liturgical.
liviandad (li·βjan'dað) *adj.* **1,** lightness. **2,** frivolity.
liviano (li'βja·no) *adj.* **1,** light; slight. **2,** frivolous.
lívido ('li·βi·ðo) *adj.* livid. —**lividez,** *n.f.* lividness.
liza ('li·θa; -sa) *n.f.* **1,** lists (*pl.*). **2,** = **lid.**
-lizar (li'θar; -'sar) *suffix* -lyze; *forming verbs from nouns ending in* **-lisis**: *paralizar,* paralyze; *analizar,* analyze.
lo (lo) *def.art. neut.sing., used with adjs. & advs.* the: *lo bueno,* the good; *a lo más temprano,* at the earliest. —*dem.pron. neut.sing.* that; that matter: *lo que deseo,* what I want; *lo de Zuriaga,* that matter of Zuriaga. —*pers.pron. masc. & neut.sing., used as dir.obj. of a verb* him; you; it. —*adverbial qualifier, used with adjs. & advs.* how: *Se ve lo hermoso que es,* One can see how beautiful it is. *Tú no sabes lo fuerte que trabajo,* You don't know how hard I'm working.
loa ('lo·a) *n.f.* praise; panegyric. —**loable,** *adj.* praiseworthy. —**loar** (lo'ar) *v.t.* to praise; extol.

loba ('lo·βa) *n.f.* she-wolf.
lobanillo (lo·βa'ni·ʎo; -jo) *n.m.* wen.
lobato (lo'βa·to) *n.m.* wolf cub.
lobero (lo'βe·ro) *adj.* wolfish. —*n.m.* wolf hunter.
lobo ('lo·βo) *n.m.* **1,** wolf. **2,** lobe.
lóbrego ('lo·βre·ɣo) *adj.* dark; tenebrous. —**lobreguez** (-'ɣeθ; -'ɣes) *n.f.* darkness; gloominess.
lóbulo ('lo·βu·lo) *n.m.* lobule; lobe.
local (lo'kal) *adj.* local. —*n.m.* place; premises (*pl.*). —**localidad,** *n.f.* locality; location.
localización (lo·ka·li·θa'θjon; -sa'sjon) *n.f.* **1,** localization. **2,** location.
localizar (lo·ka·li'θar; -'sar) *v.t.* [*pres.subjve.* **localice** (-'li·θe; -se); *pret.* **localicé** (-'θe; -'se)] **1,** to localize. **2,** to locate.
loción (lo'θjon; -'sjon) *n.f.* lotion.
loco ('lo·ko) *adj.* insane; mad. —*n.m.* madman.
loco- (lo·ko) *prefix* loco-; place; *locomoción,* locomotion.
locomoción (lo·ko·mo'θjon; -'sjon) *n.f.* locomotion.
locomotor (lo·ko·mo'tor) *also,* **locomotriz** (-'triθ; -'tris) *adj.* locomotor; locomotive. —**locomotora,** *n.f.* locomotive.
locuaz (lo'kwaθ; -'kwas) *adj.* loquacious. —**locuacidad,** (-θi'ðað; -si'ðað) *n.f.* loquacity.
locución (lo·ku'θjon; -'sjon) *n.f.* locution.
locura (lo'ku·ra) *n.f.* madness; insanity; folly.
locutor (lo·ku'tor) *n.m., radio; TV* announcer; speaker.
lodazal (lo·ða'θal; -'sal) *n.m.* muddy ground; mudhole.
lodo ('lo·ðo) *n.m.* mud; mire. —**lodoso,** *adj.* muddy; miry.
logaritmo (lo·ɣa'rit·mo) *n.m.* logarithm. —**logarítmico,** *adj.* logarithmic.
logia ('lo·xja) *n.f.* **1,** lodge (*of a fraternal order*). **2,** *archit.* loggia.
-logía (lo'xi·a) *suffix* -logy. **1,** science; doctrine; treatise: *cosmología,* cosmology. **2,** collection; group: *antología,* anthology.
lógica ('lo·xi·ka) *n.f.* logic. —**lógico,** *adj.* logical. —*n.m.* logician.
-lógico ('lo·xi·ko) *suffix* -logic; -logical; *forming adjectives from nouns ending in* **-logía:** *cosmológico,* cosmologic; cosmological.
logística (lo'xis·ti·ka) *n.f.* logistics. —**logístico,** *adj.* logistic; logistical.
logo- (lo·ɣo) *prefix* logo-; word; speech: *logotipo,* logotype.
-logo (lo·ɣo) *suffix* **1,** *forming nouns corresponding to nouns ending in* **-logía,** *denoting* expert; practitioner: *geólogo,* geologist. **2,** -logue; -log; *forming nouns denoting* speech; writing; description: *diálogo,* dialogue; *catálogo,* catalogue.
lograr (lo'ɣrar) *v.t.* to gain; attain; achieve. —*v.i.* to succeed. —**logrero,** *n.m.* usurer; profiteer.
logro ('lo·ɣro) *n.m.* **1,** profit; lucre. **2,** attainment.
loma ('lo·ma) *n.f.* hillock; slope.
lombarda (lom'bar·ða) *n.f.* red cabbage.
lombriz (lom'briθ; -'bris) *n.f.* earthworm; intestinal worm. —**lombriz solitaria,** tapeworm.
lomo ('lo·mo) *n.m.* **1,** loin; back. **2,** spine; back (*of an animal, book, etc.*). **3,** ridge between furrows.
lona ('lo·na) *n.f.* canvas.
lonche ('lon·tʃe) *n.m., Amer.* lunch. —**lonchería,** *n.f., Amer.* lunchroom.
loncha ('lon·tʃa) *n.f.* **1,** slice. **2,** thin, flat stone.
longánimo (lon'ga·ni·mo) *adj.* **1,** forbearing. **2,** magnanimous. —**longanimidad,** *n.f.* forbearance.
longaniza (lon·ga'ni·θa; -sa) *n.f.* a kind of sausage.
longevo (lon'xe·βo) *adj.* long-lived. —**longevidad,** *n.f.* longevity.
longitud (lon·xi'tuð) *n.f.* **1,** length. **2,** longitude.
longitudinal (lon·xi·tu·ði'nal) *adj.* **1,** lengthwise. **2,** longitudinal.
lonja ('lon·xa) *n.f.* **1,** exchange; stock exchange. **2,** slice; strip. **3,** thong.
lontananza (lon·ta'nan·θa; -sa) *n.f.* background; distance.
loor (lo'or) *n.m.* praise.
loquear (lo·ke'ar) *v.i.* to act foolishly.
lorán (lo'ran) *n.m.* loran.
loro ('lo·ro) *n.m.* parrot.
los (los) *def.art.masc.pl.* the. —*pers.pron.masc.pl., used as dir.obj. of a verb* them; you. —*dem.pron. masc. pl.* those.
losa ('lo·sa) *n.f.* **1,** slab. **2,** flagstone.
losar (lo'sar) *v.t.* = **enlosar.** —**losado,** *n.m.* = **enlosado.**

losange (lo'san·xe) *n.m.* lozenge; diamond-shaped figure.
loseta (lo'se·ta) *n.f.* small flagstone; tile.
lote ('lo·te) *n.m.* **1,** lot; share; portion. **2,** *Amer.* lot; plot of land.
lotear (lo·te'ar) *v.t. Amer.* to divide into lots.
lotería (lo·te'ri·a) *n.f.* lottery; raffle.
loto ('lo·to) *n.m.* lotus.
loza ('lo·θa; sa) *n.f.* crockery; porcelain.
lozanear (lo·θa·ne'ar; lo·sa-) *v.i.* **1,** to luxuriate. **2,** to be vigorous; be full of life.
lozanía (lo·θa'ni·a; lo·sa-) *n.f.* **1,** luxuriance. **2,** vigor; vitality.
lozano (lo'θa·no; -'sa·no) *adj.* **1,** luxuriant. **2,** vigorous; healthy.
lubricar (lu·βri'kar) *v.t.* [*pres. subjve.* **lubrique** (-'βri·ke); *pret.* **lubriqué** (-'ke)] to lubricate. —**lubricación,** *n.f.* lubrication. —**lubricante,** *adj.* & *n.m.* lubricant.
lubricidad (lu·βri·θi'ðað; -si·'ðað) *n.f.* **1,** slipperiness. **2,** lechery.
lúbrico ('lu·βri·ko) *adj.* **1,** slippery. **2,** lecherous.
lucerna (lu'θer·na; -'ser·na) *n.f.* **1,** chandelier. **2,** skylight.
lucero (lu'θe·ro; -'se·ro) *n.m.* **1,** bright star. **2,** brightness. **3,** *poet.* eye.
luces ('lu·θes; -ses) *n.f.pl.* **1,** culture; enlightenment. **2,** understanding.
lucido (lu'θi·ðo; -'si·ðo) *adj.* **1,** gracious, elegant. **2,** *colloq.* done for; fouled up.
lúcido ('lu·θi·ðo; 'lu·si-) *adj.* lucid. —**lucidez,** *n.f.* lucidity.
luciente (lu'θjen·te; -'sjen·te) *adj.* **1,** shining; lucid. **2,** outstanding.
luciérnaga (lu'θjer·na·ɣa; lu·'sjer-) *n.f.* firefly; glowworm.
Lucifer (lu·θi'fer; lu·si-) *n.m.* **1,** Lucifer. **2,** morning star.
lucífero (lu'θi·fe·ro; lu'si-) *adj.* shining. —*n.m., cap.* morning star.
lucimiento (lu·θi'mjen·to; lu·si-) *n.m.* **1,** brightness; brilliancy. **2,** dash; display.
lucir (lu'θir; -'sir) *v.i.* [*pres.ind.* **luzco;** *pres.subjve.* **luzca**] **1,** to shine; be bright. **2,** to befit. —*v.t.* to display; show to advantage. —**lucirse,** *v.r.* **1,** to appear to advantage. **2,** *colloq.* to appear ridiculous; make oneself a laughingstock.
lucro ('lu·kro) *n.m.* lucre; gain. —**lucrarse,** *v.r.* to profit (*in work or business*). —**lucrativo,** *adj.* lucrative.
luctuoso (luk'two·so) *adj.* mournful.
lucubrar (lu·ku'βrar) *v.i.* to lucubrate. —**lucubración,** *n.f.* lucubration.
lucha ('lu·tʃa) *n.f.* strife; struggle; battle.
luchar (lu'tʃar) *v.t.* to wrestle; struggle; contend. —**luchador,** *n.m.* wrestler.
ludibrio (lu'ði·βrjo) *n.m.* scorn; mockery.
lúe ('lu·e) *n.f.* infection.
luego ('lwe·ɣo) *adv.* **1,** immediately; directly. **2,** soon. **3,** then; thereupon. —*conj.* therefore. —**desde luego,** naturally; of course. —**hasta luego,** so long; good bye. —**luego como; luego que,** as soon as.
luengo ('lwen·go) *adj.* long.
lugar (lu'ɣar) *n.m.* **1,** place. **2,** space; room. **3,** occasion; opportunity. **4,** small village. —**en lugar de,** in lieu of; instead of. —**lugar geométrico,** locus. —**tener lugar,** to take place.
lugarteniente (lu·ɣar·te'njen·te) *n.m.* deputy; substitute.
lúgubre ('lu·ɣu·βre) *adj.* lugubrious.
lujo ('lu·xo) *n.m.* luxury; extravagance. —**lujoso,** *adj.* luxurious.
lujuria (lu'xu·rja) *n.f.* lust; lechery. —**lujurioso,** *adj.* lustful; lecherous.
lujuriante (lu·xu'rjan·te) *adj.* **1,** luxuriant. **2,** lustful.
lumbago (lum'ba·ɣo) *n.m.* lumbago.
lumbar (lum'bar) *adj.* lumbar.
lumbre ('lum·bre) *n.f.* **1,** fire; light. **2,** brightness. **3,** lucidity. **4,** space admitting light.
lumbrera (lum'bre·ra) *n.f.* **1,** luminary. **2,** louver.
luminaria (lu·mi'na·rja) *n.f.* luminary; light.
luminiscente (lu·mi·nis'θen·te; -ni'sen·te) *adj.* luminescent. —**luminiscencia,** *n.f.* luminiscence.
luminoso (lu·mi'no·so) *adj.* luminous. —**luminosidad,** *n.f.* luminosity.
luna ('lu·na) *n.f.* **1,** moon. **2,** glass; plate glass.

lunar (lu'nar) *adj.* lunar. —*n.m.* mole; blemish.
lunático (lu'na·ti·ko) *adj.* & *n.m.* lunatic.
lunes ('lu·nes) *n.m.sing.* & *pl.* Monday.
luneta (lu'ne·ta) *n.f.* **1,** eyeglass; lens. **2,** *theat.* orchestra; orchestra seat.
luni- (lu·ni) *prefix* luni-; moon: *lunisolar,* lunisolar.
lupa ('lu·pa) *n.f.* magnifying glass.
lupanar (lu·pa'nar) *n.m.* brothel.
lupino (lu'pi·no) *adj.* lupine.
lúpulo ('lu·pu·lo) *n.m., bot.* hop.
lusitano (lu·si'ta·no) *adj.* & *n.m.* Lusitanian; Portuguese.
lustrabotas (lus·tra'βo·tas) *n.m. sing.* & *pl., Amer.* bootblack.
lustrar (lus'trar) *v.t.* to polish; shine.
lustre ('lus·tre) *n.m.* **1,** polish; gloss; luster. **2,** glory; renown. —**lustroso,** *adj.* lustrous; shiny.
lutecio (lu'te·θjo; -sjo) *n.m.* lutecium.
luterano (lu·te'ra·no) *adj.* & *n.m.* Lutheran. —**luteranismo,** *n.m.* Lutheranism.
luto ('lu·to) *n.m.* mourning. —**de luto, 1,** in mourning. **2,** mourning (*attrib.*).
luz (luθ; lus) *n.f.* [*pl.* **luces**] **1,** light. **2,** lamp; candle. **3,** span (*of a bridge*). **4,** opening; clearance. **5,** headroom. —**a primera luz, 1,** at daybreak. **2,** at first sight. —**a toda luz; a todas luces,** by all means. —**dar a luz,** to give birth. —**entre dos luces, 1,** at twilight. **2,** half drunk; tipsy. **3,** confused; bewildered.
luzca ('luθ·ka; 'lus-) *v., pres. subjve. of* **lucir.**
luzco ('luθ·ko; 'lus-) *v., 1st pers. sing. pres.ind. of* **lucir.**

LL

Ll, ll ('e·ʎe; 'e·je) *n.f.* 14th letter of the Spanish alphabet.
llaga ('ʎa·ɣa; 'ja-) *n.f.* sore; ulcer.
llagar (ʎa'ɣar; ja-) *v.t.* [*pres. subjve.* **llague** ('ʎa·ɣe; 'ja-) *pret.* **llagué** (-'ɣe)] to ulcerate.
llama ('ʎa·ma; 'ja-) *n.f.* **1,** flame. **2,** llama.
llamada (ʎa'ma·ða; ja-) *n.f.* **1,** call. **2,** sign; signal. **3,** knock. **4,** reference mark.
llamamiento (ʎa·ma'mjen·to; ja-) *n.m.* **1,** call; calling. **2,** convening; convocation.
llamar (ʎa'mar; ja-) *v.t.* **1,** to call. **2,** to cite; summon. —*v.i.* to knock. —**llamarse,** *v.r.* to be named; be called: *¿Cómo se llama Vd.?* What is your name? —**llamativo,** *adj.* showy; gaudy.
llamarada (ʎa·ma'ra·ða; ja-) *n.f.* **1,** blaze; flame. **2,** *fig.* flare-up; outburst (*of temper*).
llamear (ʎa·me'ar; ja-) *v.i.* to flame; blaze.
llana ('ʎa·na; 'ja-) *n.f.* trowel.
llanada (ʎa'na·ða; ja-) *n.f.* plain.
llanero (ʎa'ne·ro; ja-) *n.m., Amer.* plainsman.
llaneza (ʎa'ne·θa; ja'ne·sa) *n.f.* plainness; simplicity.
llano ('ʎa·no; 'ja-) *adj.* **1,** plain; level; even. **2,** straightforward; simple. **3,** accented on the penultimate syllable. —*n.m.* plain; flat ground.
llanta ('ʎan·ta; 'jan-) *n.f.* **1,** tire. **2,** wheel rim.
llantén (ʎan'ten; jan-) *n.m.* plantain (*weed*).
llanto ('ʎan·to; 'jan-) *n.m.* weeping; crying.
llanura (ʎa'nu·ra; ja'nu-) *n.f.* **1,** plain; prairie. **2,** evenness; flatness.
llares ('ʎa·res; 'ja-) *n.f.pl.* pothook (*sing.*).
llave ('ʎa·βe; 'ja-) *n.f.* **1,** key. **2,** wrench. **3,** faucet; tap; spigot. —**llave inglesa,** monkey wrench.
llavero (ʎa'βe·ro; ja-) *n.m.* **1,** key ring. **2,** keymaker. **3,** turnkey.
llavín (ʎa'βin; ja-) *n.m.* small key; latchkey.
llegar (ʎe'ɣar; je-) *v.i.* [*pres. subjve.* **llegue** ('ʎe·ɣe; 'je-); *pret.* **llegué** (-'ɣe)] **1,** to arrive; come. **2,** to reach; attain. **3,** to succeed. **4,** to amount; come to. —**llegarse,** *v.r.* **1,** to approach. **2,** to go; betake oneself. —**llegada,** *n.f.* arrival; coming.
llena ('ʎe·na; 'je-) *n.f.* flood; overflow.

llenar (ʎe'nar; je-) *v.t.* **1,** to fill. **2,** to satisfy. **3,** to fill out; complete.

lleno ('ʎe·no; 'je-) *adj.* full. —*n.m.* **1,** fullness. **2,** capacity audience; full house. **3,** full moon. —**de lleno,** fully; completely.

llenura (ʎe'nu·ra; je-) *n.f.* fullness; fill.

llevadero (ʎe·βa'ðe·ro; je-) *adj.* light; easy to bear.

llevar (ʎe'βar; je-) *v.t.* **1,** to carry; transport. **2,** to wear. **3,** to keep (books, accounts, etc.). **4,** to take; lead; guide. **5,** to take off *or* away; carry off. **6,** to bear; endure. **7,** to charge (someone) for (something). **8,** to run; manage (a business, organization, etc.). **9,** to be ahead (a certain time, distance, etc.) of someone *or* something: *Este alumno lleva al otro dos años,* This student is two years ahead of the other. *Este tren lleva al otro diez kilómetros,* This train is ten kilometers ahead of the other. **10,** to be older than (someone) by: *Mi hijo lleva al suyo tres años,* My son is three years older than yours. **11,** *colloq.* to take (a certain time): *Me llevó una hora ir a la oficina,* It took me an hour to get to the office. **12,** to have been *or* gone (a certain time): *Lleva cinco días enfermo,* He has been sick five days. *Llevo tres días sin comer,* I have gone three days without eating. —**llevarse,** *v.r.* **1,** *with* **bien** *or* **mal,** to get along (well *or* badly). **2,** to be apart (*a certain time*): *Mi hijo y el suyo se llevan dos años,* My son and yours are two years apart. —**llevar a cabo,** to succeed in; bring about; accomplish. —**llevar las de perder,** to be doomed; be bound to fail. —**llevar y traer,** *colloq.* to carry gossip.

llorar (ʎo'rar; jo-) *v.i.* to weep; cry. —*v.t.* to mourn; lament.

lloriquear (ʎo·ri·ke'ar; jo-) *v.i.* to whine; whimper. —**lloriqueo** (-'ke·o) *n.m.* whining; whimpering.

lloro ('ʎo·ro; 'jo-) *n.m.* weeping.

llorón (ʎo'ron; jo-) *n.m.* weeper; whiner. —*adj.* weeping; whining.

lloroso (ʎo'ro·so; jo-) *adj.* **1,** weeping; tearful. **2,** sad; heartrending.

llovedizo (ʎo·βe'ði·θo; jo·βe'ði·so) *adj.* leaky. —**agua llovediza,** rain water.

llover (ʎo'βer; jo-) *v.impers.* [*pres.ind.* **llueve** ('ʎwe·βe; 'jwe-); *pres.subjve.* **llueva** (-βa)] to rain; pour.

llovizna (ʎo'βiθ·na; jo'βis-) *n.f.* drizzle. —**lloviznar,** *v.impers.* to drizzle.

llueca ('ʎwe·ka; 'jwe-) *n.f.* brooding hen.

lluvia ('ʎu·βja; 'ju-) *n.f.* **1,** rain; shower. **2,** *fig.* flood; deluge.—**lluvioso,** *adj.* rainy; wet.

M

M, m ('e·me) *n.f.* 15th letter of the Spanish alphabet.

maca ('ma·ka) *n.f.* **1,** bruise (*in a fruit*). **2,** *colloq.* fraud; deceit; trickery.

macabro (ma'ka·βro) *adj.* macabre.

macaco (ma'ka·ko) *n.m.* **1,** macaque. **2,** *Mex.* hobgoblin. —*adj. Amer., colloq.* ugly; ill-shaped.

macadán (ma·ka'ðan) *also,* **macádam** (-'ka·ðam) *n.m.* macadam. —**macadamizar** [*pres.subjve.* **macadamice** (-'mi·θe; -se); *pret.* **macadamicé** (-'θe; -'se)] to macadamize.

macana (ma'ka·na) *n.f., Amer.* **1,** a kind of flint axe. **2,** cudgel; club. **3,** *colloq.* nonsense.

macanudo (ma·ka'nu·ðo) *adj., Amer., colloq.* **1,** tremendous; extraordinary. **2,** superb.

macareo (ma·ka're·o) *n.m.* riptide.

macarrón (ma·ka'rron) *n.m.* **1,** macaroon. **2,** macaroni. —**macarrones,** *n.m.pl.* macaroni.

macarse (ma'kar·se) *v.r.* to begin to rot, as bruised fruit.

macerar (ma·θe'rar; ma·se-) *v.t.* to macerate. —**maceración,** *n.f., also,* **maceramiento,** *n.m.* maceration.

macero (ma'θe·ro; -'se·ro) *n.m.* mace-bearer.

maceta (ma'θe·ta; -'se·ta) *n.f.* **1,** flowerpot. **2,** small mallet.

macias ('ma·θjas; -sjas) *n.f.* mace (*spice*). *Also,* **macis** ('ma·θis; -sis).

macilento (ma·θi'len·to; ma·si-) *adj.* gaunt; withered.
macillo (ma'θi·ʎo; -'si·jo) *n.m.* hammer (*of a percussion instrument*).
macizar (ma·θi'θar; -si'sar) *v.t.* [*infl.:* **matizar**] to fill in (a hole or gap).
macizo (ma'θi·θo; -'si·so) *adj.* massive; solid. —*n.m.* mass; cluster (*of mountains, buildings, trees, flowers, etc.*). —**macicez,** *n.f.* massiveness.
macro- (ma·kro) *prefix* macro-; long; large; great: *macroscópico,* macroscopic.
macrocosmo (ma·kro'kos·mo) *n.m.* macrocosm.
macroscópico (ma·kros'ko·pi·ko) *adj.* macroscopic.
mácula ('ma·ku·la) *n.f.* stain; spot.
machacar (ma·tʃa'kar) *v.t.* [*pres. subjve.* **machaque** (-'tʃa·ke); *pret.* **machaqué** (-'ke)] to crush; pound. —*v.i., colloq.* **1,** to harp. **2,** to drill; work hard; plug.
machacón (ma·tʃa'kon) *adj., colloq.* importunate; insistent. —*n.m., colloq.* plugger.
machada (ma'tʃa·ða) *n.f.* **1,** flock of male goats. **2,** *colloq.* stupidity. **3,** *Amer., colloq.* manly, virile action.
machar (ma'tʃar) *v.t.* = **machacar.** —**macharse,** *v.r., Amer.* to get drunk.
machete (ma'tʃe·te) *n.m.* machete. —**machetazo,** *n.m.* blow with a machete. —**machetear** (-te'ar) *v.t.* to strike or cut with a machete.
machihembrar (ma·tʃi·em'brar) *v.t.* to dovetail; mortise.
machina (ma'tʃi·na) *n.f.* **1,** crane; derrick. **2,** pile-driver.
macho ('ma·tʃo) *adj.* **1,** male. **2,** *colloq.* masculine; manly. **3,** *mech.* male. —*n.m.* male.
machucar (ma·tʃu'kar) *v.t.* [*pres. subjve.* **machuque** (-'tʃu·ke); *pret.* **machuqué** (-'ke)] to crush; pound; bruise. —**machucamiento,** *n.m.* crushing; pounding; bruising.
machucho (ma'tʃu·tʃo) *adj.* **1,** staid; judicious. **2,** advancing in years.
madama (ma'ða·ma) *n.f.* madam.
madeja (ma'ðe·xa) *n.f.* **1,** hank; skein. **2,** *fig.* tangle; complication.
madera (ma'ðe·ra) *n.f.* **1,** wood. **2,** timber; lumber. —*n.m.* madeira wine.
maderamen (ma·ðe'ra·men) *also,* **maderaje,** *n.m.* timberwork; timber.
maderero (ma·ðe're·ro) *adj.* lumbering; of the lumber industry. —*n.m.* lumberman.
madero (ma'ðe·ro) *n.m.* **1,** beam; timber. **2,** *colloq.* blockhead.
madona (ma'ðo·na) *n.f.* Madonna.
madrastra (ma'ðras·tra) *n.f.* stepmother.
madre ('ma·ðre) *n.f.* **1,** mother. **2,** bed (*of a river*). —**madre de familia,** housewife. —**madre de leche,** wet nurse. —**madre política,** mother-in-law. —**sacar de madre,** to make (someone) lose patience. —**salirse de madre,** (*of a stream*) to overflow its banks.
madreperla (ma·ðre'per·la) *n.f.* mother-of-pearl.
madreselva (ma·ðre'sel·βa) *n.f.* honeysuckle.
madrigado (ma·ðri'ɣa·ðo) *adj.* **1,** (*of an animal, esp. a bull*) that has sired. **2,** (*of a woman*) twice-wed. **3,** *colloq.* experienced; versed.
madrigal (ma·ðri'ɣal) *n.m.* madrigal.
madriguera (ma·ðri'ɣe·ra) *n.f.* **1,** burrow. **2,** den; lair.
madrileño (ma·ðri'le·ɲo) *adj. & n.m.* Madrilenian.
madrina (ma'ðri·na) *n.f.* **1,** godmother. **2,** maid *or* matron of honor. **3,** patroness.
madroño (ma'ðro·ɲo) *n.m.* arbutus.
madrugada (ma·ðru'ɣa·ða) *n.f.* **1,** daybreak; dawn. **2,** early rising. —**de madrugada,** at dawn.
madrugador (ma·ðru·ɣa'ðor) *adj.* early-rising. —*n.m.* early riser.
madrugar (ma·ðru'ɣar) *v.i.* [*pres.subjve.* **madrugue** (-'ðru·ɣe); *pret.* **madrugué** (-'ɣe)] **1,** to rise early. **2,** to come *or* arrive early. —**madrugarse a,** *Amer., colloq.* to steal a march on.
madrugón (ma·ðru'ɣon) *adj.* early-rising.
madurar (ma·ðu'rar) *v.t. & i.* to ripen. —*v.i.* to mature; become mature. —**maduración,** *n.f.* ripening; aging.
madurez (ma·ðu'reθ; -'res) *n.f.* **1,** ripeness. **2,** maturity. **3,** wisdom; prudence.

maduro (ma'ðu·ro) *adj.* **1,** ripe. **2,** mature; middle-aged. **3,** wise; prudent.

maelstrom (ma·els'trom) *n.m.* maelstrom.

maestra (ma'es·tra) *n.f.* **1,** teacher. **2,** mistress.

maestría (ma·es'tri·a) *n.f.* **1,** mastery. **2,** mastership.

maestro (ma'es·tro) *adj.* master. —*n.m.* **1,** teacher. **2,** master. —**maestro de obras,** contractor; builder.

magenta (ma'xen·ta) *adj.* & *n.m.* magenta.

magia ('ma·xja) *n.f.* magic.

magiar (ma'xjar) *adj.* & *n.m.* & *f.* Magyar.

mágico ('ma·xi·ko) *adj.* magic; magical. —*n.m.* magician.

magín (ma'xin) *n.m., colloq.* imagination.

magisterial (ma·xis·te'rjal) *adj.* **1,** of or pert. to teachers or teaching. **2,** pompous; magisterial.

magisterio (ma·xis'te·rjo) *n.m.* **1,** mastery; control. **2,** professorship; professoriate. **3,** teachers collectively; teaching profession.

magistrado (ma·xis'tra·ðo) *n.m.* magistrate.

magistral (ma·xis'tral) *adj.* masterly; superb. —**obra magistral,** masterpiece; masterwork.

magistratura (ma·xis·tra'tu·ra) *n.f.* magistracy.

magnánimo (maɣ'na·ni·mo) *adj.* magnanimous. —**magnanimidad,** *n.f.* magnanimity.

magnate (maɣ'na·te) *n.m.* magnate.

magnesia (maɣ'ne·sja) *n.f.* magnesia.

magnesio (maɣ'ne·sjo) *n.m.* magnesium.

magnetismo (maɣ·ne'tis·mo) *n.m.* magnetism. —**magnético** (-'ne·ti·ko) *adj.* magnetic.

magnetita (maɣ·ne'ti·ta) *n.f.* magnetite.

magnetizar (maɣ·ne·ti'θar; -'sar) *v.t.* [*pres.subjve.* **magnetice** (-'ti·θe; -se); *pret.* **magneticé** (-'θe; -'se)] **1,** to magnetize. **2,** to hypnotize.

magneto (maɣ'ne·to) *n.m.* magneto.

magnetófono (maɣ·ne'to·fo·no) *n.m.* wire *or* tape recorder.

magni- (maɣ·ni) *prefix* magni-; large; great: *magnífico,* magnificent.

magnificar (maɣ·ni·fi'kar) *v.t.* [*pres.subjve.* **magnifique** (-'fi·ke); *pret.* **magnifiqué** (-'ke)] to magnify. —**magnificación,** *n.f.* magnification.

magnífico (maɣ'ni·fi·ko) *adj.* magnificent. —**magnificencia** (-'θen·βja; -'sen·sja) *n.f.* magnificence.

magnitud (maɣ·ni'tuð) *n.f.* magnitude.

magno ('maɣ·no) *adj.* great.

magnolia (maɣ'no·lja) *n.f.* magnolia.

mago ('ma·ɣo) *n.m.* magician; wizard. —**los reyes magos,** the Magi.

magro ('ma·ɣro) *adj.* lean; thin. —**magra,** *n.f.* slice of ham. —**magrez,** *n.f.* leanness.

maguey (ma'ɣei) *n.m.* American agave; maguey.

magullar (ma·ɣu'ʎar; -'jar) *v.t.* to bruise. —**magulladura,** *n.f.* bruise.

maharajá (ma·a·ra'xa; ma·ra·'xa) *n.m.* maharajah.

maharaní (ma·a·ra'ni; ma·ra·'ni) *n.f.* maharanee.

mahometano (ma·o·me'ta·no) *adj.* & *n.m.* Mohammedan. —**mahometismo,** *n.m.* Mohammedanism.

maicena (mai'θe·na; -'se·na) *n.f.* corn flour; corn meal.

maitines (mai'ti·nes) *n.m.pl.* matins.

maíz (ma'iθ; -'is) *n.m.* corn; maize. —**maizal,** *n.m.* cornfield.

majada (ma'xa·ða) *n.f.* **1,** sheepfold. **2,** dung; manure.

majadería (ma·xa·ðe'ri·a) *n.f.* **1,** absurdity; nonsense. **2,** importunity; bother. —**majadero,** *adj.* annoying; importunate.

majar (ma'xar) *v.t.* **1,** to pound; crush; mash. **2,** *colloq.* to annoy; importune.

majestad (ma·xes'tað) *n.f.* majesty.

majestuoso (ma·xes'two·so) *adj.* majestic. —**majestuosidad,** *n.f.* majesty; grandeur.

majo ('ma·xo) *adj.* **1,** gallant; bold. **2,** elegant; handsome. —*n.m.* gallant.

majuelo (ma'xwe·lo) *n.* white hawthorn.

mal (mal) *adj., var. of* **malo** *before a masc. noun.* —*n.m.* **1,** evil. **2,** harm; hurt; mischief. **3,** illness; disease. —*adv.* badly; bad; poorly.

—**estar mal con,** to be on bad terms with. —**mal de ojo,** evil eye. —**mal que bien,** anyhow; at any rate. —**mal que le pese (a uno),** in spite of (someone); however (someone) may dislike it. —**parar mal,** to end up badly. —**tomar a mal,** to misconstrue; take amiss.

mal- (mal) *prefix* mal-; mis-; ill-; bad; badly: *maltrato,* maltreatment; *malajustado,* maladjusted; *malgastar,* misspend; *malintencionado,* ill-intentioned.

malabarismo (ma·la·βa'ris·mo) *n.m.* [*also,* **juegos malabares**] jugglery; juggling. —**malabarista,** *n.m. & f.* juggler.

malacostumbrado (mal·a·kos·tum'bra·ðo) *adj.* pampered.

malacrianza (ma·la·kri'an·θa; -sa) *n.f., Amer.* **1,** poor manners. **2,** vulgarity; indelicacy.

malagua (ma'la·ɣwa) *n.f., Amer.* = **medusa.**

malandanza (mal·an'dan·θa; -sa) *n.f.* misfortune; misery.

malandrín (ma·lan'drin) *n.m.* rascal; scoundrel. —*adj.* rascally; scoundrelly.

malaquita (ma·la'ki·ta) *n.f.* malachite.

malar (ma'lar) *adj.* malar.

malaria (ma'la·rja) *n.f.* malaria.

malavenido (mal·a·βe'ni·ðo) *adj.* unfriendly; unsociable.

malaventura (mal·a·βen'tu·ra) *also,* **malaventuranza** (-'ran·θa; -sa) *n.f.* misfortune; unhappiness. —**malaventurado,** *adj.* unfortunate.

malayo (ma'la·jo) *adj. & n.m.* Malay; Malayan.

malbaratar (mal·βa·ra'tar) *v.t.* to squander.

malcarado (mal·ka'ra·ðo) *adj.* **1,** surly; grim. **2,** ill-looking; ugly.

malcontento (mal·kon'ten·to) *adj. & n.m.* malcontent.

malcriar (mal·kri'ar) *v.t.* [*infl.:* **criar**] to spoil; pamper. —**malcriado,** *adj.* ill-bred; spoiled; pampered. —**malcriadez,** *n.f., Amer.* brattiness; poor breeding.

maldad (mal'dað) *n.f.* wickedness; evil.

maldecir (mal·ðe'θir; -'sir) *v.t. & i.* [*infl.:* **bendecir**] to damn; curse. —**maldecir de,** to speak evil of; backbite.

maldición (mal·di'θjon; -'sjon) *n.f.* **1,** malediction; curse. **2,** damnation.

maldispuesto (mal·dis'pwes·to) *adj.* ill-disposed; reluctant.

maldito (mal'di·to) *adj.* **1,** perverse. **2,** accursed; damned. **3,** blasted; confounded.

male- (ma·le) *prefix, var. of* **mal-:** *maledicencia,* malediction.

maleable (ma·le'a·βle) *adj.* malleable. —**maleabilidad,** *n.f.* malleability.

malear (ma·le'ar) *v.t.* to spoil; corrupt. —**maleante,** *n.m.* hoodlum; bandit.

malecón (ma·le'kon) *n.m.* mole; dike; sea wall.

maledicencia (ma·le·ði'θen·θja; -'sen·sja) *n.f.* slander; evil talk.

maleficiar (ma·le·fi'θjar; -'sjar) *v.t.* **1,** to injure; harm. **2,** to cast evil spells on.

maleficio (ma·le'fi·θjo; -sjo) *n.m.* **1,** evil spell. **2,** harm; injury.

maléfico (ma'le·fi·ko) *adj.* maleficent. —**maleficencia** (-'θen·θja; -'sen·sja) *n.f.* maleficence.

malestar (ma·les'tar) *n.m.* uneasiness; discomfort; malaise.

maleta (ma'le·ta) *n.f.* suitcase. —*n.m. & f. colloq.* incompetent.

maletín (ma·le'tin) *n.m.* valise.

malévolo (ma'le·βo·lo) *adj.* malevolent. —**malevolencia,** *n.f.* malevolence.

maleza (ma'le·θa; -sa) *n.f.* **1,** thicket. **2,** growth of weeds.

malformación (mal'for·ma'θjon; -'sjon) *n.f.* malformation.

malgastar (mal·ɣas'tar) *v.t.* to misspend; squander. —**malgastador,** *adj. & n.m.* spendthrift.

malhechor (mal·e'tʃor) *n.m.* malefactor; criminal; bandit.

malhumorado (mal·u·mo'ra·ðo) *adj.* ill-humored.

malicia (ma'li·θja; -sja) *n.f.* **1,** malice. **2,** shrewdness. **3,** suspicion; inkling.

maliciar (ma·li'θjar; -'sjar) *v.t.* to suspect; mistrust.

malicioso (ma·li'θjo·so; -'sjo·so) *adj.* **1,** malicious. **2,** suspicious; distrustful. **3,** shrewd; knowing.

maligno (ma'liɣ·no) *adj.* malign; malignant. —**malignidad,** *n.f.* malignancy; malignity.

malintencionado (mal·in·ten·θjo'na·ðo; -sjo'na·ðo) *adj.* ill-intentioned; malicious.

malmandado (mal·man'da·ðo) *adj.* disobedient; unruly.

malo ('ma·lo) *adj.* **1,** bad; evil. **2,** ill. **3,** naughty. **4,** defective; poor. —*n.m.* bad one; evil one. —**a las malas,** with evil intentions. —**estar de malas, 1,** to be out of luck. **2,** to be out of sorts. —**por** *or* **a la mala,** by force; against one's will. —**por malas o por buenas, 1,** by hook or by crook. **2,** willingly or unwillingly.

malograr (ma·lo'ɣrar) *v.t.* **1,** to spoil; impair. **2,** to break; put out of order. —**malograrse,** *v.r.* **1,** to spoil. **2,** to go wrong; miscarry.

malogro (ma'lo·ɣro) *n.m.* **1,** spoiling. **2,** miscarriage; a going wrong.

maloliente (mal·o'ljen·te) *adj.* malodorous.

malón (ma'lon) *n.m.* **1,** mean trick. **2,** *Amer.* surprise attack. **3,** *Amer.* surprise party.

malparado (mal·pa'ra·ðo) *adj.* **1,** worsted. **2,** shaken up; mauled.

malparto (mal'par·to) *n.m.* miscarriage.

malquerencia (mal·ke'ren·θja; -sja) *n.f.* **1,** dislike. **2,** ill will.

malquerer (mal·ke'rer) *v.t.* [*infl.:* **querer**] **1,** to dislike. **2,** to wish (someone) ill.

malquistar (mal·kis'tar) *v.t.* to alienate.

malquisto (mal'kis·to) *adj.* **1,** alienated. **2,** disliked; unpopular.

malsano (mal'sa·no) *adj.* unwholesome.

malta ('mal·ta) *n.f.* malt.

maltosa (mal'to·sa) *n.f.* maltose.

maltraer (mal·tra'er) *v.t.* [*infl.:* **traer**] to mistreat.

maltratar (mal·tra'tar) *v.t.* to maltreat; mistreat. —**maltrato** (-'tra·to) *n.m.* mistreatment.

maltrecho (mal'tre·tʃo) *adj.* battered; in bad shape.

malva ('mal·βa) *n.f.* mallow. —*adj.* & *n.m.* mauve.

malvado (mal'βa·ðo) *adj.* perverse; bad; evil. —*n.m.* evildoer.

malvavisco (mal·βa'βis·ko) *n.m.* marsh mallow.

malvender (mal·βen'der) *v.t.* to sell unprofitably.

malversar (mal·βer'sar) *v.t.* to misappropriate. —**malversación,** *n.f.* misappropriation.

malvís (mal'βis) *n.m.* mavis.

malla ('ma·ʎa; -ja) *n.f.* **1,** mesh. **2,** coat of mail. **3,** sweater; jersey. **4,** *So.Amer.* bathing suit.

mama ('ma·ma) *n.f.* **1,** mamma; breast. **2,** = **mamá.**

mamá (ma'ma) *n.f.* mother; mamma; mama.

mamada (ma'ma·ða) *n.f.* **1,** breast feeding. **2,** *colloq.* suck; sucking.

mamadera (ma·ma'ðe·ra) *n.f.* **1,** breast pump. **2,** *Amer.* nursing bottle.

mamar (ma'mar) *v.t.* **1,** to suck. **2,** *colloq.* to gobble; gobble up. —*v.i.* to suckle. —**mamarse,** *v.r.*, *Amer.*, *slang* to get drunk. —**dar de mamar,** to breast-feed. —**mamarla,** *colloq.* to be taken in. —**mamarse a uno,** *colloq.* **1,** to get the best of someone. **2,** to do away with someone.

mamario (ma'ma·rjo) *adj.* mammary.

mamarracho (ma·ma'rra·tʃo) *n.m.*, *colloq.* **1,** mess; sight. **2,** good-for-nothing; ne'er-do-well.

mambo ('mam·bo) *n.m.* mambo.

mamífero (ma'mi·fe·ro) *n.m.* mammal. —*adj.* mammalian.

mamita (ma'mi·ta) *n.f.* mammy; mama.

mammón (ma'mon) *n.m.* Mammon.

mamola (ma'mo·la) *n.f.* chuck (*under the chin*). —**hacer la mamola a,** to chuck (someone) under the chin.

mamón (ma'mon) *adj.* & *n.m.* suckling. —*n.m.*, *bot.* shoot; sucker.

mampara (mam'pa·ra) *n.f.* screen; room divider.

mamparo (mam'pa·ro) *n.m.*, *naut.* bulkhead.

mampostería (mam·pos·te'ri·a) *n.f.* masonry.

mampuesto (mam'pwes·to) *n.m.* **1,** parapet. **2,** roughhewn stone. **3,** *Amer.* arm rest (*for firing a weapon*). —**mampuesta,** *n.f.* course (*of masonry*).

mamut (ma'mut) *n.m.* mammoth.

maná (ma'na) *n.m.* manna.

manada (ma'na·ða) *n.f.* herd; drove; pack.

manantial (ma·nan'tjal) *n.m.* spring; fountain. —*adj.* spring (*attrib.*).

manar (ma'nar) *v.i.* to flow; spring forth. —*v.i.* & *t.* to gush.

manatí (ma·na'ti) *n.m.* manatee.

manceba (man'θe·βa; -'se·βa) *n.f.* mistress; concubine.

mancebo (man'θe·βo; -'se·βo) *n.m.* 1, young man; young lad. 2, bachelor.
-mancia ('man·θja; -sja) *suffix* -mancy; divination: *nigromancia,* necromancy.
mancilla (man'θi·ʎa; -'si·ja) *n.f.* blemish; stain; dishonor. —**mancillar,** *v.t.* to stain; taint; dishonor.
manco ('man·ko) *adj.* 1, maimed; lacking one or both hands or arms. 2, crippled in one or both hands or arms.
mancomún (man·ko'mun) *n.m., in* **de mancomún,** jointly; in common.
mancomunidad (man·ko·mu·ni'ðað) *n.f.* 1, commonwealth. 2, joint authority *or* administration. —**mancomunar** (-'nar) *v.t.* to associate; unite.
mancha ('man·tʃa) *n.f.* spot; stain; blemish. —**manchado,** *adj.* spotted; stained; soiled. —**manchar,** *v.t.* to spot; stain; soil.
manchú (man'tʃu) *adj.* & *n.m.* & *f.* [*pl.* **manchús** *or* **manchúes**] Manchu.
manda ('man·da) *n.f.* 1, offer; promise; pledge. 2, legacy; donation.
mandamiento (man·da'mjen·to) *n.m.* 1, commandment. 2, *law* writ.
mandar (man'dar) *v.t.* & *i.* 1, to command; order. 2, to govern. —*v.t.* to send. —**mandarse cambiar,** *colloq.* to get out; clear out.
mandarín (man·da'rin) *n.m.* mandarin.
mandarina (man·da'ri·na) *n.f.* tangerine.
mandatario (man·da'ta·rjo) *n.m.* 1, legal representative; mandatary. 2, *Amer.* high official.
mandato (man'da·to) *n.m.* 1, mandate. 2, command; order.
mandíbula (man'di·βu·la) *n.f.* 1, jaw. 2, mandible; jawbone. —**mandibular,** *adj.* mandibular.
mandil (man'dil) *n.m.* full-length apron.
mandioca (man'djo·ka) *n.f.* manioc.
mando ('man·do) *n.m.* 1, command; authority. 2, *mech.* control; drive; steering.
mandolina (man·do'li·na) *n.f.* mandolin.
mandón (man'don) *adj.* bossy; domineering. —*n.m.* domineering person.
mandrágora (man'dra·ɣo·ra) *n.f.* mandrake.
mandril (man'dril) *n.m.* 1, *zool.* mandrill; baboon. 2, *mech.* chuck.
manducar (man·du'kar) *v.t.* [*pres.subjve.* **manduque** (-'du·ke); *pret.* **manduqué** (-'ke)] *colloq.* to eat up; gobble. —**manducatoria** (-ka'to·rja) *n.f., colloq.* food.
manear (ma·ne'ar) *v.t.* 1, to hobble (an animal). 2, = **manejar.**
manecilla (ma·ne'θi·ʎa; -'si·ja) *n.f.* 1, *dim. of* **mano.** 2, hand (*of a timepiece*). 3, pointer; needle.
manejar (ma·ne'xar) *v.t.* 1, to handle. 2, *Amer.* to manage. 3, *Amer.* to drive (a car); ride (a bicycle). 4, to operate (an instrument, machine, etc.). —**manejable,** *adj.* manageable.
manejo (ma'ne·xo) *n.m.* 1, handling. 2, *Amer.* management. 3, operation (*of a machine, device, etc.*). 4, *Amer.* driving (*of a vehicle, conveyance, etc.*). 5, intrigue; stratagem.
manera (ma'ne·ra) *n.f.* manner; way. —**de manera que,** so that. —**de todas maneras,** 1, by all means. 2, in any case; anyway. —**sobre manera,** extremely.
manga ('man·ga) *n.f.* 1, sleeve. 2, = **manguera.** 3, *Amer.* cloth strainer. 4, *naut.* beam. —**manga de agua,** squall; shower. —**manga de viento,** whirlwind; tornado. —**tener manga ancha,** *colloq.* to be easygoing.
manganeso (man·ga'ne·so) *n.m.* manganese. —**mangánico** (-'ga·ni·ko) *adj.* manganic.
mangle ('man·gle) *n.m.* mangrove.
mango ('man·go) *n.m.* 1, handle. 2, mango.
mangonear (man·go·ne'ar) *v.i., colloq.* to meddle; butt in. —*v.t., colloq.* to boss; manage.
mangosta (man'gos·ta) *n.f.* mongoose.
manguera (man'ge·ra) *n.f.* hose; water hose.
manguito (man'gi·to) *n.m.* 1, muff. 2, gas mantle.
maní (ma'ni) *n.m.* [*pl.* **maníes** (-'ni·es) *or* **manises** (-'ni·ses) peanut.
mani- (ma·ni) *prefix* mani-; hand: *manicura,* manicure.
manía (ma'ni·a) *n.f.* 1, mania. 2, whim; caprice. 3, habit. —**maníaco**

(-'ni·a·ko) *adj.* maniacal; maniac. —*n.m.* maniac.
maniatar (ma·nja'tar) *v.t.* to manacle; tie the hands of.
maniático (ma'nja·ti·ko) *adj.* & *n.m.* **1,** eccentric. **2,** = **maníaco.**
manicomio (ma·ni'ko·mjo) *n.m.* **1,** mental hospital. **2,** madhouse.
manicura (ma·ni'ku·ra) *n.f.* **1,** manicure. **2,** manicurist.
manicuro (ma·ni'ku·ro) *n.m.* manicurist. *Also, Amer.,* **manicurista** (-'ris·ta) *n.m.* & *f.*
manido (ma'ni·ðo) *adj.* worn; threadbare.
manifestación (ma·ni·fes·ta·'θjon; -'sjon) *n.f.* **1,** manifestation. **2,** public demonstration.
manifestar (ma·ni·fes'tar) *v.t.* [*pres.ind.* **manifiesto** (-'fjes·to); *pres.subjve.* **manifieste** (-te)] **1,** to manifest; evince; show. **2,** to state; declare.
manifiesto (ma·ni'fjes·to) *adj.* & *n.m.* manifest. —*n.m.* manifesto.
manija (ma'ni·xa) *n.f.* **1,** handle (*of certain tools*). **2,** crank. **3,** clamp. **4,** hobble (*for an animal.*).
manilla (ma'ni·ʎa; -ja) *n.f.* manacle.
manillar (ma·ni'ʎar; -'jar) *n.m.* handlebar.
maniobra (ma'njo·βra) *n.f.* maneuver. —**maniobrabilidad,** *n.f.* maneuverability. —**maniobrable,** *adj.* maneuverable. —**maniobrar,** *v.t.* & *i.* to maneuver.
maniota (ma'njo·ta) *n.f.* hobble.
manipular (ma·ni·pu'lar) *v.t.* to handle; manipulate. —**manipulación,** *n.f.* handling; manipulation. —**manipulador,** *n.m.* manipulator. —**manipuleo** (-'le·o) *n.m., colloq.* manipulation; hanky-panky.
maniquí (ma·ni'ki) *n.m.* manikin; mannequin.
manirroto (ma·ni'rro·to) *adj.* lavish; prodigal. —*n.m.* spendthrift.
manivela (ma·ni'βe·la) *n.f.* handle; crank.
manjar (man'xar) *n.m.* delicacy.
mano ('ma·no) *n.f.* **1,** hand. **2,** side (*right or left*). **3,** coat, as of paint. **4,** quire. **5,** *Amer., slang* pal. —**a la mano,** at hand; handy. —**a mano, 1,** by hand. **2,** at hand; handy. —**buenas manos,** skill; dexterity. —**echar mano de,** *colloq.* to have recourse to; resort to. —**llegar a las manos,** to come to blows. —**mano de obra,** labor. —**manos aguadas,** *colloq.* butterfingers. —**mano sobre mano,** idle; idly. —**ser mano,** to lead (*in a game*). —**tener mano con,** *colloq.* to have pull with.
manojo (ma'no·xo) *n.m.* handful; bunch.
manómetro (ma'no·me·tro) *n.m.* manometer. —**manométrico** (-'me·tri·ko) *adj.* manometric.
manopla (ma'no·pla) *n.f.* **1,** gauntlet; armored glove. **2,** *Amer.* brass knuckles.
manosear (ma·no·se'ar) *v.t.* to handle; finger; paw. —**manoseo** (-'se·o) *n.m.* handling; fingering; pawing.
manotada (ma·no'ta·ða) *n.f., also* **manotazo** (-θo; -so) *n.m.* blow with the hand.
manotear (ma·no·te'ar) *v.t.* **1,** to beat with the hands; cuff; buffet. **2,** *Amer.* to snatch; filch. —*v.i.* to move the hands; gesticulate.
manquear (man·ke'ar) *v.i.* **1,** to be crippled in the hand or arm. **2,** to pretend to be so crippled.
manquedad (man·ke'ðað) *also, colloq.,* **manquera** (-'ke·ra) *n.f.* lack of, or impediment in, one or both arms or hands.
mansalva (man'sal·βa) *n.f., in* **a mansalva,** without risk; from a safe position.
mansarda (man'sar·ða) *n.f.* mansard.
mansedumbre (man·se'ðum·bre) *n.f.* meekness.
mansión (man'sjon) *n.f.* **1,** dwelling; abode. **2,** mansion.
manso ('man·so) *adj.* **1,** meek; gentle. **2,** tame; domesticated. **3,** *Amer., colloq.* gullible. —*n.m.* lead animal.
manta ('man·ta) *n.f.* **1,** blanket; coverlet. **2,** mantle; cloak. **3,** *Amer.* poncho. **4,** manta ray. **5,** *colloq.* = **zurra.**
mantear (man·te'ar) *v.t.* to toss in a blanket. —**manteamiento,** *n.m.* tossing in a blanket.
manteca (man'te·ka) *n.f.* **1,** lard; fat; grease. **2,** = **mantequilla.** —**mantecoso,** *adj.* lardy; greasy.
mantecado (man·te'ka·ðo) *n.m.* **1,** biscuit made with lard. **2,** ice cream.
mantel (man'tel) *n.m.* tablecloth. —**mantelería,** *n.f.* table linen.
mantener (man·te'ner) *v.t.* [*infl.:* **tener**] to maintain; hold; keep.

—**mantenerse,** *v.r.* to sustain oneself.
mantenimiento (man·te·ni·'mjen·to) *n.m.* **1,** maintenance. **2,** sustenance.
manteo (man'te·o) *n.m.* **1,** tossing in a blanket. **2,** priest's cloak.
mantequera (man·te'ke·ra) *also, Amer.,* **mantequillera** (-ki'ʎe·ra; -'je·ra) *n.f.* **1,** churn. **2,** butter dish.
mantequilla (man·te'ki·ʎa; -ja) *n.f.* butter.
mantilla (man'ti·ʎa; -ja) *n.f.* **1,** mantilla. **2,** infant's frock. —**estar en mantillas,** to be in infancy.
mantillo (man'ti·ʎo; -jo) *n.m.* = **humus.**
mantis ('man·tis) *n.m.* mantis.
manto ('man·to) *n.m.* **1,** mantle; cloak. **2,** mantel. **3,** stratum.
mantón (man'ton) *n.m.* a large shawl, usu. of wool. —**mantón de Manila,** embroidered silk shawl.
manu- (ma·nu) *prefix* manu-; hand: *manufactura,* manufacture.
manuable (ma'nwa·βle) *adj.* easily handled.
manual (ma'nwal) *adj.* **1,** manual; hand (*attrib.*). **2,** = **manuable.** —*n.m.* manual; handbook.
manubrio (ma'nu·βrjo) *n.m.* **1,** handle; crank. **2,** *Amer.* handlebar; handlebars. **3,** *Amer.* steering wheel.
manufactura (ma·nu·fak'tu·ra) *n.f.* manufacture. —**manufacturar,** *v.t.* to manufacture. —**manufacturero,** *adj.* manufacturing. —*n.m.* manufacturer.
manumitir (ma·nu·mi'tir) *v.t.* to manumit. —**manumisión** (-'sjon) *n.f.* manumission.
manuscrito (ma·nus'kri·to) *adj.* handwritten. —*n.m.* manuscript.
manutención (ma·nu·ten'θjon; -'sjon) *n.f.* **1,** maintenance; support. **2,** sustenance.
manzana (man'θa·na; -'sa·na) *n.f.* **1,** apple. **2,** city block. **3,** *Amer.* Adam's apple. —**manzanar,** *also,* **manzanal,** *n.m.* apple orchard. —**manzano,** *n.m.* apple tree.
manzanilla (man·θa'ni·ʎa; -sa·'ni·ja) *n.f.* camomile.
maña ('ma·ɲa) *n.f.* **1,** skill; ingenuity; knack. **2,** craftiness; cunning. —**darse maña,** to contrive; manage.
mañana (ma'ɲa·na) *n.f.* morning. —*n.m.* morrow; future. —*adv.* tomorrow. —**muy de mañana,** early in the morning. —**pasado mañana,** the day after tomorrow.
mañanear (ma·ɲa·ne'ar) *v.i.* to rise early; be an early riser.
mañanero (ma·ɲa'ne·ro) *adj.* **1,** early-rising. **2,** *colloq.* morning (*attrib.*).
mañoso (ma'ɲo·so) *adj., colloq.* **1,** ingenious; facile; adroit. **2,** tricky.
mapa ('ma·pa) *n.m.* map. —**mapamundi** (-'mun·di) *n.m.* map of the world.
mapache (ma'pa·tʃe) *n.m.* raccoon.
maquiavélico (ma·kja'βe·li·ko) *adj.* Machiavellian. —**maquiavelismo,** *n.m.* Machiavellism. —**maquiavelista,** *adj.* & *n.m.* & *f.* Machiavellian.
maquillar (ma·ki'ʎar; -'jar) *v.t.* to make up; apply cosmetics to. —**maquillaje,** *n.m.* make-up.
máquina ('ma·ki·na) *n.f.* machine; machinery; contrivance. —**maquinal,** *adj.* mechanical.
maquinar (ma·ki'nar) *v.t.* & *i.* to machinate; plot; scheme. —**maquinación,** *n.f.* machination; plot. —**maquinador,** *adj.* plotting; scheming. —*n.m.* plotter; schemer.
maquinaria (ma·ki'na·rja) *n.f.* **1,** machinery. **2,** machine design; machine construction.
maquinista (ma·ki'nis·ta) *n.m.* **1,** engineer; machinist. **2,** machine designer; machine builder.
mar (mar) *n.m. or f.* sea. —**alta mar,** the high seas. —**a mares,** copiously. —**la mar de,** *colloq.* a lot of; no end of. —**mar de fondo, 1,** ocean swell; ground swell. **2,** *fig.* turmoil.
marabú (ma·ra'βu) *n.m.* marabou.
maraña (ma'ra·ɲa) *n.f.* **1,** tangle. **2,** dense growth. **3,** plot; intrigue.
marasmo (ma'ras·mo) *n.m.* **1,** *pathol.* marasmus. **2,** *fig.* torpor.
maratón (ma·ra'ton) *n.f.* marathon.
maravedí (ma·ra·βe'ði) *n.m.* [*pl.* **maravedís, -díes** *or* **-dises**] a name given to various old Spanish coins.
maravilla (ma·ra'βi·ʎa; -ja) *n.f.* **1,** marvel; wonder. **2,** *bot.* marigold. —**maravilloso,** *adj.* marvelous; wonderful.
maravillar (ma·ra·βi'ʎar; -'jar) *v.t.* to strike with wonder; delight; amaze. —**maravillarse de** *or* **con,** to marvel at; wonder at.

marbete (mar'βe·te) *n.m.* 1, label; tag; sticker. 2, border; fillet.

marca ('mar·ka) *n.f.* 1, mark. 2, brand; make; trademark. 3, brand (*of animals*). 4, *sports* record. —**de marca mayor,** outstanding; first rate. —**de marca,** of quality.

marcar (mar'kar) *v.t.* [*pres.subjve.* **marque;** *pret.* **marqué**] 1, to brand; mark. 2, to designate; point out. 3, to monogram. 4, to point to; show (the hour). 5, to dial (a telephone number). 6, *sports* to score.

marcasita (mar·ka'si·ta) *n.f.* marcasite.

marcial (mar'θjal; -'sjal) *adj.* martial.

marciano (mar'θja·no; -'sja·no) *adj.* & *n.m.* Martian.

marco ('mar·ko) *n.m.* 1, frame. 2, standard (*of weight*). 3, mark (*monetary unit*).

marcha ('mar·tʃa) *n.f.* 1, march. 2, course; progress. 3, watch movement. 4, running; functioning. —**marcha atrás,** *mech.* reverse. —**sobre la marcha,** 1, offhand; on the spot. 2, in the course of events.

marchamo (mar'tʃa·mo) *n.m.* 1, customhouse mark. 2, *fig.* mark; label.

marchar (mar'tʃar) *v.i.* 1, to march. 2, to proceed; go. 3, to run; work. —**marcharse,** *v.r.* to leave.

marchitar (mar·tʃi'tar) *v.t.* to wither; fade. —**marchitamiento,** *n.m.*, *also,* **marchitez,** *n.f.* withering; fading. —**marchito** (-'tʃi·to) *adj.* withered; faded.

marea (ma're·a) *n.f.* tide.

marear (ma·re'ar) *v.t.* 1, to make seasick; make dizzy. 2, to bother; importune. —**marearse,** *v.r.* to be seasick; be dizzy. —**mareado,** *adj.* seasick; dizzy.

marejada (ma·re'xa·ða) *n.f.* 1, ocean swell; ground swell. 2, *fig.* commotion; turmoil.

mareo (ma're·o) *n.m.* 1, [*also,* **mareamiento**] seasickness; dizziness. 2, bother; annoyance.

marfil (mar'fil) *n.m.* ivory. —**marfileño,** *adj.* ivory (*attrib.*); ivorylike.

marga ('mar·ɣa) *n.f.* loam. —**margoso,** *adj.* loamy.

margarina (mar·ɣa'ri·na) *n.f.* margarine.

margarita (mar·ɣa'ri·ta) *n.f.* daisy; marguerite.

margen ('mar·xen) *n.m.* & *f.* 1, margin. 2, verge; fringe. 3, *agric.* row. —**marginal** (-xi'nal) *adj.* marginal. —**dar margen,** to give cause *or* opportunity.

marginar (mar·xi'nar) *v.t.* 1, to make marginal notes of *or* in. 2, to leave a margin on.

mariache (ma'rja·tʃe) *n.m.* 1, a Mexican dance, similar to the fandango. 2, music for this dance. 3, ensemble that plays such music.

marica (ma'ri·ka) *n.m.* milksop; effeminate man.

maricón (ma·ri'kon) *n.m.* 1, *colloq.* sissy. 2, *vulg.* homosexual.

marido (ma'ri·ðo) *n.m.* husband.

mariguana (ma·ri'gwa·na) *n.f.* marijuana.

marimacho (ma·ri'ma·tʃo) *n.m., colloq.* hoyden; tomboy.

marimba (ma'rim·ba) *n.f.* marimba.

marina (ma'ri·na) *n.f.* 1, shore; coast. 2, fleet; navy. 3, seascape.

marinar (ma·ri'nar) *v.t.* to marinate.

marinera (ma·ri'ne·ra) *n.f.* sailor's blouse.

marinería (ma·ri·ne'ri·a) *n.f.* 1, seamanship. 2, ship's crew. 3, seamen collectively.

marinero (ma·ri'ne·ro) *n.m.* sailor. —*adj.* 1, = **marino.** 2, seaworthy.

marino (ma'ri·no) *n.m.* sailor; seaman. —*adj.* marine; nautical.

marioneta (ma·rjo'ne·ta) *n.f.* marionette.

mariposa (ma·ri'po·sa) *n.f.* 1, butterfly. 2, night light. —**mariposear,** *v.i.* to flit.

mariquita (ma·ri'ki·ta) *n.f.* ladybug; ladybird.

mariscal (ma·ris'kal) *n.m., mil.* marshal. —**mariscalato,** *n.m., also,* **mariscalía,** *n.f.* marshalship.

marisco (ma'ris·ko) *n.m.* shellfish.

marisma (ma'ris·ma) *n.f.* marsh; swamp.

marisquero (ma·ris'ke·ro) *n.m.* fisher or seller of shellfish. —**marisquería,** *n.f.* sea food shop or restaurant.

marital (ma·ri'tal) *adj.* marital.

marítimo (ma'ri·ti·mo) *adj.* maritime; marine.

marjal (mar'xal) *n.* bog; fen.

marlín (mar'lin) *n.m.* marlin.

marmita (mar'mi·ta) *n.f.* kettle.

mármol ('mar·mol) *n.m.* marble. —**marmolista,** *n.m.* marbleworker. —**marmóreo** (-'mo·re·o) *adj.* marble (*attrib.*); marmoreal.
marmolería (mar·mo·le'ri·a) *n.f.* **1,** marblework. **2,** marble works.
marmota (mar'mo·ta) *n.f.* **1,** marmot. **2,** sleepyhead.
maroma (ma'ro·ma) *n.f.* **1,** hemp rope; hawser. **2,** tightrope. **3,** *Amer.* acrobatic feat; stunt. —**maromero,** *n.m., Amer.* tightrope walker; acrobat.
marque ('mar·ke) *v., pres.subjve. of* **marcar.**
marqué (mar'ke) *v., 1st pers.sing. pret. of* **marcar.**
marqués (mar'kes) *n.m.* marquis. —**marquesa,** *n.f.* marchioness. —**marquesado,** *n.m.* marquisate.
marquesina (mar·ke'si·na) *n.f.* marquee; awning.
marquetería (mar·ke·te'ri·a) *n.f.* marquetry.
marra ('ma·rra) *n.f.* **1,** lack; deficiency. **2,** sledgehammer.
marranada (ma·rra'na·ða) *also,* **marranería,** *n.f., colloq.* **1,** filthiness. **2,** swinishness; dirty trick.
marrano (ma'rra·no) *n.m.* **1,** pig; hog. **2,** *colloq., derog.* swine.
marrar (ma'rrar) *v.i.* & *t.* to fail; miss.
marras ('ma·rras) *adv., colloq., usu. in* **de marras, 1,** aforementioned. **2,** previous.
marrasquino (ma·rras'ki·no) *n.m.* maraschino.
marro ('ma·rro) *n.m.* **1,** a game resembling prisoner's base. **2,** a game resembling quoits. **3,** *colloq.* evasion; dodge.
marrón (ma'rron) *adj.* chestnut; brown. —*n.m.* **1,** quoit. **2,** marron.
marroquín (ma·rro'kin) *n.m.* morocco (*leather*).
marrubio (ma'rru·βjo) *n.m.* horehound.
marrullería (ma·rru·ʎe'ri·a; -je·'ri·a) *n.f.* cunning; cajolery. —**marrullero,** *adj.* crafty; cunning.
Marsellesa (mar·se'ʎe·sa; -'je·sa) *n.f.* Marseillaise.
marsopa (mar'so·pa) *n.f.* porpoise.
marsupial (mar·su'pjal) *adj.* & *n.m.* & *f.* marsupial.
marta ('mar·ta) *n.f.* marten. —**marta cebellina,** sable.
Marte ('mar·te) *n.m.* Mars.
martes ('mar·tes) *n.m. sing.* & *pl.* Tuesday. —**martes de carnaval** *or* **carnestolendas,** Shrove Tuesday.
martillar (mar·ti'ʎar; -'jar) *v.t.* & *i.* to hammer. *Also,* **martillear.**
martillazo (mar·ti'ʎa·θo; -'ja·so) *n.m.* hammer blow.
martilleo (mar·ti'ʎe·o; -'je·o) *n.m.* hammering.
martillo (mar'ti·ʎo; -jo) *n.m.* **1,** hammer; claw hammer. **2,** persistent person. **3,** auction room. —**a macha** ('ma·tʃa) **martillo,** *also,* **a machamartillo, 1,** roughly made. **2,** insistently; firmly.
martinete (mar·ti'ne·te) *n.m.* **1,** a kind of heron. **2,** drop hammer. **3,** pile driver.
martingala (mar·tin'ga·la) *n.f., colloq.* **1,** trick; artifice. **2,** gambling system.
martini (mar'ti·ni) *n.m.* martini.
mártir ('mar·tir) *n.m.* & *f.* martyr. —**martirio** (mar'ti·rjo) *n.m.* martyrdom.
martirizar (mar·ti·ri'θar; -'sar) *v.t.* [*pres.subjve.* **martirice** (-'ri·θe; -se); *pret.* **martiricé** (-'θe; -'se)] to martyrize; torment.
marxismo (mark'sis·mo) *n.m.* Marxism. —**marxista,** *n.m.* & *f.* Marxist. —*adj.* Marxian.
marzo ('mar·θo; -so) *n.m.* March.
mas (mas) *conj.* but; yet.
más (mas) *adv.* **1,** more. **2,** most. **3,** longer. **4,** rather. **5,** besides; in addition. **6,** plus. —**a lo más,** at most; at best. —**a más y mejor,** copiously; to one's heart's content. —**de más,** extra; superfluous. —**más de,** more than (*fol. by a number or expression of quantity*). —**más que,** more than (*fol. by the second term of a comparison*). —**por más que,** however much. —**sin más ni más,** *colloq.* **1,** without further ado. **2,** suddenly; unexpectedly.
masa ('ma·sa) *n.f.* **1,** mass. **2,** dough. **3,** mash. **4,** populace; rabble.
masacre (ma'sa·kre) *n.f.* massacre. —**masacrar,** *v.t.* to massacre.
masaje (ma'sa·xe) *n.m.* massage. —**masajista,** *n.m.* masseur. —*n.f.* masseuse.
masajear (ma·sa·xe'ar) *v.t., Amer.* to massage.
mascar (mas'kar) *v.t.* [*pres.subjve.* **masque;** *pret.* **masqué**] to chew.
máscara ('mas·ka·ra) *n.f.* **1,** mask. **2,** disguise. —*n.m.* & *f.* masquer-

ader; mummer. —**máscaras,** *n.f.pl.* masquerade (*sing.*).

mascarada (mas·ka'ra·ða) *n.f.* masquerade; mummery; masque.

mascarilla (mas·ka'ri·ʎa; -ja) *n.f.* death mask.

mascarón (mas·ka'ron) *n.m.* stone mask. —**mascarón de proa,** figurehead.

mascota (mas'ko·ta) *n.f.* mascot.

masculino (mas·ku'li·no) *adj.* male; manly; masculine. —**masculinidad,** *n.f.* masculinity.

mascullar (mas·ku'ʎar; -'jar) *v.t.* & *i.* to mumble.

masía (ma'si·a) *n.f.* farm; farmhouse.

masilla (ma'si·ʎa; -ja) *n.f.* putty.

masón (ma'son) *n.m.* Freemason; Mason. —**masonería,** *n.f.* Freemasonry; Masonry. —**masónico,** *adj.* Masonic; Freemasonic.

masonita (ma·so'ni·ta) *n.f.* masonite.

masoquismo (ma·so'kis·mo) *n.m.* masochism. —**masoquista,** *n.m.* & *f.* masochist. —*adj.* masochistic. —**masoquístico,** *adj.* masochistic.

masque ('mas·ke) *v., pres.subjve. of* **mascar.**

masqué (mas'ke) *v., 1st pers.sing. pret. of* **mascar.**

mastelero (mas·te'le·ro) *n.m.* topmast.

masticar (mas·ti'kar) *v.t.* [*pres. subjve.* **mastique** (-'ti·ke); *pret.* **mastiqué** (-'ke)] **1,** to masticate; chew. **2,** to mull; ponder; ruminate. —**masticación,** *n.f.* mastication.

mástil ('mas·til) *n.m.* **1,** mast. **2,** stanchion. **3,** neck (*of a violin, guitar, etc.*).

mastín (mas'tin) *n.m.* mastiff.

mástique ('mas·ti·ke) *n.m.* mastic.

mastodonte (mas·to'ðon·te) *n.m.* mastodon.

mastoides (mas'toi·ðes) *adj.* & *n.f. sing.* & *pl.* mastoid. —**mastoideo** (-'ðe·o) *adj.* mastoidal. —**mastoiditis,** *n.f.* mastoiditis.

mastuerzo (mas'twer·θo; -so) *n.m.* **1,** dolt; oaf. **2,** cress.

masturbarse (mas·tur'βar·se) *v.r.* to masturbate. —**masturbación,** *n.f.* masturbation.

mata ('ma·ta) *n.f.* **1,** bush. **2,** sprig. **3,** grove. **4,** clump of grass; hassock. —**mata de pelo,** mass of hair; head of hair.

matadero (ma·ta'ðe·ro) *n.m.* slaughterhouse.

matador (ma·ta'ðor) *adj.* killing. —*n.m.* matador.

matadura (ma·ta'ðu·ra) *n.f.* sore; gall.

matamoros (ma·ta'mo·ros) *n.m. sing.* & *pl.* blusterer; fire-eater.

matamoscas (ma·ta'mos·kas) *n.m. sing.* & *pl.* fly swatter.

matanza (ma'tan·θa; -sa) *n.f.* killing; slaughter.

mataperro (ma·ta'pe·rro) *n.m., colloq.* urchin; ragamuffin; gamin. —**mataperrear,** *v.i., Amer., colloq.* to roam the streets doing mischief.

matar (ma'tar) *v.t.* **1,** to kill. **2,** to gall. **3,** to tone down; subdue; dull. —**matarse,** *v.r.* **1,** to kill oneself. **2,** to strive; strain.

matarife (ma·ta'ri·fe) *n.m.* butcher; slaughterer.

matasanos (ma·ta'sa·nos) *n.m. sing.* & *pl.* quack doctor.

match (matʃ) *n.m., sports* match.

mate ('ma·te) *n.m.* **1,** mate; checkmate. **2,** *bot.* maté. —*adj.* mat.

matemáticas (ma·te'ma·ti·kas) *n.f.pl., also, sing.,* **matemática,** mathematics. —**matemático,** *adj.* mathematical. —*n.m.* mathematician.

materia (ma'te·rja) *n.f.* matter. —**materia prima,** raw material.

material (ma·te'rjal) *adj.* & *n.m.* material. —**materialidad,** *n.f.* materiality.

materialismo (ma·te·rja'lis·mo) *n.m.* materialism. —**materialista,** *n.m.* & *f.* materialist. —*adj.* materialistic.

materializar (ma·te·rja·li'θar; -'sar) *v.t.* [*pres.subjve.* **materialice** ('li·θe; -se); *pret.* **materialicé** (-'θe; -'se)] to materialize. —**materialización,** *n.f.* materialization.

maternal (ma·ter'nal) *adj.* maternal. *Also,* **materno** (-'ter·no).

maternidad (ma·ter'ni·ðað) *n.f.* **1,** maternity. **2,** motherliness; motherly affection.

matinal (ma·ti'nal) *adj.* matinal; matutinal.

matiné (ma·ti'ne) *n.m.* & *f.* matinee.

matiz (ma'tiθ; -'tis) *n.m.* shade; tint; tone.

matizar (ma·ti'θar; -'sar) *v.t.* [*pres.subjve.* **matice** (-'ti·θe; -se); *pret.* **maticé** (-'θe; -'se)] to shade; color.

matón (ma'ton) *n.m., colloq.* bully. —**matonería,** *n.f., colloq.* braggadocio; bravado.
matorral (ma·to'rral) *n.m.* bush; scrub.
matraca (ma'tra·ca) *n.f.* **1,** noisemaker; rattle. **2,** *colloq.* annoying insistence. **3,** *colloq.* rattle; rattling. **4,** *colloq.* monotony; humdrum.
matrero (ma'tre·ro) *adj.* **1,** shrewd; cunning. **2,** *Amer.* = **arisco.**
matri- (ma·tri) *prefix* matri-; mother: *matriarcado,* matriarchy.
matriarca (ma'trjar·ka) *n.f.* matriarch. —**matriarcado,** *n.m.* matriarchy. —**matriarcal,** *adj.* matriarchal.
matricida (ma·tri'θi·ða; -'si·ða) *adj.* matricidal. —*n.m.* & *f.* matricide (*agent*). —**matricidio** (-θi·ðjo; -'si·ðjo) *n.m.* matricide (*act*).
matrícula (ma'tri·ku·la) *n.f.* **1,** matriculation; enrollment. **2,** registration.
matricular (ma·tri·ku'lar) *v.t.* **1,** to matriculate; enroll. **2,** to register; record.
matrimonio (ma·tri'mo·njo) *n.m.* **1,** matrimony; marriage. **2,** *colloq.* married couple. —**matrimonial,** *adj.* matrimonial.
matriz (ma'triθ; -'tris) *n.f.* **1,** uterus; womb. **2,** matrix. —*adj.* basic; original.
matrona (ma'tro·na) *n.f.* **1,** matron. **2,** midwife. —**matronal,** *adj.* matronly.
matute (ma'tu·te) *n.m.* **1,** smuggling. **2,** smuggled goods. —**matutear,** (-te'ar) *v.i.* to smuggle.
matutino (ma·tu'ti·no) *also,* **matutinal** (-'nal) *adj.* matutinal; morning (*attrib.*).
maullar (mau'ʎar; -'jar) *v.i.* [*pres.ind.* **maúllo** (ma'u·ʎo; -jo); *pres.subjve.* **maúlle** (-ʎe; -je)] to meow. —**maullador,** *adj.* meowing.
maullido (mau'ʎi·ðo; -'ji·ðo) *also,* **maúllo** (ma'u·ʎo; -jo) *n.m.* meow.
mausoleo (mau·so'le·o) *n.m.* mausoleum.
maxilar (mak·si'lar) *adj.* & *n.m.* maxillary.
máxima ('mak·si·ma) *n.f.* maxim.
máxime ('mak·si·me) *adv.* mainly; chiefly; especially.
máximo ('mak·si·mo) *n.m.* & *adj.* maximum. —*adj.* maximal.
máximum ('mak·si·mum) *n.m.* [*pl.* **-mums**] maximum.
maya ('ma·ja) *adj.* & *n.m.* & *f.* Mayan. —*n.m.* Maya.
mayar (ma'jar) *v.i.* = **maullar.**
mayo ('ma·jo) *n.m.* **1,** May. **2,** Maypole.
mayonesa (ma·jo'ne·sa) *n.f.* mayonnaise. *Also,* **mahonesa** (ma·o-).
mayor (ma'jor) *adj.* **A** *comp of* **grande, 1,** greater; larger. **2,** more; further. **3,** older; elder. **4,** *music* major. **B** *superl. of* **grande, 1,** greatest; largest. **2,** oldest; eldest. **3,** principal; main. —*n.m., mil.* major. —*n.f., logic* major premise; major term. —**mayores,** *n.m.pl.* ancestors. —**mayor de edad,** of age. —**por mayor; al por mayor,** wholesale.
mayoral (ma·jo'ral) *n.m.* foreman; boss.
mayorazgo (ma·jo'raθ·ɣo; -'ras·ɣo) *n.m.* **1,** primogeniture. **2,** estate inherited by primogeniture.
mayordomo (ma·jor'ðo·mo) *n.m.* **1,** majordomo. **2,** steward. **3,** manservant.
mayoría (ma·jo'ri·a) *n.f.* majority.
mayoridad (ma·jo·ri'ðað) *n.f.* legal age; majority.
mayorista (ma·jo'ris·ta) *n.m.* & *f.* wholesaler.
mayormente (ma·jor'men·te) *adv.* greatly; especially.
mayúsculo (ma'jus·ku·lo) *adj.* **1,** good-sized; great. **2,** capital; uppercase. —**mayúscula,** *n.f.* capital letter.
maza ('ma·θa; -sa) *n.f.* **1,** mace; club. **2,** hammer of a pile driver; drop hammer.
mazacote (ma·θa'ko·te; ma·sa-) *n.m.* lump; lumpy mass; mess. —**mazacotudo,** *adj.* lumpy; gooey; messy.
mazamorra (ma·θa'mo·rra; ma·sa-) *n.f.* **1,** *colloq.* hodgepodge. **2,** *Amer.* dessert made with corn starch and fruits.
mazapán (ma·θa'pan; ma·sa-) *n.m.* marzipan.
mazazo (ma'θa·θo; -'sa·so) *n.m., also,* **mazada,** *n.f.* blow with a mace or mallet.
mazmorra (maθ'mo·rra; mas-) *n.f.* dungeon.
mazo ('ma·θo; -so) *n.m.* **1,** large wooden hammer; mallet; maul. **2,** bundle; bunch. **3,** stack (*of cards*).
mazorca (ma'θor·ka; ma'sor-) *n.f.* ear of corn.
mazurca (ma'θur·ka; ma'sur-) *n.f.* mazurka.

me (me) *pers.pron. 1st pers.sing., used as obj. of a verb* me; to me; myself.
meandro (me'an·dro) *n.m.* meandering; loop.
mear (me'ar) *v.i., vulg.* to urinate, **—meada,** *n.f., vulg.* urination. **—meadero,** *n.m., vulg.* urinal.
mecánica (me'ka·ni·ka) *n.f.* mechanics. **—mecánico,** *adj.* mechanic; mechanical. **—***n.m.* mechanic. **—mecanismo,** *n.m.* mechanism.
mecanizar (me·ka·ni'θar; -'sar) *v.t.* [*pres.subjve.* **mecanice** (-'ni·θe; -se); *pret.* **mecanicé** (-'θe; -'se)] to mechanize. **—mecanización,** *n.f.* mechanization.
mecanografía (me·ka·no·ɣra·'fi·a) *n.f.* typewriting. **—mecanográfico** (-'ɣra·fi·ko) *adj.* typewriting (*attrib.*) **—mecanógrafo** (-'no·ɣra·fo) *n.m.* typist.
mecanografiar (me·ka·no·ɣra·'fjar) *v.t. & i.* [*infl.:* **telegrafiar**] to typewrite; type.
mecedor (me·θe'ðor; -se'ðor) *adj.* rocking; swinging. **—***n.m.* swing; porch glider. **—mecedora,** *n.f.* rocking chair.
mecer (me'θer; -'ser) *v.t.* [*pres.ind.* **mezo;** *pres.subjve.* **meza**] to rock; swing.
mecha ('me·tʃa) *n.f.* **1,** wick. **2,** wick fuse; fuse. **3,** = **mechón. 4,** thin strip of bacon.
mechar (me'tʃar) *v.t.* to lard with bacon strips.
mechero (me'tʃe·ro) *n.m.* **1,** burner. **2,** oil *or* gas lamp. **3,** wick lighter.
mechón (me'tʃon) *n.m.* lock; tuft of hair.
medalla (me'ða·ʎa; -ja) *n.f.* medal. **—medallón** (-'ʎon; -'jon) *n.m.* medallion; locket.
médano ('me·ða·no) *n.m.* **1,** = **duna. 2,** sand bar.
medi- (me·ði) *prefix, var. of* **medio-:** *medieval,* also, *medioeval,* medieval.
media ('me·ðja) *n.f.* **1,** stocking. **2,** *Amer.* sock. **3,** *math.* mean. **—a medias,** by halves; halfway; fifty-fifty.
mediación (me·ðja'θjon; -'sjon) *n.f.* mediation. **—mediador,** *adj.* mediating. **—***n.m.* mediator.
mediado (me'ðja·ðo) *adj.* **1,** half full. **2,** halfway; in the middle. **—a mediados de,** towards the middle of (*the month, year, etc.*).
mediana (me'ðja·na) *n.f., geom.* median.
medianamente (me·ðja·na·'men·te) *adv.* **1,** moderately; reasonably. **2,** halfway; incompletely.
medianero (me·ðja'ne·ro) *adj.* intervening; intermediate. **—***n.m.* = **mediador. —medianera,** *n.f.* party wall.
medianía (me·ðja'ni·a) *n.f.* **1,** mediocrity. **2,** mediocre person. **3,** tenant farming on a fifty-fifty basis.
mediano (me'ðja·no) *adj.* **1,** medium; average. **2,** moderate. **3,** mediocre.
medianoche (me·ðja'no·tʃe) *n.f.* midnight.
mediante (me'ðjan·te) *adj.* mediating; interceding. **—***prep.* by means of; with the help of; through. **—Dios mediante,** God willing.
mediar (me'ðjar) *v.i.* **1,** to be in the middle; be at the midpoint. **2,** to intervene. **3,** to mediate.
medicación (me·ði·ka'θjon; -'sjon) *n.f.* medication.
medicamento (me·ði·ka'men·to) *n.m.* medicament.
medicastro (me·ði'kas·tro) *n.m.* quack doctor.
medicina (me·ði'θi·na; -'si·na) *n.f.* medicine. **—medicinal,** *adj.* medicinal.
medicinar (me·ði·θi'nar; -si'nar) *v.t.* to medicate.
medición (me·ði'θjon; -'sjon) *n.f.* measurement; measuring; mensuration.
médico ('me·ði·ko) *adj.* medical. **—***n.m.* physician. **—médico de cabecera,** family physician. **—médico forense,** medical examiner.
medida (me'ði·ða) *n.f.* **1,** measure. **2,** measurement. **3,** proportion; correspondence. **—a medida de,** according to. **—a medida que,** as; while.
medidor (me·ði'ðor) *adj.* measuring. **—***n.m., Amer.* meter.
medieval (me·ðje'βal) *adj.* medieval. *Also,* **medioeval** (me·ðjo·e-).
medievo (me'ðje·βo) *n.m.* Middle Ages. *Also,* **medioevo** (me·ðjo'e-).
medio ('me·ðjo) *adj. & adv.* half. **—***adj.* **1,** middle. **2,** medium. **—***n.m.* **1,** middle; center. **2,** agency; means. **3,** medium; surroundings; environment. **4,** = **médium, 5,** *math.* one half; a half. **6,** *math.* mean. **—medios,** *n.m.pl.* means. **—a medio,** *fol. by inf.* to be half done: *a medio*

vestir, half dressed. —**de medio a medio,** 1, right on center; on the button. 2, from *a* to *z;* completely. —**de por medio,** in between; between. —**echar por en medio,** *colloq.* to go at it firmly; ride roughshod. —**en medio de,** in the midst of; amidst. —**meterse de por medio** *or* **por en medio,** to intervene. —**poner los medios,** to take steps; take measures. —**quitar de en medio,** *colloq.* to put out of the way; do away with. —**quitarse de en medio,** to get out of the way.
medio- (me·ðjo) *prefix* mid-; middle: *mediocentro,* midcenter.
mediocre (me'ðjo·kre) *adj.* mediocre. —**mediocridad,** *n.f.* mediocrity.
mediodía (me·ðjo'ði·a) *n.m.* 1, noon. 2, south.
medioevo (me·ðjo'e·βo) *n.m.* = medievo. —**medioeval,** *adj.* = medieval.
mediopensionista (me·ðjo·pen·sjo'nis·ta) *n.m.* & *f.* day student.
medir (me'ðir) *v.t.* [*infl.:* **pedir**] 1, to measure; size. 2, to fit; try on. —**¿Cuánto mide Vd.?** How tall are you?
meditabundo (me·ði·ta'βun·do) *also, Amer., colloq.* **meditativo** (-'ti·βo) *adj.* meditative.
meditar (me·ði'tar) *v.t.* & *i.* to meditate. —**meditación,** *n.f.* meditation.
mediterráneo (me·ði·te'rra·ne·o) *adj.* & *n.m.* Mediterranean.
médium ('me·ðjum) *n.m.* & *f.* [*pl.* **médium** *or* **médiums**] spiritualistic medium.
medra ('me·ðra) *n.f.* progress; improvement; thriving. *Also,* **medro,** *n.m.,* **medros,** *n.m.pl.*
medrar (me'ðrar) *v.i.* to thrive; prosper.
medroso (me'ðro·so) *adj.* 1, timorous. 2, frightful.
médula ('me·ðu·la) *n.f.* 1, medulla. 2, marrow. 3, pith. 4, *fig.* core; essence.
medular (me·ðu'lar) *adj.* 1, medullary. 2, basic; essential.
meduloso (me·ðu'lo·so) *adj.* pulpy; pithy.
medusa (me'ðu·sa) *n.f.* jellyfish.
mefítico (me'fi·ti·ko) *adj.* mephetic.
mega- (me·ɣa) *prefix* mega-. 1, large; great: *megalito,* megalith. 2, million; millionfold: *megaciclo,* megacycle.
megaciclo (me·ɣa'θi·klo; -'si·klo) *n.m.* megacycle.
megáfono (me'ɣa·fo·no) *n.m.* megaphone.
megalo- (me·ɣa·lo) *prefix* megalo-; very large: *megalocéfalo,* megalocephalic.
megalomanía (me·ɣa·lo·ma'ni·a) *n.f.* megalomania. —**megalómano** (-'lo·ma·no) *adj.* & *n.m.* megalomaniac.
megatón (me·ɣa'ton) *n.m.* megaton.
mejicano (me·xi'ka·no) *adj.* & *n.m.* Mexican. *Also,* **mexicano.**
mejilla (me'xi·ʎa; -ja) *n.f.* cheek.
mejillón (me·xi'ʎon; -'jon) *n.m.* mussel.
mejor (me'xor) *adj.* 1, *comp. of* **bueno;** better. 2, *superl. of* **bueno;** best. —*adv.* 1, *comp. of* **bien;** better. 2, *superl. of* **bien;** best. 3, rather; preferably. —**a lo mejor,** perhaps; maybe. —**mejor dicho,** rather; more exactly. —**mejor que mejor,** much better; much the better; very well. —**tanto mejor,** so much the better; all the better.
mejora (me'xo·ra) *n.f.* 1, improvement; melioration. 2, *law* special bequest.
mejoramiento (me·xo·ra'mjen·to) *n.m.* improvement; melioration.
mejorana (me·xo'ra·na) *n.f.* marjoram.
mejorar (me·xo'rar) *v.t.* 1, to improve; meliorate. 2, to outbid. 3, *law* to give a special bequest to. —*v.i.* [*also, refl.,* **mejorarse**] to improve; recover.
mejoría (me·xo'ri·a) *n.f.* improvement.
mejunje (me'xun·xe) *n.m.* hodgepodge. *Also,* **menjunje.**
melado (me'la·ðo) *adj.* honey-colored.
melancolía (me·lan·ko'li·a) *n.f.* 1, melancholy. 2, melancholia. —**melancólico,** *adj.* melancholic; melancholy.
melanesio (me·la'ne·sjo) *adj.* & *n.m.* Melanesian.
melano- (me·la·no) *prefix* melano-; black: *melanosis,* melanosis.
melaza (me'la·θa; -sa) *n.f.* molasses.
melcocha (mel'ko·tʃa) *n.f.* taffy.
melena (me'le·na) *n.f.* 1, loose hair; long hair. 2, mane.

meli- (me·li) *prefix* melli-: honeyed; sweet: *melifluo,* mellifluous.
melifluo (me'li·flwo) *adj.* mellifluous. —**melifluidad,** *n.f.* mellifluousness.
melindre (me'lin·dre) *n.m.* **1,** ladyfinger. **2,** priggishness. —**melindroso,** *adj.* & *n.m.* namby-pamby.
melo- (me·lo) *prefix* melo-; song; music: *melómano,* melomaniac.
melocotón (me·lo·ko'ton) *n.m.* peach. —**melocotonero,** *n.m.* peach tree.
melodía (me·lo'ði·a) *n.f.* melody. —**melódico** (-'lo·ði·ko) *adj.* melodic. —**melodioso** (-'ðjo·so) *adj.* melodious.
melodrama (me·lo'ðra·ma) *n.m.* melodrama. —**melodramático** (-'ma·ti·ko) *adj.* melodramatic.
melón (me'lon) *n.m.* melon; muskmelon. —**melonar,** *n.m.* melon patch. —**melonero,** *n.m.* melon vendor.
meloso (me'lo·so) *adj.* excessively sweet; unctuous. —**melosidad,** *n.f.* excessive sweetness; unctuousness.
mella ('me·ʎa; -ja) *n.f.* **1,** notch; nick; dent. **2,** hollow; gap. —**hacer mella a,** to impress; affect. —**hacer mella en,** to impair.
mellado (me'ʎa·ðo; -'ja·ðo) *adj.* **1,** jagged; notched. **2,** toothless.
mellar (me'ʎar; -'jar) *v.t.* to notch; nick; dent.
mellizo (me'ʎi·θo; -'ji·so) *adj.* & *n.m.* twin.
membrana (mem'bra·na) *n.f.* membrane. —**membranoso,** *adj.* membranous.
membrete (mem'bre·te) *n.m.* **1,** letterhead. **2,** inside address. **3,** caption; heading. **4,** *journalism* masthead.
membrillo (mem'bri·ʎo; -jo) *n.m.* **1,** quince. **2,** [*also,* **membrillero**] quince tree.
membrudo (mem'bru·ðo) *adj.* muscular; brawny.
memento (me'men·to) *n.m.* memento.
memo ('me·mo) *adj.* silly; foolish. —*n.m.* simpleton.
memorable (me·mo'ra·βle) *adj.* memorable.
memorándum (me·mo'ran·dum) *n.m.* [*pl.* **-mums**] memorandum.
memoria (me'mo·rja) *n.f.* **1,** memory. **2,** remembrance. **3,** account. **4,** note; memorandum. —**memorias,** *n.f.pl.* **1,** memoirs. **2,** regards. —**de memoria,** by heart; from memory. —**flaco de memoria,** forgetful. —**hacer memoria de,** to recall. —**memoria de gallo,** poor memory; short memory.
memorial (me·mo'rjal) *n.m.* formal petition; memorial.
memorizar (me·mo·ri'θar; -'sar) *v.t.* [*pres.subjve.* **memorice** (-'ri·θe; -se); *pret.* **memoricé** (-'θe; -'se)] to memorize.
menaje (me'na·xe) *n.m.* household furniture and furnishings.
mención (men'θjon; -'sjon) *n.f.* mention; reference. —**mencionar,** *v.t.* to mention; name.
mendaz (men'daθ; -'das) *adj.* mendacious. —**mendacidad,** *n.f.* mendacity.
mendicante (men·di'kan·te) *adj.* & *n.m.* mendicant.
mendicidad (men·di·θi'ðað; -si·'ðað) *n.f.* beggary; mendicancy.
mendigar (men·di'ɣar) *v.t.* [*pres. subjve.* **mendigue** (-'di·ɣe); *pret.* **mendigué** (-'ɣe)] to beg. —**mendigo** (-'di·ɣo) *n.m.* beggar.
mendrugo (men'dru·ɣo) *n.m.* crust of bread; bit of stale bread.
menear (me·ne'ar) *v.t.* to shake; wag. —**meneo** (-'ne·o) *n.m.* wag; wagging.
menester (me·nes'ter) *n.m.* **1,** need. **2,** task; chore. —**menesteroso,** *adj.* needy. —**es menester,** it is necessary.
menestra (me'nes·tra) *n.f.* **1,** vegetable stew. **2,** *pl.* dried vegetables.
mengua ('men·gwa) *n.f.* **1,** diminution; decrease; wane. **2,** want; lack. **3,** poverty; indigence. **4,** discredit.
menguante (men'ɣwan·te) *adj.* waning; decreasing. —*n.f.* wane.
menguar (men'ɣwar) *v.t.* & *i.* to decrease; wane. —**menguado,** *adj.* cowardly. —*n.m.* coward.
menhir (men'ir) *n.m.* menhir.
meningitis (me·nin'xi·tis) *n.f.* meningitis.
menjunje (men'xun·xe) *n.m.* = **mejunje.**
menopausia (me·no'pau·sja) *n.f.* menopause.
menor (me'nor) *adj.* **A** *comp. of* **pequeño, 1,** smaller. **2,** younger. **3,** *music* minor. **B** *superl. of* **pequeño, 1,** smallest. **2,** youngest. —*n.m.* & *f.* minor. —*n.f., logic* minor premise; minor term. —**me-**

nor de edad, under age. —**por menor; al por menor,** retail.
menos ('me·nos) *adv.* **1,** less. **2,** least. **3,** except. **4,** minus. **5,** *in expressions of time* to, before: *las dos menos cuarto,* a quarter to *or* before two. —**al menos; a lo menos,** at least. —**a menos que,** unless. —**de menos,** lacking; less. —**echar de menos,** to miss. —**menos de,** less than (*fol. by a number or expression of quantity*). —**menos que,** less than (*fol. by the second term of a comparison*). —**no poder menos de** *or* **que,** to be unable to do other than: *No pude menos que hacerlo,* I could not help doing it. —**por lo menos,** at least. —**por menos que,** however little. —**sin más ni menos** = **sin más ni más.** —**tener a** *or* **en menos,** to belittle; scorn. —**venir a menos,** to decline.
menoría (me·no'ri·a) *n.f.* **1,** inferiority. **2,** minority; condition of a minor or underage person.
menoscabar (me·nos·ka'βar) *v.t.* **1,** to reduce; diminish. **2,** to impair. **3,** to discredit; disparage.
menoscabo (me·nos'ka·βo) *n.m.* **1,** diminution. **2,** impairment. **3,** disparagement.
menospreciar (me·nos·pre'θjar; -'sjar) *v.t.* **1,** to underrate; undervalue. **2,** to belittle; scorn.
menosprecio (me·nos'pre·θjo; -sjo) *n.m.* **1,** undervaluation; underestimation. **2,** scorn.
mensaje (men'sa·xe) *n.m.* **1,** message. **2,** errand. —**mensajero,** *n.m.* messenger.
menstruar (mens'trwar) *v.t.* [*infl.*: **continuar**] to menstruate. —**menstruación,** *n.f.* menstruation. —**menstrual,** *adj.* menstrual.
menstruo ('mens·trwo) *adj.* menstrual. —*n.m.* **1,** menstruation. **2,** menstrual fluid.
mensual (men'swal) *adj.* monthly. —**mensualidad,** *n.f.* monthly salary; monthly payment.
mensurable (men·su'ra·βle) *adj.* measurable; mensurable.
menta ('men·ta) *n.f.* mint.
mentado (men'ta·ðo) *adj.* noted; famous.
mental (men'tal) *adj.* mental. —**mentalidad,** *n.f.* mentality.
mentar (men'tar) *v.t.* [*pres.ind.* **miento;** *pres.subjve.* **miente**] to mention; cite.
mente ('men·te) *n.f.* mind.
-mente ('men·te) *suffix* -ly; *forming adverbs: lentamente,* slowly.
mentecato (men·te'ka·to) *adj.* silly, stupid. —*n.m.* fool.
mentir (men'tir) *v.i.* [*infl.*: **sentir**] to lie; speak falsely.
mentira (men'ti·ra) *n.f.* lie; falsehood. —**mentira oficiosa,** white lie.
mentiroso (men·ti'ro·so) *adj.* lying; false.
mentirijillas (men·ti·ri'xi·ʎas; -jas) *n.f.pl., in* **de mentirijillas,** make-believe.
mentís (men'tis) *n.m.* flat denial. —**dar el mentís a,** give the lie to.
-mento ('men·to) *suffix* -ment; *forming nouns denoting* action; result: *armamento,* armament.
mentol (men'tol) *n.m.* menthol. —**mentolado,** *adj.* mentholated.
mentón (men'ton) *n.m.* chin.
mentor (men'tor) *n.m.* mentor.
menú (me'nu) *n.m.* menu.
menudear (me·nu·de'ar) *v.i.* **1,** to be frequent; occur often. **2,** to enumerate details or trifles. **3,** to fall abundantly, as rain. —*v.t., colloq.* to repeat; do often.
menudencia (me·nu'ðen·θja; -sja) *n.f.* **1,** smallness; minuteness. **2,** trifle; detail. —**menudencias,** *n.f.pl.* minutiae.
menudeo (me·nu'ðe·o) *n.m.* **1,** frequent occurrence. **2,** detailed account. **3,** retail. —**al menudeo,** at retail.
menudillos (me·nu'ði·ʎos; -jos) *n.m.pl.* giblets.
menudo (me'nu·ðo) *adj.* **1,** small; little; minute. **2,** petty; picayune. —*n.m.* loose change. —**a menudo,** often. —**por menudo,** minutely.
meñique (me'ɲi·ke) *n.m.* little finger.
meollo (me'o·ʎo; -jo) *n.m.* **1,** brain. **2,** marrow. **3,** essence.
mequetrefe (me·ke'tre·fe) *n.* coxcomb; busybody.
meramente (me·ra'men·te) *adv.* merely; solely.
mercachifle (mer·ka'tʃi·fle) *n.m.* **1,** peddler; hawker. **2,** *colloq.,* petty dealer; huckster.
mercader (mer·ka'ðer) *n.m.* merchant. —**mercadería,** *n.f.* merchandise.
mercado (mer'ka·ðo) *n.m.* **1,** market. **2,** marketing; shopping.
mercancía (mer·kan'θi·a; -'si·a) *n.f., usu.pl.* goods; merchandise.

—**tren mercancías** *or* **de mercancías,** freight train.
mercante (mer'kan·te) *adj.* & *n.m.* merchant.
mercantil (mer·kan'til) *adj.* mercantile. —**mercantilismo,** *n.m.* mercantilism.
mercar (mer'kar) *v.t.* [*pres.subjve.* **merque;** *pret.* **merqué**] to buy.
merced (mer'θed; -'sed) *n.f.* grace; mercy; favor. —**a merced de,** in the hands of; subject to the will of. —**merced a,** thanks to. —**vuestra merced,** your grace; your honor.
mercenario (mer·θe'na·rjo; mer·se-) *adj.* & *n.m.* mercenary.
mercería (mer·θe'ri·a; mer·se-) *n.f.* **1,** notions (*pl.*). **2,** notions store. **3,** haberdashery. —**mercero** (-'θe·ro; -'se·ro) *n.m.* mercer.
mercerizar (mer·θe·ri'θar; -se·ri'sar) *v.t.* [*infl.*: **realizar**] to mercerize.
mercurial (mer·ku'rjal) *adj.* **1,** pert. to mercury or the god Mercury. **2,** [*also,* **mercúrico** (-'ku·ri·ko)] mercuric; mercury (*attrib.*).
mercurio (mer'ku·rjo) *n.m.* **1,** mercury. **2,** *cap.* Mercury.
mercurocromo (mer·ku·ro'kro·mo) *n.m.* mercurochrome.
merecer (me·re'θer; -'ser) *v.t.* [*pres.ind.* **merezco** (-'reθ·ko; -'res·ko); *pres.subjve.* **merezca** (-ka)] **1,** to merit; deserve. **2,** to be worth; be worthy of. —*v.i.* to be worthy *or* deserving. —**merecimiento,** *n.m.* merit. —**merecedor,** *adj.* deserving; worthy. —**merecido,** *n.m.* (just) deserts (*pl.*).
merendar (me·ren'dar) *v.i.* [*pres. ind.* **meriendo** (-'rjen·do); *pres. subjve.* **meriende** (-de)] **1,** to have an afternoon snack *or* tea. **2,** to picnic. —*v.t.* to have as an afternoon snack.
merendero (me·ren'de·ro) *n.m.* **1,** patio restaurant. **2,** picnic stand.
merengue (me'ren·ge) *n.m.* **1,** meringue. **2,** merengue.
meretricio (me·re'tri·θjo; -sjo) *adj.* meretricious.
meretriz (me·re'triθ; -'tris) *n.f.* prostitute.
mergo ('mer·ɣo) *n.m.* merganser. *Also,* **mergánsar** (-'ɣan·sar).
meridiano (me·ri'ðja·no) *adj.* **1,** meridional. **2,** noon. —*n.m.* meridian. —**meridional,** *adj.* southern.
merienda (me'rjen·da) *n.f.* **1,** afternoon snack *or* tea. **2,** picnic.
merino (me'ri·no) *adj.* & *n.m.* merino.
mérito ('me·ri·to) *n.m.* **1,** merit; worth. **2,** excellence. —**meritorio,** *adj.* worthy; meritorious. —*n.m.* unpaid trainee.
merla ('mer·la) *n.f.* blackbird; merle. *Also,* **mirlo.**
merlín (mer'lin) *n.m.* marline.
merluza (mer'lu·θa; —sa) *n.f.* **1,** hake. **2,** haddock. **3,** *colloq.* drunkenness.
merma ('mer·ma) *n.f.* **1,** diminution; decrease. **2,** *comm.* leakage.
mermar (mer'mar) *v.i.* to diminish; decrease. —*v.t.* to reduce.
mermelada (mer·me'la·ða) *n.f.* marmalade.
mero ('me·ro) *adj.* **1,** pure; simple; mere. **2,** *Mex.* very; self. —*n.m.* jewfish.
merodeador (me·ro·ðe·a'ðor) *adj.* **1,** foraging. **2,** marauding. —*n.m.* **1,** forager. **2,** marauder.
merodear (me·ro·ðe'ar) *v.i.* **1,** to forage. **2,** to maraud.
merodeo (me·ro'ðe·o) *n.m.* **1,** foraging. **2,** marauding.
merque ('mer·ke) *v., pres.subjve. of* **mercar.**
merqué (mer'ke) *v., 1st pers.sing. pret. of* **mercar.**
mes (mes) *n.m.* **1,** month. **2,** monthly pay *or* payment. **3,** *colloq.* menstruation. —**mesada,** *n.f.* monthly pay. —**meses mayores,** last months of pregnancy.
mesa ('me·sa) *n.f.* **1,** table. **2,** desk; bureau. **3,** counter. **4,** executive board. **5,** = **meseta.** —**a mesa puesta,** *colloq.* without trouble or expense. —**hacer mesa limpia,** *colloq.* to make a clean sweep. —**mesa revuelta,** *colloq.* topsy-turvy.
mesana (me'sa·na) *n.f.* mizzen. —**palo de mesana,** mizzenmast.
mesar (me'sar) *v.t., usu.refl.* **mesarse,** to tear out (one's hair).
mescolanza (mes·ko'lan·θa; -sa) *n.f.* mixture; medley.
mesero (me'se·ro) *n.m.* **1,** worker paid by the month. **2,** *Mex.* waiter.
meseta (me'se·ta) *n.f.* **1,** tableland; plateau. **2,** stair landing.
Mesías (me'si·as) *n.m.* Messiah. —**mesiánico** (-'sja·ni·ko) *adj.* Messianic.
mesmerismo (mes·me'ris·mo) *n.m.* mesmerism. —**mesmeriano** (-'rja·no) *adj.* mesmeric.

mesnada (mes'na·ða) *n.f.* 1, retinue. 2, band; troupe. —**mesnadero,** *n.m.* retainer; follower.
meso- (me·so) *prefix* meso-; middle: *mesocarpio,* mesocarp.
mesón (me'son) *n.m.* 1, inn; tavern. 2, meson. —**mesonero,** *n.m.* innkeeper; tavernkeeper.
mesotrón (me·so'tron) *n.m.* mesotron.
mesozoico (me·so'θoi·ko; -'soi·ko) *adj.* Mesozoic.
mestizo (mes'ti·θo; -so) *adj.* & *n.m.* mestizo.
mesurar (me·su'rar) *v.t.* to temper; moderate. —**mesurarse,** *v.r.* to control oneself.
meta ('me·ta) *n.f.* 1, end; limit. 2, goal. 3, *sports* finish line.
meta- (me·ta) *prefix* meta-. 1, along with; after; over; in or of the middle: *metacentro,* metacenter: *metafísica,* metaphysics. 2, change; transformation: *metátesis,* metathesis.
metabolismo (me·ta·βo'lis·mo) *n.m.* metabolism. —**metabólico** (-'βo·li·ko) *adj.* metabolic.
metacarpo (me·ta'kar·po) *n.m.* metacarpus. —**metacarpiano** (-'pja·no) *adj.* metacarpal.
metafísica (me·ta'fi·si·ka) *n.f.* metaphysics. —**metafísico,** *adj.* metaphysical. —*n.m.* metaphysician.
metáfora (me'ta·fo·ra) *n.f.* metaphor. —**metafórico** (-'fo·ri·ko) *adj.* metaphoric.
metal (me'tal) *n.m.* 1, metal. 2, tone or timbre of the voice. —**metal blanco,** nickel silver.
metálico (me'ta·li·ko) *adj.* metallic. —*n.m.* coin; specie.
metalífero (me·ta'li·fe·ro) *adj.* metalliferous.
metalizarse (me·ta·li'θar·se; -'sar·se) *v.r.* [*pres.subjve.* **metalice** (-'li·θe; -se); *pret.* **metalicé** (-'θe; -'se)] to be dominated by love of money.
metaloide (me·ta'loi·ðe) *adj.* & *n.m.* metalloid.
metalurgia (me·ta'lur·xja) *n.f.* metallurgy. —**metalúrgico** (-'lur·xi·ko) *adj.* metallurgic. —*n.m.* metallurgist.
metamorfosis (me·ta·mor'fo·sis) *also,* **metamórfosis** (-'mor·fo·sis) *n.f.sing.* & *pl.* metamorphosis. —**metamórfico** (-'mor·fi·ko) *adj.* metamorphic. —**metamorfosear** (-se'ar) *v.t.* to metamorphose.
metano (me'ta·no) *n.m.* methane.
metaplasma (me·ta'plas·ma) *n.m.* metaplasm.
metástasis (me'tas·ta·sis) *n.f.* metastasis. —**metastático** (-'ta·ti·ko) *adj.* metastatic.
metatarso (me·ta'tar·so) *n.m.* metatarsus. —**metatarsiano** (-'sja·no) *adj.* metatarsal.
metazoario (me·ta·θo'a·rjo; -so·'a·rjo) *adj.* & *n.m.* Metazoan.
metazoo (me·ta'θo·o; -'so·o) *adj.* & *n.m.* Metazoan. —**metazoos,** *n.m.pl.* Metazoa.
metempsicosis (me·tem·psi'ko·sis) *also,* **metempsícosis** (-'psi·ko·sis) *n.f.sing.* & *pl.* metempsychosis.
meteorito (me·te·o'ri·to) *n.m.* meteorite.
meteoro (me·te'o·ro) *n.m.* meteor. —**meteórico,** *adj.* meteoric.
meteorología (me·te·o·ro·lo'xi·a) *n.f.* meteorology. —**meteorológico** (-'lo·xi·ko) *adj.* meteorological. —**meteorologista** (-'xis·ta) *n.m.* & *f.,* *also,* **meteorólogo** (-'ro·lo·ɣo) *n.m.* meteorologist.
meter (me'ter) *v.t.* 1, to put in; insert. 2, to bring in; introduce. 3, to raise; stir up; produce. 4, to invest; stake. 5, to put forth; utter. —**meterse,** *v.r.* 1, to interfere; meddle. 2, to become involved. —**meterse con,** *colloq.* to pick a quarrel with.
meticuloso (me·ti·ku'lo·so) *adj.* meticulous. —**meticulosidad,** *n.f.* meticulousness.
metido (me'ti·ðo) *adj.* 1, *fol. by* **en,** profuse in; abounding in. 2, *Amer.* meddlesome. —*n.m., Amer.* meddler.
metileno (me·ti'le·no) *n.m.* methylene.
metilo (me'ti·lo) *n.m.* methyl. —**metílico,** *adj.* methylic. —**alcohol metílico,** methyl alcohol.
metodista (me·to'ðis·ta) *adj.* & *n.m.* & *f.* Methodist. —**metodismo,** *n.m.* Methodism.
método ('me·to·ðo) *n.m.* method. —**metódico** (-'to·ði·ko) *adj.* methodical.
metraje (me'tra·xe) *n.m., motion pictures* length; footage.
metralla (me'tra·ʎa; -ja) *n.f.* grapeshot.

-metría (me'tri·a) *suffix* -metry; measurement: *antropometría,* anthropometry.
métrica ('me·tri·ka) *n.f.* metrics.
métrico ('me·tri·ko) *adj.* **1,** metric. **2,** metrical.
metro ('me·tro) *n.m.* **1,** meter. **2,** = **metropolitano.**
metro- (me·tro) *prefix* metro-. **1,** measure: *metrología,* metrology. **2,** womb; uterus; mother: *metrorragia,* metrorrhagia; *metrópolis,* metropolis.
-metro (me·tro) *suffix* -meter. **1,** measure: *termómetro,* thermometer, **2,** units in the metric system: *kilómetro,* kilometer. **3,** *poetry,* having a specified number of feet: *hexámetro,* hexameter.
metrónomo (me'tro·no·mo) *n.m.* metronome.
metrópoli (me'tro·po·li) *n.f.* metropolis. **—metropolitano** (-'ta·no) *adj.* & *n.m.* metropolitan. **—***n.m.* [*also,* **metro**] city transit system; subway.
mexicano (me·xi'ka·no) *adj.* & *n.m., Amer.* = **mejicano.**
meza ('me·θa; -sa) *v., pres.subjve. of* **mecer.**
mezcal (meθ'kal; mes-) *n.m.* mescal.
mezcla ('meθ·kla; 'mes-) *n.f.* mixture; mix; mixing.
mezcladora (meθ·kla'ðo·ra; mes-) *n.f.* mixing machine; mixer.
mezcladura (meθ·kla'ðu·ra; mes-) *n.f.* = **mezcla.**
mezclamiento (meθ·kla'mjen·to; mes-) *n.m.* = **mezcla.**
mezclar (meθ'klar; mes-) *v.t.* to mix. **—mezclarse,** *v.r.* to mingle.
mezcolanza (meθ·ko'lan·θa; mes·ko'lan·sa) *n.f.* mixture; hodgepodge; medley.
mezo ('me·θo; -so) *v., 1st pers. sing. pret. of* **mecer.**
mezquindad (meθ·kin'dað; mes-) *n.f.* **1,** miserliness. **2,** smallness; pettiness; meanness. **3,** meagerness. **4,** wretchedness; poverty.
mezquino (meθ'ki·no; mes-) *adj.* **1,** miserly. **2,** small; petty; mean. **3,** meager. **4,** wretched; poor.
mezquita (meθ'ki·ta; mes-) *n.f.* mosque.
mezquite (meθ'ki·te; mes-) *n.m.* mesquite.
mezzo-soprano (me·so·so'pra·no) *n.f.* mezzo-soprano.
mi (mi) *poss.adj. masc.* & *fem.sing.* [*m.* & *f.pl.* **mis**], *agreeing in number with the thing possessed* my.
mi (mi) *n.m., music* mi; E.
mí (mi) *pers.pron. 1st pers.sing., used after a prep.* me; myself.
mía ('mi·a) *poss.pron. fem.sing.* mine. **—***poss.adj.f.sing., used after a noun* my; mine; of mine.
mías ('mi·as) *poss.pron. fem.pl.* mine. **—***poss.adj fem.pl. used after a noun* my; mine; of mine.
miasma ('mjas·ma) *n.m.* miasma. **—miasmático** (-'ma·ti·ko) *adj.* miasmal; miasmatic.
miau (mjau) *n.m.* meow.
mica ('mi·ka) *n.f.* mica.
micado (mi'ka·ðo) *n.m.* mikado.
micción (mik'θjon; -'sjon) *n.f.* urination.
mico- (mi·ko) *prefix* myco-; fungus· *micología,* mycology.
micra ('mi·kra) *n.f.* micron.
micro- (mi·kro) *prefix* micro-; very small: *microcosmo,* microcosm.
microbio (mi'kro·βjo) *n.m.* microbe. **—micróbico** (-βi·ko) *adj.* microbic.
microcosmo (mi·kro'kos·mo) *n.m.* microcosm.
microfilm (mi·kro'film) *n.m.* microfilm.
micrófono (mi'kro·fo·no) *n.m.* microphone.
microfotografía (mi·kro·fo·to·ɣra'fi·a) *n.f.* **1,** microphotography. **2,** microphotograph.
micrómetro (mi'kro·me·tro) *n.m.* micrometer.
micrón (mi'kron) *n.m.* micron.
micronesio (mi·kro'ne·sjo) *adj.* & *n.m.* Micronesian.
microorganismo (mi·kro·or·ɣa'nis·mo) *n.m.* microörganism.
microscopio (mi·kros'ko·pjo) *n.m.* microscope. **—microscópico** (-'ko·pi·ko) *adj.* microscopic.
micrótomo (mi'kro·to·mo) *n.m.* microtome.
mida ('mi·ða) *v., pres.subjve. of* **medir.**
midiendo (mi'ðjen·do) *v., ger. of* **medir.**
midió (mi'ðjo) *v., 3rd pers.sing. pret. of* **medir.**
mido ('mi·ðo) *v., pres.ind. of* **medir.**
miedo ('mje·ðo) *n.m.* fear. **—miedoso,** *adj.* scary; fearful; afraid. **—miedo cerval,** animal fear; dreadful fear.

miel (mjel) *n.f.* honey. —**miel de caña,** molasses; sugar cane juice.
miembro ('mjem·bro) *n.m.* **1,** member. **2,** limb.
mienta ('mjen·ta) *v., pres.subjve. of* **mentir.**
miente ('mjen·te) *n.f., usu.pl.* mind; thought. —**parar** *or* **poner mientes en,** to consider; pay attention to. —**traer a las mientes,** to recall; bring to mind.
miente ('mjen·te) *v., pres.subjve. of* **mentar.**
miento ('mjen·to) *v., pres.ind. of* **mentir** *and* **mentar.**
-miento ('mjen·to) *suffix* -ment; *forming nouns denoting* action; result of action: *lanzamiento,* launching; *rompimiento,* breaking.
mientras ('mjen·tras) *conj.* while; as; whereas. —*prep.* during. —*adv.* meanwhile; in the meantime. —**mientras más,** the more. —**mientras menos,** the less. —**mientras que,** while; as; so long as. —**mientras tanto,** meanwhile; in the meantime.
miércoles ('mjer·ko·les) *n.m. sing. & pl.* Wednesday. —**miércoles de ceniza,** Ash Wednesday.
mierda ('mjer·ða) *n.f., vulg.* excrement; filth.
mies (mjes) *n.f.* **1,** ripe grain. **2,** harvest season. —**mieses,** *n.f.pl.* grainfields.
miga ('mi·ɣa) *n.f.* **1,** crumb. **2,** soft part of bread. **3,** *colloq.* substance; gist. —**hacer buenas (malas) migas,** to be on good (bad) terms.
migaja (mi'ɣa·xa) *n.f.* crumb.
migración (mi·ɣra'θjon: -'sjon) *n.f.* migration. —**migratorio** (-'to·rjo) *adj.* migratory.
mijo ('mi·xo) *n.m.* millet.
mil (mil) *adj.* & *n.m.* **1,** thousand. **2,** thousandth; one-thousandth. —**a las mil y quinientas,** at an unearthly hour. —**armar las mil y quinientas,** to raise a row. —**cantar las mil y quinientas, 1,** to give someone a dressing-down. **2,** to talk nonsense.
milagro (mi'la·ɣro) *n.m.* miracle. —**milagroso,** *adj.* miraculous.
milano (mi'la·no) *n.m. ornith.* kite.
mile- (mi·le) *prefix* mille-; thousand; *milépora,* millepore.
milenario (mi·le'na·rjo) *adj.* **1,** millenary. **2,** millennial. —*n.m.* millennium.
milenio (mi'le·njo) *n.m.* millennium.
milenrama (mil·en'ra·ma) *n.f.* yarrow.
milésimo (mi'le·si·mo) *adj.* & *n.m.* thousandth. —**milésima,** *n.f.* thousandth part.
milhojas (mil'o·xas) *n.f.sing. & pl.* yarrow.
mili- (mi·li) *prefix* milli-; thousandth part: *milímetro,* millimeter.
miliar (mi'ljar) *adj.* miliary. —**erupción miliar,** *n.f.* miliaria. —**poste miliar,** milepost; milestone.
milicia (mi'li·θja; -sja) *n.f.* militia. —**miliciano,** *n.m.* militiaman; armed civilian. —*adj.* militia (*attrib.*).
milico (mi'li·ko) *n.m., Amer., colloq.* **1,** rookie. **2,** cop; policeman. **3,** *derog.* soldier.
miligramo (mi·li'ɣra·mo) *n.m.* milligram.
mililitro (mi·li'li·tro) *n.m.* milliliter.
milímetro (mi'li·me·tro) *n.m.* millimeter.
militante (mi·li'tan·te) *adj.* militant. —*n.m.* active member.
militar (mi·li'tar) *adj.* military. —*n.m.* soldier; military man. —*v.i.* to be an active member; militate. —**militarismo,** *n.m.* militarism. —**militarista,** *n.m.* & *f.* militarist. —*adj.* militaristic.
militarizar (mi·li·ta·ri'θar; -'sar) *v.t.* [*pres.subjve.* **militarice** (-'ri·θe; -se); *pret.* **militaricé** (-'θe; -'se)] to militarize. —**militarización,** *n.f.* militarization.
milonga (mi'lon·ga) *n.f., Amer.* **1,** a South American dance and air. **2,** street dancing.
milpiés (mil'pjes) *n.m.sing. & pl.* millipede.
milla ('mi·ʎa; -ja) *n.f.* **1,** mile. **2,** nautical mile. —**millaje,** *n.m.* mileage.
millar (mi'ʎar; -'jar) *n.m.* a quantity of a thousand. —**millarada,** *n.f.* about a thousand.
millo ('mi·ʎo; -jo) *n.m.* = **mijo.**
millón (mi'ʎon; -'jon) *n.m.* million. —**millonada,** *n.f.* about a million.
millonario (mi·ʎo'na·rjo; mi·jo-) *n.m.* millionaire.
millonésimo (mi·ʎo'ne·si·mo; mi·jo-) *adj. & n.m.* millionth.
mimar (mi'mar) *v.t.* to pamper; pet.

mimbre ('mim·bre) *n.m.* osier. —**mimbrera** (-'bre·ra) *n.f.* osier (*plant*).

mimeógrafo (mi·me'o·ɣra·fo) *n.m.* mimeograph. —**mimeografiar** (-'fjar) *v.t.* [*infl.*: **fotografiar**] to mimeograph.

mimetismo (mi·me'tis·mo) *n.m., biol.* protective coloration; mimicry.

mímica ('mi·mi·ka) *n.f.* mimicry. —**mímico,** *adj.* mimic; imitative.

mimo ('mi·mo) *n.m.* **1,** mime. **2,** mimic. **3,** caress; pampering; petting. **4,** care; gentleness. —**mimoso,** *adj.* fastidious; delicate.

mimosa (mi'mo·sa) *n.f.* mimosa.

mina ('mi·na) *n.f.* **1,** mine. **2,** lead (*of a pencil*).

minador (mi·na'ðor) *n.m.* **1,** minelayer. **2,** demolition expert.

minar (mi'nar) *v.t.* **1,** to mine (*as for demolition*). **2,** to undermine.

minarete (mi·na're·te) *n.m.* minaret.

mineral (mi·ne'ral) *adj.* & *n.m.* mineral.

mineralogía (mi·ne·ra·lo'xi·a) *n.f.* mineralogy. —**mineralógico** (-'lo·xi·ko) *adj.* mineralogical. —**mineralogista,** *n.m.* & *f.* mineralogist.

minería (mi·ne'ri·a) *n.f.* mining.

minero (mi'ne·ro) *adj.* mining. —*n.m.* miner.

miniatura (mi·nja'tu·ra) *n.f.* miniature.

mínima ('mi·ni·ma) *n.f.* minim.

mínimo ('mi·ni·mo) *adj.* least; smallest. —*n.m.* minimum; least.

minimum ('mi·ni·mum) *n.m.* minimum.

minino (mi'ni·no) *n.m., colloq.* pussy cat.

ministerial (mi·nis·te'rjal) *adj.* **1,** ministerial. **2,** cabinet (*attrib.*).

ministerio (mi·nis'te·rjo) *n.m.* ministry.

ministrar (mi·nis'trar) *v.t.* & *i.* to minister. —*v.t.* **1,** to administer. **2,** to supply. —**ministrador,** *adj.* & *n.m.* ministrant. —**ministrante,** *adj.* & *n.m.* & *f.* ministrant. —*n.m.* & *f.* nurse; ward nurse.

ministril (mi·nis'tril) *n.m.* marshal (*law-enforcement officer*).

ministro (mi'nis·tro) *n.m.* minister.

minorar (mi·no'rar) *v.t.* = **aminorar.** —**minorativo,** *adj.* & *n.m.* laxative, esp. mild.

minoría (mi·no'ri·a) *n.f.* minority. —**minoridad,** *n.f.* minority (*of age*).

minorista (mi·no'ris·ta) *adj.* retail. —*n.m.* retailer.

mintiendo (min'tjen·do) *v., ger. of* **mentir.**

mintió (min'tjo) *v., 3rd pers.sing. pret. of* **mentir.**

minucia (mi'nu·θja; -sja) *n.f.* trifle; detail; *pl.* minutiae.

minucioso (mi·nu'θjo·so; -'sjo·so) *adj.* minute; detailed; thorough. —**minuciosidad,** *n.f.* minuteness of detail.

minué (mi'nwe) *n.m.* minuet.

minuendo (mi·nu'en·do) *n.m.* minuend.

minúsculo (mi'nus·ku·lo) *adj.* **1,** minute; tiny. **2,** minuscule. **3,** lower-case. —**minúscula,** *n.f.* lower-case letter.

minuta (mi'nu·ta) *n.f.* **1,** note; memorandum. **2,** rough draft. **3,** menu; bill of fare.

minutero (mi·nu'te·ro) *n.m.* minute hand (*of a timepiece*).

minuto (mi'nu·to) *adj.* = **diminuto.** —*n.m.* minute.

mío ('mi·o) *poss.pron. masc.sing.* [*fem.* **mía;** *pl.* **míos, mías**], *agreeing in number and gender with the thing or things possessed* mine. —*poss.adj., used after a noun* my; mine; of mine: *hermanos míos,* my brothers; brothers mine (*or* of mine).

mio- (mi·o) *prefix* myo-; muscle: *miocardio,* myocardium.

miopía (mi·o'pi·a) *n.f.* myopia; nearsightedness. —**miope** (mi'o·pe) *adj.* & *n.m.* myopic; nearsighted.

miosis (mi'o·sis) *n.f.* myosis. —**miótico** (-ti·ko) *adj.* myotic.

mira ('mi·ra) *n.f.* **1,** eyepiece; sight. **2,** aim; intent. **3,** leveling rod.

mirada (mi'ra·ða) *n.f.* glance; look.

mirador (mi·ra'ðor) *n.m.* **1,** lookout; watch tower. **2,** balcony; terrace. —*adj.* watching; looking.

miramiento (mi·ra'mjen·to) *n.m.* **1,** look; looking. **2,** consideration; regard. **3,** prudence; circumspection. **4,** misgiving; scruple.

mirar (mi'rar) *v.t.* **1,** to look at *or* upon; gaze at *or* upon; watch; observe. **2,** to regard; consider. —*v.i.* **1,** to look; gaze. **2,** to face; look (*in a certain direction*). —**mirarse en,** to look up to; follow the

example of. —**mirar por,** to look after; look out for.
miria- (mi·rja) *prefix* myria-. **1,** many: *miriápodo,* myriapod. **2,** ten thousand: *miriámetro,* myriameter.
miríada (mi'ri·a·ða) *n.f.* myriad.
mirilla (mi'ri·ʎa; -ja) *n.f.* peephole.
miriñaque (mi·ri'ɲa·ke) *n.m.* hoopskirt.
mirlo ('mir·lo) *n.m.* blackbird; merle.
mirón (mi'ron) *n.m.* **1,** looker-on; bystander. **2,** kibitzer.
mirra ('mi·rra) *n.f.* myrrh.
mirto ('mir·to) *n.m.* myrtle.
mis (mis) *poss.adj., pl. of* **mi** (*agreeing in number with the things possessed*) my.
misa ('mi·sa) *n.f.* Mass. —**misal,** *n.m.* missal. —**misa del gallo,** midnight Mass. —**misa mayor,** High Mass; principal Mass.
misantropía (mi·san·tro'pi·a) *n.f.* misanthropy. —**misantrópico** (-'tro·pi·ko) *adj.* misanthropic. —**misántropo** (-'san·tro·po) *n.m.* misanthrope.
miscelánea (mis·θe'la·ne·a; mi·se-) *n.f.* miscellany. —**misceláneo,** *adj.* miscellaneous.
miscible (mis'θi·βle; -'si·βle) *adj.* miscible. —**miscibilidad,** *n.f.* miscibility.
miserable (mi·se'ra·βle) *adj.* **1,** miserable; wretched. **2,** paltry. **3,** tightfisted; stingy. —*n.m.* **1,** wretch. **2,** tightwad; miser.
miseria (mi'se·rja) *n.f.* **1,** misery; wretchedness. **2,** stinginess; miserliness. **3,** paltry thing; paltry sum.
misericordia (mi·se·ri'kor·ðja) *n.f.* mercy; pity. —**misericordioso,** *adj.* compassionate; merciful.
mísero ('mi·se·ro) *adj.* = **miserable.**
misérrimo (mi'se·rri·mo) *adj., superl. of* **mísero.**
misión (mi'sjon) *n.f.* mission. —**misional,** *adj.* missionary.
misionario (mi·sjo'na·rjo) *n.m.* **1,** = **misionero. 2,** delegate; envoy.
misionero (mi·sjo'ne·ro) *n.m.* missionary.
misiva (mi'si·βa) *n.f.* missive; note.
mismísimo (mis'mi·si·mo) *adj. & pron., colloq., superl. of* **mismo,** very same.
mismo ('mis·mo) *adj.* same; self; very; selfsame. —*pron.* same; very same.
miso- (mi·so) *prefix* miso-; hatred; dislike: *misoginia,* mysogyny.
misogamia (mi·so'ɣa·mja) *n.f.* misogamy. —**misógamo** (-'so·ɣa·mo) *adj.* misogamous. —*n.m.* misogamist.
misoginia (mi·so'xi·nja) *n.f.* misogyny. —**misógino** (-'so·xi·no) *adj.* misogynous. —*n.m.* misogynist.
misterio (mis'te·rjo) *n.m.* mystery. —**misterioso,** *adj.* mysterious.
mística ('mis·ti·ka) *n.f.* **1,** mysticism. **2,** mystique.
místico ('mis·ti·ko) *adj.* & *n.m.* mystic. —*adj.* mystical. —**misticismo** (-'θis·mo; -'sis·mo) *n.m.* mysticism.
mitad (mi'tað) *n.f.* **1,** half. **2,** middle.
mítico ('mi·ti·ko) *adj.* mythical.
mitigar (mi·ti'ɣar) *v.t.* [*pres. subjve.* **mitigue** (-'ti·ɣe); *pret.* **mitigué** (-'ɣe)] to mitigate. —**mitigación,** *n.f.* mitigation.
mitin ('mi·tin) *n.m.* [*pl.* **mítines**] meeting; public assembly.
mito ('mi·to) *n.m.* myth.
mitología (mi·to·lo'xi·a) *n.f.* mythology. —**mitológico** (-'lo·xi·ko) *adj.* mythological.
mitón (mi'ton) *n.m.* mitt; mitten.
mitra ('mi·tra) *n.f.* **1,** miter (*bishop's headdress*). **2,** bishopric.
mixtificar (miks·ti·fi'kar) *v.t.* [*pres.subjve.* **mixtifique** (-'fi·ke); *pret.* **mixtifiqué** (-'ke)] to mystify. —**mixtificación,** *n.f.* mystification. —**mixtificador,** *adj.* mystifying.
mixto ('miks·to) *adj.* **1,** mixed; mingled. **2,** composite. —*n.m.* **1,** sulfur match. **2,** explosive.
mixtura (miks'tu·ra) *n.f.* mixture. —**mixturar,** *v.t.* to mix.
mnemotecnia (mne·mo'tek·nja) *n.f.* mnemonics. —**mnemotécnico** (-ni·ko) *adj.* mnemonic.
moaré (mo·a're) *n.f.* moire. *Also,* **muaré.**
mobiliario (mo·βi'lja·rjo) *adj., comm.* negotiable. —*n.m.* furniture; household goods.
moblaje (mo'βla·xe) *n.m.* furniture.
moca *also,* **moka** ('mo·ka) *n.f.* mocha.
mocasín (mo·ka'sin) *n.m.* moccasin.

mocear (mo·θe'ar; mo-se-) *v.i.* to sow wild oats.
mocedad (mo·θe'ðað; mo·se-) *n.f.* **1,** youth; boyhood. **2,** carefree living.
mocetón (mo·θe'ton; mo·se-) *n.m.* strapping youngster.
moción (mo'θjon; -'sjon) *n.f.* motion.
moco ('mo·ko) *n.m.* **1,** mucus. **2,** viscous substance. **3,** snuff (*of a candle*). **4,** candle drippings. —**moco del bauprés,** *naut.* martingale. —**moco de pavo, 1,** cockscomb. **2,** *colloq.* trifle.
mocoso (mo'ko·so) *adj.* **1,** snivelly. **2,** full of mucus. **3,** impudent; saucy. —*n.m.* brat; upstart youth.
mochar (mo'tʃar) *v.t.* **1,** to butt; strike with the head or horns. **2,** = **desmochar.** —**mochada,** *n.f.* butt; blow with the head or horns.
mochila (mo'tʃi·la) *n.f.* knapsack.
mocho ('mo·tʃo) *adj.* **1,** blunt; stub-pointed. **2,** cut short; cropped; lopped. **3,** stub-horned, as a bull. —*n.m.* butt; butt end; stub.
mochuelo (mo'tʃwe·lo) *n.m.* red owl. —**cargar con el mochuelo,** to get (*or* give) the worst part.
moda ('mo·ða) *n.f.* fashion; mode.
modal (mo'ðal) *adj.* modal. —**modales,** *n.m.pl.* manners.
modalidad (mo·ða·li'ðað) *n.f.* **1,** modality. **2,** *colloq.* manner; sort.
modelar (mo·ðe'lar) *v.t. & i.* to model. —**modelado,** *n.m.* modeling.
modelo (mo'ðe·lo) *n.m.* model; pattern; norm. —*n.m. & f.* artist's model; fashion model. —*adj. indecl.* model: *casa modelo,* model house.
moderar (mo·ðe'rar) *v.t.* to moderate; restrain. —**moderación,** *n.f.* moderation; temperance. —**moderado,** *adj.* moderate; restrained. —**moderador,** *n.m.* moderator.
modernizar (mo·ðer·ni'θar; -'sar) *v.t.* [*pres.subjve.* **modernice** (-'ni·θe; -se); *pret.* **modernicé** (-'θe; -'se)] to modernize. —**modernización,** *n.f.* modernization.
moderno (mo'ðer·no) *adj.* & *n.m.* modern. —**modernismo,** *n.m.* modernism. —**modernista,** *n.m.* & *f.* modernist. —*adj.* modernistic.
modesto (mo'ðes·to) *adj.* modest. —**modestia,** *n.f.* modesty.
módico ('mo·ði·ko) *adj.* **1,** frugal; sparing. **2,** moderate (*of prices*).
modificar (mo·ði·fi'kar) *v.t.* [*pres.subjve.* **modifique** (-'fi·ke); *pret.* **modifiqué** (-'ke)] to modify. —**modificación,** *n.f.* modification. —**modificador,** *n.m.* modifier. —*adj.* modifying.
modismo (mo'ðis·mo) *n.* idiom; idiomatic expression.
modista (mo'ðis·ta) *n.m. & f.* dressmaker; modiste.
modo ('mo·ðo) *n.m.* **1,** mode; manner. **2,** *gram.* mood. **3,** *music* mode. —**modoso,** *adj.* well-mannered; well-behaved. —**de modo que,** so; and so. —**de ningún modo,** by no means. —**de todos modos,** anyhow; at any rate. —**de un modo u otro,** somehow; in one way or another. —**en cierto modo,** to some extent.
modorra (mo'ðo·rra) *n.f.* drowsiness.
modular (mo·ðu'lar) *v.t. & i. to* modulate. —**modulación,** *n.f.* modulation. —**modulador,** *n.m.* modulator.
módulo ('mo·ðu·lo) *n.m.* **1,** module. **2,** *music* modulation. **3,** modulus. —**modular,** *adj.* modular.
mofa ('mo·fa) *n.f.* mockery; jeer. —**mofar,** *v.i.* [*also, refl.,* **mofarse**] to deride; mock.
mofiete (mo'fle·te) *n.m.* chubcheek. —**mofletudo,** *adj.* chubcheeked.
mogol (mo'ɣol) *n.m.* **1,** mogul. **2,** Mongol. —*adj.* [*also,* **mogólico**] Mongolian.
mogote (mo'ɣo·te) *n.* hummock.
mohín (mo'in) *n.m.* face; pout; grimace.
mohina (mo'i·na) *n.f.* displeasure.
mohino (mo'i·no) *adj.* crestfallen.
moho ('mo·o) *n.m.* **1,** rust. **2,** mildew; mold; must.
mohoso (mo'o·so) *adj.* **1,** rusty. **2,** mildewed; moldy; musty.
mojar (mo'xar) *v.t.* to wet; moisten. —*v.i., fig.* to be involved.
mojicón (mo·xi'kon) *n.m.* **1,** biscuit; bun. **2,** *colloq.* punch, esp. in the face.
mojiganga (mo·xi'ɣan·ga) *n.f.* **1,** grimace. **2,** horseplay; clowning.
mojigato (mo·xi'ɣa·to) *adj.* prudish. —*n.m.* prude. —**mojigatería,** *n.f.* prudery; prudishness.
mojón (mo'xon) *n.m.* **1,** landmark. **2,** heap. **3,** turd.
moka ('mo·ka) *n.f.* = **moca.**
molar (mo'lar) *adj.* & *n.m.* molar.

molde ('mol·de) *n.m.* **1,** mold; cast. **2,** model; example. **3,** *print.* form. **—de molde,** printed. **—venir de molde,** to come as a godsend.
moldear (mol·de'ar) *v.t.* to mold; cast. **—moldeado,** *n.m.* molding. **—moldeador,** *n.m.* molder.
moldura (mol'du·ra) *n.f.* molding.
mole ('mo·le) *adj.* soft. —*n.f.* mass; bulk. —*n.m., Mex.* fricassee of meat and chili.
molécula (mo'le·ku·la) *n.f.* molecule. **—molecular,** *adj.* molecular.
moler (mo'ler) *v.t.* [*pres.ind.* **muelo;** *pres.subjve.* **muela**] **1,** to grind; mill. **2,** to weary; wear out. **—moler a palos,** to beat up.
molestar (mo·les'tar) *v.t.* to molest; bother; disturb.
molestia (mo'les·tja) *n.f.* **1,** molestation. **2,** bother; trouble. **3,** discomfort. **4,** hardship.
molesto (mo'les·to) *adj.* **1,** annoying; bothersome. **2,** uncomfortable.
molibdeno (mo·liβ'ðe·no) *n.m.* molybdenum. **—molíbdico** (mo·'liβ·ði·ko) *adj.* molybdic.
molicie (mo'li·θje; -sje) *n.f.* **1,** softness. **2,** soft living.
molienda (mo'ljen·da) *n.f.* **1,** grinding; milling. **2,** grist. **3,** *fig.* weariness; fatigue.
molificar (mo·li·fi'kar) *v.t.* [*pres. subjve.* **molifique** (-'fi·ke); *pret.* **molifiqué** (-'ke)] to mollify; soften. **—molificación,** *n.f.* mollification. **—molificativo,** *adj.* mollifying.
molinete (mo·li'ne·te) *n.m.* **1,** windlass. **2,** pinwheel; windmill (*toy*). **3,** turnstile. **4,** exhaust fan. **5,** flourish (*with a sword, stick, etc.*).
molinillo (mo·li'ni·ʎo; -jo) *n.m.* **1,** hand mill. **2,** coffee grinder. **3,** pinwheel; windmill (*toy*).
molino (mo'li·no) *n.m.* mill. **—molinero,** *n.m.* miller. —*adj.* milling (*attrib.*).
molusco (mo'lus·ko) *n.m.* mollusk.
molla ('mo·ʎa; -ja) *n.f.* **1,** lean meat. **2,** soft part of bread. **3,** bulge of flesh.
molleja (mo'ʎe·xa; -'je·xa) *n.f.* **1,** gizzard. **2,** sweetbread.
mollera (mo'ʎe·ra; -'je·ra) *n.f.* **1,** crown of the head. **2,** *fig.* brains; intellect. **—cerrado de mollera,** *also,* **duro de mollera,** stubborn; dense.
mollete (mo'ʎe·te; -'je·te) *n.m.* muffin.
momento (mo'men·to) *n.m.* **1,** moment. **2,** momentum. **—momentáneo** (-'ta·ne·o) *adj.* momentary.
momia ('mo·mja) *n.f.* mummy.
momificar (mo·mi·fi'kar) *v.t.* [*pres.subjve.* **momifique** (-'fi·ke); *pret.* **momifiqué** (-'ke)] to mummify. **—momificación,** *n.f.* mummification.
mona ('mo·na) *n.f.* **1,** female monkey. **2,** *colloq.* drunkenness; hangover. —*adj., fem. of* **mono.**
monacal (mo·na'kal) *adj.* monastic.
monacato (mo·na'ka·to) *n.m.* monasticism.
monacillo (mo·na'θi·ʎo; -'si·jo) *n.m., colloq.* = **monaguillo.**
monada (mo'na·ða) *n.f.* **1,** grimace. **2,** *colloq.* monkeyshine. **3,** *colloq.* pretty child; charming girl.
mónada ('mo·na·ða) *n.f.* monad.
monaguillo (mo·na'ɣi·ʎo; -jo) *n.m.* acolyte; altar boy.
monarca (mo'nar·ka) *n.m.* monarch. **—monarquía** (-'ki·a) *n.f.* monarchy. **—monárquico** (-ki·ko) *adj.* monarchal. —*n.m.* monarchist. **—monarquismo** (-'kis·mo) *n.m.* monarchism.
monasterio (mo·nas'te·rjo) *n.m.* monastery.
monástico (mo'nas·ti·ko) *adj.* monastic.
monda ('mon·da) *n.f.* **1,** pruning. **2,** pruning season.
mondadientes (mon·da'ðjen·tes) *n.m.sing. & pl.* toothpick.
mondar (mon'dar) *v.t.* **1,** to prune. **2,** to hull; peel.
mondo ('mon·do) *adj.* clean; pure.
mondongo (mon'don·go) *n.m.* **1,** tripe. **2,** *colloq.* guts.
moneda (mo'ne·ða) *n.f.* **1,** money. **2,** coin. **—moneda de curso legal,** legal tender.
monedero (mo·ne'ðe·ro) *n.m.* **1,** coiner. **2,** money purse.
monería (mo·ne'ri·a) *n.f.* **1,** grimace. **2,** monkeyshine.
monetario (mo·ne'ta·rjo) *adj.* monetary.
monetizar (mo·ne·ti'θar; -'sar) *v.t.* [*pres.subjve.* **monetice** (-'ti·θe; -se); *pret.* **moneticé** (-'θe; -'se)] to monetize.
mongol (mon'gol) *adj. & n.m.* = **mogol. —mongólico,** *adj.* = **mogólico.**

-monia ('mo·nja) *suffix* -mony; *forming nouns denoting* quality; condition: *acrimonia*, acrimony.

monigote (mo·ni'ɣo·te) *n.m.* **1,** *colloq.* bumpkin. **2,** puppet.

-monio ('mo·njo) *suffix* -mony; *forming nouns denoting* quality; condition: *matrimonio*, matrimony.

monismo (mo'nis·mo) *n.m.* monism. —**monista,** *adj.* monistic. —*n.m.* monist.

monitor (mo·ni'tor) *n.m.* monitor; adviser.

monja ('mon·xa) *n.f.* nun.

monje ('mon·xe) *n.m.* monk.

monjil (mon'xil) *n.m.* widow's weeds. —*adj.* nunnish; nun's.

mono ('mo·no) *adj., colloq.* pretty; cute. —*n.m.* **1,** monkey. **2,** coveralls (*pl.*); jeans (*pl.*).

mono- (mo·no) *prefix* mono-; one; alone; single: *monoteísta*, monotheist.

monocromo (mo·no'kro·mo) *adj.* & *n.m.* monochrome. —**monocromático** (-'ma·ti·ko) *adj.* monochromatic.

monóculo (mo'no·ku·lo) *n.m.* monocle. —**monocular,** *adj.* monocular.

monogamia (mo·no'ɣa·mja) *n.f.* monogamy. —**monógamo** (mo'no·ɣa·mo) *adj.* monogamous. —*n.m.* monogamist.

monografía (mo·no·ɣra'fi·a) *n.f.* monograph. —**monográfico** (-'ɣra·fi·ko) *adj.* monographic.

monograma (mo·no'gra·ma) *n.m.* monogram.

monolito (mo·no'li·to) *n.m.* monolith. —**monolítico,** *adj.* monolithic.

monologar (mo·no·lo'ɣar) *v.i.* [*pres.subjve.* **monologue** (-'lo·ɣe); *pret.* **monologué** (-'ɣe)] to soliloquize.

monólogo (mo'no·lo·ɣo) *n.m.* monologue.

monomanía (mo·no·ma'ni·a) *n.f.* monomania. —**monomaníaco,** *adj.* & *n.m.* monomaniac.

monometalismo (mo·no·me·ta·'lis·mo) *n.m.* monometallism.

monomio (mo'no·mjo) *n.m.* monomial.

monopolio (mo·no'po·ljo) *n.m.* monopoly. —**monopolista** (-'lis·ta) *n.m.* & *f.* monopolist. —**monopolizar** (-li'θar; -li'sar) *v.t.* [*infl.:* **realizar**] to monopolize.

monosílabo (mo·no'si·la·βo) *n.m.* monosyllable. —**monosilábico** (-'la-βi·ko) *adj.* monosyllabic.

monoteísmo (mo·no·te'is·mo) *n.m.* monotheism. —**monoteísta,** *n.m.* & *f.* monotheist. —*adj.* monotheistic.

monotipia (mo·no'ti·pja) *n.f.* monotype. *Also,* **monotipo** (-po) *n.m.* & *f.*

monotonía (mo·no·to'ni·a) *n.f.* **1,** monotone. **2,** monotony.

monótono (mo'no·to·no) *adj.* monotonous.

monovalente (mo·no·βa'len·te) *adj.* monovalent.

monóxido (mo'nok·si·ðo) *n.m.* monoxide.

monseñor (mon·se'ɲor) *n.m.* monsignor.

monserga (mon'ser·ɣa) *n.f.* gibberish.

monstruo ('mons·trwo) *n.m.* monster. —*adj., colloq.* monstrous; extraordinary.

monstruoso (mons'trwo·so) *adj.* monstrous; extraordinary. —**monstruosidad,** *n.f.* monstrosity.

monta ('mon·ta) *n.f.* **1,** act of mounting. **2,** *mil.* signal or call to mount. **3,** sum; total; amount. **4,** value; worth. —**de poca monta,** of little account; insignificant.

montacargas (mon·ta'kar·ɣas) *n.m.* **1,** hoist; lift; cargo elevator. **2,** dumbwaiter.

montadura (mon·ta'ðu·ra) *n.f.* **1,** mounting. **2,** *jewelry* setting.

montaje (mon'ta·xe) *n.m.* **1,** mounting; assembly. **2,** *photog.* montage. **3,** *motion pictures* editing. **4,** *mech.* mount. —**montaje musical,** musical setting.

montante (mon'tan·te) *n.m.* **1,** broadsword. **2,** upright; post; strut. **3,** transom. **4,** sum; total; amount. —*n.f.* high *or* flood tide.

montaña (mon'ta·ɲa) *n.f.* **1,** mountain. **2,** highlands (*pl.*). —**montaña rusa,** roller coaster.

montañero (mon·ta'ɲe·ro) *n.m.* mountain climber. —*adj.* mountaineering (*attrib.*).

montañés (mon·ta'ɲes) *n.m.* mountain dweller; highlander. —*adj.* highland (*attrib.*).

montañismo (mon·ta'ɲis·mo) *n.m.* mountaineering.

montañoso (mon·ta'ɲo·so) *adj.* mountainous.

montar (mon'tar) *v.i.* **1,** to mount; to get on *or* in. **2,** to ride. —*v.t.*

1, to mount; set. 2, to ride (a horse). 3, to cock (a firearm). 4, to carry (*in a vehicle*). 5, to cover (*of animals*). —**montar en cólera**, to fly into a rage.
montaraz (mon·ta'raθ; -'ras) *adj.* 1, mountain bred. 2, wild; untamed. —*n.m.* forester; ranger.
monte ('mon·te) *n.m.* 1, mountain; mount. 2, monte (*card game*). 3, *fig.* obstruction. —**monte de piedad**, a pawnshop operated by a bank or the state.
montecillo (mon·te'θi·ʎo; -'si·jo) *n.m.* hillock; mound; knoll.
montepío (mon·te'pi·o) *n.m.* 1, pension fund. 2, emergency fund.
montera (mon'te·ra) *n.f.* bullfighter's cap.
montería (mon·te'ri·a) *n.f.* hunting; hunt. —**montero**, *n.m.* hunter; beater.
montículo (mon'ti·ku·lo) *n.m.* mound.
monto ('mon·to) *n.m.* sum; total.
montón (mon'ton) *n.m.* heap; pile; mass.
montonera (mon·to'ne·ra) *n.f.* guerrilla band. —**montonero**, *n.m.* guerrilla fighter.
montuoso (mon'two·so) *adj.* hilly.
montura (mon'tu·ra) *n.f.* 1, mount (*animal*). 2, harness; saddle. 3, mounting. 4, *jewelry* setting.
monumento (mo·nu'men·to) *n.m.* monument. —**monumental**, *adj.* monumental.
monzón (mon'θon; -'son) *n.m.* monsoon.
moño ('mo·ɲo) *n.m.* chignon; topknot.
moquillo (mo'ki·ʎo; -jo) *n.m.*, *vet.med.* distemper.
mora ('mo·ra) *n.f.* 1, blackberry. 2, mulberry.
morada (mo'ra·ða) *n.f.* abode.
morado (mo'ra·ðo) *adj.* & *n.m.* purple.
morador (mo·ra'ðor) *adj.* dwelling; residing. —*n.m.* dweller; resident.
moral (mo'ral) *adj.* moral. —*n.m.* black mulberry tree. —*n.f.* 1, ethics; morals. 2, morale.
moraleja (mo·ra'le·xa) *n.f.* moral (*of a story*).
moralidad (mo·ra·li'ðað) *n.f.* morality.
moralista (mo·ra'lis·ta) *n.m.* & *f.* moralist.
moralizar (mo·ra·li'θar; -'sar) *v.t.* & *i.* [*pres.subjve.* **moralice** (-'li·θe; -se); *pret.* **moralicé** (-'θe; -'se)] to moralize.
morar (mo'rar) *v.i.* to dwell.
moratoria (mo·ra'to·rja) *n.f.* moratorium. —**moratorio**, *adj.* moratory.
morbidez (mor·βi'ðeθ; -'ðes) *n.f.* 1, morbidity. 2, *fig.* lusciousness.
mórbido ('mor·βi·ðo) *adj.* 1, morbid; diseased. 2, *fig.* luscious; inviting.
morbo ('mor·βo) *n.m.* disease. —**morboso**, *adj.* morbid. —**morbosidad**, *n.f.* morbidity.
morcilla (mor'θi·ʎa; -'si·ja) *n.f.* 1, blood pudding. 2, *theat.* ad lib. 3, *colloq.* long-winded speech.
mordaz (mor'ðaθ; -'ðas) *adj.* 1, corrosive. 2, sarcastic; pungent. —**mordacidad**, *n.f.* sarcasm; pungency.
mordaza (mor'ða·θa; -sa) *n.f.* gag; muzzle.
mordedor (mor·ðe'ðor) *adj.* 1, biting; snapping. 2, sarcastic. —*n.m.* 1, biter; snapper. 2, carper; harsh critic.
mordelón (mor·ðe'lon) *adj.*, *Amer.* biting; given to biting. —*n.m.*, *Amer.* 1, biter; snapper. 2, grafter.
morder (mor'ðer) *v.t.* [*pres.ind.* **muerdo**; *pres.subjve.* **muerda**] 1, to bite. 2, to gnaw. 3, to corrode. —**mordedura**, *n.f.* bite.
mordida (mor'ði·ða) *n.f.*, *Amer.* 1, bite; snap. 2, graft; bribe.
mordiente (mor'ðjen·te) *also*, **mordente** (-'ðen·te) *adj.* & *n.m.* mordant.
mordiscar (mor·ðis'kar) *v.t.* [*pres.subjve.* **mordisque** (-'ðis·ke); *pret.* **mordisqué** (-'ke)] to nibble.
mordisco (mor'ðis·ko) *n.m.* bite.
morena (mo're·na) *n.f.* 1, moraine. 2, moray. 3, brunette.
moreno (mo're·no) *adj.* 1, brown; swarthy. 2, brunette. 3, *Amer.*, *colloq.* negro.
morera (mo're·ra) *n.f.* white mulberry tree.
moretón (mo·re'ton) *n.m.* livid bruise.
-mórfico ('mor·fi·ko) *suffix* -morphic; *forming adjectives denoting* likeness in form or appearance: *antropomórfico*, anthropomorphic.
morfina (mor'fi·na) *n.f.* morphine. —**morfinómano** (-'no·ma·

no) *n.m.* morphine addict; drug addict.
-morfismo (mor'fis·mo) *suffix* -morphism; *forming nouns corresponding to adjectives ending in* **-mórfico**: *antropomorfismo,* anthropomorphism.
morfo- (mor·fo) *prefix* morpho-; morph-; form: *morfología,* morphology.
-morfo ('mor·fo) *suffix* **1,** -morph; *forming nouns denoting* form; appearance: *isomorfo,* isomorph. **2,** -morphous; *forming adjectives denoting* likeness in form or appearance: *antropomorfo,* anthropomorphous.
morfología (mor·fo·lo'xi·a) *n.f.* morphology. —**morfológico** (-'lo·xi·ko) *adj.* morphological.
morfosis (mor'fo·sis) *n.f.* morphosis.
morganático (mor·ɣa'na·ti·ko) *adj.* morganatic.
morgue ('mor·ɣe) *n.f.* morgue.
moribundo (mo·ri'βun·do) *adj.* dying; moribund.
morillo (mo'ri·ʎo; -jo) *n.m.* andiron.
morir (mo'rir) *v.i.* [*pres.ind.* **muero;** *pres.subjve.* **muera;** *pret.* **morí, murió;** *ger.* **muriendo;** *p.p.* **muerto**] **1,** to die. **2,** to end; come to an end. —*v.t., colloq., in compound tenses only* to kill. —**morirse,** *v.r.* to die. —**morirse por,** to yearn for.
morisco (mo'ris·ko) *adj.* Moorish. —*n.m.* Christianized Moor.
mormón (mor'mon) *adj.* & *n.m.* Mormon. —**mormonismo,** *n.m.* Mormonism.
moro ('mo·ro) *adj.* Moorish. —*n.m.* Moor.
moroso (mo'ro·so) *adj.* slow; tardy. —**morosidad,** *n.f.* slowness; tardiness.
morral (mo'rral) *n.m.* **1,** game bag. **2,** rustic.
morriña (mo'rri·ɲa) *n.f.* **1,** sadness; blues (*pl.*); homesickness. **2,** a parasitic disease of animals; rot.
morro ('mo·rro) *n.m.* **1,** snout. **2,** round hill or cliff. —**estar de morro** *or* **morros,** *colloq.* to be on the outs. —**poner morro,** *colloq.* to pout; grimace.
morsa ('mor·sa) *n.f.* walrus.
mortaja (mor'ta·xa) *n.f.* shroud.
mortal (mor'tal) *adj.* **1,** mortal. **2,** fatal; deadly. —*n.m.* mortal; man.
mortalidad (mor·ta·li'ðað) *n.f.* **1,** mortality. **2,** death rate.
mortandad (mor·tan'dað) *n.f.* **1,** mortality. **2,** massacre.
mortecino (mor·te'θi·no; -'si·no) *adj.* **1,** dying. **2,** pale; wan. —**hacer la mortecina,** *colloq.* to play dead.
mortero (mor'te·ro) *n.m.* **1,** mortar (*mixing vessel*). **2,** mortar (*cement*). **3,** mortar (*artillery weapon*). **4,** howitzer. —**mano de mortero,** pestle.
mortífero (mor'ti·fe·ro) *adj.* death-dealing; fatal.
mortificar (mor·ti·fi'kar) *v.t.* [*pres.subjve.* **mortifique** (-'fi·ke); *pret.* **mortifiqué** (-'ke)] **1,** to mortify. **2,** *Amer., colloq.* to bother; annoy. —**mortificación,** *n.f.* mortification.
mortuorio (mor'two·rjo) *adj.* mortuary; obituary. —*n.m.* funeral.
moruno (mo'ru·no) *adj.* Moorish.
mosaico (mo'sai·ko) *adj.* & *n.m.* mosaic.
mosca ('mos·ka) *n.f.* fly. —**aflojar** *or* **soltar la mosca,** *colloq.* to fork out; shell out. —**mosca muerta,** *colloq.* **1,** milquetoast. **2,** hypocrite. —**papar moscas,** *colloq.* to gape.
moscardón (mos·kar'ðon) *n.m.* **1,** bumblebee. **2,** horsefly. **3,** = **moscón.**
moscatel (mos·ka'tel) *adj.* & *n.m.* & *f.* muscat. —*n.m.* muscatel.
mosco ('mos·ko) *n.m.* **1,** gnat. **2,** any small fly.
moscón (mos'kon) *n.m., colloq.* hanger-on. *Also,* **moscardón.**
moscovita (mos·ko'βi·ta) *adj.* & *n.m.* & *f.* Muscovite.
mosqueado (mos·ke'a·ðo) *adj.* speckled; mottled.
mosquear (mos·ke'ar) *v.t., colloq.* **1,** to elude; give the slip to. **2,** to deceive; dupe. —*v.i., colloq.* to smell fishy; look suspicious. —**mosquearse,** *v.r., colloq.* to be suspicious or distrustful.
mosquete (mos'ke·te) *n.m.* musket. —**mosquetazo,** *n.m.* musket shot.
mosquetero (mos·ke'te·ro) *n.m.* musketeer. —**mosquetería,** *n.f.* musketry.
mosquito (mos'ki·to) *n.m.* **1,** mosquito. **2,** gnat. —**mosquitero,** *n.m.* mosquito net.
mostacho (mos'ta·tʃo) *n.m.* mustache.

mostaza (mos'ta·θa; -sa) *n.f.* mustard.
mosto ('mos·to) *n.m.* wine, esp. new wine.
mostrar (mos'trar) *v.t.* [*pres.ind.* **muestro;** *pres.subjve.* **muestre**] to show; point out; demonstrate. —**mostrarse,** *v.r.* to appear. —**mostrador,** *n.m.* showcase; counter.
mostrenco (mos'tren·ko) *adj.* **1,** homeless; vagrant. **2,** dull; stupid. —**bienes mostrencos,** ownerless goods.
mota ('mo·ta) *n.f.* **1,** mote; speck. **2,** slight defect. **3,** knoll. **4,** *Amer.* powder puff.
mote ('mo·te) *n.m.* **1,** motto. **2,** nickname.
motear (mo·te'ar) *v.t.* to speckle; mottle.
motejar (mo·te'xar) *v.t., usu.fol. by* **de,** to call; brand (as).
motel (mo'tel) *n.m.* motel.
motilidad (mo·ti·li'ðað) *n.f.* motility.
motín (mo'tin) *n.m.* mutiny; uprising.
motivar (mo·ti'βar) *v.t.* **1,** to motivate; cause. **2,** to justify; explain the reason for. —**motivación,** *n.f.* motivation.
motivo (mo'ti·βo) *adj.* motive; moving. —*n.m.* **1,** cause; reason; motive. **2,** motif.
motocicleta (mo·to·θi'kle·ta; -si'kle·ta) *n.f.* motorcycle.
motón (mo'ton) *n.m., naut.* block; pulley.
motoneta (mo·to'ne·ta) *n.f.* motor scooter.
motor (mo'tor) *n.m.* **1,** motor. **2,** mover. —*adj.* motor; motive; moving.
-motor (mo'tor) *suffix* -motor; -motive; *forming nouns and adjectives denoting* motion; propulsion: *vasomotor,* vasomotor; *locomotor,* locomotive.
motora (mo'to·ra) *n.f., also,* **lancha motora,** motorboat.
motorista (mo·to'ris·ta) *n.m. & f.* **1,** motorist. **2,** *Amer.* motorman.
motorizar (mo·to·ri'θar; -'sar) *v.t.* [*pres.subjve.* **motorice** (-'ri·θe; -se); *pret.* **motoricé** (-'θe; -'se)] to motorize.
motriz (mo'triθ; -'tris) *adj.* motor; motive; moving.
-motriz (mo'triθ; -'tris) *suffix* -motive; -motor; *forming adjectives denoting* motion; propulsion: *automotriz,* automotive; *locomotriz,* locomotor.
movedizo (mo·βe'ði·θo; -so) *adj.* **1,** moving; movable. **2,** easily moved; shaky; unsteady.
mover (mo'βer) *v.t.* [*pres.ind.* **muevo;** *pres.subjve.* **mueva**] **1,** to move. **2,** to persuade; induce.
movible (mo'βi·βle) *adj.* movable; mobile; motile.
móvil ('mo·βil) *adj.* movable; mobile; motile. —*n.m.* **1,** motive. **2,** moving body.
movilidad (mo·βi·li'ðað) *n.f.* **1,** mobility; motility. **2,** unsteadiness.
movilizar (mo·βi·li'θar; -'sar) *v.t.* [*pres.subjve.* **movilice** (-'li·θe; -se); *pret.* **movilicé** (-'θe; -'se)] to mobilize. —**movilización,** *n.f.* mobilization.
movimiento (mo·βi'mjen·to) *n.m.* **1,** movement; motion. **2,** agitation; activity. **3,** *comm.* lively trade.
moza ('mo·θa; -sa) *n.f.* **1,** girl; young woman. **2,** maid. **3,** mistress. —**moza de cámara,** chambermaid.
mozalbete (mo·θal'βe·te; mo·sal-) *n.m.* lad; boy.
mozo ('mo·θo; -so) *n.m.* **1,** young man. **2,** bachelor. **3,** waiter; porter. —*adj.* **1,** young. **2,** unmarried.
mozuelo (mo'θwe·lo; -'swe·lo) *n.m.* boy; lad. —**mozuela,** *n.f.* girl; lass.
muaré (mwa're) *n.f.* = **moaré.**
mucílago (mu'θi·la·ɣo; mu'si-) *n.m.* mucilage. —**mucilaginoso,** *adj.* mucilaginous.
muco- (mu·ko) *prefix* muco-; mucous membrane; mucus: *mucoproteína,* mucoprotein.
mucoso (mu'ko·so) *adj.* mucous. —**mucosa,** *n.f.* mucous membrane. —**mucosidad,** *n.f.* mucosity; mucus.
muchacha (mu'tʃa·tʃa) *n.f.* **1,** girl; lass; young woman. **2,** maid; servant. —*adj.* girlish.
muchachada (mu·tʃa'tʃa·ða) *n.f.* **1,** boyishness; boyish behavior. **2,** group of boys; boys collectively.
muchachez (mu·tʃa'tʃeθ; -'tʃes) *n.f.* childhood.
muchacho (mu'tʃa·tʃo) *n.m.* boy. —*adj.* boyish.
muchedumbre (mu·tʃe'ðum·bre) *n.f.* crowd; multitude; swarm.
muchísimo (mu'tʃi·si·mo) *adj. & adv., superl. of* **mucho.**
mucho ('mu·tʃo) *adj., adv. & pron.* **1,** much; very much; a great deal

(of); a lot (of). 2, *colloq.* too much; overmuch. —**muchos,** *adj.* & *pron.pl.* 1, many. 2, *colloq.* too many. —**con mucho,** by far. —**ni con mucho,** *also,* **ni mucho menos,** not by any means. —**por mucho que,** however much. —**tener a** *or* **en mucho,** to hold in high esteem.
muda ('mu·ða) *n.f.* 1, change. 2, molting; molting time.
mudable (mu'ða·βle) *adj.* changeable; mutable.
mudadizo (mu·ða'ði·θo; -so) *adj.* fickle; changeable.
mudanza (mu'ðan·θa; -sa) *n.f.* 1, change; changing. 2, moving; change of residence. 3, inconstancy; fickleness.
mudar (mu'ðar) *v.t.* 1, to change. 2, to move; change the position or location of. 3, to molt. —**mudarse,** *v.r.* 1, to change. 2, to move; change residence or location.
mudez (mu'deθ; -'ðes) *n.f.* 1, dumbness; muteness. 2, silence.
mudo ('mu·ðo) *adj.* 1, dumb; mute. 2, silent.
mueblaje (mwe'βla·xe) *n.m.* furniture.
mueble ('mwe·βle) *adj.* movable; mobile. —*n.m.* piece of furniture. —**bienes muebles,** liquid assets; chattels.
mueblería (mwe·βle'ri·a) *n.f.* furniture store. —**mueblista,** *n.m.* & *f.* furniture dealer.
mueca ('mwe·ka) *n.f.* grimace.
muecín (mu·e'θin; -'sin) *n.m.* muezzin.
muela ('mwe·la) *n.f.* 1, grindstone. 2, millstone. 3, molar. —**dolor de muelas,** toothache. —**muela del juicio,** wisdom tooth.
muela ('mwe·la) *v., pres.subjve. of* **moler.**
muelo ('mwe·lo) *v., pres.ind. of* **moler.**
muellaje (mwe'ʎa·xe; -'ja·xe) *n.m.* dockage; wharfage.
muelle ('mwe·ʎe; -je) *adj.* soft; comfortable. —*n.m.* 1, *mech.* spring. 2, pier; dock. —**muelle real,** mainspring.
muera ('mwe·ra) *v., pres.subjve. of* **morir.**
muerda ('mwer·ða) *v., pres. subjve. of* **morder.**
muérdago ('mwer·ða·ɣo) *n.m.* mistletoe.
muerdo ('mwer·ðo) *v., pres.ind. of* **morder.**
muero ('mwe·ro) *v., pres.ind. of* **morir.**
muerte ('mwer·te) *n.f.* 1, death. 2, ruin; destruction. —**de mala muerte,** poor; wretched.
muerto ('mwer·to) *v., pp. of* **morir.** —*adj.* dead. —*n.m.* 1, dead person; dead body. 2, *cards* dummy. —**echarle a uno el muerto,** to put the onus on someone.
muesca ('mwes·ka) *n.f.* 1, notch. 2, mortise.
muestra ('mwes·tra) *n.f.* 1, sample. 2, sign; token. 3, sign (*of a shop, inn, etc.*). 4, face (*of a watch or clock*). —**muestrario,** *n.m.* sample book; collection of samples.
muestre ('mwes·tre) *v., pres. subjve. of* **mostrar.**
muestro ('mwes·tro) *v., pres.ind. of* **mostrar.**
mueva ('mwe·βa) *v., pres.subjve. of* **mover.**
muevo ('mwe·βo) *v., pres.ind. of* **mover.**
mufti (muf'ti) *n.m.* mufti.
mugir (mu'xir) *v.i.* [*pres.ind.* **mujo;** *pres.subjve.* **muja**] to moo; low. —**mugido,** *n.m.* moo; low.
mugre ('mu·ɣre) *n.f.* dirt; grime. —**mugriento** (-'ɣrjen·to) *adj.* dirty; grimy.
muja ('mu·xa) *v., pres.subjve. of* **mugir.**
mujer (mu'xer) *n.f.* 1, woman. 2, wife.
mujercilla (mu·xer'θi·ʎa; -'si·ja) *n.f.* floozy.
mujeriego (mu·xe'rje·ɣo) *adj.* skirt-chasing. —*n.m.* skirt-chaser.
mujeril (mu·xe'ril) *adj.* feminine; womanly.
mujerzuela (mu·xer'θwe·la; -'swe·la) *n.f.* floozy.
mujo ('mu·xo) *v., pres.ind. of* **mugir.**
mújol ('mu·xol) *n.m.* mullet.
mula ('mu·la) *n.f.* mule; she-mule.
muladar (mu·la'ðar) *n.m.* trash heap; garbage dump.
mulato (mu'la·to) *adj.* & *n.m.* mulatto.
mulero (mu'le·ro) *n.m.* mule driver; muleteer.
muleta (mu'le·ta) *n.f.* 1, crutch. 2, red flag used by bullfighters.
muletilla (mu·le'ti·ʎa; -ja) *n.f.* 1, refrain; cliché. 2, = **muleta.**
mulo ('mu·lo) *n.m.* mule. —*adj.* stubborn; mulish.

multa ('mul·ta) *n.f.* fine; penalty. —**multar,** *v.t.* to fine.
multi- (mul·ti) *prefix* multi-; many: *multimillonario,* multimillionaire.
multicolor (mul·ti·ko'lor) *adj.* multicolored; motley.
multicopista (mul·ti·ko'pis·ta) *n.m.* duplicator; duplicating machine.
multiforme (mul·ti'for·me) *adj.* multiform.
multilátero (mul·ti'la·te·ro) *adj., geom.* multilateral. *Also, fig.,* **multilateral** (-'ral).
multimillonario (mul·ti·mi·ʎo·'na·rjo; -jo'na·rjo) *n.m.* & *adj.* multimillionaire.
multipartito (mul·ti·par'ti·to) *adj.* multipartite.
múltiple ('mul·ti·ple) *adj.* multiple.
multiplicar (mul·ti·pli'kar) *v.t.* [*pres.subjve.* **multiplique** (-'pli·ke); *pret.* **multipliqué** (-'ke)] to multiply. —**multiplicación,** *n.f.* multiplication. —**multiplicador,** *adj.* multiplying. —*n.m.* multiplier. —**multiplicando** (-'kan·do) *n.m.* multiplicand.
multiplicidad (mul·ti·pli·θi·'ðað; -si'ðað) *n.f.* multiplicity.
múltiplo ('mul·ti·plo) *n.m.* & *adj.* multiple.
multitud (mul·ti'tuð) *n.f.* multitude. —**multitudinario** (-ði'na·rjo) *adj.* multitudinous.
mullido (mul'ʎi·ðo; -'ji·ðo) *adj.* soft; fluffy. —*n.m.* **1,** fluff. **2,** straw bedding.
mullir (mu'ʎir; -'jir) *v.t.* to fluff.
mundanalidad (mun·da·na·li·'ðað) *n.f.* worldliness; mundaneness. *Also,* **mundanería** (-ne'ri·a).
mundano (mun'da·no) *adj.* worldly; mundane. *Also,* **mundanal.**
mundial (mun'djal) *adj.* worldwide; world (*attrib.*).
mundo ('mun·do) *n.m.* world; earth. —**todo el mundo,** everyone.
munición (mu·ni'θjon; -'sjon) *n.f.* **1,** *often pl.* munitions. **2,** charge; load (*of a firearm*). **3,** birdshot. —**municionar,** *v.t.* to munition.
municipal (mu·ni·θi'pal; -si'pal) *adj.* municipal. —*n.m.* city policeman. —**municipalidad,** *n.f.* = **municipio.**
municipio (mu·ni'θi·pjo; -'si·pjo) *n.m.* **1,** municipality; city; township. **2,** town hall; city hall.
munificencia (mu·ni·fi'θen·θja; -'sen·sja) *n.f.* munificence. —**munificente,** *adj.* = **munífico.**
munífico (mu'ni·fi·ko) *adj.* munificent.
muñeca (mu'ɲe·ka) *n.f.* **1,** wrist. **2,** doll. **3,** *colloq.* dressmaker's form; manikin.
muñeco (mu'ɲe·ko) *n.m.* puppet; doll; manikin; dummy.
muñón (mu'ɲon) *n.m.* stump (*esp. of an amputated limb*).
murajes (mu'ra·xes) *n.m.pl.* pimpernel (*sing.*).
mural (mu'ral) *adj.* mural.
muralla (mu'ra·ʎa; -ja) *n.f.* rampart; wall.
murciélago (mur'θje·la·ɣo; mur'sje-) *n.m., zool.* bat.
murga ('mur·ɣa) *n.f., colloq.* band of street musicians. —**dar murga a,** *colloq.* to bother; annoy.
muriendo (mu'rjen·do) *v., ger. of* **morir.**
murió (mu'rjo) *v., 3rd pers.sing. pret. of* **morir.**
murmullo (mur'mu·ʎo; -jo) *n.m.* murmur.
murmurar (mur·mu'rar) *v.i.* **1,** to murmur. **2,** to grumble. **3,** to gossip. —**murmuración,** *n.f.* backbiting; gossip. —**murmurador,** *n.m.* detractor; backbite. —**murmurio** (-'mu·rjo) *n.m.* murmur.
muro ('mu·ro) *n.m.* wall, esp. a thick or supporting wall.
murria ('mu·rrja) *n.f., colloq.* melancholy; blues (*pl.*).
musa ('mu·sa) *n.f.* Muse.
musaraña (mu·sa'ra·ɲa) *n.f.* shrew; shrewmouse. —**pensar en las musarañas,** *colloq.* to be absent-minded.
músculo ('mus·ku·lo) *n.m.* muscle. —**muscular,** *adj.* muscular. —**musculatura,** *n.f.* musculature. —**musculoso,** *adj.* muscular. —**musculosidad,** *n.f.* muscularity.
muselina (mu·se'li·na) *n.f.* muslin.
museo (mu'se·o) *n.m.* museum.
musgo ('mus·ɣo) *n.m.* moss. —**musgoso,** *adj.* mossy.
música ('mu·si·ka) *n.f.* music. —**musical,** *adj.* musical.
músico ('mu·si·ko) *adj.* musical. —*n.m.* musician.
musitar (mu·si'tar) *v.i.* & *t.* to mumble; whisper; muse.
muslime (mus'li·me) *adj.* & *n.m.* Moslem. —**muslímico,** *adj.* Moslem.

muslo ('mus·lo) *n.m.* thigh.
mustango (mus'tan·go) *n.m., Amer.* mustang.
mustio ('mus·tjo) *adj.* **1,** withered; wilted. **2,** sad; melancholy.
musulmán (mu·sul'man) *adj.* & *n.m.* Moslem.
mutabilidad (mu·ta·βi·li'ðað) *n.f.* mutability.
mutación (mu·ta'θjon; -'sjon) *n.f.* change; mutation.
mutante (mu'tan·te) *adj.* & *n.m.* & *f.* mutant.
mutilar (mu·ti'lar) *v.t.* to mutilate; maim. —**mutilación,** *n.f.* mutilation.
mutis ('mu·tis) *n.m., esp. theat.* exit. —**hacer mutis,** *esp. theat.* to exit.
mutismo (mu'tis·mo) *n.m.* muteness; silence.
mutual (mu'twal) *adj.* = **mutuo.**
mutualidad (mu·twa·li'ðað) *n.f.* **1,** mutuality. **2,** credit union.
mutuo ('mu·two) *adj.* mutual; reciprocal.
muy (mui) *adv.* very; greatly; most.

N

N, n ('e·ne) *n.f.* 16th letter of the Spanish alphabet.
nabab (na'βaβ) *n.m.* nabob.
nabo ('na·βo) *n.m.* **1,** turnip. **2,** newel.
nácar ('na·kar) *n.m.* mother-of-pearl; nacre. —**nacarino,** *also,* **nacarado,** *adj.* nacreous.
nacencia (na'θen·θja; -'sen·sja) *n.f.* tumor; growth.
nacer (na'θer; -'ser) *v.i.* [*pres.ind.* **nazco;** *pres.subjve.* **nazca**] **1,** to be born; come to life. **2,** to rise; emerge; appear. —**nacer de pie,** *also, Amer.,* **nacer parado,** to be born under a lucky star.
nacida (na'θi·ða; -'si·ða) *adj. fem.* born; née.
nacido (na'θi·ðo; -'si·ðo) *adj.* **1,** born. **2,** inborn; innate. **3,** natural; proper. —*n.m.* **1,** human being. **2,** = **nacencia.** —**bien nacido,** wellborn. —**mal nacido,** lowborn; low.
naciente (na'θjen·te; -'sjen·te) *adj.* **1,** nascent. **2,** rising (*of the sun*). —*n.m.* east.
nacimiento (na·θi'mjen·to; na·si-) *n.m.* **1,** birth. **2,** Nativity scene; crèche. **3,** source (*of a river*).
nación (na'θjon; -'sjon) *n.f.* nation. —**nacional,** *adj.* & *n.m.* national. —**nacionalidad,** *n.f.* nationality.
nacionalismo (na·θjo·na'lis·mo; na·sjo-) *n.m.* nationalism. —**nacionalista,** *adj.* nationalistic. —*n.m.* & *f.* nationalist.
nacionalización (na·θjo·na·li·θa'θjon; na·sjo·na·li·sa'sjon) *n.f.* **1,** nationalization. **2,** naturalization.
nacionalizar (na·θjo·na·li'θar; -sjo·na·li'sar) *v.t.* [*pres.subjve.* **nacionalice** (-'li·θe; -se); *pret.* **nacionalicé** (-'θe; -'se)] **1,** to nationalize. **2,** to naturalize. —**nacionalizarse,** *v.r.* to become naturalized; become a citizen.
nacre ('na·kre) *n.m.* = **nácar.**
nada ('na·ða) *indef.pron.* nothing; not anything; naught. —*n.f.* **1,** nothing; nothingness. **2,** nonentity. —*adv.* not at all. —**de nada,** think nothing of it; don't mention it; not at all. —**nada de eso,** nothing of the sort. —**nada entre dos platos,** nothing of substance. —**por nada, 1,** for nothing. **2,** under no circumstances.
nadada (na'ða·ða) *n.f., Amer.* swim.
nadadera (ha·ða'ðe·ra) *n.f.* **1,** swim bladder. **2,** *pl.* water wings.
nadadero (na·ða'ðe·ro) *n.m.* swimming hole.
nadar (na'ðar) *v.i.* **1,** to swim. **2,** to fit loosely (in). —**nadador,** *n.m.* swimmer. —*adj.* swimming.
nadería (na·ðe'ri·a) *n.f.* trifle; nothing.
nadie ('na·ðje) *indef.pron.* nobody; no one. —*n.m.* & *f.* nobody; nonentity.
nadir (na'ðir) *n.m.* nadir.
nafta ('naf·ta) *n.f.* **1,** naphtha. **2,** *Amer.* gasoline.
naftalina (naf·ta'li·na) *n.f.* naphthalene.
naipe ('nai·pe) *n.m.* **1,** playing card. **2,** *pl.* cards; card games.
nalga ('nal·ɣa) *n.f.* buttock; rump. —**nalgada,** *n.f.* a blow on *or* with the buttocks; spanking.

nana ('na·na) *n.f., colloq.* **1,** grandmother. **2,** nanny; nurse. **3,** lullaby.

nao ('na·o) *n.f., archaic* = **nave.**

napoleón (na·po·le'on) *n.m.* napoleon (*coin*).

naranja (na'ran·xa) *n.f.* orange. —**naranjada,** *n.f.* orangeade. —**naranjal,** *n.m.* orange grove. —**naranjo,** *n.m.* orange tree. —**mi media naranja,** my better half.

narcisismo (nar·θi'sis·mo; nar·si-) *n.m.* narcissism. —**narcisista,** *n.m.* & *f.* narcissist. —*adj.* narcissistic.

narciso (nar'θi·so; nar'si-) *n.m.* narcissus; daffodil.

narcómano (nar'ko·ma·no) *n.m.* drug addict. —**narcomanía,** *n.f.* drug addiction.

narcosis (nar'ko·sis) *n.f.* narcosis.

narcótico (nar'ko·ti·ko) *adj.* & *n.m.* narcotic. —**narcotismo,** *n.m.* narcotism.

narcotizar (nar·ko·ti'θar; -'sar) *v.t.* [*pres.subjve.* **narcotice** (-'ti·θe; -se); *pret.* **narcoticé** (-'θe; -'se)] to drug; administer a narcotic to.

nardo ('nar·ðo) *n.m.* nard; spikenard; tuberose.

narigón (na·ri'ɣon) *n.m.* large nose. —*adj.* = **narigudo.**

narigudo (na·ri'ɣu·ðo) *adj.* large-nosed.

nariz (na'riθ; -'ris) *n.f.* **1,** nose. **2,** *usu.pl.* nostrils. —**nariz respingona** *or* **respingada,** turned-up nose. —**sonarse las narices,** *colloq.* to blow one's nose.

narrar (na'rrar) *v.t.* & *i.* to nar-
tiva, *n.f.* narrative. —**narrativo,** *adj.*
rate. —**narración,** *n.f.* narration.
—**narrador,** *n.m.* narrator. —**narra-**
narrative.

narria ('na·rrja) *n.f.* **1,** sled; sledge. **2,** heavy carriage; drag. **3,** *colloq.* corpulent woman.

narval (nar'βal) *n.m.* narwhal.

nasal (na'sal) *adj.* nasal. —**nasalidad,** *n.f.* nasality.

naso- (na·so) *prefix* naso-; nose: *nasofrontal,* nasofrontal.

nata ('na·ta) *n.f.* **1,** cream. **2,** skin that forms on milk. **3,** *fig.* cream; pick.

natación (na·ta'θjon; -'sjon) *n.f.* swimming.

natal (na'tal) *adj.* natal; native. —**natalidad,** *n.f.* birth rate.

natalicio (na·ta'li·θjo; -sjo) *adj.* & *n.m.* birthday.

natátil (na'ta·til) *adj.* natant.

natatorio (na'ta'to·rjo) *adj.* swimming (*attrib.*). —*n.m., Amer.* natatorium.

natillas (na'ti·ʎas; -jas) *n.f.pl.* custard (*sing.*).

natividad (na·ti·βi'ðað) *n.f.* nativity.

nativo (na'ti·βo) *adj.* **1,** native. **2,** natural; occurring naturally.

nato ('na·to) *adj.* by nature or birth; born.

natrón (na'tron) *n.m.* natron.

natura (na'tu·ra) *n.f.* = **naturaleza.**

natural (na·tu'ral) *adj.* natural; native. —*n.m.* & *f.* native. —*n.m.* natural inclination; nature. —**al natural,** in the raw; in the natural state. —**del natural,** from nature; from life.

naturaleza (na·tu·ra'le·θa; -sa) *n.f.* nature. —**naturaleza muerta,** still life.

naturalidad (na·tu·ra·li'ðað) *n.f.* ease; spontaneity; naturalness.

naturalismo (na·tu·ra'lis·mo) *n.m.* naturalism. —**naturalista,** *adj.* naturalistic. —*n.m.* & *f.* naturalist.

naturalizar (na·tu·ra·li'θar; -'sar) *v.t.* [*pres.subjve.* **naturalice** (-'li·θe; -se); *pret.* **naturalicé** (-'θe; -'se)] to naturalize. —**naturalizarse,** *v.r.* to become naturalized. —**naturalización,** *n.f.* naturalization.

naufragar (nau·fra'ɣar) *v.i.* [*pres.subjve.* **naufrague** (-'fra·ɣe) *pret.* **naufragué** (-'ɣe)] to be shipwrecked.

naufragio (nau'fra·xjo) *n.m.* shipwreck.

náufrago ('nau·fra·ɣo) *n.m.* castaway.

náusea ('nau·se·a) *n.f.* nausea. —**nauseabundo** (-'βun·do) *adj.* nauseous; nauseating. —**nauseado** (-'aðo) *adj.* nauseated.

nauta ('nau·ta) *n.m.* seaman.

náutica ('nau·ti·ka) *n.f.* navigation (*as an art or discipline*). —**náutico,** *adj.* nautical.

nautilo (nau'ti·lo) *n.m.* nautilus.

navaja (na'βa·xa) *n.f.* razor; jackknife; folding blade. —**navajazo,** *n.m.* razor slash; knife slash.

naval (na'βal) *adj.* naval.

nave ('na·βe) *n.f.* **1,** ship; vessel; craft. **2,** nave.

navegar (na·βe'ɣar) *v.t.* & *i.* [*pres.subjve.* **navegue** (-'βe·ɣe); *pret.* **navegué** (-'ɣe)] to navigate.

—**navegable,** *adj.* navigable. —**navegación,** *n.f.* navigation. —**navegador,** *n.m.* navigator. —*adj.* navigating. —**navegante,** *n.m.* & *f.* navigator. —*adj.* navigating.

Navidad (na·βi'ðað) *n.f.* Christmas; Nativity. —**Navidades,** *n.f.pl.* Christmas season; Yuletide.

naviero (na'βje·ro) *adj.* of ships or shipping. —*n.m.* shipowner.

navío (na'βi·o) *n.m.* ship.

náyade ('na·ja·ðe) *n.f.* naiad.

nazca ('naθ·ka; 'nas-) *v., pres. subjve. of* **nacer.**

nazco ('naθ·ko; 'nas-) *v., 1st pers. sing.pres. ind. of* **nacer.**

nazi ('na·θi; -si) *adj.* & *n.m.* Nazi. —**nazismo,** *n.m.* Nazism.

nébeda ('ne·βe·ða) *n.f.* catnip.

neblina (ne'βli·na) *n.f.* fog.

nebulosa (ne·βu'lo·sa) *n.f.* nebula. —**nebulosidad,** *n.f.* nebulosity. —**nebuloso,** *adj.* nebulous; nebular.

necear (ne·θe'ar; ne·se-) *v.i.* **1,** to utter nonsense. **2,** to behave foolishly.

necedad (ne·θe'ðað; ne·se-) *n.f.* **1,** foolishness; inanity. **2,** impertinence; nonsense. **3,** tomfoolery.

necesario (ne·θe'sa·rjo; ne·se-) *adj.* necessary.

neceser (ne·θe'ser; ne·se-) *n.m.* **1,** toilet case; vanity case. **2,** sewing kit; sewing basket.

necesidad (ne·θe·si'ðað; ne·se-) *n.f.* **1,** necessity; need. **2,** *usu.pl.* bodily needs.

necesitado (ne·θe·si'ta·ðo; ne·se-) *adj.* in need; needy. —*n.m.* needy person.

necesitar (ne·θe·si'tar; ne·se-) *v.t.* **1,** to necessitate. **2,** to need. —*v.i.* to need; be in need. —**necesitarse,** *v.r.* to be necessary.

necio ('ne·θjo; -sjo) *adj.* **1,** foolish; inane. **2,** impertinent. —*n.m.* **1,** fool. **2,** importunate person; pest.

necro- (ne·kro) *prefix* necro-; dead; death: *necrología,* necrology.

necrología (ne·kro·lo'xi·a) *n.f.* obituary. —**necrológico** (-'lo·xi·ko) *adj.* obituary.

necromancia (ne·kro'man·θja; -sja) *n.f.* necromancy.

necrópolis (ne'kro·po·lis) *n.f.* necropolis.

necrosis (ne'kro·sis) *n.f.* necrosis. —**necrótico** (-'kro·ti·ko) *adj.* necrotic.

néctar ('nek·tar) *n.m.* nectar.

neerlandés (ne·er·lan'des) *adj.* Dutch. —*n.m.* **1,** Dutchman. **2,** Dutch language.

nefando (ne'fan·do) *adj.* unspeakable; infamous.

nefario (ne'fa·rjo) *adj.* nefarious.

nefasto (ne'fas·to) *adj.* ominous; fateful.

nefritis (ne'fri·tis) *n.f.* nephritis. —**nefrítico,** *adj.* nephritic.

nefro- (ne·fro) *also, before a vowel,* **nefr-** (nefr) *prefix* nephro-; nephr-; kidney: *nefrotomía,* nephrotomy; *nefritis,* nephritis.

negación (ne·ɣa'θjon; -'sjon) *n.f.* **1,** negation. **2,** denial. **3,** *gram.* negative.

negar (ne'ɣar) *v.t.* [*pres.ind.* **niego;** *pres.subjve.* **niegue;** *pret.* **negué**] **1,** to negate; deny. **2,** to refuse. **3,** to prohibit. **4,** to disown; disclaim. —**negarse,** *v.r.* to deny oneself; sacrifice one's own interests. —**negarse a, 1,** to refuse; turn away from. **2,** *fol. by inf.* to refuse to.

negativa (ne·ɣa'ti·βa) *n.f.* negative; denial; refusal.

negativo (ne·ɣa'ti·βo) *adj.* negative. —*n.m., photog.; electricity* negative.

negligente (ne·ɣli'xen·te) *adj.* negligent. —**negligencia** (-θja; -sja) *n.f.* negligence.

negociado (ne·ɣo'θja·ðo; -'sja·ðo) *n.m.* **1,** deal; business. **2,** *Amer.* shady business; shady deal.

negociador (ne·ɣo·θja'ðor; -sja·'ðor) *adj.* negotiating. —*n.m.* negotiator.

negociar (ne·ɣo'θjar; -'sjar) *v.t.* & *i.* to negotiate. —*v.i.* to deal; trade. —**negociable,** *adj.* negotiable. —**negociación,** *n.f.* negotiation. —**negociante,** *n.m.* & *f.* dealer; businessman; tradesman.

negocio (ne'ɣo·θjo; -sjo) *n.m.* **1,** business; concern. **2,** transaction; dealing. **3,** profit; benefit; gain. **4,** *Amer.* place of business; office; store. —**negocios,** *n.m.pl.* business affairs. —**encargado de negocios,** chargé d'affaires. —**negocio redondo,** *colloq.* clearly profitable deal; sound business.

negrear (ne·ɣre'ar) *v.i.* to look black; be blackish.

negrero (ne'ɣre·ro) *adj.* of or pert. to the slave trade. —*n.m.* slaver.

negro ('ne·ɣro) *adj.* & *n.m.* **1,** black. **2,** negro. —**negra,** *n.f.* negress. —**negro de humo,** lampblack. —**pasarlas negras,** *colloq.* to have a hard time of it.
negroide (ne'ɣroi·ðe) *adj.* negroid.
negrura (ne'ɣru·ra) *n.f.* blackness. *Also,* **negror** (-'ɣror) *n.m.*
negruzco (ne'ɣruθ·ko; -'ɣrus·ko) *adj.* blackish.
negué (ne'ɣe) *v., 1st pers.sing. pret. of* **negar.**
nemato- (ne·ma·to) *prefix* nemato-; thread; threadlike: *nematocisto,* nematocyst.
némesis ('ne·me·sis) *n.m.* nemesis.
nene ('ne·ne) *n.m., colloq.* [*fem.* **nena**] baby; child.
nenúfar (ne'nu·far) *n.m.* white water lily.
neo- (ne·o) *prefix* neo-; new; recent: *neoclásico,* neoclassical.
neoceno (ne·o'θe·no; -'se·no) *adj.* Neocene.
neodimio (ne·o'ði·mjo) *n.m.* neodymium.
neófito (ne'o·fi·to) *n.m.* neophyte.
neolatino (ne·o·la'ti·no) *adj.* & *n.m.* Neo-Latin; Romance.
neolítico (ne·o'li·ti·ko) *adj.* neolithic.
neologismo (ne·o·lo'xis·mo) *n.m.* neologism.
neón (ne'on) *n.m.* neon.
neoplasma (ne·o'plas·ma) *n.m.* neoplasm.
neoyorquino (ne·o·jor'ki·no) *adj.* of New York; New York (*attrib.*). —*n.m.* New Yorker.
nepotismo (ne·po'tis·mo) *n.m.* nepotism.
neptunio (nep'tu·njo) *n.m.* neptunium.
Neptuno (nep'tu·no) *n.m.* Neptune.
nereida (ne'rei·ða) *n.f.* nereid.
nervadura (ner·βa'ðu·ra) *n.f.* **1,** nervure. **2,** nervation.
nérveo ('ner·βe·o) *adj.* neural.
nervio ('ner·βjo) *n.m.* **1,** nerve. **2,** vein (*of a leaf*).
nerviosidad (ner·βjo·si'ðað) *n.f.* **1,** nervousness. **2,** = **nervosidad.**
nervioso (ner'βjo·so) *adj.* **1,** nervous. **2,** sinewy.
nervosidad (ner·βo·si'ðað) *n.f.* **1,** force; vigor. **2,** cogency (*of an argument*). **3,** flexibility.
nervoso (ner'βo·so) *adj.* = **nervioso.**
nervudo (ner'βu·ðo) *adj.* **1,** vigorous. **2,** sinewy.
nesciencia (nes'θjen·θja; ne'sjen·sja) *n.f.* nescience.
nesga ('nes·ɣa) *n.f., sewing* gore.
neto ('ne·to) *adj.* **1,** clear; pure; clean. **2,** net.
neumático (neu'ma·ti·ko) *adj.* pneumatic. —*n.m.* tire.
neumato- (neu·ma·to) *prefix* pneumato-. **1,** air; vapor: *neumatólisis,* pneumatolysis. **2,** breathing: *neumatómetro,* pneumatometer.
neumo- (neu·mo) *prefix* pneumo-; lung; *neumoconiosis,* pneumoconiosis.
neumonía (neu·mo'ni·a) *n.f.* pneumonia.
neumono- (neu·mo·no) *prefix* pneumono-; lung: *neumonóforo,* pneumonophore.
neuralgia (neu'ral·xja) *n.f.* neuralgia. —**neurálgico** (-xi·ko) *adj.* neuralgic.
neurastenia (neu·ras'te·nja) *n.f.* neurasthenia. —**neurasténico** (-ni·ko) *adj.* & *n.m.* neurasthenic.
neuritis (neu'ri·tis) *n.f.* neuritis.
neuro- (neu·ro) *also, before a vowel,* **neur-** (neur) *prefix* neuro-; neur-; nerve: *neurología,* neurology; *neuritis,* neuritis.
neurología (neu·ro·lo'xi·a) *n.f.* neurology. —**neurológico** (-'lo·xi·ko) *adj.* neurological. —**neurólogo** (-'ro·lo·ɣo) *n.m.* neurologist.
neurona (neu'ro·na) *n.f.* neuron.
neurosis (neu'ro·sis) *n.f.* neurosis. —**neurótico** (-'ro·ti·ko) *adj.* & *n.m.* neurotic.
neutral (neu'tral) *adj.* & *n.m.* & *f.* neutral. —**neutralidad,** *n.f.* neutrality.
neutralizar (neu·tra·li'θar; -'sar) *v.t.* [*pres.subjve.* **neutralice** (-'li·θe; -se); *pret.* **neutralicé** (-'θe; -'se)] to neutralize. —**neutralización,** *n.f.* neutralization.
neutro ('neu·tro) *adj.* **1,** neuter. **2,** neutral. **3,** *gram.* intransitive.
neutrón (neu'tron) *n.m.* neutron.
nevar (ne'βar) *v.impers.* [*pres.ind.* **nieva;** *pres.subjve.* **nieve**] to snow. —**nevada,** *n.f.* snowfall. —**nevado,** *adj.* snow-covered. —*n.m.* snow-capped mountain.
nevasca (ne'βas·ka) *n.f.* snowfall; snowstorm.

nevera (ne'βe·ra) *n.f.* icebox; refrigerator.
nevisca (ne'βis·ka) *n.f.* snow flurry; light snow.
neviscar (ne·βis'kar) *v.impers.* [*pres.subjve.* **nevisque** (-'βis·ke)] to snow lightly.
nevoso (ne'βo·so) *adj.* snowy.
nexo ('nek·so) *n.m.* bond; connection; nexus.
ni (ni) *conj.* neither; nor. —**ni . . . ni**, neither . . . nor. —**ni que**, 1, as if. 2, would that. —**ni siquiera**, not even.
nicotina (ni·ko'ti·na) *n.f.* nicotine. —**nicotínico**, *adj.* nicotinic.
nicho ('ni·tʃo) *n.m.* niche.
nidada (ni'ða·ða) *n.f.* brood; covey.
nidal (ni'ðal) *n.m.* 1, nest. 2, nest egg.
nido ('ni·ðo) *n.m.* nest.
niebla ('nje·βla) *n.f.* fog; mist.
niego ('nje·ɣo) *v., pres.ind. of* **negar.**
niegue ('nje·ɣe) *v., pres.subjve. of* **negar.**
nieta ('nje·ta) *n.f.* granddaughter.
nieto ('nje·to) *n.m.* grandson.
nieva ('nje·βa) *v., pres.ind.* of **nevar.**
nieve ('nje·βe) *n.f.* 1, snow. 2, *Amer.* sherbet. —**nieve carbónica**, dry ice.
nieve ('nje·βe) *v., pres.subjve. of* **nevar.**
nigromancia (ni·ɣro'man·θja; -sja) *n.f.* necromancy. —**nigromante**, *n.m.* & *f.* necromancer.
nihilismo (ni·i'lis·mo) *n.m.* nihilism. —**nihilista**, *n.m.* & *f.* nihilist. —*adj.* nihilistic.
nilón (ni'lon) *n.m.* nylon.
nimbo ('nim·bo) *n.m.* nimbus.
nimiedad (ni·mje'ðað) *n.f.* 1, trifle. 2, meticulousness; minuteness. 3, fastidiousness.
nimio ('ni·mjo) *adj.* 1, trivial; trifling. 2, meticulous; minute. 3, fastidious.
ninfa ('nin·fa) *n.f.* nymph.
ninfomanía (nin·fo·ma'ni·a) *n.f.* nymphomania. —**ninfomaníaca**, *n.f.* nymphomaniac.
ningún (nin'gun) *adj.* = **ninguno** *before a masc. noun.* —**de ningún modo**, by no means; not at all; nowise.
ninguno (nin'gu·no) *adj.* not any; no. —*pron.* none; no one; nobody.
niña ('ni·ɲa) *n.f.* 1, girl. 2, pupil (*of the eye*).
niñada (ni'ɲa·ða) *n.f.* childishness; childish behavior.
niñera (ni'ɲe·ra) *n.f.* nursemaid.
niñería (ni·ɲe'ri·a) *n.f.* 1, = **niñada**. 2, trifle.
niño ('ni·ɲo) *adj.* childish. —*n.m.* boy; child. - **niñez**, *n.f.* childhood.
niobio ('njo·βjo) *n.m.* niobium; columbium.
nipón (ni'pon) *adj.* & *n.m.* Nipponese.
níquel ('ni·kel) *n.m.* nickel. —**niquelar**, *v.t.* to nickel-plate. —**niquelado**, *adj.* nickel-plated. —*n.m.* nickelplating.
nirvana (nir'βa·na) *n.m.* nirvana.
níspero ('nis·pe·ro) *n.m.* medlar.
nítido ('ni·ti·ðo) *adj.* clear; clean; well defined. - **nitidez**, *n.f.* clarity.
nitón (ni'ton) *n.m.* = **radón.**
nitos ('ni·tos) *adv.* & *interj., slang* nix; no.
nitrato (ni'tra·to) *n.m.* nitrate.
nítrico ('ni·tri·ko) *adj.* nitric.
nitro ('ni·tro) *n.m.* niter; saltpeter.
nitro- (ni·tro) *prefix* nitro-; nitrogen; nitrogen compounds: *nitrobencina,* nitrobenzene; *nitrocelulosa,* nitrocellulose.
nitrocelulosa (ni·tro·θe·lu'lo·sa; -se·lu'lo·sa) *n.f.* nitrocellulose.
nitrógeno (ni'tro·xe·no) *n.m.* nitrogen. —**nitrogenado**, *adj.* nitrogenous.
nitroglicerina (ni·tro·ɣli·θe'ri·na; -se'ri·na) *n.f.* nitroglycerine.
nitroso (ni'tro·so) *adj.* nitrous.
nivel (ni'βel) *n.m.* level. —**a nivel**, on a level line; level. —**a nivel con**, on a level with. —**nivel de vida**, standard of living.
nivelado (ni·βe'la·ðo) *adj.* 1, level; even. 2, horizontal.
nivelar (ni·βe'lar) *v.t.* to level; make even. —**nivelación**, *n.f.* leveling.
níveo ('ni·βe·o) *adj.* snowy; like snow.
no (no) *adv.* no; not. *Preceding nouns and adjectives, equivalent to Eng. prefix* **non-**: *no beligerante,* nonbelligerent; *no intervención,* nonintervention. —*n.m.* refusal; denial; nay; no. —**a no ser que**, unless. —**no bien**, no sooner. —**no más**, only. —**no obstante**, notwithstanding; nevertheless. —**no sea que**, lest. —**por sí o por no**, just in case. —**ya no**, no longer.

nobelio (no'βe·ljo) *n.m.* nobelium.
noble ('no·βle) *adj.* noble. —*n.m.* nobleman. —**nobleza,** *n.f.* nobility.
noción (no'θjon; -'sjon) *n.f.* notion; idea. —**nociones,** *n.f.pl.* rudiments; elements.
nocivo (no'θi·βo; -'si·βo) *adj.* noxious. —**nocividad,** *n.f.* noxiousness.
nocti- (nok·ti) *also, before a vowel,* **noct-** (nokt) *prefix* nocti-; noct-; night: *noctiluca,* noctiluca; *noctambulismo,* noctambulism.
nocturno (nok'tur·no) *adj.* nocturnal. —*n.m.* nocturne.
noche ('no·tʃe) *n.f.* **1,** night. **2,** evening. **3,** dark; darkness. —**buenas noches,** good evening; good night. —**de la noche a la mañana,** suddenly; unexpectedly. —**de noche,** at night; by night. —**es de noche,** it is night. —**hacer noche,** to stop for the night. —**pasar la noche en claro,** not to sleep a wink.
nochebuena (no·tʃe'βwe·na) *n.f.* Christmas Eve.
nodo ('no·ðo) *n.m.* node. —**nodal,** *adj.* nodal.
nodriza (no'ðri·θa; -sa) *n.f.* wet nurse.
nódulo ('no·ðu·lo) *n.m.* nodule. —**nodular,** *adj.* nodular.
nogal (no'ɣal) *n.m.* **1,** walnut tree. **2,** walnut (*wood and color*).
nómada ('no·ma·ða) *adj.* [*also,* **nómade** (-ðe)] nomadic. —*n.m.* & *f.* nomad.
nombradía (nom·bra'ði·a) *n.f.* fame; renown.
nombrado (nom'bra·ðo) *adj.* celebrated; renowned.
nombrar (nom'brar) *v.t.* **1,** to name. **2,** to appoint; nominate. —**nombramiento,** *n.m.* appointment; commission.
nombre ('nom·bre) *n.m.* **1,** name. **2,** noun. —**de nombre,** renowned. —**nombre de pila,** given name. —**no tiene nombre,** there's no word for it; unbelievable; impossible.
nomenclatura (no·men·kla'tu·ra) *n.f.* nomenclature.
nomeolvides (no·me·ol'βi·ðes) *n.m.sing.* & *pl.* forget-me-not.
-nomía (no'mi·a) *suffix* -nomy; *forming nouns denoting* **1,** science; systematized study; body of knowledge: *astronomía,* astronomy. **2,** arrangement; management; government: *taxonomía,* taxonomy; *economía,* economy; *autonomía,* autonomy.
nómina ('no·mi·na) *n.f.* list; roll, esp. payroll.
nominal (no·mi'nal) *adj.* nominal.
nominar (no·mi'nar) *v.t.* to nominate; appoint. —**nominación,** *n.f.* nomination; appointment.
nómino ('no·mi·no) *adj.* nominee; appointee.
nominativo (no·mi·na'ti·βo) *adj.* & *n.m.* nominative.
-nomo (no·mo) *suffix, forming nouns and adjectives corresponding to nouns ending in* **-nomía:** *astrónomo,* astronomer; *autónomo,* autonomous.
non (non) *adj.* odd; uneven. —*n.m.* odd number. —**nones,** *n.m.pl.* emphatic no; nix.
nonada (no'na·ða) *n.f.* trifle; nothing.
nonagenario (no·na·xe'na·rjo) *adj.* & *n.m.* nonagenarian.
nonagésimo (no·na'xe·si·mo) *adj.* & *n.m.* ninetieth.
nonágono (no'na·ɣo·no) *n.m.* nonagon.
nonato (no'na·to) *adj.* **1,** born by Cesarean section. **2,** unborn; still to come.
nonillón(no·ni'ʎon; -'jon) *n.m.* a septillion nonillion; *Brit.* nonillion.
noningentésimo (no·nin·xen'te·si·mo) *adj.* & *n.m.* nine-hundredth.
nono ('no·no) *adj.* ninth.
nopal (no'pal) *n.m.* nopal.
noquear (no·ke'ar) *v.t., slang* to knock out; kayo.
nordestal (nor·ðes'tal) *adj.* northeastern; northeasterly.
nordeste (nor'ðes·te) *n.m.* northeast. *Also,* **noreste** (no'res·te).
nórdico ('nor·ði·ko) *adj.* & *n.m.* Nordic; Norse.
noria ('no·rja) *n.f.* noria.
norma ('nor·ma) *n.f.* norm.
normal (nor'mal) *adj.* normal. —*adj.* & *n.m. or f., geom.* normal. —**normalidad,** *n.f.* normalcy; normality.
normalizar (nor·ma·li'θar; -'sar) *v.t.* [*pres.subjve.* **normalice** (-'li·θe; -se); *pret.* **normalicé** (-'θe; -'se)] to normalize.
normando (nor'man·do) *adj.* **1,** Norman. **2,** Norse. —*n.m.* **1,** Norman. **2,** Norseman; Northman; *pl.* the Norse.
noroeste (nor·o'es·te) *n.m.* northwest.

norte ('nor·te) *adj.* & *n.m.* north. —*n.m., fig.* guiding light; aim.
norteamericano (nor·te·a·me·ri'ka·no) *adj.* & *n.m.* **1,** North American. **2,** American (*of the U.S.A.*).
norteño (nor'te·ɲo) *adj.* **1,** northern (*of persons*). **2,** northerly. —*n.m.* northerner.
nos (nos) *pers.pron. 1st pers.pl., used as obj. of a verb* us; to us; ourselves.
nosotros (no'so·tros) *pers.pron. 1st pers.m.pl.* [*fem.* **nosotras**] *used as subject of a verb or object of a preposition* we; us.
nostalgia (nos'tal·xja) *n.f.* nostalgia. —**nostálgico** (-xi·ko) *adj.* nostalgic.
nota ('no·ta) *n.f.* **1,** note. **2,** grade; mark (*in school*).
notable (no'ta·βle) *adj.* notable; noteworthy. —*n.m.* notable. —**notabilidad,** *n.f.* notability.
notación (no·ta'θjon; -'sjon) *n.f.* notation.
notar (no'tar) *v.t.* **1,** to note. **2,** to notice; perceive.
notaría (no·ta'ri·a) *n.f.* **1,** notary public's office. **2,** profession of notary public.
notario (no'ta·rjo) *n.m.* notary public; notary. —**notarial,** *adj.* notarial.
notarizar (no·ta·ri'θar; -'sar) *v.t., Amer.* [*pres.subjve.* **notarice** (-'ri·θe; -se); *pret.* **notaricé** (-'θe; -'se)] to notarize.
noticia (no'ti·θja; -sja) *n.f.* news; information. —**noticias,** *n.f.pl.* news. —**noticiar,** *v.t., colloq.* to give news of.
noticiario (no·ti'θja·rjo; -'sja·rjo) *n.m.* **1,** newsreel. **2,** newscast.
noticiero (no·ti'θje·ro; -'sje·ro) *n.m.* **1,** news writer. **2,** newscaster. **3,** newsreel. —*adj.* **1,** news (*attrib.*). **2,** *colloq.* newsy.
noticioso (no·ti'θjo·so; -'sjo·so) *adj.* newsy; informative.
notificar (no·ti·fi'kar) *v.t.* [*pres. subjve.* **notifique** (-'fi·ke); *pret.* **notifiqué** (-'ke)] to notify. —**notificación,** *n.f.* notification; notice.
notorio (no'to·rjo) *adj.* notorious. —**notoriedad,** *n.f.* notoriety.
nova ('no·βa) *n.f., astron.* nova.
novatada (no·βa'ta·ða) *n.f.* **1,** hazing. **2,** beginner's blunder.
novato (no'βa·to) *n.m.* tyro; tenderfoot; greenhorn.
novecientos (no·βe'θjen·tos; -sjen·tos) *adj.* & *n.m.pl.* [*fem.* **-tas**] nine hundred. —*adj.* nine-hundredth.
novedad (no·βe'ðað) *n.f.* **1,** novelty. **2,** bit of news; latest news. —**sin novedad,** all is quiet; no news to report.
novedoso (no·βe'ðo·so) *adj.* novel; original; newfangled.
novel (no'βel) *adj.* new; beginning; inexperienced.
novela (no'βe·la) *n.f.* **1,** novel. **2,** tale; fiction; falsehood. —**novela policíaca,** detective story.
novelería (no·βe·le'ri·a) *n.f.* **1,** bit of news; gossip. **2,** fad. **3,** faddishness.
novelero (no·βe'le·ro) *adj.* **1,** fond of gossip: gossiping. **2,** faddish. —*n.m.* **1,** gossipmonger; talebearer. **2,** faddist.
novelesco (no·βe'les·ko) *adj.* **1,** fictional. **2,** romantic.
novelista (no·βe'lis·ta) *n.m.* & *f.* novelist.
novena (no'βe·na) *n.f.* **1,** *eccles.* novena. **2,** *music* ninth.
noveno (no'βe·no) *adj.* & *n.m.* ninth.
noventa (no'βen·ta) *adj.* & *n.m.* ninety. —**noventavo,** *adj.* & *n.m.* ninetieth.
novia ('no·βja) *n.f.* **1,** bride. **2,** fiancée.
noviazgo (no'βjaθ·ɣo; -'βjas·ɣo) *n.m.* betrothal; engagement.
novicio (no'βi·θjo; -sjo) *n.m.* novice. —*adj.* inexperienced. —**noviciado,** *n.m.* novitiate.
noviembre (no'βjem·bre) *n.m.* November.
novilunio (no·βi'lu·njo) *n.m.* new moon.
novillero (no·βi'ʎe·ro; -'je·ro) *n.m.* **1,** herdsman, esp. for young cattle. **2,** fighter of young bulls; novice bullfighter **3,** truant.
novillo (no'βi·ʎo; -jo) *n.m.* young bull. —**novilla,** *n.f.* heifer. —**novillada,** *n.f.* mock bullfight with young bulls. —**hacer novillos,** to play hooky.
novio ('no·βjo) *n.m.* **1,** bridegroom. **2,** fiancé.
novísimo (no'βi·si·mo) *adj., superl. of* **nuevo.**
novocaína (no·βo·ka'i·na) *n.f.* novocaine.

nube ('nu·βe) *n.f.* **1,** cloud. **2,** swarm. **3,** cataract (*in the eye*). —**nubarrón** (-βa'rron) storm cloud.

núbil ('nu·βil) *adj.* nubile; marriageable. —**nubilidad,** *n.f.* nubility; marriageability.

nubio ('nu·βjo) *adj.* & *n.m.* Nubian.

nublado (nu'βla·ðo) *adj.* cloudy. —*n.m.* cloud formation; storm clouds.

nublar (nu'βlar) *v.t.* to cloud; becloud. —**nublarse,** *v.r.* to cloud over; become cloudy.

nubloso (nu'βlo·so) *adj.* **1,** cloudy; overcast. **2,** unfortunate. *Also,* **nuboso** (-'βo·so).

nuca ('nu·ka) *n.f.* nape.

nuclear (nu·kle'ar) *adj.* nuclear.

núcleo ('nu·kle·o) *n.m.* nucleus.

nucléolo (nu'kle·o·lo) *n.m.* nucleolus.

nucleón (nu·kle'on) *n.m.* nucleon.

nudi- (nu·ði) *prefix* nudi-; bare; nude: *nudifoliado,* nudifoliate.

nudillo (nu'ði·ʎo; -jo) *n.m.* knuckle.

nudismo (nu'ðis·mo) *n.m.* nudism. —**nudista,** *adj.* & *n.m.* & *f.* nudist.

nudo ('nu·ðo) *n.m.* **1,** knot. **2,** tangle. **3,** cluster, esp. of mountains. **4,** *naut.* knot. —**nudoso,** *adj.* knotty.

nuégado ('nwe·ɣa·ðo) *n.m.* nougat.

nuera ('nwe·ra) *n.f.* daughter-in-law.

nuestro ('nwes·tro) *poss.adj.* & *pron.m.sing.* [*fem.* **nuestra;** *pl.* **nuestros, nuestras**], *agreeing in number and gender with the thing or things possessed* our; ours. —**los nuestros,** our side.

nueva ('nwe·βa) *n.f.* = **noticia.**

nueve ('nwe·βe) *adj.* & *n.m.* nine.

nuevo ('nwe·βo) *adj.* new. —**de nuevo,** again. —**¿Que hay de nuevo?,** What's new?

nuez (nweθ; nwes) *n.f.* **1,** *bot.* nut. **2,** walnut. **3,** Adam's apple. —**nuez moscada,** nutmeg.

nulidad (nu·li'ðað) *n.f.* **1,** nullity. **2,** incompetent; good-for-nothing.

nulo ('nu·lo) *adj.* **1,** null. **2,** incompetent; good-for-nothing.

numeración (nu·me·ra'θjon; -'sjon) *n.f.* **1,** numbering. **2,** numeration.

numerador (nu·me·ra'ðor) *n.m.* numerator.

numeral (nu·me'ral) *adj.* numeral.

numerar (nu·me'rar) *v.t.* **1,** to number; count. **2,** to express in numbers. **3,** to assign a number to. —**asiento numerado,** reserved seat. —**sesión numerada,** reserved-seat performance.

numerario (nu·me'ra·rjo) *n.m.* cash; specie.

numérico (nu'me·ri·ko) *adj.* numerical.

número ('nu·me·ro) *n.m.* **1,** number. **2,** numeral. —**numerosidad,** *n.f.* numerousness. —**numeroso,** *adj.* numerous.

numerología (nu·me·ro·lo'xi·a) *n.f.* numerology. —**numerólogo** (-'ro·lo·ɣo) *n.m.* numerologist.

numismática (nu·mis'ma·ti·ka) *n.f.* numismatics. —**numismático,** *adj.* numismatic. —*n.m.* numismatist.

nunca ('nun·ka) *adv.* never. —**nunca jamás,** nevermore.

nuncio ('nun·θjo; -sjo) *n.m.* **1,** nuncio. **2,** harbinger.

nupcial (nup'θjal; -'sjal) *adj.* nuptial.

nupcias ('nup·θjas; -sjas) *n.f.pl.* nuptials; wedding.

nutria ('nu·trja) *n.f.* **1,** otter. **2,** nutria.

nutrición (nu·tri'θjon; -'sjon) *n.f.* nutrition.

nutrido (nu'tri·ðo) *adj.* **1,** *fig.* abounding; abundant. **2,** *mil.* uninterrupted; thick (*of fire or firing*). —**bien nutrido,** well-fed. —**mal nutrido,** ill-fed.

nutrimento (nu·tri'men·to) *also,* **nutrimiento** (-'mjen·to) *n.m.* nutriment.

nutrir (nu'trir) *v.t.* to nourish; nurture.

nutritivo (nu·tri'ti·βo) *adj.* nutrient; nutritive; nutritious.

Ñ

Ñ, ñ ('e·ɲe) *n.f.* 17th letter of the Spanish alphabet.

ña (ɲa) *n.f., Amer., colloq.* = **doña.**

ñame ('ɲa·me) *n.m.* yam.

ñandú (ɲan'du) *n.m.* American ostrich.
ñáñigo ('ɲa·ɲi·ɣo) *adj.* & *n.m., Cuba* voodoo.
ñapa ('ɲa·pa) *n.f., Amer.* bonus; extra. **—de ñapa,** to boot; in the bargain.
ñato ('ɲa·to) *adj., Amer.* pug-nosed; flat-nosed.
ñeque ('ɲe·ke) *n.m., Amer.* vigor; enterprise.
ño (ɲo) *n.m., Amer., colloq.* = **don.**
ñongo ('ɲon·go) *adj., Amer., derog.* lazy; ignorant.
ñoño ('ɲo·ɲo) *adj., colloq.* mawkish. **—ñoñería,** *n.f.* drivel; mawkishness. **—ñoñez,** *n.f.* mawkishness.
ñu (ɲu) *n.m.* gnu.
ñudo ('ɲu·ðo) *n.m.* = **nudo. —ñudoso** = nudoso.

O

O, o (o) *n.f.* 18th letter of the Spanish alphabet.
o (o) *conj.* or; either. **—o . . . o,** either . . . or. **—o sea,** that is.
o- (o) *prefix, var. of* **ob-** *before* f, m, p: *ofuscar,* obfuscate; *omitir,* omit; *oponer,* oppose.
oasis (o'a·sis) *n.m.* oasis.
ob- (oβ) *prefix* ob-. **1,** toward; facing: *oblicuo,* oblique. **2,** against: *objetar,* object. **3,** upon; over: *observar,* observe. **4,** inversely: *obovoide,* obovoid.
obcecar (oβ·θe'kar; -se'kar) *v.t.* [*pres.subjve.* **obceque** (-'θe·ke; -'se·ke); *pret.* **obcequé** (-'ke)] to blind; obsess. **—obcecarse,** *v.r.* to be obsessed. **—obcecación,** *n.f.* obsession; blind stubbornness.
obedecer (o·βe·ðe'θer; -'ser) *v.t.* & *i.* [*pres.ind.* **obedezco** (-'ðeθ·ko; -'ðes·ko); *pres.subjve.* **obedezca** (-ka)] to obey. **—obedecer a, 1,** to yield to. **2,** to be due to; arise from.
obediente (o·βe'ðjen·te) *adj.* obedient. **—obediencia,** *n.f.* obedience.
obelisco (o·βe'lis·ko) *n.m.* obelisk.
obenques (o'βen·kes) *n.m.pl., naut.* shrouds.
obertura (o·βer'tu·ra) *n.f., music* overture.
obeso (o'βe·so) *adj.* obese. **—obesidad,** *n.f.* obesity.
óbice ('o·βi·θe; -se) *n.m.* impediment; obstacle.
obispalía (o·βis·pa'li·a) *n.f.* **1,** bishop's palace. **2,** diocese.
obispo (o'βis·po) *n.m.* bishop. **—obispado,** *n.m.* bishopric; diocese. **—obispal,** *adj.* episcopal.
obituario (o·βi'twa·rjo) *n.m.* obituary.
objeción (oβ·xe'θjon; -'sjon) *n.f.* objection.
objetar (oβ·xe'tar) *v.t.* to object.
objeto (oβ'xe·to) *n.m.* object. **—objetivo,** *adj.* & *n.m.* objective. **—objetividad,** *n.f.* objectivity.
oblación (o·βla'θjon; -'sjon) *n.f.* oblation.
oblicuo (o'βli·kwo) *adj.* oblique. **—oblicuidad,** *n.f.* obliquity.
obligación (o·βli·ɣa'θjon; -'sjon) *n.f.* **1,** obligation. **2,** *comm.* bond. **—obligacionista,** *n.m.* & *f.* bondholder.
obligar (o·βli'ɣar) *v.t.* [*pres.subjve.* **obligue** (o'βli·ɣe); *pret.* **obligué** (-'ɣe)] to obligate; compel.
obligatorio (o·βli·ɣa'to·rjo) *adj.* obligatory; compulsory.
oblongo (oβ'lon·go) *adj.* oblong.
oboe (o'βo·e) *n.m.* **1,** oboe. **2,** oboist.
óbolo ('o·βo·lo) *n.m.* mite; small contribution.
obra ('o·βra) *n.f.* **1,** work. **2,** construction. **3,** *theat.* play. **4,** *music* composition. **—obra maestra,** masterpiece.
obrar (o'βrar) *v.t.* & *i.* **1,** to work. **2,** to build. **—obrador,** *n.m.* workshop.
obrerismo (o·βre'ris·mo) *n.m.* **1,** labor movement. **2,** working class.
obrero (o'βre·ro) *adj.* working. **—***n.m.* worker.
obsceno (oβs'θe·no; oβ'se·no) *adj.* obscene. **—obscenidad,** *n.f.* obscenity.
obscurecer (oβs·ku·re'θer; -'ser) *v.t.* [*pres.ind.* **obscurezco** (-'reθ·ko; -'res·ko); *pres.subjve.* **obscurezca** (-ka)] to darken; becloud; obscure. **—***v.impers.* to grow dark.
obscuridad (oβs·ku·ri'ðað) *n.f.* **1,** darkness. **2,** obscurity.
obscuro (oβs'ku·ro) *adj.* **1,** dark. **2,** obscure. **—a obscuras,** in the dark.

obsequiar (oβ·se'kjar) *v.t.* **1,** to give; present. **2,** to treat; regale.
obsequio (oβ'se·kjo) *n.m.* gift; compliment. —**en obsequio de,** in deference to.
obsequioso (oβ·se'kjo·so) *adj.* obsequious. —**obsequiosidad,** *n.f.* obsequiousness.
observable (oβ·ser'βa·βle) *adj.* observable.
observar (oβ·ser'βar) *v.t.* to observe. —**observación,** *n.f.* observation. —**observador,** *n.m.* observer. —*adj.* observant. —**observancia,** *n.f.* observance. —**observatorio,** *n.m.* observatory.
obsesión (oβ·se'sjon) *n.f.* obsession. —**obsesionar,** *v.t.* to obsess. —**obsesivo** (-'si·βo) *adj.* obsessive.
obsidiana (oβ·si'ðja·na) *n.f.* obsidian.
obstáculo (oβs'ta·ku·lo) *n.m.* obstacle.
obstante (oβs'tan·te) *adv., in* **no obstante,** nevertheless; notwithstanding.
obstetricia (oβs·te'tri·θja; -sja) *n.f.* obstetrics. —**obstétrico** (-'te·tri·ko) *adj.* obstetrical.
obstinarse (oβs·ti'nar·se) *v.r.* to persist; be obstinate. —**obstinación,** *n.f.* obstinacy. —**obstinado,** *adj.* obstinate.
obstruccionismo (oβs·truk·θjo·'nis·mo; -sjo'nis·mo) *n.m.* obstructionism. —**obstruccionista,** *adj.* & *n.m.* & *f.* obstructionist.
obstruir (oβs·tru'ir) *v.t.* [*infl.:* **construir**] to obstruct. —**obstrucción** (-truk'θjon; -'sjon) *n.f.* obstruction. —**obstructor** (-'tor) *adj.* [*also,* **obstructivo** (-'ti·βo)] obstructive. —*n.m.* obstructionist.
obtener (oβ·te'ner) *v.t.* [*infl.:* **tener**] to get; obtain. —**obtención,** *n.f.* obtaining; attainment. —**obtenible,** *adj.* obtainable.
obturador (oβ·tu·ra'ðor) *adj.* stopping; plugging. —*n.m.* **1,** plug; stopper. **2,** *mech.* choke. **3,** *photog.* shutter.
obturar (oβ·tu'rar) *v.t.* **1,** to stop up; plug. **2,** *mech.* to choke.
obtuso (oβ'tu·so) *adj.* obtuse.
obtuve (oβ'tu·βe) *v., pret. of* **obtener.**
obús (o'βus) *n.m.* **1,** artillery shell. **2,** howitzer.
obviar (oβ'βjar) *v.t.* to obviate.
obvio ('oβ·βjo) *adj.* obvious.
oca ('o·ka) *n.f.* goose.
ocasión (o·ka'sjon) *n.f.* occasion; opportunity. —**ocasional,** *adj.* occasional; casual. —**ocasionar,** *v.t.* to occasion; provoke. —**de ocasión,** bargain (*attrib.*).
ocaso (o'ka·so) *n.m.* **1,** setting (*of a star*); sunset. **2,** *fig.* decline; fall; twilight.
occidente (ok·θi'ðen·te; ok·si-) *n.m.* west; occident. —**occidental,** *adj.* occidental; western; west (*attrib.*).
occipucio (ok·θi'pu·θjo; ok·si·'pu·sjo) *n.m.* occiput. —**occipital** (-pi'tal) *adj.* occipital.
océano (o'θe·a·no; o'se-) *n.m.* ocean. —**oceánico** (-'a·ni·ko) *adj.* oceanic.
oceanografía (o·θe·a·no·ɣra·'fi·a; o·se-) *n.f.* oceanography. —**oceanográfico** (-'ɣra·fi·ko) *adj.* oceanographic. —**oceanógrafo** (-'no·ɣra·fo) *n.m.* oceanographer.
ocelote (o·θe'lo·te; o·se-) *n.m.* ocelot.
ocio ('o·θjo; 'o·sjo) *n.m.* idleness; leisure. —**ociosidad,** *n.f.* idleness; laziness. —**ocioso,** *adj.* idle; lazy; useless.
ocluir (o·klu'ir) *v.t.* [*infl.:* **concluir**] to occlude. —**oclusión** (-'sjon) *n.f.* occlusion. —**oclusivo** (-'si·βo) *adj.* occlusive.
ocre ('o·kre) *n.m.* ocher.
octa- (ok·ta) *prefix, var. of* **octo-:** *octágono,* octagon.
octaedro (ok·ta'e·ðro) *n.m.* octahedron. —**octaédrico,** *adj.* octahedral.
octágono (ok'ta·ɣo·no) *n.m.* octagon. —**octagonal,** *adj.* octagonal.
octano (ok'ta·no) *n.m.* octane.
octante (ok'tan·te) *n.m.* octant.
octava (ok'ta·βa) *n.f.* octave.
octavilla (ok·ta'βi·ʎa; -ja) *n.f.* handbill.
octavo (ok'ta·βo) *adj.* & *n.m.* eighth. —**en octavo,** octavo.
octeto (ok'te·to) *n.m.* octet.
octillón (ok·ti'ʎon; -'jon) *n.m.* a sextillion octillion; *Brit.* octillion.
octingentésimo (ok·tin·xen'te·si·mo) *adj.* & *n.m.* eight-hundredth.
octo- (ok·to) *also,* **oct-** (okt) *before a vowel; prefix* octo-; oct-; eight: *octogenario,* octogenarian; *octeto,* octet.
octogenario (ok·to·xe'na·rjo) *adj.* & *n.m.* octogenarian.
octogésimo (ok·to'xe·si·mo) *adj.* & *n.m.* eightieth.

octubre (ok'tu·βre) *n.m.* October.

óctuple ('ok·tu·ple) *adj.* & *n.m.* & *f.* octuple. *Also,* **óctuplo** (-plo) *adj.* & *n.m.* —**octuplicar** (-pli'kar) *v.t.* [*infl.:* **tocar**] to octuple.

ocular (o·ku'lar) *adj.* ocular. —*n.m.* eyepiece.

oculista (o·ku'lis·ta) *n.m.* & *f.* oculist.

oculo- (o·ku·lo) *prefix* oculo-; eye: *oculomotor,* oculomotor.

ocultación (o·kul·ta'θjon; -'sjon) *n.f.* **1,** concealment. **2,** *astron.* occultation.

ocultar (o·kul'tar) *v.t.* to hide; conceal.

oculto (o'kul·to) *adj.* hidden; concealed; occult. —**ocultismo,** *n.m.* occultism.

ocupación (o·ku·pa'θjon; -'sjon) *n.f.* **1,** occupation. **2,** occupancy.

ocupante (o·ku'pan·te) *n.m.* & *f.* occupant. —*adj.* occupying.

ocupar (o·ku'par) *v.t.* to occupy. —**ocuparse,** *v.r.* **1,** to occupy oneself; be busy. **2,** *fol. by* **de,** to take charge of; concern oneself with; take care of.

ocurrencia (o·ku'rren·θja; -sja) *n.f.* **1,** occurrence. **2,** *fig.* bright idea. —**ocurrente,** *adj.* witty.

ocurrir (o·ku'rrir) *v.t.* to occur.

ochavo (o'tʃa·βo) *n.m.* **1,** an ancient brass coin. **2,** *Amer., colloq.* small coin; *pl.* money.

ochavón (o·tʃa'βon) *adj.* & *n.m.* octoroon.

ochenta (o'tʃen·ta) *adj.* & *n.m.* eighty. —**ochentavo,** *adj.* & *n.m.* eightieth.

ocho ('o·tʃo) *adj.* & *n.m.* eight.

ochocientos (o·tʃo'θjen·tos; -'sjen·tos) *adj.* & *n.m.pl.* [*fem.* **-tas**] eight hundred. —*adj.* eight-hundredth.

oda ('o·ða) *n.f.* ode.

-oda ('o·ða) *suffix* -ode; *forming nouns and adjectives denoting* like; in the form of: *geoda,* geode; *nematoda,* nematode.

odiar (o'ðjar) *v.t.* to hate.

odio ('o·ðjo) *n.m.* **1,** hate; hatred. **2,** odium.

odioso (o'ðjo·so) *adj.* hateful; odious. —**odiosidad,** *n.f.* hatefulness; odiousness.

odisea (o·ði'se·a) *n.f.* Odyssey.

-odo (o·ðo) *suffix* -ode; *forming nouns denoting* path; way: *cátodo,* cathode.

odómetro (o'ðo·me·tro) *n.m.* odometer.

-odonte (o'ðon·te) *suffix* -odont; tooth: *macrodonte,* macrodont.

odonto- (o·ðon·to) *also,* **odont-** (o·ðont) *before a vowel; prefix* odonto-; odont-; tooth: *odontología,* odontology; *odontalgia,* odontalgia.

odontología (o·ðon·to·lo'xi·a) *n.f.* odontology; dentistry. —**odontológico** (-'lo·xi·ko) *adj.* odontological. —**odontólogo** (-'to·lo·ɣo) *n.m.* odontologist; dentist.

odorífero (o·ðo'ri·fe·ro) *adj.* odoriferous.

odre ('o·ðre) *n.m.* **1,** wineskin. **2,** *colloq.* drunkard; tippler.

oeste (o'es·te) *n.m.* west.

ofender (o·fen'der) *v.t.* to offend. —**ofenderse,** *v.r.* to take offense.

ofensa (o'fen·sa) *n.f.* offense.

ofensiva (o·fen'si·βa) *n.f.* offensive.

ofensivo (o·fen'si·βo) *adj.* offensive.

ofensor (o·fen'sor) *adj.* offending. —*n.m.* offender.

oferta (o'fer·ta) *n.f.* offer. —**oferta y demanda,** supply and demand.

ofertorio (o·fer'to·rjo) *n.m.* offertory.

oficial (o·fi'θjal; -'sjal) *adj.* official. —*n.m.* **1,** official. **2,** officer.

oficialidad (o·fi·θja·li'ðað; -sja·li'ðað) *n.f.* **1,** officers collectively. **2,** official nature.

oficiar (o·fi'θjar; -'sjar) *v.i.* to officiate. —**oficiante,** *n.m., eccles.* celebrant.

oficina (o·fi'θi·na; -'si·na) *n.f.* office. —**oficinista,** *n.m.* & *f.* office clerk.

oficio (o'fi·θjo; -sjo) *n.m.* **1,** craft; trade. **2,** function; office. **3,** official communication. —**oficios,** *n.m.pl., eccles.* office (*sing.*); services.

oficioso (o·fi'θjo·so; -'sjo·so) *adj.* **1,** officious. **2,** helpful. —**oficiosidad,** *n.f.* officiousness.

ofrecer (o·fre'θer; -'ser) *v.t.* [*pres. ind.* **ofrezco** (-'freθ·ko; -'fres·ko); *pres.subjve.* **ofrezca** (-ka)] **1,** to offer. **2,** to present; show. —**ofrecimiento,** *n.m.* offer; offering. —**¿Qué se le ofrece?,** What do you wish?

ofrenda (o'fren·da) *n.f.* offering; gift. —**ofrendar,** *v.t.* to present.

oftálmico (of'tal·mi·ko) *adj.* ophthalmic.

oftalmo- (of'tal·mo) *prefix* ophthalmo-; eye: *oftalmología,* ophthalmology.
oftalmología (of·tal·mo·lo'xi·a) *n.f.* ophthalmology. —**oftalmólogo** (-'mo·lo·ɣo) *n.m.* ophthalmologist; oculist.
ofuscar (o·fus'kar) *v.t.* [*pres.subjve.* **ofusque** (o'fus·ke); *pret.* **ofusqué** (-'ke)] to obfuscate; bewilder. —**ofuscación,** *n.f., also,* **ofuscamiento,** *n.m.* bewilderment.
ogro ('o·ɣro) *n.m.* ogre.
¡Oh! (o) *interj.* Oh!
ohmio ('o·mjo) *n.m.* ohm. *Also,* **ohm** (om).
oíble (o'i·βle) *adj.* audible.
-oide ('oi·ðe) *suffix* -oid; resembling like: *celuloide* celluloid.
-oideo (oi'ðe·o) *suffix* -oid; *forming adjectives denoting* like; resembling: *mastoideo,* mastoid.
oído (o'i·ðo) *n.m.* **1,** ear. **2,** hearing. —**oídas,** *n.f.pl.,* in **de** *or* **por oídas,** by hearsay.
oír (o'ir) *v.t.* & *i.* [*pres.ind.* **oigo** ('oi·ɣo), **oyes, oye, oímos** (o'i·mos), **oís** (o'is), **oyen;** *pres.subjve.* **oiga** ('oi·ɣa); *impve.* **oye;** *pret.* **oí** (o'i), **oyó;** *pr.p.* **oyente;** *ger.* **oyendo**] to hear; listen. —**oír decir (que),** to hear (that). —**oír hablar (de),** to hear (about).
ojal (o'xal) *n.m.* buttonhole.
¡ojalá! (o·xa'la) *interj.* God grant . . . ! Would that . . . !
ojeada (o·xe'a·ða) *n.f.* glance.
ojear (o·xe'ar) *v.t.* to eye; ogle.
ojera (o'xe·ra) *n.f.* eyecup. —**ojeras,** *n.f.pl.* rings under the eyes.
ojeriza (o·xe'ri·θa; -sa) *n.f.* ill will; grudge.
ojeroso (o·xe'ro·so) *adj.* having rings under the eyes; haggard.
ojete (o'xe·te) *n.m.* eyelet.
ojiva (o'xi·βa) *n.f.* ogive.
ojo ('o·xo) *n.m.* **1,** eye. **2,** look; regard. **3,** opening between bridge supports. —**a ojo de buen cubero,** *colloq.* roughly; approximately. —**a ojos vistas,** clearly; openly. —**costar un ojo de la cara,** *colloq* to cost an arm and a leg. —**dar en los ojos,** *also,* **saltar a los ojos,** to be obvious. —**¡Dichosos los ojos!** You're a sight for sore eyes! —**echar el ojo a,** to set one's eye on. —**globo del ojo,** eyeball. —**mal de ojo,** evil eye. —**mirar con buenos** (*or* **malos**) **ojos,** to look favorably (*or* unfavorably) upon. —**¡mucho ojo!** *also,* **¡ojo!,** beware! —**no pegar los ojos,** *colloq.* not to sleep a wink. —**ojo amoratado,** black eye. —**ojo avizor,** sharp eye. —**ojo de buey, 1,** *bot.* oxeye. **2,** *naut.* porthole. —**ojo de la cerradura,** keyhole. —**ojos saltones,** popeyes.
-ol ('ol) *suffix, chem.* -ol; *forming nouns denoting* alcohol or phenol derivative: *mentol,* menthol.
ola ('o·la) *n.f.* wave.
olaje (o'la·xe) *n.m.* = **oleaje.**
¡olé! (o'le) *also,* **¡ole!** ('o·le) *interj.* bravo!; ole!
oleada (o·le'a·ða) *n.f.* **1,** big wave. **2,** pounding of waves. **3,** press; crush (*of a crowd*).
oleaginoso (o·le·a·xi'no·so) *adj.* oily; oleaginous.
oleaje (o·le'a·xe) *n.m.* **1,** surf. **2,** heavy sea. **3,** waves (*pl.*).
-olento (o'len·to) *suffix, forming adjectives denoting* quality; condition: *sanguinolento* bloody.
óleo ('o·le·o) *n.m.* oil.
oleo- (o·le·o) *prefix* oleo-; oil: *oleomargarina,* oleomargarine.
oleomargarina (o·le·o·mar·ɣa·'ri·na) *n.f.* oleomargarine.
oleoso (o·le'o·so) *adj.* oily.
oler (o'ler) *v.t.* [*pres.ind.* **huelo;** *pres.subjve.* **huela**] to smell; sniff. —*v.i.* to smell; stink. —**oler a,** to smell of.
olfatear (ol·fa·te'ar) *v.t.* & *i.* to smell; sniff; scent. —**olfateo** (-'te·o) *n.m* sniffing.
olfato (ol'fa·to) *n.m.* **1,** sense of smell. **2,** *fig.* perspicacity. —**olfatorio,** *adj.* olfactory.
oligarquía (o·li·ɣar'ki·a) *n.f.* oligarchy. —**oligarca** (-'ɣar·ka) *n.m.* oligarch. —**oligárquico** (-'ɣar·ki·ko) *adj.* oligarchical.
oligo- (o·li·ɣo) *also* **olig-** (o·liɣ) *before a vowel; prefix* oligo-; olig-; few; scanty *oligarquía,* oligarchy; *oliguria,* oliguria.
Olimpo (o'lim·po) *n.m.* Olympus. —**olímpico,** *adj.* Olympic. —**olimpíada** (-'pi·a·ða) *n.f.* Olympic Games; Olympiad.
oliva (o'li·βa) *n.f.* olive. —**olivar,** *n.m.* olive grove. —**olivo,** *n.m. also,* **olivera,** (-'βe·ra) *n.f.* olive tree.
olmo ('ol·mo) *n.m.* elm. —**olmeda,** *n.f.* grove of elms.
ológrafo (o'lo·ɣra·fo) *adj.* & *n.m.* holograph.
olor (o'lor) *n.m.* odor. —**oloroso,** *adj.* odorous; fragrant.

olvidar (ol·βi'ðar) *v.i.* to forget. —**olvidarse,** *v.r.* **1,** to be forgotten; slip one's mind. **2,** *fol. by* **de,** to forget. —**olvidadizo,** *adj.* forgetful.

olvido (ol'βi·ðo) *n.m.* **1,** forgetfulness. **2,** oversight. **3,** oblivion. —**echar al** *or* **en olvido,** to forget.

olla ('o·ʎa; 'o·ja) *n.f.* **1,** pot. **2,** stew. —**olla de grillos,** bedlam. —**olla podrida,** a Spanish stew.

ollar (o'ʎar; -'jar) *n.m.* nostril.

-oma ('o·ma) *suffix* -oma; morbid growth: *fibroma,* fibroma.

ombligo (om'bli·ɣo) *n.m.* navel.

omega (o'me·ɣa) *n.f.* omega.

ominoso (o·mi'no·so) *adj.* ominous. —**ominosidad,** *n.f.* ominousness.

omiso (o'mi·so) *adj.* careless; remiss. —**hacer caso omiso de,** to omit; overlook; ignore.

omitir (o·mi'tir) *v.t.* to omit. —**omisión** (-'sjon) omission.

omni- (om·ni) *prefix* omni-; all: *omnipotente,* omnipotent.

ómnibus ('om·ni·βus) *n.m.sing.* & *pl.* omnibus; bus.

omnipotente (om·ni·po'ten·te) *adj.* omnipotent. —**omnipotencia,** *n.f.* omnipotence.

omnipresente (om·ni·pre'sen·te) *adj.* omnipresent. —**omnipresencia,** *n.f.* omnipresence.

omnisciente (om·nis'θjen·te; -ni·'sjen·te) *adj.* omniscient. —**omnisciencia,** *n.f.* omniscience.

omnívoro (om'ni·βo·ro) *adj.* omnivorous.

omóplato (o'mo·pla·to) *n.m.* shoulder blade; scapula.

-ón ('on) *fem.* **-ona** ('o·na) *suffix* **1,** *forming nouns and adjectives with augmentative, and often derogatory, force: hombrón,* big man; *solterona,* spinster; *bravucón,* fourflushing; fourflusher. **2,** *affixed to numbers, denotes* of a certain age: *cincuentón,* quinquagenarian. **3,** *added to verbs, forms nouns and adjectives expressing tendency or instinct to do the action contained in the verb: acusón,* talebearing; tattletale. **4,** *forming nouns from verbs denoting* rough, sudden action: *apretón,* squeeze. **5,** *forming nouns denoting: in physics,* subatomic particles: *protón,* proton; *in chemistry,* inert gases: *argón,* argon.

-ona ('o·na) *suffix* **1,** *chem.* -one; *forming names of ketones: acetona,* acetone. **2,** *fem. of* **-ón.**

once ('on·θe; -se) *adj.* & *n.m.* eleven. —**onceavo,** *adj.* & *n.m.* = **onzavo.**

onceno (on'θe·no; -'se·no) *adj.* & *n.m.* eleventh.

-oncho ('on·tʃo) *suffix, forming augmentatives: rechoncho,* chubby.

onda ('on·da) *n.f.* wave; ripple. —**ondear,** *v.i.* to wave; ripple; flutter.

ondular (on·du'lar) *v.t.* to wave, esp. the hair. —*v.i.* to undulate; wave; wriggle. —**ondulación,** *n.f.* undulation; wave. —**ondulado,** *adj.* wavy. —**ondulante,** *adj.* waving; undulant.

oneroso (o·ne'ro·so) *adj.* onerous. —**onerosidad,** *n.f.* onerousness.

ónice ('o·ni·θe; -se) *n.m. or f.* onyx. *Also,* **ónix.**

-onimia (o'ni·mja) *suffix, forming nouns corresponding to nouns and adjectives ending in* **-ónimo:** *toponimia,* toponymy.

-ónimo ('o·ni·mo) *suffix, forming nouns and adjectives denoting* name; appellation: *sinónimo,* synonym; synonymous.

ónix ('o·niks) *n.m. or f. sing.* & *pl.* onyx.

onoma- (o·no·ma) *prefix* onoma-; name: *onomatopeya,* onomatopoeia.

onomástico (o·no'mas·ti·ko) *n.m., also,* **onomástica,** *n.f.* name day.

onomatopeya (o·no·ma·to'pe·ja) *n.f.* onomatopoeia. —**onomatopéyico,** (-'pe·ji·ko) *adj.* onomatopoetic.

onto- (on·to) *prefix* onto-; existence; being: *ontogenia,* ontogeny.

ontología (on·to·lo'xi·a) *n.f.* ontology. —**ontológico** (-'lo·xi·ko) *adj.* ontological. —**ontólogo** (-'to·lo·ɣo) *n.m.* ontologist.

onza ('on·θa; -sa) *n.f.* **1,** ounce. **2,** snow leopard; ounce.

onzavo (on'θa·βo; -'sa·βo) *adj.* & *n.m.* eleventh.

oo- (o·o) *prefix* oö-; egg: *oogénesis,* oögenesis.

opaco (o'pa·ko) *adj.* opaque. —**opacidad** (-θi'ðað; -si'ðað) *n.f.* opacity.

opalescente (o·pa·les'θen·te; -le'sen·te) *adj.* opalescent. —**opalescencia,** *n.f.* opalescence.

opalino (o·pa'li·no) *adj.* opaline.

ópalo ('o·pa·lo) *n.m.* opal.

opción (op'θjon; -'sjon) *n.f.* option. —**opcional,** *adj.* optional.

-ope ('o·pe) *suffix* -opic; -ope; *forming nouns and adjectives denoting* having a (specified) kind or defect of eye: *miope,* myopic; myope.
ópera ('o·pe·ra) *n.f.* opera.
operable (o·pe'ra·βle) *adj.* operable.
operación (o·pe·ra'θjon; -'sjon) *n.f.* operation.
operador (o·pe·ra'ðor) *adj.* operating; operative. —*n.m.* operator. —**operador cinematográfico,** 1, cameraman. 2, projectionist.
operante (o·pe'ran·te) *adj.* 1, operating; operative. 2, effective.
operar (o·pe'rar) *v.t.* & *i.*, *surg.* to operate. —*v.i.* 1, to operate; work. 2, *comm.* to speculate.
operático (o·pe'ra·ti·ko) *adj.* operatic.
operatorio (o·pe·ra'to·rjo) *adj.*, *surg.* operative.
opereta (o·pe're·ta) *n.f.* operetta.
-opía (o'pi·a) *suffix* -opia; -opy; *denoting* a (specified) kind or defect of eye: *miopía,* myopia.
opiado (o'pja·ðo) *adj.* opiate.
opiata (o'pja·ta) *n.f.* opiate. *Also,* **opiato** (-to) *n.m.*
opinar (o·pi'nar) *v.i.* to think; opine.
opinión (o·pi'njon) *n.f.* opinion.
opio ('o·pjo) *n.m.* opium.
opíparo (o'pi·pa·ro) *adj.* lavish; sumptuous.
oponer (o·po'ner) *v.t.* [*infl.:* **poner**] to oppose; place against. —**oponerse,** *v.r.* to object; be opposed.
oporto (o'por·to) *n.m.* port (*wine*).
oportunidad (o·por·tu·ni'ðað) *n.f.* 1, opportunity. 2, opportuneness.
oportuno (o·por'tu·no) *adj.* 1, opportune. 2, quick-witted. —**oportunismo,** *n.m.* opportunism. —**oportunista,** *n.m.* & *f.* opportunist. —*adj.* opportunistic.
oposición (o·po·si'θjon; -'sjon) *n.f.* 1, opposition. 2, *usu.pl.* competitive examinations. —**oposicionista,** *n.m* & *f.* oppositionist; member of the opposition. —*adj.* opposition (*attrib.*).
opositor (o·po·si'tor) *n.m.* 1, competitor, esp. in a competitive examination. 2, opponent.
opresión (o·pre'sjon) *n.f.* oppression. —**opresivo** (-'si·βo) *adj.* oppressive. —**opresor** (-'sor) *n.m.* oppressor. —*adj.* oppressive.
oprimir (o·pri'mir) *v.t.* 1, to press. 2, to oppress.
oprobio (o'pro·βjo) *n.m.* opprobrium. —**oprobioso,** *adj.* opprobrious.
optar (op'tar) *v.i.* to choose; decide.
óptica ('op·ti·ka) *n.f.* 1, optics. 2, optical shop. —**óptico,** *n.m.* optician. —*adj.* optic; optical.
optimismo (op·ti'mis·mo) *n.m.* optimism. —**optimista,** *adj.* optimistic. —*n.m.* & *f.* optimist.
óptimo ('op·ti·mo) *adj.*, *superl. of* **bueno.** —*adj.* & *n.m.* optimum.
optometría (op·to·me'tri·a) *n.f.* optometry. —**optómetra** (-'to·me·tra) *also,* **optometrista** (-'tris·ta) *n.m.* & *f.* optometrist. - **optómetro** (-'to·me·tro) *n.m.* optometer.
opuesto (o'pwes·to) *v., p.p. of* **oponer.** —*adj.* & *n.m.* opposite; contrary.
opulento (o·pu'len·to) *adj.* opulent. —**opulencia,** *n.f.* opulence.
opúsculo (o'pus·ku·lo) *n.m.* tract; booklet.
opuse (o'pu·se) *v., pret. of* **oponer.**
oquedad (o·ke'ðað) *n.f.* 1, cavity; hollow. 2, *fig.* hollowness; emptiness.
-or ('or) *suffix, forming nouns denoting* 1, -or; -er; agent: *pintor,* painter; *eyector,* ejector. 2, -or; -ness; condition; quality; *langor,* languor; *dulzor,* sweetness.
ora ('o·ra) *conj.* (*in correlative constructions*) now: *ora rico, ora pobre,* now rich, now poor.
oración (o·ra'θjon; -'sjon) *n.f.* 1, speech; oration. 2, prayer. 3, *gram.* sentence. —**partes de la oración,** parts of speech.
oráculo (o'ra·ku·lo) *n.m.* oracle. —**oracular,** *adj.* oracular.
orador (o·ra'ðor) *n.m.* orator; speaker.
oral (o'ral) *adj.* oral.
-orama (o'ra·ma) *suffix, forming nouns denoting* sight; view: *diorama,* diorama.
orangután (o·ran·gu'tan) *n.m.* orangutan.
orar (o'rar) *v.i.* to pray.
orate (o'ra·te) *n.m.* & *f.* lunatic.
oratoria (o·ra'to·rja) *n.f.* oratory; eloquence.
oratorio (o·ra'to·rjo) *n.m.* 1, small chapel; oratory. 2, oratorio. —*adj.* oratorical.
orbe ('or·βe) *n.m.* orb.

órbita ('or·βi·ta) *n.f.* orbit. —**orbital,** *adj.* orbital.
orca ('or·ka) *n.f., also,* **orco** (-ko) *n.m.* killer whale.
ordalías (or·ða'li·as) *n.f.pl., hist.* ordeal (*sing.*).
orden ('or·ðen) *n.m.* order; arrangement. —*n.f.* **1,** order; command. **2,** *comm.* order. **3,** religious order; order of knighthood; honor society. —**órdenes,** *n.f.pl.* holy orders. —**a sus órdenes,** at your service. —**orden del día,** agenda.
ordenación (or·ðe·na'θjon; -'sjon) *n.f.* **1,** *eccles.* ordination. **2,** arrangement; disposition.
ordenado (or·ðe'na·ðo) *adj.* ordered; orderly. —**ordenada,** *n.f., geom.* ordinate.
ordenancista (or·ðe·nan'θis·ta; -'sis·ta) *n.* disciplinarian; martinet.
ordenanza (or·ðe'nan·θa; -sa) *n.f.* ordinance; bylaw. —*n.m.* **1,** *mil.* orderly. **2,** office boy.
ordenar (or·ðe'nar) *v.t.* **1,** to order; command. **2,** to arrange. **3,** to direct. **4,** *eccles.* to ordain.
ordeñar (or·ðe'ɲar) *v.t.* & *i.* **1,** to milk. **2,** to strip, as olives from the branch.
ordeño (or'ðe·ɲo) *n.m.* **1,** milking. **2,** stripping, as from a branch.
ordinal (or·ði'nal) *adj.* & *n.m.* ordinal.
ordinario (or·ði'na·rjo) *adj.* **1,** ordinary; common; usual. **2,** coarse; vulgar. —*n.m.* **1,** *eccles.* bishop. **2,** delivery man; expressman. —**ordinariez,** *n.f.* vulgarity. —**de ordinario,** usually.
orégano (o're·ɣa·no) *n.m.* oregano.
oreja (o're·xa) *n.f.* **1,** ear; outer ear. **2,** *mech.* lug. —**orejera,** *n.f.* earflap; earmuff. —**calentar las orejas a,** to scold sharply; dress down. —**con las orejas caídas** *or* **gachas,** crestfallen. —**enseñar la oreja,** to show one's true colors.
orfanato (or·fa'na·to) *n.m.* orphanage.
orfandad (or·fan'dað) *n.f.* orphanhood; orphanage.
orfebre (or'fe·βre) *n.m.* goldsmith; silversmith. —**orfebrería,** *n.f.* goldsmith's *or* silversmith's trade.
orfeón (or·fe'on) *n.m.* glee club; choral society. —**orfeonista,** *n.m.* & *f.* chorister.
organdí (or·ɣan'di) *n.m.* organdy.
orgánico (or'ɣa·ni·ko) *adj.* organic.
organillo (or·ɣa'ni·ʎo; -jo) *n.m.* hand organ; barrel organ; hurdy-gurdy. —**organillero,** *n.m.* organ grinder.
organismo (or·ɣa'nis·mo) *n.m.* **1,** organism. **2,** organization.
organista (or·ɣa'nis·ta) *n.m.* & *f.* organist.
organizar (or·ɣa·ni'θar; -'sar) *v.t.* [*pres.subjve.* **organice** (-'ni·θe; -'ni·se); *pret.* **organicé** (-'θe; -'se)] to organize. —**organización,** *n.f.* organization. —**organizador,** *n.m.* organizer. —*adj.* organizing.
órgano ('or·ɣa·no) *n.m.* **1,** organ. **2,** pipe organ. **3,** *fig.* medium; instrument.
orgasmo (or'ɣas·mo) *n.m.* orgasm.
orgía (or'xi·a) *n.f.* orgy. —**orgiástico** (or'xjas·ti·ko) *adj.* orgiastic.
orgullo (or'ɣu·ʎo; -jo) *n.m.* pride; haughtiness. —**orgulloso,** *adj.* proud; haughty.
oriental (o·rjen'tal) *adj.* **1,** eastern. **2,** Oriental. —*n.m.* & *f.* **1,** easterner. **2,** Oriental.
orientar (o·rjen'tar) *v.t.* **1,** to orient. **2,** to brief; inform. —**orientación,** *n.f.* orientation.
oriente (o'rjen·te) *n.m.* **1,** east. **2,** *cap.* Orient.
orificar (o·ri·fi'kar) *v.t.* [*infl.:* **tocar**] to fill (a tooth) with gold. —**orificación,** *n.f.* gold filling.
orificio (o·ri'fi·θjo; -sjo) *n.m.* orifice.
origen (o'ri·xen) *n.m.* origin.
original (o·ri·xi'nal) *adj.* & *n.m.* & *f.* original. —**originalidad,** *n.f.* originality.
originar (o·ri·xi'nar) *v.t.* to originate; start; give rise to. —**originarse,** *v.r.* to originate; arise. —**originador,** *n.m.* originator. —*adj.* originating; causing.
originario (o·ri·xi'na·rjo) *adj.* **1,** originating. **2,** native.
orilla (o'ri·ʎa; -ja) *n.f.* **1,** edge. **2,** shore; bank. **3,** shoulder (*of a road*).
orillo (o'ri·ʎo; -jo) *n.m.* selvage.
orín (o'rin) *n.m.* **1,** rust. **2,** *usu.pl.* urine.

orina (o'ri·na) *n.f.* urine. —**orinar,** *v.i.* to urinate. —**orinal,** *n.m.* chamber pot.
-orio ('o·rjo) *fem.* **-oria** ('o·rja) *suffix.* **1,** -ing; -ory; *forming adjectives denoting, in an active or passive sense,* aptitude; suitability: *meritorio,* deserving; *transitorio,* transitory. **2,** -ory; -orium; *forming nouns denoting* place: *refectorio,* refectory; *sanatorio,* sanatorium. **3,** *forming nouns denoting* action; result of action: *velorio,* wake; *trayectoria,* trajectory.
oriol (o'rjol) *n.m.* oriole.
Orión (o'rjon) *n.m.* Orion.
oriundo (o'rjun·do) *adj.* native.
orla ('or·la) *n.f.* **1,** fringe; trimming. **2,** fillet; molding. **3,** ornamental border. **4,** mat; border for a picture.
orlar (or'lar) *v.t.* to border; edge; trim.
orlón (or'lon) *n.m.* orlon.
ornado (or'na·ðo) *adj.* ornate; adorned.
ornamento (or·na'men·to) *n.m.* **1,** ornament. **2,** *pl., eccles.* vestments. —**ornamentación,** *n.f.* ornamentation. —**ornamental,** *adj.* ornamental. —**ornamentar,** *v.t.* = **adornar.**
ornar (or'nar) *v.t.* = **adornar.**
ornato (or'na·to) *n.m.* adornment; decoration.
ornito- (or·ni·to) *prefix* ornitho-; bird: *ornitología,* ornithology.
ornitología (or·ni·to·lo'xi·a) *n.f.* ornithology. —**ornitológico** (-'lo·xi·ko) *adj.* ornithological. —**ornitólogo** (-'to·lo·ɣo) *n.m.* ornithologist.
ornitorrinco (or·ni·to'rrin·ko) *n.m.* platypus.
oro ('o·ro) *n.m.* **1,** gold. **2,** gold coin. **3,** *pl., cards* in the Spanish deck, the suit corresponding to diamonds. —**pan de oro,** gold leaf.
orondo (o'ron·do) *adj.* **1,** puffed out; puffy. **2,** *colloq.* puffed up; vain; conceited.
oropel (o·ro'pel) *n.m.* tinsel.
orquesta (or'kes·ta) *n.m.* orchestra. —**orquestal,** *adj.* orchestral.
orquestar (or·kes'tar) *v.t. & i.* to orchestrate. —**orquestación,** *n.f.* orchestration.
orquídea (or'ki·ðe·a) *n.f.* orchid.
ortiga (or'ti·ɣa) *n.f.* nettle.
orto- (or·to) *prefix* ortho-; upright; straight; correct: *ortostático,* orthostatic; *ortodoxo,* orthodox.
ortodoncia (or·to'ðon·θja; -sja) *n.f.* orthodontia.
ortodoxo (or·to'ðok·so) *adj.* orthodox. —**ortodoxia** (-'ðok·sja) *n.f.* orthodoxy.
ortogonal (or·to·ɣo'nal) *adj.* orthogonal.
ortografía (or·to·ɣra'fi·a) *n.f.* spelling; orthography. —**ortográfico** (-'ɣra·fi·ko) *adj.* orthographic.
ortopedia (or·to'pe·ðja) *n.f.* orthopedics. —**ortopédico** (-ði·ko) *adj.* orthopedic. —*n.m.* [*also,* **ortopedista,** *n.m.* & *f.*] orthopedist.
oruga (o'ru·ɣa) *n.f.* caterpillar.
orzuelo (or'θwe·lo; -'swe·lo) *n.m.* **1,** *pathol.* sty. **2,** snare.
os (os) *pers.pron. 2nd pers.pl., used as obj. of a verb* you; to you; yourselves.
osa ('o·sa) *n.f.* she-bear. —**Osa Mayor,** Ursa Major; Big Dipper. —**Osa Menor,** Ursa Minor; Little Dipper.
-osa ('o·sa) *suffix, chem.* -ose; carbohydrate: *celulosa,* cellulose.
osado (o'sa·ðo) *adj.* daring; bold. —**osadía,** *n.f.* daring; boldness.
osar (o'sar) *v.i.* to dare; venture.
osario (o'sa·rjo) *n.m.* ossuary.
oscilar (os·θi'lar; o·si-) *v.i.* to oscillate. —**oscilación,** *n.f.* oscillation. —**oscilador,** *n.m.* oscillator. —**oscilante,** *adj.* oscillating. —**oscilatorio,** *adj.* oscillating.
oscilógrafo (os·θi'lo·ɣra·fo; o·si-) *n.m.* oscillograph.
osciloscopio (os·θi·los'ko·pjo; o·si-) *n.m.* oscilloscope.
ósculo ('os·ku·lo) *n.m.* kiss.
oscurecer (os·ku·re'θer; -'ser) *v.* = **obscurecer.** —**oscuridad,** *n.f.* = **obscuridad.** —**oscuro,** *adj.* = **obscuro.**
óseo ('o·se·o) *adj.* osseous.
osezno (o'seθ·no; -'ses·no) *n.m.* bear cub.
-osidad (o·si'ðað) *suffix* -osity; *forming nouns corresponding to adjectives ending in* **-oso**: *belicosidad,* bellicosity.
osificarse (o·si·fi'kar·se) *v.r.* [*pres.subjve.* **osifique** (-'fi·ke); *pret.* **osifiqué** (-'ke)] to ossify. —**osificación,** *n.f.* ossification.
-osis (o·sis) *suffix* -osis; *forming nouns denoting* **1,** action; condi-

tion: *ósmosis,* osmosis. **2,** diseased condition: *avitaminosis,* avitaminosis.

osmio ('os·mjo) *n.m.* osmium.

ósmosis ('os·mo·sis) *also,* **osmosis** (-'mo·sis) *n.f.* osmosis. —**osmótico** (-'mo·ti·ko) *adj.* osmotic.

oso ('o·so) *n.m.* bear. —**oso blanco,** polar bear. —**oso gris,** grizzly bear. —**oso hormiguero,** anteater. —**oso marino,** fur seal. —**oso pardo,** brown bear.

-oso ('o·so) *suffix* **1,** -ose; -ous; -y: *forming adjectives denoting* full of; having; characterized by: *belicoso,* bellicose; *vicioso,* vicious; *aceitoso,* oily. **2,** *chem.* -ous; *denoting a lower valence in a compound than that denoted by* **-ico**: *sulfuroso,* sulfurous.

ostensible (os·ten'si·βle) *adj.* ostensible; apparent.

ostentar (os·ten'tar) *v.t.* to exhibit; display. —**ostentación,** *n.f.* ostentation; display. —**ostentoso,** *adj.* ostentatious.

osteo- (os·te·o) *prefix* osteo-; bone: *osteología,* osteology.

osteología (os·te·o·lo'xi·a) *n.f.* osteology. —**osteólogo** (-'o·lo·ɣo) *n.m.* osteologist.

osteopatía (os·te·o·pa'ti·a) *n.f.* osteopathy. —**osteópata** (-'o·pa·ta) *n.m. & f.* osteopath.

ostra ('os·tra) *n.f.* oyster.

ostracismo (os·tra'θis·mo; -'sis·mo) *n.m.* ostracism.

ostrón (os'tron) *n.m.* a kind of large oyster. *Also,* **ostión** (-'tjon).

osuno (o'su·no) *adj.* bearlike.

-otazo (o'ta·θo; -so) *suffix, var. of* **-azo**: *manotazo,* hard slap on the hands.

otero (o'te·ro) *n.m.* hill; hillock.

otitis (o'ti·tis) *n.f.* otitis.

oto- (o·to) *also,* **ot-** (ot) *before a vowel, prefix* oto-; ot-; ear: *otología,* otology; *otalgia,* otalgia.

otología (o·to·lo'xi·a) *n.f.* otology. —**otólogo** (o'to·lo·ɣo) otologist.

otomano (o·to'ma·no) *adj.* & *n.m.* Ottoman. —**otomana,** *n.f.* ottoman; divan.

otoño (o'to·ɲo) *n.m.* autumn; fall. —**otoñal,** *adj.* autumnal; fall (*attrib.*).

otorgar (o·tor'ɣar) *v.t.* [*pres. subjve.* **otorgue** (-'tor·ɣe); *pret.* **otorgué** (-'ɣe)] **1,** to grant. **2,** to consent to. **3,** *law* to execute (a document). —**otorgante,** *n.m.* & *f.* grantor.

otramente (o·tra'men·te) *adv.* otherwise.

otro ('o·tro) *adj.* & *pron.* other; another. —**al otro día,** on the next day. —**al otro día de,** on the day after. —**la otra vida,** the hereafter. —**otro que tal,** another such. —**otros tantos,** as many more.

otrora (o'tro·ra) *adv.* formerly.

otrosí (o·tro'si) *adv.* furthermore.

ovación (o·βa'θjon; -'sjon) *n.f.* ovation.

ovado (o'βa·ðo) *adj.* ovate.

óvalo ('o·βa·lo) *n.m.* oval. —**ovalado,** *also,* **oval** (o'βal) *adj.* oval.

ovario (o'βa·rjo) *n.m.* ovary. —**ovárico** (o'βa·ri·ko) *adj.* ovarian.

oveja (o'βe·xa) *n.f.* ewe. —**ovejero,** *n.m.* shepherd; sheep raiser. —**ovejuno,** *adj.* of sheep; sheep (*attrib.*).

overol (o·βe'rol) *n.m., Amer.* overalls (*pl.*). *Also,* **overoles,** *n.m. pl.*

ovi- (o·βi) *prefix* ovi-; egg: *oviforme,* oviform.

ovillo (o'βi·ʎo; -jo) *n.m.* skein; clew.

ovino (o'βi·no) *adj.* ovine.

ovíparo (o'βi·pa·ro) *adj.* oviparous.

ovoide (o'βoi·ðe) *adj.* & *n.m.* ovoid.

óvulo ('o·βu·lo) *n.m.* **1,** ovule. **2,** ovum. —**ovulación,** *n.f.* ovulation.

oxálico (ok'sa·li·ko) *adj.* oxalic.

oxi- (ok·si) *prefix* oxy-. **1,** oxygen: *oxisulfuro,* oxysulfide. **2,** acute; sharp: *oxicefálico,* oxycephalic.

oxiacetilénico (ok·si·a·θe·ti'le·ni·ko; ok·si·a·se-) *adj.* oxyacetylene.

óxido ('ok·si·ðo) *n.m.* oxide. —**oxidar,** *v.t.* to oxidize. —**oxidación,** *n.f.* oxidation.

oxigenar (ok·si·xe'nar) *v.t.* to oxygenate. —**oxigenación,** *n.f.* oxygenation.

oxígeno (ok'si·xe·no) *n.m.* oxygen. —**agua oxigenada,** hydrogen peroxide.

oye ('o·je) *v.* **1,** *3rd pers.sing. pres.ind. of* **oír. 2,** *impve.sing. of* **oír.**

oyen ('o·jen) *v., 3rd pers.pl. pres. ind. of* **oír.**
oyendo (o'jen·do) *v., ger. of* **oír.**
oyente (o'jen·te) *v., pr.p. of* **oír.** —*n.m.* listener; hearer.
oyes ('o·jes) *v., 2nd pers.sing. pres. ind. of* **oír.**
oyó (o'jo) *v., 3rd pers.sing. pret. of* **oír.**
ozono (o'θo·no; o'so-) *n.m.* ozone.

P

P, p (pe) *n.f.* 19th letter of the Spanish alphabet.
pa (pa) *prep., colloq.* = **para.**
pabellón (pa·βe'ʎon; -'jon) *n.m.* **1,** pavilion. **2,** flag; colors (*pl.*) **3,** canopy.
pabilo (pa'βi·lo) *n.m.* **1,** candlewick. **2,** snuff of a candle.
pábulo ('pa·βu·lo) *n.m.* nourishment; food. —**dar pábulo a,** to encourage; abet.
pacana (pa'ka·na) *n.f.* pecan. —**pacano,** *n.m.* pecan tree.
pacato (pa'ka·to) *adj.* timorous; pacific; quiet.
pacedura (pa·θe'ðu·ra; pa·se-) *n.f.* pasturage.
pacer (pa'θer; -'ser) *v.i. & t.* [*pres. ind.* **pazco;** *pres.subjve.* **pazca**] to pasture; graze.
paces ('pa·θes; -ses) *n.f., pl. of* **paz.** —**hacer las paces,** to make peace; make one's peace.
paciente (pa'θjen·te; pa'sjen-) *adj.* & *n.m.* & *f.* patient. —**paciencia,** *n.f.* patience.
pacienzudo (pa·θjen'θu·ðo; pa·sjen'su·) *adj.* patient; forbearing.
pacificar (pa·θi·fi'kar; pa·si-) *v.t.* [*infl.:* **tocar**] to pacify; appease. —**pacificarse,** *v.r.* to calm down; quiet down. —**pacificación,** *n.f.* pacification. —**pacificador,** *adj.* appeasing; peacemaking. —*n.m.* peacemaker.
pacífico (pa'θi·fi·ko; pa'si-) *adj.* pacific; peaceful. —*n.m., cap.* Pacific.
pacifismo (pa·θi'fis·mo; pa·si-) *n.m.* pacifism. —**pacifista,** *adj.* pacifistic. —*n.m.* & *f.* pacifist.
paco ('pa·ko) *n.m., Amer.* **1,** alpaca. **2,** *slang* cop; policeman.
pacotilla (pa·ko'ti·ʎa; -ja) *n.f.* bauble; bagatelle; knickknack. —**de pacotilla,** cheap; shoddy.
pactar (pak'tar) *v.t.* to agree to *or* upon.
pacto ('pak·to) *n.m.* pact; agreement; covenant.
pachá (pa'tʃa) *n.m.* pasha.
pachamanca (pa·tʃa'man·ka) *n.f. Amer.* **1,** barbecue. **2,** *slang* petting; necking.
pachorra (pa'tʃo·rra) *n.f.* sluggishness; slowness. *Also,* **pachocha** (-tʃa).
padecer (pa·ðe'θer; -'ser) *v.t.* [*pres.ind.* **padezco** (-'ðeθ·ko; -'ðes·ko); *pres.subjve.* **padezca** (-ka)] to suffer. —*v.i., fol. by* **de,** to suffer from *or* with. —**padecimiento,** *n.m.* suffering.
padilla (pa'ði·ʎa; -ja) *n.f.* **1,** small frying pan. **2,** bread oven.
padrastro (pa'ðras·tro) *n.m.* **1,** stepfather. **2,** hangnail.
padre ('pa·ðre) *n.m.* **1,** father. **2,** priest; padre. —**padres,** *n.m.pl* parents. —**armar el lío padre** *colloq.* to raise a row. —**de padre y señor mío,** *colloq.* terrific —**padre adoptivo,** foster father —**padre político** father-in-law.
padrenuestro (pa·ðre'nwes·tro) *n.m.* the Lord's Prayer.
padrinazgo (pa·ðri'naθ·ɣo; -'nas·ɣo) *n.m.* **1,** godfathership. **2,** patronage; sponsorship.
padrino (pa'ðri·no) *n.m.* **1,** godfather. **2,** second (*in a duel*). **3,** best man. **4,** patron; protector.
padrón (pa'ðron) *n.m.* **1,** pattern; model. **2,** census; registration. **3,** mark of infamy.
paella (pa'e·ʎa; -ja) *n.f.* a dish of rice with meats and seafood; paella.
¡paf! (paf) *interj.* imitating the sound of a blow, slap, fall, etc.; pow!
paga ('pa·ɣa) *n.f.* **1,** pay; payment. **2,** wages; salary. **3,** requital of love or friendship.
pagadero (pa·ɣa'ðe·ro) *adj.* **1,** payable. **2,** due. **3,** easily paid.
pagado (pa'ɣa·ðo) *adj., Amer.* self-satisfied; conceited.
pagador (pa·ɣa'ðor) *n.m.* **1,** payer. **2,** paymaster. **3,** paying teller.
pagaduría (pa·ɣa·ðu'ri·a) *n.f.*

paymaster's office; disbursement office.
pagamento (pa·ɣa'men·to) *n.m.* pay; payment.
pagano (pa'ɣa·no) *adj.* & *n.m.* pagan. —*n.m., colloq.* [*also*, **pagote** (-'ɣo·te)] fall guy; scapegoat. —**paganismo**, *n.m.* paganism.
pagar (pa'ɣar) *v.t.* [*pres.subjve.* **pague**; *pret.* **pagué**] **1,** to pay. **2,** to return; reciprocate. —**pagarse,** *v.r.* **1,** *fol. by* **de,** to become infatuated with; become fond of. **2,** to be self-satisfied; be conceited.
pagaré (pa·ɣa're) *n.m.* promissory note.
página ('pa·xi·na) *n.f.* page.
paginar (pa·xi'nar) *v.t.* to paginate. —**paginación,** *n.m.* pagination; paging.
pago ('pa·ɣo) *n.m.* **1,** payment. **2,** country district, esp. of vineyards or olive groves. **3,** hamlet. **4,** *So. Amer.* home; home town or region. —*adj., colloq.* paid.
pagoda (pa'ɣo·ða) *n.f.* pagoda.
pagro ('pa·ɣro) *n.m.* porgy.
pague ('pa·ɣe) *v., pres.subjve. of* **pagar.**
pagué (pa'ɣe) *v., 1st pers.sing. pret. of* **pagar.**
paila ('pai·la) *n.f.* **1,** washbowl; washbasin. **2,** shallow pot.
pairar (pai'rar) *v.i., naut.* to lie to with all sails set. —**pairo** ('pai·ro) *n.m., in* **al pairo,** lying to.
país (pa'is) *n.m.* country. —**del país,** domestic; national.
paisaje (pai'sa·xe) *n.m.* landscape. —**paisajista,** *n.m.* & *f.* landscape painter.
paisana (pai'sa·na) *n.f.* a country dance.
paisanaje (pai·sa'na·xe) *n.m.* **1,** peasantry; countryfolk. **2,** nationality or citizenship in common.
paisano (pai'sa·no) *adj.* **1,** of or from the same country or locality. **2,** civilian. —*n.m.* **1,** fellow countryman; compatriot. **2,** civilian.
paja ('pa·xa) *n.f.* **1,** straw; chaff. **2,** trash; refuse. —**dormirse en las pajas,** *Amer.* to let the grass grow under one's feet. —**echar paja,** *Amer., colloq.* **1,** to talk nonsense. **2,** to fib; tell tall tales. —**echar pajas,** to draw lots. —**en un quítame allá esas pajas,** *colloq.* in a jiffy. —**paja de madera,** excelsior. —**por quítame allá esas pajas,** *colloq.* for a straw; (to quarrel) over a trifle.
pajar (pa'xar) *n.m.* barn; straw loft.
pájara ('pa·xa·ra) *n.f.* **1,** female bird. **2,** = **pajarita. 3,** paper kite. **4,** crafty woman.
pajarear (pa·xa·re'ar) *v.i.* **1,** to hunt birds. **2,** to wander about; loaf. **3,** *Amer.* to be absent-minded; be bemused.
pajarera (pa·xa're·ra) *n.f.* **1,** aviary. **2,** bird cage.
pajarete (pa·xa're·te) *n.m.* fine sherry wine.
pajarita (pa·xa'ri·ta) *n.f.* folded paper figure, esp. in the form of a bird.
pájaro ('pa·xa·ro) *n.m.* **1,** bird. **2,** *colloq.* character; guy. —**pájaro mosca,** humming bird. —**pájaro bobo,** *also* **pájaro niño,** penguin. —**pájaro de cuenta,** sharper; cunning fellow.
paje ('pa·xe) *n.m.* page; groom.
pajizo (pa'xi·θo; -so) *adj.* **1,** of, resembling or filled with straw. **2,** straw-colored.
pajonal (pa·xo'nal) *n.m., Amer.* place abounding in tall grass.
pala ('pa·la) *n.f.* **1,** shovel; spade. **2,** blade (*of an oar, spade, etc.*). **3,** paddle. **4,** *colloq.* craft; cleverness. **5,** upper (*of a shoe*). —**hacer la pala,** *colloq.* to stall; speak *or* act evasively.
palabra (pa'la·βra) *n.f.* word. —**empeñar la palabra,** to pledge one's word. —**palabras mayores, 1,** serious matter. **2,** angry words; quarrel. —**pedir la palabra,** to ask for the floor. —**tener la palabra,** to have the floor. —**tratar mal de palabra,** to scold; berate.
palabrero (pa·la'βre·ro) *adj.* talkative; wordy. —*n.m.* chatterbox. —**palabrería,** *n.f.* wordiness; palaver.
palabrita (pa·la'βri·ta) *n.f.* a bit of good sense; a word of advice.
palacete (pa·la'θe·te; -'se·te) *n.m.* small palace.
palacio (pa'la·θjo; -sjo) *n.m.* **1,** palace. **2,** public building; hall. —**palaciego** (-'θje·ɣo; -'sje·ɣo) *adj.* palace (*attrib.*); court (*attrib.*). —*n.m.* courtier.
palada (pa'la·ða) *n.f.* **1,** shovelful. **2,** stroke of an oar.
paladar (pa·la'ðar) *n.m.* **1,** palate, **2,** taste.

paladear (pa·la·ðe'ar) *v.t.* **1,** to taste; savor. **2,** to relish; enjoy. —**paladeo** (-'ðe·o) *n.m.* relishing; savoring; tasting.
paladín (pa·la'ðin) *n.m.* paladin.
paladio (pa'la·ðjo) *n.m.* palladium.
palafrén (pa·la'fren) *n.m.* palfrey.
palafrenero (pa·la·fre'ne·ro) *n.m.* **1,** groom. **2,** attendant on horseback; outrider.
palanca (pa'lan·ka) *n.f.* **1,** lever. **2,** push rod; handle. **3,** *Amer., colloq.* influence; pull.
palangana (pa·lan'ga·na) *n.f.* washbowl. —*n.m., Amer., colloq.* braggart. —**palanganearse,** *v.r., Amer., colloq.* to brag.
palangre (pa'lan·gre) *n.m.* trotline.
palanqueta (pa·lan'ke·ta) *n.f.* **1,** small lever or handle. **2,** jimmy.
palanquín (pa·lan'kin) *n.m.* **1,** public porter. **2,** palanquin.
palastro (pa'las·tro) *n.m.* sheet iron; sheet steel.
palatal (pa·la'tal) *adj.* & *n.f.* palatal.
palatino (pa·la'ti·no) *adj.* palatal. —*adj.* & *n.m.* palatine. —**palatinado,** *n.m.* palatinate.
palazo (pa'la·θo; -so) *n.m.* blow with a shovel.
palco ('pal·ko) *n.m.* **1,** theater box. **2,** grandstand. —**palco escénico,** stage.
palear (pa·le'ar) *v.t.* & *i.* to shovel; stoke (coal). —**paleador,** *n.m.* shoveler; stoker.
palenque (pa'len·ke) *n.m.* **1,** barrier; palisade. **2,** lists (*pl.*); arena. **3,** *theat.* passage from pit to stage.
paleo- (pa·le·o) *prefix* paleo-; ancient; primitive: *paleología,* paleology.
paleografía (pa·le·o·ɣra'fi·a) *n.f.* paleography. —**paleográfico** (-'ɣra·fi·ko) *adj.* paleographic. —**paleógrafo** (-'o·ɣra·fo) *n.m.* paleographer.
paleolítico (pa·le·o'li·ti·ko) *adj.* paleolithic.
paleontología (pa·le·on·to·lo·'xi·a) *n.f.* paleontology. —**paleontológico** (-'lo·xi·ko) *adj.* paleontological. —**paleontólogo** (-'to·lo·ɣo) *n.m.* paleontologist.
paleozoico (pa·le·o'θoi·ko; -'soi·ko) *adj.* Paleozoic.
palero (pa'le·ro) *n.m.* **1,** maker or seller of shovels. **2,** *Amer., colloq.* weaver of tall tales; fibber.
palestino (pa·les'ti·no) *adj.* & *n.m.* Palestinian.
palestra (pa'les·tra) *n.f.* **1,** lists (*pl.*); arena. **2,** contest; struggle.
paleta (pa'le·ta) *n.f.* **1,** palette. **2,** paddle. **3,** trowel. **4,** small shovel.
paletear (pa·le·te'ar) *v.t.* to row or paddle ineffectively.
paletilla (pa·le'ti·ʎa; -ja) *n.f.* shoulderblade.
paleto (pa'le·to) *adj.* & *n.m.* rustic; yokel.
paletó (pa·le'to) *n.m.* overcoat; greatcoat.
paliar (pa'ljar) *v.t.* **1,** to palliate. **2,** to cloak; dissimulate. —**paliación,** *n.f.* palliation. —**paliativo,** *adj.* & *n.m.* palliative.
palidecer (pa·li·ðe'θer; -'ser) *v.i.* [*pres.ind.* **palidezco** (-'ðeθ·ko; -'ðes·ko); *pres.subjve.* **palidezca** (-ka)] to pale.
pálido ('pa·li·ðo) *adj.* pale; pallid. —**palidez,** *n.f.* paleness; pallor.
palillo (pa'li·ʎo; -jo) *n.m.* **1,** small stick. **2,** toothpick. **3,** *music* drumstick. **4,** knitting needle. **5,** *pl., Andal.* castanets. **6,** *pl.* chopsticks.
palio ('pa·ljo) *n.m.* **1,** pallium. **2,** canopy used in religious processions.
paliza (pa'li·θa; -sa) *n.f.* beating; drubbing.
palizada (pa·li'θa·ða; -'sa·ða) *n.f.* paling.
palma ('pal·ma) *n.f.* **1,** palm tree. **2,** palm leaf. **3,** palm of the hand. **4,** pad (*of an animal's foot*). —**batir palmas,** to clap.
palmacristi (pal·ma'kris·ti) *n.f.* = **ricino.**
palmada (pal'ma·ða) *n.f.* **1,** slap. **2,** handclap.
palmar (pal'mar) *adj.* palmar. —*n.m.* palm grove. —*v.i., colloq.* to die.
palmario (pal'ma·rjo) *adj.* plain; evident.
palmatoria (pal·ma'to·rja) *n.f.* candlestick.
palmeado (pal·me'a·ðo) *also,* **palmado** (-'ma·ðo) *adj.* webbed.
palmear (pal·me'ar) *v.t.* to pat. —*v.i.* to clap the hands.
palmera (pal'me·ra) *n.f.* palm tree. —**palmeral,** *n.m.* palm grove.
palmeta (pal'me·ta) *n.f.* **1,** ferule. **2,** [*also,* **palmetazo,** *n.m.*] slap with a ferule.

palmípedo (pal'mi·pe·ðo) *n.m.* web-footed.
palmito (pal'mi·to) *n.m.* **1,** dwarf fan palm; palmetto. **2,** heart of palm. **3,** *colloq.* woman's face.
palmo ('pal·mo) *n.m.* **1,** span of the hand. **2,** unit of length of approximately 8 inches. **—dejar con un palmo de narices,** to disappoint; leave in the cold. **—palmo a palmo,** inch by inch.
palmotear (pal·mo·te'ar) *v.i.* to clap the hands. **—*v.t.*** to pat; give pats on.
palmoteo (pal·mo'te·o) *n.m.* **1,** clapping. **2,** patting.
palo ('pa·lo) *n.m.* **1,** stick; piece of wood. **2,** club; cudgel. **3,** blow with a stick or club. **4,** *cards* clubs (*in the Spanish deck*). **5,** suit (*at cards*). **6,** *naut.* mast. **7,** hook of a letter. **8,** *Amer.* drink, esp. of liquor. **9,** *W.I.* tree. **—dar de palos,** to drub; beat. **—moler a palos,** to beat to a pulp. **—palo dulce,** licorice. **—palo mayor,** mainmast.
paloduz (pa·lo'ðuθ; -'ðus) *n.m.,* *also,* **palo dulce,** licorice.
paloma (pa'lo·ma) *n.f.* **1,** pigeon; dove. **2,** meek person. **3,** *pl.* whitecaps. **—paloma buchona,** pouter. **—paloma emigrante,** passenger pigeon. **—paloma mensajera,** carrier pigeon; homing pigeon. **—paloma moñuda,** ruff. **—paloma torcaz,** ringdove; wood pigeon; wild pigeon. **—paloma triste,** mourning dove.
palomar (pa·lo'mar) *n.m.* pigeon house; dovecot.
palomilla (pa·lo'mi·ʎa; -ja) *n.f.* **1,** nocturnal butterfly. **2,** grain moth. **3,** any small moth or butterfly. **4,** *mech.* wing nut. **5,** *Amer., colloq.* urchin; ragamuffin. **6,** palomino. **—palomillas,** *n.f.pl.* whitecaps.
palomitas (pa·lo'mi·tas) *n.f.pl., Amer.* popcorn.
palomo (pa'lo·mo) *n.m.* male pigeon.
palote (pa'lo·te) *n.m.* **1,** stick. **2,** scribble; scrawl.
palpable (pal'pa·βle) *adj.* palpable.
palpación (pal·pa'θjon; -'sjon) *n.f.* **1,** [*also,* **palpadura,** *n.f.,* **palpamiento,** *n.m.*] feeling; touching; groping. **2,** *med.* palpation.
palpar (pal'par) *v.t.* & *i.* **1,** to feel; touch. **2,** to grope. **3,** to know positively. **4,** *med.* to palpate.
palpitante (pal·pi'tan·te) *adj.* **1,** palpitating throbbing. **2,** *fig.* burning; highly controversial.
palpitar (pal·pi'tar) *v.i.* to palpitate; throb. **—palpitación,** *n.f.* palpitation; throbbing.
pálpito ('pal·pi·to) *n.m., Amer.* hunch; premonition.
palpo ('pal·po) *n.m., zool.* feeler.
palta ('pal·ta) *n.f., So.Amer.* avocado. **—palto,** *n.m., So.Amer.* avocado tree.
palúdico (pa'lu·ði·ko) *adj.* **1,** swampy; marshy. **2,** malarial. **—paludismo,** *n.m.* malaria.
palurdo (pa'lur·ðo) *adj.* rustic; rude. **—*n.m.*** rustic; boor.
palustre (pa'lus·tre) *n.m.* trowel.
palla ('pa·ja) *n.f., So.Amer.* = paya.
pallador (pa·ja'ðor) *n.m., So. Amer.* = **payador.**
pampa ('pam·pa) *n.f.* pampa.
pámpana ('pam·pa·na) *n.f.* vine leaf. **—zurrar la pámpana a,** *colloq.* to thrash.
pámpano ('pam·pa·no) *n.m.* **1,** vine leaf. **2,** vine shoot; tendril. **3,** *ichthy.* gilthead; *Amer.* pompano.
pampeano (pam·pe'a·no) *adj., So.Amer.* of or pert. to the pampas.
pampear (pam·pe'ar) *v.i., So. Amer.* to travel through the pampas.
pampero (pam'pe·ro) *n.m.* **1,** dweller of the pampas. **2,** *Amer.* violent wind blowing from the pampas. **—*adj.*** pampas (*attrib.*).
pampirolada (pam·pi·ro'la·ða) *n.f.* **1,** garlic sauce. **2,** *colloq.* nonsense.
pamplemusa (pam·ple'mu·sa) *n.f.* shaddock.
pamplina (pam'pli·na) *also,* **pamplinada,** *n.f., colloq.* nonsense.
pan (pan) *n.m.* **1,** bread. **2,** cake; loaf; patty. **3,** pastry crust. **—pan bendito,** manna. **—pan de oro,** gold leaf.
pan- (pan) *prefix* pan-; all; every; universal: *panamericano,* Pan-American; *pandemia,* pandemic.
pana ('pa·na) *n.f.* **1,** velveteen; corduroy. **2,** *Amer.* liver. **3,** *Amer., colloq.* nerve; gall.
panacea (pa·na'θe·a; -'se·a) *n.f.* panacea.
panadero (pa·na'ðe·ro) *n.m.* baker. **—panadería,** *n.f.* bakery.

panadizo (pa·na'ði·θo; -so) *n.m., pathol.* felon.
panal (pa'nal) *n.m.* **1,** honeycomb. **2,** hornet's nest.
panamá (pa·na'ma) *n.m.* panama hat.
panamericano (pan·a·me·ri'ka·no) *adj.* Pan-American. —**panamericanismo,** *n.m.* Pan-Americanism.
panatela (pa·na'te·la) *n.f.* sponge cake.
pancista (pan'θis·ta; -'sis·ta) *adj.* noncommital; politic; straddling. —*n.m.* & *f.* straddler; one who is on the fence; politician.
páncreas ('pan·kre·as) *n.m.* pancreas. —**pancreático** (-kre'a·ti·ko) *also,* **pancrático** (-'kra·ti·ko) *adj.* pancreatic.
pancromático (pan·kro'ma·ti·ko) *adj.* panchromatic.
panda ('pan·da) *n.m.* panda.
pandear (pan·de'ar) *v.i.* [*also, refl.,* **pandearse**] to bend; warp; bulge out.
pandemónium (pan·de'mo·njum) *n.m.* pandemonium.
pandereta (pan·de're·ta) *n.f., also,* **pandera** (-'de·ra) *n.f.,* **pandero** (-'de·ro) *n.m.* tambourine.
panderetear (pan·de·re·te'ar) *v.i.* to play on the tambourine.
pandereteo (pan·de·re'te·o) *n.m.* **1,** playing on the tambourine. **2,** merriment.
pandilla (pan'di·ʎa; -ja) *n.f.* **1,** gang; clique. **2,** group of merrymakers.
pandorga (pan'dor·ɣa) *n.f.* **1,** kite. **2,** *colloq.* fat, hulking woman.
panecillo (pa·ne'θi·ʎo; -'si·jo) *n.m.* bread roll.
panegírico (pa·ne'xi·ri·ko) *n.m.* panegyric. —*adj.* panegyrical.
panel (pa'nel) *n.m.* **1,** panel. **2,** pane.
panela (pa'ne·la) *n.f.* **1,** a kind of biscuit. **2,** *Amer.* unrefined sugar.
panera (pa'ne·ra) *n.f.* **1,** breadbox. **2,** breadbasket.
pánfilo ('pan·fi·lo) *n.m.* dullard; sad sack.
panfleto (pan'fle·to) *n.m.* pamphlet. —**panfletista,** *n.m.* & *f.* pamphleteer.
pánico ('pa·ni·ko) *n.m.* & *adj.* panic.
panizo (pa'ni·θo; -so) *n.m.* millet.
panoja (pa'no·xa) *n.f.* panicle; ear of grain. *Also,* **panocha** (-tʃa).
panoplia (pa'no·plja) *n.f.* panoply.
panóptico (pa'nop·ti·ko) *n.m., Amer.* penitentiary.
panorama (pa·no'ra·ma) *n.m.* panorama. —**panorámico,** *adj.* panoramic.
panoso (pa'no·so) *adj.* mealy.
panqueque (pan'ke·ke) *n.m., Amer.* pancake.
pantalón (pan·ta'lon) *n.m., also pl.,* **pantalones,** trousers; pantaloons; pants.
pantaloncito (pan·ta·lon'θi·to; -'si·to) *n.m.* panties (*pl.*).
pantalla (pan'ta·ʎa; -ja) *n.f.* **1,** lamp shade. **2,** screen.
pantano (pan'ta·no) *n.m.* **1,** swamp; marsh; bog. **2,** hindrance; obstacle. —**pantanal,** *n.m.* marshy terrain. —**pantanoso,** *adj.* marshy; swampy.
panteísmo (pan·te'is·mo) *n.m.* pantheism. —**panteísta,** *n.m.* & *f.* pantheist. —*adj.* [*also,* **panteístico**] pantheistic.
panteón (pan·te'on) *n.m.* pantheon.
pantera (pan'te·ra) *n.f.* panther.
panto- (pan·to) *prefix* panto-, *var. of* **pan-**: *pantógrafo,* pantograph.
pantógrafo (pan'to·ɣra·fo) *n.m.* pantograph.
pantomima (pan·to'mi·ma) *n.f.* pantomime. —**pantomímico,** *adj.* pantomimic. —**pantomimo,** *n.m.* mimic; pantomimist.
pantoque (pan'to·ke) *n.m., naut.* bilge.
pantorrilla (pan·to'rri·ʎa; -ja) *n.f.* calf of the leg. —**pantorrillera,** *n.f.* padded stocking. —**pantorrilludo,** *adj.* having thick calves.
pantufla (pan'tu·fla) *n.f., also,* **pantuflo,** *n.m.* slipper.
panza ('pan·θa; -sa) *n.f.* belly; paunch. —**panzudo,** *also,* **panzón,** *adj.* paunchy.
panzada (pan'θa·ða; -'sa·ða) *n.f.* **1,** push with the paunch. **2,** *colloq.* bellyful.
pañal (pa'ɲal) *n.m.* **1,** diaper. **2,** tail (*of a shirt*). —**pañales,** *n.m.pl.* swaddling clothes.
pañero (pa'ɲe·ro) *n.m.* dealer in cloth or dry goods.
paño ('pa·ɲo) *n.m.* **1,** cloth. **2,** film; opacity. —**paños calientes,** half measures. —**paños menores, 1,** underclothes. **2,** state of undress.
pañol (pa'ɲol) *n.m., naut.* store-

room. —**pañolero,** *n.m.* storekeeper; yeoman.
pañoleta (pa·ɲo'le·ta) *n.f.* triangular shawl.
pañolón (pa·ɲo'lon) *n.m.* large square shawl.
pañuelo (pa'ɲwe·lo) *n.m.* **1,** handkerchief. **2,** shawl.
papa ('pa·pa) *n.f.* **1,** Pope. **2,** *Amer.* potato. **3,** pap. **4,** = **paparrucha. 5,** = **papá.**
papá (pa'pa) *n.m.* [*pl.* **papás**] papa; dad.
papada (pa'pa·ða) *n.f.* double chin.
papado (pa'pa·ðo) *n.m.* papacy.
papagayo (pa·pa'ɣa·jo) *n.m.* parrot; macaw.
papahuevos (pa·pa'we·βos) *n.m.* & *f. sing.* & *pl.* = **papanatas.**
papal (pa'pal) *adj.* papal.
papalote (pa·pa'lo·te) *n.m., Mex.* paper kite.
papamoscas (pa·pa'mos·kas) *n.m.* & *f. sing.* & *pl.* **1,** *ornith.* flycatcher. **2,** *colloq.* = **papanatas.**
papanatas (pa·pa'na·tas) *n.m.* & *f. sing.* & *pl., colloq.* simpleton; dolt.
papar (pa'par) *v.t.* **1,** to eat without chewing (*as pap, gruel, etc.*). **2,** *colloq.* to eat. —**papar moscas,** *colloq.* to gape.
paparrucha (pa·pa'rru·tʃa) *n.f., colloq.* humbug; nonsense.
papaya (pa'pa·ja) *n.f.* papaya; papaw. —**papayo,** *n.m.* papaya tree; papaw tree.
papazgo (pa'paθ·ɣo; pa'pas-) *n.m.* papacy.
papel (pa'pel) *n.m.* **1,** paper. **2,** part; role. —**hacer buen papel,** to show to advantage; make a fine show. —**papel cuadriculado,** graph paper. —**papel de lija,** sandpaper. —**papel de oficio,** foolscap. —**papel higiénico** *or* **sanitario,** toilet paper. —**papel majado** *or* **maché** (ma'tʃe) papier-maché.
papelear (pa·pe·le'ar) *v.i.* **1,** to rummage through papers. **2,** *colloq.* to do paperwork.
papeleo (pa·pe'le·o) *n.m.* **1,** rummaging through papers. **2,** *colloq.* papers; paperwork.
papelera (pa·pe'le·ra) *n.f.* **1,** file; filing cabinet. **2,** wastebasket.
papelería (pa·pe·le'ri·a) *n.f.* **1,** heap of papers. **2,** stationery store.
papelero (pa·pe'le·ro) *adj.* paper (*attrib.*). —*n.m.* stationer.
papeleta (pa·pe'le·ta) *n.f.* **1,** card; ticket. **2,** blank form. **3,** *Amer.* traffic ticket.
papelillo (pa·pe'li·ʎo; -jo) *n.m.* **1,** packet (*for medicinal powders*). **2,** hand-rolled cigarette.
papelón (pa·pe'lon) *n.m.* **1,** pasteboard. **2,** *Amer., colloq.* ludicrous performance; howler.
papelucho (pa·pe'lu·tʃo) *n.m.* scrap of paper. *Also,* **papelote** (-'lo·te).
papera (pa'pe·ra) *n.f.* goiter. —**paperas,** *n.f.pl.* mumps.
papi ('pa·pi) *n.m., colloq.* = **papá.**
papila (pa'pi·la) *n.f.* papilla. —**papilar,** *adj.* papillary.
papilla (pa'pi·ʎa; -ja) *n.f.* **1,** pap. **2,** *colloq.* deceitful talk; cajolery.
papiro (pa'pi·ro) *n.m.* papyrus.
papirote (pa·pi'ro·te) *also,* **papirotazo,** *n.m.,* **papirotada,** *n.f.* fillip.
papismo (pa'pis·mo) *n.m.* popery. —**papista,** *n.m.* & *f.* papist. —*adj.* papist; popish.
papito (pa'pi·to) *n.m., colloq.* = **papá.**
papo ('pa·po) *n.m.* **1,** double chin. **2,** gizzard (*of fowl*). **3,** thistledown. **4,** wattle (*of animals*).
papudo (pa'pu·ðo) *adj.* double-chinned.
pápula ('pa·pu·la) *n.f.* papule.
paquebote (pa·ke'βo·te) *n.m.* packet boat; steamer.
paquete (pa'ke·te) *n.m.* package; pack; packet. —*adj., Amer.* **1,** dapper; spruce. **2,** insincere.
paquetería (pa·ke·te'ri·a) *n.f.* retail store.
paquidermo (pa·ki'ðer·mo) *n.m.* pachyderm.
par (par) *adj.* **1,** equal; on a par. **2,** alike; matching. **3,** even (*of numbers*). —*n.m.* **1,** pair; couple. **2,** mate; match. **3,** peer. **4,** *mech.* couple. —**a la par, 1,** jointly. **2,** equally. **3,** par; at par. —**a pares,** two by two; by pairs. —**de par en par,** unobstructedly; wide open (*as a door, window, etc.*). —**ir a la par,** to go halves. —**pares y nones,** the game of odds and evens. —**sin par,** peerless; matchless.
para ('pa·ra) *prep.* **1,** for. **2,** toward. **3,** to. **4,** in order to. —**para con,** toward, with. —**para eso,** for that; for that matter. —**para mí,** for my part; as far as I am concerned. —**para nunca,** *colloq.* **1,** poorly;

badly. 2, endlessly. —**para que,** so that; in order that. —**¿para qué?** what for? what is the use?

para- (pa·ra) *prefix* para-. **1,** near; beside; beyond: *paramilitar,* paramilitary; *paráfrasis,* paraphrase. **2,** *pathol.* abnormal: *paranoia,* paranoia. **3,** serving as a guard or protection: *paracaídas,* parachute; *parabrisas,* windshield.

parabién (pa·ra'βjen) *n.m.* congratulation; felicitation.

parábola (pa'ra·βo·la) *n.f.* **1,** parable. **2,** parabola. —**parabólico** (-'βo·li·ko) *adj.* parabolic.

parabrisas (pa·ra'βri·sas) *n.f. sing.* & *pl.* windshield.

paracaídas (pa·ra·ka'i·ðas) *n.m. sing.* & *pl.* parachute. —**paracaidista** (-kai'ðis·ta) *n.m.* & *f.* parachutist.

parachoques (pa·ra'tʃo·kes) *n.m.sing.* & *pl.* bumper.

parada (pa'ra·ða) *n.f.* **1,** stop (*of a vehicle*). **2,** halt. **3,** parade; review. **4,** *fencing* parry. —**parada en seco,** dead stop.

paradero (pa·ra'ðe·ro) *n.m.* **1,** whereabouts (*pl.*). **2,** stopping place; stop. **3,** end; final stop.

paradigma (pa·ra'ðiɣ·ma) *n.m.* paradigm.

paradisíaco (pa·ra·ði'si·a·ko) *adj.* paradisiacal.

parado (pa'ra·ðo) *adj.* **1,** stopped; standing still; at a standstill. **2,** slow; slack; sluggish. **3,** unemployed. **4,** *Amer.* standing. **5,** *Amer.* arrogant; standoffish. —**salir mal parado,** to come out poorly; get the worst of it.

paradoja (pa·ra'ðo·xa) *n.f.* paradox. —**paradójico,** *adj.* paradoxical.

parador (pa·ra'ðor) *n.m.* inn; road stop; motor court.

parafina (pa·ra'fi·na) *n.f.* paraffin.

parafrasear (pa·ra·fra·se'ar) *v.t.* & *i.* to paraphrase.

paráfrasis (pa'ra·fra·sis) *n.f. sing.* & *pl.* paraphrase. —**parafrástico** (-'fras·ti·ko) *adj.* paraphrastic.

paragolpes (pa·ra'ɣol·pes) *n.m. sing.* & *pl.* bumper.

parágrafo (pa'ra·ɣra·fo) *n.m.* = **párrafo.**

paraguas (pa'ra·ɣwas) *n.m.sing.* & *pl.* umbrella.

paragüero (pa·ra'ɣwe·ro) *n.m.* **1,** umbrella man. **2,** umbrella stand. —**paragüería,** *n.f.* umbrella shop.

paraíso (pa·ra'i·so) *n.m.* **1,** paradise. **2,** *theat., colloq.* upper gallery.

paraje (pa'ra·xe) *n.m.* place; spot.

paralaje (pa·ra'la·xe) *n.m.* parallax.

paralelar (pa·ra·le'lar) *v.t.* to parallel.

paralelepípedo (pa·ra·le·le'pi·pe·ðo) *n.m.* parallelepiped.

paralelo (pa·ra'le·lo) *adj.* & *n.m.* parallel. —**paralelas,** *n.f.pl.* parallel bars. —**paralelismo,** *n.m.* parallelism.

paralelogramo (pa·ra·le·lo·'ɣra·mo) *n.m.* parallelogram.

Paralipómenos (pa·ra·li'po·me·nos) *n.m.pl., Bib.* Chronicles.

parálisis (pa'ra·li·sis) *n.f.* paralysis. —**paralítico** (-'li·ti·ko) *adj.* & *n.m.* paralytic.

paralización (pa·ra·li·θa'θjon; -sa'sjon) *n.f.* **1,** paralyzation. **2,** stoppage.

paralizar (pa·ra·li'θar; -'sar) *v.t.* [*pres.subjve.* **paralice** (-'li·θe; -se); *pret.* **paralicé** (-'θe; -'se)] to paralyze.

paralogizar (pa·ra·lo·xi'θar; -'sar) *v.t.* [*pres.subjve.* **paralogice** (-'xi·θe; -se); *pret.* **paralogicé** (-'θe; -'se)] to confuse; befuddle.

paramecio (pa·ra'me·θjo; -sjo) *n.m.* paramecium.

paramento (pa·ra'men·to) *n.m.* ornament; trappings (*pl.*). —**paramentar,** *v.t.* to adorn; bedeck.

parámetro (pa'ra·me·tro) *n.m.* parameter.

páramo ('pa·ra·mo) *n.m.* **1,** flat, barren land; paramo. **2,** *Amer.* cold drizzle.

parar (pa'rar) *v.t.* & *i.* to stop; check. —*v.t.* **1,** to parry. **2,** *Amer.* to stand; stand up; place upright. —*v.i.* **1,** to end up (as *or* in). **2,** to put up; lodge. —**pararse,** *v.r.* **1,** to stop. **2,** *Amer.* to stand up. —**parar las orejas,** *Amer.* to prick up one's ears. —**pararse en,** to notice; pay attention to. —**sin parar,** at once.

parangón (pa·ran'gon) *n.m.* **1,** comparison. **2,** model; paragon. —**parangonar,** *v.t.* to compare.

paraninfo (pa·ra'nin·fo) *n.m.* auditorium, esp. in an academic institution.

paranoia (pa·ra'no·ja) *n.f.* paranoia. —**paranoico** (-'noi·ko) *adj.* & *n.m.* paranoiac.

parapetarse (pa·ra·pe'tar·se)

v.r. to take cover, as behind a parapet.
parapeto (pa·ra'pe·to) *n.m.* parapet.
paraplejía (pa·ra·ple'xi·a) *n.f.* paraplegia. —**parapléjico** (-'ple·xi·ko) *adj.* & *n.m.* paraplegic.
pararrayos (pa·ra'rra·jos) *n.m. sing.* & *pl.* lightning rod.
parásito (pa'ra·si·to) *n.m.* parasite. —*adj.* parasitic. —**parasitario,** *also,* **parasítico,** *adj.* parasitic.
parasol (pa·ra'sol) *n.m.* parasol.
paratifoide (pa·ra·ti'foi·ðe) *adj.* paratyphoid. *Also,* **paratífico** (-'ti·fi·ko). —**paratifoidea** (-'ðe·a) *n.f.* paratyphoid fever.
parca ('par·ka) *n.f., often cap.* Death.
parcamente (par·ka'men·te) *adv.* sparingly.
parcela (par'θe·la; -'se·la) *n.f.* parcel of land.
parcelar (par·θe'lar; -se'lar) *v.t.* to divide into lots; parcel. —**parcelación,** *n.f.* division into lots; parceling.
parcial (par'θjal; -'sjal) *adj.* partial. —**parcialidad,** *n.f.* partiality.
parco ('par·ko) *adj.* moderate; sparing; spare.
parchar (par'tʃar) *v.t., Amer.* to patch; mend.
parche ('par·tʃe) *n.m.* 1, plaster; poultice. 2, patch; added piece. 3, daub; blotch. 4, drumhead. 5, drum. —**pegar un parche a,** *colloq.* to swindle.
pardal (par'ðal) *adj.* rustic. —*n.m.* 1, sparrow. 2, = **pardillo.** 3, = **leopardo.** 4, *colloq.* crafty fellow.
pardear (par·ðe'ar) *v.i.* to be or become grayish brown.
¡pardiez! (par'ðjeθ; -'ðjes) *interj., colloq.* by heavens!; by Jove!
pardillo (par'ði·ʎo; -jo) *n.m.* linnet.
pardo ('par·ðo) *adj.* & *n.m.* grayish brown; dun. —*n.m.* = **leopardo.** —**pardusco** (-'ðus·ko) *adj.* brownish.
parear (pa·re'ar) *v.t.* 1, to pair. 2, to match. —**parearse,** *v.r.* to pair off.
parecer (pa·re'θer; -'ser) *v.i.* [*pres.ind.* **parezco;** *pres.subjve.* **parezca**] 1, to appear; seem. 2, to look like; appear to be. —*n.m.* 1, opinion; view. 2, countenance; mien. —**parecerse,** *v.r.* 1, to look alike; resemble each other. 2, *fol. by* **a,** to look like; resemble. —**al parecer,** *also,* **a lo que parece,** seemingly; apparently.
parecido (pa·re'θi·ðo; -'si·ðo) *adj.* like; alike; similar. —*n.m.* likeness; resemblance. —**bien parecido,** good-looking. —**mal parecido,** ill-favored; ugly.
pared (pa'reð) *n.f.* wall. —**hasta la pared de enfrente,** *colloq.* to the limit. —**pared maestra,** main wall. —**pared medianera,** party wall.
paredaño (pa·re'ða·ɲo) *adj.* having a common wall; adjoining.
paredón (pa·re'ðon) *n.m.* thick wall.
paregórico (pa·re'ɣo·ri·ko) *n.m.* paregoric.
pareja (pa're·xa) *n.f.* 1, pair. 2, couple. 3, mate; partner. —**correr parejas con,** to go hand in hand with.
parejo (pa're·xo) *adj.* 1, level; flush; even. 2, equal; like. —*n.m., W.I.* mate; partner.
parentela (pa·ren'te·la) *n.f.* kin; relations (*pl.*).
parentesco (pa·ren'tes·ko) *n.m.* relationship; kinship.
paréntesis (pa'ren·te·sis) *n.m. sing.* & *pl.* parenthesis.
paresa (pa're·sa) *n.f.* peeress.
paresia (pa're·sja) *n.f.* paresis. *Also,* **paresis** (-sis). —**parético** (-ti·ko) *adj.* & *n.m.* paretic.
parezca (pa'reθ·ka; -'res·ka) *v., pres.subjve. of* **parecer.**
parezco (pa'reθ·ko; -'res·ko) *v., 1st pers.sing.pres.ind. of* **parecer.**
parfait (par'fe) *n.m.* [*pl.* **parfaits** (-'fes)] parfait.
pargo ('par·ɣo) *n.m.* = **pagro.**
pari- (pa·ri) *prefix* pari-; equal: *paripinado,* paripinnate.
paria ('pa·rja) *n.m.* & *f.* pariah.
parida (pa'ri·ða) *adj.fem.* recently delivered.
paridad (pa·ri'ðað) *n.f.* parity.
pariente (pa'rjen·te) *n.m.* relation; relative.
parihuela (pa·ri'we·la) *n.f., usu. pl.* litter; stretcher.
parir (pa'rir) *v.t.* to give birth to. —*v.i.* to give birth; be delivered.
parla ('par·la) *n.f.* 1, loquacity. 2, talk; chatter.
parlamentar (par·la·men'tar) *v.i.* to parley; negotiate.
parlamentario (par·la·men'ta·rjo) *adj.* parliamentary. —*n.m.* 1,

parliamentarian. 2, envoy; emissary (*to a parley*).
parlamentarismo (par·la·men·ta'ris·mo) *n.m.* parliamentarism.
parlamento (par·la'men·to) *n.m.* 1, parliament. 2, parley.
parlanchín (par·lan'tʃin) *adj.* chattering. —*n.m.* chatterer; chatterbox.
parlante (par'lan·te) *adj., Amer.* talking; speaking. —*n.m., Amer.* loudspeaker.
parlar (par'lar) *v.t. & i.* 1, to talk; chatter. 2, to speak glibly.
parlero (par'le·ro) *adj.* 1, talkative. 2, gossipy.
parlotear (par·lo·te'ar) *v.i.* to prattle. —**parloteo** (-'te·o) *n.m.* prattle.
parnaso (par'na·so) *n.m.* Parnassus.
parné (par'ne) *n.m., colloq.* money.
paro ('pa·ro) *n.m.* 1, titmouse. 2, work stoppage. 3, lockout. 4, *Amer.* throw of the dice. —**paro y pinta,** *Amer.* game of dice; craps.
-paro (pa·ro) *suffix* -parous; producing; giving birth to: *ovíparo,* oviparous.
parodia (pa'ro·ðja) *n.f.* parody. —**parodiar** (-'ðjar) *v.t.* to parody. —**parodista** (-'ðis·ta) *n.m. & f.* writer of parodies.
parótida (pa'ro·ti·ða) *n.f.* 1, parotid. 2, mumps. —**parotídeo** (-'ti·ðe·o) *adj.* parotid. —**parotiditis,** *n.f.* parotiditis; mumps.
paroxismo (pa·rok'sis·mo) *n.m.* paroxysm.
parpadear (par·pa·ðe'ar) *v.i.* to blink. —**parpadeo** (-'ðe·o) *n.m.* blinking; blink.
párpado ('par·pa·ðo) *n.m.* eyelid.
parpar (par'par) *v.i.* to quack.
parque ('par·ke) *n.m.* 1, park. 2, parking field. 3, *mil.* depot; dump. 4, equipment, esp. for a public service.
parquear (par·ke'ar) *v.t. & i., Amer.* to park. —**parqueadero,** *n.m., Amer.* parking lot. —**parqueo** (-'ke·o) *n.m., Amer.* parking.
parquedad (par·ke'ðað) *n.f.* paucity.
parra ('pa·rra) *n.f.* grapevine.
parrafada (pa·rra'fa·ða) *n.f., colloq.* private talk; chat.
párrafo ('pa·rra·fo) *n.m.* paragraph. —**echar un párrafo,** to chat amicably.
parral (pa'rral) *n.m.* vine arbor; grape arbor.
parranda (pa'rran·da) *n.f.* revel; carousal. —**parrandero,** *adj.* fond of carousing. —*n.m.* [*also,* **parrandista**] carouser.
parrandear (pa·rran·de'ar) *v.i.* to revel; carouse.
parricida (pa·rri'θi·ða; -'si·ða) *n.m. & f.* parricide; patricide (*agent*). —*adj.* parricidal; patricidal. —**parricidio** (-'θi·ðjo; -'si·ðjo) *n.m.* parricide; patricide (*act*).
parrilla (pa'rri·ʎa; -ja) *n.f.* 1, gridiron; grill. 2, barbecue; grillroom.
párroco ('pa·rro·ko) *n.m.* parson.
parroquia (pa'rro·kja) *n.f.* 1, parish. 2, parish church. —**parroquial,** *adj.* parochial.
parroquiano (pa·rro'kja·no) *n.m.* 1, customer; patron; habitué. 2, parishioner. —*adj.* = **parroquial.**
parsimonia (par·si'mo·nja) *n.f.* parsimony. —**parsimonioso,** *adj.* parsimonious.
parte ('par·te) *n.f.* 1, part. 2, side; place; hand. 3, *law* party. —*n.m.* 1, dispatch; message. 2, official communication; writ. —**en parte,** in part; partly. —**dar parte,** to inform; notify. —**de algún tiempo a esta parte,** for some time past. —**de mi parte,** for my part. —**de parte a parte,** from side to side; through. —**de parte de,** 1, from; by courtesy *or* command of. 2, on the side of; favoring. —**echar a mala parte,** 1, to take amiss. 2, to misuse *or* misconstrue (a word or expression). —**en ninguna parte,** nowhere. —**por todas partes,** everywhere.
partenogénesis (par·te·no'xe·ne·sis) *n.f.* parthenogenesis.
partera (par'te·ra) *n.f.* midwife. —**partería,** *n.f.* midwifery.
parterre (par'te·rre) *n.m.* parterre.
partición (par·ti'θjon; -'sjon) *n.f.* partition; division.
participación (par·ti·θi·pa·'θjon; -si·pa'sjon) *n.f.* 1, participation. 2, notification.
participante (par·ti·θi'pan·te; -si'pan·te) *n.m. & f.* 1, participant. 2, informant.
participar (par·ti·θi'par; -si'par) *v.t.* to notify; communicate. —*v.i.* 1, *fol. by* **de,** to share in. 2, *fol. by* **en,** to participate in.

participe (par'ti·θi·pe; -si·pe) *n.m.* & *f.* & *adj.* participant.
participio (par·ti·'θi·pjo; -'si·pjo) *n.m.* participle. —**participial,** *adj.* participial.
partícula (par'ti·ku·la) *n.f.* particle.
particular (par·ti·ku'lar) *adj.* 1, particular. 2, private. 3, special; peculiar. —*n.m.* 1, *also fem.* individual; private person. 2, particular.
particularidad (par·ti·ku·la·ri·'ðað) *n.f.* 1, peculiarity. 2, detail; particular.
partida (par'ti·ða) *n.f.* 1, departure. 2, item in an account; entry. 3, lot. 4, game; match. 5, certificate (*of birth, marriage, etc.*). 6, band; gang; party. 7, start. 8, consignment. —**partida de campo,** picnic. —**partida doble,** *comm.* double entry. —**partida simple,** *comm.* single entry.
partidario (par·ti'ða·rjo) *adj.* & *n.m.* partisan. —*n.m.* follower; supporter. —**partidario de,** supporting; in favor of.
partidismo (par·ti'ðis·mo) *n.m.* partisanship. —**partidista,** *adj.* partisan.
partido (par'ti·ðo) *adj.* split; broken. —*n.m.* 1, *polit.* party. 2, match; contest; game. 3, advantage. 4, expedient; measure. 5, players (*pl.*); team. 6, odds; handicap. —**buen partido,** desirable suitor; good catch. —**mal partido,** undesirable suitor; bad catch. —**tomar partido,** to take sides; choose.
partidura (par·ti'ðu·ra) *n.f.* part (*in the hair*).
partir (par'tir) *v.t.* 1, to divide; split. 2, to crack; rend; shatter. 3, *math.* to divide. —*v.i.* 1, to depart; leave. 2, to start; set out. —**partirse,** *v.r., fig.* to be torn apart. —**a partir de,** starting from; as of.
partitivo (par·ti'ti·βo) *adj.* partitive.
partitura (par·ti'tu·ra) *n.f., music* score.
parto ('par·to) *n.m.* 1, parturition. 2, birth; delivery. 3, being or thing that is born. —**estar de parto,** to labor; be in difficulties.
parturienta (par·tu'rjen·ta) *also,* **parturiente** (-te) *adj.fem.* parturient. —*n.f.* woman in childbirth.
parva ('par·βa) *n.f.* 1, stack; rick (*of straw, hay, etc.*). 2, heap; multitude.
parvada (par'βa·ða) *n.f.* 1, row of haystacks. 2, brood; covey.
parvedad (par·βe'ðað) *n.f.* 1, smallness; sparseness. 2, light snack, esp. one taken on the morning of a fast day.
párvulo ('par·βu·lo) *n.m.* tot. —*adj.* 1, very small. 2, innocent.
pasa ('pa·sa) *n.f.* 1, raisin. 2, tight curl; kink (*of hair*).
pasable (pa'sa·βle) *adj.* 1, passable. 2, tolerable.
pasada (pa'sa·ða) *n.f.* 1, passing; pass; passage. 2, trick; trickery; chicanery. —**de pasada,** 1, in passing. 2, hastily; cursorily.
pasadera (pa·sa'ðe·ra) *n.f.* stepping stone.
pasadero (pa·sa'ðe·ro) *adj.* = pasable.
pasadizo (pa·sa'ði·θo; -so) *n.m.* passageway.
pasado (pa'sa·ðo) *adj.* 1, past. 2, last; just past. 3, stale. 4, spoiled (*of fruit*). 5, out of date; antiquated. —*n.m.* past. —**pasado mañana,** the day after tomorrow.
pasador (pa·sa'ðor) *n.m.* 1, door bolt. 2, cotter pin. 3, hairpin. 4, hatpin. 5, marlinespike.
pasagonzalo (pa·sa·ɣon'θa·lo; -'sa·lo) *n.m., colloq.* flip; flick; light rap.
pasaje (pa'sa·xe) *n.m.* 1, passage. 2, fare; ticket. 3, ship's passengers; passenger list.
pasajero (pa·sa'xe·ro) *adj.* passing; transitory. —*n.m.* passenger.
pasamano (pa·sa'ma·no) *n.m.* 1, handrail; banister. 2, trimming; passementerie.
pasante (pa'san·te) *n.m.* 1, assistant (*to a teacher, lawyer, physician, etc.*). 2, tutor.
pasaporte (pa·sa'por·te) *n.m.* passport.
pasar (pa'sar) *v.t.* & *i.* to pass. —*v.t.* 1, to pass on; convey; transmit. 2, to run through; pierce. 3, to swallow. 4, to cross; pass through. —*v.i.* 1, to last; endure. 2, to manage; get along; make do. —*v.impers.* to come to pass; happen. —**pasarse,** *v.r.* 1, to pass. 2, to go over (to); change allegiance (to). 3, to spoil (*of food*). 4, to become permeated; be soaked through. —**pasar a cuchillo,** to put to the sword. —**pasar de largo,** to go through; go by. —**pasar en blanco** *or* **claro,** to pass over; disregard.

—**pasar lista,** to call the roll. —**pasar por alto,** to overlook. —**pase lo que pase,** come what may; no matter what.
pasarela (pa·sa're·la) *n.f.* 1, gangplank; gangway. 2, footbridge. 3, catwalk.
pasatiempo (pa·sa'tjem·po) *n.m.* pastime.
pascua ('pas·kwa) *n.f.* 1, *usu.pl.* Christmas; Yuletide. 2, Easter. 3, Passover.
pascual (pas'kwal) *adj.* paschal.
pase ('pa·se) *n.m.* 1, pass; permit. 2, *fencing* thrust. 3, pass (*in certain games and sports*). 4, movement; motion; pass.
paseante (pa·se'an·te) *n.m.* promenader; stroller.
pasear (pa·se'ar) *v.i.* [*also, refl.,* **pasearse**] 1, to promenade; stroll; take a walk. 2, to take a ride. 3, *Amer., colloq.* to take a trip; travel. —*v.t.* to take out for a walk or a ride.
paseo (pa'se·o) *n.m.* 1, walk; stroll. 2, drive; ride. 3, promenade; boulevard. —**dar un paseo,** to take a walk *or* ride. —**mandar a paseo,** *colloq.* to send flying; send off; send packing.
pasillo (pa'si·ʎo; -jo) *n.m.* 1, corridor. 2, aisle. 3, *theat.* sketch; farce.
pasión (pa'sjon) *n.f.* passion.
pasional (pa·sjo'nal) *adj.* 1, of or pert. to passion. 2, passionate.
pasionaria (pa·sjo'na·rja) *n.f.* passionflower.
pasito (pa'si·to) *n.m.* short step. —*adv., colloq.* gently; softly.
pasivo (pa'si·βo) *adj.* passive. —*n.m.* liabilities (*pl.*). —**pasividad,** *n.f.* passivity.
pasmado (pas'ma·ðo) *adj.* stunned; amazed.
pasmar (pas'mar) *v.t.* 1, to stun; benumb. 2, to astound. 3, to stunt. 4, to freeze (*as a plant*). —**pasmarse,** *v.r.* 1, to freeze; become rigid. 2, to suffer from lockjaw. 3, to marvel; be astounded.
pasmo ('pas·mo) *n.m.* 1, astonishment. 2, wonder; marvel. 3, lockjaw. 4, cold; chill. —**pasmoso,** *adj.* astounding; marvelous.
paso ('pa·so) *n.m.* 1, step; pace. 2, way; path; pass. 3, predicament; tight spot. 4, an event of the life of Christ; sculptured figure or group representing such event. —*adj.* dried (*of fruit*). —**a cada paso,** frequently. —**al paso que,** while; as. —**paso a nivel,** grade crossing. —**de paso,** 1, on the way. 2, passing or traveling through. —**llevar el paso,** 1, to lead (*in dancing*). 2, to keep step. —**marcar el paso,** to mark time. —**prohibido el paso,** no trespassing.
pasquín (pas'kin) *n.m.* lampoon; pasquinade. —**pasquinar,** *v.t.* to lampoon.
pasquinada (pas·ki'na·ða) *n.f.* pasquinade; skit.
pasta ('pas·ta) *n.f.* 1, paste. 2, batter; dough. 3, metal bullion, 4, *colloq.* money.
pastadero (pas·ta'ðe·ro) *n.m.* grazing field; pasture. *Also,* **pastal** (-'tal).
pastar (pas'tar) *v.i.* to pasture; graze. —*v.t.* to lead (cattle) to graze.
pastel (pas'tel) *n.m.* 1, pie; pastry; tart. 2, *print.* pie. 3, *colloq.* jumble. —*adj.* & *n.m.* pastel.
pastelería (pas·te·le'ri·a) *n.f.* 1, pastry shop. 2, pastry.
pastelero (pas·te'le·ro) *n.m.* 1, pastry baker. 2, pastry seller.
pastelillo (pas·te'li·ʎo; -jo) *n.m.* patty; pasty.
pasteurizar (pas·teu·ri'θar; -'sar) *also,* **pasterizar** (pas·te·ri-) *v.t.* [*infl.:* **realizar**] to pasteurize. —**pasteurización,** *also,* **pasterización,** *n.f.* pasteurization.
pastilla (pas'ti·ʎa; -ja) *n.f.* 1, lozenge; pastille. 2, cake, tablet, block (*as of soap, chocolate, etc.*).
pastinaca (pas·ti'na·ka) *n.f.* 1, *ichthy.* stingray. 2, *bot.* parsnip.
pastizal (pas·ti'θal; -'sal) *n.m.* rich pasture, esp. for horses.
pasto ('pas·to) *n.m.* 1, pasture. 2, grass; herbage. 3, *fig.* food; fuel.
pastor (pas'tor) *n.m.* 1, shepherd. 2, pastor; clergyman.
pastoral (pas·to'ral) *adj.* pastoral. —*n.f.* pastorale.
pastorear (pas·to·re'ar) *v.t.* & *i.* to pasture.
pastoreo (pas·to're·o) *n.m.* 1, pasturing. 2, tending of flocks.
pastoril (pas·to'ril) *adj.* shepherd (*attrib.*).
pastoso (pas'to·so) *adj.* 1, pasty; doughy. 2, mellow. —**pastosidad,** *n.f.* pastiness; doughiness.
pastura (pas'tu·ra) *n.f.* pasture; pasturage.

pata (ˈpa·ta) *n.f.* **1,** leg or paw of an animal. **2,** *colloq.* human leg or foot. **3,** leg of a chair, table, etc. **4,** female of the drake; duck. **5,** pocket flap. **—a pata,** *colloq.* on foot. **—enseñar la pata,** *colloq.* to show one's ignorance. **—estirar la pata,** *colloq.* to die; to kick the bucket. **—meter la pata,** *colloq.* to botch; bungle. **—pata de palo,** peg leg. **—tener mala pata,** *colloq.* **1,** to be jinxed. **2,** to be churlish. **—salir, quedar** *or* **esta patas,** *colloq.* to end in a draw or tie.

-pata (pa·ta) *suffix* -path; *forming nouns denoting persons corresponding to nouns ending in* **-patía**; *psicópata,* psychopath; *homeópata,* homeopath.

patada (paˈta·ða) *n.f.* kick. **—a patadas,** *colloq.* plentifully.

patalear (pa·ta·leˈar) *v.i.* **1,** to kick about violently. **2,** to stamp the feet. **3,** *colloq.* to raise a ruckus.

pataleo (pa·taˈle·o) *n.m.* **1,** kicking. **2,** stamping of the feet. **—derecho a pataleo,** *colloq.* the right to complain.

pataleta (pa·taˈle·ta) *n.f., colloq.* **1,** convulsion; fit. **2,** tantrum.

patán (paˈtan) *adj.* **1,** rustic; churlish. **2,** unmannerly. **—*n.m.*** churl; boor. **—patanería,** *n.f.* churlishness; boorishness.

patata (paˈta·ta) *n.f.* potato. **—patatal,** *also,* **patatar,** *n.m.* potato patch. **—patatero,** *adj., colloq., often derog.* potato-eating.

patatús (pa·taˈtus) *n.m., colloq.* swoon; fainting fit.

pateadura (pa·te·aˈðu·ra) *n.f.* **1,** kicking. **2,** drubbing. **3,** *colloq.* dressing down.

patear (pa·teˈar) *v.t.* **1,** to kick; trample. **2,** to boo; hoot off. **—*v.i., colloq.*** to rage; stamp.

patentar (pa·tenˈtar) *v.t.* to patent.

patente (paˈten·te) *adj.* & *n.f.* patent.

paternal (pa·terˈnal) *adj.* fatherly; paternal. **—paternalismo,** *n.m.* paternalism. **—paternalista,** *adj.* paternalistic.

paternidad (pa·ter·niˈðað) *n.f.* **1,** paternity. **2,** title of respect used with clergymen; Reverence.

paterno (paˈter·no) *adj.* paternal; of or inherited from the father.

paternóster (pa·terˈnos·ter) *n.m. sing. & pl.* paternoster.

patético (paˈte·ti·ko) *adj.* pathetic. **—patetismo** (-ˈtis·mo) *n.m.* pathos.

pati- (pa·ti) *prefix* leg; having a (specified) kind or defect of legs: *patizambo,* knockkneed; *patilargo,* longlegged.

-patía (paˈti·a) *suffix* -pathy; -pathia. **1,** feeling; suffering: *antipatía,* antipathy. **2,** disease: *psicopatía,* psychopathy. **3,** treatment of disease: *homeopatía,* homeopathy.

patiabierto (pa·tjaˈβjer·to) *adj.* bowlegged.

patibulario (pa·ti·βuˈla·rjo) *adj.* repulsive; villainous.

patíbulo (paˈti·βu·lo) *n.m.* gallows; scaffold.

-pático (ˈpa·ti·ko) *suffix* -pathic; *forming adjectives from nouns ending in* **-patía**: *psicopático,* psychopathic; *homeopático,* homeopathic.

patilla (paˈti·ʎa; -ja) *n.f.* **1,** sideburn. **2,** *Amer., colloq.* thingumbob. **—patillas,** *n.m.pl.* Old Nick.

patín (paˈtin) *n.m.* **1,** ice skate; roller skate. **2,** child's scooter. **3,** skiff. **4,** *ornith.* petrel.

pátina (ˈpa·ti·na) *n.f.* patina.

patinadero (pa·ti·naˈðe·ro) *n.m.* skating rink; skating pond.

patinador (pa·ti·naˈðor) *n.m.* skater.

patinaje (pa·tiˈna·xe) *n.m.* skating.

patinar (pa·tiˈnar) *v.i.* **1,** to skate. **2,** to skid. **—patinamiento,** *n.m., also, Amer.,* **patinada,** *n.f.* skidding; skid.

patio (ˈpa·tjo) *n.m.* **1,** patio; courtyard. **2,** *theat.* pit; orchestra.

patitieso (pa·tiˈtje·so) *adj., colloq.* **1,** unconscious; knocked out. **2,** stunned; overwhelmed.

patituerto (pa·tiˈtwer·to) *adj.* **1,** crook-legged; bowlegged *or* knockkneed. **2,** crooked; lopsided.

patizambo (pa·tiˈθam·bo; -ˈsam·bo) *adj.* **1,** knockkneed. **2,** bowlegged.

pato (ˈpa·to) *n.m.* duck. **—pagar el pato,** *colloq.* to be the scapegoat. **—pato almizclado,** *also,* **pato turco,** Muscovy duck. **—pato negro,** mallard. **—pato silvestre,** wild duck.

pato- (pa·to) *prefix* patho-; disease: *patología,* pathology.

patochada (pa·toˈtʃa·ða) *n.f.* tomfoolery.

patógeno (paˈto·xe·no) *adj.* pathogenic.

patología (pa·to·loˈxi·a) *n.f.* pa-

thology. —**patológico** (-'lo·xi·ko) *adj.* pathological. —**patólogo** (-'to·lo·ɣo) *n.m.* pathologist.
patraña (pa'tra·ɲa) *n.f.* humbug; fib.
patri- (pa·tri) *prefix* patri-; father: *patriarcado,* patriarchate.
patria ('pa·trja) *n.f.* fatherland; native land.
patriarca (pa'trjar·ka) *n.m.* patriarch. —**patriarcado,** *n.m.* patriarchate; patriarchy. —**patriarcal,** *adj.* patriarchal.
patricio (pa'tri·θjo; -sjo) *n.m.* & *adj.* patrician.
patrimonio (pa·tri'mo·njo) *n.m.* patrimony. —**patrimonial,** *adj.* patrimonial.
patrio ('pa·trjo) *adj.* **1,** of the fatherland. **2,** = **paterno.**
patriota (pa'trjo·ta) *n.m.* & *f.* patriot. —**patriótico,** *adj.* patriotic. —**patriotismo,** *n.m.* patriotism.
patriotero (pa·trjo'te·ro) *adj.* & *n.m.* chauvinist; jingoist. —**patriotería,** *n.f.* chauvinism; jingoism.
patrocinar (pa·tro·θi'nar; -si'nar) *v.t.* to sponsor; patronize. —**patrocinador,** *adj.* sponsoring; patronizing. —*n.m.* sponsor; patron. —**patrocinio** (-'θi·njo; -'si·njo) *n.m.* sponsorship; patronage.
patrón (pa'tron) *n.m.* **1,** employer; boss. **2,** patron; sponsor. **3,** patron saint. **4,** pattern; model; standard. **5,** skipper.
patrona (pa'tro·na) *n.f.* **1,** mistress; boss. **2,** landlady; housekeeper. **3,** patroness.
patronal (pa·tro'nal) *adj.* **1,** patronal. **2,** of or pert. to an employer *or* employers.
patronato (pa·tro'na·to) *n.m.* **1,** employer's association. **2,** welfare organization. **3,** [*also,* **patronazgo**] patronage.
patronímico (pa·tro'ni·mi·ko) *adj.* & *n.m.* patronymic.
patrono (pa'tro·no) *n.m.* **1,** patron. **2,** employer; boss.
patrulla (pa'tru·ʎa; -ja) *n.f.* **1,** patrol. **2,** band; gang. —**patrullaje,** *n.m.* patrolling; patrol. —**patrullar,** *v.t.* & *i.* to patrol.
patuá (pa'twa) *n.m.* patois.
paulatino (pau·la'ti·no) *adj.* gradual; slow.
pauperismo (pau·pe'ris·mo) *n.m.* pauperism.
paupérrimo (pau'pe·rri·mo) *adj.* very poor; destitute; penniless.
pausa ('pau·sa) *n.f.* **1,** pause. **2,** *music* rest. **3,** slowness. —**pausado,** *adj.* slow; deliberate. —*adv.* slow; slowly. —**pausar,** *v.i.* to pause. —**con pausa,** slowly.
pauta ('pau·ta) *n.f.* **1,** ruler. **2,** ruled lines. **3,** norm; standard; model.
pava ('pa·βa) *n.f.* **1,** turkey hen. **2,** large furnace bellows. **3,** *Amer.* kettle. **4,** *W. I.* farmer's straw hat. **5,** *colloq.* graceless woman. —**pelar la pava,** *colloq.* to engage in amorous chat.
pavada (pa'βa·ða) *n.f.* **1,** flock of turkeys. **2,** *Amer.* foolishness; silliness; nonsense.
pavesa (pa'βe·sa) *n.f.* ember.
pavía (pa'βi·a) *n.f.* cling peach.
pavimento (pa·βi'men·to) *n.m.* pavement. —**pavimentar,** *v.t.* to pave. —**pavimentación,** *n.f.* paving. —**pavimentado,** *adj.* paved.
pavo ('pa·βo) *n.m.* **1,** turkey. **2,** *colloq.* oaf; sad sack; fool. —*adj., colloq.* oafish; foolish. —**pavo real,** peacock. —**ponerse hecho un pavo,** to blush. —**subírsele a uno el pavo,** to put on airs.
pavón (pa'βon) *n.m.* peacock.
pavonear (pa·βo·ne'ar) *v.i.* [*also, refl.,* **pavonearse**] to strut; show off.
pavor (pa'βor) *n.m.* dread. —**pavoroso,** *adj.* dreadful; awful. —**pavura,** *n.f.* dread; terror.
paya ('pa·ja) *n.f., Amer.* song improvised to the tune of the guitar —**payar,** *v.i., Amer.* to sing a *paya.* —**payador,** *n.m., Amer.* singer; improviser.
payaso (pa'ja·so) *n.m.* clown. —**payasada,** *n.f.* clownery; tomfoolery. —**payasear,** *v.i., Amer.* to clown.
payo ('pa·jo) *adj.* & *n.m.* rustic. —*n.m., slang* fellow; guy.
payuelas (pa'jwe·las) *n.f.pl.* chicken pox.
paz (paθ; pas) *n.f.* peace.
pazca ('paθ·ka; 'pas-) *v., pres. subjve. of* **pacer.**
pazco ('paθ·ko; 'pas-) *v., 1st pers. sing.pres.ind. of* **pacer.**
pazguato (paθ'ɣwa·to; pas-) *n.m.* dolt; simpleton.
pe (pe) *n.f., in* **de pe a pa,** from beginning to end; from A to Z.
peaje (pe'a·xe) *n.m.* toll. —**peajero,** *n.m.* toll collector.
peatón (pe·a'ton) *n.m.* **1,** pedestrian. **2,** rural postman.

pebete (pe'βe·te) *n.m.* 1, incense. 2, *Amer., colloq.* kid; small boy. 3, *colloq.* malodorous thing.
pebre ('pe·βre) *n.m.* or *f.* sauce of pepper, garlic and spice. —**hacer pebre,** *colloq.* to maul; beat.
peca ('pe·ka) *n.f.* freckle.
pecadillo (pe·ka'ði·ʎo; -jo) *n.m.* peccadillo.
pecado (pe'ka·ðo) *n.m.* sin. —**de mis pecados,** of mine; my own.
pecador (pe·ka'ðor) *n.m.* sinner. —*adj.* sinning.
pecaminoso (pe·ka·mi'no·so) *adj.* sinful.
pecar (pe'kar) *v.i.* [*pres.subjve.* **peque;** *pret.* **pequé**] to sin. —**pecar de** (*fol. by adj.*), to be too . . .
pecarí (pe·ka'ri) *n.m.* peccary.
pecblenda (pek'βlen·da) *n.f.* pitchblende.
pecera (pe'θe·ra; -'se·ra) *n.f.* fish bowl; fish tank.
pécora ('pe·ko·ra) *n.f.* 1, head of sheep; sheep. 2, *colloq.* hussy; minx.
pecoso (pe'ko·so) *adj.* freckly; freckled.
pectina (pek'ti·na) *n.f.* pectin.
pectoral (pek·to'ral) *adj.* pectoral; chest (*attrib.*). —*n.m., eccles.* pectoral.
pecuario (pe'kwa·rjo) *adj.* of or pert. to livestock.
peculado (pe·ku'la·ðo) *n.m.* embezzlement; peculation.
peculiar (pe·ku'ljar) *adj.* peculiar. —**peculiaridad,** *n.f.* peculiarity.
peculio (pe'ku·ljo) *n.m.* personal wealth; belongings (*pl.*); possessions (*pl.*).
pecunia (pe'ku·nja) *n.f., colloq.* hard cash; money.
pecuniario (pe·ku'nja·rjo) *adj.* pecuniary.
pechar (pe'tʃar) *v.t.* & *i.* to shoulder (a burden or responsibility). —*v.i., Amer.* to contend; struggle. —*v.t.* to breast; confront.
pechblenda (petʃ'βlen·da) *n.f.* = **pecblenda.**
pechera (pe'tʃe·ra) *n.f.* 1, shirt front. 2, chest protector. 3, *colloq.* chest; bosom.
pechicolorado (pe·tʃi-ko·lo'ra·ðo) *n.m.* linnet.
pecho ('pe·tʃo) *n.m.* 1, chest; thorax. 2, breast. 3, bosom. 4, *fig.* courage; fortitude. 5, *music* strength of the voice. —**abrir el pecho,** to open one's heart; confide. —**dar el pecho,** 1, to suckle; nurse. 2, to face; confront. —**entre pecho y espalda,** *colloq.* deep down inside. —**tomar a pecho,** to take to heart.
pechuga (pe'tʃu·ɣa) *n.f.* 1, breast (*of fowl*). 2, *colloq.* bosom; breasts (*pl.*). 3, *Amer., colloq.* nerve; gall.
pechugón (pe·tʃu'ɣon) *adj., Amer., colloq.* brazenly demanding. —*n.m., Amer., colloq.* sponger; demanding person.
ped- (peð) *prefix* ped-, *var. of* **pedi-.**
pedagogía (pe·ða·ɣo'xi·a) *n.f.* pedagogy. —**pedagógico** (-'ɣo·xi·ko) *adj.* pedagogical. —**pedagogo** (-'ɣo·ɣo) pedagogue; educator.
pedal (pe'ðal) *n.m.* pedal; treadle. —**pedalear,** *v.t.* & *i.* to pedal.
pedáneo (pe'ða·ne·o) *n.m., also,* **alcalde pedáneo,** reeve; bailiff.
pedante (pe'ðan·te) *n.m.* & *f.* pedant. —*adj.* pedantic. —**pedantear,** *v.i.* to act the pedant. —**pedantería,** *n.f.* pedantry. —**pedantesco,** *adj.* pedantic (*of style*).
pedazo (pe'ða·θo; -so) *n.m.* piece; fragrant; slice.
pederasta (pe·ðe'ras·ta) *n.m.* pederast. —**pederastia** (-tja) *n.f.* pederasty.
pedernal (pe·ðer'nal) *n.m.* flint.
pedestal (pe·ðes'tal) *n.m.* pedestal.
pedestre (pe'ðes·tre) *adj.* pedestrian.
pedi- (pe·ði) *prefix* pedi-. 1, foot: *pedicura,* pedicure; *pediforme,* pediform. 2, child: *pediatría,* pediatrics.
-pedia ('pe·ðja) *suffix* -pedia; -pedics; education; conditioning: *enciclopedia,* encyclopedia; *ortopedia,* orthopedics.
pediatría (pe·ðja'tri·a) *n.f.* pediatrics. —**pediatra** (pe'ðja·tra) *n.m.* & *f.* pediatrician. —**pediátrico** (pe·'ðja·tri·ko) *adj.* pediatric.
pedicura (pe·ði'ku·ra) *n.f.* pedicure.
pedicuro (pe·ði'ku·ro) *n.m.* chiropodist; pedicure.
pedida (pe'ði·ða) *adj.fem.* spoken for. —*n.f.* request for the hand of a woman in marriage.
pedido (pe'ði·ðo) *n.m.* 1, demand; request; call. 2, *comm.* order.
pedidor (pe·ði'ðor) *adj.* demanding. —*n.m.* demanding person.
pedigüeño (pe·ði'ɣwe·ɲo) *adj., colloq.* importunate. *Also,* **pedigón** (-'ɣon).
pedir (pe'dir) *v.t.* [*pres.ind.* **pido;** *pres.subjve.* **pida;** *pret.* **pedí, pidió;**

ger. **pidiendo**] to request; ask; beg. —**a pedir de boca,** at just the right moment; just as hoped for.

pedo ('pe·ðo) *n.m.* fart; breaking wind.

pedo- (pe·ðo) *prefix* pedo-; child: *pedodoncia,* pedodontia.

-pedo (pe·ðo) *suffix* -ped; -pede; foot; having a (specified) kind or number of feet: *cuadrupedo,* quadruped; *alípedo,* aliped.

pedorrero (pe·ðo'rre·ro) *adj.* farting; farty. —**pedorrera,** *n.f.* farting, flatulence.

pedorreta (pe·ðo'rre·ta) *n.f., colloq.* Bronx cheer.

pedrada (pe'ðra·ða) *n.f.* **1,** stone's throw. **2,** blow with a stone. **3,** *colloq.* taunt; insinuation.

pedregal (pe·ðre'ɣal) *n.m.* stony terrain. —**pedregoso,** *adj.* stony; rocky.

pedrería (pe·ðre'ri·a) *n.f.* jewelry.

pedrusco (pe'ðrus·ko) *n.m.* boulder; rough stone.

pedúnculo (pe'ðun·ku·lo) *n.m.* stem; stalk.

pega ('pe·ɣa) *n.f.* **1,** = **pegadura. 2,** *Amer., colloq.* paste glue. **3,** *Amer., colloq.* soft job; racket.

pegadizo (pe·ɣa'ði·θo -so) *adj.* **1,** sticky; adhesive **2,** catching; contagious. **3,** catchy (*of a tune*).

pegadura (pe·ɣa'ðu·ra) *n.f.* **1,** pasting; sticking. **2,** adhesion.

pegajoso (pe·ɣa'xo·so) *adj.* **1,** sticky. **2,** catching; contagious. **3,** catchy (*of a tune*) **4,** clammy. —**pegajosidad,** *n.f.* stickiness.

pegar (pe'ɣar) *v.t.* [*pres.subjve.* **pegue** ('pe·ɣe); *pret.* **pegué** (-'ɣe)] **1,** to stick; glue. **2,** to attach· fasten. **3,** to sew on. **4,** to give (a vice or disease). **5,** to strike (a blow). —*v.i.* **1,** to take root. **2,** to take; catch on. —**pegarse,** *v.r.* **1,** to stick; scorch (*of food*). **2,** to become ingrained; become fixed. —**pegársela a uno,** to dupe someone.

pegote (pe'ɣo·te) *n.* **1,** sticky mass; goo. **2,** hanger-on; leech.

peinado (pei'na·ðo) *n.m.* coiffure; hairdo. —*adj.* overnice (*of style*).

peinador (pei·na'ðor) *n.m.* peignoir.

peinar (pei'nar) *v.t.* to comb. —**peinarse,** *v.r.* to comb one's hair.

peine ('pei·ne) *n.m.* comb.

peineta (pei'ne·ta) *n.f.* ornamental comb.

peje ('pe·xe) *n.m.* **1,** fish. **2,** *colloq.* crafty fellow.

pejerrey (pe·xe'rrei) *n.m.* a variety of smelt.

pejesapo (pe·xe'sa·po) *n.m., ichthy.* angler.

peladilla (pe·la'ði·ʎa; -ja) *n.f.* **1,** candied almond **2,** small pebble.

pelado (pe'la·ðo) *adj.* **1,** plucked. **2,** bald; hairless. **3,** bare. **4,** *colloq.* penniless, broke —*n.m.* **1,** *colloq.* penniless person **2,** *Mex.* peasant. **3,** *Amer.* infant; child.

pelafustán (pe·la·fus'tan) *n.m., colloq.* ne'er-do-well; loafer.

pelagatos (pe·la'ɣa·tos) *n.m.sing. & pl., colloq.* tramp.

pelagra (pe'la·ɣra) *n.f.* pellagra.

pelaje (pe'la·xe) *n.m.* **1,** coat; hair; fur. **2,** aspect complexion.

pelambre (pe'lam·bre) *n.f.* **1,** hair; hairiness. **2,** [*also* **pelambrera**] shed hair *or* fur. **3,** [*also,* **pelambrera**] bare or bald spot.

pelar (pe'lar) *v.t.* **1,** to cut or pull off (the hair). **2,** to pluck (feathers). **3,** to peel; skin. **4,** *colloq.* to clean out; make bankrupt. —**pelarse,** *v.r.* **1,** to lose the hair. **2,** to peel off; flake. **3,** [*also* **pelárselas**] *usu.fol. by* **por,** to be eager to; be raring to; be excited about. **4,** [*also,* **pelárselas**] *usu.fol. by* **de,** to be intensely affected by.

peldaño (pel'da·ɲo) *n.m.* step (*of a staircase*).

pelea (pe'le·a) *n.f.* fight; quarrel.

pelear (pe·le'ar) *v.i.* to fight; quarrel. —**pelearse** *v.r.* **1,** to have a fight; scuffle **2,** to be on bad terms.

pelechar (pe·le'tʃar) *v.i.* to molt; shed.

pelele (pe'le·le) *n.m.* **1,** stuffed figure; dummy. **2,** *fig.* straw man.

peletero (pe·le'te·ro) *n.m.* furrier. —**peletería,** *n.f.* furrier's shop *or* trade.

peliagudo (pe·li·a'ɣu·ðo; pe·lja-) *adj.* **1,** having long, thin hair. **2,** *colloq.* difficult; tough; crucial.

pelícano (pe'li·ka·no) *n.m.* pelican.

película (pe'li·ku·la) *n.f.* film.

peligrar (pe·li'ɣrar) *v.i.* to be in danger.

peligro (pe'li·ɣro) *n.m.* danger; peril. —**peligroso,** *adj.* dangerous; perilous.

pelillo (pe'li·ʎo; -jo) *n.m.* **1,** hair; trifle. **2,** *usu.pl.* bone of contention; gripe. —**echar pelillos a la**

mar, *colloq.* to bury the hatchet. —**pararse en pelillos,** *colloq.* to quibble; haggle.

pelirrojo (pe·li'rro·xo) *adj.* redheaded. —*n.m.* redheaded person; redhead.

pelmazo (pel'ma·θo; -so) *n.m.,* *also,* **pelma** ('pel·ma) *n.m.* & *f.* **1,** thick lump. **2,** *colloq.* slow, sluggish person. **3,** *colloq.* nuisance; bore.

pelo ('pe·lo) *n.m.* hair. —**al pelo; a pelo,** just right; to a T. —**de pelo en pecho,** *colloq.* manly; virile. —**en pelo,** bareback. —**pelos y señales,** *colloq.* minute details; characteristics. —**tomar el pelo,** *colloq.* to pull one's leg; josh.

pelón (pe'lon) *adj.* hairless; bald. —*n.m.* bald person; baldhead.

pelota (pe'lo·ta) *n.f.* **1,** ball. **2,** jai alai, soccer, or any of several games of ball. —**en pelota,** naked; stripped.

pelotear (pe·lo·te'ar) *v.i.* to bandy a ball; play catch.

pelotera (pe·lo'te·ra) *n.f., colloq.* brawl; riot; tumult.

pelotón (pe·lo'ton) *n.m.* **1,** bunch; crowd. **2,** hank; knot. **3,** platoon.

peltre ('pel·tre) *n.m.* pewter.

peluca (pe'lu·ka) *n.f.* wig.

peludo (pe'lu·ðo) *adj.* hairy. —*n.m.* fiber mat.

peluquería (pe·lu·ke'ri·a) *n.f.* **1,** hairdresser's shop. **2,** barber shop.

peluquero (pe·lu'ke·ro) *n.m.* **1,** barber. **2,** hairdresser.

pelusa (pe'lu·sa) *n.f.* fuzz; down.

pelvis ('pel·βis) *n.f.* pelvis. —**pelviano** (-'βja·no) *adj.* pelvic.

pellejo (pe'ʎe·xo; -'je·xo) *n.m.* **1,** skin; pelt. **2,** wineskin.

pelliza (pe'ʎi·θa; -'ji·sa) *n.f.* pelisse.

pellizcar (pe·ʎiθ'kar; pe·jis'kar) *v.t.* [*pres.subjve.* **pellizque** (pe'ʎiθ·ke; pe'jis·ke); *pret.* **pellizqué** (-'ke)] to pinch; nip. —**pellizcarse,** *v.r.* to long; pine.

pellizco (pe'ʎiθ·ko; pe'jis-) *n.m.* pinch; nip.

pena ('pe·na) *n.f.* **1,** penalty; punishment. **2,** sorrow. **3,** suffering; pain. **4,** toil; hardship. **5,** mortification; embarrassment. **6,** *Amer.* spirit; ghost. —**a duras penas,** barely; just barely. —**dar pena,** to evoke sorrow; cause to be sorry. —**merecer** *or* **valer la pena,** to be worthwhile. —**tener pena,** to be sorry.

penacho (pe'na·tʃo) *n.m.* **1,** tuft of feathers. **2,** plume; crest.

penado (pe'na·ðo) *n.m.* convict. —*adj.* = **penoso.**

penal (pe'nal) *adj.* penal.

penalidad (pe·na·li'ðað) *n.f.* **1,** hardship. **2,** *law* penalty.

penalista (pe·na'lis·ta) *n.m.* penologist.

penalizar (pe·na·li'θar; -'sar) *v.t.* [*pres.subjve.* **penalice** (-'li·θe; -se); *pret.* **penalicé** (-'θe; -'se)] to penalize.

penar (pe'nar) *v.i.* **1,** to suffer; experience sorrow. **2,** to be in torment (*in the afterlife*). **3,** to long; pine. —*v.t.* to impose a penalty on. —**penarse,** *v.r.* to grieve; mourn; lament.

penca ('pen·ka) *n.f.* **1,** rawhide; whip. **2,** pulpy leaf of some plants, as cactus. —**coger una penca,** *Amer., colloq.* to get drunk.

penco ('pen·ko) *n.m., colloq.* nag; plug.

pendejo (pen'de·xo) *n.m.* **1,** pubic hair. **2,** *Amer., vulg.* fool; jerk.

pendencia (pen'den·θja; -sja) *n.f.* quarrel; wrangle; brawl. —**pendenciar,** *v.i.* to quarrel; wrangle. —**pendenciero,** *adj.* quarrelsome; wrangling; brawling. —*n.m.* wrangler; brawler.

pender (pen'der) *v.i.* **1,** to hang; dangle. **2,** to pend. **3,** to depend.

pendiente (pen'djen·te) *adj.* **1,** pendent; hanging. **2,** pending. —*n.f.* slope; gradient. —*n.m.* pendant; earring.

péndola ('pen·do·la) *n.f.* **1,** pendulum. **2,** pendulum clock.

pendolista (pen·do'lis·ta) *n.m.* penman.

pendón (pen'don) *n.m.* **1,** standard; banner; pennant. **2,** tiller; shoot. **3,** *colloq.* so-and-so; hussy (*if applied to a woman*).

péndulo ('pen·du·lo) *n.m.* pendulum. —*adj.* pendulous. —**pendular,** *adj.* of or like a pendulum.

pene ('pe·ne) *n.m.* penis.

penetrar (pe·ne'trar) *v.t.* to penetrate. —**penetrable,** *adj.* penetrable. —**penetración,** *n.f.* penetration.

peni- (pe·ni) *prefix* penni-; feather: *peniforme,* penniform.

penicilina (pe·ni·θi'li·na; pe·ni·si-) *n.f.* penicillin.

península (pe'nin·su·la) *n.f.* peninsula. —**peninsular,** *adj.* peninsular.

penique (pe'ni·ke) *n.m.* British penny.
penitencia (pe·ni'ten·θja; -sja) *n.f.* penitence; penance. —**penitencial,** *adj.* penitential.
penitenciaría (pe·ni·ten·θja'ri·a; -sja'ri·a) *n.f.* penitentiary. —**penitenciario** (-'θja·rjo; -'sja·rjo) *adj.* penitentiary (*attrib.*). —*n.m.*, *R.C.Ch.* penitentiary.
penitente (pe·ni'ten·te) *adj.* & *n.m.* & *f.* penitent.
penol (pe'nol) *n.m.* yardarm.
penología (pe·no·lo'xi·a) *n.f.* penology.
penoso (pe'no·so) *adj.* **1,** painful. **2,** grieving.
pensado (pen'sa·ðo) *adj.* deliberate; reasoned. —**mal pensado,** evil-minded.
pensador (pen·sa'ðor) *n.m.* thinker. —*adj.* thinking.
pensamiento (pen·sa'mjen·to) *n.m.* **1,** thought. **2,** mind. **3,** *bot.* pansy.
pensar (pen'sar) *v.t.* & *i.* [*pres.ind.* **pienso;** *pres.subjve.* **piense**] to think. —*v.t.* to forage; feed.
pensativo (pen·sa'ti·βo) *adj.* pensive.
pensión (pen'sjon) *n.f.* **1,** pension. **2,** boarding house. **3,** board; meals (*pl.*). —**pensionar** *v.t.* to pension.
pensionado (pen·sjo'na·ðo) *adj.* pensioned. —*n.m.* **1,** pensioner. **2,** boarding school.
pensionista (pen·sjo'nis·ta) *n.m.* & *f.* **1,** boarder. **2,** pensioner.
penta- (pen·ta) *prefix* penta-; five: *pentágono* pentagon.
pentaedro (pen·ta'e·ðro) *n.m.* pentahedron.
pentágono (pen'ta·ɣo·no) *n.m.* pentagon. —**pentagonal,** *adj.* pentagonal.
pentagrama (pen·ta'ɣra·ma) *n.m.*, *music* staff.
pentámetro (pen'ta·me·tro) *n.m.* pentameter.
Pentateuco (pen·ta'teu·ko) *n.m.* Pentateuch.
péntatlo ('pen·ta·tlo) *n.m.* pentathlon.
Pentecostés (pen·te·kos'tes) *n.m.* Pentecost. —**pentecostal,** *adj.* & *n.m.* & *f.* Pentecostal.
penúltimo (pe'nul·ti·mo) *adj.* penultimate. —**penúltima,** *n.f.* penult.
penumbra (pe'num·bra) *n.f.* penumbra; twilight. —**penumbroso,** *adj.* penumbral.
penuria (pe'nu·rja) *n.f.* penury.
peña ('pe·ɲa) *n.f.* rock.
peñasco (pe'ɲas·ko) *n.m.* large rock. —**peñascal** *n.m.* rocky terrain. —**peñascoso** *adj.* rocky.
peñón (pe'ɲon) *n.m.* rocky prominence.
peón (pe'on) *n.m.* **1,** laborer; peon. **2,** spinning top. **3,** *chess* pawn. **4,** *checkers* man. **5,** foot soldier. **6,** pedestrian.
peonada (pe·o'na·ða) *n.f.* **1,** day's work (*of a peon*). **2,** gang of peons. **3,** = **peonaje**
peonaje (pe·o'na·xe) *n.m.* **1,** peonage. **2,** peons collectively. **3,** foot soldiers collectively.
peonía (pe·o'ni·a) *n.f.* peony.
peonza (pe'on·θa; -sa) *n.f.* spinning top.
peor (pe'or) *adj.* & *adv.* worse; worst.
pepa ('pe·pa) *n.f.*, *Amer.* **1,** seed; pit. **2,** playing marble.
pepinillos (pe·pi'ni·ʎos; -jos) *n.m.pl.* **1,** gherkins. **2,** pickled cucumbers.
pepino (pe'pi·no) *n.m.* cucumber. —**importar un pepino** *or* **tres pepinos,** *colloq.* not to matter a bit.
pepita (pe'pi·ta) *n.f.* **1,** pip; seed. **2,** pip (*disease of fowls*). **3,** nugget.
pepitoria (pe·pi'to·rja) *n.f.* **1,** giblet fricassee. **2,** hodgepodge.
pepón (pe'pon) *n.m.* watermelon.
-pepsia ('pep·sja) *suffix* -pepsia; digestion: *dispepsia* dyspepsia.
pepsina (pep'si·na) *n.f.* pepsin.
péptico ('pep·ti·ko) *adj.* peptic.
-péptico ('pep·ti·ko) *suffix* -peptic; *forming adjectives from nouns ending in* **-pepsia:** *dispéptico,* dyspeptic.
péptido ('pep·ti·ðo) *n.m.* peptide.
peptona (pep'to·na) *n.f.* peptone.
peque ('pe·ke) *v., pres.subjve. of* **pecar.**
pequé (pe'ke) *v., 1st pers.sing. pret. of* **pecar.**
pequeñez (pe·ke'ɲeθ; -'ɲes) *n.f.* **1,** smallness. **2,** meanness; pettiness. **3,** trifle. **4,** infancy; childhood.
pequeño (pe'ke·ɲo) *adj.* **1,** small; little. **2,** petty; trifling. —*n.m.* child; tot; little one.
pequeñuelo (pe·ke'ɲwe·lo) *n.m.* baby; infant; tot. —*adj.* very small.
per- (per) *prefix* per-. **1,** through: *perenne,* perennial. **2,** thoroughly, very; completely: *persuadir,* per-

suade. 3, *chem.* maximum or high valence: *peróxido,* peroxide.

pera (ˈpe·ra) *n.f.* 1, pear. 2, goatee; imperial. 3, rubber bulb. 4, *colloq.* light bulb. —**pedir peras al olmo,** to expect the impossible. —**ponerle a uno las peras a cuarto,** to call down; reprimand.

peral (peˈral) *n.m.* pear tree.

peralte (peˈral·te) *n.m.* 1, superelevation; banking (*of curves*). 2, *archit.* rise of an arch.

perca (ˈper·ka) *n.f., ichthy.* perch.

percal (perˈkal) *n.m.* percale; muslin.

percance (perˈkan·θe; -se) *n.m.* mishap.

percatar (per·kaˈtar) *v.i.* [*usu. refl.,* **percatarse**] to perceive; apprehend; realize.

percebe (perˈθe·βe; -ˈse·βe) *n.m.* barnacle.

percepción (per·θepˈθjon; -sep·ˈsjon) *n.f.* perception.

perceptibilidad (per·θep·ti·βi·liˈðað; per·sep-) *n.f.* 1, perceptibility. 2, perceptivity.

perceptible (per·θepˈti·βle; per·sep-) *adj.* 1, perceptible; perceivable. 2, *comm.* receivable.

perceptivo (per·θepˈti·βo; per·sep-) *adj.* perceptive.

percibir (per·θiˈβir; per·si-) *v.t.* 1, to perceive. 2, to receive (salary, monies, etc.).

percudir (per·kuˈðir) *v.t.* 1, to tarnish. 2, to soil; begrime.

percusión (per·kuˈsjon) *n.f.* percussion.

percusor (per·kuˈsor) *n.m.* hammer (*of a firearm*).

percha (ˈper·tʃa) *n.f.* 1, perch; roost. 2, hat *or* clothes rack. 3, = **perca.**

perchero (perˈtʃe·ro) *n.m.* hat *or* clothes rack.

perdedor (per·ðeˈðor) *n.m.* loser. —*adj.* losing.

perder (perˈðer) *v.t.* [*pres.ind.* **pierdo;** *pres.subjve.* **pierda**] 1, to lose. 2, to waste; throw away. 3, to miss (a train, opportunity, etc.). 4, to corrupt. —*v.i.* to lose. —**perderse,** *v.r.* 1, to be lost. 2, to lose one's way. 3, to go wrong; go astray. 4, to disappear. 5, to be smitten. —**perder los estribos,** to lose one's self-control. —**¡pierda Vd. cuidado!** don't worry! forget it!

perdición (per·ðiˈθjon; -ˈsjon) *n.f.* perdition.

pérdida (ˈper·ði·ða) *n.f.* 1, loss. 2, *comm.* leakage.

perdido (perˈði·ðo) *adj.* 1, lost. 2, mislaid. —*adj.* & *n.m.* profligate.

perdigón (per·ðiˈɣon) *n.m.* 1, young partridge. 2, bird shot. —**perdigonada,** *n.f.* volley of bird shot.

perdiguero (per·ðiˈɣe·ro) *n.m.* setter; retriever.

perdiz (perˈðiθ; -ˈðis) *n.f.* partridge.

perdón (perˈðon) *n.m.* 1, pardon; forgiveness. 2, reprieve. 3, remission (*of a debt*). —*interj.* I beg your pardon; excuse me. —**con perdón,** by your leave; begging your pardon.

perdonable (per·ðoˈna·βle) *adj.* pardonable; forgivable.

perdonar (per·ðoˈnar) *v.t.* 1, to pardon; forgive. 2, to remit (a debt). 3, to excuse. 4, to overlook (a fault or mistake).

perdonavidas (per·ðo·naˈβi·ðas) *n.m. & f. sing. & pl., colloq.* bully.

perdulario (per·ðuˈla·rjo) *adj.* 1, careless; slovenly. 2, dissolute; unregenerate. —*n.m.* 1, slovenly person. 2, profligate.

perdurar (per·ðuˈrar) *v.i.* to last; endure. —**perdurable** *adj.* lasting; everlasting. —**perdurabilidad,** *n.f.* permanence.

perecedero (pe·re·θeˈðe·ro; pe·re·se-) *adj.* perishable; not lasting.

perecer (pe·reˈθer; -ˈser) *v.i.* [*pres.ind.* **perezco;** *pres.subjve.* **perezca**] to perish; die. —**perecerse,** *v.r.* to crave; pine.

peregrinación (pe·re·ɣri·naˈθjon; -ˈsjon) *n.f., also,* **peregrinaje** (-ˈna·xe) *n.m.* 1, peregrination. 2, pilgrimage.

peregrinar (pe·re·ɣriˈnar) *v.i.* 1, to roam. 2, to go on a pilgrimage.

peregrino (pe·reˈɣri·no) *adj.* 1, migratory. 2, singular; extraordinary. —*n.m.* pilgrim.

perejil (pe·reˈxil) *n.m.* 1, parsley. 2, *colloq.* dressiness; garishness.

perenne (peˈren·ne; peˈre·ne) *adj.* 1, perennial. 2, evergreen.

perentorio (pe·renˈto·rjo) *adj.* peremptory.

pereza (peˈre·θa; -sa) *n.f.* laziness; sloth.

perezca (peˈreθ·ka; -ˈres·ka) *v., pres.subjve. of* **perecer.**

perezco (peˈreθ·ko; -ˈres·ko) *v., 1st pers.sing. pres.ind. of* **perecer.**

perezoso (pe·reˈθo·so; -ˈso·so) *adj.*

lazy; slothful. —*n.m.* 1, idler; lazybones. 2, *zool.* sloth.

perfección (per·fek'θjon; -'sjon) *n.f.* 1, perfection. 2, perfect thing.

perfeccionar (per·fek·θjo'nar; -sjo'nar) *v.t.* to perfect. —**perfeccionamiento,** *n.m.* perfecting; perfection.

perfecto (per'fek·to) *adj.* perfect.

perfidia (per'fi·ðja) *n.f.* perfidy. —**pérfido** ('per·fi·ðo) *adj.* perfidious.

perfil (per'fil) *n.m.* 1, profile; outline. 2, cross section. —**perfiles,** *n.m.pl.* final touches.

perfilado (per·fi'la·ðo) *adj.* 1, elongated (*of the face*). 2, cleancut; well-shaped.

perfilar (per·fi'lar) *v.t.* 1, to draw in profile; outline. 2, to finish; polish. —**perfilarse,** *v.r.* 1, to place oneself in profile. 2, to emerge; begin to stand out. 3, *colloq.* to preen oneself; primp.

perforación (per·fo·ra'θjon; -'sjon) *n.f.* perforation.

perforador (per·fo·ra'ðor) *adj.* perforating; boring; drilling. —*n.m.* [*also,* **perforadora,** *n.f.*] borer; perforator; driller.

perforar (per·fo'rar) *v.t.* to perforate; bore; drill.

perfume (per'fu·me) *n.m.* perfume. —**perfumador,** *n.m.* atomizer. —**perfumar,** *v.t.* to perfume.

perfumista (per·fu'mis·ta) *n.m.* & *f., also,* **perfumero,** *n.m.* perfumer. —**perfumería,** *n.f.* perfumery.

perfunctorio (per·funk'to·rjo) *adj.* perfunctory.

pergamino (per·ɣa'mi·no) *n.m.* parchment.

pergeñar (per·xe'ɲar) *v.t.* to sketch; outline; frame. —**pergeño** (-'xe·ɲo) *n.m.* sketch.

peri- (pe·ri) *prefix* peri-; around; about: *periferia,* periphery.

pericia (pe'ri·θja; -sja) *n.f.* skill; expertness.

perico (pe'ri·ko) *n.m.* parakeet. —**Perico de los palotes,** John Doe.

periferia (pe·ri'fe·rja) *n.f.* periphery. —**periférico** (-'fe·ri·ko) *adj.* peripheral.

perifollos (pe·ri'fo·ʎos; -jos) *n.m. pl.* frippery (*sing.*).

perífrasis (pe'ri·fra·sis) *n.f.* periphrasis. —**perifrástico** (-'fras·ti·ko) *adj.* periphrastic.

perigeo (pe·ri'xe·o) *n.m.* perigee.

perihelio (pe·ri'e·ljo) *n.m.* perihelion.

perilla (pe'ri·ʎa; -ja) *n.f.* 1, pear-shaped ornament. 2, goatee. 3, lobe of the ear. 4, *Amer.* doorknob. —**de perilla** *or* **perillas,** most opportune *or* opportunely.

perillán (pe·ri'ʎan; -'jan) *n.m.* rascal; crafty person.

perímetro (pe'ri·me·tro) *n.m.* perimeter.

periódico (pe'rjo·ði·ko) *n.m.* 1, newspaper. 2, periodical. —*adj.* 1, periodic. 2, periodical.

periodismo (pe·rjo'ðis·mo) *n.m.* journalism. —**periodista,** *n.m.* & *f.* journalist. —**periodístico,** *adj.* journalistic.

período (pe'ri·o·ðo) *n.m.* 1, period (*of time*). 2, *rhet.; music; physics* period. 3, *electricity* cycle. 4, *colloq.* menses; menstrual period.

peripatético (pe·ri·pa'te·ti·ko) *adj.* & *n.m.* peripatetic. —*adj., colloq.* highfalutin; high-sounding; ridiculous.

peripecia (pe·ri'pe·θja; -sja) *n.f.* 1, vicissitude. 2, mischance; misadventure.

peripuesto (pe·ri'pwes·to) *adj., colloq.* dandified; foppish.

periquito (pe·ri'ki·to) *n.m.* parakeet.

periscopio (pe·ris'ko·pjo) *n.m.* periscope.

peristalsis (pe·ris'tal·sis) *n.f.sing.* & *pl.* peristalsis. —**peristáltico** (-ti·ko) *adj.* peristaltic.

peristilo (pe·ris'ti·lo) *n.m.* peristyle.

perito (pe'ri·to) *n.m.* & *adj.* expert.

peritoneo (pe·ri·to'ne·o) *n.m.* peritoneum. —**peritonitis,** *n.f.* peritonitis.

perjudicar (per·xu·ði'kar) *v.t.* [*pres.subjve.* **perjudique** (-'ði·ke); *pret.* **perjudiqué** (-'ke)] to harm; impair; jeopardize.

perjudicial (per·xu·ði'θjal; -'sjal) *adj.* harmful; prejudicial.

perjuicio (per'xwi·θjo; -sjo) *n.m.* 1, prejudice. 2, injury; damage. —**sin perjuicio de,** without affecting.

perjurar (per·xu'rar) *v.i.* 1, to commit perjury. 2, to swear; be profane. —**perjurarse,** *v.r.* to perjure oneself. —**jurar y perjurar,** to swear over and over.

perjurio (per'xu·rjo) *n.m.* perjury. —**perjuro** (-'xu·ro) *adj.* perjured. —*n.m.* perjurer.

perla ('per·la) *n.f.* pearl. —**de perlas,** *colloq.* just right; to a T.
perlado (per'la·ðo) *adj.* pearly; pearled.
perlesía (per·le'si·a) *n.f.* palsy.
permanencia (per·ma'nen·θja; -sja) *n.f.* 1, stay; sojourn. 2, permanence. —**permanente,** *adj.* & *n.f.* permanent.
permeable (per·me'a·βle) *adj.* permeable. —**permeabilidad,** *n.f.* permeability.
permisible (per·mi'si·βle) *adj.* permissible. —**permisión** (-'sjon) *n.f.* permission. —**permisivo** (-'si·βo) *adj.* permissive.
permiso (per'mi·so) *n.m.* 1, permission. 2, license; permit. —**¡con permiso!** excuse me! —**¿permiso?** may I come in?
permitir (per·mi'tir) *v.t.* to allow; permit.
permuta (per'mu·ta) *n.f.* barter; exchange.
permutación (per·mu·ta'θjon; -'sjon) *n.f.* 1, barter; exchange. 2, permutation.
permutar (per·mu'tar) *v.t.* 1, to barter; exchange. 2, to permute. —**permutable,** *adj.* exchangeable.
pernada (per'na·ða) *n.f.* 1, kick; blow with the leg. 2, shake of the leg.
pernaza (per'na·θa; -sa) *n.f.* large or thick leg.
pernetas (per'ne·tas) *n.f.pl., in* **en pernetas,** barelegged.
pernicioso (per·ni'θjo·so; -'sjo·so) *adj.* pernicious. —**perniciosidad,** *n.f.* perniciousness.
pernil (per'nil) *n.m.* 1, hock; ham (*of animals*). 2, [*also,* **pernera** (-'ne·ra)] *n.f.* trouser leg.
perno ('per·no) *n.m.* 1, bolt. 2, pin; spike. 3, hook of a door hinge. 4, *mech.* joint pin; crank pin.
pernoctar (per·nok'tar) *v.i.* to spend the night.
pero ('pe·ro) *conj.* but; except that; yet. —*n.m., colloq.* fault; objection. —**poner peros,** *colloq.* to find fault; object.
perogrullada (pe·ro·ɣru'ʎa·ða; -'ja·ða) *n.f.* 1, truism; platitude. 2, nonsense; tomfoolery.
perol (pe'rol) *n.m.* kettle.
peroné (pe·ro'ne) *n.m., anat.* fibula.
perorar (pe·ro'rar) *v.i.* 1, to orate. 2, to discourse; hold forth. —**peroración,** *n.f.* peroration. —**perorata** (-'ra·ta) *n.f., colloq.* harangue; spiel.
peróxido (pe'rok·si·ðo) *n.m.* peroxide.
perpendicular (per·pen·di·ku'lar) *adj.* & *n.f.* perpendicular.
perpetrar (per·pe'trar) *v.t.* to perpetrate. —**perpetración,** *n.f.* perpetration.
perpetua (per'pe·twa) *n.f., bot.* immortelle; everlasting.
perpetuar (per·pe'twar) *v.t.* [*infl.:* **continuar**] to perpetuate. —**perpetuación,** *n.f.* perpetuation. —**perpetuidad,** *n.f.* perpetuity.
perpetuo (per'pe·two) *adj.* perpetual.
perplejo (per'ple·xo) *adj.* perplexed; puzzled. —**perplejidad,** *n.f.* perplexity; puzzlement.
perra ('pe·rra) *n.f.* 1, female dog; bitch. 2, *colloq.* tantrum. 3, *colloq.* drunken fit. —**perra chica,** Spanish coin of 5 céntimos. —**perra gorda,** *also,* **perro gordo,** Spanish coin of 10 céntimos.
perrada (pe'rra·ða) *n.f.* 1, pack of dogs. 2, *colloq.* dastardly deed.
perrera (pe'rre·ra) *n.f.* 1, kennel; doghouse. 2, dog catcher's wagon. 3, *colloq.* tantrum. 4, drudgery; thankless job.
perrero (pe'rre·ro) *n.m.* 1, kennel; doghouse. 2, dog catcher's wagon. 3, *colloq.* tantrum.
perrería (pe·rre'ri·a) *n.f.* 1, = **perrada.** 2, churlishness.
perrito (pe'rri·to) *also,* **perrillo,** *n.m.* 1, small dog. 2, puppy.
perro ('pe·rro) *n.m.* dog. —*adj., colloq.* dastardly. —**perro braco,** pointer. —**perro de aguas,** spaniel. —**perro de lanas,** poodle. —**perro de presa,** bulldog. —**perro de Terranova,** Newfoundland dog. —**perro dogo,** bulldog. —**perro faldero,** lap dog.
perruno (pe'rru·no) *adj.* 1, canine. 2, churlish.
persa ('per·sa) *adj.* & *n.m.* & *f.* Persian.
persecución (per·se·ku'θjon; -'sjon) *n.f.* 1, persecution. 2, pursuit. *Also,* **perseguimiento** (-ɣi·'mjen·to) *n.m.*
perseguidor (per·se·ɣi'ðor) *n.m.* 1, pursuer. 2, persecutor. —**perseguidora,** *n.f., Amer., colloq.* hangover.
perseguir (per·se'ɣir) *v.t.* [*infl.:* **seguir**] 1, to persecute. 2, to pursue.

perseverancia (per·se·βe'ran·θja; -sja) *n.f.* **1,** perseverance. **2,** persistence; continuance. —**perseverante,** *adj.* persevering.
perseverar (per·se·βe'rar) *v.i.* **1,** to persevere. **2,** to persist; continue.
persiana (per'sja·na) *n.f.* **1,** shutter. **2,** louver. **3,** Venetian blind.
pérsico ('per·si·ko) *adj.* Persian. —*n.m.* **1,** peach. **2,** peach tree.
persiga (per'si·ɣa) *v., pres.subjve. of* **perseguir.**
persignarse (per·siɣ'nar·se) *v.r.* to cross oneself.
persigo (per'si·ɣo) *v., pres.ind. of* **perseguir.**
persiguiendo (per·si'ɣjen·do) *v., ger. of* **perseguir.**
persiguió (per·si'ɣjo) *v., 3rd pers.sing. pret. of* **perseguir.**
persistir (per·sis'tir) *v.i.* to persist. —**persistencia,** *n.f.* persistence. —**persistente,** *adj.* persistent.
persona (per'so·na) *n.f.* person.
personaje (per·so'na·xe) *n.m.* **1,** personage. **2,** character (*in a story, play, etc.*).
personal (per·so'nal) *adj.* personal. —*n.m.* personnel; staff.
personalidad (per·so·na·li'ðað) *n.f.* **1,** personality. **2,** *law* person. **3,** legal capacity.
personalizar (per·so·na·li'θar; -'sar) *v.t.* & *i.*[*pres.subjve.* **personalice** (-'li·θe; -se); *pret.* **personalicé** (-'θe; -'se)] to personalize.
personería (per·so·ne'ri·a) *n.f.* **1,** solicitorship. **2,** legal capacity.
personero (per·so'ne·ro) *n.m.* solicitor; agent.
personificar (per·so·ni·fi'kar) *v.t.* [*pres.subjve.* **personifique** (-'fi·ke); *pret.* **personifiqué** (-'ke)] to personify. —**personificación,** *n.f.* personification.
personilla (per·so'ni·ʎa; -ja) *n.f.* person of no importance; nonentity.
perspectiva (pers·pek'ti·βa) *n.f.* perspective.
perspicaz (pers·pi'kaθ; -'kas) *adj.* perspicacious. —**perspicacia** (-'ka·θja; -sja) *n.f.* perspicacity.
perspicuo (pers'pi·kwo) *adj.* perspicuous. —**perspicuidad,** *n.f.* perspicuity.
persuadir (per·swa'ðir) *v.t.* to persuade. —**persuadidor,** *adj.* persuading. —*n.m.* persuader.
persuasible (per·swa'si·βle) *adj.* persuasible; persuadable.
persuasión (per·swa'sjon) *n.f.* persuasion.
persuasivo (per·swa'si·βo) *adj.* persuasive. —**persuasiva,** *n.f.* persuasiveness.
pertenecer (per·te·ne'θer; -'ser) *v.i.* [*pres.ind.* **pertenezco** (-'neθ·ko; -'nes·ko); *pres.subjve.* **pertenezca** (-ka)] **1,** to belong; appertain. **2,** to pertain.
pertenencia (per·te'nen·θja; -sja) *n.f.* **1,** ownership. **2,** tenure; holding. **3,** personal belonging; property. **4,** appurtenance; accessory. **5,** *fig.* province; domain.
pértica ('per·ti·ka) *n.f.* perch (*land measure*).
pértiga ('per·ti·ɣa) *n.f.* staff; pole; rod.
pertinaz (per·ti'naθ; -'nas) *adj.* pertinacious. —**pertinacia** (-'na·θja; -sja) *n.f.* pertinacity.
pertinente (per·ti'nen·te) *adj.* pertinent. —**pertinencia,** *n.f.* pertinence.
pertrechar (per·tre'tʃar) *v.t., mil.* to stock; equip; supply.
pertrechos (per'tre·tʃos) *n.m.pl., mil.* supplies; stores.
perturbar (per·tur'βar) *v.t.* to upset; perturb. —**perturbable,** *adj.* readily perturbed. —**perturbación,** *n.f.* upset; perturbation. —**perturbador,** *adj.* perturbing; disturbing.
peruano (pe'rwa·no) *adj.* & *n.m.* Peruvian. *Also,* **peruviano** (pe·ru·'βja·no).
perulero (pe·ru'le·ro) *adj.* & *n.m., hist.* **1,** Peruvian. **2,** one returning rich from Peru.
perversión (per·βer'sjon) *n.f.* perversion.
perverso (per'βer·so) *adj.* perverse. —**perversidad,** *n.f.* perversity.
pervertir (per·βer'tir) *v.t.* [*infl.:* **advertir**] to pervert. —**pervertirse,** *v.r.* to become depraved.
pervinca (per'βin·ka) *n.f.* periwinkle (*plant*).
pesa ('pe·sa) *n.f.* **1,** weight (*used on scales*). **2,** clock weight. **3,** counterweight. **4,** dumbbell.
pesada (pe'sa·ða) *n.f.* **1,** weighing. **2,** quantity weighed.
pesadez (pe·sa'ðeθ; -'ðes) *n.f.* **1,** heaviness; weight. **2,** impertinence; importunity. **3,** bother; unpleasantness.
pesadilla (pe·sa'ði·ʎa; -ja) *n.f.* nightmare.
pesado (pe'sa·ðo) *adj.* **1,** heavy.

2, tedious; tiresome. 3, annoying; importunate. —*n.m.* 1, bore. 2, tease.

pesadumbre (pe·sa'ðum·bre) *n.f.* sorrow; grief; affliction.

pésame ('pe·sa·me) *n.m.* condolence.

pesantez (pe·san'teθ; -'tes) *n.f.* heaviness; weight.

pesar (pe'sar) *v.t.* & *i.* to weigh. —*n.m.* sorrow; regret. —**a pesar de,** in spite of; notwithstanding. —**pese a quien pese,** no matter who gets hurt; whether anybody likes it or not.

pesaroso (pe·sa'ro·so) *adj.* sorrowful; regretful.

pesca ('pes·ka) *n.f.* 1, fishing. 2, catch (*of fish*).

pescada (pes'ka·ða) *n.f.* hake.

pescadería (pes·ka·ðe'ri·a) *n.f.* fish market. —**pescadero** (-'ðe·ro) *n.m.* fishmonger.

pescado (pes'ka·ðo) *n.m.* edible fish taken from the water.

pescador (pes·ka'ðor) *n.m.* 1, fisherman. 2, = **pejesapo.** —*adj.* fishing (*attrib.*).

pescante (pes'kan·te) *n.* 1, davit. 2, boom; jib; hoist. 3, driver's seat.

pescar (pes'kar) *v.t.* & *i.* [*pres. subjve.* **pesque**; *pret.* **pesqué**] to fish. —*v.t., colloq.* 1, to grab. 2, to catch in the act.

pescozón (pes·ko'θon; -'son) *n.m.* slap on the head or neck. *Also,* **pescozada,** *n.f.*

pescozudo (pes·ko'θu·ðo; -'su·ðo) *adj.* thick-necked; bullnecked.

pescuezo (pes'kwe·θo; -so) *n.m.* 1, neck. 2, *fig.* haughtiness.

pesebre (pe'se·βre) *n.m.* manger. —**pesebrera,** *n.f.* stable.

peseta (pe'se·ta) *n.f.* 1, peseta; monetary unit of Spain. 2, *Amer.* quarter; any coin of comparable size.

pesimismo (pe·si'mis·mo) *n.m.* pessimism. —**pesimista,** *n.m.* & *f.* pessimist. —*adj.* pessimistic.

pésimo ('pe·si·mo) *adj. superl.* extremely bad.

peso ('pe·so) *n.m.* 1, weight. 2, peso; monetary unit of several Spanish-American countries. 3, *Amer., colloq.* dollar. —**caerse de su propio peso,** to be self-evident; go without saying. —**de peso,** of due weight; of importance. —**en peso,** 1, bodily. 2, wholly; in toto. 3, in the balance. —**peso bruto,** gross weight. —**peso duro,** *also,* **peso fuerte,** a silver coin weighing one ounce.

pesque ('pes·ke) *v., pres.subjve. of* **pescar.**

pesqué (pes'ke) *v., 1st pers.sing. pret. of* **pescar.**

pesquera (pes'ke·ra) *n.f.* fishing grounds.

pesquería (pes·ke'ri·a) *n.f.* 1, fishing. 2, fishery. 3, = **pesquera.**

pesquero (pes'ke·ro) *adj.* fishing (*attrib.*).

pesquis ('pes·kis) *n.m.* acumen; cleverness.

pesquisa (pes'ki·sa) *n.f.* inquiry; investigation; search. —*n.m., Amer.* police investigator; plainclothesman.

pesquisar (pes·ki'sar) *v.t.* to investigate; inquire into. —**pesquisidor** (-si'ðor) *n.m.* inquirer; investigator. —*adj.* inquiring; investigating.

pestaña (pes'ta·ɲa) *n.f.* 1, eyelash. 2, *sewing* fag end; fringe; edging. 3, cilium. 4, flange.

pestañear (pes·ta·ɲe'ar) *v.i.* to blink. —**pestañeo** (-'ɲe·o) *n.m.* blinking.

peste ('pes·te) *n.f.* 1, pest. 2, plague. 3, stench; foul smell. 4, *colloq.* swarm; lot; lots (*pl.*). 5, *usu.pl.* profanities; swearwords.

pestífero (pes'ti·fe·ro) *adj.* 1, pestiferous. 2, malodorous; stinking.

pestilencia (pes·ti'len·θja; -sja) *n.f.* 1, pestilence. 2, stench; foulness. —**pestilencial,** *adj.* = **pestilente.**

pestilente (pes·ti'len·te) *adj.* 1, pestilent. 2, malodorous.

pestillo (pes'ti·ʎo; -jo) *n.m.* door bolt; latch; bolt of a lock.

pesuña (pe'su·ɲa) *n.f.* = **pezuña.**

pesuño (pe'su·ɲo) *n.m.* each half of a cloven hoof.

petaca (pe'ta·ka) *n.f.* 1, cigar *or* cigarette case. 2, tobacco pouch. 3, *Amer., colloq.* piece of luggage; bag.

pétalo ('pe·ta·lo) *n.m.* petal.

petardo (pe'tar·ðo) *n.m.* 1, petard. 2, large firecracker. 3, fraud; swindle.

petate (pe'ta·te) *n.m., Amer.* 1, sleeping mat. 2, *colloq.* luggage; baggage. 3, *colloq.* worthless fellow. —**liar el petate,** *colloq.* 1, to pack up and go. 2, to die.

petición (pe·ti'θjon; -'sjon) *n.f.* petition. —**peticionario,** *n.m.* petitioner.

petimetre (pe·ti'me·tre) *n.m.* fop; beau; dude. —**petimetra,** *n.f.* clotheshorse.

petirrojo (pe·ti'rro·xo) *n.m.* redbreast.

petitorio (pe·ti'to·rjo) *adj.* petitionary. —*n.m., colloq.* impertinent petitioning. —**petitoria,** *n.f., colloq.* petition; petitioning.

peto ('pe·to) *n.m.* **1,** breastplate. **2,** dickey.

petrel (pe'trel) *n.m.* petrel.

pétreo ('pe·tre·o) *adj.* petrous.

petrificar (pe·tri·fi'kar) *v.t.* [*pres. subjve.* **petrifique** (-'fi·ke); *pret.* **petrifiqué** (-'ke)] to petrify. —**petrificación,** *n.f.* petrification.

petro- (pe·tro) *also,* **petri-** (pe·tri) *prefix* petro-; petri-; stone; rock: *petrografía,* petrography; *petrificar,* petrify.

petrografía (pe·tro·ɣra'fi·a) *n.f.* petrography. —**petrográfico** (-'ɣra·fi·ko) *adj.* petrographic.

petróleo (pe'tro·le·o) *n.m.* petroleum; oil.

petrolero (pe·tro'le·ro) *adj.* of or pertaining to petroleum; oil (*attrib.*). —*n.m.* **1,** tanker. **2,** *Amer.* oil man. **3,** incendiary; saboteur (esp. one using kerosene, gasoline, etc.).

petrolífero (pe·tro'li·fe·ro) *adj.* oil-bearing; oil (*attrib.*).

petroso (pe'tro·so) *adj.* **1,** rocky; stony. **2,** *anat.* petrous.

petulante (pe·tu'lan·te) *adj.* petulant. —**petulancia,** *n.f.* petulance.

petunia (pe'tu·nja) *n.f.* petunia.

peyorativo (pe·jo·ra'ti·βo) *adj.* pejorative.

pez (peθ; pes) *n.m.* **1,** fish. **2,** pitch; tar. —**pez blanca; pez griega,** rosin.

pezón (pe'θon; -'son) *n.m.* **1,** stem (*of fruits*). **2,** stalk (*of a leaf or flower*). **3,** nipple; teat.

pezuña (pe'θu·ɲa; pe'su-) *n.f.* **1,** hoof; toe of animals. **2,** *Amer., colloq.* foot odor.

pi (pi) *n.f.* pi (*Greek letter; math.*).

piache ('pja·tʃe) *in* **tarde piache,** *colloq.* too late.

piada (pi'a·ða) *n.f.* chirp; chirping. —**piador,** *adj.* chirping.

piadoso (pja'ðo·so) *adj.* **1,** pious. **2,** compassionate.

piafar (pja'far) *v.i.* to stamp (*of horses*).

pial (pjal) *n.m., So.Amer.* lasso. —**pialar,** *v.t., So.Amer.* to lasso.

piamente (pi·a'men·te) *adv.* piously.

pianísimo (pja'ni·si·mo) *adj.* & *adv.* pianissimo.

pianista (pi·a'nis·ta) *n.m.* & *f.* pianist.

piano ('pja·no) *n.m.* piano. —*adv.* slowly; step by step. —*adj.* & *adv., music* piano. —**piano de cola,** grand piano. —**piano de media cola,** baby grand. —**piano vertical** *or* **recto,** upright piano.

pianoforte (pja·no'for·te) *n.m.* pianoforte.

pianola (pja'no·la) *n.f.* pianola.

piar (pi'ar) *v.i.* [*pres.ind.* **pío** ('pi·o); *pres.subjve.* **píe** ('pi·e)] **1,** to chirp; peep. **2,** *colloq.* to plead; whine.

piara ('pja·ra) *n.f.* herd, esp. of swine.

piastra ('pjas·tra) *n.f.* piaster.

pibe ('pi·βe) *n.m., Arg.* kid; child.

pica ('pi·ka) *n.f.* **1,** pike; lance. **2,** bullfighter's goad. **3,** stonecutter's hammer. **4,** *colloq.* pique. —**poner una pica en Flandes,** to put a feather in one's cap.

picacho (pi'ka·tʃo) *n.m.* peak; mountaintop.

picada (pi'ka·ða) *n.f.* **1,** sting; stinging; bite. **2,** = **picotazo. 3,** *Amer.* trail; narrow pass. **4,** dive; swoop. **5,** *Amer.* jackrabbit start.

picadero (pi·ka'ðe·ro) *n.m.* **1,** riding school. **2,** boat skid; boat block.

picadillo (pi·ka'ði·ʎo; -jo) *n.m.* **1,** minced meat. **2,** hash.

picado (pi'ka·ðo) *adj.* **1,** perforated; stippled. **2,** minced; ground. **3,** *colloq.* piqued; irritated. **4,** *colloq.* tipsy. —*n.m.* **1,** minced meat; hash. **2,** *aero.* dive; diving.

picador (pi·ka'ðor) *n.m.* **1,** horsebreaker. **2,** bullfighter armed with a goad; picador. **3,** chopping block.

picadura (pi·ka'ðu·ra) *n.f.* **1,** prick; pricking. **2,** sting; bite. **3,** cut tobacco. **4,** cavity; decay in a tooth. **5,** pinking.

picaflor (pi·ka'flor) *n.m.* **1,** hummingbird. **2,** *Amer., colloq.* fickle person; butterfly.

picamaderos (pi·ka·ma'ðe·ros) *n.m.sing.* & *pl.* woodpecker.

picana (pi'ka·na) *n.f., Amer.* goad. —**picanear,** *v.t., Amer.* to goad.

picante (pi'kan·te) *adj.* **1,** hot; piquant; highly seasoned. **2,** risqué.

—*n.m.* 1, piquancy. 2, hot, spicy seasoning.

picapedrero (pi·ka·pe'ðre·ro) *n.m.* stonemason.

picapica (pi·ka'pi·ka) *n.f.* 1, itching powder. 2, *Amer.* any plant that causes itching.

picapleitos (pi·ka'plei·tos) *n.m. sing.* & *pl., colloq.* 1, = pleitista. 2, *Amer.* shyster; pettifogger. 3, ambulance chaser.

picaporte (pi·ka'por·te) *n.m.* 1, latch; spring lock. 2, *Amer.* slide bolt; door bolt.

picaposte (pi·ka'pos·te) *n.m.* woodpecker.

picar (pi'kar) *v.t.* [*pres.subjve.* **pique**; *pret.* **piqué**] 1, to prick; puncture. 2, to sting. 3, to bite (*said only of serpents, birds or insects*). 4, to bite (the bait). 5, to stipple. 6, to mince; chop. 7, to spur; goad. 8, to peck. 9, to strike, as with a pick. 10, *colloq.* to pique; vex. 11, to ring clearly. 12, *billiards* to strike (the ball) with english. —*v.i.* 1, to smart. 2, to itch. 3, to be hot or sharp to the taste; burn. 4, to strike; take the bait. 5, to dive; swoop. 6, *fig., fol. by* **en**, to border on; verge on. —**picarse**, *v.r.* 1, to become choppy (*as the sea*). 2, to become vexed; become annoyed. 3, to be motheaten. 4, to sour; spoil. 5, to boast. 6, *Amer.* to make a jackrabbit start. 7, *Amer.* to get tipsy. —**picar (muy) alto**, to aim (too) high.

picardía (pi·kar'ði·a) *n.f.* 1, mischievousness; impishness. 2, roguery.

picaresco (pi·ka'res·ko) *adj.* 1, picaresque. 2, mischievous; roguish.

pícaro ('pi·ka·ro) *adj.* 1, knavish; roguish. 2, mischievous. —*n.m.* rascal; knave; rogue.

picarón (pi·ka'ron) *n.m.* 1, rascal. 2, *Amer.* doughnut-shaped fritter; cruller.

picazo (pi'ka·θo; -so) *n.m.* 1, blow with a pickax or mattock. 2, insect bite.

picazón (pi·ka'θon; -'son) *n.f.* itch; itching.

picea (pi'θe·a; -'se·a) *also,* **pícea** ('pi-) *n.f.* spruce.

pico ('pi·ko) *n.m.* 1, beak. 2, pick; pickax; mattock. 3, pouring spout. 4, peak (*of a cap, mountain, etc.*). 5, *colloq.* mouth. 6, = picamaderos. —**andar de picos pardos**, *colloq.* to loaf; goof off. —**pico de oro**, *colloq.* 1, gift of gab. 2, great talker. —**sobras y picos**, odds and ends. —**y pico**, and some; and some odd; and change; a little after (*in expressions of time*).

picofeo (pi·ko'fe·o) *n.m., Amer.* toucan.

picota (pi'ko·ta) *n.f.* 1, gallows. 2, pillory.

picotazo (pi·ko'ta·θo; -so) *n.m.* peck; blow with the beak. *Also,* **picotada**, *n.f.*

picotear (pi·ko·te'ar) *v.t.* to peck; nibble. —*v.i.* 1, to bob the head up and down (*as a horse*). 2, to chatter; prattle. —**picotearse**, *v.r.* to squabble (*said of women*).

pícrico ('pi·kri·ko) *adj.* picric.

pictórico (pik'to·ri·ko) *adj.* of or pert. to painting; pictorial.

picudo (pi'ku·ðo) *adj.* 1, beaked; having a long beak. 2, pointed. 3, *colloq.* garrulous. —*n.m.* spit; skewer.

pichel (pi'tʃel) *n.m.* tankard.

pichincha (pi'tʃin·tʃa) *n.f., Amer., colloq.* very good buy; bargain.

pichón (pi'tʃon) *n.m.* 1, squab; young pigeon. 2, *colloq.* darling; dove. 3, *colloq.* babe in the woods; novice. 4, *Amer.* nestling.

pida ('pi·ða) *v., pres.subjve. of* **pedir**.

pidiendo (pi'ðjen·do) *v., ger. of* **pedir**.

pidió (pi'ðjo) *v., 3rd pers.sing. pret. of* **pedir**.

pido ('pi·ðo) *v., pres.ind. of* **pedir**.

pidón (pi'ðon) *adj., colloq.* = **pedigüeño**.

pie (pje) *n.m.* 1, foot. 2, footing; basis. 3, leg (*of a piece of furniture*). 4, stem (*of a glass*). —**al pie de la letra**, to the letter; literally. —**a pie**, on foot. —**a pie juntillas**, closely; rigidly. —**buscar tres pies al gato**, *colloq.* to go poking for trouble. —**de pie, de pies**, 1, up; out of bed. 2, standing. —**echar pie a tierra**, to dismount; alight. —**en pie = de pie**. —**no dar pie con bola**, *colloq.* to have everything go wrong with one. —**pie de grabado**, caption. —**poner pies en polvorosa**, *colloq.* to light out; take to one's heels.

piedad (pje'ðað) *n.f.* 1, piety. 2, mercy; pity.

piedra ('pje·ðra) *n.f.* stone. —**a piedra y lodo**, sealed; sealed up.

—**piedra angular,** cornerstone. —**piedra de amolar,** whetstone. —**piedra de toque,** touchstone. —**piedra imán,** lodestone. —**piedra pómez,** pumice.

piel (pjel) *n.f.* **1,** skin. **2,** hide; pelt. **3,** fur.

piélago ('pje·la·ɣo) *n.m., poet.* sea.

piense ('pjen·se) *v., pres.subjve. of* **pensar.**

pienso ('pjen·so) *v., pres.ind. of* **pensar.** —*n.m.* feed; fodder. —**ni por pienso,** *colloq.* **1,** not even in dreams. **2,** not for anything.

pierda ('pjer·ða) *v., pres.subjve. of* **perder.**

pierdo ('pjer·ðo) *v., pres.ind. of* **perder.**

pierna ('pjer·na) *n.f.* **1,** *anat.* leg. **2,** leg (*of a compass*). —**a pierna suelta,** in a carefree manner. —**dormir a pierna suelta,** to sleep soundly.

pieza ('pje·θa; -sa) *n.f.* **1,** piece; part. **2,** room (*of a house*). **3,** bag; catch (*in hunting or fishing*). **4,** bolt (*of cloth*). —**quedarse de una pieza,** to be stunned; be astonished.

pífano ('pi·fa·no) *n.m.* fife.

pifia ('pi·fja) *n.f.* **1,** *billiards* miscue. **2,** *Amer.* jeer; hiss; hoot.

pifiar (pi'fjar) *v.i.* **1,** *billiards* to miscue. **2,** *Amer.* to jeer; hiss; hoot.

pigmento (piɣ'men·to) *n.m.* pigment. —**pigmentación,** *n.f.* pigmentation.

pigmeo (piɣ'me·o) *adj.* & *n.m.* pygmy.

pijama (pi'xa·ma) *n.m., also, Amer., n.f.* pajama.

pila ('pi·la) *n.f.* **1,** basin; trough. **2,** font, esp. baptismal font. **3,** pile; heap. **4,** pilaster; pile; pier. **5,** dry cell battery.

pilar (pi'lar) *n.m.* **1,** pillar. **2,** pallbearer.

pilastra (pi'las·tra) *n.f.* pilaster.

pilcha ('pil·tʃa) *n.f., Amer., usu. pl.* **1,** various typical country garments. **2,** *colloq., derog.* clothes; clothing.

píldora ('pil·do·ra) *n.f.* pill.

pileta (pi'le·ta) *n.f.* **1,** small font; bowl. **2,** *So. Amer.* swimming pool. *Amer., n.f.,* pajama.

pilón (pi'lon) *n.m.* **1,** basin (*of a fountain*). **2,** trough; water trough. **3,** mortar (*bowl*). **4,** pylon. **5,** drop hammer. **6,** counterweight. **7,** sugar loaf.

píloro ('pi·lo·ro) *n.m.* pylorus. —**pilórico** (-'lo·ri·ko) *adj.* pyloric.

piloso (pi'lo·so) *adj.* pilose; downy; hairy.

pilotaje (pi·lo'ta·xe) *n.m.* **1,** pilotage. **2,** piles; piling.

pilotar (pi·lo'tar) *also,* **pilotear,** *v.t.* **1,** to pilot. **2,** *Amer.* to drive, esp. in racing.

pilote (pi'lo·te) *n.m.* pile (*support*).

piloto (pi'lo·to) *n.m.* **1,** pilot. **2,** *naut.* mate. **3,** *Amer.* driver, esp. racing driver.

piltrafa (pil'tra·fa) *n.f.* **1,** scum; riffraff. **2,** *Amer.* rag; tatter. **3,** *pl.* scraps; castoffs.

pillada (pi'ʎa·ða; -'ja·ða) *n.f.* **1,** rascality. **2,** *Amer., colloq.* a catching by surprise.

pillaje (pi'ʎa·xe; pi'ja-) *n.m.* pillage; plunder.

pillar (pi'ʎar; -'jar) *v.t.* **1,** to pillage; plunder. **2,** to catch; get. **3,** to grab. **4,** *colloq.* to surprise; catch by surprise.

pillastre (pi'ʎas·tre; -'jas·tre) *n.m.* = **pillo.**

pillería (pi·ʎe'ri·a; pi·je-) *n.f.* **1,** rascality. **2,** shrewdness. **3,** band of rogues.

pillo ('pi·ʎo; -jo) *adj.* **1,** roguish; rascally. **2,** shrewd. —*n.m.* rogue; rascal.

pilluelo (pi'ʎwe·lo; -'jwe·lo) *n.m.* gamin; street Arab.

pimentero (pi·men'te·ro) *n.m.* **1,** pepper bush. **2,** pepper shaker.

pimentón (pi·men'ton) *n.m.* **1,** pimento. **2,** ground red pepper.

pimienta (pi'mjen·ta) *n.f.* pepper. —**tener pimienta,** to be racy or risqué.

pimiento (pi'mjen·to) *n.m.* **1,** pimiento. **2,** red pepper.

pimpollo (pim'po·ʎo; -jo) *n.m.* **1,** sapling. **2,** shoot; sprout; bud. **3,** rosebud. **4,** *fig.* pretty girl.

pinacoteca (pi·na·ko'te·ka) *n.f.* museum of paintings.

pináculo (pi'na·ku·lo) *n.m.* pinnacle.

pinado (pi'na·ðo) *adj.* = **pinnado.**

pinar (pi'nar) *n.m.* pine grove.

pincel (pin'θel; -'sel) *n.m.* **1,** brush; paintbrush. **2,** brushwork. —**pincelada,** *n.f.* brush stroke.

pincelar (pin·θe'lar; -se'lar) *v.t.* **1,** to paint. **2,** to portray.

pincha ('pin·tʃa) *n.f.* **1,** kitchen maid. **2,** = **pincho.**

pinchadura (pin·tʃa'ðu·ra) *n.f.* 1, prick; pricking. 2, puncture.
pinchar (pin'tʃar) *v.t.* 1, to prick. 2, to puncture. —**ni pinchar ni cortar,** *colloq.* to have nothing to do (with a matter).
pinchazo (pin'tʃa·θo; -so) *n.m.* 1, prick; puncture. 2, *fig.* goading; prodding.
pinche ('pin·tʃe) *n.m.* & *f.* kitchen helper; scullion.
pincho ('pin·tʃo) *n.m.* 1, prickle; thorn. 2, skewer.
pindonguear (pin·don·ge'ar) *v.i., colloq.* = **callejear.**
pineal (pi·ne'al) *adj.* pineal.
pingajo (pin'ga·xo) *n.m., colloq.* rag; tatter.
pingar (pin'gar) *v.i.* 1, to drip. 2, to jump; skip. —*v.t., colloq.* to incline.
pingo ('pin·go) *n.m., colloq.* = **pingajo.**
pingorotudo (pin·go·ro'tu·ðo) *adj., colloq.* highfalutin.
ping-pong *also,* **pinpón** (pin'pon) *n.m.* ping-pong.
pingüe ('pin·gwe) *adj.* substantial; fat; juicy.
pingüino (pin'gwi·no) *n.m.* penguin.
pinitos (pi'ni·tos) *n.m.pl.* child's first steps.
pinnado (pin'na·ðo; pi'na·ðo) *adj., bot.* pinnate.
pino ('pi·no) *n.m.* pine. —*adj.* steep.
pinocle (pi'no·kle) *n.m.* pinochle.
pinocha (pi'no·tʃa) *n.f.* pine needle.
pinoso (pi'no·so) *adj.* piny; abounding in pines.
pinta ('pin·ta) *n.f.* 1, spot; mark. 2, distinctive mark. 3, *colloq.* appearance; looks. 4, pint.
pintado (pin'ta·ðo) *adj.* 1, colored; colorful. 2, *Amer.* like; alike. —*adv.* fitly; just right. —**el más pintado,** *colloq.* the best; the bravest.
pintar (pin'tar) *v.t.* 1, to paint. 2, to portray; depict. —*v.i.* to color with ripening (*said of fruit*). —**pintarse** *v.r.* to put on make-up. —**pintarla,** to play a part; cut a figure. —**pintarse para,** to be skilled in. —**¿Qué pintas tú aquí?,** *colloq.* What are you doing here?
pintarrajear (pin·ta·rra·xe'ar) *also,* **pintarrajar** (-'xar) *v.t., colloq.* = **pintorrear.**
pintear (pin·te'ar) *v.i.* = **lloviznar.**
pintiparado (pin·ti·pa'ra·ðo) *adj.* 1, just right; most suitable. 2, exactly like; closely resembling.
pinto ('pin·to) *adj.* & *n.m.* pinto; piebald.
pintonear (pin·to·ne'ar) *v.i., Amer.* to begin to ripen; color with ripening.
pintor (pin'tor) *n.m.* painter (*artist and tradesman*). —**pintor de brocha gorda,** 1, painter (*tradesman*). 2, dauber.
pintoresco (pin·to'res·ko) *adj.* picturesque; colorful.
pintorrear (pin·to·rre'ar) *v.t.* to daub; daub paint on. —**pintorrearse,** *v.r.* to daub make-up on.
pintura (pin'tu·ra) *n.f.* 1, paint. 2, painting. 3, portrayal.
pinza ('pin·θa; -sa) *n.f.* 1, clothespin. 2, *sewing* dart. 3, *pl.* pincers. 4, *pl.* tweezers.
pinzón (pin'θon; -'son) *n.m.* finch.
piña ('pi·ɲa) *n.f.* 1, pine cone. 2, pineapple. 3, *colloq.* crowd. 4, *Amer., colloq.* = **puñetazo.**
piñata (pi'ɲa·ta) *n.f.* 1, pot. 2, pot filled with party goodies; piñata.
piñón (pi'ɲon) *n.m.* 1, pine seed. 2, pinion.
pío ('pi·o) *adj.* pious. —*n.m.* 1, peep; chirp. 2, *colloq.* yen; craving.
piojo ('pjo·xo) *n.m.* louse. —**piojento,** *adj.* lousy. —**piojería,** *n.f.* lousiness.
piojoso (pjo'xo·so) *adj.* 1, lousy. 2, *colloq.* mean; stingy.
pión (pi'on) *adj.* 1, chirping; tweeting. 2, *colloq.* demanding; exigent.
pionero (pi·o'ne·ro) *n.m.* pioneer.
piorrea (pjo'rre·a) *n.f.* pyorrhea.
pipa ('pi·pa) *n.f.* 1, cask; butt. 2, smoking pipe. 3, reed pipe. 4, *Amer., colloq.* belly; paunch.
pipeta (pi'pe·ta) *n.f.* pipette.
pipiar (pi'pjar) *v.i.* to chirp; peep.
pipiolo (pi'pjo·lo) *n.m., colloq.* 1, beginner; greenhorn. 2, pipsqueak.
pique ('pi·ke) *n.m.* 1, pique. 2, chigger. 3, *Amer., colloq.* pickup; acceleration. —**a pique de,** close to; on the verge of. —**echar a pique,** to sink; send to the bottom. —**irse a pique,** to sink; go to the bottom.
pique ('pi·ke) *v., pres.subjve. of* **picar.**
piqué (pi'ke) *v., 1st pers.sing. pret. of* **picar.** —*n.m.* piqué.

piqueta (pi'ke·ta) *n.f.* pickax; mattock.

piquete (pi'ke·te) *n.m.* **1,** jab; prick. **2,** picket.

pira ('pi·ra) *n.f.* pyre.

piramidal (pi·ra·mi'ðal) *adj.* **1,** pyramidal. **2,** colossal.

pirámide (pi'ra·mi·ðe) *n.f.* pyramid.

pirata (pi'ra·ta) *adj.* **1,** pirate (*attrib.*). **2,** pirated. —*n.m.* & *f.* pirate. —**piratear** (-te'ar) *v.i.* to practice piracy. —**piratería** (-te'ri·a) *n.f.* piracy. —**pirático** (-'ra·ti·ko) *adj.* piratical.

pirita (pi'ri·ta) *n.f.* **1,** pyrite. **2,** pyrites.

piro- (pi·ro) *prefix* pyro-; fire: *pirómetro,* pyrometer.

piromania (pi·ro·ma'ni·a) *n.f.* pyromania. —**pirómano** (-'ro·ma·no) *also,* **piromaníaco** (-ma'ni·a·ko) *n.m.* pyromaniac.

piropo (pi'ro·po) *n.m., colloq.* compliment; gallantry. —**piropear,** *v.t.* to flatter; compliment.

pirotecnia (pi·ro'tek·nja) *n.f.* pyrotechnics. —**pirotécnico** (-'tek·ni·ko) *adj.* pyrotechnic. —*n.m.* maker *or* seller of fireworks.

piroxilina (pi·rok·si'li·na) *n.f.* pyroxylin.

pirrarse (pi'rrar·se) *v.r., colloq., fol. by* **por,** to die for; pine for.

pírrico ('pi·rri·ko) *adj.* pyrrhic.

pirueta (pi'rwe·ta) *n.f.* **1,** pirouette. **2,** prank; caper. —**piruetear** (-te'ar) *v.i.* to pirouette.

pirulí (pi·ru'li) *n.m.* sucker; lollipop.

pisa ('pi·sa) *n.f.* **1,** pressing (*of grapes, olives, etc.*). **2,** *colloq.* beating; kicking.

pisada (pi'sa·ða) *n.f.* **1,** step; footstep. **2,** footprint. **3,** stepping on the foot.

pisadura (pi·sa'ðu·ra) *n.f.* = **pisada.**

pisapapeles (pi·sa·pa'pe·les) *n.m. sing.* & *pl.* paperweight.

pisar (pi'sar) *v.t.* **1,** to step on; tread on. **2,** to crush; stamp. **3,** to overlap. **4,** to cover (*said of birds*). **5,** *colloq.* to steal (an idea, plan, etc.) —**pisarse,** *v.r., Amer., colloq.* to be fooled; be deceived.

pisaverde (pi·sa'βer·ðe) *n.m., colloq.* fop; beau. —*n.f., colloq.* clotheshorse.

piscatorio (pis·ka'to·rjo) *adj.* piscatorial.

pisci- (pis·θi; pi·si) *prefix* pisci-; fish: *piscicultura,* pisciculture.

piscina (pis'θi·na; pi'si-) *n.f.* pool; swimming pool.

Piscis ('pis·θis; 'pi·sis) *n.m.* Pisces.

piscolabis (pis·ko'la·βis) *n.m. sing.* & *pl., colloq.* light snack; tidbit.

piso ('pi·so) *n.m.* floor; story (*of a building*).

pisón (pi'son) *n.m.* tamper; rammer.

pisonear (pi·so·ne'ar) *v.t.* = **apisonar.**

pisotear (pi·so·te'ar) *v.t.* to step on; stamp on; trample. —**pisoteo,** *n.m.* trampling.

pisotón (pi·so'ton) *n.m.* stepping on the foot.

pista ('pis·ta) *n.f.* **1,** track; course. **2,** trace; trail. **3,** clue; hint.

pistacho (pis'ta·tʃo) *n.m.* pistachio.

pistilo (pis'ti·lo) *n.m.* pistil.

pisto ('pis·to) *n.m.* **1,** meat juice; broth. **2,** *Amer., colloq.* money; dough. **3,** a diced vegetable dish. —**darse pisto,** to put on airs.

pistola (pis'to·la) *n.f.* **1,** pistol. **2,** spray gun; sprayer.

pistolera (pis·to'le·ra) *n.f.* gun holster.

pistolero (pis·to'le·ro) *n.m.* gunman; armed bandit.

pistoletazo (pis·to·le'ta·θo; -so) *n.f.* gunshot; gun wound.

pistón (pis'ton) *n.m.* **1,** piston. **2,** primer (*of a shell*).

pita ('pi·ta) *n.f.* **1,** American agave; pita. **2,** *Amer.* string; cord. **3,** *colloq.* chicken. —**enredar la pita,** *Amer., colloq.* to foul up the works.

pitada (pi'ta·ða) *n.f.* whistle; whistling.

pitagórico (pi·ta'ɣo·ri·ko) *adj.* Pythagorean.

pitanza (pi'tan·θa; -sa) *n.f.* **1,** quota; ration; allowance. **2,** food allowance; ration. **3,** *colloq.* daily food consumption.

pitar (pi'tar) *v.i.* **1,** to whistle; blow a whistle. **2,** *Amer., colloq.* to smoke a cigarette. —*v.t., colloq.* to whistle *or* hoot (a performer) off the stage.

pitecántropo (pi·te'kan·tro·po) *n.m.* pithecanthropus.

pitido (pi'ti·ðo) *n.m.* whistle; hoot.

pitillo (pi'ti·ʎo; -jo) *n.m.* cigarette. —**pitillera,** *n.f.* cigarette case.

pito ('pi·to) *n.m.* **1,** whistle (*instrument*). **2,** *Amer., colloq.* fag; cigarette. —**no dársele** *or* **importársele a uno un pito,** *colloq.* not to give a hoot. —**no tocar pito,** *colloq.* to be out of place; not belong. —**pitos y flautas,** *colloq.* nonsense.

pitón (pi'ton) *n.m.* **1,** beginnings of a horn (*in an animal*). **2,** small hornlike protuberance. **3,** nozzle; spout. —*n.f.* python.

pituitario (pi·twi'ta·rjo) *adj.* pituitary.

pituso (pi'tu·so) *adj.* cute; darling (*usu. said of children*).

pivote (pi'βo·te) *n.m.* pivot.

piyama (pi'ja·ma) *n.f.* pajama.

pizarra (pi'θa·rra; pi'sa-) *n.f.* **1,** shale. **2,** slate. **3,** blackboard. —**pizarroso,** *adj.* slaty.

pizarrón (pi·θa'rron; pi·sa-) *n.m., Amer.* blackboard.

pizca ('piθ·ka; 'pis-) *n.f. colloq.* **1,** bit. **2,** dash; pinch (*of seasonings*). **3,** jot; iota.

pizpireta (piθ·pi're·ta; pis-) *adj. fem., colloq.* vivacious.

placa ('pla·ka) *n.f.* **1,** badge. **2,** plaque; plate. **3,** *photog.* plate. **4,** film; coating. **5,** shingle (*of a professional man*).

placaminero (pla·ka·mi'ne·ro) *n.m.* persimmon.

placativo (pla·ka'ti·βo) *adj.* placatory.

pláceme ('pla·θe·me; 'pla·se-) *n.m., usu.pl.* congratulation.

placenta (pla'θen·ta; pla'sen-) *n.f.* placenta. —**placentario,** *adj.* & *n.m.* placental.

placentero (pla·θen'te·ro; pla·sen-) *adj.* pleasant.

placer (pla'θer; -'ser) *v.t.* [*pres. ind.* **plazco;** *pres.subjve.* **plazca,** *also,* **plazga, plegue, plega;** *pret.* **plací, plació,** *also,* **plugo**] to please; gratify; content. —*n.m.* pleasure. —**a placer,** at one's convenience. —**que me place,** it gives me pleasure.

placero (pla'θe·ro; -'se·ro) *n.m.* **1,** dealer or seller in the marketplace. **2,** gadabout; idle fellow.

plácido ('pla·θi·ðo; 'pla·si-) *adj.* placid. —**placidez,** *n.f.* placidity.

plaga ('pla·ɣa) *n.f.* **1,** plague. **2,** *fig.* swarm; crowd.

plagar (pla'ɣar) *v.t.* [*pres.subjve.* **plague** ('pla·ɣe); *pret.* **plagué** (-'ɣe)] to plague; infest. —**plagarse,** *v.r., usu.fol. by* **de,** to be infested with; be full of; swarm with.

plagiar (pla'xjar) *v.t.* **1,** to plagiarize. **2,** *Amer.* to kidnap.

plagiario (pla'xja·rjo) *n.m.* **1,** plagiarist. **2,** *Amer.* kidnapper.

plagio ('pla·xjo) *n.m.* **1,** plagiarism. **2,** *Amer.* kidnapping.

plan (plan) *n.m.* plan. —**plan de estudios,** curriculum.

plana ('pla·na) *n.f.* **1,** page; side (*of a sheet*). **2,** flat; flatland. **3,** record; docket. —**enmendar la plana a uno,** *colloq.* **1,** to show someone up. **2,** to patch things up with someone. —**plana mayor,** *mil.* staff.

plancton *also,* **plankton** ('plank·ton) *n.m.* plankton.

plancha ('plan·tʃa) *n.f.* **1,** plate; metal plate. **2,** plank; gangplank. **3,** iron; flatiron. **4,** *print.* plate. **5,** *colloq.* ridiculous mistake; boner; howler.

planchada (plan'tʃa·ða) *n.f.* gangplank.

planchado (plan'tʃa·ðo) *n.m.* **1,** ironing; pressing. **2,** items ironed or ready for pressing. —*adj.* **1,** *Amer., colloq.* penniless; broke. **2,** *Mex.* courageous; forthright.

planchadora (plan·tʃa'ðo·ra) *n.f.* **1,** pressing machine; mangle. **2,** ironer; presser; ironing woman.

planchar (plan'tʃar) *v.t.* to iron; press. —**planchador,** *n.m.* presser.

planchear (plan·tʃe'ar) *v.t.* to plate; cover with metal sheets.

planeador (pla·ne·a'ðor) *n.m., aero.* glider.

planear (pla·ne'ar) *v.t.* & *i.* to plan. —*v.i.* to glide. —**planeo** (-'ne·o) *n.m.* gliding; glide.

planeta (pla'ne·ta) *n.m.* planet.

planetario (pla·ne'ta·rjo) *adj.* planetary. —*n.m.* planetarium.

planetoide (pla·ne'toi·ðe) *n.m.* planetoid.

plani- (pla·ni) *prefix* plani-; plane: *planimetría,* planimetry.

planicie (pla'ni·θje; -sje) *n.f.* plain; flat terrain.

planificar (pla·ni·fi'kar) *v.t.* [*pres.subjve.* **planifique** (-'fi·ke); *pret.* **planifiqué** (-'ke)] to plan. —**planificación,** *n.f.* planning.

planilla (pla'ni·ʎa; -ja) *n.f., Amer.* **1,** roll; list. **2,** blank form.

plano ('pla·no) *adj.* **1,** plane; flat. **2,** level; smooth; even. —*n.m.* **1,** plan; blueprint. **2,** map. **3,** *geom.* plane. **4,** flat; flat part. —**de plano,** flatly; plainly. —**primer plano, 1,**

foreground. 2, forefront. 3, *photog.* close-up.
plano- (pla·no) *prefix* plano-; plane: *planocóncavo,* plano-concave.
-plano ('pla·no) *suffix* -plane; aircraft; plane: *hidroplano,* hydroplane.
planta ('plan·ta) *n.f.* 1, plant. 2, sole (*of the foot*). 3, *engin.* plan; top view. 4, *archit.* floor plan. 5, position; stance; attitude. 6, disposition. —**buena planta,** good looks; handsome appearance. —**planta baja,** ground floor.
plantación (plan·ta'θjon; -'sjon) *n.f.* 1, plantation. 2, planting.
plantador (plan·ta'ðor) *n.m.* planter.
plantaina (plan'tai·na) *n.f.* plantain (*weed*).
plantar (plan'tar) *v.t.* 1, to plant. 2, to strike; land (a blow). 3, to leave in the lurch; stand up. —**plantarse,** *v.r.* 1, to stand pat. 2, to balk; refuse to move. 3, *colloq.* to dash; get to a place quickly. 4, *colloq.* to post oneself; set oneself. —**dejar plantado,** to leave in the lurch; stand up.
planteamiento (plan·te·a'mjen·to) *n.m.* 1, a stating; setting forth. 2, framing; outline. 3, setting up; establishment. 4, posing (*of a question or problem*). *Also,* **planteo** (-'te·o).
plantear (plan·te'ar) *v.t.* 1, to state; set forth. 2, to frame; outline. 3, to set up; establish. 4, to pose (a question or problem).
plantel (plan'tel) *n.m.* center (*of education or training*).
plantificar (plan·ti·fi'kar) *v.t.* [*pres.subjve.* **plantifique** (-'fi·ke); *pret.* **plantifiqué** (-'ke)] 1, to set up; establish. 2, *colloq.* to strike; land (a blow). 3, *colloq.* to put; place; plant. —**plantificarse,** *v.r.* 1, *colloq.* to dash; get to a place quickly. 2, *W.I., colloq.* to spruce up.
plantígrado (plan'ti·ɣra·ðo) *adj.* plantigrade.
plantilla (plan'ti·ʎa; -ja) *n.f.* 1, insole. 2, templet. 3, table of organization.
plantillar (plan·ti'ʎar; -'jar) *v.t.* to sole (shoes).
plantío (plan'ti·o) *n.m.* 1, plantation. 2, vegetable field. 3, planting.
plantón (plan'ton) *n.m.* 1, seedling; slip. 2, *colloq.* long wait.
planudo (pla'nu·ðo) *adj.* flat-bottomed.
plañir (pla'ɲir) *v.i.* [*pret.* **plañí, plañó** (-'ɲo); *ger.* **plañendo** (-'ɲen·do)] to make a plaintive sound; wail; moan. —**plañido,** *n.m.* plaint; wail; moan. —**plañidero,** *adj.* plaintive.
plaqué (pla'ke) *n.m.* 1, plate; plating. 2, plated ware.
plaqueta (pla'ke·ta) *n.f.* 1, small plaque; brooch. 2, platelet.
-plasia ('pla·sja) *suffix* -plasia; formation; development: *hipoplasia,* hypoplasia.
-plasis ('pla·sis) *suffix* -plasis; formation; development: *metaplasis,* metaplasis.
plasma ('plas·ma) *n.m.* plasma.
-plasma ('plas·ma) *suffix* -plasm; formation; molding; a thing molded or formed: *protoplasma,* protoplasm.
plasmar (plas'mar) *v.t.* to mold; shape; give shape to.
plasmo- (plas·mo) *prefix* plasmo-; plasma; form; mold: *plasmólisis,* plasmolysis.
plasta ('plas·ta) *n.f.* 1, mush; soft mass. 2, something flat, as a pancake. 3, *colloq.* mess; poor job.
-plastia ('plas·tja) *suffix* -plasty; *forming nouns denoting* 1, a manner of growth or development: *dermatoplastia,* dermatoplasty. 2, an operation in plastic surgery: *rinoplastia,* rhinoplasty.
plástica ('plas·ti·ka) *n.f.* plastic arts.
plástico ('plas·ti·ko) *adj.* & *n.m.* plastic. —**plasticidad** (-θi'ðað; -si·'ðað) *n.f.* plasticity.
-plasto ('plas·to) *suffix* -plast; *forming nouns denoting* a structure of protoplasm: *cromoplasto,* chromoplast.
plata ('pla·ta) *n.f.* 1, silver. 2, money. 3, silver coin. —**en plata,** briefly; in substance.
plataforma (pla·ta'for·ma) *n.f.* platform.
platal (pla'tal) *n.m.* great wealth; great quantity of money.
platanal (pla·ta'nal) *n.m.* banana plantation. *Also,* **platanar** (-'nar).
platanero (pla·ta'ne·ro) *n.m.* banana tree. —*adj., W.I.* of hurricane strength.
plátano ('pla·ta·no) *n.m.* 1, ba-

nana; plantain. **2,** banana tree; plantain tree. **3,** plane tree.

platazo (pla'ta·θo; -so) *n.m.* **1,** large dish. **2,** dishful; plateful. **3,** blow with a dish or plate.

platea (pla'te·a) *n.f., theat.* orchestra circle; parterre.

platear (pla·te'ar) *v.t.* to silver. —**plateado,** *adj.* silver (*attrib.*); silvered; silverplated. —**plateadura,** *n.f.* silvering; silver plating.

platero (pla'te·ro) *n.m.* silversmith. —**platería,** *n.f.* silversmith's shop *or* trade.

plati- (pla·ti) *prefix* platy-; broad: *platirrino,* platyrrhine.

plática ('pla·ti·ka) *n.f.* **1,** talk; chat; conversation. **2,** brief or informal lecture or sermon.

platicar (pla·ti'kar) *v.i.* [*pres. subjve.* **platique;** *pret.* **platiqué**] to chat; converse; talk informally.

platija (pla'ti·xa) *n.f.* plaice.

platillo (pla'ti·ʎo; -jo) *n.m.* **1,** small dish; saucer. **2,** pan (*of a balance*). **3,** cymbal.

platina (pla'ti·na) *n.f.* **1,** table of a microscope. **2,** = **platino.**

platinado (pla·ti'na·ðo) *adj.* **1,** platinum plated. **2,** platinum (*attrib.*). —*n.m.* platinum plating.

platinar (pla·ti'nar) *v.t.* **1,** to plate with platinum. **2,** to give a platinum sheen to.

platino (pla'ti·no) *n.m.* platinum.

platique (pla'ti·ke) *v., pres.subjve. of* **platicar.**

platiqué (-'ke) *v., 1st pers.sing. pret. of* **platicar.**

plato ('pla·to) *n.m.* **1,** dish; plate. **2,** plateful. **3,** pan (*of a balance*). **4,** turntable (*of a phonograph*). —**plato volador,** flying saucer. —**ser un plato,** *Amer., colloq.* to be a riot; be funny; be a card.

platónico (pla'to·ni·ko) *adj.* platonic.

platudo (pla'tu·ðo) *adj., Amer., colloq.* rich; loaded with money.

plausible (plau'si·βle) *adj.* plausible. —**plausibilidad,** *n.f.* plausibility.

playa ('pla·ja) *n.f.* beach; shore.

plaza ('pla·θa; -sa) *n.f.* **1,** plaza; square. **2,** local market; marketplace. **3,** position; opening; place. **4,** *mil.* fortified place. —**plaza de toros,** bull ring. —**plaza fuerte,** stronghold; fortress. **¡plaza, plaza!** clear the way! make room! —**sacar a plaza,** to publish; make public. —**sentar plaza,** *mil.* to enlist.

plazca ('plaθ·ka; 'plas-) *v., pres. subjve. of* **placer.**

plazco ('plaθ·ko; 'plas-) *v., 1st pers.sing.pres.ind. of* **placer.**

plazga ('plaθ·ɣa; 'plas-) *v., pres. subjve. of* **placer.**

plazo ('pla·θo; -so) *n.m.* **1,** term; period of time. **2,** installment. —**a corto plazo, 1,** soon. **2,** short-term. —**a largo plazo,** long-term; long-range.

plazoleta (pla·θo'le·ta; pla·so-) *n.f.* small plaza or square. *Also,* **plazuela** (-'θwe·la; -'swe·la).

pleamar (ple·a'mar) *n.f.* high water; high tide.

plebe ('ple·βe) *n.f.* common people; populace. —**plebeyo** (-'βe·jo) *adj.* & *n.m.* plebeian.

plebiscito (ple·βis'θi·to; -βi'si·to) *n.m.* plebiscite.

plectro ('plek·tro) *n.m.* **1,** plectrum. **2,** *fig.* poetic inspiration; muse.

plega ('ple·ɣa) *v., 3rd pers.sing. pres.subjve. of* **placer.**

plegable (ple'ɣa·βle) *also,* **plegadizo** (-'ði·θo; -'ði·so) *adj.* folding; that can fold or be folded.

plegado (ple'ɣa·ðo) *n.m.* **1,** plait; plaiting. **2,** fold; folding.

plegadura (ple·ɣa'ðu·ra) *n.f.* **1,** plait; pleat. **2,** fold; crease.

plegar (ple'ɣar) *v.t.* [*pres.ind.* **pliego;** *pres.subjve.* **pliegue;** *pret.* **plegué**] **1,** to fold. **2,** to pleat; plait. —**plegarse,** *v.r.* **1,** to fold up; give in; submit. **2,** to adhere; give one's support.

plegaria (ple'ɣa·rja) *n.f.* prayer; supplication.

plegue ('ple·ɣe) *v., 3rd pers.sing. pres.subjve. of* **placer.**

plegué (ple'ɣe) *v., 1st pers.sing. pret. of* **plegar.**

pleistoceno (pleis·to'θe·no; -'se·no) *n.m. & adj.* Pleistocene.

pleiteador (plei·te·a'ðor) *n.m.* **1,** [*also,* **pleiteante**] litigant; pleader. **2,** squabbler.

pleitear (plei·te'ar) *v.t.* to take to court; fight in court.

pleitesía (plei·te'si·a) *n.f.* homage; tribute.

pleitista (plei'tis·ta) *adj.* squabbling; quarrelsome. —*n.m.* & *f.* wrangler; squabbler.

pleito ('plei·to) *n.m.* **1,** lawsuit; litigation. **2,** dispute; wrangle; quarrel. —**conocer de un pleito,** to pass judgment on a lawsuit. —**contestar**

el pleito, to fight the case. —salir con el pleito, to win the case. —pleito homenaje, due homage.
-plejía (ple'xi·a) *suffix* -plegia; -plegy; stroke; paralysis: *hemiplejía*, hemiplegia.
plenamar (ple·na'mar) *n.f.* = pleamar.
plenario (ple'na·rjo) *adj.* plenary.
plenilunio (ple·ni'lu·njo) *n.m.* full moon.
plenipotenciario (ple·ni·po·ten'θja·rjo; -'sja·rjo) *adj.* & *n.m.* plenipotentiary.
plenitud (ple·ni'tuð) *n.f.* plenitude.
pleno ('ple·no) *adj.* full; complete. —*n.m.* plenary session. —**en pleno,** in the middle of; smack on center. —**a** *or* **en pleno día,** in broad daylight.
pleonasmo (ple·o'nas·mo) *n.m.* pleonasm; redundancy. —**pleonástico** (-'nas·ti·ko) *adj.* pleonastic; redundant.
plétora ('ple·to·ra) *n.f.* plethora. —**pletórico** (-'to·ri·ko) *adj.* plethoric.
pleura ('pleu·ra) *n.f.* pleura. —**pleural,** *adj.* pleural.
pleuresía (pleu·re'si·a) *n.f.* pleurisy. —**pleurítico** ('ri·ti·ko) *adj.* pleuritic.
pleuro- (pleu·ro) *prefix* pleuro-; side; rib: *pleurodonto*, pleurodont.
plexi- (plek·si) *prefix* plexi-; twining; interwoven; *plexiforme*, plexiform.
plexo ('plek·so) *n.m.* plexus.
Pléyades ('ple·ja·ðes) *n.f.pl.* Pleiades. *Also,* **Pléyadas** (-ðas).
plica ('pli·ka) *n.f.* escrow.
pliego ('plje·ɣo) *n.m.* **1,** sheet of paper. **2,** dossier. **3,** legal sheet. —**pliego de cargos,** bill of particulars.
pliego ('plje·ɣo) *v., pres.ind. of* **plegar.**
pliegue ('plje·ɣe) *n.m.* **1,** fold; crease. **2,** pleat; plait.
pliegue ('plje·ɣe) *v., pres.subjve. of* **plegar.**
plioceno (pli·o'θe·no; -'se·no) *adj.* & *n.m.* Pliocene.
plisar (pli'sar) *v.t.* to pleat; plait. —**plisado,** *adj.* plaited. —*n.m.* plait; pleat.
-ploide ('ploi·ðe) *suffix* -ploid; *forming adjectives denoting* having a specified number of chromosomes: *diploide*, diploid.
plomada (plo'ma·ða) *n.f.* **1,** plumb; plumb bob. **2,** *naut.* lead; sounding lead. **3,** *fishing* sinker.
plomazo (plo'ma·θo; -so) *n.m.* **1,** gunshot. **2,** gunshot wound.
plomería (plo·me'ri·a) *n.f.* **1,** lead sheeting. **2,** *Amer.* plumbing.
plomero (plo'me·ro) *n.m.* **1,** worker in lead. **2,** *Amer.* plumber.
plomizo (plo'mi·θo; -so) *adj.* leaden; gray.
plomo ('plo·mo) *n.m.* **1,** lead (*metal*). **2,** plumb bob. **3,** *colloq.* bullet. **4,** *colloq.* bore; dullard. —**andar con pies de plomo,** to proceed with great caution. —**a plomo,** true; plumb. —**caer a plomo,** to fall down; fall flat. —**caer como plomo,** *colloq.* to be a pain in the neck.
plugo ('plu·ɣo) *v., 3rd pers.sing. pret. of* **placer.**
pluguiera (plu'ɣje·ra) *v., impf. subjve. of* **placer.**
pluma ('plu·ma) *n.f.* **1,** feather; plume. **2,** writing pen. **3,** nib; pen point. —**pluma estilográfica; pluma fuente,** fountain pen.
plumada (plu'ma·ða) *n.f.* **1,** pen stroke. **2,** *fig.* flourish. **3,** brief writing.
plumado (plu'ma·ðo) *adj.* feathered; feathery.
plumaje (plu'ma·xe) *n.m.* plumage.
plumero (plu'me·ro) *n.m.* **1,** feather duster. **2,** *Amer.* penholder.
plumista (plu'mis·ta) *n.m.* & *f.* scrivener.
plumón (plu'mon) *n.m.* **1,** down. **2,** down quilt. **3,** plume.
plumoso (plu'mo·so) *adj.* feathery.
plural (plu'ral) *adj.* & *n.m.* plural.
pluralidad (plu·ra·li'ðað) *n.f.* plurality.
pluralizar (plu·ra·li'θar; -'sar) *v.t.* [*infl.:* **realizar**] to make plural; pluralize.
pluri- (plu·ri) *prefix* pluri-; many; several: *pluricelular*, pluricellular.
plus (plus) *n.m.* plus; extra.
pluscuamperfecto (plus·kwam·per'fek·to) *adj.* & *n.m.* pluperfect.
plusvalía (plus·βa'li·a) *n.f.* increased value or valuation.
plutocracia (plu·to'kra·θja; -sja) *n.f.* plutocracy. —**plutócrata** (-'to·kra·ta) *n.m.* & *f.* plutocrat. —**plutocrático** (-'kra·ti·ko) *adj.* plutocratic.

Plutón (plu'ton) *n.m., myth.; astron.* Pluto.
plutonio (plu'to·njo) *n.m.* plutonium.
pluvial (plu'βjal) *adj.* pluvial; rain (*attrib.*).
pobeda (po'βe·ða) *n.f.* poplar grove.
población (po·βla'θjon; -'sjon) *n.f.* **1,** population. **2,** city; town; village.
poblacho (po'βla·tʃo) *n.m.* poor village or hamlet.
poblado (po'βla·ðo) *adj.* populated; inhabited. —*n.m.* town; settlement.
poblador (po·βla'ðor) *n.m.* settler.
poblar (po'βlar) *v.t.* [*pres.ind.* **pueblo;** *pres.subjve.* **pueble**] **1,** to populate; people. **2,** to settle; colonize. **3,** to plant; stock. —*v.i.* to increase; multiply. —**poblarse,** *v.r.* **1,** to bud; leaf. **2,** to be covered (with); be overrun (with); teem (with).
pobre ('po·βre) *adj.* poor. —*n.m.* & *f.* pauper; poor person.
pobrete (po'βre·te) *adj.* poor; wretched. —*n.m.* poor fellow; poor wretch.
pobreza (po'βre·θa; -sa) *n.f.* **1,** poverty. **2,** paucity; dearth. **3,** meanness; pettiness.
pocilga (po'θil·ɣa; po'sil-) *n.f.* pigsty; pigpen.
pocillo (po'θi·ʎo; -'si·jo) *n.m.* **1,** well; container. **2,** bowl; mug.
pócima ('po·θi·ma; 'po·si-) *n.f.* potion; draught.
poción (po'θjon; -'sjon) *n.f.* potion.
poco ('po·ko) *adj.* **1,** little; not much. **2,** *pl.* few; not many. —*adv.* & *n.m.* little. —**pocos,** *n.m.* & *pron.pl.* few. —**a poco,** shortly; soon. —**a poco de,** shortly after. —**poco a poco, 1,** little by little. **2,** slow; easy. —**por poco, 1,** by a hair. **2,** almost. —**tener en poco,** to think little of; hold in low esteem.
poda ('po·ða) *n.f.* **1,** pruning. **2,** pruning season. —**podar,** *v.t.* to prune.
podadera (po·ða'ðe·ra) *n.f.* pruning hook; pruning knife.
podenco (po'ðen·ko) *n.m.* hound.
poder (po'ðer) *n.m.* **1,** power; strength. **2,** power of attorney. **3,** possession. —**poderes,** *n.m.pl.* authority (*sing.*). —**a poder de,** by dint of. —**por poderes,** by proxy.
poder (po'ðer) *v.i.* [*pres.ind.* **puedo;** *pres.subjve.* **pueda;** *pret.* **pude;** *fut.* **podré;** *ger.* **pudiendo**] to be able to; can; may. —*v.t.* to be capable of; be able to do. —*v.impers.* to be possible; may. —**a más no poder,** with all possible strength or effort. —**no poder con,** not to be able to handle. —**no poder más,** to be at the end of one's strength or patience. —**no poder menos de . . . ,** not to be able to help. . . . —**no poder ver,** not to be able to stand the sight of; loathe.
poderío (po·ðe'ri·o) *n.m.* power; might.
poderoso (po·ðe'ro·so) *adj.* **1,** powerful; mighty. **2,** influential.
podiatría (po·ðja'tri·a) *n.f.* podiatry. —**podiatra** (po'ðja·tra) *n.m.* & *f.* podiatrist.
podio ('po·ðjo) *n.m.* podium.
podo- (po·ðo) *also,* **pod-** (poð) *before a vowel; prefix* pedo-; pod-; foot: *podómetro* pedometer; *podiatra,* podiatrist.
-podo (po·ðo) *suffix* -ped; -pod; foot: *cirrópodo,* cirriped; *pseudópodo,* pseudopod.
podómetro (po'ðo·me·tro) *n.m.* pedometer.
podré (po'ðre) *v., fut. of* **poder.**
podredumbre (po·ðre'ðum·bre) *n.f.* decay; putrescence.
podredura (po·ðre'ðu·ra) *n.f.* putrescence; corruption.
podrir (po'ðrir) *v.t.* [*also, refl.,* **podrirse**] to rot; putrefy.
poema (po'e·ma) *n.m.* poem.
poesía (po·e'si·a) *n.f.* **1,** poetry. **2,** poem.
poeta (po'e·ta) *n.m.* poet.
poetastro (po·e'tas·tro) *n.m.* poetaster.
poético (po'e·ti·ko) *adj.* poetic. —**poética,** *n.f.* poetics.
poetisa (po·e'ti·sa) *n.f.* poetess.
poetizar (po·e·ti'θar; -'sar) *v.i.* [*pres.subjve.* **poetice** (-'ti·θe; -se); *pret.* **poeticé** (-'θe; -'se)] **1,** to compose poetry. **2,** to wax poetic. —*v.t.* to make poetic; lyricize.
poinsetia (poin'se·tja) *n.f.* poinsettia.
póker ('po·ker) *n.m.* poker (*card game*).
polaco (po'la·ko) *adj.* & *n.m.* Polish. —*n.m.* Pole.
polaina (po'lai·na) *n.f.* legging.
polar (po'lar) *adj.* polar. —**Estrella polar,** Polaris; polestar; North Star.

polaridad (po·la·ri'ðað) *n.f.* polarity.

polarizar (po·la·ri'θar; -'sar) *v.t.* [*pres.subjve.* **polarice** (-'ri·θe; -se); *pret.* **polaricé** (-'θe; -'se)] to polarize. —**polarización,** *n.f.* polarization.

polca ('pol·ka) *n.f.* polka. —**polcar,** *v.i.* to dance the polka.

polea (po'le·a) *n.f.* **1,** pulley. **2,** tackle block; block pulley. —**poleame** (-'a·me) *n.m.* set of pulleys; tackle.

polémica (po'le·mi·ka) *n.f.* **1,** polemic. **2,** polemics. —**polémico,** *adj.* polemical. —**polemista** (-'mis·ta) *n.m.* & *f.* polemist; polemicist.

polen ('po·len) *n.m.* pollen.

poli- (po·li) *prefix* poly-; many; *poligamia,* polygamy.

poliandria (po·li'an·drja) *n.f.* polyandry. —**poliándrico** (-'an·dri·ko) *adj.* [*also, bot.,* **poliandro** (-'an·dro)] polyandrous.

policía (po·li'θi·a; -'si·a) *n.f.* **1,** police. **2,** policeman.

policiaco (po·li'θi·a·ko; -'si·a·ko) *adj.* police (*attrib.*). —**novela policíaca,** detective story.

policial (po·li'θjal; -'sjal) *adj., Amer.* = **policíaco.**

policlínico (po·li'kli·ni·ko) *adj.* polyclinic. —**policlínica,** *n.f.* polyclinic.

policromía (po·li·kro'mi·a) *n.f.* **1,** polychrome. **2,** polychromy.

policromo (po'li·kro·mo) *also,* **policromo** (-'kro·mo) *adj.* polychrome.

polichinela (po·li·tʃi'ne·la) *n.m.* Punch; punchinello.

poliedro (po·li'e·ðro) *n.m.* polyhedron. —**poliédrico,** *adj.* polyhedral.

polígala (po'li·ɣa·la) *n.f.* milkwort.

poligamia (po·li'ɣa·mja) *n.f.* polygamy.

polígamo (po'li·ɣa·mo) *adj.* polygamous. —*n.m.* polygamist.

políglota (po'li·ɣlo·ta) *adj.* & *n.m.* & *f.* polyglot. *Also,* **poligloto** (-'ɣlo·to) *adj.* & *n.m.*

poligonal (po·li·ɣo'nal) *adj.* polygonal.

polígono (po'li·ɣo·no) *adj.* polygonal. —*n.m.* **1,** polygon. **2,** target range.

polilla (po'li·ʎa; -ja) *n.f.* **1,** moth. **2,** rot; something causing rot. **3,** *colloq.* pest; nuisance.

polimerizar (po·li·me·ri'θar; -'sar) *v.t.* [*pres.subjve.* **polimerice** (-'ri·θe; -se); *pret.* **polimericé** (-'θe; -'se)] to polymerize. —**polimerización,** *n.f.* polymerization.

polímero (po'li·me·ro) *adj.* polymeric. —*n.m.* polymer.

polinesio (po·li'ne·sjo) *adj.* & *n.m.* Polynesian.

polinizar (po·li·ni'θar; -'sar) *v.t.* [*pres.subjve.* **polinice** (-'ni·θe; -se); *pret.* **polinicé** (-'θe; -'se)] to pollinate. —**polinización,** *n.f.* pollination.

polinomio (po·li'no·mjo) *n.m.* polynomial.

poliomielitis (po·ljo·mje'li·tis) *n.f.* poliomyelitis; polio.

pólipo ('po·li·po) *n.m.* polyp.

-polis (po·lis) *suffix* -polis; city: *cosmópolis,* cosmopolis.

polisílabo (po·li'si·la·βo) *adj.* polysyllabic. —*n.m.* polysyllable.

polisón (po·li'son) *n.m.* bustle (*woman's dress*).

polista (po'lis·ta) *n.m.* polo player.

Politburó (po·lit·βu'ro) *n.m.* Politburo.

politécnico (po·li'tek·ni·ko) *adj.* polytechnic.

politeísmo (po·li·te'is·mo) *n.m.* polytheism. —**politeísta,** *n.m.* & *f.* polytheist. —*adj.* polytheistic.

política (po'li·ti·ka) *n.f.* **1,** policy. **2,** politics. **3,** polity. **4,** tact. —**política exterior,** foreign policy. —**por política,** out of courtesy.

políticamente (po·li·ti·ka'men·te) *adv.* **1,** politically. **2,** civilly.

politicastro (po·li·ti'kas·tro) *n.m.* petty politician; ward heeler.

político (po'li·ti·ko) *adj.* **1,** political. **2,** politic. **3,** tactful. **4,** in-law: *padre político,* father-in-law. —*n.m.* politician.

politiquear (po·li·ti·ke'ar) *v.i., colloq.* **1,** to politick. **2,** to talk politics. —**politiqueo** (-'ke·o) *n.m., colloq.* politicking.

politiquería (po·li·ti·ke'ri·a) *n.f., Amer., colloq.* political chicanery. —**politiquero,** *n.m., Amer., colloq.* petty politician.

póliza ('po·li·θa; -sa) *n.f.* **1,** [*also,* **póliza de seguro**] insurance policy. **2,** tax stamp. **3,** [*also,* **póliza de crédito**] letter of credit. **4,** scrip.

polizón (po·li'θon; -'son) *n.m.* **1,** vagrant. **2,** stowaway.

polizonte (po·li'θon·te; -'son·te) *n.m., colloq., derog.* cop; flatfoot.

polo ('po·lo) *n.m.* **1,** *geog.; physics* pole. **2,** polo.
polonés (po·lo'nes) *adj.* Polish. —*n.m.* Pole.
polonesa (po·lo'ne·sa) *adj., fem. of* **polonés.** —*n.f.* **1,** Polish woman. **2,** polonaise.
polonio (po'lo·njo) *n.m.* polonium.
poltrón (pol'tron) *adj.* lazy; slothful. —**poltrona,** *n.f.* easy chair. —**poltronería,** *n.f.* laziness; indolence.
polución (po·lu'θjon; -'sjon) *n.f.* pollution.
poluto (po'lu·to) *adj.* polluted; unclean.
polvareda (pol·βa're·ða) *n.f.* **1,** cloud of dust. **2,** tiff; free-for-all.
polvera (pol'βe·ra) *n.f.* **1,** powder box. **2,** compact.
polvillo (pol'βi·ʎo; -jo) *n.m.* fine dust.
polvo ('pol·βo) *n.m.* **1,** dust. **2,** powder; face powder. **3,** *pl.* toilet powder. —**hacer polvo,** *colloq.* to beat to a pulp. —**limpio de polvo y paja,** *colloq.* free of all charges; net.
pólvora ('pol·βo·ra) *n.f.* **1,** powder; gunpowder. **2,** *colloq.* fireball; spitfire.
polvorear (pol·βo·re'ar) *v.t.* = **espolvorear.**
polvoriento (pol·βo'rjen·to) *adj.* dusty; dust-covered.
polvorín (pol·βo'rin) *n.m.* **1,** powder magazine. **2,** powder flask; powder horn. **3,** *colloq.* touchy or irascible person.
polvoroso (pol·βo'ro·so) *adj.* = **polvoriento.** —**poner pies en polvorosa,** *colloq.* to take flight; take to one's heels.
polla ('po·ʎa; -ja) *n.f.* **1,** spring chicken; pullet. **2,** *So.Amer.* first prize (*in a lottery*).
pollada (po'ʎa·ða; po'ja-) *n.f.* hatch; brood; covey.
pollera (po'ʎe·ra; po'je-) *n.f.* **1,** child's walker. **2,** chicken coop. **3,** *So.Amer.* skirt.
pollino (po'ʎi·no; po'ji-) *n.m.* ass; donkey.
pollita (po'ʎi·ta; po'ji-) *n.f.* **1,** pullet. **2,** *colloq.* girl; lass.
pollito (po'ʎi·to; po'ji-) *n.m.* **1,** chick. **2,** *colloq.* boy; lad.
pollo ('po·ʎo; -jo) *n.m.* **1,** chicken. **2,** boy; lad.
polluelo (po'ʎwe·lo; -'jwe·lo) *n.m.* chick.
poma ('po·ma) *n.f.* pome.
pomada (po'ma·ða) *n.f.* pomade; salve.
pomar (po'mar) *n.f.* orchard, esp. apple orchard.
pomelo (po'me·lo) *n.m.* grapefruit.
pómez ('po meθ; -mes) *n.f.* pumice.
pomo ('po·mo) *n.m.* **1,** flask; phial. **2,** pommel; knob. **3,** bunch; cluster. **4,** *bot.* pome.
pompa ('pom·pa) *n.f.* **1,** pomp. **2,** bubble. **3,** *naut.* pump.
pompón (pom'pon) *n.m.* **1,** pompon. **2,** *Amer.* chrysanthemum.
pomposo (pom'po·so) *adj.* pompous. —**pomposidad,** *n.f.* pomposity.
pómulo ('po·mu·lo) *n.m.* cheekbone.
pon (pon) *v., impve.sing. of* **poner.** —*n.m., W.I.* lift; free ride.
ponche ('pon·tʃe) *n.m.* punch (*drink*). —**ponchera,** *n.f.* punch bowl.
poncho ('pon·tʃo) *n.m.* poncho. —*adj.* lax; lazy.
ponderable (pon·de'ra·βle) *adj.* **1,** ponderable. **2,** admirable.
ponderación (pon·de·ra'θjon; -'sjon) *n.f.* **1,** tact; prudence. **2,** praise.
ponderado (pon·de'ra·ðo) *adj.* tactful; prudent.
ponderar (pon·de'rar) *v.t.* **1,** to ponder; weigh. **2,** to praise.
ponderoso (pon·de'ro·so) *adj.* **1,** heavy; ponderous. **2,** serious; circumspect.
ponedero (po·ne'ðe·ro) *adj.* egg-laying. —*n.m.* hen's nest.
ponedor (po·ne'ðor) *adj.* egg-laying.
poner (po'ner) *v.t.* [*pres.ind.* **pongo** ('pon·go); *pres.subjve.* **ponga** (-ga); *impve.* **pon;** *fut.* **pondré** (-'dre); *pret.* **puse;** *p.p.* **puesto**] **1,** to put; place; set. **2,** to set (the table). **3,** [*also, refl.,* **ponerse**] to put on (a garment). **4,** to put up; wager; stake. **5,** to lay (eggs). **6,** to suppose; assume. **7,** to give (a name). **8,** to take (a period of time). **9,** *fol. by* **de, por** *or* **como,** to show (someone) up as. **10,** *fol. by adj.* to turn; make; cause to be or become. **11,** *fol. by* **en,** to get (someone) into. —**ponerse,** *v.r.* **1,** to become. **2,** to set, as the sun. **3,** *fol. by* **en,** to make it to; get to (a place or position). **4,** *fol. by* **de** *or* **como,** to set oneself up as. —**poner bien,** to commend; put in

a favorable light. —**poner mal,** to discredit; put in a bad light.

poniente (po'njen·te) *n.m.* west. —**sol poniente,** setting sun.

pontear (pon·te'ar) *v.t.* to bridge. —*v.i.* to build a bridge.

pontificado (pon·ti·fi'ka·ðo) *n.m.* pontificate.

pontifical (pon·ti·fi'kal) *adj.* pontifical.

pontificar (pon·ti·fi'kar) *v.i.* [*pres.subjve.* **pontifique** (-'fi·ke); *pret.* **pontifiqué** (-'ke)] to pontificate. —**pontificación,** *n.f.* pontification.

pontífice (pon'ti·fi·θe; -se) *n.m.* pontiff.

pontificio (pon·ti'fi·θjo; -sjo) *adj.* papal; pontifical.

pontón (pon'ton) *n.m.* pontoon.

ponzoña (pon'θo·ɲa; -'so·ɲa) *n.f.* venom; poison. —**ponzoñoso,** *adj.* venomous; poisonous.

popa ('po·pa) *n.f.* poop; stern.

popelina (po·pe'li·na) *n.f.* poplin.

populachería (po·pu·la·tʃe'ri·a) *n.f.* **1,** vulgar manners; vulgar behavior. **2,** crowd response. **3,** = **populacho. 4,** popular appeal; rabble rousing.

populachero (po·pu·la'tʃe·ro) *adj.* **1,** vulgar; uncouth. **2,** of or characteristic of the rabble. **3,** catering to the populace; rabble-rousing.

populacho (po·pu'la·tʃo) *n.m.* populace; rabble.

popular (po·pu'lar) *adj.* popular. —**popularidad,** *n.f.* popularity.

popularizar (po·pu·la·ri'θar; -'sar) *v.t.* [*pres. subjve.* **popularice** (-'ri·θe; -se); *pret.* **popularicé** (-'θe; -'se)] to popularize. —**popularización,** *n.f.* popularization.

populoso (po·pu'lo·so) *adj.* populous.

popurrí (po·pu'rri) *n.m.* potpourri.

poquedad (po·ke'ðað) *n.f.* **1,** shortness; paucity. **2,** timidity; pusillanimity. **3,** trifle.

póquer ('po·ker) *n.m.* = **póker.**

poquito (po'ki·to) *adj.* very little. —**a poquitos,** bit by bit. —**poquito a poco,** *also,* **a poquito,** little by little.

por (por) *prep.* **1,** by; by way of; through: *por las calles,* through the streets. **2,** throughout the extent of; over: *Los perros andan sueltos por el prado,* The dogs are running loose over the meadow. **3,** by; by means or agency of: *Fue aplastado por el auto,* He was run over by the car. **4,** *in expressions of time* in: *por la mañana,* in the morning. **5,** for; because of: *por haber hecho esto,* for having done this. **6,** for the sake of; on behalf of: *Lo hizo por mí,* He did it for my sake. **7,** to; in order to: *No llevo corbata por ir más cómodo.* I am not wearing a tie in order to be more comfortable. **8,** for; in quest of: *Fue por el médico,* He went for the doctor. **9,** by; multiplied by; times: *siete por seis,* seven times six; seven by six. **10,** *denoting price or cost* for: *Pagué cinco dólares por la camisa,* I paid five dollars for the shirt. **11,** per; a; each: *cinco por ciento,* five percent; *Pagué treinta centavos por docena,* I paid thirty cents a dozen. **12,** for; as: *La tomó por esposa,* He took her as his wife. **13,** for; instead of; in place of: *El vicepresidente firmó por el presidente,* The vice-president signed for the president. —**estar por,** *fol. by inf.* **1,** to be ready to or disposed to: *Estamos por salir,* We are ready to leave. **2,** to be; be still to be: *La casa está por barrer,* The house is still to be swept. —**por cuanto,** whereas; inasmuch as. —**por donde, 1,** where; whereabout. **2,** whereby; wherefore. —**por que** = **porque.** —**por qué,** why. —**por si acaso,** in case.

porcachón (por·ka'tʃon) *adj.* piggish; hoggish. *Also, colloq.,* **porcacho** (-'ka·tʃo).

porcelana (por·θe'la·na; por·se-) *n.f.* porcelain.

porcentaje (por·θen'ta·xe; por·sen-) *n.m.* percentage.

porcino (por'θi·no; -'si·no) *adj.* porcine.

porción (por'θjon; -'sjon) *n.f.* portion.

porche ('por·tʃe) *n.m.* porch.

pordiosear (por·ðjo·se'ar) *v.t.* & *i.* to beg.

pordiosero (por·ðjo'se·ro) *n.m.* beggar. —*adj.* mendicant; begging. —**pordiosería,** *n.f.* begging; beggary.

porfía (por'fi·a) *n.f.* **1,** stubbornness. **2,** altercation; quarrel. —**a porfía,** in competition.

porfiado (por'fja·ðo) *adj.* stubborn. —*n.m.* stubborn man.

porfiar (por'fjar) *v.i.* [*pres.subjve.* **porfíe** (-'fi·e); *pret.* **porfié** ('fje)]

1, to fight; dispute stubbornly. 2, to be stubborn; be obstinate.
pórfido ('por·fi·ðo) *n.m.* porphyry.
pormenor (por·me'nor) *n.m.* detail; particular.
pormenorizar (por·me·no·ri·'θar; -'sar) *v.t.* [*infl.:* **realizar**] 1, to detail; relate in detail. 2, to itemize.
pornografía (por·no·ɣra'fi·a) *n.f.* pornography. —**pornográfico** (-'ɣra·fi·ko) *adj.* pornographic.
poro ('po·ro) *n.m.* pore. —**poroso,** *adj.* porous. —**porosidad,** *n.f.* porosity.
poroto (po'ro·to) *n.m., So.Amer.* bean. —**apuntarse un poroto,** *So. Amer., colloq.* to make a point; hit the mark.
porque ('por·ke) *conj.* 1, because. 2, so that; in order that.
porqué (por'ke) *n.m.* reason; motive; cause; the why; the wherefore. —**los porqués y los cómos,** the whys and wherefores.
porquería (por·ke'ri·a) *n.f.* 1, filth. 2, *colloq.* mess; botch. 3, *colloq.* trifle; junk. 4, *colloq.* dirty trick.
porqueriza (por·ke'ri·θa; -sa) *n.f.* pigsty; sty. —**porquerizo,** *n.m.* swineherd.
porra ('po·rra) *n.f.* 1, mace; truncheon. 2, stick; club; bludgeon. 3, *colloq.* gall; brazenness. —*interj.* confound it! —**irse a la porra,** to go to the dickens.
porrada (po'rra·ða) *n.f.* 1, = **porrazo.** 2, *colloq.* nonsense; inanity. 3, *colloq.* heap; slew.
porrazo (po'rra·θo; -so) *n.m.* 1, blow; clubbing. 2, fall; bump.
porro ('po·rro) *adj., colloq.* dull; stupid. —*n.m., colloq.* dullard.
porrón (po'rron) *n.m.* 1, glass jug with a spout for drinking wine. 2, earthen jar.
porta- (por·ta) *prefix; forming nouns denoting* carrying; holding: *portaaviones,* aircraft carrier; *portaplumas,* penholder.
portaaviones (por·ta·a'βjo·nes; por·ta'βjo-) *n.m.sing. & pl.* aircraft carrier.
portacartas (por·ta'kar·tas) *n.m.sing. & pl.* mail pouch; mailbag.
portada (por'ta·ða) *n.f.* 1, façade; front. 2, cover (*of a book, magazine, etc.*).
portado (por'ta·ðo) *adj., in* **bien** *or* **mal portado,** well *or* poorly attired *or* behaved.
portador (por·ta'ðor) *adj.* bearing; carrying. —*n.m.* bearer; carrier.
portafolio (por·ta'fo·ljo) *n.m.* portfolio.
portafusil (por·ta·fu'sil) *n.m.* rifle sling.
portal (por'tal) *n.m.* 1, portal: entrance. 2, doorstep. 3, portico.
portalón (por·ta'lon) *n.m.* 1, large door; portal. 2, *naut.* side hatchway.
portamantas (por·ta'man·tas) *n.m. sing. & pl.* carrying straps.
portamonedas (por·ta·mo'ne·ðas) *n.m.sing. & pl.* pocketbook; purse.
portaobjetos (por·ta·oβ'xe·tos) *n.m.sing. & pl.* microscope slide.
portapapeles (por·ta·pa'pe·les) *n.m.sing. & pl.* 1, briefcase. 2, paper rack; paper holder.
portapliegos (por·ta'plje·ɣos) *n.m.sing. & pl.* briefcase.
portaplumas (por·ta'plu·mas) *n.m.sing. & pl.* penholder.
portar (por'tar) *v.t.* to carry; bear (esp. arms). —*v.i., naut.* to bear well before the wind. —**portarse,** *v.r.* to behave; comport oneself.
portátil (por'ta·til) *adj.* portable.
portaviandas (por·ta'βjan·das) *n.m.sing. & pl.* = **fiambrera.**
portavoz (por·ta'βoθ; -'βos) *n.m.* 1, megaphone. 2, spokesman. 3, organ (*publication*).
portazgo (por'taθ·ɣo; -'tas·ɣo) *n.m.* toll; road toll.
portazo (por'ta·θo; -so) *n.m.* slam *or* slamming of a door.
porte ('por·te) *n.m.* 1, transport; transportation. 2, portage. 3, shipping costs; postage. 4, carriage; demeanor. 5, deportment. 6, import; importance.
portear (por·te'ar) *v.t.* to carry; transport. —*v.i.* to slam, as a door. —**portearse,** *v.r.* to migrate, esp. as birds.
portento (por'ten·to) *n.m.* portent. —**portentoso,** *adj.* portentous.
porteño (por'te·ɲo) *adj.* inhabiting or coming from a seaport, esp. Buenos Aires, Cadiz, and other principal ports. —*n.m.* inhabitant or native of a seaport.
portería (por·te'ri·a) *n.f.* 1, porter's desk, office or quarters. 2, gatehouse. 3, *sports* goal.
portero (por'te·ro) *n.m.* 1, porter; gatekeeper; doorman. 2, goalkeeper.
portezuela (por·te'θwe·la; -'swe·la) *n.f.* small door, usu. of a vehicle.

pórtico ('por·ti·ko) *n.m.* portico.
portier (por'tjer) *n.m.* portiere.
portilla (por'ti·ʎa; -ja) *n.f.* porthole.
portillo (por'ti·ʎo; -jo) *n.m.* **1,** aperture; opening; gap. **2,** wicket; barnyard gate. **3,** *colloq.* break; crack.
portón (por'ton) *n.m.* large door; gate.
portorriqueño (por·to·rri'ke·ɲo) *adj.* & *n.m.* = **puertorriqueño.**
portuario (por'twa·rjo) *adj.* **1,** port (*attrib.*). **2,** dock (*attrib.*); docking (*attrib.*).
portugués (por·tu'ɣes) *adj.* & *n.m.* Portuguese.
porvenir (por·βe'nir) *n.m.* future.
pos (pos) *in* **en pos** *or* **en pos de,** after; following; in pursuit of.
pos- (pos) *prefix* post-; after; behind: *posponer,* postpone. *Also, in some words,* **post-.**
posada (po'sa·ða) *n.f.* **1,** inn; lodge. **2,** lodging; lodgings.
posaderas (po·sa'ðe·ras) *n.f.pl.* buttocks.
posadero (po·sa'ðe·ro) *n.m.* innkeeper.
posar (po'sar) *v.i.* **1,** to rest; repose. **2,** to lodge; room. **3,** *art; photog.* to pose. —*v.t.* **1,** to put; place. **2,** to lay down (a burden). —**posarse,** *v.r.* to light; alight; come to rest; settle.
posas ('po·sas) *n.f.pl., colloq.* = **posaderas.**
posdata (pos'ða·ta) *n.f.* postscript.
pose ('po·se) *n.f.* **1,** pose. **2,** *photog.* exposure; take.
poseedor (po·se·e'ðor) *n.m.* possessor; holder. —*adj.* possessing.
poseer (po·se'er) *v.t.* [*pret.* **poseí** (po·se'i), **poseyó;** *ger.* **poseyendo**] **1,** to possess. **2,** to master; have knowledge or command of. **3,** to seize; take possession of. —**poseerse,** *v.r.* to be self-possessed.
poseído (po·se'i·ðo) *adj.* possessed. *Also,* **poseso.**
posesión (po·se'sjon) *n.f.* possession.
posesionar (po·se·sjo'nar) *v.t.* to give possession (of something) to. —**posesionarse,** *v.r.* to take possession; seize control.
posesivo (po·se'si·βo) *adj.* & *n.m.* possessive.
poseso (po'se·so) *adj.* & *n.m.* possessed.
poseyendo (po·se'jen·do) *v., ger. of* **poseer.**
poseyó (po·se'jo) *v., 3rd pers.sing. pret. of* **poseer.**
posfecha (pos'fe·tʃa) *n.f.* postdate. —**posfechar,** *v.t.* to postdate.
posguerra (pos'ɣe·rra) *n.f.* = **postguerra.**
posible (po'si·βle) *adj.* possible. —**posibilidad,** *n.f.* possibility. —**posibilitar,** *v.t.* to make possible.
posición (po·si'θjon; -'sjon) *n.f.* position.
positivismo (po·si·ti'βis·mo) *n.m.* positivism. —**positivista,** *n.m.* & *f.* positivist. —*adj.* positivistic.
positivo (po·si'ti·βo) *adj.* & *n.m.* positive. —**positiva,** *n.f., photog.* positive. —**positividad,** *n.f.* positivity.
positrón (po·si'tron) *n.m.* positron.
posma ('pos·ma) *n.m.* & *f., colloq.* sluggard; slowpoke. —*n.f., colloq.* sluggishness; phlegm.
posmeridiano (pos·me·ri'ðja·no) *adj.* = **postmeridiano.**
poso ('po·so) *n.m.* **1,** sediment; dregs (*pl.*). **2,** quiet; repose.
posponer (pos·po'ner) *v.t.* [*infl.:* **poner**] to postpone.
post- (post) *prefix, var., in some words, of* **pos-:** *postguerra,* postwar; *postdiluviano,* postdiluvian.
posta ('pos·ta) *n.f.* **1,** relay of horses; express post. **2,** stagecoach run; distance between posts. **3,** meat repast. **4,** *gambling* pool; pot. —**a posta,** *also,* **aposta,** *adv.* on purpose.
postal (pos'tal) *adj.* postal; post (*attrib.*); postage (*attrib.*). —*n.f.* postcard.
postdata (post'ða·ta) *n.f.* = **posdata.**
postdiluviano (post·ði·lu'βja·no) *adj.* postdiluvian.
poste ('pos·te) *n.m.* post; pole. —**ser un poste, 1,** to be deaf; be impassive. **2,** to be clumsy.
postergar (pos·ter'ɣar) *v.t.* [*pres. subjve.* **postergue** (-'ter·ɣe); *pret.* **postergué** (-'ɣe)] **1,** to postpone; put off. **2,** to hold back; check. —**postergación,** *n.f.* postponement; deferment.
posteridad (pos·te·ri'ðað) *n.f.* posterity.
posterior (pos·te'rjor) *adj.* & *n.m.* posterior. —**posterioridad,** *n.f.* pos-

teriority. —**con posterioridad,** after; subsequently.

posteriormente (pos·te·rjor·'men·te) *adv.* 1, after. 2, later.

postgraduado (post·ɣra'ðwa·ðo) *adj.* & *n.m.* postgraduate.

postguerra (post'ɣe·rra) *n.f.* postwar period.

postigo (pos'ti·ɣo) *n.m.* 1, wicket. 2, shutter. 3, postern. 4, peephole.

postilla (pos'ti·ʎa; -ja) *n.f.* scab.

postillón (pos·ti'ʎon; -'jon) *n.m.* postillion.

postín (pos'tin) *n.m., colloq.* dash; cockiness.

postizo (pos'ti·θo; -so) *adj.* false; artificial.

postludio (post'lu·ðjo) *n.m.* postlude.

postmeridiano (post·me·ri'ðja·no) *adj.* postmeridian.

post mortem (post'mor·tem) postmortem.

postor (pos'tor) *n.m.* bidder. —**mejor postor,** highest bidder.

postrar (pos'trar) *v.t.* to prostrate. —**postrarse,** *v.r.* to kneel down; lie prone. —**postración,** *n.f.* prostration. —**postrador,** *adj.* prostrating.

postre ('pos·tre) *adj.* = **postrero.** —*n.m.* dessert. —**a la postre,** at last; finally.

postrer (pos'trer) *adj.* = **postrero** *before a masc. noun.*

postrero (pos'tre·ro) *adj.* & *n.m.* 1, last; last remaining. 2, hindmost.

postrimería (pos·tri·me'ri·a) *n.f., usu.pl.* end; final *or* late stages, esp. of life.

postulado (pos·tu'la·ðo) *n.m.* postulate.

postulante (pos·tu'lan·te) *adj.* requesting admission. —*n.m.* candidate for admission; postulant.

postular (pos·tu'lar) *v.t.* 1, to postulate. 2, to request; petition for.

póstumo ('pos·tu·mo) *adj.* posthumous.

postura (pos'tu·ra) *n.f.* 1, posture. 2, bid. 3, = **puesta.** 4, *Amer.* a trying on; fitting.

potable (po'ta·βle) *adj.* potable.

potaje (po'ta·xe) *n.m.* pottage; stew.

potasa (po'ta·sa) *n.f.* potash.

potasio (po'ta·sjo) *n.m.* potassium. —**potásico** (-'ta·si·ko) *adj.* potassic.

pote ('po·te) *n.m.* 1, pot. 2, jug; jar.

potencia (po'ten·θja; -sja) *n.f.* 1, power. 2, potency. —**en potencia,** potentially.

potencial (po·ten'θjal; -'sjal) *adj.* & *n.m.* potential. —**potencialidad,** *n.f.* potentiality.

potenciar (po·ten'θjar; -'sjar) *v.t.* to utilize; exploit.

potentado (po·ten'ta·ðo) *n.m.* potentate.

potente (po'ten·te) *adj.* potent; powerful.

potestad (po·tes'tað) *n.f.* jurisdiction; power. —**patria potestad,** parental jurisdiction.

potestativo (po·tes·ta'ti·βo) *adj., law* facultative.

potra ('po·tra) *n.f.* 1, young mare. 2, *colloq.* hernia. —**tener potra,** *colloq.* to have it made; be happy.

potranca (po'tran·ka) *n.f.* filly; young mare. —**potranco,** *n.m., Amer.* colt.

potrero (po'tre·ro) *n.m.* 1, grazing field for horses. 2, colt tender.

potro ('po·tro) *n.m.* 1, colt. 2, torture rack. 3, *gymnastics* horse.

poza ('po·θa; -sa) *n.f.* puddle.

pozo ('po·θo; -so) *n.m.* 1, well. 2, shaft; pit. 3, hole or dip in the bed of a river or the sea. 4, *cards* jackpot; kitty. —**pozo negro,** cesspool.

práctica ('prak·ti·ka) *n.f.* practice.

practicable (prak·ti'ka·βle) *adj.* practicable; feasible.

practicanta (prak·ti'kan·ta) *n.f.* 1, female nurse. 2, *pharm.* female clerk.

practicante (prak·ti'kan·te) *adj.* practicing. —*n.m.* 1, practitioner. 2, intern. 3, male nurse. 4, *pharm.* clerk.

practicar (prak·ti'kar) *v.t.* [*pres. subjve.* **practique** (-'ti·ke); *pret.* **practiqué** (-'ke)] to practice.

práctico ('prak·ti·ko) *adj.* 1, practical. 2, skillful; experienced. —*n.m.* harbor pilot.

pradera (pra'ðe·ra) *n.f.* prairie; meadow.

prado ('pra·ðo) *n.m.* 1, field; meadow. 2, grassy spot; park.

pragmático (praɣ'ma·ti·ko) *adj.* pragmatic. —*n.m.* interpreter of the law; jurist.

pragmatismo (praɣ·ma'tis·mo) *n.m.* pragmatism. —**pragmatista,** *n.m.* & *f.* pragmatist.

praseodimio (pra·se·o'ði·mjo) *n.m.* praseodymium.

pre- (pre) *prefix* pre-; before (*in time, place or rank*): **precedencia,**

precedence; *predecesor,* predecessor; *preeminente,* preëminent.
preámbulo (pre'am·bu·lo) *n.m.* **1,** preamble. **2,** *colloq.* evasion; circumlocution.
prebenda (pre'βen·da) *n.f.* **1,** prebend. **2,** *colloq.* soft job.
preboste (pre'βos·te) *n.m.* provost.
precario (pre'ka·rjo) *adj.* precarious.
precaución (pre·kau'θjon; -'sjon) *n.f.* precaution. —**precaucionarse,** *v.r.* to take precautions; be on guard.
precautela (pre·kau'te·la) *n.f., Amer.* caution; precaution.
precautorio (pre·kau'to·rjo) *adj.* precautionary.
precaver (pre·ka'βer) *v.t.* to forestall. —**precaverse,** *v.r., fol. by* **de** *or* **contra,** to guard against; take precautions against.
precavido (pre·ka'βi·ðo) *adj.* **1,** careful; cautious. **2,** forewarned.
precedencia (pre·θe'ðen·θja; -se·'ðen·sja) *n.f.* precedence. —**precedente,** *adj.* preceding; foregoing. —*n.m.* precedent.
preceder (pre·θe'ðer; pre·se-) *v.t.* & *i.* to precede.
precepto (pre'θep·to; pre'sep-) *n.m.* precept. —**preceptivo,** *adj.* preceptive. —**preceptor,** *n.m.* preceptor.
preceptuar (pre·θep'twar; pre·sep-) *v.t.* [*infl.:* **continuar**] **1,** to rule on; advise on. **2,** to prescribe.
preces ('pre·θes; -ses) *n.f.pl.* **1,** prayers; devotions. **2,** supplications.
preciado (pre'θja·ðo; -'sja·ðo) *adj.* **1,** valuable; precious. **2,** valued; esteemed. **3,** presumptuous; vain.
preciador (pre·θja'ðor; -sja'ðor) *n.m.* appraiser.
preciar (pre'θjar; -'sjar) *v.t.* **1,** to appraise; price. **2,** to value; appreciate. —**preciarse,** *v.r.* to take pride; boast.
precinto (pre'θin·to; -'sin·to) *n.m.* strap; strapping. —**precintar,** *v.t.* to strap; bind.
precio ('pre·θjo; -sjo) *n.m.* **1,** price. **2,** value; esteem. —**tener en precio,** to esteem; value highly.
preciosidad (pre·θjo·si'ðað; pre·sjo-) *n.f.* **1,** preciousness. **2,** precious thing. **3,** *colloq.* beauty; pretty thing; precious one.
precioso (pre'θjo·so; pre'sjo-) *adj.* **1,** precious. **2,** *colloq.* beautiful. —**preciosismo,** *n.m.* preciosity.
preciosura (pre·θjo'su·ra; pre·sjo-) *n.f., Amer.* = **preciosidad.**
precipicio (pre·θi'pi·θjo; -si'pi·sjo) *n.m.* precipice.
precipitación (pre·θi·pi·ta'θjon; -si·pi·ta'sjon) *n.f.* **1,** haste; precipitancy. **2,** precipitation.
precipitadero (pre·θi·pi·ta'ðe·ro; pre·si-) *n.m.* precipice; steep cliff.
precipitado (pre·θi·pi'ta·ðo; pre·si-) *n.m.* & *adj.* precipitate.
precipitar (pre·θi·pi'tar; pre·si-) *v.t.* & *i.* to precipitate. —**precipitarse,** *v.r.* to rush headlong; hasten.
precisar (pre·θi'sar; -si'sar) *v.t.* **1,** to fix; set; determine exactly. **2,** *Amer.* to need; have need of. —*v.i.* **1,** to be precise. **2,** *Amer.* to be necessary.
precisión (pre·θi'sjon; pre·si-) *n.f.* **1,** necessity. **2,** precision; accuracy.
preciso (pre'θi·so; -'si·so) *adj.* **1,** necessary; indispensable. **2,** precise; exact. **3,** concise. —**tiempo preciso,** just time enough.
precitado (pre·θi'ta·ðo; pre·si-) *adj.* aforesaid; aforementioned.
preclaro (pre'kla·ro) *adj.* famous; illustrious; prominent.
precisamente (pre·θi·sa'men·te; pre·si-) *adv.* **1,** precisely; exactly. **2,** necessarily; unavoidably.
precocidad (pre·ko·θi'ðað; -si·'ðað) *n.f.* precocity.
precognición (pre·koɣ·ni'θjon; -'sjon) *n.f.* precognition.
precolombino (pre·ko·lom'bi·no) *adj.* pre-Columbian.
preconcebir (pre·kon·θe'βir; -se·'βir) *v.t.* [*infl.:* **concebir**] to preconceive.
preconizar (pre·ko·ni'θar; -'sar) *v.t.* [*pres.subjve.* **preconice** (-'ni·θe; -se); *pret.* **preconicé** (-'θe; -'se)] to herald; proclaim.
preconocer (pre·ko·no'θer; -'ser) *v.t.* [*infl.:* **conocer**] to foreknow.
precoz (pre'koθ; -'kos) *adj.* precocious.
precursor (pre·kur'sor) *adj.* preceding. —*n.m.* precursor; harbinger.
predecesor (pre·ðe·θe'sor; -se·'sor) *n.m.* predecessor.
predecir (pre·ðe'θir; -'sir) *v.t.* [*infl.:* **decir**] to predict; foretell; forecast.
predestinar (pre·ðes·ti'nar) *v.t.* to predestine. —**predestinación,** *n.f.* predestination.

predeterminar (pre·ðe·ter·mi·'nar) *v.t.* to predetermine. —**predeterminación,** *n.f.* predetermination.
prédica ('pre·ði·ka) *n.f.* preachment; sermon.
predicación (pre·ði·ka'θjon; -'sjon) *n.f.* **1,** preaching. **2,** predication.
predicado (pre·ði'ka·ðo) *n.m.* predicate.
predicador (pre·ði·ka'ðor) *n.m.* preacher. —*adj.* preaching.
predicamento (pre·ði·ka'men·to) *n.m.* **1,** position; status. **2,** *logic* predicament; category.
predicar (pre·ði'kar) *v.t.* & *i.* [*pres.subjve.* **predique** (-'ði·ke); *pret.* **prediqué** (-'ke)] to preach. —*v.t.* **1,** to make public; make known. **2,** *colloq.* to lecture; reprimand. **3,** to predicate.
predicativo (pre·ði·ka'ti·βo) *adj.* predicative.
predicción (pre·ðik'θjon; -'sjon) *n.f.* prediction.
predilecto (pre·ði'lek·to) *adj.* favorite; preferred. —**predilección,** *n.f.* predilection.
predio ('pre·ðjo) *n.m.* **1,** landed property; real property. **2,** *usu.pl., Amer.* taxes on real property.
predisponer (pre·ðis·po'ner) *v.t.* [*infl.:* **poner**] to predispose. —**predisposición** (-si'θjon; -'sjon) *n.f.* predisposition.
predominar (pre·ðo·mi'nar) *v.t.* & *i.* to predominate. —**predominancia,** *also,* **predominación,** *n.f.* predominance. —**predominante,** *adj.* predominant.
predominio (pre·ðo'mi·njo) *n.m.* predominance.
preeminente (pre·e·mi'nen·te) *adj.* preëminent. —**preeminencia,** *n.f.* preëminence.
preexistir (pre·ek·sis'tir) *v.i.* to preëxist. —**preexistencia,** *n.f.* preëxistence. —**preexistente,** *adj.* preëxisting.
prefabricar (pre·fa·βri'kar) *v.t.* [*infl.:* **fabricar**] to prefabricate. —**prefabricación,** *n.f.* prefabrication.
prefacio (pre'fa·θjo; -sjo) *n.m.* preface.
prefecto (pre'fek·to) *n.m.* prefect. —**prefectura,** *n.f.* prefecture.
preferencia (pre·fe'ren·θja; -sja) *n.f.* preference. —**preferente,** *adj.* preferential. —**preferible,** *adj.* preferable.
preferir (pre·fe'rir) *v.t.* [*infl.:* **diferir**] to prefer.
prefijar (pre·fi'xar) *v.t.* **1,** to fix beforehand; predetermine. **2,** to prefix.
prefijo (pre'fi·xo) *n.m.* prefix.
pregón (pre'ɣon) *n.m.* announcement; proclamation. —**pregonero,** *adj.* proclaiming; divulging. —*n.m.* town crier.
pregonar (pre·ɣo'nar) *v.t.* **1,** to announce; proclaim. **2,** to hawk (wares). **3,** to divulge. **4,** to praise publicly.
preguerra (pre'ɣe·rra) *n.f.* prewar period.
pregunta (pre'ɣun·ta) *n.f.* question; query.
preguntar (pre·ɣun'tar) *v.t.* to ask; question. —*v.i.* to ask; inquire. —**preguntarse,** *v.r.* to wonder; ask oneself.
preguntón (pre·ɣun'ton) *adj., colloq.* nosy; inquisitive; prying.
prehistoria (pre·is'to·rja) *n.f.* prehistory. —**prehistórico** (-'to·ri·ko) *adj.* prehistoric.
prejuicio (pre'xwi·θjo; -sjo) *n.m.* prejudice; bias. —**prejuiciado,** *adj.* prejudiced; biased. —**prejuiciar,** *v.t.* to prejudice.
prejuzgar (pre·xuθ'ɣar; -xus'ɣar) *v.t.* [*infl.:* **juzgar**] to prejudge.
prelacía (pre·la'θi·a; -'si·a) *n.f.* prelacy.
prelación (pre·la'θjon; -'sjon) *n.f.* preference.
prelada (pre'la·ða) *n.f.* abbess.
prelado (pre'la·ðo) *n.m.* prelate. —**prelado doméstico,** monsignor.
preliminar (pre·li·mi'nar) *adj.* & *n.m.* preliminary.
preludio (pre'lu·ðjo) *n.m.* prelude. —**preludiar,** *v.t.* & *i.* to prelude.
prematuro (pre·ma'tu·ro) *adj.* premature.
premédico (pre'me·ði·ko) *adj.* premedical. —**premédica,** *n.f.* premedical training.
premeditar (pre·me·ði'tar) *v.t.* to premeditate. —**premeditación,** *n.f.* premeditation.
premiar (pre'mjar) *v.t.* **1,** to reward. **2,** to give an award to.
premio ('pre·mjo) *n.m.* **1,** reward. **2,** prize. **3,** premium.
premioso (pre'mjo·so) *adj.* **1,**

pressing; urging. **2,** exacting. **3,** clumsy; heavy.

premisa (pre'mi·sa) *n.f.* premise.

premonitorio (pre·mo·ni'to·rjo) *adj.* premonitory.

premura (pre'mu·ra) *n.f.* urgency; haste.

prenatal (pre·na'tal) *adj.* prenatal.

prenda ('pren·da) *n.f.* **1,** pledge; security; pawn. **2,** household or personal effect. **3,** pledge; token. **4,** *pl.* talents; natural gifts. **5,** loved one. **6,** *W.I.* jewel. —**juego de prendas,** game of forfeits.

prendar (pren'dar) *v.t.* **1,** to pledge; pawn. **2,** to charm; please. —**prendarse,** *v.r.* to become enamored; be smitten.

prendedor (pren·de'ðor) *n.m.* brooch; pin; clasp.

prender (pren'der) *v.t.* **1,** to seize; apprehend. **2,** to pin; fasten. **3,** *Amer.* to turn on (a light, gas jet, etc.); to light (a fire, match, etc.). —*v.t.* & *i.* to catch; entangle. —*v.i.* **1,** to take; take root. **2,** *Amer.* to light up; be lit; be set afire.

prendero (pren'de·ro) *n.m.* secondhand dealer.

prensa ('pren·sa) *n.f.* **1,** press; vise. **2,** printing press. **3,** press; publishing.

prensar (pren'sar) *v.t.* to press; squeeze. —**prensado,** *n.m.* press; pressing; compressing. —**prensador,** *n.m.* presser.

prensil (pren'sil) *adj.* prehensile.

prensista (pren'sis·ta) *n.m.* pressman.

preñado (pre'ɲa·ðo) *adj.* **1,** pregnant. **2,** full; loaded. —*n.m.* pregnancy.

preñar (pre'ɲar) *v.t.* to make pregnant.

preñez (pre'ɲeθ; -'ɲes) *n.f.* pregnancy.

preocupación (pre·o·ku·pa'θjon; -'sjon) *n.f.* **1,** preoccupation. **2,** worry; concern.

preocupar (pre·o·ku'par) *v.t.* **1,** to preoccupy. **2,** to worry; concern; cause anxiety to.

preordinar (pre·or·ði'nar) *v.t.* to preordain. —**preordinación,** *n.f.* preordination.

preparación (pre·pa·ra'θjon; -'sjon) *n.f.* **1,** preparation. **2,** *Amer.* education; learning.

preparado (pre·pa'ra·ðo) *adj.* **1,** prepared; concocted. **2,** ready. **3,** *Amer.* capable; learned. —*n.m.* preparation; concoction.

preparar (pre·pa'rar) *v.t.* to prepare; ready. —**preparativo,** *adj.* preparatory. —*n.m.* preparation. —**preparatorio,** *adj.* preparatory.

preponderar (pre·pon·de'rar) *v.t.* to preponderate. —**preponderancia,** *n.f.* preponderance. —**preponderante,** *adj.* preponderant.

preposición (pre·po·si'θjon; -'sjon) *n.f.* preposition. —**preposicional,** *also,* **prepositivo** (-'ti·βo) *adj.* prepositional.

prepósito (pre'po·si·to) *n.m.* chairman; president; chief officer or official.

preposterar (pre·pos·te'rar) *v.t.* to reverse; transpose; disarrange.

prepóstero (pre'pos·te·ro) *adj.* **1,** reversed; transposed; out of order. **2,** inopportune.

prepotente (pre·po'ten·te) *adj.* overpowering; dominant. —**prepotencia,** *n.f.* dominance.

prepucio (pre'pu·θjo; -sjo) *n.m.* prepuce.

prerrogativa (pre·rro·ɣa'ti·βa) *n.f.* prerogative.

presa ('pre·sa) *n.f.* **1,** prey. **2,** morsel; portion. **3,** dam. **4,** millpond. **5,** ditch; trench. **6,** booty; prize. —**hacer presa de,** to grab; seize.

presagiar (pre·sa'xjar) *v.t.* to presage; forbode. —**presagio** (-'sa·xjo) *n.m.* presage; foreboding.

presbicia (pres'βi·θja; -sja) *n.f.* farsightedness.

présbita ('pres·βi·ta) *also,* **présbite,** *adj.* farsighted.

presbiterado (pres·βi·te'ra·ðo) *n.m.* **1,** priesthood. **2,** presbytery.

presbiteriano (pres·βi·te'rja·no) *adj.* & *n.m.* Presbyterian.

presbiterio (pres·βi'te·rjo) *n.m.* **1,** presbytery. **2,** chancel.

presbítero (pres'βi·te·ro) *n.m.* presbyter.

presciencia (pres'θjen·θja; pre·'sjen·sja) *n.f.* prescience.

prescindir (pres·θin'dir; pre·sin-) *v.i., fol. by* **de,** to do without; dispense with.

prescribir (pres·kri'βir) *v.t.* & *i.* [*p.p.* **prescrito**] to prescribe.

prescripción (pres·krip'θjon; -'sjon) *n.f.* prescription.

prescripto (pres'krip·to) *adj.* & *n.m.* prescript.

presencia (pre'sen·θja; -sja) *n.f.*

1, presence. 2, appearance; bearing. —**presencia de ánimo**, presence of mind.
presencial (pre·sen'θjal; -'sjal) *adj.* present. —**testigo presencial**, eyewitness.
presenciar (pre·sen'θjar; -'sjar) *v.t.* to witness.
presentable (pre·sen'ta·βle) *adj.* presentable.
presentación (pre·sen·ta'θjon; -'sjon) *n.f.* 1, presentation. 2, personal introduction. —**a presentación**, *comm.* at sight; on demand.
presentar (pre·sen'tar) *v.t.* 1, to present. 2, to introduce. —**presentarse**, *v.r.* 1, to appear; present oneself. 2, to introduce oneself.
presente (pre'sen·te) *adj.* & *n.m.* present. —**hacer presente**, to call attention to; point out. —**por la presente**, by these presents. —**tener presente**, to bear in mind.
presentir (pre·sen'tir) *v.t.* [*infl.:* **sentir**] to have a presentiment or premonition of. —**presentimiento**, *n.m.* presentiment; premonition.
preservar (pre·ser'βar) *v.t.* to preserve; keep. —**preservación**, *n.f.* preservation. —**preservador**, *adj.* preserving. —*n.m.* preserver.
preservativo (pre·ser·βa'ti·βo) *adj.* & *n.m.* preservative. —*n.m.* prophylactic; contraceptive.
presidencia (pre·si'ðen·θja; -sja) *n.f.* 1, presidency. 2, chairmanship; chair. —**presidencial**, *adj.* presidential.
presidente (pre·si'ðen·te) *n.m.* 1, president. 2, chairman; presiding officer. —*adj.* presiding.
presidiario (pre·si'ðja·rjo) *also,* **presidario** (-'ða·rjo) *n.m.* convict.
presidio (pre'si·ðjo) *n.m.* 1, penitentiary. 2, imprisonment.
presidir (pre·si'ðir) *v.t.* to preside over. —*v.i.* to preside.
presilla (pre'si·ʎa; -ja) *n.f.* 1, loop; eye; bight. 2, buttonhole stitching.
presión (pre'sjon) *n.f.* pressure.
presionar (pre·sjo'nar) *v.t., Amer.* to press; exert pressure on.
preso ('pre·so) *adj.* imprisoned; in jail. —*n.m.* prisoner; person apprehended.
prestación (pres·ta'θjon; -'sjon) *n.f.* lending; loan.
prestador (pres·ta'ðor) *n.m.* lender.
prestamista (pres·ta'mis·ta) *n.m.* & *f.* moneylender; pawnbroker.
préstamo ('pres·ta·mo) *n.m.* loan.
prestancia (pres'tan·θja; -sja) *n.f.* 1, excellence. 2, handsomeness.
prestar (pres'tar) *v.t.* 1, to lend; loan. 2, to give (help, attention, etc.). 3, to keep (silence, patience, etc.). —**prestarse**, *v.r.* to lend oneself *or* itself. —**dar prestado**, to lend; loan. —**pedir prestado**, to borrow; ask for loan of. —**tomar prestado**, to borrow; take as a loan.
presteza (pres'te·θa; -sa) *n.f.* promptness; speed; haste.
prestidigitación (pres·ti·ði·xi·ta'θjon; -'sjon) *n.f.* prestidigitation. —**prestidigitador**, *n.m.* prestidigitator.
prestigio (pres'ti·xjo) *n.m.* prestige. —**prestigioso**, *adj.* renowned; reputable.
presto ('pres·to) *adj.* 1, quick; swift; prompt. 2, ready; prepared. —*adv.* soon; quickly. —**de presto**, promptly; swiftly.
presumible (pre·su'mi·βle) *adj.* presumable.
presumido (pre·su'mi·ðo) *adj.* conceited; presumptuous.
presumir (pre·su'mir) *v.t.* to presume; surmise; conjecture. —*v.i.* to presume; boast; be conceited.
presunción (pre·sun'θjon; -'sjon) *n.f.* 1, presumption. 2, presumptuousness; conceit.
presuntamente (pre·sun·ta·'men·te) *adv.* 1, presumptively. 2, seemingly.
presuntivo (pre·sun'ti·βo) *adj.* presumptive; supposed.
presunto (pre'sun·to) *adj.* 1, presumed; assumed. 2, presumptive.
presuntuoso (pre·sun'two·so) *adj.* presumptuous. —**presuntuosidad**, *n.f.* presumptuousness.
presuponer (pre·su·po'ner) *v.t.* [*infl.:* **poner**] 1, to presuppose. 2, to estimate; draw up a budget of.
presuposición (pre·su·po·si'θjon; -'sjon) *n.f.* presupposition.
presupuesto (pre·su'pwes·to) *n.m.* budget. —**presupuestar**, *v.t.* & *i.* to budget. —**presupuestario**, *adj.* budgetary.
presura (pre'su·ra) *n.f.* 1, anxiety. 2, promptness; haste. 3, obstinacy; persistence.
presuroso (pre·su'ro·so) *adj.* prompt; hasty.
pretencioso (pre·ten'θjo·so; -'sjo·so) *adj.* pretentious.
pretender (pre·ten'der) *v.t.* 1, to

pretend. 2, to aspire to. 3, to seek to; attempt to. 4, *Amer.* to court; woo.
pretendiente (pre·ten'djen·te) *n.m.* 1, pretender. 2, *Amer.* suitor.
pretensión (pre·ten'sjon) *n.f.* 1, pretension. 2, pretentiousness.
preter- (pre·ter) *prefix* preter-; beyond; more than: *preternatural,* preternatural.
preterir (pre·te'rir) *v.t.* [*defect., used only in inf. & p.p.*] to ignore; omit.
pretérito (pre'te·ri·to) *adj. & n.m.* preterit.
preternatural (pre·ter·na·tu'ral) *adj.* preternatural.
pretexto (pre'teks·to) *n.m.* pretext. —**pretextar,** *v.t.* to give as pretext.
pretil (pre'til) *n.m.* railing; parapet.
pretina (pre'ti·na) *n.f.* 1, waistband. 2, belt, girdle; sash.
pretor (pre'tor) *n.m.* praetor. —**pretorial,** *adj.* praetorial. —**pretoriano,** *adj.* praetorian.
prevalecer (pre·βa·le'θer; -'ser) *v.i.* [*pres.ind.* **prevalezco** (-'leθ·ko; -'les·ko); *pres.subjve.* **prevalezca** (-ka)] to prevail.
prevaler (pre·βa'ler) *v.i.* [*infl.:* **valer**] = **prevalecer.** —**prevalerse,** *v.r.* to avail oneself.
prevaricación (pre·βa·ri·ka·'θjon; -'sjon) *n.f.* 1, prevarication. 2, dereliction; inobservance.
prevaricador (pre·βa·ri·ka'ðor) *adj.* 1, prevaricating. 2, remiss; inobservant. —*n.m.* prevaricator.
prevaricar (pre·βa·ri'kar) *v.i.* [*pres.subjve.* **prevarique** (-'ri·ke); *pret.* **prevariqué** (-'ke)] 1, to prevaricate. 2, to be remiss or derelict. 3, to transgress. 4, *colloq.* to talk nonsense; ramble.
prevención (pre·βen'θjon; -'sjon) *n.f.* 1, prevention. 2, supply; store (*as of provisions*). 3, bias; prepossession. 4, police station. 5, guardhouse; guardroom. —**a prevención,** just in case.
prevenido (pre·βe'ni·ðo) *adj.* 1, ready; prepared. 2, forewarned. 3, alert; watchful; vigilant. 4, well stocked; well supplied.
prevenir (pre·βe'nir) *v.t.* [*infl.:* **venir**] 1, to prepare; make ready. 2, to forewarn. 3, to warn; admonish. 4, to forestall. —**prevenirse,** *v.r.* to prepare oneself; make ready.
preventivo (pre·βen'ti·βo) *adj.* preventive. —*adj. & n.m.* preventative.
prever (pre'βer) *v.t.* [*infl.:* **ver**] to foresee; anticipate.
previo ('pre·βjo) *adj.* previous; prior.
previsible (pre·βi'si·βle) *adj.* foreseeable.
previsión (pre·βi'sjon) *n.f.* foresight; providence. —**previsión social,** social security.
previsor (pre·βi'sor) *adj.* foresighted; provident.
prez (preθ; pres) *n.m. or f.* praise; honor.
priesa ('prje·sa) *n.f.* = **prisa.**
prieto ('prje·to) *adj.* 1, dark; black. 2, closely packed; firm. 3, miserly; tight. —*adj. & n.m., Amer.* negro.
prima ('pri·ma) *n.f.* 1, female cousin. 2, *comm.* premium. 3, bounty; allowance. 4, government grant; subsidy.
primacía (pri·ma'θi·a; -'si·a) *n.f.* primacy.
primada (pri'ma·ða) *n.f., colloq.* 1, hoax; prank. 2, naïveté; naïve act.
primado (pri'ma·ðo) *n.m.* primate; bishop.
prima donna ('pri·ma 'ðon·na; -'ðo·na) *n.f.* [*pl.* **prima donnas**] prima donna.
primar (pri'mar) *v.i.* to excel.
primario (pri'ma·rjo) *adj.* primary.
primate (pri'ma·te) *n.m., zool.* primate.
primavera (pri·ma'βe·ra) *n.f.* 1, spring; springtime; prime. 2, primrose. 3, gaiety; liveliness; color.
primaveral (pri·ma·βe'ral) *adj.* 1, spring (*attrib.*); springlike. 2, gay; lively; colorful.
primazgo (pri'maθ·ɣo; -'mas·ɣo) *n.m.* cousinship.
primer (pri'mer) *adj.* = **primero** *before a masc. noun.* —**Primer Ministro,** Prime Minister.
primera (pri'me·ra) *n.f.* 1, *mech.* first gear. 2, *fencing* first position.
primerizo (pri·me'ri·θo; -so) *adj.* 1, earliest; beginning; maiden. 2, firstborn. —*n.m.* 1, firstborn; firstling. 2, novice; beginner.
primero (pri'me·ro) *adj., adv. & n.m.* first. —*adj.* 1, foremost. 2, former; original. —*adv.* firstly. —**de buenas a primeras,** all at once; suddenly. —**de primera,** of superior

quality; firstrate. —**primera dama,** *theat.* leading lady. —**primeros auxilios,** first aid.
primicia (pri'mi·θja; -sja) *n.f.* **1,** first fruits; first pickings. **2,** *journalism, Amer.* scoop.
primitivo (pri·mi'ti·βo) *adj.* & *n.m.* primitive.
primo ('pri·mo) *adj.* **1,** prime; first. **2,** excellent; choice. —*n.m.* **1,** cousin. **2,** *colloq.* naïve person. —**primo hermano; primo carnal,** first cousin.
primogénito (pri·mo'xe·ni·to) *adj.* & *n.m.* firstborn. —**primogenitura,** *n.f.* primogeniture.
primor (pri'mor) *n.m.* **1,** artistry; delicacy. **2,** exquisite beauty. **3,** artistic gem.
primordial (pri·mor'ðjal) *adj.* primordial.
primoroso (pri·mo'ro·so) *adj.* artistic; delicate; exquisite.
princesa (prin'θe·sa; -'se·sa) *n.f.* princess.
principado (prin·θi'pa·ðo; prin·si-) *n.m.* principality.
principal (prin·θi'pal; -si'pal) *adj.* & *n.m.* & *f.* principal; main; chief.
príncipe ('prin·θi·pe; -si·pe) *n.m.* prince. —*adj.* first; foremost. —**principesco** (-'pes·ko) princely.
principiante (prin·θi'pjan·te; prin·si-) *n.m.* [*fem.* **-ta**] beginner; apprentice.
principiar (prin·θi'pjar; prin·si-) *v.t.* to begin.
principio (prin'θi·pjo; -'si·pjo) *n.m.* **1,** principle. **2,** beginning. **3,** origin.
pringar (prin'gar) *v.t.* [*pres.subjve.* **pringue** ('prin·gue) *pret.* **pringué** (-'ge)] **1,** to dip in grease. **2,** to smear. —**pringarse,** *v.r., colloq.* to profiteer; make shady profits.
pringón (prin'gon) *adj., colloq.* greasy; dirty. —*n.m., colloq.* grease stain.
pringoso (prin'go·so) *adj.* greasy; fat.
pringue ('prin·ge) *n.m.* **1,** fat; dripping. **2,** dirt; filth.
prior (pri'or; prjor) *n.m.* prior. —**priora,** *n.f.* prioress.
prioridad (pri·o·ri'ðað; prjo-) *n.f.* priority.
prisa ('pri·sa) *n.f.* haste; promptness. —**a prisa,** quickly; swiftly. —**dar prisa a,** to hurry (someone). —**darse prisa,** to hurry; make haste. —**estar de prisa; tener prisa,** to be in a hurry.
prisco ('pris·ko) *n.m.* a variety of peach.
prisión (pri'sjon) *n.f.* **1,** prison. **2,** imprisonment. **3,** shackle; fetter; bond.
prisionero (pri·sjo'ne·ro) *n.m.* prisoner.
prisma ('pris·ma) *n.m.* prism. —**prismático** (-'ma·ti·ko) *adj.* prismatic. —**prismáticos,** *n.m.pl.* binoculars.
prístino ('pris·ti·no) *adj.* pristine; primeval.
privación (pri·βa'θjon; -'sjon) *n.f.* privation.
privada (pri'βa·ða) *n.f.* privy.
privado (pri'βa·ðo) *adj.* **1,** private. **2,** unconscious; senseless; stunned. —*n.m.* confidant; favorite.
privanza (pri'βan·θa; -sa) *n.f.* favor; special regard; favoritism.
privar (pri'βar) *v.t.* **1,** to deprive. **2,** to make unconscious; render senseless. —*v.i.* to have favor; enjoy favor. —**privarse,** *v.r.* **1,** to deprive oneself. **2,** to become unconscious. —**privarse de,** to forgo; give up.
privativo (pri·βa'ti·βo) *adj.* **1,** personal; peculiar. **2,** privative.
privilegio (pri·βi'le·xjo) *n.m.* privilege. —**privilegiado,** *adj.* privileged. —**privilegiar,** *v.t.* to favor; grant privilege to.
pro (pro) *prep., adv.* & *n.m. or f.* pro. —**¡buena pro!,** hearty appetite! —**de pro,** worthy. —**el pro y el contra,** the pros and cons. —**en pro,** for; in favor.
pro- (pro) *prefix* pro-. **1,** in favor of: *profrancés,* pro-French. **2,** on behalf of; in place of: *procónsul,* proconsul. **3,** forward: *proseguir,* proceed. **4,** outward: *proyectar,* project. **5,** before (*in time or place*): *prólogo,* prologue; *proscenio,* proscenium.
proa ('pro·a) *n.f.* **1,** prow; bow. **2,** *aero.* nose.
probable (pro'βa·βle) *adj.* probable. —**probabilidad,** *n.f.* probability.
probación (pro·βa'θjon; -'sjon) *n.f.* **1,** probation. **2,** = **prueba.**
probado (pro'βa·ðo) *adj.* tried; proven.
probador (pro·βa'ðor) *n.m.* **1,** sampler; taster. **2,** fitting room. —*adj.* sampling; tasting.

probadura (pro·βa'ðu·ra) *n.f.* sampling; tasting.
probar (pro'βar) *v.t.* [*pres.ind.* **pruebo**; *pres.subjve.* **pruebe**] 1, to prove. 2, to sample; try; taste. 3, to try on. —*v.i.* 1, *fol. by* **a**, to try to; attempt to. 2, to suit; be suitable.
probatorio (pro·βa'to·rjo) *adj.* probationary.
probeta (pro'βe·ta) *n.f.* 1, test tube. 2, mercury manometer. 3, *photog.* developing pan.
probidad (pro·βi'ðað) *n.f.* probity.
problema (pro'βle·ma) *n.m.* problem. —**problemático** (-'ma·ti·ko) *adj.* problematic.
probo ('pro·βo) *adj.* upright; honest.
probóscide (pro'βos·θi·ðe; -'βo·si·ðe) *n.f.* proboscis.
procaz (pro'kaθ; -'kas) *adj.* impudent; pert. —**procacidad** (-θi'ðað; -si'ðað) *n.f.* impudence; pertness.
procedencia (pro·θe'ðen·θja; -se·'ðen·sja) *n.f.* 1, source. 2, place of origin.
procedente (pro·θe'ðen·te; pro·se-) *adj.* 1, originating. 2, fitting; apt. 3, rightful; lawful.
proceder (pro·θe'ðer; -se'ðer) *v.i.* 1, to proceed; go on. 2, to act; behave. 3, to arise; stem; originate. 4, to be fitting; be rightful. 5, *fol. by* **contra**, to bring suit against; proceed against. —*n.m.* conduct; behavior; action.
procedimiento (pro·θe·ði·'mjen·to; pro·se-) *n.m.* 1, procedure. 2, *law* proceedings (*pl.*).
prócer ('pro·θer; -ser) *adj.* exalted; lofty. —*n.m.* exalted personage; great patriot.
procesado (pro·θe'sa·ðo; pro·se-) *adj.* 1, legal; of or pert. to legal proceedings. 2, accused; indicted. —*n.m.* defendant.
procesal (pro·θe'sal; -se'sal) *adj.* of or pert. to legal proceedings; legal.
procesamiento (pro·θe·sa'mjen·to; pro·se-) *n.m.* 1, prosecution. 2, indictment.
procesar (pro·θe'sar; -se'sar) *v.t.* 1, to process. 2, to indict; prosecute.
procesión (pro·θe'sjon; -se'sjon) *n.f.* procession. —**procesional**, *adj.* processional.
proceso (pro'θe·so; -'se·so) *n.m.* 1, process. 2, *law* trial; proceedings (*pl.*).
proclama (pro'kla·ma) *n.f.* 1, announcement; public notice. 2, manifesto. 3, *usu.pl.* marriage banns.
proclamar (pro·kla'mar) *v.t.* to proclaim. —**proclamación**, *n.f.* proclamation.
proclive (pro'kli·βe) *adj.* inclined; disposed. —**proclividad**, *n.f.* proclivity.
procomún (pro·ko'mun) *n.m.* public welfare. *Also*, **procomunal**.
procónsul (pro'kon·sul) *n.m.* proconsul. —**proconsulado**, *n.m.* proconsulate. —**proconsular**, *adj.* proconsular.
procrear (pro·kre'ar) *n.f.* to procreate. —**procreación**, *n.f.* procreation. —**procreador**, *adj.* procreating. —*n.m.* procreator.
procura (pro'ku·ra) *n.f.* 1, power of attorney; commission. 2, = **procuraduría**. 3, diligence. —**en procura de**, *Amer.* 1, in search of. 2, in an attempt to.
procuración (pro·ku·ra'θjon; -'sjon) *n.f.* 1, enterprise; diligence. 2, power of attorney; commission. 3, = **procuraduría**. 4, procurement.
procurador (pro·ku·ra'ðor) *n.m.* 1, procurator. 2, solicitor; attorney. 3, agent; proctor; representative. 4, *polit.* deputy.
procuraduría (pro·ku·ra·ðu'ri·a) *n.f.* office of a legal representative, proctor, attorney, solicitor, etc.
procurar (pro·ku'rar) *v.t.* 1, to procure; secure. 2, to attempt; endeavor. 3, to manage; look after. 4, *Amer.* to cause; bring about.
prodigalidad (pro·ði·ɣa·li'ðað) *n.f.* prodigality.
prodigar (pro·ði'ɣar) *v.t.* [*pres. subjve.* **prodigue** (-'ði·ɣe); *pret.* **prodigué** (-'ɣe)] to lavish; squander.
prodigio (pro'ði·xjo) *n.m.* prodigy. —**prodigioso**, *adj.* prodigious.
pródigo ('pro·ði·ɣo) *adj.* & *n.m.* prodigal.
producción (pro·ðuk'θjon; -'sjon) *n.f.* production.
producir (pro·ðu'θir; -'sir) *v.t.* [*infl.:* **conducir**] 1, to produce. 2, to yield; bear. 3, to cause; bring about.
productivo (pro·ðuk'ti·βo) *adj.* productive; fruitful. —**productividad**, *n.f.* productivity.
producto (pro'ðuk·to) *n.m.* 1, product. 2, *often pl.* produce.
productor (pro·ðuk'tor) *adj.* pro-

ducing. —*n.m.* 1, producer. 2, worker.

proemio (pro'e·mjo) *n.m.* preface; introduction. —**proemial,** *adj.* prefatory; introductory.

proeza (pro'e·θa; -sa) *n.f.* prowess; heroic deed.

profanar (pro·fa'nar) *v.t. to* profane; defile. —**profanación,** *n.f., also,* **profanamiento,** *n.m.* profanation. —**profanador,** *adj.* profaning; defiling. —*n.m.* profaner; defiler.

profanidad (pro·fa·ni'ðað) *n.f.* 1, profanity. 2, immodesty; excess.

profano (pro'fa·no) *adj.* 1, profane. 2, secular. 3, lay; uninformed.

profecía (pro·fe'θi·a; -'si·a) *n.f.* prophecy.

proferir (pro·fe'rir) *v.t.* [*infl.:* **conferir**] to utter.

profesar (pro·fe'sar) *v.t.* 1, to profess. 2, to exercise; practice (an art or science). 3, to teach. —*v.i.* to take the vows of a religious order.

profesión (pro·fe'sjon) *n.f.* profession. —**profesional,** *adj.* & *n.m.* & *f.* professional.

profeso (pro'fe·so) *adj.* professed; avowed.

profesor (pro·fe'sor) *n.m.* professor; teacher.

profesorado (pro·fe·so'ra·ðo) *n.m.* 1, professorate. 2, professoriate. 3, professorship.

profesoral (pro·fe·so'ral) *adj.* professorial.

profeta (pro'fe·ta) *n.m.* prophet. —**profético,** *adj.* prophetic. —**profetisa,** *n.f.* prophetess.

profetizar (pro·fe·ti'θar; -'sar) *v.t.* & *i.* [*pres.subjve.* **profetice** (-'ti·θe; -se); *pret.* **profeticé** (-'θe; -'se)] to prophesy.

proficiente (pro·fi'θjen·te; -'sjen·te) *adj.* proficient. —**proficiencia,** *n.f* proficiency.

profiláctico (pro·fi'lak·ti·ko) *adj.* & *n.m.* prophylactic. —**profiláctica,** *n.f.* hygiene.

profilaxis (pro·fi'lak·sis) *n.f.* prophylaxis.

prófugo ('pro·fu·ɣo) *adj.* escaping; escaped; fugitive. —*n.m.* 1, fugitive from justice; escapee. 2, *mil.* deserter.

profundizar (pro·fun·di'θar; -'sar) *v.t.* [*pres.subjve.* **profundice** (-'di·θe; -se): *pret.* **profundicé** (-'θe; -'se)] 1, to deepen. 2, to fathom; delve into.

profundo (pro'fun·do) *adj.* deep; profound. —**profundidad,** *n.f.* depth; profundity.

profuso (pro'fu·so) *adj.* profuse. —**profusión,** *n.f.* profusion; profuseness.

progenie (pro'xe·nje) *n.f.* 1, ancestry; lineage. 2, progeny.

progenitor (pro·xe·ni'tor) *n.m.* parent; progenitor. —**progenitura,** *n.f.* primogeniture.

prognosis (proɣ'no·sis) *n.f.* prognosis.

programa (pro'ɣra·ma) *n.m.* program.

programar (pro·ɣra'mar) *v.t., electronics* to program. —**programación,** *n.f., electronics* programming.

progresar (pro·ɣre'sar) *v.i.* to progress.

progresión (pro·ɣre'sjon) *n.f.* progression.

progresista (pro·ɣre'sis·ta) *adj.* & *n.m.* & *f.* progressive.

progresivo (pro·ɣre'si·βo) *adj.* progressive.

progreso (pro'ɣre·so) *n.m.* progress.

prohibición (pro·i·βi'θjon; -'sjon) *n.f.* prohibition. —**prohibicionista,** *n.m.* & *f.* prohibitionist.

prohibir (pro·i'βir) *v.t.* to prohibit; forbid.

prohibitivo (pro·i·βi'ti·βo) *adj.* prohibitive.

prohibitorio (pro·i·βi'to·rjo) *adj.* prohibitory.

prohijar (pro·i'xar) *v.t.* to adopt. —**prohijamiento,** *n.m., also,* **prohijación,** *n.f.* adoption.

prohombre (pro'om·bre) *n.m.* great man; respected man.

prójima ('pro·xi·ma) *n.f., colloq.* woman of questionable reputation.

prójimo ('pro·xi·mo) *n.m.* fellow being; *Bib.* neighbor.

prole ('pro·le) *n.f.* offspring; progeny.

proletario (pro·le'ta·rjo) *adj.* & *n.m.* proletarian. —**proletariado,** *n.m.* proletariat.

proliferación (pro·li·fe·ra'θjon; -'sjon) *n.f.* proliferation.

prolífico (pro'li·fi·ko) *adj.* prolific.

prolijidad (pro·li·xi'ðað) *n.f.* 1, neatness; fastidiousness. 2, prolixity.

prolijo (pro'li·xo) *adj.* 1, excessively tidy or neat; fastidious. 2, prolix; tedious.

prologar (pro·lo'ɣar) *v.t.* [*pres. subjve.* **prologue** (-'lo·ɣe); *pret.*

prologué (-'ɣe)] to write a prologue or preface to; prologue; preface.
prólogo ('pro·lo·ɣo) *n.m.* prologue.
prolongación (pro·lon·ga'θjon; -'sjon) *n.f., also,* **prolongamiento,** *n.m.* prolongation; extension.
prolongado (pro·lon'ga·ðo) *adj.* **1,** elongated. **2,** prolonged; extended.
prolongar (pro·lon'gar) *v.t.* [*pres.subjve.* **prolongue** (-'lon·ge); *pret.* **prolongué** (-'ge)] to prolong; extend. —**prolongarse,** *v.r.* to last; extend.
promediar (pro·me'ðjar) *v.t.* to average. —*v.i.* **1,** to mediate. **2,** to reach the middle; be half over: *antes de promediar el mes de agosto,* before the middle of August.
promedio (pro'me·ðjo) *n.m.* **1,** average. **2,** *math.* mean.
promesa (pro'me·sa) *n.f.* promise.
prometedor (pro·me·te'ðor) *adj.* promising.
Prometeo (pro·me'te·o) *n.m.* Prometheus.
prometer (pro·me'ter) *v.t.* to promise. —*v.i.* to give promising indications. —**prometerse,** *v.r.* to become betrothed; become engaged.
prometido (pro·me'ti·ðo) *n.m.* **1,** betrothed. **2,** promise.
prometio (pro'me·tjo) *n.m.* promethium.
prominente (pro·mi'nen·te) *adj.* prominent. —**prominencia,** *n.f.* prominence.
promiscuo (pro'mis·kwo) *adj.* promiscuous. —**promiscuidad,** *n.f.* promiscuity.
promisión (pro·mi'sjon) *n.f.* promise.
promisorio (pro·mi'so·rjo) *adj.* promissory.
promoción (pro·mo'θjon; -'sjon) *n.f.* **1,** promotion. **2,** group of individuals promoted or graduated together; class.
promontorio (pro·mon'to·rjo) *n.m.* promontory.
promotor (pro·mo'tor) *adj.* promoting. —*n.m.* promoter. *Also,* **promovedor** (-βe'ðor).
promover (pro·mo'βer) *v.t.* [*infl.:* **mover**] to promote.
promulgar (pro·mul'ɣar) *v.t.* [*pres.subjve.* **promulgue** (-'mul·ɣe); *pret.* **promulgué** (-'ɣe)] to promulgate. —**promulgación,** *n.f.* promulgation. —**promulgador,** *n.m.* promulgator.
prono ('pro·no) *adj.* prone.
pronombre (pro'nom·bre) *n.m.* pronoun. —**pronominal** (-mi'nal) *adj.* pronominal.
pronosticar (pro·nos·ti'kar) *v.t.* [*pres.subjve.* **pronostique** (-'ti·ke); *pret.* **pronostiqué** (-'ke)] to prognosticate; forecast. —**pronosticación,** *n.f.* prognostication. —**pronosticador,** *adj.* prognostic; forecasting.
pronóstico (pro'nos·ti·ko) *n.m.* **1,** forecast; prediction. **2,** prognosis. —**pronóstico de vida,** life expectancy.
prontamente (pron·ta'men·te) *adv.* promptly.
prontitud (pron·ti'tuð) *n.f.* **1,** promptness. **2,** quick wit. **3,** quick temper.
pronto ('pron·to) *adj.* **1,** prompt; quick. **2,** ready; prepared. —*n.m., colloq.* sudden impulse. —*adv.* **1,** soon. **2,** promptly; quickly. —**al pronto,** at first. —**de pronto, 1,** suddenly. **2,** *comm., Mex.* down; as down payment. —**por lo pronto,** in the meantime; for the time being; provisionally. —**tan pronto como,** as soon as.
prontuario (pron'twa·rjo) *n.m.* **1,** compendium; handbook. **2,** dossier; record.
pronunciación (pro·nun·θja·'θjon; -sja'sjon) *n.f.* pronunciation.
pronunciamiento (pro·nun·θja·'mjen·to; -sja'mjen·to) *n.m.* **1,** military uprising; insurrection. **2,** *law* pronouncement of a sentence.
pronunciar (pro·nun'θjar; -'sjar) *v.t.* **1,** to pronounce; utter. **2,** to deliver (a speech). —**pronunciarse,** *v.r.* **1,** to rebel; rise in mutiny. **2,** to declare oneself; decide.
propagación (pro·pa·ɣa'θjon; -'sjon) *n.f.* **1,** propagation. **2,** dissemination; spreading.
propagador (pro·pa·ɣa'ðor) *adj.* propagating. —*n.m.* propagator.
propaganda (pro·pa'ɣan·da) *n.f.* propaganda. —**propagandista,** *n.m.* & *f.* propagandist.
propagar (pro·pa'ɣar) *v.t.* [*pres. subjve.* **propague** (-'pa·ɣe); *pret.* **propagué** (-'ɣe)] to propagate.
propalar (pro·pa'lar) *v.t.* to divulge.
propano (pro'pa·no) *n.m.* propane.

propasarse (pro·pa'sar·se) *v.r.* to overstep one's bounds; forget oneself.
propender (pro·pen'der) *v.i.* to tend; be prone; be inclined.
propensión (pro·pen'sjon) *n.f.* propensity; tendency.
propenso (pro'pen·so) *adj.* inclined; susceptible.
propiciar (pro·pi'θjar; -'sjar) *v.t.* to propitiate. —**propiciación,** *n.f.* propitiation. —**propiciatorio,** *adj.* propitiatory.
propicio (pro'pi·θjo; -sjo) *adj.* propitious; favorable.
propiedad (pro·pje'ðað) *n.f.* **1,** property. **2,** ownership. **3,** propriety. **4,** quality; peculiarity.
propietario (pro·pje'ta·rjo) *n.m.* proprietor; owner; landlord. —*adj.* proprietary.
propina (pro'pi·na) *n.f.* **1,** gratuity; tip. **2,** *Amer.* child's allowance.
propinar (pro·pi'nar) *v.t.* **1,** to give a drink to; treat to a drink. **2,** to administer (a medicine). **3,** to deliver (a blow, beating, etc.).
propincuo (pro'pin·kwo) *adj.* close; near. —**propincuidad,** *n.f.* propinquity.
propio ('pro·pjo) *adj.* **1,** one's own; peculiar. **2,** suitable; proper. **3,** characteristic; typical. **4,** natural. **5,** very same; identical. —*n.m.* **1,** municipal land or resources. **2,** messenger.
proponer (pro·po'ner) *v.t.* [*infl.:* **poner**] **1,** to propose. **2,** to propound. —**proponerse,** *v.r.* to resolve; determine. —**proponente,** *n.m.* & *f.* proponent.
proporción (pro·por'θjon; -'sjon) *n.f.* **1,** proportion. **2,** extent; scope. **3,** chance; opportunity. —**a proporción de,** in accordance with; commensurate with.
proporcionado (pro·por·θjo'na·ðo; -sjo'na·ðo) *adj.* **1,** proportionate. **2,** proportioned. **3,** convenient; suitable.
proporcional (pro·por·θjo'nal; -sjo'nal) *adj.* proportional.
proporcionar (pro·por·θjo'nar; -sjo'nar) *v.t.* **1,** to proportion. **2,** to provide; furnish. **3,** to adjust; to adapt.
proposición (pro·po·si'θjon; -'sjon) *n.f.* **1,** proposition. **2,** proposal. **3,** *gram.* sentence; clause.
propósito (pro'po·si·to) *n.m.* purpose. —**a propósito, 1,** by the way. **2,** apropos. **3,** [*also,* **de propósito**] on purpose. —**fuera de propósito,** irrelevant; beside the point.
propuesta (pro'pwes·ta) *n.f.* proposal.
propuesto (pro'pwes·to) *v., p.p. of* **proponer.**
propugnar (pro·puɣ'nar) *v.t.* to champion; support.
propulsa (pro'pul·sa) *n.f.* rejection.
propulsar (pro·pul'sar) *v.t.* to propel.
propulsión (pro·pul'sjon) *n.f.* propulsion.
propulsor (pro·pul'sor) *n.m.* propellant. —*adj.* propellent; propulsive.
prorrata (pro'rra·ta) *n.f.* quota; assessment. —**a prorrata,** in proportion.
prorratear (pro·rra·te'ar) *v.t.* to prorate. —**prorrateo** (-'te·o) *n.m.* proportioning; proration.
prórroga ('pro·rro·ɣa) *also,* **prorrogación,** *n.f.* extension of time; deferment.
prorrogar (pro·rro'ɣar) *v.t.* [*pres. subjve.* **prorrogue** (-'rro·ɣe); *pret.* **prorrogué** (-'ɣe)] to extend; defer.
prorrumpir (pro·rrum'pir) *v.i., usu.fol. by* **en,** to burst into (tears, laughter, etc.).
prosa ('pro·sa) *n.f.* **1,** prose. **2,** *colloq.* verbosity; wordiness.
prosaico (pro'sai·ko) *adj.* prosaic.
prosapia (pro'sa·pja) *n.f.* ancestry; lineage.
proscenio (pros'θe·njo; pro'se-) *n.m.* proscenium.
proscribir (pros·kri'βir) *v.t.* [*p.p.* **proscrito**] to proscribe.
proscripción (pros·krip'θjon; -'sjon) *n.f.* proscription; exile.
proscrito (pros'kri·to) *v., p.p. of* **proscribir.** —*n.m.* outlaw; exile.
prosecución (pro·se·ku'θjon; -'sjon) *n.f.* **1,** prosecution; continuance. **2,** pursuit.
proseguir (pro·se'ɣir) *v.t.* & *i.* [*infl.:* **seguir**] to continue. —*v.i.* to proceed.
prosélito (pro'se·li·to) *n.m.* proselyte.
prosista (pro'sis·ta) *n.m.* & *f.* prose writer.
prosodia (pro'so·ðja) *n.f.* prosody. —**prosódico** (-'so·ði·ko) *adj.* prosodic.
prospecto (pros'pek·to) *n.m.* **1,** prospectus. **2,** *Amer.* prospect.

prosperar (pros·pe'rar) *v.t.* & *i.* to prosper.
próspero ('pros·pe·ro) *adj.* 1, prosperous; thriving. 2, propitious. —**prosperidad,** *n.f.* prosperity.
próstata ('pros·ta·ta) *n.f.* prostate gland. —**prostático** (-'ta·ti·ko) *adj.* prostatic.
prosternarse (pros·ter'nar·se) *v.r.* to prostrate oneself.
prostíbulo (pros'ti·βu·lo) *n.m.* house of prostitution.
prostituir (pros·ti·tu'ir) *v.t.* [*infl.:* **constituir**] to prostitute. —**prostitución,** *n.f.* prostitution.
prostituta (pros·ti'tu·ta) *n.f.* prostitute.
protagonista (pro·ta·ɣo'nis·ta) *n.m.* & *f.* protagonist; star. —**protagonizar,** *v.t.* [*infl.:* **agonizar**] to star in (a play, film, etc.).
protección (pro·tek'θjon; -'sjon) *n.f.* protection. —**proteccionismo,** *n.m.* protectionism. —**proteccionista,** *adj.* & *n.m.* & *f.* protectionist.
protector (pro·tek'tor) *adj.* protecting; protective. —*n.m.* protector. —**protectora,** *n.f.* protectress.
protectorado (pro·tek·to'ra·ðo) *n.m.* protectorate.
protectriz (pro·tek'triθ; -'tris) *adj.fem.* protecting; protective. —*n.f.* protectress.
proteger (pro·te'xer) *v.t.* [*pres. ind.* **protejo** (-'te·xo); *pres.subjve.* **proteja** (-xa)] to protect.
protegido (pro·te'xi·ðo) *n.m.* protégé.
proteína (pro·te'i·na) *n.f.* protein.
protesta (pro'tes·ta) *n.f.* 1, protest. 2, protestation. *Also,* **protestación.**
protestante (pro·tes'tan·te) *adj.* & *n.m.* & *f.* Protestant. —**protestantismo,** *n.m.* Protestantism.
protestar (pro·tes'tar) *v.t.* & *i.* to protest.
protesto (pro'tes·to) *n.m., comm.* protest.
proto- (pro·to) *prefix* proto-. 1, first: *protomártir,* protomartyr. 2, *chem.* having a lower proportion than that of the other members in a series of compounds: *protocloruro,* protochloride.
protoactinio (pro·to·ak'ti·njo) *n.m.* protactinium.
protocolizar (pro·to·ko·li'θar; -'sar) *v.t.* [*pres.subjve.* **protocolice** (-'li·θe; -se); *pret.* **protocolicé** (-'θe; -'se)] 1, to incorporate in a protocol. 2, *colloq.* to make official; put official sanction on.
protocolo (pro·to'ko·lo) *n.m.* protocol. —**protocolar,** *adj.* of or pert. to protocol. —**protocolario,** *adj.* in accordance with protocol.
protón (pro'ton) *n.m.* proton.
protoplasma (pro·to'plas·ma) *n.m.* protoplasm. —**protoplasmático** (-'ma·ti·ko) *adj.* protoplasmic.
prototipo (pro·to'ti·po) *n.m.* prototype.
protozoario (pro·to·θo'a·rjo; -so'a·rjo) *adj.* & *n.m.* protozoan. *Also,* **protozoo** (-'θo·o; -'so·o).
protuberancia (pro·tu·βe'ran·θja; -sja) *n.f.* protuberance. —**protuberante,** *adj.* protuberant.
provecho (pro'βe·tʃo) *n.m.* benefit; advantage; good. —**¡buen provecho!,** *colloq.* good appetite! —**de provecho,** useful; of use.
provechoso (pro·βe'tʃo·so) *adj.* 1, profitable. 2, beneficial; good. 3, useful; advantageous.
proveedor (pro·βe·e'ðor) *n.m.* 1, purveyor; supplier. 2, caterer. 3, provider.
proveeduría (pro·βe·e·ðu'ri·a) *n.f.* 1, storehouse. 2, purveyor's shop.
proveer (pro·βe'er) *v.t.* [*pret.* **proveí, proveyó** (-'jo); *ger.* **proveyendo** (-'jen·do); *p.p.* **proveído, provisto** (-'βis·to)] 1, to provide. 2, to stock; provision. 3, to confer (a title, honor, etc.). 4, *law* to decide.
proveído (pro·βe'i·ðo) *n.m., law* judgment; decision.
proveimiento (pro·βei'mjen·to) *n.m.* supply; provisioning.
provenir (pro·βe'nir) *v.i.* [*infl.:* **venir**] 1, to arise; originate. 2, to result.
proverbio (pro'βer·βjo) *n.m.* proverb. —**proverbial,** *adj.* proverbial.
providencia (pro·βi'ðen·θja; -sja) *n.f.* 1, provision; preparation; measure. 2, foresight. 3, providence. —**providencial,** *adj.* providential.
providente (pro·βi'ðen·te) *adj.* provident.
próvido ('pro·βi·ðo) *adj.* 1, provident. 2, propitious; benevolent.
provincia (pro'βin·θja; -sja) *n.f.* province. —**provincial,** *adj.* provincial. —**provincialismo,** *n.m.* provincialism.
provinciano (pro·βin'θja·no; -'sja·no) *adj.* & *n.m.* provincial.

provisión (pro·βi'sjon) *n.f.* provision. —**provisional,** *adj.* provisional.
provisorio (pro·βi'so·rjo) *adj.* provisional; temporary.
provisto (pro'βis·to) *v., p.p.* of **proveer.**
provocador (pro·βo·ka'ðor) *adj.* **1,** provoking; provocative. **2,** inviting; tempting.
provocar (pro·βo'kar) *v.t.* [*pres. subjve.* **provoque** (-'βo·ke); *pret.* **provoqué** (-'ke)] **1,** to provoke. **2,** to move; incite. **3,** to invite; tempt. —**provocación,** *n.f.* provocation. —**provocativo,** *adj.* provocative.
proxeneta (prok·se'ne·ta) *n.m.* procurer; go-between. —*n.f.* procuress.
próximamente (prok·si·ma·'men·te) *adv.* **1,** immediately; closely. **2,** soon. **3,** approximately.
proximidad (prok·si·mi'ðað) *n.f.* proximity. —**proximidades,** *n.f.pl.* environs; vicinity (*sing.*).
próximo ('prok·si·mo) *adj.* **1,** next. **2,** close; near. —**el próximo pasado,** last month.
proyección (pro·jek'θjon; -'sjon) *n.f.* projection.
proyectar (pro·jek'tar) *v.t.* **1,** to project. **2,** to plan.
proyectil (pro·jek'til) *n.m.* projectile.
proyectista (pro·jek'tis·ta) *n.m.* & *f.* designer; planner.
proyecto (pro'jek·to) *n.m.* project; plan.
proyector (pro·jek'tor) *n.m.* projector. —**proyector cinematográfico,** movie projector.
prudencia (pru'ðen·θja; -sja) *n.f.* prudence. —**prudencial,** *adj.* prudential.
prudente (pru'ðen·te) *adj.* prudent.
prueba ('prwe·βa) *n.f.* **1,** proof. **2,** trial; test. **3,** ordeal. **4,** fitting; trying on. **5,** sample; sampling. **6,** *Amer.* sporting event. **7,** tryout. —**a prueba,** *comm.* **1,** on trial; on approval. **2,** warranted; perfect. —**a prueba de,** proof against; -proof: *a prueba de agua,* waterproof. —**de prueba,** firm; solid; durable.
pruebe ('prwe·βe) *v., pres.subjve.* of **probar.**
pruebo ('prwe·βo) *v., pres.ind.* of **probar.**
prurito (pru'ri·to) *n.m.* **1,** itch. **2,** *fig.* yen; craving.
prusiano (pru'sja·no) *adj.* & *n.m.* Prussian.
pseudo ('seu·ðo) *adj.* pseudo.
pseudo- *also,* **seudo-** (seu·ðo) *prefix* pseudo-; false; deceptive: *pseudomorfo, also, seudomorfo,* pseudomorph.
pseudónimo (seu'ðo·ni·mo) *adj.* & *n.m.* = **seudónimo.**
psico- *also,* **sico-** (si·ko) *prefix* psycho-; mind; mental process: *psicología; sicología,* psychology.
psicoanálisis (si·ko·a'na·li·sis) *n.m.* psychoanalysis. —**psicoanalista** (-'lis·ta) *n.m.* & *f.* psychoanalyst. —**psicoanalítico** (-'li·ti·ko) *adj.* psychoanalytic. —**psicoanalizar** *v.t.* [*infl.:* **analizar**] to psychoanalyze.
psicología (si·ko·lo'xi·a) *n.f.* psychology. —**psicológico** (-'lo·xi·ko) *adj.* psychological. —**psicólogo** (-'ko·lo·ɣo) *n.m.* psychologist.
psiconeurosis (si·ko·neu'ro·sis) *n.f.* psychoneurosis.
psicópata (si'ko·pa·ta) *n.m.* & *f.* psychopath. —**psicopatía** (-'ti·a) *n.f.* psychopathy. —**psicopático** (-'pa·ti·ko) *adj.* psychopathic.
psicopatología (si·ko·pa·to·lo·'xi·a) *n.f.* psychopathology.
psicosis (si'ko·sis) *n.f.* psychosis.
psicosomático (si·ko·so'ma·ti·ko) *adj.* psychosomatic.
psicoterapia (si·ko·te'ra·pja) *n.f.* psychotherapy. —**psicoterapeuta** (-'peu·ta) *n.m.* & *f.* psychotherapist.
psicótico (si'ko·ti·ko) *adj.* & *n.m.* psychotic.
psiquiatría (si·kja'tri·a) *n.f.* psychiatry. —**psiquiatra** (-'kja·tra) *n.m.* & *f.* psychiatrist. —**psiquiátrico** (-'kja·tri·ko) *adj.* psychiatric.
psíquico ('si·ki·ko) *adj.* psychic.
psiquis ('si·kis) *n.m.* or *f.* psyche.
psitacosis (si·ta'ko·sis) *n.f.* psittacosis; parrot fever.
psoríasis (so'ri·a·sis) *also,* **psoriasis** (so'rja·sis) *n.f.* psoriasis.
ptero- (te·ro) *prefix* ptero-; wing: *pterodáctilo,* pterodactyl.
-ptero (pte·ro) *suffix* -pterous; -pter; *forming adjectives and nouns denoting* having a specified number or kind of wings: *himenóptero,* hymenopterous; hymenopter.
pterodáctilo (te·ro'ðak·ti·lo) *n.m.* pterodactyl.

ptomaina (to·ma'i·na) *n.f.* ptomaine. *Also,* **tomaína.**
¡pu! (pu) *interj.* ugh!
púa ('pu·a) *n.f.* **1,** spine; quill; barb; prickle. **2,** tooth (*of a comb*). **3,** phonograph needle. **4,** plectrum. **5,** *colloq.* wily person; sharp person.
púber ('pu·βer) *also,* **púbero** ('pu·βe·ro) *adj.* pubescent.
pubertad (pu·βer'tað) *n.f.* puberty.
pubescencia (pu·βes'θen·θja; -βe'sen·sja) *n.f.* pubescence. **—pubescente,** *adj.* pubescent.
pubis ('pu·βis) *n.m.sing.* & *pl.* **1,** pubis. **2,** pubes. **—púbico** ('pu·βi·ko) *adj.* pubic.
publicación (pu·βli·ka'θjon; -'sjon) *n.f.* publication.
publicano (pu·βli'ka·no) *n.m.* publican.
publicar (pu·βli'kar) *v.t.* [*pres. subjve.* **publique** (-'βli·ke); *pret.* **publiqué** (-'ke)] **1,** to publish. **2,** to publicize; make public.
publicidad (pu·βli·θi'ðað; -si·'ðað) *n.f.* **1,** publicity. **2,** advertising. **—en publicidad,** publicly.
publicista (pu·βli'θis·ta; -'sis·ta) *n.m.* & *f.* publicist.
publicitario (pu·βli·θi'ta·rjo; -si'ta·rjo) *adj.* **1,** publicity (*attrib.*). **2,** advertising (*attrib.*).
público ('pu·βli·ko) *adj.* public. **—*n.m.*** **1,** public. **2,** audience.
puchero (pu'tʃe·ro) *n.m.* **1,** pot. **2,** pout; grimace.
puches ('pu·tʃes) *n.m. or f.pl.* pap (*sing.*); porridge (*sing.*); gruel (*sing.*).
pucho ('pu·tʃo) *n.m., Amer.* **1,** cigar or cigarette stub; butt. **2,** butt end. **3,** leftover; trash; rubbish.
pude ('pu·ðe) *v., pret. of* **poder.**
pudelar (pu·ðe'lar) *v.t.* to puddle (iron). **—pudelación,** *n.f.* puddling. **—pudelador,** *n.m.* puddler.
pudendo (pu'ðen·do) *adj., in* **partes pudendas,** private parts; pudenda.
pudibundez (pu·ði·βun'deθ; -'des) *n.f.* prudery; priggery.
pudibundo (pu·ði'βun·do) *adj.* = **pudoroso.**
pudicicia (pu·ði'θi·θja; -'si·sja) *n.f.* modesty; chastity; decorum.
púdico ('pu·ði·ko) *adj.* modest; chaste.
pudiendo (pu'ðjen·do) *v., ger. of* **poder.**
pudiente (pu'ðjen·te) *adj.* rich; well-to-do.
pudín (pu'ðin) *n.m.* = **budín.**
pudor (pu'ðor) *n.m.* modesty; decency. **—pudoroso,** *adj.* modest; decent.
pudrición (pu·ðri'θjon; -'sjon) *n.f.* = **putrefacción.**
pudrimiento (pu·ðri'mjen·to) *n.m* putrefaction; rotting.
pudrir (pu'ðrir) *v.t.* [*p.p.* **podrido**] **1,** to putrefy; rot. **2,** to pester; annoy. **—*v.i.*** [*also, refl.,* **pudrirse**] to rot; rot away.
pueble ('pwe·βle) *v., pres.subjve. of* **poblar.**
pueblerino (pue·βle'ri·no) *adj.* small-town.
pueblo ('pwe·βlo) *n.m.* **1,** small town; village. **2,** people; populace. **3,** people; nation. **4,** pueblo.
pueblo ('pwe·βlo) *v., pres.ind. of* **poblar.**
pueda ('pwe·ða) *v., pres.subjve. of* **poder.**
puedo ('pwe·ðo) *v., pres.ind. of* **poder.**
puente ('pwen·te) *n.m.* **1,** bridge. **2,** *naut.* deck.
puerca ('pwer·ka) *n.f.* **1,** sow; pig. **2,** slut.
puerco ('pwer·ko) *n.m.* **1,** pig; hog. **2,** pork. **—*adj.*** piggish. **—puerco espín,** (es'pin) porcupine.
pueril (pwe'ril) *adj.* puerile. **—puerilidad,** *n.f.* puerility.
puerperal (pwer·pe'ral) *adj.* puerperal.
puerro ('pwe·rro) *n.m.* leek.
puerta ('pwer·ta) *n.f.* door. **—puerta falsa; puerta excusada,** private door; back door.
puerto ('pwer·to) *n.m.* **1,** port. **2,** mountain pass; defile. **3,** harbor; haven. **—puerto seco,** inland port of entry.
puertorriqueño (pwer·to·rri·'ke·ɲo) *adj.* & *n.m.* Puerto Rican.
pues (pwes) *conj.* **1,** for; since; because; inasmuch as. **2,** then; therefore. **—*interj.*** well; why; well, yes. **—pues bien,** now then; well. **—pues que,** since; inasmuch as.
puesta ('pwes·ta) *n.f.* **1,** setting (*as of the sun*). **2,** stake (*at cards*). **3,** bet; amount bet. **4,** clutch of eggs. **5,** *colloq.* a putting on or wearing of a garment.
puestero (pwes'te·ro) *n.m.* vendor; seller (*at a stand or booth*).
puesto ('pwes·to) *v., p.p. of* **poner.**

—*adj.*, *usu. with* **bien** *or* **mal,** dressed; attired. —*n.m.* **1,** post; station. **2,** position; place. **3,** stand; booth. —**puesto que, 1,** though. **2,** for; since.
¡puf! (puf) *interj.* ugh!
púgil ('pu·xil) *n.m.* pugilist; boxer.
pugilato (pu·xi'la·to) *n.m.* **1,** pugilism; boxing. **2,** fight; boxing match. **3,** contention; rivalry.
pugilismo (pu·xi'lis·mo) *n.m.* pugilism; boxing. —**pugilista,** *n.m.* & *f., Amer.* pugilist; boxer.
pugna ('puɣ·na) *n.f.* struggle; strife.
pugnacidad (puɣ·na·θi'ðað; -si·'ðað) *n.f.* pugnacity.
pugnar (puɣ'nar) *v.i.* to struggle; strive.
pugnaz (puɣ'naθ; -'nas) *adj.* pugnacious.
puja ('pu·xa) *n.f.* **1,** bid; bidding. **2,** struggle.
pujador (pu·xa'ðor) *n.m.* bidder.
pujanza (pu'xan·θa; -sa) *n.f.* vigor; energy; might. —**pujante,** *adj.* vigorous; energetic.
pujar (pu'xar) *v.t.* **1,** to push; further; advance. **2,** to bid up. —*v.i.* **1,** to struggle; push. **2,** to bid (*as in an auction*). **3,** *colloq.* to snivel; pout.
pujo ('pu·xo) *n.m.* **1,** straining at stool or in urinating. **2,** irresistible impulse. **3,** craving; desire; eagerness. **4,** attempt, esp. an unsuccessful one.
pulcro ('pul·kro) *adj.* neat; tidy. —**pulcritud** (-kri'tuð) *n.f.* pulchritude.
pulchinela (pul·tʃi'ne·la) *n.m.* = **polichinela.**
pulga ('pul·ɣa) *n.f.* flea. —**juego de la pulga,** tiddlywinks. —**no aguantar pulgas,** *colloq.* to brook no nonsense. —**tener malas pulgas,** *colloq.* to have a nasty disposition; be irascible.
pulgada (pul'ɣa·ða) *n.f.* inch.
pulgar (pul'ɣar) *n.m.* thumb.
pulgoso (pul'ɣo·so) *adj.* flea-bitten; flea-ridden. *Also, Amer.,* **pulguiento** (-'ɣjen·to).
pulido (pu'li·ðo) *adj.* polished; refined. —**pulidez** (-'ðeθ; -'ðes) *n.f.* polish; refinement.
pulidor (pu·li'ðor) *n.m.* polisher. —*adj.* polishing.
pulimentar (pu·li·men'tar) *v.t.* to polish; buff.
pulimento (pu·li'men·to) *n.m.* polish; gloss.
pulir (pu'lir) *v.t.* to polish.
pulmón (pul'mon) *n.m.* lung. —**pulmonado,** *adj.* pulmonate. —**pulmonar,** *adj.* pulmonary.
pulmonía (pul·mo'ni·a) *n.f.* pneumonia.
pulmotor (pul·mo'tor) *n.m.* pulmotor.
pulóver (pu'lo·βer) *n.m.* pullover.
pulpa ('pul·pa) *n.f.* pulp.
pulpería (pul·pe'ri·a) *n.f., Amer.* general store. —**pulpero,** *n.m., Amer.* storekeeper.
púlpito ('pul·pi·to) *n.m.* pulpit.
pulpo ('pul·po) *n.m.* cuttlefish; octopus.
pulposo (pul'po·so) *adj.* pulpy.
pulque ('pul·ke) *n.m.* fermented juice of the maguey; pulque.
pulsación (pul·sa'θjon; -'sjon) *n.f.* pulsation.
pulsada (pul'sa·ða) *n.f.* pulse beat.
pulsador (pul·sa'ðor) *n.m.* push button.
pulsar (pul'sar) *v.t.* **1,** to pluck; strum. **2,** to take the pulse of. —*v.i.* to pulse; pulsate; throb.
pulsear (pul·se'ar) *v.i.* to hand-wrestle.
pulsera (pul'se·ra) *n.f.* bracelet; wristlet.
pulso ('pul·so) *n.m.* pulse. —**a pulso, 1,** by sheer exertion. **2,** freehand, as in drawing.
pulular (pu·lu'lar) *v.i.* to swarm; teem.
pulverización (pul·βe·ri·θa'θjon; -sa'sjon) *n.f.* **1,** pulverization. **2,** spraying.
pulverizar (pul·βe·ri'θar; -'sar) *v.t.* [*pres.subjve.* **pulverice** (-'ri·θe; -se); *pret.* **pulvericé** (-'θe; -'se)] **1,** to pulverize. **2,** to spray; spray with an atomizer.
pulla ('pu·ʎa; -ja) *n.f.* satirical remark; barb; gibe.
¡pum! (pum) *interj.* bang!; wham!; pop!
puma ('pu·ma) *n.m.* puma; cougar.
puna ('pu·na) *n.f., So. Amer.* **1,** highland; mountain heights. **2,** mountain sickness.
punce ('pun·θe; -se) *v., pres. subjve. of* **punzar.**
puncé (pun'θe; -'se) *v., 1st pers. sing.pret. of* **punzar.**
punción (pun'θjon; -'sjon) *n.f., med.* puncture; puncturing; lancing.

pundonor (pun·do'nor) *n.m.* honor; pride; integrity.

pundonoroso (pun·do·no'ro·so) *adj.* **1,** delicate; touchy (*in matters of honor*). **2,** upright; honorable.

punible (pu'ni·βle) *adj.* punishable.

punición (pu·ni'θjon; -'sjon) *n.f.* punishment.

punitivo (pu·ni'ti·βo) *adj.* punitive.

punta ('pun·ta) *n.f.* **1,** point; tip; end. **2,** touch; trace; tinge. **3,** grain; speck; bit. **4,** *Amer.* bunch; lot. **5,** = **colilla.** —**puntas,** *n.f.pl.* needlepoint lace. —**a punta de,** *Amer.* by dint of. —**de punta en blanco,** *colloq.* all dressed up. —**de puntas** = **de puntillas.** —**estar de punta,** to be on bad terms.

puntada (pun'ta·ða) *n.f.* **1,** stitch. **2,** hint. **3,** *Amer.* = **punzada.**

puntaje (pun'ta·xe) *n.m.* score; points (*pl.*).

puntal (pun'tal) *n.m.* **1,** prop; support. **2,** *Amer., colloq.* snack. **3,** *naut.* depth of hold.

puntapié (pun·ta'pje) *n.m.* kick.

puntazo (pun'ta·θo; -so) *n.m., Amer.* stab; jab.

punteado (pun·te'a·ðo) *n.m.* pattern of dots or stipples; stippling.

puntear (pun·te'ar) *v.t.* **1,** to dot. **2,** to stitch. **3,** to pluck; strum. —*v.i., naut.* to tack.

punteo (pun'te·o) *n.m.* strumming; plucking.

puntera (pun'te·ra) *n.f.* **1,** toecap. **2,** darn; patch (*on socks or stockings*). **3,** *colloq.* = **puntapié.**

puntería (pun·te'ri·a) *n.f.* **1,** aim. **2,** marksmanship.

puntero (pun'te·ro) *n.m.* **1,** pointer. **2,** hole punch. **3,** stonecutter's chisel. **4,** *Amer.* hand (*of a timepiece*).

puntiagudo (pun·tja'ɣu·ðo) *adj.* pointed; sharp.

puntilla (pun'ti·ʎa; -ja) *n.f.* **1,** lace; lace edging. **2,** brad. **3,** sharp, slender pick. —**dar la puntilla,** *colloq.* to finish off. —**de puntillas,** on tiptoe.

puntillazo (pun·ti'ʎa·θo; -'ja·so) *n.m., colloq.* kick.

puntillo (pun'ti·ʎo; -jo) *n.m.* punctilio. —**puntilloso,** adj. punctilious.

punto ('pun·to) *n.m.* **1,** point. **2,** dot; speck. **3,** period (*punctuation*). **4,** stitch. **5,** notch (*of a belt, strap, etc.*). **6,** catch (*in a stocking*). **7,** aim. **8,** ideal state or condition; peak. **9,** point of honor. **10,** taxi stand. **11,** *colloq.* shrewd one. —**al punto, 1,** right away; immediately. **2,** = **a punto.** —**a punto 1,** ready. **2,** just right; at the right point. **3,** to the point; pertinent. —**a punto de,** at *or* on the point of; just about to. —**a punto fijo,** exactly; with certainty. —**bajar de punto,** to cool off; calm down. —**de punto,** knit; knitted. —**de todo punto,** entirely; completely. —**dos puntos,** colon. —**en punto,** sharp; on the dot. —**poner los puntos sobre las íes,** *colloq.* to get down to brass tacks. —**por punto general,** as a rule; generally. —**por puntos, 1,** from one moment to the next. **2,** point by point; in detail. **3,** scarcely; barely. —**punto en boca,** silence; mum. —**punto final,** end; finish. —**punto menos (que),** almost; well nigh; practically. —**puntos seguidos,** *print.* leaders. —**puntos suspensivos,** suspension points. —**punto y aparte,** period (*at the end of a paragraph*). —**punto y coma,** semicolon. —**punto y seguido,** period (*at the end of a sentence, within a paragraph*). —**subir de punto,** to come up to a peak state or condition.

puntuación (pun·twa'θjon; -'sjon) *n.f.* punctuation.

puntual (pun'twal) *adj.* punctual. —**puntualidad,** *n.f.* punctuality.

puntualizar (pun·twa·li'θar; -'sar) *v.t.* [*pres.subjve.* **puntualice** (-'li·θe; -se); *pret.* **puntualicé** (-'θe; -'se)] **1,** to define; set forth in detail. **2,** to give the finishing touches to. **3,** to fix in one's memory.

puntuar (pun'twar) *v.t.* [*infl.:* **continuar**] to punctuate.

puntura (pun'tu·ra) *n.f.* puncture.

punzada (pun'θa·ða; -'sa·ða) *n.f.*, **1,** [*also,* **punzadura**] prick; pricking. **2,** sharp pain; pang.

punzar (pun'θar; -'sar) *v.t.* [*pres. subjve.* **punce;** *pret.* **puncé**] **1,** to prick; pierce. **2,** to cause a sharp pain in; hurt.

punzó (pun'θo; -'so) *n.m.* poppy red.

punzón (pun'θon; -'son) *n.m.* **1,** punch; puncheon. **2,** awl. **3,** die punch. —**punzón de trazar,** scriber.

puñada (pu'ɲa·ða) *n.f.* = **puñetazo.**

puñado (pu'ɲa·ðo) *n.m.* handful.

—a puñados, 1, by fistfuls; abundantly. 2, by handfuls; sparsely.
puñal (pu'ɲal) *n.m.* dagger. —**puñalada,** *n.f.* stab.
puñetazo (pu·ɲe'ta·θo; -so) *n.m.* blow with the fist; punch. *Also,* **puñete** (-'ɲe·te).
puño ('pu·ɲo) *n.m.* 1, fist. 2, cuff; wristband. 3, handle (*of an umbrella, cane, etc.*). 4, hilt (*of a sword, dagger, etc.*). 5, fistful. 6, *colloq.* hand. 7, *colloq.* courage; strength. 8, *Amer.* = **puñetazo.**
pupa ('pu·pa) *n.f.* 1, cold sore; chap (*of the lips*). 2, = **postilla.** 3, childish expression of pain.
pupila (pu'pi·la) *n.f.* 1, pupil; student. 2, ward. 3, *anat.* pupil.
pupilaje (pu·pi'la·xe) *n.m.* wardship.
pupilo (pu'pi·lo) *n.m.* 1, pupil; student. 2, ward.
pupitre (pu'pi·tre) *n.m.* school desk.
puré (pu're) *n.m.* purée.
pureza (pu're·θa; -sa) *n.f.* purity.
purga ('pur·ɣa) *n.f.* purge.
purgación (pur·ɣa'θjon); -'sjon) *n.f.* 1, purge; purgation. 2, *usu.pl.* gonorrhea.
purgador (pur·ɣa'ðor) *adj.* purging. —*n.m.* steam valve.
purgante (pur'ɣan·te) *adj.* & *n.m.* & *f.* purgative.
purgar (pur'ɣar) *v.t.* [*pres.subjve.* **purgue** ('pur·ɣe); *pret.* **purgué** (-'ɣe)] to purge; cleanse.
purgativo (pur·ɣa'ti·βo) *adj.* & *n.m.* purgative.
purgatorio (pur·ɣa'to·rjo) *n.m.* purgatory.
purificar (pu·ri·fi'kar) *v.t.* [*pres. subjve.* **purifique** (-'fi·ke); *pret.* **purifiqué** (-'ke)] to purify. —**purificación,** *n.f.* purification. —**purificador,** *adj.* purifying. —*n.m.* purifier.
purismo (pu'ris·mo) *n.m.* purism. —**purista,** *adj.* puristic. —*n.m.* purist.
puritano (pu·ri'ta·no) *adj.* puritanical. —*n.m.* puritan. —**puritanismo,** *n.m.* puritanism.
puro ('pu·ro) *adj.* 1, pure. 2, sheer; mere. —*n.m.* cigar. —**oro puro,** solid gold.
púrpura ('pur·pu·ra) *adj.* & *n.f.* purple.
purpúreo (pur'pu·re·o) *adj.* purple; purplish. *Also,* **purpurino** (-'ri·no).
purulento (pu·ru'len·to) *adj.* purulent. —**purulencia,** *n.f.* purulence.
pus (pus) *n.f.* pus.
puse ('pu·se) *v., pret. of* **poner.**
pusilánime (pu·si'la·ni·me) *adj.* pusillanimous. —**pusilanimidad,** *n.f.* pusillanimity.
pústula ('pus·tu·la) *n.f.* pustule. —**pustuloso,** *adj.* pustular.
puta ('pu·ta) *n.f.* whore.
putaísmo (pu·ta'is·mo) *n.m.* 1, harlotry; whoring. 2, brothel.
putativo (pu·ta'ti·βo) *adj.* putative.
putear (pu·te'ar) *v.i., colloq.* to whore.
putería (pu·te'ri·a) *n.f.* 1, = **putaísmo.** 2, [*also,* **putada** (-'ta·ða)] *colloq.* dirty trick.
putero (pu'te·ro) *adj., colloq.* lewd; lecherous. —*n.m.* lecher.
putesco (pu'tes·ko) *adj.* whorish.
putrefacción (pu·tre·fak'θjon; -'sjon) *n.f.* putrefaction.
putrefacto (pu·tre'fak·to) *adj.* putrefied; putrid.
pútrido ('pu·tri·ðo) *adj.* putrid. —**putridez** (-'ðeθ; -'ðes) *n.f.* rottenness.
puya ('pu·ja) *n.f.* 1, goad. 2, snide remark; dig.

Q

Q, q (ku) *n.f.* 20th letter of the Spanish alphabet.
quantum ('kwan·tum) *n.m.* [*pl.* **-ta**] quantum.
que (ke) *rel.pron.* who; whom; that; which. —*conj.* 1, *in subordinate clauses* that: *Él dice que lo hará,* He says that he will do it. *In subjunctive constructions denoting command or request, the clause introduced by* que *is usually rendered in Eng. by* to + inf.: *Quiero que vengas,* I want you to come. 2, *in correlative constructions* whether . . . or: *que quiera que no quiera,* whether he wants to or not. 3, *in*

coordinate clauses, indicating repetition or continuance of an action: habla que habla, talk, talk; talking and talking. **4,** *colloq.* since; for; as: *Léalo, que es interesante,* Read it, for it is interesting. **5,** *in comparisons* than: *Más vale tarde que nunca,* Better late than never. **6,** *in independent clauses expressing indirect command or request,* **que** *is rendered in Eng. by* let: *Que lo haga,* Let him do it. **7,** *colloq.* = **para que**: *Dame el dinero que te compre el libro,* Give me the money so I may buy you the book. —**por . . . que,** no matter how . . .; however . . .: *Por enfermo que esté, tiene que venir,* However sick he is, he has to come.

qué (ke) *interrog. adj. & pron.* which; what. —*adj., in exclamations* what a: *¡qué lástima!,* what a pity!; —*adv., in exclamations* how: *¡qué bonita!,* how pretty! —**a qué,** why; what for. —**¿pues y qué?,** why not?; so what? —**qué de . . .!,** how much . . .!; how many . . .!—**¿Qué más da?,** What's the difference?; What does it matter?

quebracho (ke'βra·tʃo) *n.m.* a tropical tree with very hard wood. *Also,* **quiebrahacha.**

quebrada (ke'βra·ða) *n.f.* **1,** ravine; gorge. **2,** bankruptcy; failure. **3,** *Amer.* brook.

quebrado (ke'βra·ðo) *adj.* **1,** broken. **2,** bankrupt. —*n.m., math.* fraction. —**quebradizo,** *adj.* breakable; fragile; frail.

quebradura (ke·βra'ðu·ra) *n.f.* **1,** break; fracture; rupture. **2,** hernia.

quebrantador (ke·βran·ta'ðor) *adj.* **1,** harrowing; distressing. **2,** debilitating. —*n.m.* breaker.

quebrantahuesos (ke·βran·ta·'we·sos) *n.m.* osprey.

quebrantamiento (ke·βran·ta·'mjen·to) *n.m.* **1,** breakdown; collapse. **2,** breaking; breach. **3,** violation.

quebrantar (ke·βran'tar) *v.t.* **1,** to break; breach. **2,** to crush; break down. **3,** to harrow; distress. **4,** to cool (something hot); take the chill off (something cold). —**quebrantarse,** *v.r.* **1,** to break; become broken. **2,** to break down.

quebranto (ke'βran·to) *n.m.* **1,** breakdown. **2,** despair. **3,** affliction. **4,** damage; loss. **5,** commiseration; pity.

quebrar (ke'βrar) *v.t. & i.* [*pres. ind.* **quiebro;** *pres.subjve.* **quiebre**] to break. —*v.t.* to break; bend. —*v.i.* **1,** to break down; give; fail. **2,** to fail; become bankrupt. —**quebrarse,** *v.r.* **1,** to break; become broken. **2,** to break off; end. **3,** *colloq.* to put forth great effort.

quebrazón (ke·βra'θon; -'son) *n.m.* breaking; breakage.

queche ('ke·tʃe) *n.m.* ketch.

queda ('ke·ða) *n.f.* curfew.

quedar (ke'ðar) *v.i.* **1,** to rest; remain. **2,** to stay; tarry. **3,** to be left; be *or* become; find oneself *or* itself. **4,** *fol. by* **en,** to agree. **5,** *fol. by* **en,** to come to; result in. **6,** *fol. by* **por** *or* **como,** to be taken for; come to be regarded as; seem. **7,** to fit, as clothes. **8,** to come out; turn out. **9,** *Amer.* to be; to be located. —*aux.v., fol. by p.p.* to be *or* become. —**quedarse,** *v.r.* **1,** to remain. **2,** *fol. by* **con,** to keep; hold on to.

quedo ('ke·ðo) *adj.* quiet; silent. —*adv.* softly; quietly.

quehacer (ke·a'θer; -'ser) *n.m.* occupation; chore; odd job.

queja ('ke·xa) *n.f.* **1,** plaint; plaintive cry. **2,** complaint.

quejarse (ke'xar·se) *v.r.* **1,** to cry; lament. **2,** to complain.

quejido (ke'xi·ðo) *n.m.* plaintive sound; groan; moan.

quejoso (ke'xo·so) *adj.* complaining; grumbling; disgruntled.

quejumbre (ke'xum·bre) *n.f.* constant complaining; querulousness.

quejumbroso (ke·xum'bro·so) *adj.* plaintive; querulous.

quema ('ke·ma) *n.f.* **1,** burning. **2,** fire.

quemado (ke'ma·ðo) *n.m.* **1,** something burning *or* burnt. **2,** *colloq.* burnt portion, esp. of rice.

quemador (ke·ma'ðor) *adj.* burning; scorching. —*n.m.* burner.

quemadura (ke·ma'ðu·ra) *n.f.* **1,** burn. **2,** frostbite.

quemar (ke'mar) *v.t. & i.* to burn. —**quemarse,** *v.r.* to burn; be burning.

quemazón (ke·ma'θon; -'son) *n.f.* **1,** burn; burning. **2,** burning sensation. **3,** itch; irritation.

quepa ('ke·pa) *v., pres.subjve. of* **caber.**

quepis ('ke·pis) *n.m.sing. & pl.* = **kepis.**

quepo ('ke·po) *v., 1st pers.sing. pres.ind. of* **caber.**
querella (ke're·ʎa; -ja) *n.f.* **1,** plaint; complaint. **2,** quarrel; dispute; disagreement. **3,** *law* complaint.
querellado (ke·re'ʎa·ðo; -'ja·ðo) *n.m.* defendant.
querellante (ke·re'ʎan·te; -'jan·te) *n.m. & f.* complainant.
querellarse (ke·re'ʎar·se; -'jar·se) *v.r.* to complain.
querelloso (ke·re'ʎo·so; -'jo·so) *adj.* querulous.
querencia (ke'ren·θja; -sja) *n.f.* **1,** love; fondness; affection. **2,** yearning; longing. **3,** haunt; nest; lair.
querendón (ke·ren'don) *adj.* affectionate.
querer (ke'rer) *v.t. & i.* [*pres.ind.* **quiero**; *pres.subjve.* **quiera**; *fut.* **querré** (-'rre); *pret.* **quise**] **1,** to want; wish; will. **2,** to love; like; be fond (of). —*v.impers.* to threaten; be about to. —*n.m.* love; affection. —**como quiera que,** however; no matter how. —**como quiera que sea,** in any case; no matter what. —**cuando quiera,** at any time; whenever. —**donde quiera,** anywhere; wherever. —**sin querer,** involuntarily; unwittingly.
querida (ke'ri·ða) *n.f.* **1,** darling; dear. **2,** mistress.
querido (ke'ri·ðo) *adj.* dear. —*n.m.* **1,** beloved; darling. **2,** lover.
querúbico (ke'ru·βi·ko) *adj.* cherubic.
querubín (ke·ru'βin) *n.m.* cherub. *Also,* **querube** (-'ru·βe).
quesadilla (ke·sa'ði·ʎa; -ja) *n.f.* **1,** cheese cake. **2,** a kind of tart.
quesera (ke'se·ra) *n.f.* **1,** cheese vat. **2,** cheese container. **3,** cheese dish.
quesería (ke·se'ri·a) *n.f.* **1,** cheese store. **2,** cheese dairy.
quesero (ke'se·ro) *adj.* cheese (*attrib.*). —*n.m.* maker or seller of cheese.
queso ('ke·so) *n.m.* cheese.
quevedos (ke'βe·ðos) *n.m.pl.* pince-nez.
¡quia! (kja) *interj.* come now!; you don't say!
quicio ('ki·θjo; -sjo) *n.m.* **1,** hinge post (*of a door or window*). **2,** eye of a hinge. —**fuera de quicio,** unhinged; put out. —**sacar de quicio,** to unhinge; exasperate.
quid (kið) *n.m.* gist; substance; point.
quiebra ('kje·βra) *n.f.* **1,** break; fissure. **2,** bankruptcy.
quiebre ('kje·βre) *v., pres.subjve. of* **quebrar.**
quiebro ('kje·βro) *n.m.* **1,** dodge; shift; twist. **2,** trill. **3,** break or catch in the voice. —*v., pres.ind. of* **quebrar.**
quien (kjen) *rel.pron.* [*pl.* **quienes** ('kje·nes)] who; whom; whoever; whomever; which; whichever. —**quien . . . quien . . .,** one . . . another . . .: *Quien iba a pie, quien a caballo,* One (some) went on foot, another (others) on horseback.
quién (kjen) *interrog.pron.* [*pl.* **quiénes** ('kje·nes)] who; whom; which.
quienquiera (kjen'kje·ra) *indef. pron.* [*pl.* **quienesquiera** (kje·nes-)] whoever; whosoever; whomever; whomsoever; whichever.
quiera ('kje·ra) *v., pres.subjve. of* **querer.**
quiero ('kje·ro) *v., pres.ind. of* **querer.**
quieto ('kje·to) *adj.* still; quiet; calm. —**quietud,** *n.f.* quietude; quiet; stillness.
quijada (ki'xa·ða) *n.f.* jaw; jawbone.
quijote (ki'xo·te) *n.m.* quixotic person. —**quijotada,** *n.f.* quixotic deed or undertaking. —**quijotesco,** *adj.* quixotic. —**quijotismo,** *n.m.* quixotism.
quilate (ki'la·te) *n.m.* carat.
quilo ('ki·lo) *n.m.* = **kilo.**
quilo- (ki·lo) *prefix, var. of* **kilo-:** *quilogramo,* kilogram.
quilla ('ki·ʎa; -ja) *n.f.* keel.
quimera (ki'me·ra) *n.f.* chimera. —**quimérico** (-'me·ri·ko) *adj.* chimerical.
química ('ki·mi·ka) *n.f.* chemistry.
químico ('ki·mi·ko) *adj.* chemical. —*n.m.* chemist.
quimono (ki'mo·no) *n.m.* kimono.
quina ('ki·na) *n.f.* **1,** cinchona bark. **2,** quint (*in games of chance*).
quincalla (kin'ka·ʎa; -ja) *n.f.* **1,** metalware; hardware. **2,** small wares; novelties. **3,** costume jewelry. —**quincallería,** *n.f.* shop dealing in metalware, novelties, etc. —**quincallero,** *n.m.* dealer in metalware, novelties, etc.

quince ('kin·θe; -se) *adj.* & *n.m.* fifteen.

quincena (kin'θe·na; -'se·na) *n.f.* **1,** fortnight. **2,** biweekly allowance or pay. —**quincenal,** *adj.* fortnightly; biweekly.

quinceno (kin'θe·no; -'se·no) *adj.* fifteenth.

quincuagenario (kin·kwa·xe·'na·rjo) *adj.* & *n.m.* = **cincuentón.**

quincuagésimo (kin·kwa'xe·si·mo) *adj.* & *n.m.* fiftieth. —**Quincuagésima,** *n.f.* Quinquagesima.

quindécimo (kin'de·θi·mo; -si·mo) *adj.* & *n.m.* fifteenth.

quingentésimo (kin·xen'te·si·mo) *adj.* & *n.m.* five-hundredth.

quingombó (kin·gom'bo) *n.m.* **1,** okra. **2,** gumbo.

quinientos (ki'njen·tos) *adj.* & *n.m.pl.* [*fem.* **-tas**] five hundred. —*adj.* five-hundredth.

quinina (ki'ni·na) *n.f.* quinine.

quino ('ki·no) *n.m.* cinchona tree.

quinqué (kin'ke) *n.m.* **1,** kerosene lamp; hurricane lamp. **2,** globe lamp.

quinque- (kin·ke) *prefix* quinque-; five: *quinquenal,* quinquennial.

quinquenio (kin'ke·njo) *n.m.* five-year period; quinquennium. —**quinquenal** (-'nal) *adj.* five-year; quinquennial.

quinta ('kin·ta) *n.f.* **1,** country house; villa. **2,** draft; levy. **3,** *music* fifth; quint. **4,** *cards* five of a kind.

quintaesencia (kin·ta·e'sen·θja; sja) *n.f.* quintessence.

quintal (kin'tal) *n.m.* quintal. —**quintal métrico,** 100 kilograms.

quinteto (kin'te·to) *n.m.* quintet.

quintillizo (kin·ti'ʎi·θo; -'ji·so) *adj.* & *n.m.* quintuplet.

quintillón (kin·ti'ʎon; -'jon) *n.m.* a trillion quintillion; *U.S.* nonillion; *Brit.* quintillion.

quinto ('kin·to) *adj.* & *n.m.* fifth. —*n.m.* draftee; conscript.

quintuple ('kin·tu·ple) *n.m.* & *f.*, *Amer.* quintuplet.

quintuplicar (kin·tu·pli'kar) *v.t.* [*pres.subjve.* **quintuplique** (-'pli·ke); *pret.* **quintupliqué** (-'ke)] to quintuple; multiply by five.

quíntuplo ('kin·tu·plo) *adj.* & *n.m.* quintuple.

quinzavo (kin'θa·βo; -'sa·βo) *adj.* & *n.m.* fifteenth.

quiosco *also,* **kiosco** ('kjos·ko) *n.m.* kiosk; stand; booth.

quiro- (ki·ro) *prefix* chiro-; hand: *quiromancia,* chiromancy.

quirófano (ki'ro·fa·no) *n.m.* **1,** operating room. **2,** surgical amphitheater.

quiromancia (ki·ro'man·θja; -sja) *n.f.* chiromancy; palmistry. —**quiromántico** (-ti·ko) *adj.* of or pert. to chiromancy or palmistry. —*n.m.* chiromancer; palmist.

quiropráctica (ki·ro'prak·ti·ka) *n.f.* chiropractic. —**quiropráctico,** *adj.* chiropractic. —*n.m.* chiropractor.

quirúrgico (ki'rur·xi·ko) *adj.* surgical.

quise ('ki·se) *v., pret. of* **querer.**

quisquilla (kis'ki·ʎa; -ja) *n.f.* **1,** petty nuisance. **2,** = **camarón.**

quisquilloso (kis·ki'ʎo·so; -'jo·so) *adj.* **1,** fastidious. **2,** touchy; skittish.

quiste ('kis·te) *n.m.* cyst.

quisto ('kis·to) *adj., in* **bien quisto,** well-liked; **mal quisto,** disliked.

quita ('ki·ta) *n.f.* acquittance; release (*from debt*).

¡quita! ('ki·ta) *interj., colloq.* get out!; get off it!; come on!

quitamanchas (ki·ta'man·tʃas) *n.m.sing.* & *pl.* **1,** spot remover; cleaning fluid. **2,** dry cleaner.

quitanieves (ki·ta'nje·βes) *n.m. sing.* & *pl.* snow plow; snow remover.

quitanza (ki'tan·θa; -sa) *n.f.* quittance.

quitar (ki'tar) *v.t.* **1,** to remove; take away; take off. **2,** to prevent; preclude. —**quitarse,** *v.r.* **1,** to remove; take off, as clothing. **2,** *fol. by* **de,** to quit; abstain from. —**(de) quita y pon, 1,** removable; detachable. **2,** (*of clothing*) casual; slip-on. **3,** *also,* **juego de quita y pon,** the game of put and take. —**quitar del medio** *or* **de en medio,** to get out of the way; to get rid of. —**quitarse de encima,** to get rid of; get off one's shoulders.

quitasol (ki·ta'sol) *n.m.* parasol; sunshade.

quite ('ki·te) *n.m.* **1,** side-stepping; dodge. **2,** parry.

quizás (ki'θas; -'sas) *adv.* maybe; perhaps. *Also,* **quizá.**

quórum ('kwo·rum) *n.m.sing.* & *pl.* quorum.

R

R, r ('e·rre; 'e·re) *n.f.* 21st letter of the Spanish alphabet.
rabada (ra'βa·ða) *n.f.* rump.
rabadán (ra·βa'ðan) *n.m.* head shepherd.
rabadilla (ra·βa'ði·ʎa; -ja) *n.f.* **1,** coccyx; small of the back. **2,** tail end of a bird.
rábano ('ra·βa·no) *n.m.* radish. **—tomar el rábano por las hojas,** *colloq.* to be off the track; get one's wires crossed.
rabí (ra'βi) *n.m.* rabbi.
rabia ('ra·βja) *n.f.* **1,** rage; fury. **2,** rabies.
rabiar (ra'βjar) *v.i.* **1,** to rage; be mad. **2,** to be rabid; have rabies. **—a rabiar,** *colloq.* madly; exceedingly. **—rabiar por,** *colloq.* to crave; be eager for.
rabicorto (ra·βi'kor·to) *adj.* stub-tailed; short-tailed.
rábido ('ra·βi·ðo) *adj.* rabid.
rabieta (ra'βje·ta) *n.f., colloq.* tantrum; fit.
rabillo (ra'βi·ʎo; -jo) *n.m., dim. of* **rabo. —rabillo del ojo,** corner of the eye.
rabínico (ra'βi·ni·ko) *adj.* rabbinical.
rabino (ra'βi·no) *n.m.* rabbi.
rabioso (ra'βjo·so) *adj.* **1,** mad; rabid. **2,** furious; raging.
rabo ('ra·βo) *n.m.* **1,** tail. **2,** tail end. **3,** corner of the eye.
rabona (ra'βo·na) *n.f., in* **hacer rabona,** *also* **hacerse la rabona,** to play hooky.
rabotada (ra·βo'ta·ða) *n.f.* insolent remark; grossness.
racial (ra'θjal; -'sjal) *adj.* racial.
racimo (ra'θi·mo; -'si·mo) *n.m.* **1,** bunch; cluster. **2,** *bot.* raceme.
raciocinar (ra·θjo·θi'nar; ra·sjo·si-) *v.i.* to reason; ratiocinate. **—raciocinación,** *n.f.* ratiocination.
raciocinio (ra·θjo'θi·njo; ra·sjo·'si-) *n.m.* reasoning; ratiocination.
ración (ra'θjon; -'sjon) *n.f.* ration.
racional (ra·θjo'nal; -sjo'nal) *adj.* rational. **—***n.m. or f.* rationale. **—racionalidad,** *n.f.* rationality.
racionalismo (ra·θjo·na'lis·mo; ra·sjo-) *n.m.* rationalism. **—racionalista,** *adj.* rationalistic. **—***n.m.* & *f.* rationalist.
racionar (ra·θjo'nar; ra·sjo-) *v.t.* to ration. **—racionamiento,** *n.m.* rationing.
racismo (ra'θis·mo; -'sis·mo-) *n.m.* racism. **—racista,** *adj.* & *n.m.* & *f.* racist.
racha ('ra·tʃa) *n.f.* **1,** gust of wind. **2,** *colloq.* gush; spate. **3,** *colloq.* streak (*of luck*).
rada ('ra·ða) *n.f.* small bay; inlet; roadstead.
radar (ra'ðar) *n.m.* radar.
radiación (ra·ðja'θjon; -'sjon) *n.f.* radiation.
radiactivo (ra·ði·ak'ti·βo) *adj.* radioactive. **—radiactividad,** *n.f.* radioactivity.
radiado (ra'ðja·ðo) *adj.* radiate.
radiador (ra·ðja'ðor) *n.m.* radiator.
radial (ra'ðjal) *adj.* radial.
radián (ra'ðjan) *n.m.* radian.
radiante (ra'ðjan·te) *adj.* radiant.
radiar (ra'ðjar) *v.t.* & *i.* **1,** to radiate. **2,** to broadcast.
radical (ra·ði'kal) *adj.* & *n.m.* & *f.* radical. **—***n.m., math.; chem.; gram.* radical.
radicalismo (ra·ði·ka'lis·mo) *n.m.* radicalism.
radicar (ra·ði'kar) *v.i.* [*pres.subjve.* **radique;** *pret.* **radiqué**] **1,** to settle; be or become rooted. **2,** to reside; have roots. **—radicarse,** *v.r.* to settle; establish residence.
radio ('ra·ðjo) *n.m.* **1,** radius. **2,** [*also,* **rádium**] radium. **3,** *also fem.* radio set; radio. **4,** spoke; ray. **—***n.f.* = **radiodifusión.**
radio- (ra·ðjo) *prefix* radio-. **1,** radio: *radiotelegrafía;* radiotelegraphy. **2,** radium; radioactive: *radioterapia,* radiotherapy.
radioactivo (ra·ðjo·ak'ti·βo) *adj.* radioactive. **—radioactividad,** *n.f.* radioactivity.
radiocomunicación (ra·ðjo·ko·mu·ni·ka'θjon; -'sjon) *n.f.* radio communication.
radiodifundir (ra·ðjo·ði·fun'dir) *v.i.* to broadcast.
radiodifusión (ra·ðjo·ði·fu'sjon) *n.f.* radio broadcasting.
radiodifusora (ra·ðjo·ði·fu'so·ra) *n.f.* [*also,* **estación radiodifusora**] broadcasting station.

radiodirigido (ra·ðjo·ði·ri'xi·ðo) *adj.* radio-controlled.
radioemisor (ra·ðjo·e·mi'sor) *adj.* transmitting. —*n.m.* radio transmitter. —**radioemisora,** *n.f.* = **radiodifusora.**
radioescucha (ra·ðjo·es'ku·tʃa) *n.m.* & *f.* **1,** radio listener. **2,** radio monitor. **3,** short-wave listener.
radiofonía (ra·ðjo·fo'ni·a) *n.f.* = **radiotelefonía.**
radiofrecuencia (ra·ðjo·fre·'kwen·θja; -sja) *n.f.* radio frequency.
radiografía (ra·ðjo·ɣra'fi·a) *n.f.* **1,** X-ray photograph; radiograph. **2,** radiography. —**radiográfico** (-'ɣra·fi·ko) *adj.* of or for X-rays; X-ray (*attrib.*).
radiograma (ra·ðjo'ɣra·ma) *n.m.* radiogram.
radiolocutor (ra·ðjo·lo·ku'tor) *n.m.* radio announcer.
radiología (ra·ðjo·lo'xi·a) *n.f.* radiology. —**radiológico** (-'lo·xi·ko) *adj.* radiological. —**radiólogo** (ra·'ðjo·lo·ɣo) *n.m.* radiologist.
radiorreceptor (ra·ðjo·rre·θep·'tor; -sep'tor) *adj.* receiving. —*n.m.* radio receiver.
radioscopia (ra·ðjos'ko·pja) *n.f.* radioscopy.
radiotécnico (ra·ðjo'tek·ni·ko) *n.m.* radio technician. —**radiotecnia** (-'tek·nja) *n.f.* radio technology; radio repair.
radiotelefonía (ra·ðjo·te·le·fo·'ni·a) *n.f.* **1,** radiotelephony. **2,** radio; radio communication. —**radioteléfono** (-'le·fo·no) *n.m.* radiotelephone.
radiotelefotografía (ra·ðjo·te·le·fo·to·ɣra'fi·a) *n.f.* **1,** telephotography. **2,** telephotograph.
radiotelegrafía (ra·ðjo·te·le·ɣra'fi·a) *n.f.* wireless telegraphy. —**radiotelegrafista,** *n.m.* & *f.* wireless operator.
radioterapia (ra·ðjo·te'ra·pja) *n.f.* radiotherapy.
radiotransmisor (ra·ðjo·trans·mi'sor) *n.m.* radio transmitter.
radioyente (ra·ðjo'jen·te) *n.m.* & *f.* radio listener.
radique (ra'ði·ke) *v., pres.subjve. of* **radicar.**
radiqué (ra·ði'ke) *v., 1st pers.sing. pret. of* **radicar.**
rádium ('ra·ðjum) *n.m.* radium.
radón (ra'ðon) *n.m.* radon.
raer (ra'er) *v.t.* [*pres.ind.* **raigo;** *pres.subjve.* **raiga,** *also,* **raya;** *pret.* **raí, rayó;** *ger.* **rayendo**] to abrade; wear away; fray.
ráfaga ('ra·fa·ɣa) *n.f.* **1,** gust of wind. **2,** flash. **3,** burst; volley.
rafia ('ra·fja) *n.f.* raffia.
raglán (ra'ɣlan) *n.m.* raglan.
raído (ra'i·ðo) *adj.* **1,** abraded; worn out. **2,** frayed; threadbare. **3,** disreputable; seedy.
raiga ('rai·ɣa) *v., pres.subjve. of* **raer.**
raigambre (rai'ɣam·bre) *n.f.* **1,** *lit.* & *fig.* root; roots (*pl.*). **2,** intertwining of roots.
raigo ('rai·ɣo) *v., pres.ind. of* **raer.**
raigón (rai'ɣon) *n.m.* root (*of a tooth*).
rail (rail) *n.m., R. R.* rail; track.
raíz (ra'iθ; -'is) *n.f.* root. —**a raíz de,** following upon. —**de raíz,** by the roots; entirely. —**echar raíces,** to take root; grow roots.
raja ('ra·xa) *n.f.* **1,** crack; split. **2,** slice. **3,** splinter; split piece of wood.
rajá (ra'xa) *n.m.* rajah.
rajadura (ra·xa'ðu·ra) *n.f.* crack; split; fissure.
rajar (ra'xar) *v.t.* to split; crack. —*v.i., colloq.* to boast; brag. —**rajarse,** *v.r., colloq.* **1,** to quit; give up. **2,** *Amer.* to get out; scram. **3,** to jabber; prattle.
ralea (ra'le·a) *n.f.* sort; breed.
ralear (ra·le'ar) *v.i.* **1,** to thin out; become sparse. **2,** to show one's true colors.
ralo ('ra·lo) *adj.* **1,** sparse. **2,** *Amer.* thin; weak; watery. —**raleza,** *n.f.* sparseness; thinning out.
rallador (ra·ʎa'ðor; ra·ja-) *n.m.* grater.
ralladura (ra·ʎa'ðu·ra; ra·ja-) *n.f.* **1,** shavings (*pl.*); gratings (*pl.*). **2,** scrape; scratch.
rallar (ra'ʎar; -'jar) *v.t.* to grate; shred.
rallo ('ra·ʎo; -jo) *n.m.* = **rallador.**
rama ('ra·ma) *n.f.* **1,** branch. **2,** *print.* chase. —**andarse por las ramas,** to beat around the bush. —**de rama en rama,** shifting; changing. —**en rama,** in unfinished state; unprocessed.
ramada (ra'ma·ða) *n.f.* **1,** = **ramaje. 2,** = **enramada.**
ramaje (ra'ma·xe) *n.m.* branches (*pl.*); boughs (*pl.*); mass of branches.
ramal (ra'mal) *n.m.* **1,** branch;

spur. **2,** ramification; offshoot. **3,** strand (*of a rope*).

ramalazo (ra·ma'la·θo; -so) *n.m.* lash; blow.

ramera (ra'me·ra) *n.f.* whore; harlot.

ramificarse (ra·mi·fi'kar·se) *v.r.* [*pres.subjve.* **ramifique** (-'fi·ke); *pret.* **ramifiqué** (-'ke)] to ramify; branch off. —**ramificación,** *n.f.* ramification; branching off.

ramillete (ra·mi'ʎe·te; -'je·te) *n.m.* **1,** bouquet (*of flowers*). **2,** centerpiece. **3,** bevy of young girls.

ramilletero (ra·mi·ʎe'te·ro; ra·mi·je-) *n.m.* **1,** maker or seller of bouquets. **2,** flower vase. —**ramilletera,** *n.f.* flower girl.

ramo ('ra·mo) *n.m.* **1,** small branch. **2,** bunch; cluster. **3,** sprig; spray. **4,** bouquet. **5,** branch (*of knowledge, study, etc.*). **6,** line (*of trade, business, etc.*). —**Domingo de Ramos,** Palm Sunday.

ramojo (ra'mo·xo) *n.m.* brushwood.

rampa ('ram·pa) *n.f.* ramp.

rampante (ram'pan·te) *adj.* rampant.

ramplón (ram'plon) *adj.* rude; gross; vulgar. —*n.m.* calk (*of a horseshoe*). —**ramplonería,** *n.f.* vulgarity; grossness.

rana ('ra·na) *n.f.* frog. —**no ser rana,** *colloq.* to be no slouch.

rancio ('ran·θjo; -sjo) *adj.* **1,** rancid. **2,** age-old; ancient. **3,** aged. —**ranciarse** (-'θjar·se; -'sjar·se) *v.r.* to become rancid. —**rancidez** (-θi·'ðeθ; -si'ðes) *also,* **ranciedad** (-θje·'ðað; -sje'ðað) *n.f.* rancidity.

ranchería (ran·tʃe'ri·a) *n.f.* group of huts or cabins; small settlement.

ranchero (ran'tʃe·ro) *n.m., Amer.* rancher; ranchman.

rancho ('ran·tʃo) *n.m.* **1,** mess. **2,** large hut or cabin. **3,** *Amer.* ranch. —**hacer rancho,** *colloq.* to make room; move aside. —**hacer rancho aparte,** *colloq.* to go one's own way.

rango ('ran·go) *n.m.* **1,** rank; position. **2,** *Amer.* high social rank. **3,** *Amer.* airs (*pl.*); stateliness; pomposity. —**de rango,** *Amer.* high-class.

rani (ra'ni) *n.f.* ranee.

ranura (ra'nu·ra) *n.f.* **1,** groove. **2,** slot; slit.

rapacería (ra·pa·θe'ri·a; -se'ri·a) *n.f.* **1,** = **rapacidad. 2,** mischievous prank.

rapacidad (ra·pa·θi'ðað; -si'ðað) *n.f.* rapacity.

rapador (ra·pa'ðor) *adj.* shaving. —*n.m., colloq.* barber.

rapadura (ra·pa'ðu·ra) *n.f.* shaving; shave; cropping.

rapapolvo (ra·pa'pol·βo) *n.m., colloq.* sharp reproof; dressing down.

rapar (ra'par) *v.t.* **1,** to shave. **2,** to crop (the hair). **3,** *colloq.* to clean out; rob.

rapaz (ra'paθ; -'pas) *adj.* **1,** rapacious. **2,** predatory. —*n.m.* young boy; lad. —**ave rapaz,** bird of prey.

rape ('ra·pe) *n.m., colloq.* shave; cropping; trimming. —**al rape,** clean; bald.

rapé (ra'pe) *n.m.* snuff.

rápido ('ra·pi·ðo) *adj.* quick; swift; rapid. —*n.m.* **1,** *usu.pl.* rapids. **2,** express train. —**rapidez,** *n.f.* rapidity; swiftness.

rapiña (ra'pi·ɲa) *n.f.* pillage; rapine. —**de rapiña,** of prey.

raposa (ra'po·sa) *n.f.* = **zorra.**

raposear (ra·po·se'ar) *v.i.* to be foxy.

raposera (ra·po'se·ra) *n.f.* foxhole.

raposo (ra'po·so) *n.m.* = **zorro.**

rapsoda (rap'so·ða) *n.m.* bard; reciter of poetry.

rapsodia (rap'so·ðja) *n.f.* rhapsody. —**rapsódico** (-'so·ði·ko) rhapsodic.

raptar (rap'tar) *v.t.* to abduct; kidnap. —**raptor,** *n.m.* abductor; kidnapper.

rapto ('rap·to) *n.m.* **1,** abduction; kidnapping. **2,** rapture. **3,** seizure; spell.

raqueta (ra'ke·ta) *n.f.* **1,** racket (*used in games*). **2,** snowshoe. **3,** croupier's rake.

raquis ('ra·kis) *n.m.sing.* & *pl.* backbone; spine. —**raquídeo** (ra·'ki·ðe·o) *adj.* spinal.

raquítico (ra'ki·ti·ko) *adj.* **1,** rachitic. **2,** rickety; weak. —**raquitismo,** *n.m.* rickets.

raramente (ra·ra'men·te) *adv.* **1,** rarely. **2,** oddly.

rarefacción (ra·re·fak'θjon; -'sjon) *n.f.* rarefaction.

rareza (ra're·θa; -sa) *n.f.* **1,** rarity. **2,** oddity.

raro ('ra·ro) *adj.* **1,** rare; uncommon. **2,** strange; odd. —**rara vez,** *also,* **raras veces,** seldom.

ras (ras) *n.m.* level. —**a ras de,** level with; even with.
rasar (ra'sar) *v.t.* 1, to skim; graze. 2, to level off; make even.
rascacielos (ras·ka'θje·los; 'sje·los) *n.m.sing.* & *pl.* skyscraper.
rascar (ras'kar) *v.t.* [*pres.subjve.* **rasque;** *pret.* **rasqué**] 1, to scratch; scrape. —**rascador,** *n.m.* scratcher; scraper. —**rascadura,** *n.f.* scratching; scraping.
rascatripas (ras·ka'tri·pas) *n.m.* & *f.sing.* & *pl.* poor violinist; fiddler.
rascón (ras'kon) *adj.* tart; sour. —*n.m., ornith.* rail.
rasero (ra'se·ro) *n.m.* 1, leveling stick; skimmer. 2, [*also,* **rasera,** *n.f.*] egg turner; spatula. —**medir con el mismo rasero,** to treat impartially.
rasgado (ras'ɣa·ðo) *adj.* 1, torn; rent. 2, almond-shaped (*of the eyes*). 3, wide (*of the mouth*). —*n.m.* = **rasgón.**
rasgar (ras'ɣar) *v.t.* [*pres.subjve.* **rasgue** ('ras·ɣe); *pret.* **rasgué** (-'ɣe)] to tear; rend; rip.
rasgo ('ras·ɣo) *n.m.* 1, pen stroke; flourish. 2, trait; feature. 3, gesture; act. —**a grandes rasgos,** broadly; in outline.
rasgón (ras'ɣon) *n.m.* rent; tear; rip.
rasguear (ras·ɣe'ar) *v.i.* to strum; pluck; stroke. —**rasgueo** (ras'ɣe·o) *n.m.* stroking; strumming.
rasguñar (ras·ɣu'ɲar) *v.t.* 1, to scratch. 2, to sketch. —**rasguño** (-'ɣu·ɲo) *n.m.* scratch.
raso ('ra·so) *adj.* 1, clear; open. 2, plain. 3, flat. —*n.m.* satin. —**al raso,** in the open; outdoors. —**cielo raso,** 1, flat ceiling. 2, clear sky. —**soldado raso,** private soldier.
raspa ('ras·pa) *n.f.* 1, rasp. 2, fishbone; spine of a fish. 3, *Amer., colloq.* dressing down; scolding.
raspador (ras·pa'ðor) *n.m.* scraper.
raspadura (ras·pa'ðu·ra) *n.f.* 1, scraping. 2, scrape; scratch. 3, erasure. 4, *usu.pl.* shavings.
raspar (ras'par) *v.t.* 1, to rasp; scrape. 2, to graze.
rasque ('ras·ke) *v., pres.subjve. of* **rascar.**
rasqué (ras'ke) *v., 1st pers.sing. pret. of* **rascar.**
rasqueta (ras'ke·ta) *n.f.* scraper.
rasquetear (ras·ke·te'ar) *v.t., Amer.* to scrape; scratch.
rastra ('ras·tra) *n.f.* 1, rake. 2, *agric.* harrow; drag. 3, *naut.* drag; grapnel. 4, string (*as of dried fruit*). 5, trace; sign. —**a la rastra; a rastra; a rastras,** 1, dragging. 2, crawling. 3, *fig.* unwillingly.
rastreador (ras·tre·a'ðor) *n.m.* 1, drag; dredge. 2, tracker; scout.
rastrear (ras·tre'ar) *v.t.* to track; trail. —*v.t.* & *i.* 1, to rake; harrow. 2, to drag; dredge. —*v.i.* to skim *or* hug the ground.
rastreo (ras'tre·o) *n.m.* dragging; dredging.
rastrero (ras'tre·ro) *adj.* 1, creeping; crawling. 2, abject; groveling.
rastrillar (ras·tri'ʎar; -'jar) *v.t.* & *i.* 1, to hackle; comb (flax). 2, to rake. —**rastrillador,** *n.m.* flax dresser.
rastrillo (ras'tri·ʎo; -jo) *n.m.* 1, hackle; flax brake. 2, rake. 3, portcullis.
rastro ('ras·tro) *n.m.* 1, track; trail. 2, rake. 3, slaughterhouse. 4, vestige; trace. 5, [*also, Amer.,* **rastrillo**] open-air bargain market, esp. that of Madrid. 6, harrow.
rastrojo (ras'tro·xo) *n.m.* stubble. —**rastrojera,** *n.f.* stubble field.
rasurar (ra·su'rar) *v.t.* to shave. —**rasuración,** *also,* **rasura** (ra'su·ra) *n.f.* shaving.
rata ('ra·ta) *n.f.* rat. —*n.m., colloq.* = **ratero.**
rataplán (ra·ta'plan) *n.m.* sound of a drum; rub-a-dub.
ratear (ra·te'ar) *v.i.* to pick pockets; filch.
ratería (ra·te'ri·a) *n.f.* 1, petty theft. 2, pettiness; skulduggery.
ratero (ra'te·ro) *adj.* 1, low; mean; contemptible. 2, thieving. —*n.m.* pickpocket; petty thief.
ratificar (ra·ti·fi'kar) *v.t.* [*pres. subjve.* **ratifique** (-'fi·ke); *pret.* **ratifiqué** (-'ke)] to ratify; confirm. —**ratificación,** *n.f.* ratification; confirmation.
rato ('ra·to) *n.m.* period of time; moment; while. —**a ratos perdidos,** in spare time. —**de rato en rato,** *also,* **a ratos,** occasionally.
ratón (ra'ton) *n.m.* mouse.
ratonar (ra·to'nar) *v.t.* to gnaw.
ratonera (ra·to'ne·ra) *n.f.* 1, mouse-trap. 2, mousehole. 3, *fig., colloq.* rathole; hole in the wall.
ratonil (ra·to'nil) *adj.* of *or* pert. to mice; mousy. *Also,* **ratonesco** (-'nes·ko).

raudal (rau'ðal) *n.m.* stream; torrent; flood.
raudo ('rau·ðo) *adj.* rapid; impetuous.
raya ('ra·ja) *n.f.* **1,** stroke; dash; streak; stripe. **2,** boundary; limit. **3,** part (*of the hair*). **4,** *ichthy.* ray; skate. **—a raya,** within bounds. **—pasar de la raya, 1,** [*also, refl.,* **pasarse . . .**] to overstep oneself. **2,** to top it; be the last straw. **—(juego de las) tres en raya,** ticktacktoe.
raya ('ra·ja) *v., pres.subjve. of* **raer.**
rayadillo (ra·ja'ði·ʎo; -jo) *n.m.* striped cotton duck.
rayado (ra'ja·ðo) *adj.* lined; ruled. **—*n.m.*** ruling; lines (*pl.*).
rayar (ra'jar) *v.t.* **1,** to draw lines in *or* on; rule. **2,** to scratch; score. **3,** to underline. **—*v.i.*** **1,** to stand out; excel. **2,** to break, as the dawn. **3,** to border; verge.
rayendo (ra'jen·do) *v., ger. of* **raer.**
rayo ('ra·jo) *n.m.* **1,** beam; ray. **2,** spoke. **3,** thunderbolt. **4,** *fig.* wit; live wire. **—echar rayos,** *colloq.* to blow up; make the sparks fly.
rayó (ra'jo) *v., 3rd pers.sing.pret. of* **raer.**
rayón (ra'jon) *n.m.* rayon.
raza ('ra·θa; -sa) *n.f.* **1,** race. **2,** lineage. **3,** breed; sort. **—de raza,** thoroughbred.
razón (ra'θon; -'son) *n.f.* **1,** reason. **2,** reasoning; argument. **3,** cause; motive. **4,** right; justification. **5,** *math.* ratio. **—a razón de,** at the rate of. **—dar razón de, 1,** to inform of. **2,** to give account of. **—en razón de** *or* **a,** concerning; regarding. **—meter (a uno) en razón,** to enjoin reason (upon someone). **—no tener razón,** to be wrong. **—razón comercial,** business, concern; trade name. **—razón social,** company; firm; company name. **—tener razón,** to be right. **—tomar razón de, 1,** to note down; make a note of. **2,** to record; register.
razonable (ra·θo'na·βle; ra·so-) *adj.* **1,** reasonable. **2,** moderate.
razonamiento (ra·θo·na'mjen·to; ra·so-) *n.m.* reasoning; argument.
razonar (ra·θo'nar; ra·so-) *v.i.* to reason; argue. **—*v.t.*** **1,** to reason out; explain. **2,** to corroborate; support with evidence.
re (re) *n.m., music* re; D.
re- (re) *prefix* re-. **1,** back; reverse action: *reacción,* reaction. **2,** again; anew: *reelegir,* reelect. **3,** resistance; opposition: *rechazar,* reject. **4,** emphasis; intensification: *refuerzo,* reinforcement.
reabrir (re·a'βrir) *v.t.* [*p.p.* **reabierto** (-'βjer·to)] to reopen.
reacción (re·ak'θjon; -'sjon) *n.f.* reaction. **—reaccionar,** *v.i.* to react.
reaccionario (re·ak·θjo'na·rjo; re·ak·sjo-) *adj.* & *n.m.* reactionary.
reacio (re'a·θjo; -sjo) *adj.* obstinate; stubborn.
reactivo (re·ak'ti·βo) *adj.* reactive. **—*n.m.*** reagent.
reactor (re·ak'tor) *n.m.* reactor.
real (re'al) *adj.* **1,** real. **2,** royal; kingly. **3,** fine; splendid. **—*n.m.*** **1,** *mil.* camp. **2,** fair grounds. **3,** a Spanish coin; real. **—sentar los reales,** to encamp. **—levantar los reales,** to break camp.
realce (re'al·θe; -se) *n.m.* **1,** embossment. **2,** splendor; magnificence. **3,** highlight. **4,** emphasis. **5,** enhancement.
realengo (re·a'len·go) *adj.* **1,** royal. **2,** unappropriated, as land. **—*n.m.*** royal patrimony.
realeza (re·a'le·θa; -sa) *n.f.* royalty.
realidad (re·a·li'ðað) *n.f.* **1,** reality; fact. **2,** truth; sincerity.
realismo (re·a'lis·mo) *n.m.* **1,** royalism. **2,** realism.
realista (re·a'lis·ta) *adj.* & *n.m.* & *f.* **1,** royalist. **2,** realist. **—*adj.*** realistic.
realizable (re·a·li'θa·βle; -'sa·βle) *adj.* **1,** realizable. **2,** *comm.* liquid.
realización (re·a·li·θa'θjon; -sa·'sjon) *n.f.* **1,** realization; fulfillment. **2,** *comm.* sale; liquidation.
realizar (re·a·li'θar; -'sar) *v.t.* [*pres.subjve.* **realice** (-'li·θe; -se); *pret.* **realicé** (-'θe; -'se)] **1,** to realize; fulfill. **2,** *comm.* to sell; liquidate.
realzar (re·al'θar; -'sar) *v.t.* [*infl.:* **alzar**] **1,** to emboss. **2,** to highlight. **3,** to enhance; heighten.
reanimar (re·a·ni'mar) *v.t.* **1,** to cheer; to comfort. **2,** to reanimate; resuscitate.
reanudar (re·a·nu'ðar) *v.t.* to resume; continue.
reaparecer (re·a·pa·re'θer; -'ser) *v.i.* [*infl.:* **parecer**] to reappear.
reaparición (re·a·pa·ri'θjon; -'sjon) *n.f.* reappearance.

rearmar (re·ar'mar) *v.t.* to rearm. —**rearme** (-'ar·me) *n.m.* rearmament.
reasumir (re·a·su'mir) *v.t.* to resume. —**reasunción** (-sun'θjon; -'sjon) *n.f.* resumption.
reata (re'a·ta) *n.f.* 1, rope; tether. 2, string of mules or asses.
reavivar (re·a·βi'βar) *v.t.* to revive; revivify.
rebaba (re'βa·βa) *n.f.* 1, burr; mold mark; rough seam. 2, flange; rim.
rebaja (re'βa·xa) *n.f.* 1, abatement; diminution. 2, *comm.* discount; rebate.
rebajar (re·βa'xar) *v.t.* 1, to lessen; diminish; abate. 2, to reduce. 3, to lower. 4, to deduct; discount. 5, *mil.* to relieve *or* excuse (*from a detail*). 6, to abase; demean. 7, to make paler; lighten (a color).
rebanar (re·βa'nar) *v.t.* to slice; cut. —**rebanada,** *n.f.* slice. —**rebanador,** *adj.* slicing. —*n.m.* [*also,* **rebanadora,** *n.f.*] slicer.
rebañar (re·βa'ɲar) *v.t.* to sop up.
rebaño (re'βa·ɲo) *n.m.* flock.
rebasar (re·βa'sar) *v.t.* 1, to exceed; go beyond. 2, *naut.* to skirt; sail past. —*v.i., Amer.* to escape; dodge.
rebate (re'βa·te) *n.m.* fight; encounter.
rebatir (re·βa'tir) *v.t.* 1, to repel; resist. 2, to refute. —**rebatible,** *adj.* refutable; vulnerable.
rebato (re'βa·to) *n.m.* 1, alarm; tocsin. 2, commotion. 3, *mil.* surprise attack.
rebelarse (re·βe'lar·se) *v.r.* 1, to revolt; rebel. 2, to resist.
rebelde (re'βel·de) *adj.* 1, rebellious. 2, stubborn. —*n.m.* & *f.* rebel.
rebeldía (re·βel'di·a) *n.f.* 1, rebelliousness. 2, stubbornness. 3, *law* default; contempt.
rebelión (re·βe'ljon) *n.f.* rebellion; revolt; insurrection.
rebenque (re'βen·ke) *n.m.* whip; lash. —**rebencazo** (-'ka·θo; -so) *n.m.* blow with a lash.
rebisabuelo (re·βis·a'βwe·lo) *n.m.* great-great-grandfather. —**rebisabuela,** *n.f.* great-great-grandmother.
rebisnieto (re·βis'nje·to) *n.m.* great-great-grandson. —**rebisnieta,** *n.f.* great-great-granddaughter.
reblandecer (re·βlan·de'θer; -'ser) *v.t.* [*pres.ind.* **reblandezco** (-'deθ·ko; -'des·ko); *pres.subjve.* **reblandezca** (-ka)] to soften. —**reblandecimiento,** *n.m.* softening.
reborde (re'βor·ðe) *n.m.* rim; edge; flange.
rebosar (re·βo'sar) *v.i.* 1, to run over; overflow. 2, to abound; teem. —**rebosamiento,** *n.m.* overflow; overflowing.
rebotar (re·βo'tar) *v.i.* to rebound. —*v.t.* 1, to cause to rebound. 2, to clinch (a spike or nail). 3, to repel. 4, to raise the nap of. 5, *colloq.* to annoy.
rebote (re'βo·te) *n.m.* rebound. —**de rebote,** 1, indirectly; incidentally. 2, on the rebound.
rebotica (re·βo'ti·ka) *n.f.* back room in a pharmacy.
rebozar (re·βo'θar; -'sar) *v.t.* [*pres.subjve.* **reboce** (-'βo·θe; -se); *pret.* **rebocé** (-'θe; -'se)] 1, to muffle up. 2, *cooking* to coat with batter.
rebozo (re'βo·θo; -so) *n.m.* 1, shawl; muffler. 2, muffling up. 3, pretext. —**de rebozo,** secretly. —**sin rebozo,** frankly; candidly.
rebujo (re'βu·xo) *n.m.* 1, muffler; wrapper. 2, clumsy bundle.
rebullir (re·βu'ʎir; -'jir) *v.i.* [*infl.:* **bullir**] to stir; boil up. *Also, refl.,* **rebullirse.**
rebusca (re'βus·ka) *n.f.* 1, gleaning. 2, gleanings (*pl.*). 3, *colloq.* rummaging; searching.
rebuscado (re·βus'ka·ðo) *adj.* 1, affected; precious. 2, recherché. —**rebuscamiento,** *n.m.* affectation.
rebuscar (re·βus'kar) *v.t.* [*infl.:* **buscar**] 1, to rummage; search through. 2, to glean. —**rebuscárselas,** *colloq.* to contrive; manage.
rebuznar (re·βuθ'nar; re·βus-) *v.i.* to bray. —**rebuzno** (-'βuθ·no; -'βus·no) *n.m.* bray; braying.
recabar (re·ka'βar) *v.t.* to request; obtain by request.
recado (re'ka·ðo) *n.m.* 1, message. 2, errand. 3, gift; compliment. 4, daily shopping *or* marketing. 5, advice; warning. 6, *pl.* compliments; regards. 7, implements (*pl.*); tools (*pl.*). —**recado de escribir,** writing materials.
recaer (re·ka'er) *v.i.* [*infl.:* **caer**] 1, to relapse. 2, to fall upon; befall. —**recaída** (-ka'i·ða) *n.f.* relapse.
recalar (re·ka'lar) *v.i. naut.* to reach land. —*v.t.* to soak; drench. —**recalada,** *n.f.* landfall.
recalcar (re·kal'kar) *v.t.* [*pres.*

subjve. **recalque** (-'kal·ke); *pret.* **recalqué** (-'ke)] **1,** to emphasize. **2,** to bear down on. —*v.i., naut.* to heel; list. —**recalcarse,** *v.r.* to speak emphatically.

recalcitrar (re·kal·θi'trar; -si'trar) *v.i.* to resist; be recalcitrant. —**recalcitrante,** *adj.* recalcitrant.

recalentamiento (re·ka·len·ta·'mjen·to) *n.m.* **1,** reheating. **2,** overheating.

recalentar (re·ka·len'tar) *v.t.* [*infl.:* **calentar**] **1,** to reheat. **2,** to overheat. —**recalentarse,** *v.r.* **1,** to become overheated. **2,** to be spoiled by heat.

recamar (re·ka'mar) *v.t.* to embroider with raised work. —**recamado,** *n.m.* raised embroidery.

recámara (re'ka·ma·ra) *n.f.* **1,** antechamber. **2,** dressing room. **3,** breech (*of a gun*). **4,** chamber (*of a firearm*). **5,** *Mex.* bedroom.

recambiar (re·kam'bjar) *v.t.* **1,** to exchange anew. **2,** *comm.* to redraw.

recambio (re'kam·bjo) *n.m.* **1,** *comm.* reexchange. **2,** *mech.* [*also,* **pieza de recambio**] replacement part.

recamo (re'ka·mo) *n.m.* **1,** = **recamado. 2,** frog (*ornamental fastening*).

recapacitar (re·ka·pa·θi'tar; -si·'tar) *v.t.* **1,** to think over; consider. **2,** *Amer.* to rehabilitate.

recapitular (re·ka·pi·tu'lar) *v.t.* to recapitulate. —**recapitulación,** *n.f.* recapitulation.

recargar (re·kar'ɣar) *v.t.* [*infl.:* **cargar**] **1,** to overload. **2,** to overburden. **3,** to reload; recharge. **4,** to surcharge. **5,** to bear down on. **6,** *law* to increase (the sentence of a convict). **7,** to overadorn. —**recargarse,** *v.r., med.* to suffer an increase in temperature.

recargo (re'kar·ɣo) *n.m.* **1,** extra load; extra burden. **2,** overload; overloading. **3,** surcharge. **4,** *med.* rise in temperature. **5,** *law* new or additional charge.

recatado (re·ka'ta·ðo) *adj.* **1,** circumspect; cautious. **2,** modest; decorous.

recatar (re·ka'tar) *v.t.* **1,** to cloak; conceal. **2,** to sample or taste again. —**recatarse,** *v.r.* to be circumspect; be cautious.

recato (re'ka·to) *n.m.* **1,** circumspection; caution. **2,** modesty; decorousness.

recauchar (re·kau'tʃar) *v.t.* to retread (a tire). *Also,* **recauchutar** (-tʃu'tar). —**recauchaje,** *n.m.* retread; retreading.

recaudación (re·kau·ða'θjon; -'sjon) *n.f.* **1,** collection, esp. of taxes. **2,** collector's office.

recaudar (re·kau'ðar) *v.t.* **1,** to collect, esp. rents or taxes. **2,** to set aside; put in reserve. —**recaudador,** *n.m.* tax collector. —**recaudamiento,** *n.m.* tax collection.

recaudo (re'kau·ðo) *n.m.* **1,** collection, esp. of taxes. **2,** precaution. **3,** reserve; store. **4,** *law* bail; security. —**a buen recaudo, 1,** in safekeeping. **2,** present in one's mind; well in mind.

rece ('re·θe; -se) *v., pres.subjve. of* **rezar.**

recé (re'θe; -'se) *v., 1st pers.sing. pret. of* **rezar.**

recelar (re·θe'lar; re·se-) *v.t.* to fear; suspect; distrust. —**recelarse,** *v.r.* to be afraid; be suspicious. —**recelo** (-'θe·lo; -'se·lo) *n.m.* fear; suspicion; distrust. —**receloso,** *adj.* suspicious; distrustful.

recental (re·θen'tal; re·sen-) *adj.* milk-fed; suckling.

recentísimo (re·θen'ti·si·mo; re·sen-) *adj., superl. of* **reciente.**

recepción (re·θep'θjon; -sep'sjon) *n.f.* **1,** reception. **2,** admission; acceptance. **3,** receiving; receipt. —**recepcionista,** *n.m.* & *f.* receptionist.

receptáculo (re·θep'ta·ku·lo; re·sep-) *n.m.* receptacle.

receptar (re·θep'tar; re·sep-) *v.t.* **1,** to receive; welcome. **2,** to harbor (a fugitive). **3,** to receive (stolen goods).

receptivo (re·θep'ti·βo; re·sep-) *adj.* receptive. —**receptividad,** *n.f.* receptivity; receptiveness.

receptor (re·θep'tor; re·sep-) *adj.* receiving. —*n.m.* receiver.

receso (re'θe·so; re'se-) *n.m.* adjournment; recess.

receta (re'θe·ta; re'se-) *n.f.* **1,** prescription. **2,** recipe.

recetar (re·θe'tar; re·se-) *v.t.* to prescribe.

recetario (re·θe'ta·rjo; re·se-) *n.m.* **1,** prescription book. **2,** recipe book.

recibí (re·θi'βi; re·si-) *n.m., comm.* receipt; payment received.

recibidero (re·θi·βi'ðe·ro; re·si-) *adj.* receivable.
recibidor (re·θi·βi'ðor; re·si-) *n.m.* 1, parlor; drawing room. 2, reception room; waiting room. 3, receiver; recipient. —*adj.* receiving.
recibimiento (re·θi·βi'mjen·to; re·si-) *n.m.* 1, reception. 2, hall; salon. 3, anteroom; reception room.
recibir (re·θi'βir; re·si-) *v.t.* 1, to receive; admit; accept. 2, to meet; greet; welcome. 3, to suffer; sustain. —**recibirse,** *v.r.* 1, to graduate. 2, to be admitted or received.
recibo (re'θi·βo; re'si-) *n.m.* 1, reception. 2, receiving; receipt. —**acusar recibo,** *comm.* to acknowledge receipt. —**estar de recibo,** to be at home to callers.
recidiva (re·θi'ði·βa; re·si-) *n.f., med.* relapse.
reciedumbre (re·θje'ðum·bre; re·sje-) *n.f.* strength; vigor.
recién (re'θjen; -'sjen) *adv.* = **recientemente** *before a p.p.*
reciente (re'θjen·te; re'sjen-) *adj.* recent; new; fresh. —**recientemente,** *adv.* recently; newly; lately.
recinto (re'θin·to; re'sin-) *n.m.* enclosure; precinct; confines (*pl.*).
recio ('re·θjo; -sjo) *adj.* 1, strong; robust. 2, thick; stout; sturdy. 3, rude; coarse. 4, hard; severe; rigorous. 5, loud. 6, sudden; violent. —*adv.* 1, strongly. 2, suddenly; violently. 3, loud; loudly.
recipiente (re·θi'pjen·te; re·si-) *adj.* receiving. —*n.m.* 1, recipient. 2, container; receptacle.
recíproca (re'θi·pro·ka; re'si-) *n.f., math.* reciprocal.
reciprocar (re·θi·pro'kar; re·si-) *v.t.* [*pres.subjve.* **reciproque** (-'pro·ke); *pret.* **reciproqué** (-'ke)] to reciprocate; match. —**reciprocación,** *n.f.* reciprocation.
recíproco (re'θi·pro·ko; re'si-) *adj.* reciprocal. —**reciprocidad** (-θi·'ðað; -si'ðað) *n.f.* reciprocity.
recital (re·θi'tal; re·si-) *n.m.* recital.
recitar (re·θi'tar; re·si-) *v.t.* & *i.* to recite. —**recitación,** *n.f.* recitation. —**recitado,** *n.m.* recitative.
reclamación (re·kla·ma'θjon; -'sjon) *n.f.* 1, demand; claim; complaint. 2, reclamation.
reclamar (re·kla'mar) *v.t.* 1, to claim; reclaim; demand. 2, to decoy (birds). 3, to call; attract. —*v.i.* to protest; complain. —**reclamante,** *n.m.* claimant.
reclamo (re'kla·mo) *n.m.* 1, decoy bird. 2, bird call. 3, allurement; attraction. 4, advertisement. 5, catchword. 6, demand; claim; complaint.
reclinar (re·kli'nar) *v.t.* to rest; lean; recline. —**reclinación,** *n.f.* reclining; recumbency. —**reclinado,** *adj.* reclining; recumbent.
reclinatorio (re·kli·na'to·rjo) *n.m.* prie-dieu.
recluir (re·klu'ir) *v.t.* [*infl.:* **incluir**] to seclude; shut in; confine.
reclusión (re·klu'sjon) *n.f.* seclusion; confinement.
recluso (re'klu·so) *n.m.* inmate; prisoner.
recluta (re'klu·ta) *n.m.* recruit. —*n.f.* [*also,* **reclutamiento,** *n.m.*] recruiting; recruitment. —**reclutar,** *v.t.* to recruit.
recobrar (re·ko'βrar) *v.t.* to recover; regain; recoup. —**recobrarse,** *v.r.* to recover; recuperate. —**recobro** (-'ko·βro) *n.m.* recovery; recuperation.
recocer (re·ko'θer; -'ser) *v.t.* [*infl.:* **cocer**] 1, to recook. 2, to overcook. 3, to anneal. —**recocerse,** *v.r.* to be consumed with passion.
recocido (re·ko'θi·ðo; -'si·ðo) *adj.* veteran; experienced. —*n.m.* 1, overcooking. 2, reheating. 3, annealing.
recodo (re'ko·ðo) *n.m.* turn; bend; twist.
recoger (re·ko'xer) *v.t.* [*infl.:* **coger**] 1, to get back; receive in return. 2, to gather; pick up. 3, to harvest; reap. 4, to shrink; contract. 5, to lock up. 6, to shelter. 7, to call back; withdraw from distribution. —**recogerse,** *v.r.* 1, to take shelter. 2, to go to bed; retire. 3, to shut oneself off; withdraw.
recogida (re·ko'xi·ða) *n.f.* 1, withdrawal. 2, harvest; reaping. 3, gathering; collection. 4, a picking up; pickup.
recogido (re·ko'xi·ðo) *adj.* shy; withdrawn. —*n.m.* inmate.
recogimiento (re·ko·xi'mjen·to) *n.m.* 1, withdrawal; seclusion. 2, absorption; raptness. 3, house of correction for women.
recolección (re·ko·lek'θjon; -'sjon) *n.f.* 1, reaping; harvest. 2, collection; gathering.

recolectar (re·ko·lek'tar) *v.t.* to collect; gather.
recoleto (re·ko'le·to) *adj.* retired; secluded.
recomendable (re·ko·men'da·βle) *adj.* 1, advisable. 2, commendable.
recomendación (re·ko·men·da·'θjon; -'sjon) *n.f.* 1, recommendation; advice. 2, commendation; praise.
recomendar (re·ko·men'dar) *v.t.* [*pres.ind.* **recomiendo** (-'mjen·do); *pres.subjve.* **recomiende** (-de)] 1, to recommend; advise. 2, to commend.
recompensa (re·kom'pen·sa) *n.f.* recompense; reward. —**recompensar,** *v.t.* to recompense; reward.
recomponer (re·kom·po'ner) *v.t.* [*infl.:* **poner**] to mend; repair.
reconcentrar (re·kon·θen'trar; -sen'trar) *v.t.* 1, to concentrate. 2, *fig.* to store up, as feelings. —**reconcentrarse,** *v.r.* to be absorbed or engrossed.
reconciliar (re·kon·θi'ljar; -si'ljar) *v.t.* to reconcile. —**reconciliación,** *n.f.* reconciliation.
reconcomio (re·kon'ko·mjo) *n.m.* 1, urge; itch. 2, *colloq.* gnawing suspicion; misgiving.
recóndito (re'kon·di·to) *adj.* recondite; hidden. —**reconditez,** *n.f.* *colloq.* reconditeness; obscurity.
reconocer (re·ko·no'θer; -'ser) *v.t.* [*infl.:* **conocer**] 1, to recognize. 2, to acknowledge. 3, to confess; admit; avow. 4, to reconnoiter. —**reconocible,** *adj.* recognizable.
reconocido (re·ko·no'θi·ðo; -'si·ðo) *adj.* 1, acknowledged. 2, grateful.
reconocimiento (re·ko·no·θi·'mjen·to; -si'mjen·to) *n.m.* 1, recognition. 2, acknowledgment. 3, gratitude. 4, reconnaissance.
reconquistar (re·kon·kis'tar) *v.t.* to reconquer. —**reconquista** (-'kis·ta) *n.f.* reconquest.
reconstituir (re·kons·ti·tu'ir) *v.t.* [*infl.:* **constituir**] to reconstitute. —**reconstitución,** *n.f.* reconstitution. —**reconstituyente,** *adj.* & *n.m.* reconstituent.
reconstruir (re·kons·tru'ir) *v.t.* [*infl.:* **construir**] to reconstruct. —**reconstrucción,** *n.f.* reconstruction.
recontar (re·kon'tar) *v.t.* [*infl.:* **contar**] 1, to tell; retell. 2, to recount; count again.
reconvención (re·kon·βen'θjon; -'sjon) *n.f.* 1, reproof; reproach. 2, remonstrance.
reconvenir (re·kon·βe'nir) *v.t.* [*infl.:* **venir**] 1, to reproach; reprove. 2, to remonstrate.
recopilación (re·ko·pi·la'θjon; -'sjon) *n.f.* 1, compendium; abridgment; summary. 2, compilation; digest.
recopilar (re·ko·pi'lar) *v.t.* 1, to abridge; summarize. 2, to compile.
récord ('re·korð) *n.m.,* *sports* record.
recordación (re·kor·ða'θjon; -'sjon) *n.f.* remembering; remembrance.
recordar (re kor'ðar) *v.t.* [*infl.:* **acordar**] 1, to remember; recall. 2, to remind; call to mind. —**recordativo,** *adj.* reminding. —**recordatorio,** *n.m.* reminder; memento.
recorrer (re·ko'rrer) *v.t.* 1, to traverse; pass over or through. 2, to travel; go over. 3, to examine. 4, to glance through; scan.
recorrido (re·ko'rri·ðo) *n.m.* 1, route; course. 2, a going over. *Also,* **recorrida** (-ða) *n.f.*
recortar (re·kor'tar) *v.t.* 1, to cut away; clip; trim. 2, to outline; mark out. —**recortado,** *n.m.* paper cutout. —*adj.* jagged; irregular in outline.
recorte (re'kor·te) *n.m.* 1, cutting; clipping; trimming. 2, item (*in a newspaper*).
recoser (re·ko'ser) *v.t.* to resew; mend.
recostado (re·kos'ta·ðo) *adj.* reclining; recumbent.
recostar (re·kos'tar) *v.t.* [*infl.:* **acostar**] to rest; recline. —**recostarse,** *v.r.* 1, to lie down; rest. 2, to lean back.
recoveco (re·ko'βe·ko) *n.m.* 1, turning; winding. 2, nook; cranny. 3, ruse; artifice.
recrear (re·kre'ar) *v.t.* 1, to amuse; delight. 2, to re-create; create anew. —**recreación,** *n.f.* recreation. —**recreativo,** *adj.* recreative.
recrecer (re·kre'θer; -'ser) *v.t.* & *i.* [*infl.:* **crecer**] to increase; grow.
recreo (re'kre·o) *n.m.* recreation; leisure.
recriminar (re·kri·mi'nar) *v.t.* to

recriminate. —**recriminación**, *n.f.* recrimination.

recrudecer (re·kru·ðe'θer; -'ser) *v.i.* [*pres.ind.* **recrudezco** (-'ðeθ·ko; -'ðes·ko); *pres.subjve.* **recrudezca** (-ka)] to recrudesce. —**recrudecimiento**, *n.m.* recrudescence.

recrudescente (re·kru·ðes'θen·te; -ðe'sen·te) *adj.* recrudescent. —**recrudescencia**, *n.f.* recrudescence.

recrujir (re·kru'xir) *v.i.* to creak loudly.

rect- (rekt) *prefix, var. of* **recti-**: *rectángulo,* rectangle.

recta ('rek·ta) *n.f.* **1,** straightaway. **2,** straight line.

rectal (rek'tal) *adj.* rectal.

rectángulo (rek'tan·gu·lo) *adj.* right; right-angled. —*n.m.* rectangle. —**rectangular**, *adj.* rectangular.

recti- (rek·ti) *prefix* recti-; straight: *rectilíneo,* rectilinear.

rectificar (rek·ti·fi'kar) *v.t.* [*pres. subjve.* **rectifique** (-'fi·ke); *pret.* **rectifiqué** (-'ke)] to rectify. —**rectificación**, *n.f.* rectification; rectifying. —**rectificador**, *adj.* rectifying. —*n.m.* rectifier. —**rectificativo**, *adj.* & *n.m.* corrective.

rectitud (rek·ti'tuð) *n.f.* **1,** rectitude. **2,** straightness; directness.

recto ('rek·to) *adj.* **1,** straight. **2,** upright; honest. **3,** *geom.* right. —*n.m.* rectum.

rector (rek'tor) *n.m.* rector. —**rectorado**, *n.m.* rectorate.

rectoría (rek·to'ri·a) *n.f.* **1,** rectorate. **2,** rectory.

recua ('re·kwa) *n.f.* **1,** string of pack animals. **2,** *fig.* string; pack; slew.

recuadro (re'kwa·ðro) *n.m.* square section; panel.

recubrir (re·ku'βrir) *v.t.* [*infl.:* **cubrir**] **1,** to cover; coat. **2,** to recover. —**recubrimiento**, *n.m.* cover; covering; coating.

recuento (re'kwen·to) *n.m.* **1,** recount. **2,** inventory.

recuerde (re'kwer·ðe) *v., pres. subjve. of* **recordar**.

recuerdo (re'kwer·ðo) *v., pres.ind. of* **recordar**.

recuerdo (re'kwer·ðo) *n.m.* **1,** remembrance; memory. **2,** memento; keepsake; souvenir. —**recuerdos**, *n.m.pl.* regards; best wishes.

recuestar (re·kwes'tar) *v.t.* to request. —**recuesta** (-'kwes·ta) *n.f.* request.

recueza (re'kwe·θa; -sa) *v., pres. subjve. of* **recocer**.

recuezo (re'kwe·θo; -so) *v., 1st pers.sing. pres.ind. of* **recocer**.

reculada (re·ku'la·ða) *n.f.* **1,** rearing back; recoil. **2,** *colloq.* backing down; backing out.

recular (re·ku'lar) *v.i.* **1,** to rear back; recoil. **2,** *colloq.* to back down; back out.

reculones (re·ku'lo·nes) *n.m.pl.* *in* **a reculones**, *colloq.* rearing back; recoiling.

recuperar (re·ku·pe'rar) *v.t.* to recover; regain; recoup. —**recuperarse**, *v.r.* to recover; recuperate. —**recuperación**, *n.f.* recovery; recuperation. —**recuperativo**, *adj.* recuperative; restorative.

recurrir (re·ku'rrir) *v.i.* **1,** to resort; have recourse. **2,** to recur. **3,** to return; repair; revert. —**recurrente**, *adj.* recurrent. —*n.m.* & *f.* petitioner.

recurso (re'kur·so) *n.m.* **1,** recourse; resort. **2,** resource; *pl.* means. **3,** petition; appeal.

recusar (re·ku'sar) *v.t.* to disallow; refuse; deny. —**recusación**, *n.f.* refusal; denial; recusancy. —**recusante**, *adj.* & *n.m.* & *f.* recusant.

rechazar (re·tʃa'θar; -'sar) *v.t.* [*pres.subjve.* **rechace** (-'tʃa·θe; -se); *pret.* **rechacé** (-'θe; -'se)] **1,** to reject. **2,** to repel; repulse.

rechazo (re'tʃa·θo; -so) *n.m.* **1,** rebound. **2,** rejection; rebuff. —**de rechazo**, incidentally; accidentally.

rechifla (re'tʃi·fla) *n.f.* catcall; hoot; razz. —**rechiflar**, *v.t.* & *i.* to catcall; hoot; razz.

rechinamiento (re·tʃi·na'mjen·to) *n.m.* **1,** grating; grinding; grating or grinding sound. **2,** gnashing of the teeth. *Also,* **rechinido** (-'ni·ðo), **rechino** (re'tʃi·no).

rechinar (re·tʃi'nar) *v.i.* to grate; grind. —*v.t.* & *i.* to gnash (the teeth).

rechistar (re·tʃis'tar) *v.i., usu. with* **sin** *or* **no**, to protest; grumble.

rechoncho (re'tʃon·tʃo) *adj., colloq.* chubby.

rechupete (re·tʃu'pe·te) *n.m., in* **de rechupete**, *colloq.* wonderful; fine; exquisite.

red (reð) *n.f.* **1,** net. **2,** netting. **3,** network. **4,** snare; trap.

redacción (re·ðak'θjon; -'sjon) *n.f.* **1,** writing; editing; redaction.

2, editorial staff. 3, newsroom. 4, editorial office.
redactar (re·ðak'tar) *v.t.* to write; edit; redact.
redactor (re·ðak'tor) *n.m.* writer; editor.
redada (re'ða·ða) *n.f.* 1, cast *or* casting of a net. 2, catch; haul.
redar (re'ðar) *v.t.* to net; catch.
redecilla (re·ðe'θi·ʎa; -'si·ja) *n.f.* 1, small net. 2, hairnet. 3, netting; mesh.
rededor (re·ðe'ðor) *n.m.* 1, contour; outline. 2, immediate vicinity or surroundings. —**al** *or* **en rededor** = **alrededor.**
redención (re·ðen'θjon; -'sjon) *n.f.* redemption.
redentor (re·ðen'tor) *n.m.* redeemer. —*adj.* redeeming.
redicho (re'ði·tʃo) *adj.* affected or over-precise in speech.
redil (re'ðil) *n.m.* fold; sheepfold.
redimir (re·ði'mir) *v.t.* to redeem. —**redimible,** *adj.* redeemable.
redingote (re·ðin'go·te) *n.m.* 1, riding coat. 2, overcoat; greatcoat.
rédito ('re·ði·to) *n.m.* interest; return; income. —**reditual** (-'twal) *adj.* interest-bearing; income-producing.
redituar (re·ði'twar) *v.t.* [*infl.:* **habituar**] to yield (interest or income).
redivivo (re·ði'βi·βo) *adj.* risen; resurrected.
redoblado (re·ðo'βla·ðo) *adj.* 1, redoubled. 2, double-folded. 3, double-quick. 4, thickset. —*n.m.* double fold.
redoblar (re·ðo'βlar) *v.t.* 1, to redouble. 2, to double-fold. 3, to clinch (*as a nail or with nails*). —*v.t.* & *i.* to roll (*as a drum*).
redoble (re'ðo·βle) *n.m.* 1, redoubling; redouble. 2, drum roll.
redoblona (re·ðo'βlo·na) *n.f., So. Amer.* combination bet; parlay.
redolente (re·ðo'len·te) *adj.* aching; suffering a dull pain.
redolor (re·ðo'lor) *n.m.* dull ache or pain; afterpain.
redoma (re'ðo·ma) *n.f.* flask; phial.
redomado (re·ðo'ma·ðo) *adj.* artful; crafty; cunning.
redomón (re·ðo'mon) *adj., So. Amer.* half-tamed.
redonda (re'ðon·da) *n.f.* 1, surrounding neighborhood. 2, *music* semibreve. —**a la redonda,** around; in a circle; about.
redondear (re·ðon·de'ar) *v.t.* 1, to round; round off. 2, to settle; pay off; discharge; clear. —**redondearse,** *v.r., colloq.* to be or become well-off.
redondel (re·ðon'del) *n.m., colloq.* 1, circle; ring. 2, arena.
redondez (re·ðon'deθ; -'des) *n.f.* 1, roundness. 2, curvature. 3, round or curved surface.
redondilla (re·ðon'di·ʎa; -ja) *n.f.* quatrain.
redondo (re'ðon·do) *adj.* 1, round. 2, *typog.* roman. —*n.m.* 1, roundness; round shape. 2, *colloq.* coin; cash. —**en redondo,** around; round; full circle.
redopelo (re·ðo'pe·lo) *n.m.* hassle; squabble. —**a** *or* **al redopelo,** the wrong way; against the grain.
reducir (re·ðu'θir; -'sir) *v.t.* [*infl.:* **conducir**] to reduce. —**reducirse,** *v.r.* 1, to be or become reduced; confine oneself. 2, *fol. by* **en,** to cut down on. —**reducción,** *n.f.* reduction. —**reducible,** *also* **reductible,** *adj.* reducible. —**reducido,** *adj.* reduced; small; confined.
reducto (re'ðuk·to) *n.m.* redoubt.
redundante (re·ðun'dan·te) *adj.* redundant. —**redundancia,** *n.f.* redundancy.
redundar (re·ðun'dar) *v.i.* 1, to redound. 2, to be redundant. 3, to overflow; run over.
reduplicar (re·ðu·pli'kar) *v.t.* [*infl.:* **duplicar**] 1, to reduplicate. 2, to redouble. —**reduplicación,** *n.f.* reduplication.
reelegir (re·e·le'xir) *v.t.* [*infl.:* **elegir**] to reelect. —**reelección,** *n.f.* reelection. —**reelegible,** *adj.* eligible for reelection.
reembarcar (re·em·bar'kar) *v.t.* [*infl.:* **embarcar**] to reship. —**reembarcarse,** *v.r.* to reembark.
reembarque (re·em'bar·ke) *n.m.* 1, reshipment. 2, [*also,* **reembarco** (-ko).] reembarkation.
reembolsar (re·em·bol'sar) *v.t.* to reimburse. —**reembolso** (-'bol·so) *n.m.* reimbursement. —**a** *or* **contra reembolso,** cash on delivery.
reemplazar (re·em·pla'θar; -'sar) *v.t.* [*infl.:* **emplazar**] to replace; substitute. —**reemplazo** (-'pla·θo; -so) *n.m.* replacement; substitution.
reencarnar (re·en·kar'nar) *v.i.* to

be reincarnated. —**reencarnación,** *n.f.* reincarnation.
reentrar (re·en'trar) *v.i.* to reenter.
reenviar (re·en·βi'ar) *v.t.* [*infl.:* **enviar**] to forward; send on.
reenvío (re·en'βi·o) *n.m.* forwarding; reshipment.
reexpedir (re·eks·pe'ðir) *v.t.* to forward; reship. —**reexpedición,** *n.f.* forwarding; reshipment.
refacción (re·fak'θjon; -'sjon) *n.f.* **1,** refection; repast. **2,** repair; repairing. —**refaccionar,** *v.t., Amer.* to repair; remake; do over.
refajo (re'fa·xo) *n.m.* underskirt.
refección (re·fek'θjon; -'sjon) *n.f.* = **refacción.**
refectorio (re·fek'to·rjo) *n.m.* refectory.
referencia (re·fe'ren·θja; -sja) *n.f.* **1,** reference. **2,** account; report.
referendum (re·fe'ren·dum) *n.m.* referendum.
referente (re·fe'ren·te) *adj.* referring; relating.
referir (re·fe'rir) *v.t.* [*infl.:* **conferir**] **1,** to refer. **2,** to tell; relate. —**referirse,** *v.r.* to refer; relate; have reference.
refilón (re·fi'lon) *n.m., colloq.* glancing blow. —**de refilón,** obliquely; aslant; glancing.
refinar (re·fi'nar) *v.t.* to refine. —**refinación,** *n.f.* refining. —**refinado,** *adj.* refined. —**refinamiento,** *n.m.* refinement. —**refinería,** *n.f.* refinery.
reflectar (re·flek'tar) *v.t.* to reflect (light, sound, etc.).
reflector (re·flek'tor) *adj.* reflecting. —*n.m.* **1,** reflector. **2,** searchlight. **3,** headlight.
reflejar (re·fle'xar) *v.t.* **1,** to reflect. **2,** to mirror.
reflejo (re·fle'xo) *adj.* **1,** reflected. **2,** reflex. **3,** *gram.* reflexive. —*n.m.* **1,** reflection; reflected light. **2,** reflex.
reflexión (re·flek'sjon) *n.f.* reflection.
reflexionar (re·flek·sjo'nar) *v.i.* to reflect; ponder.
reflexivo (re·flek'si·βo) *adj.* **1,** thoughtful; considerate. **2,** *gram.* reflexive.
refluir (re·flu'ir) *v.i.* [*infl.:* **fluir**] **1,** to flow back. **2,** to redound; come back; react.
reflujo (re'flu·xo) *n.m.* **1,** reflux; ebbing. **2,** ebb tide.
refocilar (re·fo·θi'lar; -si'lar) *v.t.* to please; bring enjoyment to. —**refocilarse,** *v.r.* to enjoy oneself. —**refocilación,** *n.f.* enjoyment; pleasure.
reforma (re'for·ma) *n.f.* **1,** reform. **2,** reformation; *cap.* Reformation.
reformación (re·for·ma'θjon; -'sjon) *n.f.* reformation; reforming; reform.
reformar (re·for'mar) *v.t.* **1,** to reform. **2,** to reshape; remake; alter. —**reformarse,** *v.r.* to reform; be reformed. —**reformador,** *adj.* reforming. —*n.m.* reformer.
reformatorio (re·for·ma'to·rjo) *n.m.* reformatory.
reformista (re·for'mis·ta) *adj.* reform; reformist. —*n.m. & f.* advocate of reform; reformist.
reforzar (re·for'θar; -'sar) *v.t.* [*infl.:* **forzar**] to reinforce; strengthen; fortify.
refracción (re·frak'θjon; -'sjon) *n.f.* refraction.
refractar (re·frak'tar) *v.t.* to refract.
refractario (re·frak'ta·rjo) *adj.* refractory; unyielding.
refractor (re·frak'tor) *n.m.* refractor.
refrán (re'fran) *n.m.* **1,** proverb; saying. **2,** refrain. —**refranero,** *n.m.* collection of sayings.
refregadura (re·fre·ɣa'ðu·ra) *n.f.* **1,** rub; rubbing. **2,** scratch; bruise; abrasion.
refregar (re·fre'ɣar) *v.t.* [*infl.:* **fregar**] to rub; rub in. —**refregamiento,** *n.m.* rub; rubbing.
refregón (re·fre'ɣon) *n.m.* = **refregadura.**
refreír (re·fre'ir) *v.t.* [*infl.:* **freír**] **1,** to refry. **2,** to overfry.
refrenar (re·fre'nar) *v.t.* to restrain; curb; rein. —**refrenamiento,** *n.m.* restraining; restraint.
refrendar (re·fren'dar) *v.t.* **1,** to countersign. **2,** to visé. **3,** to approve; sanction. **4,** to support; corroborate. —**refrendata** (-'da·ta) *n.f.* countersignature.
refrescar (re·fres'kar) *v.t. & i.* [*pres.subjve.* **refresque** (-'fres·ke); *pret.* **refresqué** (-'ke)] to refresh. —*v.i.* **1,** to become cool, as weather. **2,** to cool off; take refreshment. —**refrescarse,** *v.r.* **1,** to cool off; take refreshment. **2,** to become brisk (*said of the wind*). —**refrescante,** *adj.* refreshing.

refresco (re'fres·ko) *n.m.* refreshment. —**de refresco, 1,** relief; fresh. **2,** refreshed; renewed.
refresquería (re·fres·ke'ri·a) *n.f., Amer.* refreshment stand.
refriega (re'frje·ɣa) *n.f.* fray; affray; battle.
refrigerador (re·fri·xe·ra'ðor) *adj.* refrigerating; cooling. —*n.m.* [*also,* **refrigeradora,** *n.f.*] refrigerator; ice box; cooler.
refrigerar (re·fri·xe'rar) *v.t.* to refrigerate. —**refrigeración,** *n.f.* refrigeration. —**refrigerante,** *adj.* & *n.m.* refrigerant.
refrigerio (re·fri'xe·rjo) *n.m.* **1,** refreshment; snack. **2,** relief; solace.
refringir (re·frin'xir) *v.t.* [*infl.:* **infringir**] to refract. —**refringente,** *adj.* refracting; refractive.
refrito (re'fri·to) *v., p.p. of* **refreír.** —*adj., Amer., colloq.* done; fouled up; done for. —*n.m., colloq.* rehash.
refuerzo (re'fuer·θo; -so) *n.m.* reinforcement.
refugiar (re·fu'xjar) *v.t.* to shelter; harbor; give refuge to. —**refugiarse,** *v.r.* to take refuge; take shelter. —**refugiado,** *n.m.* refugee.
refugio (re'fu·xjo) *n.m.* **1,** refuge. **2,** shelter.
refulgencia (re·ful'xen·θja; -sja) *n.f.* refulgence. —**refulgente,** *adj.* refulgent.
refulgir (re·ful'xir) *v.i.* to shine; glow.
refundición (re·fun·di'θjon; -'sjon) *n.f.* recasting; revision; abridgment.
refundir (re·fun'dir) *v.t.* **1,** to remelt. **2,** to recast; revise; abridge. **3,** to contain; include. **4,** *Amer., colloq.* to lose; misplace; bury among assorted things.
refunfuñar (re·fun·fu'ɲar) *v.i.* to grumble. —**refunfuño** (-'fu·ɲo) *n.m.* grumble; grumbling. —**refunfuñón** (-'ɲon) *adj.* grumbling; grumbly. —*n.m.* grumbler.
refutar (re·fu'tar) *v.t.* to refute. —**refutación,** *n.f.* refutation.
regadera (re·ɣa'ðe·ra) *n.f.* **1,** watering pot. **2,** sprinkler.
regadío (re·ɣa'ði·o) *adj.* irrigable. —*n.m.* [*also,* **tierras de regadío**] irrigated land.
regalado (re·ɣa'la·ðo) *adj.* **1,** delicate; exquisite. **2,** pleasing; delightful. **3,** easy; pleasant. **4,** *colloq.* fond of being waited upon; fond of easy living. **5,** free; gratis. **6,** cheap; bargain-priced.
regalar (re·ɣa'lar) *v.t.* **1,** to give; present. **2,** to regale; entertain. —**regalarse,** *v.r.* to regale oneself.
regalía (re·ɣa'li·a) *n.f.* **1,** royal prerogative. **2,** exemption; privilege. **3,** bonus; *pl.* perquisites. **4,** *Amer.* muff.
regaliz (re·ɣa'liθ; -'lis) *n.m.* licorice. *Also,* **regaliza** (-'li·θa; -sa) *n.f.*
regalo (re'ɣa·lo) *n.m.* **1,** present; gift. **2,** pleasure; comfort. **3,** regalement.
regalón (re·ɣa'lon) *adj., Amer., colloq.* pampered; spoiled.
regañar (re·ɣa'ɲar) *v.i.* **1,** to grumble; gripe. **2,** *colloq.* to bicker; squabble. —*v.t., colloq.* to scold. —(**a**) **regañadientes** (re·ɣa·ɲa·'ðjen·tes) reluctantly; grumblingly.
regaño (re'ɣa·ɲo) *n.m.* **1,** grumble; gripe. **2,** *colloq.* scolding.
regañón (re·ɣa'ɲon) *adj., colloq.* **1,** grumbly; griping. **2,** scolding. —*n.m., colloq.* grouch. —**regañona,** *n.f.* scold; nag.
regar (re'ɣar) *v.t.* [*pres.ind.* **riego;** *pres.subjve.* **riegue;** *pret.* **regué**] **1,** to water. **2,** to spread; strew.
regata (re'ɣa·ta) *n.f.* regatta.
regate (re'ɣa·te) *n.m.* dodge; evasion.
regatear (re·ɣa·te'ar) *v.t.* **1,** to dicker *or* haggle over (price). **2,** to sell (bargain goods); sell at retail. **3,** *colloq.* to shirk. **4,** to begrudge. —*v.i.* **1,** to bargain. **2,** to dodge. **3,** to engage in a boat race.
regateo (re·ɣa'te·o) *n.m.* haggling; dickering; bargaining.
regatero (re·ɣa'te·ro) *n.m.* **1,** hawker. **2,** *colloq.* haggler; bargain hunter.
regato (re'ɣa·to) *n.m.* **1,** rill; rivulet. **2,** pool; puddle. *Also,* **regajo** (-xo).
regazo (re'ɣa·θo; -so) *n.m.* lap.
regencia (re'xen·θja; -sja) *n.f.* regency.
regenerar (re·xe·ne'rar) *v.t.* to regenerate. —**regeneración,** *n.f.* regeneration. —**regenerativo,** *adj.* regenerative.
regentar (re·xen'tar) *v.t.* to rule, esp. as regent.
regente (re'xen·te) *adj.* ruling; regent. —*n.m.* & *f.* **1,** regent. **2,** [*fem.* **regenta**] manager of a small establishment.

regentear (re·xen·te'ar) *v.t.* **1,** to rule sternly or arbitrarily; boss. **2,** to manage (a small establishment, store, etc.).

regicida (re·xi'θi·ða; -'si·ða) *n.m.* & *f.* regicide (*agent*). —**regicidio** (-'θi·ðjo; -'si·ðjo) *n.m.* regicide (*act*).

regidor (re·xi'ðor) *adj.* ruling; governing. —*n.m.* alderman; councilman. —**regiduría** (-ðu'ri·a) *n.f.* office or dignity of an alderman or councilman.

régimen ('re·xi·men) *n.m.* [*pl.* **regímenes** (re'xi·me·nes)] **1,** regime. **2,** regimen; order; plan. **3,** diet. **4,** *gram.* government.

regimental (re·xi·men'tal) *adj.* regimental.

regimentar (re·xi·men'tar) *v.t.* [*pres.ind.* **regimiento** (-'mjen·to); *pres.subjve.* **regimiente** (-te)] to regiment. —**regimentación,** *n.f.* regimentation.

regimiento (re·xi'mjen·to) *n.m.* **1,** regiment. **2,** ruling; rule. **3,** council; board of aldermen.

regio ('re·xjo) *adj.* regal.

región (re'xjon) *n.f.* region. —**regional,** *adj.* regional.

regionalismo (re·xjo·na'lis·mo) *n.m.* regionalism. —**regionalista,** *adj.* regionalistic. —*n.m.* & *f.* regionalist.

regir (re'xir) *v.t.* [*pres.ind.* **rijo,** *pres.subjve.* **rija;** *pret.* **regí, rigió;** *ger.* **rigiendo**] **1,** to rule; govern. **2,** *gram.* to govern. —*v.i.* **1,** to be in force or effect. **2,** to govern; prevail.

registrador (re·xis·tra'ðor) *adj.* registering. —*n.m.* **1,** register; cash register. **2,** registering device; meter. **3,** registrar; recorder.

registrar (re·xis'trar) *v.t.* **1,** to register. **2,** to search; inspect. **3,** to rummage; rummage through. —**registrarse,** *v.r.* to register.

registro (re'xis·tro) *n.m.* **1,** register. **2,** registry. **3,** registration. **4,** record; entry. **5,** search; inspection. **6,** *mech.* regulator. **7,** bookmark.

regla ('re·ɣla) *n.f.* **1,** rule. **2,** ruler; straightedge. **3,** period; menses. —**en regla,** in order; properly.

reglamentación (re·ɣla·men·ta'θjon; -'sjon) *n.f.* **1,** rule; regulation. **2,** set of rules or regulations.

reglamentar (re·ɣla·men'tar) *v.t.* to set rules or regulations for.

reglamentario (re·ɣla·men'ta·rjo) *adj.* **1,** regulation (*attrib.*); prescribed by regulation. **2,** ruling; regulatory. **3,** mandatory; necessary.

reglamento (re·ɣla'men·to) *n.m.* **1,** collection of rules, regulations or bylaws. **2,** regulation; rule; bylaw. —**de reglamento** = **reglamentario.**

reglar (re'ɣlar) *v.t.* **1,** to rule; draw lines on. **2,** to regulate; order. —*v.i., Arg.* to menstruate. —*adj., eccles.* regular. —**reglarse,** *v.r.* to restrict oneself; limit oneself.

regleta (re'ɣle·ta) *n.f., print.* lead. —**regletear,** *v.t.* to lead.

regocijar (re·ɣo·θi'xar; -si'xar) *v.t.* to gladden; rejoice. —**regocijarse,** *v.r.* to rejoice; be gladdened.

regocijo (re·ɣo'θi·xo; -'si·xo) *n.m.* **1,** joy. **2,** rejoicing.

regodearse (re·ɣo·ðe'ar·se) *v.r.* **1,** to enjoy oneself; delight. **2,** *colloq.* to frolic. **3,** *colloq.* to coddle oneself.

regodeo (re·ɣo'ðe·o) *n.m., colloq.* **1,** coddling; pampering; indulgence. **2,** frolic.

regojo (re'ɣo·xo) *n.m.* **1,** bread crumb. **2,** *colloq.* small boy; shaver.

regoldar (re·ɣol'dar) *v.i., colloq.* [*pres.ind.* **regüeldo;** *pres.subjve.* **regüelde**] to belch.

regordete (re·ɣor'ðe·te) *adj., colloq.* pudgy; chubby.

regresar (re·ɣre'sar) *v.i.* **1,** to return; go *or* come back. **2,** to regress.

regresión (re·ɣre'sjon) *n.f.* regression. —**regresivo** (-'si·βo) *adj.* regressive.

regreso (re'ɣre·so) *n.m.* **1,** return; going *or* coming back. **2,** regress.

regué (re'ɣe) *v., 1st pers.sing. pret. of* **regar.**

regüelde (re'ɣwel·de) *v., pres. subjve. of* **regoldar.**

regüeldo (re'ɣwel·do) *v., pres.ind. of* **regoldar.** —*n.m., colloq.* belch.

reguera (re'ɣe·ra) *n.f.* ditch; irrigation ditch.

reguero (re'ɣe·ro) *n.m.* **1,** trail (*of something spilled* or *scattered*). **2,** trickle; thin stream. **3,** irrigation ditch.

regulación (re·ɣu·la'θjon; -'sjon) *n.f.* regulation.

regulador (re·ɣu·la'ðor) *adj.* regulating. —*n.m.* **1,** regulator. **2,** throttle.

regular (re·ɣu'lar) *adj.* **1,** regular. **2,** medium; average. —*adj.* & *adv., colloq.* so-so. —*n.m.* & *f.* regular. —*v.t.* to regulate; adjust. —**por lo regular,** usually; ordinarily.

regularidad (re·ɣu·la·ri'ðað) *n.f.* regularity.
regularizar (re·ɣu·la·ri'θar; -'sar) *v.t.* [*pres.subjve.* **regularice** (-'ri·θe; -se); *pret.* **regularicé** (-'θe; -'se)] to regularize. —**regularización,** *n.f.* regularization.
regulativo (re·ɣu·la'ti·βo) *adj.* regulating.
régulo ('re·ɣu·lo) *n.m.* **1,** petty king; kinglet. **2,** *ornith.* kinglet. **3,** = **basilisco.**
regurgitar (re·ɣur·xi'tar) *v.i.* to regurgitate. —**regurgitación,** *n.f.* regurgitation.
rehabilitar (re·a·βi·li'tar) *v.t.* to rehabilitate. —**rehabilitación,** *n.f.* rehabilitation.
rehacer (re·a'θer; -'ser) *v.t.* [*infl.:* **hacer**] **1,** to redo; do over. **2,** to remake; make over. **3,** to rebuild. **4,** to revive; restore. —**rehacerse,** *v.r.* **1,** to recover; get back on one's feet. **2,** to reorganize; reassemble.
rehacimiento (re·a·θi'mjen·to; re·a·si-) *n.m.* **1,** recovery; recovering. **2,** remaking; rebuilding.
rehecho (re'e·tʃo) *v., p.p. of* **rehacer.** —*adj.* heavy-set.
rehén (re'en) *n.m.* hostage. —**en rehenes, 1,** in *or* as hostage. **2,** in *or* as pledge.
rehervir (re·er'βir) *v.t.* [*infl.:* **hervir**] to reboil. —*v.i.* to burn with love. —**rehervirse,** *v.r.* to ferment.
rehogar (re·o'ɣar) *v.t.* [*pres. subjve.* **rehogue** (-'o·ɣe); *pret.* **rehogué** (-'ɣe)] to cook slowly in a covered pan.
rehuir (re·u'ir) *v.t.* [*infl.:* **huir**] **1,** to shirk; avoid; shrink from. **2,** to refuse; decline. —**rehuída** (-'i·ða) *n.f.* shirking; avoidance.
rehusar (re·u'sar) *v.t.* to refuse.
reidor (re·i'ðor) *adj.* laughing; jolly.
reimprimir (re·im·pri'mir) *v.t.* [*p.p.* **reimpreso** (-'pre·so)] to reprint. —**reimpresión** (-pre'sjon) *n.f.* reprint.
reina ('rei·na) *n.f.* queen.
reinado (rei'na·ðo) *n.m.* reign.
reinar (rei'nar) *v.i.* to reign.
reincidir (re·in·θi'ðir; -si'ðir) *v.i.* to relapse; repeat an error or offense. —**reincidencia,** *n.f.* relapse; recidivism. —**reincidente,** *adj.* relapsing; recidivous. —*n.m.* & *f.* recidivist.
reingresar (re·in·gre'sar) *v.i.* to reenter; rejoin. —**reingreso** (-'gre·so) *n.m.* reentry; rejoining.
reino ('rei·no) *n.m.* **1,** kingdom. **2,** reign.
reinstalar (re·ins·ta'lar) *v.t.* to reinstate; reinstall. —**reinstalación,** *n.f.* reinstatement; reinstallation.
reintegración (re·in·te·ɣra'θjon; -'sjon) *n.f.* **1,** return; restitution. **2,** reimbursement.
reintegrar (re·in·te'ɣrar) *v.t.* **1,** to restore; return. **2,** to refund; reimburse. —**reintegrarse,** *v.r.* **1,** to return; rejoin. **2,** to reimburse oneself.
reintegro (re·in'te·ɣro) *n.m.* **1,** = **reintegración. 2,** *comm.* withdrawal.
reír (re'ir) *v.i.* [*also, refl.,* **reírse**] [*pres.ind.* **río;** *pres.subjve.* **ría;** *pret.* **reí, rió;** *ger.* **riendo**] **1,** to laugh. **2,** to sneer; scoff. —*v.t.* to laugh at; laugh about.
reiterar (re·i·te'rar; rei-) *v.t.* to reiterate. —**reiteración,** *n.f.* reiteration.
reivindicación (re·i·βin·di·ka·'θjon; -'sjon) *n.f.* **1,** vindication. **2,** assertion (*of a legal right*). **3,** repossession.
reivindicar (re·i·βin·di'kar) *v.t.* [*infl.:* **vindicar**] **1,** to vindicate. **2,** to assert (a legal right). **3,** to regain possession of.
reja ('re·xa) *n.f.* **1,** grille; grating, esp. in a window. **2,** plowshare. —**entre rejas,** behind bars; in prison.
rejado (re'xa·ðo) *n.m.* = **verja.**
rejilla (re'xi·ʎa; -ja) *n.f.* **1,** lattice; grating. **2,** grate. **3,** luggage rack. **4,** rattan or cane for chair backs, seats, etc.
rejo ('re·xo) *n.m.* **1,** spike; goad. **2,** sting; barb. **3,** *Amer.* lash; whip.
rejón (re'xon) *n.m.* **1,** spear; lance. **2,** dagger.
rejonear (re·xo·ne'ar) *v.t.* to spear or lance (a bull). —**rejoneo** (-'ne·o) *n.m.* lancing; spearing.
rejuvenecer (re·xu·βe·ne'θer; -'ser) *v.t.* [*pres.ind.* **rejuvenezco** (-'neθ·ko; -'nes·ko); *pres.subjve.* **rejuvenezca** (-ka)] to rejuvenate. —*v.i.* [*also, refl.,* **rejuvenecerse**] to be or become rejuvenated. —**rejuvenecedor,** *adj.* rejuvenating. —**rejuvenecimiento,** *n.m.* rejuvenation.
relación (re·la'θjon; -'sjon) *n.f.* **1,** relation. **2,** account; report. —**tener relaciones con,** to be engaged to.
relacionar (re·la·θjo'nar; -sjo'nar)

v.t. to relate. —**relacionarse,** *v.r.* **1,** to be or become related. **2,** to become involved; become acquainted.
relajación (re·la·xa'θjon; -'sjon) *n.f.* **1,** relaxation. **2,** laxity. **3,** hernia.
relajado (re·la'xa·ðo) *adj.* morally lax; dissolute; licentious.
relajamiento (re·la·xa'mjen·to) *n.m.* = **relajación.**
relajar (re·la'xar) *v.t.* **1,** to relax. **2,** to weaken morally. **3,** *law* to release. —**relajarse,** *v.r.* **1,** to be or become lax or relaxed. **2,** to become morally lax; become dissolute.
relamer (re·la'mer) *v.t.* to lick over; lick again. —**relamerse,** *v.r.* to smack the lips.
relamido (re·la'mi·ðo) *adj.* **1,** prim; overnice; affected. **2,** *Amer.* blasé.
relámpago (re'lam·pa·ɣo) *n.m.* lightning; lightning flash. —**relampaguear** (-ɣe'ar) *v.i.* to flash as with lightning. —**relampagueo** (-'ɣe·o) *n.m.* flashing; flash of lightning.
relapso (re'lap·so) *adj.* relapsed into error. —*n.m.* relapse.
relatar (re·la'tar) *v.t.* to tell; relate; report.
relativo (re·la'ti·βo) *adj.* relative. —**relatividad,** *n.f.* relativity. —**relativismo,** *n.m.* relativism.
relato (re'la·to) *n.m.* **1,** statement; report. **2,** story; narrative.
relator (re·la'tor) *n.m.* narrator.
releer (re·le'er) *v.t.* [*infl.:* **leer**] to reread.
relegar (re·le'ɣar) *v.t.* [*infl.:* **legar**] to relegate. —**relegación,** *n.f.* relegation.
relente (re'len·te) *n.m.* night dew.
relevación (re·le·βa'θjon; -'sjon) *n.f.* **1,** relief; release. **2,** enhancement; enhancing.
relevante (re·le'βan·te) *adj.* prominent; excellent.
relevar (re·le'βar) *v.t.* **1,** to relieve (*as from duty or a duty*). **2,** to put or bring into relief. **3,** to overrate; overpraise. **4,** to give relief to; succor. **5,** to release; absolve. —*v.i.* to be in relief; stand out.
relevo (re'le·βo) *n.m.* **1,** relief; replacement. **2,** change of watch, guard, shift, etc. **3,** *pl.* [*also,* **carrera de relevos**] relay race.
relicario (re·li'ka·rjo) *n.m.* **1,** shrine. **2,** reliquary. **3,** locket.
relieve (re'lje·βe) *n.m.* **1,** relief. **2,** prominence; importance. —**de** *or* **en relieve,** in relief.
religa (re'li·ɣa) *n.f.* alloy; metal added to an alloy.
religión (re·li'xjon) *n.f.* religion.
religiosidad (re·li·xjo·si'ðað) *n.f.* **1,** religiousness. **2,** religiosity. **3,** scrupulousness.
religioso (re·li'xjo·so) *adj.* religious. —*n.m.* member of a religious order.
relimpio (re'lim·pjo) *adj., colloq.* very clean.
relinchar (re·lin'tʃar) *v.i.* to neigh; whinny. —**relincho** (-'lin·tʃo) *n.m.* neigh; whinny.
relindo (re'lin·do) *adj.* very pretty.
reliquia (re'li·kja) *n.f.* **1,** relic. **2,** vestige; trace.
reloj (re'lox; re'lo) *n.m.* **1,** clock. **2,** watch. —**reloj despertador,** alarm clock. —**reloj de pulsera,** wristwatch.
relojera (re·lo'xe·ra) *n.f.* **1,** watchcase. **2,** watch pocket.
relojería (re·lo·xe'ri·a) *n.f.* **1,** clockmaking; watchmaking. **2,** watchmaker's shop.
relojero (re·lo'xe·ro) *n.m.* watchmaker; clockmaker.
relucir (re·lu'θir; -'sir) *v.i.* [*infl.:* **lucir**] **1,** to shine; glow. **2,** to stand out; excel. —**sacar a relucir,** to bring out; bring to view. —**salir a relucir,** to come out; come to view.
reluctancia (re·luk'tan·θja; -sja) *n.f., electricity* reluctance.
reluctante (re·luk'tan·te) *adj.* recalcitrant; intractable.
relumbrar (re·lum'brar) *v.i.* to sparkle; shine; glare. —**relumbre** (-'lum·bre) *n.m.* glare; brilliance.
relumbro (re'lum·bro) *n.m.* **1,** flash. **2,** tinsel.
relumbrón (re·lum'bron) *n.m.* = **relumbro.** —**de relumbrón,** tinsel; showy; gaudy.
rellenar (re·ʎe'nar; re·je-) *v.t.* **1,** to refill. **2,** to fill completely; cram. **3,** to stuff. —**rellenarse,** *v.r., colloq.* to be stuffed; be satiated.
relleno (re'ʎe·no; re'je-) *adj.* **1,** stuffed. **2,** *colloq.* satiated; full. —*n.m.* **1,** stuffing. **2,** padding. **3,** meatball; dumpling.
remachado (re·ma'tʃa·ðo) *n.m.* riveting; clinching.
remachar (re·ma'tʃar) *v.t.* to clinch; rivet; nail down.
remache (re'ma·tʃe) *n.m.* **1,** clinch-

ing; riveting. 2, rivet. 3, *colloq.* clincher.
remada (re'ma·ða) *n.f.* 1, stroke of the oar. 2, *colloq.* rowing; row.
remador (re·ma'ðor) *n.m.* = **remero.**
remanente (re·ma'nen·te) *adj.* residual; remaining. —*n.m.* residue; remnant.
remangar (re·man'gar) *v.t.* [*pres. subjve.* **remangue** (-'man·ge); *pret.* **remangué** (-'ge)] to roll up, esp. the sleeves.
remanso (re'man·so) *n.m.* 1, river pond; backwater. 2, *fig.* haven; oasis. —*adj., So.Amer., colloq.* timorous; timid.
remar (re'mar) *v.i.* to row; paddle.
rematado (re·ma'ta·ðo) *adj.* 1, finished; ended; lost. 2, hopeless; irremediable. —**loco rematado,** stark mad.
rematar (re·ma'tar) *v.t.* 1, to end; finish; close; terminate. 2, to finish off; give the final stroke to. 3, to auction; knock down.
remate (re'ma·te) *n.m.* 1, end. 2, auction. 3, crown; top piece; topping. 4, *cards* bidding.
remecer (re·me'θer; -'ser) *v.t.* [*infl.:* **mecer**] to rock; swing back and forth.
remedar (re·me'ðar) *v.t.* to imitate; mimic; ape. —**remedable,** *adj.* imitable. —**remedador,** *n.m.* imitator; mimic.
remediar (re·me'ðjar) *v.t.* to remedy; help. —**remediable,** *adj.* remediable.
remedio (re'me·ðjo) *n.m.* remedy; help. —**No hay remedio,** It can't be helped.
remedo (re'me·ðo) *n.m.* imitation; parody.
remembranza (re·mem'bran·θa; -sa) *n.f.* remembrance.
rememorar (re·me·mo'rar) *v.t.* to remember; recall. —**rememorativo,** *adj.* reminding; recalling.
remendar (re·men'dar) *v.t.* [*pres. ind.* **remiendo** (-'mjen·do); *pres. subjve.* **remiende** (-de)] to patch; mend; darn.
remendón (re·men'don) *n.m.* 1, patcher; mender. 2, cobbler.
remero (re'me·ro) *n.m.* rower; oarsman.
remesa (re'me·sa) *n.f.* 1, shipment. 2, remittance.
remesar (re·me'sar) *v.t.* 1, to pull (the hair). 2, *comm.* to send; remit.
remeter (re·me'ter) *v.t.* to take in (a garment); to take up (a hem).
remiendo (re'mjen·do) *n.m.* 1, patch; mend; darn. 2, patching; mending; darning.
remilgarse (re·mil'ɣar·se) *v.r.* [*pres.subjve.* **remilgue** (-'mil·ɣe); *pret.* **remilgué** (-'ɣe)] to fuss; be fussy. —**remilgado,** *adj.* fussy; overfastidious.
remilgo (re'mil·ɣo) *n.m.* 1, primness; priggishness. 2, fastidiousness.
reminiscencia (re·mi·nis'θen·θja; -ni'sen·sja) *n.f.* reminiscence.
remirar (re·mi'rar) *v.t.* to recheck; look at again; review. —**remirarse,** *v.r.* 1, to take great pains. 2, to primp.
remisión (re·mi'sjon) *n.f.* remission.
remiso (re'mi·so) *adj.* remiss.
remitente (re·mi'ten·te) *n.m.* & *f.* sender.
remitido (re·mi'ti·ðo) *n.m.* personal notice.
remitir (re·mi'tir) *v.t.* 1, to remit; send. 2, to forgive. 3, to defer; postpone. 4, to refer. —*v.i.* [*also, refl.,* **remitirse**] to abate, as the wind. —**remitirse,** *v.r.* 1, to submit. 2, to abide; hold fast.
remo ('re·mo) *n.m.* 1, oar; paddle. 2, rowing. 3, *usu.pl., zool.* leg; *ornith.* wing; *colloq.* limbs.
remoce (re'mo·θe; -se) *v., pres. subjve. of* **remozar.**
remocé (re·mo'θe; -'se) *v., 1st pers.sing. pret. of* **remozar.**
remoción (re·mo'θjon; -'sjon) *n.f.* removal.
remojar (re·mo'jar) *v.t.* 1, to steep; soak. 2, to wet; wet down. —**remojo** (-'mo·xo) *n.m.* steeping; soaking.
remolacha (re·mo'la·tʃa) *n.f.* beet.
remolcador (re·mol·ka'ðor) *adj.* towing. —*n.m.* tug; towboat.
remolcar (re·mol'kar) *v.t.* [*pres. subjve.* **remolque** (-'mol·ke); *pret.* **remolqué** (-'ke)] to tow; haul.
remolino (re·mo'li·no) *n.m.* 1, whirl; swirl. 2, whirlwind. 3, whirlpool. 4, cowlick. 5, crowd; throng. 6, disturbance; commotion.
remolón (re·mo'lon) *adj.* indolent; lazy. —*n.m.* loiterer; idler; sluggard. —**remolonear,** *v.i.* to lag; loiter; shirk.
remolque (re'mol·ke) 1, towing; tow. 2, trailer. —**a remolque,** in tow.
remontar (re·mon'tar) *v.t.* 1, to

raise; lift; bear aloft. 2, to mount (a stream); go upstream. 3, to surmount; overcome. 4, to repair (a saddle). 5, to resole (a shoe). —**remontarse,** *v.r.* 1, to soar. 2, to go back to (in time); date from.

remonte (re'mon·te) *n.m.* 1, repairing. 2, remounting. 3, soaring.

remoque (re'mo·ke) *n.m., colloq.* jibe; scoff.

remoquete (re·mo'ke·te) *n.m.* 1, nickname; epithet. 2, witticism; sally.

rémora ('re·mo·ra) *n.f.* 1, *ichthy.* remora. 2, hindrance; obstacle.

remorder (re·mor'ðer) *v.t.* [*infl.:* **morder**] 1, to gnaw; corrode. 2, to prick; pierce; sting. —**remorderse,** *v.r.* to show worry, remorse, etc. —**remordimiento,** *n.m.* remorse.

remoto (re'mo·to) *adj.* remote.

remover (re·mo'βer) *v.t.* [*infl.:* **mover**] 1, to remove. 2, to stir. —**removimiento,** *n.m.* removal.

remozar (re·mo'θar; -'sar) *v.t.* [*pres.subjve.* **remoce;** *pret.* **remocé**] to give a fresh look to; renovate. —**remozarse,** *v.r.* to look young *or* new. —**remozamiento,** *n.m.* new appearance; renovation.

rempujar (rem·pu'xar) *v.t.* to push; shove. —**rempujo** (-'pu·xo) *also,* **rempujón** (-'xon) *n.m.* push; shove.

remudar (re·mu'ðar) *v.t.* to change; replace. —**remuda** (-'mu·ða) *n.f.* change; replacement.

remunerar (re·mu·ne'rar) *v.t.* to remunerate. —**remuneración,** *n.f.* remuneration. —**remuneratorio,** *adj.* remunerative.

renacer (re·na'θer; -'ser) *v.i.* [*infl.:* **nacer**] to be born again; spring up anew. —**renaciente,** *adj.* renascent.

renacimiento (re·na·θi'mjen·to; re·na·si-) *n.m.* renascence; renaissance.

renacuajo (re·na'kwa·xo) *n.m.* 1, tadpole. 2, *colloq.* runt.

renal (re'nal) *adj.* renal.

rencilla (ren'θi·ʎa; -'si·ja) *n.f.* quarrel; falling out. —**rencilloso,** *adj.* peevish; quarrelsome.

renco ('ren·ko) *adj.* lame in the hip.

rencor (ren'kor) *n.m.* rancor. —**rencoroso,** *adj.* rancorous.

rendición (ren·di'θjon; -'sjon) *n.f.* 1, surrender; submission. 2, yield.

rendido (ren'di·ðo) *adj.* 1, obsequious; devoted. 2, exhausted; worn out.

rendija (ren'di·xa) *n.f.* crack; fissure; split.

rendimiento (ren·di'mjen·to) *n.m.* 1, exhaustion; fatigue. 2, submission. 3, tribute. 4, yield. 5, *mech.* efficiency.

rendir (ren'dir) *v.t.* [*pres.ind.* **rindo;** *pres.subjve.* **rinda;** *pret.* **rendí, rindió;** *ger.* **rindiendo**] 1, to overcome; subdue. 2, to yield. 3, to exhaust; fatigue. 4, to render; pay; give. 5, to give back; return. —**rendirse,** *v.r.* 1, to surrender; submit; yield. 2, to collapse; give way.

renegado (re·ne'ɣa·ðo) *n.m.* 1, renegade. 2, ombre (*card game*). —*adj.* renegade.

renegar (re·ne'ɣar) *v.t.* [*infl.:* **negar**] 1, to deny vehemently. 2, *often fol. by* **de,** to disown; renounce, 3, to execrate. —*v.i.* 1, to apostatize. 2, to blaspheme. 3, to swear. 4, *colloq.* to rant; rave.

renegón (re·ne'ɣon) *adj., colloq.* 1, profane; swearing. 2, ranting; raving.

renegrido (re·ne'ɣri·ðo) *adj.* livid; black and blue.

renglón (ren'glon) 1, line (*of writing or printing*). 2, *comm.* line (*of merchandise*). 3, *bookkeeping* item. 4, *colloq.* affair; matter. —**renglonadura,** *n.f.* ruling (*of paper*). —**a renglón seguido,** immediately following; below.

rengo ('ren·go) *adj.* 1, lame in the hip. 2, *Amer.* lame. —**renguear** (-ge'ar) *v.i., Amer.* to limp.

reni- (re·ni) *prefix* reni-; kidney: *reniforme,* reniform.

reniego (re'nje·ɣo) *n.m.* 1, blasphemy. 2, *colloq.* swearing; curse; cursing.

renio ('re·njo) *n.m.* rhenium.

reno ('re·no) *n.m.* reindeer.

renombre (re'nom·bre) *n.m.* renown. —**renombrado** (-'bra·ðo) *adj.* renowned.

renovación (re·no·βa'θjon; -'sjon) *n.f.* 1, renewal. 2, renovation.

renovar (re·no'βar) *v.t.* [*pres.ind.* **renuevo** (-'nwe·βo); *pres.subjve.* **renueve** (-βe)] 1, to renew; restore. 2, to renovate.

renquear (ren·ke'ar) *v.i.* to limp.

renta ('ren·ta) *n.f.* 1, rent. 2, rental. 3, income; return. 4, revenue. 5,

annuity. —**rentado,** *adj.* living on an income.
rentar (ren'tar) *v.t.* to yield; return (income).
rentista (ren'tis·ta) *n.m.* **1,** financier. **2,** bondholder. **3,** one living on an income.
renuente (re·nu'en·te) *adj.* reluctant; unwilling. —**renuencia,** *n.f.* reluctance; unwillingness.
renuevo (re'nwe·βo) *n.m.* **1,** sprout; shoot. **2,** renewal. **3,** renovation.
renuncia (re'nun·θja; -sja) *n.f.* resignation (*of a right or an office*).
renunciar (re·nun'θjar; -'sjar) *v.t.* **1,** to renounce. **2,** to resign. —*v.i., cards* to revoke. —**renunciación,** *n.f.* renunciation.
renuncio (re'nun·θjo; -sjo) *n.m., cards* revoke.
reñido (re'ɲi·ðo) *adj.* **1,** on bad terms; on the outs. **2,** hard-fought; bitter.
reñidor (re·ɲi'ðor) *adj.* **1,** quarrelsome. **2,** scolding; nagging.
reñir (re'ɲir) *v.t.* & *i.* [*pres.ind.* **riño;** *pres.subjve.* **riña;** *pret.* **reñí, riñó;** *ger.* **riñendo**] to fight. —*v.i.* to quarrel. —*v.t.* to scold.
reo ('re·o) *n.m.* & *f.* **1,** offender; culprit. **2,** defendant. —*adj.* culpable; guilty.
reo- (re·o) *prefix* rheo-; flow; current: *reómetro,* rheometer.
reojo (re'o·xo) *n.m., in* **de reojo,** sideways; out of the corner of one's eye.
reorganizar (re·or·ɣa·ni'θar; -'sar) *v.t.* [*infl.:* **organizar**] to reorganize. —**reorganización,** *n.f.* reorganization.
reóstato (re'os·ta·to) *n.m.* rheostat.
repagar (re·pa'ɣar) *v.t.* [*infl.:* **pagar**] **1,** to repay. **2,** to overpay.
repantigarse (re·pan·ti'ɣar·se) *v.r.* [*pres.subjve.* **repantigue** (-'ti·ɣe); *pret.* **repantigué** (-'ɣe)] to stretch out; slump down.
reparable (re·pa'ra·βle) *adj.* **1,** reparable. **2,** noticeable; noteworthy.
reparación (re·pa·ra'θjon; -'sjon) *n.f.* **1,** reparation. **2,** reparations (*pl.*). **3,** repair.
reparador (re·pa·ra'ðor) *adj.* **1,** repairing; restorative. **2,** faultfinding. —*n.m.* repairer; repairman.
reparar (re·pa'rar) *v.t.* **1,** to repair. **2,** to restore. **3,** to make amends for. **4,** to observe; note; mark. —*v.i.* **1,** *fol. by* **en,** to notice; take note of. **2,** to stop. —**repararse,** *v.r.* to refrain; forbear.
reparo (re'pa·ro) *n.m.* **1,** repair; restoration. **2,** remark; advice; warning. **3,** objection; difficulty. **4,** defense; protection.
repartimiento (re·par·ti'mjen·to) *n.m.* partition; apportionment; distribution.
repartir (re·par'tir) *v.t.* **1,** to divide; distribute; apportion. **2,** to deal (cards). —**repartición,** *n.f.* division; distribution.
reparto (re'par·to) *n.m.* **1,** = **repartimiento. 2,** *theat.* cast. **3,** delivery; delivery route.
repasar (re·pa'sar) *v.t.* **1,** *also intr.* to repass; pass again. **2,** to review. **3,** to go over; look over. **4,** to mend (clothes).
repaso (re'pa·so) *n.m.* **1,** review. **2,** *colloq.* reprimand.
repatriar (re·pa'trjar) *v.t.* to repatriate. —*v.i.* [*also, refl.,* **repatriarse**] to return to one's own country. —**repatriación,** *n.f.* repatriation.
repechar (re·pe'tʃar) *v.i.* to go uphill.
repecho (re'pe·tʃo) *n.m.* **1,** short, steep slope. **2,** window sill. **3,** *colloq.* mantelpiece. —**a repecho,** uphill.
repelar (re·pe'lar) *v.t.* **1,** to pull the hair of. **2,** to trim; crop. **3,** to gnaw down; gnaw clean.
repeler (re·pe'ler) *v.t.* to repel; repulse. —**repelente,** *adj.* repellent; repelling; repulsive.
repelo (re'pe·lo) *n.m.* **1,** anything that goes against the grain. **2,** cross grain. **3,** *colloq.* spat; set-to.
repelón (re·pe'lon) *n.m.* **1,** pulling of the hair. **2,** torn piece; tatter. —**a repelones,** *colloq.* **1,** by degrees; little by little. **2,** by fistfuls. —**de repelón,** *colloq.* **1,** in passing. **2,** quick as a flash.
repeloso (re·pe'lo·so) *adj.* **1,** rough-grained. **2,** *colloq.* touchy; peevish.
repensar (re·pen'sar) *v.t.* [*infl.:* **pensar**] to reconsider.
repente (re'pen·te) *n.m., colloq.* sudden movement; outburst. —**de repente,** suddenly.
repentino (re·pen'ti·no) *adj.* sudden; abrupt.
repercutir (re·per·ku'tir) *v.i.* **1,** to rebound. **2,** to resound; echo. **3,** to have repercussions. —**repercusión** (-'sjon) *n.f.* repercussion.

repertorio (re·per'to·rjo) *n.m.* repertory; repertoire.
repetidor (re·pe·ti'ðor) *adj.* 1, repeating. 2, repetitious. —*n.m.* repeater.
repetir (re·pe'tir) *v.t.* [*pres.ind.* **repito**; *pres.subjve.* **repita**; *pret.* **repetí, repitió**; *ger.* **repitiendo**] to repeat. —*v.i.* to repeat; have an aftertaste. —**repetición** (-'θjon; -'sjon) *n.f.* repetition.
repicar (re·pi'kar) *v.t.* [*infl.:* **picar**] 1, to chop; mince. 2, to peal, as a bell. —**repicarse,** *v.r.* to boast.
repique (re'pi·ke) *n.m.* 1, chopping, mincing. 2, peal of a bell. 3, spat; set-to.
repiquetear (re·pi·ke·te'ar) *v.t.* to ring or sound rapidly. —**repiquetearse,** *v.r.* to quarrel. —**repiqueteo** (-'te·o) *n.m.* ringing; sounding.
repisa (re'pi·sa) *n.f.* 1, shelf; ledge. 2, mantelpiece. 3, bracket. 4, sill.
repita (re'pi·ta) *v., pres.subjve. of* **repetir.**
repitiendo (re·pi'tjen·do) *v., ger. of* **repetir.**
repitió (re·pi'tjo) *v., 3rd pers.sing. pret. of* **repetir.**
repito (re'pi·to) *v., pres.ind. of* **repetir.**
repizcar (re·piθ'kar; re·pis-) *v.t.* [*infl.:* **pellizcar**] to pinch. —**repizco** (-'piθ·ko; -'pis·ko) *n.m.* pinch.
repleción (re·ple'θjon; -'sjon) *n.f.* repletion.
replegar (re·ple'ɣar) *v.t.* [*infl.:* **plegar**] to refold; fold over and over. —**replegarse,** *v.r., mil.* to retire in good order.
repleto (re'ple·to) *adj.* replete; full.
réplica ('re·pli·ka) *n.f.* 1, reply; answer. 2, retort; repartee. 3, objection. 4, replica.
replicar (re·pli'kar) *v.i.* [*infl.:* **aplicar**] 1, to reply; answer. 2, to retort. 3, to object.
repliegue (re'plje·ɣe) *n.m.* 1, folding. 2, *mil.* withdrawal.
repoblación (re·po·βla'θjon; -'sjon) *n.f.* 1, repopulation. 2, reforestation. 3, restocking (with fish or game).
repoblar (re·po'βlar) *v.t.* [*infl.:* **poblar**] 1, to repopulate. 2, to reforest. 3, to restock (with fish or game).
repollo (re'po·ʎo; -jo) *n.m.* 1, cabbage. 2, head (*of cabbage, lettuce, etc.*).
reponer (re·po'ner) *v.t.* [*infl.:* **poner**] 1, to replace; restore. 2, *theat.* to revive. —**reponerse,** *v.r.* to recover; regain one's health or composure.
reportaje (re·por'ta·xe) *n.m.* 1, reportage. 2, report.
reportar (re·por'tar) *v.t.* 1, to repress; restrain. 2, to attain; obtain. 3, to bring; carry. —**reportarse,** *v.r.* to restrain oneself.
reporte (re'por·te) *n.m.* 1, report; news. 2, gossip; rumor.
reportero (re·por'te·ro) *n.m.* reporter. *Also,* **repórter** (re'por·ter).
reposar (re·po'sar) *v.i.* to rest; repose. —**reposarse,** *v.r.* to settle, as liquids. —**reposado,** *adj.* quiet; peaceful; calm.
reposición (re·po·si'θjon; -'sjon) *n.f.* 1, replacement. 2, *theat.* revival.
repositorio (re·po·si'to·rjo) *n.m.* repository.
reposo (re'po·so) *n.m.* rest; repose.
repostada (re·pos'ta·ða) *n.f., Amer.* sharp answer; retort.
repostar (re·pos'tar) *v.t.* to refuel; reprovision.
repostería (re·pos·te'ri·a) *n.f.* 1, pastry; confectionery. 2, pastry shop. —**repostero** (-'te·ro) *n.m.* pastry baker; confectioner.
reprender (re·pren'der) *v.t.* to reprehend; reprimand; scold. —**reprensible** (-'si·βle) *adj.* reprehensible. —**reprensión** (-'sjon) *n.f.* reprehension. —**reprensor** (-'sor) *adj.* reprehensive.
represa (re'pre·sa) *n.f.* dam.
represalia (re·pre'sa·lja) *n.f.* reprisal.
represar (re·pre'sar) *v.t.* 1, to bank; dam. 2, to repress.
representación (re·pre·sen·ta·'θjon; -'sjon) *n.f.* 1, representation. 2, *theat.* performance. 3, authority; dignity.
representante (re·pre·sen'tan·te) *n.m.* 1, representative. 2, *comm.* agent; salesman.
representar (re·pre·sen'tar) *v.t.* 1, to represent. 2, *theat.* to perform. —**representarse,** *v.r.* to imagine. —**representativo,** *adj.* representative.
represión (re·pre'sjon) *n.f.* repression. —**represivo** (-'si·βo) *also,* **represor** (-'sor) *adj.* repressive.
reprimenda (re·pri'men·da) *n.f.* reprimand.

reprimir (re·pri'mir) *v.t.* to repress; restrain.
reprobar (re·pro'βar) *v.t.* [*infl.:* **probar**] to reprove.
réprobo ('re·pro·βo) *adj.* & *n.m.* reprobate; damned.
reprochar (re·pro'tʃar) *v.t.* to reproach (someone) with. —**reproche** (-'pro·tʃe) *n.m.* reproach.
reproducir (re·pro·ðu'θir; -'sir) *v.t.* [*infl.:* **producir**] to reproduce. —**reproducción** (-ðuk'θjon; -'sjon) *n.f.* reproduction. —**reproductivo** (-'ti·βo) *adj.* reproductive. —**reproductor** (-'tor) *adj.* reproducing. —*n.m.* reproducer.
repropiarse (re·pro'pjar·se) *v.r.* to balk; be restive, as a horse. —**repropio** (-'pro·pjo) *adj.* balky; restive.
reptil (rep'til) *n.m.* reptile. —*adj.* reptilian.
república (re'pu·βli·ka) *n.f.* republic. —**republicano,** *adj.* & *n.m.* republican. —**republicanismo,** *n.m.* republicanism.
repudiar (re·pu'ðjar) *v.t.* to repudiate. —**repudio** (-'pu·ðjo) *n.m., also,* **repudiación,** *n.f.* repudiation.
repudrirse (re·pu'ðrir·se) *v.r., colloq.* [*infl.:* **pudrir**] to pine away.
repuesto (re'pwes·to) *v., pp. of* **reponer.** —*n.m.* replacement part; spare part. —**de repuesto,** extra; spare.
repugnar (re·puɣ'nar) *v.t.* to disgust; revolt. —*v.i.* to be repugnant. —**repugnancia,** *n.f.* repugnance. —**repugnante,** *adj.* repugnant.
repujar (re·pu'xar) *v.t.* to work (metal) in repoussé; emboss (leather). —**repujado,** *adj.* & *n.m.* repoussé; embossing.
repulgado (re·pul'ɣa·ðo) *adj., colloq.* affected.
repulgar (re·pul'ɣar) *v.t.* [*pres. subjve.* **repulgue** (-'pul·ɣe); *pret.* **repulgué** (-'ɣe)] to hem; border.
repulgo (re'pul·ɣo) *n.m.* **1,** hem. **2,** edging (*of pie or pastry*).
repulir (re·pu'lir) *v.t.* **1,** to repolish; refurbish. **2,** to dress up. —**repulido,** *adj.* slick; shiny.
repulsar (re·pul'sar) *v.t.* to repulse. —**repulsa** (-'pul·sa) *n.f.* repulse. —**repulsión** (-'sjon) *n.f.* repulsion; repugnance. —**repulsivo** (-'si·βo) *adj.* repulsive.
repullo (re'pu·ʎo; -jo) *n.m.* start; jump.
reputar (re·pu'tar) *v.t.* to esteem; repute. —**reputación,** *n.f.* reputation.
requebrar (re·ke'βrar) *v.t.* [*infl.:* **quebrar**] to flatter; address gallantries to.
requemar (re·ke'mar) *v.t.* **1,** to burn again. **2,** to overcook; scorch. **3,** to parch. —**requemarse,** *v.r.* to smolder.
requerir (re·ke'rir) *v.t.* [*pres.ind.* **requiero;** *pres.subjve.* **requiera;** *pret.* **requerí, requirió;** *ger.* **requiriendo**] **1,** to require; need; call for. **2,** to demand; request. **3,** to court; woo. —**requerimiento,** *n.m.* demand; request.
requesón (re·ke'son) *n.m.* cottage cheese.
requiebro (re'kje·βro) *n.m.* flattery; gallantry.
réquiem ('re·kjem) [*pl.* **réquiems**] *n.m.* requiem.
requiera (re'kje·ra) *v., pres.subjve. of* **requerir.**
requiero (re'kje·ro) *v., pres.ind. of* **requerir.**
requilorios (re·ki'lo·rjos) *n.m.pl., colloq.* hemming and hawing; beating about the bush.
requiriendo (re·ki'rjen·do) *v., ger. of* **requerir.**
requirió (re·ki'rjo) *v., 3rd pers. sing.pret. of* **requerir.**
requisa (re'ki·sa) *n.f.* **1,** tour of inspection. **2,** requisition. **3,** confiscation; expropriation.
requisar (re·ki'sar) *v.t.* **1,** to requisition. **2,** to confiscate; expropriate.
requisición (re·ki·si'θjon; -'sjon) *n.f.* requisition.
requisito (re·ki'si·to) *n.m.* requisite.
res (res) *n.f.* **1,** head, esp. of cattle. **2,** bovine animal.
resabiar (re·sa'βjar) *v.t.* to incline to bad habits; give bad habits to. —**resabiarse,** *v.r.* **1,** to spoil; acquire bad taste. **2,** to be miffed; be piqued. **3,** to fester.
resabio (re'sa·βjo) *n.m.* **1,** unpleasant aftertaste. **2,** touch; tinge. **3,** bad habit or tendency.
resaca (re'sa·ka) *n.f.* **1,** undertow; backflow. **2,** hangover. **3,** *comm.* redraft.
resalado (re·sa'la·ðo) *adj., colloq.* **1,** very graceful; charming. **2,** amusing; spicy.
resalir (re·sa'lir) *v.i.* [*infl.:* **salir**] to jut out; project.

resaltar (re·sal'tar) *v.i.* 1, to stand out; show up clearly. 2, to be evident; be clear. 3, to jut out; project.
resalto (re'sal·to) *n.m., also,* **resalte** (-te) 1, jutting part; projection. 2, prominence; conspicuousness.
resarcir (re·sar'θir; -'sir) *v.t.* [*pres.ind.* **resarzo** (-'sar·θo; -so); *pres.subjve.* **resarza** (-θa; -sa)] to compensate; repay; indemnify. —**resarcirse,** *v.r., fol. by* **de,** to recover; recoup. —**resarcimiento,** *n.m.* compensation; indemnification.
resbalar (res·βa'lar) *v.i.* 1, to slip; slide. 2, to err; fall into error. —**resbaladizo,** *also,* **resbaloso,** *adj.* slippery. —**resbalón** (-'lon) *n.m.* slip.
rescatar (res·ka'tar) *v.t.* 1, to rescue; free; save. 2, to extricate; disentangle. 3, to ransom. 4, to redeem; recover.
rescate (res'ka·te) *n.m.* 1, rescue. 2, ransom. 3, redemption.
rescindir (res·θin'dir; re·sin-) *v.t.* to rescind. —**rescisión** (res·θi'sjon; re·si-) *n.f.* rescission.
rescoldo (res'kol·do) *n.m.* 1, ember; embers (*pl.*). 2, grudge; sore spot; rankling. 3, scruple; qualm; misgiving.
rescripto (res'krip·to) *n.m.* rescript; edict.
resecar (re·se'kar) *v.t.* [*infl.:* **secar**] 1, to dry up. 2, to wither; shrivel. —**resecación,** *n.f.* a drying up.
reseco (re'se·ko) *adj.* dried up. —*n.m.* dried-up part.
reseda (re'se·ða) *n.f.* mignonette.
resentido (re·sen'ti·ðo) *adj.* 1, sore; tender. 2, angry; annoyed; resentful.
resentirse (re·sen'tir·se) *v.r.* [*infl.:* **sentir**] 1, to be or become sore or tender. 2, to be resentful; be annoyed or angry. —**resentir,** *v.t., colloq.* to resent. —**resentimiento,** *n.m.* resentment.
reseña (re'se·ɲa) *n.f.* 1, brief description; note; sketch. 2, review.
reseñar (re·se'ɲar) *v.t.* 1, to make a review of; review. 2, to outline; sketch.
resero (re'se·ro) *n.m., Amer.* 1, cowboy; cattle herder. 2, livestock dealer.
reserva (re'ser·βa) *n.f.* 1, reserve. 2, *mil.* reserve; reserves (*pl.*). 3, reservation; qualification.
reservación (re·ser·βa'θjon; -'sjon) *n.f.* reservation.
reservado (re·ser'βa·ðo) *adj.* 1, reserved. 2, private; confidential. —*n.m.* compartment or room reserved for special use or occasion.
reservar (re·ser'βar) *v.t.* 1, to reserve. 2, to keep; hold back, retain. —**reservarse,** *v.r.* 1, to become reserved. 2, to hold back; hold off.
reservista (re·ser'βis·ta) *n.m.* reservist.
resfriado (res·fri'a·ðo) *n.m.* cold; catarrh. *Also,* **resfrío** (-'fri·o).
resfriarse (res·fri'ar·se) *v.r.* [*infl.:* **enfriar**] to catch cold.
resguardar (res·ɣwar'ðar) *v.t.* to guard; shield; protect. —**resguardarse,** *v.r.* 1, to shield oneself. 2, to take shelter.
resguardo (res'ɣwar·ðo) *n.m.* 1, guard; shield; protection. 2, *comm.* guaranty; security.
residencia (re·si'ðen·θja; -sja) *n.f.* residence. —**residencial,** *adj.* residential. —**residente,** *adj.* & *n.m.* & *f.* resident.
residir (re·si'ðir) *v.i.* to reside.
residuo (re'si·ðwo) *n.m.* 1, residue. 2, *math.* remainder. —**residual,** *adj.* residual.
resignar (re·siɣ'nar) *v.t.* & *i.* to resign. —**resignarse,** *v.r.* to resign oneself; be resigned. —**resignación,** *n.f.* resignation.
resina (re'si·na) *n.f.* 1, resin. 2, rosin. —**resinoso,** *adj.* resinous.
resistencia (re·sis'ten·θja; -sja) *n.f.* resistance. —**resistente,** *adj.* resistant.
resistible (re·sis'ti·βle) *adj.* resistible.
resistir (re·sis'tir) *v.t.* & *i.* 1, to resist; withstand. 2, to endure; bear. —**resistirse,** *v.r.* 1, to resist. 2, *fol. by* **a,** to refuse.
resistor (re·sis'tor) *n.m.* resistor.
resma ('res·ma) *n.f.* ream.
resobrino (re·so'βri·no) *n.m.* grandnephew; great-nephew. —**resobrina,** *n.f.* grandniece; great-niece.
resol (re'sol) *n.m.* sun glare.
resolución (re·so·lu'θjon; -'sjon) *n.f.* 1, resolution. 2, resolve. —**en resolución,** in short; by way of concluding.
resoluto (re·so'lu·to) *adj.* resolute.
resolver (re·sol'βer) *v.t.* [*infl.:* **absolver**] 1, to resolve. 2, to solve. —**resolverse,** *v.r.* to resolve; make up one's mind.
resollar (re·so'ʎar; -'jar) *v.i.*

[*pres.ind.* **resuello**; *pres.subjve.* **resuelle**] **1,** to breathe noisily or heavily. **2,** *colloq.* to breathe. **3,** *colloq.* to talk; make a peep.

resonador (re·so·na'ðor) *adj.* resonating. —*n.m.* resonator.

resonante (re·so'nan·te) *adj.* **1,** resonant. **2,** resounding. —**resonancia,** *n.f.* resonance.

resonar (re·so'nar) *v.i.* [*infl.:* **sonar**] to resound.

resoplar (re·so'plar) *v.i.* to breathe noisily; snort; puff. —**resoplido** *also,* **resoplo** (-'so·plo) *n.m.* snort; puff.

resorte (re'sor·te) *n.m.* **1,** *mech.* spring. **2,** springiness. **3,** recourse; resort.

respaldar (res·pal'dar) *v.t.* to back; support. —*n.m.* back (*of a seat*). —**respaldarse,** *v.r.* **1,** to find support; be backed. **2,** to sit back.

respaldo (res'pal·do) *n.m.* **1,** back (*of a seat*). **2,** backing; support. **3,** back of a sheet of paper.

respectar (res·pek'tar) *v.t.* to concern; relate to.

respectivo (res·pek'ti·βo) *adj.* respective.

respecto (res'pek·to) *n.m.* concern; relation; bearing; respect. —**al respecto,** in that respect; in that regard. —**con respecto a; respecto a,** as concerns; respecting; with respect to.

résped ('res·peð) *n.f.* **1,** serpent's tongue. **2,** barb; sting.

respetable (res·pe'ta·βle) *adj.* respectable. —**respetabilidad,** *n.f.* respectability.

respetar (res·pe'tar) *v.t.* to respect.

respeto (res'pe·to) *n.m.* respect. —**respetuoso** (-'two·so) *adj.* respectful.

respingado (res·pin'ga·ðo) *adj.* turned up, as the nose. *Also,* **respingón** (-'gon).

respingar (res·pin'gar) *v.i.* [*pres. subjve.* **respingue** (-'pin·ge); *pret.* **respingué** (-'ge)] **1,** to buck; rear. **2,** *colloq.* to wince.

respingo (res'pin·go) *n.m.* **1,** buck; bucking. **2,** *colloq.* wince.

respiración (res·pi·ra'θjon; -'sjon) *n.f.* respiration; breathing. —**sin respiración,** breathless; panting.

respiradero (res·pi·ra'ðe·ro) *n.m.* **1,** vent; air hole. **2,** small window or skylight. **3,** *colloq.* breather; respite. **4,** *colloq.* respiratory system.

respirador (res·pi·ra'ðor) *adj.* **1,** breathing. **2,** respiratory. —*n.m.* respirator.

respirar (res·pi'rar) *v.i.* & *t.* to breathe. —*v.i.* to breathe freely; rest; relax.

respiratorio (res·pi·ra'to·rjo) *adj* respiratory.

respiro (res'pi·ro) *n.m.* **1,** breath. **2,** pause; respite.

resplandecer (res·plan·de'θer; 'ser) *v.i.* [*pres.ind.* **resplandezco** (-'deθ·ko; -'des·ko); *pres.subjve.* **resplandezca** (-ka)] to shine; glow; glitter. —**resplandeciente,** *adj.* resplendent.

resplandor (res·plan'dor) *n.m.* shine; glitter; glow; resplendence.

respondedor (res·pon·de'ðor) *adj.* **1,** respondent. **2,** responsive. —*n.m.* respondent.

responder (res·pon'der) *v.t.* & *i.* to answer. —*v.i.* to respond.

respondón (res·pon'don) *adj., colloq.* cheeky; impertinent; saucy.

responsabilizar (res·pon·sa·βi·li'θar; -'sar) *v.t.* [*pres.subjve.* **responsabilice** (-'li·θe; -se); *pret.* **responsabilicé** (-'θe; -'se)] to make responsible. —**responsabilizarse,** *v.r.* to be responsible; take responsibility. —**responsabilizarse de,** to take responsibility for.

responsable (res·pon'sa·βle) *adj.* responsible. —**responsabilidad,** *n.f.* responsibility.

responsar (res·pon'sar) *v.i.* to recite prayers for the dead. —*v.t.* **1,** to say prayers for (a dead person). **2,** *colloq.* to scold; lecture. *Also, colloq.,* **responsear** (-se'ar).

responsivo (res·pon'si·βo) *adj.* responsive.

responso (res'pon·so) *n.m.* **1,** prayer for the dead. **2,** *colloq.* scolding; lecture.

respuesta (res'pwes·ta) *n.f.* answer; reply; response.

resquebradura (res·ke·βra'ðu·ra) *n.f.* crack; cracking. *Also,* **resquebrajadura** (-xa'ðu·ra) *n.f.,* **resquebrajo** (-'βra·xo) *n.m.*

resquebrajar (res·ke·βra'xar) *v.t.* to crack; damage; break. —**resquebrajarse,** *v.r.* to crack; break. —**resquebrajadizo,** *adj.* brittle; fragile.

resquebrar (res·ke'βrar) *v.t.* [*infl.:* **quebrar**] to cause to give way; crack; split.

resquemar (res·ke'mar) *v.t.* & *i.*

1, to sting; bite (the tongue). 2, to itch.
resquemor (res·ke'mor) *n.m.* 1, burn; bite; smarting. 2, *fig.* itch; restlessness.
resquicio (res'ki·θjo; -sjo) *n.m.* 1, chink; crack; slit. 2, chance; opening.
resta ('res·ta) *n.f., math.* 1, subtraction. 2, difference; remainder.
restablecer (res·ta·βle'θer; -'ser) *v.t.* [*infl.:* **establecer**] to reestablish; restore. —**restablecerse,** *v.r.* to recuperate; recover.
restablecimiento (res·ta·βle·θi·'mjen·to; -si'mjen·to) *n.m.* 1, reestablishment; restoration. 2, recovery; recuperation.
restallar (res·ta'ʎar; -'jar) *v.i.* to crack, as a whip; snap. —**restallido,** *n.m.* snap; crack.
restante (res'tan·te) *n.m.* rest; remainder.
restañar (res·ta'ɲar) *v.t.* to stanch.
restar (res'tar) *v.t.* & *i.* to subtract. —*v.i.* to be left; be left over; remain.
restaurante (res·tau'ran·te) *n.m.* restaurant.
restaurar (res·tau'rar) *v.t.* to restore. —**restauración,** *n.f.* restoration. —**restaurativo,** *adj.* & *n.m.* restorative.
restituir (res·ti·tu'ir) *v.t.* [*infl.:* **constituir**] to return; restore. —**restituirse,** *v.r.* to go back; return. —**restitución,** *n.f.* restitution.
resto ('res·to) *n.m.* rest; remainder. —**restos,** *n.m.pl.* 1, remains. 2, leftovers. —**echar el resto,** to do one's best.
restorán (res·to'ran) *n.m., Amer.* restaurant.
restregar (res·tre'ɣar) *v.t.* [*infl.:* **estregar**] to scrub; rub. —**restregadura,** *n.f., also,* **restregón** (-'ɣon) *n.m.* scrubbing; rubbing.
restringir (res·trin'xir) *v.t.* [*pres. ind.* **restrinjo** (-'trin·xo); *pres.subjve.* **restrinja** (-xa)] to restrict. —**restricción** (-trik'θjon; -'sjon) *n.f.* restriction. —**restrictivo** (-'ti·βo) *adj.* restrictive.
resucitar (re·su·θi'tar; -si'tar) *v.t.* & *i.* to resuscitate; revive. —*v.t.* to resurrect. —*v.i.* to rise from the dead. —**resucitación,** *n.f.* resuscitation.
resudar (re·su'ðar) *v.i.* to perspire lightly. —**resudor** (-'ðor) *n.m.* light sweat.
resuelto (re'swel·to) *v., pp. of* **resolver.** —*adj.* resolute.
resuelva (re'swel·βa) *v., pres. subjve. of* **resolver.**
resuelvo (re'swel·βo) *v., pres.ind. of* **resolver.**
resuelle (re'swe·ʎe; -je) *v., pres. subjve. of* **resollar.**
resuello (re'swe·ʎo; -jo) *v., pres. ind. of* **resollar.** —*n.m.* 1, breath; breathing. 2, pant; panting.
resuene (re'swe·ne) *v., pres. subjve. of* **resonar.**
resueno (re'swe·no) *v., pres.ind. of* **resonar.**
resulta (re'sul·ta) *n.f.* result; consequence. —**de resultas,** as a result.
resultado (re·sul'ta·ðo) *n.m.* result.
resultante (re·sul'tan·te) *adj.* & *n.f.* resultant. —*adj.* resulting.
resultar (re·sul'tar) *v.i.* 1, to result. 2, to come out; turn out.
resumen (re'su·men) *n.m.* summary; abridgment; résumé. —**en resumen,** in short.
resumidero (re·su·mi'ðe·ro) *n.m., Amer.* = **sumidero.**
resumir (re·su'mir) *v.t.* 1, to summarize; abridge. 2, *incorrect* = **reasumir.**
resurgir (re·sur'xir) *v.i.* [*pres.ind.* **resurjo** (-'sur·xo); *pres.subjve.* **resurja** (-xa)] 1, to resurge. 2, to revive; be revived or resurrected. —**resurgimiento,** *n.m.* resurgence.
resurrección (re·su·rrek'θjon; -'sjon) *n.f.* resurrection.
retablo (re'ta·βlo) *n.m.* 1, altarpiece; retable. 2, tableau.
retaco (re'ta·ko) *adj., colloq.* stubby. —*n.m.* 1, short, stubby shotgun. 2, stubby person.
retador (re·ta'ðor) *n.m.* challenger.
retaguardia (re·ta'ɣwar·ðja) *n.f.* 1, rear guard. 2, rearward sector; rear.
retahila (re·ta'i·la) *n.f.* slew; string.
retal (re'tal) *n.m.* remnant.
retama (re'ta·ma) *n.f., bot.* broom; furze.
retar (re'tar) *v.t.* 1, to challenge. 2, *colloq.* to scold; reprimand.
retardar (re·tar'ðar) *v.t.* to retard; delay. —**retardarse,** *v.r.* to be delayed; be late. —**retardo** (-'tar·ðo) *n.m., also,* **retardación,** *n.f.* retardation; delay.

retazo (re'ta·θo; -so) *n.m.* **1,** remnant; strip. **2,** part; fragment.
retemblar (re·tem'blar) *v.i.* [*infl.:* **temblar**] to tremble or shake violently and repeatedly.
retén (re'ten) *n.m.* **1,** provision; reserve. **2,** reserve troops. **3,** house of detention; city jail.
retener (re·te'ner) *v.t.* [*infl.:* **tener**] **1,** to retain. **2,** to detain; confine. **3,** to contain; hold back. —**retención,** *n.f.* retention.
retentivo (re·ten'ti·βo) *adj.* retentive. —**retentiva,** *n.f.* retentiveness; memory.
reticencia (re·ti'θen·θja; -'sen·sja) *n.f.* reticence. —**reticente,** *adj.* reticent.
retina (re'ti·na) *n.f.* retina.
retintín (re·tin'tin) *n.m.* **1,** tinkling. **2,** *colloq.* ironic tone. **3,** ringing in the ears.
retiñir (re·ti'ɲir) *v.i.* [*infl.:* **bruñir**] **1,** to tinkle; jingle. **2,** to ring, as the ears.
retirada (re·ti'ra·ða) *n.f.* retreat; withdrawal.
retirado (re·ti'ra·ðo) *adj.* **1,** retired. **2,** distant; removed; remote. —*n.m., mil.* retired officer.
retirar (re·ti'rar) *v.t.* **1,** to retire. **2,** to take back; withdraw; remove. —**retirarse,** *v.r.* **1,** to withdraw. **2,** to retire.
retiro (re'ti·ro) *n.m.* **1,** retirement. **2,** retreat.
reto ('re·to) *n.m.* challenge.
retocar (re·to'kar) *v.t.* [*infl.:* **tocar**] to retouch.
retoño (re'to·ɲo) *n.m.* **1,** sprout; shoot. **2,** *colloq.* child; offspring. —**retoñar,** *v.i.* to sprout; shoot.
retoque (re'to·ke) *n.m.* **1,** beat; beating; pounding. **2,** retouching. **3,** finishing touch. **4,** touch; mild attack, as of a disease.
retorcer (re·tor'θer; -'ser) *v.t.* [*infl.:* **torcer**] **1,** to twist. **2,** to wring (the hands). —**retorcerse,** *v.r.* to twist; writhe. —**retorcimiento,** *n.m.* twist; twisting.
retórica (re'to·ri·ka) *n.f.* **1,** rhetoric. **2,** *usu.pl., colloq.* sophistries; roundabout talk. —**retórico,** *adj.* rhetorical. —*n.m.* rhetorician.
retornar (re·tor'nar) *v.i.* **1,** to return. **2,** to recede. —*v.t.* to give back; return; restore. —**retorno** (-'tor·no) *n.m.* return.
retorta (re'tor·ta) *n.f., chem.* retort.
retortero (re·tor'te·ro) *n.m.* twirl; whirl; twist. —**andar al retortero,** to bustle around; hover about.
retortijar (re·tor·ti'xar) *v.t.* to twist; curl. —**retortijón** (-'xon) *n.m.* twisting. —**retortijón de tripas,** *colloq.* bellyache.
retozar (re·to'θar; -'sar) *v.i.* [*pres. subjve.* **retoce** (-'to·θe; -se); *pret.* **retocé** (-'θe; -'se)] to romp; frolic. —**retozo** (-'to·θo; -so) *n.m.* romping; frolicking. —**retozo de la risa,** titter; snicker.
retozón (re·to'θon; -'son) *adj.* playful; frolicsome.
retractar (re·trak'tar) *v.t.* to retract. —**retractarse,** *v.r.* to retract; recant. —**retracción,** *n.f.* retraction. —**retractación,** *n.f.* recantation.
retractor (re·trak'tor) *n.m.* retractor.
retraer (re·tra'er) *v.t.* [*infl.:* **traer**] to dissuade. —**retraerse,** *v.r.* to retire; withdraw. —**retraído,** *adj.* shy; retiring.
retraimiento (re·tra·i'mjen·to) *n.m.* **1,** shyness; reserve. **2,** retreat; withdrawal.
retraqueo (re·tra'ke·o) *n.m., archit.* setback.
retrasar (re·tra'sar) *v.t.* **1,** to defer; delay. **2,** to set back, as a clock. —*v.i.* to go back; retrogress. —**retrasarse,** *v.r.* **1,** to be backward. **2,** to be late.
retraso (re'tra·so) *n.m.* **1,** delay. **2,** slowness. **3,** backwardness.
retratar (re·tra'tar) *v.t.* **1,** to portray; describe. **2,** to photograph.
retrato (re'tra·to) *n.m.* **1,** portrait; description. **2,** resemblance; likeness. —**retratista,** *n.m.* & *f.* portrait painter.
retrechar (re·tre'tʃar) *v.i.* to move backward.
retrechero (re·tre'tʃe·ro) *adj., colloq.* **1,** sly; cunning; evasive. **2,** bewitching; attractive.
retreta (re'tre·ta) *n.f., mil.* retreat.
retrete (re'tre·te) *n.m.* toilet; rest room.
retribuir (re·tri·βu'ir) *v.t.* [*infl.:* **contribuir**] to recompense. —**retribución,** *n.f.* retribution. —**retributivo** (-'ti·βo) *adj.* retributive.
retro- (re·tro) *prefix* retro-. **1,** back; backwards (in space or time): *retrospección,* retrospection; *retrogresión,* retrogression. **2,** anterior; prior: *retroactivo,* retroactive.
retroactivo (re·tro·ak'ti·βo) *adj.*

retroactive. —**retroactividad,** *n.f.* retroactivity.
retroceder (re-tro·θe'ðer; -se·ðer) *v.i.* to turn back; recede.
retroceso (re·tro'θe·so; -'se·so) *n.m.* **1,** setback. **2,** backward movement; recession. **3,** *med.* relapse.
retrogradar (re·tro·ɣra'ðar) *v.i.* **1,** to retrogress. **2,** *astron.* to retrograde. —**retrogradación,** *n.f., astron.* retrogradation.
retrógrado (re'tro·ɣra·ðo) *adj.* **1,** retrograde. **2,** retrogressive. —*adj.* & *n.m., polit.* reactionary.
retrogresión (re·tro·ɣre'sjon) *n.f.* retrogression.
retronar (re·tro'nar) *v.i.* [*infl.:* **tronar**] to thunder; rumble.
retrospección (re·tros·pek'θjon; -'sjon) *n.f.* **1,** retrospect. **2,** retrospection. —**retrospectivo** (-'ti·βo) *adj.* retrospective.
retrotraer (re·tro·tra'er) *v.t.* [*infl.:* **traer**] to antedate.
retruécano (re'trwe·ka·no) *n.m.* pun; play on words.
retuerza (re'twer·θa; -sa) *v., pres. subjve. of* **retorcer.**
retuerzo (re'twer·θo; -so) *v., 1st pers.sing. pres.ind. of* **retorcer.**
retumbar (re·tum'bar) *v.i.* to resound; reverberate; rumble. —**retumbo** (-'tum·bo) *n.m.* reverberation; rumble.
reuma ('reu·ma) *n.m. or f.* = **reumatismo.**
reumatismo (reu·ma'tis·mo) *n.m.* rheumatism. —**reumático** (-'ma·ti·ko) *adj.* & *n.m.* rheumatic.
reunión (re·u'njon) *n.f.* **1,** reunion. **2,** gathering; assembly.
reunir (re·u'nir) *v.t.* [*pres.ind.* **reúno** (-'u·no); *pres.subjve.* **reúna** (-na)] **1,** to reunite. **2,** to unite; join. **3,** to gather. —**reunirse,** *v.r.* to meet; gather.
revalidar (re·βa·li'ðar) *v.t.* to confirm; validate. —**revalidación,** *n.f.* confirmation; validation. —**reválida** (-'βa·li·ða) *n.f.* final examination for an academic degree.
revancha (re'βan·tʃa) *n.f.* **1,** revenge; retaliation. **2,** return game or match.
revelar (re·βe'lar) *v.t.* **1,** to reveal. **2,** *photog.* to develop. —**revelación,** *n.f.* revelation. —**revelado,** *n.m., photog.* developing. —**revelador,** *adj.* revealing. —*n.m.* **1,** revealer. **2,** *photog.* developer.
revendedor (re·βen·de'ðor) *n.m.* **1,** retailer. **2,** *colloq.* ticket scalper.
revender (re·βen'der) *v.t.* to resell; retail. —**revendedor,** *n.m.* **1,** retailer. **2,** *colloq.* ticket scalper.
revenirse (re·βe'nir·se) *v.r.* [*infl.:* **venir**] to become shriveled; spoil; turn.
reventa (re'βen·ta) *n.f.* **1,** resale. **2,** retail.
reventar (re·βen'tar) *v.i.* [*pres.ind.* **reviento**; *pres.subjve.* **reviente**] **1,** to burst; blow up; blow out. **2,** to break, as waves. **3,** to blossom; burst into bloom. **4,** *colloq. fol. by* **por,** to crave; long. **5,** *slang* to die; croak. —*v.t.* **1,** to burst; crack open. **2,** to break down (a horse). **3,** *colloq.* to ruin; destroy; smash. **4,** *colloq.* to overburden; crush. **5,** *colloq.* to tire; exhaust.
reventón (re·βen'ton) *adj.* bursting. —*n.m.* **1,** burst; explosion. **2,** blowout; flat tire. **3,** *colloq.* backbreaking job.
reverberar (re·βer·βe'rar) *v.i.* to reverberate. —**reverbero** (-'βe·ro) *n.m., also,* **reverberación,** *n.f.* reverberation.
reverdecer (re·βer·ðe'θer; -'ser) *v.i.* [*pres.subjve.* **reverdezca** (-'ðeθ·ka; -'ðes·ka)] to grow green again; regain freshness.
reverencia (re·βe'ren·θja; -sja) *n.f.* **1,** reverence. **2,** curtsy; bow. —**reverencial,** *adj.* reverential; awesome.
reverenciar (re·βe·ren'θjar; -'sjar) *v.t.* to revere. —**reverenciable,** *adj.* venerable.
reverendo (re·βe'ren·ðo) *adj.* & *n.m.* reverend.
reverente (re·βe'ren·te) *adj.* reverent.
reversible (re·βer'si·βle) *adj.* reversible. —**reversibilidad,** *n.f.* reversibility.
reversión (re·βer'sjon) *n.f.* reversion.
reverso (re'βer·so) *n.m.* reverse. —**el reverso de la medalla,** the exact opposite.
reverter (re·βer'ter) *v.i.* [*infl.:* **verter**] to overflow.
revertir (re·βer'tir) *v.i.* [*infl.:* **advertir**] to revert.
revés (re'βes) *n.m.* **1,** other side; reverse. **2,** backhanded slap or blow. **3,** setback; reverse. —**al revés,** backwards; inside out; wrong side out (*or* up); the opposite way.

revesado (re·βe'sa·ðo) *adj.* **1,** complex; intricate. **2,** wild; unruly.
revestir (re·βes'tir) *v.t.* [*infl.:* **vestir**] **1,** to dress; clothe. **2,** to invest; endow. **3,** to cover; coat; face. **—revestirse,** *v.r.* to gird oneself. **—revestimiento,** *also,* **revestido,** *n.m.* facing; coating.
reviente (re'βjen·te) *v., pres. subjve. of* **reventar.**
reviento (re'βjen·to) *v., pres.ind. of* **reventar.**
revisar (re·βi'sar) *v.t.* **1,** to review. **2,** to inspect; examine; check. **3,** to revise. **4,** to audit.
revisión (re·βi'sjon) *n.f.* **1,** review. **2,** inspection; examination; check. **3,** revision. **4,** audit.
revisor (re·βi'sor) *n.m.* **1,** inspector; examiner. **2,** reviser. **3,** auditor.
revista (re'βis·ta) *n.f.* **1,** review. **2,** magazine; journal; review. **3,** *theat.* revue. **—pasar revista,** *also,* **revistar,** *v.t.* to review; inspect.
revivir (re·βi'βir) *v.i.* to revive.
revocable (re·βo'ka·βle) *adj.* revocable.
revocador (re·βo·ka'ðor) *n.m.* **1,** revoker. **2,** plasterer; whitewasher; painter.
revocar (re·βo'kar) *v.t.* [*pres. subjve.* **revoque;** *pret.* **revoqué**] **1,** to revoke. **2,** to repaint or refinish, esp. the walls of a building. **—revocación,** *n.f.* revocation. **—revocadura,** *n.f.* refinishing; repainting.
revolcar (re·βol'kar) *v.t.* [*infl.:* **volcar**] to knock down; trample; drag in the dust. **—revolcarse,** *v.r.* **1,** to wallow, as in mud. **2,** to roll over and over on the ground. **—revolcadero,** *n.m.* wallow.
revolcón (re·βol'kon) *n.m., colloq.* **1,** a rolling over; writhing in the dust. **2,** trampling; mauling. **3,** wallowing; tumbling. **4,** *colloq.* rebuff; rebuke. **5,** *colloq.* bawling-out; dressing-down.
revolotear (re·βo·lo·te'ar) *v.i.* **1,** to flutter; flit. **2,** to tumble through the air.
revoloteo (re·βo·lo'te·o) *n.m.* **1,** fluttering; flitting. **2,** tumbling through the air.
revolqué (re·βol'ke) *v., 1st pers. sing. pret. of* **revolcar.**
revoltijo (re·βol'ti·xo) *also,* **revoltillo,** *n.m.* **1,** jumble; mess; scramble. **2,** hodgepodge.
revoltoso (re·βol'to·so) *adj.* **1,** mischievous; unruly. **2,** turbulent; riotous.
revolución (re·βo·lu'θjon; -'sjon) *n.f.* revolution. **—revolucionar,** *v.t.* to revolutionize. **—revolucionario,** *adj.* & *n.m.* revolutionary. **—***n.m.* revolutionist.
revólver (re'βol·βer) *n.m.* revolver.
revolver (re·βol'βer) *v.t.* [*infl.:* **volver**] **1,** to mix; stir. **2,** to turn over; rummage through. **3,** to mix up; confuse. **4,** to arouse; stir up. **5,** to turn; turn over; revolve. **—revolverse,** *v.r.* **1,** to turn; turn around; wheel. **2,** to toss and turn. **3,** to squirm; wriggle.
revoque (re'βo·ke) *n.m.* **1,** = **revocadura. 2,** whitewash; plaster; finishing materials. **—***v., pres.subjve. of* **revocar.**
revoqué (re·βo'ke) *v., 1st pers. sing. pret. of* **revocar.**
revuelco (re'βwel·ko) *n.m.* **1,** upset; tumble. **2,** wallow; wallowing.
revuelo (re'βwe·lo) *n.m.* **1,** circling in flight. **2,** uproar; commotion. **—de revuelo,** in passing.
revuelque (re'βwel·ke) *v., pres. subjve. of* **revolcar.**
revuelta (re'βwel·ta) *n.f.* **1,** turn; return. **2,** revolt. **3,** turn; turning.
revuelto (re'βwel·to) *v., p.p. of* **revolver. —***adj.* **1,** disordered; upset. **2,** jumbled; scrambled. **3,** churned up; rough. **4,** mischievous; unruly.
revuelva (re'βwel·βa) *v., pres. subjve. of* **revolver.**
revuelvo (re'βwel·βo) *v., pres.ind. of* **revolver.**
revulsión (re·βul'sjon) *n.f.* revulsion.
rey ('rei) *n.m.* king.
reyerta (re'jer·ta) *n.f.* quarrel; dispute.
reyezuelo (re·je'θwe·lo; -'swe·lo) *n.m.* kinglet; wren.
rezagar (re·θa'ɣar; re·sa-) *v.t.* [*pres.subjve.* **rezague** (-'θa·ɣe; -'sa·ɣe); *pret.* **rezagué** (-'ɣe)] **1,** to leave behind; outstrip. **2,** to put off. **—rezagarse,** *v.r.* to fall behind; lag. **—rezagado,** *adj.* & *n.m.* laggard. **—rezago** (-'θa·ɣo; -'sa·ɣo) *n.m.* residue; remainder. **—venta de rezagos,** rummage sale.
rezar (re'θar; -'sar) *v.t.* [*pres. subjve.* **rece;** *pret.* **recé**] **1,** to say or recite (prayers, mass., etc.) **2,** *colloq.* to say; state. **—***v.i.* **1,** to pray; recite prayers. **2,** *colloq.* to

say; read. **3,** *colloq.* to grumble; whine. —**rezar con,** to concern; pertain to.

rezo ('re·θo; -so) *n.m.* **1,** prayer. **2,** prayers (*pl.*); devotions (*pl.*).

rezongar (re·θon'gar; re·son-) *v.i.* [*pres.subjve.* **rezongue** (-'θon·ge; -'son·ge); *pret.* **rezongué** (-'ge)] to grumble. —**rezongador,** *adj.* grumbling. —*n.m.* grumbler. *Also, colloq.* **rezongón** (-'gon).

rezumar (re·θu'mar; re·su-) *v.t.* & *i.* **1,** to ooze; exude. **2,** to percolate. —**rezumarse,** *v.r.* **1,** to seep; leak. **2,** *fig.* to leak out; be divulged.

ría ('ri·a) *n.f.* mouth of a river.

ría ('ri·a) *v., pres.subjve. of* **reír.**

¡riá! (ri'a) *interj.* haw!

riachuelo (ri·a'tʃwe·lo) *n.m.* stream; rivulet. *Also,* **riacho** (ri'a·tʃo).

riada (ri'a·ða) *n.f.* freshet; flood.

ribazo (ri'βa·θo; -so) *n.m.* embankment.

ribera (ri'βe·ra) *n.f.* shore; bank.

ribereño (ri·βe're·ɲo) *adj.* of or by the riverside. —*n.m.* riverside dweller.

ribero (ri'βe·ro) *n.m.* dike; levee.

ribete (ri'βe·te) *n.m.* **1,** edge; binding; border. **2,** trimming. **3,** embellishment. —**ribetes,** *n.m.pl.,* signs; indications.

ribetear (ri·βe·te'ar) *v.t.* **1,** to edge; bind; border. **2,** to trim; adorn.

ricacho (ri'ka·tʃo) *adj.* & *n.m., colloq., derog.* nouveau riche; filthy rich. *Also,* **ricachón.**

rice ('ri·θe; -se) *v., pres.subjve. of* **rizar.**

ricé (ri'θe; -'se) *v., 1st pers.sing. pret. of* **rizar.**

ricino (ri'θi·no; ri'si-) *n.m.* castor oil plant.

rico ('ri·ko) *adj.* **1,** rich; wealthy. **2,** delicious; exquisite. —*n.m., colloq., as a term of endearment* cutie; precious.

ridiculez (ri·ði·ku'leθ; -'les) *n.f.* **1,** ridiculousness. **2,** extravagance; oddity. **3,** excessive nicety; squeamishness.

ridiculizar (ri·ði·ku·li'θar; -'sar) *v.t.* [*pres.subjve.* **ridiculice** (-'li·θe; -se); *pret.* **ridiculicé** (-'θe; -'se)] to ridicule.

ridículo (ri'ði·ku·lo) *adj.* **1,** ridiculous. **2,** extravagant; odd. **3,** excessively nice; squeamish. —*n.m.* **1,** ridiculousness. **2,** ridicule.

riego ('rje·ɣo) *v., pres.ind. of* **regar.** —*n.m.* irrigation.

riegue ('rje·ɣe) *v., pres.subjve. of* **regar.**

riel (rjel) *n.m.* rail.

rielar (rje'lar) *v.i., poet.* to gleam; glitter.

rienda ('rjen·da) *n.f.* rein. —**rienda suelta,** free rein.

riendo ('rjen·do) *v., ger. of* **reír.**

riente ('rjen·te) *adj.* laughing; cheerful.

riesgo ('rjes·ɣo) *n.m.* danger; risk.

rifa ('ri·fa) *n.f.* raffle. —**rifar,** *v.t.* to raffle.

rifle ('ri·fle) *n.m.* rifle.

riflero (ri'fle·ro) *n.m* rifleman.

riges ('ri·xes) *v., 2nd pers.sing. pres.ind. of* **regir.**

rígido ('ri·xi·ðo) *adj.* rigid; inflexible. —**rigidez,** *n.f.* rigidity; inflexibility.

rigiendo (ri'xjen·do) *v., ger. of* **regir.**

rigió (ri'xjo) *v., 3rd pers.sing.pret. of* **regir.**

rigor (ri'ɣor) *n.m.* rigor; strictness. —**de rigor,** strictly required. —**en rigor,** *also,* **en rigor de verdad,** strictly speaking; as a matter of fact.

rigoroso (ri·ɣo'ro·so) *adj.* = **riguroso.** —**rigorosidad,** *n.f.* = **rigurosidad.**

riguroso (ri·ɣu'ro·so) *adj.* rigorous; strict; severe. —**rigurosidad,** *n.f.* rigorousness; severity.

rija ('ri·xa) *v., pres.subjve. of* **regir.** —*n.f.* lachrymal fistula.

rijo ('ri·xo) *v., 1st pers.sing.pres. ind. of* **regir.**

rima ('ri·ma) *n.f.* rhyme; *pl.* poems. —**rimar,** *v.t.* & *i.* to rhyme.

rimbombante (rim·bom'ban·te) *adj.* resounding; bombastic.

rimero (ri'me·ro) *n.m.* heap; pile.

rincón (rin'kon) *n.m.* corner; nook.

rinconada (rin·ko'na·ða) *n.f.* corner; angle.

rinconera (rin·ko'ne·ra) *n.f.* corner cupboard; corner table.

rinda ('rin·da) *v., pres.subjve. of* **rendir.**

rindiendo (rin'djen·do) *v., ger. of* **rendir.**

rindió (rin'djo) *v., 3rd pers.sing. pret. of* **rendir.**
rindo ('rin·do) *v., pres.ind. of* **rendir.**
ringlera (rin'gle·ra) *n.f.* row; file; line.
ringorrango (rin·go'rran·go) *n.m., colloq.* frill; fanciness.
rino- (ri·no) *prefix* rhino-; nose: *rinoplastia,* rhinoplasty.
rinoceronte (ri·no·θe'ron·te; ri·no·se-) *n.m.* rhinoceros.
riña ('ri·ɲa) *n.f.* quarrel; squabble. —*v., pres.subjve. of* **reñir.**
riñendo (ri'ɲen·do) *v., ger. of* **reñir.**
riño ('ri·ɲo) *v., pres.ind. of* **reñir.**
riñó (ri'ɲo) *v., 3rd pers.sing.pret. of* **reñir.**
riñón (ri'ɲon) *n.m.* **1,** kidney. **2,** *fig.* heart; core. —**tener el riñón cubierto,** *colloq.* to be well-off.
río ('ri·o) *n.m.* river. —**a río revuelto,** in confusion.
río('ri·o) *v., pres.ind. of* **reír.**
rió (rjo) *v., 3rd pers.sing.pret. of* **reír.**
riostra ('rjos·tra) *n.f., archit.* brace; stay.
ripio ('ri·pjo) *n.m.* **1,** refuse; debris; rubble. **2,** superfluous word or words; padding.
riqueza (ri'ke·θa; -sa) *n.f.* **1,** riches (*pl.*); wealth. **2,** richness. **3,** abundance.
risa ('ri·sa) *n.f.* laugh; laughter.
risada (ri'sa·ða) *n.f.* = **risotada.**
risco ('ris·ko) *n.m.* crag; cliff. —**riscoso,** *adj.* steep; craggy.
risible (ri'si·βle) *adj.* risible; laughable. —**risibilidad,** *n.f.* risibility.
risita (ri'si·ta) *also,* **risica,** *n.f.* giggle; titter.
risotada (ri·so'ta·ða) *n.f.* guffaw; loud laugh.
ristra ('ris·tra) *n.f.* **1,** string (*of onions, garlic, sausage, etc.*). **2.** row; file.
risueño (ri'swe·ɲo) *adj.* **1,** smiling; cheerful. **2,** favorable; promising. **3,** optimistic.
ritmo ('rit·mo) *n.m.* rhythm. —**rítmico,** *adj.* rhythmical.
rito ('ri·to) *n.m.* rite; ceremony. —**ritual** (-'twal) *adj. & n.m.* ritual. —**ritualista,** *adj.* ritualistic.
rival (ri'βal) *n.m. & f.* rival. —**rivalidad,** *n.f.* rivalry. —**rivalizar,** *v.i.* [*pres.subjve.* **rivalice** (-'li·θe; -se); *pret.* **rivalicé** (-'θe; -'se)] to compete. —**rivalizar con,** to rival; compete against.
rizar (ri'θar; -'sar) *v.t.* [*pres. subjve.* **rice**; *pret.* **ricé**] **1,** to curl. **2,** to crinkle; frizzle. **3,** to ripple, as water. —**rizador,** *n.m.* curler; curling iron.
rizo ('ri·θo; -so) *adj.* curly. —*n.m.* **1,** curl; ringlet. **2,** *aero.* loop. **3,** *naut.* reef. **4,** ripple.
rizo- (ri·θo; -so) *prefix* rhizo-; root: *rizópodo,* rhizopod.
roano (ro'a·no) *adj.* = **ruano.**
róbalo ('ro·βa·lo) *also,* **robalo** (ro'βa·lo) *n.m., ichthy.* bass; sea bass.
robar (ro'βar) *v.t.* **1,** to rob; steal. **2,** to abduct. **3,** to erode. **4,** *cards* to draw.
roble ('ro·βle) *n.m.* **1,** oak. **2,** *fig.* very strong person. —**roblizo,** *adj.* hard; strong.
robledal (ro·βle'ðal) *n.m.* oak woods. *Also,* **robleda,** *n.f.,* **robledo,** *n.m.*
robo ('ro·βo) *n.m.* robbery; theft.
robot (ro'βot) *n.m.* [*pl.* **robots**] robot.
robustecer (ro·βus·te'θer; -'ser) *v.t.* [*pres.ind.* **robustezco** (-'teθ·ko; -'tes·ko); *pres.subjve.* **robustezca** (-ka)] to strengthen; fortify.
robusto (ro'βus·to) *adj.* robust. —**robustez,** *n.f.* robustness.
roca ('ro·ka) *n.f.* rock. —**rocalla** (-'ka·ʎa; -ja) *n.f.* pebbles.
roce ('ro·θe; -se) *n.m.* **1,** friction. **2,** contact; intimacy. —*v., pres. subjve. of* **rozar.**
rocé (ro'θe; -'se) *v., 1st pers.sing. pret. of* **rozar.**
rociada (ro'θja·ða; -'sja·ða) *n.f.* **1,** sprinkle; spray; splash. **2,** *colloq.* scolding; dressing down.
rociar (ro'θjar; -'sjar) *v.i.* [*pres. ind.* **rocío** (-'θi·o; -'si·o); *pres. subjve.* **rocíe** (-'θi·e; -'si·e)] to fall as dew. —*v.t.* to spray; sprinkle; spatter. —**rociadera,** *n.f. also* **rociador,** *n.m.* watering can; sprinkler; sprayer.
rocín (ro'θin; -'sin) *n.m.* nag; jade.
rocío (ro'θi·o; -'si·o) *n.m.* dew.
rococó (ro·ko'ko) *adj. & n.m.* rococo.
rocoso (ro'ko·so) *adj.* rocky.
roda ('ro·ða) *n.f.* stem (*of a ship*).
rodaballo (ro·ða'βa·ʎo; -jo) *n.m.*

a fish resembling the turbot or the brill.

rodada (ro'ða·ða) *n.f.* **1,** rut; wheel track. **2,** *Amer.* fall; tumble.

rodadura (ro·ða'ðu·ra) *n.f.* rolling; wheeling.

rodado (ro'ða·ðo) *adj.* **1,** dappled. **2,** well-beaten; well-traveled; easy.

rodaja (ro'ða·xa) *n.f.* **1,** small wheel or disk. **2,** caster. **3,** round slice. **4,** rowel.

rodaje (ro'ða·xe) *n.m.* **1,** wheels; set of wheels; wheelwork. **2,** filming; shooting (*of a film*).

rodar (ro'ðar) *v.i.* [*pres.ind.* **ruedo;** *pres.subjve.* **ruede**] **1,** to roll; run on wheels. **2,** to spin; turn. **3,** to fall; tumble. **4,** to wander; drift. **5,** to follow in quick succession. —*v.t.* to film; shoot (a film).

rodear (ro·ðe'ar) *v.i.* **1,** to go around. **2,** to take the long way around. —*v.t.* **1,** to surround; encircle. **2,** to circle; go around. **3,** *Amer.* to round up (cattle).

rodeo (ro'ðe·o) *n.m.* **1,** turn. **2,** roundabout way. **3,** *Amer.* rodeo. **4,** corral. **5,** circumlocution; beating about the bush.

rodilla (ro'ði·ʎa; -ja) *n.f.* knee. —**rodillazo,** *n.m.* thrust with the knee. —**de rodillas,** on one's knees; kneeling.

rodillera (ro·ði'ʎe·ra; -'je·ra) *n.f.* **1,** kneecap. **2,** knee guard. **3,** bagging of trousers at the knees.

rodillo (ro'ði·ʎo; -jo) *n.m.* **1,** roller. **2,** rolling pin.

rodio ('ro·ðjo) *n.m.* rhodium.

rododendro (ro·ðo'ðen·dro) *n.m.* rhododendron.

rodrigar (ro·ðri'ɣar) *v.t.* [*pres. subjve.* **rodrigue** (-'ðri·ɣe); *pret.* **rodrigué** (-'ɣe)] to prop up (vines). —**rodrigazón,** *n.m.* propping season.

rodrigón (ro·ðri'ɣon) *n.m.* **1,** vine prop. **2,** *hist.* a male retainer who accompanied ladies.

roedor (ro·e'ðor) *adj.* gnawing. —*n.m.* rodent.

roedura (ro·e'ðu·ra) *n.f.* **1,** gnawing; gnawed part. **2,** corrosion; corroded part.

roer (ro'er) *v.t.* [*pret.* **roí, royó;** *ger.* **royendo**] **1,** to gnaw. **2,** to corrode.

rogación (ro·ɣa'θjon; -'sjon) *n.f.* request; petition. —**rogaciones,** *n.f.pl.* =**rogativa.**

rogar (ro'ɣar) *v.t.* [*pres.ind.* **ruego;** *pres.subjve.* **ruegue;** *pret.* **rogué** (-'ɣe)] **1,** to pray; ask. **2,** to beg; plead.

rogativa (ro·ɣa'ti·βa) *n.f., eccles.* rogation; Rogation Days.

rojo ('ro·xo) *adj.* **1,** red. **2,** ruddy; reddish. —**rojez,** *n.f.* redness. —**rojizo,** *adj.* reddish. —**rojura,** *n.f.* redness.

rollizo (ro'ʎi·θo; -'ji·so) *adj.* plump; robust. —*n.m.* log.

rollo ('ro·ʎo; -jo) *n.m.* **1,** roll. **2,** roller. **3,** log.

romadizo (ro·ma'ði·θo; -so) *n.m.* head cold.

romana (ro'ma·na) *n.f.* **1,** steelyard. **2,** scale; balance.

romance (ro'man·θe; -se) *adj.* Romance. —*n.m.* **1,** Romance language, esp. Spanish. **2,** romance; tale. **3,** historical ballad. **4,** *pl., colloq.* excuses; evasions. —**hablar en romance,** to speak plainly.

romancero (ro·man'θe·ro; -'se·ro) *n.m.* **1,** romancer. **2,** collection of ballads, esp. Spanish. **3,** *colloq.* fibber. —*adj., colloq.* evasive; fibbing.

románico (ro'ma·ni·ko) *adj.* **1,** Romanesque. **2,** Romanic; Romance.

romanista (ro·ma'nis·ta) *n.m.* Romanist.

romano (ro'ma·no) *adj.* & *n.m.* Roman.

romántico (ro'man·ti·ko) *adj.* romantic. —*n.m.* romanticist. —**romanticismo** (-'θis·mo; -'sis·mo) *n.m.* romanticism.

romanza (ro'man·θa; -sa) *n.f., music* romance; song.

romaza (ro'ma·θa; -sa) *n.f., bot.* dock.

rombo ('rom·bo) *n.m.* rhombus.

romboide (rom'boi·ðe) *n.m.* rhomboid. —**romboidal,** *also,* **rombóideo** (-'boi·ðe·o) *adj.* rhomboidal.

romero (ro'me·ro) *n.m.* **1,** pilgrim. **2,** *bot.* rosemary. —**romería,** *n.f.* pilgrimage; religious excursion.

romo ('ro·mo) *adj.* **1,** blunt; stubby. **2,** flat-nosed.

rompecabezas (rom·pe·ka'βe·θas; -sas) *n.m.sing.* & *pl.* **1,** a kind of mace; slung shot. **2,** puzzle; riddle; brain teaser. **3,** jigsaw puzzle.

rompehielos (rom·pe'je·los) *n.m.sing.* & *pl.* icebreaker.

rompehuelgas (rom·pe'wel·ɣas) *n.m.sing. & pl.* strikebreaker; scab.
rompeolas (rom·pe'o·las) *n.m. sing. & pl.* breakwater; mole; jetty.
romper (rom'per) *v.t.* [*p.p.* **roto**] **1,** to break. **2,** to rend; rip; tear. —*v.i.* **1,** to break; come apart; burst. **2,** to break; break forth (into action, utterance, etc.). **3,** to start; begin; open. **4,** *fol. by* **con,** to break with. **5,** to break, as the day. —**romperse,** *v.r., colloq.* to give one's all. —**de rompe y rasga,** confidently; resolutely.
rompiente (rom'pjen·te) *n.m.* reef; rocky shore; shoal; surf.
rompimiento (rom·pi'mjen·to) *n.m.* **1,** break; breaking; breakage. **2,** a breaking off; estrangement. **3,** break; opening.
ron (ron) *n.m.* rum.
roncador (ron·ka'ðor) *adj.* **1,** snoring. **2,** growling; roaring; bellowing. —*n.m.* **1,** snorer. **2,** *ichthy.* small bass.
roncar (ron'kar) *v.i.* [*pres.subjve.* **ronque;** *pret.* **ronqué**] **1,** to snore. **2,** to growl; roar; bellow. **3,** *colloq.* to be or act important; cut a figure.
roncear (ron·θe'ar; -se'ar) *v.i.* **1,** to shilly-shally; drag one's heels. **2,** to flatter; cajole. **3,** *naut.* to move slowly; make slow headway.
roncería (ron·θe'ri·a; -se'ri·a) *n.f.* **1,** shilly-shallying; heel-dragging. **2,** *colloq.* flattery; blandishment.
roncero (ron'θe·ro; -'se·ro) *adj.* **1,** slow; lazy; reluctant. **2,** uncooperative; malingering.
ronco ('ron·ko) *adj.* hoarse; raucous.
roncha ('ron·tʃa) *n.f.* **1,** welt; wale. **2,** *colloq.* brazen swindle. **3,** round slice. —**levantar** *or* **sacar ronchas,** *colloq.* to annoy; rankle.
ronda ('ron·da) *n.f.* **1,** round; circuit; regular course. **2,** watch; patrol. **3,** *colloq.* round, as of drinks. **4,** group of revelers. **5,** round of reveling; carousing. —**coger la ronda a,** to catch in the act. —**hacer la ronda a,** to court.
rondalla (ron'da·ʎa; -ja) *n.f.* **1,** tale; fib. **2,** making the rounds; carousing.
rondar (ron'dar) *v.t. & i.* **1,** to prowl. **2,** to circle; move around. **3,** to roam, as the streets. **4,** to make the rounds (of); go the rounds (of).
rondín (ron'din) *n.m.* **1,** round of inspection. **2,** *So. Amer.* night watchman.
rondó (ron'do) *n.m.* rondo.
ronque ('ron·ke) *v., pres.subjve. of* **roncar.**
ronqué (ron'ke) *v., 1st pers.sing. pret. of* **roncar.**
ronquedad (ron·ke'ðað) *n.f.* raucousness.
ronquera (ron'ke·ra) *n.f.* hoarseness.
ronquido (ron'ki·ðo) *n.m.* **1,** snore. **2,** hoarse sound.
ronronear (ron·ro·ne'ar) *v.i.* to purr. —**ronroneo** (-'ne·o) *n.m.* purr; purring.
ronzal (ron'θal; -'sal) *n.m.* halter.
roña ('ro·ɲa) *n.f.* **1,** rust. **2,** scabies; mange. **3,** grime. **4,** rot; rottenness; decay. **5,** *colloq.* stinginess; miserliness.
roñería (ro·ɲe'ri·a) *n.f., colloq.* miserliness; stinginess.
roñoso (ro'ɲo·so) *adj.* **1,** rusty. **2,** moldy. **3,** scabby; mangy. **4,** grimy. **5,** *colloq.* miserly; stingy.
ropa ('ro·pa) *n.f.* clothes (*pl.*); clothing. —**a quema ropa,** point-blank; at close range. —**ropa blanca, 1,** underwear; underclothes. **2,** linen. —**ropa de quita y pon,** knockabout clothes; casual wear. —**ropa hecha,** ready-made clothes.
ropaje (ro'pa·xe) *n.m.* **1,** dress; garb. **2,** wardrobe.
ropavejero (ro·pa·βe'xe·ro) *n.m.* old-clothes dealer. —**ropavejería,** *n.f.* secondhand clothing shop.
ropería (ro·pe'ri·a) *n.f.* **1,** clothier's trade. **2,** clothing shop. **3,** wardrobe; clothes room.
ropero (ro'pe·ro) *n.m.* **1,** clothier; clothes dealer. **2,** clothes cabinet; wardrobe; clothes closet.
roque ('ro·ke) *n.m., chess* rook.
roqueño (ro'ke·ɲo) *adj.* = **rocoso.**
rorcual (ror'kwal) *n.m.* rorqual.
rorro ('ro·rro) *n.m., colloq.* babe in arms.
rosa ('ro·sa) *n.f. & adj.* rose. —**rosa de los vientos; rosa náutica,** mariner's compass.
rosáceo (ro'sa·θe·o; -se·o) *adj.* **1,** rose-colored. **2,** rosaceous.
rosada (ro'sa·ða) *n.f.* rime.

rosado (ro'sa·ðo) *adj.* **1,** rosy; rose-colored; pink. **2,** frosted, as a drink.
rosal (ro'sal) *n.m.* rosebush.
rosaleda (ro·sa'le·ða) *n.f.* rose patch; rose thicket. *Also,* **rosalera.**
rosario (ro'sa·rjo) *n.m.* **1,** rosary. **2,** *fig.* series; train; chain.
rosbif (ros'bif) *n.m.* roast beef.
rosca ('ros·ka) *n.f.* **1,** bolt and nut. **2,** loop; twist; coil. **3,** thread (*of a screw, bolt, nut, etc.*). **4,** pastry ring; ring-shaped bread or roll. **5,** roll of fat, esp. of children. **6,** *So.Amer., colloq.* hassle; commotion.
roscado (ros'ka·ðo) *adj.* **1,** threaded; having threads. **2,** looped; coiled.
róseo ('ro·se·o) *adj.* rosy; roseate; rose-colored.
roseta (ro'se·ta) *n.f.* **1,** rosette. **2,** small rose. **3,** *pl.* [*also,* **rositas**] popcorn.
rosetón (ro·se'ton) *n.m.* rose window.
rosillo (ro'si·ʎo; -jo) *adj.* **1,** light red. **2,** roan.
rosquilla (ros'ki·ʎa; -ja) *n.f.* ring-shaped pastry or roll.
rostro ('ros·tro) *n.m.* face; visage; countenance. **—hacer rostro a,** to face; face up to.
rota ('ro·ta) *n.f.* **1,** rout; utter defeat. **2,** rattan; rattan palm.
rotación (ro·ta'θjon; -'sjon) *n.f.* rotation.
rotativo (ro·ta'ti·βo) *adj.* rotary. *—n.m., So.Amer.* continuous show.
rotatorio (ro·ta'to·rjo) *adj.* rotatory.
rotén (ro'ten) *also* **roten** ('ro·ten) *n.m.* **1,** rattan; rattan palm. **2,** rattan cane or stick.
roto ('ro·to) *v., p.p. of* **romper.** *—adj.* **1,** broken; broken down. **2,** ragged; raggedy.
rotonda (ro'ton·da) *n.f.* rotunda.
rotor (ro'tor) *n.m.* rotor.
rotoso (ro'to·so) *adj., So.Amer.* ragged; raggedy.
rótula ('ro·tu·la) *n.f.* kneepan; kneecap.
rotular (ro·tu'lar) *v.t.* **1,** to label. **2,** to put a heading on; place an inscription on. **—rotulación,** *n.f.* labeling.
rótulo ('ro·tu·lo) *n.m.* **1,** identifying label. **2,** poster; sign. **3,** title; heading.
rotundo (ro'tun·do) *adj.* **1,** rotund. **2,** round; complete. **—rotundidad,** *n.f.* rotundity.
rotura (ro'tu·ra) *n.f.* **1,** break; breaking; crack. **2,** tear; rip. **3,** rupture.
roturar (ro·tu'rar) *v.t.* to break up (ground) for cultivation. **—roturación,** *n.f.* breaking of ground.
royendo (ro'jen·do) *v., ger. of* **roer.**
royó (ro'jo) *v., 3rd pers.sing.pret. of* **roer.**
rozadura (ro·θa'ðu·ra; ro·sa-) *n.f.* **1,** light touch in passing; brush. **2,** scrape; abrasion; graze.
rozamiento (ro·θa'mjen·to; ro·sa-) *n.m.* friction.
rozar (ro'θar; -'sar) *v.t.* [*pres. subjve.* **roce;** *pret.* **rocé**] **1,** to touch or brush lightly. **2,** to scrape; scuff; graze. **—rozarse,** *v.r.* **1,** to be scuffed. **2,** to have contact; come into contact; meet. **3,** to come close; be similar.
-rragia ('ra·xja) *suffix* -rrhage; abnormal or excessive flow: *hemorragia,* hemorrhage.
-rrea ('re·a) *suffix* -rrhea; flow; discharge: *diarrea,* diarrhea.
-rrino ('ri·no) *suffix* -rrhine; nose: *platirrino,* platyrrhine.
rúa ('ru·a) *n.f.* road; lane.
ruana ('rwa·na) *n.f., So.Amer.* = **poncho.**
ruano (ru'a·no; 'rwa·no) *adj.* roan.
rúbeo ('ru·βe·o) *adj.* ruddy; reddish.
rubéola (ru'βe·o·la) *n.f.* rubella; German measles.
rubí (ru'βi) *n.m. & adj.* ruby.
rubia ('ru·βja) *adj. & n.f.* blonde. *—n.f., bot.* madder.
rubicundo (ru·βi'kun·do) *adj.* rubicund; ruddy. **—rubicundez,** *n.f.* rubicundity; ruddiness.
rubidio (ru'βi·ðjo) *n.m.* rubidium.
rubio ('ru·βjo) *adj.* blond; fair. *—n.m.* **1,** blond. **2,** *ichthy.* roach.
rublo ('ru·βlo) *n.m.* ruble.
rubor (ru'βor) *n.m.* blush. **—ruboroso,** *adj.* blushing.
ruborizar (ru·βo·ri'θar; -'sar) *v.t.* [*pres.subjve.* **ruborice** (-'ri·θe; -se); *pret.* **ruboricé** (-'θe; -'se)] to

cause to blush. —**ruborizarse,** *v.r.* to blush.

rúbrica ('ru·βri·ka) *n.f.* **1,** fancy or distinctive signature marked by a flourish. **2,** rubric. —**de rúbrica,** *colloq.* by the letter of the word; in accordance with standard procedure.

rubricar (ru·βri'kar) *v.t.* [*pres. subjve.* **rubrique** (-'βri·ke); *pret.* **rubriqué** (-'ke)] **1,** to sign with a flourish. **2,** to put one's mark of approval on; subscribe to.

rucio ('ru·θjo; -sjo) *adj.* **1,** (*of animals*) grayish; whitish. **2,** (*of persons*) grayhaired; graying.

ruda ('ru·ða) *n.f., bot.* rue.

rudeza (ru'ðe·θa; -sa) *n.f.* rudeness; roughness.

rudimento (ru·ði'men·to) *n.m.* rudiment. —**rudimentario,** *also,* **rudimental,** *adj.* rudimentary.

rudo ('ru·ðo) *adj.* rude; rough.

rueca ('rwe·ka) *n.f.* distaff.

rueda ('rwe·ða) *n.f.* **1,** wheel. **2,** roller; caster. **3,** circular arrangement; circle. **4,** turn; sequence. **5,** round slice. **6,** group; circle; ring. **7,** *ichthy.* sunfish. —**hacer la rueda a,** *colloq.* **1,** to flatter; wheedle. **2,** to pursue; run after. —**rueda de presos** *or* **sospechosos,** police lineup.

ruede ('rwe·ðe) *v., pres.subjve. of* **rodar.**

ruedo ('rwe·ðo) *v., pres.ind. of* **rodar.**

ruedo ('rwe·ðo) *n.m.* **1,** hem; border; edge. **2,** perimeter; circumference. **3,** ring; arena.

ruego ('rwe·ɣo) *n.m.* plea; entreaty; supplication. —*v., pres.ind. of* **rogar.**

ruegue ('rwe·ɣe) *v., pres.subjve. of* **rogar.**

ruejo ('rwe·xo) *n.m.* mill-wheel.

rufián (ru'fjan) *n.m.* ruffian. —**rufianería,** n.f. ruffianism. —**rufianesco,** *adj.* ruffianly.

rugir (ru'xir) *v.i.* [*pres.ind.* **rujo;** *pres.subjve.* **ruja**] to roar; rumble; growl. —**rugido,** *n.m.* roar; rumble; growl.

rugoso (ru'ɣo·so) *adj.* wrinkled; corrugated. —**rugosidad,** *n.f.* wrinkle; corrugation.

ruibarbo (ru·i'βar·βo) *n.m.* rhubarb.

ruido ('rwi·ðo) *n.m.* **1,** noise. **2,** fuss; clamor.

ruidoso (rwi'ðo·so) *adj.* **1,** noisy. **2,** sensational.

ruin (ru'in; rwin) *adj.* **1,** base; vile. **2,** mean; wretched. **3,** stingy; miserly, paltry.

ruina ('rwi·na) *n.f.* ruin. —**ruinar,** *v.t.* = **arruinar.**

ruindad (rwin'dað) *adj.* **1,** baseness; vileness. **2,** meanness; wretchedness. **3,** stinginess; miserliness.

ruinoso (rwi'no·so) *adj.* ruinous.

ruiseñor (rwi·se'ɲor) *n.m.* nightingale

ruja ('ru·xa) *v., pres.subjve. of* **rugir**

rujo ('ru·xo) *v., 1st pers.sing.pres. ind. of* **rugir.**

ruleta (ru'le·ta) *n.f.* roulette.

rulo ('ru·lo) *n.m.* **1,** round object; ball. **2,** roller. **3,** *Amer.* lock; curl.

ruma ('ru·ma) *n.f., So.Amer., colloq* heap; bunch.

rumba ('rum·ba) *n.f.* **1,** rumba. **2,** *Amer* spree.

rumbear (rum·be'ar) *v.i.* **1,** *Amer.* to dance the rumba. **2,** *W. I., colloq.* to go on a spree. **3,** *So. Amer., colloq.* to take a course; choose a direction.

rumbo ('rum·bo) *n.m.* **1,** direction; course; bearing. **2,** *colloq.* lavishness; pomp; show. —**rumboso,** *adj., colloq.* lavish; openhanded.

rumia ('ru·mja) *n.f.* rumination. *Also,* **rumiadura.**

rumiar (ru'mjar) *v.t. & i.* to ruminate. —**rumiante,** *adj. & n.m.* ruminant.

rumor (ru'mor) *n.m.* **1,** rumor. **2,** murmur. —**rumoroso,** *adj.* murmuring; murmurous.

rumorear (ru·mo·re'ar) *v.t.* [*also, Amer.,* **rumorar** (-'rar)] to rumor. —**rumorearse,** *also, Amer.,* **rumorarse,** *v.r.* to be rumored.

runfla ('run·fla) *n.f.* **1,** *cards* sequence. **2,** *colloq.* series; row.

runrún (run'run) *n.m., colloq.* murmur: purr. —**runrunearse,** *v.r., colloq.* = **rumorearse.**

rupia ('ru·pja) *n.f.* rupee.

rupicabra (ru·pi'ka·βra) *n.f.* chamois. *Also,* **rupicapra** (-pra).

ruptura (rup'tu·ra) *n.f.* rupture.

rural (ru'ral) *adj.* rural.

ruso ('ru·so) *adj. & n.m.* Russian.

rústico ('rus·ti·ko) *adj.* & *n.m.* rustic. —**rusticidad** (-θi'ðað; -si'ðað) *n.f.* rusticity. —**en rústica; a la rústica,** paperbound; paperback.
ruta ('ru·ta) *n.f.* route.
rutenio (ru'te·njo) *n.m.* ruthenium.
rutilar (ru·ti'lar) *v.i., poet* to twinkle, sparkle; shine.
rutina (ru'ti·na) *n.f.* routine. —**rutinario,** *adj.* routine.

S

S, s ('e·se) *n.f.* 22nd letter of the Spanish alphabet.
sábado ('sa·βa·ðo) *n.m.* Saturday.
sábalo ('sa·βa·lo) *n.m.* shad.
sabana (sa'βa·na) *n.f.* savanna.
sábana ('sa·βa·na) *n.f.* sheet; bedsheet.
sabandija (sa·βan'di·xa) *n.f.* vermin; small noxious animal.
sabañón (sa·βa'ɲon) *n.m.* chilblain.
sabático (sa'βa·ti·ko) *adj.* 1, Sabbath (*attrib.*). 2, sabbatical.
sabatino (sa·βa'ti·no) *adj.* Saturday (*attrib.*). —**sabatina,** *n.f.* Saturday devotions to the Virgin Mary.
sabedor (sa·βe'ðor) *adj.* informed; aware.
sábelotodo (sa·βe·lo'to·ðo) *n.m.* & *f. sing. & pl., colloq.* know-it-all.
saber (sa'βer) *v.t.* & *i.* [*pres.ind.* **sé, sabes**; *pres.subjve.* **sepa**; *fut.* **sabré**; *pret.* **supe**] **1,** to know; have knowledge (of). **2,** *fol. by inf.* to know how to; can. —*v.i., fol. by* **a,** to taste of; have the flavor of. —*n.m.* knowledge; wisdom; learning. —**a saber.** that is; to wit.
sabido (sa'βi·ðo) *adj.* **1,** learned; well-informed. **2,** *colloq.* shrewd; cunning. —**de** *or* **por sabido,** surely; of course.
sabiduría (sa·βi·ðu'ri·a) *n.f.* wisdom; learning.
sabiendas (sa'βjen·das) *in* **a sabiendas**, knowingly; consciously.
sabiente (sa'βjen·te) *adj.* informed; knowing.
sabihondo *also,* **sabiondo** (sa'βjon·do) *adj.* & *n.m., colloq.* know-it-all.
sabio ('sa·βjo) *adj.* sage; wise. —*n.m.* sage.
sablazo (sa'βla·θo; -so) *n.m.* **1,** blow or wound with a saber. **2,** *colloq.* a cadging of money; touch.
sable ('sa·βle) *n.m.* saber; cutlass. —*adj.* & *n.m., heraldry* sable; black.
sablista (sa'βlis·ta) *n.m., colloq.* sponger; cadger. *Also,* **sableador** (sa·βle·a'ðor).
sabor (sa'βor) *n.m.* taste; savor; flavor. —**saborear,** *v.t.* to savor; enjoy the flavor of.
sabotaje (sa·βo'ta·xe) *n.m.* sabotage. —**saboteador,** *n.m.* saboteur. —**sabotear,** *v.t.* to sabotage.
sabré (sa'βre) *v., fut. of* **saber.**
sabroso (sa'βro·so) *adj.* savory; flavorful, tasty.
sabueso (sa'βwe·so) *n.m.* **1,** hound; bloodhound; beagle. **2,** *colloq.* investigator; sleuth.
sábulo ('sa·βu·lo) *n.m.* coarse sand.
saburra (sa'βu·rra) *n.f.* coating *or* fur on the tongue. —**saburroso,** *adj.* furred *or* coated, as the tongue
saca ('sa·ka) *n.f.* **1,** extraction, taking out. **2,** sack; bag.
sacabocados (sa·ka·βo'ka·ðos) *n.m.sing. & pl., mech.* punch.
sacacorchos (sa·ka'kor·tʃos) *n.m.sing. & pl.* corkscrew.
sacamiento (sa·ka'mjen·to) *n.m.* removal.
sacamuelas (sa·ka'mwe·las) *n.m. & f. sing. & pl., colloq.* **1,** dentist. **2,** charlatan; quack.
sacapuntas (sa·ka'pun·tas) *n.m.sing. & pl.* pencil sharpener.
sacar (sa'kar) *v.t.* [*pres.subjve* **saque**; *pret.* **saqué**] **1,** to take out; withdraw. **2,** to bring out; get out. **3,** to take off; remove. **4,** to get; gain; acquire. **5,** to show; bring to notice. **6,** to make (a copy). **7,** to take (photographs). **8,** to take; take down (notes, information, etc.). **9,** to figure out; find out; get at. **10,** to give or apply (a name or nickname. —*v.t.* & *i., sports* to serve. —**sacar adelante, 1,** to further; advance. **2,** to rear; bring up. —**sacar a luz,** to publish. —**sacar el cuerpo,** to dodge; duck. —**sacar a uno de sí,** to drive one out of

one's mind; drive one mad. —**sacar en limpio** *or* **claro, 1,** to understand; deduce. **2,** to gain; benefit.
sacarina (sa·ka'ri·na) *n.f.* saccharin. —**sacarino,** *adj.* saccharine.
sacerdote (sa·θer'ðo·te; sa·ser-) *n.m.* priest. —**sacerdocio** (-'ðo·θjo; -sjo) *n.m.* priesthood. —**sacerdotal,** *adj.* sacerdotal. —**sacerdotisa,** *n.f.* priestess.
saciar (sa'θjar; -'sjar) *v.t. to* satiate; sate. —**saciable,** *adj.* satiable. —**saciedad,** *n.f.* satiety; satiation. —**sacio** ('sa·θjo; -sjo) *adj.* satiated; sated.
saco ('sa·ko) *n.m.* **1,** sack; bag. **2,** *anat.; bot.; zool.* sac. **3,** plunder; loot; sack. **4,** *Amer.* jacket. **5,** *colloq.* pack; bunch. —**saco de noche,** overnight bag.
sacramento (sa·kra'men·to) *n.m.* sacrament. —**sacramental,** *adj.* sacramental. —**sacramentar,** *v.t.* to administer the last rites to.
sacratísimo (sa·kra'ti·si·mo) *adj.* most sacred.
sacrificar (sa·kri·fi'kar) *v.t.* [*pres.subjve.* **sacrifique** (-'fi·ke); *pret.* **sacrifiqué** (-'ke)] **1,** to sacrifice. **2,** to slaughter (animals) for use.
sacrificatorio (sa·kri·fi·ka'to·rjo) *adj.* sacrificial.
sacrificio (sa·kri'fi·θjo; -sjo) *n.m.* sacrifice.
sacrilegio (sa·kri'le·xjo) *n.m.* sacrilege. —**sacrílego** (sa'kri·le·ɣo) *adj.* sacrilegious.
sacristán (sa·kris'tan) *n.m.* sexton; sacristan. —**sacristía,** *n.f.* sacristy; vestry.
sacro ('sa·kro) *n.m., also,* **hueso sacro,** sacrum. —*adj.* **1,** sacred. **2,** sacral.
sacrosanto (sa·kro'san·to) *adj.* sacrosanct.
sacudir (sa·ku'ðir) *v.t.* **1,** to shake; jerk back and forth. **2,** to jolt. **3,** to shake off; dust off. **4,** to beat; strike repeatedly; pound. —**sacudirse,** *v.r., colloq.* get out; get off. —**sacudida,** *n.f.* shake; jerk; jolt. —**sacudidura,** *n.f.* a shaking off; dusting. —**sacudimiento,** *n.m.* jolt; jolting; shaking. —**sacudón,** *n.m.* jerk; jolt; shock.
sachar (sa'tʃar) *v.t.* to weed. —**sacho** ('sa·tʃo) *n.m.* hoe; weeder.
sadismo (sa'ðis·mo) *n.m.* sadism. —**sádico** ('sa·ði·ko) *also,* **sadista,** *n.m.* sadist. —*adj.* sadistic.
saeta (sa'e·ta) *n.f.* **1,** arrow; dart. **2,** hand of a clock. **3,** poignant religious song of Holy Week; saeta. —**saetazo,** *n.m.* stroke or wound of a dart or arrow.
safari (sa'fa·ri) *n.m.* safari.
saga ('sa·ɣa) *n.f.* saga.
sagaz (sa'ɣaθ; -'ɣas) *adj.* sagacious. —**sagacidad** (-'θi'ðað; -si'ðað) *n.f.* sagacity.
Sagitario (sa·xi'ta·rjo) *n.m.* Sagittarius.
sagrado (sa'ɣra·ðo) *adj.* sacred.
sagrario (sa'ɣra·rjo) *n.m.* **1,** sanctuary. **2,** *R.C.Ch.* tabernacle.
sahina (sa'i·na) *n.f.* = **zahina.**
sahumar (sa·u'mar) *v.t.* to perfume (a room) by burning aromatic substances.
sahumerio (sa·u'me·rjo) *n.m.* **1,** perfuming by burning of aromatic substances. **2,** a substance so used.
sainete (sa·i'ne·te) *n.m.* **1,** one-act farce. **2,** morsel; tidbit. **3,** tang; flavor.
sajar (sa'xar) *v.t.* to slit; cut. —**saja** ('sa·xa) *also,* **sajadura,** *n.f.* slit; cut; incision.
sajón (sa'xon) *adj.* & *n.m.* Saxon.
sal (sal) *n.f.* **1,** salt. **2,** wit; grace; charm. **3,** *colloq.* color; spice; zest. —**sal de Higuera,** Epsom salts.
sala ('sa·la) *n.f.* **1,** living room; parlor. **2,** hall; room; gallery. **3,** auditorium; theater. —**sala de fiestas,** cabaret.
saladar (sa·la'ðar) *n.m.* **1,** salt marsh. **2,** barren, saline soil. **3,** salt lick.
salado (sa'la·ðo) *adj.* **1,** salt; salty. **2,** witty; graceful; charming. **3,** colorful; spicy; zestful. **4,** *Amer., colloq.* unlucky.
salamandra (sa·la'man·dra) *n.f.* **1,** salamander. **2,** coal stove.
salar (sa'lar) *v.t.* **1,** to salt; cure by salting. **2,** to make salty. **3,** *Amer., colloq.* to give bad luck to; make unlucky. **4,** *Amer., colloq.* to spoil; ruin.
salario (sa'la·rjo) *n.m.* salary; pay.
salaz (sa'laθ; -'las) *adj.* salacious. —**salacidad** (-θi'ðað; -si'ðað) *n.f.* salaciousness.
salazón (sa·la'θon; -'son) *n.m.* **1,** salt meat or fish. **2,** salt meat and fish trade.

salcochar (sal·ko'tʃar) *v.t.* to boil (meat, fish, etc.).
salchicha (sal'tʃi·tʃa) *n.f.* small sausage. —**salchichón,** *n.m.* salami.
saldar (sal'dar) *v.t.* **1,** to pay in full; close; settle (an account). **2,** to liquidate; close out. **3,** to settle (a question or dispute).
saldo ('sal·do) *n.m.* **1,** *comm.* balance; difference. **2,** closeout; bargain.
saldré (sal'dre) *v., fut. of* **salir.**
saledizo (sa·le'ði·θo; -so) *adj.* projecting; jutting. —*n.m.* = **salidizo.**
salero (sa'le·ro) *n.m.* **1,** salt shaker; salt cellar. **2,** wit; piquancy; charm. —**saleroso,** *adj.* witty; charming; piquant.
salga ('sal·ɣa) *v., pres.subjve. of* **salir.**
salgo ('sal·ɣo) *v., 1st pers.sing. pres. ind. of* **salir.**
salicilato (sa·li·θi'la·to; -si'la·to) *n.m.* salicylate. —**salicílico** (-'θi·li·ko; -'si·li·ko) *adj.* salicylic.
salida (sa'li·ða) *n.f.* **1,** exit; way out. **2,** a going or coming out. **3,** leaving; departure. **4,** outset; start. **5,** expenditure. **6,** sally. **7,** outlet. **8,** = **saliente. 9,** *colloq.* remark; crack. —**salida de baño,** bathrobe. —**salida de teatro,** *Amer.* evening wrap. —**tener salida,** to sell well.
salidizo (sa·li'ði·θo; -so) *n.m.* projection; ledge.
saliente (sa'ljien·te) *adj.* salient; jutting. —*n.f.* projection; protuberance; salient.
salina (sa'li·na) *n.f., usu.pl.* salt pit; salt mine.
salino (sa'li·no) *adj.* saline; salt.
salir (sa'lir) *v.i.* [*pres.ind.* **salgo, sales;** *pres.subjve.* **salga;** *fut.* **saldré**] **1,** to go out; get out. **2,** to come out. **3,** to emerge; arise. **4,** to open; give access; lead. **5,** to leave; depart. **6,** to project; protrude. **7,** to flow out. **8,** *games* to open; lead; begin. —**salirse,** *v.r.* to overflow; leak out. —**salir a,** to resemble —**salir de, 1,** to escape; get out of. **2,** to get rid of; dispose of. —**salirse con la suya,** to have one's way.
salitre (sa'li·tre) *n.m.* saltpeter. —**salitral,** *adj.* nitrous. —*n.m.* [*also,* **salitrera,** *n.f.*] nitrate bed. —**salitrero,** *also,* **salitroso,** *adj.* nitrous.
saliva (sa'li·βa) *n.f.* saliva. —**salival,** *adj.* salivary.
salivar (sa·li'βar) *v.i.* to salivate. —**salivación,** *n.f.* salivation. —**salivazo,** *n.m.* spit; spitting.
salmo ('sal·mo) *n.m.* psalm. —**salmista,** *adj.* psalmist. —**salmodia** (-'mo·ðja) *n.f.* psalmody.
salmodiar (sal·mo'ðjar) *v.t.* & *i.* to chant; sing or speak monotonously.
salmón (sal'mon) *n.m.* salmon.
salmonete (sal·mo'ne·te) *n.m.* red mullet.
salmuera (sal'mwe·ra) *n.f.* brine; pickle.
salobral (sa·lo'βral) *n.m.* **1,** barren, saline soil. **2,** salt lick. —*adj.* = **salobre.**
salobre (sa'lo·βre) *adj.* salty; briny; brackish. —**salobridad,** *n.f.* saltiness; brackishness.
salón (sa'lon) *n.m.* **1,** salon; parlor. **2,** drawing room. **3,** hall; room; saloon. **4,** gallery; art exhibit.
salpicar (sal·pi'kar) *v.t.* [*pres. subjve.* **salpique** (-'pi·ke); *pret.* **salpiqué** (-'ke)] to spatter; sprinkle; splash. —**salpicadura,** *n.f.* spattering; sprinkling; splashing.
salpicón (sal·pi'kon) *n.m.* **1,** splash; spatter. **2,** salmagundi. **3,** hash; mincemeat. **4,** *colloq.* hodgepodge; jumble. **5,** *So.Amer.* cold fruit drink.
salpullido (sal·pu'ʎi·ðo; -'ji·ðo) *n.m.* rash; skin rash.
salsa ('sal·sa) *n.f.* sauce; gravy; dressing. —**salsera,** *n.f.* gravy boat; sauce dish or tray.
saltador (sal·ta'ðor) *adj.* jumping; leaping. —*n.m.* **1,** jumper. **2,** jump rope; skipping rope.
saltamontes (sal·ta'mon·tes) *n.m. sing.* & *pl.* grasshopper.
saltar (sal'tar) *v.t.* & *i.* **1,** to jump; leap; spring; bounce. **2,** to skip. **3,** to break; snap; crack. —*v.i.* **1,** to stand out; be evident. **2,** to shift or change suddenly; start. —**saltar a la vista; saltar a los ojos,** to be obvious.
saltarín (sal·ta'rin) *adj.* gamboling; frolicking. —*n.m.* restless boy; jumping jack.
saltear (sal·te'ar) *v.t.* **1,** to assault; rob; hold up. **2,** to sauté. —**salteador,** *n.m.* bandit; robber. —**salteo** (-'te·o) *n.m.* = **asalto.**
saltimbanqui (sal·tim'ban·ki)

also, **saltimbanco** (-ko) *n.m.* **1,** mountebank; charlatan; quack. **2,** tumbler; acrobat. **3,** *colloq.* ne'er-do-well.
salto ('sal·to) *n.m.* **1,** leap; jump; spring. **2,** gap; hiatus. **3,** cliff; precipice. —**salto de agua,** waterfall. —**salto mortal,** somersault.
saltón (sal'ton) *adj.* jumping; hopping. —*n.m.* **1,** grasshopper. **2,** maggot.
salubre (sa'lu·βre) *adj.* salubrious; healthful.
salubridad (sa·lu·βri'ðað) *n.f.* **1,** salubriousness; salubrity. **2,** public health.
salud (sa'luð) *n.f.* health. —**vender salud,** *colloq.* to be the picture of health.
saludable (sa·lu'ða·βle) *adj.* **1,** salutary; healthful. **2,** healthy.
saludar (sa·lu'ðar) *v.t.* to greet; salute. —**saludador,** *adj.* salutatory. —*n.m.* salutatorian.
saludo (sa'lu·ðo) *n.m.* **1,** greeting; salutation. **2,** salute.
salutación (sa·lu·ta'θjon; -'sjon) *n.f.* **1,** salutation. **2,** salutatory.
salva ('sal·βa) *n.f.* salvo; burst.
salvación (sal·βa'θjon; -'sjon) *n.f.* salvation.
salvado (sal'βa·ðo) *n.m.* bran.
salvador (sal·βa'ðor) *n.m.* savior. —*adj.* saving.
salvaguardar (sal·βa·ɣwar'ðar) *v.t.* to safeguard; protect.
salvaguardia (sal·βa'ɣwar·ðja) *n.m.* **1,** guard; watchman. **2,** safeguard; protection. —*n.f.* **1,** token of immunity or privilege. **2,** = **salvoconducto.**
salvaje (sal'βa·xe) *adj.* savage; wild. —*n.m.* savage. —**salvajada,** *n.f.* wild action; vandalism. —**salvajismo,** *n.m.* savagery; atrocity.
salvamanteles (sal·βa·man'te·les) *n.m.sing.* & *pl.* place mat.
salvamento (sal·βa'men·to) *n.m.* **1,** salvage. **2,** salvation; rescue. **3,** refuge; retreat.
salvar (sal'βar) *v.t.* **1,** to save; rescue. **2,** to salvage. **3,** to pass; leap over; clear. **4,** to except; exclude. **5,** to skip; omit.
salvavidas (sal·βa'βi·ðas) *n.m. sing.* & *pl.* life preserver. —**lancha salvavidas,** lifeboat.
salve ('sal·βe) *interj.* hail! —*n.f., R.C.Ch.* Salve Regina.
salvia ('sal·βja) *n.f., bot.* sage.
salvo ('sal·βo) *adj.* **1,** safe; saved. **2,** left out; omitted; excepted. —*prep.* save; except. —**a salvo,** safe; safely; in safety. —**dejar a salvo,** to except; make an exception of. —**en salvo, 1,** at liberty. **2,** safe; out of danger. —**salvo que,** save that; unless.
salvoconducto (sal·βo·kon'duk·to) *n.m.* safe-conduct; pass.
sallar (sa'ʎar; -'jar) *v.t.* to weed.
samario (sa'ma·rjo) *n.m.* samarium.
samaritano (sa·ma·ri'ta·no) *adj.* & *n.m.* Samaritan.
samba ('sam·ba) *n.f.* samba.
samovar (sa·mo'βar) *n.m.* samovar.
sampán (sam'pan) *n.m.* sampan.
samurai (sa·mu'rai) *n.m.* samurai.
san (san) *adj., contr. of* **santo,** *used before masculine names of saints, except* Tomás, Tomé, Toribio *and* Domingo.
sánalotodo (sa·na·lo'to·ðo) *n.m.* [*pl.* **–do**] cure-all.
sanamente (sa·na'men·te) *adv.* sincerely; candidly.
sanar (sa'nar) *v.t.* to heal; cure; make whole. —*v.i.* to heal; be cured; recover.
sanatorio (sa·na'to·rjo) *n.m.* sanatorium; sanitarium; *Amer.* hospital.
sanción (san'θjon; -'sjon) *n.f.* **1,** sanction. **2,** *sports* penalty. —**sancionar,** *v.t.* to sanction.
sancochar (san·ko'tʃar) *v.t.* to parboil. —**sancocho** (-'ko·tʃo) *n.m., Amer.* stew.
sandalia (san'da·lja) *n.f.* sandal.
sándalo ('san·da·lo) *n.m.* sandalwood.
sandez (san'deθ; -'des) *n.f.* silliness; foolishness.
sandía (san'di·a) *n.f.* watermelon.
sandio ('san·djo) *adj.* foolish; silly. —*n.m.* fool; simpleton.
sandunga (san'dun·ga) *n.f.* **1,** *colloq.* grace; charm. **2,** *Amer.* spree. —**sandunguero** (-'ge·ro) *adj., colloq.* charming.
sandwich ('san·dwitʃ) *n.m.* sandwich.
saneamiento (sa·ne·a'mjen·to) *n.m.* **1,** sanitation; cleansing. **2,** improvement, as of land. **3,** *law* reparation; indemnification.
sanear (sa·ne'ar) *v.t.* **1,** to make

sanitary; cleanse. 2, to improve (land, swampy terrain, etc.). 3, *law* to pay damages or reparations to.
sangre ('san·gre) *n.f.* blood. —**sangrar,** *v.t.* & *i.* to bleed. —**estar sangrando,** to be recent; to be still painfully present in memory.
sangría (san'gri·a) *n.f.* 1, bleeding; bloodletting. 2, *colloq.* cold drink of wine and fruits; wine cooler.
sangriento (san'grjen·to) *adj.* bloody.
sangüesa (san'gwe·sa) *n.f.* raspberry.
sangui- (san·gi) *prefix* sangui-; blood: *sanguífero,* sanguiferous.
sanguijuela (san·gi'xwe·la) *n.f.* leech.
sanguinario (san·gi'na·rjo) *adj.* sanguinary; bloodthirsty.
sanguíneo (san'gi·ne·o) *adj.* sanguine.
sanguinolento (san·gi·no'len·to) *adj.* bloody; sanguinolent.
sanidad (sa·ni'ðað) *n.f.* public health; sanitation.
sanitario (sa·ni'ta·rjo) *adj.* sanitary.
sano ('sa·no) *adj.* healthy; sound; whole. —**sano y salvo,** safe and sound.
sánscrito ('sans·kri·to) *adj.* & *n.m.* Sanskrit.
sanseacabó (san·se·a·ka'βo) *also,* **sansacabó** (san·sa-) *interj., colloq.* that's the end!; that does it!
santabárbara (san·ta'βar·βa·ra) *n.f.* powder magazine.
santiamén (san·tja'men) *n.m., colloq.* instant; jiffy.
santidad (san·ti'ðað) *n.f.* 1, sanctity; holiness; saintliness. 2, sainthood.
santificar (san·ti·fi'kar) *v.t.* [*pres.subjve.* **santifique** (-'fi·ke); *pret.* **santifiqué** (-'ke)] to sanctify. —**santificación,** *n.f.* sanctification.
santiguarse (san·ti'ɣwar·se) *v.r.* to cross oneself.
santísimo (san'ti·si·mo) *adj.* most holy. —*n.m.* the Holy Sacrament. —**todo el santísimo día,** the livelong day.
santo ('san·to) *adj.* saintly; holy. —*n.m.* 1, saint. 2, saint's day; name day. 3, *colloq.* holy card or stamp. —**santa voluntad,** one's own will. —**¿a santo de qué?,** *colloq.* why on earth? —**santo y seña,** watchword; password. —**todo el santo día,** the livelong day.
santón (san'ton) *n.m.* 1, dervish. 2, = **santurrón.**
santoral (san·to'ral) *n.m.* calendar of saints.
santuario (san'twa·rjo) *n.m.* 1, shrine. 2, sanctuary.
santurrón (san·tu'rron) *adj.* sanctimonious. —*n.m., colloq.* hypocrite. —**santurronería,** *n.f.* sanctimony.
saña ('sa·ɲa) *n.f.* 1, rage; fury. 2, vindictive cruelty; malice. —**sañoso,** *also,* **sañudo,** *adj.* vindictive; cruel.
sápido ('sa·pi·ðo) *adj.* sapid. —**sapidez,** *n.f.* sapidity.
sapiencia (sa'pjen·θja; -sja) *n.f.* sapience. —**sapiente,** *adj.* sapient.
sapo ('sa·po) *n.m.* toad. —**echar sapos y culebras,** *colloq.* to pour forth abuse. —**sapo marino,** *ichthy.* angler.
saponaria (sa·po'na·rja) *n.f.* soapwort.
saque ('sa·ke) *v., pres.subjve. of* **sacar.** —*n.m., sports* 1, serve; service. 2, taking away (*of a ball*).
saqué (sa'ke) *v., 1st pers.sing.pret. of* **sacar.**
saquear (sa·ke'ar) *v.t.* to sack; plunder. —**saqueo** (-'ke·o) *n.m.* sacking; plunder.
saquillo (sa'ki·ʎo; -jo) *n.m.* handbag; satchel.
sarampión (sa·ram'pjon) *n.m.* measles.
sarao (sa'ra·o) *n.m.* soirée; informal dance.
sarape (sa'ra·pe) *n.m., Amer.* serape; shawl.
sarcasmo (sar'kas·mo) *n.m.* sarcasm. —**sarcástico** (-ti·ko) *adj.* sarcastic.
sarco- (sar·ko) *prefix* sarco-; flesh: *sarcófago,* sarcophagus.
sarcófago (sar'ko·fa·ɣo) *n.m.* sarcophagus.
sarcoma (sar'ko·ma) *n.f.* sarcoma.
sardina (sar'di·na) *n.f.* sardine.
sardineta (sar·ði'ne·ta) *n.f.* 1, small sardine. 2, chevron.
sardónico (sar'ðo·ni·ko) *adj.* sardonic.
sarga ('sar·ɣa) *n.f.* 1, serge. 2, willow.

sargazo (sar'ɣa·θo; -so) *n.m.* sargasso.
sargento (sar'xen·to) *n.m.* sergeant.
sarmiento (sar'mjen·to) *n.m.* **1,** shoot or branch of a grapevine. **2,** *fig.* offshoot.
sarna ('sar·na) *n.f.* mange; scabies. —**sarnoso,** *adj.* mangy.
sarong (sa'roŋ) *n.m.* sarong.
sarpullido (sar·pu'ʎi·ðo; -'ji·ðo) *n.m.* = **salpullido.**
sarraceno (sa·rra'θe·no; -'se·no) *adj.* & *n.m.* Saracen.
sarro ('sa·rro) *n.m.* **1,** crust; sediment. **2,** tartar (*on teeth*). **3,** coating or fur on the tongue. —**sarroso,** *adj.* furred or coated, as the tongue.
sarta ('sar·ta) *n.f.* string; row; series.
sartén (sar'ten) *n.f.* frying pan.
sasafrás (sa·sa'fras) *n.m.* sassafras.
sastre ('sas·tre) *n.m.* tailor.
sastrería (sas·tre'ri·a) *n.f.* **1,** tailor shop. **2,** tailoring.
Satán (sa'tan) *also,* **Satanás** (-'nas) *n.m.* Satan. —**satánico,** *adj.* satanic.
satélite (sa'te·li·te) *n.m.* satellite.
satén (sa'ten) *also,* **satín** (-'tin) *n.m.* sateen. —**satinar,** *v.t.* to glaze; make glossy.
satín (sa'tin) *n.m.* **1,** satinwood. **2,** = **satén.**
sátira ('sa·ti·ra) *n.f.* satire. —**satírico** (-'ti·ri·ko) *adj.* satirical. —*n.m.* & *f.* satirist. —**satirizar,** *v.t.* [*pres.subjve.* **satirice** (-'ri·θe; -se); *pret.* **satiricé** (-'θe, -'se)] to satirize.
sátiro ('sa·ti·ro) *n.m.* satyr.
satisfacer (sa·tis·fa'θer; -'ser) *v.t.* [*infl.*: **hacer**] to satisfy. —**satisfacción** (-fak'θjon; -'sjon) *n.f.* satisfaction. —**satisfactorio** (-fak·'to·rjo) *adj.* satisfactory.
satisfecho (sa·tis'fe·tʃo) *v., p.p. of* **satisfacer.** —*adj.* satisfied.
sátrapa ('sa·tra·pa) *n.m.* satrap. —**satrapía** (-'pi·a) *n.f.* satrapy.
saturar (sa·tu'rar) *v.t.* to saturate. —**saturación,** *n.f.* saturation.
Saturno (sa'tur·no) *n.m.* Saturn. —**saturnino,** *adj.* saturnine.
sauce ('sau·θe; -se) *n.m.* willow. —**sauce llorón,** weeping willow.
saúco (sa'u·ko) *n.m., bot.* elder.
sauro- (sau·ro) *prefix* sauro-; lizard; lizardlike: *saurópodo,* sauropod.
-sauro (sau·ro) *suffix* -saur; lizard; lizardlike: *dinosauro,* dinosaur.
savia ('sa·βja) *n.f.* sap.
saxofonista (sak·so·fo'nis·ta) *n.m.* & *f.* saxophonist.
saxófono (sak'so·fo·no) *n.m.* saxophone. *Also,* **saxofón** (-'fon).
saya ('sa·ja) *n.f.* **1,** skirt. **2,** halfslip; petticoat.
sazón (sa'θon; -'son) *n.f.* **1,** maturity; ripeness. **2,** seasoning; flavoring. **3,** ripe moment; right time. —**a la sazón,** at the time; at the moment; then. —**en sazón, 1,** in season; ripe. **2,** opportunely; in due season.
sazonar (sa·θo'nar; sa·so-) *v.t.* **1,** to season. **2,** to ripen. —**sazonado,** *adj.* witty; pithy.
-scopia ('sko·pja) *suffix* -scopy; viewing or observing through optical instruments: *fluoroscopia,* fluoroscopy.
-scopio ('sko·pjo) *suffix* -scope; *forming nouns denoting* instrument or means for viewing: *fluoroscopio,* fluoroscope. *Also, in some words,* **-scopo** (sko·po): *giróscopo,* gyroscope.
se (se) *pers.pron. 3rd pers.m. & f. sing. & pl.refl., used as obj. of a verb* oneself; yourself; himself; herself; itself; yourselves; themselves; each other; one another. —*pers. pron., used to replace a 3rd pers. ind.obj.pron. when fol. by a 3rd pers.dir.obj.pron.*: *se lo doy,* I give it to him (to her, to it, to them, to you).
sé (se) *v., 1st pers.sing.pres.ind. of* **saber.**
sea ('se·a) *v., pres.subjve. of* **ser.**
sebáceo (se'βa·θe·o; -se·o) *adj.* sebaceous.
sebo ('se·βo) *n.m.* tallow; suet; fat. —**seboso,** *adj.* greasy; fatty.
seca ('se·ka) *n.f.* drought; dry period or season. —**a secas, 1,** simply; baldly. **2,** drily; curtly; coldly.
secano (se'ka·no) *n.m.* dry or unwatered land.
secante (se'kan·te) *adj.* blotting; drying. —*n.m.* blotter; drier. —*n.f.* secant.
secar (se'kar) *v.t.* [*pres.subjve.* **seque;** *pret.* **sequé**] to dry; —**se-**

carse, *v.r.* to dry; dry up. —**secamiento,** *n.m.* drying up; withering.
sección (sek'θjon; -'sjon) *n.f.* section. —**seccional,** *adj.* sectional. —**seccionar,** *v.t.* to section.
secesión (se·θe'sjon; se·se-) *n.f.* secession. —**secesionismo,** *n.m.* secessionism. —**secesionista,** *adj.* & *n.m.* & *f.* secessionist.
seco ('se·ko) *adj.* **1,** dry. **2,** withered; parched. **3,** *fig.* curt; aloof.
secoya (se'ko·ja) *n.f.* sequoia.
secreción (se·kre'θjon; -'sjon) *n.f.* secretion.
secretar (se·kre'tar) *v.t., biol.* to secrete.
secretaría (se·kre·ta'ri·a) *n.f.* **1,** secretary's office. **2,** secretaryship. **3,** secretariat.
secretario (se·kre'ta·rjo) *n.m.* secretary.
secretear (se·kre·te'ar) *v.i.* to whisper; talk in secret.
secreto (se'kre·to) *adj.* secret. —*n.m.* **1,** secret. **2,** secrecy. —**secreto a voces,** open secret.
secretor (se·kre'tor) *adj.* secretory. *Also,* **secretorio** (-to'rjo).
secta ('sek·ta) *n.f.* sect. —**sectario,** *adj.* & *n.m.* sectarian. —**sectarismo,** *n.m.* sectarianism.
sector (sek'tor) *n.m.* sector.
secuaz (se'kwaθ; -'kwas) *n.m.* & *f.* **1,** adherent; follower. **2,** henchman.
secuela (se'kwe·la) *n.f.* sequel; continuation.
secuencia (se'kwen·θja; -sja) *n.f.* sequence.
secuestrar (se·kwes'trar) *v.t.* **1,** to sequester. **2,** to kidnap.
secuestro (se'kwes·tro) *n.m.* **1,** sequestration. **2,** kidnapping.
secular (se·ku'lar) *adj.* & *n.m.* secular. —**secularismo,** *n.m.* secularism. —**secularista,** *adj.* secularistic. —*n.m.* & *f.* secularist.
secularizar (se·ku·la·ri'θar; -'sar) *v.t.* [*pres.subjve.* **secularice** (-'ri·θe; -se); *pret.* **secularicé** (-'θe, -'se)] to secularize. —**secularización,** *n.f.* secularization.
secundar (se·kun'dar) *v.t.* to second; support.
secundario (se·kun'da·rjo) *adj.* secondary.
sed (seð) *n.f.* thirst.
seda ('se·ða) *n.f.* silk.
sedal (se'ðal) *n.m.* fishline.
sedán (se'ðan) *n.m.* sedan.
sedar (se'ðar) *v.t.* **1,** to calm; pacify. **2,** to allay; soothe. —**sedación,** *n.f.* sedation. —**sedante,** *also,* **sedativo,** *adj.* & *n.m.* sedative.
sede ('se·ðe) *n.f.* **1,** see. **2,** seat (*of government or authority*). **3,** *fig.* seat; center; heart.
sedentario (se·ðen'ta·rjo) *adj.* sedentary.
sedición (se·ði'θjon; -'sjon) *n.f.* sedition. —**sedicioso,** *adj.* seditious.
sediento (se'ðjen·to) *adj.* **1,** thirsty. **2,** eager; craving.
sedimento (se·ði'men·to) *n.m.* sediment. —**sedimentar,** *v.t.* to cause sedimentation of. —**sedimentarse,** *v.r.* to be deposited as sediment. —**sedimentación,** *n.f.* sedimentation. —**sedimentario,** *adj.* sedimentary.
sedoso (se'ðo·so) *adj.* silky.
seducir (se·ðu'θir; -'sir) *v.t.* [*infl.:* **conducir**] to seduce. —**seducción** (se·ðuk'θjon; -'sjon) *n.f.* seduction.
seductor (se·ðuk'tor) *adj.* seductive; charming. —*n.m.* seducer. —**seductivo,** *adj.* seductive.
segada (se'ɣa·ða) *n.f.* = **siega.**
segadera (se·ɣa'ðe·ra) *n.f.* sickle.
segar (se'ɣar) *v.t.* [*pres.ind.* **siego;** *pres.subjve.* **siegue;** *pret.* **segué**] to reap; harvest; mow. —**segador,** *n.m.* reaper; harvester. —**segadora,** *n.f.* reaper; harvester (*machine*).
seglar (seɣ'lar) *adj.* secular; worldly. —*n.m.* layman.
segmento (seɣ'men·to) *n.m.* segment. —**segmental,** *adj.* segmental.
segregación (se·ɣre·ɣa'θjon; -'sjon) *n.f.* **1,** segregation. **2,** *biol.* secretion.
segregar (se·ɣre'ɣar) *v.t.* [*pres. subjve.* **segregue** (-'ɣre·ɣe); *pret.* **segregué** (-'ɣe)] **1,** to segregate; separate. **2,** *biol.* to secrete.
segué (se'ɣe) *v., 1st pers.sing.pret. of* **segar.**
segueta (se'ɣe·ta) *n.f.* **1,** hacksaw. **2,** jigsaw.
seguida (se'ɣi·ða) *n.f.* **1,** pursuit. **2,** continuance; continuation; succession. *Obs. except in the following phrases:* **de seguida, 1,** one after another; in succession. **2,** at once; immediately. —**en seguida,** at once; immediately.
seguido (se'ɣi·ðo) *adj.* **1,** con-

tinued; successive. **2,** straight; direct. —*adv.* **1,** at once; immediately. **2,** straight; directly. **3,** in quick succession; thick and fast.
seguidor (se·ɣi'ðor) *n.m.* follower.
seguimiento (se·ɣi'mjen·to) *n.m.* pursuit; chase; quest.
seguir (se'ɣir) *v.t. & i.* [*pres.ind.* **sigo, sigues;** *pres.subjve.* **siga;** *pret.* **seguí, siguió;** *ger.* **siguiendo**] **1,** to follow. **2,** to continue. —**seguirse,** *v.r.* to follow as a consequence; arise; spring.
según (se'ɣun) *prep.* according to; in accordance with. —*adv.* accordingly; correspondingly; depending. —*conj.* [*also,* **según que; según lo que**] **1,** according to how *or* what; depending upon how *or* what. **2,** as; in the same way as. **3,** to the degree that. —**según y como; según y conforme, 1,** in the same way or manner. **2,** it depends.
segunda (se'ɣun·da) *n.f., music* second.
segundar (se·ɣun'dar) *v.t.* **1,** to do again; repeat. **2,** to second; be second to.
segundario (se·ɣun'da·rjo) *adj.* secondary. —*n.m., So.Amer.* second hand (*of a timepiece*).
segundero (se·ɣun'de·ro) *n.m.* second hand (*of a timepiece*). *Also, So.Amer.,* **segundario.**
segundo (se'ɣun·do) *adj. & n.m.* second. —**de segunda mano,** secondhand. —**segunda intención,** double meaning; ulterior motive; malice. —**sin segundo,** without equal; without peer.
segur (se'ɣur) *n.m.* **1,** ax. **2,** sickle.
seguridad (se·ɣu·ri'ðað) *n.f.* **1,** security; safety. **2,** certainty.
seguro (se'ɣu·ro) *adj.* **1,** safe; secure. **2,** sure; certain. —*adv., colloq.* sure; for sure. —*n.m.* **1,** insurance. **2,** lock; safety lock. —**de seguro,** surely; assuredly. —**sobre seguro,** with full assurance.
seis (seis) *adj. & n.m.* six.
seisavo (sei'sa·βo) *adj. & n.m.* sixth.
seiscientos (seis'θjen·tos; sei·'sjen-) *adj. & n.m.* [*fem.* **-tas**] six hundred.
seiseno (sei'se·no) *adj.* sixth.
seísmo (se'is·mo) *n.m.* = **sismo.**
selección (se·lek'θjon; -'sjon) *n.f.* selection. —**seleccionar,** *v.t.* to select.
selecto (se'lek·to) *adj.* select. —**selectividad,** *n.f.* selectivity. —**selectivo,** *adj.* selective.
selenio (se'le·njo) *n.m.* selenium.
seltz (selts) *n.f., also,* **agua de seltz,** seltzer.
selva ('sel·βa) *n.f.* forest; jungle. —**selvático** (-'βa·ti·ko) *adj.* forest (*attrib.*); sylvan.
sellar (se'ʎar; -'jar) *v.t.* **1,** to seal. **2,** to stamp.
sello ('se·ʎo; -jo) *n.m.* **1,** seal; stamp. **2,** postage stamp. **3,** *pharm.* wafer.
semáforo (se'ma·fo·ro) *n.m.* **1,** semaphore. **2,** traffic signal.
semana (se'ma·na) *n.f.* week.
semanal (se·ma'nal) *adj.* weekly. —**semanalmente,** *adv.* weekly.
semanario (se·ma'na·rjo) *adj. & n.m.* weekly.
semántica (se'man·ti·ka) *n.f.* semantics. —**semántico,** *adj.* semantic.
semblante (sem'blan·te) *n.m.* **1,** semblance; countenance; aspect. **2,** face.
semblanza (sem'blan·θa; -sa) *n.f.* **1,** likeness. **2,** biographical sketch.
sembrado (sem'bra·ðo) *n.m.* cultivated field. *Also, So.Amer.,* **sembrío** (-'bri·o).
sembrar (sem'brar) *v.t.* [*pres.ind.* **siembro;** *pres.subjve.* **siembre**] to sow; seed; plant.
semejante (se·me'xan·te) *adj.* **1,** similar; like. **2,** such; such a. —*n.m.* fellow man; like.
semejanza (se·me'xan·θa; -sa) *n.f.* similarity; resemblance. —**semejar** (-'xar) *v.i.* [*also, refl.,* **semejarse**] to resemble; be similar.
semen ('se·men) *n.m.* semen.
semental (se·men'tal) *adj.* breeding. —*n.m.* breeding male animal.
semestre (se'mes·tre) *n.m.* semester. —**semestral,** *adj.* semiannual.
semi- (se·mi) *prefix* semi-. **1,** half: *semicírculo,* semicircle. **2,** partly: *semidormido,* half-asleep.
semibreve (se·mi'βre·βe) *n.f.* semibreve; whole note.
semicírculo (se·mi'θir·ku·lo; se·mi'sir-) *n.m.* semicircle. —**semicircular,** adj. semicircular.
semidiós (se·mi'ðjos) *n.m.* demigod.

semifinal (se·mi·fi'nal) *adj.* & *n.m.* semifinal.
semilunio (se·mi'lu·njo) *n.m.* half moon.
semilla (se'mi·ʎa; -ja) *n.f.* seed.
semillero (se·mi'ʎe·ro; -'je·ro) *n.m.* **1,** seed bed. **2,** plant nursery. **3,** *fig.* hotbed.
seminal (se·mi'nal) *adj.* seminal.
seminario (se·mi'na·rjo) *n.m.* **1,** seminary. **2,** seminar. —**seminarista,** *n.m.* theological student.
semita (se'mi·ta) *n.m.* & *f.* Semite. —**semítico,** *adj.* Semitic.
sempiterno (sem·pi'ter·no) *adj.* perpetual; eternal.
sena ('se·na) *n.f.* a six at dice.
senado (se'na·ðo) *n.m.* senate. —**senador,** *n.m.* senator. —**senaduría** (-ðu'ri·a) *n.f.* senatorship. —**senatorial** (-to'rjal) *also,* **senatorio** (-'to·rjo) *adj.* senatorial.
sencillo (sen'θi·ʎo; -'si·jo) *adj.* **1,** simple. **2,** plain; unadorned. —*n.m., Amer.* change; silver. —**sencillez,** *n.f.* simplicity.
senda ('sen·da) *n.f.* path; trail; way. *Also,* **sendero** (-'de·ro) *n.m.*
sendos ('sen·dos) *adj.m.pl.* [*fem.* **-das**] one each; one for each.
senectud (se·nek'tuð) *n.f.* old age; senescence.
senescal (se·nes'kal) *n.m.* seneschal.
senil (se'nil) *adj.* senile. —**senilidad,** *n.f.* senility.
seno ('se·no) *n.m.* **1,** bosom; breast. **2,** *fig.* womb. **3,** sinus. **4,** *geom.* sine.
sensación (sen·sa'θjon; -'sjon) *n.f.* sensation. —**sensacional,** *adj.* sensational. —**sensacionalismo,** *n.m.* sensationalism.
sensato (sen'sa·to) *adj.* sensible; reasonable; wise. —**sensatez,** *n.f.* good sense; wisdom.
sensibilizar (sen·si·βi·li'θar; -'sar) *v.t.* [*pres.subjve.* **sensibilice** (-'li·θe; -se); *pret.* **sensibilicé** (-'θe; -'se)] to sensitize.
sensible (sen'si·βle) *adj.* **1,** sensible; perceptible. **2,** sensitive; readily affected. **3,** regrettable; grievous. —**sensibilidad,** *n.f.* sensitivity; sensibility.
sensiblería (sen·si·βle'ri·a) *n.f.* sentimentality; mawkishness. —**sensiblero,** *adj.* maudlin; mawkish; sentimental.
sensitivo (sen·si'ti·βo) *adj.* sensitive. —**sensitiva,** *n.f.* mimosa.
sensorio (sen'so·rjo) *adj.* sensory. *Also,* **sensorial.**
sensual (sen'swal) *adj.* sensual; sensuous. —**sensualidad,** *n.f.* sensuality; sensuousness. —**sensualismo,** *n.m.* sensualism. —**sensualista,** *adj.* sensualistic. —*n.m.* & *f.* sensualist.
sentado (sen'ta·ðo) *adj.* **1,** steady; quiet; sedate. **2,** settled. —**dar por sentado,** to assume; take for granted. —**dejar por sentado,** to establish; fix; set.
sentar (sen'tar) *v.t.* [*pres.ind.* **siento**; *pres.subjve.* **siente**] to seat; sit. —*v.i.* to agree (with); go well (with). —**sentarse,** *v.r.* to sit; sit down.
sentencia (sen'ten·θja; -sja) *n.f.* **1,** *law* sentence. **2,** maxim. —**sentenciar,** *v.t.* to sentence. —**sentencioso,** *adj.* sententious.
sentido (sen'ti·ðo) *adj.* **1,** heartfelt. **2,** sensitive; touchy. **3,** offended; hurt. —*n.m.* **1,** sense. **2,** direction.
sentimental (sen·ti·men'tal) *adj.* sentimental. —**sentimentalismo,** *n.m.* sentimentalism; sentimentality.
sentimiento (sen·ti'mjen·to) *n.m.* **1,** sentiment; feeling. **2,** regret.
sentina (sen'ti·na) *n.f.* **1,** bilge. **2,** *fig.* cesspool; sink.
sentir (sen'tir) *v.t.* [*pres.ind.* **siento**; *pres.subjve.* **sienta**; *pret.* **sentí, sintió**; *ger.* **sintiendo**] **1,** to feel; experience. **2,** to sense; perceive. **3,** to hear; be aware of (a sound). **4,** to regret; be sorry for. —*n.m.* feeling. —**sentirse,** *v.r.* **1,** to feel. **2,** to be sensitive to the touch; pain; hurt. **3,** to take offense; feel hurt.
seña ('se·ɲa) *n.f.* **1,** sign; mark. **2,** password. —**señas,** *n.f.pl.* address (*sing.*). —**señas personales,** personal description. —**por (más) señas,** *colloq.* to put it more plainly.
señal (se'ɲal) *n.f.* **1,** signal. **2,** sign; mark. **3,** indication; token.
señalado (se·ɲa'la·ðo) *adj.* signal; eminent.
señalar (se·ɲa'lar) *v.t.* **1,** to mark; put a mark on. **2,** to signal; indicate; point out. **3,** to signalize. **4,** to single out; point to. —*v.t.* &

i. to point. —**señalarse,** *v.r.* to distinguish oneself.
señero (se'ɲe·ro) *adj.* **1,** singular; rare. **2,** solitary; alone.
señor (se'ɲor) *n.m.* **1,** mister; sir. **2,** lord; master. **3,** gentleman.
señora (se'ɲo·ra) *n.f.* **1,** mistress; madam. **2,** lady.
señorear (se·ɲo·re'ar) *v.t.* to command; be master of. —**señorearse,** *v.r.* **1,** to take command; become master. **2,** to look imposing; put on grandiose manners.
señoría (se·ɲo'ri·a) *n.f.* lordship. —**señorial** (-'rjal) *adj.* lordly. —**señoril** (-'ril) *adj.* lordly; noble.
señorío (se·ɲo'ri·o) *n.m.* **1,** noble rank; nobility. **2,** dominion; domain. **3,** lordliness.
señorita (se·ɲo'ri·ta) *n.f.* miss; young lady.
señorito (se·ɲo'ri·to) *n.m.* **1,** young master. **2,** young gentleman. **3,** *colloq.* fop; dandy.
señuelo (se'ɲwe·lo) *n.m.* lure; bait; decoy.
seó (se'o) *n.m., colloq., contr. of* **señor.** *Also,* **seor** (se'or).
seora (se'o·ra) *n.f., colloq., contr. of* **señora.**
sepa ('se·pa) *v., pres.subjve. of* **saber.**
sépalo ('se·pa·lo) *n.m.* sepal.
separar (se·pa'rar) *v.t.* **1,** to separate. **2,** to set aside; set apart; remove. —**separarse,** *v.r.* **1,** to separate; come apart. **2,** to part company; sever connections. —**separable,** *adj.* separable. —**separación,** *n.f.* separation. —**separado,** *adj.* separate; apart.
separatismo (se·pa·ra'tis·mo) *n.m.* separatism. —**separatista,** *adj. & n.m. & f.* separatist.
sepelio (se'pe·ljo) *n.m.* burial.
sepia ('se·pja) *n.f.* **1,** sepia. **2,** cuttlefish.
sepsis ('sep·sis) *n.f.* sepsis.
sept- (sept) *prefix* sept-; seven: *septeto,* septet.
septeno (sep'te·no) *adj. & n.m.* seventh.
septentrional (sep·ten·trjo'nal) *adj.* north; northern; northerly. —**septentrión** (-'trjon) *n.m.* north.
septeto (sep'te·to) *n.m.* septet.
septi- (sep·ti) *prefix* septi-. **1,** seven: *septilateral,* septilateral. **2,** decomposition: *septicemia,* septicemia. **3,** septum; partition: *septífraga,* septifragal.
séptico ('sep·ti·ko) *adj.* septic.
septiembre (sep'tjem·bre) *n.m.* September. *Also,* **setiembre.**
septillón (sep·ti'ʎon; -'jon) *n.m.* a quintillion septillion; *Brit.* septillion.
séptimo ('sep·ti·mo) *adj. & n.m.* seventh. —**séptima,** *n.f., music* seventh.
septingésimo (sep·tin'xe·si·mo) *adj. & n.m.* seven-hundredth.
septo ('sep·to) *n.m.* septum.
septuagenario (sep·twa·xe'na·rjo) *adj. & n.m.* septuagenarian.
septuagésimo (sep·twa'xe·si·mo) *adj. & n.m.* seventieth. —**Septuagésima,** *n.f.* Septuagesima.
séptuplo ('sep·tu·plo) *adj.* septuple. —**septuplicar** (-pli'kar) *v.t.* [*infl.:* **duplicar**] to septuple.
sepulcro (se'pul·kro) *n.m.* sepulcher. —**sepulcral,** *adj.* sepulchral.
sepultar (se·pul'tar) *v.t.* to bury. —**sepultador,** *n.m.* gravedigger. —**sepulto** (se'pul·to) *adj.* buried.
sepultura (se·pul'tu·ra) *n.f.* **1,** grave. **2,** burial. —**sepulturero,** *n.m.* gravedigger.
seque ('se·ke) *v., pres.subjve. of* **secar.**
sequé (se'ke) *v., 1st pers. sing. pret. of* **secar.**
sequedad (se·ke'ðað) *n.f.* **1,** dryness. **2,** asperity; brusqueness.
sequía (se'ki·a) *n.f.* drought.
séquito ('se·ki·to) *n.m.* retinue; following.
ser (ser) *v.i.* [*pres.ind.* **soy, eres, es, somos, sois, son;** *pres.subjve.* **sea;** *impf.* **era;** *pret.* **fui, fue;** *p.p.* **sido;** *ger.* **siendo**] **1,** *copulative* to be; have the intrinsic quality, property, nature or status of. **2,** to happen; come about. **3,** *expressing identity or equality* to be; make; be the same as; be equal to: *Dos y dos son cuatro,* Two and two are (*or* make) four; *Amar es sufrir,* To love is to suffer. **4,** *expressing existence; fact; reality:* to be; exist; *Esto no puede ser,* This cannot be. **5,** *fol. by* **de,** *denoting origin* to be from; come from: *¿De dónde eres?,* Where are you from?; *denoting material* to be of; be made of: *La mesa es de madera,* The table is (made) of wood. **6,** *fol. by* **de**

or poss.adj. or pronoun to belong to; pertain to: *La pluma es de Pedro,* The pen is Peter's; *La pluma es mía,* The pen is mine. **7,** *fol. by* **de** *and inf., expressing tendency or expectation: Es de esperar,* It is to be expected. **—***aux.v., used with p.p. to form the passive voice: Es temido por todos,* He is feared by all. **—***n.m.* **1,** being. **2,** nature. **—a no ser por,** were it not for. **—a no ser que,** unless. **—¡cómo es eso!,** *colloq.,* how's that!; what's the idea! **—¡Cómo ha de ser!, 1,** How can it be? **2,** That's the way it is. **—de ser Vd.,** if I were you; in your place. **—érase que se era,** once upon a time there was. **—no sea que,** lest. **—no ser para menos,** to have good cause; be justified: *Ella lloró y no era para menos,* She cried, and with good cause. **—sea lo que sea; sea lo que fuere; sea como sea, 1,** come what may. **2,** be that as it may; anyhow. **—sea o no sea,** be that as it may. **—ser de lo que no hay,** *colloq.* to be unbelievable; be unheard of. **—ser para,** *fol. by inf.* **1,** *colloq.* to make one want to . . . : *Es para matarlo,* It makes you want to kill him. **2,** to be . . . ; be meant to be . . . : *Estos papeles son para tirar* or *tirarlos,* These papers are to be thrown away. **—si yo fuera Vd.,** if I were you; if I were in your place. **—soy con Vd.,** *colloq.* I'll be right with you.

sera ('se·ra) *n.f.* basket, usu. without handles.

serafín (se·ra'fin) *n.m.* seraph. **—seráfico** (-'ra·fi·ko) *adj.* seraphic.

serenar (se·re'nar) *v.t.* to make serene; calm. **—***v.i.* [*also, refl.,* **serenarse**] to become serene; calm.

serenata (se·re'na·ta) *n.f.* serenade.

sereno (se're·no) *adj.* serene; unruffled. **—***n.m.* **1,** night watchman. **2,** night cold; night air; night dew. **—serenidad,** *n.f.* serenity.

serial (se'rjal) *n.f.* serial.

sérico ('se·ri·ko) *adj.* silken.

serie ('se·rje) *n.f.* series; sequence.

serio ('se·rjo) *adj.* **1,** serious. **2,** serious-minded; sober. **—seriedad,** *n.f.* seriousness.

sermón (ser'mon) *n.m.* sermon. **—sermonear,** *v.i. & t.* to sermonize; lecture.

sero- (se·ro) *prefix* sero-; serum: *serología,* serology.

seroja (se'ro·xa) *n.f., also,* **serojo,** *n.m.* **1,** dry leaf. **2,** brushwood.

serón (se'ron) *n.m.* large basket, usu. without handles.

seroso (se'ro·so) *adj.* serous. **—serosidad,** *n.f.* serosity.

serpentear (ser·pen·te'ar) *v.i.* to wind; meander; twist.

serpentín (ser·pen'tin) *n.m.* cooling coil; coil of a still.

serpentina (ser·pen'ti·na) *n.f.* **1,** paper streamer; festoon. **2,** = **serpentín.**

serpentino (ser·pen'ti·no) *adj.* serpentine.

serpiente (ser'pjen·te) *n.f.* serpent.

serpollo (ser'po·ʎo; -jo) *n.m.* shoot; tiller.

serrado (se'rra·ðo) *adj.* serrate.

serrador (se·rra'ðor) *n.m.* sawyer.

serrallo (se'rra·ʎo; -jo) *n.f.* seraglio.

serrano (se'rra·no) *adj.* highland; mountain (*attrib.*). **—***n.m.* highlander. **—serranía,** *n.f.* mountain region; highlands (*pl.*).

serrar (se'rrar) *v.t.* [*pres.ind.* **sierro;** *pres.subjve.* **sierre**] to saw.

serrín (se'rrin) *n.m.* sawdust.

serrucho (se'rru·tʃo) *n.m.* handsaw; carpenter's saw.

servible (ser'βi·βle) *adj.* serviceable; useful.

servicio (ser'βi·θjo; -sjo) *n.m.* **1,** service. **2,** help; servants. **3,** tableware. **4,** *Amer.* toilet; water closet. **—servicial,** *adj.* helpful; obliging.

servidor (ser·βi'ðor) *n.m.* servant. **—servidor de Vd.** your servant; at your service.

servidumbre (ser·βi'ðum·bre) *n.f.* **1,** servants collectively; help. **2,** serfdom; servitude. **—servidumbre de paso** *or* **de vía,** right of way.

servil (ser'βil) *adj.* servile. **—servilismo,** *n.m.* servility.

servilleta (ser·βi'ʎe·ta; -'je·ta) *n.f.* serviette; napkin. **—servilletero,** napkin ring; napkin holder.

servio ('ser·βjo) *adj. & n.m.* Serbian; Serb.

servir (ser'βir) *v.t. & i.* [*pres.ind.* **sirvo;** *pres.subjve.* **sirva;** *pret.* **serví,**

sirvió; *ger.* **sirviendo**] **1,** to serve. **2,** to be of use (to); avail. —**servirse,** *v.r.* **1,** to be willing; be pleased. **2,** to help oneself; take. **3,** *fol. by* **de,** to make use of. —**sírvase** ('sir·βa·se) *fol. by inf.* please. —**ir servido; ir bien servido,** to get one's due; get one's just deserts.

servocroata (ser·βo·kro'a·ta) *adj. & n.m.* Serbo-Croatian.

sésamo ('se·sa·mo) *n.m.* sesame.

sesear (se·se'ar) *v.i.* to pronounce (s) for *z* and for *c* before *e* or *i.* —**seseo** (-'se·o) pronunciation as (s) of *z* and *c* before *e* or *i.*

sesenta (se'sen·ta) *adj. & n.m.* sixty. —**sesentavo,** *adj. & n.m.* sixtieth.

sesentón (se·sen'ton) *adj. & n.m., colloq., usu. derog.* = **sexagenario.**

sesgar (ses'ɣar) *v.t.* [*pres.subjve.* **sesgue** ('ses·ɣe); *pret.* **sesgué** (-'ɣe)] **1,** to cut on a bias; cut or tear obliquely. **2,** to bevel. **3,** to pass or cross at a slant or at an angle. **4,** to skew; slant. —**sesgado,** *adj.* aslant; askew; oblique; beveled. —**sesgadura,** *n.f.* slanting or oblique cut.

sesgo ('ses·ɣo) *n.m.* **1,** slant; skew; bevel; bias. **2,** *fig.* grimace; bad face. **3,** *fig.* course; direction; way. —**al sesgo, 1,** obliquely; slantingly. **2,** through; across.

sesión (se'sjon) *n.f.* **1,** session. **2,** conference; consultation.

seso ('se·so) *n.f.* brain; brains. —**devanarse los sesos,** to rack one's brain.

sesqui- (ses·ki) *prefix* sesqui-; one and a half: *sesquicentenario,* sesquicentennial.

sestear (ses·te'ar) *v.i.* to nap; take a siesta.

sesudo (se'su·ðo) *adj.* **1,** intelligent; wise; brainy. **2,** *Amer.* stubborn.

seta ('se·ta) *n.f.* **1,** mushroom. **2,** bristle.

setecientos (se·te'θjen·tos; -'sjen·tos) *adj. & n.m.* [*fem.* **-tas**] seven hundred.

setenta (se'ten·ta) *adj. & n.m.* seventy. —**setentavo,** *adj. & n.m.* seventieth.

setentón (se·ten'ton) *adj. & n.m., colloq.* = **septuagenario.**

setiembre (se'tjem·bre) *n.m.* = **septiembre.**

sétimo ('se·ti·mo) *adj. & n.m.* = **séptimo.**

seto ('se·to) *n.m.* fence; garden fence; hedge.

seudo ('seu·ðo) *adj.* pseudo.

seudo- (seu·ðo) *prefix, var. of* **pseudo-.**

seudónimo (seu'ðo·ni·mo) *n.m.* pseudonym.

severo (se'βe·ro) *adj.* severe. —**severidad,** *n.f.* severity.

sevicia (se'βi·θja; -sja) *n.f.* excessive cruelty.

sex- (seks) *prefix* sex-; six: *sexenio,* sexennial.

sexagenario (sek·sa·xe'na·rjo) *adj. & n.m.* sexagenarian.

sexagésimo (sek·sa'xe·si·mo) *adj. & n.m.* sixtieth. —**Sexagésima,** *n.f.* Sexagesima.

sexagonal (sek·sa·ɣo'nal) *adj.* = **hexagonal.**

sexcentésimo (seks·θen'te·si·mo; sek·sen-) *adj. & n.m.* six-hundredth.

sexo ('sek·so) *n.m.* sex.

sexta ('seks·ta) *n.f., music* sixth.

sextante (seks'tan·te) *n.m.* sextant.

sexteto (seks'te·to) *n.m.* sextet.

sextillón (seks·ti'ʎon; -'jon) *n.m.* a quadrillion sextillion; *Brit.* sextillion.

sexto ('seks·to) *adj. & n.m.* sixth.

séxtuplo ('seks·tu·plo) *adj.* sextuple. —**sextuplicar** (-pli'kar) *v.t.* [*infl.*: **duplicar**] to sextuple.

sexual (sek'swal) *adj.* sexual. —**sexualidad,** *n.f.* sexuality.

si (si) *conj.* **1,** if. **2,** whether. **3,** *archaic* although. —**por si,** in case; in the event that. —**si bien,** while; though. —**si no, 1,** otherwise. **2,** unless.

si (si) *n.m., music* si; B.

sí (si) *adv.* yes; indeed. —*n.m.* assent; consent; yea; aye; yes. —**por sí o por no,** in any case. —**sí que,** certainly. —**sí tal,** yes indeed.

sí (si) *refl.pron. 3rd pers.m. & f. sing. & pl., used after a prep.* oneself; yourself; yourselves; himself; herself; itself; themselves. —**de por sí,** by itself. —**sobre sí,** on guard.

siamés (si·a'mes) *adj. & n.m.* Siamese.

sibarita (si·βa'ri·ta) *n.m.* sybarite. —*adj.* sybaritic. —**sibarítico,** *adj.* sybaritic.

sibila (si'βi·la) *n.f.* sibyl.
sibilante (si·βi'lan·te) *adj. & n.f.* sibilant.
sicario (si'ka·rjo) *n.m.* **1,** hired assassin. **2,** henchman.
siclo ('si·klo) *n.m.* shekel.
sico- (si·ko) *prefix, var. of* **psico-**.
sicoanálisis *n.m.* = **psicoanálisis.** —**sicoanalista,** *n.m. & f.* = **psicoanalista.** —**sicoanalítico,** *adj.* = **psicoanalítico.** —**sicoanalizar,** *v.t.* = **psicoanalizar.**
sicofante (si·ko'fan·te) *also,* **sicofanta** (-ta) *n.m.* sycophant.
sicología *nf.* = **psicología.** —**sicológico,** *adj.* = **psicológico.** —**sicólogo,** *n.m.* = **psicólogo.**
sicómoro (si'ko·mo·ro) *n.m.* sycamore.
sicópata *n.m.* = **psicópata.** —**sicopatía,** *n.f.* = **psicopatía.** —**sicopático,** *adj.* = **psicopático.**
sicopatología *n.f.* = **psicopatología.**
sicosis *n.f.* = **psicosis.**
sicosomático *adj.* = **psicosomático.**
sicoterapia *n.f.* = **psicoterapia.**
sideral (si·ðe'ral) *adj.* sidereal. *Also,* **sidéreo** (-'ðe·re·o).
siderurgia (si·ðe'rur·xja) *n.f.* iron or steel metallurgy. —**siderúrgico** (-xi·ko) *adj.* of or pert. to the iron or steel industry; steel (*attrib.*).
sido ('si·ðo) *v., p.p. of* **ser.**
sidra ('si·ðra) *n.f.* cider.
siega ('sje·ɣa) *n.f.* harvest; harvesting; reaping.
siego ('sje·ɣo) *v., pres. ind. of* **segar.**
siegue ('sje·ɣe) *v., pres.subjve. of* **segar.**
siembra ('sjem·bra) *n.f.* **1,** sowing. **2,** sowing season. **3,** = **sembrado.**
siembre ('sjem·bre) *v., pres. subjve. of* **sembrar.**
siembro (-'bro) *v., pres.ind. of* **sembrar.**
siempre ('sjem·pre) *adv.* **1,** always; ever; forever. **2,** *Amer.* anyway; in any case. —**de siempre,** accustomed; usual. —**por siempre jamás,** forever and ever. —**siempre que, 1,** whenever. **2,** [*also,* **siempre y cuando que**] provided.
siempreviva (sjem·pre'βi·βa) *n.f., bot.* everlasting; immortelle.
sien (sjen) *n.f., anat.* temple.
siena ('sje·na) *n.f.* sienna.
siendo ('sjen·do) *v., ger. of* **ser.**
sienta ('sjen·ta) *v.* **1,** *pres.subjve. of* **sentir. 2,** *3rd pers.sing.pres.ind. of* **sentar.**
siente ('sjen·te) *v.* **1,** *pres.subjve. of* **sentar. 2,** *3rd pers.sing.pres.ind. of* **sentir.**
siento ('sjen·to) *v., 1st pers.sing. pres.ind. of* **sentar** *and* **sentir.**
sierpe ('sjer·pe) *n.f.* serpent.
sierra ('sje·rra) *n.f.* **1,** saw. **2,** mountain range. **3,** sawfish.
sierre ('sje·rre) *v., pres.subjve. of* **serrar.**
sierro ('sje·rro) *v., pres.ind. of* **serrar.**
siervo ('sjer·βo) *n.m.* **1,** serf; slave. **2,** servant.
siesta ('sjes·ta) *n.f.* siesta.
siete ('sje·te) *adj. & n.m.* seven. —*n.m.* a V-shaped rent or tear.
sífilis ('si·fi·lis) *n.f.* syphilis. —**sifilítico** (-'li·ti·ko) *adj. & n.m.* syphilitic.
sifón (si'fon) *n.m.* siphon.
siga ('si·ɣa) *v., pres.subjve. of* **seguir.**
sigilar (si·xi'lar) *v.t.* **1,** to conceal; secrete. **2,** *archaic* to seal.
sigilo (si'xi·lo) *n.m.* **1,** secrecy. **2,** stealth. **3,** caution; reserve. **4,** *archaic* seal.
sigiloso (si·xi'lo·so) *adj.* **1,** secretive. **2,** stealthy. **3,** reticent; reserved.
siglo ('si·ɣlo) *n.m.* **1,** century. **2,** age; epoch. **3,** *fig.* world; worldly affairs.
signar (siɣ'nar) *v.t.* **1,** to stamp; mark. **2,** *archaic* to sign. —**signarse,** *v.r.* to cross oneself three times (on the brow, on the mouth, and on the breast) invoking divine deliverance from enemies.
signatario (siɣ·na'ta·rjo) *adj. & n.m.* signatory.
signatura (siɣ·na'tu·ra) *n.f.* **1,** sign; mark. **2,** signing; signature. **3,** *print.* signature.
significado (siɣ·ni·fi'ka·ðo) *adj.* important; significant; eminent. —*n.m.* **1,** meaning; significance. **2,** [*also,* **significación,** *n.f.*] signification.
significar (siɣ·ni·fi'kar) *v.t.* [*pres.subjve.* **signifique** (-'fi·ke); *pret.* **signifiqué** (-'ke)] to signify; mean. —*v.i.* to have importance;

be significant. —**significativo,** *adj.* significant.
signo ('siɣ·no) *n.m.* sign; mark; character; symbol.
sigo ('si·ɣo) *v., 1st pers.sing.pres. ind. of* **seguir.**
siguiendo (si'ɣjen·do) *v., ger. of* **seguir.**
siguiente (si'ɣjen·te) *adj.* following; next.
siguió (si'ɣjo) *v., 3rd pers.sing. pret. of* **seguir.**
sílaba ('si·la·βa) *n.f.* syllable. —**silabario** (-'βa·rjo) *n.m.* spelling book. —**silábico** (si'la·βi·ko) *adj.* syllabic.
silabear (si·la·βe'ar) *v.t.* to syllabicate. —*v.i.* to speak in syllables. —**silabeo** (-'βe·o) *n.m.* syllabication.
sílabo ('si·la·βo) *n.m.* syllabus.
silbar (sil'βar) *v.t. & i.* to whistle. —*v.t.* to hiss (a performance). —**silbato** (-'βa·to) *n.m.* whistle (*device*). —**silbido** (-'βi·ðo) *n.m.* whistling; whistle; hiss.
silenciar (si·len'θjar; -'sjar) *v.t.* to silence. —**silenciador,** *n.m.* silencer; muffler.
silencio (si'len·θjo; -sjo) *n.m.* silence. —**silencioso,** *adj.* silent.
sílfide ('sil·fi·ðe) *n.f.* sylph.
silfo ('sil·fo) *n.m.* sylph.
silicato (si·li'ka·to) *n.m.* silicate.
sílice ('si·li·θe; -se) *n.m.* silica.
silíceo (si'li·θe·o; -se·o) *adj.* siliceous.
silicio (si'li·θjo; -sjo) *n.m.* silicon.
silicón (si·li'kon) *n.m.* silicone.
silicosis (si·li'ko·sis) *n.f.* silicosis.
silo ('si·lo) *also,* **silero** (si'le·ro) *n.m.* silo.
silogismo (si·lo'xis·mo) *n.m.* syllogism.
silueta (si'lwe·ta) *n.f.* silhouette.
silvestre (sil'βes·tre) *adj.* wild; uncultivated.
silla ('si·ʎa; -ja) *n.f.* **1,** chair. **2,** saddle. **3,** *eccles.* see. —**silleta,** *n.f.* folding chair. —**sillón,** *n.m.* armchair.
sillín (si'ʎin; -'jin) *n.m.* **1,** light riding saddle. **2,** bicycle *or* motorcycle seat.
sima ('si·ma) *n.f.* abyss; chasm.
simbiosis (sim'bjo·sis) *n.f.* symbiosis.
símbolo ('sim·bo·lo) *n.m.* symbol; token. —**simbólico** (-'bo·li·ko) *adj.* symbolic. —**simbolismo,** *n.m.* symbolism. —**simbolizar** (-li'θar; -'sar) *v.t.* [*pres.subjve.* **simbolice** (-'li·θe; -se); *pret.* **simbolicé** (-'θe; -'se)] to symbolize.
simetría (si·me'tri·a) *n.f.* symmetry. —**simétrico** (-'me·tri·ko) *adj.* symmetrical.
símico ('si·mi·ko) *adj.* simian.
simiente (si'mjen·te) *n.f.* seed.
simiesco (si'mjes·ko) *adj.* simian.
símil ('si·mil) *adj.* similar; like. —*n.m.* **1,** similarity. **2,** simile. —**similar,** *adj.* similar. —**similitud,** *n.f.* similitude.
similor (si·mi'lor) *n.m.* imitation gold; ormolu.
simio ('si·mjo) *n.m.* male ape or monkey; simian.
simonía (si·mo'ni·a) *n.f.* simony.
simpatía (sim·pa'ti·a) *n.f.* **1,** sympathy. **2,** congeniality.
simpático (sim'pa·ti·ko) *adj.* **1,** sympathetic. **2,** congenial; likable. **3,** pleasant; agreeable.
simpatizar (sim·pa·ti'θar; -'sar) *v.i.* [*pres.subjve.* **simpatice** (-'ti·θe; -se); *pret.* **simpaticé** (-'θe; -'se)] **1,** to sympathize. **2,** to be congenial; get along.
simple ('sim·ple) *adj.* **1,** simple; plain. **2,** single. **3,** silly; foolish.
simpleza (sim'ple·θa; -sa) *n.f.* **1,** simpleness; plainness. **2,** silliness; foolishness. **3,** trifle.
simplicidad (sim·pli·θi'ðað; -si'ðað) *n.f.* **1,** simplicity. **2,** candor; ingenuousness.
simplificar (sim·pli·fi'kar) *v.t.* [*pres.subjve.* **simplifique** (-'fi·ke); *pret.* **simplifiqué** (-'ke)] to simplify. —**simplificación,** *n.f.* simplification.
simplón (sim'plon) *n.m.* simpleton.
simulacro (si·mu'la·kro) *n.m.* **1,** image. **2,** sham; parody. **3,** *mil.* training exercise; combat drill.
simular (si·mu'lar) *v.t.* to simulate. —**simulación,** *n.f.* simulation.
simultáneo (si·mul'ta·ne·o) *adj.* simultaneous. —**simultaneidad,** *n.f.* simultaneousness.
simún (si'mun) *n.m.* simoom.
sin (sin) *prep.* without. —**sin que,** without: *Salió sin que lo viéramos,* He left without our seeing him.
sin- (sin) *prefix* **1,** syn-; with; together with: *sincrónico,* synchronic. **2,** without: *sinrazón,* unreason; injustice.

sinagoga (sina'ɣo·ɣa) *n.f.* synagogue.
sinapismo (si·na'pis·mo) *n.m.* **1,** mustard plaster. **2,** = **cataplasma.**
sincerarse (sin·θe'rar·se; sin·se-) *v.r.* to speak candidly; unbosom oneself.
sincero (sin'θe·ro; -'se·ro) *adj.* sincere. —**sinceridad,** *n.f.* sincerity.
síncopa ('sin·ko·pa) *n.f.* **1,** *gram.* syncope. **2,** *music* syncopation. —**sincopar,** *v.t.* to syncopate.
síncope ('sin·ko·pe) *n.m.* **1,** *gram.* = **síncopa. 2,** *med.* syncope; fainting spell.
sincrónico (sin'kro·ni·ko) *adj.* synchronous.
sincronizar (sin·kro·ni'θar; -'sar) *v.t.* [*pres.subjve.* **sincronice** (-'ni·θe; -se); *pret.* **sincronicé** (-'θe; -'se)] to synchronize. —**sincronización,** *n.f.* synchronization.
sindicalismo (sin·di·ka'lis·mo) *n.m.* unionism. —**sindicalista,** *n.m. & f.* unionist.
sindicar (sin·di'kar) *v.t.* [*pres. subjve.* **sindique** (-'di·ke); *pret.* **sindiqué** (-'ke)] to syndicate; unionize. —**sindicación,** *n.f.* syndication; unionization. —**sindicato** (-'ka·to) *n.m.* syndicate; union.
síndico ('sin·di·ko) *n.m.* **1,** *law* receiver. **2,** trustee; board member.
sindiós (sin'djos) *adj. & n.m. & f. sing. & pl.* godless.
sinecura (si·ne'ku·ra) *n.f.* sinecure.
sinfonía (sin·fo'ni·a) *n.f.* symphony. —**sinfónico** (-'fo·ni·ko) *adj.* symphonic.
singlón (sin'glon) *n.m.* yardarm.
singular (sin·gu'lar) *adj.* singular; unique. —**singularidad,** *n.f.* singularity. —**singularizarse** (-ri·'θar·se; -'sar·se) *v.r.* [*pres. subjve.* **singularice** (-'ri·θe; -se); *pret.* **singularicé** (-'θe; -'se)] to distinguish oneself.
siniestro (si'njes·tro) *adj.* **1,** sinister. **2,** left. —*n.m.* disaster. —**siniestra,** *n.f.* left hand; left side.
sinistro- (si·nis·tro) *prefix* sinistro-; left: *sinistrorso,* sinistrorse.
sinnúmero (sin'nu·me·ro) *n.m.* countless number. —**un sinnúmero de . . . ,** countless . . .
sino ('si·no) *conj.* but; except; only. —*n.m.* fate.
sino- (si·no) *prefix* Sino-; Chinese: *sinología,* Sinology.
sínodo ('si·no·ðo) *n.m.* synod. —**sinodal,** *adj.* synodal.
sinónimo (si'no·ni·mo) *adj.* synonymous. —*n.m.* synonym.
sinopsis (si'nop·sis) *n.f. sing. & pl.* synopsis. —**sinóptico** (-'nop·ti·ko) *adj.* synoptic.
sinrazón (sin·ra'θon; -'son) *n.f.* **1,** unreason. **2,** injustice; wrong.
sinsabor (sin·sa'βor) *n.m.* **1,** insipidity. **2,** *fig.* trouble; worry.
sinsonte (sin'son·te) *n.m.* mockingbird.
sintaxis (sin'tak·sis) *n.f.* syntax. —**sintáctico** (-'tak·ti·ko) *adj.* syntactical.
síntesis ('sin·te·sis) *n.f. sing. & pl.* synthesis. —**sintético** (-'te·ti·ko) *adj.* synthetic. —**sintetizar** (-ti'θar; -'sar) *v.t.* [*pres.subjve.* **sintetice** (-'ti·θe; -se); *pret.* **sinteticé** (-'θe; -'se)] to synthesize.
sintiendo (sin'tjen·do) *v., ger. of* **sentir.**
sintió (sin'tjo) *v., 3rd pers.sing. pret. of* **sentir.**
sintoísmo (sin·to'is·mo) *n.m.* Shinto; Shintoism. —**sintoísta,** *adj.* Shinto; Shintoist. —*n.m. & f.* Shintoist.
síntoma ('sin·to·ma) *n.m.* symptom; sign. —**sintomático** (-'ma·ti·ko) *adj.* symptomatic.
sintonizar (sin·to·ni'θar; -'sar) *v.t.* [*pres.subjve.* **sintonice** (-'ni·θe; -se); *pret.* **sintonicé** (-'θe; -'se)] to tune in. —**sintonización,** *n.f.* tuning. —**sintonizador,** *n.m.* tuner.
sinuoso (si'nwo·so) *adj.* sinuous. —**sinuosidad,** *n.f.* sinuosity.
sinusitis (si·nu'si·tis) *n.f.* sinusitis.
sinvergonzonería (sin·βer·ɣon·θo·ne'ri·a; -so·ne'ri·a) *n.f., colloq.* **1,** shamelessness; brazenness. **2,** low trick; dastardly act. —**sinvergonzón** (-'θon; -'son) *n.m., colloq.* scamp; so-and-so.
sinvergüenza (sin·βer'ɣwen·θa; -sa) *adj.* shameless; brazen. —*n.m.* rascal; scoundrel. —*n.f.* wanton; hussy. —**sinvergüenzada,** *n.f., colloq.* low trick; dastardly act. —**sinvergüencería** (-θe'ri·a; -se'ri·a) *n.f., colloq.* = **sinvergonzonería.** —**sinvergüenzón** (-'θon; -'son) *n.m.* = **sinvergonzón.**
Sión (si'on) *n.f.* Zion. —**sionismo,** *n.m.* Zionism. —**sionista,** *adj. & n.m. & f.* Zionist.
-sión (sjon) *suffix* -sion; *forming*

nouns denoting act; result of; quality; condition: *admisión*, admission; *confusión*, confusion.
sique *n.f.* = **psique.**
siquiatría *n.f.* = **psiquiatría.** —**siquiatra,** *n.m.* & *f.* = **psiquiatra.** —**siquiátrico,** *adj.* = **psiquiátrico.**
síquico *adj.* = **psíquico.**
siquiera (si'kje·ra) *adv.* at least. —*conj.* though; although. —**ni siquiera,** not even.
siquis *n.f.* = **psiquis.**
sirena (si're·na) *n.f.* siren.
sirga ('sir·ɣa) *n.f.* tow rope; tow line.
Sirio ('si·rjo) *n.m.* Dog Star; Sirius.
siroco (si'ro·ko) *n.m.* sirocco.
sirsaca (sir'sa·ka) *n.f.* seersucker.
sirva ('sir·βa) *v., pres.subjve. of* **servir.**
sirviendo (sir'βjen·do) *v., ger. of* **servir.**
sirviente (sir'βjen·te) *n.m.* [*fem.* **sirvienta**] servant; domestic.
sirvió (sir'βjo) *v., 3rd pers.sing. pret. of* **servir.**
sirvo ('sir·βo) *v., pres.ind.of* **servir.**
sisa ('si·sa) *n.f.* **1,** pilferage; cheating, esp. in domestic accounts. **2,** dart in a garment.
sisal (si'sal) *n.m., Amer.* sisal; sisal hemp.
sisar (si'sar) *v.t.* **1,** to cheat; pilfer. **2,** to take in (a garment).
sisear (si·se'ar) *v.t.* & *i.* to hiss. —**siseo** (-'se·o) *n.m.* hissing.
sísmico ('sis·mi·ko) *adj.* seismic.
sismo ('sis·mo) *n.m.* earthquake.
sismógrafo (sis'mo·ɣra·fo) *n.m.* seismograph.
sistema (sis'te·ma) *n.m.* system. —**sistemático** (-'ma·ti·ko) *adj.* systematic. —**sistematizar** (-ti'θar; -'sar) *v.t.* [*infl.:* **realizar**] to systematize.
sístole ('sis·to·le) *n.m.* systole. —**sistólico** (-'to·li·ko) *adj.* systolic.
sitial (si'tjal) *n.m.* seat of honor.
sitiar (si'tjar) *v.t.* to besiege; surround.
sitio ('si·tjo) *n.m.* **1,** place; site; location. **2,** siege.
sito ('si·to) *adj.* situated; located.
situación (si·twa'θjon; -'sjon) *n.f.* **1,** situation; position; location. **2,** condition; circumstances (*pl.*).
situar (si'twar) *v.t.* [*infl.:* **continuar**] to situate; locate; place.

smoking ('smo·kin) *n.m.* [*pl.* **smokings** (-kins)] dinner jacket; tuxedo.
snob (snob) *n.m.* & *f.* = **esnob.** —**snobismo,** *n.m.* = **esnobismo.**
so (so) *prep.* under; below. —*interj.* whoa!
so- (so) *prefix* **1,** below; under: *socavar*, undermine. **2,** expressing partial or incomplete performance of an action: *soasar*, roast lightly.
soba ('so·βa) *n.f.* **1,** squeezing; pressing; kneading. **2,** rub; rubbing; massage. **3,** *colloq.* pawing; fondling. **4,** *colloq.* fawning; servile flattery. **5,** *colloq.* drubbing. **6,** *colloq.* bother; annoyance.
sobaco (so'βa·ko) *n.m.* armpit.
sobado (so'βa·ðo) *adj.* trite; hackneyed; stale. —*n.m.* = **sobadura.**
sobadura (so·βa'ðu·ra) *n.f.* **1,** rub; rubbing; massage. **2,** squeezing; pressing; kneading.
sobajar (so·βa'xar) *v.t.* **1,** to handle; paw. **2,** *Amer.* to degrade; humiliate.
sobajear (so·βa·xe'ar) *v.t., Amer.* to handle; paw. —**sobajeo** (-'xe·o) *n.m.* handling; pawing.
sobaquera (so·βa'ke·ra) *n.f.* **1,** armhole. **2,** shield for the armpit. **3,** *Amer.* = **sobaquina.**
sobaquina (so·βa'ki·na) *n.f.* underarm perspiration.
sobar (so'βar) *v.t.* **1,** to squeeze; press; knead. **2,** to rub; massage. **3,** *colloq.* to paw; fondle. **4,** *colloq.* to fawn on; toady to. **5,** *colloq.* to beat; give a drubbing to. **6,** *colloq.* to displease; molest.
soberano (so·βe'ra·no) *n.m.* & *adj.* sovereign. —**soberanía,** *n.f.* sovereignty.
soberbia (so'βer·βja) *n.f.* **1,** arrogance; haughtiness. **2,** magnificence.
soberbio (so'βer·βjo) *adj.* **1,** arrogant; haughty; overbearing. **2,** magnificent; superb.
sobina (so'βi·na) *n.f.* wooden pin; peg.
sobón (so'βon) *adj., colloq.* fawning; obsequious. —*n.m., colloq.* toady.
sobornal (so·βor'nal) *n.m.* surcharge.
sobornar (so·βor'nar) *v.t.* to suborn; bribe. —**sobornación,** *n.f.* bribing; subornation. —**soborno** (so'βor·no) *n.m.* bribe; bribing; subornation.
sobra ('so·βra) *n.f.* excess; re-

mainder. —**sobras**, *n.f.pl.* leftovers. —**de sobra**, **1**, ample; amply; more than enough. **2**, redundant; unnecessary; superfluous.
sobrado (so'βra·ðo) *adj.* **1**, redundant, superfluous; excessive. **2**, well-provided; well-off. **3**, intemperate; immoderate. —*adv.* **1**, amply; well. **2**, too; too much. —*n.m.* **1**, attic; garret. **2**, *usu.pl., Amer.* leftovers.
sobrante (so'βran·te) *adj.* excess; extra; leftover. —*n.m.* excess; remainder.
sobrar (so'βrar) *v.t.* **1**, to exceed. **2**, to excel. —*v.i.* **1**, to be ample; be more than sufficient. **2**, to be unnecessary; be superfluous. **3**, to be left over; remain.
sobre ('so·βre) *prep. & adv.* over; above. —*prep.* **1**, on; upon; on top of. **2**, about; concerning. **3**, after; following. **4**, beyond; besides. —*n.m.* **1**, envelope. **2**, = **sobrescrito**.
sobre- (so·bre) *prefix*, over; beyond; extra: *sobrealimentación*, overfeeding; extra nourishment; *sobrepasar*, go beyond; surpass.
sobreabundante (so·βre·a·βun'dan·te) *adj.* superabundant. —**sobreabundancia**, *n.f.* superabundance
sobreagudo (so·βre·a'ɣu·ðo) *adj. & n.m., music* treble.
sobrealiento (so·βre·a'ljen·to) *n.m.* labored breathing.
sobrealzar (so·βre·al'θar; -'sar) *v.t.* [*infl.:* **alzar**] to extol; laud.
sobrecama (so·βre'ka·ma) *n.f.* bedspread.
sobrecarga (so·βre'kar·ɣa) *n.f.* overload; surcharge. —**sobrecargar**, *v.t.* [*infl.:* **cargar**] to overload; surcharge.
sobrecargo (so·βre'kar·ɣo) *n.m.* supercargo.
sobreceja (so·βre'θe·xa; -'se·xa) *n.f.* ridge of the brow.
sobreceño (so·βre'θe·ɲo; -'se·ɲo) *n.m.* frown.
sobrecincha (so·βre'θin·tʃa; -'sin·tʃa) *n.f.* surcingle. *Also,* **sobrecincho**, *n.m.*
sobrecoger (so·βre·ko'xer) *v.t.* [*infl.:* **coger**] to catch up with; overtake. —**sobrecogerse**, *v.r.* **1**, to be overcome; be overwhelmed. **2**, to be seized with fear or apprehension. —**sobrecogimiento**, *n.m.* fear.
sobrecubierta (so·βre·ku'βjer·ta) *n.f.* **1**, double wrapper. **2**, dust jacket. **3**, *naut.* upper deck.
sobredicho (so·βre'ði·tʃo) *adj.* aforesaid.
sobreentender (so·βre·en·ten·'der) *v.t.* = **sobrentender.**
sobreestimar (so·βre·es·ti'mar) *v.t.* to overestimate. —**sobreestimación**, *n.f.* overestimation.
sobreexceder (so·βre·eks·θe'ðer; -ek·se'ðer) *v.t.* = **sobrexceder.**
sobreexcitar (so·βre·eks·θi'tar; -ek·si'tar) *v.t.* to overexcite.
sobreexponer (so·βre·eks·po·'ner) *v.t.* [*infl.:* **poner**] to overexpose. —**sobreexposición** (-po·si·'θjon; -'sjon) *n.f.* overexposure.
sobregirar (so·βre·xi'rar) *v.t. & i., comm.* to overdraw. —**sobregiro** (-'xi·ro) *n.m.* overdraft.
sobrehilar (so·βre·i'lar) *v.t., sewing* to overcast. —**sobrehilado**, *adj. & n.m.* overcast.
sobrehumano (so·βre·u'ma·no) *adj.* superhuman.
sobrellenar (so·βre·ʎe'nar; -je·'nar) *v.t.* to overfill; overflow.
sobrellevar (so·βre·ʎe'βar; -je·'βar) *v.t.* to endure; put up with.
sobremanera (so·βre·ma'ne·ra) *adv.* exceedingly.
sobremarcha (so·βre'mar·tʃa) *n.f., mech.* overdrive.
sobremesa (so·βre'me·sa) *n.f.* **1**, tablecloth; table cover. **2**, after-dinner amenities. —**de sobremesa**, after-dinner.
sobrenadar (so·βre·na'ðar) *v.i.* to float; swim on the surface.
sobrenatural (so·βre·na·tu'ral) *adj.* supernatural.
sobrenombre (so·βre'nom·bre) *n.m.* nickname; cognomen.
sobrentender (so·βren·ten'der) *v.t.* [*infl.:* **entender**] to understand; assume; take for granted.
sobrepasar (so·βre·pa'sar) *v.t.* to surpass. —**sobrepasarse**, *v.r.* to overstep one's bounds.
sobrepelliz (so·βre·pe'ʎiθ; -'jis) *n.f.* surplice.
sobrepeso (so·βre'pe·so) *n.m.* overweight; excess weight.
sobreponer (so·βre·po'ner) *v.t.* [*infl.:* **poner**] to superimpose. —**sobreponerse**, *v.r., fol. by* **a**, to overcome; master.
sobrepuesto (so·βre'pwes·to) *v., p.p. of* **sobreponer.** —*adj. & n.m.* appliqué. —*n.m., Amer.* patch; mend.

sobrepujar (so·βre·pu'xar) *v.t.* to outdo; outstrip.
sobresaliente (so·βre·sa'ljen·te) *adj.* **1,** outstanding; excellent. **2,** projecting; protruding. —*n.m.* [*fem.* **sobresalienta**] substitute; understudy.
sobresalir (so·βre·sa'lir) *v.i.* [*infl.:* **salir**] **1,** to stand out; excel. **2,** to project; protrude.
sobresaltar (so·βre·sal'tar) *v.t.* to startle; frighten. —*v.i.* to stand out; show up clearly. —**sobresaltarse,** *v.r.* to take fright; be startled. —**sobresalto** (-'sal·to) *n.m.* start; fright. —**de sobresalto,** suddenly.
sobrescribir (so·βres·kri'βir) *v.t.* [*p.p.* **sobrescrito** (-'kri·to)] **1,** to superscribe. **2,** to address (a letter or package). —**sobrescrito,** *n.m.* address (*on a letter or package*).
sobrestante (so·βres'tan·te) *n.m.* foreman; supervisor.
sobresueldo (so·βre'swel·do) *n.m.* extra pay; bonus.
sobretodo (so·βre'to·ðo) *n.m.* overcoat.
sobrevenir (so·βre·βe'nir) *v.i.* [*infl.:* **venir**] to befall; happen; supervene.
sobrevivir (so·βre·βi'βir) *v.t.* & *i.* to survive. —**sobreviviente,** *adj.* & *n.m.* & *f.* survivor.
sobrexceder (so·βreks·θe'ðer; so·βrek·se'ðer) *v.t.* to exceed; outdo; excel; surpass.
sobriedad (so·βrje'ðað) *n.f.* **1,** sobriety. **2,** frugality.
sobrina (so'βri·na) *n.f.* niece. —**sobrino,** *n.m.* nephew.
sobrio ('so·βrjo) *adj.* **1,** sober. **2,** sparing; frugal.
socaire (so'kai·re) *n.m.* lee; shelter. —**estar** *or* **ponerse al socaire,** *colloq.* to shirk.
socapa (so'ka·pa) *n.f.* pretense; pretext; cloak. —**a socapa,** surreptitiously.
socarrar (so·ka'rrar) *v.t.* to singe. —**socarra** (-'ka·rra) *n.f.* singe; singeing.
socarrón (so·ka'rron) *adj.* **1,** ironic; jesting; mocking. **2.** cunning; roguish; rascally.
socarronería (so·ka·rro·ne'ri·a) *n.f.* **1,** irony; mockery; jest. **2,** roguishness; cunning.
socavar (so·ka'βar) *v.t.* to undermine; dig under. —**socavación,** *also,* **socava** (-'ka·βa) *n.f.* undermining; digging under. —**socavón** (-'βon) *n.m.* tunnel; dugout.
sociable (so'θja·βle; -'sja·βle) *adj.* sociable. —**sociabilidad,** *n.f.* sociability.
social (so'θjal; -'sjal) *adj.* **1,** social. **2,** of or pert. to a company or association. **3,** *colloq.* sociable.
socialismo (so·θja'lis·mo; so·sja-) *n.m.* socialism. —**socialista,** *adj.* & *n.m.* & *f.* socialist. —*adj.* socialistic.
socializar (so·θja·li'θar; -sja·li·'sar) *v.t.* [*pres.subjve.* **socialice** (-'li·θe; -se); *pret.* **socialicé** (-'θe; -'se)] to socialize. —**socialización,** *n.f.* socialization.
sociedad (so·θje'ðað; so·sje-) *n.f.* **1,** society. **2,** high society; the fashionable world. **3,** partnership. **4,** corporation; company; organization. —**sociedad anónima,** stock company; corporation.
socio ('so·θjo; -sjo) *n.m.* partner; member; associate. —**socio fundador,** charter member.
sociología (so·θjo·lo'xi·a; so·sjo-) *n.f.* sociology. —**sociológico** (-'lo·xi·ko) *adj.* sociological. —**sociólogo** (so'θjo·lo·ɣo; -'sjo·lo·ɣo) *n.m.* sociologist.
socolor (so·ko'lor) *n.m.* guise; pretense.
socorrer (so·ko'rrer) *v.t.* **1,** to succor; give help or relief to. **2,** to favor.
socorrido (so·ko'rri·ðo) *adj.* **1,** well-stocked; well-supplied. **2,** hackneyed; worn; trite.
socorro (so'ko·rro) *n.m.* succor; help; aid.
soda ('so·ða) *n.f.* soda.
sodio ('so·ðjo) *n.m.* sodium.
sodomía (so·ðo'mi·a) *n.f.* sodomy. —**sodomita,** *n.m.* & *f.* sodomite.
soez (so'eθ; -'es) *adj.* low; vulgar.
sofá (so'fa) *n.m.* sofa.
sófbol ('sof·βol) *n.m.* softball.
-sofía (so'fi·a) *suffix* -sophy; knowledge; thought: *filosofía,* philosophy.
sofisma (so'fis·ma) *n.m.* sophism. —**sofista,** *adj.* sophistic. —*n.m.* & *f.* sophist. —**sofistería,** *n.f.* sophistry.
sofisticar (so·fis·ti'kar) *v.t.* [*pres.subjve.* **sofistique** (-'ti·ke); *pret.* **sofistiqué** (-'ke)] to sophisticate. —**sofisticación,** *n.f.* sophistication.
soflama (so'fla·ma) *n.f.* **1,** flicker;

glow. 2, blush. 3, *derog.* bombastic speech.
sofocar (so·fo'kar) *v.t.* [*pres. subjve.* **sofoque** (-'fo·ke); *pret.* **sofoqué** (-'ke)] to suffocate; smother. —**sofocarse,** *v.r.* 1, to suffocate. 2, to be discomfited or embarrassed. —**sofocante,** *adj.* suffocating; oppressive.
sofoco (so'fo·ko) *n.m.* 1, suffocation. 2, shame; embarrassment. 3, shock; jolt; upset.
sofreír (so·fre'ir) *v.t.* [*infl.:* **freír**] to fry lightly.
sofrenar (so·fre'nar) *v.t.* to curb; check; restrain.
sofrito (so'fri·to) *v., p.p. of* **sofreír.** —*n.m.* fry.
soga ('so·ɣa) *n.f.* rope.
sois (sois) *v., 2nd pers.pl.pres.ind. of* **ser.**
soja ('so·xa) *n.f.* = **soya.**
sojuzgar (so·xuθ'ɣar; so·xus-) *v.t.* [*infl.:* **juzgar**] to subjugate; subdue.
sol (sol) *n.m.* 1, sun. 2, sunshine; sunlight. 3, *music* sol; G. 4, monetary unit of Peru; sol. —**hacer sol,** to be sunny.
solacear (so·la·θe'ar; -se'ar) *v.t.* = **solazar.**
solamente (so·la'men·te) *adv.* only; merely; just; solely. —**solamente que,** only that; unless.
solana (so'la·na) *n.f.* 1, sun parlor. 2, sunny spot.
solano (so'la·no) *n.m.* nightshade.
solapa (so'la·pa) *n.f.* 1, lapel. 2, *fig.* pretext; cloak. —**solapado,** *adj.* deceitful; underhanded. —**de solapa,** underhandedly; deceitfully.
solar (so'lar) *n.m.* 1, lot; plot of ground. 2, ancestry; lineage; house. 3, heritage. —*adj.* solar.
solar (so'lar) *v.t.* [*pres.ind.* **suelo;** *pres.subjve.* **suele**] 1, to sole (shoes). 2, to pave; floor.
solariego (so·la'rje·ɣo) *adj.* ancestral. —**casa solariega,** family home; homestead; manor.
solario (so'la·rjo) *n.m.* solarium.
solaz (so'laθ; -'las) *n.m.* 1, solace. 2, enjoyment; recreation.
solazar (so·la'θar; -'sar) *v.t.* [*pres.subjve.* **solace** (-'la·θe; -se); *pret.* **solacé** (-'θe; -'se)] to solace.
soldado (sol'da·ðo) *n.m.* soldier. —**soldadesca,** *n.f.* soldiery. —**soldadesco,** *adj.* soldierly. —**soldado raso,** private.
soldador (sol·da'ðor) *n.m.* 1, welder; solderer. 2, soldering iron; soldering gun.
soldadura (sol·da'ðu·ra) *n.f.* 1, solder. 2, soldering. 3, weld.
soldar (sol'dar) *v.t.* [*pres.ind.* **sueldo;** *pres.subjve.* **suelde**] to solder; weld.
solear (so·le'ar) *v.t.* to sun.
solecismo (so·le'θis·mo; -'sis·mo) *n.m.* solecism.
soledad (so·le'ðað) *n.f.* solitude; loneliness.
solemne (so'lem·ne) *adj.* solemn. —**solemnidad,** *n.f.* solemnity. —**solemnizar** (-ni'θar, -'sar) *v.t.* [*pres.subjve.* **solemnice** (-'ni·θe; -se); *pret.* **solemnicé** (-'θe; -'se)] to solemnize.
solenoide (so·le'noi·ðe) *n.m.* solenoid.
soler (so'ler) *v.i., defective, used only in pres.ind.* [**suelo**], *pres. subjve.* [**suela**], *and impf.* [**solía**] to be used (to); be accustomed (to); be customary (to); do often.
solera (so'le·ra) *n.f.* crossbeam.
solevantar (so·le·βan'tar) *v.t.* 1, to agitate; stir; stir up. 2, = **solevar.** —**solevantado,** *adj.* restless; excited. —**solevantamiento,** *n.m.* upheaval; uprising.
solevar (so·le'βar) *v.t.* to raise; lift.
solfa ('sol·fa) *n.f.* 1, solmization. 2, *fig.* music. 3, *colloq.* beating; drubbing. 4, *colloq.* reprimand; scolding. 5, *colloq.* harping; ranting. —**poner en solfa,** to set to music.
solfear (sol·fe'ar) *v.t. & i.* 1, to sing or play in solmization. 2, **colloq.** to harp (on); rant. —**solfeo** (-'fe·o) *n.m.* solmization.
solferino (sol·fe'ri·no) *adj.* reddish-purple.
-soli- (so·li) *prefix* soli-; single; alone: *soliloquio,* soliloquy.
solicitar (so·li·θi'tar; -si'tar) *v.t.* 1, to solicit; entreat. 2, to request; demand. 3, to further; promote. —**solicitación,** *n.f.* solicitation. —**solicitado,** *adj.* in demand; sought after. —**solicitador,** *n.m.* solicitor. —**solicitante,** *n.m. & f.* applicant; petitioner.
solícito (so'li·θi·to; -si·to) *adj.* solicitous.
solicitud (so·li·θi'tuð; -si'tuð) *n.f.* 1, solicitude. 2, application; request; appeal; demand.
solidar (so·li'ðar) *v.t.* 1, =

consolidar. 2, to affirm; establish.
solidario (so·li'ða·rjo) *adj.* 1, solidary. 2, united; unanimous; at one. —**solidaridad,** *n.f.* solidarity.
solidarizar (so·li·ða·ri'θar; -'sar) *v.i.* [*pres.subjve.* **solidarice** (-'ri·θe; -se); *pret.* **solidaricé** (-'θe; -'se)] *fol. by* **con,** to make common cause with; stand together with.
solidificar (so·li·ði·fi'kar) *v.t.* [*pres.subjve.* **solidifique** (-'fi·ke); *pret.* **solidifiqué** (-'ke)] to solidify. —**solidificación,** *n.f.* solidification.
sólido ('so·li·ðo) *adj.* & *n.m.* solid. —**solidez,** *n.f.* solidity.
soliloquio (so·li'lo·kjo) *n.m.* soliloquy. —**soliloquiar,** *v.i., colloq.* to soliloquize.
solista (so'lis·ta) *n.m.* & *f.* soloist.
solitaria (so·li'ta·rja) *n.f.* tapeworm.
solitario (so·li'ta·rjo) *adj.* & *n.m.* solitary. —*n.m.* solitaire.
sólito ('so·li·to) *adj.* accustomed; usual.
solitud (so·li'tuð) *n.f.* solitude.
soliviantar (so·li·βjan'tar) *v.t.* to arouse; incite. —**soliviantado,** *adj.* restless; excited; aroused.
soliviar (so·li'βjar) *v.t.* to raise; prop; lift.
solo ('so·lo) *adj.* 1, alone. 2, single; only; sole. 3, lonely. —*n.m.* solo. —**sólo,** *adv.* = **solamente.**
solomillo (so·lo'mi·ʎo; -jo) *also,* **solomo** (so'lo·mo) *n.m.* loin; sirloin.
solsticio (sols'ti·θjo; -sjo) *n.m.* solstice.
soltar (sol'tar) *v.t* [*pres.ind.* **suelto;** *pres.subjve.* **suelte**] 1, to untie. 2, to loosen; let out. 3, to let go; loose; release. —**soltarse,** *v.r.* 1, to loosen; become loose. 2, to come off. 3, to lose restraint. —**soltar a,** *fol. by inf.* to begin; set out.
soltería (sol·te'ri·a) *n.f.* 1, bachelorhood. 2, spinsterhood.
soltero (sol'te·ro) *adj.* unmarried. —*n.m.* bachelor; unmarried man. —**soltera,** *n.f.* spinster. —**solterón,** *n.m.* confirmed bachelor. —**solterona,** *n.f.* old maid.
soltura (sol'tu·ra) *n.f.* 1, loosing. 2, ease; freedom. 3, fluency.
soluble (so'lu·βle) *adj.* soluble. —**solubilidad,** *n.f.* solubility.
solución (so·lu'θjon; -'sjon) *n.f.* solution. —**solucionar,** *v.t.* to solve.
solventar (sol·βen'tar) *v.t.* 1, to pay; settle (an account). 2, to resolve; solve.
solvente (sol'βen·te) *adj.* & *n.m.* solvent. —**solvencia,** *n.f.* solvency.
sollastría (so·ʎas'tri·a; so·jas-) *n.f.* scullery.
sollo ('so·ʎo; -jo) *n.m.* sturgeon.
sollozar (so·ʎo'θar; -jo'sar) *v.i.* [*pres.subjve.* **solloce** (-'ʎo·θe; -'jo·se); *pret.* **sollocé** (-'θe; -'se)] to sob. —**sollozo** (-'ʎo·θo; -'jo·so) *n.m.* sob.
-soma (so·ma) *suffix* -some; body: *cromosoma,* chromosome.
somanta (so'man·ta) *n.f., colloq.* beating; drubbing.
somático (so'ma·ti·ko) *adj.* somatic.
somato- (so·ma·to) *prefix* somato-; body: *somatología;* somatology.
sombra ('som·bra) *n.f.* 1, shade; shadow. 2, protection; shelter. 3, image. 4, umbra. —**a la sombra,** *colloq.* in jail. —**tener mala sombra,** *colloq.* 1, (of persons) [*also,* **ser un mala sombra**] to be baneful; be detestable. 2, (of things) to be a jinx. —**tierra de sombra,** umber.
sombraje (som'bra·xe) *n.m.* shade; awning.
sombrear (som·bre'ar) *v.t.* to shade (a drawing or painting). —**sombreado,** *n.m.* shading.
sombrero (som'bre·ro) *n.m.* hat. —**sombrerera,** *n.f.* hatbox. —**sombrerería,** *n.f.* hat shop. —**sombrerero,** *n.m.* hatter. —**sombrero de copa,** high hat; top hat. —**sombrero de jipijapa; sombrero panamá,** Panama hat. —**sombrero de muelles,** opera hat. —**sombrero de pelo,** *Amer.* high hat. —**sombrero hongo,** derby.
sombrilla (som'bri·ʎa; -ja) *n.f.* 1, parasol; sunshade. 2, umbrella.
sombrío (som'bri·o) *adj.* somber; gloomy.
somero (so'me·ro) *adj.* superficial; summary.
someter (so·me'ter) *v.t.* 1, to subject. 2, to submit; propose. 3, to entrust; commit. —**someterse,** *v.r.* to submit; yield.
sometimiento (so·me·ti'mjen·to) *n.m.* 1, subjection; subjugation. 2, submission.

sommier (so'mjer) *n.m.* bedspring.
somnambulismo (som·nam·bu'lis·mo) *n.m.* = **sonambulismo.** —**somnámbulo** (som'nam·bu·lo) *n.m.* = **sonámbulo.**
somnífero (som'ni·fe·ro) *adj.* somniferous. —*n.m.* sleeping pill or potion.
somnolencia (som·no'len·θja; -sja) *n.f.* somnolence.
somorgujar (so·mor·ɣu'xar) *v.t. & i.* to dip; dunk. —*v.i.* to dive; duck. —**somorgujo** (-'ɣu·xo) *n.m.* merganser; loon.
somos ('so·mos) *v., 1st pers.pl. pres.ind. of* ser.
son (son) *n.m.* **1,** sound. **2,** tune. **3,** fame; report. **4,** *fig.* manner; guise; tenor. —**¿a son de qué?,** *also,* **¿a qué son?** why?; for what reason? —**sin son,** *also,* **sin ton ni son,** *colloq.* without rhyme or reason.
son (son) *v., 3rd pers.pl.pres.ind. of* ser.
sonado (so'na·ðo) *adj.* **1,** noted; famous. **2,** notorious.
sonaja (so'na·xa) *n.f.* **1,** tambourine. **2,** noisemaker. **3,** [*also,* **sonajero,** *n.m.*] baby rattle.
sonambulismo (so·nam·bu'lis·mo) *n.m.* somnambulism. —**sonámbulo** (so'nam·bu·lo) *n.m.* sleepwalker; somnambulist.
sonante (so'nan·te) *adj.* sounding; ringing. —**dinero sonante,** *also,* **dinero contante y sonante,** hard cash.
sonar (so'nar) *v.t.* [*pres.ind.* **sueno;** *pret.* **suene**] **1,** to sound; ring. **2,** to blow (the nose). —*v.i.* **1,** to sound; ring. **2,** to sound familiar. **3,** to strike (*of the clock or the hour*). **4,** *colloq.* to be finished; be done for. —**sonarse,** *v.r.* **1,** to blow one's nose. **2,** to be rumored. —**sonar a,** to sound like.
sonar (so'nar) *n.m.* sonar.
sonata (so'na·ta) *n.f.* sonata.
sonda ('son·da) *n.f.* **1,** sounding. **2,** sounding line. **3,** borer; drill. **4,** *med.* catheter. **5,** *surg.* probe.
sondear (son·de'ar) *also,* **sondar** (-'dar) *v.t.* to sound; probe.
sondeo (son'de·o) *n.m.* **1,** sounding. **2,** boring.
sonetista (so·ne'tis·ta) *n.m. & f.* sonneteer.
soneto (so'ne·to) *n.m.* sonnet. —**sonetillo,** *n.m.* light sonnet.
sónico ('so·ni·ko) *adj.* sonic.
sonido (so'ni·ðo) *n.m.* sound.
soniquete (so·ni'ke·te) *n.m.* click; clack; rattle.
sonorizar (so·no·ri'θar; -'sar) *v.t.* [*infl.:* **realizar**] *phonet.* to voice. —**sonorización,** *n.f.* voicing.
sonoro (so'no·ro) *adj.* **1,** sonorous. **2,** *phonet.* voiced. —**sonoridad,** *n.f.* sonority.
sonreír (son·re'ir) *v.i.* [*infl.:* **reír**] to smile; grin. —**sonrisa** (-'ri·sa) *n.f.* smile; grin.
sonrojar (son·ro'xar) *v.t.* to cause to blush. —**sonrojarse,** *v.r.* to blush. —**sonrojo** (-'ro·xo) *n.m.* blush; blushing.
sonrosado (son·ro'sa·ðo) *adj.* pink; rosy.
sonsacar (son·sa'kar) *v.t.* [*infl.:* **sacar**] to cajole; get by cajolery; wheedle. —**sonsaca** (-'sa·ka) *n.f.,* *also,* **sonsaque** (-'sa·ke) *n.m.* cajolery; wheedling.
sonsonete (son·so'ne·te) *n.m.* **1,** clicking; clacking; rattle. **2,** ironic tone of the voice. **3,** singsong.
soñar (so'ɲar) *v.t.* [*pres.ind.* **sueño;** *pres.subjve.* **sueñe**] to dream. —**soñador,** *adj.* dreaming. —*n.m.* dreamer. —**soñar con,** to dream of or about.
soñoliento (so·ɲo'ljen·to) *adj.* sleepy; somnolent. —**soñolencia,** *n.f.* sleepiness; somnolence.
sopa ('so·pa) *n.f.* soup. —**sopas,** *n.f.pl.* sops; pieces of bread soaked in soup or milk. —**a la sopa boba,** sponging; without effort or exertion. —**estar hecho una sopa,** to be soaking wet.
sopaipa (so'pai·pa) *n.f.* **1,** honey fritter. **2,** *colloq.* gooey mass.
sopanda (so'pan·da) *n.f.* brace; joist.
sopapo (so'pa·po) *n.m. colloq.* slap; box; blow. —**sopapina,** *n.f., Amer., colloq.* drubbing.
sopera (so'pe·ra) *n.f.* tureen. —**sopero,** *n.m., also,* **plato sopero,** soup plate.
sopetear (so·pe·te'ar) *v.t., colloq.* to sop; dip; dunk. —*v.i., colloq.* to snoop around. —**sopeteo** (-'te·o) *n.m., colloq.* sopping; dipping; dunking.
sopetón (so·pe'ton) *n.m.* slap; box; blow. —**de sopetón,** suddenly.
soplado (so'pla·ðo) *adj., colloq.*

1, dapper; neat. 2, conceited; vain. —*n.m.* deep crevice.
soplar (so'plar) *v.t. & i.* to blow; puff. —*v.t.* 1, to inflate; blow up. 2, to blow out (a flame). 3, to blow away. 4, *colloq.* to disclose; inform of or about. 5, *colloq.* to whisper (information, answers to examination questions, etc.). 6, *checkers* to take (a piece) for failing to jump. 7, *slang* to filch. —**soplarse,** *v.r.* to be puffed up; swell with pride. —¡**sopla!,** wow! —**soplador,** *adj.* blowing. —*n.m.* blower; fire bellows.
soplete (so'ple·te) *n.m.* 1, blowtorch. 2, blowpipe.
soplido (so'pli·ðo) *n.m.* blowing; puffing; puff.
soplillo (so'pli·ʎo; -jo) *n.m.* 1, ventilator; blower. 2, chiffon; gauze. 3, chiffon cake.
soplo ('so·plo) *n.m.* 1, blow; blowing; puff. 2, *colloq.* instant; moment. 3, *colloq.* informing; squealing. —**en un soplo,** in a twinkling of the eye.
soplón (so'plon) *adj., colloq.* 1, tattling; gossiping. 2, informing; squealing. —*n.m., colloq.* 1, tattletale. 2, informer.
soplonería (so·plo·ne'ri·a) *n.f., colloq.* 1, tattling; gossip. 2, informing; squealing.
soponcio (so'pon·θjo; -sjo) *n.m., colloq.* faint; swoon.
sopor (so'por) *n.m.* 1, stupor. 2, drowsiness.
soporífico (so·po'ri·fi·ko) *adj. & n.m.* soporific. *Also,* **soporífero** (-fe·ro).
soportal (so·por'tal) *n.m.* 1, porch. 2, portico. 3, arcade.
soportar (so·por'tar) *v.t.* 1, to support. 2, to tolerate; bear; endure. —**soportable,** *adj.* tolerable; bearable. —**soporte** (-'por·te) *n.m.* prop; support.
soprano (so'pra·no) *n.m. & f.* soprano.
sopuntar (so·pun'tar) *v.t.* to underscore with dots.
sor (sor) *n.f., eccles.* sister.
sorber (sor'βer) *v.t.* 1, to sip; suck. 2, to sniff; sniffle. 3, to soak up; absorb. —**sorber los vientos por,** *colloq.* to be crazy about.
sorbete (sor'βe·te) *n.m.* sherbet.
sorbo ('sor·βo) *n.m.* 1, sip; gulp. 2, sniff; sniffle.
sordera (sor'ðe·ra) *n.f.* deafness; hardness of hearing. *Also, colloq.,* **sordez.**
sordez (sor'ðeθ; -'ðes) *n.f.* 1, *phonet.* voicelessness. 2, = **sordera.**
sórdido ('sor·ði·ðo) *adj.* sordid. —**sordidez,** *n.f.* sordidness.
sordina (sor'ði·na) *n.f., music* mute.
sordo ('sor·ðo) *adj.* 1, deaf; hard of hearing. 2, silent; muffled. 3, *phonet.* voiceless. —**a sordas; a la sorda,** silently.
sordomudo (sor·ðo'mu·ðo) *n.m.* deafmute.
sorgo ('sor·ɣo) *n.m.* sorghum.
soríasis (so'ri·a·sis) *also,* **soriasis** (so'rja·sis) *n.f.* = **psoríasis.**
sorna ('sor·na) *n.f.* 1, irony; sarcasm; scorn. 2, malingering; heel-dragging.
soroche (so'ro·tʃe) *n.m., So.Amer.* 1, mountain sickness. 2, *colloq.* blush.
sorprender (sor·pren'der) *v.t.* 1, to surprise. 2, to amaze; astound. —**sorprendente** (-'den·te) *adj.* surprising; amazing. —**sorpresa** (-'pre·sa) *n.f.* surprise. —**sorpresivo** (-'si·βo) *adj.* sudden; surprise (*attrib.*).
sortear (sor·te'ar) *v.i.* 1, to raffle; choose or assign by lot. 2, to dodge; elude. —**sorteo** (-'te·o) *n.m.* raffle; drawing or casting of lots.
sortija (sor'ti·xa) *n.f.* ring.
sortilegio (sor·ti'le·xjo) *n.m.* 1, sorcery. 2, magic spell. —**sortílego** (-'ti·le·ɣo) *n.m.* sorcerer.
sosa ('so·sa) *n.f., chem.* soda.
sosegar (so·se'ɣar) *v.t.* [*pres.ind.* **sosiego** (-'sje·ɣo); *pres.subjve.* **sosiegue** (-'sje·ɣe); *pret.* **sosegué** (-se'ɣe)] to assuage; calm. —*v.i.* to rest. —**sosegarse,** *v.r.* to calm down; become calm. —**sosiego** (-'sje·ɣo) *n.m.* peace; stillness; calm.
sosería (so·se'ri·a) *n.f.* insipidity. *Also, colloq.,* **sosera** (so'se·ra).
soslayar (sos·la'jar) *v.t.* 1, to avoid; sidestep. 2, to put or place obliquely.
soslayo (sos'la·jo) *adj.* oblique. —**al soslayo,** obliquely; on the bias. —**de soslayo,** obliquely; sideways; askance.
soso ('so·so) *adj.* insipid.
sospecha (sos'pe·tʃa) *n.f.* suspicion. —**sospechar,** *v.t.* to suspect. —*v.i.* to be suspicious. —**sospe-**

choso, *adj.* suspicious; suspect. —*n.m.* suspect.
sosquín (sos'kin) *n.m.* treacherous blow.
sostén (sos'ten) *n.m.* **1,** support. **2,** brassiere.
sostener (sos·te'ner) *v.t.* [*infl.:* **tener**] **1,** to support; sustain; maintain. **2,** to endure; suffer. —**sostenido,** *adj. & n.m., music* sharp. —**sostenimiento,** *n.m.* support; sustenance; maintenance.
sota ('so·ta) *n.f., cards* jack.
sotabanco (so·ta'βan·ko) *n.m.* garret; attic.
sotana (so'ta·na) *n.f.* cassock.
sótano ('so·ta·no) *n.m.* cellar; basement.
sotavento (so·ta'βen·to) *n.m.* leeward; lee.
sotechado (so·te'tʃa·ðo) *n.m.* shed.
soterrar (so·te'rrar) *v.t.* [*infl.:* **enterrar**] to bury.
soto ('so·to) *n.m.* thicket; grove.
sotrozo (so'tro·θo; -so) *n.f.* cotter pin; axle pin.
soviet (so'βjet) *n.m.* [*pl.* **soviets**] soviet. —**soviético,** *adj. & n.m.* soviet.
soy (soi) *v., 1st pers.sing.pres.ind. of* **ser.**
soya ('so·ja) *n.f.* soy; soybean.
-sperma ('sper·ma) *suffix* -sperm; seed; sperm: *gimnosperma,* gymnosperm.
-sporo (spo·ro) *suffix* -sporous; having spores: *gimnosporo,* gymnosporous.
staccato (sta'ka·to) *adj., music* staccato.
-stática ('sta·ti·ka) *suffix* -statics; *forming names of sciences dealing with the equilibrium of physical forces: hidrostática,* hydrostatics.
-stático ('sta·ti·ko) *suffix* -static; *forming adjectives corresponding to nouns ending in* **-stática** *or* **-stato**: *hidrostático,* hydrostatic; *fotostático,* photostatic.
-stato (sta·to) *suffix* -stat; *forming nouns denoting* equilibrium; stationary position or condition: *aeróstato,* aerostat.
su (su) *poss.adj.m. & f. sing.* [*m. & f.pl.* **sus**], *agreeing in number with the thing possessed* his; her; its; one's; your; their.
su- (su) *prefix, var. of* **sub-** *before* p: *suponer,* suppose.
suave ('swa·βe) *adj.* **1,** soft; smooth. **2,** mild; gentle.
suavidad (swa·βi'ðað) *n.f.* **1,** softness; smoothness. **2,** gentleness.
suavizar (swa·βi'θar; -'sar) *v.t.* [*pres.subjve.* **suavice** (-'βi·θe; -se); *pret.* **suavicé** (-'θe; -'se)] **1,** to soften; smooth. **2,** to mitigate; temper. —**suavizador,** *adj.* softening; smoothing. —*n.m.* **1,** softener. **2,** razor strop.
sub- (sub) *prefix* sub-. **1,** under; below; beneath: *subsuelo,* subsoil. **2,** lesser in degree: *subtropical,* subtropical. **3,** inferior to; lower in rank or position: *subordinado,* subordinate. **4,** forming a division; formed by division: *subgrupo,* subgroup; *subarrendar,* sublease.
subalterno (suβ·al'ter·no) *adj. & n.m.* subaltern; subordinate.
subarrendar (suβ·a·rren'dar) *v.t.* [*infl.:* **arrendar**] to sublease. —**subarriendo** (-'rrjen·do) *n.m.* sublease.
subastar (su·βas'tar) *v.t.* to auction. —**subasta** (su'βas·ta) *n.f.* auction.
subcomisión (suβ·ko·mi'sjon) *n.f.* subcommittee. *Also,* **subcomité** (-'te) *n.m.*
subconsciente (suβ·kons'θjen·te; -kon'sjen·te) *adj. & n.m.* subconscious. —**subconsciencia,** *n.f.* subconscious; subconsciousness.
subcontratar (suβ·kon·tra'tar) *v.t. & i.* to subcontract. —**subcontrato** (-'tra·to) *n.m.* subcontract. —**subcontratista** (-'tis·sta) *n.m. & f.* subcontractor.
subcutáneo (suβ·ku'ta·ne·o) *adj.* subcutaneous.
subdesarrollado (suβ·ðe·sa·rro'ʎa·ðo; -'ja·ðo) *adj.* underdeveloped.
subdirector (suβ·ði·rek'tor) *n.m.* assistant director; manager; editor, etc.
súbdito ('suβ·ði·to) *adj.* subject. —*n.m.* subject; citizen; national.
subdividir (suβ·ði·βi'ðir) *v.t.* to subdivide. —**subdivisión** (-'sjon) *n.f.* subdivision.
subestimar (suβ·es·ti'mar) *v.t.* to underestimate. —**subestimación,** *n.f.* underestimation.
subida (su'βi·ða) *n.f.* **1,** rise; rising. **2,** raise; raising. **3,** upgrade; rising slope. **4,** climbing; mounting; ascent. **5,** increase.

subido (su'βi·ðo) *adj.* **1,** raised; high. **2,** bright; deep; loud (*of color*).
subilla (su'βi·ʎa; -ja) *n.f.* awl.
subir (su'βir) *v.t.* to raise; lift. —*v.i.* **1,** to rise. **2,** *comm.* to amount to; come to. —*v.t.* & *i.* **1,** to climb; mount; ascend. **2,** to increase. —**subirse,** *v.r., usu.fol.by* **a,** to get on; go up on *or* into.
súbitamente (su·βi·ta'men·te) *adv.* suddenly.
súbito ('su·βi·to) *adj.* sudden. —*adv.* = **súbitamente.** —**de súbito,** suddenly.
subjefe (suβ'xe·fe) *n.m.* assistant chief; assistant manager.
subjetivo (suβ·xe'ti·βo) *adj.* subjective. —**subjetividad,** *n.f.* subjectivity.
subjuntivo (suβ·xun'ti·βo) *adj.* subjunctive.
sublevar (suβ·le'βar) *v.t.* **1,** to incite to rebellion. **2,** to arouse; excite. —**sublevarse,** *v.r.* to rise up; rebel. —**sublevación,** *n.f., also,* **sublevamiento,** *n.m.* revolt; insurrection.
sublimar (su·βli'mar) *v.t.* to sublimate. —**sublimación,** *n.f.* sublimation. —**sublimado,** *n.m.* sublimate.
sublime (su'βli·me) *adj.* sublime. —**sublimidad,** *n.f.* sublimity.
submarino (suβ·ma'ri·no) *adj.* & *n.m.* submarine.
suboficial (suβ·o·fi'θjal; -'sjal) *n.m.* **1,** noncommissioned officer. **2,** warrant officer.
subordinar (suβ·or·ði'nar) *v.t.* to subordinate. —**subordinación,** *n.f.* subordination. —**subordinado,** *adj.* & *n.m.* subordinate.
subrayar (suβ·ra'jar) *v.t.* to underline; underscore.
subrepticio (suβ·rep'ti·θjo; -sjo) *adj.* surreptitious. —**subrepción** (-'θjon; -'sjon) *n.f.* underhandedness.
subrogar (suβ·ro'ɣar) *v.t.* [*infl.:* **rogar**] to subrogate. —**subrogación,** *n.f.* subrogation.
subsanar (suβ·sa'nar) *v.t.* to remedy; put right; set aright.
subscribir (suβs·kri'βir) *v.t.* = **suscribir.** —**subscripción,** *n.f.* = **suscripción.** —**subscriptor, subscritor,** *n.m.* = **suscriptor, suscritor.**
subsecretario (suβ·se·kre'ta·rjo) *n.m.* undersecretary.
subsecuente (suβ·se'kwen·te) *adj.* subsequent.
subsidiario (suβ·si'ðja·rjo) *adj.* & *n.m.* subsidiary.
subsidio (suβ'si·ðjo) *n.m.* subsidy.
subsiguiente (suβ·si'ɣjen·te) *adj.* subsequent; following.
subsistir (suβ·sis'tir) *v.i.* to subsist. —**subsistencia,** *n.f.* subsistence. —**subsistente,** *adj.* subsisting.
subsónico (suβ'so·ni·ko) *adj.* subsonic.
substancia (suβs'tan·θja; -sja) *n.f.* = **sustancia.** —**substancial,** *adj.* = **sustancial.** —**substanciar,** *v.t.* = **sustanciar.** —**substancioso,** *adj.* = **sustancioso.**
substantivo (suβs·tan'ti·βo) *adj.* & *n.m.* = **sustantivo.**
substituir (suβs·ti·tu'ir) *v.t.* = **sustituir.** —**substitución,** *n.f.* = **sustitución.** —**substituto,** *adj.* & *n.m.* = **sustituto.**
substraer (suβs·tra'er) *v.t.* = **sustraer.** —**substracción,** *n.f.* = **sustracción.** —**substraendo,** *n.m.* = **sustraendo.**
subsuelo (suβ'swe·lo) *n.m.* subsoil.
subsumir (suβ·su'mir) *v.t.* to subsume.
subteniente (suβ·te'njen·te) *n.m.* second lieutenant.
subter- (sub·ter) *prefix* subter-; below: *subterfugio,* subterfuge.
subterfugio (suβ·ter'fu·xjo) *n.m.* subterfuge.
subterráneo (suβ·te'rra·ne·o) *adj.* subterranean. —*n.m.* underground passage; subway.
subtítulo (suβ'ti·tu·lo) *n.m.* subtitle.
suburbio (su'βur·βjo) *n.m.* suburb. —**suburbano** (-'βa·no) *adj.* suburban. —*n.m.* suburbanite.
subvención (suβ·βen'θjon; -'sjon) *n.f.* subsidy. —**subvencionar,** *v.t.* to subsidize.
subvenir (suβ·βe'nir) *v.t.* [*infl.:* **venir**] to aid; assist; provide for.
subvertir (suβ·βer'tir) *v.t.* [*infl.:* **advertir**] to subvert. —**subversión** (-'sjon) *n.f.* subversion. —**subversivo** (-'si·βo) *adj.* subversive. —**subversor** (-'sor) *n.m.* subversive; subverter.
subyacente (suβ·ja'θen·te; -'sen·te) *adj.* underlying.
subyugar (suβ·ju'ɣar) *v.t.* [*pres.*

subjve. **subyugue** (-'ju·ɣe); *pret.* **subyugué** (-'ɣe)] to subjugate. —**subyugación,** *n.f.* subjugation.
succión (suk'θjon; -'sjon) *n.f.* suction. —**succionar,** *v.t.* to suck.
suceder (su·θe'ðer; su·se-) *v.i.* to follow; succeed. —*v.impers.* to happen; occur. —**sucedido,** *n.m.* event; happening.
sucesión (su·θe'sjon; su·se-) *n.f.* **1,** succession. **2,** issue; offspring. **3,** *law* estate. —**sucesivo** (-'si·βo) *adj.* successive; next. —**en lo sucesivo,** from now on; hereafter.
suceso (su'θe·so; su'se-) *n.m.* **1,** event; occurrence. **2,** outcome; issue.
sucesor (su·θe'sor; su·se-) *n.m.* successor.
sucinto (su'θin·to; su'sin-) *adj.* succinct.
sucio ('su·θjo; -sjo) *adj.* **1,** dirty; soiled; filthy. **2,** obscene. —**suciedad,** *n.f.* dirt; filth.
sucre ('su·kre) *n.m.* monetary unit of Ecuador; sucre.
sucrosa (su'kro·sa) *n.f.* sucrose.
súcula ('su·ku·la) *n.f.* windlass.
suculento (su·ku'len·to) *adj.* succulent. —**suculencia,** *n.f.* succulence.
sucumbir (su·kum'bir) *v.i.* to succumb.
sucursal (su·kur'sal) *adj.* subsidiary; branch. —*n.f.* branch office.
sud (suð) *n.m.* = **sur.**
sudamericano (suð·a·me·ri'ka·no) *adj.* & *n.m.* South American.
sudar (su'ðar) *v.t.* & *i.* to sweat.
sudario (su'ða·rjo) *n.m.* shroud.
sudeste (suð'es·te) *adj.* & *n.m.* southeast; southeastern; southeasterly.
sudoeste (suð·o'es·te) *adj.* & *n.m.* southwest; southwestern; southwesterly.
sudor (su'ðor) *n.m.* sweat. —**sudoroso,** *adj.* sweating; sweaty. —**sudoso** (-'ðo·so) *adj.* sweaty.
sudsudeste (suð·suð'es·te) *adj.* & *n.m.* south southeast.
sudsudoeste (suð·suð·o'es·te) *adj.* & *n.m.* south southwest.
sueco ('swe·ko) *adj.* Swedish. —*n.m.* **1,** Swede. **2,** Swedish (*language*). —**hacerse el sueco,** *colloq.* to play dumb; pretend not to understand.
suegra ('swe·ɣra) *n.f.* mother-in-law. —**suegro,** *n.m.* father-in-law.
suela ('swe·la) *n.f.* sole of a shoe.
suela ('swe·la) *v., pres.subjve. of* **soler.**
suelde ('swel·de) *v., pres.subjve. of* **soldar.**
sueldo ('swel·do) *n.m.* salary.
sueldo ('swel·do) *v., pres.ind. of* **soldar.**
suele ('swe·le) *v., pres.subjve. of* **solar.**
suelo ('swe·lo) *n.m.* **1,** floor. **2,** ground.
suelo ('swe·lo) *v., pres.ind. of* **solar** *and* **soler.**
suelta ('swel·ta) *n.f.* release.
suelte ('swel·te) *v., pres.subjve. of* **soltar.**
suelto ('swel·to) *adj.* **1,** loose. **2,** nimble. **3,** easy; flowing. —*n.m.* **1,** change; small change; silver. **2,** bit of news; item.
suelto ('swel·to) *v., pres.ind. of* **soltar.**
suene ('swe·ne) *v., pres.subjve. of* **sonar.**
sueno ('swe·no) *v., pres.ind. of* **sonar.**
sueñe ('swe·ɲe) *v., pres.subjve. of* **soñar.**
sueño ('swe·ɲo) *n.m.* **1,** sleep; sleeping. **2,** desire to sleep; sleepiness. **3,** dream. —*v., pres.ind. of* **soñar.** —**en** *or* **entre sueños,** in one's sleep; dreaming. —**ni por sueños,** by no means. —**tener sueño,** to be sleepy.
suero ('swe·ro) *n.m.* **1,** serum. **2,** whey.
suerte ('swer·te) *n.f.* **1,** luck. **2,** fate; lot. **3,** chance; share of luck. **4,** kind; sort. **5,** manner; way. **6,** trick; maneuver. —**de suerte que,** so that; in such a way that. —**echar suertes,** to cast or draw lots.
suertudo (swer'tu·ðo) *adj., colloq.* lucky. —*n.m., colloq.* lucky fellow.
suéter ('swe·ter) *n.m. or f.* sweater.
suficiente (su·fi'θjen·te; -'sjen·te) *adj.* sufficient. —**suficiencia,** *n.f.* sufficiency.
sufijo (su'fi·xo) *adj.* suffixed; affixed. —*n.m.* suffix.
sufragar (su·fra'ɣar) *v.t.* [*pres. subjve.* **sufrague** (-'fra·ɣe); *pret.* **sufragué** (-'ɣe)] to defray; pay;

bear the costs of. —*v.i., So.Amer., fol. by* **por,** to vote (for).
sufragio (su'fra·xjo) *n.m.* **1,** suffrage. **2,** aid; help; support. **3,** mass or prayers for the dead.
sufragista (su·fra'xis·ta) *adj. & n.m. & f.* suffragist. —*n.f.* suffragette.
sufrimiento (su·fri'mjen·to) *n.m.* **1,** suffering. **2,** sufferance; forbearance.
sufrir (su'frir) *v.t. & i.* to suffer. —*v.t.* **1,** to bear; endure. **2,** to undergo. —**sufrido,** *adj.* patient; forbearing.
sufusión (su·fu'sjon) *n.f.* suffusion.
sugerir (su·xe'rir) *v.t.* [*pres.ind.* **sugiero** (-'xje·ro); *pres.subjve.* **sugiera** (-'xje·ra); *pret.* **sugerí, sugirió** (-xi'rjo); *ger.* **sugiriendo** (-xi'rjen·do)] to suggest. —**sugerencia,** *n.f.* suggestion. —**sugerente,** *adj.* suggesting; suggestive.
sugestión (su·xes'tjon) *n.f.* suggestion. —**sugestionar,** *v.t.* to influence or impress by suggestion. —**sugestionable,** *adj.* suggestible; impressionable.
sugestivo (su·xes'ti·βo) *adj.* suggestive.
suicida (sui'θi·ða; -'si·ða) *adj.* suicidal. —*n.m. & f.* suicide (*agent*). —**suicidarse** (-'ðar·se) *v.r.* to commit suicide. —**suicidio** (-'θi·ðjo; -'si·ðjo) *n.m.* suicide (*act*).
sujeción (su·xe'θjon; -'sjon) *n.f.* subjection; restraint.
sujetapapeles (su·xe·ta·pa'pe·les) *n.m.sing. & pl.* paper clip.
sujetar (su·xe'tar) *v.t.* **1,** to hold; grasp; **2,** to fasten; secure. **3,** to subject; subdue. —**sujetarse,** *v.r.* **1,** to subject oneself; submit. **2,** *fol. by* **a,** to abide by; hold to.
sujeto (su'xe·to) *adj.* subject; liable. —*n.m.* **1,** subject; theme. **2,** *philos.; logic; gram.* subject. **3,** individual; person. **4,** *derog.* character; guy.
sulfa ('sul·fa) *n.f. & adj.* sulfa.
sulfato (sul'fa·to) *n.m.* sulfate.
sulfurar (sul·fu'rar) *v.t.* **1,** to sulfurate. **2,** to anger; annoy. —**sulfurarse,** *v.r.* to be angry; be annoyed.
sulfuro (sul'fu·ro) *n.m.* sulfide. —**sulfúrico,** *adj.* sulfuric. —**sulfuroso,** *adj.* sulfurous.
sultán (sul'tan) *n.m.* sultan. —**sultana,** *n.f.* sultana. —**sultanía,** *n.f., also,* **sultanato,** *n.m.* sultanate.
suma ('su·ma) *n.f.* **1,** sum. **2,** *math.* addition. —**en suma,** in short; summing up; in sum.
sumadora (su·ma'ðo·ra) *n.f., also,* **máquina de sumar,** adding machine.
sumamente (su·ma'men·te) *adv.* extremely; exceedingly.
sumando (su'man·do) *n.m.* addend.
sumar (su'mar) *v.t. & i., math.* to add. —*v.t.* **1,** to add up to; reach a total of. **2,** to summarize; sum up. —**sumarse,** *v.r., usu. fol. by* **a,** to join; become part of.
sumario (su'ma·rjo) *adj.* summary. —*n.m.* **1,** summary. **2,** *law* indictment.
sumergir (su·mer'xir) *v.t.* [*pres. ind.* **sumerjo** (-'mer·xo); *pres. subjve.* **sumerja** (-xa)] to submerge. —**sumergible,** *adj.* submersible. —*n.m.* submarine. —**sumersión** (su·mer'sjon) *n.f.* submersion.
sumidero (su·mi'ðe·ro) *n.m.* sewer; drain.
suministrar (su·mi·nis'trar) *v.t.* **1,** to supply; furnish; provide. **2,** to give; administer. —**suministro** (-'nis·tro) *n.m.* supply.
sumir (su'mir) *v.t.* to sink; plunge. —**sumirse,** *v.r.* **1,** to sink. **2,** *Amer.* to shrink; shrivel. **3,** *Amer.* to cringe; cower.
sumiso (su'mi·so) *adj.* submissive; meek; humble. —**sumisión** (-'sjon) *n.f.* submission.
sumo ('su·mo) *adj.* highest; supreme. —**a lo sumo,** at most. —**de sumo,** thoroughly; perfectly.
suntuoso (sun'two·so) *adj.* sumptuous. —**suntuosidad,** *n.f.* sumptuousness.
supe ('su·pe) *v., pret. of* **saber.**
supeditar (su·pe·ði'tar) *v.t.* **1,** to make subservient or subordinate. **2,** to subject; subdue.
super- (su·per) *prefix* super-; over; above; beyond; superior: *supereminencia,* supereminence.
superable (su·pe'ra·βle) *adj.* **1,** surmountable. **2,** improvable. **3,** surpassable.
superabundante (su·per·a·βun'dan·te) *adj.* superabundant. —**superabundancia,** *n.f.* superabundance.

superar (su·pe'rar) *v.t.* **1,** to surpass; exceed; excel. **2,** to overcome; surmount; prevail over. **3,** to improve; improve upon.

superávit (su·pe'ra·βit) *n.m.* surplus.

supercheria (su·per·tʃe'ri·a) *n.f.* **1,** deceit; fraud. **2,** superstition; mumbo jumbo. —**superchero** (-'tʃe·ro) *adj.* deceitful; fraudulent.

super ego ('su·per'e·ɣo) superego.

superentender (su·per·en·ten·'der) *v.t.* [*infl.:* **entender**] to supervise; manage.

superestructura (su·per·es·truk'tu·ra) *n.f.* superstructure.

superficie (su·per'fi·θje; -sje) *n.f.* **1,** surface. **2,** area. —**superficial,** *adj.* superficial. —**superficialidad,** *n.f.* superficiality.

superfino (su·per'fi·no) *adj.* superfine.

superfluo (su'per·flwo) *adj.* superfluous. —**superfluidad,** *n.f.* superfluity.

superheterodino (su·per·e·te·ro'ði·no) *adj.* superheterodyne.

superhombre (su·per'om·bre) *n.m.* superman.

superintendente (su·per·in·ten'den·te) *n.m.* & *f.* superintendent. —**superintendencia,** *n.f.* superintendency.

superior (su·pe'rjor) *adj.* & *n.m.* superior. —*adj.* higher; highest; upper; uppermost. —**superioridad,** *n.f.* superiority.

superiora (su·pe'rjo·ra) *n.f.* superior, esp. mother superior.

superlativo (su·per·la'ti·βo) *adj.* & *n.m.* superlative.

superno (su'per·no) *adj.* supreme; supernal.

supernumerario (su·per·nu·me'ra·rjo) *adj.* & *n.m.* supernumerary.

superponer (su·per·po'ner) *v.t.* [*infl.:* **poner**] to superpose; superimpose.

superposición (su·per·po·si·'θjon; -'sjon) *n.f.* superposition; superimposition.

supersónico (su·per'so·ni·ko) *adj.* supersonic.

superstición (su·pers·ti'θjon; -'sjon) *n.f.* superstition. —**supersticioso,** *adj.* superstitious.

superveniencia (su·per·βe'njen·θja; -sja) *n.f.* supervention. —**supervenir** (-βe'nir) *v.i.* = **sobrevenir.**

supervisar (su·per'βi·sar) *v.t.* & *i.* to supervise. —**supervisión,** *n.f.* supervision.

supervisión (su·per·βi'sjon) *n.f.* supervision.

supervisor (su·per·βi'sor) *n.m.* **1,** overseer. **2,** controller; examiner.

superviviente (su·per·βi'βjen·te) *adj.* & *n.m.* & *f.* = **sobreviviente.** —**supervivencia** (-'βen·θja; -sja) *n.f.* survival.

supino (su'pi·no) *adj.* **1,** supine. **2,** crass; gross.

suplantar (su·plan'tar) *v.t.* to supplant.

suplemento (su·ple'men·to) *n.m.* supplement. —**suplementar,** *v.t.* to supplement. —**suplementario,** *adj.* supplementary; supplemental.

suplente (su'plen·te) *adj.* & *n.m.* & *f.* substitute.

suplicar (su·pli'kar) *v.t.* [*pres. subjve.* **suplique** (-'pli·ke); *pret.* **supliqué** (-'ke)] to supplicate; beseech; entreat. —**súplica** ('su·pli·ka) *n.f.* supplication. —**suplicante,** *adj.* & *n.m.* & *f.* supplicant; suppliant.

suplicio (su'pli·θjo; -sjo) *n.m.* **1,** torture; torment. **2,** execution.

suplir (su'plir) *v.t.* **1,** to supply. **2,** to take the place of; substitute for. **3,** to supplement. —**suplidor,** *adj.* & *n.m.* = **suplente.**

suponer (su·po'ner) *v.t.* [*infl.:* **poner**] to suppose. —**suposición** (-si'θjon; -'sjon) *n.f.* supposition.

supositorio (su·po·si'to·rjo) *n.m.* suppository.

supra- (su·pra) *prefix* supra-; over; above: *suprarrenal,* suprarenal.

supremo (su'pre·mo) *adj.* supreme —**supremacía** (-ma'θi·a; -'si·a) *n.f.* supremacy.

supresión (su·pre'sjon) *n.f.* suppression.

suprimir (su·pri'mir) *v.t.* **1,** to suppress; abolish; cancel. **2,** to omit; leave out.

supuesto (su'pwes·to) *v., p.p of* **suponer.** —*adj.* supposed; assumed. —*n.m.* supposition; assumption. —**por supuesto,** certainly.

supurar (su·pu'rar) *v.i.* to suppurate. —**supuración,** *n.f.* suppuration. —**supurante,** *adj.* suppurating.

sur (sur) *n.m.* south. *Also,* **sud.**
surcar (sur'kar) *v.t.* [*pres.subjve.* **surque** ('sur·ke); *pret.* **surqué** (-'ke)] **1,** to furrow. **2,** to cleave through; plow through.
surco ('sur·ko) *n.m.* furrow; groove; wrinkle.
sureño (su're·ɲo) *adj., Amer.* southern; of or from the South.
surgir (sur'xir) *v.i.* [*pres.ind.* **surjo** ('sur·xo); *pres.subjve.* **surja** (-xa)] **1,** to surge; rise; spurt out; squirt out. **2,** to emerge; appear. —**surgimiento,** *n.m.* emergence.
surrealismo (su·rre·a'lis·mo) *n.m.* surrealism. —**surrealista** *adj.* & *n.m.* & *f.* surrealist. —*adj.* surrealistic.
surtidor (sur·ti'ðor) *n.m.* waterspout; jet; fountain.
surtir (sur'tir) *v.t.* to supply; provide. —**surtido,** *adj.* assorted. —*n.m.* assortment.
sus (sus) *poss.adj., pl. of* **su** (*agreeing in number with the things possessed*).
¡sus! (sus) *interj.* forward!; get on!; *hunting* halloo!
sus- (sus) *prefix. var. of* **sub-** *before* c: *susceptible,* susceptible.
susceptible (sus·θep'ti·βle; su·sep-) *adj.* susceptible. —**susceptibilidad,** *n.f.* susceptibility.
suscitar (sus·θi'tar; su·si-) *v.t.* to stir up; arouse.
suscribir (sus·kri'βir) *v.t.* [*p.p.* **suscrito** (-'kri·to)] **1,** to subscribe. **2,** to subscribe to; endorse; adhere to. —**suscribirse,** *v.r.* to subscribe.
suscripción (sus·krip'θjon; -sjon) *n.f.* subscription. —**suscriptor** (-krip'tor) *also,* **suscritor** (-kri'tor) *n.m.* subscriber.
susodicho (su·so'ði·tʃo) *adj.* aforesaid.
suspender (sus·pen'der) *v.t.* to suspend.
suspensión (sus·pen'sjon) *n.f.* suspension. —**suspensivo** (-'si·βo) *adj.* suspensive; suspension (*attrib.*).
suspenso (sus'pen·so) *adj.* **1,** suspended. **2,** astonished; enthralled. —*n.m.* suspense.
suspensores (sus·pen'so·res) *n.m.pl., Amer.* suspenders.
suspensorio (sus·pen'so·rjo) *adj.* & *n.m.* suspensory.
suspicaz (sus·pi'kaθ; -'kas) *adj.* suspicious. —**suspicacia** (-'ka·θja; -sja) *n.f.* suspiciousness.
suspirar (sus·pi'rar) *v.i.* **1,** to sigh. **2,** to pine; long.
suspiro (sus'pi·ro) *n.m.* **1,** sigh. **2,** *music* quarter rest. **3,** a kind of meringue.
sustancia (sus·tan·θja; -sja) *n.f.* substance. —**sustancial,** *adj.* substantial. —**sustanciar,** *v.t.* to substantiate.
sustancioso (sus·tan'θjo·so; -'sjo·so) *adj.* **1,** substantial. **2,** nourishing.
sustantivo (sus·tan'ti·vo) *adj.* substantive. —*n.m., gram.* substantive.
sustentar (sus·ten'tar) *v.t.* to sustain; support; maintain. —**sustento** (-'ten·to) *n.m.* sustenance; support.
sustituir (sus·ti·tu'ir) *v.t.* [*infl.:* **constituir**] to substitute; replace. —**sustitución,** *n.f.* substitution; replacement. —**sustituto** (-'tu·to) *adj.* & *n.m.* substitute; replacement.
susto ('sus·to) *n.m.* fright; scare.
sustracción (sus·trak'θjon; -'sjon) *n.f.* subtraction.
sustraendo (sus·tra'en·do) *n.m.* subtrahend.
sustraer (sus·tra'er) *v.t.* [*infl.:* **traer**] **1,** to subtract; deduct. **2,** to remove; withdraw. —**sustraerse,** *v.r.* to withdraw. —**sustraerse a** *or* **de,** to evade; avoid; dodge.
susurrar (su·su'rrar) *v.i.* **1,** to whisper. **2,** to rustle. —**susurrarse,** *v.r.* to be rumored.
susurro (su'su·rro) *n.m.* **1,** whisper. **2,** rustle.
sutura (su'tu·ra) *n.f.* suture.
sutil (su'til) *adj.* **1,** subtle. **2,** thin; slender. **3,** fine; sheer; delicate. —**sutileza,** *n.f.* subtlety; subtleness.
sutilizar (su·ti·li'θar; -'sar) *v.i.* [*infl.:* **realizar**] to cavil; quibble. —*v.t.* **1,** to make thin; taper. **2,** to file; smooth; rub smooth. **3,** to cavil at *or* about; find fault with.
suyo ('su·jo) *poss.pron.m.sing.* [*fem.* **suya;** *pl.* **suyos, suyas**], *agreeing in number and gender with the thing or things possessed* his; hers; its own; one's own; yours; theirs. —**de suyo,** by itself. —**hacer de las suyas,** to be up to one's tricks. —**una de las suyas,** one of his tricks.
svástica ('sβas·ti·ka) *n.f.* swastika.

T

T, t (te) *n.f.* 23rd letter of the Spanish alphabet.

¡ta! (ta) *interj.* **1,** tut, tut! **2,** rat-tat-tat.

tabaola (ta·βa'o·la) *n.f., colloq.* = **batahola.**

tabaco (ta'βa·ko) *n.m.* **1,** tobacco. **2,** cigar. **3,** snuff. —**tabacal,** *n.m.* tobacco plantation. —**tabacalero,** *adj.* tobacco (*attrib.*). —*n.m.* tobacco grower.

tabalear (ta·βa·le'ar) *v.t.* to shake; rock. —*v.i.* to drum; beat; tap, as with the fingers.

tabanco (ta'βan·ko) *n.m.* market stand.

tábano ('ta·βa·no) *n.m.* gadfly; horsefly.

tabaquera (ta·βa'ke·ra) *n.f.* **1,** cigar case. **2,** tobacco pouch. **3,** pipe bowl. **4,** snuff box. —**tabaquería,** *n.f.* cigar store. —**tabaquero,** *n.m.* tobacconist; cigar maker or dealer.

tabardillo (ta·βar'ði·ʎo; -jo) *n.m.* **1,** malignant fever. **2,** *colloq.* sunstroke. **3,** *colloq.* pest; nuisance.

tabasco (ta'βas·ko) *n.m.* tabasco.

taberna (ta'βer·na) *n.f.* **1,** tavern. **2,** bar; pub.

tabernáculo (ta·βer'na·ku·lo) *n.m.* tabernacle.

tabernero (ta·βer'ne·ro) *n.m.* **1,** tavern keeper. **2,** bartender.

tabes ('ta·βes) *n.m.* tabes.

tabicar (ta·βi'kar) *v.t.* [*pres. subjve.* **tabique** (-'βi·ke); *pret.* **tabiqué** (-'ke)] **1,** to wall up; seal. **2,** to partition; divide with partitions.

tabique (ta'βi·ke) *n.m.* **1,** thin wall; partition. **2,** septum.

tabla ('ta·βla) *n.f.* **1,** board. **2,** table (*list, tabular arrangement, etc.*). **3,** slab; tablet. **4,** flat, broad part of anything. —**a raja tabla,** *colloq.* at any cost; all out. —**hacer tabla rasa de, 1,** to omit; ignore. **2,** *Amer.* to clear the way for. —**tabla de salvación,** salvation; lifesaver.

tablado (ta'βla·ðo) *n.m.* **1,** flooring. **2,** wooden platform; scaffold. **3,** stage; stage floor. **4,** boarding; boards (*pl.*). —**tablaje** (-'βla·xe) *n.m.* boarding; boards (*pl.*).

tablas ('ta·βlas) *n.f.pl.* **1,** draw (*sing.*); tie (*sing.*). **2,** *theat.* stage (*sing.*). —**estar** *or* **quedar tablas,** *colloq.* **1,** to be tied. **2,** to be even; be quits.

tablazón (ta·βla'θon; -'son) *n.f.* **1,** boards (*pl.*); planks (*pl.*); planking. **2,** *naut.* deck; decking.

tablero (ta'βle·ro) *n.m.* **1,** instrument or control panel; dashboard. **2,** playing board, esp. for chess or checkers. **3,** thin board. **4,** board of a table. **5,** writing slate. —**poner** *or* **traer al tablero,** to risk; hazard.

tableta (ta'βle·ta) *n.f.* tablet; lozenge.

tablilla (ta'βli·ʎa; -ja) *n.f.* **1,** splint; slat. **2,** wooden tablet. **3,** bulletin board.

tablón (ta'βlon) *n.m.* **1,** plank; board. **2,** *colloq.* drunkenness; intoxication. —**coger un tablón,** *colloq.* to get drunk.

tabú (ta'βu) *adj. & n.m.* taboo.

tabular (ta·βu'lar) *adj.* tabular. —*v.t.* to tabulate. —**tabulación,** *n.f.* tabulation. —**tabulador,** *n.m.* tabulator.

taburete (ta·βu're·te) *n.m.* stool; taboret.

tac (tak) *interj. & n.m.* tick; tick-tock.

taca ('ta·ka) *n.f.* small cupboard.

tacaño (ta'ka·ɲo) *adj.* stingy. —**tacañería,** *n.f.* stinginess.

tacita (ta'θi·ta; -'si·ta) *n.f.* small cup; demitasse.

tácito ('ta·θi·to; -si·to) *adj.* tacit.

taciturno (ta·θi'tur·no; ta·si-) *adj.* taciturn. —**taciturnidad,** *n.f.* taciturnity.

taco ('ta·ko) *n.m.* **1,** plug; slug. **2,** wedge; stopper. **3,** wad; wadding. **4,** billiard cue. **5,** ramrod; rammer. **6,** drink, esp. of wine. **7,** pea shooter. **8,** *colloq.* snack. **9,** *colloq.* tangle; jam. **10,** *So.Amer.* heel of a shoe. **11,** *Amer., colloq.* stumpy person or thing. **12,** *colloq.* swear word; profanity. —**darse taco,** *Amer., colloq.* to put on airs. —**soltar tacos,** *colloq.* to swear; use profanity.

tacómetro (ta'ko·me·tro) *n.m.* tachometer.
tacón (ta'kon) *n.m.* heel of a shoe. —**taconazo,** *n.m.* thump or kick with the heel.
taconear (ta·ko·ne'ar) *v.i.* **1,** to tap the heels. **2,** to strut. —**taconeo** (-'ne·o) *n.m.* tapping of the heels, esp. in dancing.
táctica ('tak·ti·ka) *n.f.* **1,** tactic. **2,** tactics.
táctico ('tak·ti·ko) *adj.* tactical. —*n.m.* **1,** tactic. **2,** tactician.
táctil ('tak·til) *adj.* tactile.
tacto ('tak·to) *n.m.* **1,** touch; sense of touch. **2,** tact.
tacha ('ta·tʃa) *n.f.* **1,** flaw; fault. **2,** stain; smirch.
tachable (ta'tʃa·βle) *adj.* exceptionable; censurable.
tachadura (ta·tʃa'ðu·ra) *n.f.* erasure; deletion.
tachar (ta'tʃar) *v.t.* **1,** to find fault; censure. **2,** to label; depict. **3,** to cross off *or* out; delete.
tacho ('ta·tʃo) *n.m., Amer.* large, cylindrical can, esp. a garbage can.
tachón (ta'tʃon) *n.m.* **1,** erasure; scratch; blot. **2,** braid; trimming. **3,** stud; boss. —**tachonar,** *v.t.* to stud.
tachuela (ta'tʃwe·la) *n.f.* **1,** tack. **2,** hobnail. **3,** thumbtack.
-tad ('tað) *suffix* -ty; *forming abstract nouns denoting* quality; state; condition: *lealtad,* loyalty; *enemistad,* enmity.
tafetán (ta·fe'tan) *n.m.* taffeta.
tafilete (ta·fi'le·te) *n.m.* morocco; morocco leather.
tagalo (ta'ɣa·lo) *adj.* & *n.m.* Tagalog.
tagarote (ta·ɣa'ro·te) *n.m.* **1,** sparrow hawk. **2,** lanky, gawky person.
tahona (ta'o·na) *n.f.* **1,** bakery. **2,** grist mill.
tahonero (ta·o'ne·ro) *n.m.* **1,** baker. **2,** miller.
tahur (ta'ur) *n.m.* gambler; cardsharp.
taimado (tai'ma·ðo) *adj.* sly; crafty. —**taimarse,** *v.r., Amer.* to sulk; become stubborn.
taita ('tai·ta) *n.m., Amer., colloq.* dad; daddy.
taja ('ta·xa) *n.f.* **1,** incision; cut. **2,** = **tajada.**
tajada (ta'xa·ða) *n.f.* slice; cut.
tajado (ta'xa·ðo) *adj.* **1,** sliced; cut. **2,** steep; sheer.
tajador (ta·xa'ðor) *n.m.* **1,** cutter; chopper; slicer. **2,** *Amer.* = **tajalápiz.**
tajalápiz (ta·xa'la·piθ; -pis) *n.m., also,* **tajalápices,** *n.m.sing.* & *pl.* pencil sharpener.
tajamar (ta·xa'mar) *n.m.* cutwater.
tajar (ta'xar) *v.t.* **1,** to cut; chop; cleave; slash. **2,** to sharpen (a pencil). —**tajadura,** *n.f.* cut; slash. —**tajante,** *adj.* cutting; incisive.
tajo ('ta·xo) *n.m.* **1,** cut. **2,** gash; slash. **3,** sheer cliff. **4,** cutting edge. **5,** chopping block.
tal (tal) *adj.* such; such a. —*indef. pron.* such; such a one; so-and-so. —*adv.* thus; so. —**con tal que,** provided that. —**el tal,** that person; the so-called. —**¿qué tal?** how are you? —**tal cual, 1,** such as; just as. **2,** just so; so-so. —**tal para cual,** exactly alike; exactly suited. —**un tal por cual,** a no-account person.
tala ('ta·la) *n.f.* felling; cutting down.
talabarte (ta·la'βar·te) *n.m.* sword belt.
talabartería (ta·la·βar·te'ri·a) *n.f.* **1,** saddlery. **2,** harness shop.
taladrar (ta·la'ðrar) *v.t.* to drill; bore; pierce.
taladro (ta'la·ðro) *n.m.* **1,** drill; borer; auger. **2,** drill hole.
tálamo ('ta·la·mo) *n.m.* **1,** bridal bed. **2,** thalamus. —**talámico** (ta·'la·mi·ko) *adj.* thalamic.
talán (ta'lan) *interj.* & *n.m.* dingdong.
talanquera (ta·lan'ke·ra) *n.f.* breastwork; parapet; fence.
talante (ta'lan·te) *n.m.* **1,** disposition; will; mood. **2,** looks; appearance.
talar (ta'lar) *v.t.* **1,** to fell (trees). **2,** to desolate; destroy; ravage. —*adj.* full length; reaching to the ankles: *traje talar,* cassock.
talco ('tal·ko) *n.m.* talc; talcum.
talega (ta'le·ɣa) *n.f.* bag; sack; moneybag.
talego (ta'le·ɣo) *n.m.* **1,** bag; sack; duffel bag. **2,** *colloq.* dumpy person; rolypoly.
talento (ta'len·to) *n.m.* talent. —**talentoso,** *adj.* talented.
talio ('ta·ljo) *n.m.* thallium.

talismán (ta·lis'man) *n.m.* talisman; charm.
talmud (tal'muð) *n.m.* Talmud.
talón (ta'lon) *n.m.* **1,** heel. **2,** stub; coupon. **3,** talon.
talonario (ta·lo'na·rjo) *n.m.* **1,** book of stubs; coupon book. **2,** checkbook.
taltuza (tal'tu·θa; -sa) *n.f., Amer.* gopher.
talud (ta'luð) *n.m.* talus; slope; embankment.
talla ('ta·ʎa; -ja) *n.f.* **1,** height; stature. **2,** size (*of a garment*). **3,** carving; cutting. **4,** ransom. **5,** reward for the capture of a criminal or a fugitive.
tallar (ta'ʎar; -'jar) *v.t.* **1,** to cut; carve. **2,** to engrave. **3,** *cards* to have (the deck) as dealer. **4,** to evaluate; appraise. —*v.i., Amer., colloq.* to figure; have a say. —**tallado,** *adj.* carved; cut. —*n.m.* carving; cutting. —**talladura,** *n.f.* carving; cutting.
tallarín (ta·ʎa'rin; ta·ja-) *n.m.* noodle.
talle ('ta·ʎe; -je) *n.m.* **1,** waist, esp. a slender waist. **2,** form; figure; shape. **3,** fit (*of a garment*). **4,** *Amer.* bodice.
taller (ta'ʎer; -'jer) *n.m.* **1,** workshop; factory; mill. **2,** studio.
tallo ('ta·ʎo; -jo) *n.m.* **1,** stem; stalk. **2,** sprout; shoot.
tamal (ta'mal) *n.m.* tamale.
tamaño (ta'ma·ɲo) *n.m.* size. —*adj.* **1,** great; large; big. **2,** *colloq.* such a big . . . : *tamaño error,* such a big mistake.
tamarindo (ta·ma'rin·do) *n.m.* tamarind.
tambalear (tam·ba·le'ar) *v.i.* to stagger; totter. —**tambaleo** (-'le·o) *n.m.* staggering; tottering.
también (tam'bjen) *adv.* also; too; as well; besides.
tambo ('tam·bo) *n.m., So.Amer.* trading post.
tambor (tam'bor) *n.m.* **1,** drum. **2,** drummer. **3,** eardrum. —**tambor mayor,** drum major.
tambora (tam'bo·ra) *n.f.* bass drum.
tamborilear (tam·bo·ri·le'ar) *v.i.* **1,** to play the tambourine or tabor. **2,** to drum, beat or tap as with the fingers.
tamborín (tam·bo'rin) *n.m.* tambourine; tabor. *Also,* **tamboril** (-'ril).
tamiz (ta'miθ; -'mis) *n.f.* sifter; fine sieve. —**tamizar** (-'θar; -'sar) *v.t.* [*pres.subjve.* **tamice** (-'mi·θe; -se); *pret.* **tamicé** (-'θe; -'se)] to sift; strain.
tamo ('ta·mo) *n.m.* fuzz; fluff; lint.
tampoco (tam'po·ko) *adv.,* neither; not either; nor.
tam-tam (tam'tam) *n.m.* tom-tom.
tan (tan) *adv.* as; so; so much. —**tan . . . como,** as . . . as; so . . . as. —**tan siquiera,** at least.
tanda ('tan·da) *n.f.* **1,** turn; round. **2,** shift; relay. **3,** series; string. **4,** *colloq.* great deal; lot. **5,** *Amer.* performance; showing (*of a play or movie*). **6,** *colloq.* drubbing; beating.
tándem ('tan·dem) *n.m.* tandem.
tángara ('tan·ga·ra) *n.f.* tanager.
tangente (tan'xen·te) *adj. & n.m.* tangent. —**tangencia,** *n.f.* tangency. —**tangencial,** tangential.
tangible (tan'xi·βle) *adj.* tangible.
tango ('tan·go) *n.m.* tango.
tanino (ta'ni·no) *n.m.* tannin. —**tánico** ('ta·ni·ko) *adj.* tannic.
tanque ('tan·ke) *n.m.* **1,** tank. **2,** *Amer.* pool; reservoir. **3,** *mil.* tank.
tantalio (tan'ta·ljo) *n.m.* tantalum.
tantán (tan'tan) *n.m.* **1,** gong. **2,** clang; clanging.
tantarantán (tan·ta·ran'tan) *n.m.* sound of a drum; rub-a-dub.
tantear (tan·te'ar) *v.t.* **1,** to feel; probe. **2,** to feel out; sound out. **3,** to try out; test. **4,** to sketch; outline. **5,** *Amer., colloq.* to estimate; calculate.
tanteo (tan'te·o) *n.m.* **1,** test; trial. **2,** estimate; calculation. **3,** score (*of a game*). **4,** *Amer., colloq.* groping; feeling. —**al tanteo,** by guess; by feel; by eye.
tanto ('tan·to) *adj. & pron.* so much; as much; *pl.* so many; as many. —*adv.* so; so much; so long; in such a manner. —*n.m.* **1,** a certain amount; so much; *pl.* a certain number; so many. **2,** point (*in a game*). **3,** counter (*in games*). **4,** copy; duplicate. —**a tantos de mayo,** on such-and-such day in May. —**en su tanto,** within proper

bounds; within rights. —**en tanto**; **entre tanto**, meanwhile. —**estar al tanto**, 1, to be *or* keep informed; be aware; be in the know. 2, to look out; be on the lookout. —**las tantas**, a late hour. —**mientras tanto**, meanwhile. —**otro tanto**, 1, the same; equally. 2, as much more. —**poner al tanto**, to inform; brief. —**por tanto**; **por lo tanto**, therefore. —**por tanto que**, inasmuch as; since. —**tanto por ciento**, percentage. —**un tanto**, *fol. by adj. or adv.* somewhat. —**y tantos**, and some; and some odd.

tañer (ta'ɲer) *v.t.* [*pret.* **tañí**, **tañó** (ta'ɲo); *ger.* **tañendo** (-'ɲen·do)] to pluck (a stringed instrument). —*v.t. & i.* 1, to twang; sound, as strings. 2, to peal; toll, as a bell.

tañido (ta'ɲi·ðo) *n.m.* 1, pluck; plucking; twang. 2, peal; toll (*of a bell*).

tapa ('ta·pa) *n.f.* 1, lid; cover; cap; top. 2, pocket flap. 3, *usu.pl.* tidbits; hors d'oeuvres.

tapabarro (ta·pa'βa·rro) *n.m., Amer.* mudguard.

tapada (ta'pa·ða) *n.f.* veiled woman.

tapadera (ta·pa'ðe·ra) *n.f.* cover; lid.

tapado (ta'pa·ðo) *n.m., Amer.* 1, cloak; cape. 2, buried treasure.

tapar (ta'par) *v.t.* 1, to cover; cover up. 2, to plug; stop up. 3, to cap; put a lid on. 4, *Amer.* to fill (a tooth).

taparrabo (ta·pa'rra·βo) *n.m.* loin cloth. *Also*, **taparrabos**, *n.m. sing. & pl.*

tapete (ta'pe·te) *n.m.* 1, small carpet; runner. 2, table cover; table mat. —**sobre el tapete**, on the carpet.

tapia ('ta·pja) *n.f.* adobe wall. —**tapiar**, *v.t.* to wall up; wall in.

tapicería (ta·pi·θe'ri·a; -se'ri·a) *n.f.* 1, tapestries (*pl.*). 2, upholstery. 3, tapestry shop and trade. 4, upholstery shop.

tapicero (ta·pi'θe·ro; -'se·ro) *n.m.* 1, carpet maker. 2, tapestry maker. 3, upholsterer.

tapioca (ta'pjo·ka) *n.f.* tapioca.

tapir (ta'pir) *n.m.* tapir.

tapiz (ta'piθ; -'pis) *n.m.* tapestry.

tapizar (ta·pi'θar; -'sar) *v.t.* [*pres.subjve.* **tapice** (-'pi·θe; -se); *pret.* **tapicé** (-'θe; -'se)] 1, to cover with tapestry. 2, to carpet; cover over. 3, to upholster.

tapón (ta'pon) *n.m.* 1, plug; stopper; cap. 2, tampon. 3, fuse. 4, *W.I.* traffic jam. —**taponazo**, *n.m.* pop (*of a cap or cork*).

taponamiento (ta·po·na'mjen·to) *n.m.* 1, act of corking or stopping up. 2, bottleneck.

taponar (ta·po'nar) *v.t.* to plug; stopper; cap.

tapujo (ta'pu·xo) *n.m.* 1, muffler; scarf; face wrap. 2, *colloq.* concealment; subterfuge.

taquigrafía (ta·ki·ɣra'fi·a) *n.f.* stenography; shorthand. —**taquigrafiar**, *v.t.* [*infl.*: **fotografiar**] to take down in shorthand. —**taquigráfico** (-'ɣra·fi·ko) *adj.* stenographic. —**taquígrafo** (-'ki·ɣra·fo) *n.m.* stenographer.

taquilla (ta'ki·ʎa; -ja) *n.f.* 1, ticket office. 2, box office. 3, ticket rack. 4, letter file. 5, *Amer.* barroom; tavern.

tara ('ta·ra) *n.f.* 1, *comm.* tare. 2, defect; handicap.

tarabilla (ta·ra'βi·ʎa; -ja) *n.f.* fastener; catch.

tarambana (ta·ram'ba·na) *n.m. & f., colloq.* madcap; flighty person.

tarantela (ta·ran'te·la) *n.f.* tarantella.

tarántula (ta'ran·tu·la) *n.f.* tarantula.

tararear (ta·ra·re'ar) *v.t. & i.* to hum (a tune). —**tarareo** (-'re·o) *n.m.* hum; humming.

tarasca (ta'ras·ka) *n.f., colloq.* 1, gluttony. 2, *Amer.* mouth; big mouth.

tarascar (ta·ras'kar) *v.t.* [*pres. subjve.* **tarasque** (-'ras·ke); *pret.* **tarasqué** (-'ke)] to bite; snap.

tardanza (tar'ðan·θa; -sa) *n.f.* delay; tardiness.

tardar (tar'ðar) *v.i.* to delay; be late; take time; be long. —*v.t.* to take (a certain time). —**a más tardar**, at the latest.

tarde ('tar·ðe) *n.f.* afternoon. —*adv.* late; too late. —**de tarde en tarde**, from time to time. —**mas tarde**, later. —**tarde o temprano**, sooner or later.

tardío (tar'ði·o) *adj.* tardy.

tardo ('tar·ðo) *adj.* 1, tardy; slow; sluggish. 2, retarded.

tarea (ta're·a) *n.f.* task; job; assignment.
tarifa (ta'ri·fa) *n.f.* tariff.
tarima (ta'ri·ma) *n.f.* **1,** platform; stand. **2,** low bench or stool.
-tario ('ta·rjo) *suffix, forming nouns and adjectives denoting* the person for whose benefit an action is performed: *arrendatario,* tenant; lessee.
tarjeta (tar'xe·ta) *n.f.* **1,** card. **2,** label. —**tarjetero,** *n.m.* card file; card case. —**tarjeta postal,** postcard.
taro ('ta·ro) *n.m.* taro.
tarpón (tar'pon) *n.m.* tarpon.
tarquín (tar'kin) *n.m.* mud; silt.
tarraya (ta'rra·ja) *n.f.* casting net.
tarro ('ta·rro) *n.m.* **1,** can; jar. **2,** pail. **3,** *Amer.* high hat; top hat.
tarso ('tar·so) *n.m.* tarsus.
tarta ('tar·ta) *n.f.* tart.
tartajear (tar·ta·xe'ar) *v.i.* to stammer; stutter. —**tartajeo** (-'xe·o) *n.m.* stammering; stuttering.
tartalear (tar·ta·le'ar) *v.i., colloq.* **1,** to fumble; dawdle; dodder. **2,** to be dumfounded.
tartamudear (tar·ta·mu·ðe'ar) *v.i.* to stutter. —**tartamudeo** (-'ðe·o) *n.m.* stammering; stuttering.
tartamudo (tar·ta'mu·ðo) *adj.* stuttering. —*n.m.* stutterer. —**tartamudez,** *n.f.* affliction with stuttering.
tartán (tar'tan) *n.m.* tartan.
tártaro ('tar·ta·ro) *adj. & n.m.* Tartar. —*n.m.* **1,** hell. **2,** tartar. —**tártrico** ('tar·tri·ko) *also,* **tartárico** (-'ta·ri·ko) *adj.* tartaric.
tartera (tar'te·ra) *n.f.* **1,** baking pan; pie pan. **2,** lunch basket.
tarugo (ta'ru·ɣo) *n.m.* **1,** peg; pin. **2,** plug; bung. **3,** *Amer., colloq.* cheat.
tasa ('ta·sa) *n.f.* **1,** assessment; appraisal; estimate. **2,** rate. **3,** price, esp. fixed price. **4,** measure; moderation.
tasación (ta·sa'θjon; -'sjon) *n.f.* appraisal; assessment.
tasador (ta·sa'ðor) *n.m.* appraiser; assessor.
tasajo (ta'sa·xo) *n.m.* **1,** jerked beef. **2,** piece of meat.
tasar (ta'sar) *v.t.* **1,** to appraise; assess; evaluate. **2,** to fix (a price, quota, etc.).
tasca ('tas·ka) *n.f.* gambling den; dive.
tascar (tas'kar) *v.t.* [*pres.subjve.* **tasque** ('tas·ke); *pret.* **tasqué** (-'ke)] **1,** to crunch; chew noisily. **2,** to champ.
tata ('ta·ta) *n.m., Amer., colloq.* dad.
tatarabuelo (ta·ta·ra'βwe·lo) *n.m.* great-great-grandfather. —**tatarabuela,** *n.f.* great-great-grandmother.
tataranieto (ta·ta·ra'nje·to) *n.m.* great-great-grandson. —**tataranieta,** *n.f.* great-great-granddaughter.
¡tate! ('ta·te) *interj.* **1,** easy!; careful! **2,** that's it!; I have it!
tato ('ta·to) *n.m.* stutterer with a lisp.
tatuar (ta'twar) *v.t.* [*infl.:* **continuar**] to tattoo. —**tatuaje,** *n.m.* tattoo.
taumaturgo (tau·ma'tur·ɣo) *n.m.* miracle worker.
taurino (tau'ri·no) *adj.* taurine.
tauro ('tau·ro) *n.m.* Taurus.
tauromaquia (tau·ro'ma·kja) *n.f.* the art of bullfighting. —**taurómaco** (-'ro·ma·ko) *adj.* bullfighting (*attrib.*) —*n.m.* expert in bullfighting.
taurófilo (tau'ro·fi·lo) *n.m.* bullfight fan.
tautología (tau·to·lo'xi·a) *n.f.* tautology. —**tautológico** (-'lo·xi·ko) *adj.* tautological.
taxativo (tak·sa'ti·βo) *adj.* limiting; restrictive.
taxear (tak·se'ar) *v.i., aero.* to taxi.
taxi ('tak·si) *n.m.* taxi; taxicab.
taxi- (tak·si) *prefix* taxi-; arrangement; order: *taxidermia,* taxidermy.
taxidermia (tak·si'ðer·mja) *n.f.* taxidermy. —**taxidermista** (-'mis·ta) *n.m. & f.* taxidermist.
taxímetro (tak'si·me·tro) *n.m.* **1,** taximeter. **2,** taxicab.
-taxis ('tak·sis) *suffix* -taxis; order; arrangement: *termotaxis,* thermotaxis.
taxista (tak'sis·ta) *n.m. & f.* taxi driver.
taxonomía (tak·so·no'mi·a) *n.f.* taxonomy. —**taxonómico** (-'no·mi·ko) *adj.* taxonomic. —**taxonomista** (-'mis·ta) *n.m. & f.* taxonomist.

taza ('ta·θa; -sa) *n.f.* **1,** cup. **2,** toilet bowl.
tazón (ta'θon; -'son) *n.m.* large cup; bowl.
te (te) *pers.pron. 2nd pers.sing., used as obj. of a verb* you; to you; yourself; thee; to thee; thyself.
té (te) *n.m.* tea.
tea ('te·a) *n.f.* torch; firebrand.
teatro (te'a·tro) *n.m.* **1,** theater. **2,** theatrics. **—teatral** (-'tral) *adj.* theatrical.
teca ('te·ka) *n.f.* teak.
tecla ('te·kla) *n.f.* key (*of a keyboard*). **—teclado,** *n.m.* keyboard. **—dar en (la) tecla,** to hit the mark; hit the nail on the head.
teclear (te·kle'ar) *v.i.* **1,** to operate a keyboard. **2,** *colloq.* to thrum; drum the fingers. **3,** to click; clack. *—v.t., colloq.* to try out; feel out.
tecleo (te'kle·o) *n.m.* **1,** fingering (*of a keyboard*). **2,** *colloq.* thrumming; drumming the fingers. **3,** clicking; clacking.
tecnecio (tek'ne·θjo; -sjo) *n.m.* technetium.
-tecnia ('tek·nja) *suffix* -technics; *forming nouns denoting* art; science; industry: *electrotecnia,* electrotechnics.
técnica ('tek·ni·ka) *n.f.* **1,** technique. **2,** technics. **—técnico,** *adj.* technical. *—n.m.* technician.
tecnicismo (tek·ni'θis·mo; -'sis·mo) *n.m.* technicality.
-técnico ('tek·ni·ko) *suffix* -technic; *forming adjectives corresponding to nouns ending in* **-tecnia:** *electrotécnico,* electrotechnic.
tecnicolor (tek·ni·ko'lor) *n.m.* technicolor.
tecnocracia (tek·no'kra·θja; -sja) *n.f.* technocracy. **—tecnócrata** (-'no·kra·ta) *n.m. & f.* technocrat. **—tecnocrático** (-'kra·ti·ko) *adj.* technocratic.
tecnología (tek·no·lo'xi·a) *n.f.* technology. **—tecnológico** (-'lo·xi·ko) *adj.* technological. **—tecnólogo** (-'no·lo·ɣo) *n.m.* technologist.
tectónica (tek'to·ni·ka) *n.f.* tectonics. **—tectónico,** *adj.* tectonic.
techado (te'tʃa·ðo) *n.m.* roof; roofing. *Also,* **techumbre** (te'tʃum·bre) *n.f.*
techo ('te·tʃo) *n.m.* **1,** roof. **2,** ceiling. **—techar,** *v.t.* to roof.
tedio ('te·ðjo) *n.m.* tedium; boredom. **—tedioso,** *adj.* tedious.
tee (ti) *n.m., golf* tee.
tegumento (te·ɣu'men·to) *n.m.* tegument.
teísmo (te'is·mo) *n.m.* theism. **—teísta,** *n.m. & f.* theist. *—adj.* theistic.
teja ('te·xa) *n.f.* roof tile. **—tejado,** *n.m.* roof. esp. tiled roof. **—tejar,** *v.t.* to tile; roof with tiles. *—n.m.* tile works.
tejamaní (te·xa·ma'ni) *n.m., Amer.* roof shingle. *Also,* **tejamanil** (-'nil).
tejeduría (te·xe·ðu'ri·a) *n.f.* **1,** weaving art or trade. **2,** weaving mill.
tejemaneje (te·xe·ma'ne·xe) *n.m., colloq.* **1,** knack; cleverness. **2,** scheming; maneuvering.
tejer (te'xer) *v.t. & i.* **1,** to weave. **2,** to spin (a web, cocoon, etc.). **3,** *colloq.* to knit; crochet. **—tejedor,** *adj.* weaving; spinning. *—n.m.* weaver; spinner. **—tejedura,** *n.f.* weave; weaving.
tejido (te'xi·ðo) *n.m.* **1,** fabric; textile. **2,** weave. **3,** tissue.
tejo ('te·xo) *n.m.* **1,** quoit; disk. **2,** metal disk. **3,** yew; yew tree.
tejón (te'xon) *n.m.* **1,** badger. **2,** disk; round slug.
tela ('te·la) *n.f.* **1,** cloth; fabric. **2,** skin; membrane. **3,** *painting* canvas. **4,** insect web; cobweb. **5,** subject matter; material. **—en tela de juicio,** in doubt; in question. **—tela metálica,** wire mesh; wire netting.
telar (te'lar) *n.m.* **1,** loom; weaving machine. **2,** frame, as for weaving. **3,** *theat.* flies (*pl.*).
telaraña (te·la'ra·ɲa) *n.f., also,* **tela de araña,** cobweb; spider web.
tele- (te·le) *prefix* tele-; far off; distant: *telescopio,* telescope.
teléfono (te'le·fo·no) *n.m.* telephone. **—telefonazo** (-'na·θo; -so) *n.m., colloq.* telephone call. **—telefonear** (-ne'ar) *v.t. & i.* to telephone. **—telefonía,** *n.f.* telephony. **—telefónico** (-'fo·ni·ko) *adj.* telephonic. **—telefonista,** *n.m. & f.* telephone operator.
telefoto (te·le'fo·to) *n.m.* telephoto. **—telefotografía** (-ɣra'fi·a) *n.f.* telephotography. **—telefotográfico** (-'ɣra·fi·ko) *adj.* telephotographic.

telégrafo (te'le·ɣra·fo) *n.m.* telegraph. —**telegrafía** (-'fi·a) *n.f.* telegraphy. —**telegrafiar** (-'fjar) *v.t.* [*infl.:* **fotografiar**] to telegraph. —**telegráfico** (-'ɣra·fi·ko) *adj.* telegraphic. —**telegrafista,** *n.m.* & *f.* telegraph operator; telegrapher.
telegrama (te·le'ɣra·ma) *n.m.* telegram.
telémetro (te'le·me·tro) *n.m.* telemeter; range finder. —**telemetría,** *n.f.* telemetry.
teleología (te·le·o·lo'xi·a) *n.f.* teleology. —**teleológico** (-'lo·xi·ko) *adj.* teleological.
telepatía (te·le·pa'ti·a) *n.f.* telepathy. —**telepático** (-'pa·ti·ko) *adj.* telepathic.
telescopio (te·les'ko·pjo) *n.m.* telescope. —**telescópico** (-'ko·pi·ko) *adj.* telescopic.
teletipo (te·le'ti·po) *n.m.* teletype.
televidente (te·le·βi'ðen·te) *n.m.* & *f.* television viewer; televiewer.
televisión (te·le·βi'sjon) *n.f.* television. —**televisar** (-'sar) *v.t.* to televise. —**televisor** (-'sor) *n.m.* television set. —*adj.* television (*attrib.*).
telilla (te'li·ʎa; -ja) *n.f.* **1,** thin, light fabric. **2,** thin membrane; film.
telón (te'lon) *n.m.* theater curtain; drop curtain. —**telón de boca,** front curtain. —**telón de foro** *or* **fondo,** backdrop.
telurio (te'lu·rjo) *n.m.* tellurium.
tema ('te·ma) *n.m.* **1,** theme; subject. **2,** *gram.* stem; base. —*n.f.* mania; obsession. —**temático** (te'ma·ti·ko) *adj.* thematic.
temblar (tem'blar) *v.i.* [*pres.ind.* **tiemblo;** *pres.subjve.* **tiemble**] **1,** to tremble; shake; quake. **2,** to shiver; shudder. —**tembladera,** *n.f., Amer., colloq.* fit of shakes. —**tembladero,** *n.m.* = **tremedal.**
tembleque (tem'ble·ke) *adj.* **1,** shaky. **2,** trembling; quaking. —**temblequear,** *v.i., colloq.* to shiver; quiver; have the shakes.
temblón (tem'blon) *adj., colloq.* **1,** shaky. **2,** quaking; trembling.
temblor (tem'blor) *n.m.* **1,** tremor; trembling. **2,** quake; earth tremor.
tembloroso (tem·blo'ro·so) *adj.* quaking; trembling; tremulous.
temer (te'mer) *v.t.* to fear. —*v.i.* to be afraid; fear.
temerario (te·me'ra·rjo) *adj.* temerarious; rash. —**temeridad** (-ri'ðað) *n.f.* temerity.
temeroso (te·me'ro·so) *adj.* **1,** fearful; afraid. **2,** timorous.
temible (te'mi·βle) *adj.* fearful; fearsome.
temor (te'mor) *n.m.* fear; dread.
témpano ('tem·pa·no) *n.m.* **1,** kettledrum; tympanum. **2,** drumskin. **3,** block of ice; ice floe. **4,** [*also,* **témpano de hielo**] iceberg. **5,** barrelhead. **6,** thick slice, as of bacon.
temperado (tem·pe'ra·ðo) *adj.* = **templado.**
temperamento (tem·pe·ra'men·to) *n.m.* temperament.
temperancia (tem·pe'ran·θja; -sja) *n.f.* temperance.
temperante (tem·pe'ran·te) *adj.* **1,** temperate; moderate. **2,** tempering; moderating.
temperar (tem·pe'rar) *v.t.* to temper; moderate; calm.
temperatura (tem·pe·ra'tu·ra) *n.f.* temperature.
temperie (tem'pe·rje) *n.f.* weather; state of the weather.
tempestad (tem·pes'tað) *n.f.* tempest; storm. —**tempestuoso** (-'two·so) *adj.* tempestuous; stormy.
templa ('tem·pla) *n.f.* tempera.
templado (tem'pla·ðo) *adj.* **1,** temperate; moderate. **2,** tempered. **3,** tepid; lukewarm. **4,** *Amer., colloq.* drunk.
templanza (tem'plan·θa; -sa) *n.f.* temperance.
templar (tem'plar) *v.t.* **1,** to temper. **2,** to take the chill out of; warm; make lukewarm. **3,** to stretch; make taut. **4,** to tune; put in tune. **5,** *naut.* to trim or adjust (the sails) to the wind. —*v.i.* to warm up; become warmer. —**templarse,** *v.r.* **1,** to become temperate; exercise temperance. **2,** *Amer., colloq.* to become tipsy; get drunk.
temple ('tem·ple) *n.m.* **1,** temperature. **2,** temper, as of metals. **3,** disposition; mood; temperament. **4,** courage. **5,** *music* tuning; tempering. —**al temple,** *painting* in tempera.
templete (tem'ple·te) *n.m.* canopy; pavilion.
templo ('tem·plo) *n.m.* temple; sanctuary.

temporada (tem·po'ra·ða) *n.f.* time; period of time; season.
temporal (tem·po'ral) *adj.* **1,** temporal; secular. **2,** temporary; transitory. **3,** *anat.* temporal. —*n.m.* **1,** tempest; storm. **2,** temporal bone.
temporario (tem·po'ra·rjo) *adj.* temporary. *Also,* **temporáneo** (-'ra·ne·o).
temporero (tem·po're·ro) *adj.* provisional; temporary.
temporizar (tem·po·ri'θar; -'sar) *v.i.* [*pres.subjve.* **temporice** (-'ri·θe; -se); *pret.* **temporicé** (-'θe; -'se)] to temporize.
tempranero (tem·pra'ne·ro) *adj.* early.
tempranito (tem·pra'ni·to) *adv., colloq.* early; very early.
temprano (tem'pra·no) *adj. & adv.* early.
tenacidad (te·na·θi'ðað; -si'ðað) *n.f.* tenacity.
tenacillas (te·na'θi·ʎas; -'si·jas) *n.f.pl.* **1,** tweezers; pincers; small tongs. **2,** sugar tongs. **3,** curling irons.
tenada (te'na·ða) *n.f.* shed.
tenaz (te'naθ; -'nas) *adj.* tenacious.
tenaza (te'na·θa; -sa) *n.f., also pl.* **tenazas, 1,** pincers; claws. **2,** tongs. **3,** pliers. **4,** pincer-like hold. —**tenazuelas,** *n.f.pl.* tweezers.
tenca ('ten·ka) *n.f.* tench.
tendal (ten'dal) *n.m.* **1,** awning. **2,** clothes spread out for drying. **3,** cloth spread out to catch fruit. **4,** *So.Amer.* apron.
tendalera (ten·da'le·ra) *n.f., colloq.* slew; scattered lot; litter. *Also, Amer.,* **tendalada** (-'la·ða).
tendencia (ten'den·θja; -sja) *n.f.* **1,** tendency. **2,** tendentiousness. —**tendencioso,** *adj.* tendentious.
ténder ('ten·der) *n.m., R.R.* tender.
tender (ten'der) *v.t.* [*infl.:* **entender**] **1,** to stretch; lay out. **2,** to hang out (laundry) for drying. **3,** to lay down. **4,** to extend; tender; offer. —*v.i.* to tend.
tenderete (ten·de're·te) *n.m.* **1,** = **tendalera. 2,** market stall.
tendero (ten'de·ro) *n.m.* storekeeper.
tendido (ten'di·ðo) *adj.* accelerated; at full speed. —*n.m.* **1,** laying out; laying down. **2,** bleachers (*pl.*).
tendón (ten'don) *n.m.* tendon.
tendré (ten'dre) *v., fut. of* **tener.**
tenebroso (te·ne'βro·so) *adj.* dark; gloomy. —**tenebrosidad,** *n.f.* darkness; gloom.
tenedor (te·ne'ðor) *n.m.* **1,** fork; table fork. **2,** holder; keeper. —**tenedor de libros,** bookkeeper.
teneduría (te·ne·ðu'ri·a) *n.f., also,* **teneduría de libros,** bookkeeping.
tenencia (te'nen·θja; -sja) *n.f.* **1,** tenure; holding. **2,** lieutenancy.
tener (te'ner) *v.t.* [*pres.ind.* **tengo** ('ten·go); **tienes;** *pres.subjve.* **tenga** (-ga); *fut.* **tendré;** *pret.* **tuve**] **1,** to have. **2,** to hold; take or have hold of. **3,** to contain. **4,** to have or experience the feeling of, as cold, hunger, etc.: *tener sed, calor, etc.,* to be thirsty, warm, etc. **5,** to be (a certain age): *tiene cinco años,* he is five years old. —*aux.v., sometimes used in place of* **haber:** *tengo dicho,* I have said. *When the p.p. is construed as a participial adjective, it agrees in gender and number with the object: Tengo escritos dos libros,* I have written two books (i.e., I have two books written). *The combination of aux.v. and p.p. is sometimes equivalent to the simple form of the verb: Tengo entendido que irás,* I understand you will go; *Tengo pensado comprar una casa,* I intend to buy a house. —**tenerse,** *v.r.* to hold (oneself *or* itself); keep (oneself *or* itself). —**no tener en qué** (or **donde**) **caerse muerto,** to be penniless; be destitute. —**no tenerlas todas consigo,** to be scared; be worried. —**tener lugar,** to take place; occur; happen. —**tener que,** *fol. by inf.* to have to; must: *Tengo que salir,* I have to go out. —**tener (algo) que . . .** to have (something) to . . .: *Tengo mucho que decir,* I have much to say. —**tener que ver,** to be pertinent. —**tener que ver con,** to have to do with; be concerned with.
tenería (te·ne'ri·a) *n.f.* tannery.
tenia ('te·nja) *n.f.* tapeworm.
teniente (te'njen·te) *n.m.* lieutenant. —*adj.* **1,** having; holding. **2,** *colloq.* hard of hearing. —**teniente de alcalde,** deputy mayor.
tenis ('te·nis) *n.m.* tennis. —**tenista,** *n.m. & f.* tennis player.

tenor (te'nor) *n.m.* **1,** tenor; purport. **2,** *music* tenor. **3,** kind; nature; sort.
tenorio (te'no·rjo) *n.m.* Don Juan; rake.
tensar (ten'sar) *v.t.* to tauten; tighten.
tensión (ten'sjon) *n.m.* **1,** tension. **2,** tensity.
tenso ('ten·so) *adj.* tense.
tensor (ten'sor) *n.m.* tensor. —*adj.* **1,** tensile. **2,** producing tension.
tentación (ten·ta'θjon; -'sjon) *n.f.* temptation.
tentáculo (ten'ta·ku·lo) *n.m.* tentacle.
tentador (ten·ta'ðor) *adj.* tempting. —*n.m.* tempter.
tentalear (ten·ta·le'ar) *v.t.* to feel; grope about for.
tentar (ten'tar) *v.t.* [*pres.ind.* **tiento**; *pres.subjve.* **tiente**] **1,** to tempt. **2,** to try; attempt. **3,** to touch; feel. **4,** to grope for. **5,** to probe.
tentativa (ten·ta'ti·βa) *n.f.* attempt; trial. —**tentativo,** *adj.* tentative.
tenue ('te·nwe) *adj.* **1,** thin; light; slender. **2,** tenuous. —**tenuidad** (te·nwi'ðað) *n.f.* tenuousness.
teñir (te'ɲir) *v.t.* [*pres.ind.* **tiño**; *pres.subjve.* **tiña**; *pret.* **teñí, tiñó**; *ger.* **tiñendo**] to dye; stain. —**teñido,** *n.m.* dyeing.
teo– (te·o) *prefix* theo–; god; divine: *teología,* theology.
teocracia (te·o'kra·θja; -sja) *n.f.* theocracy. —**teocrático** (-'kra·ti·ko) *adj.* theocratic.
teologal (te·o·lo'ɣal) *adj.* theological. —**virtudes teologales,** theological virtues.
teología (te·o·lo'xi·a) *n.f.* theology. —**teológico** (-'lo·xi·ko) *adj.* theological. —**teólogo** (te'o·lo·ɣo) *n.m.* theologian.
teorema (te·o're·ma) *n.m.* theorem.
teoría (te·o'ri·a) *n.f.* theory. —**teórica** (te'o·ri·ka) *n.f.* theoretics. —**teórico,** *adj.* theoretical. —*n.m.* theorist.
teorizar (te·o·ri'θar; -'sar) *v.i.* [*pres.subjve.* **teorice** (-'ri·θe; -se); *pret.* **teoricé** (-'θe; -'se)] to theorize. —*v.t.* to treat theoretically.
teosofía (te·o·so'fi·a) *n.f.* theosophy. —**teosófico** (-'so·fi·ko) *adj.* theosophical. —**teósofo** (te'o·so·fo) *n.m.* theosophist.
tepe ('te·pe) *n.m.* block of turf or sod.
tequila (te'ki·la) *n.f.* tequila.
terapéutica (te·ra'peu·ti·ka) *n.f.* **1,** therapeutics. **2,** therapy. —**terapeuta** (-'peu·ta) *n.m.* & *f.* therapist. —**terapéutico** (-'peu·ti·ko) *adj.* therapeutic.
-terapia (te'ra·pja) *suffix* therapy; treatment of diseases: *hidroterapia,* hydrotherapy.
terbio ('ter·βjo) *n.m.* terbium.
tercer (ter'θer; -'ser) *adj.* = **tercero** *before a masc. noun.*
tercera (ter'θe·ra; -'se·ra) *n.f.* **1,** *music* third. **2,** procuress.
tercería (ter·θe'ri·a; -se'ri·a) *n.f.* **1,** mediation. **2,** *law* right of third party. **3,** one-third interest or partnership.
tercero (ter'θe·ro; -'se·ro) *adj.* & *n.m.* third. —*n.m.* **1,** third party. **2,** mediator; go-between.
terciana (ter'θja·na; -'sja·na) *n.f., usu.pl.* tertian fever.
terciar (ter'θjar; -'sjar) *v.t.* **1,** to divide into thirds. **2,** to slant; place aslant. **3,** *mil.* to port (a rifle). —*v.i.* **1,** to mediate; intercede. **2,** to take part; participate. **3,** to come up; happen; intervene. —**terciarse,** *v.r.* **1,** to be fitting; be propitious. **2,** *colloq.* to accede; come around; agree.
terciario (ter'θja·rjo; -'sja·rjo) *adj.* & *n.m.* tertiary. —*n.m.* member of a tertiary order.
tercio ('ter·θjo; -sjo) *adj.* & *n.m.* third. —**hacer tercio,** to take equal share; join in as an equal.
terciopelo (ter·θjo'pe·lo; ter·sjo-) *n.m.* velvet. —**terciopelado,** *adj.* = **aterciopelado.** —*n.m.* velours.
terco ('ter·ko) *adj.* obstinate; stubborn.
tergiversar (ter·xi·βer'sar) *v.t., fig.* to distort; twist. —**tergiversación,** *n.f., fig.* distortion.
termal (ter'mal) *adj.* thermal.
termas ('ter·mas) *n.f.pl.* **1,** thermal waters; hot springs. **2,** Roman baths.
termes ('ter·mes) *n.m.* termite.
-termia ('ter·mja) *suffix* -thermy; heat: *diatermia,* diathermy.
térmico ('ter·mi·ko) *adj.* thermal; thermic.

terminable (ter·mi'na·βle) *adj.* terminable.
terminal (ter·mi'nal) *adj.* & *n.m.* terminal.
terminante (ter·mi'nan·te) *adj.* 1, definite; unequivocal. 2, definitive; final.
terminar (ter·mi'nar) *v.t.* & *i.* to finish; terminate; end. —**terminación**, *n.f.* termination. —**terminado**, *adj.* finished. —*n.m.* finish; polish.
término ('ter·mi·no) *n.m.* 1, term. 2, end. 3, boundary; limit; terminus. 4, place; position. 5, terminal. —**primer término**, foreground. —**término medio**, average. —**término municipal**, township.
terminología (ter·mi·no·lo'xi·a) *n.f.* terminology.
termita (ter'mi·ta) *n.f.* 1, thermit. 2, termite.
termo- (ter·mo) *also*, **term-** (term) *before a vowel; prefix* thermo-; heat: *termonuclear*, thermonuclear.
termodinámica (ter·mo·ði'na·mi·ka) *n.f.* thermodynamics. —**termodinámico**, *adj.* thermodynamic.
termómetro (ter'mo·met·ro) *n.m.* thermometer. —**termométrico** (-'me·tri·ko) *adj.* thermometric.
termonuclear (ter·mo·nu·kle'ar) *adj.* thermonuclear.
termos ('ter·mos) *n.m.sing.* & *pl.* thermos bottle.
termosifón (ter·mo·si'fon) *n.m.* water heater.
termostático (ter·mos'ta·ti·ko) *adj.* thermostatic.
termóstato (ter'mos·ta·to) *n.m.* thermostat.
terna ('ter·na) *n.f.* 1, group or set of three. 2, slate of three candidates.
ternario (ter'na·rjo) *adj.* & *n.m.* ternary.
ternera (ter'ne·ra) *n.f.* 1, female calf. 2, veal. —**ternero**, *n.m.* calf; male calf.
terneza (ter'ne·θa; -sa) *n.f.* 1, = **ternura.** 2, *usu.pl.* sweet nothings.
ternilla (ter'ni·ʎa; -ja) *n.f.* cartilage.
terno ('ter·no) *n.m.* 1, suit of clothes, usu. including a vest. 2, swear word; profanity. 3, group or set of three.
ternura (ter'nu·ra) *n.f.* tenderness.
terquear (ter·ke'ar) *v.i.* to be stubborn.
terquedad (ter·ke'ðað) *n.f.* obstinacy; stubbornness.
terracota (te·rra'ko·ta) *n.f.* terra cotta.
terrado (te'rra·ðo) *n.m.* flat roof; terrace.
terramicina (te·rra·mi'θi·na; -'si·na) *n.f.* terramycin.
terraplén (te·rra'plen) *n.m.* embankment; terrace.
terraplenar (te·rra·ple'nar) *v.t.* 1, to level (land). 2, to terrace by cut or fill. 3, to embank.
terráqueo (te'rra·ke·o) *adj.* 1, terraqueous. 2, terrestrial.
terrateniente (te·rra·te'njen·te) *n.m.* landholder; landowner.
terraza (te'rra·θa; -sa) *n.f.* terrace.
terregoso (te·rre'ɣo·so) *adj.* 1, lumpy; full of clods. 2, paved with dirt.
terremoto (te·rre'mo·to) *n.m.* earthquake.
terrenal (te·rre'nal) *adj.* worldly; earthly; mundane.
terreno (te'rre·no) *n.m.* 1, terrain; ground. 2, grounds (*pl.*). 3, plot of land. —*adj.* 1, terrestrial. 2, = **terrenal.**
terrestre (te'rres·tre) *adj.* 1, terrestrial. 2, land (*attrib.*).
terrible (te'rri·βle) *adj.* terrible. —**terribilidad**, *n.f.* terribleness.
terrier (te'rrjer) *n.m.* terrier.
terrífico (te'rri·fi·ko) *adj.* terrific; terrifying.
territorio (te·rri'to·rjo) *n.m.* territory. —**territorial**, adj. territorial.
terrón (te'rron) *n.m.* lump; clod.
terror (te'rror) *n.m.* terror. —**terrorífico** (-'ri·fi·ko) *adj.* = **terrífico.**
terrorismo (te·rro'ris·mo) *n.m.* terrorism. —**terrorista**, *n.m.* & *f.* terrorist. —*adj.* terroristic.
terruño (te'rru·ɲo) *n.m.* soil; land, esp. native land.
terso ('ter·so) *adj.* 1, smooth. 2, terse.
tersura (ter'su·ra) *n.f.* 1, smoothness. 2, terseness.
tertulia (ter'tu·lja) *n.f.* 1, social gathering; tea party; salon. 2, conversation; talk. 3, *So. Amer.* orches-

tra; parquet (*of a theater*). —**salón de tertulia**, lounge.
tesar (te'sar) *v.t., naut.* to make taut.
tesauro (te'sau·ro) *n.m.* thesaurus.
tesis ('te·sis) *n.f.sing. & pl.* thesis.
teso ('te·so) *adj.* = **tieso.**
tesón (te'son) *n.m.* tenacity; firmness. —**tesonería**, *n.f.* stubbornness; pertinacity. —**tesonero**, *adj.* pertinacious; tenacious.
tesoro (te'so·ro) *n.m.* **1**, treasure. **2**, treasury. —**tesorería**, *n.f.* treasury. —**tesorero**, *n.m.* treasurer.
test (test) *n.m.* test.
testa ('tes·ta) *n.f.* head.
testaferro (tes·ta'fe·rro) *n.m.* figurehead; dummy. *Also*, **testaférrea** (-rre·a).
testamentaría (tes·ta·men·ta'ri·a) *n.f.* **1**, testamentary execution. **2**, inheritance; estate.
testamento (tes·ta'men·to) *n.m.* **1**, testament. **2**, will. —**testamentaria**, *n.f.* executrix. —**testamentario**, *adj.* testamentary. —*n.m.* executor.
testar (tes'tar) *v.i.* to make a will. —**testación**, *n.f.* making of a will. —**testado**, *adj.* testate. —**testador**, *n.m.* testator. —**testadora**, *n.f.* testatrix.
testarudo (tes·ta'ru·ðo) *adj.* stubborn. —**testarudez**, *n.f.* stubbornness.
teste ('tes·te) *n.m.* testicle. —**testes**, *n.m.pl.* testes.
testículo (tes'ti·ku·lo) *n.m.* testicle.
testificar (tes·ti·fi'kar) *v.t. & i.* [*pres.subjve.* **testifique** (-'fi·ke); *pret.* **testifiqué** (-'ke)] to testify. —**testificación**, *n.f.* testifying; attestation.
testigo (tes'ti·ɣo) *n.m. & f.* witness. —*n.m.* proof; evidence. —**testigo de cargo**, witness for the prosecution. —**testigo de descargo**, witness for the defense. —**testigo de vista; testigo ocular**, eyewitness.
testimonio (tes·ti'mo·njo) *n.m.* testimony. —**testimonial**, *adj.* confirmatory; attesting; testifying. —*n.f.* testimonial. —**testimoniar**, *v.t. & i.* to testify; attest.
testosterona (tes·tos·te'ro·na) *n.f.* testosterone.
testuz (tes'tuθ; -'tus) *n.m.* **1**, nape. **2**, forehead (*of animals*).
teta ('te·ta) *n.f.* teat. —**tetar**, *v.t.* to suckle; nurse.
tétano ('te·ta·no) *n.m.* tetanus. *Also*, **tétanos.**
tetera (te'te·ra) *n.f.* teapot; teakettle.
tetero (te'te·ro) *n.m., So.Amer.* nursing bottle.
tetilla (te'ti·ʎa; -ja) *n.f.* nipple.
tetra- (te·tra) *prefix* tetra-; four: *tetraedro*, tetrahedron.
tetraedro (te·tra'e·ðro) *n.m.* tetrahedron. —**tetraédrico**, *adj.* tetrahedral.
tetrágono (te'tra·ɣo·no) *n.m.* tetragon. —**tetragonal**, *adj.* tetragonal.
tetrarca (te'trar·ka) *n.m.* tetrarch. —**tetrarquía** (-'ki·a) *n.f.* tetrarchy.
tétrico ('te·tri·ko) *adj.* sad; gloomy; dark.
teutón (teu'ton) *n.m.* Teuton. —**teutónico** (-'to·ni·ko) *adj. & n.m.* Teutonic.
textil (teks'til) *adj. & n.m.* textile.
texto ('teks·to) *n.m.* **1**, text. **2**, textbook. —**textual** (-'twal) *adj.* textual.
textura (teks'tu·ra) *n.f.* **1**, texture. **2**, weave.
tez (teθ; tes) *n.f.* complexion.
tezado (te'θa·ðo; -'sa·ðo) *adj.* = **atezado.**
ti (ti) *pers.pron. 2nd pers.sing., used after a prep.* you; yourself; thee; thyself.
tía ('ti·a) *n.f.* **1**, aunt. **2**, *derog.* woman; female. —**no hay tu tía**, *colloq.* there's nothing to be done about it. —**quedarse para tía**, to remain an old maid. —**tía abuela**, great-aunt.
tiamina (ti·a'mi·na) *n.f.* thiamine.
tiara ('tja·ra) *n.f.* tiara.
tibia ('ti·βja) *n.f.* tibia.
tibio ('ti·βjo) *adj.* tepid; lukewarm. —**tibieza**, *n.f.* tepidity; tepidness; lukewarmness.
tiburón (ti·βu'ron) *n.m.* shark.
tic (tik) *n.m.* **1**, [*pl.* **tiques** ('ti·kes)] tic. **2**, [*also*, **tictac** (tik'tak)] tick; ticking.
ticket ('ti·ket) *n.m.* [*pl.* **tickets**] ticket.
tiemble ('tjem·ble) *v., pres.subjve. of* **temblar.**

tiemblo ('tjem·blo) *v., pres.ind. of* **temblar.**

tiempo ('tjem·po) *n.m.* **1,** time. **2,** epoch; age; times (*pl.*). **3,** period; season. **4,** weather. **5,** *gram.* tense. **6,** *music* tempo. **7,** phase; measure. —**a tiempo,** in time; at the right time. —**a su tiempo,** in good time. —**a un tiempo,** in unison; at once. —**cargarse** *or* **cerrarse el tiempo,** to cloud over; become cloudy. —**con tiempo 1,** in time; eventually. **2,** ahead of time; with foresight. —**cuanto tiempo,** how long. —**de un tiempo a esta parte,** for some time; for some time now. —**fuera de tiempo,** untimely.

tienda ('tjen·da) *n.f.* **1,** store; shop. **2,** tent. —**tienda de campaña,** army tent.

tienda ('tjen·da) *v., pres.subjve. of* **tender.**

tiendo ('tjen·do) *v., pres.ind. of* **tender.**

tienes ('tje·nes) *v., 2nd pers.sing. pres.ind. of* **tener.**

tienta ('tjen·ta) *n.f.* **1,** probe. **2,** shrewdness. —**a tientas,** gropingly; groping one's way.

tiente ('tjen·te) *v., pres.subjve. of* **tentar.**

tiento ('tjen·to) *n.m.* **1,** touch; feel. **2,** tact. **3,** care; caution. **4,** steady hand. **5,** feeler. **6,** try; test. **7,** blind man's stick. **8,** *colloq.* slap; blow; poke. **9,** *colloq.* swig; swallow. —**dar un tiento a,** *colloq.* to have a try at; take a crack at.

tiento ('tjen·to) *v., pres.ind. of* **tentar.**

tierno ('tjer·no) *adj.* tender.

tierra ('tje·rra) *n.f.* **1,** earth. **2,** land; soil. **3,** ground. —**tierra adentro,** inland. —**tierra firme, 1,** mainland. **2,** terra firma.

tieso ('tje·so) *adj.* stiff. —*adv.* stiffly. —**tiesura,** *n.f.* stiffness.

tiesto ('tjes·to) *n.m.* pot; flowerpot.

tifo ('ti·fo) *adj., colloq.* full; satiated. —*n.m.* typhus. —**tifo asiático,** cholera. —**tifo de América,** yellow fever. —**tifo de Oriente,** bubonic plague.

tifoideo (ti·foi'ðe·o) *adj.* typhoid. —**tifoidea,** *n.f.* typhoid fever.

tifón (ti'fon) *n.m.* typhoon.

tifus ('ti·fus) *n.m.sing. & pl.* typhus.

tigre ('ti·ɣre) *n.m.* **1,** tiger. **2,** *Amer.* jaguar. —**tigra,** *n.f., Amer.* female jaguar. —**tigresa,** *n.f.* tigress.

tijeras (ti'xe·ras) *n.f.pl., also sing.* **tijera,** scissors; shears. —**tijerada,** *n.f.* = **tijeretazo.** —**(de) tijera,** folding; scissor (*attrib.*).

tijeretear (ti·xe·re·te'ar) *v.t.* to snip; cut with scissors. —**tijeretazo** (-'ta·θo; -so) *n.m.* snip or cut with scissors. —**tijereteo** (-'te·o) *n.m.* snipping; cutting.

tila ('ti·la) *n.f.* **1,** linden flower. **2,** tea made of linden flowers.

tildar (til'dar) *v.t.* **1,** to put a tilde on. **2,** *usu.fol. by* **de,** to brand as; label as. **3,** strike out; erase.

tilde ('til·de) *n.m. or f.* **1,** tilde. **2,** flaw; blemish. **3,** brand; stigma. —*n.f.* jot; speck.

tilín (ti'lin) *n.m.* tinkle. —**hacer tilín,** to be likable; be well-liked.

tilo ('ti·lo) *n.m.* **1,** linden tree. **2,** tea made of linden flowers.

tilla ('ti·ʎa; -ja) *n.f.* deck board, esp. of a small boat. —**tillado,** *n.m.* wood floor. —**tillar,** *v.t.* to floor.

timar (ti'mar) *v.t.* to cheat; swindle. —**timarse,** *v.r., colloq.* to make eyes at each other. —**timador,** *n.m., colloq.* cheat; swindler.

timbal (tim'bal) *n.f.* **1,** kettledrum. **2,** tabor; drum. —**timbalero,** *n.m.* tympanist.

timbrado (tim'bra·ðo) *adj.* **1,** stamped. **2,** sonorous.

timbrar (tim'brar) *v.t.* to stamp; affix a stamp to. —*v.t. & i., Amer., colloq.* to ring.

timbre ('tim·bre) *n.m.* **1,** stamp; seal. **2,** official stamp; tax stamp. **3,** *Amer.* postage stamp. **4,** timbre. **5,** electric bell; buzzer; call bell; doorbell. —**timbre de gloria, 1,** milestone of glory; outstanding achievement. **2,** pride; object of pride.

tímido ('ti·mi·ðo) *adj.* timid; bashful; shy. —**timidez,** *n.f.* timidity; bashfulness; shyness.

timo ('ti·mo) *n.m.* **1,** thymus. **2,** *colloq.* cheat; swindle.

timón (ti'mon) *n.m.* **1,** helm; rudder. **2,** steering wheel. **3,** beam of a plow. —**timonear,** *v.t. & i.* to steer (a vessel). —**timonel,** *also,* **timonero,** *n.m.* helmsman; boatsman;

yachtsman. —**timón de profundidad,** *aero.* elevator.
timorato (ti·mo'ra·to) *adj.* timorous.
tímpano ('tim·pa·no) *n.m.* **1,** *anat.* tympanum; eardrum. **2,** *archit.* tympanum; pediment. **3,** drum; kettledrum.
tina ('ti·na) *n.f.* **1,** = **tinaja. 2,** bathtub.
tinaja (ti'na·xa) *n.f.* large earthen jar.
tinajero (ti·na'xe·ro) *n.m.* **1,** maker or seller of water jars. **2,** stand for water jars.
tinglado (tin'gla·ðo) *n.m.* **1,** shed; tent. **2,** wooden stand or platform. **3,** trick; scheme. **4,** *colloq.* brawl; scramble.
tiniebla (ti'nje·βla) *n.f., usu.pl.* **1,** darkness. **2,** abysmal ignorance.
tino ('ti·no) *n.m.* **1,** good sense; good judgment. **2,** accuracy; precision; good aim. **3,** tact. —**sacar de tino,** *colloq.* to drive (someone) mad.
tinta ('tin·ta) *n.f.* **1,** ink. **2,** dye; color. —**de buena tinta,** on good authority. —**media tinta,** halftone. —**tinta china,** India ink. —**tinta simpática,** invisible ink.
tintar (tin'tar) *v.t.* to dye; tint; stain.
tinte ('tin·te) *n.m.* **1,** hue; tint; tinge. **2,** dye; stain; color. **3,** dyeing; coloring; staining.
tinterillo (tin·te'ri·ʎo; -jo) *n.m., Amer.* shyster; pettifogger.
tintero (tin'te·ro) *n.m.* inkwell; inkstand. —**dejar en el tintero,** *colloq.* to forget.
tintinar (tin·ti'nar) *v.i.* = **tintinear.**
tintinear (tin·ti·ne'ar) *v.i.* to tinkle; jingle. —**tintineo** (-'ne·o) *n.m.* tinkling; jingling; tintinnabulation.
tinto ('tin·to) *adj.* **1,** dyed; tinted. **2,** deep-colored. —**vino tinto,** red wine. —**café tinto,** *Amer.* black coffee.
tintorería (tin·to·re'ri·a) *n.f.* **1,** dyer's shop or trade. **2,** dry cleaning store. —**tintorero** (-'re·ro) *n.m.* dyer.
tintura (tin'tu·ra) *n.f.* **1,** tincture. **2,** dye; tint; stain. **3,** dyeing; staining. **4,** smattering. —**tinturar,** *v.t.* to tincture; tinge.
tiña ('ti·ɲa) *n.f.* **1,** mange. **2,** scalp ringworm. **3,** *colloq.* stinginess.
tiña ('ti·ɲa) *v., pres.subjve. of* **teñir.**
tiñendo (ti'ɲen·do) *v., ger. of* **teñir.**
tiño ('ti·ɲo) *v., pres.ind. of* **teñir.**
tiñó (ti'ɲo) *v., 3rd pers.sing.pret. of* **teñir.**
tiñoso (ti'ɲo·so) *adj.* **1,** mangy; scabby. **2,** stingy.
tío ('ti·o) *n.m.* **1,** uncle. **2,** *colloq.* guy; fellow; bloke. —**tío abuelo,** great-uncle.
tiovivo (ti·o'βi·βo) *n.m.* merry-go-round.
tipejo (ti'pe·xo) *n.m., derog.* insignificant person; jerk.
-tipia ('ti·pja) *suffix* -typy; -type; printing; printing process: *electrotipia,* electrotypy; *linotipia,* linotype.
tipiador (ti·pja'ðor) *n.m.* = **mecanógrafo.** —**tipiadora,** *n.f.* typewriter. —**tipiar** (ti'pjar) *v.t. & i., Amer.* to type; typewrite.
típico ('ti·pi·ko) *adj.* typical.
tiple ('tip·le) *n.m.* treble; soprano. —*n.m. & f.* soprano singer.
tipo ('ti·po) *n.m.* **1,** type. **2,** presence; bearing; appearance. **3,** *colloq.* guy; fellow. **4,** *Amer.* rate (*of interest, discount, exchange, etc.*).
tipo- (ti·po) *prefix* typo-; type: *tipografía,* typography.
-tipo ('ti·po) *suffix* -type. **1,** example; representative form: *prototipo,* prototype. **2,** print; stamp: *daguerrotipo,* daguerrotype.
tipografía (ti·po·ɣra'fi·a) *n.f.* typography. —**tipográfico** (-'ɣra·fi·ko) *adj.* typographical. —**tipógrafo** (-'po·ɣra·fo) *n.m.* typographer.
tipómetro (ti'po·me·tro) *n.m.* type gauge.
tiquete (ti'ke·te) *n.m., Amer., colloq.* ticket.
tiquismiquis (ti·kis'mi·kis) *n.m.pl., colloq.* **1,** squeamishness; fastidiousness. **2,** priggishness; affectation.
tira ('ti·ra) *n.f.* strip. —**tiras,** *n.f. pl., Amer.* tatters; shreds.
tirabuzón (ti·ra·βu'θon; -'son) *n.m.* **1,** curl; corkscrew curl. **2,** corkscrew. **3,** *aero.* spin.
tirada (ti'ra·ða) *n.f.* **1,** throw. **2,** distance; stretch. **3,** space or lapse of time. **4,** issue; printing; edition.

5, outpouring; tirade. 6, string; series. —**de** *or* **en una tirada**, at one stroke; all at once.

tirado (ti'ra·ðo) *adj.* 1, thrown away; discarded. 2, *colloq.* cheap; dirt-cheap. 3, *colloq.* plentiful; abundant.

tirador (ti·ra'ðor) *n.m.* 1, thrower. 2, shooter. 3, marksman. 4, pull cord; pull chain. 5, slingshot. 6, pea shooter. 7, = **tiralíneas.**

tiralíneas (ti·ra'li·ne·as) *n.m. sing. & pl.* ruling pen.

tiranía (ti·ra'ni·a) *n.f.* tyranny. —**tiránico** (ti'ra·ni·ko) *adj.* tyrannical.

tiranizar (ti·ra·ni'θar; -'sar) *v.t. & i.* [*pres.subjve.* **tiranice** (-'ni·θe; -se); *pret.* **tiranicé** (-'θe; -'se)] to tyrannize.

tirano (ti'ra·no) *adj.* tyrannical. —*n.m.* tyrant.

tirante (ti'ran·te) *adj.* 1, taut; tight; pulling. 2, tense; strained. —*n.m.* 1, harness trace. 2, brace; joist; truss. 3, guy rope. —**tirantes,** *n.m.pl.* suspenders.

tirantez (ti·ran'teθ; -'tes) *n.f.* 1, tautness; tightness. 2, tension; strain.

tirar (ti'rar) *v.i.* 1, to pull; draw; exert a pull or attraction. 2, to tend; bear (*in a given direction*). 3, to bear up; hold out. 4, to fire; shoot. —*v.t.* 1, to throw; cast; fling. 2, to throw away; cast off. 3, to shoot; shoot off; fire. 4, to squander. 5, to stretch; draw. 6, to draw (a line). 7, to give (a blow, pinch, kick, etc.). 8, to knock down; throw down. 9, to print; draw from the presses. —**tirarse,** *v.r.* to throw oneself; lunge; plunge; jump. —**tirarse a,** *Amer., colloq.* to finish off; polish off. —**a todo tirar,** at the most; at the outmost. —**tirar a,** 1, to shade toward. 2, to resemble; look like. 3, to aim at or toward. —**tirar de,** 1, to pull out; draw (a weapon). 2, to pull on; tug at. —**tirarla de,** *also,* **tirárselas de,** to boast of; boast of being. —**tira y afloja,** give and take; blowing hot and cold.

tiritar (ti·ri'tar) *v.i.* to shiver. —**tiritón,** *n.m.* shiver.

tiro ('ti·ro) *n.m.* 1, shot. 2, throw; cast. 3, trajectory. 4, shooting range. 5, team (*of draft animals*). 6, draft; chimney draft. 7, length (*of a piece of cloth*). 8, *Amer., colloq.* run; sweep. —**a tiro,** within range. —**de tiros largos,** *colloq.* all dressed up.—**ni a tiros,** *colloq.* not by wild horses. —**salir el tiro por la culata,** *colloq.* to backfire; boomerang. —**tiro al blanco,** target shooting. —**tiro de pichón,** trapshooting.

tiroides (ti'roi·ðes) *n.m. sing. & pl.* thyroid gland. —**tiroideo** (-'ðe·o) *adj.* thyroid.

tirón (ti'ron) *n.m.* 1, pull; tug. 2, stretch. —**de un tirón,** all at once; at one blow.

tirotear (ti·ro·te'ar) *v.t.* to shoot; shoot at. —**tirotearse,** *v.r.* to exchange shots. —**tiroteo** (-'te·o) *n.m.* shooting.

tirria ('ti·rrja) *n.f., colloq.* antipathy; aversion.

tisana (ti'sa·na) *n.f.* herb tea.

tisis ('ti·sis) *n.f.* tuberculosis; consumption. —**tísico** ('ti·si·ko) *adj. & n.m.* consumptive.

tisú (ti'su) *n.m.* gold or silver lamé.

titán (ti'tan) *n.m.* titan. —**titánico,** *adj.* titanic.

titanio (ti'ta·njo) *n.m.* titanium. —*adj.* = **titánico.**

titano (ti'ta·no) *n.m.* = **titanio.**

títere ('ti·te·re) *n.m.* 1, puppet. 2, *colloq.* clown; buffoon. —**títeres,** *n.m.pl.* jugglers' show. —**titerotada** (-'ta·ða) *n.f., colloq.* clowning; buffoonery.

tití (ti'ti) *n.m.* a small So.Amer. monkey; titi.

titilar (ti·ti'lar) *v.i.* 1, to quiver. 2, to twinkle. —**titilación,** *n.f.* = **titileo.**

titileo (ti·ti'le·o) *n.m.* 1, quiver; quivering; titillation. 2, twinkle; twinkling.

titiritar (ti·ti·ri'tar) *v.t.* = **tiritar.**

titiritero (ti·ti·ri'te·ro) *n.m.* 1, puppeteer. 2, ropewalker. 3, juggler.

titubear (ti·tu·βe'ar) *v.i.* 1, to vacillate; hesitate. 2, to toddle. *Also,* **titubar** (-'βar).

titubeo (ti·tu'βe·o) *n.m.* 1, vacillation; hesitation. 2, toddling; toddle.

titular (ti·tu'lar) *adj.* titular. —*n.m.* 1, holder; bearer. 2, incumbent. 3, large type capital letter. 4, headline. —*v.t.* to title. —**titularse,** *v.r.* to be called; call oneself.

título ('ti·tu·lo) *n.m.* **1,** title. **2,** diploma. **3,** academic degree. **4,** bond; certificate. **5,** qualification; requisite. —**a título de, 1,** by way of; as. **2,** by right of being; as.
tiza ('ti·θa; -sa) *n.f.* chalk.
tizne ('tiθ·ne; 'tis-) *n.m. or f.* **1,** soot. **2,** black smudge; smut. —*n.m.* charred stick used for blacking. —**tiznar,** *v.t.* to soot; cover with or as with soot.
tizón (ti'θon; -'son) *n.m.* **1,** smudge; smut. **2,** charred stick used for blacking. **3,** flaming stick; brand. **4,** *fig.* stigma; dishonor.
tizona (ti'θo·na; -'so·na) *n.f., colloq.* sword.
toalla (to'a·ʎa; -ja) *n.f.* towel. —**toallero,** *n.m.* towel rack.
tobillo (to'βi·ʎo; -jo) *n.m.* ankle. —**tobillera,** *n.f.* ankle support; ankle guard.
tobogán (to·βo'ɣan) *n.m.* toboggan.
toca ('to·ka) *n.f.* **1,** toque. **2,** coif.
tocadiscos (to·ka'ðis·kos) *n.m. sing. & pl.* pickup; record player.
tocado (to'ka·ðo) *n.m.* coiffure; headdress. —*adj.* **1,** touched; slightly unbalanced. **2,** spoiled; bruised, esp. of fruits.
tocador (to·ka'ðor) *n.m.* **1,** player (*of a musical* instrument). **2,** dressing room; boudoir. **3,** dresser; vanity. **4,** vanity case.
tocar (to'kar) *v.t. & i.* [*pres.subjve.* **toque**; *pret.* **toqué**] **1,** to touch. **2,** to play (music, an instrument, etc.); perform. **3,** to knock; rap. **4,** to ring; toll; peal; sound (*a bell, buzzer, etc.*); strike (*the hour*); blow (*a whistle, horn, etc.*). —*v.t.* **1,** to knock on; rap on. **2,** to touch up. **3,** to do (the hair). **4,** to concern. —*v.i.* **1,** to fall; befall. **2,** to be one's turn. **3,** to be due; be one's share or portion. **4,** to fall to one's lot (*as something inherited, won, etc.*). **5,** *usu.fol. by* **a,** to behoove; be incumbent (upon); be fitting. **6,** to be related; be kin: *¿Qué le toca Juan? Es mi primo,* What is John to you? He is my cousin. —**tocarse,** *v.r.* **1,** to touch (oneself or each other). **2,** to cover one's head; put on a hat. **3,** *fol. by* **de,** to become touched (with); have a touch (of).
tocayo (to'ka·jo) *n.m.* namesake.
tocino (to'θi·no; -'si·no) *n.m.* bacon; salt pork. *Also, W.I. & C. A.,* **tocineta,** *n.f.*
tocología (to·ko·lo'xi·a) *n.f.* obstetrics. —**tocólogo** (-'ko·lo·ɣo) *n.m.* obstetrician.
tocón (to'kon) *n.m.* tree stump. —*adj., colloq.* fond of touching.
tocuyo (to'ku·jo) *n.m., Amer.* a coarse cotton cloth.
tocho ('to·tʃo) *adj.* rustic; homespun.
todavía (to·ða'βi·a) *adv.* still; yet; even. —**todavía no,** not yet.
todo ('to·ðo) *adj.* **1,** all. **2,** every; each and every. **3,** all of; the whole (of). **4,** full: *a todo correr,* at full speed. —*pron.* everything; all. —*n.m.* all; whole. —**todos,** *pron. m.pl.* all; everybody; everyone. —**ante todo,** first of all. —**con todo,** still; however; all in all. —**del todo,** entirely; completely. —**por todo,** throughout. —**todo el que,** everybody who. —**todos cuantos,** all those that.
todopoderoso (to·ðo·po·ðe'ro·so) *adj.* almighty.
toga ('to·ɣa) *n.f.* toga.
tojino (to'xi·no) *n.m.* cleat.
tojo ('to·xo) *n.m.* furze.
toldilla (tol'di·ʎa; -ja) *n.f., naut.* **1,** poop deck. **2,** roundhouse.
toldo ('tol·do) *n.m.* **1,** awning; canopy; tilt. **2,** *Amer.* hut; shelter.
tolemaico (to·le'mai·ko) *adj.* Ptolemaic.
tolerante (to·le'ran·te) *adj.* tolerant. —**tolerancia,** *n.f.* tolerance; toleration.
tolerar (to·le'rar) *v.t.* to tolerate. —**tolerable,** *adj.* tolerable.
tolete (to'le·te) *n.m., Amer.* **1,** club; cudgel. **2,** *colloq.* blow; rap.
tolmo ('tol·mo) *n.m.* boulder; outcropping of rock.
tolondro (to'lon·dro) *also,* **tolondrón** (-'dron) *adj.* giddy; scatterbrained; reckless. —*n.m.* **1,** scatterbrain. **2,** = **chichón.**
tolteca (tol'te·ka) *adj. & n.m. & f.* Toltec.
tolueno (to'lwe·no) *n.m.* toluene.
tolva ('tol·βa) *n.f.* **1,** mill hopper. **2,** slot; box with a slot.
tolvanera (tol·βa'ne·ra) *n.f.* **1,** whirling dust; dust storm. **2,** *fig.* whirlwind; tempest.
tollo ('to·ʎo; -jo) *n.m.* **1,** dogfish. **2,** *hunting* blind.
toma ('to·ma) *n.f.* **1,** take; taking.

2, seizure; capture. 4, dose. 5, tap. 6, intake. 7, outlet; source. —*interj., colloq.* 1, Well, how about that!; You don't say! 2, There!

tomaína (to·ma'i·na) *n.f.* = **ptomaína.**

tomar (to'mar) *v.t.* 1, to take; get. 2, to take hold of; grasp. 3, to seize; capture. 4, to take in; receive. 5, to take on; hire. 6, to drink. 7, to have; partake of, as food or drink. —*v.i.* 1, to proceed; go; head (*in a given direction*). 2, to drink; have a drink or drinks; *Amer.* to tipple. 3, *Amer.* to take; catch (*as a fire, flame, etc.*); take effect (*as a vaccine*). —**tomarse,** *v.r.* 1, to become rusty; rust. 2, to be scorched, as food, clothing, etc. —**tomador,** *n.m., Amer.* drinker; tippler. —**tomar a bien, a mal, etc.,** to take (something) well, ill, etc. —**tomar el pelo a,** *colloq.* to poke fun at; tease; pull the leg of. —**tomarla con (uno),** to pick on; take it out on. —**tomarla con (algo),** *colloq.* to get into the habit of. —**toma y daca,** *colloq.* give and take.

tomate (to'ma·te) *n.m.* tomato. —**tomatera** (-'te·ra) *n.f.* tomato plant.

tómbola ('tom·bo·la) *n.f.* 1, raffle. 2, charity bazaar.

-tomía (to'mi·a) *suffix* -tomy. 1, a cutting, dividing: *dicotomía,* dichotomy. 2, surgical operation: *apendectomía,* appendectomy.

tomillo (to'mi·ʎo; -jo) *n.m.* thyme.

tomo ('to·mo) *n.m.* 1, tome; volume. 2, importance; consequence; weight. —**de tomo y lomo,** 1, of great importance or moment. 2, *colloq.* tremendous.

-tomo (to·mo) *suffix* -tome; *forming nouns denoting* cutter; cutting instrument: *micrótomo,* microtome.

ton (ton) *n.m., contr. of* **tono.** —**sin ton ni son,** without rhyme or reason.

tonada (to'na·ða) *n.f.* air; tune; song. —**tonadilla,** *n.f.* light tune.

tonal (to'nal) *adj.* tonal. —**tonalidad,** *n.f.* tonality.

tonante (to'nan·te) *adj.* thundering; thunderous.

tonel (to'nel) *n.m.* barrel; cask. —**tonelero,** *n.m.* cooper. —**tonelería,** *n.f.* cooperage.

tonelada (to·ne'la·ða) *n.f.* ton. —**tonelaje,** *n.m.* tonnage.

tongo ('ton·go) *n.m.* 1, fix; rigging (*of a contest*); throwing (*of a race, game, etc.*); dive (*in boxing*). 2, *So.Amer.* derby hat.

tónica ('to·ni·ka) *n.f.* 1, *music* tonic. 2, *fig.* keynote.

tónico ('to·ni·ko) *adj.* & *n.m.* tonic. —**tonicidad** (-θi'ðað; -si'ðað) *n.f.* tonicity.

tonificar (to·ni·fi'kar) *v.t.* [*pres. subjve.* **tonifique** (-'fi·ke); *pret.* **tonifiqué** (-'ke)] to give tone or tonicity to; invigorate. —**tonificación,** *n.f.* strengthening; invigoration. —**tonificador,** *adj.* strengthening; invigorating.

tonina (to'ni·na) *n.f.* tunny.

tono ('to·no) *n.m.* 1, tone. 2, *music* pitch. 3, *music* key. 4, tune; accord; agreement. —**darse tono,** *colloq.* to put on airs. —**de buen (mal) tono,** in or of good (bad) taste. —**subirse de tono,** to assume a lofty attitude; be supercilious.

tonsila (ton'si·la) *n.f.* = **amígdala.** —**tonsilectomía,** *n.f.* tonsillectomy. —**tonsilitis,** *n.f.* tonsillitis.

tonsura (ton'su·ra) *n.f.* tonsure. —**tonsurar,** *v.t.* to tonsure.

tontería (ton·te'ri·a) *n.f.* foolishness; nonsense. *Also,* **tontera.**

tonto ('ton·to) *adj.* foolish. —*n.m.* fool. —**a tontas y a locas,** recklessly.

topacio (to'pa·θjo; -sjo) *n.m.* topaz.

topar (to'par) *v.t.* & *i.* 1, to butt; ram with the head. 2, to bump (into); run (into). 3, to hit upon; come upon.

tope ('to·pe) *n.m.* 1, top; summit. 2, butt; collision; bump.

topetazo (to·pe'ta·θo; -so) *n.m.* butt; bump; collision. *Also,* **topetada,** *n.f.,* **topetón,** *n.m.*

tópico ('to·pi·ko) *adj.* topical; local. —*n.m.* topic; subject.

topo ('to·po) *n.m.* mole. —**topinera** (-pi'ne·ra) *n.f.* molehill; mole hole.

topo- (to·po) *prefix* topo-; place: *toponimia,* toponymy.

topografía (to·po·ɣra'fi·a) *n.f.* topography. —**topográfico** (-'ɣra·fi·ko) *adj.* topographical. —**topógrafo** (-'po·ɣra·fo) *n.m.* topographer.

toque ('to·ke) *n.m.* 1, touch. 2,

knock. 3, beat, as of a drum. 4, ring; peal. 5, test; crucial point. 6, *mil.* call. 7, *Amer.* painting (*of the throat*). —**piedra de toque**, touchstone. —**toque de diana**, reveille. —**toque de queda**, curfew.
toque ('to·ke) *v., pres.subjve. of* **tocar**.
toqué (to'ke) *v., 1st pers.sing. pret. of* **tocar**.
toquilla (to'ki·ʎa; -ja) *n.f.* 1, hatband. 2, bandanna.
-tor ('tor) *suffix* -tor; *forming nouns and adjectives denoting* agency: *director*, director; directing.
Tora *also*, **Torah** ('to·ra) *n.f.* Torah.
tórax ('to·raks) *n.m. sing. & pl.* thorax. —**torácico** (-'ra·θi·ko; si·ko) *adj.* thoracic.
torbellino (tor·βe'ʎi·no; -'ji·no) *n.m.* whirlwind; vortex.
torcaz (tor'kaθ; -'kas) *adj.* ring-necked (*esp. of birds*). *See* **paloma torcaz**.
torcedura (tor·θe'ðu·ra; tor·se-) *n.f.* twisting; sprain.
torcer (tor'θer; -'ser) *v.t.* [*pres.ind.* **tuerzo, tuerces**; *pres.subjve.* **tuerza**] 1, to twist. 2, to bend; put a bend in; make crooked. 3, to turn; change the course or direction of. 4, to sprain. 5, to distort; pervert. —*v.i.* to twist; bend; turn; swerve. —**torcerse**, *v.r.* 1, to twist; turn; writhe. 2, to turn sour, esp. milk or wine. 3, to go astray; fall into evil ways. 4, to go awry; come to naught; fail.
torcido (tor'θi·ðo; -'si·ðo) *adj.* twisted; crooked; bent. —*n.m.* twist, as of yarn or pastry. —**torcida**, *n.f.* wick.
torcijón (tor·θi'xon; tor·si-) *n.m.* colic; stomach cramp; cramps (*pl.*).
tordillo (tor'ði·ʎo; -jo) *adj.* gray; dapple-gray. —*n.m.* dapple-gray horse.
tordo ('tor·ðo) *n.m.* 1, thrush. 2, dapple-gray horse. —*adj.* dapple-gray.
torear (to·re'ar) *v.t. & i.* 1, to fight (bulls). 2, to tease. —**toreador**, *n.m.* toreador.
toreo (to're·o) *n.m.* bullfighting.
torero (to're·ro) *n.m.* bullfighter. —*adj.* bullfighting; bullfighter (*attrib.*).
toril (to'ril) *n.m.* bull pen.
torio ('to·rjo) *n.m.* thorium.
-torio ('to·rjo) *suffix, var. of* **-orio**.
tormenta (tor'men·ta) *n.f.* 1, storm; tempest. 2, misfortune; trouble.
tormento (tor'men·to) *n.m.* torment; torture.
torna ('tor·na) *n.f.* 1, return. 2, small dam placed in an irrigation ditch for diverting the flow of water. —**volver las tornas**, to turn tables; return tit for tat: *Se volvieron las tornas,* The worm turned.
tornadizo (tor·na'ði·θo; -so) *adj.* changeable; fickle.
tornado (tor'na·ðo) *n.m.* tornado.
tornapunta (tor·na'pun·ta) *n.f.* brace; strut.
tornar (tor'nar) *v.t. & i.* to return. —*v.t.* to turn; make; cause to become. —**tornarse**, *v.r.* to turn; become. —**tornar a**, *fol. by inf.* to go back to (doing something); do again.
tornasol (tor·na'sol) *n.m.* 1, sunflower. 2, litmus. 3, iridescence. —**tornasolado**, *adj.* changing colors; iridescent. —**tornasolar**, *v.t.* to make iridescent.
tornavía (tor·na'βi·a) *n.f., R.R.* turntable.
tornavoz (tor·na'βoθ; -'βos) *n.m.* sounding board.
tornear (tor·ne'ar) *v.t.* to shape in a lathe. —*v.i.* to compete in a tourney or tournament. —**torneado**, *adj.* turned; shaped. —*n.m.* turning; shaping; shape. —**tornero** (-'ne·ro) *n.m.* turner; lathe operator.
torneo (tor'ne·o) *n.m.* 1, tourney; tournament. 2, turning (*on a lathe*).
tornillo (tor'ni·ʎo; -jo) *n.m.* 1, screw. 2, bolt. 3, clamp; vise. —**faltarle a uno un tornillo; tener flojos los tornillos**, *colloq.* to have a screw loose. —**tornillo de mariposa**, wing bolt.
torniquete (tor·ni'ke·te) *n.m.* 1, tourniquet. 2, turnbuckle.
torno ('tor·no) *n.m.* 1, lathe. 2, winch. 3, turnstile. 4, wheel (*for spinning, potterymaking, etc.*). 5, turn; gyration. —**en torno**, around.
toro ('to·ro) *n.m.* bull. —**toros**, *n.m.pl.* bullfight. —**plaza de toros**, bullring; arena.
torón (to'ron) *n.m.* thoron.

toronja (to'ron·xa) *n.f.* grapefruit. —**toronjo,** *n.m.* grapefruit tree.

toronjil (to·ron'xil) *n.m., bot.* a kind of balm.

torpe ('tor·pe) *adj.* **1,** dull; stupid; torpid. **2,** clumsy. **3,** lewd; obscene.

torpedo (tor'pe·ðo) *n.m.* torpedo. —**torpedear** (-ðe'ar) *v.t.* to torpedo. —**torpedero,** *n.m.* torpedo boat.

torpeza (tor'pe·θa; -sa) *n.f.* **1,** dullness; stupidity. **2,** clumsiness. **3,** lewdness; turpitude.

torpor (tor'por) *n.m.* torpor. —**tórpido** ('tor·pi·ðo) *adj.* torpid.

torrar (to'rrar) *v.t.* **1,** to toast. **2,** to parch; burn. —**torrado,** *n.m.* toasted chick pea.

torre ('to·rre) *n.f.* **1,** tower. **2,** turret. **3,** *chess* rook. **4,** steeple. **5,** villa. —**torre del homenaje,** keep. —**torre de perforación,** oil derrick.

torrecilla (to·rre'θi·ʎa; -'si·ja) *n.f.* turret.

torrefacción (to·rre·fak'θjon; -'sjon) *n.f.* roasting; toasting. —**torrefacto** (-'fak·to) *adj.* roasted; toasted.

torrentada (to·rren'ta·ða) *n.f.* flash flood; cloudburst.

torrente (to'rren·te) *n.m.* torrent. —**torrencial** (-'θjal; -'sjal) *adj.* torrential.

torrentera (to·rren'te·ra) *n.f.* bed of a torrent; gully.

torrentoso (to·rren'to·so) *adj., Amer.* torrential (*of streams and rivers*).

torreón (to·rre'on) *n.m.* fortified tower; watchtower.

torrero (to'rre·ro) *n.m.* lighthouse keeper.

tórrido ('to·rri·ðo) *adj.* torrid.

torrija (to'rri·xa) *n.f.* a kind of French toast.

torsión (tor'sjon) *n.f.* torsion. —**torsional,** *adj.* torsional.

torso ('tor·so) *n.m.* torso.

torta ('tor·ta) *n.f.* **1,** cake. **2,** tart; patty. **3,** *print.* font. **4,** *colloq.* slap; buffet.

tortera (tor'te·ra) *n.f.* baking pan; pie pan.

tortícolis (tor'ti·ko·lis) *n.f.* stiff neck.

tortilla (tor'ti·ʎa; -ja) *n.f.* **1,** omelet. **2,** *Mex.* tortilla.

tórtola ('tor·to·la) *n.f.* turtledove. —**tortolos** (-los) *n.m.pl., colloq.* lovebirds.

tortuga (tor'tu·ɣa) *n.f.* tortoise; turtle.

tortuoso (tor'two·so) *adj.* tortuous. —**tortuosidad,** *n.f.* tortuousness.

tortura (tor'tu·ra) *n.f.* torture. —**torturar,** *v.t.* to torture.

torvo ('tor·βo) *n.m.* grim; fierce.

torzal (tor'θal; -'sal) *n.m.* cord; silk twist.

tos (tos) *n.f.* cough. —**tos ferina,** whooping cough.

tosco ('tos·ko) *adj.* coarse; rough.

toser (to'ser) *v.i.* to cough. —*v.t., colloq.* to match; outdo (*esp. in courage*). —**toser fuerte,** to boast.

tósigo ('to·si·ɣo) *n.m.* poison.

tosquedad (tos·ke'ðað) *n.f.* coarseness; roughness.

tostada (tos'ta·ða) *n.f.* toast. —**dar** *or* **pegar la tostada a,** *colloq.* to cheat; dupe.

tostado (tos'ta·ðo) *adj.* **1,** toasted. **2,** roasted. **3,** tanned; sunburnt. **4,** tan; brown. —*n.m.* **1,** toasting. **2,** roasting. **3,** toasted or roasted part.

tostador (tos·ta'ðor) *adj.* toasting. —*n.m.* [*also,* **tostadora,** *n.f.*] toaster.

tostar (tos'tar) *v.t.* [*pres.ind.* **tuesto;** *pres.subjve.* **tueste**] **1,** to toast. **2,** to roast. **3,** to tan. —**tostarse,** *v.r.* **1,** to tan; become tanned. **2,** to roast.

tostón (tos'ton) *n.m.* **1,** toasted corn. **2,** roast suckling. **3,** *colloq.* nuisance; bore. **4,** *Amer.* fried plantain.

total (to'tal) *adj.* & *n.m.* total. —**totalidad,** *n.f.* totality; entirety.

totalitario (to·ta·li'ta·rjo) *adj.* totalitarian. —**totalitarismo,** *n.m.* totalitarianism.

tótem ('to·tem) *n.m.* [*pl.* **tótems**] totem. —**totémico** (-'te·mi·ko) *adj.* totem. —**totemismo,** *n.m.* totemism.

totuma (to'tu·ma) *n.f., Amer.* = **güira.**

toxemia (tok'se·mja) *n.f.* toxemia.

tóxico ('tok·si·ko) *adj.* toxic. —*n.m.* toxicant; poison. —**toxicidad** (-θi'ðað; -si'ðað) *n.f.* toxicity.

toxico- (tox·si·ko) *prefix* toxico-; toxic; poison: *toxicógeno,* toxicogenic.

toxicología (tok·si·ko·lo'xi·a) *n.f.* toxicology. —**toxicológico** (-'lo·xi·ko) *adj.* toxicological.

—**toxicólogo** (-'ko·lo·ɣo) *n.m.* toxicologist.
toxicómano (tok·si'ko·ma·no) *adj.* addicted to drugs. —*n.m.* drug addict. —**toxicomanía,** *n.f.* drug addiction.
toxina (tok'si·na) *n.f.* toxin.
toxo- (tox·so) *also,* **tox-** (toks) *before vowel; prefix* toxo-; poison: *toxoplasmosis,* toxoplasmosis; *toxemia,* toxemia.
toza ('to·θa; -sa) *n.f.* **1,** log; stump; wooden block. **2,** piece of bark.
tozo ('to·θo; -so) *adj.* dwarfish; stumpy.
tozudo (to'θu·ðo; to'su-) *adj.* stubborn. —**tozudez,** *n.f.* stubbornness.
tra- (tra) *prefix, var. of* **trans-**.
traba ('tra·βa) *n.f.* **1,** bond; tie. **2,** lock; trammel; shackle. **3,** impediment; obstacle.
trabado (tra'βa·ðo) *adj.* **1,** connected; joined. **2,** blocked; trammeled; inhibited. **3,** strong; sinewy. **4,** *Amer.* tongue-tied; slurred; slurring. **5,** *phonet.* closed (*syllable*).
trabajar (tra·βa'xar) *v.t.* & *i.* to work. —*v.t.* to mold; shape; form. —**trabajador,** *adj.* industrious. —*n.m.* worker; laborer.
trabajo (tra'βa·xo) *n.m.* **1,** work. **2,** occupation; employment. **3,** task; undertaking; duty. **4,** work; product of work. **5,** workmanship. **6,** labor. **7,** *mech.* work. —**trabajos,** *n.m.pl.* **1,** hardships; tribulations. **2,** works; construction.
trabajoso (tra·βa'xo·so) *adj.* difficult; laborious.
trabalenguas (tra·βa'len·gwas) *n.m.sing.* & *pl.* tongue twister.
trabar (tra'βar) *v.t.* & *i.* **1,** to join; bind; fasten. **2,** to engage; lock. **3,** to grab; grasp; seize. **4,** to tie in (with); mesh. —*v.t.* **1,** to entangle. **2,** to shackle; fetter. **3,** to enter upon; engage in. —**trabarse,** *v.r.* **1,** to become entangled; catch; lock. **2,** to tangle (with). —**trabarse la lengua,** to stammer; stutter.
trabazón (tra·βa'θon; -'son) *n.f.* **1,** bond; connection; union. **2,** thickness; consistency.
trabilla (tra'βi·ʎa; -ja) *n.f.* **1,** strap. **2,** loose stitch; end stitch.
trabucar (tra·βu'kar) *v.t.* [*pres. subjve.* **trabuque** (-'βu·ke); *pret.* **trabuqué** (-'ke)] to jumble; garble; confuse.
trabuco (tra'βu·ko) *n.m.* blunderbuss.
tracalada (tra·ka'la·ða) *n.f.*, *Amer. colloq.* slew; scads (*pl.*).
tracción (trak'θjon; -'sjon) *n.f.* traction.
trace ('tra·θe; -se) *v., pres.subjve. of* **trazar.**
tracé (tra'θe; -'se) *v., 1st pers. sing.pret. of* **trazar.**
tracoma (tra'ko·ma) *n.f.* trachoma.
tracto ('trak·to) *n.m.* stretch; extent; tract.
tractor (trak'tor) *n.m.* tractor.
tradición (tra·ði'θjon; -'sjon) *n.f.* tradition. —**tradicional,** *adj.* traditional. —**tradicionalismo,** *n.m.* traditionalism. —**tradicionalista,** *adj.* & *n.m.* & *f.* traditionalist.
traducir (tra·ðu'θir; -'sir) *v.t.* [*infl.*: **conducir**] to translate; render. —**traducción** (-ðuk'θjon; -'sjon) *n.f.* translation; rendering. —**traductor** (-ðuk'tor) *n.m.* translator.
traer (tra'er) *v.t.* [*pres.ind.* **traigo, traes;** *pres.subjve.* **traiga;** *pret.* **traje;** *ger.* **trayendo**] **1,** to bring. **2,** to fetch; carry. **3,** to bring on; bring about; cause. **4,** to have; hold; bear. **5,** to have on; wear. **6,** to bring up; introduce; bring forward. **7,** *fol. by adj. denoting state or condition,* to have (one) . . . , cause (one) to be . . . . : *Esto me trae aburrido,* This has me bored. —**traerse,** *v.r.* **1,** *fol. by adv. of manner,* to dress. **2,** to comport oneself. **3,** to be up to; be doing. —**traérselas, 1,** to be up to something. **2,** to have more than meets the eye. —**traer a mal traer,** to put (someone) in a bad way. —**traer y llevar,** *colloq.* to carry gossip.
traeres (tra'e·res) *n.m.pl.* finery.
trafagar (tra·fa'ɣar) *v.i.* [*pres. subjve.* **trafague** (-'fa·ɣe); *pret.* **trafagué** (-'ɣe)] **1,** to trade; traffic. **2,** to travel; rove.
tráfago ('tra·fa·ɣo) *n.m.* **1,** traffic; trade. **2,** hustle and bustle. **3,** drudgery.
traficar (tra·fi'kar) *v.i.* [pres. *subjve.* **trafique** (-'fi·ke): *pret.* **trafiqué** (-'ke)] **1,** to traffic; trade. **2,**

to travel; roam; rove. —**traficante,** *n.m.* trafficker; trader.
tráfico ('tra·fi·ko) *n.m.* **1,** traffic. **2,** trade.
tragaderas (tra·ɣa'ðe·ras) *n.f.pl.* gullet (*sing.*). —**tener (buenas) tragaderas,** *colloq.* **1,** to be gullible. **2,** to be lax; be indulgent.
tragadero (tra·ɣa'ðe·ro) *n.m.* **1,** gullet. **2,** drain.
tragaldabas (tra·ɣal'da·βas) *n.m. & f.sing. & pl., colloq.* **1,** big eater; glutton. **2,** gullible person; gull.
tragaluz (tra·ɣa'luθ; -'lus) *n.f.* skylight.
tragamonedas (tra·ɣa·mo'ne·ðas) *n.m.sing. & pl., colloq.* slot machine. *Also,* **traganíqueles** (-'ni·ke·les).
tragar (tra'ɣar) *v.t.* [*pres.subjve.* **trague** ('tra·ɣe); *pret.* **tragué** (-'ɣe)] **1,** to swallow; gulp. **2,** *fig., colloq.* to stomach; be able to bear; be able to put up with.
tragedia (tra'xe·ðja) *n.f.* tragedy.
trágico ('tra·xi·ko) *adj.* tragic. —*n.m.* tragedian. —**trágica,** *n.f.* tragedienne.
tragicomedia (tra·xi·ko'me·ðja) *n.f.* tragicomedy. —**tragicómico** (-'ko·mi·ko) *adj.* tragicomic.
trago ('tra·ɣo) *n.m.* **1,** drink. **2,** swallow; gulp. **3,** *fig.* calamity; misfortune. —**a tragos,** little by little.
tragón (tra'ɣon) *adj., colloq.* gluttonous; voracious. —*n.m., colloq.* glutton.
traición (trai'θjon; -'sjon) *n.f.* treason; treachery. —**traicionar,** *v.t.* to betray. —**traicionero,** *adj.* treacherous. —*n.m.* treacherous person; double-dealer.
traída (tra'i·ða) *n.f.* bringing in; carrying in. —**traída de aguas,** water supply.
traído (tra'i·ðo) *adj.* threadbare; worn out.
traidor (trai'ðor) *n.m.* traitor. —*adj.* traitorous; treacherous.
traiga ('trai·ɣa) *v., pres.subjve. of* **traer.**
traigo ('trai·ɣo) *v., 1st pers.sing. pres.ind. of* **traer.**
traílla (tra'i·ʎa; -ja) *n.f.* **1,** leash. **2,** road scraper. **3,** lash. —**traillar,** *v.t.* to level.
traje ('tra·xe) *n.m.* **1,** dress. **2,** suit. **3,** gown; costume. —*v., pret. of* **traer.** —**traje de etiqueta** *or* **ceremonia,** formal wear. —**traje de luces,** bullfighter's costume. —**traje de montar,** riding habit. —**traje sastre,** lady's tailored suit.
trajear (tra·xe'ar) *v.t.* to dress; clothe.
trajín (tra'xin) *n.m.* bustle; activity.
trajinar (tra·xi'nar) *v.t.* **1,** to carry; cart (merchandise). **2,** *colloq.* to push; peddle. —*v.i.* to run or travel back and forth; bustle.
tralla ('tra·ʎa; -ja) *n.f.* lash; whip. —**trallazo,** *n.m.* lash; crack of a whip.
trama ('tra·ma) *n.f.* **1,** weave; woof; texture. **2,** plot; scheme.
tramar (tra'mar) *v.t.* **1,** to weave. **2,** to plot; scheme.
tramilla (tra'mi·ʎa; -ja) *n.f.* twine.
tramitar (tra·mi'tar) *v.t.* to negotiate; arrange; expedite. —**tramitación,** *n.f.* procedure; arrangement; expediting.
trámite ('tra·mi·te) *n.m.* procedure; formality; step.
tramo ('tra·mo) *n.m.* **1,** stretch; lap; span. **2,** flight (*of stairs*). **3,** *fig.* literary passage.
tramoya (tra'mo·ja) *n.f.* **1,** stage machinery. **2,** sham; artifice; contrivance. **3,** plot (*of a play, novel, etc.*).
tramoyista (tra·mo'jis·ta) *n.m.* **1,** stage machinist. **2,** scene shifter; stagehand. —*n.m. & f.* schemer; swindler; humbug. —*adj.* scheming; swindling.
trampa ('tram·pa) *n.f.* **1,** trap; snare. **2,** trapdoor. **3,** trick; fraud. —**hacer trampa,** to cheat.
trampear (tram·pe'ar) *v.t. & i., colloq.* to cheat.
trampería (tram·pe'ri·a) *n.f.* cheating; trickery.
trampero (tram'pe·ro) *n.m.* trapper.
trampista (tram'pis·ta) *adj. & n.m. & f.* = **tramposo.**
trampolín (tram·po'lin) *n.m.* springboard.
tramposo (tram'po·so) *adj.* cheating; swindling. —*n.m.* cheat; swindler.
tranca (tran·ka) *n.f.* **1,** bar; crossbar; bolt. **2,** club; stick. **3,** *Amer.* drunk; spree.
trancar ('tran·kar) *v.t.* [*pres. subjve.* **tranque;** *pret.* **tranqué**] **1,**

to bolt; bar. **2,** to block; obstruct. **—trancarse,** *v.r., colloq.* **1,** to seclude oneself. **2,** *Amer.* to stuff oneself; gorge.

trancazo (tran'ka·θo; -so) *n.m.* blow with a stick or club.

trance ('tran·θe; -se) *n.m.* **1,** strait; predicament. **2,** *law* seizure. **—a todo trance,** at any cost. **—en trance de,** at the point of; in the act of. **—trance de armas,** feat of arms. **—último trance,** last moment; death throes.

trance ('tran·θe; -se) *v., pres. subjve. of* **tranzar.**

trancé (tran'θe; -'se) *v., 1st pers. sing.pret. of* **tranzar.**

tranco ('tran·ko) *n.m.* **1,** stride; long step. **2,** threshold. **—a trancos,** at a stride; hurriedly. **—a un tranco,** one step away; on the threshold.

tranque ('tran·ke) *v., pres.subjve. of* **trancar.**

tranqué (tran'ke) *v., 1st pers.sing. pret. of* **trancar.**

tranquear (tran·ke'ar) *v.i., colloq.* to walk with long strides.

tranquera (tran'ke·ra) *n.f.* **1,** stockade; palisade. **2,** *Amer.* fence gate; corral gate.

tranquilo (tran'ki·lo) *adj.* **1,** tranquil; calm. **2,** easygoing. **—tranquilidad,** *n.f.* tranquillity; calm. **—tranquilizar** (-li'θar; -'sar) *v.t.* [*pres.subjve.* **tranquilice** (-'li·θe; -se); *pret.* **tranquilicé** (-'θe; -'se)] to tranquilize; calm. **—tranquilizarse,** *v.r.* to calm down. **—tranquilizante,** *n.m.* tranquilizer.

trans– (trans) *prefix* trans–. **1,** across; over; beyond: *transatlántico,* transatlantic. **2,** through: *translúcido,* translucent. **3,** change: *transformar,* transform. *Also, usu. less correctly,* **tras–**: *trasformador,* transformer. *In some words, in variant form* **tra–**: *tramitar,* arrange; expedite.

transacción (tran·sak'θjon; -'sjon) *n.f.* **1,** transaction. **2,** compromise; accommodation.

transar (tran'sar) *v.t., Amer.* to compromise; settle; adjust.

transatlántico (trans·a'tlan·ti·ko) *adj.* transatlantic. **—*n.m.*** ocean liner.

transbordador (trans·βor·ða·'ðor) *n.m.* **1,** ferry. **2,** funicular; cable car; aerial car.

transbordar (trans·βor'ðar) *v.t.* to transship; transfer. **—*v.i.*** to transfer; change vehicles. **—transbordo** (-'βor·ðo) *n.m.* transshipment; transfer.

transcender (trans·θen'der; tran·sen-) *v.t.* = **trascender. —transcendencia,** *n.f.* = **trascendencia. —transcendental,** *adj.* = **trascendental. —transcendente,** *adj.* = **trascendente.**

transcontinental (trans·kon·ti·nen'tal) *adj.* transcontinental.

transcribir (trans·kri'βir) *v.t.* [*infl.:* **escribir**] to transcribe. **—transcripción** (-krip'θjon; -'sjon) *n.f.* transcription; transcript. **—transcrito** (-'kri·to) *also,* **transcripto** (-'krip·to) *adj.* transcribed. **—*n.m., Amer.*** transcript. **—transcriptor** (-krip'tor) *n.m.* transcriber.

transcurrir (trans·ku'rrir) *v.i.* to elapse; pass. **—transcurso** (-'kur·so) *n.m.* course (*as of time*).

transeúnte (tran·se'un·te) *adj.* transient; transitory. **—*n.m. & f.*** **1,** passerby. **2,** transient.

transferencia (trans·fe'ren·θja; -sja) *n.f.* **1,** transference. **2,** transfer.

transferir (trans·fe'rir) *v.t.* [*infl.:* **conferir**] to transfer. **—transferible,** *adj.* transferable.

transfigurar (trans·fi·ɣu'rar) *v.t.* to transfigure. **—transfigurarse,** *v.r.* to be transfigured. **—transfiguración,** *n.f.* transfiguration; transfigurement.

transfixión (trans·fik'sjon) *n.f.* transfixion. **—transfijo** (-'fi·xo) *adj.* transfixed.

transflorar (trans·flo'rar) *v.i.* to show through. **—*v.t.*** **1,** to trace against the light. **2,** to paint (metal).

transformar (trans·for'mar) *v.t.* to transform. **—transformación** *n.f.* transformation. **—transformador,** *n.m.* transformer. **—*adj.*** transforming.

transformista (trans·for'mis·ta) *n.m. & f.* **1,** quick-change artist. **2,** transformist. **—transformismo,** *n.m.* transformism.

tránsfuga ('trans·fu·ɣa) *n.m. & f.* fugitive; deserter; turncoat.

transfundir (trans·fun'dir) *v.t.* to transfuse. **—transfusión** (-fu·'sjon) *n.f.* transfusion.

transgredir (trans·ɣre'ðir) *v.t.* [*defective: used only in tenses with terminations beginning with* i] to transgress. —**transgresión** (-'sjon) *n.f.* transgression. —**transgresor** (-'sor) *n.m.* transgressor.

transición (tran·si'θjon; -'sjon) *n.f.* transition.

transido (tran'si·ðo) *adj.* overcome; overwhelmed (*with fear, emotion, etc.*); pierced (*with pain, suffering, etc.*)

transigir (tran·si'xir) *v.i. & t.* [*pres.ind.* **transijo** (-'si·xo); *pres. subjve.* **transija** (-xa)] to compromise; concede; yield. —**transigencia,** *n.f.* tolerance. —**transigente,** *adj.* tolerant; accommodating.

transistor (tran·sis'tor) *n.m.* transistor.

transitar (tran·si'tar) *v.i.* to travel; pass. —**transitable,** *adj.* passable; capable of bearing traffic. —**transitado,** *adj.* bearing traffic; traveled.

tránsito ('tran·si·to) *n.m.* **1,** transit. **2,** traffic.

transitivo (tran·si'ti·βo) *adj. & n.m.* transitive.

transitorio (tran·si'to·rjo) *adj.* **1,** transitory; transient; passing. **2,** transitional. —**transitoriedad** (-rje·'ðað) *n.f.* transitoriness; transience.

translación (trans·la'θjon; -'sjon) *n.f.* = **traslación.**

translimitar (trans·li·mi'tar) *v.t.* to go beyond; cross over; overstep.

transliteración (trans·li·te·ra·'θjon; -'sjon) *n.f.* transliteration.

translúcido (trans'lu·θi·ðo; -si·ðo) *adj.* translucent. —**translucidez,** *n.f.* translucence.

transmigrar (trans·mi'ɣrar) *v.i.* to transmigrate. —**transmigración,** *n.f.* transmigration.

transmisión (trans·mi'sjon) *n.f.* **1,** transmission. **2,** transmittal. **3,** broadcast.

transmisor (trans·mi'sor) *n.m.* transmitter. —*adj.* transmitting.

transmitir (trans·mi'tir) *v.t.* to transmit. —**transmisible** (-'si·βle) *adj.* transmissible. —**transmisibilidad,** *n.f.* transmissibility.

transmutar (trans·mu'tar) *v.t.* to transmute. —**transmutación,** *n.f.* transmutation.

transónico (tran'so·ni·ko) *adj.* transsonic.

transparentarse (trans'pa·ren·'tar·se) *v.r.* **1,** to become transparent. **2,** to be visible; show through.

transparente (trans·pa'ren·te) *adj.* transparent. —**transparencia,** *n.f.* transparency.

transpirar (trans·pi'rar) *v.i.* **1,** to perspire. **2,** to transpire.

transpiración (trans·pi·ra'θjon; -'sjon) *n.f.* **1,** perspiration. **2,** transpiration.

transplantar (trans·plan'tar) *v.t.* = **trasplantar.** —**transplante,** *n.m.* = **trasplante.**

transponer (trans·po'ner) *v.t.* [*infl.:* **poner**] to transpose.

transportación (trans·por·ta·'θjon; -'sjon) *n.f.* **1,** transportation. **2,** *music* transposition.

transportador (trans·por·ta'ðor) *adj.* transporting. —*n.m.* **1,** transporter. **2,** protractor.

transportar (trans·por'tar) *v.t.* **1,** to transport. **2,** *music* to transpose. —**transportarse,** *v.r.* to be transported; be rapt.

transporte (trans'por·te) *n.m.* **1,** transport. **2,** transportation.

transposición (trans·po·si'θjon; -'sjon) *n.f.* transposition.

transpuesto (trans'pwes·to) *v., p.p. of* **transponer.**

transversal (trans·βer'sal) *adj.* **1,** transverse. **2,** intersecting. —*n.f.* **1,** transversal. **2,** cross street. —**corte** *or* **sección transversal,** cross section.

transverso (trans'βer·so) *adj.* transverse.

transvertir (trans·βer'tir) *v.t.* [*infl.:* **advertir**] to change; change over; transform.

transvestismo (trans·βes'tis·mo) *also,* **transvestitismo** (-ti'tis·mo) *n.m.* transvestism. —**transvestista,** *adj.* transvestic. —*n.m. & f.* transvestite.

tranvía (tran'βi·a) *n.f.* **1,** streetcar. **2,** tramway; trolley system.

tranzar (tran'θar; -'sar) *v.t.* [*pres. subjve.* **trance;** *pret.* **trancé**] = **tronchar.**

trapacear (tra·pa·θe'ar; -se'ar) *v.t.* to deceive; swindle; cheat. —**trapacería,** *n.f.* fraud; swindle. —**trapacero,** *also,* **trapacista,** *adj.* cheating; swindling. —*n.m.* cheater; swindler.

trapajo (tra'pa·xo) *n.m.* rag; tatter. —**trapajoso,** *adj.* ragged; tattered.

trapalear (tra·pa·le'ar) *v.i., colloq.* **1,** to clatter; patter. **2,** to jabber; babble. **3,** to cheat.

trapear (tra·pe'ar) *v.t., Amer.* to mop; swab. —**trapeador,** *n.m., Amer.* mop; swab.

trapecio (tra'pe·θjo; -sjo) *n.m.* **1,** trapeze. **2,** *anat.* trapezium. **3,** *geom.* trapezoid.

trapense (tra'pen·se) *adj. & n.m.* Trappist.

trapezoide (tra·pe'θoi·ðe; -'soi·ðe) *n.m.* **1,** *geom.* trapezium. **2,** *anat.* trapezoid. —**trapezoidal,** *adj.* trapezoidal.

trapiche (tra'pi·tʃe) *n.m.* **1,** sugar mill. **2,** *So.Amer.* ore crusher. **3,** press; juice extractor. **4,** *colloq.* wringer.

trapichear (tra·pi·tʃe'ar) *v.i., colloq.* **1,** to deal at retail. **2,** to scheme; wangle.

trapisonda (tra·pi'son·da) *n.f., colloq.* **1,** brawl; uproar. **2,** prank.

trapo ('tra·po) *n.m.* **1,** rag. **2,** sails (*pl.*) —**trapos,** *n.m.pl.* duds. —**a todo trapo,** *colloq.* at full speed; full sail. —**soltar el trapo,** *colloq.* to burst out (laughing *or* crying).

traposo (tra'po·so) *adj., Amer.* ragged; tattered.

traque ('tra·ke) *n.m.* clack; crack; crackle.

tráquea ('tra·ke·a) *n.f.* trachea. —**traqueal** (tra·ke'al) *adj.* tracheal.

traquear (tra·ke'ar) *v.i.* = **traquetear.**

traquearteria (tra·ke·ar'te·rja) *n.f.* = **tráquea.**

traqueo- (tra·ke·o) *also,* **traque-** (tra·ke) *prefix* tracheo-; trachea: *traqueotomía,* tracheotomy; *traqueítis,* tracheitis.

traquetear (tra·ke·te'ar) *v.t. & i.* **1,** to shake; rattle. **2,** to clack; crack; crackle.

traqueteo (tra·ke'te·o) *n.m.* **1,** shaking; rattling. **2,** clacking; cracking; crackling. **3,** *Amer.* uproar; racket; din.

traquido (tra'ki·ðo) *n.m.* **1,** report (*of a firearm*). **2,** crack; snap.

tras (tras) *prep.* **1,** after; behind. **2,** beyond. —**tras de, 1,** after; behind. **2,** besides; in addition to.

tras- (tras) *prefix, var. of* **trans-.**

¡tras! (tras) *interj.* knock!—**¡tras, tras!** knock, knock!

trasbordador (tras·βor·ða'ðor) *n.m.* = **transbordador.** —**trasbordar,** *v.t. & i.* = **transbordar.** —**trasbordo,** *n.m.* = **transbordo.**

trasca ('tras·ka) *n.f.* leather thong.

trascendencia (tras·θen'den·θja; tra·sen'den·sja) *n.f.* **1,** importance; consequence. **2,** transcendence; transcendency.

trascendental (tras·θen·den'tal; tra·sen-) *adj.* **1,** important; momentous. **2,** transcendental. —**trascendente** (-'den·te) *adj.* transcendent.

trascender (tras·θen'der; tra·sen-) *v.i.* [*infl.:* **ascender**]**1,** to come to be known; become known. **2,** to spread. **3,** to be transcendent. —*v.t.* **1,** to transcend. **2,** to penetrate; fathom.

trascocina (tras·ko'θi·na; -'si·na) *n.f.* scullery.

trascolar (tras·ko'lar) *v.t.* [*infl.:* **colar**] to percolate; strain.

trascurrir (tras·ku'rrir) *v.i.* = **transcurrir.** —**trascurso** (-'kur·so) *n.m.* = **transcurso.**

trasechar (tras·e'tʃar) *v.t.* to waylay.

trasegar (tra·se'ɣar) *v.t.* [*infl.:* **segar**] **1,** to pour; decant. **2,** to upset; turn topsy-turvy.

trasero (tra'se·ro) *adj.* rear; hind; back. —*n.m.* rump; posterior.

trasgo ('tras·ɣo) *n.m.* sprite; goblin.

trasgredir (tras·ɣre'ðir) *v.t.* = **transgredir.** —**trasgresión,** *n.f.* = **transgresión.** —**trasgresor,** *n.m.* = **transgresor.**

trashojar (tras·o'xar) *v.t.* to leaf through; skim.

traslación (tras·la'θjon; -'sjon) *n.f.* **1,** conveying; moving; transfer. **2,** *mech.* translation.

trasladar (tras·la'ðar) *v.t.* **1,** to move; convey. **2,** to transfer; relocate. **3,** to postpone; reschedule (*for an earlier or later date*). —**trasladarse,** *v.r.* to move; change residence or location.

traslado (tras'la·ðo) *n.m.* **1,** moving; conveying. **2,** transfer; relocation. **3,** *law* notification.

traslucir (tras·lu'θir; -'sir) *v.t.* [*infl.:* **lucir**] to show up; bring to light; evince. —**traslucirse,** *v.r.* **1,**

to show up; be seen; show through. **2,** to be translucent.

trasluz (tras'luθ; -'lus) *n.m.* diffuse light. —**al trasluz,** against the light.

trasmallo (tras'ma·ʎo; -jo) *n.m.* trammel net.

trasnochada (tras·no'tʃa·ða) *n.f.* **1,** long night; sleepless night. **2,** last night. —**darse la trasnochada,** *colloq.* to make a night of it.

trasnochado (tras·no'tʃa·ðo) *adj.* **1,** weary; haggard (*from lack of sleep*). **2,** stale; old. **3,** passé.

trasnochar (tras·no'tʃar) *v.i.* **1,** to stay up all night; go without sleep. **2,** to spend the night. **3,** to keep late hours. —**trasnochador,** *adj. & n.m.* night owl.

trasnoche (tras'no·tʃe) *n.m.* [*also,* **trasnocho** (-tʃo)] long night; sleepless night. —*n.f., Amer., colloq.* night before last.

traspapelar (tras·pa·pe'lar) *v.t.* to misplace (a letter or papers) among other papers.

traspasar (tras·pa'sar) *v.t.* **1,** to cross; cross over; pass over. **2,** to pierce; run through; transfix. **3,** to transfer; turn over. **4,** to trespass; transgress. —**traspasarse,** *v.r.* to overstep one's bounds.

traspaso (tras'pa·so) *n.m.* **1,** transfer. **2,** trespass; transgression. **3,** grief; pain.

traspié (tras'pie) *n.m.* trip; stumble; slip. —**dar traspiés,** *also,* **dar un traspié,** to trip; stumble; slip.

trasplantar (tras·plan'tar) *v.t.* to transplant.

trasplante (tras'plan·te) *n.m.* **1,** transplanting; transplantation. **2,** transplant.

trasponer (tras·po'ner) *v.t.* = **transponer.**

trasportación (tras·por·ta'θjon; -'sjon) *n.f.* = **transportación.** —**trasportador,** *adj. & n.m.* = **transportador.** —**trasportar,** *v.t.* = **transportar.** —**trasporte,** *n.m.* = **transporte.**

trasposición (tras·po·si'θjon; -'sjon) *n.f.* = **transposición.** —**traspuesto,** *p.p.* = **transpuesto.**

traspunte (tras'pun·te) *n.m.* **1,** prompter. **2,** prompting.

trasquilar (tras'ki·lar) *v.t.* to shear; crop; cut; clip. —**trasquila** (-'ki·la) *also,* **trasquilada, trasquiladura,** *n.f., colloq.* cropping; trim; clipping.

trasquilón (tras·ki'lon) *n.m., colloq.* **1,** scissor slash. **2,** swindle; something swindled. **3,** = **trasquila.**

trastabillar (tras·ta·βi'ʎar; -'jar) *v.i.* **1,** to stumble. **2,** to stagger; reel. —**trastabillón,** *n.m., Amer.* = **traspié.**

trastada (tras'ta·ða) *n.f., colloq.,* low trick; bad turn.

trastazo (tras'ta·θo; -so) *n.m., colloq.* **1,** blow; whack. **2,** bump; thump.

traste ('tras·te) *n.m.* **1,** fret (*of a stringed instrument*). **2,** *chiefly Amer.* = **trasto. 3,** *Amer., colloq.* = **trasero.** —**dar al traste con,** to ruin; undo; spoil.

trastear (tras'te·ar) *v.i.* to move or change things around. —*v.t.* **1,** to strum. **2,** to make passes at (a bull) with the *muleta.* **3,** *colloq.* to handle; manage. —**trastearse,** *v.r., colloq.* to move; move one's belongings.

trastera (tras'te·ra) *n.f.* [*also,* **cuarto trastero** *or* **de los trastos**] attic; storeroom; junk room.

trastienda (tras'tjen·da) *n.f.* back or back room of a store.

trasto ('tras·to) *n.m.* **1,** piece; thing. **2,** piece of junk. **3,** *colloq.* good-for-nothing. —**trastos,** *n.m. pl.* **1,** things; personal belongings. **2,** odds and ends; junk; rummage.

trastornar (tras·tor'nar) *v.t.* **1,** to upset; disturb. **2,** to unbalance; derange.

trastorno (tras'tor·no) *n.m.* **1,** upset; disturbance. **2,** derangement.

trastrabillar (tras·tra·βi'ʎar; -'jar) *v.i.* = **trastabillar.**

trastrocar (tras·tro'kar) *v.t.* [*infl.:* **trocar**] to reverse; invert; change the order of.

trasudar (tra·su'ðar) *v.i.* to perspire lightly. —**trasudor** (-'ðor) *n.m.* light perspiration.

trasunto (tra'sun·to) *n.m.* likeness; image; copy.

trasversal (tras·βer'sal) *adj. & n.f.* = **transversal.** —**trasverso,** *adj.* = **transverso.**

trasverter (tras·βer'ter) *v.i.* [*infl.:* **verter**] to overflow; run over.

trata ('tra·ta) *n.f.* trade; traffic. —**trata de blancas,** white slavery. —**trata de esclavos,** slave trade.

tratable (tra'ta·βle) *adj.* **1,** tractable. **2,** approachable; accessible.
tratado (tra'ta·ðo) *n.m.* **1,** treaty; agreement. **2,** treatise.
tratamiento (tra·ta'mjen·to) *n.m.* **1,** treatment. **2,** form of address; title.
tratante (tra'tan·te) *n.m.* trader; dealer; merchant.
tratar (tra'tar) *v.t.* **1,** to treat. **2,** to handle; manage. **3,** to discuss. **4,** *also v.i., fol. by* **de** *or* **sobre,** to deal with; have to do with; be about. **5,** *fol. by* **de,** to call; address (someone) as. —*v.i.* **1,** to try; attempt. **2,** *fol. by* **en,** to deal (in); trade (in). —**tratarse,** *v.r.* **1,** *fol. by* **de,** to deal with; have to do with; be about. **2,** *fol. by* **con,** to have dealings with; have to do with.
trato ('tra·to) *n.m.* **1,** treatment. **2,** trade; dealings (*pl.*). **3,** manner; behavior. **4,** *colloq.* agreement; deal. **5,** form of address; title. **6,** [*also,* **trato de gentes**] social intercourse; social graces. —**trato hecho,** *colloq.* it's a deal; agreed.
trauma ('trau·ma) *n.f.* trauma. —**traumático** (-'ma·ti·ko) *adj.* traumatic. —**traumatismo** (-'tis·mo) *n.m.* traumatism.
través (tra'βes) *n.m.* **1,** bias; slant; diagonal. **2,** reverse; misfortune. —**al través; a través,** through; across. —**al través; de través, 1,** transversely; diagonally. **2,** askance; sideways.
travesaño (tra·βe'sa·ɲo) *n.m.* **1,** crossbeam; crossbar. **2,** bolster.
travesear (tra·βe·se'ar) *v.i.* **1,** to misbehave; be naughty or mischievous. **2,** to frolic; romp.
travesía (tra·βe'si·a) *n.f.* **1,** crossing; traversing. **2,** cross street; crossroad.
travesura (tra·βe'su·ra) *n.f.* mischief; prank.
traviesa (tra'βje·sa) *n.f.* railroad tie.
travieso (tra'βje·so) *adj.* **1,** mischievous; naughty. **2,** frolicsome.
trayecto (tra'jek·to) *n.m.* **1,** course; route. **2,** journey; passage. **3,** distance; stretch.
trayectoria (tra·jek'to·rja) *n.f.* trajectory.
trayendo (tra'jen·do) *v., ger. of* **traer.**
traza ('tra·θa; -sa) *n.f.* **1,** plan; sketch; drawing. **2,** aspect; appearance. **3,** indication; sign. **4,** way; means (*pl.*). —**darse trazas (de),** to manage (to); find a way (to). —**tener trazas de,** to look like.
trazado (tra'θa·ðo; -'sa·ðo) *n.m.* **1,** trace; outline; contour. **2,** tracing; outlining. —**bien trazado,** handsome; good-looking. —**mal trazado,** homely; ill-looking.
trazar (tra'θar; -'sar) *v.t.* [*pres. subjve.* **trace;** *pret.* **tracé**] to trace; outline. —**trazante,** *adj.* tracer (*attrib.*); tracing.
trazo ('tra·θo; -so) *n.m.* **1,** line; trace. **2,** outline; contour.
trazumar (tra·θu'mar; -su'mar) *v.i.* to ooze; seep.
trébedes ('tre·βe·ðes) *n.f.pl.* trivet (*sing.*).
trebejo (tre'βe·xo) *n.m.* **1,** thing; piece. **2,** utensil; implement. —**trebejos,** *n.m.pl.* **1,** things; personal belongings. **2,** pots and pans. **3,** odds and ends; rummage. **4,** stuff; nonsense.
trébol ('tre·βol) *n.m.* **1,** trefoil; clover. **2,** *cards* club.
trece ('tre·θe; -se) *adj. & n.m.* thirteen. —**estar** *or* **seguir en sus trece,** to stick to one's guns.
treceno (tre'θe·no; -'se·no) *adj. & n.m.* thirteenth.
trecientos (tre'θjen·tos; tre'sjen-) *adj. & n.m.* = **trescientos.**
trecho ('tre·tʃo) *n.m.* distance; space; stretch. —**a trechos,** at intervals. —**de trecho en trecho,** from time to time; here and there.
tregua ('tre·ɣwa) *n.f.* **1,** truce. **2,** rest; respite.
treinta ('trein·ta) *adj. & n.m.* thirty.
treintavo (trein'ta·βo) *adj. & n.m.* thirtieth.
treintena (trein'te·na) *n.f.* **1,** a quantity of thirty. **2,** a thirtieth part.
treinteno (trein'te·no) *adj.* thirtieth.
tremebundo (tre·me'βun·do) *adj.* dreadful; fearful.
tremedal (tre·me'ðal) *n.m.* marsh; bog; quagmire.
tremendo (tre'men·do) *adj.* **1,** tremendous. **2,** terrible; awful.
trementina (tre·men'ti·na) *n.f.* turpentine.
tremolar (tre·mo'lar) *v.t.* to wave; fly, as a flag.
trémolo ('tre·mo·lo) *n.m.* tremolo.

tremor (tre'mor) *n.m.* tremor; trembling.
trémulo ('tre·mu·lo) *adj.* tremulous; trembling.
tren (tren) *n.m.* 1, train. 2, retinue. 3, gear; equipment; outfit. 4, pace; speed. 5, show; pomp. —**en tren de**, in the garb of; ready for. —**tren de aterrizaje**, landing gear. —**tren de vida**, mode of living.
trencilla (tren'θi·ʎa; -'si·ja) *n.f.* braid.
trenza ('tren·θa; -sa) *n.f.* 1, braid; tress. 2, pastry twist.
trenzar (tren'θar; -'sar) *v.t.* [*pres. subjve.* **trence** ('tren·θe; -se) *pret.* **trencé** (-'θe; -'se)] to braid; plait. —**trenzarse**, *v.r.*, *Amer.*, *colloq.* to tangle; get into a fight.
trepa ('tre·pa) *n.f.* 1, climb; climbing. 2, *colloq.* somersault; turn. 3, *colloq.* beating; drubbing.
trepador (tre·pa'ðor) *adj.* climbing. —*n.m.* climber.
trepanar (tre·pa'nar) *v.t.* to trepan. —**trepanación**, *n.f.* trepanning.
trépano ('tre·pa·no) *n.m.* trepan.
trepar (tre'par) *v.t.* & *i.* 1, to climb. 2, to creep up.
trepidar (tre·pi'ðar) *v.i.* 1, to tremble; shake; vibrate. 2, *Amer.* to fear; be fearful. —**trepidación**, *n.f.* trepidation.
tres (tres) *adj.* & *n.m.* three.
trescientos (tres'θjen·tos; tre·'sjen-) *adj.* & *n.m.pl.* [*fem.* **-tas**] three hundred. —*adj.* three-hundredth.
tresillo (tre'si·ʎo; -jo) *n.m.* 1, ombre (*card game*). 2, *music* triplet. 3, trio; ensemble of three.
treta ('tre·ta) *n.f.* trick; wile; ruse.
trezavo (tre'θa·βo; -'sa·βo) *adj.* & *n.m.* thirteenth.
tri- (tri) *prefix tri-*. 1, three: *triciclo*, tricycle. 2, three times: *triplicar*, triplicate. 3, every third: *trienio*, triennial.
tríada ('tri·a·ða) *n.f.* triad.
triángulo ('trjan·gu·lo) *n.m.* triangle. —*adj.* triangular. —**triangulación**, *n.f.* triangulation. —**triangular**, *adj.* triangular. —*v.t.* to triangulate.
tribu ('tri·βu) *n.m.* tribe. —**tribual** (tri'βwal) *also*, **tribal** (-'βal) *adj.* tribal.
tribulación (tri·βu·la'θjon; -'sjon) *n.f.* tribulation.
tribuna (tri'βu·na) *n.f.* 1, tribune; dais; rostrum. 2, stand; grandstand. —**tribuna de la prensa**, press box. —**tribuna de los acusados**, dock.
tribunal (tri·βu'nal) *n.m.* tribunal; court.
tribuno (tri'βu·no) *n.m.* tribune.
tributario (tri·βu'ta·rjo) *adj.* & *n.m.* tributary.
tributo (tri'βu·to) *n.m.* tribute. —**tributar**, *v.t.* to pay; render (homage, admiration, etc.).
trice ('tri·θe; -se) *v.*, *pres.subjve. of* **trizar**.
tricé (tri'θe; -'se) *v.*, *1st pers.sing. pret. of* **trizar**.
tricentenario (tri·θen·te'na·rjo; tri·sen-) *n.m.* tercentenary.
tricentésimo (tri·θen'te·si·mo; tri·sen-) *adj.* & *n.m.* three-hundredth.
tríceps ('tri·θeps; -seps) *n.m.* triceps.
triciclo (tri'θi·klo; -'si·klo) *n.m.* tricycle.
tricolor (tri·ko'lor) *adj.* & *n.m.* tricolor.
tricornio (tri'kor·njo) *adj.* & *n.m.* tricorn.
tricot (tri'ko) *n.m.* tricot.
tricota (tri'ko·ta) *n.f.* turtleneck sweater.
tricúspide (tri'kus·pi·ðe) *adj.* & *n.f.* tricuspid.
tridente (tri'ðen·te) *adj.* & *n.m.* trident.
triedro (tri'e·ðro) *adj.* trihedral. —*n.m.* trihedron.
trifásico (tri'fa·si·ko) *adj.* three-phase.
trifoliado (tri·fo'lja·ðo) *adj.* trifoliate.
trifulca (tri'ful·ka) *n.f.*, *colloq.* free-for-all; brawl; row.
trifurcar (tri·fur'kar) *v.t.* [*pres. subjve.* **trifurque** (-'fur·ke) *pret.* **trifurqué** (-'ke)] to trifurcate. —**trifurcación**, *n.f.* trifurcation. —**trifurcado**, *adj.* trifurcate.
trigésimo (tri'xe·si·mo) *adj.* & *n.m.* thirtieth.
trigo ('tri·ɣo) *n.m.* wheat. —**trigal** (-'ɣal) *n.m.* wheat field.
trigonometría (tri·ɣo·no·me·'tri·a) *n.f.* trigonometry. —**trigonométrico** (-'me·tri·ko) *adj.* trigonometric.
trigueño (tri'ɣe·ɲo) *adj.* brunet; olive-skinned; swarthy.
trilátero (tri'la·te·ro) *adj.* trilateral; three-sided.

trilogía (tri·lo'xi·a) *n.f.* trilogy.
trilla ('tri·ʎa; -ja) *n.f.* **1,** threshing. **2,** threshing time.
trillado (tri'ʎa·ðo; -'ja·ðo) *adj.* **1,** threshed; beaten. **2,** hackneyed.
trillar (tri'ʎar; -'jar) *v.t.* **1,** to thresh. **2,** *colloq.* to mistreat. —**trillador,** *adj.* threshing. —*n.m.* thresher. —**trilladora,** *n.f.* threshing machine. —**trilladura,** *n.f.* threshing.
trillizo (tri'ʎi·θo; -'ji·so) *n.m.* triplet.
trillo ('tri·ʎo; -jo) *n.m.* **1,** thresher; threshing machine. **2,** *Amer.* trail; footpath.
trillón (tri'ʎon; -'jon) *n.m.* a million trillion; *U.S.* quintillion; *Brit.* trillion. —**trillonésimo,** *adj. & n.m., U.S.* quintillionth; *Brit.* trillionth.
trimensual (tri·men'swal) *adj.* thrice monthly.
trimestre (tri'mes·tre) *n.m.* trimester; quarter. —**trimestral,** *adj.* quarterly.
trimotor (tri·mo'tor) *adj.* three-engined. —*n.m.* three-engined airplane.
trinar (tri'nar) *v.i.* **1,** to trill; warble. **2,** *colloq.* to be angry; rage; rave.
trinca ('trin·ka) *n.f.* **1,** triad. **2,** *naut.* rope; cable; lanyard. **3,** binding; fastening. **4,** *colloq.* pinioning. **5,** *Amer., colloq.* drunk; drunkenness; spree.
trincar (trin'kar) *v.t.* [*pres.subjve.* **trinque;** *pret.* **trinqué**] **1,** to cut into pieces. **2,** to fasten; bind. **3,** to pinion. —*v.t. & i., colloq.* to drink; tipple.
trinchar (trin'tʃar) *v.t. & i.* **1,** to carve; slice. **2,** *colloq.* to decide; dispose; settle. —**trinchante,** *n.m.* carving fork. —*adj.* carving. —**trinche,** *n.m., Amer., colloq.* fork.
trinchera (trin'tʃe·ra) *n.f.* **1,** trench. **2,** trench coat.
trineo (tri'ne·o) *n.m.* sled; sleigh.
trinidad (tri·ni'ðað) *n.f.* trinity.
trinitrotolueno (tri·ni·tro·to·'lwe·no) *n.m.* trinitrotoluene; TNT.
trino ('tri·no) *n.m.* **1,** trill; warble. **2,** *music* trill.
trinomio (tri'no·mjo) *n.m.* trinomial.
trinque ('trin·ke) *v., pres.subjve. of* **trincar.**
trinqué (trin'ke) *v., 1st pers.sing. pret. of* **trincar.**
trinquete (trin'ke·te) *n.m.* **1,** foremast. **2,** foreyard. **3,** foresail. **4,** ratchet; pawl. **5,** rackets (*game*). —**a cada trinquete,** *colloq.* at every turn.
trinquis ('trin·kis) *n.m.sing. & pl., colloq.* swig; drink.
trío ('tri·o) *n.m.* trio.
tríodo ('tri·o·ðo) *n.m.* triode.
tripa ('tri·pa) *n.f.* **1,** intestine; gut. **2,** *often pl.* tripe. **3,** *pl.* entrails. —**hacer de tripas corazón,** *colloq.* to pluck up courage; make the best of it. —**tener malas tripas,** *colloq.* to be cruel.
tripartito (tri·par'ti·to) *adj.* tripartite. —**tripartir,** *v.t.* to divide into three parts. —**tripartición,** *n.f.* division into three parts.
tripe ('tri·pe) *n.m.* shag (*fabric*).
triplano (tri'pla·no) *n.m.* triplane.
triple ('tri·ple) *adj. & n.m.* triple; triplex.
triplicación (tri·pli·ka'θjon; -'sjon) *n.f.* **1,** tripling; trebling. **2,** triplication.
triplicado (tri·pli'ka·ðo) *adj. & n.m.* triplicate. —**por** *or* **en triplicado,** in triplicate.
triplicar (tri·pli'kar) *v.t.* [*pres. subjve.* **triplique** (-'pli·ke); *pret.* **tripliqué** (-'ke)] **1,** to triple; treble. **2,** to triplicate.
tríplice ('tri·pli·θe; -se) *adj.* = **triple.**
trípode ('tri·po·ðe) *n.m.* tripod.
tríptico ('trip·ti·ko) *n.m.* triptych.
triptongo (trip'ton·go) *n.m.* triphthong.
tripulación (tri·pu·la'θjon; -'sjon) *n.f.* crew (*of a ship or aircraft*). —**tripulante,** *n.m.* crew member. —**tripular,** *v.t.* to man (a ship or aircraft).
trique ('tri·ke) *n.m.* **1,** click; crack; clack. **2,** *Amer.* trinket. —**a cada trique,** at every turn.
triquina (tri'ki·na) *n.f.* trichina. —**triquinosis,** *n.f.* trichinosis.
triquiñuela (tri·ki'ɲwe·la) *n.f., colloq.* chicanery; subterfuge; trick.
triquitraque (tri·ki'tra·ke) *n.m.* **1,** click; clack; clacking. **2,** *colloq.* noisemaker.
trirreme (tri'rre·me) *n.m.* trireme.

tris (tris) *n.m.* **1,** crack; crackle. **2,** *colloq.* trice; instant. **3,** *colloq.* trifle; bit. —**en un tris,** within an ace; within an inch.

trisar (tri'sar) *v.t., So.Amer.* to crack; chip (glass, porcelain, etc.).

trisca ('tris·ka) *n.f.* **1,** crunch; crunching; crackle. **2,** ruckus; uproar. **3,** *Amer., colloq.* bit; speck.

triscar (tris'kar) *v.i.* [*pres.subjve.* **trisque** ('tris·ke); *pret.* **trisqué** (-'ke)] **1,** to crunch; crackle. **2,** to romp; frolic. —*v.t.* **1,** to set (the teeth of a saw). **2,** *colloq.* to ball up; foul.

trisecar (tri·se'kar) *v.t.* to trisect. —**trisección** (-sek'θjon; -'sjon) *n.f.* trisection.

trisílabo (tri'si·la·βo) *adj.* trisyllabic. —*n.m.* trisyllable.

triste ('tris·te) *adj.* sad; gloomy. —**tristeza,** *n.f.* sadness; gloom.

tristón (tris'ton) *adj.* somewhat sad; somewhat gloomy.

tritio ('tri·tjo) *n.m.* tritium.

tritón (tri'ton) *n.m.* triton; merman.

triturar (tri·tu'rar) *v.t.* to triturate; crush; grind. —**trituración,** *n.f.* trituration. —**triturador,** *adj.* triturating; crushing. —*n.m.* crusher. —**trituradora,** *n.f.* crushing machine.

triunfar (trjun'far) *v.i.* **1,** to triumph. **2,** *cards* to trump. —**triunfal,** *adj.* triumphal. —**triunfador,** *n.m.* victor; winner. —**triunfante,** *adj.* triumphant.

triunfo ('trjun·fo) *n.m.* **1,** triumph. **2,** *cards* trump. —**costar un triunfo,** to cost a great effort. —**sin triunfo,** no trump.

triunvirato (trjun·βi'ra·to) *n.m.* triumvirate. —**triunviro** (-'βi·ro) *n.m.* triumvir.

trivial (tri'βjal) *adj.* trivial. —**trivialidad,** *n.f.* triviality.

-triz ('triθ; 'tris) *suffix* -ess; -trix; *forming fem. nouns of agency corresponding to some masc. nouns ending in* **-tor** *and* **-dor**: *actriz,* actress; *emperatriz,* empress; *bisectriz,* bisectrix.

triza ('tri·θa; -sa) *n.f.* shred; fragment; bit. —**hacer trizas,** to shatter; break to bits.

trizar (tri'θar; -'sar) *v.t.* [*pres. subjve.* **trice;** *pret.* **tricé**] to shatter.

trocaico (tro'kai·ko) *adj.* & *n.m.* trochaic.

trocar (tro'kar) *v.t.* [*pres.ind.* **trueco;** *pres.subjve.* **trueque;** *pret.* **troqué**] **1,** to change; exchange. **2,** to barter. **3,** to transform; convert. —**trocable,** *adj.* changeable; exchangeable.

trocatinta (tro·ka'tin·ta) *n.f., colloq.* mixup.

troce ('tro·θe; -se) *v., pres.subjve. of* **trozar.**

trocé (tro'θe; -'se) *v., 1st pers. sing.pret. of* **trozar.**

trocla ('tro·kla) *n.f.* pulley.

trocha ('tro·tʃa) *n.f.* **1,** trail; path. **2,** *Amer., R.R.* gauge. **3,** *Amer.* wheelbase.

trochemoche (tro·tʃe'mo·tʃe) *n.m.,* in **a trochemoche,** *also,* **a troche y moche,** helter-skelter; pell-mell.

trofeo (tro'fe·o) *n.m.* trophy.

-trofia ('tro·fja) *suffix* -trophy; nutrition: *atrofia,* atrophy.

trófico ('tro·fi·ko) *adj.* trophic.

-trófico ('tro·fi·ko) *suffix* -trophic; *forming adjectives corresponding to nouns ending in* **-trofia**: *hipertrófico,* hypertrophic.

trofo- (tro·fo) *prefix* tropho-; nutrition: *trofoplasma,* trophoplasm.

troglodita (tro·ɣlo'ði·ta) *n.m.* **1,** troglodyte. **2,** *colloq.* glutton. —*adj.* [*also,* **troglodítico** (-'ði·ti·ko)] troglodytic.

troica ('troi·ka) *n.f.* troika.

troj (trox) *n.f.* **1,** granary; barn. **2,** bin. *Also,* **troje** ('tro·xe).

trole ('tro·le) *n.m.* trolley.

trolebús (tro·le'βus) *n.m.* trolley bus.

tromba ('trom·ba) *n.f.* **1,** [*also,* **tromba marina**] waterspout. **2,** [*also,* **tromba de viento**] whirlwind; tornado.

trombón (trom'bon) *n.m.* **1,** trombone. **2,** trombonist.

trombosis (trom'bo·sis) *n.f.* thrombosis.

trompa ('trom·pa) *n.f.* **1,** horn; French horn. **2,** elephant's trunk. **3,** proboscis. **4,** snout. **5,** *colloq.* mouth; puss. **6,** *med.* tube; canal; duct: *trompa de Eustaquio,* Eustachian tube; *trompa de Falopio,* Fallopian tube.

trompada (trom'pa·ða) *n.f., colloq.* blow with the fist; punch. *Also,* **trompazo** (-'pa·θo; -so) *n.m.*

trompearse (trom·pe'ar·se) *v.r.,*

Amer., colloq. to have a fist fight.

trompeta (trom'pe·ta) *n.f.* **1,** trumpet; bugle. **2,** *also masc.* trumpeter; bugler. **3,** *colloq.* good-for-nothing; scamp. —**trompetazo,** *n.m., also,* **trompetada,** *n.f., colloq.* trumpet blast. —**trompetero,** *n.m.* trumpeter.

trompetear (trom·pe·te'ar) *v.i., colloq.* to trumpet. —**trompeteo** (-'te·o) *n.m.* trumpeting.

trompetilla (trom·pe'ti·ʎa; -ja) *n.f.* **1,** ear trumpet. **2,** *Amer., colloq.* Bronx cheer.

trompicar (trom·pi'kar) *v.t.* [*pres.subjve.* **trompique** (-'pi·ke); *pret.* **trompiqué** (-'ke)] to trip; cause to stumble. —**trompicón** (-'kon) *n.m.* stumble.

trompis ('trom·pis) *n.m., colloq.* = **trompada.**

trompo ('trom·po) *n.m.* top; spinning top.

tronada (tro'na·ða) *n.f.* thunderstorm.

tronar (tro'nar) *v.i.* [*pres.ind.* **trueno**; *pres.subjve.* **truene**] **1,** to thunder. **2,** *colloq.* to collapse; be finished; be ruined. —*v.t., Amer., colloq.* to finish off; kill. —**por lo que pueda tronar,** *colloq.* just in case. —**tronar** *or* **tronarse con,** *colloq.* to fall out with; quarrel with. —**tronar los dedos,** to snap the fingers.

troncal (tron'kal) *adj.* trunk.

troncar (tron'kar) *v.t.* [*pres. subjve.* **tronque;** *pret.* **tronqué**] to truncate; lob. —**tronca** ('tron·ka) *n.f.* = **truncamiento.**

tronce ('tron·θe; -se) *v., pres. subjve. of* **tronzar.**

troncé (tron'θe; -'se) *v., 1st pers. sing. pret. of* **tronzar.**

tronco ('tron·ko) *n.m.* **1,** trunk (*of a tree, body, etc.*). **2,** main trunk or stem. **3,** log. **4,** team (*of animals*). **5,** frustum. —**estar hecho un tronco,** *colloq.* **1,** to be dead to the world; be out cold. **2,** to be fast asleep; be sleeping like a log.

troncha ('tron·tʃa) *n.f., Amer., colloq.* slice; cut; hunk.

tronchar (tron'tʃar) *v.t.* **1,** to snap; break. **2,** to twist; wrench. **3,** to mutilate; damage.

tronera (tro'ne·ra) *n.f.* **1,** porthole. **2,** small opening or window. **3,** *billiards* pocket. **4,** *also masc., colloq.* fly-by-night; scatterbrain.

tronido (tro'ni·ðo) *n.m.* thunder; thunderous sound.

trono ('tro·no) *n.m.* throne.

tronque ('tron·ke) *v., pres.subjve. of* **troncar.**

tronqué (tron'ke) *v., 1st pers.sing. pret. of* **troncar.**

tronzar (tron'θar; -'sar) *v.t.* [*pres. subjve.* **tronce**; *pret.* **troncé**] **1,** = **tronchar.** **2,** to pleat (a skirt). **3,** to exhaust; fatigue.

tropa ('tro·pa) *n.f.* **1,** troop; troops (*pl.*). **2,** *Amer.* herd; drove; troop.

tropel (tro'pel) *n.m.* **1,** rush; rushing; bustle. **2,** gang; crowd; pack.

tropelía (tro·pe'li·a) *n.f.* **1,** abuse; outrage. **2,** confusion.

tropezar (tro·pe'θar; -'sar) *v.i.* [*pres.ind.* **tropiezo**; *pres.subjve.* **tropiece**; *pret.* **tropecé** (-'θe; -'se)] to stumble; trip. —**tropezar con,** *colloq.* to chance upon; stumble upon; meet.

tropezón (tro·pe'θon; -'son) *n.m.* **1,** stumble. **2,** slip; error.

-tropía (tro'pi·a) *suffix* -tropy; change; transformation: *entropía,* entropy.

trópico ('tro·pi·ko) *n.m.* tropic. —**tropical,** *adj.* tropical.

-trópico ('tro·pi·ko) *suffix* -tropic; -tropal; -tropous; *forming adjectives corresponding to nouns ending in* **-tropismo**: *heliotrópico,* heliotropic.

tropiece (tro'pje·θe; -se) *v., pres. subjve. of* **tropezar.**

tropiezo (tro'pje·θo; -so) *n.m.* **1,** stumble. **2,** trouble; difficulty. **3,** obstacle; stumbling block. **4,** slip; error. **5,** mishap. —*v., pres.ind. of* **tropezar.**

tropismo (tro'pis·mo) *n.m.* tropism.

-tropismo (tro'pis·mo) *suffix* -tropism; tendency to turn toward; turning: *heliotropismo,* heliotropism.

tropo ('tro·po) *n.m.* figure of speech; trope.

tropo- (tro·po) *prefix* tropo-; change; transformation: *troposfera,* troposphere.

troposfera (tro·pos'fe·ra) *n.f.* troposphere.

troqué (tro'ke) *v., 1st pers.sing. pret. of* **trocar.**

troquel (tro'kel) *n.m.* die; stamp. —**troquelar,** *v.t.* to die-stamp.

troqueo (tro'ke·o) *n.m.* trochee.

trotamundos (tro·ta'mun·dos) *n.m. & f.sing. & pl.* globetrotter.

trotar (tro'tar) *v.i.* **1,** to trot. **2,** *colloq.* to be on the run; hustle. —**trotón,** *adj.* trotting —*n.m.* horse, esp. a trotter.

trote ('tro·te) *n.m.* **1,** trot. **2,** *colloq.* chore; hard task. —**al trote, 1,** on the double; fast. **2,** at a trot.

troupe ('tru·pe) *n.f.* troupe.

trousseau (tru'so) *n.m. or f.* trousseau.

trova ('tro·βa) *n.f.* song; ballad; lyric; love song. —**trovador,** *n.m.* troubadour. —**trovar,** *v.i. & t.* to versify; lyricize.

Troya ('tro·ja) *n.f.* Troy, *in* **ahí, allí** *or* **aquí fué Troya,** *colloq.* that's when (*or* where) the fireworks started. —**ardió Troya,** *colloq.* the fireworks started; all hell broke loose.

troza ('tro·θa; -sa) *n.f.* log; timber.

trozar (tro'θar; -'sar) *v.t.* [*pres. subjve.* **troce;** *pret.* **trocé**] to cut off; lop.

trozo ('tro·θo; -so) *n.m.* **1,** piece; chunk; bit. **2,** passage; excerpt.

truco ('tru·ko) *n.m.* trick; legerdemain. —**trucos,** *n.m.pl.* pool (*game*).

truculento (tru·ku'len·to) *adj.* truculent. —**truculencia,** *n.f.* truculence.

trucha ('tru·tʃa) *n.f.* trout.

trueco ('trwe·ko) *v., pres.ind. of* **trocar.** —*n.m.* = **trueque.**

truene ('trwe·ne) *v., pres.subjve. of* **tronar.**

trueno ('trwe·no) *n.m.* **1,** thunder. **2,** thunderclap. —*v., pres.ind. of* **tronar.**

trueque ('trwe·ke) *n.m.* **1,** exchange. **2,** barter; bartering. **3,** change; transformation. —*v., pres. subjve. of* **trocar.** —**a trueque de,** instead of. —**a** *or* **en trueque,** in exchange.

trufa ('tru·fa) *n.f.* **1,** truffle. **2,** lie; fib.

truhán (tru'an) *adj.* scoundrelly; rascally. —*n.m.* scoundrel; rascal. —**truhanesco,** *adj.* rascally; knavish.

truhanada (tru·a'na·ða) *n.f.* **1,** rascally act. **2,** gang of crooks.

truhanería (tru·a·ne'ri·a) *n.f.* **1,** knavery; rascality. **2,** mischievousness; buffoonery. **3,** gang of rascals.

trujamán (tru·xa'man) *also,* **trujimán** (tru·xi-) *n.m.* wizard; whiz; expert.

trullo ('tru·ʎo; -jo) *n.m.* teal.

truncar (trun'kar) *v.t.* [*pres. subjve.* **trunque** ('trun·ke); *pret.* **trunqué** (-'ke)] **1,** to truncate; lop. **2,** to make or leave incomplete. **3,** to block; hinder; disrupt. —**truncamiento,** *n.m.* truncation.

trusa ('tru·sa) *n.f., Amer.* bathing suit; trunks (*pl.*).

tsetsé (tse'tse) *n.f.* tsetse.

tu (tu) *poss.adj.m. & f.sing.* [*m. & f.pl.* **tus**], *agreeing in number with the thing possessed* your; thy; thine.

tú (tu) *pers.pron.2ndpers.sing.* you; thou. —**de tú por tú,** on intimate terms.

tualet (twa'let) *n.m.* [*pl.* **tualets**] toilet; lavatory.

tuba ('tu·βa) *n.f.* tuba.

tuberculina (tu·βer·ku'li·na) *n.f.* tuberculin.

tubérculo (tu'βer·ku·lo) *n.m.* **1,** tubercle. **2,** tuber.

tuberculosis (tu·βer·ku'lo·sis) *n.f.* tuberculosis. —**tuberculoso,** *adj.* tuberculous; tubercular. —*n.m.* tubercular.

tubería (tu·βe'ri·a) *n.f.* **1,** pipes (*pl.*); tubing. **2,** plumbing. **3,** pipeline.

tuberosa (tu·βe'ro·sa) *n.f.* tuberose.

tuberoso (tu·βe'ro·so) *adj.* tuberous.

tubo ('tu·βo) *n.m.* **1,** tube. **2,** pipe. —**tubular** (-βu'lar) *adj.* tubular.

tucán (tu'kan) *n.m.* toucan.

-tud ('tuð) *suffix* -tude; -ness; *forming abstract nouns denoting* quality; condition; state: *verosimilitud,* verisimilitude; *acritud,* acridness.

tudesco (tu'ðes·ko) *adj.* Teutonic; German. —*n.m.* Teuton; German.

tuerca ('twer·ka) *n.f., mech.* nut. —**tuerca de mariposa,** wing nut.

tuerces ('twer·θes; -ses) *v., 2nd pers.sing.pres.ind. of* **torcer.**

tuerto ('twer·to) *adj.* **1,** one-eyed. **2,** crosseyed. —*n.m.* **1,** one-eyed person. **2,** crosseyed person. **3,** *obs.* wrong; injustice. —**a tuertas,** wrongly; contrariwise. —**a tuertas o a derechas,** *also,* **a tuerto o a derecho,** rightly or wrongly.

tuerza ('twer·θa; -sa) *v., pres. subjve. of* **torcer.**
tuerzo ('twer·θo; -so) *v., 1st pers. sing.pres.ind. of* **torcer.**
tueste ('twes·te) *v., pres.subjve. of* **tostar.**
tuesto ('twes·to) *v., pres.ind. of* **tostar.**
tuétano ('twe·ta·no) *n.m.* marrow.
tufo ('tu·fo) *n.f.* **1,** fume; vapor. **2,** *colloq.* unpleasant odor; reek. **3,** *often pl., colloq.* haughtiness; airs (*pl.*). **4,** lock of hair; tuft; bang.
tugurio (tu'ɣu·rjo) *n.m.* **1,** shepherd's hut. **2,** *colloq.* hovel; dump.
tul (tul) *n.m.* **1,** tulle. **2,** = **tule.**
tule ('tu·le) *n.m., Amer.* a kind of reed used in making cane chairs, straw hats, etc. *Also,* **tul.**
tulio ('tu·ljo) *n.m.* thulium.
tulipa (tu'li·pa) *n.f.* light globe.
tulipán (tu·li'pan) *n.m.* tulip.
tullido (tu'ʎi·ðo; -'ji·ðo) *adj.* crippled; lame. —*n.m.* cripple.
tullir (tu'ʎir; -'jir) *v.t.* to cripple; lame. —**tullirse,** *v.r.* to become crippled.
tumba ('tum·ba) *n.f.* **1,** tomb. **2,** *Amer.* felling, as of trees. **3,** *Amer.* forest clearing.
tumbar (tum'bar) *v.t.* to fell; knock down; tumble. —**tumbarse,** *v.r., colloq.* to lie down.
tumbo ('tum·bo) *n.m.* tumble; tumbling.
tumefacción (tu·me·fak'θjon; -'sjon) *n.f.* tumefaction; tumidity. —**tumefacto** (-'fak·to) *adj.* tumid.
tumescente (tu·mes'θen·te; -me·'sen·te) *adj.* tumescent. —**tumescencia,** *n.f.* tumescence.
túmido ('tu·mi·ðo) *adj.* tumid; swollen.
tumor (tu'mor) *n.m.* tumor.
túmulo ('tu·mu·lo) *n.m.* **1,** burial mound; tomb. **2,** catafalque. **3,** mound.
tumulto (tu'mul·to) *n.m.* tumult. —**tumultuoso** (-'two·so) *adj.* tumultuous.
tumultuar (tu·mul'twar) *v.t.* to incite to riot. —**tumultuarse,** *v.r.* to riot.
tuna ('tu·na) *n.f.* **1,** prickly pear. **2,** *colloq.* dissolute life. —**tunal,** *n.m.* prickly pear cactus.
tunanta (tu'nan·ta) *n.f.* hussy; wench.
tunante (tu'nan·te) *n.m.* rogue; scoundrel.
tunar (tu'nar) *v.i.* to bum around; be a hobo.
tunda ('tun·da) *n.f., colloq.* beating; whipping.
tundir (tun'dir) *v.t.* to beat; whip; drub.
tundra ('tun·dra) *n.f.* tundra.
tunear (tu·ne'ar) *v.i.* to live or behave as a scoundrel.
túnel ('tu·nel) *n.m.* tunnel.
tungsteno (tunɣs'te·no) *n.m.* tungsten.
túnica ('tu·ni·ka) *n.f.* tunic; robe.
tuno ('tu·no) *adj.* scoundrelly; rascally. —*n.m.* scoundrel; rascal.
tuntún (tun'tun) *n.m., in* **al (buen) tuntún,** *colloq.* **1,** gropingly; by trial and error. **2,** blindly; helter-skelter.
tupé (tu'pe) *n.m.* **1,** toupee. **2,** nerve; audacity.
tupido (tu'pi·do) *adj.* **1,** thick; dense. **2,** obstructed; blocked; stopped up. **3,** filled; crammed.
tupir (tu'pir) *v.t.* **1,** to fill; cram. **2,** to obstruct; block; stop up. —**tupirse,** *v.r.* **1,** to become full; be gorged. **2,** to become obstructed. **3,** *Amer.* to become morose; become stultified. **4,** *Amer.* to be astonished.
turba ('tur·βa) *n.f.* **1,** mob; crowd. **2,** peat; turf.
turbante (tur'βan·te) *n.m.* turban.
turbar (tur'βar) *v.t.* to disturb; trouble; upset; discomfit. —**turbación,** *n.f.* perturbation; discomfiture.
turbidez (tur·βi'ðeθ; -'ðes) *n.f.* turbidity.
turbina (tur'βi·na) *n.f.* turbine.
turbio ('tur·βjo) *adj.* **1,** turbid; murky. **2,** muddled; confused. —**turbios,** *n.m.pl.* dregs, esp. oil dregs.
turbión (tur'βion) *n.m.* **1,** squall; thunderstorm. **2,** maelstrom. **3,** *fig.* hail; avalanche.
turbonada (tur·βo'na·ða) *n.f.* squall; pelting shower.
turbulento (tur·βu'len·to) *adj.* turbulent. —**turbulencia,** *n.f.* turbulence.
turco ('tur·ko) *adj.* & *n.m.* Turkish. —*n.m.* Turk.
turf (turf) *n.m., sports* turf.

turgente (tur'xen·te) *adj.* turgid. —**turgencia,** *n.f.* turgidity.
turista (tu'ris·ta) *n.m. & f.* tourist. —**turismo,** *n.m.* touring; tourism. —**turístico,** *adj.* tourist (*attrib.*).
turmalina (tur·ma'li·na) *n.f.* tourmaline.
turnar (tur'nar) *v.i.* **1,** to alternate; take turns. **2,** to work shifts.
turno ('tur·no) *n.m.* **1,** turn. **2,** shift. —**de turno,** on duty; open (*said of a drugstore*).
turquesa (tur'ke·sa) *n.f.* turquoise.
turquí (tur'ki) *adj. & n.m.* deep blue.
turrón (tu'rron) *n.m.* **1,** nougat. **2,** *fig.* toothsome morsel. —**romper el turrón,** *Amer.* to switch from polite to informal address.
turulato (tu·ru'la·to) *adj., colloq.* stunned; agape; dumfounded.
tus (tus) *poss.adj., pl. of* **tu** (*agreeing in number with the things possessed*) your; thy; thine.
tusa ('tu·sa) *n.f., Amer.* **1,** corncob. **2,** corn husk. **3,** *fig.* rubbish.
tusar (tu'sar) *v.t., Amer.* to cut; crop; shear.
tutear (tu·te'ar) *v.t. & i.* to use the familiar pronouns **tú** and **te** in addressing someone. —**tuteo** (-'te·o) *n.m.* use of **tú** and **te.**
tutela (tu'te·la) *n.f.* **1,** tutelage; guardianship. **2,** tutorage. —**tutelar,** *adj.* tutelary.
tutiplén (tu·ti'plen) *n.m., in* **a tutiplén,** in abundance.
tutor (tu'tor) *n.m.* tutor. —**tutora,** *n.f.* female tutor. —**tutoría,** *n.f.* tutelage.
tutti-frutti ('tu·ti'fru·ti) *n.m.* tutti-frutti.
tuturuto (tu·tu'ru·to) *adj., Amer., colloq.* = **turulato.**
tuturutú (tu·tu·ru'tu) *n.m.* trumpet or bugle call.
tuve ('tu·βe) *v., pret. of* **tener.**
tuyo ('tu·jo) *poss.pron.m.sing.* [*fem.* **tuya;** *pl.* **tuyos, tuyas**] yours; thine. —*poss.adj.m.sing., used after a noun* your; of yours; thy; of thine.
tuza ('tu·θa; -sa) *n.f., Amer.* gopher.

U

U, u (u) *n.f.* 24th letter of the Spanish alphabet.
U. *abbr. of* **usted.**
u (u) *conj.* or. *Used in place of* **o** *before words beginning with* o *or* ho.
ubérrimo (u'βe·rri·mo) *adj.* extremely fruitful, fertile or abundant.
ubicación (u·bi·ka'θjon; -'sjon) *n.f.* **1,** location; situation. **2,** *Amer.* placing; placement.
ubicar (u·βi'kar) *v.i.* [*pres.subjve.* **ubique** (u'βi·ke); *pret.* **ubiqué** (-'ke)] to lie; be situated. —*v.t., Amer.* to locate; situate; place. —**ubicarse,** *v.r.* **1,** to lie; be situated. **2,** *Amer.* to orient oneself; take one's bearings.
ubicuo (u'βi·kwo) *adj.* ubiquitous. —**ubicuidad** (-kwi'ðað) *n.f.* ubiquity.
ubre ('u·βre) *n.f.* udder; teat.
ubrera (u'βre·ra) *n.f.* thrush (*disease*).
-ucho ('u·tʃo) *fem.* **-ucha** ('u·tʃa) *suffix, forming diminutives, usu. derog.: cuartucho,* hut; *debilucho,* feeble.
Ud. *abbr. of* **usted.**
-udo ('u·ðo) *fem.* **-uda** ('u·ða) *suffix, forming adjectives denoting* strongly characterized by; having abundance of: *barbudo,* heavy-bearded.
Uds. *abbr. of* **ustedes.**
-uelo ('we·lo) *fem.* **-uela** (-la) *suffix, forming diminutives: mozuelo,* youngster.
-ueño ('we·ɲo) *fem.* **-ueña** (-ɲa) *suffix, forming adjectives denoting* tendency; characteristic: *risueño,* smiling; cheerful.
¡uf! (uf) *interj.* ugh! (*denoting weariness or annoyance*).
ufanarse (u·fa'nar·se) *v.r.* to boast; brag.
ufanía (u·fa'ni·a) *n.f.* **1,** conceit; airs (*pl.*). **2,** airiness; jauntiness. **3,** contentment; satisfaction.
ufano (u'fa·no) *adj.* **1,** conceited; haughty. **2,** airy; jaunty. **3,** content; satisfied.
ujier (u'xjer) *n.m.* usher; doorman.

ukase *also,* **ucase** (u'ka·se) *n.m.* ukase.
ukulele (u·ku'le·le) *n.m.* ukulele.
-ula (u·la) *suffix* -ule; *forming diminutives: espórula,* sporule.
úlcera ('ul·θe·ra; 'ul·se-) *n.f.* ulcer. —**ulceroso,** *adj.* ulcerous.
ulcerar (ul·θe'rar; ul·se-) *v.t.* to ulcerate. —**ulcerarse,** *v.r.* to ulcerate; become ulcerated. —**ulceración,** *n.f.* ulceration.
-ulento (u'len·to) *fem.* **-ulenta** (-ta) *suffix* -ulent; *forming adjectives denoting* abounding in: *virulento,* virulent.
-ulo (u·lo) *fem.* **-ula** (-la) *suffix* -ulous; tending to; full of; characterized by: *trémulo,* tremulous; *crédulo,* credulous.
ulterior (ul·te'rjor) *adj.* ulterior.
últimamente (ul·ti·ma'men·te) *adv.* **1,** finally; lastly. **2,** lately.
ultimar (ul·ti'mar) *v.t.* to finish; end; finish off.
ultimatum (ul·ti'ma·tum) *n.m. sing. & pl.* **1,** ultimatum. **2,** *colloq.* last say; final say.
último ('ul·ti·mo) *adj.* last; final; ultimate. —**a la última (moda),** in the latest (fashion). —**a la última hora,** at the last moment; at the eleventh hour. —**a últimos de,** at the end of (a month). —**estar en las últimas,** to be at one's (*or* its) end; be on one's (*or* its) last legs. —**por último,** in the end; at last; finally.
ultra ('ul·tra) *adj.* ultra; extreme. —*n.m. & f.* ultra; extremist.
ultra- (ul·tra) *prefix* ultra-; **1,** on the other side of; beyond: *ultravioleta,* ultraviolet. **2,** extreme; excessive: *ultranacionalismo,* ultranationalism.
ultraje (ul'tra·xe) *n.m.* outrage. —**ultrajar,** *v.t.* to outrage. —**ultrajante,** *adj.* outrageous.
ultramar (ul·tra'mar) *n.m.* land beyond the sea. —**de ultramar,** overseas.
ultramarino (ul·tra·ma'ri·no) *adj. & n.m.* ultramarine. —**tienda de ultramarinos,** delicatessen.
ultranza (ul'tran·θa; -sa) *in* **a ultranza,** to the end; to the utmost.
ultratumba (ul·tra'tum·ba) *adv.* beyond the grave.
ultravioleta (ul·tra·βjo'le·ta) *adj.* ultraviolet.
ulular (u·lu'lar) *v.i.* to ululate. —**ululación,** *n.f., also,* **ululato,** *n.m.* ululation.
umbilical (um·bi·li'kal) *adj.* umbilical.
umbral (um'bral) *n.m.* **1,** threshold; doorsill. **2,** lintel.
-umbre ('um·bre) *suffix, forming abstract nouns denoting* quality; condition: *muchedumbre,* swarm; *pesadumbre,* sorrow.
umbría (um'bri·a) *n.f.* shade; shadow.
umbrío (um'bri·o) *adj.* shady; dark.
umbroso (um'bro·so) *adj.* shady; umbrageous.
un (un) *indef.article m.sing.* a; an. —*adj.m.sing.* one.
una ('u·na) *indef.article, adj. & pron., fem. of* **un** *or* **uno.** —**a una, 1,** jointly; together. **2,** at one; of one accord. —**la una,** one o'clock.
unánime (u'na·ni·me) *adj.* unanimous. —**unanimidad,** *n.f.* unanimity. —**por unanimidad,** unanimously.
unas ('u·nas) *indef.pron. & adj., fem. of* **unos.**
unción (un'θjon; -'sjon) *n.m.* unction.
uncir (un'θir; -'sir) *v.t.* [*pres.ind.* **unzo, unces;** *pres.subjve.* **unza**] to yoke.
undécimo (un'de·θi·mo; -si·mo) *adj. & n.m.* eleventh.
-undo ('un·do) *suffix, forming adjectives denoting* quality; condition: *rubicundo,* rubicund; *rotundo,* rotund.
undular (un·du'lar) *v.i.* = **ondular.** —**undulación,** *n.f.* = **ondulación.**
ungir (un'xir) *v.t.* [*pres.ind.* **unjo, unges;** *pres.subjve.* **unja**] to anoint. —**ungimiento,** *n.m.* anointment.
ungüento (un'gwen·to) *n.m.* ointment.
uni- (u·ni) *prefix* uni-; one; single: *unísono,* unison; *unicornio,* unicorn.
unicameral (u·ni·ka·me'ral) *adj.* unicameral.
unicelular (u·ni·θe·lu'lar; u·ni·se-) *adj.* unicellular.
unicidad (u·ni·θi'ðað; -si'ðað) *n.f.* singleness.
único ('u·ni·ko) *adj.* **1,** only; sole; single. **2,** unique. —**únicamente,** *adv.* only; solely.

unicornio (u·ni'kor·njo) *n.m.* unicorn.
unidad (u·ni'ðað) *n.f.* **1,** unity. **2,** unit.
unidamente (u·ni·ða'men·te) *adv.* jointly; together; unitedly.
unido (u'ni·ðo) *adj.* **1,** united; joined. **2,** close.
unificar (u·ni·fi'kar) *v.t.* [*pres. subjve.* **unifique** (-'fi·ke); *pret.* **unifiqué** (-'ke)] to unify. —**unificación,** *n.f.* unification.
uniformar (u·ni·for'mar) *v.t.* **1,** to make uniform. **2,** to uniform; furnish with a uniform. —**uniforme** (-'for·me) *adj. & n.m.* uniform. —**uniformidad,** *n.f.* uniformity.
unigénito (u·ni'xe·ni·to) *adj.* only-begotten.
unilateral (u·ni·la·te'ral) *adj.* unilateral.
unión (u'njon) *n.f.* **1,** union. **2,** joining; uniting. **3,** unity; concord. **4,** combination; fusion. **5,** junction; juncture. **6,** joint; seam. **7,** merging; merger.
unionismo (u·njo'nis·mo) *n.m.* unionism. —**unionista,** *n.m. & f.* unionist.
unipersonal (u·ni·per·so'nal) *adj.* **1,** unipersonal. **2,** *gram.* impersonal.
unir (u'nir) *v.t.* **1,** to unite. **2,** to join; connect; merge. —**unirse,** *v.r.* **1,** to unite; join; merge. **2,** *fol. by* **a,** to join; become a member of. **3,** to wed; be married.
unisexual (u·ni·sek'swal) *adj.* unisexual.
unisón (u·ni'son) *adj.* = **unísono.** —*n.m.* unison.
unísono (u'ni·so·no) *adj.* **1,** sounding alike; of like sound. **2,** sounding together; in unison. —**al unísono,** in unison.
unitario (u·ni'ta·rjo) *adj.* **1,** unitary; unit (*attrib.*). **2,** unitarian. **3,** *polit.* centralized; advocating centralization. —*n.m.* **1,** unitarian. **2,** *polit.* advocate of centralization.
univalente (u·ni'βa'len·te) *adj.* univalent.
univalvo (u·ni'βal·βo) *adj. & n.m.* univalve.
universal (u·ni·βer'sal) *adj.* **1,** universal. **2,** world (*attrib.*). —**universalidad,** *n.f.* universality.
universalismo (u·ni·βer·sa'lis·mo) *n.m.* universalism. —**universalista,** *adj. & n.m. & f.* universalist.
universalizar (u·ni·βer·sa·li·'θar; -'sar) *v.t.* [*pres.subjve.* **universalice** (-'li·θe; -se); *pret.* **universalicé** (-'θe; -'se)] to universalize.
universidad (u·ni·βer·si'ðað) *n.f.* **1,** university. **2,** = **universalidad.** —**universitario,** *adj.* university (*attrib.*). —*n.m.* university student.
universo (u·ni'βer·so) *n.m.* universe. —*adj.* universal.
unja ('un·xa) *v., pres.subjve. of* **ungir.**
unjo ('un·xo) *v., 1st pers.sing. pres.ind. of* **ungir.**
uno ('u·no) *indef.pron.* **1,** one. **2,** oneself. **3,** someone; somebody. —*adj. & n.m.* one. —**de uno en uno; uno a uno,** one by one. —**uno a otro,** each other; one another. —**uno de tantos,** one of many; one of the lot. —**uno que otro,** one here and there; some; a few. —**uno y otro,** both.
-uno ('u·no) *fem.* **-una** ('u·na) *suffix, forming adjectives denoting* having the characteristic of; like: *gatuno,* catlike; feline.
unos ('u·nos) *indef.pron.pl.* some: *Unos cantan, otros lloran,* Some sing, some weep. —*indef.adj.pl.* **1,** some; several; a few: *Compré unos libros,* I bought some books. **2,** *fol. by a numeral* some; approximately; about; more or less: *unos veinte libros,* about twenty books. —**unos cuantos,** a few; some; several.
untar (un'tar) *v.t.* **1,** to spread; smear; daub. **2,** *colloq.* to tip; bribe; grease: *untar las manos,* to grease the palm. —**untarse,** *v.r.* **1,** to spread or daub oneself with ointment, grease, etc. **2,** to line one's pockets; engage in pilferage. —**untadura,** *n.f.* = **untura.** —**untamiento,** *n.m.* daubing; smearing.
unto ('un·to) *n.m.* ointment; pomade.
untuoso (un'two·so) *also,* **untoso** (-'to·so) *adj.* unctuous; greasy. —**untuosidad,** *n.f.* unctuousness.
untura (un'tu·ra) *n.f.* **1,** ointment; pomade. **2,** daubing; smearing.
unza ('un·θa; -sa) *v., pres.subjve. of* **uncir.**
unzo ('un·θo; -so) *v., 1st pers. sing.pres.ind. of* **uncir.**
uña ('u·ɲa) *n.f.* **1,** nail; fingernail; toenail. **2,** hoof. **3,** claw; hook. **4,**

plectrum. **5,** *colloq.* greed; itchy fingers. —**a uña de caballo,** at full gallop. —**enseñar** *or* **mostrar las uñas,** to show one's claws. —**ser uña y carne,** to be very close friends; be hand in glove. —**tener uñas largas,** to have itchy fingers.
uñada (u'ɲa·ða) *n.f.* scratch.
uñero (u'ɲe·ro) *n.m.* ingrown toenail.
uñir (u'ɲir) *v.t., dial.* [*pret.* **uñí, uñó** (u'ɲo); *ger.* **uñendo** (u'ɲen·do)] = **uncir.**
¡upa! ('u·pa) *interj.* up, up!; hoopla!
-ura ('u·ra) *suffix* -ure; *forming nouns denoting* **1,** quality; condition: *compostura,* composure; *bravura,* bravery. **2,** action; result of action; process: *pintura,* picture; painting. **3,** means; instrument: *embocadura,* mouthpiece; opening. **4,** art: *escultura,* sculpture. **5,** office; function: *prefectura,* prefecture.
uranálisis (u·ra'na·li·sis) *n.m. or f.sing. & pl.* urinalysis.
uranio (u'ra·njo) *n.m.* uranium.
Urano (u'ra·no) *n.m.* Uranus.
urbanidad (ur·βa·ni'ðað) *n.f.* urbanity; civility; manners (*pl.*).
urbanismo (ur·βa'nis·mo) *n.m.* city planning.
urbanización (ur·βa·ni·θa'θjon; -sa'sjon) *n.f.* **1,** urbanization. **2,** *chiefly Amer.* housing development.
urbanizar (ur·βa·ni'θar; -'sar) *v.t.* [*pres.subjve.* **urbanice** (-'ni·θe; -se); *pret.* **urbanicé** (-'θe; -'se)] **1,** to urbanize. **2,** to develop (land).
urbano (ur'βa·no) *adj.* **1,** urban. **2,** urbane; polite.
urbe ('ur·βe) *n.f.* city; metropolis.
urdimbre (ur'ðim·bre) *also,* **urdiembre** (-'ðjem·bre) *n.f.* **1,** *weaving* warp. **2,** *lit. & fig.* weave.
urdir (ur'ðir) *v.t.* **1,** to twine; warp; weave. **2,** *fig.* to weave; concoct; plot.
urea (u're·a) *n.f.* urea.
uremia (u're·mja) *n.f.* uremia. —**urémico** (u're·mi·ko) *adj.* uremic.
uréter (u're·ter) *n.m.* ureter.
uretra (u're·tra) *n.f.* urethra.
urgente (ur'xen·te) *adj.* urgent. —**urgencia,** *n.f.* urgency. —**de urgencia,** **1,** urgent. **2,** urgently.
urgir (ur'xir) *v.i.* [*pres.ind.* **urjo** (-xo), **urges;** *pres.subjve.* **urja** (-xa)] **1,** to be urgent. **2,** to urge; insist. —*v.t., Amer.* to urge.
-uria ('u·rja) *suffix* -uria; urine; a diseased condition of the urine: *albuminuria,* albuminuria.
úrico ('u·ri·ko) *adj.* uric.
urinación (u·ri·na'θjon; -'sjon) *n.f.* urination.
urinal (u·ri'nal) *adj.* urinary. —*n.m.* urinal.
urinálisis (u·ri'na·li·sis) *n.m. or f.sing. & pl.* urinalysis.
urinario (u·ri'na·rjo) *adj.* urinary. —*n.m.* urinal.
urna ('ur·na) *n.f.* **1,** urn. **2,** showcase. **3,** ballot box; *pl.* polls.
uro- (u·ro) *prefix* uro-; urine; urinary tract: *uroscopia,* uroscopy; *urología,* urology.
-uro ('u·ro) *suffix, chem.* -ide; *forming names of binary compounds: cloruro,* chloride.
urología (u·ro·lo'xi·a) *n.f.* urology. —**urológico** (-'lo·xi·ko) *adj.* urological. —**urólogo** (u'ro·lo·ɣo) *n.m.* urologist.
urraca (u'rra·ka) *n.f.* magpie.
-urrón (u'rron) *fem.* **-urrona** (u'rro·na) *suffix, forming adjectives and nouns, usu.derog.: beaturrón,* prudish; prude.
úrsido ('ur·si·ðo) *adj.* ursine; bear (*attrib.*). —*n.m.* member of the bear family.
ursino (ur'si·no) *adj.* ursine.
urticaria (ur·ti'ka·rja) *n.f., pathol.* hives (*pl.*).
usado (u'sa·ðo) *adj.* **1,** used; worn. **2,** customary. **3,** second-hand. **4,** experienced; skilled.
usanza (u'san·θa; -sa) *n.f.* usage; custom; fashion.
usar (u'sar) *v.t.* **1,** to use. **2,** *fol. by* **de,** to make use of; take advantage of. **3,** to wear. **4,** to exercise; practice; follow. —*v.i., fol. by inf.* to be accustomed to; be used to; be wont to. —**usarse,** *v.r.* **1,** to be used; be employed. **2,** to be usual; be in fashion or usage; be customary.
-usco ('us·ko) *suffix, var. of* **-uzco.**
usía (u'si·a) *pers.pron., contr. of* **vuestra señoría,** your lordship.
usina (u'si·na) *n.f., Amer.* **1,** powerhouse. **2,** gas works. **3,** industrial plant.
uso ('u·so) *n.m.* **1,** use. **2,** usage; custom; fashion. **3,** habit; practice.

4, wearing; wear. 5, wear and tear. **—en buen uso,** *colloq.* in good condition. **—uso de razón,** discernment; understanding.
usted (us'teð) *pers.pron.* [*pl.* **ustedes**] you; yourself (*or* yourselves). *Used as subject of a verb or object of a preposition in polite or formal address. Construed with the verb in the third person.*
usual (u'swal) *adj.* usual. **—usualmente,** *adv.* usually.
usufructo (u·su'fruk·to) *n.m.* 1, usufruct. 2, benefits (*pl.*); advantage; profit.
usufructuar (u·su·fruk'twar) [*infl.:* **continuar**] *v.t.* 1, to have the usufruct of. 2, to make use of; turn to account; enjoy the benefits of.
usura (u'su·ra) *n.f.* usury. **—usurario,** *adj.* usurious. **—usurero,** *n.m.* usurer.
usurpar (u·sur'par) *v.t.* to usurp. **—usurpación,** *n.f.* usurpation. **—usurpador,** *adj.* usurping. **—*n.m.*** usurper.
utensilio (u·ten'si·ljo) *n.m.* utensil.
útero ('u·te·ro) *n.m.* uterus. **—uterino** (-'ri·no) *adj.* uterine.
útil ('u·til) *adj.* 1, useful; usable. 2, *law* allowable (time). **—*n.m.*** 1, *usu. pl.* utensils; tools. 2, usefulness.
utilidad (u·ti·li'ðað) *n.f.* 1, utility. 2, profit. 3, usefulness.
utilitario (u·ti·li'ta·rjo) *adj.* utilitarian. **—utilitarismo** (-'ris·mo) *n.m.* utilitarianism. **—utilitarista** (-'ris·ta) *adj. & n.m. & f.* utilitarian.
utilizar (u·ti·li'θar; -'sar) *v.t.* [*pres.subjve.* **utilice** (-'li·θe; -se); *pret.* **utilicé** (-'θe; -'se)] to utilize. **—utilizable,** *adj.* utilizable. **—utilización,** *n.f.* utilization.
utopía (u·to'pi·a) *also,* **utopia** (u'to·pja) *n.f.* Utopia. **—utópico** (u'to·pi·ko) *adj.* Utopian. **—utopismo,** *n.m.* utopianism. **—utopista,** *adj. & n.m. & f.* Utopian.
utrero (u'tre·ro) *n.m.* calf between two and three years old.
UU. *abbr. of* **ustedes.**
uva ('u·βa) *n.f.* 1, grape. 2, bunch of grapes. 3, grapes collectively. **—uvero,** *adj.* grape (*attrib.*). **—*n.m.*** grape vendor.
úvula ('u·βu·la) *n.f.* uvula. **—uvular,** *adj.* uvular.
uxoricidio (uk·so·ri'θi·ðjo; -'si·ðjo) *n.m.* uxoricide (*act*). **—uxoricida** (-'θi·ða; -'si·ða) *n.m.* uxoricide (*agent*).
-uzco ('uθ·ko; 'us·ko) *also,* **-usco** ('us·ko) *suffix, forming adjectives, esp. relating to colors, denoting* likeness; tendency toward: *blancuzco,* whitish; *verdusco,* greenish.
-uzo ('u·θo; -so) *fem.* **-uza** ('u·θa; -sa) *suffix, forming nouns and adjectives, often of derog. meaning: carnuza,* coarse cheap meat; *lechuzo,* suckling mule.

V

V,v (be) *n.f.* 25th letter of the Spanish alphabet.
V. *abbr. of* **usted.**
va (ba) *v., 3rd pers.sing.pres.ind. of* **ir.**
vaca ('ba·ka) *n.f.* 1, cow. 2, beef. 3, cowhide. **—hacerse la vaca; hacer vacas,** *Amer., colloq.* to play hooky. **—vaca marina,** sea cow.
vacación (ba·ka'θjon; -'sjon) *n.f., usu.pl.* vacation.
vacada (ba'ka·ða) *n.f.* drove of cattle.
vacancia (ba'kan·θja; -sja) *n.f.* vacancy; unfilled position; opening.
vacante (ba'kan·te) *adj.* vacant; unoccupied. **—*n.f.*** 1, vacancy; unfilled position; opening. 2, vacation.
vacar (ba'kar) *v.i.* [*pres.subjve.* **vaque;** *pret.* **vaqué**] 1, to be idle; be not working. 2, to be vacant, as a position. **—*v.t.*** to vacate.
vaciado (ba'θja·ðo; -'sja·ðo) *n.m.* cast; casting; molding.
vaciar (ba'θjar; -'sjar) *v.t.* [*infl.:* **enviar**] 1, to empty. 2, to vacate. 3, to hollow. 4, to cast; mold. 5, to grind; put a cutting edge on. **—*v.i.*** to discharge; empty; flow out or away. **—vaciarse,** *v.r.* 1, to become empty or vacant. 2, *colloq.* to unbosom oneself. 3, *colloq.* to let the cat out of the bag. 4, *Amer.,*

colloq. to come to naught; be foiled.

vaciedad (ba·θje'ðað; -sje'ðað) *n.f.* empty statement; tomfoolery.

vacilación (ba·θi·la'θjon; -si·la'sjon) *n.f.* **1,** swaying; tottering. **2,** hesitation; vacillation.

vacilar (ba·θi'lar; -si'lar) *v.i.* **1,** to vacillate; waver; hesitate. **2,** to sway; totter.

vacío (ba'θi·o; -'si·o) *adj.* **1,** empty; void. **2,** vacuous. **3,** unoccupied; untenanted. **4,** idle. **5,** concave; hollow. **6,** vain; presumptuous. —*n.m.* **1,** void; emptiness. **2,** vacuum. **3,** vacancy. **4,** concavity; hollowness. **5,** blank; gap. —**hacer el vacío a, 1,** to ignore; shun. **2,** to isolate.

vacuidad (ba·kwi'ðað) *n.f.* emptiness; vacuity.

vacuna (ba'ku·na) *n.f.* **1,** cowpox. **2,** vaccine.

vacunar (ba·ku'nar) *v.t.* to vaccinate. —**vacunación,** *n.f.* vaccination.

vacuno (ba'ku·no) *adj.* bovine. —**ganado vacuno,** cattle.

vacuo ('ba·kwo) *adj.* empty; vacuous.

vacuola (ba'kwo·la) *n.f.* vacuole.

vadear (ba·ðe'ar) *v.t.* **1,** to wade; ford. **2,** to get around; circumvent. **3,** to get through; get over. —**vadearse,** *v.r.* to behave; conduct oneself.

vado ('ba·ðo) *n.m.* ford.

vagabundear (ba·ɣa·βun·de·'ar) *v.i.* **1,** to wander; rove. **2,** to loaf; idle. —**vagabundeo** (-'de·o) *n.m.* vagabondage; vagrancy.

vagabundo (ba·ɣa'βun·do) *adj.* & *n.m.* vagabond; vagrant.

vagamente (ba·ɣa'men·te) *adv.* vaguely.

vagancia (ba'ɣan·θja; -sja) *n.f.* vagrancy. —**vagante,** *adj.* & *n.m.* & *f.* vagrant.

vagar (ba'ɣar) *v.i.* [*pres.subjve.* **vague**; *pret.* **vagué**] **1,** to roam; wander. **2,** to idle; loiter. —*n.m.* **1,** wandering; roaming. **2,** idleness.

vagaroso (ba·ɣa'ro·so) *adj.* flitting.

vagido (ba'xi·ðo) *n.m.* wail, esp. of a newborn child.

vagina (ba'xi·na) *n.f.* vagina. —**vaginal,** *adj.* vaginal.

vago ('ba·ɣo) *adj.* **1,** roaming; wandering. **2,** vague; indistinct. **3,** lax; loose. **4,** lazy; slothful. **5,** *painting* misty; hazy. —*n.m.* loafer; vagrant.

vagón (ba'ɣon) *n.m.* **1,** railroad car. **2,** wagon; van. —**vagón de cola,** caboose. —**vagón de mercancías,** freight car.

vagonada (ba·ɣo'na·ða) *n.f.* wagonload; carload.

vagoneta (ba·ɣo'ne·ta) *n.f.* **1,** *R.R.* gondola. **2,** dump car. **3,** station wagon. **4,** *Amer.* delivery truck; pickup.

vague ('ba·ɣe) *v., pres.subjve. of* **vagar.**

vagué (ba'ɣe) *v., 1st pers.sing. pret. of* **vagar.**

vaguear (ba·ɣe'ar) *v.i.* = **vagar.**

vaguedad (ba·ɣe'ðað) *n.f.* vagueness; ambiguity.

vaharada (ba·a'ra·ða) *n.f.* breath; puff.

vahido (ba'i·ðo) *n.m.* dizziness; fainting spell.

vaho ('ba·o) *n.m.* **1,** breath; exhalation. **2,** vapor; condensation. **3,** reek; stench.

vaina ('bai·na) *n.f.* **1,** scabbard; sheath. **2,** pod. **3,** *colloq.* bother; nuisance. **4,** *colloq.* tripe; humbug. **5,** *Amer., colloq.* luck. —**salirse de la vaina,** *Amer., colloq.* to fly off the handle.

vainica (bai'ni·ka) *n.f.* hemstitch.

vainilla (bai'ni·ʎa; -ja) *n.f.* **1,** vanilla. **2,** = **vainica.**

vais (bais) *v., 2nd pers.pl.pres.ind. of* **ir.**

vaivén (bai'βen) *n.m.* **1,** swinging; swaying. **2,** coming and going. **3,** *usu.pl.* ups and downs.

vajilla (ba'xi·ʎa; -ja) *n.f.* table service; set of dishes. —**vajilla de plata,** silverware. —**vajilla de porcelana,** chinaware.

val (bal) *n.m., contr. of* **valle.** *Used chiefly in place names.*

valdré (bal'dre) *v., fut. of* **valer.**

vale ('ba·le) *n.m.* **1,** bond; promissory note. **2,** voucher; coupon. **3,** farewell. —*n.m.* & *f., Amer.* pal; chum.

valedero (ba·le'ðe·ro) *adj.* worthy; valuable.

valedor (ba·le'ðor) *n.m.* **1,** defender; protector. **2,** *Amer.* comrade.

valencia (ba'len·θja; -sja) *n.f., chem.* valence.

-valente (βa'len·te) *suffix, chem.* -valent; *forming adjectives denoting* valence: *monovalente,* monovalent.

valentía (ba·len'ti·a) *n.f.* valor; courage; bravery.

valentón (ba·len'ton) *adj.* blustering; swaggering. —*n.m.* swaggerer; blusterer; braggart. —**valentonada,** *n.f.* boast; boasting; bluster. —**valentonería,** *n.f.* bravado; bluster.

valer (ba'ler) *v.i.* [*pres.ind.* **valgo, vales;** *pres.subjve.* **valga;** *fut.* **valdré**] **1,** to be worth. **2,** to be worthy; have value. **3,** to cost. **4,** to avail; be effective; be useful or helpful. **5,** to have power or authority. **6,** to be valid; count. **7,** to be good; be acceptable. —*v.t.* to produce; yield; bring about. —*n.m.* **1,** worth; value. **2,** power; influence. —**hacer valer, 1,** to assert. **2,** to make good; make effective. —**no poder valerse,** to be helpless. —**valer la pena,** to be worthwhile; be worth the trouble. —**valer más,** to be better; be preferable. —**valer por, 1,** to be good for; be sufficient for. **2,** to be worth; be equal to; be as good as. —**valerse de,** to take advantage of; avail oneself of. —**¡Válgame Dios!,** Bless my soul!

valeroso (ba·le'ro·so) *adj.* brave; courageous; valorous. —**valerosidad,** *n.f.* courage.

valga ('bal·ɣa) *v., pres.subjve. of* **valer.**

valgo ('bal·ɣo) *v., 1st pers.sing. pres.ind. of* **valer.**

valía (ba'li·a) *n.f.* **1,** value; worth. **2,** favor; influence. **3,** political sympathy.

validar (ba·li'ðar) *v.t.* to validate. —**validación,** *n.f.* validation.

valido (ba'li·ðo) *adj.* accepted; credited. —*n.m.* favorite; protégé.

válido ('ba·li·ðo) *adj.* valid. —**validez** (-'ðeθ; -'ðes) *n.f.* validity.

valiente (ba'ljen·te) *adj.* **1,** valiant; brave; courageous. **2,** *usu. ironic* great; big. —*n.m.* **1,** brave man. **2,** = **valentón.**

valija (ba'li·xa) *n.f.* **1,** valise; suitcase. **2,** mail bag; pouch. **3,** *Amer.* brief case; leather case.

valimiento (ba·li'mjen·to) *n.m.* **1,** benefit; advantage. **2,** favor; influence.

valioso (ba'ljo·so) *adj.* **1,** valuable. **2,** influential; powerful.

valor (ba'lor) *n.m.* **1,** value. **2,** worth. **3,** valor; courage. **4,** staunchness. **5,** effrontery; audacity. **6,** *pl.* securities; stocks; bonds.

valoración (ba·lo·ra'θjon; -'sjon) *n.f.* **1,** valuation; appraisal. **2,** increase in value.

valorar (ba·lo'rar) *v.t.* **1,** to appraise; evaluate. **2,** to value; prize. **3,** to increase the value of.

valorización (ba·lo·ri·θa'θjon; -sa'sjon) *n.f.* **1,** valuation; appraisal. **2,** increase in value or price.

valorizar (ba·lo·ri'θar; -'sar) *v.t.* [*pres.subjve.* **valorice** (-'ri·θe; -se); *pret.* **valoricé** (-'θe; -'se)] **1,** to appraise; evaluate. **2,** to increase the value or price of. —**valorizarse,** *v.r.* to increase in value or price.

vals (bals) *n.m.* waltz. —**valsar,** *v.i.* to waltz.

valuar (ba'lwar) *v.t.* [*pres.ind.* **valúo** (-'lu·o); *pres.subjve.* **valúe** (-'lu·e)] to appraise; evaluate; value. —**valuación,** *n.f.* valuation.

valva ('bal·βa) *n.f., bot.; zool.* valve.

válvula ('bal·βu·la) *n.f.* **1,** valve. **2,** *electronics* tube. —**valvular,** *adj.* valvular.

valla ('ba·ʎa; -ja) *n.f.* **1,** paling; fence; stockade. **2,** barrier; barricade. **3,** obstacle; impediment. **4,** *sports* hurdle.

valle ('ba·ʎe; -je) *n.m.* valley; vale.

vamos ('ba·mos) *v., 1st pers.pl. pres.ind. & impve. of* **ir.** —*interj.* well!; come, now!; why!; go on!; let's go!; stop!

vampiresa (bam·pi're·sa) *n.f.* vamp.

vampiro (bam'pi·ro) *n.m.* **1,** vampire. **2,** vampire bat.

van (ban) *v., 3rd pers.pl.pres.ind. of* **ir.**

vanadio (ba'na·ðjo) *n.m.* vanadium.

vanguardia (ban'gwar·ðja) *n.f.* vainglory. —**vanagloriarse** (-'rjar·se) *v.r.* to boast. —**vanaglorioso,** *adj.* vainglorious.

vanamente (ba·na'men·te) *adv.* vainly.

vándalo ('ban·da·lo) *adj. & n.m.* vandal. —**vandálico** (-'da·li·ko) *adj.* vandal. —**vandalismo,** *n.m.* vandalism.

vanguardia (ban'gwar·ðja) *n.f.* vanguard; van.
vanidad (ba·ni'ðað) *n.f.* vanity; conceit. —**vanidoso** (-'ðo·so) *adj.* vain; conceited.
vano ('ba·no) *adj.* vain. —*n.m.* bay; recess; door *or* window opening. —**en vano,** in vain.
vapor (ba'por) *n.m.* **1,** vapor; steam. **2,** exhalation; fume. **3,** steamboat; steamer. **4,** *usu.pl.* vertigo; faintness.
vaporizar (ba·po·ri'θar; -'sar) *v.t. & i.* [*pres.subjve.* **vaporice** (-'ri·θe; -se); *pret.* **vaporicé** ('θe; -'se)] to vaporize. —**vaporización,** *n.f.* vaporization. —**vaporizador,** *n.m.* vaporizer. —*adj.* vaporizing.
vaporoso (ba·po'ro·so) *adj.* vaporous. —**vaporosidad,** *n.f.* vaporousness.
vapulear (ba·pu·le'ar) *v.t.* to thrash; beat. —**vapuleo** (-'le·o) *n.m.* thrashing; beating.
vaque ('ba·ke) *v., pres.subjve. of* **vacar.**
vaqué (ba'ke) *v., 1st pers.sing. pret. of* **vacar.**
vaquería (ba·ke'ri·a) *n.f.* **1,** = **vacada. 2,** dairy.
vaquerizo (ba·ke'ri·θo; -so) *adj.* cattle (*attrib.*). —*n.m.* cattle tender; herdsman. —**vaqueriza,** *n.f.* winter stable for cattle.
vaquero (ba'ke·ro) *adj.* cattle (*attrib.*). —*n.m.* cowboy; cowhand.
vaqueta (ba'ke·ta) *n.f.* cowhide; calfskin.
vara ('ba·ra) *n.f.* **1,** rod; stick; shaft. **2,** wand; staff. **3,** a measure of length of about 33 inches; vara. **4,** influence; power; authority.
varada (ba'ra·ða) *n.f.* **1,** a running aground; grounding; stranding. **2,** *colloq.* frustrating experience.
varadero (ba·ra'ðe·ro) *n.m.* boatyard; graving beach.
varadura (ba·ra'ðu·ra) *n.f.* grounding; stranding.
varar (ba'rar) *v.i.* **1,** to run aground. **2,** to halt; come to a standstill. —*v.t.* **1,** to strand. **2,** to beach.
varear (ba·re'ar) *v.t.* **1,** to beat; club. **2,** to goad (a bull). **3,** to measure or sell by the vara. —**varearse,** *v.r.* to weaken; flag.
variable (ba'rja·βle) *adj. & n.f.* variable. —*adj.* changeable; fickle. —**variabilidad,** *n.f.* variability.
variación (ba·rja'θjon; -'sjon) *n.f.* **1,** variation. **2,** variance; divergence.
variado (ba'rja·ðo) *adj.* **1,** varied. **2,** variegated.
variante (ba'rjan·te) *adj.* variant; variable; changeable. —*n.f.* variant; variation.
variar (ba'rjar) *v.t. & i.* [*pres.ind.* **varío** (-'ri·o); *pres.subjve.* **varíe** (-'ri·e)] to vary; change.
várice ('ba·ri·θe; -se) *n.f.* varicosity; varicose vein.
varicela (ba·ri'θe·la; -'se·la) *n.f.* varicella; chicken pox.
varicocela (ba·ri·ko'θe·la, -'se·la) *n.f.* varicocele.
varicosis (ba·ri'ko·sis) *n.f.* varicose veins. —**varicoso,** *adj.* varicose. —**varicosidad,** *n.f.* varicosity.
variedad (ba·rje'ðað) *n.f.* variety. —**variedades,** *n.f.pl.* variety show.
varilla (ba'ri·ʎa; -ja) *n.f.* **1,** thin rod or stick. **2,** wand. **3,** rib, as of a fan, umbrella, etc. —**varillaje,** *n.m.* ribs (*pl.*); ribbing.
vario ('ba·rjo) *adj.* **1,** varied; various. **2,** variegated. **3,** fickle; variable. —**varios,** *adj.pl.* several; various.
variola (ba'rjo·la) *n.f.* variola.
varón (ba'ron) *n.m.* **1,** male person; male. **2,** man; adult man. —**varonil** (ba·ro'nil) *adj.* manly.
vas (bas) *v., 2nd pers.sing.pres.ind. of* **ir.**
vasallo (ba'sa·ʎo; -jo) *adj. & n.m.* vassal. —**vasallaje,** *n.m.* vassalage.
vascular (bas·ku'lar) *adj.* vascular.
vaselina (ba·se'li·na) *n.f.* vaseline.
vasija (ba'si·xa) *n.f.* **1,** vessel; receptacle. **2,** pottery; vessels collectively.
vaso ('ba·so) *n.m.* **1,** glass; drinking glass. **2,** glassful. **3,** vase. **4,** *anat.; bot.* vessel. **5,** vessel; container. **6,** washbowl; toilet bowl; urinal bowl.
vaso- (ba·so) *prefix* vaso-; vessel: *vasomotor,* vasomotor.
vástago ('bas·ta·ɣo) *n.m.* **1,** shoot; sprout. **2,** offspring; descendant; scion. **3,** *mech.* driving rod, esp. piston rod.
vasto ('bas·to) *adj.* vast. —**vastedad,** *n.f.* vastness.

vate ('ba·te) *n.m.* **1,** prophet. **2,** poet.
vatiaje (ba'tja·xe) *n.m.* wattage.
Vaticano (ba·ti'ka·no) *n.m.* Vatican. **—vaticano,** *adj.* Vatican.
vaticinio (ba·ti'θi·njo; -'si·njo) *n.m.* prophecy; prediction. **—vaticinar** (-θi'nar; -si'nar) *v.t.* to prophesy; predict. **—vaticinador,** *adj.* prophetic. **—***n.m.* seer.
vatímetro (ba'ti·me·tro) *n.m.* watt meter. *Also,* **vatiómetro** (ba·'tjo-).
vatio ('ba·tjo) *n.m.* watt.
vaya ('ba·ja) *v., pres.subjve. of* **ir.** **—***interj.* well now!; look here!; you don't say! **—¡vaya una idea!,** what an idea! **—***n.f.* scoff; jest.
Vd. *abbr. of* **usted.**
Vds. *abbr. of* **ustedes.**
ve (be) *v.* **1,** *2nd pers.sing.impve. of* **ir. 2,** *3rd pers.sing.pres.ind. of* **ver.**
vea ('be·a) *v., pres.subjve. of* **ver.**
vecinal (be·θi'nal; -si'nal) *adj.* neighborhood (*attrib.*); local.
vecindad (be·θin'dað; -sin'dað) *n.f.* **1,** vicinity. **2,** neighborhood.
vecindario (be·θin'da·rjo; be·sin-) *n.m.* neighborhood; community.
vecino (be'θi·no; -'si·no) *adj.* **1,** neighboring; near. **2,** like. **—***n.m.* **1,** neighbor. **2,** local resident. **—vecino a,** close to; bordering on or upon.
vector (bek'tor) *adj. & n.m.* vector. **—vectorial,** *adj.* vector (*attrib.*).
veda ('be·ða) *n.f.* **1,** prohibition. **2,** closed season.
vedado (be'ða·ðo) *n.m.* game park; game preserve.
vedar (be'ðar) *v.t.* to prohibit; forbid.
vedeja (be'ðe·xa) *n.f.* = **guedeja.**
vedette (be'ðet; *pl.* be'ðets) *n.f.* principal actress in musical shows.
vedija (be'ði·xa) *n.f.* **1,** mat or tangle of hair. **2,** curl of smoke.
veedor (be·e'ðor) *adj.* peering; prying; observant. **—***n.m.* **1,** inquisitive, observant person. **2,** overseer; inspector.
vega ('be·ɣa) *n.f.* **1,** fertile plain. **2,** *Amer.* tobacco plantation.
vegetación (be·xe·ta'θjon; -sjon) *n.f.* vegetation.
vegetal (be·xe'tal) *adj.* vegetal; vegetable. **—***n.m.* plant; vegetable.
vegetar (be·xe'tar) *v.i.* to vegetate.
vegetariano (be·xe·ta'rja·no) *adj. & n.m.* vegetarian.
vegetativo (be·xe·ta'ti·βo) *adj.* vegetative.
vehemente (be·e'men·te) *adj.* vehement. **—vehemencia,** *n.f.* vehemence.
vehículo (be'i·ku·lo) *n.m.* vehicle.
veintavo (bein'ta·βo) *adj. & n.m.* twentieth.
veinte ('bein·te) *adj. & n.m.* twenty.
veintena (bein'te·na) *n.f.* score; quantity of twenty.
veinteno (bein'te·no) *adj. & n.m.* twentieth.
veintésimo (bein'te·si·mo) *adj. & n.m.* = **vigésimo.**
vejación (be·xa'θjon; -'sjon) *n.f.* **1,** vexation. **2,** abuse; ill-treatment.
vejamen (be'xa·men) *n.m.* **1,** ill-treatment; abuse. **2,** taunt; sarcasm.
vejancón (be·xan'kon) *adj., colloq.* old; oldish. **—***n.m., colloq.* oldster; old fellow.
vejar (be'xar) *v.t.* **1,** to vex; annoy. **2,** to criticize; censure.
vejatorio (be·xa'to·rjo) *adj.* vexatious; annoying.
vejestorio (be·xes'to·rjo) *n.m., derog.* old man; relic.
vejete (be'xe·te) *n.m., colloq.* old codger.
vejez (be'xeθ; -'xes) *n.f.* **1,** old age. **2,** oldness; age. **3,** trite story; old story. **4,** senile act or behavior.
vejiga (be'xi·ɣa) *n.f.* **1,** bladder. **2,** blister.
vela ('be·la) *n.f.* **1,** wakefulness. **2,** vigil; watch. **3,** candle. **4,** sail. **—dar vela (a uno) en un entierro,** *colloq.* to let (someone) in on a matter; let (someone) have a say. **—en vela,** awake; wakeful **—estar a dos velas,** *colloq.* **1,** to be broke. **2,** to be blissfully ignorant. **—hacerse a la vela,** to sail; set sail. **—no tener vela en un entierro,** to have no say in a matter.
velaciones (be·la'θjo·nes; -'sjo·nes) *n.f.pl., also,* **misa de velaciones,** nuptial Mass.
velada (be'la·ða) *n.f.* **1,** evening. **2,** soirée. **—velada musical,** musicale.
velado (be'la·ðo) *adj.* **1,** veiled. **2,** fogged; blurred.
velador (be·la'ðor) *n.m.* **1,**

watcher; watchman; guard. 2, pedestal table; café table. 3, *Amer.* night table.
velamen (be'la·men) *n.m.* sail; sails (*pl.*); rigging. *Also,* **velaje** (-xe).
velar (be'lar) *v.t.* 1, to veil. 2, to fog; blur (the eyes, a photograph, etc.). 3, to hold a wake over. 4, to watch; watch over; take care of. 5, to keep vigil over. —*v.i.* 1, to be awake; stay awake. 2, to keep watch; keep vigil. —**velar por que** . . . . to take care that . . . ; be on the watch that . . . .
velar (be'lar) *adj.* velar.
velatorio (be·la'to·rjo) *n.m.* wake; vigil over the deceased.
veleidad (be·lei'ðað) *n.f.* 1, whim; whimsy. 2, fickleness; inconstancy. —**veleidoso,** *adj.* fickle; inconstant.
velero (be'le·ro) *adj.* 1, sail (*attrib.*); sailing. 2, swift; swift-sailing. —*n.m.* 1, sailboat. 2, sailmaker. 3, candlemaker.
veleta (be'le·ta) *n.f.* 1, vane; weather vane; weathercock. 2, bob; float. —*n.m.* & *f.* fickle person; weathercock.
velís (be'lis) *n.m., Amer.* valise.
velo ('be·lo) *n.m.* 1, veil. 2, veiling; curtain. 3, [*also,* **velo del paladar**] velum.
velocidad (be·lo·θi'ðað; -si'ðað) *n.f.* velocity; speed.
velocímetro (be·lo'θi·me·tro; -'si·me·tro) *n.m.* speedometer.
velocípedo (be·lo'θi·pe·ðo; -'si·pe·ðo) *n.m.* velocipede.
velódromo (be'lo·ðro·mo) *n.m.* velodrome.
velorio (be'lo·rjo) *n.m.* = **velatorio.**
veloz (be'loθ; -'los) *adj.* swift; speedy; fleet.
vello ('be·ʎo; -jo) *n.m.* 1, body hair. 2, fuzz; down.
vellón (be'ʎon; -'jon) *n.m.* 1, fleece. 2, tuft of wool. 3, an ancient Spanish coin. 4, *W.I.* dime.
vellonera (be·ʎo'ne·ra; be·jo-) *n.f., W.I.* 1, juke box. 2, vending machine.
velloso (be'ʎo·so; -'jo·so) *adj.* 1, fuzzy; downy. 2, hairy.
velludillo (be·ʎu'ði·ʎo; be·ju·'ði·jo) *n.m.* velveteen.
velludo (be'ʎu·ðo; -'ju·ðo) *adj.* hairy. —*n.m.* velvet; plush.
vena ('be·na) *n.f.* vein. —**estar en** *or* **de vena,** to be in the mood.
venablo (be'na·βlo) *n.m.* a short javelin or spear.
venado (be'na·ðo) *n.m.* 1, deer; stag. 2, venison. —**pintar venado,** *Amer.* to play hooky.
venal (be'nal) *adj.* 1, venal. 2, venous. —**venalidad,** *n.f.* venality.
venático (be'na·ti·ko) *adj. colloq.* eccentric; erratic.
vencedor (ben·θe'ðor; -se'ðor) *adj.* winning; victorious. —*n.m.* winner; victor.
vencejo (ben'θe·xo; -'se·xo) *n.m., ornith.* martin; swift.
vencer (ben'θer; -'ser) *v.t.* [*pres. ind.* **venzo;** *pres.subjve.* **venza**] 1, to vanquish; defeat. 2, to conquer; overcome; surmount. 3, to best. 4, to force; strain (a mechanism). 5, to impair through use or misuse. —*v.i.* 1, to win; be victorious. 2, to fall due; mature. 3, to expire; terminate. 4, to sag; twist or bend out of shape. —**vencerse,** *v.r.* to control oneself.
vencida (ben'θi·ða; -'si·ða) *n.f., in* **a la tercera va la vencida,** the third time does it. —**ir de vencida,** 1, to be losing; be getting the worst of it. 2, to be nearly over.
vencido (ben'θi·ðo; -'si·ðo) *adj.* 1, defeated; frustrated. 2, broken; worn; sagging. 3, due; overdue. 4, expired.
vencimiento (ben·θi'mjen·to; ben·si-) *n.m.* 1, expiration. 2, maturity. 3, due date. 4, defeat.
venda ('ben·da) *n.f.* 1, bandage. 2, blindfold.
vendaje (ben'da·xe) *n.m.* bandage; dressing. —**vendaje de yeso,** *surg.* plaster cast.
vendar (ben'dar) *v.t.* 1, to bandage. 2, to blindfold.
vendaval (ben·da'βal) *n.m.* strong, blustery wind.
vendedor (ben·de'ðor) *adj.* vending; selling. —*n.m.* 1, seller; vendor. 2, salesman.
vender (ben'der) *v.t.* & *i.* to sell; vend. —*v.t.* to sell out; betray —**venderse,** *v.r.* 1, to sell; be sold; be for sale. 2, to sell oneself; sell out. 3, *usu.fol. by* **por,** to offer one's all for; give all for. 4, *usu.fol. by* **por,** to pose as; pass oneself off as.

vendetta (ben'de·ta) *n.f.* vendetta.
vendible (ben'di·βle) *adj.* salable; marketable.
vendimia (ben'di·mja) *n.f.* grape harvest; vintage.
vendré (ben'dre) *v., fut. of* **venir.**
venduta (ben'du·ta) *n.f., Amer.* **1,** auction. **2,** vegetable shop.
veneciano (be·ne'θja·no; -'sja·no) *adj. & n.m.* Venetian. —**veneciana,** *n.f.* Venetian blind.
veneno (be'ne·no) *n.m.* poison; venom. —**venenoso,** *adj.* poisonous.
venerable (be·ne'ra·βle) *adj.* venerable. —**venerabilidad,** *n.f.* venerability; venerableness.
venerar (be·ne'rar) *v.t.* to venerate; honor. —**veneración;** *n.f.* veneration. —**venerando,** *adj.* venerable.
venéreo (be'ne·re·o) *adj.* venereal.
venero (be'ne·ro) *n.m.* **1,** water spring. **2,** origin; source. **3,** *mining* lode.
venga ('ben·ga) *v., pres.subjve. of* **venir.**
venganza (ben'gan·θa; -sa) *n.f.* vengeance; revenge.
vengar (ben'gar) *v.t.* [*pres.subjve.* **vengue** ('ben·ge); *pret.* **vengué** (-'ge)] to avenge; revenge. —**vengarse,** *v.r.* to take vengeance; avenge oneself. —**vengador,** *adj.* avenging. —*n.m.* avenger.
vengativo (ben·ga'ti·βo) *adj.* vengeful; vindictive.
vengo ('ben·go) *v., 1st pers.sing. pres.ind. of* **venir.**
venia ('be·nja) *n.f.* **1,** pardon; forgiveness. **2,** leave; permission. **3,** bow of the head; nod.
venial (be'njal) *adj.* venial. —**venialidad,** *n.f.* veniality.
venida (be'ni·ða) *n.f.* **1,** coming. **2,** coming back.
venidero (be·ni'ðe·ro) *adj.* future; coming.
venido (be'ni·ðo) *adj.* come; arrived. —**bien venido,** welcome.
venir (be'nir) *v.i.* [*pres.ind.* **vengo, vienes;** *pres.subjve.* **venga;** *fut.* **vendré;** *pret.* **vine;** *ger.* **viniendo**] **1,** to come. **2,** to suit; fit; befit. **3,** to concern; be of interest: *Eso no me va ni me viene,* That doesn't concern me one way or the other. —*aux. v., used with the gerund to form the progressive tenses: Vengo diciéndolo desde hace un año,* I have been saying it for a year. —**¿A qué viene esto?,** To what purpose is this? —**lo por venir,** the future. —**que viene,** coming; next: *el mes que viene,* next month. —**venir al caso; venir a cuento,** to be to the point; be appropriate. —**venirse abajo; venirse al suelo,** to fall; collapse.
venoso (be'no·so) *adj.* **1,** venous. **2,** veiny; veined.
venta ('ben·ta) *n.f.* **1,** sale. **2,** selling. **3,** roadside inn.
ventada (ben'ta·ða) *n.f.* gust of wind.
ventaja (ben'ta·xa) *n.f.* **1,** advantage. **2,** lead (*in a race or contest*): *Llevaba dos cuerpos de ventaja,* He had a two-length lead. **3,** odds given at play: *Te doy seis puntos de ventaja,* I spot you six points.
ventajista (ben·ta'xis·ta) *n.m. & f.* opportunist.
ventajoso (ben·ta'xo·so) *adj.* advantageous.
ventana (ben'ta·na) *n.f.* **1,** window. **2,** [*also,* **ventana de la nariz**] nostril. **3,** *anat.* fenestra.
ventanal (ben·ta'nal) *n.m.* large window; multiple window; bay window; church window.
ventanilla (ben·ta'ni·ʎa; -ja) *n.f.* **1,** small window; opening. **2,** window (*of a conveyance*). **3,** window offering information, service, etc. to the public.
ventarrón (ben·ta'rron) *n.m.* stiff wind; windstorm.
ventear (ben·te'ar) *also,* **ventar** (-'tar) *v.impers.* to blow, as wind. —*v.t.* **1,** to sniff; scent. **2,** to air. —*v.i.* = **ventosear.**
ventero (ben'te·ro) *n.m.* innkeeper.
ventilador (ben·ti·la'ðor) *n.m.* **1,** ventilator. **2,** fan; blower.
ventilar (ben·ti'lar) *v.t.* **1,** to ventilate; air. **2,** *fig.* to thrash out. —**ventilación,** *n.f.* ventilation.
ventisca (ben'tis·ka) *n.f.* **1,** snowstorm; blizzard. **2,** wind-driven snow.
ventiscar (ben·tis'kar) *v.impers.* [*pres.subjve.* **ventisque** (-'tis·ke)] **1,** to blow, as a blizzard. **2,** to be driven by the wind, as snow. *Also,* **ventisquear** (-ke'ar).

ventisquero (ben·tis'ke·ro) *n.m.* **1,** mountain glacier. **2,** = ventisca.

ventolera (ben·to'le·ra) *n.f.* **1,** gust of wind. **2,** *colloq.* draft; breeze. **3,** *colloq.* airs (*pl.*). **4,** *colloq.* caprice; whim.

ventosa (ben'to·sa) *n.f.* **1,** *zool.* sucker. **2,** cupping glass.

ventosear (ben·to·se'ar) *v.i.* to break wind.

ventoso (ben'to·so) *adj.* **1,** windy. **2,** flatulent. **—ventosidad,** *n.f.* flatulence.

ventral (ben'tral) *adj.* ventral.

ventrículo (ben'tri·ku·lo) *n.m.* *anat.* ventricle. **—ventricular,** *adj.* ventricular.

ventrílocuo (ben'tri·lo·kwo) *n.m.* ventriloquist. **—ventriloquia** (-'lo·kja) *n.f.* ventriloquism.

ventura (ben'tu·ra) *n.f.* **1,** felicity; bliss. **2,** chance; luck; fortune. **3,** hazard; risk. **—venturoso,** *adj.* lucky; fortunate. **—a la ventura,** aimlessly; at random. **—buena ventura,** fortune; fortunetelling. **—por ventura,** by chance; perchance. **—probar ventura,** to try one's luck; venture.

Venus ('be·nus) *n.f.* Venus; beautiful woman. **—***n.m., astron.* Venus.

venza ('ben·θa; -sa) *v., pres. subjve. of* **vencer.**

venzo ('ben·θo; -so) *v., 1st pers. sing. pres.ind. of* **vencer.**

ver (ber) *v.t. & i.* [*pres.ind.* **veo** ('be·o), **ves;** *pres.subjve.* **vea;** *pret.* **vi;** *ger.* **viendo;** *p.p.* **visto**] to see. **—***v.t.* **1,** to look into; examine. **2,** *fol. by* **de** *+inf.* to see about; try to: *Veré de hacerlo,* I will see about doing it; I will try to do it. **—***n.m.* **1,** sight. **2,** appearance; looks (*pl.*). **3,** view; opinion. **—verse,** *v.r.* **1,** to appear; seem; look. **2,** to be visible. **3,** to be obvious; be evident. **4,** to find oneself; happen to be. **—a** *or* **hasta más ver,** *colloq.* so long. **—allá veremos,** we shall see. **—a ver,** let's see. **—estar por ver,** to remain to be seen. **—no poder ver a (uno)** not to be able to stand (someone); hate the sight of. **—no tener nada que ver con,** to have nothing to do with; be irrelevant to. **—ser de ver,** to be worth seeing. **—tener que ver con,** to have to do with; deal with. **—vérselas con,** to come face to face with; confront. **—ver y creer,** seeing is believing. **—ya se ve,** of course; it is obvious.

vera ('be·ra) *n.f.* edge; border; side. **—a la vera de,** by the side of; near; beside.

veracidad (be·ra·θi'ðað; -si'ðað) *n.f.* veracity.

veranda (be'ran·da) *n.f.* veranda.

veranear (be·ra·ne'ar) *v.i.* to summer; spend the summer. **—veraneo** (-'ne·o) *n.m.* summering; summer vacation.

veraniego (be·ra'nje·ɣo) *adj.* summer (*attrib.*).

veranillo (be·ra'ni·ʎo; -jo) *n.m.* Indian summer.

verano (be'ra·no) *n.m.* **1,** summer. **2,** *Amer.* dry season.

veras ('be·ras) *n.f.pl.* fact (*sing.*); truth (*sing.*). **—de veras,** truly; really.

veraz (be'raθ; -'ras) *adj.* veracious; truthful.

verba ('ber·βa) *n.f.* eloquence; fluency.

verbal (ber'βal) *adj.* verbal.

verbatim (ber'βa·tim) *adj. & adv.* verbatim.

verbena (ber'βe·na) *n.f.* **1,** evening festival. **2,** *bot.* verbena.

verbigracia (ber·βi'ɣra·θja; -sja) for example; that is.

verbo ('ber·βo) *n.m.* **1,** verb. **2,** *cap., theol.* Word.

verborrea (ber·βo'rre·a) *n.f., colloq.* verbosity; verbiage.

verboso (ber'βo·so) *adj.* verbose. **—verbosidad,** *n.f.* verbosity.

verdad (ber'ðað) *n.f.* truth **—a decir verdad; a la verdad,** to be truthful; truthfully. **—de verdad, 1,** true; real. **2,** in fact; truly; really. **—¿es verdad?,** is it (*or* that) so? **—¿no es verdad?,** *also,* **¿verdad?,** isn't it (*or* that) so?

verdadero (ber·ða'ðe·ro) *adj.* **1,** true. **2,** real; genuine. **3,** truthful. **—verdaderamente,** *adv.* truly; verily.

verde ('ber·ðe) *adj.* **1,** green. **2,** verdant. **3,** unripe. **4,** off-color; risqué. **5,** *colloq.* unpromising; improbable. **—***n.m.* **1,** green. **2,** greenery. **—estar verde,** *colloq.* **1,** to be annoyed. **—poner verde,** *colloq.* **1,** to scold. **2,** *Amer.* to annoy. **—viejo verde,** *colloq.* old fop.

verdear (ber·ðe'ar) *v.i.* **1,** to tend to green; look greenish. **2,** to sprout; begin to grow; turn green. **—verdeante,** *adj.* verdant.

verdete (ber'ðe·te) *n.m.* verdigris.
verdolaga (ber·ðo'la·ɣa) *n.f.* purslane.
verdor (ber'ðor) *n.m.* **1,** verdure; verdancy. **2,** greenness.
verdoso (ber'ðo·so) *adj.* greenish.
verdugo (ber'ðu·ɣo) *n.m.* **1,** executioner. **2,** = **verdugón. 3,** *hortic.* shoot; sucker. **4,** *fig.* torment. **5,** rapier.
verdugón (ber·ðu'ɣon) *n.m.* **1,** welt; wale. **2,** whip; lash.
verdulería (ber·ðu·le'ri·a) *n.f.* vegetable shop. —**verdulero** (-'le·ro) *n.m.* vegetable man; vegetable vendor. —**verdulera,** *n.f., colloq.* hussy; fishwife.
verdura (ber'ðu·ra) *n.f.* **1,** verdure; verdancy. **2,** greenness. **3,** green; vegetable. **4,** greenery.
verdusco (ber'ðus·ko) *adj.* greenish; dark-green.
vereda (be're·ða) *n.f.* **1,** path; trail. **2,** *Amer.* sidewalk. —**poner en vereda,** to set aright; put on the right path.
veredicto (be·re'ðik·to) *n.m.* verdict.
verga ('ber·ɣa) *n.f.* **1,** *naut.* yard; spar. **2,** penis (*of animals; also, vulg., of the human male*).
vergajo (ber'ɣa·xo) *n.m.* **1,** short whip, esp. one made from a bull's penis. **2,** *colloq.* wretch; scoundrel.
vergel (ber'xel) *n.f.* garden; garden spot.
vergonzante (ber·ɣon'θan·te; -'san·te) *adj.* shameful.
vergonzoso (ber·ɣon'θo·so; -'so·so) *adj.* **1,** shameful. **2,** bashful; modest.
vergüenza (ber'ɣwen·θa; -sa) *n.f.* **1,** shame. **2,** bashfulness; modesty. **3,** embarrassment. **4,** *pl.* pudenda. —**tener vergüenza,** to be ashamed.
vericueto (be·ri'kwe·to) *n.m.* **1,** rough, difficult ground. **2,** *often pl.* twists and turns; maze.
verídico (be'ri·ði·ko) *adj.* true; truthful.
verificar (be·ri·fi'kar) *v.t.* [*pres. subjve.* **verifique** (-'fi·ke); *pret.* **verifiqué** (-'ke)] **1,** to verify. **2,** to fulfill; cause to take place; carry out. —**verificarse,** *v.r.* **1,** to be verified; prove true. **2,** to take place. —**verificable,** *adj.* verifiable. —**verificación,** *n.f.* verification.
verija (be'ri·xa) *n.f.* **1,** pubic parts; pubes. **2,** *Amer.* groin.
verja ('ber·xa) *n.f.* **1,** railing; fence. **2,** grating.
verme ('ber·me) *n.m.* intestinal worm.
vermi- (ber·mi) *prefix* vermi-; worm: *vermicida,* vermicide.
vermicida (ber·mi'θi·ða; -'si·ða) *n.m.* vermicide. —*adj.* vermicidal.
vermicular (ber·mi·ku'lar) *adj.* vermiculate; vermicular.
vermiforme (ber·mi'for·me) *adj.* vermiform.
vermífugo (ber'mi·fu·ɣo) *adj.* & *n.m.* vermifuge.
verminoso (ber·mi'no·so) *adj.* verminous.
vermut (ber'mut) *n.m.* vermouth.
vernáculo (ber'na·ku·lo) *adj.* & *n.m.* vernacular.
vernal (ber'nal) *adj.* vernal; spring (*attrib.*).
vernier (ber'njer) *n.m.* vernier.
verónica (be'ro·ni·ka) *n.f.* **1,** *bot.* veronica. **2,** a pass in bullfighting; veronica.
verosímil (be·ro'si·mil) *adj.* **1,** probable; likely. **2,** credible. *Also,* **verisímil** (be·ri-).
verosimilitud (be·ro·si·mi·li'tuð) *n.f.* verisimilitude. *Also,* **verisimilitud** (be·ri-).
verraco (be'rra·ko) *n.m.* male hog; domestic boar.
verriondo (be'rrjon·do) *adj.* in rut; rutting; in heat.
verruga (be'rru·ɣa) *n.f.* wart. —**verrugoso,** *adj.* warty.
versado (ber'sa·ðo) *adj.* versed; informed.
versar (ber'sar) *v.i., fol. by* **sobre** or **acerca de,** to be about; treat of; deal with. —**versarse,** *v.r.* to become versed; become informed.
versátil (ber'sa·til) *adj.* **1,** turning easily. **2,** fickle; inconstant. **3,** *bot.; zool.* versatile.
versatilidad (ber·sa·ti·li'ðað) *n.f.* **1,** ability to turn easily. **2,** fickleness; inconstancy. **3,** *bot.; zool.* versatility.
versículo (ber'si·ku·lo) *n.m.* verse, esp. of the Bible.
versificar (ber·si·fi'kar) *v.t.* & *i.* [*pres.subjve.* **versifique** (-'fi·ke); *pret.* **versifiqué** (-'ke)] to versify. —**versificación,** *n.f.* versification.
versión (ber'sjon) *n.f.* version.

verso ('ber·so) *n.m.* **1,** verse. **2,** verso.
versus ('ber·sus) *prep.* versus.
vértebra ('ber·te·βra) *n.f.* vertebra. —**vertebrado,** *adj.* & *n.m.* vertebrate. —**vertebral,** *adj.* vertebral.
vertedero (ber·te'ðe·ro) *n.m.* **1,** dumping ground; dump. **2,** spillway.
verter (ber'ter) *v.t.* [*pres.ind.* **vierto**; *pres.subjve.* **vierta**] **1,** to pour; spill; shed. **2,** to tip (a container). **3,** to translate. —*v.i.* to flow; empty; run.
vertical (ber·ti'kal) *adj.* & *n.f.* vertical.
vértice ('ber·ti·θe; -se) *n.m.* vertex.
vertiente (ber'tjen·te) *n.m. or f.* **1,** watershed. **2,** slope. —*n.f., Amer.* spring; fount.
vertiginoso (ber·ti·xi'no·so) *adj.* vertiginous.
vértigo ('ber·ti·ɣo) *n.m.* **1,** dizziness; vertigo. **2,** fit of insanity. **3,** *fig.* whirl; bustle.
ves (bes) *v., 2nd pers.sing.pres.ind. of* **ver.**
vesícula (be'si·ku·la) *n.f.* vesicle. —**vesicular,** *adj.* vesicular. —**vesiculoso,** *adj.* vesiculate.
vespasiana (bes·pa'sja·na) *n.f., So.Amer.* public urinal.
vespertino (bes·per'ti·no) *adj.* evening (*attrib.*).
vestal (bes'tal) *adj.* & *n.f.* vestal.
vestíbulo (bes'ti·βu·lo) *n.m.* vestibule; hall; lobby.
vestido (bes'ti·ðo) *n.m.* **1,** dress; suit. **2,** clothing; clothes (*pl.*); attire.
vestidura (bes·ti'ðu·ra) *n.f.* dress; garment; vestment.
vestigio (bes'ti·xjo) *n.m.* vestige. —**vestigial,** *adj.* vestigial.
vestiglo (bes'ti·ɣlo) *n.m.* monster.
vestimenta (bes·ti'men·ta) *n.f.* **1,** clothing; clothes (*pl.*). **2,** garment. **3,** *usu.pl.* vestments.
vestir (bes'tir) *v.t.* [*pres.ind.* **visto**; *pres.subjve.* **vista**; *pret.* **vestí, vistió**; *ger.* **vistiendo**] **1,** to clothe; dress. **2,** to deck; adorn. **3,** to cover; cloak. **4,** to wear. —*v.i.* **1,** to dress. **2,** to be dressy; be decorative. —**vestirse,** *v.r.* **1,** to dress oneself. **2,** to be clothed. **3,** *fol. by* **de,** to put on; assume.
vestuario (bes'twa·rjo) *n.m.* **1,** wardrobe; supply of clothing. **2,** uniform. **3,** cloakroom. **4,** vestry. **5,** clothing allowance. **6,** *theat.* wardrobe; dressing room.
veta ('be·ta) *n.f.* **1,** *mining* vein; seam; lode. **2,** grain; streak; vein, as in wood or marble. —**vetado,** *adj.* veined; streaked.
vetar (be'tar) *v.t.* to veto.
vetear (be·te'ar) *v.t.* to grain; streak. —**veteado,** *adj.* veined; streaked. —*n.m.* veining; graining; streaks (*pl.*).
veterano (be·te'ra·no) *adj.* & *n.m.* veteran.
veterinario (be·te·ri'na·rjo) *adj.* veterinary. —*n.m.* veterinary; veterinarian. —**veterinaria,** *n.f.* veterinary medicine.
veto ('be·to) *n.m.* veto.
vetusto (be'tus·to) *adj.* ancient; hoary. —**vetustez,** *n.f.* great age; antiquity; hoariness.
vez (beθ; bes) *n.f.* [*pl.* **veces** ('be·θes; -ses)] **1,** time; occasion. **2,** turn. —**a la vez,** at once; at one time; at the same time. —**a la vez que,** while; at the same time as. —**algunas veces,** at times; some times; occasionally. —**alguna vez,** some time; at some time. —**alguna vez que otra** = **de vez en cuando.** —**a veces,** at times; sometimes. —**cada vez,** each time; every time. —**de una vez, 1,** all at once. **2,** [*also,* **de una vez para siempre**] once and for all. —**de vez en cuando,** from time to time; once in a while; occasionally. —**en vez de,** instead of; in place of; in lieu of. —**érase una vez,** once upon a time. —**hacer las veces de,** to substitute for; take the place of. —**las más veces,** most of the time; in most cases. —**muchas veces,** often. —**otra vez, 1,** again; once more. **2,** at another time. —**pocas veces,** seldom. —**rara vez; raras veces,** very seldom; once in a great while. —**tal vez,** perhaps; maybe. —**tomar la vez a,** to steal a march on. —**una que otra vez, 1,** a few times. **2,** once in a while. —**unas veces,** at times; sometimes. —**una vez, 1,** once; one time. **2,** at one time; at some time. **3,** once upon a time.
vi (bi) *v., pret. of* **ver.**
vía ('bi·a) *n.f.* **1,** way; road; street. **2,** path; route; way. **3,** *R. R.* track. **4,** *R. R.* gauge. **5,** method;

procedure. 6, *law* process. 7, *anat.* canal; passage; tract. —*prep.* via; by way of. —**en vías de**, in the process of. —**vía crucis** ('kru·θis; -sis) 1, Way of the Cross. 2, [*also,* **viacrucis**, *n.m.*] affliction; burden. —**vía férrea**, railroad; railway; track; rail.

viabilidad (bi·a·βi·li'ðað) *n.f.* 1, feasibility; practicability. 2, viability.

viable (bi'a·βle) *adj.* 1, feasible; practicable. 2, viable.

viaducto (bi·a'ðuk·to) *n.m.* viaduct.

viajante (bja'xan·te) *adj.* traveling. —*n.m.* 1, traveler. 2, traveling salesman.

viajar (bja'xar) *v.t.* & *i.* to travel; journey.

viaje ('bja·xe) *n.m.* 1, journey; voyage; trip. 2, passage; fare. —**viaje de ida y vuelta**, round trip.

viajero (bja'xe·ro) *adj.* traveling. —*n.m.* 1, traveler. 2, passenger.

vianda ('bjan·da) *n.f.* 1, food; viand; victuals (*pl.*). 2, *W. I.* staple; starchy food, esp. tubers.

viandante (bjan'dan·te) *n.m.* & *f.* passerby.

viático ('bja·ti·ko) *n.m.* 1, *eccles.* viaticum. 2, travel allowance; viaticum.

víbora ('bi·βo·ra) *n.f.* viper.

vibración (bi·βra'θjon; -'sjon) *n.f.* 1, vibration. 2, vibrancy.

vibrante (bi'βran·te) *adj.* 1, vibrating. 2, vibrant.

vibrar (bi'βrar) *v.t.* & *i.* to vibrate. —*v.t.* 1, to brandish. 2, to throw; hurl. —**vibrador**, *adj.* vibrating; vibratory. —*n.m.* vibrator.

vibrátil (bi'βra·til) *adj.* vibratile. —**vibratorio** (-'to·rjo) *adj.* vibratory.

vicaría (bi·ka'ri·a) *n.f.* 1, vicarage. 2, vicarship; vicariate.

vicario (bi'ka·rjo) *adj.* 1, vicarial. 2, vicarious. —*n.m.* vicar. —**vicariato**, *n.m.* vicarship; vicariate.

vice- (bi·θe; -se) *prefix* vice- 1, one who takes the place of; substitute: *vicepresidente,* vice-president. 2, one second in rank; subordinate: *vicecónsul,* vice-consul. *Also,* **viz-**, in *vizconde,* viscount; **vi-**, in *virrey,* viceroy.

vicealmirante (bi·θe·al·mi'ran·te; bi·se-) *n.m.* vice-admiral.

vicepresidente (bi·θe·pre·si·'ðen·te; bi·se-) *n.m.* vice-president. —**vicepresidencia**, *n.f.* vice-presidency.

viceversa (bi·θe'βer·sa; bi·se-) *adv.* vice versa.

viciar (bi'θjar; -'sjar) *v.t.* 1, to vitiate; spoil; corrupt. 2, to foul; contaminate. 3, to misconstrue; distort. —**viciación**, *n.f.* vitiation.

vicio ('bi·θjo; -sjo) *n.m.* 1, vice. 2, habit, esp. bad habit. 3, defect.

vicioso (bi'θjo·so; -'sjo·so) *adj.* 1, vicious. 2, given to vice; depraved. 3, defective.

vicisitud (bi·θi·si'tuð; bi·si-) *n.f.* vicissitude.

víctima ('bik·ti·ma) *n.f.* 1, victim. 2, scapegoat. 3, underdog.

victoria (bik'to·rja) *n.f.* 1, victory. 2, Victoria (*carriage*). —**victorioso**, adj. victorious.

victoriano (bik·to'rja·no) *adj.* Victorian.

vicuña (bi'ku·ɲa) *n.f.* vicuña; vicuna.

vid (bið) *n.f.* vine; grapevine.

vida ('bi·ða) *n.f.* 1, life. 2, living. 3, vitality. —**hacer vida**, to live together; cohabit. —**vida mía**; **mi vida**, dearest; darling.

vidente (bi'ðen·te) *adj.* seeing. —*n.m.* seer. —*n.f.* seeress.

video (bi'ðe·o) *n.m.* video.

vidriado (bi'ðrja·ðo) *adj.* 1, glassy. 2, glazed. —*n.m.* 1, glaze; glazing. 2, glazed earthenware.

vidriar (bi'ðrjar) *v.t.* to glaze.

vidriera (bi'ðrje·ra) *n.f.* 1, glass window or partition. 2, *Amer.* glass case; showcase; show window. 3, [*also,* **vidriera de colores**] stained-glass window.

vidriero (bi'ðrje·ro) *n.m.* 1, glazier. 2, glass blower. 3, glass maker. 4, glass dealer.

vidrio ('bi·ðrjo) *n.m.* 1, glass. 2, piece of glass; something made of glass. 3, pane of glass. —**vidrioso**, *adj.* glassy. —**pagar los vidrios rotos**, to be the scapegoat.

viejo ('bje·xo) *adj.* 1, old. 2, aged. 3, ancient. 4, stale. —*n.m.* 1, old man. 2, *Amer., colloq.* term of endearment applied to parents, spouses, etc. —**viejos**, *n.m.pl., Amer., colloq.* parents; folks.

viendo ('bjen·do) *v., ger. of* **ver**.

vienes ('bje·nes) *v., 2nd pers. sing.pres.ind. of* **venir**.

viento ('bjen·to) *n.m.* 1, wind.

2, vanity; airs (*pl.*). 3, brace; guy; bracing rope. 4, *naut.* course. 5, scent; smell. —**beber los vientos por,** *colloq.* to be head over heels for. —**contra viento y marea,** come hell or high water; against all odds. —**viento en popa,** 1, before the wind. 2, *fig.* very successfully.

vientre ('bjen·tre) *n.m.* 1, abdomen; belly; bowels (*pl.*). 2, womb.

viernes (bjer'nes) *n.m.sing.* & *pl.* Friday. —**comer de viernes,** to fast.

vierta ('bjer·ta) *v., pres.subjve. of* **verter.**

vierto ('bjer·to) *v., pres.ind. of* **verter.**

viga ('bi·ɣa) *n.f.* beam; girder; joist; rafter.

vigente (bi'xen·te) *adj.* in force; in effect; standing. —**vigencia,** *n.f.* force; effect.

vigésimo (bi'xe·si·mo) *adj.* & *n.m.* twentieth. —**vigesimal,** *adj.* vigesimal.

vigía (bi'xi·a) *n.f.* 1, watchtower. 2, watch; watching. 3, *naut.* jutting rock; reef. —*n.m. or f.* lookout.

vigilar (bi·xi'lar) *v.t.* & *i.* to watch; guard. —**vigilancia,** *n.f.* vigilance; watchfulness. —**vigilante,** *adj.* vigilant; watchful. —*n.m.* 1, watchman; guard. 2, vigilante.

vigilia (bi'xi·lja) *n.f.* 1, vigil. 2, *esp. eccles.* = **víspera.** 3, *eccles.* fast; fasting. 4, *esp.mil.* & *naut.* period of duty; watch; division of the night.

vigor (bi'ɣor) *n.m.* vigor. —**vigoroso,** *adj.* vigorous. —**en vigor,** in force; in effect.

vigorizar (bi·ɣo·ri'θar; -'sar) *v.t.* [*pres.subjve.* **vigorice** (-'ri·θe; -se); *pret.* **vigoricé** (-'θe; -'se)] to strengthen; invigorate. —**vigorización,** *n.f.* invigoration. —**vigorizador,** *adj.* invigorating. —*n.m.* invigorant; tonic.

vihuela (bi'we·la) *n.f.* a medieval type of guitar.

viking ('bi·king) *n.m.* [*pl.* **vikings**] viking.

vil (bil) *adj.* vile; mean.

vileza (bi'le·θa; -sa) *n.f.* vileness; meanness.

vilipendiar (bi·li·pen'djar) *v.t.* to vilify; revile. —**vilipendio** (-'pen·djo) *n.m.* vilification; revilement.

vilo ('bi·lo) *n.m., in* **en vilo,** 1, up in the air; hanging. 2, in suspense.

villa ('bi·ʎa; -ja) *n.f.* 1, country house; villa. 2, village. 3, *chiefly hist.* city; town.

villadiego (bi·ʎa'ðje·ɣo; bi·ja-) *n.m., in* **coger** *or* **tomar las de villadiego,** to turn tail; sneak out.

villanada (bi·ʎa'na·ða; bi·ja-) *n.f.* villainous act; villainy.

villancico (bi·ʎan'θi·ko; bi·jan·'si·ko) *n.m.* Christmas carol.

villanía (bi·ʎa'ni·a; bi·ja-) *n.f.* villainy.

villano (bi'ʎa·no; -'ja·no) *adj.* 1, villainous. 2, *hist.* boorish; rustic. —*n.m.* 1, villain. 2, *hist.* rustic; peasant; villager.

villorrio (bi'ʎo·rrjo; bi'jo-) *n.m.* hamlet; one-horse town.

vinagre (bi'na·ɣre) *n.m.* vinegar. —**vinagreta,** *n.f.* vinegar sauce.

vinagrera (bi·na'ɣre·ra) *n.f.* 1, cruet. 2, *So.Amer.* acid stomach.

vinatero (bi·na'te·ro) *adj.* wine (*attrib.*). —*n.m.* vintner.

vincular (bin·ku'lar) *v.t.* 1, to bind; tie. 2, to relate; associate; refer. 3, *law* to entail. —**vinculación,** *n.f., law* entailment.

vínculo ('bin·ku·lo) *n.m.* 1, tie; bond; relationship. 2, *law* entailment.

vindicar (bin·di'kar) *v.t.* [*pres. subjve.* **vindique** (-'di·ke); *pret.* **vindiqué** (-'ke)] to vindicate. —**vindicación,** *n.f.* vindication. —**vindicativo,** *also,* **vindicatorio,** *adj.* vindicatory.

vine ('bi·ne) *v., pret. of* **venir.**

vinícola (bi'ni·ko·la) *adj.* wine (*attrib.*).

vinicultor (bi·ni·kul'tor) *n.m.* winegrower. —**vinicultura** (-'tu·ra) *n.f.* winegrowing.

viniendo (bi'njen·do) *v., ger. of* **venir.**

vinilo (bi'ni·lo) *n.m.* vinyl.

vino ('bi·no) *n.m.* wine. —*v., 3rd pers.sing.pret. of* **venir.**

vinoso (bi'no·so) *adj.* of or like wine; winy.

viña ('bi·ɲa) *n.f.* vineyard. *Also,* **viñedo** (-'ɲe·ðo) *n.m.*

viñeta (bi'ɲe·ta) *n.f.* vignette.

vió (bjo) *v., 3rd pers.sing.pret. of* **ver.**

viola ('bjo·la) *n.f.* 1, viol. 2, viola. —*n.m.* & *f.* violist.

violáceo (bjo'la·θe·o; -se·o) *adj.* purplish; resembling violet. *Also,* **violado** (-ðo).

violar (bjo'lar) *v.t.* **1,** to violate. **2,** to ravish; rape. **3,** to profane; desecrate; defile. —**violación,** *n.f.* violation.
violencia (bjo'len·θja; -sja) *n.f.* violence.
violentar (bjo·len'tar) *v.t.* **1,** to do violence to. **2,** to break into; force. —**violentarse,** *v.r.* to force oneself; control one's unwillingness.
violento (bjo'len·to) *adj.* **1,** violent; furious. **2,** forced; distorted. **3,** shocking; repugnant.
violeta (bjo'le·ta) *adj.* & *n.f.* violet.
violín (bjo'lin) *n.m.* violin. —**violinista,** *n.m.* & *f.* violinist.
violón (bjo'lon) *n.m.* bass; double bass. —**tocar el violón,** *colloq.* to dawdle.
violoncelo (bjo·lon'θe·lo; -'se·lo) *n.m.* violoncello; cello. —**violoncelista,** *n.m.* & *f.* violoncellist.
viperino (bi·pe'ri·no) *adj.* **1,** viperine. **2,** viperous; viperish.
vira ('bi·ra) *n.f.* **1,** dart; arrow. **2,** welt of a shoe.
virada (bi'ra·ða) *n.f.* turn; sudden turn; veer.
virago (bi'ra·ɣo) *n.f.* virago.
viraje (bi'ra·xe) *n.m.* turn.
virar (bi'rar) *v.t.* & *i.* **1,** to turn; veer. **2,** *naut.* to tack.
virazón (bi·ra'θon; -'son) *n.f.* **1,** sea breeze. **2,** change of wind.
virgen ('bir·xen) *adj.* & *n.f.* virgin. —**virginidad,** *n.f.* virginity. —**virginal,** *adj.* virginal. —*n.m., music* virginal.
virgo ('bir·ɣo) *n.m.* **1,** maidenhead. **2,** *cap., astron.* Virgo.
viril (bi'ril) *adj.* virile. —**virilidad,** *n.f.* virility.
virola (bi'ro·la) *n.f.* metal collar or clasp.
virolento (bi·ro'len·to) *adj.* **1,** of or pert. to smallpox. **2,** afflicted with smallpox. **3,** pockmarked.
virreina (bi'rrei·na) *n.f.* wife of a viceroy.
virreinal (bi'rrei'nal) *adj.* viceregal.
virrey (bi'rrei) *n.m.* viceroy. —**virreinato** (-'na·to) *also,* **virreino** (-'rrei·no) *n.m.* viceroyalty; viceroyship.
virtual (bir'twal) *adj.* virtual.
virtud (bir'tuð) *n.f.* **1,** virtue. **2,** quality; property. **3,** power; capacity.
virtuoso (bir'two·so) *adj.* virtuous. —*n.m.* virtuoso. —**virtuosidad,** *n.f.* virtuousness. —**virtuosismo,** *n.m.* virtuosity.
viruela (bi'rwe·la) *n.f.* **1,** pock; pockmark. **2,** *often pl.* smallpox. —**viruelas locas,** chicken pox.
virulento (bi·ru'len·to) *adj.* virulent. —**virulencia,** *n.f.* virulence.
virus ('bi·rus) *n.m.sing.* & *pl.* virus.
viruta (bi'ru·ta) *n.f.* shaving (*of wood or metal*).
vis (bis) *n.f.,* *in* **vis cómica,** comic verve or dash.
visa ('bi·sa) *n.f., Amer.* visa.
visado (bi'sa·ðo) *n.m.* **1,** visa. **2,** visaing.
visaje (bi'sa·xe) *n.m.* **1,** gesture; grimace. **2,** visage.
visar (bi'sar) *v.t.* **1,** to visa. **2,** to endorse; check.
víscera ('bis·θe·ra; 'bi·se-) *n.f., usu.pl.* viscera; vitals. —**visceral,** *adj.* visceral.
viscosa (bis'ko·sa) *n.f.* viscose.
viscoso (bis'ko·so) *adj.* viscous. —**viscosidad,** *n.f.* viscosity.
visera (bi'se·ra) *n.f.* visor.
visible (bi'si·βle) *adj.* **1,** visible. **2,** conspicuous; evident. —**visibilidad,** *n.f.* visibility.
visigodo (bi·si'ɣo·ðo) *n.m.* Visigoth. —*adj.* & *n.m.* Visigothic. —**visigótico,** *adj.* Visigothic.
visillo (bi'si·ʎo; -jo) *n.m.* a sheer window curtain.
visión (bi'sjon) *n.f.* **1,** vision. **2,** sight. **3,** grotesque figure. —**quedarse (uno) como quien ve visiones,** *colloq.* to be agape *or* aghast. —**ver visiones,** to see things.
visionario (bi·sjo'na·rjo) *adj.* & *n.m.* visionary.
visir (bi'sir) *n.m.* vizier.
visita (bi'si·ta) *n.f.* **1,** visit. **2,** visitor; caller; company. **3,** call; house call; social call.
visitar (bi·si'tar) *v.t.* to visit; call on *or* at. —**visitación,** *n.f.* visitation. —**visitador,** *n.m.* visiting inspector. —**visitante,** *adj.* visiting. —*n.m.* & *f.* visitor; visitant.
vislumbrar (bis·lum'brar) *v.t.* **1,** to glimpse. **2,** to foresee; envisage.
vislumbre (bis'lum·bre) *n.m.* **1,** glimmer; glimpse. **2,** hint; surmise.
viso ('bi·so) *n.m.* **1,** shimmer; sheen. **2,** gleam; glitter. **3,** indication; appearance. **4,** ladies' slip.

visón (bi'son) *n.m.* mink.
visor (bi'sor) *n.m.* **1,** sight; sighting device. **2,** *photog.* view finder.
visorio (bi'so·rjo) *adj.* visual. —*n.m.* expert examination.
víspera ('bis·pe·ra) *n.f.* eve. —**vísperas,** *n.f.pl.* vespers. —**en vísperas de,** near; close to.
vista ('bis·ta) *n.f.* **1,** sight. **2,** vision; eyesight. **3,** view. **4,** vista. **5,** looks (*pl.*); appearance. **6,** = **vistazo. 7,** *law* hearing. —*n.m.* customs inspector. —**a la vista, 1,** at *or* on sight. **2,** in plain view; evident. —**corto de vista,** shortsighted; nearsighted. —**de vista,** by sight. —**en vista de,** in view of; because of. —**hacer la vista gorda,** to close one's eyes; pretend not to see. —**hasta la vista,** until we meet again; goodbye; so long.
vista ('bis·ta) *v., pres.subjve. of* **vestir.**
vistaria (bis'ta·rja) *n.f.* wisteria.
vistazo (bis'ta·θo; -so) *n.m.* look; glance.
vistiendo (bis'tjen·do) *v., ger. of* **vestir.**
vistió (bis'tjo) *v., 3rd pers.sing. pret. of* **vestir.**
visto ('bis·to) *v.* **1,** *p.p. of* **ver. 2,** *pres.ind. of* **vestir.**
visto ('bis·to) *adj.* **1,** obvious; evident; clear. **2,** considered; thought out. —**bien** (*or* **mal**) **visto,** well (*or* poorly) regarded. —**visto bueno, 1,** approved; passed. **2,** approval; endorsement. —**visto que,** whereas; since; seeing that.
vistoso (bis'to·so) *adj.* attractive; showy. —**vistosidad,** *n.f.* attractiveness; showiness.
visual (bi'swal) *adj.* visual. —*n.f.* line of sight.
visualizar (bi·swa·li'θar; -'sar) *v.t.* [*pres.subjve.* **visualice** (-'li·θe; -se); *pret.* **visualicé** (-'θe; -'se)] to visualize. —**visualización,** *n.f.* visualization.
vital (bi'tal) *adj.* vital. —**vitalidad,** *n.f.* vitality.
vitalicio (bi·ta'li·θjo; -sjo) *adj.* lifelong; life (*attrib.*); for life.
vitalismo (bi·ta'lis·mo) *n.m.* vitalism. —**vitalista,** *adj.* vitalistic. —*n.m.* vitalist.
vitalizar (bi·ta·li'θar; -'sar) *v.t.* [*pres.subjve.* **vitalice** (-'li·θe; -se); *pret.* **vitalicé** (-'θe; -'se)] to vitalize. —**vitalización,** *n.f.* vitalization.
vitamina (bi·ta'mi·na) *n.f.* vitamin. —**vitamínico** (-'mi·ni·ko) *adj.* vitamin (*attrib.*).
vitela (bi'te·la) *n.f.* vellum.
vitorear (bi·to·re'ar) *v.t.* to cheer; acclaim.
vítreo ('bi·tre·o) *adj.* vitreous.
vitrificar (bi·tri·fi'kar) *v.t.* [*pres.subjve.* **vitrifique** (-'fi·ke); *pret.* **vitrifiqué** (-'ke)] to vitrify. —**vitrificación,** *n.f.* vitrification.
vitrina (bi'tri·na) *n.f.* **1,** showcase; show window. **2,** glass cabinet.
vitriolo (bi'trjo·lo) *n.m.* vitriol. —**vitriólico** (-'trjo·li·ko) *adj.* vitriolic.
vitualla (bi'twa·ʎa; -ja) *n.f., usu. pl.* victuals.
vituperar (bi·tu·pe'rar) *v.t.* to vituperate. —**vituperación,** *n.f.* vituperation.
vituperio (bi·tu'pe·rjo) *n.m.* insult; vituperation. —**vituperioso,** *adj.* vituperative.
viuda ('bju·ða) *n.f.* widow.
viudedad (bju·ðe'ðað) *n.f.* widow's inheritance; dower.
viudez (bju'ðeθ; -'ðes) *n.f.* **1,** widowhood. **2,** condition of a widower.
viudo ('bju·ðo) *adj.* widowed. —*n.m.* widower.
viva ('bi·βa) *n.m.* cheer; acclamation. —*interj.* long live!; hurrah!
vivac (bi'βak) *n.m.* [*pl.* **vivaques** (-kes)] = **vivaque.**
vivacidad (bi·βa·θi'ðað; -si'ðað) *n.f.* vivacity.
vivamente (bi·βa'men·te) *adv.* **1,** energetically. **2,** vividly; clearly. **3,** to the quick.
vivandero (bi·βan'de·ro) *n.m.* sutler.
vivaque (bi'βa·ke) *n.m.* bivouac. —**vivaquear,** *v.i.* to bivouac.
vivar (bi'βar) *n.m.* **1,** warren; burrow. **2,** fish hatchery. —*v.t., Amer.* to cheer; acclaim.
vivaracho (bi·βa'ra·tʃo) *adj., colloq.* gay; sprightly.
vivaz (bi'βaθ; -'βas) *adj.* **1,** vivacious; lively. **2,** *bot.* perennial.
víveres ('bi·βe·res) *n.m.pl.* provisions; food supplies.
vivero (bi'βe·ro) *n.m.* **1,** warren. **2,** hatchery. **3,** plant nursery. **4,** *fig.* hotbed.
viveza (bi'βe·θa; -sa) *n.f.* **1,** alacrity. **2,** alertness; sharpness. **3,** live-

liness; animation; sparkle. **4,** vividness. **5,** clever ruse; sharp trick.
vívido ('bi·βi·ðo) *adj.* vivid.
vivido (bi'βi·ðo) *adj.* personally experienced; firsthand.
vividor (bi·βi'ðor) *adj.* **1,** fond of good or high living. **2,** *colloq.* opportunistic; sponging. —*n.m.* **1,** one fond of good or high living. **2,** *colloq.* opportunist; sponger.
vivienda (bi'βjen·da) *n.f.* dwelling; house; abode.
viviente (bi'βjen·te) *adj.* living.
vivificar (bi·βi·fi'kar) *v.t.* [*pres. subjve.* **vivifique** (-'fi·ke); *pret.* **vivifiqué** (-'ke)] **1,** to vivify. **2,** to refresh; revivify. —**vivificación,** *n.f.* vivification. —**vivificador,** *adj.* vivifying.
vivíparo (bi'βi·pa·ro) *adj.* viviparous.
vivir (bi'βir) *v.i.* & *t.* to live. —*n.m.* living; life. —**¿Quién vive?,** Who goes there? —**¡Vive Dios!,** By God! —**vivir para ver,** live and learn.
vivisección (bi·βi·sek'θjon; -'sjon) *n.f.* vivisection.
vivo ('bi·βo) *adj.* **1,** alive; living. **2,** vivid; intense. **3,** lively; brisk. **4,** sharp; quick. **5,** expressive; forceful. **6,** *colloq.* foxy; sly; cunning. —*n.m.* **1,** edge; sharp edge. **2,** edging; fringe; trimming. **3,** *colloq.* sly fox. —**carne viva,** raw flesh; quick. —**en lo vivo,** to the quick.
vizcaíno (biθ·ka'i·no; bis-) *adj.* & *n.m.* Biscayan. —**vizcainada** (-kai'na·ða) *n.f.* ungrammatical speech.
vizconde (biθ'kon·de; bis-) *n.m.* viscount. —**vizcondado,** *n.m.* viscountship.
vocablo (bo'ka·βlo) *n.m.* word; term; vocable.
vocabulario (bo·ka·βu'la·rjo) *n.m.* vocabulary.
vocación (bo·ka'θjon; -'sjon) *n.f.* vocation. —**vocacional,** *adj.* vocational.
vocal (bo'kal) *adj.* vocal. —*n.f., gram.* vowel. —*n.m.* & *f.* board member; director. —**vocálico** (-'ka·li·ko) *adj.* vocalic; vowel (*attrib.*).
vocalista (bo·ka'lis·ta) *n.m.* & *f.* vocalist.
vocalizar (bo·ka·li'θar; -'sar) *v.t.* & *i.* [*pres.subjve.* **vocalice** (-'li·θe; -se); *pret.* **vocalicé** (-'θe; -'se)] **1,** to vocalize. **2,** to enunciate; articulate. —**vocalización,** *n.f.* vocalization.
vocativo (bo·ka'ti·βo) *adj.* & *n.m.* vocative.
vocear (bo·θe'ar; -se'ar) *v.t.* & *i.* to cry; shout. —*v.t.* **1,** to proclaim; announce. **2,** to hail. **3,** to boast of; brag about. —**voceador,** *n.m.* town crier. —**voceo** (-'θe·o; -'se·o) *n.m.* crying; shouting.
vocería (bo·θe'ri·a; bo·se-) *n.f.* **1,** = **vocerío. 2,** spokesmanship.
vocerío (bo·θe'ri·o; bo·se-) *n.m.* shouting; uproar.
vocero (bo'θe·ro; bo'se-) *n.m.* spokesman.
vociferar (bo·θi·fe'rar; bo·si-) *v.i.* to vociferate; be vociferous. —*v.t.* to boast loudly of. —**vociferación,** *n.f.* vociferation. —**vociferador,** *adj.* [*also,* **vociferante**] vociferous. —*n.m.* barker; hawker.
vocinglero (bo·θin'gle·ro; bo·sin-) *adj.* **1,** loud; loud-voiced. **2,** garrulous; verbose; windy. —**vocinglería,** *n.f. also,* **vocingleo** (-'gle·o) *n.m.* loud chatter; shouting.
vodevil (bo·ðe'βil) *n.m.* vaudeville.
vodka ('boð·ka) *n.f.* vodka.
vodú (bo'ðu) *n.m.* & *adj.* voodoo. —**voduismo** (bo·ðu'is·mo) *n.m.* voodooism. —**voduista,** *n.m.* & *f.* voodooist.
volada (bo'la·ða) *n.f.* flight; short flight. —**de una volada,** *Amer., colloq.* = **de un vuelo.**
voladero (bo·la'ðe·ro) *adj.* flying; fleeting. —*n.m.* precipice.
volado (bo'la·ðo) *adj.* **1,** *print.* superior. **2,** *Amer., colloq.* absent-minded. —*n.m., So.Amer.* frill; ruffle.
volador (bo·la'ðor) *adj.* flying. —*n.m.* skyrocket.
voladura (bo·la'ðu·ra) *n.f.* blast; blasting.
volandas (bo'lan·das) *n.f.pl., in* **en volandas, 1,** through the air; suspended. **2,** *colloq.* speedily; flying.
volandero (bo·lan'de·ro) *adj.* **1,** poised, as for flight. **2,** flighty. **3,** occurring by chance; fortuitous.
volante (bo'lan·te) *adj.* hovering; fluttering; flying. —*n.m.* **1,** frill; ruffle. **2,** flier; leaflet. **3,** flywheel. **4,** balance wheel. **5,** steering wheel. **6,** shuttlecock. **7,** the game of battledore and shuttlecock; bad-

minton. **8,** crack driver; auto racer.
volantín (bo·lan'tin) *n.m., Amer.* **1,** paper kite. **2,** = **volatín.**
volar (bo'lar) *v.i. & t* [*pres.ind.* **vuelo;** *pres.subjve.* **vuele**] to fly. —*v.i.* **1,** to flutter; hover. **2,** to vanish; disappear. **3,** to blow up; explode. —*v.t.* **1,** to blast; blow up. **2,** to make angry; enrage.
volátil (bo'la·til) *adj.* volatile. —**volatilidad,** *n.f.* volatility.
volatilizar (bo·la·ti·li'θar; -'sar) *v.t.* [*pres.subjve.* **volatilice** (-'li·θe; -se); *pret.* **volatilicé** (-'θe; 'se)] to volatilize; vaporize.
volatín (bo·la'tin) *n.m.* acrobatic feat; tumble.
volatinero (bo·la·ti'ne·ro) *n.m.* tumbler; acrobat; aerialist.
volcán (bol'kan) *n.m.* volcano. —**volcánico,** *adj.* volcanic.
volcar (bol'kar) *v.t.* [*pres.ind.* **vuelco;** *pres.subjve.* **vuelque;** *pret.* **volqué**] **1,** to tip over; upset; overturn. **2,** to capsize. **3,** to pour; spill.
volear (bo·le'ar) *v.t.* **1,** *games* to volley. **2,** to throw; let fly.
voleo (bo'le·o) *n.m.* **1,** *games* volley. **2,** blow; strike. —**al voleo,** overhand.
volframio (bol'fra·mjo) *n.m.* wolfram.
volibol (bo·li'βol) *n.m.* volleyball.
volición (bo·li'θjon; -'sjon) *n.f.* volition. —**volitivo** (-'ti·βo) *adj.* volitional; volitive.
volqué (bol'ke) *v., 1st pers.sing. pret. of* **volcar.**
volt (bolt) *n.m.* [*pl.* **volts** (bolts)] volt.
voltaico (bol'tai·ko) *adj.* voltaic. —**voltaísmo** (-ta'is·mo) *n.m.* voltaism.
voltaje (bol'ta·xe) *n.m.* voltage.
voltear (bol·te'ar) *v.t. & i.* **1,** to turn; turn over. **2,** to turn around. **3,** to overturn; upset. —*v.t.* **1,** to swing; spin; whirl. **2,** to arch; vault. **3,** to peal (a bell). **4,** *Amer., colloq.* to knock over; knock down.
volteo (bol'te·o) *n.m.* **1,** whirling; revolving; turning. **2,** overturning; upsetting. **3,** tumbling. **4,** peal (*of a bell*). **5,** *Amer., colloq.* knocking down; felling.
voltereta (bol·te're·ta) *n.f.* tumble; somersault.
voltímetro (bol'ti·me·tro) *n.m.* voltmeter.
voltio ('bol·tjo) *n.m.* volt.
volubilidad (bo·lu·βi·li'ðað) *n.f.* **1,** changeableness; fickleness; inconstancy. **2,** volubility.
voluble (bo'lu·βle) *adj.* **1,** changeable; fickle; inconstant. **2,** voluble.
volumen (bo'lu·men) *n.m.* volume.
voluminoso (bo·lu·mi'no·so) *adj.* voluminous. —**voluminosidad,** *n.f.* voluminousness.
voluntad (bo·lun'tað) *n.f.* **1,** will. **2,** [*also,* **buena voluntad**] good will. **3,** disposition; inclination. **4,** [*also,* **fuerza de voluntad**] will power. **5,** free will. —**mala voluntad,** ill will.
voluntariedad (bo·lun·ta·rje·'ðað) *n.f.* **1,** voluntariness. **2,** willfulness; stubbornness.
voluntario (bo·lun'ta·rjo) *adj.* voluntary. —*n.m.* volunteer.
voluntarioso (bo·lun·ta'rjo·so) *adj.* **1,** willful; self-willed; stubborn. **2,** tenacious; determined.
voluptuoso (bo·lup'two·so) *adj.* voluptuous. —*n.m.* voluptuary. —**voluptuosidad,** *n.f.* voluptuousness.
voluta (bo'lu·ta) *n.f.* **1,** volute. **2,** wisp or curl of smoke.
volver (bol'βer) *v.t.* [*pres.ind.* **vuelvo;** *pres.subjve.* **vuelva;** *p.p.* **vuelto**] **1,** to turn; turn over. **2,** = **devolver. 3,** to put back; replace; restore. **4,** to change; convert; turn: *Volvió el agua en vino,* He changed water into wine. **5,** to make; cause to become. —*v.i.* **1,** *fol. by* **a** + *inf.* to do again (the action expressed by the verb): *Volvió a salir,* He went out again. **2,** to return; go or come back. **3,** to turn; change direction. —**volverse,** *v.r.* **1,** to turn; turn into; become. **2,** to return. —**volver en sí,** to come to. —**volverse atrás, 1,** to turn back; go back. **2,** to back out; withdraw. —**volverse contra,** to turn on; turn against.
vomitado (bo·mi'ta·ðo) *adj., colloq.* pale; sickly.
vomitar (bo·mi'tar) *v.t.* **1,** to vomit. **2,** to disgorge; belch forth.
vomitivo (bo·mi'ti·βo) *adj. & n.m.* emetic.
vómito ('bo·mi·to) *n.m.* vomit.
voracidad (bo·ra·θi'ðað; -si'ðað) *n.f.* voracity; voraciousness.
vorágine (bo'ra·xi·ne) *n.f.* vortex; maelstrom.

voraz (bo'raθ; -'ras) *adj.* voracious.

-voro (βo·ro) *suffix* -vorous; -vore; *forming adjectives and nouns denoting* eating; eater: *carnívoro,* carnivorous; carnivore.

vórtice ('bor·ti·θe; -se) *n.m.* vortex.

vos (bos) *pers.pron. 2nd pers.sing. & pl., used as subj. or obj. of a verb or obj. of a prep., in addressing God, a saint or an important personage; in Amer.colloq. usage often replacing* **tú, te, ti,** you; to you; ye; yourself; thou; thee; to thee; thyself.

vosear (bo·se'ar) *v.t. & i.* to use vos in addressing a person or persons. —**voseo** (-'se·o) *n.m.* use of vos.

vosotros (bo'so·tros) *pers.pron. 2nd pers.m.pl.* [*fem.* **vosotras**] you; ye; yourselves.

votación (bo·ta'θjon; -'sjon) *n.f.* **1,** voting; balloting. **2,** vote; number of votes cast.

votar (bo'tar) *v.i. & t.* **1,** to vote. **2,** to vow. —*v.i.* to swear; utter an oath. —**votante,** *n.m. & f.* voter. —*adj.* voting.

votivo (bo'ti·βo) *adj.* votive.

voto ('bo·to) *n.m.* **1,** vote. **2,** vow. **3,** oath; curse. —**hacer votos por,** to pray for; wish that. —**¡voto a tal!,** confound it!

voy (boi) *v., 1st pers.sing.pres.ind. of* **ir.**

voz (boθ; bos) *n.f.* **1,** voice. **2,** shout; cry. **3,** clamor; outcry. **4,** *gram.* voice. **5,** word; expression; vocable. —**a voces,** shouting; crying loudly. —**a voz en cuello; a voz en grito,** at the top of one's voice. —**correr la voz (que),** to be rumored (that). —**dar voces,** to shout; cry out. —**en voz alta,** aloud.

vozarrón (bo·θa'rron; -sa'rron) *n.m.* strong, deep voice.

vudú (bu'ðu) *adj. & n.m.* = **vodú.**

vuecencia (bwe'θen·θja; -'sen·sja) *n.m. & f., contr. of* **vuestra excelencia,** your excellency. *Also,* **vuecelencia** (bwe·θe'len·θja; -se·'len·sja).

vuelco ('bwel·ko) *n.m.* **1,** upset; overturn. **2,** a tumbling; tumble; somersault. —**darle a uno un vuelco el corazón,** *colloq.* **1,** to feel one's heart leap. **2,** to have a foreboding or premonition.

vuelco ('bwel·ko) *v., pres.ind. of* **volcar.**

vuele ('bwe·le) *v., pres.subjve. of* **volar.**

vuelo ('bwe·lo) *n.m.* **1,** flight; flying. **2,** flare, as of a skirt. **3,** *fig.* scope; breadth; reach. **4,** *Amer.* take-off distance; running start. —**al vuelo, 1,** at once; in a jiffy. **2,** on the wing; on the fly. —**alzar el vuelo,** to take flight. —**de un vuelo,** in one fell swoop. —**echar a vuelo las campanas,** to set the bells ringing; ring a full peal. —**levantar el vuelo,** to take off; take flight. —**tomar vuelo, 1,** to grow; grow wings; progress. **2,** *Amer.* to take a running start.

vuelo ('bwe·lo) *v., pres.ind. of* **volar.**

vuelque ('bwel·ke) *v., pres.subjve. of* **volcar.**

vuelta ('bwel·ta) *n.f.* **1,** turn; turning; a turning around. **2,** bend; twist. **3,** walk; stroll. **4,** ride; trip. 5, outing; excursion. **6,** tour. **7,** other side; reverse. **8,** return. **9,** return trip. **10,** change; money returned. —**a la vuelta, 1,** on or upon returning. **2,** *colloq.* around the corner; close by. —**a la vuelta de, 1,** at the end of; after. **2,** around; just off; just past. —**a vuelta de, 1,** after; following upon. **2,** about to; on the point of. —**a vuelta de correo,** by return mail. —**dar una vuelta,** to take a stroll, walk, ride, etc. —**dar vuelta,** to turn. —**dar vueltas, 1,** to circle. **2,** to go around and around. —**de vuelta,** on returning. —**estar de vuelta,** to be back. —**media vuelta,** about-face. —**no tiene vuelta,** that's that; no two ways about it. —**poner a uno de vuelta y media,** to give a tongue-lashing to. —**vuelta de campana,** tumble; somersault.

vuelto ('bwel·to) *n.m.* **1,** verso. **2,** *Amer.* change; money returned. —*v., p.p. of* **volver.**

vuelva ('bwel·βa) *v., pres.subjve. of* **volver.**

vuelvo ('bwel·βo) *v., pres.ind. of* **volver.**

vuestro ('bwes·tro) *poss.adj & pron.m.sing.* [*fem.* **vuestra;** *pl.* **vuestros, vuestras**], *agreeing in number and gender with the thing or things possessed* your; yours.

vulcanita (bul·ka'ni·ta) *n.f.* vulcanite.
vulcanizar (bul·ka·ni'θar; -'sar) *v.t.* 1, [*pres.subjve.* **vulcanice** (-'ni·θe; -se); *pret.* **vulcanicé** (-'θe; -'se)] to vulcanize. —**vulcanización,** *n.f.* vulcanization.
vulgacho (bul'ɣa·tʃo) *n.m.* rabble; riffraff.
vulgar (bul'ɣar) *adj.* 1, vulgar. 2, common; ordinary. —**vulgaridad,** *n.f.* vulgarity. —**vulgarismo,** *n.m.* vulgarism. —**idioma** *or* **lengua vulgar,** vernacular. —**vulgar y corriente,** run-of-the mill.
vulgarizar (bul·ɣa·ri'θar; -'sar) *v.t.* [*pres.subjve.* **vulgarice** (-'ri·θe; -se); *pret.* **vulgaricé** (-'θe; -'se)] to vulgarize. —**vulgarización,** *n.f.* vulgarization.
Vulgata (bul'ɣa·ta) *n.f.* Vulgate.
vulgo ('bul·ɣo) *n.m.* 1, common people; populace. 2, laymen collectively; the uninitiated.
vulnerable (bul·ne'ra·βle) *adj.* vulnerable. —**vulnerabilidad,** *n.f.* vulnerability.
vulpino (bul'pi·no) *adj.* vulpine.
vultuoso (bul'two·so) *adj.* bloated, as the face.
vulva ('bul·βa) *n.f.* vulva.
V.V., VV *abbr. of* **ustedes.**

W

W, w (be'ðo·βle; 'u·βe'ðo·βle) *n.f.* w; *not properly a letter of the Spanish alphabet; found only in foreign words.*
wagogo (wa'ɣo·ɣo) *n.m.* African arrow poison.
wagón (va'gon) *n.m.* = **vagón.**
wat (wat) *n.m.* [*pl.* **wats** (wats)] = **vatio.**
water-closet ('va·ter 'klo·set) *n.m.* water closet; lavatory. *Abbr.* **W. C.**
watt (wat) *n.m.* = wat.
whig (wig) *n.m.* wig.
whisky ('wis·ki) *n.m.* whiskey.
whist (wist) *n.m.* whist.
wigwam ('wig·wam) *n.m.* wigwam.
winche ('win·tʃe) *n.m., Amer.* winch.
wolfram ('vol·fram) *n.m.* = **volframio.**

X

X, x ('e·kis) *n.f.* 26th letter of the Spanish alphabet.
xanteína (ksan·te'i·na) *n.f.* xanthein.
xantina (ksan'ti·na) *n.f.* xanthin.
xanto– (ksan·to) *prefix* xantho–; yellow: *xantofilia,* xanthophilia.
xenia ('kse·nja) *n.f.* xenia.
xeno ('kse·no) *n.m.* = **xenón.**
xeno– (kse·no) *prefix* xeno–; strange; foreign: *xenofobia,* xenophobia.
xenofobia (kse·no'fo·βja) *n.f.* xenophobia. —**xenófobo** (-'no·fo·βo) *adj.* xenophobic. —*n.m.* xenophobe.
xenón (kse'non) *n.m.* xenon.
xero– (kse·ro) *prefix* xero–; dry: *xeroftalmia,* xerophthalmia.
xilema (ksi'le·ma) *n.m.* xylem.
xilo– (ksi·lo) *prefix* xylo–; wood: *xilófono,* xylophone.
xilófago (ksi'lo·fa·ɣo) *adj.* xylophagous.
xilófono (ksi'lo·fo·no) *n.m.* xylophone.
xilografía (ksi·lo·ɣra'fi·a) *n.f.* 1, xylography. 2, xylograph.

Y

Y, y (i'ɣrje·ɣa; *also,* je) *n.f.* 27th letter of the Spanish alphabet.
y (i) *conj.* and.
ya (ja) *adv.* 1, already: *Ya comí,* I have already eaten. 2, now; at once: *Hazlo ya,* Do it now. 3, *in*

questions yet: *¿Está ya en casa tu padre?*, Is your father at home yet? **4,** presently; in a while; eventually: *Ya saldrá,* He will come out presently; *Ya vendrá,* He will come eventually. **5,** *intensifying the immediacy of an action: Ya voy,* I'm coming; *Ya lo veré,* I'll see to it. —*interj.* yes!; of course!; I see!; so! —**no ya .... sino,** not only .... but also: *no ya los vivos, sino los muertos,* not only the living but also the dead. —**si ya,** if only; so long as; provided: *Lo haré si ya no me molestas,* I will do it if only you will not bother me. —**ya ..... ya, 1,** whether .... or; as well ... as: *Ya en política ya en letras, es un maestro,* Whether in politics or in letters, he is an expert; As well in politics as in letters he is an expert. **2,** now ..... now: *ya rico, ya pobre,* now rich, now poor. —**¡ya lo creo!,** of course! —**ya no,** no longer. —**ya que,** as long as; since: *Lo haré ya que lo dije,* I will do it as long as I have said so.

yacer (ja'θer; -'ser) *v.i.* [*pres.ind.* **yazco,** *also,* **yazgo, yago**; *pres. subjve.* **yazca,** *also,* **yazga, yaga**; *impve.* **yace,** *also,* **yaz**] to lie; rest.

yacimiento (ja·θi'mjen·to; ja·si-) *n.m., geol.* deposit.

yaga ('ja·ɣa) *v., pres.subjve. of* **yacer.** —**yago** (-ɣo) *v., 1st pers. sing.pres.ind. of* **yacer.**

yagua ('ja·ɣwa) *n.f., W.I.* **1,** royal palm. **2,** palm leaf, used for thatching.

yaguar (ja'ɣwar) *n.m.* = **jaguar.**

yak (jak) *n.m.* yak.

yambo ('jam·bo) *n.m.* iamb; iambic. —**yámbico,** *adj.* iambic.

yanqui ('jan·ki) *adj. & n.m. & f.* Yankee.

yantar (jan'tar) *v.t., rare* to eat; dine. —*n.m.* food.

yapa ('ja·pa) *n.f., Amer.* bonus; extra.

yarda ('jar·ða) *n.f.* **1,** yard (*measure*). **2,** yardstick.

yate ('ja·te) *n.m.* yacht.

yautía (jau'ti·a) *n.f., W.I.* a tropical tuber; yautia.

yaz (jaθ; jas) *v., impve. of* **yacer.** —**yazca** ('jaθ·ka; 'jas-) *also,* **yazga** (-ɣa) *v., pres.subjve. of* **yacer.** —**yazco** ('jaθ·ko; 'jas-) *also,* **yazgo** (-ɣo) *v., 1st pers.sing.pres.ind. of* **yacer.**

yedra ('je·ðra) *n.f.* = **hiedra.**

yegua ('je·ɣwa) *n.f.* mare. —**yeguada,** *n.f.* herd of mares or horses.

yelmo ('jel·mo) *n.m.* helmet.

yema ('je·ma) *n.f.* **1,** yolk. **2,** bud. **3,** candied egg yolk. —**yema del dedo,** finger tip.

yen (jen) *n.m.* yen (*monetary unit*).

yendo ('jen·do) *v., ger. of* **ir.**

yerba ('jer·βa) *n.f.* = **hierba.** —**yerba mate,** maté.

yerbajo (jer'βa·xo) *n.m.* useless plant; weed.

yerga ('jer·ɣa) *v., pres.subjve. of* **erguir.** —**yergo** (-ɣo) *v., pres.ind. of* **erguir.**

yermo ('jer·mo) *adj.* **1,** lifeless; desolate. **2,** barren; waste. —*n.m.* wasteland.

yerno ('jer·no) *n.m.* son-in-law.

yerre ('je·rre) *v., pres.subjve. of* **errar.**

yerro ('je·rro) *v., pres.ind. of* **errar.** —*n.m.* mistake; error.

yerto ('jer·to) *adj.* inert; rigid.

yesal (je'sal) *n.m.* gypsum pit; gypsum quarry. *Also,* **yesar** (-'sar).

yesca ('jes·ka) *n.f.* **1,** tinder; kindling. **2,** *fig.* incentive to passion.

yeso ('je·so) *n.m.* **1,** gypsum. **2,** plaster. **3,** plaster cast. —**yeso blanco,** finishing plaster. —**yeso mate,** *also,* **yeso de París,** plaster of Paris. —**yeso negro,** coarse plaster.

yesoso (je'so·so) *adj.* of or like gypsum or plaster; chalky.

yiddish ('ji·ðiʃ) *adj. & n.m.* Yiddish.

yo (jo) *pers.pron.* I. —*n.m.* ego; self.

yodo ('jo·ðo) *n.m.* iodine.

yodoformo (jo·ðo'for·mo) *n.m.* iodoform.

yoduro (jo'ðu·ro) *n.m.* iodide. —**yodurar,** *v.t.* to iodize.

yoga ('jo·ɣa) *n.m.* yoga. —**yogi** (-ɣi) *n.m.* yogi.

yogurt (jo'ɣurt) *n.m.* yogurt.

yola ('jo·la) *n.f.* yawl.

yuan (ju'an) *n.m.* yuan.

yuca ('ju·ka) *n.f.* **1,** cassava. **2,** yucca.

yugo ('ju·ɣo) *n.m.* yoke.

yugoslavo (ju·ɣos'la·βo) *also,* **yugoeslavo** (-es'la·βo) *adj.* & *n.m.* Yugoslav; Yugoslavian.
yugular (ju·ɣu'lar) *adj.* jugular.
yunque ('jun·ke) *n.m.* anvil.
yunta ('jun·ta) *n.f.* yoke of draft animals, esp. oxen. —**yuntero,** *n.m.* plowboy.
yute ('ju·te) *n.m.* jute.
yuxta– (juks·ta) *prefix* juxta–; near; together; in close proximity: *yuxtaposición,* juxtaposition.
yuxtaponer (juks·ta·po'ner) *v.t.* [*infl.:* **poner**] to juxtapose. —**yuxtaposición** (-si'θjon; -'sjon) *n.f.* juxtaposition.
yuyo ('ju·jo) *n.m., So.Amer.* = **yerbajo.**

Z

Z, z ('θe·ta; 'se·ta, *also,* 'θe·ða; 'se·ða) *n.f.* 28th letter of the Spanish alphabet.
zacate (θa'ka·te; sa-) *n.m., Amer.* hay; fodder.
zafacoca (θa·fa'ko·ka; sa-) *n.f., Amer., colloq.* row; melée.
zafado (θa'fa·ðo; sa-) *adj., Amer.* **1,** brazen; barefaced. **2,** alert; wide-awake. **3,** out of joint; dislocated. **4,** *colloq.* screwloose; daft.
zafar (θa'far; sa-) *v.t.* **1,** to free; release; disengage. **2,** *Amer.* to dislocate; put out of joint. —**zafarse,** *v.r., fol. by* **de, 1,** to get out of; avoid. **2,** to get rid of; shake off. **3,** to become loose. **4,** *Amer., colloq.* to go out of one's mind.
zafarrancho (θa·fa'rran·tʃo; sa-) *n.m.* **1,** a clearing for action. **2,** *colloq.* melée; row. **3,** *Amer., colloq.* mess; confusion.
zafio ('θa·fjo; sa-) *adj.* rustic; coarse; uncouth. —*n.m.* rustic; boor. —**zafiedad,** *n.f.* coarseness; uncouthness.
zafiro (θa'fi·ro; sa-) *n.m.* sapphire. —**zafirino** (-'ri·no) *also,* **zafíreo** (-'fi·re·o) *adj.* sapphirine; sapphire-colored.
zafra ('θa·fra; sa-) *n.f.* **1,** sugar harvest. **2,** sugar making. **3,** *Sp.* olive harvest. **4,** oil jar or vat.
zaga ('θa·ɣa; 'sa-) *n.f.* end; rear; back. —**a la zaga,** *also,* **en zaga, a zaga,** *usu.fol. by* **de,** behind; after; following.
zagal (θa'ɣal; sa-) *n.m.* **1,** youth; lad. **2,** [*also,* **zagalejo** (-'le·xo)] shepherd boy.
zagala (θa'ɣa·la; sa-) *n.f.* **1,** girl; lass. **2,** [*also,* **zagaleja** (-'le·xa)] shepherd girl.
zagalejo (θa·ɣa'le·xo; sa-) *n.m.* **1,** shepherd boy. **2,** peasant skirt.
zaguán (θa'ɣwan; sa-) *n.m.* entrance; entrance hall; vestibule.
zaguero (θa'ɣe·ro; sa-) *adj.* rear; back; hind. —*n.m., sports* back.
zaherir (θa·e'rir; sa-) *v.t.* [*infl.:* **herir**] **1,** to blame; censure; scold. **2,** to hurt; offend.
zahína (θa'i·na; sa-) *n.f.* a variety of sorghum.
zahones (θa'o·nes; sa-) *n.m.pl.* leather trousers; hunting breeches.
zahorí (θa·o'ri; sa-) *n.m.* **1,** diviner; clairvoyant. **2,** perspicacious person.
zaino ('θai·no; 'sai-) *adj.* **1,** untrustworthy; tricky. **2,** chestnut-colored (*of a horse*). —*n.m.* chestnut-colored horse.
zalagarda (θa·la'ɣar·ða; sa-) *n.f.* **1,** row; rumpus. **2,** trap; snare; ambush.
zalamero (θa·la'me·ro; sa-) *adj.* sugary; flattering; fawning. —**zalamería,** *n.f.* fawning; adulation.
zalea (θa'le·a; sa-) *n.f.* unsheared sheepskin; fur of sheep.
zalema (θa'le·ma; sa-) *n.f.* **1,** salaam. **2,** = **zalamería.**
zamarra (θa'ma·rra; sa-) *n.f.* **1,** sheepskin jacket. **2,** sheepskin.
zamarrear (θa·ma·rre'ar; sa-) *v.t.* **1,** to shake violently. **2,** to jolt; jar. **3,** to drub; trounce. *Also,* **zamarronear** (-rro·ne'ar).
zamarro (θa'ma·rro; sa-) *adj., Amer., colloq.* sly; shrewd. —*n.m.* **1,** = **zamarra. 2,** *pl., So.Amer.* chaps.
zambo ('θam·bo; 'sam-) *adj.* knockneed. —*adj.* & *n.m., Amer.* halfbreed of Indian and Negro ancestry.
zambomba (θam'bom·ba; sam-) *n.f.* a kind of rustic drum. —*interj.* wow!

zambra ('θam·bra; 'sam-) *n.f.* a gypsy dance.

zambullir (θam·bu'ʎir; sam·bu'jir) *v.t.* to dip; plunge. —**zambullirse,** *v.r.* to dive; plunge. —**zambullida,** *n.f.* dive; plunge.

zampar (θam'par; sam-) *v.t.* **1,** to thrust in; jam. **2,** to gobble; devour. **3,** *Amer., colloq.* to give (a blow). —**zamparse,** *v.r.* **1,** to rush in; barge in. **2,** *colloq.* to slip in; crash the gate.

zanahoria (θa·na'o·rja; sa-) *n.f.* carrot.

zanca ('θan·ka; 'san-) *n.f.* leg; long leg. —**zancada,** *n.f.* long step; stride. —**en dos zancadas,** *colloq.* in a jiffy.

zancadilla (θan·ka'ði·ʎa; san·ka'ði·ja) *n.f.* trip; a tripping up. —**echar una zancadilla a,** to trip; trip up.

zanco ('θan·ko; 'san-) *n.m.* stilt.

zancón (θan'kon; san-) *adj.* **1,** *colloq.* long-legged. **2,** *Amer.* too short, as a skirt or dress.

zancudo (θan'ku·ðo; san-) *adj.* **1,** long-legged. **2,** *ornith.* wading. —*n.m., Amer.* mosquito. —**zancuda,** *n.f., also,* **ave zancuda,** wading bird.

zángano ('θan·ga·no; 'san-) *n.m.* **1,** *entom.* drone. **2,** *colloq.* loafer; good-for-nothing. —**zanganada,** *n.f., colloq.* impertinence; nuisance. —**zanganear,** *v.i., colloq.* to loaf.

zangolotear (θan·go·lo·te'ar; san-) *v.t., colloq.* to shake; rattle. —*v.i., colloq.* to fuss about; fidget. —**zangolotearse,** *v.r., colloq.* to be loose; move about; rattle.

zanguango (θan'gwan·go; san-) *n.m., colloq.* lazybones. —**zanguanga,** *n.f., colloq.* malingering.

zanja ('θan·xa; 'san-) *n.f.* ditch.

zanjar (θan'xar; san-) *v.t.* **1,** to open ditches in. **2,** to settle; resolve.

zanquilargo (θan·ki'lar·ɣo; san-) *adj.* long-legged; lanky.

zapa ('θa·pa; 'sa-) *n.f., mil.* **1,** sapper's spade. **2,** sap; trench. —**zapador,** *n.m., mil.* sapper. —**labor de zapa,** undermining; subversion.

zapallo (θa'pa·ʎo; sa'pa·jo) *n.m., So.Amer.* **1,** pumpkin; squash; gourd. **2,** *colloq.* stroke of luck; chance.

zapapico (θa·pa'pi·ko; sa-) *n.m.* pick mattock.

zapateado (θa·pa·te'a·ðo; sa-) *n.m.* **1,** a typical Spanish clog dance. **2,** *Amer.* tap dance.

zapatear (θa·pa·te'ar; sa-) *v.i.* to tap or stamp with the feet. —**zapateo** (-'te·o) *n.m.* tapping or stamping with the feet.

zapatería (θa·pa·te'ri·a; sa-) *n.f.* **1,** shoe store; bootery. **2,** shoemaking; bootmaking. **3,** cobbler's shop; shoe repair shop.

zapatero (θa·pa'te·ro; sa-) *n.m.* **1,** shoemaker; cobbler. **2,** *games* player who fails to score a point, or take a trick. —**zapatero a tus zapatos,** mind your own business.

zapatilla (θa·pa'ti·ʎa; sa·pa'ti·ja) *n.f.* **1,** slipper; pump. **2,** leather or rubber washer.

zapato (θa'pa·to; sa-) *n.m.* shoe.

¡zape! ('θa·pe; 'sa·pe) *interj.* **1,** scat! **2,** gee!; gee whiz!

zaquizamí (θa·ki·θa'mi; sa·ki·sa-) *n.m.* **1,** attic; garret. **2,** hole in the wall; rathole. **3,** *fig., colloq.* scrape; tight spot.

zar (θar; sar) *n.m.* czar; tsar. —**zarevitz** (θa·re'βits; sa-) *n.m.* czarevitch. —**zarevna** (θa'reβ·na; sa-) *n.f.* czarevna.

zarabanda (θa·ra'βan·da; sa-) *n.f.* saraband.

zarandaja (θa·ran'da·xa; sa-) *n.f., usu.pl.* trivia.

zarandear (θa·ran·de'ar; sa-) *v.t.* **1,** to sift. **2,** to shake; move to and fro. —**zarandearse,** *v.r., Amer.* to strut; swagger; sway the hips.

zaraza (θa'ra·θa; sa'ra·sa) *n.f.* chintz; printed cotton.

zarcillo (θar'θi·ʎo; sar'si·jo) *n.m.* **1,** tendril. **2,** drop earring.

zarco ('θar·ko; 'sar-) *adj.* light blue.

zarigüeya (θa·ri'ɣwe·ja; sa-) *n.f.* opossum.

zarina (θa'ri·na; sa-) *n.f.* czarina.

zarpa ('θar·pa; 'sar-) *n.f.* paw; claw. —**echar la zarpa a,** *colloq.* to grab; nab.

zarpada (θar'pa·ða; sar-) *n.f.* **1,** blow with the paw. **2,** grabbing; grab. *Also,* **zarpazo** (-θo; -so) *n.m.*

zarpar (θar'par; sar-) *v.i.* to weigh anchor; sail.

zarrapastroso (θa·rra·pas'tro·so; sa-) *adj.* ragged; tattered. —*n.m.* ragamuffin.

zarria ('θa·rrja; 'sa-) *n.f.* **1,** dirt; grime. **2,** rag; tatter. **3,** leather thong.
zarza ('θar·θa; 'sar·sa) *n.f.* **1,** bramble; brier. **2,** blackberry; dewberry.
zarzal (θar'θal; sar'sal) *n.m.* **1,** brier patch; brambles (*pl.*). **2,** blackberry patch; dewberry patch.
zarzamora (θar·θa'mo·ra; sar·sa-) *n.f.* brambleberry; blackberry.
zarzaparrilla (θar·θa·pa'rri·ʎa; sar·sa·pa'rri·ja) *n.f.* sarsaparilla.
zarzo ('θar·θo; 'sar·so) *n.m.* wattle.
zarzoso (θar'θo·so; sar'so-) *adj.* brambly.
zarzuela (θar'θwe·la; sar'swe-) *n.f.* traditional Spanish musical drama; zarzuela.
¡zas! (θas; sas) *interj.* pow!; smack!
zeda ('θe·ða; 'se-) *n.f.* name of the letter *z*; zed.
zenit (θe'nit; se-) *n.m.* = **cenit.**
zeta ('θe·ta; 'se-) *n.f.* **1,** zeta. **2,** name of the letter *z*; zed.
zigzag (θiɣ'θaɣ; siɣ'saɣ) *n.m.* zigzag. **—zigzaguear** (-ɣe'ar) *v.i.* to zigzag. **—zigzagueo** (-'ɣe·o) *n.m.* zigzag; zigzagging.
zinc (θink; sink) *n.m.* zinc.
zinia ('θi·nja; 'si-) *n.f.* zinnia.
zipizape (θi·pi'θa·pe; si·pi'sa·pe) *n.m. colloq.* rumpus.
¡zis, zas! ('θis'θas; 'sis'sas) *interj.* **1,** wham! bam! **2,** swish! swish!
zócalo ('θo·ka·lo; 'so-) *n.m.* **1,** base of a column, pedestal, etc. **2,** dado. **3,** baseboard. **4,** *Amer.* public square.
zodíaco (θo'ði·a·ko; so-) *n.m.* zodiac. **—zodiacal** (-ðja'kal) *adj.* zodiacal.
-zoico ('θoi·ko; 'soi·ko) *suffix* -zoic; *forming adjectives denoting* **1,** animal; animal life: *fanerozoico,* phanerozoic. **2,** *geol.* fossil era: *mesozoico,* Mesozoic.
zombi ('θom·bi; 'som-) *n.m. & f.* zombi.
-zón ('θon; 'son) *suffix, forming nouns and adjectives, usu. with augmentative force: tropezón,* big stumble; *cabezón,* big-headed; stubborn.
zona ('θo·na; 'so-) *n.f.* **1,** zone. **2,** *pathol.* shingles.
zonzo ('θon·θo; 'son·so) *adj.* **1,** insipid; inane. **2,** slow-witted; dull. *—n.m.* boob; fool; ninny. **—zoncería** (-θe'ri·a; -se'ri·a) *also, Amer.,* **zoncera** (-'θe·ra; -'se·ra) *n.f.* inanity; foolishness.
zoo- (θo·o; so·o) *prefix* zoo-; animal; *zoología,* zoölogy.
-zoo ('θo·o; 'so·o) *suffix* -zoon; animal: *espermatozoo,* spermatozoon.
zoología (θo·o·lo'xi·a; so-) *n.f.* zoölogy. **—zoológico** (-'lo·xi·ko) *adj.* zoölogical. **—zoólogo** (-'o·lo·ɣo) *n.m.* zoölogist.
zopenco (θo'pen·ko; so-) *n.m., colloq.* blockhead. *—adj., colloq.* stupid.
zopilote (θo·pi'lo·te; so-) *n.m., Amer.* turkey buzzard.
zopo ('θo·po; 'so-) *adj.* crippled; deformed. *—n.m.* cripple.
zoquete (θo'ke·te; so-) *n.m.* **1,** stub; chunk; stump (*of wood, bread, etc.*). **2,** *colloq.* stumpy or stubby fellow. **3,** *colloq.* blockhead; dolt. *—adj.* doltish.
zoroástrico (θo·ro'as·tri·ko; so-) *adj.* Zoroastrian. **—zoroastrismo,** *n.m.* Zoroastrianism.
zorra ('θo·rra; 'so-) *n.f.* **1,** fox. **2,** she-fox; vixen. **3,** *colloq.* drunkenness. **4,** *colloq.* prostitute. **5,** heavy truck; dray.
zorrero (θo'rre·ro; so-) *n.m., also,* **perro zorrero,** foxhound.
zorrillo (θo'rri·ʎo; so'rri·jo) *n.m., Amer.* skunk.
zorro ('θo·rro; 'so-) *n.m.* **1,** fox; male fox. **2,** *fig.* sly, crafty person. **—estar hecho un zorro,** to be drowsy. **—hacerse el zorro,** to play dumb; play deaf.
zorruno (θo'rru·no; so-) *adj.* fox (*attrib.*); foxlike.
zorzal (θor'θal; sor'sal) *n.m.* **1,** thrush. **2,** *colloq.* sharp fellow; fox. **3,** *So.Amer., colloq.* booby; dupe.
zote ('θo·te; 'so-) *n.m. colloq.* blockhead.
zozobra (θo'θo·βra; so'so-) *n.f.* **1,** shipwreck; danger of shipwreck. **2,** anguish; anxiety. **—zozobrar,** *v.i.* to founder; sink.
zuavo ('θwa·βo; 'swa-) *n.m.* Zouave.
zucarino (θu·ka'ri·no; su-) *adj.* = **sacarino.**
zueco ('θwe·ko; 'swe-) *n.m.* sabot.
-zuelo ('θwe·lo; 'swe-), *fem.* **-zuela** (-la) *suffix, forming diminutives: bribonzuelo,* little rascal.

zulú (θu'lu; su-) *adj.* & *n.m.* & *f.* Zulu.

zumaque (θu'ma·ke; su-) *n.m.* sumac.

zumba ('θum·ba; 'sum-) *n.f.* **1,** banter; raillery. **2,** *colloq.* jeer; hiss; hoot. **3,** *Amer., colloq.* beating.

zumbar (θum'bar; sum-) *v.i.* to buzz; hum. —*v.t.* **1,** *colloq.* to throw (a punch, blow, missile, etc.). **2,** *Amer., colloq.* to put out; throw out. —**zumbarse,** *v.r.* **1,** *colloq.* to become sassy. **2,** *Amer., colloq.* to scram; clear out.

zumbido (θum'bi·ðo; sum-) *n.m.* hum; buzz.

zumbón (θum'bon; sum-) *adj.* waggish; jesting. —*n.m.* wag.

zumo ('θu·mo; 'su-) *n.m.* juice. —**zumoso,** *adj.* juicy.

zuncho ('θun·tʃo; 'sun-) *n.m.* **1,** hoop; metal strap. **2,** ferrule. —**zunchar,** *v.t.* to strap; bind with hoops or straps.

zunzún (θun'θun; sun'sun) *n.m., Amer.* a kind of hummingbird.

zurcir (θur'θir; sur'sir) *v.t.* [*pres. ind.* **zurzo, zurces;** *pres.subjve.* **zurza**] to darn. —**zurcido,** *n.m., also,* **zurcidura,** *n.f.* darn; patch.

zurdo ('θur·ðo; 'sur-) *adj.* **1,** lefthanded. **2,** gauche. —**a zurdas, 1,** lefthandedly. **2,** clumsily.

zuro ('θu·ro; 'su-) *n.m.* corncob. —*adj.* wild (*of doves or pigeons*).

zurra ('θu·rra; 'su-) *n.f.* **1,** flogging; beating; trouncing. **2,** *colloq.* continuous task; grind. **3,** fight; brawl. **4,** treating; curing (*of hides*).

zurrapa (θu'rra·pa; su-) *n.f.* dregs (*pl.*).

zurrar (θu'rrar; su-) *v.t.* **1,** to flog; beat; trounce. **2,** to berate; upbraid. **3,** to treat; cure (hides). —**zurrarse,** *v.r.* **1,** to befoul oneself. **2,** *colloq.* to be scared stiff.

zurrón (θu'rron; su-) *n.m.* **1,** game bag; shepherd's pouch; shoulder bag. **2,** membranous covering; sac.

zurullo (θu'ru·ʎo; su'ru·jo) *n.m.* round lump; gob.

zurza ('θur·θa; 'sur·sa) *v., pres. subjve. of* **zurcir.**

zurzo ('θur·θo; 'sur·so) *v., 1st pers.sing.pres.ind. of* **zurcir.**

zutano (θu'ta·no; su-) *n.m.* See **fulano.**

SUMMARY OF SPANISH GRAMMAR

I. *The Alphabet*

The Spanish alphabet consists of the following 28 letters.

Letter	*Name*	*Pronunciation*
a	a	(a)
b	be	(be)
c	ce	(θe; se)
ch	che	(tʃe)
d	de	(de)
e	e	(e)
f	efe	('e·fe)
g	ge	(xe)
h	hache	('a·tʃe)
i	i	(i)
j	jota	('xo·ta)
l	ele	('e·le)
ll	elle	('e·ʎe; -je)
m	eme	('e·me)
n	ene	('e·ne)
ñ	eñe	('e·ɲe)
o	o	(o)
p	pe	(pe)
q	cu	(ku)
r	ere	('e·re)
rr	erre	('e·rre)
s	ese	('e·se)
t	te	(te)
u	u	(u)
v	ve, uve	(be; 'u·βe)
x	equis	('e·kis)
y	i griega	(i'ɣrje·ɣa)
z	zeda *or* zeta	('θe·ða; -ta 'se·ða; -ta)

k (ka) and **w** (doble u) are found only in words of foreign origin. The letters **ch**, **ll**, **ñ**, and **rr** are counted as separate letters and (except for **rr**) are so treated in the alphabetization of Spanish words.

II. *Key to Spanish Pronunciation*

The center dot (·) is used to divide syllables. This is the *phonetic* division of syllables, which may often not agree with the orthographic rules for division of syllables. The stress mark (') is used instead of the center dot to mark the stresses. It is placed at the beginning of the stressed syllable. The symbol (ˌ) denoting secondary stress, which appears in the pronunciation of many words in the English-Spanish section of this dictionary, is not used in the Spanish pronunciations, since the Spanish speech level is quite even in all syllables except the syllable bearing primary stress.

If a pronunciation is broken at the end of a line, the center dot is placed after the syllable that ends the line. This is done even when the syllable beginning the next line is preceded by the stress mark, which would otherwise replace the center dot.

VOWELS

Phonetic Symbol	*Approximate English Sound*	*Examples*
a	like *a* in *what, father*	**bala** ('ba·la) **acá** (a'ka)
e	when followed by a single consonant or any vowel, or standing at the end of a word, pronounced like *é* in *café*	**pelo** ('pe·lo) **peor** (pe'or) **ante** ('an·te)
	when followed by more than one consonant, or by a single consonant at the end of a word, pronounced like *e* in *let*	**vengo** ('ben·go) **perro** ('pe·rro) **hotel** (o'tel)
i	when not preceded or followed by a vowel, or when stressed even though preceded or followed by a vowel, pronounced like *i* in *machine*	**misa** ('mi·sa) **ibis** ('i·βis) **país** (pa'is) **río** ('ri·o)
	when preceded by a vowel (except **u**) in the same syllable, pronounced like *y* in *day, boy* (See the diphthongs **ai**, **ei**, **oi**, and the triphthongs **jai**, **jei**, **wai**, **wei**)	**reino** ('rei·no) **boina** ('boi·na) **fraile** ('frai·le)
o	when followed by a single consonant or any vowel, or standing at the end of a word, pronounced like *o* in *note, going, piano,* but only about half as long and without the *w* sound usually heard at the end of the English vowel	**moda** ('mo·ða) **coágulo** (ko'a·ɣu·lo) **paso** ('pa·so)
	when followed by more than one consonant, or by a single consonant at the end of a word, pronounced like *o* in *order*	**bolsa** ('bol·sa) **farol** (fa'rol)
u	when not preceded or followed by a vowel, or when stressed even though preceded or followed by a vowel, pronounced like *u* in *June*	**ruta** ('ru·ta) **unir** (u'nir) **ataúd** (a·ta'uð) **falúa** (fa'lu·a)
	when preceded by another vowel (except **i**) in the same syllable, pronounced like *w* in *how* (See the diphthongs **au, eu**)	**pausa** ('pau·sa) **deuda** ('deu·ða)

DIPHTHONGS

Phonetic Symbol	*Approximate English Sound*	*Examples*
ai	like *i* in *site*	**baile** ('bai·le) **hay** (ai)
au	like *ow* in *brow*	**fauna** ('fau·na)
ei	like *a* in *gate*	**reino** ('rei·no) **ley** (lei)
eu	like *ayw* in *wayward*	**deuda** ('deu·ða)
oi	like *oi* in *boil*	**boina** ('boi·na) **estoy** (es'toi)
ja	like *ya* in *yacht*	**enviamos** (en'βja·mos) **guayaba** (gwa'ja·βa)
je	like *ye* in *yes*	**tiene** ('tje·ne) **huye** ('u·je)
jo	like *yo* in *yore*	**biombo** ('bjom·bo) **peyote** (pe'jo·te)
ju	like *u* in *use*	**viuda** ('bju·ða) **ayuda** (a'ju·ða)
wa	like *wa* in *watch*	**cuanto** ('kwan·to)
we	like *wa* in *wake*	**bueno** ('bwe·no)
wi	like *wee* in *weed*	**cuidado** (kwi'ða·ðo)
wo	like *uo* in *quorum*	**cuota** ('kwo·ta)

TRIPHTHONGS

jai	like *yi* in the exclamation *yikes!*	**cambiáis** (kam'bjais)
jei	like the English word *yea*	**cambiéis** (kam'bjeis)
wai	like *wi* in *wide*	**uai** between consonants: **insinuáis** (in·si'nwais) **uay** at the end of a word: **Paraguay** (pa·ra'ɣwai)
wei	like *wai* in *wait*	**uei** between consonants: **insinuéis** (in·si'nweis) **uey** at the end of a word: **buey** (bwei)

CONSONANTS

b	like *b* in *cabin*	**b** or **v** at the beginning of a word: **bola** ('bo·la) **vaya** ('ba·ja) **b** following **m:** **rumbo** ('rum·bo)

Phonetic Symbol	Approximate English Sound	Examples
β	like *v* in *ever*, but with both lips nearly touching (not, as in English *v*, with the lower lip between the upper and lower teeth)	**b** in all positions except at the beginning of a word or following **m**: **cabo** ('ka·βo) **sobre** ('so·βre) **alba** ('al·βa) **v** in all positions except at the beginning of a word: **envío** (en'βi·o) **vivir** (bi'βir) **tuve** ('tu·βe) **salvo** ('sal·βo)
p	like *p* in *tepid*	**pata** ('pa·ta) **supe** ('su·pe)
f	like *f* in *knife*	**fonda** ('fon·da) **gafa** ('ga·fa)
m	like *m* in *some*	**mana** ('ma·na) **lomo** ('lo·mo)
t	like *t* in *satin*, but with the tip of the tongue touching the upper teeth, not (as in English) the alveolar ridge	**toma** ('to·ma) **meta** ('me·ta)
θ	like *th* in *think*	**c** (in *ceceo* pronunciation) before **e** or **i**: **cena** ('θe·na) **cita** ('θi·ta) **acción** (ak'θjon) **z** in all positions (in *ceceo* pronunciation): **zumo** ('θu·mo) **moza** ('mo·θa) **caz** (kaθ)
d	like *d* in *day*, but with the tip of the tongue touching the upper teeth, not (as in English) the alveolar ridge	**d** at the beginning of a word, or following **l** or **n**: **damos** ('da·mos) **falda** ('fal·da) **hondo** ('on·do)
ð	like *th* in *rather*	**d** between vowels, or following a consonant other than **l** or **n**, or preceded by a vowel and followed by **r**, or at the end of a word: **modelo** (mo'ðe·lo) **nardo** ('nar·ðo) **madre** ('ma·ðre)

Phonetic Symbol	*Approximate English Sound*	*Examples*
		pared (pa'reð)
n	like *n* in *unity*	**nada** ('na·ða) **hongo** ('on·go)
s	like *s* in *see*	**s** in all positions: **seso** ('se·so) **estar** (es'tar) **lunes** ('lu·nes) **c** (in *seseo* pronunciation) before **e** or **i**: **cena** ('se·na) **cita** ('si·ta) **acción** (ak'sjon) **z** in all positions (in *seseo* pronunciation): **zumo** ('su·mo) **moza** ('mo·sa) **caz** (kas)
k	like *c* in *care* or *k* in *keen*	**c** before **a, o, u** or a consonant: **caber** (ka'βer) **cosa** ('ko·sa) **cuna** ('ku·na) **activo** (ak'ti·βo) **qu** (always followed by **e** or **i**): **queda** ('ke·ða) **quinta** ('kin·ta) **quiosco** ('kjos·ko) **x** (the first element): **exacto** (ek'sak·to) **sexo** ('sek·so) **k** in some words of foreign origin: **kilogramo** (ki·lo'ɣra·mo)
g	like *g* in *go*	**g** at the beginning of a word and followed by **a, o,** or **u**, or in the middle of a word and preceded by **n**: **gato** ('ga·to) **gorra** ('go·rra) **gusano** (gu'sa·no) **mango** ('man·go)
ɣ	like *g* in *cigar*, but with greatly reduced tension and with vibration of the uvula	**g** in the middle of a word and followed by **a, o,** or **u** and not preceded by **n**:

Phonetic Symbol	*Approximate English Sound*	*Examples*
		paga ('pa·ɣa) **digo** ('di·ɣo) **laguna** (la'ɣu·na) **cargo** ('kar·ɣo) **vulgar** (bul'ɣar)
x	like *ch* in Scottish *loch* or German *ach*	**j** in all positions, except sometimes at the end of a word: **justo** ('xus·to) **traje** ('tra·xe) **reloj** (re'lo) *but* **relojes** (re'lo·xes)
		g followed by **e** or **i**: **gemir** (xe'mir) **angina** (an'xi·na)
		x in a few words: **México** ('me·xi·ko)
		h in some words, as a variant pronunciation (**h** is usually silent): **holgorio** (ol'ɣo·rjo) *or* (xol'ɣo·rjo)
tʃ	like *ch* in *chat*	**ch** in all positions: **chino** ('tʃi·no) **mucho** ('mu·tʃo) **cancha** ('kan·tʃa)
ɲ	like *ny* in *canyon*	**ñ** in all positions: **caña** (ka·ɲa) **ñame** ('ɲa·me)
ʎ	like *lli* in *million*	**ll** in all positions: **llamar** (ʎa'mar) **pollo** ('po·ʎo)
j	like *y* in *yet*	**y** in all positions except at the end of a word: **ya** (ja) **huyo** ('u·jo) *but* **carey** (ka'rei)
		i as first element in a diphthong (see **ja, je, jo, ju**) or triphthong (see **jai, jei**)
		ll as a variant pronunciation in many regions: **llamar** (ja'mar)

Phonetic Symbol	*Approximate English Sound*	*Examples*
		pollo ('po·jo)
l	like *l* in *love*	**l** in all positions: **lata** ('la·ta) **calma** ('kal·ma) **útil** ('u·til)
r	at the end of a word, or in the middle of a word and not preceded by **l**, **n**, or **s**, pronounced with a single flap of the tongue, somewhat like the British pronunciation of *r* in *very* or the relaxed pronunciation of *dd* in *ladder*	**deber** (de'βer) **pero** ('pe·ro) **otro** ('o·tro) **forma** ('for·ma)
	at the beginning of a word, or in the middle of a word and preceded by **l**, **n**, or **s**, strongly trilled, like *rr*	**roto** ('ro·to) **alrededor** (al·re·ðe'ðor) **enredo** (en're·ðo) **israelita** (is·ra·e'li·ta)
rr	strongly trilled, like the Scottish burr	**rr** (so written only between vowels): **perro** ('pe·rro) **corro** ('ko·rro)
w	like *w* in *wet*	**u** as first element in a diphthong (see **wa, we, wi, wo**) or triphthong (see **wai, wei**)
		w or **wh** in some foreign words: **wat** (wat) **whiskey** ('wis·ki)

FURTHER REMARKS ON SPANISH PRONUNCIATION

1. Regional and variant pronunciations. The following are regularly shown in our notation:

a. *Ceceo* and *seseo* alternates. *Ceceo* (θe'θe·o) and the related verb *cecear* (θe·θe'ar) are used to refer to speakers of Spanish who regularly use (θ) for **z** in all positions and for **c** before **e** or **i**; see (θ) in the pronunciation table. *Ceceo* speakers are concentrated largely in central and northern Spain, notably in Castile. Also, certain areas of the New World, particularly Peru, Colombia, and Ecuador, have a considerable number of *ceceo* speakers, especially among the more conservative or aristocratic classes. Furthermore, a number of educated speakers in all regions deliberately cultivate *ceceo,* in the belief that it is the truer and nobler form of Spanish.

Seseo (se'se·o) and the related verb *sesear* (se·se'ar) are used to refer to speakers of Spanish who regularly use (s) for **z** in all positions and for **c** before **e** or **i**; see (s) in the pronunciation table. *Seseo* is almost universal in the New World and in insular Spain (Canary

Islands, etc.) as well as over most of southern Spain. The speakers of Judeo-Spanish, or Ladino, also regularly use *seseo.*

b. *Yeísmo* (je'is·mo) and the related noun *yeísta* (je'is·ta) are used to refer to speakers of Spanish who do not distinguish between **ll** and **y**, pronouncing both as (j); see (ʎ) and (j) in the pronunciation table. *Yeísmo* has gradually encroached upon the use of (ʎ) to the extent that today it may be said to be universal in all regions except among the more conservative or scholarly groups. In some regions not only have both sounds been merged but they have been further evolved to (ʒ) or (dʒ); see **2a**, below.

2. Regional and variant pronunciations not shown in our notation:

a. Variant pronunciation—chiefly in Argentina, Uruguay, Paraguay, and parts of Chile—of **ll** and also of **y** as (ʒ) or (dʒ):

calle ('ka·ʎe) *or* ('ka·je) *or* ('ka·ʒe)
yo (jo) *or* (ʒo) *or* (dʒo)

b. Common variant pronunciation of **s** as (z), especially before a voiced consonant:

mismo ('mis·mo) *or* ('miz·mo)
sesgo ('ses·ɣo) *or* ('sez·ɣo)

c. Common variant pronunciation of **nv** as (mb):

convenir (kon·βe'nir) *or* (kom·be'nir)

d. Common variant pronunciation of **x** as (s), especially before consonants:

extático (eks'ta·ti·ko) *or* (es'ta·ti·ko)

also sometimes between vowels:

exacto (ek'sak·to) *or* (e'sak·to)

another variant between vowels is (ɣz):

existe (ek'sis·te) *or* (eɣ'zis·te)

e. Common variant pronunciation of **j** and of **g** before **e** and **i** as (h):

justo ('xus·to) *or* ('hus·to)
traje ('tra·xe) *or* ('tra·he)

f. Syntactical phonetics: the treatment of groups of words in spoken utterance as a unit. In this dictionary, we naturally give the pronunciation of each word as if standing alone or at the beginning of an utterance. In normal speech, the initial sound of a word will often undergo certain modifications, as though it were in the middle of a word.

d at the beginning of a word may be pronounced as (ð) rather than (d) if it follows closely upon a word ending in a vowel or in a consonant other than **l** or **n**:

vamos a dormir ('ba·mo·sa·ðor'mir)

b at the beginning of a word may be pronounced as (β) rather than (b) if it follows closely upon a word ending in a vowel or in a consonant other than **m**:

agua bien fría (ˈa·ɣwa·βjenˈfri·a)

s at the end of a word may be pronounced as (z) rather than (s) if the next word begins with a voiced consonant:

los dientes (lozˈðjen·tes)

g. Aspiration, or loss of **s**. In many regions, and especially in the West Indies, **s** at the end of a word or preceded by a vowel and followed by a consonant may be pronounced as a mere aspiration (h) or may be elided altogether; in the latter case, however, there is usually lengthening of the preceding vowel:

bonitos (boˈni·tos) *or* (boˈni·toh) *or* (boˈni·to:)
postre (ˈpos·tre) *or* (ˈpoh·tre) *or* (ˈpo:·tre)

III. Stress and Accentuation

Spanish uses regularly only one written accent, the "acute" accent (´). The following simple rules govern its use:

1. Words ending in a vowel (not including **y**) or **n** or **s** are stressed on the syllable before the last: hablado, vinieron, españoles.

2. Words ending in a consonant other than **n** or s (but including **y**) are stressed on the last syllable: entender, arrabal, codorniz, estoy.

3. Words not stressed according to one or the other of the above rules must have the written accent over the vowel of the stressed syllable: rubí, acá, cayó, nación, cortés, carácter, fácil, páramo.

4. The orthographic accent often serves to distinguish words that are spelled alike but differ in meaning:

se, reflexive pronoun
sé, I know

tu, possessive adjective
tú, personal pronoun

este, demonstrative adjective
éste, demonstrative pronoun

como, declarative
¿cómo?, interrogative; **¡cómo!**, exclamatory

In most cases, the written accent represents a genuine stress, or preserves a historic stress, on the words so marked. Its use is nevertheless governed by orthographic rather than phonetic rule.

5. Adjectives that have a written accent retain the accent when adding **-mente** to form adverbs, even though the stress shifts to the syllable before the last: fácilmente, últimamente, cortésmente.

Words that have a written accent often retain the accent when joined to other words to form compounds: décimotercio or decimotercio; décimoséptimo or decimoséptimo.

Verb forms that have a written accent retain the accent when an object pronoun is added: déme, el acabóse.

6. The written accent over the vowel **i** or **u** serves to show that the sound does not form a diphthong with an adjacent vowel or a triphthong with two adjacent vowels: hacían, veíamos, evalúo. The vowels **i** and **u** (commonly called "weak" vowels) would otherwise form a

diphthong with an adjacent **a**, **e**, or **o** ("strong" vowels)—averiguo, hacia—or a triphthong with any two adjacent vowels—cambiáis, evaluáis. When the vowels **i** and **u** come together and do not form a diphthong, one of them must have a written accent: destruís, flúido.

The written accent is always placed over the strong vowel in a diphthong or triphthong whenever it is required to mark the stressed syllable, in accordance with rules (1), (2), and (3) above: cantáis, habéis, continuáis, evaluéis.

7. The pronouncements of the Spanish Royal Academy issued in 1952 permit departures from the rules hitherto in effect in the following classes of words:

a. The combination **ui** is considered always to form a diphthong, and neither vowel needs to be marked orthographically unless otherwise required by rules (1), (2), and (3) above. Thus, without accent: jesuita, huido, juicio, construido, fluido; with accent: benjuí, casuístico.

b. The silent letter **h** between vowels does not prevent these vowels from forming a diphthong: desahucio (de'sau·θjo). Consequently, when such vowels do not form a diphthong, the stressed vowel of the pair may be written with or without accent: vahído, búho, rehúso *or* vahido, buho, rehuso.

c. Monosyllabic verb forms do not require a written accent: fue, fui, vio, dio. This rule is even extended to include infinitives, which now are often written without accent: oir, reir, huir.

IV. *Punctuation and Capitalization*

Spanish punctuation differs from English in the following respects:

1. The **question mark** and the **exclamation mark** are used at both the beginning and the end of interrogative and exclamatory sentences, respectively, the first sign being inverted:

¿Dónde está Juan?
¡Qué bueno!

In longer sentences in which only a part of the sentence is a question or exclamation the signs are placed only at the beginning and the end of that part:

Dime: ¿que harás en mi lugar?

Cuando salí de la Habana ¡Válgame Dios!
Nadie me ha visto salir si no fui yo . . .

2. Quotation marks (« ») are used to indicate direct quotations or citations from a text:

«Veo que las leyes son contra los flacos, dice Luis Mejía, como las telarañas contra las moscas.»

Dialogue, however, is set off by the use of dashes. The dash precedes each change of speaker:

——¡Qué barbaridad! Se me olvidó la cartera.
——María, ¿necesitas dinero?
——Sí, tengo que comprarle un regalo a mi hermano.
——¿Cuánto piensas gastar?
——Como cinco dólares.

3. Capitalization is more restricted in Spanish than in English. Nouns and adjectives denoting nationality, religion, language, etc., names of the days of the week, the months of the year, and the pronoun *yo* are usually not capitalized: un francés, la nación rusa, el idioma inglés, un presbiteriano, martes, junio, yo.

V. *Division of Syllables in Spanish*

CONSONANTS

1. **ch, ll, rr** count as single letters and are never separated:

pe·cho o·lla pe·rro

2. Single consonants between vowels go with the second vowel:

ca·be·za pa·re·cer

Note: **y** is treated as a consonant when it is followed by a vowel; in other cases it is treated as a vowel.

3. The groups **pr, pl, br, bl, fr, fl, tr, dr, cr, cl, gr, gl** go with the following vowel and are never separated:

re·pri·mir co·pla te·cla

4. In other groups of two consonants, whether identical or different, the consonants are divided between the preceding and the following vowel:

res·pi·ro hon·ra ac·ción in·noble at·las

5. In groups of three consonants, the first two go with the preceding vowel and the third with the following vowel:

ins·tin·to obs·tá·cu·lo

Exception: The groups listed in (3), above, are not separated:

en·tre com·pra tem·plo ins·tru·men·to

Note: A group of four consonants that does not contain one of the groups listed in (3), above, is rarely found, if at all.

VOWELS

6. In any combination of two of the following: **a, e, o,** the syllable is divided between the two vowels:

ca·o·ba i·de·a·ción

7. In any combination of two vowels in which one is **a, e,** or **o** and the other is **i** or **u,** and there is no accent mark on the **i** or **u,** the vowels form a diphthong and are not separated:

jo·fai·na vian·da em·bau·car men·guan·te
vi·rrei·na con·tien·da en·deu·dar·se con·sue·lo
co·loi·dal na·cio·nal duo·de·no

If there is an accent mark on the **a, e,** or **o** of the group, the two vowels still form a diphthong and are not separated:

es·táis es·co·géis cuán·do

If the accent mark falls on the **i** or **u** of the group, the two vowels do not form a diphthong and are separated:

ca·í·da pen·sa·rí·a·mos a·ta·úd re·ú·ne

8. In any combination of **i** and **u**, that is **ui** or **iu**, no division of syllables is made between these two vowels. This holds whether there is an accent mark or not:

ciu·dad rui·do ca·suís·ti·co

9. In any combination of three vowels (more than three do not occur), there is no division of syllables between any two vowels of the group. This holds whether there is an accent mark on any of the vowels or not:

a·pre·ciáis

VI. *Nouns*

1. *Gender*

Spanish nouns have grammatical rather than natural gender. Consequently, the gender of a noun may have nothing to do with the fact that it denotes a male or female being or something inanimate. Nouns have either masculine or feminine gender. The neuter gender in Spanish is limited to the neuter pronouns.

In this dictionary all nouns and pronouns are labeled to show gender. To determine the gender of nouns not included in this dictionary, some general rules (though there are exceptions) may be applied:

a. Nouns denoting male human beings or animals are generally masculine: el señor, el caballo. *But:* la guardia, la centinela.

Nouns ending in **-o** are generally masculine: el cuarto, el mexicano. *But:* la mano.

Days of the week, months, rivers, lakes, seas, oceans, mountains are generally masculine: el lunes, el marzo, el Paraná, el Atlántico, los Pirineos.

Nouns of Greek origin ending in **-ma** are masculine: el tema, el drama.

b. Nouns denoting female human beings or animals are generally feminine: la señora, la vaca.

Nouns ending in **-a** are generally feminine. *But:* el mapa, el día.

Nouns ending in **-ez**, **-dad**, **-ion**, **-tad**, **-tud**, **-umbre** are generally feminine: la vejez, la humanidad, la nación, la dificultad, la juventud, la certidumbre.

Abstract nouns ending in **-ón** are generally feminine: la razón, la comezón. *But:* nouns with augmentative suffix **-ón** are masculine: el montón (the feminine augmentative suffix is **-ona**: la regañona).

Letters of the alphabet and phonetic sounds or symbols are feminine: la b, la g, la ð.

c. Abstract nouns formed from adjectives are neuter and take the article lo: lo bueno, lo largo.

d. Some nouns are either masculine or feminine, with little or no difference in meaning: el *or* la azúcar, el *or* la mar.

e. Some nouns have different meanings in the masculine and in the feminine: el guía (the guide), la guía (guidebook, directory); el capital (money), la capital (seat of government).

f. Nouns denoting persons and ending in **-ista**, **-ante**, **-cida**, etc. have only one form for the masculine and the feminine, the gender being shown only in the article: et *or* la artista, el *or* la paciente, el *or* la estudiante, el *or* la homicida.

2. *Formation of the Plural*

a. Nouns ending in an unstressed vowel add **s**: el palo, los palos; la casa, las casas.

b. Nouns ending in a consonant or **y** add **es**: la mujer, las mujeres; el cristal, los cristales; el buey, los bueyes; la ley, las leyes.

c. Nouns ending in a stressed vowel (except **é**) usually add **es**, but sometimes **s**: el rubí, los rubíes; el cebú, los cebúes; el bajá, los bajaes; el paletó, los paletoes. *But:* el papá, los papás; la mamá, las mamás; el bongó, los bongós.

d. Nouns ending in stressed **e** add **s**: el bebé, los bebés; el café, los cafés.

e. Nouns of more than one syllable ending in **s** preceded by an unstressed vowel remain unchanged in the plural: la crisis, las crisis; el jueves, los jueves. *But:* el mes, los meses; el dios, los dioses.

f. Foreign nouns or recent borrowings ending in a consonant may form the plural by adding **s** or **es**, though usage tends more and more to favor **s**: el club, los clubs (*or* clubes); el complot, los complots (*or* complotes); el album, los álbums (*or* álbumes).

g. Spelling and accentuation of plural forms.

1) Nouns ending in **z** change the **z** to **c** when adding **es** to form the plural: el lápiz, los lápices; la raíz, las raíces.

2) With but few exceptions, the stressed vowel of the singular is stressed also in the plural. Consequently a written accent may have to be dropped or added, in accordance with the rules of Spanish accentuation:

written accent dropped	la nación, las naciones el mohín, los mohines
written accent added	el crimen, los crímenes el joven, los jóvenes
Exceptions: the stress shifts to a different syllable in the plural	el carácter, los caracteres el régimen, los regímenes

3. *Formation of the Feminine*

a. Nouns ending in **o** change the **o** to **a**: el muchacho, la muchacha; el tío, la tía.

b. Nouns ending in **-án**, **-ón**, **-or**, **-ol**, **-és**, **-ín**, add **a** to form the feminine:

el haragán, la haragana
el burlón, la burlona
el profesor, la profesora
el español, la española
el francés, la francesa
el bailarín, la bailarina

c. Nouns ending in **-ista, -ante, -ente, -cida,** etc. do not change in the feminine (see **1f**, above).

A few nouns ending in **-ante** or **-ente** change the **e** to **a** in the feminine: el asistente, la asistenta; el ayudante, la ayudanta; el practicante, la practicanta; el sirviente, la sirvienta.

d. Some nouns have a different suffix in the feminine: el poeta, la poetisa; el actor, la actriz; el díacono, la diaconisa; el emperador, la emperatriz; el duque, la duquesa; el abad, la abadesa.

VII. *Adjectives*

1. *Agreement of Adjectives*

a. Formation of the Feminine

1) Adjectives ending in **o** change the **o** to **a** in the feminine: bueno, buena; malo, mala.

2) Adjectives ending in a consonant or a vowel other than **o** have the same form for the masculine and the feminine: débil, familiar, común, verde, elegante, egoísta, etc.

3) Adjectives of nationality ending in a consonant add **a** to form the feminine: español, española; inglés, inglesa.

4) Adjectives ending in **-án, -ón,** and **-or** (except comparatives) add **a** to form the feminine: holgazán, holgazana; querendón, querendona.

5) Comparatives ending in **-or** do not change in the feminine: mejor, peor, mayor, menor, inferior, superior, etc.

b. Formation of the Plural

Adjectives follow in general the same rules for formation of the plural as nouns (see **VI 2**, above).

2. *Comparison of Adjectives*

a. The comparative of most adjectives (and adverbs) is formed by placing **más** (or **menos**) before the adjective or adverb. The superlative is the same as the comparative, except that it usually requires the definite article or a possessive adjective before it.

fácil, easy *más fácil,* easier *el* (*la*) *más fácil,* (the) easiest

tarde, late *más tarde,* later (*lo*) *más tarde,* (the) latest

b. Some adjectives (and adverbs) have special forms for the comparative and superlative. (Most of these permit also the regularly formed comparative and superlative.)

bueno, good *mejor,* better *el* (*la*) *mejor,* (the) best
malo, bad *peor,* worse *el* (*la*) *peor,* (the) worst

grande, large *mayor,* larger, older *el* (*la*) *mayor,* (the) largest, oldest

pequeño, small *menor,* smaller, younger *el* (*la*) *menor,* (the) smallest, youngest

alto, high *superior,* higher, upper *el* (*la*) *superior,* (the) highest, uppermost *bajo*, low *inferior*, lower, nether *el* (*la*) *inferior*, (the) lowest, nethermost

bien, well *mejor*, better *mejor*, best
mal, badly *peor*, worse *peor*, worst

mucho, much / *muchos*, many } *más*, more *más*, most

poco, little *menos*, less *menos*, least
pocos, few *menos*, fewer *menos*, fewest

3. *The Absolute Superlative*

The superlative described in **a** and **b**, above, is known as the **relative superlative**. It signifies a quality possessed by a person or thing in a higher degree than any of the other persons or things with which it is compared. The **absolute superlative**, on the other hand, signifies only a quality possessed by a person or thing in a very high degree, without direct comparison with any other persons or things.

The absolute superlative is formed by adding the suffix **-ísimo** to the stem of the adjective:

rapidísimo, most rapid, very rapid
facilísimo, most easy, very easy

Adverbs ending in **-mente** form the absolute superlative by inserting **-ísima** between the stem of the adjective and the suffix **-mente**: *bravísimamente*, most bravely, very bravely.

Other adverbs form the absolute superlative in the same way as adjectives:

muchísimo, most, very much
poquísimo, least, very little

4. *Irregular Superlatives*

bueno—óptimo, bonísimo (*or* buenísimo)
malo—pésimo, malísimo
grande—máximo, grandísimo
pequeño—mínimo, pequeñísimo
acre—acérrimo
antiguo—antiquísimo
pobre—paupérrimo
mísero—misérrimo
probable—probabilísimo (similarly all adjectives ending in **-ble**)

VIII. Adverbs

1. *Regular Adverbs*

These are formed in Spanish from nearly all adjectives by adding the suffix **-mente** to the *feminine* form of the adjective:

solo, solamente
feliz, felizmente
rápido, rápidamente

(Adjectives that have an orthographic accent retain the accent when adding **-mente** even though the principal stress moves to the penultimate syllable.)

2. *Special Forms*

Adjective	*Adverb*
bueno, good	*bien*, well
malo, bad	*mal*, badly, ill
mucho, much (adj. & adv.)	
poco, little (adj. & adv.)	
tardío, tardy	*tarde*, late
cercano, near, neighboring	*cerca*, near, close by
lejano, far, remote	*lejos*, far, far off

3. *Comparison of Adverbs*
(See *Comparison of Adjectives*, **VII 2**, above.)

IX. *Verbs*

1. *Regular Conjugations*

Spanish has three regular classes of verbs, with infinitives ending in **-ar** (1st conjugation), **-er** (2nd conjugation), and **-ir** (3rd conjugation).

The regular tenses are formed by dropping the ending **-ar**, **-er**, or **-ir** of the infinitive and adding the endings shown below in boldface type.

	Infinitive	*Gerund*	*Past Participle*
1st conjugation	am**ar**	am**ando**	am**ado**
2nd conjugation	tem**er**	tem**iendo**	tem**ido**
3rd conjugation	viv**ir**	viv**iendo**	viv**ido**

PRESENT INDICATIVE

	1st Conjugation	*2nd Conjugation*	*3rd Conjugation*
yo	am**o**	tem**o**	viv**o**
tú	am**as**	tem**es**	viv**es**
él, ella, Vd.	am**a**	tem**e**	viv**e**
nosotros	am**amos**	tem**emos**	viv**imos**
vosotros	am**áis**	tem**éis**	viv**ís**
ellos, ellas, Vds.	am**an**	tem**en**	viv**en**

IMPERATIVE

The imperative is normally used only in the second person singular, second person plural, and first person plural. Of these, the first two are properly imperatives; the last is the subjunctive form used as an imperative. There are furthermore no negative forms in Spanish. The negative imperative is expressed by the appropriate subjunctive forms.

1st Conjugation	*2nd Conjugation*	*3rd Conjugation*
am**a** (tú)	tem**e** (tú)	viv**e** (tú)
no am**es**	no tem**as**	no viv**as**
am**ad** (vosotros)	tem**ed** (vosotros)	viv**id** (vosotros)
no am**áis**	no tem**áis**	no viv**áis**

amemos (nosotros)	temamos (nosotros)	vivamos (nosotros)
no amemos	no temamos	no vivamos

IMPERFECT INDICATIVE

	1st Conjugation	*2nd Conjugation*	*3rd Conjugation*
yo	**amaba**	**temía**	**vivía**
tú	**amabas**	**temías**	**vivías**
él, ella, Vd.	**amaba**	**temía**	**vivía**
nosotros	**amábamos**	**temíamos**	**vivíamos**
vosotros	**amabais**	**temíais**	**vivíais**
ellos, ellas, Vds.	**amaban**	**temían**	**vivían**

FUTURE INDICATIVE

yo	**amaré**	**temeré**	**viviré**
tú	**amarás**	**temerás**	**vivirás**
él, ella, Vd.	**amará**	**temerá**	**vivirá**
nosotros	**amaremos**	**temeremos**	**viviremos**
vosotros	**amaréis**	**temeréis**	**viviréis**
ellos, ellas, Vds.	**amarán**	**temerán**	**vivirán**

CONDITIONAL

yo	**amaría**	**temería**	**viviría**
tú	**amarías**	**temerías**	**vivirías**
él, ella, Vd.	**amaría**	**temería**	**viviría**
nosotros	**amaríamos**	**temeríamos**	**viviríamos**
vosotros	**amaríais**	**temeríais**	**viviríais**
ellos, ellas, Vds.	**amarían**	**temerían**	**vivirían**

PRETERIT INDICATIVE

	1st Conjugation	*2nd Conjugation*	*3rd Conjugation*
yo	**amé**	**temí**	**viví**
tú	**amaste**	**temiste**	**viviste**
él, ella, Vd.	**amó**	**temió**	**vivió**
nosotros	**amamos**	**temimos**	**vivimos**
vosotros	**amasteis**	**temisteis**	**vivisteis**
ellos, ellas, Vds.	**amaron**	**temieron**	**vivieron**

PRESENT SUBJUNCTIVE

yo	**ame**	**tema**	**viva**
tú	**ames**	**temas**	**vivas**
él, ella, Vd.	**ame**	**tema**	**viva**
nosotros	**amemos**	**temamos**	**vivamos**
vosotros	**améis**	**temáis**	**viváis**
ellos, ellas, Vds.	**amen**	**teman**	**vivan**

IMPERFECT SUBJUNCTIVE

yo	**amara** **amase**	**temiera** **temiese**	**viviera** **viviese**
tú	**amaras** **amases**	**temieras** **temieses**	**vivieras** **vivieses**
él, ella, Vd.	**amara** **amase**	**temiera** **temiese**	**viviera** **viviese**
nosotros	**amáramos** **amásemos**	**temiéramos** **temiésemos**	**viviéramos** **viviésemos**
vosotros	**amarais** **amaseis**	**temierais** **temieseis**	**vivierais** **vivieseis**
ellos, ellas, Vds.	**amaran** **amasen**	**temieran** **temiesen**	**vivieran** **viviesen**

FUTURE SUBJUNCTIVE

	1st Conjugation	*2nd Conjugation*	*3rd Conjugation*
yo	**amare**	**temiere**	**viviere**
tú	**amares**	**temieres**	**vivieres**
él, ella, Vd.	**amare**	**temiere**	**viviere**
nosotros	**amáremos**	**temiéremos**	**viviéremos**
vosotros	**amareis**	**temiereis**	**viviereis**
ellos, ellas, Vds.	**amaren**	**temieren**	**vivieren**

2. *Auxiliary Verbs*

The principal auxiliary verbs of Spanish are **haber**, to have; **ser**, to be; and **estar**, to be. **Haber** has little use as an independent verb and functions largely as the auxiliary verb in forming (with the past participle) the **compound tenses** of all verbs. **Ser**, in addition to its other uses, functions as the auxiliary verb in forming (with the past participle) the **passive voice. Estar**, in addition to its other uses, functions as the auxiliary in forming (with the gerund) the **progressive tenses**. The conjugations of **haber**, **ser**, and **estar** are given below. A few other verbs, principally **tener** and **ir**, are used occasionally as auxiliaries. **Tener** is sometimes used in place of **haber** as a more emphatic auxiliary in forming the compound tenses.

tengo dicho . . ., I have said . . .
(that is, authoritatively)

Ir is sometimes used in place of **estar** in forming the progressive tenses:

va creciendo, it is growing
(that is, keeps on growing)

CONJUGATIONS OF AUXILIARY VERBS

Infinitive	*Gerund*	*Past Participle*
haber	habiendo	habido
ser	siendo	sido
estar	estando	estado

PRESENT INDICATIVE

haber	**ser**	**estar**
he	soy	estoy
has	eres	estás
ha	es	está
hemos (*also*, habemos)	somos	estamos
habéis	sois	estáis
han	son	están

IMPERATIVE

(*impve. rarely used*)

hé (tú)	sé (tú)	está (tú)
no hayas	no seas	no estés
habed (vosotros)	sed (vosotros)	estad (vosotros)
no hayáis	no seáis	no estéis
hayamos (nosotros)	seamos (nosotros)	estemos (nosotros)
no hayamos	no seamos	no estemos

IMPERFECT INDICATIVE

había	era	estaba
habías	eras	estabas
había	era	estaba
habíamos	éramos	estábamos
habíais	erais	estabais
habían	eran	estaban

FUTURE INDICATIVE

habré	seré	estaré
habrás	serás	estarás
habrá	será	estará
habremos	seremos	estaremos
habréis	seréis	estaréis
habrán	serán	estarán

CONDITIONAL

habría	sería	estaría
habrías	serías	estarías
habría	sería	estaría
habríamos	seríamos	estaríamos
habríais	seríais	estaríais
habrían	serían	estarían

PRETERIT INDICATIVE

hube	fui	estuve
hubiste	fuiste	estuviste
hubo	fue	estuvo
hubimos	fuimos	estuvimos
hubisteis	fuisteis	estuvisteis
hubieron	fueron	estuvieron

PRESENT SUBJUNCTIVE

haya	sea	esté
hayas	seas	estés
haya	sea	esté
hayamos	seamos	estémos
hayáis	seáis	estéis
hayan	sean	estén

IMPERFECT SUBJUNCTIVE

yo	hubiera / hubiese	fuera / fuese	estuviera / estuviese
tú	hubieras / hubieses	fueras / fueses	estuvieras / estuvieses
él, ella, Vd.	hubiera / hubiese	fuera / fuese	estuviera / estuviese
nosotros	hubiéramos / hubiésemos	fuéramos / fuésemos	estuviéramos / estuviésemos
vosotros	hubierais / hubieseis	fuerais / fueseis	estuvierais / estuvieseis
ellos, ellas, Vds.	hubieran / hubiesen	fueran / fuesen	estuvieran / estuviesen

FUTURE SUBJUNCTIVE

hubiere	fuere	estuviere
hubieres	fueres	estuvieres
hubiere	fuere	estuviere
hubiéremos	fuéremos	estuviéremos
hubiereis	fuereis	estuviereis
hubieren	fueren	estuvieren

3. *Compound Tenses*

These are normally formed with the appropriate tense of **haber** followed by the past participle. Only the first person singular of each tense is given below.

	amar	**temer**	**vivir**
Perfect infinitive	haber amado	haber temido	haber vivido
Perfect gerund	habiendo amado	habiendo temido	habiendo vivido

Perfect indicative	he amado	he temido	he vivido
Pluperfect indicative	había amado	había temido	había vivido
Future perfect indicative	habré amado	habré temido	habré vivido
Conditional perfect	habría amado	habría temido	habría vivido
Past anterior	hube amado	hube temido	hube vivido
Perfect subjunctive	haya amado	haya temido	haya vivido
Pluperfect subjunctive	hubiera amado hubiese amado	hubiera temido hubiese temido	hubiera vivido hubiese vivido
Future perfect subjunctive	hubiere amado	hubiere temido	hubiere vivido

4. *Irregular Verbs*

a. Radical-Changing Verbs

These are the true irregular verbs. The orthographic-changing verbs described in the following section are on the whole phonetically regular, and the changes in their inflected forms affect only the spelling. Radical-changing verbs, on the other hand, exhibit irregularities in their stem vowels under the influence of the shifting pattern of stress. These inflectional changes date back to the earliest stages in the development of the Spanish language from the parent Latin. Consequently, many of the most basic and most common verbs will be found to have irregularities of one kind or another. It is entirely possible furthermore for a verb to be both radical-changing and orthographic-changing. The radical-changing verbs may conveniently be grouped into three classes, according to the kind of change that is undergone by the stem vowel (that is, the last vowel before the infinitive ending **-ar**, **-er**, or **-ir**).

Class I consists of verbs of the 1st and 2nd conjugations in which the stem vowels **e** and **o** change to the diphthongs **ie** and **ue**, respectively, whenever they are stressed. This change affects the 1st, 2nd, and 3rd persons singular and the 3rd person plural of the present indicative and present subjunctive, and the 2nd person singular affirmative imperative. These are shown in the table below in boldface type.

	pensar		**perder**	
present indicative	**pienso**	pensamos	**pierdo**	perdemos
	piensas	pensáis	**pierdes**	perdéis
	piensa	**piensan**	**pierde**	**pierden**

present subjunctive	**piense**	pensemos	**pierda**	perdamos
	pienses	penséis	**pierdas**	perdáis
	piense	**piensen**	**pierda**	**pierdan**
imperative	**piensa**		**pierde**	

	acostar		**mover**	
present indicative	**acuesto**	acostamos	**muevo**	movemos
	acuestas	acostáis	**mueves**	movéis
	acuesta	**acuestan**	**mueve**	**mueven**
present subjunctive	**acueste**	acostemos	**mueva**	movamos
	acuestes	acostéis	**muevas**	mováis
	acueste	**acuesten**	**mueva**	**muevan**
imperative	**acuesta**		**mueve**	

Class II consists of verbs of the 3rd conjugation in which the stem vowels **e** and **o** change to **ie** and **ue**, respectively, whenever they are stressed, just as in Class I. In addition, the stem vowels **e** and **o** change to **i** and **u**, respectively, whenever they are unstressed and followed by an ending containing **a**, **ió**, or **ie**. This second change affects the gerund, the 1st and 2nd persons plural of the present subjunctive, the 3rd person singular and plural of the preterit indicative, and the entire imperfect subjunctive and future subjunctive. The irregular forms showing either of these changes are in boldface type in the table below.

	sentir		**morir**	
gerund	**sintiendo**		**muriendo**	
present indicative	**siento**	sentimos	**muero**	morimos
	sientes	sentís	**mueres**	morís
	siente	**sienten**	**muere**	**mueren**
present subjunctive	**sienta**	**sintamos**	**muera**	**muramos**
	sientas	**sintáis**	**mueras**	**muráis**
	sienta	**sientan**	**muera**	**mueran**
preterit indicative	sentí	sentimos	morí	morimos
	sentiste	sentisteis	moriste	moristeis
	sintió	**sintieron**	**murió**	**murieron**
imperfect subjunctive	**sintiera**, etc.		**muriera**, etc.	
	sintiese, etc.		**muriese**, etc.	
future subjunctive	**sintiere**, etc.		**muriere**, etc.	

Class III consists of verbs of the 3rd conjugation in which the stem vowel **e** changes to **i** whenever it is stressed. This change affects the 1st, 2nd, and 3rd persons singular and the 3rd person plural of the present indicative and present subjunctive, and the 2nd person singular affirmative imperative. In addition, the stem vowel **e** changes to **i** whenever it is unstressed and followed by an ending containing **a**, **ió**, or **ie**, just as in Class II. The irregular forms showing either of these changes are in boldface type in the following table.

pedir

gerund	**pidiendo**	*preterit indicative*	pedí pedimos pediste pedisteis **pidió pidieron**
present indicative	**pido** pedimos **pides** pedís **pide piden**	*imperfect subjunctive*	**pidiera**, etc. **pidiese**, etc.
present subjunctive	**pida pidamos** **pidas pidáis** **pida pidan**	*future subjunctive*	**pidiere**, etc.

b. Orthographic-Changing Verbs

In the conjugation of some regular as well as irregular verbs, it is necessary to change the final letters of the stem before adding certain personal endings. Such verbs are on the whole phonetically regular, but require the indicated changes in order to preserve the same sound of the final stem consonant throughout and still conform to the rules of Spanish spelling.

RULES FOR ORTHOGRAPHIC-CHANGING VERBS

Infinitive Ending	*Change Required*		*Tenses Affected*	*Examples*
-car	**c** to **qu**	before **e**	1st pers. sing. pret. ind.; entire pres. subjve.	tocar: toqué; toque, toques, etc.
-gar	insert **u**	before **e**	1st pers. sing. pret. ind.; entire pres. subjve.	pagar: pagué; pague, pagues, etc.
-guar	change **u** to **ü**	before **e**	1st pers. sing. pret. ind.; entire pres. subjve.	averiguar: averigüé; averigüe, averigües, etc.
-zar	change **z** to **c**	before **e**	1st pers. sing. pret. ind.; entire pres. subjve.	rezar: recé; rece, reces, etc.
-cer preceded by a consonant	change **c** to **z**	before **a** or **o**	1st pers. sing. pres. ind.; entire pres. subjve.	vencer: venzo; venza, venzas, etc.
-cir preceded by a consonant	change **c** to **z**	before **a** or **o**	1st pers. sing. pres. ind.; entire pres. subjve.	esparcir: esparzo; esparza, esparzas, etc.
-cer preceded by a vowel	insert **z** before **c**	before **a** or **o**	1st pers. sing. pres. ind.; entire pres. subjve.	conocer: conozco; conozca, conozcas, etc.
-cir preceded by a vowel	insert **z** before **c**	before **a** or **o**	1st pers. sing. pres. ind.; entire pres. subjve.	lucir: luzco; luzca, luzcas, etc.

(Exceptions: **mecer**, to rock; **cocer**, to cook; **escocer**, to smart, which follow the model of **vencer**, above, and **decir** and **hacer** and their compounds, which are irregular.)

Infinitive Ending	*Change Required*		*Tenses Affected*	*Examples*
-ger, **-gir**	change **g** to **j**	before **a** or **o**	1st pers. sing. pres. ind.; entire pres. subjve.	coger: cojo; coja, cojas, etc. dirigir: dirijo; dirija, dirijas, etc.
-quir	change **qu** to **c**	before **a** or **o**	1st pers. sing. pres. ind.; entire pres. subjve.	delinquir: delinco; delinca, delincas, etc.
-guir	drop the **u** of **gu**	before **a** or **o**	1st pers. sing. pres. ind.; entire pres. subjve.	distinguir: distingo; distinga, distingas, etc.
-ller	drop the **i** from the ending **-ió** and from all endings beginning with **-ie**		gerund; 3rd pers. sing. and 3rd pers. pl. of pret. ind.; entire impf. subjve. and fut. subjve.	empeller: empellendo; empelló, empelleron; empellera; empellese; empellere
-llir				bullir: bullendo; bulló, bulleron; bullera; bullese; bullere
-ñer				tañer: tañendo; tañó, tañeron; tañera; tañese; tañere
-ñir				gruñir: gruñendo; gruñó, gruñeron; gruñera; gruñese; gruñere

(The preceding rule affects also certain verbs that have **j** in the stem of some tenses in which the **i** is dropped from endings beginning with **-ie-**: **decir**: 3rd pers. pl. pret. ind., **dijeron**; impfv. subjve., **dijera, dijese**; fut. subjve., **dijere**.)

-iar	the **i** or **u** of the stem adds a written accent when stressed before one-syllable endings	1st, 2nd, 3rd pers. sing. and 3rd pers. pl. of the pres. ind. and pres. subjve; 2nd pers. sing. impve.	enviar: envío, envías, envía, envían; envíe, envíes, envíe, envíen; envía
-uar			continuar: continúo, continúas, continúa, continúan; continúe, continúes, continúe, continúen; continúa

The rules of Spanish spelling require that the vowel **i** when unstressed and standing at the beginning of a word and followed by a vowel, or in the middle of a word between two other vowels, become phonetically a consonant and be written **y** [see the vowel (i), the diphthongs (ja), (je), (jo), (ju), and the consonant (j) in the pronunciation section]. This rule affects verb forms in all tenses in which the stem ends in a vowel and the ending begins with an unstressed **i** followed by another vowel. In all such cases **i** must be changed in writing to **y**. This rule affects verbs of the following types:

creer *ger.* creyendo; *3rd pers. sing. & pl. pret. ind.* creyó, creyeron; *impf. subjve.* creyera, etc., creyese, etc.; *fut. subjve.* creyere, etc.

oír *ger.* oyendo; *2nd pers. sing., 3rd pers. sing. & pl. pres. ind.* oyes, oye, oyen (the 1st pers. sing. is irregular: oigo, not oyo); *3rd pers. sing. & pl. pret. ind.* oyó, oyeron; *impf. subjve.* oyera, etc., oyese, etc.; *fut. subjve.* oyere, etc.

huir *ger.* huyendo; *entire sing. and 3rd pl. pres. ind.* huyo, huyes, huye, huyen (but huímos, huís); *entire pres. subjve.* huya, huyas, etc.; *3rd pers. sing. & pl. pret. ind.* huyó, huyeron; *impf. subjve.* huyera, etc., huyese, etc.; *fut. subjve.* huyere, etc.

ir *ger.* yendo.

The New World
SPANISH-ENGLISH and ENGLISH-SPANISH
Dictionary

ENGLISH-SPANISH SECTION

(*Parte Inglesa-Española*)

A

A, a (ei) **1,** primera letra del alfabeto inglés. **2,** *música* la. **3,** *denota* primera clase; mejor calidad; primer grado; excelencia.

a (ə; ei *bajo acento*) *adj., art. indef.* un; *fem.* una. *También* (*ante vocal o* h *muda*) **an.**

a- (ə) *prefijo* **1,** *contracción preposicional* en; a; hacia: *abed,* en cama; *aside,* al lado; *astern,* a popa. **2,** *contracción de* **of:** *akin,* afín. **3,** *denota intensidad: arouse,* animar. **4,** *dial., indica acción progresiva: agoing,* listo para marchar. **5,** *indica parte en la acción: awake,* despertar. **6,** *forma de* **ab-:** *avert,* apartar. **7,** *forma de* **ad-:** *ascribe,* ascribir. **8,** negación; carencia: *acatholic,* acatólico; *amoral,* amoral.

ab- (æb; əb) *prefijo* ab-. **1,** separación; cese; alejamiento: *abduction,* abducción; *abjure,* abjurar. *Se convierte en* **a-** *ante* m, p, v: *amentia,* demencia; *frecuentemente en* **abs-** *ante* c, t: *abstract,* abstracto. **2,** origen: *aborigines,* aborígenes.

aback (ə'bæk) *adv.* atrás; detrás; al fondo. **—taken aback,** desconcertado; aturdido.

abacus ('æb·ə·kəs) *n.* ábaco.

abandon (ə'bæn·dən) *v.t.* abandonar; dejar; desechar; desistir de. **—***n.* desenfado; indiferencia. **—abandoned,** *adj.* abandonado; indiferente; descuidado. **—abandonment,** *n.* abandono; desamparo.

abase (ə'beis) *v.t.* degradar; rebajar; humillar. **—abasement,** *n.* abatimiento; humillación.

abash (ə'bæʃ) *v.t.* avergonzar; desconcertar; aturdir.

abate (ə'beit) *v.t.* **1,** (reduce) reducir; disminuir; rebajar. **2,** *law* suprimir; condonar; suspender. **—***v.i.* mermar; menguar. **—abatement,** *n.* rebaja; disminución.

abbé (æ'be) *n.* abate.

abbess ('æb·ɛs) *n.* abadesa; superiora; prelada.

abbey ('æb·i) *n.* abadía; monasterio.

abbot ('æb·ət) *n.* abad.

abbreviate (ə'bri·vi·eit) *v.t.* abreviar; acortar; compendiar. **—abbreviation,** *n.* abreviación; abreviatura.

abc's (ei·bi'siːz) *n.* abecé; rudimentos.

abdicate ('æb·də·keit) *v.t.* & *i.* abdicar; renunciar. **—abdication,** *n.* abdicación; renuncia.

abdomen ('æb·də·mən) *n.* abdomen; vientre. **—abdominal** (æb·'dam·ɪ·nəl) *adj.* abdominal.

abduct (æb'dʌkt) *v.t.* secuestrar. **—abduction** (-'dʌk·ʃən) *n.* secuestro. **—abductor,** *n.* secuestrador.

abeam (ə'biːm) *adv., naut.* a través; por el lado; en dirección lateral.

abed (ə'bɛd) *adv.* en cama; acostado.

aberrant (æb'ɛr·ənt) *adj.* errado; irregular; anómalo. **—aberrance, aberrancy,** *n.* error; equivocación; extravío.

aberration (æb·ə'rei·ʃən) *n.* **1,** (displacement; deviation) error; extravío; desviación. **2,** *astron.; optics* aberración.

abet (ə'bɛt) *v.t.* **[abetted, -ting]** instigar; inducir; animar. **—abetter, abettor,** *n.* instigador; cómplice. **—abetment,** *n.* instigación.

abeyance (ə'bei·əns) *n.* suspensión; expectación; dilación.

abhor (æb'hoːr) *v.t.* **[abhorred, abhorring]** aborrecer; detestar; odiar.

abhorrence (æb'har·əns) *n.* aborrecimiento; aversión; odio. **—abhorrent,** *adj.* aborrecible; detestable.

abide (ə'baid) *v.t.* soportar; aguantar. **—***v.i.* [*pret. & p.p* **abode**] **1,** (remain) permanecer. **2,** (continue) continuar; seguir. **3,** (dwell) morar. **4,** (stand firm) permanecer; sostenerse.

ability (ə'bɪl·ə·ti) *n.* **1,** (capacity) habilidad; capacidad. **2,** (skill) ingenio; competencia; aptitud.

-ability (ə'bɪl·ə·ti) *sufijo* -abilidad; *forma nombres de los adjetivos con terminación* **-able:** *probability,* probabilidad.

abject ('æb·dʒɛkt) *adj.* abyecto; vil; despreciable. **—abjectness,** *n.* abyección.

abjure (æb'dʒʊr) *v.t.* abjurar; renunciar. **—abjuration** (ˌæb·dʒə·'rei·ʃən) *n.* abjuración.

ablative ('æb·lə·tɪv) *n.* ablativo.

ablaze (ə'bleiz) *adv.* en llamas. —*adj.* **1,** (afire) encendido. **2,** (lit up) iluminado; alumbrado.

able ('ei·bəl) *adj.* **1,** (capable) apto; capaz. **2,** (talented) competente; hábil; talentoso. —**ably** ('ei·bli) *adv.* hábilmente.

-able (ə·bəl) *sufijo* -able; -ible: *forma adjetivos denotando* capacidad; habilidad: *excitable,* excitable; *punishable,* punible.

able-bodied ('ei·bəl'ba·did) *adj.* robusto; fuerte; sano.

-ably (ə·bli) *sufijo* -ablemente; *forma adverbios de los adjetivos teminados en* **-able**: *amicably,* amigablemente.

abnegate ('æb·nə·geit) *v.t.* renunciar a; privarse de; negar. —**abnegation,** *n.* abnegación; renunciación.

abnormal (æb'nor·məl) *adj.* **1,** (unusual) anormal; desusado; raro. **2,** (deviating) abnormal; contranatural. —**abnormality** (ˌæb·nor·'mæl·ə·ti) *n.* anormalidad; anomalía.

aboard (ə'bord) *adv.* & *prep.* a bordo (de). —**all aboard!,** ¡pasajeros al tren!

abode (ə'boːd) *v., pret.* & *p.p. de* **abide.** —*n.* **1,** (dwelling place) domicilio; morada. **2,** (sojourn) estancia; permanencia.

abolish (ə'bal·ɪʃ) *v.t.* abolir; derogar; suprimir. —**abolishment,** *n.* abolición; anulamiento; derogación.

abolition (ˌæb·ə'lɪʃ·ən) *n.* abolición; supresión; derogación. —**abolitionism,** *n.* abolicionismo. —**abolitionist,** *n.* abolicionista.

A-bomb ('eiˌbam) *n.* bomba atómica.

abominable (ə'bam·ɪ·nə·bəl) *adj.* abominable; odioso.

abominate (ə'bam·ɪ·neit) *v.t.* abominar; aborrecer; odiar. —**abomination,** *n.* abominación; repugnancia; odio.

aboriginal (ˌæb·ə'rɪdʒ·ɪ·nəl) *adj.* aborigen; indígena. —**aborigines** (-niz) *n.pl.* [*sing.* **-ne** (-ni)] aborígenes; indígenas.

abort (ə'bort) *v.i.* abortar. —*v.t.* **1,** (deliver prematurely) abortar. **2,** (produce abortion in) hacer abortar. —**abortive,** *adj.* abortivo. —**abortion** (ə'bor·ʃən) *n.* aborto.

abound (ə'baund) *v.i.* abundar. —**abound in,** tener en cantidad; abundar en *o* de.

about (ə'baut) *adv.* alrededor; poco más o menos; aproximadamente. —*prep.* en *o* con referencia a; acerca de; por. —**about to,** a punto de.

about-face *n.* media vuelta.

above (ə'bʌːv) *prep.* sobre; encima de; superior a. —*adv.* arriba; antes. —*adj.* antedicho; ya mencionado. —**above all,** sobre todo; principalmente.

aboveboard (ə'bʌvˌbord) *adj.* franco; sincero. —*adv.* al descubierto; sin rodeos.

abracadabra (ˌæb·rə·kə'dæb·rə) *n.* abracadabra.

abrade (ə'breid) *v.t.* raer; raspar.

abrasion (ə'brei·ʒən) *n.* raedura; raspadura; abrasión. —**abrasive** (-sɪv) *adj.* & *n.* abrasivo.

abreast (ə'brɛst) *adv.* **1,** (side by side) de frente. **2,** (in marching) en fondo.

abridge (ə'brɪdʒ) *v.t.* **1,** (shorten) condensar; resumir; compendiar. **2,** (curtail) cortar; privar. —**abridgement,** *n.* compendio; resumen.

abroad (ə'brɔːd) *adv.* **1,** (in a foreign country) en el extranjero. **2,** (in circulation) entre el público. **3,** (outdoors) afuera.

abrogate ('æb·rəˌgeit) *v.t.* revocar por ley; abolir; abrogar. —**abrogation,** *n.* abrogación.

abrupt (ə'brʌpt) *adj.* **1,** (suddenly changing) repentino; brusco; impensado. **2,** (precipitous) abrupto; escarpado; áspero. —**abruptness,** *n.* aspereza.

abs- (æbs) *prefijo, forma de* **ab-** *ante* c, t: *abstract,* abstracto.

abscess ('æb·sɛs) *n.* absceso.

abscissa (æb'sɪs·ə) *n., geom.* abscisa.

abscond (æb'skand) *v.i.* evadirse; esconderse; desaparecer.

absence ('æb·səns) *n.* ausencia; falta.

absent ('æb·sənt) *adj.* ausente; no presente. —**absentee** (ˌæb·sən'tiː) *n.* ausente. —**absenteeism,** *n.* absentismo. —**absent oneself,** ausentarse; irse; retirarse.

absentminded ('æb·səntˌmain·dɪd) *adj.* abstraído; distraído; olvidadizo. —**absentmindedness,** *n.* distracción; olvido.

absinthe ('æb·sɪnθ) *n.* absintio; ajenjo.

absolute (æb·sə'lut) *adj.* **1,** (unqualified) absoluto; perfecto. **2,**

(complete) completo; total. —**absoluteness,** *n.* lo absoluto. —**absolutely,** *adv.* en absoluto; terminantemente.
absolution (æb·sə'lu·ʃən) *n.* absolución; perdón.
absolutism ('æb·sə·lu·tɪz·əm) *n.* absolutismo.
absolve (æb'salv) *v.t.* absolver; perdonar; justificar.
absorb (æb'sorb) *v.t.* **1,** (suck up or in) absorber. **2,** (assimilate) asimilar. **3,** (engulf completely) preocupar. —**absorbed,** *adj.* absorto; absorbido. —**absorbent,** *adj.* absorbente. —**absorbency,** *n.* absorbencia. —**absorbing,** *adj.* absorbente; interesante.
absorption (æb'sorp·ʃən) *n.* **1,** (a sucking in) absorción. **2,** (assimilation) asimilación. **3,** (preoccupation) preocupación. —**absorptive** (-tɪv) *adj.* absorbente.
abstain (æb'stein) *v.i.* abstenerse; retraerse; privarse. —**abstainer,** *n.* abstinente.
abstemious (æb'stiː·mi·əs) *adj.* abstemio; sobrio; parco. —**abstemiousness,** *n.* sobriedad.
abstention (æb'stɛn·ʃən) *n.* abstención. —**abstentious,** *adj.* abstinente.
abstinence ('æb·stɪ·nəns) *n.* abstinencia. —**abstinent,** *adj.* abstinente.
abstract (æb'strækt) *v.t.* **1,** (consider) considerar; abstraer. **2,** (take away) separar; alejar. **3,** (epitomize) compendiar; resumir; extractar. —*n.* ('æb·strækt) **1,** (summary) resumen; extracto. **2,** (essential aspect) extracto; meollo. —*adj.* abstracto. —**abstracted,** *adj.* abstraído; desatento; preocupado.
abstraction (æb'stræk·ʃən) *n.* **1,** abstracción. **2,** (absentmindedness) descuido; desatención.
abstruse (æb'strus) *adj.* abstruso; oscuro. —**abstruseness,** *n.* oscuridad.
absurd (æb'sʌɹd) *adj.* absurdo; ilógico; ridículo; disparatado. —**absurdity,** *n.* disparate; ilógica; absurdo.
abundance (ə'bʌn·dəns) *also,* **abundancy,** *n.* abundancia; plenitud; afluencia. —**abundant,** *adj.* abundante; lleno; copioso.
abuse (ə'bjuːz) *v.t.* **1,** (misapply) usar mal. **2,** (do wrong to) abusar de. **3,** (injure) maltratar; ultrajar. **4,** (revile) denostar; ofender. —*n.* (ə'bjus) abuso; maltrato; insulto. —**abusive** (-sɪv) *adj.* abusivo.
abut (ə'bʌt) *v.t.* [**abutted, -ting**] limitar con; colindar con; confinar.
abutment (ə'bʌt·mənt) *n.* **1,** (juxtaposition) contigüidad; yuxtaposición. **2,** *archit.* contrafuerte; estribo.
abysmal (ə'bɪz·məl) *adj.* abismal; insondable.
abyss (ə'bɪs) *n.* abismo; sima.
ac- (æk; ək) *prefijo, forma de* **ad-** *ante* c, q *y a veces* k: *accept,* aceptar; *acquit,* absolver; *acknowledge,* reconocer.
-ac (æk; ək) *sufijo* -aco; *forma adjetivos que denotan* **1,** característica: *elegiac,* elegíaco. **2,** relación; pertenencia: *cardiac,* cardíaco. *Generalmente estos adjetivos pueden usarse como nombres.*
acacia (ə'kei·ʃə) *n.* acacia.
academy (ə'kæd·ə·mi) *n.* academia; centro de enseñanza. —**academic** (ˌæk·ə'dɛm·ɪk) *adj.* académico. —**academician** (əˌkæd·ə·'mɪʃ·ən) *n.* académico.
acanthus (ə'kæn·θəs) *n.* acanto.
accede (æk'siːd) *v.i.* acceder; asentir; consentir.
accelerate (æk'sɛl·ə·reit) *v.t.* acelerar; precipitar. —*v.i.* acelerarse; precipitarse; apresurarse. —**acceleration,** *n.* aceleración; precipitación. —**accelerator,** *n.* acelerador.
accent ('æk·sɛnt) *n.* acento; énfasis. —*v.t.* (*también,* æk'sɛnt) acentuar.
accentuate (æk'sɛn·tʃu·eit) *v.t.* acentuar; hacer énfasis en. —**accentuation,** *n.* acentuación.
accept (æk'sɛpt) *v.t.* **1,** (take in a formal way) aceptar; acoger bien. **2,** (agree to) aceptar; admitir.
acceptable (æk'sɛp·tə·bəl) *adj.* aceptable. —**acceptability,** *n.* aceptabilidad.
acceptance (æk'sɛp·təns) *n.* aceptación; admisión.
acceptation (ˌæk·sɛp'tei·ʃən) *n., gram.* acepción.
access ('æk·sɛs) *n.* acceso. —**accessible** (æk'sɛs·ə·bəl) *adj.* accesible. —**accessibility,** *n.* accesibilidad.
accession (æk'sɛʃ·ən) *n.* **1,** (attainment) accesión; advenimiento. **2,** (increase) incremento. **3,** (consent) consentimiento; asentimiento.
accessory (æk'sɛs·ə·ri) *n.* **1,** (sub-

ordinate part) accesorio; secundario. **2,** *law* cómplice. —*adj.* **1,** (belonging to) accesorio; adjunto. **2,** (contributory) contribuyente. —**accessories,** *n.pl.* accesorios; extras; repuestos.

accident ('æk·sɪ·dənt) *n.* accidente; contratiempo; percance.

accidental (ˌæk·sɪ'dɛn·təl) *adj.* **1,** (occurring by chance) accidental; casual. **2,** (subsidiary) secundario. —*n., music* acorde accidental.

acclaim (ə'kleim) *v.t.* aclamar; vitorear; aplaudir. —*n.* aplauso. —**acclamation** (æk·lə'mei·ʃən) *n.* aclamación.

acclimate (ə'klai·mət) *también,* **acclimatize** *v.t.* aclimatar; acostumbrar. —*v.i.* aclimatarse; acostumbrarse. —**acclimation** (ˌæk·lə'mei·ʃən), **acclimatization** (əˌklai·mə·tɪ'zei·ʃən) *n.* aclimatación.

accommodate (ə'kam·ə·deit) *v.t.* **1,** (adapt) acomodar; arreglar; ordenar. **2,** (lodge) acomodar; hospedar. **3,** (serve) ayudar. **4,** (please; satisfy) complacer. —**accommodating,** *adj.* complaciente.

accommodation (əˌkam·ə'dei·ʃən) *n.* **1,** (adaptation) arreglo; acomodo. **2,** (readiness to serve) servicio; favor. **3,** *pl.* (facilities) facilidades; conveniencias.

accompany (ə'kʌm·pə·ni) *v.t.* acompañar. —**accompanist,** *n.* acompañador. —**accompaniment,** *n.* acompañamiento.

accomplice (ə'kam·plɪs) *n.* cómplice.

accomplish (ə'kam·plɪʃ) *v.t.* **1,** (do) realizar; cumplir. **2,** (achieve) lograr; conseguir. **3,** (complete) concluir; culminar. —**accomplishment,** *n.* resultado; logro; éxito.

accomplished (ə'kam·plɪʃt) *adj.* **1,** (done) realizado; cumplido. **2,** (talented) perfecto; consumado; diestro.

accord (ə'kord) *v.t.* **1,** (agree) acordar; pactar; convenir. **2,** (concede) conceder; acceder. —*v.i.* avenirse. —*n.* acuerdo; pacto. —**of one's own accord,** espontáneamente. —**with one accord,** unánimemente.

accordance (ə'kord·əns) *n.* conformidad. —**accordant,** *adj.* acorde; conforme. —**in accordance with,** de acuerdo con; de conformidad a *o* con.

according (ə'kor·dɪŋ) *adv.* acorde; según. —**accordingly,** *adv.* por lo tanto; por consiguiente. —**according to,** de acuerdo con; conforme a.

accordion (ə'kor·di·ən) *n.* acordeón. —**accordionist,** *n.* acordeonista.

accost (ə'kɔst) *v.t.* abordar; acercarse a.

account (ə'kaunt) *n.* **1,** (business record) cuenta. **2,** (enumeration) enumeración; cuenta; relato. **3,** (explanation) explicación; razón. —*v.t.* estimar; calificar; imputar. —**account for,** explicar; responder de. —**on account,** *comm.* a cuenta. —**on account of, 1,** (because of) porque. **2,** (for the sake of) en favor de; por. —**on no account,** de ninguna manera. —**take account of,** *también,* **take into account,** considerar; tener *o* tomar en cuenta.

accountable (ə'kaun·tə·bəl) *adj.* **1,** (explicable) explicable. **2,** (responsible) responsable.

accountant (ə'kaunt·ənt) *n.* contador; tenedor de libros. —**accountancy; accounting,** *n.* contabilidad; teneduría de libros.

accredit (ə'krɛd·ɪt) *v.t.* **1,** (believe) dar crédito a; creer. **2,** (attribute to) atribuir a. **3,** (bring into favor) acreditar; abonar. **4,** (confer authority upon) dar credenciales a; autorizar.

accretion (ə'kri·ʃən) *n.* acreción; acrecencia.

accrue (ə'kruː) *v.i.* **1,** (come about) provenir; resultar. **2,** (increase) acrecentarse; aumentar; crecer. —**accrual,** *n.* acrecencia; acrecentamiento.

accumulate (ə'kju·mjə·leit) *v.t.* acumular; amasar. —*v.i.* acumularse; amontonarse. —**accumulation,** *n.* acumulación; acopio. —**accumulative** (-lə·tɪv) *adj.* acumulador.

accuracy ('æk·ju·rə·si) *n.* precisión; minuciosidad; exactitud.

accurate ('æk·ju·rət) *adj.* correcto; verdadero; exacto. —**accurateness,** *n.* precisión; esmero.

accursed (ə'kʌɹ·səd) *también,* **accurst** (ə'kʌɹst) *adj.* maldito; maldecido; perverso; detestable. —**accursedness,** *n.* maldición; desventura; infamia.

accusative (ə'kju·zə·tɪv) *adj.* & *n., gram.* acusativo.

accuse (ə'kjuːz) *v.t.* acusar; incul-

par; denunciar. —**accusation** (ˌæk·ju'zei·ʃən) *n.* acusación; denuncia; cargo.
accustom (ə'kʌs·təm) *v.t.* acostumbrar; habituar. —**accustomed,** *adj.* acostumbrado; usual.
ace (eis) *n.* as. —*adj.* experto; sobresaliente. —**within an ace of,** a dos dedos de.
-acea ('ei·ʃi·ə; 'ei·ʃə) *también,* **-aceae** ('ei·si·i) *sufijo, zool.; bot.* -áceos; -áceas; *forma nombres de órdenes, familias y clases: crustacea,* crustáceos; *graminaceae,* gramináceas.
-aceous ('ei·ʃəs) *sufijo* -áceo; *forma adjetivos, especialmente con los nombres terminando en* **-acea** *o* **-aceae**: *cetaceous,* cetáceo; *orchidaceous,* orquidáceo.
acerbity (ə'sʌɹ·bə·ti) *n.* acerbidad; amargura.
acetanilide (ˌæs·ɪ'tæn·ə·lɪd) *n.* acetanilida.
acetate ('æs·ə·teit) *n.* acetato. —**cellulose acetate,** *n.* acetato de celulosa.
acetic (ə'si·tɪk) *adj.* acético. —**acetic acid,** ácido acético.
acetone ('æs·ə·ton) *n.* acetona.
acetylene (ə'sɛt·ə·lɪn; -liːn) *n.* acetileno.
ache (eik) *n.* dolor. —*v.i.* **1,** (cause pain) doler. **2,** (suffer pain) tener dolor. —**ache for,** *colloq.* desear; anhelar.
achieve (ə'tʃiːv) *v.t.* conseguir; realizar; lograr. —**achievement,** *n.* resultado; logro.
acid ('æs·ɪd) *n.* ácido. —*adj.* ácido; agrio. —**acidity** (æ'sɪd·ə·ti) *n.* acidez.
-acious ('ei·ʃəs) *sufijo* -az; *forma adjetivos indicando* característica; posesión: *audacious,* audaz.
-acity ('æs·ə·ti) *sufijo* -acidad: *forma nombres expresando* cualidad: *pugnacity,* pugnacidad.
acknowledge (æk'nal·ɪdʒ) *v.t.* **1,** (admit) reconocer; admitir; aceptar. **2,** (certify receipt of) acusar recibo de. —**acknowledgment; acknowledgement,** *n.* reconocimiento; aceptación; admisión.
acme ('æk·mi) *n.* cima; cumbre; colmo.
acne ('æk·ni) *n.* acné.
acolyte ('æk·ə·lait) *n.* acólito; monaguillo.
aconite ('æk·əˌnait) *n.* acónito.
acorn ('ei·korn) *n.* bellota.
acoustic (ə'kus·tɪk) *adj.* acústico. —**acoustics,** *n.pl.* acústica (*sing.*).
acquaint (ə'kweint) *v.t.* **1,** (make familiar with) familiarizar. **2,** (inform) enterar; informar.
acquaintance (ə'kwein·təns) *n.* **1,** (knowledge) conocimiento; noción. **2,** (person) conocido. —**acquaintanceship,** *n.* conocimiento; relación.
acquiesce (ˌæk·wi'ɛs) *v.i.* consentir; acceder. —**acquiesce in,** aprobar; admitir.
acquiescent (ˌæk·wi'ɛs·ənt) *adj.* condescendiente; conforme; acorde. —**acquiescence,** *n.* aquiescencia; consentimiento; aprobación.
acquire (ə'kwair) *v.t.* adquirir; conseguir; alcanzar; obtener. —**acquirement,** *n.* obtención.
acquisition (æk·wə'zɪʃ·ən) *n.* adquisición.
acquisitive (ə'kwɪz·ə·tɪv) *adj.* avaricioso; codicioso. —**acquisitiveness,** *n.* avaricia; codicia.
acquit (ə'kwɪt) *v.t.* [**acquitted, -ting**] **1,** (absolve) exonerar; absolver. **2,** (settle, as debts) pagar; cancelar. —**acquit oneself,** conducirse; comportarse.
acquittal (ə'kwɪt·əl) *n.* **1,** (discharge of duty) descargo; licencia. **2,** *law* exoneración; absolución.
acre ('ei·kər) *n.* acre (40.469 áreas).
acrid ('æk·rɪd) *adj.* acre; amargo; agrio. —**acridity** (ə'krɪd·ə·ti); **acridness,** *n.* acritud; acidez; mordacidad.
acrimony ('æk·rə·mo·ni) *n.* acrimonia; aspereza. —**acrimonious** (-'mo·ni·əs) *adj.* acrimonioso; áspero.
acro- (æk·ro) *prefijo* acro-; altura; cima; borde: *acropolis,* acrópolis; *acrobatics,* acrobacia.
acrobat ('æk·rə·bæt) *n.* acróbata. —**acrobatic** (-'bæt·ɪk) *adj.* acrobático. —**acrobatics,** *n.* acrobacia; acrobatismo.
across (ə'krɔs) *adv.* a través; de través; al otro lado; transversalmente. —*prep.* al otro lado de; por; a través de.
acrylic (ə'krɪl·ɪk) *adj.* acrílico.
act (ækt) *v.i.* **1,** (do something) actuar; hacer; obrar. **2,** (behave) comportarse; conducirse. **3,** *theat.* representar; actuar. —*v.t.* **1,** (do) actuar; obrar. **2,** *theat.* actuar; representar *o* desempeñar el papel

de. —*n.* **1,** (deed) acto; acción; hecho. **2,** *law* decreto. **3,** *theat.* acto. —**put on an act,** *colloq.* hacer escenas.

acting (ˈækt·ɪŋ) *n.* **1,** *theat.* actuación; representación. **2,** (affected behavior) simulación; fingimiento. —*adj.* interino; provisional; suplente.

actinic (ækˈtɪn·ɪk) *adj.* actínico.

actinium (ækˈtɪn·i·əm) *n.* actinio.

actinon (ˈæk·tɪ·nən) *n.* actinón.

action (ˈæk·ʃən) *n.* **1,** (act) acción; hecho; obra. **2,** (behavior) acto; gesto. **3,** *mil.* acción; batalla. **4,** (of a play or narrative) acción; desarrollo; argumento. **5,** *law* demanda; proceso. —**actionable,** *adj.* litigable; procesable. —**bring action,** demandar; procesar. —**in action, 1,** (operating) obrando; actuando; activo. **2,** *mil.* en el combate; en campaña. —**take action, 1,** *law* procesar. **2,** (begin to act) comenzar a actuar; obrar.

activate (ˈæk·təˌveit) *v.t.* activar. —**activation,** *n.* activación. —**activator,** *n.* activador.

active (ˈæk·tɪv) *adj.* **1,** (brisk) activo; enérgico. **2,** *gram.* activo; transitivo. —**activeness; activity** (-ˈtɪv·ə·ti) *n.* actividad; viveza. —**activities,** *n.pl.* ocupaciones.

actor (ˈæk·tər) *n.* actor. —**actress** (-trɪs) *n.* actriz.

actual (ˈæk·tʃu·əl) *adj.* **1,** (real) real; verdadero. **2,** (present) actual; presente; existente. —**actuality** (-ˈæl·ə·ti) *n.* realidad. —**actually,** *adv.* realmente; en realidad.

actuary (ˈæk·tʃuˌɛr·i) *n.* actuario. —**actuarial** (-ˈɛr·i·əl) *adj.* actuarial.

actuate (ˈæk·tʃu·eit) *v.t.* actuar; activar; impulsar; mover. —**actuation,** *n.* actuación; impulso.

acuity (əˈkju·ə·ti) *n.* agudeza.

acumen (əˈkju·mən) *n.* cacumen; acumen; perspicacia.

acute (əˈkjut) *adj.* **1,** (sharp) agudo; penetrante. **2,** (perceptive) ingenioso; vivo; sutil. —**acuteness,** *n.* agudeza.

-acy (ə·si) *sufijo* -acia; *forma nombres que indican* calidad; condición: *bureaucracy,* burocracia.

ad (æd) *n., colloq.* = **advertisement.**

ad- (æd; əd) *prefijo* ad-; *indica* adición; dirección; tendencia: *adhere,* adherirse.

-ad (æd) *sufijo* **1,** *forma nombres indicando un determinado grupo de unidades: triad,* grupo de tres. **2,** = **-ade.**

adage (ˈæd·ɪdʒ) *n.* adagio; proverbio.

adagio (əˈdaːʒo) *n., music* adagio.

adamant (ˈæd·ə·mənt) *adj.* reacio; porfiado; duro; inflexible. —*n.* diamante.

Adam's apple (ˈæd·əmz) nuez.

adapt (əˈdæpt) *v.t.* adaptar; convertir; arreglar. —*v.i.* adaptarse. —**adaptable,** *adj.* adaptable; transformable; convertible. —**adaptation** (ˌæd·əpˈtei·ʃən) *n.* adaptación; arreglo.

add (æːd) *v.t.* añadir; agregar; unir. —*v.i.* sumar.

adder (ˈæd·ər) *n.* serpiente; víbora.

addict (ˈæd·ɪkt) *n.* **1,** (enthusiast) adicto; adepto; partidario. **2,** (drug addict) vicioso de drogas; morfinómano. —**addicted** (əˈdɪk·tɪd) *adj.* adicto; aficionado.

addiction (əˈdɪk·ʃən) *n.* **1,** inclinación; tendencia; propensión. **2,** afición a las drogas; morfinomanía.

adding machine máquina de sumar; calculadora.

addition (əˈdɪʃ·ən) *n.* **1,** *arith.* suma; adicion. **2,** (something added) añadidura. —**in addition (to),** además (de).

additional (əˈdɪʃ·ən·əl) *adj.* adicional; aditicio.

additive (ˈæd·ə·tɪv) *adj. & n.* aditivo.

addle (ˈæd·əl) *adj.* huero. —*v.t.* **1,** (make rotten) enhuerar. **2,** (confuse) ofuscar; enturbiar. —*v.i.* enhuerarse.

address (əˈdrɛs) *v.t.* **1,** (speak or write to) hablar con *o* a; escribir a; dirigirse a. **2,** (pay court to) piropear; galantear. —*n.* **1,** (speech) alocución; discurso. **2,** (dwelling or mailing place) señas; domicilio; dirección. **3,** (formal utterance) petición. —**address oneself to,** volverse a; aplicarse a; dedicarse a. —**addressee,** *n.* destinatario. —**addresser; addressor,** *n.* remitente.

adduce (əˈdjus) *v.t.* aducir; alegar.

-ade (eid) *sufijo* -ado; -ada. **1,** *forma nombres de acción, efecto o resultado de la acción: ambuscade,* emboscada. **2,** *compone nombres de bebidas: lemonade,* limonada. **3,** *var. de* **-ad:** *decade,* década.

adenoid (ˈæd·ə·noid) *n.* adenoide.

—**adenoidal** (-'nɔid·əl) *adj.* adenoideo.
adept *n.* ('æd·ɛpt) & *adj.* (ə'dɛpt) adepto; eficiente. —**adeptness** (ə'dɛpt·nəs) *n.* eficiencia; pericia.
adequate ('æd·ɪ·kwət) *adj.* adecuado; apto; oportuno. —**adequacy**, *n.* oportunidad; pertinencia.
adhere (æd'hɪːr) *v.i.* adherirse; pegarse; unirse. —**adherence**, *n.* adherencia. —**adherent**, *adj.* & *n.* adherente.
adhesion (æd'hiː·ʒən) *n.* adhesión.
adhesive (æd'hiː·sɪv) *adj.* adhesivo; pegajoso; pertinaz. —*n.* adhesivo. —**adhesive tape**, esparadrapo.
adieu (ə'djuː) *interj.* adiós. —*n.* [*pl.* **adieus**; **adieux** (ə'djuːz)] despedida; adiós.
adipose ('æd·ɪ·pos) *adj.* adiposo.
adjacent (ə'dʒei·sənt) *adj.* adyacente; contiguo; colindante. —**adjacency**, *n.* contigüidad; colindancia.
adjective ('ædʒ·ək·tɪv) *n.* & *adj.* adjetivo. —**adjectival** (-'tai·vəl) *adj.* adjetival.
adjoin (ə'dʒɔin) *v.t.* & *i.* yuxtaponer; lindar; colindar. —**adjoining**, *adj.* contiguo.
adjourn (ə'dʒʌɹn) *v.t.* aplazar; diferir; dilatar. —**adjournment**, *n.* aplazamiento; dilación.
adjudge (ə'dʒʌdʒ) *v.t.* **1,** (decree) decretar; juzgar. **2,** (award) adjudicar; conferir.
adjudicate (ə'dʒu·dɪ·ket) *v.t.* & *i.* juzgar.
adjunct ('æ·dʒʌŋkt) *n.* & *adj.* anexo; adjunto; asociado.
adjuration (ˌædʒ·ə'rei·ʃən) *n.* **1,** (command) orden imperiosa. **2,** (entreaty) conjuro; ruego.
adjure (ə'dʒʊr) *v.t.* **1,** (command) ordenar. **2,** (entreat) conjurar; rogar.
adjust (ə'dʒʌst) *v.t.* **1,** (adapt) ajustar; adaptar. **2,** (put in order) acomodar; arreglar; ordenar. **3,** (settle) asegurar; ajustar; asentar. —*v.i.* ajustarse. —**adjustment**, *n.* ajuste; arreglo.
adjutant ('ædʒ·ə·tənt) *n.* ayudante; asistente.
administer (æd'mɪn·ɪs·tər) *v.t.* **1,** (manage) administrar; regentar; conducir. **2,** (supply) proveer; suplir; dispensar. —**administer to**, ayudar; socorrer.
administration (ædˌmɪn·ɪ'strei·ʃən) *n.* administración.
administrative (æd'mɪn·ɪˌstre·tɪv) *adj.* administrativo.
administrator (æd'mɪn·ɪˌstre·tər) *n.* administrador.
administratrix (ædˌmɪn·ɪs'trei·trɪks) *n.* [*pl.* **-trices** (-trəˌsiːz)] administradora.
admirable ('æd·mə·rə·bəl) *adj.* admirable; excelente; estupendo.
admiral ('æd·mə·rəl) *n.* almirante. —**admiralty**, *n.* almirantazgo.
admiration (æd·mə'rei·ʃən) *n.* admiración.
admire (æd'mair) *v.t.* admirar; apreciar; estimar.
admirer (æd'mair·ər) *n.* **1,** (one who admires) admirador. **2,** *colloq.* (suitor) pretendiente; enamorado.
admissible (æd'mɪs·ə·bəl) *adj.* admisible; aceptable; válido. —**admissibility**, *n.* validez; aceptabilidad.
admission (æd'mɪʃ·ən) *n.* **1,** (acknowledgment; act of admitting) admisión; confesión. **2,** (entrance fee) entrada; admisión.
admit (æd'mɪt) *v.t.* [**admitted, -ting**] **1,** (allow to enter) admitir; permitir entrar. **2,** (acknowledge) admitir; reconocer; confesar. —**admittance**, *n.* entrada.
admonish (æd'man·ɪʃ) *v.t.* **1,** (reprove mildly) amonestar; censurar. **2,** (exhort) exhortar; aconsejar. —**admonishment**, *n.* amonestación; reprensión; consejo.
admonition (æd·mə'nɪʃ·ən) *n.* **1,** (reproof) admonición; amonestación; reprensión. **2,** (warning) consejo; aviso.
ado (ə'duː) *n.* alharaca; trabajo; dificultad.
adobe (ə'do·bi) *n.* adobe. —*adj.* de adobe.
adolescent (æd·ə'lɛs·ənt) *n.* & *adj.* adolescente. —**adolescence**, *n.* adolescencia.
adopt (ə'dapt) *v.t.* **1,** (take as one's own) adoptar; prohijar. **2,** (vote to accept) aceptar; tomar; resolver. —**adoption** (ə'dap·ʃən) *n.* adopción; aceptación. —**adoptive**, *adj.* adoptivo.
adorable (ə'dor·ə·bəl) *adj.* adorable.
adore (ə'doːr) *v.t.* adorar; venerar. —**adoration** (æd·ə'rei·ʃən) *n.* adoración; veneración.
adorn (ə'dorn) *v.t.* adornar; em-

bellecer. —**adornment**, *n.* adorno; gala; ornato.

adrenal (ə'dri·nəl) *adj.* suprarrenal.

adrenalin (ə'drɛn·ə·lɪn) *n.* adrenalina.

adrift (ə'drɪft) *adj.* flotante. —*adv.* a la deriva; al pairo.

adroit (ə'drɔit) *adj.* experto; hábil; diestro. —**adroitness**, *n.* habilidad; destreza.

adulate ('æd·ju·let) *v.t.* adular. —**adulation**, *n.* adulación.

adult (ə'dʌlt) *n.* & *adj.* adulto; crecido; mayor. —**adulthood**, *n.* edad adulta.

adulterant (ə'dʌl·tə·rənt) *adj.* & *n.* adulterante.

adulterate (ə'dʌl·tə·reit) *v.t.* adulterar; falsear; viciar. —**adulteration**, *n.* adulteración; falseamiento; corrupción.

adulterer (ə'dʌl·tər·ər) *n.* adúltero. —**adulteress** (-tər·əs; -trɪs) *n.* adúltera.

adultery (ə'dʌl·tə·ri) *n.* adulterio. —**adulterous**, *adj.* adúltero.

advance (æd'væns) *v.t.* **1,** (bring forward) avanzar; adelantar. **2,** (suggest) sugerir; insinuar; ofrecer. **3,** *comm.* adelantar; anticipar. **4,** (promote) promover; mejorar. —*v.i.* **1,** (move forward) adelantarse; avanzar. **2,** (make progress) progresar; adelantar. **3,** (rise in price) subir. —*n.* **1,** (a move forward) avance; adelanto. **2,** (improvement) progreso; mejora. **3,** *comm.* anticipo; adelanto. —**in advance, 1,** *comm.* anticipado; por adelantado. **2,** (in front) al frente. **3,** (beforehand) antes; de antemano.

advancement (æd'væns·mənt) *n.* **1,** (forward movement) adelantamiento. **2,** (promotion) ascenso; promoción. **3,** (improvement) mejoría; prosperidad.

advantage (æd'væn·tɪdʒ) *n.* **1,** (favorable circumstance) ventaja; facilidad. **2,** (gain) beneficio; ganancia. **3,** (superiority) superioridad; preponderancia. **4,** *tennis* ventaja. —**advantageous** (ˌæd·vən'tei·dʒəs) *adj.* ventajoso. —**be of advantage to,** favorecer. —**have the advantage of,** llevar ventaja a. —**take advantage of, 1,** (for one's benefit) aprovecharse de; valerse de. **2,** (impose upon) imponerse a.

advent ('æd·vɛnt) *n.* **1,** (arrival) llegada; venida; advenimiento. **2,** *cap., eccles.* Adviento.

adventure (æd'vɛn·tʃər) *n.* **1,** (remarkable event) aventura; incidente. **2,** (hazardous undertaking) aventura; riesgo; percance. —*v.t.* aventurar; arriesgar. —*v.i.* aventurarse; arriesgarse. —**adventurer**, *n.* aventurero; explorador. —**adventuress**, *n.* aventurera. —**adventurous**, *adj.* aventurado; arriesgado.

adverb ('æd·vʌɹb) *n.* adverbio. —**adverbial** (æd·vʌɹb·i·əl) *adj.* adverbial.

adversary ('æd·vər·sɛr·i) *n.* adversario; enemigo; contrincante.

adverse (æd'vʌɹs) *adj.* adverso; hostil; desfavorable.

adversity (æd'vʌɹ·sə·ti) *n.* adversidad; infortunio; malaventura.

advertise *también,* **advertize** ('æd·vər·taiz) *v.t.* & *i.* anunciar; avisar. —**advertisement** (-'taiz·mənt) *n.* anuncio; aviso; noticia. —**advertising**, *n.* publicidad. —*adj.* publicitario.

advice (æd'vais) *n.* aviso; consejo; advertencia. —**take advice,** aconsejarse; orientarse.

advisable (æd'vai·zə·bəl) *adj.* aconsejable; recomendable; conveniente.

advise (æd'vaiz) *v.t.* **1,** (give counsel to) avisar; aconsejar. **2,** (give information to) advertir; orientar. **3,** (recommend) recomendar. —**advised**, *adj.* avisado; advertido; aconsejado. —**adviser; advisor** (-zər) *n.* aconsejador; consejero. —**advisement**, *n.* parecer; opinión; consideración. —**advisory**, *adj.* consultor; consejero.

advocacy ('æd·və·kə·si) *n.* defensa; vindicación.

advocate ('æd·vəˌkeit) *v.t.* abogar por; defender; interceder por. —*n.* (-kət) abogado; defensor.

adz *también,* **adze** (æːdz) *n.* azuela.

-ae (i) *sufijo* -as; *terminación plural de algunos nombres femeninos derivados del latín: alumnae,* alumnas. *A veces, es una alternativa para el plural regular: formulae* o *formulas,* fórmulas.

aegis *también,* **egis** ('iː·dʒɪs) *n.* égida.

aerate ('e·ərˌet; 'eːr-) *v.t.* **1,** (expose to air) airear; ventilar. **2,** (charge with air) impregnar *o*

saturar con aire. —**aeration,** *n.* aeración. —**aerator,** *n.* aparato para aeración; fumigadora.
aerial *adj.* ('eːr·i·əl; e'ɪr-) **1,** *lit.* aéreo. **2,** *fig.* etéreo; sutil; leve. —*n.* ('eːr·i·əl) antena. —**aerialist,** *n.* trapecista.
aerie ('eːr·i; 'ɪr·i) *n.* = **eyrie.**
aero- ('eːr·o) *también,* **aer-** (eːr), **aeri-** ('eːr·i) *prefijo* aero-; aeri-: *aeronaut,* aeronauta.
aerodrome ('eːr·əˌdrom) *n.* = **airdrome.**
aerodynamics (ˌer·o·dai'næm·ɪks) *n.pl.* aerodinámica (*sing.*) —**aerodynamic,** *adj.* aerodinámico.
aeronaut ('eːr·əˌnɔt) *n.* aeronauta. —**aeronautic; aeronautical,** *adj.* aeronáutico. —**aeronautics,** *n.pl.* & *sing.* aeronáutica (*sing.*).
aerostat ('eːr·əˌstæt) *n.* aeróstato.
aerostatic (ˌeːr·ə'stæt·ɪk) *adj.* aerostático. —**aerostatics,** *n.* aerostática.
af- (æf; əf) *prefijo, var. de* **ad-** *ante* f: *affirm,* afirmar.
afar (ə'far) *adv.* lejos; distante.
affable ('æf·ə·bəl) *adj.* afable; cariñoso; condescendiente. —**affability,** *n.* afabilidad; condescendencia.
affair (ə'feːr) *n.* **1,** (event; matter) suceso; acontecimiento; hecho. **2,** *colloq.* (involvement of love) aventura. **3,** *pl.* (business) asuntos; cosas; negocios.
affect (ə'fɛkt) *v.t.* **1,** (change) afectar; cambiar; influenciar. **2,** (feign) simular; fingir. **3,** (make a show of) impresionar; conmover.
affectation (ˌæf·ɛk'tei·ʃən) *n.* afectación; amaneramiento; pretensión; presunción.
affected (ə'fɛk·tɪd) *adj.* **1,** (influenced) afectado; influenciado; influido. **2,** (artificial in manner) amanerado; afectado. **3,** (moved by emotion) conmovido. **4,** (afflicted) afectado; atacado; afligido.
affecting (ə'fɛk·tiŋ) *adj.* conmovedor; emocionante; tierno.
affection (ə'fɛk·ʃən) *n.* afección; afecto; cariño. —**affectionate,** *adj.* afecto; afectuoso; cariñoso.
affective (ə'fɛk·tɪv) *adj.* afectivo.
affidavit (ˌæf·ɪ'dei·vɪt) *n.* aval; garantía; declaración jurada.
affiliate (ə'fɪl·i·eit) *v.i.* afiliarse; asociarse. —*v.t.* afiliar; asociar; incorporar. —*n.* (-ət) afiliado; asociado; socio. —**affiliation,** *n.* afiliación; asociación.
affinity (ə'fɪn·ə·ti) *n.* afinidad.
affirm (ə'fʌɹm) *v.t.* **1,** (assert) afirmar; aseverar; sostener. **2,** (confirm) confirmar; ratificar. **3,** *law* jurar. —**affirmation** (ˌæf·ər'mei·ʃən) *n.* afirmación; ratificación. —**affirmative** (ə'fʌɹ·mə·tɪv) *adj.* & *n.* afirmativo; aseverativo.
affix (ə'fɪks) *v.t.* **1,** (add; append) añadir; juntar. **2,** (fasten) fijar; pegar. —*n.* ('æf·ɪks) **1,** *gram.* afijo. **2,** (an addition) añadidura.
afflatus (ə'flei·təs) *n.* soplo; inspiración.
afflict (ə'flɪkt) *v.t.* afligir; acongojar; angustiar. —**afflicting,** *adj.* aflictivo. —**affliction** (ə'flɪk·ʃən) *n.* aflicción; congoja; pena.
affluence ('æf·lu·əns) *n.* afluencia. —**affluent,** *adj.* & *n.* afluente.
afford (ə'ford) *v.t.* **1,** (be able to) poder. **2,** (have the means for) proporcionar. **3,** (yield) dar; producir; deparar.
affront (ə'frʌnt) *n.* afrenta; agravio; ofensa. —*v.t.* afrentar; agraviar; ofender.
Afghan ('æf·gæn) *n.* **1,** (dog) perro afgano. **2,** [*también adj.*] (native of Afghanistan) afgano; afganistaní. **3,** *l.c.* (woolen blanket or shawl) cubrecama *o* manta de estambre.
afield (ə'fild) *adv.* lejos de casa; por el campo; en la campiña.
afire (ə'fair) *adv.* en llamas. —*adj.* ardiente; encendido.
aflame (ə'fleim) *adv.* en llamas; en ascuas. —*adj.* ardiente; inflamado.
afloat (ə'flot) *adv.* a flote; flotando. —*adj.* flotante.
aflutter (ə'flʌt·ər) *adj.* agitado. —*adv.* agitadamente.
afoot (ə'fʊt) *adv.* & *adj.* **1,** (walking) a pie; moviéndose; andando. **2,** (underway) en preparación.
aforementioned (ə'forˌmɛn·ʃənd) *adj.* antepuesto; ya mencionado.
aforesaid (ə'for·sɛd) *adj.* antedicho; ya mencionado.
afoul (ə'faul) *adv.* en colisión. —*adj.* enredado. —**run afoul of,** enredarse con; tener una pelea *o* altercado con.
afraid (ə'freid) *adj.* atemorizado; amedrentado; temeroso. —**be afraid,** tener miedo.

African ('æf·rɪ·kən) *n.* & *adj.* africano.
aft (æft) *adv.* a popa.
after ('æf·tər) *prep.* después (de); tras (de); detrás. —*conj.* después que; después de que. —*adv.* después; detrás; atrás. —*adj.* siguiente; posterior.
afterbirth *n.* placenta.
aftereffect *n.* efecto subsiguiente.
afterlife *n.* vida futura.
aftermath ('æf·tər·mæθ) *n.* consecuencias (*pl.*); resultados (*pl.*).
afternoon (æf·tər'nu:n) *n.* tarde.
afterpains *n.pl.* entuertos.
afterthought *n.* idea tardía; segundo *o* nuevo pensamiento.
afterward ('æf·tər·wərd) *también,* **afterwards** (-wərdz) *adv.* después; más tarde; posteriormente.
ag- (æg; əg) *prefijo, var. de* **ad-** *ante* g: *aggregate,* agregado.
again (ə'gɛn) *adv.* además; otra vez; de nuevo; asimismo. —**again and again**, una y otra vez; muchas veces. —**now and again**, de cuando en cuando; a veces.
against (ə'gɛnst) *prep.* **1,** (in opposite direction to; hostile to) contra. **2,** (toward) frente; enfrente. **3,** (in provision for) por. **4,** (adjoining) junto a; contra.
agate ('æg·ət) *n.* ágata.
age (eidʒ) *n.* **1,** (years since birth) edad; años. **2,** (stage of life) edad; época; período. **3,** (lifetime) vida; existencia. **4,** *hist.; geol.* época; era; período. **5,** *colloq.* [*también,* **ages**] (a long time) mucho tiempo. —*v.i.* envejecer; envejecerse. —*v.t.* madurar; curar; envejecer. —**aged** ('ei·dʒed; eidʒd) *adj.* viejo; anciano; senil. —**ageless,** *adj.* inmutable; perenne. —**coming of age,** mayoría de edad. —**of age,** mayor de edad. —**under age,** menor de edad.
-age (ɪdʒ) *sufijo* -aje; *forma nombres denotando:* **1,** acción: *pillage,* pillaje. **2,** resultado: *cartage,* carretaje. **3,** colectividad: *foliage,* follaje. **4,** estado; condición: *bondage,* esclavitud. **5,** domicilio; sitio: *parsonage,* rectoría. **6,** derechos; coste: *wharfage,* muellaje.
agency ('ei·dʒən·si) *n.* **1,** (means) acción; gestión. **2,** (office) agencia. **3,** (government bureau) organismo; departamento.
agenda (ə'dʒɛn·də) *n.* [*sing.* **agendum** (-dəm)] agenda; diario.
agent ('ei·dʒənt) *n.* agente.
agglomerate (ə'glam·ə·reit) *v.t.* aglomerar; amontonar; hacinar. —*v.i.* aglomerarse; amontonarse; hacinarse. —*adj.* (-rət) aglomerado; amontonado. —**agglomeration,** *n.* aglomeración; amontonamiento.
agglutinate (ə'glu·tə,neit) *v.t.* aglutinar. —**agglutinant,** *adj.* & *n.* aglutinante. —**agglutination,** *n.* aglutinación.
aggrandize ('æg·rən,daiz) *v.t.* **1,** (increase; extend) engrandecer; exaltar; agrandar; ensanchar. **2,** (exaggerate) exagerar; aumentar.
aggrandizement (ə'græn·dɪz·mənt) *n.* **1,** (increase) engrandecimiento; ensanche. **2,** (exaggeration) exageración.
aggravate ('æg·rə,veit) *v.t.* **1,** (make worse) agravar; empeorar; deteriorar. **2,** *colloq.* (vex) irritar; provocar. —**aggravation,** *n.* agravación; agravamiento.
aggregate ('æg·rə·gət) *n.* agregado. —*adj.* en bruto; en total. —**aggregation,** *n.* agregación.
aggression (ə'grɛʃ·ən) *n.* agresión; ataque; provocación.
aggressive (ə'grɛs·ɪv) *adj.* **1,** (hostile) agresivo; provocador; hostil. **2,** (vigorous) agresivo; emprendedor; vigoroso. —**aggressiveness,** *n.* agresividad.
aggressor (ə'grɛs·ər) *n.* agresor; atacante; enemigo.
aggrieved (ə'gri:vd) *adj.* agraviado; ofendido; oprimido.
aghast (ə'gæst) *adj.* espantado; aterrorizado; atónito.
agile ('ædʒ·əl) *adj.* ágil; vivo; ligero; rápido. —**agility** (ə'dʒɪl·ə·ti) *n.* agilidad; ligereza.
agitate ('ædʒ·ɪ·teit) *v.t.* **1,** (shake briskly) agitar; mover; sacudir. **2,** (perturb) agitar; perturbar. —*v.i.* inquietar el ánimo; alborotar; perturbar al público. —**agitation,** *n.* agitación; alboroto.
agitator ('ædʒ·ɪ,te·tər) *n.* **1,** (person) agitador; perturbador. **2,** (device) agitador.
aglow (ə'glo:) *adj.* fulgurante.
agnostic (æg'nas·tɪk) *n.* & *adj.* agnóstico. —**agnosticism** (-tɪ,siz·əm) *n.* agnosticismo.
ago (ə'go:) *adv.* & *adj.* hace (*often contracted to* ha): *a short time ago,* hace poco; *long ago,*

hace mucho tiempo; *two years ago,* hace dos años *or* dos años ha.

agonize ('æg·ə·naiz) *v.i.* agonizar; extinguirse; languidecer. —*v.t.* angustiar; causar gran pena.

agony ('æg·ə·ni) *n.* agonía; congoja; lucha.

agrarian (ə'grɛːr·i·ən) *adj.* agrario; rural; campesino.

agree (a'griː) *v.i.* **1,** (give assent) asentir; consentir. **2,** (arrive at a settlement) entenderse; ponerse de acuerdo; convenir. **3,** (be similar) corresponder. **4,** (be in accord) estar de acuerdo. **5,** *gram.* concordar. —**agree on,** convenir en. —**agree that,** coincidir en que. —**agree to,** consentir en.

agreeable (ə'gri·ə·bəl) *adj.* **1,** (pleasing) agradable; satisfactorio. **2,** (conformable) conveniente; oportuno; lógico. **3,** (willing to consent) complaciente; condescendiente.

agreement (ə'gri·mənt) *n.* **1,** (concord) acuerdo; armonía. **2,** (arrangement) contrato; acuerdo. **3,** (among nations) pacto; convenio.

agriculture ('æg·rɪ,kʌl·tʃər) *n.* agricultura. —**agricultural** (-'kʌl·tʃər·əl) *adj.* agrícola.

agriculturist (-'kʌl·tʃər·ɪst) *n.* **1,** (expert) perito agrícola. **2,** (farmer) agricultor.

agronomy (ə'gran·ə·mi) *n.* agronomía. —**agronomist,** *n.* agrónomo.

aground (ə'graund) *adv.* & *adj.* varado; encallado.

ah (aː) *interj.* ¡ah!

aha (a'haː) *interj.* ¡ajá!

ahead (ə'hɛd) *adv.* **1,** (in front) adelante; al frente; delante. **2,** (in advance) antes; delante.

ahem (ə'hɛm) *interj.* ¡ejem!

aid (eid) *v.t.* **1,** (help) ayudar; asistir; socorrer. **2,** (facilitate) facilitar; favorecer; promover. —*n.* **1,** (assistance) ayuda; asistencia; auxilio. **2,** (helper) ayudante; auxiliar; colaborador.

aide (eid) *n.* ayudante.

aide-de-camp ('eid·də'kæmp) *n.* ayuda de campo; edecán.

ail (eil) *v.t.* afligir; padecer; molestar. —*v.i.* indisponerse; sentirse mal.

aileron ('ei·lə·ran) *n.* alerón.

ailment ('eil·mənt) *n.* dolencia; enfermedad; padecimiento.

aim (eim) *n.* **1,** (direction) trayectoria; mira; dirección. **2,** (act of aiming) apuntamiento. **3,** (intention; purpose) objetivo; intención; mira. —*v.t.* apuntar; dirigir. —*v.i.* aspirar; pretender; luchar (por). —**aimless,** *adj.* desorientado; despistado; sin norte.

air (eːr) *n.* **1,** (atmosphere) aire; atmósfera. **2,** (light breeze) aire; brisa. **3,** (outward appearance) aire; impresión; sensación. **4,** (personal bearing) aire; semblante; talante. **5,** *pl.* (affected manners) aires; ínfulas; presunción (*sing.*). **6,** *music* aire; tonada; melodía. —*v.t.* **1,** (ventilate) airear; ventilar. **2,** (bring to public notice) airear; sacar a relucir; pregonar. —*adj.* **1,** (by or in the air) aéreo; de aire. **2,** (operated by air) neumático. —**put on airs,** darse aires; darse ínfulas. —**up in the air, 1,** (undecided) en la luna; indeciso. **2,** *colloq.* (excited) enojado; enfadado.

air base base aérea.

airborne ('ɛr,born) *adj.* **1,** (aloft) en vuelo. **2,** (transported by air) aéreo; llevado por aire.

air brake freno neumático.

aircoach ('ɛr,kotʃ) *n.* clase turista.

air conditioner acondicionador de aire. —**air conditioned,** refrigerado; climatizado. —**air conditioning,** acondicionamiento de aire; aire acondicionado.

aircraft ('ɛr,kræft) *n.* aeronave; avión; aeroplano. —**aircraft carrier,** portaaviones.

airdrome ('ɛr,drom) *también,* **aerodrome** ('ɛr·ə·drom) *n.* aeródromo; aeropuerto.

airfield ('ɛr,fiːld) *n.* aeropuerto; campo de aviación.

air force fuerza aérea militar; fuerzas de aviación; aviación militar.

air hole respiradero.

airiness ('ɛr·i·nəs) *n.* **1,** (ventilation) ventilación; aire. **2,** *fig.* (jauntiness) ligereza; viveza.

airing ('ɛr·ɪŋ) *n.* **1,** (exposure to air) aireo; ventilación. **2,** (walk) paseo.

airlift ('ɛr,lɪft) *n.* ayuda aérea.

airline ('ɛr,lain) *n.* compañía *o* línea aérea; aerolínea.

air mail correo aéreo. —**by air mail,** por avión.

airman ('ɛr,mən) *n.* [*pl.* **-men**] aviador; aeronauta; soldado de la aviación militar.
airplane ('ɛr,plein) *n.* aeroplano; avión.
airport ('ɛr,port) *n.* aeropuerto.
air pressure presión atmosférica.
air raid bombardeo; ataque aéreo.
airship ('ɛr,ʃɪp) *n.* nave aérea; avión; aeroplano; aeronave.
airsick ('ɛr,sɪk) *adj.* mareado. —**airsickness,** *n.* mal de altura.
airstrip ('ɛr,strɪp) *n.* pista de aterrizaje.
airtight ('ɛr,tait) *adj.* hermético.
airway ('ɛr·we) *n.* aerovía; vía aérea.
airy ('ɛr·i) *adj.* **1,** (like air) ligero; sutil; etéreo. **2,** (well-ventilated) aireado; ventilado. **3,** (unreal) idealista; visionario. **4,** (pretentious) vanidoso; pretencioso.
aisle (ail) *n.* pasillo; paso.
ajar (ə'dʒar) *adj.* entreabierto; entornado. —*adv.* a medio abrir.
akimbo (ə'kɪm·bo) *adj.* & *adv.* de *o* en jarras.
akin (ə'kɪn) *adj.* **1,** (related) consanguíneo. **2,** (similar) parecido; semejante.
al- (æl; əl) *prefijo, var. de* **ad-** *ante* l: *alliteration,* aliteración.
-al (əl) *sufijo* -al. **1,** *forma adjetivos denotando* relación; pertenencia; calidad: *national,* nacional. **2,** *forma nombres expresando* acción *o* efecto: *acquittal,* exoneración.
alabaster ('æl·ə·bæs·tər) *n.* alabastro. —*adj.* alabastrino.
a la carte (a·lə'kart) a la carta.
alacrity (ə'læk·rə·ti) *n.* presteza; prontitud; alacridad.
a la mode (a·lə'mo:d) a la moda; de moda.
alarm (ə'larm) *v.t.* **1,** (frighten) alarmar; atemorizar; inquietar. **2,** (warn of danger) avisar; dar la alarma a. —*n.* **1,** (warning of danger) alarma; aviso. **2,** (device) alarma. **3,** (apprehension of danger) ansiedad; temor; inquietud. —**alarming,** *adj.* alarmante. —**alarmist,** *n.* alarmista. —**alarm clock,** despertador.
alas (ə'læs) *interj.* ¡ay! ¡ay de mí!
albacore ('æl·bə,kor) *n.* albacora.
albatross ('æl·bə,trɔs) *n.* albatros.
albeit (ɔl'bi·ɪt) *conj.* a pesar de que; aunque.
albinism ('æl·bə·nɪz·əm) *n.* albinismo.
albino (æl'bai·no) *n.* & *adj.* albino.
album ('æl·bəm) *n.* álbum.
albumen (æl'bju·mən) *n.* **1,** (white of egg) clara. **2,** *chem.* albumen.
albumin (æl'bju·mɪn) *n.* albúmina.
alchemy ('æl·kə·mi) *n.* alquimia. —**alchemist,** *n.* alquimista.
alcohol ('æl·kə·hɔl; -hal) *n.* alcohol. —**alcoholic** (-'hal·ɪk) *adj.* & *n.* alcohólico. —**alcoholism,** *n.* alcoholismo; dipsomanía.
alcove ('æl·ko:v) *n.* alcoba; recámara.
aldehyde ('æl·də,haid) *n.* aldehído.
alder ('ɔl·dər) *n.* aliso.
alderman ('ɔl·dər·mən) *n.* [*pl.* **-men**] concejal.
ale (eil) *n.* cerveza inglesa.
alert (ə'lʌɹt) *n.* alerta; aviso. —*adj.* **1,** (watchful) vigilante. **2,** (nimble) vivo; despierto; inteligente. —*v.t.* alertar; avisar; prevenir. —**alertness,** *n.* vigilancia; atención. —**on the alert,** vigilante; alerta.
alfalfa (æl'fæl·fə) *n.* alfalfa.
alga ('æl·gə) [*pl.* **algae** (-dʒi)] *n.* alga.
algebra ('æl·dʒə·brə) *n.* álgebra. —**algebraic** (-'brei·ɪk) *adj.* algebraico.
alias ('ei·li·əs) *n.* alias. —*adv.* conocido como.
alibi ('æl·ə·bai) *n.* **1,** *law* coartada. **2,** *colloq.* excusa; pretexto.
alien ('eil·jən) *n.* & *adj.* extranjero; forastero. —*adj.* extraño; ajeno; diferente.
alienable ('eil·jə·nə·bəl) *adj.* alienable; enajenable; transferible.
alienate ('eil·jə·neit) *v.t.* **1,** (estrange) enajenar; alejar; malquistar. **2,** *law* enajenar.
alienation (eil·jə'nei·ʃən) *n.* **1,** (estrangement) enajenación; desunión; desapego; desvío. **2,** (mental aberration) enajenación; locura; desvarío.
alienist ('eil·jə·nɪst) *n.* alienista; psiquiatra.
alight (ə'lait) *v.i.* bajar; desmontar; descender; apearse. —*adj.* brillante; luminoso.
align *también,* **aline** (ə'lain) *v.t.* alinear. —**alignment,** *n.* alineamiento; alineación.
alike (ə'laik) *adv.* igualmente; a

semejanza; de igual forma. —*adj.* igual; semejante; parecido.
alimentary (æl·ə'mɛn·tə·ri) *adj.* alimenticio.
alimony ('æl·ɪ·mo·ni) *n.* alimentos; manutención.
-ality ('æl·ə·ti) *sufijo* -alidad; *forma nombres indicando* calidad; condición: *rationality,* racionalidad.
alive (ə'laiv) *adj.* **1,** (living) vivo; existente. **2,** (active) animado; activo. **3,** (susceptible) impresionable; susceptible.
alkali (æl·kə·lai) *n., chem.* álcali. —**alkaline,** (-lain) *adj.* alcalino. —**alkalinity** (-'lɪn·ə·ti) *n.* alcalinidad. —**alkalize** (-laiz) *v.t.* & *i.* alcalizar. —**alkalization** (-lɪ'zei·ʃən) *n.* alcalización.
alkaloid ('æl·kə·lɔid) *n.* alcaloide.
all (ɔːl) *n., adj.* & *pron.* todo. —*adv.* completamente; por entero; totalmente. —**above all,** sobre todo; ante todo. —**after all,** después de todo. —**all in all,** en conjunto. —**all the better** *o* **worse,** tanto mejor *o* peor. —**all the more,** tanto más. —**all the same,** a pesar de todo. —**at all,** en absoluto; de ninguna forma. —**not at all,** de ninguna manera; por nada. —**once and for all,** por última vez.
Allah ('aː·la) *n.* Alá.
all-around *también,* **all-round,** *adj.* completo; cabal; versátil.
allay (æ'lei) *v.t.* **1,** (pacify) aquietar; pacificar. **2,** (mitigate) aliviar; mitigar; calmar.
allegation (ˌæl·ə'gei·ʃən) *n.* alegación; alegato.
allege (ə'lɛdʒ) *v.t.* alegar; sostener.
allegiance (ə'li·dʒəns) *n.* fidelidad; devoción; lealtad.
allegory ('æl·əˌgor·i) *n.* alegoría; figura; símbolo. —**allegorical** (-'gar·ɪ·kəl) *adj.* alegórico; simbólico.
allegro (ə'lɛg·ro) *adv.* & *n., music* alegro; allegro.
alleluia (æl·ə'luː·jə) *n.* & *interj.* aleluya.
allergen ('æl·ər·dʒən) *n.* alergeno. —**allergenic** (-'dʒɛn·ɪk) *adj.* que produce alergia.
allergy ('æl·ər·dʒi) *n.* alergia. —**allergic** (ə'lʌɹ·dʒɪk) *adj.* alérgico.
alleviate (ə'liː·vi·eit) *v.t.* aliviar; aligerar; mitigar. —**alleviation,** *n.* alivio; mitigación; desahogo.
alley ('æl·i) *n.* callejón; travesía; pasadizo. —**blind alley,** callejón sin salida.
alliance (ə'lai·əns) *n.* alianza; pacto; unión.
allied (ə'laid; 'æl·aid) *adj.* aliado; socio; unido.
alligator ('æl·ɪˌgei·tər) *n.* caimán; *Mex.* lagarto.—**alligator pear,** aguacate.
alliteration (əˌlɪt·ə'rei·ʃən) *n.* aliteración. —**alliterative** (ə'lɪt·əˌrei·tɪv) *adj.* aliterado.
allo- ('æl·o) *prefijo* alo-; variación; alejamiento; diferencia: *allopathy,* alopatía.
allocate ('æl·ə·keit) *v.t.* colocar; distribuir. —**allocation,** *n.* colocación; distribución.
allopathy (ə'lap·ə·θi) *n.* alopatía. —**allopathic** (æl·ə'pæθ·ɪk) *adj.* alopático.
allot (ə'lat) *v.t.* [**allotted, -ting**] **1,** (parcel out) parcelar; distribuir; prorratear. **2,** (appoint for a purpose; assign) señalar; asignar.
allotment (ə'lat·mənt) *n.* **1,** (portion) parcela; trozo; prorrateo. **2,** (appointment) asignación.
allotrope ('æl·ə·trop) *n.* alótropo. —**allotropic** (-'trap·ɪk) *adj.* alotrópico. —**allotropy** (ə'lat·rə·pi), **allotropism,** *n.* alotropía.
all-out ('ɔlˌaut) *adj.* completo; vigoroso.
allow (ə'lau) *v.t.* **1,** (permit) autorizar; permitir. **2,** (yield) ceder; condescender. **3,** (admit) admitir; confesar. **4,** *comm.* descontar. —**allow for, 1,** (leave room for) dejar sitio *o* espacio para. **2,** (reckon with) tener en cuenta.
allowance (ə'lau·əns) *n.* **1,** (permission) autorización; permiso. **2,** (allotment, as of money) asignación; subvención. **3,** *comm.* descuento; deducción. **4,** (compensation, as for weight) margen.
alloy ('æl·ɔi) *n.* aleación; mezcla. —*v.t.* (ə'loi) alear; ligar; mezclar.
all right 1, (satisfactory) bueno; satisfactorio. **2,** (unhurt) bien. **3,** (expression of assent) muy bien; por seguro; de acuerdo.
All Saints' Day Día de Todos los Santos.
All Souls' Day Día de los Difuntos.
allude (ə'luːd) *v.i.* aludir; mencionar; referirse.
allure (ə'lʊr) *v.t.* atraer; seducir; tentar. —*n.* [*también,* **allurement**]

atracción; seducción. **—alluring,** *adj.* seductor; atrayente; fascinante.
allusion (ə'luː·ʒən) *n.* alusión; referencia. **—allusive** (-sɪv) *adj.* alusivo; referente.
alluvium (ə'lu·vi·əm) *n.* aluvión. **—alluvial,** *adj.* aluvial.
ally (ə'lai) *v.t.* unir; ligar; enlazar. *—v.i.* aliarse; unirse. *—n.* (*también,* 'æl·ai) aliado.
almanac ('ɔl·mə·næk) *n.* almanaque.
almighty (ɔl'mai·ti) *adj.* omnipotente; todopoderoso. **—the Almighty,** Dios; el Todopoderoso.
almond ('a·mənd) *n.* **1,** (tree) almendro. **2,** (fruit) almendra.
almoner ('æl·mən·ər) *n.* limosnero.
almost ('ɔl·most) *adv.* casi.
alms (aːmz) *n.* limosna; caridad.
almshouse *n.* asilo; hospicio.
aloe ('æl·o) *n.* áloe. **—aloes,** *n. sing.* áloe.
aloft (ə'lɔft) *adj.* flotante; aéreo. *—adv.* en el aire; en alto.
alone (ə'loːn) *adj.* solo; único. *—adv.* tan solo; aparte; solitariamente.
along (ə'lɔŋ) *prep.* por; a lo largo de. *—adv.* a lo largo; junto; en compañía. **—all along,** desde el principio; todo el tiempo. **—along with,** junto con; en compañía de.
alongside (ə'lɔŋ·said) *adv.* & *prep.* a lo largo (de).
aloof (ə'luːf) *adv.* a distancia; desde lejos. *—adj.* retraído; apartado; huraño. **—aloofness,** *n.* reserva; retraimiento.
aloud (ə'laud) *adv.* fuerte; con fuerza; en voz alta.
alpaca (æl'pæk·ə) *n.* alpaca.
alpha ('æl·fə) *n.* alfa.
alphabet ('æl·fə·bɛt) *n.* alfabeto. **—alphabetical** (-'bɛt·ɪ·kəl); **alphabetic,** *adj.* alfabético. **—alphabetize** (-bə·taiz) *v.t.* alfabetizar.
alpine ('æl·pain) *adj.* alpino. **—alpinism** ('æl·pə·nɪz·əm) *n.* alpinismo. **—alpinist** ('æl·pə·nɪst) *n.* alpinista.
already (ɔl'rɛd·i) *adv.* ya; con anterioridad; anteriormente.
also ('ɔl·so) *adv.* además; también; asimismo.
altar ('ɔl·tər) *n.* altar. **—altar boy,** acólito; monaguillo.
altarpiece *n.* retablo.
alter ('ɔl·tər) *v.t.* alterar; cambiar; variar. *—v.i.* alterarse; cambiarse; modificarse.
alteration (ɔl·tər'ei·ʃən) *n.* **1,** (change) alteración; cambio. **2,** (renovation) arreglo.
altercate ('ɔl·tər,keit) *v.t.* altercar. **—altercation,** *n.* altercación; altercado.
alternate ('ɔl·tər,neit) *v.t.* alternar; hacer turnos de. *—v.i.* alternarse; turnarse; *electricity* alternar. *—n.* (-nət) substituto; suplente. *—adj.* (-nət) alterno. **—alternation,** *n.* alternación; turno. **—alternating current,** corriente alterna.
alternative (ɔl'tʌɹ·nə·tɪv) *n.* alternativa; dilema. *—adj.* alternativo.
although (ɔl'ðoː) *conj.* aunque; si bien.
alti- (æl·tɪ) *prefijo* alti-; alto; altura: *altimeter,* altímetro.
altimeter (æl'tɪm·ə·tər) *n.* altímetro.
altitude ('æl·tɪ·tud) *n.* altitud; altura.
alto ('æl·toː) *adj.* & *n.* [*pl.* **-tos**] **1,** *music* alto. **2,** (voice) contralto.
alto- (æl·to) *prefijo* alto-; alta; altura: *alto-cumulus,* alto-cúmulo.
altogether (ɔl·tə'gɛð·ər) *adv.* completamente; del todo. **—in the altogether,** *colloq.* desnudo; en cueros.
altruism ('æl·tru·ɪz·əm) *n.* altruísmo. **—altruist,** *n.* altruísta. **—altruistic,** *adj.* altruísta.
alum ('æl·əm) *n.* alumbre.
alumina (ə'luː·mə·nə) *n.* alúmina.
aluminum (ə'luː·mɪn·əm) *también, Brit.,* **aluminium** (,æl·ju'mɪn·i·əm) *n.* aluminio.
alumnus (ə'lʌm·nəs) *n.* [*pl.* **-ni** (-nai)] graduado. **—alumna** (-nə) *n.* [*pl.* **-nae** (-ni)] graduada.
alveolus (æl'vi·ə·ləs) *n.* [*pl.* **-li** (-lai)] alvéolo. **—alveolar,** *adj.* alveolar.
always ('ɔl·wiz; -wez) *adv.* siempre; por siempre.
am (æm) *v., primera persona del sing. del pres. de* **be.**
amalgam (ə'mæl·gəm) *n.* amalgama; compuesto; mezcla.
amalgamate (ə'mæl·gə,meit) *v.t.* amalgamar; mezclar; combinar. *—v.i.* mezclarse; combinarse; amalgamarse. **—amalgamation,** *n.* amalgamación.
amanuensis (ə,mæn·ju'ɛn·sɪs) *n.* amanuense.

amaranth ('æm·ə·rænθ) *n.* amaranto.
amaryllis (æm·ə'rɪl·ɪs) *n.* **1,** *bot.* amarilis. **2,** *cap., poet.* Amarilis.
amass (ə'mæs) *v.t.* amasar; amontonar; acumular.
amateur ('æm·ə·tʃʊr; -tʌɪ) *n. & adj.* aficionado; principiante. —**amateurish,** *adj.* de aficionado; inexperto. —**amateurism,** *n.* inexperiencia; impericia.
amatory ('æm·əˌtor·i) *adj.* amatorio.
amaze (ə'meiz) *v.t.* asombrar. —**amazement,** *n.* asombro. —**amazing,** *adj.* asombroso.
amazon ('æm·ə·zan) *n.* amazona.
ambassador (æm'bæs·ə·dər) *n.* embajador. —**ambassadorial** (-'dor·i·əl) *adj.* de la embajada; del embajador. —**ambassadress** (-drəs) *n.* embajadora.
amber ('æm·bər) *n.* ámbar. —*adj.* ambarino.
ambergris ('æm·bərˌgris) *n.* ámbar gris.
ambi- (æm·bɪ) *prefijo* ambi-. **1,** ambos; por ambos lados: *ambidextrous,* ambidiestro. **2,** alrededor: *ambient,* ambiente.
ambidexterity (ˌæm·bɪ·dɛk·'stɛr·ə·ti) *n.* **1,** (skill with both hands) habilidad *o* destreza con ambas manos. **2,** *fig.* (duplicity) doblez.
ambidextrous (æm·bɪ'dɛks·trəs) *adj.* **1,** (apt with both hands) ambidextro; ambidiestro. **2,** *fig.* (deceitful) falso; engañoso.
ambiguity (ˌæm·bɪ'gju·ə·ti) *n.* ambigüedad; equívoco; oscuridad. —**ambiguous** (-'bɪg·ju·əs) *adj.* ambiguo; equívoco; confuso.
ambit ('æm·bɪt) n. ámbito; ambiente; contorno.
ambition (æm'bɪʃ·ən) *n.* ambición; aspiración; codicia. —**ambitious** (-əs) *adj.* ambicioso.
ambivalent (æm'bɪv·ə·lənt) *adj.* ambivalente. —**ambivalence,** *n.* ambivalencia.
amble ('æm·bəl) *v.i.* amblar.
ambrosia (æm'broː·ʒə) *n.* ambrosía. —**ambrosial** (-ʒəl) *adj.* superior; delicioso.
ambulance ('æm·bjə·ləns) *n.* ambulancia.
ambush ('æm·bʊʃ) *v.t.* acechar; emboscar. —*n.* emboscada; celada.
ameba *también,* **amoeba** (ə'mi·bə) *n.,* ameba; amiba.
ameliorate (ə'miːl·jə·reit) *v.t.* mejorar; perfeccionar. —*v.i.* mejorarse. —**ameliorable** (-rə·bəl) *adj.* mejorable; perfeccionable. —**amelioration,** *n.* mejoría; adelanto; progreso. —**ameliorative** (-rə·tɪv) *adj.* mejorador; perfeccionador.
amen ('ei'mɛn; 'a-) *adv., n. & interj.* amén.
amenable (ə'miː·nə·bəl; ə'mɛn-) *adj.* **1,** (tractable) sumiso; dócil. **2,** (answerable) responsable.
amend (ə'mɛnd) *v.t.* **1** (correct) enmendar; corregir; mejorar. **2,** (alter) enmendar; alterar; cambiar. —*v.i.* enmendarse; corregirse; mejorarse. —**amends,** *n.pl.* compensación; reparación; enmienda. —**make amends (for)** compensar; enmendar.
amendment (ə'mɛnd·mənt) *n.* enmienda; cambio; corrección.
amenity (ə'mɛn·ə·ti) *n.* amenidad.
ament ('æm·ənt; 'ei·mənt) *n.* amento; candelilla.
American (ə'mɛr·ɪ·kən) *n. & adj.* americano. —**American plan,** pensión completa; plan americano.
Americanism (ə'mɛr·ɪ·kanˌɪz·əm) *n.* americanismo.
Americanize (ə'mɛr·ɪ·kəˌnaiz) v.t. americanizar. —**Americanization** (-nɪ'zei·ʃən) *n.* americanización.
americium (æm·ə'rɪs·i·əm; -'rɪʃ·jəm) *n.* americio; américo.
amethyst ('æm·ə·θɪst) *n. & adj.* amatista.
amiable ('ei·mi·ə·bəl) *adj.* amable; cordial; afable. —**amiability, amiableness,** *n.* cordialidad; amabilidad; afabilidad.
amicable ('æm·ɪ·kə·bəl) *adj.* amistoso; sociable; afectuoso. —**amicability,** *n.* cordialidad; sociabilidad.
amid (ə'mɪd) *también,* **amidst** (ə'mɪdst) *prep.* entre; en medio de.
amiss (ə'mɪs) *adv.* impropiamente; equivocadamente; fuera de sitio *o* de tono; demás. —*adj.* impropio; inoportuno. —**take amiss,** llevar *o* tomar a mal.
amity ('æm·ə·ti) *n.* amistad; cordialidad; concordia.
ammeter ('æm·mi·tər) *n.* amperímetro.
ammonia (ə'moːn·jə) *n., chem.* amoníaco.
ammoniate (ə'mo·ni·eit) *v.t.* tratar con amoníaco. —*n.* (-ət) amoniuro.

ammonium (ə'mo·ni·əm) *n.* amonio.
ammunition (ˌæm·ju'nɪʃ·ən) *n.* munición.
amnesia (æm'niː·ʒə) *n.* amnesia. —**amnesic** (-zɪk) *adj.* & *n.* amnésico.
amnesty ('æm·nəs·ti) *n.* amnistía; indulto; perdón.
amoeba *n.* = **ameba.**
among (ə'mʌŋ) *también,* **amongst** (ə'mʌŋst) *prep.* entre; en medio de.
amoral (ei'mar·əl) *adj.* amoral. —**amorality** (ˌei·mə'ræl·ə·ti) *n.* amoralidad.
amorous ('æm·ə·rəs) *adj.* amoroso; apasionado. —**amorousness,** *n.* enamoramiento; apasionamiento.
amorphous (ə'mor·fəs) *adj.* amorfo.
amortize ('æm·ərˌtaiz; ə'mor-) *v.t.* amortizar. —**amortization** (-tɪ·'zei·ʃən) *n.* amortización.
amount (ə'maunt) *n.* cantidad; suma; importe. —*v.i.* sumar; ascender; importar.
ampere ('æm·pɪr) *n.* amperio. —**amperage,** *n.* amperaje.
amphi- (æm·fɪ) *prefijo* anfi-. **1,** ambos; doble: *amphibious,* anfibio. **2,** alrededor de: *amphitheater,* anfiteatro. **3,** de ambas especies: *amphibology,* anfibología.
amphibian (æm'fɪb·i·ən) *n.* anfibio. —**amphibious,** *adj.* anfibio.
amphitheater ('æm·fəˌθi·ə·tər) *n.* anfiteatro.
amphora ('æm·fə·rə) *n.* [*pl.* **-rae** (-ri) *o* **-ras** (-rəz)] ánfora.
ample ('æm·pəl) *adj.* **1,** (large) amplio; capaz; suficiente. **2,** (plentiful) abundante; copioso; bastante.
amplifier ('æm·plɪˌfai·ər) *n.* amplificador.
amplify ('æm·plɪ·fai) *v.t.* amplificar; ampliar. —**amplification** (-fɪ'kei·ʃən) *n.* amplificación; ampliación.
amplitude ('æm·plɪ·tud) *n.* amplitud. —**amplitude modulation,** *también,* **AM** ('ei'ɛm) modulación dilatada *o* de extensión.
ampoule ('æm·pul) *n.* ampolla; ampolleta.
amputate ('æm·pjə·teit) *v.t.* amputar; cortar un miembro. —**amputation,** *n.* amputación. —**amputee** (-'tiː) *n.* amputado.
amuck (ə'mʌk) *adv.* con frenesí; con rabia. —**run amuck,** correr *o* ir a troche y moche.
amulet ('æm·ju·lɛt) *n.* amuleto.
amuse (ə'mjuːz) *v.t.* divertir; entretener; recrear. —**amusement,** *n.* diversión; distracción; entretenimiento. —**amusing,** *adj.* divertido. —**amusement park,** parque de atracciones *o* diversiones.
an (ən; æn *bajo acento*) *adj., art. indef., var. de* **a** *ante vocal o* **h** *muda.*
an- (æn; ən) *prefijo* an-. **1,** negación; carencia; *var. de* **a-** *ante vocal: anarchy,* anarquía; *anaphrodisiac,* anafrodisíaco. **2,** *var. de* **ad-** *ante* **n**: *annul,* anular. **3,** *var. de* **ana-** *ante vocal: anode,* ánodo.
-an (ən) *sufijo* -ano; -ana; *forma nombres y adjetivos denotando* relación; calidad; pertenencia: *American,* americano; *Christian,* cristiano; *diocesan,* diocesano.
ana- (æn·ə) *prefijo* ana-. **1,** en alto; hacia arriba: *anathema,* anatema. **2,** contra; hacia atrás: *anagram,* anagrama; *anachronism,* anacronismo. **3,** de nuevo: *Anabaptist,* anabaptista. **4,** del todo; completo: *analysis,* análisis. **5,** conforme; similar: *analogy,* analogía.
anabolism (ə'næb·əˌlɪz·əm) *n.* anabolismo. —**anabolic** (ˌæn·ə·'bal·ɪk) *adj.* anabólico.
anachronism (ə'næk·rə·nɪz·əm) *n.* anacronismo. —**anachronistic** (-'nɪs·tɪk) *adj.* anacrónico.
anaconda (æn·ə'kan·də) *n.* anaconda.
anaerobe ('æn·əˌrob) *n.* anaerobio. —**anaerobic** (-'ro·bɪk) *adj.* anaerobio.
anagram ('æn·əˌgræm) *n.* anagrama.
anal ('ei·nəl) *adj.* anal.
analogous (ə'næl·ə·gəs) *adj.* análogo; similar; semejante.
analogue ('æn·əˌlɔg) *n.* término análogo.
analogy (ə'næl·ə·dʒi) *n.* analogía. —**analogical** (ˌæn·ə'ladʒ·ɪ·kəl) *adj.* analógico.
analysis (ə'næl·ə·sɪs) *n.* [*pl.* **-ses** (-siz)] análisis; estudio. —**analyst** ('æn·ə·lɪst) *n.* analista; analizador. —**analytical** (æn·ə'lɪt·ɪ·kəl); **analytic,** *adj.* analítico.
analyze ('æn·ə·laiz) *v.t.* analizar; estudiar.
anamorphosis (ˌæn·ə'mor·fə·sɪs) *n.* [*pl.* **-ses** (-siz)] anamorfosis.
anapest ('æn·ə·pɛst) *n.* anapesto.

—**anapestic** (-ˈpɛst·ɪk) *adj.* anapéstico.

anarchism (ˈæn·ər·kɪz·əm) *n.* anarquismo. —**anarchist** (-kɪst) *n.* anarquista. —**anarchistic** (-ˈkɪs·tɪk) *adj.* anarquista.

anarchy (ˈæn·ər·ki) *n.* anarquía. —**anarchic** (ænˈark·ɪk), **anarchical,** *adj.* anárquico.

anathema (əˈnæθ·ə·mə) *n.* anatema. —**anathematize** (-taiz) *v.t.* & *i.* anatematizar.

anatomist (əˈnæt·ə·mɪst) *n.* anatomista.

anatomize (əˈnæt·əˌmaiz) *v.t.* anatomizar.

anatomy (əˈnæt·ə·mi) *n.* anatomía. —**anatomical** (ˌæn·əˈtam·ɪ·kəl) *adj.* anatómico.

-ance (əns) *sufijo* -ancia; -encia; *forma nombres de adjetivos terminados en* **-ant**: *abundance,* abundancia; *assistance,* asistencia.

ancestor (ˈæn·sɛs·tər) *n.* antepasado; ascendiente. —**ancestress** (-trəs) *n.* antepasada.

ancestral (ænˈsɛs·trəl) *adj.* ancestral; atávico; antiguo.

ancestry (ˈæn·sɛs·tri) *n.* ascendencia; genealogía; linaje.

anchor (ˈæŋ·kər) *n.* ancla. —*v.t.* asegurar; sujetar; amarrar. —*v.i.* anclar; echar anclas; fondear. —**anchorage,** *n.* anclaje; ancladero; fondeadero.

anchovy (ˈæn·tʃo·vi) *n.* anchoa.

ancient (ˈein·ʃənt) *adj.* antiguo; remoto.

-ancy (ən·si) *sufijo, var. de* **-ance**: *occupancy,* ocupación.

and (ænd) *conj.* y; e (*before a word beginning with* i *or* hi).

andante (anˈdan·ti) *n., music* andante.

Andean (ænˈdi·ən) *adj.* andino.

andiron (ˈændˌai·ərn) *n.* morillo.

andro- (æn·dro) *prefijo* andro-. **1,** hombre; varón: *androgynous,* andrógino. **2,** *bot.* estambre: *androecium,* androceo.

-androus (æn·drəs) *sufijo* -andro; macho: *monandrous,* monandro.

-ane (ein) *sufijo* -ano; **1,** *quím., terminación de los hidrocarburos saturados: methane,* metano. **2,** *var. de* **-an** *para diferenciarse de otro vocablo terminado en* **-an**: *urbane, urban,* urbano.

anecdote (ˈæn·ɛk·dot) *n.* anécdota.

anemia (əˈniː·mi·ə) *n.* anemia. —**anemic,** *adj.* & *n.* anémico.

anemometer (ˌæn·əˈmam·ə·tər) *n.* anemómetro.

anemone (əˈnɛm·ə·ni) *n.* anémona.

-aneous (ˈei·ni·əs) *sufijo* -áneo; *forma adjetivos denotando* relación; pertenencia: *instantaneous,* instantáneo.

aneroid (ˈæn·ər·ɔid) *adj.* aneroide.

anesthesia (ˌæn·əsˈθiː·ʒə) *n.* anestesia. —**anesthetic** (-ˈθɛt·ɪk) *n.* & *adj.* anestésico. —**anesthetist** (əˈnɛs·θə·tɪst), **anesthetician** (-ˈtɪʃ·ən) *n.* anestesista. —**anesthetize** (əˈnɛs·θəˌtaiz) *v.t.* anestesiar.

aneurysm *también,* **aneurism** (ˈæn·jəˌrɪz·əm) *n.* aneurisma.

anew (əˈnjuː) *adv.* de nuevo; nuevamente; otra vez.

angel (ˈein·dʒəl) *n.* ángel. —**angelic** (ænˈdʒɛl·ɪk), **angelical,** *adj.* angélico; angelical.

anger (ˈæŋ·gər) *n.* furia; cólera; enfado. —*v.t.* encolerizar; enfurecer; irritar.

angina (ænˈdʒai·nə) *n.* angina. —**angina pectoris** (ˈpɛk·tə·rɪs) angina de pecho.

angle (ˈæŋ·gəl) *n.* **1,** *geom.* ángulo. **2,** (corner) ángulo; rincón. **3,** (point of view) aspecto; faceta. —*v.t.* & *i.* **1,** (form an angle) hacer *o* formar ángulo. **2,** *colloq.* (focus; direct) enfocar. —*v.i.* **1,** (fish) pescar con caña. **2,** (scheme) maquinar; intrigar. —**angler** (-glər) *n.* pescador de caña. —**angling** (-glɪŋ) *n.* pesca.

Angle (ˈæŋ·gəl) *n.* anglo. —**Anglian** (ˈæŋ·gli·ən) *adj.* anglo.

angleworm *n.* lombriz.

Anglican (ˈæŋ·glɪ·kən) *n.* & *adj.* anglicano. —**Anglicanism,** *n.* anglicanismo.

Anglicism (ˈæŋ·glɪˌsɪz·əm) *n.* anglicismo.

Anglicize (ˈæŋ·glɪˌsaiz) *v.t.* inglesar; hacer inglés. —**Anglicization** (-sɪˈzei·ʃən) *n.* anglicización.

Anglo- (æŋ·glo) *prefijo* anglo-; inglés; de *o* referente a Inglaterra: *Anglo-American,* angloamericano; *Anglophobe,* anglófobo.

Anglo-American *adj.* & *n.* angloamericano.

Anglophile (ˈæŋ·gloˌfail) *n.* & *adj.* anglófilo.

Anglophobe ('æŋ·glo,fob) *n.* anglófobo.
Anglo-Saxon (,æŋ·glo'sæk·sən) *adj.* & *n.* anglo-sajón.
angry ('æŋ·gri) *adj.* airado; colérico; violento; inflamado.
anguish ('æŋ·gwɪʃ) *n.* angustia; congoja; ansia. —*v.t.* angustiar; acongojar; aquejar. —*v.i.* angustiarse; acongojarse.
angular ('æŋ·gju·lər) *adj.* **1,** (forming angles) angular. **2,** (bony; gaunt) angular; anguloso; huesudo. —**angularity** (-'lær·ə·ti) *n.* lo angular; calidad de angular.
aniline ('æn·ə·lɪn) *n.* anilina.
animadversion (,æn·ɪ·mæd·'vʌɹ·ʒən) *n.* **1,** (criticism) animadversión; censura. **2,** (bias) animadversión; animosidad; antipatía.
animal ('æn·ə·məl) *n.* & *adj.* animal; bestia; bruto. —**animality** (-'mæl·ə·ti) *n.* animalidad.
animate ('æn·ɪ·meit) *v.t.* **1,** (give life to) animar; dar vida a; vivificar. **2,** (incite to action) alentar; impulsar; dar ánimo a. —*adj.* (-mət) animado; viviente. —**animated,** *adj.* vivaz; vivo. —**animation,** *n.* animación; viveza.
animism ('æn·ə·mɪz·əm) *n.* animismo. —**animist,** *n.* animista. —**animistic** (-'mɪs·tɪk) *adj.* animista.
animosity (,æn·ɪ'mas·ə·ti) *n.* animosidad; enemistad.
anion ('æn,ai·ən) *n.* anión.
anise ('æn·ɪs) *n.* anís.
aniseed ('æn·ə,sid) *n.* anís; grano de anís.
anisette (æn·ɪ'sɛt) *n.* anisete; anisado.
ankle ('æŋ·kəl) *n.* tobillo. —**ankle bone,** hueso del tobillo.
annals ('æn·əlz) *n.* *pl.* anales. —**annalist** (-əl·ɪst) *n.* analista.
anneal (ə'niːl) *v.t.* **1,** (treat glass, metals, etc.) recocer. **2,** *fig.* (strengthen) fortalecer; vigorizar.
annex (ə'nɛks) *v.t.* anexar; añadir; agregar. —*n.* ('æn·ɛks) anexo; adjunto; apéndice. —**annexation** (,æn·ɛk'sei·ʃən) *n.* anexión.
annihilate (ə'nai·ə·leit) *v.t.* aniquilar; destruir; arrasar. —**annihilation,** *n.* aniquilación; destrucción.
anniversary (,æn·ə'vʌɹ·sə·ri) *n.* & *adj.* aniversario.
annotate ('æn·ə·teit) *v.t.* & *i.* anotar; explicar; comentar. —**annotation,** *n.* anotación; nota; apunte.
announce (ə'nauns) *v.t.* anunciar; proclamar; avisar.
announcement (ə'nauns·mənt) *n.* **1,** (information) anuncio; comunicación. **2,** (public notice) aviso; prospecto.
announcer (ə'naun·sər) *n.* anunciador; *radio; TV* locutor.
annoy (ə'nɔi) *v.t.* enojar; incomodar; irritar. —**annoyance** (-əns) *n.* enojo; disgusto.
annual ('æn·ju·əl) *adj.* anual. —*n.* anuario.
annuity (ə'nju·ə·ti) *n.* anualidad; prima anual.
annul (ə'nʌl) *v.t.* [**annulled, -nulling**] anular; revocar; suprimir. —**annulment,** *n.* anulación; cancelación; revocación.
annunciation (ə,nʌn·si'ei·ʃən) *n., usu.cap.* anunciación.
anode ('æn·od) *n.* ánodo.
anodyne ('æn·ə,dain) *adj.* & *n.* anodino.
anoint (ə'nɔint) *v.t.* ungir. —**anointment,** *n.* ungimiento.
anomaly (ə'nam·ə·li) *n.* anomalía; anormalidad; irregularidad. —**anomalous** (-ləs) *adj.* anómalo; anormal; irregular.
anonymity (,æn·ə'nɪm·ə·ti) *n.* anonimato. —**anonymous** (ə'nan·ə·məs) *adj.* anónimo; desconocido.
anopheles (ə'naf·ə,liz) *n.sing.* & *pl.* anofeles.
another (ə'nʌð·ər) *adj.* & *pron.* otro; diferente. —**one another,** uno a otro; entre sí.
answer ('æn·sər) *n.* **1,** (reply) respuesta; contestación. **2,** (solution) solución; resultado. **3,** *law* defensa; refutación. —*v.i.* **1,** *también, v.t.* (reply) contestar; replicar; responder. **2,** (be responsible) ser responsable; responder. **3,** (be in conformity) responder; concordar. —*v.t.* **1,** (comply with) servir; satisfacer. **2,** (refute) refutar. **3,** (suit) corresponder a; responder a.
answerable ('æn·sər·ə·bəl) *adj.* **1,** (that can be answered) explicable. **2,** (responsible) responsable.
ant (ænt) *n.* hormiga.
ant- (ænt) *prefijo, var. de* **anti-** *ante vocal: antacid,* antiácido.
-ant (ənt) *sufijo* -ante; -ente. **1,** *forma adjetivos equivalentes al participio en* **-ing**: *reliant,* confiado; *defiant,* desafiador. **2,** *forma nom-*

bres indicando actividad; ocupación: *accountant,* contador; *servant,* sirviente.
antacid (ænt'æs·ɪd) *n.* & *adj.* antiácido.
antagonism (æn'tæg·əˌnɪz·əm) *n.* antagonismo; oposición; enemistad. —**antagonist** (-nɪst) *n.* antagonista; adversario; contrincante. —**antagonistic** (-'nɪs·tɪk) *adj.* antagónico; opuesto; hostil.
antagonize (æn'tæg·ə'naiz) *v.t.* antagonizar; contrariar.
antalkali (ænt'æl·kə·lai) *n.* antialcalino.
antarctic (ænt'ark·tɪk) *adj.* antártico. —*n., cap.* Antártica.
ante ('æn·ti) *n.* **1,** *cards* puesta. **2,** (share) cuota. —*v.t.* **1,** *cards* apostar. **2,** [*también,* **ante up**] (pay) pagar. —*v.i.* **1,** *cards* poner su apuesta. **2,** [*también,* **ante up**] (pay one's share) pagar su cuota.
ante- (æn·ti) *prefijo* ante-; antes (*en tiempo o en espacio*): *antediluvian,* antediluviano; *antechamber,* antecámara.
anteater ('ænt,i·tər) *n.* oso hormiguero.
antecedent (ˌæn·tə'si·dənt) *n.* antecedente. —*adj.* antecedente; anterior; precedente. —**antecedence,** *n.* precedencia; anterioridad.
antechamber *n.* antecámara.
antedate ('æn·tiˌdeit) *v.t.* antedatar. —*n.* antedata.
antelope ('æn·tə·lop) *n.* antílope.
antenna (æn'tɛn·ə) *n.* **1,** *radio* antena. **2,** *zoöl.* [*pl.* **-nae** (-i)] antena.
anterior (æn'tɪr·i·ər) *adj.* **1,** (in space) delantero; del frente. **2,** (in time) anterior; precedente; previo.
anteroom ('æn·tiˌrum) *n.* antesala; vestíbulo; recibimiento.
anthem ('æn·θəm) *n.* **1,** *eccles.* antífona. **2,** (national) himno nacional.
anther ('æn·θər) *n.* antera.
anthill ('ænt,hɪl) *n.* hormiguero.
antho- ('æn·θo) *prefijo* anto-; flor: *anthology,* antología.
anthology (æn'θal·ə·dʒi) *n.* antología.
-anthous ('æn·θəs) *sufijo* -anto; flor: *monanthous,* monanto.
anthracite ('æn·θrə·sait) *n.* antracita. —*adj.* color carbón.
anthrax ('æn·θræks) *n.* ántrax.
anthropo- (æn·θrə·po) *prefijo* antropo-; hombre: *anthropology,* antropología.
anthropoid ('æn·θrə·poid) *adj.* & *n.* antropoideo; antropoide.
anthropology (æn·θrə'pal·ə·dʒi) *n.* antropología. —**anthropological** (-pə'ladʒ·ɪ·kəl) *adj.* antropológico. —**anthropologist** (-'pal·ə·dʒɪst) *n.* antropólogo.
anti- (æn·ti; -tɪ; -tai) *prefijo* anti-. **1,** contra: *antislavery,* antiesclavitud. **2,** falso; rival: *antipope,* antipapa. **3,** opuesto; contrario: *antigrammatical,* antigramatical; *antipode,* antípoda. **4,** *med.* curativo; preventivo: *antidote,* antídoto. *Delante de vocales, generalmente* **ant-**: *antacid,* antiácido.
antiaircraft ('æn·ti'ɛrˌkræft) *adj.* antiaéreo.
antibiotic (ˌæn·tɪ·bai'at·ɪk) *n.* & *adj.* antibiótico.
antibody ('æn·tɪˌbad·i) *n.* anticuerpo.
antic ('æn·tɪk) *adj.* extraño; ridículo. —*n., usu.pl.* bufonadas. —*v.i.* bufonear; bufonearse.
Antichrist ('æn·tiˌkraist) *n.* Anticristo.
anticipate (æn'tɪs·ɪ·peit) *v.t.* **1,** (expect) esperar. **2,** (foresee) anticipar; prever. **3,** (forestall) impedir; frustrar. **4,** (be ahead of) anticiparse a; adelantarse a. —**anticipation,** *n.* anticipación; antelación. —**anticipatory** (-pəˌtor·i) *adj.* anticipante.
anticlerical (ˌæn·ti'klɛr·ɪ·kəl) *adj.* anticlerical.
anticlimax (ˌæn·tɪ'klai·mæks) *n.* anticlímax.
antidote ('æn·tɪ·dot) *n.* antídoto; remedio.
antimony ('æn·təˌmo·ni) *n.* antimonio.
antipathy (æn'tɪp·ə·θi) *n.* antipatía; antagonismo. —**antipathetic** (ˌæn·tɪ·pə'θɛt·ɪk) *adj.* antipático.
antiphon ('æn·təˌfan) *n.* antífona.
antipode ('æn·təˌpod) *n.* antípoda. —**antipodal** (æn'tɪp·ə·dəl) *adj.* antípoda.
antipope ('æn·ti·pop) *n.* antipapa.
antiquary ('æn·tɪˌkwɛr·i) *n.* anticuario. —**antiquarian** (-'kwe:r·i·ən) *n.* & *adj.* anticuario.
antiquated ('æn·tɪ·kwei·tɪd) *adj.* anticuado; arcaico; desusado.
antique (æn'tik) *adj.* antiguo; pa-

sado de moda. —*n.* antigualla; *pl.* antigüedades.
antiquity (æn'tɪk·wə·ti) *n.* antigüedad; vetustez.
anti-Semite (ˌæn·ti'sɛm·ait) *n.* antisemita. —**anti-Semitic** (-sə'mɪt·ɪk) *adj.* antisemítico; anti-judío. —**anti-Semitism** (-'sɛm·ə·tiz·əm) *n.* antisemitismo.
antiseptic (æn·tɪ'sɛp·tɪk) *adj.* & *n.* antiséptico; desinfectante. —**antisepsis** (-sɪs) *n.* antisepsia.
antisocial (ˌæn·ti'so·ʃəl) *adj.* antisocial.
anti-tank *adj.* antitanque.
antithesis (æn'tɪθ·ə·sɪs) *n.* [*pl.* **-ses** (-siz)] antítesis. —**antithetical** (æn·tɪ'θɛt·ɪ·kəl) *adj.* antitético.
antitoxin (ˌæn·tɪ'tak·sɪn) *n.* antitoxina. —**antitoxic,** *adj.* antitóxico.
antler ('ænt·lər) *n.* asta *o* cuerno de venado.
antonym ('æn·tə·nɪm) *n.* antónimo; vocablo opuesto.
antonymous (æn'tan·ə·məs) *adj.* antónimo.
anus ('ei·nəs) *n.* ano.
anvil ('æn·vəl) *n.* yunque.
anxiety (æŋ'zai·ə·ti) *n.* ansiedad; angustia; zozobra.
anxious ('æŋk·ʃəs) *adj.* **1,** (worried) preocupado; intranquilo. **2,** (eager) ansioso; deseoso.
anxiousness ('æŋk·ʃəs·nəs) *n.* **1,** (yearning) ansiedad; anhelo. **2,** (impatience) impaciencia; intranquilidad.
any ('ɛn·i) *adj.* & *pron.* algún; alguno; cualquiera. —*adv.* más.
anybody ('ɛn·iˌbad·i) *pron.* alguien; alguno; cualquiera.
anyhow ('ɛn·iˌhau) *adv.* de cualquier forma; de todos modos; como sea.
anyone ('ɛn·iˌwʌn) *pron.* alguien; alguno; cualquiera.
anything ('ɛn·iˌθɪŋ) *pron.* algo; cualquier cosa; alguna cosa.
anyway ('ɛn·iˌwei) *adv.* **1,** = **anyhow. 2,** (carelessly) descuidadamente; no importa como.
anywhere ('ɛn·iˌhwɛr) *adv.* en *o* por cualquier sitio; doquiera; dondequiera.
aorta (ei'or·tə) *n.* aorta.
ap- (æp; əp) *prefijo.* **1,** *var. de* **ad-** *ante* p: *approve,* aprobar. **2,** *var. de* **apo-** *ante vocal o* h: *aphelion,* afelio.
apache (ə'pæʃ) *n.* apache.
Apache (ə'pætʃ·i) *n.* apache.
apart (ə'part) *adv.* aparte; separadamente.
apartment (ə'part·mənt) *n.* apartamiento; piso; *Arg.* departamento.
apathy ('æp·ə·θi) *n.* apatía; insensibilidad; flema. —**apathetic** (-'θɛt·ɪk) *adj.* apático; indolente; indiferente.
ape (eip) *n.* **1,** (animal) mono. **2,** *fig.* (mimic) imitador; parodista. —*v.t.* imitar; remedar; parodiar.
aperitif (ə·pɛr·ə'tif) *n.* aperitivo.
aperture ('æp·ər·tʃur) *n.* **1,** (opening) apertura; abertura. **2,** (hole) agujero; vacío.
apex ('ei·pɛks) *n.* ápice; cima.
aphelion (ə'fi·li·ən) *n.* afelio.
aphorism ('æf·ə·rɪz·əm) *n.* aforismo. —**aphoristic** (-'rɪs·tɪk) *adj.* aforístico.
aphrodisiac (ˌæf·rə'diz·i·æk) *adj.* & *n.* afrodisíaco.
apiary ('ei·piˌɛr·i) *n.* abejera.
apiece (ə'pis) *adv.* cada uno; por persona.
aplomb (ə'plam) *n.* aplomo.
apo- (æp·o) *prefijo* apo-. **1,** separado de: *apogee,* apogeo. **2,** de: *aponeurosis,* aponeurosis. **3,** desde: *apothem,* apotema.
apocalypse (ə'pak·ə·lɪps) *n.* **1,** *cap., Bib.* Apocalipsis. **2,** (revelation) revelación; profecía. —**apocalyptic** (-'lɪp·tɪk) *adj.* apocalíptico.
Apocrypha (ə'pak·rə·fə) *n.pl., Bib.* libros apócrifos. —**apocryphal** (-fəl) *adj.* apócrifo; falso.
apogee ('æp·ə·dʒiː) *n.* apogeo.
apologetic (əˌpal·ə'dʒɛt·ɪk) *adj.* **1,** (regretful) pesaroso; compungido. **2,** (defending) apologético.
apologist (ə'pal·ə·dʒɪst) *n.* apologista.
apologize (ə'pal·ə·dʒaiz) *v.i.* **1,** (express regret) excusarse; disculparse. **2,** (make a formal defense) apologizar; defenderse; justificarse.
apology (ə'pal·ə·dʒi) *n.* **1,** (formal defense) apología; defensa; elogio. **2,** (expression of regret) excusa; disculpa. **3,** (makeshift) expediente.
apoplexy ('æp·ə·plɛk·si) *n.* apoplejía. —**apoplectic** (-'plɛk·tɪk) *adj.* apoplético.
apostasy (ə'pas·tə·si) *n.* apostasía; repudio. —**apostate** (-teit) *n.* & *adj.* apóstata; renegado. —**apostatize** (-tə·taiz) *v.i.* apostatar; repudiar; renegar.
apostle (ə'pas·əl) *n.* apóstol.

—**apostolic** (ˌæp·əˈstal·ɪk) *adj.* apostólico.
apostolate (əˈpas·təˌleit; -lɪt) *n.* apostolado.
apostrophe (əˈpas·trə·fi) *n.* **1,** (direct address) apóstrofe. **2,** *gram.* apóstrofo. —**apostrophize** (-faiz) *v.t.* & *i.* apostrofar.
apothecary (əˈpaθ·əˌkɛr·i) *n.* boticario. —**apothecary's shop,** botica.
appall *también,* **appal** (əˈpɔl) *v.t.* horrorizar; aterrar; espantar.
apparatus (ˌæp·əˈrei·təs) *n.* aparato; aparejo.
apparel (əˈpær·əl) *n.* **1,** (clothing) vestidos; trajes; ropa. **2,** (outward aspect) aspecto; apariencia. —*v.t.* vestir; ataviar.
apparent (əˈpær·ənt) *adj.* **1,** (obvious) patente; evidente; indudable. **2,** (seeming) aparente; presunto.
apparently (əˈpær·ənt·li) *adv.* **1,** (clearly) evidentemente; claramente; sin duda. **2,** (seemingly) aparentemente; presuntamente.
apparition (ˌæp·əˈrɪʃ·ən) *n.* aparición; espectro; fantasma.
appeal (əˈpiːl) *v.i.* **1,** (seek help) acudir; pedir ayuda; implorar. **2,** (resort) volverse; recurrir. **3,** (be attractive) atraer; interesar. —*v.t.* & *i., law* apelar; recurrir a un tribunal superior. —*n.* **1,** (call for aid) llamamiento; súplica. **2,** (attractiveness) atracción. **3,** *law* apelación; instancia. —**appealing,** *adj.* atractivo; atrayente.
appear (əˈpɪr) *v.i.* **1,** (become visible) aparecer; aparecerse. **2,** (seem to be) parecer; figurar; asemejar; asemejarse. **3,** (be known) manifestarse. **4,** (be published) aparecer. **5,** *law* comparecer.
appearance (əˈpɪr·əns) *n.* **1,** (act of appearing) aparición. **2,** (outward aspect) aspecto; porte; apariencia. **3,** (presence) comparecencia.
appease (əˈpiːz) *v.t.* **1,** (placate) apaciguar; aplacar. **2,** (satisfy) aplacar; calmar. —**appeasement,** *n.* apaciguamiento; pacificación.
appellate (əˈpɛl·ət) *adj.* de apelación.
appellation (ˌæp·əˈlei·ʃən) *n.* apelativo; nombre.
appellative (əˈpɛl·ə·tɪv) *n.* & *adj.* apelativo.
append (əˈpɛnd) *v.t.* añadir; agregar; fijar; acompañar. —**appendage** (-ɪdʒ) *n.* añadidura; adición; accesorio.
appendectomy (ˌæp·ənˈdɛk·tə·mi) *n.* apendectomía.
appendicitis (əˌpɛn·dɪˈsai·tɪs) *n.* apendicitis.
appendix (əˈpɛn·dɪks) *n.* [*pl.* **-dixes, -dices** (-dəˌsiz)] **1,** (of a document or book) apéndice; suplemento. **2,** *anat.* apéndice.
appertain (æp·ərˈtein) *v.i.* pertenecer; relacionarse.
appetite (ˈæp·ə·tait) *n.* **1,** (readiness to eat) apetito. **2,** (strong desire) apetencia; deseo; anhelo.
appetizing (ˈæp·ə·taiz·ɪŋ) *adj.* apetecible; sabroso; apetitoso; deleitable. —**appetizer** (-ər) *n.* aperitivo; apetito.
applaud (əˈplɔːd) *v.t.* aplaudir; aclamar. —*v.i.* ovacionar; aprobar.
applause (əˈplɔːz) *n.* aplauso; aclamación; ovación.
apple (ˈæp·əl) *n.* manzana; poma.
applesauce *n.* **1,** (food) compota de manzana. **2,** *slang* (nonsense) tontería; disparate.
appliance (əˈplai·əns) *n.* **1,** (tool; utensil) utensilio; instrumento. **2,** (act of putting to use) aplicación; uso.
applicable (ˈæp·lɪ·kə·bəl) *adj.* aplicable; pertinente. —**applicability,** *n.* aplicabilidad.
applicant (ˈæp·lɪ·kənt) *n.* aspirante; candidato; solicitante.
application (ˌæp·lɪˈkei·ʃən) *n.* **1,** (act of applying; thing applied) aplicación. **2,** (request) solicitud; instancia; petición; *Mex.* ocurso. **3,** (diligence) aplicación; diligencia; estudio.
applicator (ˈæp·lɪˌkei·tər) *n.* instrumento que sirve para aplicar alguna cosa.
appliqué (ˌæp·ləˈkei) *adj.* & *n.* sobrepuesto.
apply (əˈplai) *v.t.* **1,** (lay on) aplicar. **2,** (put to use) usar; aplicar. **3,** (concentrate on) applicarse a *o* en. —*v.i.* **1,** (be applicable or pertinent) aplicarse; atribuirse. **2,** (request) pedir; solicitar.
appoint (əˈpɔint) *v.t.* **1,** (assign) nombrar; designar. **2,** (prescribe) ordenar; decretar. **3,** (rig) surtir; equipar. —**appointive,** *adj.* electivo; elegible.
appointment (əˈpɔint·mənt) *n.* **1,** (act) nombramiento; elección. **2,** (position) puesto; cargo; posi-

ción. **3,** (scheduled meeting) cita. **4,** *pl.* (furnishings) equipo (*sing.*).

apportion (ə'por·ʃən) *v.t.* prorratear; dividir proporcionalmente. —**apportionment,** *n.* prorrateo; división.

apposite ('æp·ə·zɪt) *adj.* adecuado; apropiado; oportuno. —**apposition** (-'zɪʃ·ən) *n.* adición; añadidura; *gram.* aposición.

appraisal (ə'prei·zəl) *n.* valuación; tasación; cálculo.

appraise (ə'preiz) *v.t.* valorar; estimar; apreciar. —**appraiser** (-ər) *n.* tasador; estimador.

appreciable (ə'priː·ʃə·bəl) *adj.* apreciable; estimable; considerable.

appreciate (ə'priː·ʃi·eit) *v.t.* apreciar; estimar; valorar. —*v.i.* subir (de precio *o* valor).

appreciation (əˌpri·ʃi'ei·ʃən) *n.* **1,** (esteem) apreciación. **2,** (grateful recognition) reconocimiento. **3,** (sensitive awareness) percepción; apreciación. **4,** (estimate) valuación. **5,** (rise in value) alza.

appreciative (ə'priː·ʃə·tɪv) *adj.* agradecido.

apprehend (æp·ri'hɛnd) *v.t.* **1,** (seize physically) prender; detener. **2,** (understand) comprender; entender; percibir. **3,** (fear) temer; recelar; sospechar.

apprehension (æp·ri'hɛn·ʃən) *n.* **1,** (seizure) aprehensión; presa; captura. **2,** (understanding) comprensión; percepción. **3,** (fear) aprensión; temor; recelo.

apprehensive (ˌæp·ri'hɛn·sɪv) *adj.* aprensivo; receloso. —**apprehensiveness,** *n.* aprensión; sospecha; recelo.

apprentice (ə'prɛn·tɪs) *n.* aprendiz; principiante. —*v.t.* poner de aprendiz. —**apprenticeship** (-ʃɪp) *n.* aprendizaje.

apprize (ə'praiz) *v.t.* informar.

approach (ə'protʃ) *v.t.* **1,** (draw near) acercar. **2,** (resemble) parecerse a. **3,** (make advances or proposals to) abordar. —*v.i.* acercarse; aproximarse. —*n.* **1,** (act of approaching) acercamiento. **2,** (avenue) acceso; vía. **3,** (nearness) proximidad; cercanía.

approbation (æp·rə'bei·ʃən) *n.* aprobación; autorización; consentimiento.

appropriate (ə'pro·pri·eit) *v.t.* **1,** (allot) asignar. **2,** (take possession of) apropiarse de. **3,** (steal) robar. —*adj.* (-ət) apropiado; adecuado. —**appropriateness,** *n.* propiedad; lo adecuado.

appropriation (əˌpro·pri'ei·ʃən) *n.* **1,** (allotment) asignación. **2,** (act of appropriating) apropiación.

approve (ə'pruːv) *v.t.* **1,** (pronounce good) sancionar; confirmar. **2,** (ratify) aprobar; asentir. —*v.i.* aprobar; sancionar. —**approval** (-əl) *n.* aprobación; consentimiento.

approximate (ə'prak·sɪ·mət) *adj.* **1,** (nearly correct) parecido; aproximado. **2,** (close together) cercano; inmediato. —*v.t.* (-meit) **1,** (approach) aproximarse a; acercarse a. **2,** (resemble) parecerse a. —**approximately,** *adv.* aproximadamente; más o menos. —**approximation,** *n.* aproximación.

appurtenance (ə'pʌɹ·tə·nəns) *n.* **1,** *law* adjunto. **2,** (accessory) accesorio. **3,** (appendage) añadidura; apéndice. **4,** (that which appertains) pertenencia. **5,** *pl.* (furnishings) accesorios; instrumentos. —**appurtenant,** *adj.* perteneciente.

apricot ('ei·prɪ·kat) *n.* **1,** (fruit) albaricoque. **2,** (tree) albaricoquero.

April ('ei·prəl) *n.* abril. —**April fool,** inocente; tonto; burlado. —**April Fool's Day,** Día de Inocentes (in the Spanish world, December 28).

apron ('ei·prən) *n.* delantal; mandil.

apropos (æp·rə'poː) *adv.* a propósito. —*adj.* adecuado; oportuno. —**apropos of,** con referencia a.

apse (æps) *n.* ábside.

apt (æpt) *adj.* **1,** (suited) apto; adecuado. **2,** (quick to learn) vivo; listo. **3,** (inclined) propenso; inclinado. —**aptness,** *n.* aptitud; competencia.

aptitude ('æp·tɪ·tud) *n.* aptitud; habilidad; competencia.

aquamarine (ˌæk·wə·mə'riːn) *n.* aguamarina. —*adj.* de color aguamarina.

aquarium (ə'kweːr·i·əm) *n.* acuario.

Aquarius (ə'kweːr·i·əs) *n., astron.* Acuario.

aquatic (ə'kwæt·ɪk) *adj.* acuático.

aquatint ('æk·wə·tɪnt) *n.* acuatinta.

aqueduct ('æk·wɪ·dʌkt) *n.* acueducto; *Mex.* cañería.
aqueous ('ei·kwi·əs) *adj.* ácueo; acuoso.
aquiline ('æk·wə·lɪn) *adj.* aguileño; *poet.* aquilino.
ar- (ər; ær) *prefijo, var. de* **ad-** *ante* r: *arrest,* arrestar.
-ar (ər) *sufijo* -al; -ar; *forma adjetivos y nombres que indican* modo; relación; pertenencia: *linear,* lineal; *regular,* regular.
Arab ('ær·əb) *n.* & *adj.* árabe.
arabesque (ær·ə'bɛsk) *n.* arabesco.
Arabian (ə'rei·bi·ən) *n.* árabe. —*adj.* árabe; arábico; arábigo.
Arabic ('ær·ə·bɪk) *adj.* árabe; arábico; arábigo. —*n.* árabe; arábigo.
arable ('ær·ə·bəl) *adj.* arable; labrable; cultivable.
arachnid (ə'ræk·nɪd) *n.* arácnido.
Aramaic (ær·ə'mei·ɪk) *n.* & *adj.* arameo.
arbiter ('ar·bɪ·tər) *n.* árbitro; juez.
arbitrary ('ar·bɪˌtrɛr·i) *adj.* **1,** (not regulated by rule) arbitrario; voluble. **2,** (despotic) absoluto; despótico. **3,** (unreasonable) injusto; irrazonable. —**arbitrariness,** *n.* arbitrariedad.
arbitrate ('ar·bɪ·treit) *v.t.* & *i.* arbitrar; mediar; intervenir. —**arbitration,** *n.* arbitraje; mediación; —**arbitrator** (-tər) *n.* árbitro; mediador; intermediario.
arbor ('ar·bər) *n.* **1,** [*también,* **arbour**] (bower) emparrado; pérgola; enramada. **2,** *mech.* eje; árbol. —**arboreal** (ar'bor·i·əl) *adj.* arbóreo.
arbutus (ar'bju·təs) *n.* arbusto; madroño.
arc (ark) *n.* arco. —**arc lamp; arc light,** lámpara de arco.
arcade (ar'keid) *n.* arcada; galería *o* pasadizo abovedado.
arch (artʃ) *n.* arco. —*v.t.* arquear; enarcar. —*v.i.* hacer un arco *o* arcos. —*adj.* **1,** (preëminent) principal; prominente. **2,** (sly) travieso; pícaro.
arch- (artʃ; ark) *prefijo* archi-; arqui-; arz-; preeminencia; prioridad: *archbishop,* arzobispo; *archduke,* archiduque; *archdiocese,* archidiócesis *o* arquidiócesis.
-arch (ark) *sufijo* -arca; gobernante: *monarch,* monarca; *tetrarch,* tetrarca.
archaeo- *también,* **archeo-** (ar·ki·o) *prefijo* arqueo-; antigüedad: *archaeology,* arqueología.
archaeology (ar·ki'al·ə·dʒi) *n.* arqueología. —**archaeological** (-ə·'ladʒ·ɪ·kəl) *adj.* arqueológico. —**archaeologist** (-'al·ə·dʒɪst) *n.* arqueólogo.
archaic (ar'kei·ɪk) *adj.* arcaico; antiguo; vetusto. —**archaism** ('ar·ki·ɪz·əm) *n.* arcaísmo.
archangel (ark'ein·dʒəl) *n.* arcángel.
archbishop ('artʃˌbɪʃ·əp) *n.* arzopispo. —**archbishopric** (-rɪk) *n.* arzobispado.
archdeacon ('artʃˌdi·kən) *n.* arcediano; archidiácono.
archdiocese (artʃ'dai·ə·sɪs) *n.* archidiócesis.
archduke ('artʃˌduk) *n.* archiduque. —**archducal** (-'du·kəl) *adj.* archiducal. —**archduchess** (-ˌdʌtʃ·əs) *n.* archiduquesa. —**archduchy** (-ˌdʌtʃ·i) *n.* archiducado.
arche- (ar·kɪ) *prefijo, var. de* **arch-; archi-:** *archetype,* arquetipo.
archer ('ar·tʃər) *n.* arquero. —**archery,** *n.* tiro al arco.
archetype ('ar·kɪ·taip) *n.* arquetipo; prototipo; modelo.
archi- *también,* **arche-** (ar·kɪ) *prefijo, var. de* **arch-;** *archimandrite,* archimandrita.
archiepiscopal (ˌar·ki·ɪ'pɪs·kə·pəl) *adj.* arzobispal.
archipelago (ar·kə'pɛl·ə·go) *n.* archipiélago.
architect ('ar·kə·tɛkt) *n.* arquitecto. —**architecture** (-ˌtɛk·tʃər) *n.* arquitectura. —**architectural** (-'tɛk·tʃər·əl) *adj.* arquitectónico.
archives ('ar·kaivz) *n.pl.* archivos. —**archivist** ('ar·kɪ·vɪst; 'ar·ˌkai·vɪst) *n.* archivero.
archpriest ('artʃˌprist) *n.* arcipreste.
archway ('artʃ·wei) *n.* arcada; bóveda; pasaje abovedado.
-archy (ar·ki; ər·ki) *sufijo* -arquía; gobierno; mando: *autarchy,* autarquía.
arctic ('ark·tɪk) *n.* & *adj.* ártico.
-ard (ərd) *también,* **-art** (ərt) *sufijo; forma nombres, generalmente con sentido despectivo: drunkard,* borracho; *braggart,* fanfarrón.

ardent (ˈar·dənt) *adj.* **1,** (burning) ardiente; en llamas. **2,** (passionate) fogoso; apasionado. —**ardency,** *n.* ardor; incandescencia.
ardor *también,* **ardour** (ˈar·dər) *n.* ardor; pasión.
arduous (ˈar·dju·əs) *adj.* arduo; difícil; penoso. —**arduousness,** *n.* arduidad; dificultad.
are (ar) *v., segunda persona del sing. y todas las personas del pl. del pres. de* **be.**
are (eːr) *n.* área.
area (ˈeːr·i·ə) *n.* **1,** (surface) área; superficie. **2,** (region) región. **3,** (scope) área; extensión; alcance.
arena (əˈriː·nə) *n.* **1,** (enclosure for sports) anfiteatro; arena; estadio. **2,** (bull ring) plaza de toros; redondel.
argon (ˈar·gan) *n.* argo; argón.
argot (ˈar·go) *n.* argot; jerga.
argue (ˈar·gju) *v.i.* argüir; disputar. —*v.t.* **1,** (discuss) argüir; discutir; debatir. **2,** (try to prove) razonar; probar.
argument (ˈar·gju·mənt) *n.* **1,** (debate) discusión; debate. **2,** (reasoning) razonamiento. **3,** (summary) argumento. —**argumentation** (-mənˈtei·ʃən) *n.* argumentación; razonamiento; debate. —**argumentative** (-ˈmɛn·tə·tɪv) *adj.* argumentativo; disputador; contencioso.
argyrol (ˈar·dʒɪ·rol) *n.* argirol.
aria (ˈar·i·ə) *n.* aria.
-aria (ɛr·i·ə) *sufijo* -aria; *forma el plural de nombres que:* **1,** *expresan* clasificación; género: *cineraria,* cineraria. **2,** *terminan el singular en* **-arium:** *honoraria,* honorarios.
-arian (ɛr·i·ən) *sufijo* -ario; *forma nombres y adjetivos denotando:* **1,** edad: *centenarian,* centenario. **2,** doctrina; relación: *sectarian,* sectario; *disciplinarian,* disciplinario. **3,** ocupación: *antiquarian,* anticuario.
arid (ˈær·ɪd) *adj.* **1,** (dry) árido; reseco; estéril. **2,** *fig.* (dull) árido; aburrido. —**aridity** (əˈrɪd·ə·ti) aridez; sequedad.
Aries (ˈeːr·iz) *n., astron.* Aries.
aright (əˈrait) *adv.* rectamente; justamente. —**set aright,** rectificar.
-arious (ɛr·i·əs) *sufijo* -ario; *forma adjetivos expresando* relación; pertenencia: *precarious,* precario.
arise (əˈraiz) *v.i.* [**arose, arisen** (əˈriz·ən)] **1,** (move upward) surgir; elevarse. **2,** (get up; come into being or action) levantarse; sublevarse.
aristocracy (ˌær·ɪsˈtak·rə·si) *n.* aristocracia. —**aristocrat** (əˈrɪs·tə·kræt) *n.* aristócrata; noble. —**aristocratic** (-ˈkræt·ɪk) *adj.* aristocrático; distinguido.
arithmetic (əˈrɪθ·mə·tɪk) *n.* aritmética. —**arithmetical** (ˌær·ɪθ·ˈmɛt·ɪ·kəl), **arithmetic,** *adj.* aritmético. —**arithmetician,** (əˌrɪθ·mə·ˈtɪʃ·ən) *n.* aritmético.
-arium (ɛr·i·əm) *sufijo* -ario; *forma nombres denotando:* **1,** *lugares especiales: aquarium,* acuario. **2,** *relación con otra cosa: honorarium,* honorario.
ark (ark) *n.* arca.
arm (arm) *n.* **1,** *anat.* brazo. **2,** (of a river) brazo. **3,** (weapon) arma. **4,** *fig.* (helpful person or thing) rama. —*v.t.* armar. —*v.i.* armarse. —**arm in arm,** de *o* del brazo; de bracero; de bracete. —**with open arms,** con los brazos abiertos.
armada (arˈma·də) *n.* armada; flota.
armadillo (ar·məˈdɪl·o) *n.* [*pl.* **-los**] armadillo.
armament (ˈar·mə·mənt) *n.* armamento.
armature (ˈar·mə·tʃʊr) *n.* **1,** (armor) armadura. **2,** (for horses) arnés. **3,** *electricity* (of a magnet) armadura; (of a dynamo) inducido.
armband *n.* brazal.
armchair *n.* sillón; butaca.
armed (armd) *adj.* armado. —**armed forces,** fuerzas armadas; ejército.
armful (ˈarmˌful) *n.* brazada.
armhole (ˈarmˌhol) *n.* sobaquera.
armistice (ˈar·mɪ·stɪs) *n.* armisticio.
armlet (ˈarm·lət) *n.* brazal; brazalete.
armor (ˈar·mər) *n.* armadura; coraza; blindaje. —*v.t.* blindar; acorazar. —*v.i.* acorazarse; ponerse coraza. —**armored,** *adj.* blindado. —**armor plate,** plancha blindada; blindaje.
armory (ˈar·mə·ri) *n.* **1,** (arsenal) armería; arsenal. **2,** (heraldry) heráldica; blasones; armas.
armpit (ˈarmˌpɪt) *n.* axila; sobaco.
arms (armz) *n.pl.* **1,** (weapons) armas. **2,** *heraldry* armas; blasones. —**bear arms,** estar armado; cargar

armas. —**be up in arms,** levantarse en armas. —**lay down one's arms,** rendir las armas; rendirse. —**take up arms,** tomar las armas. —**to arms!,** ¡a las armas!.
army ('ar·mi) *n.* 1, *mil.* ejército. 2, *fig.* multitud.
arnica ('ar·nɪk·ə) *n.* árnica.
aroma (ə'ro·mə) *n.* aroma; fragancia. —**aromatic** (ær·ə'mæt·ɪk) *adj.* aromático; fragante; oloroso.
arose (ə'roːz) *v., pret. de* **arise.**
around (ə'raund) *adv.* a la redonda; en derredor; alrededor; a la vuelta; por todos lados. —*prep.* cerca; en; alrededor de.
arouse (ə'rauz) *v.t.* excitar; impulsar; despertar.
arraign (ə'rein) *v.t.* procesar; acusar. —**arraignment,** *n.* procesamiento; proceso; acusación.
arrange (ə'reindʒ) *v.t.* 1, (put in order) ordenar; arreglar. 2, (settle) ajustar; acordar. 3, (plan) preparar; planear. 4, *music* arreglar; adaptar.
arrangement (ə'reindʒ·mənt) *n.* 1, (order) orden; arreglo; colocación. 2, (settlement) acuerdo; arreglo. 3, *pl.* (plans) medidas; preparativos. 4, *music* adaptación; arreglo.
arrant ('ær·ənt) *adj.* 1, (notorious) conocido; manifiesto. 2, (downright) absoluto; categórico.
array (ə'rei) *n.* 1, (arrangement) orden; colocación. 2, *mil.* formación. 3, (apparel) vestido; indumentaria. —*v.t.* 1, (place in order) ordenar; organizar. 2, (bedeck) vestir; adornar.
arrears (ə'rɪrz) *n.pl.* atrasos; deudas vencidas. —**in arrears,** atrasado.
arrest (ə'rɛst) *v.t.* 1, (capture) arrestar; capturar. 2, (stop forcibly) detener; impedir. —*n.* 1, (detention) arresto; detención. 2, (capture) captura. 3, *mech.* interrupción. —**arresting,** *adj.* impresionante.
arrival (ə'rai·vəl) *n.* 1, (act of arriving) arribo; llegada. 2, (person or thing that arrives) llegada; arribado.
arrive (ə'raiv) *v.i.* 1, (reach) llegar; arribar. 2, (occur) suceder; ocurrir; acontecer. 3, (attain success) lograr; llegar.
arrogant ('ær·ə·gənt) *adj.* arrogante; altanero; despectivo. —**arrogance,** *n.* arrogancia; altanería.
arrogate ('ær·ə,geit) *v.t.* arrogarse; atribuirse; usurpar. —**arrogation,** *n.* arrogación.
arrow ('ær·o) *n.* flecha; saeta.
arrowhead *n.* punta de flecha.
arroyo (ə'rɔi·o) *n.* arroyo.
arsenal ('ar·sə·nəl) *n.* arsenal.
arsenic ('ar·sə·nɪk) *n.* arsénico. —**arsenical** (-'sɛn·ɪ·kəl) *adj.* arsenical; de arsénico.
arson ('ar·sən) *n.* incendio premeditado.
art (art) *n.* arte.
art (art) *v., arcaico, segunda persona del sing. del pres. de* **be.**
-art (ərt) *sufijo, var. de* **-ard:** *braggart,* fanfarrón.
arteriosclerosis (ar,tɪr·i·o·sklɛ'ro·sɪs) *n.* arteriosclerosis.
artery ('ar·tə·ri) *n.* arteria. —**arterial** (-'tɪr·i·əl) *adj.* arterial.
artesian well (ar'tiː·ʒən) pozo artesiano.
artful ('art·fəl) *adj.* 1, (wily) engañoso; artificial. 2, (skillful) diestro; ingenioso.
artfulness ('art·fəl·nəs) *n.* 1, (cunning) engaño; artificio. 2, (skill) habilidad; destreza.
arthritis (ar'θrai·tɪs) *n.* artritis. —**arthritic** (-'θrɪt·ɪk) *adj.* artrítico.
arthropod ('ar·θro·pad) *n., zool.* artrópodo.
artichoke ('ar·tɪ,tʃok) *n.* alcachofa; *Sp.* alcacil.
article ('ar·tɪ·kəl) *n.* artículo.
articulate (ar'tɪk·ju·leit) *v.t. & i.* 1, (enunciate) articular; enunciar. 2, (join) enlazar; unir. —*adj.* (-lət) 1, (expressive) claro. 2, (having joints) articulado. —**articulation,** *n.* articulación.
artifact ('ar·tə,fækt) *n.* artefacto.
artifice ('ar·tɪ·fɪs) *n.* 1, (crafty device) artificio. 2, (trickery) treta; engaño; ardid.
artificer (ar'tɪf·ə·sər) *n.* artífice.
artificial (ar·tɪ'fɪʃ·əl) *adj.* 1, (man-made) artificial. 2, (pretended) falso; postizo. 3, (fictitious) ficticio; fingido; artificioso. 4, (affected) afectado; artificial. —**artificiality** (-,fɪʃ·i'æl·ə·ti) *n.* artificialidad.
artillery (ar'tɪl·ə·ri) *n.* artillería. —**artilleryman** (-mən) *n.* [*pl.* **-men**] artillero.
artisan ('ar·tɪ·zən) *n.* artesano.

artist ('ar·tɪst) *n.* artista. —**artistic** (-'tɪs·tɪk) *adj.* artístico. —**artistry** (-ri) *n.* arte; maña; habilidad artística.

artless ('art·ləs) *adj.* natural; simple; sincero. —**artlessness,** *n.* naturalidad; sencillez.

-ary (ɛr·i; ə·ri) *sufijo* -ario; -aria. **1,** *forma adjetivos que denotan* relación; pertenencia: *secondary,* secundario; *disciplinary,* disciplinario. **2,** *forma nombres que denotan* profesión: *notary,* notario. **3,** *forma nombres indicando* cesión de algo: *beneficiary,* beneficiario; *concessionary,* concesionario.

Aryan *también,* **Arian** ('eːr·i·ən; 'ær-) *n.* & *adj.* ario.

as (æz) *adv.* **1,** (to the same degree) tan; como. **2,** (for example) como; por ejemplo. —*conj.* **1,** (to the same degree that) así como; como; a medida que. **2,** (in the same manner that) como; según. **3,** (while) cuando; mientras; a la vez que. **4,** (because) porque; puesto que; ya que. **5,** (though) aunque; aun. —*rel.pron.* que; lo que; como. —*prep.* como; por. —**as . . . . . as,** tan . . . . . como. —**as for,** en cuanto a. —**as if,** como si. —**as if to,** como para. —**as is,** tal cual; sin condición. —**as it were,** por decirlo así. —**as though,** como si. —**as to, 1,** (concerning) en cuanto a. **2,** = **as if to.** —**as well,** también. —**as well as,** así como. —**as yet,** todavía; aún. —**so . . . . . as,** tan . . . . . como. —**such as, 1,** (the same as) tal cual; como. **2,** (who) quien (*o* quienes); los (*o* las) que. —**the same as,** el mismo que.

as- (æs; əs) *prefijo, var. de* **ad-** *ante* s: *associate,* asociar.

asafetida (ˌæs·ə'fɛt·ɪ·də) *n.* asafétida.

asbestos (æz'bɛs·təs) *n.* asbesto; amianto.

ascend (ə'sɛnd) *v.i.* ascender; elevarse. —*v.t.* escalar; subir.

ascendant (ə'sɛn·dənt) *adj.* **1,** (rising) ascendente. **2,** (dominant) superior; predominante. —*n.* predominio; influjo. —**ascendancy,** *n.* ascendiente; poder.

ascension (ə'sɛn·ʃən) *n.* **1,** (ascent) subida; ascensión. **2,** *cap., relig.* Ascensión.

ascent (ə'sɛnt) *n.* **1,** (upward movement) ascenso; ascensión; subida. **2,** (upward slope) pendiente; cuesta.

ascertain (æs·ər'tein) *v.t.* indagar; inquirir; averiguar. —**ascertainment,** *n.* indagación; averiguación.

ascetic (ə'sɛt·ɪk) *adj.* ascético. —*n.* asceta; eremita. —**asceticism** (-ɪˌsɪz·əm) *n.* ascetismo.

ascribe (ə'skraib) *v.t.* adscribir; atribuir; imputar. —**ascription** (ə'skrɪp·ʃən) *n.* adscripción.

-ase (eis) *sufijo* -asa; *en química indica la relación con enzimas: diastase,* diastasa.

asepsis (ə'sɛp·sɪs) *n.* asepsia. —**aseptic** (-tɪk) *adj.* aséptico.

asexual (ei'sɛk·ʃu·əl) *adj.* asexual; ambiguo; indeterminado.

ash (æʃ) *n.* **1,** (residue) ceniza. **2,** (tree) fresno. **3,** *pl.* (human remains) cenizas; despojos. —**ash tray,** cenicero. —**ash can, 1,** (for trash) cubo de basura; basurero. **2,** *slang* (depth charge) carga de profundidad.

ashamed (ə'ʃeimd) *adj.* avergonzado; abochornado; confundido.

ashen ('æʃ·ən) *adj.* ceniciento; pálido; exangüe.

ashore (ə'ʃor) *adv.* en *o* a tierra.

Ash Wednesday miércoles de Ceniza.

ashy ('æʃ·i) *adj.* ceniciento; gris. —**ashiness,** *n.* palidez; cualidad de ceniza.

Asiatic (ei·ʒi'æt·ɪk) *adj.* asiático. —*n.* [*también,* **Asian** ('ei·ʒən)] asiático. —**Asiatic flu; Asian flu,** gripe asiática.

aside (ə'said) *adv.* **1,** (on or to one side) al lado; aparte; a un lado. **2,** (regardless) sin consideración *o* atención. —*n., theat.* aparte. —**aside from,** aparte de; además de.

asinine ('æs·ə·nain) *adj.* asnal; estúpido; idiota. —**asininity** (-'nɪn·ə·ti) *n.* asnada; asnería; estupidez.

-asis (ə·sɪs) *sufijo, med.* -asis; *forma nombres de enfermedades: elephantiasis,* elefantíasis.

ask (æsk) *v.t.* **1,** (interrogate) preguntar; interrogar. **2,** (request) solicitar; rogar; pedir. **3,** (invite) invitar; convidar.

askance (ə'skæns) *adv.* desconfiadamente; con recelo.

askew (ə'skjuː) *adv.* oblicuamente; de soslayo. —*adj.* oblicuo; sesgado.

aslant (ə'slænt) *adv.* oblicuamente. —*adj.* oblicuo; inclinado.
asleep (ə'sli:p) *adj.* **1,** (sleeping) dormido. **2,** (numb) insensible. —*adv.* dormidamente.
-asm (æz·əm) *sufijo* -asmo; *forma nombres indicando* acción; tendencia; calidad: *spasm,* espasmo; *enthusiasm,* entusiasmo.
asp (æsp) *n.* áspid; serpiente venenosa.
asparagus (ə'spær·ə·gəs) *n.* **1,** (plant) espárrago. **2,** (shoots used as food) espárragos (*pl.*).
aspect ('æs·pɛkt) *n.* **1,** (viewpoint) aspecto. **2,** (appearance) semblante; aspecto; talante; cariz. **3,** (view) vista.
aspen ('æs·pən) *n.* álamo temblón.
asperity (æs'pɛr·ə·ti) *n.* aspereza; severidad.
asperse (ə'spʌɹs) *v.t.* difamar; inculpar; calumniar.
aspersion (ə'spʌɹ·ʒən) *n.* **1,** (sprinkling) aspersión. **2,** (defamation) calumnia; difamación.
asphalt ('æs·fɔlt) *n.* asfalto.
asphodel ('æs·fə·dɛl) *n.* asfódelo; gamón.
asphyxia (æs'fɪk·si·ə) *n.* asfixia; sofocación; ahogo.
asphyxiate (æs'fɪk·si·eit) *v.t.* asfixiar; sofocar; ahogar. —*v.i.* asfixiarse; sofocarse; ahogarse. —**asphyxiation,** *n.* asfixia; sofocación.
aspic ('æs·pɪk) *n.* jalea de carne *u* hortalizas.
aspirant ('æs·pər·ənt) *n.* aspirante; candidato.
aspirate ('æs·pə·reit) *v.t.* aspirar. —*n.* & *adj.* (-rət) aspirado.
aspiration (ˌæs·pə'rei·ʃən) *n.* **1,** (desire) aspiración; deseo; anhelo. **2,** (breathing) aspiración.
aspire (ə'spair) *v.i.* aspirar; anhelar; desear.
aspirin ('æs·pə·rɪn) *n.* aspirina.
ass (æs; as) *n.* **1,** (donkey) asno; burro. **2,** *slang* (dunce) burro; idiota.
assail (ə'seil) *v.t.* asaltar; atacar; acometer. —**assailant** (-ənt) *n.* atacador; agresor.
assassin (ə'sæs·ɪn) *n.* asesino; homicida.
assassinate (ə'sæs·ə·neit) *v.t.* asesinar. —**assassination,** *n.* asesinato.
assault (ə'sɔlt) *v.t.* **1,** (attack physically) asaltar; atacar; agredir. **2,** (attack verbally) asaltar; abusar. —*n.* asalto; agresión; ataque.
assay (ə'sei) *v.t.* examinar; probar; *metall.* ensayar; analizar; *chem.* analizar. —*n.* ('æs·ei) prueba; examen; *metall.* ensayo; análisis; *chem.* análisis.
assemblage (ə'sɛm·blɪdʒ) *n.* **1,** (gathering of persons) asamblea; reunión. **2,** (group of things) grupo; conjunto. **3,** *mech.* montaje.
assemble (ə'sɛm·bəl) *v.t.* **1,** (persons) convocar; reunir. **2,** (things) montar; unir; ensamblar. —*v.i.* congregarse; reunirse; agruparse.
assembly (ə'sɛm·bli) *n.* **1,** (meeting) asamblea; reunión; junta. **2,** *mech.* juego de piezas.
assent (ə'sɛnt) *v.i.* asentir; consentir; aprobar. —*n.* ('æs·ɛnt) asenso; consentimiento; aprobación.
assert (ə'sʌɹt) *v.t.* **1,** (aver) aseverar; afirmar; ratificar. **2,** (claim and defend) defender; sostener; mantener. —**assert oneself,** hacer valer sus derechos.
assertion (ə'sʌɹ·ʃən) *n.* aserción; afirmación; aseveración.
assertive (ə'sʌɹ·tɪv) *adj.* aseverativo; afirmativo.
assess (ə'sɛs) *v.t.* **1,** (evaluate) tasar; evaluar; valorar. **2,** (tax) fijar *o* poner impuestos. **3,** (require a contribution of) imponer contribución a.
assessment (ə'sɛs·mənt) *n.* **1,** (evaluation) tasación; valoración. **2,** (amount of tax) impuesto; contribución.
assessor (ə'sɛs·ər) *n.* **1,** (tax appraiser) tasador. **2,** (adviser) asesor.
asset ('æs·ɛt) *n.* **1,** (anything advantageous) ventaja. **2,** *usu.pl., comm.* capital (*sing.*); activo (*sing.*).
assiduous (ə'sɪdʒ·u·əs) *adj.* asiduo; constante; diligente. —**assiduousness, assiduity** (ˌæs·ɪ'dju·ə·ti) *n.* asiduidad; diligencia; constancia.
assign (ə'sain) *v.t.* **1,** (allot) asignar; repartir; distribuir. **2,** (appoint) asignar; designar; nombrar. **3,** *law* consignar; ceder. —*v.i., law* hacer cesión. —*n., law* cesionario.
assignation (ˌæs·ɪg'nei·ʃən) *n.* **1,** *law* asignación; cesión. **2,** (tryst) cita amorosa ilícita.
assignee (ˌæs·ə'ni:; əˌsai'ni:) *n., law* cesionario.
assignment (ə'sain·mənt) *n.* **1,** (allotment) asignación. **2,** (appoint-

ment) designación. **3,** (task) tarea; misión. **4,** *law* documento de cesión *o* traspaso.

assimilate (ə'sɪm·ə·leit) *v.t.* **1,** (absorb) asimilar; absorber. **2,** (adapt) asimilar; adaptar; asemejar. —*v.i.* asemejarse; asimilarse. —**assimilation,** *n.* asimilación.

assist (ə'sɪst) *v.t.* asistir; ayudar; atender. —*v.i.* asistir; concurrir; atender.

assistance (ə'sɪs·təns) *n.* asistencia; ayuda; auxilio. —**assistant,** *n.* asistente; ayudante.

associate (ə'so·ʃi·eit) *v.t.* unir; juntar; asociar. —*v.i.* asociarse; juntarse; unirse. —*n.* (-ət) asociado; socio; consocio. —*adj.* (-ət) asociado.

association (əˌso·si'ei·ʃən) *n.* **1,** (act of associating) unión; reunión. **2,** (a society) asociación; sociedad; compañía. **3,** (of ideas) asociación.

assonance ('æs·ə·nəns) *n.* asonancia. —**assonant,** *adj.* asonante.

assort (ə'sort) *v.t.* **1,** (classify) arreglar; clasificar; distribuir. **2,** (supply with various goods) surtir; proveer; suministrar. —**assort with,** asociarse con.

assortment (ə'sort·mənt) *n.* **1,** (classification) arreglo; clasificación. **2,** (variety) surtido; variedad.

assuage (ə'sweidʒ) *v.t.* **1,** (lessen) aminorar; mitigar. **2,** (calm) pacificar; sosegar; calmar. —**assuagement,** *n.* mitigación.

assume (ə'sum) *v.t.* **1,** (believe without proof) asumir; presumir. **2,** (take for oneself) usurpar; apropiarse de. **3,** (undertake) asumir; tomar. **4,** (pretend to have) presumir de. **5,** (take for granted) presumir; dar por sentado *o* descontado.

assumption (ə'sʌmp·ʃən) *n.* **1,** (belief without proof) asunción. **2,** (acceptance on faith) presunción; hipótesis. **3,** *cap., R.C.Ch.* Asunción de María.

assurance (ə'ʃur·əns) *n.* **1,** (confidence) seguridad; confianza. **2,** (certainty) certeza; convicción. **3,** (boldness) valor; arrojo. **4,** (impudence) descaro. **5,** (insurance) seguro.

assure (ə'ʃur) *v.t.* **1,** (make certain) asegurar; afirmar. **2,** (make confident) inspirar confianza en.

Assyrian (ə'sɪr·i·ən) *adj.* & *n.* asirio.

-ast (æst; əst) *sufijo* -asta; *indica la persona o cosa en nombres correspondiendo a nombres terminados en* **-asm**: *enthusiast,* entusiasta.

astatine ('æs·təˌtin) *n.* astacio.

aster ('æs·tər) *n.* aster.

-aster (æs·tər) *sufijo* -astro; -astra; -astre; *forma nombres diminutivos y despectivos: oleaster,* oleastro; *poetaster,* poetastro.

asterisk ('æs·tər·ɪsk) *n.* asterisco.

astern (ə'stʌɹn) *adv.* & *adj.* a popa.

asteroid ('æs·tər·ɔid) *n.* asteroide.

asthma ('æz·mə) *n.* asma. —**asthmatic** (-'mæt·ɪk) *adj.* & *n.* asmático.

astigmatism (ə'stig·mə·tɪz·əm) *n.* astigmatismo. —**astigmatic** (ˌæs·tɪg'mæt·ɪk) *adj.* astigmático.

astir (ə'stʌɹ) *adv.* **1,** (actively) afanosamente; vivamente. **2,** (out of bed) fuera de la cama. —*adj.* activo; laborioso.

astonish (ə'stan·ɪʃ) *v.t.* asombrar; sorprender; pasmar. —**astonishment,** *n.* asombro; pasmo; sorpresa.

astound (ə'staund) *v.t.* aturdir; espantar; aterrar.

astraddle (ə'stræd·əl) *adv.* a horcajadas. —*prep.* a horcajadas en.

astral ('æs·trəl) *adj.* astral.

astray (ə'strei) *adv.* desviadamente; fuera del camino. —*adj.* extraviado; perdido; descarriado.

astride (ə'straid) *adv.* a horcajadas. —*prep.* a horcajadas en.

astringe (ə'strɪndʒ) *v.t.* astringir; constreñir; contraer.

astringent (ə'strɪn·dʒənt) *n.* astringente; constringente. —*adj.* **1,** (tending to constrict) astringente; constringente. **2,** (severe) severo; riguroso; áspero. —**astringency** (-dʒən·si) *n.* astringencia; contracción.

astro- (æs·tro) *prefijo* astro-; estrella: *astrology,* astrología; *astronomy,* astronomía.

astrology (ə'stral·ə·dʒi) *n.* astrología. —**astrologer** (-dʒər) *n.* astrólogo. —**astrological** (ˌæs·trə·'ladʒ·ɪ·kəl) *adj.* astrológico.

astronaut ('æs·trə·nɔt) *n.* astronauta. —**astronautics** (-'nɔː·tɪks) *n.* astronáutica.

astronomy (ə'stran·ə·mi) *n.* astronomía. —**astronomer** (-mər) *n.* astrónomo. —**astronomical** (ˌæs·trə'nam·ɪ·kəl) *adj.* astronómico.

astrophysics (ˌæs·tro'fɪz·ɪks) *n.* astrofísica. —**astrophysical** (-ɪ·kəl) *adj.* astrofísico.
astute (ə'stut) *adj.* astuto; sagaz; taimado. —**astuteness,** *n.* astucia; sagacidad.
asunder (ə'sʌn·dər) *adj.* separado; dividido; desunido. —*adv.* aparte; por separado; desunidamente.
asylum (ə'sai·ləm) *n.* asilo.
asymmetry (e'sɪm·ə·tri) *n.* asimetría. —**asymmetrical** (ˌe·sə·'mɛt·rɪk·əl) *adj.* asimétrico.
at (æt) *prep.* **1,** (expressing location) a. **2,** (expressing direction or goal) a. **3,** (in the state of) en. **4,** (by; near) por. **5,** (expressing price, speed, etc.) a.
at- (æt; ət) *prefijo, var. de* **ad-** *ante* t: *attract,* atraer.
-atary (ə·tɛr·i) *prefijo* -atario; *forma nombres que denotan* agencia; relación: *mandatary,* mandatario.
atavism ('æt·ə·vɪz·əm) *n.* atavismo. —**atavistic** (-'vɪs·tɪk) *adj.* atávico.
ataxia (ə'tæk·si·ə) *n.* ataxia.
ate (eit) *v., pret. de* **eat.**
-ate (eit; ət) *sufijo* **1,** *forma verbos: accumulate,* acumular. **2,** *forma adjetivos: innate,* innato. **3,** *a veces, equivale al participio usado como adjetivo: desolate, desolated,* desolado. **4,** *expresa la forma sustantiva del verbo: precipitate,* precipitado; *mandate,* mandato. **5,** *quím.* -ato; *terminación de los nombres de sales formadas por ácidos: acetate,* acetato. **6,** *biol.* -ado: *vertebrate,* vertebrado. **7,** -ato; *forma nombres denotando* dignidad; cargo: *cardinalate,* cardenalato.
atheism ('ei·θi·ɪz·əm) *n.* ateísmo. —**atheist,** *n.* ateo; ateísta. —**atheistic** (-'ɪs·tɪk) *adj.* ateo; ateísta; ateístico.
athenium (æ'θiː·ni·əm) *n., chem.* atenio.
athlete ('æθ·lit) *n.* atleta. —**athlete's foot,** pie de atleta; infección entre los dedos de los pies.
athletic (æθ'lɛt·ɪk) *adj.* atlético. —**athletics,** *n.pl.* deportes; atletismo (*sing.*).
athwart (ə'θwort) *prep.* **1,** (across) a *o* de través de. **2,** (against) contra; en oposición a. —*adv.* **1,** (crosswise) oblicuamente; contrariamente. **2,** (perversely) aviesamente; perversamente.
-atic ('æt·ɪk) *también,* **-atical** ('æt·ɪ·kəl) *sufijo* -ático; *forma adjetivos que denotan* estado; relación: *aquatic,* acuático; *sabbatical,* sabático; sabática.
-ation ('ei·ʃən) *sufijo* -ación; *expresa acción o efecto en nombres verbales: concentration,* concentración; *generation,* generación.
-atious ('ei·ʃəs) *sufijo; forma adjetivos de nombres terminados en* **-ation:** *vexatious,* vejatorio; *disputatious,* disputador.
-ative (ə·tɪv) *sufijo* -ativo; -itivo; *forma adjetivos usados frecuentemente como sustantivos que expresan* relación; tendencia: *demonstrative,* demostrativo.
Atlantic (æt'læn·tɪk) *adj.* atlántico. —*n., cap.* Atlántico.
atlas ('æt·ləs) *n.* atlas.
atmosphere ('æt·məsˌfɪr) *n.* **1,** (air) atmósfera. **2,** *fig.* (environment) ambiente; medio. —**atmospheric** (-'fɛr·ɪk) *adj.* atmosférico.
atoll ('æ·tal) *n.* atolón.
atom ('æ·təm) *n.* átomo. —**atomic** (ə'tam·ɪk) *adj.* atómico. —**atom bomb; atomic bomb,** bomba atómica. —**atomic pile,** reactor atómico.
atomize ('æt·ə·maiz) *v.t.* pulverizar; rociar; atomizar. —**atomizer,** *n.* pulverizador; atomizador.
atonal (e'to·nəl) *adj.* atonal. —**atonality** (ˌe·to'næl·ə·ti) *n.* atonalidad.
atone (ə'toːn) *v.i.* arrepentirse; enmendarse; expiar. —**atonement,** *n.* expiación; arrepentimiento; enmienda.
atop (ə'tap) *adj.* elevado; alto. —*adv.* encima; en la cima. —*prep.* sobre; encima de.
-atory (ə·tor·i) *sufijo* -atorio; -atario; *forma adjetivos y nombres que denotan* pertenencia; sitio; agente: *amatory,* amatorio; *laboratory,* laboratorio; *signatory,* signatario.
atrium ('ei·tri·əm) *n.* atrio.
atrocious (ə'tro·ʃəs) *adj.* atroz; cruel; perverso. —**atrociousness,** *n.* perversidad; crueldad.
atrocity (ə'tras·ə·ti) *n.* atrocidad; brutalidad.
atrophy ('æt·rə·fi) *n.* atrofia. —*v.i.* atrofiarse.

atropine ('æt·rə,pin) *n.* atropina.

attach (ə'tætʃ) *v.t.* **1,** (fasten) adherir; sujetar; fijar. **2,** *law* embargar. **3,** (appoint) designar; nombrar. **4,** (associate) unir; asociar; enlazar. —*v.i.* pegarse; unirse; adherirse.

attaché (æt·ə'ʃei) *n.* agregado diplomático. —**attaché case,** portafolio; cartera.

attachment (ə'tætʃ·mənt) *n.* **1,** (adhesion) adhesión; adherencia. **2,** (devotion) afición; afecto. **3,** *mech.* accesorio.

attack (ə'tæk) *v.t.* **1,** (assault) atacar; agredir; asaltar. **2,** (assail) acusar; acometer. —*n.* **1,** (assault) ataque; agresión. **2,** *mil.* ataque; combate. **3,** (illness) ataque; acometida.

attain (ə'tein) *v.t.* obtener; conseguir; lograr; realizar.

attainment (ə'tein·mənt) *n.* **1,** (acquisition) obtención; logro; realización. **2,** (acquired honor or ability) conocimiento; don.

attar ('æt·ər) *n.* aceite esencial.

attempt (ə'tɛmpt) *v.t.* intentar; procurar; probar. —*n.* intento; tentativa; esfuerzo.

attend (ə'tɛnd) *v.t.* **1,** (be present at) asistir a; concurrir a. **2,** (take care of) cuidar; atender. **3,** (go with) acompañar. **4,** (heed) atender; escuchar.

attendance (ə'tɛn·dəns) *n.* **1,** (presence) concurrencia; asistencia. **2,** (help) asistencia; ayuda.

attendant (ə'tɛn·dənt) *n.* **1,** (one who serves) asistente; sirviente. **2,** (one who is present) asistente. **3,** (follower) acompañante; seguidor. —*adj.* **1,** (serving or being present) asistente. **2,** (accompanying) concomitante; acompañante.

attention (ə'tɛn·ʃən) *n.* **1,** (mindfulness; care) atención; cuidado. **2,** (act of civility) cortesía; fineza; atención. —*interj., mil.* ¡atención! ¡firmes!

attentive (ə'tɛn·tɪv) *adj.* **1,** (intent) atento; aplicado. **2,** (polite) atento; educado; cortés. —**attentiveness,** *n.* atención; fijeza; finura.

attenuate (ə'tɛn·ju·eit) *v.t.* atenuar; disminuir; aminorar. —*v.i.* atenuarse; disminuirse; aminorarse. —**attenuation,** *n.* atenuación; disminución.

attest (ə'tɛst) *v.t.* **1,** (testify) atestiguar; declarar. **2,** (prove) probar; garantizar; confirmar. **3,** *law* deponer; declarar.

attestation (,æt·ɛs'tei·ʃən) *n.* atestación; deposición; declaración.

attic ('æt·ɪk) *n.* ático; desván.

Attic ('æt·ɪk) *adj.* ático.

attire (ə'tair) *n.* atavío; traje; vestido. —*v.t.* vestir; adornar; ataviar.

attitude ('æt·ɪ·tud) *n.* **1,** (feeling; opinion) actitud; gesto; posición. **2,** (posture) actitud; postura.

attorney (ə'tʌɹ·ni) *n.* abogado. —**attorney at law,** procurador. —**attorney general,** ministro de justicia; fiscal de la nación. —**power of attorney,** poder.

attract (ə'trækt) *v.t.* atraer.

attraction (ə'træk·ʃən) *n.* atracción.

attractive (ə'træk·tɪv) *n.* atrayente; seductor.

attribute (ə'trɪb·jut) *v.t.* atribuir; achacar; imputar. —*n.* ('æt·rɪ·bjut) atributo; característica. —**attribution** (,æt·rɪ'bju·ʃən) *n.* atribución. —**attributive** (ə'trɪb·ju·tɪv) *adj.* & *n.* atributivo.

attrition (ə'trɪʃ·ən) *n.* desgaste; rozadura; *fig.* agotamiento.

attune (ə'tu:n) *v.t.* **1,** (tune) afinar; templar. **2,** (bring into accord) armonizar; poner de acuerdo.

atypical (ei'tɪp·ɪ·kəl) *adj.* desusado; anormal.

auburn ('ɔ·bərn) *adj.* castaño-rojizo.

auction ('ɔk·ʃən) *n.* subasta; remate. —*v.t.* subastar. —**auctioneer** (-'ɪ:r) *n.* subastador; rematador.

audacious (ɔ'dei·ʃəs) *adj.* **1,** (daring) audaz; intrépido; valiente. **2,** (unrestrained) atrevido; insolente; descarado.

audacity (ɔ'dæs·ə·ti) *n.* **1,** (daring) audacia; intrepidez. **2,** (impudence) atrevimiento; insolencia.

audible ('ɔ·də·bəl) *adj.* audible; oíble; perceptible. —**audibility,** *n.* sonoridad; perceptibilidad.

audience ('ɔ·di·əns) *n.* **1,** (listeners) oyentes (*pl.*). **2,** (assembly) auditorio; concurso. **3,** (formal interview) audiencia.

audio- (ɔ·di·o) *también,* **audi-** (ɔ·di) *prefijo* audio-; audi-; oír; oído: *audio-visual,* audiovisual; *audiphone,* audífono.

audion ('ɔ·di·an) *n.* audión.
audiphone ('ɔ·də,fon) *n.* audífono.
audit ('ɔ·dɪt) *n.* inspección. —*v.t.* inspeccionar.
audition (ɔ'dɪʃ·ən) *n.* **1,** (act of hearing) audición. **2,** (test performance) audición; *music* recital. —*v.t.* dar audición a. —*v.i.* dar una audición.
auditor ('ɔ·dɪ·tər) *n.* **1,** (listener) oyente. **2,** *comm.* contador; revisor *o* inspector de contabilidad.
auditorium (ɔ·də'tor·i·əm) *n.* **1,** (for a small group) paraninfo. **2,** (for the public) sala de espectáculos.
auditory ('ɔ·də·tor·i) *adj.* auditivo.
auger ('ɔ·gər) *n.* barrena; taladro.
aught (ɔt) *n.* algo; alguna cosa; (*en proposiciones negativas*) nada. —*adv.* de cualquier forma; en absoluto.
augment (ɔg'mɛnt) *v.t.* aumentar; incrementar. —*v.i.* crecer; hacerse más grande. —*n.* ('ɔg·mɛnt) aumento. —**augmentation** (,ɔg·mɛn'tei·ʃən) *n.* aumentación; aumento; incremento. —**augmentative** (ɔg'mɛn·tə·tɪv) *adj.* aumentativo.
augur ('ɔ·gər) *v.t.* & *i.* predecir; presagiar; augurar. —*n.* augur; agorero; adivino.
augury ('ɔ·gjʊ·ri) *n.* **1,** (omen) augurio; presagio. **2,** (bad omen) mal agüero.
august (ɔ'gʌst) *adj.* augusto; solemne; impresionante.
August ('ɔ·gəst) *n.* agosto.
auk (ɔk) *n.* alca.
aunt (ant; ænt) *n.* tía.
aura ('ɔ·rə) *n.* aura.
aureole ('or·i·ol) *n.* aureola.
aureomycin (,or·i·o'mai·sɪn) *n.* aureomicina.
auricle ('ɔ·rə·kəl) *n.* **1,** (outer ear) oreja. **2,** (chamber of the heart) aurícula. —**auricular** (ɔ'rɪk·jə·lər) *adj.* auricular.
auriferous (ɔ'rɪf·ər·əs) *adj.* aurífero.
aurora (ɔ'ror·ə) *n.* **1,** (dawn) amanecer; alborada. **2,** (atmospheric phenomenon) aurora. —**aurora borealis** (bor·i'æl·ɪs) aurora boreal. —**aurora australis** (ɔ'strei·lɪs) aurora austral.
auscultate ('ɔs·kəl,teit) *v.t.* auscultar. —**auscultation,** *n.* auscultación.
auspice ('ɔ·spɪs) *n.,* *usu.pl.* auspicios; protección (*sing.*). —**auspicious** (ɔ'spɪʃ·əs) *adj.* favorable; propicio; benigno. —**auspiciousness,** *n.* benignidad; prosperidad.
austere (ɔ'stɪːr) *adj.* **1,** (unadorned) austero; sobrio. **2,** (severe) severo; estricto; riguroso. —**austerity** (ɔ'stɛr·ə·ti) *n.* austeridad.
austral ('ɔ·strəl) *adj.* austral.
autarchy ('ɔ·tar·ki) *n.* autarquía. —**autarchic** (ɔ'tar·kɪk) *adj.* autárquico.
autarky ('ɔ·tar·ki) *n.* autarquía. —**autarkic** (ɔ'tar·kɪk); **autarkical,** *adj.* autárquico.
authentic (ɔ'θɛn·tɪk) *adj.* auténtico; genuino; verdadero. —**authenticity** (,ɔ·θɛn'tɪs·ə·ti) *n.* autenticidad.
authenticate (ɔ'θɛn·tɪ·keit) *v.t.* autenticar; validar; autorizar. —**authentication,** *n.* autenticación.
author ('ɔ·θər) *n.* autor. —**authoress** (-əs) *n.* autora.
authoritative (ə'θar·ə·tei·tɪv) *adj.* **1,** (official) autoritario. **2,** (based on authority) autorizado.
authority (ə'θar·ə·ti) *n.* autoridad; poder; mando. —**authoritarian** (-'teːr·i·ən) *n.* & *adj.* autoritario.
authorize ('ɔ·θə·raiz) *v.t.* autorizar; permitir; sancionar. —**authorization** (-rɪ'zei·ʃən) *n.* autorización; licencia; permiso.
auto ('ɔ·to) *n.,* *colloq.* auto; automóvil; coche; *Amer.* carro.
auto- (ɔ·to) *prefijo* auto-; mismo; propio: *automobile,* automóvil; *autobiography,* autobiografía.
autobiography (,ɔ·to·bai'ag·rə·fi) *n.* autobiografía. —**autobiographical** (-ə'græf·ɪ·kəl) *adj.* autobiográfico.
autocracy (ɔ'tak·rə·si) *n.* autocracia. —**autocrat** ('ɔ·tə·kræt) *n.* autócrata. —**autocratic** (-'kræt·ɪk) *adj.* autocrático.
autogiro (,ɔ·tə'dʒai·ro) *n.* autogiro.
autograph ('ɔ·tə·græf) *n.* autógrafo.
automat ('ɔ·tə·mæt) *n.* restaurante automático.
automate ('ɔ·tə,meit) *v.t.* automatizar.
automatic (,ɔ·tə'mæt·ɪk) *adj.* **1,** *mech.* automático. **2,** *fig.* habitual;

reflejo; automático. —*n.* (pistola) automática.

automation (ˌɔ·tə'mei·ʃən) *n.* automatización.

automaton (ɔ'tam·ə·tan) *n.* autómata.

automobile *n.* ('ɔ·tə·mə,bil) & *adj.* (-'moː·bəl) automóvil.

automotive (ˌɔ·tə'mo·tɪv) *adj.* automotor.

autonomic (ˌɔ·tə'nam·ɪk) *adj.* autonómico.

autonomy (ɔ'tan·ə·mi) *n.* autonomía. —**autonomous** (-məs) *adj.* autónomo.

autopsy ('ɔˌtap·si) *n.* autopsia.

autosuggestion *n.* autosugestión.

autumn ('ɔ·təm) *n.* otoño. —**autumnal** (ɔ'tʌm·nəl) *adj.* otoñal; autumnal.

auxiliary (ɔg'zɪl·jə·ri) *adj.* **1,** (assisting) auxiliar; ayudante. **2,** (subordinate) asistente; subordinado. **3,** (additional) adicional; suplementario. —*n.* ayudante; asistente; auxiliar.

avail (ə'veil) *v.t.* aprovechar; servir; ayudar. —*v.i.* ser ventajoso; ser de provecho. —*n.* provecho. —**avail oneself of,** aprovecharse de; valerse de. —**to no avail,** inútilmente.

available (ə'veil·ə·bəl) *adj.* disponible. —**availability,** *n.* disponibilidad.

avalanche ('æv·əˌlæntʃ) *n.* avalancha; alud.

avant-garde (æ·vaɴ'gard) *n.* vanguardia.

avarice ('æv·ə·rɪs) *n.* avaricia; codicia. —**avaricious** (-'rɪʃ·əs) *adj.* avaricioso; codicioso.

Ave Maria ('a·və·ma'ri·ə; 'a·ve-) ave-maría.

avenge (ə'vɛndʒ) *v.t.* vengar; vindicar.

avenue ('æ·və·nju) *n.* **1,** (wide street) avenida. **2,** *fig.* (approach) entrada; acceso; vía.

aver (ə'vʌɹ) *v.t.* [**averred, averring**] **1,** (assert) afirmar; aseverar. **2,** *law* (prove) confirmar; justificar.

average ('æv·ə·rɪdʒ) *n.* promedio. —*adj.* promedio; ordinario; normal. —*v.i.* calcular el promedio; ser *o* tener el promedio de. —*v.t.* hacer un promedio de; promediar; prorratear.

averse (ə'vʌɹs) *adj.* contrario; opuesto.

aversion (ə'vʌɹ·ʒən) *n.* aversión; repulsión; antipatía.

avert (ə'vʌɹt) *v.t.* **1,** (ward off) prevenir; evitar. **2,** (turn away) alejar; desviar.

avi- (ei·vi) *prefijo* avi-; ave; pájaro: *aviculture,* avicultura.

aviary ('ei·vi·ɛr·i) *n.* pajarera; jaula.

aviation (e·vi'ei·ʃən) *n.* aviación.

aviator ('ei·vi·e·tər) *n.* aviador. —**aviatrix** (-'e·trɪks) *n.* [*pl.* **-trices** (-trɪ·siz)] aviadora; aviatriz.

avid ('æv·ɪd) *adj.* ávido; ansioso; codicioso.

avidity (ə'vɪd·ə·ti) *n.* avidez; ansiedad; codicia.

avocado (æv·ə'ka·do) *n.* [*pl.* **-dos**] aguacate.

avocation (æv·ə'kei·ʃən) *n.* afición; entretenimiento; pasatiempo.

avoid (ə'vɔid) *v.t.* evitar; esquivar; eludir. —**avoidance** (-əns) *n.* evasión; escape.

avoirdupois (ˌæv·ər·də'pɔiz) *n.* **1,** (measure) sistema de peso basado en la libra de 16 onzas. **2,** *colloq.* (obesity) gordura.

avouch (ə'vautʃ) *v.t.* **1,** (vouch for) justificar; garantizar. **2,** (assert) afirmar; sostener.

avow (ə'vau) *v.t.* declarar abiertamente; admitir; confesar; reconocer. —**avowal** (-əl) *n.* reconocimiento; confesión; admisión.

await (ə'weit) *v.t.* aguardar; esperar.

awake (ə'weik) *v.* [*pret.* & *p.p.* **awoke** *o* **awaked**] —*v.t.* **1,** (rouse) despertar. **2,** (call into action) despabilar; animar. —*v.i.* despertarse. —*adj.* despierto; despabilado; alerta.

awaken (ə'wei·kən) *v.t.* & *i.* = **awake.** —**awakening,** *n.* el despertar; el abrir los ojos.

award (ə'wɔrd) *v.t.* premiar; conceder; *law* adjudicar. —*n.* **1,** (prize) premio; galardón. **2,** *law* adjudicación.

aware (ə'weːr) *adj.* enterado; consciente; informado.

awash (ə'waʃ) *adj.* anegado en agua; inundado. —*adv.* a flor de agua.

away (ə'wei) *adv.* **1,** (off) lejos. **2,** (aside) aparte. **3,** (at once) en seguida. **4,** (out of one's presence, etc.) afuera; fuera. —*adj.* **1,** (absent) ausente. **2,** (distant) lejano; distante.

awe (ɔː) *n.* pavor; temor reverencial. —*v.t.* impresionar.
aweigh (ə'wei) *adj., naut.* levado.
awesome ('ɔː·səm) *adj.* impresionante; pavoroso.
awestruck ('ɔː·strʌk) *adj.* despavorido; espantado; impresionado.
awful ('ɔː·fəl) *adj.* **1,** (inspiring awe) tremendo; abrumador. **2,** (terrifying) horripilante; terrible. **3,** *colloq.* (very bad) detestable; muy malo; desagradable. **4,** *colloq.* (great) grande; excesivo.
awfully ('ɔf·li) *adv.* **1,** (horribly) horriblemente. **2,** *colloq.* (very) muy.
awhile (ə'hwail) *adv.* (por) un rato; (por) un momento.
awkward ('ɔk·wərd) *adj.* **1,** (unskilled) torpe; poco diestro. **2,** (clumsy) desmañado; tosco. **3,** (ill-adapted) indócil. **4,** (difficult to handle) delicado; peligroso. —**awkwardness,** *n.* tosquedad; torpeza.
awl (ɔːl) *n.* lezna; punzón.
awn (ɔːn) *n.* arista.
awning (ɔː·nɪŋ) *n.* toldo.
awoke (ə'woːk) *v., pret. de* **awake.**
awry (ə'rai) *adv.* oblicuamente; al través. —*adj.* desviado; perverso.
ax *también,* **axe** (æks) *n.* hacha. —*v.t.* **1,** (cut with an ax) hachear. **2,** *slang* (dismiss) despedir. —**have an ax to grind,** tener fines interesados.
axial ('æk·si·əl) *adj.* axial.
axiom ('æk·si·əm) *n.* axioma. —**axiomatic** (-ə'mæt·ɪk) *adj.* axiomático.
axis ('æk·sɪs) *n.* [*pl.* **-es** (-siz)] **1,** (pivot) eje. **2,** *anat.* axis.
axle ('æk·səl) *n.* **1,** (of a wheel) eje. **2,** (of a machine) árbol.
ay 1, [*también,* **aye**] (ei) *adv., poet.* siempre. **2,** (ai) *adv.* & *n.* = **aye.**
aye 1, [*también,* **ay**] (ai) *adv.* & *n.* sí. **2,** (ei) *adv., poet.* = **ay.**
azalea (ə'zeil·jə) *n.* azalea.
azimuth ('æz·ə·məθ) *n.* azimut; acimut.
azoic (ə'zo·ɪk) *adj.* azoico.
Aztec ('æz·tɛk) *n.* & *adj.* azteca.
azure ('æʒ·ər) *n.* & *adj.* azur.

B

B, b (biː) **1,** segunda letra del alfabeto inglés. **2,** *musica* si. **3,** *denota* segunda clase; segundo grado; suficiencia.
baa (baː) *v.i.* [**baaed** (baːd), **baaing**] balar. —*n.* balido.
babble ('bæb·əl) *v.i.* **1,** (chatter) charlar; parlotear. **2,** (utter words imperfectly) balbucear; balbucir. **3.** (murmur) murmurar. —*v.t.* **1,** (utter incoherently) mascullar; barbotar. **2,** (murmur) murmurar. —*n.* **1,** (prattle) balbuceo; barboteo. **2,** (murmur) murmullo.
babe (beib) *n.* **1,** = **baby. 2,** *slang* (girl) muchachita; chiquita.
babel ('bei·bəl) *n.* babel; confusión; *cap.* Babel.
baboon (bæ'buːn) *n.* babuino.
baby ('bei·bi) *n.* **1,** (infant) bebé; niño; criatura; nene (*fem.* nena). **2,** (youngest child) menor. **3,** (young of an animal) pequeño. **4,** *slang* (pet) monada. —*adj.* **1,** (infantile) infantil; de *o* para niños. **2,** (small) pequeño. —*v.t.* mimar; tratar como niño. —**babyhood,** *n.* niñez; infancia. —**babyish,** *adj.* pueril; aniñado. —**baby talk,** habla infantil.
Babylon ('bæb·əˌlan) *n.* Babilonia. —**Babylonian** (-'lo·ni·ən) *adj.* babilonio; babilónico.
babysit ('bei·bi·sɪt) *v.i.* cuidar niños. —**babysitter,** *n.* quien cuida niños; niñera.
baccalaureate (bæk·ə'lar·i·ət) *n.* bachillerato.
baccarat ('bæk·əˌra) *n.* bacará.
bacchanal ('bæk·ə·nəl; -nal) *n.* **1,** (orgy) bacanal. **2,** (reveler) calavera; borracho. —**bacchanalia** (-'nei·li·ə) *n.pl.* bacanales. —**bacchanalian,** *adj.* bacanal; ebrio.
bachelor ('bætʃ·ə·lər) *n.* **1,** (unmarried man) soltero. **2,** (college graduate) bachiller. —**bachelorhood,** *n.* soltería.
bacillus (bə'sɪl·əs) *n.* [*pl.* **-li** (-lai)] bacilo.
back (bæk) *n.* **1,** (of an animal) lomo; espinazo. **2,** (of a person) espalda. **3,** (rear or hind part) trasero; respaldo. **4,** (of a book) lomo. **5,** (support; stiffening) respaldo. **6,** (reverse side) **reverso;**

revés. —*adj.* 1, (behind) trasero; posterior. 2, (distant) distante; lejano. 3, (of past time) atrasado; retrasado. —*v.t.* 1, (support) respaldar; apoyar; sostener. 2, (cause to move backward) hacer retroceder; mover hacia atrás; dar marcha atrás a. —*v.i.* retroceder; retirarse; moverse hacia atrás; dar marcha atrás. —*adv.* 1, (toward the rear) atrás; detrás. 2, (again) otra vez; de nuevo. 3, (returned or restored) de vuelta. 4, (ago) hace: *three months back,* hace tres meses. —**back and fill,** vacilar; dudar. —**back and forth,** de una parte a otra; de aquí para allá. —**back down,** ceder; rendirse; acobardarse. —**back entrance,** puerta trasera. —**back out,** retractarse; volverse atrás; desertar. —**back water,** 1, *naut.* recular. 2, (withdraw) retirarse. —**be back,** estar de vuelta. —**come back,** volver. —**go back on,** *colloq.* desertar; abandonar; faltar a. —**slap** *o* **pat on the back,** espaldarazo.

backache ('bæk·eik) *n.* dolor de espalda.

backbite ('bæk·bait) *v.t.* & *i.* calumniar; desacreditar.

backbone ('bæk·boːn) *n.* 1, (spine) espina dorsal; columna vertebral; espinazo. 2, (mainstay) nervio; fundamento. 3, (firmness) firmeza; resolución.

backbreaking ('bæk·breik·ɪŋ) *adj.* abrumador; extenuante.

backfire ('bæk·fair) *n.* 1, *mech.* explosión prematura de un motor *o* fusil. 2, (fire to check another fire) cinturón de cenizas; claro abierto. 3, (undesired outcome) resultado contrario *u* opuesto. —*v.i.* 1, (explode) explotar prematuramente. 2, (go awry) tener resultado contrario.

backgammon ('bæk,gæm·ən) *n.* chaquete.

background ('bæk,graund) *n.* 1, (setting) fondo. 2, (past history) antecedentes (*pl.*).

backhand ('bæk,hænd) *n.* 1, (writing) escritura inclinada a la izquierda. 2, *tennis; jai-alai* revés.

backing ('bæk·ɪŋ) *n.* 1, (supporting material) respaldo. 2, (endorsement; aid) sostén; apoyo; ayuda.

backlash *n.* contragolpe.

backward ('bæk·wərd) *también,* **backwards** (-wərdz) *adv.* 1, (toward the rear) para *o* hacia atrás. 2, (with back foremost) de espaldas. 3, (in reverse order) invertidamente. 4, (inside out) al revés. 5, (in past time) con atraso; retrasadamente. —*adj.* 1, (retarded) atrasado; retrasado. 2, (shy) retraído; esquivo.

bacon ('bei·kən) *n.* tocino; *W.I.; C.A.* tocineta.

bacteria (bæk'tɪr·i·ə) *n.* [*sing.* **-um** (əm)] bacteria. —**bacterial,** *adj.* bacterial; bactérico. —**bacterial warfare,** guerra bacteriológica.

bacteriology (bæk,tɪr·i'al·ə·dʒi) *n.* bacteriología. —**bacteriological** (-ə'ladʒ·ɪ·kəl) *adj.* bacteriológico. —**bacteriologist,** *n.* bacteriólogo.

bad (bæːd) *adj.* [**worse, worst**] 1, (wicked) malo; perverso. 2, (defective) defectuoso; dañado. 3, (noxious) nocivo; dañino. 4, (unfavorable) desfavorable; desafortunado. 5, (sick) malo; enfermo; indispuesto. —*n.* el mal; lo malo. —**in a bad way,** de mala manera.— **in bad,** *colloq.* en desgracia. —**be to the bad** (financially or morally) resultar *o* salir perdiendo.

bade (bæːd) *v., pret. de* **bid.**

badge (bæːdʒ) *n.* divisa; distintivo; emblema.

badger ('bæ·dʒər) *n.* tejón. —*v.t.* fastidiar; molestar; importunar.

badly ('bæd·li) *adv.* 1, (poorly) mal; malamente. 2, (seriously) gravemente. 3, *colloq.* (very much) muy; mucho; muchísimo.

badminton ('bæd·mɪn·tən) *n.* juego del volante.

badness ('bæd·nəs) *n.* maldad.

baffle ('bæf·əl) *v.t.* 1, (impede) frustrar; impedir. 2, (bewilder) confundir; aturdir. —*n.* deflector. —**bafflement,** *n.* confusión; aturdimiento.

bag (bæːg) *n.* 1, (portable receptacle) bolsa; saco. 2, (suitcase) maleta. 3, (purse) bolso; cartera. 4, (hunter's catch) morral. 5, *slang* (money collected) bolsa. 6, (udder) ubre; teta. —*v.t.* [**bagged, bagging**] capturar; cazar. —*v.i.* 1, (swell) inflamarse; hincharse. 2, (hang loosely) hacer bolsas; abolsarse. —**baggy,** *adj.* abolsado.

bagasse (bə'gæs) *n.* bagazo.

bagatelle (,bæg·ə'tɛl) *n.* bagatela.

baggage ('bæg·ɪdʒ) *n.* **1,** (luggage) equipaje. **2,** *mil.* bagaje. **3,** (lewd woman) ramera; bagasa.
bagpipe ('bæg·paip) *n.* gaita.
bah! (baː) *interj.* ¡bah!
bail (beil) *n., law* **1,** (money or credit) fianza. **2,** (person) fiador. —*v.t.* **1,** (deliver in trust for) poner como fianza. **2,** [*también,* **bail out**] libertar *o* poner en libertad bajo fianza. **3,** (pay money for release of) poner fianza *o* salir fiador de *o* por. —**bail out, 1,** *naut.* desaguar; achicar. **2,** *aero.* tirarse *o* saltar con paracaídas.
bailiff ('bei·lɪf) *n.* alguacil.
bailiwick ('bei·lə·wɪk) *n.* bailía.
bait (beit) *n.* cebo; anzuelo. —*v.t.* **1,** (provide with a lure) cebar; poner cebo a. **2,** (tease) molestar; enojar.
baize (beiz) *n.* bayeta.
bake (beik) *v.t.* cocer al horno; hornear. —*v.i.* (be baked) hornearse; cocerse; endurecerse al horno.
bakelite ('bei·kə,lait) *n.* baquelita; bakelita.
baker ('bei·kər) *n.* panadero. —**baker's dozen,** docena del fraile.
baking ('bei·kɪŋ) *n.* cocimiento; hornada. —**baking powder,** levadura en polvo. —**baking soda,** bicarbonato de sosa.
balance ('bæl·əns) *n.* **1,** (scale) balanza. **2,** (equal distribution of weight) balance; equilibrio. **3,** (mental stability) buen juicio **4,** *comm.* saldo; balance. **5,** (remainder) resto. —*v.t.* **1,** (equalize) equilibrar; igualar. **2,** (weigh) pesar. **3,** (estimate) ponderar; comparar. **4,** *comm.* saldar. —*v.i.* equilibrarse; contrarrestarse; balancear. —**balance beam,** balancín. —**balance of trade,** balanza de comercio. —**balance sheet,** balance. —**balancing pole,** balancín.
balcony ('bæl·kə·ni) *n.* **1,** *archit.* balcón. **2,** *theat.* galería; paraíso.
bald (bɔːld) *adj.* **1,** (hairless) calvo. **2,** (without covering) descubierto. **3,** (bare) soso; desnudo. **4,** (unqualified) puro; mero; escueto.
balderdash ('bɔl·dər,dæʃ) *n.* jerigonza; jerga.
baldness ('bɔld·nəs) *n.* **1,** (lack of hair) calvicie. **2,** (bareness) desnudez; simplicidad.
bale (beil) *n.* bala. —*v.t.* embalar; empacar.
baleen (bə'liːn) *n.* ballena.
baleful ('beil·fəl) *adj.* **1,** (menacing) amenazante; peligroso. **2,** (malign) nocivo; maligno. —**balefulness,** *n.* malignidad.
balk (bɔːk) *n.* **1,** (obstacle) obstáculo; impedimento. **2,** (blunder) derrota; fracaso. **3,** (piece of timber) viga. **4,** *sports* falta. —*v.t.* impedir; frustrar. —*v.i.* resistirse; rebelarse. —**balky,** *adj.* porfiado; obstinado.
Balkan ('bɔl·kən) *adj.* balcánico. —**the Balkans,** los Balcanes.
ball (bɔl) *n.* **1,** (round body) bola; esfera; globo. **2,** *sports* pelota; balón. **3,** (bullet) bala. **4,** (dance) baile. **5,** (of yarn) ovillo. **6,** (of the finger) yema del dedo. —**ball up,** *slang* desordenar; enredar.
ballad ('bæl·əd) *n.* balada.
ballast ('bæl·əst) *n.* **1,** (stabilizing material) lastre. **2,** *R.R.* balasto.
ball bearing cojinete.
ballerina (bæl·ə'ri·nə) *n.* bailarina de ballet.
ballet (bæl'eiː) *n.* baile; ballet.
ballistics (bə'lɪs·tɪks) *n. sing. o pl.* balística. —**ballistic,** *adj.* balístico.
balloon (bə'luːn) *n.* **1,** (inflated sphere) globo. **2,** *aero.* globo aerostático; aeróstato. —*v.i.* hincharse; inflarse. —**ballooning,** *n.* aerostación. —**balloonist,** *n.* aeronauta; ascensionista.
ballot ('bæl·ət) *n.* **1,** (voting ticket) balota; papeleta *o* cédula de votación; voto. **2,** (voting; total vote) voto; votación. —*v.i.* votar; balotar.
ballpoint pen bolígrafo.
ballroom ('bɔl·rum) *n.* salón de baile.
ballyhoo ('bæl·i,hu) *n., slang* alharaca; bombo. —*v.t.* dar bombo a.
balm (baːm) *n.* bálsamo; ungüento.
balmy ('ba·mi) *adj.* **1,** (mild) suave. **2,** (fragrant) fragante; balsámico. **3,** *slang* (mildly demented) alocado. —**balminess,** *n.* untuosidad; suavidad; fragancia.
baloney (bə'lo·ni) *n.* **1,** *slang* (nonsense) tontería; disparate. **2,** = **bologna.**
balsa ('bɔl·sə) *n.* balsa.
balsam ('bɔl·səm) *n.* bálsamo.

Baltic ('bɔl·tɪk) *adj.* báltico. —*n.* Báltico.
baluster ('bæl·əs·tər) *n.* balaustre. —**balustrade** (-treid) *n.* balaustrada; barandilla.
bamboo (bæm'buː) *n.* bambú.
ban (bæːn) *v.t.* [**banned, banning**] proscribir; prohibir; suprimir. —*n.* **1,** (prohibition) prohibición; supresión; proscripción. **2,** (medieval proclamation) bando; proclama; pregón. **3,** *eccles.* excomunión.
banal ('bei·nəl) *adj.* banal; trivial. —**banality** (bə'næl·ə·ti) *n.* banalidad; trivialidad.
banana (bə'næn·ə) *n.* banana; *Sp.* plátano; *W.I., C.A., northern So. Amer.* guineo.
band (bæːnd) *n.* **1,** (strip) banda; faja; franja. **2,** (metal strip) fleje; abrazadera. **3,** (zone marked off) precinto; tira. **4,** (group of persons) cuadrilla; grupo; pandilla. **5,** (group of musicians) banda. **6,** *radio* banda. —*v.t.* **1,** (mark or fasten with a band) zunchar. **2,** (group together) unir; reunir; juntar. —*v.i.* [*también,* **band together**] unirse; reunirse; juntarse.
bandage ('bæn·dɪdʒ) *n.* vendaje; venda. —*v.t.* vendar.
bandanna (bæn'dæn·ə) *n.* pañuelo grande.
banderilla (ˌbæn·də'ri·jə) *n.* banderilla. —**banderillero** (-ri'je·ro) *n.* banderillero.
bandit ('bæn·dɪt) *n.* bandido; bandolero; ladrón. —**banditry,** *n.* bandolerismo; bandidaje.
bandoleer (ˌbæn·də'lɪr) *n.* bandolera.
bandstand ('bænd·stænd) *n.* quiosco *o* concha de música.
bandwagon *n.* carro de banda. —**get on the bandwagon,** *colloq.* adherirse al partido que gana.
bandy ('bæn·di) *v.t.* cambiar; tirar *o* pasar de una parte a otra. —*adj.* zambo; combado. —**bandy a ball,** pelotear. —**bandy words,** trocar palabras.
bandylegged *adj.* patizambo; patituerto.
bane (bein) *n.* **1,** (poison) veneno. **2,** (destroyer) ruina; azote; calamidad. —**baneful,** *adj.* dañino; pernicioso.
bang (bæːŋ) *n.* **1,** (noise) ruido; golpe seco; porrazo. **2,** *slang* (energy) energía; vigor. **3,** *slang* (thrill) emoción; fascinación. **4,** (hair over the forehead) flequillo. —*v.t.* golpear ruidosamente; arrojar. —*v.i.* dar golpes; hacer estrépito. —*adv.* de repente; de golpe.
bangle ('bæŋ·gəl) *n.m.* ajorca.
banish ('bæn·ɪʃ) *v.t.* **1** (exile) desterrar; proscribir. **2,** (dismiss) expulsar; expeler; desechar. —**banishment,** *n.* destierro; proscripción.
banister ('bæn·ɪs·tər) *n.* pasamano; barandal.
banjo ('bæn·dʒo) *n.* [*pl.* **-jos**] banjo. —**banjoist,** *n.* banjoísta.
bank (bæŋk) *n.* **1,** (mound; ridge) banco; loma; montón de tierra *o* nubes. **2,** (river edge) orilla; ribera; margen. **3,** (shoal) bajío. **4,** (financial establishment) banco. **5,** (row; tier) hilera; fila. **6,** *music* teclado. **7,** *aero.* inclinación lateral. **8,** *gambling* banca. **9,** (sloping curve, as of a road) peralte. —*v.t.* **1,** (pile up) amontonar; apilar. **2,** (dam; hold back, as water) represar. **3,** (cover, as a fire) cubrir; soterrar. **4,** (deposit in a bank) depositar *o* guardar en un banco. **5,** *aero.* ladear. —*v.i.* **1,** (engage in banking) ocuparse en banca; ser banquero. **2,** (maintain a bank account) tener su cuenta (en *o* con). —**bank on,** *colloq.* confiar en; contar con.
banker ('bæŋk·ər) *n.* banquero. —**banking,** *n.* banca.
banknote ('bæŋk·not) *n.* billete; billete de banco.
bankrupt ('bæŋk·rʌpt) *n.* & *adj.* quebrado; fallido; insolvente. —*v.t.* quebrar. —**bankruptcy,** *n.* bancarrota.
banner ('bæn·ər) *n.* **1,** (flag) bandera; enseña. **2,** (symbol; standard) estandarte; enseña. **3,** (newspaper headline) titular. —*adj.* sobresaliente; primero.
banns (bæːnz) *n.pl.* amonestaciones.
banquet ('bæŋ·kwɪt) *n.* banquete; festín. —*v.t.* & *i.* banquetear.
bantam ('bæn·təm) *n.* gallo Bantam; gallo de India.
banter ('bæn·tər) *n.* chanza; zumba. —*v.t.* chancearse con; chotearse de. —*v.i.* hacer zumba; chancear; chotear.
banyan ('bæn·jən) *n.* higuera india; baniano.
baptism ('bæp·tɪz·əm) *n.* bautismo.

—**baptismal** (-ˈtɪz·məl) *adj.* bautismal.
Baptist (ˈbæp·tɪst) *adj.* & *n.* bautista.
baptistery *también,* **baptistry** (ˈbæp·tɪst·ri) *n.* bautisterio; baptisterio.
baptize (ˈbæp·taiz) *v.t.* **1,** (consecrate) bautizar; cristianar. **2,** (name) poner nombre.
bar (baːr) *n.* **1,** (rod) barra; palanca. **2,** (crossbar; bolt) tranca. **3,** (obstruction) impedimento; obstáculo. **4,** [*también,* **barroom**] (place serving liquor) bar; cantina. **5,** (counter) mostrador. **6,** (lawyers collectively) abogacía. **7,** (tribunal) tribunal; foro. **8,** *music* barra. —*v.t.* [**barred, barring**] **1,** (block) impedir; prohibir. **2,** (close; bolt) cerrar; trancar. **3,** (shut out) excluir. —*prep.* con excepción de; excepto. —**bar none,** sin excepción.
barb (baːrb) *n.* **1,** (points bent backward, as on a fishhook) lengüeta; púa; punta. **2,** (beardlike growth) barba.
barbarian (barˈbɛr·i·ən) *adj.* & *n.* bárbaro. —**barbarism** (ˈbar·bə·rɪz·əm) *n.* barbarismo.
barbaric (barˈbær·ɪk) *adj.* barbárico; bárbaro.
barbarity (barˈbær·ə·ti) *n.* barbaridad.
barbarous (ˈbar·bə·rəs) *adj.* bárbaro. —**barbarousness,** *n.* barbaridad.
barbecue (ˈbar·bə·kju) *n.* barbacoa. —*v.t.* hacer barbacoa.
barbed (baːrbd) *adj.* **1,** (having a sharp point) erizado; barbado. **2,** *fig.* (stinging) punzante; mordaz. —**barbed wire,** alambrada.
barber (ˈbar·bər) *n.* barbero. —*v.t.* afeitar; hacer la barba a; cortar el pelo a. —**barber shop** [*también,* **barbershop,** *n.*] barbería; peluquería.
barbiturate (barˈbɪt·jʊˌreit) *n.* barbiturato. —**barbituric** (ˌbar·bɪ·ˈtjʊr·ɪk) *adj.* barbitúrico.
barcarole (ˈbar·kə·rol) *n.* barcarola.
bard (baːrd) *n.* bardo; juglar; poeta.
bare (beir) *adj.* **1,** (naked) desnudo; en cueros. **2,** (empty; unequipped) pelado; desnudo. **3,** (unadorned) simple; sencillo. **4,** (open to view) descubierto; público. **5,** (just sufficient) escaso; solo. —*v.t.* **1,** (uncover) desnudar; desposeer. **2,** (open to view) descubrir. —**bareness,** *n.* desnudez.
bareback *adj.* & *adv.* en pelo; sin silla.
barefaced (ˈbeir·feist) *adj.* descarado; insolente.
barefoot (ˈbeir·fʊt) *adj.* descalzo.
bareheaded *adj.* descubierto; en cabellos.
barely (ˈbeir·li) *adv.* **1,** (scarcely) apenas. **2,** (openly) abiertamente.
bargain (ˈbar·gən) *n.* **1,** (agreement) convenio; contrato. **2,** (advantageous purchase) ganga. —*v.i.* **1,** (discuss terms) negociar; tratar. **2,** (haggle) regatear. —*adj.* barato. —**bargain sale,** baratillo; barato; *Amer.* barata.
barge (baːrdʒ) *n.* gabarra; barcaza; lanchón. —*v.i.* moverse pesadamente. —**barge in,** entremeterse; irrumpir. —**barge into,** chocar con.
bari- (bær·ə) *prefijo* bari-; pesado: *baritone,* barítono.
baritone (ˈbær·ə·ton) *n.* & *adj.* barítono.
barium (ˈbær·i·əm) *n.* bario.
bark (baːrk) *n.* **1,** (cry of a dog, animal or person) ladrido. **2,** (tree covering) corteza. **3,** (small ship) barca; barqueta. —*v.i.* ladrar. —*v.t.* descortezar; desollar.
barker (ˈbar·kər) *n.* vociferador.
barley (ˈbar·li) *n.* cebada.
barmaid (ˈbar·med) *n.* camarera.
barman (ˈbar·mən) *n.* [*pl.* **-men**] cantinero; tabernero.
barn (baːrn) *n.* **1,** (storage place for fodder) almiar; pajar. **2,** (granary) granero; troj; troje. **3,** (stable) cuadra; establo. **4,** (depot; garage) cochera.
barnacle (ˈbar·nə·kəl) *n.* percebe.
barnyard *n.* corral.
baro- (bær·o) *prefijo* baro-; presión; peso: *barometer,* barómetro; *baroscope,* baroscopio.
barometer (bəˈram·ə·tər) *n.* barómetro. —**barometric** (ˌbæ·rə·ˈmɛt·rɪk) *adj.* barométrico.
baron (ˈbær·ən) *n.* barón. —**baroness,** *n.* baronesa. —**baronial** (bə·ˈro·ni·əl) *adj.* del barón. —**barony,** *n.* baronía.

baroque (bə'roːk) *n.* & *adj.* barroco.
barrack ('bær·ək) *n., usu.pl.* cuartel; barraca.
barracuda (ˌbær·ə'ku·də) *n.* barracuda.
barrage (bə'raːʒ) *n.* **1,** *mil.* cortina de fuego. **2,** *engin.* presa *o* dique (de contención).
barratry ('bær·ə·tri) *n.* baratería.
barrel ('bær·əl) *n.* barril; barrica; tonel. —**barrel organ,** organillo.
barren ('bær·ən) *adj.* estéril; árido; improductivo. —**barrenness,** *n.* esterilidad; aridez; improductividad.
barricade ('bær·ə·keid) *n.* **1,** (barrier) empalizada; cerca. **2,** *mil.* barricada; trinchera. —*v.t.* obstruir; impedir.
barring ('bar·iŋ) *prep.* con excepción de; excepto; salvo.
barrister ('bær·ɪs·tər) *n., Brit.* abogado.
barroom *n.* bar; cantina.
barrow ('bær·o) *n.* **1,** (hand barrow) angarillas. **2,** (wheelbarrow) carretón; carretilla. **3,** (burial mound) túmulo.
bartender ('baːrˌtɛn·dər) *n.* cantinero.
barter ('bar·tər) *v.t.* trocar; cambiar. —*v.i.* traficar. —*n.* trueque; cambio.
basal ('bei·səl) *adj.* basal.
bascule ('bæs·kjul) *n.* balanza oscilante; balancín. —**bascule bridge,** puente levadizo de contrapeso.
basalt (bə'sɔlt) *n.* basalto.
base (beis) *n.* **1,** (bottom) base; fondo. **2,** (fundamental) fundamento. **3,** *chem.; math.* base. **4,** (depot) base. **5,** *music* contrabajo; bajo grave. **6,** *baseball* base. —*v.t.* **1,** (found) establecer; poner base a. **2,** (establish as fact) basar; apoyar; fundamentar. —*adj.* **1,** (mean) bajo; ruin; vil. **2,** (low in rank) inferior; secundario. **3,** (almost worthless, esp. of metals) bajo de ley. —**baseness,** *n.* bajeza; vileza; ruindad. —**baseless,** *adj.* infundado. —**basely,** *adv.* bajamente. —**base metal,** metal común.
baseball ('beisˌbɔl) *n.* **1,** (game) béisbol. **2,** (ball) pelota.
baseboard ('beisˌbord) *n.* friso; zócalo.
basement ('beis·mənt) *n.* sótano.
bases ('be·siz) *n., pl. de* **basis.**
bashful ('bæʃ·fəl) *adj.* vergonzoso; tímido. —**bashfulness,** *n.* timidez; cortedad.
basic ('bei·sɪk) *adj.* **1,** (standard) básico; fundamental; corriente. **2,** *chem.* básico.
basil ('be·zəl) *n.* albahaca.
basilica (bə'sɪl·ə·kə) *n.* basílica.
basilisk ('bæs·ə·lɪsk) *n.* basilisco.
basin ('bei·sən) *n.* **1,** (bowl for liquids) palangana; jofaina; *W.I.* ponchera. **2,** (lowland) valle; cuenca; *Amer.* hoya. **3,** (pond; pool) estanque; represa. **4,** (hollow of a fountain) pilón.
basis ('bei·sɪs) *n.* [*pl.* **-ses** (-siz)] **1,** (fundamental principle) base; fundamento; principio. **2,** (chief ingredient) base; elemento principal.
bask (bæsk) *v.i.* calentarse. —**bask in the sun,** tomar el sol; asolearse.
basket ('bæs·kɪt) *n.* **1,** (small container) cesto; cesta; canasta. **2,** (large container) espuerta. **3,** *basketball* cesta.
basketball ('bæs·kɪtˌbɔl) *n.* baloncesto; básquetbol.
basketwork *n.* cestería.
basketry ('bæs·kɪt·ri) *n.* cestería.
Basque (bæsk) *adj.* & *n.* vasco; vascuence. —*n., l.c.* (blouse) blusa ajustada; jubón.
bas-relief ('ba·rəˌlif) *n.* bajorrelieve.
bass (beis) *adj.* & *n., music* bajo. —**bass clef,** clave de fa. —**bass drum,** bombo. —**bass viol** [*también,* **bass; double bass**] violón; contrabajo.
bass (bæs) *n.* **1,** *ichthy.* róbalo. **2,** = **basswood.**
basso ('bæs·o) *n., music* bajo.
bassoon (bæ'suːn) *n.* fagot; bajón. —**bassoonist,** *n.* fagotista; bajonista.
basswood *n.* tilo.
bastard ('bæs·tərd) *n.* bastardo. —*adj.* **1,** (of illegitimate birth) bastardo; ilegítimo. **2,** (impure) espurio; impuro; degenerado. —**bastardy,** *n.* bastardía.
bastardize ('bæs·tərd·aiz) *v.t.* **1,** (make bastard of) probar la bastardía de; bastardear. **2,** (debase) adulterar; degenerar; depravar.
baste (beist) *v.t.* **1,** (sew) embastar; hilvanar. **2,** (moisten meat)

untar *or* pringar la carne; lardear. 3, (beat) golpear con un palo. —**basting**, *n.* baste; basta.

bastion ('bæs·tʃən) *n.* bastión; baluarte.

bat (bæt) *n.* **1,** (heavy club) estaca; garrote. **2,** *sports* bate. **3,** *zoöl.* murciélago. —*v.t.* [**batted, batting**] **1,** *sports* batear. **2,** *colloq.* (blink) pestañear. —**go on a bat,** *slang* ir de parranda. —**go to bat for,** *colloq.* salir a la defensa de.

batch (bætʃ) *n.* **1,** (quantity made at one time) cochura; hornada. **2,** (mound of dough) masa. **3,** *slang* (lot) montón; cantidad.

bath (bæθ) *n.* **1,** (a washing) baño. **2,** (bathroom) cuarto de baño. **3,** *fig.* baño; inundación.

bathe (beið) *v.t.* bañar. —*v.i.* bañarse. —**bathing suit,** traje de baño.

bathhouse *n.* caseta de baños.

batho- (bæθ·o) *prefijo* bato-; profundo; profundidad: *bathometer,* batómetro.

bathrobe ('bæθ·rob) *n.* albornoz; bata de baño.

bathtub ('bæθ·tʌb) *n.* bañera; *Amer.* bañadera.

bathy- (bæθ·ɪ) *prefijo* bati-; profundo; profundidad: *bathysphere,* batisfera; *bathyscaphe,* batiscafo.

bathyscaphe ('bæθ·ɪˌskeif) *también,* **bathyscaph** (-ˌskæf) *n.* batiscafo.

bathysphere ('bæθ·ɪ·sfir) *n.* batisfera.

batiste (bə'tist) *n.* batista.

baton (bæ'tan) *n.* **1,** (symbol of authority) bastón de mando. **2,** *music* batuta.

battalion (bə'tæl·jən) *n., mil.* batallón.

batten ('bæt·ən) *v.i.* **1,** (overeat) engordar; cebar. **2,** (grow fat) engordar; engruesar; ponerse obeso. **3,** (thrive) medrar; prosperar. —*v.t.* **1,** (overfeed) cebar. **2,** *carpentry* construir con listones *o* latas. **3,** *naut.* (fasten with battens) tapar (las escotillas) con listones. —*n.* listón.

batter ('bæt·ər) *v.i.* & *t.* batir; golpear. —*n.* **1,** (dough) masa; pasta; batido. **2,** *baseball* bateador.

battery ('bæt·ə·ri) *n.* **1,** (for cars) batería; acumulador. **2,** (for flashlight) pila. **3,** *mil.* batería. **4,** *law* agresión.

batting ('bæt·ɪŋ) *n.* **1,** (stuffing) relleno. **2,** *baseball* bateo.

battle ('bæt·əl) *n.* batalla; lucha; pelea. —*v.i.* batallar; luchar; pelear. —*v.t.* luchar con.

battledore ('bæt·əlˌdor) *n.* raqueta. —**battledore and shuttlecock,** volante; raqueta y volante.

battlefield *también,* **battleground** *n.* campo de batalla.

battlement ('bæt·əl·mənt) *n.* muralla almenada.

battleship ('bæt·əl·ʃɪp) *n.* acorazado.

bauble ('bɔ·bəl) *n.* bagatela; chuchería; fruslería.

bauxite ('bɔks·ait) *n.* bauxita.

bawd (bɔːd) *n.* alcahueta.

bawdy ('bɔ·di) *adj.* indecente; obsceno; sucio. —**bawdiness,** *n.* obscenidad; indecencia.

bawl (bɔːl) *n.* **1,** (howl) berrido; bramido. **2,** *colloq.* (loud weeping) llanto. —*v.i.* gritar; vocear; chillar. —*v.t.* vocear. —**bawl out,** *colloq.* regañar; reprender.

bay (bei) *n.* **1,** (inlet) bahía. **2,** (protruding turret) mirador; ventana salediza; balcón. **3,** (niche; alcove) receso. **4,** *bot.* laurel. **5,** (animal bark) ladrido; aullido. **6,** (reddish-brown horse) caballo bayo. —*v.i.* ladrar; aullar. —**at bay,** acosado; acorralado. —**bay leaf,** hoja de laurel. —**bay rum,** ron con aceite esencial de laurel.

bayberry *n.* arrayán.

bayonet ('be·jə·nɛt) *n.* bayoneta. —*v.t.* cargar *o* herir a bayoneta.

bay window mirador; ventana salediza.

bazaar (bə'zaːr) *n.* bazar.

bazooka (bə'zu·kə) *n., mil.* cañón antitanques.

be (biː) *v.i. & copulativo* [*p.pr.* **being;** *p.p.* **been;** *pres. de ind.:* I **am,** thou **art** (*arcaico*), he, she, it **is,** we, you, they **are;** *pret.:* I, he, she, it **was,** we, you, they **were,** thou **wert** (*arcaico*), he, she, it **wast** (*arcaico*)] **1,** (expressing permanent condition; ownership; source; material; time; impersonal state) ser. **2,** (expressing temporary condition; location; date, etc.) estar.

be- (bi) *prefijo* **1,** *hállase en muchas palabras derivadas del anglo-sajón y apenas modifica el sentido: belong,* pertenecer. **2,** *forma verbos transitivos: belittle,* rebajar. **3,** *con algunos verbos expresa carácter pasivo o reflexivo: bemused,* pasmado. **4,** alrededor: *becloud,* oscurecer; *beset,* sitiar.

beach (bitʃ) *n.* playa; ribera. —*v.t.* varar.

beachhead ('bitʃ·hɛd) *n.* desembarco armado; cabeza de puente.

beacon ('bi·kən) *n.* faro; señal luminosa.

bead (biːd) *n.* **1,** (small ball) cuenta; abalorio. **2,** *pl.* (rosary) rosario (*sing.*). **3,** (bubble) gota; burbuja. **4,** (small globular body) glóbulo. —*v.t.* adornar con abalorios. —**draw a bead on,** apuntar con arma de fuego.

beadle ('bi·dəl) *n.* bedel. —**beadleship,** *n.* bedelía.

beagle ('bi·gəl) *n.* sabueso.

beak (bik) *n.* **1,** (of bird) pico. **2,** (of animal) hocico. **3,** *hist.* (prow of a warship) espolón.

beaker ('bi·kər) *n.* **1,** (drinking vessel) vaso; copa. **2,** *chem.* vaso picudo.

beam (biːm) *n.* **1,** (structural member) viga; vigueta. **2,** (crossbar) astil; brazo de balanza. **3,** *naut.* manga. **4,** (light ray) rayo de luz. **5,** (smile) sonrisa. —*v.i.* **1,** (shine brightly) destellar; irradiar. **2,** (smile warmly) rebosar (de alegría). —*v.t.* **1,** (shed light) emitir rayos de luz. **2,** *aero.* (guide by radio) dirigir por radio. —**on the beam,** *colloq.,* en el buen camino.

bean (biːn) *n.* habichuela; haba; judía; frijol.

bear (beːr) *v.t.* [**bore, borne**] **1,** (hold up) sostener. **2,** (support) soportar; llevar. **3,** (endure) aceptar; tolerar. **4,** (bring forward) producir; rendir. **5,** (possess) tener; poseer. **6,** (show) mostrar; enseñar. **7,** (exercise) ejercitar; desempeñar. **8,** (give birth) dar a luz; alumbrar; parir. —*v.i.* **1,** (remain firm) aguantar; soportar. **2,** (press) apretar; oprimir. **3,** (be productive) fructificar. **4,** (go in a given direction) llevar rumbo *o* dirección. —*n.* **1,** (animal) oso. **2,** *finance* bajista. —**bear down,** apretar; ejercer presión; hacer esfuerzo. —**bear in mind,** tener presente; recordar; tener en cuenta. —**bear off, 1,** (carry away) quitar; llevarse. **2,** *naut.* salvar; esquivar. —**bear on,** referirse a. —**bear out, 1,** (support) apoyar; sostener. **2,** (confirm) confirmar. —**bear up,** sostener; resistir. —**bear with,** tolerar; soportar; tener paciencia con.

bearable ('bɛr·ə·bəl) *adj.* soportable; tolerable.

beard (bɪːrd) *n.* **1,** (hair on the face) barba. **2,** (tuft of hair) mechón.

bearer ('bɛr·ər) *n.* **1,** (carrier) portador; dador; mensajero. **2,** (pallbearer) pilar. **3,** (productive tree) árbol fructífero.

bearing ('bɛr·iŋ) *n.* **1,** (behavior) comportamiento; modales; actuación. **2,** (ability to produce) fertilidad; producción. **3,** (support) apoyo; sostén; soporte. **4,** (relation of parts) conexión; relación. **5,** (compass direction) orientación. **6,** *pl.* (position) rumbo (*sing.*); posición (*sing.*). **7,** *archit.* apoyo; apuntalamiento. **8,** *mech.* cojinete.

beast (bist) *n.* bestia; animal; bruto. —**beastly,** *adj.* bestial; brutal; animal. —**beast of burden,** animal de carga. —**beast of prey,** animal de presa.

beat (bit) *v.t.* & *i.* [**beat, beaten, beating**] **1,** (strike repeatedly) golpear; sacudir. **2,** *colloq.,* (defeat) superar; vencer. —*v.t.* **1,** (overcome) sobrepasar; superar. **2,** (whip, as eggs or metal) batir. **3,** *music* marcar (el compás). **4,** *mil.* batir; abatir. **5,** (move the wings) aletear. **6,** (force) abrirse paso. —*v.i.* latir; palpitar. —*n.* **1,** (blow) golpe; sonido repetido. **2,** (throb) latido; palpitación; pulsación. **3,** (stress) fuerza; énfasis. **4,** (habitual path) ronda; recorrido.

beatify (bi'æt·ə·fai) *v.t.* beatificar. —**beatific** (ˌbi·ə'tɪf·ɪk) *adj.* beatífico. —**beatification** (-fɪ'kei·ʃən) *n.* beatificación.

beatitude (bi'æt·ə·tud) *n.* **1,** (bliss) beatitud; bienaventuranza. **2,** *cap., usu.pl., Bib.* Bienaventuranzas. **3,** *cap., R.C.Ch.* (title of the Pope) Beatitud.

beatnik ('bit·nɪk) *n., slang* bohemio.

beau (boː) *n.* [*pl.* **beaus, beaux**] **1,** (male admirer) galán. **2,** (fop) petimetre.

beauteous ('bju·ti·əs) *adj.* hermoso; bello. —**beauteousness,** *n.* belleza; hermosura; donaire.

beautician (bju'tɪʃ·ən) *n.* peluquero de señoras.

beautiful (ˈbju·tɪ·fəl) *adj.* hermoso; bello; encantador.
beautify (ˈbju·tɪ·fai) *v.t.* hermosear; embellecer; adornar. —*v.i.* hermosearse; acicalarse.
beauty (ˈbju·ti) n. belleza. —**beauty shop,** salón de belleza.
beaux (boːz) *n., pl. de* **beau.**
beaver (ˈbi·vər) *n.* **1,** *zool.* castor. **2,** (hat) castor. **3,** (high silk hat) sombrero de copa.
becalm (biˈkaːm) *v.t.* calmar; tranquilizar; sosegar. —**becalmed,** *adj., naut.* encalmado; al pairo.
because (biˈkɔːz) *conj.* porque; pues; puesto que. —*adv.* a causa de; por.
beck (bɛk) *n.* seña. —**at the beck and call of,** a disposición de; a las órdenes de.
beckon (ˈbɛk·ən) *v.t.* hacer señas a; llamar con señas. —*v.i.* hacer señas.
becloud (biˈklaud) *v.t.* obscurecer; anublar.
become (biˈkʌm) *v.i.* [**became, becoming**] convertirse en; hacerse. —*v.t.* quedar, sentar *o* caer bien. —**becoming,** *adj.* atractivo; apropiado; que cae bien.
bed (bɛːd) *n.* **1,** (furniture) lecho; cama. **2,** (foundation) cimientos (*pl.*). **3,** *geol.* capa; estrato. **4,** (bottom of a river, lake, etc.) madre; lecho. **5,** (plot for planting) tabla; cuadro. —*v.t.* [**bedded, -ding**] **1,** (put to bed) acostar; dar cama a. **2,** (place in a bed) asentar. —*v.i.* **1,** (go to bed) acostarse; descansar. **2,** (have sexual intercourse) cohabitar.
bedbug (ˈbɛd·bʌg) *n.* chinche.
bedchamber *n.* = **bedroom.**
bedclothes (ˈbɛdˌkloːz) *también,* **bedding** (ˈbɛd·ɪŋ) *n.* ropa de cama.
bedeck (biˈdɛk) *v.t.* decorar; adornar; engalanar.
bedevil (biˈdɛv·əl) *v.t.* **1,** (torment maliciously) enloquecer; maleficiar. **2,** (bewitch) embrujar. **3,** (harass) endiablar; atormentar.
bedfellow *n.* compañero de cama.
bedlam (ˈbɛd·ləm) *n.* **1,** (lunatic asylum) manicomio. **2,** *fig.* (uproar) confusión; desbarajuste; babel.
Bedouin (ˈbɛ·du·ɪn) *n.* & *adj.* beduino.
bedpan *n.* chata.
bedridden (ˈbɛd·rɪd·ən) *adj.* imposibilitado; postrado en cama.
bedrock *n.* lecho de roca.
bedroom *también,* **bedchamber** *n.* alcoba; dormitorio; *Mex.* recámara.
bedside *n.* lado de cama.
bedspread (ˈbɛd·sprɛd) *n.* cubrecama; colcha.
bedspring *n.* colchón de muelles; sommier.
bedstead (ˈbɛd·stɛd) *n.* cuja; armazón de cama.
bedtime (ˈbɛd·taim) *n.* hora de dormir.
bee (biː) *n.* **1,** (insect) abeja. **2,** (social gathering) reunión; tertulia.
beech (bitʃ) *n.* haya. —**beechen** (-ən) *adj.* de haya.
beechnut *n.* hayuco; nuez de haya.
beef (bif) *n.* **1,** (meat) carne de res. **2,** [*pl.* **beeves**] (steer) novillo. **3,** *colloq.* (muscle) fuerza; músculo. **4,** *colloq.* (complaint) queja. —*v.i., colloq.* quejarse; dar quejas. —**beefy,** *adj.* muscular. —**beef tea,** caldo de res. —**roast beef,** rosbif.
beefsteak *n.* bistec.
beekeeping *n.* apicultura. —**beekeeper,** *n.* apicultor.
been (bɪn) *v., p.p. de* **be.**
beep (bip) *n.* señal de bocina o de diversos aparatos.
beer (bɪr) *n.* **1,** (alcoholic) cerveza. **2,** (non-alcoholic) gaseosa.
beet (bit) *n.* remolacha.
beetle (ˈbi·təl) *n.* **1,** (insect) escarabajo. **2,** (mallet) mazo. **3,** *slang* (slow racehorse) jamelgo. —*v.t.* martillar con un mazo. —*v.i.* sobresalir.
beeves (biːvz) *n., pl. de* **beef.**
befall (biˈfɔl) *v.i.* suceder; ocurrir; acontecer. —*v.t.* suceder *o* pasar a.
befit (biˈfɪt) *v.t.* [**befitted, -ting**] cuadrar; convenir; acomodarse a.
before (biˈfoːr) *prep.* **1,** (earlier than) antes de *o* que. **2,** (in front of) delante de; enfrente de. **3,** (in presence of) ante; frente a. **4,** (in preference to) antes que. —*conj.* **1,** (previous to) primero que. **2,** (rather than) antes que. —*adv.* **1,** (ahead) antes; delante. **2,** (previously) previamente; anteriormente. —**beforehand,** *adv.* de antemano; con antelación.
befriend (biˈfrɛnd) *v.t.* **1,** (act as a friend to) tener amistad con; brindar amistad a. **2,** (favor) favorecer; patrocinar; proteger.

befuddle (bi'fʌd·əl) *v.t.* aturdir; confundir.
beg (bɛg) *v.t.* [**begged, begging**] rogar; suplicar; pedir. —*v.i.* **1,** (ask for alms) pedir limosna. **2,** (live by asking alms) mendigar.
began (bɪ'gæn) *v., pret. de* **begin.**
begat (bi'gæt) *v., arcaico, pret. de* **beget.**
beget (bi'gɛt) *v.t.* [**begot, begot** *o* **begotten, begetting**] **1,** (procreate) engendrar; procrear. **2,** (result in) causar; resultar en.
beggar ('bɛg·ər) *n.* limosnero; pordiosero. —*v.t.* empobrecer; arruinar. —**beggary,** *n.* mendicidad.
begin (bɪ'gɪn) *v.t.* [**began, begun, beginning**] comenzar; empezar; iniciar. —*v.i.* **1,** (come into existence) nacer; tomar forma. **2,** (arise) levantarse; surgir. —**beginner,** *n.* principiante; novicio.
beginning (bɪ'gɪn·ɪŋ) *n.* **1,** (early stage) comienzo; fuente. **2,** (origin) principio; origen.
begone (bi'gaːn) *interj.* fuera; afuera. —*v.i., en el imperativo,* irse; marcharse.
begonia (bɪ'go·ni·ə) *n.* begonia.
begot (bi'gat) *v., pret. & p.p. de* **beget.**
begotten (bi'gat·ən) *v., p.p. de* **beget.**
begrime (bi'graim) *v.t.* embarrar; enlodar; encenagar.
begrudge (bi'grʌdʒ) *v.t.* **1,** (be disinclined to) refunfuñar; rezongar. **2,** (envy) envidiar; codiciar.
beguile (bi'gail) *v.t.* **1,** (delude) defraudar; engañar. **2,** (divert) divertir; entretener. —**beguilement,** *n.* engaño.
begun (bɪ'gʌn) *v., p.p. de* **begin.**
behalf (bi'hæːf) *n.* interés; favor. —**in, on** *o* **upon behalf of,** por; en *o* a nombre de; en *o* a favor de.
behave (bi'heiv) *v.i.* **1,** (conduct oneself) comportarse; conducirse. **2,** (act) proceder; actuar.
behavior (bi'heiv·jər) *n.* comportamiento; conducta; modales.
behaviorism (bi'heiv·jər·ɪz·əm) *n.* behaviorismo. —**behaviorist,** *n.* & *adj.* behaviorista. —**behavioristic,** *adj.* behaviorista.
behead (bi'hɛːd) *v.t.* decapitar; degollar.
beheld (bi'hɛld) *v., pret. & p.p. de* **behold.**
behemoth ('bi·ə·məθ; bə'hi-) *n.* bestia colosal; cualquier cosa enorme; *Bib.* behemot.
behind (bi'haind) *prep.* **1,** (in the rear of) detrás de; tras. **2,** (inferior to) después de; tras; inferior a. **3,** (later than) más tarde que *o* de. —*adv.* **1,** (toward the back) detrás; atrás. **2,** (slow) con atraso; retrasadamente. —*adj.* atrasado; retrasado.
behindhand (bi'haind·hænd) *adv.* atrasadamente; con retraso.
behold (bi'hold) *v.t.* [**beheld, beholding**] observar; mirar; vigilar. —*interj.* ¡he aquí!; ¡aquí está!
behoove (bi'huːv) *v.i. impers.* **1,** (be fitting) corresponder a; cuadrar a. **2,** (be necessary) corresponder; necesitar; tocar.
being ('bi·ɪŋ) *n.* **1,** (existence) existencia; vida. **2,** (a human) ser; ente; criatura. —*v., p.pr. de* **be.**
bejewel (bi'ju·əl) *v.t.* enjoyar; alhajar.
belabor (bi'lei·bər) *v.t.* **1,** (thump) apalear; dar de puñadas. **2,** (scold) criticar; acusar.
belated (bi'lei·tɪd) *adj.* retrasado; demorado; tardío.
belch (bɛltʃ) *v.i.* **1,** (eructate) eructar; regoldar. **2,** (spurt) vomitar. —*v.t.* vomitar; despedir. —*n.* eructo; regüeldo.
beleaguer (bi'li·gər) *v.t.* sitiar; asediar; bloquear.
belfry ('bɛl·fri) *n.* campanario.
Belgian ('bɛl·dʒən) *adj.* & *n.* belga.
belie (bi'lai) *v.t.* **1,** (misrepresent) mentir; engañar. **2,** (disguise) disfrazar; falsear. **3,** (contradict) contradecir; desmentir.
belief (bi'lif) *n.* creencia; convicción.
believe (bi'liːv) *v.t.* & *i.* creer. —**believable,** *adj.* creíble. —**believer,** *n.* creyente.
belittle (bi'lɪt·əl) *v.t.* rebajar; disminuir; atenuar.
bell (bɛl) *n.* **1,** (device emitting sound) campana. **2,** *electricity* timbre. **3,** *naut.* campanada. —*v.i.* crecer *o* hincharse como campana. —*v.t.* poner campana a.
belladonna (bɛl·ə'dan·ə) *n.* belladona.
bellboy *n.* botones. *También,* **bellhop.**
bellflower *n.* campanilla.
bellicose ('bɛl·ə·kos) *adj.* belicoso; beligerante. —**bellicosity** (-'kas·ə·ti) *n.* belicosidad.

belligerent (bəˈlɪdʒ·ə·rənt) *adj.* **1,** (pert. to war) beligerante. **2,** (bellicose) belicoso; peleante. **3,** (at war) beligerante; en guerra. —*n.* beligerante. —**belligerence,** *n.* beligerancia.

bellow (ˈbɛ·lo) *v.i.* & *t.* rugir; bramar; mugir. —*n.* bramido; alarido.

bellows (ˈbɛ·loz) *n.* fuelle.

belly (ˈbɛl·i) *n.* **1,** (stomach) vientre; abdomen; estómago. **2,** (the inside of anything) entrañas. —*v.i.* hartarse; hincharse. —*v.t.* inflar; hinchar.

belong (biˈlɔːŋ) *v.i.* pertenecer. —**belong to,** pertenecer a; ser de. —**belong with** *o* **among,** pertenecer a.

belongings (biˈlɔŋ·ɪŋz) *n.pl.* posesiones; pertenencias; propiedad (*sing.*).

beloved (bɪˈlʌv·ɪd) *n.* & *adj.* amado; querido.

below (biˈloː) *adv.* **1,** (in a lower place) abajo; debajo. **2,** (coming later in a writing) más adelante; más abajo. —*prep.* **1,** (under) bajo. **2,** (beneath) bajo; *o* debajo de. **3,** (inferior to) después de.

belt (bɛlt) *n.* **1,** (strap) correa; cinturón. **2,** *geog.* zona. **3,** *slang* (blow) porrazo; zurra. **4,** *slang* (swig) trago. —*v.t.* **1,** (gird) ceñir. **2,** *slang* (beat) aporrear; zurrar.

bemire (biˈmair) *v.t.* enlodar; embarrar.

bemoan (biˈmoːn) *v.t.* deplorar; lamentar.

bemused (biˈmjuːzd) *adj.* confundido; aturdido.

bench (bɛntʃ) *n.* **1,** (seat) banco; asiento. **2,** *law* judicatura. **3,** (shelf) estante; tabla.

bend (bɛnd) *v.t.* [*pret.* & *p.p.* **bent**] **1,** (curve) doblar; combar. **2,** (turn) doblar. **3,** (force into submission) doblegar; vencer; doblar. —*v.i.* **1,** (become curved) doblarse; combarse. **2,** (yield) someterse; doblegarse. —*n.* **1,** (curve) curva; curvatura; codo. **2,** *naut.* nudo. **3,** *pl.* (sickness) calambres.

beneath (biˈniθ) *adv.* debajo; abajo. —*prep.* bajo; debajo de.

Benedictine (bɛn·əˈdɪk·tɪn; -tin) *adj.* & *n.* benedictino.

benediction (bɛn·əˈdɪk·ʃən) *n.* bendición.

benefaction (bɛn·əˈfæk·ʃən) *n.* **1,** (good deed) beneficencia; bondad. **2,** (benefit; charity) beneficio; merced; gracia. —**benefactor,** n. benefactor; bienhechor.

benefice (ˈbɛn·ə·fɪs) *n.* beneficio.

beneficent (bəˈnɛf·ɪ·sənt) *adj.* benéfico; caritativo. —**beneficence,** *n.* beneficencia; caridad.

beneficial (bɛn·əˈfɪʃ·əl) *adj.* beneficioso; benéfico; provechoso.

beneficiary (bɛn·əˈfɪʃ·i·ɛr·i) *n.* beneficiario.

benefit (ˈbɛn·ə·fɪt) *n.* **1,** (profit) beneficio; utilidad. **2,** (kind act) beneficio; ventaja. **3,** *theat.* función de beneficio; beneficio. —*v.i.* [**-fitted, -ting**] beneficiarse; aprovecharse. —*v.t.* beneficiar; aprovechar; mejorar.

benevolent (bəˈnɛv·ə·lənt) *adj.* benévolo; bondadoso. —**benevolence** (-ləns) *n.* benevolencia.

benign (biˈnain) *adj.* **1,** (gracious) gracioso; benigno. **2,** (favorable) propicio; favorable. **3,** *med.* ligero; leve; benigno. —**benignity** (biˈnɪg·nə·ti) *n.* benignidad; dulzura.

benignant (biˈnig·nənt) *adj.* bondadoso; afable. —**benignancy,** *n.* benignidad; bondad; afabilidad.

bent (bɛnt) *adj.* **1,** (curved) doblado; curvado. **2,** (determined) decidido; resuelto. —*n.* tendencia; inclinación. —*v., pret.* & *p.p. de* **bend.**

benumb (biˈnʌm) *v.t.* entumecer; paralizar.

benzedrine (ˈbɛn·zəˌdrin) *n.* bencedrina.

benzene (ˈbɛn·zin) *n.* benceno.

benzine (ˈbɛn·zin) *n.* bencina.

benzoate (ˈbɛn·zo·ət) *n.* benzoato.

benzoic (bɛnˈzo·ɪk) *adj.* benzoico.

benzoin (ˈbɛn·zo·ɪn) *n.* benjuí.

benzol (ˈbɛn·zol) *n.* benzol.

bequeath (biˈkwiθ) *v.t.* legar; dejar (en testamento).

bequest (biˈkwɛst) *n.* legado; donación.

berate (biˈreit) *v.t.* regañar; reñir; reprender.

Berber (ˈbʌɹ·bər) *n.* & *adj.* bereber; berberí.

bereave (biˈriːv) *v.t.* [*pret.* & *p.p. a veces* **bereft**] despojar; desposeer; arrebatar.

bereavement *n.* **1,** (deprivation) despojo; privación. **2,** (loss through death) aflicción; duelo; luto.

bereft (biˈrɛft) *v., p.p. de* **bereave.**

—*adj.* despojado; privado; desposeído.
beret (bə'rei) *n.* boina.
beriberi ('bɛr·i'bɛr·i) *n.* beriberi.
berkelium ('bʌɹk·li·əm) *n.* berkelio.
berry ('bɛr·i) *n.* baya; grano. —*v.i.* echar bayas. —*v.t.* recoger *o* coger bayas.
berserk (bər'sʌɹk) *adj.* frenético; colérico.
berth (bʌɹθ) *n.* **1,** (bed on a train or ship) camarote. **2,** (bunk) litera. **3,** (dock) amarradero. **4,** (job) empleo; trabajo. —*v.t.* **1,** dar litera *o* empleo. **2,** *naut.* atracar. —*v.i.* tener *u* ocupar una litera.
beryl ('bɛr·əl) *n.* berilo.
beryllium (bə'rɪ·li·əm) *n.* berilio.
beseech (bi'sitʃ) *v.t.* [*pret.* & *p.p.* **besought**] suplicar; rogar; implorar.
beset (bi'sɛt) *v.t.* [**beset, besetting**] **1,** (attack) sitiar; acosar; rodear. **2,** (harass) importunar; fastidiar; fatigar.
beside (bi'said) *prep.* **1,** (at the side of) al lado de; junto a. **2,** (near) cerca de. **3,** [*también,* **besides**] (in addition to) además de. **4,** (unconnected with) aparte de. —*adv.* [*también,* **besides**] **1,** (moreover) además; también. **2,** (in addition) aparte; por otra parte. —**beside oneself,** loco; fuera de sí.
besiege (bi'si:dʒ) *v.t.* **1,** (lay siege to) asediar; sitiar. **2,** (harass) asediar; demandar; acosar.
besmirch (bi'smʌɹtʃ) *v.t.* manchar; escarnecer.
besotted (bi'sat·ɪd) *adj.* **1,** (foolish) embrutecido; entontecido. **2,** (intoxicated) embriagado; emborrachado.
besought (bi'sɔt) *v., pret.* & *p.p. de* **beseech.**
best (bɛst) *adj., superl. de* **good;** óptimo; mejor; superior. —*adv., superl. de* **well;** bien; mejor. —*n.* lo sumo; lo más; lo mayor: lo mejor. —*v.t.* derrotar; vencer; ganar. —**at best,** a lo más; a lo mejor —**get the best of, 1,** (outdo) vencer; ganar. **2,** (outwit) ser más listo que; sobrepasar a. —**make the best of,** aprovecharse de. —**best man,** padrino de boda. —**best seller,** el de más venta; éxito de librería.
bestial ('bɛs·tʃəl) *adj.* **1,** (beastlike) brutal; irracional. **2,** (pert. to beasts) bestial. —**bestiality,** *n.* bestialidad; brutalidad.
bestow (bi'sto:) *v.t.* **1,** (give) dar; conferir; otorgar. **2,** (give in marriage) dar *o* entregar en matrimonio. —**bestowal,** *n.* dádiva; donación.
bestride (bi'straid) *v.t.* [**bestrode, bestridden**] **1,** (straddle) montar a horcajadas. **2,** (step over) cruzar de un salto; saltar a.
bet (bɛt) *v.t.* & *i.* [**bet, betting**] apostar. —*n.* apuesta; envite. —**better; bettor,** *n.* apostador.
beta ('be·tə) *n.* beta.
betake (bi'teik) *v.t., usu.refl.* irse; marcharse; dirigirse.
betel ('bi·təl) *n.* betel. —**betel nut,** fruto del betel.
betide (bi'taid) *v.i.* acontecer; suceder; pasar. —*v.t.* indicar; presagiar.
betoken (bi'to·kən) *v.t.* señalar; representar; denotar.
betray (bi'trei) *v.t.* traicionar; denunciar. —**betrayal** (-əl) *n.* traición; denuncia.
betroth (bi'trɔθ; bi'tro:ð) *v.t.* desposar; contraer esponsales; prometer en matrimonio. —**betrothal,** *n.* desposorios (*pl.*); esponsales (*pl.*); compromiso. —**betrothed,** *n.* novio; prometido.
better ('bɛt·ər) *adj., comp. de* **good;** mejor. —*adv., comp. de* **well;** mejor; más bien. —*v.t.* **1,** (improve) mejorar. **2,** (surpass) aventajar. —*v.i.* mejorarse. —*n.* **1,** (superior thing) lo mejor. **2,** (superior person) el mejor. **3,** (advantage) ventaja; superioridad. —**get the better of, 1,** (outdo) sobrepasar a. **2,** (outwit) ser más listo que. —**think better of,** considerar; reconsiderar. —**better oneself,** mejorar; adelantar. —**betterment,** *n.* mejora; mejoría.
between (bi'twi:n) *prep.* entre. —*adv.* en medio; entremedias.
bevel ('bɛv·əl) *n.* **1,** (instrument) cartabón. **2,** (angle) ángulo agudo *u* obtuso. **3,** (sloping part) bisel; chaflán. —*v.i.* & *t.* biselar; achaflanar. —*adj.* biselado; oblicuo.
beverage ('bɛv·ər·ɪdʒ) *n.* bebida.
bevy ('bɛv·i) *n.* bandada.
bewail (bi'weil) *v.t.* & *i.* lamentar.
beware (bi'we:r) *v.i.* precaverse; guardarse. —*v.t.* vigilar; tener cuidado con.
bewilder (bi'wɪl·dər) *v.t.* confundir; aturdir; aturullar. —**bewilder-**

ment, *n.* aturdimiento; perplejidad.
bewitch (bi'wɪtʃ) *v.t.* **1,** (charm) encantar; fascinar; hechizar. **2,** (cast a spell upon) embrujar; maleficiar. —**bewitching,** *adj.* encantador; hechicero.
beyond (bi'ja:nd) *adv.* más lejos; más allá. —*prep.* tras; superior a; más allá de.
bi- (bai) *prefijo* bi-. **1,** dos: *biconvex,* biconvexo. **2,** dos veces: *biyearly,* semestral; dos veces al año. **3,** una vez de cada dos: *bimonthly,* bimestral. **4,** doble: *bicephalous,* bicéfalo.
bias ('bai·əs) *n.* **1,** (oblique direction) oblicuidad; inclinación. **2,** (prejudice) prejuicio; propensión. —*v.t.* prejuzgar; predisponer; inclinar. —*adj.* inclinado; sesgado; diagonal.
bib (bɪb) *n.* babero.
Bible ('bai·bəl) *n.* Biblia. —**Biblical** ('bɪb·lɪ·kəl) *adj.* bíblico.
biblio- (bɪb·li·o) *prefijo* **1,** biblio-; libro: *bibliography,* bibliografía. **2,** Biblia: *bibliolatry,* adoración de la Biblia.
bibliography (ˌbɪb·li'ag·rə·fi) *n.* bibliografía. —**bibliographical** (-ə'græf·ɪ·kəl) *adj.* bibliográfico.
bibliomania (bɪb·li·o'mei·ni·ə) *n.* bibliomanía. —**bibliomaniac** (-æk) *n.* bibliómano.
bibliophile ('bɪb·li·o·fail) *n.* bibliófilo.
bibulous ('bɪb·jə·ləs) *adj.* **1,** (highly absorbent) poroso; absorbente. **2,** (addicted to liquor) borrachín; bebedor. —**bibulousness,** *n.* porosidad; absorbencia.
bicameral (bai'kæm·ər·əl) *adj.* bicameral; de dos cámaras legislativas.
bicarbonate of soda (bai'kar·bə·nət) bicarbonato de soda.
bicentennial (bai·sɛn'tɛn·i·əl) *n.* & *adj.* bicentenario.
biceps ('bai·sɛps) *n.* bíceps.
bichloride (bai'klo·raid) *n.* bicloruro.
bicker ('bɪk·ər) *n.* altercado; camorra. —*v.i.* argumentar; disputar.
bicolor ('bai,kʌl·ər) *adj.* bicolor. *También,* **bicolored.**
bicuspid (bai'kʌs·pɪd) *adj.* bicúspide. —*n.* gran molar.
bicycle ('bai·sɪk·əl) *n.* bicicleta.
bid (bɪd) *v.t.* **[bade, bidden, -ding] 1,** (command) mandar; ordenar. **2,** [*pret.* & *p.p.* **bid]** (invite) invitar; convidar. **3,** (offer a price of) proponer; ofrecer. —*v.i.* pujar. —*n.* **1,** (offer) oferta; postura; puja. **2,** (attempt) ensayo; prueba. **3,** (invitation) invitación; oferta. —**bidder,** *n.* postor; licitador; pujador.
bidding *n.* **1,** (command) orden; mandato. **2,** (request) ruego; favor. **3,** *cards or auction* apuesta; puja; (in bridge) remate.
bide (baid) *v.t.* **[bided *o* bode, biding]** aguantar; soportar. —*v.i.* **1,** (dwell) residir; vivir. **2,** (stay) continuar; permanecer. **3,** (wait) esperar; aguardar.
biennial (bai'ɛn·i·əl) *adj.* bienal. —**biennium** (-əm) *n.* bienio.
bier (bɪr) *n.* túmulo; estrado funeral.
bifocal (bai'fo·kəl) *adj.* bifocal. —**bifocals,** *n.pl.* bifocales.
bifurcate ('bai·fər,keit) *adj.* [*también,* **bifurcated]** bifurcado. —*v.i.* bifurcarse. —*v.t.* dividir en dos ramales. —**bifurcation,** *n.* bifurcación.
big (bɪg) *adj.* **[bigger, -gest] 1,** (large) grande; enorme. **2,** (important) importante; principal; sobresaliente. **3,** (generous) generoso; magnánimo. **4,** (fullgrown) mayor. —**big game, 1,** (hunting) caza mayor. **2,** *colloq.* empresa peligrosa.
bigamist ('bɪg·ə·mɪst) *n.* bígamo.
bigamy ('bɪg·ə·mi) *n.* bigamia. —**bigamous** (-məs) *adj.* bígamo.
big-hearted *adj.* de gran corazón; generoso.
bigot ('bɪg·ət) *n.* intolerante; fanático; beatón. —**bigoted,** *adj.* fanático. —**bigotry,** *n.* fanatismo; intolerancia.
bigwig ('bɪg·wɪg) *n., colloq.* persona importante; pájaro de cuenta.
bilateral (bai'læt·ər·əl) *adj.* bilateral.
bile (bail) *n.* **1,** (secretion) bilis. **2,** (peevishness) cólera; mal humor; mal genio.
bilge (bɪldʒ) *n.* **1,** *naut.* pantoque. **2,** (bulge of a barrel) barriga. **3,** *slang* (nonsense) tontería. —**bilge water,** agua de pantoque.
bilingual (bai'lɪŋ·gwəl) *adj.* bilingüe. —**bilingualism,** *n.* bilingüismo.
bilious ('bɪl·jəs) *adj.* bilioso. —**biliousness,** *n.* biliosidad.
-bility ('bɪl·ə·ti) *sufijo* -bilidad;

forma nombres de los adjetivos con terminaciones **-ble, -able** *e* **-ible:** *solubility,* solubilidad; *ability,* habilidad; *responsibility,* responsabilidad.

bill (bɪl) *n.* **1,** (account of money owed) factura; cuenta. **2,** *comm.* letra; giro; pagaré. **3,** (money) billete. **4,** (proposed law) proyecto de ley. **5,** (handbill) prospecto; aviso. **6,** *theat.* espectáculo; representación. **7,** (beak) pico. —*v.t.* **1,** (send a bill to) facturar. **2,** (enter on a bill) entrar; cargar; adeudar. **3,** *theat.* anunciar. —**bill and coo,** arrullarse. —**bill of fare,** menú. —**bill of sale,** escritura de venta. —**bill of lading,** conocimiento de embarque.

billboard ('bɪl,bord) *n.* cartelera.

billet ('bɪl·ɪt) *n.* **1,** *mil.* cuartel; alojamiento militar. **2,** (assignment) trabajo; tarea; empleo. **3,** (ticket) billete; boleto; entrada. **4,** (written note) billete; esquela. **5,** (stick) zoquete de leña. —*v.t.* **1,** *mil.* alojar; aposentar. **2,** (assign) designar; señalar.

billet-doux ('bɪl·i'du:) *n.* [*pl.* **billets-doux** ('bɪl·i'du:z)] esquela amorosa.

billfold *n.* cartera; *Amer.* billetera.

billiards ('bɪl·jərdz) *n.* billar. —**billiard,** *n.* carambola.

billing ('bɪl·ɪŋ) *n., theat.* elenco; reparto.

billion ('bɪl·jən) *n.* (*U.S.*) mil millones; (*Brit.*) un millón de millones; billón. —**billionaire** (-jə·'ne:r) *n.* billonario. —**billionth,** *adj.* & *n.* (*U.S.*) mil millonésimo; (*Brit.*) billonésimo.

billow ('bɪl·o) *n.* ola; oleada. —*v.i.* crecer *o* hincharse como ola. —**billowy,** *adj.* hinchado como ola.

billygoat ('bɪl·i,got) *n.* macho cabrío; cabrón.

bimonthly (bai'mʌnθ·li) *adj.* bimestral; bimestre. —*adv.* bimestralmente.

bin (bɪn) *n.* depósito; hucha; arca.

bin- (bɪn; bain) *prefijo, var. de* **bi-:** *binocular,* binocular.

binary ('bai·nə·ri) *adj.* binario.

bind (baind) *v.t.* [*pret.* & *p.p.* **bound**] **1,** (tie) atar; ligar; apretar. **2,** (wrap) envolver. **3,** (bandage) vendar. **4,** (hem) ribetear; galonear. **5,** (obligate) obligar; precisar; exigir. —*v.i.* **1,** (cohere) pegarse; endurecerse. **2,** (be necessary) ser obligatorio.

binder ('bain·dər) *n.* **1,** (wrapper) atador; encuadernador. **2,** (cord) atadura; lazo. **3,** (adhesive) adhesivo; pegante. —**bindery,** *n.* taller de encuadernación.

binding ('bain·dɪŋ) *n.* **1,** (fastening; wrapping) ligadura; faja; venda. **2,** (covering of a book) encuadernación.

binnacle ('bɪn·ə·kəl) *n.* bitácora.

binocular (bɪ'nak·jə·lər) *adj.* binocular. —**binoculars,** *n.pl.* anteojos; gemelos.

binomial (bai'no·mi·əl) *adj.* binómico. —*n.* binomio.

bio- (bai·o) *prefijo* bio-; vida: *biography,* biografía; *biology,* biología.

biochemistry (,bai·o'kɛm·ɪs·tri) *n.* bioquímica. —**biochemical,** *adj.* bioquímico. —**biochemist,** *n.* bioquímico.

biography (bai'ag·rə·fi) *n.* biografía. —**biographer,** *n.* biógrafo. —**biographical** (,bai·ə'græf·ɪ·kəl) *adj.* biográfico.

biology (bai'al·ə·dʒi) *n.* biología. —**biological** (-ə'ladʒ·ɪ·kəl) *adj.* biológico. —**biologist** (-'al·ə·dʒɪst) *n.* biólogo.

biopsy ('bai·ap·si) *n.* biopsia.

-biosis (bi'o·sɪs) *sufijo* -biosis; medios de vida *o* subsistencia: *symbiosis,* simbiosis.

bipartisan (bai'par·tɪ·zən) *adj.* de dos (*o* ambos) partidos políticos.

biped ('bai·pɛd) *n.* bípedo. —*adj.* bípede; bípedo.

biplane ('bai·plein) *n.* biplano.

birch (bʌɹtʃ) *n.* abedul. —*v.t.* varear.

bird (bʌɹd) *n.* ave; pájaro. —**bird's-eye,** *adj.* general; global; superficial. —**bird shot,** perdigón.

biretta (bə'rɛt·ə) *n.* birreta.

birth (bʌɹθ) *n.* **1,** (act of being born) nacimiento; alumbramiento. **2,** (descent) linaje; ascendencia; descendencia. **3,** (beginning) origen; principio.

birth control control de los nacimientos.

birthday ('bʌɹθ·dei) *n.* cumpleaños.

birthmark ('bʌɹθ·mark) *n.* marca de nacimiento.

birthplace ('bʌɹθ·pleis) *n.* sitio o lugar de nacimiento.
birthright ('bʌɹθ·rait) *n.* **1,** (rights conferred by birth) derechos de nacimiento. **2,** (right of the first-born) primogenitura.
bis- (bɪs) *prefijo, var. de* **bi-** *ante vocal o* s: *bisaxillary,* biaxilar; *bissextile,* bisiesto.
Biscayan (bɪs'kei·ən) *adj.* & *n.* vizcaíno.
biscuit ('bɪs·kɪt) *n.* galleta; bizcocho.
bisect (bai'sɛkt) *v.* bisecar. —**bisection** (-'sɛk·ʃən) *n.* bisección.
bisector (bai'sɛk·tər) *n.* bisectriz. *También,* **bisectrix** (-trɪks) [*pl.* **-trices** (-'trai·siz)].
bishop ('bɪ·ʃəp) *n.* **1,** *eccles.* obispo. **2,** *chess* alfil. —**bishopric** (-rɪk) *n.* obispado.
bismuth ('bɪz·məθ) *n.* bismuto.
bison ('bai·sən) *n.* bisonte.
bisque (bɪsk) *n.* **1,** (thick soup) sopa espesa. **2,** *ceramics* bizcocho. **3,** *games* (handicap) ventaja.
bissextile (bɪ'sɛks·tɪl) *adj.* bisiesto.
bit (bɪt) *v., pret. de* **bite.** —*n.* **1,** (small piece) pizca; trocito; ardite. **2,** (small coin) monedita. **3,** (mouthpiece) bocado del freno. **4,** (tool) taladro; hoja.
bitch (bɪtʃ) *n.* **1,** (dog) perra. **2,** (malicious woman) ramera. **3,** *slang* (complaint) queja. —*v.i., slang* quejarse. —*v.t., slang* estropear; chapucear.
bite (bait) *v.t.* [**bit, bitten, biting**] **1,** (grip with the teeth) morder; mordiscar; picar. **2,** (grasp) apresar; agarrar. **3,** (corrode) comer; corroer. —*v.i.* **1,** (take a bait) picar. **2,** (be duped) ser engañado. **3,** (take hold) hacer presa. —*n.* **1,** (act or effect of biting) mordedura; picadura. **2,** (small piece) mordisco. **3,** *slang* (extortion) exacción; extorsión. **4,** *slang* (graft) concusión; *Amer.* mordida.
bitten ('bɪt·ən) *v., p.p. de* **bite.**
bitter ('bɪt·ər) *adj.* **1,** (harsh-tasting) amargo; áspero. **2,** *fig.* (grievous) doloroso; penoso; desagradable. **3,** *fig.* (piercing) mordaz. **4,** *fig.* (severe) encarnizado. —**bitters,** *n.pl.* licor amargo (*sing.*) —**to the bitter end,** hasta la muerte; hasta el extremo.
bittern ('bɪt·ərn) *n.* avetoro.
bitterness ('bɪt·ər·nəs) *n.* **1,** (harsh taste) amargura; amargor. **2,** (grief) dolor; pena. **3,** (severity) encarnizamiento.
bittersweet *adj.* & *n.* agridulce.
bitumen (bɪ'tu·mən) *n.* betún; —**bituminous** (-mɪn·əs) *adj.* bituminoso.
bivalent (bai'vei·lənt) *adj.* bivalente. —**bivalence,** *n.* bivalencia.
bivalve ('bai·vælv) *n.* & *adj.* bivalvo.
bivouac ('bɪv·wæk) *n.* vivac; vivaque. —*v.i.* [**bivouacked, -acking**] vivaquear.
bizarre (bɪ'za:r) *adj.* raro; caprichoso; grotesco.
blab (blæ:b) *v.t.* [**blabbed, blabbing**] revelar; divulgar. —*v.i.* chismear.
blabbermouth ('blæb·ər,mauθ) *n.* bocaza.
black (blæk) *n.* negro. —*adj.* **1,** (dark) negro; obscuro. **2,** *fig.* (wicked) atroz; horrible. **3,** *fig.* (sad) triste; calamitoso. —*v.t.* & *i.* = **blacken.** —**black and blue,** lívido; amoratado. —**black sheep,** garbanzo negro; oveja descarriada.
blackball ('blæk·bɔl) *v.t.* rechazar; votar en contra.
blackberry ('blæk·bɛr·i) *n.* zarzamora.
blackbird ('blæk·bʌɹd) *n.* mirlo.
blackboard *n.* pizarra; encerado.
blacken ('blæk·ən) *v.t.* **1,** (make black) ennegrecer; obscurecer; betunar. **2,** (defame) difamar; denigrar; calumniar. —*v.i.* ennegrecerse; obscurecerse.
blackguard ('blæg·ərd) *n.* tunante; pillo; pelagatos.
blackhead *n.* comedón; espinilla.
blackjack ('blæk·dʒæk) *n.* **1,** (heavy club) cachiporra; porra. **2,** (card game) veintiuna. —*v.t.* **1,** (strike) aporrear. **2,** (coerce) coaccionar; obligar; forzar.
blacklist ('blæk·lɪst) *n.* lista negra. —*v.t.* votar en contra; rechazar.
blackmail ('blæk·meil) *n.* chantaje. —*v.t.* chantajear. —**blackmailer,** *n.* chantajista.
Black Maria (mə'rai·ə) *colloq.* coche celular; camión de policía.
black market mercado negro; estraperlo. —**black marketeer,** estraperlista.
blackout ('blæk·aut) *n.* **1,** (extinction of lights) apagón. **2,** (fainting spell) inconsciencia; desvane-

cimiento. **3,** (loss of memory) amnesia.

blacksmith ('blæk·smɪθ) *n.* herrador; herrero; forjador.

bladder ('blæd·ər) *n.* vejiga.

blade (bleid) *n.* **1,** (weapon) espada. **2,** (cutting edge) hoja; cuchilla. **3,** (plant leaf) hoja. **4,** *colloq.* (rakish man) calavera.

blame (bleim) *v.t.* acusar; culpar; censurar. —*n.* censura; acusación; culpa; reproche. —**blameless,** *adj.* inculpable.

blameworthy *adj.* culpable.

blanch (blæntʃ) *v.t.* emblanquecer; blanquear. —*v.i.* palidecer.

bland (blæ:nd) *adj.* suave; dulce; blando. —**blandness,** *n.* suavidad; blandura.

blandish ('blænd·ɪʃ) *v.t.* ablandar; halagar; lisonjear; engatusar. —**blandishment,** *n.* halago; lisonja; engatusamiento.

blank (blæŋk) *adj.* **1,** (bare) vacío; sin adorno. **2,** (without marks) sin llenar; en blanco. **3,** (utter) completo; total. **4,** (colorless) pálido; descolorido. —*n.* **1,** (vacant space) blanco; espacio en blanco; libre. **2,** (form) impreso en blanco. **3,** *mech.* madera *o* metal para ser trabajado. —*v.t.* **1,** [*también,* **blank out**] (cancel) anular; borrar. **2,** *colloq.* (prevent from scoring) confundir.

blanket ('blæŋk·ət) *n.* manta; frazada; cobertor de lana; *fig.* manto. —*adj.* comprensivo; general. —*v.t.* **1,** (cover) cubrir con manta; mantear. **2,** (overwhelm) suprimir; cubrir; oscurecer.

blankness *n.* **1,** (empty space) hueco; espacio. **2,** (mental confusion) turbación; confusión.

blare (ble:r) *v.t.* trompetear; publicar. —*v.i.* vociferar; bramar. —*n.* **1,** (trumpet sound) trompeteo. **2,** (blatant sound, color, etc.) trompetada; estridencia.

blarney ('blar·ni) *n.* adulación; lisonja. —*v.t.* & *i.* lisonjear.

blasé (bla'zei) *adj.* hastiado; cansado; aburrido.

blaspheme (blæs'fi:m) *v.i.* blasfemar. —*v.t.* maldecir; vilipendiar. —**blasphemer,** *n.* blasfemador; blasfemante; blasfemo.

blasphemy ('blæs·fə·mi) *n.* blasfemia. —**blasphemous,** *adj.* blasfemo; blasfemador.

blast (blæst) *n.* **1,** (gust of air) golpe de viento; ráfaga de aire. **2,** (blowing of a horn) resoplido; soplo. **3,** (explosion) explosión; estallido. —*v.t.* **1,** (explode) explotar; estallar. **2,** (destroy) arruinar; destruir. —**blast furnace,** alto horno.

blast-off *n.* despegue (*de un cohete*). —**blast off,** despegar un cohete.

blatancy ('blei·tən·si) *n.* **1,** (noise) vocinglería. **2,** (obtrusiveness) lo entremetido; lo intruso.

blatant ('blei·tənt) *adj.* **1,** (noisy) vocinglero; bramante; ruidoso. **2,** (obtrusive) entremetido; intruso.

blaze (bleiz) *n.* **1,** (fire) llama; fuego. **2,** (brilliant light) luz brillante. **3,** (outburst) llamarada; hoguera. **4,** (mark on an animal's face) mancha; señal. —*v.i.* quemarse; encenderse; brillar. —*v.t.* **1,** (enflame) encender; inflamar **2,** (proclaim) pregonar; proclamar.

blazon ('blei·zən) *n.* **1,** (heraldry) blasón; escudo de armas. **2,** (display) divulgación; proclamación. —*v.t.* **1,** *heraldry* blasonar. **2,** (embellish) adornar. **3,** (proclaim) divulgar; proclamar. —**blazonry,** *n.* heráldica; blasón.

bleach (blitʃ) *v.t.* blanquear; decolorar. —*v.i.* palidecer; decolorarse; empalidecer. —*n.* lejía.

bleachers ('blitʃ·ərz) *n.pl.* gradas descubiertas.

bleak (blik) *adj.* **1,** (desolate) desolado; desierto; yermo. **2,** (cold) frío; helado; desabrigado. **3,** (dreary) apático; indiferente; sin entusiasmo. —**bleakness,** *n.* desolación; frialdad.

blear (blɪr) *v.t.* nublar; ofuscar. —*adj.* [*también,* **bleary**] legañoso; ofuscado; nublado.

bleat (blit) *n.* (of a sheep or goat) balido; (of a calf) mugido. —*v.i.* balar; mugir.

bleed (bli:d) *v.i.* [*pret.* & *p.p.* **bled**] **1,** (emit blood) sangrar; echar sangre. **2,** (flow from a plant) exudar. **3,** *fig.* (pity) apiadarse; compadecerse; angustiarse. —*v.t.* **1,** (draw blood from) sangrar a. **2,** *colloq.* (extort money from) dar un sablazo. **3,** *print.* sangrar.

blemish ('blɛm·ɪʃ) *v.t.* **1,** (mar) afear; manchar. **2,** (defame) denigrar; infamar. —*n.* tacha; mancha.

blend (blɛ:nd) *v.t.* mezclar; combinar. —*v.i.* **1,** (harmonize) armonizar. **2,** (mix paints) casar colores. —*n.* mezcla; combinación.

bless (blɛs) *v.t.* **1,** (consecrate) bendecir; santificar. **2,** (make happy) hacer feliz. **3,** (extol) alabar; glorificar. —**blessed** ('blɛs·ɪd) *adj.* bendito; feliz. —**blessedness,** *n.* felicidad.

blessing ('blɛs·ɪŋ) *n.* **1,** (benediction) bendición; bien; gracia. **2,** (approval) bendición; aprobación; consentimiento.

blew (bluː) *v., pret. de* **blow.**

blight (blait) *n.* plaga. —*v.t.* **1,** (cause to decay) plagar; marchitar; agostar. **2,** (ruin) arruinar; frustrar.

blimp (blɪmp) *n.* globo dirigible.

blind (blaind) *adj.* **1,** (sightless) ciego. **2,** (unaware) ignorante; insensato. **3,** (heedless) irrazonable; descuidado. **4,** (secret) oculto; secreto. —*v.t.* **1,** (deprive of sight) cegar; quitar la vista a. **2,** (conceal) oscurecer; esconder. —*n.* **1,** (obstruction) obstáculo. **2,** (ruse) evasiva; pretexto. **3,** (deceit) disfraz; engaño. **4,** (hunters' shelter) refugio para cazadores. **5,** (window shade) transparente. —**blind alley,** callejon sin salida. —**blind date,** *slang* cita a ciegas. —**Venetian blind,** celosía.

blindfold ('blaind·fold) *n.* venda ocular. —*adj.* que tiene vendados los ojos. —*v.t.* vendar los ojos a.

blink (blɪŋk) *v.i.* **1,** (wink rapidly) parpadear; pestañear. **2,** (flash) destellar; fulgurar. —*n.* **1,** (wink) guiño; parpadeo; pestañeo. **2,** (flash) destello. **3,** (glimpse) mirada. —**blink at,** ignorar; disimular.

blinker ('blɪŋk·ər) *n.* **1,** (flashing light) parpadeo luminoso. **2,** *pl.,* (shades for a horse's eyes) anteojeras.

blip (blɪp) *n.* centella que aparece en la pantalla del radar.

bliss (blɪs) *n.* **1,** (supreme joy) bienaventuranza; gloria. **2,** (delight) deleite; alegría; felicidad. —**blissful,** *adj.* dichoso; bienaventurado; contento.

blister ('blɪs·tər) *n.* ampolla; vejiga. —*v.t.* **1,** (cause to swell) ampollar. **2,** *fig.* (vituperate) mortificar; vituperar. —*v.i.* ampollarse.

blithe (blaið) *también,* **blithesome** (-səm) *adj.* contento; feliz; alegre; gozoso. —**blitheness,** *n.* gozo; alegria; júbilo.

blitz (blɪts) *n.* **1,** *mil.* ataque blindado. **2,** (sudden onslaught) matanza; aniquilación. —*v.t.* atacar violentamente. *También,* **blitzkrieg** (-ˌkriːg).

blizzard ('blɪz·ərd) *n.* **1,** (snowstorm) nevada. **2,** (windstorm with sleet) ventisca.

bloat (blot) *v.t.* **1,** (cause to swell) hinchar; entumecer. **2,** (smoke, as fish) curar; ahumar. —*v.i.* hincharse; abotagarse. —*n., vet.med.* inflamación del abdomen.

bloater ('blot·ər) *n.* pescado ahumado.

blob (blaːb) *n.* burbuja; pompa.

bloc (blak) *n.* grupo político; bloc; unión.

block (blak) *n.* **1,** (solid mass) bloque. **2,** (obstacle) obstáculo; impedimento. **3,** (city block) manzana; *Amer.* cuadra. **4,** (base for work) mesa; bloque. **5,** (auction platform) plataforma. **6,** *mech.* bloque de cilindros. **7,** *print.* bloque de grabado. **8,** *R.R.* tramo; sección. **9,** *naut.* motón; sistema de poleas. —*v.t.* **1,** (mount on a block) montar. **2,** [*usu.,* **block out**] (plan) delinear; esbozar. **3,** (obstruct) bloquear; obstruir. **4,** (shape, as a hat) conformar.

blockade (bla'keid) *n.* **1,** (barrier) bloqueo. **2,** (obstruction) obstrucción; impedimento. —*v.t.* bloquear.

blockbuster ('blakˌbʌs·tər) *n.* bomba rompemanzanas.

blockhead ('blak·hɛd) *n.* necio; estúpido; bruto. —**blockheaded,** *adj.* estúpido; lerdo.

blond (blaːnd) *n.* & *adj.* [*fem.* **blonde**] blondo; rubio; *Amer.* güero (*o* huero).

blood (blʌd) *n.* **1,** (body fluid) sangre. **2,** (plant sap) savia. **3,** (lineage) ascendencia; linaje; parentesco. —**blood bank,** banco de sangre. —**blood count,** suma de glóbulos rojos y blancos por unidad de volumen. —**blood relation,** parentesco directo. —**blood vessel,** vena; arteria.

bloodhound ('blʌd·haund) *n.* perro sabueso.

bloodless ('blʌd·ləs) *adj.* **1,** (without blood) desangrado; exangüe; incruento. **2,** (pale) pálido; lívido. **3,** (cowardly) indeciso; apático; sin sangre.

bloodshed ('blʌd·ʃɛd) *n.* matanza; carnicería; degollina.

bloodshot ('blʌd·ʃat) *adj.* inyectado en sangre; sanguinolento.
bloodsucker ('blʌd·sʌk·ər) *n.* **1,** (leech) sanguijuela. **2,** *slang* (extortionist) usurero.
bloodthirsty ('blʌd·θʌɹst·i) *adj.* sanguinario; cruel. —**bloodthirstiness,** *n.* encarnizamiento; sed de sangre.
bloody ('blʌ·di) *adj.* **1,** (gory) sangriento; ensangrentado. **2,** (marked by bloodshed) sanguinario; cruel. —*v.t.* ensangrentar. —**bloodiness,** *n.* sanguinolencia; ensangrentamiento.
bloom (bluːm) *n.* **1,** (flower) flor. **2,** (foliage) floración; florecimiento. **3,** (healthful glow) flor; frescura; juventud. **4,** (fuzz on fruit) pelusilla. **5,** *metall.* lingote. —*v.i.* **1,** (flower) florecer. **2,** (keep young) ser joven; disfrutar de salud. **3,** (glow) brillar vivamente. —**bloomer,** *n.* desatino; disparate.
bloomers ('blum·ərz) *n.pl.* pantalones de mujer holgados.
blossom ('bla·səm) *n.* **1,** (flower) flor. **2,** (foliage) floración. —*v.i.* **1,** (bloom) florecer; echar flor. **2,** (ripen) desarrollarse; madurar.
blot (blat) *n.* **1,** (spot) borrón; mancha. **2,** (moral stain) mancilla; mancha. —*v.t.* [**blotted, -ting**] **1,** (stain) manchar; ensuciar. **2,** (spot with ink; scribble) emborronar. **3,** (dry; soak up) secar. —*v.i.* mancharse; emborronarse; empañarse; ensuciarse.
blotch (blatʃ) *n.* pintarrajo; mancha; borrón. —*v.t.* manchar; pintarrajear; empañar.
blotter (bla·tər) *n.* **1,** (absorbent paper) papel secante. **2,** (police journal) libro registro *o* borrador.
blouse (blaus) *n.* blusa.
blow (bloː) *v.i.* [**blew, blown** (bloːn), **blowing**] **1,** (send forth air) soplar; hacer viento. **2,** (produce sound) sonar. **3,** (breathe hard) respirar fuerte. **4,** (pant) jadear. **5,** (explode; burst) explotar; estallar; reventarse. **6,** (be carried by the wind) llevarse por el viento. **7,** *colloq.* (boast) jactarse. **8,** (bloom) florecer. **9,** *slang* (leave) irse; marcharse. **10,** (burn out, as a fuse) quemarse. —*v.t.* **1,** (drive by air) soplar. **2,** (cause to sound) sonar; tocar. **3,** (scatter) limpiar *o* diseminar a chorro. **4,** (explode) hacer estallar. **5,** (burn out, as a fuse) quemar. **6,** *slang* (waste) disipar; malgastar. —*n.* **1,** (blast) golpe de aire; vendaval; borrasca. **2,** (stroke) golpe; manotazo; puñetazo. **3,** (disaster) desastre; desdicha; calamidad. **4,** (bloom) florescencia. **5,** *slang* (boast) jactancia. —**blow down,** derribar. —**blow hot and cold,** vacilar; estar indeciso. —**blow in,** *slang* **1,** (arrive) llegar. **2,** (spend) gastar; disipar. —**blow off, 1,** (let out pressure) descargar; descargarse; escaparse. **2,** *slang* (boast) jactarse. —**blow off steam,** *slang* desahogarse. —**blow out, 1,** (extinguish) apagar. **2,** (burst) reventar; reventarse. **3,** (escape suddenly) escaparse. **4,** (burn out, as a fuse) quemar; quemarse. —**blow over,** pasar; disiparse; olvidarse. —**blow up, 1,** (inflate) inflar. **2,** (swell) hinchar; hincharse. **3,** (explode; burst) explotar; estallar; saltar; reventar. **4,** (become stormy) emborrascarse. **5,** (lose one's temper) reventar de ira; enfurecerse.
blowgun *n.* cerbatana.
blowout ('blo·aut) *n.* **1,** (rupture) escape; reventón; estallido. **2,** *colloq.* (spree) juerga.
blowpipe *n.* soplete.
blowtorch *n.* soplete; antorcha a soplete.
blubber ('blʌb·ər) *n.* grasa (*de ballena u otro animal*). —*v.i.* gimotear. —*v.t.* hablar con lágrimas; llorar. —**blubber lip,** bezo.
bludgeon ('blʌdʒ·ən) *n.* cachiporra; garrote; porra. —*v.t.* **1,** (strike) aporrear. **2,** (bully) obligar; coaccionar.
blue (bluː) *n.* azul. —*adj.* **1,** (color) azul. **2,** (pallid in face) lívido; exangüe. **3,** (depressed) triste; melancólico; abatido. **4,** (morally strict) puritano; exigente; riguroso. —*v.t.* azular.
bluebell ('blu·bɛl) *n.* campanilla; coronilla.
blueberry ('blu·bɛr·i) *n.* mora azul.
bluebird *n.* pájaro cantor; pájaro azul.
blueblood ('blu·blʌd) *n., colloq.* aristócrata; sangre azul.
bluefish *n.* pez azul.
blueprint ('blu·prɪnt) *n.* plano. —*v.t.* hacer un plano de; levantar un plano de.

blues (bluːz) *n.pl.* **1,** *music* variedad de música de jazz. **2,** (sadness) tristeza; melancolía.
bluff (blʌf) *v.t.* & *i.* alardear; baladronear. —*n.* **1,** (deception) fanfarronada; alarde; baladronada. **2,** (hill) colina *o* risco escarpado. —*adj.* **1,** (abrupt) rudo; áspero. **2,** (broad) abierto; ancho.
bluish ('blu·ɪʃ) *adj.* azulado; azulino.
blunder ('blʌn·dər) *n.* disparate; dislate; estupidez. —*v.i.* **1,** (err grossly) disparatar; desbarrar. **2,** (move blindly) emperezarse. —*v.t.* **1,** (confuse) confundir. **2,** (bungle) chapucear.
blunderbuss ('blʌn·dər·bʌs) *n.* trabuco.
blunt (blʌnt) *adj.* **1,** (not sharp) obtuso; romo. **2,** (abrupt) bronco; brusco; abrupto. —*v.t.* **1,** (dull) embotar; enervar. **2,** (lessen pain) calmar un dolor. —**bluntness,** *n.* embotadura; brusquedad.
blur (blʌɹ) *v.t.* [**blurred, blurring**] **1,** (obscure) empañar; hacer borroso. **2,** (stain) manchar; ensuciar. —*v.i.* empañarse. —*n.* mancha; borrón; trazo borroso. —**blurry,** *adj.* emborronado; confuso. —**blurriness,** *n.* emborronamiento; ensuciamiento.
blurt (blʌɹt) *v.t.* decir *o* hablar abruptamente; hablar a tontas y a locas.
blush (blʌʃ) *v.i.* sonrojarse; ruborizarse; avergonzarse. —*n.* rubor; sonrojo.
bluster ('blʌs·tər) *v.i.* **1,** (swagger) fanfarronear; bravear. **2,** (bellow) bramar; rugir. —*n.* rugido; bramido.
boa ('bo·ə) *n.* boa.
boar (boːr) *n.* jabalí; verraco.
board (boːrd) *n.* **1,** (wooden strip) tabla; tablero. **2,** (table) mesa. **3,** (meals) pensión; alimentos. **4,** (group of officials) consejo; junta. **5,** *naut.* bordo; borde. —*v.t.* **1,** (cover with wood) entablar; enmaderar. **2,** (give meals) tomar a pupilaje. **3,** (embark) abordar. —*v.i.* estar de pupilo. —**boarding house,** pensión; casa de huéspedes.
boast (bost) *v.i.* **1,** (brag) jactarse; alardear. **2,** (be justly proud) alabarse. —*v.t.* **1,** (exult) exaltar. **2,** (show off) ostentar. —*n.* jactancia; alarde; ostentación. —**boastful,** *adj.* jactancioso; fanfarrón.
boat (bot) *n.* **1,** (vessel) bote; barca. **2,** (gravy dish) salsera. —*v.i.* navegar; embarcarse. —**be in the same boat,** correr la misma suerte.
boat hook bichero.
boatman ('bot·mən) *n.* [*pl.* **-men**] barquero.
boatswain ('bo·sən) *n.* contramaestre.
bob (bab) *n.* **1,** (jerk) sacudida; tirón; sacudimiento. **2,** (pendant) colgante. **3,** (plumb line) plomada. **4,** (fishing float) flotador de pesca. **5,** (haircut) pelo corto. **6,** *colloq.* (shilling) chelín. —*v.i.* [**bobbed, bobbing**] sacudirse; bambolear. —*v.t.* **1,** (cut short) cortar corto (el pelo). **2,** (rap) dar con el codo *o* la mano.
bobbin ('bab·ɪn) *n.* bobina; carrete.
bode (boːd) *v.t.* & *i.* presagiar; pronosticar; vaticinar.
bode (boːd) *v., pret.* & *p.p. de* **bide.**
bodice ('bad·ɪs) *n.* corpiño; jubón.
bodily ('bad·ə·li) *adj.* corpóreo; corporal.
body ('ba·di) *n.* **1,** *anat.* cuerpo. **2,** (group) corporación; gremio; cuerpo. **3,** (collection) colección. **4,** (density) espesor; consistencia. **5,** (of a car) carrocería. **6,** (of a truck) caja.
bodyguard ('ba·di,gard) *n.* **1,** (personal guard) guardia de corps. **2,** (escort) guardaespaldas.
Boer (boːr) *n.* & *adj.* bóer.
bog (baːg) *n.* pantano; ciénaga; fangal. —*v.t.* & *i.* [**bogged, bogging**] empantanar(se); enfangar(se).
bogus ('bo·gəs) *adj.* engañoso; falso; fingido.
bogy ('bo·gi) *también,* **bogie** *n.* fantasma; espectro; coco; bu.
Bohemian (bo'hi·mi·ən) *n.* & *adj., también l.c.* bohemio.
boil (bɔil) *v.i.* **1,** (become hot) hervir; bullir. **2,** *fig.* (be excited) agitarse; excitarse; airarse. —*v.t.* **1,** (cook) hervir; cocer. **2,** [*usu.,* **boil down**] (condense) condensar. —*n.* **1,** (boiling state) hervor; ebullición. **2,** (skin sore) furúnculo; divieso.
boiler ('bɔi·lər) *n.* **1,** (caldron) caldera. **2,** (water heater) termosifón.
boilermaker *n.* calderero.

boisterous (ˈbɔi·stə·rəs) *adj.* ruidoso; tempestuoso; vocinglero. —**boisterousness,** *n.* turbulencia; vocinglería; impetuosidad.

bold (boːld) *adj.* **1,** (daring) valiente; bravo; audaz. **2,** (impudent) impudente; temerario; descarado. **3,** (conspicuous) prominente; sobresaliente. —**boldness,** *n.* valentía; audacia.

bolero (boˈlɛr·o) *n.* [*pl.* **-ros**] bolero.

boll (boːl) *n.* cápsula. —**boll weevil,** gorgojo.

bologna (bəˈlo·njə; **-ni**) *n.* boloña.

bolo knife (ˈbo·lo) bolo.

boloney (bəˈlo·ni) *n., slang* = **baloney.**

Bolshevik (ˈbol·ʃə·vɪk) *n.* [*pl.* **-viki** (-vi·ki)] bolchevique. —**Bolshevism,** *n.* bolchevismo; bolcheviquismo. —**Bolshevist,** *n.* bolchevique.

bolster (ˈbol·stər) *n.* **1,** (long pillow) almohadón cilíndrico. **2,** (support) soporte; travesero. —*v.t.* soportar; reforzar.

bolt (bolt) *n.* **1,** (metal pin) perno. **2,** (bar in a lock) pernio. **3,** (arrow) dardo; flecha. **4,** (roll of material) pieza *o* rollo de tela. **5,** (stroke of thunder or lightning) rayo. **6,** (flight) fuga; deserción. **7,** (lock) cerrojo; pestillo. —*v.t.* **1,** (lock) acerrojar; empernar. **2,** (swallow) engullir; tragar. **3,** (sift) cerner. —*v.i.* desertar; escapar. —*adv.* repentinamente; abruptamente.

bomb (bam) *n.* **1,** (missile) bomba. **2,** (lava mass) masa de lava. —*v.t.* & *i.* bombardear. —**bomber,** *n.* bombardero.

bombard (bamˈbaːrd) *v.t.* bombardear. —**bombardier** (-bərˈdɪr) *n.* bombardero. —**bombardment,** *n.* bombardeo.

bombast (ˈbam·bæst) *n.* palabras altisonantes. —**bombastic** (bamˈbæs·tɪk) *adj.* bombástico; altisonante ampuloso.

bombshell *n.* **1,** (bomb) bomba. **2,** *slang, fig.* catástrofe; estallido.

bona fide (ˈbo·nə·faid) buena fe. —*adj.* sincero; franco; genuino.

bonanza (boˈnæn·zə) *n.* bonanza.

bonbon (ˈban·ban) *n.* bombón.

bond (baːnd) *n.* **1,** (binder) lazo; vínculo; unión. **2,** (duty) obligación. **3,** *comm.* bono; obligación. **4,** (binding substance) adhesivo. **5,** (type of paper) papel de tina *o* marca. —*v.t.* **1,** (give in trust) depositar. **2,** (pledge) empeñar. **3,** (form into a mass) ligar; trabar. —*v.i.* adherirse; juntarse.

bondage (ˈban·dɪdʒ) *n.* esclavitud; servidumbre; cautiverio.

bondholder *n.* obligacionista.

bondsman (ˈbandz·mən) *n.* [*pl.* **-men**] fiador; fianza.

bone (boːn) *n.* **1,** *anat.* hueso. **2,** (of fish) espina. **3,** (ivory) marfil. **4,** (corset stiffening) ballena. —*v.t.* **1,** (remove bones) desosar; deshuesar. **2,** (stiffen) emballenar. —*v.i., slang* empollar.

bonehead *n.* estúpido; ignorante.

bonfire (ˈban·fair) *n.* fogata; hoguera.

bongo drum (ˈbaŋ·go) bongó.

bonito (bəˈni·to) *n., ichthy.* bonito.

bonnet (ˈban·ɪt) *n.* cofia; sombrero de cofia.

bonus (ˈbo·nəs) *n.* bono; gratificación económica.

bony (ˈbo·ni) *adj.* **1,** (with or like bones) huesudo; anguloso. **2,** (thin) delgado. —**boniness,** *n.* delgadez; flacura.

boo (buː) *interj.* **1,** (to frighten) ¡bu! **2,** (to express disapproval) ¡fuera! —*n.* chifla; rechifla. —*v.t.* & *i.* rechiflar.

booby (ˈbu·bi) *n.* **1,** (stupid person) estúpido. **2,** (person with the worst score) bobo. —**booby trap,** matasuegras; sorpresa desagradable.

boodle (ˈbu·dəl) *n.* **1,** (bribe; graft) soborno. **2,** (loot) botín.

book (bʊk) *n.* **1,** (printed work) libro. **2,** (notebook) libreta. **3,** *theat.* libreto. —*v.t.* inscribir; registrar; reservar; planear.

bookbinder *n.* encuadernador. —**bookbindery,** *n.* taller de encuadernación. —**bookbinding,** *n* encuadernación.

bookcase *n.* armario para libros; biblioteca.

bookie (ˈbʊk·i) *n., colloq.* = **bookmaker.**

bookkeeper (ˈbʊk·kip·ər) *n.* contador; tenedor de libros —**bookkeeping,** *n.* contabilidad; teneduría de libros.

booklet (ˈbʊk·lət) *n.* folleto; opúsculo.

ookmaker *n.* corredor de apuestas.
ookworm ('buk·wʌɹm) *n.* **1,** (insect) polilla de libros. **2,** (diligent reader) ratón de biblioteca; empollón.
oom (buːm) *n.* **1,** (sound) estampido. **2,** (increase) alza; auge. **3,** *naut.* botalón; botavara. **4,** (arm of a derrick) brazo de grúa *o* de taladro. **5,** (underwater trap) barrera de puerto. —*v.t.* **1,** (announce loudly) anunciar a bombo y platillo. **2,** (promote) promover. —*v.i.* **1,** (emit a sound) hacer estampido. **2,** (flourish) estar en auge.
oomerang ('bu·məˌræŋ) *n.* bumerang. —*v.i.* tener resultado malo, opuesto al que se esperaba.
oon (buːn) *n.* **1,** (welcome gift) dádiva; donación; regalo. **2,** (favor) gracia; favor. —*adj.* convival; festivo.
oor (buːr) *n.* **1,** (rude person) zafio; tosco. **2,** (peasant) patán; aldeano. —**boorish,** *adj.* tosco; grosero.
oost (buːst) *v.t.* **1,** (raise) empujar hacia arriba; alzar. **2,** *colloq.* (promote) ayudar; favorecer; alentar. —*n.* **1,** (lift) empujón hacia arriba; alza. **2,** (help) asistencia; ayuda.
ooster ('bust·ər) *n.* **1,** *electricity* elevador de potencial. **2,** (supporter) partidario; entusiasta.
oot (but) *n.* **1,** (footwear) bota. **2,** (kick) puntapié; patada. **3,** *slang* (dismissal) patada. —*v.t.* **1,** (kick) dar puntapiés; patear. **2,** *slang* (expel) despedir; echar. **3,** *colloq.* (botch) chapucear. **4,** (put shoes on) calzar. —**to boot,** además.
ootblack ('but·blæk) *n.* limpiabotas.
ooth (buθ) *n.* casilla; cabina.
ootleg ('but·lɛg) *n.* licor de contrabando. —*v.t.* & *i.* [**bootlegged, -legging**] contrabandear en licores. —**bootlegger,** *n.* contrabandista de licores.
ootmaker *n.* botinero.
ooty ('bu·ti) *n.* botín.
ooze (buːz) *n., colloq.* licor. —*v.i.* emborracharse; beber inmoderadamente. —**boozy,** *adj.* borrachín.
orate ('bor·et) *n.* borato. —**borated,** *adj.* boratado.
orax ('bor·æks) *n.* bórax.
order ('bor·dər) *n.* **1,** (edge) borde; orilla; margen. **2,** (boundary) frontera; límite. **3,** (ornament) franja; banda; ribete; orla. —*v.i.* **1,** (touch upon) aproximarse; acercarse. **2,** (confine) confinar; lindar. —*v.t.* ribetear; repulgar.
bore (boːr) *n.* **1,** (drill) taladro; barrena. **2,** (hole) agujero. **3,** *firearms* calibre. **4,** *mech.* diámetro interno de cilindro. **5,** (tiresome person) pelma; cargante; jorobón. —*v.t.* **1,** (drill) taladrar; barrenar; perforar. **2,** (tire) aburrir; fastidiar. —*v.i.* **1,** (drill) hacer agujeros. **2,** (push ahead) avanzar; adelantarse.
bore (boːr) *v., pret. de* **bear.**
boreal ('bor·i·əl) *adj.* boreal; nórdico.
boredom ('bor·dəm) *n.* tedio; fastidio; aburrimiento.
boric ('bor·ɪk) *adj.* bórico. —**boric acid,** ácido bórico.
born (boːrn) *adj.* nato; congénito.
borne (boːrn) *v., p.p. de* **bear.** —*adj.* **1,** (carried) llevado; sostenido. **2,** (endured) sobrellevado; resistido.
boron ('bor·an) *n.* boro.
borough ('bʌɹ·o) *n.* villa; municipio incorporado; división administrativa (*esp. de una ciudad*).
borrow ('ba·ro) *v.t.* **1,** (take temporarily) tomar prestado; tomar fiado. **2,** (plagiarize) apropiar. —*v.i.* conseguir un préstamo.
borsch (boːrʃ) *también,* **borsht** (boːrʃt) *n.* sopa de remolachas.
bosh (baʃ) *n., slang* nadería; tontería.
bosom ('bʊ·zəm) *n.* **1,** *anat.* seno; pecho. **2,** *fig.* (heart) amor; cariño; corazón. **3,** (dress front) pechera. —*adj.* familiar; querido; íntimo. —*v.t.* **1,** (cherish) abrazar; estimar; acariciar. **2,** (hide) ocultar; esconder.
boss (bɔs) *n.* **1,** *colloq.* (supervisor) jefe; patrón; dueño. **2,** *colloq.* (political chief) jefe; cacique. **3,** (protuberance) nudo; protuberancia; joroba. —*v.t., colloq.* mandar; ordenar; dirigir. —**bossy,** *adj.* dominante.
botany ('bat·ə·ni) *n.* botánica. —**botanical** (bə'tæn·ɪ·kəl) *adj.* botánico. —**botanist,** *n.* botánico; botanista.
botch (batʃ) *v.t.* chapucear; estropear por ineptitud. —*n.* chapucería.
both (boθ) *adj.* & *pron.* ambos; los dos; entrambos. —*adv.* & *conj.*

tanto como; así como; a la vez; igualmente.

bother ('ba·ðər) *v.t.* molestar; fastidiar; incomodar. —*v.i.* molestarse; incomodarse. —*n.* fastidio; molestia; enojo. —*interj., colloq.* ¡joroba! —**bothersome,** *adj.* enojoso; fastidioso; importuno.

bottle ('ba·təl) *n.* botella; frasco. —*v.t.* embotellar; enfrascar; envasar. —**bottle up,** contener; refrenar.

bottleneck *n.* taponamiento; congestión; obstáculo.

bottom ('bat·əm) *n.* **1,** (base) fondo; base; cimiento; asiento. **2,** (bed of a river) lecho fluvial. **3,** *naut.* quilla; buque; barco. **4,** (buttocks) asiento; asentaderas. —*adj.* **1,** (lowest) inferior; hondo. **2,** (basic) fundamental; básico. —*v.t.* **1,** (furnish with a bottom) cimentar; asentar; apoyar. **2,** (fathom) repasar; profundizar; escudriñar. —*v.i.* **1,** (be based; rest) apoyarse; reclinarse. **2,** (run aground) encallar.

botulism ('batʃ·ə·lɪz·əm) *n.* botulismo.

boudoir ('bu·dwar) *n.* tocador; gabinete de señora.

bougainvillea (ˌbu·gən'vɪl·jə) *n.* buganvilla.

bough (bau) *n.* rama.

bought (bɔt) *v., pret. & p.p. de* **buy.**

bouillon ('bʊl·jan) *n.* caldo; consomé; consumado.

boulder *también,* **bowlder** ('bol·dər) *n.* peña; roca; canto rodado.

boulevard ('bʊl·əˌvard) *n.* avenida; paseo; bulevar.

bounce (bauns) *v.i.* botar; rebotar; brincar; saltar. —*v.t.* **1,** (toss up and down) hacer saltar *o* botar; **2,** *slang* (dismiss) despedir; expulsar. —*n.* **1,** (motion) bote; salta; brinco. **2,** *slang* (discharge) expulsión; despido. **3,** (impudence) jactancia; fanfarronada.

bound (baund) *v.i., pret. & p.p. de* **bind.** saltar; dar saltos; rebotar. —*v.t.* **1,** (cause to bounce or leap) hacer saltar *o* botar. **2,** (limit) limitar; lindar. —*n.* **1,** (leap) salto; bote; brinco. **2,** (limit) límite; lindero. **3,** *pl.* (limited area) territorio fronterizo (*sing.*); limítrofe (*sing.*). —*adj.* **1,** (tied) atado; sujeto; ligado. **2,** (covered as a book) encuadernado. **3,** (obliged) obligado; forzado. **4,** (determined) determinado; resuelto. **5,** (traveling to) destinado; con destino a.

bountiful ('baun·ti·fəl) *adj.* dadivoso; generoso; munífico. —**bountifulness,** *n.* munificencia; liberalidad; generosidad.

bounty ('baun·ti) *n.* **1,** (generosity) generosidad; largueza. **2,** (favor) dádiva; gracia. **3,** (premium) prima; premio.

bouquet (bu'kei) *n.* **1,** (bunch of flowers) buqué; ramillete. **2** (of wine) buqué; aroma del vino.

bourbon ('bʌɹ·bən) *n.* **1,** *cap* (French royal family) Borbón. **2** (corn whiskey) whisky.

bourgeois (bʊr'ʒwa) *n. & adj* burgués. —**bourgeoisie** (-'zi) *n* burguesía.

bout (baut) *n.* **1,** (contest) combate; pelea; lucha. **2,** (period of struggle) ataque; crisis. **3,** (round turn) turno; vez.

bovine ('bo·vain) *adj.* **1,** (oxlike) bovino; vacuno. **2,** (stolid) bruto estúpido. —*n.* bovino.

bow (bau) *v.i.* **1,** (bend) doblarse inclinarse; arquearse. **2,** (yield) ceder; someterse. **3,** (worship; salute) hacer reverencia; inclinarse —*v.t.* **1,** (cause to bend) doblar arquear; inclinar. **2,** (subdue) someter; forzar; obligar. —*n.* **1** (bend) inclinación; reverencia; saludo. **2,** *naut.* proa.

bow (boː) *n.* **1,** (weapon) arco **2,** *music* arco. **3,** (knot) lazo. **4** (curve) curva. —*adj.* arqueado curvado; doblado. —*v.i.* doblarse arquearse. —*v.t.* doblar; arquear —**bow compass,** bigotera. —**bow tie,** corbata de lazo.

bowel ('bau·əl) *n.* intestino; *p* tripas; entrañas. —**bowel movement, 1,** (passing of waste) defecación. **2,** (feces) heces; excremento

bower ('bau·ər) *n.* **1,** (shaded retreat) emparrado; glorieta. **2,** *poe* (rustic cottage) enramada; cenador **3,** *cards* sota.

bowl (boːl) *n.* **1,** (deep dish) cuenco; plato hondo; escudilla. **2** (basin) palangana; jofaina. **3** (large cup) tazón. **4,** (cup of a tobacco pipe) hornillo de pipa. **5** (of a toilet) taza. **6,** (ball) bola —*v.i.* **1,** (play at bowls) bolear jugar a bolos. **2,** [*usu.,* **bowl along**] (glide) deslizarse. —*v.t.* **1,** roda **2,** [*usu.,* **bowl over** *o* **down**] (up

set) desconcertar; (knock down) derribar.
bowlder *n.* = **boulder.**
bowleg ('bo:·lɛg) *n.* pierna corva; pata zamba. —**bowlegged** (-əd) *adj.* patizambo; patiabierto.
bowling ('bo:l·ɪŋ) *n.* juego de bolos; bolos (*pl.*); boliche. —**bowling alley**, bolera; boliche.
bowls (bo:lz) *n.sing.* juego de bolos; bolos (*pl.*).
bowsprit ('bau·sprɪt; 'bo-) *n.* bauprés.
bowwow ('bau'wau) *n.* ladrido. —*v.i.* ladrar.
box (baks) *n.* **1,** (container) caja; (small box) estuche; (large box) cajón. **2,** *theat.* palco. **3,** (outdoor booth or privy) garita; casilla. **4,** (socket; pit) caja. **5,** (enclosed area) cuadro; cuadrado. **6,** (blow) bofetón; bofetada. **7,** *bot.* boj. —*v.t.* **1,** (put in a box) encajonar; guardar; almacenar. **2,** (strike) abofetear; dar puñetazos. —*v.i.* boxear. —**box office**, taquilla.
boxer ('bak·sər) *n.* **1,** (pugilist) boxeador; púgil. **2,** (dog) bóxer.
boxing ('baks·ɪŋ) *n.* **1,** (sport) boxeo; pugilismo. **2,** (packing) embalaje; empaque.
boxwood *n.* boj.
boy (bɔi) *n.* **1,** (male child) niño; chico; muchacho. **2,** (servant) mozo; sirviente; criado. —**boyhood,** *n.* niñez; infancia. —**boyish,** *adj.* aniñado. —**boy friend, 1,** *colloq.* (escort) amigo; íntimo. **2,** *colloq.* (sweetheart) novio.
boycott ('bɔi·kat) *n.* boicot; boicoteo. —*v.t.* boicotear.
Boy Scout explorador.
bra (bra:) *n., colloq.* = **brassiere.**
brace (breis) *n.* **1,** (fastener) abrazadera; grapa; traba. **2,** (support, as for guy wire) tirante; refuerzo. **3,** *archit.* riostra. **4,** *dent.* mordaza. **5,** *carpentry,* berbiquí. **6,** *pl.* (suspenders) tirantes. **7,** *music* corchete. **8,** (couple) par; pareja. —*v.t.* **1,** (join) juntar; ligar. **2,** (make tense) reforzar; fortalecer. —**brace up**, resolverse; decidirse.
bracelet ('breis·lət) *n.* **1,** (wrist band) brazalete; pulsera. **2,** (handcuff) esposas (*pl.*).
brachial ('brei·ki·əl) *adj.* braquial.
brachy- (bræk·ɪ) *prefijo* braqui-; corto: *brachycephalic,* braquicéfalo.
bracket ('bræk·ɪt) *n.* **1,** (shelf support) ménsula; brazo; soporte. **2,** (small shelf) repisa. **3,** *print.* paréntesis angulares. **4,** (category) categoría; clase. —*v.t.* **1,** (support) aguantar; sostener. **2,** *print.* poner paréntesis a. **3,** (classify) clasificar; agrupar.
brackish ('bræk·ɪʃ) *adj.* salado; salobre. —**brackishness,** *n.* salobridad.
brag (bræ:g) *v.i.* [**bragged, bragging**] fanfarronear; jactarse; vanagloriarse. —*n.* **1,** (boast) fanfarronada; jactancia. **2,** (boaster) fanfarrón; petulante.
braggadocio (ˌbræg·ə'do·ʃiˌo) *n.* [*pl.* **-os** (-ˌo:z)] **1,** (vain boasting) fanfarronada. **2,** (braggart) fanfarrón.
braggart ('bræg·ərt) *n.* fanfarrón; petulante; jactancioso.
Brahman ('bra:·mən) *también,* **Brahmin** (-mɪn) *n.* brahmán. —**Brahmanism,** *n.* brahmanismo.
braid (breid) *v.t.* **1,** (plait) entrelazar; trenzar. **2,** (weave) entretejer. —*n.* **1,** (ornamental tape) galón; fleco; cordoncillo. **2,** (braided hair) trenza.
Braille (breil) *n.* Braille.
brain (brein) *n.* **1,** *anat.* cerebro. **2,** *usu.pl.,* (intelligence) inteligencia (*sing.*); conocimiento (*sing.*). —*v.t.* descrismar; descerebrar. —**brainy,** *adj.* inteligente; entendido; listo.
brainsick ('brein·sɪk) *adj.* loco; chiflado. —**brainsickness,** *n.* chifladura; desvarío.
brainstorm ('brein·storm) *n., colloq.* ocurrencia; idea.
brain teaser rompecabezas.
brain trust *slang* grupo de especialistas consejeros.
braise (breiz) *v.t.* asar a la brasa.
brake (breik) *n.* **1,** (stopping device) freno. **2,** (thicket) matorral; maleza. —*v.t.* frenar; parar.
brakeman ('breik·mən) *n.* [*pl.* **-men**] guardafrenos.
bramble ('bræm·bəl) *n.* zarza; espino. —**brambly** (-bli) *adj.* zarzoso; espinoso.
bran (bræ:n) *n.* salvado; afrecho; bren.
branch (bræntʃ) *n.* **1,** (limb of a tree) rama; (of a vine) sarmiento. **2,** (offshoot) rama; sección; división. **3,** (arm of a river) riachuelo; tributario; brazo. **4,** *comm.* sucursal. —*v.i.* **1,** (put forth branches)

enramar. **2,** (extend) ramificarse; extenderse. —**branch off,** bifurcarse; apartarse. —**branch out,** extenderse; ramificarse.

branchial ('bræŋk·i·əl) *adj.* branquial.

brand (bræːnd) *n.* **1,** (flaming stick) tizón. **2,** (identifying mark) marca a fuego. **3,** (marking iron) marcador. **4,** (label; make) marca; nombre. **5,** (quality) calidad; clase. **6,** (stigma) estigma; baldón. —*v.t.* **1,** (mark) marcar. **2,** (stigmatize) infamar; tildar; manchar. —**brand new,** sin usar; nuevo.

brandish ('bræn·dɪʃ) *v.t.* blandir; sacudir; mover.

brandy ('bræn·di) *n.* coñac. —*v.t.* aromar con *o* mojar en coñac. —**brandied,** *adj.* con coñac.

brash (bræʃ) *adj.* **1,** (reckless) impetuoso; temerario. **2,** (impudent) desvergonzado; impudente.

brashness ('bræʃ·nəs) *n.* **1,** (recklessness) impetuosidad. **2,** (impudence) impudicia.

brass (bræs) *n.* **1,** (alloy) latón. **2,** *music* metales (*pl.*); instrumentos metálicos de viento. **3,** *colloq.* (impudence) desvergüenza; impudicia. **4,** *slang* (persons in authority) peces gordos.

brassard ('bræs·ard) *n.* brazal.

brass band charanga.

brassiere (brə'ziːr) *n.* sostén; corpiño; *Amer.* ajustador.

brassiness ('bræs·i·nəs) *n.* **1,** (brassy quality) bronceamiento. **2,** *colloq.* (impudence) desfachatez; desvergüenza; descaro.

brassy ('bræs·i) *adj.* **1,** (of brass) de latón. **2,** *colloq.* (impudent) desvergonzado; desfachatado.

brat (bræt) *n.* chiquillo; rapaz.

bravado (brə'va·do) *n.* bravata; bravuconería.

brave (breiv) *adj.* bravo; valiente; intrépido. —*n.* guerrero indio. —*v.t.* arrostrar; desafiar. —**braveness, bravery,** *n.* bravura; valor; coraje.

bravo ('bra·vo) *interj.* ¡bravo!

brawl (brɔːl) *n.* **1,** (quarrel) pendencia; disputa; camorra. **2,** *slang* (noisy party) juerga; alboroto; jaleo. —*v.i.* **1,** (quarrel noisily) pendenciar; disputar. **2,** *slang* (carouse) jaranear; alborotar.

brawn (brɔːn) *n.* **1,** (muscular strength) músculo; vigor. **2,** (meat) carne dura; carne de jabalí. —**brawny,** *adj.* muscular; membrudo; fuerte.

bray (brei) *n.* rebuzno. —*v.i.* rebuznar. —*v.t.* triturar; pulverizar; moler.

braze (breiz) *v.t.* **1,** (solder) soldar con latón. **2,** (cover with brass) broncear.

brazen ('brei·zən) *adj.* **1,** (of brass) de latón. **2,** (shameless) insolente; descarado. —*v.t.,* [*usu.,* **brazen out**] sostener descaradamente; encarar con insolencia. —**brazenness,** *n.* desvergüenza; desfachatez.

brazier ('brei·ʒər) *n.* **1,** (worker in brass) latonero; calderero. **2,** (iron vessel) brasero; calentador.

breach (britʃ) *n.* **1,** (break) brecha; abertura. **2,** *law* infracción; violación. **3,** (disagreement) interrupción; brecha; disensión. —*v.t.* romper; quebrar.

bread (brɛd) *n.* **1,** (food) pan. **2,** *fig.* (necessities of life) sustento; comida; alimentos (*pl.*). —*v.t.* empanar.

breadstuff *n.* harina; cereal.

breadth (brɛdθ) *n.* **1,** (width) anchura; ancho. **2,** (liberality) amplitud; liberalidad. **3,** (broadness) holgura.

breadwinner ('brɛd·wɪn·ər) *n.* productor; trabajador; quien gana el pan.

break (breik) *v.t.* [**broke, broken, breaking**] **1,** (shatter) romper; quebrar; destrozar. **2,** (interrupt) interrumpir. **3,** (discontinue) suspender; discontinuar. **4,** (change) cambiar. **5,** (tame) adiestrar; entrenar; amansar. **6,** (violate) infringir; violar. **7,** (make known) descubrir. **8,** (demote) degradar; destituir. **9,** (soften; weaken) amortiguar; debilitar. **10,** (surpass) batir; exceder. **11,** (bankrupt) arruinar; quebrar. **12.** [*usu.,* **break down**] (analyze) dividir; separar; analizar. **13,** [*usu.,* **break off**] (discontinue) suspender; cesar. —*v.i.* **1,** (be shattered) romperse; quebrarse. **2,** (change) cambiar; variar. **3,** (discharge, as a sore) reventar. **4,** (come into being) rayar; apuntar. **5,** [*usu.,* **break in**] (force one's way) forzar; entrar violentamente. **6,** [*usu.,* **break down**] (fall ill) enfermarse; quebrantarse. **7,** (give way to emotions) desfallecer; desanimarse. **8,** [*usu.,* **break up** *o*

with] (quarrel; disband) pelear; separarse; romper. —*n.* 1, (breach) brecha; abertura; grieta. 2, (interruption) pausa; descanso; suspensión; interrupción. 3, (sudden change) desviación. —**breakable,** *n.* & *adj.* frágil.
breakage ('breik·ɪdʒ) *n.* 1, (break) rotura; fractura. 2, (indemnity) indemnización.
breakdown ('breik·daun) *n.* 1, *med.* trastorno; agotamiento; colapso. 2, *mech.* parada; derrumbamiento.
breaker ('breik·ər) *n.* 1, (tool; worker) roturador; rompedor. 2, (ocean wave) ola rompiente.
breakfast ('brɛk·fəst) *n.* desayuno. —*v.i.* desayunar.
breakneck ('breik·nɛk) *adj.* precipitado; peligroso; apresurado.
breakthrough ('breik·θru) *n.* brecha; abertura.
break-up ('breik·ʌp) *n.* ruptura.
breakwater ('breik·wat·ər) *n.* escollera; rompeolas.
bream (briːm) *n., ichthy.* brema.
breast (brɛst) *n.* 1, (chest) pecho. 2, (mammary gland) pezón. 3, *fig.* (seat of emotions) corazón. —*v.t.* 1, (move forward against) empujar con el pecho. 2, (face) arrostrar; encarar; *colloq.,* apechugar.
breastbone *n.* esternón.
breastwork *n.* parapeto; barricada.
breath (brɛθ) *n.* 1, (air inhaled or exhaled) aliento. 2, (light breeze) hálito; soplo. 3, (moment) instante; segundo. 4, (faint scent) vaharada. 5, (trifle) fruslería; friolera; trivialidad. —**catch one's breath,** 1, (pant) jadear; palpitar. 2, (rest) recuperarse; recobrar el aliento. —**in one breath,** en seguida; de un tirón. —**under one's breath,** en voz baja; en un murmullo.
breathe (briːð) *v.i.* 1, (respire) respirar; alentar. 2, (live) vivir. 3, (rest) descansar; reposar. —*v.t.* 1, (inhale and exhale) respirar; inhalar; exhalar. 2, (whisper) susurrar; murmurar. —**breather,** *n., colloq.* respiro; descanso.
breathless ('brɛθ·ləs) *adj.* 1, (panting) jadeante; sofocado; sin aliento. 2, (thrilled) emocionante; impresionante; tenso. —**breathlessness,** *n.* sofocación; desaliento.
breathtaking ('brɛθ·teik·iŋ) *adj.* impresionante; excitante; emocionante.
bred (brɛd) *v., pret.* & *p.p. de* **breed.**
breech (britʃ) *n.* 1, (of a gun) culata. 2, (buttocks) trasero; nalgas; posaderas.
breechcloth *n.* taparrabo.
breeches ('brɪtʃ·əz) *n.* calzones.
breed (briːd) *v.t.* [*pret.* & *p.p.* **bred**] 1, (beget) engendrar; procrear. 2, (produce) producir; crear. 3, (rear) criar; educar. —*v.i.* 1, (be produced) producirse; criarse. 2, (reproduce) reproducirse; desarrollarse. —*n.* raza; casta.
breeder ('briː·dər) *n.* 1, (reproducing plant or animal) generador; (person) criador. 2, (source) causa; fuente; origen.
breeding ('bri·dɪŋ) *n.* 1, (upbringing) crianza. 2, (gentility) modales (*pl.*); educación.
breeze (briːz) *n.* 1, (light wind) brisa; soplo. 2, *colloq.* (disturbance) conmoción; barullo. —*v.i.* 1, (blow lightly) soplar. 2, *colloq.* (move briskly) volar.
breezy ('briz·i) *adj.* 1, (mildly windy) refrescado con brisas. 2, (brisk) animado; vivo. 3, *colloq.* (pert) descarado; atrevido.
brethren ('brɛð·rən) *n.pl.* 1, (brothers) hermanos. 2, (associates) compañeros; *relig.* correligionarios.
Breton ('brɛt·ən) *adj.* & *n.* bretón.
breve (briːv) *n.* 1, *music* breve. 2, *print.; gram.* marca de brevedad.
brevet (brə'vɛt) *adj.* graduado; honorario. —*n.* grado honorario; comisión honoraria. —*v.t.* dar un ascenso honorífico; dar una comisión honoraria.
brevi- (brɛv·i) *prefijo* brevi-; breve; corto: *brevipennate,* brevipenne.
breviary ('bri·vi·ɛr·i) *n.* breviario.
brevity ('brɛv·ə·ti) *n.* brevedad; concisión.
brew (bruː) *v.t.* 1, (ferment) fermentar. 2, (steep, as tea) hervir. —*v.i.* (gather) formarse; fraguarse. —*n.* mezcla; cocción.
brewer ('bru·ər) *n.* cervecero. —**brewery,** *n.* cervecería; fábrica de cerveza.
bribe (braib) *n.* soborno; cohecho. —*v.t.* sobornar; cohechar. —**bribery,** *n.* soborno; cohecho.
bric-a-brac ('brɪk·ə·bræk) *n.* bric-a-brac; chucherías; curiosidades.

brick (brɪk) *n.* **1,** (block) ladrillo; loseta; *Mex.* adobe. **2,** *colloq.* (good fellow) buen chico. —*adj.* de ladrillos. —*v.t.* [*usu.,* **brick up**] enladrillar.
brickbat *n.* ladrillo; teja.
bricklayer *n.* enladrillador.
brickwork *n.* enladrillado.
bridal ('brai·dəl) *adj.* **1,** (of or pert. to a bride or bridal couple) de novia; de novios. **2,** (nuptial) nupcial. —*n.* boda.
bride (braid) *n.* **1,** (before marriage) novia. **2,** (after marriage) desposada.
bridegroom *n.* novio.
bridesmaid ('braidz·meid) *n.* madrina de boda.
bridge (brɪdʒ) *n.* **1,** (structure) puente. **2,** (of the nose) caballete; puente. **3,** *naut.; music* puente. **4,** (card game) bridge. **5,** *electricity* paralelo. **6,** *dent.* puente. —*v.t.* **1,** (build a bridge across) tender un puente sobre. **2,** (span; get across) salvar; cruzar.
bridgehead *n.* cabeza de puente.
bridle (brai·dəl) *n.* **1,** (of a horse) brida. **2,** (restraint) freno; coto; sujeción. —*v.t.* embridar; refrenar; controlar. —*v.i.* erguirse; alterarse. —**bridle path,** camino de herradura.
brief (brif) *adj.* breve; corto; conciso. —*n.* sumario; resumen. —*v.t.* **1,** (epitomize) condensar; resumir. **2,** (inform) informar; dar cuenta a *o* de. —**briefing,** *n.* resumen; información breve. —**briefness,** *n.* brevedad.
briefcase ('brif·keis) *n.* cartera; portafolio.
brier *también,* **briar** ('brai·ər) *n.* **1,** (prickly shrub) zarza. **2,** (tree heath, used for making pipes) brezo. —**briar patch,** zarzal. —**brier pipe,** pipa hecha de madera de brezo.
brig (brɪg) *n.* **1,** (ship) bergantín. **2,** (ship's prison) calabozo (de un buque).
brigade (brɪ'geid) *n.* brigada.
brigadier (ˌbrɪg·ə'dɪr) *n.* brigadier. —**brigadier general,** general de brigada; brigadier.
brigand ('brɪg·ənd) *n.* bandido; salteador; bandolero. —**brigandage,** *n.* bandidaje; bandolerismo.
brigantine ('brɪg·ən·tin; -tain) *n.* bergantín.
bright (brait) *adj.* **1,** (shining) claro; brillante; reluciente. **2,** (sunny) asoleado; luminoso. **3,** (clever) despejado; vivaz; despierto. **4,** (vivacious) alegre; feliz; vivaz. **5,** (illustrious) eminente; preclaro; ilustre.
brighten ('brait·ən) *v.t.* **1,** (make bright) abrillantar; aclarar. **2,** (cheer up) alegrar; animar. —*v.i.* **1,** (become bright) aclararse; despejarse. **2,** (gladden) alegrarse; animarse.
brightness ('brait·nəs) *n.* **1,** (quality) brillo; esplendor. **2,** (cleverness) agudeza; viveza.
brilliance ('brɪl·jəns) *n.* **1,** (luster) brillantez; lustre; magnificencia. **2,** (mental superiority) inteligencia; brillantez. **3,** (vivacity) agudeza; viveza. —**brilliant,** *adj.* brillante. —*n.* brillante; diamante.
brim (brɪm) *n.* **1,** (edge) borde; orilla. **2,** (rim of a hat) ala. —**brimful,** *adj.* rebosante; colmado.
brimstone ('brɪm·ston) *n.* azufre. —*adj.* azufroso; sulfuroso.
brine (brain) *n.* **1,** (salt solution) salmuera. **2,** (the sea) mar. —**briny** (-ni) *adj.* salobre; salado.
bring (brɪŋ) *v.t.* [*pret.* & *p.p.* **brought**] **1,** (carry) traer; llevar. **2,** (yield) producir; dar. **3,** [*usu.,* **bring around**] (induce) inducir; persuadir. **4,** (command as a price) tener; alcanzar. **5,** [*usu.,* **bring up**] (raise) criar; educar. **6,** [*usu.,* **bring about**] (cause) resultar; causar. **7,** *law* presentar. —**bring forth, 1,** (give birth to) parir; dar a luz. **2,** (produce) producir; dar. **3,** (disclose) descubrir; poner de manifiesto. —**bring in, 1,** (import) importar; traer. **2,** (produce as income) producir; entrar; obtener. **3,** (give a verdict) dar un fallo; **4,** (report) informar; presentar. —**bring off,** completar; realizar. —**bring on,** causar; comenzar. —**bring to, 1,** (revive) reanimar. **2,** *naut.* ponerse a la capa. —**bring up, 1,** (raise) educar; criar. **2,** (introduce) traer a colación; introducir.
brink (briŋk) *n.* borde; margen.
brioche (bri'ɔʃ) *n.* bollo; brioche.
briquette (brɪ'kɛt) *n.* briqueta.
brisk (brɪsk) *adj.* vivo; fuerte; enérgico. —**briskness,** *n.* animación; viveza; energía.

bristle ('brɪs·əl) *n.* **1,** (of hair) cerda. **2,** (of a brush) cerda; púa. —*v.i.* erizarse. —**bristly** (-li) *adj.* erizado.
bristling ('brɪs·lɪŋ) *adj.* **1,** (prickly) espinoso; erizado. **2,** (resentful) rencoroso; resentido.
Britain ('brɪt·ən) *n.* Bretaña; la gran Bretaña.
Britannia (brɪ'tæn·i·ə) *n.* = **Britain.** —**britannia metal,** metal británico.
Britannic (brɪ'tæn·ɪk) *adj.* británico.
British ('brɪt·ɪʃ) *adj.* británico; britano; inglés. —**the British,** los britanos; los ingleses.
Briton ('brɪt·ən) *n.* britano; inglés.
brittle ('brɪt·əl) *adj.* **1,** (fragile) frágil; quebradizo. **2,** (crisp) tieso; crespo. —**brittleness,** *n.* fragilidad.
broach (brotʃ) *n.* **1,** (tool) broca; lezna. **2,** (brooch) broche; prendedor. —*v.t.* **1,** (pierce) taladrar; agujerear. **2,** (bring up) introducir; presentar; abordar.
broad (brɔːd) *adj.* **1,** (wide) ancho; amplio. **2,** (widespread) abierto; claro. **3,** (liberal) tolerante; liberal. **4,** (pronounced openly) abierto. **5,** (extensive) general; amplio. **6,** (indelicate) descomedido; rudo.
broadcast ('brɔd·kæst) *adj.* conocido; público. —*n.* emisión; radiodifusión. —*v.t.* [*pret.* & *p.p.* **-cast** *o* **-casted**] **1,** (scatter) diseminar; esparcir. **2,** *radio* emitir; radiar. —*v.i.* radiar; radiodifundir; dar emisiones. —*adv.* por todas partes. —**broadcasting,** *n.* emisión; radiodifusión.
broadcloth *n.* paño fino.
broadminded ('brɔd,main·dɪd) *adj.* liberal; tolerante; comprensivo.
broad-shouldered *adj.* espaldudo; ancho de espaldas.
broadside ('brɔd·said) *n.* **1,** *naut.* (side of a ship) costado. **2,** *naut.* (discharge of guns) andanada. **3,** *fig.* ataque; andanada. **4,** *colloq.* (announcement) anuncio impreso.
broadsword ('brɔd,sord) *n.* montante.
brocade (bro'keid) *n.* brocado. —**brocaded,** *adj.* brocado.
broccoli ('brak·ə·li) *n.* bróculi; brécol.
brochure (bro'ʃʊr) *n.* folleto.
brogue (broːg) *n.* **1,** [*también,* **brogan** ('bro·gən)] (shoe) zapato fuerte y pesado, muchas veces con perforaciones decorativas. **2,** (accent) acento regional, esp. irlandés.
broil (brɔil) *v.t.* asar en parrillas; soasar. —*v.i.* asarse; torrarse. —*n.* soasado; carne soasada.
broiler ('brɔil·ər) *n.* **1,** (cooking appliance) parrilla. **2,** (fowl) ave para asar.
broke (brok) *v., pret. de* **break.** —*adj., slang* pelado; sin dinero; arruinado.
broken (brok·ən) *v., p.p. de* **break.** —*adj.* **1,** (rough; hilly) quebrado; áspero; irregular. **2,** (shattered) roto; avenado. **3,** (imperfectly spoken) chapurreado; imperfecto. **4,** (sick) enfermo; débil; agotado. **5,** (breached; violated) quebrantado; roto. **6,** (tamed) amaestrado; domado. **7,** (subdued) desanimado; desalentado.
broken-hearted *adj.* angustiado; destrozado; desesperado.
broker (brok·ər) *n., finance* corredor de comercio. —**brokerage** (-ɪdʒ) *n.* corretaje; comisión.
bromide ('bro·maid) *n.* **1,** *chem.* bromuro. **2,** *colloq.* (cliché) perogrullada; trivialidad. —**bromidic** (-'mɪd·ɪk) *adj., colloq.,* trillado; trivial.
bromine ('bro·min) *n.* bromo.
bronch- (brank) *prefijo, var. de* **broncho-** *ante vocal: bronchitis,* bronquitis.
bronchial ('braŋ·ki·əl) *adj.* bronquial.
bronchitis (braŋ'kai·tɪs) *n.* bronquitis.
broncho ('braŋ·ko) *n.* [*pl.* **-chos**] = **bronco.**
broncho- (bran·ko) *prefijo* bronco-; *denota relación con los bronquios: bronchoscope,* broncoscopio.
bronchoscope ('braŋ·ko·skop) *n.* broncoscopio.
bronchus ('braŋ·kəs) *n.* [*pl.* **-chi** (-kai)] bronquio.
bronco ('braŋ·ko) *n.* [*pl.* **-cos**] potro *o* caballo bronco.
broncobuster *n.* domador; *Amer.* chalán.
brontosaurus (,bran·tə'sor·əs) *n.* brontosauro.
Bronx cheer (braŋks) pedorreta; *Amer.* trompetilla.
bronze (braːnz) *n.* bronce. —*v.t.* broncear. —*adj.* broncíneo.

brooch (brotʃ; brutʃ) *n.* broche; prendedor. *También,* **broach** (brotʃ).

brood (bruːd) *n.* **1,** (litter of animals) cría; (of birds) nidada. **2,** (breed; kind) tipo; clase. —*v.i.* **1,** (hatch eggs) empollar. **2,** (ponder) ponderar; cavilar. —*v.t.* **1,** (sit on, as eggs) empollar. **2,** (protect) cobijar; amparar. —**broody,** *adj.* preocupado; intranquilo.

brook (brʊk) *n.* arroyo; arroyuelo; *Amer.* quebrada. —*v.t.* tolerar; sufrir; aguantar.

broom (bruːm) *n.* **1,** (brush) escoba. **2,** *bot.* retama.

broomstick *n.* palo de escoba.

broth (brɔθ) *n.* caldo.

brothel (ˈbrað·əl) *n.* burdel; prostíbulo.

brother (ˈbrʌð·ər) *n.* hermano. —**brotherhood,** *n.* fraternidad; hermandad; cofradía. —**brotherly,** *adj.* fraternal. —**brotherliness,** *n.* fraternidad.

brother-in-law *n.* [*pl.* **brothers-in-law**] cuñado; hermano político.

brought (brɔt) *v., pret.* & *p.p. de* **bring.**

brow (brau) *n.* **1,** (eyebrow) ceja. **2,** (forehead) frente; sienes (*pl.*). **3,** (edge of a cliff) cresta.

browbeat (ˈbrau·bit) *v.t.* intimidar; atemorizar; mirar mal.

brown (braun) *n.* color castaño. —*adj.* pardo; castaño; moreno. —*v.t.* broncearse; *cookery* dorar. —**in a brown study,** preocupado.

brownie (ˈbrau·ni) *n.* **1,** (elf) duendecillo. **2,** (kind of cake) galleta de chocolate.

brownstone *n.* piedra arenisca.

browse (brauz) *n.* pimpollos; renuevos. —*v.t.* ramonear; mordiscar. —*v.i.* **1,** (feed; graze) ramonear; mordiscar. **2,** (read cursorily) hojear. **3,** (look around idly) mirar; curiosear.

bruin (ˈbru·ɪn) *n.* oso.

bruise (bruːz) *n.* contusión; golpe. —*v.t.* magullar; golpear.

bruiser (ˈbru·zər) *n.* **1,** (fight) pelea. **2,** (fighter) púgil.

brunch (brʌntʃ) *n., colloq.* almuerzo.

brunette (bruˈnɛt) *n.* & *adj. fem.* trigueña; morena. —**brunet** (-ˈnɛt) *n.* & *adj. masc.* trigueño; moreno.

brunt (brʌnt) *n.* choque; esfuerzo.

brush (brʌʃ) *n.* **1,** (shrub) matorral; maleza. **2,** (bristled cleaning tool) escobilla; cepillo. **3,** (for painting) pincel; brocha. **4,** (for shaving) brocha. **5,** (light touch) roce; rozadura. **6,** *electricity* escobilla. **7,** (skirmish) pelea; discusión. —*v.t.* **1,** (sweep) barrer; limpiar. **2,** (rub) frotar; restregar. **3,** (touch lightly) rozar. —*v.i.* **1,** [*usu.,* **brush by**] (sweep past) pasar rápidamente. **2,** [*usu.,* **brush up**] (clean up) limpiar. **3,** [*usu.,* **brush up**] (refresh one's memory) acordarse; recordarse. —**brush stroke,** brochada; brochazo.

brushwood *n.* broza.

brusque (brʌsk) *adj.* brusco; rudo; abrupto. —**brusqueness,** *n.* brusquedad; rudeza.

Brussels sprouts (ˈbrʌs·əlz·ˈsprauts) *n.* bretones; col de Bruselas.

brutal (ˈbru·təl) *adj.* brutal; cruel; bárbaro. —**brutality** (bruˈtæl·ə·ti) *n.* brutalidad; barbarie.

brute (brut) *n.* & *adj.* bruto; bestia; animal. —**brutish,** *adj.* brutal; bestial. —**brutishness,** *n.* brutalidad; salvajismo.

bubble (ˈbʌb·əl) *n.* **1,** (gas or air film) burbuja. **2,** (unsound idea) tontería; bagatela. —*v.i.* **1,** (effervesce) burbujear. **2,** (boil) bullir; hervir. —**bubble gum,** goma hinchable.

bubo (ˈbju·bo) *n.* bubón. —**bubonic** (-ˈban·ɪk) *adj.* bubónico. —**bubonic plague,** peste bubónica.

buccaneer (ˌbʌk·əˈnɪr) *n.* bucanero.

buck (bʌk) *n.* **1,** (male of various animals) macho. **2,** *slang* (dollar) dólar; *Amer.* peso. **3,** (sawhorse) cabrilla; caballete de aserrar. **4,** *colloq.* (young man) petimetre. **5,** (leap, as of a horse) corcovo. —*v.i.* **1,** (make twisting leaps) corcovear. **2,** (suddenly demur) embestir. —*v.t.* **1,** (unseat by leaping) despedir por la cerviz. **2,** *colloq.* (go against) oponerse a. —**pass the buck,** *colloq.* pasar el bulto; no responsabilizarse. —**buck up,** *colloq.* animarse; reanimarse.

buckaroo (ˌbʌk·əˈruː) *n.* vaquero.

bucket (ˈbʌk·ɪt) *n.* **1,** (pail) pozal;

cubo; balde. 2, (scoop of a dredge) cangilón. —**bucket shop**, oficina ilegal de transacciones ficticias.

buckle ('bʌk·əl) *n.* 1, (belt clasp) hebilla. 2, (clasp of a strap) presilla; grapa. 3, (kink in metal) horquilla; hebilla. —*v.t.* 1, (fasten) hebillar; engrapar. 2, (crumple) doblar; arrugar. —*v.i.* 1, [*usu.*, **buckle down**] (work hard) empeñarse; decidirse. 2, (warp) combarse; doblarse.

buckram ('bʌk·rəm) *n.* bucarán.

buckshot ('bʌkˌʃat) *n.* balines (*pl.*).

buckskin ('bʌk·skɪn) *n.* piel de gamo; ante; *pl.* artículos de ante.

bucktooth ('bʌk·tuθ) *n.* diente saliente. —**bucktoothed** (-ˌtuːðd) *adj.* con *o* de diente saliente.

buckwheat ('bʌk·hwit) *n.* 1, (cereal) alforfón; trigo moro. 2, (flour) harina de alforfón.

bucolic (bju'ka·lɪk) *adj.* bucólico. —*n.* bucólica.

bud (bʌːd) *n.* 1, (unopened leaf) botón; yema; (unopened flower) capullo. 2, (undeveloped thing or person) brote; germen. 3, *colloq.* (debutante) joven presentada en sociedad. —*v.i.* [**budded, -ding**] florecer; germinar; brotar.

Buddha ('bud·ə) *n.* Buda. —**Buddhism**, *n.* budismo. —**Buddhist**, *n.* & *adj.* budista.

buddy ('bʌd·i) *n.*, *colloq.* camarada; compañero; amigo.

budge (bʌːdʒ) *v.t.* mover; revolver. —*v.i.* moverse; revolverse.

budget ('bʌdʒ·ɪt) *n.* presupuesto. —*v.t.* & *i.* presuponer. —**budgetary**, *adj.* presupuestario.

buff (bʌf) *n.* 1, (kind of leather) piel de ante. 2, (tan color) color de ante. 3, *colloq.*, (enthusiast) aficionado; seguidor; entusiasta. —*v.t.* 1, (polish) pulimentar; adelgazar. 2, (deaden) amortiguar.

buffalo ('bʌf·ə·lo) *n.* búfalo.

buffer ('bʌf·ər) *n.* 1, (polisher) lustrador. 2, (mitigator) amortiguador. —**buffer state**, nación parachoques; estado neutral.

buffet ('bʌf·ɪt) *n.* golpe; bofetón. —*v.t.* 1, (beat) golpear. 2, (contend against) contender con; pelear contra.

buffet (bə'fei) *n.* 1, (sideboard) aparador; mostrador. 2, (food for self-service) bufet; refrigerio. —*adj.* informal; sin etiqueta.

buffoon (bə'fuːn) *n.* bufón. —**buffoonery**, *n.* bufonería; bufonada.

bug (bʌːg) *n.* 1, (insect) chinche. 2, *colloq.* (germ) microbio. 3, *slang* (zealot) fanático; intransigente. 4, *slang* (difficulty) defecto; dificultad; tropiezo.

bugaboo ('bʌg·ə·bu) *también*, **bugbear** ('bʌgˌbeːr) *n.* espantajo; fantoche; coco; bu.

buggy ('bʌg·i) *n.* cabriolé; birlocho.

bugle ('bju·gəl) *n.* corneta. —**bugler** (-glər) *n.* corneta.

build (bɪːld) *v.t.* [*pret.* & *p.p.* **built**] 1, (erect) construir; edificar; fabricar. 2, (found) fundar; establecer. 3, (strengthen) reforzar; rigorizar. —*v.i.* edificar. —*n.* estructura; (of a person) talle. —**builder**, *n.* constructor. —**building**, *n.* edificio.

build-up *n.* refuerzo; vigorizacion; *colloq.* propaganda.

built (bɪlt) *v.*, *pret.* & *p.p.* de **build**.

built-in *adj.* incorporado; estructural.

bulb (bʌːlb) *n.* 1, (plant root) bulbo. 2, (light bulb) bombilla; *Amer.* foco; bombillo; bombita. —**bulbous**, *adj.* bulboso.

bulge (bʌːldʒ) *n.* comba; pandeo; panza. —*v.t.* combar. —*v.i.* pandearse; combarse.

bulk (bʌlk) *n.* 1, (mass) bulto; grueso; volumen. 2, (the major part) mayoría. —*v.t.* abultar; pesar. —**bulky**, *adj.* abultado; voluminoso.

bulkhead ('bʌlk·hɛd) *n.* mamparo.

bull (bʊl) *n.* 1, (ox) buey; (fighting bull) toro. 2, *finance* alcista. 3, *R.C.Ch.* (edict) bula. 4, (blunder) disparate; desatino. 5, *cap.*, *astron.* Tauro.

bulldog ('bʊl·dɔg) *n.* bulldog; perro de presa. —*adj.* testarudo; tenaz.

bulldoze ('bʊl·doz) *v.t.* intimidar; atemorizar. —**bulldozer**, *n.* niveladora *o* removedora a tracción.

bullet ('bʊl·ɪt) *n.* bala.

bulletin ('bʊl·ə·tən) *n.* boletín.

bullfight *n.* lidia; corrida de toros. —**bullfighter**, *n.* torero; toreador. —**bullfighting**, *n.* toreo;

tauromaquia. —*adj.* torero; taurómaco.

bullion ('bʊl·jən) *n.* oro *o* plata en lingotes.

bullish ('bʊl·ɪʃ) *adj.* **1,** (of or like a bull) taurino. **2,** *finance* alcista. **3,** *colloq.* (foolish) disparatado.

bullnecked *adj.* pescozudo.

bullock ('bʊl·ək) *n.* buey; ternero.

bull ring plaza de toros.

bull's-eye ('bʊlz·ai) *n.* **1,** (round window) claraboya; tragaluz. **2,** (convex lens) linterna sorda. **3,** (target) diana.

bully ('bʊl·i) *n.* camorrista; matón. —*v.t.* intimidar; amedrentar. —*adj.* & *interj., colloq.* excelente; estupendo.

bulrush ('bʊl·rʌʃ) *n.* enea; junco; *Bib.* planta del papiro.

bulwark ('bʊl·wərk) *n.* parapeto; defensa; baluarte.

bum (bʌm) *n.* & *adj., slang* holgazán; pordiosero. —*v.i.* *slang* [**bummed, bumming**] haraganear; holgazanear. —*v.t.* pordiosear; mendigar.

bumblebee ('bʌm·bəl·biː) *n.* abejarrón; moscardón.

bump (bʌmp) *n.* **1,** (shock) choque; colisión; topetón. **2,** (protuberance) giba; joroba; protuberancia. **3,** (swelling) chichón; *Amer.* bodoque. —*v.t.* topar; chocar. —*v.i.* chocar; estrellarse. —**bumpy,** *adj.* abollado; traqueteado.

bumper ('bʌm·pər) *n.* **1,** (protective bar) parachoques. **2,** (filled glass) vaso *o* copa colmada. —*adj., colloq.* enorme.

bumpkin ('bʌmp·kɪn) *n.* zafio; patán; rústico.

bun (bʌːn) *n.* **1,** (biscuit) bollo. **2,** (roll of hair) relleno.

bunch (bʌntʃ) *n.* (cluster of flowers) manojo; ramo; (of fruits) ramo; racimo. —*v.t.* arracimar; agrupar. —*v.i.* arracimarse; juntarse.

bundle ('bʌn·dəl) *n.* (loose package) atado; bulto; envoltorio; (neat package) paquete; bulto. —*v.t.* **1,** (tie) atar; envolver; empaquetar. **2,** [*usu.,* **bundle off**] *colloq.* (send away) deshacerse de. —*v.i.* **1,** *colloq.* [*usu.,* **bundle off**] (depart) marcharse. **2,** (lie in bed fully clothed) acostarse vestido.

bung (bʌŋ) *n.* bitoque.

bungalow ('bʌŋ·gə·lo) *n.* bungalow; casa de una planta.

bunghole *n.* boca de tonel.

bungle ('bʌŋ·gəl) *v.t.* estropear; chapucear. —*v.i.* hacer chapucerías. —**bungler** (-glər) *n.* chapucero.

bunion ('bʌn·jən) *n.* juanete.

bunk (bʌŋk) *n.* **1,** (bed) litera. **2,** *slang* (nonsense) tontería; banalidad. —*v.i., colloq.* acostarse.

bunker ('bʌŋk·ər) *n.* **1,** (storage bin) depósito. **2,** (coal bin) pañol del carbón; carbonera. **3,** *mil.* fortín. **4,** *golf* hoya de arena.

Bunsen burner ('bʌn·sən) mechero Bunsen.

bunting ('bʌn·tiŋ) *n.* **1,** (fabric) estameña; lanilla. **2,** *ornith.* calandria. **3,** (infant's garment) capa cerrada con capucha.

buoy ('bu·i) *n.* boya; baliza. —*v.t.,* [*usu.,* **buoy up**] **1,** (keep afloat) mantener a flote. **2,** *fig.* (encourage) apoyar; sostener; alentar.

buoyancy ('bɔi·ən·si) *n.* **1,** (floating) flotación. **2,** *fig.* (exuberance) animación; alegría.

buoyant ('bɔi·ənt) *adj.* **1,** (floating) boyante; flotante. **2,** (lighthearted) alegre; vivaz; animado.

bur *también* **burr** (bʌɹ) *n.* erizo.

burble ('bʌɹ·bəl) *n.* burbujeo. —*v.i.* burbujear.

burden ('bʌɹ·dən) *también,* **burthen** (-ðən) *n.* **1,** (load) carga; peso. **2,** *comm.* porte. **3,** (main theme) tema; estribillo. **4,** (encumbrance) estorbo; embarazo; obstáculo. **5,** *music* bordón. —*v.t.* cargar; agobiar; imponer. —**burdensome,** *adj.* gravoso; oneroso; pesado; molesto.

bureau ('bjʊr·o) *n.* **1,** (dresser) tocador; cómoda. **2,** (government agency) oficina; agencia; departamento.

bureaucracy (bjʊ'rak·rə·si) *n.* burocracia. —**bureaucrat** ('bjʊ·rə·kræt) *n.* burócrata. —**bureaucratic** (-rə'kræt·ɪk) *adj.* burocrático.

-burger (bʌɹ·gər) *sufijo* de un bocadillo de albondigón (carne picada y asada de res) y otro comestible: *cheeseburger,* albondigón con queso.

burglar ('bʌɹg·lər) *n.* escalador. —**burglarize,** *v.t.* escalar; robar. —**burglary,** *n.* escalo; robo.

Burgundy ('bʌɹ·gən·di) *n.* borgoña.
burial ('bɛr·i·əl) *n.* entierro; funeral.
burin ('bjʊr·ɪn) *n.* buril.
burlap ('bʌɹ·læp) *n.* arpillera.
burlesque (bʌɹ'lɛsk) *n.* **1,** *theat.* parodia. **2,** (satire) sátira. —*v.t.* parodiar; remedar. —*adj.* burlesco; satírico.
burly ('bʌɹ·li) *adj.* musculoso; robusto; firme.
burn (bʌɹn) *v.t.* [*pret.* & *p.p.* **burned** *o* **burnt**] **1,** (destroy by fire) quemar; incendiar. **2,** (scorch) socarrar; chamuscar. **3,** (consume as fuel) quemar; consumir. **4,** (inflame) inflamar. —*v.i.* **1,** (be on fire) quemarse; incendiarse. **2,** (be charred) chamuscarse; socarrarse. **3,** *fig.* (become inflamed) inflamarse; abrasarse; consumirse. —*n.* quemadura; *Amer.* quemada.
burner ('bʌɹ·nər) *n.* **1,** (heating unit) mechero. **2,** (apparatus for burning) quemador. **3,** (worker) quemador.
burnish ('bʌɹ·nɪʃ) *v.t.* bruñir; pulir.
burnoose (bʌɹ'nuːs) *n.* albornoz.
burnt (bʌɹnt) *v., pret.* & *p.p. de* **burn.**
burp (bʌɹp) *n., slang* eructo; regüeldo. —*v.i., slang* eructar; regoldar.
burr (bʌːɹ) *n.* **1,** (roughness after cutting) viruta; rebaba. **2,** = **bur.** **3,** *dent.* buril. **4,** *phonet.* pronunciación gutural de la *r.* —*v.t.* **1,** (make rough or jagged) poner serrado *o* dentado. **2,** (pronounce with a burr) pronunciar con sonido gutural (la *r*).
burro ('bʌɹ·o) *n.* [*pl.* **-ros**] burro.
burrow ('bʌɹ·o) *n.* madriguera. —*v.t.* minar; agujerear.
bursa ('bʌɹ·sə) *n., anat.* [*pl.* **-sas** (-səz) *o* **-sae** (-si)] bolsa.
bursitis (bʌɹ'sai·tɪs) *n.* bursitis.
burst (bʌɹst) *v.i.* **1,** (break) estallar; explotar; reventar. **2,** [*usu.,* **burst into**] (display suddenly) deshacerse en; prorrumpir en; desatarse en. **3,** (appear suddenly) irrumpir. —*v.t.* reventar; quebrar; explotar. —*n.* **1,** (outburst) explosión; reventón. **2,** (rush) carrera; precipitación. **3,** (firearms) andanada.
burthen *n.* & *v.t., arcaico* = **burden.**
bury ('bɛr·i) *v.t.* **1,** (inter) sepultar; enterrar. **2,** (conceal) ocultar; esconder. —**bury oneself,** abstraerse; concentrarse.
bus (bʌs) *n.* autobús; ómnibus; *W.I.; C.A.* guagua; *Mex.* camión. —**bus driver,** conductor de autobús.
busboy *n.* ayudante de camarero.
busby ('bʌz·bi) *n.* sombrero de húsar; birretina.
bush (bʊʃ) *n.* **1,** (shrub) zarza; arbusto. **2,** (uncleared land) matorral; chaparral. —**bushed,** *adj. colloq.* cansado; exhausto.
bushing ('bʊʃ·ɪŋ) *n., mech.* forro; abrazadera.
bushy ('bʊʃ·i) *adj.* **1,** (like a bush) espeso; tupido. **2,** (hairy) peludo. —**bushiness,** *n.* espesura.
business ('biz·nəs) *n.* **1,** (occupation) profesión; trabajo; oficio. **2,** (enterprise) empresa; compañía. **3,** *comm.* negocio. **4,** (aim) deber; obligación. **5,** (affair) asunto; cosa. **6,** *theat.* actuación.
businesslike ('bɪz·nəs·laik) *adj.* metódico; ordenado.
businessman ('bɪz·nəs·mæn) *n.* [*pl.* **-men**] hombre de negocios.
buskin ('bʌs·kɪn) *n.* borceguí.
busman ('bʌs·mən) *n.* [*pl.* **-men**] conductor de autobús. —**busman's holiday,** vacación tonta.
bust (bʌst) *n.* **1,** *anat.* busto; pecho. **2,** *sculp.* busto. **3,** *slang* (failure) fallo; fracaso. **4,** *slang* (spree) juerga; parranda. —*v.i., slang.* **1,** (burst) reventar; estallar. **2,** (fail) fallar; fracasar. —**busted,** *adj., slang* sin dinero; tronado.
buster ('bʌs·tər) *n., slang* **1,** (something noteworthy) maravilla; sensación. **2,** (spree) francachela; juerga. **3,** *often cap., usu. derog.* (boy) chico; muchacho.
bustle ('bʌs·əl) *v.i.* pulular; bullir. —*n.* **1,** (stir) agitación; ruido; bulla. **2,** (pad on the back of a skirt) caderilla; almohadillas (*pl.*).
busy ('bɪz·i) *adj.* atareado; ocupado. —*v.t.* ocupar; atarear. —**busy oneself,** atarearse; ocuparse.
busybody ('bɪz·i·bad·i) *n.* chismoso; entrometido; enredador.
but (bʌt) *adv.* sólo; simplemente. —*conj.* mas; pero; no obstante; sin embargo. —*prep.* excepto; salvo.

—**all but**, casi todo. —**but for**, a excepción de; salvo; si no es por *o* si no fuese por.
butane (bju'tein) *n.* butano.
butcher ('butʃ·ər) *n.* **1,** (cutter or seller of meat) carnicero. **2,** *fig.* (assassin) asesino. —*v.t.* **1,** (slaughter) matar. **2,** *fig.* (murder) asesinar. —**butchery,** *n.* matanza; carnicería. —**butcher shop,** carnicería.
butler ('bʌt·lər) *n.* mayordomo.
butt (bʌt) *n.* **1,** (cask) tonel; barril; pipa. **2,** (thick end) extremo; mango. **3,** (target) blanco. **4,** (cigarette end) colilla. **5,** (blow with the head) topetazo. **6,** (of a gun) culata. —*v.t.* **1,** (strike with the head) topar; embestir; chocar con; arremeter contra. **2,** (abut on) confinar con; lindar con. —**butt in,** *slang* interferir; entremeterse.
butter ('bʌt·ər) *n.* mantequilla; *Sp.* manteca de vaca. —*v.t.* **1,** (put butter on) untar con mantequilla. **2,** *colloq.* [*también,* **butter up**] (flatter) adular; halagar. —**buttery,** *adj.* con *o* de mantequilla.
buttercup ('bʌt·ər·kʌp) *n.* ranúnculo; botón de oro.
butterfly ('bʌt·ər·flai) *n.* **1,** (insect) mariposa. **2,** *colloq.* (flirtatious girl) mujer alegre.
buttermilk ('bʌt·ər·mɪlk) *n.* nata agria *o* suero agrio de la leche.
buttocks ('bʌt·əks) *n.pl.* (of a person) nalgas; asentaderas; trasero (*sing.*); asiento (*sing.*); (of an animal) ancas.
button ('bʌt·ən) *n.* botón. —*v.t.* abotonar; abrochar.
buttonhole ('bʌt·ən·hol) *n.* ojal. —*v.t.* **1,** (slit) hacer ojales; abrir ojales. **2,** *colloq.* (grasp by the lapel) coger por las solapas.
buttonwood *n.* plátano.
buttress ('bʌt·rɪs) *n.* **1,** *archit.* contrafuerte. 2, *fig.* (prop) refuerzo; apoyo. —*v.t.* reforzar; entibar.
butyl ('bju·tɪl) *n.* butilo. —**butylene** (-tə'liːn) *n.* butileno.
buxom ('bʌk·səm) *adj.* robusto; fuerte; desarrollado. —**buxomness,** *n.* robustez; desarrollo.
buy (bai) *v.t.* [**bought, buying**] **1,** (purchase) comprar. **2,** (win by striving) lograr; obtener; alcanzar. **3,** (bribe) comprar; sobornar. —*n.*, *colloq.* compra.
buyer ('bai·ər) *n.* **1,** *comm.* (purchasing agent) comprador. **2,** (purchaser) cliente; parroquiano.
buzz (bʌːz) *n.* **1,** (hum) zumbido. **2,** *slang* (telephone call) telefonazo. —*v.i.* **1,** (hum) zumbar; sonar. **2,** (gossip) chismorrear; cuchichear. **3,** (bustle) atarearse; afanarse. —*v.t., slang* **1,** *aero.* volar muy bajo por encima de. **2,** (telephone) telefonear. —**buzzer,** *n.* zumbador; vibrador.
buzzard ('bʌz·ərd) *n.* busardo.
by (bai) *prep.* **1,** (beside; near) a; en; cerca a *o* de; junto a. **2,** (along; over) por; hacia. **3,** (past; beyond) después de; tras. **4,** (through the action or agency of) por; con. **5,** (in or to amount or degree of) a; por. **6,** (before; no later than) a; en; de; por. **7,** (with permission of) por. **8,** (according to; in) de acuerdo a *o* con; según; por; a **9,** (with respect to) por. —*adv.* **1,** (beside) cerca; al lado. **2,** (aside) aparte; a un lado. **3,** (past) ya. —**by oneself,** solo; por sí mismo; sin ayuda. —**by the way,** a propósito; entre paréntesis; de paso. —**by way of,** por medio de. —**by and large,** en general; en conjunto.
by- (bai) *prefijo* **1,** secundario: *by-product,* producto parcial; subproducto. **2,** cerca; alrededor: *bystander,* espectador. **3,** aparte; separado: *by-street,* callejuela; calle lateral.
bygone ('bai·gan) *adj.* pasado; anterior. —*adv.* anteriormente. —**bygones,** *n.pl.* cosas pasadas; hechos pasados; sucesos.
bylaw ('bai,lɔ) *n.* estatuto; reglamento; ordenanza.
by-line *n.* nombre de autor.
by-pass ('bai·pæs) *n.* **1,** (detour) desviación; desvío; **2,** (of a pipe) derivación. —*v.t.* rodear.
bypath ('bai·pæθ) *n.* **1,** (side road) sendero. **2,** (detour) desviación; desvío.
by-product *n.* sub-producto; residuo.
byroad *n.* camino vecinal.
bystander *n.* espectador; mirón.
byway ('bai·wei) *n.* camino accesorio.
byword ('bai,wʌɹd) *n.* **1,** (axiom) proverbio; refrán. **2,** (slogan) mote. **3,** (nickname) apodo.
Byzantine ('bɪz·ən,tin) *n.* & *adj.* bizantino.

C

C, c (siː) tercera letra del alfabeto inglés. —*n.*, *music* do.
cab (kæːb) *n.* **1,** (hired vehicle) taxímetro; taxi; coche. **2,** (driver's compartment) cabina. —**cab driver; cabman,** *n.* taxista; cochero; chófer.
cabal (kə'bæl) *n.* cábala. —*v.i.* intrigar; maquinar. —**cabalist** ('kæb·ə,lɪst) *n.* cabalista. —**cabalistic,** *adj.* cabalístico; oculto.
cabaret (kæ·bə'rei) *n.* sala de fiestas; cabaret.
cabbage ('kæb·ɪdʒ) *n.* col; berza; repollo. —**cabbage patch,** berzal.
cabin ('kæ·bɪn) *n.* **1,** (house) cabaña; choza; barraca; *W.I.* bohío. **2,** (stateroom on a ship) camarote; cabina; cámara. **3,** (airplane compartment) cabina.
cabinet ('kæb·ɪ·nət) *n.* **1,** (cupboard) alacena. **2,** (for medicines) botiquín. **3,** (of a radio) caja; mueble. **4,** (advisory body) gabinete; ministerio.
cabinetmaker *n.* ebanista.
cabinetwork *n.* ebanistería.
cable ('kei·bəl) *n.* **1,** (rope) maroma; cuerda. **2,** (wire) cable. **3,** *naut.* (hawser) amarra. **4,** = **cablegram. 5,** (measure of 120 fathoms) cable. —*v.t.* & *i.* cablegrafiar. —**cable address,** dirección cablegrafica.
cablegram ('kei·bəl,græm) *n.* cablegrama.
caboose (kə'bus) *n.*, *R.R.* furgón de cola.
cabriolet (,kæb·ri·ə'lei) *n.* cabriolé.
cacao (kə'ka·o) *n.*, cacao.
cachalot ('kæʃ·ə,lat; -,lo) *n.* cachalote.
cache (kæʃ) *n.* **1,** (hiding place) escondrijo; escondite. **2,** (hidden supply) depósito; repuesto. —*v.t.* esconder; ocultar.
cackle ('kæk·əl) *n.* **1,** (sound of fowl) cacareo. **2,** (chatter) charla; cháchara. **3,** (laughter) risotada; carcajada. —*v.i.* **1,** (of fowl) cacarear. **2,** (chatter) charlar. **3,** (laugh raucously) dar risotadas *o* carcajadas; reír estrepitosamente.
cacophony (kə'kaf·ə·ni) *n.* cacofonía. —**cacophonous,** *adj.* cacofónico.
cactus ('kæk·təs) *n.* [*pl.* **-ti** (-tai)] cacto.
cad (kæːd) *n.* sinvergüenza; canalla. —**caddish** ('kæd·ɪʃ) *adj.* canallesco; inescrupuloso.
cadaver (kə'dæv·ər) *n.* cadáver. —**cadaverous,** *adj.* cadavérico.
caddie *también,* **caddy** ('kæd·i) *n.* muchacho de golf. —*v.i.* ser *o* servir de muchacho de golf.
cadence ('kei·dəns) *n.* cadencia; ritmo.
cadenza (kə'dɛn·zə) *n.*, *music* cadencia.
cadet (kə'dɛt) *n.* **1,** *mil.* (student) cadete. **2,** (younger brother) hermano menor. **3,** (younger son) hijo menor.
cadmium ('kæd·mi·əm) *n.* cadmio.
cadre ('ka·dər) *n.* **1,** (nucleus) núcleo. **2,** *mil.* (officer corps) cuadro de jefes.
caduceus (kə'du·si·əs) *n.* [*pl.* **-cei** (-si·ai)] caduceo.
caecum ('si·kəm) *n.* intestino ciego.
Caesarean (sɪ'zɛr·i·ən) *adj.* cesáreo; imperial. —**Caesarean operation** *o* **section,** operación cesárea; cesárea.
caesura (sɪ'ʒur·ə) *n.* cesura.
café (kæ'fei) *n.* café.
cafeteria (,kæf·ə'tɪr·i·ə) *n.* restaurante de autoservicio; *Amer.* cafetería.
caffeine ('kæf·in) *n.* cafeína.
cage (keidʒ) *n.* jaula; alambrera. —*v.t.* enjaular.
caisson ('kei·sən) *n.* **1,** *mil.* cajón. **2,** *engin.* cajón hidráulico. **3,** *naut.* camello; cajón de suspensión.
cajole (kə'dʒoːl) *v.t.* & *i.* halagar; lisonjear; adular. —**cajolery,** *n.* lisonja; adulación.
cake (keik) *n.* **1,** (pastry) bizcocho; pastel; torta. **2,** (loaflike mass) pastilla.
calabash ('kæl·ə,bæʃ) *n.* calabaza.

calaboose ('kæl·ə·bus) *n., slang* calabozo.
calamine ('kæl·əˌmain) *n.* calamina.
calamity (kə'læm·ə·ti) *n.* calamidad; desastre; desgracia. —**calamitous**, *adj.* calamitoso; desastroso.
calcareous (kæl'kɛr·i·əs) *adj.* calcáreo; calizo.
calcify ('kæl·sɪˌfai) *v.t.* calcificar. —*v.i.* calcificarse. —**calcification** (-fɪ'kei·ʃən) *n.* calcificación.
calcimine *también,* **kalsomine** ('kæl·səˌmain) *n.* lechada. —*v.t.* dar lechada a.
calcine ('kæl·sain) *v.t. & i.* calcinar.
calcium ('kæl·si·əm) *n.* calcio.
calculate ('kæl·kju·leit) *v.t.* **1,** *math.* calcular; computar. **2,** (plan) proyectar; planear. **3,** *colloq.* (guess) pretender; creer; suponer. —*v.i.* hacer cálculos. —**calculable,** *adj.* calculable. —**calculation,** *n.* cálculo; calculación. —**calculator,** *n.* calculador.
calculus ('kæl·kju·ləs) *n.* **1,** *math.* cálculo. **2,** [*pl.* **-li** (-lai)] *pathol.* cálculo; piedra.
caldron *también,* **cauldron** ('kɔl·drən) *n.* caldera.
calendar ('kæl·ən·dər) *n.* **1,** (list or table of dates) calendario. **2,** *law* orden del día; lista de pleitos. —*v.t.* incluir en el calendario; poner en lista.
calendula (kə'lɛnd·jə·lə) *n.* caléndula.
calf (kæf) *n.* [*pl.* **calves**] **1,** (young animal) ternero (*masc.*); ternera (*fem.*); becerro. **2,** (calfskin) piel de becerro. **3,** *anat.* pantorrilla.
caliber *también,* **calibre** ('kæl·ə·bər) *n.* **1,** (diameter) calibre. **2,** (ability) calibre; aptitud; capacidad.
calibrate ('kæl·ə·breit) *v.t.* calibrar; graduar. —**calibration,** *n.* calibración; graduación.
calico ('kæl·ɪˌko) *n.* calicó.
californium (ˌkæl·ə'for·ni·əm) *n.* californio.
caliper *también,* **calliper** ('kæl·ɪ·pər) *n.* calibrador. —*v.t. & i.* medir el calibre; calibrar.
caliph ('kei·lɪf) *n.* califa. —**caliphate** ('kæl·ɪ·feit) *n.* califato.
calisthenics (kæl·əs'θɛn·ɪks) *n.pl.* calistenia (*sing.*). —**calisthenic,** *adj.* calisténico.
calk (kɔk) *n.* ramplón. —*v.t.* [*también,* **caulk**] calafatear.
call (kɔl) *v.t.* **1,** (speak loudly) llamar; anunciar; proclamar. **2,** (demand the attention of) atraer. **3,** (summon) citar; llamar. **4,** (designate) nombrar; designar. **5,** (telephone) telefonear; llamar por teléfono. —*v.i.* **1,** (shout) gritar; dar voces. **2,** (visit) hacer una visita; visitar. —*n.* **1,** (cry; shout) llamada; grito. **2,** (call of an animal, bird, bugle, etc.) llamada; reclamo. **3,** (notice; summons; invitation) aviso; citación; invitación. **4,** (visit) visita. **5,** *comm.* demanda. —**close call,** escape por un pelo.
calla ('kæl·ə) *n.* cala. *También,* **calla lily.**
caller ('kɔl·ər) *n.* **1,** (device) llamador. **2,** (visitor) visitante; visita.
call girl prostituta que uno solicita por teléfono.
calligraphy (kə'lɪg·rə·fi) *n.* caligrafía. —**calligrapher,** *n.* calígrafo. —**calligraphic** (ˌkæl·ə'græf·ɪk) *adj.* caligráfico.
calling (kɔl·ɪŋ) *n.* **1,** (vocation) profesión; oficio; vocación. **2,** (summons) invitación.
callous ('kæl·əs) *adj.* **1,** (hardened) calloso; endurecido. **2,** *fig.* (insensitive) insensible; duro; seco. —**callousness,** *n.* callosidad. —**callosity** (kə'las·ə·ti) *n.* callosidad; dureza.
callow ('kæl·o) *adj.* **1,** (immature) inexperto; joven; inmaturo. **2,** (unfledged) desplumado; pelado. —**callowness,** *n.* inexperiencia.
callus ('kæl·əs) *n.* callo; dureza.
calm (kaːm) *adj.* tranquilo; sereno; quieto. —*n.* calma; tranquilidad; serenidad. —*v.t.* aquietar; tranquilizar. —*v.i.* [*también,* **calm down**] calmarse; tranquilizarse. —**calmness,** *n.* quietud; serenidad.
calomel ('kæl·ə·məl) *n.* calomel.
calorie ('kæl·ə·ri) *n.* caloría. —**caloric** (kə'lor·ɪk) *adj.* calórico.
calumniate (kə'lʌm·ni·eit) *v.t.* calumniar. —**calumniation,** *n.* calumnia. —**calumnious,** *adj.* calumnioso.
calumny ('kæl·əm·ni) *n.* calumnia.
calvary ('kæl·və·ri) *n.* calvario.
calve (kæːv) *v.i.* parir una vaca.
calves (kæːvz) *n., pl. de* **calf.**
calyx ('kei·lɪks) *n.* [*pl.* **calyxes** (-ɪz) *o* **calyces** ('kei·ləˌsiz)] cáliz.

cam (kæm) *n., mech.* leva.
camaraderie (ˌka·məˈra·də·ri) *n.* camaradería.
cambric (ˈkeim·brɪk) *n.* cambray; batista.
came (keim) *v., pret. de* **come.**
camel (ˈkæm·əl) *n.* camello.
camellia (kəˈmil·jə) *n.* camelia.
cameo (ˈkæm·i·o) *n.* [*pl.* **-os**] camafeo.
camera (ˈkæm·ə·rə) *n.* cámara fotográfica.
cameraman *n.* [*pl.* **-men**] operador.
camomile (ˈkæm·əˌmail) *n.* camomila; manzanilla.
Camorra (kəˈmor·ə) *n.* Camorra.
camouflage (ˈkæm·ə·flaʒ) *n.* **1,** (disguise) disfraz; *mil.* camuflaje. **2,** (false pretense) engaño; fingimiento. —*v.t.* disfrazar; *mil.* camuflar.
camp (kæmp) *n.* **1,** (shelter) campamento; campo; colonia. **2,** *fig.* (group) partido; agrupación; cuerpo; clase. —*v.i.* acampar. —**camper,** *n.* acampado; quien va a acampar.
campaign (kæmˈpein) *n.* campaña. —*v.i.* hacer campaña.
campanile (ˌkæm·pəˈni·li) *n.* campanario.
campfire *n.* fuego u hoguera de campamento.
camphor (ˈkæm·fər) *n.* alcanfor. —**camphorate** (-eit) *v.t.* alcanforar.
campus (ˈkæm·pəs) *n.* jardines *o* terrenos de un centro universitario.
can (kæːn) *v.aux.* [*pret.* **could**] **1,** (be able) poder. **2,** *colloq.* (may) tener permiso para; poder. —*n.* lata; bote. —*v.t.* [**canned, canning**] **1,** (preserve) enlatar. **2,** *slang* (dismiss) despedir; dejar cesante. —**can opener,** abrelatas.
Canadian (kəˈnei·di·ən) *adj.* & *n.* canadiense.
canal (kəˈnæːl) *n.* canal.
canalize (ˈkæn·əˌlaiz) *v.t.* canalizar. —**canalization** (-lɪˈzei·ʃən) *n.* canalización.
canapé (ˈkæn·ə·pi; -ˌpe) *n.* entremés; aperitivo; bocadito.
canard (kəˈnaːrd) *n.* decepción; engaño; burla.
canary (kəˈnɛr·i) *n.* **1,** (bird) canario. **2,** (color) amarillo canario.
canasta (kəˈnæs·tə) *n.* canasta.
cancan (ˈkæn·kæn) *n.* cancán.
cancel (ˈkæn·səl) *v.t.* & *i.* **1,** (strike out) cancelar; anular; invalidar. **2,** *math.; print.* suprimir. —**cancellation,** *n.* cancelación; invalidación; (of stamps or currency) inutilización.
cancer (ˈkæn·sər) *n.,* **1,** *pathol.* cáncer. **2,** *cap., astron.* Cáncer. —**cancerous,** *adj.* canceroso.
candelabrum (kæn·dəˈla·brəm) *n.* [*pl.* **-bra** (-brə)] candelabro.
candid (ˈkæn·dɪd) *adj.* sincero; franco. —**candidness,** *n.* sinceridad; franqueza.
candidate (ˈkæn·də·det) *n.* candidato; aspirante. —**candidacy** (-də·si) *n.* candidatura.
candied (ˈkæn·did) *adj.* azucarado; almibarado; confitado.
candle (ˈkæn·dəl) *n.* candela; vela; bujía. —*v.t.* examinar; probar (huevos). —**candle power,** fuerza de iluminación; bujía.
candlemaker *n.* velero; cerero.
candlestick *n.* candelero.
candor *también,* **candour** (ˈkæn·dər) *n.* candor; sinceridad; integridad.
candy (ˈkæn·di) *n.* dulce; bombón; caramelo. —*v.t.* **1,** (cook) almibarar; garapiñar. **2,** *fig.* (make agreeable) endulzar; suavizar. —**candy dish; candy box,** bombonera.
cane (kein) *n.* **1,** (stick) bastón; caña; palo. **2,** *bot.* caña. **3,** (woody fiber) mimbre; junco. —*v.t.* **1,** (flog) apalear. **2,** (weave) tejer con mimbre *o* junco.
canebrake (ˈkeinˌbreik) *n.* cañaveral.
canine (ˈkei·nain) *n.* & *adj.* canino. —**canine tooth,** diente canino.
canister (ˈkæn·ɪs·tər) *n.* bote; lata; frasco.
canker (ˈkæŋ·kər) *n.* llaga ulcerosa *o* gangrenosa. —*v.t.* **1,** (ulcerate) gangrenar; ulcerar; **2,** *fig.* (corrupt) corromper; emponzoñar. —*v.i.* gangrenarse; ulcerarse. —**cankerous,** *adj.* gangrenoso.
canner (ˈkæn·ər) *n.* enlatador; envasador. —**cannery,** *n.* fábrica de conservas.
cannibal (ˈkæn·ə·bəl) *n.* caníbal; antropófago. —**cannibalism,** *n.* canibalismo. —**cannibalistic,** *adj.* caníbal.
cannon (ˈkæn·ən) *n.* **1,** (gun) cañón. **2,** (carom) carambola. —**cannonade** (ˌkæn·əˈneid) *n.* ca-

ñoneo. —*v.t.* & *i.* cañonear. —**cannonry** (-ri) *n.* cañonería.
cannot ('kæn·at) = **can not.**
cannula ('kæn·jə·lə) *n.* [*pl.* **-lae** (-li)] cánula.
canny ('kæn·i) *adj.* prudente; sagaz; sensato. —**canniness,** *n.* sagacidad; sensatez.
canoe (kə'nuː) *n.* canoa. —*v.i.* navegar *o* ir en canoa. —**canoeist,** *n.* canoero.
canon ('kæn·ən) *n.* **1,** (rule; law) canon; regla; ley eclesiástica. **2,** *Bib.* libros canónicos. **3,** (church official) canónigo. —**canon law,** *n.* derecho canónico.
cañon ('kæn·jən) *n.* = **canyon.**
canonical (kə'nan·ɪ·kəl) *adj.* canónico. —**canonicals,** *n.pl.* vestiduras.
canonicity (ˌkæ·nə'nɪs·ə·ti) *n.* canonicidad.
canonist ('kæn·ən·ɪst) *n.* canonista.
canonize ('kæn·əˌnaiz) *v.t.* canonizar. —**canonization** (-nɪ'zei·ʃən) *n.* canonización.
canonry ('kæn·ən·ri) *n.* canonjía.
canopy ('kæn·ə·pi) *n.* dosel; pabellón; *fig.* cielo.
cant (kæːnt) *n.* **1,** (insincerity) hipocresía. **2,** (jargon) jerga; jerigonza; argot. **3,** (slant) inclinación; sesgo. **4,** (salient angle) esquina; canto. —*v.i.* hablar en jerga. —*v.t.* achaflanar; inclinar; poner al sesgo.
can't (kæːnt; kant) *v., contr. de* **cannot.**
cantaloupe ('kæn·təˌlop) *n.* cantalupo.
cantankerous (kæn'tæŋ·kər·əs) *adj.* pendenciero; camorrista; mal inclinado. —**cantankerousness,** *n.* camorra; pendencia.
cantata (kən'ta·tə) *n.* cantata.
canteen (kæn'tiːn) *n.* **1,** (shop) cantina. **2,** (container) cantimplora.
canter ('kæn·tər) *n.* medio galope. —*v.i.* ir a medio galope.
cantilever ('kæn·təˌli·vər) *n.* modillón; soporte. —*adj.* a modillones.
canto ('kæn·to) *n.* canto.
canton ('kæn·tən) *n.* cantón. —*v.t.* cantonar; acantonar. —**cantonment** (-'tan·mənt) *n.* acantonamiento; acuartelamiento.
cantor ('kæn·tər) *n.* cantor, esp. de sinagoga.
canvas ('kæn·vəs) *n.* **1,** (cloth) lona; cañamazo; lienzo. **2,** (sail) vela; lona. **3,** (painting) óleo; cuadro.
canvass ('kæn·vəs) *v.t.* **1,** (solicit votes) recorrer pidiendo votos. **2,** (investigate) examinar; discutir; averiguar. —*v.i.* pedir *o* solicitar votos, opiniones, impresiones, etc. —*n.* **1,** (campaign) campaña para pedir votos. **2,** (survey) examen; investigación; encuesta.
canyon ('kæn·jən) *n.* cañón.
cap (kæp) *n.* **1,** (hat) gorro; gorra. **2,** (top) tapadera; tapa. **3,** (peak; summit) cima; cumbre; pináculo. **4,** (explosive device) fulminante. —*v.t.* [**capped, capping**] **1,** (cover) tapar; cubrir. **2,** (culminate) completar; finalizar; coronar. **3,** (surpass) mejorar; aventajar.
capable ('kei·pə·bəl) *adj.* capaz; competente; eficiente. —**capability,** *n.* capacidad; competencia; eficiencia.
capacious (kə'pei·ʃəs) *adj.* capaz; amplio; holgado; espacioso. —**capaciousness,** *n.* capacidad; espaciosidad.
capacity (kə'pæs·ə·ti) *n.* **1,** (volume) capacidad; cabida; volumen. **2,** (ability) capacidad; aptitud; idoneidad. **3,** (function) capacidad; facultad; poder.
caparison (kə'pær·ɪ·sən) *n.* **1,** (trappings) caparazón. **2,** (clothing) equipo; vestido fastuoso. —*v.t.* enjaezar.
cape (keip) *n.* **1,** (garment) capa. **2,** (point of land) cabo.
caper ('kei·pər) *v.i.* cabriolear; cabriolar. —*n.* **1,** (leap) cabriola; voltereta. **2,** (bud) alcaparra.
capillary ('kæp·əˌlɛr·i) *adj.* capilar. —*n.* capilar; vaso capilar. —**capillarity** (-'lær·ə·ti) *n.* capilaridad.
capital ('kæp·ɪ·təl) *n.* **1,** (city) capital. **2,** (letter) mayúscula. **3,** *archit.* capitel; chapitel. **4,** *econ.* capital. —*adj.* **1,** (chief) principal; capital; excelente. **2,** *law* capital. —**capital punishment,** pena capital; pena de muerte. —**capital ship,** acorazado grande.
capitalism ('kæp·ɪ·təlˌɪz·əm) *n.* capitalismo. —**capitalist,** *n.* capitalista. —**capitalistic,** *adj.* capitalista.
capitalization (ˌkæp·ɪ·tə·lɪ'zei·ʃən) *n.* **1,** *finance* capitalización. **2,** (profitable use) aprovechamiento. **3,** *orthography* escritura en mayúsculas.

capitalize ('kæp·ɪ·tə,laiz) *v.t.* **1,** *finance* capitalizar. **2,** [*usu.*, **capitalize on**] (use to advantage) sacar provecho de. **3,** *orthography* poner en mayúsculas.
capitol ('kæp·ɪ·təl) *n.* capitolio.
capitular (kə'pɪt·jə·lər) *adj.* capitular. *También,* **capitulary** (-,lɛr·i).
capitulate (kə'pɪtʃ·ə·leit) *v.i.* capitular; rendirse. —**capitulation,** *n.* capitulación.
capon ('ke·pan) *n.* capón.
caprice (kə'pris) *n.* capricho; antojo; veleidad. —**capricious** (-'priʃ·əs) *adj.* caprichoso; veleidoso.
Capricorn ('kæp·rɪ,korn) *n.* Capricornio.
capsize (kæp'saiz) *v.t.* volcar; zozobrar. —*v.i.* volcarse.
capstan ('kæp·stən) *n.* cabrestante.
capsule ('kæp·səl) *n.* cápsula. —*adj.* capsular. —**capsular,** *adj.* capsular.
captain ('kæp·tən) *n.* capitán. —*v.t.* mandar; gobernar; dirigir. —**captaincy,** *n.* capitanía. —**captainship,** *n.* capitanía.
caption ('kæp·ʃən) *n.* titular; título; encabezamiento; pie de grabado.
captious ('kæp·ʃəs) *adj.* capcioso; quisquilloso. —**captiousness,** *n.* capciosidad.
captivate ('kæp·tɪ·veit) *v.t.* cautivar; fascinar. —**captivation,** *n.* fascinación.
captive ('kæp·tɪv) *n.* & *adj.* cautivo; prisionero.
captivity (kæp'tɪv·ə·ti) *n.* **1,** (physical) cautividad; esclavitud; cautiverio. **2,** (mental) sujeción; fascinación.
captor ('kæp·tər) *n.* aprehensor; apresador.
capture ('kæp·tʃər) *v.t.* capturar; apresar; detener. —*n.* **1,** (act) captura; aprehensión; detención. **2,** (prey) presa; botín.
Capuchin ('kæp·ju·ʃɪn) *adj. & n., eccles.* capuchino. —*n., zool.* [*también,* **capuchin monkey**] (mono) capuchino.
car (kar) *n.* **1,** (automobile) automóvil; coche. **2,** (elevator) caja de ascensor. **3,** *R.R.* vagón. —**closed car,** sedán.
caracul ('kær·ə·kəl) *n.* caracul.
carabao (,kar·ə'ba·o) *n.* carabao.
carafe (kə'ræf) *n.* garrafa; botella de cristal.
caramel ('kær·ə·məl) *n.* caramelo.
caramelize ('kær·ə·mə,laiz) *v.t.* acaramelar. —*v.i.* acaramelarse.
carapace ('kær·ə,pes) *n.* carapacho.
carat *también,* **karat** ('kær·ət) *n.* quilate.
caravan ('kær·ə·væn) *n.* **1,** (group) caravana. **2,** (vehicle) camión de mudanzas.
caravel ('kær·ə,vɛl) *n.* carabela.
caraway ('kær·ə·wei) *n.* alcaravea.
carbide ('kar·baid) *n.* carburo.
carbine ('kar·bain) *n.* carabina.
carbohydrate (,kar·bo'hai·dret) *n.* hidrato de carbono; carbohidrato.
carbolic (kar'bal·ɪk) *adj.* carbólico.
carbon ('kar·bən) *n.* **1,** *chem.* carbono. **2,** *electricity* carbón (de filamento, de batería). **3,** (paper) papel carbón. **4,** (copy) copia al *o* de carbón.
carbonaceous (,kar·bə'nei·ʃəs) *adj.* carbonoso.
carbonate ('kar·bə·neit) *v.t.* carbonatar. —*n.* (-nət) carbonato. —**carbonated water,** aqua de soda.
carbon dioxide anhídrido *o* ácido carbónico.
carbonic (kar'ban·ɪk) *adj.* carbónico.
carboniferous (,kar·bə'nɪf·ər·əs) *adj.* carbonífero.
carbonize ('kar·bə,naiz) *v.t.* carbonizar. —*v.i.* carbonizarse. —**carbonization** (-nɪ'zei·ʃən) *n.* carbonización.
carbon monoxide monóxido de carbono.
carbon tetrachloride tetracloruro de carbón.
carborundum (,kar·bə'rʌn·dəm) *n.* carborundo.
carboy ('kar·bɔi) *n.* bombona.
carbuncle ('kar·bʌŋ·kəl) *n.* **1,** *jewelry* carbúnculo. **2,** *pathol.* carbunco.
carburetor ('kar·bə,re·tər) *n.* carburador.
carcass ('kar·kəs) *n.* animal muerto.
carcinoma (,kar·sə'no·mə) *n.* carcinoma.
card (kard) *n.* **1,** (social) tarjeta. **2,** (for games) carta; naipe. **3,**

(program) anuncio; papeleta; aviso. **4,** (bill of fare) carta. **5,** (cardboard) tarjeta; cartulina. **6,** (tool) carda; cardencha. **7,** *colloq.* (amusing person) chistoso; bromista; —*v.t.* **1,** (comb) cardar. **2,** (schedule) señalar; designar; preparar. —**lay one's cards on the table,** descubrir el juego.

cardboard *n.* cartón.

cardi- (kar·di) *prefijo, var. de* **cardio-** *ante vocal: cardialgia,* cardialgia.

cardiac ('kar·di·æk) *adj.* & *n.* cardíaco.

cardialgia (ˌkar·di'æl·dʒi·ə) *n.* cardialgia.

cardinal ('kar·də·nəl) *adj.* **1,** (fundamental) cardinal; principal; fundamental. **2,** (color) púrpura; violeta; cardenal. —*n., eccles.; ornith.* cardenal. —**cardinalate,** *n.* cardenalato.

cardio- (kar·di·o) *prefijo* cardio-; corazón: *cardiogram,* cardiograma.

cardiology (ˌkar·di'al·ə·dʒi) *n.* cardiología. —**cardiological** (-ə·'ladʒ·ɪ·kəl) *adj.* cardiológico. —**cardiologist,** *n.* cardiólogo.

carditis (kar'dai·tɪs) *n.* carditis.

cardsharp *también,* **cardsharper** *n.* tahur.

care (keːr) *n.* **1,** (heed) cuidado; atención; solicitud. **2,** (anxiety) zozobra; ansiedad. **3,** (protection) custodia; cargo —*v.i.* preocuparse; cuidarse; hacer caso. —**care for, 1,** (tend) cuidar; cuidar de; proteger. **2,** (be fond of) querer; estimar; apreciar. **3,** (desire) desear; gustar. —**in care of,** al cuidado de; a cargo de. —**take care,** tener cuidado.

careen (kə'riːn) *v.t.* inclinar; volcar. —*v.i.* volcarse; echarse de costado.

career (kə'rɪr) *n.* **1,** (course of events) curso. **2,** (speed) carrera. **3,** (calling) carrera; profesión. —*v.i.* correr a carrera tendida *o* a toda marcha.

carefree *adj.* sin preocupaciones; libre de cuidados.

careful ('kɛr·fəl) *adj.* cuidadoso; cauteloso; prudente. —**carefulness,** *n.* prudencia; cautela; atención.

careless ('kɛr·ləs) *adj.* **1,** (reckless) descuidado; desatento; negligente. **2,** (unworried) despreocupado. —**carelessness,** *n.* descuido; negligencia; despreocupación.

caress (kə'rɛs) *v.t.* acariciar; mimar. —*n.* caricia; mimo; terneza.

caret ('kær·ət) *n.* signo de intercalación (^).

caretaker ('kɛr·tek·ər) *n.* guardián; celador; vigilante.

careworn *adj.* agobiado; abatido; cansado.

cargo (kar·go) *n.* carga; cargamento.

Carib ('kær·ɪb) *adj.* & *n.* caribe.

Caribbean (ˌkær·ə'bi·ən; kə·'rɪb·i-) *adj.* caribe. —*n.* mar Caribe.

caricature ('kær·i·kəˌtʃʊr) *n.* caricatura. —*v.t.* caricaturizar. —**caricaturist,** *n.* caricaturista.

caries ('keːr·iz) *n.* caries.

carillon ('kær·əˌlan) *n.* carillón. —**carillonneur** (-lə'nʌːɹ) *n.* campanero.

cariole ('kar·iˌol) *n.* carriola.

carious ('keːr·i·əs) *adj.* cariado.

carload *n.* **1,** *R.R.* vagonada; carga de un vagón. **2,** *fig.* (load) cargamento.

carmine ('kar·mɪn) *n.* & *adj.* carmín; color carmín.

carnage ('kar·nɪdʒ) *n.* carnicería; matanza.

carnal ('kar·nəl) *adj.* carnal; impúdico; lascivo. —**carnality** (-'næl·ə·ti) *n.* carnalidad; lascivia.

carnation (kar'nei·ʃən) *n.* clavel. —*adj.* encarnado; rosado.

carnival ('kar·nə·vəl) *n.* **1,** (festival) carnaval. **2,** (amusement park) feria. —*adj.* carnavalesco.

carnivore ('kar·nə·vor) *n.* carnívoro. —**carnivorous** (kar'nɪv·ə·rəs) *adj.* carnívoro.

carob ('kær·əb) *n.* **1,** (fruit) algarroba. **2,** (tree) algarrobo; algarrobera.

carol ('kær·əl) *n.* canción alegre; villancico. —*v.t. & i.* cantar (villancicos); cantar alegremente.

carom ('kær·əm) *n.* carambola. —*v.t.* & *i.* carambolear.

carotid (kə'rat·ɪd) *adj.* & *n.* carótida.

carouse (kə'rauz) *v.i.* parrandear; jaranear. —**carousal,** *n.* parranda; holgorio.

carp (karp) *n., ichthy.* carpa. —*v.i.* criticar; censurar.

-carp (karp) *sufijo* -carpio; fruta: *endocarp,* endocarpio.

carpel ('kar·pəl) *n.* carpelo.

carpenter ('kar·pən·tər) *n.* carpintero. —**carpentry** (-tri) *n.* carpintería.

carpet ('kar·pɪt) *n.* alfombra; tapiz. —*v.t.* alfombrar. —**carpeting,** *n.* tejido de alfombras; alfombrado. —**on the carpet,** *colloq.* **1,** (under consideration) en consideración. **2,** (being reprimanded) castigado; reprendido.

carpo- (kar·po) *prefijo* carpo-; fruta: *carpology,* carpología.

carriage ('kær·ɪdʒ) *n.* **1,** (vehicle) carruaje; coche. **2,** (posture) presencia; modales; porte. **3,** *mech.* soporte; jinete. **4,** (transport) acarreo; porte.

carrier ('kær·i·ər) *n.* **1,** (person) portador; mensajero; ordinario. **2,** *naval* portaaviones. **3,** (transporter) acarreador.

carriole ('kær·iˌol) *n.* = **cariole.**

carrion ('kær·i·ən) *n.* carroña.

carrot ('kær·ət) *n.* zanahoria.

carrousel *también,* **carousel** (ˌkær·ə'sɛl) *n.* tiovivo.

carry ('kær·i) *v.t.* **1,** (convey) transportar; acarrear; llevar. **2,** (support) aguantar; sostener. **3,** (pass as legislation) adoptar; aprobar; aceptar. **4,** (win the votes of) ganar; conseguir; lograr. **5,** *comm.* (stock) vender; tener surtido de. **6,** (transfer) trasladar; pasar. —*v.i.* alcanzar; llegar. —*n.* **1,** (distance) alcance. **2,** (portage) porteo. —**carry away, 1,** (remove) quitar; llevarse. **2,** *fig.* (delight) entusiasmar; encantar; llevar violentamente. —**carry forward,** *comm.* pasar a la cuenta; llevar. —**carried forward,** *comm.* suma y sigue. —**carry off, 1,** (win) ganar; lograr. **2,** *colloq.* (kill) llevar; matar. —**carry on, 1,** (engage in) ocuparse en; practicar. **2,** (persist) proseguir; continuar. **3,** *colloq.* (act foolishly) tontear; hacer el oso. —**carry out, 1,** (put into practice) aplicar. **2,** (accomplish) realizar; llevar a cabo. —**carry over,** aplazar; posponer. —**carry through, 1,** (accomplish) realizar; ejecutar. **2,** (sustain) ayudar; sostener hasta el final.

carryall *n.* carriola.

cart (kart) *n.* **1,** (small) carretilla; carrito. **2,** (medium) carretón. **3,** (big) carro; carreta; carromato. —*v.t.* & *i.* acarrear.

cartage ('kart·ɪdʒ) *n.* carretaje; acarreo.

carte blanche (kart'blanʃ) carta blanca.

cartel (kar'tɛl) *n.* cartel; reglamento; sociedad para un monopolio.

carter ('kar·tər) *n.* carretero.

cartilage ('kar·tə·lɪdʒ) *n.* cartílago. —**cartilaginous** (ˌkar·tə·'lædʒ·ə·nəs) *adj.* cartilaginoso.

cartography (kar'tag·rə·fi) *n.* cartografía. —**cartographer,** *n.* cartógrafo. —**cartographic** (ˌkar·tə·'græf·ɪk) *adj.* cartográfico.

carton ('kar·tən) *n.* caja de cartón.

cartoon (kar'tuːn) *n.* **1,** (caricature) caricatura; dibujo; boceto; historieta. **2,** (motion picture) dibujos animados; dibujo. —**cartoonist,** *n.* dibujante; caricaturista.

cartridge ('kar·trɪdʒ) *n.* **1,** (of ammunition) cartucho; bala; munición. **2,** (for a phonograph) cartucho. **3,** (of film) rollo.

carve (karv) *v.t.* & *i.* **1,** (sculpture) tallar; esculpir; cincelar. **2,** (slice food) trinchar.

cascade (kæs'keid) *n.* cascada; catarata; salto de agua.

case (keis) *n.* **1,** (event) caso. **2,** (condition; problem) caso; problema. **3,** *law* causa; pleito; caso. **4,** *med.* (disease) caso; (person) paciente. **5,** *gram.* caso. **6,** (box) caja; estuche; (of a knife) vaina. **7,** *print.* caja. **8,** *mech.* forro; cubierta. —*v.t.* **1,** (enclose) embalar; cubrir. **2,** *slang* (investigate) inspeccionar; registrar; examinar. —**upper case,** letra mayúscula. —**lower case,** letra minúscula.

casein ('kei·si·ɪn) *n.* caseína.

casement ('keis·mənt) *n.* marco de ventana; puerta ventana.

cash (kæʃ) *n.* **1,** (currency) dinero; efectivo. **2,** (immediate payment) contado; dinero contante y sonante. —*v.t.* cobrar; hacer efectivo; cambiar. —**cash and carry,** compra al contado. —**cash in, 1,** (convert to cash) cobrar; cambiar. **2,** *slang* (die) morirse; terminar. —**cash on delivery,** contra reembolso. —**cash register,** registradora; caja.

cashbook *n.* libro de caja.

cashew ('kæʃ·uː) *n.* anacardo.

cashier (kæ'ʃɪːr) *n.* cajero. —*v.t.,* *slang* degradar; destituir.

cashmere ('kæʃ·mɪr) *n.* casimir.

casino (kə'si·no) *n.* [*pl.* **-nos**] casino.

cask (kæsk) *n.* barril; tonel; cuba.

casket ('kæs·kət) *n.* **1,** (small box) joyero; estuche; cofrecito. **2,** (coffin) ataúd; féretro.
cassava (kə'sa·və) *n.* cazabe.
casserole ('kæs·ə·rol) *n.* cacerola.
cassia ('kæʃ·ə) *n.* casia.
cassock ('kæs·ək) *n.* **1,** (clerical garment) sotana. **2,** (coat) balandrán.
cast (kæst; kast) *v.t.* [*pret.* & *p.p.* **cast**] **1,** (hurl) tirar; lanzar. **2,** (shed) despedir; echar. **3,** (arrange) calcular; planear; computar. **4,** *theat.* (as[illegible] roles) elegir (actores); repartir (papeles de una obra). **5,** (mold) vaciar; moldear. —*v.i.* **1,** (throw) tirar. **2,** (conjecture) idear; pronosticar; conjeturar. —*n.* **1,** (throw) tiro; lanzamiento. **2,** [*también,* **casting**] (thing made from a mold) molde. **3,** *theat.* (the company) reparto. **4,** (tendency) inclinación; tendencia. **5,** (computation) recuento; computación. —**cast a ballot,** votar. —**cast away, 1,** (discard) abandonar; desechar. **2,** *naut.* naufragar. —**cast down, 1,** (project downward) abatir; derribar. **2,** (sadden) abatir; desanimar. —**cast off, 1,** (abandon) desechar; abandonar. **2,** (free) libertar; librar. **3,** *naut.* desamarrar.
castanets (kæs·tə'nɛts) *n.* castañuelas; palillos.
castaway ('kæst·ə·wei) *n.* abandonado; náufrago.
caste (kæst; kast) *n.* casta; clase social.
caster ('kæs·tər) *n.* **1,** (molder) fundidor; vaciador; moldeador. **2,** *fig.* (guesser) adivino. **3,** (small wheel) rodaja de mobiliario. **4,** (cruet) vinagrera.
castigate ('kæs·tɪˌgeit) *v.t.* castigar; reprender; corregir. —**castigation,** *n.* castigo; corrección.
Castilian (kæs'tɪl·jən) *adj.* & *n.* castellano.
casting ('kæst·ɪŋ) *n.* **1,** (molding) fundición; vaciado. **2,** [*también,* **cast**] (thing molded) molde.
cast-iron *adj.* **1,** *lit.* de hierro colado. **2,** *fig.* (hardy) inflexible; duro; rígido. —**cast iron,** hierro fundido; hierro colado.
castle ('kæs·əl) *n.* **1,** (fortress) castillo; fortaleza. **2,** *chess* castillo. —*v.i.* & *t., chess* enrocar.
castoff ('kæst·af) *adj.* & *n.* abandonado; desechado.
castor oil ('kæs·tər'ɔil) *n.* aceite de ricino; aceite de castor.
castrate ('kæs·treit) *v.t.* capar; castrar. —**castration,** *n.* castración.
casual ('kæʒ·u·əl) *adj.* **1,** (offhand) casual; eventual; fortuito. **2,** (careless) negligente; sin cuidado. —*n.* trabajador temporero *o* eventual. —**casualness,** *n.* casualidad; contingencia.
casualty ('kæʒ·u·əl·ti) *n.* **1,** (injury; death) accidente. **2,** (person) accidentado. **3,** *mil.* baja.
casuist ('kæʒ·u·ɪst) *n.* casuista. —**casuistic,** *adj.* casuista; casuístico. —**casuistry,** *n.* casuística.
cat (kæt) *n.* **1,** (domesticated) gato. **2,** (wild) felino. **3,** *colloq.* (spiteful woman) mujer despreciable. —**cat nap,** siesta corta.
cata- (kæt·ə) *prefijo* cata-; *forma nombres y adjetivos denotando* **1,** oposición: *catapult,* catapulta. **2,** abajo; hacia abajo: *catabolism,* catabolismo. **3,** disolución; destrucción: *cataclysm,* cataclismo.
catabolism (kə'tæb·əˌlɪz·əm) *n.* catabolismo. —**catabolic** (ˌkæt·ə'bal·ɪk) *adj.* catabólico.
cataclysm ('kæt·ə·klɪz·əm) *n.* cataclismo. —**cataclysmic** (-'klɪz·mɪk) *adj.* de cataclismo.
catacomb ('kæt·ə·kom) *n.* catacumba.
catafalque ('kæt·əˌfælk) *n.* catafalco.
catalepsy ('kæt·ə·lɛp·si) *n.* catalepsia. —**cataleptic** (-'lɛp·tɪk) *adj.* cataléptico.
catalog *también,* **catalogue** ('kæt·ə·lag) *n.* catálogo; lista; índice. —*v.t.* catalogar; registrar; inventariar; clasificar.
Catalan ('kæt·əˌlæn) *adj.* & *n.* catalán.
Catalonian (ˌkæt·ə'lo·ni·ən) *adj.* & *n.* catalán.
catalpa (kə'tæl·pə) *n.* catalpa.
catalysis (kə'tæl·ə·sɪs) *n.* catálisis. —**catalyst** ('kæt·ə·lɪst) *n.* catalizador. —**catalytic** (-'lɪt·ɪk) *adj.* catalítico.
catamount ('kæt·ə·maunt) *n.* gato montés.
catapult ('kæt·ə·pʌlt) *n.* catapulta. —*v.t.* arrojar como catapulta. —*v.i.* saltar *o* brincar repentinamente.
cataract ('kæt·əˌrækt) *n.* **1,** (water) catarata; cascada. **2,** *pathol.* catarata.

catarrh (kə'taːr) *n.* catarro. —**catarrhal,** *adj.* catarral.
catastrophe (kə'tæs·trə·fi) *n.* catástrofe; desastre. —**catastrophic** (ˌkæt·ə'straf·ɪk) *adj.* catastrófico; desastroso.
catcall *n.* chifla; rechifla. —*v.t. & i.* chiflar; rechiflar.
catch (kætʃ) *v.t.* [*pret. & p.p.* **caught**] **1,** (seize) atrapar; agarrar; capturar. **2,** (overtake) atajar; interceptar. **3,** (halt) detener; controlar. **4,** (entrap) engañar. **5,** (get) coger; obtener. **6,** *colloq.* (understand) comprender; entender. —*v.i.* enredarse; pegarse; engancharse. —*n.* **1,** (act) captura; detención; prendimiento. **2,** (thing caught) presa; botín. **3,** *mech.* freno; tope; pestillo. **4,** *colloq.* (trick) trampa; engaño. **5,** *colloq.* (desirable thing) atractivo; ventaja. —**catch on, 1,** (become popular) prender; popularizarse. **2,** *colloq.* (understand) comprender; entender. —**catch up,** ponerse al día.
catch-all *n.* **1,** (box) arca; cofre. **2,** (room) ático; desván.
catchup ('kætʃ·əp) *n.* salsa de setas *o* tomate. *También,* **catsup, ketchup.**
catchword *n.* **1,** (key word) reclamo. **2,** *theat.* (cue) pie.
catchy ('kætʃ·i) *adj., colloq.* atrayente; agradable.
catechetical (ˌkæt·ə'kɛt·ɪ·kəl) *adj.* catequístico.
catechism ('kæt·ə·kɪz·əm) *n.* catecismo. —**catechist,** *n.* catequista; catequizante. —**catechize,** *v.t.* catequizar; adoctrinar.
catechumen (ˌkæt·ə'kju·mən) *n.* catecúmeno.
category ('kæt·ə·gor·i) *n.* categoría; clase. —**categorical** (-'gor·ɪ·kəl) *adj.* categórico; absoluto.
cater ('kei·tər) *v.i.* proveer; abastecer. —**caterer,** *n.* abastecedor; proveedor; despensero.
cater-cornered ('kæt·ərˌkor·nərd) *adj.* diagonal. —*adv.* diagonalmente.
caterpillar ('kæt·ər·pɪl·ər) *n.* **1,** (larva) oruga; larva. **2,** (tractor) tractor oruga.
catgut ('kætˌgʌt) *n.* cuerda de tripa.
catharsis (kə'θar·sɪs) *n., med.* catarsis; purga. —**cathartic** (-tɪk) *n. & adj.* catártico; purgante.
cathedra (kə'θi·drə) *n., eccles.* cátedra.
cathedral (kə'θiː·drəl) *n.* catedral.
catheter ('kæθ·ə·tər) *n.* catéter.
cathode ('kæθ·od) *n.* cátodo.
catholic ('kæθ·ə·lɪk) *adj.* **1,** (universal) católico; universal. **2,** *cap., relig.* católico. —**Catholicism** (kə'θal·ə·sɪz·əm) *n.* catolicismo. —**catholicity** (ˌkæθ·ə'lɪs·ə·ti) *n.* catolicidad.
cation ('kætˌai·ən) *n.* catión.
catkin ('kæt·kɪn) *n.* amento; candelilla.
catnip ('kæt·nɪp) *n.* nébeda.
cat-o'-nine-tails (ˌkæt·ə'nain·teilz) *n.* disciplina con nueve azotes.
catsup ('kæt·səp; 'kætʃ·əp) = **catchup.**
cattle ('kæt·əl) *n.* ganado vacuno.
catty ('kæt·i) *también,* **cattish,** *adj.* malicioso; felino.
Caucasian (ko'kei·ʒən) *n. & adj.* caucásico.
caucus ('ko·kəs) *n.* junta política *o* electoral. —*v.i.* reunirse en camarilla política.
caudal ('koː·dəl) *adj.* caudal.
caught (cot) *v., pret. & p.p. de* **catch.**
cauliflower ('ko·lɪˌflau·ər) *n.* coliflor.
causal ('ko·zəl) *adj.* causal. —**causality** (ko'zæl·ə·ti) *n.* causalidad.
causation (ko'zei·ʃən) *n.* causa; origen. —**causative** ('koː·zə·tɪv) *adj.* causante.
cause (koːz) *n.* **1,** (source of a result) causa; motivo. **2,** *law* causa; litigio; proceso. —*v.t.* causar; hacer.
causeway ('koːzˌwei) *n.* calzada; calzada elevada.
caustic ('kos·tɪk) *n. & adj.* cáustico.
cauterize ('ko·tərˌaiz) *v.t.* cauterizar. —**cauterization** (-ɪ'zei·ʃən) *n.* cauterización.
caution ('ko·ʃən) *n.* **1,** (prudence) cautela; cuidado, precaución. **2,** (warning) advertencia; aviso. —*v.t.* avisar; aconsejar; advertir.
cautious ('ko·ʃəs) *adj.* precavido; cauto; cauteloso.
cavalcade ('kæv·əl·keid) *n.* cabalgata.
cavalier (ˌkæv·ə'lɪr) *n.* **1,** (knight) caballero. **2,** (escort) caballero; galán. —*adj.* **1,** (gay) alegre; caballeroso. **2,** (haughty) arrogante; altivo.

cavalry ('kæv·əl·ri) *n.*, *mil.* caballería. —**mechanized cavalry,** cuerpo motorizado.
cave (keiv) *n.* cueva; caverna. —*v.t.* cavar. —**cave in,** hundirse; *fig.* rendirse. —**cave man,** cavernícola.
cavern ('kæv·ərn) *n.* caverna; cueva. —**cavernous,** *adj.* cavernoso.
caviar ('kæv·i,ar) *n.* caviar; cavial.
cavil ('kæv·əl) *v.i.* sutilizar; rodear. —*n.* sutileza; rodeo. —**cavil at** *o* **about,** sutilizar.
cavity ('kæv·ə·ti) *n.* **1,** (hole) cavidad; hueco. **2,** *dent.* caries.
cavort (kə'vort) *v.i.* cabriolear; corvetear.
caw (kɔː) *n.* graznido.
cease (sis) *v.i.* cesar; desistir; pararse. —*v.t.* suspender; parar. —**ceaseless,** *adj.* incesante; sin descanso.
cedar ('si·dər) *n.* cedro.
cede (sid) *v.t.* ceder; transferir; traspasar.
cedilla (sɪ'dɪl·ə) *n.* cedilla.
ceiling ('si·lɪŋ) *n.* **1,** (in a room) techo. **2,** *aero.* máxima altitud. —**ceiling price,** tope legal de precios.
celebrate ('sɛl·ə·breit) *v.t.* **1,** (commemorate; perform) celebrar; solemnizar. **2,** (praise) encomiar; alabar; elogiar. —*v.i.* estar de fiesta. —**celebrant** (-brənt) *n.* celebrante; oficiante. —**celebrated,** *adj.* famoso; conocido; célebre. —**celebration,** *n.* celebración.
celebrity (sə'lɛb·rə·ti) *n.* **1,** (fame) celebridad; renombre; fama. **2,** (person) celebridad.
celerity (sə'lɛr·ə·ti) *n.* celeridad; rapidez; ligereza.
celery ('sɛl·ə·ri) *n.* apio.
celestial (sə'lɛs·tʃəl) *adj.* **1,** (sky) celeste. **2,** (divine) celestial; divino; angélico.
celestite ('sɛl·əs,tait) *n.* celestina. *También,* **celestine** (-tɪn).
celibacy ('sɛl·ə·bə·si) *n.* celibato. —**celibate** (-bət) *n.* & *adj.* célibe.
cell (sɛl) *n.* **1,** (prison) celda; calabozo. **2,** (small room) cuarto; celda. **3,** (mouth) alvéolo. **4,** (group; protoplasm) célula. **5,** *electricity* célula eléctrica. **6,** (honeycomb) celdilla. **7,** (hole) nicho; cavidad.
cellar ('sɛl·ər) *n.* sótano; bodega.
cello ('tʃɛl·o) *n.* [*pl.* **-los**] violoncelo. —**cellist,** *n.* violoncelista.
cellophane ('sɛl·ə·fein) *n.* celofán.
cellular ('sɛl·jə·lər) *adj.* celular.
celluloid ('sɛl·jə·lɔid) *n.* celuloide.
cellulose ('sɛl·jə·los) *n.* celulosa.
cellulous ('sɛl·jə·ləs) *adj.* celuloso.
Celt (sɛlt) *también,* **Kelt** (kɛlt) *n.* celta.
Celtic ('sɛl·tɪk) *también,* **Keltic** ('kɛl-) *adj.* celta; céltico. —*n.* celta.
cement (sɪ'mɛnt) *n.* **1,** (adhesive) aglutinante; adhesivo; pegamento. **2,** (powdered lime) cemento. —*v.t.* pegar; aglutinar; asegurar. —*v.i.* pegarse; aglutinarse.
cemetery ('sɛm·ə·tɛr·i) *n.* cementerio.
-cene (sin) *sufijo* -ceno; reciente; nuevo: *Miocene,* mioceno.
ceno- (si·no; sɛn·o) *prefijo* ceno-. **1,** [*también,* **coeno-**] común: *cenobite,* cenobita. **2,** nuevo; reciente: *Cenozoic,* cenozoico.
cenotaph ('sɛn·ə,taf; -,tæf) *n.* cenotafio.
censor ('sɛn·sər) *n.* **1,** (examiner) censor. **2,** (faultfinder) crítico; censurador. —*v.t.* censurar; criticar. —**censorship,** *n.* censura.
censorial (sɛn'sor·i·əl) *adj.* censorio.
censorious (sɛn'sor·i·əs) *adj.* crítico; severo. —**censoriousness,** *n.* predisposición a censurar.
censure ('sɛn·ʃər) *v.t.* censurar; reprobar; criticar. —*n.* censura; reprobación.
census ('sɛn·səs) *n.* censo; padrón; empadronamiento.
cent (sɛnt) *n.* centavo; *Sp.* céntimo.
cent- (sɛnt) *prefijo, var. de* **centi-** *ante vocal: centennial,* centenario.
centaur ('sɛn·tor) *n.* centauro.
centenarian (,sɛn·tə'nɛr·i·ən) *n.* centenario. —**centenary** ('sɛn·tə·nɛr·i) *n.* & *adj.* centenario.
centennial (sɛn'tɛn·i·əl) *n.* & *adj.* centenario.
center *también,* **centre** ('sɛn·tər) *n.* centro. —*v.t.* centrar. —*v.i.* centrarse; concentrarse.
centesimal (sɛn'tɛs·ə·məl) *adj.* centésimo.
centi- (sɛn·ti) *prefijo* centi-; ciento; centésima parte: *centigrade,* centígrado; *centimeter,* centímetro.
centiare ('sɛn·ti,eːr) *n.* centiárea.
centigrade ('sɛn·tə,greid) *adj.* centígrado.

centigram (ˈsɛn·tə,græm) *n.* centigramo.
centiliter (ˈsɛn·tə,li·tər) *n.* centilitro.
centime (ˈsan·tim) *n.* céntimo.
centimeter (ˈsɛn·tə,mi·tər) *n.* centímetro.
centipede (ˈsɛn·tə·pid) *n.* ciempiés.
central (ˈsɛn·trəl) *n.* central. —*adj.* central; céntrico.
centralize (ˈsɛn·trə,laiz) *v.t.* centralizar. —*v.i.* centralizarse. —**centralization** (-lɪˈzei·ʃən) *n.* centralización.
centri- (sɛn·tri) *prefijo, var. de* **centro-**: *centrifugal,* centrífugo.
centrifugal (sɛnˈtrɪf·jə·gəl) *adj.* centrífugo.
centrifuge (ˈsɛn·trɪ,fjudʒ) *n.* máquina centrífuga.
centripetal (sɛnˈtrɪp·ə·təl) *adj.* centrípeto.
centro- (sɛn·tro) *prefijo* centro-; centro; central: *centrobaric,* centrobárico; *centrosome,* centrosoma.
centuple (ˈsɛn·tjʊ·pəl) *adj.* céntuplo. —*v.t.* centuplicar.
centurion (sɛnˈtjʊr·i·ən) *n.* centurión.
centurium (sɛnˈtjʊr·i·əm) *n.* centurio.
century (ˈsɛn·tʃə·ri) *n.* centuria; siglo.
cephalic (səˈfæl·ɪk) *adj.* cefálico.
cephalopod (ˈsɛf·ə·lə,pad) *n.* & *adj.* cefalópodo.
ceramics (səˈræm·ɪks) *n.sing.* cerámica. —*n.pl.* objetos de cerámica. —**ceramic,** *adj.* cerámico.
cereal (ˈsɪr·i·əl) *n.* cereal; grano. —*adj.* cereal.
cerebellum (,sɛr·əˈbɛl·əm) *n.* cerebelo.
cerebral (ˈsɛr·ə·brəl) *adj.* cerebral. —**cerebral palsy,** parálisis cerebral.
cerebro- (sɛr·ə·bro) *prefijo* cerebro-; cerebro; mente: *cerebrospinal,* cerebroespinal.
cerebrum (ˈsɛr·ə·brəm) *n.* cerebro.
ceremonial (sɛr·əˈmo·ni·əl) *adj.* ceremonial. —*n.* ceremonial; rito externo.
ceremony (ˈsɛr·ə,mo·ni) *n.* **1,** (rite) ceremonia; rito. **2,** (politeness) etiqueta; formalidad. —**ceremonious** (-ˈmo·ni·əs) *adj.* ceremonioso. —**stand on ceremony,** estar de etiqueta; estar de ceremonia.
cerium (ˈsɪr·i·əm) *n.* cerio.
certain (ˈsʌɪ·tən) *adj.* **1,** (sure) cierto; seguro; inevitable. **2,** (unspecified) algún; cierto. —**certainty** (-ti) *n.* certidumbre; certeza.
certificate (sərˈtɪf·ɪ·kət) *n.* **1,** (legal document) certificado. **2,** (written testimonial) atestado; certificación. **3,** *comm.* obligación; título; bono. —*v.t.* (-,keit) certificar. —**certification,** *n.* certificación.
certify (ˈsʌɪ·tə,fai) *v.t.* certificar; atestiguar; darse.
certitude (ˈsʌɪ·tɪ·tjud) *n.* certitud; certeza; certidumbre.
cerulean (səˈru·li·ən) *adj.* cerúleo.
cerumen (səˈru·mən) *n.* cerilla; cerumen.
cervine (ˈsʌɪ·vain) *adj.* cervino.
cervix (ˈsʌɪ·vɪks) *n.* cerviz; nuca. —**cervical** (-vɪ·kəl) *adj.* cervical.
cesium (ˈsiː·zi·əm) *n.* cesio.
cessation (sɛˈsei·ʃən) *n.* cesación; cesamiento; cese.
cession (ˈsɛʃ·ən) *n.* **1,** (act of ceding) cesión; traspaso; transferencia. **2,** (surrender) rendición.
cesspool (ˈsɛs,pul) *n.* pozo negro.
cetacean (səˈtei·ʃən) *n.* cetáceo.
cetaceous (səˈtei·ʃəs) *adj.* cetáceo.
chafe (tʃeif) *v.t.* **1,** (rub) escoriar; raer; escaldar. **2,** *fig.* (annoy) irritar; enojar. —*v.i.* **1,** (be roughened) escoriarse; raerse; desgastarse. **2,** *fig.* (be annoyed) acalorarse; enojarse; irritarse.
chaff (tʃæf) *n.* **1,** (husk) hollejo; cascabillo. **2,** (fodder) broza; desperdicios (*pl.*); pienso. **3,** (raillery) burla; zumba. —*v.t.* molestar; burlarse de. —*v.i.* burlarse.
chafing dish chofeta.
chagrin (ʃəˈgrɪn) *n.* mortificación; desazón. —*v.t., usu. pasivo* mortificar; disgustar.
chain (tʃein) *n.* **1,** (connected links) cadena. **2,** *pl.* (fetters) cautiverio (*sing.*); esclavitud (*sing.*); servidumbre (*sing.*). **3,** (connected events, objects) encadenamiento; sucesión. **4,** (measuring device) cadena de medir. —*v.t.* encadenar; enlazar. —**chain gang,** cuadrilla de malhechores encadenados. —**chain reaction,** reacción en cadena. —**chain store,** tienda de cadena.
chair (tʃɛːr) *n.* **1,** (seat) silla; asiento. **2,** *fig.* (leadership) presidencia. **3,** (professorship) cátedra.

chairlift *n.* ascensor funicular con sillas para esquiadores.
chairman ('tʃɛr·mən) *n.* [*pl.* **-men**] presidente. —**chairwoman,** *n.fem.* [*pl.* **-women**] presidenta.
chaise (ʃeiz) *n.* calesa; calesín.
chaise longue (ʃeiz 'lɔŋ) *n.* cheslón.
chalet (ʃa'lei) *n.* chalet.
chalice ('tʃæl·ɪs) *n.* cáliz.
chalk (tʃɔk) *n.* **1,** (limestone) creta. **2,** (crayon) tiza; clarión. —*v.t.* enyesar. —**chalk up, 1,** (write; draw) escribir *o* dibujar con tiza. **2,** (score; record) llevar cuenta; apuntar.
challenge ('tʃæl·əndʒ) *n.* **1,** (defiance) desafío; reto. **2,** *mil.* contraseña; santo y seña. **3,** *law* recusación. **4,** (objection) oposición; objeción. —*v.t.* **1,** (invite to fight or debate) desafiar; retar. **2,** (demand explanation of) demandar; exigir. **3,** *law* recusar. **4,** (object to) contradecir; disputar; objetar. —**challenger,** *n.* retador.
chamber ('tʃeim·bər) *n.* **1,** (room) cámara. **2,** (bedroom) habitación; dormitorio. **3,** (legislature) cámara. **4,** *law* tribunal. **5,** (cavity) cámara. **6,** (of a firearm) recámara. —**chamber music,** música de cámara. —**chamber pot,** orinal.
chamberlain ('tʃeim·bər·lɪn) *n.* chambelán; camarlengo.
chambermaid *n.* doncella; camarera.
chameleon (kə'mi·li·ən) *n.* camaleón.
chamfer ('tʃæm·fər) *n.* chaflán. —*v.t.* achaflanar.
chamois ('ʃæm·i) *n.* **1,** (antelope) gamuza; ante. **2,** (skin) piel de gamuza *o* ante.
champ (tʃæmp) *v.t.* & *i.* mordiscar; morder; mascar. —*n., colloq.* = **champion.**
champagne (ʃæm'pein) *n.* champaña.
champion ('tʃæm·pi·ən) *n.* **1,** (winner) campeón. **2,** (defender) paladín; defensor. —*adj.* campeón. —*v.t.* defender; apoyar; propugnar.
championship ('tʃæm·pi·ən·ˌʃɪp) *n.* **1,** (supremacy) campeonato. **2,** (support) apoyo; defensa.
chance (tʃæns) *n.* **1,** (fortuity) casualidad; azar. **2,** (risk) peligro; riesgo. **3,** (opportunity) oportunidad. **4,** (unexpected event) contingencia. **5,** *usu. pl.* (probability) probabilidad (*sing.*). —*v.t.* (hazard) arriesgar; probar. —*v.i.* (befall) acaecer; acontecer; suceder. —*adj.* casual; fortuito.
chancel ('tʃæn·səl) *n.* entrecoro; presbiterio.
chancellery ('tʃæn·sə·lə·ri) *n.* cancillería.
chancellor ('tʃæn·sə·lər) *n.* canciller. —**chancellorship,** *n.* cancillería.
chancery ('tʃæn·sə·ri) *n.* cancillería. —**in chancery,** en posición difícil *o* embarazosa.
chancre ('ʃæŋ·kər) *n.* chancro.
chandelier (ˌʃæn·də'lɪr) *n.* araña de luces.
chandler ('tʃænd·lər) *n.* **1,** (dealer) tendero; abacero. **2,** (candlemaker) velero; cerero.
change (tʃeindʒ) *v.t.* **1,** (alter) cambiar; mudar. **2,** (replace) substituir; reemplazar. **3,** (exchange) cambiar; convertir; intercambiar. —*v.i.* alterarse; cambiarse. —*n.* **1,** (modification) modificación; alteración; transformación. **2,** (substitution) cambio; substitución. **3,** (money) cambio; vuelta. —**changeless,** *adj.* inmutable; invariable. —**change of life,** menopausia.
changeable ('tʃeindʒ·ə·bəl) *adj.* **1,** (liable to change) cambiable; variable. **2,** (changing readily) cambiadizo; mudable.
changeling ('tʃeindʒ·lɪŋ) *n.* niño trocado por otro.
channel ('tʃæn·əl) *n.* **1,** (waterway) canal. **2,** (river bed) cauce; lecho. **3,** *fig.* (route) conducto; vía; canal; medio. **4,** (groove) surco; estría. **5,** *radio; TV* canal; estación. **6,** *pl., slang* (involved routing) conducto reglamentario. —*v.t.* **1,** (direct) conducir; encauzar. **2,** (groove) estriar; acanalar.
chant (tʃænt; tʃant) *n.* canto; salmodia. —*v.t.* & *i.* cantar monótonamente; salmodiar.
chaos ('kei·as) *n.* caos. —**chaotic** (ke'at·ɪk) *adj.* caótico.
chap (tʃæp) *v.t.* [**chapped, chapping**] **1,** (harm the skin) agrietar; resquebrajar. **2,** (roughen) hender; rajar. —*v.i.* agrietarse; resquebrajarse; henderse. —*n., colloq.* chico; mozo; amigo.
chapel ('tʃæp·əl) *n.* capilla.
chaperon ('ʃæp·ə·ron) *n.* acompañante de señoritas; rodrigón.

—*v.t.* & *i.* acompañar *o* proteger a.
chaplain (ˈtʃæp·lɪn) *n.* capellán.
chaps (tʃæps) *n.pl.* zahones; *Amer.* chaparreras.
chapter (ˈtʃæp·tər) *n.* **1,** (part of a book; council; branch of an association) capítulo. **2,** *eccles.* cabildo.
char (tʃar) *v.t.* [**charred, charring**] **1,** (burn to charcoal) carbonizar; hacer carbón. **2,** (scorch) socarrar; chamuscar. —*v.i.* **1,** (become charcoal) carbonizarse; hacerse carbón. **2,** (perform domestic work) trabajar a jornal.
character (ˈkær·ɪk·tər) *n.* **1,** (personality) carácter; personalidad. **2,** (trait) índole; genio. **3,** (reputation) reputación; fama. **4,** *colloq.* (an eccentric) persona; tipo. **5,** *theat.* (role) personaje; parte; papel. **6,** (symbol) tipo de letra; tipo.
characteristic (ˌkær·ɪk·təˈrɪs·tɪk) *adj.* característico; peculiar. —*n.* característica.
characterize (ˈkær·ɪk·təˌraiz) *v.t.* caracterizar; señalar. —**characterization** (-rɪˈzei·ʃən) *n.* caracterización.
charade (ʃəˈreid) *n.* charada.
charcoal (ˈtʃar·kol) *n.* **1,** (burnt wood) carbón. **2,** (for drawing) carbón; carboncillo.
chard (tʃard) *n.* acelga.
charge (tʃardʒ) *v.t.* **1,** (load) cargar. **2,** (command) mandar; comisionar. **3,** (accuse) censurar; acusar. **4,** (ask as a price) poner precio; pedir. **5,** (defer payment) cargar en cuenta. **6,** (attack) acometer; atacar. **7,** (prepare arms) apuntar; preparar. —*v.i.* (attack) embestir; atacar. —*n.* **1,** (load) carga; peso. **2,** (command) mandato; orden; encargo. **3,** (duty) obligación; deber. **4,** (accusation) cargo; acusación. **5,** (price) coste; precio. **6,** (professional fee) honorario. **7,** (violent onslaught) embestida; ataque. —**in charge, 1,** (responsible) encargado. **2,** (substitute) suplente; interino. **3,** *Brit.* (under arrest) bajo arresto; arrestado. —**in charge of,** a cargo de.
chargé d'affaires (ʃarˈʒei da·ˈfeːr) *n.* [*pl.* **chargés d'affaires** (ʃarˈʒei)] encargado de negocios.
charger (ˈtʃar·dʒər) *n.* **1,** (war horse) caballo de guerra; corcel. **2,** (tray) fuente *o* plato grande. **3,** *electricity* cargador.
chariot (ˈtʃær·i·ət) *n.* carro de guerra *o* combate; carro. —**charioteer** (-əˈtɪr) *n.* auriga.
charity (ˈtʃær·ə·ti) *n.* **1,** (benevolence) caridad; tolerancia; amor. **2,** (alms) caridad; limosna. —**charitable,** *adj.* caritativo; benéfico.
charlatan (ˈʃar·lə·tən) *n.* charlatán. —**charlatanism,** *n.* charlatanería.
charm (tʃarm) *n.* **1,** (attractiveness) atractivo; encanto; hechizo. **2,** (amulet) talismán; amuleto; dije. —*v.t.* encantar; hechizar; atraer. —*v.i.* embelesar; arrobar. —**charming,** *adj.* atrayente; atractivo; encantador.
chart (tʃart) *n.* **1,** (map) mapa; *naut.* carta hidrográfica *o* de navegación. **2,** (record) gráfico; cuadro. —*v.t.* poner en *o* hacer una carta hidrográfica *o* gráfico.
charter (ˈtʃar·tər) *n.* **1,** (grant of rights) cédula; título. **2,** (constitution) reglamento; estatutos (*pl.*); carta. **3,** (lease) alquiler. —*v.t.* **1,** (authorize) estatuir; incorporar *o* instituir legítimamente. **2,** (hire) alquilar; fletar. —**charter member,** socio fundador.
charwoman *n.* [*pl.* **-women**] asalariada; criada a jornal.
chary (ˈtʃɛr·i) *adj.* precavido; cauteloso. —**chariness,** *n.* cautela; precaución; circunspección.
chase (tʃeis) *v.t.* **1,** (hunt; pursue) cazar; perseguir; acosar. **2,** (drive away) espantar; ahuyentar. **3,** (of jewelry) cincelar; montar; engastar. —*v.i.* corretear. —*n.* **1,** (chasing) caza; persecución. **2,** (quarry) caza. **3,** (sport) caza; montería. **4,** *print.* rama.
chaser (ˈtʃei·sər) *n.* **1,** (one who chases) cazador. **2,** *colloq.* (drink) bebida que sigue a un trago fuerte. **3,** *colloq.* (licentious person) libertino.
chasm (ˈkæz·əm) *n.* **1,** (fissure) abismo; grieta; hendedura. **2,** *fig.* (difference) divergencia; laguna; separación.
chassis (ˈʃæs·i) *n.* [*pl.* **chassis**] **1,** (framework) armazón; cuerpo; bastidor. **2,** *mech.* chasis.
chaste (tʃeist) *adj.* **1,** (pure) casto; puro. **2,** (restrained in style) puro; castizo. —**chasteness,** *n.* = **chastity.**
chasten (ˈtʃei·sən) *v.t.* **1,** (punish) reprimir; castigar; corregir. **2,** (make chaste) purificar; limpiar.

chastise (tʃæs'taiz) *v.t.* castigar; disciplinar. —**chastisement,** *n.* castigo; corrección; disciplina.
chastity ('tʃæs·tə·ti) *n.* castidad; continencia; pureza.
chasuble ('tʃæz·ju·bəl) *n.* casulla.
chat (tʃæt) *v.i.* [**chatted, chatting**] charlar; conversar. —*n.* charla; conversación íntima. —**chatty,** *adj., colloq.* locuaz; hablador; charlador.
chattel ('tʃæt·əl) *n.* bienes muebles (*pl.*).
chatter ('tʃæt·ər) *v.i.* **1,** (rattle; vibrate noisily) traquetear; golpetear. **2,** (click together, as the teeth) castañetear. **3,** (prattle) parlotear; chacharear; cotorrear. —*n.* **1,** (noisy vibration) traqueteo; golpeteo. **2,** (clicking, as of the teeth) castañeteo. **3,** (prattle) parloteo; cháchara; cotorreo.
chatterbox *n.* hablador; parlanchín.
chauffeur ('ʃo·fər) *n.* chofer; conductor.
chauvinism ('ʃo·və·nɪz·əm) *n.* chauvinismo; patriotería. —**chauvinist,** *n.* chauvinista; patriotero. —**chauvinistic,** *adj.* chauvinista; patriotero.
cheap (tʃip) *adj.* **1,** (low-priced) barato; asequible. **2,** *fig.* (vulgar) de poco precio; despreciable; mezquino. —**cheapness,** *n.* baratura; *fig.* mezquindad.
cheapen ('tʃi·pən) *v.t.* abaratar; rebajar. —*v.i.* rebajar de precio; regatear.
cheat (tʃit) *v.t.* **1,** (mislead) engañar; equivocar; defraudar. **2,** (swindle) timar; chasquear. —*v.i.* cometer fraude *o* engaño. —*n.* **1,** (swindler) timador; tramposo. **2,** (act of fraud) engaño; timo; trampa.
check (tʃɛk) *n.* **1,** (obstruction) obstáculo; impedimento. **2,** (brake) freno; tope. **3,** (rebuff) contratiempo; descalabro. **4,** [*usu.,* **check-up**] (test) verificación; comprobación. **5,** (mark) contraseña. **6,** [*también,* **cheque**] (money order) cheque; talón de cuenta corriente. **7,** (receipt; token) talón; billete de reclamo. **8,** (square) escaque; cuadrito. **9,** (restaurant bill) cuenta; factura. **10,** *chess* jaque. **11,** (chip) ficha. —*v.t.* **1,** (impede) impedir; reprimir; parar. **2,** (test) investigar; comprobar; verificar. **3,** (mark) hacer una contraseña; marcar. **4,** (put in temporary custody) dar a guardar; dejar en consigna. **5,** (send baggage) facturar. **6,** *chess* dar jaque. —*v.i.* **1,** (prove to be accurate) concordar; estar de acuerdo. **2,** (stop) pararse; detenerse. —*interj., slang* ¡muy bien! —**check in,** registrarse; inscribirse. —**check out,** despedirse; *slang* (die) morir. —**check up,** comprobar. —**in check,** controlado; *chess* en jaque.
checkbook *n.* talonario de cheques.
checker ('tʃɛk·ər) *n.* **1,** (record-keeper) archivista. **2,** (store clerk) cajero. **3,** (tester; watcher) verificador; examinador; vigilante. **4,** (playing piece) pieza de damas. —**checkered,** *adj.* a *o* de cuadros; ajedrezado.
checkerboard *n.* tablero de damas.
checkers ('tʃɛk·ərz) *n.* juego de damas.
checkmate ('tʃɛk·meit) *n.* **1,** *chess* jaque mate; mate. **2,** (defeat) derrota. —*v.t.* **1,** *chess* dar mate a. **2,** (overthrow) derrotar; deshacer; destruir.
checkroom *n.* guardarropía; guardarropa; *R.R.* consigna.
check-up *n.* **1,** = **check,** *n.* 4. **2,** (medical) reconocimiento médico.
cheek (tʃik) *n.* **1,** *anat.* mejilla; carrillo. **2,** *colloq.* (impudence) descaro; atrevimiento. —**cheeky,** *adj., colloq.* atrevido; descarado.
cheekbone *n.* pómulo.
cheep (tʃip) *n.* pío; chirrido. —*v.t.* & *i.* piar; chirriar.
cheer (tʃɪːr) *n.* **1,** (joyful feeling) alegría; regocijo; buen humor. **2,** (shout of joy) viva; aplauso; vítores (*pl.*). —*v.t.* & *i.* animar; alentar; aplaudir. —**cheers!** *interj.* ¡a la salud!
cheerful ('tʃɪr·fəl) *adj.* jovial; alegre; animado. —**cheerfulness,** *n.* jovialidad; animación; alegría.
cheery ('tʃɪr·i) *adj.* alegre; jubiloso. —**cheeriness,** *n.* júbilo; animación.
cheese (tʃiːz) *n.* queso.
cheesecloth *n.* estopilla de algodón.
cheetah ('tʃi·tə) *n.* leopardo cazador.
chef (ʃɛf) *n.* primer cocinero.
chemical ('kɛm·ɪ·kəl) *adj.* químico. —*n.* producto químico.
chemise (ʃə'miːz) *n.* camisa; camisola; camisón.

chemist ('kɛm·ɪst) *n.* químico.
chemistry ('kɛm·ɪs·tri) *n.* química.
chenille (ʃə'ni:l) *n.* felpilla.
cheque (tʃɛk) *n., Brit.* = **check,** *n.* 6.
chequer ('tʃɛk·ər) *n., Brit.* = **checker. —chequered,** *adj., Brit.* = **checkered.**
cherish ('tʃɛr·ɪʃ) *v.t.* **1,** (hold dear) estimar; apreciar. **2,** *fig.* (take care of) acariciar; alimentar; abrigar.
cherry ('tʃɛr·i) *n.* **1,** (tree and wood) cerezo. **2,** (fruit; color) cereza.
cherub ('tʃɛr·əb) *n.* [*pl.* **cherubim** ('tʃɛr·ə·bɪm)] querube; querubín. **—cherubic** (tʃə'ru·bɪk) *adj.* querúbico.
chess (tʃɛs) *n.* ajedrez. **—chessboard,** *n.* tablero de ajedrez. **—chessman,** *n.* [*pl.* **-men**] pieza de ajedrez.
chest (tʃɛst) *n.* **1,** (box) cofre; arca; baúl. **2,** *anat.* pecho; tórax. **—get off one's chest,** *colloq.* descargarse (de).
chestnut ('tʃɛs·nʌt) *n.* **1,** (tree and wood) castaño. **2,** (nut) castaña. **3,** (color) color castaño; marrón. **4,** *slang* (cliché) broma *o* frase gastada. —*adj.* castaño.
chetah ('tʃi·tə) *n.* = **cheetah.**
chevalier (ˌʃɛv·ə'lɪr) *n.* caballero.
cheviot ('ʃɛv·i·ət) *n.* lanilla; paño de lana; cheviot.
chevron ('ʃɛv·rən) *n.* galón; sardineta.
chew (tʃu:) *v.t.* **1,** (grind) masticar; mascar. **2,** *fig.* (consider) rumiar; considerar; meditar. —*n.* mascadura; *Chile* & *Arg.* mascada. **—chew the rag,** *slang* hablar mucho. **—chewing gum,** chicle; goma de mascar.
chic (ʃik) *adj.* elegante; bien hecho; de moda.
chicanery (ʃɪ'kei·nə·ri) *n.* embrollo; trampa legal; sofistería.
chick (tʃɪk) *n.* **1,** (fowl) polluelo; pichón. **2,** *slang* (girl) jovencita; *Amer.* gallina.
chicken ('tʃɪk·ən) *n.* **1,** (fowl) pollo. **2,** *slang* = **chick.**
chickenhearted *adj.* tímido; cobarde.
chicken pox *n.* varicela.
chickpea ('tʃɪkˌpi) *n.* garbanzo.
chicle ('tʃɪk·əl) *n.* chicle; goma para *o* de mascar.
chicory ('tʃɪk·ə·ri) *n.* achicoria.
chide (tʃaid) *v.t.* [*pret.* & *p.p.* **chid** (tʃɪd), *p.p. también,* **chidden** ('tʃɪd·ən) reprobar; echar en cara; culpar; increpar. —*v.i.* regañar; refunfuñar.
chief (tʃif) *n.* jefe; líder. —*adj.* principal; el más importante; primero. **—chiefly,** *adv.* principalmente; ante todo.
chieftain ('tʃif·tən) *n.* **1,** (of a tribe) jefe. **2,** (of a clan or band) jefe; capitán; caudillo.
chiffon (ʃɪ'fan) *n.* gasa; soplillo.
chigger ('tʃɪg·ər) *n.* garrapata; pique. *También,* **chigoe** (-o).
chignon ('ʃin·jan) *n.* moño.
chilblain ('tʃɪl·blein) *n.* sabañón.
child (tʃaild) *n.* [*pl.* **children**] niño; infante; hijo. **—with child,** embarazada; preñada. **—child's play,** juego de niños.
childbirth *n.* parto; alumbramiento.
childhood ('tʃaild·hʊd) *n.* niñez; infancia.
childish ('tʃail·dɪʃ) *adj.* pueril; aniñado. **—childishness,** *n.* puerilidad; niñería.
childless ('tʃaild·ləs) *adj.* sin hijos.
childlike *adj.* pueril; aniñado.
children ('tʃɪl·drən) *n., pl. de* **child.**
chili ('tʃɪl·i) *n.* chile; chili.
chill (tʃɪl) *n.* **1,** (sensation) escalofrío; estremecimiento. **2,** (degree of cold) frío. —*v.t.* **1,** (make cold) enfriar; helar. **2,** *fig.* (repulse) desanimar; desalentar; enfriar. —*v.i.* desanimarse; desalentarse. **—chilly** *adj.* frío; helado.
chime (tʃaim) *n.* **1,** (bell or set of bells) campana; juego de campanas. **2,** (ringing sound) repique; campaneo. **3,** *fig.* (concord) armonía; conformidad. —*v.t.* **1,** (cause to ring) repicar; tañer; tocar. **2,** (say in chorus) decir al unísono. —*v.i.* **1,** (ring) tañer; sonar. **2,** *fig.* (harmonize) armonizar; concordar. **—chime in,** *colloq.* **1,** (agree) convenir; consentir; estar de acorde. **2,** (interrupt) interrumpir; entremeterse.
chimera (kɪ'mɪr·ə) *n.* quimera. **—chimerical** (kɪ'mɛr·ɪ·kəl) *adj.* quimérico.
chimney ('tʃɪm·ni) *n.* chimenea.

chimpanzee (tʃɪm'pæn·zi) *n.* chimpancé.
chin (tʃɪn) *n.* barbilla. —*v.i.* [**chinned, chinning**] *slang* charlar; hablar.
china ('tʃai·nə) *n.* porcelana; loza fina. —**china closet**, chinero; cristalera.
Chinaman ('tʃai·nə·mən) *n.* [*pl.* **-men**] chino.
chinaware *n.* vajilla de porcelana.
chinchilla (tʃɪn'tʃɪl·ə) *n.* chinchilla.
Chinese (tʃai'niːz) *adj.* chino; chinesco. —*n.* **1,** (person) chino. **2,** (language) idioma chino.
chink (tʃɪŋk) *n.* grieta; raja; hendedura. —*v.i.* **1,** (crack) hender; rajar. **2,** (ring) sonar; resonar. —*v.t.* **1,** (split) hender; partir, rajar. **2,** (fill cracks) rellenar hendiduras; calafatear.
chintz (tʃɪnts) *n.* zaraza.
chip ('tʃɪp) *n.* **1,** (fragment of wood) astilla. **2,** (counter; bus token) ficha. —*v.t.* [**chipped, chipping**] astillar. —*v.i.* astillarse. —**chip in**, contribuir; ayudar.
chipmunk ('tʃɪp·mʌŋk) *n.* ardilla norteamericana.
chipper ('tʃɪp·ər) *v.i.* gorjear; piar. —*adj., colloq.* jovial; alegre.
chiro- (kai·ro) *prefijo* quiro-; mano: *chiromancy*, quiromancia.
chiropody (kai'rap·ə·di) *n.* pedicura. —**chiropodist** (-dɪst) *n.* pedicuro; callista.
chiropractic (ˌkai·ro'præk·tɪk) *n.* quiropráctica. —*adj.* quiropráctico. —**chiropractor**, *n.* quiropráctico.
chirp (tʃʌɹp) *n.* **1,** (of birds) gorjeo. **2,** (of insects) chirrido. —*v.i.* **1,** gorjear. **2,** chirriar.
chisel ('tʃɪz·əl) *n.* cincel; formón; escoplo. —*v.t.* & *i.* **1,** (cut) cincelar; esculpir. **2,** *slang* (cheat) engañar; defraudar; conseguir engañando.
chit (tʃɪt) *n.* **1,** (memo) comunicación; esquela. **2,** (girl) chiquilla. **3,** (animal) cachorro; cría.
chitchat ('tʃɪt·tʃæt) *n., colloq.* cháchara; charla; plática.
chivalry ('ʃɪv·əl·ri) *n.* **1,** (medieval knighthood) caballería. **2,** *fig.* (knightly manners) caballerosidad; hidalguía. —**chivalrous** (-rəs); **chivalric** (-rɪk) *adj.* caballeresco.
chive (tʃaiv) *n.* cebollina.
chlorate ('klor·et) *n.* clorato.
chloride ('klor·aid) *n.* cloruro.
chlorine ('klor·in) *n.* cloro.
chloroform ('klor·ə·form) *n.* cloroformo. —*v.t.* cloroformizar.
chlorophyll ('klor·ə·fɪl) *n.* clorofila.
chock (tʃak) *n.* cuña; calzo. —**chock-full**, *adj.* lleno; colmado.
chocolate ('tʃak·lɪt; -ə·lɪt) *n.* & *adj.* chocolate.
choice (tʃɔis) *n.* **1,** (act of choosing) elección; preferencia. **2,** (option) oportunidad; opción. **3,** (thing chosen) lo elegido; lo escogido. **4,** (the best part) lo mejor; lo más escogido. —*adj.* selecto; superior; excelente. —**choiceness**, *n.* discernimiento; gusto; delicadeza.
choir (kwair) *n.* coro.
choke (tʃok) *v.t.* **1,** (strangle) ahogar; estrangular; sofocar. **2,** (obstruct) tapar; obstruir. —*v.i.* **1,** (suffocate) sofocarse; ahogarse; atorarse. **2,** (be overcrowded) rebosar; estar de bote en bote. —*n.* **1,** (obstruction) opresión; sofocamiento; ahogo. **2,** *mech.* obstrucción.
cholera ('kal·ər·ə) *n.* cólera morbo.
choleric ('kal·ər·ɪk) *adj.* colérico.
choose (tʃuːz) *v.t.* [**chose, chosen, choosing**] elegir; escoger; decidir. —*v.i.* preferir.
chop (tʃap) *v.t.* [**chopped, chopping**] **1,** (hew) tajar; hender; rajar. **2,** (mince) picar; desmenuzar. —*v.i.* **1,** (hew) hachear; dar tajos. **2,** (turn; shift) virar; cuartearse. —*n.* **1,** (cut of meat) chuleta. **2,** *usu.pl.* (jaw) quijada (*sing.*); labios. **3,** (act of chopping) tajo; corte. **4,** (ocean wave) oleada. —**chopper**, *n.* hacha; cuchilla (de carnicería).
choppy ('tʃap·i) *adj.* adusto; violento.
chopsticks ('tʃapˌstɪks) *n.pl.* palillos.
choral ('kor·əl) *adj.* coral.
chorale (kə'ræːl) *n.* coral.
chord (kord) *n.* **1,** (cord) cordón; cordel. **2,** *music* acorde. **3,** *geom.; anat.; aero.* cuerda. **4,** *engin.* viga de celosía *o* reticulada.
chore (tʃoːr) *n.* tarea.
choreographer (ˌkor·i'ag·rə·fər) *n.* coreógrafo.
choreography (ˌkor·i'ag·rə·fi) *n.* coreografía.
chorine ('kor·in) *n., colloq.* corista.

chorister ('kor·ɪs·tər) *n.* corista.

chorus ('kor·əs) *n.* **1,** (group of singers) coro. **2,** (refrain) estribillo; coro. —*v.i.* cantar en *o* a coro. —*v.t.* corear.

chorus girl (*o* **boy**) corista.

chose (tʃoːz) *v., pret. de* **choose.**

chosen ('tʃo·zən) *v., p.p. de* **choose.**

chow (tʃau) *n.* **1,** (dog) perro chino. **2,** *slang* (food) comida; alimentos.

chowder ('tʃau·dər) *n.* sancocho *o* sopa, esp. de pescado *o* almejas.

Christ (kraist) *n.* Cristo.

christen ('krɪs·ən) *v.t.* bautizar. —**christening,** *n.* bautizo; bautismo.

Christendom ('krɪs·ən·dəm) *n.* cristiandad; cristianismo.

Christian ('krɪs·tʃən) *n.* & *adj.* cristiano. —**Christian name,** nombre de pila; nombre.

Christianity (ˌkrɪs·tʃi'æn·ə·ti) *n.* cristianismo.

Christmas ('krɪs·məs) *n.* Navidad. —**Christmas carol,** villancico. —**Christmas Eve,** Nochebuena. —**Christmas tree,** árbol de Navidad. —**Merry Christmas,** felices Pascuas.

chrom- (krom) *prefijo, var. de* **chromo-** *ante vocal: chromopsia,* cromatopsia.

chromatic (kro'mæt·ɪk) *adj.* cromático.

chromato- (kro·mə·to) *prefijo* cromato-. **1,** color: *chromatology,* cromatología. **2,** cromatina: *chromatolysis,* cromatólisis.

chrome (kroːm) *n.* & *adj.* cromado.

-chrome (krom) *sufijo* -cromo. **1,** color: *polychrome,* polícromo. **2,** *quím.* cromo: *mercurochrome,* mercuro-cromo.

chromi- (kro·mi) *prefijo, var. de* **chromo-**: *chromiferous,* cromífero.

chromium ('kro·mi·əm) *n.* cromo.

chromo- (kro·mo) *prefijo* cromo-. **1,** color: *chromolithography,* cromolitografía. **2,** *quím.* cromo: *chromo-arsenate,* cromo-arseniato.

chromosome ('kro·mə·som) *n.* cromosoma.

chronic ('kran·ɪk) *adj.* crónico; habitual; inveterado; continuo.

chronicle ('kran·ɪ·kəl) *n.* **1,** (history) crónica. **2,** *pl., cap., Bib.* Paralipómenos; Crónicas. —*v.t.* escribir una crónica. —**chronicler** (-klər) *n.* cronista.

chrono- (kran·o) *prefijo* crono-; tiempo: *chronology,* cronología.

chronology (krə'nal·ə·dʒi) *n.* cronología. —**chronological** (ˌkran·ə'ladʒ·ɪ·kəl) *adj.* cronológico.

chronometer (krə'nam·ə·tər) *n.* cronómetro.

chrysalis ('krɪs·ə·lɪs) *n.* crisálida.

chrysanthemum (krɪ'sæn·θə·məm) *n.* crisantemo.

chubby ('tʃʌb·i) *adj.* gordezuelo; gordiflón; rechoncho.

chuck (tʃʌk) *n.* **1,** *mech.* mandril. **2,** (wedge) calzo; cuña. **3,** (cut of beef) carne del cuello del buey. **4,** (tap, esp. under the chin) mamola. —*v.t.* **1,** (tap under the chin) hacer la mamola **a. 2,** (toss) tirar. **3,** [*usu.,* **chuck out**] *colloq.* (throw away) echar; arrinconar. —*v.i.* (cackle) cloquear.

chuckle ('tʃʌk·əl) *v.i.* reír contenidamente. —*n.* risita; risa ahogada.

chug (tʃʌg) *n.* ruido explosivo corto. —*v.i.* [**chugged, chugging**] hacer *o* moverse con ruidos explosivos cortos.

chum (tʃʌm) *n., colloq.* compañero; compinche. —*v.i.* [**chummed, chumming**] ser compañero; ser compinche.

chunk (tʃʌŋk) *n.* **1,** (piece) trozo; pedazo grande. **2,** *colloq.* (large piece) cantidad importante. —**chunky,** *adj.* grueso; carnoso; rechoncho.

church (tʃʌɹtʃ) *n.* iglesia.

churchman ('tʃʌɹtʃ·mən) *n.* [*pl.* **-men**] **1,** (clergyman) eclesiástico. **2,** (church member) hombre de iglesia; militante.

churchyard *n.* patio *o* jardín de iglesia.

churl (tʃʌɹl) *n.* **1,** (boor) patán. **2,** (rustic) rústico. —**churlish,** *adj.* patán; zafio.

churn (tʃʌɹn) *n.* **1,** (for making butter) mantequera. **2,** (agitator) batidora; agitadora. —*v.t.* (stir) batir; agitar. —*v.i., fig.* (be stirred up) agitarse; alterarse.

chute (ʃut) *n.* **1,** (inclined duct) canal; conducto. **2,** (mail duct) tubo del correo. **3,** (parachute) paracaídas.

cicada (sɪ'kei·də) *n.* chicharra; cigarra.

cicerone (ˌsɪs·ə'ro·ni) *n.* cicerone.

-cidal (sai·dəl) *sufijo* cida-; *forma adjetivos de los nombres terminando en* **-cide**: *suicidal,* suicida.
-cide (said) *sufijo* **1,** -cida; que mata: *suicide,* suicida. **2,** -cidio; acción de matar: *homicide,* homicidio.
cider ('sai·dər) *n.* sidra.
cigar (sɪ'gar) *n.* puro; habano; *Amer.* cigarro; tabaco.
cigarette *también,* **cigaret** (ˌsɪg·ə'rɛt) *n.* cigarrillo; cigarro.
cilia ('sɪl·i·ə) *n.pl.* [*sing.* **cilium** (-əm)] cilios. —**ciliary,** *adj.* ciliar. —**ciliate,** *adj.* ciliado.
cinch (sɪntʃ) *n.* **1,** (girth; strap) cincha; cincho. **2,** *slang* (easy task) ganga. **3,** (sure thing) cosa asegurada. —*v.t.* **1,** (tighten) cinchar. **2,** (assure) asegurar; afianzar.
cinder ('sɪn·dər) *n.* **1,** (burnt particle) cernada; pavesa. **2,** *pl.* (ashes) cenizas.
Cinderella (sɪn·də'rɛl·ə) *n.* Cenicienta.
cinema ('sɪn·ə·mə) *n.* cinema; cine. —**cinematic** (sɪn·ə'mæt·ɪk); **cinematographic** (ˌsɪn·əˌmæt·ə·'græf·ɪk) *adj.* cinematográfico. —**cinematograph** (sɪn·ə'mæt·ə·græf) *n.* cinematógrafo; cine. —**cinematography** (ˌsɪn·ə·mə'tag·rə·fi) *n.* cinematografía.
cingulum ('sɪŋ·gjə·ləm) *n.* cíngulo.
cinnabar ('sɪn·əˌbar) *n.* cinabrio.
cinnamon ('sɪn·ə·mən) *n.* **1,** (tree) canelo; árbol de la canela. **2,** (spice) canela.
cipher ('sai·fər) *n.* **1,** (zero) cero. **2,** (numeral) cifra. **3,** (code; its key) clave. —*v.t.* **1,** (calculate) calcular. **2,** (write in code) cifrar.
circle ('sʌɹ·kəl) *n.* **1,** *geom.* círculo; circunferencia; **2,** (ring) anillo. **3,** (cycle) ciclo; círculo. **4,** (social group) círculo; grupo; clase. —*v.t.* circundar; rodear. —*v.i.* dar vueltas.
circuit ('sʌɹ·kɪt) *n.* **1,** *electricity* circuito. **2,** (boundary) radio; contorno. **3,** (itinerary) itinerario.
circuit breaker cortacircuitos.
circuitous (sər'kju·ɪ·təs) *adj.* tortuoso; indirecto. —**circuitousness,** *n.* tortuosidad; rodeo.
circular ('sʌɹ·kjə·lər) *adj.* **1,** (round) circular; redondo. **2,** (indirect) tortuoso; sinuoso. —*n.* circular; aviso.
circulate ('sʌɹ·kju·leit) *v.i.* circular; moverse. —*v.t.* propalar; divulgar; esparcir. —**circulatory** (-lə·ˌtor·i) *adj.* circulatorio.
circulation (ˌsʌɹ·kju'lei·ʃən) *n.* circulación.
circum- (sʌɹ·kəm) *prefijo* circum-; circun-; alrededor: *circumscribe,* circumscribir.
circumcision ('sʌɹ·kəmˌsɪʒ·ən) *n.* circuncisión. —**circumcise** ('sʌɹ·kəm·saiz) *v.t.* circuncidar.
circumference (sʌɹ'kʌm·fər·əns) *n.* circunferencia.
circumflex ('sʌɹ·kəm·flɛks) *n.* circunflejo; acento circunflejo (^).
circumlocution (ˌsʌɹ·kəm·lo·'kju·ʃən) *n.* circunlocución; circunloquio; rodeo.
circumnavigate *v.t.* circunnavegar. —**circumnavigation,** *n.* circunnavegación.
circumscribe (ˌsʌɹ·kəm'skraib) *v.t.* circunscribir; limitar. —**circumscription** (-'skrɪp·ʃən) *n.* circunscripción; limitación.
circumspect ('sʌɹ·kəm·spɛkt) *adj.* circunspecto; discreto. —**circumspection** (-'spɛk·ʃən) *n.* circunspección: recato; discreción.
circumstance ('sʌɹ·kəmˌstæns) *n.* circunstancia. —**in easy circumstances,** en buena posición; acomodado. —**under no circumstances,** de ninguna manera.
circumstantial (ˌsʌɹ·kəm'stæn·ʃəl) *adj.* circunstancial.
circumstantiate (ˌsʌɹ·kəm·'stæn·ʃiˌet) *v.t.* comprobar en todos los detalles.
circumvent (sʌɹ·kəm'vɛnt) *v.t.* **1,** (evade) esquivar. **2,** (outwit) engañar; embaucar.
circus ('sʌɹ·kəs) *n.* circo.
cirrhosis (sɪ'ro·sɪs) *n.* cirrosis.
cirrus ('sɪr·əs) *n.* [*pl.* **cirri** (-ai)] cirro.
cistern ('sɪs·tərn) *n.* cisterna.
citadel ('sɪt·ə·dəl) *n.* ciudadela; fortaleza.
citation (sai'tei·ʃən) *n.* **1,** (quotation) cita. **2,** (commendation) citación; mención. **3,** *law* emplazamiento.
cite (sait) *v.t.* **1,** (mention) citar; mencionar; referirse a. **2,** *law* emplazar.
cithara ('sɪθ·ə·rə) *n.* cítara.
citified ('sɪt·ɪˌfaid) *adj., colloq.* urbano; con costumbres de ciudad.

citizen ('sɪt·ə·zən) *n.* ciudadano. —**citizenry** (-ri) *n.* nación; gente; población. —**citizenship,** *n.* ciudadanía; nacionalidad. —**fellow citizen,** conciudadano.
citrate ('sai·tret; 'sɪt·ret) *n.* citrato.
citric ('sɪt·rɪk) *adj.* cítrico.
citron ('sɪt·rən) *n.* **1,** (tree) cidro. **2,** (fruit) cidra.
citrus ('sɪt·rəs) *n.* cidro. —*adj.* [*también,* **citrous**] cítrico.
city ('sɪt·i) *n.* ciudad. —**city hall,** ayuntamiento; alcaldía; municipio.
civet ('sɪv·ɪt) *n.* civeto. —**civet cat,** civeta.
civic ('sɪv·ɪk) *adj.* cívico. —**civics,** *n.* ciencia del gobierno civil.
civil ('sɪv·əl) *adj.* **1,** (pert. to citizens) civil. **2,** (polite) civil; educado; cortés. —**civil defense,** defensa civil. —**civil engineering,** ingeniería civil; *Sp.* ingeniería de caminos, canales y puertos. —**civil law,** derecho civil. —**civil marriage,** matrimonio civil. —**civil servant,** funcionario; empleado de administración pública. —**civil service,** servicio civil *o* de administración pública. —**civil war,** guerra civil.
civilian (sə'vɪl·jən) *n.* ciudadano. —*adj.* civil.
civility (sə'vɪl·ə·ti) *n.* civilidad; sociabilidad; urbanidad.
civilization (ˌsɪv·ə·lɪ'zei·ʃən) *n.* civilización.
civilize ('sɪv·əˌlaiz) *v.t.* civilizar.
clack (klæk) *n.* chasquido; ruido seco. —*v.t.* chasquear. —*v.i.* chascar.
clad (klæːd) *v., pret.* & *p.p. de* **clothe.** —*adj.* vestido; cubierto.
claim (kleim) *v.t.* **1,** (demand) demandar; reclamar. **2,** *colloq.* (assert) pretender; debatir; contender. —*n.* demanda; reclamación. —**claimant,** *n.* demandante; peticionario.
clairvoyance (klɛr'vɔi·əns) *n.* clarividencia; lucidez. —**clairvoyant,** *n.* & *adj.* clarividente.
clam (klæm) *n.* **1,** (mollusk) almeja. **2,** *fig.* (reticent person) ostra. —**clam up,** *slang* callarse.
clamber ('klæm·bər) *v.i.* gatear; encaramarse; trepar.
clammy ('klæm·i) *adj.* pegajoso; pastoso; gelatinoso. —**clamminess,** *n.* viscosidad; pegajosidad.
clamor *también,* **clamour** ('klæm·ər) *n.* clamor; alboroto; vocería. —*v.i.* clamorear; gritar; vociferar. —**clamorous,** *adj.* clamoroso; vociferante; vocinglero.
clamp (klæmp) *n.* grapa; abrazadera. —*v.t.* sujetar; afianzar; coser con grapas. —**clamp down (on),** *colloq.* ponerse serio (con); volverse riguroso (con).
clan (klæn) *n.* **1,** (tribe) clan; tribu. **2,** *fig.* (kin) familia. **3,** (clique) camarilla; pandilla. —**clannish** (-ɪsh) *adj.* gregario.
clandestine (klæn'dɛs·tɪn) *adj.* clandestino; furtivo. —**clandestineness,** *n.* clandestinidad.
clang (klæŋ) *n.* retintín. —*v.t.* hacer sonar; resonar. —*v.i.* sonar *o* vibrar metálicamente.
clank (klæŋk) *n.* chirrido *o* golpe metálico. —*v.i.* rechinar; chirriar.
clansman ('klænz·mən) *n.* [*pl.* **-men**] pariente; miembro de un clan.
clap (klæp) *v.t.* [**clapped, clapping**] **1,** (strike the hands) palmotear; aplaudir. **2,** *slang* (place or dispose of swiftly) empujar; tirar; arrojar. —*v.i.* batir; aplaudir. —*n.* **1,** (applause) aplauso; ovación. **2,** (a blow) palmada.
clapboard ('klæb·ərd) *n.* chilla.
clapper ('klæp·ər) *n.* badajo.
claptrap ('klæpˌtræp) *n.* engañifa.
claque (klæk) *n.* claque.
claret ('klær·ət) *n.* vino clarete.
clarify ('klær·əˌfai) *v.t.* **1,** (make clear) clarificar; aclarar. **2,** *fig.* (explain) esclarecer. —*v.i.* aclararse; clarificarse. —**clarification** (-fɪ'kei·ʃən) *n.* clarificación; aclaración.
clarinet (klær·ə'nɛt) *n.* clarinete. —**clarinetist,** *n.* clarinete.
clarion ('klær·i·ən) *n.* clarín.
clarity ('klær·ə·ti) *n.* claridad.
clash (klæʃ) *v.i.* **1,** (collide) chocar; entrechocar. **2,** *fig.* (oppose) encontrarse; oponerse; antagonizar. —*v.t.* golpear violentamente. —*n.* **1,** (collision) choque; colisión. **2,** *fig.* (conflict) encuentro; disputa.
clasp (klæsp) *n.* **1,** (latch) abrazadera; broche; hebilla. **2,** (embrace) abrazo; apretón. —*v.t.* **1,** (lock) abrochar; enganchar; asegurar. **2,** (embrace) apretar; abrazar.
class (klæs) *n.* **1,** (category) clase; categoría; rango; condición. **2,** (academic) clase. **3,** *colloq.* (refinement) elegancia; belleza; madera. —*v.t.* clasificar.
classic ('klæs·ɪk) *n.* clásico; obra

clásica; autor clásico. —*adj.* [*también*, **classical**] clásico.
classicism ('klæs·ə·sɪz·əm) *n.* clasicismo. —**classicist**, *n.* clasicista.
classification (ˌklæs·ɪ·fɪ'kei·ʃən) *n.* clasificación.
classified ('klæs·ɪˌfaid) *adj.* **1,** (grouped) clasificado. **2,** *mil.* secreto; confidencial.
classify ('klæs·ɪˌfai) *v.t.* clasificar.
classless ('klæs·ləs) *adj.* sin clase; sin categoría.
classroom *n.* sala *o* salón de clase; aula.
clatter ('klæt·ər) *n.* estruendo; ruido; martilleo. —*v.t.* hacer retumbar. —*v.i.* resonar; hacer ruido.
clause (klɔːz) *n.* **1,** *gram.* cláusula; período. **2,** (stipulation) cláusula; condición.
claustrophobia (ˌklɔs·trə'fo·bi·ə) *n.* claustrofobia.
clavicle ('klæv·ɪ·kəl) *n.* clavícula.
claw (klɔː) *n.* **1,** *anat.* garra. **2,** (tool) garfio; gancho; diente. —*v.t.* & *i.* desgarrar; arañar; despedazar.
clay (klei) *n.* **1,** (earth) arcilla. **2,** *fig.* (human body) barro; el cuerpo humano. —**potter's clay,** barro de alfarero.
clayey ('kle·i) *adj.* arcilloso.
-cle (kəl) *sufijo, var. de* **-cule**: *particle,* partícula; *article,* artículo.
clean (kliːn) *adj.* **1,** (free from dirt) limpio; nítido; aseado. **2,** *fig.* (pure) puro; honrado. **3,** (innocent) inocente. **4,** (fastidious) meticuloso. —*v.t.* **1,** (remove dirt from) limpiar; asear. **2,** (rid of superfluous material) depurar. —*adv.* completamente. —**clean up,** *colloq.* **1,** (make clean) limpiar; lavar. **2,** (tidy) arreglar; asear. **3,** (finish) completar; terminar. **4,** (make money) ganar mucho. —**come clean,** *slang* confesar; desahogarse.
clean-cut *adj.* **1,** (shapely) definido; claro. **2,** *fig.* (neat) agradable; bien portado; límpido.
cleaner ('kli·nər) *n.* **1,** (person who cleans) limpiador. **2,** (cleaning agent) limpiador: quitamanchas.
cleanly ('klin·li) *adv.* limpiamente. —*adj.* ('klɛn·li) limpio. —**cleanliness** ('klɛn-) *n.* limpieza.
cleanness ('klin·nəs) *n.* limpieza; aseo.
cleanse (klɛnz) *v.t.* **1,** (clean) limpiar; quitar manchas. **2,** *fig.* (purge) depurar; purificar. —**cleanser,** *n.* limpiador; quitamanchas; *fig.* purificador.
clean-shaven *adj.* apurado; bien afeitado; bien rasurado.
clear (klɪr) *adj.* **1,** (easily understood) claro; evidente; palpable. **2,** (transparent) transparente; claro; lúcido; despejado. **3,** (innocent) inocente; libre; limpio. —*v.t.* **1,** (unburden) desembarazar; limpiar; aclarar. **2,** (make a profit) ganar; sacar. **3,** (jump over) saltar; salvar. **4,** [*también,* **clear up**] (solve) solucionar; dilucidar. **5,** [*también,* **clear away** *o* **off**] (empty) quitar; desembarazar. —*v.i.* **1,** [*usu.,* **clear up**] (brighten) aclararse; despejarse. **2,** (be paid, as a check) pasar, **3,** [*usu.,* **clear out**] (leave) marcharse; escabullirse. —**clearness,** *n.* claridad; limpidez.
clearance ('klɪr·əns) *n.* **1,** *comm.* despacho de aduana; utilidad líquido. **2,** (space) espacio libre; paso. —**clearance sale,** venta de liquidación.
clearcut *adj.* obvio; claro; definido.
clearing ('klir·ɪŋ) *n.* raso; claro. —**clearing house,** cámara de compensación.
cleat (klit) *n.* abrazadera; tojino.
cleavage ('kliv·ɪdʒ) *n.* hendidura; raja.
cleave (kliːv) *v.i.* **1,** (adhere) adherirse; pegarse; unirse. **2,** (split) henderse; rajarse; partirse. —*v.t.* hender; rajar; partir.
cleaver ('kli·vər) *n.* cuchillo; destral; hacha.
clef (klɛf) *n.* clave. —**bass** *o* **F clef,** clave de fa. —**tenor** *o* **C clef,** clave de do. —**treble** *o* **G clef,** clave de sol.
cleft (klɛft) *n.* grieta; rajadura; hendidura. —*v., pret.* & *p.p. de* **cleave.** —*adj.* agrietado; hendido; rajado.
clematis ('klɛm·ə·tɪs) *n.* clemátide.
clemency ('klɛm·ən·si) *n.* clemencia; indulgencia; piedad. —**clement,** *adj.* clemente; piadoso; indulgente.
clench (klɛntʃ) *v.t.* **1,** (close tightly) apretar. **2,** (grip tightly) asir; agarrar; atenazar.
clergy ('klʌɹ·dʒi) *n.* clerecía; clero.
clergyman ('klʌɹ·dʒi·mən) *n.* [*pl.* **-men**] clérigo; eclesiástico; sacerdote; pastor.
cleric ('klɛr·ɪk) *n.* & *adj.* clérigo.

clerical ('klɛr·ə·kəl) *adj.* **1,** *eccles.* clerical; eclesiástico. **2,** (administrative) de oficina.
clerk (klʌɹk) *n.* **1,** (shop employee) dependiente. **2,** (office worker) oficinista. —*v.i.* trabajar de oficinista *o* dependiente. —**clerkship,** *n.* oficio de dependiente *o* oficinista.
clever ('klɛv·ər) *adj.* listo; inteligente; alerta; hábil; ingenioso. —**cleverness,** *n.* agudeza; listeza.
clew (kluː) *n.* **1,** (ball of yarn) madeja; ovillo. **2,** = **clue.**
cliché (kli'ʃei) *n.* frase trillada.
click (klɪk) *n.* golpe seco. —*v.t.* & *i.* (sound) sonar secamente. —*v.i., colloq.* (succeed) triunfar; prosperar.
client ('klai·ənt) *n.* cliente. —**clientele** (kli·ən'tɛl; klai-) *n.* clientela.
cliff (klɪf) *n.* farallón; escarpadura.
climacteric (klai'mæk·tər·ɪk) *adj.* climatérico. —*n.* período climatérico.
climactic (klai'mæk·tɪk) *adj.* culminante.
climate ('klai·mɪt) *n.* clima. —**climatic** (klai'mæt·ɪk) *adj.* climático.
climax ('klai·mæks) *n.* clímax; culminación. —*v.t.* & *i.* culminar.
climb (klaim) *v.t.* & *i.* escalar; trepar; subir. —*n.* ascenso; subida. —**climb down,** descender; bajar.
clime (klaim) *n., poet.* región.
clinch (klɪntʃ) *v.t.* **1,** (fasten) remachar. **2,** (clench) apretar; consolidar. **3,** *fig.* (settle) afirmar; confirmar. —*v.i.* **1,** *colloq.* (hug) abrazar. **2,** *boxing* echar un gancho. —*n.* **1,** (fastening) remache. **2,** *boxing* gancho. **3,** *colloq.* (hug) abrazo.
clincher ('klɪntʃ·ər) *n.* **1,** (person; tool) remachador. **2,** *colloq.* (decisive statement) argumento decisivo; remache.
cling (klɪŋ) *v.i.* [**clung, clinging**] adherirse; pegarse.
clingstone *n.* albérchigo; pavía. *También,* **cling peach.**
clinic ('klɪn·ɪk) *n.* clínica. —**clinical,** *adj.* clínico.
clink (klɪŋk) *n.* **1,** (sharp sound) retintín; sonido agudo. **2,** *slang* (jail) cárcel. —*v.i.* tintinar. —*v.t.* hacer tintinar.
clip (klɪp) *n.* **1,** (fastener) pinza; grapa. **2,** *colloq.* (rapid pace) galope. —*v.t.* [**clipped, clipping**] **1,** (fasten) poner pinzas *o* grapas a; asegurar; unir. **2,** (shear) cortar; recortar. **3,** (cut short, as hair) esquilar; trasquilar. **4,** *colloq.* (strike) pegar; golpear. —**paper clip,** sujetapapeles.
clipper ('klɪp·ər) *n.* **1,** (cutting tool) recortador; trasquilador; *pl.* tijeras. **2,** (ship) clíper.
clipping ('klɪp·ɪŋ) *n.* recorte.
clique (klik) *n.* camarilla; círculo. —**cliquish,** *adj.* exclusivista.
clitoris ('klɪt·ə·rɪs; 'klai·tə-) *n.* clítoris.
cloak (klok) *n.* **1,** (garment) capa; manto. **2,** *fig.* (disguise) capa; pretexto; excusa. —*v.t.* **1,** (cover) cubrir; encubrir. **2,** (conceal) ocultar.
clobber ('klab·ər) *v.t., slang* aporrear; golpear.
clock (klak) *n.* **1,** (timepiece) reloj. **2,** (design on hose) cuadrado de medias. —*v.t.* calcular *o* medir el tiempo de.
clockface *n.* esfera del reloj.
clockmaker *n.* relojero.
clockwise ('klak,waiz) *adj.* & *adv.* según las manecillas del reloj.
clockwork *n.* movimiento de reloj. —**like clockwork,** como un reloj; muy regular.
clod (klad) *n.* **1,** (turf) terrón; tierra. **2,** *fig.* (dolt) estúpido; zoquete; idiota. —**cloddish,** *adj.* estúpido; idiota.
clog (klag) *n.* **1,** (block) obstrucción; obstáculo; traba. **2,** (thick-soled shoe) galocha; chanclo. **3,** (dance) zapateado. —*v.t.* [**clogged, clogging**] **1,** (impede) obstaculizar; entorpecer; embarazar. **2,** (stop up) atorar. —*v.i.* **1,** (become obstructed) atorarse. **2,** (dance) zapatear; bailar el zapateado.
cloister ('klɔis·tər) *n.* **1,** (arcade) claustro. **2,** (religious retreat) monasterio.
close (kloːz) *v.t.* **1,** (shut) cerrar; clausurar. **2,** (fill) cerrar; tapar. **3,** (finish) terminar; concluir; acabar. —*v.i.* **1,** [*usu.,* **close in**] (draw near) acercarse; aproximarse. **2,** (join) unirse; juntarse. **3,** (end) finalizar; concluir. **4,** (complete a transaction) ponerse de acuerdo; saldar. **5,** (grapple) agarrarse; pelearse. —*n.* conclusión; terminación; fin. —**close out,** liquidar. —**close up, 1,** (shut) cerrar por completo; terminar. **2,** (fill a gap in) acercarse más.
close (klos) *adj.* **1,** (near) cercano; junto; inmediato. **2,** (airless)

cerrado; sofocante. **3,** (dense) denso; compacto; pesado. **4,** (reticent) reticente; secreto; oculto. **5,** *colloq.* (penurious) tacaño; interesado. —*adv.* cerca. —*n.* cercado; vallado. —**close quarters, 1,** (narrow space) cuchitril; lugar estrecho. **2,** (encounter with an enemy) lucha cuerpo a cuerpo. —**close shave; close call,** *colloq.* escape por un pelo.
closed shop taller de unión obligatoria; taller cerrado.
closefisted (klos'fɪst·ɪd) *adj.* miserable; cicatero; tacaño.
closefitting (klos'fɪt·ɪŋ) *adj.* ajustado; apretado.
closeness ('klos·nəs) *n.* **1,** (nearness) proximidad. **2,** (airlessness) falta de aire.
closet ('klaz·ɪt) *n.* **1,** (place for storage) armario. **2,** (small room) gabinete. **3,** (toilet) excusado; retrete; lavabo. —*v.t.* encerrar. —**closeted,** *adj.* encerrado.
close-up ('klos,ʌp) *n.* vista de cerca.
closure ('klo·ʒər) *n.* **1,** (act) cierre; clausura. **2,** (state) encierro. **3,** (thing that closes) cierre. **4,** (end) conclusión; fin; término.
clot (klat) *n.* coágulo; grumo. —*v.t.* [**clotted, clotting**] coagular; cuajar. —*v.i.* coagularse; cuajarse.
cloth (klɔθ) *n.* **1,** (fabric) tejido; paño; tela. **2,** (clerical robe) traje clerical; sotana. **3,** *fig.* (the clergy) clero. —*adj.* de tejido; de tela.
clothe (klo:ð) *v.t.* vestir; arropar; trajear.
clothes (klo:z) *n.pl.* **1,** (for men) traje. **2,** (for women) vestido. **3,** (for a bed) ropa de cama; cobertor. —**clothes closet,** ropero. —**clothes tree,** perchero.
clotheshorse *n., slang* petimetra; pisaverde.
clothesline *n.* cordel de tender.
clothier ('kloð·jər) *n.* ropero.
cloture ('klo·tʃər) *n.* clausura (*de un debate*).
clothing ('klo·ðɪŋ) *n.* vestuario; ropa. —**clothing shop** *o* **store,** ropería.
cloud (klaud) *n.* **1,** (sky vapor) nube; nublado. **2,** (dark spot) nube; mancha. **3,** *fig.* (mass) nube; multitud. —*v.t.* & *i.* (obscure) anublar; nublar; oscurecer; empañar. —*v.t.* (sully) difamar; manchar. —**cloudiness,** *n.* nublosidad; obscuridad. —**cloudless,** *adj.* sin nubes; despejado. —**cloudy,** *adj.* nublado.
cloudburst *n.* aguacero; turbión.
clout (klaut) *n.* golpe; bofetada. —*v.t.* abofetear; golpear con la mano.
clove (klov) *n.* **1,** (segment, as of garlic) diente. **2,** (spice) clavo. —*v., pret. de* **cleave.**
cloven ('klo·vən) *v., p.p. de* **cleave.**
cloven hoof pie hendido. —**cloven-hoofed,** *adj.* bisulco; *fig.* diabólico.
clover ('klo·vər) *n.* trébol.
clown (klaun) *n.* payaso. —*v.i.* payasear; hacer el payaso *o* el bufón; parodiar. —**clownish,** *adj.* grotesco; apayasado.
cloy (klɔi) *v.t.* & *i.* hartar; saciar. —*v.i.* empalagarse.
club (klʌb) *n.* **1,** (weapon) porra; garrote; palo. **2,** (association) club; círculo. **3,** *cards* trébol (*in the French deck*); basto (*in the Spanish deck*). —*v.t.* [**clubbed, clubbing**] golpear; aporrear. —**club together,** unirse; congregarse.
clubfoot *n.* [*pl.* **-feet**] patituerto. —**clubfooted,** *adj.* patituerto.
cluck (klʌk) *n.* **1,** (of a person) chasquido de la lengua. **2,** (of a hen) cloqueo. —*v.i.* cloquear.
clue (klu:) *n.* pista; guía; indicio.
clump (klʌmp) *n.* **1,** (lump) trozo; masa. **2,** (cluster, as of trees) macizo; grupo. —*v.i.* andar pesadamente.
clumpy ('klʌm·pi) *adj.* **1,** (heavy) macizo; pesado. **2,** (awkward) desmañado; torpe.
clumsy ('klʌm·zi) *adj.* zafio; ordinario; tosco; inadaptado. —**clumsiness,** *n.* zafiedad; ordinariez; desmañamiento.
clung (klʌŋ) *v., pret.* & *p.p. de* **cling.**
cluster ('klʌs·tər) *n.* **1,** (of persons) grupo; pelotón. **2,** (of things) racimo; ramo. —*v.t.* agrupar; arracimar. —*v.i.* arracimarse; agruparse.
clutch (klʌtʃ) *v.t.* agarrar; asir. —*v.i.* [*usu.,* **clutch at**] intentar agarrar *o* apresar. —*n.* **1,** *usu. pl.* (grip) control; poder; mando. **2,** *mech.* embrague. **3,** (brood of chickens) nidada; pollada. —**fall into the clutches of,** caer en las garras de. —**engage the clutch,** embragar.
clutter ('klʌt·ər) *n.* desorden; con-

fusión. —*v.t.* [*también,* **clutter up**] alborotar; desordenar.

co- (ko) *prefijo, var. de* **com- 1,** asociación: *coadjutor,* coadjutor. **2,** acción conjunta: *cooperation,* cooperación. **3,** *matem.* complemento de: *cosine,* coseno.

coach (kotʃ) *n.* **1,** (carriage) carruaje; coche; vehículo. **2,** (instructor) instructor; entrenador. —*v.t.* instruir; entrenar; aconsejar.

coachman ('kotʃ·mən) *n.* [*pl.* **-men**] cochero.

coagulate (ko'æg·jə,leit) *v.t.* coagular. —*v.i.* coagularse. —**coagulation,** *n.* coagulación.

coal (koːl) *n.* **1,** (mineral) hulla; carbón de piedra. **2,** (lump) brasa; carbón. —**coal mine,** mina de carbón; mina de hulla. —**coal tar,** alquitrán de hulla.

coalesce (ko·ə'lɛs) *v.i.* incorporarse; juntarse; integrarse. —**coalescence,** *n.* coalición; unión. —**coalescent,** *adj.* integrante.

coalition (ko·ə'lɪʃ·ən) *n.* coalición.

coarse (kors) *adj.* **1,** (rough) basto; ordinario. **2,** *fig.* (vulgar) rudo; soez; vulgar. —**coarsen** ('kor·sən) *v.t.* hacer ordinario. —**coarseness,** *n.* rudeza; ordinariez.

coast (kost) *n.* costa; litoral. —*v.i.* deslizarse; correr por la gravedad. —**coastal,** *adj.* costero. —**coast guard,** cuerpo de guardacostas.

coastline *n.* litoral.

coat (kot) *n.* **1,** (outer garment) chaqueta; americana; *Amer.* saco. **2,** (hair; fur) pelo. **3,** (layer, as of paint) mano. —*v.t.* **1,** (cover) cubrir; vestir. **2,** (paint) dar una mano a. —**coat of mail,** cota de malla.

coating ('ko·tɪŋ) *n.* **1,** (covering) capa; revestimiento. **2,** (plating) baño.

coax (koks) *v.t. & i.* engatusar; halagar. —**coaxing,** *n.* engatusamiento; halago.

coaxial (ko'æk·si·əl) *adj.* coaxial.

cob (kaːb) *n.* **1,** (of corn) mazorca; *Amer.* tusa. **2,** (horse) jaca. **3,** (male swan) cisne.

cobalt ('ko·bɔlt) *n.* cobalto. —*adj.* de cobalto.

cobble ('kab·əl) *v.t. & i.* remendar (zapatos).

cobbler ('kab·lər) *n.* **1,** (shoemaker) zapatero remendón. **2,** (fruit pie or drink) postre *o* bebida con frutas.

cobblestone *n.* guijarro.

cobra ('ko·brə) *n.* cobra.

cobweb ('kab·wɛb) *n.* tela de araña; telaraña.

coca ('ko·kə) *n., bot.* coca.

cocaine (ko'kein) *n.* cocaína.

coccus ('kak·əs) *n.* [*pl.* **cocci** (-sai)] **1,** (bacterium) coco. **2,** *bot.* carpelo.

coccyx ('kak·sɪks) *n.* [*pl.* **coccyges** (-sɪ,dʒiz)] cóccix; rabadilla.

cock (kak) *n.* **1,** (male fowl) gallo; macho. **2,** (leader) capitán; líder; caudillo. **3,** (conical pile) pajar; henil. **4,** (tilt, as of a hat) vuelta (del ala); inclinación. **5,** (weathercock) veleta. —*v.t.* **1,** (turn up on one side) ladear; inclinar. **2,** (ready a gun) amartillar; montar. **3,** (raise) levantar. —**cock and bull story,** cuento increíble.

cochineal (,katʃ·ə'niːl) *n.* cochinilla.

cochlea ('kak·li·ə) *n.* [*pl.* **cochleae** (-i)] caracol (*del oído*).

cockatoo (,kak·ə'tuː) *n.* cacatúa.

cockboat *n.* barquichuelo.

cocked hat tricornio; sombrero de tres picos.

cockfight *n.* pelea de gallos.

cockle ('kak·əl) *n.* **1,** (weed) maleza; cizaña. **2,** (mollusk) coquina; caracol de mar. **3,** (boat) barquichuelo. —*v.t. & i.* arrugar; doblar. —**cockles of the heart,** las entrañas.

cockleshell *n.* coquina.

cockney ('kak·ni) *n.* londinense bajo.

cockpit *n.* **1,** *aero.* carlinga. **2,** (place for cockfighting) gallera.

cockroach *n.* cucaracha.

cockscomb *n.* cresta de gallo.

cocksure ('kak'ʃʊr) *adj.* seguro; confiado.

cocktail ('kak·tel) *n.* coctel. —**cocktail shaker,** coctelera.

cocky ('kak·i) *adj.* vanidoso; presumido. —**cockiness,** *n.* presunción.

cocoa ('ko·ko) *n.* cacao; chocolate. —**cocoa butter,** manteca de cacao.

coconut *también,* **cocoanut** ('ko·kə,nʌt) *n.* **1,** (fruit) coco. **2,** (tree) coco; cocotero. —**coconut grove** *o* **plantation,** cocotal.

cocoon (kə'kuːn) *n.* capullo (de gusanos).

cod (kaːd) *n.* bacalao. *También,* **codfish.**

coda ('ko·də) *n.* coda.
coddle ('kad·əl) *v.t.* **1,** (pamper) consentir; mimar. **2,** (cook) mediococer; mediohervir.
code (koːd) *n.* **1,** (set of laws or rules) código. **2,** (system of signals) código; clave; cifra.
codeine ('ko·din) *n.* codeína.
codex ('ko·dɛks) *n.* códice.
codger ('kadʒ·ər) *n.* vejete.
codicil ('kad·ə·səl) *n.* codicilo.
codify ('kad·ɪˌfai) *v.t.* codificar; compilar. **—codification** (-fɪ'kei·ʃən) *n.* codificación.
coeducation (ˌko·ɛd·jə'kei·ʃən) *n.,* coeducación. **—coeducational,** *adj.* coeducativo.
coefficient (ˌko·ə'fɪʃ·ənt) *n.* & *adj.* coeficiente.
coeno- (si·no) *prefijo, var. de* **ceno-**: *coenobite,* cenobita.
coequal *adj.* & *n.* igual; semejante.
coerce (ko'ʌɹs) *v.t.* coercer; obligar; forzar. **—coercion** (-'ʌɹ·ʃən) *n.* coerción.
coeval (ko'i·vəl) *adj.* coevo; contemporáneo.
coexist (ˌko·ɛg'zɪst) *v.i.* coexistir; convivir. **—coexistence,** *n.* coexistencia.
coffee ('kɔf·i) **1,** (tree) cafeto. **2,** (drink) café. **—coffee pot,** cafetera. **—coffee shop,** café.
coffee break pausa para tomar café.
coffeehouse *n.* café.
coffer ('kɔf·ər) *n.* cofre; arca.
coffin ('kɔf·ɪn) *n.* ataúd; féretro; caja.
cog (kaːg) *n.* diente de rueda.
cogent ('ko·dʒənt) *adj.* convincente; poderoso; urgente. **—cogency,** *n.* evidencia; fuerza.
cogitate ('kadʒ·ə·teit) *v.t.* & *i.* pensar; planear; meditar; reflexionar.
cognac ('kon·jæk) *n.* coñac.
cognate ('kag·net) *adj.* & *n.* cognado.
cognition (kag'nɪʃ·ən) *n.* conocimiento; entendimiento.
cognizance ('kag·nɪ·zəns) *n.* **1,** (awareness) conocimiento; noticia; percepción. **2,** (range of knowledge) comprensión. **3,** *law* jurisdicción; competencia. **4,** *heraldry* divisa; mote. **—cognizant,** *adj.* sabedor; conocedor; informado. **—take cognizance of,** reconocer oficialmente.
cognomen (kag'no·mən) *n.* **1,** (surname) apellido. **2,** (nickname) mote; apodo. **3,** (Roman family name) cognomen.
cogwheel *n.* rueda dentada.
cohabit (ko'hæb·ɪt) *v.i.* cohabitar; vivir maritalmente. **—cohabitation,** *n.* cohabitación.
coheir *n.* coheredero.
cohere (ko'hɪr) *v.i.* **1,** (adhere) unirse; adherirse; pegarse. **2,** (conform) conformarse; ajustarse. **—coherence,** *n.* coherencia. **—coherent,** *adj.* coherente.
cohesion (ko'hi·ʒən) *n.* cohesión; coherencia. **—cohesive** (-sɪv) *adj.* adherente; coherente.
cohort ('ko·hort) *n.* cohorte; banda.
coif (kɔif) *n.* **1,** (tight cap) cofia. **2,** (nun's cap) toca.
coiffure (kwa'fjʊr) *n.* peinado; tocado. **—coiffeur** (-'fʌɹ) *n.* peluquero.
coil (kɔil) *v.t.* & *i.* enrollar; arrollar. **—*n.*** **1,** (roll) rollo. **2,** *electricity* bobina.
coin (kɔin) *n.* moneda. **—*v.t.*** **1,** (mint) acuñar. **2,** (invent) acuñar; inventar.
coinage ('kɔin·ɪdʒ) *n.* **1,** (minting) acuñación. **2,** (currency) moneda; dinero; sistema monetario. **3,** (invention) acuñación; invención.
coincide (ˌko·ɪn'said) *v.i.* **1,** (take up the same space) coincidir. **2,** (occur at the same time) coincidir; concurrir. **3,** (agree) convenir; estar *o* ponerse de acuerdo.
coincidence (ko'ɪn·sɪ·dəns) *n.* coincidencia; casualidad.
coincident (ko'ɪn·sɪ·dənt) *adj.* coincidente.
coincidental (koˌɪn·sɪ'dɛn·təl) *adj.* coincidente; de coincidencia; por casualidad.
coitus ('ko·ɪ·təs) *n.* coito. *También,* **coition** (ko'ɪʃ·ən).
coke (kok) *n.* **1,** (fuel) cok; coque. **2,** *slang* = **cocaine. 3,** *colloq.* Coca-Cola.
col- (kal) *prefijo, var. de* **com-** *ante* l: *collateral,* colateral.
colander ('kal·ən·dər) *n.* colador; coladera; escurridor.
cold (koːld) *adj.* **1,** (lacking warmth) frío. **2,** *fig.* (unfeeling) frío; tibio; indiferente; insensible. **—*n.*** **1,** (lack of warmth) frío. **2,** (ailment) catarro; constipado; resfrío. **—catch, take** *o* **get a cold,** acatarrarse; resfriarse; tomar frío. **—cold feet,** *colloq.* miedo; temor;

desánimo. —**cold meat; cold cuts,** fiambre.
cold front frente frío.
coldblooded *adj.* inhumano; cruel; de sangre fría; atroz. —**coldbloodedness,** *n.* sangre fría; crueldad; inhumanidad.
coldhearted *adj.* duro; frío; insensible.
coldness ('kold·nəs) *n.* **1,** (lack of warmth) frío; frigidez. **2,** (indifference) frialdad; insensibilidad; indiferencia.
cole (kol) *n.* col; berza.
coleslaw ('kol·slɔː) *n.* ensalada de col.
colic ('kal·ɪk) *n.* & *adj.* cólico. —**colicky,** *adj.* que padece cólico.
coliseum (kal·ə'si·əm) *n.* coliseo.
colitigant (ˌko'lɪt·ə·gənt) *n., law* consorte.
colitis (ko'lai·tɪs) *n.* colitis.
collaborate (kə'læb·ə·reit) *v.i.* colaborar. —**collaboration,** *n.* colaboración. —**collaborationist,** *n.* colaboracionista. —**collaborator,** *n.* colaborador.
collapse (kə'læps) *n.* colapso. —*v.i.* **1,** (become broken) romperse. **2,** (fail) desplomarse; derrumbarse. **3,** (break down physically) debilitarse; prostrarse. —*v.t.* plegar; cerrar. —**collapsible,** *adj.* plegable.
collar ('kal·ər) *n.* **1,** (of a garment) cuello. **2,** (of an animal) collar; collera. —*v.t.* **1,** (put a collar on) poner cuello *o* collar a. **2,** (grasp by the collar) coger por el cuello. **3,** *slang* (seize; arrest) agarrar; capturar.
collarbone *n.* clavícula.
collate (kə'leit) *v.t.* **1,** (compare) comparar; cotejar. **2,** (assemble in order) ordenar.
collateral (kə'læt·ə·rəl) *adj.* **1,** (supplementary) accesorio; subordinado. **2,** (side by side) paralelo. **3,** *genealogy* colateral. —*n.* garantía.
collation (ko'lei·ʃən) *n.* **1,** (act of collating) cotejo; comparación. **2,** (light meal) colación.
colleague ('kal·ig) *n.* colega; compañero.
collect (kə'lɛkt) *v.t.* **1,** (assemble) congregar; reunir; juntar. **2,** (obtain payment for) cobrar; recaudar. **3,** (acquire) coleccionar; juntar. —*n.* ('kal·ɛkt) colecta. —**collect oneself,** volver en sí; reponerse; tranquilizarse. —**collectedness,** *n.* calma. —**collectible,** *adj.* cobrable.
collection (kə'lɛk·ʃən) *n.* **1,** (things collected) colección. **2,** (money collected) colecta. **3,** (mass) conjunto; acumulación.
collective (kə'lɛk·tɪv) *adj.* colectivo. —**collectively,** *adv.* en conjunto. —**collectivism,** *n.* colectivismo. —**collectivity** (ˌkal·ɛk'tɪv·ə·ti) *n.* colectividad.
collector (kə'lɛk·tər) *n.* **1,** (one who collects as a hobby) coleccionista. **2,** (one who collects money due) recaudador.
college ('kal·ɪdʒ) *n.* colegio.
collegian (kə'lɪː·dʒən) *n.* colegial; universitario.
collegiate (kə'liː·dʒi·ət) *adj.* **1,** (of a college) colegiado; colegial. **2,** *eccles.* colegial.
collide (kə'laid) *v.i.* chocar; topar.
collie ('kal·i) *n.* perro de pastor escocés.
collier ('kal·jər) *n.* **1,** (coal miner) minero de carbón. **2,** (vessel) barco carbonero; carbonero. —**colliery,** *n.* mina de carbón.
collision (kə'lɪʒ·ən) *n.* **1,** (clash) colisión; choque. **2,** (encounter) encuentro.
collodion (kə'lo·di·ən) *n.* colodión.
colloid ('kal·ɔid) *n.* coloide. —**colloidal** (kə'lɔi·dəl) *adj.* coloideo.
colloquial (kə'lo·kwi·əl) *adj.* familiar. —**colloquialism,** *n.* expresión familiar.
colloquy ('kal·ə·kwi) *n.* coloquio; conversación.
collusion (kə'lu·ʒən) *n.* colusión. —**collusive** (-sɪv) *adj.* colusorio.
cologne (kə'loːn) *n.* colonia; agua de colonia.
colon ('ko·lən) *n.* **1,** *anat.* colon. **2,** *gram.* dos puntos (:).
colonel ('kʌɹ·nəl) *n.* coronel. —**colonelcy** (-si) *n.* coronelía.
colonial (kə'lo·ni·əl) *adj.* colonial. —*n.* colono. —**colonialism,** *n.* colonialismo.
colonist ('kal·ə·nɪst) *n.* colono.
colonize ('kal·əˌnaiz) *v.t.* colonizar. —**colonization** (-nɪ'zei·ʃən) *n.* colonización.
colonnade (kal·ə'neid) *n.* columnata.
colony ('kal·ə·ni) *n.* colonia.
color *también,* **colour** ('kʌl·ər) *n.* **1,** (hue) color. **2,** *fig.* (appearance)

complexión; color de la piel; apariencia; constitución. 3, *pl.* (flag) colores; bandera (*sing.*). —*v.t.* 1, (dye) teñir; colorar. 2, (misrepresent) falsear; desfigurar. —*v.i.* enrojecerse; ruborizarse. —**coloration,** *n.* coloración. —**show one's colors,** descubrirse; declararse. —**with flying colors,** con lucimiento; a banderas desplegadas.

color-blind *adj.* daltoniano. —**color blindness,** daltonismo.

colored ('kʌl·ərd) *adj.* 1, (having color) de *o* con color. 2, (Negro) negro. 3, (biased) prejuiciado; predispuesto; influenciado.

colorful ('kʌl·ər·fəl) *adj.* vistoso; lleno de color; pintoresco.

coloring ('kʌl·ər·iŋ) *n.* tinte; colorante; colorido.

colorless ('kʌl·ər·ləs) *adj.* 1, (without color) incoloro; descolorido. 2, *fig.* (dull) sin atractivo.

colossal (kə'las·əl) *adj.* colosal; gigantesco.

colossus (kə'las·əs) *n.* coloso.

colt (kolt) *n.* potro.

columbium (kə'lʌm·bi·əm) *n.* columbio.

column ('kal·əm) *n.* columna. —**columnar** (kə'lʌm·nər) *adj.* columnario.

columnist ('kal·əm·ɪst) *n.* articulista; columnista.

com- (kam) *prefijo* com-; con; juntamente; por entero. *Tiene la forma* **com-** *ante* b, m, p, *y a veces* f: *combine,* combinar; *commit,* cometer; *compose,* componer; *comfort,* confortar. *Por asimilación fonética, tiene la forma* **col-** *ante* l; **cor-** *ante* r; **con-** *ante toda consonante con excepción de* b, h, l, m, p, r *y* w. *Tiene la forma* **co-** *ante vocal, ante* h, w, *y a veces otras consonantes: coalition,* coalición; *cohabit,* cohabitar; *coworker,* colaborador.

coma ('ko·mə) *n.* coma; letargo. —**comatose** (-tos) *adj.* comatoso; letárgico.

comb (kom) *n.* 1, (for hair) peine; peineta; *Amer.* peinilla. 2, (for fibers) carda; cardencha; rastrillo. 3, (of a rooster) cresta. 4, (honeycomb) panal. —*v.t.* 1, (dress hair) peinar. 2, (card fibers) cardar; rastrillar. 3, (search thoroughly) registrar; revolver.

combat ('kam·bæt) *n.* combate; batalla; lucha. —*v.t.* & *i.* (kəm'bæt) combatir; pelear; batallar; luchar. —**combatant** ('kam·bə·tənt) *n.* & *adj.* combatiente. —**combative** (kəm'bæt·ɪv) *adj.* peleador; luchador.

combination (ˌkam·bɪ'nei·ʃən) *n.* combinación.

combine (kəm'bain) *v.t.* & *i.* combinar; mezclar; unir. —*n.* ('kam·bain) 1, (harvesting machine) segadora; trilladora. 2, *colloq.* (union) combinación; unión de personas *o* empresas.

combustion (kəm'bʌs·tʃən) *n.* combustión. —**combustible** (-tə·bəl) *n.* & *adj.* combustible.

come (kʌm) *v.i.* [**came, come, coming**] 1, (approach) acercarse; aproximarse. 2, (arrive) llegar; venir; aparecer. 3, (be derived) provenir; proceder. 4, (become) convertirse; hacerse. 5, (happen) ocurrir; acontecer. 6, (extend to) acercarse; llegar. 7, (be obtainable) conseguirse; venir. —**come about,** acaecer; suceder; pasar. —**come across,** 1, *colloq.* (meet) encontrarse con. 2, *slang* (deliver) entregar. —**come apart,** separarse; desmontarse; despegarse. —**come around,** *colloq.* 1, (recover) recuperar. 2, (yield) someterse. —**come back,** 1, (recur to mind) recordar; acordarse de. 2, (return) volver. 3, *slang* (retort) responder; contestar. —**come between,** interponerse en; separar; desunir. —**come by,** conseguir; obtener. —**come down,** 1, (descend) bajar; descender. 2, (lose caste) descender. 3, (be inherited) transmitirse. —**come down with,** enfermarse de. —**come forth,** salir. —**come forward,** 1, (advance) avanzar; adelantarse. 2, (appear) presentarse. 3, (volunteer) ofrecerse. —**come in,** 1, (enter) entrar. 2, (arrive) llegar. 3, (begin) empezar. —**come in!,** ¡adelante! —**come into,** 1, (enter) entrar en. 2, (acquire) conseguir; obtener; recibir. 3, (inherit) heredar. —**come off,** 1, (become separated) separarse; soltarse; salir. 2, (occur) ocurrir; suceder. 3, *colloq.* (result) salir; resultar. —**come on,** 1, (make progress) mejorar; adelantar. 2, (find; meet) encontrar; encontrarse con; hallar. 3, (attack) caerle encima a uno. —**come on!,** ¡vamos!; ¡vaya!; ¡adelante! —**come out**, **1,** (leave; exit) salir. **2,** (be disclosed) salir a luz. **3,** (make a debut) debutar; estrenarse. **4,** (be presented to society) ponerse de largo. **5,** (result) salir; resultar. **6,** (take a stand) declararse. —**come over**, **1,** (happen to) pasarle a uno. **2,** (seize) asir; coger. **3,** (be persuaded) convencerse. —**come through**, **1,** (survive) sobrevivir. **2,** (do as expected) acceder; convenir. **3,** (perform well) triunfar. —**come to; come to oneself**, recobrarse; volver en sí. —**come true**, realizarse. —**come up**, **1,** (ascend) subir. **2,** (arise; come under consideration) surgir; presentarse. —**come upon**, **1,** (meet) tropezar con; encontrarse con. **2,** (attack) atacar. —**come up to**, **1,** (reach) alcanzar. **2,** (approach) acercarse a. **3,** (ascend to) subir a. **4,** (be equal to) ser igual a; estar a la altura de. —**come up with**, **1,** (overtake) alcanzar. **2,** (propose) proponer. —**how come?**, *slang* ¿cómo pudo?

comeback ('kʌm·bæk) *n.*, *colloq.* **1,** (recovery) rehabilitación. **2,** (return) reaparición; retorno. **3,** (retort) respuesta mordaz.

comedian (kə'mi·di·ən) *n.* actor; cómico; comediante. —**comedienne** (-'ɛn) *n.fem.* actriz; cómica; comedianta.

comedown *n.*, *slang* revés.

comedy ('kam·ə·di) *n.* comedia.

comely ('kʌm·li) *adj.* gracioso; gentil; guapo. —**comeliness**, *n.* gentileza; donosura.

comet ('kam·ɪt) *n.* cometa.

comfort ('kʌm·fərt) *v.t.* confortar; animar; consolar. —*n.* **1,** (solace) consuelo; ánimo. **2,** (well-being) bienestar; consuelo; alivio. **3,** (ease) comodidad; satisfacción. **4,** *pl.* (conveniences) comodidades.

comfortable ('kʌm·fərt·ə·bəl) *adj.* **1,** (affording ease; at ease) confortable; cómodo. **2,** (free from distress) tranquilo; sereno.

comforter ('kʌm·fər·tər) *n.* **1,** (bed covering) edredón; cubrecama almohadillado. **2,** (muffler) bufanda; tapado. **3,** (consoler) consolador.

comic ('kam·ɪk) *adj.* cómico; divertido. —*n.* **1,** (comedian) cómico. **2,** *pl.* (cartoon strips) historietas; dibujos. —**comical**, *adj.* cómico; divertido; gracioso. —**comic opera**, ópera bufa.

coming ('kʌm·ɪŋ) *adj.* **1,** (approaching) venidero; futuro. **2,** *colloq.* (progressing) en camino; prometedor. —*n.* venida; llegada; advenimiento.

comity ('kam·ə·ti) *n.* cortesía; deferencia.

comma ('kam·ə) *n.* coma (,).

command (kə'mænd) *v.t.* **1,** (order) ordenar; mandar; dirigir. **2,** (rule) gobernar; regir. **3,** (look down on) dominar. —*v.i.* imponerse; mandar. —*n.* **1,** (order) mandato; mandamiento; orden. **2,** (authority) autoridad; mandato; poder. **3,** (mastery) recursos; habilidad; facilidad. **4,** *mil.* comando. —**command performance**, actuación magistral.

commandant (ˌkam·ən'dant) *n.* comandante.

commandeer (ˌkam·ən'dɪr) *v.t.* **1,** (recruit persons) reclutar a la fuerza. **2,** (seize things) requisar; confiscar.

commander (kə'mæn·dər) *n.* **1,** *mil.* comandante. **2,** *naval* teniente de navío. —**commander in chief**, comandante en jefe; jefe supremo.

commandment (kə'mænd·mənt) *n.* **1,** mandato; orden; precepto. **2,** *cap.*, *Bib.* mandamiento.

commemorate (kə'mɛm·ə·reit) *v.t.* conmemorar. —**commemoration**, *n.* conmemoración. —**commemorative** (-re·tɪv) *adj.* conmemorativo.

commence (kə'mɛns) *v.t.* & *i.* comenzar; empezar.

commencement (kə'mɛns·mənt) *n.* **1,** (beginning) principio; comienzo. **2,** (graduation) distribución de diplomas.

commend (kə'mɛnd) *v.t.* **1,** (praise) alabar; elogiar. **2,** (recommend) recomendar; aconsejar. **3,** (entrust) confiar.

commendation (ˌkam·ən'dei·ʃən) *n.* elogio; loa.

commensurable (kə'mɛn·ʃə·rə·bəl) *adj.* conmensurable.

commensurate (kə'mɛn·ʃə·rət) *adj.* proporcionado; adecuado; conmensurado.

comment ('ka·mɛnt) *n.* comentario; observación. —*v.i.* comentar; glosar.

commentary ('kam·ənˌtɛr·i) *n.* comentario; explicación. —**com-**

mentator (-tei·tər) *n.* comentador.
commerce ('ka·mʌɹs) *n.* comercio.
commercial (kə'mʌɹ·ʃəl) *adj.* comercial; mercantil. —*n.* anuncio publicitario. —**commercialism,** *n.* mercantilismo. —**commercialize,** *v.t.* comercializar.
commiserate (kə'mɪz·ə·reit) *v.t.* & *i.* compadecer. —*v.i.* apiadarse. —**commiseration,** *n.* conmiseración; piedad.
commissar ('kam·ɪˌsar) *n.* comisario. —**commissariat** (-'sɛr·i·ət) *n.* comisariado.
commissary ('kam·əˌsɛr·i) **1,** (store) comisaría; intendencia. **2,** (deputy) comisario; delegado.
commission (kə'mɪʃ·ən) *n.* **1,** (act of committing) cometido; acción. **2,** (warrant) patente; nombramiento. **3,** (group of persons) comisión; junta; misión. **4,** (assignment) misión; tarea; deber. **5,** (fee) comisión; corretaje. **6,** *mil.; naval* nombramiento. —*v.t.* **1,** (appoint) nombrar. **2,** (give authority) comisionar. **3,** (equip) poner en servicio activo. —**commissioned officer,** oficial; oficial destinado.
commissioner (kə'mɪʃ·ən·ər) *n.* jefe; delegado; comisionado.
commit (kə'mɪt) *v.t.* [**committed, -mitting**] **1,** (entrust) confiar; depositar. **2,** (do) cometer; perpetrar. **3,** (venture) aventurar. **4,** (consign to custody) encerrar; internar. —**commit oneself,** comprometerse; obligarse. —**commit to memory,** aprender de memoria. —**commit to paper,** poner por escrito.
commitment (kə'mɪt·mənt) *n.* **1,** (act of committing) cometido. **2,** (pledge) promesa; obligación; compromiso. **3,** (consignment to custody) encierro; internación.
committee (kə'mɪt·i) *n.* comisión; comité.
commodious (kə'mo·di·əs) *adj.* holgado; amplio; cómodo. —**commodiousness,** *n.* comodidad; amplitud.
commodity (kə'mad·ə·ti) *n.* **1,** *comm.* mercancía. **2,** (useful thing) comodidad.
commodore ('kam·ə·dor) *n.* comodoro.
common ('kam·ən) *adj.* **1,** (shared) común; mutuo. **2,** (public) general; público. **3,** (familiar) familiar; usual; común. **4,** (ordinary) ordinario; corriente. **5,** (coarse) vulgar; bajo. —*n.* **1,** (public land) ejido. **2,** (public square) plaza. **3,** *pl., cap.* (Brit. parliament) los Comunes. —**common law,** derecho común. —**common stock,** acciones ordinarias. —**in common,** en común.
commoner ('kam·ən·ər) *n.* plebeyo.
commonplace *adj.* ordinario; corriente. —*n.* cosa común.
commonwealth *n.* mancomunidad. —**Commonwealth of Puerto Rico,** Estado libre asociado de Puerto Rico.
commotion (kə'mo·ʃən) *n.* **1,** (agitation) conmoción; perturbación. **2,** (public unrest) tumulto; desorden.
communal ('kam·ju·nəl) *adj.* comunal; público.
commune (kə'mjuːn) *v.i.* comunicarse; conversar; hablar. —*n.* ('kam·jun) comuna; comunidad.
communicant (kə'mju·nɪ·kənt) *n.* **1,** (one who communicates) comunicante. **2,** (one who takes Communion) comulgante.
communicate (kə'mju·nɪ·keit) *v.t.* comunicar; notificar. —*v.i.* comunicarse; tener comunicación.
communication (kəˌmju·nɪ'kei·ʃən) *n.* **1,** (act of communicating) comunicación; participación. **2,** (message) comunicación; noticia. **3,** (passage) comunicación; acceso.
communicative (kə'mju·nɪ·kə·tɪv) *adj.* comunicativo; hablador; franco.
communion (kə'mjun·jən) *n.* **1,** (sharing) comunión; contacto. **2,** (fellowship) amistad; confraternidad; trato. **3,** *cap.* (Eucharist) comunión.
communiqué (kə·mju·nɪ'kei) *n.* comunicado *o* boletín oficial.
communism ('kam·jə·nɪz·əm) *n.* comunismo. —**communist,** *n.* & *adj.* comunista. —**communistic,** *adj.* comunista.
community (kə'mju·nə·ti) *n.* **1,** (group of persons; locality) comunidad; público; colectividad; sociedad. **2,** (joint sharing) comunidad; colectividad.
communize ('kam·jəˌnaiz) *v.t.* comunizar.
commutation (ˌkam·ju'tei·ʃən) *n.* conmutación; permuta. —**commutation ticket,** billete de abono.
commute (kə'mjut) *v.t.* conmutar;

cambiar. —*v.i.* viajar diariamente. —**commuter,** *n.* viajero diario.

compact (kəm'pækt) *adj.* **1,** (solid) compacto; sólido. **2,** (closely packed) apretado; cerrado. **3,** (concise) compacto; breve; conciso. —*n.* ('kam·pækt) **1,** (agreement) convenio; acuerdo. **2,** (cosmetic container) polvera.

companion (kəm'pæn·jən) *n.* **1,** (comrade) compañero; camarada. **2,** (paid attendant) acompañante. —**companionable,** *adj.* sociable; amistoso. —**companionship,** *n.* compañerismo; camaradería.

companionway *n.* escalera de cámara.

company ('kʌm·pə·ni) *n.* **1,** (group) compañía. **2,** (guest *or* guests) invitados; visita; visitantes. **3,** *comm.* compañía; sociedad; empresa. **4,** *mil.* compañía. **5,** *naut.; aero.* tripulación. —**have company,** tener visita. —**keep company,** acompañar; *colloq.* cortejar; galantear. —**part company,** separarse; desunirse.

comparable ('kam·pə·rə·bəl) *adj.* comparable; semejante.

comparative (kəm'pær·ə·tɪv) *adj.* comparativo; relativo. —*n., gram.* comparativo.

compare (kəm'pe:r) *v.t.* comparar; cotejar. —*v.i.* poder compararse.

comparison (kəm'pær·ɪ·sən) *n.* comparación.

compartment (kəm'part·mənt) *n.* compartimiento; división.

compass ('kʌm·pəs) *n.* **1,** (extent; range) circuito; ámbito. **2,** (instrument) brújula. **3,** *también pl.* (dividers) compás. —*v.t.* **1,** (encircle) circundar. **2,** (accomplish) lograr; obtener; conseguir.

compassion (kəm'pæʃ·ən) *n.* compasión. —**compassionate** (-ət) *adj.* compasivo.

compatible (kəm'pæt·ə·bəl) *adj.* compatible. —**compatibility,** *n.* compatibilidad.

compatriot (kəm'pei·tri·ət) *n.* & *adj.* compatriota.

compel (kəm'pɛl) *v.t.* [**compelled, -pelling**] compeler; forzar; obligar.

compendium (kəm'pɛn·di·əm) *n.* compendio.

compensate ('kam·pən,seit) *v.t.* & *i.* **1,** (offset) compensar; resarcir. **2,** (recompense) remunerar; recompensar. —**compensation,** *n.* compensación; reparación.

compensatory (kəm'pɛns·ə·tor·i) *adj.* compensatorio; compensativo.

compete (kəm'pit) *v.i.* competir; emular.

competence ('kam·pɪ·təns) *n.* **1,** (fitness) competencia; habilidad; aptitud. **2,** (sufficient means) suficiencia; bienestar.

competent ('kam·pə·tənt) *adj.* hábil; competente.

competition (,kam·pə'tɪʃ·ən) *n.* **1,** (rivalry) competición; competencia. rivalidad. **2,** (contest) concurso; competición; pugna; contienda.

competitive (kəm'pɛt·ə·tɪv) *adj.* competidor; que compite.

competitor (kəm'pɛt·ə·tər) *n.* competidor; rival.

compilation (,kam·pə'lei·ʃən) *n.* compilación; recopilación.

compile (kəm'pail) *v.t.* compilar; recopilar. —**compiler,** *n.* compilador; recopilador.

complacency (kəm'plei·sən·si) *también,* **complacence,** *n.* complacencia; satisfacción. —**complacent,** *adj.* complaciente.

complain (kəm'plein) *v.i.* **1,** (express dissatisfaction) quejarse; lamentarse. **2,** *law* demandar; querellarse. —**complainant,** *n.* demandante; querellante.

complaint (kəm'pleint) *n.* **1,** (expression of discontent) queja; lamento. **2,** (ailment) mal; dolencia. **3,** *law* querella; demanda.

complaisant (kəm'plei·zənt) *adj.* complaciente; condescendiente.

complement ('kam·plə·mənt) *n.* complemento. —*v.t.* complementar; completar. —**complementary** (-'mɛn·tə·ri) *adj.* complementario.

complete (kəm'plit) *adj.* **1,** (whole) completo; total. **2,** (finished) completo; terminado. —*v.t.* completar; acabar; terminar. —**completion** (-'pli·ʃən) *n.* terminación; fin.

complex (kəm'plɛks) *adj.* **1,** (of many parts) complejo; compuesto. **2,** (complicated) complejo; difícil. —*n.* ('kam·plɛks) complejo. —**complexity** (kəm'plɛks·ə·ti) *n.* complejidad.

complexion (kəm'plɛk·ʃən) *n.* **1,** (skin) tez; complexión. **2,** (aspect) complexión; constitución; apariencia.

compliant (kəm'plai·ənt) *adj.*

1, (acquiescent) condescendiente; complaciente. 2, (submissive) sumiso; rendido; servicial. —**compliance**, *n.* obediencia; sumisión. —**in compliance with**, de acuerdo con; según; accediendo a.
complicate ('kam·plɪ·keit) *v.t.* complicar; enredar; embrollar. —**complication**, *n.* complicación.
complicity (kəm'plɪs·ə·ti) *n.* complicidad.
compliment ('kam·plə·mənt) *n.* 1, (praise) elogio; cumplido; fineza. 2, (gallantry) piropo; galantería. 3, *pl.* (greetings) saludos; respetos. —*v.t.* felicitar.
complimentary (ˌkam·plə'mɛn·tə·ri) *adj.* 1, (laudatory) lisonjero; obsequioso. 2, (free) gratuito; como obsequio; de regalo.
comply (kəm'plai) *v.i.* someterse; cumplir. —**comply with**, acatar; obedecer.
component (kəm'po·nənt) *n.* componente; parte. —*adj.* componente.
comport (kəm'port) *v.t.* proceder; obrar. —*v.i.* convenir; acordar. —**comport oneself**, portarse; comportarse.
comportment (kəm'port·mənt) *n.* comportamiento; conducta.
compose (kəm'poːz) *v.t.* 1, (form) componer; formar. 2, (create, esp. music) componer. 3, (calm) calmar; sosegar. 4, (settle differences) apaciguar; sosegar; serenar. 5, (set) arreglar; *printing* ajustar. —*v.i.* componer. —**composed**, *adj.* compuesto; tranquilo; sereno. —**composer**, *n.* compositor.
composite (kəm'paz·ɪt) *n.* & *adj.* compuesto.
composition (kam·pə'zɪʃ·ən) *n.* composición.
compositor (kəm'paz·ɪ·tər) *n.* cajista.
compost ('kam·post) *n.* abono.
composure (kəm'po·ʒər) *n.* compostura; calma; serenidad.
compote ('kam·pot) *n.* 1, (stewed fruit) compota. 2, (small dish) compotera.
compound (kəm'paund) *v.t.* componer; combinar. —*n.* ('kam·paund) 1, (mixture) compuesto. 2, (enclosure) recinto. —*adj.* compuesto. —**compound fracture**, fractura abierta. —**compound interest**, interés compuesto.
comprehend (ˌkam·pri'hɛnd) *v.t.* 1, (include) comprender; contener; incluir. 2, (understand) comprender; entender. —**comprehensible** (-'hɛn·sə·bəl) *adj.* comprensible; inteligible. —**comprehensibility**, *n.* comprensibilidad.
comprehension (ˌkam·pri'hɛn·ʃən) *n.* comprensión. —**comprehensive** (-sɪv) *adj.* comprensivo. —**comprehensiveness**, *n.* comprensión; alcance; perspicacia.
compress (kəm'prɛs) *v.t.* 1, (press) comprimir; apretar. 2, (condense) condensar; abreviar. —*n.* ('kam·prɛs) compresa. —**compression** (kəm'prɛʃ·ən) *n.* compresión. —**compressor** (kəm'prɛs·ər) *n.* compresor.
comprise (kəm'praiz) *v.t.* 1, (include) comprender; abarcar; incluir. 2, (consist of) consistir de.
compromise ('kam·prəˌmaiz) *n.* 1, (settlement) compromiso; convenio; acuerdo. 2, (middle course) compromiso; termino medio. —*v.t.* 1, (settle) comprometer; acordar; arreglar. 2, (expose to suspicion) comprometer; exponer. —*v.i.* comprometerse; convenir; transigir.
comptroller *también*, **controller** (kən'trol·ər) *n.* interventor. —**comptrollership**, *n.* intervención.
compulsion (kəm'pʌl·ʃən) *n.* 1, (coercion) impulso; impulsión; coerción. 2, *law* compulsión. —**compulsive** (-sɪv) *adj.* compulsivo. —**compulsory** (-sə·ri) *adj.* obligatorio.
compunction (kəm'pʌŋk·ʃən) *n.* compunción; remordimiento.
compute (kəm'pjut) *v.t.* computar; calcular; contar. —**computation** (ˌkam·pju'tei·ʃən) *n.* computación; cómputo; recuento.
computer (kəm'pju·tər) *n.* 1, (person) calculador. 2, (machine) calculadora.
comrade ('kam·ræd) *n.* camarada; compañero. —**comradeship**, *n.* camaradería; compañerismo.
con (kaːn) *v.t.* [**conned, conning**] 1, (study) estudiar; escudriñar. 2, *slang* (swindle) estafar; embaucar. 3, (steer, as a ship) gobernar; dirigir. —*adv.* & *n.* contra.
con- (kan) *prefijo, var. de* **com-** *ante* c, d, f, g, j, n, q, s, t, v: *concave*, cóncavo; *condone*, condonar; *confide*, confiar; *congress*, congreso; *conjunct*, conjunto; *connote*, connotar; *conquest*, conquista; *consent*,

consentir; *contact,* contacto; *convert,* convertir.

concatenation (kan,kæt·ə'nei·ʃən) *n.* encadenamiento.

concave (kan'keiv) *adj.* cóncavo. —**concavity** (kən'kæv·ə·ti) *n.* concavidad; hueco.

conceal (kən'si:l) *v.t.* ocultar; esconder; encubrir.

concealment (kən'sil·mənt) *n.* **1,** (act of concealing) encubrimiento; secreto. **2,** (hiding place) escondite; escondrijo.

concede (kən'si:d) *v.t.* **1,** (grant) conceder; otorgar. **2,** (admit) aceptar; admitir. —*v.i.* conceder.

conceit (kən'sit) *n.* **1,** (vanity) presunción; engreimiento. **2,** (quaint idea or object) fantasía; imaginación. —**conceited,** *adj.* presuntuoso; vano; engreído.

conceivable (kən'siv·ə·bəl) *adj.* concebible.

conceive (kən'si:v) *v.t.* **1,** (form in the mind) concebir; inventar; formar. **2,** (believe) creer; comprender; concebir. —*v.i.* concebir. —**conceive of,** imaginar; formar idea de.

concentrate ('kan·sən·treit) *v.t.* reunir; concentrar. —*v.i.* **1,** (meet) concentrarse; encontrarse. **2,** (focus attention) concentrarse; pensar detenidamente; enfocar.

concentration (,kan·sən'trei·ʃən) *n.* concentración. —**concentration camp,** campo de concentración.

concentric (kən'sɛn·trɪk) *adj.* concéntrico. —**concentricity** (,kan·sən'trɪs·ə·ti) *n.* concentricidad.

concept ('kan·sɛpt) *n.* concepto; idea; noción. —**conceptual** (kən·'sɛp·tʃu·əl) *adj.* conceptual.

conception (kən'sɛp·ʃən) *n.* concepción; concepto; noción.

concern (kən'sʌɹn) *v.t.* **1,** (interest) concernir; afectar; interesar; importar. **2,** (disturb) preocupar; inquietar. —*n.* **1,** (matter of interest) asunto; negocio. **2,** (anxiety) preocupación; inquietud. **3,** (business firm) empresa; firma. —**concerning,** *prep.* con referencia a; respecto a.

concert ('kan·sərt) *n.* **1,** (agreement) concierto; convenio. **2,** (musical performance) concierto. **3,** (unison) concierto; armonía. —*v.t.* & *i.* (kən'sʌɹt) concertar; aunar; ajustar. —**concerted** (kən'sʌɹ·tɪd) *adj.* concertado; armonioso.

concertina (,kan·sər'ti·nə) *n.* concertina.

concerto (kən'tʃɛr·to) *n.* [*pl.* **-tos**] concierto.

concession (kən'sɛʃ·ən) *n.* concesión. —**concessionaire** (-'e:r) *n.* concesionario.

conch (kantʃ; kaŋk) *n.* concha; caracol de mar.

concierge (kan'sjɛrʒ) *n.,* conserje; portero.

conciliate (kən'sɪl·i·eit) *v.t.* conciliar; pacificar. —**conciliation,** *n.* conciliación. —**conciliatory** (-ə·tor·i) *adj.* conciliatorio; conciliador.

concise (kən'sais) *adj.* conciso. —**conciseness; concision** (kən'sɪʒ·ən) *n.* concisión.

conclave ('kan·kleiv) *n.* cónclave.

conclude (kən'klu:d) *v.t.* **1,** (finish) concluir; terminar; acabar. **2,** (deduce) inferir; deducir. **3,** (decide; settle) decidir; determinar. —*v.i.* **1,** (finish) finalizar; acabarse. **2,** (decide) resolver; decidir.

conclusion (kən'klu·ʒən) *n.* conclusión; final; resultado. —**conclusive** (-sɪv) *adj.* concluyente; conclusivo.

concoct (kən'kakt) *v.t.* **1,** (combine and cook) preparar mezclando; combinar. **2,** (devise) planear; proyectar.

concoction (kən'kak·ʃən) *n.* **1,** (thing prepared) preparación; combinación. **2,** (thing devised) trama; maquinación.

concomitant (kan'kam·ə·tənt) *adj.* & *n.* concomitante. —**concomitance,** *n.* concomitancia.

concord ('kan·kord) *n.* **1,** (harmony) concordia; armonía; unanimidad. **2,** (agreement) acuerdo; paz; convenio.

concordance (kən'kor·dəns) *n.* **1,** (agreement) concordancia; concordia. **2,** (word index) concordancias (*pl.*).

concordant (kən'kor·dənt) *adj.* concordante; armonioso; conforme.

concourse ('kan·kors) *n.* **1,** (throng) concurso; concurrencia; gentío. **2,** (thoroughfare) bulevar; avenida. **3,** (flowing together) confluencia.

concrete (kan'krit) *adj.* **1,** (real; specific) concreto; definido. **2,** (made of concrete) de cemento; de hormigón. —*n.* ('kan·krit) cemento; hormigón. —**concrete-**

ness, *n.* calidad de concreto. —**concretion** (kən'kri·ʃən) *n.* concreción.

concubine ('kaŋ·kju,bain) *n.* concubina. —**concubinage** (kən·'kju·bɪ·nɪdʒ) *n.* concubinato.

concupiscent (kan'kju·pə·sənt) *adj.* concupiscente. —**concupiscence**, *n.* concupiscencia.

concur (kən'kʌɹ) *v.i.* [**concurred, concurring**] **1,** (coincide) concurrir; coincidir. **2,** (agree) concurrir; convenir; ponerse de acuerdo. —**concurrence**, *n.* concurrencia; coincidencia. —**concurrent**, *adj.* concurrente; coincidente; simultáneo.

concussion (kən'kʌʃ·ən) *n.* concusión; golpe.

condemn (kən'dɛm) *v.t.* **1,** (censure) condenar; censurar; reprobar. **2,** (sentence) condenar; castigar; sentenciar. **3,** (declare unfit) condenar; cerrar. **4,** (claim for public use) expropiar. —**condemnation** (ˌkan·dɛm'nei·ʃən) *n.* condenación.

condense (kən'dɛns) *v.t.* **1,** (compress) condensar; comprimir. **2,** (abridge) condensar; resumir; compendiar. —*v.i.* condensarse. —**condensation** (ˌkan·dən'sei·ʃən) *n.* condensación. —**condenser**, *n.* condensador.

condescend (ˌkan·dɪ'sɛnd) *v.i.* **1,** (adjust) condescender; avenirse; transigir. **2,** (deign) dignarse. **3,** (deal patronizingly) prestarse; contemporizar. —**condescension** (-'sɛn·ʃən) *n.* condescendencia.

condign (kən'dain) *adj.* condigno; adecuado; merecido.

condiment ('kan·də·mənt) *n.* condimento.

condition (kən'dɪʃ·ən) *n.* **1,** (state of being) condición; circunstancia. **2,** (social rank) condición; categoría; clase. **3,** (state of health) salud. **4,** (stipulation) condición; requisito; estipulación. —*v.i.* poner condiciones. —*v.t.* **1,** (limit) condicionar; estipular. **2,** (put into condition) subordinar; supeditar. —**conditional**, *adj.* condicional. —**on condition that**, a condición de; a condición que; con la condición de que.

condole (kən'doːl) *v.i.* condolerse. —**condolence**, *n.* condolencia.

condominium (ˌkan·də'mɪn·i·əm) *n.* condominio.

condone (kən'doːn) *v.t.* condonar; perdonar; olvidar. —**condonement; condonation** (ˌkan·də'nei·ʃən) *n.* condonación; perdón.

condor ('kan·dər) *n.* cóndor.

conduce (kən'dus) *v.i.* conducir; llevar; tender. —**conducive**, *adj.* conducente; tendente.

conduct (kən'dʌkt) *v.t.* **1,** (guide; lead) conducir; dirigir. **2,** (manage) dirigir; administrar; manejar. —*n.* ('kan·dʌkt) **1,** (behavior) comportamiento. **2,** (management) dirección. —**conduct oneself**, portarse; comportarse.

conductible (kən'dʌk·tə·bəl) *adj.* conductible. —**conductibility**, *n.* conductibilidad.

conduction (kən'dʌk·ʃən) *n.* conducción.

conductive (kən'dʌk·tɪv) *adj.* conductivo. —**conductivity** (ˌkan·dʌk'tɪv·ə·ti) *n.* conductividad.

conductor (kən'dʌk·tər) *n.* **1,** (orchestra leader) director. **2,** *R.R.* revisor; cobrador. **3,** *electricity* conductor.

conduit ('kan·dɪt) *n.* **1,** (channel for fluids) conducto. **2,** *electricity* tubo.

cone (kon) *n.* cono.

confect (kən'fɛkt) *v.t.* confeccionar; preparar; hacer.

confection (kən'fɛk·ʃən) *n.* **1,** (a sweet) confitura; dulce. **2,** *fig.* (dress) confección. —**confectioner**, *n.* confitero; dulcero. —**confectionery**, *n.* confitería; dulcería.

confederacy (kən'fɛd·ə·rə·si) *n.* confederación.

confederate (kən'fɛd·ə·reit) *v.t.* & *i.* confederar. —*adj.* (-rət) confederado. —*n.* (-rət) **1,** (ally) confederado. **2,** (accomplice) socio; compinche. —**confederation**, *n.* confederación; liga.

confer (kən'fʌɹ) *v.t.* [**conferred, -ferring**] conferir; otorgar. —*v.i.* conferenciar; consultar.

conference ('kan·fər·əns) *n.* **1,** (meeting) conferencia; consulta. **2,** (league) conferencia; junta; asamblea.

confess (kən'fɛs) *v.t.* **1,** (acknowledge) confesar; admitir; reconocer. **2,** *eccles.* confesar. —*v.i.* confesarse.

confession (kən'fɛʃ·ən) *n.* confesión.

confessional (kən'fɛʃ·ən·əl) *n.* **1,** (enclosure) confesonario; confesionario. **2,** (book of confession)

confesionario. 3, (act of confessing) confesión. —*adj.* confesional.
confessor (kən'fɛs·ər) *n.* confesor.
confetti (kən'fɛt·i) *n.* confeti.
confidant (ˌkan·fɪ'dant) *n.* confidente. —**confidante** (-'dant) *n. fem.* confidente.
confide (kən'faid) *v.t.* confiar. —*v.i.* 1, (have trust) tener confianza. 2, (entrust a secret) confiarse; fiarse.
confidence ('kan·fɪ·dəns) *n.* 1, (faith) confianza; fe; seguridad. 2, (self-assurance) ánimo; creencia. 3, (state of mind) tranquilidad; certeza. 4, (intimacy) intimidad; familiaridad. 5, (secret) confidencia. —**confidence man**, estafador; timador.
confident ('kan·fɪ·dənt) *adj.* confiado; seguro.
confidential (ˌkan·fɪ'dɛn·ʃəl) *adj.* 1, (secret) confidencial; secreto; privado. 2, (intimate) íntimo; privado. 3, (trusted) confidencial; de confianza.
configuration (kənˌfɪg·jə'rei·ʃən) *n.* configuración; forma; aspecto.
confine (kən'fain) *v.t.* 1, (restrict) limitar. 2, (put to bed, as in illness or childbirth) confinar. 3, (shut in) encerrar. 4, (imprison) encarcelar. —**be confined**, estar de parto.
confinement (kən'fain·mənt) *n.* 1, (restriction) limitación. 2, (childbirth) parto. 3, (imprisonment) encarcelamiento.
confines ('kan·fainz) *n.pl.* confines; límites.
confirm (kən'fʌɹm) *v.t.* 1, (strengthen) confirmar; afirmar. 2, (verify) verificar; corroborar. 3, (make valid) confirmar; sancionar; ratificar. 4, *eccles.* confirmar. —**confirmation** (ˌkan·fər'mei·ʃən) *n.* confirmación. —**confirmatory** (kən·'fʌɹ·mə·tor·i) *adj.* confirmatorio; confirmativo.
confirmed (kən'fʌɹmd) *adj.* 1, (settled) confirmado; comprobado; demostrado. 2, (chronic) inveterado; crónico; consumado.
confiscate ('kan·fɪsˌkeit) *v.t.* confiscar; expropiar. —**confiscation**, *n.* confiscación.
conflagration (ˌkan·flə'grei·ʃən) *n.* conflagración.
conflict (kən'flɪkt) *v.i.* chocar; estar en pugna. —*n.* ('kan·flɪkt) 1, (combat) conflicto; lucha; combate. 2, *fig.* (opposition) discordia; contradicción.
confluence ('kan·flu·əns) *n.* 1, (of rivers) confluente. 2, (of a crowd) concurrencia; concurso. —**confluent**, *adj.* confluente.
conform (kən'form) *v.t.* conformar; concordar; adaptar. —*v.i.* obedecer; conformarse; acatar.
conformable (kən'for·mə·bəl) *adj.* conforme.
conformation (ˌkan·fər'mei·ʃən) *n.* 1, (structure) configuración; forma; estructura. 2, (adaptation) conformación; adaptación.
conformist (kən'for·mɪst) *n.* conformista.
conformity (kən'for·mə·ti) *n.* conformidad.
confound (kan'faund) *v.t.* 1, (perplex) aturdir; embrollar; desordenar. 2, (mistake for another) confundir; equivocar. —**confounded**, *adj., colloq.* endemoniado; maldito. —**confound it!**, ¡diablo!
confraternity *n.* confraternidad; cofradía.
confront (kən'frʌnt) *v.t.* 1, (face) confrontar; encontrar. 2, (meet boldly) afrontar; hacer frente a; desafiar. 3, [*usu.*, **confront with**] (force to face) carear. 4, (compare) cotejar; comparar. —**confrontation** (ˌkan·frən'tei·ʃən) *n.* confrontación; careo.
confuse (kən'fjuːz) *v.t.* 1, (confound) confundir; desordenar; embrollar. 2, (mistake) confundir; equivocar. —**confusion** (-'fju·ʒən) *n.* confusión.
confutation (ˌkan·fju'tei·ʃən) *n.* confutación; desaprobación; refutación.
confute (kən'fjut) *v.t.* confutar; desaprobar; refutar.
congeal (kən'dʒiːl) *v.t.* congelar. —*v.i.* congelarse.
congenial (kən'dʒin·jəl) *adj.* 1, (kindred) semejante; parecido; congénere. 2, (agreeable) congenial; simpático; afable.
congeniality (kənˌdʒi·ni'æl·ə·ti) *n.* 1, (likeness) parecido; semejanza. 2, (affability) afabilidad; simpatía.
congenital (kən'dʒɛn·ɪ·təl) *adj.* congénito.

congest (kən'dʒɛst) *v.t.* **1,** (overcrowd) amontonar; apiñar. **2,** (overfill, as with blood) congestionar. —**congestion** (-'dʒɛs·tʃən) *n.* congestión.

conglomerate (kən'glam·ər·ət) *n.* & *adj.* conglomerado. —*v.t.* & *i.* (-ˈreit) conglomerar; aglomerar. —**conglomeration,** *n.* conglomeración.

Congolese (ˌkaŋ·go'liːz) *adj.* & *n.* congoleño; congolés.

congratulate (kən'grætʃ·əˌleit) *v.t.* congratular; felicitar. —**congratulation,** *n.* congratulación; felicitación.

congregate ('kaŋ·grɪˌgeit) *v.t.* & *i.* congregar; juntar; reunir; convocar.

congregation (ˌkaŋ·grɪ'gei·ʃən) *n.* reunión; asamblea; *relig.* congregación.

congregational (ˌkaŋ·grɪ'gei·ʃən·əl) *adj.* congregacionalista.

congress ('kaŋ·grəs) *n.* **1,** (meeting) congreso; asamblea. **2,** *cap.* (U.S. legislative body) Congreso. —**congressional** (kən'grɛʃ·ə·nəl) *adj.* del congreso.

congressman ('kaŋ·grəs·mən) *n.* [*pl.* **-men**] diputado; *U.S.* congresista.

congruent ('kan·gru·ənt) *adj.* congruente. —**congruence,** *n.* congruencia.

congruity (kən'gru·ə·ti) *n.* congruidad.

congruous ('kaŋ·gru·əs) *adj.* congruente; congruo; apropiado. —**congruousness,** *n.* congruencia; congruidad; armonía.

conic ('kan·ɪk) *también,* **conical,** *adj.* cónico.

conifer ('kan·ɪ·fər) *n.* conífera. —**coniferous** (kə'nɪf·ər·əs) *adj.* conífero.

conjecture (kən'dʒɛk·tʃər) *n.* conjetura; presunción. —*v.t.* & *i.* conjeturar; presumir. —**conjectural,** *adj.* conjetural.

conjoin (kən'dʒɔin) *v.t.* & *i.* asociar; unir; federarse. —**conjoint** (-'dʒɔint) *adj.* conjunto; unido; asociado.

conjugal ('kan·dʒə·gəl) *adj.* conyugal; matrimonial.

conjugate ('kan·dʒəˌgeit) *v.t.* conjugar. —*adj.* (-gət) apareado; en pares; a pares.

conjugation (ˌkan·dʒə'gei·ʃən) *n.* **1,** *gram.* conjugación. **2,** (conjunction) unión; conjunción.

conjunct (kən'dʒʌŋkt) *adj.* conjunto; unido. —**conjunctive,** *adj.* conjuntivo; conjunto.

conjunction (kən'dʒʌŋk·ʃən) *n.* **1,** (act of joining) conjunción. **2,** (union) unión; conexión; liga. **3,** *gram.* conjunción.

conjunctivitis (kənˌdʒʌŋk·tə·'vai·tɪs) *n.* conjuntivitis.

conjuncture (kən'dʒʌŋk·tʃər) *n.* **1,** (concurrence) coyuntura; oportunidad. **2,** (crisis) crisis.

conjure ('kan·dʒər) *v.t.* & *i.* **1,** (practice magic) conjurar; imprecar. **2,** (entreat) conjurar; conspirar. —**conjuration** (ˌkan·dʒə'rei·ʃən) *n.* conjuración. —**conjurer** *también,* **conjuror** *n.* mago; brujo.

connect (kə'nɛkt) *v.t.* **1,** (associate mentally) conectar; coordinar; relacionar. **2,** (join) unir; reunir; conectar. —*v.i.* **1,** (join; be joined) unirse; conectarse; juntarse. **2,** (be related) relacionarse. **3,** (meet, as trains) empalmar. **4,** *slang* (hit the mark; succeed) dar en el blanco; tener éxito.

connecting rod biela.

connection (kə'nɛk·ʃən) *n.* **1,** (union) conexión; unión; enlace. **2,** (kin) parentesco. **3,** (relation *or* coherence) ilación; coherencia. **4,** *pl.* (associates) asociados; compañía (*sing.*). **5,** *usu. pl.* (meeting, as of trains) conexiones; empalme.

connective (kə'nɛk·tɪv) *n.* conjunción. —*adj.* conectivo.

conning tower *n.* torre de mando.

connive (kə'naiv) *v.i.* **1,** (tolerate) tolerar; disimular; permitir. **2,** (conspire) conspirar; atentar. —**connivance,** *n.* connivencia.

connoisseur (kan·ə'sʌɹ) *n.* experto; conocedor; crítico.

connotation (ˌkan·ə'tei·ʃən) *n.* connotación.

connote (kə'not) *v.t.* connotar; sugerir; implicar.

conquer ('kaŋ·kər) *v.t.* **1,** (defeat) conquistar; vencer. **2,** *fig.* (overcome) triunfar; superar. —**conqueror,** *n.* conquistador; vencedor.

conquest ('kan·kwɛst) *n.* conquista; triunfo; victoria.

consanguineous (ˌkan·sæŋ·'gwɪn·i·əs) *adj.* consanguíneo.

—**consanguinity** (-ə·ti) *n.* consanguinidad.
conscience ('kan·ʃəns) *n.* conciencia. —**clear conscience,** conciencia limpia; manos limpias (*pl.*). —**guilty conscience,** complejo de culpabilidad. —**have a guilty conscience,** sentirse culpable. —**on one's conscience,** en la conciencia.
conscientious (ˌkan·ʃi'ɛn·ʃəs) *adj.* concienzudo; recto; justo. —**conscientiousness,** *n.* escrupulosidad; rectitud.
conscionable ('kan·ʃən·ə·bəl) *adj.* razonable; prudente.
conscious ('kan·ʃəs) *adj.* **1,** (aware) consciente. **2,** (awake) despierto. —*n.* consciente. —**be conscious of,** darse cuenta de. —**become conscious,** recobrar el sentido.
consciousness ('kan·ʃəs·nəs) *n.* **1,** (awareness) conocimiento. **2,** *psychol.* (self-awareness) consciencia. —**lose consciousness,** perder el sentido; desvanecerse. —**regain consciousness,** volver en sí.
conscript ('kan·skrɪpt) *n.* conscripto; recluta. —*v.t.* (kən'skrɪpt) reclutar. —**conscription** (kən·'skrɪp·ʃən) *n.* conscripción; reclutamiento.
consecrate ('kan·sɪ·kreit) *v.t.* consagrar. —**consecration,** *n.* consagración.
consecutive (kən'sɛk·jə·tɪv) *adj.* consecutivo; sucesivo.
consensus (kən'sɛn·səs) *n.* consenso; asentimiento; opinión.
consent (kən'sɛnt) *v.i.* consentir; aceptar; acceder. —*n.* consentimiento; permiso.
consequence ('kan·sɪˌkwɛns) *n.* **1,** (result) consecuencia; derivación; efecto. **2,** (importance) importancia; valor.
consequent ('kan·sɪˌkwɛnt) *adj.* consecuente; consiguiente.
consequential (ˌkan·sɪ'kwɛn·ʃəl) *adj.* **1,** (important) importante. **2,** (consequent) consiguiente; lógico.
conservation (ˌkan·sər'vei·ʃən) *n.* conservación; preservación.
conservative (kən'sʌɹ·və·tɪv) *adj.* **1,** (opposed to change) conservador; moderado. **2,** (protecting) preservativo. —*n.* conservador. —**conservatism,** *n.* calidad de conservador.
conservatory (kən'sʌɹ·və·tor·i) *n.* **1,** (greenhouse) invernadero. **2,** (school) conservatorio.
conserve (kən'sʌɹv) *v.t.* conservar; preservar. —*n.* conserva.
consider (kən'sɪd·ər) *v.t.* **1,** (study) considerar; ponderar; estudiar. **2,** (esteem) considerar; apreciar; estimar. **3,** (judge) creer; opinar; juzgar. —*v.i.* pensar (en); reflexionar.
considerable (kən'sɪd·ər·ə·bəl) *adj.* considerable; importante; notable.
considerate (kən'sɪd·ər·ət) *adj.* considerado; respetuoso.
consideration (kənˌsɪd·ə'rei·ʃən) *n.* **1,** (reflection) consideración; deliberación; reflexión. **2,** (factor to be considered) consideración; factor. **3,** (thoughtfulness of others) consideración; atención; miramiento. **4,** (compensation) remuneración; retribución.
considered (kən'sɪd·ərd) *adj.* **1,** (deliberated) considerado; deliberado. **2,** (respected) considerado; estimado; respetado.
considering (kən'sɪd·ər·ɪŋ) *prep.* visto que; en vista de; en atención a.
consign (kən'sain) *v.t.* **1,** (hand over) consignar; entregar. **2,** (assign) señalar; asignar. **3,** *comm.* (allot) consignar. —**consignee** (ˌkan·sai'niː) *n.* consignatario. —**consignor** (kən'sai·nər) *n.* consignador.
consignment (kən'sain·mənt) *n.* **1,** (act of consigning) consignación. **2,** (thing consigned) partida.
consist (kən'sɪst) *v.i.* **1,** [*usu.,* **consist of**] (be made of) consistir; componerse. **2,** [*usu.,* **consist in**] (exist) estribar; contenerse; radicar.
consistency (kən'sɪst·ən·si) *n.* **1,** (viscosity) consistencia; solidez. **2,** [*también,* **consistence**] (harmony) correspondencia; compatibilidad.
consistent (kən'sɪst·ənt) *adj.* **1,** (congruous) congruente; conforme. **2,** (steady; uniform) consistente; firme.
consolation (ˌkan·sə'lei·ʃən) *n.* consolación; consuelo.
console (kən'soːl) *v.t.* consolar; confortar; reanimar.
console ('kan·sol) *n.* **1,** (of an organ) caja. **2,** (cabinet) consola. **3,** (bracket) cartela.
consolidate (kən'sal·ə·deit) *v.t.* **1,** (strengthen) consolidar; reforzar. **2,** (combine) unir; fusionar. —**consolidation,** *n.* consolidación.

consomme (ˌkan·səˈmei) *n.* caldo; consumado; consomé.
consonant (ˈkan·sə·nənt) *adj.* **1,** (harmonious) consonante; acorde. **2,** (consistent) consonante; consistente. —*n.* consonante. —**consonance,** *n.* consonancia; armonía.
consort (ˈkan·sort) *n.* consorte. —*v.i.* (kənˈsort) [*usu.,* **consort with**] asociarse; juntarse.
conspicuous (kənˈspɪk·ju·əs) *adj.* sobresaliente; conspicuo.
conspiracy (kənˈspɪr·ə·si) *n.* conspiración. —**conspirator** (-tər) *n.* conspirador.
conspire (kənˈspair) *v.i.* **1,** (plot) conspirar; atentar; tramar. **2,** (work together) concurrir; converger.
constable (ˈkan·stə·bəl) *n.* alguacil.
constabulary (kənˈstæb·jə·lɛr·i) *n.* cuerpo de alguaciles *o* policías.
constancy (ˈkan·stən·si) *n.* constancia; fidelidad; lealtad.
constant (ˈkan·stənt) *adj.* **1,** (recurring; ceaseless) invariable; constante; incesante. **2,** (steadfast) firme; resuelto. —*n.* constante.
constellation (ˌkan·stəˈlei·ʃən) *n.* constelación.
consternate (ˈkan·stərˌnet) *v.t.* consternar.
consternation (ˌkan·stərˈnei·ʃən) *n.* consternación.
constipate (ˈkan·stɪˌpeit) *v.t.* estreñir. —**constipation,** *n.* estreñimiento.
constituent (kənˈstɪ·tʃu·ənt) *n.* **1,** (component) componente; ingrediente. **2,** (voter) elector. —*adj.* constitutivo. —**constituency,** *n.* distrito electoral.
constitute (ˈkan·stɪˌtut) *v.t.* **1,** (form) constituir; establecer; formar. **2,** (appoint) nombrar; dar poder a.
constitution (ˌkan·stɪˈtu·ʃən) *n.* constitución. —**constitutional,** *adj.* constitucional; básico; esencial. —**take a constitutional,** dar un paseo (de salud).
constrain (kənˈstrein) *v.t.* **1,** (oblige) constreñir; compeler. **2,** (bind) apretar; estrechar. **3,** (restrain) impedir; restringir. —**constraint** (-ˈstreint) *n.* coerción; impedimento; restricción.
constrict (kənˈstrɪkt) *v.t.* **1,** (shrink) encoger. **2,** (bind) apretar; reducir. —**constriction** (-ˈstrik·ʃən) *n.* constricción; encogimiento.
constrictive (kənˈstrɪk·tɪv) *adj.* constrictor.
constrictor (kənˈstrɪk·tər) *n.* **1,** (binder) constrictor. **2,** (snake) boa.
construct (kənˈstrʌkt) *v.t.* **1,** (build) construir; fabricar. **2,** (contrive) idear; planear; imaginar. —**constructor,** *n.* constructor.
construction (kənˈstrʌk·ʃən) *n.* **1,** (building) construcción; obra; estructura. **2,** (explanation) interpretación; sentido. **3,** *gram.* construcción.
constructive (kənˈstrʌk·tɪv) *adj.* constructivo.
construe (kənˈstruː) *v.t.* **1,** *gram.* construir. **2,** (translate) traducir. **3,** (interpret) interpretar.
consul (ˈkan·səl) *n.* cónsul. —**consular,** *adj.* consular. —**consulate,** *n.* consulado. —**consulship,** *n.* consulado.
consult (kənˈsʌlt) *v.t.* **1,** (ask advice from) consultar. **2,** (consider) considerar. —*v.i.* asesorarse.
consultant (kənˈsʌl·tənt) *n.* **1,** (person asking advice) consultante. **2,** (advisor) asesor; consultor.
consultation (ˌkan·səlˈtei·ʃən) *n.* **1,** (act of consulting) consulta. **2,** (conference) consultación; deliberación; conferencia. —**consultative** (kənˈsʌlt·ə·tɪv) *adj.* consultivo.
consume (kənˈsuːm) *v.t.* **1,** (eat) consumir. **2,** (waste) desperdiciar. —**consumer,** *n.* consumidor.
consummate (ˈkan·sə·meit) *v.t.* consumar; completar; perfeccionar. —*adj.* (kənˈsʌm·ət) consumado; excelente; perfecto. —**consummation** (ˌkan·səˈmei·ʃən) *n.* consumación; final; término.
consumption (kənˈsʌmp·ʃən) *n.* **1,** (using up) consunción; extinción. **2,** *econ.* consumo. **3,** *pathol.* tuberculosis; tisis.
consumptive (kənˈsʌmp·tɪv) *n.* & *adj.* tuberculoso; tísico.
contact (ˈkanˌtækt) *n.* **1,** (meeting; touching) contacto. **2,** *colloq.* (personal connection) relación. —*v.t.* & *i.* relacionarse (con); ponerse en contacto (con). —**contact man,** *colloq.* intermediario.
contagion (kənˈtei·dʒən) *n.* contagio; contaminación. —**contagious,**

adj. contagioso. —**contagiousness,** *n.* contagiosidad.
contain (kən'tein) *v.t.* **1,** (hold) contener; encerrar; incluir. **2,** (have capacity) contener; tener cabida. **3,** *math.* ser divisible por. —**container,** *n.* envase; receptáculo; caja.
contaminate (kən'tæm·ɪ·neit) *v.t.* **1,** (taint) contaminar; corromper. **2,** (corrupt) pervertir; depravar. —**contamination,** *n.* contaminación.
contemplate ('kan·təm,pleit) *v.t.* **1,** (study) contemplar; considerar; estudiar. **2,** (intend) planear; esperar. —*v.i.* meditar; contemplar.
contemplation (,kan·təm'plei·ʃən) *n.* **1,** (study) contemplación; meditación. **2,** (intention) esperanza; intención.
contemplative ('kan·tɛm,ple·tɪv) *adj.* contemplativo.
contemporaneous (kən,tɛm·pə·'rei·ni·əs) *adj.* contemporáneo.
contemporary (kən'tɛm·pə·rɛr·i) *n.* & *adj.* contemporáneo; coetáneo.
contempt (kən'tɛmpt) *n.* **1,** (scorn) desprecio; desdén; menosprecio. **2,** *law* rebeldía; contumacia; desacato. —**contemptible,** *adj.* despreciable; menospreciable. —**contemptibility,** *n.* desprecio; menosprecio.
contemptuous (kən'tɛmp·tʃu·əs) *adj.* desdeñoso; despectivo; altivez. —**contemptuousness,** *n.* desdén; altanería; altivez.
contend (kən'tɛnd) *v.i.* **1,** (struggle) contender; luchar; pelear. **2,** (assert) afirmar; asentir.
content (kən'tɛnt) *adj.* [*también,* **contented**] contento; satisfecho; tranquilo. —*v.t.* satisfacer; contentar.
content ('kan·tɛnt) *n.* **1,** (gist; substance) tema; asunto; objeto. **2,** (capacity) volumen; capacidad. **3,** *pl.* (of a receptacle) contenido; cabida. **4,** *pl.* (of a book) asunto; materia.
contention (kən'tɛn·ʃən) *n.* **1,** (oral strife) contienda; disputa; debate. **2,** (struggle) contienda; lucha; pelea.
contentious (kən'tɛn·ʃəs) *adj.* contencioso; litigioso. —**contentiousness,** *n.* tendencia a litigar.
contentment (kən'tɛnt·mənt) *n.* contentamiento; satisfacción.
contest ('kan·tɛst) *n.* **1,** (fight) encuentro; lucha; pugna; pelea. **2,** (competition) concurso; competición. —*v.t.* (kən'tɛst) desafiar; disputar; oponer; *law* rebatir. —**contestant** (kən'tɛs·tənt) *n.* contendiente; contrincante.
context ('kan·tɛkst) *n.* contexto; contenido. —**contextual** (kən·'tɛkst·ju·əl) *adj.* perteneciente al contexto.
contiguity (,kan·tɪ'gju·ə·ti) *n.* contigüidad; inmediación.
contiguous (kən'tɪg·ju·əs) *adj.* contiguo; inmediato.
continence ('kan·tɪ·nəns) *n.* continencia.
continent ('kan·tɪ·nənt) *n.* continente. —*adj.* continente; casto; puro. —**continental** (-'nɛnt·əl) *adj.* continental.
contingency (kən'tɪn·dʒən·si) *n.* contingencia; casualidad; circunstancia.
contingent (kən'tɪn·dʒənt) *adj.* contingente; accidental. —*n.* contingente; cuota.
continual (kən'tɪn·ju·əl) *adj.* **1,** (continuing) continuo. **2,** (repeated) reiterado. **3,** (unceasing) incesante.
continuance (kən'tɪn·ju·əns) *n.* continuación; *law* aplazamiento.
continuation (kən,tɪn·ju'ei·ʃən) *n.* continuación; prolongación.
continue (kən'tɪn·ju) *v.t.* **1,** (prolong) continuar; prolongar; extender. **2,** (resume) continuar; proseguir. **3,** (retain, as in office) continuar; retener. —*v.i.* **1,** (persist) persistir; perseverar. **2,** (resume) proseguir; seguir. **3,** (stay) permanecer; quedarse. **4,** (endure) prolongarse; durar.
continuity (,kan·tɪ'nju·ə·ti) *n.* **1,** (unbroken sequence) continuidad. **2,** (script, as for radio) guión.
continuous (kən'tɪn·ju·əs) *adj.* continuo; ininterrumpido; incesante. —**continuously,** *adv.* continuamente; de continuo.
continuum (kən'tɪn·ju·əm) *n.* continuo.
contort (kən'tort) *v.t.* retorcer. —**contortion** (-'tor·ʃən) *n.* contorsión; retorcimiento. —**contortionist,** *n.* contorsionista.
contour ('kan·tʊr) *n.* contorno; perímetro.
contra- (kan·trə) *prefijo* contra-; contra; oposición: *contravene,* contravenir.

contraband ('kan·trə·bænd) *n.* contrabando. —*adj.* de contrabando; prohibido.
contraception (kan·trə'sɛp·ʃən) *n.* prevención del embarazo; anticoncepción. —**contraceptive** (-tɪv) *n.* & *adj.* anticonceptivo.
contract ('kan·trækt) *n.* **1,** contrato; escritura. **2,** *cards* mayor apuesta. —*v.t.* (kən'trækt) **1,** (condense) contraer; condensar; encoger. **2,** (acquire; incur) contraer; incurrir. —*v.i.* **1,** (shrink) encogerse; contraerse. **2,** (agree formally) comprometerse; hacer contrato.
contraction (kən'træk·ʃən) *n.* **1,** (shrinkage) encogimiento; contracción. **2,** *gram.* contracción.
contractor (kən'træk·tər) *n.* contratista.
contractual (kən'træk·tʃu·əl) *adj.* contractual.
contradict (kan·trə'dɪkt) *v.t.* **1,** (deny) contradecir; negar. **2,** (be contrary to) oponerse a. —**contradiction** (-'dɪk·ʃən) *n.* contradicción. —**contradictory,** *adj.* contradictorio.
contralto (kən'træl·to) *n.* contralto. —*adj.* de *o* para contralto.
contrapuntal (kan·trə'pʌnt·əl) *adj., music* referente al contrapunto.
contrary ('kan·trɛr·i) *adj.* **1,** (opposite) contrario; opuesto. **2,** (conflicting) contradictorio. **3,** (perverse) terco; porfiado. —*n.* lo contrario; lo opuesto. —**contrariness,** *n.* terquedad; oposición.
contrast (kən'træst) *v.t.* & *i.* contrastar. —*n.* ('kan·træst) contraste; diferencia.
contravene (ˌkan·trə'viːn) *v.t.* contravenir; infringir; romper. —**contravention** (-'vɛn·ʃən) *n.* contravención.
contretemps ('kan·trəˌtɔɴ) *n.* contratiempo; *Amer.* broma.
contribute (kən'trɪb·jut) *v.t.* contribuir. —*v.i.* cooperar; colaborar. —**contributor,** *n.* contribuyente; contribuidor; colaborador. —**contributory** (-jə·tor·i) *adj.* cooperante; que contribuye; contribuidor.
contribution (ˌkan·tri'bju·ʃən) *n.* contribución; colaboración.
contrite (kən'trait) *adj.* contrito; arrepentido. —**contrition** (-'trɪʃ·ən) *n.* contrición.
contrivance (kən'trai·vəns) *n.* **1,** (device) artefacto; aparato; utensilio. **2,** (scheme) plan; estratagema.
contrive (kən'traiv) *v.t.* planear; imaginar; maquinar; tramar. —*v.i.* **1,** (scheme) urdir; idear. **2,** *con inf.* (manage) ingeniarse para; darse maña para.
control (kən'trol) *v.t.* [**controlled, -trolling**] **1,** (govern) dominar; gobernar. **2,** (regulate) inspeccionar; revisar. **3,** (restrain) refrenar; cohibir. —*n.* **1,** (authority) dominio; supremacía; dirección. **2,** *mech.* regulador; control. **3,** (restraint) freno; limitación. —**controllable,** *adj.* sujeto a dirección *o* registro.
controller (kən'tro·lər) *n.* = **comptroller.**
controversial (ˌkan·trə'vʌɹ·ʃəl) *adj.* controversial; discutible; polémico.
controversy ('kan·trəˌvʌɹ·si) *n.* controversia; polémica.
controvert (ˌkan·trə'vʌɹt) *v.t.* controvertir; debatir. —**controvertible,** *adj.* controvertible.
contumacy ('kan·tju·mə·si) *n.* contumacia. —**contumacious** (-'me·ʃəs) *adj.* contumaz.
contumely ('kan·tju·mə·li) *n.* contumelia; injuria; ultraje. —**contumelious** (-'mi·li·əs) *adj.* contumelioso; injurioso; ultrajante.
contusion (kən'tu·ʒən) *n.* contusión.
conundrum (kə'nʌn·drəm) *n.* adivinanza, esp. la que termina con juego de palabras.
convalesce (kan·və'lɛs) *v.i.* convalecer; recuperarse. —**convalescence,** *n.* convalecencia. —**convalescent,** *n.* & *adj.* convaleciente.
convene (kən'viːn) *v.t.* convocar; congregar. —*v.i.* congregarse; reunirse; juntarse.
convenience (kən'vin·jəns) *n.* **1,** (suitability; advantage) conveniencia; comodidad; oportunidad. **2,** *usu. pl.* (comforts) comodidades. —**convenient,** *adj.* conveniente; adecuado.
convent ('kan·vənt) *n.* convento.
convention (kən'vɛn·ʃən) *n.* **1,** (meeting) asamblea; convención. **2,** (agreement) convención. **3,** (custom) conformidad; conveniencia; regla.

conventional (kən'vɛn·ʃən·əl) *adj.* **1,** (customary) convencional. **2,** (stipulated) estipulado; convenido. —**conventionality** (-'æl·ə·ti) *n.* convencionalismo.
converge (kən'vʌɹdʒ) *v.i.* converger. —**convergence,** *n.* convergencia. —**convergent,** *adj.* convergente.
conversant (kən'vʌɹ·sənt) *adj.* **1,** (acquainted with) versado. **2,** (informed) enterado.
conversation (ˌkan·vər'sei·ʃən) *n.* conversación; charla. —**conversational,** *adj.* de conversación.
converse (kən'vʌrs) *v.i.* conversar; platicar; charlar. —*n.* ('kan·vʌɹs) charla; plática.
converse ('kan·vʌɹs) *adj.* traspuesto; inverso. —*n.* **1,** (the opposite) lo opuesto; lo contrario. **2,** *philos.* (a proposition) recíproca.
conversion (kən'vʌɹ·ʒən) *n.* **1,** (act of converting) conversión. **2,** (change) transformación; cambio. **3,** *finance* (exchange) cambio.
convert (kən'vʌɹt) *v.t.* **1,** (change) convertir; transformar. **2,** *comm.* (exchange) convertir; cambiar. **3,** *law* apropiar ilícitamente. —*n.* ('kan·vʌɹt) converso. —**converter; convertor,** *n.* convertidor.
convertible (kən'vʌɹt·ə·bəl) *adj.* **1,** (alterable) convertible; transformable. **2,** (automobile) descapotable. —*n.* descapotable. —**convertibility,** *n.* condición de convertible; capacidad de transformación.
convex (kan'vɛks) *adj.* convexo. —**convexity** (-ə·ti) *n.* convexidad.
convey (kən'vei) *v.t.* **1,** (carry) transportar; llevar. **2,** (send) transmitir; transferir. **3,** (communicate) comunicar; impartir. **4,** *law* traspasar; transferir.
conveyance (kən'vei·əns) *n.* **1,** (transportation) transporte; conducción. **2,** (vehicle) vehículo. **3,** (transfer of ownership) cesión de propiedad. **4,** (deed) escritura de traspaso.
conveyor (kən'vei·ər) *n.* transportador; correa de transmisión.
convict (kən'vɪkt) *v.t.* condenar. —*n.* ('kan·vɪkt) convicto; reo. —**convicted,** *adj.* convicto.
conviction (kən'vɪk·ʃən) *n.* **1,** (act of convincing) convencimiento. **2,** (act of convicting) convicción. **3,** (belief) convicción; creencia.
convince (kən'vɪns) *v.t.* convencer; persuadir. —**convincing,** *adj.* convincente.
convivial (kən'vɪv·i·əl) *adj.* convival; alegre; divertido; jovial. —**conviviality** (-'æl·ə·ti) *n.* jovialidad.
convocation (ˌkan·vo'kei·ʃən) *n.* **1,** (summons) convocación; convocatoria. **2,** (assembly) asamblea.
convoke (kən'vok) *v.t.* convocar; llamar.
convoy (kən'vɔi) *v.t.* convoyar. —*n.* ('kan·vɔi) convoy.
convulse (kən'vʌls) *v.t.* & *i.* **1,** (cause spasms) producir convulsiones; convulsionar; crispar. **2,** (agitate) agitar; trastornar; disturbar. —*v.i.* (shake with laughter) morirse de risa; reír con convulsiones.
convulsion (kən'vʌl·ʃən) *n.* **1,** *pathol.* convulsión; espasmo. **2,** *fig.* (agitation) conmoción; alboroto. —**convulsive** (-sɪv) *adj.* convulsivo; espasmódico.
coo (kuː) *v.i.* arrullar. —*n.* [*también,* **cooing**] arrullo; mimo.
cook (kʊk) *v.t.* & *i.* cocer; cocinar. —*n.* cocinero. —**cookery** (-ər·i) *n.* arte de cocinar; cocina. —**cook up,** *slang,* fraguar; planear; tramar.
cookie *también,* **cooky** ('kʊk·i) *n.* galleta; pasta.
cool (kuːl) *adj.* **1,** (not very cold) frío; fresco. **2,** (calm) sereno; tranquilo. **3,** (not cordial) frío; tibio; indiferente. —*v.t.* **1,** (make cool) enfriar; refrescar. **2,** (calm) calmar; sosegar. —*v.i.* **1,** (become cool) enfriarse. **2,** (calm down) apaciguarse.
cooler ('kuː·lər) *n.* **1,** enfriadera; refrigerador. **2,** *slang* (prison) cárcel; prisión.
cool-headed *adj.* sereno; sensato.
coolie ('kuː·li) *n.* peón chino.
coolness ('kul·nəs) *n.* **1,** (of temperature) frescura. **2,** (calmness) calma; tranquilidad. **3,** (indifference) frialdad; indiferencia.
coop (kup) *n.* **1,** (for fowl) pollera; jaula. **2,** (cramped place) jaula; ratonera; cárcel. —*v.t.* [*usu.,* **coop up**] confinar; encerrar.
co-op (ko'ap) *n., slang* = **coöperative.**
cooper ('ku·pər) *n.* barrilero; tonelero.
coöperate (ko'ap·əˌreit) *v.i.* cooperar; colaborar. —**coöperation,**

n. cooperación; ayuda; colaboración.
coöperative (ko'ap·ə·rə·tɪv) *adj.* cooperante; cooperativo. —*n.* [*también, slang,* **co-op**] cooperativa.
coördinate (ko'or·də,neit) *v.t.* coordinar. —*adj.* (-nət) coordinado; *math.* coordenado. —*n., math.* coordenada. —**coördination**, *n.* coordinación.
coot (kut) *n. ornith.* fúlica.
cootie ('ku·ti) *n., slang* piojo.
cop (kap) *n., slang* policía. —*v.t.* [**copped, copping**] *slang* **1,** (steal) robar. **2,** (catch) atrapar; coger.
cope (kop) *n.* **1,** *eccles.* capa pluvial. **2,** (arch, as of the sky) bóveda; arco. **3,** [*también,* **coping**] (sloping ridge) albardilla. —*v.t.* cubrir. —*v.i.* competir; hacer frente. —**cope with,** hacer frente a; competir con.
copious ('ko·pi·əs) *adj.* copioso; abundante. —**copiousness,** *n.* abundancia; profusión.
copper ('kap·ər) *n.* **1,** (metal) cobre. **2,** *fig.* (coin) cobre; centavo. **3,** *slang* (policeman) policía; guardia. —*adj.* de cobre; cobrizo. —**coppery; copperish,** *adj.* de cobre; cobrizo.
copperhead *n., zoöl.* víbora norteamericana muy venenosa, con cabeza de color cobrizo.
coppersmith *n.* calderero.
coppice ('kap·ɪs) *n.* = **copse.**
copra ('kap·rə) *n.* copra.
copse (kaps) *n.* matorral; soto.
Coptic ('kap·tɪk) *adj.* cóptico; copto. —*n.* copto. —**Copt** (kapt) *n.* copto.
copula ('kap·jə·lə) *n.* cópula.
copulate ('kap·jə·leit) *v.i.* copular; copularse. unirse. —**copulation,** *n.* copulación; unión. —**copulative** (-lə·tɪv) *adj.* copulativo.
copy ('kap·i) *n.* **1,** (reproduction) copia; imitación; reproducción. **2,** (magazine, book, etc.) ejemplar; número. **3,** *print.* original. —*v.t.* **1,** (reproduce) copiar; reproducir. **2,** (imitate) imitar. —**copyist,** *n.* copista.
copyright *n.* propiedad literaria *o* artística. —*v.t.* patentar; registrar.
coquette (ko'kɛt) *n.* coqueta. —**coquettish,** *adj.* coquetón. —**coquetry** (-ri) *n.* coquetería.
cor- (kor) *prefijo, var. de* **com-** *ante* r: *correspond,* corresponder.
coral ('kor·əl) *n.* coral. —*adj.* **1,** (of or like coral) coralino. **2,** (of coral color) acoralado. —**coral snake,** coral.
cord (kord) *n.* **1,** (string) cordón; cordel. **2,** *anat.* tendón. **3,** (cubic measure) cuerda. **4,** (rib in fabric) pana; cordoncillo. —*v.t.* encordelar. —**cordage** ('kor·dɪdʒ) *n.* cordaje; cordelería.
cordial ('kor·dʒəl) *adj.* cordial; abierto; afable. —*n.* cordial; licor. —**cordiality** (-'dʒæl·ə·ti) *n.* cordialidad; afabilidad.
cordillera (kor·dɪ'lɛr·ə) *n.* cordillera.
cordon ('kord·ən) *n.* **1,** *mil.* (defensive line) cordón. **2,** (badge) cíngulo. **3,** *archit.* (projection) parapeto.
cordovan ('kor·də·vən) *n.* cordobán. —*adj.* de cordobán.
corduroy ('kor·də·rɔi) *n.* pana.
core (kor) *n.* **1,** (pith) corazón; meollo; esencia. **2,** (center of fruit) pepita; corazón; hueso. —*v.t.* despepitar.
coreligionist (,ko·rɪ'lɪdʒ·ən·ɪst) *n.* correligionario.
co-respondent *n.* codemandado.
cork (kork) *n.* corcho. —*v.t.* encorchar; taponar.
corkscrew *n.* sacacorchos; tirabuzón. —*adj.* retorcido; tortuoso. —*v.i., fig.* zigzaguear; serpentear.
corn (korn) *n.* **1,** (cereal) maíz. **2,** (callus) callo; dureza. **3,** *slang* (triteness) trivialidad; vulgaridad. —*v.t.* acecinar; salar; curar.
corncob *n.* mazorca de maíz; carozo; *Amer.* tusa.
cornea ('kor·ni·ə) *n.* córnea.
corner ('kor·nər) *n.* **1,** (angle; street crossing) esquina; rincón. **2,** (nook) escondrijo. **3,** (awkward position) aprieto; apuro. **4,** (region) región apartada. **5,** *comm.* monopolio. —*v.t.* **1,** (trap) arrinconar; apretar; acosar. **2,** *comm.* monopolizar.
cornerstone *n.* piedra angular; primera piedra.
cornet (kor'nɛt) *n., music* corneta. —**cornetist,** *n.* el corneta.
corn flour maicena.
cornflower *n.* aciano.
cornice ('kor·nɪs) *n.* cornisa.
cornstarch *n.* almidón de maíz.
cornucopia (,korn·ju'ko·pi·ə) *n.* cuerno de la abundancia.
corolla (kə'ra·lə) *n., bot.* corola.

corollary ('kar·ə·lɛr·i) *n.* corolario.
corona (kə'ro·nə) *n.* corona; halo. —**coronal** ('kor·ə·nəl) *adj.*, coronal.
coronary ('kar·ə,nɛr·i) *adj.* coronario.
coronation (,kar·ə'nei·ʃən) *n.* coronación.
coroner ('kar·ə·nər) *n.* pesquisidor (en una encuesta).
coronet ('kar·ə·nɛt) *n.* **1,** (crown) corona. **2,** (headdress) diadema.
corporal ('kor·pə·rəl) *n.* cabo. —*adj.* corporal; físico. —**corporal punishment**, castigo físico.
corporate ('kor·pə·rət) *adj.* **1,** (of or like a corporation) incorporado. **2,** (joint; common) colectivo.
corporation (,kor·pə'rei·ʃən) *n.* **1,** (company; association) corporación; sociedad. **2,** *slang* (paunch) panza; barriga; *Amer.* pipa.
corporeal (kor'por·i·əl) *adj.* corpóreo; físico; material.
corps (kor) *n.* [*pl.* **corps** (kor *o* korz)] cuerpo.
corpse (korps) *n.* cadáver.
corpulence ('kor·pjə·ləns) *n.* corpulencia; robustez; obesidad. —**corpulent**, *adj.* corpulento; robusto.
corpus ('kor·pəs) *n.* **1,** (body) cuerpo. **2,** (collection, as of laws) cuerpo; conjunto.
corpuscle ('kor·pəs·əl) *n.* **1,** (small particle) corpúsculo. **2,** (blood cell) glóbulo.
corral (kə'ræl) *n.* corral. —*v.t.* acorralar; acosar; cazar.
correct (kə'rɛkt) *v.t.* **1,** (note errors in) corregir. **2,** (rectify) rectificar; enmendar. **3,** (discipline) reprender; castigar. —*adj.* **1,** (true) correcto; exacto; justo. **2,** (ethical) propio; bien hecho. —**corrective**, *adj.* correctivo; correccional. —**correctness**, *n.* corrección; exactitud.
correction (kə'rɛk·ʃən) *n.* **1,** (act of correcting) corrección; rectificación; enmienda. **2,** (rebuke) castigo; escarmiento.
corregidor (kə'rɛg·ə,dor) *n.* corregidor.
correlate ('kar·ə,leit) *v.t.* correlacionar; relacionar. —**correlation**, *n.* correlación; relación.
correlative (kə'rɛl·ə·tɪv) *n.* & *adj.* correlativo.
correspond (kar·ə'spand) *v.i.* **1,** (match) corresponder; tener proporción (con). **2,** (write) escribirse; tener *o* mantener correspondencia. —**correspondence** (-əns) *n.* correspondencia.
correspondent (kar·ə'spand·ənt) *n.* corresponsal; correspondiente. —*adj.* correspondiente.
corridor ('kar·ɪ·dər) *n.* corredor; pasillo; galería.
corroborate (kə'rab·ə·reit) *v.t.* corroborar; confirmar. —**corroboration**, *n.* corroboración. —**corroborative**, *adj.* corroborativo; que corrobora.
corrode (kə'ro:d) *v.t.* corroer. —*v.i.* corroerse.
corrosion (kə'ro·ʒən) *n.* corrosión. —**corrosive** (-sɪv) *n.* & *adj.* corrosivo.
corrugate ('kar·ə,geit) *v.t.* & *i.* arrugar; acanalar; plegar. —**corrugation**, *n.* acanalamiento. —**corrugated paper**, cartón acanalado.
corrupt (kə'rʌpt) *adj.* **1,** (evil) corrompido; degenerado; depravado. **2,** (tainted) putrefacto; pútrido. —*v.t.* **1,** (pervert) corromper; pervertir. **2,** (bribe) sobornar; cohechar. **3,** (taint) podrir; infectar. —**corruptible**, *adj.* corruptible. —**corruptness**; **corruption** (kə'rʌp·ʃən) *n.* corrupción.
corsage (kor'sa:ʒ) *n.* ramillete para llevar al hombro *o* a la cintura.
corsair (kor'se:r) *n.* corsario.
corset ('kor·sət) *n.* corsé.
cortege (kor'tɛ:ʒ) *n.* **1,** (procession) cortejo; procesión. **2,** (retinue) comitiva; séquito.
cortex ('kor·tɛks) *n.* [*pl.* **cortices** ('kor·tə,siz)] *anat.; bot.* corteza. —**cortical** (-tɪ·kəl) *adj.* cortical.
cortisone ('kor·tɪ,son) *n.* cortisona.
corvette (kor'vɛt) *n.* corbeta.
cosecant (ko'si·kənt) *n.* cosecante.
cosine ('ko·sain) *n.* coseno.
cosmetic (kaz'mɛt·ɪk) *n.* & *adj.* cosmético.
cosmic ('kaz·mɪk) *adj.* **1,** (pert. to the universe) cósmico. **2,** *fig.* (vast; ordered) vasto; metódico; ordenado. —**cosmic rays**, rayos cósmicos.
cosmo- (kaz·mo) *prefijo* cosmo-; cosmos: *cosmography*, cosmografía.
cosmogony (kaz'mag·ə·ni) *n.* cosmogonía.
cosmography (kaz'mag·rə·fi) *n.* cosmografía.

cosmology (kaz'mal·ə·dʒi) *n.* cosmología.
cosmopolitan (kaz·mə'pal·ɪ·tən) *adj.* cosmopolita. —*n.* [*también,* **cosmopolite** (kaz'map·ə·lait)] cosmopolita.
cosmos ('kaz·məs) *n.* **1,** (universe) cosmos; universo. **2,** *bot.* flor cosmos.
Cossack ('kas·æk) *n.* & *adj.* cosaco.
cost (kɔːst) *n.* **1,** (price) coste; costo; precio. **2,** (expense) expensas (*pl.*); gastos (*pl.*). **3,** (loss; suffering) pérdida; daño. **4,** *pl., law* costas. —*v.t.* & *i.* costar. —**at all costs,** a toda costa.
costly ('kɔst·li) *adj.* **1,** (expensive) costoso; caro. **2,** (very valuable) suntuoso; magnífico. —**costliness,** *n.* lo costoso; suntuosidad; magnificencia.
costume ('kas·tjum) *n.* **1,** (garb) vestido; traje. **2,** (fancy dress) disfraz. **3,** *theat.* (clothes) indumentaria; atavío.
cot (kat) *n.* catre; camita.
cotangent (ko'tæn·dʒənt) *n.* cotangente.
coterie ('ko·tə·ri) *n.* grupo; círculo; corrillo.
cotillion (ko'tɪl·jən) *n.* cotillón.
cottage ('kat·ɪdʒ) *n.* **1,** (small house) cabaña. **2,** (country house) quinta. —**cottage cheese,** requesón.
cotter pin ('kat·ər) chaveta.
cotton ('kat·ən) *n.* **1,** (fiber; cloth) algodón. **2,** (plant) algodonero. —*adj.* de algodón; algodonero. —**cotton field; cotton plantation,** algodonal.
cottonseed *n.* semilla de algodón.
cotyledon (ˌkat·ə'li·dən) *n.* cotiledón.
couch (kautʃ) *n.* **1,** (sofa) poltrona; diván; sofá. **2,** (small bed) camita; lecho. —*v.t.* **1,** (lay) recostar; reclinar. **2,** (express) indicar; expresar. —*v.i.* **1,** (to lie down) recostarse; reclinarse. **2,** (wait in ambush) agacharse; encorvarse.
cougar ('ku·gər) *n.* cuguar; puma.
cough (kɔf) *v.i.* toser. —*n.* tos. —**cough up, 1,** (expel from the throat) esputar. **2,** *slang* (hand over) rendir; entregar.
could (kʊd) *v., pret. de* **can.**
coulomb (kʊ'lam) *n.* culombio.
council ('kaun·səl) *n.* **1,** (assembly) consejo; junta. **2,** (municipal body) concejo. **3,** *eccles.* concilio.
councilman ('kaun·səl·mən) *n.* [*pl.* **-men**] concejal.
councilor *también,* **councillor** ('kaun·səl·ər) *n.* consejero; concejal.
counsel ('kaun·səl) *n.* **1,** (consultation) consejo; consulta. **2,** (advice) parecer; aviso; guía. **3,** (plan) trama; deliberación; plan. **4,** *law* abogado; consultor. —*v.t.* & *i.* aconsejar; consultar; dirigir; asesorar. —**keep one's own counsel,** callarse la boca; reservarse la opinión. —**take counsel,** aconsejarse; pedir consejo.
counselor *también,* **counsellor** ('kaun·sə·lər) *n.* **1,** (lawyer) abogado. **2,** (adviser) consejero; asesor; confidente.
count (kaunt) *v.t.* **1,** (enumerate) contar; enumerar. **2,** (deem) considerar; reputar; estimar. —*v.i.* **1,** (enumerate) contar; numerar. **2,** (be of value) importar. —*n.* **1,** (enumeration) cuenta; enumeración; cálculo. **2,** *law* cargo; demanda. **3,** *cap.* (title) conde. —**count in,** incluir. —**count off,** contar separando. —**count on** *o* **upon,** depender de; contar con. —**count out, 1,** (omit) omitir. **2,** *colloq., polit.* falsear una elección. **3,** *boxing* declarar vencido.
countdown *n.* conteo.
countenance ('kaun·tə·nəns) *n.* **1,** (face) cara; faz. **2,** (facial expression) aspecto; semblante; expresión. **3,** (favor) apoyo; favor; protección. —*v.t.* ayudar; apoyar; favorecer; fomentar.
counter ('kaun·tər) *n.* **1,** (device) contador. **2,** (token) ficha; tanto. **3,** (display table) mostrador. **4,** (enumerator) contador. **5,** (the opposite) lo opuesto; lo contrario. —*adj.* contrario; opuesto. —*adv.* contra; al revés. —*v.t.* & *i.* **1,** (oppose) oponer; contradecir. **2,** (attack) oponerse; contraatacar.
counter- (kaun·tər) *prefijo* contra-; contra; oposición: *counterweight,* contrapeso.
counteract *v.t.* contrarrestar; estorbar; neutralizar; impedir.
counterattack *v.t.* & *i.* contraatacar. —*n.* contraataque.
counterbalance *v.t.* contrabalancear. —*n.* contrapeso.
counterclockwise *adj.* & *adv.* contrario a las manecillas del reloj.

counterespionage *n.* contraespionaje.
counterfeit ('kaun·tər,fɪt) *adj.* falsificado; espurio. —*n.* **1,** (imitation) falsificación; imitación. **2,** (false money) moneda falsa. —*v.t.* falsificar; falsear. —*v.i.* fingir; pretender; disimular. —**counterfeiter,** *n.* falsario; falsificador.
countermand ('kaun·tər,mænd) *v.t.* contramandar; revocar; cancelar. —*n.* contramandato; contraorden.
countermark *n.* contramarca. —*v.t.* contramarcar.
counteroffensive *n.* contraofensiva.
counterpane ('kaun·tər,pein) *n.* cubrecama; colcha.
counterpart *n.* **1,** (complement) contraparte. **2,** (copy) duplicado; facsímil.
counterpoint *n., music* contrapunto.
counterpoise *n.* contrapeso.
counterrevolution *n.* contrarrevolución. —**counterrevolutionary** (-ɛr·i) *adj.* & *n.* contrarrevolucionario.
countersign *v.t.* refrendar; visar. —*n.* contraseña; santo y seña.
countersignature *n.* refrendata.
countersink *v.t.* [*pret.* & *p.p.* **-sunk**] avellanar. —*n.* **1,** (tool) avellanador. **2,** (countersunk hole) agujero avellanado.
counterweight *n.* contrapeso.
countess ('kaun·tɪs) *n.* condesa.
countless ('kaunt·ləs) *adj.* incontable; innumerable.
country ('kʌn·tri) *n.* **1,** (expanse of land) región; tierra; país. **2,** (nation) país; nación. **3,** (rural region) campiña; campo. —*adj.* campestre; rústico; rural. —**country club,** club de campo.
countryman ('kʌn·tri·mən) *n.* [*pl.* **-men**] **1,** (compatriot) compatriota. **2,** (rustic) campesino.
countryside *n.* paisaje campestre; campiña; campo.
county ('kaun·ti) *n.* condado; distrito. —*adj.* del condado.
coup (kuː) *n.* golpe. —**coup d'etat** ('ku·de'taː) golpe de estado.
coupe *también,* **coupé** (ku'pei) *n.* **1,** (automobile) cupé. **2,** (closed carriage) berlina.
couple ('kʌp·əl) *n.* **1,** (pair) par; pareja. **2,** (man and wife) matrimonio. —*v.t.* acoplar; ensamblar; juntar.
couplet ('kʌp·lət) *n.* copla.
coupling ('kʌp·lɪŋ) *n.* acoplamiento; *R.R.* enganche.
coupon ('ku·pan) *n.* cupón.
courage ('kʌɹ·ɪdʒ) *n.* coraje; valentía; bravura. —**courageous** (kə·'rei·dʒəs) *adj.* intrépido; valeroso; bravo.
courier ('kʊr·i·ər) *n.* **1,** (messenger) correo; mensajero; ordinario. **2,** (travel guide) acompañante; encargado.
course (kors) *n.* **1,** (passage) vía; pasaje; pasadizo. **2,** (direction) recorrido; dirección. **3,** *sports* campo; terreno. **4,** (progressive phases) curso; marcha; rumbo. **5,** (series, as of classes) curso; serie. **6,** (behavior) conducta; comportamiento. **7,** (succession of acts, procedures, etc.) sistema; método. **8,** (part of a meal) plato. **9,** *naut.* rumbo. —*v.t.* correr; perseguir; cazar; ir detrás de. —*v.i.* corretear. —**in due course,** a su debido tiempo; oportunamente. —**matter of course,** cosa común; de cajón. —**of course,** desde luego; naturalmente; por supuesto.
courser ('kor·sər) *n., poet.* corcel; caballo de guerra.
court (kort) *n.* **1,** (patio) patio; atrio. **2,** (sports area) cancha; frontón. **3,** (royal) corte; palacio. **4,** *law* tribunal; sala de justicia. —*v.t.* **1,** (seek the favor of) cortejar. **2,** (woo) enamorar; cortejar; galantear. **3,** (aspire to) solicitar; buscar; —*v.i.* hacer la corte.
courteous ('kʌɹ·ti·əs) *adj.* cortés; atento; educado.
courtesan ('kor·tə·zən) *n.* cortesana.
courtesy ('kʌɹ·tə·si) *n.* **1,** (politeness) cortesía; atención; finura. **2,** (indulgence) favor.
courthouse *n.* audiencia; tribunal; palacio de justicia.
courtier ('kor·ti·ər) *n.* cortesano; palaciego.
courtly ('kort·li) *adj.* cortesano; cortés.
court-martial (kort'mar·ʃəl) *n.* [*pl.* **courts-martial**] *mil.* consejo de guerra. —*v.t.* someter a consejo de guerra.
courtship ('kort·ʃɪp) *n.* cortejo; corte; noviazgo.
courtyard *n.* atrio; patio.

cousin (ˈkʌz·ən) *n.* primo; prima (*fem.*).

cove (koːv) *n.* 1, (inlet) caleta; ensenada. 2, *Brit. slang* (fellow) hombre; tipo.

covenant (ˈkʌv·ə·nənt) *n.* pacto; convenio. —*v.t.* prometer; estipular. —*v.i.* pactar; comprometerse.

cover (ˈkʌv·ər) *v.t.* 1, (place something on) cubrir; encubrir; proteger; abrigar. 2, (hide) ocultar; tapar. 3, (traverse) andar; recorrer. 4, (include) comprender; incluir. 5, (aim at) apuntar a; cubrir. 6, *comm.* remesar *o* cubrir fondos. 7, *colloq.* (report on) informar de; cubrir. —*v.i.* 1, (spread over) correrse; esparcirse. 2, (put one's hat on) cubrirse; taparse; tocarse. —*n.* 1, (lid) tapadera; tapa. 2, (protective layer) funda; forro; tapete. 3, (envelope) cubierta. 4, (disguise) pretexto; pretensión; velo. 5, (shelter) refugio; abrigo; albergue. 6, (table setting) cubierto. —**cover charge,** precio de admisión. —**from cover to cover,** de cabo a rabo. —**take cover,** ponerse a cubierto; ocultarse. —**under cover,** 1, (sheltered) a cubierto; a seguro. 2, (hidden) secreto; oculto; escondido. 3, (by pretense) so pretexto (de); con la excusa (de).

coverage (ˈkʌv·ər·ɪdʒ) *n.* 1, (insurance) protección. 2, (reporting) información; reportaje.

covering (ˈkʌv·ər·ɪŋ) *n.* cubierta; tapadera; envoltura.

coverlet (ˈkʌv·ər·lɪt) *n.* colcha; cobertor; cubrecama.

covert (ˈkʌv·ərt) *adj.* 1, (hidden) secreto; escondido. 2, (sheltered) cubierto; tapado; resguardado. —*n.* refugio; guarida; escondite.

covet (ˈkʌv·ɪt) *v.t.* 1, (aspire to) ambicionar. 2, (desire) codiciar. —**covetous** (ˈkʌv·ə·təs) *adj.* ambicioso; codicioso; envidioso; interesado. —**covetousness,** *n.* codicia.

covey (ˈkʌv·i) *n.* bandada; nidada.

cow (kau) *n.* vaca. —*v.t.* acobardar; intimidar; amedrentar.

coward (ˈkau·ərd) *n.* cobarde. —**cowardice** (ˈkau·ər·dɪs) *n.* cobardía. —**cowardly,** *adj.* cobarde; miedoso. —*adv.* cobardemente.

cowbell *n.* cencerro.

cowboy *n.* vaquero. *También,* **cowhand, cowpuncher.**

cower (ˈkau·ər) *v.i.* agacharse; achicarse; derrumbarse.

cowherd *n.* boyero.

cowl (kaul) *n.* 1, (monk's hood) capucha; capuz; cogulla. 2, *auto.* cubretablero.

cowling (ˈkau·lɪŋ) *n., aero; auto.* cubierta *o* caja del motor.

cowpox *n.* vacuna.

coxcomb (ˈkaks·kom) *n.* 1, *lit.* cresta de gallo. 2, *fig.* (vain man) farol; presumido; mequetrefe. 3, (jester's cap) gorro de bufón.

coy (kɔi) *adj.* 1, (shy) tímido; vergonzoso; recatado. 2, (feigning shyness) hipócrita; esquivo. —**coyness,** *n.* timidez; recato.

coyote (kaiˈo·ti; ˈkai·ot) *n.* coyote.

cozen (ˈkʌz·ən) *v.t.* & *i.* engañar; defraudar; embaucar. —**cozenage** (-ɪdʒ) *n.* engaño; embaucamiento.

cozy (ˈko·zi) *adj.* 1, (of things) cálido; acogedor. 2, (of persons) cómodo; a gusto.

crab (kræb) *n.* 1, (shellfish) cangrejo; *Amer.* jaiba. 2, *colloq.* (irascible person) iracundo; mal genio; cascarrabias. 3, *cap., astron.* Cáncer. —*v.i.* [**crabbed, crabbing**] *colloq.* quejarse; culpar. —**crabby,** *adj.* espinoso.

crabapple *n.* 1, (tree) manzano silvestre. 2, (fruit) manzana silvestre.

crabbed (ˈkræb·ɪd) *adj.* 1, (cramped) obscuro; difícil. 2, (cross) áspero; espinoso. —*v., pret. & p.p. de* **crab.**

crack (kræk) *v.t.* 1, (split) quebrar; hender; rajar. 2, (damage) romper; destruir. 3, (distill) someter a destilación fraccionada. —*v.i.* 1, (split) quebrarse; rajarse; reventarse. 2, (break, as a voice) dar chasquidos. 3, *colloq.* (lose one's effectiveness) desquiciarse; trastornarse. 4, *colloq.* (tell, as a joke) bromear; hacer chistes. —*n.* 1, (sound) chasquido; crujido; estallido. 2, (fissure) grieta; raja; hendedura. 3, *slang* (attempt) golpe; atentado. 4, *slang* (gibe) escarnio; burla. 5, (voice break) mudanza *o* cambio de la voz. —*adj., colloq.* excelente; estupendo; superior. —**crack down on,** *colloq.* castigar; tratar con rigor. —**crack up,** *colloq.* 1, (crash) estrellarse. 2, (break down) quebrantarse; enfermarse.

cracked (krækt) *adj.* 1, (split) roto; quebrado. 2, *colloq.* (brainless) chiflado; alocado; loco.

cracker ('kræk·ər) *n.* **1,** (biscuit) galleta. **2,** (firecracker) petardo; cohete.
crackle ('kræk·əl) *v.i.* crujir; dar chasquidos. —*n.* crepitación.
crackpot ('kræk·pat) *n., slang* chiflado; excéntrico.
crack-up *n.* **1,** (crash) choque. **2,** (collapse) trastorno; agotamiento.
-cracy (krə·si) *sufijo* -cracia; *forma nombres indicando* **1,** mando; autoridad: *autocracy,* autocracia. **2,** clase gobernadora: *aristocracy,* aristocracia. **3,** forma de gobierno: *democracy,* democracia.
cradle ('krei·dəl) *n.* **1,** (crib) cuna. **2,** *fig.* (origin; infancy) origen; infancia; nacimiento. —*v.t.* acunar; mecer.
craft (kræft) *n.* **1,** [*pl.* **craft**] (vessel) nave; barco; buque. **2,** (trade) profesión; oficio. **3,** (guild) gremio. **4,** (skill) destreza; habilidad; maña. **5,** (guile) astucia; artificio.
craftsman ('kræfts·mən) *n.* [*pl.* **-men**] artesano; artífice. —**craftsmanship,** *n.* artesanía.
crafty ('kræft·i) *adj.* astuto; taimado; avieso. —**craftiness,** *n.* astucia; maña.
crag (kræ:g) *n.* risco; despeñadero. —**craggy** *adj.* escarpado; riscoso.
cram (kræ:m) *v.t.* [**crammed, cramming**] **1,** (fill overfull) rellenar; atestar; embutir. **2,** (eat greedily) hartar; atracar. —*v.i.* **1,** (stuff oneself) llenarse; hartarse; atracarse. **2,** *colloq.* (study) empollar; darse un atracón.
cramp (kræmp) *n.* **1,** (of a muscle) calambre. **2,** *pl.* (in the abdomen) retortijones. **3,** (clamp) grapa; abrazadera. **4,** (hindrance) traba; impedimento. —*v.t.* **1,** (give cramps to) dar calambres. **2,** (fasten) sujetar; trabar. **3,** (constrict) constreñir; apretar. **4,** (hinder) impedir; estorbar. —**cramped,** *adj.* dificultoso; apretado; diminuto.
cranberry *n.* arandano agrio.
crane (krein) *n.* **1,** (bird) grulla. **2,** (derrick) grúa. —*v.t.* **1,** (stretch, as the neck) estirar; alargar. **2,** (raise or move by crane) levantar con grúa.
cranium ('krei·ni·əm) *n.* cráneo. —**cranial,** *adj.* craneal.
crank (kræŋk) *n.* **1,** (device) manivela; manubrio. **2,** *colloq.* (zealot) maniático; extravagante. —*v.t.* & *i.* dar a *o* voltear (la manivela).
crankshaft *n.* cigüeñal.
cranky ('kræŋ·ki) *adj.* irritable; maniático; caprichoso. —**crankiness,** *n.* manía; chifladura.
cranny ('kræn·i) *n.* grieta; raja; hendedura.
craps (kræps) *n.* juego de dados.
crash (kræʃ) *n.* **1,** (sound) estampido; estallido. **2,** (collision) choque; colisión. **3,** (financial failure) fracaso; quiebra; bancarrota. **4,** (rough fabric) cutí; tela basta. —*v.t.* **1,** (smash) estallar; despedazar. **2,** *slang* (burst into) irrumpir; abrirse paso. —*v.i.* chocar; estrellarse.
crass (kræs) *adj.* craso; torpe; tosco; obtuso. —**crassness,** *n.* crasitud.
-crat (kræt) *sufijo* -crata; *forma nombres denotando personas, correspondiendo a los nombres terminados en* **-cracy**: *autocrat,* autócrata; *aristocrat,* aristócrata.
crate (kreit) *n.* banasta; envase *o* embalaje de madera; *Amer.* guacal. —*v.t.* poner en banasta; embalar con tablas de madera.
crater ('krei·tər) *n.* cráter.
-cratic ('kræt·ɪk) *sufijo* -crático; *forma adjetivos de los nombres terminados en* **-crat** *o* **-cracy**: *autocratic,* autocrático.
cravat (krə'væt) *n.* corbata; *W.I.* chalina.
crave (kreiv) *v.t.* **1,** (desire) anhelar; desear; ambicionar. **2,** (beg for) pedir humildemente.
craven ('krei·vən) *adj.* & *n.* cobarde.
craving ('krei·vɪŋ) *n.* deseo; ansia; anhelo.
crawfish ('krɔ·fɪʃ) *n.* langostino. *También,* **crayfish** ('krei-).
crawl (krɔ:l) *v.i.* **1,** (creep) arrastrarse; gatear; serpentear. **2,** (advance slowly) andar a paso de tortuga. **3,** (humiliate oneself) rebajarse; humillarse. —*n.* **1,** (creeping movement) gateo. **2,** (slow progress) marcha lenta; paso de tortuga. **3,** (swimming stroke) crawl.
crayon ('krei·an) *n.* clarión; tiza de color.
craze (kreiz) *v.t.* & *i.* enloquecer. —*n.* manía; capricho; moda.
crazy ('krei·zi) *adj.* **1,** (insane) loco; demente; enfurecido. **2,** *slang* (excited) extravagante; insensato.

—**craziness,** *n.* locura; demencia; extravío. —**be crazy about,** *colloq.* sorber los vientos por. —**crazy bone,** nervio ulnar. —**crazy quilt,** centón.

creak (krik) *v.i.* rechinar; chirriar. —*n.* chirrido; rechinamiento. —**creakiness** ('kri·ki·nəs) *n.* rechinamiento. —**creaky,** *adj.* rechinante.

cream (kriːm) *n.* **1,** (of milk) crema; nata. **2,** *fig.* (the best part) la flor y nata; lo mejor. —*v.t.* desnatar; hacer nata. —**creamy,** *adj.* de *o* con crema *o* nata.

creamer ('kri·mər) *n.* cremera.

creamery ('kri·mə·ri) *n.* lechería; granja.

crease (kris) *n.* **1,** (pressed fold) pliegue; doblez. **2,** (trouser fold) raya. **3,** (wrinkle) arruga. —*v.t.* **1,** (make a crease in) sacar la raya a. **2,** (wrinkle) plegar; arrugar. —*v.i.* arrugarse; plegarse.

create (kri'eit) *v.t.* **1,** (bring into being) crear; engendrar; hacer; producir. **2,** (give a new rank) constituir; elegir. **3,** (originate) causar; ocasionar.

creation (kri'ei·ʃən) *n.* creación.

creative (kri'ei·tɪv) *adj.* creador; inventor. —**creativeness,** *n.* genio; capacidad de crear.

creator (kri'ei·tər) *n.* creador.

creature ('kri·tʃər) *n.* criatura.

creche (krɛʃ) *n.* belén; nacimiento; pesebre.

credence ('kri·dəns) *n.* creencia; crédito; fe.

credentials (krɪ'dɛn·ʃəlz) *n.pl.* credenciales.

credible ('krɛd·ə·bəl) *adj.* creíble; verosímil. —**credibility,** *n.* credibilidad; verosimilitud.

credit ('krɛd·ɪt) *n.* **1,** (belief) crédito; fe. **2,** (credibility) credibilidad. **3,** (acknowledgement) mérito; reconocimiento. **4,** *comm.* crédito. **5,** *bookkeeping* haber. —*v.t.* **1,** (believe) creer; tener fe. **2,** (acknowledge) reconocer; atribuir; acreditar. **3,** *comm.* acreditar; abonar. —**creditable,** *adj.* creíble; fidedigno; loable. —**creditor,** *n.* acreedor. —**credit (someone) with,** hacer justicia a; atribuir el mérito a. —**do credit to,** acreditar. —**give credit for,** conceder el mérito de *o* por. —**letter of credit,** carta de crédito. —**on credit,** *comm.* a crédito; fiado. —**to the credit of,** para mérito de.

credo ('kri·do) *n.* [*pl.* **-dos**] credo; creencia.

credulity (krɛ'dju·lə·ti) *n.* credulidad. —**credulous** ('krɛd·jə·ləs) *adj.* crédulo.

creed (kriːd) *n.* **1,** (belief) credo; doctrina. **2,** (sect) creencia; secta.

creek (krik) *n.* riachuelo; arroyo.

creel (kriːl) *n.* cesta para pescados; chistera.

creep (krip) *v.i.* [*pret.* & *p.p.* **crept**] **1,** (crawl) gatear; arrastrarse; deslizarse. **2,** (move slowly) moverse a paso de tortuga. **3,** *fig.* (debase oneself) humillarse. **4,** (grow along a surface) trepar; correrse; expandirse. —*n.* **1,** (crawl) arrastramiento. **2,** (slow pace) paso de tortuga. 3, *slang* (repulsive person) pendejo. —**creep up (on),** acercarse furtivamente (a).

creeper ('kri·pər) *n.* **1,** (vine) enredadera; planta trepadora. **2,** (infant's garment) traje de niño hecho todo de una pieza.

creeps (krips) *n.pl., colloq.* pavor (*sing.*); crispamiento (*sing.*).

creepy ('kri·pi) *adj.* pavoroso; horroroso. —**creepiness,** *n.* pavor; horror.

cremate ('kri·meit) *v.t.* incinerar. —**cremation,** *n.* incineración. —**crematory** (-mə,tor·i) [*también,* **crematorium** (-mə'tor·i·əm)] *n.* crematorio.

crenelated ('krɛn·ə,le·tɪd) *adj.* almenado.

creole ('kri·ol) *adj.* & *n.* criollo.

creosote ('kri·ə·sot) *n.* creosota.

crêpe *también,* **crape** (kreip) *n.* crepé; crespón. —**crêpe de chine** (də'ʃiːn) crepé; crespón; burato. —**crêpes Suzette** (,kreip·su'zɛt) panqueques Suzette.

crept (krɛpt) *v., pret.* & *p.p. de* **creep.**

crescendo (krə'ʃɛn·do) *n., adj.* & *adv., music* crescendo.

crescent ('krɛs·ənt) *adj.* creciente. —*n.* media luna; luneta.

cress (krɛs) *n.* mastuerzo.

crest (krɛst) *n.* **1,** (of fowl) cresta; copete. **2,** *heraldry* cimera; timbre. **3,** (the top) cima; cumbre. —*v.t.* coronar. —*v.i.* formar cresta.

crestfallen ('krɛst,fɔl·ən) *adj.* abatido; amilanado; caído.

cretin ('kri·tɪn) *n.* cretino. —**cretinism,** *n.* cretinismo.

cretonne (krɪ'taːn) *n.* cretona.

crevasse (krə'væs) *n.* brecha; hendidura.
crevice ('krɛv·ɪs) *n.* raja; hendedura; grieta.
crew (kruː) *n.* personal; *naut.* tripulación; dotación; *aero.* tripulación. —*v., pret. alt. de* **crow.**
crib (krɪb) *n.* **1,** (infant's bed) cuna. **2,** (bin) arca; pesebre; granero. —*v.t.* [**cribbed, cribbing**] **1,** (confine) confinar; enjaular; encerrar. **2,** *colloq.* (plagiarize) plagiar; (for an examination) hurtar. —**cribber** (-ər) *n.* plagiario.
cribbage ('krɪb·ɪdʒ) *n.* un juego inglés de naipes.
crick (krɪk) *n.* calambre; espasmo; (in the neck) tortícolis.
cricket ('krɪk·ɪt) *n.* **1,** (insect) grillo. **2,** (game) cricket.
crier ('krai·ər) *n.* pregonero.
crime (kraim) *n.* crimen.
criminal ('krɪm·ɪ·nəl) *n.* & *adj.* criminal. —**criminality** (-'næl·ə·ti) *n.* criminalidad.
criminology (ˌkrɪ·mɪ'na·lə·dʒi) *n.* criminología. —**criminologist** (-dʒɪst) *n.* criminalista.
crimp (krɪmp) *v.t.* rizar; plegar; ondear. —*n.* rizo; onda; ondulación.
crimson ('krɪm·zən) *n.* & *adj.* carmesí.
cringe (krɪndʒ) *v.i.* rebajarse; encogerse; adular. —**cringing** ('krɪn·dʒɪŋ) *adj.* bajo; rastrero.
crinkle ('krɪŋ·kəl) *v.t.* & *i.* **1,** (ripple) rizar; arrugar; ondular. **2,** (twist) retorcerse; serpentear.
crinoline ('krɪn·ə·lɪn) *n.* **1,** (fabric) crinolina; **2,** (hoop skirt) miriñaque.
cripple ('krɪp·əl) *n.* inválido; lisiado. —*v.t.* lisiar; baldar; tullir.
crisis ('krai·sɪs) *n.* crisis.
crisp (krɪsp) *adj.* **1,** (brittle) crespo; quebradizo; tostado. **2,** (fresh) fresco; lozano. **3,** *fig.* (terse) terso. **4,** (pithy) enérgico; eficaz. **5,** (tightly curled) rizado. —*v.t.* rizar. —**crispness,** *n.* frescura; lozanía.
crisscross ('krɪsˌkrɔs) *adj.* cruzado. —*adv.* en cruz. —*n.* cruz.
criterion (krai'tɪr·i·ən) *n.* [*pl.* **criteria** (-ə)] criterio.
critic ('krɪt·ɪk) *n.* crítico. —**critical** (-ɪ·kəl) *adj.* crítico.
criticism ('krɪt·ɪ·sɪz·əm) *n.* crítica.
criticize ('krɪt·ɪˌsaiz) *v.t.* & *i.* criticar; censurar.
critique (krɪ'tik) *n.* crítica.
croak (krok) *n.* **1,** (of a frog) canto de rana. **2,** (of a raven) graznido. —*v.i.* **1,** (utter a hoarse cry) croar; groznar. **2,** *slang* (die) morirse.
Croat ('kro·æt) *n.* croata. —**Croatian** (kro'ei·ʃən) *n.* & *adj.* croata.
crochet (kro'ʃei) *n.* gancho; ganchillo; punto *o* labor de croché. —*v.t.* & *i.* hacer ganchillo; hacer punto *o* labor de croché.
crock (krak) *n.* olla *o* cazuela de barro; cacharro.
crockery ('krak·ə·ri) *n.* loza; vasijas de barro; loza vidriada.
crocodile ('krak·əˌdail) *n.* cocodrilo. —**crocodile tears,** lágrimas de cocodrilo.
crocus ('kro·kəs) *n.* azafrán.
crony ('kro·ni) *n.* compadre; compinche.
crook (krʊk) *n.* **1,** (a bend) curva; curvatura; doble. **2,** (hook) gancho; garfio. **3,** (bent staff) cayado; báculo. **4,** *slang* (a cheat) pícaro; fullero; tramposo.
crooked ('krʊk·ɪd) *adj.* **1,** (bent) doblado; torcido; sinuoso. **2,** *slang* (dishonest) tramposo; fullero; deshonesto.
crookedness ('krʊk·ɪd·nəs) *n.* **1,** curvatura; corvadura. **2,** *slang* (dishonesty) picardía; perversión; deshonestidad.
croon (krun) *v.t.* & *i.* canturrear.
crop (krap) *n.* **1,** (harvest) cosecha; producción. **2,** (plants growing) siembra. **3,** (riding whip) fusta. **4,** (bird's gullet) buche. **5,** (haircut) cabello corto. —*v.t.* [**cropped, cropping**] **1,** (trim; pare) cortar; recortar. **2,** (bite off) mordisquear; roer (la hierba); pacer. **3,** (cut short) trasquilar. **4,** (reap) segar; cosechar. —**crop up,** surgir; aparecer; aflorar.
cropper ('krap·ər) *n., usu. in* **come a cropper,** fracasar; caerse.
croquette (kro'kɛt) *n.* croqueta.
crosier ('kro·ʒər) *n.* = **crozier.**
cross (krɔs) *n.* **1,** (symbol) cruz. **2,** *fig.* (burden) carga; peso; revés; desgracia. **3,** (crossing of breeds) cruce. —*adj.* **1,** (intersecting) cruzado; atravesado; transversal. **2,** (contrary) contrario; opuesto. **3,** (peevish) malhumorado; serio. **4,** (hybrid) cruzado; híbrido. —*v.t.* & *i.* **1,** (intersect) cruzar. **2,** (go across) cruzar; atravesar. **3,** (meet and pass) encontrar a. **4,** (cross-

breed) cruzar. —*v.t.* (thwart) oponer; contradecir; frustrar. —**crossly,** *adv.* con enfado. —**crossness,** *n.* enfado; enojo. —**cross fire,** fuego cruzado. —**cross off** *o* **out,** borrar; tachar; cruzar. —**cross oneself,** cruzarse; santiguarse. —**cross reference,** comprobación; contrarreferencia. —**cross section,** corte *o* sección transversal.
crossbar *n.* travesaño; tranca.
crossbeam *n.* travesaño; balancín.
crossbones (ˈkrɔsˌbonz) *n.* huesos cruzados; bandera pirata.
crossbow (ˈkrɔsˌboː) *n.* ballesta.
crossbreed *v.t.* [*pret.* & *p.p.* **-bred** (-brɛd)] cruzar. —*v.i.* cruzarse. —*n.* híbrido; mestizo.
cross-country *adj.* & *adv.* a campo traviesa.
cross-examine *v.t.* interrogar. —**cross-examination,** *n.* interrogatorio.
crosseyed (ˈkrɔsˌaid) *adj.* bizco; bisojo.
crossing (ˈkrɔs·ɪŋ) *n.* **1,** (intersection) cruce; intersección. **2,** (place to cross) travesía; paso; cruce. **3,** (ford) vado. **4,** (act of opposing) oposición; resistencia.
cross-purpose *n.* propósito contrario. —**at cross-purposes,** por caminos opuestos; en pugna involuntaria.
cross-question *v.t.* interrogar.
crossroads *n.* encrucijada; cuatro caminos.
crosswise (ˈkrɔs·waiz) *adv.* en cruz; a, al, *o* de través. *También,* **crossways** (-weiz).
crossword puzzle (ˈkrɔs·wərd) *n.* crucigrama.
crotch (kratʃ) *n.* **1,** (juncture, as of branches) bifurcación; cruz. **2,** *anat.* ingle. **3,** (of trousers) entrepierna.
crotchety (ˈkratʃ·ɪt·i) *adj.* excéntrico; chiflado; extravagante.
crouch (krautʃ) *v.i.* agacharse; ponerse en cuclillas. —*n.* inclinación del cuerpo; posición agachada.
croup (krup) *n.* **1,** (ailment) tos ferina. **2,** (rump) anca; grupa. —**croupy,** *adj.* con *o* de tos ferina.
croupier (ˈkru·pi·ər) *n.* crupié.
crouton (ˈkru·tan) *n.* cuscurro.
crow (kroː) *v.i.* **1,** [*pret.* **crowed** *o* **crew**] (cry, as a rooster) cantar el gallo; cacarear. **2,** (brag) gallear; alardear; presumir. —*n.* **1,** (rooster's cry) canto del gallo; cacareo. **2,** (bird) cuervo; corneja.
crowbar *n.* palanca de hierro.
crowd (kraud) *n.* **1,** (throng) muchedumbre; gentío; multitud. **2,** (the populace) populacho; plebe. **3,** *colloq.* (coterie) círculo; pandilla; grupo. —*v.t.* **1,** (cram) apretar; estrechar. **2,** (fill to excess) amontonar; agolpar; apiñar. —*v.i.* pulular; amontonarse; agolparse. —**be crowded,** estar de bote en bote.
crown (kraun) *n.* **1,** (of a monarch) corona. **2,** (wreath for the head) diadema. **3,** (summit) corona; cima; cumbre. **4,** (of a tooth) colmo *o* corona del diente. **5,** (English coin) corona. —*v.t.* **1,** (put a crown on) coronar. **2,** (confer honor upon) premiar; recompensar; honrar. **3,** (finish) coronar; culminar; completar. **4,** *colloq.* (hit on the head) golpear en la cabeza. —**crown jewels,** joyas de la corona. —**crown prince,** príncipe heredero. —**crown princess,** princesa heredera.
crozier (ˈkro·ʒər) *n., eccles.* cayado.
crucial (ˈkru·ʃəl) *adj.* crucial; decisivo; crítico.
crucible (ˈkru·sə·bəl) *n.* crisol.
crucifer (ˈkru·sɪ·fər) *n.* crucero.
crucifix (ˈkru·sɪ·fɪks) *n.* crucifijo. —**crucifixion** (-ˈfɪk·ʃən) *n.* crucifixión.
crucify (ˈkru·sɪˌfai) *v.t.* **1,** (nail to a cross) crucificar; clavar en la cruz. **2,** *fig.* (mortify) mortificar.
crude (kruːd) *adj.* **1,** (raw) crudo; bruto. **2,** (unrefined) tosco; sin refinar. —**crudeness; crudity,** *n.* crudeza; aspereza; tosquedad.
cruel (ˈkru·əl) *adj.* cruel; implacable. —**cruelty,** *n.* crueldad.
cruet (ˈkru·ɪt) *n.* vinagrera.
cruise (kruːz) *v.i.* vagar; navegar. —*n.* crucero; viaje marítimo de placer.
cruiser (ˈkru·zər) *n.* crucero.
cruller (ˈkrʌl·ər) *n.* buñuelo; churro.
crumb (krʌm) *n.* **1,** (particle) migaja; miga. **2,** *slang* (insignificant person) don nadie; don pizca. —**crumby,** *adj.* de migajas.
crumble (ˈkrʌm·bəl) *v.t.* desmigajar; desmenuzar; hacer migas. —*v.i.* desmigajarse; desmenuzarse;

desmoronarse. —**crumbly** (-bli) *adj.* susceptible de desmigajarse.
crummy ('krʌm·i) *adj.*, *slang* asqueroso; despreciable.
crumpet ('krʌm·pɪt) *n.* mollete.
crumple ('krʌm·pəl) *v.t.* arrugar; ajar; encoger. —*v.i.* arrugarse; encogerse.
crunch (krʌntʃ) *v.t.* & *i.* mascar; tascar; cascar.
crusade (kru'seid) *n.* cruzada. —*v.i.* participar en una cruzada. —**crusader**, *n.* cruzado.
crush (krʌʃ) *v.t.* **1,** (mash) majar. **2,** (grind) moler; triturar. **3,** (conquer) arrollar; aplastar; vencer. —*v.i.* aplastarse; triturarse. —*n.* **1,** (pressure) trituración; aplastamiento. **2,** (crowd) agolpamiento; apiñamiento. **3,** *slang* (infatuation) apasionamiento.
crust (krʌst) *n.* **1,** (outer coating, as of bread or pie) costra; corteza. **2,** *slang* (insolence) nervio; descaro; insolencia.
crustacean (krʌs'tei·ʃən) *n.* & *adj.* crustáceo.
crusty ('krʌs·ti) *adj.* **1,** (having a crust) costroso; cortezoso. **2,** *fig.* (hard) duro; rudo; brusco.
crutch (krʌtʃ) *n.* **1,** (staff) muleta. **2,** *fig.* (support) ayuda; soporte.
crux (krʌks) *n.* **1,** (puzzling thing) enigma; misterio. **2,** (essential part) esencial; meollo.
cry (krai) *v.i.* **1,** (call loudly) gritar; exclamar; vocear. **2,** (weep) llorar; lamentarse. **3,** (call, as an animal) chillar; aullar; bramar. —*v.t.* **1,** (proclaim) promulgar; proclamar. **2,** (hawk wares) pregonar; vocear. —*n.* **1,** (outcry) grito; exclamación; alarido. **2,** (fit of weeping) lamento; lloro; clamor. —**a far cry,** mucho; lejos.
crybaby *n.*, *colloq.* llorón.
crypt (krɪpt) *n.* **1,** (cave) cripta; gruta. **2,** (secret code) clave; cifra.
cryptic ('krɪp·tɪk) *adj.* secreto; misterioso; oculto.
crypt- (krɪpt) *prefijo, var. de* **crypto-** *ante vocal: cryptanalysis,* criptoanálisis.
crypto- (krɪp·to) *prefijo* cripto-; oculto: *cryptogram,* criptograma.
cryptograph ('krɪp·tə·græf) *n.* **1,** (device) criptógrafo. **2,** [*también,* **cryptogram** (-græm)] (message) criptograma.
cryptographer (krɪp'tag·rə·fər) *n.* criptógrafo.
cryptographic (ˌkrɪp·tə'græf·ɪk) *adj.* criptográfico.
cryptography (krɪp'tag·rə·fi) *n.* criptografía.
crystal ('krɪs·təl) *n.* cristal. —**crystalline** (-tə·lɪn) *adj.* cristalino.
crystallize ('krɪs·təˌlaiz) *v.t.* & *i.* cristalizar. —**crystallization** (-lɪ'zei·ʃən) *n.* cristalización.
cub (kʌb) *n.* **1,** (young animal) cachorro. **2,** *fig.* (child) cachorro; criatura. **3,** *colloq.*, (tyro) novato; principiante. —*adj.* sin experiencia.
cubbyhole ('kʌb·iˌhoːl) *n.* **1,** (small room) cubículo; aposento. **2,** (compartment) casilla; compartimiento.
cube (kjuːb) *n.* cubo. —*v.t.* **1,** *math.* cubicar; elevar al cubo. **2,** (cut into cubes) hacer *o* cortar en cubos. **3,** (measure) cubicar. —**cube root,** raíz cúbica.
cubic ('kju·bɪk) *adj.* cúbico.
cubicle ('kju·bə·kəl) *n.* cubículo.
cubism ('kju·bɪz·əm) *n.* cubismo. —**cubist,** *n.* & *adj.* cubista.
cuckold ('kʌk·əld) *n.* & *adj.* cornudo. —*v.t.* poner cuernos a.
cuckoo ('ku·ku) *n.* cuco. —*adj.*, *slang* alocado; loco. —**cuckoo clock,** reloj de cuco.
cucumber ('kju·kʌm·bər) *n.* pepino; cohombro.
cud (kʌd) *n.* bolo de alimento a medio mascar. —**chew the cud,** rumiar.
cuddle ('kʌd·əl) *v.t.* abrazar; acariciar; acunar. —*v.i.* estar abrazado. —**cuddly** (-li) [*también,* **cuddlesome** (-səm)] *adj.* querendón.
cudgel ('kʌdʒ·əl) *n.* porra. —*v.t.* aporrear; dar golpes de *o* con porra. —**cudgel one's brains,** devanarse los sesos.
cue (kjuː) *n.* **1,** (hint) sugerencia; idea. **2,** *theat.* apunte. **3,** *billiards* taco. **4,** (pigtail) rabo; cola. **5,** (queue; line) cola; fila. —*v.t.*, *theat.* apuntar.
cuff (kʌf) *n.* **1,** (end, as of a sleeve) puño; bocamanga. **2,** (slap) bofetón; bofetada; puñetazo. —*v.t.* abofetear. —**on the cuff,** *slang* a plazos; a crédito.
cuff links gemelos.
cuirass (kwɪ'ræs) *n.* coraza.
cuisine (kwɪ'ziːn) *n.* cocina.
-cule (kjul) *sufijo* -culo; -cula; *forma diminutivos de nombres y*

adjetivos: minuscule, minúsculo; *molecule,* molécula.
culinary ('kju·lə·nɛr·i) *adj.* culinario.
cull (kʌl) *n.* desperdicio. —*v.t.* escoger; elegir lo mejor.
culminate ('kʌl·mɪ·neit) *v.i.* culminar. —**culmination**, *n.* culminación.
culottes (kju'lats) *n.pl.* falda pantalón (*sing.*).
culpable ('kʌl·pə·bəl) *adj.* culpable. —**culpability**, *n.* culpabilidad.
culprit ('kʌl·prɪt) *n.* ofensor; reo; delincuente.
cult (kʌlt) *n.* culto.
cultivate ('kʌl·tə·veit) *v.t.* **1,** (till) cultivar; labrar. **2,** (foster) cultivar; promover; favorecer; impulsar. **3,** (refine) cultivar; estudiar. **4,** (develop) desarrollar; perfeccionar. —**cultivation**, *n.* cultivo; educación.
cultivated ('kul·tə,ve·tɪd) *adj.* **1,** (tilled) cultivado. **2,** (trained; refined) educado; instruido.
cultivator ('kul·tə,vei·tər) *n.* **1,** (grower) cultivador. **2,** (machine) cultivadora.
culture ('kʌl·tʃər) *n.* **1,** (civilization) cultura. **2,** (growth of bacteria) cultivo. **3,** (tillage) cultivo; labranza; labor. **4,** (refinement) cultura; conocimiento; educación. —**cultural**, *adj.* cultural.
cultured ('kʌl·tʃərd) *adj.* **1,** (tilled) cultivado. **2,** (refined) culto; instruido.
cumbersome ('kʌm·bər·səm) *adj.* pesado; incómodo; fastidioso; molesto. *También,* **cumbrous** (-brəs).
cumulative ('kju·mjə·le·tɪv) *adj.* acumulativo.
cumulus ('kju·mjə·ləs) *n.* [*pl.* **cumuli** (-lai)] cúmulo.
cuneiform (kju'ni·ə·form) *n.* & *adj.* cuneiforme.
cunning ('kʌn·ɪŋ) *adj.* ingenioso; astuto; socarrón. —*n.* astucia; ardid; marrullería.
cup (kʌp) *n.* **1,** (vessel) copa; taza; jícara. **2,** (chalice) cáliz. —**cupful**, *n.* una taza. —**cupped** (kʌpt) *adj.* en forma de copa. —**in one's cups**, ebrio.
cupboard ('kʌb·ərd) *n.* aparador; chinero.
cupid ('kju·pɪd) *n.* cupido; Cupido.
cupidity (kju'pɪd·ə·ti) *n.* codicia; avaricia.
cupola ('kju·pə·lə) *n.* cúpula.
cur (kʌɹ) *n.* **1,** (dog) perro de mala casta. **2,** *colloq.* (evil man) perro; canalla.
curable ('kjʊr·ə·bəl) *adj.* curable.
curate ('kjʊr·ɪt) *n.* cura. —**curacy** (-ə·si) *n.* curato.
curative ('kjʊr·ə·tɪv) *adj.* curativo. —*n.* curativa.
curator (kju'rei·tər) *n.* curador; conservador.
curb (kʌɹb) *v.t.* refrenar; poner freno; contener; sujetar. —*n.* **1,** (restraint) sujeción; freno; restricción. **2,** (bridle) freno; barbada. **3,** [*también,* **curbstone**] bordillo *o* borde de acera. **4,** (minor securities market) lonja; bolsín.
curd (kʌɹd) *n.* cuajada; requesón.
curdle ('kʌɹ·dəl) *v.t.* cuajar; coagular. —*v.i.* cuajarse; coagularse. —**curdle one's blood**, helarse la sangre.
cure (kjʊr) *n.* **1,** (healing) curación. **2,** (treatment) cura. **3,** (remedy) remedio. —*v.t.* **1,** (heal) curar; sanar. **2,** (remedy) remediar. **3,** (dry or salt, as meat) curar.
curé (kju're:) *n.* cura; párroco.
cure-all *n.* cúralotodo.
curfew ('kʌɹ·fju) *n.* toque de queda.
curie (kjʊ'ri) *n., physics* curie.
curio ('kjʊ·ri·o) *n.* [*pl.* **-os**] objeto curioso; curiosidad.
curiosity (,kjʊr·i'as·ə·ti) *n.* curiosidad; rareza.
curious ('kjʊr·i·əs) *adj.* **1,** (inquisitive) curioso; deseoso. **2,** (strange) raro; curioso; extraño.
curium ('kjʊr·i·əm) *n.* curio.
curl (kʌɹl) *n.* **1,** (of hair) rizo; bucle; *Amer.* crespo. **2,** (spiral) rollo; espiral; ondulación; sinuosidad. —*v.t.* & *i.* rizar; enrollar; ondular. —**curler**, *n.* rizador. —**curly**, *adj.* rizado; enrollado; rizo.
curlew (kʌɹ'lu:) *n.* chorlito.
curmudgeon (kər'mʌdʒ·ən) *n.* erizo; cicatero; camorrista.
currant ('kʌr·ənt) *n.* **1,** (bush) grosellero; **2,** (berry) grosella. **3,** (raisin) pasa de Corinto.
currency ('kʌr·ən·si) *n.* **1,** (currentness) circulación; uso corriente. **2,** (money) moneda en circulación.
current ('kʌr·ənt) *adj.* **1,** (prevalent) corriente; común; ordinario. **2,** (contemporary) actual; presente.

—*n.* 1, (stream) corriente. 2, (trend) corriente; curso; marcha.
curriculum (kəˈrɪk·jə·ləm) *n.* 1, (study plan) plan de estudios. 2, (routine) plan; programa. —**curriculum vitae** (ˈvai·ti) historial. —**curricular** (-lər) *adj.* de un plan de estudios.
curry (ˈkʌɹ·i) *v.t.* 1, (comb) almohazar. 2, (dress leather) curtir; adobar. —*n.* cari. —**curry favor,** pedir favores adulando.
currycomb *n.* almohaza. —*v.t.* almohazar.
curse (kʌɹs) *n.* 1, (invocation of evil) maldición; anatema. 2, (profane oath) imprecación; blasfemia. 3, (bane) aflicción; azote; castigo; ruina. —*v.t.* 1, (invoke evil on) maldecir; anatematizar. 2, (swear at) renegar de. 3, (blaspheme) blasfemar. 4, (harm) dañar; ofender. —*v.i.* jurar en vano; blasfemar. —**cursed** (ˈkʌɹ·sɪd) *adj.* maldecido; maldito; abominable. —**cursedness,** *n.* maldición.
cursive (ˈkʌɹ·sɪv) *adj.* cursivo.
cursory (ˈkʌɹ·sə·ri) *adj.* precipitado; rápido; superficial.
curt (kʌɹt) *adj.* 1, (short) corto; sucinto; breve. 2, (abrupt) rudo; abrupto; tosco.
curtail (kərˈteil) *v.t.* 1, (cut short) cortar; abreviar; reducir. 2, (deprive of) privar de; restringir; circunscribir. —**curtailment,** *n.* abreviación; reducción.
curtain (ˈkʌɹ·tən) *n.* 1, (drape) cortina. 2, *theat.* telón. —*v.t.* 1, (drape) poner cortinas a. 2, (conceal) ocultar; encubrir. —**curtain call,** salida *o* llamada a las candilejas. —**curtain off,** separar con cortinas. —**curtain raiser,** entremés.
curtness (ˈkʌɹt·nəs) *n.* 1, (shortness) brevedad; concisión. 2, (abruptness) tosquedad; rudeza.
curtsy *también,* **curtsey** (ˈkʌɹt·si) *n.* reverencia; cortesía.
curvature (ˈkʌɹ·və·tʃur) *n.* curvatura.
curve (kʌɹv) *n.* curva. —*v.t.* & *i.* curvar; torcer.
cushion (ˈkuʃ·ən) *n.* 1, (pillow) cojín; almohadón; almohadilla. 2, (rim of billiard table) banda. —*v.t.* 1, (pillow) poner cojines a; cubrir con cojines. 2, (absorb the shock of) amortiguar; suavizar.
cusp (kʌsp) *n.* cúspide.
cuspid (ˈkʌs·pɪd) *n.* cúspide.
custard (ˈkʌs·tərd) *n.* flan.
custard apple anón; anona.
custodian (kəsˈto·di·ən) *n.* custodio; guardián; encargado.
custody (ˈkʌs·tə·di) *n.* 1, (guardianship) custodia; cuidado; guardia. 2, *law* (arrest) seguridad; prisión; arresto.
custom (ˈkʌs·təm) *n.* 1, (habit) costumbre; usanza; uso. 2, (patronage) clientela; parroquia. 3, *pl.* (import taxes) derechos de aduana. —**customhouse,** aduana. —**custom-made,** hecho a la medida.
customary (ˈkʌs·təˌmɛr·i) *adj.* acostumbrado; usual.
customer (ˈkʌs·tə·mər) *n.* cliente; parroquiano.
cut (kʌt) *v.t.* [**cut, cutting**] 1, (sever) cortar; partir. 2, (trim) recortar; desbastar. 3, (reap) segar. 4, (intersect) cortar; cruzar. 5, (divide into parts) cortar; dividir. 6, (insult) lastimar; herir; insultar. 7, *slang* (hit) golpear. 8, (abridge) reducir; abreviar. 9, (ignore) extrañar; ignorar; negar el saludo a. 10, *colloq.* (fail to attend) faltar a; dejar de ir. —*v.i.* 1, (slit) hacer corte *o* incisión; cortar. 2, (admit of being cut) cortarse; poderse cortar. 3, (go by a shorter route) atajar. —*n.* 1, (incision) corte; cortadura; *Amer.* cortada. 2, *print.* grabado. —*adj.* 1, (made by cutting) cortado. 2, (carved) tallado. 3, (lessened) rebajado; reducido. —**cut and dried,** preparado. —**cut back,** 1, (turn back) cambiar; volver. 2, (shorten) acortar. —**cut down,** 1, (kill) matar. 2, (fell) talar; derribar. 3, (abridge) condensar; resumir. —**cut in,** 1, (move in sharply) cortar; introducirse rápidamente. 2, (interrupt) intercalar; introducir. —**cut off,** 1, (intercept) cortar; interrumpir; interceptar. 2, (shut out) excluir; abandonar; olvidar. 3, (halt suddenly) parar repentinamente; suspender. 4, (disinherit) desheredar. —**cut out,** 1, (apt; suited) adecuado; apto. 2, *slang* (cease) dejar; dejarse de. —**cut up,** *slang* hacer el tonto; bromear.
cutaway *n.* chaqué. *También,* **cutaway coat.**
cute (kjut) *adj., colloq.* mono; lindo; atractivo. —**cuteness,** *n.* monería; lindeza; atractivo.
cuticle (ˈkju·tə·kəl) *n.* cutícula.

cutlass ('kʌt·ləs) *n.* alfanje.
cutler ('kʌt·lər) *n.* cuchillero.
cutlery ('kʌt·lə·ri) *n.* cuchillería.
cutlet ('kʌt·lət) *n.* **1,** (slice of meat) chuleta. **2,** (croquette) croqueta.
cutter ('kʌt·ər) *n.* **1,** (person or thing that cuts) cortador. **2,** *naval* cúter. **3,** (sleigh) trineíllo.
cutthroat ('kʌt,θrot) *n.* asesino; criminal. —*adj.* implacable; criminal; asesino.
cuttlefish ('kʌt·əl·fɪʃ) *n.* jibia; calamar.
cutwater *n.* tajamar.
-cy (si) *sufijo* -cia; *forma nombres denotando* **1,** cualidad: *expediency,* conveniencia. **2,** entes abstractos: *autocracy,* autocracia. **3,** artes; profesiones: *necromancy,* nigromancia. **4,** empleo: *captaincy,* capitanía.
cyanide ('sai·ə,naid) *n.* cianuro.
cyanogen (sai'æn·ə·dʒən) *n.* cianógeno.
cyanosis (,sai·ə'no·sɪs) *n.* cianosis.
cycle ('sai·kəl) *n.* **1,** (era) ciclo; período. **2,** (series) curso. —*v.i.* montar en bicicleta. —**cycling** (-klɪŋ) *n.* ciclismo.
cyclic ('sai·klɪk; 'sɪ-) *adj.* cíclico. *También,* **cyclical.**
cyclist ('sai·klɪst) *n.* ciclista.
cyclo- (sai·klo) *prefijo* ciclo-; círculo; circular: *cyclorama,* ciclorama.
cycloid ('sai·klɔid) *n.* cicloide. —**cycloidal** (-'klɔi·dəl) *adj.* cicloidal; cicloideo.
cyclone ('sai·klon) *n.* ciclón; huracán. —**cyclonic** (-'klan·ɪk) *adj.* ciclónico; ciclonal.
cyclopedia (,sai·klə'pi·di·ə) *n.* enciclopedia. —**cyclopedic,** *adj.* enciclopédico.
Cyclops ('sai·klaps) *n.* Cíclope. —**Cyclopean** (-klə'pi·ən) *adj.* ciclópeo.
cyclorama (,sai·klə'ræm·ə) *n.* ciclorama.
cyclotron ('sai·klə,tran) *n.* ciclotrón.
cylinder ('sɪl·ɪn·dər) *n.* cilindro. —**cylindrical** (sə'lɪn·drɪ·kəl) *adj.* cilíndrico.
cymbal ('sɪm·bəl) *n.* címbalo. —**cymbalist,** *adj.* cimbalista; cimbalero.
cynic ('sɪn·ɪk) *n.* cínico. —**cynicism** (-ɪ,sɪz·əm) *n.* cinismo. —**cynical** (-ɪ·kəl) *adj.* cínico.
cynosure ('sai·nə,ʃur) *n.* **1,** (center of attention) cinosura; centro de atracción. **2,** *cap., astron.* Osa Menor.
cypher ('sai·fər) *n.* & *v.t.* & *i.* = **cipher.**
cypress ('sai·prəs) *n.* ciprés.
Cyrillic (sɪ'rɪl·ɪk) *adj.* & *n.* cirílico.
cyst (sɪst) *n.* quiste. —**cystic,** *adj.* cístico; del quiste.
cystitis (sɪs'tai·tɪs) *n.* cistitis.
cystology (sɪs'tal·ə·dʒi) *n.* cistología.
cystoscope ('sɪs·tə,skop) *n.* cistoscopio.
-cyte (sait) *sufijo* -cito; célula: *thrombocyte,* trombocito.
cyto- (sai·to) *prefijo* cito-; célula: *cytology,* citología.
cytology (sai'tal·ə·dʒi) *n.* citología. —**cytological** (-tə'ladʒ·ɪ·kəl) *adj.* citológico. —**cytologist,** *n.* citólogo.
cytoplasm ('sai·tə,plæz·əm) *n.* citoplasma.
czar *también,* **tsar** (zaːr; tsaːr) *n.* **1,** (emperor) zar. **2,** *fig.* (dictator) déspota; autócrata. —**czarevitch** (-ə·vɪtʃ) *n.* zarevitz. —**czarevna** (zar'ɛv·nə) *n.* zarevna. —**czarina** (zar'i·nə) *n.* zarina.
Czech (tʃɛk) *n.* & *adj.* checo.
Czechoslovak (,tʃɛk·o'slo·vak) *n.* & *adj.* [*también,* **Czechoslovakian** (,tʃɛk·ə·slo'vak·i·ən)] checoslovaco; checoeslovaco.

D

D, d (diː) cuarta letra del alfabeto inglés. —*n., music* re.
dab (dæb) *v.t.* & *i.* [**dabbed, dabbing**] **1,** (pat) frotar suavemente; golpear levemente. **2,** (moisten) humedecer. —*n.* **1,** (pat) golpe suave; sopapo. **2,** (bit) trocito; salpicadura.
dabble ('dæb·əl) *v.i.* **1,** (splash in water) salpicar; rociar. **2,** (do in a superficial way) chapucear. —**dabbler** (-lər) *n.* chapucero.

dachshund ('daks·hund) *n.* perro pachón.
dactyl ('dæk·təl) *n.* dáctilo. —**dactylic** (-'tɪl·ɪk) *adj.* dactílico.
dad (dæːd) *n., colloq.* papá; padre. *También,* **daddy** ('dæd·i).
dado ('dei·do) *n.* friso; zócalo.
daffodil ('dæf·ə·dɪl) *n.* narciso.
daffy ('dæf·i) *adj., slang* loco; tonto; bobo. —**daffiness,** *n., slang* bobería; tontería.
daft (dæft) *adj.* loco; tonto.
dagger ('dæg·ər) *n.* **1,** (knife) daga; estilete; puñal. **2,** *print.* (†) cruz.
daguerreotype (də'gɛr·əˌtaip) *n.* daguerrotipo.
dahlia ('dæl·ja; 'dal-) *n.* dalia.
daily ('dei·li) *adj.* diario; cotidiano. —*adv.* diariamente; todos los días. —*n.* diario; periódico.
dainty ('dein·ti) *adj.* **1,** (delicate) delicado; fino; precioso. **2,** (of refined taste) gustoso; sabroso; exquisito. **3,** (fastidious) melindroso; afectado. —*n.* confitura; golosina. —**daintiness,** *n.* exquisitez.
dairy ('dɛr·i) *n.* **1,** (milk farm) granja; vaquería. **2,** (enterprise) compañía de productos lácteos.
dairymaid *n.* lechera.
dairyman ('dɛr·i·mən) *n.* [*pl.* **-men**] lechero.
dais ('dei·ɪs) *n.* tribuna; estrado.
daisy ('dei·zi) *n.* margarita.
dale (deil) *n.* valle.
dally ('dæl·i) *v.i.* **1,** (trifle) juguetear; entretener. **2,** (idle) tardar; dilatar.
Dalmation (dæl'mei·ʃən) *adj.* & *n.* dálmata. —*n.* (dog) perro dálmata.
Daltonism ('dɔl·təˌnɪz·əm) *n.* daltonismo.
dam (dæːm) *n.* **1,** (wall to stop water) presa; pantano. **2,** (mare) yegua. —*v.t.* [**dammed, damming**] **1,** (build a dam) estancar; represar. **2,** (confine) detener; contener. **3,** (shut up) cerrar.
damage ('dæm·ɪdʒ) *n.* **1,** (injury) daño; estropeo. **2,** *pl., law* indemnización (*sing.*); daños y perjuicios. —*v.t.* perjudicar; ofender.
damask ('dæm·əsk) *n.* damasco. —*adj.* adamascado.
dame (deim) *n.* **1,** (a woman) dama; señora. **2,** *cap., Brit.* baronesa.
damn (dæːm) *v.t.* **1,** (condemn) condenar. **2,** (curse) maldecir. **3,** (censure) vituperar. —*n.* juramento; maldición. —*interj.* ¡maldito sea! —**damnable** ('dæm·nə·bəl) *adj.* condenable; detestable. —**damned** (dæːmd) *adj.* maldito; condenado.
damnation (dæm'nei·ʃən) *n.* condenación.
damp (dæmp) *adj.* húmedo; mojado. —*n.* **1,** (moisture) humedad. **2,** (poisonous vapor) emanación. —*v.t.* **1,** (moisten) humedecer; remojar. **2,** (dispirit) desanimar; enfriar. **3,** (smother) extinguir; apagar. —**dampness,** *n.* humedad.
dampen ('dæm·pən) *v.t.* **1,** (wet) humedecer; remojar. **2,** (dishearten) desanimar; desalentar.
damper ('dæm·pər) *n.* **1,** (of a flue) regulador de tiro. **2,** (of a piano) sordina. **3,** *fig.* (disheartening person or thing) desalentador; aguafiestas.
damsel ('dæm·zəl) *n.* damisela; señorita.
damson ('dæm·zən) *n.* damasco. *También,* **damson plum.**
dance (dæns) *v.i.* **1,** (move rhythmically) danzar; bailar. **2,** (quiver) saltar; brincar. **3,** (bounce) botar; brincar. —*v.t.* **1,** (make dance) hacer bailar; llevar a bailar. **2,** (perform, as a dance) bailar. **3,** (bounce up and down) balancear; hacer saltar. —*n.* danza; baile. —**dancer,** *n.* bailarín; *fem.* bailarina.
dandelion ('dæn·diˌlai·ən) *n.* diente de león.
dandruff ('dæn·drəf) *n.* caspa.
dandy ('dæn·di) *n.* **1,** (fop) petimetre; presumido. **2,** *colloq.* (an excellent thing) belleza; primor. —*adj., colloq.* perfecto; estupendo.
Dane (dein) *n.* danés; dinamarqués.
danger ('dein·dʒər) *n.* peligro; riesgo. —**dangerous,** *adj.* peligroso; arriesgado. —**be in danger,** correr peligro.
dangle ('dæŋ·gəl) *v.t.* colgar; suspender. —*v.i.* colgarse; bambolearse; quedar *o* estar colgado.
Danish ('dei·nɪʃ) *adj.* & *n.* danés; dinamarqués.
dank (dæŋk) *adj.* viscoso; húmedo; mojado. —**dankness,** *n.* viscosidad; humedad.
dapper ('dæp·ər) *adj.* **1,** (trim) impecable; nítido; apuesto. **2,** (small and lively) vivaracho; vivaz.
dapple ('dæp·əl) *v.t.* motear; salpicar. —**dappled,** *adj.* rodado.

dare (deːr) *v.t.* **1,** (challenge) desafiar; retar. **2,** (face boldly) enfrentar; hacer frente a. —*v.i.* [*pret.* **dared** *o* **durst** (dʌɹst)] atreverse; arriesgarse.

daredevil (ˈdɛrˌdɛv·əl) *n.* atrevido; aventurero; temerario. —*adj.* intrépido; valeroso; aventurado. —**daredeviltry** (-tri) *n.* intrepidez; temeridad.

daring (ˈdɛr·ɪŋ) *n.* valentía; intrepidez. —*adj.* intrépido; temerario.

dark (dark) *adj.* **1,** (unlighted) oscuro; apagado. **2,** (deep in color, as skin) moreno; oscuro; trigueño. **3,** (dreary) desconsolador; triste. **4,** (concealed) oscuro; oculto. **5,** (sinister) difícil; siniestro; amenazador. —*n.* **1,** (absence of light) oscuridad; tenebrosidad. **2,** (nightfall) noche. **3,** (secrecy) secreto; enigma. **4,** (ignorance) oscuridad; ignorancia; desconocimiento. **5,** *painting* (shadow) sombra. —**be in the dark,** ofuscarse. —**become** [*o, colloq.,* **get**] **dark,** anochecer.

darken (ˈdar·kən) *v.t.* **1,** (make dark) oscurecer. **2,** (shut off) apagar. **3,** (blacken) ennegrecer. **4,** (conceal) ocultar. **5,** (sadden) contristar; deprimir. **6,** (harm) manchar; denigrar. **7,** (confound) confundir; ofuscar. —*v.i.* **1,** (become dark) oscurecerse. **2,** (be shut off) apagarse. **3,** (become blackened) ennegrecerse. **4,** (be concealed) no verse claro; estar oculto. **5,** (become dreary) deprimirse; desfallecer. **6,** (be harmed) mancharse. **7,** (be confused) ofuscarse; confundirse.

dark horse **1,** (candidate) candidato inesperado. **2,** (winner) vencedor inesperado.

darkness (ˈdark·nɪs) *n.* oscuridad.

darkroom *n.* cámara oscura.

darling (ˈdar·lɪŋ) *n.* querido; cariño. —*adj.* querido; amado; favorito.

darn (darn) *v.t.* **1,** (mend) zurcir; repasar. **2,** *colloq.* (damn) maldecir. —*adj., colloq.* [*también,* **darned**] maldito; condenado. —*n.* **1,** (mend) zurcido; cosido. **2,** (oath) juramento *o* maldición leve.

darnel (ˈdar·nəl) *n., bot.* cizaña.

dart (dart) *n.* **1,** (missile) dardo; flecha. **2,** *pl.* (game) dardos. **3,** (dash) salpicadura; rociadura. —*v.t.* **1,** (thrust) echar; tirar. **2,** (start) arrancar; flechar. —*v.i.* disparar como dardo.

dash (dæʃ) *v.t.* **1,** (smash) disparar. **2,** (sprinkle) rociar; salpicar. **3,** (season lightly) sazonar. **4,** (frustrate) malograr; frustrar. —*v.i.* **1,** (crash) chocar; estrellarse. **2,** (rush) lanzarse; abalanzarse. —*n.* **1,** (sudden thrust) arranque; embestida. **2,** (bit, as a flavor) condimento; *W.I.; C.A.; Mex.* sazón. **3,** *slang* (vigorous or dramatic behavior) gran papel. **4,** (punctuation) guión. **5,** *teleg.* raya. **6,** (rush) embestida; arranque. —**cut a dash,** *colloq.* hacer un gran papel. —**dash off** (a letter, etc.) escribir rápidamente; (a sketch) esbozar. —**dash one's hopes to the ground,** dejar a uno con un palmo de narices. —**dash to pieces,** estrellar; estrellarse.

dashboard *n.* **1,** (splashboard) guardafangos; cristal. **2,** (in a vehicle) tablero de instrumentos.

dasher (ˈdæʃ·ər) *n., mech.* agitador.

dashing (ˈdæʃ·ɪŋ) *adj.* atrayente; vistoso.

dastard (ˈdæs·tərd) *n.* cobarde. —**dastardly,** *adj.* cobarde.

data (ˈdei·tə) *n.pl.* [*sing.* **datum** (-təm)] hechos; datos.

date (deit) *n.* **1,** (point in time) fecha; día. **2,** *law* fecha; plazo. **3,** *colloq.* (engagement) cita. **4,** (a fruit) dátil. —*v.t.* **1,** (mark with a time) fechar; poner fecha a. **2,** (note the date of) computar; contar. **3,** *colloq.* (meet with) salir con. —*v.i.* datar. —**out of date,** antiguo; pasado. —**to date,** hasta la fecha; hasta hoy. —**up to date,** **1,** (current; informed) al día. **2,** (in vogue) del día.

dated (ˈdei·tɪd) *adj.* **1,** (marked with a date) fechado. **2,** *colloq.* (old-fashioned) pasado; antiguo.

dative (ˈdei·tɪv) *n.* & *adj.* dativo.

datum (ˈdei·təm) *n.* [*pl.* **data**] dato.

daub (dɔːb) *v.t.* **1,** (smear) embarrar; manchar. **2,** (paint coarsely) pintorrear; pintarrajar. —*n.* **1,** (smear) mancha; embarradura. **2,** (inartistic painting) mamarracho; mamarrachada. —**dauber,** *n.* pintor de brocha gorda.

daughter (ˈdɔ·tər) *n.* hija.

daughter-in-law *n.* [*pl.* **daughters-in-law**] nuera; hija política.
daughterly (ˈdɔ·tər·li) *adj.* filial; de *o* como hija.
daunt (dɔnt) *v.t.* **1,** (make afraid) amedrentar; intimidar. **2,** (discourage) desalentar; desanimar. —**dauntless,** *adj.* intrépido; valiente.
dauphin (ˈdɔ·fɪn) *n.* delfín.
davenport (ˈdæv·ən,port) *n.* sofá cama; canapé.
davit (ˈdæv·ɪt) *n.* pescante de bote.
dawdle (ˈdɔ·dəl) *v.t.* & *i.* holgazanear; perder el tiempo; tontear.
day (dei) *n.* **1,** (division of time) día. **2,** *usu. pl.* (epoch) tiempos; días; época (*sing.*). **3,** *slang* (a hard time) lid; jornada. —**by day,** de día. —**day after day,** día tras día. —**day after tomorrow,** pasado mañana. —**day before,** víspera. —**day before yesterday,** anteayer. —**day by day,** día a día. —**every other day,** un día sí y otro no. —**from day to day,** de día en día. —**the next day,** el día siguiente.
day bed sofá cama.
daybreak *n.* amanecer; aurora.
daydream *n.* sueño. —*v.t.* soñar despierto.
daylight *n.* luz natural; luz diurna.
day school 1, (school with daytime hours) escuela diurna. **2,** (school whose pupils live at home) externado.
daytime *n.* día. —**in the daytime,** de día.
daze (deiz) *n.* ofuscación; ofuscamiento; aturdimiento. —*v.t.* ofuscar; aturdir.
dazzle (ˈdæz·əl) *v.t.* deslumbrar; ofuscar.
de- (di) *prefijo* de-; des-. **1,** disminución: *degrade,* degradar. **2,** privación: *dethrone,* destronar. **3,** sentido contrario: *decentralize,* descentralizar. **4,** negación: *demerit,* demérito. **5,** intensificación: *decompound,* volver a componer.
deacon (ˈdi·kən) *n.* diácono. —**deaconess,** *n.* diaconisa.
dead (dɛd) *adj.* **1,** (deceased) muerto; fallecido; difunto. **2,** (numb) insensible. **3,** (inert) inerte; inmóvil. **4,** (complete) completo; total; absoluto. **5,** (useless) inútil; inactivo; inservible. **6,** (unprofitable) improductivo; baldío. **7,** *slang* (tired) cansado; entregado; exhausto. —*adv.* por completo; totalmente. —*n.* **1,** (that which no longer exists) muerto; fallecido; difunto. **2,** (culminating point) profundidad. —**dead reckoning,** estima. —**dead weight,** peso muerto; *fig.* (heavy burden) carga onerosa.
deaden (ˈdɛd·ən) *v.t.* **1,** (muffle) amortiguar; parar. **2,** (retard) retardar; retrasar. **3,** (dull) apagar; embotar.
dead end 1, (street without an exit) camino sin salida. **2,** *colloq.* (impasse) punto muerto. —**dead-end,** *adj.* sin salida.
dead letter carta no reclamada; *fig.* costumbre *o* ley desusada.
deadline *n.* límite; término; plazo.
deadlock *n.* punto muerto; estancamiento. —*v.t.* estancar. —*v.i.* estancarse.
deadly (ˈdɛd·li) *adj.* **1,** (lethal) mortal; letal. **2,** *fig.* (relentless) implacable. **3,** *colloq.* (dull) pesado; soso; aburrido. —**deadliness,** *n.* calidad de mortífero; peligro mortal.
deadpan *adj., slang* inmutable; inescrutable. —*n., slang* cara inexpresiva.
deaf (dɛf) *adj.* sordo. —**deafness,** *n.* sordera.
deafen (ˈdɛf·ən) *v.t.* **1,** (make deaf) ensordar. **2,** (seem too loud) ensordecer. —**deafening,** *adj.* ensordecedor.
deafmute *n.* sordomudo.
deal (di:l) *v.t.* [*pret.* & *p.p.* **dealt**] **1,** (apportion; distribute) distribuir; repartir. **2,** (administer, as a blow) asestar. **3,** (distribute, as cards) dar. —*v.i.* **1,** [*usu.,* **deal with**] (negotiate) entenderse (con); (transact business) tratar (con). **2,** [*usu.,* **deal with**] (cope) ocuparse (de *o* en); tratar (con *o* de). **3,** (comport oneself) comportarse; portarse. **4,** [*usu.,* **deal in**] (trade; conduct a business) comerciar; negociar; traficar. **5,** (distribute cards) dar cartas. —*n.* **1,** (portion) porción; parte; trozo. **2,** (transaction) trato; negocio. **3,** *colloq.* (private pact) acuerdo. **4,** (distribution of cards) reparto de cartas. **5,** (wood) madero de pino *o* abeto. —**deal dishonestly with,** abusar de; engañar. —**a good deal** (a large quantity) bastante. —**a great deal** (a very large quantity) mucho.
dealer (ˈdi·lər) *n.* **1,** *comm.* (tradesman) comerciante; negociante. **2,**

(distributor) repartidor. —**dealership**, *n.* exclusiva.

dealing ('di·liŋ) *n.* **1,** (treatment of others) comportamiento; proceder; trato. **2,** *comm.* (distribution) distribución. **3,** *comm., usu.pl.* (transactions) transacciones.

dealt (dɛlt) *v., pret. & p.p. de* **deal.**

dean (din) *n.* **1,** *eccles.* deán. **2,** (senior member of a group) decano. —**deanship,** *n.* decanato.

dear (dɪːr) *adj.* **1,** (beloved) querido; caro; estimado. **2,** (valuable) valioso; estimable. **3,** (costly) caro; costoso. —*n.* querido; persona querida. —**Dear Sir,** Muy señor mío; Estimado señor. —**oh dear!**; **dear me!**, ¡válgame Dios!

dearness ('dɪr·nəs) *n.* **1,** (closeness) cariño; afecto. **2,** (kindness) benevolencia. **3,** (value) costo; valor; precio alto.

dearth (dʌɹθ) *n.* carestía; escasez.

death (dɛθ) *n.* **1,** (dying) muerte; fallecimiento. **2,** (plague) estrago; plaga. —**deathless,** *adj.* inmortal. —**death house,** capilla. —**death rate,** mortalidad; índice de mortalidad. —**be at death's door,** estar a la muerte. —**on pain of death,** bajo pena de muerte.

debacle (de'ba·kəl) *n.* **1,** (disaster; rout) desastre; derrota. **2,** (icebreaking) deshielo. **3,** (rush of waters) inundación.

debar (dɪ'bar) *v.t.* [**debarred, -barring**] **1,** (shut out) expulsar; despedir. **2,** (exclude) excluir; prohibir. —**debarment,** *n.* expulsión; exclusión.

debark (di'bark) *v.t. & i.* desembarcar.

debarkation (ˌdi·bar'kei·ʃən) *n.* **1,** (of passengers) desembarco. **2,** (of cargo) desembarque.

debase (di'beis) *v.t.* **1,** (degrade) degradar; rebajar; **2,** (adulterate) degenerar; envilecer. **3,** (lower in value) depreciar. —**debasement,** *n.* degradación; envilecimiento; depreciación.

debate (di'beit) *v.t. & i.* **1,** (argue) debatir; discutir; disputar. **2,** (consider) considerar; reflexionar; deliberar. —*n.* debate; discusión; controversia. —**debatable,** *adj.* debatible; disputable.

debauch (di'bɔtʃ) *v.t.* corromper; destruir; pervertir. —*v.i.* entregarse al vicio *o* al libertinaje. —*n.* libertinaje; corrupción; licencia. —**debauchee** (ˌdi·bɔ'tʃiː) *n.* libertino. —**debaucher,** *n.* seductor. —**debauchery** (-ə·ri) *n.* libertinaje; licencia; corrupción.

debilitate (dɪ'bɪl·ə·teit) *v.t.* debilitar. —**debilitation,** *n.* debilitación.

debility (dɪ'bɪl·ə·ti) *n.* debilidad.

debit ('dɛb·ɪt) *n., finance* **1,** (a charge) debe. **2,** (entry) cargo; adeudo. —*v.t.* adeudar; cargar.

debonair (ˌdɛb·ə'neːr) *adj.* **1,** (gay) alegre; vivaz. **2,** (courteous) afable; cortés; educado.

debris (də'briː) *n.* partícula; fragmento; residuo; *geol.* despojos (*pl.*).

debt (dɛt) *n.* deuda; obligación. —**debtor,** *n.* deudor.

debut (dɪ'bju) *n.* debut; estreno; primera presentación. —**debutante** (ˌdɛb·ju'tant) *n.* presentada en sociedad; puesta de largo; debutante.

deca- (dɛk·ə) *prefijo* deca-; diez: *decameter,* decámetro.

decade ('dɛk·eid) *n.* década.

decadence (dɪ'kei·dəns; 'dɛk·ə-) *n.* decadencia. —**decadent,** *adj.* decadente.

decagon ('dɛk·əˌgan) *n.* decágono.

decagram *n.* decagramo.

decahedron (dɛk·ə'hi·drən) *n.* decaedro.

decalcomania (dɪˌkæl·kə'mein·jə) *también, colloq.,* **decal** (di'kæl) *n.* calcomanía.

decaliter *n.* decalitro.

decalogue ('dɛk·əˌlɔg) *n.* decálogo.

decameter *n.* decámetro.

decamp (di'kæmp) *v.i.* **1,** (break camp) decampar. **2,** *slang* (depart) despedirse a la francesa.

decant (dɪ'kænt) *v.t.* decantar. —**decanter,** *n.* frasco; botella.

decapitate (dɪ'kæp·ɪ·teit) *v.t.* decapitar. —**decapitation,** *n.* decapitación.

decare ('dɛk·ɛr) *n.* decárea.

decastere ('dɛk·əˌstɪr) *n.* decastéreo.

decasyllable *n.* decasílabo. —**decasyllabic,** *adj.* decasílabo.

decathlon (dɪ'kæθ·lan) *n.* decatlon.

decay (dɪ'kei) *v.t.* podrir; corromper. —*v.i.* **1,** (decline) decaer; declinar. **2,** (rot) podrirse. **3,** *dent.* cariarse. —*n.* **1,** (decline) de-

caimiento. **2,** (rottenness) podredumbre. **3,** *dent.* caries.
decease (dɪ'sis) *n.* fallecimiento; muerte; óbito. —*v.i.* fallecer; morir. —**deceased** (-'sist) *n.* & *adj.* muerto; fallecido.
deceit (dɪ'sit) *n.* fraude; mentira; engaño. —**deceitful**, *adj.* mentiroso; fraudulento; engañoso. —**deceitfulness**, *n.* falsedad; duplicidad.
deceive (dɪ'si:v) *v.t.* engañar. —*v.i.* mentir.
decelerate (ˌdi'sɛl·ə·reit) *v.t.* retardar; disminuir. —*v.i.* retardarse. —**deceleration**, *n.* retardación; disminución.
December (di'sɛm·bər) *n.* diciembre.
decency ('di·sən·si) *n.* decencia.
decennial (dɪ'sɛn·i·əl) *n.* decenio. —*adj.* decenal.
decent ('di·sənt) *adj.* **1,** (proper) decente; honesto. **2,** (honest) honrado. **3,** (fair) razonable.
decentralize (ˌdi'sɛn·trəˌlaiz) *v.t.* descentralizar. —*v.i.* descentralizarse. —**decentralization** (-lɪ'zei·ʃən) *n.* descentralización.
deception (dɪ'sɛp·ʃən) *n.* **1,** (act of deceiving) decepción; engaño. **2,** (misrepresentation) fraude. —**deceptive** (-tɪv) *adj.* engañoso; falaz.
deci- (dɛs·i) *prefijo* deci-. **1,** diez: *decipolar,* que tiene diez polos. **2,** décima parte: *deciliter,* decilitro.
decibel ('dɛs·ə·bɛl) *n.* decibel; decibelio.
decide (dɪ'said) *v.t.* & *i.* decidir; determinar; resolver.
decided (dɪ'sai·dɪd) *adj.* **1,** (unmistakable) decidido; **2,** (determined) determinado; resuelto.
deciduous (dɪ'sɪd·dʒu·əs) *adj.* deciduo.
decigram *n.* decigramo.
deciliter *n.* decilitro.
decillion (dɪ'sɪl·jən) *n.* (*U.S.*) mil quintillones; (*Brit.*) un millón de nonillones; decillón.
decimal ('dɛs·ɪ·məl) *n.* & *adj.* decimal. —**decimal point**, coma de decimal.
decimate ('dɛs·ɪˌmeit) *v.t.* diezmar. —**decimation**, *n.* gran mortandad.
decimeter *n.* decímetro.
decipher (di'sai·fər) *v.t.* descifrar. —**decipherable**, *adj.* descifrable. —**decipherment**, *n.* descifre.
decision (dɪ'sɪʒ·ən) *n.* **1,** (selection) decisión. **2,** (determination) determinación; resolución. **3,** *law* (judgment) decisión; sentencia.
decisive (dɪ'sai·sɪv) *adj.* decisivo. —**decisiveness**, *n.* fuerza decisiva.
deck (dɛk) *n.* **1,** *naut.* cubierta. **2,** *cards* baraja. —*v.t.* [*también,* **deck out**] adornar; engalanar.
declaim (dɪ'kleim) *v.t.* & *i.* declamar; recitar.
declamation (ˌdɛk·lə'mei·ʃən) *n.* declamación. —**declamatory** (dɪ'klæm·ə·tor·i) *adj.* declamatorio.
declaration (ˌdɛk·lə'rei·ʃən) *n.* declaración.
declarative (dɪ'klær·ə·tɪv) *adj., gram.* aseverativo.
declare (dɪ'kle:r) *v.t.* & *i.* declarar.
declassify (di'klæs·ɪˌfai) *v.t.* hacer público.
declension (dɪ'klɛn·ʃən) *n.* **1,** (descent) declive. **2,** (deterioration) decadencia; deterioro. **3,** *gram.* declinación.
declination (ˌdɛk·lɪ'nei·ʃən) *n.* **1,** (bending) declive; inclinación. **2,** (refusal) excusa; rechazamiento.
decline (dɪ'klain) *v.t.* & *i.* **1,** (bend) inclinar; descender; bajar. **2,** (refuse) declinar; rehusar. —*v.t., gram.* declinar. —*v.i.* **1,** (approach the end) ponerse. **2,** (deteriorate) desmejorarse; decaer. —*n.,* **1,** (slope) declinación. **2,** (decay) decadencia. **3,** (deterioration) menoscabo.
declining (dɪ'klai·nɪŋ) *adj.* **1,** (bending) pendiente. **2,** (ending) final. **3,** (refusing) rehusante.
declivity (dɪ'klɪv·ə·ti) *n.* declive; pendiente.
decoct (dɪ'kakt) *v.t.* extraer por decocción. —**decoction** (-'kak·ʃən) *n.* decocción.
decode (di'ko:d) *v.t.* descifrar. —**decoding**, *n.* descifre.
décolleté (ˌde·kal'te:) *adj.* descotado; escotado. —**décolletage** (-'ta:ʒ) *n.* descote; escote.
decompose (ˌdi·kəm'po:z) *v.t.* descomponer. —*v.i.* descomponerse. —**decomposition** (ˌdi·kam·pə'ʒɪʃ·ən) *n.* descomposición.
decontaminate (ˌdi·kən'tæm·ɪ·ˌneit) *v.t.* purificar. —**decontamination**, *n.* purificación.
decontrol (di·kən'trol) *n.* descontrol. —*v.t.* descontrolar.
decorate ('dɛk·ə·reit) *v.t.* **1,** (ornament) decorar; adornar; engalanar. **2,** (award a medal, etc., to) con-

decorar. 3, (paint) pintar; enlucir. 4, (furnish) decorar. —**decorator**, *n.* decorador.
decoration (ˌdɛk·əˈrei·ʃən) *n.* 1, (ornament) decoración. 2, (award) condecoración.
decorative (ˈdɛk·ə·re·tɪv) *adj.* decorativo; adornante.
decorum (dɪˈkor·əm) *n.* decoro. —**decorous** (ˈdɛk·ə·rəs) *adj.* decoroso.
decoy (diˈkɔi) *n.* 1, (a lure) trampa. 2, *hunting* reclamo. 3, (stratagem) añagaza; estratagema. 4, (person used as lure) entruchón. —*v.t.* & *i.* atraer; entruchar.
decrease (dɪˈkris) *v.i.* decrecer; reducirse; bajar. —*v.t.* disminuir; reducir. —*n.* (ˈdi·kris) reducción; disminución.
decree (dɪˈkriː) *n.* decreto; ley; edicto; orden. —*v.t.* & *i.* decretar; ordenar; mandar.
decrement (ˈdɛk·rə·mənt) *n.* decremento.
decrepit (dɪˈkrɛp·ɪt) *adj.* decrépito; viejo. —**decrepitude** (-ɪˌtud) *n.* decrepitud.
decry (diˈkrai) *v.t.* 1, (blame) vituperar; acusar. 2, (deplore) deplorar; lamentar.
decuple (ˈdɛk·ju·pəl) *adj.* décuplo. —*v.t.* decuplicar; decuplar.
dedicate (ˈdɛd·ɪˌkeit) *v.t.* dedicar. —**dedication**, *n.* dedicación. —**dedicatory** (-kəˌtor·i) *adj.* dedicatorio.
deduce (diˈdus) *v.t.* deducir; colegir. —**deducible**, *adj.* deducible; colegible.
deduct (dɪˈdʌkt) *v.t.* deducir; substraer; descontar. —**deductible**, *adj.* deducible; descontable.
deduction (dɪˈdʌk·ʃən) *n.* 1, (subtraction) substracción. 2, (reasoning) deducción. —**deductive** (-tɪv) *adj.* deductivo.
deed (diːd) *n.* 1, (act) hecho; acción; acto. 2, (exploit) proeza; gesta. 3, *law* (title) escritura. —*v.t.* hacer escritura de cesión *o* traspaso; ceder *o* traspasar por escritura.
deem (diːm) *v.t.* & *i.* estimar; creer; juzgar.
deep (dip) *adj.* 1, (extending far down, back, or into) hondo; profundo. 2, (absorbed) embebecido; absorto. 3, (abstruse) oscuro; difícil; complicado. 4, (extreme) tremendo; grande. 5, *music* (low-pitched) grave; profundo. 6, (intense) subido; intenso. 7, (heartfelt) sentido; profundo. —*n.* 1, (the sea) el mar. 2, (hell) abismo; infierno. 3, (the farthest point) lo profundo. —**deepness**, *n.* profundidad; hondura; intensidad.
deepen (ˈdi·pən) *v.t.* 1, (make deeper) profundizar; ahondar. 2, (intensify) intensificar. —*v.i.* 1, (grow deeper) profundizarse. 2, (grow more intense) intensificarse.
deepseated (ˈdipˌsit·əd) *adj.* incrustado; firmemente fijo.
deer (dɪːr) *n.* [*pl.* **deer**] ciervo. —**deerskin**, *n.* gamuza.
deface (diˈfeis) *v.t.* desfigurar; estropear. —**defacement**, *n.* desfiguración; estropeo; mutilación.
de facto (diˈfæk·to) *adv.* de hecho.
defalcate (dɪˈfæl·ket) *v.i.* desfalcar. —**defalcation**, *n.* desfalco.
defame (diˈfeim) *v.t.* difamar; calumniar. —**defamation** (ˌdɛf·əˈme·ʃən) *n.* difamación; calumnia. —**defamatory** (dɪˈfæm·ə·tor·i) *adj.* difamatorio.
default (dɪˈfɔlt) *v.t.* 1, (fail to do) faltar; no cumplir. 2, *sports* perder por incomparecencia. 3, *law* condenar en rebeldía. —*v.i.* 1, (fail to appear) no aparecer; no presentarse. 2, (lose) perder por incomparecencia. 3, *law* caer en rebeldía. —*n.* 1, (voluntary failure) falta; incumplimiento. 2, (involuntary failure) omisión; descuido; falta. 3, *law* rebeldía. —**in default of**, 1, *law* en rebeldía. 2, (through lack of) por ausencia de.
defeat (dɪˈfit) *v.t.* 1, (overcome) derrotar; vencer; ganar. 2, (thwart) frustrar; impedir. —*n.* derrota. —**defeatism**, *n.* derrotismo. —**defeatist**, *adj.* & *n.* derrotista.
defecate (ˈdɛf·ə·keit) *v.t.* & *i.* defecar. —**defecation**, *n.* defecación.
defect (dɪˈfɛkt) *n.* 1, (imperfection) defecto; imperfección. 2, (deficiency) omisión. —*v.i.* desertar. —**defector**, *n.* desertor.
defection (dɪˈfɛk·ʃən) *n.* deserción; defección.
defective (dɪˈfɛk·tɪv) *adj.* defectuoso; deficiente; *gram.* defectivo. —*n.* persona anormal *o* de inteligencia poco desarrollada.
defend (dɪˈfɛnd) *v.t.* 1, (protect) defender. 2, (uphold) mantener; sostener. —**defender**, *n.* defensor.

defendant (dɪ'fɛn·dənt) *n.* **1,** (in criminal proceedings) acusado; reo. **2,** (in civil proceedings) demandado.
defense *también,* **defence** (dɪ'fɛns) *n.* defensa. —**defenseless,** *adj.* indefenso; inerme.
defensible (dɪ'fɛns·ə·bəl) *adj.* **1,** (that can be defended) defendible. **2,** (that can be upheld) sostenible.
defensive (dɪ'fɛn·sɪv) *adj.* defensivo. —*n.* defensiva.
defer (dɪ'fʌɹ) *v.t.* [**deferred, -ferring**] diferir; aplazar; retrasar. —*v.i.* ceder; acceder; deferir.
deference ('dɛf·ə·rəns) *n.* deferencia; acatamiento.
deferent ('dɛf·ə·rənt) *adj.* deferente.
deferential (dɛf·ə'rɛn·ʃəl) *adj.* deferente; respetuoso.
deferment (dɪ'fʌɹ·mənt) *n.* aplazamiento.
defiance (dɪ'fai·əns) *n.* **1,** (resistance) desafío; oposición. **2,** (contempt) contumacia; obstinación. —**defiant,** *adj.* desafiador; provocador.
deficient (dɪ'fɪʃ·ənt) *adj.* **1,** (incomplete) defectuoso. **2,** (insufficient) deficiente. —**deficiency,** *n.* deficiencia.
deficit ('dɛf·ə·sɪt) *n.* déficit.
defile (di'fail) *v.t.* manchar; corromper; profanar. —*v.i.* desfilar; marchar. —*n.* desfiladero. —**defilement,** *n.* corrupción; profanación; violación.
define (dɪ'fain) *v.t.* **1,** (limit) definir; prescribir. **2,** (explain) explicar; definir; describir. —**definable,** *adj.* definible.
definite ('dɛf·ə·nɪt) *adj.* definido; cierto; preciso. —**definiteness,** *n.* exactitud; precisión.
definition (dɛf·ə'nɪʃ·ən) *n.* definición.
definitive (dɪ'fɪn·ə·tɪv) *adj.* definitivo; final. —**definitiveness,** *n.* lo definitivo.
deflate (di'fleit) *v.t.* **1,** (remove gas or air from) desinflar. **2,** (lower, as prices) rebajar; disminuir.
deflation (di'flei·ʃən) *n.* **1,** (act of deflating) desinflación. **2,** (devaluation of currency) disminución; desinflación.
deflect (dɪ'flɛkt) *v.t.* desviar; apartar. —*v.i.* desviarse; apartarse.
deflection (dɪ'flɛk·ʃən) *n.* desviación; deflexión.
deflective (dɪ'flɛk·tɪv) *adj.* desviador.
deflector (dɪ'flɛk·tər) *n.* deflector.
defloration (ˌdɛf·lə'rei·ʃən) *n.* desfloración.
deflower (dɪ'flau·ər) *v.t.* desflorar.
defoliate (dɪ'fo·liˌet) *v.t.* deshojar. —**defoliation,** *n.* defoliación.
deform (di'form) *v.t.* deformar; estropear. —**deformation** (ˌdi·for·'mei·ʃən) *n.* deformación.
deformed (di'formd) *adj.* **1,** (misshapen) deformado. **2,** (ugly) deforme.
deformity (di'form·ə·ti) *n.* deformidad.
defraud (di'frɔːd) *v.t.* defraudar; estafar.
defray (dɪ'frei) *v.t.* sufragar; costear. —**defrayal,** *n.* pago; sufragación.
defrost (di'frɔst) *v.t.* descongelar; deshelar. —**defroster,** *n.* descongelador.
deft (dɛft) *adj.* diestro; [illegible]o; hábil.
defunct (di'fʌŋkt) *adj.* difunto; fallecido; muerto.
defy (dɪ'fai) *v.t.* **1,** (challenge) desafiar; retar. **2,** (show contempt for) despreciar; resistir.
degenerate (di'dʒɛn·ə·reit) *v.i.* degenerar; degradar. —*adj.* & *n.* (-rət) degenerado. —**degeneration,** *n.* degeneración.
degrade (di'greid) *v.t.* **1,** (demote) degradar; deponer. **2,** (debase) reducir; rebajar. **3,** (corrupt) degradar; depravar. —**degradation** (dɛg·rə'dei·ʃən) *n.* degradación. —**degrading,** *adj.* degradante.
degree (dɪ'griː) *n.* **1,** (stage in a series; unit of temperature; *mil., geom., physics*) grado. **2,** (condition) estado. **3,** (academic rank won by study) licencia. —**by degrees,** poco a poco. —**take a degree,** licenciarse.
dehydrate (di'hai·dreit) *v.t.* deshidratar. —*v.i.* deshidratarse. —**dehydration** (ˌdi·hai'drei·ʃən) *n.* deshidratación.
deify ('di·əˌfai) *v.t.* deificar; endiosar. —**deification** (-fɪ'kei·ʃən) *n.* endiosamiento; deificación.
deign (dein) *v.i.* dignarse; condescender. —*v.t.* conceder; dar.
deism ('diː·ɪz·əm) *n.* deísmo. —**deist,** *n.* deísta. —**deistic,** *adj.* deísta.

deity ('di·ə·ti) *n.* deidad; *cap.* Dios.

deject (dɪ'dʒɛkt) *v.t.* abatir; desanimar; descorazonar. **—dejected,** *adj.* abatido; descorazonado.

dejection (di'dʒɛk·ʃən) *n.* **1,** (gloom) melancolía; desánimo. **2,** *med.* (evacuation) deposición.

deka- (dɛk·ə) *prefijo, var. de* **deca-.**

delay (dɪ'lei) *v.t.* dilatar; retrasar; hacer esperar. **—*v.i.*** dilatarse; tardar; demorarse. **—*n.*** dilación; tardanza; retraso.

delectable (dɪ'lɛk·tə·bəl) *adj.* deleitable; delicioso. **—delectability,** *n.* delectación.

delectation (ˌdi·lɛk'tei·ʃən) *n.* delectación.

delegate ('dɛl·ɪ·gət) *n.* delegado. **—*v.t.*** (-geit) **1,** (empower) autorizar; comisionar. **2,** (send as a representative) delegar. **—delegation,** *n.* delegación; comisión

delete (dɪ'lit) *v.t.* borrar; suprimir. **—deletion** (-'li·ʃən) *n.* supresión.

deleterious (dɛl·ə'tɪr·i·əs) *adj.* deletéreo. **—deleteriousness,** *n.* daño; agravio.

deliberate (dɪ'lɪb·ər·eit) *v.t.* & *i.* deliberar. **—*adj.*** (-ət) **1,** (careful) cauto; circunspecto. **2,** (unhurried) lento; calmo. **3,** (intentional) reflexionado; pensado; premeditado. **—deliberation,** *n.* deliberación.

deliberative (dɪ'lɪb·əˌre·tɪv) *adj.* **1,** (discussing) deliberante. **2,** (considered) deliberado.

delicacy ('dɛl·ɪ·kə·si) *n.* **1,** (fineness) delicadeza; sensibilidad. **2,** (fragility) fragilidad; cuidado. **3,** (food) golosina; exquisitez.

delicate ('dɛl·ɪ·kət) *adj.* **1,** (fragile; requiring care) delicado. **2,** (tactful; sensitive) fino; sensible. **3,** (choice, as food) exquisito; de buen gusto *o* sabor.

delicatessen (ˌdɛl·ɪ·kə'tɛs·ən) *n.* **1,** (delicacies) ultramarinos; gollerías. **2,** (store) tienda de ultramarinos.

delicious (dɪ'lɪʃ·əs) *adj.* delicioso; sabroso. **—deliciousness,** *n.* lo delicioso; lo sabroso.

delight (dɪ'lait) *n.* delicia; deleite. **—*v.t.*** & *i.* deleitar; encantar; agradar. **—delightful,** *adj.* delicioso; deleitoso.

delineate (dɪ'lɪn·i·eit) *v.t.* **1,** (outline) delinear; esbozar. **2,** (describe) describir. **—delineation,** *n.* delineación; esbozo.

delinquent (dɪ'lɪŋ·kwənt) *adj.* **1,** (tardy) delincuente. **2,** (failing in duty) culpable; reo. **—*n.*** delincuente. **—delinquency,** *n.* delincuencia.

deliquesce (ˌdɛl·ɪ'kwɛs) *v.i.* derretirse; licuarse. **—deliquescence,** *n.* licuación; delicuescencia. **—deliquescent,** *adj.* delicuescente.

delirious (də'lɪr·i·əs) *adj.* delirante. **—deliriousness,** *n.* delirio.

delirium (də'lɪr·i·əm) *n.* delirio. **—delirium tremens,** delirium tremens.

deliver (dɪ'lɪv·ər) *v.t.* **1,** (transmit; send) entregar; repartir. **2,** (deal, as a blow) dar; asestar. **3,** (throw, as a ball) tirar; lanzar. **4,** (give birth to) parir. **5,** *obstetrics* asistir en el nacimiento de. **6,** (utter) pronunciar. **7,** (set free) liberar; librar; libertar.

deliverance (dɪ'lɪv·ər·əns) *n.* **1,** (rescue) rescate; liberación. **2,** (pronouncement) discurso; alocución.

delivery (dɪ'lɪv·ə·ri) *n.* **1,** (handing over) entrega; reparto. **2,** *obstetrics* parto. **3,** (rescue) liberación. **4,** (manner of speaking) estilo. **5,** (act of throwing) tiro; lanzamiento.

dell (dɛl) *n.* vallecito.

delouse (di'laus) *v.t.* espulgar.

delta ('dɛl·tə) *n.* delta.

delude (dɪ'luːd) *v.t.* deludir; burlar; engañar.

deluge ('dɛl·judʒ) *n.* **1,** (heavy rain) diluvio. **2,** (flood) inundación. **—*v.t.*** inundar.

delusion (dɪ'lu·ʒən) *n.* **1,** (mistaken belief) error. **2,** (false conception) ilusión; engaño. **—delusive** (-sɪv) [*también,* **delusory** (-sə·ri)] *adj.* ilusorio; engañoso.

de luxe (də'lʌks; -'lʊks) de lujo.

delve (dɛːlv) *v.i.* cavar; ahondar. **—delve into,** profundizar; sondear.

demagnetize (di'mæg·nəˌtaiz) *v.t.* desimantar.

demagogue *también,* **demagog** ('dɛm·ə·gɔg) *n.* demagogo. **—demagoguery** (-ˌgɔg·ər·i) *n.* demagogia. **—demagogic** (-'gadʒ·ɪk) *adj.* demagógico.

demand (dɪ'mænd) *v.t.* **1,** (ask) demandar; preguntar. **2,** (request urgently) pedir. **3,** (claim by right) reclamar. **4,** (require) exigir. **—*n.***

1, (request) demanda. 2, (requirement) exigencia. 3, *comm.* (sales potential) demanda. 4, *law* (claim) petición jurídica. —**be in demand**, ser solicitado. —**in demand**, en demanda; solicitado. —**on demand**, a instancia; a solicitud; a la presentación.
demanding (dɪ'mæn·dɪŋ) *adj.* 1, (difficult) perentorio; apremiante. 2, (exacting) exigente.
demarcate (dɪ'mar·ket) *v.t.* demarcar; deslindar. —**demarcation**, *n.* demarcación; deslinde.
demarche (di'marʃ) *n.* gestión.
demean (dɪ'min) *v.t.* & *i.* rebajar; degradar.
demeanor *también,* **demeanour** (dɪ·'min·ər) *n.* comportamiento; conducta.
demented (dɪ'mɛn·tɪd) *adj.* demente; loco. —**dementia** (-ʃə) *n.* demencia; locura.
demerit (di'mɛr·ɪt) *n.* demérito.
demi- (dɛm·i) *prefijo* semi-. 1, mitad: *demisemiquaver,* semifusa. 2, inferior: *demigod,* semidiós.
demigod ('dɛm·iˌgad) *n.* semidiós.
demijohn ('dɛm·iˌdʒan) *n.* garrafa; garrafón; damajuana.
demilitarize (di'mɪl·ɪ·təˌraiz) *v.t.* desmilitarizar. —**demilitarization** (-rɪ'zei·ʃən) *n.* desmilitarización.
demimonde ('dɛm·iˌmand) *n.* mujeres mundanas. —**demimondaine** (-mon'dein) *n.* mujer mundana.
demise (dɪ'maiz) *n.* 1, (death) fallecimiento; muerte. 2, *law* (transfer) traslación de dominio, poderes *o* soberanía. —*v.t.* 1, (transfer) transferir; pasar. 2, (rent) arrendar. 3, (yield) ceder.
demitasse ('dɛm·iˌtæs) *n.* tacita.
demobilize(di'mo·bəˌlaiz) *v.t.* & *i.* desmovilizar. —**demobilization** (-lɪ'zei·ʃən) *n.* desmovilización.
democracy (dɪ'mak·rə·si) *n.* democracia.
democrat ('dɛm·ə·kræt) *n.* demócrata. —**democratic** (-'kræt·ɪk) *adj.* demócrata; democrático.
democratize (dɪ'mak·rəˌtaiz) *v.t.* democratizar. —**democratization** (-tɪ'zei·ʃən) *n.* democratización.
demography (dɪ'mag·rə·fi) *n.* demografía. —**demographer** (-fər) *n.* demógrafo. —**demographic** (ˌdi·mə·'græf·ɪk) demográfico.
demolish (di'mal·ɪʃ) *v.t.* demoler; destruir; arruinar. —**demolition** (dɛm·ə'lɪʃ·ən) *n.* demolición.
demon ('di·mən) *n.* demonio; diablo. —**demoniac** (dɪ'mo·ni·æk) [*también,* **demoniacal** (ˌdi·mə'nai·ə·kəl)] *adj.* demoníaco.
demonstrable (dɪ'man·strə·bəl) *adj.* demostrable.
demonstrate ('dɛm·ən·streit) *v.t.* demostrar; probar. —*v.i.* demostrarse.
demonstration (ˌdɛm·ən'strei·ʃən) *n.* 1, (act of demonstrating) demostración; prueba. 2, (display) prueba; exhibición. 3, *mil.* (show of force) alarde. 4, (protest) manifestación.
demonstrative (dɪ'man·strə·tɪv) *adj.* demostrativo.
demonstrator ('dɛm·ən·stre·tər) *n.* 1, (person or thing that displays) demostrador. 2, (noisy person) alborotador. 3, *colloq.* (automobile) vehículo de demostración.
demoralize (di'mar·əˌlaiz) *v.t.* desmoralizar. —**demoralization** (-lɪ'zei·ʃən) *n.* desmoralización.
demote (di'mot) *v.t.* degradar. —**demotion** (-'mo·ʃən) *n.* degradación.
demur (dɪ'mʌɹ) *v.i.* [**demurred, -murring**] 1, (object) objetar; poner dificultades. 2, (hesitate) dudar; vacilar. 3, *law* (enter a demurrer) aceptar con excepciones. —*n.* 1, (objection) objeción. 2, (hesitation) duda; vacilación.
demure (dɪ'mjʊːr) *adj.* 1, (prim) gazmoño; relamido. 2, (sedate) formal; grave; serio.
demureness (dɪ'mjʊr·nəs) *n.* 1, (primness) gazmoñería. 2, (sedateness) seriedad.
demurrage (dɪ'mʌɹ·ɪdʒ) *n.*, *comm.* estadía.
demurrer (dɪ'mʌɹ·ər) *n.* 1, (irresolute person) persona irresoluta. 2, *law* excepción perentoria.
den (dɛn) *n.* 1, (cave) madriguera; guarida. 2, (retreat) guarida; cuchitril. 3, (room) estudio; cuartito.
denaturalize (di'nætʃ·ə·rəˌlaiz) *v.t.* desnaturalizar.
denature (ˌdi'nei·tʃər) *v.t.* adulterar; desnaturalizar.
dendro- (dɛn·dro) *prefijo* dendro-; árbol: *dendrography,* dendrografía.
-dendron (dɛn·drən) *sufijo* -den-

dro; árbol: *rhododendron,* rododendro.

dengue ('dɛŋ·gei) *n.* dengue.

denial (dɪ'nai·əl) *n.* 1, (refusal) negativa. 2, (contradiction) negación. 3, (self-restraint) abnegación.

denigrate ('dɛn·ə,gret) *v.t.* denigrar. —**denigration,** *n.* denigración.

denim ('dɛn·əm) *n.* tela de mono; dril.

denizen ('dɛn·ɪ·zən) *n.* 1, (inhabitant) habitante. 2, (naturalized foreigner) ciudadano naturalizado. 3, (naturalized thing) naturalizado.

denominate (dɪ'nam·ɪ,neit) *v.t.* denominar; designar; nombrar.

denomination (di,nam·ɪ'nei·ʃən) *n.* 1, (type) denominación; nombre. 2, (sect) denominación; secta.

denominative (dɪ'nam·ə,ne·tɪv) *adj.* denominativo.

denominator (dɪ'nam·ɪ,ne·tər) *n., math.* denominador.

denote (dɪ'not) *v.t.* 1, (designate) señalar; marcar. 2, (mean) significar; denotar; indicar. —**denotation** (,di·no'tei·ʃən) *n.* denotación; indicación.

denouement (,de·nu'mant; -'mɔɴ) *n.* desenlace.

denounce (dɪ'nauns) *v.t.* 1, (stigmatize) denunciar; censurar. 2, (inform against) delatar. 3, (repudiate, as a treaty) denunciar. —**denouncement,** *n.* = **denunciation.**

dense (dɛns) *adj.* 1, (compact) denso; espeso; compacto. 2, (stupid) torpe. —**denseness** [*también,* **density** (-ə·ti)] *n.* densidad; opacidad.

dent (dɛnt) *n.* abolladura. —*v.t.* abollar. —*v.i.* abollarse.

dental ('dɛn·təl) *adj.* dental.

denti- (dɛn·ti) *también,* **dent-** (dɛnt), **dento-** (dɛn·to) *prefijo* denti-; diente: *dentifrice,* dentífrico.

dentine ('dɛn·tin) *también,* **dentin** (-tɪn) *n.* dentina.

dentist ('dɛn·tɪst) *n.* dentista. —**dentistry,** *n.* odontología.

dentition (dɛn'tɪʃ·ən) *n.* dentición.

denture ('dɛn·tʃər) *n.* dentadura postiza.

denude (di'nuːd) *v.t.* 1, (strip of clothing) desnudar; desvestir. 2, (despoil) despojar; privar. —**denudation,** *n.* denudación.

denunciation (dɪ,nʌn·si'ei·ʃən) *n.* denuncia; acusación.

deny (dɪ'nai) *v.t.* & *i.* 1, (contradict) negar; contradecir. 2, (refuse; reject) rehusar. 3, (renounce) abjurar; renunciar.

deodorant (di'o·də·rənt) *n.* & *adj.* desodorante.

deodorize (di'o·də·raiz) *v.t.* desodorizar. —**deodorization** (-rɪ'zei·ʃən) *n.* desodorización.

depart (dɪ'part) *v.i.* 1, (leave) partir; marchar; irse. 2, (deviate) apartarse; desviarse. 3, (die) morir. —**departed,** *adj.* & *n.* difunto; fallecido; muerto.

department (dɪ'part·mənt) *n.* 1, (section) departamento; sección. 2, (government bureau) ministerio. 3, (area) distrito; provincia. —**departmental** (-'mɛn·təl) *adj.* departamental; ministerial. —**department store,** galerías (*pl.*); almacén.

departure (dɪ'par·tʃər) *n.* 1, (leaving) partida; marcha. 2, (deviation) desviación.

depend (dɪ'pɛnd) *v.i.* (hang) pender; colgar. —**depend on** *o* **upon,** 1, (trust in) contar con; confiar en. 2, (rely on) depender de; descansar en. 3, (be contingent on) depender de.

dependable (dɪ'pɛn·də·bəl) *adj.* confiable; seguro; digno de confianza.

dependence (dɪ'pɛn·dəns) *n.* dependencia; pertenencia.

dependency (dɪ'pɛn·dən·si) *n.* 1, = **dependence.** 2, (dependent territory) dependencia; posesión.

dependent (dɪ'pɛn·dənt) *adj.* 1, (hanging) pendiente; colgante. 2, (contingent) dependiente; contingente; condicional. 3, (subordinate) dependiente; subordinado; subalterno. —*n.* dependiente; carga de familia. —**dependent** *or* **depending upon,** 1, (according to) según. 2, (contingent on) si . . . permite.

depict (dɪ'pɪkt) *v.t.* describir; representar; pintar. —**depiction** (-'pɪk·ʃən) *n.* descripción; representación; pintura.

depilate ('dɛp·ə,let) *v.t.* depilar. —**depilation,** *n.* depilación. —**depilatory** (dɪ'pɪl·ə,tor·i) *adj.* & *n.* depilatorio.

deplete (dɪ'plit) *v.t.* consumir; agotar; depauperar. —**depletion** (-'pli·ʃən) *n.* agotamiento; depauperación.

deplore (dɪ'plor) *v.t.* deplorar; lamentar. —**deplorable,** *adj.* deplorable; lamentable.
deploy (dɪ'plɔi) *v.t.* desplegar. —*v.i.* desplegarse. —**deployment,** *n.* despliegue.
deponent (dɪ'po·nənt) *n.* & *adj.* deponente.
depopulate (di'pap·jə,let) *v.t.* despoblar.
deport (di'port) *v.t.* (exile) deportar; desterrar. —**deport oneself,** comportarse; conducirse.
deportation (,di·por'tei·ʃən) *n.* deportación.
deportment (di'port·mənt) *n.* comportamiento; conducta; modales (*pl.*).
depose (di'poːz) *v.t.* **1,** (unseat) deponer. **2,** *law* (testify) atestiguar. —*v.i., law* (bear witness) ser testigo.
deposit (dɪ'paz·ɪt) *v.t.* **1,** (put) depositar; poner; colocar. **2,** (pledge) dar como señal. —*n.* **1,** (deposited thing) depósito. **2,** *banking* ingreso. **3,** (part payment) señal. **4,** *geol.* (residue) depósito; residuo.
depositary (dɪ'paz·ə,tɛr·i) *adj.* depositario. —*n.* **1,** (trustee) depositario. **2,** = **depository.**
deposition (,dɛp·ə'zɪʃ·ən) *n.* **1,** (displacement) deposición. **2,** *law* (testimony) declaración; testimonio; deposición.
depositor (dɪ'paz·ə·tər) *n.* depositador.
depository (dɪ'paz·ɪ,tor·i) *n.* **1,** (storage place) depósito; almacén; depositaría. **2,** = **depositary.** —*adj.* depositario.
depot ('di·po) *n.* **1,** (warehouse) depósito; almacén. **2,** *R.R.* estación. **3,** *mil.* depósito.
deprave (dɪ'preiv) *v.t.* depravar; degenerar; pervertir.
depravity (dɪ'præv·ə·ti) *n.* depravación; perversión.
deprecate ('dɛp·rə·keit) *v.t.* desaprobar; lamentar; rechazar. —**deprecation,** *n.* desaprobación.
deprecatory ('dɛp·rə·kə,tor·i) *adj.* desaprobante; desaprobador.
depreciate (dɪ'pri·ʃi·eit) *v.i.* depreciarse. —*v.t.* **1,** (lessen value of) depreciar. **2,** (belittle) desestimar; despreciar. —**depreciation,** *n.* depreciación.
depredate ('dɛp·rə,deit) *v.t.* & *i.* depredar. —**depredation,** *n.* depredación.
depress (dɪ'prɛs) *v.t.* **1,** (press or move down) bajar; rebajar. **2,** (sadden) deprimir; abatir; desanimar. **3,** (weaken) desalentar; descorazonar. —**depressive** (-ɪv) *adj.* depresivo; deprimente. —**depressor,** *n.* depresor. —**depressant** (-ənt) *n.* & *adj.* sedante.
depression (dɪ'prɛʃ·ən) *n.* **1,** (concavity) concavidad; depresión. **2,** (melancholy) desánimo; melancolía. **3,** (market decline) depresión; crisis.
deprivation (,dɛp·rɪ'vei·ʃən) *n.* **1,** (removal) privación. **2,** (loss) pérdida. **3,** (poverty) carencia.
deprive (dɪ'praiv) *v.t.* **1,** (divest) privar. **2,** (strip) despojar. **3,** (withhold) retener; impedir; excluir.
depth (dɛpθ) *n.* **1,** (deepness) profundidad; hondura; hondo. **2,** (intensity) intensidad; fuerza; viveza. **3,** (profundity) gravedad. —**depth charge,** carga *o* bomba de profundidad. —**in the depths of** (winter, etc.) en pleno (invierno). —**out of one's depth,** en honduras.
deputation (,dɛp·ju'tei·ʃən) *n.* **1,** (mission) delegación; comisión. **2,** (group of emissaries) diputación.
depute (dɪ'pjut) *v.t.* diputar.
deputize ('dɛp·jə,taiz) *v.t.* diputar; delegar.
deputy ('dɛp·jə·ti) *n.* diputado; delegado. —*adj.* teniente.
derail (di'reil) *v.t., R.R.* hacer descarrilar. —*v.i.* descarrilar. —**derailment,** *n.* descarrilamiento.
derange (dɪ'reindʒ) *v.t.* **1,** (disarrange) descomponer; desordenar. **2,** (make insane) volver loco; enloquecer. —**deranged,** *adj.* loco.
derangement (dɪ'reindʒ·mənt) *n.* **1,** (disorder) desarreglo. **2,** (insanity) locura.
derby ('dʌɹ·bi) *n.* **1,** (hat) hongo. **2,** *cap.* (a race) derby.
derelict ('dɛr·ə,lɪkt) *adj.* **1,** (forsaken) derrelicto; abandonado; desamparado. **2,** (remiss) negligente; remiso. —*n.* **1,** *naut.* (abandoned ship) derrelicto. **2,** (outcast) deshecho.
dereliction (dɛr·ə'lɪk·ʃən) *n.* derrelicción; abandono; negligencia.
deride (dɪ'raid) *v.t.* ridiculizar; hacer burla de.

derision (dɪ'rɪʒ·ən) *n.* irrisión; burla.
derisive (dɪ'rai·sɪv) *adj.* irrisorio.
derivation (ˌdɛr·ɪ'vei·ʃən) *n.* 1, (act of deriving) derivación. 2, (source) fuente; origen. 3, (etymology) etimología.
derivative (də'rɪv·ə·tɪv) *adj.* derivativo; derivado. —*n.* derivado.
derive (dɪ'raiv) *v.t.* 1, (receive) derivar. 2, (deduce) inferir; deducir. —*v.i.* derivarse.
derm- (dʌɹm) *prefijo, var. de* **dermo-** *ante vocal: dermalgia,* dermalgia.
-derm (dərm) *sufijo* -dermo; piel: *pachyderm,* paquidermo.
dermat- (dʌɹ·mət) *prefijo, var. de* **dermato-** *ante vocal: dermathemia,* dermatemia.
dermatitis ('dʌɹ·mə'tai·tɪs) *n.* dermatitis.
dermato- (dʌɹ·mə·to) *prefijo* dermato-; piel: *dermatology,* dermatología.
dermatology (ˌdʌɹ·mə'tal·ə·dʒi) *n.* dermatología. —**dermatological** (-tə'ladʒ·ɪ·kəl) *adj.* dermatológico. —**dermatologist,** *n.* dermatólogo.
dermis ('dʌɹ·mɪs) *n.* dermis; piel; cutis.
dermo- (dʌɹ·mo) *prefijo-;* dermo-; piel: *dermoblast,* dermoblasto.
derogate ('dɛr·əˌgeit) *v.t.* derogar. —*v.i.* [*usu.,* **derogate from**] 1, detract) disminuir; desmerecer; menospreciar. 2, (degenerate) degenerar; quitar mérito (a). —**derogation,** *n.* derogación; desmerecimiento; menosprecio.
derogatory (dɪ'rag·əˌtor·i) *adj.* despectivo; menospreciativo. *También,* **derogative** (-tɪv).
derrick ('dɛr·ɪk) *n.* 1, (crane) grúa. 2, (oil derrick) torre de perforación.
dervish ('dʌɹ·vɪʃ) *n.* derviche.
desalt (di'sɔːlt) *v.t.* desalar.
descend (dɪ'sɛnd) *v.t.* & *i.* descender; bajar. —*v.i.* 1, (lower oneself) rebajarse. 2, *music* (lower) bajar. 3, (derive from) descender; provenir; venir. —**descendant,** *n.* descendiente. —**descendent,** *adj.* descendiente.
descent (dɪ'sɛnt) *n.* 1, (downward progress) descenso. 2, (downward slope) bajada; declive. 3, (ancestry) descendencia; origen; alcurnia.
describe (dɪ'skraib) *v.t.* 1, (portray) describir; representar. 2, (explain) definir; explicar. 3, (delineate) trazar; delinear.
description (dɪ'skrɪp·ʃən) *n.* 1, (a describing) descripción; representación. 2, (kind) clase; género. —**descriptive** (-tɪv) *adj.* descriptivo.
desecrate ('dɛs·ɪˌkreit) *v.t.* violar; profanar. —**desecration,** *n.* profanación.
desert ('dɛz·ərt) *n.* desierto.
desert (dɪ'zʌɹt) *v.t.* desertar; abandonar; desamparar. —*v.i.* desertar. —*n., usu. pl.* merecido (*sing.*) —**deserted,** *adj.* despoblado; desierto. —**deserter,** *n.* desertor.
desertion (dɪ'zʌɹ·ʃən) *n.* 1, (dishonorable departure) deserción. 2, (abandonment) abandono.
deserve (dɪ'zʌɹv) *v.t.* merecer. —*v.i.* tener merecimientos. —**deserved** (-'zʌɹvd) *adj.* merecido. —**deservedly** (-'zʌɹ·vəd·li) *adv.* merecidamente; justamente. —**deserving** (-'zʌɹ·vɪŋ) *adj.* meritorio; valioso; digno; merecedor.
desiccate ('dɛs·əˌket) *v.t.* desecar. —*v.i.* desecarse. —**desiccant,** *adj.* & *n.* desecante. —**desiccation,** *n.* desecación.
design (dɪ'zain) *v.t.* 1, (sketch) diseñar; trazar. 2, (contrive) proyectar; planear. 3, (intend) intentar; tener intención de. —*n.* 1, (art work) diseño; trazado; bosquejo. 2, *pl.,* (scheme) planes; designios; intenciones. 3, (decorative arrangement) diseño; composición.
designate ('dɛz·ɪgˌneit) *v.t.* 1, (point out) indicar; señalar. 2, (name) denominar. 3, (appoint) designar; elegir. —*adj.* designado.
designation (ˌdɛz·ɪg'nei·ʃən) *n.* 1, (indication) indicación; señalamiento. 2, (name; naming) denominación. 3, (appointing) designación; elección.
designer (dɪ'zai·nər) *n.* 1, (one who designs) diseñador; (of machinery) proyectista. 2, (plotter) maquinador.
designing (dɪ'zai·nɪŋ) *adj.* 1, (making a design) del diseño. 2, (crafty) intrigante; astuto. —*n.* (art work) diseño.
desire (dɪ'zair) *v.t.* 1, (want) desear; anhelar. 2, (request) suplicar; rogar. —*n.* deseo. —**desirable,** *adj.*

deseable; apetecible. —**desirous,** *adj.* deseoso; anhelante.
desist (dɪ'zɪst) *v.i.* desistir; cesar. —**desistance,** *n.* desistimiento.
desk (dɛsk) *n.* **1,** (writing table) escritorio. **2,** (for messages) mesa (de despacho). **3,** (school desk) pupitre. **4,** *fig.* (editorial office) redacción. —**desk work,** trabajo de oficina.
desolate ('dɛs·ə·lət) *adj.* **1,** (forlorn) desolado. **2,** (solitary) solitario. **3,** (miserable) infeliz; triste. **4,** (deserted) desierto; despoblado. **5,** (ravaged) asolado. —*v.t.* (-ˌleit) **1,** (make desolate) desolar. **2,** (depopulate) despoblar. **3,** (devastate) asolar; devastar; arrasar.
desolation (ˌdɛs·ə'lei·ʃən) *n.* **1,** (barren waste) desolación. **2,** (loneliness) soledad.
despair (dɪ'spɛːr) *v.i.* desesperar. —*n.* desesperación. —**despairing,** *adj.* desesperanzado.
despatch (dɪ'spætʃ) *n.* & *v.* = **dispatch.**
desperado (dɛs·pə'rei·do) *n.* criminal desesperado; bandido.
desperate ('dɛs·pər·ət) *adj.* **1,** (impelled by despair) desesperado; perdido. **2,** (reckless) violento; terrible. **3,** (hopeless) irremediable. **4,** (drastic) heroico. **5,** (brutal; bloody) encarnizado.
desperation (ˌdɛs·pə'rei·ʃən) *n.* desesperación.
despicable ('dɛs·pɪ·kə·bəl) *adj.* despreciable; bajo; vil.
despise (dɪ'spaiz) *v.t.* **1,** (scorn) despreciar. **2,** (hate) detestar.
despite (dɪ'spait) *n.* **1,** (insult) insulto; afrenta. **2,** (malice) malicia. —*prep.* a pesar de; a despecho de; no obstante. —**in despite of,** a pesar de; a despecho de; no obstante.
despoil (dɪ'spɔil) *v.t.* despojar; robar; saquear. —**despoilment,** *n.* despojo.
despond (dɪ'spand) *v.t.* desanimarse; desesperarse. —**despondent,** *adj.* desanimado; abatido. —**despondency,** *n.* desánimo.
despot ('dɛs·pət) *n.* déspota. —**despotic** (dɛ'spat·ɪk) *adj.* despótico. —**despotism** ('dɛs·pə·tɪz·əm) *n.* despotismo.
dessert (dɪ'zʌɹt) *n.* postre; dulces.
destination (ˌdɛs·tɪ'nei·ʃən) *n.* **1,** (aim; goal) destinación. **2,** (place or condition to be reached) destino.
destine ('dɛs·tɪn) *v.t.* **1,** (intend) destinar; dedicar. **2,** (predetermine unalterably) predeterminar.
destiny ('dɛs·tə·ni) *n.* destino.
destitute ('dɛs·tɪˌtut) *adj.* **1,** [*con* **of**] (lacking) desprovisto de. **2,** (indigent) destituido; pobre; indigente. —**destitution** (-'tu·ʃən) *n.* pobreza; indigencia.
destroy (dɪ'strɔi) *v.t.* destruir; aniquilar.
destroyer (dɪ'strɔi·ər) *n.* **1,** (demolisher) destructor. **2,** *naval* cazatorpedero; destructor.
destructible (dɪ'strʌk·tə·bəl) *adj.* destruible.
destruction (dɪ'strʌk·ʃən) *n.* destrucción. —**destructive** (-tɪv) *adj.* destructivo.
desultory (dɛs·əl·tor·i) *adj.* deshilvanado; incoherente; inconexo.
detach (dɪ'tætʃ) *v.t.* **1,** (unfasten) despegar; desprender; separar. **2,** *mil.* (send on a mission) destacar.
detached (dɪ'tætʃt) *adj.* **1,** (separate) separado; suelto. **2,** (impartial) imparcial; desinteresado. **3,** (aloof) despreocupado.
detachment (dɪ'tætʃ·mənt) *n.* **1,** (separation) despegadura. **2,** (aloofness) separación. **3,** *mil.* destacamento.
detail (dɪ'teil) *v.t.* **1,** (describe minutely) detallar. **2,** *mil.* (assign) destacar. —*n.* **1,** (item) detalle. **2,** *mil.* (assigned group) destacamento. —**detailed,** *adj.* detallado; completo.
detain (dɪ'tein) *v.t.* **1,** (delay) detener. **2,** (arrest) arrestar. —**detainer,** *n., law* orden de arresto.
detect (dɪ'tɛkt) *v.t.* **1,** (discover) percibir; descubrir. **2,** *radio* detectar; rectificar. —**detectable,** *adj.* averiguable. —**detector,** *n.* detector.
detection (di'tɛk·ʃən) *n.* **1,** (discovery) descubrimiento. **2,** *radio* detección.
detective (dɪ'tɛk·tɪv) *n.* detective.
detention (dɪ'tɛn·ʃən) *n.* detención.
deter (dɪ'tʌɹ) *v.t.* [**deterred, -terring**] detener; refrenar. —**determent,** *n.* freno; impedimento.
detergent (dɪ'tʌɹ·dʒənt) *n.* & *adj.* detergente; limpiador.
deteriorate (dɪ'tɪr·i·əˌreit) *v.t.* deteriorar. —*v.i.* deteriorarse. —**deterioration,** *n.* deterioración; deterioro.

determinate (dɪˈtʌɹ·mə·nət) *adj.* determinado.
determination (dɪˌtʌɹ·mɪˈnei·ʃən) *n.* determinación.
determine (dɪˈtʌɹ·mɪn) *v.t.* **1,** (resolve) determinar; resolver; solucionar. **2,** (end) terminar; acabar; *law* concluir. **3,** (restrict) limitar. **4,** (ordain) decretar. —*v.i.* determinarse; resolverse. —**determined,** *adj.* determinado.
deterrent (dɪˈtʌɹ·ənt) *adj.* impeditivo; disuasivo. —*n.* freno; impedimento.
detest (dɪˈtɛst) *v.t.* detestar; aborrecer; odiar. —**detestable,** *adj.* detestable.
detestation (ˌdi·tɛsˈtei·ʃən) *n.* **1,** (hatred) detestación; aborrecimiento. **2,** (object of hatred) lo detestado; persona *o* cosa detestada.
dethrone (diˈθron) *v.t.* destronar. —**dethronement,** destronamiento.
detonate (ˈdɛt·əˌneit) *v.i.* detonar. —*v.t.* hacer detonar. —**detonation,** *n.* detonación. —**detonator,** *n.* detonador.
detour (ˈdi·tʊr) *n.* desvío; rodeo. —*v.t.* desviar. —*v.i.* desviarse; dar rodeos.
detract (dɪˈtrækt) *v.t.* & *i.* [*usu.,* **detract from**] detraer; reducir; disminuir; denigrar. —**detractor,** *n.* detractor; enemigo; denigrador.
detraction (dɪˈtræk·ʃən) *n.* detracción; maledicencia. —**detractive** (-tɪv) *adj.* difamatorio.
detriment (ˈdɛt·rɪ·mənt) *n.* detrimento. —**detrimental** (-ˈmɛn·təl) *adj.* perjudicial; nocivo.
detritus (dɪˈtrai·təs) *n.* detritus.
deuce (dus) *n.* **1,** *cards; dice* dos; *tennis* a dos. **2,** (in exclamations) diablo.
deuced (dust; ˈdu·sɪd) *adj., slang* diabólico, excesivo. —*adv.* [*también,* **deucedly** (ˈdus·əd·li)] diabólicamente; en demasía.
deuter- (du·tər) *prefijo, var. de* **deutero-** *ante vocal: deuteragonist,* deuteragonista.
deuterium (djuˈtɪr·i·əm) *n.* deuterio.
deutero- (du·tər·o) *prefijo* deutero-; segundo; posterior: *Deuteronomy,* Deuteronomio.
deuteron (ˈdu·tə·ran) *n.* deuterión.
deuto- (du·to) *prefijo* deuto-; segundo; posterior: *deutoplasm,* deutoplasma.
devaluate (diˈvæl·juˌeit) *v.t.* desvalorar; desvalorizar. *También,* **devalue.** —**devaluation,** *n.* devaluación; desvalorización.
devastate (ˈdɛv·ə·steit) *v.t.* devastar; asolar; arrasar. —**devastation,** *n.* devastación.
develop (dɪˈvɛl·əp) *v.t.* **1,** (expand) desarrollar. **2,** (train) entrenar; adiestrar. **3,** (disclose) desplegar; revelar; descubrir. **4,** (improve) perfeccionar; mejorar. **5,** *photog.* revelar. **6,** (real estate) urbanizar. —*v.i.* **1,** (evolve) desarrollarse. **2,** (grow) crecer. **3,** (be disclosed) revelarse; descubrirse.
development (dɪˈvɛl·əp·mənt) *n.* **1,** (growth; expansion) desarrollo; desenvolvimiento. **2,** *photog.* revelado. **3,** (real estate) urbanización. **4,** (undertaking; venture) empresa. **5,** (accomplishment) creación; realización.
deviate (ˈdi·viˌeit) *v.t.* desviar. —*v.i.* desviarse; dar vueltas. —*n.* (-ət) excéntrico. —**deviation,** *n.* desviación.
device (dɪˈvais) *n.* **1,** (apparatus) artefacto; dispositivo; utensilio. **2,** (scheme) treta; ardid. **3,** *heraldry* mote; blasón; lema. **4,** *pl.* (desires) deseos; antojos.
devil (ˈdɛv·əl) *n.* **1,** (evil spirit) demonio; diablo. **2,** *cap.* el Diablo; Satán. —*v.t.* **1,** (torment) atormentar; martirizar; molestar. **2,** (season) condimentar.
devilfish *n.* **1,** (octopus) octópodo; pulpo. **2,** (ray) manta.
devilish (ˈdɛv·əl·ɪʃ) *adj.* **1,** (fiendish) diabólico; perverso. **2,** (roguish) excesivo.
devilment (ˈdɛv·əl·mənt) *también,* **deviltry,** *n.* **1,** (evil act) perversidad. **2,** (mischief) diablura.
devious (ˈdi·vi·əs) *adj.* desviado; tortuoso. —**deviousness,** *n.* desviación; extravío.
devise (dɪˈvaiz) *v.t.* **1,** (concoct) proyectar; planear. **2,** *law* (bequeath) legar. —*v.i.* hacer planes *o* proyectos. —*n., law* **1,** (bequest) legado; manda. **2,** (will) testamento. —**devisee** (-ˌvaiˈziː) *n.* legatorio. —**deviser,** *n.* autor; inventor. —**devisor,** *n., law* testador.
devoid (dɪˈvɔid) *adj.* vacío; desprovisto; carente.
devolution (dɛv·əˈlu·ʃən) *n.* **1,** (transmission) traspaso; transmisión. **2,** *biol.* degeneración.

devolve (dɪ'valv) *v.t.* transferir; traspasar; transmitir. —*v.i.* pasar (a); incumbir (a).
devote (dɪ'vot) *v.t.* **1,** (give) dedicar; aplicar. **2,** (consecrate) consagrar. —**devoted** (-ɪd) *adj.* dedicado; devoto; ferviente. —**devotee** (dɛv·ə'ti) *n.* devoto.
devotion (dɪ'vo·ʃən) *n.* **1,** (affection) devoción; dedicación. **2,** *pl.* (prayers) oraciones; preces; plegarias. —**devotional,** *adj.* devoto; piadoso.
devour (dɪ'vaur) *v.t.* devorar; destruir.
devout (dɪ'vaut) *adj.* **1,** (pious) devoto; piadoso. **2,** (heartfelt) sincero; cordial. —**devoutness,** *n.* devoción; piedad.
dew (djuː) *n.* rocío.
dewberry ('du,bɛr·i) *n.* zarza.
dewy ('dju·i) *adj.* **1,** (moist) rociado. **2,** *fig.* (fresh) fresco; joven; hermoso.
dexterity (dɛk'stɛr·ə·ti) *n.* destreza; habilidad; —**dexterous** ('dɛks·tər·əs) *adj.* diestro; hábil.
dextro- (dɛks·tro) *prefijo* dextro-; derecha; que está a la derecha: *dextrogyrate,* dextrógiro.
dextrose ('dɛks·tros) *n.* dextrosa.
di- (dai) *prefijo* **1,** dos; dos veces; el doble: *digraph,* dígrafo; *dichloride,* dicloruro; *dichromatic,* dicromático. **2,** *var. de* **dis-**: *divest,* despojar. **3,** *var. de* **dia-**: *diactinic,* diactínico.
dia- (dai·ə) *prefijo* dia-. **1,** separación: *diacritical,* diacrítico. **2,** oposición: *diamagnetic,* diamagnético. **3,** a través: *diagonal,* diagonal.
diabetes (,dai·ə'bi·tɪs) *n.* diabetes. —**diabetic** (-'bɛt·ɪk) *n.* & *adj.* diabético.
diabolic (,dai·ə'bal·ɪk) *adj.* diabólico; infernal; demoníaco. *También,* **diabolical.**
diacritical (,dai·ə'krɪt·ɪ·kəl) *adj.* diacrítico. —**diacritical mark,** signo diacrítico.
diadem ('dai·ə,dɛm) *n.* diadema.
diagnose (,dai·æg'nos) *v.t.* diagnosticar.
diagnosis (,dai·æg'no·sɪs) [*pl.* **-ses** (-siz)] *n.* diagnosis; diagnóstico.
diagnostic (,dai·æg'nas·tɪk) *adj.* diagnóstico. —**diagnostician** (-nas·'tɪʃ·ən) *n.* médico experto en diagnosticar.
diagonal (dai'æg·ə·nəl) *adj.* & *n.* diagonal.
diagram ('dai·ə,græm) *n.* diagrama. —*v.t.* esquematizar. —**diagrammatic** (-grə'mæt·ɪk) *adj.* diagramático.
dial ('dai·əl) *n.* **1,** (clock face) esfera. **2,** (sundial) cuadrante. **3,** (telephone device) disco. **4,** *radio* (station finder) cuadrante; dial. —*v.t.* **1,** (use telephone device) marcar. **2,** *radio* (tune in) sintonizar. —**dial tone,** señal para marcar.
dialect ('dai·ə,lɛkt) *n.* dialecto. —**dialectal** (-'lɛk·təl) *adj.* dialectal.
dialectic (,dai·ə'lɛk·tɪk) *adj.* [*también,* **dialectical**] dialéctico. —*n.* [*también,* **dialectics**] dialéctica.
dialectician (,dai·ə·lɛk'tɪʃ·ən) *n.* dialéctico.
dialogue *también,* **dialog** ('dai·ə,lɔg) *n.* diálogo.
diameter (dai'æm·ɪ·tər) *n.* diámetro. —**diametrical** (,dai·ə'mɛt·rɪ·kəl) *adj.* diametral.
diamond ('dai·mənd) *n.* **1,** (gem) diamante. **2,** (rhombus or lozenge [◇]) rombo; losange. **3,** (playing-card symbol) rombo; diamante; *Amer.* carró. **4,** (baseball field) losange.
diapason (,dai·ə'pei·zən) *n.* diapasón.
diaper ('dai·pər) *n.* **1,** (infant's breech cloth) pañal. **2,** (pattern) adamasca. **3,** (patterned cloth) lienzo adamascado.
diaphanous (dai'æf·ə·nəs) *adj.* diáfano.
diaphragm ('dai·ə,fræm) *n.* diafragma.
diarrhea (dai·ə'ri·ə) *n.* diarrea.
diarrhetic (dai·ə'rɛt·ɪk) *adj.* diarreico. —*n.* purgante.
diary ('dai·ə·ri) *n.* diario.
Diaspora (dai'æs·pə·rə) *n.* Diáspora.
diastole (dai'æs·tə·li) *n.* diástole. —**diastolic** (,dai·ə'stal·ɪk) *adj.* diastólico.
diathermy ('dai·ə,θʌɹ·mi) *n.* diatermia. —**diathermic** (-'θʌɹ·mɪk) *adj.* diatérmico.
diatom ('dai·ə·təm) *n.* diatomea.
diatonic (,dai·ə'tan·ɪk) *adj.* diatónico.
diatribe ('dai·ə,traib) *n.* diatriba.
dice (dais) *n.* **1,** (game) dados. **2,** *pl. de* **die.** —*v.t.* cortar en cubitos.

dichotomy (dai'kat·ə·mi) *n.* dicotomía.
dicker ('dɪk·ər) *v.t.* & *i., colloq.* regatear. —*n.* regateo.
dickey ('dɪk·i) *n.* **1,** (child's bib) babero; (shirt front) pechera. **2,** (bird) pajarito; **3,** (back seat) asiento trasero. **4,** (driver's seat) asiento del conductor.
dicta ('dɪk·tə) *n., pl. de* **dictum.**
Dictaphone ('dɪk·təˌfon) *n., marca registrada* dictáfono.
dictate ('dɪk·teit) *v.t.* & *i.* **1,** (tell what to write) dictar. **2,** (decree; command) ordenar; mandar; dictar. —*n.* dictado; mandato. —**dictation,** *n.* dictado.
dictator ('dɪk·tei·tər) *n.* dictador. —**dictatorship,** *n.* dictadura.
dictatorial (dɪk·tə'tor·i·əl) *adj.* dictatorial.
diction ('dɪk·ʃən) *n.* dicción.
dictionary ('dɪk·ʃə·nɛr·i) *n.* diccionario.
dictum ('dɪk·təm) *n.* [*pl.* **-ta** (-tə)] **1,** (order) dictamen; sentencia. **2,** (saying) dicho; máxima; aforismo.
did (dɪd) *v., pret. de* **do.**
didactic (dai'dæk·tɪk) *adj.* didáctico. —**didactics,** *n.* didáctica.
didymium (dɪ'dɪm·i·əm) *n.* didimio.
die (dai) *v.i.* [**died, dying**] **1,** (cease living) morir; fallecer. **2,** *fig.* (come to an end) acabarse; terminarse. **3,** [*usu.,* **die away** *o* **out**] (fade away) desaparecer lentamente; morir poco a poco. **4,** (lose sparkle, as wine) desvirtuarse. **5,** *colloq.* (desire) morirse. —*n.* **1,** (engraving stamp) troquel; plancha; matriz. **2,** *sing. de* **dice,** dado. **3,** *mech.* (various tools) tuerca; cojinete *o* hembra de terraja. **4,** *archit.* (dado) cubo.
diehard *n.* & *adj.* intransigente.
dielectric (ˌdai·ə'lɛk·trɪk) *adj.* & *n.* dieléctrico.
dieresis (dai'ɛr·ə·sɪs) *n.* [*pl.* **-ses** (-siz)] diéresis; crema.
die-stamp *v.t.* troquelar; acuñar.
diet ('dai·ət) *n.* **1,** (food restriction) dieta; régimen. **2,** (assembly) dieta. —*v.i.* adietar; estar a dieta. —*v.t.* poner a dieta.
dietary ('dai·ə·tɛr·i) *adj.* dietético.
dietetic (ˌdai·ə'tɛt·ɪk) *adj.* dietético. —**diatetics,** *n.* dietética.
dietician (ˌdai·ə'tɪʃ·ən) *n.* especialista en dietética.
dif- (dɪf) *prefijo, var. de* **dis-** *ante* f: *difference,* diferencia.
differ ('dɪf·ər) *v.i.* **1,** [**differ from**] (be dissimilar) diferir; no parecerse a. **2,** [**differ with**] (disagree) diferir de; no estar de acuerdo; discutir.
difference ('dɪf·ər·əns) *n.* diferencia. —**what difference does it make?,** ¿qué más da?
different ('dɪf·ər·ənt) *adj.* diferente; distinto.
differential (dɪf·ə'rɛn·ʃəl) *adj.* & *n.* diferencial.
differentiate (ˌdɪf·ə'rɛn·ʃiˌet) *v.t.* diferenciar —*v.i.* diferenciarse. —**differentiation,** *n.* diferenciación.
difficult ('dɪf·ɪ·kəlt) *adj.* difícil.
difficulty ('dɪf·ɪˌkʌl·ti) *n.* **1,** (obstacle) dificultad. **2,** *pl.* (troubles, esp. economic) aprietos; apuros económicos. —**be in difficulties,** hallarse en un apuro.
diffidence ('dɪf·ɪ·dəns) *n.* apocamiento; vergüenza; timidez. —**diffident,** *adj.* apocado; vergonzoso; tímido.
diffract (dɪ'frækt) *v.t.* difractar; descomponer. —**diffraction** (-'fræk·ʃən) *n.* difracción.
diffuse (dɪ'fjuːz) *v.t.* difundir; esparcir; derramar. —*v.i.* difundirse; esparcirse; derramarse. —*adj.* (-'fjus) **1,** (scattered) difundido; extendido. **2,** (verbose) difuso; prolijo.
diffusion (dɪ'fju·ʃən) *n.* difusión. —**diffusive** (-sɪv) *adj.* difusor.
dig (dɪg) *v.t.* [**dug, digging**] **1,** (excavate) cavar; excavar. **2,** *colloq.* (work hard) ahondar; trabajar mucho. **3,** *slang* (understand) comprender. —*v.i.* **1,** (excavate) cavar. **2,** *colloq.* (work hard) sudar la gota gorda. **3,** *mil.* (dig trenches) abrir trincheras. **4,** [**dig through** *o* **into**] (penetrate) abrirse camino. —*n., colloq.* **1,** (hole) cava. **2,** (poke) empuje; empellón. **3,** *colloq.* (jeer) pulla; puya. —**dig in,** (entrench) atrincherar.
digest (dɪ'dʒɛst) *v.t.* **1,** (absorb) digerir. **2,** (assimilate) digerir; meditar. **3,** (epitomize) condensar. —*n.* ('dai·dʒɛst) compendio; resumen; *law* digesto. —**digestible** (dɪ·'dʒɛs·tə·bəl) *adj.* digestible; digerible. —**digestion** (-'dʒɛs·tʃən) *n.* digestión. —**digestive,** *adj.* digestivo.
digger ('dɪg·ər) *n.* **1,** (person digging) excavador; cavador. **2,**

(tool) azada; azadón. **3,** (machine) excavadora.
diggings ('dɪg·ɪŋz) *n.pl.* **1,** (excavations) excavaciones. **2,** *slang* (abode) domicilio; morada.
digit ('dɪdʒ·ɪt) *n.* **1,** (finger; toe) dedo. **2,** (number) dígito. **—digital,** *adj.* dígito; digital.
digitalis (dɪdʒ·ə'tæl·ɪs) *n., bot.; pharm.* digital.
dignify ('dɪg·nɪˌfai) *v.t.* dignificar; ennoblecer; honrar. **—dignified,** *adj.* digno; grave; noble.
dignitary ('dɪg·nɪˌtɛr·i) *n.* dignatario.
dignity ('dɪg·nə·ti) *n.* **1,** (worthiness) dignidad. **2,** (rank) ocupación; cargo. **3,** (stateliness) gravedad; nobleza.
digress (dɪ'grɛs) *v.i.* desviarse; divagar. **—digression** (-'grɛʃ·ən) *n.* digresión. **—digressive** (-'grɛs·ɪv) *adj.* digresivo.
dihedral (dai'hiː·drəl) *adj.* diedro.
dike (daik) *n.* dique; represa.
dilapidate (dɪ'læp·ə·deit) *v.t.* dilapidar. **—*v.i.*** arruinarse; desmantelarse. **—dilapidated,** *adj.* arruinado; destartalado.
dilapidation (dɪˌlæp·ə'dei·ʃən) *n.* dilapidación; derroche; arruinado.
dilate ('dai·leit) *v.t.* & *i.* dilatar; extender. **—dilation** [*también,* **dilatation** (ˌdɪl·ə'tei·ʃən)] *n.* dilatación. **—dilator,** *n.* dilatador.
dilatory ('dɪl·ə·tor·i) *adj.* dilatorio; tardo; lento; *law* dilatorio.
dilemma (dɪ'lɛm·ə) *n.* dilema; alternativa; disyuntiva.
dilettante (ˌdɪl·ə'tan·ti; -'tant) *n.* diletante; aficionado; entusiasta.
diligence ('dɪl·ɪ·dʒəns) *n.* diligencia. **—diligent,** *adj.* diligente.
dill (dɪl) *n.* eneldo.
dillydally ('dɪl·i'dæl·i) *v.i.* malgastar el tiempo.
dilute (dɪ'lut) *v.t.* diluir; desleír. **—*adj.*** diluido; desleído.
dilution (dɪ'lu·ʃən) *n.* dilución; desleimiento.
diluvial (dɪ'lu·vi·əl) *adj.* diluvial; diluviano.
dim (dɪm) *adj.* **1,** (almost dark) mortecino; difuso; débil. **2,** (vague) oscuro; confuso. **3,** (dull) tardo; torpe; lento. **—*v.t.*** [**dimmed, dimming**] amortiguar; oscurecer. **—*v.i.*** amortiguarse; oscurecerse.
dime (daim) *n., U.S.* moneda de 10 centavos.
dimension (dɪ'mɛn·ʃən) *n.* dimensión. **—dimensional,** *adj.* dimensional.
diminish (dɪ'mɪn·ɪʃ) *v.t.* & *i.* disminuir; rebajar.
diminuendo (dɪˌmɪn·ju'ɛn·do) *n., adj.* & *adv., music* diminuendo.
diminution (ˌdɪ·mɪ'nju·ʃən) *n.* disminución; diminución.
diminutive (dɪ'mɪn·jʊ·tɪv) *adj.* diminutivo; diminuto. **—*n.* 1,** (small thing) cosa diminuta. **2,** *gram.* diminutivo.
dimness ('dɪm·nəs) *n.* oscuridad.
dimple ('dɪm·pəl) *n.* hoyuelo. **—*v.i.*** formarse hoyuelos.
dimwit ('dɪm·wɪt) *n., slang* lerdo; tonto.
din (dɪn) *n.* clamor; estrépito.
dine (dain) *v.i.* cenar; comer. **—*v.t.*** dar de comer; ofrecer una comida a.
diner ('dai·nər) *n.* **1,** (person who dines) comensal. **2,** (eating place) restaurante; café. **3,** *R.R.* coche-comedor; coche-restaurante.
ding (dɪŋ) *n.* repique; sonido. **—*v.i.* 1,** (clang) repicar; sonar. **2,** *slang* (repeat) insistir; repetir insistentemente. **—ding-dong** ('dɪŋ·'daŋ) *n.* din-dán; tintín.
dinghy ('dɪŋ·gi) *n.* bote de remos.
dingy ('dɪn·dʒi) *adj.* deslucido; manchado. **—dinginess,** *n.* deslustre; suciedad.
dining room *n.* comedor.
dinky ('dɪŋ·ki) *adj.* diminuto; pequeño. **—*n.*** [*también,* **dinkey**] locomotora de maniobras.
dinner ('dɪn·ər) *n.* **1,** (meal) cena; comida. **2,** (banquet) banquete. **—dinner coat,** smoking. **—dinner napkin,** servilleta. **—dinner party,** convite.
dinosaur ('dai·nəˌsor) *n.* dinosauro.
dint (dɪnt) *n.* **1,** (dent) abolladura. **2,** (power) fuerza. **—by dint of,** a fuerza de.
diocese ('dai·ə·sis) *n.* diócesis. **—diocesan** (dai'as·ɪ·sən) *adj.* diocesano.
diode ('dai·od) *n.* díodo.
diorama (ˌdai·ə'ræm·ə) *n.* diorama. **—dioramic,** *adj.* diorámico.
dioxide (dai'ak·said) *n.* dióxido.
dip (dɪp) *v.t.* [**dipped, dipping**] **1,** (immerse) sumergir. **2,** (lower and

raise) subir y bajar rápidamente. **3,** (scoop up) sacar. —*v.i.* **1,** (plunge) sumergirse; zambullirse. **2,** [*usu.,* **dip into**] (investigate) investigar; buscar; (be interested in) empeñarse en; interesarse en; (browse) hojear. **3,** (bend down) inclinarse hacia abajo. **4,** *fig.* (sink) hundirse; penetrar. **5,** *geol.; mining* buzar. —*n.* **1,** (immersion) inmersión; zambullida. **2,** (downward slope) inclinación; declive; *aero.* bache. **3,** (bath, to dye or disinfect) tinte. **4,** *geol.; mining* buzamiento. —**dip the flag,** saludar con la bandera.

diphtheria (dɪf'θɪr·i·ə) *n.* difteria.

diphthong ('dɪf·θaŋ) *n.* diptongo.

diploma (dɪ'plo·mə) *n.* diploma.

diplomacy (dɪ'plo·mə·si) *n.* **1,** (international relations) diplomacia. **2,** (tact) tacto.

diplomat ('dɪp·lə·mæt) *n.* diplomático. —**diplomatic** (-'mæt·ɪk) *adj.* diplomático.

diplomatist (dɪ'plo·mə·tɪst) *n.* diplomático.

dipper ('dɪp·ər) *n.* **1,** (ladle) cucharón; cazo; (of a machine) cuchara; pala. **2,** *cap., astron.* Carro.

dippy ('dɪp·i) *adj., slang* loco; excéntrico.

dipsomania (ˌdɪp·sə'mei·ni·ə) *n.* dipsomanía. —**dipsomaniac** (-ˌæk) *n.* & *adj.* dipsomaníaco.

dire (dair) *adj.* horrible; horroroso; lamentable. —**direful** (-fəl) *adj.* horrendo; deplorable.

direct (dɪ'rɛkt) *v.t.* **1,** (aim) dirigir. **2,** (guide) guiar; ordenar. **3,** (command) mandar. —*adj.* **1,** (straightforward) directo; franco; abierto. **2,** (firsthand) personal; fidedigno.

direct current corriente continua.

direction (dɪ'rɛk·ʃən) *n.* **1,** (relative position) dirección. **2,** (regulation) orden; mandato. **3,** *usu.pl.* (instruction) instrucción. —**directional,** *adj.* direccional.

directive (dɪ'rɛk·tɪv) *n.* directiva. —*adj.* directivo.

directly (dɪ'rɛkt·li) *adv.* **1,** (without deviating) derecho. **2,** (immediately) en seguida.

direct object *gram.* complemento directo.

director (dɪ'rɛk·tər) *n.* director. —**directorate** (-ət) [*también,* **directorship**] *n.* dirección; directorio.

directory (dɪ'rɛk·tə·ri) *n.* **1,** (list of names, etc.) directorio. **2,** (telephone book) guía telefónica. **3,** *cap., hist.* Directorio.

dirge (dʌɹdʒ) *n.* **1,** (sad music or poem) endecha. **2,** *eccles.* (hymn) canto fúnebre; (mass) oficio de difuntos.

dirigible ('dɪr·ɪ·dʒə·bəl) *adj.* & *n.* dirigible.

dirt (dʌɹt) *n.* **1,** (dust) polvo; (mud) lodo; barro. **2,** (earth; soil) tierra; suelo; terreno. **3,** (filth) suciedad; porquería. **4,** *slang* (gossip) trapos sucios. —*adj.* de tierra. —**dirt cheap,** *colloq.* muy barato.

dirtiness ('dʌɹ·ti·nəs) *n.* **1,** (uncleanliness) suciedad; porquería. **2,** (baseness) bajeza; vileza.

dirty ('dʌɹ·ti) *adj.* **1,** (soiled) enlodado; sucio; con polvo. **2,** (base) bajo; vil; menospreciable. —*v.t.* ensuciar. —**dirty look,** *slang* mirada despectiva.

dis- (dɪs) *prefijo* dis-; des-; di-. **1,** negación: *discontinuous,* discontinuo; descontinuo. **2,** oposición; contraste: *dissimilar,* disímil; desemejante. **3,** separación: *dissident,* disidente.

disable (dɪs'ei·bəl) *v.t.* inhabilitar; incapacitar. —**disability** (dɪs·ə'bɪl·ə·ti) *n.* incapacidad; impedimento.

disabuse (dɪs·ə'bjuːz) *v.t.* desengañar.

disaccord (ˌdɪs·ə'kord) *n.* desacuerdo. —*v.i.* estar en desacuerdo.

disadvantage (ˌdɪs·əd'væn·tɪdʒ) *n.* **1,** (unfavorable condition) desventaja. **2,** (drawback) detrimento; menoscabo. —*v.t.* perjudicar. —**disadvantageous,** *adj.* desventajoso.

disaffect (dɪs·ə'fɛkt) *v.t.* enemistar; indisponer. —**disaffection** (-'fɛk·ʃən) *n.* desafección; desafecto; descontento.

disaffirm (dɪs·ə'fʌɹm) *v.t.* negar; contradecir; *law* impugnar; anular.

disagree (dɪs·ə'griː) *v.i.* **1,** (have different opinions) no estar de acuerdo; diferir; disentir. **2,** (be incompatible or unsuitable) no sentar bien (a); no ir bien (con).

disagreeable (ˌdɪs·ə'gri·ə·bəl) *adj.* desagradable.

disagreement (ˌdɪs·ə'gri·mənt) *n.* **1,** (difference of opinion) desacuerdo; disensión. **2,** (quarrel) contienda; altercado. **3,** (discrepancy) discrepancia; diferencia.

disallow (dɪs·ə'lau) *v.t.* **1,** (disapprove) desaprobar. **2,** (deny; reject) denegar; rechazar.
disappear (dɪs·ə'pɪr) *v.i.* desaparecer. —**disappearance,** *n.* desaparición.
disappoint (dɪs·ə'pɔint) *v.t.* **1,** (fail to satisfy) defraudar; decepcionar; desilusionar. **2,** (thwart) chasquear; frustrar; desbaratar. —**disappointing,** *adj.* desilusionante. —**disappointment,** *n.* decepción; desilusión; chasco.
disapprove (dɪs·ə'pruv) *v.t.* & *i.* desaprobar. —**disapproval,** *n.* desaprobación.
disarm (dɪs'arm) *v.t.* & *i.* desarmar. —**disarming,** *adj.* conciliador; amistoso.
disarmament (dɪs'ar·mə·mənt) *n.* desarme.
disarrange (dɪs·ə'reindʒ) *v.t.* desarreglar; descomponer.
disarray (dɪs·ə'rei) *v.t.* **1,** (disrobe) desnudar; desvestir. **2,** (rout) derrotar; desordenar. —*n.* **1,** (confusion) desorden; desarreglo; confusión. **2,** (disorderly dress) desatavío; trapillo.
disassemble (dɪs·ə'sɛm·bəl) *v.t.* desarmar; desmontar; desacoplar.
disassociate (dɪs·ə'so·si·eit) *v.t.* disociar; desunir; separar.
disaster (dɪ'zæs·tər) *n.* desastre. —**disastrous** (-trəs) *adj.* desastroso.
disavow (dɪs·ə'vau) *v.t.* **1,** (deny approval of) desautorizar; repudiar. **2,** (disown) negar; repudiar. **3,** (deny knowledge of) desconocer; ignorar. —**disavowal,** *n.* negación; desconocimiento; repudiación.
disband (dɪs'bænd) *v.t.* **1,** (dissolve, as a group) disolver. **2,** *mil.* (dismiss) licenciar. —*v.i.* desbandarse. —**disbandment,** *n.* desbandada; disolución; *mil.* licenciamiento.
disbelief (dɪs·bə'lif) *n.* incredulidad.
disbelieve (dɪs·bə'liːv) *v.t.* & *i.* descreer; dudar.
disburse (dɪs'bʌɹs) *v.t.* desembolsar. —**disbursement,** *n.* desembolso.
disc (dɪsk) *n.* = **disk.**
discard (dɪs'kard) *v.t.* & *i.* descartar. —*n.* ('dɪs·kard) descarte.
discern (dɪ'sʌɹn) *v.t.* & *i.* discernir; distinguir; percibir. —**discerning,** *adj.* perspicaz; sagaz. —**discernment,** n. discernimiento; percepción.
discharge (dɪs'tʃardʒ) *n.* **1,** (act of unloading; shooting) descarga. **2,** (payment, as of a debt) descargo; cumplimiento. **3,** (release, as of a prisoner) liberación; absolución; (as of a defendant) exoneración; (as of a soldier) licenciamiento; licencia; (as of a patient) alta; (as from a duty) descargo. **4,** (dismissal) despedida; remoción. **5,** (emission) derrame. **6,** (performance) desempeño; cumplimiento. **7,** *electricity* descarga. —*v.t.* **1,** (unload) descargar. **2,** (emit, as water) desaguar; (suppurate) arrojar; echar; emitir. **3,** (release) libertar; absolver; (as from suspicion) exonerar; (as from obligations) eximir; (as from the army) licenciar; (as a patient) dar de alta. **4,** (dismiss) despedir; echar. **5,** (perform) desempeñar; cumplir. **6,** (fire) disparar; descargar. **7,** (pay [a debt]) saldar; cancelar. **8,** *electricity* descargar. —*v.i.* descargar; descargarse.
disciple (dɪ'sai·pəl) *n.* discípulo.
discipline ('dɪs·ə·plɪn) *n.* **1,** (training; obedience) disciplina. **2,** (punishment) disciplina; corrección; castigo. —*v.t.* **1,** (train) disciplinar. **2,** (punish) castigar; disciplinar. —**disciplinarian** (-plɪ'nɛr·i·ən) *n.* ordenancista. —*adj.* disciplinario. —**disciplinary,** *adj.* disciplinario.
disclaim (dɪs'kleim) *v.t.* **1,** (disown) renunciar; rehusar. **2,** (refuse to acknowledge) rechazar; repudiar. **3,** (deny) negar. **4,** *law* renunciar. —**disclaimer,** *n.* renuncia; rechazo; repudio.
disclose (dɪs'kloːz) *v.t.* descubrir; revelar; exponer. —**disclosure** (-'kloː·ʒər) *n.* revelación; descubrimiento.
discolor (dɪs'kʌl·ər) *v.t.* descolorar; desteñir. —*v.i.* descolorarse; desteñirse. —**discoloration,** *n.* decoloración.
discomfit (dɪs'kʌm·fɪt) *v.t.* frustrar; desconcertar. —**discomfiture** (-fɪ·tʃər) *n.* desconcierto; frustración.
discomfort (dɪs'kʌm·fərt) *n.* incomodidad; malestar. —*v.t.* incomodar; molestar.
discompose (ˌdɪs·kʌm'poːz) *v.t.* descomponer; desconcertar. —**discomposure** (-'po·ʒər) *n.* descomposición; desconcierto.

disconcert (dɪs·kən'sʌɹt) *v.t.* 1, (confuse) desconcertar; confundir; perturbar. 2, (throw into disorder) desconcertar; desordenar.
disconnect (dɪs·kə'nɛkt) *v.t.* desconectar; desunir.
disconsolate (dɪs'kan·sə·lət) *adj.* desconsolado; inconsolable.
discontent (dɪs·kən'tɛnt) *n.* descontento. —*v.t.* descontentar. —**discontented,** *adj.* descontento.
discontinue (dɪs·kən'tɪn·ju) *v.t.* & *i.* descontinuar *o* discontinuar; interrumpir. —**discontinuation; discontinuance,** *n.* discontinuación. —**discontinuous,** *adj.* discontinuo; interrumpido.
discontinuity (dɪsˌkan·tə'nju·ə·ti) *n.* discontinuidad.
discord ('dɪs·kord) *n.* 1, (disagreement) desacuerdo; discordia. 2, *music* discordancia; disonancia.
discordant (dɪs'kor·dənt) *adj.* discordante; discorde; desacorde; *music* disonante. —**discordance,** *n.* discordancia; discordia; desacuerdo; *music* disonancia.
discount ('dɪs·kaunt) *v.t.* 1, (deduct) descontar. 2, (disregard) considerar exagerado; desestimar. 3, *comm.* descontar; deducir; rebajar. —*n.* descuento; rebaja.
discountenance (dɪs'kaun·tə·nəns) *v.t.* 1, (abash) avergonzar; humillar. 2, (discourage) desaprobar; desanimar.
discourage (dɪs'kʌɹ·ɪdʒ) *v.t.* 1, (lessen one's hopes) desanimar; desalentar. 2, (urge to refrain) disuadir. 3, (try to prevent) oponerse a. —**discouraging,** *adj.* desalentador.
discouragement (dɪs'kʌɹ·ɪdʒ·mənt) *n.* 1, (dejection) desánimo; desaliento. 2, (dissuasion) disuasión. 3, (hindrance) oposición.
discourse ('dɪs·kors) *n.* discurso. —*v.i.* (dɪs'kors) discurrir.
discourteous (dɪs'kʌɹ·ti·əs) *adj.* descortés; mal educado. —**discourtesy** (-tə·si) *n.* descortesía.
discover (dɪs'kʌv·ər) *v.t.* descubrir. —**discoverer,** *n.* descubridor. —**discovery,** *n.* descubrimiento.
discredit (dɪs'krɛd·ɪt) *v.t.* 1, (destroy the reputation of) desacreditar. 2, (mistrust) descreer. —*n.* descrédito. —**discreditable,** *adj.* deshonroso; vergonzoso.
discreet (dɪs'krit) *adj.* discreto; comedido. —**discreetness,** *n.* discreción; comedimiento.
discrepancy (dɪs'krɛp·ən·si) *n.* discrepancia; contradicción.
discrete (dɪs'krit) *adj.* distinto; descontinuo; discreto. —**discreteness,** *n.* distinción.
discretion (dɪs'krɛʃ·ən) *n.* 1, (prudence) discreción. 2, (power to decide) albedrío. —**discretionary** (-ə·nɛr·i) *adj.* discrecional.
discriminate (dɪs'krɪm·ɪ·neit) *v.t.* distinguir; separar; discriminar. —*v.i.* diferenciarse. —**discriminating,** *adj.* discerniente; de buen gusto. —**discrimination,** *n.* distinción; diferencia; discriminación. —**discriminative** (-ˌne·tɪv); **discriminatory** (-nəˌtor·i) *adj.* injusto; parcial.
discursive (dɪs'kʌɹ·sɪv) *adj.* digresivo; divagante.
discus ('dɪs·kəs) *n.* disco.
discuss (dɪs'kʌs) *v.t.* discutir; debatir; tratar de. —**discussion** (-'kʌʃ·ən) *n.* discusión.
disdain (dɪs'dein) *v.t.* & *i.* desdeñar. —*n.* desdén. —**disdainful** (-fəl) *adj.* desdeñoso.
disease (dɪ'ziːz) *n.* enfermedad. —*v.t.* enfermar.
disembark (ˌdɪs·ɛm'bark) *v.i.* desembarcar.
disembarrass (dɪs·əm'bær·əs) *v.t.* desembarazar.
disembody (dɪs·ɛm'ba·di) *v.t.* libertar; desencarnar.
disembowel (ˌdɪs·ɛm'bau·əl) *v.t.* destripar; desentrañar.
disenchant (dɪs·ɛn'tʃænt) *v.t.* desencantar; desilusionar. —**disenchantment,** *n.* desencantamiento.
disencumber (dɪs·ɛn'kʌm·bər) *v.t.* descombrar; liberar. —**disencumbrance** (-brəns) *n.* descombro.
disengage (ˌdɪs·ɛn'geidʒ) *v.t.* 1, (free) librar; soltar. 2, (detach) desunir. 3, (disentangle) desenredar. 4, *mech.* desembragar; desengranar.
disentangle (ˌdɪs·ɛn'tæŋ·gəl) *v.t.* desenredar. —**disentanglement,** *n.* desenredo.
disestablish (ˌdɪs·ɛs'tæb·lɪʃ) *v.t.* separar (la Iglesia) del Estado.
disfavor (dɪs'fei·vər) *v.t.* desfavorecer; desairar. —*n.* disfavor; desgracia.

disfigure (dɪs'fɪg·jər) *v.t.* desfigurar. —**disfigurement,** *n.* desfiguración; desfiguramiento.
disfranchise (dɪs'fræn·tʃaiz) *v.t.* privar de derechos (de ciudadanía).
disgorge (dɪs'gordʒ) *v.t.* arrojar; vomitar. —*v.i.* vaciarse. —**disgorgement,** *n.* vómito.
disgrace (dɪs'greis) *n.* desgracia; deshonra. —*v.t.* deshonrar. —**disgraceful** (-fəl) *adj.* deshonroso; lamentable.
disgruntled (dɪs'grʌn·təld) *adj.* disgustado; descontento; enfadado. —**disgruntle,** *v.t.* disgustar; descontentar. —**disgruntlement,** *n.* disgusto; enfado; descontento.
disguise (dɪs'gaiz) *v.t.* **1,** (mask) disfrazar. **2,** (hide) encubrir; ocultar. **3,** (obscure) desfigurar. —*n.* disfraz; falsa apariencia.
disgust (dɪs'gʌst) *n.* asco; repugnancia. —*v.t.* asquear; repugnar. —**disgusting,** *adj.* repugnante; asqueroso.
dish (dɪʃ) *n.* **1,** (plate) plato. **2,** *pl.* (set of dishes) vajilla (*sing.*). —*v.t.* **1,** (serve) servir. **2,** (shape like a dish) formar una concavidad en. —**dish out, 1,** [*también,* **dish up**] (serve) sevir. **2,** *slang* (administer; inflict) echar (una afrenta); pegar (un castigo) —**do the dishes,** lavar *o* fregar los platos.
disharmony (dɪs'har·mə·ni) *n.* **1,** (discord) discordancia; discordia. **2,** *music* disonancia.
dishcloth *n.* paño de cocina.
dishearten (dɪs'har·tən) *v.t.* descorazonar; desanimar.
dishevel (dɪ'ʃɛv·əl) *v.t.* desmelenar; desgreñar. —**dishevelment,** *n.* desmelenamiento.
dishonest (dɪs'an·əst) *adj.* fraudulento; engañador; deshonesto; ímprobo. —**dishonesty,** *n.* deshonestidad; improbidad.
dishonor *también,* **dishonour** (dɪs·'an·ər) *v.t.* **1,** (shame) deshonrar. **2,** *comm.* (refuse to pay) no aceptar; no pagar. —*n.* deshonra; deshonor.
dishonorable (dɪs'an·ər·ə·bəl) *adj.* **1,** (not honorable) deshonroso; vergonzoso. **2,** (disgraceful) deshonrado.
dishpan *n.* paila para lavar platos.
dishtowel *n.* paño de secar.
dishwasher *n.* **1,** (person) lavaplatos. **2,** (machine) lavadora de platos; máquina de lavar platos.
dishwater *n.* agua de cocina.
disillusion (dɪs·ɪ'lu·ʒən) *n.* desilusión; desencantamiento. —*v.t.* desilusionar; desencantar.
disinclination (dɪs,ɪn·klɪ'nei·ʃən) *n.* mala gana; repugnancia; aversión.
disincline (,dɪs·ɪn'klain) *v.t.* desinclinar. —*v.i.* desinclinarse.
disinfect (dɪs·ɪn'fɛkt) *v.t.* desinfectar. —**disinfectant,** *n.* & *adj.* desinfectante. —**disinfection,** (-'fɛk·ʃən) *n.* desinfección.
disingenuous (dɪs·ɪn'dʒɛn·ju·əs) *adj.* falso; disimulado. —**disingenuousness,** *n.* disimulación; mala fe.
disinherit (dɪs·ɪn'hɛr·ɪt) *v.t.* desheredar. —**disinheritance,** *n.* desheredación.
disintegrate (dɪs'ɪn·tə,greit) *v.t.* desintegrar. —*v.i.* desintegrarse. —**disintegration,** *n.* desintegración.
disinter (,dɪs·ɪn'tʌɹ) *v.t.* [**-interred, -terring**] **1,** (dig up) desenterrar. **2,** *fig.* (bring to light) descubrir. —**disinterment,** *n.* desenterramiento.
disinterest (dɪs'ɪn·tə·rɪst) *n.* desinterés. —**disinterested** (-rɛs·tɪd) *adj.* desinteresado; imparcial.
disjoin (dɪs'dʒoin) *v.t.* desunir; separar.
disjoint (dɪs'dʒoint) *v.t.* **1,** (dislocate) dislocar; desarticular. **2,** (dismember) descoyuntar; desmembrar.
disjointed (dɪs'dʒoin·tɪd) *adj.* **1,** (dislocated) descoyuntado; dislocado. **2,** (disconnected) desarticulado.
disjunction (dɪs'dʒʌŋk·ʃən) *n.* disyunción.
disjunctive (dɪs'dʒʌŋk·tɪv) *adj.* disyuntivo. —*n.* **1,** *gram.* conjunción disyuntiva. **2,** *logic* disyuntiva.
disk *también,* **disc** (dɪsk) *n.* disco.
disk jockey radiolocutor (que toca discos).
dislike (dɪs'laik) *v.t.* disgustar; no gustar de. —*n.* aversión; antipatía. —**dislikable,** *adj.* antipático.
dislocate (dɪs·lo'keit) *v.t.* dislocar. —**dislocation,** *n.* dislocación.
dislodge (dɪs'ladʒ) *v.t.* desalojar. —**dislodgment,** *n.* desalojamiento.
disloyal (dɪs'loi·əl) *adj.* desleal. —**disloyalty** (-ti) *n.* deslealtad.

dismal ('dɪz·məl) *adj.* 1, (miserable) triste; oscuro; miserable. 2, (dreary) tenebroso. —**dismalness,** *n.* tristeza; melancolía.
dismantle (dɪs'mæn·təl) *v.t.* desmantelar.
dismay (dɪs'mei) *v.t.* 1, (cause unexpected alarm) consternar; desanimar. 2, (frighten) espantar. —*n.* miedo; desánimo; consternación.
dismember (dɪs'mɛm·bər) *v.t.* desmembrar. —**dismemberment,** *n.* desmembramiento.
dismiss (dɪs'mɪs) *v.t.* 1, (send away) despedir. 2, (order or permit to depart) autorizar para marcharse. 3, (remove from office) destituir. 4, (discard) descartar. 5, (put out of mind) echar en olvido. 6, *law* (discontinue; reject) rechazar.
dismissal (dɪs'mɪs·əl) *n.* 1, (act of dismissing) despido; despedida. 2, (order to depart) autorización; permiso. 3, (removal from office) destitución; deposición. 4, *law* rechazamiento. 5, *mil.* licenciamiento.
dismount (dɪs'maunt) *v.t.* & *i.* desmontar.
disobedience (dɪs·ə'bi·di·əns) *n.* desobediencia. —**disobedient,** *adj.* desobediente.
disobey (dɪs·ə'bei) *v.t.* & *i.* desobedecer.
disoblige (ˌdɪs·ə'blaidʒ) *v.t.* desobligar.
disorder (dɪs'or·dər) *n.* 1, (disarray) desorden; confusión. 2, (riot) alboroto; tumulto. 3, (irregularity) desarreglo; irregularidad. 4, (disease) enfermedad; (mental) enajenación mental. —*v.t.* desordenar; revolver; desarreglar. —**disordered** (-dərd) *adj.* desordenado; desarreglado; revuelto.
disorderly (dɪs'or·dər·li) *adj.* 1, (irregular; illegal) desordenado. 2, (untidy) desarreglado. 3, (unruly) violento; turbulento. 4, (immoral) inmoral; escandaloso. —**disorderly conduct,** perturbación del orden público; *Amer.* conducta escandalosa. —**disorderly house,** burdel.
disorganize (dɪs'or·gəˌnaiz) *v.t.* desorganizar. —**disorganization** (-nɪ'zei·ʃən) *n.* desorganización.
disorient (dɪs'or·i·ɛnt) *v.t.* desorientar. —**disorientation,** *n.* desorientación.
disown (dɪs'oːn) *v.t.* repudiar; desconocer; negar.
disparage (dɪs'pær·ɪdʒ) *v.t.* desacreditar. —**disparagement,** *n.* descrédito; infamia; desprecio.
disparate ('dɪs·pə·rət) *adj.* disparejo; dispar. —**disparity** (-'pær·ə·ti) *n.* disparidad.
dispassion (dɪs'pæʃ·ən) *n.*, desapasionamiento; imparcialidad. —**dispassionate** (-ət) *adj.* desapasionado; imparcial.
dispatch *también,* **despatch** (dɪs·'pætʃ) *v.t.* 1, (send off or away) despachar; expedir; remitir. 2, (transact) despachar; apresurar. 3, (kill) concluir; rematar; acabar. —*n.* 1, (sending away) despacho; envío; expedición. 2, (message) despacho; parte; comunicación. 3, (speed) prontitud; celeridad. —**dispatcher,** *n.* despachador.
dispel (dɪs'pɛl) *v.t.* [**dispelled, -pelling**] hacer desaparecer.
dispensable (dɪs'pɛn·sə·bəl) *adj.* dispensable.
dispensary (dɪs'pɛns·ər·i) *n.* dispensario.
dispensation (dɪs·pən'sei·ʃən) *n.* 1, (distribution) dispensación. 2, *law; R.C.Ch.* (release) dispensa. 3, (divine act) decreto *o* designio divino.
dispense (dɪs'pɛns) *v.t.* 1, (distribute) dispensar; distribuir. 2, (administer) administrar. 3, (excuse) eximir. —**dispenser,** *n.* dispensador. —**dispense with,** pasar sin; hacer caso omiso de.
disperse (dɪs'pʌɹs) *v.t.* 1, (scatter) dispersar; difundir. 2, (cause to vanish) disipar. 3, *optics* descomponer. —*v.i.* desbandarse. —**dispersion** (-'pʌɹ·ʒən) *n.* dispersión.
dispirit (dɪs'pɪr·ɪt) *v.t.* desanimar; desalentar.
displace (dɪs'pleis) *v.t.* 1, (put out) desplazar; 2, (replace) reemplazar. 3, (remove from office) destituir. —**displaced person,** persona sin hogar.
displacement (dɪs'pleis·mənt) *n.* 1, (dislocation) desalojamiento; mudanza. 2, (removal) destitución. 3, (weight or volume displaced) desplazamiento. 4, *chem.* (filtration) coladura. 5, *geol.* (slide) falla.
display (dɪs'plei) *v.t.* 1, (spread out) desplegar; abrir. 2, (show) mostrar; exhibir. 3, (show off) ostentar. —*v.i.* desplegarse; exhibirse.

—*n.* **1,** (array) despliegue; presentación. **2,** (exhibition) exposición; exhibición. **3,** (ostentatious show) espectáculo; manifestación. **4,** *mil.* (parade) parada. —**display the flag,** enarbolar la bandera.

displease (dɪs'pliːz) *v.t.* desplacer; desagradar; disgustar. —**displeasure** (-'plɛʒ·ər) *n.* desplacer; desagrado; disgusto.

disport (dɪs'port) *v.i.* divertirse; juguetear.

disposable (dɪs'po·zə·bəl) *adj.* disponible.

disposal (dɪs'poz·əl) *n.* **1,** (arrangement) disposición; posición; arreglo. **2,** (settlement) ajuste; arreglo. **3,** *comm.* (transfer) venta; distribución. **4,** (bestowal) cesión; donación. —**at one's disposal,** a la disposición de uno. —**have at one's disposal,** disponer de; poder disponer de.

dispose (dɪs'poːz) *v.t.* **1,** (arrange) disponer; componer; arreglar. **2,** (regulate) disponer; decidir; mandar. **3,** (make willing) inducir; mover. —**dispose of, 1,** (get rid of) deshacerse de; disponer de. **2,** (control) disponer de. **3,** (pass on, as by gift or sale) traspasar; ceder.

disposition (dɪs·pə'zɪʃ·ən) *n.* **1,** (arrangement) disposición; orden. **2,** (settlement) arreglo; acuerdo. **3,** (innate temper) natural; índole; genio. **4,** (tendency) propensión; disposición; tendencia.

dispossess (dɪs·pə'zɛs) *v.t.* desposeer; desalojar; *law* desahuciar. —**dispossession** (-'zɛʃ·ən) *n.* desposeimiento; *law* desahucio.

disproof (dɪs'pruf) *n.* refutación.

disproportion (dɪs·prə'por·ʃən) *n.* desproporción; disparidad. —*v.t.* desproporcionar. —**disproportionate** (-ət) *adj.* desproporcionado.

disprove (dɪs'pruv) *v.t.* refutar.

disputation (ˌdɪs·pju'tei·ʃən) *n.* disputa; debate. —**disputatious** (-ʃəs) *adj.* disputador.

dispute (dɪs'pjut) *v.t.* & *i.* disputar; argüir. —*n.* disputa. —**disputable,** *adj.* disputable. —**disputant** ('dɪs·pju·tənt) *n.* & *adj.* disputador.

disqualify (dɪs'kwal·ɪˌfai) *v.t.* descalificar. —**disqualification** (-fɪ·'kei·ʃən) *n.* descalificación.

disquiet (dɪs'kwai·ət) *v.t.* inquietar; desasosegar. —*n.* [*también,* **disquietude** (-ə·tud)] inquietud; desasosiego.

disquisition (dɪs·kwɪ'zɪʃ·ən) *n.* disquisición.

disregard (ˌdɪs·rɪ'gard) *v.t.* **1,** (ignore) pasar por alto; ignorar. **2,** (disdain) desairar; ignorar; desatender. —*n.* omisión; desaire.

disrepair (ˌdɪs·rɪ'peːr) *n.* desconcierto; estado destartalado.

disrepute (ˌdɪs·rɪ'pjut) *n.* descrédito; mala fama. —**disreputable** (dɪs'rɛp·jə·tə·bəl) *adj.* desacreditado; deshonroso.

disrespect (ˌdɪs·rɪ'spɛkt) *v.t.* desacatar. —*n.* desacato. —**disrespectful** (-fəl) *adj.* irrespetuoso.

disrobe (dɪs'roːb) *v.t.* desnudar; desvestir. —*v.i.* desnudarse; desvestirse.

disrupt (dɪs'rʌpt) *v.t.* & *i.* romper; desbaratar.

disruption (dɪs'rʌp·ʃən) *n.* **1,** (break-up) rompimiento; ruptura; separación. **2,** (turmoil) desorganización. **3,** *electricity* interrupción.

disruptive (dɪs'rʌp·tɪv) *adj.* **1,** (destructive) rompedor. **2,** (disturbing) desorganizador. **3,** *electricity* disruptivo.

dissatisfy (dɪs'sæt·ɪsˌfai) *v.t.* desagradar; descontentar. —**dissatisfaction** (-'fæk·ʃən) *n.* desagrado; descontento.

dissect (dɪ'sɛkt) *v.t.* **1,** (divide) disecar. **2,** *fig.* (analyze) analizar.

dissection (dɪ'sɛk·ʃən) *n.* **1,** (division) disección; *anat.* anatomía. **2,** (analysis) análisis.

dissector (dɪ'sɛk·tər) *n.* disector.

dissemble (dɪ'sɛm·bəl) *v.t.* & *i.* disimular; encubrir; fingir. —**dissemblance** (-bləns) *n.* disimulo; fingimiento.

disseminate (dɪ'sɛm·ɪ·neit) *v.t.* diseminar. —**dissemination,** *n.* diseminación.

dissent (dɪ'sɛnt) *v.i.* disentir. —*n.* disensión; desavenencia. —**dissenter,** *n.* disidente. —**dissension** (-'sɛn·ʃən) *n.* disensión.

dissertation (ˌdɪs·ər'tei·ʃən) *n.* disertación.

disservice (dɪs'sʌɹ·vɪs) *n.* deservicio.

dissidence ('dɪs·ɪ·dəns) *n.* disidencia. —**dissident,** *n.* & *adj.* disidente.

dissimilar (dɪ'sɪm·ɪ·lər) *adj.* disímil; disparejo; diferente. —**dissimilarity** (-'lær·ə·ti) *n.* disimilitud; disparidad.

dissimilate (dɪ'sɪm·ə,leit) *v.t.* disimilar. —*v.i.* disimilarse. —**dissimilation**, *n.* disimilación.

dissimilitude (,dɪs·sɪ'mɪl·ɪ·tud) *n.* disimilitud; disparidad.

dissimulate (dɪ'sɪm·ju,leit) *v.t.* & *i.* disimular. —**dissimulation**, *n.* disimulación; disimulo.

dissipate ('dɪs·ɪ·peit) *v.t.* disipar. —*v.i.* disiparse; desvanecerse. —**dissipation**, *n.* disipación.

dissociate (dɪ'so·ʃi·eit) *v.t.* disociar; separar. —**dissociation**, *n.* disociación.

dissolute ('dɪs·ə·lut) *adj.* disoluto; depravado; relajado. —**dissoluteness**, *n.* disipación; relajación.

dissolution (,dɪs·ə'lu·ʃən) *n.* disolución.

dissolve (dɪ'salv) *v.t.* **1,** (melt; terminate) disolver. **2,** *law* (revoke) anular; revocar. **3,** *photog.* (fade out) disolver; mezclar. —*v.i.* disolverse. —**dissolvent**, *adj.* & *n.* disolvente.

dissonance ('dɪs·ə·nəns) *n.* **1,** disonancia. **2,** (discord) discordia; desacuerdo. —**dissonant**, *adj.* disonante.

dissuade (dɪ'sweid) *v.t.* disuadir. —**dissuasion** (-'swei·ʒən) *n.* disuasión. —**dissuasive** (-sɪv) *adj.* disuasivo.

dissyllable (dɪ'sɪl·ə·bəl) *n.* = **disyllable.** —**dissyllabic** (,dɪs·ɪ·'læb·ɪk) *adj.* = **disyllabic.**

dissymmetry (dɪs'sɪm·ə·tri) *n.* disimetría. —**dissymmetrical** (,dɪs·ɪ'mɛt·rɪ·kəl) *adj.* disimétrico.

distaff ('dɪs·tæf) *n.* **1,** (rod for flax) rueca. **2,** (woman's work) labores femeninas. **3,** (the female sex) el sexo femenino. —**distaff side,** lado materno.

distance ('dɪs·təns) *n.* **1,** (intervening space) distancia. **2,** (remoteness) lontananza. **3,** *music* (interval) intervalo. **4,** *fig.* (haughtiness) esquivez. —**at a distance**, a lo lejos. —**from a distance**, desde lejos. —**keep at a distance**, tratar con indiferencia; mantener a distancia. —**keep one's distance**, mantenerse a distancia; mantenerse en su lugar.

distant ('dɪs·tənt) *adj.* **1,** (remote) distante; lejano; remoto. **2,** (cold; indifferent) esquivo; reservado; frío.

distaste (dɪs'teist) *n.* **1,** (dislike) disgusto. **2,** (aversion) antipatía; aversión. —**distasteful**, *adj.* desagradable.

distemper (dɪs'tɛm·pər) *n.* **1,** (bad humor) destemplanza. **2,** *vet.med.* moquillo. **3,** (disorder) alboroto; tumulto. **4,** *painting* temple. —*v.t.* **1,** (disorder) destemplar; desconcertar; desordenar. **2,** *painting* pintar al temple.

distend (dɪs'tɛnd) *v.t.* distender; dilatar. —*v.i.* distenderse; inflamarse. —**distention**; **distension** (-'stɛn·ʃən) *n.* distensión.

distill (dɪs'tɪl) *v.t.* & *i.* destilar.

distillation (,dɪs·tɪ'lei·ʃən) *n.* destilación. —**fractional distillation**, destilación fraccionada.

distillery (dɪs'tɪl·ə·ri) *n.* destilería.

distinct (dis'tɪŋkt) *adj.* **1,** (different) distinto; diferente. **2,** (well-defined) claro; preciso. **3,** (unmistakable) inequívoco; indudable. —**distinctness**, *n.* distinción; claridad.

distinction (dɪs'tɪŋk·ʃən) *n.* **1,** (differentiation; characteristic) diferencia; distintivo. **2,** (honor) distinción.

distinctive (dɪs'tɪŋk·tɪv) *adj.* **1,** (different) distintivo; diferente. **2,** (characteristic) característico.

distinctiveness (dɪs'tɪŋk·tɪv·nəs) *n.* **1,** (difference) diferencia. **2,** (characteristic quality) característica.

distinguish (dɪs'tɪŋ·gwɪʃ) *v.t.* **1,** (mark; recognize) distinguir; diferenciar. **2,** (discern) discernir; distinguir. **3,** (honor) distinguir; honrar. —*v.i.* distinguirse; destacarse; singularizarse. —**distinguishable**, *adj.* distinguible; destacable. —**distinguished**, *adj.* distinguido; destacado; eminente.

distort (dɪs'tort) *v.t.* **1,** (twist) retorcer; distorsionar. **2,** (falsify) falsear; pervertir. —**distortion** (-'tor·ʃən) *n.* distorsión; falseamiento.

distract (dɪs'trækt) *v.t.* **1,** (divert) distraer; interrumpir. **2,** (bewilder) aturullar; alborotar. **3,** (derange) enloquecer.

distracted (dɪs'træk·tɪd) *adj.* **1,** (diverted) distraído. **2,** (bewildered) aturullado.

distraction (dɪs'træk·ʃən) *n.* **1,** (diversion) distracción. **2,** (bewil-

derment) alboroto. **3,** *colloq.* (madness) locura; frenesí.
distrait (dɪs'treit) *adj.* distraído.
distraught (dɪs'trɔt) *adj.* **1,** (bewildered) aturdido; perplejo. **2,** (irrational) demente.
distress (dɪs'trɛs) *n.* **1,** (pain; suffering) dolor; pena; angustia. **2,** (adversity) revés; infortunio; apuro. **3,** (danger) peligro. **4,** *law* (property seizure) embargo. —*v.t.* afligir; angustiar.
distribute (dɪs'trɪb·jut) *v.t.* **1,** (apportion) distribuir. **2,** (classify) clasificar. **3,** (spread out) esparcir. —**distribution,** *n.* distribución. —**distributive** (-ju·tɪv) *n.* & *adj.* distributivo. —**distributor,** *n.* distributor.
district ('dɪs·trɪkt) *n.* distrito. —**district attorney,** fiscal de distrito.
distrust (dɪs'trʌst) *n.* desconfianza; recelo. —*v.t.* desconfiar; recelar. —**distrustful** (-fəl) *adj.* desconfiado; receloso; sospechoso.
disturb (dɪs'tʌɹb) *v.t.* **1,** (disquiet) turbar; perturbar; alborotar. **2,** (disarrange) desordenar; revolver. **3,** (molest) molestar. —**disturbance,** *n.* disturbio; perturbación.
disunion (dɪs'jun·jən) *n.* desunión.
disunite (ˌdɪs·ju'nait) *v.t.* desunir; separar. —*v.i.* desunirse; separarse. —**disunity** (dɪs'ju·nə·ti) *n.* desunión.
disuse (dɪs'jus) *n.* desuso. —*v.t.* (dɪs'juːz) desusar.
disyllable (dɪ'sɪl·ə·bəl) *n.* disílabo; bisílabo. —**disyllabic** (ˌdɪs·ɪ'læb·ɪk) *adj.* disílabo; bisílabo.
ditch (dɪtʃ) *n.* **1,** (channel) zanja. **2,** (gutter) cuneta. **3,** *mil.* (trench) foso. **4,** (channel for drainage) badén. **5,** *slang* (the sea) charco. —*v.t.* **1,** (surround or drain by a ditch) zanjar. **2,** (throw into a ditch) echar en una zanja. **3,** (run, as a vehicle into a ditch) embarrancar. **4,** (land, as an aircraft in the sea) amerizar por emergencia. **5,** *slang* (abandon) sacudir; desembarazarse de.
ditto ('dɪt·o) *n.* [*pl.* **-os**] **1,** (the same) dicho; ídem. **2,** (duplicate) copia; duplicado. —*v.t.* copiar; duplicar. —*adv., colloq.* igualmente; así como.
ditty ('dɪt·i) *n.* cancioncilla.
diuretic (ˌdai·ju'rɛt·ɪk) *adj.* & *n.* diurético. —**diuresis** (-'ri·sɪs) *n.* diuresis.
diurnal (dai'ʌɹ·nəl) *adj.* diurno; diario.
diva ('di·va) *n.* diva.
divalent (dai'vei·lənt) *adj.* bivalente.
divan ('dai·væn) *n.* diván.
dive (daiv) *v.i.* **1,** (plunge) bucear; zambullirse. **2,** *fig.* (interest oneself) enfrascarse; sumergirse. **3,** *naut.* (submerge) sumergirse. **4,** *aero.* (descend) picar. —*v.t.* zambullir; sumergir. —*n.* **1,** (plunge) zambullida; inmersión. **2,** *colloq.* (disreputable place) tasca; garito. **3,** (plunge) *naut.* inmersión; *aero.* picado. —**dive bomber,** bombardero en picado.
diver ('dai·vər) *n.* **1,** *swimming* zambullidor. **2,** (skindiver; deepsea diver) buzo; buceador. **3,** (diving bird) somorgujo.
diverge (dɪ'vʌɹdʒ) *v.i.* divergir. —**divergence; divergency,** *n.* divergencia. —**divergent,** *adj.* divergente.
diverse (dɪ'vʌɹs; 'dai·vərz) *también,* **divers** ('dai·vərz) *adj.* diverso; vario. —**diverseness,** *n.* diversidad; variedad.
diversify (dɪ'vʌɹs·əˌfai) *v.t.* diversificar. —*v.i.* diversificarse. —**diversification** (-ɪ·fɪ'kei·ʃən) *n.* diversificación.
diversion (dɪ'vʌɹ·ʒən) *n.* **1,** (change of direction) desvío; desviación. **2,** (amusement) diversión; entretenimiento. —**diversionary,** *adj.* de diversión.
diversity (dɪ'vʌɹs·ə·ti) *n.* diversidad; variedad.
divert (dɪ'vʌɹt) *v.t.* **1,** (turn away) desviar; apartar. **2,** (amuse) divertir; entretener.
divest (dɪ'vɛst) *v.t.* **1,** (strip) desvestir; desnudar. **2,** (deprive) despojar; desposeer. —**divestment,** *n.* despojo.
divestiture (dɪ'vɛs·tɪ·tʃər) *n.* despojo; desposeimiento.
divide (dɪ'vaid) *v.t.* **1,** (separate) dividir. **2,** (sever) desunir. **3,** (apportion) compartir. —*v.i.* dividirse; separarse. —*n.* (watershed) vertiente; línea divisoria. —**dividers,** *n.pl.* compás (*sing.*).
dividend ('dɪv·ə·dɛnd) *n.* dividendo.
divination (ˌdɪv·ə'nei·ʃən) *n.* adivinación.
divine (dɪ'vain) *adj.* divino. —*n.* clérigo. —*v.t.* & *i.* adivinar. —**divining rod,** vara de adivinar.

diviner (dɪˈvai·nər) *n.* **1,** (clairvoyant) adivinador. **2,** (magical device) vara mágica. **3,** (divining rod) buscador.
diving (ˈdai·vɪŋ) *adj.* zambullidor; sumergible. —*n.* zambullida; buceo. —**diving suit,** escafandra.
divinity (dɪˈvɪn·ə·ti) *n.* **1,** (divine nature; deity) divinidad. **2,** (study of religion) teología. **3,** *cap.* (God) Dios.
divisible (dɪˈvɪz·ə·bəl) *adj.* divisible. —**divisibility,** *n.* divisibilidad.
division (dɪˈvɪʒ·ən) *n.* división. —**divisional,** *adj.* divisional.
divisive (dɪˈvai·sɪv) *adj.* divisivo.
divisor (dɪˈvai·zər) *n.* divisor.
divorce (dɪˈvors) *n.* divorcio. —*v.t.* divorciar. —*v.i.* divorciarse. —**divorcé** [*fem.* **divorcée**] (-ˈsei) *n.* divorciado; *fem.* divorciada.
divulge (dɪˈvʌldʒ) *v.t.* divulgar; revelar; publicar. —**divulgence,** *n.* divulgación.
Dixie (ˈdɪk·si) *n.* el sur de EE.UU.
dizzy (ˈdɪz·i) *adj.* **1,** (giddy) vertiginoso; mareado; aturdido. **2,** (causing dizziness) mareante. **3,** *slang* (silly) atontado; mentecato; tonto. —*v.t.* marear; aturdir —**dizziness,** *n.* mareo; vértigo; aturdimiento.
do (duː) *v.t.* [**did, done, doing**] **1,** (carry out) hacer; (perform) realizar; ejecutar. **2,** (cause) hacer; causar. **3,** (render) tributar; rendir. **4,** (work at) trabajar en; ocuparse de *o* en. **5,** (finish) terminar; acabar. **6,** (solve) solucionar; resolver. **7,** *slang* (tour) ver; visitar. **8,** (cover, as distance) recorrer. **9,** (translate) traducir. **10,** *colloq.* (cheat; swindle) chasquear; engañar. **11,** *colloq.* (serve, as a jail term) cumplir (una condena). —*v.i.* **1,** (behave) comportarse; conducirse. **2,** (fare) estarse; ir; hallarse. **3,** (suffice; be suitable) servir; bastar. —*v. aux.* **1,** *formando preguntas: Do you like this?,* ¿Le gusta a Vd. esto? **2,** *formando oraciones negativas: I do not like this,* No me gusta esto. **3,** *dando énfasis: Yes, I do like this,* Sí, esto me gusta. **4,** *reemplazando un verbo ya expresado o sobrentendido: Work hard; if you do, you will succeed,* Trabaja; si lo haces, triunfarás. **5,** *en orden invertido tras adverbio: Rarely do things turn out as we expect,* Es raro que salgan las cosas tal cual se espera. —**do away with, 1,** (get rid of) suprimir; desembarazarse de. **2,** (destroy) matar; destrozar. —**do for,** *colloq.* **1,** (destroy) destrozar; arruinar. **2,** (provide for) tratar; cuidar. —**do in,** *slang* **1,** (kill) matar. **2,** (swindle) engañar; timar. —**do up,** *colloq.* **1,** (wrap) envolver; atar. **2,** (dress) arreglar; componer. —**do without,** prescindir de; pasar sin.
do (do) *n., music* do.
docile (ˈdas·əl) *adj.* dócil; sumiso. —**docility** (daˈsɪl·ə·ti) *n.* docilidad; sumisión.
dock (dak) *n.* **1,** (pier) dársena; muelle. **2,** (prisoner's stand) banquillo de los acusados. **3,** (plant) romaza. **4,** (cut tail) muñón de la cola. —*v.t.* **1,** (cut, as a tail) derrabar; cercenar. **2,** (deduct from, as wages) reducir; descontar. **3,** (settle at a pier) atracar. —*v.i.* arrive at a pier) entrar en muelle.
dockage (ˈdak·ɪdʒ) *n.* **1,** *naut.* (docking) entrada en muelle; (docking fee) muellaje; (docking rights) derecho de dique. **2,** (curtailment) rebaja; reducción.
docket (ˈdak·ɪt) *n., law* **1,** (agenda) orden del día; lista de causas pendientes. **2,** (registry of judgments) sumario; lista. —*v.t.* poner en el orden del día.
dockyard *n.* arsenal; dársena.
doctor (ˈdak·tər) *n.* doctor. —*v.t.* **1,** (treat medicinally) medicinar; recetar. **2,** *colloq.* (patch up) componer; reparar. **3,** (adulterate) adulterar. —**doctorate** *n.* doctorado.
doctrine (ˈdak·trɪn) *n.* doctrina. —**doctrinal,** *adj.* doctrinal. —**doctrinaire** (ˌdak·trɪˈneːr) *n.* & *adj.* doctrinario.
document (ˈdak·jə·mənt) *n.* documento. —*v.t.* documentar. —**documental** (-ˈmɛn·təl) *adj.* documental. —**documentation** (-mɛnˈtei·ʃən) *n.* documentación. —**documentary** (-ˈmɛn·tə·ri) *n.* & *adj.* documental.
dodder (ˈdad·ər) *v.i.* **1,** (tremble) temblar. **2,** (totter) tambalear.
dodge (dadʒ) *v.t.* escapar; evadir. —*v.i.* escabullirse; regatear; zafarse. —*n.* **1,** (evasion) regate; evasión. **2,** *colloq.* (trick) esquinazo; evasiva.
dodo (ˈdo·do) *n.* **1,** (extinct bird) dodo; dodó. **2,** (simpleton) necio; bodoque. **3,** (fogy) vejestorio; vejete.

doe (doː) *n.* **1,** (deer) cierva. **2,** (antelope) antílope hembra. **3,** (hare) liebre. **4,** (rabbit) coneja.
doer ('du·ər) *n.* **1,** (performer) hacedor. **2,** (effective person) persona activa.
does (dʌz) *v., tercera persona del sing. del pres. de ind. de* **do.**
doeskin *n.* **1,** (leather) piel de ante. **2,** (woolen cloth) tejido fino de lana.
doff (daf) *v.t.* quitar; quitarse.
dog (dɔg) *n.* **1,** (canine) perro. **2,** (mechanical device) morillo. **3,** (mean fellow) perro; tunante. **4,** *cap., astron.* Can. —*v.t.* [**dogged** (dɔgd), **dogging**] *colloq.* (track; pursue) rastrear; perseguir; seguir las huellas de. —**a dog's age,** una eternidad. —**a dog's life,** vida de perros. —**dog days,** días de perros. —**dog in the manger,** perro de hortelano. —**dog Latin,** latinajo. —**dog tag,** placa. —**dog tired,** cansado como perro; extenuado. —**go to the dogs,** arruinarse; estar perdido. —**house dog,** perro guardián. —**lap dog,** perrito faldero. —**put on the dog,** *slang* presumir; darse ínfulas. —**rain cats and dogs,** llover a cántaros.
dogcatcher *n.* cazaperros.
dog collar dogal.
dogear ('dɔgˌɪr) *n.* orejón. —*v.t.* doblar la punta de.
dogfight *n.* **1,** (fight of dogs) lucha de perros. **2,** (any violent fight) refriega. **3,** *aero.* combate de cazas.
dogfish *n.* cazón; tollo.
dogged ('dag·ɪd) *adj.* emperrado; terco. —**doggedness,** *n.* emperramiento; terquedad.
doggerel ('dag·ər·əl) *n.* aleluyas (*pl.*); coplas de ciego.
doggone (dɔg'gɔn) *adj., colloq.* maldito. —*interj., colloq.* ¡maldicion!
doghouse *n.* perrera. —**in the doghouse,** *slang* en desgracia.
dogma ('dɔg·mə) *n.* dogma. —**dogmatism** (-tɪz·əm) *n.* dogmatismo. —**dogmatic** (-'mæt·ɪk) *adj.* dogmático.
Dog Star Sirio.
dogtooth *n.* [*pl.* **-teeth**] **1,** (eyetooth) colmillo. **2,** *archit.* diente de perro. —**dogtooth violet,** *n.* diente de perro.
dog track canódromo.
dogwatch *n., naut.* guardia de cuartillo.
dogwood *n.* cornejo.
doily ('dɔi·li) *n.* pañito de adorno.
doings ('du·ɪŋs) *n.pl.* **1,** (actions) acciones; actos; hechos. **2,** (behavior) conducta; proceder.
doldrums ('dal·drəmz) *n.pl.* **1,** *naut.* (calm) zona de calmas tropicales. **2,** *fig.* (low spirits) abatimiento (*sing.*).
dole (doːl) *n.* dádiva; limosna; *Brit.* subsidio *o* socorro de desempleo. —*v.t.* [*usu.,* **dole out**] distribuir; repartir.
doll (daːl) *n.* muñeca. —*v.t.* [*usu.,* **doll up**] engalanar; ataviar.
dollar ('da·lər) *n.* dólar.
dolly ('da·li) *n.* **1,** (doll) muñequita. **2,** (truck) plataforma de rodillos.
dolor *también,* **dolour** ('do·lər) *n.* dolor. —**dolorous,** *adj.* doloroso; triste. —**dolorousness,** *n.* dolor; tristeza.
dolphin ('dal·fɪn) *n.* delfín.
dolt (doːlt) *n.* mentecato; bobo.
-dom (dəm) *sufijo; forma nombres indicando:* **1,** dominio; jurisdicción; dignidad: *kingdom,* reino; *earldom,* marquesado. **2,** condición; estado: *martyrdom,* martirio. **3,** colectividad: *Christendom,* cristiandad.
domain (do'mein) *n.* **1,** (territory) dominio. **2,** (scope) campo.
dome (dom) *n.* **1,** (cupola) domo; cúpula. **2,** *slang* (head) cabeza.
domestic (də'mɛs·tɪk) *adj.* **1,** (of the home) doméstico. **2,** (internal) interno. —*n.* doméstico; criado. —**domesticate** (-tɪˌkeit) *v.t.* domesticar. —**domesticity** (ˌdo·mɛs·'tɪs·ə·ti) *n.* domesticidad; *pl.* asuntos domésticos.
domicile ('dom·ə·sɪl) *n.* domicilio. —*v.t.* domiciliar. —*v.i.* domiciliarse.
dominate ('dam·ə·neit) *v.t.* & *i.* dominar; mandar. —**dominance;** **domination,** *n.* dominación. —**dominant,** *adj.* dominante.
domineer (da·mɪ'nɪːr) *v.t.* & *i.* dominar; tiranizar. —**domineering,** *adj.* dominante; tiránico.
dominical (də'mɪn·ə·kəl) *adj.* dominical.
Dominican (də'mɪn·ɪ·kən) *adj.* & *n.* **1,** (of the Dominican Republic) dominicano. **2,** (of the order of St. Dominic) dominico.
dominion (də'mɪn·jən) *n.* dominio.
domino ('dam·ɪ·no) *n.* **1,** (masquerade costume) máscara;

dominó. **2,** *pl.* (game) dominós; dominó. **3,** (tile used in game) dominó; ficha.
don (dan) *v.t.* [**donned, donning**] vestir; poner. —*n.* **1,** *cap.* (Spanish title) don; señor. **2,** *Brit.* (fellow) socio; (tutor) preceptor.
donate ('do·neit) *v.t.* donar; dar; regalar. —**donation,** *n.* donativo; donación.
done (dʌn) *v., p.p. de* **do.** —*adj., cooking* cocinado; cocido; hecho.
donee (do'niː) *n.* donatario.
donkey ('daŋ·ki) *n.* burro; asno.
donor ('do·nər) *n.* donador; donante.
doodle ('du·dəl) *v.i.* borrajear; borronear; garabatear. —*n.* garabato; borrón.
doom (dum) *n.* **1,** (destiny) destino; hado; ruina. **2,** (judgment) juicio; condena; sentencia. —*v.t.* predestinar a la ruina; condenar.
doomsday ('dumʒ·de) *n.* día del juicio final *o* universal.
door (doːr) *n.* puerta; entrada. —**back door,** puerta trasera. —**street door,** puerta de entrada. —**throw open one's doors,** dar hospitalidad.
doorbell *n.* campanilla; timbre.
doorkeeper *n.* portero.
doorknob *n.* tirador; pomo.
doorman *n.* [*pl.* **-men**] portero.
doorsill *n.* umbral.
doorstep *n.* escalón.
doorway *n.* portal; jamba.
dope (dop) *n.* **1,** (viscous substance) pasta; lubricante. **2,** (narcotic) narcótico; droga. **3,** *slang* (information) informe. **4,** *slang* (stupid person) idiota; bobo. —*v.t. slang* [*usu.,* **dope out**] **1,** (solve) solucionar. **2,** (predict) pronosticar. —**dopey; dopy** ('do·pi) atontado.
Doric ('dor·ɪk) *adj.* dórico.
dormant ('dor·mənt) *adj.* adormilado; inactivo; latente. —**dormancy** ('dor·mən·si) *n.* adormilamiento; letargo.
dormer ('dor·mər) *n.* buhardilla; buharda.
dormitory ('dor·mə,tor·i) *n.* dormitorio.
dormouse ('dor,maus) *n.* [*pl.* **-mice**] lirón.
dorsal ('dor·səl) *adj.* dorsal.
dory ('dor·i) *n.* **1,** (dinghy) bote. **2,** (fish) gallo; dorado.
dosage ('do·sɪdʒ) *n.* **1,** (act of dosing) dosificación. **2,** (dose) dosis.
dose (dos) *n.* dosis. —*v.t.* **1,** (give a dose to) dar *or* administrar una dosis; medicinar. **2,** (give in doses) dosificar.
dossier (dɔ'sje) *n.* expediente.
dot (dat) *n.* **1,** *printing* (period) punto. **2,** (speck) lunar. **3,** (dowry) dote. —*v.t.* [**dotted, dotting**] **1,** (mark with a dot) puntear. **2,** (cover with dots) motear; salpicar. —**on the dot,** puntualmente; con exactitud.
dote (dot) *v.i.* chochear. —**dotage** ('do·tɪdʒ) *n.* chochez. —**dotard** ('do·tərd) *n.* viejo chocho.
double ('dʌb·əl) *adj.* doble. —*v.t.* doblar. —*v.i.* doblarse. —**doubly** (-li) *adv.* doblemente; dos al mismo tiempo. —**double chin,** papada. —**double meaning,** doble intención.
double bass *music* contrabajo.
double-breasted *adj.* cruzado.
double-cross *v.t., slang* traicionar. —*n., slang* traición.
double-dealing *n.* doblez; trato de dos caras. —*adj.* doblado; de dos caras.
double-header *n.* **1,** *baseball* doble encuentro. **2,** *R.R.* tren con dos locomotoras.
doubles ('dʌb·əlʒ) *n.pl., games* juego de dobles.
doublet ('dʌb·lɪt) *n.* **1,** (jacket) jubón. **2,** (couple; one of a pair) par; pareja.
doubletalk *n.* jerigonza.
doubt (daut) *n.* duda. —*v.t. & i.* dudar. —**doubtful** (-fəl) *adj.* dudoso. —**doubtless** (-ləs) *adj.* indudable; cierto.
douche (duʃ) *n.* **1,** (spray) ducha; irrigación. **2,** (syringe) ducha; bolsa; jeringa. —*v.t.* duchar. —*v.i.* darse una ducha.
dough (doː) *n.* **1,** (flour paste) pasta; masa. **2,** *slang* (money) pasta; dinero.
doughnut *n.* buñuelo.
dour (dʊr) *adj.* **1,** (grim) austero; inflexible; duro. **2,** (gloomy) triste; melancólico. —**dourness,** *n.* dureza; inflexibilidad; tristeza.
douse (daus) *v.t.* **1,** (immerse) zambullir. **2,** (soak) empapar. **3,** *colloq.* (extinguish) apagar. —*v.i.* **1,** (dive) zambullirse. **2,** (soak) empaparse.
dove (dʌːv) *n.* paloma.
dove (doːv) *v., pret. & p.p. de* **dive.**

dovecot (ˈdʌvˌkat) *n.* palomar. *También,* **dovecote** (-ˌkot).
dovetail (ˈdʌvˌteil) *v.t.* ensamblar; ajustar; machihembrar. —*v.i.* ajustarse.
dowager (ˈdau·ə·dʒər) *n.* **1,** (widow) viuda. **2,** *colloq.* (elderly lady) matrona; anciana.
dowdy (ˈdau·di) *adj.* descuidado; desaliñado. —**dowdiness,** *n.* descuido; desaliño.
dowel (ˈdau·əl) *n.* clavija.
dower (ˈdau·ər) *n.* **1,** (dowry) dote. **2,** (widow's inheritance) viudedad. **3,** (endowment) prenda. —*v.t.* **1,** (give a dowry to) dotar. **2,** (endow, as a widow) señalar *o* dar viudedad a.
down (daun) *adv.* **1,** (descending) para abajo; hacia abajo. **2,** (at the bottom) abajo. **3,** (in written form) por escrito; en papel. **4,** (at a lower rate) a precio reducido. **5,** (as the first payment) al contado; de pronto; *Mex.* pronto. **6,** (completely) por completo. —*adj.* **1,** (downward) descendente; pendiente. **2,** (lower) de abajo. **3,** *colloq.* (dejected) desanimado; abatido; desalentado. **4,** *colloq.* (prostrate; ill) enfermo; agotado. —*prep.* bajo; bajo de. —*n.* **1,** (downward movement) bajada; descenso. **2,** *football* colocación de pelota. **3,** (fuzz, as of birds) plumón; (of fruits) pelusa; pelusilla; (of persons) vello. **4,** *usu.pl.* (hill; dune) colina; duna. —*v.t.* derribar; hacer caer. —*v.i.* caerse; bajarse. —**down and out, 1,** *boxing* fuera de combate. **2,** (in bad shape) arruinado; vencido. —**down with . . . !,** ¡muera!; ¡abajo!
downcast *adj.* abatido; desanimado.
downfall *n.* caída; derrota.
downfallen *adj.* caído; arruinado.
downgrade *n.* pendiente; declive; bajada. —*adj.* pendiente; inclinado. —*adv.* en pendiente; en declive. —*v.t.* degradar.
downhearted *adj.* deprimido; desalentado.
downhill *adj.* inclinado; pendiente. —*adv.* en pendiente; cuesta abajo.
down payment pago inicial.
downpour *n.* aguacero; chaparrón.
downright *adj.* **1,** (absolute) categórico; absoluto. **2,** (clear; complete) claro; patente; completo. —*adv.* completamente; directamente.
downstairs *adj.* de abajo. —*adv.* abajo: en *o* al piso de abajo. —*n.* piso inferior; piso bajo.
downstream *adv.* río abajo; aguas abajo. —*adj.* de río abajo; que va río abajo; descendente.
downtown *adj.* del sector comercial de la ciudad; céntrico. —*adv.* en, al *o* del centro. —*n.* centro de la ciudad.
downtrodden (ˈdaunˌtrad·ən) *adj.* **1,** (trampled) pisoteado. **2,** (oppressed) oprimido.
downward (ˈdaun·wərd) *adv.* [*también,* **downwards** (-wərdz)] **1,** (going lower) hacia abajo. **2,** (more recent) más atrás. —*adj.* descendente.
downy (ˈdau·ni) *adj.* **1,** (covered with down) velloso. **2,** (soft) blando; suave. **3,** (fluffy) felpudo. —**downiness,** *n.* vellosidad; suavidad.
dowry (ˈdau·ri) *n.* dote.
doxology (dakˈsal·ə·dʒi) *n.* doxología.
doze (doːz) *n.* sueño ligero; sopor. —*v.i.* dormitar.
dozen (ˈdʌz·ən) *n.* docena. —**baker's dozen,** docena del fraile.
drab (dræb) *adj.* **1,** (yellow-gray) parduzco. **2,** (dull) monótono; soso. —*n.* **1,** (color) gris amarillento; parduzco. **2,** (slattern) puta; ramera. —**drabness,** *n.* monotonía.
drachma (ˈdræk·mə) *n.* dracma.
draft (dræft; draft) *n.* **1,** (hauling) tiro; tirón. **2,** (load) carga. **3,** (drink) trago; bebida. **4,** (heavy demand) demanda. **5,** (conscription) llamamiento a filas; quinta. **6,** *comm.* giro; libranza; letra de cambio. **7,** *naut.* calado. **8,** (current of air) corriente (de aire). **9,** (device to regulate air intake) tiro. **10,** (outline; preliminary copy) borrador; bosquejo; apunte. —*adj.* **1,** (for hauling) de tiro; de arrastre. **2,** (drawn from a cask) de grifo; de barril. —*v.t.* **1,** (conscript) llamar a quintas *o* al servicio. **2,** (sketch; outline) bosquejar; hacer un borrador de. *También, Brit.,* **draught.**
draftsman (ˈdræfts·mən) *n.* [*pl.* **-men**] delineante; dibujante.
drafty (ˈdræf·ti) *adj.* con *o* de corrientes de aire.
drag (dræg) *v.t.* [**dragged, drag-**

ging] **1,** (haul) arrastrar; tirar. **2,** (dredge) rastrear; dragar. **3,** (harrow) rastillar. —*v.i.* **1,** (trail) arrastrarse. **2,** (move slowly) avanzar lentamente. **3,** (lag) retrasarse. **4,** (decline) decaer. —*n.* **1,** (harrow) rastrillo. **2,** (carriage) narria. **3,** (hindrance) carga; impedimento; freno; obstáculo. **4,** (act of dragging) arrastre; tirón. **5,** *naut.* (slipping of the anchor) rastra; dragado. **6,** *aero.* resistencia al aire. **7,** *slang* (influence) poder; influencia. **8,** *slang* (draw, as on a cigarette) vaharada; fumada. **9,** *slang* (street; district) calle; barrio.

dragnet ('dræg,nɛt) *n.* red barredera.

dragon ('dræg·ən) *n.* dragón.

dragonfly *n.* caballito del diablo.

dragoon (drə'gun) *n.* dragón. —*v.t.* acosar.

drain (drein) *v.t.* **1,** (draw off) desaguar; escurrir; vaciar. **2,** *surg.* drenar; desangrar. **3,** (empty) vaciar; disipar. **4,** *fig.* (exhaust gradually) consumir. —*v.i.* **1,** (run; flow out or into) desaguarse; escurrirse. **2,** (be exhausted gradually) escaparse. —*n.* **1,** (channel; pipe) desaguadero; desagüe. **2,** *surg.* drenaje; desangre. **3,** (drawing off of resources) desangramiento; agotamiento.

drainage ('drei·nɪdʒ) *n.* **1,** (draining) desagüe; desaguadero. **2,** *surg.* drenaje. **3,** (sewerage) alcantarillado. **4,** (area drained) arroyada.

drake (dreik) *n.* pato.

dram (dræm) *n.* **1,** (1/16 ounce) dracma. **2,** (small drink) trago de licor.

drama ('dræ·mə; 'dra-) *n.* drama. —**dramatist** (-tɪst) *n.* dramaturgo.

dramatic (drə'mæt·ɪk) *adj.* dramático. —**dramatics,** *n.* dramática.

dramatize ('dræm·ə,taiz) *v.t.* dramatizar. —**dramatization** (-tɪ'zei·ʃən) *n.* dramatización.

drank (dræŋk) *v.*, *pret. de* **drink.**

drape (dreip) *v.t.* **1,** (cover with fabric) engalanar; ornar. **2,** (arrange in folds) adornar con pliegues; arreglar los pliegues de. —*n.* colgadura; *pl.* = **drapery.** —**draper,** *n.* tapicero; pañero.

drapery ('drei·pə·ri) *n.* paño; tejido; *pl.* [*también,* **drapes**] cortinas; colgaduras.

drastic ('dræs·tɪk) *adj.* drástico.

draught (dræft; draft) *n.* = **draft.**

draughts (drafts) *n.pl.* (game) juego de damas.

draw (drɔː) *v.t.* [**drew, drawn, drawing**] **1,** (pull) tirar; arrastrar. **2,** (take out) sacar; retirar. **3,** (derive) obtener; conseguir. **4,** (induce; attract) incitar; mover; atraer. **5,** (infer) deducir; derivar. **6,** (inhale) inspirar; aspirar; respirar. **7,** (suck) chupar; mamar. **8,** (drain) desaguar; vaciar. **9,** *sports* (tie) empatar. **10,** (lengthen) estirar; alargar; extender. **11,** (attenuate) atenuar. **12,** (obtain, as salary) cobrar. **13,** (sketch; outline) trazar; dibujar; esbozar. **14,** *comm.* (write, as a check or draft) librar; girar; extender. **15,** *comm.* (earn, as interest) devengar. **16,** (pull, as curtains) correr; descorrer. **17,** *naut.* calar. **18,** (win in a lottery) ganar. **19,** *cards* robar. —*v.i.* **1,** (move nearer) acercarse; venir. **2,** (move away) alejarse; irse. **3,** (attract an audience) atraer público. **4,** (sketch) dibujar; esbozar. **5,** *comm.* girar. **6,** (create an air current) tirar bien. **7,** (unsheathe a weapon) desenvainar; sacar. **8,** (tie the score) empatar; (in chess or checkers) hacer tablas. **9,** (shrink) encogerse; contraerse. —*n.* **1,** (pulling) tirada; tiro; (tugging) tracción; arrastre. **2,** (tie score) empate; (in chess or checkers) tablas. **3,** (lift of a drawbridge) compuerta; piso. —**draw out, 1,** (encourage to talk) sonsacar; sacar. **2,** = **draw,** *v.t.* 10.

drawback *n.* desventaja; inconveniente.

drawbridge *n.* (bridge with rising section) puente levadizo; (with turning section) puente giratorio.

drawer (dror; 'drɔ·ər) *n.* **1,** (sliding tray) cajón; gaveta. **2,** (draftsman) dibujante; delineante. **3,** *comm.* librador. **4,** *pl.* (undergarment) calzoncillos; *Amer.* pantaloncillos.

drawing ('drɔ·ɪŋ) *n.* **1,** (art) dibujo. **2,** (plan) esbozo; plan. **3,** (selection by lot) sorteo.

drawing room *n.* sala; recibidor; recibimiento.

drawl (drɔːl) *v.i.* arrastrar las palabras. —*v.t.* pronunciar lentamente. —*n.* arrastre de palabras; pronunciación lenta.

drawn (drɔːn) *adj.* **1,** (disemboweled) destripado; desentrañado. 2, (pulled out) desenvainado; sacado. 3, (tied) empatado. 4, (strained) agotado; cansado. 5, (melted, as butter) fundido; derretido. —*v.*, *p.p. de* **draw.**

dray (drei) *n.* carro; carreta. —**drayage** (-ɪdʒ) *n.* acarreo.

drayhorse *n.* caballo de tiro.

drayman ('drei·mən) *n.* [*pl.* **-men**] acarreador; carretero.

dread (drɛd) *v.t.* temer. —*v.i.* tener miedo. —*n.* pavor; temor; sobrecogimiento. —*adj.* **1,** (frightening) espantoso. **2,** (awesome) impresionante.

dreadful ('drɛd·fəl) *adj.* **1,** (horrible) terrible; horrible; espantoso. **2,** (awesome) impresionante. **3,** *colloq.* (extreme) desagradable. —**dreadfulness,** *n.* horror.

dreadnought ('drɛd·nɔːt) *n.* acorazado grande.

dream (driːm) *n.* **1,** (thoughts while asleep) sueño. **2,** (fancy) ensueño. —*v.i.* & *t.* [*pret.* & *p.p.* **dreamed** *o* **dreamt**] soñar. —**dream of** *o* **about,** soñar con.

dreamer ('dri·mər) *n.* soñador; *fig.* visionario.

dreamland *n.* tierra de hadas; región de los sueños.

dreamt (drɛmt) *v., pret.* & *p.p. de* **dream.**

dreamy ('dri·mi) *adj.* **1,** (vague) desvariado; vago. **2,** (fanciful) soñador; lleno de sueños. **3,** *colloq.* (delightful) encantador; delicioso.

dreary ('drɪr·i) *adj.* triste; cansado; fastidioso. *También,* **drear.** —**dreariness,** *n.* tristeza; fastidio; cansancio.

dredge (drɛdʒ) *n.* draga; rastra. —*v.t.* & *i.* **1,** (drag) dragar; rastrear. **2,** (cover with flour) espolvorear.

dregs (drɛgz) *n.pl.* **1,** (residue) heces; poso (*sing.*); impurezas. **2,** *fig.* (worst portion) heces; escoria (*sing.*).

drench (drɛntʃ) *v.t.* **1,** (soak) ensopar; empapar. **2,** *vet.med.* purgar. —*n.* **1,** (large dose) tragantada; purgante. **2,** (soaking) mojada.

dress (drɛs) *v.t.* **1,** (clothe) vestir; trajear; (adorn) adornar; engalanar. **2,** *med.* (bandage) vendar. **3,** (prepare for cooking) preparar; aderezar; adobar. **4,** (put in order) arreglar. —*v.i.* **1,** (clothe oneself) vestirse; (wear clothes) vestir. **2,** *mil.* (come into alignment) alinearse. —*n.* **1,** (garment) vestido; traje. **2,** (apparel) indumentaria. —**dress coat,** frac. —**dress down,** *colloq.* **1,** (reprimand) reñir; amonestar. **2,** (thrash) azotar; zurrar. —**dress parade,** desfile. —**dress rehearsal,** ensayo general. —**dress suit,** traje de etiqueta.

dresser ('drɛs·ər) *n.* **1,** (one who dresses another person) ayuda de cámara; camarera; doncella. **2,** (preparer, as of meat, leather, etc.) aliñador; adobador. **3,** (furniture) cómoda; tocador; *Amer.* gavetero.

dressing ('drɛs·ɪŋ) *n.* **1,** (act of clothing) aderezo; adorno. **2,** (bandage) venda; hila. **3,** (sauce) aderezo; aliño; condimento; (stuffing) relleno. **4,** (sizing for leather) adobo; (for fabrics) aderezo. —**dressing gown,** bata; peinador. —**dressing room,** tocador; *theat.* camarín; camerino.

dressing-down *n., colloq.* **1,** (reprimand) regaño; reprimenda. **2,** (thrashing) zurra; aporreo.

dressmaker *n.* modista; sastre (*fem.* sastresa).

dressy ('drɛs·i) *adj., colloq.* **1,** (formal; stylish) elegante; de gala. **2,** (showy) acicalado.

drew (droo) *v., pret. de* **draw.**

dribble ('drɪb·əl) *v.i.* **1,** (drip) gotear. **2,** (drool) babear. —*v.t.* **1,** (let fall in drops) derramar gota a gota. **2,** *sports* (bounce, as a ball) driblar. —*n.* **1,** (dripping) goteo. **2,** *colloq.* (drizzle) llovizna. **3,** *sports* dribling.

driblet ('drɪb·lɪt) *n.* gota; trozo; pedacito; (of money) pico.

drier *también,* **dryer** ('drai·ər) *n.* **1,** (person; device) secador. **2,** (substance) secante. —*adj., comp. de* **dry.**

driest ('drai·ɪst) *adj., superl. de* **dry.**

drift (drɪft) *n.* **1,** (direction) corriente; rumbo. **2,** (snow, etc., driven by wind) ventisquero; alud. **3,** (trend) inclinación; impulso; tendencia. **4,** *naut.; aero.* deriva. **5,** *colloq.* (meaning) intención; sentido. **6,** *geol.* terrenos de acarreo. **7,** *mech.* (tool) mandril de ensanchar. **8,** *mining* galería; socavón. —*v.i.* **1,** *naut.; aero.* ir a la deriva. **2,** (be heaped up) amontonarse. **3,** *fig.* (move aimlessly) vagar; ir sin rumbo.

driftwood *n.* despojo del mar.
drill (drɪl) *n.* **1,** (tool) taladro; barrena. **2,** (training exercise) instrucción. **3,** (teaching) disciplina; repetición; (test) ejercicio; simulacro. **4,** (agricultural machine) sembradora mecánica. **5,** (fabric) dril. **6,** = **mandrill.** —*v.t.* **1,** (pierce) taladrar; barrenar. **2,** *mil.* enseñar la instrucción a. **3,** (train) insistir; repetir. **4,** (sow in rows) plantar en hileras.
drillmaster *n.* maestro de ejercicios *o* en instrucción.
drink (drɪŋk) *v.t.* [**drank, drunk, drinking**] **1,** (swallow) beber; tragar. **2,** *fig.* [*usu.*, **drink in**] (absorb) embeber; empapar. —*v.i.* **1,** (imbibe) beber. **2,** (drink a toast) brindar. —*n.* **1,** (beverage; liquor) bebida; trago. **2,** *slang* (body of water) océano; charco. —**drinkable,** *adj.* potable; bebible.
drinker ('drɪŋk·ər) *n.* **1** (one who drinks) bebedor. **2,** (drunkard) borrachín.
drip (drɪp) *v.i.* [**dripped, dripping**] gotear; chorrear. —*v.t.* verter gota a gota; hacer gotear. —*n.* **1,** (dropping) goteo. **2,** (roof leak) gotera. **3,** *archit.* (rain catch) alero. **4,** *slang* (unattractive person) mastuerzo; pelma. —**drippings,** *n.pl.* (juices from roasting) pringue (*sing.*); grasa (*sing.*).
drive (draiv) *v.t.* [**drove, driven, driving**] **1,** (impel) impulsar; impeler. **2,** (urge) empujar; forzar. **3,** (direct, as a vehicle) conducir; guiar. **4,** (transport in a vehicle) transportar; accarrear; llevar. **5,** (carry forward) ejecutar; actuar. **6,** (chase, as game; hunt) acosar; acorralar. **7,** (lead, as animals) acarrear; conducir. **8,** (force to work) forzar; empujar. **9,** *sports* (hit; cast) lanzar; golpear fuerte. **10,** (cause to go through or penetrate) atornillar (*a screw*); clavar (*a nail*) hincar (*a stick*). —*v.i.* **1,** (dash) lanzarse; arrojarse. **2,** (go in a vehicle) ir en coche *o* auto. **3,** (operate a vehicle) guiar; conducir. **4,** (aim; tend) pretender; proponerse. **5,** (work energetically) afanarse. —*n.* **1,** (trip, as by car) paseo *o* viaje en auto. **2,** (road; driveway) calzada para autos. **3,** (animal roundup) manada. **4,** (campaign) campaña. **5,** (extreme haste) urgencia; exigencia. **6,** (energy; ambition) energía; vigor; ambición. **7,** *mech.* mecanismo de transmisión *o* dirección.
drive-in *adj.* para automovilistas. —*n.* cine, restaurante, ventanilla de banco, etc., para automovilistas.
drivel ('drɪv·əl) *v.i.* **1,** (drool) babear; babosear. **2,** (talk foolishly) bobear; hablar tonterías. —*n.* baba.
driven ('drɪv·ən) *v., p.p. de* **drive.**
driver ('drai·vər) *n.* **1,** (one who drives) conductor. **2,** (golf club) conductor. **3,** *mech.* pieza *o* rueda motriz.
driveshaft *n.* eje motor; árbol de mando.
driveway *n.* entrada de coches.
driving ('drai·viŋ) *v., p.pr. de* **drive.** —*n.* conducción. —*adj.* **1,** (compelling) impulsor; motriz. **2,** (moving forcefully) devastador; violento.
drizzle ('drɪz·əl) *v.i.* lloviznar. —*n.* llovizna.
droll (dro:l) *adj.* gracioso; chocante; festivo; jocoso. —**drollery** ('dro·lə·ri) *n.* chocarrería; bufonería.
dromedary ('dram·ə·dɛr·i) *n.* dromedario.
drone (dro:n) *v.i.* **1,** (hum) zumbar. **2,** (speak monotonously) salmodiar. **3,** (idle) haraganear; zanganear. —*n.* **1,** (sound) zumbido. **2,** (bee) zángano. **3,** (idler) zángano; haragán.
drool (dru:l) *v.i.* **1,** (slobber) babear. **2,** (talk nonsense) bobear. —*n.* **1,** (slobbering) baba. **2,** (nonsense) bobería.
droop (drup) *v.t.* hundir; inclinar. —*v.i.* **1,** (sag) caer; desplomarse. **2,** (languish) desanimarse; consumirse. —*n.* hundimiento; decaimiento.
drop (drap) *n.* **1,** (liquid globule) gota. **2,** (small quantity) gota; poquito; pizca. **3,** (fall) caída; bajada; (from an airplane) lanzamiento. **4,** (decrease) baja. **5,** *theat.* (curtain) telón de boca. **6,** (mail box) buzón. **7,** (trap door) escotillón. —*v.t.* **1,** (let fall) dejar caer. **2,** (lower) bajar. **3,** (drip) echar; tirar. **4,** (let drip) poner *o* echar a gotas. **5,** *colloq.* (utter, as a hint) indicar; sugerir. **6,** (send, as a note) mandar; enviar. **7,** (put aside; dismiss) descartar. **8,** (let off, as from a conveyance) dejar. **9,** (knock down) derribar; abatir. **10,** (omit) omitir;

suprimir. —*v.i.* 1, (fall; descend) caer; bajar; descender. 2, (drip) gotear. 3, (cease) parar; cesar. —**drop by drop**, gota a gota. —**drop in**, visitar de paso; entrar al pasar. —**drop in the bucket**, nada; pelillos a la mar. —**drop off**, 1, (diminish) disminuir. 2, (fall asleep) caer dormido; quedarse dormido. —**drop out**, retirarse; darse de baja.

ropper ('drap·ər) *n.* cuentagotas.

roppings (drap·ıŋz) *n.pl.* excrementos; heces.

ropsy ('drap·si) *n.* hidropesía. —**dropsical** (-sı·kəl) *adj.* hidrópico.

ross (drɔs) *n.* 1, (waste from metal) escoria. 2, *fig.* (refuse) desecho; hez.

rought (draut) *n.* 1, (dryness) sequedad; aridez. 2, (prolonged dry weather) sequía. *También,* **drouth** (drauθ).

rove (dro:v) *n.* (of cattle or horses) manada; (of sheep) rebaño; (of mules) recua; (of pigs) piara. —*v., pret. de* **drive.** —**in droves**, en masa.

rover ('dro·vər) *n.* ganadero.

rown (draun) *v.t.* 1, (suffocate with water) ahogar. 2, (drench) inundar; anegar. 3, [*también,* **drown out**] (deaden) sofocar; apagar. 4, *fig.* (dispel, as sorrow) ahogar; olvidar. —*v.i.* 1, (be suffocated) ahogarse. 2, (be soaked) anegarse; inundarse.

rowse (drauz) *v.i.* amodorrarse; adormecerse. —*n.* siestita; siestecita.

rowsy ('drau·zi) *adj.* amodorrado; adormilado; adormecido. —**drowsiness**, *n.* modorra; somnolencia.

rub (drʌb) *v.t.* [**drubbed, drubbing**] 1, (beat) golpear; sacudir; apalear. 2, (defeat) ganar; vencer; derrotar. —**drubbing** (-ıŋ) *n.* paliza; zurra.

rudge (drʌdʒ) *v.i.* afanarse. —*n.* esclavo (del trabajo). —**drudgery**, *n.* faena; afán; trabajo penoso.

rug (drʌg) *n.* 1, *pharm.* medicina. 2, (narcotic) droga; narcótico. —*v.t.* 1, (add a drug to) poner narcótico en. 2, (administer a drug to) narcotizar. —**drug on the market**, artículo difícil de vender.

ruggist ('drʌg·ıst) *n.* farmacéutico; boticario.

rugstore *n.* farmacia; botica.

druid ('dru·ıd) *n.* druida.

drum (drʌm) *n.* tambor. —*v.i.* [**drummed, drumming**] 1, (play a drum) tocar el tambor. 2, (tap with the fingers) teclear; tamborilear. 3, (resound) resonar. —*v.t.* 1, *mil.* [*usu.,* **drum out**] expulsar a tambor batiente. 2, [*usu.,* **drum into**] (instill) machacar; repetir. —**drum major**, tambor mayor. —**drum up**, fomentar; avivar.

drumbeat *n.* redoble; toque de tambor.

drumhead *n.* piel de tambor; parche.

drummer ('drʌm·ər) *n.* 1, (drum player) tambor. 2, (traveling salesman) viajante.

drumstick *n.* 1, (baton) palillo. 2, (leg of fowl) muslo.

drunk (drʌŋk) *v., p.p. de* **drink.** —*n.* = **drunkard.** —*adj.* borracho; ebrio; beodo.

drunkard ('drʌŋk·ərd) *n.* borracho; borrachón; beodo.

drunken ('drʌŋk·ən) *adj. atributivo* = **drunk.** —**drunkenness,** *n.* embriaguez; borrachera.

dry (drai) *adj.* 1, (not wet) seco. 2, (sterile) estéril. 3, (thirsty) seco; sediento. 4, (arid) árido; sediento. 5, (dull) monótono; árido; aburrido. 6, (grave but humorous) incisivo; satírico; agudo. 7, (not sweet, as wine) seco. 8, (plain) escueto; frío. —*v.t.* secar. —*v.i.* secarse. —**dry cell**, pila seca. —**dry dock**, dique seco *o* de carena. —**dry goods**, telas; tejidos. —**dry ice**, hielo seco; nieve carbónica. —**dry measure**, medida para áridos.

dryad ('drai·æd) *n.* dríada.

dry-clean *v.t.* limpiar en seco. —**dry cleaning**, limpieza en seco.

dry-cleaner *n.* quitamanchas. —**dry-cleaner's**, *n.sing.* tintorería; quitamanchas.

dryness (drai·nəs) *n.* sequedad; aridez.

dual ('du·əl) *adj.* binario; dual; *gram.* dual.

dualism ('du·ə,lız·əm) *n.* dualismo. —**dualistic** (-'lıs·tık) *adj.* dualístico.

duality (du'æl·ə·ti) *n.* dualidad.

dub (dʌb) *v.t.* [**dubbed, dubbing**] 1, (knight) armar caballero a. 2, (name) apellidar. 3, (confer a title on) dar título a. 4, (make smooth) alisar. 5, (in sound recording) doblar. —*n.*, *colloq.* (inept person) desmañado; torpe.

dubiety (du'bai·ə·ti) *n.* incertidumbre; duda.

dubious ('du·bi·əs) *adj.* **1,** (doubtful) dudoso; incierto. **2,** (of doubtful value) sospechoso; ambiguo. —**dubiousness,** *n.* duda; incertidumbre.

ducal ('du·kəl) *adj.* ducal.

ducat ('dʌk·ət) *n.* **1,** (old coin) ducado. **2,** *slang* (money) dinero; pasta.

duchess ('dʌtʃ·əs) *n.* duquesa.

duchy ('dʌtʃ·i) *n.* ducado.

duck (dʌk) *n.* **1,** (fowl) pato. **2,** (fabric) dril; *pl.*, pantalones de dril. **3,** (evasive action) agachada. **4,** (dip; immersion) zambullida. —*v.t.* **1,** (immerse) sumergir. **2,** (bow) agachar rápidamente. **3,** (dodge) evitar agachándose. **4,** (avoid) evadir; evitar. —*v.i.* **1,** (submerge) zambullirse. **2,** (lower the head or body) agacharse. **3,** *colloq.* (escape) evadirse; escaparse.

duckling ('dʌk·lɪŋ) *n.* anadeja.

duct (dʌkt) *n.* conducto; canal; tubo. —**ductless gland,** glándula cerrada.

ductile ('dʌk·təl) *adj.* dúctil; maleable. —**ductility** (-'tɪl·ə·ti) *n.* ductilidad.

dud (dʌd) *n.*, *colloq.* **1,** (false coin) ochavo falso. **2,** (faulty explosive) bomba, granada *o* cohete que no estalla. **3,** (failure) fracaso; calamidad. **4,** *pl.* (clothes) trapos. —*adj.* falso; inútil.

dude (duːd) *n.* caballerete. —**dude ranch,** rancho de veraneo.

due (dju; duː) *adj.* **1,** (owed) debido; vencido; (payable) pagadero. **2,** (expected) esperado. **3,** (attributable) debido. **4,** (suitable) propio; apto. —*n.* **1,** (debt) deuda. **2,** *pl.* (fee) derechos. —**due bill,** pagaré. —**due to,** debido a. —**give (someone) his due,** ser justo hacia *o* con. —**in due time,** a su debido tiempo.

duel ('du·əl) *n.* duelo; desafío. —*v.t.* desafiar; combatir en duelo. —*v.i.* tener un duelo; batirse. —**duelist,** *n.* duelista.

duenna (dju'ɛn·ə) *n.* dueña; doña; acompañante de señoritas.

duet (du'ɛt) *n.* dueto.

duffel ('dʌf·əl) *n.* **1,** (woolen cloth) paño de lana basta. **2,** (outfit) equipo; pertrechos. —**duffel bag,** talego.

duffer ('dʌf·ər) *n.* **1,** (peddler) buhonero. **2,** (inept person) desmañado; torpe.

dug (dʌg) *v.*, *pret.* & *p.p.* *de* **dig**. —*n.* teta; pezón.

dugout *n.* **1,** (boat) canoa; piragua. **2,** (shelter) refugio subterráneo.

duke (duk) *n.* duque. —**dukedom** (-dəm) *n.* ducado.

dulcet ('dʌl·sət) *adj.* dulce; suave; armonioso; melodioso.

dull (dʌl) *adj.* **1,** (stupid) estúpido; lerdo. **2,** (tedious; boring) árido; tedioso; fastidioso; aburrido. **3,** (dismal) lánguido; triste; desanimado. **4,** (dim) empañado; nebuloso. **5,** (blunt) obtuso; romo. **6,** (slack) inactivo; muerto; paralizado. —*v.t.* **1,** (blunt) embotar. **2,** (benumb) entorpecer.

dullard ('dʌl·ərd) *n.* lerdo; estúpido; idiota.

dullwitted *adj.* boto; estúpido; lerdo.

duly ('du·li) *adv.* **1,** (as owed) debidamente; propiamente. **2,** (on time) puntualmente. **3,** (as required) exactamente.

dumb (dʌm) *adj.* **1,** (mute) mudo. **2,** (silent) callado; silencioso. **3,** *colloq.* (moronic) estúpido; lerdo. —**dumbness,** *n.* mudez; silencio; estupidez.

dumbbell *n.* **1,** (weight for exercise) bola gimnástica. **2,** *slang* (dolt) estúpido.

dumbwaiter *n.* montacargas.

dumfound *también,* **dumbfound** (dʌm'faund) *v.t.* dejar mudo; confundir; pasmar.

dummy ('dʌm·i) *n.* **1,** (mute) mudo. **2,** (model) maniquí; (figurehead) testaferro; figurón. **3,** (effigy) efigie; imagen. **4,** *cards* muerto. **5,** *print.* modelo *o* copia (en blanco). **6,** (sham) imitación; remedo. —*adj.* falso; de imitación; fingido.

dump (dʌmp) *v.t.* **1,** (unload) descargar. **2,** (spill) verter. **3,** (throw away) tirar; arrojar. **4,** *comm.* vender (exceso de productos) al extranjero más barato que en el mercado nacional. —*n.* **1,** (field for rubbish) vertedero; basurero. **2,** *mil.* (storage place) depósito de municiones. **3,** *slang* (hovel; shack) cuchitril. —**in the dumps,** melancólico; desanimado.

dumpling ('dʌmp·liŋ) *n.* relleno; bola de pasta rellena de fruta *o* carne.
dumpy ('dʌm·pi) *adj., colloq.* regordete; rollizo.
dun (dʌn) *v.t.* [**dunned, dunning**] importunar; apremiar. —*n.* apremio. —*adj.* & *n.* (color) pardo; bruno.
dunce (dʌns) *n.* torpe; ignorante; zopenco. —**dunce cap,** gorro de tonto.
dune (dun) *n.* duna.
dung (dʌŋ) *n.* estiércol; excremento. —*v.t.* estercolar.
dungaree (ˌdʌŋ·gə'riː) *n.* 1, (coarse fabric) tela de mono. 2, *pl.* (work clothes) mono (*sing.*); traje de faena (*sing.*).
dungeon ('dʌn·dʒən) *n.* calabozo; mazmorra.
dunghill ('dʌŋˌhɪl) *n.* estercolar; estercolero.
dunk (dʌŋk) *v.t.* ensopar; empapar; remojar.
duo ('du·o) *n.* dúo; dueto; pareja.
duo- (du·o) *prefijo* duo-; dos: *duologue,* diálogo.
duodecimal (ˌdu·o'dɛs·ɪ·məl) *adj.* duodecimal.
duodenum (ˌdu·o'di·nəm) *n.* duodeno. —**duodenal** (-nəl) *adj.* duodenal.
dupe (dup) *v.t.* engañar; embaucar. —*n.* primo; incauto; bobo. —**dupery** ('du·pə·ri) *n.* engaño; embaucamiento.
duplex ('du·plɛks) *adj.* doble; duplo. —*n.* apartamento de dos pisos.
duplicate ('du·plɪ·kət) *n.* & *adj.* duplicado. —*v.t.* (-ˌkeit) duplicar. —**duplication** (-'kei·ʃən) *n.* duplicación. —**duplicator** (-ˌke·tər) *n.* multicopista.
duplicity (du'plɪs·ə·ti) *n.* doblez; duplicidad.
durable ('dʊr·ə·bəl) *adj.* durable; duradero. —**durability,** *n.* durabilidad.
dura mater ('djʊr·ə'mei·tər) duramadre.
duration (dʊ'rei·ʃən) *n.* duración.
duress (dʊ'rɛs; 'djʊr·əs) *n.* 1, (imprisonment) encierro; prisión. 2, (coercion) coacción.
during ('dʊr·iŋ) *prep.* durante; mientras.
durst (dʌɹst) *v., pret de* **dare.**
dusk (dʌsk) *n.* 1, (twilight) anochecida; crepúsculo. 2, (partial darkness) penumbra.
dusky ('dʌsk·i) *adj.* 1, (dim) oscuro. 2, (swarthy) moreno; atezado. —**duskiness,** *n.* atezamiento.
dust (dʌst) *n.* 1, (tiny bits, as of earth) polvo. 2, *fig.* (remains) cenizas; restos. —*v.t.* 1, (rid of dust) quitar el polvo a; desempolvar. 2, (sprinkle) empolvar; espolvorear. —**dust bowl,** cuenca polvorienta. —**dust jacket,** sobrecubierta.
duster ('dʌs·tər) *n.* 1, (cloth for dusting) paño del polvo; (feather duster) plumero. 2, (protective coat) guardapolvo.
dustpan *n.* pala de recoger la basura.
dusty ('dʌs·ti) *adj.* polvoriento.
Dutch (dʌtʃ) *n.* & *adj.* 1, (of Holland) holandés. 2, *U.S. slang* alemán. —**Dutch oven,** horno portátil. —**Dutch treat,** *colloq.* convite a escote. —**Dutch uncle,** mentor severo. —**in Dutch,** *slang* 1, (in disfavor) en desgracia. 2, (in trouble) en apuros.
duteous ('du·ti·əs) *adj.* = **dutiful.**
dutiable ('du·ti·ə·bəl) *adj.* sujeto a derechos de aduana.
dutiful ('du·tɪ·fəl) *adj.* 1, (obedient) obediente; respetuoso. 2, (diligent) meticuloso; diligente.
duty ('du·ti) *n.* 1, (obligation) deber; obligación. 2, (responsibility) faena; tarea; obligación. 3, (tax) impuesto; derecho. —**duty free,** exento de impuestos. —**off duty,** libre (de servicio). —**on duty,** de servicio.
dwarf (dworf) *n.* & *adj.* enano. —*v.t.* 1, (stunt the growth of) impedir crecer; parar. 2, (make to seem smaller) empequeñecer; achicar. —**dwarfish,** *adj.* enano; diminuto.
dwell (dwɛːl) *v.i.* [*pret.* & *p.p.* **dwelt** *o* **dwelled**] 1, (remain) estar. 2, (reside) vivir; morar. —**dweller,** *n.* habitante; morador; residente. —**dwelling,** *n.* morada; vivienda. —**dwell on** *o* **upon,** explayarse en.
dwindle ('dwɪn·dəl) *v.i.* disminuirse; achicarse; encogerse. —*v.t.* disminuir; acortar; encoger.
dyad ('dai·æd) *n.* elemento bivalente. —*adj.* bivalente.
dye (dai) *n.* tinte; colorante. —*v.t.*

[dyed, dyeing] teñir. —dyer, *n.* tintorero.
dyestuff *n.* materia colorante.
dying ('dai·ɪŋ) *v., p.pr. de* die. —*adj.* moribundo; agonizante. —*n.* muerte.
dyna- (dai·nə) *también,* dyn- (dain) *prefijo* dina-; fuerza: *dynatron,* dinatrón.
dynamic (dai'næm·ɪk) *adj.* dinámico; enérgico.
dynamics (dai'næm·ɪks) *n.* dinámica; *pl.* fuerzas dinámicas.
dynamism ('dai·nə,mɪz·əm) *n.* dinamismo.
dynamite ('dai·nə,mait) *n.* dinamita. —*v.t.* dinamitar.
dynamo ('dai·nə·mo) *n.* [*pl.* -mos] dínamo. —**dynamometer** (-'mam·ɪ·tər) *n.* dinamómetro.
dynamo- *prefijo* dinamo-; fuerza: *dynamometer,* dinamómetro.
dynasty ('dai·nəs·ti) *n.* dinastía. —**dynast** (-,næst) *n.* dinasta. —**dynastic** (-'næs·tɪk) *adj.* dinástico.
dyne (dain) *n., physics* dina.
-dyne (dain) *sufijo* -dino; fuerza: *superheterodyne,* superheterodino.
dys- (dɪs) *prefijo, med.* dis-; dificultad; mal: *dyspepsia,* dispepsia.
dysentery ('dɪs·ən·tɛr·i) *n.* disentería.
dyspepsia (dɪs'pɛp·ʃə) *n.* dispepsia.
dyspeptic (dɪs'pɛp·tɪk) *adj.* **1,** (suffering from indigestion) dispéptico. **2,** (irritable) melancólico; irritable.
dysprosium (dis'pro·si·əm) *n.* disprosio.

E

E, e (iː) quinta letra del alfabeto inglés. —*n., music* mi.
e- (i; ɪ; ɛ) *prefijo, var. de* **ex-**: *emanation,* emanación.
each (itʃ) *adj.* cada; todo. —*pron.* cada uno; cada cual. —*adv.* por persona; por cabeza; por pieza. —**each other,** mútuamente; uno a otro.
eager ('i·gər) *adj.* ansioso; anhelante; afanoso. —**eagerness,** *n.* ansia; anhelo; afán.
eagle ('i·gəl) *n.* águila. —**eaglet** (-glət) *n.* aguilucho.
-ean (i·ən) *sufijo, forma nombres y adjetivos denotando* relación; pertenencia: *Mediterranean,* mediterráneo.
ear (ɪːr) *n.* **1,** (outer ear) oreja. **2,** (inner ear) oído. **3,** (hearing) oído. **4,** (of corn) mazorca. **5,** (of wheat, etc.) espiga. —*v.i.* espigar. —**turn a deaf ear,** hacerse sordo.
eardrum *n.* tímpano.
earl (ʌɹl) *n.* conde. —**earldom** (-dəm) *n.* condado.
earliness ('ʌɹ·li·nəs) *n.* **1,** (punctualness) prontitud. **2,** (prematureness) precocidad.
early ('ʌɹ·li) *adj. & adv.* (near the beginning of a stated time) temprano. —*adj.* **1,** (ancient) primitivo; antiguo. **2,** (before expected) precoz; prematuro. **3,** (in the near future) próximo; cercano. —*adv.* **1,** (soon) pronto. **2,** (at an early time) temprano. **3,** (before expected) temprano; con anticipación; precozmente. —**early bird; early riser,** madrugador. —**early in the morning,** muy de mañana. —**rise early,** madrugar.
early-rising *adj.* madrugador; madrugón.
earmark *n.* señal de identificación. —*v.t.* asignar; señalar.
earn (ʌɹn) *v.t.* **1,** (as wages) ganar. **2,** (as interest) devengar. **3,** (deserve) merecer; ganar. —**earnings,** *n.pl.* sueldo (*sing.*); salario (*sing.*); jornal (*sing.*).
earnest ('ʌɹ·nəst) *adj.* **1,** (serious) serio; formal; sincero. **2,** (diligent) activo; celoso. —*n.* prenda; señal; arras (*pl.*). —**earnestness,** *n.* formalidad; seriedad. —**in earnest,** en serio.
earphone *n.* auricular; audífono.
earring ('ɪr,riŋ) *n.* pendiente; arete; zarcillo.
earshot *n.* alcance del oído.
earth (ʌɹθ) *n.* **1,** *often cap.* (planet) tierra; globo terráqueo; orbe. **2,** (soil) suelo. **3,** (people of the world) gente; mundo.
earthen ('ʌɹθ·ən) *adj.* térreo; terrizo. —**earthenware,** *n.* loza de barro; alfarería.
earthiness ('ʌɹ·θi·nəs) *n.* **1,** (quality of earth) terrosidad. **2,** (coarseness) tosquedad.
earthling ('ʌɹθ·lɪŋ) *n.* habitante

de la tierra; mortal; mundano.
earthly ('ʌɪθ·li) *adj.* terreno; terrestre; terrenal; mundano. —**earthliness,** *n.* terrenidad; mundanalidad.
earthquake *n.* terremoto; temblor de tierra.
earthworks *n.pl.* terraplén (*sing.*)
earthworm *n.* lombriz de tierra.
earthy ('ʌɪ·θi) *adj.* **1,** (of earth) terrizo; terroso. **2,** (coarse) grosero; tosco.
earwax *n.* cerumen; cerilla.
ease (iːz) *n.* **1,** (comfort) comodidad. **2,** (mental calm) tranquilidad; sosiego. **3,** (facility) facilidad. **4,** (unaffectedness) naturalidad; desenvoltura. —*v.t.* **1,** (put at ease) aliviar; descansar. **2,** (mitigate) aligerar; descargar. **3,** (facilitate) facilitar. —*v.i.* **1,** (be mitigated) aliviarse; disminuir. **2,** (move slowly) moverse lentamente. —**at ease,** cómodo; *mil.* ¡en su lugar descansen! —**take one's ease,** descansar.
easel ('iː·zəl) *n.* caballete de pintor.
easement ('iːz·mənt) *n.* **1,** (easing) alivio; descarga. **2,** *law* servidumbre.
east (ist) *n.* este; oriente. —*adj.* este; del este; oriental. —*adv.* hacia el este; al este.
Easter ('is·tər) *n.* Pascua de Resurrección. —**Easter Day,** día de Pascua; domingo de gloria. —**Easter Eve,** sábado santo.
easterly ('iːs·tər·li) *adj.* este; del este; hacia el este. —*adv.* hacia el este.
eastern ('iːs·tərn) *adj.* este; del este; oriental. —**easterner,** *n.* oriental; habitante del este.
eastward ('ist·wərd) *adj.* en *o* de dirección este. —*adv.* hacia el este.
easy ('iː·zi) *adj.* **1,** (not difficult) fácil. **2,** (comfortable; tranquil) cómodo; tranquilo. **3,** (not oppressive) complaciente; condescendiente; razonable. —**easiness,** *n.* facilidad; comodidad; tranquilidad; soltura. —**easy chair,** butaca; sillón; poltrona.
easygoing *adj.* lento; tranquilo; despreocupado.
eat (it) *v.t.* [**ate, eaten, eating**] **1,** (consume) comer. **2,** (corrode) corroer; consumir. —*v.i.* comer; alimentarse; sustentarse. —**eatables,** *n.pl., colloq.* comestibles; víveres; vituallas. —**eat one's words,** desdecirse. —**eat out,** comer fuera. —**eats,** *n.pl., slang* alimentos.
eaves (iːvz) *n.pl.* alero (*sing.*).
eavesdrop *v.i.* [**-dropped, -dropping**] escuchar a las puertas; escuchar a escondidas. —**eavesdropper,** *n.* escucha. —**eavesdropping,** *n.* escucha.
ebb (ɛb) *v.i.* **1,** (recede) bajar. **2,** *fig.* (decline) decaer; disminuir. —*n.* decaimiento; disminución. —**ebb tide,** marea menguante; bajamar.
ebony ('ɛb·ə·ni) *n.* ébano. —*adj.* **1,** (made of ebony) de ébano. **2,** (black) negro.
ebullient (ɪ'bʌl·jənt) *adj.* **1,** (boiling) hirviente. **2,** (excited) apasionado; entusiasta.
ebullition (ˌɛb·ə'lɪʃ·ən) *n.* **1,** (boiling) ebullición. **2,** *fig.* (excitement) agitación; conmoción.
ec- (ɛk) *prefijo, var. de* **ex-**: *ecstasy,* éxtasis.
eccentric (ɛk'sɛn·trɪk) *adj.* **1,** (off center) excéntrico. **2,** (unusual) extraño; extravagante; excéntrico; estrafalario; raro. —*n.* **1,** (eccentric person) excéntrico; persona excéntrica. **2,** (device) excéntrica. —**eccentricity** (ˌɛk·sən·'trɪs·ə·ti) *n.* excentricidad.
ecclesiastic (ɛˌkli·zi'æs·tɪk) *n.* eclesiástico; clérigo. —*adj.* [*también,* **ecclesiastical**] eclesiástico.
echelon ('ɛʃ·əˌlan) *n., mil.* **1,** (level of command) escalón. **2,** (deployment) despliegue escalonado.
echo ('ɛk·oː) *n.* eco. —*v.i.* hacer eco; repercutir; reverberar; resonar. —*v.t.* repetir.
eclectic (ɛk'lɛk·tɪk) *adj.* & *n.* ecléctico.
eclipse (ɪ'klɪps) *n.* eclipse. —*v.t.* eclipsar. —**ecliptic** (ɪ'klɪp·tɪk) *n.* eclíptica. —*adj.* eclíptico.
eclogue ('ɛk·lag) *n.* écloga.
ecology (ɪ'kal·ə·dʒi) *n.* ecología. —**ecological** (-'ladʒ·ɪ·kəl) ecológico. —**ecologist,** *n.* ecólogo.
economic (ˌi·kə'nam·ɪk; ˌɛk·ə-) *adj.* económico. —**economics,** *n.pl.* economía (*sing.*).
economical (ˌi·kə'nam·ɪ·kəl; ˌɛk·ə-) *adj.* económico; ahorrativo; frugal; parco.
economy (ɪ'ka·nə·mi) *n.* economía; ahorro. —**economist** (-mɪst) *n.m.* & *f.* economista. —**economize** (-maiz) *v.i.* economizar; ahorrar.

ecstasy ('ɛk·stə·si) *n.* éxtasis; rapto; transporte. **—ecstatic** (ɛk·'stæt·ɪk) *adj.* extático.
ecto- (ɛk·to) *prefijo* ecto-; externo: *ectoderm,* ectodermo.
-ectomy (ɛk·tə·mi) *sufijo, med.* -ectomía; extirpación: *appendectomy,* apendectomía.
ectoplasm ('ɛk·tə,plæz·əm) *n.* ectoplasma.
ecumenical (,ɛk·jʊ'mɛn·ɪ·kəl) *adj.* ecuménico.
eczema ('ɛk·sə·mə; 'ɛg·zə-) *n.* eczema.
-ed (ɪd *o* d *o* t) *prefijo* **1,** *forma pretéritos de verbos: I wanted,* quise. **2,** *forma participios pasivos: talked,* hablado; *rained,* llovido. **3,** *forma adjetivos de nombres denotando* característica; formación; posesión: *bearded,* barbudo; *armored,* blindado; *armed,* armado.
eddy ('ɛd·i) *n.* remolino. *—v.t.* arremolinar. *—v.i.* arremolinarse.
Eden ('i·dən) *n.* Edén.
edge (ɛdʒ) *n.* **1,** (border) borde; orilla; margen. **2,** (sharp side) filo; corte; canto. **3,** *geom.* arista. **4,** *colloq.* (advantage) ventaja. *—v.t.* **1,** (trim) orlar; ribetear; bordear. **2,** (sharpen) afilar; aguzar. *—v.i.* avanzar de lado. **—edgy,** *adj.* impaciente; irritable; nervioso.
edging ('ɛdʒ·ɪŋ) *n.* orilla; ribete; pestaña.
edgewise *adj.* & *adv.* de filo; de canto.
edible ('ɛd·ə·bəl) *adj.* & *n.* comestible. **—edibility,** *n.* calidad de comestible.
edict ('i·dɪkt) *n.* edicto.
edifice ('ɛd·ə·fɪs) *n.* edificio.
edify ('ɛd·ɪ,fai) *v.t.* & *i.* edificar. **—edification** (-fɪ'kei·ʃən) *n.* edificación.
edit ('ɛ·dɪt) *v.t.* **1,** (revise) redactar; revisar; corregir. **2,** (supervise publication of) dirigir.
edition (ɪ'dɪʃ·ən) *n.* edición; tirada.
editor ('ɛd·ɪ·tər) *n.* redactor; compilador; director (de un periódico).
editorial (,ɛd·ɪ'tor·i·əl) *adj.* editorial. *—n.* editorial; artículo de fondo. **—editorialize** (-ə,laiz) *v.i.* escribir editoriales.
educate ('ɛd·jʊ,keit) *v.t.* educar; instruir; enseñar. **—educated** (-,ke·tɪd) *adj.* culto; instruido. **—educator** (-,ke·tər) *n.* educador; pedagogo.
education (,ɛd·jʊ'kei·ʃən) *n.* educación; instrucción; enseñanza. **—educational,** *adj.* educativo.
-ee (iː) *sufijo* **1,** *forma nombres denotando* objeto *o* recipiente de una acción: *lessee,* arrendatario; *payee,* tenedor; portador. **2,** *forma nombres con sentido diminutivo: goatee,* perilla.
eel (iːl) *n.* anguila.
e'en (iːn) *adv., poet.* = **even.** *—n., poet.* = **even** (*evening*).
e'er (eːr) *adv., poet.* = **ever.**
-eer ('ɪːr) *sufijo* **1,** -ero; -ario; *forma nombres denotando* profesión; actividad: *engineer,* ingeniero; *volunteer,* voluntario. **2,** *forma verbos derivados de nombres: electioneer,* solicitar votos.
eerie ('ɪːr·i) *adj.* espectral; misterioso.
efface (ɛ'feis) *v.t.* **1,** (erase) borrar; raspar; tachar. **2,** (make inconspicuous) apagar. **—effacement,** *n.* tachadura; raspadura; destrucción.
effect (ɛ'fɛkt) *n.* **1,** (result) efecto; resultado; impresión. **2,** (force) efecto; eficacia; eficiencia; validez. **3,** *pl.* (personal property) efectos; bienes muebles. *—v.t.* efectuar. **—effective,** *adj.* eficaz; válido; fuerte. **—effectiveness,** *n.* eficacia.
effectual (ɛ'fɛk·tʃu·əl) *adj.* eficaz.
effectuate (ɛ'fɛk·tʃu·eit) *v.t.* efectuar.
effeminate (ə'fɛm·ɪ·nət) *adj.* afeminado. **—effeminacy** (-ɪ·nə·si) *n.* afeminamiento; afeminación.
effervesce (ɛf·ər'vɛs) *v.i.* fermentar; estar en efervescencia. **—effervescence,** *n.* efervescencia. **—effervescent,** *adj.* efervescente.
effete (ə'fit) *adj.* usado; gastado; agotado.
efficacious (,ɛf·ɪ'kei·ʃəs) *adj.* eficaz. **—efficacy** ('ɛf·ɪ·kə·si) *n.* fuerza; validez; eficacia.
efficiency (ɪ'fɪʃ·ən·si) *n.* eficiencia; competencia.
efficient (ɪ'fɪʃ·ənt) *adj.* **1,** (competent) eficiente; competente. **2,** *mech.* (productive) de buen rendimiento.
effigy ('ɛf·ə·dʒi) *n.* efigie.
efflorescence (,ɛf·lo'rɛs·əns) *n.* eflorescencia. **—efflorescent,** *adj.* eflorescente.
effluvium (ɪ'flu·vi·əm) *n.* efluvio.
effort ('ɛf·ərt) *n.* **1,** (exertion) esfuerzo. **2,** (achievement) obra. **—effortless,** *adj.* sin esfuerzo. **—effortlessly,** *adv.* fácilmente.

effrontery (ɪˈfrʌn·tə·ri) *n.* desfachatez; descaro; desvergüenza.

effulgent (ɪˈfʌl·dʒənt) *adj.* fulgente; resplandeciente. —**effulgence,** *n.* fulgor; fulgencia.

effuse (ɛˈfjuːz) *v.t.* derramar; verter. —*v.i.* emanar; exudar. —*adj.* (ɛˈfjus) esparcido. —**effusion** (ɪˈfju·ʒən) *n.* efusión; derrame. —**effusive** (ɪˈfju·sɪv) *adj.* efusivo; expansivo; comunicativo.

egad (iˈgæːd) *interj.* ¡Dios mío!

egg (ɛg) *n.* huevo; *Mex.* postura *o* blanquillo. —*v.t.* incitar; provocar a.

eggplant *n.* berenjena.

eggshell *n.* cáscara de huevo; cascarón.

egis *también,* **aegis** (ˈiː·dʒɪs) *n.* égida.

eglantine (ˈɛg·lən,tain) *n.* eglantina.

ego (ˈi·go) *n.* **1,** [*pl.* **-gos**] (self) ego; yo. **2,** *colloq.* = **egotism.**

egoism (ˈi·go,ɪz·əm) *n.* egoísmo. —**egoist,** *n.* egoísta. —**egoistic,** *adj.* egoísta.

egotism (ˈi·gə,tɪz·əm) *n.* egotismo. —**egotist,** *n.* egotista. —**egotistic; egotistical,** *adj.* egotista.

egregious (ɪˈgri·dʒəs) *adj.* **1,** (utter; complete) perfecto; cabal. **2,** (flagrant) atroz; escandaloso; enorme.

egress (ˈiː·grɛs) *n.* salida.

egret (ˈiː·grɛt) *n.* arión.

Egyptian (ɪˈdʒɪp·ʃən) *adj.* & *n.* egipcio.

eh (ei) *interj.* ¡eh! —**eh?,** ¿qué?; ¿eh?; ¿no?

eider (ˈai·dər) *n.* [*también,* **eider duck**] eíder; pato de flojel. —**eider down,** edredón.

eight (eit) *n.* & *adj.* ocho.

eighteen (ˈeˈtin) *n.* & *adj.* diez y ocho; dieciocho. —**eighteenth** (-tinθ) *n.* & *adj.* décimoctavo; dieciochavo.

eightfold *adj.* & *n.* óctuple; ocho veces (más). —*adv.* ocho veces; en un óctuple.

eighth (eitθ) *adj.* octavo. —*n.* octavo; octava parte; *music* octava.

eight hundred ochocientos. —**eight-hundredth,** *adj.* & *n.* octingentésimo.

eighty (ˈe·ti) *n.* & *adj.* ochenta. —**eightieth** (-əθ) *n.* & *adj.* octogésimo; ochentavo.

einsteinium (ˈain,stain·i·əm) *n.* einsteinio.

either (ˈi·ðər; ˈai-) *adj.* & *pron.* uno u otro; cualquiera de los dos; uno y otro. —*conj.* o. —*adv.* tampoco. —**either . . . or,** o . . . o.

ejaculate (ɪˈdʒæk·jə·leit) *v.t.* **1,** (exclaim) exclamar; proferir. **2,** (emit forcibly) eyacular.

ejaculation (ɪ,dʒæk·jəˈlei·ʃən) **1,** (exclamation) exclamación. **2,** (discharge) eyaculación. **3,** (short prayer) jaculatoria.

eject (ɪˈdʒɛkt) *v.t.* echar; arrojar; expeler; expulsar. —**ejection** (ɪˈdʒɛk·ʃən) *n.* expulsión. —**ejector,** *n.* eyector; expulsor.

eke (ik) *v.t.* [*usu.,* **eke out**] **1,** (obtain with difficulty) ganar a duras penas. **2,** (supplement) suplementar; suplir.

elaborate (ɪˈlæb·ə·rət) *adj.* **1,** (carefully worked out) detallado; primoroso. **2,** (intricate; involved) complicado; intrincado. —*v.t.* (-reit) elaborar; complicar; detallar. —*v.i.* dar detalles. —**elaborateness,** *n.* primor; complicación. —**elaboration** (-ˈrei·ʃən) *n.* elaboración.

elapse (ɪˈlæps) *v.i.* mediar; pasar; transcurrir.

elastic (ɪˈlæs·tɪk) *adj.* & *n.* elástico. —**elasticity** (,i·læsˈtɪs·ə·ti) *n.* elasticidad.

elate (ɪˈleit) *v.t.* regocijar. —**elation,** *n.* júbilo; alborozo; regocijo.

elbow (ˈɛl·boː) *n.* **1,** *anat.* codo. **2,** (angle) recodo; ángulo. —*v.t.* dar codazos a; dar con el codo a. —*v.i.* abrirse paso con el codo; codear. —**elbow room,** *colloq.* amplio espacio; libertad de acción.

elder (ˈɛl·dər) *adj.* mayor; de más edad. —*n.* **1,** (older person) mayor; anciano. **2,** (person of authority) dignatario. **3,** (shrub) saúco. —**elderly** (-li) *adj.* mayor; de edad madura. —**elderliness,** *n.* ancianidad. —**eldest** (-dəst) *adj.* el mayor.

elect (ɪˈlɛkt) *v.t.* **1,** (select by vote) elegir. **2,** (choose) elegir; escoger. —*adj.* **1,** (elected) electo; elegido. **2,** (chosen) escogido. —*n.* elegido; electo; *theol.* predestinado.

election (ɪˈlɛk·ʃən) *n.* elección. —**electioneer** (-ʃəˈnɪːr) *v.i.* solicitar votos.

elective (ɪˈlɛk·tɪv) *adj.* **1,** (chosen by election) electivo. **2,** (optional) facultativo; potestativo.

elector (ɪˈlɛkt·ər) *n.* elector.

electoral (ɪ'lɛk·tə·rəl) *adj.* electoral.
electorate (ɪ'lɛk·tə·rət) *n.* electorado.
electric (ɪ'lɛk·trɪk) *adj.* **1,** [*también,* **electrical**] eléctrico. **2,** *fig.* (exciting) vivo; ardiente.
electrician (ɪ,lɛk'trɪʃ·ən) *n.* electricista.
electricity (ɪ,lɛk'trɪs·ə·ti) *n.* electricidad.
electrification (ɪ,lɛk·trə·fɪ'kei·ʃən) *n.* **1,** (providing with electricity) electrificación. **2,** (stimulation) electrización.
electrify (ɪ'lɛk·trɪ,fai) *v.t.* **1,** (charge with electricity) electrizar. **2,** (equip for electricity) electrificar. **3,** (startle; thrill) avivar; inflamar.
electro- (ɪ'lɛk·tro) *prefijo* electro-; electricidad: *electrostatics,* electrostática.
electrocute (ɪ'lɛk·trə·kjut) *v.t.* electrocutar. —**electrocution** (-'kju·ʃən) *n.* electrocución. —**electrocutionist,** *n.* electrocutor.
electrode (ɪ'lɛk·trod) *n.* electrodo.
electrolysis (ɪ,lɛk'tral·ə·sɪs) *n.* electrólisis. —**electrolytic** (-trə'lɪt·ɪk) *adj.* electrolítico.
electrolyte (ɪ'lɛk·trə·lait) *n.* electrólito.
electrolyze (ɪ'lɛk·trə,laiz) *v.t.* electrolizar.
electromagnetic (ɪ,lɛk·tro·mæg'nɛt·ɪk) *adj.* electromagnético. —**electromagnetism** (-'mæg·nə·,tɪz·əm) *n.* electromagnetismo.
electromotive (ɪ,lɛk·trə'mo·tɪv) *adj.* electromotriz.
electron (ɪ'lɛk·tran) *n.* electrón.
electronic (ɪ,lɛk'tran·ɪk) *adj.* electrónico. —**electronics,** *n.* electrónica.
electrostatic (ɪ,lɛk·trə'stæt·ɪk) *adj.* electrostático. —**electrostatics,** *n.* electrostática.
electrotype (ɪ'lɛk·trə·taip) *n.* electrotipo.
electrum (ɪ'lɛk·trəm) *n.* electro.
elegant ('ɛl·ɪ·gənt) *adj.* elegante. —**elegance,** *n.* elegancia.
elegiac (ɛ'li;·dʒi·æk) *adj.* elegíaco.
elegy ('ɛl·ə·dʒi) *n.* elegía. —**elegize** (-dʒaiz) *v.t. & i.* lamentar.
element ('ɛl·ə·mənt) *n.* **1,** *chem.* cuerpo simple; elemento. **2,** (component) elemento; componente; ingrediente. **3,** (environment) medio; ambiente. **4,** *pl.* (fundamentals) nociones; elementos; principios. **5,** *pl.* (weather) elementos; fuerzas naturales. —**elemental** (ɛl·ə'mɛn·təl) *adj.* elemental.
elementary (,ɛl·ɪ'mɛn·tə·ri) *adj.* elemental; rudimentario. —**elementary school,** escuela primaria.
elephant ('ɛl·ə·fənt) *n.* elefante. —**elephantine** (-'fæn·tɪn) *adj.* elefantino.
elephantiasis (,ɛl·ə·fən'tai·ə·sɪs) *n.* elefancía; elefantiasis.
elevate ('ɛl·ə·veit) *v.t.* elevar; alzar; levantar. —**elevated,** *adj. & n.* elevado.
elevation (,ɛl·ɪ'vei·ʃən) *n.* **1,** (raising) elevación. **2,** (altitude) altura; altitud. **3,** (high place) altura; eminencia. **4,** (in mechanical drawing) alzado; proyección vertical.
elevator ('ɛl·ɪ,ve·tər) *n.* **1,** (conveyance) ascensor; montacargas; elevador. **2,** (storehouse for grain) depósito de granos. **3,** *aero.* timón de profundidad; elevador.
eleven (ɪ'lɛv·ən) *n. & adj.* once. —**eleventh** (-ənθ) *n. & adj.* undécimo; onceno; onceavo.
elf (ɛlf) *n.* [*pl.* **elves**] elfo; duende. —**elfin** ('ɛl·fɪn) *adj.* de duende.
elicit (ɪ'lɪs·ɪt) *v.t.* sonsacar; evocar. —**elicitation,** *n.* sonsacamiento; evocación.
elide (ɪ'laid) *v.t.* elidir. —**elision** (ɪ'lɪʒ·ən) *n.* elisión.
eligible ('ɛl·ə·dʒə·bəl) *adj.* elegible. —**eligibility** (-'bɪl·ə·ti) *n.* elegibilidad.
eliminate (ɪ'lɪm·ə,neit) *v.t.* eliminar. —**elimination,** *n.* eliminación.
elite (e'lit) *n.* flor y nata; lo selecto; lo escogido.
elixir (ɪ'lɪk·sər) *n.* elíxir; elixir.
elk (ɛlk) *n.* anta; alce.
ell (ɛl) *n.* **1,** (wing) ala. **2,** (measure) ana.
ellipse (ɪ'lɪps) *n.* elipse.
ellipsis (ɪ'lɪp·sɪs) *n.* [*pl.* **-ses** (siz)] elipsis.
elliptical (ɪ'lɪp·tɪ·kəl) *adj.* elíptico.
elm (ɛlm) *n.* olmo.
elocution (ɛl·ə'kju·ʃən) *n.* elocución; declamación. —**elocutionary** (-ʃə,nɛ·ri) *adj.* declamatorio. —**elocutionist** (-ɪst) *n.* declamador.
elongate (ɪ'lɔŋ·geit) *v.t.* alargar; extender. —*v.i.* alargarse; prolongarse. —**elongation,** *n.* alargamiento.

elope (ɪ'lop) *v.i.* escaparse; fugarse. —**elopement,** *n.* fuga.
eloquent ('ɛl·ə·kwənt) *adj.* elocuente. —**eloquence,** *n.* elocuencia.
else (ɛls) *adj.* otro; diferente; más. —*adv.* **1,** (more) más. **2,** (also) además. **3,** (otherwise) de otro modo; de otra manera.
elsewhere *adv.* en, a *o* de otra parte.
elucidate (ɪ'lu·sɪ,deit) *v.t.* elucidar; dilucidar; aclarar. —**elucidation,** *n.* elucidación; dilucidación; aclaración.
elude (ɪ'luːd) *v.t.* eludir; esquivar; evitar; evadir.
elusion (ɪ'lu·ʃən) *n.* evasión.
elusive (ɪ'lu·sɪv) *adj.* evasivo. *También,* **elusory** (-sə·ri).
elves (ɛlvz) *n., pl. de* **elf.**
em- (ɛm) *prefijo, var. de* **en-** *ante* b, p, m: *embellish,* embellecer; *empiric,* empírico.
emaciate (ɪ'mei·ʃi,eit) *v.t.* adelgazar; enflaquecer; extenuar. —**emaciation,** *n.* adelgazamiento; enflaquecimiento; extenuación.
emanate ('ɛm·ə·neit) *v.i.* emanar; derivar; proceder. —**emanation,** *n.* emanación; exhalación.
emancipate (ɪ'mæn·sɪ,peit) *v.t.* emancipar; libertar. —**emancipation,** *n.* emancipación. —**emancipator,** *n.* emancipador; libertador.
emasculate (ɪ'mæs·kju,leit) *v.t.* castrar; capar; mutilar. —**emasculation,** *n.* castradura; castración; mutilación.
embalm (ɛm'baːm) *v.t.* embalsamar. —**embalmer,** *n.* embalsamador. —**embalmment,** *n.* embalsamamiento.
embank (ɛm'bæŋk) *v.t.* represar; terraplenar. —**embankment,** *n.* malecón; dique; terraplén.
embargo (ɛm'bar·go) *v.t.* embargar. —*n.* embargo.
embark (ɛm'bark) *v.i.* embarcarse.
embarkation (,ɛm·bar'kei·ʃən) *n.* **1,** (of passengers) embarco; embarcación. **2,** (of freight) embarque.
embarrass (ɛm'bær·əs) *v.t.* **1,** (abash) turbar; desconcertar. **2,** (perplex) desconcertar. **3,** (hamper; impede) estorbar; poner en un aprieto.
embarrassment (ɛm'bær·əs·mənt) *n.* **1,** (abashment) turbación; desconcierto. **2,** (perplexity) desconcierto; perplejidad. **3,** (impediment) estorbo; embarazo.
embassy ('ɛm·bə·si) *n.* embajada.
embattled (ɛm'bæt·əld) *adj.* **1,** (engaged in battle) empeñado en la lucha. **2,** (fortified) almenado.
embed (ɛm'bɛd) *v.t.* = **imbed.**
embellish (ɛm'bɛl·ɪʃ) *v.t.* **1,** (beautify) hermosear; embellecer. **2,** (add fiction to fact) adornar. —**embellishment,** *n.* embellecimiento.
ember ('ɛm·bər) *n.* ascua; pavesa. —**embers,** *n.pl.* rescoldo (*sing.*).
embezzle (ɛm'bɛz·əl) *v.t.* desfalcar. —**embezzlement,** *n.* desfalco. —**embezzler** (-lər) *n.* desfalcador.
embitter (ɛm'bɪt·ər) *v.t.* amargar; agriar. —**embitterment,** *n.* resentimiento; enojo.
emblem ('ɛm·bləm) *n.* emblema; símbolo; insignia. —**emblematic** (ɛm·blə'mæt·ɪk) *adj.* emblemático.
embodiment (ɛm'ba·di·mənt) *n.* **1,** (incarnation) encarnación; personificación. **2,** (expression) expresión; fórmula. **3,** (inclusion) inclusión.
embody (ɛm'ba·di) *v.t.* **1,** (incarnate) encarnar; personificar. **2,** (express concretely) formular; fijar. **3,** (comprise) incluir; comprender; englobar.
embolism ('ɛm·bə·lɪz·əm) *n.* embolia.
embolus ('ɛm·bə·ləs) *n.* émbolo.
emboss (ɛm'bɔs) *v.t.* abollonar; repujar; realzar; imprimir en relieve. —**embossment,** *n.* abolladura; realce; relieve.
embrace (ɛm'breis) *v.t.* **1,** (hug) abrazar. **2,** (enclose; comprise) abarcar; contener; comprender; encerrar. **3,** (accept) admitir; aceptar; adoptar. —*n.* abrazo.
embroider (ɛm'brɔi·dər) *v.t.* **1,** (decorate with needlework) bordar; recamar. **2,** (embellish) adornar; embellecer. —**embroiderer,** *n.* bordador. —**embroidery,** *n.* bordado; recamado.
embroil (ɛm'brɔil) *v.t.* embrollar; enredar. —**embroilment,** *n.* embrollo; intriga; lío.
embryo ('ɛm·bri·o) *n.* **1,** *biol.* embrión. **2,** (rudimentary stage) rudimento; germen; principio. —**embryonic** (-'an·ɪk) *adj.* embrionario; rudimentario.
embryology (,ɛm·bri'al·ə·dʒi) *n.*

embriología. —**embryologist**, *n.* embriólogo.
emend (i'mɛnd) *v.t.* enmendar; corregir. —**emendation** (ˌɛm·ən·'dei·ʃən) *n.* enmienda; corrección.
emerald ('ɛm·ər·əld) *n.* esmeralda. —*adj.* de esmeralda; esmeraldino.
emerge (ɪ'mʌɹdʒ) *v.i.* **1,** (rise, as from water) emerger. **2,** (come out) salir; surgir. **3,** (grow out) brotar. **4,** (appear) aparecer.
emergence (ɪ'mʌɹ·dʒəns) *n.* emergencia; salida; surgimiento; aparición.
emergency (ɪ'mʌɹ·dʒən·si) *n.* emergencia. —*adj.* **1,** (of or for extremity) de emergencia. **2,** (of or for rescue) de socorro; de auxilio.
emeritus (ɪ'mɛr·ɪ·təs) *adj.* emérito; retirado; jubilado.
emery ('ɛm·ə·ri) *n.* esmeril.
emetic (ɪ'mɛt·ɪk) *n.* & *adj.* emético; vomitivo.
-emia ('i·mi·ə) *también,* **-aemia** (i·mi·ə), **-hemia** *o* **haemia** (hi·mi·ə) *sufijo* -emia; *forma nombres denotando* cierta condición de la sangre: *anemia,* anemia.
emigrate ('ɛm·ɪˌgreit) *v.i.* emigrar; expatriarse. —**emigrant** (-grənt) *n.* emigrante; expatriado. —**emigration**, *n.* emigración.
emigré ('ɛm·ɪˌgre) *n.* emigrado.
eminence ('ɛm·ɪ·nəns) *n.* **1,** (high repute) eminencia; encumbramiento; distinción. **2,** (hill) altura; cima. **3,** *cap.* (title of a cardinal) eminencia.
eminent ('ɛm·ɪ·nənt) *adj.* **1,** (distinguished) eminente. **2,** (conspicuous) sobresaliente; relevante; supremo. —**eminent domain**, dominio eminente.
emir (ɛ'mɪr) *n.* emir; amir.
emissary ('ɛm·ɪ·sɛ·ri) *n.* emisario.
emission (ɪ'mɪʃ·ən) *n.* emisión.
emit (ɪ'mɪt) *v.t.* [**emitted, -mitting**] emitir; arrojar; despedir; exhalar.
emollient (ɪ'mal·jənt) *adj.* & *n.* emoliente.
emolument (ɪ'mal·jə·mənt) *n.* emolumento.
emotion (ɪ'mo·ʃən) *n.* emoción.
emotional (ɪ'mo·ʃən·əl) *adj.* **1,** (showing emotion) emocional; emotivo. **2,** (easily stirred) impresionable; sensible.
emotive (ɪ'mo·tɪv) *adj.* emotivo.
empathy ('ɛm·pə·θi) *n.* empatía.
emperor ('ɛm·pər·ər) *n.* emperador.
emphasis ('ɛm·fə·sɪs) *n.* [*pl.* **-ses** (siz)] énfasis; relieve; realce.
emphasize ('ɛm·fəˌsaiz) *v.t.* recalcar; acentuar; poner de relieve; insistir en; subrayar.
emphatic (ɛm'fæt·ɪk) *adj.* enfático; categórico.
empire ('ɛm·pair) *n.* imperio.
empiric (ɛm'pɪr·ɪk) *n.* & *adj.* empírico. —**empirical**, *adj.* empírico. —**empiricism** (-ɪˌsɪz·əm) *n.* empirismo.
emplacement (ɛm'pleis·mənt) *n., mil.* colocación; emplazamiento.
employ (ɛm'plɔi) *v.t.* **1,** (use) usar; aplicar; dedicar. **2,** (hire) emplear; encargar; dar trabajo a. —*n.* empleo. —**employee** (-iː) *n.* empleado; obrero; dependiente. —**employer**, *n.* amo; dueño; jefe; patrón; patrono; empresario.
employment (ɛm'plɔi·mənt) *n.* **1,** (use) uso; aplicación. **2,** (work; occupation) empleo.
emporium (ɛm'por·i·əm) *n.* [*pl.* **-a** (-ə)] emporio.
empower (ɛm'pau·ər) *v.t.* **1,** (authorize) autorizar. **2,** (enable) habilitar; dar poderes. —**empowerment**, *n.* autorización; facultad; apoderamiento.
empress ('ɛm·prəs) *n.* emperatriz.
empty ('ɛmp·ti) *adj.* **1,** (unfilled) vacío; desocupado; vacante. **2,** (futile) vano; inútil. —*v.t.* & *i.* vaciar; evacuar; desocupar; descargar. —*v.i.* desaguar; desembocar. —**emptiness**, *n.* vacío; vacuidad; vaciedad.
empty-headed *adj.* tonto; casquivano.
emulate ('ɛm·ju·leit) *v.t.* emular; rivalizar con; imitar. —**emulation**, *n.* emulación; rivalidad. —**emulous** (-ləs) *adj.* émulo; rival.
emulsify (ɪ'mʌl·sɪˌfai) *v.t.* emulsionar. —**emulsification** (-fɪ'kei·ʃən) *n.* emulsionamiento. —**emulsifier**, *n.* emulsor.
emulsion (ɪ'mʌl·ʃən) *n.* emulsión.
en- (ɛn) *prefijo* en-. **1,** en; dentro; *forma verbos indicando* colocación del objeto en un lugar, condición, etc.: *enclose,* encerrar; *enrich,* enriquecer. **2,** *intensifica la acción de ciertos verbos transitivos: entangle,* enmarañar. **3,** en; *especialmente en palabras de origen griego: endemic,* endémico.

-en (ən) *sufijo* **1,** *forma verbos de adjetivos: weaken,* debilitar; debilitarse; *o de nombres: frighten,* atemorizar. **2,** *forma la terminación del participio pasivo de muchos verbos fuertes: written,* escrito. **3,** *forma adjetivos denotando* sustancia; apariencia: *golden,* dorado. **4,** *forma el plural de algunos nombres: oxen,* bueyes; *children,* niños. **5,** *forma diminutivos o nombres femeninos: maiden,* doncella; *vixen,* zorra. **6,** *indica* personas, clases, etc.: *citizen,* ciudadano.

enable (ɛn'ei·bəl) *v.t.* habilitar; capacitar; permitir.

enact (ɛn'ækt) *v.t.* **1,** (make into law) establecer; realizar; estatuir; promulgar; decretar. **2,** (perform) representar; desempeñar; (un papel). **—enactment,** *n.* estatuto; promulgación.

enamel (ɪ'næm·əl) *n.* esmalte. *—v.t.* esmaltar.

enamor (ɪ'næm·ər) *v.t.* enamorar; encantar; cautivar.

encamp (ɛn'kæmp) *v.i.* acampar.

encampment (ɛn'kæmp·mənt) *n.* **1,** (act of camping) acampamiento. **2,** (camp) campamento.

encase (ɛn'keis) *v.t.* encajar; encajonar.

-ence (əns) *sufijo* -encia; *forma nombres indicando* acción; cualidad; condición, *que corresponden a adjetivos terminados en* **-ent:** *violence,* violencia.

encephalitis (ɛn,sɛf·ə'lai·tɪs) *n.* encefalitis.

encephalo- (ɛn'sɛf·ə·lo) *prefijo* encefalo-; cerebro: *encephalogram,* encefalograma.

enchant (ɛn'tʃænt) *v.t.* **1,** (put under a spell) hechizar; encantar; ensalmar. **2,** (charm) encantar; deleitar; embelesar. **—enchantment,** *n.* encantamiento; hechicería; encanto.

enchantress (ɛn'tʃænt·rɪs) *n.* **1,** (witch) bruja; hechicera. **2,** (charmer) encantadora.

enchilada (,ɛn·tʃɪ'la·də) *n.* enchilada.

encircle (ɛn'sʌɹ·kəl) *v.t.* **1,** (surround) cercar; circuir; circundar. **2,** (move around) rodear; circunvalar; circunscribir. **—encirclement,** *n.* circunvalación; encerramiento.

enclave ('ɛn·kleiv) *n.* enclavado; enclave.

enclose (ɛn'klo:z) *v.t.* **1,** (surround) cercar; rodear; circundar. **2,** (confine) encerrar. **3,** (include) incluir; adjuntar. *También,* **inclose.**

enclosure (ɛn'klo·ʒər) *n.* **1,** (act of enclosing) cercamiento. **2,** (enclosed area) cercado; coto; recinto. **3,** (fence, wall, etc.) cerca; valla. *También,* **inclosure.**

encomium (ɛn'ko·mi·əm) *n.* encomio.

encompass (ɛn'kʌm·pəs) *v.t.* **1,** (encircle) cercar; circundar; rodear. **2,** (include) encerrar; abarcar; incluir. **—encompassment,** *n.* cerco; rodeo; encierro.

encore ('an·kor) *interj., theat.* ¡bis!; ¡que se repita! *—n., theat.* repetición.

encounter (ɛn'kaun·tər) *v.t.* **1,** (meet) encontrar; topar con; tropezar con. **2,** (engage) batirse con. *—n.* encuentro; choque; combate.

encourage (ɛn'kʌɹ·ɪdʒ) *v.t.* **1,** (incite) animar; alentar; estimular. **2,** (support) fortalecer; estimular; aprobar. **—encouraging,** *adj.* animador; alentador; favorable. **—encouragement,** *n.* aliento; estímulo; ánimo; incentivo.

encroach (ɛn'kro:tʃ) *v.i.* [*usu.,* **encroach on** *o* **upon**] **1,** (trespass; make inroads) adentrarse; meterse; invadir. **2,** (violate) violar; abusar. **—encroachment,** *n.* intrusión; invasión; abuso.

encumber (ɛn'kʌm·bər) *v.t.* **1,** (hinder) impedir; embarazar; estorbar. **2,** (burden) cargar; gravar.

encumbrance (ɛn'kʌm·brəns) *n.* **1,** (hindrance) impedimento; estorbo. **2,** (burden) carga. **3,** (financial obligation) gravamen.

-ency (ən·si) *sufijo, var. de* **-ence:** *constituency,* distrito electoral.

encyclical (ɛn'sɪk·lə·kəl) *adj.* encíclico. *—n.* encíclica.

encyclopedia *también,* **encyclopaedia** (ɛn,sai·klə'pi:·di·ə) *n.* enciclopedia. **—encyclopedic** (-dɪk) *adj.* enciclopédico. **—encyclopedist** (-dɪst) *n.* enciclopedista.

end (ɛnd) *n.* **1,** (finish) final; extremidad; punta; cola. **2,** (boundary) remate; final. **3,** (final moment) conclusión; desenlace; final. **4,** (death; extinction) fin; muerte. **5,** (purpose) finalidad; objeto; propósito. **6,** (outcome; result) resultado; desenlace. *—v.t. & i.* acabar; concluir; terminar; cesar; morir. *—adj.* final; terminal; último; de cola. **—at loose ends,** en desorden; desarreglado. **—come to an end,** acabarse; terminarse. **—come to a bad end,** acabar mal. **—end over end,** de cabeza; dando traspiés *o* volatines. **—end to end,** punta a punta; cabeza con cabeza. **—end up, 1,** (upright) de cabeza; de pie; derecho; *Amer.* parado. **2,** (finish) acabar. **—in the end,** al fin; a la larga; al fin y al cabo. **—make an end of,** acabar con. **—make ends meet,** pasar con lo que se tiene. **—on end, 1,** (upright) de pie; de punta; derecho. **2,** (one after the other) sucesivamente; uno después de otro. **—put an end to,** acabar con; poner fin a.

endanger (ɛn'dein·dʒər) *v.t.* poner en peligro; arriesgar; comprometer. **—endangerment,** *n.* arriesgo; compromiso.

endear (ɛn'dɪr) *v.t.* hacer querer. **—endearing,** *adj.* cariñoso. **—endearment,** *n.* encariñamiento; cariño.

endeavor *también,* **endeavour** (ɛn·'dɛv·ər) *v.i.* intentar; probar (a *o* de); tratar (de); esforzarse (a, en *o* por). **—***n.* esfuerzo.

endemic (ɛn'dɛm·ɪk) *adj.* endémico.

ending ('ɛn·dɪŋ) *n.* **1,** (termination) fin; conclusión; cesación; suspensión. **2,** (final part) desenlace; final.

endive ('ɛn·daiv) *n.* endibia.

endless ('ɛnd·ləs) *adj.* fin; infinito; perpetuo; interminable; continuo. **—endlessness,** *n.* perpetuidad.

endmost *adj.* extremo; último.

endo- (ɛn·do) *prefijo* endo-; dentro; interno: *endocrine,* endocrino.

endocrine ('ɛn·do,krain) *adj.* & *n.* endocrino.

endorse (ɛn'dors) *v.t.* **1,** (sign) endosar. **2,** (support) apoyar; aprobar. **—endorsee,** *n.* endosatario. **—endorser,** *n.* endosante.

endorsement (ɛn'dors·mənt) *n.* **1,** (signature) endoso. **2,** (support) apoyo; aprobación.

endow (ɛn'dau) *v.t.* dotar; fundar. **—endowment,** *n.* dote; dotación; fundación. **—endowment policy,** póliza dotal.

endurance (ɛn'djur·əns) *n.* paciencia; resistencia; perduración. **—beyond endurance,** insoportable.

endure (ɛn'djur) *v.t.* **1,** (bear; suffer) sufrir; soportar; sobrellevar. **2,** (sustain without harm) resistir; aguantar; tolerar. **—***v.i.* durar; perdurar.

endways ('ɛnd·weiz) *adv.* **1,** (erect) de punta; de pie; *Amer.* parado. **2,** (lengthwise) a lo largo; de largo; longitudinalmente. **3,** (end to end) punta a punta; cabeza con cabeza. *También,* **endwise** (-waiz).

-ene (iːn) *sufijo, quím.* -eno; *forma los nombres de algunos hidrocarburos: ethylene,* etileno.

enema ('ɛn·ə·mə) *n.* enema.

enemy ('ɛn·ə·mi) *n.* & *adj.* enemigo; adversario; antagonista.

energetic (ɛn·ər'dʒɛt·ɪk) *adj.* enérgico; vigoroso.

energy ('ɛn·ər·dʒi) *n.* **1,** (vigor) energía; vigor. **2,** (activity) energía; acción; actividad. **3,** *mech.* (power) energía; fuerza; potencia. **—energize** (-dʒaiz) *v.t.* excitar; dar energía a.

enervate ('ɛn·ər,veit) *v.t.* enervar; debilitar; desvirtuar. **—enervation,** *n.* enervación; debilidad.

enfilade (,ɛn·fə'leid) *n.* enfilada. **—***v.t.* enfilar.

enforce (ɛn'fors) *v.t.* **1,** ejecutar; dar fuerza *o* vigor a; poner en vigor; cumplimentar; hacer cumplir. **—enforceable,** *adj.* ejecutable. **—enforcement,** *n.* ejecución; coacción; compulsión.

enfranchise (ɛn'fræn·tʃaiz) *v.t.* **1,** (grant a franchise to) conceder franquicia. **2,** (accord voting rights to) concedar sufragio. **3,** (liberate) emancipar.

enfranchisement (ɛn'fræn·tʃaiz·mənt) *n.* **1,** (franchise) franquicia. **2,** (voting) concesión del sufragio. **3,** (emancipation) emancipación.

engage (ɛn'geidʒ) *v.t.* **1,** (hire) emplear; contratar; tomar a su servicio. **2,** (bind by a pledge) apalabrar; comprometer. **3,** (attract) atraer. **4,** (meet in conflict) trabar con; entrar en lucha con. **5,** *mech.* (interlock) engranar.

engaged (ɛn'geidʒd) *adj.* **1,** (busy) ocupado. **2,** (betrothed) prometido; comprometido. **—become engaged (to),** comprometerse (con); prometerse (a).

engagement (ɛn'geidʒ·mənt) *n.* **1,** (pledge) ajuste; contrato; obligación. **2,** (betrothal) compromiso; noviazgo. **3,** *mech.* engranaje; ajuste. **4,** (conflict) acción; batalla.

engaging (ɛn'geidʒ·ɪŋ) *adj.* atractivo; agraciado; simpático.
engender (ɛn'dʒɛn·dər) *v.t.* **1,** (generate) engendrar; producir. **2,** (beget) procrear. **3,** (cause) causar.
engine ('ɛn·dʒən) *n.* **1,** (machine) máquina; motor; ingenio. **2,** *R.R.* locomotora.
engineer (ɛn·dʒə'nɪːr) *n.* **1,** (engine operator) maquinista; mecánico. **2,** (graduate in engineering) ingeniero. —*v.t.* **1,** (act as engineer for) hacer de ingeniero *o* maquinista de. **2,** *colloq.* (contrive) ingeniar; gestionar; manejar; dirigir. —**engineering,** *n.* ingeniería.
English ('ɪŋ·glɪʃ) *n.* & *adj.* inglés.
Englishman ('ɪŋ·glɪʃ·mən) *n.* [*pl.* **-men**] inglés. —**Englishwoman,** *n.* [*pl.* **-women**] inglesa.
engrave (ɛn'greiv) *v.t.* **1,** (carve) esculpir; cincelar; burilar. **2,** (etch) grabar. —**engraver,** *n.* esculpidor. —**engraving,** *n.* grabado; lámina; estampa.
engross (ɛn'groːs) *v.t.* **1,** (absorb) absorber; abstraer. **2,** (write) transcribir caligráficamente.
engrossing (ɛn'gro·sɪŋ) *adj.* muy interesante; fascinante. —*n.* = **engrossment.**
engrossment (ɛn'gros·mənt) *n.* **1,** (absorption) abstracción; ensimismamiento. **2,** (writing) transcripción caligráfica.
engulf (ɛn'gʌlf) *v.t.* **1,** (swallow) tragar. **2,** (submerge) sumergir; hundir. **3,** (overwhelm) abrumar.
enhance (ɛn'hæns) *v.t.* realzar; mejorar; acrecentar; aumentar el valor de. —**enhancement,** *n.* realce; acrecentamiento; mejoría.
enigma (ɪ'nɪg·mə) *n.* enigma. —**enigmatic** (ˌɛn·ɪg'mæt·ɪk) *adj.* enigmático.
enjoin (ɛn'dʒɔin) *v.t.* **1,** (command; prescribe) mandar; ordenar; prescribir. **2,** (restrain by injunction) prohibir.
enjoy (ɛn'dʒɔi) *v.t.* **1,** (take pleasure in) gozar de; gozarse en; gustar de. **2,** (possess) disfrutar de; tener; poseer. —**enjoyable,** *adj.* deleitable; agradable.
enjoyment (ɛn'dʒɔi·mənt) *n.* **1,** (pleasure) goce; disfrute; placer. **2,** (possession) uso; usufructo.
enlarge (ɛn'lardʒ) *v.t.* **1,** (make larger) agrandar; aumentar; ensanchar; ampliar. **2,** (amplify) ampliar; amplificar. —*v.i.* **1,** (become larger) ensancharse; agrandarse. **2,** (expatiate) explayarse; tratar detalladamente.
enlargement (ɛn'lardʒ·mənt) *n.* **1,** (enlarging) agrandamiento; ensanchamiento. **2,** (expansion) aumento; dilatación; expansión. **3,** *photog.* ampliación.
enlighten (ɛn'lai·tən) *v.t.* **1,** (give knowledge to) ilustrar; iluminar; instruir. **2,** (inform) informar.
enlightenment (ɛn'lai·tən·mənt) *n.* **1,** (knowledge) instrucción; civilización; cultura. **2,** (information) información. **3,** *cap., hist.* el siglo de las luces.
enlist (ɛn'lɪst) *v.t.* alistar; enrolar; *mil.* reclutar. —*v.i.* alistarse; enrolarse; *mil.* sentar plaza. —**enlistment,** *n.* alistamiento; enganche; enrolamiento. —**enlisted man,** recluta; soldado.
enliven (ɛn'laiv·ən) *v.t.* **1,** (give life to) vivificar; animar. **2,** (in spirit) alegrar; regocijar.
enmesh (ɛn'mɛʃ) *v.t.* enredar.
enmity ('ɛn·mə·ti) *n.* enemistad.
ennoble (ɛn'no·bəl) *v.t.* ennoblecer. —**ennoblement,** *n.* ennoblecimiento.
enormity (ɪ'nor·mə·ti) *n.* atrocidad; enormidad.
enormous (ɪ'nor·məs) *adj.* enorme; descomunal. —**enormousness,** *n.* demasía; exceso.
enough (ɪ'nʌf) *adj.* bastante; suficiente. —*adv.* suficientemente; bastante. —*n.* (lo) suficiente. —*interj.* ¡basta!
enquire (ɪn'kwair) *v.i.* & *t.* = **inquire.** —**enquiry,** *n.* = **inquiry.**
enrage (ɛn'reidʒ) *v.t.* enfurecer; encolerizar.
enrapture (ɛn'ræp·tʃər) *v.t.* arrebatar; embelesar; extasiar.
enrich (ɛn'rɪtʃ) *v.t.* **1,** (make rich) enriquecer. **2,** (improve, as soil) abonar; fertilizar; beneficiar. —**enrichment,** *n.* enriquecimiento; abono; beneficio.
enroll *también,* **enrol** (ɛn'roːl) *v.t.* alistar. —*v.i.* alistarse; inscribirse; matricularse. —**enrollment; enrolment,** *n.* alistamiento; inscripción; matriculación; registro.
ensconce (ɛn'skans) *v.t.* **1,** (settle firmly) acomodar; situar. **2,** (cover; hide) ocultar; esconder; poner en seguro.

ensemble (an'sam·bəl) *n.* **1,** (group) conjunto; grupo. **2,** (costume) traje.
enshrine (ɛn'ʃrain) *v.t.* **1,** (place in a shrine) guardar como reliquia. **2,** *fig.* (cherish) apreciar; estimar.
enshroud (ɛn'ʃraud) *v.t.* **1,** (wrap) amortajar; envolver. **2,** (conceal) ocultar; tapar.
ensign ('ɛn·sain) *n.* **1,** (flag) bandera; pabellón; enseña. **2,** (emblem) insignia; divisa. **3,** (-sɪn) *mil.; naval* alférez.
ensile (ɛn'sail) *v.t.* ensilar. **—ensilage** ('ɛn·sə·lɪdʒ) *n.* ensilaje.
enslave (ɛn'sleiv) *v.t.* esclavizar; avasallar. **—enslavement,** *n.* esclavitud; esclavización.
ensnare (ɛn'sneːr) *v.t.* atrapar; enredar; engañar. **—ensnarement,** *n.* atrapamiento; enredo; engaño.
ensue (ɛn'suː) *v.i.* **1,** (follow) seguir; suceder. **2,** (result) sobrevenir.
ensure (ɛn'ʃʊr) *v.t.* asegurar.
-ent (ənt) *sufijo* -ente; -iente. **1,** *forma adjetivos equivalentes al participio activo: different,* diferente; *ardent,* ardiente. *Algunos se usan como nombres: deterrent,* deterrente. **2,** *forma nombres indicando* agente; actor: *regent,* regente.
entail (ɛn'teil) *v.t.* **1,** (bring about) ocasionar. **2,** (involve) envolver. **3,** (impose as a burden) imponer. **4,** *law* vincular. **—entailment,** *n., law* vinculación.
entangle (ɛn'tæŋ·gəl) *v.t.* **1,** (involve in difficulties) enredar; embrollar; enmarañar. **2,** (complicate) intrincar; implicar. **—entanglement,** *n.* enredo; embrollo; complicación.
entente (an'taːnt) *n.* pacto; alianza.
enter ('ɛn·tər) *v.t.* **1,** (come into) entrar en *o* a; penetrar. **2,** (insert) introducir; insertar. **3,** (join, as a class or club) ingresar en; alistarse en; matricularse en; afiliarse a. **4,** (record) asentar; anotar; registrar. **—*v.i.* 1,** (come or go in) entrar; introducirse; ingresar. **2,** (take part) participar; interesarse.
entero- (ˌɛn·tə·ro) *prefijo* entero-; intestino: *enterocolitis,* enterocolitis.
enterprise ('ɛn·tər·praiz) *n.* **1,** (project; business) empresa. **2,** (boldness; initiative) arresto; actividad. **—enterprising,** *adj.* emprendedor; acometedor; esforzado.
entertain (ɛn·tər'tein) *v.t.* **1,** (amuse) festejar; agasajar; entretener; divertir. **2,** (have as a guest) hospedar. **3,** (have in mind) tomar en consideración; acariciar; abrigar. **—*v.i.*** invitar; dar fiestas, comidas, etc. **—entertaining,** *adj.* divertido; entretenido.
entertainment (ˌɛn·tər'tein·mənt) *n.* **1,** (receiving of guests) recepción; recibimiento. **2,** (amusement) entretenimiento; diversión. **3,** (show) espectáculo.
enthrall (ɛn'θrɔl) *v.t.* **1,** (captivate; charm) dominar; cautivar. **2,** (enslave) esclavizar; sojuzgar. **—enthrallment,** *n.* dominación; esclavización; sojuzgación.
enthrone (ɛn'θroːn) *v.t.* entronar; entronizar. **—enthronement,** *n.* entronización.
enthusiasm (ɛn'θuː·zi·æz·əm) *n.* entusiasmo. **—enthusiast** (-ˌæst) *n.* entusiasta; aficionado. **—enthusiastic** (-'æs·tɪk) *adj.* entusiástico.
entice (ɛn'tais) *v.t.* tentar; seducir; atraer. **—enticement,** *n.* tentación; seducción; añagaza.
entire (ɛn'tair) *adj.* entero; completo; íntegro; total. **—entireness,** *n.* entereza. **—entirety** (-ti) *n.* entereza; totalidad; integridad; todo.
entirely (ɛn'tair·li) *adv.* **1,** (wholly) del todo; enteramente. **2,** (solely) solamente; exclusivamente.
entitle (ɛn'tai·təl) *v.t.* **1,** (authorize) dar derecho; habilitar; autorizar. **2,** (name) titular.
entity ('ɛn·tə·ti) *n.* **1,** (individual reality) entidad. **2,** (being) ser; ente.
ento- (ɛn·to) *prefijo* ento-; dentro; interior: *entophyte,* entofita.
entomb (ɛn'tuːm) *v.t.* enterrar; sepultar. **—entombment,** *n.* entierro; sepultura.
entomo- (ɛn·tə·mo) *prefijo* entomo-; insecto: *entomology,* entomología.
entomology (ɛn·tə'mal·ə·dʒi) *n.* entomología. **—entomological** (-mə'la·dʒɪ·kəl) *adj.* entomológico. **—entomologist,** *n.* entomólogo.
entourage (an·tʊ'raːʒ) *n.* compañía; cortejo; séquito.
entrails ('ɛn·trəlz; -treilz) *n.pl.* entrañas; vísceras.
entrance ('ɛn·trəns) *n.* **1,** (the act of entering) entrada; ingreso. **2**

(place to enter) entrada; puerta; portal; embocadura.
entrance (ɛn'træns) *v.t.* extasiar; fascinar; embelesar; hechizar.
entrant ('ɛn·trənt) *n.* principiante; *sports* competidor.
entrap (ɛn'træp) *v.t.* [**entrapped, -trapping**] atrapar con trampa; entrampar. —**entrapment,** *n.* entrampamiento.
entreat (ɛn'trit) *v.t.* rogar; suplicar; implorar; impetrar.
entreaty (ɛn'tri·ti) *n.* **1,** (request) ruego; súplica. **2,** (petition) rogación; rogativa.
entrée (an'tre) *n.* **1,** (right of entering) entrada; privilegio de entrar. **2,** (main dish) principio; entrada.
entrench (ɛn'trɛntʃ) *v.t.* atrincherar. —*v.i.* invadir; infringir. —**entrenchment,** *n.* atrincheramiento.
entrepreneur (ˌan·trə·prə'nʌːɹ) *n.* empresario.
entrust (ɛn'trʌst) *v.t.* confiar; encomendar; encargar.
entry ('ɛn·tri) *n.* **1,** (act of entering; entrance) entrada; acceso; ingreso. **2,** (opening) vestíbulo; portal; zaguán. **3,** (item recorded) asiento; anotación; inscripción; *comm.* partida.
entwine (ɛn'twain) *v.t.* & *i.* entrelazar.
enumerate (ɪ'nu·mə·reit) *v.t.* **1,** (name one by one) enumerar. **2,** (count) enumerar; contar. —**enumeration,** *n.* enumeración; recuento.
enunciate (ɪ'nʌn·si·eit) *v.t.* & *i.* pronunciar; enunciar; articular. —**enunciation,** *n.* pronunciación; enunciación; articulación.
envelop (ɛn'vɛl·əp) *v.t.* envolver; cubrir. —**envelopment,** *n.* envolvimiento.
envelope ('ɛn·və·lop) *n.* **1,** (covering) cubierta; envolvedor. **2,** (for a letter) sobre.
envenom (ɛn'vɛn·əm) *v.t.* envenenar.
enviable ('ɛn·vi·ə·bəl) *adj.* envidiable.
envious ('ɛn·vi·əs) *adj.* envidioso. —**enviousness,** *n.* envidia.
environment (ɛn'vai·rən·mənt) *n.* cercanía; medio ambiente. —**environmental** (-'mɛn·təl) *adj.* ambiente.
environs (ɛn'vai·rənz) *n.pl.* **1,** (surroundings) alrededores; cercanías; inmediaciones. **2,** (outlying areas) afueras.
envoy ('ɛn·vɔi) *n.* (representative) enviado; agente diplomático; mensajero.
envy ('ɛn·vi) *v.t.* envidiar; codiciar. —*n.* envidia.
enzyme ('ɛn·zaim) *n.* enzima.
eo- (ˌi·o) *prefijo* eo-; temprano; primitivo: *eolithic,* eolítico.
eon ('i·ən; 'i·an) *n.* eón.
ep- (ɛp) *prefijo, var. de* **epi-.**
epaulet *también,* **epaulette** ('ɛp·ə·lɛt) *n., mil.* charretera.
ephemeral (ɪ'fɛm·ər·əl) *adj.* efímero; transitorio.
epi- (ˌɛp·ɪ) *prefijo* epi-; sobre; entre; hasta; contra: *epicenter,* epicentro.
epic ('ɛp·ɪk) *adj.* épico. —*n.* poema épico; epopeya.
epicure ('ɛp·ɪˌkjʊr) *n.* **1,** (gourmet) epicúreo; gastrónomo. **2,** (sensualist) epicúreo; sibarita. —**epicurean** (-kjʊ'ri·ən) *adj.* epicureo.
epidemic (ˌɛp·ɪ'dɛm·ɪk) *adj.* epidémico. —*n.* epidemia; plaga; peste.
epidermis (ˌɛp·ə'dʌɹ·mɪs) *n.* epidermis; cutícula; piel.
epiglottis (ˌɛp·ə'glat·ɪs) *n.* epiglotis; lengüeta.
epigram ('ɛp·ɪˌgræm) *n.* epigrama. —**epigrammatic** (-grə'mæt·ɪk) *adj.* epigramático. —**epigrammatist** (-'græm·ə·tɪst) *n.* epigramista; epigramatista.
epilepsy ('ɛp·ə·lɛp·si) *n.* epilepsia. —**epileptic** (-'lɛp·tɪk) *adj.* & *n.* epiléptico.
epilogue ('ɛp·ə·lɔg) *n.* epílogo.
Epiphany (ɪ'pɪf·ə·ni) *n.* Epifanía; día de los Reyes.
episcopacy (ɪ'pɪs·kə·pə·si) *n.* episcopado.
episcopal (ɪ'pɪs·kə·pəl) *adj.* episcopal; obispal.
Episcopalian (ɪˌpɪs·kə'peil·jən) *adj.* & *n.* episcopalista; episcopaliano.
episcopate (ɪ'pɪs·kə·pɪt; -ˌpeit) *n.* episcopado.
episode ('ɛp·ɪ·sod) *n.* **1,** (event) episodio; lance; peripecia. **2,** *music* (digressive passage) digresión. —**episodic** (-'sad·ɪk) *adj.* episódico.
epistle (ɪ'pɪs·əl) *n.* epístola; carta. —**epistolary** (-tə·lɛr·i) *adj.* epistolar. —*n.* epistolario.
epitaph ('ɛp·ɪˌtæf) *n.* epitafio.
epithet ('ɛp·ə·θɛt) *n.* epíteto.

epitome (ɪ'pɪt·ə·mi) *n.* epítome; sumario; compendio. **—epitomize** (-ˌmaiz) *v.t.* epitomar; compendiar.
epoch ('ɛp·ək) *n.* época; edad; período; era. **—epochal,** *adj.* trascendental; memorable.
equable ('ɛk·wə·bəl) *adj.* **1,** (uniform) igual; uniforme; ecuable. **2,** (stable) estable. **3,** (calm) tranquilo. **—equability** [*también,* **equableness**] *n.* igualdad; uniformidad.
equal ('i·kwəl) *adj.* **1,** (same) igual. **2,** (balanced; level) igual; parejo. **—*n.*** igual. **—*v.t.*** **1,** (be equal to) ser igual a; equivaler; valer. **2,** (make equal) igualar. **3,** (become equal to) igualarse a. **4,** (adjust) compensar. **—equal to, 1,** (sufficient for) suficiente para. **2,** (competent for) con fuerzas para. **—equal out,** igualar; igualarse. **—feel equal to,** sentirse con fuerzas para.
equality (i'kwal·ə·ti) *n.* igualdad; uniformidad; paridad.
equalize ('iː·kwə·laiz) *v.t.* igualar; compensar. **—equalization** (ˌi·kwə·lɪ'zei·ʃən) *n.* igualamiento; igualación; compensación.
equanimity (i·kwə'nɪm·ə·ti) *n.* ecuanimidad.
equate (ɪ'kweit) *v.t.* igualar; poner en ecuación.
equation (ɪ'kwei·ʃən) *n.* ecuación.
equator (ɪ'kwei·tər) *n.* ecuador. **—equatorial** (i·kwə'tor·i·əl) *adj.* ecuatorial.
equestrian (ɪ'kwɛs·tri·ən) *adj.* ecuestre. **—*n.*** jinete. **—equestrienne** (-'ɛn) *n.* amazona.
equi- (ɛk·wɪ; i·kwɪ) *prefijo* equi-; igual: *equivalent,* equivalente.
equidistant (i·kwə'dɪs·tənt) *adj.* equidistante.
equilateral (i·kwə'læt·ər·əl) *adj.* equilátero.
equilibrate (ˌi·kwə'lai·bret) *v.t.* equilibrar.
equilibrist (ɪ'kwɪl·ə·brɪst) *n.* equilibrista.
equilibrium (i·kwə'lɪb·ri·əm) *n.* equilibrio; balance.
equinox ('i·kwəˌnaks) *n.* equinoccio. **—equinoctial** (-'nak·ʃəl) *adj.* equinoccial.
equip (ɪ'kwɪp) *v.t.* [**equipped, equipping**] **1,** (fit out) equipar; pertrechar. **2,** *naut.* (fit) aprestar.
equipment (ɪ'kwɪp·mənt) *n.* equipo; aparatos; material.
equitable ('ɛk·wɪ·tə·bəl) *adj.* equitativo; justo. **—equitableness,** *n.* equidad; imparcialidad; justicia.
equity ('ɛk·wə·ti) *n.* **1,** (fairness) equidad; imparcialidad. **2,** *law* equidad; justicia. **3,** *finance* valor; título; acción.
equivalent (ɪ'kwɪv·ə·lənt) *n.* & *adj.* equivalente. **—equivalence,** *n.* equivalencia.
equivocal (ɪ'kwɪv·ə·kəl) *adj.* equívoco; ambiguo.
equivocate (ɪ'kwɪv·əˌkeit) *v.t.* & *i.* tergiversar. **—equivocation,** *n.* equívoco.
-er (ər) *sufijo* **1,** *añadido a verbos forma nombres de personas o cosas con sentido de* agente: *driver,* conductor. **2,** *unido a nombres denota* ocupación; conexión: *philosopher,* filósofo; *prisoner,* prisionero. **3,** *con nombres de lugar indica* habitante: *Londoner,* londinense. **4,** *denota* característica: *three-master,* velero de tres palos. **5,** *forma el comparativo de adjetivos y adverbios: greener,* más verde; *slower,* más despacio. **6,** *forma nombres de acción, esp. en derecho: waiver,* renuncia. **7,** *forma verbos frecuentativos: patter,* golpetear.
era ('ɪr·ə) *n.* era; época; edad.
eradicate (ɪ'ræd·ɪ·keit) *v.t.* desarraigar; erradicar; extirpar. **—eradication,** *n.* erradicación; desarraigo; extirpación. **—eradicator,** *n.* desarraigador; erradicador; extirpador.
erase (ɪ'reis) *v.t.* borrar; tachar; raer. **—eraser,** *n.* borrador; goma de borrar.
erasure (ɪ'rei·ʃər) *n.* borradura.
erbium ('ʌɹ·bi·əm) *n.* erbio.
ere (eir) *prep., poet.* antes de. **—*conj.*** antes que.
erect (ɪ'rɛkt) *v.t.* **1,** (build) erigir; edificar; construir; levantar. **2,** (establish) montar; instalar. **3,** (place upright) erguir; poner de pie; *Amer.* parar. **—*adj.*** erguido; enhiesto; de pie; *Amer.* parado. **—erection** (ɪ'rɛk·ʃən) *n.* erección; montaje; instalación.
erg (ʌɹg) *n.* erg; ergio.
ergot ('ʌɹ·gət) *n.* **1,** *bot.; pharm.* cornezuelo. **2,** *plant pathol.* ergotismo. **—ergotism,** *n., pathol.* ergotismo.
ergotine ('ʌɹ·gət·ɪn) *n.* ergotina.
ermine ('ʌɹ·mɪn) *n.* **1,** (animal; fur) armiño. **2,** *fig.* (judge's office or dignity) toga; judicatura.

-ern (ərn) *sufijo* **1,** -erna; *terminación de nombres: lantern,* linterna. **2,** -erno; *terminación de adjetivos: modern,* moderno.
erode (ɪ'roːd) *v.t.* corroer; roer; comer. —*v.i.* desgastarse.
erosion (ɪ'roː·ʒən) *n.* corrosión; desgaste; *geol.* erosión. —**erosive** (-sɪv) *adj.* erosivo.
erotic (ɪ'rat·ɪk) *adj.* erótico. —**eroticism** (-əˌsɪz·əm) *n.* erotismo. —**erotism** ('ɛr·əˌtɪz·əm) *n.* erotismo.
err (ʌɹ) *v.t.* **1,** (blunder) errar; equivocarse. **2,** (go astray) descarriarse. **3,** (sin) pecar.
errand ('ɛr·ənd) *n.* encargo; recado; mandado.
errant ('ɛr·ənt) *adj.* **1,** (roving) errante; andante. **2,** (erring) errado.
erratic (ə'ræt·ɪk) *adj.* excéntrico; irregular.
erratum (ɪ'rat·əm) *n.* [*pl.* **-ta** (-tə)] errata.
erroneous (ɪ'roː·ni·əs) *adj.* errado; erróneo; falso. —**erroneousness,** *n.* error; falsedad.
error ('ɛr·ər) *n.* **1,** (mistake) error; equivocación; yerro. **2,** (sin) engaño; pecado. **3,** (deviation) error.
Erse (ʌɹs) *n.* & *adj.* gaélico; erso.
erstwhile ('ʌɹst·hwail) *adj.* antiguo; de otro tiempo. —*adv.* antes; primeramente.
eruct (ɪ'rʌkt) *v.t.* & *i.* eructar; regoldar. *También,* **eructate** (ɪ'rʌk·teit). —**eructation** (ɪˌrʌk'tei·ʃən) *n.* eructación; eructo; regüeldo.
erudition (ˌɛr·ʊ'dɪʃ·ən) *n.* erudición; conocimientos. —**erudite** (-dait) *adj.* erudito.
erupt (ɪ'rʌpt) *v.i.* erumpir; hacer erupción. —**eruption** (ɪ'rʌp·ʃən) *n.* erupción. —**eruptive** (-tɪv) *adj.* eruptivo.
-ery (ə·ri) *sufijo* -ería; *forma nombres denotando* **1,** colectividad: *pottery,* alfarería. **2,** condición; estado: *drudgery,* afán. **3,** agregación: *finery,* atavíos. **4,** ocupación: *surgery,* cirugía. **5,** utensilios; productos: *cutlery,* cuchillería. **6,** lugares de actividad mercantil: *haberdashery,* camisería. **7,** lugares donde se recoge *o* cría: *piggery,* pocilga.
erysipelas (ˌɛr·ə'sɪp·ə·ləs) *n.* erisipela.
-es (ɪz) *sufijo* **1,** *forma la tercera persona singular del presente de indicativo tras sibilantes: he wishes,* desea; *he crushes,* aplasta. **2,** *forma el plural de nombres terminados en sibilante* (s, sh, ch, *etc.*): *dresses,* vestidos; *watches,* relojes.
escalator ('ɛs·kə·le·tər) *n.* escalera móvil. —*adj., law* de ajuste automático.
escallop *también,* **escalop** (ɛs'kal·əp) *v.t.* **1,** *cookery* cocer en salsa. **2,** (serrate) ondear. —*n.* = **scallop.**
escapade ('ɛs·kə·peid) *n.* escapada; travesura; aventura.
escape (ɛs'keip) *v.i.* **1,** (flee) escaparse; fugarse; huir. **2,** (leak out) escaparse; salirse; filtrarse. —*v.t.* evadir; evitar; eludir. —*n.* escapada; huida; fuga; envasión. —**escape hatch,** escotilla de emergencia. —**have a narrow escape,** salvarse por un pelo.
escapism (ɛs'kei·pɪz·əm) *n.* escapismo. —**escapist,** *adj.* & *n.* escapista.
escapement (ɛs'keip·mənt) *n.* escape.
escarole ('ɛs·kəˌrol) *n.* escarola.
escarpment (ɛs'karp·mənt) *n.* escarpa; escarpadura; frontón.
-esce (ɛːs) *sufijo; terminación de verbos incoativos: convalesce,* convalecer; *deliquesce,* derretirse.
-escence ('ɛs·əns) *sufijo* -escencia; *forma nombres de verbos terminados en* **-esce** *o de adjetivos terminados en* **-escent**: *convalescence,* convalencencia.
-escent ('ɛs·ənt) *sufijo* -escente; *forma adjetivos, usados a veces como nombres, de verbos terminados en* **-esce** *o de nombres terminados en* **-escence**: *convalescent,* convaleciente.
eschew (ɛs'tʃuː) *v.t.* huir de; evitar.
escort (ɛs'kort) *v.t.* escoltar; acompañar; convoyar. —*n.* ('ɛs·kort) escolta; acompañante; convoy.
escrow ('ɛs·kroː) *n.* plica.
escudo (ɛs'ku·do) *n.* escudo.
escutcheon (ɛs'kʌtʃ·ən) *n.* escudo de armas.
-ese (iːz; is) *sufijo* -és; *forma adjetivos y nombres expresando* relación geográfica; idioma; nacionalidad, etc.: *Portuguese,* portugués.
Eskimo ('ɛs·kə·mo) *n.* [*pl.* **-mos**] & *adj.* esquimal.
eso- (ɛs·o) *prefijo* eso-; en; interno; oculto: *esoteric,* esotérico.
esophagus (ɪ'saf·ə·gəs) *n.* [*pl.* **-gi** (-dʒai)] esófago.

esoteric (ɛs·ə'tɛr·ɪk) *adj.* esotérico; secreto; oculto.
esparto (ɛs'par·to) *n.* esparto.
especial (ɛs'pɛʃ·əl) *adj.* **1,** (particular) especial; particular. **2,** (exceptional) notable; sobresaliente. *También,* **special.**
espionage (ˌɛs·pi·ə'naʒ) *n.* espionaje.
esplanade (ɛs·plə'nad; -'neid) *n.* explanada.
espouse (ɛs'pauz) *v.t.* **1,** (wed) casarse con; contraer matrimonio con. **2,** (advocate) defender; abogar por; abrazar.
esprit de corps (ɛsˌpri·də'koːr) compañerismo.
espy (ɛs'pai) *v.t.* divisar; alcanzar a ver; columbrar.
-esque ('ɛsk) *sufijo* -esco; parecido; en forma *o* modo de: *picturesque,* pintoresco; *arabesque,* arabesco.
esquire (ɛs'kwair) *n.* **1,** (courtesy title) señor *o* don. **2,** (knight's attendant) escudero.
-ess (ɛs; ɪs) *sufijo; forma nombres femeninos: hostess,* anfitriona; *authoress,* autora; *princess,* princesa.
essay ('ɛs·ei) *n.* **1,** (composition) ensayo. **2,** (attempt) conato; esfuerzo. —*v.t.* (ɛ'sei) ensayar; tratar. —**essayist** ('ɛs·e·jɪst) *n.* ensayista.
essence ('ɛs·əns) *n.* **1,** (characteristic) esencia. **2,** (nature) ser; substancia; médula. **3.** (distillate) esencia; perfume. —**in essence,** en el fondo.
essential (ə'sɛn·ʃəl) *adj.* **1,** (indispensable) esencial; vital; indispensable; imprescindible. **2,** (basic) esencial; constitutivo; substancial. **3,** *chem.* esencial. —*n.* parte *o* elemento esencial.
-est (əst) *sufijo* **1,** *forma el superlativo de adjetivos y adverbios: coldest,* el más frío; *latest,* lo más tarde. **2,** *arcaico; poét.; forma presente y pretérito de verbos con el pronombre* **thou**: *thou goest,* tú vas; *thou madest,* tú hiciste.
establish (ɛs'tæb·lɪʃ) *v.t.* **1,** (set up; found) establecer; fundar; crear; constituir. **2,** (install) establecer; instalar; radicar. **3,** (prove) establecer; determinar; dejar sentado. —**establishment,** *n.* establecimiento.
estate (ɛs'teit) *n.* **1,** (residence) hacienda; heredad. **2,** (possessions) propiedad; bienes. **3,** (inheritance) herencia. **4,** (class; condition) estado; clase; condición.
esteem (ɛs'tiːm) *v.t.* **1,** (respect) estimar; apreciar. **2,** (rate) juzgar; reputar. —*n.* **1,** (respect) estima; aprecio. **2,** (estimate) juicio; opinión.
ester ('ɛs·tər) *n.* éster.
-esthesia (ɛs'θi·ʒə) *sufijo* -estesia; sensación; sensibilidad: *hyperesthesia,* hiperestesia.
esthete *también,* **aesthete** ('ɛs·θit) *n.* esteta. —**esthetic; aesthetic** (ɛs·'θɛt·ɪk) *adj.* estético. —**esthetics; aesthetics,** *n.pl.* estética (*sing.*).
estimable ('ɛs·tɪ·mə·bəl) *adj.* **1,** (worthy of esteem) benemérito; estimable. **2,** (calculable) calculable.
estimate ('ɛs·tə·meit) *v.t.* apreciar; computar; calcular aproximadamente. —*n.* (-mət) estimación; tasación; cálculo aproximado; *comm.* presupuesto. —**estimation,** *n.* cálculo; opinión; suposición.
estrange (ɛs'treindʒ) *v.t.* alejar; malquistar; enajenar. —**estrangement,** *n.* desvío; alejamiento; enajenamiento.
estuary ('ɛs·tjuˌɛr·i) *n.* estuario; ría.
-et (ɛt; ɪt; ət) *sufijo; forma nombres diminutivos: islet,* islita; *fillet,* filete.
et cetera (ɛt 'sɛt·ər·ə) etcétera.
etch (ɛtʃ) *v.t.* **1,** (cut with acid) grabar al aguafuerte. **2,** (cut with stylus) cincelar. —**etching,** *n.* aguafuerte; grabado al aguafuerte.
eternal (ɪ'tʌɹ·nəl) *adj.* eterno; eternal; inmortal.
eternity (ɪ'tʌɹ·nə·ti) *n.* eternidad.
-eth (əθ; ɛθ) *sufijo* **1,** *forma números ordinales y fraccionarios: twentieth,* vigésimo; veintavo. **2,** *arcaico; poét.; forma la tercera persona singular del presente: he goeth,* él va.
ethane ('ɛθ·ein) *n.* etano.
ether ('i·θər) *n.* éter.
ethereal *también,* **aethereal** (ɪ·'θɪr·i·əl) *adj.* etéreo.
ethical ('ɛθ·ɪ·kəl) *también,* **ethic** ('ɛθ·ɪk) *adj.* ético; moral.
ethics ('ɛθ·ɪks) *n.pl., también,* **ethic,** *n.sing.* ética (*sing.*); moral (*sing.*).
Ethiopian (ˌi·θi'o·pi·ən) *adj.* etíope; etiópico. —*n.* etíope.

Ethiopic (ˌi·θi'ap·ɪk) *adj.* etiópico. —*n.* lengua etiópica.
ethnic ('ɛθ·nɪk) *adj.* étnico. *También,* **ethnical.**
ethno- (ɛθ·nə) *prefijo* -etno; pueblo; raza: *ethnography,* etnografía.
ethnology (ɛθ'nal·ə·dʒi) *n.* etnología. —**ethnological** (ɛθ·nə'ladʒ·ɪ·kəl) *adj.* etnológico. —**ethnologist** (-dʒɪst) *n.* etnólogo.
ethyl ('ɛθ·əl) *n.* etilo.
ethylene ('ɛθ·əˌlin) *n.* etileno.
etiology (ˌi·ti'al·ə·dʒi) *n.* etiología.
etiquette ('ɛt·ɪ·kɛt) *n.* etiqueta.
etymology (ɛt·ɪ'mal·ə·dʒi) *n.* etimología. —**etymological** (-mə·'ladʒ·ɪ·kəl) *adj.* etimológico. —**etymologist** (-dʒɪst) *n.* etimologista; etimólogo.
eu- (ju) *prefijo* eu-; bien; bueno; *euphony,* eufonía.
eucalyptus (ju·kə'lɪp·təs) *n.* eucalipto.
Eucharist ('ju·kə·rɪst) *n.* eucaristía. —**Eucharistic** (-'rɪs·tɪk) *adj.* eucarístico.
eugenics (ju'dʒɛn·ɪks) *n.pl.* eugenesia (*sing.*). —**eugenic,** *adj.* eugenésico.
eulogy ('ju·lə·dʒi) *n.* elogio; encomio; panegírico; apología. —**eulogistic** (-'dʒɪs·tɪk) *adj.* laudatorio; encomiástico. —**eulogize** (-dʒaiz) *v.t.* elogiar; loar; encomiar; ensalzar.
eunuch ('ju·nək) *n.* eunuco.
euphemism ('ju·fə·mɪz·əm) *n.* eufemismo. —**euphemistic** (-'mɪs·tɪk) *adj.* eufemístico.
euphonious (ju'foː·ni·əs) *adj.* eufónico. —**euphoniousness,** *n.* eufonía.
euphony ('ju·fə·ni) *n.* eufonía. —**euphonic** (ju'fan·ɪk) *adj.* eufónico.
euphoria (ju'for·i·ə) *n.* euforia. —**euphoric** (-ɪk) *adj.* eufórico.
Eurasian (jʊ'rei·ʒən) *n.* & *adj.* eurásico.
European (ˌjʊr·ə·'pi·ən) *n.* & *adj.* europeo. —**European plan,** hospedaje *o* habitación sin comidas.
europium (jʊ'ro·pi·əm) *n.* europio.
euthanasia (ˌju·θə'nei·ʒə) *n.* **1,** (mercy-killing) eutanasia. **2,** (painless death) muerte tranquila.
evacuate (ɪ'væk·ju·eit) *v.t.* **1,** (empty) evacuar; vaciar. **2,** (withdraw from) desocupar; sacar. **3,** (excrete) evacuar; excretar. —**evacuation,** *n.* evacuación; desocupación. —**evacuee** (-iː) *n.* evacuado.
evade (ɪ'veid) *v.t.* & *i.* evadir; eludir; huir.
evaluate (ɪ'væl·ju·eit) *v.t.* evaluar; valorar; tasar. —**evaluation,** *n.* evaluación; valoración; tasación.
evanesce (ɛv·ə'nɛs) *v.i.* desaparecer; disiparse; desvanecerse. —**evanescence,** *n.* disipación; desvanecimiento; evanescencia. —**evanescent,** *adj.* evanescente.
evangel (ɪ'væn·dʒəl) *n.* evangelio.
evangelical (ˌi·væn'dʒel·ɪ·kəl) *adj.* evangélico.
evangelism (ɪ'væn·dʒə·lɪz·əm) *n.* evangelismo. —**evangelist,** *n.* evangelista. —**evangelize,** *v.t.* evangelizar.
evaporate (ɪ'væp·ə·reit) *v.t.* evaporar; vaporizar. —*v.i.* evaporarse; disiparse; desvanecerse. —**evaporation,** *n.* evaporación; vaporización.
evasion (ɪ'vei·ʒən) *n.* **1,** (avoidance) evasión; fuga; escape. **2,** (subterfuge; equivocation) evasiva; equívoco. —**evasive** (-sɪv) *adj.* evasivo; ambiguo.
eve (iːv) *n.* **1,** (night before) vigilia; víspera. **2,** (time preceding an event) víspera. **3,** *poet.* (evening) noche.
even ('i·vən) *adj.* **1,** (level; smooth) llano; plano; nivelado. **2,** (uniform) igual; uniforme; inmutable. **3,** (equal) igual; parejo; al mismo nivel. **4,** (divisible by 2) par. **5,** *math.* (having no fraction) justo. **6,** (placid) apacible; ecuánime. —*adv.* **1,** (equally; wholly) uniformemente; precisamente; llanamente; inmutablemente. **2,** (exactly; moreover) exactamente; aún; hasta; incluso; siquiera. —*v.t.* **1,** (make equal) igualar; emparejar. **2,** (make smooth) allanar; nivelar. **3,** (adjust evenly) ajustar cuentas. —*n., poet.* = **evening.** —**break even,** salir en paz; cubrir los gastos. —**even if** *o* **though,** aun cuando; aunque. —**even so,** no obstante. —**even with,** al nivel de. —**get even with,** vengarse de. —**not even,** ni siquiera.
evening ('iːv·nɪŋ) *n.* **1,** (late day; early night) tarde; noche; vísperas. **2,** *fig.* (decline) terminación. —*adj.* vespertino. —**evening clothes** *o*

dress, traje *o* vestido de etiqueta. —**good evening!** (before sundown) buenas tardes; (after dark) buenas noches.
evenness ('i·vən·nəs) *n.* **1,** (uniformity) igualdad; uniformidad. **2,** (smoothness) llanura; lisura. **3,** (fairness) imparcialidad.
event (ɪ'vɛnt) *n.* **1,** (occurrence) suceso; ocurrencia. **2,** (notable occasion) acontecimiento; acaecimiento. **3,** (result) éxito; consecuencia; resultado. —**at all events** *o* **in any event,** en todo caso; de cualquier modo; sea lo que fuere. —**in the event of,** en caso de.
even-tempered *adj.* tranquilo; apacible; ecuánime.
eventful (ɪ'vɛnt·fəl) *adj.* lleno de acontecimientos; memorable.
eventide ('i·vən·taid) *n., poet.* crepúsculo; caída de la tarde.
eventual (ɪ'vɛn·tju·əl) *adj.* **1,** (ultimate) consiguiente; eventual. **2,** (contingent) contingente; fortuito. —**eventuality** (-'æl·ə·ti) *n.* eventualidad.
eventuate (ɪ'vɛn·tju·eit) *v.i.* acontecer; acaecer.
ever ('ɛv·ər) *adv.* **1,** (always) siempre; constantemente. **2,** (at any time) en cualquier tiempo. **3,** (in any degree) nunca; jamás; en la, mi, *o* su vida.
evergreen *adj.* de hojas perennes. —*n.* árbol *o* planta de hojas perennes.
evergreen oak encina.
everlasting *adj.* eterno; perdurable; perpetuo. —*n.* perpetua; siempreviva.
evermore (ˌɛv·ər'mor) *adv.* eternamente; de todo tiempo.
every ('ɛv·ri) *adj.* **1,** (each) cada. **2,** (all) todos los . . . (*pl.*). —**every now and then,** de vez en cuando. —**every once in a while,** una que otra vez. —**every other,** cada dos; uno sí y otro no. —**every which way,** en toda dirección.
everybody *n.* todos; todo el mundo; cada uno; cada cual.
everyday *adj.* de cada día; cotidiano; diario.
everyone *n.* todo el mundo; todos (*pl.*).
everything *n.* todo; toda cosa.
everywhere *adv.* en, a *o* por todas partes; por dondequiera.
evict (ɪ'vɪkt) *v.t.* desahuciar; desalojar; expulsar. —**eviction** (ɪ'vɪk·ʃən) *n.* desahucio; desalojamiento; expulsión.
evidence ('ɛv·ɪ·dəns) *n.* **1,** (manifestness) evidencia. **2,** *law* prueba; *Amer.* evidencia. —*v.t.* evidenciar; patentizar. —**give evidence,** deponer. —**in evidence,** a la vista; manifiesto.
evident ('ɛv·ɪ·dənt) *adj.* evidente; claro; manifiesto; patente. —**be evident,** resaltar.
evil ('iː·vəl) *adj.* **1,** (wicked) malo; maligno; perverso. **2,** (harmful) nocivo; perjudicial. —*n.* **1,** (improper conduct) maldad; perversidad. **2,** (harm) mal; desgracia. —**evilness,** *n.* maldad. —**evil eye,** aojo; mal de ojo.
evildoing *n.* maldad. —**evildoer,** *n.* malhechor.
evil-minded *adj.* malicioso; mal intencionado.
evince (ɪ'vɪns) *v.t.* hacer patente; revelar; indicar. —**evincible,** *adj.* demostrable.
eviscerate (ɪ'vɪs·ə·reit) *v.t.* destripar; desentrañar; eviscerar. —**evisceration,** *n.* destripamiento; evisceración.
evocation (ɛv·ə'kei·ʃən) *n.* evocación; llamamiento. —**evocative** (ɪ'vak·ə·tɪv) *adj.* evocador.
evoke (ɪ'voːk) *v.t.* evocar; llamar.
evolution (ɛv·ə'lu·ʃən) *n.* **1,** (natural growth) evolución; desarrollo. **2,** (progress) progreso; marcha. —**evolutionary,** *adj.* evolucionista; evolutivo. —**evolutionism,** *n.* evolucionismo. —**evolutionist,** *n.* evolucionista.
evolve (ɪ'valv) *v.t.* **1,** (develop) desenvolver; desarrollar. **2,** (emit, as a gas) despedir; emitir. —*v.i.* desarrollarse; evolucionar.
ewe (juː) *n.* oveja.
ex- (ɛks) *prefijo* ex-. **1,** fuera; fuera de; más allá: *export,* exportar. **2,** antes; que ha sido: *ex-president,* expresidente.
exacerbate (ɛg'zæs·ərˌbeit) *v.t.* exacerbar; irritar. —**exacerbation,** *n.* exacerbación; irritación; exasperación.
exact (ɛg'zækt) *v.t.* exigir; imponer. —*adj.* (ɪg-) **1,** (accurate) exacto; cabal; correcto. **2,** (strict) estrecho; estricto; riguroso. —**exacting,** *adj.* exigente. —**exactness,** *n.* = **exactitude.**
exaction (ɪg'zæk·ʃən) *n.* exacción; extorsión.

exactitude (ɪg'zæk·tɪˌtuːd) *n.* exactitud; precisión; rectitud.
exactly (ɪg'zækt·li) *adv.* exactamente; precisamente. —*interj.* ¡justo!; ¡exacto!
exaggerate (ɛg'zædʒ·əˌreit) *v.t.* & *i.* exagerar. —**exaggeration**, *n.* exageración.
exalt (ɛg'zɔlt) *v.t.* **1,** (elevate) exaltar; elevar. **2,** (praise; extol) exaltar; enaltecer; ensalzar; sublimar. **3,** (inspire; elate) alegrar; regocijar.
exaltation (ˌɛg·zɔl'tei·ʃən) *n.* **1,** (elevation) exaltación; enaltecimiento. **2,** (praise) ensalzamiento; sublimación. **3,** (elation) regocijo.
examination (ɛgˌzæm·ɪ'nei·ʃən) *n.* examen; investigación; inspección; *law* interrogatorio.
examine (ɛg'zæm·ɪn) *v.t.* **1,** (inspect) inspeccionar; revisar; explorar. **2,** (inquire into) inquirir; interrogar. **3,** (test) examinar.
example (ɪg'zæm·pəl) *n.* **1,** (sample) ejemplo; dechado. **2,** (illustration) ejemplo; paradigma. **3,** (model) modelo; muestra. **4,** (precedent; analogy) ejemplar. **5,** (warning; lesson) ejemplar; escarmiento.
exasperate (ɛg'zæs·pə·reit) *v.t.* exasperar. —**exasperation**, *n.* exasperación.
excavate ('ɛks·kə·veit) *v.t.* **1,** (dig into) excavar; cavar. **2,** (form by digging) ahondar; vaciar. **3,** (unearth) desenterrar. —**excavation**, *n.* excavación. —**excavator**, *n.* excavador (*person*); excavadora (*machine*).
exceed (ɛk'siːd) *v.t.* **1,** (go beyond) exceder; aventajar; rebasar. **2,** (surpass) sobrepasar; superar. —**exceedingly**, *adv.* excesivamente; sumamente; muy.
excel (ɛk'sɛl) *v.t.* [**excelled, -celling**] aventajar; superar. —*v.i.* sobresalir.
excellence ('ɛk·sə·ləns) *n.* excelencia. —**excellent** (-lənt) *adj.* excelente; sobresaliente.
excellency ('ɛk·sə·lən·si) *n., usu. con mayúscula* excelencia.
except (ɪk'sɛpt) *prep.* [*también,* **excepting**] excepto; con excepción de; salvo; menos. —*conj.* sino; fuera de que. —*v.t.* exceptuar; excluir; omitir. —*v.i., law* recusar. —**except for**, si no fuera porque; salvo.
exception (ɪk'sɛp·ʃən) *n.* **1,** (exclusion) excepción; salvedad. **2,** (objection) objeción; *law* recusación. —**take exception, 1,** (object) oponerse; objetar. **2,** (be offended) ofenderse.
exceptionable (ɪk'sɛp·ʃə·nə·bəl) *adj.* recusable; objetable; tachable.
exceptional (ɪk'sɛp·ʃə·nəl) *adj.* excepcional.
excerpt ('ɛk·sərpt) *n.* extracto; excerta. —*v.t.* (ɛk'sʌɹpt) extractar.
excess (ɛk'sɛs) *n.* **1,** (superfluity) exceso; demasía. **2,** (surplus; remainder) excedente; sobrante; superávit. **3,** (immoderation) inmoderación; destemplanza. —*adj.* excesivo; desmedido.
excessive (ɛk'sɛs·ɪv) *adj.* excesivo; inmoderado; superfluo. —**excessiveness**, *n.* demasía; inmoderación; destemplanza.
exchange (ɛks'tʃeindʒ) *v.t.* & *i.* **1,** (give and take) cambiar; canjear. **2,** (barter; trade) permutar; trocar. —*n.* **1,** (act of exchanging) cambio; permuta; (of prisoners, etc.) canje. **2,** (thing exchanged) cambio. **3,** (stock exchange) bolsa. **4,** (telephone exchange) central telefónica.
excise ('ɛk·saiz) *n.* impuesto sobre consumos. —*v.t.* **1,** (cut out) extirpar. **2,** (tax) someter a impuesto. —**excision** (ɛk'sɪʒ·ən) *n.* excisión.
excitable (ɛk'sai·tə·bəl) *adj.* excitable. —**excitability**, *n.* excitabilidad.
excitation (ˌɛk·sai'tei·ʃən) *n.* excitación.
excite (ɛk'sait) *v.t.* excitar. —**excited**, *adj.* excitado; agitado. —**exciter**, *n.* excitante.
excitement (ɛk'sait·mənt) *n.* excitación; agitación; conmoción.
exciting (ɛk'sai·tɪŋ) *adj.* excitante; estimulante; emocionante.
exclaim (ɛk'skleim) *v.i.* exclamar; clamar. —*v.t.* gritar; proferir.
exclamation (ˌɛks·klə'mei·ʃən) *n.* exclamación; grito. —**exclamation point**, signo de admiración (!).
exclamatory (ɛk'sklæm·ə·tor·i) *adj.* **1,** (spoken vehemently) exclamativo; exclamatorio. **2,** *gram.* admirativo.
exclude (ɛk'skluːd) *v.t.* **1,** (shut out) excluir. **2,** (omit) omitir. —**exclusion** (ɪk'skluː·ʒən) *n.* exclusión; eliminación.
exclusive (ɪk'sklu·sɪv) *adj.* exclusivo; exceptuado; privativo. —**ex-**

clusiveness, *n.* exclusividad; —**exclusive of**, exclusive; con exclusión de.
excommunicate (ˌɛks·kə'mju·nɪ·keit) *v.t.* excomulgar. —**excommunication**, *n.* excomunión.
excoriate (ɛk'skor·i·eit) *v.t.* **1,** (denounce) excoriar; flagelar. **2,** (strip the skin off) desollar; despellejar. —**excoriation**, *n.* desolladura; excoriación.
excrement ('ɛks·krə·mənt) *n.* excremento; heces (*pl.*).
excrescence (ɪk'skrɛs·əns) *n.* excrecencia. —**excrescent**, *adj.* excrecente; superfluo.
excrete (ɛk'skrit) *v.t.* excretar. —**excretion** (-'skri·ʃən) *n.* excreción.
excruciating (ɪk'skru·ʃiˌei·tɪŋ) *adj.* agudísimo; penosísimo. —**excruciation** (-'ei·ʃən) *n.* tormento.
exculpate (ɛk'skʌl·peit) *v.t.* disculpar; justificar; exonerar. —**exculpation** (ˌɛks·kəl'pei·ʃən) *n.* disculpa; exoneración. —**exculpatory** (ɛk'skʌlp·ə·tor·i) *adj.* disculpador; justificador.
excursion (ɪk'skʌɹ·ʒən) *n.* **1,** (journey) excursión. **2,** (digression) digresión; desviación. —**excursionist** (-ɪst) *n.* excursionista.
excuse (ɛk'skjuːz) *v.t.* **1,** (forgive) excusar; dispensar; disculpar. **2,** (justify) sincerar; justificar. **3,** (release from a duty) excusar; exentar. **4.** (refrain from exacting; remit) perdonar; condonar. —*n.* (ɛk'skjus) **1,** (plea; reason) excusa; justificación. **2,** (pretext) disculpa; pretexto. —**excusable**, *adj.* excusable; disculpable.
execrable ('ɛk·sɪ·krə·bəl) *adj.* execrable; aborrecible; abominable.
execrate ('ɛk·sɪ·kreit) *v.t.* **1,** (detest) execrar; aborrecer. **2,** (denounce) execrar; abominar; maldecir. —**execration**, *n.* execración; aborrecimiento; maldición.
execute ('ɛk·sɪ·kjut) *v.t.* **1,** (perform) ejecutar; realizar; llevar a cabo. **2,** (effect) legalizar; formalizar; otorgar (un documento). **3,** (put to death) ejecutar; ajusticiar.
execution (ˌɛk·sɪ'kju·ʃən) *n.* ejecución. —**executioner**, *n.* verdugo; ejecutor de la justicia.
executive (ɪg'zɛk·jə·tɪv) *adj.* ejecutivo. —*n.* ejecutivo; director; administrador; *U.S.*, *con* **the**, poder ejecutivo; el ejecutivo. —**Chief Executive**, jefe de estado; *U.S.* Presidente.
executor (ɪg'zɛk·jə·tər) *n.* **1,** (administrator) ejecutivo; ejecutor. **2,** *law* albacea. —**executorship**, *n.*, *law* albaceazgo.
executory (ɪg'zɛk·jəˌtor·i) *adj.* **1,** (administrative) ejecutivo; administrativo. **2,** *law* (in force) ejecutorio.
executrix (ɪg'zɛk·jəˌtrɪks) *n.* **1,** (administrator) ejecutora. **2,** *law* albacea.
exegesis (ɛk·sə'dʒi·sɪs) *n.* [*pl.* **-ses**] exégesis. —**exegete** ('ɛk·sə·dʒit) *n.* exégeta. —**exegetic** (-'dʒɛt·ɪk) *adj.* [*también*, **exegetical**] exegético.
exemplary (ɪg'zɛm·plə·ri) *adj.* ejemplar.
exemplify (ɛg'zɛm·plɪ·fai) *v.t.* ejemplificar. —**exemplification** (-fɪ·'kei·ʃən) *n.* ejemplificación.
exempt (ɛg'zɛmpt) *v.t.* eximir; franquear. —*adj.* exento; libre; franco; inmune. —**exemption** (ɛg·'zɛmp·ʃən) *n.* exención; franquicia; dispensa; inmunidad.
exercise ('ɛk·sərˌsaiz) *n.* **1,** (exertion; drill) ejercicio. **2,** (performance; use) ejercicio; uso **3,** *usu.pl.* (ceremonies) ceremonia (*sing.*). —*v.t.* **1,** (perform; use) ejercer; ejercitar. **2,** (train) adiestrar; ejercitar. —*v.i.* hacer ejercicios.
exert (ɛg'zʌɹt) *v.t.* esforzar; ejercer. —**exert oneself**, empeñarse; esforzarse; hacer esfuerzo. —**exertion** (ɪg'zʌɹ·ʃən) *n.* esfuerzo; ejercicio.
exhalation (ɛks·ə'lei·ʃən) *n.* **1,** *physiol.* (act of exhaling) exhalación; espiración; evaporación; **2,** (what is exhaled) exhalación; efluvio; emanación; vapor.
exhale (ɛks'heil) *v.t.* exhalar; emitir; espirar. —*v.i.* vahear; disiparse.
exhaust (ɛg'zɔst) *v.t.* **1,** (empty) vaciar. **2,** (consume) agotar; consumir. **3,** (fatigue) fatigar; agotar. —*n.* escape. —**exhaustible**, *adj.* agotable. —**exhaustive**, *adj.* cabal; completo.
exhaustion (ɛg'zɔs·tʃən) *n.* **1,** (repletion) agotamiento. **2,** (fatigue) extenuación.
exhibit (ɛg'zɪb·ɪt) *v.t.* **1,** (display) exhibir; presentar. **2,** (manifest) manifestar; mostrar. —*v.i.* dar una exhibición. —*n.* **1,** (display) exhibición. **2,** *law* (item of evidence) prueba material.

exhibition (ˌɛk·zəˈbɪʃ·ən) *n.* exhibición; exposición. —**exhibitionism,** *n.* exhibicionismo. —**exhibitionist,** *n.* exhibicionista.
exhibitor (ɛgˈzɪb·ɪ·tər) *n.* **1,** (one who exhibits) expositor. **2,** *motion pictures* empresario de teatro.
exhilarate (ɛgˈzɪl·ə·reit) *v.t.* regocijar; alborozar. —**exhilaration,** *n.* regocijo; alborozo.
exhort (ɛgˈzort) *v.t.* exhortar; dar admonestación *o* consejo a. —**exhortation** (ˌɛk·sərˈtei·ʃən) *n.* exhortación; consejo. —**exhortative** (ɛgˈzor·tə·tɪv) [*también,* **exhortatory** (-tor·i)] *adj.* exhortatorio.
exhume (ɛksˈhjuːm) *v.t.* exhumar; desenterrar. —**exhumation** (ˌɛk·sjuˈmei·ʃən) *n.* exhumación.
exigency (ˈɛk·sɪ·dʒən·si) *n.* exigencia; requisito urgente. —**exigent,** *adj.* exigente; urgente.
exiguous (ɪgˈzɪg·ju·əs) *adj.* exiguo. —**exiguousness,** *n.* exigüidad.
exile (ˈɛg·zail; ˈɛk·sail) *n.* **1,** (expatriation) destierro; expatriación. **2,** (expatriate) desterrado; expatriado. —*v.t.* desterrar; expatriar.
exist (ɛgˈzɪst) *v.i.* existir; subsistir; encontrarse. —**existence,** *n.* existencia; ser; vida. —**existent,** *adj.* existente.
existential (ˌɛg·zɪsˈtɛn·ʃəl) *adj.* existencial. —**existentialism,** *n.* existencialismo. —**existentialist,** *n.* & *adj.* existencialista.
exit (ˈɛk·sɪt; ˈɛg·zɪt) *n.* **1,** (avenue of departure) salida. **2,** (departure) partida; marcha; salida. **3,** *fig.* (death) muerte. —*v.i.* salir.
exo- (ɛk·so) *prefijo* exo-; externo; fuera: *exosmosis,* exósmosis.
exodus (ˈɛk·sə·dəs) *n.* **1,** (a going out) éxodo; salida; emigración. **2,** *cap., Bib.* Éxodo.
exonerate (ɛgˈzan·ə·reit) *v.t.* exonerar; descargar; disculpar. —**exoneration,** *n.* exoneración; exculpación; descargo.
exorbitant (ɪgˈzor·bɪ·tənt) *adj.* exorbitante; excesivo. —**exorbitance,** *n.* exorbitancia; exceso.
exorcise (ˈɛk·sor·saiz) *v.t.* exorcisar; conjurar. —**exorcism** (-sɪz·əm) *n.* exorcismo; conjuro.
exoteric (ˌɛk·səˈtɛr·ɪk) *adj.* exotérico.
exotic (ɪgˈzat·ɪk) *adj.* **1,** (foreign; strange) exótico; forastero; extraño. **2,** *colloq.* (striking in appearance) extraño; raro. —**exoticism** (ɪgˈzat·əˌsɪz·əm) *n.* exotismo.
expand (ɛkˈspæːnd) *v.t.* **1,** (increase) dilatar; ensanchar; agrandar; ampliar. **2,** (spread; unfold) extender; tender; desarrollar.
expanse (ɪkˈspæns) *n.* extensión; espacio.
expansible (ɪkˈspæn·sə·bəl) *adj.* expansible.
expansile (ɪkˈspæn·sɪl) *adj.* expansivo.
expansion (ɪkˈspæn·ʃən) *n.* expansión. —**expansive** (-sɪv) *adj.* expansivo.
expatiate (ɪkˈspei·ʃiˌet) *v.i.* espaciarse; explayarse; extenderse.
expatriate (ɛksˈpei·tri·ət) *n.* & *adj.* expatriado; exilado; desnaturalizado; proscrito. —*v.t.* (-eit) desnaturalizar; desterrar; expatriar. —**expatriation,** *n.* expatriación.
expect (ɛkˈspɛkt) *v.t.* **1,** (anticipate; await) esperar; aguardar. **2,** (rely on) contar con. **3,** *colloq.* (suppose) suponer.
expectancy (ɛkˈspɛk·tən·si) *n.* **1,** (expectation) expectativa; esperanza. **2,** (contingency) contingencia; eventualidad; casualidad.
expectant (ɛkˈspɛk·tənt) *adj.* **1,** (awaiting) expectante. **2,** (pregnant) preñada; encinta. —**expectant mother,** madre en ciernes.
expectation (ˌɛk·spɛkˈtei·ʃən) *n.* expectación; esperanza.
expectorate (ɛkˈspɛk·təˌreit) *v.t.* & *i.* expectorar; esputar. —**expectorant,** *adj.* & *n.* expectorante. —**expectoration,** *n.* expectoración; esputo.
expedient (ɪkˈspiː·di·ənt) *adj.* oportuno; conveniente; propio. —*n.* expediente; medio; recurso. —**expediency** [*también,* **expedience**] *n.* propiedad; conveniencia; comodidad; oportunidad.
expedite (ˈɛks·pəˌdait) *v.t.* **1,** (accelerate) acelerar; apresurar; dar prisa a. **2,** (dispatch) facilitar; despachar; expedir. —**expediter,** *n.* despachador; expedidor.
expedition (ɛks·pəˈdɪʃ·ən) *n.* expedición. —**expeditionary** (-ə·nɛr·i) *adj.* expedicionario.
expeditious (ɛks·pəˈdiʃ·əs) *adj.* pronto; expeditivo. —**expeditiousness,** *n.* prontitud; despacho.
expel (ɛkˈspɛl) *v.t.* [**expelled, -pelling**] expeler; expulsar; echar.

—**expellant** (-ənt) *adj.* & *n.* expelente; expulsivo.
expend (ɛk'spɛnd) *v.t.* expender; gastar.
expenditure (ɛk'spɛn·dɪ·tʃər) *n.* desembolso; gasto; salida.
expense (ɪk'spɛns) *n.* **1,** (cost) costo; coste. **2,** (expenditure) gasto. **3,** (loss) detrimento; pérdida. —**at any expense,** a toda costa. —**at the expense of,** a costa de. —**expense account,** cuenta de gastos.
expensive (ɪk'spɛn·sɪv) *adj.* costoso; caro.
experience (ɪk'spɪr·i·əns) *n.* experiencia. —*v.t.* experimentar; sufrir. —**experienced,** *adj.* experimentado.
experiment (ɪk'spɛr·ə·mənt) *n.* experimento; ensayo. —*v.i.* experimentar; hacer una prueba. —**experimental** (-'mɛn·təl) *adj.* experimental; de prueba. —**experimentation** (-mɛn'tei·ʃən) *n.* experimento; experimentación.
expert ('ɛks·pʌɹt) *adj.* experimentado; experto; diestro; hábil. —*n.* experto; perito; juez. —**expertness,** *n.* destreza; habilidad; pericia.
expiate ('ɛks·pi·eit) *v.t.* expiar; purgar; reparar. —**expiation,** *n.* expiación.
expiration (ˌɛk·spə'rəi·ʃən) *n.* **1,** (termination) expiración; terminación; cumplimiento. **2,** (exhalation) espiración.
expire (ɛk'spair) *v.i.* **1,** (come to an end) expirar; acabarse; cumplirse; terminar. **2,** (die) fallecer; morir. **3,** (exhale) espirar; exhalar.
explain (ɛk'splein) *v.t.* & *i.* explicar.
explanation (ˌɛk·splə'nei·ʃən) *n.* explicación.
explanatory (ɛk'splæn·ə·tor·i) *adj.* explicativo.
expletive ('ɛks·plə·tɪv) *adj.* expletivo. —*n.* interjección; reniego.
explicable ('ɛks·plɪ·kə·bəl) *adj.* explicable.
explicit (ɪk'splɪs·ɪt) *adj.* **1,** (definite) explícito; claro; inequívoco. **2,** (outspoken) franco; abierto. —**explicitness,** *n.* claridad; franqueza.
explode (ɛk'splo:d) *v.i.* volar; estallar; detonar; hacer explosión; reventar. —*v.t.* **1,** (cause to burst) hacer estallar; fulminar. **2,** *fig.* (disprove) refutar; desbaratar; confundir.
exploit ('ɛks·plɔit) *n.* hazaña; proeza. —*v.t.* (ɛk'splɔit) explotar; aprovechar. —**exploitation** (ˌɛks·plɔi'tei·ʃən) *n.* explotación; aprovechamiento.
exploration (ˌɛks·plə'rei·ʃən) *n.* exploración. —**exploratory** (ɪk·'splor·ə·tor·i) *adj.* exploratorio; explorador.
explore (ɛk'splor) *v.t.* & *i.* **1,** (traverse, for discovery) explorar. **2,** (investigate) averiguar. —**explorer,** *n.* explorador.
explosion (ɛks'plo:·ʒən) *n.* explosión; reventón.
explosive (ɛks'plos·ɪv) *n.* & *adj.* explosivo; fulminante.
exponent (ɛk'spo:·nənt) *n.* **1,** (expounder) exponente; expositor. **2,** (representative; symbol) representante; símbolo. **3,** *math.* (power) exponente.
export (ɛk'sport) *v.t.* exportar. —*n.* ('ɛks·port) **1,** [*también,* **exportation**] (shipment) exportación. **2,** (something exported) artículo de exportación. —**exportable,** *adj.* exportable. —**exporter,** *n.* exportador. —**exporting,** *adj.* exportador. —**export trade,** comercio exterior.
expose (ɛk'spo:z) *v.t.* **1,** (exhibit) exponer; mostrar; descubrir; revelar. **2,** (reveal the truth about) desenmascarar; descubrir. **3,** (leave unprotected) exponer; arriesgar; poner en peligro.
exposé (ˌɛk·spo'ze) *n.* revelación; descubrimiento; desenmascaramiento.
exposition (ɛks·pə'zɪʃ·ən) *n.* exposición; exhibición.
expositor (ɪk'spaz·ə·tər) *n.* comentador; expositor.
expository (ɛk'spaz·ə·tor·i) *adj.* expositivo; explicativo.
expostulate (ɛk'spas·tʃə·leit) *v.i.* protestar; altercar; contender. —**expostulation,** *n.* protesta; reconvención; disuasión.
exposure (ɛk'spo:·ʒər) *n.* **1,** (act or effect of exposing) exposición. **2,** (direction faced) orientación. **3,** *photog.* exposición; toma. **4,** (lack of shelter or cover) desabrigo. **5,** (unmasking) desenmascaramiento. —**exposure meter,** fotómetro.
expound (ɛk'spaund) *v.t.* exponer; explicar.
express (ɛk'sprɛs) *v.t.* **1,** (reveal in words, etc.) expresar; representar. **2,** (manifest) expresar; mani-

festar; explicar. 3, (press) exprimir; prensar; extraer el jugo de. 4, (send by express) enviar *o* expedir por expreso. —*adj.* 1, (clear; explicit) expreso; claro; explícito. 2, (special; fast) especial; pronto; rápido. —*n.* expreso; tren expreso. —**expressible,** *adj.* expresable; exprimible. —**expressly,** *adv.* expresamente.

expression (ɛk'sprɛʃ·ən) *n.* 1, (act or manner of expressing) expresión. 2, (word or phrase) vocablo; palabra; voz; locución. 3, (manifestation) expresión; gesto; cara.

expressive (ɛk'sprɛs·ɪv) *adj.* expresivo. —**expressiveness,** *n.* significación; expresión; energía.

expropriate (ɛks'pro·pri·eit) *v.t.* expropiar. —**expropriation,** *n.* expropiación. —**expropriator,** *n.* expropiador.

expulsion (ɪk'spʌl·ʃən) *n.* expulsión.

expunge (ɛx'pʌndʒ) *v.t.* 1, (strike out) borrar; cancelar. 2, (destroy) aniquilar; destruir.

expurgate ('ɛks·pər,geit) *v.t.* expurgar; purificar. —**expurgation,** *n.* expurgación; expurgo; purificación.

exquisite ('ɛks·kwɪ·zɪt) *adj.* 1, (dainty; elegant) exquisito; delicado; primoroso. 2, (intense; keen) vivo; agudo; excesivo. —**exquisiteness,** *n.* exquisitez; primor; delicadeza; perfección.

extant ('ɛks·tənt) *adj.* existente; viviente.

extemporaneous (ɛk,stɛm·pə·'rei·ni·əs) *adj.* improvisado. *También,* **extemporary** (-,rɛr·i). —**extemporaneousness,** *n.* improvisación.

extemporize (ɛk'stɛm·pə·raiz) *v.t.* & *i.* improvisar; repentizar.

extend (ɛk'stɛnd) *v.t.* 1, (stretch) extender. 2, (enlarge) ampliar. 3, (extend in time) prorrogar. 4, (defer; postpone) diferir. 5, (offer; bestow) ofrecer. —*v.i.* extenderse. —**extend to,** llegar a; alcanzar a.

extensible (ɛk'stɛn·sə·bəl) *adj.* extensible.

extension (ɛk'stɛn·ʃən) *n.* 1, (extending) extensión; dilatación; expansión; ensanche. 2, (addition) aumento; adición; prolongación; anexo. 3, (scope; extent) alcance; proporción; grado.

extensive (ɛk'stɛn·sɪv) *adj.* extendido; dilatado; amplio. —**extensiveness,** *n.* extensión; amplitud; grado; alcance.

extent (ɪk'stɛnt) *n.* 1, (expanse) extensión. 2, (limit) alcance; límite. 3, (degree) grado. —**to a certain extent,** hasta cierto punto. —**to the full extent,** en toda su extensión. —**to a great extent,** en sumo grado.

extenuate (ɛk'stɛn·ju·eit) *v.t.* 1, (attenuate) atenuar. 2, (mitigate) mitigar; paliar. —**extenuated,** *adj.* mermado; delgado. —**extenuating,** *adj.* paliativo; atenuante. —**extenuation,** *n.* atenuación; paliación; mitigación.

exterior (ɪk'stɪr·i·ər) *adj.* exterior; externo. —*n.* exterior; aspecto; exterioridad.

exterminate (ɛk'stʌɹ·mɪ·neit) *v.t.* exterminar. —**extermination,** *n.* exterminio; extirpación. —**exterminator,** *n.* exterminador.

external (ɪk'stʌɹ·nəl) *adj.* 1, (exterior) externo; exterior. 2, (outside and apart) extraño; extranjero.

extinct (ɪk'stɪŋkt) *adj.* 1, (extinguished) extinto; extinguido; apagado. 2, (no longer existing) extinto; desaparecido. —**extinction,** *n.* extinción; desaparición. —**become extinct,** extinguirse.

extinguish (ɛk'stɪŋ·gwɪʃ) *v.t.* 1, (quench) extinguir; apagar; sofocar. 2, (put an end to) extinguir; suprimir; destruir. —**extinguishment,** *n.* extinción; apagamiento. —**fire extinguisher,** extintor.

extirpate ('ɛk·stər·peit) *v.t.* extirpar; desarraigar; arrancar. —**extirpation,** *n.* extirpación; arrancamiento.

extol (ɛk'sto:l) *v.t.* [**extolled, -tolling**] ensalzar; enaltecer; exaltar.

extort (ɛk'stort) *v.t.* extorsionar; sacar *u* obtener por fuerza; arrancar. —**extortion** (ɛk'stor·ʃən) *n.* extorsión; exacción; concusión. —**extortionate** (-ət) *adj.* opresivo; injusto; gravoso.

extra ('ɛks·trə) *adj.* extraordinario; suplementario; adicional; de más; de sobra; sobrante; de repuesto; de recambio; de reserva. —*adv.* excepcionalmente. —*n.* 1, (addition) exceso; recargo. 2, (additional cost) gasto extraordinario. 3, (newspaper) extra; edición *o* número extraordinario. 4, *theat.* (supernumerary) extra. 5, (spare) repuesto.

extra- (ɛks·trə) *prefijo* extra-; más

allá; fuera: *extraterritorial,* extraterritorial.
extract (ɛk'strækt) *v.t.* **1,** (remove) extraer; sacar; arrancar. **2,** (separate) extraer; separar. **3,** (select) seleccionar; extractar; compendiar. **—*n.*** ('ɛks·trækt) **1,** (thing extracted) extracto. **2,** (excerpt) excerta.
extraction (ɛk'stræk·ʃən) *n.* **1,** (removal) extracción; saca. **2,** (derivation) descendencia; origen.
extractor (ɛk'stræk·tər) *n.* **1,** (abstractor) extractador. **2,** (device) exprimidera; extractor.
extradite ('ɛks·trə·dait) *v.t.* entregar por extradición; obtener la extradición de. **—extradition** (-'dɪ·ʃən) *n.* extradición.
extraneous (ɛk'strei·ni·əs) *adj.* extraño; externo; extranjero; ajeno.
extraordinary (ɛk'stror·də·nɛr·i) *adj.* extraordinario; raro; singular; especial; descomunal.
extraterritorial (ˌɛks·trəˌtɛr·ɪ'tor·i·əl) *adj.* extraterritorial.
extravagant (ɪk'stræv·ə·gənt) *adj.* **1,** (wasteful) pródigo; manirroto; gastador. **2,** (high-priced) exorbitante; disparatado. **3,** (irregular; fantastic) extravagante; estrafalario. **—extravagance,** *n.* lujo exagerado; derroche; profusión; extravagancia.
extravaganza (ɪk·stræv·ə'gæn·zə) *n., theat.* obra *o* composición extravagante.
extreme (ɪk'striːm) *adj.* **1,** (utmost) extremo; extremado. **2,** (final) último; postrero. **3,** (exact; strict) riguroso; estricto; severo. **4,** (immoderate) extremado; extremoso. **—*n.* 1,** (greatest degree) extremo. **2,** (something immoderate) extremosidad. **3,** (the first or last) extremidad; ápice; fin; cabo. **4,** (exactness) rigurosidad; severidad. **—extremely,** *adv.* extremadamente; sumamente. **—extremeness,** *n.* extremosidad; rigurosidad; severidad.
extremist (ɛk'striː·mɪst) *n.* extremista; radical.
extremity (ɛk'strɛm·ə·ti) *n.* **1,** (terminal) extremidad. **2,** *a veces pl.* (distress) necesidad (*sing.*); apuro (*sing.*).
extricable ('ɛks·trɪ·kə·bəl) *adj.* fácil de desenredar.
extricate ('ɛks·trɪ·keit) *v.t.* desenredar; desembrollar; sacar. **—extrication,** *n.* desembarazo; desenredo.
extrinsic (ɛk'strɪn·zɪk) *adj.* extrínseco.
extro- (ɛks·tro) *prefijo, var. de* **extra-:** *extrovert,* extrovertido.
extroversion (ˌɛks·trə'vʌɹ·ʒən) *n.* extraversión; extroversión.
extrovert ('ɛks·trə·vʌɹt) *n.* extrovertido. **—extroverted,** *adj.* extrovertido.
extrude (ɛk'struːd) *v.t.* **1,** (eject) forzar hacia fuera; echar; arrojar. **2,** *metall.; plastics* fabricar por extrusión. **—*v.i.*** salir fuera; sobresalir.
extrusion (ɛk'struː·ʒən) *n.* **1,** (extruding) expulsión; resalto. **2,** *metall.; plastics* extrusión. **3,** *geol.* efusión de lava por grietas de rocas.
exuberant (ɛg'zu·bə·rənt) *adj.* exuberante; lujuriante; profuso. **—exuberance,** *n.* exuberancia.
exude (ɛg'zuːd) *v.t.* exudar; sudar; transpirar. **—*v.i.*** rezumarse; revenirse. **—exudation** (ˌɛks·ju'dei·ʃən) *n.* exudación; exudado.
exult (ɛg'zʌlt) *v.i.* exultar; regocijarse; alegrarse. **—exultant,** *adj.* triunfante; regocijado; alborozado. **—exultation** (ˌɛks·əl'tei·ʃən) *n.* exultación; regocijo; transporte.
-ey (i) *sufijo, var. de* **-y,** *en las palabras terminadas en* y: *clayey,* arcilloso.
eye (ai) *n.* **1,** (organ of vision) ojo. **2,** (view) vista; aspecto. **3,** (opinion) talante; juicio; discernimiento. **4,** *mech.* (hole) anillo; aro. **5,** *bot.* (bud; shoot) yema; botón. **6,** (hurricane's center) vórtice. **—*v.t.*** mirar de hito en hito; observar. **—an eye for an eye,** ojo por ojo. **—black eye,** ojo amoratado. **—blind in one eye,** tuerto. **—have a cast in one eye,** ser bisojo. **—have an eye on,** echar el ojo a. **—have an eye to,** intentar; proponerse. **—keep an eye on,** vigilar. **—keep one's eyes open,** abrir el ojo. **—make eyes at,** mirar amorosamente *o* con codicia. **—see eye to eye,** estar de acuerdo; ver con el mismo ojo. **—with an eye to,** con la intención de.
eyeball *n.* globo del ojo.
eyebrow *n.* ceja.
eyecup *n.* ojera; lavaojos.
eyeful *n., slang* cuadro completo.
eyeglass *n.* **1,** (lens) ocular; anteojo. **2,** *pl.* (spectacles) lentes; anteojos; gafas; quevedos.

eyelash *n.* pestaña.
eyeless ('ai·ləs) *adj.* sin ojos; ciego.
eyelet ('ai·lət) *n.* resquicio; abertura; ojete.
eyelid *n.* párpado.
eye opener **1,** (surprise) revelación; sorpresa. **2,** (drink) copa temprana; trago temprano.
eyepiece *n.* ocular.
eyesight *n.* vista; alcance de la vista.
eyesore *n.* cosa que ofende a la vista; esperpento.
eyestrain *n.* vista cansada.
eyetooth *n.* colmillo; diente canino.
eyewitness *n.* testigo ocular *o* presencial.
eyrie *también,* **aerie** ('ei·ri; 'ai·ri) *n.* **1,** (eagle's nest) nido de águila; aguilera. **2,** (dwelling on a height) vivienda elevada.

F

F, f (ɛf) sexta letra del alfabeto inglés. —*n., music* fa.
fa (faː) *n., music* fa.
fable ('fei·bəl) *n.* fábula; cuento. —**fabled,** *adj.* legendario; ficticio.
fabric ('fæb·rɪk) *n.* **1,** (frame; structure) estructura; trama; fábrica. **2,** (cloth) tejido; tela; género.
fabricate ('fæb·rɪˌkeit) *v.t.* **1,** (build; manufacture) fabricar. **2,** (invent) inventar; elaborar.
fabrication (ˌfæb·rɪ'kei·ʃən) *n.* **1,** (manufacture) fabricación; manufactura. **2,** (invention) invención; mentira.
fabulist ('fæb·ju·lɪst) *n.* fabulista.
fabulous ('fæb·ju·ləs) *adj.* fabuloso.
façade (fə'saːd) *n.* fachada; frente.
face (feis) *n.* **1,** (front of the head; countenance) cara; faz; rostro. **2,** (expression; look) expresión; cara. **3,** (outward aspect) aspecto; cariz. **4,** (reputation) prestigio. **5,** (effrontery) descaro; desfachatez. **6,** (surface) superficie; lado; cara. **7,** (front) fachada; frente. **8,** *typog.* carácter. —*v.t.* **1,** (have the face or front toward) dar a; mirar a *o* hacia. **2,** (meet boldly) afrontar; enfrentar; encarar. **3,** (cover the surface of) revestir; cubrir. —*v.i.* mirar. —**face card,** figura. —**face down,** boca abajo; cara abajo. —**to face down,** apocar; desconcertar. —**face lifting, 1,** *surgery* cirugía plástica de la cara. **2,** (refurbishing) arreglo. —**face the music,** afrontar las consecuencias. —**face up,** boca arriba; cara arriba. —**face up to, 1,** (confront boldly) arrostrar; dar cara a; enfrentar. **2,** (resign oneself to) amoldarse a; avenirse a. —**face value,** *comm.* valor nominal. —**at face value,** como tal; en su valor; por lo que vale. —**in the face of,** encarando; en presencia de. —**lose face,** desprestigiarse. —**on the face of it,** por lo manifiesto; por lo que se ve. —**save face,** salvar las apariencias.
facet ('fæs·ɪt) *n.* faceta.
facetious (fə'si·ʃəs) *adj.* gracioso; chistoso. —**facetiousness,** *n.* chiste; gracia.
facial ('fei·ʃəl) *adj.* facial.
-facient ('fei·ʃənt) *sufijo* -faciente; causante: *stupefacient,* estupefaciente.
facile ('fæs·əl) *adj.* **1,** (ready; quick; easy) fácil; vivo. **2,** (affable); agradable.
facilitate (fə'sɪl·əˌteit) *v.t.* facilitar. —**facilitation,** *n.* facilitación.
facility (fə'sɪl·ə·ti) *n.* **1,** (ease) facilidad. **2,** (talent; skill) facilidad; destreza. **3,** *pl.* (conveniences) comodidades; acomodaciones.
facing ('fei·sɪŋ) *n.* **1,** (outer covering) paramento. **2,** (trim) guarnición. **3,** *sewing* falso.
facsimile (fæk'sɪm·ə·li) *n.* facsímile.
fact (fækt) *n.* **1,** (something done or known) hecho. **2,** (reality) realidad. —**in fact,** en realidad; de hecho.
faction ('fæk·ʃən) *n.* facción. —**factious** (-ʃəs) *adj.* faccioso.
factitious (fæk'tɪʃ·əs) *adj.* facticio.
factor ('fæk·tər) *n.* **1,** *comm.* factor; corredor. **2,** (contributing element) elemento; factor. **3,** *math.*

factor. —*v.t., math.* descomponer en factores. —**factorial** (fæk'tor·i·əl) *adj.* factorial. —**factoring,** *n., comm.* factoraje; factoría.
factory ('fæk·tə·ri) *n.* fábrica; taller.
factual ('fæk·tʃu·əl) *adj.* **1,** (of facts) basado en hechos; objetivo. **2,** (real; actual) real; verdadero.
facultative ('fæk·əl,tei·tɪv) *adj.* facultativo; *law* potestativo.
faculty ('fæk·əl·ti) *n.* **1,** (aptitude; ability) facultad; aptitud. **2,** (academic) facultad; claustro.
fad (fæd) *n.* novedad; moda; manía. —**faddish,** *adj.* novelero. —**faddishness,** *n.* novelería. —**faddist,** *n.* novelero; aficionado a novedades.
fade (feid) *v.i.* **1,** (lose color) descolorarse; desteñirse. **2,** (wither) marchitarse. **3,** (grow dim; die gradually) disminuir; apagarse; desvanecerse. —*v.t.* **1,** (cause to fade) descolorar; desteñir. **2,** (wither) marchitar. **3,** (accept, as a bet) cubrir (una apuesta). —**fade in,** aclararse gradualmente. —**fade out,** borrarse gradualmente; desvanecerse.
fag (fæg) *v.t.* [**fagged, fagging**] fatigar; cansar. —*v.i.* trabajar como esclavo; fatigarse; cansarse. —*n., slang* cigarrillo.
fagot *también,* **faggot** ('fæg·ət) *n.* haz de leña.
fagoting *también,* **faggoting** ('fæg·ət·ɪŋ) *n.* vainicas (*pl.*).
Fahrenheit ('fær·ən·hait) *adj.* Fahrenheit.
fail (feil) *v.i.* **1,** (fall short; be deficient or lacking) faltar. **2,** (weaken; diminish) decaer; menguar. **3,** (be exhausted or spent) acabarse. **4,** (be unsuccessful) fallar; fracasar. **5,** (cease to function) fallar. **6,** (go bankrupt) quebrar; arruinarse. **7,** *educ.* ser suspendido; ser desaprobado. —*v.t.* **1,** (disappoint) desilusionar; decepcionar; defraudar. **2,** *educ.* suspender; desaprobar. —**without fail,** sin falta.
failing ('fei·lɪŋ) *n.* falta; defecto. —*prep.* a falta de; sin.
failure ('feil·jər) *n.* **1,** (unsuccessful deed or attempt) fracaso. **2,** (unsuccessful person) fracasado; fracaso. **3,** (bankruptcy) quiebra; bancarrota. **4,** (nonperformance; neglect) omisión. **5,** (ceasing of function) falla. **6,** *educ.* suspenso; desaprobado; *Amer.* aplazado.
faint (feint) *adj.* **1,** (feeble; weak) débil. **2,** (dim; subdued) pálido; apagado; tenue. **3,** (dizzy) desfallecido; desfalleciente. —*n.* desmayo; desvanecimiento. —*v.i.* desmayarse; privarse; desvanecerse.
fainthearted *adj.* medroso; apocado; pusilánime.
faintness ('feint·nəs) *n.* **1,** (weakness) debilidad. **2,** (dimness) tenuidad; palidez. **3,** (dizziness) desfallecimiento; languidez; desmayo.
fair (feːr) *adj.* **1,** (handsome; comely) hermoso; bello. **2,** (blond) rubio. **3,** (light-skinned) blanco; de tez blanca. **4,** (unblemished) intachable; limpio. **5,** (just; honest) justo; recto. **6,** (valid) legal; válido. **7,** (clear; sunny) claro; despejado. **8,** (good; of good size or quality) buen; bueno. **9,** (average) regular; pasable. —*n.* **1,** (exposition) feria; exposición. **2,** (sale; bazaar) bazar. **3,** (market) mercado; feria. —*adv.* **1,** (according to rule) imparcialmente; justamente; legalmente. **2,** (favorably) bien. **3,** (squarely) justo; redondamente. —**bid fair,** tener buen cariz; prometer. —**fair and square,** *colloq.* muy justo *o* justamente; limpio *o* limpiamente. —**fair play,** juego limpio. —**fair sex,** sexo débil; sexo bello. —**fair to middling,** *colloq.* regular; pasable.
fairhaired *adj.* **1,** (having blond hair) rubio. **2,** *slang* (unduly favored) favorito; preferido.
fairly ('fɛr·li) *adv.* **1,** (according to rule) imparcialmente, justamente; legalmente. **2,** (moderately; somewhat) moderadamente; bastante. **3,** (squarely) justo; redondamente.
fairness ('fɛr·nəs) *n.* **1,** (handsomeness) hermosura; belleza. **2,** (justness) justicia; imparcialidad. **3,** (light color) blancura.
fairspoken *adj.* bien hablado; comedido.
fairy ('fɛr·i) *n.* hada. —**fairy tale,** cuento de hadas.
fairyland *n.* país de las hadas.
faith (feiθ) *n.* fe. —**in faith,** en realidad; realmente. —**in good** (*o* **bad**) **faith,** de buena (*o* mala) fe.
faithful ('feiθ·fəl) *adj.* fiel. —**faithfulness,** *n.* fidelidad.
faithless ('feiθ·ləs) *adj.* **1,** (not

keeping faith) desleal; infiel. 2, (untrustworthy) falaz; falso. 3, (unbelieving) descreído; incrédulo; sin fe. —**faithlessness**, *n.* infidelidad; deslealtad.
fake (feik) *v.t.* & *i.* 1, (feign) fingir. 2, (falsify) falsificar. —*adj.* 1, (feigned) fingido. 2, (false) falso; falsificado. —*n.* 1, (counterfeit) falsificación. 2, (deception) engaño; mentira. 3, (impostor) farsante; impostor.
faker ('fei·kər) *n.* 1, (one who fakes) falsario; farsante; impostor. 2, (swindler) estafador; engañabobos.
fakir (fə'kɪr) *n.* faquir.
Falange (fə'landʒ) *n.* Falange. —**Falangist**, *n.* falangista.
falcon ('fɔl·kən) *n.* halcón. —**falconry**, *n.* halconería; cetrería.
fall (fɔːl) *v.i.* [**fell, fallen, falling**] 1, (drop) caer. 2, (come down; tumble) caerse. 3, (descend) bajar. 4, (occur; take place) caer. —*n.* 1, (drop; dropping) caída. 2, (autumn) otoño. 3, (waterfall) salto de agua; catarata. —**fall away**, 1, (become estranged) alejarse; apartarse. 2, (decline) debilitarse; desintegrarse. —**fall back**, echarse atrás; retroceder. —**fall back on** *o* **upon**, 1, (count on) contar con; apoyarse en. 2, (retreat to) retroceder a; replegarse a. —**fall behind**, 1, (lag; drop back) quedarse atrás; rezagarse. 2, (be in arrears) atrasarse. —**fall flat**, fallar; fracasar; no surtir efecto. —**fall for**, *slang* 1, (fall in love with) enamorarse de; prendarse de; estar colado por. 2, (be taken in by) engañarse con; ser engañado por. —**fall in**, 1, (line up) alinearse; ponerse en línea. 2, (agree) ajustarse; concordar. 3, (cave in) desplomarse; hundirse. —**fall off**, 1, (drop) declinar; caer. 2, (fade) debilitarse; decaer. —**fall out**, 1, (quarrel) reñir; pelearse; enemistarse. 2, (break ranks) romper filas; salirse de la fila. —**fall short**, quedarse corto; faltar; ser insuficiente. —**fall through**, fracasar; quedar en nada. —**fall to**, 1, (begin) comenzar; partir; empezar. 2, (move into position) caer *o* entrar en marco. —**fall to one's lot**, tocar *o* venir en suerte. —**falling out**, desavenencia; desacuerdo. —**falling star**, estrella fugaz.
fallacious (fə'lei·ʃəs) *adj.* falaz.
fallacy ('fæl·ə·si) *n.* falacia.
fallible ('fæl·ə·bəl) *adj.* falible. —**fallibility**, *n.* falibilidad.
fallout ('fɔlˌaut) *n.* lluvia radioactiva. —**fallout shelter**, refugio atómico.
fallow ('fæl·o) *adj.* 1, (plowed but unseeded) barbechado. 2, (idle; untended) eriazo; sin cultivo. 3, (color) melado; amarillo pálido. —*n.* barbecho. —*v.t.* barbechar. —**fallow deer**, gamo.
false (fɔls) *adj.* falso. —**falseness**, *n.* falsedad. —**false front**, fachada engañosa. —**false step**, paso en falso.
falsehood *n.* falsedad; embuste; mentira.
falsetto (fɔl'sɛt·o) *n.* [*pl.* **-tos**] falsete.
falsify ('fɔl·sɪˌfai) *v.t.* falsear; falsificar. —**falsification** (-fɪ'kei·ʃən) *n.* falsificación.
falsity ('fɔl·sə·ti) *n.* falsedad; falsía.
falter ('fɔl·tər) *v.i.* vacilar; titubear.
fame (feim) *n.* fama. —**famed**, *adj.* afamado; famoso.
familiar (fə'mɪl·jər) *adj.* 1, (friendly; intimate) familiar; íntimo; amistoso. 2, (overfree; presuming) confianzudo; presuntuoso. 3, (well known) familiar; muy conocido. 4, (well versed) familiarizado. —*n.* familiar; íntimo.
familiarity (fəˌmɪl'jær·ə·ti) *n.* 1, (quality of being well known) familiaridad. 2, (knowledge) conocimiento.
familiarize (fə'mɪl·jəˌraiz) *v.t.* familiarizar.
family ('fæm·ə·li) *n.* familia. —**family tree**, árbol genealógico.
famine ('fæm·ɪn) *n.* hambre; *Amer.* hambruna.
famish ('fæm·ɪʃ) *v.t.* matar de hambre; hacer pasar hambre. —*v.i.* morirse de hambre; pasar hambre. —**famished**, *adj.* famélico; hambriento; muerto de hambre. —**famishment**, *n.* hambre.
famous ('fei·məs) *adj.* famoso; célebre.
fan (fæn) *n.* 1, (manual device) abanico. 2, (machine) ventilador. 3, *slang* (devotee) entusiasta; aficionado; hincha. —*v.t.* [**fanned, fanning**] 1, (drive air into or upon) abanicar; soplar. 2, (rouse; excite)

atizar. **3,** (spread out) desplegar en abanico.
fanatic (fə'næt·ɪk) *n.* fanático. —*adj.* [*también,* **fanatical**] fanático. —**fanaticism** (-ɪˌsɪz·əm) *n.* fanatismo.
fancied ('fæn·sid) *adj.* imaginado; imaginario.
fanciful ('fæn·sɪ·fəl) *adj.* fantástico; extravagante; caprichoso.
fancy ('fæn·si) *n.* **1,** (imagination) fantasía; imaginación. **2,** (whim) antojo; capricho. **3,** (fondness; liking) inclinación; afecto. —*adj.* **1,** (imaginative; whimsical) fantástico; imaginativo; caprichoso. **2,** (of best quality) fino; de calidad. **3,** (extravagant) extravagante; rebuscado. **4,** (done with skill) primoroso; refinado. —*v.t.* **1,** (imagine) imaginar. **2,** (like; wish for) gustar; gustar de. —**fancy dress,** traje de máscara. —**fancy free,** libre; desembarazado.
fandango (fæn'dæŋ·go) *n.* [*pl.* **-gos**] fandango.
fanfare ('fæn·fɛr) *n.* **1,** (ceremony; ostentation) fanfarria. **2,** (trumpet flourish) toque de clarines; fanfarria.
fang (fæŋ) *n.* colmillo.
fantastic (fæn'tæs·tɪk) *adj.* fantástico.
fantasy *también,* **phantasy** ('fæn·tə·si) *n.* fantasía.
far (faːr) *adj.* lejano; remoto; distante. —*adv.* **1,** (a long way) lejos. **2,** *in comparisons* (by a great deal) mucho; por mucho; *Amer.* lejos. —**a far cry,** muy lejos; muy diferente. —**as far as; so far as,** hasta. —**by far,** mucho; por mucho; *Amer.* lejos. —**far and away,** muchísimo; por un mucho. —**far and near; far and wide,** por *o* en todas partes. —**far off,** a lo lejos; muy lejos. —**in so far as,** en lo que; en cuanto. —**not by far,** ni con mucho. —**so far, 1,** (up to now) hasta este momento; hasta ahora. **2,** (to that point) hasta ese punto; hasta allá.
farad ('fær·əd) *n.* faradio; farad.
faraway ('far·əˌwei) *adj.* **1,** (distant) lejano. **2,** (dreamy) abstraído.
farce (fars) *n.* farsa; sainete. —**farcical** ('far·sɪ·kal) *adj.* burlesco; de reír; de farsa.
fare (feːr) *v.i.* **1,** (proceed; go; travel) ir; viajar. **2,** (get along) pasarlo (bien *o* mal); irle a uno (bien *o* mal). —*n.* **1,** (charge; rate) pasaje; tarifa. **2,** (paying passenger) pasajero. **3,** (food) comida.
farewell (fɛr'wɛl) *interj.* adiós; que (le) vaya bien. —*n.* despedida.
farfetched *adj.* rebuscado; traído por los cabellos.
farflung *adj.* muy extenso; vasto.
farinaceous (ˌfær·ə'nei·ʃəs) *adj.* farináceo.
farm (farm) *n.* hacienda; cortijo; granja; *So.Amer.* estancia; *Mex.* rancho. —*v.t. & i.* cultivar *o* labrar (la tierra). —**farm hand,** campesino; peón. —**farm out,** dar *o* ceder (un contrato, trabajo, etc.) a consignación.
farmer ('far·mər) *n.* **1,** (small farm owner or operator) agricultor; granjero; labrador; *Mex.* ranchero. **2,** (large landowner) latifundista; *So.Amer.* estanciero. **3,** (rustic) rústico; campesino.
farmhouse *n.* alquería; cortijo; casa de una granja.
farming ('far·mɪŋ) *n.* agricultura; cultivo; labranza.
farmyard *n.* corral.
faro ('fɛr·o) *n.* faraón; faro.
far-off *adj.* lejano; remoto.
far-reaching *adj.* de gran alcance; de vasta proyección.
farsighted *adj.* **1,** *optics* présbita. **2,** [*también,* **far-seeing**] (having foresight) de visión; previsor.
farsightedness *n.* **1,** *optics* presbicia. **2,** (foresight) visión.
farther ('far·ðər) *comp. de* **far.** —*adj.* más lejano; más alejado. —*adv.* más lejos; más allá; más adelante.
farthermost *adj.* más lejano; más alejado.
farthest ('far·ðəst) *superl. de* **far.** —*adj.* **1,** (most distant) más lejano; más alejado. **2,** (longest) más largo. —*adv.* más lejos.
farthing ('far·ðɪŋ) *n.* **1,** (coin) cuarto de penique. **2,** *fig.* (trifle) ardite; comino.
fascicle ('fæs·ɪ·kəl) *n.* fascículo.
fascinate ('fæs·ɪˌneit) *v.t.* fascinar. —**fascination,** *n.* fascinación.
fascism ('fæʃ·ɪz·əm) *n.* fascismo.
fascist ('fæʃ·ɪst) *n.* fascista. —*adj.* [*también,* **fascistic** (fə'ʃɪs·tɪk)] fascista.
fashion ('fæʃ·ən) *n.* **1,** (prevailing mode or custom) moda. **2,** (kind; sort) clase; suerte. **3,** (manner; way) manera; forma. **4,**

(shape; form) forma; estilo. —*v.t.* formar; hacer. —**fashion plate,** figurín. —**high fashion,** alta costura.

fashionable ('fæʃ·ən·ə·bəl) *adj.* **1,** (stylish) de moda; a la moda; en boga. **2,** (favored by society) elegante; de buen tono.

fast (fæst; fast) *adj.* **1,** (swift) veloz; ligero; rápido. **2,** (of a clock) adelantado. **3,** (morally lax) disoluto. **4,** (firmly fixed; tight) firme; seguro; fuerte. **5,** (of colors) fijo; sólido; permanente. —*adv.* **1,** (rapidly) rápidamente; *Amer.* ligero. **2,** (firmly) fuertemente; firmemente; seguro. **3,** (soundly) profundamente. —*n.* ayuno. —*v.i.* ayunar. —**fasting,** *adj.* & *n.* ayuno.

fasten ('fæs·ən) *v.t.* & *i.* asegurar; sujetar; abrochar. —**fastener,** *n.* cierre; broche. —**fastening,** *n.* cierre; atadura; sujetador.

fastidious (fæs'tɪd·i·əs) *adj.* quisquilloso; prolijo; nimio; difícil de complacer. —**fastidiousness,** *n.* prolijidad; nimiedad.

fastness ('fæst·nəs) *n.* **1,** (firmness) firmeza; seguridad. **2,** (of colors) solidez. **3,** (speed) celeridad; rapidez; velocidad. **4,** (stronghold) fortaleza; plaza fuerte.

fat (fæt) *adj.* **1,** (plump) gordo; grueso; obeso. **2,** (fatty; greasy) grasoso; mantecoso. **3,** (rich; fertile) fértil; abundante; rico. —*n.* **1,** (fat part) gordo. **2,** (grease; fatty substance) grasa. —**fatness,** *n.* gordura; grasa.

fatal ('fei·təl) *adj.* fatal.

fatalism ('fei·tə·lɪz·əm) *n.* fatalismo. —**fatalist,** *n.* fatalista. —**fatalistic,** *adj.* fatalístico; fatalista.

fatality (fə'tæl·ə·ti) *n.* fatalidad.

fate (feit) *n.* destino; suerte; sino; estrella. —**fated,** *adj.* predestinado.

fateful ('feit·fəl) *adj.* **1,** (momentous) trascendente; decisivo. **2,** (predestined) fatal; inevitable. **3,** (ominous) fatídico. **4,** (disastrous) funesto; aciago.

fathead *n.,* *colloq.* lerdo; torpe; tardo.

father ('fa·ðər) *n.* **1,** (male parent; creator) padre. **2,** *pl.* (ancestors) antepasados. —*v.t.* **1,** (beget) engendrar; procrear. **2,** (foster) servir de padre; tratar como hijo. **3,** (found; originate) fundar; crear. —**fatherhood,** *n.* paternidad. —**fatherly,** *adj.* paternal; paterno.

father-in-law *n.* [*pl.* **fathers-in-law**] suegro; padre político.

fatherland *n.* patria.

fathom ('fæð·əm) *n.* braza. —*v.t.* **1,** (measure in fathoms; reach the bottom of) sondar; sondear. **2,** (understand thoroughly) profundizar; penetrar. —**fathomless,** *adj.* insondable; impenetrable.

fatigue (fə'tiːg) *n.* fatiga; cansancio. —*v.t.* fatigar; cansar; rendir.

fatten (fæt·ən) *v.t.* **1,** (feed to make fat) cebar; engordar. **2,** (enrich; increase) enriquecer. —*v.i.* engordar.

fatty ('fæt·i) *adj.* grasoso; graso; grasiento. —*n.,* *slang* gordinflón; gordito.

fatuous ('fætʃ·u·əs) *adj.* fatuo. —**fatuity** (fə'tu·ə·ti); **fatuousness,** *n.* fatuidad.

faucet ('fɔ·sɪt) *n.* espita; canilla; grifo; llave.

fault (fɔːlt) *n.* **1,** (deflect; flaw) falta; defecto; tacha. **2,** (blame) culpa. **3,** *geol.* falla. **4,** *sports* falta. —**faultless,** *adj.* perfecto; cabal; intachable. —**faulty,** *adj.* defectuoso; imperfecto.

faultfinding *adj.* criticón.

faun (fɔːn) *n.* fauno.

fauna ('fɔ·nə) *n.* fauna.

favor *también,* **favour** ('fei·vər) *n.* **1,** (preferment) favor; gracia. **2,** (act of kindness) favor. **3,** (acceptance; approval) aceptación; aprobación. **4,** (small gift; token) obsequio; agasajo. **5,** *comm.* atenta; estimada. —*v.t.* **1,** (prefer; advocate) favorecer; preferir. **2,** *colloq.* (resemble) parecerse a. —**favored,** *adj.* favorecido. —**find favor,** tener aceptación *o* aprobación. —**out of favor,** caído en desgracia.

favorable ('fei·vər·ə·bəl) *adj.* favorable; propicio. —**favorableness,** *n.* lo favorable.

favorite ('fei·vər·ɪt) *adj.* & *n.* favorito; preferido; predilecto. —**favoritism** (-əˌtɪz·əm) *n.* favoritismo.

fawn (fɔːn) *n.* **1,** (young deer) cervato. **2,** (color) color ciervo *o* cervato. —*v.i.* arrastrarse. —**fawn on** *o* **upon,** adular.

faze (feiz) *v.t.,* *colloq.* **1,** (disturb) perturbar; molestar. **2,** (daunt) desanimar.

fear (fɪr) *n.* **1,** (fright) miedo; terror. **2,** (anxiety) aprensión; temer; recelo. **3,** (awe) respeto; temor. —*v.t.* & *i.* temer; recelar; tener miedo *o* aprensión. —**fearless,** *adj.* sin temor; sin miedo.

fearful ('fɪr·fəl) *adj.* **1,** (timid; apprehensive) tímido; temeroso. **2,** = **fearsome.** —**fearfulness,** *n.* temor; miedo.

fearsome ('fɪr·səm) *adj.* temible; espantoso.

feasible ('fiz·ə·bəl) *adj.* **1,** (possible) factible; posible. **2,** (suitable) apropiado; adecuado. —**feasibility,** *n.* factibilidad; posibilidad.

feast (fist) *n.* **1,** (sumptuous meal) banquete; festín. **2,** (festival) fiesta. —*v.t.* **1,** (entertain) festejar; agasajar. **2,** (gratify; delight) regalar; recrear. —*v.i.* **1,** (have a feast) darse un banquete. **2,** (dwell with delight) gozarse; deleitarse.

feat (fit) *n.* hazaña; proeza.

feather ('fɛð·ər) *n.* **1,** (of a bird) pluma. **2,** *fig.* (kind) clase; condición. —*v.t.* **1,** (put feathers on) emplumar. **2,** *aero.* emplumar; poner (la hélice) vertical. **3,** *naut.* poner (el remo) horizontal. —*v.i.* pelechar. —**feathery,** *adj.* plumoso. —**in fine** (*también,* **good** *o* **high**) **feather,** en buena condición; de muy buen ánimo.

feather duster plumero.

feature ('fi·tʃər) *n.* **1,** (part of the face) rasgo; facción. **2,** (distinctive characteristic) rasgo; característica. **3,** *journalism* artículo, noticia *o* sección especial. **4,** *motion pictures* película principal; película de largo metraje. —*v.t.* **1,** (give prominence to) hacer resaltar; destacar; ofrecer principalmente. **2,** *motion pictures* presentar como estrella.

febri- ('fɛb·rə) *prefijo* febri-; fiebre: *febrifuge,* febrífugo.

February ('fɛb·ru,ɛr·i) *n.* febrero.

feces *también,* **faeces** ('fi·siz) *n.pl.* heces. —**fecal** (-kəl) *adj.* fecal.

fecund ('fi·kʌnd) *adj.* fecundo. —**fecundity** (fɪ'kʌn·də·ti) *n.* fecundidad.

fecundate ('fi·kən,deit) *v.t.* fecundar. —**fecundation,** *n.* fecundación.

fed (fɛd) *v., pret.* & *p.p de* **feed.**

federal ('fɛd·ə·rəl) *adj.* federal. —**federalism,** *n.* federalismo. —**federalist,** *n.* federalista.

federate ('fɛd·ə,reit) *v.t.* federar. —*v.i.* federarse. —**federation,** *n.* federación.

fedora (fə'dor·ə) *n.* sombrero de fieltro; fieltro.

fee (fiː) *n.* **1,** (charge for services, privileges, etc.) pago; abono; derechos (*pl.*); (*esp. for professional services*) honorarios (*pl.*). **2,** (tip; gratuity) gratificación; regalía; propina. **3,** (fief) feudo. **4,** *law* (property; estate) heredad; hacienda; (ownership) feudo. —**fee simple,** dominio absoluto.

feeble ('fi·bəl) *adj.* **1,** (weak; ineffective) débil; vacilante. **2,** (frail) endeble. —**feebleness,** *n.* debilidad.

feebleminded *adj.* imbécil; falto de seso.

feed (fiːd) *v.t.* **1,** (give food to) dar de comer a; alimentar. **2,** (to provide as food) dar de comer; alimentar con *o* de. **3,** (nourish) nutrir; alimentar. **4,** (supply, as with fuel or material) surtir; proveer. **5,** (satisfy; gratify) dar pábulo a; nutrir. —*v.i.* alimentarse; comer. —*n.* **1,** (food for cattle) forraje; pienso; alimento. **2,** *colloq.* (meal) comida.

feedback *n.* regeneración; retroalimentación. —**feed-back,** *adj.* regenerativo.

feedbag *n.* morral; caparazón.

feeder ('fi·dər) *n.* **1,** (mechanism) mecanismo de alimentación; alimentador. **2,** (tributary) tributario; afluente. **3,** (branch line) ramal; ensamble.

feedline *n.* línea *o* fuente de alimentación. *También,* **feeder line.**

feel (fiːl) *v.t.* [*pret.* & *p.p.* **felt**] **1,** (perceive; be aware of) sentir. **2,** (touch; handle) tocar; palpar. **3,** (be moved or affected by) sentir. **4,** (believe) pensar; intuir; considerar. **5,** (grope) tentar; tantear. —*v.i.* **1,** (have physical sensation) percibir; sentir. **2,** (seem, as to the touch) sentirse; parecer. **3,** (grope) tantear. **4,** (perceive oneself to be) sentirse.

feeler ('fi·lər) *n., lit.* & *fig.* tiento.

feeling ('fi·lɪŋ) *n.* **1,** (sense of touch) tacto. **2,** (sensation) sensación. **3,** (emotion) sentimiento; emoción; sensibilidad. **4,** (premoni-

tion) presentimiento. —*adj.* sensible; sensitivo.
feet (fit) *n., pl. de* **foot.**
feign (fein) *v.i. & t.* fingir.
feint (feint) *n.* amago; finta. —*v.t. & i.* amagar.
feldspar ('fɛld·spar) *n.* feldespato.
felicitate (fə'lɪs·ɪˌteit) *v.t.* felicitar. —**felicitation,** *n.* felicitación.
felicitous (fə'lɪs·ə·təs) *adj.* feliz; acertado; apropiado; oportuno. —**felicitousness,** *n.* felicidad.
felicity (fə'lɪs·ə·ti) *n.* **1,** (bliss) felicidad; dicha. **2,** (aptness; grace) gracia; felicidad.
feline ('fi·lain) *n. & adj.* felino.
fell (fɛl) *v.t.* derribar; talar. —*v.i., pret. de* **fall.** —*adj.* cruel; fiero.
fellow ('fɛl·o) *n.* **1,** (comrade) compañero; camarada; colega; compadre. **2,** (one of a pair; mate) pareja; compañero. **3,** *colloq.* (person) hombre; sujeto; tipo. **4,** (member of a society) socio; compañero. **5,** (graduate student) becario. —*adj.* asociado; compañero.
fellowship ('fɛl·oˌʃɪp) *n.* **1,** (body of associates) cuerpo; sociedad. **2,** (comradeship) fraternidad; confraternidad; compañerismo. **3,** (grant of money for further study) beca.
felon ('fɛl·ən) *n.* **1,** (criminal) criminal; felón. **2,** *pathol.* panadizo. —**felony,** *n.* crimen. —**felonious** (fə'lo·ni·əs) *adj.* criminal.
felt (fɛlt) *n.* fieltro. —*v., pret. & p.p. de* **feel.**
female ('fi·mel) *adj.* **1,** (of women) femenino. **2,** (of animals) hembra; de hembra. **3,** *mech.* hembra. —*n.* hembra.
feminine ('fɛm·ɪ·nɪn) *adj.* femenino. —**femininity,** *n.* femineidad; feminidad.
feminism ('fɛm·ɪ·nɪz·əm) *n.* feminismo. —**feminist,** *n.* feminista.
femur ('fi·mər) *n.* fémur. —**femoral** ('fɛm·ər·əl) *adj.* femoral.
fen (fɛn) *n.* marjal; fangal.
fence (fɛns) *n.* **1,** (enclosure) cerca; valla; empalizada. **2,** *slang* (receiver of stolen goods) traficante en efectos robados. —*v.t.* cercar; vallar; empalizar. —*v.i.* **1,** (practice fencing) conocer *o* practicar la esgrima. **2,** *fig.* (parry; avoid argument) hacer el quite. —**fencer,** *n.* esgrimidor; *So.Amer.* esgrimista. —**on the fence,** *colloq.* indeciso; entre dos fuegos.
fencing ('fɛn·sɪŋ) *n.* **1,** (swordplay) esgrima. **2,** (system of fences) cercados (*pl.*); vallados (*pl.*). **3,** (material for fences) cercado.
fend (fɛnd) *v.t.* [*también,* **fend off**] rechazar; parar; defenderse de. —*v.i.* defenderse. —**fend for oneself,** componérselas; arreglárselas.
fender ('fɛn·dər) *n.* **1,** (of an automobile) guardabarros; guardafango. **2,** (of a fireplace) guardafuegos.
fenestra (fɪ'nɛs·trə) *n., anat.* [*pl.* **-trae** (-tri)] ventana.
fennel ('fɛn·əl) *n.* hinojo.
fermata (fɛr'ma·ta) *n., music* calderón (𝄐).
ferment ('fʌɹ·mɛnt) *n.* fermento. —*v.t. & i.* (fər'mɛnt) fermentar. —**fermentation** (ˌfʌɹ·mɛn'tei·ʃən) *n.* fermentación.
fermium ('fʌɹ·mi·əm) *n.* fermio.
fern (fʌɹn) *n.* helecho.
ferocious (fə'ro·ʃəs) *adj.* feroz; fiero. —**ferocity** (fə'ras·ə·ti) *n.* ferocidad.
-ferous (fər·əs) *sufijo* -fero; que tiene, lleva o produce: *coniferous,* conífero.
ferret ('fɛr·ɪt) *n.* hurón. —*v.t.* **1,** (seek by searching) buscar; andar tras de. **2,** (find by searching) encontrar; capturar. **3,** (elicit, as information) sonsacar; extraer.
ferri- (fɛr·ɪ) *prefijo* ferri-; hierro: *ferriferous,* ferrífero.
ferro- (fɛr·o) *prefijo* ferro-; hierro: *ferrochromium,* ferrocromo.
ferrotype ('fɛr·o·taip) *n.* ferrotipo.
ferrous ('fɛr·əs) *adj.* ferroso.
ferruginous (fə'ru·dʒɪ·nəs) *adj.* ferruginoso.
ferrule ('fɛr·əl; -ul) *n.* contera; virola.
ferry ('fɛr·i) *n.* transbordador; barco de transbordo. —*v.t. & i.* transbordar.
fertile ('fʌɹ·tɪl) *adj.* fértil; feraz. —**fertility** (fər'tɪl·ə·ti) *n.* fertilidad; feracidad.
fertilize ('fʌɹ·tɪ·laiz) *v.t.* **1,** (make fertile) fertilizar. **2,** (spread fertilizer on) abonar; fer-

tilizar con abono. 3, *biol.* fecundar. —**fertilization** (-lɪ'zei·ʃən) *n.* fertilización; fecundación. —**fertilizer,** *n.* abono; fertilizante.
ferule ('fɛr·əl) *n.* palmeta; férula.
fervent ('fʌɹ·vənt) *adj.* fervoroso; ferviente. —**fervency,** *n.* fervor.
fervid ('fʌɹ·vɪd) *adj.* férvido. —**fervidness,** *n.* fervor.
fervor *también,* **fervour** ('fʌɹ·vər) *n.* fervor.
festal ('fɛs·təl) *adj.* festivo; de gala.
fester ('fɛs·tər) *v.t.* enconar. —*v.i.* enconarse.
festival ('fɛs·tɪ·vəl) *n.* festival; fiesta.
festive ('fɛs·tɪv) *adj.* festivo. —**festivity** (fɛs'tɪv·ə·ti) *n.* fiesta; festividad.
festoon (fɛs'tuːn) *n.* festón. —*v.t.* festonear.
fetal ('fi·təl) *adj.* fetal.
fetch (fɛtʃ) *v.t.* 1, (bring) traer; ir por. 2, (deal, as a stroke or blow) dar; pegar. 3, (sell for) traer; venderse por.
fetching ('fɛtʃ·ɪŋ) *adj., colloq.* atrayente; atractivo.
fête (feit) *n.* fiesta. —*v.t.* festejar.
fetid ('fɛt·ɪd) *adj.* fétido; hediondo. —**fetidness,** *n.* fetidez; hediondez.
fetish ('fɛt·ɪʃ) *n.* fetiche. —**fetishism,** *n.* fetichismo. —**fetishist,** *n.* fetichista. —**fetishistic,** *adj.* fetichista.
fetlock ('fɛt·lak) *n.* espolón.
fetter ('fɛt·ər) *n.* 1, *usu.pl.* (shackle) grilletes; grillos; cadenas. 2, (check; restraint) traba; freno. —*v.t.* engrillar; encadenar; trabar.
fettle ('fɛt·əl) *n.* condición; disposición.
fetus ('fi·təs) *n.* feto.
feud (fjuːd) *n.* riña; pelea; vendetta. —*v.i.* reñir; pelear. —**feudist,** *n.* disputante.
feudal ('fju·dəl) *adj.* feudal. —**feudalism,** *n.* feudalismo.
fever ('fi·vər) *n.* fiebre; calentura.
feverish ('fi·vər·ɪʃ) *adj.* 1, (having fever) afiebrado; calenturiento. 2, (excited; hectic) febril. —**feverishness,** *n.* fiebre; estado febril.
few (fjuː) *adj. & pron.* pocos. —**a few,** unos pocos; unos cuantos; algunos. —**quite a few,** *colloq.* bastantes; una buena cantidad.
fez (fɛz) *n.* fez.
fiancé (ˌfi·an'sei) *n.* prometido; novio. —**fiancée,** *n.fem.* prometida; novia.
fiasco (fi'æs·ko) *n.* fiasco; fracaso.
fiat ('fai·ət) *n.* mandato; decreto.
fib (fɪb) *n.* mentirilla; embuste; bola. —*v.i.* [**fibbed, fibbing**] mentir; decir embustes. —**fibber,** *n.* mentiroso; embustero.
fiber *también,* **fibre** ('fai·bər) *n.* fibra. —**fibrous** (-brəs) *adj.* fibroso.
fiberboard *n.* tablero de fibra.
fibula ('fɪb·ju·lə) *n., anat.* [*pl.* **-lae** (-li)] peroné.
-fic (fɪk) *sufijo* -fico; causante; que crea: *terrific,* terrorífico.
-fication (fɪ'kei·ʃən) *sufijo* -ficación; *forma nombres de los verbos terminados en* **-fy**: *glorification,* glorificación.
fickle ('fɪk·əl) *adj.* voluble; inconstante; veleidoso. —**fickleness,** *n.* volubilidad; inconstancia; veleidad.
fiction ('fɪk·ʃən) *n.* 1, literature) novelística; novela. 2, (statement contrary to fact) ficción. —**fictional,** *adj.* ficticio; imaginario; de novela.
fictitious (fɪk'tɪʃ·əs) *adj.* ficticio.
fiddle ('fɪd·əl) *n.* violín. —*v.i.* 1, *colloq.* (play the fiddle) tocar el violín. 2, (trifle) jugar; enredar. —*v.t.* 1, (play on the fiddle) tocar en el violín. 2, (waste; fritter, as time) perder; desperdiciar. —**fiddler** (-lər) *n.* violinista. —**fit as a fiddle,** en forma; en perfecta condición. —**play second fiddle,** tener un papel secundario.
fidelity (fɪ'dɛl·ɪ·ti) *n.* 1, (faithfulness) fidelidad. 2, (accuracy) fidelidad; exactitud.
fidget ('fɪdʒ·ət) *v.i.* 1, (move restlessly) moverse nerviosamente. 2, (be nervously uneasy) estar inquieto o nervioso. —**fidgety,** *adj.* inquieto; nervioso; desasosegado. —**to have the fidgets,** estar inquieto.
fiduciary (fɪ'du·ʃi·ɛ·ri) *adj. & n.* fiduciario.
fie (fai) *interj.* ¡vergüenza!
fief (fif) *n.* feudo.
field (fiːld) *n.* 1, (open space or

area; sphere or scope) campo. **2,** (background) fondo; campo. **3,** (group of competitors, as in a race) participantes (*pl.*). —*v.t.* **1,** (put into competition or combat) entrar (un equipo); situar (un ejercito). **2,** (catch and return, as a ball) parar y devolver (la pelota). —**field day,** día de ejercicios (atléticos); *fig.* día de gran actividad. —**field glass,** prismáticos de campaña.

fiend (fiːnd) *n.* demonio; diablo. —**fiendish,** *adj.* diabólico; perverso.

fierce (fɪrs) *adj.* fiero; feroz. —**fierceness,** *n.* ferocidad; fiereza.

fiery ('faiː·ri) *adj.* **1,** (glowing; burning; hot) ardiente. **2,** (spirited) ardiente; fogoso. —**fieriness,** *n.* ardor; fogosidad.

fiesta (fi'ɛs·tə) *n.* fiesta.

fife (faif) *n.* pífano.

fifteen (ˌfɪf'tin) *adj. & n.* quince.

fifteenth (ˌfɪf'tinθ) *adj.* décimoquinto. —*n.* quinzavo; décimoquinta parte.

fifth (fɪfθ) *adj.* quinto. —*n.* quinto; quinta parte; *music* quinta.

fiftieth ('fɪf·ti·əθ) *n. & adj.* quincuagésimo; cincuentavo.

fifty ('fɪf·ti) *n & adj.* cincuenta.

fig (fɪg) *n.* **1,** (tree) higuera. **2,** (fruit) higo. **3,** (bit; small amount) ardite; comino; bledo.

fight (fait) *v.i.* [*pret. & p.p.* **fought**] luchar; pelear; batirse. —*v.t.* **1,** (oppose; struggle against) combatir. **2,** (wage; carry on) sostener (una guerra); librar (una batalla). —*n.* **1,** (struggle; battle) pelea; lucha; contienda. **2,** (fighting spirit) espíritu combativo. —**fight it out,** resolverlo luchando. —**fight off,** deshacerse de. —**fight one's way,** abrirse paso *o* camino.

fighter ('fai·tər) *n.* **1,** (warrior) guerrero. **2,** (combative person) luchador; combatiente. **3,** (boxer) boxeador; pugilista. **4,** (fighter plane) avión de caza.

figment ('fɪg·mənt) *n.* invención; ficción.

figurative ('fɪg·jə·rə·tɪv) *adj.* figurativo; figurado.

figure ('fig·jər) *n.* **1,** (form; shape) figura; forma. **2,** (bodily form) talle; cuerpo; tipo. **3,** *rhet.* figura. **4,** (personage) figura; personaje. **5,** (number) cifra; número. **6,** (price) precio. —*v.t.* **1,** (calculate) calcular; computar. **2,** (portray) representar. **3,** (visualize) imaginar; suponer. **4,** (ornament) adornar con figuras. —*v.i.* **1,** (take prominent part) figurar. **2,** *colloq.* (deduce) suponer; deducir; inferir.

figurehead *n.* figurón; *naut.* mascarón de proa.

figurine (ˌfɪg·ju'riːn) *n.* estatuilla; estatuita.

filament ('fɪl·ə·mənt) *n.* filamento.

filbert ('fɪl·bərt) *n.* avellana.

filch (fɪltʃ) *v.t.* ratear; escamotear.

file (fail) *n.* **1,** (folder) carpeta; ficha; pliego. **2,** (case or cabinet) archivador; fichero. **3,** (dossier; record) ficha; expediente; archivo. **4,** (classified collection) archivo. **5,** (row; line) fila; hilera; columna. **6,** (tool) lima; escofina. —*v.t.* **1,** (put in a file; record) archivar; registrar. **2,** (present formally or officially) presentar; registrar. **3,** (smooth or cut with a file) limar. —*v.i.* **1,** (march in file) marchar en fila. **2,** (apply) solicitar; presentar solicitud.

filet (fɪ'lei; 'fɪl·ət) *n.* filete. —**filet mignon** (fɪˌlei·mi'njan) filete de solomillo.

filial ('fɪl·i·əl) *adj.* filial.

filibuster ('fɪl·əˌbʌs·tər) *n.* **1,** *polit.* táctica de obstruir la aprobación de un proyecto de ley con discursos prolongados. **2,** = **freebooter.** —*v.i.* **1,** *polit.* emplear la táctica del *filibuster.* **2,** (be a freebooter) piratear.

filigree ('fɪl·ə·gri) *n.* filigrana.

filing ('fai·lɪŋ) *n., usu. pl.* limaduras.

filing cabinet archivo; fichero.

fill (fɪl) *v.t.* **1,** (make full) llenar. **2,** (puff; swell) henchir; hinchar. **3,** (plug up; close, as cracks, ruts, etc.) rellenar; tapar. **4,** (satisfy the hunger of) llenar; saciar. **5,** (occupy, as a position) ocupar; desempeñar. **6,** (supply or satisfy, as an order for merchandise) llenar; despachar. **7,** (put a filling in, as a tooth) empastar; *So.Amer.* tapar. —*v.i.* llenarse. —*n.* **1,** (full supply) carga. **2,** (filling; filling material) relleno. **3,** (dental filling) empaste; *So.Amer.* tapadura. —**filler,** *n.* relleno. —**fill in, 1,** (fill or complete) llenar. **2,** (substitute) substituir. —**fill one in on,** *colloq.* informar a uno sobre. —**fill out, 1,** (become fuller) llenarse. **2,** (complete, as a document) llenar. —**have** (eat, drink) **one's fill,** hartarse; saciarse; darse un hartazgo (de).

fillet ('fɪl·ət) *n.* **1,** (band for the hair) banda para el pelo. **2,** (molding; strip) filete; orla. **3,** [*también,* **filet**] (cut of meat or fish) filete.

filling ('fɪl·ɪŋ) *n.* relleno; (of a tooth) empaste; *So.Amer.* tapadura.

filling station puesto *o* estacion de gasolina.

fillip ('fɪl·əp) *n.* capirotazo; papirotazo.

filly ('fɪl·i) *n.* potra; potranca.

film (fɪlm) *n.* **1,** (thin layer or coating) película; capa. **2,** *photog.* película; film. **3,** (mist; haze) nube. —*v.t. & i.* filmar; rodar.

filmy ('fɪl·mi) *adj.* **1,** (thin; light) delgado; delicado; leve. **2,** (misty) empañado.

filter ('fɪl·tər) *n.* filtro. —*v.t. & i.* filtrar.

filth (fɪlθ) *n.* suciedad; inmundicia. —**filthy,** *adj.* sucio; inmundo.

fin (fɪn) *n.* aleta. —**finned; finny,** *adj.* con aletas.

final ('fai·nəl) *adj.* **1,** (last; ultimate) último; final. **2,** (conclusive) definitivo; terminante. —*n.pl.* finales. —**finalist,** *n.* finalista. —**finally,** *adv.* finalmente; por fin; al fin; por último.

finale (fɪ'na·li) *n.* final.

finality (fɪ'næl·ə·ti) *n.* ultimidad. —**with finality,** en forma concluyente.

finance (fɪ'næns; 'fai-) *n.* finanzas (*pl.*); (*in government*) hacienda; hacienda pública. —*v.t.* costear; financiar.

financial (fɪ'næn·ʃəl) *adj.* financiero.

financier (fɪ·næn'sɪr) n. financiero.

finch (fɪntʃ) *n.* pinzón.

find (faind) *v.t.* [*pret. & p.p* **found**] **1,** (locate; discover) encontrar; hallar. **2,** *law* declarar. —*v.i., law* fallar. —*n.* hallazgo. —**finder,** *n.* visor; enfocador. —**find out,** averiguar; enterarse de.

finding ('fain·dɪŋ) *n.* **1,** *usu. pl.* (results, as of study or inquiry) conclusiones; resultado (*sing.*). **2,** (verdict) fallo; decisión. **3,** *pl.* (accessories) accesorios.

fine (fain) *adj.* **1,** (excellent; superior) muy bueno; excelente; fino. **2,** (thin; slender; delicate) fino. **3,** (sharp; keen) afilado; fino. **4,** (discriminating; subtle) fino. **5,** (good-looking; handsome) hermoso; guapo. **6,** (pure; refined; unalloyed) fino. —*n.* multa. —*v.t.* multar. —*adv., colloq.* bien; muy bien. —**fine arts,** bellas artes.

fineness ('fain·nəs) *n.* fineza; finura; (*of metals*) ley.

finery ('fai·nə·ri) *n.* adornos (*pl.*); galas (*pl.*).

finesse (fɪ'nɛs) *n.* **1,** (delicacy of execution; subtlety) finura. **2,** (tact) tino; tacto; habilidad. **3,** *cards* jugada por bajo; *Amer.* fineza.

finger ('fiŋ·gər) *n.* dedo. —*v.t.* tocar; palpar; manosear. —**fingering,** *n., music* digitación. —**finger board,** diapasón (*of a stringed instrument*); teclado (*of a piano*). —**finger bowl,** lavafrutas; aguamanil.

fingernail *n.* uña (*del dedo*).

fingerprint *n.* huella dactilar *o* digital.

fingertip *n.* punta del dedo. —**have at one's fingertips,** saber al dedillo; tener muy a mano.

finical ('fɪn·ə·kəl) *adj.* melindroso; quisquilloso. *También,* **finicky** (-ki).

finish ('fɪn·ɪʃ) *v.t. & i.* acabar; terminar. —*n.* **1,** (end) fin. **2,** (final work done upon an object) acabado; terminado. **3,** (social polish) refinamiento. —**finished,** *adj.* acabado; terminado.

finite ('fai·nait) *adj.* finito; limitado. —**finiteness,** *n.* limitación; lo finito; lo limitado.

fiord *también,* **fjord** (fjord) *n.* fiordo.

fir (fʌɹ) *n.* abeto.

fire (fai;r) *n.* **1,** (heat and light caused by burning) fuego. **2,** (conflagration) incendio; fuego. **3,** (shooting) fuego. **4,** *fig.* (zeal) fuego; ardor. —*v.t.* **1,** (set ablaze, ignite) encender. **2,** (excite; inflame) enardecer; inflamar. **3,** (shoot) disparar; descargar. **4,** *colloq.* (dismiss from a job) despedir; echar. —**catch fire,** encenderse. —**catch on fire,** incendiarse. —**fire department,** servicio de bomberos; cuerpo de bomberos. —**fire drill,** simulacro de incendio. —**fire engine,** bomba de incendios. —**fire**

escape, escalera de incendios. —**fire plug**, boca de agua; *Amer.* hidrante. —**firing squad**, piquete *o* pelotón de fusilamiento. —**on fire**, ardiendo. —**set fire to; set on fire**, encender; pegar fuego a; quemar. —**under fire**, bajo fuego; *fig.* acosado.

firearm *n.* arma de fuego.

firebrand *n. lit. & fig.* tea.

firecracker *n.* petardo; triquitraque; *Amer.* cohete.

firefly *n.* luciérnaga; *Amer.* cocuyo.

firelight *n.* luz de fuego; flama.

fireman ('fair·mən) *n.* [*pl.* **-men**] **1,** (one employed to prevent or extinguish fires) bombero. **2,** (stoker) fogonero.

fireplace *n.* hogar; chimenea.

fireproof *adj.* a prueba de incendios; refractario; incombustible.

fireside *n.* hogar.

firewood *n.* leña.

fireworks *n.pl.* fuegos artificiales.

firm (fʌɹm) *adj.* **1,** (steady; rigid) firme; fuerte; fijo. **2,** (stanch; loyal) firme; fiel. **3,** (positive; unalterable) tenaz; inflexible. —*n.* firma; razón social. —**firmness,** *n.* firmeza; consistencia.

firmament ('fʌɹ·mə·mənt) *n.* firmamento.

first (fʌɹst) *adj.* primero; anterior; delantero. —*adv.* primero; en primer lugar; al principio; antes. —*n.* el primero; el principio. —**first aid,** primeros auxilios; primer socorro. —**first finger,** (dedo) índice.

firstclass *adj.* de primera clase; de calidad.

firsthand *adj.* directo; personal.

firstrate *adj.* excelente; de primera clase. —*adv., colloq.* muy bien.

fiscal ('fɪs·kəl) *adj.* fiscal. —**fiscal year,** ejercicio *o* año económico.

fish (fɪʃ) *n.* [*pl.* **fishes** *o* **fish**] **1,** *zool.* pez. **2,** (fish caught) pescado. **3,** *slang* (dupe) primo. —*v.i. & t.* **1,** (catch, as fish) pescar. **2,** (search) buscar. **3,** (seek indirectly) sonsacar. —**fish bowl; fish tank,** pecera. —**fish market,** pescadería. —**fish story,** mentira *o* cuento de marca mayor.

fisherman ('fɪʃ·ər·mən) *n.* [*pl.* **-men**] **1,** (man) pescador. **2,** (ship; vessel) barca de pesca.

fishery ('fɪʃ·ə·ri) *n.* **1,** (business of fishing) pesca. **2,** (fishing ground) pesquería.

fishhook *n.* anzuelo.

fishing ('fɪʃ·ɪŋ) *adj.* pesquero; pescador; de pescar. —*n.* pesca; pesquería. —**fishing grounds,** pesquera; pesquería. —**fishing rod,** caña de pescar.

fishline *n.* sedal.

fishmonger *n.* pescadero.

fishy ('fɪʃ·i) *adj.* **1,** (of or like fish) de, a *o* como pescado. **2,** *colloq.* (suspect) sospechoso; increíble; que huele a chamusquina. **3,** (expressionless) pasmado; sin expresión.

fission ('fɪʃ·ən) *n.* fisión. —**fissionable,** *adj.* fisionable.

fissure ('fɪʃ·ər) *n.* fisura; grieta.

fist (fɪst) *n.* puño. —**fistfight,** riña a puñadas *o* puñetazos.

fisticuffs ('fɪs·tɪ·kʌfs) *n.pl.* lucha a puñetazos.

fistula ('fɪs·tʃu·lə) *n.* fístula.

fit (fɪt) *adj.* **1,** (proper; suitable) apto; adecuado; apropiado; conveniente. **2,** (ready; prepared) dispuesto; listo; en forma. —*v.t.* [**fitted, fitting**] **1,** (adapt) adaptar; ajustar; acomodar. **2,** (equip; supply) surtir; proveer; equipar. **3,** (adjust to shape, as a garment) entallar; ajustar. **4,** (agree with) cuadrar con. **5,** (be suitable for) servir para. **6,** (be of the right shape, size, etc. for) servirle a uno; venirle bien a uno, —*v.i.* **1,** (be proper) convenir; venir bien; corresponder. **2,** (be of the right shape, size, etc.) ajustar; encajar; (*esp. of garments*) servir; venir bien. **3,** (be able to be contained) caber. —*n.* **1,** (manner of fitting) ajuste; encaje; (*esp. of garments*) corte; caída. **2,** (something that fits) lo que viene bien; lo apropiado. **3,** (convulsion; outburst) acceso; ataque. —**fitness,** *n.* aptitud; conveniencia; buena condición. —**by fits and starts,** a empujones; a tropezones. —**throw** *o* **have a fit,** darle a uno una pataleta.

fitful ('fɪt·fəl) *adj.* irregular; vacilante.

fitter ('fɪt·ər) *n.* ajustador; (*esp. of garments*) entallador.

fitting ('fɪt·ɪŋ) *adj.* propio; adecuado; conveniente. —*n.* **1,** (act of fitting) ajuste; (*esp. of garments*) prueba. **2,** *pl.* (furnishings) accesorios.

five (faiːv) *n.* & *adj.* cinco.
fivefold *adj.* quíntuplo; cinco veces (más). —*adv.* cinco veces; en un quíntuplo.
five hundred quinientos. —**five-hundredth**, *adj.* & *n.* quingentésimo.
fix (fɪks) *v.t.* **1,** (fasten) sujetar; asegurar; fijar. **2,** (settle; establish, as a time or place) precisar; señalar. **3,** *chem.; photog.* fijar. **4,** (arrange; repair) arreglar. **5,** *slang* (bribe) arreglar (*mediante soborno o influencia*). —*n.* **1,** *colloq.* (predicament) apuro; aprieto. **2,** *slang* (bribery) chanchullo. —**fixings**, *n.pl.*, *colloq.* accesorios; (*of foods*) aderezos. —**fix up**, arreglar.
fixation (fɪk'sei·ʃən) *n.* **1,** (act or result of fixing) fijación. **2,** *psychoanal.* idea fija. **3,** *photog.* fijado.
fixed (fɪkst) *adj.* **1,** (fast; firm; rigid) fijo. **2,** (resolved) decidido; resuelto. **3,** *chem.; photog.* fijado. **4,** (put in order; arranged) arreglado.
fixity ('fɪk·sə·ti) *n.* fijeza.
fixture ('fɪks·tʃər) *n.* **1,** (attached article of furniture) artículo; accesorio. **2,** (person or thing that cannot be removed) institución.
fizz (fɪz) *v.i.* efervescer. —*n.* **1,** (effervescence) efervescencia. **2,** (drink) gaseosa.
fizzle ('fɪz·əl) *v.i.* **1,** (make a hissing sound) chisporrotear. **2,** *colloq.* (fail) fallar; fracasar. —*n.* **1,** (hissing sound) chisporroteo. **2,** *colloq.* (failure) fracaso; fiasco.
flabbergast ('flæb·ər·gæst) *v.t.*, *colloq.* confundir; pasmar; dejar mudo.
flabby ('flæb·i) *adj.* blando; flojo; débil. —**flabbiness**, *n.* blandura; flojedad; debilidad.
flaccid ('flæk·sɪd) *adj.* fláccido. —**flaccidity** (flæk'sɪd·ə·ti) [*también,* **flaccidness**] n. flaccidez.
flag (flæg) *n.* **1,** (banner) bandera; estandarte; pabellón. **2,** *bot.* lirio. —*v.t.* [**flagged, flagging**] **1,** (signal to) hacer señales a. **2,** (pave with flagstones) pavimentar. —*v.i.* flaquear; decaer. —**flag officer,** jefe de escadra.
flagon ('flæg·ən) *n.* frasco; pomo.
flagpole *n.* asta; mástil.
flagrant ('flei·grənt) *adj.* flagrante. —**flagrancy**, *n.* flagrancia.
flagship *n.* capitana.
flagstaff *n.* asta; mástil.
flagstone *n.* losa; laja.
flail (fleil) *n.* mayal; mangual. —*v.t.* **1,** (thresh) desgranar con mayal. **2,** (beat) batir; sacudir.
flair (fleːr) *n.* **1,** (talent) instinto; talento. **2,** (liking; bent) afición; inclinación.
flak (flæk) *n.* fuego antiaéreo.
flake (fleik) *n.* escama; hojuela. —*v.t.* cortar en hojuelas; desmenuzar. —*v.i.* formar escamas *u* hojuelas; descascararse. —**flaky**, *adj.* escamoso.
flamboyant (flæm'bɔi·ənt) *adj.* ostentoso; vistoso.
flame (fleim) *n.* **1,** (light produced by burning) llama; candela. **2,** (burning zeal; ardor) vehemencia; ardor; llama. **3,** *slang* (sweetheart) pasión. —*v.i.* **1,** (blaze) llamear. **2,** (shine) brillar; fulgurar. **3,** (break out in anger or passion) inflamarse; apasionarse.
flaming ('flei·mɪŋ) *adj.* **1,** (blazing) llameante. **2,** (passionate; violent) ardiente; vehemente.
flamingo (flə'mɪŋ·go) *n.* flamenco.
flange (flændʒ) *n.* pestaña; borde; reborde.
flank (flæŋk) *n.* flanco. —*v.t.* flanquear.
flannel ('flæn·əl) *n.* franela.
flap (flæp) *n.* **1,** (broad hanging piece) falda; faldilla; aleta; (*of a pocket*) cartera. **2,** (flapping motion or sound) aleteo; aletazo. **3,** (slap) bofetada; cachetada. —*v.t.* [**flapped, flapping**] batir; sacudir; golpear. —*v.i.* colgar suelto; aletear; golpear.
flapjack *n.* hojuela; *Amer.* panqueque.
flapper ('flæp·ər) *n.* **1,** (thing that flaps) aleta. **2,** (young bird) pollo; polluelo. **3,** *colloq.* (brash girl) polla; pollita.
flare (fleːr) *n.* **1,** (glaring light) llamarada; fulgor; destello. **2,** (signal) cohete luminoso; bengala. **3,** [*también,* **flare-up**] (outburst) explosión; arrebato (de ira). **4,** (of a garment) vuelo. —*v.i.* **1,** (burst into flame) encenderse; echar llamaradas. **2,** (spread out, as a garment) tener vuelo. —**flare up, 1,** (burst into flames) encenderse;

prender fuego. **2,** (become angry) arrebatarse de ira; encenderse.

flash (flæʃ) *n.* **1,** (blaze of light) golpe de luz; relumbrón. **2,** (gun flash; camera flash) fogonazo. **3,** (lightning) rayo. **4,** (gleam) destello. **5,** (glimpse) golpe de vista; ojeada. **6,** (instant) momento; instante. **7,** (burst; spurt; brief display) arranque; golpe; destello. **8,** (ostentation) ostentación; relumbrón. **9,** (brief bulletin) noticia de último momento; noticia súbita; fogonazo. —*v.i.* **1,** (shine; sparkle) destellar; fulgurar. **2,** (move quickly) pasar como un rayo. —*v.t.* **1,** (make gleam; shine) hacer destellar. **2,** (send, as a signal) trasmitir; telegrafiar. **3,** *colloq.* (show off) ostentar; hacer alarde de. —**flash bulb,** bombilla de magnesio. —**flash flood,** torrentada. —**flash gun,** lámpara de magnesio. —**flash in the pan,** relumbrón.

flashback *n.* mirada atrás; retrospección.

flashlight *n.* linterna.

flashy ('flæʃ·i) *adj.* ostentoso; llamativo; de relumbrón. —**flashiness,** *n.* ostentación; relumbrón.

flask (flæsk; flask) *n.* frasco; pomo.

flat (flæt) *adj.* **1,** (level; smooth) plano; llano. **2,** (spread out) extendido; tendido; plano. **3,** (categorical; positive) categórico; tajante. **4,** (deflated, as a tire) reventado; desinflado. **5,** (dull; insipid) insulso; insípido. **6,** *slang* (penniless) pelado; sin blanca; *Amer.* planchado. **7,** *music* (below pitch) desentonado; desafinado; (lowered in pitch) bemol. —*adv.* **1,** (extended; spread out) tendido. **2,** (categorically) de plano; categóricamente. **3,** *music* bajo tono. —*n.* **1,** (plain) planicie; llanura. **2,** (shoal) bajo; bajío. **3,** (flat part) parte plana *o* llana. **4,** (apartment) apartamiento. **5,** *colloq.* (deflated tire) reventón; llanta desinflada. —*v.t.* bajar en *o* de tono. —*v.i.* bajar el tono; cantar *o* tocar bajo tono.

flatboat *n.* chalana.

flat-bottomed *adj.* planudo.

flatcar *n.* vagón de plataforma; batea; *Amer.* chata.

flatfish *n.* pez plano, como el lenguado.

flatfoot *n.* [*pl.* **-feet**] **1,** (deformity of the foot) pie plano. **2,** *slang* (policeman) policía. —**flatfooted,** *adj.* de pies planos.

flatiron *n.* plancha.

flatness ('flæt·nəs) *n.* **1,** (evenness) calidad de plano; llanura. **2,** (dullness) insulsez; insipidez.

flatten ('flæt·ən) *v.t.* **1,** (make flat) aplanar; aplastar. **2,** (crush) apabullar; aplastar. **3,** (knock down) tirar al suelo; derribar. —*v.i.* aplanarse; aplastarse.

flatter ('flæt·ər) *v.t.* **1,** (praise excessively) adular; lisonjear; halagar. **2,** (show to advantage) favorecer; dar realce; lucir. —**flattering,** *adj.* adulador; lisonjero; halagüeño; favorecedor. —**flattery,** *n.* adulación; lisonja; halago.

flattop ('flæt,tap) *n.* portaaviones.

flatulent ('flæ·tʃə·lənt) *adj.* flatulento. —**flatulence,** *n.* flatulencia.

flaunt (flɔnt) *v.t.* hacer ostentación de; hacer alarde de. —*v.i.* hacer alarde; pavonearse. —*n.* alarde; gesto desafiante.

flavor *también,* **flavour** ('flei·vər) *n.* **1,** (quality affecting taste) sabor; gusto. **2,** = **flavoring.** —*v.t.* sazonar; dar sabor *o* gusto a. —**flavoring,** *n.* condimento; sazón; sabor.

flaw (flɔː) *n.* **1,** (fault) falta; defecto; tacha; falla. **2,** (crack) grieta; raja; rajadura. —**flawless,** *adj.* sin tacha; sin falla; intachable; perfecto.

flax (flæks) *n.* lino. —**flaxseed,** *n.* linaza.

flaxen ('flæk·sən) *adj.* **1,** (made of flax) de lino. **2,** (light yellow) blondo.

flay (flei) *v.t.* despellejar; desollar.

flea (fliː) *n.* pulga. —**flea-ridden,** *adj.* pulgoso; *Amer.* pulguiento.

fleabite *n.* picadura de pulga. —**fleabitten,** *adj.* picado de pulgas; *Amer.* pulguiento.

fleck (flɛk) *n.* mancha; salpicón. —*v.t.* manchar; salpicar; vetear.

fledgling *también,* **fledgeling** ('flɛdʒ·lɪŋ) *n.* **1,** (young bird) pajarito. **2,** (novice) novato.

flee (fliː) *v.t.* [*pret.* & *p.p.* **fled** (flɛd)] huir de; escaparse de. —*v.i.* huir; fugarse; escaparse.

fleece (flis) *n.* vellón; vedija;

lana. —*v.t.* esquilar; pelar. —**fleecy,** *adj.* lanudo.

fleet (flit) *adj.* veloz; rápido; ligero. —*n.* flota; armada; escuadra. —**fleeting,** *adj.* fugaz; transitorio. —**fleetness,** *n.* velocidad; rapidez; ligereza.

Fleming ('flɛm·ɪŋ) *n.* flamenco. —**Flemish** (-ɪʃ) *adj.* & *n.* flamenco.

flesh (flɛʃ) *n.* carne. —*adj.* de color carne. —**fleshless,** *adj.* descarnado. —**fleshly,** *adj.* carnal. —**fleshy,** *adj.* carnoso.

fleur-de-lis (ˌflʌɹ·də'liː) *n.* [*pl.* **fleurs-de-lis** (ˌflʌɹ·də'liːz)] **1,** (royal emblem of France) flor de lis. **2,** *bot.* (iris) lirio.

flew (fluː) *v., pret. de* **fly.**

flex (flɛks) *v.t.* flexionar; doblar. —**flexion** ('flɛk·ʃən) *n.* flexión.

flexible ('flɛk·sɪ·bəl) *adj.* flexible. —**flexibility,** *n.* flexibilidad.

flick (flɪk) *n.* golpe o movimiento ligero; sacudida. —*v.t.* **1,** (strike lightly) dar un golpe ligero. **2,** (move or remove with a flick) sacudir.

flicker ('flɪk·ər) *v.i.* **1,** (quiver) oscilar; temblar; vacilar. **2,** (blink) parpadear. —*n.* **1,** (flickering) parpadeo. **2,** (wavering light) luz trémula. **3,** (large woodpecker) picamaderos norteamericano. **4,** *slang* (motion picture) película.

flier *también,* **flyer** ('flai·ər) *n.* **1,** (aviator) aviador. **2,** (handbill) volante. **3,** *colloq.* (risk; financial venture) albur.

flies (flaiz) *n., pl. de* **fly.**

flight (flait) *n.* **1,** (act of flying) vuelo. **2,** (unit of aircraft) escuadrilla. **3,** (number of creatures flying together) bandada. **4,** (imaginative excursion or soaring) vuelo. **5,** (hasty departure) huida; fuga. **6,** (series of steps or stairs) tramo (de escaleras). **7,** (story; floor) piso.

flighty ('flai·ti) *adj.* veleidoso; inconstante. —**flightiness,** *n.* veleidad; inconstancia.

flimsy ('flɪm·zi) *adj.* débil; endeble; insubstancial. —**flimsiness,** *n.* endeblez; inconsistencia.

flinch (flɪntʃ) *v.i.* dar un respingo; respingar; arrugarse; echarse atrás.

fling (flɪŋ) *v.t.* [*pret.* & *p.p.* **flung**] arrojar; tirar; lanzar. —*n.* **1,** (act of flinging) lanzamiento; tiro. **2,** *colloq.* (try) prueba; lance. —**go on a fling,** echar una cana al aire. —**have a fling at,** probar; ensayar; tirarse un lance con.

flint (flɪnt) *n.* pedernal; (*of a lighter*) piedra. —**flinty,** *adj.* empedernido; duro.

flintlock *n.* fusil de chispa.

flip (flɪp) *n.* **1,** (flick; snap) tirón; golpe seco. **2,** (mixed drink) vino, sidra *o* cerveza con ron y azúcar. —*v.t.* [**flipped, flipping**] **1,** (toss) lanzar *o* tirar con un golpe seco. **2,** (tap; shove) dar un golpe seco a. —*adj., colloq.* descarado; impertinente; fresco.

flippant ('flɪp·ənt) *adj.* petulante; impertinente; frívolo. —**flippancy,** *n.* petulancia; impertinencia; frivolidad.

flipper ('flɪp·ər) *n.* **1,** (limb of turtles, whales, etc.) aleta. **2,** *slang* (hand) mano.

flirt (flʌɹt) *v.i.* **1,** (play at being in love) coquetear; flirtear. **2,** (trifle, as with an idea) acariciar (una idea). —*n.* coqueta.

flirtation (flʌɹ'tei·ʃən) *n.* coqueteo; flirteo.

flirtatious (flʌɹ'tei·ʃəs) *adj.* galanteador; coquetón. —**flirtatiousness,** *n.* coquetería.

flit (flɪt) *v.i.* [**flitted, flitting**] volar; revolotear.

float (flot) *v.i.* flotar. —*v.t.* **1,** (cause to float) poner a flote; poner a flotar. **2,** (start; launch) lanzar. **3,** *comm.* (offer for sale) emitir. —*n.* **1,** (something that floats) flotador. **2,** (decorated vehicle in a parade) carroza alegórica.

floater ('flo·tər) *n.* **1,** (person that floats) persona sin meta fija; vagabundo. **2,** (insurance policy) póliza flotante.

floating ('flo·tɪŋ) *adj.* flotante; *comm.* en circulación.

flock (flak) *n.* **1,** (of animals) manada; rebaño; (of birds) bandada. **2,** (congregation) rebaño; grey. **3,** (crowd) muchedumbre; multitud. **4,** (tuft) copo; vedija. **5,** (fibers of wool, etc.) borra; pelusilla. —*v.i.* congregarse; reunirse.

floe (floː) *n.* témpano.

flog (flɔg) *v.t.* [**flogged, flogging**] azotar.

flood (flʌd) *n.* **1,** (overflowing) riada; desbordamiento. **2,** (inundation) inundación; diluvio. **3,** (superfluity) abundancia; exceso.

4, (inflow of the tide) pleamar. —*v.t.* inundar; anegar. —*v.i.* inundarse; anegarse; desbordarse.
floodlight *n.* reflector.
floor (flor) *n.* **1,** (bottom surface) suelo; piso. **2,** (bottom of the sea) fondo. **3,** (story of a building) piso. **4,** (right to speak) palabra. —*v.t.* **1,** (furnish with a floor) solar; poner suelo o piso a. **2,** *colloq.* (knock down) derribar; echar al suelo. —**flooring,** *n.* (of wood) entablado; piso; entarimado; (of tile) embaldosado. —**floor show,** espectáculo de cabaret; show.
floorwalker *n.* encargado *o* jefe de sección.
floozy ('flu·zi) *n., slang* mujercilla; mujerzuela.
flop (flap) *v.i.* [**flopped, flopping**] **1,** (flap) aletear; sacudir. **2,** (fall clumsily) caer como saco. **3,** *slang* (fail) fracasar. —*n., slang* fracaso. —**floppy,** *adj.* flojo.
flora ('flo·rə) *n.* flora.
floral ('flo·rəl) *adj.* floral.
flori- ('flo·rə) *prefijo* flori-; flor: *floriculturist,* floricultor.
floriculture ('flo·rə,kʌl·tʃər) *n.* floricultura. —**floriculturist** (-'kʌl·tʃər·ɪst) *n.* floricultor.
florid ('flor·ɪd) *adj.* **1,** (ruddy) encarnado; rojo. **2,** (highly ornate) florido.
florist ('flor·ɪst) *n.* florista.
-florous (flo·rəs) *sufijo* -floro; que tiene o produce cierta especie o número de flores: *uniflorous,* unífloro.
floss (flɔs) *n.* seda floja; seda.
flossy ('flɔs·i) *adj.* **1,** (like floss) sedoso. **2,** *slang* (ornate) historiado; recargado.
flotation (flo'tei·ʃən) *n.* flotación; *comm.* lanzamiento.
flotilla (flo'tɪl·ə) *n.* flotilla.
flotsam ('flat·səm) *n.* restos de naufragio; despojos flotantes.
flounce (flauns) *n.* **1,** (ruffle) volante; fleco. **2,** (abrupt twist or jerk of the body) salto; bote. —*v.i.* saltar; ir *o* salir de un bote.
flounder ('flaun·dər) *v.i.* **1,** (move or speak awkwardly) desorientarse; desconcertarse; andar a tropezones. **2,** (struggle helplessly) forcejear; debatirse. —*n.* lenguado.
flour ('flau·ər) *n.* harina. —**floury,** *adj.* harinoso.
flourish ('flʌɹ·ɪʃ) *v.i.* florecer; prosperar. —*v.t.* **1,** (brandish; wave about) hacer molinetes con. **2,** (flaunt) hacer alarde de. —*n.* **1,** (brandishing; waving) floreo; molinete. **2,** (pen stroke) rasgo; rúbrica. **3,** (of trumpets) toque de clarines; fanfarria.
flout (flaut) *v.t.* burlar; burlarse de; mofarse de; escarnecer. —*n.* burla; mofa; escarnio.
flow (floː) *v.i.* **1,** (move as a stream) correr; fluir. **2,** (issue forth) manar. **3,** (fall in waves, as the hair) caer en ondas; caer con soltura. —*n.* corriente; flujo; caudal.
flower ('flau·ər) *n.* flor. —*v.i.* florecer. —**flowered,** *adj.* floreado.
flowerpot *n.* tiesto; maceta.
flowery ('flau·ə·ri) *adj.* florido. —**floweriness,** *n.* abundancia de flores; floreo (*de palabras*).
flown (floːn) *v., p.p. de* **fly.**
flu (fluː) *n.* influenza; gripe.
fluctuate ('flʌk·tʃu·et) *v.i.* fluctuar. —**fluctuation,** *n.* fluctuación.
flue (fluː) *n.* cañón *o* tubo de chimenea.
fluent ('flu·ənt) *adj.* fluido; suelto. —**fluency,** *n.* fluidez; soltura; facilidad. —**fluently,** *adv.* con soltura; con facilidad; fluidamente.
fluff (flʌf) *n.* **1,** (light down) plumón; mullido. **2,** (puff of dust, nap, etc.) pelusa; pelusilla. **3,** *slang* (mistake; bungle) equivocación; chapuz; desatino. —*v.t.* **1,** (make fluffy) mullir. **2,** *slang* (mistake; bungle) equivocar; chapucear. —*v.i.* **1,** (become fluffy) mullirse. **2,** (blunder) cometer un chapuz; desatinar. —**fluffy,** *adj.* blando; mullido.
fluid ('flu·ɪd) *adj.* & *n.* fluido. —**fluidity** (flu'ɪd·ə·ti) *n.* fluidez.
fluke (fluk) *n.* **1,** (anchor blade; barb of an arrow, harpoon, etc.) uña; punta. **2,** (lobe of a whale's tail) aleta (de la cola de una ballena). **3,** (fish) especie de lenguado. **4,** (parasitic worm) lombriz intestinal. **5,** *slang* (lucky chance) chiripa. —**fluky,** *adj., slang* de *o* por chiripa.
flung (flʌŋ) *v., pret. & p.p. de* **fling.**
flunk (flʌŋk) *v.t., colloq.* colgar; catear. —*v.i., colloq.* salir mal.
flunky *también,* **flunkey** ('flʌŋ·

ki) *n.* **1,** (manservant) lacayo. **2,** (toady) adulón; tiralevitas.

fluorescence (ˌflu·əˈrɛs·əns) *n.* fluorescencia. —**fluorescent,** *adj.* fluorescente.

fluorine (ˈflu·ə·rin) *n.* flúor. —**fluoride** (-ˌraid) *n.* fluoruro. —**fluoridation** (-rɪˈdei·ʃən) *n.* fluorización.

fluoroscope (ˈflʊr·ə·skop) *n.* fluoroscopio. —**fluoroscopic** (-ˈskap·ɪk) *adj.* fluoroscópico. —**fluoroscopy** (flʊˈras·kə·pi) *n.* fluoroscopía.

flurry (ˈflʌɹ·i) *n.* **1,** (sudden gust of wind) ráfaga; racha. **2,** (whir, as of activity; commotion) remolino; conmoción. —*v.t.* confundir; turbar; aturullar.

flush (flʌʃ) *v.i.* **1,** (blush) sonrojarse; ruborizarse; ponerse colorado. **2,** (flow rapidly; rush suddenly) afluir; fluir. **3,** (fly off, as game) saltar; levantarse; espantarse. —*v.t.* **1,** (cause to blush) sonrojar; ruborizar. **2,** (cause to glow) iluminar; hacer brillar. **3,** (wash; cleanse) enjuagar; hacer pasar agua sobre. **4,** (empty out) pasar; vaciar. **5,** (infuse, as with emotion) llenar (de gozo o excitación). **5,** (drive from cover) levantar; espantar; hacer saltar. —*n.* **1,** (blush) sonrojo; rubor. **2,** (glow) brillo; fulgor. **3,** (sudden rush; rapid flow) aflujo; flujo. **4,** (washing; cleansing) irrigación; riego; enjuague. **5,** (excitement) excitación; animación. **6,** (heat; fever) calor; fiebre. **7,** *cards* color; flux. —*adj.* **1,** (even; level) al ras; parejo. **2,** (full; filled) lleno; rebosante. **3,** (glowing; rosy) sonrosado; colorado. **4,** *colloq.* (well supplied, as with money) bien provisto. —*adv.* **1,** (level; in alignment) al ras. **2,** (directly; squarely) directamente; al centro.

fluster (ˈflʌs·tər) *v.t.* confundir; aturullar; descompaginar. —*n.* aturullamiento; confusión.

flute (flut) *n.* **1,** (musical instrument) flauta. **2,** (groove) estría; acanaladura. —**fluted,** *adj.* estriado; acanalado. —**flutist,** *n.* flautista.

flutter (ˈflʌt·ər) *v.i.* **1,** (flap, as wings) aletear; batir rapidamente. **2,** (move or beat irregularly) batir *o* latir descompasadamente. **3,** (wave, flap, as a flag) tremolar; ondear. **4,** (quiver, as with excitement) estar trémulo. **5,** (flutter about; bustle) revolotear. —*v.t.* batir; agitar; sacudir. —*n.* **1,** (fluttering movement) aleteo; movimiento trémulo. **2,** (agitation; stir) agitación; conmoción. **3,** (condition of the heart) palpitación acelerada. —**fluttery,** *adj.* trémulo.

fluvial (ˈflu·vi·əl) *adj.* fluvial.

flux (flʌks) *n.* **1,** (flow; continual change) flujo. **2,** *metall.* fundente.

fly (flai) *v.i.* [**flew, flown, flying**] **1,** (move through or in the air; move or pass swiftly) volar. **2,** (flee) huir; volar; escaparse. **3,** *baseball* [*pret. & p.p.* **flied**] *usu.* **fly out,** batear en alto una pelota que se recoge al vuelo. —*v.t.* **1,** (cause to fly) volar; hacer volar. **2,** (travel over) volar; volar por. **3,** (flee from) huir de; volarse de; escaparse de. —*n.* [*pl.* **flies**] **1,** (insect) mosca. **2,** (fishing lure) mosca artificial; señuelo. **3,** (flap in a pair of trousers) bragueta. **4,** (flap or roof of a tent) toldo; capota; volante. **5,** *pl., theat.* bambalina (*sing.*). **6,** *baseball* pelota recogida al vuelo. —**flying fish,** pez volador. —**flying saucer,** platillo volador. —**fly at,** atacar; abalanzarse contra. —**fly in the face of,** encarer desafiante *o* atrevidamente. —**fly into (a rage),** montar en (cólera). —**fly off,** huir. —**let fly,** soltar; mandar; tirar. —**on the fly,** al vuelo. —**with flying colors,** triunfante.

flycatcher *n.* papamoscas.

flyer (ˈflai·ər) *n.* = **flier.**

flyleaf *n.* [*pl.* **-leaves**] guarda.

flywheel *n.* volante.

foal (foːl) *n.* **1,** (young horse) potro; potrillo. **2,** (young ass) pollino. —*v.i. & t.* parir (una yegua o burra).

foam (foːm) *n.* espuma. —*v.t.* hacer espuma. —*v.i.* espumar. —**foamy,** *adj.* espumoso. —**foam at the mouth,** echar espumarajos. —**foam rubber,** caucho esponjoso.

foci (ˈfo·sai) *n., pl. de* **focus.**

focus (ˈfo·kəs) *n.* [*pl.* **focuses** *o* **foci**] foco. —*v.t. & i.* enfocar. —**focal,** *adj.* focal.

fodder (ˈfad·ər) *n.* forraje.

foe (foː) *n.* enemigo; antagonista; adversario. —**foeman** (-mən) *n.* enemigo.

fog (fɔːg; faːg) *n.* **1,** (mist) niebla; neblina; bruma. **2,** *fig.* (confusion; muddle) confusión; perplejidad; niebla. —*v.t.* [**fogged, fogging**] **1,** (surround by fog) nublar. **2,** (cover with a fog or vapor) empañar. **3,** *fig.* (obscure; muddle) obscurecer; nublar. **4,** *photog.* velar.

foggy ('fɔg·i; 'fag·i) *adj.* **1,** (full of fog; misty) nublado. **2,** (dim; murky) nebuloso. **3,** (confused; muddled) confuso; perplejo. **4,** *photog.* velado.

foghorn *n.* sirena *o* bocina de niebla.

fogy ('fo·gi) *n.* vejestorio; vejete.

foible ('fɔi·bəl) *n.* debilidad; flaqueza.

foil (fɔil) *v.t.* frustrar. —*n.* **1,** (thin sheet of metal) papel metálico; hoja metálica. **2,** (person or thing furnishing contrast) persona o casa que da realce; marco. **3,** (fencing sword) espada de esgrima; florete.

foist (fɔist) *v.t.* pasar (con maña); colar; endosar.

fold (foːld) *v.t.* **1,** (bend double) plegar; doblar. **2,** (draw together and cross, as the arms) cruzar. **3,** (draw close to the body, as wings) plegar. **4,** (envelop; embrace) envolver. —*v.i.* **1,** (double together) plegarse; doblarse. **2,** *slang* (fail; cease to function) fracasar; venirse abajo. —*n.* **1,** (crease; folded layer) pliegue; doblez. **2,** (pen for sheep) redil. **3,** (flock) rebaño.

-fold (fold) *sufijo; denota* multiplicación; veces: *tenfold,* diez veces.

folder ('fol·dər) *n.* **1,** (booklet) folleto. **2,** (holder for papers or records) carpeta; ficha; pliego.

folding ('fol·dɪŋ) *adj.* plegable, plegadizo.

foliage ('fol·i·ɪdʒ) *n.* follaje.

folio ('fo·li·o) *n.* [*pl.* **-os**] **1,** (sheet of paper; page number) folio. **2,** (book) libro en folio.

folk (foːk) *n.* **1,** (people) gente. **2,** *pl., colloq.* (relatives) parientes; familiares; (parents) padres. —*adj.* popular; del pueblo.

folklore ('fok,lor) *n.* folklore. —**folkloristic,** *adj.* folklórico.

folkways *n.pl.* costumbres tradicionales.

follow ('fa·lo) *v.t.* **1,** (come or go after) seguir; ir detrás de; venir después de. **2,** (pursue) perseguir. **3,** (understand) entender. **4,** (imitate) imitar; copiar. **5,** (adhere or conform to; obey) seguir; obedecer. —*v.i.* **1,** (go or come after another) seguir; ir detrás; venir después. **2,** (result) seguirse; resultar. —**follow through,** seguir; rematar. —**follow up,** continuar; insistir.

follower ('fa·lo·ər) *n.* seguidor; discípulo; secuaz.

following ('fa·lo·ɪŋ) *n.* **1,** (entourage) séquito; acompañamiento. **2,** (group of followers) partidarios; seguidores. **3,** (clientele) clientela. —*adj.* siguiente.

followthrough *n.* remate; continuación.

followup *n.* continuación; insistencia.

folly ('fal·i) *n.* locura; disparate; desatino.

foment (fo'mɛnt) *v.t.* fomentar. —*n.* ('fo·mɛnt) [*también,* **fomentation** (,fo·mɛn'tei·ʃən)] fomento.

fond (fand) *adj.* **1,** (loving) encariñado; apegado. **2,** (inclined toward) aficionado. **3,** (doting) condescendiente; indulgente.

fondle ('fan·dəl) *v.t.* mimar; acariciar.

fondness ('fand·nəs) *n.* **1,** (affection) afecto; cariño; apego. **2,** (inclination) afición. **3,** (doting) condescendencia; indulgencia.

font (fant) *n.* **1,** *eccles.* pila. **2,** *typog.* fundición; tipo de letra.

food (fuːd) *n.* comida; alimento.

foodstuff *n., usu.pl.* comestibles; víveres; productos alimenticios.

fool (fuːl) *n.* **1,** (stupid person) tonto; bobo; necio. **2,** (court jester) bufón. —*v.t.* engañar; defraudar; embaucar. —*v.i.* bromear; tontear. —**fool around,** *colloq.* **1,** (jest) bromear; chancear. **2,** (idle) haraganear; zanganear. —**fool away,** malgastar; perder (el tiempo). —**fool with,** *colloq.* meterse en; tontear con; entretenerse con. —**make a fool of,** poner en ridículo.

foolhardy *adj.* temerario. —**foolhardiness,** *n.* temeridad.

foolish ('fu·lɪʃ) *adj.* bobo; tonto; necio. —**foolishness,** *n.* bobería; tontería; necedad.

foolproof *adj., colloq.* **1,** (easily

understood) muy fácil; inequívoco. **2,** (surely effective) cierto; seguro.

foolscap *n.* papel de oficio.

foot (fʊt) *n.* [*pl.* **feet**] **1,** *anat.* (of humans) pie; (of animals) pata. **2,** (part resembling a foot) pata. **3,** (bottom or lowest point) pie; base. **4,** [*pl. también* **foot**] (measure of length) pie. **5,** (step; pace) paso; movimiento. **6,** (infantry) infantería. **7,** *pros.* pie. —*v.t.* **1,** (add up) sumar. **2,** *colloq.* (pay, as a bill) pagar. —**on foot,** a pie. —**put one's foot down,** plantarse en sus trece. —**put one's foot in it,** meter la pata.

footage ('fʊt·ɪdʒ) *n.* largo (*en pies*); metraje.

football *n.* **1,** (game) fútbol; balompié. **2,** (ball) balón; pelota de fútbol.

footboard *n.* **1,** (of a vehicle) estribo. **2,** (of a bed) pie de cama.

footgear *n.* calzado.

foothill *n.* estribación; falda.

foothold *n.* posición; base.

footing ('fʊt·ɪŋ) *n.* **1,** (foothold) posición; base. **2,** (foundation) base; fundamento. **3,** (basis; relative standing) pie; relación; —**lose one's footing,** perder el pie.

footlights *n.pl.* candilejas; batería (*sing.*).

footloose *adj.* libre; desembarazado.

footman ('fʊt·mən) *n.* [*pl.* **-men**] lacayo.

footnote *n.* nota (*al pie de página*).

footprint *n.* huella; pisada.

footrest *n.* **1,** (footstool) escabel. **2,** (support for the foot) apoyo *o* descanso para los pies.

footstep *n.* paso; pisada.

footstool *n.* banqueta; escabel.

foot warmer calientapiés.

footwear *n.* calzado.

footwork *n.* juego de pies.

fop (fap) *n.* petimetre; pisaverde. —**foppery,** *n.* afectación en el vestir. —**foppish,** *adj.* peripuesto; afectado.

for (for) *prep.* **1,** (intended for; for the use of) para: *a book for children,* un libro para niños. **2,** (destined for; to be given to) para: *a gift for Louis,* un regalo para Luis. **3,** (for the purpose of; appropriate to) para: *a box for handkerchiefs,* una caja para pañuelos. **4,** (with inclination or tendency toward) para: *a good ear for music,* buen oído para la música. **5,** (toward, as a destination) para: *He left for Washington,* Salió para Washington. **6,** (with the purpose or goal of) para: *He is training for policeman,* Se prepara para policía. **7,** (for the benefit or advantage of) para: *Wine is good for the digestion,* El vino es bueno para la digestión. **8,** (with reference or relation to) para: *He is tall for his age,* Es alto para su edad. **9,** (in quest of; in order to get) por: *I went for the doctor,* Fui por el médico. **10,** (in request of; requesting) por: *a suit for damages,* un pleito por daños. **11,** (in return for; in compensation for) por: *I paid five dollars for a hat,* Pagué cinco dólares por un sombrero. **12,** (in spite of, notwithstanding) aun con; a pesar de: *He is a fool for all his learning,* Es un idiota aun con toda su ciencia. **13,** (over the space or time of) en; por: *I have not seen him in two years,* No lo he visto en *o* por dos años. **14,** (in favor of) por: *I vote for an honest policy,* Voto por una política recta. **15,** (in place of; in substitution for) por; en vez de: *The vice-president signed for the president,* El vicepresidente firmó por el presidente. **16,** (on behalf of) por: *I act for my brother,* Actúo por mi hermano. **17,** (for the sake of) por: *I did it for you,* Lo hice por ti. **18,** (corresponding to; in proportion to) por: *mile for mile,* milla por milla. **19,** (in token or recognition of) por: *He was given a medal for bravery,* Le concedieron una medalla por su valentía. **20,** (in honor of) por: *He was named Albert for his uncle,* Se le llamó Alberto por su tío. **21,** (because of; by reason of) por: *for having done this,* por haber hecho esto. **22,** (as; in the character or capacity of) por; como: *He took her for his wife,* La tomó por *o* como esposa. **23,** (mistakenly as or for) por: *He took* (*o mistook*) *me for someone else,* Me tomó por otro. **24,** (*denotando una hora determinada*) de: *It is time for lunch,* Es hora de almorzar. —*conj.* porque; pues; puesto que. —**as for me,** por mi parte. —**but for,** a no ser por. —**for hire,** de alquiler. —**for**

rent, se alquila. —**for sale,** en venta; se vende.
for- (for) *prefijo* **1,** lejos; aparte: *forget,* olvidar. **2,** negación: *forbid,* prohibir. **3,** intensidad: *forlorn,* abandonado.
forage ('for·ɪdz) *n.* forraje. —*v.t. & i.* forrajear.
foray ('for·e) *n.* correría; saqueo; pillaje.
forbear (for'beːr) *v.t.* [**forbore, forborne, forbearing**] abstenerse de. —*v.i.* reprimirse; contenerse.
forbearance (for'bɛr·əns) *n.* **1,** (abstinence) abstención. **2,** (patient endurance) paciencia; indulgencia. —**forbearing,** *adj.* paciente; sufrido; indulgente.
forbid (for'bɪd) *v.t.* [**forbade** *o* **forbid, forbidden, forbidding**] **1,** (prohibit) prohibir; vedar. **2,** (prevent) impedir.
forbidding (for'bɪd·ɪŋ) *adj.* **1,** (threatening; dark) amenazante; sombrío. **2,** (disagreeable) desagradable; adusto.
force (fors) *n.* **1,** (power; might; strength) fuerza. **2,** (operation; effect, as of laws) vigor; vigencia. **3,** (meaning; import) valor; significado. **4,** (body of men prepared for action) fuerza; tropa. **5,** (staff of workers) personal. —*v.t.* forzar. —**forceful,** *adj.* fuerte; poderoso; enérgico.
forced (forst) *adj.* **1,** (compulsory) forzoso. **2,** (strained; unnatural) forzado; artificial; afectado. **3,** (caused by an emergency) forzado; obligado.
forceps ('for·sɛps) *n.* fórceps.
forcible ('for·sə·bəl) *adj.* **1,** (powerful) fuerte; poderoso. **2,** (convincing) de peso; concluyente. **3,** (effected by force) forzado. **4,** (marked by force) vigoroso; enérgico.
ford (ford) *n.* vado. —*v.t.* vadear.
fore (for) *n.* frente. —*adv.* de proa. —*adj.* anterior; delantero; *naut.* de proa. —*interj., golf* ¡ojo!; ¡atención!
fore- (for) *prefijo* **1,** anterior (*en tiempo o lugar*): *forenoon,* mañana; *forepaw,* pata delantera. **2,** superior en rango: *foreman,* capataz.
fore-and-aft *adj.* de popa a proa. —**fore-and-aft sail,** cangreja; vela cangreja.
forearm *n.* antebrazo.
forebear ('for,bɛr) *n.* antepasado.
forebode (for'boːd) *v.t.* **1,** (presage) pronosticar; presagiar. **2,** (have a premonition of) presentir. —**foreboding,** *n.* pronóstico; presagio; presentimiento.
forecast ('for·kæst) *n.* **1,** (prediction) pronóstico. **2.** (foresight) previsión. —*v.t.* (for'kæst) [*pret. & p.p. también* **forecast**] **1,** (predict) pronosticar. **2,** (foresee) prever.
forecastle ('foːk·səl) *n.* castillo de proa.
foreclose (for'kloːz) *v.t. & i.* anular por orden judicial el derecho de redimir (una hipoteca). —**foreclosure** (-'klo·ʒər) *n.* anulación del derecho de redimir una hipoteca.
forefather *n.* antepasado; ascendiente.
forefinger *n.* (dedo) índice.
forefoot *n.* pata delantera.
forefront *n.* frente; primer lugar.
forego (for'goː) *v.t.* = **forgo.**
foregoing (for'go·ɪŋ) *adj.* anterior; precedente.
foregone *adj.* **1,** (past) pasado. **2,** (settled in advance) predeterminado; decidido de antemano. —**to be foregone,** darse por sentado.
foreground *n.* primer plano; frente.
forehead ('for·hɛd) *n.* frente.
foreign ('far·ən) *adj.* **1,** (situated outside one's own land) extranjero. **2,** (relating to or dealing with other countries) exterior. **3,** (alien; not native; strange) extraño; exótico. **4,** (extraneous; external) extraño; ajeno. —**foreigner,** *n.* extranjero.
foreleg *n.* pata delantera.
forelock *n.* **1,** (lock of hair on the forehead) mechón. **2,** (of a horse) copete. **3,** *mech.* chaveta.
foreman ('for·mən) *n.* [*pl.* **-men**] **1,** (superintendent of workers) encargado (capataz; mayoral, etc.). **2,** (spokesman of a jury) portavoz del jurado.
foremost *adj.* **1,** (in place) delantero; más avanzado. **2,** (in rank or importance) primero; principal. —*adv.* primero; principalmente.
forenoon *n.* mañana.
forensic (fə'rɛn·sɪk) *adj.* forense.
forerunner *n.* antecesor; precursor.

foresee (for'siː) *v.t.* [**foresaw, forseen**] prever. —**foreseeable,** *adj.* previsible.
foreshadow *v.t.* presagiar; preconizar.
foresight *n.* previsión.
foreskin *n.* prepucio.
forest ('far·əst) *n.* bosque; selva; floresta. —**forester,** *n.* guardabosque. —**forestry,** *n.* silvicultura.
forestall *v.t.* prevenir; precaver; anticipar; anticiparse a.
foretell *v.t. & i.* [*pret. & p.p.* **foretold**] predecir.
forethought *n.* prevención; providencia; premeditación.
foretoken (for'to·kən) *v.t.* presagiar. —*n.* ('for-) presagio.
forever *adv.* siempre; para siempre; por siempre.
forewarn *v.t.* prevenir; advertir. —*v.i.* presagiar. —**forewarning,** *n.* presagio.
foreword *n.* prólogo; introducción.
forfeit ('for·fɪt) *n.* **1,** (something forfeited) pérdida. **2,** (fine; penalty) multa; pena. —*v.t. & i.* perder. —*v.t.* perder el derecho a. —*adj.* perdido. —**forfeits,** *n.pl.* juego de prendas. —**forfeiture** ('for·fɪ·tʃər) *n.* pérdida.
forge (fordʒ) *v.t.* **1,** (shape; fashion) forjar; fraguar. **2,** (counterfeit) falsificar. —*v.i.* abrirse *o* labrarse camino; seguir avanzando. —*n.* forja; fragua.
forger ('for·dʒər) *n.* **1,** (counterfeiter) falsificador. **2,** (worker in metals) forjador.
forgery ('for·dʒə·ri) *n.* falsificación.
forget (fər'gɛt) *v.t.* [**forgot, forgotten** *o* **forgot, forgetting**] olvidar; olvidarse de; olvidársele (a uno) una cosa. —**forget oneself 1,** (be unselfish) olvidarse de sí. **2,** (act or speak unseemly) olvidarse de lo que uno es.
forgetful (fər'gɛt·fəl) *adj.* **1,** (given to forgetting) olvidadizo. **2,** (unmindful; inconsiderate) desconsiderado; olvidado. —**forgetfulness,** *n.* olvido.
forget-me-not *n.* nomeolvides.
forgive (fər'gɪv) *v.t.* [**forgave, forgiven, forgiving**] perdonar. —**forgiveness,** *n.* perdón; clemencia. —**forgiving,** *adj.* indulgente; clemente; misericordioso.
forgo *también,* **forego** (for'goː) *v.t.* [**forwent, forgone, forgoing**] privarse de; renunciar.
fork (fork) *n.* **1,** (utensil for eating) tenedor. **2,** (of a tree) horqueta; horquilla. **3,** (pitchfork) horca; horquilla. **4,** (branching, as of a road or river) bifurcación. **5,** (anything forked or fork-shaped) horquilla; horqueta. —*v.t.* **1,** (pierce or handle with a fork) pinchar, sujetar o mover con tenedor, trinchante u horquilla. **2,** (make fork-shaped) bifurcar; ahorquillar. —*v.i.* bifurcarse; ahorquillarse. —**forked,** *adj.* bifurcado; ahorquillado. —**fork over** *o* **out,** *slang* entregar; pasar.
forlorn (for'loːrn) *adj.* **1,** (forsaken) abandonado; desamparado. **2,** (desolate) triste; desolado. **3,** (hopeless) desesperado. —**forlornness,** *n.* desamparo; desolación; desesperación. —**forlorn hope,** acción o empresa desesperada.
form (form) *n.* **1,** (shape; style; pattern) forma. **2,** (condition) condición; forma. **3,** (blank document) formulario. —*v.t.* formar. —*v.i.* formarse.
-form (form) *sufijo* -forme; con o en forma de: *cuneiform,* cuneiforme.
formal ('for·məl) *adj.* **1,** (of or relating to form) formal. **2,** (stiff) formal; ceremonioso; tieso. **3,** (ceremonial; gala) de etiqueta. —*n., colloq.* función (o vestido) de etiqueta.
formaldehyde (for'mæl·də·haid) *n.* formaldehído.
formalism ('for·mə,lɪz·əm) *n.* formalismo. —**formalist,** *n.* formalista. —**formalistic,** *adj.* formalista.
formality (for'mæl·ə·ti) *n.* formalidad.
formalize ('for·mə·laiz) *v.t.* formalizar.
format ('for·mæt) *n.* formato; forma.
formation (for'mei·ʃən) *n.* formación.
formative ('form·ə·tɪv) *adj.* formativo.
former ('for·mər) *adj.* **1,** (preceding in time) anterior; pasado; precedente. **2,** (first mentioned of two) anterior; primero. —**formerly,** *adv.* antes; anteriormente. —**the former . . . the latter,** aquél . . . éste.

formidable ('for·mɪ·də·bəl) *adj.* formidable.
formless ('form·ləs) *adj.* informe; sin forma.
formula ('form·ju·lə) *n.* fórmula.
formulate ('form·ju,leit) *v.t.* formular. —**formulation,** *n.* formulación.
fornicate ('for·nɪ,keit) *v.i.* fornicar. —**fornication,** *n.* fornicación.
forsake (for'seik) *v.t.* [**forsook, forsaken, forsaking**] **1,** (abandon) abandonar; desamparar. **2,** (renounce) dejar; renunciar.
forswear (for'swe:r) *v.t.* [*pret. & p.p.* **forsworn**] renegar. —*v.i.* jurar en falso; perjurar.
fort (fort) *n.* fuerte; fortaleza.
forte ('for·ti; -te) *n.* fuerte. —*adj. & adv., music* fuerte.
forth (forθ) *adv.* **1,** (onward or forward) adelante; hacia adelante. **2,** (out; away) fuera; afuera; hacia afuera. —**and so forth,** y (lo) demás; etcétera.
forthcoming *adj.* **1,** (approaching in time) próximo; que viene. **2,** (available) disponible.
forthright *adj.* franco; abierto; directo. —*adv.* **1,** (directly) francamente; directamente; abiertamente. **2,** (immediately) inmediatamente; en el acto. —**forthrightness,** *n.* franqueza; sinceridad.
forthwith *adv.* en el acto; en seguida.
fortieth ('for·ti·əθ) *adj. & n.* cuadragésimo; cuarentavo.
fortification (,for·tɪ·fɪ'kei·ʃən) *n.* fortificación.
fortify ('for·tɪ,fai) *v.t.* **1,** (provide with defenses) fortificar. **2,** (strengthen) fortalecer. **3,** (reinforce) reforzar.
fortissimo (for'tɪs·ɪ,mo) *adj. & adv.* fortísimo.
fortitude ('for·tɪ·tud; -tjud) *n.* fortaleza; entereza.
fortnight ('fort,nait; -nɪt) *n.* quincena; dos semanas. —**fortnightly,** *adj.* quincenal. —*adv.* quincenalmente.
fortress ('fort·rəs) *n.* fortaleza; fuerte.
fortuitous (for'tu·ɪ·təs) *adj.* fortuito; casual; accidental. —**fortuitousness; fortuity,** *n.* casualidad.
fortunate ('for·tʃə·nət) *adj.* afortunado; feliz.
fortune ('for·tʃən) *n.* fortuna.
fortuneteller *n.* vidente; adivino; adivinador.
forty ('for·ti) *n. & adj.* cuarenta.
forum ('for·əm) *n.* foro.
forward ('for·wərd) *adj.* **1,** (near or toward the front) delantero; anterior. **2,** (well-advanced) adelantado. **3,** (eager; ready) entusiasta; emprendedor. **4,** (bold) atrevido; descarado. —*adv.* **1,** (onward; ahead; toward the front) adelante; hacia delante. **2,** (forth; into view) fuera; afuera; hacia fuera. —*v.t.* **1,** (send; dispatch) enviar; expedir; transmitir. **2,** (send to a further destination) reexpedir. **3,** (promote) promover; adelantar.
forwardness ('for·wərd·nəs) *n.* **1,** (boldness) audacia; descaro. **2,** (drive; energy) empuje; entusiasmo.
fossil ('fas·əl) *n. & adj.* fósil. —**fossilize,** *v.t.* fosilizar. —*v.i.* fosilizarse.
foster ('fɔs·tər) *v.t.* **1,** nourish; bring up) criar. **2,** (cherish) alentar; alimentar. **3,** (promote; sponsor) patrocinar. —*adj.* adoptivo; de crianza.
fought (fɔt) *v., pret. & p.p. de* **fight.**
foul (faul) *adj.* **1,** (filthy) sucio; inmundo; **2,** (of offensive odor) apestoso; pestilente. **3,** (stale, as air) viciado. **4,** (inclement, as weather) malo. **5,** (clogged) atorado; obstruido. **6,** (entangled) enredado; enmarañado. **7,** (in violation of rules) ilegal; inválido. **8,** (base; vicious; scurrilous) sucio; bajo; vil. —*n.* infracción; falta. —*v.t.* **1,** (defile) ensuciar; manchar. **2,** (clog) atorar; obstruir. **3,** (entangle) enredar; enmarañar. —*v.i.* **1,** (become soiled) ensuciarse. **2,** (become clogged) obstruirse; atorarse. **3,** (become entangled) enmarañarse; enredarse. **4,** (violate a rule) cometer una infracción *o* falta. —**foulness,** *n.* asquerosidad. —**fall foul of; run foul of,** enredarse con; chocarse con; chocar contra. —**foul blow; foul punch,** golpe bajo. —**foul up,** embarrar; embarullar; embrollar.
foulard (fu'la:rd) *n.* fular.
foul-mouthed *adj.* deslenguado; desbocado.
found (faund) *v.t.* **1,** (lay the foundation of; establish) fundar; establecer. **2,** (support; base) asen-

tar (en); fundar (en); basar (en). 3, (cast) fundir.
found (faund) *v., pret. & p.p. de* **find.**
foundation (faun'dei·ʃən) *n.* **1,** (base) cimiento. **2,** (basis) base; fundamento; principio. **3,** (endowed institution) fundación. **4,** (act of founding) fundación.
founder ('faun·dər) *v.i.* **1,** (sink) hundirse; irse a pique. **2,** (go lame, as a horse) derrengarse. **3,** (fail) fracasar; hundirse. —*n.* **1,** (originator) fundador. **2,** (caster of metals) fundidor.
founding ('faun·dıŋ) *n.* fundición.
foundling ('faund·lıŋ) *n.* (niño) expósito; echadillo. —**foundling hospital; foundling home,** inclusa; hospicio.
foundry ('faun·dri) *n.* fundición.
fountain ('faun·tən) *n.* fuente. —**fountainhead,** nacimiento; fuente; origen. —**fountain pen,** estilográfica; pluma fuente.
four (for) *n. & adj.* cuatro. —**on all fours,** a *o* en cuatro patas; gateando.
fourfold *adj.* cuádruplo; cuatro veces (más). —*adv.* cuatro veces; en un cuádruplo.
four-footed *adj.* cuadrúpedo.
four hundred cuatrocientos. —**four-hundredth,** *adj. & n.* cuadringentésimo.
four-in-hand *n.* **1,** (necktie) corbata de nudo. **2,** (team of horses) tiro de cuatro caballos.
foursome ('for·səm) *n.* grupo de *o* a cuatro. —*adj.* de a cuatro.
foursquare *adj.* **1,** (steady) firme; constante. **2,** (frank) franco; abierto.
fourteen (for'tin) *n. & adj.* catorce. —**fourteenth,** *adj.* décimocuarto. —*n.* décimocuarto; décimocuarta parte.
fourth (forθ) *adj.* cuarto. —*n.* cuarto; cuarta parte; *music* cuarta.
fowl (faul) *n.* ave; (*collectively*) volatería. —**fowler,** *n.* cazador (de aves). —**fowling,** *n.* caza (de aves). —**fowling piece,** escopeta.
fox (faks) *n.* zorra (*masc.* zorro); raposa. —*v.t., slang* engañar.
foxhole *n., mil.* pozo *u* hoyo de tirador.
foxhound *n.* perro zorrero.
foxy ('fak·si) *adj.* astuto; listo.
foyer ('fɔi·ər) *n.* vestibulo.
Fra (fra) *n.* fray.
fracas ('frei·kəs) *n.* riña; bronca.
fraction (fræk·ʃən) *n.* fracción. —**fractional,** *adj.* fraccionario; fraccionado. —**fractional distillation,** destilación fraccionada. —**fractional motor,** motor de menos de un caballo.
fractious (fræk·ʃəs) *adj.* **1,** (cross; peevish) enojadizo; arisco. **2,** (unruly) reacio; rebelde. —**fractiousness,** *n.* indocilidad; mal genio.
fracture ('fræk·tʃər) *n.* rotura; *surg.* fractura. —*v.t.* fracturar; quebrar; romper.
fragile ('frædʒ·əl) *adj.* frágil. —**fragility** (fra'dʒıl·ə·ti) *n.* fragilidad.
fragment ('fræg·mənt) *n.* fragmento; trozo. —*v.t.* fragmentar. —*v.i.* fragmentarse. —**fragmentary,** *adj.* fragmentario. —**fragmentation** (-mən'tei·ʃən) *n.* fragmentación.
fragrant ('frei·grənt) *adj.* fragante; oloroso. —**fragrance,** *n.* fragancia; olor.
frail (freil) *adj.* **1,** (fragile) frágil; quebradizo. **2,** (weak) débil; delicado; endeble. —**frailty,** *n.* fragilidad; debilidad.
frame (freim) *v.t.* **1,** (construct; fit together) armar; fabricar; formar. **2,** (compose; devise) componer; inventar; forjar; idear. **3,** (surround with a frame) poner marco a. **4,** *slang* (incriminate) fraguar; incriminar. —*n.* **1,** (ornamental border) marco. **2,** (structure for enclosing or holding something) armadura; armazón; bastidor. **3,** (bodily structure) esqueleto. **4,** (state of mind) talante; disposición. —**frame house,** casa de madera.
framework *n.* armazón; *fig.* cuadro.
franc (fræŋk) *n.* franco.
franchise ('fræn·tʃaiz) *n.* **1,** (right to vote) sufragio. **2,** (special right granted) franquicia; exclusiva.
francium ('fræn·si·əm) *n.* francio.
Franco- ('fræŋ·ko) *prefijo* franco-; francés: *Franco-American,* francoamericano.
frank (fræŋk) *adj.* franco; abierto. —*n.* franquicia postal; carta franca. —*v.t.* enviar con franquicia. —**frankness,** *n.* franqueza.
frankfurter ('frænk,fʌɹ·tər) *n.* salchicha.

frankincense ('fræŋk·ɪn·sɛns) *n.* incienso.
frantic (fræn·tɪk) *adj.* frenético.
fraternal (frə'tʌɹ·nəl) *adj.* fraternal.
fraternity (frə'tʌɹ·nə·ti) *n.* fraternidad; hermandad.
fraternize ('fræt·ər,naiz) *v.i.* fraternizar. —**fraternization** (-nɪ·'zei·ʃən) *n.* fraternización.
fratricide ('fræt·rɪ,said) *n.* **1,** (act) fratricidio. **2,** (agent) fratricida. —**fratricidal,** *adj.* fratricida.
fraud (frɔːd) *n.* **1,** (deceit; trick) fraude; engaño; timo. **2,** *law* fraude. **3,** *colloq.* (cheat) timador; trapalón.
fraudulent ('frɔd·jə·lənt) *adj.* fraudulento. —**fraudulence,** *n.* fraude; fraudulencia.
fraught (frɔt) *adj.* lleno; atestado.
fray (frei) *n.* riña; disputa; querella. —*v.t.* deshilachar; desgastar; raer. —*v.i.* deshilacharse; desgastarse; raerse.
frazzle (fræz·əl) *v.t., colloq.* **1,** (fray) rozar; raer; deshilachar. **2,** (exhaust) cansar; fatigar; abrumar. —*n.* **1,** (shred) hilacha. **2,** (exhaustion) cansancio; fatiga; extenuación.
freak (friːk) *n.* **1,** (monster) monstruo; aborto; engendro. **2,** (whim; odd notion) capricho; rareza.
freakish ('fri·kɪʃ) *adj.* **1,** (odd; unusual) raro; extravagante. **2,** (monstrous) monstruoso.
freckle ('frɛk·əl) *n.* peca. —*v.t.* poner pecoso. —*v.i.* ponerse pecoso. —**freckly** (-li); **freckled,** *adj.* pecoso.
free (friː) *adj.* **1,** (independent; self-determining) libre; independiente. **2,** (unrestricted; unbound; loose) libre; suelto. **3,** (exempt) libre; exento. **4,** (free of charge) gratuito; gratis. **5,** (not literal or exact) libre. **6,** (open to all) abierto. **7,** (unoccupied; unengaged) libre; disponible; desocupado. **8,** (lavish; profuse) liberal. —*adv.* gratis; de balde. —*v.t.* **1,** (release; liberate) liberar; libertar. **2,** (save; rescue) librar; rescatar. **3,** (exempt) eximir. **4,** (loose; let go) soltar. **5,** (rid; disencumber) desembarazar. **6,** (clear; purify) limpiar. —**free and clear,** libre de hipoteca y cargos. —**free and easy,** desenvuelto; desembarazado. —**free hand,** mano libre; carta blanca. —**free lance,** quien trabaja por su cuenta. —**free on board,** franco a bordo. —**free port,** puerto franco. —**free will,** propia voluntad; libre albedrío. —**make free with,** tomarse libertades con; abusar de; disponer de.
-free (fri) *sufijo* exento: *taxfree,* exento de impuestos.
freebooter ('friː·bu·tər) *n.* filibustero; pirata.
freeborn *adj.* nacido libre.
freedman ('frid·mən) *n.* liberto.
freedom ('fri·dəm) *n.* libertad.
free-for-all *n.* **1,** (brawl) trifulca; pelotera. **2,** (open contest) carrera o concurso abierto a todos. —*adj.* abierto; general.
freehand *adj. & adv.* a pulso.
freehanded *adj.* generoso; liberal; dadivoso.
freehold *n.* feudo franco.
freeman ('fri·mən) *n.* hombre libre; ciudadano.
Freemason *n.* masón; francmasón. —**Freemasonic,** *adj.* masónico; francmasónico. —**Freemasonry,** *n.* masonería; francmasonría.
freethinker *n.* librepensador. —**free thought,** libre pensamiento.
freewill *adj.* voluntario.
freeze (friːz) *v.t.* [**froze, frozen, freezing**] **1,** (congeal; chill) congelar; helar. **2,** (block; hinder) bloquear; congelar. —*v.i.* helarse; helar; escarchar. —*n.* hielo; escarcha.
freezer ('fri·zər) *n.* congeladora; congelador.
freight (freit) *n.* **1,** (transportation of goods) transporte. **2,** (cargo; shipment) carga; cargamento. **3,** (charge for handling) flete. **4,** *R.R.* tren de carga o mercancías. —*v.t.* **1,** (load) cargar. **2,** (ship by freight) embarcar. —**freighter,** *n.* buque de carga.
French (frɛntʃ) *adj. & n.* francés. —**Frenchman,** *n.* francés. —**French doors,** puertas de alas. —**French windows,** ventanas de alas. **French horn,** trompa. —**French leave,** despedida a la francesa. —**French toast,** torrija.
Frenchify ('frɛn·tʃə·fai) *v.t.* afrancesar.
frenetic (frə'nɛt·ɪk) *adj.* frenético.
frenum ('fri·nəm) *n.* frenillo.

frenzy ('frɛn·zi) *n.* frenesí. —**frenzied,** *adj.* frenético.

frequency ('fri·kwən·si) *n.* frecuencia. —**frequency modulation,** frecuencia modulada.

frequent ('fri·kwənt) *adj.* frecuente. —*v.t.* (fri'kwɛnt) frecuentar. —**frequentation** (-kwən'tei·ʃən) frecuentación. —**frequentative** (fri'kwɛn·tə·tɪv) *adj.* frecuentativo.

fresco ('frɛs·ko) *n.* fresco.

fresh (frɛʃ) *adj.* **1,** (having its original qualities) fresco. **2,** (not salt, as water) dulce. **3,** (recently made) acabado de hacer; recién hecho; fresco. **4,** (recent; new) reciente; nuevo. **5,** (clean, as clothing) limpio. **6,** (not tired) descansado. **7,** (healthy; youthful) sano; lozano; joven. **8,** (inexperienced) inexperto; novato. **9,** (cool; brisk; refreshing) fresco. **10,** *slang* (impudent) fresco; descarado. —**freshen,** *v.t.* refrescar.

freshet ('frɛʃ·ɪt) n. crecida; aluvión.

freshman ('frɛʃ·mən) *n.* [*pl.* **-men**] estudiante de primer año.

freshness ('frɛʃ·nəs) *n.* **1,** (newness) novedad. **2,** (coolness) fresco; frescura; frescor. **3,** (impudence) frescura. **4,** (vigor; vitality) lozanía.

freshwater *adj.* **1,** (of inland waters) de agua dulce. **2,** (inexperienced) novato; inexperto. **3,** (rural; rustic) rural; de provincias.

fret (frɛt) *v.i.* [**fretted, fretting**] **1,** (be distressed) atormentarse; desesperarse. **2,** (become worn or corroded) raerse; desgastarse; corroerse. —*v.t.* **1,** (vex; irritate) irritar; desesperar. **2,** (chafe; rub) raer; desgastar. —*n.* **1,** (irritation) irritación; enojo. **2,** (carved pattern) calado; greca. **3,** (of a stringed instrument) traste.

fretful ('frɛt·fəl) *adj.* **1,** (distressing) enojoso; molesto. **2,** (peevish) enojadizo. **3,** (perturbed; restless) inquieto; perturbado.

fretwork *n.* calado; greca.

friar ('frai·ər) *n.* fraile; fray.

fricassee ('frɪk·ə·si) *n.* fricasé. —*v.t.* hacer un fricasé de; preparar al fricasé.

friction ('frɪk·ʃən) *n.* **1,** (a rubbing together) fricción; rozamiento; roce. **2,** (disagreement; conflict) rozamiento; fricción. **3,** *mech.* rozamiento. —**frictional,** *adj.* de rozamiento.

Friday ('frai·de) *n.* viernes. —**Good Friday,** viernes santo.

fried (fraid) *v., pret. & p.p. de* **fry.** —*adj.* frito.

friend (frɛnd) *n.* **1,** (close acquaintance; supporter) amigo. **2,** *cap.* (Quaker) cuáquero.

friendly ('frɛnd·li) *adj.* **1,** (of or like a friend) amistoso; amigo. **2,** (not hostile; amicable) amigable; cordial. **3,** (supporting; helping; favorable) favorable; amigo. **4,** (desiring friendship) cariñoso; amistoso. —**friendliness,** *n.* amistad.

friendship ('frɛnd·ʃɪp) *n.* amistad.

frieze (friːz) *n.* **1,** *archit.* friso. **2,** (cloth) frisa.

frigate ('frɪg·ət) *n.* fragata.

fright (frait) *n.* **1,** (sudden terror) espanto; susto. **2,** *colloq.* (grotesque person or thing) esperpento; espantajo.

frighten ('frai·tən) *v.t.* **1,** (terrify; startle) espantar; asustar. **2,** (intimidate) amedrentar; atemorizar. —*v.i.* asustarse; amedrentarse.

frightful ('frait·fəl) *adj.* **1,** (terrifying; shocking) espantoso; horrible; pavoroso. **2,** *colloq.* (unpleasant) desagradable; atroz; horrible. —**frightfulness,** *n.* espanto.

frigid ('frɪdʒ·ɪd) *adj.* frígido; glacial; frío.

frigidity (frɪ'dʒɪd·ə·ti) *n.* frialdad; frigidez.

frill (frɪl) *n.* **1,** (ruffle) faralá; volante. **2,** *usu.pl., colloq.* (affectations) faralá (*sing.*); faramallas. **3,** (fancy detail) ringorrango; *Amer.* firulete. —**frilly,** *adj.* alechugado; escarolado.

fringe (frɪndʒ) *n.* **1,** (trimming) fleco; orla. **2,** (border; margin) borde; linde; margen. —*adj.* al linde; marginal.

frippery ('frɪp·ə·ri) *n.* **1,** (cheap finery) perifollos (*pl.*); cursilerías (*pl.*). **2,** (ostentation) perejil; cursilería.

frisk (frɪsk) *v.i.* retozar; brincar; dar cabriolas. —*v.t., slang* cachear; registrar; *Amer.* esculcar. —**frisky,** *adj.* vivaracho; retozón; juguetón.

fritter ('frɪt·ər) *v.t.* derrochar;

desperdiciar. —*n.* fritura; frito; fritada.

frivolity (frɪ'val·ə·ti) *n.* frivolidad.

frivolous ('frɪv·ə·ləs) *adj.* frívolo. —**frivolousness,** *n.* frivolidad.

frizzle ('frɪz·əl) *v.t.* **1,** (form into tight curls; crimp) encrespar; rizar. **2,** (make crisp, as by frying) achicharrar; churruscar. —*v.i.* **1,** (curl; crimp) encresparse; rizarse. **2,** (become crisp) achicharrarse; churruscarse. —**frizzly** (-li); **frizzy,** *adj.* rizado; encrespado.

fro (fro:) *adv.* atrás; hacia atrás. —**to and fro,** de un lado a otro; de aquí para allí.

frock (frak) *n.* **1,** (dress) vestido; sayo. **2,** (monk's habit) sayo. —**frock coat,** levita.

frog (frɔg; frag) *n.* **1,** *zool.; R.R.* rana. **2,** (ornamental fastening) alamar; recamo. —**frog in the throat,** carraspera. —**frogs' legs,** ancas de rana.

frogman *n.* buzo; hombre rana.

frolic ('fral·ɪk) *v.i.* [**frolicked, frolicking**] **1,** (make merry) jaranear; divertirse. **2,** (gambol) retozar; juguetear. —*n.* holgorio; diversión. —**frolicsome,** *adj.* retozón; juguetón; travieso.

from (frʌm) *prep.* **1,** (distant or separated in time, space, order, etc.) de: *ten miles from here,* a diez millas de aquí. **2,** (beginning at; starting with) de; desde: *from here to there,* desde aquí hasta allá. **3,** (out of; drawn or derived from) de: *This wine comes from Spain,* Este vino viene de España. **4,** (coming from; emanating from, as a message, order, etc.) de; de parte de: *This message comes from the judge,* Este mensaje viene del (*o* de parte del) juez. **5,** (because of; by reason of) de; por: *suffering from love,* sufriendo de *o* por amor. **6,** (removed, released, prevented, absent, different, etc. from) de: *He took the money from his savings,* Sacó el dinero de sus ahorros; *This house is different from the other,* Esta casa es distinta de la otra.

frond (frand) *n.* fronda.

front (frʌnt) *n.* **1,** (foremost part or position) frente. **2,** (outward appearance or aspect) fachada; apariencia. **3,** *mil.* frente. **4,** *colloq.* (ostentation of wealth, importance, etc.) fachenda; ostentación. **5,** (business firm, noted individual, etc., used as a cover up) pantalla; tapujo. **6,** (front part of a shirt) pechera. **7,** (front part of a book) comienzo; principio. —*adj.* delantero; de adelante; de frente; anterior. —*v.t.* hacer frente a; dar *o* caer a. —*v.i.* estar al frente *o* de frente; dar frente. —**front door,** puerta de entrada. —**front page,** primera plana. —**in front of,** al *o* en frente *de;* frente a; delante de.

frontage ('frʌn·tɪdʒ) *n.* frente; frontis; fachada.

frontal ('frʌn·təl) *adj.* frontal.

frontier (frʌn'tɪr) *n.* frontera. —*adj.* fronterizo. —**frontiersman** (-'tɪrz·mən) *n.* hombre de la frontera; colonizador.

frontispiece ('frʌn·tɪs·pis) *n.* frontispicio.

frost (frɔst) *n.* **1,** (frozen dew) escarcha. **2,** (freezing weather) helada. **3,** (frozen or icy state) hielo. **4,** (coldness of manner) hielo; frialdad. **5,** *slang* (failure) fracaso; plancha. —*v.t.* **1,** (cover with frost) cubrir de escarcha. **2,** (injure by freezing) helar; dañar la helada las mieses, frutas, etc. **3,** (cover with frosting) escarchar; garapiñar. **4,** (give a frosty finish to, as glass) escarchar; esmerilar.

frostbite *n.* congelación; congelamiento; quemadura. —**frostbitten,** *adj.* quemado por el frío.

frosting ('frɔs·tɪŋ) *n.* **1,** (sugar coating) escarchado; garapiña. **2,** (finish, as on glass) escarchado; esmerilado.

frosty ('frɔs·ti) *adj.* **1,** (cold; freezing) helado; frígido; frío. **2,** (covered with or as with frost) escarchado. **3,** (cold in manner or feeling) frío. **4,** (gray, as from age) canoso.

froth (frɔθ) *n.* espuma. —*v.t.* hacer espumar. —*v.i.* espumar; echar espuma.

frothy ('frɔθ·i) *adj.* **1,** (foamy) espumante; espumoso. **2,** (insubstantial) ligero; insubstancial.

froward ('fro·wərd) *adj.* indócil; díscolo. —**frowardness,** *n.* indocilidad.

frown (fraun) *n.* ceño. —*v.i.* fruncirse; arrugar el entrecejo. —**frown on** *o* **upon,** desaprobar de; mirar con malos ojos.

frowzy ('frau·zi) *adj.* desaliñado. —**frowziness,** *n.* desaliño.
froze (fro:z) *v., pret. de* **freeze.**
frozen ('fro·zən) *adj.* **1,** (frigid; cold) helado. **2,** (congealed; preserved by freezing) congelado. **3,** (stiff; rigid) helado; rígido. **4,** (not liquid, as assets) congelado. —*v., p.p. de* **freeze.**
fructify ('frʌk·tɪˌfai) *v.i.* fructificar. —*v.t.* hacer fructificar. —**fructification** (-fɪ'kei·ʃən) *n.* fructificación.
frugal ('fru·gəl) *adj.* frugal. —**frugality** (fru'gæl·ə·ti) *n.* frugalidad.
fruit (frut) *n.* **1,** (yield; seed of a plant) fruto. **2,** (sweet fruit of certain plants) fruta. **3,** (result; consequence) fruto; resultado. —**fruitful,** *adj.* fructífero; fructuoso. —**fruitless,** *adj.* estéril; infructuoso.
fruiterer ('fru·tər·ər) *n.* frutero.
fruition (fru'ɪʃ·ən) *n.* **1,** (state of bearing fruit) fructificación. **2,** (attainment; realization) realización; consecución. **3,** (enjoyment of use or possession) fruición.
frump (frʌmp) *n.* vieja desastrada y regañona. —**frumpish,** *adj.* regañón; a mal traer.
frustrate ('frʌs·tret) *v.t.* frustrar. —**frustration,** *n.* frustración.
frustum ('frʌs·təm) *n.* tronco.
fry (frai) *v.t.* freír. —*v.i.* freírse; achicharrarse. —*n.* **1,** (young fish) pececillo; (young frog) renacuajo. **2,** (swarm or brood of young) cría; cardumen de pececillos *o* renacuajos. **3,** (children collectively) chiquillería; enjambre de niños. **4,** (fried food) frito; fritada; fritura. —**frying pan,** sartén.
fuchsia ('fju·ʃə) *n.* fucsia.
fuddle ('fʌd·əl) *v.t.* **1,** (intoxicate) emborrachar. **2,** (confuse) confundir; aturdir.
fudge (fʌdʒ) *n.* **1,** (candy) melcocha. **2,** (nonsense) tontera; tontería; paja. —*v.t.* **1,** (botch) chapucear. **2,** (perform dishonestly) hacer con trampa. —*v.i.* (cheat) trampear.
fuel ('fju·əl) *n.* **1,** (combustible material) combustible. **2,** (means of increasing passion, etc.) pábulo; leña. —*v.t.* abastecer de combustible. —*v.i.* abastecerse de combustible.
-fuge (fjudʒ) *sufijo* -fugo; que aleja; que echa fuera: *centrifuge,* centrífugo; *vermifuge,* vermífugo.
fugitive ('fju·dʒə·tɪv) *adj.* **1,** (fleeing) fugitivo; prófugo. **2,** (evanescent; transitory) fugaz; efímero; fugitivo. —*n.* fugitivo; prófugo.
fugue (fju:g) *n., music* fuga.
-ful (fəl) *sufijo* **1,** -oso; *forma adjetivos expresando* lleno de; característico de; tendente a: *beautiful,* hermoso; *careful,* cuidadoso; *harmful,* peligroso. **2,** -ada; *forma nombres denotando* contenido: *spoonful,* cucharada.
fulcrum ('fʌl·krəm) *n.* [*pl. también* **fulcra** (-krə)] fulcro; punto de apoyo.
fulfill *también,* **fulfil** (fʊl'fɪl) *v.t.* **1,** (carry out; complete) cumplir; llevar a cabo; consumar. **2,** (perform, as a duty) cumplir; desempeñar. **3,** (satisfy, as a desire) colmar; satisfacer. —**fulfillment** [*también,* **fulfilment**] *n.* cumplimiento; realización; consumación.
fulgent ('fʌl·dʒənt) *adj.* fulgente; resplandeciente.
full (fʊl) *adj.* **1,** (filled to capacity; filled or rounded out; rich; abounding; sated) lleno. **2,** (complete; entire) completo; entero; cabal. **3,** (with loose, wide folds; ample) lleno; amplio; de mucho vuelo. **4,** (having reached full development, size, intensity, etc.) pleno; máximo; todo. **5,** (entirely visible) pleno; completo. **6,** (sonorous) lleno; sonoro. **7,** (filled, as with emotions, thoughts, ideas) lleno; pleno; colmado. —*adv.* **1,** (entirely) enteramente; del todo. **2,** (directly) de pleno; de lleno. **3,** (very) muy. —*n.* tope; plenitud. —*v.t.* abatanar; enfurtir. —**at the full,** pleno; lleno; en (su) plenitud. —**full dress,** vestido *o* traje de etiqueta. —**full house,** *poker* fulján. —**full stop, 1,** (of a vehicle) parada; alto. **2,** *gram.* punto aparte; *Amer.* punto acápite. —**in full,** por completo; por entero; en (su) totalidad; sin abreviar. —**to the full,** completamente; enteramente; de pleno.
fullblast *adj. & adv.* a todo vapor; embalado; con toda fuerza; a todo volumen.
fullblooded *adj.* **1,** (of unmixed ancestry) de pura raza. **2,** (virile) vigoroso; robusto.

fullblown *adj.* **1,** (in full bloom) en (plena) flor. **2,** (fully developed) cabal; pleno.
fullbodied *adj.* de (mucho) cuerpo; que tiene cuerpo; rico.
fuller ('fʊl·ər) *n.* **1,** (one who treats cloth) batanero. **2,** (hammer) mazo de batán. —**fuller's earth,** tierra de batán; greda.
fullfledged ('fʊl,flɛdʒd) *adj.* acabado; cabal; completo; hecho y derecho.
fullgrown *adj.* maduro; completamente desarrollado.
fullness ('fʊl·nəs) *n.* **1,** (state of being full) plenitud. **2,** (satiety) hartura; llenura. **3,** (completeness; entirety) integridad; totalidad.
fully ('fʊl·i) *adv.* **1,** (completely) completamente; enteramente. **2,** (copiously) llenamente; abundantemente.
fulminate ('fʌl·mɪ,neit) *v.t.* & *i.* **1,** (detonate) detonar. **2,** (denounce; thunder forth) fulminar. —*n.* fulminante. —**fulmination,** *n.* fulminación.
fulsome ('fʊl·səm) *adj.* burdo; torpe; grosero. —**fulsomeness,** *n.* torpeza; grosería.
fumble ('fʌm·bəl) *v.t.* & *i.* **1,** (grope clumsily) tentar *o* tantear a ciegas; buscar a tientas. **2,** (bungle) chapucear. **3,** *sports* perder (la pelota). —*n.* **1,** (bungle) chapuz. **2,** *sports* pérdida (*de la pelota*). —**fumbling** (-blɪŋ) *adj.* chapucero. —*n.* tanteo; tentativa.
fume (fjum) *n., usu.pl.* humo; gas; vapor; vaho. —*v.i.* **1,** (emit fumes) humear; exhalar vahos o vapores. **2,** (be vexed; fret) echar humo; encolerizarse; enojarse. —*v.t.* ahumar; sahumar; fumigar. —**fumed,** *adj.* ahumado.
fumigate ('fju·mɪ,geit) *v.t.* fumigar; sahumar. —**fumigation,** *n.* fumigación. —**fumigator,** *n.* fumigador.
fun (fʌn) *n.* diversión. —**in fun,** en *o* de broma; por *o* como chiste. —**make fun of; poke fun at,** burlarse de; mofarse de.
function ('fʌŋk·ʃən) *n.* función. —*v.i.* funcionar. —**functional,** *adj.* funcional. —**functioning,** *n.* funcionamiento.
functionary ('fʌŋk·ʃə,nɛr·i) *n.* funcionario.
fund (fʌnd) *n.* **1,** (stock or supply, esp. of money) fondo; caudal. **2,** (store of anything, as of knowledge) acopio; reserva. —*v.t.* consolidar (una deuda).
fundamental (,fʌn·də'mɛn·təl) *adj.* fundamental. —*n.* fundamento.
funeral ('fju·nə·rəl) *n.* funeral; funerales; exequias. —*adj.* funerario; fúnebre. —**funeral director,** funerario. —**funeral parlor,** funeraria.
funereal (fju'nɪr·i·əl) *adj.* fúnebre; funeral.
fungicide ('fʌn·dʒɪ,said) *n.* fungicida. —**fungicidal,** *adj.* fungicida.
fungous ('fʌŋ·gəs) *adj.* fungoso.
fungus ('fʌŋ·gəs) *n.* [*pl.* **fungi** ('fʌn·dʒai)] fungo; hongo.
funicular (fju'nɪk·ju·lər) *adj.* & *n.* funicular.
funk (fʌŋk) *n., colloq.* **1,** (fear) temor; miedo; pánico. **2,** (coward) miedoso; cobarde. —*v.i., colloq.* [*también,* **funk it**] acobardarse; amilanarse. —*v.t., colloq.* sacar el cuerpo a; hacer el quite a.
funnel (fʌn·əl) *n.* **1,** (device for pouring) embudo. **2,** (smokestack) chimenea. **3,** (shaft for ventilation) tubo *o* caño de ventilación. —*v.t.* enfocar; concentrar; hacer converger. —*v.i.* enfocarse; concentrarse; converger.
funny ('fʌn·i) *adj.* **1,** (amusing) cómico; divertido; gracioso. **2,** *colloq.* (odd) extraño; raro; curioso. —*n., usu.pl., colloq.* (comic strips) historietas; dibujos. —**funniness,** *n.* comicidad; gracia.
funnybone *n.* **1,** (nerve in the elbow) nervio ulnar. **2,** (sense of humor) sentido del humor.
fur (fʌɹ) *n.* **1,** (animal hide) piel; pelaje. **2,** (coating on the tongue) saburra; sarro. —**fur shop,** peletería.
furbelow ('fʌɹ·bə·lo) *n.* **1,** (ruffle) fleco; orla. **2,** (fancy detail) ringorrango; *Amer.* firulete.
furbish ('fʌɹ·bɪʃ) *v.t.* acicalar; pulir.
furious ('fjʊr·i·əs) *adj.* furioso; violento. —**furiousness,** *n.* furia; violencia.
furl (fʌɹl) *v.t.* plegar; recoger (una bandera o vela).
furlong ('fʌɹ·lɔŋ) *n.* medida de longitud de 220 yardas *o* 1/8 de milla.
furlough ('fʌɹ·lo) *n.* licencia.
furnace ('fʌɹ·nɪs) *n.* horno.

furnish ('fʌɹ·nɪʃ) *v.t.* **1,** (supply; provide; give) surtir; suministrar; proporcionar. **2,** (equip) equipar. **3,** (put furniture into) amueblar; amoblar.
furnishings ('fʌɹ·nɪʃ·ɪŋz) *n.pl.* **1,** (furniture) moblaje (*sing.*); mobiliario (*sing.*). **2,** (equipment) avíos; enseres. **3,** (accessories) accesorios. **4,** (house furnishings) ajuar doméstico; enseres domésticos.
furniture ('fʌɹ·nɪ·tʃər) *n.* muebles (*pl.*); mobiliario.
furor ('fjʊr·or) *n.* furor.
furred (fʌɹd) *adj.* **1,** (made, trimmed, or lined with fur) de piel. **2,** (having fur) que tiene piel o pelaje; peludo. **3,** (coated, as the tongue) sucio; saburroso; sarroso.
furrier ('fʌɹ·i·ər) *n.* peletero. —**furriery,** *n.* peletería.
furring ('fʌɹ·ɪŋ) *n.* **1,** (fur for a garment) piel; pieles (*pl.*) **2,** (in building) enlistonado.
furrow ('fʌɹ·o) *n.* surco. —*v.t.* surcar.
furry ('fʌɹ·i) *adj.* peludo; velludo; velloso. —**furriness,** *n.* vellosidad.
further ('fʌɹ·ðər) *adj.* **1,** (more remote or extended) más lejano; más distante. **2,** (additional) adicional; otro; mayor; más. —*adv.* **1,** (to a greater distance or extent) más lejos; más allá; más adelante. **2,** (also) además; aún; por añadidura. —*v.t.* promover; adelantar; ayudar. —**furtherance,** *n.* adelantamiento; promoción; medra.
furthermore *adv.* además.
furthermost *adj.* más lejano.
furthest (fʌɹ·ðɪst) *adj.* más lejano; más distante. —*adv.* más lejos; más allá.
furtive ('fʌɹ·tɪv) *adj.* furtivo. —**furtiveness,** *n.* sigilo; secreto.
furuncle ('fjʌɹ·ʌŋ·kəl) *n.* furúnculo.
fury ('fjʊ·ri) *n.* furia.
furze (fʌɹz) *n.* tojo; aulaga.
fuse (fju:z) *n.* **1,** (powder wick) mecha. **2,** (detonating device) espoleta. **3,** *electricity* fusible; cortacircuitos. —*v.t.* fundir. —*v.i.* fundirse.
fuselage ('fju·sə·lɪdʒ) *n.* fuselaje.
fusible ('fju·zɪ·bəl) *adj.* fusible; fundible. —**fusibility,** *n.* fusibilidad.
fusilier (fju·zə'lɪr) *n.* fusilero.
fusillade (ˌfju·zə'leid) *n.* descarga de fusilería.
fusion ('fju·ʒən) *n.* fusión.
fuss (fʌs) *n.* **1,** (bustle; ado) aspavientos (*pl.*); bulla; alharacas (*pl.*). **2,** *colloq.* (petty quarrel) riña; reyerta; pleito. —*v.i.* agitarse; hacer aspavientos *o* alharacas. —*v.t.* turbar; fastidiar.
fussy ('fʌs·i) *adj.* **1,** (fretful; peevish) quisquilloso. **2,** (bustling) aspaventero; alharaquiento. **3,** (fastidious) prolijo; nimio; difícil de complacer. **4,** (bothersome) fastidioso; molesto.
fustian ('fʌs·tʃən) *n.* **1,** (coarse cotton fabric) fustán. **2,** (highflown language) altisonancia; grandilocuencia.
fusty ('fʌs·ti) *adj.* **1,** (musty; stuffy) rancio. **2,** (oldfashioned) anticuado; del tiempo de Maricastaña. —**fustiness,** *n.* ranciedad.
futile ('fju·təl) *adj.* fútil. —**futility** (fju'tɪl·ə·ti) *n.* futilidad.
future ('fju·tʃər) *adj.* futuro. —*n.* futuro; porvenir.
futurism ('fju·tʃər·ɪz·əm) *n.* futurismo. —**futuristic,** *adj.* futurista.
futurity (fju'tjʊr·ə·ti) *n.* futuro; porvenir.
fuzz (fʌz) *n.* pelusa; pelusilla; vello. —**fuzzy,** *adj.* velloso; cubierto de pelusa. —**fuzziness,** *n.* vellosidad.
-fy (fai) *sufijo* -ficar; hacer; hacerse: *purify,* purificar; *intensify,* intensificar; intensificarse.

G

G, g (dʒi) séptima letra del alfabeto inglés. —*n., music* sol.
gab (gæb) *n., colloq.* parloteo; locuacidad. —*v.i., colloq.* [**gabbed, gabbing**] parlotear. —**gabby,** *adj., colloq.* parlanchín. —**gift of gab,** labia; elocuencia.
gabardine ('gæb·ərˌdin) *n.* gabardina. —*adj.* de gabardina.
gabble ('gæb·əl) *n.* parloteo; co-

torrreo; cháchara. —*v.i.* parlotear; cotorrear.

gable ('gei·bəl) *n.* gablete; faldón. —**gable roof**, tejado a dos aguas.

gad (gæd) *n.* aguijón; aguijada; rejo. —*v.i.* [**gadded, gadding**] vagar; callejear. —*interj., slang* ¡Dios! —**gadder** [*también,* **gadabout**] *n.* callejero; vagabundo.

gadfly *n.* tábano; moscardón.

gadget ('gædʒ·ɪt) *n.* artefacto.

gadolinium (ˌgæd·ə'lɪn·i·əm) *n.* gadolinio.

Gaelic ('gei·lɪk) *adj.* & *n.* gaélico.

gaff (gæf) *n.* **1,** (hook) garfio. **2,** *naut.* (spar) cangrejo; botavara; pico. **3,** *slang* (nuisance) vaina; *Amer.* friega. —**stand the gaff,** *slang* ser de aguante.

gag (gæg) *n.* **1,** (silencer) mordaza. **2,** *slang* (joke) broma; burla; chiste. —*v.t.* [**gagged, gagging**] **1,** (silence) amordazar; silenciar. **2,** (cause to retch) atragantar. —*v.i.* atragantarse.

gaiety *también,* **gayety** ('gei·ə·ti) *n.* alegría; alborozo; júbilo.

gaily *también,* **gayly** ('gei·li) *adv.* **1,** (merrily) alegremente. **2,** (showily) vistosamente.

gain (gein) *n.* **1,** (profit) ganancia. **2,** (improvement); adelanto; mejora. **3,** (benefit) beneficio; provecho; utilidad. **4,** (increase) aumento; acrecentamiento. —*v.t.* **1,** (get; obtain) ganar; obtener. **2,** (win; earn) ganar. **3,** (reach; achieve) ganar; alcanzar. **4,** (acquire as an increase or addition) aumentar (en). —*v.i.* **1,** (benefit) aprovechar; ganar. **2,** (progress; improve) adelantar; mejorar. **3,** (put on weight) aumentar de peso. **4,** (run fast, as a watch) adelantarse. —**gain on** *o* **upon,** ir alcanzando a; ganar terreno; acercarse a.

gainful ('gein·fəl) *adj.* remunerativo; útil; provechoso.

gainsay ('gein'sei) *v.t.* [*pret.* & *p.p.* **ganisaid**] contradecir; negar; desmentir.

gait (geit) *n.* paso; andar; modo de andar.

gaiter ('gei·tər) *n.* polaina corta.

gala ('gei·lə; 'gæl·ə) *n.* fiesta; gala. —*adj.* festivo; de gala; de fiesta.

galaxy ('gæl·ək·si) *n.* galaxia. —**galactic** (gə'læk·tɪk) *adj.* galáctico.

gale (geil) *n.* **1,** (strong wind) ventarrón. **2,** (outburst, as of laughter) explosión.

galena (ga'li·nə) *n.* galena.

gall (gɔːl) *n.* **1,** (liver secretion) bilis; hiel. **2,** (something bitter or distasteful) hiel. **3,** (rancor; bitter feeling) rencor; inquina. **4,** (sore, as on a horse) matadura. **5,** *bot.* agalla. **6,** *colloq.* (impudence) desfachatez; descaro; agallas (*pl.*). —*v.t.* & *i.* **1,** (chafe) irritar; desollar. **2,** (annoy; vex) irritar; molestar; *Amer.* fregar. —**gall bladder,** vesícula biliar.

gallant ('gæl·ənt) *adj.* **1,** (brave; daring) gallardo; bizarro. **2,** (courtly) galante; galán. **3,** (stately; impressive) impresionante; fastuoso. —*n.* (gə'laːnt) galán.

gallantry ('gæl·ən·tri) *n.* **1,** (bravery) gallardía; bizarría. **2,** (courtly act or manner) galantería; galanteo.

galleon ('gæl·i·ən) *n.* galeón.

gallery ('gæl·ə·ri) *n.* galería.

galley ('gæl·i) *n.* **1,** (ship) galera. **2,** (ship's kitchen) cocina de un barco. **3,** *print.* galera. —**galley slave,** galeote.

Gallic ('gæl·ɪk) *adj.* galo.

Gallicism ('gæl·ə·sɪz·əm) *n.* galicismo. —**Gallicize,** *v.t.* afrancesar.

gallium ('gæl·i·əm) *n.* galio.

gallivant ('gæl·ɪˌvænt) *v.i.* callejear; vagar.

gallnut ('gɔlˌnʌt) *n.* agalla; bugalla.

Gallo- ('gæl·o) *prefijo* galo-; francés; galo: *Gallophile,* galófilo; francófilo.

gallon ('gæl·ən) *n.* medida para líquidos equivalente a 4.5 litros; galón.

gallop ('gæl·əp) *n.* galope. —*v.i.* galopar.

gallows ('gæl·oz) *n.* horca; patíbulo.

gallstone *n.* cálculo biliar.

galore (gə'loːr) *adv.* en abundancia; por montones.

galosh (gə'laʃ) *n.* chanclo; galocha.

galvanic (gæl'væn·ɪk) *adj.* **1,** *electricity* galvánico. **2,** *fig.* (startling) electrizante.

galvanism ('gæl·və·nɪz·əm) *n.* galvanismo.

galvanize ('gæl·vəˌnaiz) *v.t.* galvanizar. —**galvanization** (-nɪ'zei·ʃən) *n.* galvanización.

galvano- (gæl·və·no) *prefijo*

galvano-; electricidad: *galvanometer*, galvanómetro.
galvanometer (ˌgæl·vəˈnam·ə·tər) *n.* galvanómetro.
gambit (ˈgæm·bɪt) *n.* gambito.
gamble (ˈgæm·bəl) *v.i.* **1,** (play games of chance) jugar. **2,** (take a risk) arriesgarse. —*v.t.* **1,** (bet; wager) apostar; jugar. **2,** [*también,* **gamble away**] (lose in gambling) perder; jugarse. —*n.* albur; riesgo. —**gambler** (-blər) *n.* jugador. —**gambling** (-blɪŋ) *n.* juego. —**gambling den,** casa de juego; garito.
gambol (ˈgæm·bəl) *n.* retozo; cabriola. —*v.i.* retozar; dar cabriolas.
game (geim) *n.* **1,** (play; sport) juego. **2,** (contest) partido. **3,** (trick; scheme) jugada. **4,** (in hunting) caza. —*adj.* **1,** (of animals) de caza. **2,** (plucky; willing) animoso; resuelto. **3,** (lame) cojo. —**gameness,** *n.* ánimo; resolución. —**game bag,** morral. —**make game of,** reírse de; burlarse de. —**play the game,** seguir el juego.
gamecock *n.* gallo de pelea.
gamin (ˈgæm·ɪn) *n.* pilluelo; golfillo.
gaming (ˈgei·miŋ) *n.* juego.
gamma (ˈgæm·ə) *n.* gamma. —**gamma rays,** rayos gamma.
gammon (ˈgæm·ən) *n.* **1,** (smoked ham) jamón ahumado; pernil. **2,** (trickery) engaño; añagaza.
gamo- (gæm·o) *prefijo, biol.* gamo-; unión: *gamopetalous,* gamopétalo.
-gamous (gæm·əs) *sufijo* -gamo; *forma adjetivos denotando* unión; matrimonio: *monogamous,* monógamo.
gamut (ˈgæm·ət) *n.* gama.
-gamy (gə·mi) *sufijo* -gamia; *forma nombres denotando* matrimonio: unión: *monogamy,* monogamia.
gander (ˈgæn·dər) *n.* ganso.
gang (gæŋ) *n.* cuadrilla; pandilla. —*v.i.* **1,** (band together) unirse; organizarse. **2,** (pile up) amontonarse. —**gang up on,** unrise *o* organizarse contra.
gangling (ˈgæŋ·glɪŋ) *adj.* desgarbado.
ganglion (ˈgæŋ·gli·ən) *n.* ganglio.
gangplank *n.* pasarela; plancha.
gangrene (ˈgæŋ·grin) *n.* gangrena. —**gangrenous** (-grə·nəs) *adj.* gangrenoso.
gangster (ˈgæŋ·stər) *n.* pistolero; gangster.
gangue (gæŋ) *n.* ganga.
gangway *n.* **1,** (passageway) paso; pasadizo. **2,** *naut.* pasarela; portalón. —*interj.* ¡a un lado!; ¡abran paso!; ¡paso!
gannet (ˈgæn·ɪt) *n.* bubia.
gantlet (ˈgɔnt·lət; ˈgænt-) *n.* (punishment) baqueta. *También,* **gauntlet.** —**run the gantlet,** correr la baqueta.
gantry (ˈgæn·tri) *n.* **1,** (framework) armazón. **2,** (movable bridge of a crane) puente corredizo de grúa. *También,* **gauntry** (ˈgɔn·tri).
gaol (dʒeil) *n.* = **jail.**
gap (gæp) *n.* **1,** (opening; breach) brecha; boquete; hendidura. **2,** (interruption of continuity) hueco; vacío; laguna. **3,** (difference) diferencia; discrepancia; laguna. **4,** (distance that separates) distancia; luz.
gape (geip) *v.i.* **1,** (yawn; open the mouth) bostezar; abrir la boca. **2,** (open wide) abrirse. **3,** (stare openmouthed) quedarse boquiabierto; embobarse. —*n.* **1,** (yawn) bostezo. **2,** (openmouthed stare) boca abierta. **3,** (breach; gap) brecha; hendidura.
gar (gaːr) *n.* pez aguja. *También,* **garfish.**
garage (gəˈraːʒ) *n.* garaje. —*v.t.* meter en garaje.
garb (garb) *n.* **1,** (clothing) vestido; indumentaria. **2,** *fig* (guise) aspecto; apariencia. —*v.t.* vestir; ataviar.
garbage (ˈgar·bɪdʒ) *n.* basura.
garble (ˈgar·bəl) *v.t.* **1,** (jumble) hacer confuso; hacer un revoltijo de. **2,** (distort; misrepresent) torcer; tergiversar. —*n.* confusión; revoltijo.
garden (ˈgar·dən) *n.* jardín. —*v.i.* cuidar un jardín. —**gardener,** *n.* jardinero. —**gardening,** *n.* jardinería.
gardenia (garˈdi·njə) *n.* gardenia.
garfish *n.* = **gar.**
Gargantuan (garˈgænt·ju·ən) *adj.* enorme; gigantesco.
gargle (ˈgar·gəl) *n.* gárgara; gargarismo. —*v.i.* gargarizar; hacer gárgaras.

gargoyle ('gar·gɔil) *n.* gárgola.
garish ('gɛr·ɪʃ) *adj.* llamativo; chillón. —**garishness,** *n.* lo llamativo; lo chillón.
garland ('gar·lənd) *n.* guirnalda. —*v.t.* enguirnaldar; adornar con guirnaldas.
garlic ('gar·lɪk) *n.* ajo. —**garlicky,** *adj.* de *o* con ajo.
garment ('gar·mənt) *n.* vestido; traje. —**garments,** *n.pl.* ropa (*sing.*).
garner ('gar·nər) *v.t.* **1,** (gather; reap) cosechar; recoger. **2,** (store) almacenar. —*n.* **1,** (granary) granero. **2,** (storage place) depósito; almacén.
garnet ('gar·nɪt) *n.* granate.
garnish ('gar·nɪʃ) *n.* adorno; aderezo. —*v.t.* **1,** (adorn) adornar; aderezar. **2,** *law* = **garnishee.** —**garnishment,** *n., law* embargo.
garnishee (ˌgar·nɪ'ʃiː) *v.t.* [**-sheed, -sheeing**] *law* embargar.
garret ('gær·ət) *n.* desván; buhardilla.
garrison ('gær·ə·sən) *n.* guarnición. —*v.t.* **1,** (provide with a garrison) guarnecer. **2,** (station, as troops) acuartelar.
garrote *también,* **garotte, garrotte** (gə'rot) *n.* garrote. —*v.t.* agarrotar.
garrulity (gə'ru·lə·ti) *n.* garrulidad; locuacidad. *También,* **garrulousness.**
garrulous ('gær·jə·ləs) *adj.* gárrulo; locuaz.
garter ('gar·tər) *n.* liga. —**Order of the Garter,** Orden de la Jarretera.
gas (gæs) *n.* **1,** (vapor) gas. **2,** *colloq.* (gasoline) gasolina. **3,** *slang* (idle talk) vaciedad. —*v.t.* [**gassed, gassing**] **1,** (supply with gas) suministrar gas a. **2,** (attack, poison or kill by gas) atacar, envenenar *o* matar con gases. —*v.i., slang* (talk idly) decir vaciedades. —**gas burner,** mechero *o* quemador de gas. —**gas chamber,** cámara de gas. —**gas mask,** careta antigás.
gaseous ('gæs·i·əs) *adj.* gaseoso.
gash (gæʃ) *n.* tajo. —*v.t.* dar un tajo *o* tajos a.
gasket ('gæs·kɪt) *n.* empaquetadura.
gasoline *también,* **gasolene** (ˌgæs·ə'lin) *n.* gasolina.
gasp (gæsp) *n.* **1,** (labored breath) jadeo; boqueada. **2,** (convulsive utterance) grito sofocado. —*v.t.* **1,** (breathe out) exhalar. **2,** (utter convulsively) decir jadeando. —*v.i.* jadear; dar boqueadas.
gastric ('gæs·trɪk) *adj.* gástrico.
gastritis (gæs'trai·tɪs) *n.* gastritis.
gastro- (gæs·tro) *prefijo* gastro-; estómago: *gastronome,* gastrónomo.
gastronomy (gæs'tran·ə·mi) *n.* gastronomía. —**gastronomic** (ˌgæs·trə'nam·ɪk) [*también,* **gastronomical**] *adj.* gastronómico. —**gastronome** ('gæs·trəˌnom) *n.* gastrónomo.
gate (geit) *n.* **1,** (opening; entrance) portón; puerta. **2,** (barrier) barrera. **3,** *slang* (gate receipts) entrada; taquilla. **4,** *slang* (dismissal) despedida. —**give the gate to,** *slang* largar; mandar a paseo.
gatehouse *n.* portería.
gatekeeper *n.* portero; *R.R.* guardabarreras.
gateway *n.* entrada; puerta.
gather ('gæð·ər) *v.t.* **1,** (pick; cull; pick up) recoger. **2,** (accumulate; amass) acumular; amasar. **3,** (assemble) juntar; reunir. **4,** (infer) deducir; inferir; colegir. **5,** (pleat; draw into folds) plegar; recoger. **6,** (prepare or collect, as oneself) aprestarse; aprontarse. **7,** (regain one's composure) reponerse; recobrarse. **8,** (gain, as speed) coger; cobrar; tomar (velocidad, vuelo, etc.). **9,** (wrinkle, as the brow) arrugar. —*v.i.* **1,** (assemble) reunirse; congregarse. **2,** (accumulate) acumularse; amontonarse. —*n.* pliegue.
gathering ('gæð·ər·ɪŋ) *n.* **1,** (meeting; assembly) reunión. **2,** (collection) recogida; recolección. **3,** (heap; crowd) amontonamiento; montón.
gauche (goʃ) *adj.* torpe; desmañado.
gaucho ('gau·tʃo) *n.* [*pl.* **–chos**] gaucho.
gaudy ('gɔ·di) *adj.* charro; llamativo. —**gaudiness,** *n.* charrada.
gauge (geidʒ) *n.* **1,** (measure) medida; tamaño; dimensión. **2,** (caliber) calibre. **3,** (thickness, as of wire) grosor; calibre. **4,** *R.R.* vía. **5,** (calibrator) calibrador. **6,** (indicator) indicador. —*v.t.* medir; calibrar; estimar; calcular.
Gaul (gɔːl) *n.* **1,** (country) Galia. **2,** (person) galo.

gaunt (gɔnt) *adj.* **1,** (thin; emaciated) flaco; demacrado. **2,** (desolate; grim) desolado; sombrío. —**gauntness,** *n.* flacura.

gauntlet ('gɔnt·lət) *n.* **1,** (glove) guantelete; manopla. **2,** *fig.* (challenge) reto. **3,** = **gantlet.** —**throw down the gauntlet,** retar. —**take up the gauntlet,** recoger el guante; aceptar el reto.

gauze (gɔːz) *n.* gasa; cendal.

gave (geiv) *v., pret. de* **give.**

gavel ('gæv·əl) *n.* mazo.

gavotte (gə'vat) *n.* gavota.

gawk (gɔk) *n.* ganso; bobo. —*v.i.* papar moscas; mirar como bobo. —**gawky,** *adj.* desmañado; desgarbado.

gay (gei) *adj.* alegre; jovial; festivo. —**gayety** (-ə·ti) *n.* = **gaiety.** —**gayly,** *adv.* = **gaily.** —**gayness,** jovialidad; viveza; alegría.

gaze (geiz) *v.i.* mirar. —*n.* mirada. —**gaze at** *o* **on,** mirar; contemplar.

gazelle (gə'zɛl) *n.* gacela.

gazette (gə'zɛt) *n.* gaceta. —*v.t.* publicar en la gaceta.

gazetteer (ˌgæz·ə'tɪr) *n.* diccionario *o* índice geográfico.

gear (gɪr) *n.* **1,** (apparel) atavío; indumentaria. **2,** (equipment; rigging) equipo; avíos (*pl.*); aparejo; aparejos (*pl.*). **3,** (harness) arneses (*pl.*); arreos (*pl.*). **4,** *mech.* (gear system) engranaje; sistema de engranaje; *auto.* embrague; cambio; cambio de velocidades. **5,** *mech.* (specific gear adjustment) velocidad; cambio. **6,** *mech.* (gearwheel) rueda dentada *o* de engranaje. **7,** *mech.* (mechanism) mecanismo; aparato; sistema. —*v.t.* **1,** (equip; fit out) equipar. **2,** (adapt) ajustar; adaptar; acomodar. **3,** *mech.* (furnish with gears) poner engranajes a. **4,** *mech.* (put into gear) hacer engranar; embragar. —*v.i.* engranar. —**high gear,** tercera *o* alta (velocidad). —**in high gear,** en tercera *o* alta (velocidad); *fig., colloq.* embalado; a toda máquina. —**in gear,** embragado. —**low gear,** primera (velocidad). —**in low gear,** en primera (velocidad); *fig., colloq.* lentamente; despacio. —**out of gear,** desembragado, desengranado; *fig., colloq.* desajustado; en desajuste. —**reverse gear,** marcha atrás. —**shift gears,** cambiar (de velocidad). —**throw into gear,** embragar; hacer engranar. —**throw out of gear,** desembragar; desengranar.

gearbox *n.* caja de cambios; caja de engranajes.

gearing ('gɪr·ɪŋ) *n.* engranaje.

gearshift *n.* embrague; cambio de velocidades. —**gearshift lever,** palanca de cambios.

gee (dʒiː) *v.t.* & *i.* [**geed, geeing**] volver a derecha. —*interj., colloq.* ¡cielos!; ¡Jesús! —**gee up!,** ¡arre!

geese (giːs) *n., pl. de* **goose.**

geisha ('gei·ʃə) *n.* geisha.

gelatine ('dʒɛl·ə·tɪn) *n.* gelatina. —**gelatinous** (dʒə'læt·ɪ·nəs) *adj.* gelatinoso.

geld (gɛld) *v.t.* castrar; capar. —**gelding,** *n.* caballo castrado.

gelid ('dʒɛl·ɪd) *adj.* gélido; helado. —**gelidity** (dʒə'lɪd·ə·ti); **gelidness,** *n.* frialdad.

gem (dʒɛm) *n.* gema; joya. —*v.t.* enjoyar; engastar de joyas.

geminate ('dʒɛm·ə·nət) *adj.* & *n.* geminado. —*v.t.* (-ˌneit) geminar. —*v.i.* geminarse. —**gemination,** *n.* geminación.

Gemini ('dʒɛm·əˌnai) *n.* Géminis.

-gen (dʒɪn) *sufijo* -geno; *forma nombres indicando* **1,** *quím.* engendrador; generador: *hydrogen,* hidrógeno. **2,** *biol.* lo engendrado o generado: *exogen,* exógeno.

gendarme ('ʒan·darm) *n.* gendarme.

gender ('dʒɛn·dər) *n.* género.

gene (dʒiːn) *n.* gen; gene.

gene- (dʒɪn) *prefijo* gene-; generación; descendencia: *genealogy,* genealogía.

genealogy (ˌdʒi·ni'æl·ə·dʒi) *n.* genealogía. —**genealogical** (-ə·'ladʒ·ɪ·kəl) *adj.* genealógico. —**genealogist,** *n.* genealogista.

genera ('dʒɛn·ə·rə) *n., pl. de* **genus.**

general ('dʒɛn·ər·əl) *adj.* & *n.* general. —**in general,** en general; por lo general. —**general staff,** estado major. —**general store,** tienda de comestibles y ultramarinos; *Amer.* tienda de abarrotes; *Amer.* pulpería; *Amer.* almacén.

generality (ˌdʒɛn·ər'æl·ə·ti) *n.* generalidad.

generalize ('dʒɛn·ər·əˌlaiz) *v.i.* generalizar. —**generalization** (-lɪ·'zei·ʃən) *n.* generalización.

generalship ('dʒɛn·ər·əlˌʃɪp) *n.* **1,** (rank) generalato. **2,** (leader-

ship) capacidad directiva; dotes de general. 3, (tactics) táctica.
generate ('dʒɛn·ə,reit) *v.t.* generar; engendrar. —**generative,** *adj.* generativo.
generation (,dʒɛn·ə'rei·ʃən) *n.* generación.
generator ('dʒɛn·ə,rei·tər) *n.* generador.
generic (dʒɪ'nɛr·ɪk) *adj.* genérico.
generous ('dʒɛn·ər·əs) *adj.* generoso. —**generosity** (-ə'ras·ə·ti) *n.* generosidad.
genesis ('dʒɛn·ə·sɪs) *n.* [*pl.* -ses (-siz)] génesis.
genetic (dʒɪ'nɛt·ɪk) *adj.* 1, (of genetics or reproduction) genésico. 2, (of genesis or origin) genético.
genetics (dʒɪ'nɛt·ɪks) *n.* genética.
genial ('dʒin·jəl) *adj.* 1, (amiable) afable; cordial. 2, (mild, as a climate) suave; agradable.
-genic (dʒɛn·ɪk) *sufijo* -génico; *forma adjetivos que corresponden a los nombres terminados en* **-gen** *o* **-geny**: *photogenic,* fotogénico.
genie (dʒi·ni) *n.* genio.
genital ('dʒɛn·ə·təl) *adj.* genital. —**genitals,** *n.pl.* genitales.
genitive ('dʒɛn·ə·tɪv) *n.* & *adj.* genitivo.
genito- ('dʒɛn·ə·to) *prefijo* genito-; perteneciente a los genitales: *genito-urinary,* genitourinario.
genius ('dʒin·jəs) *n.* genio.
genocide ('dʒɛn·ə·said) *n.* genocidio. —**genocidal,** *adj.* genocida.
-genous (dʒɪ·nəs) *sufijo* -geno; -gena; *forma adjetivos denotando* engendrado; generado: *nitrogenous,* nitrógeno; nitrogenado; *indigenous,* indígena.
genre ('ʒan·rə) *n.* género; clase.
genteel (dʒɛn'til) *adj.* 1, (wellbred; refined) gentil. 2, (elegant; fashionable) elegante; distinguido. 3, (affected) afectado; cursi.
gentian ('dʒɛn·ʃən) *n.* genciana.
gentile ('dʒɛn·tail) *adj.* & *n.* 1, (pagan) gentil. 2, (non-Jewish) no judío; cristiano. 3, *gram.* gentilicio.
gentility (dʒɛn'tɪl·ə·ti) *n.* 1, (nobility) nobleza. 2, (gentleness) gentileza.
gentle ('dʒɛn·təl) *adj.* 1, wellborn) noble. 2, (wellbred; refined) gentil; fino; delicado. 3, (light) leve; ligero; liviano. 4, (kind; generous) gentil; amable. 5, (tame) manso; dócil. 6, (mild; soft) apacible; suave.
gentleman ('dʒɛn·təl·mən) *n.* [*pl.* **-men**] caballero; señor. —**gentlemanly,** *adj.* caballeroso. —**gentlewoman,** *n.* dama; señora.
gentleness ('dʒɛn·təl·nəs) *n.* 1, (lightness; mildness) suavidad; delicadeza. 2, (kindness) gentileza. 3, (tameness) docilidad; mansedumbre.
gentry ('dʒɛn·tri) *n.* clase acomodada; alta burguesía.
genuflect ('dʒɛn·ju,flɛkt) *v.i.* hacer genuflexión. —**genuflection; genuflexion** (-'flɛk·ʃən) *n.* genuflexión.
genuine ('dʒɛn·ju·ɪn) adj. genuino.
genuineness ('dʒɛn·ju·ɪn·nəs) *n.* 1, (authenticity) legitimidad; autenticidad. 2, (sincerity) sinceridad; pureza.
genus ('dʒi·nəs) *n.* [*pl.* **genera**] género.
-geny (dʒɪ·ni) *sufijo* -genia; *forma nombres indicando* origen: *ontogeny,* ontogenia.
geo- (dʒi·o) *prefijo* geo-; tierra: *geocentric,* geocéntrico.
geocentric (,dʒi·o'sɛn·trɪk) *adj.* geocéntrico.
geodesy (dʒi'ad·ə·si) *n.* geodesia. —**geodetic** (,dʒi·ə'dɛt·ɪk) *adj.* geodésico.
geography (dʒi'ag·rə·fi) *n.* geografía. —**geographer,** geógrafo. —**geographic** (,dʒi·ə'græf·ɪk); **geographical,** *adj.* geográfico.
geology (dʒi'al·ə·dʒi) *n.* geología. —**geological** (,dʒi·ə'ladʒ·ɪ·kəl) *adj.* geológico. —**geologist,** *n.* geólogo.
geometry (dʒi'am·ə·tri) *n.* geometría. —**geometric** (,dʒi·ə'mɛt·rɪk); **geometrical,** *adj.* geométrico. —**geometrician** (,dʒi·ə·mə'trɪʃ·ən) *n.* geómetra.
geopolitics (,dʒi·o'pal·ə·tɪks) *n.pl.* geopolítica (*sing.*).
geranium (dʒə'rei·ni·əm) *n.* geranio.
geriatrics (,dʒɛr·i'æt·rɪks) *n.* geriatría. —**geriatric,** *adj.* geriátrico.
germ (dʒʌɹm) *n.* germen.
German ('dʒʌɹ·mən) *n.* & *adj.* alemán; germano. —**Germanic** (dʒər'mæn·ɪk) *adj.* germánico. —**German measles,** viruelas locas; rubéola.

germane (dʒər'mein) *adj.* relacionado; afín.
germanium (dʒər'mei·ni·əm) *n.* germanio.
germicide ('dʒʌɹ·mɪ·said) *n.* germicida. —**germicidal,** *adj.* germicida.
germinal ('dʒʌɹ·mə·nəl) *adj.* germinal.
germinate ('dʒʌɹ·mə,neit) *v.i.* germinar. —**germination,** *n.* germinación.
gerund ('dʒɛr·ənd) *n.* gerundio.
gestation (dʒɛs'tei·ʃən) *n.* gestación.
gesticulate (dʒɛs'tɪk·jə,leit) *v.i.* gesticular. —**gesticulation,** *n.* gesticulación.
gesture ('dʒɛs·tʃər) *n.* gesto; ademán. —*v.i.* gesticular; hacer gestos. —*v.t.* indicar por *o* con gestos.
get (gɛt) *v.t.* [**got** *o* **gotten, getting**] **1,** (receive) recibir. **2,** (obtain; acquire) conseguir; lograr; obtener. **3,** (gain; earn) ganar. **4,** (reach; contact) comunicarse con; ponerse en contacto con. **5,** *radio; TV* (tune in) sintonizar; captar. **6,** (fetch; bring) traer. **7,** (catch; seize; take hold of) agarrar; coger. **8,** (learn; commit to memory) aprender. **9,** (obtain as a result) tener; obtener (como resultado): *When you add one and one you get two,* Cuando sumas uno y uno, tienes dos. **10,** (cause to do or be done; bring about) hacer (que); conseguir (que); lograr (que); componérselas (para que): *Can you get the door to close?,* ¿Puedes hacer que la puerta se cierre? **11,** (cause to be or become) poner; volver: *The smoke gets your face dirty,* El humo te pone sucia la cara. **12,** (carry; take; convey) llevar: *Get him to the doctor,* Llévelo al médico. **13,** (cause to go; send) enviar; mandar: *I will get the bill to you tomorrow,* Le enviaré la cuenta mañana. **14,** (cause to be carried or conveyed; cause to arrive) hacer llegar; hacer que llegue: *Get this letter to the manager,* Haz llegar esta carta a manos del gerente. **15,** (prepare) preparar: *Will you get dinner for us?,* ¿Puedes prepararnos la comida? **16,** *archaic* = **beget. 17,** *colloq.* (overpower; get control of) dominar; esclavizar; hacer un esclavo de: *Liquor will get him,* El trago hará de él un esclavo. **18,** *colloq.* (puzzle; baffle) confundir; dejar confuso. **19,** *colloq.* (kill; destroy; finish off) acabar con; aniquilar; matar. **20,** *slang* (perceive) captar; coger: *Did you get his expression?* ¿Captaste su expresión? **21,** *colloq.* (irritate) irritar; molestar; *Amer.* fregar. **22,** *colloq.* (strike; hit) dar; pegar: *He got him in the nose,* Le dio (*o* pegó) en la nariz. **23,** *colloq.* (understand; comprehend) comprender; entender. —*v.i.* **1,** (come; arrive) llegar: *When will we get to Lima?* ¿Cuándo llegaremos a Lima? **2,** (be; become; come to be) ponerse; volverse: *He got angry,* Se puso furioso; se enfureció. *Los modismos consistiendo de* get *y un adjetivo se expresan muchas veces en español por un verbo intransitivo o reflexivo: get married,* casarse; *get sick,* enfermarse; *get old,* envejecer. **3,** *en la voz pasiva* (be; become) *I got caught in the rain,* Me cogió la lluvia; *My suit got wet,* Se me mojó el traje. **4,** (begin, as to acquire skills, knowledge, attitudes, habits, etc.) empezar a; comenzar a; llegar a: *He is getting to dance well,* Empieza a bailar bien; *He has got to be a big chatterbox,* Ha llegado a ser un gran parlanchín. **5,** (manage; contrive) lograr; conseguir; arreglárselas para: *Could I get to see the president?,* ¿Podría arreglármelas para ver al presidente? —*n.* prole; cría. —**get about, 1,** (move from place to place) andar; moverse; andar por aquí y por allá. **2,** (circulate; spread) circular; difundirse. —**get across, 1,** (cross; reach the opposite side) cruzar; atravesar; pasar. **2,** *colloq.* (transmit; impart) hacer comprender *o* entender. **3,** *colloq.* (be clear; be understood) comprenderse; entenderse; estar claro. **4,** *colloq.* (succeed; gain acceptance) tener aceptación; tener éxito. —**get ahead,** tener éxito; progresar. —**get ahead of,** adelantarse a. —**get along, 1,** (proceed; move on) seguir adelante. **2,** (fare; progress) seguir; irle a uno. **3,** (manage) arreglárselas; componérselas; manejárselas. **4,** (agree) llevarse; entenderse. **5,** (grow older) envejecer; entrar en

años. —**get around**, **1**, (move about) andar; moverse; andar por aquí y por allá. **2**, (circumvent; avoid) eludir; hacer el quite a; evitar. **3**, (influence; cajole) engatusar; manejar. —**get around to**, **1**, (reach) llegar a. **2**, (be ready for) estar listo para. **3**, (attend to) ocuparse de; atender. —**get at**, **1**, (reach; approach) alcanzar. **2**, (find out; ascertain) averiguar; llegar a conocer. **3**, *colloq.* (imply; hint) pretender; implicar. **4**, (apply oneself to; attend to) aplicarse a; ocuparse de. **5**, *colloq.* (influence, as by bribery or intimidation) sobornar; intimidar. —**get away**, **1**, (leave; start) salir; partir. **2**, (escape) escaparse. **3**, (slip out) zafarse. —**get away with**, *slang* salirse con (la suya); zafarse de; escaparse de. —**get back**, **1**, (return) volver; regresar. **2**, (move back) retroceder; echarse atrás. **3**, (recover) recobrar. **4**, *slang*. [*usu.* **get at**] (get revenge) vengarse (de); desquitarse (con). —**get behind**, **1**, (give support to) apoyar; prestar apoyo a; ayudar. **2**, = **fall behind**. —**get by**, **1**, (pass) pasar. **2**, *colloq.* (escape notice; sneak past) colarse; pasarse; pasar desapercibido. **3**, *colloq.* (survive; manage) arreglárselas; manejárselas; componérselas. —**get down**, bajar; descender. —**get down to**, considerar; abocar; enfrentarse con. —**get even**, **1**, (recover one's losses) recuperar; desquitarse. **2**, (retaliate) desquitarse (con). —**get in**, **1**, (enter) entrar. **2**, (arrive) llegar. **3**, *colloq.* [*usu.* **get in with**] (ingratiate oneself) hacer amistad con; ganarse la voluntad de. —**get lost!**, *slang* ¡lárgate!; ¡mándate cambiar! —**get nowhere**, *colloq.* no llegar (*o* llevar) a ninguna parte. —**get off**, **1**, (come down from) bajar de; apearse de. **2**, (leave; go away) marcharse. **3**, (take off; remove) sacar; quitar. **4**, (escape) escaparse; zafarse. **5**, (start; commence) partir; salir; arrancar; comenzar. **6**, (utter, as a joke) salir con *o* decir (un chiste); tener (una ocurrencia *o* salida). —**get on**, **1**, (go on *o* into) subir (a); montar (en). **2**, = **get along**. —**get out**, **1**, (go out) salir. **2**, (go away) irse; marcharse. **3**, (take out) sacar. **4**, (become known, as a secret) salir a la luz; descubrirse. **5**, (publish) dar a luz; publicar. —**get out of**, **1**, (go out from) salir de. **2**, (escape from; avoid) salir de; escapar de; evitar; zafarse de. **3**, (go beyond the reach of, as of sight, hearing, etc.) perderse de; ponerse fuera del alcance de: *to get out of sight*, perderse de vista. **4**, (elicit from) sonsacar de; sacar de. —**get over**, **1**, (recover from) recobrarse de; recuperarse de. **2**, = **get across**. **3**, (forget) olvidarse de. —**get ready**, preparar; disponer. —**get rid of**, deshacerse de; zafarse de; sacarse de encima (una cosa o persona). —**get round** = **get around**. —**get there**, *colloq.* triunfar; tener éxito. —**get through**, **1**, (finish) terminar. **2**, (manage to survive) sobrevivir; arreglárselas (en); pasar. **3**, *colloq.* = **get across**. **4**, (make contact) ponerse en contacto; establecer comunicación. —**get to**, **1**, (make contact with) comunicarse con; ponerse en contacto con. **2**, (influence; persuade) convencer; persuadir; influir en el ánimo de. **3**, = **get at**. —**get together**, **1**, (bring together; accumulate) acumular; juntar. **2**, (come together) juntarse; reunirse. **3**, *colloq.* (reach agreement) ponerse de acuerdo. —**get up**, **1**, (rise) levantarse. **2**, (raise) levantar. **3**, (assemble; organize) levantar; organizar. **4**, (dress up) vestir; ataviar. **5**, (advance; make progress) avanzar; adelantar. **6**, (climb; mount) subir; montar.

getaway *n.*, *colloq.* **1**, (escape) fuga; huida; escapada. **2**, (start) partida; arranque.

get-together *n.*, *colloq.* reunión; tertulia.

getup *también*, **get-up** *n.*, *colloq.* **1**, (makeup; appearance) apariencia; hechura; facha. **2**, (costume) ropaje; vestimenta.

geyser ('gai·zər) *n.* géiser.

ghastly ('gæst·li; 'gast-) *adj.* **1**, (horrible; frightful) horrible; espantoso. **2**, (ghostlike; haggard) cadavérico; lívido. **3**, *colloq.* (very bad) horrible; pésimo. —*adv.* horriblemente.

gherkin ('gʌɹ·kın) *n.* pepinillo.

ghetto ('gɛt·o) *n.* [*pl.* **ghettos**] judería; ghetto.

ghost (gost) *n.* fantasma; espíritu. —**ghostly**, *adj.* espectral.

—**ghost writer,** autor de escritos que aparecen con firma de otro; escritor anónimo.
ghoul (guːl) *n.* vampiro. —**ghoulish,** *adj.* vampiresco.
giant ('dʒai·ənt) *n.* gigante. —*adj.* gigante; gigantesco. —**giantess,** *n.f.* giganta.
gibber ('dʒɪb·ər) *v.i.* chapurrear. —**gibberish,** *n.* jerigonza; cháchara; chapurreo.
gibbet ('dʒɪb·ət) *n.* horca; patíbulo. —*v.t.* ahorcar.
gibbon ('gɪb·ən) *n.* gibón.
gibe (dzaib) *v.t.* burlarse de; mofarse de; tirar pullas a. —*v.i.* burlarse; mofarse. —*n.* mofa; burla; pulla.
giblets ('dʒɪb·ləts) *n.pl.* menudillos.
giddap (gɪ'dæp) *interj.* ¡arre!
giddiness ('gɪd·i·nəs) *n.* **1,** (dizziness) mareo; vértigo. **2,** (frivolity) frivolidad; atolondramiento.
giddy ('gɪd·i) *adj.* **1,** (dizzy; dazed) mareado; aturdido. **2,** (causing giddiness, as a height) que da mareo o vértigo. **3,** (frivolous) alocado; atolondrado; frívolo.
gift (gɪft) *n.* **1,** (present) regalo; obsequio. **2,** (donation) donación; donativo. **3,** (talent) don; talento. —**gifted,** *adj.* de talento; talentoso. —**gift wrap,** papel de regalo. —**gift-wrap,** *v.t.* envolver como regalo.
gig (gɪg) *n.* **1,** (carriage) calesa; cabriolé. **2,** *naut.* lancha; falúa. **3,** (toy) trompo; peonza. **4,** *slang* (demerit) demérito; falta.
gigantic (dʒai'gæn·tɪk) *adj.* gigantesco; gigante.
giggle ('gɪg·əl) *v.i.* reír tonta o nerviosamente. —*n.* risita; risa tonta o nerviosa.
gigolo ('dʒɪg·ə·lo) *n.* [*pl.* **-los**] hombre que por profesión acompaña a mujeres.
gigot ('dʒɪg·ət) *n.* **1,** (leg of mutton) pierna de carnero. **2,** [*también,* **gigot sleeve**] (puffed sleeve) manga ajamonada.
gigue (ʒig) *n.* giga.
gild (gɪld) *v.t.* [*pret. & p.p.* **gilded** *o* **gilt**] dorar. —**gilding,** *n.* dorado.
gill (gɪl) *n.* **1,** (fish organ) agalla; branquia. **2,** (dʒɪl) (liquid measure) cuarto de pinta.
gillyflower ('dʒɪl·i,flau·ər) *n.* alhelí; alelí.
gilt (gɪlt) *adj. & n.* dorado. —*v., pret. & p.p. alt. de* **gild.**
gimlet ('gɪm·lɪt) *n.* barrena; barrena de mano.
gimmick ('gɪm·ɪk) *n., slang* treta; truco; martingala.
gin (dʒɪn) *n.* **1,** (liquor) ginebra. **2,** (trap; snare) trampa. **3,** = **cotton gin.** —*v.t.* [**ginned, ginning**] alijar; desmotar (algodón). —**gin fizz,** ginebra con gaseosa. —**gin rummy,** cierto juego de cartas. —**cotton gin,** alijadora; desmotadora.
ginger ('dʒɪn·dʒər) *n.* **1,** (spice) jengibre. **2,** *colloq.* (vigor) vivacidad; energía. —**ginger ale,** gaseosa de jengibre.
gingerbread *n.* **1,** (cake) pan de jengibre. **2,** (fancy decoration) decorado excesivo.
gingerly ('dʒɪn·dʒər·li) *adj.* tímido; cuidadoso. —*adv.* tímidamente; cuidadosamente. —**gingerliness,** *n.* cuidado.
gingham ('gɪŋ·əm) *n.* guinga.
gingivitis (,dʒɪn·dʒə'vai·tɪs) *n.* gingivitis.
gipsy ('dʒɪp·si) *n. & adj.* = **gypsy.**
giraffe (dʒə'ræf) *n.* jirafa.
gird (gʌɹd) *v.t.* [*pret. & p.p.* **girt** *o* **girded**] **1,** (fasten with a belt) ceñir. **2,** (encircle; enclose) circundar; rodear. **3,** (prepare for action) preparar; aprestar.
girder ('gʌɹ·dər) *n.* viga; durmiente.
girdle ('gʌɹ·dəl) *n.* faja; ceñidor. —*v.t.* ceñir; rodear; circundar.
girl (gʌɹl) *n.* **1,** (young lady) niña; muchacha; chica. **2,** (servant) moza; criada; servienta. **3,** *colloq.* (sweetheart) amiga; novia. —**girlhood,** *n.* niñez; mocedad. —**girlish,** *adj.* de niña; de muchacha.
Girl Scout exploradora.
girt (gʌɹt) *v., pret. & p.p. de* **gird.**
girth (gʌɹθ) *n.* **1,** (cinch) cincha; cinto. **2,** (circumference) circunferencia; (*of the waist*) talle. —*v.t.* ceñir.
gist (dʒɪst) *n.* sustancia; esencia; médula; quid; meollo.
give (gɪv) *v.t.* [**gave, given, giving**] dar. —*v.i.* **1,** (make gifts) hacer regalos; dar. **2,** (yield) ceder; dar; dar de sí. **3,** (be soft or resilient) tener elasticidad; ser muelle. —*n.* elasticidad. —**give away, 1,** (give

freely) donar; regalar; dar de balde. **2,** (give in marriage) dar en matrimonio. **3,** (reveal) revelar; dar a conocer. **4,** (betray) traicionar; vender. —**give back**, devolver; restituir. —**give birth**, dar a luz; parir. —**give ear**, escuchar; prestar oídos. —**give forth**, emitir; dar. —**give ground**, retroceder. —**give heed**, atender; hacer caso. —**give in, 1,** (hand in) entregar; presentar. **2,** (yield) ceder; rendirse. —**give it to**, *colloq.* dar una paliza a; zurrarle una a. —**give leave**, dar permiso. —**give off,** emitir; dar. —**give out, 1,** (send forth; emit) emitir; dar. **2,** (make public) dar a conocer. **3,** (distribute) dar; distribuir. **4,** (fail; cease; be exhausted or worn out) terminarse; acabarse; agotarse. —**give over,** entregar. —**give the lie to,** dar (el) mentís a. —**give up, 1,** (hand over; relinquish) entregar; dar. **2,** (surrender) rendirse; darse por vencido. **3,** (cease; stop) dejar; desistir de. **4,** (abandon) abandonar. **5,** (devote wholly) dedicar. **6,** (sacrifice) sacrificar; renunciar. —**give warning**, avisar; advertir. —**give way**, ceder.

give-and-take *n.* toma y daca; tira y afloja.

giveaway *n., colloq.* **1,** (unintentional betrayal) indicio revelador; revelación. **2,** (gift; premium) obsequio; regalo. —*adj., colloq.* de regalo; de cesión.

given ('gɪv·ən) *p.p. de* **give.** —*adj.* **1,** (bestowed; presented) dado; regalado. **2,** (prone; accustomed) dado; adicto; inclinado. **3,** (stated; specified) dado; determinado; especificado. **4,** *math.; logic* dado; supuesto. —**given name,** nombre de pila.

giver ('gɪv·ər) *n.* dador; donador. —**giving,** *n.* donación; presentación.

gizzard ('gɪz·ərd) *n.* molleja.

glacé (glæ'sei) *adj.* **1,** (having a glossy surface) lustroso; pulido; glaseado. **2,** (candied) acaramelado; garapiñado.

glacial ('glei·ʃəl) *adj.* glacial.

glacier ('glei·ʃər) *n.* glaciar; ventisquero.

glad (glæd) *adj.* **1,** (happy; pleased) alegre; contento; dichoso. **2,** (pleasing; bright) alegre. —**gladden,** *v.t.* regocijar; alegrar. —*v.i.* regocijarse; alegrarse. —**gladness,** *n.* alegría; gozo; regocijo. —**gladly,** *adv.* alegremente; con (mucho) gusto; gustosamente. —**be glad,** alegrarse; tener mucho gusto; estar gustoso.

glade (gleid) *n.* claro (*de un bosque o floresta*).

gladiator ('glæd·iˌei·tər) *n.* gladiador.

gladiolus (glæd·i'o·ləs) *n.* estoque; gladiolo; *Amer.* gladiola. *También,* **gladiola** (-lə).

gladsome ('glæd·səm) *adj.* alegre; festivo.

glamour *también,* **glamor** ('glæm·ər) *n.* encanto; fascinación; embrujo. —**glamourous; glamorous,** *adj.* encantador; fascinador; hechicero. —**glamour girl,** *slang* moza maja y bien puesta; *Amer.* mujer chula. —**glamorize,** *v.t.* prestar atracción o atractivo a; embellecer; acicalar.

glance (glæns) *n.* mirada; vistazo; ojeada. —*v.i.* **1,** (strike and be deflected) dar *o* pegar de refilón. **2,** (give a quick look) echar una ojeada *o* vistazo. **3,** (flash; gleam) destellar; centellear. —**glancing,** *adj.* de refilón. —**glance off,** rebotar; salir de refilón.

gland (glænd) *n.* glándula. —**glandular** ('glæn·djə·lər) *adj.* glandular.

glans (glænz) *n., anat.* bálano.

glare (gleːr) *n.* **1,** (dazzling light) destello; reflejo; brillo deslumbrante. **2,** (fierce stare) mirada furiosa. —*adj.* lustroso; vidrioso. —*v.i.* **1,** (shine) destellar; relumbrar; brillar. **2,** (look fiercely) mirar con enojo *o* furiosamente.

glaring ('glɛr·ɪŋ) *adj.* **1,** (dazzlingly bright) destellante; deslumbrante. **2,** (flagrant; obvious) muy evidente; que salta a la vista.

glass (glæs) *n.* **1,** (material) vidrio; cristal. **2,** (container) vaso. **3,** (pane or sheet of glass) luna; vidrio; cristal. **4,** *pl.* (eyeglasses; binoculars) anteojos. —*adj.* de vidrio; de cristal. —*v.t.* encerrar entre vidrios; poner vidrios a. —**glassful** (-ful) *n.* vaso; vaso lleno. —**cut glass,** cristal tallado. —**glass blower,** soplador de vidrio. —**glass case,** vitrina.

glasshouse *n.* invernáculo; invernadero.

glassware *n.* vajilla de cristal; cristalería.
glassy ('glæs·i) *adj.* vidrioso. —**glassiness,** *n.* vidriosidad.
glaucoma (glɔ'ko·ma) *n.* glaucoma.
glaze (gleiz) *n.* **1,** [*también,* **glazing**] (glassy coating) vidriado; lustre. **2,** (film, as on the eyes) vidriosidad. **3,** (sugar coating) garapiña. —*v.t.* **1,** (furnish with glass) encristalar; poner vidrios a. **2,** (put a glaze on or in) vidriar. **3,** (coat with sugar) acaramelar; garapiñar; confitar. —*v.i.* vidriarse.
glazier ('glei·ʒər) *n.* vidriero.
gleam (gliːm) *n.* destello. —*v.i.* destellar; fulgurar; centellear.
glean (gliːn) *v.t.* & *i.* **1,** (collect, as grain) espigar. **2,** (gather, as information) colegir; recoger; espigar. —**gleaner,** *n.* espigadora. —**gleanings,** *n.pl.* espigaduras.
glee (gliː) *n.* **1,** (gaiety) regocijo; júbilo; alegría. **2,** *music* especie de canción para tres o más voces sin acompañamiento. —**gleeful,** *adj.* alegre; gozoso; jubiloso. —**glee club,** grupo coral; coral.
glen (glɛn) *n.* cañada; vallecito.
glib (glɪb) *adj.* desenvuelto; desparpajado; desembarazado. —**glibness,** *n.* desenvoltura; desparpajo; desenfado; facilidad.
glide (glaid) *n.* **1,** (sliding) deslizamiento; desliz; movimiento gracioso y fluido. **2,** (in flight) planeo. **3,** *music* ligadura. —*v.i.* **1,** (slide) deslizarse. **2,** (in flight) planear. —*v.t.* deslizar; resbalar. —**glider,** *n.* planeador.
glimmer ('glɪm·ər) *n.* **1,** (faint, flickering light) centelleo; titileo; luz trémula. **2,** (glimpse) vislumbre. —*v.i.* **1,** (shine faintly) centellear; titilar; dar una luz trémula. **2,** (be seen dimly) vislumbrarse.
glimmering ('glɪm·ər·ɪŋ) *n.* = **glimmer.**
glimpse (glɪmps) *n.* vislumbre; vistazo. —*v.t.* vislumbrar.
glint (glɪnt) *n.* destello; centelleo. —*v.i.* destellar; centellear.
glisten ('glɪs·ən) *v.i.* relucir; brillar; tener lustre.
glitter ('glɪt·ər) *n.* **1,** (sparkling light; brightness) brillo; resplandor; lustre. **2,** (showiness; splendor) brillo; oropel; esplendor. —*v.i.* brillar; resplandecer.
gloaming ('glo·mɪŋ) *n.* anochecer; anochecida.
gloat (glot) *v.i.* gozar con malicia; refocilarse.
global ('glo·bəl) *adj.* global.
globe (glob) *n.* globo.
globetrotter *n.* trotamundos.
globular ('glab·jə·lər) *adj.* globular. —**globularity** (-'lær·ə·ti) *n.* redondez; esfericidad.
globule ('glab·jul) *n.* glóbulo.
gloom (gluːm) *n.* **1,** (darkness) oscuridad; sombra; lobreguez. **2,** (melancholy feeling) abatimiento; melancolía; tristeza.
gloomy ('glu·mi) *adj.* **1,** (dark; dim) oscuro; sombrío; lóbrego. **2,** (sad; morose) abatido; melancólico; triste. —**gloominess,** *n.* = **gloom.**
glorify ('glor·ɪˌfai) *v.t.* glorificar. —**glorification** (-fɪ'kei·ʃən) *n.* glorificación.
glorious ('glor·i·əs) *adj.* glorioso.
glory ('glor·i) *n.* gloria. —*v.i.* gloriarse.
gloss (glɔs) *n.* **1,** (shine) lustre; brillo. **2,** (specious appearance) barniz; pátina. **3,** (comment; explanation) glosa. —*v.t.* **1,** (make lustrous) lustrar; dar lustre a. **2,** [*usu.* **gloss over**] (cover up, as by a specious argument) arreglar; adornar; disfrazar. **3,** (comment on; explain) glosar.
glossary ('glas·ə·ri) *n.* glosario.
glossy ('glɔs·i) *adj.* lustroso; brillante; satinado.
-glot (glat) *sufijo* -glota; idioma; lengua: *polyglot,* políglota.
glottis ('glat·ɪs) *n.* glotis.
glove (glʌv) *n.* guante. —*v.t.* enguantar. —**glover,** *n.* comerciante en guantes. —**handle with kid gloves,** tratar con delicadeza.
glow (gloː) *v.i.* **1,** (shine; gleam) brillar; lucir; resplandecer. **2,** (be flushed; redden) encenderse; ruborizarse. **3,** *fig.* (radiate health or high spirits) resplandecer; brillar. —*n.* **1,** (luminosity) brillo; luz. **2,** (vividness) brillo; viveza. **3,** (ardor) calor; ardor. **4,** (flush; redness) rubor; color. **5,** (pervading feeling) calor; euforia.
glower ('glau·ər) *v.i.* poner mala cara; fruncir el ceño.
glowworm *n.* luciérnaga.
glucinium (glu'sɪn·i·əm) *n.* glucinio.

glucose ('glu·kos) *n.* glucosa.
glue (gluː) *n.* goma; cola. —*v.t.* encolar; pegar. —**gluey,** *adj.* pegajoso.
glum (glʌm) *adj.* hosco; triste; sombrío. —**glumness,** *n.* hosquedad; tristeza.
glut (glʌt) *n.* **1,** (surfeit) hartura; saciedad. **2,** (supply exceeding demand) saturación; inundación. —*v.t.* [**glutted, glutting**] **1,** (surfeit) hartar; saciar; llenar. **2,** *comm.* saturar; inundar; *Amer.* abarrotar. —*v.i.* hartarse; saciarse; llenarse.
gluten ('glu·tən) *n.* gluten. —**glutinous,** *adj.* glutinoso.
glutton ('glʌt·ən) *n.* glotón; tragón; *zool.* glotón. —**gluttonous,** *adj.* glotón. —**gluttony,** *n.* gula; glotonería.
glycerin ('glɪs·ər·ɪn) *n.* glicerina.
gnarl (narl) *n.* nudo; nudosidad. —*v.t.* retorcer. —*v.i.* gruñir. —**gnarled,** *adj.* nudoso; retorcido; deforme.
gnash (næʃ) *v.t.* rechinar; hacer crujir (los dientes).
gnat (næt) *n.* mosquito; *Amer.* jején.
gnaw (nɔː) *v.t.* & *i.* roer. —**gnawing,** *n.* roedura; *fig.* carcoma.
gnome (noːm) *n.* gnomo.
gnostic ('nas·tɪk) *adj.* & *n.* gnóstico. —**gnosticism** (-tɪˌsɪz·əm) *n.* gnosticismo.
gnu (nuː) *n.* ñu.
go (goː) *v.i.* [**went, gone, going**] **1,** (move off or along; proceed; be moving) ir. **2,** (operate; work) marchar; funcionar; caminar. **3,** (behave in a specified way) hacer: *The bottle went "pop",* La botella hizo "pop". **4,** (result; turn out) salir; resultar: *All went well,* Todo salió bien. **5,** (be guided or regulated) guiarse (por); sujetarse (a); ir de acuerdo (con): *I will go by what you say,* Me guiaré por lo que digas. **6,** (take its course; proceed) ir: *How is the work going?,* ¿Cómo va el trabajo? **7,** (pass, as time) pasar; irse: *Time went quickly,* El tiempo pasó rápidamente. **8,** (circulate; get around) circular; correr: *The news went through the town,* Las noticias circularon por el pueblo. **9,** (be known or named) conocerse; llevar el nombre (de): *He goes by the name of González,* Se le conoce como González. **10,** (move about; be in a certain condition or state) andar; ir; estar: *He goes in rags,* Anda en harapos. **11,** (become; turn or change to) volverse: *He went mad,* Se volvió loco. **12,** (follow a certain plan or arrangement) ir; ser: *How does the story go?,* ¿Cómo va el cuento? **13,** (be fitting or suitable) ir: *This goes well with that,* Esto va bien con aquello. **14,** (put oneself) meterse; pasar; verse: *He went to a lot of trouble to do it,* Pasó (*o* se vio en) muchas dificultades para hacerlo. **15,** (leave; depart) ir; salir; partir. **16,** (cease) cesar; pasar; irse: *The pain went,* Se fue el dolor. **17,** (die) morir: *His wife went first,* Su esposa murió primero. **18,** (be done away with; be eliminated) terminarse; acabarse. **19,** (break away; be carried away or broken off) perderse; romperse; irse: *The oars went in the storm,* Los remos se perdieron en la tormenta. **20,** (fail; give way) fallar; perderse: *His eyesight is going,* Le está fallando la vista. **21,** (be allotted or given) tocar; corresponder: *The medal goes to John,* La medalla le toca a Juan. **22,** (be sold) venderse: *The chair went for ten dollars,* La silla se vendió por diez dólares. **23,** (extend; lead) ir; llevar: *This road goes to Mexico,* Este camino va a México. **24,** (reach; extend) alcanzar; llegar: *The carpet didn't go to the wall,* La alfombra no llegó a la pared. **25,** (enter; attend; engage in) ir: *They have gone fishing,* Han ido a pescar. **26,** (resort; have recourse) ir; dirigirse (a): *You must go to the judge,* Tienes que dirigirte al juez. **27,** (carry one's activity to certain lengths) ir; llegar; alcanzar: *How far will you go with this plan?,* ¿Hasta dónde llegarás con este plan? **28,** (endure; last; hold out) ir: *I can go no further,* No puedo ir más lejos. **29,** (have a particular place or position; belong) ir: *The ties go in this box,* Las corbatas van en esta caja. **30,** (fit; be contained) caber; ir. **31,** (count; be valid; be acceptable) valer; contar; ir. **32,** (be accepted; be successful) tener aceptación; tener éxito. —*v.t., colloq.* **1,** (bet; wager) apostar; ir. **2,** *colloq.* (put up with) tolerar;

soportar; aguantar. —*n.* **1,** (act of going) ida; partida; salida. **2,** *colloq.* (success) éxito. **3,** *colloq.* (animation; energy) empuje; energía. **4,** *colloq.* (state of affairs) estado de cosas; situación. **5,** *colloq.* (try; attempt) tentativa; intentona. —**go about, 1,** (be busy at; do) ocuparse de; atender. **2,** (move from place to place) ir por aquí y por allí; dar vueltas. **3,** (circulate) circular; correr. **4,** *naut.* (turn) virar; cambiar de bordada. —**go after,** *colloq.* perseguir; ir detrás de. —**go along, 1,** (proceed) seguir; proseguir. **2,** (agree) estar de acuerdo; avenirse. **3,** (coöperate) cooperar. **4,** (accompany) ir (con); acompañar. —**go around, 1,** (enclose; surround) circundar; rodear; circunvalar. **2,** (provide a share for each) alcanzar; bastar. **3,** (move from place to place; circulate) circular; ir por aquí y por allí; dar vueltas. —**go at,** atacar. —**go away,** irse; marcharse. —**go back, 1,** (return) volver; regresar. **2,** (move back) retroceder; echarse atrás. —**go back on,** *colloq.* **1,** (break, as a promise) quebrar; quebrantar; faltar a. **2,** (betray) traicionar. —**go beyond, 1,** (go past) pasar; ir más allá de. **2,** (exceed) exceder. —**go by, 1,** (pass) pasar; pasar por; pasar de largo por. **2,** (be overlooked; slip past) pasar por alto; pasar desapercibido. —**go down, 1,** (descend) descender; bajar. **2,** (sink) hundirse. **3,** (set, as the sun) ponerse. **4,** (fall; suffer defeat) caer. **5,** (be put on record) inscribirse; anotarse. —**go for, 1,** (try to get) ir por; tratar de conseguir. **2,** *colloq.* (attack) atacar; cargar contra. **3,** *slang* (regard with favor) gustar; entusiasmarse de *o* con *o* por. —**go halves,** *colloq.* ir a medias. —**go in, 1,** (enter) entrar. **2,** (be contained) caber. —**go in for,** *colloq.* gustar de; ser aficionado a. —**go into, 1,** (enter) entrar en. **2,** (inquire into) investigar; indagar. **3,** (take up, as a study or occupation) tomar; seguir. **4,** (be contained in) caber en. —**go in with,** asociarse con. —**go off, 1,** (leave; depart) irse; marcharse; salir. **2,** (explode) explotar; detonar. **3,** (happen) pasar; ocurrir; suceder. **4,** (be extinguished) apagarse. —**go on, 1,** (continue) continuar; seguir. **2,** (behave) comportarse. **3,** (happen) pasar; tener lugar. **4,** *theat.* (come on stage) entrar (en escena). **5,** (be turned on, as a light) prenderse; encenderse. —**go (someone) one better,** superar; aventajar. —**go out, 1,** (leave; go out of doors) salir. **2,** (be extinguished) apagarse. **3,** (be outdated) pasar (de moda). **4,** (go on strike) declararse (en huelga) —**go over, 1,** (examine thoroughly) examinar; escudriñar. **2,** (do again) rehacer; volver a hacer. **3,** (review) repasar. —**go through, 1,** (carry out; perform) actuar; desempeñar. **2,** (suffer; undergo) sufrir; experimentar. **3,** (search; look through) examinar; investigar. **4,** (win approval) pasar; aprobarse. **5,** (spend) gastar; dilapidar. —**go through with,** concluir; terminar. —**go together, 1,** (combine suitably) combinar; ir bien. **2,** *colloq.* (be sweethearts) salir *o* ir juntos. —**go under,** hundirse. —**go up,** subir. —**go without,** pasar sin; arreglárselas sin. —**it's no go,** *colloq.* es imposible; no hay tu tía. —**let go, 1,** (set free; release) soltar. **2,** (give up) dejar pasar; abandonar. —**let oneself go,** dejarse; abandonarse. —**on the go,** en movimiento; activo; atareado. —**to go,** *slang* para llevar.

goad (goːd) *n.* aguijón; aguijada; rejo. —*v.t.* aguijonear.

goal (goːl) *n.* **1,** *sports* gol; meta. **2,** (aim) gol; meta; objetivo. —**goalie** (-i) *n.* = **goalkeeper.**

goalkeeper *n.* guardameta. *También,* **goaltender.**

goat (got) *n.* **1,** (she-goat) cabra; chiva. **2,** (male goat) chivo; macho cabrío; *Amer.* cabro. **3,** *slang* (scapegoat) pagano; víctima. —**be the goat,** *colloq.* ser la víctima; ser el pagano; pagar el pato. —**get one's goat,** *colloq.* molestar; enojar. —**wild goat,** cabra montés.

goatee (go'tiː) *n.* perilla; pera; *Amer.* chiva.

goatherd *n.* cabrero.

goatish ('got·ɪʃ) *adj.* cabrío.

goatskin *n.* cabritilla.

gob (gaːb) *n.* **1,** (mass; lump) mazacote; pelmazo. **2,** *colloq.* (sailor) marinero.

gobble ('gab·əl) *n.* voz del pavo;

gluglú. —*v.t.* tragar; engullir; devorar. —*v.i.* gluglutear.
gobbler ('gab·lər) *n.* **1,** (male turkey) pavo. **2,** *colloq.* (glutton) tragón; glotón; engullidor.
go-between *n.* **1,** (mediator) intermediario; mediador. **2,** (between lovers) alcahuete.
goblet ('gab·lɪt) *n.* copa.
goblin ('gab·lɪn) *n.* duende.
god (ga:d) *n.* dios. —**goddess,** *n.f.* diosa.
godchild *n.* ahijado.
goddaughter *n.* ahijada.
godfather *n.* padrino.
godhead *n.* divinidad; deidad.
godless ('gad·ləs) *adj.* sindiós; impío. —**godlessness,** *n.* impiedad.
godlike *adj.* divino.
godly ('gad·li) *adj.* piadoso; devoto. —**godliness,** *n.* piedad.
godmother *n.* madrina.
godsend *n.* bendición de Dios.
godson *n.* ahijado.
go-getter (go'gɛt·ər) *n., slang* buscavidas; hombre de empuje.
goggle ('gag·əl) *v.i.* saltársele a uno los ojos; poner los ojos saltones; mirar con ojos saltones. —**goggles,** *n.pl.* anteojos de protección o seguridad.
going ('go·ɪŋ) *n.* **1,** (departure) ida; salida; partida. **2,** (manner or conditions of movement) camino; marcha. **3,** *colloq.* (circumstances) estado *o* marcha de las cosas. —*adj.* en marcha. —**be going to,** ir a; estar por *o* para. —**get going,** *colloq.* marcharse; irse. —**goings on,** *colloq.* enredos; pasos.
goiter ('gɔi·tər) *n.* papera; bocio.
gold (go:ld) *n.* oro. —*adj.* de oro; dorado; áureo.
gold brick 1, (worthless object) gato por liebre. **2,** *slang* (shirker of duty) zángano.
goldbrick ('gold,brɪk) *v.t.* (swindle) dar *o* vender gato por liebre. —*v.i.* (loaf) escurrir el bulto; hacer el zángano. —*n.* [*también,* **goldbricker**] zángano.
gold digger *slang* vampiresa.
golden ('gol·dən) *adj.* de oro; dorado; áureo.
goldenrod *n.* vara de oro; vara de San José.
golden rule norma o regla de conducta.
gold-filled *adj.* chapado *o* enchapado en oro.
goldfinch *n.* cardelina.
goldfish *n.* carpa dorada; pez de color.
gold leaf pan de oro.
gold plate 1, (coating of gold) dorado. **2,** (tableware) vajilla de oro. —**gold-plated,** *adj.* dorado.
goldsmith *n.* orfebre.
gold standard patrón oro.
golf (galf) *n.* golf. —*v.i.* jugar al golf.
golly ('gal·i) *interj.* ¡cielos!; ¡caramba!
-gon (gan) *sufijo* -gono; *forma nombres denotando figuras planas geométricas con determinado número de ángulos: polygon,* polígono.
gonad ('go·næd) *n.* gonado.
gondola ('gan·də·lə) *n.* **1,** (boat) góndola. **2,** *aero.* barquilla. **3,** *R.R.* (open freight car) vagón descubierto.
gondolier (,gan·də'lɪr) *n.* gondolero.
gone (gɔ:n) *v., p.p. de* **go.** —*adj.* **1,** (departed) ido. **2,** (ruined; lost) arruinado; perdido. **3,** (dying; dead) muerto. **4,** (used up) agotado; consumido. **5,** (past) pasado; ido. —**goner,** *n., slang* persona *o* cosa perdida *o* acababa. —**far gone, 1,** (deeply involved) muy comprometido *o* envuelto. **2,** (far advanced) muy avanzado. **3,** (exhausted) exhausto; agotado. —**gone on,** *colloq.* loco por; chalado por.
gong (gɔŋ) *n.* gong; batintín.
gono- (gan·ə) *prefijo* gono-; perteneciente al sexo *o* a la reproducción sexual: *gonorrhea,* gonorrea.
gonorrhea (,gan·ə'ri·ə) *n.* gonorrea; blenorragia.
-gony (gə·ni) *sufijo* -gonía; génesis; origen: *cosmogony,* cosmogonía.
goo (gu:) *n., slang* masa pegajosa; mazacote; pegote.
good (gud) *adj.* [**better, best**] bueno. —*n.* **1,** (virtue; merit) bondad; bien. **2,** (benefit; advantage) bien. —*interj.* ¡bien!; ¡bueno! —**come to no good,** terminar mal; fracasar. —**for good; for good and all,** para siempre; por siempre. —**good afternoon,** buenas tardes. —**good and . . . ,** *colloq.* bien; muy. —**good evening,** buenas noches. —**good for, 1,** (able to last or hold out for) que puede durar o

servir por. 2, (worth; valid for) válido por. 3, (able to give or repay) capaz de dar *o* pagar. —**Good Friday**, Viernes Santo. —**good morning**, buenos días. —**good night**, buenas noches. —**good will**, buena voluntad. —**have a good time**, divertirse; pasar un buen rato. —**in good time**, a tiempo; a su tiempo. —**make good**, 1, (be successful) tener éxito. 2, (fulfill) cumplir. 3, (repay; replace) reponer; pagar. 4, (prove) demostrar; probar. —**no good**, 1, (bad) malo. 2, (worthless) sin valor. 3, (useless) inútil; que no sirve. —**to the good**, 1, (to advantage) para bien. 2, (representing credit or profit) de ganancia; sobrante.

goodbye *también*, **goodby** (gʊd'bai) *n.* & *interj.* adiós.

good-for-nothing *adj.* & *n.* inútil; zángano.

good-hearted *adj.* de buen corazón; bondadoso.

goodies ('gʊd·iz) *n.pl.* golosinas.

good-looking *adj.* bien parecido; guapo; hermoso.

goodly ('gʊd·li) *adj.* 1, (good-looking) bien parecido; hermoso. 2, (of good quality) excelente; bueno. 3, (pleasing) atractivo; agradable. 4, (rather large) considerable; bueno.

good-natured *adj.* afable; bondadoso; benévolo.

goodness ('gʊd·nəs) *n.* bondad. —*interj.* ¡Dios mío!

goods (gʊdz) *n.pl.* 1, (personal property) bienes. 2, (merchandise; wares) artículos; mercancías; efectos. 3, (fabric) géneros.

goody ('gʊd·i) *interj.* ¡bueno!; ¡muy bien! —**goody-goody**, *adj.* & *n.* mojigato; santurrón.

gooey ('gu·i) *adj.* pegajoso; mazacotudo.

goof (guf) *n.*, *slang* bobo; tonto; mentecato. —*v.i.*, *slang* meter la pata. —**goofy**, *adj.*, *slang* tonto; necio; disparatado.

goose (gus) *n.* [*pl.* **geese**] ganso. —**goose flesh; goose pimples**, carne de gallina. —**goose step**, paso de ganso.

gooseberry ('gus,bɛr·i; -bə·ri) *n.* grosella blanca *o* silvestre.

gooseneck *n.* herramienta *o* soporte en forma de cuello de ganso.

gopher ('go·fər) *n.* tuza; taltuza.

gore (goːr) *n.* 1, (blood) cuajo de sangre; sangre. 2, *sewing* nesga. —*v.t.* 1, (pierce, as with a horn or tusk) acornear; cornear; dar cornadas *o* colmillazos a. 2, *sewing* poner nesgas a.

gorge (gordʒ) *n.* 1, (ravine) garganta; cañón; barranco. 2, (gluttonous eating; feast) atracón; empacho. 3, (disgust; revulsion) bilis; asco. —*v.t.* 1, (stuff with food; glut) atracar; atiborrar. 2, (swallow greedily) engullir. —*v.i.* atracarse; atiborrarse.

gorgeous ('gor·dʒəs) *adj.* espléndido; magnífico; hermosísimo. —**gorgeousness**, *n.* esplendor; magnificencia; hermosura.

gorilla (gə'rɪl·ə) *n.* gorila.

gorse (gors) *n.* aulaga; tojo.

gory ('gor·i) *adj.* 1, (covered with blood) sangriento; ensangrentado; sanguinolento. 2, (involving bloodshed) cruento; sangriento. —**goriness**, *n.* sanguinolencia; sangre.

gosh (gaʃ) *interj.* ¡caramba!; ¡Dios mío!

goshawk ('gas,hɔk) *n.* azor.

gosling ('gaz·lɪŋ) *n.* ganso joven; ansarino.

gospel ('gas·pəl) *n.* evangelio.

gossamer ('gas·ə·mər) *n.* 1, (cobweb) telaraña. 2, (fabric) gasa; tul. —*adj.* sutil; delicado; tenue.

gossip ('gas·ɪp) *n.* 1, (chatter; rumor) chisme; murmuración; habladuría. 2, [*también*, **gossiper**] (person who chatters) chismoso; murmurador. —*v.i.* chismear; murmurar. —**gossipy**, *adj.* chismoso.

got (gat) *v.* 1, *pret. & p.p. de* **get**. 2, *U.S. colloq. & Brit., con el v.aux.* **have** (hold; own; possess) tener: *Have you got a pencil?*, ¿Tiene Vd. un lápiz?

Goth (gaθ) *n.* godo.

Gothic ('gaθ·ɪk) *adj.* gótico; godo. —*n.* gótico.

gotten ('gat·ən) *v.*, *p.p. de* **get**.

gouge (gaudʒ) *v.t.* 1, (make grooves in) acanalar; hacer surcos en. 2, (remove; scoop out) vaciar; sacar. 3, (rip or tear out) arrancar. 4, (nick; notch) mellar; hacer muescas en. 5, *colloq.* (swindle; cheat) estafar; robar. —*n.* 1, (tool) gubia; escoplo. 2, (groove) estría; surco; escopladura. 3, (nick; notch) mella; muesca. 4, *colloq.* (swindle) estafa; robo.

goulash ('gu·laʃ) *n.* estofado; guiso de carne; guisado.
gourd (gord) *n.* calabaza.
gourmand ('gʊr·mand) *n.* **1,** (glutton) glotón; comilón. **2,** = **gourmet.**
gourmet (gʊr'mei) *n.* gastrónomo; gourmet; epicúreo.
gout (gaut) *n.* gota. —**gouty,** *adj.* gotoso.
govern ('gʌv·ərn) *v.t.* **1,** (rule) gobernar; regir. **2,** *gram.* pedir; regir. —*v.i.* gobernar.
governess ('gʌv·ər·nəs) *n.* institutriz; aya.
government ('gʌv·ərn·mənt) *n.* **1,** (rule) gobierno; régimen. **2,** *gram.* régimen. —**governmental** (-'mɛn·təl) *adj.* gubernativo; gubernamental.
governor ('gʌv·ər·nər) *n.* **1,** *polit.* gobernador. **2,** *mech.* regulador.
gown (gaun) *n.* **1,** (woman's garment) vestido; traje. **2,** (nightgown; dressing gown) bata; salto de cama. **3,** *law; educ.* toga. **4,** *eccles.* sotana; traje talar. —*v.t.* vestir.
grab (græ;b) *v.t.* **[grabbed, grabbing] 1,** (seize) agarrar; coger; asir; empuñar. **2,** (snatch) arrebatar; arrancar; *Amer.* arranchar. —*n.* **1,** (act of grabbing) tirón; agarrón. **2,** (something grabbed) presa; botín. **3,** (hook; grapple) gancho; garfio. —**up for grabs,** *slang* para disputar; para quien lo coja.
grace (greis) *n.* **1,** (favor) gracia; favor. **2,** (charm) gracia; garbo; donaire. **3,** (prayer at meals) bendición de la mesa. **4,** *cap.* (title of respect) Señoría. —*v.t.* adornar; agraciar. —**fall from grace,** caer en desgracia. —**say grace,** bendecir la mesa.
graceful ('greis·fəl) *adj.* agraciado; gracioso; donoso.
gracious ('grei·ʃəs) *adj.* **1,** (affable; courteous) afable; grato. **2,** (merciful) indulgente; benévolo. —*interj.* ¡válgame Dios!
gradation (gre'dei·ʃən) *n.* gradación.
grade (greid) *n.* **1,** (degree) grado. **2,** (rank; class) grado; rango; categoría. **3,** *educ.* nota; calificación. **4,** (slope) cuesta; pendiente; declive. —*v.t.* **1,** (classify) clasificar. **2,** (give a grade to) calificar. **3,** (graduate) graduar. **4,** (level) aplanar; nivelar. —**grade crossing,** paso *o* cruce a nivel. —**grade school,** escuela primaria.
-grade (greid) *sufijo* -grado; *forma adjetivos denotando* **1,** movimiento; andar: *digitigrade,* digitígrado. **2,** gradación: *centigrade,* centígrado.
gradient ('grei·di·ənt) *n.* **1,** (slope) pendiente; declive. **2,** (degree of slope) inclinación.
gradual ('græ·dʒu·əl) *adj.* gradual.
graduate ('græ·dʒu·ət) *n.* **1,** *educ.* graduado. **2,** *chem.* probeta graduada. —*adj.* graduado. —*v.t.* (-et) **1,** *educ.* conferir un grado *o* diploma a; graduar. **2,** (calibrate) calibrar; graduar. —*v.i.* **1,** *educ.* graduarse. **2,** (change by degrees) cambiar gradualmente; ir en gradaciones. —**graduation,** *n.* graduación.
Graeco- (gri·ko; grɛ-; gre-) *prefijo, var. de* **Greco-.**
graft (græft) *n.* **1,** (transplant) injerto. **2,** (political corruption) malversación; soborno; *Amer.* coima. **3,** (extortion by a public official) concusión; *Amer.* mordida. —*v.t. & i.* **1,** (transplant) injertar. **2,** (gain dishonestly) malversar; obtener ilícitamente; *Amer.* coimear.
grail (greil) *n.* grial.
grain (grein) *n.* **1,** (seed) grano. **2,** (texture) vena; veta; veteado. **3,** (particle) pizca; grano. **4,** (unit of weight) grano. **5,** (of leather) grano. —*v.t.* vetear. —**against the grain,** a contrapelo.
grainy ('grei·ni) *adj.* **1,** (streaked; veined) veteado. **2,** (granular) granular.
gram (græm) *n.* gramo.
-gram (græm) *sufijo; forma nombres indicando* **1,** -grama; escritura; dibujo: *telegram,* telegrama; *diagram,* diagrama. **2,** -gramo; unidades de peso del sistema métrico: *kilogram,* kilogramo.
grammar ('græm·ər) *n.* gramática. —**grammar school,** escuela primaria.
grammarian (grə'mɛr·i·ən) *n.* gramático.
grammatical (grə'mæt·ɪ·kəl) *adj.* gramatical; gramático.

gramophone ('græm·ə·fon) *n.* gramófono.
granary ('græn·ə·ri) *n.* granero.
grand (grænd) *adj.* 1, (great) grande; gran. 2, (principal; chief) principal. 3, (magnificent; grandiose) grandioso; grande; gran. 4, (complete; comprehensive) grande; gran; general. 5, (pretentious; haughty) pomposo; ostentoso. —**grandness,** *n.* grandeza.
grand- (grænd) *prefijo, denotando relación de ascendencia o descendencia remontándose una generación: grandfather,* abuelo; *grandson,* nieto.
grandaunt *n.* tía abuela.
grandchild *n.* nieto.
granddad *n., colloq.* abuelo.
granddaughter *n.* nieta.
grand duke gran duque. —**grand duchess,** gran duquesa. —**grand duchy,** gran ducado.
grandee (græn'di) *n.* grande (*de España o Portugal*).
grandeur ('græn·dʒər) *n.* grandeza; grandiosidad.
grandfather *n.* abuelo.
grandiloquent (græn'dɪl·ə·kwənt) *adj.* grandilocuente. —**grandiloquence,** *n.* grandilocuencia.
grandiose ('græn·di·os) *adj.* grandioso. —**grandiosity** (-'as·ə·ti) *n.* grandiosidad.
grand jury gran jurado.
grand larceny robo de mayor cuantía.
grandma *n., colloq.* abuela; abuelita. *También,* **grandmamma.**
grandmother *n.* abuela.
grandnephew *n.* resobrino. —**grandniece,** *n.* resobrina.
grand opera ópera.
grandpa ('grænd,pa; 'græm-) *n., colloq.* abuelo; abuelito. *También,* **grandpapa** (-,pa·pə; -pə,paː).
grandparent *n.* abuelo.
grand piano piano de cola.
grand slam *cards* bola.
grandson *n.* nieto.
grandstand *n.* tribuna. —**grandstand play,** *slang* jugada llamativa; lance ostentoso.
granduncle *n.* tío abuelo.
grange (greindʒ) *n.* granja.
granite (græn·ɪt) *n.* granito.
granny ('græn·i) *n., colloq.* 1, (grandmother) abuela; abuelita. 2, (old woman) viejita; viejecita; anciana. 3, (fussy person) melindroso; remilgado.
grant (grænt) *n.* donación; concesión. —*v.t.* 1, (give; bestow) dar; otorgar; conceder. 2, (convey by deed) ceder; transferir. 3, (concede; allow) conceder. —**take for granted,** dar por descontado *o* seguro.
grantee (græn'ti) *n.* cesionario; donatario.
grantor (græn'tor) *n.* cesionista; donante; otorgante.
granular ('græn·jə·lər) *adj.* granular.
granulate ('græn·jə,leit) *v.t.* granular. —**granulation,** *n.* granulación.
granule ('græn·jul) *n.* gránulo.
grape (greip) *n.* uva.
grapefruit *n.* toronja; pomelo.
grapeshot *n.* metralla.
grapevine *n.* 1, (plant) vid; parra. 2, *colloq.* (secret channel of communication) fuente o vía de rumores; correo de las brujas.
graph (græf) *n.* gráfica. —*v.t.* hacer una gráfica de. —**graph paper,** papel cuadriculado.
-graph (græf) *sufijo; forma nombres indicando* 1, -grafía; escrito; grabado: *monograph,* monografía; *lithograph,* litografía. 2, -grafo; medio *o* instrumento para escribir, dibujar, grabar, etc.: *telegraph,* telégrafo; *phonograph,* fonógrafo.
graphic ('græf·ɪk) *adj.* gráfico. *También,* **graphical.**
-graphic ('græf·ɪk) *también,* **-graphical,** *sufijo* -gráfico; *forma adjetivos correspondientes a nombres terminados en* **-graphy**: *stenographic,* estenográfico.
graphite ('græf·ait) *n.* grafito.
grapho- (græf·o) *prefijo* grafo-; escritura; dibujo: *graphology,* grafología.
-graphy (græf·i) *sufijo* -grafía; *forma nombres indicando:* 1, ciencias; estudios: *geography,* geografía. 2, bellas artes: *choreography,* coreografía. 3, arte, facultad *o* medio de escribir, grabar, dibujar, etc.: *telegraphy,* telegrafía; *calligraphy,* caligrafía. 4, escritura; representación por escrito: *orthography,* ortografía.
grapple ('græp·əl) *n.* arpeo; gancho. —*v.i.* luchar. —*v.t.* agarrar; asir; aferrar. —**grappling iron** ('græp·lɪŋ) arpeo.

grasp (græsp) *n.* **1,** (grip; clasp) apretón; agarrón. **2,** (reach) alcance. **3,** (grab; attempt to seize) agarrón. **4,** (hold; possession) posesión; poder; mano. **5,** (understanding) comprensión. —*v.t.* **1,** (seize) agarrar; coger; asir; empuñar. **2,** (grip; clasp) apretar. **3,** (understand) comprender. —**grasping,** *adj.* codicioso.

grass (græs) *n.* **1,** (plant; greenery) hierba. **2,** (lawn) césped. **3,** (pasture) pasto.

grasshopper ('græs·hap·ər) *n.* saltamontes.

grass widow mujer divorciada o separada.

grassy ('græs·i) *adj.* **1,** (covered with grass) herboso; con *o* de hierba. **2,** (like grass) herbáceo.

grate (greit) *n.* **1,** (grating) reja; verja; enrejado. **2,** (fireplace) parrilla. —*v.t.* **1,** (reduce to particles) rallar. **2,** (rub harshly) crujir; rechinar. —*v.i.* **1,** (creak) crujir; rechinar. **2,** [*usu.* **grate on** *o* **upon**] (annoy) enoajar; irritar.

grateful ('greit·fəl) *adj.* agradecido.

grater ('grei·tər) *n.* rallador; raspador; rallo.

gratify ('græt·ɪ·fai) *v.t.* agradar; complacer; satisfacer. —**gratification** (-fɪ'kei·ʃən) *n.* agrado; satisfacción; placer.

grating ('grei·tɪŋ) *n.* reja; enrejado; verja. —*adj.* irritante; áspero.

gratis ('grei·tɪs; 'græt·ɪs) *adv.* gratis; de balde.

gratitude ('græt·ɪ·tud) *n.* gratitud; reconocimiento; agradecimiento.

gratuitous (grə'tu·ɪ·təs) *adj.* gratuito.

gratuity (grə'tu·ɪ·ti) *n.* gratificación; propina.

grave (greiv) *n.* **1,** (excavation) fosa. **2,** (tomb) tumba; sepultura. —*adj.* grave; serio. —*v.t.* & *i.* = **engrave.** —**graveness,** *n.* seriedad; gravedad.

gravedigger *n.* sepulturero.

gravel ('græv·əl) *n.* grava; cascajo. —*v.t.* enarenar; cubrir con grava.

graven ('grei·vən) *v., p.p. var. de* **grave.** —*adj.* grabado.

gravestone *n.* lápida.

graveyard *n.* cementerio; camposanto.

gravitate ('græv·ɪˌteit) *v.i.* gravitar. —**gravitation,** *n.* gravitación.

gravity ('græv·ə·ti) *n.* gravedad. —**specific gravity,** peso específico; gravedad específica.

gravy ('grei·vi) *n.* **1,** (sauce) salsa. **2,** (juice given off by meat) jugo. **3,** *slang* (unearned profit) extra; miel sobre buñuelos.

gray *también,* **grey** (grei) *adj.* & *n.* gris. —*v.t.* poner gris. —*v.i.* encanecer. —**grayish,** *adj.* grisáceo. —**gray matter,** *lit.* & *fig.* materia gris.

grayhaired *adj.* cano; canoso.

graze (greiz) *n.* **1,** (light touch; brush) roce; rozamiento. **2,** (scratch; scrape) raspadura; rasguño. —*v.t.* **1,** (brush lightly) rozar. **2,** (scratch; scrape) raspar; arañar. **3,** (put to pasture) pastorear; apacentar. —*v.i.* pacer; pastar. —**grazing,** *n.* pasto.

grease (gris) *n.* grasa. —*v.t.* engrasar. —**grease the palm,** *slang* untar la mano.

greasy ('gri·zi; -si) *adj.* grasiento; grasoso. —**greasiness,** *n.* lo grasiento; calidad de grasiento; grasa.

great (greit) *adj.* **1,** (large) grande. **2,** (eminent) grande; gran; eminente. **3,** *colloq.* (fine; excellent) magnífico; estupendo. —**greatness,** *n.* grandeza.

great- (greit) *prefijo; denota relación de ascendencia o descendencia remontándose una generación; úsase antepuesto al prefijo* **grand-,** *o en vez de éste: great-uncle,* también, *granduncle,* tío abuelo; *great-grandfather,* bisabuelo. *Se repite para indicar ascendencia o descendencia más remota: great-great-grandfather,* tatarabuelo.

greatcoat *n.* paletó.

great-grandchild *n.* bisnieto. —**great-granddaughter,** *n.* bisnieta. —**great-grandfather,** *n.* bisabuelo. —**great-grandmother,** *n.* bisabuela. —**great-grandparent,** *n.* bisabuelo. —**great-grandson,** *n.* bisnieto.

great-great-grandfather *n.* tatarabuelo; rebisabuelo. —**great-great-grandmother,** *n.* tatarabuela; rebisabuela.

great-great-grandson *n.* rebisnieto. —**great-great-granddaughter,** *n.* rebisnieta.

great-nephew *n.* resobrino. —**great-niece,** *n.* resobrina.

Grecian ('gri·ʃən) *adj.* & *n.* griego.
Greco- (gri·ko; grɛ-, gre-) *prefijo* greco-; griego: *Greco-Roman*, grecorromano.
Greco-Roman *adj.* grecorromano.
greed (griːd) *n.* codicia; avaricia. —**greedy**, *adj.* codicioso; avariento.
Greek (grik) *n.* & *adj.* griego.
green (griːn) *adj.* **1,** (color) verde. **2,** (unripe; inexperienced) verde. **3,** (new, fresh) reciente; fresco. **4,** (wan) demudado; verde. **5,** [*también,* **green-eyed**] *colloq.* (envious) amarillo de envidia. —*n.* **1,** (color) verde. **2,** (common) prado; pradera. **3,** *pl.* (evergreens) ramos verdes. **4,** *pl.* (green vegetables) verduras; hortalizas. **5,** *golf* césped. —**greenish**, *adj.* verdoso.
greenback *n.*, *U.S.* papel moneda.
greenery ('gri·nə·ri) *n.* verde; verdura.
greenhorn *n.*, *colloq.* novato; bisoño.
greenhouse *n.* invernadero.
greenness ('grin·nəs) *n.* **1,** (green color) verdor. **2,** (immaturity; inexperience) inmadurez; inexperiencia.
greensward ('grin·sword) *n.* césped.
greet (grit) *v.t.* saludar; recibir.
greeting ('gri·tɪŋ) *n.* saludo; salutación; bienvenida. —**greetings**, *n.pl.* saludos. —**greeting card**, tarjeta de saludo *o* felicitación.
gregarious (grɪ'gɛr·i·əs) *n.* gregario. —**gregariousness**, *n.* gregarismo.
gremlin ('grɛm·lɪn) *n.* duende; diablillo.
grenade (grɪ'neid) *n.* granada.
grenadier (ˌgrɛn·ə'dɪr) *n.* granadero.
grenadine (ˌgrɛn·ə'din) *n.* granadina.
grew (gruː) *v.*, *pret. de* **grow.**
grey (grei) *n.*, *adj.* & *v.* = **gray.**
greyhound *n.* galgo.
grid (grɪd) *n.* **1,** (grate; gridiron) reja; enrejado. **2,** *electricity* rejilla; grilla.
griddle ('grɪd·əl) *n.* tortera; plancha.
gridiron *n.* **1,** *cookery* parrilla. **2,** (football field) campo; cancha.
grief (grif) *n.* dolor; pesar; pesadumbre. —**come to grief**, venir a menos; parar mal.
grievance ('gri·vəns) *n.* queja; querella.
grieve (griːv) *v.t.* afligir; apenar; acongojar. —*v.i.* estar apenado *o* afligido. —**grieve for** *o* **over**, lamentar; llorar.
grievous ('gri·vəs) *adj.* **1,** (causing pain or grief) doloroso; penoso. **2,** (severe; serious) grave.
griffin ('grɪf·ɪn) *n.* grifo.
grill (grɪl) *n.* **1,** (gridiron) parrilla. **2,** (grilled food) asado; *So. Amer.* parrillada. **3,** (grillroom) parrilla. —*v.t.* **1,** (broil) asar a la parrilla. **2,** *colloq.* (question) asar *o* acribillar a preguntas.
grille (grɪl) *n.* reja; verja; enrejado; *auto.* parrilla.
grillwork *n.* enrejado.
grim (grɪm) *adj.* **1,** (forbidding) torvo; hosco. **2,** (frightful; cruel) siniestro; cruel.
grimace (grɪ'meis, 'grɪ·məs) *n.* mueca; gesto. —*v.i.* hacer muecas; hacer gestos.
grime (graim) *n.* mugre; *Amer.* caca. —**grimy**, *adj.* mugriento.
grin (grɪn) *n.* sonrisa. —*v.i.* [**grinned, grinning**] sonreír.
grind (graind) *v.t.* [*pret.* & *p.p.* **ground**] **1,** (crush; pulverize) moler; triturar. **2,** (sharpen) afilar; amolar. **3,** (polish) pulir. **4,** (grate) rallar. **5,** (rub harshly) refregar; restregar. **6,** (crush; oppress) aplastar; oprimir. **7,** (grate together; grit, as the teeth) rechinar. **8,** (operate by turning) dar vueltas a. —*v.i.*, *slang* (work hard) echar los bofes; sudar. —*n.* **1,** (act or result of grinding) molienda. **2,** (tedious routine) rutina; matraca; monotonía. **3,** *slang* (industrious student) empollón; machacón. —**grind to a stop** *o* **halt**, frenar *o* parar en seco.
grinder ('grain·dər) *n.* **1,** (machine for sharpening) amoladera; (for coffee) molino *o* molinillo. **2,** (person that sharpens) amolador; afilador.
grindstone *n.* piedra de amolar.
gringo ('grɪŋ·go) *n.* gringo.
grip (grɪp) *n.* **1,** (handle) mango; agarradero; *Amer.* agarradera. **2,** (secure grasp) agarrón; apretón. **3,** (power of one's clasp) fuerza en la mano; pulso. **4,** (control; command) control; dominio. **5,** *colloq.* (valise) maletín; valija. —*v.t.* [**gripped, gripping**] **1,** (grasp firmly) agarrar; aferrar; sujetar;

apretar. **2,** (take hold upon, as the emotions, attention, etc.) coger; dominar. —**come to grips,** agarrarse; llegar a las manos. —**come to grips with,** atacar; tratar de resolver. —**get a grip on oneself,** dominarse.

gripe (graip) *v.t.* **1,** (grip; squeeze) apretar; oprimir. **2,** (distress; oppress) afligir; oprimir; acongojar. —*v.i.* **1,** (have pain in the bowels) tener cólico. **2,** *slang* (complain) quejarse; lamentarse. —*n.* **1,** (colic) cólico. **2,** *slang* (complaint) queja; querella. —**griper,** *n., slang* gruñón.

grippe (grɪp) *n.* gripe; influenza.

grisly ('grɪz·li) *adj.* **1,** (somewhat gray) grisáceo; entregris. **2,** (gruesome) horripilante; espantoso.

grist (grɪst) *n.* molienda. —**be grist to one's mill,** ser de provecho propio; servir de experiencia.

gristle ('grɪs·əl) *n.* cartílago. —**gristly** (-li) *adj.* cartilaginoso; correoso.

grit (grɪt) *n.* **1,** (sand; tiny particles) arena; polvillo áspero. **2,** (courage; pluck) valor; aguante; firmeza. **3,** *pl.* (ground corn) sémola; maíz molido. —*v.t.* & *i.* [**gritted, gritting**] crujir; rechinar.

gritty ('grɪt·i) *adj.* **1,** (coarse) áspero; rasposo. **2,** (plucky) valeroso; firme; de aguante.

grizzled ('grɪz·əld) *adj.* canoso; cano.

grizzly ('grɪz·li) *adj.* grisáceo; pardusco. —**grizzly bear,** oso pardo *o* gris.

groan (groːn) *n.* gemido; quejido. —*v.i.* gemir; quejarse.

groats (grots) *n.pl.* sémola; avena *o* trigo molido.

grocer ('gro·sər) *n.* abacero; *Amer.* bodeguero; *Amer.* almacenero; *Amer.* abarrotero. —**grocery,** *n.* abacería; *Amer.* bodega; *Amer.* almacén; *Amer.* tienda de abarrotes. —**groceries,** *n.pl.* comestibles; *Amer.* abarrotes.

grog (graːg) *n.* bedida de ron y agua; brebaje. —**groggy,** *adj.* mareado; turulato; atontado.

groin (grɔin) *n.* **1,** *anat.* ingle. **2,** *archit.* arista de bóveda.

grommet ('gram·ɪt) *n.* ojete; hembrilla; *naut.* estrobo; amura.

groom (gruːm) *n.* **1,** (stableman) caballerizo; mozo de cuadra; palafrenero. **2,** (bridegroom) novio. **3,** (attendant in a royal household) encargado de palacio. —*v.t.* **1,** (tend, as horses) atender; cuidar de. **2,** (make neat) arreglar; acicalar. **3,** (train) adiestrar; preparar. —**grooming,** *n.* arreglo; acicalado.

groomsman ('grumz·mən) *n.* padrino de boda.

groove (gruːv) *n.* **1,** (notch) muesca. **2,** (furrow) surco. **3,** (hollow cut) acanaladura; estría. **4,** (slit) ranura; hendidura. —*v.t.* acanalar; estriar. —**in the groove,** en las mismas de siempre.

grope (grop) *v.i.* & *t.* tantear; tentar. —**grope for,** buscar a ciegas *o* a tientas; tantear.

grosgrain ('gro·gren) *n.* gro.

gross (gros) *adj.* **1,** (fat; heavy) grueso; gordo. **2,** (thick; dense) espeso; denso. **3,** (coarse) burdo; tosco. **4,** (vulgar) grosero; vulgar; rudo. **5,** (stupid) bruto. **6,** (flagrant; glaring) grande; tremendo; enorme. **7,** (total) total. **8,** (without deductions) bruto. **9,** (raw; unfinished) en bruto. —*n.* gruesa. —*v.t.* sacar *o* hacer en total *o* en bruto. —**gross weight,** peso bruto.

grossness ('gros·nəs) *n.* **1,** (vulgarity) vulgaridad; rudeza. **2,** (thickness) espesor; densidad. **3,** (fatness; heaviness) gordura.

grotesque (gro'tɛsk) *adj.* grotesco. —**grotesqueness,** *n.* extravagancia; lo grotesco.

grotto ('grat·o) *n.* gruta.

grouch (grautʃ) *n., colloq.* **1,** (morose person) gruñón; refunfuñón; cascarrabias. **2,** (sullen mood) mal humor. **3,** (complaint) queja. —*v.i.* quejarse; gruñir; refunfuñar. —**grouchy,** *adj.* gruñón; refunfuñón; malhumorado.

ground (graund) *n.* **1,** (earth; soil) tierra; suelo. **2,** (area) terreno. **3,** *usu. pl.* (basis; justification) fundamento; base; razón. **4,** *usu. pl.* (plot of land) tierra; solar; terreno. **5,** *usu. pl.* (land used for a special purpose) terreno; terrenos; campo. **6,** *pl.* (meal; coarse particles) harina (*sing.*); polvo (*sing.*). **7,** *pl.* (dregs; sediment) poso; posos. **8,** *electricity* tierra; conductor a tierra. —*adj.* **1,** (prepared by grinding) molido. **2,** (at ground level) a nivel del terreno *o* de tierra. —*v.t.* **1,** (set on the ground) poner en tierra. **2,** (base; found) basar; cimentar; fundar.

3, *aero.* prohibir *o* detener el vuelo de; detener en tierra. 4, *electricity* conectar a tierra. 5, (run aground) varar. 6, *pret. & p.p. de* **grind.** —*v.i.* 1, (run aground) encallar; embarrancar; varar. 2, (alight; land) aterrizar. —**above ground,** vivo; vivito y coleando. —**break ground,** 1, (begin digging) comenzar una obra. 2, (plow) arar. 3, (prepare the way) preparar el camino. —**cut the ground from under one's feet,** echar la zancadilla a. —**give ground,** ceder. —**ground floor,** 1, *lit.* planta baja; piso bajo. 2, *fig.* posición ventajosa; ventaja. —**ground swell,** marejada; mar de fondo. —**hold** *o* **stand one's ground,** mantener *o* sostener su posición. —**lose ground,** perder terreno. —**on the grounds of,** basado en; por razón de. —**run into the ground,** *colloq.* agotar; acabar (con). —**shift one's ground,** cambiar de actitud or posición.

ground hog marmota de América.

groundless ('graund·ləs) *adj.* infundado; sin base *o* fundamento.

groundwork *n.* base; fundamento.

group (grup) *n.* grupo. —*v.t.* agrupar. —*v.i.* agruparse.

grouper ('gru·pər) *n., ichthy.* cabrilla.

grouse (graus) *n.* 1, [*pl.* **grouse**] (bird) ave silvestre (perdiz, faisán, etc.). 2, [*pl.* **grouses**] *slang* (complaint) queja. —*v.i., slang* refunfuñar; gruñir; quejarse.

grout (graut) *n.* lechada; argamasa clara.

grove (groːv) *n.* arboleda.

grovel ('grʌv·əl) *v.i.* arrastrarse; humillarse.

grow (groː) *v.i.* [**grew, grown, growing**] 1, (sprout; spring up) brotar. 2, (develop) crecer; desarrolarse. 3, (increase) crecer. 4, (become) ponerse; volverse. —*v.t.* 1, (cultivate; raise) cultivar; producir. 2, (cause or allow to grow) hacer crecer; dejar(se) crecer. —**grow old,** envejecer. —**grow on,** conquistar; apoderarse de. —**grow out of,** 1, (develop from) provenir de; surgir de. 2, (outgrow) dejar atrás; perder (la costumbre de). —**grow up,** 1, (reach maturity) crecer; llegar a la madurez. 2, (develop; arise) brotar; surgir. —**grow young,** rejuvenecerse.

growl (graul) *n.* gruñido; ronquido. —*v.i.* gruñir; roncar. —*v.t.* proferir gruñendo. —**growler,** *n.* gruñón.

grown (groːn) *v., p.p. de* **grow.** —*adj.* 1, (mature) crecido; desarrollado. 2, (covered over) lleno; cubierto.

grownup ('gron,ʌp) *n.* adulto; persona mayor.

growth (groθ) *n.* 1, (development) crecimiento; desarrollo. 2, (increase) aumento. 3, (something growing or grown) brote; cultivo; vegetación. 4, *med.* tumor.

grub (grʌb) *v.t.* [**grubbed, grubbing**] 1, (dig up by the roots) sacar de raíz; arrancar; desarraigar. 2, (clear, as earth) quitar la maleza de; *Amer.* desmalezar. 3, *slang* (sponge; beg) gorrear. —*v.i.* 1, (dig) escarbar. 2, (toil) afanarse; trabajar asiduamente. —*n.* 1, (larva) larva; gorgojo. 2, *slang* (food) comida; manducatoria.

grubby ('grʌb·i) *adj.* 1, (dirty) sucio; mugriento. 2, (covered with vermin) piojento; piojoso. 3, (ragged; shabby) desaliñado; desharrapado.

grudge (grʌdʒ) *n.* rencor; ojeriza. —*v.t.* 1, (envy) envidiar. 2, (grant reluctantly) escatimar; escasear. —**grudging,** *adj.* dado o hecho de mala gana o con repugnancia.

gruel ('gru·əl) *n.* gachas (*pl.*); puches (*pl.*). —*v.t.* cansar; agotar. —**grueling,** *adj.* arduo; agotador.

gruesome ('gru·səm) *adj.* repulsivo; horrible; horripilante.

gruff (grʌf) *adj.* 1, (hoarse) ronco; áspero. 2, (surly; rude) hosco; rudo. —**gruffness,** *n.* aspereza; sequedad; hosquedad.

grumble ('grʌm·bəl) *n.* refunfuño; gruñido; queja. —*v.i.* refunfuñar; gruñir; quejarse.

grumpy ('grʌm·pi) *adj.* malhumorado; gruñón.

grunt (grʌnt) *n.* gruñido. —*v.i.* gruñir.

guanaco (gwə'na·ko) *n.* guanaco.

guano ('gwa·no) *n.* [*pl.* **-nos**] guano.

guarantee (,gær·ən'tiː) *n.* garantía. —*v.t.* [**-teed, -teeing**] garantizar; garantir.

guarantor ('gær·ən,tor; -tər) *n.* fiador; garante; garantizador.

guaranty ('gær·ən·ti) *n.* 1, = guarantee. 2, = guarantor. —*v.t.* = guarantee.

guard (gard) *v.t.* 1, (defend; protect) proteger; guardar; defender. 2, (keep watch on; keep in check) cuidar; atender. 3, (keep watch over) custodiar; guardar; vigilar. 4, (provide with a safeguard) cubrir; resguardar; poner resguardo a. —*v.i.* 1, (take precautions) resguardarse (de *o* contra); precaverse (de *o* contra). 3, (keep watch) hacer guardia; velar. —*n.* 1, (act or duty of guarding) guardia. 2, (precaution; safeguard) resguardo; protección. 3, (defensive posture) guardia. 4, (protective device) protector; resguardo; guarda; guarnición. 5, (sentry) guardia; guarda. 6, *sports* defensa. —**mount guard**, montar guardia. —**off guard**, desprevenido. —**on (one's) guard**, en guardia; prevenido. —**stand guard**, hacer guardia.

guarded ('gar·dɪd) *adj.* 1, (protected; defended) protegido; resguardado; defendido. 2, (supervised; watched) cuidado; vigilado. 3, (cautious; careful; restrained) cuidadoso; comedido; receloso.

guardhouse *n.* prevención; cuartel de guardia.

guardian ('gar·di·ən) *n.* 1, (person who guards) guardián. 2, *law* tutor; encargado. —*adj.* custodio; de la guarda.

guardroom *n.* calabozo; prevención.

guava ('gwa·və) *n.* 1, (fruit) guayaba. 2, (tree) guayabo.

gubernatorial (ˌgu·bər·nə'tor·i·əl) *adj.* de *o* del gobernador.

gudgeon ('gʌdʒ·ən) *n.* 1, *ichthy.* gobio. 2, (bait) cebo. 3, *mech.* gorrón; espiga. 4, (dupe; gull) cándido; inocentón; pazguato. —*v.t.* engatusar; engañar.

guerrilla *también,* **guerilla** (gə·'rɪl·ə) *n.* (guerrilla fighter) guerrillero. —*adj.* de guerrillas. —**guerrilla band**, guerrilla.

guess (gɛs) *v.t.* & *i.* conjeturar; adivinar. —*n.* [*también,* **guesswork**] conjetura; adivinación.

guest (gɛst) *n.* 1, (visitor) visita; invitado; convidado. 2, (lodger, as at a hotel) huésped.

guffaw (gʌ'fɔː) *n.* risotada; carcajada. —*v.i.* dar risotadas; reír a carcajadas.

guidance ('gai·dəns) *n.* guía; dirección.

guide (gaid) *v.t.* guiar; dirigir. —*n.* guía. —**guided missile**, proyectil dirigido.

guidebook *n.* guía.

guidepost *n.* hito; poste indicador.

guild (gɪld) *n.* gremio.

guile (gail) *n.* astucia; maña; engaño. —**guileless**, *adj.* inocente; sincero; cándido.

guillotine ('gɪl·əˌtin) *n.* guillotina. —*v.t.* guillotinar.

guilt (gɪlt) *n.* culpa; delito. —**guiltless**, *adj.* inocente; sin culpa.

guilty ('gɪl·ti) *adj.* culpable. —**guiltiness**, *n.* culpabilidad.

guinea ('gɪn·i) *n.* guinea. —**guinea hen**, gallina de guinea; guinea. —**guinea pig**, conejillo de Indias; *So.Amer.* cuy.

guise (gaiz) *n.* 1, (attire; dress) vestido; traje. 2, (appearance) aspecto; apariencia.

guitar (gɪ'taːr) *n.* guitarra. —**guitarist**, *n.* guitarrista.

gulch (gʌltʃ) *n.* barranca; quebrada.

gulden ('gʊl·dən) *n.* florín.

gulf (gʌlf) *n.* 1, *geog.* golfo. 2, (chasm) abismo.

gull (gʌl) *n.* 1, (bird) gaviota. 2, (dupe) bobo; pazguato. —*v.t.* embaucar; engatusar.

gullet ('gʌl·ɪt) *n.* gaznate; garganta.

gullible ('gʌl·ə·bəl) *adj.* crédulo; simplón. —**gullibility**, *n.* credulidad; simplonería.

gully ('gʌl·i) *n.* barranca; garganta; quebrada.

gulp (gʌlp) *v.t.* tragar; engullir; echarse (algo) al coleto. —*v.i.* atragantarse. —*n.* trago.

gum (gʌm) *n.* 1, *anat.* encía. 2, (sticky substance) goma; pegamento. —*v.t.* [**gummed, gumming**] engomar; pegar. —*v.i.* ponerse pegajoso. —**chewing gum**, goma de mascar; chicle. —**gum arabic**, goma arábiga. —**gum up**, *colloq.* estropear; *Amer.* embarrar.

gumbo ('gʌm·bo) *n.* [*pl.* **-bos**] quingombó.

gumdrop *n.* pastilla de goma.

gummy ('gʌm·i) *adj.* 1, (of or like gum) gomoso. 2, (sticky) pegajoso. —**gumminess**, *n.* pegajosidad.

gumption (ˈgʌmp·ʃən) *n., colloq.* **1,** (initiative) iniciativa; empuje; nervio. **2,** (common sense) sentido común.
gumshoe (ˈgʌmˌʃu) *n.* **1,** *colloq.* (overshoe) chanclo. **2,** *slang* (detective) detective.
gun (gʌn) *n.* **1,** (weapon) arma de fuego (pistola, escopeta, cañón, etc.). **2,** (discharge of a gun, as in a salute) cañonazo. —*v.t.* [**gunned, gunning**] **1,** (shoot) disparar. **2,** [*usu.* **gun for**] (pursue) cazar; perseguir; ir en busca de. **3,** (accelerate) acelerar. —**stick to one's guns,** mantenerse en sus trece.
gunboat *n.* cañonero; lancha cañonera.
guncotton *n.* pólvora de algodón; algodón pólvora.
gunfire *n.* fuego; tiros (*de armas de fuego*).
gunman (ˈgʌn·mən) *n.* [*pl.* **-men**] pistolero.
gunner (ˈgʌn·ər) *n.* artillero.
gunnery (ˈgʌn·ər·i) *n.* artillería.
gunpowder *n.* pólvora.
gunshot (ˈgʌn·ʃat) *n.* balazo; escopetazo. —**gunshot wound,** balazo; escopetazo.
gunsmith *n.* armero.
gunwale (ˈgʌn·əl) *n.* borda.
gurgle (ˈgʌɹ·gəl) *v.i.* **1,** (flow noisily) gluglutear. **2,** (utter inarticulate sounds) hacer gorgoritos; gorjear. —*n.* **1,** (noise of flowing) gluglú; gorgoteo. **2,** (inarticulate sound) gorgorito; gorjeo.
gush (gʌʃ) *n.* **1,** (flow) chorro; borbotón; borbollón. **2,** *colloq.* (effusiveness) efusión; sensiblería. —*v.i.* borbollar; hacer borbollones; manar a borbotones. —*v.t.* echar a borbollones *o* borbotones.
gusher (ˈgʌʃ·ər) *n.* **1,** (oil well) pozo surgente. **2,** (effusive person) persona efusiva.
gushy (ˈgʌʃ·i) *adj., colloq.* efusivo. —**gushiness,** *n., colloq.* efusividad.
gusset (ˈgʌs·ɪt) *n.* **1,** *sewing* escudete. **2,** (connecting metal plate) codo de metal; escuadra metálica.
gust (gʌst) *n.* **1,** (blast of wind) ráfaga; racha. **2,** (outburst) arrebato; explosión.
gustatory (ˈgʌs·təˌtor·i) *adj.* gustativo; del gusto.
gusto (ˈgʌs·to) *n.* gusto; placer; satisfacción.
gusty (ˈgʌs·ti) *adj.* ventoso; impetuoso; de *o* con ventoleras.
gut (gʌt) *n.* **1,** *usu.pl.* (intestine) intestino; tripas. **2,** *naut.* (channel) canal; estrecho; paso. **3,** *pl., slang* (courage) agallas. **4,** *slang* (belly) barriga; panza. **5,** = **catgut.** —*v.t.* [**gutted, gutting**] destripar; desentrañar.
gutta-percha (ˈgʌt·əˈpʌɹ·tʃə) *n.* gutapercha.
gutter (ˈgʌt·ər) *n.* **1,** (of a road) cuneta. **2,** (of a roof) canal; canalón.
guttersnipe *n.* pillo; pilluelo; granuja.
guttural (ˈgʌt·ər·əl) *n.* gutural.
guy (gai) *n.* **1,** (rope or cable for steadying something) tirante. **2,** *slang* (fellow) tipo; sujeto; individuo. —*v.t., colloq.* burlarse de; mofarse de.
guzzle (ˈgʌz·əl) *v.t. & i.* beber mucho *o* con rapidez; tragar.
gym (dʒɪm) *n., colloq.* = **gymnasium.**
gymnasium (dʒɪmˈnei·zi·əm) *n.* gimnasio.
gymnast (ˈdʒɪm·næst) *n.* gimnasta. —**gymnastic** (dʒɪmˈnæs·tɪk) *adj.* gimnástico. —**gymnastics,** *n.pl.* gimnasia; gimnástica.
gyn- (dʒain) *prefijo* gin-; mujer; hembra: *gynandrous,* ginandro.
gyne- (dʒai·nə) *prefijo* gine-; *var. de* **gyn-**: *gyneolatry,* gineolatría.
gyneco- (dʒai·ni·co; -nə-) *prefijo* gineco-; mujer: *gynecology,* ginecología.
gynecology (ˌdʒai·nəˈkal·ə·dʒi) *n.* ginecología. —**gynecological** (-kəˈladʒ·ɪ·kəl) *adj.* ginecológico. —**gynecologist,** *n.* ginecólogo.
gyno- (dʒai·nə) *prefijo* gino-; *var. de* **gyn-**: *gynophore,* ginóforo.
-gynous (dʒɪ·nəs) *sufijo* -gino; mujer; hembra: *androgynous,* andrógino.
-gyny (dʒɪ·ni) *sufijo* -ginia; *forma nombres de los adjetivos terminados en* **-gynous**: *androgyny,* androginia.
gyp (dʒɪp) *n., slang* **1,** (swindler) tramposo; estafador. **2,** (swindle) estafa; timo. —*v.t., slang* estafar; timar.

gypsum (ˈdʒɪp·səm) *n.* yeso.
gypsy *también,* **gipsy** (dʒɪp·si) *n.* gitano. —*adj.* gitano; gitanesco.
gyrate (ˈdʒai·ret) *v.i.* girar; dar vueltas. —**gyration,** *n.* giro; vuelta.
gyro- (dʒai·ro; -rə) *prefijo* giro-; círculo; giro; vuelta: *gyroscope,* giróscopo.
gyroscope (ˈdʒai·rə·skop) *n.* giroscopio; giróscopo.

H

H, h (eitʃ) octava letra del alfabeto inglés.
ha (ha) *interj.* ¡ja!
haberdasher (ˈhæb·ərˌdæʃ·ər) *n.* camisero. —**haberdashery,** *n.* camisería.
habilitate (həˈbɪl·əˌteit) *v.t.* habilitar.
habit (ˈhæb·ɪt) *n.* hábito. —*v.t.* vestir. —**be in the habit of,** tener el hábito de; acostumbrar; soler. —**get into the habit of,** habituarse a; coger el hábito de.
habitable (ˈhæb·ɪt·ə·bəl) *adj.* habitable.
habitat (ˈhæb·əˌtæt) *n.* habitat; habitación; medio; elemento.
habitation (ˌhæb·əˈtei·ʃən) *n.* residencia; habitación.
habitual (hæˈbɪtʃ·u·əl) *adj.* habitual; acostumbrado.
habituate (hæˈbɪtʃ·uˌeit) *v.t.* habituar; acostumbrar. —**habituation,** *n.* costumbre; hábito.
habitué (həˈbɪtʃ·uˌei) *n.* parroquiano *o* concurrente asiduo; habitué.
hacienda (ˌha·siˈɛn·də) *n.* hacienda.
hack (hæk) *n.* **1,** (gash) tajo; corte. **2,** (tool) azuela; hacha. **3,** (cough) tos seca. **4,** (old horse) jamelgo. **5,** (car for hire) taxi. **6,** (hired writer) escritor mercenario; rutinero. —*adj.* **1,** (hired) alquilado; de alquiler. **2,** = **hackneyed.** —*v.t.* **1,** (chop) dar tajos a. **2,** = **hackney.** —*v.i.* **1,** (chop) dar *o* hacer tajos. **2,** (cough) tener una tos seca; toser. **3,** (drive a taxicab) conducir o manejar un taxi. **4,** (write for hire) escribir por un precio. —**hack out,** producir por rutina.
hackle (ˈhæk·əl) *n.* **1,** (comb for dressing flax, hemp, etc.) rastrillo. **2,** *usu.pl.* (bristling hair) pelo erizado. —*v.t.* & *i.* **1,** (dress flax, hemp, etc.) rastrillar. **2,** (hack roughly) hacer pedazos; cortar a machetazos *o* hachazos.
hackman (ˈhæk·mən) *n.* [*pl.* **-men**] conductor de taxi; chofer.
hackney (ˈhæk·ni) *n.* **1,** (horse) caballo. **2,** (hired horse or carriage) caballo o carruaje de alquiler. —*v.t.* **1,** (hire out) alquilar. **2,** (make trite) repetir hasta el cansancio; usar demasiado. —*adj.* alquilado; de alquiler. —**hackneyed,** *adj.* trillado; manoseado; gastado.
hacksaw *n.* sierra para metales.
had (hæd) *v., pret.* & *p.p. de* **have.**
haddock (ˈhæd·ək) *n.* bacalao de Escocia; merluza.
Hades (ˈhei·diz) *n.* infierno; averno.
haema- *también,* **haemo-** (hi·mə) *prefijo, var. de* **hema-, hemo-.**
-haemia (hi·mi·ə) *prefijo, var. de* **-hemia.**
hafnium (ˈhæf·ni·əm) *n.* hafnio.
haft (hæft) *n.* empuñadura; puño.
hag (hæg) *n.* **1,** (ugly woman; witch) vieja fea; bruja. **2,** = **hagfish.**
hagfish *n.* lamprea glutinosa.
haggard (ˈhæg·ərd) *adj.* demacrado; ojeroso; extenuado. —**haggardness,** *n.* fatiga; demacración.
haggle (ˈhæg·əl) *v.i.* & *t.* **1,** (bargain) regatear. **2,** (wrangle) disputar; altercar. —*n.* **1,** (bargaining) regateo. **2,** (wrangle) disputa; altercado. —**haggler** (-lər) *n.* regatero.
haha (haˈha) *interj.* ¡ja, ja! —*n.* risa; risoteo.
hail (heil) *v.t.* **1,** (acclaim) aclamar. **2,** (call to) llamar de un grito a; dar una voz a; llamar. **3,** (salute) saludar; dar la bienvenida a. **4,** (shower; pour) llover; granizar; dar a granel. —*v.impers.* (fall, as hail) granizar. —*n.* **1,** (shout) grito; llamada. **2,** (greeting; salutation) saludo; bienvenida. **3,** (hailstone) granizo. **4,** (downpour) granizada. **5,** (hail-

ing distance) grito. —*interj.* ¡salud!; ¡salve! —**hail from**, venir de; ser de. —**Hail Mary**, Ave María. —**within hail**, a un grito (de aquí o allí); al habla.

hailstone *n.* granizo; piedra.

hailstorm *n.* granizada.

hair (heːr) *n.* **1,** (on the head) pelo; cabello. **2,** (on the body) vello; pelo. **3,** (covering or coat of hair) pelambre; pelaje; pelo. **4,** (head of hair) cabellera. **5,** *bot.* filamento. **6,** (bit; small amount) pelo; cabello. —*adj.* de del *o* para el pelo. — **get in one's hair,** *slang* fastidiar; disgustar; *Amer.* fregar. —**let one's hair down,** *slang* andar sin formalidades; ponerse a sus anchas. —**make one's hair stand on end,** ponérsele a uno el pelo de punta. —**not turn a hair,** no inmutarse. —**split hairs,** pararse en pelillos. —**to a hair,** exactamente; perfectamente.

hairbreadth *n.* pelo; suspiro; tris. —*adj.* estrecho; de *o* por un pelo.

hairbrush *n.* cepillo para el pelo.

haircut *n.* corte del pelo.

hairdo *n., colloq.* peinado; tocado.

hairdresser *n.* peluquero.

hairless (ˈhɛr·ləs) *adj.* pelón; pelado.

hairline *n.* raya.

hairnet *n.* redecilla; cofia.

hairpin *n.* horquilla; gancho. —*adj.* con vueltas y revueltas.

hair-raising *adj.* espeluznante.

hairsbreadth *también,* **hair's-breadth** (ˈhɛrzˌbrɛdθ) *n.* & *adj.* = **hairbreadth.**

hairsplitting *n.* un pararse en pelillos; nimiedades (*pl.*). —*adj.* nimio; que repara en pelillos.

hairspring *n.* muelle; espiral.

hairy (ˈhɛr·i) *adj.* peludo; piloso; velludo; velluso. —**hairiness,** *n.* vellosidad; pelambre.

hake (heik) *n.* merluza; pescada.

halberd (ˈhæl·bərd) *n.* alabarda. —**halberdier** (-bərˈdɪr) *n.* alabardero.

halcyon (ˈhæl·si·ən) *n., ornith.* martín pescador. —*adj.* tranquilo; quieto; apacible.

hale (heil) *adj.* sano; saludable; robusto. —*v.t.* tirar; halar; arrastrar. —**hale and hearty,** sano y fuerte.

half (hæf) *n.* [*pl.* **halves**] mitad; medio. —*adj.* medio. —*adv.* medio; a medio; a medias. —**by half,** por un mucho. —**in half,** por la mitad.

half-and-half *adj., adv.* & *n.* mitad y mitad.

half-baked *adj.* a medio cocer.

halfblood *adj.* & *n.* = **halfbreed.**

halfbreed *n.* & *adj.* mestizo.

half brother hermanastro.

half-caste *adj.* & *n.* mestizo.

halfhearted *adj.* sin entusiasmo; desganado. —**halfheartedly,** *adv.* desganadamente; a desgano.

half-length *adj.* de medio cuerpo. —*n.* retrato de medio cuerpo.

half life período medio.

half-mast *n.* media asta. —*v.t.* poner a media asta.

half moon media luna.

half note mínima.

halfpenny (ˈhei·pə·ni) *n.* medio penique.

half sister hermanastra.

half sole media suela. —**half-sole,** *v.t.* poner media suela a.

half-staff *n.* & *v.t.* = **half-mast.**

half step **1,** *music* semitono; medio tono. **2,** *mil.* paso corto.

halftone *n.* media tinta. —*adj.* de media tinta.

half tone *music* semitono; medio tono.

half-truth *n.* verdad a medias.

halfway *adv.* **1,** (to or at the midpoint) hasta la mitad; hasta el medio; a mitad de camino; a medio camino. **2,** (partially) medio; a medio; a medias; en parte. —*adj.* **1,** (situated at the midpoint) medio; a mitad del camino. **2,** (partial) parcial; medio; a medio hacer.

half-wit *n.* imbécil; tonto de capirote. —**half-witted,** *adj.* imbécil; tonto.

halibut (ˈhæl·ə·bət) *n.* halibut.

halitosis (ˌhæl·əˈto·sɪs) *n.* halitosis; mal aliento.

hall (hɔːl) *n.* **1,** (large or principal room) sala; salón. **2,** (building) edificio. **3,** (mansion) mansión. **4,** (vestibule) vestíbulo. **5,** (corridor) pasillo; corredor. —**town** *o* **city hall,** ayuntamiento; alcaldía.

hallelujah (ˌhæl·əˈlu·ja) *n.* & *interj.* aleluya.

hallmark *n.* sello de calidad; sello distintivo.

halloo (hæˈluː) *interj.* ¡busca!; ¡sus! —*n.* grito; llamada. —*v.t.* &

i. 1, (call; shout) dar voces; llamar a voces. 2, (incite) azuzar.
hallow ('hæl·o) *v.t.* santificar; consagrar.
Halloween (ˌhæl·ə'wi:n) *n.* víspera de Todos los Santos.
hallucinate (hə'lu·səˌneit) *v.t.* alucinar. —**hallucination,** *n.* alucinación. —**hallucinatory,** *adj.* alucinante; alucinador.
hallway *n.* 1, (vestibule) vestíbulo. 2, (corridor) corredor; pasillo.
halo ('hei·lo) *n.* [*pl.* **halos**] halo.
halo- (hæl·ə) *prefijo* halo-; sal: *halogen,* halógeno.
halogen ('hæl·ə·dʒən) *n.* halógeno.
halt (hɔlt) *v.i.* 1, (stop) pararse; detenerse. 2, (waver; hesitate) vacilar; titubear. —*v.t.* parar; detener. —*n.* parada; alto; pausa. —*adj., archaic* cojo. —**halting,** *adj.* vacilante; entrecortado.
halter ('hɔl·tər) *n.* 1, (strap for tying or leading) cabestro; ronzal. 2, (hangman's noose) dogal. 3, (garment) especie de corpiño que deja la espalda al descubierto. —*v.t.* encabestrar; poner cabestro a.
halve (hæv) *v.t.* dividir en dos *o* por mitad.
halves (hævz) *n., pl. de* **half.** —**by halves,** por mitad. —**go halves,** ir a medias.
halyard ('hæl·jərd) *n.* driza.
ham (hæm) *n.* 1, (cut of meat) jamón; pernil. 2, (part behind the knee) corva. 3, (buttock) anca; nalga. 4, *slang* (actor who overacts) actor exagerado; aspaventero. 5, *slang* (amateur, esp. in radio) aficionado.
hamburger ('hæm·bʌɹ·gər) *n.* 1, (meat) carne molida *o* picada. 2, (sandwich) sandwich *o* emparedado de carne molida; *Amer.* hamburguesa.
Hamite ('hæm·ait) *n. & adj.* camita. —**Hamitic** (hæ'mɪt·ɪk) *adj.* camítico.
hamlet ('hæm·lɪt) *n.* caserío; aldea; villorrio.
hammer ('hæm·ər) *n.* 1, (tool) martillo. 2, (of a firearm) percusor. 3, (of a piano) macillo. 4, *anat.* martillo. 5, (gavel; mallet) mazo; martillo. 6, (drop hammer) maza; martinete; martillo pilón. —*v.t. & i.* martillear; martillar. —*v.t.* 1, (drive with or as with a hammer) clavar; meter. 2, (shape with a hammer) batir; formar a martillazos. —**hammering,** *n.* martilleo. —**hammer and tongs,** con vehemencia; con energía. —**hammer (away) at,** 1, (work diligently at) trabajar con empeño en. 2, (insist on) esforzarse en; insistir en. —**hammer out,** 1, (remove dents from) desabollar. 2, (fashion laboriously) crear trabajosamente; conseguir con esfuerzo.
hammerhead *n., ichthy.* cornuda; cornudilla; pez martillo.
hammock ('hæm·ək) *n.* hamaca.
hamper ('hæm·pər) *v.t.* estorbar; impedir. —*n.* canasta; cesto.
hamster ('hæm·stər) *n.* hámster.
hamstring *n.* tendón de la corva. —*v.t.* [*pret. & p.p.* **hamstrung**] desjarretar; *fig.* incapacitar.
hand (hænd) *n.* 1, (part of the body) mano. 2, (side) lado; mano. 3, (manner of doing or dexterity) mano. 4, (handwriting) caligrafía; escritura; letra. 5, (applause) aplauso. 6, (help; aid) ayuda; mano. 7, (employee; laborer) obrero; trabajador. 8, (pointer; indicator) manecilla; aguja. 9, (handbreadth) mano. 10, *cards* mano. —*adj.* 1, (of or with the hand) de mano; a mano. 2, (manual) manual. —*v.t.* 1, (pass; give) pasar; dar. 2, (deliver) entregar. 3, (help; conduct; steady) ayudar; asistir. —**all hands,** todos; todo el mundo. —**at first hand,** directamente. —**at hand,** a mano. —**at the hand** (*o* **hands**) **of,** a las manos de. —**by hand,** a mano. —**eat out of one's hand,** ser manso *o* dócil. —**from hand to hand,** de mano en mano. —**hand and foot,** 1, (securely tied) de pies y manos. 2, (diligently) con diligencia. —**hand down,** 1, (bequeath; pass on) legar; transmitir. 2, (announce, as an order or decision) dar; emitir. —**hand in,** entregar; presentar. —**hand in glove; hand and glove,** uña y carne. —**hand in hand,** 1, (holding hands) cogidos de la mano. 2, (together) de la mano. —**hand it to (someone)** *slang* reconocérselo (a uno). —**hand on,** transmitir; legar. —**hand out,** distribuir; dar. —**hand over,** pasar; dar; entregar. —**hand over fist,** *colloq.* a manos llenas. —**hands down,** sin dificultad; sin

esfuerzo. —**hands off**, no tocar; no meterse. —**hands up**!, ¡manos arriba!; ¡arriba las manos! —**hand to hand**, cuerpo a cuerpo. —**in hand**, **1**, (under control) dominado; controlado; bajo rienda. **2**, (in posession) en poder. **3**, (being attended to) entre manos. —**join hands**, unirse. —**lay hands on**, **1**, (get hold of) echar la mano a; poner las manos en. **2**, (attack) caer encima. **3**, (find) encontrar. **4**, (touch, as in blessing) imponer las manos. —**live from hand to mouth**, ir tirando. —**not lift a hand**, no levantar un dedo. —**on every hand**, por todas partes; por todos lados. —**on hand**, a mano. —**on one's hands**, a cargo de uno. —**on the one hand**, por un lado. —**on the other hand**, por otro lado. —**out of hand**, **1**, (out of control) imposible; fuera decontrol. **2**, (immediately) de súbito; sin más ni más. —**shake hands**, dar(se) la mano; estrechar (se) la mano. —**take in hand**, encargarse de. —**take** (*o* **get**) **off one's hands**, quitar de encima. —**throw up one's hands**, darse por vencido; rendirse; entregarse. —**to hand**, a mano. —**turn** (*o* **put**) **one's hand to**, dedicarse a. —**upper hand**, ventaja; posición ventajosa. —**have a hand in**, tener que ver con; tener que hacer con.

handbag *n.* **1**, (purse) bolso; *Amer.* cartera. **2**, (case; satchel) maletín; bolsa *o* saco de mano.

handball *n.* pelota; juego de frontón.

hand barrow *n.* angarillas (*pl.*).

handbill *n.* volante; impreso.

handbook *n.* manual; guía; prontuario.

handcar *n.*, *R.R.* vagoneta; zorra.

handclasp *n.* apretón de mano.

handcuff *v.t.* esposar; maniatar. —**handcuffs**, *n.pl.* esposas; manillas.

-handed (hæn·dɪd) *sufijo, forma adjetivos relacionados con* mano: *left-handed,* zurdo; *heavy-handed,* de *o* con mano fuerte; *four-handed game,* partida de cuatro jugadores.

handful ('hænd,ful) *n.* [*pl.* **handfuls**] **1**, (fistful) puñado. **2**, *slang* (difficult task) hueso.

handicap ('hæn·di,kæp) *n.* **1**, (hindrance; disadvantage) desventaja; handicap. **2**, (race or contest) handicap. **3**, (advantage given to an inferior contestant) ventaja; margen. —*v.t.* [**-capped**, **-capping**] **1**, (impede) estorbar; impedir; poner trabas a; poner en desventaja. **2**, (put a handicap on) poner handicap a.

handicraft ('hæn·di·kræft) *n.* artesanía. *También,* **handcraft.** —**handcraftsman**, *n.* artesano.

handily ('hæn·dɪ·li) *adv.* con soltura; con facilidad.

handiness ('hæn·di·nəs) *n.* **1**, (convenience) comodidad; conveniencia. **2**, (skill) facilidad; destreza.

handiwork ('hæn·di,wʌɪk) *n.* **1**, (hand work) labor manual. **2**, (work; creation) obra.

handkerchief ('hæŋ·kər·tʃɪf; -tʃif) *n.* pañuelo.

handle ('hæn·dəl) *v.t.* **1**, (touch) tocar; manosear. **2**, (manipulate) manipular; manejar. **3**, (have charge of) encargarse de; ocuparse de; atender. **4**, (treat; deal with) tratar. **5**, (manage; control) dirigir; manejar. **6**, *comm.* (deal in) negociar en; tener negocios de; vender. —*v.i.* trabajar; manejarse. —*n.* **1**, (of a tool or utensil) mango; asa. **2**, (of a door) tirador. **3**, (lever) manubrio. —**fly off the handle**, *colloq.* salirse (uno) de sus casillas; perder los estribos. —**handle with care**, trátese con cuidado.

handlebar *n.* manillar; *Amer.* manubrio.

handler ('hæn·dlər) *n.* **1**, (person or thing that handles) persona o cosa que maneja o controla. **2**, (trainer; coach) entrenador.

handmade *adj.* hecho a mano.

handmaid *n.* sirvienta; criada; moza.

hand-me-down *n.*, *colloq.* prenda o cosa usada. —*adj.* de segunda mano.

hand organ organillo.

handout *n.* **1**, *slang* (gift) limosna. **2**, *slang* (favor; reward) favor; premio. **3**, (handbill) volante. **4**, (press release) comunicado.

hand-picked *adj.* escogido; seleccionado.

handsaw *n.* serrucho.

handshake *n.* apretón de manos.

handsome ('hæn·səm) *adj.* **1**, (large; considerable) importante; considerable. **2**, (gracious; seemly) gentil; generoso. 3, (good-looking) hermoso; guapo; apuesto; buen mozo. 4, (impressive; pleasing) hermoso; atractivo. —**handsomeness**, *n.* belleza; hermosura.

handspring *n.* voltereta sobre las manos.

handwriting *n.* escritura; caligrafía; letra.

handy ('hæn·di) *adj.* 1, (accessible) cerca; a (la) mano. 2, (skillful) hábil; diestro. 3, (adaptable) cómodo; fácil de uso.

handyman *n.* [*pl.* **-men**] ayudante; persona que en una casa o establecimiento desempeña oficios menudos.

hang (hæŋ) *v.t.* [*pret.* & *p.p.* **hung**] 1, (suspend from a support) colgar. 2, (attach, as to a hinge) suspender. 3, [*pret.* & *p.p.* **hanged**] (put to death by hanging) ahorcar; colgar. 4, (decorate or cover with hangings) decorar; adornar *o* cubrir (con cuadros *o* colgaduras). 5, (deadlock, as a jury) inmovilizar; obstruir (un jurado). —*v.i.* 1, (be suspended) pender; colgar. 2, (fall or flow, as a coat) caer. 3, (lean; droop) inclinarse. 4, [*pret.* & *p.p.* **hanged**] (die by hanging) morir ahorcado. 5, (hesitate) vacilar. 6, (come to a standstill) estar suspendido. —*n.* 1, (way that a thing hangs) caída; vuelo. 2, (way of doing or using) manera; forma. 3, (significance) significado. 4, (pause in motion) pausa; alto. —**hang around** (*o* **about**), 1, (cluster around) agruparse alrededor (de). 2, *colloq.* (loiter) rondar; vagar. —**hang back**, echarse para atrás; amilanarse. —**hang fire**, 1, (be slow in firing, as a gun) retardarse en disparar. 2, (be slow in acting) retrasarse; demorarse; quedar en ciernes. 3, (be undecided) estar *o* quedar en duda. —**hang it!**, ¡al diablo! —**hang on**, 1, (keep hold) agarrarse; sujetarse. 2, (go on doing; persevere) seguir; continuar; perseverar. 3, (depend on) depender de. 4, (lean on) apoyarse en; recostarse contra. 5, (listen attentively to) estar pendiente a. —**hang on to**, no soltar; guardar. —**hang out**, 1, (lean out) asomarse. 2, *slang* (reside; frequent) residir; parar. —**hang over**, 1, (project; overhang) extenderse sobre; proyectarse sobre. 2, (hover or loom over) cernirse sobre. 3, (be left over; remain) quedar. —**hang together**, 1, (be united) estar *o* ir unidos. 2, (be coherent) concordar; tener coherencia. —**hang up**, 1, (put on a hook, hanger, etc.) colgar. 2, (delay; suspend) demorar; dilatar; suspender.

hangar ('hæŋ·ər) *n.* hangar.

hangdog *adj.* abyecto; ruin; abatido.

hanger ('hæŋ·ər) *n.* percha; colgador; *Amer.* gancho.

hanger-on *n.* [*pl.* **hangers-on**] pegote; gorrón; *Amer.* lapa.

hangfire *n.* tiro retardado.

hanging ('hæŋ·ɪŋ) *adj.* 1, (suspended; pendulous) colgante. 2, (overhanging) sobresaliente; salido. 3, (unsettled; inconclusive) en ciernes; en suspenso; pendiente. 4, (deserving the death penalty) que merece la horca. —*n.* 1, (a suspending or being suspended) colgamiento; colgado. 2, (execution) ahorcadura; horca; muerte en la horca. 3, *usu.pl.* (drapings) colgaduras.

hangman ('hæŋ·mən) *n.* [*pl.* **-men**] verdugo.

hangnail *n.* padrastro.

hangout *n.*, *slang* guarida; paraje.

hangover ('hæŋ·o·vər) *n.* 1, (carryover; survival) remanente; sobreviviente. 2, *colloq.* (aftereffect of intoxication) resaca; *Amer.* flato; *Amer.* perseguidora.

hank (hæŋk) *n.* madeja; ovillo.

hanker ('hæŋ·kər) *v.i.* [*usu.* **hanker after** *o* **for**] ansiar; apetecer; anhelar. —**hankering**, *n.* ansia; anhelo.

hanky-panky ('hæŋ·ki'pæŋ·ki) *n.*, *colloq.* escamoteo; tramoya; manipuleo; enredo.

hansom ('hæn·səm) *n.* cabriolé Hansom.

haphazard (hæp'hæz·ərd) *adj.* casual; accidental; fortuito. —*adv.* al azar; a lo loco; a la diabla. —*n.* suerte; casualidad.

hapless ('hæp·ləs) *adj.* desafortunado; infeliz; desgraciado. —**haplessness**, *n.* desventura; desgracia.

haplo- (hæp·lo) *prefijo* haplo-; único; simple; *haplology*, haplología.

happen ('hæp·ən) *v.i.* suceder; acaecer; acontecer; ocurrir. —**hap-**

pening, *n.* acontecimiento; suceso.

happenstance ('hæp·ən,stæns) *n.* casualidad.

happy ('hæp·i) *adj.* feliz. —**happiness,** *n.* felicidad; dicha. —**happy-go-lucky,** *adj.* despreocupado; alegre.

harakiri ('ha·rə'kɪr·i) *n.* harakiri.

harangue (hə'ræŋ) *n.* arenga. —*v.t. & i.* arengar.

harass ('hær·əs; hə'ræs) *v.t.* acosar; hostigar. —**harassment,** *n.* acosamiento; hostigamiento.

harbinger ('har·bɪn·dʒər) *n.* precursor; heraldo; nuncio. —*v.t.* anunciar; presagiar.

harbor *también,* **harbour** ('har·bər) *n.* **1,** (shelter) albergue; refugio; asilo. **2,** (inlet; port) rada; bahía; puerto. —*v.t.* **1,** (shelter) albergar; refugiar; asilar. **2,** (hold, as in the mind) albergar; guardar. —*v.i.* refugiarse.

harborage ('har·bər·ɪdʒ) *n.* **1,** (port; anchorage) puerto; fondeadero. **2,** (shelter) albergue.

hard (ha:rd) *adj.* **1,** (stiff; strong; harsh) duro. **2,** (difficult) difícil. **3,** (callous; unfeeling) duro. **4,** (arduous) arduo; duro. **5,** (steady; persistent) asiduo; empeñoso. **6,** (containing much alcohol) fuerte. **7,** *phonet.* sordo. —*adv.* duro; fuerte. —**be hard on,** ser duro para (con). —**go hard with,** irle mal a. —**hard and fast,** estricto; inflexible; inamovible. —**hard by,** cerca; muy cerca. —**hard cash** (*o* **money**) efectivo. —**hard of hearing,** medio sordo; duro de oído. —**(be) hard put to it,** vérselas difíciles; verse en apuros. —**hard up,** *colloq.* en apuros; en trances apurados; arrancado.

hardbitten *adj.* endurecido.

hard-boiled *adj.* **1,** (of eggs) duro. **2,** *colloq.* (unfeeling) duro; endurecido.

hard-bound *adj.* encuadernado en pasta. *También,* **hard-cover.**

harden ('har·dən) *v.t.* endurecer; (*of metals*) templar. —*v.i.* endurecerse.

hardening ('har·dən·ɪŋ) *n.* endurecimiento; (*of metals*) templado.

hardhead *n.* cabeza dura.

hardheaded *adj.* obstinado; terco.

hardhearted *adj.* empedernido; de corazón duro.

hardihood ('har·di·hʊd) *n.* audacia; temeridad; atrevimiento.

hardily ('har·də·li) *adv.* sufridamente; con entereza.

hardiness ('har·di·nəs) *n.* **1,** (endurance; vigor) aguante; vigor. **2,** = **hardihood.**

hard labor trabajo forzado.

hardly ('hard·li) *adv.* **1,** (with difficulty) con dificultad; penosamente. **2,** (severely) severamente; ásperamente. **3,** (scarcely) apenas; a duras penas; difícilmente.

hardness ('hard·nəs) *n.* dureza.

hard-set *adj.* **1,** (in trouble) en apuros. **2,** (rigid; fixed; firm) fijo; firme. **3,** (stubborn) obstinado; emperrado.

hardship ('hard·ʃɪp) *n.* adversidad; desgracia; penalidad; privación.

hardtack ('hard,tæk) *n.* galleta de munición; pan de tropa; rosca.

hardware *n.* **1,** (tools, nails, fittings, etc.) ferretería; herraje; utensilios de metal. **2,** (gear; equipment) equipo. —**hardware store,** ferretería.

hard water agua cruda; agua dura.

hardy ('har·di) *adj.* robusto; resistente; de aguante.

hare (he:r) *n.* liebre.

harebrained *adj.* atolondrado; atronado; sin pies ni cabeza.

harelip *n.* labio leporino. —**harelipped,** *adj.* labihendido.

harem ('hɛr·əm) *n.* harén.

hark *también,* **heark** (hark) *v.i.* escuchar; oír atentamente; atender. —*interj.* ¡oiga!; ¡escuche!; ¡atienda! —**hark back,** revertir; volver.

harken ('har·kən) *v.i.* = **hearken.**

harlequin ('har·lə·kwɪn) *n.* arlequín.

harlequinade (,har·lə·kwɪ'neid) *n.* arlequinada.

harlot ('har·lət) *n.* prostituta; ramera; meretriz. —**harlotry,** *n.* prostitución.

harm (harm) *n.* daño; mal; perjuicio. —*v.t.* dañar; hacer daño a; perjudicar.

harmful ('harm·fəl) *adj.* dañino; perjudicial; nocivo. —**harmfulness,** *n.* lo malo; lo dañino; nocividad.

harmless ('harm·ləs) *adj.* inofensivo; innocuo. —**harmlessness,** *n.* innocuidad.

harmonic (har'man·ɪk) *adj. & n.* armónico. —**harmonics,** *n.pl.* armonía (*sing.*).
harmonica (har'man·ɪ·kə) *n.* armónica.
harmonious (har'mo·ni·əs) *adj.* armonioso. —**harmoniousness,** *n.* armonía.
harmonize ('har·mə,naiz) *v.t. & i.* armonizar.
harmony ('har·mə·ni) *n.* armonía.
harness ('har·nəs) *n.* arneses (*pl.*); arreos (*pl.*); *Amer.* aperos (*pl.*); aparejo. —*v.t.* **1,** (put harness on) aparejar; *Amer.* aperar. **2,** (bring into fruitful control) controlar; dominar. —**in harness,** empleado; activo.
harp (harp) *n.* arpa. —*v.i.* **1,** (play the harp) tocar el arpa. **2,** [*usu.* **harp on** *o* **upon**] (insist; persist) insistir; machacar. —**harpist,** *n.* arpista.
harpoon (har'pu:n) *n.* arpón. —*v.t.* arponear.
harpsichord ('harp·sɪ·kord) *n.* clavicordio.
harpy ('har·pi) *n.* arpía.
harquebus ('har·kwə·bəs) *n.* arcabuz.
harridan ('hær·ə·dən) *n.* bruja; vieja taimada.
harrow ('hær·o) *n.* grada; rastro; rastra. —*v.t.* **1,** (draw a harrow over) gradar; pasar el rastro a. **2,** (wound; lacerate) herir; desgarrar; lacerar. **3,** (distress; torment) perturbar; atormentar.
harrowing ('hær·o·ɪŋ) *adj.* angustioso; desgarrador.
harry ('hær·i) *v.t.* acosar; hostigar.
harsh (harʃ) *adj.* **1,** (strident) estridente; chillón. **2,** (glaring) intenso; crudo. **3,** (rough; unpleasant) áspero. **4,** (severe; rigorous) severo; riguroso; inclemente.
harshness ('harʃ·nəs) *n.* **1,** (stridency) estridencia. **2,** (glare) intensidad; crudeza. **3,** (roughness; unpleasantness) aspereza. **4,** (severity) severidad; rigor; inclemencia.
hart (hart) *n.* ciervo; venado.
harum-scarum ('hɛr·əm'skɛr·əm) *adj.* atolondrado; desordenado. —*adv.* a la diabla; a lo loco; desordenadamente; atolondradamente. —*n.* atolondrado; desordenado; tarambana.
harvest ('har·vɪst) *n.* cosecha; recogida; recolección; (*of grain*) siega. —*v.t. & i.* cosechar; recoger; (*of grain*) segar.
harvester ('har·vɪs·tər) *n.* **1,** (worker) jornalero; (*of grain*) segador. **2,** (machine) segadora; trilladora.
has (hæz) *v., tercera persona del sing. del pres. de ind. de* **have.**
has-been *n., colloq.* persona que ha visto mejores tiempos.
hash (hæʃ) *n.* **1,** (food) picadillo; salpicón. **2,** (mess) lío; enredo; *Amer.* sancocho. —*v.t.* **1,** (mince) picar; hacer picadillo. **2,** [*también,* **hash up; make a hash of**] (bungle) enredar; embrollar. —**make hash of** (defeat; crush) triturar; pulverizar.
hashish ('hæʃ·iʃ) *n.* haxix.
hasp (hæsp) *n.* aldaba; (*of a book*) broche. —*v.t.* cerrar con aldaba.
hassle ('hæs·əl) *n., colloq.* lío; bronca; agarrada. —*v.i., colloq.* pelearse; armar bronca.
hassock ('hæs·ək) *n.* **1,** (stool) banqueta almohadillada. **2,** (clump of grass) mata.
hast (hæst) *v., arcaico, segunda persona del sing. del pres. de ind. de* **have.**
haste (heist) *n.* prisa. —**be in haste,** tener prisa. —**make haste,** apresurarse.
hasten ('hei·sən) *v.t.* apresurar; acelerar. —*v.i.* apresurarse.
hasty ('heis·ti) *adj.* apresurado; precipitado. —**hastily,** *adv.* de prisa; apresuradamente. —**hastiness,** *n.* apresuramiento; precipitación.
hat (hæt) *n.* sombrero. —*v.t.* cubrir con sombrero. —**hat shop,** sombrerería. —**take one's hat off to,** descubrirse ante. —**talk through one's hat,** *colloq.* decir tonterias; hablar sandeces. —**throw one's hat into the ring,** entrar en la lid.
hatband *n.* cintillo.
hatbox *n.* sombrerera.
hatch (hætʃ) *v.t.* **1,** (incubate) empollar; incubar. **2,** (devise; plan; plot) idear; maquinar. **3,** (mark with lines, as for shading) sombrear. —*v.i.* **1,** (bring forth young, as an egg) empollar. **2,** (come forth, as from the egg) salir del cascarón; empollar. **3,** (take shape; be realized) resultar; cuajar. —*n.*

1, (brood) cría; pollada. 2, *naut.* (hatchway) escotilla. 3, (trapdoor) escotillón. 4, (floodgate) compuerta. 5, (small door) portillo; portezuela. 6, (outcome; result) resultado; fruto. —**hatchery,** *n.* criadero.

hatchet ('hætʃ·ɪt) *n.* hacha. —**bury the hatchet,** hacer las paces.

hatchetman *n., slang* pistolero; asesino.

hatchway *n.* 1, (trapdoor) trampa; escotillón 2, *naut.* escotilla.

hate (heit) *v.t. & i.* odiar; aborrecer; detestar. —*n.* odio; aborrecimiento.

hateful ('heit·fəl) *adj.* detestable; odioso; aborrecible. —**hatefulness,** *n.* odio; inquina.

hath (hæθ) *v., arcaico, tercera persona del sing. del pres. de ind. de* **have.**

hatrack *n.* percha.

hatred ('hei·trəd) *n.* odio; inquina.

hatter ('hæt·ər) *n.* sombrerero.

haughty ('hɔ·ti) *adj.* altanero; altivo; orgulloso. —**haughtiness,** *n.* altanería; altivez; orgullo.

haul (hɔːl) *v.t.* 1, (tug; drag) tirar de; arrastrar; halar. 2, (transport) acarrear; transportar. —*v.i.* 1, (pull) tirar. 2, *naut.* (change course) virar. —*n.* 1, (pull; tug) tirón. 2, (catch; gain) redada; cosecha; ganancia. 3, (distance covered) trayecto; recorrido; *Amer.* tiro. 4, (load transported) carga; cargamento. 5, *slang* (booty) botín; tajada. —**haulage,** *n.* acarreo; transporte. —**hauler,** *n.* acarreador; porteador. —**haul off,** 1, (retreat) retirarse; largarse. 2, *naut.* (change direction) virar. 3, *colloq.* (prepare to strike a blow) aprestarse a pegar un golpe.

haunch (hɔntʃ) *n.* 1, (human) cadera. 2, (animal) anca.

haunt (hɔnt) *v.t.* 1, (visit or inhabit as a ghost) rondar como alma en pena. 2, (recur too persistently; obsess) perseguir; obsesionar. 3, (visit frequently) frecuentar. —*n.* cubil; guarida. —**haunted,** *adj.* embrujado.

have (hæv) *v.t.* [*pres.ind: I* **have,** *you* **have** (*arcaico, thou* **hast**), *he, she, it* **has** (*arcaico,* **hath**), *we, you, they* **have**; *pret. & p.p.* **had**; *ger.* **having**] 1, (hold; possess; contain) tener. 2, (experience; undergo) tener: *She has a cold,* Tiene un resfrío. 3, (believe; maintain) mantener; sostener: *Public opinion has it that business is good,* La opinión pública mantiene que los negocios van bien. 4, (engage in; carry on) tener: *We had a fight,* Tuvimos una pelea. 5, (cause to do or be done) hacer: *I had the roof fixed,* Hice arreglar el techado. 6, *colloq.* (perform; realize in action) echar; dar: *Have a look at this,* Échele una ojeada a esto. 7, (bear; beget) tener: *She had a baby boy,* Tuvo un niño. 8, (permit; tolerate; admit) permitir; tolerar; soportar; admitir. 9, (take; get) tomar: *Have a cigarette,* Tome un cigarrillo. 10, (hold at a disadvantage) tener; tener dominado; tener aviado: *I have you now,* Ya te tengo; *This problem has me,* Este problema me tiene aviado. 11, [*usu.* **have on**] (wear) tener puesto. 12, *slang* (cheat; deceive) estafar; embaucar; engañar: *I've been had,* Me han estafado. —*v.aux.* 1, (*con el p.p., formando los tiempos pasados*) haber: *I have finished,* He terminado. 2, (*con el inf., expresa obligación o necesidad*) tener que: *I have to write to him,* Tengo que escribirle. —*n., usu.pl.* ricos; los que tienen. —**had as good** (*o* **well**), valerle tanto a uno; dar lo mismo: *I had as well lost the money as spent it that way,* Me hubiera dado lo mismo perder el dinero que gastarlo en esa forma. —**had as soon; had sooner,** valerle más a uno; preferir; ser mejor: *I had as soon die as face him,* Prefiero morir a enfrentarme con él. —**had better** (*o* **best**), ser mejor (que); convenir (que): *We had better* (o *best*) *consent,* Conviene que consintamos. —**had rather,** preferir: *I had rather leave at once,* Prefiero salir en seguida. —**have at,** atacar; acometer. —**have done,** terminar: *Let's have done with it,* Terminemos con esto. —**have it coming,** merecérselo. —**have it in for,** *colloq.* tenérsela jurada a; tenerle tirria a. —**have it out,** decidir; resolver; zanjar (la cuestión, el problema, etc.). —**have none of,** no tolerar; no aguantar. —**have to do with,** tener que ver con.

haven (ˈhei·vən) *n.* **1,** (shelter) asilo; refugio. **2,** (harbor) puerto.
have-not *n., colloq.* pobre; desposeído; destituído.
haversack (ˈhæv·ər·sæk) *n.* mochila; alforja.
havoc (ˈhæv·ək) *n.* estrago; devastación. —**play havoc with,** perjudicar; estropear. —**wreak havoc (on** *o* **upon),** devastar; hacer estragos (en).
haw (hɔː) *v.t. & i.* (turn left) tirar *o* virar a la izquierda. —*v.i.* (hesitate) vacilar; titubear. —*n.* **1,** hesitation) titubeo. **2,** (laugh) risa; carcajada. **3,** = **hawthorn berry.** —*interj.* ¡riá!
hawk (hɔk) *n.* **1,** (bird) ave de presa; halcón. **2,** (cough) carraspeo. —*v.t. & i.* (hunt) cazar con halcones. —*v.t.* (peddle) pregonar; ofrecer. —*v.i.* (clear the throat) carraspear.
hawker (ˈhɔ·kər) *n.* **1,** (falconer) halconero. **2,** (peddler) buhonero; vendedor ambulante.
hawk-eyed *adj.* que tiene ojos de lince.
hawking (ˈhɔ·kɪŋ) n. halconería; cetrería.
hawser (ˈhɔ·zər) *n.* maroma; cable.
hawthorn (ˈhɔ·θorn) *n.* acerolo; espino. —**hawthorn berry,** acerola.
hay (hei) *n.* heno; forraje. —**hay fever,** fiebre del heno; alergia. —**hit the hay,** *colloq.* irse a dormir; tumbarse. —**that's not hay,** *colloq.* no es paja; no es comino.
hayfield *n.* henar.
hayloft *n.* henil.
hayseed *adj. & n.* rústico; patán.
haystack *n.* almiar; montón de heno; parva de paja. *También,* **hayrick.**
haywire (ˈhei·wair) *adj., slang* **1,** (out of order) malogrado; descompuesto. **2,** (crazy) loco; fuera de sus casillas.
hazard (ˈhæz·ərd) *n.* **1,** (peril) riesgo; peligro. **2,** (chance) azar; suerte. **3,** (hindrance) obstáculo. **4,** (game) juego de azar. —*v.t.* arriesgar. —**hazardous,** *adj.* peligroso; azaroso; arriesgado. —**at all hazards,** a toda costa.
haze (heiz) *n.* bruma; neblina. —*v.i.* [*usu.* **haze over**] empañarse.
haze (heiz) *v.t.* dar *o* hacer novatadas a. —**hazing,** *n.* novatada.
hazel (ˈhei·zəl) *n.* **1,** (tree and wood) avellano. **2,** (nut; color) avellana. —*adj.* de avellano; de color avellana.
hazelnut *n.* avellana.
hazy (ˈhei·zi) *adj.* brumoso; nebuloso. —**haziness,** *n.* nebulosidad.
H-bomb *n.* bomba de hidrógeno.
he (hiː) *pron. pers.* él. —*adj. & n.* varón; macho.
head (hɛd) *n.* **1,** *anat.* cabeza. **2,** (intelligence; aptitude) cabeza. **3,** (unit; individual) cabeza. **4,** (chief; director) jefe; cabeza. **5,** (top, as of a page, article, etc.) tope; cabecera. **6,** (heading) encabezamiento; título. **7,** (headline) titular. **8,** (of a coin) cara. **9,** (of a bed) cabecera. **10,** (front; lead) cabeza. **11,** (extremity; end) punta; cabeza; extremo. **12,** (headland) cabo; punta. **13,** (source) fuente. **14,** (pressure) presión; nivel de presión. **15,** (froth, as on a liquid) espuma. **16,** (handle of a cane, umbrella, etc.) puño. —*adj.* **1,** (main; principal) principal; primero. **2,** (at the top or front) primero; delantero. **3,** (striking against the front) de frente; *naut.* de proa. —*v.t.* **1,** (command; lead) encabezar. **2,** (direct) dirigir. —*v.i.* **1,** (travel; set out) dirigirse; encaminarse. **2,** (originate) nacer. —**come to a head, 1,** (reach the bursting point) estar para reventar *o* estallar. **2,** (culminate) culminar. —**give one his head,** soltarle a uno las riendas; dejarle hacer. —**go to one's head,** irse *o* subirse a la cabeza. —**hang one's head,** bajar la cabeza. —**head first,** la cabeza primero. —**head off, 1,** (overtake) interceptar; atrapar. **2,** (prevent) prevenir; evitar. —**head on,** de frente. —**head over heels, 1,** (tumbling) patas arriba; dando traspiés *o* volatines. **2,** (completely) locamente; perdidamente. —**heads up!,** ¡cuidado!; ¡alerta! —**hit the nail on the head,** dar en el clavo. —**keep one's head,** mantener la calma. —**lose one's head,** perder la cabeza. —**make head,** avanzar; adelantar. —**make head or tail of,** comprender; entender; cansancio. —**out of** (*o* **off**) **one's head,** fuera de sí. —**over one's head, 1,** (too difficult) fuera del alcance. **2,** (without consulting one) por encima de uno. —**take it into one's head,** metérsele a uno

en la cabeza; darle a uno (por). —**talk** (**yell**, *etc.*) **one's head off**, hablar (gritar, *etc.*) hasta el cansancio. —**turn one's head**, **1**, (make dizzy) marear. **2**, (make vain) trastornar. **3**, (inveigle; cajole) engatusar.
-head (hɛd) *sufijo.* **1**, *forma nombres relacionados con* cabeza: *redhead,* pelirrojo; *blockhead,* zoquete. **2**, *var. antigua de* **-hood**: *godhead,* divinidad.
headache ('hɛd·ek) *n.* dolor de cabeza; jaqueca.
headband *n.* cinta *o* banda para el pelo; cintillo.
headboard *n.* cabecera.
headdress *n.* tocado.
-headed (hɛd·ɪd) *sufijo; forma adjetivos relacionados con* cabeza: *thick-headed,* cabezón; *three-headed,* tricéfalo.
headfirst *adv.* = **headlong.**
headgear *n.* **1**, (head covering) tocado. **2**, (for a horse) cabezada. **3**, *sports* (protective helmet) casco.
headiness ('hɛd·i·nəs) *n.* **1**, (recklessness) impetuosidad; temeridad. **2**, (intoxicating quality) lo espirituoso.
heading ('hɛd·ɪŋ) *n.* encabezamiento; título.
headless ('hɛd·ləs) *adj.* sin cabeza.
headlight *n.* farol; faro.
headline *n.* titular; cabecera. —*v.t.* anunciar; poner en titulares.
headlong *adj.* **1**, (rash) temerario; impetuoso; arriesgado. **2**, (with head forward) de cabeza. —*adv.* **1**, (rashly) temerariamente; impetuosamente. **2**, (headfirst; violently) de cabeza.
headmaster *n.* director. —**headmistress**, *n.* directora.
head-on *adj.* de frente.
headphone *n.* = **headset.**
headpiece *n.* **1**, = **headgear. 2**, = **headset. 3**, *print.* cabecera.
headquarters ('hɛd,kwor·tərz) *n.* **1**, (center of operations) jefatura; *esp.mil.* cuartel general. **2**, (main office) oficina principal.
headroom *n.* espacio libre; luz.
headset *n.* auricular; audífono.
headsman ('hɛdz·mən) *n.* [*pl.* **-men**] verdugo.
headstone *n.* **1**, (tombstone) lápida. **2**, (cornerstone) piedra fundamental; primera piedra.
headstrong *adj.* obstinado; terco; testarudo.
headwaiter *n.* jefe de camareros.
headwaters *n.pl.* manantiales; fuentes.
headway *n.* **1**, (progress) avance; adelanto. **2**, (headroom) espacio libre; luz. **3**, *R.R.* intervalo entre dos trenes. —**make headway**, avanzar; adelantar.
heady ('hɛd·i) *adj.* **1**, (impetuous; reckless) impetuoso; osado; temerario. **2**, (intoxicating) intoxicante; turbador; espirituoso.
heal (hiːl) *v.t.* **1**, (make sound; cure) sanar; curar. **2**, (free from troubles) sanear; remediar. **3**, (reconcile) reconciliar; reparar. —*v.i.* sanar; curar; (*of a wound*) cicatrizar.
healer ('hi·lər) *n.* **1**, (person) curandero. **2**, (remedy) curativo.
healing ('hi·lɪŋ) *adj.* curativo. —*n.* curación; cura; (*of a wound*) cicatrización.
health (hɛlθ) *n.* salud; sanidad; salubridad. —**bill of health**, certificado de salud. —**health officer**, oficial de sanidad. —**to your health!**, ¡a su salud!
healthful ('hɛlθ·fəl) *adj.* sano; saludable; salubre. —**healthfulness**, *n.* salubridad; sanidad.
healthy ('hɛl·θi) *adj.* saludable; sano. —**healthiness**, *n.* estado sano; buena salud.
heap (hip) *n.* montón; pila. —*v.t.* amontonar; apilar. —**heaping**, *adj.* lleno hasta el borde; rebozante.
hear (hɪr) *v.t.* [*pret.* & *p.p.* **heard** (hʌɹd)] **1**, (perceive by the ear) oír. **2**, (listen) escuchar; oír. —*v.i.* oír. —**hearer**, *n.* oyente.
hearing ('hɪr·ɪŋ) *n.* **1**, (sense) oído. **2**, (earshot) alcance del oído. **3**, (opportunity to be heard) audiencia. **4**, *law* vista.
hearing aid audífono.
hearken *también,* **harken** ('har·kən) *v.i.* escuchar; atender.
hearsay *n.* rumor; habladuría. —**by hearsay**, de *o* por oídas.
hearse (hʌɹs) *n.* carroza fúnebre.
heart (hart) *n.* corazón. —**after one's own heart**, que llena los deseos del corazón. —**at heart**, en el fondo. —**by heart**, de memoria. —**change of heart**, cambio de parecer. —**do one's heart good**, halagar; contentar; agradar. —**eat one's heart out**, atormentarse; remorderse. —**have a heart**, ser bueno; ser compasivo. —**in one's heart of hearts**, en lo más recóndi-

to de uno. —**lose heart**, desanimarse; descorazonarse. —**set one's heart at rest**, sosegarse; calmarse; perder la ansiedad. —**set one's heart on**, ansiar; apetecer; desear con ansia. —**take heart**, animarse; alentarse. —**take to heart**, tomar a pecho. —**to one's heart's content**, hasta la saciedad; a la completa satisfacción de uno. —**wear one's heart on one's sleeve**, tener el corazón en la mano; ser sincero o abierto. —**with half a heart**, de mala gana; sin ánimo.

heartache *n.* pesar; congoja; aflicción.

heartbreak *n.* gran pena; pena honda. —**heartbreaking**, *adj.* doloroso; angustioso; acongojante.

heartburn *n.* acedía; acidez estomacal.

-hearted (har·tɪd) *sufijo; forma adjetivos denotando* cierta calidad de carácter, disposición, etc.: *half-hearted,* tímido; *bighearted,* magnánimo.

hearten ('hart·ən) *v.t.* animar; alentar.

heartfelt *adj.* sincero; cordial; sentido.

hearth (harθ) *n.* hogar; chimenea.

heartless ('hart·ləs) *adj.* cruel; insensible; sin corazón. —**heartlessness**, *n.* crueldad; insensibilidad; falta de corazón.

heartrending *adj.* desgarrador; conmovedor.

heartsick *adj.* afligido; acongojado.

heartstrings *n.pl.* entrañas; compasión. —**tug at the** (*o* **one's**) **heartstrings**, conmover; ser conmovedor.

heart-to-heart *adj.* íntimo; confidencial.

hearty ('har·ti) *adj.* **1,** (sincere; cordial) sincero; cordial; sentido. **2,** (unrestrained) abierto; franco. **3,** (healthy; healthful) sano; saludable. **4,** (nourishing; satisfying) substancioso; nutritivo; reconfortante. **5,** (large; substantial) grande; substancial; de consideración.

heat (hit) *n.* **1,** (hotness) calor. **2,** (heating system) calefacción. **3,** (excitement; ardor) ardor; vehemencia; calor. **4,** (burning sensation) ardor; quemazón. **5,** *sports* prueba. **6,** (sexual excitement) excitación sexual; celo. **7,** *slang* (pressure; coercion) presión; coerción. —*v.t.* calentar. —*v.i.* calentarse.

heated ('hi·tɪd) *adj.* **1,** (made hot; warmed) calentado. **2,** (angry; vehement) acalorado.

heater ('hi·tər) *n.* calentador; calefactor.

heath (hiθ) *n.* brezal; páramo.

heathen ('hi·ðən) *n. & adj.* pagano.

heather ('hɛð·ər) *n.* brezo.

heating ('hi·tiŋ) *n.* **1,** (act of heating) calentamiento. **2,** (warming, as by a stove, furnace, etc.) calefacción. —*adj.* de calentamiento; calentador; calefactor. —**heating pad**, almohadilla eléctrica.

heave (hi:v) *v.t.* [*pret. & p.p.* **heaved** *o* **hove**; *ger.* **heaving**] **1,** (lift; raise) levantar pesadamente; levantar con esfuerzo. **2,** (throw) lanzar; arrojar. **3,** (throw up; vomit) arrojar; vomitar. **4,** (utter, as a sigh or groan) lanzar (un quejido, suspiro, etc.). **5,** (pull; haul) tirar de; halar de. **6,** *naut.* (turn, as a ship) virar. —*v.i.* **1,** (lift; swell up) solevarse; levantarse. **2,** (pant; gasp) acezar; jadear. **3,** (retch; vomit) tener bascas; dar *o* tener arcadas. **4,** (tug, as on a cable) tirar; halar. **5,** *naut.* (move; proceed) avanzar. —*n.* **1.** (effort or act of throwing or lifting) tirón; tiro; empujón; esfuerzo. **2,** *usu. pl.* (retch; vomit) bascas; arcadas. **3,** (upheaval) levantamiento. **4,** *geol.* desplazamiento horizontal de una falla. —**heave ho!**, ¡halen fuerte!; ¡tiren fuerte! —**heave to,** ponerse al pairo; detenerse.

heaven ('hɛv·ən) *n.* cielo. —**heavens!**, *interj.* ¡cielos!

heavenly ('hɛv·ən·li) *adj* .**1,** (of the heavens) celeste. **2,** (divine; sublime) celestial; divino. —**heavenliness**, *n.* felicidad suprema; hermosura divina.

heavenward ('hɛv·ən·wərd) *adj. & adv.* hacia el cielo; en alto.

heaviness ('hɛv·i·nəs) *n.* **1,** (weightiness) peso; pesadez; pesantez. **2,** (forcefulness) fuerza; peso. **3,** (thickness; denseness) densidad; espesor. **4,** (coarseness) dureza. **5,** (stoutness) peso. **6,** (burdensomeness; burden) pesadez; peso. **7,** (clumsiness) pesadez. **8,** (gloominess) pesadez. **9,** (languidness) languidez. **10,** (drowsiness) modorra.

heavy ('hɛv·i) *adj.* **1,** (weighty) pesado. **2,** (forceful; intense) pesado; fuerte; recio; duro. **3,** (resounding) estruendoso; pesado. **4,** (rough, as the sea) grueso. **5,** (thick; dense) denso; espeso. **6,** (coarse; rough) grueso; duro. **7,** (stout) grueso; gordo; de peso. **8,** (grave; important) grave; de peso; importante. **9,** (burdened) cargado. **10,** (burdensome; difficult) pesado. **11,** (clumsy; unwieldy) pesado. **12,** (somber; gloomy) pesado; sombrío. **13,** (slow; languid) lánguido. **14,** (drowsy) amodorrado. —*n., theat.* villano. —*adv.* pesadamente; fuerte. —**hang heavy,** pesar; aplastar; abrumar. —**heavy fire,** fuego nutrido *o* pesado. —**heavy with child,** encinta; embarazada; grávida.

heavy-duty *adj.* extrafuerte; de gran resistencia.

heavy-handed *adj.* pesado; opresivo.

heavy-hearted *adj.* apesadumbrado; acongojado.

heavy-set *adj.* rehecho; fornido.

Hebraic (hi'brei·ɪk) *adj.* hebreo; hebraico.

Hebrew ('hi·bru) *n.* hebreo. —*adj.* hebraico; hebreo.

hecatomb ('hɛk·ə,tom) *n.* hecatombe.

heck (hɛk) *interj., slang* ¡al diablo!; qué diablos!

heckle ('hɛk·əl) *v.t.* importunar; acosar.

hectare ('hɛk·tər) *n.* hectárea.

hectic ('hɛk·tɪk) *adj.* **1,** (turbulent) arrebatado; tumultuoso. **2,** (feverish) febril.

hecto- (hɛk·tə) *prefijo* hecto-; cien: *hectogram,* hectogramo.

hectogram ('hɛk·tə,græm) *n.* hectogramo.

hectoliter ('hɛk·tə,li·tər) *n.* hectolitro.

hectometer ('hɛk·tə,mi·tər) *n.* hectómetro.

he'd (hiːd) *contr. de* **he had** *o* **he would.**

hedge (hɛdʒ) *n.* **1,** (closely planted shrubs) seto; seto vivo. **2,** (evasion) rodeo. —*v.t.* **1,** (place a hedge around or along) poner un seto **a. 2,** (surround with a barrier) cercar; rodear; limitar. **3,** (protect; cover against loss) cubrir; proteger; asegurar. —*v.i.* **1,** (hide or protect oneself) protegerse; cubrirse; esconderse. **2,** (practice evasions) andarse con rodeos; eludir la cuestión. **3,** (cover oneself, as against loss) cubrirse; protegerse; asegurarse.

hedgehog ('hɛdʒ,hɔg) *n.* erizo; puerco espín.

hedonism ('hi·də,nɪz·əm) *n.* hedonismo. —**hedonist,** *n.* hedonista. —**hedonistic,** *adj.* hedonista.

-hedral (hi·drəl) *sufijo* **-édrico;** *forma adjetivos de los nombres terminados en* **-hedron:** *polyhedral,* poliédrico.

-hedron (hi·drən) *sufijo* **-edro;** *forma nombres denotando figuras sólidas geométricas con determinado número de caras: tetrahedron,* tetraedro.

heed (hiːd) *v.t. & i.* atender; escuchar; hacer caso (de *o* a). —*n.* atención; caso.

heedful ('hid·fəl) *adj.* atento. —**heedfulness,** *n.* atención.

heedless ('hid·ləs) *adj.* descuidado. —**heedlessness,** *n.* descuido; falta de atención.

heehaw ('hi,hɔ) *n.* rebuzno. —*v.i.* rebuznar.

heel (hiːl) *n.* **1,** *anat.* talón. **2,** (of hose) talón. **3,** (of a shoe) tacón; *Amer.* taco. **4,** (tilt) inclinación; ladeo. **5,** *slang* (cad) canalla; sinvergüenza. —*v.t.* **1,** (put heels on) poner tacones o tapas **a. 2,** (follow) seguir; perseguir; pisar los talones **a. 3,** *slang* (furnish, esp. with money) pertrechar. —*v.i.* **1,** (follow closely) seguir. **2,** (list; tilt) inclinarse; ladearse; *naut.* escorar. —**at heel,** a un paso; pisando los talones. —**cool one's heels,** quedarse esperando. —**down (*o* out) at the heels,** hecho un pordiosero. —**drag one's heels,** estar irresoluto; vacilar; roncear. —**kick up one's heels,** saltar de contento; estar de fiesta. —**lay by the heels, 1,** (arrest) arrestar; encarcelar. **2,** (overcome) superar. —**on (*o* upon) the heels of,** pisando los talones a. —**show one's heels; take to one's heels,** poner pies en polvorosa. —**to heel, 1,** (close; just behind) pisando los talones; un paso detrás. **2,** (under control) bajo rienda; dominado.

heel-dragging *n.* vacilación; irresolución; roncería.

heft (hɛft) *v.t., colloq.* **1,** (lift; heave) levantar; alzar. **2,** (try the weight of) pesar; sopesar. —*n., colloq.* **1,** (weight) peso. **2,** (larger part) mayor parte; gran parte.
hefty ('hɛf·ti) *adj.* **1,** (weighty) grueso; pesado. **2,** (brawny) musculoso; membrudo.
hegemony (hɪ'dʒɛm·ə·ni) *n.* hegemonía.
hegira (hɛ'dʒai·rə) *n.* huida; fuga.
heifer ('hɛf·ər) *n.* novilla.
heigh (hei; hai) *interj.* ¡eh!; ¡ea!; ¡oiga! —**heigh-ho,** *interj.* ¡ay!; ¡ea!
height (hait) *n.* **1,** (of a person) estatura; talla. **2,** (tallness) altura; alto. **3,** *a veces pl.* (high place or position) altura; eminencia; cumbre. **4,** (elevation; altitude) altura; elevación. **5,** (top) lo alto; tope; cima. **6,** (greatest degree; highest limit) colmo; cumbre. —**at its height,** en su apogeo.
heighten ('hai·tən) *v.t.* **1,** (raise) levantar; elevar. **2,** (intensify) aumentar; intensificar; acrecentar. —*v.i.* **1,** (rise) levantarse; elevarse. **2,** (increase; intensify) crecer; aumentar; intensificarse.
heinous ('hei·nəs) *adj.* odioso; aborrecible. —**heinousness,** *n.* lo odioso; lo aborrecible.
heir (eːr) *n.* heredero. —**heiress,** *n.* heredera. —**heir apparent,** heredero forzoso. —**heir presumptive,** presunto heredero.
heirloom ('ɛrˌlum) *n.* reliquia *o* herencia de familia.
held (hɛld) *v., pret. & p.p. de* **hold.**
helical ('hɛl·ɪ·kəl) *adj.* espiral; en espiral.
helico- (hɛl·ə·ko) *prefijo* helico-; espiral; hélice: *helicopter,* helicóptero.
helicopter ('hɛl·əˌkap·tər) *n.* helicóptero.
helio- (hi·li·o; -ə) *prefijo* helio-; sol: *heliograph,* heliógrafo.
heliocentric (ˌhi·li·o'sɛn·trɪk) *adj.* heliocéntrico.
heliograph ('hi·li·əˌgræf) *n.* heliógrafo.
heliotrope ('hi·li·əˌtrop) *n.* heliotropo.
helium ('hi·li·əm) *n.* helio.
helix ('hi·lɪks) *n.* hélice; espiral.
held (hɛld) *v., pret. & p.p. de* **hold.**
he'll (hil) *contr. de* **he will** *o* **he shall.**
hell (hɛl) *n.* infierno. —*interj.* ¡cuernos!; ¡diantre!
hellbent *adj., slang* empeñado; embestido; desenfrenado.
hellcat *n.* bruja; furia.
Hellenic (hɛ'lɛn·ɪk) *adj.* helénico; griego.
hellfire *n.* fuego del infierno.
hellhound *n.* demonio.
hellion ('hɛl·jən) *n., colloq.* enredador; alborotador.
hellish ('hɛl·ɪʃ) *adj.* infernal; diabólico. —**hellishness,** *n.* infierno; lo infernal.
hello (hɛ'loː) *interj.* ¡hola!; (*in answering the telephone*) ¡diga!; ¡qué hay!; *Amer.* ¡bueno!
helm (hɛlm) *n.* timón; gobierno.
helmet ('hɛl·mɪt) *n.* casco; *hist.* yelmo; celada.
helmsman ('hɛlmz·mən) *n.* [*pl.* **-men**] timonel; timonero.
help (hɛlp) *v.t.* **1,** (aid; assist) ayudar. **2,** (further) favorecer; facilitar. **3,** (alleviate; relieve) aliviar; mejorar. **4,** (avoid; prevent) evitar; remediar. **5,** (attend; minister to the needs of) asistir; atender. **6,** (serve; wait on) servir; atender. **7,** (serve, give a helping of, as food or drink) servirle *u* ofrecerle algo a uno. **8,** (come to the aid of) socorrer; asistir. —*v.i.* **1,** (aid; be useful) ayudar; contribuir. **2,** (serve) servir. —*n.* **1,** (aid) ayuda; socorro. **2,** (remedy) remedio. **3,** (relief) alivio. **4,** (employee; *collectively* employees) empleado(s); obrero(s); sirviente(s). **5,** (service, esp. domestic) servicio; servidumbre. —*interj.* ¡socorro! —**be unable to help** (*doing something*) no poder dejar de; no poder remediar *o* evitar. —**be unable to help but** (*do something*) no poder menos que. —**cry for help,** pedir socorro. —**help oneself to, 1,** (serve oneself with) servirse; tomar. **2,** (take without asking) tomar *o* usar sin permiso. —**help out,** ayudar. —**so help me God,** por Dios; (*in swearing an oath*) que Dios me ayude.
helper ('hɛl·pər) *n.* **1,** (assistant) ayudante; asistente. **2,** (supporter) apoyo; auxilio.
helpful ('hɛlp·fəl) *adj.* **1,** (useful; beneficial) útil; provechoso.

2, (inclined to help) servicial. —**helpfulness**, *n.* utilidad; ayuda.

helping ('hɛl·pɪŋ) *n.* porción.

helpless ('hɛlp·ləs) *adj.* 1, (feeble; powerless) incapacitado; impotente. 2, (defenseless) desamparado; desvalido; indefenso. 3, (incompetent) incompetente; incapaz. —**helplessness**, *n.* impotencia; incapacidad.

helpmate *n.* 1, (companion; helper) compañero de trabajos; auxiliar. 2, (wife) cónyuge. *También*, **helpmeet** ('hɛlp,mit).

helter-skelter ('hɛl·tər'skɛl·tər) *adv.* desordenadamente; sin ton ni son; sin orden ni concierto. —*adj.* desordenado. —*n.* confusión; desorden.

hem (hɛm) *n.* 1, (border, as on a garment) doble; dobladillo; bastilla; *Amer.* ruedo. 2, (edge) borde. —*v.t.* [**hemmed, hemming**] 1, (put a hem on) hacer el doble a; bastillar. 2, (encircle) cercar; rodear. 3, [*usu.*, **hem in, about** *o* **around**] (confine; restrain) confinar; limitar. —*interj.* ¡ejem! —**hem and haw**, vacilar; andar con rodeos.

hema- (hɛm·ə) *también*, **hemo-** (hi·mə) *prefijo* hema-; hemo-; sangre: *hemachrome*, hemacroma; *hemorrhage*, hemorragia.

hemato- (hi·mə·to; hɛm·ə-) *también*, **hemat-** (hi·mət; hɛm·ət) *ante vocal; prefijo* **hemato-**; **hemat-**; sangre: *hematolysis*, hematólisis; *hematemesis*, hematémesis.

hemi- (hɛm·i) *prefijo* hemi-; medio: *hemicycle*, hemiciclo.

-hemia (hi·mi·ə) *sufijo, var. de* **-emia**.

hemiplegia (,hɛm·ɪ'pliː·dʒi·ə) *n.* hemiplejía. —**hemiplegic**, *n.* & *adj.* hemipléjico.

hemisphere ('hɛm·ə·sfɪr) *n.* hemisferio. —**hemispheric** (-'sfɛr·ɪk); **hemispherical** (-'sfɛr·ə·kəl) *adj.* hemisférico.

hemlock ('hɛm·lak) *n.* 1, (poisonous herb) cicuta. 2, (evergreen tree) abeto americano.

hemo- (hi·mə) *prefijo, var. de* **hema-**.

hemoglobin (,hi·mə'glo·bɪn) *n.* hemoglobina.

hemophilia (,hi·mə'fɪl·i·a) *n.* hemofilia. —**hemophiliac** (-æk) *n.* hemofílico. —**hemophilic**, *adj.* hemofílico.

hemorrhage ('hɛm·ə·rɪdʒ) *n.* hemorragia.

hemorrhoid ('hɛm·ə,rɔid) *n.*, *usu.pl.* hemorroides; almorranas.

hemp (hɛmp) *n.* cáñamo.

hemstitch ('hɛm,stɪtʃ) *n.* vainica. —*v.t.* hacer vainica en.

hen (hɛn) *n.* gallina.

henbane *n.* beleño.

hence (hɛns) *adv.* 1, (away; from this place) fuera de aquí; fuera. 2, (from this time) de aquí a; cuando pase. 3, (from this life) de *o* desde aquí. 4, (therefore) por tanto; por lo tanto; por consiguiente. 5, (from this origin or source) de aquí; de donde.

henceforth *adv.* de aquí en adelante; en lo futuro.

henchman ('hɛntʃ·mən) *n.* [*pl.* **-men**] secuaz; sicario.

henna ('hɛn·ə) *n.* alheña. —*v.t.* alheñar.

hennery ('hɛn·ə·ri) *n.* gallinero. *También*, **hencoop, henhouse.**

henpeck ('hɛn,pɛk) *v.t.* dominar; tiranizar.

hepatic (hɪ'pæt·ɪk) *adj.* hepático. —**hepatitis** (,hɛp·ə'tai·təs) *n.* hepatitis.

hepatica (hɪ'pæt·ɪ·kə) *n.* hepática.

hepta- (hɛp·tə) *prefijo* hepta-; siete: *heptagon*, heptágono.

her (hʌɹ) *pron.pers.fem.sing.* 1, (*complemento directo de verbo*) la; a ella. 2, (*complemento indirecto de verbo*) le; a ella. 3, (*complemento de prep.*) ella. 4, (*tras* **than**, *en comparaciones*) ella; a ella. —*adj. pos.* su (*pl.* sus); de ella.

herald ('hɛr·əld) *n.* heraldo. —*v.t.* anunciar; preconizar. —**heraldic** (hɛ'ræl·dɪk) *adj.* heráldico. —**heraldry**, *n.* heráldica.

herb (ʌɹb; hʌɹb) *n.* hierba. —**herbaceous** (hʌɹ'bei·ʃəs) *adj.* herbáceo. —**herbage**, *n.* herbaje; pasto; hierba.

herbal ('ʌɹ·bəl; 'hʌɹ-) *adj.* & *n.* herbario.

herbarium (hʌɹ'bɛr·i·əm) *n.* [*pl.* **-ums** *o* **-a** (ə)] herbario.

herbivorous (hər'bɪv·ə·rəs) *adj.* herbívoro.

herb tea tisana.

Herculean (hər'kju·li·ən) *adj.* hercúleo.

herd (hʌɹd) *n.* 1, (of cattle) manada; (of sheep) hato; rebaño;

(of swine) piara. 2, (throng) hato; manada; muchedumbre. —*v.t.* reunir; juntar. —*v.i.* ir juntos; ir en manada.
herdsman ('hʌɹdz·mən) *n.* [*pl.* **-men**] vaquero; pastor; porquerizo.
here (hɪr) *adv.* aquí; acá. —*interj.* ¡presente!; ¡aquí!; (*in handing something*) ¡tenga! —**here's to you!**, ¡a su salud!
hereabout ('hɪr·ə,baut) *adv.* aquí cerca; por aquí. *También,* **hereabouts.**
hereafter (hɪr'æf·tər) *adv.* en lo futuro; de aquí en adelante. —*n.* el más allá; la otra vida.
hereat (hɪr'æt) *adv.* a esto.
hereby ('hɪr,bai) *adv.* por éstas; por la(s) presente(s); con *o* por esto.
hereditary (hə'rɛd·ə,tɛr·i) *adj.* hereditario.
heredity (hə'rɛd·ə·ti) *n.* herencia.
herein (hɪr'ɪn) *adv.* 1, (enclosed, as in a letter) adjunto. 2, (in this place) aquí. —**hereinafter,** *adv.* en adelante.
hereof (hɪr'ʌv) *adv.* de esto; de eso.
hereon (hɪr'an) *adv.* sobre esto; en esto.
heresy ('hɛr·ə·si) *n.* herejía.
heretic ('hɛr·ə·tɪk) *n.* hereje. —**heretical** (hə'rɛt·ɪ·kəl) *adj.* herético.
hereto (hɪr'tu) *adv.* a esto.
heretofore (,hɪr·tə'for) *adv.* antes; hasta ahora; hasta hoy; hasta aquí.
hereunder (hɪr'ʌn·dər) *adv.* 1, (below) más abajo; más adelante. 2, (by this authority) en virtud de esto.
hereupon ('hɪr·ə·pan) *adv.* sobre esto; en esto.
heritable ('hɛr·ə·tə·bəl) *adj.* heredable.
heritage ('hɛr·ə·tɪdʒ) *n.* herencia.
hermaphrodite (hər'mæf·rə·,dait) *n.* hermafrodita. —**hermaphroditic** (-'dɪt·ɪk) *adj.* hermafrodita.
hermetic (hər'mɛt·ɪk) *adj.* hermético.
hermit ('hʌɹ·mɪt) *n.* eremita; ermitaño.
hermitage ('hʌɹ·mɪ·tɪdʒ) *n.* ermita.
hernia ('hʌɹ·ni·ə) *n.* hernia.
hero ('hɪr·o) *n.* héroe.
heroic (hɪ'ro·ɪk) *adj.* heroico.
heroics (hɪ'ro·ɪks) *n.pl.* rimbombancia (*sing.*); lenguaje rimbombante.
heroin ('hɛr·o·ɪn) *n.* heroína.
heroine ('hɛr·o·ɪn) *n.* heroína.
heroism ('hɛr·o·ɪz·əm) *n.* heroísmo.
heron ('hɛr·ən) *n.* garza.
herpetology (,hʌɹ·pə'tal·ə·dʒi) *n.* herpetología. —**herpetologist,** *n.* herpetólogo.
herring ('hɛr·ɪŋ) n. arenque.
hers (hʌɹz) *pron.pos.* el suyo; la suya; lo suyo; los suyos; las suyas; el, la, lo, los *o* las de ella.
herself (hʌɹ'sɛlf) *pron.pers. fem. sing.* ella; ella misma. —*pron.refl.* 1, (*complemento directo o indirecto de verbo*) se: *She washed herself,* Se lavó; *She put it on herself,* Se lo puso. 2, (*complemento de prep.*) sí; sí misma: *She bought it for herself,* Se lo compró para sí. —**to herself,** para sí: *She said to herself, "I'm not going",* Dijo para sí: no voy. —**with herself,** consigo.
he's (his) *contr. de* **he is** *o* **he has.**
hesitant ('hɛz·ɪ·tənt) *adj.* vacilante; titubeante; indeciso; irresoluto. —**hesitancy,** *n.* vacilación; indecisión; irresolución.
hesitate ('hɛz·ɪ,teit) *v.i.* vacilar; titubear. —**hesitation,** *n.* vacilación; titubeo.
hetero- (hɛt·ər·ə) *prefijo* hetero-; diferente; disconforme: *heterosexual,* heterosexual.
heterodox ('hɛt·ər·ə,daks) *adj.* heterodoxo. —**heterodoxy,** *n.* heterodoxia.
heterogeneous (,hɛt·ər·ə'dʒi·ni·əs) *adj.* heterogéneo.
hew (hjuː) *v.t. & i.* [*p.p.* **hewed** *o* **hewn**] 1, (sever) tajar; hender; partir. 2, (carve) tallar; esculpir; cincelar.
hex (hɛks) *v.t., colloq.* embrujar; maleficiar. —*n., colloq.* hechizo; maleficio.
hexa- (hɛk·sə) *prefijo* hexa-; seis: *hexagon,* hexágono.
hexagon ('hɛks·ə·gan) *n.* hexágono. —**hexagonal** (hɛks'æg·ə·nəl) *n. adj.* hexagonal.
hey (hei) *interj.* ¡eh!; ¡oiga!; ¡ea!; *Amer.* ¡epa!
heyday ('hei,dei) *n.* apogeo; cúspide; momento cumbre.
hiatus (hai'ei·təs) *n.* 1, (lacuna)

laguna; hueco; omisión. **2,** (pause) pausa; hiato.

hibernal (hai'bʌɹ·nəl) *adj.* hibernal; invernal.

hibernate ('hai·bər,neit) *v.i.* hibernar; invernar. —**hibernation,** *n.* hibernación.

hibiscus (hai'bɪs·kəs) *n.* hibisco.

hiccup ('hɪk·ʌp) *n.* hipo. —*v.i.* hipar. *También,* **hiccough** ('hɪk·ʌp).

hick (hɪk) *n.* rústico; palurdo; *Amer.* jíbaro. —*adj., colloq.* rústico; de campo.

hickory ('hɪk·ə·ri) *n.* nogal americano.

hid (hɪd) *v., pret. & p.p. de* **hide.**

hidden ('hɪd·ən) *v., p.p. de* **hide.** —*adj.* escondido; oculto.

hide (haid) *v.t.* [**hid, hid** *o* **hidden, hiding**] **1,** (put or keep out of sight) esconder; ocultar. **2,** (conceal; keep secret) ocultar; encubrir; disimular. —*v.i.* esconderse; ocultarse. —*n.* cuero; piel; pellejo. —**neither hide nor hair,** ni señal; nada.

hide-and-seek *n.* juego del escondite. —**play hide and seek,** jugar al escondite.

hidebound *adj.* cerrado; rígido; inveterado; empedernido.

hideous ('hɪd·i·əs) *adj.* horrendo; espantoso; deforme. —**hideousness,** *n.* horror; deformidad.

hide-out *n., colloq.* escondite; refugio; guarida.

hiding ('hai·dɪŋ) *n.* **1,** (concealment) ocultación. **2,** *slang* (whipping) zurra; paliza. —**in hiding,** escondido. —**hiding place,** escondite; escondrijo.

hie (hai) *v.i.* apurarse; correr; precipitarse.

hierarch ('hai·ər·ark) *n.* jerarca. —**hierarchal,** *adj.* jerárquico. —**hierarchic; hierarchical,** *adj.* jerárquico. —**hierarchy,** *n.* jerarquía.

hieroglyphic (,hai·ər·ə'glɪf·ɪk) *n. & adj.* jeroglífico.

high (hai) *adj.* **1,** (lofty; elevated) alto. **2,** (having a specified height) de alto; de altura: *a tree fifty feet high,* un árbol de cincuenta pies de alto; *That tree is fifty feet high,* Ese árbol tiene cincuenta pies de alto. **3,** (situated at a specified height) a una altura de . . . : *Mexico City is 7400 feet high;* La Ciudad de México está a una altura de 7400 pies. **4,** (great; greater than usual in size, amount, price, importance, etc.) alto; grande. **5,** (sharp; shrill) alto; agudo. **6,** (superior; excellent) alto; superior. **7,** (haughty; overbearing) altanero; arrogante. **8,** (fully advanced or developed) pleno. **9,** (smelly; tainted) pasado; rancio. **10,** *slang* (exhilarated; slightly intoxicated) borracho; alegre. —*adv.* **1,** (in a high manner) a lo grande. **2,** (at or to a high level) alto. **3,** (at a high price) caro. —*n.* **1,** (high level or point) altura; lo alto. **2,** (highest level or point) tope; cumbre. **3,** (high gear) tercera *o* alta (velocidad). **4,** (center of high pressure) presión; centro de alta presión. —**fly high,** ambicionar mucho. —**high and dry, 1,** (beached) varado. **2,** (in the lurch) plantado. —**high and low,** por todas partes. —**high and mighty,** *colloq.* altanero; arrogante. —**high command,** alto mando; alto comando. —**high days,** festividades; días de fiesta. —**high explosive,** explosivo fulminante *o* de alta potencia. —**high hat,** sombrero de copa. —**high life,** gran mundo; alta sociedad. —**high living,** la buena vida; la gran vida; el buen vivir. —**High Mass,** misa mayor. —**high priest,** gran sacerdote; sumo sacerdote. —**high sea** *o* **seas,** alta mar. —**high spirits,** buen humor; contento. —**high tide,** pleamar; marea alta. —**the Most High,** el Altísimo.

highball ('hai,bɔl) *n.* **1,** (drink) highball; jaibol. **2,** *R.R.* vía libre. —*v.i., colloq.* ir disparado *o* embalado.

highborn *adj.* noble; de noble alcurnia.

highbred *adj.* de buena familia; refinado.

highbrow *n. & adj., colloq.* intelectual.

high chair sillita para niños.

high-class *adj.* de calidad; de alto copete.

higher education educación *o* instrucción superior; educación universitaria.

higher-up *n., colloq.* superior; jefe.

highfalutin (,hai·fə'lu·tən) *adj., colloq.* pretencioso; fachendoso; (*of language*) altisonante.

highflown *adj.* **1,** (ambitious) ambicioso; desmedido. **2,** (bombastic) altisonante.
high-grade *adj.* de calidad; superior.
highhanded *adj.* arbitrario; despótico; tiránico. —**highhandedness,** *n.* arbitrariedad.
high-hat *adj., slang* de alto copete; encopetado. —*n., slang* esnob. —*v.t. & i., slang* menospreciar; mirar con menosprecio o condescendencia.
highjack ('hai,dʒæk) *v.t. & i., slang* = **hijack.**
highland ('hai·lənd) *adj.* serrano; montañés; de las montañas. —*n., usu.pl.* montañas; serranías. —**highlander,** *n.* montañés; serrano.
highlight *n.* [*también,* **high light**] **1,** (outstanding part; feature) punto culminante; punto más destacado. **2,** (brightly lighted part) toque de luz; matiz de resalte. —*v.t.* hacer resaltar; dar énfasis a.
high-minded *adj.* de miras elevadas; idealista.
highness ('hai·nəs) *n.* **1,** (loftiness) altura; elevación. **2,** *cap.* (title of honor) Alteza.
high-pressure *adj.* **1,** (of or for high pressure) de alta presión. **2,** (strongly persuasive) insistente; enérgico; persuasivo. —*v.t., colloq.* empujar; apretar; hacer presión (a *o* en); *Amer.* presionar.
high-priced *adj.* caro; costoso.
highroad *n.* camino principal; camino real.
high school escuela superior *o* secundaria; instituto de segunda enseñanza.
high-sounding *adj.* altisonante.
high-spirited *adj.* animoso; fogoso.
highstrung *adj.* nervioso; tenso; excitable.
high time **1,** *slang* (revel; spree) fiesta; juerga. **2,** (late hour) hora: *It's high time you were in bed,* (Ya) es hora de que estés en cama.
high-toned *adj.* **1,** (high-pitched) agudo; de tono alto. **2,** *fig.* (lofty) de mucho tono; de alto copete. **3,** *colloq.* (stylish) de buen tono; elegante.
high water **1,** (of a river or stream) nivel superior de las aguas. **2,** (high tide) pleamar; marea alta. —**high-water mark, 1,** *lit.* cota superior de las aguas. **2,** *fig.* apogeo; punto culminante.
highway *n.* carretera; camino.
highwayman ('hai·we·mən) *n.* [*pl.* **-men**] salteador; bandolero.
hijack *también,* **highjack** ('hai,dʒæk) *v.t. & i., slang* asaltar *o* robar en tránsito.
hike (haik) *v.i.* dar un paseo; dar *o* echar una caminata. —*v.t., colloq.* levantar; subir. —*n.* caminata; paseo.
hilarious (hɪ'lɛr·i·əs) *adj.* hilarante; divertido; alegre. —**hilarity,** *n.* hilaridad; alegría; risa.
hill (hɪl) *n.* cerro; colina; loma. —*v.t.* apilar; amontonar. —**down hill,** cuesta abajo. —**up hill,** cuesta arriba.
hillbilly ('hɪl,bɪl·i) *n. & adj.* patán; rústico.
hillock ('hɪl·ək) *n.* montecillo; loma.
hillside *n.* ladera; falda.
hilltop *n.* cima; cumbre.
hilly ('hɪl·i) *adj.* con *o* de muchas colinas *o* lomas. —**hilliness,** *n.* abundancia de colinas *o* lomas.
hilt (hɪlt) *n.* empuñadura; puño.
him (hɪm) *pron.pers. masc.sing.* **1,** (*complemento directo de verbo*) lo; le; a él. **2,** (*complemento indirecto de verbo*) le; a él. **3,** (*complemento de prep.*) él. **4,** (*tras* **than,** *en comparaciones*) él; a él.
himself (hɪm'sɛlf) *pron.pers. masc.sing.* él; él mismo. —*pron.refl.* **1,** (*complemento directo o indirecto de verbo*) se: *He washed himself,* Se lavó; *He put it on himself,* Se lo puso. **2,** (*complemento de prep.*) sí; sí mismo: *He bought it for himself,* Se lo compró para sí. —**to himself,** para sí: *He said to himself, "I'm not going",* Dijo para sí: no voy. —**with himself,** consigo.
hind (haind) *adj.* de atrás; trasero; posterior. —*n.* cierva; venado hembra.
hinder ('hɪn·dər) *v.t. & i.* impedir; obstruir; estorbar.
hinder ('hain·dər) *adj.* tasero; posterior.
hindmost ('haind·most) *adj.* último; postrero. *También,* **hindermost** ('hain·dər-).
hindrance ('hɪn·drəns) *n.* impedimento; obstáculo; estorbo.
hindsight ('haind·sait) *n.* mirada retrospectiva; mirada atrás; retrospección.

Hindu ('hɪn·du) *n. & adj.* hindú. —**Hinduism**, *n.* hinduismo.
hinge (hɪndʒ) *n.* **1,** (joint) bisagra; charnela; gozne. **2,** *fig.* (controlling principle) fundamento; base; punto cardinal. —*v.t.* poner bisagras o goznes a; engoznar. —*v.i.* girar; depender.
hint (hɪnt) *n.* **1,** (clue; indication) indicación; sugerencia. **2,** (intimation; innuendo) indirecta; insinuación; alusión. —*v.t.* indicar; sugerir. —*v.i.* aludir; hacer alusión. —**hint at**, insinuar; hacer alusión a.
hinterland ('hɪn·tər,lænd) *n.* tierra adentro; interior.
hip (hɪp) *n.* **1,** *anat.* cadera. **2,** *zool.* anca. **3,** *archit.* caballete.
hipbone *n.* cía.
hippo- (hɪp·ə) *prefijo* hipo-; caballo: *hippodrome,* hipódromo.
hippodrome ('hɪp·ə,drom) *n.* hipódromo.
hippopotamus (,hɪp·ə'pat·ə·məs) *n.* hipopótamo.
hire (hair) *v.t.* **1,** (employ) emplear. **2,** (rent) alquilar. —*n.* **1,** (salary) salario; paga. 2, (rental) alquiler. **3,** (act of hiring or being hired) empleo. —**for hire**, de alquiler. —**hire out**, emplearse.
hireling ('hair·lɪŋ) *n.* empleaducho.
hirsute (hʌɹ'sut) *adj.* hirsuto.
his (hɪz) *adj.pos.* su; (*pl.* sus); de él. —*pron.pos.* el suyo; la suya; lo suyo; los suyos; las suyas; el, la, lo, los *o* las de él.
Hispanic (hɪs'pæn·ɪk) *adj.* hispánico.
hiss (hɪs) *v.i. & t.* sisear; silbar. —*n.* siseo; silbido.
hist (hɪst) *interj.* ¡chito!; ¡chitón!; ¡silencio!
histamine ('hɪs·tə,min) *n.* histamina.
histo- (hɪs·tə) *prefijo* histo-; tejido: *histology,* histología.
histology (hɪs'tal·ə·dʒi) *n.* histología. —**histological** (hɪs·tə'la·dʒɪ·kəl) *adj.* histológico. —**histologist**, *n.* histólogo.
historian (hɪs'tor·i·ən) *n.* historiador.
historic (hɪs'tor·ɪk) *adj.* histórico. *También,* **historical**. —**historicity** (,hɪs·tə'rɪs·ə·ti) *n.* historicidad.
history ('hɪs·tə'ri) *n.* historia. —**case history**, historial.
histrionic (,hɪs·tri'an·ɪk) *adj.* histriónico; teatral. —**histrionics**, *n.pl.* histrionismo (*sing.*); teatro (*sing*).
hit (hɪt) *v.t.* [**hit, hitting**] **1,** (strike against) chocar contra; pegar contra. **2,** (give a blow to) golpear; pegar. **3,** (give, as a blow) dar; pegar; asestar. **4,** (strike, as a mark) pegar en; dar en. **5,** [*también,* **hit on** *o* **against**] (cause to bump) golpearse (la cabeza, el pie, etc.) contra. **6,** *fig.* (affect strongly) afectar; impresionar. **7,** (come upon; find) encontrar; hallar. **8,** (reach; come to or upon) llegar a. **9,** *baseball* batear; conseguir. —*v.i.* **1,** (strike) golpear; chocar. **2,** [*usu.* **hit on** *o* **upon**] (find) encontrar; hallar. **3,** *baseball* conseguir una base. —*n.* **1,** (blow; stroke) golpe. **2,** (collision) choque. **3,** *colloq.* (success; successful event) éxito. **4,** *baseball* bola bateada con éxito. —**be a hit**, *colloq.* ser un éxito; hacer sensación. —**hit it off**, *colloq.* llevarse bien; congeniar. —**hit or miss**, a la diabla; a la buena de Dios. —**hit the nail on the head**, dar en el clavo. —**hit (out) at**, atacar.
hitch (hɪtʃ) *v.t.* **1,** (fasten) sujetar; atar; amarrar. **2,** [*usu.* **hitch up**] (raise) subir; levantar. **3,** (harness) enganchar. —*v.i.* **1,** (become caught or entangled) engancharse; enredarse. **2,** (move jerkily) andar a saltos *o* tropezones. **3,** (limp) cojear. —*n.* **1,** (fastening) enganche. **2,** (kind of knot) vuelta de cabo. **3,** (obstacle) dificultad; obstáculo. **4,** (jerk; limping gait) tropezón; tirón. **5,** *colloq.* (period, as of duty, imprisonment, etc.) estancia.
hitchhike ('hɪtʃ,haik) *v.i., colloq.* gorrear un viaje en automóvil; viajar de gorra en un auto.
hitching post atadero.
hither ('hɪð·ər) *adv.* aquí; hacia aquí. —*adj.* más cercano. —**hithermost**, *adj.* más cercano.
hitherto ('hɪð·ər·tu) *adv.* hasta ahora; hasta aquí; hasta hoy.
hive (haiv) *n.* **1,** (beehive) colmena. **2,** (swarm) enjambre.
hives (haivz) *n.pl.* urticaria (*sing.*).
ho (hoː) *interj.* **1,** (calling attention) ¡eh!; ¡ea!; ¡oiga! **2,** (express-

ing surprise, exultation, etc.) ¡oh!; ¡ay!; ¡ja!
hoar (hoːr) *adj.* 1, (whitish; gray) blanquecino; blancuzco. 2, (gray-haired) cano; canoso.
hoard (hoːrd) *n.* cúmulo; montón. —*v.t.* & *i.* 1, (accumulate) acumular; amontonar. 2, (monopolize) acaparar.
hoarfrost *n.* escarcha.
hoarhound *n.* = **horehound.**
hoariness ('hor·i·nəs) *n.* 1, (whitishness) blancura. 2, (grayness of hair) canicie. 3, (antiquity) vejez.
hoarse (hors) *adj.* ronco; bronco; áspero. —**hoarseness,** *n.* ronquera; bronquedad; aspereza. —**make hoarse,** enronquecer; poner ronco.
hoary (hor·i) *adj.* 1, = **hoar.** 2, (ancient) viejo.
hoax (hoks) *n.* decepción; engaño; burla. —*v.t.* engañar; burlar.
hob (haːb) *n.* 1, (ledge of a fireplace) anaquel *o* repisa de chimenea. 2, (elf) duende. —**play** (*o* **raise**) **hob with,** *colloq.* dar al traste con; trastornar.
hobble ('hab·əl) *n.* 1, (limp) cojera; renquera. *Amer.* renguera. 2, (fetter) maniota; traba. —*v.i.* 1, (move haltingly) moverse a duras penas; avanzar con dificultad. 2, (limp) cojear; renquear; *Amer.* renguear. —*v.t.* poner maniota a; trabar.
hobby ('hab·i) *n.* afición; pasatiempo; manía. —**hobbyist,** *n.* aficionado.
hobbyhorse *n.* caballito mecedor; caballito de palo.
hobgoblin ('hab,gab·lın) *n.* duende.
hobnail ('hab·nel) *n.* tachuela; tachón.
hobnob ('hab·nab) *v.i., colloq.* tratarse con familiaridad; codearse.
hobo ('ho·bo) *n., colloq.* [*pl.* **-bos**] vagabundo.
hock (hak) *n.* 1, (joint above the hoof) jarrete; corvejón. 2, *slang* (pawn) empeño. —*v.t.* 1, (hamstring) desjarretar. 2, *slang* (pawn) empeñar.
hockey ('hak·i) *n.* hockey.
hockshop *n., slang* = **pawnshop.**
hocus ('ho·kəs) *v.t.* 1, (to fool) engañar. 2, (to drug) narcotizar.
hocus-pocus ('ho·kəs'po·kəs) *n.* 1, (incantation) palabras cabalísticas; abracadabra; cábala. 2, (meaningless jargon) jerigonza. 3, (trickery) cábala; engañifa. —*v.t., colloq.* engañar; engatusar.
hod (had) *n.* 1, (device for carrying bricks or mortar) capacho. 2, (coal scuttle) cubo para carbón.
hodgepodge ('hadʒ,padʒ) *n.* mescolanza; baturrillo. *También,* **hotchpotch.**
hoe (hoː) *n.* azada; azadón. —*v.t.* & *i.* azadonar; cavar *o* escardar con azada.
hog (haːg) *n.* puerco; cerdo; cochino. —*v.t., slang* [**hogged, hogging**] cogerse lo mejor de; acaparar; tragar. —**go the whole hog,** *slang* ir *o* seguir hasta el fin; entregarse sin reservas. —**hog wild,** *slang* fuera de sí; loco.
hoggish ('hag·ɪʃ) *adj.* 1, (hoglike) porcino. 2, (selfish; gluttonous) puerco; cerdo; glotón; *Amer.* angurriento. —**hoggishness,** *n.* glotonería; *Amer.* angurria.
hogshead ('hagz,hɛd) *n.* tonel; pipa; bocoy.
hogtie ('hag,tai) *v.t.* atar de pies y manos.
hogwash ('hag,waʃ) *n.* bazofia.
hoi polloi (,hɔi·pə'lɔi) plebe; vulgo.
hoist (hɔist) *v.t.* alzar; levantar; izar. —*n.* 1, (a hoisting) tirón; esfuerzo hacia arriba; alzamiento. 2, (elevator) elevador. 3, (lifting apparatus) cabria; pescante.
hokum ('ho·kəm) *n., slang* 1, (mawkishness) ñoñerías (*pl.*); sensiblería. 2, (nonsense) tontería; boberías (*pl.*).
hold (hold) *v.t.* [*pret.* & *p.p.* **held**] 1, (grasp; seize) coger; agarrar. 2, (clutch; keep fast) tener; sujetar; apretar. 3, (detain; delay) retener; detener. 4, (keep; save) guardar. 5, (keep in a certain place or condition) tener; mantener. 6, (possess; own) poseer; tener. 7, (occupy, as a job) desempeñar; ocupar. 8, (support; bear the weight of) sostener; soportar; aguantar. 9, (restrain) contener; reprimir; refrenar. 10, (have or keep control of) sujetar; mantener. 11, (have; carry on, as a meeting, social function, etc.) tener; dar; celebrar. 12, (consider) considerar; estimar. 13, (maintain) sostener; mantener. 14, (contain; have within) contener; tener. 15, (contain; have room for)

poder contener; tener capacidad para; acomodar. —*v.i.* **1,** (keep on; continue) mantenerse; continuar; seguir. **2,** (remain unyielding) aguantar; resistir; no ceder. **3,** (be true or valid) ser válido; tener fuerza. **4,** (halt; stop) aguantarse; detenerse; parar. —*n.* **1,** (act or manner of holding) agarrón; apretón. **2,** (handle) agarradera; mango. **3,** (of a ship) bodega. **4,** (influence; control) influencia; poder; mano. **5,** *wrestling* llave. —*interj.* ¡para!; ¡pare! —**catch hold of,** agarrar. —**get hold of, 1,** (grasp) agarrar. **2,** (acquire; attain; reach) conseguir. —**hold down, 1,** (restrain; keep down) sujetar; reprimir. **2,** *colloq.* (keep, as a job) mantenerse en; ocupar. —**hold forth, 1,** (speak; preach) hablar; perorar. **2,** (offer; propose) proponer; ofrecer. —**hold in,** contener; sujetar. —**hold off, 1,** (keep at bay) contener; mantener a distancia. **2,** (refrain) contenerse; aguantarse. —**hold on, 1,** (keep one's hold) mantenerse; afirmarse. **2,** (persist) persistir. **3,** *colloq., usu.impve.* (stop; wait) parar. —**hold one's own,** mantenerse; mantenerse firme; no quedarse atrás —**hold out, 1,** (last; endure) aguantar; durar. **2,** (stand firm) aguantar; resistir. **3,** (offer) ofrecer. **4,** *slang* (refuse to give) resistirse *o* negarse a dar. —**hold over, 1,** (postpone) aplazar; posponer. **2,** (stay or keep for an additional period) continuar; seguir. **3,** (keep as a threat) amenazar (con). —**hold up, 1,** (support) soportar; aguantar. **2,** (show; exhibit) mostrar; exhibir. **3,** (last; endure; continue) durar; aguantar; resistir. **4,** (stop; delay; impede) demorar; detener. **5,** (rob) asaltar; atracar; robar. —**hold with,** estar de acuerdo con. —**lay hold of, 1,** (seize) agarrar. **2,** (get possession or control of) apoderarse de. **3,** (acquire; attain) conseguir. —**take hold (of), 1,** (grasp) coger; agarrar. **2,** (get control of) apoderarse de. **3,** (take root) arraigar.

holder ('hol·dər) *n.* **1,** (possessor, as of a title or record in sports) poseedor. **2,** (bearer, as of a title, passport, etc.) titular. **3,** (tenant; lessee) arrendatario. **4,** *comm.* tenedor; portador. **5,** (handle) agarradera; mango. **6,** (base; support) pie; base; soporte. **7,** (case; container) caja; estuche. *Muchas veces* **holder** *se expresa en español por el prefijo* porta- *en los compuestos: penholder,* portaplumas.

holding ('hol·dɪŋ) *n.* **1,** *usu.pl.* (property) bienes; posesiones. **2,** (lease; tenure) arrendamiento; tenencia.

holdover *n.* persona o cosa que queda; resto; remanente.

holdup *n., colloq.* **1,** (robbery) atraco; robo. **2,** (delay) demora; retraso.

hole (hoːl) *n.* **1,** (pit; hollow) hoyo; cavidad. **2,** (pool; deep place in water) pozo; hoya. **3,** (den; lair) madriguera; guarida. **4,** (opening) vano; hueco. **5,** (tear; rent) roto; agujero. **6,** *colloq.* (flaw; defect) fallo; defecto. **7,** *colloq.* (predicament) aprieto; apuro. **8,** *golf* hoyo. **9,** (prison cell) calabozo. —*v.t.* **1,** (pierce; perforate) agujerear; perforar. **2,** (put or drive into a hole) meter; introducir. **3,** (make by digging a hole) cavar; excavar. —*v.i.* meterse; encerrarse. —**be in the hole,** *colloq.* estar *o* quedar en deuda. —**hole up, 1,** (hibernate) invernar; hibernar. **2,** (shut oneself in) enclaustrarse; recluirse. **3,** *slang* (find lodgings) meterse; alojarse.

holiday ('hal·ə·dei) *n.* **1,** (special day) fiesta; día de fiesta. **2,** *often pl.* (vacation) vacaciones. —*adj.* festivo.

holiness ('ho·li·nəs) *n.* santidad.

holler ('hal·ər) *v.i. & t., colloq.* gritar. —*n., colloq.* grito.

hollow ('hal·o) *adj.* **1,** (empty) vacío; hueco. **2,** (concave) cóncavo. **3,** (insincere) falso; vacío; hueco. **4,** (deep-toned) hueco. —*n.* **1,** (pit) hueco; hoyo; cavidad. **2,** (valley; depression) hondonada; hoya. —*v.t.* [*también,* **hollow out**] ahuecar; excavar. —*v.i.* ahuecarse. —**beat all hollow,** *colloq.* ganar *o* superar por mucho; *Amer.* ganar lejos.

hollow-eyed *adj.* de *o* con ojos hundidos; ojeroso; demacrado.

hollowness ('hal·o·nəs) *n.* **1,** (emptiness) vacío. **2,** (empty place or space) hueco. **3,** (insincerity) vacuidad; falsedad; falsía.

holly ('hal·i) *n.* acebo.

hollyhock ('hal·i,hak) *n.* malva loca.
holmium ('hol·mi·əm) *n.* holmio.
holo- (hal·ə) *prefijo* holo-; entero; todo: *holocaust,* holocausto.
holocaust ('hal·ə·kɔst) *n.* holocausto.
holograph ('hal·ə,græf) *n.* & *adj.* ológrafo; hológrafo.
holster ('hol·stər) *n.* pistolera.
holy ('ho·li) *adj.* sagrado; santo; sacro. —**holy day,** fiesta; día de fiesta. —**Holy Ghost; Holy Spirit,** Espíritu Santo. —**Holy Office,** Santo Oficio. —**holy oil,** crisma. —**holy water,** agua bendita. —**Holy Week,** Semana Santa.
homage ('ham·ɪdʒ) *n.* homenaje.
homburg ('ham·bʌɪg) *n.* cierto sombrero de fieltro.
home (hoːm) *n.* **1,** (house) casa. **2,** (residence) casa; domicilio. **3,** (family abode) hogar. **4,** (dwelling) vivienda; habitación. **5,** (place or country of origin) lugar de origen; patria; país *o* pueblo natal. **6,** (asylum; poorhouse; orphanage) asilo; hospicio. **7,** (habitat) medio; habitat; habitación. **8,** (focal point; center) capital; centro. **9,** (place of initial development; cradle) cuna; fuente; lugar de origen. **10,** (finish line; goal) meta. **11,** *baseball* base. —*adj.* **1,** (of the house; domestic) doméstico; casero. **2,** (of one's own country) nacional; interno. **3,** (local) local. **4,** (effective; to the point) efectivo; certero. —*adv.* **1,** (to or toward home) a casa. **2,** (at home) en casa. **3,** (to the mark) en el blanco; a su meta; a *o* en su lugar. **4,** (deeply; directly) a fondo; en lo vivo; de pleno. —*v.i.* **1,** (go to or toward home) dirigirse a casa; orientarse hacia su destino. **2,** (reside) vivir; habitar. —**at home,** en casa; como en su casa. —**be at home (in),** conocer bien *o* a fondo; estar en su elemento. —**bring home to,** hacer comprender; hacer darse cuenta de. —**home office,** oficina central. —**home rule,** gobierno autónomo; autonomía. —**home run,** *baseball* cuadrangular; jonrón. —**home town,** ciudad *o* pueblo natal. —**strike home,** *colloq.* dar en el blanco.
home-bred *adj.* **1,** (native; peculiar to a given locality) casero; propio *o* característico del lugar. **2,** (unsophisticated; crude) burdo; basto; poco refinado.
home brew preparación casera.
homecoming *n.* vuelta (a casa); retorno; regreso.
homeless ('hom·ləs) *adj.* sin hogar; desamparado.
homely ('hom·li) *adj.* **1,** (domestic) casero. **2,** (plain; simple) simple; familiar; sencillo. **3,** (ugly) feo; basto.
homemade *adj.* casero; hecho en casa; de fabricación casera.
homeo- (ho·mi·ə) *prefijo* homeo-; igual; semejante: *homeopathy,* homeopatía.
homeopathy (,ho·mi'ap·ə·θi) *n.* homeopatía. —**homeopath** ('ho·mi·ə,pæθ) *n.* homeópata. —**homeopathic** (-ə'pæθ·ɪk) *adj.* homeopático.
homer ('ho·mər) *n.* **1,** = **homing pigeon. 2,** = **home run.**
homesick *adj.* nostálgico; que tiene morriña. —**homesickness,** *n.* nostalgia; morriña. —**be homesick (for),** añorar; tener nostalgia *o* morriña (por); *Amer.* extrañar.
homespun *adj.* **1,** (made at home) casero; de fabricación casera. **2,** (simple; crude) burdo; tosco. —*n.* tela casera.
homestead ('hom,stɛd) *n.* heredad; casa solariega.
homework *n.* tarea; trabajo en la casa.
homey *también,* **homy** ('ho·mi) *adj., colloq.* hogareño.
homicide ('ham·ə·said) *n.* **1,** (act) homicidio. **2,** (agent) homicida. —**homicidal** (-'sai·dəl) *adj.* homicida.
homiletic (,ham·ə'lɛt·ɪk) *adj.* homilético. —**homiletics,** *n.pl.* homilética (*sing.*).
homily ('ham·ə·li) *n.* homilía.
homing pigeon paloma mensajera.
homo- (hom·ə) *prefijo* homo-; mismo; igual: *homogeneous,* homogéneo.
homogeneous (,ho·mə'dʒi·ni·əs) *adj.* homogéneo. —**homogeneity** (-dʒə'ni·ə·ti) *n.* homogeneidad.
homogenize (ho'madʒ·ə,naiz) *v.t.* homogeneizar. —**homogenization** (-nɪ'zei·ʃən) *n.* homogeneización.
homologous (ho'mal·ə·gəs) *adj.*

homólogo. —**homology** (-dʒi) *n.* homología.

homonym ('ham·ə·nɪm) *n.* homónimo. —**homonymous** (ho·'man·ə·məs) *adj.* homónimo.

homophone ('ham·əˌfon) *n.* homófono. —**homophonic** (-'fan·ɪk) *adj.* homófono. —**homophonous** (hə'maf·ə·nəs) *adj.* homófono. —**homophony** (hə'maf·ə·ni) *n.* homofonía.

homosexual (ˌhom·ə'sɛk·ʃu·əl) *n.* & *adj.* homosexual. —**homosexuality** (-ˌsɛk·ʃu'æl·ə·ti) *n.* homosexualidad.

homy ('ho·mi) *adj.* = **homey.**

hone (hoːn) *n.* piedra de afilar. —*v.t.* afilar. —*v.i., dial.* anhelar; ansiar.

honest ('an·ɪst) *adj.* honrado; honesto; justo.

honesty ('an·ɪs·ti) *n.* honradez; honestidad.

honey ('hʌn·i) *n.* **1,** (sweet substance) miel. **2,** *colloq.* (term of endearment) querido; amorcito. —**honeyed,** *adj.* dulce; meloso; melifluo.

honeybee *n.* abeja de miel.

honeycomb *n.* **1,** (beehive) panal; bresca. **2,** (maze) laberinto; red. —*v.t.* **1,** (riddle, as with tunnels) llenar *o* tupir de perforaciones, canales, etc.; atravesar; calar. **2,** (permeate; undermine) penetrar; llenar; saturar; minar. —*v.i.* volverse un laberinto. —*adj.* de *o* como un panal; laberíntico.

honeydew *n.* exudación o secreción dulce. —**honeydew melon,** cierto melón muy dulce.

honeymoon *n.* luna de miel.

honeysuckle *n.* madreselva.

honk (haŋk) *n.* **1,** (call of the goose) grito del ganso; trompetazo. **2,** (sound of a horn) toque de sirena o bocina; bocinazo. —*v.t.* & *i.* **1,** (cry, as a goose) gritar el ganso. **2,** (sound, as a horn) tocar (la bocina).

honor *también,* **honour** ('an·ər) *n.* **1,** (quality or distinction) honor; honra. **2,** *cap.* (title of respect) señoría. —*v.t.* **1,** (respect greatly; confer honor upon) honrar. **2,** (accept; credit) aceptar; dar buena acogida a. **3,** *comm.* aceptar; pagar. —**do honor to,** honrar. —**do the honors,** hacer los honores. —**on** (*o* **upon**) **one's honor,** por el honor de uno.

honorable ('an·ər·ə·bəl) *adj.* **1,** (noble; illustrious) honorable; noble; ilustre. **2,** *cap.* (title of respect) honorable. **3,** (upright; honest) honrado; honesto; pundonoroso. **4,** (conferring honor) honroso.

honorarium (ˌan·ə'rɛr·i·əm) *n.* [*pl.* **honoraria** (-i·ə)] honorarios (*pl.*).

honorary ('an·ər·ɛr·i) *adj.* honorario; honorífico.

hood (hʊd) *n.* **1,** (head covering) caperuza; capucha; capirote; capilla. **2,** (cover of an engine) cubierta; capota. **3,** (folding cover, as of a carriage) toldo; capota. **4,** *zool.* (crest) cresta. **5,** (chimney cowl) sombrerete; caperuza. **6,** *slang* = **hoodlum.** —*v.t.* **1,** (cover with a hood, as the head or body) encapuchar. **2,** (put a hood on or over) entoldar; proveer de capota. **3,** (hide) encubrir; ocultar; esconder.

-hood (hʊd) *sufijo; forma nombres indicando* **1,** cualidad; condición; estado: *bachelorhood,* soltería. **2,** conjunto de personas; categoría: *knighthood,* caballería.

hoodlum ('hud·ləm) *n., colloq.* rufián; maleante; matón de barrio.

hoodoo ('hu·du) *n.* **1,** (voodoo) magia negra; brujería. **2,** *colloq.* (bad luck) aojo; mala suerte. **3,** *colloq.* (jinx) pájaro de mal agüero; persona *o* cosa que trae mala suerte. —*v.t.* maldecir; embrujar; aojar.

hoodwink ('hʊdˌwɪŋk) *v.t.* engatusar; engañar; pasar gato por liebre.

hooey ('hu·i) *n.* tontería; farfolla; pamplinas (*pl.*).

hoof (hʊf) *n.* [*pl.* **hoofs** *o* **hooves**] casco; uña; pezuña. —*v.t.* & *i.* **1,** (trample) pisotear; patear. **2,** *colloq.* (walk) andar; caminar; ir a pie. **3,** *slang* (dance) bailar. —**hoofer,** *n., slang* bailarín. —**on the hoof,** en pie; vivo.

hoof-and-mouth disease fiebre aftosa.

hoofbeat *n.* ruido de cascos.

hook (hʊk) *n.* **1,** (device for catching, pulling, etc.) gancho. **2,** (gaff) garfio. **3,** (part of a hook and eye) corchete. **4,** (bend; turn) curva; recodo; vuelta. **5,** (fishhook) anzuelo. **6,** (curved course, as of a ball) curva. **7,** *boxing* gancho. —*v.t.* **1,** (attach; catch) enganchar. **2,** (gore) acornear. **3,** (bend) doblar; curvar. **4,** (hit or throw in a curve, as a ball) dar curva a. **5,** *boxing* dar un gancho a. **6,** *slang* (filch) birlar. —*v.i.* **1,** (curve) curvarse; doblarse. **2,** (be fastened or caught) engancharse. —**by hook or by crook,** de todos modos; de cualquier manera; a toda costa. —**hook it,** *slang* huir; salir corriendo. —**hook, line, and sinker,** *colloq.* completamente; todo. —**hooks and eyes,** corchetes. —**hook up, 1,** (attach, as with hooks) enganchar. **2,** (connect; assemble) conectar; montar. —**on one's own hook,** por cuenta propia.

hooked (hʊkt) *adj.* **1,** (shaped like a hook) ganchudo; corvo. **2,** (having a hook or hooks) con gancho *o* ganchos. **3,** (caught) cogido; enganchado.

hook-nosed *adj.* de nariz ganchuda, corva *o* aguileña.

hookup *n.* **1,** (assembly) montaje; conexiones (*pl.*). **2,** (connection, in communications) conexión; conexión en cadena. **3,** *colloq.* (alliance) alianza; acuerdo.

hookworm *n.* lombriz intestinal.

hooky ('hʊk·i) *n.,* *in* **play hooky,** hacer novillos; hacerse la rabona.

hooligan ('hu·lə·gən) *n.* & *adj.* rufián; matón de barrio; camorrista.

hoop (hup) *n.* aro; argolla; zuncho. —*v.t.* **1,** (provide with hoops) poner aros a; enzunchar. **2,** (encircle) cercar; rodear.

hoopla ('hup·la) *n.,* *colloq.* baraúnda. —*interj.* ¡upa!

hoopskirt *n.* miriñaque.

hooray (hə'rei) *interj., n.* & *v.* = **hurrah.**

hoot (hut) *n.* **1,** (cry, esp. of an owl) grito (del búho); alarido. **2,** (shout of disapproval) pitido; chifla; rechifla; *Amer.* pifia. **3,** (thing of no value) ardite; comino. —*v.i.* **1,** (cry, esp. as an owl) gritar; ulular. **2,** (shout in disapproval) dar pitidos; rechiflar; *Amer.* pifiar. —*v.t.* pitar; rechiflar; *Amer.* pifiar.

hooves (huːvz) *n., pl. de* **hoof.**

hop (hap) *v.i.* [**hopped, hopping**] **1,** (jump) saltar; brincar. **2,** (leap on one foot) saltar a la pata coja *o* en un pie. **3,** *colloq.* (dance) bailotear. —*v.t.* **1,** (jump) saltar. **2,** (get on; jump on) subirse a; saltar a. —*n.* **1,** (a hopping) salto; brinco. **2,** *colloq.* (dance) bailoteo. **3,** *bot.* lúpulo. —**hop off,** *colloq.* **1,** (take off) despegar; salir volando. **2,** (get down, jump down) bajarse; saltar de.

hope (hop) *v.t.* & *i.* esperar. —*n.* esperanza.

hopeful ('hop·fəl) *adj.* **1,** (feeling hope) esperanzado. **2,** (giving hope) prometedor. —**hopefully,** *adv.* con esperanza. —**hopefulness,** *n.* esperanza; promesa.

hopeless ('hop·ləs) *adj.* **1,** (without hope) desesperanzado; desilusionado. **2,** (beyond hope) desesperado. —**hopelessly,** *adv.* sin esperanza. —**hopelessness,** *n.* desesperación.

hophead ('hap,hɛd) *n., slang* morfinómano; narcómano.

hopped up *slang* **1,** (drugged) embriagado; eufórico. **2,** (supercharged) hecho más potente; de mayor potencia.

hopper ('hap·ər) *n.* **1,** (jumper) saltarín; saltador. **2,** (bin) tolva.

hopscotch ('hap,skatʃ) *n.* juego a la pata coja.

horde (hord) *n.* horda. —*v.i.* reunirse en hordas.

horehound *también,* **hoarhound** ('hor,haund) *n.* marrubio.

horizon (hə'rai·zən) *n.* horizonte.

horizontal (,har·ɪ'zan·təl) *adj.* & *n.* horizontal.

hormone ('hor·mon) *n.* hormona.

horn (horn) *n.* **1,** (bonelike growth) cuerno; asta. **2,** (anything made of or shaped like a horn) cuerno. **3,** *music* trompa. **4,** (sounding device) bocina. **5,** (loudspeaker) altavoz; *Amer.* altoparlante. —*v.t.* **1,** (put horns on) poner cuernos a. **2,** (gore) acornear. —*adj.* de cuerno; de asta. —**horned,** *adj.* con cuerno *o* cuernos. —**blow one's horn,** *colloq.* alabarse; jactarse. —**horn in,** *slang* entremeterse. —**on the horns of a dilemma,** entre la espada y la pared. —**pull, draw** *o* **haul in one's horns,** echarse para atrás.

hornet ('hor·nɪt) *n.* avispón.

hornpipe *n.* chirimía.

hornswoggle ('horn,swag·əl) *v.t., slang* engañar; engatusar.

horny ('hor·ni) *adj.* **1,** (made of or resembling horn) de cuerno; de asta. **2,** (having horns) con cuerno

o cuernos. 3, (hard like horn) calloso; duro.
horology (ho'ral·ə·dʒi) *n.* horología. —**horologist,** *n.* horólogo.
horoscope ('hor·ə,skop) *n.* horóscopo.
horrendous (hə'rɛn·dəs) *adj.* horrendo.
horrible ('har·ə·bəl) *adj.* horrible.
horrid ('har·ɪd) *adj.* horroroso; horrendo; espantoso.
horrify ('har·ɪ·fai) *v.t.* horrorizar; horripilar. —**horrifying,** *adj.* horripilante; horroroso.
horror ('har·ər) *n.* horror.
hors d'oeuvres (or'dʌɹvr) *n.pl.* entremeses.
horse (hors) *n.* 1, (animal) caballo. 2, (frame) caballete. 3, *gymnastics* potro. —*v.t.* equipar con caballos *o* monturas; montar. —*v.i.* montar *o* ir a caballo. —*adj.* 1, (of a horse or horses) de caballo *o* caballos; hípico. 2, (mounted) a caballo; *mil.* de caballería. 3, *muchas veces en los compuestos* (large; coarse) grande; basto. —**back** (*o* **bet on**) **the wrong horse,** jugar al caballo que pierde; *fig.* respaldar al que pierde. —**be** *o* **get on one's high horse,** *colloq.* dárselas de mucho. —**hold one's horses,** *colloq.* contenerse; aguantarse. —**horse around,** *slang* hacer el zángano; zanganear. —**horse of another** (*o* **different**) **color,** *colloq.* otro asunto; otra cosa; harina de otro costal.
horseback *n.* lomo del caballo. —*adv.* a caballo.
horsecar *n.* carruaje tirado por caballos.
horse chestnut 1, (tree) castaño de Indias. 2, (nut) castaña de Indias.
horsefly *n.* tábano; moscardón.
horsehair *n.* crin; tejido de crin.
horselaugh *n.* carcajada; risotada.
horseman ('hors·mən) *n.* [*pl.* **-men**] jinete. —**horsemanship,** *n.* 1, (art of riding) equitación. 2, (skill in handling horses) dotes de jinete.
horseplay *n.* chacota; chacoteo; payasada.
horsepower *n.* caballo de fuerza.
horseradish *n.* rábano picante.
horse sense *colloq.* sentido común.
horseshoe *n.* herradura; *pl.* juego de herraduras. —**horseshoe crab,** cangrejo bayoneta *o* de las Molucas.
horsewhip *n.* fusta; látigo; *Amer.* fuete. —*v.t.* dar *o* pegar con la fusta *o* el látigo.
horsewoman *n.* [*pl.* **-women**] amazona.
horsy ('hor·si) *adj.* 1, (of or like a horse or horses) de caballo *o* caballos. 2, (concerned with or fond of horses) hípico; de caballos.
hortatory ('hor·tə,tor·i) *adj.* exhortatorio.
horticulture ('hor·tɪ,kʌl·tʃər) *n.* horticultura. —**horticultural** (-'kʌl·tʃər·əl) *adj.* hortícola; de horticultura. —**horticulturist** (-'kʌl·tʃər·ɪst) *n.* horticultor.
hosanna (ho'zæn·ə) *interj.* & *n.* hosanna.
hose (ho;z) *n.* 1, (pipe) manguera. 2, [*pl.* **hose**] (stockings; socks) medias; calcetines. —*v.t.* regar con manguera.
hosier ('ho·ʒər) *n.* calcetero. —**hosiery,** *n.* calcetería; medias (*pl.*); calcetines (*pl.*).
hospitable ('has·pɪ·tə·bəl) *adj.* hospitalario. —**hospitableness,** *n.* hospitalidad.
hospital ('has·pɪ·təl) *n.* hospital.
hospitality (,has·pə'tæl·ə·ti) *n.* hospitalidad.
hospitalize ('has·pɪ·tə,laiz) *v.t.* hospitalizar. —**hospitalization** (-lɪ·'zei·ʃən) *n.* hospitalización.
host (host) *n.* 1, (one who entertains or presides) anfitrión. 2, (innkeeper) posadero; mesonero; hostelero. 3, (army) hueste; ejército. 4, (crowd) multitud; muchedumbre. 5, *cap., eccles.* hostia. 6, *biol.* huésped.
hostage ('has·tɪdʒ) *n.* rehén.
hostel ('has·təl) *n.* hostería; albergue.
hostess ('hos·tɪs) *n.* 1, (one who entertains or presides) anfitriona; (in a restaurant) encargada de mesas. 2, (stewardess) camarera; azafata; auxiliar de a bordo; *Amer.* aeromoza.
hostile ('has·təl) *adj.* hostil. —**hostility** (has'tɪl·ə·ti) *n.* hostilidad.
hot (hat) *adj.* 1, (very warm) caliente; caluroso. 2, (pungent) picante; acre. 3, (violent) violento; furioso. 4, (impassioned; excited)

apasionado; vehemente. —**hotness,** *n.* calentura; lo caliente. —**be in hot water**, estar con el agua al cuello. —**hot air,** *slang* palabrería.
hotbed *n.* vivero; *fig.* foco.
hotblooded *adj.* ardiente; impetuoso.
hot cake = **pancake.** —**sell like hot cakes**, venderse como pan bendito.
hotchpotch ('hatʃ,patʃ) *n.* = **hodgepodge.**
hot dog *colloq.* perro caliente; salchicha.
hotel (ho'tɛl) *n.* hotel. —*adj.* hotelero. —**hotel manager,** hotelero.
hotfoot *adv.* a toda prisa. —*v.i., colloq.* ir a toda prisa; correr.
hotheaded *adj.* vehemente; excitable; arrebatado. —**hotheadedness,** *n.* vehemencia; excitabilidad.
hothouse *n.* invernáculo.
hound (haund) *n.* **1,** (dog) perro; can. **2,** (hunting dog) perro de caza; sabueso. —*v.t.* **1,** (pursue; harass) perseguir; acosar; importunar. **2,** (urge on) urgir; azuzar.
hour (aur) *n.* hora. —**hour by hour,** de hora en hora; cada hora. —**hour hand,** horario. —**keep late hours,** trasnochar; acostarse tarde. —**late hours,** altas horas de la noche. —**man of the hour,** hombre del momento. —**strike the hour,** dar la hora. —**small** (*o* **wee**) **hours,** primeras horas de la mañana.
hourglass *n.* reloj de arena; clepsidra.
hourly ('aur·li) *adj.* **1,** (occurring every hour) cada hora; de cada hora; de hora en hora. **2,** (per hour; occupying an hour) por hora; en cada hora. **3,** (often; continual) frecuente; continuo. —*adv.* **1,** (once an hour; every hour) cada hora. **2,** (at any hour) a toda hora; de hora en hora. **3,** (often; continually) a todas horas; continuamente.
house (haus) *n.* [*pl.* **houses** ('hau·zɪz)] **1,** (dwelling; abode) casa. **2,** (building; residence) casa; residencia; edificio. **3,** (family; lineage) casa. **4,** (chamber; assembly) cámara; asamblea. **5,** (assembly room; hall) cámara; sala de asambleas. **6,** (theater) teatro; sala de espectáculos. **7,** (audience) concurrencia; entrada. **8,** (business establishment) establecimiento; firma; casa. **9,** (small shelter or building) caseta. —*v.t.* (hauz) **1,** (provide lodgings for) alojar; proveer de casa o vivienda. **2,** (store) almacenar; acomodar. **3,** (shelter) albergar. **4,** (cover; enclose) cubrir; encerrar. —*adj.* de casa; de la casa. —**clean house, 1,** (do housecleaning) limpiar la casa; hacer la limpieza. **2,** (get rid of undesirable persons or things) hacer una limpieza; hacer un barrido. —**keep house,** cuidar de la casa; hacer los oficios domésticos. —**on the house,** a expensas del dueño *o* establecimiento. —**play house,** *colloq.* jugar a ser dueños de casa; jugar al papá y a la mamá.
housebreaker *n.* ladrón; escalador. —**housebreaking,** *n.* robo; escalo.
housebroken *adj.* enseñado (a comportarse en casa).
housecoat *n.* bata (de entrecasa).
housefly *n.* mosca doméstica.
household ('haus·hold) *n.* casa; familia. —*adj.* casero; doméstico; de familia; de casa; para la casa. —**householder,** *n.* dueño de casa; jefe de familia.
housekeeper *n.* **1,** (housewife) ama de casa. **2,** (person in charge of a house) ama de llaves.
housekeeping *n.* quehaceres domésticos; manejo de la casa. —*adj.* doméstico.
housemaid *n.* sirvienta; criada.
housetop *n.* techo; tejado.
housewares *n.pl.* enseres domésticos.
housewarming *n.* tertulia para estrenar un nuevo domicilio.
housewife *n.* [*pl.* **-wives**] ama de casa.
housework *n.* faenas domésticas.
housing ('hau·zɪŋ) *n.* **1,** lodging; sheltering) alojamiento. **2,** (houses collectively) casas (*pl.*); viviendas (*pl.*). **3,** *archit.* nicho; empotrado. **4,** (cover) cubierta; *mech.* cárter; **5,** (frame) bastidor; armazón. **6,** (covering for a horse; caparison) caparazón.
hove (ho:v) *v., pret. & p.p de* **heave.**
hovel ('hʌv·əl) *n.* casucha; choza; cuchitril.
hover ('hʌv·ər) *v.i.* **1,** (stay suspended; flutter in the air) cernerse. **2,** (linger about) revolotear; ron-

dar. **3,** (waver; be uncertain) vacilar.

how (hau) *adv.* **1,** (in what way or manner; by what means) cómo; de qué manera *o* modo; en qué forma. **2,** (in what state or condition) cómo; qué tal. **3,** (at what price) a cuánto; a cómo: *How do you sell these oranges?*, ¿A cómo vende estas naranjas? **4,** (for what reason or purpose) cómo; por qué: *How is it that you arrived late?*, ¿Cómo es que llegastes tarde? **5,** (with what meaning; to what effect) cómo; en qué forma; en qué sentido. **6,** (*en cláusulas relativas, en expresiones de admiración y como intensivo*) cuán; cuánto; qué: *How pretty she looks!*, ¡Cuán linda se ve! —*n.* cómo. —**how do you do?**, ¿Cómo está Vd.? —**how many?**, ¿cuántos? —**how much?**, ¿cuánto? —**how now?**, ¿cómo así? —**how so?**, ¿cómo así?; ¿por qué? —**how then? 1,** (what is the meaning of this) ¿Qué es esto?; ¿Qué significa esto? **2,** (how else) ¿Cómo entonces?

howdy ('hau·di) *interj., colloq.* ¡Qué tal!; ¡hola!

however (hau'ɛv·ər) *conj.* sin embargo; no obstante; empero; pero. —*adv.* **1,** (no matter how) de cualquier modo; en todo caso; pese a todo. **2,** (to whatever degree or extent) por muy; por mucho; como quiera que.

howitzer ('hau·ɪt·sər) *n.* obús; mortero.

howl (haul) *v.i.* **1,** (wail) aullar; ulular (*esp. of the wind*). **2,** (laugh or shout in scorn, mirth, etc.) dar risotadas; morirse de risa. —*v.t.* **1,** (utter with howls) aullar; gritar. **2,** (drive or force by howling) sacar a gritos. —*n.* **1,** (wail) aullido; alarido; el ulular (*esp. of the wind*). **2,** (loud laugh) risotada. **3,** (shouting) griterío. —**howl down,** ahogar a gritos; hacer callar.

howler ('hau·lər) *n.* **1,** (person or thing that howls) gritón; chillón. **2,** (howling monkey) mono aullador. **3,** *colloq.* (boner) plancha.

howsoever (ˌhau·so'ɛv·ər) *adv.* **1,** (to whatever degree or extent) por muy; por mucho; como quiera que. **2,** (in whatever manner) como quiera que.

hoyden ('hɔi·dən) *n.* marimacho.

hub (hʌb) *n.* **1,** (of a wheel) cubo. **2,** (center; focal point) centro; foco.

hubbub ('hʌb·ʌb) *n.* tumulto; barullo; alboroto.

hubby ('hʌb·i) *n., colloq.* marido.

hubcap *n.* plato *o* platillo del cubo.

huckleberry ('hʌk·əlˌbɛr·i) *n.* arándano.

huckster ('hʌk·stər) *n.* **1,** (hawker) buhonero; vendedor ambulante. **2,** (peddler of produce) verdulero. **3,** (petty dealer; haggler) mercachifle. —*v.t. & i.* vender.

huddle ('hʌd·əl) *v.i.* **1,** (crowd together) apelotonarse; amontonarse. **2,** (hunch into a heap) encogerse; acurrucarse. —*v.t.* **1,** (crowd or jumble together) apelotonar; amontonar. **2,** (hunch) encoger. —*n.* **1,** (crowd; heap) pelotón; montón; masa. **2,** (confusion; muddle) confusión; baraúnda. **3,** *slang* (private conference) conferencia privada.

hue (hjuː) *n.* **1,** (color) color. **2,** (shade) matiz. —**hue and cry,** clamor; griterío.

huff (hʌf) *v.t.* **1,** (make angry) enojar; enfadar; ofender. **2,** (bully; hector) abusar; atropellar. —*v.i.* soplar; bufar; dar resoplidos. —*n.* bufido; resoplido. —**in a huff,** disgustado; enfadado.

huffy ('hʌf·i) *adj.* **1,** (touchy) susceptible. **2,** (sulky) resentido.

hug (hʌg) *v.t.* [**hugged, hugging**] **1,** (embrace) abrazar; apretar. **2,** (go or get close to) arrimarse a. —*v.i.* abrazarse. —*n.* abrazo.

huge (hjuːdʒ) *adj.* enorme; inmenso. —**hugeness,** *n.* enormidad; inmensidad.

hulk (hʌlk) *n.* **1,** (shell; skeleton) esqueleto; armazón. **2,** (clumsy person or thing) armatoste. —*v.i.* [*usu.* **hulk up**] levantarse; abultar. —**hulking,** *adj.* tosco; pesado.

hull (hʌl) *n.* **1,** (shell; husk) cáscara; vaina; hollejo. **2,** (outer covering) envoltura; cubierta; corteza. **3,** (body of a ship) casco. **4,** *aero.* (frame) armazón. —*v.t.* descascarar; mondar.

hullabaloo ('hʌl·ə·bəˌlu) *n.* alboroto; algarabía.

hum (hʌm) *v.i.* [**hummed, humming**] **1,** (drone; buzz; murmur) zumbar; ronronear. **2,** (sing without words) tararear. **3,** *colloq.* (be full of activity or excitement) vibrar; zumbar con actividad; parecer una colmena. —*v.t.* tararear. —*n.* **1,** (drone; buzz; murmur) zumbido; runrún. **2,** (singing without words) tarareo. —*interj.* ¡ejem! —**hum to sleep,** arrullar.

human ('hju·mən) *adj.* humano. —*n.* [*también,* **human being**] ser humano.

humane (hju'mein) *adj.* humano; compasivo; generoso. —**humaneness,** *n.* humanidad; benevolencia; compasión.

humanism ('hju·mə·nɪz·əm) *n.* humanismo. —**humanist,** *n.* humanista. —**humanistic,** *adj.* humanista.

humanitarian (hju,mæn·ə'tɛr·i·ən) *adj.* humanitario. —*n.* filántropo; persona humanitaria.

humanity (hju'mæn·ə·ti) *n.* humanidad. —**humanities,** *n.pl.* humanidades; letras humanas.

humanize ('hju·mə,naiz) *v.t.* humanizar.

humankind *n.* humanidad; género humano.

humble ('hʌm·bəl) *adj.* humilde. —*v.t.* humillar; hacer sentir humilde. —**humbleness,** *n.* humildad.

humbug ('hʌm·bʌg) *n.* **1,** (deception) patraña; embuste; farsa. **2,** (charlatan) charlatán; farsante; embustero. —*v.t.* [**-bugged, -bugging**] engañar; embaucar.

humdinger (hʌm'dɪŋ·ər) *n., slang* maravilla; fenómeno.

humdrum ('hʌm,drʌm) *adj.* monótono; rutinario; banal. —*n.* **1,** (monotony) monotonía; rutina; matraca. **2,** (dull, boring person) persona rutinaria; plomo.

humerus ('hju·mər·əs) *n.* húmero.

humid ('hju·mɪd) *adj.* húmedo.

humidify (hju'mɪd·ə·fai) *v.t.* humidificar. —**humidification** (-fɪ·'kei·ʃən) *n.* humidificación.

humidity (hju'mɪd·ə·ti) *n.* humedad.

humidor ('hju·mə,dor) *n.* caja humedecida para guardar tabaco.

humiliate (hju'mɪl·i,eit) *v.t.* humillar. —**humiliation,** *n.* humillación.

humility (hju'mɪl·ə·ti) *n.* humildad.

humming ('hʌm·ɪŋ) *adj.* **1,** (buzzing; droning) zumbante; roncante. **2,** *colloq.* (active; brisk) activo; furioso; febril. —*n.* = **hum.**

hummingbird ('hʌm·ɪŋ,bʌɹd) *n.* colibrí; picaflor.

hummock ('hʌm·ək) *n.* mogote; loma.

humor *también,* **humour** ('hju·mər) *n.* **1,** (mood; disposition) humor; disposición. **2,** (body fluid) humor. **3,** (comicality) humor; comicidad; gracia. **4,** (humorous style or works) humorismo. —*v.t.* complacer; seguirle la cuerda a. —**out of humor,** malhumorado; destemplado.

humorist ('hju·mər·ɪst) *n.* humorista. —**humoristic,** *adj.* humorístico.

humorous ('hju·mər·əs) *adj.* cómico; gracioso; chistoso; humorístico.

hump (hʌmp) *n.* **1,** (fleshy protuberance) joroba; giba. **2,** (mound) loma; montículo; corcovo. —*v.t.* arquear; encorvar. —*v.i.* combarse; arquearse.

humpback *n.* **1,** (hump on the back) joroba; giba; corcova. **2,** (person with a hump) jorobado. —**humpbacked,** *adj.* jorobado; giboso; corcovado.

humph (hʌmf) *interj.* ¡uf!; ¡quia!

humus ('hju·məs) *n.* humus.

hunch (hʌntʃ) *n.* **1,** (hump) joroba; giba. **2,** *colloq.* (intuition) presentimiento; corazonada. —*v.t.* encorvar; arquear. —*v.i.* andar a empujones *o* empellones.

hunchback *n.* = **humpback.**

hundred ('hʌn·drɪd) *adj.* cien; ciento. —*n.* ciento; centena; centenar. —**hundredth,** *adj.* & *n.* centésimo.

hundredfold ('hʌn·drɪd,fold) *adj.* céntuplo; cien veces (más). —*adv.* cien veces; en un céntuplo.

hundredweight *n.* quintal.

hung (hʌŋ) *v., pret.* & *p.p. de* **hang.**

hunger ('hʌŋ·gər) *n.* **1,** (craving for food) hambre. **2,** (strong desire) deseo intenso; hambre; anhelo. —*v.i.* tener hambre. —**hunger for** *o* **after,** desear con ansia; anhelar; ansiar.

hungry ('hʌŋ·gri) *adj.* hambriento. —**be** *o* **feel hungry,** tener hambre. —**go hungry,** pasar hambre.

hunk (hʌŋk) *n., colloq.* pedazo grande; buen pedazo; lonja.

hunky ('hʌŋ·ki) *adj., slang* magnífico; bonísimo. *También*, **hunky-dory** (-'dor·i).

hunt (hʌnt) *v.t. & i.* 1, (chase, as game) cazar. 2, (search) buscar. 3, (pursue) perseguir; ir en búsqueda (de). —*n.* 1, (chase; hunting) caza; cacería. 2, (search) búsqueda; busca. 3, (pursuit) persecución; búsqueda. 4, (hunting party) partida de caza; cazadores (*pl.*). —**go hunting (for)**, ir de caza; ir a la caza (de). —**hunt down**, buscar o perseguir hasta encontrar. —**hunt up**, buscar.

hunter ('hʌn·tər) *n.* 1, [*también*, **huntsman** ('hʌntz·mən)] (one who hunts game) cazador. 2, (pursuer) perseguidor.

hunting ('hʌn·tɪŋ) *n.* 1, (sport or occupation) caza; montería. 2, = **hunt**.

hurdle ('hʌɹ·dəl) *n.* 1, (fence; barrier, as used in sports) valla; barrera. 2, (obstacle; difficulty) obstáculo; dificultad. —*v.t.* 1, (jump over) saltar sobre. 2, (overcome, as a difficulty) superar. —**hurdler** (-dlər) *n.* saltador de vallas.

hurdy-gurdy ('hʌɹ·di,gʌɹ·di) *n.* organillo.

hurl (hʌɹl) *v.t.* lanzar; arrojar. —*n.* tiro.

hurly-burly (,hʌɹ·li'bʌɹ·li) *n.* tumulto; alboroto; batahola. —*adj.* confuso; tumultuoso; alborotado.

hurrah (hə'raː) *interj. & n.* viva; hurra. —*v.t. & i.* aclamar; dar vivas *o* hurras. *También*, **hurray** (hə'rei).

hurricane ('hʌɹ·ə,kein) *n.* huracán. —**hurricane lamp**, quinqué.

hurry ('hʌɹ·i) *v.i.* [*también*, **hurry up**] apresurarse; darse prisa; *Amer.* apurarse. —*v.t.* acelerar; apurar; apresurar; meter prisa a. —*n.* prisa; *Amer.* apuro. —**be in a hurry**, tener prisa; estar de prisa.

hurry-scurry *también*, **hurry-skurry** ('hʌɹ·i'skʌɹ·i) *n.* pelotera; baraúnda; idas y venidas. —*v.i.* ir *o* correr de un lado para otro; precipitarse; andar como loco. —*adj.* confuso y precipitado. —*adv.* confusa y precipitadamente.

hurt (hʌɹt) *v.t.* [**hurt, hurting**] 1, (wound) herir; lastimar. 2, (be detrimental to; damage) perjudicar; estropear; dañar. 3, (wound the feelings of; offend) herir; ofender. —*v.t. & i.* (cause pain) doler; hacer daño. —*n.* 1, (pain) dolor. 2, (wound) herida. 3, (damage; harm) daño; perjuicio. —**hurtful**, *adj.* perjudicial; nocivo.

hurtle ('hʌɹ·təl) *v.i.* 1, [*usu.* **hurtle against** *o* **together**] (collide; crash) chocar; estrellarse. 2, (clatter; resound) retumbar; resonar. 3, (rush violently) ir disparado; ir como bólido. —*v.t.* arrojar; lanzar.

husband ('hʌz·bənd) *n.* marido; esposo. —*v.t.* conservar; cuidar de. —**husbandman** (-mən) *adj.* agricultor; granjero.

husbandry ('hʌz·bən·dri) *n.* 1, (thrift; economy) economía. 2, (farming) labranza; labores agrícolas. 3, (management) manejo; cuidado.

hush (hʌʃ) *v.t.* 1, (silence) silenciar; hacer callar. 2, (calm; quiet) acallar; aquietar. —*v.i.* enmudecer; callarse; aquietarse. —*n.* silencio; quietud. —*interj.* ¡silencio!; ¡chito!

hush-hush *adj.* secreto.

husk (hʌsk) *n.* 1, (outer covering, as of fruits or seeds) corteza; cáscara; vaina; hollejo. 2, (any dry, hard covering) corteza; cáscara. —*v.t.* descascarar; pelar; mondar.

huskiness ('hʌs·ki·nəs) *n.* 1, (hoarseness) ronquera; aspereza. 2, (strength; robustness) fuerza; robustez.

husky ('hʌs·ki) *adj.* 1, (hoarse) ronco; áspero. 2, (robust) fornido; robusto. —*n.* perro esquimal.

hussar (hʊ'zaːr) *n.* húsar.

hussy ('hʌz·i; 'hʌs-) *n.* pícara; buena pieza.

hustle ('hʌs·əl) *v.t.* 1, (shove; jostle) empujar; dar empujones. 2, *colloq.* (hurry; press) empujar; apurar. —*v.i.* 1, (move hurriedly) apresurarse; *Amer.* apurarse. 2, (act or work energetically) ajetrearse; afanarse; trabajar afanosamente. —*n.* 1, (a shoving; a pushing) empujón. 2, *colloq.* (drive; push) empuje. —**hustler** (-lər) *n.* buscavidas.

hut (hʌt) *n.* choza; barraca; cabaña; *Amer.* bohío.

hutch (hʌtʃ) *n.* 1, (bin; chest) arca; cofre. 2, (cupboard) alacena; aparador. 3, (pen; coop) pollera; conejera. 4, (hut) choza; barraca.

huzza (hə'zaː) *interj., n. & v.* = **hurrah**.

hyacinth ('hai·ə·sɪnθ) *n.* jacinto.

hybrid ('hai·brɪd) *n.* & *adj.* híbrido. —**hybridism,** *n.* hibridismo. —**hybridize,** *v.t.* cruzar. —*v.i.* producir híbridos.
hydrangea (hai'drein·dʒə) *n.* hortensia.
hydrant ('hai·drənt) *n.* boca de riego; boca de agua; toma de agua.
hydrate ('hai·dreit) *n.* hidrato. —*v.t.* hidratar. —**hydration,** *n.* hidratación.
hydraulic (hai'drɔ·lɪk) *adj.* hidráulico. —**hydraulics,** *n.* hidráulica.
hydro- (hai·dro) *prefijo* hidro-. **1,** agua: *hydroelectric,* hidroeléctrico. **2,** *quím.* hidrógeno: *hydrocarbon,* hidrocarbono.
hydrodynamic (ˌhai·dro·dai'næm·ɪk) *adj.* hidrodinámico. —**hydrodynamics,** *n.* hidrodinámica.
hydroelectric (ˌhai·dro·ə'lɛk·trɪk) *adj.* hidroeléctrico. —**hydroelectrics,** *n.* hidroeléctrica.
hydrogen ('hai·drə·dʒən) *n.* hidrógeno.
hydrogenate ('hai·drə·dʒə·ˌneit) *v.t.* hidrogenar. —**hydrogenation,** *n.* hidrogenación.
hydrometer (hai'dram·ɪ·tər) *n.* hidrómetro.
hydrophobia (ˌhai·drə'fo·bi·ə) *n.* hidrofobia; rabia. —**hydrophobe** ('hai·drəˌfob) *n.* hidrófobo. —**hydrophobic,** *adj.* hidrófobo.
hydroplane ('hai·drəˌplein) *n.* hidroavión; hidroplano.
hydrous ('hai·drəs) *adj.* acuoso.
hyena (hai'i·na) *n.* hiena.
hygiene ('hai·dʒin) *n.* higiene.
hygienic (ˌhai·dʒi'ɛn·ɪk) *adj.* higiénico. —**hygienics,** *n.* higiene.
hygienist ('hai·dʒi·ən·ɪst) *n.* higienista.
hygrometer (hai'gram·ə·tər) *n.* higrómetro. —**hygrometric** (ˌhai·grə'mɛt·rɪk) *adj.* higrométrico.
hymen ('hai·mən) *n.* **1,** *anat.* himen. **2,** (marriage) himeneo. —**hymeneal** (-mə'ni·əl) *adj.* nupcial.
hymn (hɪm) *n.* himno.
hymnal ('hɪm·nəl) *n.* himnario.
hyper- (hai·pər) *prefijo* hiper-; sobre; superior; excesivo: *hypersensitive,* hipersensitivo.
hyperbola (hai'pʌɹ·bə·lə) *n.* hipérbola.
hyperbole (hai'pʌɹ·bə·li) *n.* hipérbole.
hyperbolic (ˌhai·pər'bal·ɪk) *adj.* hiperbólico.
hypertrophy (hai'pʌɹ·trə·fi) *n.* hipertrofia. —*v.i.* hipertrofiarse.
hyphen ('hai·fən) *n.* guión.
hyphenate ('hai·fəˌneit) *v.t.* separar con guión. —**hyphenation,** *n.* separación con guiones.
hypnosis (hɪp'no·sis) *n.* hipnosis. —**hypnotic** (-'nat·ɪk) *adj.* hipnótico.
hypnotism ('hɪp·nə·tɪz·əm) *n.* hipnotismo. —**hypnotist,** *n.* hipnotizador.
hypnotize ('hɪp·nəˌtaiz) *v.t.* hipnotizar.
hypo ('hai·po) *n.* **1,** *photog.* (fixative) fijador. **2,** *slang* = **hypodermic. 3,** *slang* = **hypochondriac.**
hypo- (hai·po; -pə) *prefijo* hipo-. **1,** bajo; inferior; escaso: *hypodermic,* hipodérmico; *hypotaxis,* hipotaxis; *hypoplasia,* hipoplasia. **2,** *quím.* grado menor de oxidación: *hyposulfite,* hiposulfuro.
hypochondriac (hai·pə'kan·dri·æk) *n.* & *adj.* hipocondríaco. —**hypochondria** (-ə) *n.* hipocondría.
hypocrisy (hɪ'pak·rə·si) *n.* hipocresía.
hypocrite ('hɪp·ə·krɪt) *n.* hipócrita. —**hypocritical** (-'krɪt·ɪ·kəl) *adj.* hipócrita.
hypodermic (ˌhai·pə'dʌɹ·mɪk) *adj.* & *n.* hipodérmico.
hypotenuse (hai'pat·ə·nus) *n.* hipotenusa.
hypothesis (hai'paθ·ə·sɪs) *n.* hipótesis.
hypothesize (hai'paθ·əˌsaiz) *v.i.* asumir una hipótesis. —*v.t.* postular; asumir.
hypothetical (ˌhai·pə'θɛt·ɪ·kəl) *adj.* hipotético.
hyssop ('hɪs·əp) *n.* hisopo.
hysterectomy (ˌhɪs·tə'rɛk·tə·mi) *n.* histerectomía.
hysteria (hɪs'tɪr·i·ə) *n.* histeria; histerismo.
hysteric (hɪs'tɛr·ɪk) *n.* **1,** (person) histérico. **2,** *pl.* (attack) histerismo (*sing.*); histeria (*sing.*). —**hysterical,** *adj.* histérico.
hystero- (hɪs·tər·o) *prefijo* histero-. **1,** útero; matriz: *hysterotomy,* histerotomía. **2,** histeria: *hysterogenic,* histerógeno.

I

I, i (ai) novena letra del alfabeto inglés.
I (ai) *pron.pers.* yo.
-ia (i·ə; jə) *sufijo; forma nombres indicando* **1,** plurales latinos y colectivos: *bacteria,* bacterias. **2,** países: *Australia,* Australia. **3,** enfermedades: *diphtheria,* difteria. **4,** géneros de plantas: *gardenia,* gardenia.
-ial (i·əl) *sufijo* -ial; *forma adjetivos denotando* relación; pertenencia: *ministerial,* ministerial.
iambic (ai'æm·bɪk) *n.* yambo. —*adj.* yámbico.
-iasis (ai·ə·sɪs) *sufijo* -iasis; enfermedad: *elephantiasis,* elefantiasis.
-iatrics (i'æt·rɪks) *sufijo* -iatría; ciencia o tratamiento de enfermedades: *pediatrics,* pediatría.
-iatry (ai·ə·tri) *sufijo* -iatría; ciencia o tratamiento de enfermedades: *psychiatry,* psiquiatría.
Iberian (ai'bɪr·i·ən) *adj.* ibérico. —*adj.* & *n.* íbero.
ibex ('ai·bɛks) *n.* íbice.
-ibility (ə'bɪl·ə·ti) *sufijo* -ibilidad; *forma nombres de los adjetivos terminados en* **-ible**: *audibility,* audibilidad.
ibis ('ai·bɪs) *n.* ibis.
-ible (ə·bəl) *sufijo* -ible; *forma adjetivos expresando* capacidad; habilidad: *legible,* legible.
-ic (ɪk) *sufijo* -ico; *forma adjetivos indicando* **1,** relación; cualidad; pertenencia; característica: *poetic,* poético. **2,** *quím.* presencia de uno de los componentes en valencia mayor: *nitric,* nítrico.
-ical (ɪ·kəl) *sufijo* -ico; -ical; *forma adjetivos de nombres o sus radicales: angelical,* angélico.
ice (ais) *n.* **1,** (frozen water) hielo. **2,** (sherbet) helado de agua; sorbete. **3,** = **icing. 4,** (reserve; formality) frialdad. —*v.t.* **1,** (cool with ice) poner en hielo; enfriar. **2,** (freeze) helar. **3,** *cooking* (frost) garapiñar; acaramelar: confitar. —*v.i.* helarse. —*adj.* [*también,* **iced**] helado; congelado; de *o* como hielo. —**ice box,** nevera. —**ice cream,** helado. —**ice cream parlor,** salón de refrescos; *Amer.* heladería. —**ice water,** agua fría *o* helada.
-ice (ɪs) *sufijo* -icio; -icia; *forma nombres denotando* acción; cualidad; condición: *sacrifice,* sacrificio; *justice,* justicia.
iceberg ('ais,bʌɹg) *n.* iceberg; témpano de hielo.
icebreaker *n.* rompehielos.
iceman *n.* [*pl.* **-men**] vendedor *o* repartidor de hielo.
ichthyo- (ɪk·θi·o; -ə) *prefijo* ictio-; pez: *ichthyosaur,* ictiosauro.
ichthyology (,ɪk·θi'al·ə·dʒi) *n.* ictiología. —**ichthyological** (-ə'la·dʒə·kəl) *adj.* ictiológico. —**ichthyologist,** *n.* ictiólogo.
-ician (ɪʃ·ən) *sufijo; forma nombres denotando* profesión: *mortician,* director de funeraria.
icicle ('ai·sɪ·kəl) *n.* carámbano.
icing ('ai·sɪŋ) *n.* baño *o* capa de pasta confitada; escarchado.
-icious (ɪʃ·əs) *sufijo* -icioso; *forma adjetivos denotando* cualidad; relación: *pernicious,* pernicioso.
icon ('ai·kan) *n.* icono.
iconoclast (ai'kan·ə,klæst) *n.* iconoclasta. —**iconoclastic** (-'klæs·tɪk) *adj.* iconoclasta.
-ics (ɪks) *sufijo* -ica; *forma nombres denotando* arte; ciencia: *athletics,* atlética; *physics,* física.
icy ('ai·si) *adj.* **1,** (cold; frozen) helado; frío; frígido. **2,** (slippery) resbaladizo.
I'd (aid) *contr. de* **I should, I would** *o* **I had.**
-id (ɪd) *sufijo* -ido. **1,** *forma nombres y adjetivos denotando* cualidad; relación: *torrid,* tórrido; *fluid,* flúido. **2,** *zool.* miembro de una familia o grupo: *arachnid,* arácnido.
-idae (ɪ·dei) *sufijo* -idos, *zool.; forma nombres de familias o grupos: Canidae,* cánidos.
-ide (aid) *sufijo* -uro, *quím.; forma nombres de compuestos binarios: sulfide,* sulfuro.
idea (ai'di·a) *n.* idea.
ideal (ai'di·əl) *n.* & *adj.* ideal. —**idealism,** *n.* idealismo. —**idealist,** *n.* idealista. —**idealistic,** *adj.* idealista.
idealize (ai'di·ə·laiz) *v.t.* idealizar. —**idealization** (-lɪ'zei·ʃən) *n.* idealización.

ideate (ai'di·eit) *v.t.* idear; imaginar. —**ideation**, *n.* ideación.
idem ('ɪd·əm) *pron.* ídem.
identical (ai'dɛn·tɪ·kəl) *adj.* idéntico.
identify (ai'dɛn·tɪ·fai) *v.t.* identificar. —**identification** (-fɪ'kei·ʃən) *n.* identificación.
identity (ai'dɛn·tə·ti) *n.* identidad.
ideo- (ɪ·di·o; ai-) *prefijo,* ideo-; idea: *ideology,* ideología.
ideology (ˌai·di'al·ə·dʒi) *n.* ideología. —**ideological** (-ə'ladʒ·ɪ·kəl) *adj.* ideológico.
ides (aidz) *n.pl.* idus.
idio- (ɪ·di·o; -ə) *prefijo* idio-; personalidad; peculiaridad: *idiosyncrasy,* idiosincrasia.
idiocy ('ɪd·i·ə·si) *n.* idiotez.
idiom ('ɪd·i·əm) *n.* **1,** (idiomatic expression) modismo. **2,** (language) lenguaje; idioma. **3,** (style) estilo. —**idiomatic** (-ə'mæt·ɪk) *adj.* idiomático.
idiosyncrasy (ˌɪd·i·ə'sɪn·krə·si) *n.* idiosincrasia. —**idiosyncratic** (-'kræt·ɪk) *adj.* idiosincrásico.
idiot ('ɪd·i·ət) *n.* idiota. —**idiotic** (-'at·ɪk) *adj.* idiota.
idle ('ai·dəl) *adj.* **1,** (useless; futile) ocioso; inútil; fútil. **2,** (baseless; unfounded) sin fundamento; sin base. **3,** (unemployed; without work) desocupado; sin trabajo. **4,** (inactive) inactivo. **5,** (not filled with activity) de ocio. **6,** (lazy) ocioso; holgazán. —*v.i.* **1,** (loaf) holgazanear. **2,** (operate without transmitting power) dar vueltas *o* funcionar sin efectuar trabajo; funcionar desconectado *o* en neutro. —*v.t.* **1,** (waste; squander) perder; malgastar. **2,** (cause to idle, as a motor) desconectar; poner en neutro; hacer funcionar en neutro. —**idleness,** *n.* ociosidad.
idler ('ai·dlər) *n.* **1,** (loafer) ocioso; holgazán. **2,** *mech.* rueda *o* polea loca.
idling ('ai·dlɪŋ) *n.* **1,** (loafing) holgazanería. **2,** *mech.* funcionamiento *o* marcha en neutro.
idly ('ai·dli) *adv.* ociosamente.
idol ('ai·dəl) *n.* ídolo. —**idolize,** *v.t.* idolatrar.
idolater (ai'dal·ə·tər) *n.* idólatra.
idolatry (ai'dal·ə·tri) *n.* idolatría. —**idolatrous,** *adj.* idólatra.
idyl *también,* **idyll** ('ai·dəl) *n.* idilio. —**idyllic** (ai'dɪl·ɪk) *adj.* idílico.
-ie (i) *sufijo, formando diminutivos: kiddie,* nenito.
-ier (ɪr) *sufijo* -ero; *forma nombres denotando* profesión: *bombardier,* bombardero.
if (ɪf) *conj.* si. —*n.* punto dudoso; supuesto. —**as if,** como si.—**even if,** aun cuando; aunque; aun si. —**if so,** si es así.
igloo ('ɪg·lu) *n.* iglú.
igneous ('ɪg·ni·əs) *adj.* ígneo.
ignite (ɪg'nait) *v.t. & i.* encender; prender.
ignition (ɪg'nɪʃ·ən) *n.* **1,** (burning) ignición. **2,** *mech.* encendido; ignición.
ignoble (ɪg'no·bəl) *adj.* innoble; bajo. —**ignobility; ignobleness,** *n.* bajeza.
ignominious (ˌɪg·nə'mɪn·i·əs) *adj.* ignominioso. —**ignominy** ('ɪg·nəˌmɪn·i) *n.* ignominia.
ignoramus (ˌɪg·nə'rei·məs) *n.* ignorante.
ignorant ('ɪg·nə·rənt) *adj.* **1,** (untutored) ignorante. **2,** (of or through ignorance) de ignorante; torpe. —**ignorance,** *n.* ignorancia.
ignore (ɪg'noːr) *v.t.* no hacer caso de; no tener en cuenta; pasar por alto.
iguana (ɪ'gwa·nə) *n.* iguana.
il- (ɪl) *prefijo, var. de* **-in** *ante* **l**: *illiterate,* iliterato.
-il (ɪl) *sufijo, var. de* **-ile**: *civil,* civil.
-ile (əl) *sufijo* -il; *forma adjetivos denotando* tendencia; relación: *fragile,* frágil; *docile,* dócil.
iliac ('ɪl·i·æk) *adj.* ilíaco; iliaco.
-ility (ɪl·ə·ti) *sufijo* -ilidad; *forma nombres de los adjetivos terminados en* **-il** *o* **-ile**: *civility,* civilidad; *docility,* docilidad.
ilk (ɪlk) *n.* jaez; clase; especie.
I'll (ail) *contr. de* **I shall** *o* **I will.**
ill (ɪl) *adj.* **1,** (evil; bad) malo. **2,** (sick) enfermo; malo. **3,** (faulty; poor) malo; inadecuado. —*n.* mal. —*adv.* **1,** (badly) malamente; mal. **2,** (scarcely) difícilmente; mal. —**go ill with,** irle mal; venirle *o* caerle mal. —**ill at ease,** incómodo; desasosegado. —**take ill, 1,** (take offense at) tomar a mal. **2,** (take sick) enfermarse; caer enfermo.
ill- (ɪl) *prefijo* mal-; mal: *ill-treat,* maltratar; *ill-disposed,* maldispuesto.

ill-advised (ˌɪl·æd'vaizd) *adj.* imprudente.
ill-bred ('ɪlˌbrɛd) *adj.* malcriado; mal educado. —**ill breeding**, mala educación.
ill-considered *adj.* poco prudente; de incauto.
ill-defined *adj.* obscuro; indefinido.
ill-disposed *adj.* maldispuesto.
illegal (ɪ'li·gəl) *adj.* ilegal. —**illegality** (ˌɪl·lɪ'gæl·ə·ti) *n.* ilegalidad.
illegible (ɪ'lɛdʒ·ə·bəl) *adj.* ilegible. —**illegibility**, *n.* lo ilegible.
illegitimate (ˌɪl·ɪ'dʒɪt·ə·mət) *adj.* ilegítimo. —**illegitimacy** (-mə·si) *n.* ilegitimidad.
ill-fated *adj.* desgraciado; infausto; aciago.
ill-favored *adj.* feo; malcarado.
ill-fed *adj.* desnutrido; hambriento.
ill-founded *adj.* mal fundado.
ill-gotten *adj.* mal adquirido.
ill-humored *adj.* malhumorado. —**ill humor**, mal humor.
illiberal (ɪ'lɪb·ə·rəl) *adj.* iliberal. —**illiberality** (ɪˌlɪb·ə'ræl·ə·ti) *n.* iliberalidad.
illicit (ɪ'lɪs·ɪt) *adj.* ilícito.
illinium (ɪ'lɪn·i·əm) *n.* ilinio.
ill-intentioned *adj.* malintencionado.
illiterate (ɪ'lɪt·ə·rət) *adj.* analfabeto. —**illiteracy** (-ər·ə·si) *n.* analfabetismo.
ill-kept *adj.* desatendido; desaseado.
ill-looking *adj.* malcarado; feo.
ill-mannered *adj.* de malos modales; descortés.
ill-natured *adj.* maldispuesto; atravesado.
illness ('ɪl·nəs) *n.* enfermedad.
illogical (ɪ'ladʒ·ɪ·kəl) *adj.* ilógico. —**illogicality** (-'kæl·ə·ti) *n.* falta de lógica; lo ilógico.
ill-omened *adj.* de mal agüero.
ill-spent *adj.* malgastado.
ill-starred *adj.* desastrado; malaventurado.
ill-tempered *adj.* de mal genio; malhumorado. —**ill temper**, mal genio; mal humor.
ill-timed *adj.* inoportuno.
ill-treat *v.t.* maltratar. —**ill-treatment**, *n.* maltrato.
illuminate (ɪ'lu·məˌneit) *v.t.* iluminar. —**illumination**, *n.* iluminación. —**illuminator**, *n.* lámpara; fuente de iluminación.
illusion (ɪ'lu·ʒən) *n.* ilusión. —**illusive** (-sɪv) *adj.* ilusivo. —**illusory** (-sə·ri) *adj.* ilusorio.
illustrate ('ɪl·əˌstreit) *v.t.* ilustrar. —**illustration**, *n.* ilustración. —**illustrative** (ɪ'lʌs·trə·tɪv) *adj.* ilustrativo. —**illustrator**, *n.* ilustrador.
illustrious (ɪ'lʌs·tri·əs) *adj.* ilustre. —**illustriousness**, *n.* fama; grandeza.
ill will mala voluntad; ojeriza; malquerencia.
ill-wisher *n.* malintencionado.
I'm (aim) *contr. de* **I am.**
im- (ɪm) *prefijo, var. de* **in-** *ante* m, b *y* p: *immaculate*, inmaculado; *imbibe*, embeber; *impoverish*, empobrecer.
image ('ɪm·ɪdʒ) *n.* imagen. —*v.t.* **1,** (portray; depict) representar; describir. **2,** (reflect; mirror) reflejar. **3,** (imagine) imaginar. —**imagery**, *n.* imágenes (*pl.*).
imaginary (ɪ'mædʒ·ɪ·nɛr·i) *adj.* imaginario.
imagination (ɪˌmædʒ·ɪ'nei·ʃən) *n.* imaginación.
imaginative (ɪ'mædʒ·ɪˌnei·tɪv) *adj.* imaginativo.
imagine (ɪ'mædʒ·ɪn) *v.t. & i.* imaginar. —**imaginable**, *adj.* imaginable.
imbalance (ɪm'bæl·əns) *n.* desequilibrio.
imbecile ('ɪm·bə·sɪl) *n. & adj.* imbécil. —**imbecilic** (-'sɪl·ɪk) *adj.* imbécil. —**imbecility** (-'sɪl·ə·ti) *n.* imbecilidad.
imbed (ɪm'bɛd) *v.t.* [**-bedded, -bedding**] **1,** (encase; inlay) encajar; incrustar; embutir; empotrar. **2,** (plant; fix) plantar; fijar.
imbibe (ɪm'baib) *v.t.* **1,** (drink) beber. **2,** (absorb) absorber; embeber.
imbroglio (ɪm'brol·jo) *n.* embrollo; enredo; lío.
imbue (ɪm'bjuː) *v.t.* **1,** (dye) teñir. **2,** (infuse) imbuir. —**imbuement**, *n.* imbuimiento.
imitate ('ɪm·əˌteit) *v.t.* imitar. —**imitable**, *adj.* imitable. —**imitation**, *n.* imitación; copia. —*adj.* imitado; de imitación. —**imitative**, *adj.* imitativo. —**imitator**, *n.* imitador.
immaculate (ɪ'mæk·jə·lɪt) *adj.*

inmaculado. —**immaculateness,** *n.* pureza; perfección.

immanent ('ɪm·ə·nənt) *adj.* inmanente. —**immanence,** *n.* inmanencia.

immaterial (ˌɪm·ə'tɪr·i·əl) *adj.* **1,** (incorporeal) inmaterial. **2,** (unimportant) sin importancia; indiferente. —**immaterialness; immateriality** (-'æl·ə·ti) *n.* inmaterialidad.

immature (ˌɪm·ə'tjʊr) *adj.* inmaduro; sin madurez. —**immaturity,** *n.* inmadurez; falta de madurez.

immeasurable (ɪ'mɛʒ·ər·ə·bəl) *adj.* inmensurable.

immediacy (ɪ'mi·di·ə·si) *n.* urgencia.

immediate (ɪ'mi·di·ət) *adj.* inmediato. —**immediateness,** *n.* lo inmediato.

immediately (ɪ'mi·di·ət·li) *adv.* inmediatamente; de inmediato. —*conj., Brit.* tan pronto como.

immemorial (ˌɪm·ə'mor·i·əl) *adj.* inmemorial.

immense (ɪ'mɛns) *adj.* inmenso. —**immenseness; immensity,** *n.* inmensidad; lo inmenso.

immerse (ɪ'mʌɹs) *v.t.* sumergir. —**immersion** (ɪ'mʌɹ·ʃən) *n.* inmersión; sumersión.

immigrant ('ɪm·ə·grənt) *n.* & *adj.* inmigrante.

immigrate ('im·əˌgreit) *v.i.* inmigrar. —**immigration,** *n.* inmigración.

imminent ('ɪm·ə·nənt) *adj.* inminente. —**imminence,** *n.* inminencia.

immobile (ɪ'mo·bɪl) *adj.* inmóvil. —**immobility,** *n.* inmovilidad.

immobilize (ɪ'mo·bəˌlaiz) *v.t.* inmovilizar. —**immobilization** (-lɪ·'zei·ʃən) *n.* inmovilización.

immoderate (ɪ'mad·ər·ət) *adj.* inmoderado. —**immoderation** (-ə'rei·ʃən) *n.* inmoderación.

immodest (ɪ'mad·ɪst) *adj.* inmodesto. —**immodesty,** *n.* inmodestia.

immolate ('ɪm·əˌleit) *v.t.* inmolar. —**immolation,** *n.* inmolación.

immoral (ɪ'mor·əl) *adj.* inmoral. —**immorality** (ˌɪm·ə'ræl·ə·ti) *n.* inmoralidad.

immortal (ɪ'mor·təl) *adj.* & *n.* inmortal. —**immortality** (-'tæl·ə·ti) *n.* inmortalidad.

immortalize (ɪ'mor·təˌlaiz) *v.t.* inmortalizar. —**immortalization** (-lɪ·'zei·ʃən) *n.* inmortalización.

immortelle (ˌɪm·or'tɛl) *n.* perpetua.

immovable (ɪ'muv·ə·bəl) *adj.* inamovible; inmovible.

immune (ɪ'mjuːn) *adj.* inmune. —**immunity** (ɪ'mju·nə·ti) *n.* inmunidad.

immunize ('ɪm·jəˌnaiz) *v.t.* inmunizar. —**immunization** (-nɪ'zei·ʃən) *n.* inmunización.

immutable (ɪ'mju·tə·bəl) *adj.* inmutable. —**immutability,** *n.* inmutabilidad.

imp (ɪmp) *n.* diablillo.

impact ('ɪm·pækt) *n.* impacto. —*v.t.* (ɪm'pækt) encajar; embutir. —**impacted,** *adj.* embutido; apretado; *dent.* impactado.

impair (ɪm'peːr) *v.t.* **1,** (spoil; damage) dañar; malograr; perjudicar. **2,** (hinder) dificultar; estorbar.

impairment (ɪm'pɛr·mənt) *n.* **1,** (damage) daño; perjuicio. **2,** (hindrance) dificultad; estorbo; traba.

impale (ɪm'peil) *v.t.* **1,** (transfix) empalar. **2,** (fence in) cercar. —**impalement,** *n.* empalamiento.

impalpable (ɪm'pæl·pə·bəl) *adj.* impalpable. —**impalpability,** *n.* impalpabilidad.

impanel (ɪm'pæn·əl) *v.t.* convocar como jurado. —**impanelment,** *n.* convocación.

impart (ɪm'part) *v.t.* impartir.

impartial (ɪm'par·ʃəl) *adj.* imparcial. —**impartiality** (-ʃi'æl·ə·ti) *n.* imparcialidad.

impassable (ɪm'pæs·ə·bəl) *adj.* impasable; intransitable. —**impassability,** *n.* calidad de impasable *o* intransitable.

impasse (ɪm'pæs) *n.* atolladero.

impassion (ɪm'pæʃ·ən) *v.t.* apasionar. —**impassioned,** *adj.* apasionado.

impassive (ɪm'pæs·ɪv) *adj.* impasible. —**impassiveness,** *n.* impasibilidad.

impaste (ɪm'peist) *v.t.* empastar. —**impasto** (ɪm'pas·to) *n.* empaste.

impatient (ɪm'pei·ʃənt) *adj.* impaciente. —**impatience,** *n.* impaciencia.

impeach (ɪm'pitʃ) *v.t.* **1,** (call in question) disputar; poner en duda; poner en tela de juicio. **2,** (accuse) acusar; procesar. —**impeachable,** *adj.* censurable; disputable.

impeachment (ɪm'pitʃ·mənt)

n. **1,** (public accusation) acusación; procesamiento. **2,** (discredit) descrédito.
impeccable (ɪm'pɛk·ə·bəl) *n.* impecable. —**impeccability,** *n.* impecabilidad.
impecunious (ˌɪm·pə'kju·ni·əs) *adj.* sin recursos; sin peculio; pobre. —**impecuniousness,** *n.* falta de recursos; pobreza.
impede (ɪm'piːd) *v.t.* impedir. —**impediment** (ɪm'pɛd·ə·mənt) *n.* impedimento.
impedimenta (ɪmˌpɛd·ɪ'mɛn·tə) *n.pl.* impedimenta (*sing.*).
impel (ɪm'pɛl) *v.t.* [**-pelled, -pelling**] impeler.
impend (ɪm'pɛnd) *v.i.* **1,** (be suspended) pender; cernerse. **2,** (be imminent) amenazar; ser inminente.
impenetrable (ɪm'pɛn·ə·trə·bəl) *adj.* impenetrable. —**impenetrability,** *n.* impenetrabilidad.
impenitent (ɪm'pɛn·ɪ·tənt) *adj.* impenitente. —**impenitence,** *n.* impenitencia. —**impenitently,** *adv.* sin contrición.
imperative (ɪm'pɛr·ə·tɪv) *adj.* & *n.* imperativo.
imperceptible (ˌɪm·pər'sɛp·tə·bəl) *adj.* imperceptible. —**imperceptibility,** *n.* imperceptibilidad.
imperfect (ɪm'pʌɹ·fɪkt) *adj.* & *n.* imperfecto. —**imperfection** (ˌɪm·pər'fɛk·ʃən) *n.* defecto; imperfección.
imperial (ɪm'pɪr·i·əl) *adj.* **1,** (of an empire or emperor) imperial. **2,** (superior) superior; de primera. —*n.* **1,** (beard) barba estilo imperio; perilla. **2,** (top of a bus, carriage, etc.) imperial.
imperialism (ɪm'pɪr·i·əˌlɪz·əm) *n.* imperialismo. —**imperialist,** *n.* imperialista. —**imperialistic,** *adj.* imperialista.
imperil (ɪm'pɛr·əl) *v.t.* hacer peligrar; poner en peligro. —**imperilment,** *n.* peligro; el poner en peligro.
imperious (ɪm'pɪr·i·əs) *adj.* imperioso. —**imperiousness,** *n.* imperiosidad.
imperishable (ɪm'pɛr·ɪʃ·ə·bəl) *adj.* imperecedero. —**imperishability,** *n.* indestructibilidad; durabilidad.
impermanent (ɪm'pʌɹ·mə·nənt) *adj.* transitorio; efímero. —**impermanence,** *n.* transitoriedad; lo efímero.
impermeable (ɪm'pʌɹ·mi·ə·bəl) *adj.* impermeable. —**impermeability,** *n.* impermeabilidad.
impersonal (ɪm'pʌɹ·sə·nəl) *adj.* impersonal; *gram.* unipersonal; impersonal.
impersonate (ɪm'pʌɹ·səˌneit) *v.t.* **1,** (represent) representar; personificar. **2,** (imitate; pretend to be) imitar; hacerse pasar por.
impersonation (ɪmˌpʌɹ·sə'nei·ʃən) *n.* **1,** (representation) representación; personificación. **2,** (imitation) imitación. **3,** (imposture) impostura.
impersonator (ɪm'pʌɹ·səˌnei·tər) *n.* **1,** (actor) actor. **2,** (imitator) imitador. **3,** (impostor) impostor.
impertinent (ɪm'pʌɹ·tə·nənt) *adj.* impertinente. —**impertinence,** *n.* impertinencia.
imperturbable (ˌɪm·pər'tʌɹb·ə·bəl) *adj.* imperturbable. —**imperturbability,** *n.* imperturbabilidad.
impervious (ɪm'pʌɹ·vi·əs) *adj.* **1,** (impermeable) impermeable; impenetrable. **2,** (resistant) resistente. **3,** (unheeding; insensible) sordo; ciego. —**imperviousness,** *n.* impermeabilidad; impenetrabilidad.
impetuous (ɪm'pɛtʃ·u·əs) *adj.* impetuoso. —**impetuousness; impetuosity** (-'as·ə·ti) *n.* impetuosidad.
impetus ('ɪm·pə·təs) *n.* ímpetu.
impiety (ɪm'pai·ə·ti) *n.* impiedad.
impinge (ɪm'pɪndʒ) *v.i.* **1,** (touch) tocar; incidir; hacer contacto. **2,** (encroach; invade) invadir; estar *o* caer dentro.
impingement (ɪm'pɪndʒ·mənt) *n.* **1,** (incidence) incidencia. **2,** (encroachment) invasión; transgresión.
impious ('ɪm·pi·əs) *adj.* impío. —**impiousness,** *n.* impiedad.
impish ('ɪmp·ɪʃ) *adj.* travieso; malicioso; de diablillo.
implacable (ɪm'plei·kə·bəl) *adj.* implacable. —**implacableness; implacability,** *n.* implacabilidad.
implant (ɪm'plænt) *v.t.* **1,** (fix; set) implantar. **2,** (imbed) plantar; enterrar. **3,** (graft) injertar. —*n.* ('ɪm·plænt) injerto.
implausible (ɪm'plɔz·ə·bəl)

adj. no plausible; improbable; increíble.

implement ('ɪm·plə·mənt) *n.* **1,** (tool) herramienta; utensilio. **2,** (means) medio; instrumento. —*v.t.* (-ˌmɛnt) **1,** (carry out) realizar; llevar a cabo; efectuar. **2,** (provide with means) ayudar; secundar.

implicate ('ɪm·plɪˌkeit) *v.t.* implicar.

implication (ˌɪm·plɪ'kei·ʃən) *n.* **1,** (involvement) complicidad; implicación. **2,** (meaning; intimation) intimación; significación.

implicit (ɪm'plɪs·ɪt) *adj.* implícito. —**implicitness,** *n.* calidad de implícito.

implied (ɪm'plaid) *adj.* implícito.

implore (ɪm'ploːr) *v.t.* implorar.

imply (ɪm'plai) *v.t.* **1,** (involve; entail) implicar. **2,** (suggest) sugerir; intimar.

impolite (ˌɪm·pə'lait) *adj.* descortés. —**impoliteness,** *n.* descortesía; falta de cortesía.

impolitic (ɪm'pal·ə·tɪk) *adj.* impolítico.

imponderable (ɪm'pan·dər·ə·bəl) *adj.* imponderable.

import (ɪm'port) *v.t.* importar. —*v.i.* importar; tener importancia. —*n.* ('ɪm·port) **1,** (importation) importación. **2,** (importance) importancia. **3,** (significance) significado; significación. —**importation** (ˌɪm·por'tei·ʃən) *n.* importación. —**importer,** *n.* importador.

important (ɪm'por·tənt) *adj.* importante. —**importance,** *n.* importancia.

importune (ˌɪm·por'tjuːn) *v.t.* importunar. —**importunate** (ɪm·'port·ju·nət) *adj.* importuno. —**importunity,** *n.* importunidad.

impose (ɪm'poːz) *v.t.* **1,** (lay on or upon) imponer. **2,** (palm off) pasar (con maña); colar; endosar. —**imposing,** *adj.* imponente. —**imposition** (ˌɪm·pə'zɪʃ·ən) *n.* imposición. —**impose on** *o* **upon** (trouble; annoy) molestar; importunar; incomodar.

impossible (ɪm'pas·ə·bəl) *adj.* imposible. —**impossibility,** *n.* imposibilidad.

impost ('ɪm·post) *n.* impuesto.

impostor (ɪm'pas·tər) *n.* impostor. —**imposture** (-tʃər) *n.* impostura.

impotent ('ɪm·pə·tənt) *n.* impotente. —**impotence; impotency,** *n.* impotencia.

impound (ɪm'paund) *v.t.* **1,** (shut in a pen) encerrar; encorralar; meter en perrera. **2,** (seize; keep in custody) embargar; retener. —**impoundage; impoundment,** *n.* embargo.

impoverish (ɪm'pav·ər·ɪʃ) *v.t.* empobrecer. —**impoverishment,** *n.* empobrecimiento.

impracticable (ɪm'præk·tɪ·kə·bəl) *adj.* impracticable. —**impracticability,** *n.* impracticabilidad.

impractical (ɪm'præk·tɪ·kəl) *adj.* impráctico. —**impracticalness; impracticality** (-'kæl·ə·ti) *n.* lo impráctico; impractibilidad.

imprecate ('ɪm·prəˌkeit) *v.t.* imprecar. —**imprecation,** *n.* imprecación.

impregnable (ɪm'prɛg·nə·bəl) *adj.* **1,** (unassailable) inexpugnable. **2,** (fecund) fecundable. **3,** (saturable) impregnable; saturable.

impregnate (ɪm'prɛg·net) *v.t.* **1,** (fecundate) fecundar; preñar. **2,** (saturate) impregnar; saturar.

impregnation (ˌɪm·prɛg'nei·ʃən) *n.* **1,** (fecundation) fecundación. **2,** (saturation) impregnación; saturación.

impresario (ˌɪm·prə'sar·i·o) *n.* empresario.

impress (ɪm'prɛs) *v.t.* **1,** (affect deeply) impresionar. **2,** (stamp; fix firmly) imprimir; estampar. **3,** (urge) urgir. **4,** (recruit) reclutar. **5,** (requisition) requisar; requisicionar. —*n.* ('ɪm·prɛs) impresión.

impression (ɪm'prɛʃ·ən) *n.* impresión. —**impressionable,** *adj.* impresionable.

impressionism (ɪm'prɛʃ·ə·nɪz·əm) *n.* impresionismo. —**impressionist,** *n.* impresionista. —**impressionistic,** *adj.* impresionista.

impressive (ɪm'prɛs·ɪv) *adj.* impresionante. —**impressiveness,** *n.* lo impresionante.

impressment (ɪm'prɛs·mənt) *n.* **1,** (recruiting) reclutamiento. **2,** (requisition) requisición.

imprint (ɪm'prɪnt) *v.t.* imprimir; estampar. —*n.* ('ɪm·prɪnt) **1,** (publisher's mark) pie de imprenta. **2,** (impression) impresión. **3,** (distinctive sign) marca; señal; huella.

imprison (ɪm'prɪz·ən) *v.t.* encarcelar. —**imprisonment,** *n.* encarcelamiento.

improbable (ɪm'prab·ə·bəl) *adj.* improbable. —**improbability,** *n.* improbabilidad.
improbity (ɪm'prob·ə·ti) *n.* improbidad.
impromptu (ɪm'pramp·tu) *adj.* improvisado; extemporáneo. —*adv.* improvisadamente; extemporáneamente. —*n., music* improvisación.
improper (ɪm'prap·ər) *adj.* impropio. —**impropriety** (ˌɪm·prə·'prai·ə·ti) *n.* impropiedad.
improve (ɪm'pruːv) *v.t.* mejorar. —*v.i.* mejorarse. —**improvement,** *n.* mejora; mejoramiento; (*esp. of health*) mejoría.
improvident (ɪm'prav·ɪ·dənt) *adj.* impróvido. —**improvidence,** *n.* improvidencia.
improvise ('ɪm·prəˌvaiz) *v.t.* improvisar. —**improvisation** (ɪm·ˌprav·ɪ'zei·ʃən) *n.* improvisación.
imprudent (ɪm'pru·dənt) *adj.* imprudente. —**imprudence,** *n.* imprudencia.
impudent ('ɪm·pjə·dənt) *adj.* insolente; atrevido, impudente. —**impudence,** *n.* insolencia; atrevimiento; impudencia.
impugn (ɪm'pjuːn) *v.t.* impugnar; poner en tela de juicio. —**impugnment,** *n.* impugnación.
impulse ('ɪm·pʌls) *n.* impulso. —**impulsive** (ɪm'pʌl·sɪv) *adj.* impulsivo. —**impulsiveness,** *n.* impulsividad.
impunity (ɪm'pju·nə·ti) *n.* impunidad.
impure (ɪm'pjur) *adj.* impuro. —**impureness,** *n.* impureza. —**impurity,** *n.* impureza.
impute (ɪm'pjut) *v.t.* imputar. —**imputable,** *adj.* imputable. —**imputation** (ˌɪm·pju'tei·ʃən) *n.* imputación.
in (ɪn) *prep.* **1,** (*expresando inclusión o localidad*) en: *in the room,* en el cuarto. **2,** (*expresando estado o condición*) en; de; con: *in good spirits,* en, de *o* con buen humor. **3,** (*con el gerundio, expresando acción*) al (+ inf.) *o* el mero gerundio español: *in writing this,* al escribir esto; escribiendo esto. **4,** (*expresando modo o manera*) en; de; con: *in silence,* en silencio; *in good faith,* de *o* con buena fe. **5,** (*expresando tiempo o época en que o al fin de que sucede algo*) en; dentro de: *in these times,* en estos tiempos; *in a little while,* dentro de poco. **6,** (*expresando movimiento, dirección o cambio*) en: *set in motion,* poner en movimiento; *break in two,* partir en dos. **7,** (during) de; en: *in the daytime,* de día; *in the summer,* en el verano. **8,** (wearing; clothed in) de; con; en: *the lady in red,* la dama de rojo. **9,** (*expresando relación o respecto*) de; en: *a change in policy,* un cambio de política; *We agreed in this matter,* Convinimos en este asunto. **10,** (*expresando colocación o disposición*) en: *in a group,* en grupo. **11,** (*expresando distribución*) por; a: *in dozens,* por docenas. **12,** (made of or with) en; de: *in marble,* en *o* de mármol. **13,** (because of) de: *She sighed in relief,* Suspiró de alivio. **14,** (into) en; a; dentro de: *come in the house,* entra en *o* a casa. —*adv.* dentro; adentro; hacia dentro. —*adj.* de dentro; de adentro. —*n.* **1,** *usu.pl.* (persons in power or favor) los de arriba; los de adentro. **2,** *colloq.* (influence) mano. —**be in for,** buscarse (algo); merecer; no poder escapar. —**be in with,** tener intimidad con; ser íntimo de. —**ins and outs,** pormenores; minucias. —**in that,** porque; puesto que.
in- (ɪn) *prefijo* **1,** in-; *forma nombres y adjetivos denotando* privación; negación: *incautious,* incauto. **2,** in-; en; dentro; hacia: *inborn,* innato. **3,** in-; en-; *forma verbos expresando* existencia, movimiento *o* dirección hacia dentro: *inclose,* incluir. *A veces tiene una función puramente intensiva: inwrap,* envolver.
-in (ɪn) *sufijo* -ina; *forma nombres denotando* compuestos y elementos químicos; preparaciones farmacéuticas; minerales: *glycerin,* glicerina; *lanolin,* lanolina. *La mayoría de estos nombres aparecen hoy en la forma* **-ine.**
inability (ˌɪn·ə'bɪl·ə·ti) *n.* incapacidad.
inaccessible (ˌɪn·æk'sɛs·ə·bəl) *adj.* inaccesible. —**inaccessibility,** *n.* inaccesibilidad.
inaccurate (ɪn'æk·jə·rət) *adj.* inexacto. —**inaccuracy,** *n.* inexactitud.
inaction (ɪn'æk·ʃən) *n.* inacción.
inactive (ɪn'æk·tɪv) *adj.* inactivo.

—**inactivity** (ˌɪn·ækˈtɪv·ə·ti) *n.* inactividad.
inadequate (ɪnˈæd·ə·kwət) *adj.* inadecuado; insuficiente. —**inadequacy,** *n.* insuficiencia.
inadmissible (ɪn·ædˈmɪs·ə·bəl) *adj.* inadmisible. —**inadmissibility,** *n.* inadmisibilidad.
inadvertent (ɪn·ədˈvʌɹ·tənt) *adj.* inadvertido. —**inadvertence; inadvertency,** *n.* inadvertencia.
inadvisable (ɪn·ədˈvaiz·ə·bəl) *adj.* no aconsejable; imprudente. —**inadvisability,** *n.* imprudencia.
inalienable (ɪnˈeil·i·ən·ə·bəl) *adj.* inalienable; inajenable.
inane (ɪnˈein) *adj.* inane; vacío; huero. —**inanity** (ɪnˈæn·ə·ti) *n.* inanidad.
inanimate (ɪnˈæn·ɪ·mət) *adj.* inanimado; inánime. —**inanimateness; inanimation** (-ˈmei·ʃən) *n.* calidad de inanimado o inánime.
inanition (ˌɪn·əˈnɪʃ·ən) *n.* inanición.
inapplicable (ɪnˈæp·lɪk·ə·bəl) *adj.* inaplicable. —**inapplicability,** *n.* inaplicabilidad.
inappreciable (ˌɪn·əˈpriʃ·ə·bəl) *adj.* inapreciable.
inappropriate (ˌɪn·əˈpro·pri·ət) *adj.* inadecuado; impropio; improcedente. —**inappropriateness,** *n.* impropiedad; improcedencia.
inapt (ɪnˈæpt) *adj.* inepto.
inaptitude (inˈæp·tə·tud) *n.* ineptitud.
inarticulate (ˌɪn·arˈtɪk·jə·lət) *adj.* **1,** (not articulated) inarticulado. **2,** (unable to articulate) balbuciente.
inartistic (ˌɪn·arˈtɪs·tɪk) *adj.* inartístico.
inasmuch as (ˌɪn·ɪzˈmʌtʃ) **1,** (since) en vista de que; ya que; puesto que. **2,** (in so far as; to such a degree that) en cuanto; tanto como; hasta donde.
inattention (ˌɪn·əˈtɛn·ʃən) *n.* desatención; falta de atención. —**inattentive** (-tɪv) *adj.* desatento.
inaudible (ɪnˈɔ·də·bəl) *adj.* inaudible. —**inaudibleness; inaudibility,** *n.* calidad de inaudible.
inaugurate (ɪnˈɔ·gjəˌreit) *v.t.* inaugurar. —**inaugural** (-gjʊ·rəl) *adj.* inaugural. —**inauguration,** *n.* inauguración.
inauspicious (ˌɪn·ɔˈspɪʃ·əs) *adj.* desfavorable; poco propicio.
inborn *adj.* innato.
inbred *adj.* **1,** (inborn) ingénito. **2,** (produced by inbreeding) resultado de *o* producido por uniones de consanguinidad.
inbreeding *n.* procreación por uniones de consanguinidad.
Inca (ˈɪŋ·kə) *adj.* & *n.* inca. —**Incan** (ˈɪŋ·kən) *adj.* incaico.
incalculable (ɪnˈkæl·kjə·lə·bəl) *adj.* incalculable.
incandescent (ˌɪn·kənˈdɛs·ənt) *adj.* incandescente. —**incandescence,** *n.* incandescencia.
incantation (ˌɪn·kænˈtei·ʃən) *n.* encantamiento; conjuro.
incapable (ɪnˈkei·pə·bəl) *adj.* incapaz. —**incapability,** *n.* incapacidad.
incapacitate (ˌɪn·kəˈpæs·əˌteit) *v.t.* incapacitar; inhabilitar. —**incapacitation,** *n.* inhabilitación.
incapacity (ˌɪn·kəˈpæs·ə·ti) *n.* incapacidad; inutilidad.
incarcerate (ɪnˈkar·səˌreit) *v.t.* encarcelar. —**incarceration,** *n.* encarcelación.
incarnate (ɪnˈkar·nət) *adj.* encarnado. —*v.t.* (-ˌneit) encarnar. —**incarnation,** *n.* encarnación.
incautious (ɪnˈkɔ·ʃəs) *adj.* incauto. —**incautiousness,** *n.* imprudencia.
incendiary (ɪnˈsɛn·di·ɛr·i) *adj.* & *n.* incendiario. —**incendiarism** (-ə·rɪz·əm) *n.* condición *o* acto de incendiario.
incense (ˈɪn·sɛns) *n.* incienso.
incense (ɪnˈsɛns) *v.t.* enfurecer; encolerizar; enojar.
incentive (ɪnˈsɛn·tɪv) *n.* incentivo; aliciente. —*adj.* estimulante; alentador.
inception (ɪnˈsɛp·ʃən) *n.* comienzo; principio; iniciación. —**inceptive** (-tɪv) *adj.* inicial; *gram.* incoativo.
incertitude (ɪnˈsʌɹ·təˌtud) *n.* incertidumbre.
incessant (ɪnˈsɛs·ənt) *adj.* incesante. —**incessancy,** *n.* calidad de incesante; persistencia.
incest (ˈɪn·sɛst) *n.* incesto. —**incestuous** (ɪnˈsɛs·tʃu·əs) *adj.* incestuoso.
inch (ɪntʃ) *n.* **1,** (measure) pulgada. **2,** (small amount) tris; pelo. —*v.t.* & *i.* avanzar poquito a poco; avanzar de a poquitos. —**by inches; inch by inch,** de a poquitos. —**every inch,** todo; en todo; enteramente.

inchoate (ɪn'ko·ət) *adj.* incipiente. —**inchoative,** *adj., gram.* incoativo.
incidence ('ɪn·sɪ·dəns) *n.* incidencia.
incident ('ɪn·sɪ·dənt) *n. & adj.* incidente.
incidental (ˌɪn·si'dɛn·tal) *adj.* incidental; incidente. —*n.* incidente. —**incidentals,** *n.pl.* imprevistos; gastos contingentes.
incinerate (ɪn'sɪn·əˌreit) *v.t.* incinerar. —**incineration,** *n.* incineración. —**incinerator,** *n.* incinerador.
incipient (ɪn'sɪp·i·ənt) *adj.* incipiente. —**incipience; incipiency,** *n.* principio; comienzo.
incise (ɪn'saiz) *v.t.* **1,** (cut into) cortar. **2,** (engrave) grabar. —**incision** (ɪn'sɪʒ·ən) *n.* incisión. —**incisor,** *n.* incisivo.
incisive (ɪn'sai·sɪv) *adj.* incisivo. —**incisiveness,** *n.* calidad de incisivo.
incite (ɪn'sait) *v.t.* incitar. —**incitement,** *n.* incitación.
incivility (ˌɪn·sə'vɪl·ə·ti) *n.* descortesía; incivilidad.
inclement (ɪn'klɛm·ənt) *adj.* inclemente. —**inclemency,** *n.* inclemencia.
inclination (ˌɪn·klə'nei·ʃən) *n.* inclinación.
incline (ɪn'klain) *v.t. & i.* inclinar. —*n.* ('ɪn·klain) declive; cuesta; gradiente.
inclose (ɪn'kloːz) *v.t.* = **enclose.**
include (ɪn'kluːd) *v.t.* incluir; comprender; abarcar. —**inclusion** (ɪn'klu·ʒən) *n.* inclusión; comprensión.
inclusive (ɪn'klu·sɪv) adj. inclusivo; comprensivo. —**inclusiveness,** *n.* comprensión; calidad de inclusivo *o* comprensivo.
incognito (ɪn'kag·nɪ·to)) *adj.* incógnito. —*adv.* de incógnito.
incoherent (ˌɪn·ko'hɪr·ənt) *adj.* incoherente. —**incoherence,** *n.* incoherencia.
incombustible (ˌɪn·kəm'bʌst·ə·bəl) *adj.* incombustible.
income ('ɪn·kʌm) *n.* entrada; ingreso. —**income tax,** impuesto sobre la renta; impuesto de utilidades. —**income tax return,** declaración de utilidades *o* de ingresos.
incoming *adj.* que llega; que entra.
incommensurable (ˌɪn·kə'mɛn·ʃə·rə·bəl) *adj.* inconmensurable. —**incommensurability,** *n.* inconmensurabilidad.
incommensurate (ˌɪn·kə'mɛn·ʃə·rət) *adj.* desproporcionado.
incommode (ˌɪn·kə'moːd) *v.t.* incomodar; fastidiar. —**incommodious** (-'mo·di·əs) *adj.* incómodo. —**incommodiousness,** *n.* incomodidad.
incommunicable (ˌɪn·kə'mju·nɪ·kə·bəl) *adj.* incomunicable.
incommunicado (ˌɪn·kəˌmju·nɪ'ka·do) *adj.* incomunicado.
incomparable (ɪn'kam·pə·rə·bəl) *adj.* incomparable. —**incomparability,** *n.* excelencia.
incompatible (ˌɪn·kəm'pæt·ə·bəl) *adj.* incompatible. —**incompatibility,** *n.* incompatibilidad.
incompetent (ɪn'kam·pə·tənt) *adj.* incompetente. —**incompetence; incompetency,** *n.* incompetencia.
incomplete (ˌɪn·kəm'plit) *adj.* incompleto. —**incompleteness,** *n.* lo incompleto.
incomprehensible (ɪnˌkam·pri'hɛn·sə·bəl) *adj.* incomprensible.
incomprehensive (ɪnˌkam·pri'hɛn·sɪv) *adj.* limitado; restringido.
inconceivable (ˌɪn·kən'si·və·bəl) *adj.* inconcebible.
inconclusive (ˌɪn·kən'klu·sɪv) *adj.* no concluyente; no definitivo; sin fuerza.
incongruent (ɪn'kaŋ·gru·ənt) *adj.* incongruente. —**incongruence,** *n.* incongruencia.
incongruous (ɪn'kaŋ·gru·əs) *adj.* incongruente; incongruo. —**incongruousness,** *n.* incongruencia; incongruidad. —**incongruity** (ˌɪn·kən'gru·ə·ti) *n.* incongruidad.
inconsequent (ɪn'kan·sə·kwənt) *adj.* inconsecuente.
inconsequential (ɪnˌkan·sə'kwɛn·ʃəl) *adj.* sin importancia; insignificante.
inconsiderable (ˌɪn·kən'sɪd·ər·ə·bəl) *adj.* insignificante.
inconsiderate (ˌɪn·kən'sɪd·ər·ət) *adj.* inconsiderado. —**inconsiderateness,** *n.* inconsideración.
inconsistent (ˌɪn·kən'sɪs·tənt) *adj.* inconsistente. —**inconsistency,** *n.* inconsistencia.
inconsolable (ˌɪn·kən'sol·ə·bəl) *adj.* inconsolable.
inconspicuous (ˌɪn·kən'spɪk·ju·əs) *adj.* poco llamativo; poco aparente; obscuro. —**inconspicuousness,** *n.* obscuridad.

inconstant (ɪn'kan·stənt) *adj.* inconstante. —**inconstancy**, *n.* inconstancia.
incontestable (ˌɪn·kən'tɛst·ə·bəl) *adj.* incontestable.
incontinent (ɪn'kan·tə·nənt) *adj.* incontinente. —**incontinence**, *n.* incontinencia.
incontrovertible (ˌɪn·kan·trə·'vʌɹt·ə·bəl) *adj.* incontrovertible. —**incontrovertibility**, *n.* incontrovertibilidad.
inconvenience (ɪn·kən'vin·jəns) *n.* inconveniencia; molestia. —*v.t.* molestar; incomodar. —**inconvenient**, *adj.* inconveniente; molesto.
incorporate (ɪn'kor·pəˌreit) *v.t.* incorporar; constituir (una sociedad). —*v.i.* asociarse; incorporarse. —**incorporation**, *n.* incorporación; formación (de una sociedad).
incorporeal (ˌɪn·kor'por·i·əl) *adj.* incorpóreo.
incorrect (ˌɪn·kə'rɛkt) *adj.* incorrecto. —**incorrectness**, *n.* incorrección.
incorrigible (ɪn'kar·ɪ·dʒə·bəl) *adj.* incorregible. —**incorrigibility**, *n.* incorregibilidad.
incorruptible (ˌɪn·kə'rʌp·tə·bəl) *adj.* incorruptible. —**incorruptibility**, *n.* incorruptibilidad.
increase (ɪn'kris) *v.t.* & *i.* aumentar. —*n.* ('ɪn·kris) aumento; incremento. —**increasingly**, *adv.* cada vez más; progresivamente.
incredible (ɪn'krɛd·ə·bəl) *adj.* increíble. —**incredibility**, *n.* incredibilidad.
incredulous (ɪn'krɛdʒ·ə·ləs) *adj.* incrédulo. —**incredulity** (ˌɪn·krə'dju·lə·ti) *n.* incredulidad.
increment ('ɪn·krə·mənt) *n.* incremento.
incriminate (ɪn'krɪm·əˌneit) *v.t.* incriminar. —**incrimination**, *n.* incriminación.
incrust (ɪn'krʌst) *v.t.* incrustar. —**incrustation** (ˌɪn·krʌs'tei·ʃən) *n.* incrustación.
incubate ('ɪn·kjəˌbeit) *v.t.* & *i.* incubar. —**incubation**, *n.* incubación. —**incubator**, *n.* incubadora.
incubus ('ɪn·kjə·bəs) *n.* íncubo.
inculcate (ɪn'kʌlˌkeit) *v.t.* inculcar. —**inculcation**, *n.* inculcación.
inculpate (ɪn'kʌlˌpeit) *v.t.* inculpar. —**inculpation**, *n.* inculpación.
incumbency (ɪn'kʌm·bən·si) *n.* 1, (obligation) incumbencia. 2, (tenure of office) tenencia.
incumbent (ɪn'kʌm·bənt) *adj.* 1, (obligatory) obligatorio. 2, (leaning) apoyado. —*n.* titular. —**be incumbent (upon)**, incumbir (a).
incur (ɪn'kʌɹ) *v.t.* incurrir en. —**incurrence**, *n.* obligación.
incurable (ɪn'kjur·ə·bəl) *adj.* incurable.
incursion (ɪn'kʌɹ·ʒən) *n.* incursión. —**incursive** (-sɪv) *adj.* invasor.
indebted (ɪn'dɛt·ɪd) *adj.* 1, (in debt) endeudado. 2, (owing gratitude) en deuda; obligado. —**indebtedness**, *n.* deuda.
indecent (ɪn'di·sənt) *adj.* indecente. —**indecency**, *n.* indecencia.
indecision (ˌɪn·dɪ'sɪʒ·ən) *n.* indecisión.
indecisive (ˌɪn·dɪ'sai·sɪv) *adj.* indeciso. —**indecisiveness**, *n.* indecisión.
indecorous (ɪn'dɛk·ə·rəs) *adj.* indecoroso. —**indecorousness; indecorum** (ˌɪn·dɪ'kor·əm) *n.* indecoro; falta de decoro.
indeed (ɪn'di:d) *adv.* claro; desde luego; de veras. —*interj.* ¡de veras!
indefatigable (ˌɪn·dɪ'fæt·ə·gə·bəl) *adj.* infatigable. —**indefatigability**, *n.* lo infatigable.
indefensible (ˌɪn·dɪ'fɛn·sə·bəl) *adj.* indefendible.
indefinable (ˌɪn·dɪ'fain·ə·bəl) *adj.* indefinible.
indefinite (ɪn'dɛf·ə·nɪt) *adj.* indefinido. —**indefiniteness**, *n.* lo indefinido.
indelible (ɪn'dɛl·ə·bəl) *adj.* indeleble. —**indelibility**, *n.* lo indeleble.
indelicate (ɪn'dɛl·ə·kət) *adj.* falto de delicadeza. —**indelicacy**, *n.* falta de delicadeza.
indemnify (ɪn'dɛm·nəˌfai) *v.t.* indemnizar. —**indemnification** (-fɪ'kei·ʃən) *n.* indemnización.
indemnity (ɪn'dɛm·nə·ti) *n.* 1, (compensation) indemnización. 2, (security against loss; exemption from liability) indemnidad.
indent (ɪn'dɛnt) *v.t.* 1, (notch) dentar; cortar muescas en; mellar. 2, (space in from the regular margin) empezar más adentro; *print.* sangrar. —*n.* mella; diente; muesca.
indentation (ˌɪn·dɛn'tei·ʃən) *n.* 1, (notch) muesca. 2, (additional

margin) margen adicional; *print.* sangría.

indenture (ɪn'dɛn·tʃər) *n.* contrato. —*v.t.* contratar.

independent (ˌɪn·di'pɛn·dənt) *adj.* independiente. —**independence,** *n.* independencia.

indescribable (ˌɪn·dɪ'skraib·ə·bəl) *adj.* indescriptible.

indestructible (ˌɪn·dɪ'strʌkt·ə·bəl) *adj.* indestructible.

indeterminable (ˌɪn·dɪ'tʌɹ·mə·nə·bəl) *adj.* indeterminable.

indeterminate (ˌɪn·dɪ'tʌɹ·mə·nət) *adj.* indeterminado.

index ('ɪn·dɛks) *n.* índice. —*v.t.* **1,** (list the contents of) poner índice a. **2,** (put in the index) poner en el índice. **3,** (indicate) indicar; señalar. —**card index,** fichero. —**index card,** ficha. —**index finger,** (dedo) índice.

India ink ('ɪn·di·ə) tinta china.

Indian ('ɪn·di·ən) *adj.* & *n.* indio. —**Indian summer,** veranillo.

indicate ('ɪn·dɪˌkeit) *v.t.* indicar. —**indication,** *n.* indicación. —**indicative** (ɪn'dɪk·ə·tɪv) *adj.* indicativo. —**indicator,** *n.* indicador.

indict (ɪn'dait) *v.t.* acusar. —**indictment,** *n.* acusación.

indifferent (ɪn'dɪf·ər·ənt) *adj.* indiferente. —**indifference,** *n.* indiferencia.

indigenous (ɪn'dɪdʒ·ə·nəs) *adj.* indígena; nativo.

indigent ('ɪn·dɪ·dʒənt) *adj.* indigente. —**indigence,** *n.* indigencia.

indigestible (ˌɪn·dɪ'dʒɛs·tə·bəl) *adj.* indigestible.

indigestion (ˌɪn·dɪ'dʒɛs·tʃən) *n.* indigestión.

indignant (ɪn'dɪg·nənt) *adj.* indignado. —**indignation** (ˌɪn·dɪg'nei·ʃən) *n.* indignación.

indignity (ɪn'dɪg·nə·ti) *n.* indignidad.

indigo ('ɪn·dɪ·go) *n.* índigo; añil.

indirect (ˌɪn·dɪ'rɛkt) *adj.* indirecto. —**indirectness,** *n.* rodeos (*pl.*); lo indirecto.

indirection (ˌɪn·dɪ'rɛk·ʃən) *n.* indirecta; rodeo.

indiscernible (ˌɪn·dɪ'sʌɹn·ə·bəl) *adj.* indiscernible.

indiscreet (ˌɪn·dɪs'krit) *adj.* indiscreto. —**indiscreetness,** *n.* indiscreción.

indiscretion (ˌɪn·dɪs'krɛʃ·ən) *n.* indiscreción.

indiscriminate (ˌɪn·dɪs'krɪm·ə·nət) *adj.* **1,** (random; haphazard) indistinto; sin discriminación. **2,** (promiscuous) promiscuo; poco exigente. —**indiscriminateness,** *n.* lo indistinto. —**indiscrimination** (-'nei·ʃən) *n.* falta de discriminación.

indispensable (ˌɪn·dɪ'spɛn·sə·bəl) *adj.* indispensable.

indispose (ˌɪn·dɪ'spoz) *v.t.* indisponer. —**indisposed,** *adj.* indispuesto. —**indisposition** (ˌɪn·dɪs·pə'zɪʃ·ən) *n.* indisposición.

indisputable (ˌɪn·dɪs'pju·tə·bəl) *adj.* indisputable.

indissoluble (ˌɪn·dɪ'sal·jə·bəl) *adj.* indisoluble. —**indissolubility,** *n.* indisolubilidad.

indistinct (ˌɪn·dɪ'stɪŋkt) *adj.* indistinto; impreciso. —**indistinctness,** *n.* imprecisión.

indistinguishable (ˌɪn·dɪ'stɪŋ·gwɪʃ·ə·bəl) *adj.* indistinguible.

indium ('ɪn·di·əm) *n.* indio.

individual (ˌɪn·dɪ'vɪdʒ·u·əl) *adj.* individual. —*n.* individuo. —**individualism,** *n.* individualismo. —**individualist,** *n.* individualista. —**individualistic,** *adj.* individualista. —**individuality** (-'æl·ə·ti) *n.* individualidad.

indivisible (ɪn·dɪ'vɪz·ə·bəl) *adj.* indivisible. —**indivisibility,** *n.* indivisibilidad.

Indo- (ɪn·do) *prefijo* indo-; indio: *Indo-European,* indoeuropeo.

indoctrinate (ɪn'dak·trɪˌneit) *v.t.* adoctrinar. —**indoctrination,** *n.* adoctrinamiento; saturación.

Indo-European *adj.* & *n.* indoeuropeo.

indolent ('ɪn·də·lənt) *adj.* indolente. —**indolence,** *n.* indolencia.

indomitable (ɪn'dam·ɪ·tə·bəl) *adj.* indómito; bravo. —**indomitability,** *n.* lo indómito.

indoor *adj.* interior; de casa. —**indoors,** *adv.* adentro; a *o* en casa.

indorse (ɪn'dors) *v.t.* = **endorse.** —**indorsee,** *n.* = **endorsee.** —**indorsement,** *n.* = **endorsement.** —**indorser,** *n.* = **endorser.**

indubitable (ɪn'du·bɪ·tə·bəl) *adj.* indudable. —**indubitableness,** *n.* certeza.

induce (ɪn'djus) *v.t.* inducir.

inducement (ɪn'djus·mənt) *n.* **1,** (persuasion) inducción; inducimiento. **2,** (incentive) incentivo.

induct (ɪn'dʌkt) *v.t.* instalar; iniciar; *mil.* alistar.

induction (ɪn'dʌk·ʃən) *n.* **1,** (installation) instalación; *mil.* alistamiento. **2,** *physics; logic* inducción. —**inductive** (-tɪv) *adj.* inductivo.
indulge (ɪn'dʌldʒ) *v.t.* **1,** (gratify) satisfacer. **2,** (allow) permitir. **3,** (yield to; humor) consentir. —**indulge in, 1,** (take pleasure in) recrearse en. **2,** (allow oneself) permitirse.
indulgence (ɪn'dʌl·dʒəns) *n.* **1,** (gratification) satisfacción. **2,** (leniency) complacencia; indulgencia. **3,** *comm.* (extension of time) moratoria. **4,** *eccles.* indulgencia.
indulgent (ɪn'dʌl·dʒənt) *adj.* condescendiente; indulgente.
induration (ˌɪn·djʊ'rei·ʃən) *n.* induración.
industrial (ɪn'dʌs·tri·əl) *adj.* industrial.
industrialism (ɪn'dʌs·tri·əˌlɪz·əm) *n.* industrialismo. —**industrialist,** *n.* industrial; *Amer.* industrialista.
industrialize (ɪn'dʌs·tri·əˌlaiz) *v.t.* industrializar. —**industrialization** (-lɪ'zei·ʃən) *n.* industrialización.
industrious (ɪn'dʌs·tri·əs) *adj.* diligente; industrioso. —**industriousnesss,** *n.* diligencia.
industry ('ɪn·dəs·tri) *n.* **1,** (business; trade) industria. **2,** (diligence) diligencia.
-ine (ain; ɪn; iːn) *sufijo* **1,** -ino; *forma adjetivos denotando* cualidad; relación: *canine,* canino; *opaline,* opalino. **2,** -ina; *forma nombres abstractos: discipline,* disciplina; *medicine,* medicina. **3,** -ina; *forma nombres femeninos: heroine,* heroína; *Christine,* Cristina. **4,** *quim.; forma nombres denotando* elementos químicos; preparaciones farmacéuticas; minerales: *chlorine,* cloro; *vasaline,* vaselina.
inebriate (ɪn'i·briˌeit) *v.t.* embriagar; emborrachar. —**inebriation,** *n.* embriaguez. —**inebriety** (ˌɪn·ɪ'brai·ə·ti) *n.* embriguez.
inedible (ɪn'ɛd·ə·bəl) *adj.* no comestible; incomible.
ineffable (ɪn'ɛf·ə·bəl) *adj.* inefable. —**ineffability,** *n.* inefabilidad.
ineffective (ˌɪn·ɪ'fɛk·tɪv) *adj.* ineficaz. —**ineffectiveness,** *n.* ineficacia.
ineffectual (ˌɪn·ɪ'fɛk·tʃu·əl) *adj.* ineficaz.
inefficacy (ɪn'ɛf·ɪ·kə·si) *n.* ineficacia. —**inefficacious** (-'kei·ʃəs) *adj.* ineficaz.
inefficient (ˌɪn·ə'fɪʃ·ənt) *adj.* ineficiente. —**inefficiency,** *n.* ineficiencia; ineficacia.
inelastic (ˌɪn·ə'læs·tɪk) *adj.* sin elasticidad. —**inelasticity** (-'tɪs·ə·ti) *n.* falta de elasticidad.
inelegant (ɪn'ɛl·ɪ·gənt) *adj.* sin elegancia; inelegante. —**inelegance; inelegancy,** *n.* inelegancia.
ineligible (ɪn'ɛl·ɪ·dʒə·bəl) *adj.* inelegible. —**ineligibility,** *n.* inelegibilidad.
ineluctable (ɪn·ɪ'lʌk·tə·bəl) *adj.* ineluctable.
inept (ɪn'ɛpt) *adj.* inepto. —**ineptness; ineptitude** ('ɪn'ɛp·tə·tud) *n.* ineptitud.
inequality (ˌɪn·i'kwal·ə·ti) *n.* desigualdad.
inequitable (ɪn'ɛk·wɪ·tə·bəl) *adj.* injusto; no equitativo.
inequity (ɪn'ɛk·wə·ti) *n.* injusticia.
ineradicable (ˌɪn·ɪ'ræd·ɪ·kə·bəl) *adj.* inextirpable.
inert (ɪn'ʌɹt) *adj.* inerte. —**inertness,** *n.* inercia.
inertia (ɪn'ʌɹ·ʃə) *n.* inercia.
inescapable (ˌɪn·ɛs'kei·pə·bəl) *adj.* ineludible.
inestimable (ɪn'ɛs·tə·mə·bəl) *adj.* inestimable.
inevitable (ɪn'ɛv·ɪ·tə·bəl) *adj.* inevitable. —**inevitability,** *n.* inevitabilidad.
inexact (ˌɪn·ɛg'zækt) *adj.* inexacto. —**inexactness,** *n.* inexactitud.
inexcusable (ˌɪn·ɛk'skjuz·ə·bəl) *adj.* inexcusable.
inexhaustible (ˌɪn·ɛg'zɔs·tə·bəl) *adj.* inagotable.
inexorable (ɪn'ɛk·sə·rə·bəl) *adj.* inexorable. —**inexorableness; inexorability,** *n.* inexorabilidad.
inexpedient (ˌɪn·ɪk'spi·di·ənt) *adj.* inconveniente; inoportuno. —**inexpediency,** *n.* inconveniencia; inoportunidad.
inexpensive (ˌɪn·ɪk'spɛn·sɪv) *adj.* barato.
inexperience (ˌɪn·ɪk'spɪr·i·əns) *n.* inexperiencia. —**inexperienced,** *adj.* inexperto.
inexpert (ɪn'ɛk·spʌɹt) *adj.* inexperto.

inexpiable (ɪn'ɛk·spi·ə·bəl) *adj.* inexpiable.
inexplicable (ɪn'ɛk·splɪk·ə·bəl) *adj.* inexplicable.
inexpressible (ˌɪn·ɪk'sprɛs·ə·bəl) *adj.* inexplicable.
inexpressive (ˌɪn·ɪk'sprɛs·ɪv) *adj.* inexpresivo.
inextinguishable (ˌɪn·ɪk'stɪŋ·gwɪʃ·ə·bəl) *adj.* inextinguible.
inextricable (ɪn'ɛks·trə·kə·bəl) *adj.* inextricable.
infallible (ɪn'fæl·ə·bəl) *adj.* infalible. —**infallibility**, *n.* infalibilidad.
infamous ('ɪn·fə·məs) *adj.* infame. —**infamy**, *n.* infamia.
infancy ('ɪn·fən·si) *n.* infancia.
infant ('ɪn·fənt) *n.* **1,** (child) niño (*fem.* niña); nene (*fem.* nena); criatura. **2,** *law* menor de edad.
infanta (ɪn'fæn·tə) *n.* infanta.
infante (ɪn'fæn·te) *n.* infante.
infanticide (ɪn'fæn·təˌsaid) *n.* **1,** (act) infanticidio. **2,** (agent) infanticida.
infantile ('ɪn·fənˌtail) *adj.* infantil.
infantry ('ɪn·fən·tri) *n.* infantería. —**infantryman** (-mən) *n.* infante; soldado de infantería.
infatuate (ɪn'fætʃ·uˌeit) *v.t.* infatuar. —**infatuation,** *n.* infatuación.
infect (ɪn'fɛkt) *v.t.* **1,** *pathol.* infectar. **2,** *fig.* (contaminate) contaminar; inficionar.
infection (ɪn'fɛk·ʃən) *n.* infección. —**infectious** (-ʃəs) *adj.* infeccioso. —**infectiousness,** *n.* calidad de infeccioso.
infecund (ɪn'fi·kʊnd) *adj.* infecundo. —**infecundity** (ˌɪn·fɪ'kʌn·də·ti) *n.* infecundidad.
infer (ɪn'fʌɹ) *v.t.* & *i.* inferir.
inference ('ɪn·fə·rəns) *n.* inferencia; ilación.
inferior (ɪn'fɪr·i·ər) *adj.* & *n.* inferior. —**inferiority** (-'ar·ə·ti) *n.* inferioridad.
inferno (ɪn'fʌɹ·no) *n.* infierno. —**infernal** (-nəl) *adj.* infernal.
infertile (ɪn'fʌɹ·təl) *adj.* infecundo; estéril. —**infertility** (ˌɪn·fər'tɪl·ə·ti) *n.* infecundidad; esterilidad.
infest (ɪn'fɛst) *v.t.* infestar.
infestation (ˌɪn·fɛs'tei·ʃən) *n.* infestación.
infidel ('ɪn·fə·dəl) *adj.* & *n.* infiel. —**infidelity** (-'dɛl·ə·ti) *n.* infidelidad.
infiltrate (ɪn'fɪlˌtreit) *v.t.* infiltrar. —*v.i.* infiltrarse. —**infiltration,** *n.* infiltración.
infinite ('ɪn·fə·nɪt) *adj.* & *n.* infinito.
infinitesimal (ˌɪn·fɪn·ɪ'tɛs·ə·məl) *adj.* infinitesimal.
infinitive (ɪn'fɪn·ə·tɪv) *adj.* & *n.* infinitivo.
infinity (ɪn'fɪn·ə·ti) *n.* **1,** (quality or state of being infinite) infinito. **2,** (infinite or great amount) infinidad.
infirm (ɪn'fʌɹm) *adj.* **1,** (of feeble health) achacoso; enfermizo. **2,** (weak; unsound) enfermizo; débil.
infirmary (ɪn'fʌɹ·mə·ri) *n.* enfermería.
infirmity (ɪn'fʌɹ·mə·ti) *n.* **1,** (ailment) achaque. **2,** (weakness) debilidad; calidad de enfermizo. **3,** (moral weakness or defect) flaqueza.
infix (ɪn'fɪks) *v.t.* plantar; implantar; fijar. —*n.* ('ɪn·fɪks) afijo.
inflame (ɪn'fleim) *v.t.* inflamar.
inflammable (ɪn'flæm·ə·bəl) *adj.* inflammable.
inflammation (ˌɪn·flə'mei·ʃən) *n.* inflamación.
inflammatory (ɪn'flæm·ə·tor·i) *adj.* inflamatorio.
inflate (ɪn'fleit) *v.t.* inflar. —*v.i.* inflarse.
inflation (ɪn'flei·ʃən) *n.* inflación. —**inflationary,** *adj.* inflacionista.
inflect (ɪn'flɛkt) *v.t.* dar inflexión a.
inflection (ɪn'flɛk·ʃən) *n.* inflexión. —**inflectional,** *adj.*, *gram.* desinencial.
inflexible (ɪn'flɛk·sə·bəl) *adj.* inflexible. —**inflexibility,** *n.* inflexibilidad.
inflict (ɪn'flɪkt) *v.t.* infligir.
infliction (ɪn'flɪk·ʃən) *n.* **1,** (act of inflicting) imposición. **2,** (something inflicted) pena; castigo.
inflow *n.* flujo (que entra); afluencia; entrada.
influence ('ɪn·flu·əns) *n.* influencia. —*v.t.* influir en. —**influential** (-'ɛn·ʃəl) *adj.* influyente.
influenza (ˌɪn·flu'ɛn·zə) *n.* influenza.
influx ('ɪnˌflʌks) *n.* **1,** (inflow) flujo (que entra); afluencia; en-

trada. **2,** (point of inflow) entrada; punto *o* boca de entrada.
inform (ɪn'form) *v.t. & i.* informar. **—inform on** *o* **against,** delatar; denunciar. **—informer,** *n.* delator; soplón.
informal (ɪn'for·məl) *adj.* informal. **—informality** (ˌɪn·for'mæl·ə·ti) *n.* informalidad.
informant (ɪn'for·mənt) *n.* informante; informador.
information (ˌɪn·for'mei·ʃən) *n.* información.
informative (ɪn'for·mə·tɪv) *adj.* informativo.
infra- (ɪn·frə) *prefijo* infra-; bajo; inferior: *infrared,* infrarrojo.
infraction (ɪn'fræk·ʃən) *n.* infracción.
infrangible (ɪn'fræn·dʒə·bəl) *adj.* infrangible.
infrared (ˌɪn·frə'rɛd) *adj.* infrarrojo.
infrequent (ɪn'fri·kwənt) *adj.* infrecuente. **—infrequency,** *n.* infrecuencia.
infringe (ɪn'frɪndʒ) *v.t.* infringir; violar. **—infringe on** *o* **upon,** invadir; disturbar. **—infringement,** *n.* infracción; violación; invasión.
infuriate (ɪn'fjʊr·iˌeit) *v.t.* enfurecer; irritar.
infuse (ɪn'fjuːz) *v.t.* **1,** (instill; imbue) instilar; infundir; imbuir. **2,** (steep) poner en infusión; infundir. **—infusion** (ɪn'fju·ʃən) *n.* infusión.
-ing (ɪŋ) *sufijo* **1,** *forma gerundios: teaching,* enseñanza; *reading,* el leer; lectura. **2,** *forma el participio presente de los verbos: he is reading,* está leyendo. *Estos participios se usan también como adjetivos: a striking story,* una historia impresionante.
ingenious (ɪn'dʒin·jəs) *adj.* ingenioso. **—ingeniousness,** *n.* ingeniosidad.
ingenuity (ˌɪn·dʒə'nju·ə·ti) *n.* inventiva; ingenio; ingeniosidad.
ingenuous (ɪn'dʒɛn·ju·əs) *adj.* ingenuo. **—ingenuousness,** *n.* ingenuidad.
ingest (ɪn'dʒɛst) *v.t.* ingerir. **—ingestion** (ɪn'dʒɛs·tʃən) *n.* ingestión.
inglorious (ɪn'glor·i·əs) *adj.* ignominioso; innoble.
ingoing *adj.* entrante; que entra; que llega.
ingot ('ɪŋ·gət) *n.* lingote.
ingrain (ɪn'grein) *v.t.* arraigar; fijar profundamente.
ingrate ('ɪn·greit) *n.* ingrato.
ingratiate (ɪn'grei·ʃiˌeit) *v.t.* congraciar. **—ingratiating,** *adj.* atractivo; congraciador.
ingratitude (ɪn'græt·ɪ·tud) *n.* ingratitud.
ingredient (ɪn'gri·di·ənt) *n.* ingrediente.
ingrown *adj.* **1,** (grown into the flesh) encarnado. **2,** (inborn) congénito; ingénito.
inhabit (ɪn'hæb·ɪt) *v.t.* habitar. **—inhabitable,** *adj.* habitable. **—inhabitant** (-ə·tənt) *n.* habitante.
inhalant (ɪn'hei·lənt) *n.* **1,** (inhalator) inhalador. **2,** (medicinal vapor) inhalante; inhalación.
inhalation (ˌɪn·hə'lei·ʃən) *n.* inhalación.
inhalator ('ɪn·həˌlei·tər) *n.* inhalador.
inhale (ɪn'heil) *v.t. & i.* inhalar; aspirar. **—inhaler,** *n.* inhalador.
inharmonious (ˌɪn·har'mo·ni·əs) *adj.* inarmónico.
inherent (ɪn'hɪr·ənt) *v.t.* inherente. **—inherence,** *n.* inherencia.
inherit (ɪn'hɛr·ɪt) *v.t. & i.* heredar. **—inheritance,** *n.* herencia. **—inheritor,** *n.* heredero.
inhibit (ɪn'hɪb·ɪt) *v.t.* inhibir. **—inhibition** (ˌɪn·ə'bɪʃ·ən) *n.* inhibición.
inhospitable (ɪn'has·pɪt·ə·bəl) *adj.* inhospitalario. **—inhospitability,** *n.* inhospitalidad.
inhuman (ɪn'hju·mən) *adj.* inhumano. **—inhumanity** (ˌɪn·hju'mæn·ə·ti) *n.* inhumanidad.
inhumane (ˌɪn·hju'mein) *n.* inhumano; cruel.
inimical (ɪn'ɪm·ɪ·kəl) *adj.* **1,** (harmful) perjudicial. **2,** (hostile) hostil.
inimitable (ɪn'ɪm·ə·tə·bəl) *adj.* inimitable.
iniquitous (ɪ'nɪk·wə·təs) *adj.* inicuo. **—iniquity,** *n.* iniquidad.
initial (ɪ'nɪʃ·əl) *adj. & n.* inicial. **—***v.t.* poner sus iniciales a *o* en.
initiate (ɪ'nɪʃ·iˌeit) *v.t.* iniciar. **—***adj. & n.* (-ət) iniciado **—initiating,** *adj.* iniciador; iniciativo. **—initiation,** *n.* iniciación.
initiative (ɪ'nɪʃ·i·ə·tɪv) *n.* iniciativa.
inject (ɪn'dʒɛkt) *v.t.* inyectar. **—injection** (ɪn'dʒɛk·ʃən) *n.* inyeccion. **—injector** *n.* inyector.

injudicious (ˌɪn·dʒuˈdɪʃ·əs) *adj.* indiscreto; imprudente; poco juicioso. —**injudiciousness,** *n.* falta de discreción *o* juicio.
injunction (ɪnˈdʒʌŋk·ʃən) *n.* mandato; *law* prohibición judicial.
injure (ˈɪn·dʒər) *v.t.* **1,** (wound; hurt) herir; lastimar. **2,** (do wrong or injustice to) perjudicar. **3,** (offend) ofender.
injurious (ɪnˈdʒʊr·i·əs) *adj.* dañino; dañoso; perjudicial. —**injuriousness,** *n.* calidad de dañino.
injury (ˈɪn·dʒə·ri) *n.* **1,** (lesion) lesión. **2,** (harm) daño. **3,** (wrong) perjuicio; daño.
injustice (ɪnˈdʒʌs·tɪs) *n.* injusticia.
ink (ɪŋk) *n.* tinta. —*v.t.* **1,** (spread ink on) entintar. **2,** (mark or draw in ink) hacer *o* trazar en tinta.
inkling (ˈɪŋk·lɪŋ) *n.* indicio; intimación; indicación.
inkstand *n.* tintero; base para tintero.
inkwell *n.* tintero.
inky (ˈɪŋk·i) *adj.* **1,** (dark; black) negro; de *o* como tinta. **2,** (covered or stained with ink) entintado.
inlaid (ˈɪnˌleid) *v., pret. & p.p. de* **inlay.** —*adj.* embutido; encajado; incrustado.
inland (ˈɪn·lənd) *adj.* del interior; de tierra adentro. —*adv.* tierra adentro. —*n.* interior. —**inlander,** *n.* habitante del interior.
in-law *n.* pariente por afinidad; afín.
inlay (ɪnˈlei) *v.t.* [**inlaid, inlaying**] embutir; incrustar; taracear. —*n.* (ˈɪn·lei) **1,** (inlaid work) incrustación; embutido; taracea. **2,** *dent.* empaste; *Amer.* tapadura.
inlet (ˈɪn·lɛt) *n.* **1,** (small bay) cala; caleta; ensenada. **2,** (entrance; mouth) entrada; boca.
inmate (ˈɪnˌmeit) *n.* **1,** (resident) residente; ocupante. **2,** (confined person, as in a prison) preso; recluso; (in an asylum) asilado; (in a hospital) enfermo.
inmost (ˈɪnˌmost) *adj.* más íntimo; más recóndito; más profundo.
inn (ɪn) *n.* posada; mesón; fonda.
innate (ɪˈneit) *adj.* innato. —**innateness,** *n.* lo innato.
inner (ˈɪn·ər) *adj.* **1,** (interior) interior. **2,** (private; intimate) privado; íntimo. —**inner tube,** cámara; tubo.
innermost *adj.* = **inmost.**
inning (ˈɪn·ɪŋ) *n.* **1,** *baseball* inning; turno de juego. **2,** (turn; chance) turno; oportunidad.
innkeeper *n.* posadero; mesonero.
innocent (ɪn·ə·sənt) *adj. & n.* inocente. —**innocence,** *n.* inocencia.
innocuous (ɪˈnak·ju·əs) *adj.* innocuo. —**innocuousness,** *n.* innocuidad.
innominate (ɪˈnam·ə·nɪt) *adj.* innominado.
innovate (ˈɪn·əˌveit) *v.t. & i.* innovar. —**innovation,** *n.* innovación. —**innovator,** *n.* innovador.
innuendo (ˌɪn·juˈɛn·do) *n.* indirecta; insinuación.
innumerable (ɪˈnum·ər·ə·bəl) *adj.* innumerable.
inoculate (ɪˈnak·jəˌleit) *v.t.* inocular. —**inoculation,** *n.* inoculación.
inoffensive (ˌɪn·əˈfɛn·sɪv) *adj.* inofensivo. —**inoffensiveness,** *n.* lo inofensivo.
inoperable (ɪnˈap·ər·ə·bəl) *adj.* inoperable.
inoperative (ɪnˈap·ər·ə·tɪv) *adj.* inoperante.
inopportune (ɪnˌap·ərˈtjun) *adj.* inoportuno. —**inopportuneness,** *n.* inoportunidad.
inordinate (ɪnˈor·də·nət) *adj.* excesivo; inmoderado; desmesurado. —**inordinateness; inordinacy,** *n.* exceso; inmoderación.
inorganic (ˌɪn·orˈgæn·ɪk) *adj.* inorgánico.
input *n.* suministro; inversión.
inquest (ˈɪn·kwɛst) *n.* encuesta.
inquire (ɪnˈkwair) *v.t. & i.* **1,** (ask) preguntar; indagar. **2,** (investigate) investigar; inquirir; indagar.
inquiry (ɪnˈkwai·ri; ˈɪn·kwə·ri) *n.* **1,** (question) pregunta; indagación. **2,** (investigation) investigación; encuesta; indagación.
inquisition (ˌɪn·kwəˈzɪʃ·ən) *n.* inquisición.
inquisitive (ɪnˈkwɪz·ə·tɪv) *adj.* inquisitivo. —**inquisitiveness,** *n.* lo inquisitivo.
inquisitor (ɪnˈkwɪz·ɪ·tər) *n.* inquisidor.
inroad *n.* **1,** (incursion) incursión. **2,** *usu.pl.* (encroachment) mella.
insalubrious (ˌɪn·səˈlu·bri·əs) *adj.* insalubre.
insane (ɪnˈsein) *adj.* insano; loco. —**insane asylum,** manicomio.

insanitary (ɪn'sæn·ə,tɛr·i) *adj.* insaluble.
insanity (ɪn'sæn·ə·ti) *n.* locura.
insatiable (ɪn'sei·ʃə·bəl) *adj.* insaciable. —**insatiability,** *n.* insaciabilidad.
inscribe (ɪn'skraib) *v.t.* inscribir.
inscription (ɪn'skrɪp·ʃən) *n.* inscripción.
inscrutable (ɪn'skru·tə·bəl) *adj.* inescrutable. —**inscrutability,** *n.* inescrutabilidad.
insect ('ɪn·sɛkt) *n.* insecto.
insecticide (ɪn'sɛk·tɪ,said) *n.* insecticida.
insecure (,ɪn·sɪ'kjʊr) *adj.* inseguro. —**insecurity,** *n.* inseguridad.
insensate (ɪn'sɛn·set) *adj.* **1,** (insensible; insensitive) insensible. **2,** (unreasoning) insensato.
insensible (ɪn'sɛn·sə·bəl) *adj.* insensible. —**insensibility,** *n.* insensibilidad.
insensitive (ɪn'sɛn·sɪ·tɪv) *adj.* insensible.
inseparable (ɪn'sɛp·ər·ə·bəl) *adj.* inseparable.
insert (ɪn'sʌɹt) *v.t.* insertar. —*n.* ('ɪn·sʌɹt) inserción. —**insertion** (ɪn·'sʌɹ·ʃən) *n.* inserción.
inset *n.* inserción. —*v.t.* insertar.
inside (ɪn'said) *prep.* en; dentro de. —*adv.* dentro; adentro. —*n.* **1,** (inner part; interior) parte *o* lado de adentro; interior. **2,** *pl., colloq.* (viscera) entrañas. —*adj.* **1,** (interior; internal) de adentro; interno; interior. **2,** (private; secret) privado; íntimo; secreto. **3,** (specially privileged) confidential. —**insider,** *n., colloq.* privilegiado. —**inside out,** al revés. —**inside track,** *colloq.* ventaja.
insidious (ɪn'sɪd·i·əs) *adj.* insidioso. —**insidiousness,** *n* insidia.
insight ('ɪn·sait) *n.* **1,** (perspicacity) perspicacia. **2,** (sudden awareness) visión.
insignia (ɪn'sɪg·ni·ə) *n.sing.* & *pl.* [*sing., también,* **insigne** (-ni)] insignia; insignias.
insignificant (,ɪn·sɪg'nɪf·ə·kənt) *adj.* insignificante. —**insignificance,** *n.* insignificancia.
insincere (,ɪn·sɪn'sɪr) *adj.* insincero. —**insincerity** (-'sɛr·ə·ti) *n.* insinceridad.
insinuate (ɪn'sɪn·ju,eit) *v.t.* insinuar. —**insinuation,** *n.* insinuación.
insipid (ɪn'sɪp·ɪd) *adj.* insípido. —**inspidity** (,ɪn·sɪ'pɪd·ə·ti) *n.* insipidez.
insist (ɪn'sɪst) *v.i.* insistir. —**insistence,** *n.* insistencia. —**insistent,** *adj.* insistente.
insobriety (,ɪn·so'brai·ə·ti) *n.* falta de sobriedad.
insofar (,ɪn·sə'far) *adv.* hasta ahí *o* allí. *También,* **in so far.** —**insofar as,** en cuanto.
insole *n.* plantilla.
insolent ('ɪn·sə·lənt) *adj.* insolente. —**insolence,** *n.* insolencia.
insoluble (ɪn'sal·jə·bəl) *adj.* insoluble. —**insolubility,** *n.* insolubilidad.
insolvent (ɪn'sal·vənt) *adj.* insolvente. —**insolvency,** *n.* insolvencia.
insomnia (ɪn'sam·ni·ə) *n.* insomnio. —**insomniac** (-æk) *n.* quien padece de insomnio.
insomuch (,ɪn·so'mʌtʃ) *adv.* **1,** (to such an extent or degree) tanto; de tal manera. **2,** = **inasmuch.**
inspect (ɪn'spɛkt) *v.t.* inspeccionar. —**inspection** (ɪn'spɛk·ʃən) *n.* inspección. —**inspector,** *n.* inspector.
inspire (ɪn'spair) *v.t.* inspirar. —**inspiration** (,ɪn·spə'rei·ʃən) *n.* inspiración. —**inspirational,** *adj.* que inspira.
instability (,ɪn·stə'bɪl·ə·ti) *n.* inestabilidad.
install (ɪn'stɔːl) *v.t.* instalar. —**installation** (,ɪn·stə'lei·ʃən) *n.* instalación.
installment *también,* **instalment** (ɪn'stɔl·mənt) *n.* **1,** (periodic payment) plazo. **2,** (chapter in a serial) serie; entrega. **3,** (installation) instalación.
instance ('ɪn·stəns) *n* **1,** (case; example) caso; ejemplo. **2,** (occasion) momento; ocasión. —**for instance,** por ejemplo.
instant (ɪn·stənt) *n.* instante. —*adj.* **1,** (immediate) inmediato; instantáneo. **2,** (of present time) actual; corriente. **3,** (quickly prepared) al instante; instantáneo. —**instantaneous** (,ɪn·stən'tei·ni·əs) *adj.* instantáneo.
instead (ɪn'stɛd) *adv.* **1,** (in place [of]) en lugar (de); en vez (de). **2,** (contrary to expectation) en cambio.
instep ('ɪn·stɛp) *n.* empeine.
instigate ('ɪn·stɪ,geit) *v.t.* instigar. —**instigation,** *n.* instigación.

—**instigator**, *n.* instigador.
instill (m'stɪl) *v.t.* instilar. —**instillation** (ˌm·stɪ'lei·ʃən) *n.* instilación.
instinct ('m·stɪŋkt) *n.* instinto. —*adj.* (m'stɪŋkt) cargado; lleno. —**instinctive** (m'stɪŋk·tɪv) *adj.* instintivo.
institute ('m·stɪ·tut) *v.t.* instituir. —*n.* instituto.
institution (ˌm·stɪ'tu·ʃən) *n.* institución. —**institutional**, *adj.* institucional.
instruct (m'strʌkt) *v.t.* instruir. —**instructor**, *n.* instructor.
instruction (m'strʌk·ʃən) *n.* instrucción.
instructive (m'strʌk·tɪv) *adj.* instructivo. —**instructiveness**, *n.* lo instructivo.
instrument ('m·strə·mənt) *n.* instrumento. —**instrumental** (-'mɛn·təl) *adj.* instrumental. —**instrumentality** (-mən'tæl·ə·ti) *n.* agencia. —**instrumentation** (-mɛn'tei·ʃən) *n.* instrumentación.
insubordinate (ˌm·sə'bor·də·nət) *adj.* & *n.* insubordinado. —**insubordination** (-'nei·ʃən) *n.* insubordinación.
insubstantial (ˌm·səb'stæn·ʃəl) *adj.* insubstancial.
insufferable (m'sʌf·ər·ə·bəl) *adj.* insufrible; intolerable.
insufficient (ˌm·sə'fɪʃ·ənt) *adj.* insuficiente. —**insufficiency**, *n.* insuficiencia.
insular ('m·sju·lər) *adj.* **1,** (of or pert. to an island) insular. **2,** (narrow-minded) estrecho de miras; provinciano.
insularity (ˌm·sju'lær·ə·ti) *n.* **1,** (being or living on an island) insularidad. **2,** (narrow-mindedness) estrechez de miras.
insulate ('m·səˌleit) *v.t.* aislar. —**insulation**, *n.* aislamiento. —**insulator**, *n.* aislador.
insulin ('m·sə·lm) *n.* insulina.
insult (m'sʌlt) *v.t.* insultar. —*n.* ('m·sʌlt) insulto.
insuperable (m'su·pər·ə·bəl) *adj.* insuperable. —**insuperability**, *n.* calidad de insuperable.
insupportable (ˌm·sə'por·tə·bəl) *adj.* insoportable.
insurance (m'ʃʊr·əns) *n.* **1,** (protection against loss) seguro. **2,** (insurance business) seguros (*pl.*).
insure (m'ʃʊr) *v.t.* asegurar. —**insurable**, *adj.* asegurable; que se puede asegurar.
insurgent (m'sʌɹ·dʒənt) *n.* & *adj.* insurgente. —**insurgence; insurgency**, *n.* insurgencia.
insurmountable (ˌm·sər·'maunt·ə·bəl) *adj.* insuperable; infranqueable.
insurrection (ˌm·sə'rɛk·ʃən) *n.* insurrección. —**insurrectionist**, *n.* insurrecto.
intact (m'tækt)) *adj.* intacto. —**intactness**, *n.* calidad de intacto.
intake *n.* **1,** (place of intake) toma. **2,** (quantity or thing taken in) consumo; toma. **3,** (a taking in) toma; admisión.
intangible (m'tæn·dʒə·bəl) *adj.* intangible. —**intangibility**, *n.* intangibilidad.
integer ('m·tə·dʒər) *n.* entero; número entero.
integral ('m·tə·grəl) *adj.* & *n.* integral.
integrate ('m·təˌgreit) *v.t.* integrar. —*v.i.* integrarse. —**integration**, *n.* integración.
integrity (m'tɛg·rə·ti) *n.* integridad.
integument (m'tɛg·jə·mənt) *n.* integumento.
intellect ('m·tə·lɛkt) *n.* intelecto. —**intellectual** (-'lɛk·tʃu·əl) *adj.* & *n.* intelectual.
intelligence (m'tɛl·ɪ·dʒəns) *n.* **1,** (mind; understanding) inteligencia. **2,** (news; information) información; datos (*pl.*). **3,** (gathering of secret information) servicio secreto; servicio de inteligencia. —**intelligence quotient**, cociente intelectual.
intelligent (m'tɛl·ɪ·dʒənt) *adj.* inteligente.
intelligentsia (mˌtɛl·ɪ'dʒɛn·si·ə) *n.pl.* intelectualidad (*sing.*).
intelligible (m'tɛl·ə·dʒə·bəl) *adj.* inteligible. —**intelligibility**, *n.* inteligibilidad.
intemperate (m'tɛm·pər·ət) *adj.* intemperante. —**intemperance; intemperateness**, *n.* intemperancia.
intend (m'tɛnd) *v.t.* **1,** (have in mind; plan) pensar; proponerse; tener la intención (de). **2,** (destine; design; mean) destinar; señalar.
intended (m'tɛn·dɪd) *adj.* **1,** (intentional) de propósito; intencional. **2,** (prospective; future) futuro. —*n.*, *colloq.* prometido; futuro.
intense (m'tɛns) *adj.* intenso.

—**intensity,** *n.* intensidad. —**intensive,** *adj.* intensivo.
intensify (ɪn'tɛn·sɪˌfai) *v.t.* intensificar. —*v.i.* intensificarse. —**intensification** (-fɪ'kei·ʃən) *n.* intensificación.
intent (ɪn'tɛnt) *n.* intento; intención. —*adj.* 1, (firm; earnest) atento; firme; fijo. 2, (engrossed) preocupado; absorto; ensimismado. 3, (firmly resolved) decidido. —**to all intents and purposes,** en todo caso; de cualquier manera.
intention (ɪn'tɛn·ʃən) *n.* intención. —**intentional,** *adj.* intencional.
inter (ɪn'tʌɹ) *v.t.* enterrar.
inter- (ɪn·tər) *prefijo* inter-; entre-; entre; durante: *international,* internacional; *interregnum,* interregno.
interact *v.i.* actuar entre sí; afectarse mutuamente; reaccionar entre sí. —**interaction,** *n.* acción recíproca; interacción.
intercalate (ɪn'tʌɹ·kəˌleit) *v.t.* intercalar. —**intercalation,** *n.* intercalación.
intercede (ˌɪn·tər'siːd) *v.i.* interceder.
intercept (ˌɪn·tər'sɛpt) *v.t.* interceptar. —**interception** (-'sɛp·ʃən) *n.* interceptación; intercepción. —**interceptor,** *n.* interceptor; *aero.* avión de caza; avión interceptor.
intercession (ˌɪn·tər'sɛʃ·ən) *n.* intercesión. —**intercessor** (-'sɛs·ər) *n.* intercesor.
interchange (ˌɪn·tər'tʃeindʒ) *v.t.* 1, (exchange; transpose) intercambiar; trocar. 2, (alternate) alternar. —*v.i.* 1, (alternate) alternarse. 2, (change places) trocarse. —*n.* ('ɪn·tər·tʃeindʒ) 1, (exchange; transposition) intercambio; trueque. 2, (alternation) alternación. 3, (highway ramp system) intercambio. —**interchangeable,** *adj.* intercambiable.
intercollegiate (ˌɪn·tər·kə'li·dʒət) *adj.* entre universidades *o* universitarios; universitario.
intercom ('ɪn·tərˌkam) *n., colloq.* sistema de intercomunicación.
intercommunicate (ˌɪn·tər·kə·'mju·nɪˌkeit) *v.i.* intercomunicarse. —**intercommunication,** *n.* intercomunicación.
interconnect (ˌɪn·tər·kə'nɛkt) *v.t.* & *i.* conectar entre sí. —**interconnection** (-'nɛk·ʃən) *n.* conexión mutua; interdependencia.
intercourse ('ɪn·tər·kors) *n.* 1, (exchange; communication) intercambio. 2, (copulation) cópula; coito.
interdependent *adj.* interdependiente. —**interdependence,** *n.* interdependencia.
interdict ('ɪn·tərˌdɪkt) *v.t.* prohibir; vedar; interdecir. —*n.* entredicho; interdicto. —**interdiction** (-'dɪk·ʃən) *n.* interdicción.
interest ('ɪn·tər·ɪst) *n.* interés. —*v.t.* interesar. —**interesting,** *adj.* interesante. —**lose interest (in),** desinteresarse (de).
interfere (ˌɪn·tər'fɪr) *v.i.* interferir; *fig.* entremeterse. —**interference,** *n.* interferencia; *fig.* entremetimiento. —**interfering,** *adj.* entremetido.
interim ('ɪn·tər·ɪm) *n.* ínterin. —*adj.* provisional; interino.
interior (ɪn'tɪr·i·ər) *n.* & *adj.* interior.
interject (ˌɪn·tər'dʒɛkt) *v.t.* & *i.* interponer; insertar; interpolar.
interjection (ˌɪn·tər'dʒɛk·ʃən) *n.* 1, (act of interjecting) interposición. 2, *gram.* interjección.
interlace *v.t.* entrelazar.
interline (ɪn·tər'lain) *v.t.* 1, (write between) interlinear. 2, (put interlining in) poner entretela a. —**interlining,** *n.* entretela.
interlinear (ˌɪn·tər'lɪn·i·ər) *adj.* interlineal.
interlock *v.t.* & *i.* trabar; ensamblar; *mech.* engranar.
interlocution (ˌɪn·tər·lo'kju·ʃən) *n.* interlocución; diálogo.
interlocutor (ˌɪn·tər'lak·jʊ·tər) *n.* interlocutor.
interlocutory (ˌɪn·tər'lak·jʊ·tor·i) *adj.* 1, (conversational) de *o* en el diálogo. 2, (interpolated) interpolado; interpuesto. 3, *law* interlocutorio.
interlope (ˌɪn·tər'lop) *v.i.* inmiscuirse; entremeterse. —**interloper,** *n.* intruso; advenedizo; entremetido.
interlude ('ɪn·tərˌlud) n. 1, (intervening time) intervalo. 2, *theat.* entremés. 3, *music* interludio.
intermarry (ˌɪn·tər'mær·i) *v.i.* casarse entre sí. —**intermarriage** (-'mær·ɪdʒ) *n.* casamiento entre parientes *o* entre personas de distintas razas.
intermediary (ˌɪn·tər'mi·di·ɛr·i) *adj.* & *n.* intermediario.

intermediate (ɪn·tər'mi·di·ət) *adj.* intermedio. —*v.i.* (-eit) mediar; intermediar.
interment (ɪn'tʌɹ·mənt) *n.* entierro.
intermezzo (ˌɪn·tər'mɛt·so) *n.* interludio.
interminable (ɪn'tʌɹ·mə·nə·bəl) *adj.* interminable; inacabable.
intermingle (ˌɪn·tər'mɪŋ·gəl) *v.t.* mezclar; entremezclar. —*v.i.* mezclarse; entremezclarse.
intermission (ˌɪn·tər'mɪʃ·ən) *n.* intermisión; descanso; *theat.* entreacto.
intermittent (ˌɪn·tər'mɪt·ənt) *adj.* intermitente. —**intermittence; intermittency,** *n.* intermitencia.
intermix (ˌɪn·tər'mɪks) *v.t.* mezclar; entremezclar. —*v.i.* mezclarse; entremezclarse.
intern (ɪn'tʌɹn) *v.t.* internar. —*n.* ('ɪn·tʌɹn) = **interne.** —**internment,** *n.* reclusión; internamiento.
internal (ɪn'tʌɹ·nəl) *adj.* interno.
international (ˌɪn·tər'næʃ·ən·əl) *adj.* internacional. —**internationalism,** *n.* internacionalismo. —**internationalist,** *n.* internacionalista. —**internationalistic,** *adj.* internacionalista.
interne ('ɪn·tʌɹn) *n.* interno; médico interno. —**interneship,** *n.* internado.
internecine (ˌɪn·tər'ni·sɪn) *adj.* encarnizado; sanguinario.
interplay ('ɪn·tər·plei) *n.* interacción; juego.
interpolate (ɪn'tʌɹ·pəˌleit) *v.t.* interpolar. —**interpolation,** *n.* interpolación.
interpose (ˌɪn·tər'poːz) *v.t.* interponer. —*v.i.* interponerse. —**interposition** (-pə'zɪʃ·ən) *n.* interposición.
interpret (ɪn'tʌɹ·prɪt) *v.t.* interpretar.
interpretation (ɪnˌtʌɹ·prə'tei·ʃən) *n.* interpretación.
interpretative (ɪn'tʌɹ·prəˌtei·tɪv) *también,* **interpretive** (-tɪv) *adj.* interpretativo.
interpreter (ɪn'tʌɹ·prɪ·tər) *n.* intérprete.
interrogate (ɪn'tɛr·əˌgeit) *v.t.* & *i.* interrogar. —**interrogation,** *n.* interrogación; interrogatorio. —**interrogator,** *n.* interrogador.
interrogative (ˌɪn·tə'rag·ə·tɪv) *adj.* interrogativo.
interrogatory (ˌɪn·tə'rag·ə·tor·i) *adj.* interrogativo. —*n.* interrogatorio.
interrupt (ˌɪn·tə'rʌpt) *v.t.* interrumpir. —**interruption** (-'rʌp·ʃən) *n.* interrupción.
interscholastic *adj.* entre escuelas; escolar.
intersect (ˌɪn·tər'sɛkt) *v.t.* cortar. —*v.i.* cortarse; cruzarse; intersecarse. —**intersection** (-'sɛk·ʃən) *n.* intersección.
intersperse (ˌɪn·tər'spʌɹs) *v.t.* diseminar; esparcir.
interstice (ɪn'tʌɹ·stɪs) *n.* intersticio.
intertwine *v.t.* entrelazar; entretejer. —*v.i.* entrelazarse; entretejerse.
interval ('ɪn·tər·vəl) *n.* intervalo.
intervene (ˌɪn·tər'viːn) *v.i.* intervenir. —**intervention** (-'vɛn·ʃən) *n.* intervención.
interview ('ɪn·tər·vju) *n.* entrevista; interviú. —*v.t.* entrevistar.
interweave *v.t.* [*infl.:* **weave**] entretejer. —*n.* [*también,* **interweaving**] entretejido. —**interwoven,** *adj.* entretejido.
intestate (ɪn'tɛs·teit) *n.* & *adj.* intestado. —**intestacy** (-tə·si) *n.* falta de testamento.
intestine (ɪn'tɛs·tɪn) *n.* intestino. —**intestinal,** *adj.* intestinal.
intimate ('ɪn·tə·mət) *n.* & *adj.* íntimo. —**intimacy,** *n.* intimidad.
intimate ('ɪn·təˌmeit) *v.t.* insinuar; intimar. —**intimation,** *n.* insinuación; intimación.
intimidate (ɪn'tɪm·əˌdeit) *v.t.* intimidar. —**intimidation,** *n.* intimidación.
into ('ɪn·tu) *prep.* en; a; dentro de.
intolerable (ɪn'tal·ər·ə·bəl) *adj.* intolerable. —**intolerability; intolerableness,** *n.* intolerabilidad.
intolerant (ɪn'tal·ər·ənt) *adj.* intolerante. —**intolerance,** *n.* intolerancia.
intone (ɪn'toːn) *v.t.* & *i.* entonar. —**intonation** (ˌɪn·tə'nei·ʃən) *n.* entonación.
intoxicant (ɪn'tak·sɪ·kənt) *n.* tóxico.
intoxicate (ɪn'tak·sɪˌkeit) *v.t.* **1,** (inebriate; elate) embriagar; emborrachar. **2,** (poison) intoxicar. —**intoxicated,** *adj.* borracho.

intoxication (ɪn,tak·sɪ'kei·ʃən) *n.* 1, (drunkenness) embriaguez. 2, (poisoning) intoxicación.
intra- (ɪn·trə) *prefijo* intra-; dentro: *intravenous,* intravenoso.
intractable (ɪn'træk·tə·bəl) *adj.* intratable. —**intractability,** *n.* intratabilidad.
intramural (,ɪn·trə'mjʊr·əl) *adj.* interior.
intransigent (ɪn'træn·sə·dʒənt) *n.* & *adj.* intransigente. —**intransigence,** *n.* intransigencia.
intransitive (ɪn'træn·sə·tɪv) *adj.* intransitivo.
intravenous (,ɪn·trə'vi·nəs) *adj.* intravenoso.
intrench (ɪn'trɛntʃ) *v.t.* & *i.* = **entrench.** —**intrenchment,** *n.* = **entrenchment.**
intrepid (ɪn'trɛp·ɪd) *adj.* intrépido. —**intrepidity** (,ɪn·trə'pɪd·ə·ti) *n.* intrepidez.
intricate ('ɪn·trɪ·kət) *adj.* intrincado. —**intricacy,** *n.* intrincación; lo intrincado; complejidad.
intrigue (ɪn'triːg) *v.t.* & *i.* intrigar. —*n.* intriga.
intrinsic (ɪn'trɪn·zɪk) *adj.* intrínseco.
intro- (ɪn·trə) *prefijo* intro-; dentro; hacia adentro: *introduce,* introducir; *introvert,* introvertido.
introduce (,ɪn·trə'djus) *v.t.* 1, (bring in; begin) introducir. 2, (present) presentar.
introduction (,ɪn·trə'dʌk·ʃən) *n.* 1, (act or result of beginning) introducción. 2, (presentation) presentación. 3, (foreword) prólogo; introducción. —**introductory** (-tə·ri) *adj.* preliminar.
introspection (,ɪn·trə'spɛk·ʃən) *n.* introspección. —**introspective** (-tɪv) *adj.* introspectivo.
introversion (,ɪn·trə'vʌɹ·ʒən) *n.* introversión.
introvert ('ɪn·trə,vʌɹt) *n.* introvertido. —*v.t.* volver hacia adentro; volver sobre sí. —**introverted,** *adj.* introvertido.
intrude (ɪn'truːd) *v.t.* insertar; introducir; entremeter. —*v.i.* [*también refl.* **intrude oneself**] molestar; estorbar; entremeterse; ser intruso.
intruder (ɪn'tru·dər) *n.* intruso.
intrusion (ɪn'tru·ʃən) *n.* intrusión. —**intrusive** (-sɪv) *adj.* intruso.
intrust (ɪn'trʌst) *v.t.* = **entrust.**
intuition (,ɪn·tu'ɪʃ·ən) *n.* intuición. —**intuitive** (ɪn'tu·ə·tɪv) *adj.* intuitivo.
inundate ('ɪn·ʌn,deit) *v.t.* inundar. —**inundation,** *n.* inundación.
inure (ɪn'jʊr) *v.t.* endurecer; acostumbrar. —*v.i.* 1, (take effect) tener efecto. 2, (accrue) pasar; redundar.
invade (ɪn'veid) *v.t.* invadir. —**invader,** *n.* invasor.
invalid ('ɪn·və·lɪd) *n.* & *adj.* inválido.
invalid (ɪn'væl·ɪd) *adj.* inválido.
invalidate (ɪn'væl·ɪ,deit) *v.t.* invalidar. —**invalidation,** *n.* invalidación. —**invalidity** (,ɪn·və'lɪd·ə·ti) *n.* invalidez.
invaluable (ɪn'væl·ju·ə·bəl) *adj.* inestimable; inapreciable.
invariable (ɪn'vɛr·i·ə·bəl) *adj.* invariable. —**invariability,** *n.* invariabilidad.
invasion (ɪn'vei·ʒən) *n.* invasión. —**invasive** (-sɪv) *adj.* agresivo; de invasión.
invective (ɪn'vɛk·tɪv) *n.* invectiva. —*adj.* vituperativo.
inveigh (ɪn'vei) *v.i.* lanzar invectivas.
inveigle (ɪn'vei·gəl) *v.t.* engatusar; embaucar. —**inveiglement,** *n.* engañifa; embaucamiento. —**inveigler** (-glər) *n.* embaucador.
invent (ɪn'vɛnt) *v.t.* inventar.
invention (ɪn'vɛn·ʃən) *n.* invención; invento.
inventive (ɪn'vɛn·tɪv) *adj.* inventivo. —**inventiveness,** *n.* inventiva.
inventory ('ɪn·vən,tor·i) *n.* inventario. —*v.t.* inventariar.
inverse (ɪn'vʌɹs) *adj.* inverso. —**inversion** (ɪn'vʌɹ·ʃən) *n.* inversión.
invert (ɪn'vʌɹt) *v.t.* invertir. —*adj.* & *n.* ('ɪn·vʌɹt) invertido.
invertebrate (ɪn'vʌɹ·tə·brət) *adj.* & *n.* invertebrado.
invest (ɪn'vɛst) *v.t.* 1, (install in office; endow, as with authority) investir. 2, (put to use, as money) invertir. 3, (cover; surround) cubrir; envolver. 4, (besiege) sitiar. —*v.i.* invertir dinero; hacer inversión. —**investment,** *n.* inversión.
investigate (ɪn'vɛs·tɪ,geit) *v.t.* investigar. —**investigation,** *n.* investigación.
investiture (ɪn'vɛs·tɪ·tʃər) *n.* investidura.
inveterate (ɪn'vɛt·ər·ət) *adj.* in-

veterado. —**inveteracy,** *n.* calidad de inveterado; hábito inveterado.
invidious (ɪn'vɪd·i·əs) *adj.* **1,** (malicious) malicioso; envidioso. **2,** (odious) odioso.
invidiousness (ɪn'vɪd·i·əs·nəs) *n.* **1,** (maliciousness) malicia; envidia. **2,** (odiousness) odiosidad.
invigorate (ɪn'vig·əˌreit) *v.t.* vigorizar; dar vigor; tonificar. —**invigoration,** *n.* vigorización; tonificación.
invincible (ɪn'vɪn·sə·bəl) *adj.* invencible. —**invincibility,** *n.* invencibilidad.
inviolable (ɪn'vai·əˌ·lə·bəl) *adj.* inviolable.
inviolate (ɪn'vai·ə·lət) *adj.* **1,** (not violated) inviolado. **2,** = **inviolable.**
invisible (ɪn'vɪz·ə·bəl) *adj.* & *n.* invisible. —**invisibility,** *n.* invisibilidad.
invite (ɪn'vait) *v.t.* invitar. —**invitation** (ˌɪn·vɪ'tei·ʃən) *n.* invitación. —**inviting,** *adj.* atrayente; invitante; provocativo.
invoice ('ɪn·vɔis) *n.* factura. —*v.t.* facturar.
invoke (ɪn'vok) *v.t.* invocar. —**invocation** (ˌɪn·və'kei·ʃən) *n.* invocación.
involute ('ɪn·vəˌlut) *adj.* **1,** (spiral) enrollado en espiral. **2,** (intricate) intrincado. —**involution** (-'lu·ʃən) *n.* involución.
involve (ɪn'vaːlv) *v.t.* **1,** (complicate) complicar; embrollar. **2,** (entangle; implicate) enredar; implicar; comprometer. **3,** (include; entail) comprender; implicar; envolver. **4,** (occupy the attention of) enfrascar; ocupar; preocupar.
involvement (ɪn'valv·mənt) *n.* **1,** (an involving or being involved) compromiso; implicación; envolvimiento. **2,** (complicated state of affairs) enredo; embrollo; complicación.
invulnerable (ɪn'vʌl·nər·ə·bəl) *adj.* invulnerable. —**invulnerability,** *n.* invulnerabilidad.
inward ('ɪn·wərd) *adj.* **1,** (situated within; internal) de adentro; interno; interior. **2,** (ingoing) hacia dentro. —*adv.* [*también,* **inwards** (-wərdz)] hacia dentro; hacia el interior. —**inwardly,** *adv.* interiormente.
iodide ('ai·əˌdaid) *n.* yoduro.
iodine ('ai·əˌdain) *n.* yodo.
iodize ('ai·əˌdaiz) *v.t.* yodurar; tratar con yodo o yoduro.
iodiform (ai'o·dəˌform) *n.* yodoformo.
ion ('ai·ən) *n.* ión.
-ion (i·ən) *sufijo* -ión. **1,** *forma nombres abstractos: option,* opción; *fusion,* fusión. **2,** *forma nombres concretos denotando personas o cosas: centurion,* centurión.
Ionic (ai'an·ɪk) *adj.* jónico.
ionium (ai'o·ni·əm) *n.* ionio.
ionosphere (ai'an·ə·sfɪr) *n.* ionosfera.
iota (ai'o·tə) *n.* ápice; jota.
I.O.U. (ˌai·o'juː) *n., abr. de* **I owe you,** pagaré.
-ious (i·əs) *sufijo; forma adjetivos denotando* cualidad; relación: *rebellious,* rebelde.
ipecac ('ɪp·əˌkæk) *n.* ipecacuana.
I.Q. ('ai'kjuː) *n., abr. de* **intelligence quotient,** cociente intelectual.
ir- (ɪr) *prefijo, var. de* **in-** *ante* r: *irrational,* irracional.
irascible (ɪ'ræs·ə·bəl) *adj.* irascible. —**irascibility,** *n.* irascibilidad.
irate ('ai·ret) *adj.* airado; irritado.
ire (air) *n.* ira. —**ireful,** *adj.* iracundo.
iridescent (ˌɪr·ə'dɛs·ənt) *adj.* iridiscente —**iridescence,** *n.* iridiscencia.
iridium (ɪ'rɪd·i·əm) *n.* iridio.
iris ('ai·rɪs) *n.* **1,** *anat.; optics* iris. **2,** *bot.* flor de lis; iris. **3,** (rainbow) iris; arco iris.
Irish ('ai·rɪʃ) *adj.* & *n.* irlandés. —**Irishman** (-mən) *n.* irlandés.
irk (ʌɹk) *v.t.* fastidiar; molestar; enfadar. —**irksome** ('ʌɹk·səm) *adj.* fastidioso; molesto; enfadoso.
iron ('ai·ərn) *n.* **1,** (metal) hierro. **2,** (iron object, device, etc.) instrumento de hierro; herramienta. **3,** *pl.* (shackles) grillos; grilletes. **4,** (flatiron) plancha. **5,** (strength; power) hierro; acero. —*adj.* de hierro; férreo. —*v.t.* & *i.* planchar. —**have (too) many irons in the fire,** *colloq.* abarcar mucho; traer muchos asuntos entre manos. —**iron out,** allanar. —**strike while the iron is hot,** aprovechar la ocasión.
ironclad *adj.* **1,** (armored) acorazado; blindado. **2,** (unassailable) irrefutable. **3,** (inviolable) inviolable.

ironing ('ai·ər·nɪŋ) *n.* planchado. —**ironing board,** tabla de planchar.
iron lung respirador.
ironwork *n.* herraje. —**ironworks,** *n.pl.* talleres metalúrgicos.
irony ('ai·rə·ni) *n.* ironía. —**ironic** (ai'ran·ɪk); **ironical** (ai·'ran·ə·kəl) *adj.* irónico.
irradiate (ɪ'rei·di·et) *v.t.* irradiar. —**irradiation,** *n.* irradiación.
irrational (ɪ'ræʃ·ən·əl) *adj.* irracional. —**irrationality** (-ə'næl·ə·ti) *n.* irracionalidad.
irreconcilable (ɪ,rɛk·ən'sail·ə·bəl) *adj.* irreconciliable.
irrecoverable (,ɪr·i'kʌv·ər·ə·bəl) *adj.* irrecuperable.
irreducible (,ɪr·i'djus·ə·bəl) *adj.* irreducible; irreductible.
irrefutable (ɪ'rɛf·ju·tə·bəl) *adj.* irrefutable; irrebatible.
irregular (ɪ'rɛg·jə·lər) *adj.* irregular. —**irregularity** (-'lær·ə·ti) *n.* irregularidad.
irrelevant (ɪ'rɛl·ə·vənt) *adj.* ajeno *o* extraño al caso; fuera de propósito. —**irrelevance; irrelevancy,** *n.* lo ajeno *o* extraño; cosa ajena o extraña.
irreligious (,ɪr·ɪ'lɪdʒ·əs) *adj.* irreligioso. —**irreligiousness,** *n.* irreligiosidad.
irremediable (,ɪr·ɪ'miː·di·ə·bəl) *adj.* irremediable.
irreparable (ɪ'rɛp·ə·rə·bəl) *adj.* irreparable.
irreplaceable (,ɪr·ɪ'plei·sə·bəl) *adj.* irreemplazable.
irrepressible (,ɪr·ɪ'prɛs·ə·bəl) *adj.* irreprimible.
irreproachable (,ɪr·ɪ'pro·tʃə·bəl) *adj.* irreprochable.
irresolute (ɪ'rɛz·ə·lut) *adj.* irresoluto. —**irresoluteness; irresolution** (-'lu·ʃən) *n.* irresolución.
irrespective (,ɪr·ɪ'spɛk·tɪv) *adj.* independiente; imparcial. —**irrespective of,** independiente de; sin fijarse en; sin hacer caso de.
irresponsible (,ɪr·ɪ'span·sə·bəl) *adj.* irresponsable. —**irresponsibility,** *n.* irresponsabilidad.
irretrievable (,ɪr·ɪ'tri·və·bəl) *adj.* irrecuperable.
irreverent (ɪ'rɛv·ər·ənt) *adj.* irreverente. —**irreverence,** *n.* irreverencia.
irrevocable (ɪ'rɛv·ə·kə·bəl) *adj.* irrevocable. —**irrevocability,** *n.* irrevocabilidad.
irrigate ('ɪr·ə,geit) *v.t.* **1,** (provide with water) regar. **2,** *med.* irrigar. —**irrigable,** *adj.* de regadío.
irrigation (,ɪr·ə'gei·ʃən) *n.* **1,** (watering) riego. **2,** *med.* irrigación.
irritable ('ɪr·ə·tə·bəl) *adj.* irritable. —**irritability,** *n.* irritabilidad.
irritant ('ɪr·ə·tənt) *n.* & *adj.* irritante.
irritate ('ɪr·ə,teit) *v.t.* irritar. —**irritation,** *n.* irritación.
is (ɪz) *v., tercera persona del sing. del pres. de ind. de* **be.**
-ise (aiz) *sufijo* **1,** *var. de* **-ice,** *formando nombres: merchandise,* mercancías. **2,** *var. de* **-ize,** *formando verbos: organise,* organizar.
-ish (ɪʃ) *sufijo; forma adjetivos* **1,** *perteneciente o relacionado con una nación o grupo: Spanish,* español; *Polish,* polaco. **2,** parecido; característico: *devilish,* endiablado; *boyish,* aniñado. **3,** más bien; bastante: *tallish,* más bien alto; *bluish,* azulado. **4,** *colloq.* aproximadamente: *thirtyish,* de unos treinta.
isinglass ('ai·zɪŋ,glæs) *n.* **1,** (gelatin) cola de pescado. **2,** (mica) mica.
Islam ('ɪs·ləm) *n.* Islam. —**Islamic** (ɪs'læm·ɪk) *adj.* islámico.
island ('ai·lənd) *n.* isla. —**islander,** *n.* isleño.
isle (ail) *n.* isla; islote.
ism ('ɪz·əm) *n.* ismo.
-ism (ɪz·əm) *sufijo* -ismo; *forma nombres indicando* doctrina; práctica; sistema: *socialism,* socialismo.
iso- (ai·so) *prefijo* iso-; igual: *isotherm,* isoterma.
isolate ('ai·sə,leit) *v.t.* aislar.
isolation (,ai·sə'lei·ʃən) *n.* aislamiento. —**isolationism,** *n.* aislacionismo. —**isolationist,** *n.* aislacionista.
isometric (,ai·sə'mɛt·rɪk) *adj.* isométrico.
isosceles (ai'sas·ə·liz) *adj.* isósceles.
isotope ('ai·sə,top) *n.* isótopo.
Israeli (ɪz'rei·li) *adj.* & *n.* israelí. —**Israelite** ('ɪz·ri·ə,lait) *adj.* & *n.* israelita.
issuance ('ɪʃ·u·əns) *n.* emisión.
issue ('ɪʃ·u) *n.* **1,** (sending out; putting forth) emisión. **2,** (result; outcome) producto; resultado. **3,** (outlet; exit) salida. **4,** (point in question) disputa; controversia. **5,**

(matter of importance) problema; punto. **6,** (publication; edition) número; edición. **7,** (progeny) sucesión; hijos (*pl.*). —*v.t.* **1,** (put or send forth) emitir. **2,** (publish) publicar. —*v.i.* emanar; salir. —**at issue,** en disputa. —**join issue,** tomar posiciones opuestas. —**take issue (with),** oponerse (a).

-ist (ɪst) *sufijo* -ista; *forma nombres de los verbos terminando en* **-ize** *y nombres en* **-ism,** *que definen a la persona que* estudia, tiene profesión, cree, propaga, etc.: *anthropologist,* antropólogo; *physicist,* físico; *Methodist,* metodista.

isthmus (ˈɪs·məs) *n.* istmo.

-istic (ˈɪs·tɪk) *también,* **-istical** (ˈɪs·tɪk·əl) *sufijo* -ístico; *forma adjetivos frecuentemente derivados de nombres terminando en* **-ist**: *artistic,* artístico; *casuistical,* casuístico.

-istics (ˈɪs·tɪks) *sufijo* -ística; *forma nombres de adjetivos terminados en* **-istic** *y denota* práctica *o* ciencia de: *ballistics,* balística.

it (ɪt) *pron.pers. neutro* **1,** (*sujeto de verbo*) él; ella; ello. **2,** (*complemento directo de verbo*) lo; la. **3,** (*complemento indirecto de verbo*) le. **4,** (*complemento de prep.*) él; ella; ello. **5,** *como sujeto en las construcciones impersonales* (*no se expresa en español*): *It is raining,* Llueve. —*n., colloq.* **1,** (person singled out, as in games) a quien le toca; *You're it,* A ti te toca; Tú eres. **2,** (center of attraction) persona *o* cosa que da el golpe. **3,** (indefinable appeal) eso.

Italian (ɪˈtæl·jən) *adj. & n.* italiano.

Italic (ɪˈtæl·ɪk) *adj.* itálico.

italic (ɪˈtæl·ɪk) *n. & adj.* bastardilla. —**italicize** (-əˌsaiz) *v.t.* poner en bastardilla.

itch (ɪtʃ) *v.t. & i.* picar. —*v.i.* (yearn) desear; anhelar. —*n.* **1,** (tingling sensation) picazón; comezón. **2,** (skin disease) sarna. **3,** (yearning) deseo; anhelo. —**itchy,** *adj.* picante.

it'd (ˈɪt·əd) *contr. de* **it had** *o* **it would.**

-ite (ait) *sufijo* **1,** -ita; *forma nombres indicando* origen; procedencia: *Israelite,* israelita. **2,** -ita; seguidor; discípulo: *Carmelite,* carmelita. **3,** -ita; -ito; roca; mineral: *dolomite,* dolomita; *graphite,* grafito. **4,** *quím.* -ito; compuesto, esp. la sal de un ácido con la desinencia **-ous**: *sulfite,* sulfito. **5,** fósil: *trilobite,* trilobites. **6,** *forma adjetivos y nombres derivados de adjetivos: erudite,* erudito; *opposite,* opuesto. **7,** *forma verbos de acción: ignite,* encender.

item (ˈai·təm) *n.* artículo; ítem; *bookkeeping* partida. —**itemize,** *v.t.* detallar.

iterate (ˈɪt·əˌreit) *v.t.* iterar; reiterar; repetir. —**iteration,** *n.* iteración; reiteración; repetición.

itinerant (aiˈtɪn·ə·rənt) *adj. & n.* ambulante. —**itinerancy,** *n.* rotación.

itinerary (aiˈtɪn·ə·rər·i) *n. & adj.* itinerario.

-ition (ˈɪʃ·ən) *sufijo* -ición; *forma nombres verbales denotando* acción; efecto: *composition,* composición; *definition,* definición.

-itious (ˈɪʃ·əs) *sufijo* -icio; -icioso; *forma adjetivos que frecuentemente corresponden a nombres terminados en* **-ition**: *fictitious,* ficticio.

-itis (ˈai·təs) *sufijo* -itis; inflamación: *bronchitis,* bronquitis.

-itive (ɪ·tɪv; ə-) *sufijo* -itivo; *forma adjetivos expresando* relación; tendencia: *sensitive,* sensitivo.

it'll (ˈɪt·əl) *contr. de* **it will** *o* **it shall.**

it's (ɪts) *contr. de* **it is** *o* **it has.**

its (ɪts) *adj.pos., concordándose en género y en número con el poseedor* su (*pl.* sus); de él, ella *o* ello. —*pron.pos., concordándose en género y en número con el poseedor* el suyo; la suya; lo suyo; los suyos; las suyas; el, la, lo, los *o* las de él, ella *o* ello.

itself (ɪtˈsɛlf) *pron.pers. neutro* el mismo; la misma. —*pron.refl.* **1,** (*complemento directo o indirecto de verbo*) se. **2,** (*complemento de prep.*) sí; sí mismo; sí misma.

-ity (ə·ti) *sufijo* -idad; *forma nombres denotando:* cualidad; condición: *activity,* actividad.

-ium (i·əm) *sufijo* -io; *forma nombres de terminología científica: actinium,* actinio.

I've (aiv) *contr. de* **I have.**

-ive (ɪv) *sufijo* -ivo; *forma adjetivos verbales denotando* función; tendencia; disposición: *formative,* formativo; *passive,* pasivo.

ivory ('ai·və·ri) *n.* marfil. —*adj.* de marfil; marfileño.
ivy ('ai·vi) *n.* hiedra.
-ization (ɪ'zei·ʃən; ə-) *sufijo* -ización; *forma nombres de verbos terminados en* **-ize**: *organization,* organización.
-ize (aiz) *sufijo* -izar; *forma verbos de nombres y adjetivos denotando* **1,** *en verbos transitivos* hacer, rendir, suministrar, desempeñar *o* tratar en cierta forma: *realize,* realizar; *civilize,* civilizar. **2,** *en verbos intransitivos* actuar, funcionar *o* practicar en forma determinada: *economize,* economizar; *crystallize,* cristalizar.

J

J, j (dzei) décima letra del alfabeto inglés.
jab (dʒæb) *v.t.* & *i.* **1,** (thrust; poke) hincar; clavar. **2,** (pierce; stab) punzar; picar. **3,** (punch; strike short blows) dar golpes cortos. —*n.* **1,** (stab; thrust) punzada; piquete. **2,** (blow) golpe corto.
jabber ('dʒæb·ər) *v.t.* & *i.* chapurrear. —*n.* chapurreo; cháchara.
jack (dʒæk) *n.* **1,** *mech.* gato. **2,** *cards* sota. **3,** *colloq.* (fellow) sujeto; tipo; fulano. **4,** (sailor) marinero. **5,** *electricity* enchufe; jack. **6,** (flag) bandera; pabellón. **7,** *slang* (money) dinero; parné. —*v.t.* [*usu.* **jack up**] levantar; subir.
jackal ('dʒæk·əl) *n.* chacal.
jackass ('dʒæk·æs) *n.* asno; burro; jumento.
jackdaw ('dʒæk,dɔ) *n.* **1,** (crow) corneja. **2,** (grackle) estornino.
jacket ('dʒæk·ɪt) *n.* **1,** (coat) chaqueta. **2,** (covering) cubierta; funda. —*v.t.* poner cubierta o funda a.
jack-in-the-box *n.* caja de sorpresa; muñeco en cajón.
jackknife *n.* **1,** (large knife) cuchilla; navaja. **2,** (kind of dive) salto de carpa. —*v.i.* doblarse en dos.
jack-of-all-trades *n.* aprendiz de todo y oficial de nada.
jack-o'-lantern ('dʒæk·o,læn·tərn) *n.* linterna hecha de una calabaza hueca.
jackpot *n.* **1,** *cards* pozo. **2,** *colloq.* (large prize) premio mayor; premio gordo.
jackrabbit *n.* liebre grande norteamericana.
jade (dʒeid) *n.* **1,** (mineral) jade. **2,** (color) color jade. **3,** (dissolute woman) mujerzuela. **4,** (old horse) jaco; jamelgo. —*adj.* de jade. —*v.t.* **1,** (exhaust; wear out) cansar; agotar; desgastar. **2,** (surfeit) saciar; embotar.
jaded ('dʒei·dɪd) *adj.* **1,** (tired; worn-out) cansado; agotado; gastado. **2,** (surfeited; satiated) saciado; embotado.
jag (dʒæg) *n.* **1,** (notch; nick) muesca; recorte. **2,** (toothlike projection) diente; saliente; pico. **3,** *slang* (drunk) borrachera. —**jagged,** *adj.* dentado; serrado; quebrado.
jaguar ('dʒæg·war) *n.* jaguar.
jai alai (,hai·ə'lai) *n.* pelota; jai alai.
jail (dʒeil) *n.* cárcel. —*v.t.* encarcelar. —**jailer,** *n.* carcelero.
jailbird *n., slang* **1,** (prisoner) preso. **2,** (habitual lawbreaker) delincuente empedernido.
jalopy (dʒə'lap·i) *n., slang* automóvil desvencijado.
jalousie ('dʒæl·ə·si) *n.* celosía.
jam (dʒæm) *v.t.* **1,** (squeeze; press) apretar; apiñar. **2,** (crowd into; fill up) atestar; atiborrar. **3,** (clog; choke) atascar; obstruir. **4,** (cause to stick) atascar; trancar. **5,** (catch fast; crush) coger; pillar. **6,** *radio* interferir; perturbar. —*v.i.* **1,** (become stuck) atascarse; encajarse; trancarse. **2,** (crowd together) apiñarse; aglomerarse. —*n.* **1,** (congestion) congestión; *W.I.* tapón; *So. Amer.* taco. **2,** *colloq.* (predicament) apuro; lío; aprieto. **3,** (preserve) compota; mermelada.
jamb (dʒæm) *n.* jamba; quicio.
jamboree (,dʒæm·bə'riː) *n., slang* holgorio; fiesta; verbena.
jangle ('dʒæŋ·gəl) *v.i.* sonar como cencerro; sonar estridentemente. —*v.t.* **1,** (cause to sound harshly) hacer sonar destempladamente. **2,** (jar, as the nerves) destemplar.

—*n.* sonido estridente; estridencia.
janitor ('dʒæn·ə·tər) *n.* portero; conserje.
January ('dʒæn·juˌɛr·i) *n.* enero.
japan (dʒə'pæn) *n.* laca; barniz.
Japanese (ˌdʒæp·ə'niːz) *adj.* & *n.* japonés.
jar (dʒaːr) *v.t.* & *i.* **1,** (jolt; rattle) sacudir. **2,** (grate; sound harshly) destemplar. **3,** (upset; disturb) turbar; desconcertar. —*n.* **1,** (jolt) sacudida. **2,** (vessel) jarra; pote; vasija; frasco.
jardinière (ˌdʒar·də'nɪr) *n.* jardinera.
jargon ('dʒar·gən) *n.* jerga; jerigonza.
jasmine ('dʒæs·mɪn) *n.* jazmín.
jasper ('dʒæs·pər) *n.* jaspe.
jaundice ('dʒɔn·dɪs) *n.* **1,** *pathol.* ictericia. **2,** (embitterment) resentimiento; amargura.
jaundiced ('dʒɔn·dɪst) *adj.* **1,** *pathol.* que tiene o padece ictericia; ictérico. **2,** (embittered) resentido; amargado.
jaunt (dʒɔnt) *n.* paseo; excursión.
jaunty ('dʒɔn·ti) *adj.* **1,** (sprightly) vivo; animado. **2,** (stylish) elegante; de buen gusto.
javelin ('dʒæv·lɪn) *n.* jabalina.
jaw (dʒɔː) *n.* mandíbula; (*esp. of animals*) quijada.
jawbone *n.* mandíbula; quijada.
jawbreaker ('dʒɔˌbrei·kər) *n., colloq.* **1,** (tongue-twister) trabalenguas. **2,** (hard candy) rompemuelas; pirulí; caramelo.
jay (dʒei) *n.* arrendajo.
jaywalk ('dʒeiˌwɔk) *v.i., colloq.* cruzar una calle en contravención a las ordenanzas. —**jaywalker,** *n.* peatón imprudente.
jazz (dʒæz) *n.* **1,** *music* jazz. **2,** *slang* (liveliness) animación. **3,** *slang* (rumpus; tumult) jaleo; bochinche. **4,** *slang* (nonsense) tontería. —*v.t.* [*también,* **jazz up**] **1,** *music* arreglar, tocar *o* cantar en estilo de jazz. **2,** *slang* (enliven) animar; dar animación.
jealous ('dʒɛl·əs) *adj.* **1,** possessive) celoso. **2,** (envious) envidioso.
jealousy ('dʒɛl·ə·si) *n.* **1,** (possessiveness) celos (*pl.*). **2,** (envy) envidia.
jean (dʒiːn) *n.* **1,** (fabric) dril. **2,** *pl.* (trousers or overalls) pantalones de dril; overoles; mono (*sing.*).
jeep (dʒip) *n.* jeep.
jeer (dʒɪr) *v.i.* [*usu.* **jeer at**] mofarse (de); burlarse (de). —*n.* befa; mofa.
Jehovah (dʒə'ho·və) *n.* Jehová.
jejune (dʒɪ'dʒuːn) *adj.* insípido; insulso.
jell (dʒɛl) *v.i.* cuajar.
jelly ('dʒɛl·i) *n.* jalea; gelatina. —**jellied,** *adj.* con gelatina; convertido en gelatina.
jellyfish ('dʒɛl·iˌfɪʃ) *n.* medusa; aguamala; *Amer.* malagua.
jenny ('dʒɛn·i) *n.* **1,** (spinning machine) máquina de hilar. **2,** (female ass) burra; asna. —*adj.* hembra.
jeopardy ('dʒɛp·ər·di) *n.* riesgo; peligro. —**jeopardize,** *v.t.* arriesgar; hacer peligrar; comprometer.
jeremiad (ˌdʒɛr·ə'mai·æd) *n.* jeremiada.
jerk (dʒʌɹk) *v.t.* **1,** (pull sharply) tirar *o* mover bruscamente; tironear. **2,** [*usu.* **jerk out**] (gasp; ejaculate) exclamar; decir bruscamente. —*v.i.* **1,** (move abruptly) moverse bruscamente; sacudirse. **2,** (twitch) saltar; dar un tic. —*n.* **1,** (quick pull) tirón. **2,** (jar; jolt) sacudida. **3,** (twitch) tic; espasmo. **4,** *slang* (fool) tonto; imbécil; cretino. —**jerky,** *adj.* irregular; espasmódico; abrupto. —**jerkiness,** *n.* irregularidad; calidad de espasmódico.
jerked beef cecina; tasajo; *Amer.* charqui.
jerkin ('dʒʌɹ·kɪn) *n.* jubón.
jerry-built ('dʒɛr·iˌbɪlt) *adj.* mal construido.
jersey ('dʒʌɹ·zi) *n.* jersey.
Jesuit ('dʒɛʒ·ju·ɪt) *n.* & *adj.* jesuita.
jest (dʒɛst) *v.i.* burlarse; bromear; chancearse. —*n.* broma; chanza; chiste. —**jester,** *n.* bufón. —**jesting,** *n.* bufonería.
jet (dʒɛt) *n.* **1,** (gush) chorro. **2,** (spout) pitón; caño; surtidor. **3,** (mineral) azabache. **4,** (plane) avión a *o* de reacción. —*v.t.* lanzar con fuerza *o* a chorros. —*v.i.* salir a chorros. —*adj.* **1,** (of or like jet) de azabache; azabachado. **2,** (jet propelled) a *o* de chorro; de propulsión a chorro; a *o* de reacción.
jet-black *adj.* azabachado.
jetsam ('dʒɛt·səm) *n.* echazón; desechos (*pl.*).
jetty ('dʒɛt·i) *n.* **1,** (breakwater)

escollera; rompeolas. **2,** (wharf) muelle.

jettison ('dʒɛt·ə·sən) *v.t.* arrojar al mar. —*n.* echazón.

Jew (dʒuː) *n.* judío. —**Jewish,** *adj.* judío. —**Jewry,** *n.* judíos (*pl.*); pueblo judío.

jewel ('dʒu·əl) *n.* joya. —*v.t.* adornar con joyas; enjoyar. —**jeweler,** *n.* joyero.

jewelry ('dʒu·əl·ri) *n.* joyas (*pl.*); pedrería. —**jewelry shop,** joyería. —**jewelry trade,** joyería.

jewfish *n.* mero.

jew's-harp *n.* birimbao.

jib (dʒɪb) *n.* **1,** (sail) foque. **2,** (boom) brazo de grúa; pescante.

jibe (dʒaib) *v.t.* & *i.,* *naut.* virar. —*v.i.* **1,** *colloq.* (agree) concordar. **2,** = gibe. —*n.* = gibe.

jiffy ('dʒɪf·i) *n., colloq.* instante; santiamén.

jig (dʒɪg) *n.* **1,** *mech.* guía. **2,** (dance) giga. —*v.i.* bailar la giga.

jiggle ('dʒɪg·əl) *v.t.* zangolotear; zarandear. —*v.i.* zarandearse; zangolotearse. —*n.* zangoloteo.

jigsaw ('dʒɪg,sɔ) *n.* sierra de vaivén. —**jigsaw puzzle,** rompecabezas.

jilt (dʒɪlt) *v.t.* dejar plantado; plantar; dar calabazas.

jimmy ('dʒɪm·i) *n.* palanqueta. —*v.t.* forzar.

jingle ('dʒɪŋ·gəl) *v.i.* & *t.* tintinar; retiñir. —*n.* **1,** (sound) tintineo; retintín; cascabeleo. **2,** (ditty) estribillo; sonsonete. —**jingle bell,** cascabel.

jingo ('dʒɪŋ·go) *n.* jingo. —**jingoism,** *n.* jingoísmo. —**jingoist,** *n.* & *adj.* jingoísta.

jinks (dʒɪŋks) *n.pl., colloq.* travesuras; bromas.

jinrikisha (dʒɪn'rɪk·ʃɔ) *n.* jinrikisha.

jinx (dʒɪŋks) *n., colloq.* cenizo; gafe. —*v.t., colloq.* traer mala suerte; dar cenizo.

jitney ('dʒɪt·ni) *n.* **1,** *colloq.* (small bus) vehículo de pasajeros con trayecto fijo. **2,** *slang* (*U.S.* nickel) níquel.

jitter ('dʒɪt·ər) *v.i., slang* estar nervioso. —*n., usu. pl.* nerviosidad. —**jittery,** *adj. slang,* agitado; nervioso.

jitterbug ('dʒɪt·ər·bʌg) *n.* persona que baila jazz con movimientos exagerados. —*v.i.* bailar de esta forma.

jive (dʒaiv) *n., slang* **1,** (rhythm) ritmo de jazz o de swing. **2,** (jargon) jerga de músicos.

job (dʒaːb) *n.* **1,** (piece of work) obra; labor; trabajo. **2,** (task; chore) tarea; trabajo. **3,** (duty) obligación; tarea; deber. **4,** (employment; work) trabajo; empleo. **5,** (office; post) puesto; cargo. **6,** *colloq.* (matter) asunto; cosa. —*v.i.* [**jobbed, jobbing**] trabajar a destajo. —*v.t.* **1,** (portion out, as an order or contract) repartir. **2,** (buy or sell wholesale) comprar *o* vender al por mayor. —**jobber,** *n.* mayorista. —**by the job,** a destajo. —**odd jobs,** trabajos menudos. —**on the job,** *colloq.* en el trabajo; en su sitio.

jockey ('dʒak·i) *v.t.* & *i.* **1,** (maneuver) componérselas; maniobrar para obtener ventaja. **2,** (swindle) embaucar. —*n.* jockey. —**disk jockey,** locutor musical.

jocose (dʒo'kos) *adj.* jocoso. —**jocosity** (-'kas·ə·ti) *n.* jocosidad.

jocular ('dʒak·jə·lər) *adj.* jocoso. —**jocularity** (-'lær·ə·ti) *n.* jocosidad.

jocund ('dʒak·ənd) *adj.* jocundo. —**jocundity** (dʒo'kʌn·də·ti) *n.* jocundidad.

jodhpurs ('dʒad·pərz) *n.pl.* pantalones de equitación.

jog (dʒag) *v.t.* [**jogged, jogging**] **1,** (shove; push) empujar; mover de un empujón *o* tirón. **2,** (shake) sacudir; remecer. **3,** (stimulate) estimular; despertar. —*v.i.* **1,** (shake; jolt) remecerse; dar una sacudida; sacudirse. **2,** (move or travel joltingly) moverse dando sacudidas; traquetear. **3,** (trudge; plod) ir pausadamente; ir a paso de buey. —*n.* **1,** (shove; nudge) empujoncito. **2,** (shake) sacudida. **3,** (trot) trote lento. **4,** (projection) saliente. **5,** (recessed part) entrante.

John Doe Fulano de Tal; Juan Pérez.

join (dʒɔin) *v.t.* **1,** (bring together; unite) unir. **2,** (fasten; fit together) juntar; unir; *carpentry* ensamblar. **3,** (become a member of) ingresar en; hacerse socio de; *mil.* alistarse en. **4,** (ally or associate oneself with) unirse *o* asociarse a *o* con. **5,** (accompany) acompañar. **6,** (connect with) unirse *o* juntarse a *o* con. 7, (meet) encontrar; alcanzar. 8, (return to) volver *o* reunirse a *o* con. —*v.i.* 1, (come together; unite) unirse. 2, (become a member) ingresar. 3, (take part) tomar parte; participar. —*n.* unión; juntura.

joiner ('dʒɔi·nər) *n.* 1, (person or thing that joins) persona *o* cosa que une. 2, (woodworker) ensamblador. 3, *colloq.* (person given to joining organizations) persona muy dada a pertenecer a distintas asociaciones.

joint (dʒɔint) *n.* 1, *anat.; zool.* articulación; coyuntura. 2, *bot.* articulación; nudo. 3, (place or manner of joining) juntura; empalme. 4, (coupling) articulación; unión. 5, (section) parte; sección. 6, (cut of meat) cuarto; sección. 7, *slang* (place) cuchitril. 8, *slang* (cheap restaurant) figón. —*adj.* 1, (done or executed in common) conjunto; colectivo; común. 2, (held or shared in common) común; en común. 3, (concurrent) concurrente. —*v.t.* 1, (fasten with joints) juntar; empalmar; *carpentry* ensamblar. 2, (form into joints) articular. 3, (cut into joints) descoyuntar; desmembrar. —**joint account,** cuenta indistinta; *Amer., también,* cuenta conjunta; común *o* en común. —**joint session,** sesión plenaria. —**joint-stock company,** sociedad anónima.

joist (dʒɔist) *n.* viga; cabio.

joke (dʒok) *n.* broma; chiste. —*v.i.* bromear; chancear. —**bad joke,** broma pesada. —**crack a joke,** soltar un chiste. —**practical joke,** bromazo.

joker ('dʒo·kər) *n.* 1, (one who jokes) bromista. 2, *cards* comodín. 3, (insidious clause in a document) cláusula capciosa.

jolly ('dʒal·i) *adj.* alegre; jovial. —**jolliness; jollity,** *n.* alegría; jovialidad.

jolt (dʒolt) *v.t.* sacudir bruscamente. —*v.i.* sacudirse; moverse dando sacudidas; traquetear. —*n.* sacudida.

jonquil ('dʒaŋ·kwɪl) *n.* junquillo.

josh (dʒaʃ) *v.t.* & *i., slang* tomar el pelo (a); gastar bromas (a).

jostle ('dʒas·əl) *v.t.* empujar. —*v.i.* moverse a empujones. —*n.* empujón.

jot (dʒat) *n.* jota; ápice. —*v.t.* anotar; apuntar.

joule (dʒaul) *n.* julio; joule.

jounce (dʒauns) *v.t.* & *i.* traquetear. —*n.* traqueteo.

journal ('dʒʌɹ·nəl) *n.* 1, (daily record; diary) diario. 2, (newspaper) diario; periódico. 3, (periodical) revista; gaceta. —**journalism,** *n.* periodismo. —**journalist,** *n.* periodista. —**journalistic,** *adj.* periodístico.

journey ('dʒʌɹ·ni) *n.* viaje. —*v.i.* viajar.

journeyman ('dʒʌɹ·ni·mən) *n.* [*pl.* **-men**] oficial.

joust (dʒaust) *n.* justa; torneo. —*v.i.* pelear; luchar.

jovial ('dʒo·vi·əl) *adj.* jovial; alegre. —**joviality** (-'æl·ə·ti) *n.* jovialidad.

jowl (dʒaul) *n.* cachete; carrillo.

joy (dʒɔi) *n.* gozo; júbilo; alegría. —**joyful; joyous,** *adj.* jubiloso; alegre; gozoso. —**joyfulness; joyousness,** *n.* gozo; júbilo; alegría.

joyless ('dʒɔi·ləs) *adj.* triste. —**joylessness,** *n.* tristeza.

joy stick palanca de mando.

jubilant ('dʒu·bə·lənt) *adj.* jubiloso. —**jubilation** (-'lei·ʃən) *n.* júbilo.

jubilee ('dʒu·bə·li) *n.* jubileo.

Judaism ('dʒu·də·ɪz·əm) *n.* judaísmo. —**Judaic** (dʒu'dei·ɪk) *adj.* judaico.

judge (dʒʌdʒ) *v.t.* & *i.* juzgar. —*n.* juez. —**judgeship,** *n.* magistratura.

judge advocate auditor (de guerra *o* de marina).

judgment ('dʒʌdʒ·mənt) *n.* 1, (act or ability of judging) juicio. 2, (decision) fallo; sentencia.

judicature ('dʒu·də·kə·tʃər) *n.* judicatura.

judicial (dʒu'dɪʃ·əl) *adj.* judicial.

judiciary (dʒu'dɪʃ·i·ɛr·i) *n.* judicatura. —*adj.* judicial.

judicious (dʒu'dɪʃ·əs) *adj.* juicioso. —**judiciousness,** *n.* juicio.

judo ('dʒu·do) *n.* judo.

jug (dʒʌg) *n.* 1, (vessel) jarro; cántaro. 2, *slang* (jail) cárcel. —*v.t., slang* (imprison) encarcelar.

juggernaut ('dʒʌg·ər·nɔt) *n.* cosa *o* fuerza ineluctable.

juggle ('dʒʌg·əl) *v.i.* 1, (perform tricks) hacer juegos malabares. 2, (practice deception) engañar; em-

baucar. —*v.t.* **1,** (perform tricks with) hacer juegos malabares con. **2,** (manipulate) manipular. —**juggler** (-lər) *n.* malabarista. —**jugglery** (-lə·ri); **juggling** (-lɪŋ) *n.* malabarismo; juegos malabares.
jugular ('dʒʌg·jə·lər) *adj.* yugular.
juice (dʒus) *n.* **1,** (liquid) jugo; zumo. **2,** *slang* (gasoline) gasolina. **3,** *slang* (electricity) electricidad. —**juicy,** *adj.* jugoso.
jujitsu (dʒu'dʒɪt·su) *n.* jiu-jitsu.
juke box (dʒuk) *n., slang* tocadiscos; tragamonedas; *W.I.* vellonera.
julep ('dʒu·lɪp) *n.* julepe.
July (dʒu'lai) *n.* julio.
jumble (dʒʌm·bəl) *v.t.* mezclar; revolver. —*v.i.* mezclarse; revolverse. —*n.* revoltijo.
jumbo ('ʒʌm·bo) *n.* [*pl.* **-bos**] persona *o* cosa muy grande; coloso. —*adj.* grande.
jump (dʒʌmp) *v.i.* & *t.* saltar. —*v.t.* hacer saltar. —*n.* salto. —**jumpy,** *adj.* nervioso; excitado. —**jumpiness,** *n.* nerviosidad. —**jump rope,** comba.
jumper ('dʒʌm·pər) *n.* **1,** (person or thing that jumps) saltador. **2,** *electricity* alambre de cierre. **3,** (loose garment) guardapolvo. **4,** (sleeveless dress) vestido sin mangas. **5,** *pl.* = **rompers.**
junction ('dʒʌŋk·ʃən) *n.* **1,** (act or result of joining) unión; juntura. **2,** (place of joining) empalme; (*of rivers*) confluencia.
juncture ('dʒʌŋk·tʃər) *n.* **1,** (place of joining; seam) juntura. **2,** (point of time) coyuntura.
June (dʒu:n) *n.* junio.
jungle ('dʒʌŋ·gəl) *n.* jungla.
junior ('dʒun·jər) *n.* **1,** (younger person) persona más joven que otra. **2,** (namesake son) hijo. **3,** (subordinate) subalterno. **4,** (third-year college student) estudiante de penúltimo. año. —*adj.* **1,** (younger) menor. **2,** (of lower rank) de grado inferior; de menor grado. **3,** (more recent) más reciente. **4,** [*abr.* **Jr.**] (designating the son of the same name) hijo: *David Jones, Jr.,* David Jones, hijo. —**junior high school,** escuela intermedia. —**junior college,** colegio que enseña los dos primeros años universitarios.
juniper ('dʒu·nə·pər) *n.* **1,** (shrub) enebro. **2,** (fruit) enebrina.
junk (dʒʌŋk) *n.* **1,** (trash) basura. **2,** (worthless objects) trastos (*pl.*); trastos viejos. **3,** (scrap metal) chatarra; hierro viejo. **4,** (boat) junco. **5,** *slang* (narcotics) narcóticos (*pl.*). —*v.t., colloq.* **1,** (throw away) descartar; desechar; tirar. **2,** (sell for scrap) vender por chatarra.
junket ('dʒʌŋ·kɪt) *n.* **1,** (dessert) especie de cuajada. **2,** (excursion) jira. —*v.i.* ir *o* andar de jira.
junta ('dʒʌn·ta) *n.* junta.
junto ('dʒʌn·to) *n.* [*pl.* **-tos**] camarilla; facción.
Jupiter ('dʒu·pɪ·tər) *n.* Júpiter.
juridical (dʒu'rɪd·ə·kəl) *adj.* jurídico.
jurisdiction (ˌdʒur·ɪs'dɪk·ʃən) *n.* jurisdicción. —**jurisdictional,** *adj.* jurisdiccional.
jurisprudence (ˌdʒur·ɪs'pru·dəns) *n.* jurisprudencia.
jurist ('dʒur·ɪst) *n.* jurista.
juror ('dʒur·ər) *también,* **juryman** ('dʒur·i·mən) *n.* jurado.
jury (dʒur·i) *n.* jurado. —*adj., naut.* provisional.
just (dʒʌst) *adj.* justo. —*adv.* **1,** (precisely) justamente; precisamente; exactamente. **2,** (barely) apenas; casi no. **3,** (only; merely) simplemente; sólo. **4,** *colloq.* (completely) completamente; absolutamente. —**justness,** *n.* justicia. —**have just,** acabar de: *I have just arrived,* Acabo de llegar. —**just now,** ahora mismo.
justice ('dʒʌs·tɪs) *n.* justicia. —**justice of the peace,** juez de paz; juez municipal.
justify ('dʒʌs·təˌfai) *v.t.* justificar. —*v.i.* justificarse. —**justifiable,** *adj.* justificable. —**justification** (-fɪ'kei·ʃən) *n.* justificación.
jut (dʒʌt) *v.i.* sobresalir; proyectarse. —*n.* saliente.
jute (dʒut) *n.* yute.
juvenile ('dʒu·və·nəl) *adj.* juvenil. —*n.* joven. —**juvenility** (-'nɪl·ə·ti) *n.* juventud; mocedad.
juxta- (dʒʌks·tə) *prefijo* yuxta-; cerca; junto; cercano: *juxtaposition,* yuxtaposición.
juxtapose (ˌdʒʌks·tə'po:z) *v.t.* yuxtaponer. —**juxtaposition** (-pə·'ziʃ·ən) yuxtaposición.

K

K, k (kei) undécima letra del alfabeto inglés.
Kaiser ('kai·zər) *n.* káiser.
kale (keil) *n.* berza; col.
kaleidoscope (kə'lai·də,skop) *n.* calidoscopio. —**kaleidoscopic** (-'skap·ɪk) *adj.* calidoscópico.
kalsomine ('kæl·sə,main) *n.* lechada. —*v.t.* blanquear.
kangaroo (,kæŋ·gə'ruː) *n.* canguro. —**kangaroo court,** tribunal anómalo y arbitrario.
kapok ('kei·pak) *n.* kapok; algodón de ceiba.
kaput (ka'put) *adj., slang* perdido.
katydid ('kei·ti·dɪd) *n.* saltamontes americano.
kayak ('kai·æk) *n.* kajak; kayak.
kayo ('kei·o) *v.t., slang* noquear; poner fuera de combate. —*n.* knockout.
kedge (kɛdʒ) *v.t. & i., naut.* halar (una embarcación) por el anclote. —*n.* anclote.
keel (kiːl) *n.* quilla. —**keel over,** *colloq.* **1,** (upset; turn over) dar(se) vuelta; volcar; voltear. **2,** (fall down, as in a faint) desplomarse. —**on an even keel,** estable.
keen (kiːn) *adj.* **1,** (sharp; acute) agudo. **2,** (eager; enthusiastic) entusiasmado; muy interesado. **3,** *slang* (excellent) excelente. —**keenness,** *n.* agudeza.
keep (kip) *v.t.* [*pret. & p.p.* **kept**] **1,** (observe; pay regard to) guardar; observar. **2,** (fulfill, as a promise) cumplir. **3,** (guard; watch over) guardar; cuidar. **4,** (maintain) mantener. **5,** (preserve) preservar. **6,** (maintain, as a record) llevar; llevar apuntes en. **7,** (have; hold) tener. **8,** (retain in one's possession) quedarse con; guardar. **9,** (detain; delay) detener; retener; demorar. **10,** (hold back; restrain) contener; aguantar. **11,** (prevent) impedir. **12,** (care for; support) mantener; cuidar de. —*v.i.* **1,** (stay) mantenerse. **2,** (continue) continuar; seguir. **3,** (abstain; refrain) abstenerse. **4,** (stay in good condition; last) conservarse; preservarse; durar. **5,** *colloq.* (wait; remain in abeyance) esperar; guardarse. —*n.* **1,** (livelihood; support) sustento; manutención; subsistencia. **2,** (stronghold of a castle) torre del homenaje. —**for keeps,** *colloq.* **1,** (in earnest) en serio; de veras. **2,** (forever) para siempre. —**keep at,** continuar en; seguir con. —**keep back, 1,** (contain; restrain) contener; sujetar; mantener apartado. **2,** (conceal) ocultar. —**keep down, 1,** (repress) reprimir. **2,** (limit) limitar. —**keep from** (+ *ger.*) evitar (+ *inf.*); abstenerse de. —**keep** (**someone** *o* **something**) **from** (+ *ger.*) evitar que; prevenir que; cuidar de que no. —**keep in with,** *colloq.* llevarse bien con. —**keep off,** mantener(se) a distancia; apartar(se). —**keep on,** continuar; seguir. —**keep out,** impedir la entrada a *o* de; apartar(se). —**keep to oneself, 1,** (avoid company) ser retraído; andar solo. **2,** (not divulge) guardar; ocultar; no contar. —**keep up, 1,** (maintain) mantener. **2,** (continue) seguir con; continuar con. **3,** (maintain the pace; not lag behind) ir a la par; no rezagarse. —**keep up with the Joneses,** llevar el mismo tren de vida que los vecinos.
keeper ('ki·pər) *n.* cuidador; guarda; guardián; encargado.
keeping ('ki·pɪŋ) *n.* **1,** (observance) observancia. **2,** (care; custody) cargo; custodia; cuidado. **3,** (maintenance; keep) manutención; subsistencia. **4,** (agreement; conformity) acuerdo; conformidad. **5,** (preservation) preservación.
keepsake ('kip,seik) *n.* recuerdo.
keg (kɛg) *n.* barril pequeño; barrilito.
kelp (kɛlp) *n.* alga marina grande.
Kelt (kɛlt) *n.* = **Celt.** —**Keltic,** *n. & adj.* = **Celtic.**
ken (kɛn) *n.* alcance del conocimiento; visión.
kennel ('kɛn·əl) *n.* perrera. —*v.t.* meter *o* tener en una perrera.
kepi ('kɛp·i) *n.* kepis; quepis.
kept (kɛpt) *v., pret. & p.p. de* **keep.**
kerb (kʌɹb) *v.t. & n., Brit.* = **curb.**
kerchief ('kʌɹ·tʃɪf) *n.* pañuelo.

kernel (ˈkʌɹ·nəl) *n.* **1,** (seed) semilla. **2,** (essence; core) esencia; meollo; médula.
kerosene (ˈkɛr·əˌsin) *n.* kerosina; *Amer.* kerosén, kerosene.
ketch (kɛtʃ) *n.* queche.
ketchup (ˈkɛtʃ·əp) *n.* = **catchup.**
ketone (ˈki·ton) *n.* cetona.
kettle (ˈkɛt·əl) *n.* caldero; perol; (*teakettle*) tetera. **—kettle of fish,** enredo; embrollo; lío.
kettledrum (ˈkɛt·əlˌdrʌm) *n.* atabal; timbal.
key (kiː) *n.* **1,** (device to turn a lock, bolt, etc.) llave. **2,** (lever, as of a piano, accordion, typewriter, etc.) tecla. **3,** (lever of wind instruments) llave. **4,** (peg; pin) clavija; chaveta; cuña. **5,** (controlling factor) clave. **6,** (clue; explanation) clave. **7,** (code; reference system) clave. **8,** (pitch; tone) tono. **9,** *music* clave. **10,** (reef; low island) cayo. **—*v.t.* 1,** (adjust; regulate) ajustar; arreglar; regular. **2,** (regulate the pitch of) templar; afinar. **3,** (relate to a reference system) clasificar *o* relacionar con *o* por clave. **—*adj.*** clave; *key position,* posición clave. **—key up,** excitar; acalorar.
keyboard *n.* teclado.
keyhole *n.* bocallave; ojo de la cerradura.
keynote *n.* **1,** *music* (tonic) clave; llave. **2,** (basic idea) punto *o* tema principal; tenor.
keystone *n.* clave.
khaki (ˈkæk·i) *n.* caqui; kaki.
khan (kæn) *n.* kan. **—khanate** (-eit) *n.* kanato.
khedive (kəˈdiːv) *n.* jedive.
kibitzer (ˈkɪb·ɪt·sər) *n.* mirón; entremetido. **—kibitz** (-ɪts) *v.t. & i.* hacer de mirón (en).
kick (kɪk) *v.i.* **1,** (strike out with the foot or feet) dar puntapiés *o* patadas; *Amer.* patear. **2,** (thrash about with the feet) patalear. **3,** (recoil) retroceder; recular; *Amer.* patear. **4,** *colloq.* (complain; grumble) rezongar; patalear; refunfuñar. **—*v.t.* 1,** (strike or drive with the foot or feet) dar puntapiés *o* patadas; *Amer.* patear. **2,** (recoil against) retroceder contra; dar un culatazo a *o* en; recular contra; *Amer.* patear. **3,** (force, as one's way, by kicking) abrir a patadas. **—*n.* 1,** (blow with the foot) patada; puntapié; coz. **2,** (recoil) culatazo; coz; *Amer.* patada. **3,** *colloq.* (complaint) queja; motivo de queja. **4,** *slang* (thrill) gusto; placer. **—kick around** (*o* **about**) **1,** (treat roughly) maltratar; castigar; patear. **2,** (move about) ir de aquí para allí; vagar. **3,** (think about; discuss) considerar; discutir. **—kick back, 1,** *colloq.* (recoil unexpectedly) rebotar; dar de rechazo. **2,** *slang* (give back, as part of money received) devolver. **—kick in,** *slang* **1,** (pay, as one's share) pagar; pagar a escote. **2,** (die) estirar la pata; morirse. **—kick off, 1,** (put a football into play) hacer el saque. **2,** *slang* (die) estirar la pata; morirse. **—kick up, 1,** (raise by kicking) levantar a puntapiés *o* patadas. **2,** *slang* (stir up, as trouble) armar (un bochinche). **3,** *slang* (flare up) reventar.
kickback *n.* **1,** *colloq.* (reaction) coz; reacción violenta. **2,** *slang* (return, as of money from one's earnings) devolución.
kid (kɪd) *n.* **1,** (young goat) cabrito. **2,** (leather) cabritilla. **3,** *colloq.* (child) niño; chiquillo; muchacho. **4,** *slang* (hoax) broma; burla. **—*adj.* 1,** (made of kidskin) de cabritilla. **2,** *colloq.* (younger) menor; más joven. **—*v.t.*** [**kidded, kidding**] *slang* **1,** (deceive; fool) engañar; embaucar. **2,** (tease) reírse de; tomar el pelo a; chacotear con. **—*v.i.*** bromear; chancear; chacotear.
kidnap (ˈkɪd·næp) *v.t.* secuestrar; raptar. **—kidnaper,** *n.* secuestrador; raptor. **—kidnaping,** *n.* secuestro; rapto.
kidney (ˈkɪd·ni) *n.* riñón. **—kidney bean,** judía; habichuela; frijol; fréjol; *So.Amer.* poroto.
kidskin *n.* cabritilla. **—*adj.*** de cabritilla.
kill (kɪl) *v.t.* **1,** (slay) matar. **2,** (put out; turn off) apagar; matar. **3,** (put an end to; ruin) destrozar; arruinar. **4,** (spend, as time) pasar; perder; matar. **5,** (veto; defeat) vetar; derrotar. **6,** (suppress; cancel) suprimir; cancelar. **—*n.* 1,** (act of killing) matanza. **2,** (animal or animals killed) caza; piezas (*pl.*). **—be in at the kill,** estar presente en el momento crítico; ser testigo presencial.
killer (ˈkɪl·ər) *n.* asesino.
killing (ˈkɪl·ɪŋ) *adj.* **1,** (deadly)

mortal. **2,** (exhausting; fatiguing) agotador; extenuante; matador. **3,** *colloq.* (very comical) de morirse de risa; muy divertido. **4,** *colloq.* (very attractive) guapísimo. —*n.* **1,** (slaughter) matanza. **2,** (murder) asesinato. **3,** *colloq.* (quick profit) golpe; negocio redondo.

killjoy ('kɪl,dʒɔi) *n.* aguafiestas.

kiln (kɪl) *n.* horno. —*v.t.* cocer *o* secar al horno.

kilo- (kɪl·ə) *prefijo* kilo-; mil: *kilogram,* kilogramo.

kilocycle *n.* kilociclo.

kilogram *n.* kilogramo.

kiloliter *n.* kilolitro.

kilometer ('kɪl·ə,mi·tər, kɪ'lam·ə·tər) *n.* kilómetro. —**kilometric** (,kɪl·ə'mɛt·rɪk) *adj.* kilométrico.

kilowatt *n.* kilovatio.

kilt (kɪlt) *n.* falda escocesa.

kilter ('kɪl·tər) *n., en* **in** *o* **out of kilter,** en *o* fuera de quicio; en buena (*o* mala) condición.

kimono (kə'mo·nə) *n.* quimono; kimono.

kin (kɪn) *n.* **1,** (family; relatives) parientes; familia; parentela. **2,** (family relationship) parentesco. —*adj.* emparentado —**of kin,** emparentado; pariente.

-kin (kɪn) *sufijo, formando diminutivos: lambkin,* corderito.

kind (kaind) *n.* clase. —*adj.* **1,** (gentle; friendly) bondadoso; bueno; benévolo. **2,** (cordial) cordial. —**be kind enough to; be so kind as to,** tener la bondad de. —**in kind, 1,** (in goods) en especie; en géneros. **2,** (in like manner) con la misma moneda; en la misma forma. —**kind of,** *colloq.* como; algo. —**of a kind, 1,** (alike) de la misma clase. **2,** (mediocre) mediocre; de poca monta.

kindergarten ('kɪn·dər,gar·tən) *n.* jardín de infancia; kindergarten.

kindhearted *adj.* bondadoso. —**kindheartedness,** *n.* bondad.

kindle ('kɪn·dəl) *v.t.* encender. —*v.i.* encenderse. —**kindling** (-dlɪŋ) *n.* leña menuda.

kindly ('kaind·li) *adj.* **1,** (kind; benevolent) bondadoso; benévolo; bueno. **2,** (agreeable; pleasant) agradable; cordial. —*adv.* **1,** (in a kind manner) con bondad; bondadosamente. **2,** (agreeably; cordially) agradablemente; cordialmente. **3,** (please) por favor; sírvase. —**kindliness,** *n.* bondad; benevolencia. —**take kindly to,** adaptarse a; aceptar; ver con buenos ojos.

kindness ('kaind·nəs) *n.* bondad.

kindred ('kɪn·drəd) *n.* = **kin.** —*adj.* **1,** (related by blood) emparentado. **2,** (like; similar) afín; parecido; similar.

kinescope ('kɪn·ə,skop) *n.* kinescopio.

kinetic (kɪ'nɛt·ɪk) *adj.* cinético. —**kinetics,** *n.* cinética.

kinfolk ('kɪn,fok) *n.pl.* parientes; familia (*sing.*); parentela (*sing.*).

king (kɪŋ) *n.* rey. —**kingdom,** *n.* reino.

kingfisher ('kɪŋ,fɪʃ·ər) *n.* martín pescador.

kinglet ('kɪŋ·lət) *n.* reyezuelo; régulo.

kingly ('kɪŋ·li) *n.* **1,** (royal) real. **2,** (resembling or befitting a king) majestuoso; de rey; digno de un rey. —**kingliness,** *n.* majestad.

kingpin *n.* **1,** *mech.* pivote de dirección; gorrón; espiga. **2,** *slang* (chief) jefe; el que manda.

kingship ('kɪŋ·ʃɪp) *n.* majestad.

king-size ('kɪŋ·saiz) *adj., colloq.* grande.

kink (kɪŋk) *n.* **1,** (crimp; crinkle) pliegue; torcedura. **2,** (twist; knot) vuelta; nudo. **3,** (curl) rizo; *So.Amer.* mota. **4,** (cramp; crick) calambre. **5,** (eccentricity) rareza. **6,** (difficulty) problema; dificultad. —*v.t. & i.* **1,** (crimp) doblar (se); plegar(se). **2,** (twist; knot) enmarañar(se); enredar(se). **3,** (curl) encrespar(se); rizar(se). —**kinky,** *adj.* ensortijado; rizado.

kinsfolk (kɪnz,fok) *n.pl.* = **kinfolk.**

kinship ('kɪn·ʃɪp) *n.* **1,** (family relationship) parentesco. **2,** (affinity) afinidad.

kinsman ('kɪnz·mən) *n.* [*pl.* **-men**] pariente. —**kinswoman,** *n.* [*pl.* **-women**] pariente.

kiosk (ki'ask) *n.* quiosco; kiosco.

kipper ('kɪp·ər) *v.t.* curar; ahumar. —*n.* pescado ahumado.

kismet ('kɪz·mɛt) *n.* suerte; destino; sino.

kiss (kɪs) *v.t. & i.* besar. —*n.* **1,** (caress) beso. **2,** (candy) dulce; confite. —**kisser,** *n., slang* trompa; hocico.

kit (kɪt) *n.* **1,** (equipment) equipo.

2, (case) estuche; caja. **3,** (kitten) gatito. **—kit and caboodle** (ˌkɪt·ən·kəˈbu·dəl) *colloq.* todo; todos.

kitchen (ˈkɪtʃ·ən) *n.* cocina. **—kitchenette** (-əˈnɛt) *n.* cocina pequeña.

kite (kait) *n.* **1,** (toy) cometa; *Amer.* volantín. **2,** *ornith.* milano.

kith (kɪθ) *n.* amigos (*pl.*)

kitten (ˈkɪt·ən) *n.* gatito; minino. **—kittenish,** *adj.* travieso; juguetón.

kitty (ˈkɪt·i) *n.* **1,** (stakes; pool) pozo; puestas; posta. **2,** (kitten) gatito; minino.

kiwi (ˈki·wi) *n.* kiwi.

kleptomania (ˌklɛp·təˈmei·ni·ə) *n.* cleptomanía. **—kleptomaniac** (-æk) *n.* cleptómano; cleptomaníaco.

knack (næk) *n.* aptitud; habilidad; destreza.

knapsack (ˈnæpˌsæk) *n.* mochila; morral.

knave (neiv) *n.* **1,** (rascal) bribón; pícaro. **2,** *cards* sota. **—knavery,** *n.* bribonería; bribonada. **—knavish,** *adj.* pícaro; picaresco; de bribón.

knead (niːd) *v.t.* amasar; sobar. **—kneading,** *n.* amasijo.

knee (niː) *n.* **1,** (part of the body, of a garment, etc.) rodilla. **2,** (bend) codo; curva. **—***v.t.* dar un rodillazo a; dar con la rodilla a.

kneecap *n.* **1,** *anat.* rótula. **2,** (knee protector) rodillera.

kneel (niːl) *v.i.* [*pret.* & *p.p.* **knelt** *o* **kneeled**] arrodillarse.

knell (nɛl) *n.* tañido; toque; doble. **—***v.t.* & *i.* doblar; tañer; tocar.

knelt (nɛlt) *v., pret.* & *p.p. de* **kneel.**

knew (nuː) *v., pret. de* **know.**

knickers (ˈnɪk·ərz) *n.pl.* pantalones bombachos; *Amer.* bombachas. *También,* **knickerbockers** (-ˌbak·ərz).

knickknack (ˈnɪkˌnæk) *n.* chuchería.

knife (naif) *n.* cuchillo; cuchilla. **—***v.t.* acuchillar; apuñalar.

knight (nait) *n.* caballero; *chess* caballo. **—***v.t.* armar *o* nombrar caballero. **—knightly,** *adj.* caballeresco.

knight-errant (ˈnaitˌɛr·ənt) *n.* [*pl.* **knights-errant**] caballero andante. **—knight-errantry,** *n.* caballería andante.

knighthood (ˈnait·hʊd) *n.* **1,** (rank of a knight) rango de caballero. **2,** (knights collectively) caballeros (*pl.*); caballería.

knit (nɪt) *v.t.* & *i* [**knitted, -ing**] **1,** (weave) tejer. **2,** (join closely) unir; ligar; trabar. **3,** (wrinkle; contract) arrugar; fruncir. **—***n.* tejido de punto. **—***adj.* de punto. **—knitting,** *n.* tejido de punto.

knitwear *n.* géneros de punto.

knob (naːb) *n.* **1,** (lump; protuberance) bulto; protuberancia. **2,** (handle of a door, drawer, etc.) pomo; *Amer.* perilla. **3,** (controlling or regulating device) botón. **4,** (hill; knoll) loma; mota.

knobby (ˈnab·i) *adj.* **1,** (covered with knobs) nudoso; con bultos *o* protuberancias. **2,** (like a knob) redondo; redondeado.

knock (nak) *v.t.* **1,** (hit; strike) golpear; pegar. **2,** [*usu.* **knock down** *o* **off**] (strike down) derribar; tumbar. **3,** *colloq.* (criticize) criticar; rebajar. **—***v.i.* **1,** (strike; pound) dar un golpe; dar golpes; golpear. **2,** (rap on the door) tocar *o* llamar a la puerta. **3,** (collide; clash) golpearse; chocar. **—***n.* **1,** (blow) golpe; porrazo. **2,** (rap, as on a door) golpe; llamada; toque. **3,** (thump; pounding) golpe; golpeteo. **4,** *colloq.* (censure) crítica; censura. **—knock about** *o* **around,** *colloq.* **1,** (wander about; roam) vagar; andar. **2,** (treat roughly) golpear; maltratar. **—knock down, 1,** (dismount; take apart) desmontar; desarmar. **2,** (sell, as at auction) rematar; adjudicar (en subasta). **—knock off, 1,** *colloq.* (stop working) dejar *o* parar de trabajar. **2,** *colloq.* (deduct) rebajar; descontar. **3,** *colloq.* (do; accomplish) hacer; acabar; terminar. **4,** *slang* (kill) matar; asesinar. **5,** *slang* (cease; desist from) dejar; acabar; parar. **—knock out, 1,** *boxing* noquear. **2,** (defeat; destroy) poner fuera de combate; aniquilar. **3,** *colloq.* (do; make) hacer. **—knock up,** *colloq.* (exhaust) cansar; extenuar.

knockabout *n.* balandro. **—***adj.* **1,** (rough; boisterous) vocinglero; escandaloso. **2,** (suitable for rough use) de *o* para uso diario.

knockdown *adj.* **1,** (overwhelming) terrible; violento. **2,** (easily taken apart) desarmable; desmontable. **—***n.* tumbo; golpe.

knocker ('nak·ər) *n.* aldaba; llamador.
knockkneed *adj.* patizambo.
knockout *n.* **1,** *boxing* knockout. **2,** *slang* (sensation) sensación. —*adj.* terrible; violento.
knoll (noːl) *n.* loma; mota.
knot (nat) *n.* **1,** (enlacement; entanglement) nudo. **2,** (lump; protuberance) bulto. **3,** (tough grain in wood) nudo. **4,** (tie; bond) lazo. **5,** *naut.* nudo. **6,** (muscular spasm) calambre. **7,** (bunch; cluster) puñado; grupo. —*v.t.* anudar. —*v.i.* anudarse; formar nudo *o* nudos.
knothole *n.* agujero (del nudo).
knotty ('nat·i) *adj.* **1,** (full of knots) nudoso; con nudos. **2,** (difficult) difícil; complicado.
knout (naut) *n.* knut.
know (noː) *v.t.* [**knew, known**] **1,** (be cognizant of; have knowledge of) saber; saber de. **2,** (be acquainted with; discern) conocer. —*v.i.* saber; estar enterado. —**in the know,** *colloq.* enterado; informado; *Amer.* interiorizado.
knowable ('no·ə·bəl) *adj.* conocible.
know-all *adj., colloq.* sabihondo. —*n., colloq.* sabelotodo. *También,* **know-it-all.**
know-how *n., colloq.* **1,** (knowledge) conocimiento. **2,** (skill) habilidad; destreza.
knowing ('kno·ɪŋ) *adj.* **1,** (well-informed) entendido; informado. **2,** (shrewd; understanding) ducho; astuto; inteligente. **3,** (deliberate; intentional) deliberado; intencional. —**knowingly,** *adv.* a sabiendas; con conocimiento de causa.
knowledge ('nal·ɪdʒ) *n.* conocimiento; saber. —**knowledgeable,** *adj., colloq.* inteligente; de conocimientos. —**to (the best of) one's knowledge,** al entender de uno; en cuanto uno sabe; por lo que uno sabe.
known (noːn) *v., p.p. de* **know.**
know-nothing *n. & adj.* ignorante.
knuckle ('nʌk·əl) *n.* **1,** (joint of the finger) nudillo. **2,** (animal joint used as food) pata; patita. **3,** (hinge) charnela. —**knuckle down, 1,** (work energetically) afanarse; esmerarse. **2,** [*también,* **knuckle under**] (submit) someterse; rendirse.
knurl (nʌɹl) *n.* **1,** (knot; knob) nudo. **2,** (milling, as on a coin) cordoncillo. —*v.t.* acordonar; cerreillar.
koala (ko'a·lə) *n.* koala.
kohlrabi ('kol,ra·bi) *n.* colinabo.
kopeck ('ko·pɛk) *n.* copec; kopek.
Koran (ko'raːn) *n.* Corán; Alcorán.
kosher ('ko·ʃər) *adj.* **1,** *relig.* hecho *o* preparado conforme a la ley dietética judía. **2,** *slang* (authentic) genuino: legítimo.
kowtow (ˌkau'tau) *v.i.* humillarse. —*n.* reverencia.
kraal (kraːl) *n.* **1,** (So. Afr. village) craal. **2,** (cattle pen) redil; corral.
Kremlin ('krɛm·lɪn) *n.* kremlin.
krona ('kro·nə) *n.* moneda sueca; corona.
krone ('kro·nə) *n.* moneda de varios países; corona.
krypton ('krɪp·tan) *n.* criptón.
kulak (ku'lak) *n.* kulak.

L

L, l (ɛl) duodécima letra del alfabeto inglés.
la (laː) *n., music* la. —*interj.* ¡ah!; ¡oh!; ¡mira!
lab (læb) *n., colloq.* laboratorio.
label ('lei·bəl) *n.* **1,** (tag; tab) etiqueta; marbete. **2,** (appellation; name) apelativo; nombre; clasificación; (*usu. despectivo*) mote. —*v.t.* **1,** (attach a label to) poner etiqueta *o* marbete a. **2,** (classify as; call) clasificar de *o* como; llamar; motejar.
labial ('lei·bi·əl) *adj.* labial.
labor *también,* **labour** (lei·bər) *n.* **1,** (work; toil) trabajo; labor. **2,** (piece of work; task) labor; trabajo; faena. **3,** (working class) trabajo. **4,** (manual work or workers) mano de obra. **5,** (childbirth) parto. —*v.i.* **1,** (work; toil) trabajar; laborar. **2,** (strive; work hard) laborar; pujar; esforzarse. **3,** (undergo childbirth) estar de parto. —*v.t.* insistir demasiado en *o* sobre; elaborar mucho.

laboratory ('læb·rə·tor·i) *n.* laboratorio.
labored ('lei·bərd) *adj.* **1,** (elaborate) muy elaborado; complicado; rebuscado. **2,** (requiring great effort) trabajoso; pesado; penoso.
laborer ('lei·bər·ər) *n.* trabajador; obrero.
laborious (lə'bor·i·əs) *adj.* laborioso. —**laboriousness,** *n.* laboriosidad.
Laborite ('lei·bər,ait) *n.* laborista. —**Labor party,** partido laborista.
labor union sindicato; gremio; unión de trabajadores.
laburnum (lə'bʌɹ·nəm) *n.* laburno; codeso.
labyrinth ('læb·ə·rɪnθ) *n.* laberinto. —**labyrinthine** (-'rɪn·θɪn) *adj.* laberíntico.
lac (læk) *n.* laca.
lace (leis) *n.* **1,** (openwork fabric) encaje. **2,** (ornamental braid) galón. **3,** (cord; fastening) cordón; lazo; atadura. —*v.t.* **1,** (bind; tie) atar; anudar; amarrar. **2,** (entwine) enlazar; entrelazar. **3,** *colloq.* (thrash; whip) azotar; dar de azotes. **4,** (put liquor in; spike) añadir licor a. —**lace into,** *colloq.* arremeter contra; atacar.
lacerate ('læs·ə,reit) *v.t.* lacerar. —**laceration,** *n.* laceración.
lacework *n.* **1,** (lace) encaje. **2,** (fretwork; openwork) calado.
lachrymal *también,* **lacrimal** ('læk·rə·məl) *adj.* lacrimal; *anat.* lagrimal.
lachrymose ('læk·rə,mos) *adj.* lacrimoso; lagrimoso.
lacing ('lei·sɪŋ) *n.* **1,** (act of fastening) atadura. **2,** (cord; binding) cordón; lazo. **3,** *colloq.* (thrashing) azotaina; zurra. **4,** *colloq.* (scolding) reprimenda. **5,** (ornamental braid) galón.
lack (læk) *n.* **1,** (shortage) falta; escasez. **2,** (absence) falta; carencia. **3,** (what is needed) lo que falta; falta. —*v.t.* **1,** (have not enough; need) no tener suficiente; necesitar. **2,** (be without; have no) carecer de; no tener. —*v.i.* **1,** (be wanting or missing) faltar; hacer falta; no haber. **2,** (be short; be in need) necesitar; tener necesidad. **3,** (be in short supply) escasear.
lackadaisical (,læk·ə'dei·zi·kəl) *adj.* lánguido; indiferente; apático.
lackey ('læk·i) *n.* lacayo.
lackluster ('læk,lʌs·tər) *adj.* insípido; insulso.
laconic (lə'kan·ɪk) *adj.* lacónico.
lacquer ('læk·ər) *n.* laca; barniz. —*v.t.* laquear; barnizar.
lacrosse (lə'krɔs) *n.* juego de pelota canadiense; lacrosse.
lactation (læk'tei·ʃən) *n.* lactación; lactancia.
lacteal ('læk·ti·əl) *adj.* lácteo.
lactic ('læk·tɪk) *adj.* láctico.
lacto- (læk·to) *también,* **lacti-** (-tɪ) *prefijo* lacto-; lacti-; leche: *lactometer,* lactómetro; *lactiferous,* lactífero.
lactose ('læk,tos) *n.* lactosa; lactina.
lacuna (lə'kju·nə) *n.* laguna.
lacy ('lei·si) *adj.* de *o* como encaje.
lad (læd) *n.* muchacho; niño; mozo.
ladder ('læd·ər) *n.* **1,** (frame with rungs) escalera; escalera de mano. **2,** (way, as to fame) escalones (*pl.*); escala. **3,** (run, as in hose) carrera.
laddie ('læd·i) *n., dim. de* **lad.**
lade (leid) *v.t.* **1,** (load) cargar; *fig.* abrumar. **2,** (ladle) servir *o* sacar con cucharón. **3,** (bail) achicar.
laden ('lei·dən) *v., p.p. de* **lade.**
lading ('lei·dɪŋ) *n.* carga. —**bill of lading,** conocimiento *o* manifiesto de embarque.
ladle ('lei·dəl) *n.* cucharón; cazo. —*v.t.* servir *o* sacar con cucharón.
lady ('lei·di) *n.* **1,** (any woman) mujer. **2,** (woman of good breeding or standing) dama; señora. **3,** (title of nobility or respect) dama. **4,** (wife) señora; esposa. **5,** (mistress) señora. —*adj.* mujer; hembra. —**Our Lady,** Nuestra Señora.
ladybug, *n.* mariquita. *También,* **ladybird.**
ladyfinger *n.* melindre.
lady in waiting azafata; camarera.
lady-killer *n., slang* tenorio; don Juan.
ladylike ('lei·di,laik) *adj.* femenino; delicado.
ladylove *n.* novia; amada; amor.
ladyship ('lei·di,ʃɪp) *n.* señoría.
lag (læg) *v.i.* atrasarse; retrasarse. —*n.* atraso; retraso.
lager ('la·gər) *n.* cerveza reposada.
laggard ('læg·ərd) *adj.* moroso;

lento; perezoso. —*n.* posma; perezoso.
lagoon (lə'gu:n) *n.* laguna.
laic ('lei·ɪk) *adj.* laico.
laid (leid) *v., pret. & p.p de* **lay.**
lain (lein) *v., p.p. de* **lie.**
lair (le:r) *n.* cubil; guarida.
laity ('lei·ə·ti) *n.* **1,** (laymen) seglares (*pl.*). **2,** (lay brothers) legos (*pl.*). **3,** (non-professionals) legos (*pl.*).
lake (leik) *n.* lago.
lam (læm) *v.t.* [**lammed, lamming**] *slang* azotar; pegar. —*v.i., slang* escapar; largarse. —**on the lam,** *slang* huyendo; escapando. —**take it on the lam,** *slang* poner pies en polvorosa.
lama ('la·mə) *n.* lama. —**Lamaism,** *n.* lamaísmo. —**Lamaist,** *n. & adj.* lamaísta. —**lamasery** (-sɛr·i) *n.* lamasería.
lamb (læm) *n.* cordero. —**lambkin,** *n.* corderito. —**lambskin,** *n.* piel de cordero.
lambaste (læm'beist) *v.t., slang* zurrar; dar una zurra a; vapulear.
lame (leim) *adj.* **1,** (crippled) lisiado; cojo. **2,** (ineffectual) débil; ineficaz; flaco. —*v.t.* lisiar; volver cojo. —**lame duck,** *colloq.* **1,** (ineffectual person) pelma; inútil. **2,** *polit.* funcionario sin influencia por estar próximo su reemplazo.
lamé (læ'mei) *n.* lamé; lama.
lameness ('leim·nəs) *n.* **1,** (disability) cojera. **2,** (weakness) debilidad; ineficacia.
lament (lə'mɛnt) *v.t. & i.* lamentar. —*n.* lamento. —**lamentable** ('læm·ən·tə·bəl) *adj.* lamentable. —**lamentation** (ˌlæm·ən'tei·ʃən) *n.* lamentación.
laminate ('læm·əˌneit) *v.t.* laminar. —*adj.* (-nət) laminado. —**lamination,** *n.* laminado; laminación.
lamp (læmp) *n.* **1,** (lighting device) lámpara. **2,** *slang, usu. pl.* (eyes) ojos; faroles.
lampblack *n.* negro de humo.
lampoon (læm'pu:n) *n.* pasquín; sátira. —*v.t.* pasquinar; satirizar.
lampost *n.* poste de farol.
lamprey ('læm·pri) *n.* lamprea.
lampshade *n.* pantalla de lámpara.
lance (læns) *n.* lanza; *surg.* lanceta. —*v.t.* lancear; *surg.* abrir con lanceta; dar una lancetada. —**lancer,** *n.* lancero.
lancet ('læn·sɪt) *n.* lanceta.
land (lænd) *n.* tierra. —*v.t.* **1,** (put ashore) desembarcar. **2,** (take, as to a destination) llevar (a); dejar (en). **3,** (put or cause to get into) meter; poner de patitas en. **4,** (set down, as an aircraft) hacer aterrizar. **5,** (catch, as a fish) coger; pescar. **6,** *colloq.* (get; secure) obtener; conseguir. **7,** *colloq.* (deliver, as a blow) dar; asestar. —*v.i.* **1,** (go ashore) desembarcar. **2,** (arrive; reach port) llegar; arribar. **3,** *colloq.* (end up; wind up) terminar; encontrarse; ir a parar. **4,** (alight; come to rest) aterrizar.
landed ('læn·dɪd) *adj.* **1,** (owning land) latifundista; terrateniente. **2,** (consisting of land) de tierras; inmueble.
landfall *n.* **1,** (sight of land) recalada; vista de tierra. **2,** (land sighted) tierra avistada. **3,** (arrival in port) arribo; llegada. **4,** (alighting) aterrizaje.
landholder *n.* terrateniente.
landing ('læn·dɪŋ) *n.* **1,** (debarkation) desembarco; desembarque. **2,** (place for unloading or loading) embarcadero. **3,** (platform, as on stairs) descanso; descansillo. **4,** (act of alighting) aterrizaje. —**landing gear,** tren de aterrizaje. —**landing strip,** pista de aterrizaje.
landlady *n.* **1,** (landowner) propietaria; dueña; *Amer.* patrona. **2,** (owner of a hotel, rooming house, etc.) patrona; dueña.
landlocked *adj.* sin acceso al mar.
landlord *n.* **1,** (landowner) propietario; dueño; *Amer.* patrón. **2,** (owner of a hotel, rooming house, etc.) patrón; dueño.
landlubber ('lændˌlʌb·ər) *n.* marinero de agua dulce.
landmark *n.* **1,** (boundary mark; milestone) hito; mojón. **2,** (conspicuous object on land) marca; guía. **3,** (point of interest) sitio destacado; sitio de interés. **4,** (memorable event) hito; momento culminante.
landowner *n.* terrateniente; propietario.
landscape ('lændˌskeip) *n.* paisaje. —*v.t. & i.* arreglar como jardín; arreglar el paisaje (de).
landslide *n.* avalancha; alud.
lane (lein) *n.* **1,** (byroad) callejón; callejuela. **2,** (path; opening) paso; senda; vereda. **3,** *naut.; aero.* (fixed route) derrotero; ruta. **4,**

(designated path, as for traffic) vía; pista; *Amer.* carril.
language ('læŋ·gwɪdʒ) *n.* **1,** (idiom; tongue) idioma; lengua. **2,** (form or manner of expression) lenguaje.
languid ('læŋ·gwɪd) *adj.* lánguido. —**languidness,** *n.* languidez.
languish ('læŋ·gwɪʃ) *v.i.* languidecer. —**languishment,** *n.* languidecimiento.
languor ('læŋ·gər) *n.* languidez. —**languorous,** *adj.* lánguido.
lank (læŋk) *adj.* **1,** (lean; gaunt) delgado; flaco; enjuto. **2,** (straight, as hair) lacio. —**lanky,** *adj.* larguirucho; desgarbado.
lanolin ('læn·ə·lɪn) *n.* lanolina.
lantern ('læn·tərn) *n.* **1,** (lamp; globe) linterna; farol. **2,** (skylight) tragaluz. —**lantern-jawed,** *adj.* chupado de cara.
lanthanum ('læn·θə·nəm) *n.* lantano.
lanyard *también,* **laniard** ('læn·jərd) *n.* trinca.
lap (læp) *n.* **1,** (portion between waist and knees) rodillas (*pl.*); regazo; *W.I.* falda. **2.** (hollow; fold) regazo; seno. **3,** (flap, as of clothing) falda; faldón; faldillas (*pl.*). **4,** (overlap) traslapo; solapo. **5,** (single turn; circuit) vuelta. **6,** (lick) lengüetada. **7,** (sound of lapping) golpeteo; batido. —*v.t.* **1,** (fold over or about; wind) envolver; dar una vuelta *o* vueltas a. **2,** (wrap; enfold) envolver. **3,** (cause to overlap) traslapar; solapar. **4,** (get a turn ahead of) llevar una vuelta de ventaja a. **5,** (polish; grind) pulir; labrar. **6,** (wash against, as waves) lamer. —*v.i.* **1,** (overlap) traslaparse; solaparse. **2,** (extend beyond) extenderse en parte; incluir parcialmente; proyectarse. —**lap dog,** perro faldero. —**lap up, 1,** (lick up, as food) tomar *o* comer a lengüetadas. **2,** *colloq.* (eat or drink greedily) comer a dos carrillos; engullir; tragar de golpe. **3,** *colloq.* (absorb eagerly) absorber; embeber.
lapel (lə'pɛl) *n.* solapa.
lapidary ('læp·ə·dɛr·i) *n.* & *adj.* lapidario.
lapin ('læp·ɪn) *n.* conejo; piel de conejo.
lapis lazuli ('læp·ɪs'læz·ju,li) lapislázuli.
Lapp (læp) *n.* & *adj.* lapón.
lappet (læp·ɪt) *n.* **1,** (flap) faldillas (*pl.*); faldón. **2,** (wattle) papo; carnosidad. **3,** (lobe of the ear) lóbulo.
lapse (læps) *n.* lapso; *comm.; law* caducidad. —*v.i.* **1,** (slip; fall) caer; recaer. **2,** (pass away; elapse) pasar; correr; transcurrir. **3,** (retrogress) retroceder; recaer. **4,** *comm.; law* (expire) caducar; vencer; vencerse.
larboard ('lar·bərd) *n.* babor. —*adj.* de babor. —*adv.* a babor.
larceny ('lar·sə·ni) *n.* robo; hurto. —**larcenist,** *n.* ladrón. —**larcenous,** *adj.* ladrón; de ladrón.
larch (lartʃ) *n.* alerce.
lard (lard) *n.* manteca. —*v.t.* **1,** (grease) poner manteca a *o* en. **2,** (stuff with bacon strips) mechar. **3,** (garnish) adornar.
larder ('lar·dər) *n.* despensa.
large (lardʒ) *adj.* grande. —**largeness,** *n.* extensión; amplitud. —**at large, 1,** (not confined) libre; en libertad. **2,** (fully) extensamente; sin limitación. **3,** *polit.* general; de representación general.
largely ('lardʒ·li) *adv.* **1,** (in great amount) grandemente; ampliamente; mucho. **2,** (mainly) por la mayor parte; en su mayor parte; en gran parte.
largess ('lar·dʒɛs) *n.* largueza.
largo ('lar·go) *adj.* & *adv.* largo.
lariat ('lær·i·ət) *n.* reata.
lark (lark) *n.* **1,** (bird) alondra. **2,** *colloq.* (frolic) juerga; parranda. —*v.i.* ir de parranda *o* juerga.
larkspur ('lark,spʌɹ) *n.* espuela de caballero.
larva ('lar·və) *n.* [*pl.* **larvae** (-vi)] larva. —**larval,** *adj.* larval.
larynx ('lær·ɪŋks) *n.* laringe. —**laryngeal** (lə'rɪn·dʒi·əl) *adj.* laríngeo. —**laryngitis** (,lær·ɪn'dʒai·tɪs) *n.* laringitis.
lascivious (lə'sɪv·i·əs) *adj.* lascivo. —**lasciviousness,** lascivia.
lash (læʃ) *n.* **1,** (whip) látigo. **2,** (blow with a whip) latigazo. **3,** *fig.* (censure; sarcasm) latigazo. **4,** (eyelash) pestaña. —*v.t.* **1,** (flog) azotar. **2,** (beat or dash against) golpear. **3,** (move or switch sharply) sacudir; agitar. **4,** (assail) fustigar. **5,** (tie) atar; amarrar. —*v.i.* [*usu.* **lash out**] arremeter; embestir; desatarse.
lashing ('læʃ·ɪŋ) *n.* **1,** (bind-

ing) atadura; *naut.* amarra. **2,** (strong rebuke) invectiva. **3,** (beating) latigazos (*pl.*); azotes (*pl.*).

lass (læs) *n.* moza; muchacha; niña. *También,* **lassie.**

lassitude ('læs·ɪ·tjud) *n.* lasitud.

lasso ('læs·o) *n.* lazo. —*v.t.* lazar.

last (læst) *v.i.* **1,** (endure) durar. **2,** (continue) continuar; seguir. —*n.* **1,** (person or thing coming latest or at the end) el, la *o* lo último; el fin. **2,** (shoe mold) horma. —*adj.* **1,** (latest; hindmost; final) último. **2,** (immediately before the present) pasado. —*adv.* **1,** (after all others; at the end) al final; a lo último. **2,** (finally) finalmente. **3,** (on the most recent occasion) por última vez; la última vez. —**lasting,** *adj.* duradero; permanente. —**at last,** al fin; por fin. —**before (the) last, 1,** (before the most recent) antepasado. **2,** (just preceding the endmost) penúltimo. —**breathe one's last,** expirar; exhalar el último suspiro. —**last but not least,** lo último pero no menos importante. —**last name,** apellido. —**last night,** anoche. —**last quarter,** cuarto menguante. —**last straw,** el colmo. —**last word,** *colloq.* lo último. —**next to (the) last,** penúltimo. —**of the last importance,** trascendental; de máxima importancia.

lastly ('læst·li) *adv.* finalmente; por último.

latch (lætʃ) *n.* pestillo; aldaba. —*v.t.* echar *o* correr el pestillo *o* aldaba a. —**latch on to,** *slang* agarrar; coger.

late (leit) *adj.* **1,** (tardy; delayed) retrasado; atrasado. **2,** (protracted in time) prolongado; que dura hasta tarde. **3,** (coming near the end) de fines (de); de finales (de). **4,** (recent) último; reciente. **5,** (occurring after the expected time) tardío. **6,** (occurring at the last moment) de último momento; postrero. **7,** (former) ex; que ha sido. **8,** (bygone) pasado. **9,** (deceased) difunto. **10,** (advanced, as the hour) avanzado; entrado. —*adv.* **1,** (tardily) tarde. **2,** (toward the end of a stated period of time) a fines (de); en las últimas horas (de); tarde (en). **3,** (at or until an advanced hour) tarde; hasta tarde; a *o* hasta hora avanzada. **4,** = **lately.** —**lately,** *adv.* recientemente; últimamente; poco ha. —**later,** *adv.* luego; más tarde. —**be late, 1,** (of the hour) ser tarde. **2,** (of arrival) llegar tarde; llegar con atraso *o* retraso; estar atrasado *o* retrasado. —**of late,** recientemente; últimamente.

lateen sail (lə'tiːn) vela latina.

lateness ('leit·nəs) *n.* **1,** (delay) atraso; retraso. **2,** (advanced time) lo avanzado. **3,** (tardiness) lo tardío.

latent ('lei·tənt) *adj.* latente. —**latency,** *n.* lo latente; estado latente.

-later (lə·tər) *sufijo* -latra; adorador: *idolater,* idólatra.

lateral ('læt·ər·əl) *adj.* lateral.

latex ('lei·tɛks) *n.* látex.

lath (læθ) *n.* listón. —*v.t.* poner listones a *o* en. —**lathing,** *n.* enlistonado; listonado.

lathe (leið) *n.* torno. —*v.t.* tornear.

lather ('læð·ər) *n.* espuma. —*v.t.* **1,** (cover with foam) enjabonar; jabonar. **2,** (cause to foam) hacer espumar. **3,** *collog.* (flog) zurrar; dar una zurra. —**lathery,** *adj.* espumoso.

lathwork ('læθˌwʌɹk) *n.* enlistonado; listonado.

Latin ('læt·ɪn) *n.* **1,** (language) latín. **2,** (person) latino. —*adj.* latino. —**Latinize,** *v.t. & i.* latinizar.

Latin-American *adj. & n.* latinoamericano.

latitude ('læt·ɪ·tjud) *n.* latitud. —**latitudinal** (-'tju·dɪ·nəl) *adj.* latitudinal.

latrine (lə'triːn) *n.* letrina.

-latry (lə·tri) *sufijo* -latría; adoración: *idolatry,* idolatría.

latter ('læt·ər) *adj.* **1,** (last mentioned of two) último; segundo. **2,** (more recent) más reciente. **3,** (near or nearer to the end) último; final. —**the former . . . the latter,** aquél . . . éste.

latter-day *adj.* actual; de hoy; moderno. —**Latter-day Saints,** mormones.

latterly ('læt·ər·li) *adv.* **1,** (recently) últimamente; recientemente. **2,** (toward the end) hacia el fin; a lo último.

lattice ('læt·ɪs) *n.* enrejado; rejilla; celosía. —*v.t.* enrejar con listones; poner celosías a; hacer un enrejado de.

laud (lɔːd) *v.t.* alabar; elogiar.

—**laudable,** *adj.* laudable. —**laudatory** (-ə·tor·i) *adj.* laudatorio.
laudanum ('lɔ·də·nəm) *n.* láudano.
laugh (læf) *v.i.* reír; reírse. —*v.t.* reírse de; mover con risa; sacar a risotadas; decir *o* expresar riendo. —*n.* risa. —**laughable,** *adj.* risible. —**laugh at,** reírse de. —**laughing gas,** gas hilarante.
laughingstock *n.* hazmerreír.
laughter ('læf·tər) *n.* risa; risas.
launch (lɔntʃ) *v.t.* **1,** (set afloat) botar. **2,** (begin) iniciar; inaugurar. **3,** (hurl) lanzar; arrojar. —*v.i.* lanzarse. —*n.* lancha. —**launching,** *n.* botadura.
launder ('lɔn·dər) *v.t.* & *i.* lavar. —**launderer,** *n.* lavandero. —**laundress** (-drɪs) *n.* lavandera.
laundry ('lɔn·dri) *n.* **1,** (establishment) lavandería. **2,** (what is laundered) lavado.
laureate ('lɔ·ri·ət) *adj.* & *n.* laureado.
laurel ('lar·əl) *n.* laurel.
lava ('la·və) *n.* lava.
lavatory ('læv·ə·tor·i) *n.* lavabo; excusado; retrete.
lave (leiv) *v.t.* lavar; bañar. —*v.i.* lavarse; bañarse.
lavender ('læv·ən·dər) *n.* **1,** *bot.* espliego; lavanda. **2,** (color; scent) lavanda.
lavish ('læv·ɪʃ) *adj.* pródigo; suntuoso. —*v.t.* prodigar. —**lavishness,** *n.* prodigalidad; suntuosidad.
law (lɔː) *n.* **1,** (rule; set of rules) ley. **2,** (jurisprudence) derecho; jurisprudencia. **3,** *colloq.* (police) policía. —**law-abiding,** *adj.* que respeta la ley. —**lawful,** *adj.* legal; lícito. —**lawfulness,** *n.* legalidad. —**go to law,** ir a juicio; litigar.
lawless ('lɔ·ləs) *adj.* **1,** (contrary to law) ilegal. **2,** (without law; defiant of law) sin ley. —**lawlessness,** *n.* desorden.
lawmaker *n.* legislador.
lawn (lɔːn) *n.* **1,** (grass) césped. **2,** (fabric) linón.
lawn mower segadora.
lawsuit *n.* juicio; pleito; demanda.
lawyer ('lɔi·jər) *n.* abogado; *Amer.* licenciado.
lax (læks) *adj.* **1,** (loose; relaxed) laxo; flojo. **2,** (careless; remiss) descuidado. **3,** (not strict) relajado. **4,** (vague) vago; indeterminado. —**laxity; laxness,** *n.* laxitud.
laxative ('læk·sə·tɪv) *n.* & *adj.* laxante; purgante.
lay (lei) *v.t.* [*pret.* & *p.p* **laid**] **1,** (put; set) poner. **2,** (allay; appease) calmar; apaciguar. **3,** (overcome) vencer; superar. **4,** (devise) hacer; trazar. **5,** (locate; situate) situar. **6,** (bet) apostar. **7,** (impute; ascribe) imputar; atribuir. —*v.i.* poner (huevos). —*v., pret. de* **lie.** —*n.* **1,** (arrangement) disposición; situación. **2,** (poem; song) lay. —*adj.* **1,** (secular) secular; seglar. **2,** (non-clerical; non-professional) lego. —**lay about (one),** dar golpes a diestra y siniestra. —**lay aside, away** *o* **by,** poner a un lado; guardar. —**lay claim to,** reclamar. —**lay down, 1,** (place in a reclining position) acostar; recostar. **2,** (give up, as one's life) dar *u* ofrecer (la vida). **3,** (surrender) rendir; entregar. **4,** (set; establish) fijar; establecer. —**lay in,** almacenar; guardar. —**lay off, 1,** (take off) quitar; quitarse. **2,** (discharge) despedir. **3,** (mark off) marcar. **4,** (cease; desist) parar; dejar. —**lay oneself open,** arriesgarse; exponerse. —**lay out, 1,** (arrange) arreglar; disponer. **2,** (spend) gastar. **3,** (advance, as funds) adelantar. —**lay over,** hacer alto; detenerse. —**lay the blame,** culpar; echar la culpa. —**lay up, 1,** (store up) amontonar; almacenar. **2,** (make inactive) inutilizar. **3,** (incapacitate) inhabilitar; incapacitar.
layer ('lei·ər) *n.* **1,** (thickness of some material laid on another) capa. **2,** (stratum) estrato; cama. **3,** (egg-producing fowl) ave ponedora.
layette (lei'ɛt) *n.* canastilla; ajuar de niño.
layman ('lei·mən) *n.* **1,** (nonprofessional) lego. **2,** (non-clerical) seglar.
layoff *n.* **1,** (suspension of employment) suspensión; despido. **2,** (period of suspension) cesantía.
layout *n.* **1,** (plan) plan. **2,** (arrangement) arreglo; disposición. **3,** (equipment) equipo; aparatos (*pl.*). **4,** (format) formato; presentación.
laze (leiz) *v.i.* holgazanear; flojear.
lazy ('lei·zi) *adj.* perezoso; flojo. —**laziness,** *n.* pereza; flojedad; flojera. —**lazybones,** *n.* holgazán.

leach (litʃ) *v.t.* & *i.* filtrar; pasar; colar.

lead (lɛd) *n.* **1,** (metal, or something made of it) plomo. **2,** (graphite) grafito; (*of a pencil*) mina. **3,** *print.* regleta. **4,** *naut.* sonda. —*v.t.* **1,** (fill or line with lead) emplomar. **2,** *print.* regletear. **3,** (weight with lead) cargar con pesas de plomo. —*adj.* de plomo.

lead (liːd) *v.t.* & *i.* [*pret.* & *p.p* **led**] **1,** (guide) guiar. **2,** (conduct) llevar; conducir. **3,** (direct; control) dirigir. **4,** (command) mandar. —*v.t.* **1,** (go or be first in; head) encabezar. **2,** *cards* salir con. —*v.i.* **1,** (go or be first) ir *o* ser primero; preceder. **2,** *en* **lead to** (be the cause of) llevar a; resultar en; traer como consecuencia. **3,** *cards* ser mano; salir. **4,** *boxing* salir. —*n.* **1,** (role of a leader) posición de mando; dirección. **2,** (initiative) iniciativa. **3,** (example) ejemplo. **4,** (first or front place) delantera. **5,** (distance ahead) ventaja; delantera. **6,** (clue) indicio; pista. **7,** (indication; suggestion) indicación; dato. **8,** *cards* salida. **9,** *boxing* golpe. **10,** *electricity* conductor. **11,** *theat.* papel principal. **12,** *journalism* primer párrafo. —*adj.* primero; principal. —**lead off** *o* **out,** comenzar; empezar; iniciar. —**lead on, 1,** (go ahead) seguir adelante; continuar. **2,** (lure) dar cuerda a; embelecar. —**lead the way,** mostrar el camino; tomar la delantera. —**lead up to,** conducir *o* llevar a.

leaden ('lɛd·ən) *adj.* **1,** (made of lead) de plomo. **2,** (color) plomizo. **3,** (heavy) pesado; de *o* como plomo.

leader ('li·dər) *n.* **1,** (chief) jefe; líder. **2,** (ringleader) cabecilla. **3,** (director) director. **4,** (editorial) artículo de fondo.

leadership ('li·dər·ʃɪp) *n.* **1,** (position or function of a leader) dirección; jefatura; mando. **2,** (ability to lead) cualidades de mando.

leading lady primera dama; primera actriz. —**leading man,** galán; primer actor.

leaf (lif) *n.* [*pl.* **leaves**] hoja. —*v.i.* echar hojas. —*v.t.* [*también,* **leaf through**] hojear. —**leafage,** *n.* follaje. —**leafy,** *adj.* frondoso; con hojas.

leaflet ('lif·lət) *n.* volante; folleto.

league (liːg) *n.* **1,** (alliance) liga. **2,** (distance) legua. —*v.t.* & *i.* ligar(se); unir(se).

leak (lik) *n.* gotera; escape; *naut.* vía de agua. —*v.i.* gotear; escaparse; rezumar; (*esp. of news*) trascender; *naut.* hacer agua. —**leakage,** *n.* goteo; escape; *comm.* merma. —**leaky,** *adj.* con goteras *o* escapes; llovedizo; *naut.* que hace agua.

lean (liːn) *v.i.* **1,** (incline) inclinarse. **2,** (rest on) descansar; apoyarse. —*v.t.* apoyar. —*n.* **1,** (inclination) inclinación. **2,** (lean part of meat) molla. —*adj.* **1,** (thin) flaco; magro. **2,** (scanty) pobre. **3,** (not fatty, as meat) magro. —**leaning,** *adj.* inclinado. —*n.* inclinación; tendencia. —**lean over backward,** exagerar la imparcialidad; esmerarse hasta la exageración.

leanness ('lin·nəs) *n.* **1,** (thinness) magrez; flacura. **2,** (scarcity) pobreza.

lean-to ('lin,tu) *n.* [*pl.* **-to**] colgadizo.

leap (lip) *v.i.* brincar; saltar. —*v.t.* saltar. —*n.* salto. —**leap year,** año bisiesto.

leapfrog *n.* la una la mula.

learn (lʌɹn) *v.t.* & *i.* **1,** (acquire knowledge [of] or skill [in]) aprender. **2,** (become aware [of]) saber; enterarse (de). —**learned** ('lʌɹ·nɪd) *adj.* erudito. —**learner,** *n.* principiante; estudiante; aprendiz.

learning ('lʌɹ·nɪŋ) *n.* **1,** (acquiring knowledge or skill) estudios (*pl.*); el aprender. **2,** (erudition) erudición.

lease (lis) *v.t.* arrendar. —*n.* arrendamiento; arriendo. —**take** (*o* **get**) **a new lease on life,** volver a vivir.

leasehold *n.* arrendamiento; arriendo.

leash (liʃ) *n.* traílla. —*v.t.* sujetar con traílla.

least (list) *adj.* menor; mínimo. —*adv.* menos. —*n.* (lo) menos; (el) menor. —**at least,** al menos; por lo menos. —**not in the least,** de ningún modo; de ninguna manera.

leather ('lɛð·ər) *n.* cuero; piel. —*v.t.* forrar con cuero. —*adj.* [*también,* **leathern** (-ərn)] de cuero. —**leatherette** (-ɛt) *n.* cuero artifi-

cial; imitación cuero. —**leathery,** *adj.* como cuero.
leave (liːv) *v.t.* [*pret. & p.p* **left**] dejar. —*v.i.* irse; marcharse; salir. —*n.* permiso; licencia. —**leave off,** dejar (de); dejarse de. —**take leave,** despedirse.
leaven ('lɛv·ən) *n.* **1,** (dough) levadura. **2,** (stimulating influence) fermento. —*v.t.* fermentar. —**leavening,** *n.* fermento; levadura.
leaves (liːvz) *n., pl. de* **leaf.**
leave-taking *n.* despedida.
leavings ('li·vɪŋz) *n.pl.* restos; residuos.
lecher ('lɛtʃ·ər) *n.* libertino. —**lecherous,** *adj.* lascivo; lujurioso. —**lechery,** *n.* lascivia; lujuria.
lectern ('lɛk·tərn) *n.* atril.
lecture ('lɛk·tʃər) *n.* **1,** (discourse) conferencia; disertación. **2,** (reprimand) lección; reprensión. —*v.t. & i.* **1,** (teach; instruct) dar una conferencia; explicar. **2,** (scold) dar una lección; amonestar. —**lecturer,** *n.* conferenciante.
led (lɛd) *v., pret. & p.p.* **lead.**
ledge (lɛdʒ) *n.* repisa; borde.
ledger ('lɛdʒ·ər) *n.* libro mayor. —**ledger line,** línea suplementaria del pentagrama.
lee (liː) *n.* **1,** (shelter) abrigo; socaire. **2,** *naut.* sotavento. —*adj.* de sotavento.
leech (litʃ) *n.* sanguijuela.
leek (lik) *n.* puerro.
leer (lɪːr) *v.i.* mirar de reojo. —*n.* mirada de reojo. —**leery,** *adj., slang* suspicaz.
lees (liːz) *n.pl.* poso (*sing.*); heces.
leeward ('li·wərd) *n.* sotavento. —*adj.* de sotavento. —*adv.* a sotavento.
leeway ('liˌwei) *n.* **1,** *naut.* deriva. **2,** *fig.* (margin) margen; espacio.
left (lɛft) *v., pret. & p.p. de* **leave.** —*adj.* izquierdo. —*n.* izquierda.
lefthand *adj.* izquierdo; de *o* a la izquierda.
lefthanded *adj.* **1,** (preferring the left hand) zurdo. **2,** (done with the left hand) con la zurda *o* izquierda. **3,** (toward the left) a la izquierda. **4,** *colloq.* (insincere) insincero; malicioso. —*adv.* con la zurda *o* izquierda.
leftist ('lɛf·tɪst) *adj. & n.* izquierdista.
leftover *adj. & n.* sobrante; residuo. —**leftovers,** *n.pl.* sobras; restos; residuos.
leftwing *adj.* izquierdista.
leg (lɛg) *n.* **1,** (limb) pierna; (*esp. of animals*) pata. **2,** (furniture support) pata. **3,** (part of a garment) pernera; pierna. **4,** *geom.* cateto. **5,** (stage, as of a journey or course) etapa. —**have not a leg to stand on,** no tener fundamento. —**leg it,** *colloq.* andar; caminar. —**on one's last legs,** en las últimas. —**pull one's leg,** tomar el pelo a. —**shake a leg,** darse prisa; *Amer.* apurarse.
legacy ('lɛg·ə·si) *n.* legado; herencia.
legal ('li·gəl) *adj.* legal. —**legalize,** *v.t.* legalizar. —**legal tender,** moneda de curso legal.
legality (lɪ'gæl·ə·ti) *n.* legalidad.
legate ('lɛg·ət) *n.* legado. —**legateship,** *n.* legacía.
legatee ('lɛg·ə·ti) *n.* legatario.
legation (lɪ'gei·ʃən) *n.* legación.
legato (lɪ'ga·to) *adj. & adv.* ligado.
legend ('lɛdʒ·ənd) *n.* leyenda. —**legendary,** *adj.* legendario.
legerdemain (ˌlɛdʒ·ər·də'mein) *n.* prestidigitación; juego de manos.
leggings ('lɛg·ɪŋz) *n.pl.* polainas.
leggy ('lɛg·i) *adj.* **1,** (long-legged) zanquilargo. **2,** (having shapely legs) de piernas torneadas.
legible ('lɛdʒ·ə·bəl) *adj.* legible. —**legibility,** *n.* legibilidad.
legion ('li·dʒən) *n.* legión. —**legionary,** *adj.* legionario.
legionnaire (ˌli·dʒə'neːr) *n.* legionario.
legislate ('lɛdʒ·ɪsˌleit) *v.t. & i.* legislar; decretar. —**legislation,** *n.* legislación. —**legislative,** *adj.* legislativo. —**legislator,** *n.* legislador.
legislature ('ledʒ·ɪsˌlei·tʃər) *n.* cuerpo legislativo; legislatura.
legitimate (lə'dʒɪt·ɪ·mət) *adj.* legítimo. —*v.t.* (-ˌmeit) legitimar. —**legitimacy,** *n.* legitimidad. —**legitimation,** *n.* legitimación.
legitimize (lə'dʒɪt·əˌmaiz) *v.t.* [*también,* **legitimatize** (-məˌtaiz)] legitimar. —**legitimization** (-mə·'zei·ʃən) *n.* legitimación.
legume ('lɛg·jum) *n.* legumbre. —**leguminous** (lɛ'gju·mɪ·nəs) *adj.* leguminoso.
leisure ('li·ʒər; 'lɛʒ·ər) *n.* tiempo libre; ocio. —*adj.* libre; ocioso; desocupado. —**at leisure, 1,** (free; not busy) libre; desocupado. **2,** (without hurry) sin prisa *o* apuro;

descansadamente. —**at one's leisure,** a su conveniencia.
leisurely ('li·ʒər·li) *adj.* reposado; pausado; tranquilo. —*adv.* reposadamente; despacio.
lemming ('lɛm·ɪŋ) *n.* conejo de Noruega.
lemon ('lɛm·ən) *n.* **1,** (fruit) limón. **2,** (tree) limonero. **3,** *slang* (failure) clavo. —*adj.* **1,** (color) limón. **2,** (made of or with lemon) de limón. —**lemonade** (-'eid) *n.* limonada.
lemur ('li·mər) *n.* lémur.
lend (lɛnd) *v.t.* [*pret.* & *p.p.* **lent**] **1,** (let have, as for use) prestar; hacer un préstamo *o* empréstito de. **2,** (give; impart) dar; impartir. —*v.i.* prestar; hacer préstamos *o* empréstitos. —**lend a hand (to),** ayudar; echar una mano. —**lend oneself (*o* itself),** prestarse.
lender ('lɛn·dər) *n.* prestador; quien presta.
length (lɛŋθ) *n.* **1,** (dimension) largo; longitud; extensión. **2,** (duration) espacio; tiempo. **3,** *racing* cuerpo. **4,** (extreme) extremo; punto. —**at length, 1,** (finally) por fin; finalmente. **2,** (in detail) con gran detalle; por completo. —**keep at arm's length,** mantener a distancia.
lengthen ('lɛŋ·θən) *v.t.* alargar; extender; prolongar. —*v.i.* alargarse; extenderse; prolongarse.
lengthwise ('lɛŋθˌwaiz) *adj.* longitudinal. —*adv.* longitudinalmente; a lo largo; a la larga.
lengthy ('lɛŋ·θi) *adj.* muy largo. —**lengthiness,** *n.* lo largo.
lenient ('li·ni·ənt) *adj.* blando; indulgente. —**leniency; lenity** ('lɛn·ə·ti) *n.* lenidad.
lens (lɛnz) *n.* **1,** (glass) lente. **2,** *anat.* cristalino.
Lent (lɛnt) *n.* cuaresma. —**Lenten** ('lɛn·tən) *adj.* de cuaresma.
lent (lɛnt) *v., pret.* & *p.p. de* **lend.**
lenticular (lɛn'tɪk·jə·lər) *adj.* lenticular.
lentil ('lɛn·təl) *n.* lenteja.
lento ('lɛn·to) *adj.* & *adv.* lento.
Leo ('li·o) *n., astron.* Leo.
leonine ('li·ə·nain) *adj.* leonino.
leopard ('lɛp·ərd) *n.* leopardo.
leper ('lɛp·ər) *n.* leproso. —**leprosy** (-rə·si) *n.* lepra. —**leprous** (-rəs) *adj.* leproso.
leporine ('lɛp·əˌrain) *adj.* lebruno; leporino.
Lesbian ('lɛz·bi·ən) *n.* & *adj.* lesbiano.
lese majesty (liz) lesa majestad.
lesion ('li·ʒən) *n.* lesión.
less (lɛs) *adv., prep.* & *n.* menos. —*adj.* [**lesser, least**] menor.
-less (ləs) *sufijo; forma adjetivos indicando* carencia; ausencia: *restless,* inquieto; *sleeveless,* sin mangas.
lessee (lɛ'siː) *n.* arrendatario.
lessen ('lɛs·ən) *v.t.* & *i.* disminuir.
lesser ('lɛs·ər) *adj.* menor.
lesson ('lɛs·ən) *n.* lección.
lessor ('lɛs·or) *n.* arrendador.
lest (lɛst) *conj.* **1,** (that . . . not; so that . . . not) para que no; no sea que. **2,** (for fear that) de *o* por miedo que. **3,** *tras expresiones de temor, duda, peligro, etc.* (that) que: *I fear lest he is lost,* Temo que se haya perdido.
let (lɛt) *v.t.* [**let, letting**] **1,** (leave) dejar. **2,** (rent; lease) alquilar; arrendar. **3,** (assign) asignar. **4,** (draw, as blood) sangrar; sacar. **5,** (allow; permit) permitir; dejar. —*v.i.* alquilarse; arrendarse. —*v.aux., úsase en las exhortaciones; se expresa en el español con el subjuntivo: let us drink,* bebamos; *let him come in,* que entre. —*n., usu. en* **without let or hindrance,** sin estorbo ni embarazo. —**let alone, 1,** [*también,* **let be**] (not interfere with) dejar tranquilo; dejar en paz; no molestar. **2,** (not to mention; much less) para qué decir; aún menos. —**let by,** dejar pasar. —**let down, 1,** (lower) bajar. **2,** (slacken; relax) no pujar tanto; andar más despacio. **3,** (disappoint) desilusionar; decepcionar. —**let go,** soltar; aflojar; dejar escapar. —**let in,** dejar entrar. —**let in for,** exponer; comprometer. —**let loose,** soltar. —**let know,** advertir; enterar; hacer saber. —**let off, 1,** (emit) lanzar; soltar. **2,** (release) dejar salir; soltar. **3,** (deal leniently with) soltar; dejar escapar; perdonar. —**let on,** *colloq.* **1,** (pretend) fingir. **2,** (give to understand) dar a entender. **3,** (divulge) dar a conocer; divulgar. —**let oneself go,** dejarse ir; abandonarse. —**let out, 1,** (release) soltar. **2,** (rent out) alquilar; arrendar. —**let up, 1,** (slacken; relax) cejar; dejar de pujar. **2,** (cease)

cesar; desistir. —**let well** (*o* **bad**) **enough alone,** más vale no meneallo.
-let (lət) *sufijo, formando nombres diminutivos: booklet,* folleto.
letdown *n.* **1,** (decrease in tension) relajamiento. **2,** *colloq.* (disappointment) desilusión; decepción.
lethal ('li·θəl) *adj.* letal.
lethargy ('lɛθ·ər·dʒi) *n.* letargo. —**lethargic** (lə'θar·dʒɪk) *adj.* letárgico.
letter ('lɛt·ər) *n.* **1,** (written character) letra. **2,** (missive) carta. **3,** *print.* carácter; letra. **4,** (literal meaning) letra. **5,** *pl.* (literature) letras. —*v.t.* & *i.* **1,** (inscribe) escribir *o* inscribir (con letras). **2,** (mark with letters) rotular; poner inscripción en. —**letter carrier,** cartero. —**letter of credit,** letra; carta de crédito. —**letter of exchange,** letra de cambio. —**letter box,** buzón. —**to the letter,** al pie de la letra.
lettered ('lɛt·ərd) *adj.* **1,** (literate) que sabe leer y escribir. **2,** (learned) instruido; letrado. **3,** (marked with letters) rotulado; marcado con letras.
letterhead *n.* membrete.
lettering ('lɛt·ər·ɪŋ) *n.* inscripción; letras (*pl.*).
letter-perfect *adj.* exacto; correcto; al pie de la letra.
lettuce ('lɛt·əs) *n.* lechuga.
letup *n., colloq.* descanso; pausa.
leucocyte ('lu·kə,sait) *n.* leucocito.
leukemia (lu'ki·mi·ə) *n.* leucemia.
Levant (lɪ'vænt) *n.* levante. —**Levantine** (lɪ'væn·tɪn) *adj.* & *n.* levantino.
levee ('lɛv·i) *n.* **1,** (dike) ribero. **2,** (reception) recepción.
level ('lɛv·əl) *adj.* **1,** (flat; even) llano; plano; raso; igual. **2,** (not sloping) nivelado. **3,** (even; on the same plane) a nivel; igual; nivelado. —*n.* nivel. —*adv.* al mismo nivel; a la par. —*v.t.* **1,** (make level or even) nivelar. **2,** (knock down; raze) arrasar. **3,** (direct; aim) dirigir; apuntar. —*v.i.* **1,** (become level) nivelarse. **2,** (take aim) apuntar. **3,** *colloq.* (be candid) ser franco; abrirse. —**levelness,** *n.* igualdad.
levelheaded *adj.* juicioso; sensato.
lever ('lɛv·ər) *n.* palanca.
leverage ('lɛv·ər·ɪdʒ) *n.* **1,** (action of a lever) acción de palanca. **2,** (mechanical advantage) brazo de palanca. **3,** (influence) palanca.
leviathan (lɪ'vai·ə·θən) *n.* leviatán.
levis ('li·vaiz) *n.pl.* overoles; pantalones de trabajo.
levitate ('lɛv·ə,teit) *v.t.* suspender en el aire. —*v.i.* flotar en el aire. —**levitation,** *n.* levitación.
Levite ('li·vait) *n.* levita. —**Levitical** (lɪ'vɪt·ə·kəl) *adj.* levítico.
levity ('lɛv·ə·ti) *n.* frivolidad; ligereza.
levo- (li·vo) *prefijo* levo-; izquierda: *levogyrate,* levógiro.
levy ('lɛv·i) *n.* **1,** (assessment; collection) recaudación. **2,** (conscription) leva; recluta. **3,** *law* embargo. —*v.t.* **1,** (assess; collect) recaudar. **2,** (conscript) reclutar; enganchar. **3,** (demand; exact) exigir. **4,** *law* embargar; poner embargo sobre.
lewd (lu:d) *adj.* indecente; lascivo; lujurioso. —**lewdness,** *n.* lujuria; lascivia.
lexicography (,lɛk·sɪ'kag·rə·fi) *n.* lexicografía. —**lexicographer,** *n.* lexicógrafo. —**lexicographic** (-ko'græf·ɪk) *adj.* lexicográfico.
lexicon ('lɛk·sɪ·kən) *n.* léxico. —**lexical,** *adj.* léxico.
liability (,lai·ə'bɪl·ə·ti) *n.* **1,** (responsibility) responsabilidad. **2,** (risk) riesgo. **3,** *usu.pl.* (debts; obligations) deudas; obligaciones; debe (*sing.*). **4,** (disadvantage) desventaja; tara.
liable ('lai·ə·bəl) *adj.* **1,** (responsible) responsable. **2,** (susceptible) susceptible; propenso. **3,** (vulnerable; exposed) expuesto; sujeto. **4,** *colloq.* (likely) capaz (de).
liaison ('li·ə,zan) *n.* **1,** (intercommunication) enlace. **2,** (link) lazo; relación; vínculo. **3,** *colloq.* (love affair) amorío; lío.
liar ('lai·ər) *n.* mentiroso; embustero.
libation (lai'bei·ʃən) *n.* libación.
libel ('lai·bəl) *n.* libelo; difamación; calumnia. —*v.t.* difamar; calumniar. —**libeler,** *n.* libelista; difamador; calumniador. —**libelous,** *adj.* difamatorio.

liberal ('lɪb·ə·rəl) *adj.* **1,** (generous) liberal; generoso. **2,** *polit.* liberal. —*n., polit.* liberal. —**liberalism,** *n.* liberalismo.
liberality (ˌlɪb·əˈræl·ə·ti) *n.* liberalidad.
liberalize ('lɪb·ər·əˌlaiz) *v.t.* liberalizar. —**liberalization** (-lɪˈzei·ʃən) *n.* liberalización.
liberate ('lɪb·əˌreit) *v.t.* libertar; liberar. —**liberation,** *n.* liberación. —**liberator,** *n.* libertador.
libertine ('lɪb·ərˌtin) *n. & adj.* libertino.
liberty ('lɪb·ər·ti) *n.* libertad. —**at liberty,** en libertad; libre; desocupado.
libido (lɪˈbi·do) *n.* libido. —**libidinous** (lɪˈbɪd·ə·nəs) *adj.* libidinoso.
Libra ('lai·brə) *n., astron.* Libra.
library ('laiˌbrɛr·i) *n.* biblioteca. —**librarian** (laiˈbrɛr·i·ən) *n.* bibliotecario.
libretto (lɪˈbrɛt·o) *n.* libreto. —**librettist,** *n.* libretista.
lice (lais) *n., pl. de* **louse.**
license ('lai·səns) *n.* licencia. —*v.t.* licenciar; dar licencia. —**licensee** (-sənˈsiː) *n.* concesionario. —**licenser,** *n.* persona *u* organismo que expide licencias.
licentious (lɪˈsɛn·ʃəs) *adj.* licencioso. —**licentiousness,** *n.* libertinaje; licencia.
lichen ('lai·kən) *n.* liquen.
licit ('lɪs·ɪt) *adj.* lícito.
lick (lɪk) *v.t.* **1,** (lap) lamer. **2,** *colloq.* (whip; thrash) dar una zurra; dar una tunda. **3,** *colloq.* (overcome) vencer; derrotar. —*n.* **1,** (stroke with the tongue) lamedura; lengüetada; lengüetazo. **2,** *colloq.* (blow) golpe. **3,** (salt deposit) salobral; saladar. **4,** (small quantity) pizca. **5,** *colloq.* (gait) paso; marcha. —**give a lick and a promise,** hacer mal y pronto.
lickety-split ('lɪk·ə·tiˈsplɪt) *adv., colloq.* a todo correr; a toda marcha.
licorice ('lɪk·ə·rɪs) *n.* regaliz.
lid (lɪd) *n.* **1,** (cover) tapa. **2,** (eyelid) párpado. **3,** *slang* (hat) sombrero. **4,** *fig., colloq.* (curb; restraint) freno.
lie (lai) *v.i.* [**lay, lain, lying**] **1,** (recline; rest) estar echado; descansar. **2,** [*también,* **lie down**] (put oneself in a reclining position) echarse; acostarse; tenderse. **3,** (be; remain) estar. **4,** (be situated) estar; estar situado; hallarse; encontrarse. **5,** (extend; stretch) extenderse. **6,** (be buried) descansar; yacer. **7,** [**lied, lying**] (make false statements; deceive) mentir. —*n.* **1,** (disposition; arrangement) disposición; situación; posición. **2,** (deception) mentira. —**give the lie to, 1,** (deny; belie) dar el mentís a. **2,** (accuse of lying) acusar de mentiroso. —**lie down on the job,** *colloq.* flojear; remolonear. —**lie in,** estar de parto. —**lie in wait (for),** acechar. —**lie over,** aplazarse; demorarse; quedar en suspenso. —**lie to,** *naut.* ponerse al pairo. —**take lying down,** *colloq.* aceptar *o* someterse sin protestar.
liege (liːʒ) *adj. & n.* vasallo.
lien (liːn) *n.* gravamen; obligación.
lieu (luː) *n.* lugar. —**in lieu of,** en lugar de; en vez de.
lieutenant (luˈtɛn·ənt) *n.* **1,** (deputy) lugarteniente. **2,** (military officer) teniente. —**lieutenancy,** *n.* tenencia. —**lieutenant colonel,** teniente coronel. —**lieutenant commander,** capitán de corbeta. —**lieutenant general,** teniente general. —**lieutenant governor,** vicegobernador.
life (laif) *n.* vida. —**lifeless,** *adj.* sin vida; muerto. —**lifelessness,** *n.* falta de vida; muerte.
lifeboat *n.* lancha *o* bote salvavidas.
life buoy boya salvavidas.
lifeguard *n.* guardia de piscina.
life insurance seguro sobre la vida.
lifelike ('laifˌlaik) *adj.* natural; real.
lifeline *n.* **1,** (cable or rope) cable *o* cuerda salvavidas. **2,** *palmistry* línea de la vida. **3,** (vital route) ruta vital; línea vital.
lifelong *adj.* de *o* para toda la vida.
life net red de bomberos.
life preserver salvavidas.
life size (de) tamaño natural.
life span duración de vida; vida.
lifetime *n.* **1,** (life span) vida. **2,** *colloq.* (long time) mucho tiempo; eternidad. —*adj.* de toda la vida; de por vida.
lifework *n.* obra de toda la vida; obra de una vida; carrera.
lift (lɪft) *v.t.* **1,** (raise) levantar;

alzar. 2, (elevate; exalt) elevar; exaltar. 3, *colloq.* (plagiarize) plagiar. 4, *slang* (steal) robar; alzarse con. —*v.i.* 1, (rise; go up) levantarse; elevarse. 2, (be dispelled) disiparse. 3, (tug upward) tirar hacia arriba. —*n.* 1, (act of raising) levantamiento; alzamiento. 2, (elevation) elevación. 3, (uplift; encouragement) ánimo; aliento. 4, (lifting force) fuerza de sustentación. 5, (help) ayuda. 6, (free ride) viaje gratis *o* de gorra; *W.I.* pon. 7, (heel wedge) tapa. 8, (cargo elevator) montacargas; elevador. 9, *Brit.* (elevator) ascensor; elevador. —**give (someone) a lift,** llevar.

ligament ('lɪg·ə·mənt) *n.* ligamento.

ligature ('lɪg·əˌtʃur) *n.* 1, (binding) ligadura. 2, *music* (slur) ligadura; (tie; bind) ligado. 3, *printing* ligado.

light (lait) *n.* 1, (illumination or source) luz. 2, (means of igniting) fuego; candela; lumbre. 3, *usu.pl.* (understanding) luces. —*adj.* 1, (having light; bright) bien iluminado; claro. 2, (pale; not dark) claro; pálido. 3, (fair; whitish) blanco; claro. 4, (not heavy) ligero; liviano; leve. 5, (gay; buoyant) alegre. 6, (fickle; frivolous) inconstante; ligero. 7, (morally loose) libre; inmoral. 8, (soft; spongy) esponjoso; ligero. 9, (swift; nimble) ligero; ágil. 10, (not serious) ligero; poco serio. 11, (graceful; delicate) delicado; gracioso; fino. —*adv.* = **lightly.** —*v.t.* [*pret. & p.p.* **lighted** *o* **lit**] 1, (ignite; turn on) encender; prender. 2, (illuminate) iluminar; dar luz. 3, [*usu.* **light up**] (animate; brighten) animar; iluminar. 4, (guide, as by a beacon) mostrar el camino a; guiar. —*v.i.* 1, (catch fire) prenderse; encenderse. 2, [*usu.* **light up**] (brighten; be animated) animarse; iluminarse. 3, (alight) aterrizar; posarse. 4, [*usu.* **light on** *o* **upon**] (come upon; find) encontrar; dar con. 5, (fall; strike suddenly) caer; golpear; dar. —**light in the head,** 1, (dizzy) mareado. 2, (simple; foolish) tonto; zonzo. —**light into,** *colloq.* arremeter contra; atacar. —**light out,** *slang,* salir corriendo; largarse. —**light up,** 1, (make or become light) iluminar(se). 2, (make or become cheerful; brighten) animar(se); iluminar(se). 3, (ignite; set to burning; begin smoking) encender; prender. —**make light of,** tratar con ligereza; no parar muchas mientes en; no dar importancia a.

lighten ('lai·tən) *v.t.* 1, (illuminate; shed light on) aclarar; iluminar. 2, (make paler) aclarar; hacer más pálido. 3, (make less heavy) aligerar. 4, (relieve) aliviar. 5, (gladden) alegrar. —*v.i.* 1, (become light; grow brighter) aclararse; iluminarse. 2, (grow paler) palidecer; aclararse.

lighter ('lai·tər) *n.* 1, (igniting device) encendedor. 2, (barge) lanchón; barcaza; chalana; gabarra. 3, (flash, as lightning) relampaguear. 4, (become less heavy) aligerarse.

light-footed *adj.* ligero de pies; ágil.

lightheaded *adj.* 1, (dizzy) mareado. 2, (delirious) delirante; desatado. 3, (thoughtless; frivolous) frívolo; tarambana; ligero de cascos.

lighthearted *adj.* alegre; despreocupado.

lighthouse *n.* faro.

lighting ('lai·tɪŋ) *n.* alumbrado; iluminación.

lightly ('lait·li) *adv.* 1, (with little pressure; gently) ligeramente. 2, (to a small degree or amount) poco. 3, (cheerfully) alegremente. 4, (indifferently; frivolously) con despego; con indiferencia.

lightness ('lait·nəs) *n.* 1, (lack of weight; insubstantiality) ligereza. 2, (delicacy) delicadeza; finura. 3, (mildness) suavidad. 4, (cheerfulness) alegría. 5, (nimbleness) agilidad. 6, (brightness) luz; iluminación. 7, (paleness) palidez. 8, (whiteness) blancura.

lightning ('lait·nɪŋ) *n.* rayo; relámpago.

light year año luz.

lignite ('lɪg·nait) *n.* lignito.

likable ('lai·kə·bəl) *adj.* simpático; agradable.

like (laik) *v.t.* 1, (wish; desire) querer; desear. 2, (have a taste or fondness for) gustarle a uno; placerle a uno. —*v.i.* querer; desear. —*adj.* 1, (similar) similar; parecido; semejante. 2, (characteristic of) propio de; característico de.

—*adv.*, *colloq.* **1,** (as though) como; igual que. **2,** (likely) probablemente; con toda probabilidad. **3,** (nearly) como. —*prep.* **1,** (similar to; similarly to) como. **2,** (in the mood of; desirous of) con ganas de. —*conj.*, *colloq.* **1,** (as) tal como; tal cual; como. **2,** (as if) como si; como que. —*n.* **1,** (something equal) cosa semejante *o* parecida; cosa *o* persona igual. **2,** *pl.* (preferences) gustos. —**feel like,** tener ganas (de). —**like as not,** con toda probabilidad. —**look like, 1,** (resemble) parecerse a. **2,** (seem as if) parecer que.

-like (laik) *sufijo; forma adjetivos denotando* semejanza: *birdlike,* como pájaro.

likely ('laik·li) *adj.* **1,** (credible) creíble; verosímil. **2,** (probable) probable. **3,** (due; apparently destined) supuesto; destinado. **4,** (promising) prometedor; que promete. **5,** (suitable) apropiado; adecuado. —*adv.* probablemente. —**likelihood,** *n.* probabilidad.

liken ('lai·kən) *v.t.* comparar; asemejar.

likeness ('laik·nəs) *n.* **1,** (similarity) similitud; parecido; semejanza. **2,** (semblance) figura; apariencia. **3,** (copy; image) copia fiel; vivo retrato.

likewise ('laik,waiz) *adv.* **1,** (in the same manner) lo mismo; igualmente; del mismo modo. **2,** (too; also) también; asimismo.

liking ('lai·kɪŋ) *n.* **1,** (preference; taste) gusto; preferencia; predilección. **2,** (fondness) cariño; afecto. —**take a liking to,** inclinarse a; aficionarse a; enamorarse de.

lilac ('lai·lək) *n.* lila.

lilt (lɪlt) *n.* ritmo; ritmo alegre.

lily ('lɪl·i) *n.* lirio; azucena. —*adj.* de lirio; de azucena. —**lily of the valley,** lirio de los valles; muguete. —**lily pad,** hoja de nenúfar. —**water lily,** nenúfar.

Lima bean ('lai·mə) haba de Lima.

limb (lɪm) *n.* **1,** (leg; arm) miembro; extremidad. **2,** (branch) rama. **3,** (offshoot; outgrowth) vástago; brazo. —**out on a limb,** en situación arriesgada.

limber ('lim·bər) *adj.* **1,** (flexible) flexible. **2,** (agile) ágil. —*v.t. & i.* poner(se) *o* hacer(se) flexible *o* ágil; entonar(se).

limbo ('lɪm·bo) *n.* limbo.

lime (laim) *n.* **1,** (fruit tree) limero. **2,** (fruit) lima; lima agria. **3,** (calcium oxide) cal. **4,** (linden tree) tilo. —*adj.* **1,** (of limes) de lima. **2,** (of quicklime) de cal. —**limeade,** *n.* bebida hecha con agua, azúcar y zumo de lima agria.

limelight ('laim,lait) *n.* luz (de un reflector). —**be in the limelight,** estar en el candelero.

limestone *n.* piedra caliza.

limewater *n.* agua de cal.

limit ('lɪm·ɪt) *n.* límite. —*v.t.* limitar. —**limitless,** *adj.* sin límites; ilimitado.

limitation (,lɪm·ə'tei·ʃən) *n.* limitación.

limited ('lɪm·ɪt·ɪd) *adj.* limitado. —*n.* tren expreso.

limousine ('lɪm·ə,zin) *n.* automóvil cerrado; limousine.

limp (lɪmp) *v.i.* **1,** (walk lamely) cojear. **2,** (move laboriously) avanzar *o* moverse con dificultad. —*n.* cojera. —*adj.* **1,** (flaccid) fláccido; lacio. **2,** (wilted) mustio; marchito; ajado. **3,** (lacking vigor) flojo; inerte; sin vigor.

limpet ('lɪm·pət) *n.* lapa.

limpid ('lɪm·pɪd) *adj.* límpido. —**limpidity** (lɪm'pɪd·ə·ti); **limpidness,** *n.* limpidez.

limpness ('lɪmp·nəs) *n.* **1,** (lameness) cojera. **2,** (flaccidity) flaccidez; laxitud. **3,** (wilted condition) lo mustio; marchitez. **4,** (lack of vigor) flojedad; inercia; languidez.

limy ('lai·mi) *adj.* **1,** (of or resembling lime) calizo; de cal. **2,** (sticky) pegajoso.

linden ('lɪn·dən) *n.* tilo.

line (lain) *n.* **1,** (cord; rope) cordel; cuerda; *naut.* cabo; *fishing* sedal. **2,** (length of wire) alambre. **3,** (means or agency of communication or transportation) línea. **4,** (pipe; tubing) tubería; cañería. **5,** (thin mark or crease) línea. **6,** (limit; border) línea de demarcación. **7,** (delineation; outline) figura; delineación. **8,** (path; course) línea. **9,** (occupation) ocupación; profesión. **10,** (stock of goods) renglón; línea. **11,** (specialty) especialidad. **12,** (row; file) línea. **13,** (series; succession) serie; sucesión. **14,** (lineage) línea; linaje. —*v.t.* **1,** (draw lines on or in) trazar líneas sobre *o* en; linear;

regular; rayar. **2,** [*usu.* **line up**] (align) alinear. **3,** (put a lining in) forrar; revestir. **4,** (form a line along; edge) bordear; formar línea a lo largo de. —*v.i.,* [*usu.* **line up**] alinearse; colocarse en fila. —**all along the line, 1,** (throughout) en toda la línea; en todas partes. **2,** (at every turn) a cada paso. —**bring into line, 1,** (align) alinear. **2,** (make conform) hacer conformar; hacer entrar en línea. —**come into line, 1,** (line up) alinearse. **2,** *colloq.* (correspond; agree) concordar; corresponder. **3,** *colloq.* (behave properly) encarrilarse; *Amer.* enrielarse. —**draw the** (*o* **a**) **line,** poner límite. —**get a line on,** *colloq.* inquirir *o* indagar sobre. —**hold the line, 1,** (stand firmly) aguantar; mantenerse firme. **2,** (wait; keep the line open) esperar; no cortar; mantener la línea abierta. —**in line, 1,** (in alignment) en línea. **2,** (in harmony) de acuerdo; conforme. **3,** (in readiness) listo; pronto; preparado. —**line up, 1,** (form a line) alinearse. **2,** (organize effectively) organizar; encarrilar. —**on a line,** en línea; alineado; nivelado. —**out of line, 1,** (not aligned) fuera de línea. **2,** (not in agreement) en desacuerdo. **3,** (behaving improperly) en falta; errado; portándose mal. —**stand in line,** hacer cola. —**toe the line,** andar derecho; seguir la norma; ajustarse a la norma.

lineage ('lɪn·i·ɪdʒ) *n.* linaje.

lineal ('lɪn·i·əl) *adj.* **1,** (in direct line of descent) en línea recta; lineal. **2,** (linear) lineal. —**lineally,** *adv.* en línea recta.

lineament ('lɪn·i·ə·mənt) *n.* lineamento; rasgo.

linear ('lɪn·i·ər) *adj.* lineal. —**linear measure,** medida de longitud.

lineman ('lain·mən) *n.* [*pl.* **-men**] **1,** *R.R.* inspector *o* reparador de vías. **2,** (telephone repairman) reparador de líneas. **3,** *sports* jugador de línea.

linen ('lɪn·ən) *n.* **1,** (yarn or fabric) lino. **2,** (bedclothes) ropa de cama. **3,** (shirts, underwear, etc.) ropa blanca. **4,** (table coverings) mantelería. —*adj.* de lino. —**linen shop,** lencería.

liner ('lai·nər) *n.* **1,** (ship) transatlántico. **2,** (aircraft) avión comercial. **3,** (drawing instrument) tiralíneas. **4,** (lining) forro.

linesman ('lainz·mən) *n.* [*pl.* **-men**] **1,** *sports* juez de línea. **2,** = **lineman.**

-liness (li·nəs) *sufijo; forma nombres de adjetivos terminados en* **-ly**: *manliness,* virilidad.

lineup ('lain,ʌp) *n.* **1,** (order; array) formación. **2,** (grouping) agrupación; composición. **3,** *sports* formación. **4,** (display of suspects) rueda (de sospechosos).

-ling (lɪŋ) *sufijo* **1,** *forma nombres indicando* persona *o* cosa relacionada con, *generalmente con tono despectivo: hireling,* mercenario. **2,** *forma diminutivos: duckling,* patito; anadeja. **3,** *forma adverbios de modo*: *darkling,* a oscuras.

linger ('lɪŋ·gər) *v.i.* **1,** (stay on) quedarse; detenerse; demorarse. **2,** [*también,* **linger on**] (continue) durar; persistir. **3,** (delay; loiter) demorarse; remolonear.

lingerie (,læn·ʒə'riː) *n.* ropa interior femenina.

lingual ('lɪŋ·gwəl) *adj.* lingual.

linguist ('lɪŋ·gwɪst) *n.* lingüista. —**linguistic** (lɪŋ'gwɪs·tɪk) *adj.* lingüístico. —**linguistics,** *n.* lingüística.

liniment ('lɪn·ə·mənt) *n.* linimento.

lining ('lai·nɪŋ) *n.* forro; revestimiento.

link (lɪŋk) *n.* **1,** (part of a chain) eslabón. **2,** (connection; tie) vínculo; lazo. **3,** *mech.* biela; conexión. **4,** (measure) medida de longitud de unos 201 *mm.* —*v.t.* unir; conectar; acoplar. —*v.i.* unirse; conectarse. —**linkage,** *n.* eslabonamiento; conexión. —**links,** *n.pl.* campo *o* cancha de golf.

linnet ('lɪn·ɪt) *n.* jilguero; pardillo.

linoleum (lɪ'no·li·əm) *n.* linóleo.

linotype ('lai·nə,taip) *n.* **1,** (machine) linotipia. **2,** (plate) linotipo. —**linotypist,** *n.* linotipista.

linseed ('lɪn,sid) *n.* linaza.

lint (lɪnt) *n.* pelusa; hilachas (*pl.*).

lintel ('lɪn·təl) *n.* dintel.

lion ('lai·ən) *n.* **1,** (animal; person of courage) león. **2,** (celebrity) celebridad. —**lioness,** *n.* leona. —**lionize,** *v.t.* poner por las alturas; agasajar.

lionhearted *adj.* valiente; bravo.

lip (lɪp) *n.* **1,** *anat.* labio. **2,** (rim) borde. **3,** *slang* (impertinence) insolencia; impertinencia. —**lip service,** sólo palabras. —**lip-read,** *v.t.* & *i.* leer (en) los labios.

lipstick *n.* lápiz para los labios *o* de labios; lápiz labial.

liquefy ('lɪk·wɪ,fai) *v.t.* licuar. —*v.i.* licuarse. —**liquefaction** (-'fæk·ʃən) *n.* licuación; licuefacción.

liqueur (lɪ'kʌɹ) *n.* licor.

liquid ('lɪk·wɪd) *n.* & *adj.* líquido. —**liquidity** (lɪ'kwɪd·ə·ti) lo líquido. —**liquid assets,** valores realizables.

liquidate ('lɪk·wɪ,deit) *v.t.* & *i.* liquidar. —**liquidation,** *n.* liquidación.

liquor ('lɪk·ər) *n.* licor.

lira ('li·ra) *n.* lira.

lisle (lail) *n.* hilo de Escocia.

lisp (lɪsp) *n.* ceceo. —*v.i.* cecear. —*v.t.* pronunciar ceceando *o* con ceceo. —**lisper,** *n.* ceceoso. —**lisping,** *adj.* ceceoso. —*n.* ceceo.

lissome ('lɪs·əm) *adj.* esbelto.

list (lɪst) *n.* **1,** (roll; roster) lista. **2,** (slant) inclinación; *naut.* escora. **3,** (selvage) orillo. **4,** (ridge of a furrow) lomo. **5,** *pl.* (jousting arena) liza (*sing.*). —*v.t.* alistar; incluir en una lista; hacer una lista de. —*v.i.* **1,** *naut.* escorar. **2,** *poet.* = **listen. 3,** *archaic* (wish) desear; querer. —**be listed,** figurar *o* aparecer inscrito.

listen ('lɪs·ən) *v.i.* **1,** (attend closely) escuchar. **2,** (pay heed) hacer caso; escuchar. —**listen in,** escuchar a hurtadillas. —**listener,** *n.* oyente.

listing ('lɪs·tɪŋ) *n.* alistamiento; inclusión *o* aparición en una lista.

listless ('lɪst·ləs) *adj.* sin ánimo; indiferente. —**listlessness,** *n.* falta de ánimo; indiferencia.

lit (lɪt) *v., pret.* & *p.p. de* **light.**

litany ('lɪt·ə·ni) *n.* letanía.

-lite (lait) *sufijo* -lita; *forma nombres de minerales: cryolite,* criolita.

liter *también,* **litre** ('li·tər) *n.* litro.

literacy ('lɪt·ə·rə·si) *n.* capacidad de leer y escribir.

literal ('lɪt·ər·əl) *adj.* literal. —**literally,** *adv.* al pie de la letra.

literal-minded *adj.* sin imaginación; prosaico.

literary ('lɪt·ə·rɛr·i) *adj.* literario; de letras; de literatura.

literate ('lɪt·ər·ət) *adj.* **1,** (able to read and write) capaz de leer y escribir. **2,** (learned) literato.

literati (,lɪt·ə'ra·ti) *n.pl.* eruditos; literatos.

literature ('lɪt·ər·ə,tʃur) *n.* literatura.

-lith (lɪθ) *sufijo* -lito; piedra: *monolith,* monolito.

lithe (laið) *adj.* **1,** (flexible) flexible; cimbreante. **2,** (agile) ágil. —**litheness,** *n.* flexibilidad; agilidad.

-lithic ('lɪθ·ɪk) *sufijo* -lítico, *formando adjetivos* **1,** *derivados de nombres terminados en* **-lith**: *monolithic,* monolítico. **2,** *denotando* períodos arqueológicos: *neolithic,* neolítico.

lithium ('lɪθ·i·əm) *n.* litio.

litho- (lɪθ·ə) *prefijo* lito-; piedra: *lithography,* litografía.

lithograph ('lɪθ·ə·græf) *n.* litografía. —*v.t.* litografiar. —**lithographic,** *adj.* litográfico. —**lithography** (lɪ'θag·rə·fi) *n.* litografía. —**lithographer** (lɪ'θag·rə·fər) *n.* litógrafo.

lithosphere ('lɪθ·ə·sfɪr) *n.* litosfera.

litigate ('lɪt·ɪ,geit) *v.t.* & *i.* litigar. —**litigant,** *n.* & *adj.* litigante. —**litigation,** *n.* litigación; litigio.

litmus paper ('lɪt·məs) *n.* papel de tornasol.

litter ('lɪt·ər) *n.* **1,** (animals born at one time) camada; lechigada. **2,** (stretcher) camilla. **3,** (straw bedding) mullido; cama; lecho. **4,** (kind of palanquin) litera. **5,** (rubbish) basura; desperdicio. **6,** (disorder; disarray) desorden; confusión. —*v.t.* **1,** [*también,* **litter up**] (make untidy) tirar basura en; cubrir de basura; ensuciar. **2,** (scatter; throw about) esparcir; tirar. —*v.i.* parir; dar cría.

little ('lɪt·əl) *adj.* **1,** (small in size) pequeño; chico. **2,** (small in amount or degree) poco. **3,** (short in duration or distance) corto. **4,** (trifling; trivial) nimio; pequeño; trivial. —*adv.* **1,** (not much) poco. **2,** (scarcely) apenas; escasamente. —*n.* poco. —**littleness,** *n.* pequeñez; lo pequeño. —**little by little,** poco a poco; poquito a poco. —**little finger** (dedo) meñique. —**make little of,** no dar mayor importancia a; tomar a la ligera. —**not a little,** no poco;

muy; mucho. —**think little of, 1,** (despise) tener a menos; mirar en menos. **2,** (have no hesitancy about) no vacilar en.

littoral ('lɪt·ə·rəl) *n.* & *adj.* litoral.

liturgy ('lɪt·ər·dʒi) *n.* liturgia. —**liturgical** (lɪ'tʌɹ·dʒɪ·kəl) *adj.* litúrgico.

livable *también,* **liveable** ('lɪv·ə·bəl) *adj.* **1,** (habitable) habitable. **2,** (endurable) soportable. **3,** (pleasant to live with) agradable; amistoso; cordial.

live (lɪv) *v.i.* & *t.* vivir. —*adj.* (laiv) **1,** (alive; living) vivo. **2,** (alert; wide-awake) alerta; despierto; vivo. **3,** (charged, as with explosives, electricity, etc.) cargado. **4,** (burning) candente; encendido. **5,** (bright; vivid) vivo. **6,** (filled with activity) lleno de vida; animado. **7,** (fresh; refreshing) fresco. **8,** (of immediate interest) de actualidad. **9,** *radio; TV* simultáneo. —*adv., radio; TV* simultáneamente. —**live down,** hacer enmiendas por; recobrarse de; borrar. —**live high,** vivir como rey; darse buena vida. —**live out,** durar; pasar de. —**live steam,** vapor a presión. —**live through,** soportar; sobrellevar. —**live up to,** vivir de acuerdo a *o* con; cumplir con.

-lived (laivd) *sufijo; forma adjetivos, generalmente unidos por guión, denotando* duración: *long-lived,* longevo.

livelihood ('laiv·li·hud) *n.* subsistencia; vida.

livelong ('lɪv,lɔŋ) *adj.* todo; entero.

lively ('laiv·li) *adj.* vivaz. —*adv.* vivazmente; vivamente. —**liveliness,** *n.* vivacidad; vida.

liven ('lai·vən) *v.t.* animar; avivar. —*v.i.* animarse; avivarse.

liver ('lɪv·ər) *n.* hígado. —**liverish,** *adj., colloq.* bilioso.

liverwurst ('lɪv·ər,wʌɹst) *n.* embutido de hígado.

livery ('lɪv·ə·ri) *n.* **1,** (uniform) librea. **2,** (uniformed help) criados de librea. **3,** (livery stable) caballeriza. **4,** (keeping of vehicles for hire; rental company) alquiler de vehículos; *So.Amer.* cochería. —**liveried,** *adj.* de librea; en librea.

lives (laivz) *n., pl. de* **life.**

livestock ('laiv,stak) *n.* ganado; animales de cría.

live wire (laiv) **1,** *electricity* alambre cargado. **2,** *slang* (go-getter) buscavidas.

livid ('lɪv·ɪd) *adj.* lívido. —**lividness,** *n.* lividez.

living ('lɪv·ɪŋ) *n.* vida; subsistencia. —*adj.* **1,** (alive) vivo; viviente. **2,** (for the maintenance of life) de subsistencia; para poder vivir. —**living quarters,** habitación; vivienda. —**living room,** sala; salón.

lizard ('lɪz·ərd) *n.* lagarto.

llama ('la·mə) *n.* llama.

llano ('la·no) *n.* llano.

lo (loː) *interj.* ¡he aquí!; ¡he allí!; ¡mira!

load (loːd) *n.* **1,** (charge; burden) carga. **2,** *slang* (drunk) borrachera. —*v.t.* & *i.* cargar. —**get a load of,** *slang* mirar; escuchar.

loadstar *n.* = **lodestar.**

loadstone *n.* = **lodestone.**

loaf (lof) *n.* [*pl.* **loaves**] pan; bollo. —*v.i.* haraganear; holgazanear.

loafer ('lo·fər) *n.* **1,** (idler) holgazán. **2,** (casual shoe) zapato de sport.

loam (loːm) *n.* **1,** (soil) marga. **2,** (material for making molds) tierra de moldeo. —**loamy,** *adj.* margoso.

loan (loːn) *n.* préstamo; empréstito. —*v.t.* & *i., colloq.* prestar; hacer un préstamo *o* empréstito (de). —**loan shark,** *colloq.* usurero; *Amer.* garrotero.

loath (loθ) *adj.* poco dispuesto; desinclinado.

loathe (loːð) *v.t.* odiar; detestar; aborrecer. —**loathing,** *n.* aversión; repugnancia; aborrecimiento. —**loathsome,** *adj.* repugnante; aborrecible. —**loathsomeness,** *n.* lo repugnante; lo aborrecible.

loaves (loːvz) *n., pl. de* **loaf.**

lob (laːb) *v.t.* volear; arrojar al voleo. —*n.* voleo.

lobby ('lab·i) *n.* **1,** (building entrance) vestíbulo; sala de entrada. **2,** (political pressure group) cabilderos (*pl.*). —*v.i.* cabildear. —**lobbying,** *n.* cabildeo. —**lobbyist,** *n.* cabildero.

lobe (loːb) *n.* lóbulo.

lobster ('lab·stər) *n.* langosta.

lobule ('lab·jul) *n.* lóbulo.

local ('lo·kəl) *adj.* local. —*n.* **1,** (train, bus, etc.) tren ómnibus; tren, autobús, etc. que hace todas las paradas. **2,** (chapter; branch) junta *u* organización local.

locale (lo'kæl) *n.* local; sitio.
locality (lo'kæl·ə·ti) *n.* localidad.
localize ('lo·kə,laiz) *v.t.* localizar. —**localization** (-lɪ'zei·ʃən) *n.* localización.
locate ('lo·keit; lo'keit) *v.t.* **1,** (situate) situar; localizar; *Amer.* ubicar. **2,** (find; discover) localizar; encontrar. **3,** (assign; place) asignar; poner; colocar.
location (lo'kei·ʃən) *n.* **1,** (act of locating) emplazamiento; colocación; localización. **2,** (position; situation) ubicación; situación; posición. **3,** (site) sitio.
loci ('lo·sai) *n., pl. de* **locus.**
lock (lak) *n.* **1,** (device for closing) cerradura. **2,** (bolt) cerrojo. **3,** (safety) seguro. **4,** (padlock) candado. **5,** (barring or stopping device) traba. **6,** (sluice; canal lock) esclusa. **7,** (curl of hair) bucle; rizo; mechón. **8,** (wrestling hold) llave. **9,** (a locking together) trabazón; enganche. —*v.t.* **1,** (secure with a key) cerrar con llave; echar llave a. **2,** [*también,* **lock up**] (close) cerrar. **3,** [*usu.* **lock up**] (put in safekeeping) guardar bajo llave. **4,** (shut in) encerrar. **5,** [*usu.* **lock up**] (jail) encarcelar. **6,** (grip; embrace) aprisionar; encerrar. **7,** *en* **lock out** (shut out) dejar afuera; cerrar la puerta a; dejar en la calle. **8,** (join or link together) enganchar; unir. **9,** (bar or stop from moving) trabar. **10,** (jam) trabar; atrancar. —*v.i.* **1,** (become locked) cerrarse. **2,** (become fixed) clavarse; trancarse; trabarse. —**lock on,** fijarse en; centrarse en. —**lock, stock and barrel,** entero; todo. —**under lock and key,** bajo llave.
locker ('lak·ər) *n.* **1,** (closet) ropero; armario. **2,** (filing cabinet) casillero; clasificador. **3,** (compartment with a lock) compartimento con llave; casillero; casilla. **4,** (drawer) gaveta; cajón.
locket ('lak·ɪt) *n.* relicario; medallón.
lockjaw *n.* tétano.
lockout *n.* paro.
locksmith *n.* cerrajero.
loco ('lo·ko) *adj., slang* loco.
loco- (lo·ko; -kə) *prefijo* loco-; lugar: *locomotion,* locomoción.
locomotion (,lo·kə'mo·ʃən) *n.* locomoción.
locomotive (,lo·kə'mo·tɪv) *adj.* locomotor. —*n.* locomotora.
locomotor (,lo·kə'mo·tər) *adj.* locomotor; locomotriz. —**locomotor ataxia,** ataxia locomotriz.
locus ('lo·kəs) *n.* [*pl.* **loci**] lugar; *geom.* lugar geométrico.
locust ('lo·kəst) *n.* **1,** *entom.* langosta; *U.S.* cicada. **2,** *bot.* acacia falsa.
locution (lo'kju·ʃən) *n.* locución.
lode (lo:d) *n.* veta; filón.
lodestar *n.* estrella (de guía); *fig.* norte.
lodestone *n.* piedra imán.
lodge (la:dʒ) *n.* **1,** (gatehouse; porter's lodge) garita; portería. **2,** (small adjoining house) casita; pabellón. **3,** (country or summer cottage) casa de campo; casa de veraneo; chalet. **4,** (cabin; hut) cabaña. **5,** (boarding house) casa de huéspedes; pensión. **6,** (fraternal society) logia. —*v.t.* **1,** (provide lodging for) alojar; hospedar. **2,** (deposit, as for safekeeping) depositar; confiar. **3,** (place; insert) alojar; meter. **4,** (present formally) presentar formalmente. —*v.i.* **1,** (have lodging) alojar; hospedarse; aposentarse. **2,** (be or remain fixed) alojarse. —**lodger,** *n.* huésped.
lodging ('ladʒ·ɪŋ) *n.* [*también pl.* **lodgings**] alojamiento; habitación.
loft (lɔft) *n.* **1,** (attic) desván; mansarda. **2,** (hayloft) pajar. **3,** (floor space in a warehouse or factory) piso; local. **4,** (lifting stroke) tiro por lo alto. —*v.t.* tirar por lo alto. —*v.i.* elevarse; remontarse.
lofty ('lɔf·ti) *adj.* alto; elevado. —**loftiness,** *n.* altura; elevación.
log (lɔ:g) *n.* **1,** (piece of timber) tronco; madero; leño. **2,** (record) anotación; crónica; registro; *naut.* diario de navegación; cuaderno de bitácora. **3,** = **logarithm.** —*v.t.* [**logged, logging**] **1,** (cut into logs) aserrar; serrar. **2,** (record) hacer crónica de; registrar; anotar. —*v.i.* serrar y transportar maderos. —**logger,** *n.* cortador de árboles; maderero; leñador. —**logging,** *n.* extracción de maderas.
-log (lɔg; lag) *sufijo, var. de* **-logue:** *catalog,* catálogo.
logarithm ('lag·ə·rɪð·əm) *n.*

logaritmo. —**logarithmic** (-'rɪð·rɪk) *adj.* logarítmico.
loge (loːʒ) *n.* palco.
loggerhead ('lɔg·ər,hɛd) *n.* zopenco; mentecato. —**at loggerheads**, en riña; en disputa.
loggia ('ladʒ·ə) *n.* logia; galería.
logic ('ladʒ·ɪk) *n.* lógica. —**logical**, *adj.* lógico.
-logic ('ladʒ·ɪk) *también,* **-logical** ('ladʒ·ɪk·əl) *sufijo* -logico; *forma adjetivos de nombres terminados en* **-logy**: *analogic; analogical,* analógico.
logician (lo'dʒɪʃ·ən) *n.* lógico.
logistics (lo'dʒɪs·tɪks) *n.* logística (*sing.*). —**logistic; logistical**, *adj.* logístico.
logo- (lɔg·ə; lag-) *prefijo* logo-; palabra: *logotype,* logotipo.
-logue *también,* **-log** (lɔg; lag) *sufijo* -logo; *forma nombres denotando* conversación; escrito; descripción: *dialogue,* diálogo; *Decalogue,* decálogo; *catalogue,* catálogo.
logy ('lo·gi) *adj.* lerdo; torpe; pesado.
-logy (lə·dʒi) *sufijo* **-logía**; *forma nombres denotando* **1,** ciencia; doctrina: *cosmology,* cosmología. **2,** colección; grupo: *anthology,* antología.
loin (lɔin) *n.* lomo. —**loins**, *n.pl.* riñones.
loincloth *n.* taparrabos (*pl.*).
loiter ('lɔi·tər) *v.i.* **1,** (linger idly) holgazanear; perder el tiempo. **2,** (dally) remolonear.
loiterer ('lɔi·tər·ər) *n.* holgazán; remolón; vago.
loitering ('lɔi·tər·ɪŋ) *n.* holgazanería; remoloneo; vagancia. —*adj.* holgazán; remolón; vago.
loll (laːl) *v.i.* **1,** (recline; lounge) arrellanarse; tenderse; recostarse. **2,** (hang; droop) caer; pender; colgar. —*v.t.* dejar caer *o* colgar.
lollipop ('lal·i,pap) *n.* pirulí; *Amer.* chupete.
lone (loːn) *adj.* **1,** (solitary) solitario; solo. **2,** (single; unwed) soltero.
lonely ('lon·li) *adj.* **1,** (isolated) solitario; aislado. **2,** [*también,* **lonesome**] (alone) solo; solitario. —**loneliness; lonesomeness**, *n.* soledad.
long (lɔːŋ) *adj.* **1,** (of great extent) largo. **2,** (of a specified length) de largo. **3,** (far-reaching) amplio; extenso. **4,** (large; big) grande. **5,** (tall) largo; alto. **6,** *en* **long on, in** *o* **of** (well provided with) que tiene mucho . . . ; de mucho . . . ; luengo en. . . . —*adv.* **1,** (for a long time) mucho; mucho tiempo; en *o* por mucho tiempo. **2,** (for the duration of) todo el . . . en todo el . . . : *all day long,* (en) todo el día. —*n.* largo; longitud. —*v.i.* ansiar; desear; anhelar. —**as** (*o* **so**) **long as, 1,** (since) puesto que; ya que. **2,** (provided that) con tal que; siempre que. **3,** (while) mientras. —**be long**, tardar mucho. —**before long**, pronto. —**how long**, cuánto tiempo; cuánto. —**long ago**, hace mucho (tiempo). —**long for**, morirse por. —**long since**, mucho ántes. —**the long and the short of (it)**, en dos palabras.
-long (lɔŋ)) *sufijo; forma adjetivos y adverbios denotando* extensión; dirección: *sidelong,* de costado; *headlong,* de cabeza.
long-distance *adj.* de larga distancia; interurbano.
long-drawn *adj.* prolongado; largo.
longevity (lɔn'dʒɛv·ə·ti) *n.* longevidad.
longhand *n.* escritura a mano.
longing ('lɔŋ·ɪŋ) *n.* anhelo; ansia. —**longingly**, *adv.* con anhelo; con ansia.
longitude ('lɔn·dʒə,tjud) *n.* longitud. —**longitudinal** (-'tju·dɪ·nəl) *adj.* longitudinal.
long-lived ('lɔŋ'laivd) *adj.* longevo.
longshoreman ('lɔŋ,ʃor·mən) *n.* [*pl.* **-men**] estibador; cargador de muelle.
long ton tonelada grande (*2,240 libras*).
longwinded ('lɔŋ,wɪn·dɪd) *adj.* palabrero. —**longwindedness**, *n.* palabrería; lata.
look (lʊk) *v.i.* **1,** [*usu. en* **look at** *o* **upon**] (see; behold) mirar; ver. **2,** (search) buscar; mirar. **3,** (seem; appear) parecer; tener apariencia. **4,** (face or be turned in a given direction) dar (a); mirar (a). **5,** [*en* **look to** *o* **for**] (hope; expect) esperar; confiar. **6,** (keep watch; take heed) mirar; tener cuidado. —*v.t.* **1,** [*en* **look up**] (try to find) buscar. **2,** (suggest by appearance) parecer; parecer tener (cierta

edad). —*n.* 1, (act of looking) mirada. 2, [*también pl.* **looks**] (appearance; aspect) apariencia; aspecto. —**look after**, cuidar (de); encargarse de. —**look alive**, *colloq.* estar alerta; despabilarse. —**look daggers**, mirar con ira; echar rayos por los ojos. —**look down on** (*o* **upon**), tener a menos; menospreciar. —**look for**, 1, (seek) buscar. 2, (expect; hope for) esperar; confiar. —**look forward to**, esperar; confiar; esperar gozar de. —**look in** (**on**), hacer una visita corta (a). —**look into**, investigar; examinar. —**look like**, 1, (resemble) parecerse a. 2, (seem to be) parecer. 3, *colloq.* (seem as if) parecer que: *It looks like rain,* Parece que va a llover. —**look on**, observar; mirar; ver. —**look oneself**, parecerse uno; parecer él mismo. —**look out**, tener cuidado. —**look out for**, cuidar (de); encargarse de. —**look over**, examinar; repasar. —**look through**, repasar; mirar por. —**look to**, 1, (take care of; give attention to) mirar por; cuidar de. 2, (resort to) acudir a. 3, (expect; look forward to) esperar; confiar. —**look up**, 1, (try to find) buscar. 2, (consult) consultar. 3, *colloq.* (call on; visit) ir a visitar. 4, *colloq.* (improve) mejorar; tomar buen cariz. —**look up to**, admirar.

looker ('lʊk·ər) *n.* 1, (watcher) espectador. 2, *slang* (handsome person) bombón.

looker-on *n.* espectador; mirón.

looking glass espejo.

lookout *n.* 1, (watch) guardia; vigilancia. 2, (person who keeps watch) vigía; centinela. 3, (vantage point) puesto de observación. 4, *colloq.* (care; concern) problema; asunto. —**on the lookout** (**for**), alerta (para); a la mira (de).

loom (lu:m) *n.* telar; *fig.* urdimbre. —*v.i.* 1, (appear dimly) vislumbrarse. 2, *fig.* (impend) cernerse. —**loom large**, proyectarse ampliamente.

loon (lu:n) *n.* 1, *ornith.* somorgujo. 2, *slang* (dolt) bobo.

loony ('lu·ni) *adj.* & *n.*, *slang* lunático.

loop (lup) *n.* 1, (doubled cord) lazo. 2, (fastening) alamar; presilla. 3, (turn; bend) recodo; vuelta. 4, *aero.* rizo. —*v.t.* 1, (fasten) enlazar. 2, (form loops) hacer lazos. —*v.i.* dar vueltas. —**loop the loop**, hacer el rizo.

loophole *n.* escapatoria; salida.

loose (lus) *adj.* 1, (free; unattached) libre; suelto. 2, (roomy; loose-fitting) holgado. 3, (not tight; slack) flojo. 4, (diffuse) difuso; impreciso. 5, (morally lax) relajado; libre. —*v.t.* 1, (set free; release) soltar; dejar escapar *o* ir. 2, (unfasten; slacken) desatar; aflojar. 3, (let fly; fire) disparar; lanzar. —**at a loose end**, sin nada que hacer. —**at loose ends**, en desorden. —**break loose**, soltarse; escaparse. —**cast loose**, soltar; dejar suelto. —**cut loose**, 1, (make or become unfastened) romper los lazos; soltar las amarras. 2, (make or become free) librar(se); soltar(se). 3, *colloq.* (go on a spree) ir *o* estar de juerga. —**loose ends**, cabos sueltos. —**on the loose**, suelto; libre. —**turn, let** *o* **set loose**, soltar; dejar suelto.

loosen ('lu·sən) *v.t.* aflojar; soltar. —*v.i.* aflojarse; soltarse.

looseness ('lus·nəs) *n.* 1, (roominess) holgura. 2, (diffuseness) imprecisión. 3, (slackness) lo flojo. 4, (moral laxity) relajación; libertad.

loot (lut) *n.* botín. —*v.t.* saquear. —**looter**, *n.* saqueador.

lop (lap) *v.t.* [**lopped, lopping**] 1, (trim; cut off) cortar; cercenar. 2, (let droop) inclinar; dejar colgar. —*v.i.* pender; colgar.

lope (lop) *v.i.* andar a paso largo. —*n.* medio galope; paso largo.

lopsided ('lap,sai·dɪd) *adj.* desequilibrado. —**lopsidedness**, *n.* desequilibrio.

loquacious (lo'kwei·ʃəs) *adj.* locuaz. —**loquacity** (lo'kwæs·ə·ti); **loquaciousness**, *n.* locuacidad.

loran ('lor·ən) *n.* lorán.

lord (lord) *n.* señor. —**lord it over**, imponerse a; dominar. —**Lord's Prayer**, padrenuestro. —**Lord's Supper**, Eucaristía.

lordly ('lord·li) *adj.* 1, (of or befitting a lord) de señor; señorial. 2, (imperious) imperioso. 3, (haughty) altivo; altanero. —**lordliness**, *n.* señorío.

lordship ('lord·ʃɪp) *n.* señoría.

lore (lo:r) *n.* ciencia; saber.

lorgnette (lor'njɛt) *n.* impertinentes (*pl.*).
lorry ('lor·i) *n.* camión.
lose (luːz) *v.t.* & *i.* [*pret.* & *p.p.* **lost**] perder. —*v.i.* (run slow, as a watch) atrasarse. —**loser,** *n.* perdedor.
loss (lɔs) *n.* pérdida. —**at a loss,** perplejo; confundido.
lost (lɔst) *v., pret.* & *p.p. de* **lose.** —*adj.* perdido.
lot (lat) *n.* **1,** (chance; destiny) suerte. **2,** (parcel of land) solar; parcela; *Amer.* lote. **3,** (unit quantity) cantidad. **4,** *colloq.,* [*también pl.* **lots**] (much; many) gran cantidad *o* número; mucho *o* muchos. —**cast lots,** echar suertes.
lotion ('lo·ʃən) *n.* loción.
lottery ('lat·ə·ri) *n.* lotería.
lotus ('lo·təs) *n.* loto.
loud (laud) *adj.* **1,** (strongly audible) fuerte; (*esp. of the voice*) alto. **2,** (noisy; clamorous) ruidoso; fuerte. **3,** *colloq.* (garish) chillón. **4,** *colloq.* (vulgar) bullanguero. —*adv.* fuerte; alto. —**loudness,** *n.* volumen; intensidad; fuerza.
loudmouth *n.m.* barbullón. —**loudmouthed** (-mauðd) *adj.* barbullón; vocinglero.
loudspeaker *n.* altavoz; *Amer.* altoparlante.
lounge (laundʒ) *v.i.* **1,** (loll) arrellanarse; ponerse *o* estar a sus anchas. **2,** (rest; idle) descansar. **3,** (loiter) holgazanear; estar de vago. —*n.* **1,** (public room) salón (de fumar, de espera, etc.). **2,** (sofa) canapé. **3,** (slovenly gait or posture) holgazanería; descuido. —**lounger,** *n.* ocioso; holgazán.
louse (laus) *n.* [*pl.* **lice**] piojo.
lousy ('lau·zi) *adj.* **1,** (infested with lice) piojoso. **2,** *slang* (mean; contemptible) asqueroso; horrible. **3,** *slang, en* **lousy with** (well supplied) colmado (de); nadando (en). —**lousiness,** *n.* piojería; asquerosidad.
lout (laut) *n.* patán; zafio. —**loutish,** *adj.* patán; zafio.
louver ('lu·vər) *n.* lumbrera (de tablillas); persiana.
lovable *también,* **loveable** ('lʌv·ə·bəl) *adj.* encantador; simpático.
love (lʌv) *n.* **1,** (affection; object of affection) amor; cariño. **2,** *sports* (no score) cero; nada. —*v.t.* **1,** (have affection for) amar; querer. **2,** (like; enjoy) encantarle a uno. —*v.i.* amar; querer; estar enamorado. —**be in love (with)** estar enamorado (de). —**fall in love (with),** enamorarse (de). —**love potion,** filtro (de amor).
lovebird *n.* **1,** (bird) periquito. **2,** *pl.* (lovers) tórtolos.
lovelorn ('lʌvˌlorn) *adj.* suspirando de amor.
lovely ('lʌv·li) *adj.* encantador; bonito. —**loveliness,** *n.* encanto; belleza.
lover ('lʌv·ər) *n.* amante.
love seat confidente; canapé de dos asientos.
lovesick *adj.* enamorado; chalado. —**lovesickness,** *n.* mal de amor *o* amores.
loving ('lʌv·ɪŋ) *adj.* **1,** (feeling love; devoted) cariñoso; amoroso. **2,** (expressing love) de cariño; de amor. —*n.* amor; cariño. —**loving cup,** copa de la amistad.
low (loː) *adj.* **1,** (not high) bajo. **2,** (inferior) inferior. **3,** (base; mean) bajo; vil. **4,** (not loud; soft) bajo. **5,** (deep) profundo. **6,** (vulgar; coarse) vulgar. **7,** (humble) humilde. **8,** (not many in number) pocos. **9,** (short; in short supply) poco; escaso. **10,** (dejected) abatido; desanimado. **11,** (weak; enfeebled) postrado; débil. —*adv.* **1,** (in a low position, manner, degree, etc.) bajo. **2,** (cheaply) barato. —*n.* **1,** (something low) bajo. **2,** (low point or degree) mínimo. **3,** (low gear) primera (velocidad). **4,** *meteorol.* depresión. **5,** (sound of cattle) mugido. —*v.i.* mugir. —**lay low, 1,** (fell) derribar; derrotar. **2,** (kill) matar. —**lie low,** esconderse; estar *o* quedarse escondido. —**Low Mass,** misa rezada. —**low spirits,** abatimiento; falta de ánimo. —**low tide,** bajamar; marea baja.
lowborn *adj.* de origen humilde; plebeyo.
lowbred *adj.* tosco; grosero.
lowbrow *n.* & *adj., colloq.* ignorante; poco refinado.
low-class *adj.* de clase baja.
low-down *n., slang* datos (*pl.*); información. —*adj., colloq.* bajo; vil; despreciable.
lower ('lo·ər) *v.t.* **1,** (move or let down) bajar. **2,** (reduce) bajar; rebajar; disminuir. **3,** (degrade) humillar; rebajar. —*v.i.*

bajar; menguar; disminuir. —*adj.* más bajo; inferior. —*adv.* más bajo; más abajo.
lower ('lau·ər) *v.i.* **1,** (scowl) fruncir el ceño; mirar con mal ceño. **2,** (become overcast) encapotarse. —**lowering,** *adj.* ceñudo; encapotado.
lower berth litera baja.
lower case caja baja; (letra) minúscula; letra de caja baja. —**lower-case,** *adj.* de caja baja; minúscula; de *o* con minúsculas.
lowerclassman ('lo·ər'klæs·mən) *n.* [*pl.* **-men**] alumno universitario de los dos primeros años.
lower house cámara baja.
low-grade *adj.* de poca calidad; de calidad inferior.
lowland ('lo·lənd) *n.* tierra baja. —**lowlander,** *n.* habitante de tierras bajas.
lowly ('lo·li) *adj.* humilde. —*adv.* con humildad; humildemente. —**lowliness,** *n.* humildad.
low-necked *adj.* escotado.
low-pressure *adj.* **1,** (of or for low pressure) de baja presión. **2,** (subdued; mild) suave; de *o* con poca insistencia.
low-priced *adj.* barato.
low-spirited *adj.* desanimado; sin humor.
low water **1,** (of a river or stream) estiaje. **2,** (low tide) bajamar. —**low-water mark, 1,** *lit.* nivel de bajamar *o* estiaje. **2,** *fig.* punto más bajo.
loyal ('lɔi·əl) *adj.* leal. —**loyalty,** *n.* lealtad.
loyalist ('lɔi·əl·ɪst) *n.* **1,** (monarchist) realista. **2,** (republican) republicano.
lozenge ('laz·əndʒ) *n.* **1,** (pastille) pastilla. **2,** (diamond-shaped figure) rombo; losange.
lubber ('lʌb·ər) *n.* tonto; marinero de agua dulce. —**lubberly,** *adj.* tonto; zafio.
lubricate ('lu·brɪ,keit) *v.t.* lubricar; engrasar. —**lubricant,** *n.* & *adj.* lubricante. —**lubrication,** *n.* lubricación; engrase.
lucerne (lu'sʌɹn) *n.* alfalfa.
lucid ('lu·sɪd) *adj.* lúcido.
lucidity (lu'sɪd·ə·ti) *n.* lucidez.
luck (lʌk) *n.* suerte; fortuna. —**luckless,** *adj.* desafortunado. —**lucky,** *adj.* afortunado. —**luckiness,** *n.* buena suerta; buena fortuna.
lucrative ('lu·krə·tɪv) *adj.* lucrativo.
lucre ('lu·kər) *n.* lucro.
lucubrate ('lu·kjʊ,breit) *v.i.* lucubrar. —**lucubration,** *n.* lucubración.
ludicrous ('lu·dɪ·krəs) *adj.* ridículo; risible. —**ludicrousness,** *n.* ridiculez; lo risible.
lug (lʌg) *v.t.* [**lugged, lugging**] arrastrar; tirar (de); cargar con. —*n.* **1,** (tug) tirón. **2,** (projecting part) saliente. **3,** *colloq.* (sluggish fellow) zángano; posma.
luggage ('lʌg·ɪdʒ) *n.* equipaje; maletas (*pl.*).
lugubrious (lu'gu·bri·əs) *adj.* lúgubre. —**lugubriousness,** *n.* lo lúgubre.
lukewarm ('luk,worm) *adj.* tibio. —**lukewarmness,** *n.* tibieza.
lull (lʌl) *v.t.* arrullar; adormecer. —*v.i.* calmarse; sosegarse. —*n.* momento de calma *o* de silencio.
lullaby ('lʌl·ə·bai) *n.* arrullo.
lumbago (lʌm'bei·go) *n.* lumbago.
lumbar ('lʌm·bər) *adj.* lumbar.
lumber ('lʌm·bər) *n.* madera. —*v.i.* andar *o* moverse pesadamente.
lumbering ('lʌm·bər·ɪŋ) *adj.* **1,** (clumsy) pesado; tardo. **2,** (pert. to the lumber industry) maderero; de la madera. —*n.* industria de la madera; industria maderera.
lumberjack *n.* leñador.
lumberman ('lʌm·bər·mən) *n.* [*pl.* **-men**] **1,** = **lumberjack. 2,** (lumber dealer) maderero.
lumberyard *n.* almacén de maderas.
luminary ('lu·mə·nɛr·i) *n.* lumbrera; luminaria.
luminescence (,lu·mə'nɛs·əns) *n.* luminiscencia. —**luminescent,** *adj.* luminiscente.
luminosity (lu·mɪ'nas·ə·ti) *n.* luminosidad.
luminous ('lu·mə·nəs) *adj.* luminoso.
lummox ('lʌm·əks) *n., colloq.* tonto; bobo.
lump (lʌmp) *n.* **1,** (shapeless mass) pedazo; masa. **2,** (lump of sugar; clod of earth) terrón. **3,** (swelling; bump) bulto; chichón; hinchazón. **4,** (clot) grumo. **5,** (dolt) bobo. —*adj.* en forma de

terrón. —*v.t.* poner junto; agrupar. —*v.i.* 1, (swell) hincharse. 2, (form lumps) hacer grumos. 3, (move heavily) andar pesadamente. —**lump it**, *colloq.* tragarlo. —**lump sum**, suma total.

lumpy ('lʌm·pi) *adj.* 1, (swollen) hinchado. 2, (bumpy) abollado. 3, (containing lumps) con grumos; que tiene grumos. 4, [*también*, **lumpish**] (doltish) bobo; necio.

lunacy ('lu·nə·si) *n.* locura.

lunar ('lu·nər) *adj.* lunar.

lunatic ('lu·nə·tɪk) *n.* & *adj.* lunático; loco.

lunch (lʌntʃ) *n.* 1, (midday meal) almuerzo. 2, (any light meal) refrigerio. —*v.i.* almorzar.

luncheon ('lʌn·tʃən) *n.* almuerzo. —**luncheonette** (-'ɛt) *n.* cantina.

lunchroom *n.* comedor.

lung (lʌŋ) *n.* pulmón. —**at the top of one's lungs**, a grito pelado; a pulmón tendido. —**iron lung**, pulmón artificial.

lunge (lʌndʒ) *n.* 1, (thrust) estocada; golpe a fondo. 2, (onslaught) acometida; arremetida. 3, (forward plunge) impulso; movimiento brusco. —*v.i.* 1, (thrust) irse a fondo; dar una estocada. 2, (attack; charge) acometer; arremeter. 3, (plunge forward) abalanzarse; tirarse.

luni- (lu·nɪ; -nə) *prefijo* luni-; luna: *lunisolar*, lunisolar.

lupine ('lu·pɪn) *adj.* lupino.

lurch (lʌɹtʃ) *v.i.* dar sacudidas *o* tirones; *naut.* dar bandazos. —*n.* sacudida; tirón; *naut.* bandazo. —**in the lurch**, 1, (far behind) a la cola. 2, (forsaken) colgado; plantado.

lure (lur) *n.* 1, (bait) cebo; anzuelo; señuelo. 2, (decoy) reclamo. 3, (enticement) atracción; atractivo. —*v.t.* atraer; tentar.

lurid ('lur·ɪd) *adj.* 1, (glowing) ardiente. 2, (sensational) sensacional; escandaloso.

lurk (lʌɹk) *v.i.* 1, (be concealed) estar escondido *o* oculto. 2, (lie in wait) acechar; estar en acecho.

luscious ('lʌʃ·əs) *adj.* delicioso; exquisito; sabroso. —**lusciousness**, *n.* exquisitez.

lush (lʌʃ) *adj.* 1, (fresh; juicy) lozano; jugoso. 2, (luxuriant) exuberante. —*n.*, *slang* (drunkard) borrachón. —**lushness**, *n.* lozanía; exuberancia.

lust (lʌst) *n.* 1, (strong desire) deseo; ansia. 2, (carnal appetite) lujuria; concupiscencia. —*v.i.* codiciar; desear. —**lustful**, *adj.* lujurioso. —**lusty**, *adj.* fuerte; vigoroso. —**lustiness**, *n.* fuerza; vigor.

luster *también*, **lustre** ('lʌs·tər) *n.* lustre. —**lustrous** (-trəs) *adj.* lustroso.

lute (lut) *n.* laúd.

lutecium (lu'ti·ʃi·əm) *n.* lutecio.

Lutheran ('lu·θə·rən) *n.* & *adj.* luterano. —**Lutheranism**, *n.* luteranismo.

luxuriate (lʌg'ʒur·i,eit) *v.i.* 1, (grow profusely) abundar; crecer con abundancia. 2, [*usu.* **luxuriate in**] (enjoy) deleitarse (en); disfrutar (de). —**luxuriant**, *adj.* abundante; lujuriante; *fig.* recargado. —**luxuriance**, *n.* abundancia; profusión.

luxury ('lʌk·ʃə·ri) *n.* lujo. —**luxurious** (lʌg'ʒur·i·əs) *adj.* lujoso. —**luxuriousness**, *n.* lujo; lo lujoso.

-ly (li) *sufijo; forma* 1, *adjetivos denotando* relación; pertenencia: *manly*, varonil. 2, *adverbios de modo: quickly*, de prisa; *slowly*, despacio. 3, *adverbios de tiempo: weekly*, semanalmente; por semana; a la semana.

lyceum (lai'si·əm) *n.* liceo; ateneo.

lye (lai) *n.* lejía.

lying ('lai·ɪŋ) *v.*, *ger. de* **lie.** —*n.* mentira. —*adj.* 1, (recumbent) recostado; acostado. 2, (located) situado. 3, (false) mentiroso.

lying-in *n.* parto. —**lying-in hospital**, clínica de maternidad.

lymph (lɪmf) *n.* linfa. —**lymphatic** (lɪm'fæt·ɪk) *adj.* linfático.

lynch (lɪntʃ) *v.t.* linchar. —**lynching**, *n.* linchamiento.

lynx (lɪŋks) *n.* lince.

lyre (lair) *n.* lira.

lyric ('lɪr·ɪk) *adj.* lírico. —*n.* 1, (lyric poem) poema lírico. 2, (lyric poetry) lírica. 3, *colloq.* (words of a song) letra. —**lyrical**, *adj.* lírico. —**lyricism** ('lɪr·ɪ·sɪz·əm) *n.* lirismo.

-lysis (lə·sɪs) *sufijo* -lisis; desintegración; destrucción: *analysis*, análisis; *paralysis*, parálisis.

-lyte (lait) *sufijo* -lito; *forma nombres denotando* resultado *o* producto de desintegración *o* destrucción: *electrolyte,* electrolito.
-lytic ('lɪt·ɪk) *sufijo* -lítico; *forma adjetivos de nombres terminados en* **-lysis**: *analytic,* analítico. *paralytic,* paralítico.
-lyze (laiz) *sufijo* -lizar; *forma verbos de nombres terminados en* **-lysis**: *paralyze,* paralizar; *analyze,* analizar.

M

M, m (ɛm) decimotercera letra del alfabeto inglés.
ma'am (mæm) *n., colloq.* = **madam.**
macabre (mə'ka·brə) *también,* **macaber** (-bər) *adj.* macabro.
macadam (mə'kæd·əm) *n.* macadán; macádam. —**macadamize,** *v.t.* macadamizar.
macaque (mə'kak) *n.* macaco.
macaroni (ˌmæk·ə'ro·ni) *n.* macarrón; macarrones (*pl.*).
macaroon (ˌmæk·ə'ruːn) *n.* almendrado; macarrón.
macaw (mə'kɔː) *n.* guacamayo; papagayo.
mace (meis) *n.* **1,** (club; staff) maza; clava; porra. **2,** (spice) macias; macis.
macerate ('mæs·əˌreit) *v.t.* macerar. —**maceration,** *n.* maceración.
machete (ma'tʃe·te; mə'ʃɛt; mə'ʃɛt·i) *n.* machete.
Machiavellian (ˌmæk·i·ə'vɛl·i·ən) *adj.* maquiavélico; maquiavelista. —*n.* maquiavelista. —**Machiavellism,** *n.* maquiavelismo.
machinate ('mæk·əˌneit) *v.t.* & *i.* maquinar. —**machination,** *n.* maquinación.
machine (mə'ʃiːn) *n.* **1,** (mechanical device) máquina; aparato. **2,** *polit.* camarilla. **3,** = **automobile.** —*v.t.* trabajar a máquina. —**machine gun,** ametralladora. —**machine gun,** *v.t.* [**-gunned, -gunning**] ametrallar. —**machine gunner,** ametrallador.
machinery (mə'ʃi·nə·ri) *n.* maquinaria; mecanismo.
machinist (mə'ʃi·nɪst) *n.* maquinista.
mackerel ('mæk·ər·əl) *n.* caballa; escombro.
mackinaw ('mæk·ə·nɔ) *n.* chaquetón; chamarra.
mackintosh ('mæk·ɪnˌtaʃ) *n.* impermeable.
macro- (mæk·ro; -rə) *prefijo* macro-; largo; grande: *macroscopic,* macroscópico.
macrocosm ('mæk·rəˌkaz·əm) *n.* macrocosmo.
macron ('mei·kran) *n.* signo de vocal larga: ā.
macroscopic (ˌmæk·rə'skap·ɪk) *adj.* macroscópico.
mad (mæd) *adj.* **1,** (insane) loco. **2,** (rabid) rabioso. **3,** *colloq.* (angry) furioso. —**be mad about,** *colloq.* estar loco por. —**get mad,** *colloq.* enfadarse. —**go mad,** enloquecer.
madam ('mæd·əm) *n.* señora. *También,* **madame** (ma'daːm).
madcap ('mædˌkæp) *n.* & *adj.* tarambana.
madden ('mæd·ən) *v.t.* **1,** (drive mad) enloquecer. **2,** (make furious) enfurecer. —**maddening,** *adj.* exasperante; enloquecedor.
madder ('mæd·ər) *n.* rubia. —*adj., comp. de* **mad.**
made (meid) *v., pret.* & *p.p. de* **make.** —*adj.* **1,** (artificially produced) hecho; fabricado. **2,** *colloq.* (assured of success) hecho; asegurado.
mademoiselle (ˌmæd·mwə'zɛl) *n.* [*pl.* **mesdemoiselles** (ˌmed·mwə'zɛl)] señorita.
made-up *adj.* **1,** (contrived) artificial; ficticio. **2,** (assembled) compuesto. **3,** (with cosmetics applied) maquillado.
madhouse *n.* manicomio.
madman *n.* [*pl.* **-men**] loco. —**madwoman,** *n.* [*pl.* **-women**] loca.
madness ('mæd·nɪs) *n.* **1,** (insanity; folly; excitement) locura. **2,** (fury) furor; ira. **3,** (rabies) rabia.
Madonna (mə'dan·ə) *n.* madona; Nuestra Señora.
madrigal ('mæd·rɪ·gəl) *n.* madrigal.
maelstrom ('meil·strəm) *n.* maelstrom; remolino; vorágine.

maestro ('mai·stro) *n.* maestro.
magazine (ˌmæg·əˈziːn) *n.* **1,** (publication) revista. **2,** (supply receptacle, as of a firearm) cargador. **3,** (depository for powder) polvorín. **4,** (storage place) almacén.
magenta (məˈdʒɛn·tə) *n. & adj.* magenta.
maggot ('mæg·ət) *n.* cresa; gusano.
Magi ('mei·dʒai) *n.pl.* magos; *Bib.* reyes magos.
magic ('mædʒ·ɪk) *n.* magia. —*adj.* [*también,* **magical**] mágico. —**magician** (məˈdʒɪʃ·ən) *n.* mago; brujo. —**by magic,** por ensalmo; por arte de magia.
magisterial (ˌmædʒ·ɪsˈtɪr·i·əl) *adj.* **1,** (masterly; authoritative) magistral. **2,** (of or pert. to a magistrate) de magistrado. **3,** (pompous) magisterial.
magistrate ('mædʒ·ɪsˌtreit) *n.* magistrado. —**magistracy** (-trə·si) *n.* magistratura.
Magna Charta *o* **Carta** ('mæg·nəˈkar·tə) *n.* Carta Magna.
magnanimous (mægˈnæn·ə·məs) *adj.* magnánimo. —**magnanimity** (ˌmæg·nəˈnɪm·ə·ti) *n.* magnanimidad.
magnate ('mæg·neit) *n.* magnate.
magnesia (mægˈni·ʒə) *n.* magnesia.
magnesium (mægˈni·ʒi·əm) *n.* magnesio.
magnet ('mæg·nɪt) *n.* imán. —**magnetic** (mægˈnɛt·ɪk) *adj.* magnético. —**magnetism,** *n.* magnetismo. —**magnetize,** *v.t.* magnetizar.
magnetite ('mag·nəˌtait) *n.* magnetita.
magneto (mægˈni·to) *n.* magneto.
magni- (mag·nɪ) *prefijo* magni-; grande: *magnificent,* magnífico.
magnificent (mægˈnɪf·ə·sənt) *adj.* magnífico. —**magnificence,** *n.* magnificencia.
magnify ('mæg·nəˌfai) *v.t.* magnificar; agrandar. —**magnification** (-fɪˈkei·ʃən) *n.* magnificación. —**magnifying,** *adj.* de aumento. —**magnifying glass,** lupa; vidrio *o* luna de aumento.
magniloquent (mægˈnɪl·ə·kwənt) *adj.* grandilocuente. —**magniloquence,** *n.* grandilocuencia.
magnitude ('mæg·nəˌtjud) *n.* magnitud.
magnolia (mægˈno·li·ə) *n.* magnolia.
magnum ('mæg·nəm) *n.* botella grande; botellón.
magpie ('mægˌpai) *n.* **1,** (bird) urraca; cotorra. **2,** (chatterbox) cotorra; parlanchín.
maguey ('mæg·we) *n.* pita; maguey.
Magyar ('ma·gjar) *n. & adj.* magiar.
maharajah (ˌma·həˈra·dʒə) *n.* maharajá. —**maharanee** (-ni) *n.* maharaní.
mahogany (məˈhag·ə·ni) *n.* **1,** (tree) caobo; caoba. **2,** (wood) caoba.
Mahometan (məˈham·ə·tən) *n. & adj.* = **Mohammedan.**
maid (meid) *n.* **1,** (young woman) doncella; moza. **2,** (servant) criada; sirvienta. —**maid of honor,** madrina de boda.
maiden ('mei·dən) *n.* virgen; doncella; joven soltera. —*adj.* **1,** (virginal) virginal. **2,** (unmarried) soltera. **3,** (first) inicial. —**maidenhood,** *n.* doncellez; virginidad. —**maidenly,** *adj.* virginal; modesto; pudoroso.
maidenhead ('mei·dən·hɛd) *n.* **1,** = **maidenhood. 2,** (hymen) virgo; himen.
mail (meil) *n.* **1,** (post) correo. **2,** (letters) correspondencia; correo. **3,** (armor) malla. —*v.t.* enviar por correo; echar al correo. —**mail order,** pedido postal. —**mail-order house,** casa de ventas por correo; casa de pedidos postales.
mailbag *n.* portacartas. *También,* **mail pouch.**
mailbox *n.* buzón.
mailman *n.* [*pl.* **-men**] cartero.
maim (meim) *v.t.* **1,** (mutilate) mutilar. **2,** (cripple; damage) estropear; lisiar.
main (mein) *adj.* **1,** (chief) principal. **2,** (sheer) puro. —*n.* **1,** (pipe) cañería maestra. **2,** (ocean) alta mar; piélago. **3,** (strength) fuerza. —**mainly,** *adv.* principalmente; sobre todo. —**by main force** (*o* **strength**), a puro pulso; a pura fuerza. —**with might and main,** con toda fuerza.
mainland ('mein·lənd) *n.* continente; tierra firme.

mainmast ('mein,mæst; -məst) *n.* palo mayor.
mainsail ('mein,seil; -səl) *n.* vela mayor.
mainspring *n.* **1,** (of a watch) muelle real. **2,** (chief source or motive) móvil *o* causa principal; fuente.
mainstay *n.* base; soporte principal.
main stem *slang* calle principal.
mainstream *n.* corriente común; corriente principal.
maintain (mein'tein) *v.t.* mantener. —**maintenance** ('mein·tə·nəns) *n.* mantenimiento; manutención.
maize (meiz) *n.* maíz.
majesty ('mædʒ·ɪs·ti) *n.* majestad. —**majestic** (mə'dʒɛs·tɪk) adj. majestuoso.
major ('mei·dʒər) *adj & n.* mayor. —*v.i.* especializarse. —**major general,** general de división.
majordomo (,mei·dʒər'do·mo) *n.* mayordomo.
majority (mə'dʒar·ə·ti) *n.* mayoría.
make (meik) *v.t.* **1,** (bring into being; shape; build) hacer. **2,** (cause; bring about) traer; ocasionar; causar: *This made trouble,* Esto trajo dificultades. **3,** (cause to; force to) hacer; obligar. **4,** (establish, as a rule) establecer; imponer. **5,** (cause to be or become) hacer; poner: *That noise makes me nervous,* Ese ruido me pone nervioso. **6,** (turn out to be; become) ser; hacer: *He will make a good hunter,* Hará un buen cazador. **7,** (arrange, as a bed) hacer; arreglar. **8,** (cause to seem) hacer aparecer; hacer: *This picture makes her younger,* Este retrato la hace (aparecer) más joven. **9,** (get; acquire) hacer; hacerse de: *He made many enemies,* Se hizo de muchos enemigos. **10,** (earn) ganar. **11,** (do; perform) hacer. **12,** (amount to; add up to) hacer; sumar. **13,** [*en* **make of**] (understand; infer) sacar; sacar en limpio; pensar. **14,** (estimate to be; regard as) tener por; considerar (como). **15,** (deliver, as a speech) pronunciar. **16,** (utter) proferir; emitir. **17,** (traverse, as a distance) cubrir; recorrer. **18,** (go or move at a certain speed) hacer; correr: *This train makes 60 miles an hour,* Este tren corre 60 millas por hora. **19,** (arrive at; reach) llegar a. **20,** (arrive in time for; catch) llegar a tiempo a *o* para. **21,** *games* (score) hacer. **22,** *slang* (win; succeed in getting) lograr; conseguir. **23,** *colloq.* (gain admission or acceptance in) figurar en. —*v.i.* **1,** *con inf.* (start; attempt) hacer ademán de. **2,** (head; proceed) ir; dirigirse. **3,** (behave) portarse; comportarse. —*n.* **1,** (manufacture) manufactura. **2,** (brand) marca. —**make after,** seguir; perseguir. —**make as if** (*o* **as though**) hacer como que; hacer ademán de. —**make away with, 1,** (steal) robar; birlar. **2,** (get rid of) eliminar; sacar de en medio. —**make believe,** hacer creer. —**make for, 1,** (head for; go toward) ir a *o* hacia; dirigirse a *o* hacia. **2,** (tend toward; promote) fomentar; promover; contribuir a. —**make good, 1,** (succeed) tener éxito; triunfar. **2,** (fulfill) cumplir. **3,** (accept responsibility) responder (por). **4,** (recoup) recobrar. **5,** (compensate; overcome) vencer; superar. **6,** (pay) pagar. —**make it,** *colloq.* conseguirlo; triunfar. —**make off,** salir corriendo. —**make out, 1,** (discern; distinguish) poder ver; distinguir. **2,** (understand) comprender. **3,** (write out; draw up) hacer; extender. **4,** (pretend to be; pass off as) hacer; pasar por. **5,** *colloq.* (manage; get along) arreglárselas. —**make over, 1,** (renovate) renovar; cambiar. **2,** (transfer; sign over) transferir; traspasar. —**make up, 1,** (put together; compose) componer; hacer. **2,** (invent; concoct) inventar; imaginar. **3,** (supply what is lacking) completar; suplir. **4,** (compensate) compensar; pagar. **5,** (arrange) arreglar; hacer. **6,** (recover) recobrar; ganar. **7,** (be reconciled) arreglarse; hacer las paces. **8,** (apply cosmetics) arreglar; maquillar. **9,** (resolve, as one's mind) resolver(se); decidir(se). **10,** (take again, as an examination) volver a examinarse (de). —**make up to,** halagar.
make-believe *adj.* fingido; ficticio; de mentirijillas. —*n.* artificio; pretexto.
maker ('mei·kər) *n.* **1,** (creator; designer) creador; modelador. **2,**

(manufacturer) fabricante. **3,** *cap.* (God) Creador; Hacedor.
makeshift *adj.* provisional; interino. —*n.* expediente.
make-up *n.* **1,** (composition) composición; construcción; arreglo. **2,** (nature; disposition) carácter; disposición; naturaleza. **3,** (cosmetics) maquillaje. **4,** *print.* imposición.
mal- (mæl) *prefijo* mal-; malo; mal; imperfecto: *maladjusted,* desajustado; *maltreatment,* maltrato.
malachite ('mæl·ə·kait) *n.* malaquita.
maladjusted (ˌmæl·ə'dʒʌs·tɪd) *adj.* desajustado; *psychol.* inadaptado. —**maladjustment** (-'dʒʌst·mənt) *n.* desajuste; inadaptación.
maladroit (ˌmæl·ə'drɔit) *adj.* torpe; desmañado.
malady ('mæl·ə·di) *n.* enfermedad; mal.
malaise (mæ'leiz) *n.* malestar; desazón.
malapropism ('mæl·əˌprap·ɪz·əm) *n.* despropósito.
malapropos (ˌmæl·æp·rə'poː) *adj.* impropio; inoportuno; inapropiado.
malar ('mei·lər) *adj.* malar.
malaria (mə'lɛr·i·ə) *n.* malaria.
Malay (mə'lei; 'mei-) *n.* & *adj.* malayo.
malcontent ('mæl·kənˌtɛnt) *n.* & *adj.* malcontento; descontento.
male (meil) *adj.* **1,** (of or pert. to the masculine sex) masculino; (*chiefly of animals*) macho; (*of persons*) varón. **2,** *mech.* macho. **3,** (composed of males) de hombres; masculino. —*n.* **1,** (male person) hombre; varón. **2,** (male animal) macho.
malediction (ˌmæl·ə'dɪk·ʃən) *n.* maldición.
malefactor ('mæl·əˌfæk·tər) *n.* malhechor. —**malefaction** (-'fæk·ʃən) *n.* delito.
maleficent (mə'lɛf·ə·sənt) *adj.* maléfico. —**maleficence,** *n.* maleficencia.
malevolent (mə'lɛv·ə·lənt) *adj.* malévolo. —**malevolence,** *n.* malevolencia.
malfeasance (mæl'fi·zəns) *n.* mal proceder; mala conducta; corrupción.
malformation (ˌmæl·for'mei·ʃən) *n.* malformación.
malice ('mæl·ɪs) *n.* malicia. —**malicious** (mə'lɪʃ·əs) *adj.* malicioso.
malign (mə'lain) *v.t.* calumniar; difamar. —*adj.* maligno; pernicioso.
malignancy (mə'lɪg·nən·si) *n.* malignidad.
malignant (mə'lɪg·nənt) *adj.* maligno.
malignity (mə'lɪg·nə·ti) *n.* malignidad.
malinger (mə'lɪŋ·gər) *v.i.* fingirse enfermo; hacerse el (*o* la) calandria. —**malingerer,** *n.* calandria.
malingering (mə'lɪŋ·gər·ɪŋ) *n.* enfermedad fingida. —*adj.* remolón.
mall (mɔːl) *n.* **1,** (mallet) mazo. **2,** (public walk) alameda.
mallard ('mæl·ərd) *n.* pato silvestre; ánade común.
malleable ('mæl·i·ə·bəl) *adj.* maleable. —**malleability,** *n.* maleabilidad.
mallet ('mæl·ɪt) *n.* mazo.
mallow ('mæl·o) *n.* malva.
malnutrition (ˌmæl·nu'trɪʃ·ən) *n.* desnutrición.
malodorous (mæl'o·dər·əs) *adj.* maloliente; hediondo.
malpractice (mæl'præk·tɪs) *n.* descuido *o* inmoralidad profesional.
malt (mɔlt) *n.* malta.
maltose ('mɔl·tos) *n.* maltosa.
maltreat (mæl'trit) *v.t.* maltratar. —**maltreatment,** *n.* maltrato.
mama ('ma·mə; mə'ma) *n.* mamá. *También,* **mamma.**
mambo ('mam·bo) *n.* mambo.
mamma ('ma·mə; mə'ma) *n.* **1,** (mother) mamá. **2,** *anat.* ('mæm·ə) [*pl.* **-mae** (-mi)] mama.
mammal ('mæm·əl) *n.* mamífero. —**mammalian** (mæ'mei·li·ən) *adj.* mamífero.
mammary ('mæm·ə·ri) *adj.* mamario.
mammon ('mæm·ən) *n.* **1,** (wealth) dinero; riquezas (*pl.*). **2,** *cap.* (personification of riches) mammón.
mammoth ('mæm·əθ) *adj.* enorme; gigantesco. —*n.* mamut.
mammy ('mæm·i) *n., colloq.* **1,** (mother) mamita. **2,** (nursemaid) niñera; nana.
man (mæn) *n.* [*pl.* **men**] **1,** (human being) hombre. **2,** (servant) criado. **3,** *chess* pieza. —*adj.* varón. —*v.t.*

[**manned, manning**] **1,** (furnish with men) dotar de hombres; *mil.* guarnecer; *naut.; aero.* tripular. **2,** (make up the crew or staff of) constituir la dotación, el personal, etc. de. **3,** (tend; have charge of) atender; tomar *o* hacerse cargo de. **4,** *usu.refl.* (brace; fortify) aprestar(se); aprontar(se); hacer acopio de fuerzas. —**be one's own man,** campar por sus respetos; ser libre; ser independiente. —**man in the street,** hombre común; hombre corriente. —**man Friday,** criado de confianza; mano derecha. —**to a man,** todos a una; como un solo hombre.

-man (mæn; mən) *sufijo* [*pl.* **-men**] hombre; persona; *forma* **1,** *nombres gentilicios: Frenchman.* francés. **2,** *nombres de personas dedicadas a una determinada actividad: mailman,* cartero; *motorman,* motorista.

manacle ('mæn·ə·kəl) *n.* manilla; esposas (*pl.*). —*v.t.* maniatar; esposar.

manage ('mæn·ɪdʒ) *v.t.* **1,** (handle) manejar. **2,** (have charge of) dirigir; administrar. **3,** (arrange; contrive) arreglar; tramitar. —*v.i.* arreglárselas. —**manageable,** *adj.* manejable; dócil. —**management,** *n.* administración; dirección.

manager ('mæn·ɪdʒ·ər) *n.* administrador; director; gerente. —**managerial** (ˌmæn·ə'dʒɪr·i·əl) *adj.* administrativo; de gerente.

man-at-arms *n.* [*pl.* **men-at-arms**] soldado; hombre de guerra.

manatee (ˌmæn·ə'ti) *n.* manatí; vaca marina.

Manchu (mæn'tʃuː) *n.* & *adj.* manchú.

-mancy (mæn·si) *sufijo* -mancia; adivinación: *necromancy,* nigromancia.

mandarin ('mæn·də·rɪn) *n.* **1,** (official; language) mandarín. **2,** (citrus fruit) naranja mandarina. **3,** (long coat) traje mandarín. **4,** (color) color mandarín.

mandate ('mæn·deit) *n.* mandato. —**mandatary** (-də·tɛr·i) *n.* mandatario. —**mandatory** (-də·tor·i) *adj.* preceptivo; obligatorio.

mandible ('mæn·də·bəl) *n.* mandíbula.

mandibular (mæn·'dɪb·jə·lər) *adj.* mandibular.

mandolin ('mæn·dəˌlɪn) *n.* mandolina; bandola.

mandrake ('mæn·dreik) *n.* mandrágora.

mandrel ('mæn·drəl) *n.* mandril.

mandrill ('mæn·drɪl) *n.* mandril.

mane (mein) *n.* melena; (*esp. of horses*) crin.

man-eater *n.* **1,** (cannibal) caníbal; antropófago. **2,** (animal dangerous to man) devorador de hombres.

maneuver *también,* **manoeuvre** (mə'nu·vər) *n.* maniobra. —*v.t.* & *i.* maniobrar. —**maneuverable,** *adj.* maniobrable. —**maneuverability,** *n.* maniobrabilidad.

manful ('mæn·fəl) *adj.* bravo; varonil; resuelto. —**manfulness,** *n.* valor; resolución.

manganese ('mæŋ·gəˌnis) *n.* manganeso. —**manganic** (mæn·'gæn·ɪk) *adj.* mangánico.

mange (meindʒ) *n.* sarna; roña. —**mangy,** *adj.* sarnoso; roñoso.

manger ('mein·dʒər) *n.* pesebre.

mangle ('mæŋ·gəl) *v.t.* destrozar; estropear; mutilar. —*n.* calandria; planchadora.

mango ('mæŋ·go) *n.* mango.

mangrove ('mæn·grov) *n.* mangle.

manhandle *v.t.* **1,** (treat roughly) maltratar. **2,** (move by hand) mover a brazo.

manhole *n.* boca de alcantarillado.

manhood ('mænˌhʊd) *n.* **1,** (manliness) hombría. **2,** (age of maturity) edad viril. **3,** (men collectively) los hombres.

manhunt *n.* persecución; búsqueda (*de un criminal*).

mani- (mæn·ɪ) *prefijo* mani-; mano; *manicure,* manicura.

mania ('mei·ni·ə) *n.* manía. —**maniac,** *n.* maniático; loco.

maniacal (mə'nai·ə·kəl) *adj.* maníaco.

manic ('mæn·ɪk) *adj.* maníaco.

manicure ('mæn·ə·kjʊr) *n.* manicura. —*v.t.* hacer la manicura a. —**manicurist,** *n.* manicuro; *Amer.* manicurista.

manifest ('mæn·ə·fɛst) *v.t.* manifestar. —*adj.* manifiesto; claro. —*n.* manifiesto. —**manifestation** (-fɛs'tei·ʃən) *n.* manifestación. —**make manifest,** poner de manifiesto.

manifesto (ˌmæn·əˈfɛs·to) *n.* manifiesto; proclama.
manifold (ˈmæn·ə·fold) *adj.* múltiple; amplio; diverso; variado. —*n.* **1,** (something complex) complejo. **2,** (copy) copia. **3,** (onionskin) papel cebolla. **4,** *mech.* tubo múltiple. —*v.t.* **1,** (multiply) multiplicar. **2,** (make copies of) sacar copias de.
manikin (ˈmæn·ə·kɪn) *n.* **1,** (model) maniquí; modelo. **2,** (dwarf) enano.
manila (məˈnɪl·ə) *n.* **1,** (hemp) cáñamo de Manila. **2,** (paper) papel (de) Manila.
manioc (ˈmæn·i·ak) *n.* mandioca.
manipulate (məˈnɪp·jəˌleit) *v.t.* manipular. —**manipulation,** *n.* manipulación. —**manipulator,** *n.* manipulador.
mankind (ˈmænˌkaind) *n.* humanidad; género humano.
manlike (ˈmæn·laik) *adj.* **1,** (resembling a man) parecido al hombre; casi humano. **2,** = **manly.**
manly (ˈmæn·li) *adj.* de hombre; varonil; viril. —**manliness,** *n.* hombría; virilidad.
manna (ˈmæn·ə) *n.* maná.
mannequin (ˈmæn·ə·kɪn) *n.* maniquí; modelo.
manner (ˈmæn·ər) *n.* **1,** (way of doing or being) manera; modo; forma. **2,** (custom; usage) costumbre; usanza. **3,** (sort) clase; género. **4,** *pl.* (social ways) modales. —**by all manner of means,** de todos modos.
mannered (ˈmæn·ərd) *adj.* amanerado.
mannerism (ˈmæn·əˌrɪz·əm) *n.* **1,** (affectation) amaneramiento. **2,** (idiosyncrasy) costumbre; hábito; *derog.* vicio.
mannerly (ˈmæn·ər·li) *adj.* cortés; educado. —**mannerliness,** *n.* urbanidad.
mannish (ˈmæn·ɪʃ) *adj.* masculino; varonil.
manoeuvre (məˈnu·vər) *n.* & *v.* = **maneuver.**
man-of-war *n.* [*pl.* **men-of-war**] buque de guerra.
manometer (məˈnam·ə·tər) *n.* manómetro. —**manometric** (ˌmæn·əˈmɛt·rɪk) *adj.* manométrico.
manor (ˈmæn·ər) *n.* finca *o* casa solariega. —**manorial** (məˌnor·i·əl) *adj.* señorial; solariego.
manpower *n.* **1,** (human resources) recursos humanos. **2,** *mil.* fuerzas disponibles. **3,** (manual power) mano de obra; brazo.
mansard (ˈmæn·sard) *n.* mansarda.
manse (mæns) *n.* rectoría.
manservant *n.* [*pl.* **menservants**] criado; sirviente.
mansion (ˈmæn·ʃən) *n.* mansión.
manslaughter (ˈmænˌslɔ·tər) *n.* homicidio casual *o* involuntario.
manta (ˈmæn·tə) *n.* manta.
mantel (ˈmæn·təl) *n.* manto; chimenea. —**mantelpiece,** *n.* repisa de chimenea.
mantilla (mænˈtɪl·ə) n. mantilla.
mantis (ˈmæn·tɪs) *n.* mantis.
mantle (ˈmæn·təl) *n.* **1,** (cloak; covering) capa; manto. **2,** (incandescent hood) manguito. —*v.t.* cubrir.
manual (ˈmæn·ju·əl) *adj.* & *n.* manual.
manufacture (ˌmæn·jəˈfæk·tʃər) *n.* manufactura. —*v.t.* manufacturar; fabricar. —**manufacturer,** *n.* fabricante; manufacturero.
manufacturing (ˌmæn·jəˈfæk·tʃər·ɪŋ) *n.* fabricación; manufactura. —*adj.* manufacturero.
manumission (ˌmæn·jəˈmɪʃ·ən) *n.* manumisión. —**manumit** (-ˈmɪt) *v.t.* manumitir.
manure (məˈnjʊr) *n.* abono; estiércol. —*v.t.* abonar; estercolar.
manuscript (ˈmæn·jəˌskrɪpt) *n.* & *adj.* manuscrito; *print.* original.
Manx (mæŋks) *adj.* & *n.* de la isla de Man.
many (ˈmɛn·i) *adj.* & *pron.* muchos. —*n.* gran número. —**a good many,** un buen número. —**a great many,** muchos; gran número. —**as many as,** tantos como; (*ante un número*) hasta. —**as many more,** otros tantos. —**be one too many,** ser uno más de la cuenta. —**how many,** cuántos. —**many a,** muchos. —**so many,** tantos. —**the many,** los más. —**too many,** demasiados; (*precedido de un número*) de más: *ten too many,* diez de más.
many-sided *adj.* **1,** (having many sides or faces) poligonal. **2,** (complex) de muchos aspectos. **3,** (having many talents) versátil.
map (mæp) *n.* mapa. —*v.t.* [**mapped, mapping**] **1,** (chart the geography of) trazar *o* dibujar el mapa de. **2,** (plan) planear; pro-

yectar. —**map maker**, cartógrafo. —**map making**, cartografía.
maple ('mei·pəl) *n.* arce.
mar (maːr) *v.t.* [**marred, marring**] desfigurar; estropear.
marabou ('mær·əˌbu) *n.* marabú.
maraschino (ˌmær·ə'ski·no) *n.* marrasquino.
marasmus (mə'ræz·məs) *n., pathol.* marasmo.
marathon ('mær·əˌθan) *n.* maratón.
maraud (mə'rɔːd) *v.t.* & *i.* merodear. —**marauder**, *n.* merodeador. —**marauding**, *n.* merodeo. —*adj.* merodeador.
marble ('mar·bəl) *n.* **1,** (mineral) mármol. **2,** (little ball) bola; bolita. —*adj.* marmóreo; de *o* como mármol. —*v.t.* jaspear. —**marbled**, *adj.* jaspeado. —**marbling** (-blɪŋ) *n.* jaspeado.
marblework *n.* marmolería. —**marbleworker**, *n.* marmolista.
marcasite ('mar·kəˌsait) *n.* marcasita.
marcel (mar'sɛl) *n.* ondulación Marcel. —*v.t.* ondular (el pelo).
march (martʃ) *v.i.* marchar. —*v.t.* hacer marchar. —*n.* marcha. —**marches**, *n.pl.* distritos fronterizos. —**marching**, *n.* marcha; paso de tropas. —*adj.* de *o* en marcha. —**march in**, entrar. —**march off**, marcharse. —**march out**, marcharse; salir. —**march up**, avanzar. —**steal a march on**, ganarle el quien vive a; *Amer.* madrugarse a.
March (martʃ) *n.* marzo.
marchioness ('mar·ʃəˌnɛs) *n.* marquesa.
Mardi gras ('mar·di'gra) *n.* carnaval.
mare (meːr) *n.* yegua.
margarine ('mar·dʒə·rin) *n.* margarina.
margin ('mar·dʒɪn) *n.* margen. —**marginal**, *adj.* marginal.
marguerite (ˌmar·gə'rit) *n.* margarita.
marigold ('mær·ɪˌgold) *n.* maravilla; flor de muerto.
marijuana (ˌmær·ə'hwa·nə) *n.* mariguana.
marimba (mə'rɪm·bə) *n.* marimba.
marina (mə'ri·nə) *n.* atracadero; dársena.
marinade (ˌmær·ə'neid) *n.* escabeche.
marinate ('mær·əˌneit) *v.t.* escabechar; marinar. —**marinated**, *adj.* en escabeche.
marine (mə'riːn) *adj.* marino; marinero; marítimo. —*n.* **1,** (seagoing soldier) marino; soldado de marina. **2,** (fleet; shipping) marina. **3,** (seascape) marina. —**mariner** ('mær·ə·nər) *n.* marinero; marino.
marionette (ˌmær·i·ə'nɛt) *n.* marioneta.
marital ('mær·ɪ·təl) *adj.* marital; matrimonial.
maritime ('mær·ɪˌtaim) *adj.* marítimo.
marjoram ('mar·dʒə·rəm) *n.* mejorana. —**wild marjoram**, orégano.
mark (mark) *v.t.* marcar; señalar. —*v.i.* advertir; notar. —*n.* **1,** (sign; trace) marca; señal. **2,** (monetary unit) marco. —**hit the mark**, dar en el blanco. —**mark down**, rebajar (de precio). —**mark time**, marcar el paso; *fig.* hacer tiempo. —**mark up**, aumentar de precio. —**toe the mark**, entrar *o* ponerse en vereda; andar derecho.
markdown *n.* rebaja (de precio).
marked (markt) *adj.* **1,** (having a mark; singled out) marcado; señalado. **2,** (doomed) condenado. **3,** (notable) notable; considerable.
marker ('mar·kər) *n.* **1,** (instrument or device for marking) marcador. **2,** (indicator; sign) indicador; señal. **3,** (chip; counter) ficha. **4,** *slang* = **I.O.U.**
market ('mar·kɪt) *n.* mercado. —*v.t.* vender. —*v.i.* comprar *o* vender en el mercado. —**marketable**, *adj.* vendible; comerciable. —**marketing**, *n.* mercados (*pl.*). —**be in the market for**, pensar *o* querer comprar. —**market woman**, placera.
marksman ('marks·mən) *n.* [*pl.* **-men**] tirador. —**marksmanship**, *n.* puntería.
markup *n.* beneficio bruto; monto de la diferencia entre el precio de costo y el de venta.
marlin ('mar·lɪn) *n.* marlín.
marline ('mar·lɪn) *n.* merlín. —**marlinespike**, *n.* pasador.
marmalade ('mar·məˌleid) *n.* mermelada.
marmoreal (mar'mor·i·əl) *adj.* marmóreo.

marmoset ('mar·mə,zɛt) *n.* mono pequeño de la América del Sur.
marmot ('mar·mət) *n.* marmota.
maroon (mə'ruːn) *v.t.* abandonar (en una costa desierta). —*n.* color castaño. —*adj.* castaño.
marquee (mar'kiː) *n.* marquesina.
marquetry ('mar·kə·tri) *n.* marquetería.
marquis *también, Brit.,* **marquess** ('mar·kwɪs) *n.* marqués. —**marquisate** (-kwɪz·ɪt) *n.* marquesado. —**marquise** (mar'kiz) *n.* marquesa.
marriage ('mær·ɪdʒ) *n.* matrimonio. —*adj.* matrimonial. —**marriageable,** *adj.* casadero.
married ('mær·id) *adj.* **1,** (wedded) casado (*fem.* casada). **2,** (of or pert. to marriage) matrimonial; conyugal. —**married couple,** casados; esposos; cónyuges.
marron ('mær·ən) *n.* marrón.
marrow ('mær·o) *n.* médula; tuétano.
marry ('mær·i) *v.t.* **1,** (wed) casarse con. **2,** (give or join in marriage) casar. —*v.i.* casarse.
Mars (maːrz) *n.* Marte.
Marseillaise (,mar·sə'leiz) *n.* Marsellesa.
marsh (marʃ) *n.* pantano; ciénaga. —**marshy,** *adj.* pantanoso.
marshal ('mar·ʃəl) *n.* **1,** *mil.* mariscal. **2,** *U.S.* (law-enforcement officer) alguacil; ministril. —*v.t.* ordenar; poner en orden; disponer. —**marshalship,** *n., mil.* mariscalato; mariscalía.
marshmallow ('marʃ,mæl·o) *n.* confite de malvavisco. —**marsh mallow,** malvavisco; altea.
marsupial (mar'su·pi·əl) *n.* & *adj.* marsupial.
mart (mart) *n.* mercado.
marten ('mar·tən) *n.* marta.
martial ('mær·ʃəl) *adj.* marcial.
Martian ('mar·ʃən) *adj.* & *n.* marciano.
martin ('mar·tən) *n.* vencejo.
martinet (,mar·tə'nɛt) *n.* ordenancista.
martingale ('mar·tən,geil) *n.* **1,** (harness) gamarra. **2,** *naut.* moco del bauprés. **3,** (betting system) martingala.
martini (mar'ti·ni) *n.* martini.
martyr ('mar·tər) *n.* mártir. —*v.t.* martirizar. —**martyrdom,** *n.* martirio.
marvel ('mar·vəl) *n.* maravilla. —*v.i.* maravillarse. —**marvelous,** *adj.* maravilloso.
Marxism ('mark·sɪz·əm) *n.* marxismo. —**Marxist,** *n.* & *adj.* marxista. —**Marxian,** *adj.* marxista.
marzipan ('mar·zə,pæn) *n.* mazapán.
mascara (mæs'kær·ə) *n.* tinte para las pestañas.
mascot ('mæs·kət) *n.* mascota.
masculine ('mæs·kjə·lɪn) *adj.* masculino. —**masculinity** (-'lɪn·ə·ti) *n.* masculinidad.
mash (mæʃ) *n.* masa. —*v.t.* majar; machacar; macerar.
masher ('mæʃ·ər) *n.* **1,** (crushing device) majador. **2,** *slang* (flirt) galanteador.
mask (mæsk) *n.* **1,** (covering for the face) máscara. **2,** (disguise) disfraz. **3,** (death mask) mascarilla. —*v.t.* **1,** (cover with a mask) enmascarar. **2,** (disguise; conceal) disfrazar; disimular. —*v.i.* enmascararse.
masochism ('mæs·ə·kɪz·əm) *n.* masoquismo. —**masochist,** *n.* masoquista. —**masochistic,** *adj.* masoquista; masoquístico.
mason ('mei·sən) *n.* **1,** (worker in stone) albañil. **2,** *cap.* = **Freemason.**
Masonic (mə'san·ɪk) *adj.* masónico.
masonite ('mei·sə,nait) *n.* masonita.
masonry ('mei·sən·ri) *n.* **1,** (work in stone) albañilería; mampostería. **2,** *cap.* = **Freemasonry.**
masque (mæsk) *n.* **1,** *hist.* (dramatic form) representación dramática alegórica. **2,** (revel) mascarada; máscaras (*pl.*). **3,** = **mask.**
masquerade (,mæs·kə'reid) *n.* **1,** (masked ball) mascarada; máscaras (*pl.*). **2,** (disguise) disfraz. —*v.i.* disfrazarse; enmascararse. —**masquerader,** *n.* máscara.
mass (mæs) *n.* **1,** (body of matter) masa. **2,** (aggregation) masa; montón. **3,** *cap., eccles.* misa. —*adj.* en masa. —*v.t.* juntar; agrupar; reunir. —*v.i.* agruparse; reunirse; apiñarse. —**in the mass,** en conjunto. —**mass production,** fabricación en serie.
massacre ('mæs·ə·kər) *n.* matanza; masacre. —*v.t.* hacer una matanza de; masacrar.
massage (mə'saːʒ) *n.* masaje;

soba. —*v.t.* dar masaje; sobar; *Amer.* masajear.
masseur (mæ'sʌɹ) *n.* masajista. —**masseuse** (-'suz) *n.* masajista.
massive ('mæs·ɪv) *adj.* **1,** (bulky; heavy) macizo; sólido. **2,** (imposing) imponente. —**massiveness,** *n.* masa; lo macizo.
mast (mæst) *n.* mástil; palo.
master ('mæs·tər) *n.* **1,** (lord; ruler; owner) amo; dueño; patrón; señor. **2,** (head; chief) maestro; jefe. **3,** (skilled workman or practitioner) maestro; perito. **4,** (teacher) maestro; profesor. **5,** (holder of a master's degree) licenciado; doctor. **6,** *naut.* capitán. —*v.t.* **1,** (subdue) dominar; vencer. **2,** (rule) señorear. **3,** (know thoroughly) saber a fondo; dominar. —*adj.* maestro. —**master's degree,** grado de maestro; licenciatura; doctorado. —**master mind,** inteligencia superior. —**master stroke,** golpe maestro. —**meet one's master,** encontrar la horma de su zapato.
masterful ('mæs·tər·fəl) *adj.* **1,** (domineering) imperioso; dominante. **2,** (expert) perito; experto. —**masterfulness,** *n.* maestría; dominio.
masterly ('mæs·tər·li) *adj.* maestro; magistral. —*adv.* con maestría; magistralmente. —**masterliness,** *n.* maestría.
masterpiece *n.* obra maestra. *También,* **masterwork.**
mastership ('mæs·tər·ʃɪp) *n.* **1,** (mastery) maestría. **2,** (position of a teacher) magisterio.
mastery ('mæs·tə·ri) *n.* **1,** (control; authority) dominio; control; poder. **2,** (expertness) maestría; dominio.
masthead *n.* **1,** *naut.* tope del mástil; espiga. **2,** *journalism* membrete de periódico.
mastic ('mæs·tɪk) *n.* almáciga; mástique. —**mastic tree,** almácigo.
masticate ('mæs·tə,keit) *v.t.* & *i.* **1,** (chew) masticar; mascar. **2,** (crush to pulp) hacer pulpa de; machacar. —**mastication,** *n.* masticación.
mastiff ('mæs·tɪf) *n.* mastín.
mastodon ('mæs·tə,dan) *n.* mastodonte.
mastoid ('mæs·tɔid) *n.* & *adj.* mastoides. —**mastoidal** (mæs'tɔi·dəl) *adj.* mastoideo. —**mastoiditis** (-tɔi'dai·tɪs) *n.* mastoiditis.
masturbate ('mæs·tər,beit) *v.i.* masturbarse. —**masturbation,** *n.* masturbación.
mat (mæt) *n.* **1,** (small rug) estera; esterilla; *Amer.* felpudo. **2,** (place mat) salvamanteles. **3,** (border for a picture) orla; marco. **4,** (for gymnastics) colchoneta. **5,** (tangled mass, as of hair) mata de pelo; greña. **6,** (dull finish) terminado *o* acabado mate. —*adj.* mate. —*v.t.* [**matted, matting**] **1,** (cover with a mat) poner estera *o* felpudo en. **2,** (tangle) enmarañar. **3,** (put a dull finish on) matar. —*v.i.* enmarañarse.
matador ('mæt·ə·dor) *n.* matador.
match (mætʃ) *n.* **1,** (equal; peer) igual; par; rival. **2,** (counterpart; facsimile) réplica. **3,** (companion; one of a pair) compañero; pareja. **4,** (pair) par; pareja. **5,** (set; combination) juego; combinación. **6,** (contest; bout) partido; partida; encuentro. **7,** (suitable or possible mate) partido. **8,** (alliance) alianza. **9,** (device for igniting) fósforo; cerilla. —*v.t.* **1,** (give or join in marriage) casar. **2,** (mate; pair) hacer pareja de *o* con; poner juntos; unir. **3,** (compete with successfully) competir con; rivalizar con. **4,** (compare) comparar. **5,** (provide or obtain a counterpart or equivalent to) dar *o* conseguir el igual de *o* el mismo que. **6,** (pit; oppose) enfrentar; poner frente a frente; oponer. **7,** (fit or go together with) hacer juego con; combinar con. **8,** (be equal to) ser igual a. —*v.i.* **1,** (get married; mate) casarse; aparearse. **2,** (harmonize) armonizar; hacer juego. **3,** (be equal) ser iguales.
matchless ('mætʃ·ləs) *adj.* sin par; incomparable.
matchmaker *n.* **1,** (arranger of marriages) casamentero. **2,** (sports promoter) promotor.
mate (meit) *n.* **1,** (spouse; companion; one of a pair or set) compañero; pareja. **2,** *chess* mate. **3,** *naut.* piloto; segundo de a bordo. —*v.t.* **1,** (couple; join as a pair) casar; unir. **2,** *chess* dar mate. —*v.i.* casarse; unirse.
maté ('ma·te; 'mæt·e) *n.* mate; yerba mate.

material (mə'tɪr·i·əl) *adj.* **1,** (physical) material. **2,** (important; essential) esencial; substancial. —*n.* material. —**material witness,** testigo de causa. —**raw material,** materia prima.

materialism (mə'tɪr·i·ə·lɪz·əm) *n.* materialismo. —**materialist,** *n.* materialista. —**materialistic,** *adj.* materialista.

materiality (məˌtɪr·i'æl·ə·ti) *n.* materialidad.

materialize (mə'tɪr·i·əˌlaiz) *v.t.* materializar. —*v.i.* **1,** (be realized) llevarse a cabo; realizarse. **2,** (assume physical form) materializarse; hacerse palpable *o* visible; tomar cuerpo. —**materialization** (-lɪ'zei·ʃən) *n.* materialización; realización.

materially (mə'tɪr·i·ə·li) *adv.* materialmente.

matériel (mə·tɪr·i'ɛl) *n.* material; materiales (*pl.*); pertrechos (*pl.*).

maternal (mə'tʌɹ·nəl) *adj.* maternal.

maternity (mə'tʌɹ·nə·ti) *n.* maternidad. —*adj.* de maternidad.

mathematical (ˌmæθ·ə'mæt·ɪ·kəl) *adj.* matemático.

mathematics (ˌmæθ·ə'mæt·ɪks) *n.* matemática; matemáticas. —**mathematician** (-mə'tɪʃ·ən) *n.* matemático.

matinal ('mæt·ə·nəl) *adj.* matinal.

matinee (ˌmæt·ə'nei) *n.* matiné.

matins ('mæt·ɪnz) *n.pl.* maitines.

matri- (mei·tri; mæt·rə) *prefijo* matri-; madre: *matriarchate,* matriarcado.

matriarch ('mei·tri·ark) *n.* matriarca. —**matriarchal** (-'ar·kəl) *adj.* matriarcal. —**matriarchy,** *n.* matriarcado.

matricide ('mæ·trəˌsaid) *n.* **1,** (act) matricidio. **2,** (agent) matricida. —**matricidal** (-'sai·dəl) *adj.* matricida.

matriculate (mə'trɪk·jəˌleit) *v.t.* matricular. —*v.i.* matricularse. —**matriculation,** *n.* matrícula.

matrimony ('mæt·rəˌmo·ni) *n.* matrimonio. —**matrimonial** (-'mo·ni·əl) *adj.* matrimonial.

matrix ('mei·trɪks) *n.* [*pl.* **-trices** (-trɪ·siz)] matriz.

matron ('mei·trən) *n.* matrona. —**matronly,** *adj.* matronal; de matrona.

matted ('mæt·ɪd) *adj.* **1,** (covered with a mat) esterado. **2,** (tangled) enmarañado.

matter ('mæt·ər) *n.* **1,** (material) materia. **2,** (affair) asunto; cosa; cuestión. **3,** (importance; moment) importancia. **4,** (pus) pus. —*v.i.* **1,** (be important) importar. **2,** (form pus) formar pus; supurar. —**as a matter of fact,** a decir verdad; en realidad. —**for that matter,** en cuanto a eso; respecto a eso. —**no matter,** no importa. —**no matter how,** por mucho que. —**What is the matter?**, ¿Qué pasa?; ¿Qué hay? —**What is the matter with you?**, ¿Qué tienes?; ¿Qué te pasa?

matter of course cosa natural; cosa de cajón. —**matter-of-course,** *adj.* de cajón; natural. —**as a matter of course,** como *o* por rutina.

matter of fact cosa positiva; hecho; realidad. —**matter-of-fact,** *adj.* prosaico; sin imaginación. —**as a matter of fact,** en realidad; de hecho.

matting ('mæt·ɪŋ) *n.* esterado.

mattock ('mæt·ək) *n.* piqueta; pico.

mattress ('mæt·rɪs) *n.* colchón.

maturation (ˌmætʃ·ʊ'rei·ʃən) *n.* maduración; *med.* supuración.

mature (mə'tjʊr) *adj.* **1,** (full-grown) maduro. **2,** *comm.* vencido. —*v.t.* madurar. —*v.i.* madurarse; *comm.* vencerse. —**maturity,** *n.* madurez; *comm.* vencimiento.

matutinal (mə'tju·tə·nəl) *adj.* matutino; matinal.

maudlin ('mɔd·lɪn) *adj.* sensiblero.

maul (mɔːl) *n.* mazo. —*v.t.* maltratar; magullar.

maunder ('mɔn·dər) *v.i.* hablar *u* obrar sin ton ni son.

Maundy Thursday ('mɔn·di) Jueves Santo.

mausoleum (ˌmɔ·sə'li·əm) *n.* mausoleo.

mauve (moːv) *n.* & *adj.* malva.

maverick ('mæv·ər·ɪk) *n.* **1,** (unbranded animal) animal mostrenco. **2,** (dissenter) rebelde; independiente.

mavis ('mei·vɪs) *n.* malvís.

maw (mɔː) *n.* buche; gaznate.

mawkish ('mɔ·kɪʃ) *adj.* **1,** (nauseating) asqueroso. **2,** (maudlin) sensiblero. —**mawkishness,** *n.* sensiblería.

maxilla (mæk'sɪl·ə) *n.* [*pl.* **-lae**

(-i)] mandíbula (*of persons*); quijada (*of animals*). —**maxillary** ('mæk·sə·lɛr·i) *adj.* & *n.* maxilar.
maxim ('mæk·sɪm) *n.* máxima.
maximal ('mæk·sɪ·məl) *adj.* maximo.
maximize ('mæk·sə,maiz) *v.t.* llevar al máximo; exagerar.
maximum ('mæk·sə·məm) *adj.* máximo. —*n.* máximo; máximum.
may (mei) *v.aux.* [*pret.* **might**] **1,** *expresando posibilidad o contingencia,* poder; ser posible: *I may do it now,* Puedo hacerlo ahora; Es posible que lo haga ahora; Puede que lo haga ahora. **2,** *expresando permiso,* poder: *You may come out now,* Puedes salir ahora. **3,** *denotando deseo, esperanza o súplica; se expresa en español con el subjuntivo: May you be happy,* Que seas feliz. —**come what may,** pase lo que pase. —**I may go,** puede que vaya. —**who may he be?,** ¿quién será?
May (mei) *n.* mayo. —**May Day,** primero de mayo.
Maya ('ma·jə) *n.* maya. —**Mayan** ('ma·jən) *n.* & *adj.* maya.
maybe ('mei·bi) *adv.* tal vez; acaso; quizá; a lo mejor.
mayflower ('mei,flau·ər) *n.* nombre de varias plantas que florecen en mayo: *en los EE.UU.,* hepática; anémona; *en las Islas Británicas,* espino; majuelo.
May fly mosca de mayo.
mayhem ('mei·hɛm) *n.* **1,** *law* mutilación *o* lesión criminal. **2,** (violence) violencia; tropelía.
mayonnaise (,mei·ə'neiz) *n.* mayonesa.
mayor ('mei·ər) *n.* alcalde. —**mayoralty,** *n.* alcaldía. —**mayoress,** *n.* alcaldesa.
Maypole ('mei,pol) *n.* mayo; árbol de mayo.
maze (meiz) *n.* laberinto. —**be in a maze,** estar perplejo.
mazurka (mə'zʌɹ·kə) *n.* mazurca.
me (miː) *pron.pers.* **1,** *complemento directo o indirecto de verbo* me. **2,** *complemento de prep.* mi. **3,** *tras* **than,** *en las comparaciones* yo. —**with me,** conmigo.
mead (miːd) *n.* **1,** (drink) aguamiel; hidromiel. **2,** = **meadow.**
meadow ('mɛd·o) *n.* pradera; prado. —**meadowland,** *n.* pradera.
meager ('mi·gər) *adj.* **1,** (lean) flaco; magro; enjuto. **2,** (poor; scarce) escaso; mezquino. —**meagerness,** *n.* escasez; mezquindad.
meal (miːl) *n.* **1,** (repast) comida. **2,** (ground grain) harina.
mealy ('mi·li) *adj.* **1,** (of or containing meal) harinoso; farináceo. **2,** (like meal; pasty) pastoso.
mealymouthed ('mi·li,mauðd) *adj.* pacato; timorato; apocado en el hablar.
mean (miːn) *v.t.* [*pret.* & *p.p.* **meant**] **1,** (intend; have as a purpose) pensar; intentar; pretender; tener intención (*o* intenciones) de. **2,** (intend; destine) destinar: *She was meant for the stage,* Estaba destinada para el escenario. **3,** (signify; indicate) significar; indicar. **4,** (intend to express) querer decir. —*v.i.* tener intención *o* intenciones. —*adj.* **1,** (low; small; base; poor; miserly) mezquino. **2,** (of low estate) humilde. **3,** *colloq.* (ill-natured) malo; avieso; cruel. **4,** *colloq.* (unpleasant; distasteful) malo; desagradable. **5,** *colloq.* (ashamed) abochornado. **6,** (middle; average) medio; del medio. —*n.* **1,** (average) promedio. **2,** *math.* (middle term) media. **3,** *pl.* (resources) medios; recursos; posibilidades. —**by all means, 1,** (without fail) sin falta; de todos modos. **2,** (of course) por supuesto. —**by any means,** de cualquier modo *o* manera; a toda costa. —**by means of,** por medio de. —**by no (manner of) means,** de ninguna manera; de ningun modo. —**mean well (*o* ill),** tener buena (*o* mala) intención. —**no mean . . . ,** un . . . de cierta importancia *o* de cierto valor. —**not by any means,** ni pensarlo; ni por pienso. —**to mean business,** hacer *o* decir (algo) en serio; hablar en serio.
meander (mi'æn·dər) *v.i.* **1,** (take a winding course) serpentear. **2,** (ramble; wander) dar vueltas. —*n.* [*también,* **meandering**] **1,** (bend; turn) meandro; vuelta; recodo. **2,** (a ramble) vueltas (*pl.*). —**meandering,** *adj.* serpenteante; tortuoso.
meaning ('mi·nɪŋ) *n.* significado; sentido. —*adj.* expresivo; significativo.
meaningful ('mi·nɪŋ·fəl) *adj.* **1,** (having significance) significativo; expresivo. **2,** (understandable)

comprensible; inteligible. **3,** (useful; productive) útil; provechoso.
meaningless ('mi·nɪŋ·ləs) *adj.* sin sentido.
meanness ('min·nɪs) *n.* **1,** (baseness; shabbiness; miserliness) mezquindad. **2,** (ill nature) maldad; crueldad.
mean-spirited *adj.* pequeño; estrecho de miras.
meant (mɛnt) *v., pret. & p.p. de* **mean.**
meantime ('min,taim) *adv.* mientras tanto; entretanto; a todo esto. —*n.* ínterin. *También,* **meanwhile** (-,hwail).
measles ('mi·zəlz) *n.* sarampión.
measly ('mi·zli) *adj.* mezquino; insignificante; despreciable. —**measliness,** *n.* insignificancia; mezquindad.
measurable ('mɛʒ·ər·ə·bəl) *adj.* **1,** (allowing of measurement) mensurable. **2,** (perceptible) perceptible.
measure ('mɛʒ·ər) *n.* **1,** (size; extent; capacity) medida. **2,** (unit or standard of measurement) medida. **3,** (system of measurement) sistema de medidas. **4,** (criterion) criterio. **5,** (action; step; means) medida. **6,** (quantity; degree) parte; proporción; **7,** *pros.* (meter) metro; medida. **8,** *music* compás. —*v.t.* **1,** (determine the size or extent of) medir. **2,** (bring into comparison) comparar; cotejar. —*v.i.* medir. —**beyond measure,** fuera de toda medida; sin tasa. —**for good measure,** para mayor seguridad *o* comodidad; por lo que toque. —**full measure,** el todo; el total. —**in full measure,** enteramente; todo. —**in a** (*o* **some**) **measure,** hasta cierto punto; en parte. —**in great measure,** en sumo grado; en gran parte. —**made to measure,** hecho a (la) medida. —**measure one's length,** medir el suelo; caerse. —**measure up to,** estar, llegar *o* ponerse a la altura de. —**tread a measure,** bailar.
measured ('mɛʒ·ərd) *adj.* **1,** (ascertained; determined) medido. **2,** (regular; steady; uniform) regular; uniforme. **3,** (slow; deliberate) mesurado. **4,** (restrained; calculated) medido; comedido; moderado.
measureless ('mɛʒ·ər·ləs) *adj.* sin límites; inmensurable.
measurement ('mɛʒ·ər·mənt) *n.* **1,** (measuring) medición. **2,** (dimension) medida.
meat (mit) *n.* **1,** (flesh) carne. **2,** (substance; pith) sustancia.
meatball *n.* albóndiga.
meat pie empanada; pastel de carne.
meaty ('mi·ti) *adj.* **1,** (fleshy) carnoso. **2,** (pithy) sustancioso.
mechanic (mə'kæn·ɪk) *adj. & n.* mecánico.
mechanical (mə'kæn·ə·kəl) *adj.* **1,** (of machinery or tools) mecánico. **2,** (automatic; reflex) maquinal; automático.
mechanics (mə'kæn·ɪks) *n.* mecánica.
mechanism ('mɛk·ə·nɪz·əm) *n.* mecanismo.
mechanize ('mɛk·ə,naiz) *v.t.* mecanizar. —**mechanization** (-nɪ'zei·ʃən) *n.* mecanización.
medal ('mɛd·əl) *n.* medalla.
medallion (mə'dæl·jən) *n.* medallón.
meddle ('mɛd·əl) *v.i.* entremeterse; inmiscuirse. —**meddler** (-lər) *n.* entremetido. —**meddlesome; meddling** (-liŋ) *adj.* entremetido; *Amer.* metido.
media ('mi·di·ə) *n., pl. de* **medium.**
medial ('mi·di·əl) *adj.* medio; del centro.
median ('mi·di·ən) *adj.* medio; del medio; intermedio. —*n.* punto *o* plano intermedio; *geom.* mediana.
mediate ('mi·di,eit) *v.i.* mediar. —*v.t.* **1,** (intervene in) mediar en; terciar en. **2,** (settle; adjust) dirimir. **3,** (effect by mediation) mediar en la promoción de. —**mediation,** *n.* mediación. —**mediator,** *n.* mediador.
medical ('mɛd·ɪ·kəl) *adj.* médico. —**medical examiner,** médico forense.
medicament (mə'dɪk·ə·mənt) *n.* medicamento.
medicate ('mɛd·ɪ,keit) *v.t.* medicinar. —**medication,** *n.* medicación.
medicine ('mɛd·ə·sən) *n.* medicina. —**medicinal** (mə'dɪs·ə·nəl) *adj.* medicinal. —**medicine ball,** pelota *o* balón de fisioterapia. —**medicine chest,** botiquín. —**medicine man,** curandero; médico brujo. —**take one's medicine,**

colloq. hacer(se) espaldas.
medieval *también,* **mediaeval** (ˌmi·di'i·vəl) *adj.* medieval; medioeval.
mediocre ('mi·diˌo·kər) *adj.* mediocre. —**mediocrity** (-'ak·rə·ti) *n.* mediocridad.
meditate ('mɛd·ɪˌteit) *v.t.* & *i.* meditar. —**meditation**, *n.* meditación. —**meditative**, *adj.* meditabundo; *Amer.* meditativo.
Mediterranean (ˌmɛd·ɪ·tə'rei·ni·ən) *n.* & *adj.* mediterráneo.
medium ('mi·di·əm) *n.* [*pl.* **media**] **1,** (mean) medio; punto medio. **2,** (means; agency) medio. **3,** (spiritualist) médium. —*adj.* medio; intermedio; mediano. —*adv.* a medias; a medio hacer; medianamente.
medlar ('mɛd·lər) *n.* níspero.
medley ('mɛd·li) *n.* mescolanza; popurrí. —*adj.* mezclado; mixto.
medulla (mɪ'dʌl·ə) *n.* médula. —**medullar**, *adj.* medular.
meek (mik) *adj.* manso; sumiso. —**meekness**, *n.* mansedumbre.
meerschaum ('mɪr·ʃəm) *n.* espuma de mar.
meet (mit) *v.t.* **1,** (come into contact with; join) encontrarse con. **2,** (receive; greet) recibir; acoger. **3,** (conform to; satisfy) cumplir con; satisfacer. **4,** (face; deal with) hacer frente a. **5,** (make the acquaintance of) conocer. —*v.i.* **1,** (gather) reunirse. **2,** (come into contact) juntarse; encontrarse. —*n.* reunión; encuentro. —*adj.* adecuado; a propósito. —**have (someone) meet (someone)**, presentarle a uno (una persona): *I would like to have you meet my wife,* Me gustaría presentarle a mi esposa.
meeting ('mi·tɪŋ) *n.* **1,** (encounter) encuentro. **2,** (gathering) reunión. —**meeting of minds**, acuerdo.
mega- (mɛg·ə) *prefijo* mega-. **1,** grande: *megalith,* megalito. **2,** millón: *megacycle,* megaciclo.
megacycle ('mɛg·əˌsai·kəl) *n.* megaciclo.
megalo- (mɛg·ə·lo; -lə) *prefijo* megalo-; enorme; muy grande: *megalocephalic,* megalocéfalo.
megalomania (ˌmɛg·ə·lə'mei·ni·ə) *n.* megalomanía. —**megalomaniac**, *n.* & *adj.* megalómano.
megaphone ('mɛg·əˌfon) *n.* megáfono.
megaton ('mɛg·əˌtʌn) *n.* megatón.
melancholia (ˌmɛl·ən'ko·li·ə) *n.* melancolía.
melancholy ('mɛl·ənˌkal·i) *n.* melancolía. —*adj.* melancólico. —**melancholic** (-'kal·ɪk) *adj.* melancólico.
Melanesian (ˌmɛl·ə'ni·ʒən) *adj.* & *n.* melanesio.
melange (mɛ'la:nʒ) *n.* mezcla; mescolanza; mejunje.
melano- (mɛl·ə·no) *prefijo* melano-; negro: *melanosis,* melanosis.
melée ('mei·lei; 'mɛl·ei) *n.* pelotera; trifulca.
meliorate ('mil·jəˌreit) *v.t.* mejorar. —*v.i.* mejorarse. —**melioration**, *n.* mejoramiento; mejoría.
melli- (mə·lɪ) *prefijo* meli-; dulce; miel: *mellifluous,* melifluo.
mellifluous (mə'lɪf·lu·əs) *adj.* melifluo. —**mellifluousness**, *n.* melifluidad.
mellow ('mɛl·o) *adj.* **1,** (soft; tender) dulce; tierno. **2,** (smooth) suave. **3,** (ripe) maduro. **4,** *colloq.* (jovial) jovial; genial. —*v.t.* & *i.* **1,** (soften) suavizar. **2,** (sweeten) endulzar. **3,** (ripen) madurar.
melo- (mɛl·ə) *prefijo* melo-; canción; música: *melomaniac,* melómano.
melodic (mə'lad·ɪk) *adj.* melódico.
melodious (mə'lo·di·əs) *adj.* melodioso. —**melodiousness**, *n.* lo melodioso; melodía.
melodrama ('mɛl·əˌdra·ma) *n.* melodrama. —**melodramatic** (-drə·'mæt·ɪk) *adj.* melodramático.
melody ('mɛl·ə·di) *n.* melodía.
melon ('mɛl·ən) *n.* melón.
melt (mɛlt) *v.t.* **1,** (liquefy by heating) fundir; derretir. **2,** (dissolve) deshacer; disolver. **3,** (soften emotionally) ablandar; deshacer. —*v.i.* **1,** (become liquid) fundirse; derretirse. **2,** (dissolve) deshacerse; disolverse. **3,** (fade away; dwindle) esfumarse; desaparecer. **4,** (become softened in feeling) ablandarse; deshacerse. —**melting pot**, crisol; *fig.* lugar de fusión de pueblos *o* razas.
member ('mɛm·bər) *n.* miembro.
membership ('mɛm·bər·ʃɪp) *n.* **1,** (status as a member) calidad de

socio; afiliación. 2, (members collectively) miembros; socios.
membrane ('mɛm·brein) *n.* membrana. —**membranous** ('mɛm·brə·nəs) *adj.* membranoso.
memento (mə'mɛn·to) *n.* recuerdo; memento.
memo ('mɛm·o) *n.* [*pl.* **-os**] *colloq.* = **memorandum.**
memoir ('mɛm·war) *n.* memoria.
memorable ('mɛm·ə·rə·bəl) *adj.* memorable.
memorandum (ˌmɛm·ə'ræn·dəm) *n.* memorándum; minuta.
memorial (mə'mor·i·əl) *n.* 1, (monument) monumento. 2, (remembrance) memoria; recuerdo. 3, (petition) memorial; instancia; petición. —*adj.* conmemorativo.
memorialize (mə'mor·i·əˌlaiz) *v.t.* 1, (commemorate) conmemorar. 2, (petition) presentar un memorial a *o* ante.
memorize ('mɛm·əˌraiz) *v.t.* aprender de memoria; memorizar.
memory ('mɛm·ə·ri) *n.* memoria.
men (mɛn) *n., pl. de* **man.**
menace ('mɛn·ɪs) *n.* amenaza. —*v.t. & i.* amenazar.
ménage *también,* **menage** (me·'naʒ) *n.* 1, (household) casa; hogar. 2, (housekeeping) economía doméstica.
menagerie (mə'nædʒ·ə·ri) *n.* colección de fieras; casa de fieras.
mend (mɛnd) *v.t.* 1, (repair) componer; arreglar. 2, (correct; improve) corregir; mejorar. —*v.i.* mejorar. —*n.* arreglo. —**mend one's ways,** reformarse; corregirse. —**on the mend,** mejorando.
mendacious (mɛn'dei·ʃəs) *adj.* mendaz; mentiroso. —**mendacity** (mɛn'dæs·ə·ti) *n.* mendacidad.
mendelevium (ˌmɛn·də'li·vi·əm) *n.* mendelevio.
mendicant ('mɛn·di·kənt) *adj. & n.* mendicante. —**mendicancy,** *n.* mendicidad.
menhir (mɛn'hir) *n.* menhir.
menial ('mi·ni·əl) *n.* sirviente; criado. —*adj.* servil; bajo; de criado.
meningitis (ˌmɛn·ɪn'dʒai·tɪs) *n.* meningitis.
menopause ('mɛn·əˌpɔz) *n.* menopausia.
menses ('mɛn·siz) *n.pl.* menstruación (*sing.*); regla (*sing.*).
menstruate ('mɛn·struˌeit) *v.i.* menstruar. —**menstruation,** *n.* menstruación. —**menstrual,** *adj.* menstrual.
mensurable ('mɛn·ʃər·ə·bəl) *adj.* mensurable.
mensuration (ˌmɛn·ʃə'rei·ʃən) *n.* medida; medición.
-ment (mənt) *sufijo* -mento: *forma nombres denotando* acción; resultado: *experiment,* experimento.
mental ('mɛn·təl) *adj.* mental. —**mentality** (mɛn'tæl·ə·ti) *n.* mentalidad.
menthol ('mɛn·θal) *n.* mentol. —**mentholated** (-θəˌleit·ɪd) *adj.* mentolado.
mention ('mɛn·ʃən) *v.t.* mencionar. —*n.* mención; alusión. —**don't mention it,** no hay de qué; de nada.
mentor ('mɛn·tor) *n.* mentor.
menu ('mɛn·ju) *n.* menú.
meow (mi'au) *v.i.* maullar. —*n.* miau; maullido.
mephitis (mɪ'fai·tɪs) *n.* vapor fétido. —**mephitic** (mɪ'fɪt·ɪk) *adj.* mefítico.
mercantile ('mʌɹ·kən·tɪl) *adj.* mercantil. —**mercantilism,** *n.* mercantilismo.
mercenary ('mʌɹ·səˌnɛr·i) *adj. & n.* mercenario.
mercer ('mʌɹ·sər) *n.* mercero.
mercerize ('mʌɹ·səˌraiz) *v.t.* mercerizar.
merchandise ('mʌɹ·tʃənˌdaiz) *n.* mercadería; mercancía(s). —*v.t. & i.* traficar (en); comerciar (en). —**merchandising,** *n.* ventas (*pl.*).
merchant ('mʌɹ·tʃənt) *n.* comerciante; mercader. —**merchant marine,** marina mercante.
merchantman ('mʌɹ·tʃənt·mən) *n.* [*pl.* **-men**] barco *o* buque mercante.
merciful (ˌmʌɹ·sɪ·ʃəl) *adj.* clemente; misericordioso. —**mercifulness,** *n.* clemencia; misericordia.
merciless ('mʌɹ·sɪ·ləs) *adj.* despiadado; inclemente; cruel. —**mercilessness,** *n.* crueldad; falta de compasión.
mercurial (mər'kjur·i·əl) *adj.* 1, [*también,* **mercuric** (-ɪk)] (of mercury) mercurial; mercúrico. 2, (changeable) volátil; mudable.
mercurochrome (mər'kjʊr·əˌkrom) *n.* mercurocromo.
mercury ('mʌɹ·kjə·ri) *n.* mercurio; *cap.* Mercurio.

mercy ('mʌɹ·si) *n.* clemencia; misericordia; piedad; compasión. —*interj.* ¡Dios santo!; ¡Dios mío!
mere (mɪr) *adj.* mero; simple; solo; puro. —*n., poet.* lago; mar.
merengue (mə'rɛn·ge) *n.* merengue.
meretricious (ˌmɛr·ə'trɪʃ·əs) *adj.* meretricio; interesado. —**meretriciousness,** *n.* lo meretricio.
merganser (mər'gæn·sər) *n.* mergo; mergánsar; somorgujo.
merge (mʌɹdʒ) *v.t. & i.* unir(se); fundir(se); fusionar(se).
merger ('mʌɹ·dʒər) *n.* fusión. —**form a merger,** fusionarse.
meridian (mə'rɪd·i·ən) *n. & adj.* meridiano. —**meridional,** *adj.* meridional; meridiano.
meringue (mə'ræŋ) *n.* merengue.
merino (mə'ri·no) *n. & adj.* merino.
merit ('mɛr·ɪt) *n.* mérito. —*v.t.* merecer; ser digno de.
meritorious (ˌmɛr·ɪ'tor·i·əs) *adj.* meritorio. —**meritoriousness,** *n.* mérito.
merle (mʌɹl) *n.* mirlo; merla.
merlin ('mʌɹ·lɪn) *n.* esmerejón.
mermaid ('mʌɹˌmeid) *n.* sirena.
merman ('mʌɹˌmæn; -mən) *n.* [*pl.* **-men**] tritón.
merry ('mɛr·i) *adj.* alegre; festivo; risueño. —**merriment,** *n.* alegría; júbilo. —**make merry,** regodearse; jaranear.
merry-andrew (ˌmɛr·i'æn·dru) *n.* bufón; chocarrero; payaso.
merry-go-round ('mɛr·i·go·ˌraund) *n.* tiovivo; caballitos (*pl.*); *Amer.* carrusel.
merrymaker *n.* parrandero; fiestero. —**merrymaking,** *n.* parranda; jarana.
mesa ('mei·sə) *n.* meseta; mesa.
mesalliance (mei'zæl·i·əns) *n.* matrimonio desigual.
mescal (mɛs'kæl) *n.* mezcal.
mesh (mɛʃ) *n.* **1,** (open space of a net) malla; ojo de red. **2,** (net; network) red. —*v.t. & i.* **1,** (tangle) enredar(se). **2,** *mech.* (engage) engranar.
mesmerism ('mɛs·mə·rɪz·əm) *n.* mesmerismo. —**mesmeric** (mɛs·'mɛr·ɪk) *adj.* mesmeriano. —**mesmerist,** *n.* hipnotizador. —**mesmerize,** *v.t.* hipnotizar.
meso- (mɛs·ə) *prefijo* meso-; medio: *mesocarp,* mesocarpio.
meson ('mei·san) *n.* mesón.
mesotron 'mɛs·əˌtran) *n.* mesotrón.
Mesozoic (ˌmɛs·ə'zo·ɪk) *adj.* mesozoico.
mesquite (mɛs'kit) *n.* mezquite.
mess (mɛs) *n.* **1,** (disorder) desorden; revoltijo. **2,** (trouble; entanglement) embrollo; lío. **3,** (dirt; filth) suciedad; porquería. **4,** (sticky mass) plasta; mazamorra; mazacote. **5,** *colloq.* (bunch; group) montón. **6,** (group taking meals together; a meal so taken) rancho. —*v.t.* **1,** (make untidy) desordenar; desarreglar. **2,** (confuse) embrollar; complicar. **3,** (spoil; ruin) estropear; dañar. **4,** (dirty) ensuciar. —*v.i.* **1,** (take meals together) comer *o* tomar rancho. **2,** (cause dirt or filth) ensuciarse. **3,** *colloq.* (putter; bungle) chapucear.
message ('mɛs·ɪdʒ) *n.* mensaje.
messenger ('mɛs·ən·dʒər) *n.* mensajero.
Messiah (mə'sai·ə) *n.* Mesías. —**Messianic** (ˌmɛs·i'æn·ɪk) *adj.* mesiánico.
messieurs ('mɛs·ərz; me'sjʊ) *n., pl. de* **monsieur.**
messmate ('mɛsˌmeit) *n.* compañero de mesa *o* rancho.
messy ('mɛs·i) *adj.* **1,** (untidy) desarreglado; desaliñado; desbarajustado. **2,** (dirty) sucio. **3,** (muddled) embrollado; enredado. **4,** (gooey) mazacotudo; apelmazado.
mestizo (mɛs'ti·zo) *n. & adj.* mestizo.
met (mɛt) *v., pret. & p.p. de* **meet.**
meta- (mɛt·ə) *prefijo* meta-. **1,** junto con; del *o* en el centro; más allá; después: *metacenter,* metacentro; *metaphysics,* metafísica. **2,** cambio; transformación: *metathesis,* metátesis.
metabolism (mə'tæb·ə·lɪz·əm) *n.* metabolismo. —**metabolic** (ˌmɛt·ə'bal·ɪk) *adj.* metabólico.
metacarpus (ˌmɛt·ə'kar·pəs) *n.* metacarpo. —**metacarpal,** *adj.* metacarpiano.
metal ('mɛt·əl) *n.* metal. —**metallic** (mə'tæl·ɪk) *adj.* metálico.
metalliferous (ˌmɛt·ə'lɪf·ə·rəs) *adj.* metalífero.
metalloid ('mɛt·əˌlɔid) *n. & adj.* metaloide.
metallurgy ('mɛt·əˌlʌɹ·dʒi) *n.* metalurgia. —**metallurgic** (-'lʌɹ·

dʒɪk) *adj.* metalúrgico. —**metallurgist,** *n.* metalúrgico.
metamorphosis (ˌmɛt·əˈmor·fə·sɪs) *n.* [*pl.* **-ses** (siz)] metamorfosis. —**metamorphic** (-fɪk) *adj.* metamórfico. —**metamorphose** (-foz) *v.t.* metamorfosear.
metaphor (ˈmɛt·əˌfor; -fər) *n.* metáfora. —**metaphoric** (-ˈfor·ɪk); **metaphorical,** *adj.* metafórico.
metaphysics (ˌmɛt·əˈfɪz·ɪks) *n.* metafísica. —**metaphysical,** *adj.* metafísico. —**metaphysician** (-fɪ·ˈzɪʃ·ən) *n.* metafísico.
metaplasm (ˈmɛt·əˌplæz·əm) *n.* metaplasma.
metastasis (məˈtæs·tə·sɪs) *n.* metástasis. —**metastatic** (ˌmɛt·ə·ˈstæt·ɪk) *adj.* metastático.
metatarsus (ˌmɛt·əˈtar·sʌs) *n.* metatarso. —**metatarsal,** *adj.* metatarsiano.
Metazoa (ˌmɛt·əˈzo·ə) *n.pl.* metazoos. —**Metazoan,** *n.* & *adj.* metazoo; metazoario.
mete (mit) *v.t.* asignar; repartir; distribuir.
metempsychosis (məˌtɛmp·sə·ˈko·sɪs) *n.* [*pl.* **-ses** (siz)] metempsicosis.
meteor (ˈmi·ti·ər) *n.* meteoro. —**meteoric** (-ˈar·ɪk) *adj.* meteórico. —**meteorite,** *n.* meteorito.
meteorology (ˌmi·ti·əˈral·ə·dʒi) *n.* meteorología. —**meteorological** (-ər·əˈladʒ·ɪ·kəl) *adj.* meteorológico. —**meteorologist,** *n.* meteorologista; meteorólogo.
meter (ˈmi·tər) *n.* **1,** (unit of length) metro. **2,** (measuring instrument) contador; *Amer.* medidor. **3,** *pros.* metro. **4,** *music* compás; tiempo.
-meter (mi·tər; mə-) *sufijo* -metro. **1,** instrumento para medir: *voltmeter,* voltímetro. **2,** metro: *kilometer,* kilómetro. **3,** medida poética: *hexameter,* hexámetro.
methane (ˈmɛθ·ein) *n.* metano.
method (ˈmɛθ·əd) *n.* método. —**methodical** (məˈθad·ə·kəl) *adj.* metódico.
Methodist (ˈmɛθ·ə·dɪst) *n.* & *adj.* metodista. —**Methodism,** *n.* metodismo.
methyl (ˈmɛθ·ɪl) *n.* metilo. —**methylic** (məˈθɪl·ɪk) *adj.* metílico. —**methyl alcohol,** alcohol metílico.
methylene (ˈmɛθ·əˌlin) *n.* metileno.
meticulous (məˈtɪk·jə·ləs) *adj.* meticuloso. —**meticulousness,** *n.* meticulosidad.
métier (mɛˈtjei) *n.* oficio; profesión.
metric (ˈmɛt·rɪk) *adj.* métrico.
metrical (ˈmɛt·rɪ·kəl) *adj.* métrico.
metrics (ˈmɛt·rɪks) *n.* métrica.
metro- (mɛt·ro; -rə) *prefijo* metro-. **1,** medida: *metrology,* metrología. **2,** matriz; madre: *metrorrhagia,* metrorragia; *metropolis,* metrópolis.
metronome (ˈmɛt·rəˌnom) *n.* metrónomo.
metropolis (məˈtrap·ə·lɪs) *n.* metrópoli.
metropolitan (ˌmɛt·rəˈpal·ə·tən) *adj.* & *n.* metropolitano.
-metry (mə·tri) *sufijo* -metría; ciencia *o* proceso de medir: *anthropometry,* antropometría.
mettle (ˈmɛt·əl) *n.* temple; fibra. —**mettlesome,** *adj.* de temple; de fibra.
mew (mjuː) *n.* **1,** (sound of a cat) maullido. **2,** (enclosure) cercado. **3,** (cage) jaula. **4,** (secret place) escondite; refugio. **5,** (sea gull) gaviota. **6,** *pl.* (stables) cuadras; caballerizas. —*v.t.* encerrar. —*v.i.* maullar.
mewl (mjuːl) *v.i.* lloriquear.
Mexican (ˈmɛk·sɪ·kən) *adj.* & *n.* mejicano; mexicano.
mezzanine (ˈmɛz·əˌnin) *n.* entresuelo.
mezzo-soprano (ˈmɛt·so·sə·ˈpræn·o) *n.* mezzo-soprano.
mezzotint (ˈmɛt·soˌtɪnt) *n.* media tinta.
mi (miː) *n., music* mi.
miasma (maiˈæz·mə) *n.* miasma. —**miasmal; miasmatic** (ˌmai·æz·ˈmæt·ɪk) *adj.* miasmático.
mica (ˈmai·kə) *n.* mica.
mice (mais) *n., pl. de* **mouse.**
micro- (mai·kro; -krə) *prefijo* micro-; muy pequeño: *microcosm,* microcosmo.
microbe (ˈmai·krob) *n.* microbio. —**microbic** (maiˈkro·bɪk) *adj.* micróbico.
microcosm (ˈmai·krəˌkaz·əm) *n.* microcosmo.
microfilm *n.* microfilm.
micrometer (maiˈkram·ə·tər) *n.* micrómetro.
micron (ˈmai·kran) *n.* micra; micrón.

Micronesian (ˌmai·krəˈni·ʒən) *n. & adj.* micronesio.

microörganism (ˌmai·kroˈor·gə·nɪz·əm) *n.* microorganismo.

microphone (ˈmai·krəˌfon) *n.* micrófono.

microphotograph (ˌmai·kroˈfo·tə·græf) *n.* microfotografía. —**microphotography** (-fəˈtag·rə·fi) *n.* microfotografía.

microscope (ˈmai·krəˌskop) *n.* microscopio. —**microscopic** (-ˈskap·ɪk) *adj.* microscópico.

microtome (ˈmai·krəˌtom) *n.* micrótomo.

mid (mɪd) *adj.* medio. —*prep.* entre; en medio de. —**in mid air,** en el aire.

mid- (mɪd) *prefijo* medio-; medio; centro; a mediados de: *midday,* mediodía; *midweek,* a mediados de semana.

midday (ˈmɪdˌdei) *n.* mediodía. —*adj.* de *o* a mediodía; de *o* a la tarde.

middle (ˈmɪd·əl) *adj.* **1,** (halfway between; in the center) del medio; del centro; entremedio. **2,** (medium) medio; mediano. **3,** (intermediate; intervening) intermedio; medio. —*n.* **1,** (central point or part) medio; centro; mitad. **2,** (waist) cintura. —**Middle Ages,** edad media. —**middle finger,** (dedo) corazón. —**towards** *o* **about the middle of** (*the month, year, etc.*), a mediados de (*mes, año, etc.*).

middle-aged *adj.* de mediana edad. —**middle age,** edad mediana.

middle-class *adj.* de clase media; burgués.

middleman *n.* [*pl.* **-men**] intermediario.

middle-of-the-road *adj.* moderado; del centro. —**middle-of-the-roader,** *n.* moderado.

middling (ˈmɪd·lɪŋ) *adj.* regular; pasadero; pasable; mediano.

middy (ˈmɪd·i) *n.* **1,** (sailor's blouse) marinera. **2,** *colloq.* = **midshipman.**

midge (mɪdʒ) *n.* **1,** (gnat) mosquito; *Amer.* jején. **2,** (midget) enano.

midget (ˈmɪdʒ·ɪt) *adj. & n.* enano.

midland (ˈmɪd·lənd) *n.* interior. —*adj.* de tierra adentro; del interior.

midnight (ˈmɪdˌnait) *n.* medianoche. —*adj.* de *o* a medianoche.

midriff (ˈmɪd·rɪf) *n.* diafragma. —*adj.* con abertura en la parte del diafragma.

midshipman (ˈmɪdˌʃɪp·mən) *n.* guardia marina.

midst (mɪdst) *n.* medio. —*prep., poet.* entre; en medio de.

midstream (ˈmɪdˌstrim) *n.* el medio de una corriente. —**in midstream,** a mitad de camino; a medio camino.

midway (ˈmɪdˌwei) *n.* avenida de atracciones (*de una feria*). —*adj.* a *o* de medio camino; a *o* en mitad del camino. —*adv.* (a) medio camino; a *o* en mitad del camino.

midweek *n.* mediados de semana. —*adj.* a *o* de mediados de semana.

Midwest *n., U.S.* el medio oeste.

midwife (ˈmɪdˌwaif) *n.* comadrona; partera. —**midwifery,** *n.* partería.

midyear *n.* mediados de año. —*adj.* a *o* de mediados de año.

mien (miːn) *n.* semblante; aire.

miff (mɪf) *v.t., colloq.* enfadar; enojar. —*n., colloq.* enfado; enojo.

might (mait) *n.* fuerza; poder; poderío. —**with might and main,** con todas sus fuerzas.

might (mait) *aux.v.* **1,** *pret.de* **may. 2,** *expresando duda, permiso o posibilidad en el presente o en el futuro; equivalente al condicional en español: Might I go now?* ¿Podría ir ahora?; *We might arrive in time,* Podríamos llegar a tiempo.

mighty (ˈmai·ti) *adj.* **1,** (powerful) potente; poderoso. **2,** (great; momentous) importante; grande. —*adv., colloq.* muy.

mignonette (ˌmɪn·jəˈnɛt) *n.* reseda.

migraine (ˈmai·grein) *n.* jaqueca.

migrant (ˈmai·grənt) *n. & adj.* emigrante.

migrate (ˈmai·gret) *v.i.* emigrar. —**migration,** *n.* migración; emigración. —**migratory** (-grəˌtor·i) *adj.* migratorio; peregrino; (*of birds*) de paso.

mikado (mɪˈka·do) *n.* micado.

mike (maik) *n., slang* = **microphone, micrometer,** etc.

mil (mɪl) *n.* **1,** (measure of diameter) milésima de pulgada. **2,** *artillery* unidad de medida de ángulos

de tiro (1/6400 de la circunferencia).
milch (mɪltʃ) *adj.* lechera; de leche.
mild (maild) *adj.* **1,** (kind; gentle) apacible; dulce. **2,** (not harsh; bland) leve; ligero. **3,** (soft or pleasant to the taste) suave. **4,** (temperate) templado. —**mildness,** *n.* suavidad; lo suave; lo templado.
mildew ('mɪl·du) *v.t. & i.* enmohecer(se); cubrir(se) de moho. —*n.* moho.
mile (mail) *n.* milla.
mileage ('mai·lɪdʒ) *n.* **1,** (distance traversed) distancia en millas *o* kilómetros; millaje. **2,** (charge per mile) derecho por milla.
milepost *n.* poste miliar.
miler ('mai·lər) *n.* corredor de una milla.
milestone *n.* **1,** = **milepost. 2,** (important event) hito; acontecimiento.
milfoil ('mɪlˌfɔil) *n.* milenrama; milhojas.
miliaria (ˌmɪl·i'ɛr·i·ə) *n.* erupción miliar.
miliary ('mɪl·i·ɛr·i) *adj.* miliar.
milieu (mi'ljʊ) *n.* medio; medio ambiente.
militant ('mɪl·ə·tənt) *adj.* militante. —**militancy,** *n.* lo militante.
militarism ('mɪl·ə·təˌrɪz·əm) *n.* militarismo. —**militarist,** *n.* militarista. —**militaristic,** *adj.* militarista.
militarize ('mɪl·ə·təˌraiz) *v.t.* militarizar. —**militarization** (-rɪ·'zei·ʃən) *n.* militarización.
military ('mɪl·əˌtɛr·i) *adj.* militar. —*n.* ejército.
militate ('mɪl·əˌteit) *v.i.* militar.
militia (mɪ'lɪʃ·ə) *n.* milicia; guardia nacional. —**militiaman** (-mən) *n.* [*pl.* **-men**] miliciano.
milk (mɪlk) *n.* leche. —*v.t.* **1,** (extract milk from) ordeñar. **2,** (squeeze out; drain) exprimir; agotar; sacar el jugo de. —*v.i.* dar leche. —**milker,** *n.* ordeñador; ordeñadora. —**milking,** *n.* ordeño; el ordeñar. —**milk fever,** fiebre de lactancia. —**milk leg,** flebitis puerperal. —**milk tooth,** diente de leche; diente mamón.
milkmaid *n.* lechera.
milkman *n.* [*pl.* **-men**] lechero.
milk shake batido (de leche).
milksop *n.* hombre afeminado.
milkweed *n.* hierba lechera.
milkwort *n.* polígala.
milky ('mɪl·ki) *adj.* lechoso; como leche; lácteo. —**Milky Way,** Vía Láctea.
mill (mɪl) *n.* **1,** (machine or establishment for grinding) molino. **2,** (factory) fábrica; taller. **3,** (machine for rolling metal) laminadora. **4,** (U.S. monetary unit) milésimo de dólar. —*v.i.* arremolinarse; dar vueltas. —*v.t.* **1,** (grind) moler. **2,** (roll, as metal) laminar. **3,** (shape by grinding, as metal) fresar. **4,** (put grooves on, as coins) acordonar. **5,** (manufacture; process) manufacturar; fabricar. —**go through the mill,** *colloq.* pasar las de San Quintín (*o* las de Caín); pasarlas todas. —**put through the mill,** *colloq.* hacer pasar las de San Quintín (*o* las de Caín); poner a prueba.
mille- (mɪl·ə) *prefijo* mile-; mil: *millepore,* milépora.
millenary ('mɪl·əˌnɛr·i) *adj.* milenario.
millenium (mɪ'lɛn·i·əm) *n.* **1,** (period of a thousand years) milenio. **2,** (thousandth anniversary) milenario. —**millennial,** *adj.* milenario.
miller ('mɪl·ər) *n.* **1,** (operator of a mill) molinero. **2,** (moth) mariposa nocturna blanquecina.
millet ('mɪl·ɪt) *n.* mijo.
milli- (mɪl·ə) *prefijo* mili-; milésima parte: *millimeter,* milímetro.
milliard ('mɪl·jərd) *n., Brit.* mil millones.
milligram *n.* miligramo.
milliliter *n.* mililitro.
millimeter *n.* milímetro.
milliner ('mɪl·ə·nər) *n.* sombrerero; modista de sombreros.
millinery ('mɪl·əˌnɛr·i) *n.* **1,** (women's hats) sombreros de señora. **2,** (milliner's shop or trade) sombrerería (de señoras).
milling ('mɪl·ɪŋ) *n.* **1,** (crushing; grinding) molienda. **2,** (grooves cut in coins) acordonamiento; cordoncillo. **3,** (lamination) laminación. **4,** (processing) manufactura; fabricación.
million ('mɪl·jən) *n.* millón. —**millionth,** *adj. & n.* millonésimo.
millionaire (ˌmɪl·jə'neːr) *n.* millonario.
millipede ('mɪl·əˌpiːd) *n.* milpiés.

millpond *n.* alberca; presa *o* represa de molino.
millrace *n.* canal de molino; caz.
millstone *n.* piedra de molino; muela.
milquetoast ('mılk,tost) *n., slang* pacato.
milt (mılt) *n., ichthy.* lecha.
mime (maim) *n.* **1,** (comic actor) pantomimo; cómico; mimo. **2,** (farce) pantomima; farsa. —*v.t. & i.* remedar; imitar.
mimeograph ('mım·i·ə,græf) *n.* mimeógrafo. —*v.t.* copiar a mimeógrafo; mimeografiar.
mimic ('mım·ık) *v.t.* [**mimicked, mimicking**] remedar; imitar; copiar. —*n.* imitador; pantomimo. —*adj.* **1,** (imitative) mímico; imitativo. **2,** (mock; simulated) simulado; de mentirijillas.
mimicry ('mım·ık·ri) *n.* mímica; imitación; remedo; *biol.* mimetismo.
mimosa (mı'mo·sə) *n.* mimosa; sensitiva.
minaret (,mın·ər'ɛt) *n.* minarete.
minatory ('mın·ə,tor·i) *adj.* amenazador.
mince (mıns) *v.t.* **1,** (chop) picar; cortar en pedacitos. **2,** (express or do with affectation) usar de afectación *o* remilgo en; poner afectación en. **3,** (weaken; soften, as words) comedirse en; medirse *o* moderarse en. —*v.i.* **1,** (speak or behave daintily) andarse con remilgos *o* mojigaterías. **2,** (walk daintily or affectedly) moverse con afectación *o* delicadeza afectada. —**mincing,** *adj.* afectado. —**not to mince words** (*o* **matters**), no pararse en pelillos; no andar por las ramas; hablar francamente. —**mince pie,** pastel hecho con pasas y especias.
mincemeat ('mıns,mit) *n.* **1,** (chopped meat) carne picada. **2,** (anything chopped fine) picadillo. **3,** (pie filling) pasas y especias. —**make mincemeat of,** hacer pedazos.
mind (maind) *n.* **1,** (mental faculty) mente; cerebro. **2,** (opinion) parecer; juicio; opinión. **3,** (reason; sanity) razón; cabeza; juicio. **4,** (intention) propósito; intención; ánimo. —*v.t.* **1,** (pay attention to) fijarse en. **2,** (heed) hacer caso de *o* a. **3,** (attend to; look after) cuidar; atender; ocuparse de. **4,** (be careful about) tener cuidado con. **5,** (care about; object to) importarle a uno. **6,** *colloq.* (keep in mind) tener presente; tener en cuenta. —*v.i.* **1,** (pay attention; give heed) prestar atención; atender; hacer caso. **2,** (be careful) tener cuidado. **3,** (care; be concerned) importarle a uno. —**bear in mind,** tener presente; tener en cuenta. —**be in one's right mind,** estar en sus cabales. —**be of one mind,** estar de acuerdo; ser de la misma opinión. —**be of two minds,** estar indeciso. —**be out of one's mind,** estar fuera de sí; estar loco. —**call to mind,** recordar; traer a (las) mientes. —**change one's mind,** cambiar de idea *o* pensamiento. —**give (someone) a piece of one's mind,** decirle a uno lo que piensa. —**go out of one's mind,** perder el juicio; salirse de sus casillas. —**have a good (** *o* **great) mind to,** tener muchas ganas de. —**have in mind,** pensar (en); acordarse de. —**keep in mind,** tener presente. —**keep one's mind on,** fijarse en; atender a; prestar atención a. —**make up one's mind,** decidirse; resolverse. —**never mind,** no importa; no se moleste. —**set one's mind on,** empeñarse en; decidirse a. —**slip one's mind,** olvidársele a uno; escapársele a uno. —**to one's mind,** para uno; en la opinión de uno.
minded ('main·dıd) *adj.* inclinado; dispuesto.
-minded (main·dıd) *sufijo; forma adjetivos denotando* inclinación o disposición de la mente: *like-minded,* del mismo parecer; *strong-minded,* testarudo.
mindful ('maind·fəl) *adj.* atento; cuidadoso. —**mindfulness,** *n.* atención; cuidado.
mindless ('maind·ləs) *adj.* **1,** (senseless) necio; insensato. **2,** (heedless; unmindful) despreocupado; desatento.
mine (main) *poss.pron.* el mío; la mía; lo mío; los míos; las mías.
mine (main) *n.* mina. —*v.t. & i.* minar. —**miner,** *n.* minero.
mine-layer *n.* minador.
mineral ('mın·ər·əl) *n. & adj.* mineral.
mineralogy (,mın·ər'æl·ə·dʒi) *n.* mineralogía. —**mineralogical** (-ə'ladʒ·ı·kəl) *adj.* mineralógico.

—**mineralogist,** *n.* mineralogista.
mine sweeper dragaminas; barreminas.
mingle ('mɪŋ·gəl) *v.t.* mezclar; juntar. —*v.i.* mezclarse; juntarse.
miniature ('mɪn·i·ə·tʃər) *n.* miniatura. —*adj.* en miniatura.
minim ('mɪn·əm) *n.* mínima.
minimal ('mɪn·ə·məl) *adj.* mínimo.
minimize ('mɪn·əˌmaiz) *v.t.* **1,** (reduce to a minimum) reducir al mínimo. **2,** (undervalue; belittle) atenuar; menospreciar.
minimum ('mɪn·ə·məm) *n.* mínimo; mínimum.
mining ('mai·nɪŋ) *n.* minería. —*adj.* minero.
minion ('mɪn·jən) *n.* **1,** (favorite) valido; favorito. **2,** (henchman) esbirro; sicario.
minister ('mɪn·ɪs·tər) *n.* ministro. —*v.i.* servir. —**minister to,** servir; atender; asistir.
ministerial (ˌmɪn·ɪs'tɪr·i·əl) *adj.* ministerial.
ministration (ˌmɪn·ə'strei·ʃən) *n.* oficio; servicio; atención.
ministry ('mɪn·ɪs·tri) *n.* ministerio.
mink (mɪŋk) *n.* visón.
minnow ('mɪn·o) *n.* nombre de varios peces de la familia de la carpa.
minor ('mai·nər) *adj.* & *n.* menor.
minority (mɪ'nar·ə·ti) *n.* minoría; (*of age*) minoridad.
minstrel ('mɪn·strəl) *n.* trovador; juglar; *Amer.* payador. —**minstrelsy** (-si) *n.* juglaría.
mint (mɪnt) *n.* **1,** (plant) menta; hierbabuena. **2,** (place where money is coined) casa de moneda. **3,** *colloq.* (vast amount) mina; montón. —*v.t.* acuñar.
mintage ('mɪnt·ɪdʒ) *n.* acuñación.
minuend ('mɪn·ju·ɛnd) *n.* minuendo.
minuet (ˌmɪn·ju'ɛt) *n.* minué.
minus ('mai·nəs) *prep.* **1,** (less) menos. **2,** (lacking) sin; falto de. —*adj.* **1,** (denoting subtraction) menos. **2,** (negative) negativo.
minuscule (mɪ'nʌs·kjul) *adj.* minúsculo. —*n.* minúscula.
minute ('mɪn·ɪt) *n.* **1,** (sixtieth part of an hour or degree) minuto. **2,** (moment) minuto; momento. **3,** *pl.* (record) minutas; acta (*sing.*). **4,** (memorandum) minuta. —**minute hand,** minutero. —**up to the minute,** de última hora; de último momento; al corriente.
minute (mai'njut) *adj.* **1,** (very small; tiny) minúsculo; muy menudo. **2,** (exact; attentive to detail) minucioso.
minuteman ('mɪn·ɪtˌmæn) *n., U.S.* [*pl.* **-men**] miliciano listo a tomar armas.
minuteness (mai'njut·nəs) *n.* **1,** (smallness) pequeñez; menudencia. **2,** (exactness) minuciosidad.
minutiae (mɪ'nju·ʃi·i) *n.pl.* minucias; menudencias.
minx (mɪŋks) *n.* tunanta; moza descarada.
miracle ('mɪr·ə·kəl) *n.* milagro.
miraculous (mɪ'ræk·jə·ləs) *adj.* milagroso.
mirage (mɪ'ra:ʒ) *n.* espejismo.
mire (mair) *n.* cieno; fango; lodo. —*v.t.* **1,** (bog down) atascar; atollar. **2,** (make muddy) enlodar. —*v.i.* atascarse; atollarse. —**miry,** *adj.* fangoso; barroso.
mirror ('mɪr·ər) *n.* espejo. —*v.t.* reflejar.
mirth (mʌɹθ) *n.* alegría; regocijo. —**mirthful,** *adj.* alegre; regocijado. —**mirthless,** *adj.* triste; abatido.
mis- (mɪs) *prefijo.* **1,** malo; equivocado; *mispronunciation,* mala pronunciación. **2,** sentido negativo u opuesto: *mischance,* contratiempo. **3,** *var. de* **miso-**: *misanthrope,* misántropo.
misadventure (ˌmɪs·əd'vɛn·tʃər) *n.* mala suerte; desgracia; contratiempo.
misanthrope ('mɪs·ənˌθrop) *también,* **misanthropist** (mɪs'æn·θrə·pɪst) *n.* misántropo. —**misanthropic** (-'θrap·ɪk) *adj.* misantrópico. —**misanthropy** (mɪs'æn·θrə·pi) *n.* misantropía.
misapprehend *v.t.* entender mal. —**misapprehension,** *n.* error; equivocación.
misappropriate *v.t.* malversar; distraer (fondos). —**misappropriation,** *n.* malversación.
misbegotten *adj.* ilegítimo; bastardo.
misbehave *v.i.* portarse *o* conducirse mal. —**misbehavior,** *n.* mala conducta; mal comportamiento.

misbelieve *v.i.* estar errado; vivir en el error. —*v.t.* no creer. —**misbeliever,** *n.* infiel; descreído.
miscalculate (mɪsˈkæl·kjəˌleit) *v.t.* & *i.* calcular mal. —**miscalculation,** *n.* error; mal cálculo.
miscarriage (mɪsˈkær·ɪdʒ) *n.* **1,** (mismanagement) extravío; desmán. **2,** (failure to reach a destination) pérdida; extravío. **3,** (abortion) malparto; aborto.
miscarry (mɪsˈkær·i) *v.i.* **1,** (go wrong; fail) fracasar; abortar. **2,** (go astray; fail to arrive) extraviarse; perderse. **3,** (abort) abortar.
miscast (mɪsˈkæst) *v.t.* dar (a un actor) un papel inapropiado; hacer un mal reparto de actores en (una obra).
miscegenation (ˌmɪs·ɪ·dʒəˈnei·ʃən) *n.* mezcla de razas.
miscellaneous (ˌmɪs·əˈlei·ni·əs) *adj.* misceláneo.
miscellany (ˈmɪs·əˌlei·ni) *n.* miscelánea.
mischance (mɪsˈtʃæns) *n.* percance; desgracia; mala suerte.
mischief (ˈmɪs·tʃɪf) *n.* **1,** (harm; damage; injury) daño; perjuicio; mal. **2,** (noxious behavior) maldad; mal proceder. **3,** (naughtiness) travesura; diablura.
mischievous (ˈmɪs·tʃə·vəs) *adj.* **1,** (injurious) dañoso; dañino; malo. **2,** (full of tricks) trapacero; embrollón; malicioso. **3,** (naughty) travieso; revoltoso.
mischievousness (ˈmɪs·tʃə·vəs·nəs) *n.* **1,** (evil; harmfulness) maldad. **2,** (malice; trickery) malicia; trapacería. **3,** (naughtiness) travesura; diablura.
miscible (ˈmɪs·ə·bəl) *adj.* miscible. —**miscibility,** *n.* miscibilidad.
misconceive *v.t.* formar concepto erróneo de; entender mal. —**misconception,** *n.* concepto erróneo.
misconduct (mɪsˈkan·dʌkt) *n.* desafuero; mal proceder; acción *o* conducta impropia. —*v.t.* (ˌmɪs·kənˈdʌkt) **1,** (mismanage) errar en; proceder sin acierto en. **2,** *usu.refl.* (misbehave) conducirse mal.
misconstrue *v.t.* interpreter mal; torcer el sentido de. —**misconstruction,** *n.* mala interpretación; error.
miscreant (ˈmɪs·kri·ənt) *adj.* & *n.* malandrín; bribón; sinvergüenza.
miscue (mɪsˈkjuː) *n.* **1,** *billiards* pifia. **2,** *theat.* equivocación en el apunte. —*v.i.* **1,** *billiards* pifiar. **2,** *theat.* equivocarse de apunte.
misdeal (mɪsˈdiːl) *v.t.* & *i.* dar *o* repartir mal (las cartas). —*n.* repartición mal hecha.
misdeed (mɪsˈdiːd) *n.* mala acción; delito.
misdemeanor (ˌmɪs·dəˈmi·nər) *n.* **1,** (misbehavior) mala conducta. **2,** *law* delito de menor cuantía.
misdirect *v.t.* encaminar mal. —**misdirection,** *n.* mala dirección; malas instrucciones.
misdoing (mɪsˈdu·ɪŋ) *n.* delito; mala acción.
miser (ˈmai·zər) *n.* avaro; miserable; tacaño. —**miserliness,** *n.* avaricia; tacañería. —**miserly,** *adj.* avariento; miserable; tacaño.
miserable (ˈmɪz·ər·ə·bəl) *adj.* miserable.
misery (ˈmɪz·ə·ri) *n.* miseria.
misfeasance (mɪsˈfi·zəns) *n.* abuso de autoridad.
misfire (mɪsˈfair) *v.i.* fallar el tiro. —*n.* tiro fallo.
misfit (ˈmɪsˌfɪt) *n.* **1,** (poor fit) mal ajuste *o* calce. **2,** (badly adjusted person) inadaptado. **3,** (ill-fitting thing) cosa que no ajusta bien; prenda que no calza *o* queda bien. —*v.t.* & *i.* (mɪsˈfɪt) no ajustar bien; no quedar bien; no calzar.
misfortune (mɪsˈfor·tʃun) *n.* mala suerte; desgracia; desventura.
misgiving (mɪsˈgɪv·ɪŋ) *n.* **1,** (suspicion; doubt) recelo; duda. **2,** (foreboding) mal presentimiento; aprensión.
misguide (mɪsˈgaid) *v.t.* descaminar; descarriar.
misguided (mɪsˈgai·dɪd) *adj.* **1,** (mistaken) equivocado; erróneo. **2,** (led astray) descaminado; descarriado.
mishap (ˈmɪs·hæp) *n.* percance; contratiempo.
mishmash (ˈmɪʃˌmæʃ) *n.* mezcolanza; mejunje; mazacote.
misinform *v.t.* informar mal. —**misinformation,** *n.* información equivocada *o* errónea.
misinterpret *v.t.* interpretar mal. —**misinterpretation,** *n.* mala interpretación.
misjudge (mɪsˈdʒʌdʒ) *v.t.* **1,** (miscalculate) calcular mal. **2,** (judge unfairly) juzgar mal *o* injustamente. —**misjudgment,** *n.* juicio equivocado.

mislay (mɪs'lei) *v.t.* [*pret. & p.p.* **mislaid**] **1,** (lay away and forget) extraviar. **2,** (place incorrectly) colocar mal.
mislead (mɪs'liːd) *v.t.* **1,** (lead astray) descarriar; extraviar. **2,** (deceive) engañar. —**misleading,** *adj.* engañador.
mismanage (mɪs'mæn·ɪdʒ) *v.t.* manejar *o* administrar mal. —**mismanagement,** *n.* mal manejo; mala administración.
mismatch (mɪs'mætʃ) *v.t.* unir *o* emparejar mal. —*n.* unión mal hecha; casamiento mal hecho; casorio.
misnomer (mɪs'no·mər) *n.* nombre inapropiado.
miso- (mɪs·o) *prefijo* miso-; odio; repulsión: *misogynous,* misógino.
misogamy (mɪ'sag·ə·mi) *n.* misogamia. —**misogamist,** *n.* misógamo. —**misogamous,** *adj.* misógamo.
misogyny (mɪ'sadʒ·ə·ni) *n.* misoginia. —**misogynist,** *n.* misógino. —**misogynous,** *adj.* misógino.
misplace (mɪs'pleis) *v.t.* **1,** (put in a wrong place) colocar mal; poner fuera de sitio. **2,** (bestow unwisely) entregar *o* poner equivocadamente. **3,** *colloq.* (mislay; lose) extraviar; perder.
misprint ('mɪs·prɪnt) *n.* errata; error de imprenta. —*v.t.* (mɪs·'prɪnt) imprimir con erratas; imprimir *o* escribir incorrectamente.
mispronounce *v.t. & i.* pronunciar mal. —**mispronunciation,** *n.* pronunciación incorrecta.
misquote (mɪs'kwot) *v.t.* citar falsa *o* equivocadamente; torcer las palabras de. —**misquotation** (ˌmɪs·kwo'tei·ʃən) *n.* cita falsa *o* equivocada; tergiversación.
misread (mɪs'riːd) *v.t.* leer mal; interpretar mal al leer.
misrepresent *v.t.* tergiversar; falsear. —**misrepresentation,** *n.* tergiversación; falsedad.
misrule (mɪs'ruːl) *v.t.* gobernar mal. —*n.* mal gobierno; desorden.
miss (mɪs) *v.t.* **1,** (fail to hit) errar; marrar; no acertar en. **2,** (fail to meet, reach or find) perder; no alcanzar; no encontrar. **3,** (overlook) pasar por alto; no darse cuenta de. **4,** (feel the absence of) echar de menos; *Amer.* extrañar. **5,** (escape; avoid, as a mishap) escaparse de; evitar; eludir. **6,** (fail to be present at) no asistir a; no estar presente a; perder. **7,** (fail to perceive) no ver; no captar. **8,** (lack) faltar; hacerle falta a uno. —*v.i.* fallar. —*n.* **1,** (failure) falla; tiro fallo; error. **2,** (young lady) señorita. —**a miss is as good as a mile,** tanto da errar por un pelo que por una cuadra. —**miss fire,** fallar el tiro. —**miss out,** errar el tiro; fracasar en el intento. —**miss the mark,** errar el tiro; errar el blanco.
missal ('mɪs·əl) *n.* misal.
misshapen (mɪs'ʃei·pən) *adj.* deforme. —**misshapenness,** *n.* deformidad.
missile ('mɪs·əl) *n.* proyectil.
missing ('mɪs·ɪŋ) *adj.* **1,** (lost) extraviado; perdido. **2,** (absent) ausente. **3,** (lacking) falto. —**be missing,** faltar.
mission ('mɪʃ·ən) *n.* misión.
missionary ('mɪʃ·ə·nɛr·i) *n.* misionero; misionario. —*adj.* misional.
missis *también,* **missus** ('mɪs·ɪz) *n., colloq.* señora; esposa.
missive ('mɪs·ɪv) *n.* misiva.
misspell (mɪs'spɛl) *v.t.* deletrear mal. —**misspelt** (mɪs'spɛlt) *adj.* mal deletreado. —**misspelling,** *n.* falta de ortografía.
misspend (mɪs'spɛnd) *v.t.* malgastar.
misstate (mɪs'steit) *v.t.* tergiversar; relatar falsamente. —**misstatement,** *n.* tergiversación; relación falsa.
misstep (mɪs'stɛp) *n.* **1,** (stumble) paso en falso; tropezón. **2,** (mistake in conduct) desliz; falta.
missus ('mɪs·ɪz) *n.* = **missis.**
mist (mɪst) *n.* **1,** (haze; fog) neblina; niebla; bruma. **2,** (firm, as of moisture) vaho. **3,** (drizzle) llovizna. **4,** (fine spray; vapor) vapor. —*v.t.* nublar; empañar. —*v.i.* nublarse; empañarse.
mistakable *también,* **mistakeable** (mɪs'teik·ə·bəl) *adj.* susceptible de error *o* equivocación.
mistake (mɪs'teik) *v.t.* [*infl.:* **take**] **1,** (take wrongly) equivocar; tomar equivocadamente. **2,** (misinterpret) entender *o* interpretar mal. —*v.i.* equivocarse. —*n.* error; equivocación. —**make a mistake,** equivocarse. —**no mistake about it,** *colloq.* sin duda.
mistaken (mɪs'tei·kən) *adj.* **1,**

(in error) equivocado. 2, (erroneous) erróneo.

mister ('mɪs·tər) *n.* señor.

mistime (mɪs'taim) *v.t.* decir *o* hacer a destiempo.

mistletoe ('mɪs·əl,to) *n.* muérdago.

mistook (mɪs'tʊk) *v., pret. de* **mistake.**

mistreat (mɪs'trit) *v.t.* maltratar. —**mistreatment,** *n.* maltrato.

mistress ('mɪs·trɪs) *n.* 1, (lady of the house; owner) señora; ama; dueña. 2, (paramour) querida; amante. 3, (skilled woman) maestra. —**be mistress of,** dominar.

mistrial (mɪs'trai·əl) *n.* causa *o* juicio anulado.

mistrust (mɪs'trʌst) *n.* desconfianza; recelo. —*v.t.* desconfiar de; recelar de. —**mistrustful,** *adj.* desconfiado; receloso.

misty ('mɪs·ti) *adj.* 1, (covered with or resembling mist) brumoso; nublado. 2, (obscure; vague) nebuloso; indistinto. 3, (filmed over) empañado. —**mistiness,** *n.* nebulosidad; brumosidad.

misunderstand *v.t. & i.* [*infl.:* **stand**] entender *o* comprender mal. —**misunderstanding,** *n.* mal entendido.

misunderstood *v., pret. & p.p. de* **misunderstand.** —*adj.* mal comprendido; incomprendido.

misusage (mɪs'jus·ɪdʒ) *n.* abuso; mal uso.

misuse (mɪs'juːz) *v.t.* 1, (maltreat) maltratar; abusar. 2, (misapply) emplear mal; desperdiciar. —*n.* (mɪs'jus) mal uso; abuso.

mite (mait) *n.* 1, *zool.* ácaro. 2, (bit; small amount) pizca; moto. 3, (small coin) óbolo.

miter *también,* **mitre** ('mai·tər) *n.* 1, *eccles.* mitra. 2, (beveled joint) inglete. —*v.t.* cortar *o* ensamblar en ingletes. —**miter box,** caja de ingletes. —**miter gear,** engranaje cónico. —**miter joint,** inglete.

mitigate ('mɪt·ə,geit) *v.t.* mitigar. —**mitigation,** *n.* mitigación.

mitt (mɪt) *n.* mitón; *sports* guante.

mitten ('mɪt·ən) *n.* mitón.

mix (mɪks) *v.t.* mezclar; juntar; unir. —*v.i.* mezclarse; juntarse. —*n.* mezcla. —**mix up,** 1, (mix thoroughly) mezclar. 2, (confuse) confundir. 3, (involve) meter; enredar.

mixed (mɪkst) *adj.* 1, (blended) mezclado. 2, (assorted) variado. 3, (heterogeneous) mixto. —**mixed up,** *colloq.* confundido.

mixer ('mɪk·sər) *n.* mezclador; mezcladora.

mixture ('mɪks·tʃər) *n.* mixtura; mezcla; mescolanza.

mix-up *n.* confusión; lío.

mizzen ('mɪz·ən) *n.* mesana. —**mizzenmast** (-mæst; -məst) *n.* palo de mesana.

mnemonic (nɪ'man·ɪk) *adj.* mnemotécnico. —**mnemonics,** *n.* mnemotecnia.

moan (moːn) *n.* gemido; quejido. —*v.i.* gemir; quejarse.

moat (mot) *n.* foso.

mob (maːb) *n.* turba; chusma; populacho. —*v.t.* [**mobbed, mobbing**] asaltar; atropellar. —**mobocracy** (mab'ak·rə·si) *n.* gobierno de la chusma.

mobile ('mo·bəl) *adj.* 1, (easily moving; movable) móvil; movible. 2, (changing easily) variable. —**mobility** (mo'bɪl·ə·ti) *n.* movilidad.

mobilize ('mo·bə,laiz) *v.t.* movilizar. —*v.i.* movilizarse.—**mobilization** (-lɪ'zei·ʃən) *n.* movilización.

moccasin ('mak·ə·sən) *n.* mocasín.

mocha ('mo·kə) *n.* moca; café moca.

mock (mak) *v.t.* 1, (ridicule; deride) escarnecer; mofarse de; burlarse de. 2, (scoff at) despreciar; no hacer caso de. 3, (mimic) imitar; remedar. 4, (deceive) decepcionar; engañar. —*v.i.* mofarse; burlarse. —*adj.* fingido; falso.

mockery ('mak·ə·ri) *n.* 1, (ridicule; derision) burla; mofa. 2, (laughingstock) hazmerreír. 3, (travesty) remedo grotesco.

mockingbird ('mak·ɪŋ,bʌɹd) *n.* sinsonte: pájaro burlón.

mock-up *n.* modelo; réplica.

modal ('mo·dəl) *adj.* modal. —**modality** (mo'dæl·ə·ti) *n.* modalidad.

mode (moːd) *n.* 1, (manner; style) modo; manera; forma. 2, (custom) moda. 3, *music; gram.* modo.

model ('mad·əl) *n.* modelo. —*adj.* modelo (*indecl.*): *model home,* casa modelo. —*v.t. & i.* modelar.

—**modeling**, *n.* modelado. —**model on** (*o* **after**), hacer *o* formar a imitación de.
moderate ('mad·ər·ɪt) *adj.* **1,** (restrained) moderado. **2,** (medium) mediano. **3,** (reasonable, as of prices) módico; razonable. —*n.* moderado. —*v.t.* ('mad·ə,reit) **1,** (restrain) moderar; refrenar; reprimir. **2,** (preside over) servir de moderador *o* árbitro en. —*v.i.* **1,** (tone down) moderarse; refrenarse. **2,** (act as moderator) servir de moderador *o* árbitro. —**moderation**, *n.* moderación.
moderator ('mad·ə,rei·tər) *n.* **1,** (one who presides) árbitro; moderador. **2,** *mech.* regulador; moderador.
modern ('mad·ərn) *adj.* & *n.* moderno. —**modernism**, *n.* modernismo. —**modernist**, *n.* modernista. —**modernistic**, *adj.* modernista.
modernize ('mad·ər,naiz) *v.t.* modernizar. —**modernization** (-nɪ·'zei·ʃən) *n.* modernización.
modest ('mad·ɪst) *adj.* modesto. —**modesty** ('mad·əs·ti) *n.* modestia.
modicum ('mad·ə·kəm) *n.* cantidad módica.
modify ('mad·ə,fai) *v.t.* **1,** (change) modificar. **2,** (moderate) moderar; atenuar. **3,** *gram.* modificar. —**modification** (-fɪ'kei·ʃən) *n.* modificación. —**modifier**, *n.* modificador.
modish ('mo·dɪʃ) *adj.* de moda; elegante. —**modishly**, *adv.* a la moda.
modiste (mo'dist) *n.* modista.
modulate ('madʒ·ə,leit) *v.t.* modular. —**modulation**, *n.* modulación. —**modulator**, *n.* modulador.
module ('madʒ·ul) *n.* módulo. —**modular**, *adj.* modular.
modulus ('madʒ·ə·ləs) *n.* módulo.
mogul ('mo·gəl) *n.* **1,** (oriental ruler) mogol. **2,** (magnate) magnate.
mohair ('mo,hɛr) *n.* lana *o* tela de Angora.
Mohammedan (mo'hæm·ə·dən) *n.* & *adj.* mahometano. —**Mohammedanism**, *n.* mahometismo.
moil (mɔil) *v.i.* bregar; afanarse. —*n.* afán.
moire (mwaːr) *n.* moaré; muaré.
—**moiré** (mwa'rei) *adj.* de moaré (*o* muaré).
moist (mɔist) *adj.* húmedo. —**moistness**, *n.* humedad.
moisten ('mɔis·ən) *v.t.* humedecer.
moisture ('mɔis·tʃər) *n.* humedad.
molar ('mol·ər) *n.* muela; molar. —*adj.* molar.
molasses (mo'læs·ɪz) *n.* melaza.
mold *también,* **mould** (moːld) *n.* **1,** (form; matrix) molde. **2,** (fungus) moho. **3,** (rich earth) mantillo; humus. —*v.t.* **1,** (shape) moldear. **2,** (make moldly) enmohecer. —*v.i.* enmohecerse; (*esp. de alimentos*) florecerse. —**moldy**, *adj.* mohoso; enmohecido; (*esp. de alimentos*) florecido.
molder ('mol·dər) *v.t.* desmoronar. —*v.i.* desmoronarse. —*n.* moldeador.
molding ('mol·dɪŋ) *n.* moldeado; moldura.
mole (moːl) *n.* **1,** (blemish) lunar. **2,** *zool.* topo. **3,** (breakwater) rompeolas. **4,** (harbor) dársena.
molecule ('mal·ə,kjul) *n.* molécula. —**molecular** (mə'lɛk·jə·lər) *adj.* molecular.
molehill *n.* topinera. —**make a mountain out of a molehill**, hacer una montaña de un grano de arena.
moleskin *n.* **1,** (fur) piel de topo. **2,** (cloth) especie de fustán.
molest (mə'lɛst) *v.t.* molestar; importunar. —**molestation** (,mo·lɛs'tei·ʃən) *n.* importunación; molestias (*pl.*).
mollify ('mal·ə,fai) *v.t.* molificar; ablandar; aplacar. —**mollification** (-fɪ'kei·ʃən) *n.* molificación.
mollusk ('mal·əsk) *n.* molusco.
mollycoddle ('mal·i,kad·əl) *v.t., colloq.* mimar; engreír. —*n.* alfeñique; engreído.
molt *también,* **moult** (molt) *v.i.* pelechar.
molten ('mol·tən) *adj.* fundido; derretido.
molybdenum (mə'lɪb·də·nəm) *n.* molibdeno. —**molybdic** (-dɪk) *adj.* molíbdico.
mom (maːm) *n., colloq.* mamá.
moment ('mo·mənt) *n.* momento.
momentarily (,mo·mən'tɛr·ə·li) *adv.* **1,** (for a short time) mo-

mentáneamente. **2,** (from moment to moment) de un momento a otro.
momentary ('mo·mən,tɛr·i) *adj.* momentáneo.
momentous (mo'mɛn·təs) *adj.* trascendental; de gran momento. —**momentousness,** *n.* trascendencia; importancia.
momentum (mo'mɛn·təm) *n.* ímpetu; fuerza; *mech.* momento.
monad ('man·æd) *n.* mónada.
monarch ('man·ərk) *n.* monarca. —**monarchal** (mə'nar·kəl) *adj.* monárquico.
monarchism ('man·ər,kɪz·əm) *n.* monarquismo. —**monarchist,** *n.* monárquico.
monarchy ('man·ər·ki) *n.* monarquía.
monastery ('man·əs,tɛr·i) *n.* monasterio.
monastic (mə'næs·tɪk) *adj.* monástico; monacal. —**monasticism** (-tə,sɪz·əm) *n.* monacato.
Monday ('mʌn·de) *n.* lunes.
monetary ('man·ə,tɛr·i) *adj.* monetario.
monetize ('man·ə,taɪz) *v.t.* **1,** (legalize as money) monetizar. **2,** (coin into money) acuñar.
money ('mʌn·i) *n.* dinero. —**in the money,** *slang* **1,** (among the winners) entre los primeros; entre los ganadores. **2,** (wealthy) acaudalado; adinerado. —**money broker,** cambista. —**money order,** giro. —**paper money,** papel moneda.
moneybag *n.* **1,** (sack for money) bolsa; saco. **2,** *pl., slang* (rich man) ricachón.
moneychanger *n.* cambista.
moneyed ('mʌn·id) *adj.* adinerado; acaudalado.
moneylender *n.* prestamista.
money-maker *n.* persona que gana buen dinero; artículo o negocio lucrativo.
money-making *adj.* lucrativo.
monger ('mʌŋ·gər) *n.* tratante; traficante.
Mongol ('maŋ·gəl) *n.* mogol; mongol. —*adj.* mogólico; mongólico. *También,* **Mongolian** (maŋ·'go·li·ən).
mongoose ('maŋ·gus) *n.* mangosta.
mongrel ('maŋ·grəl) *n.* & *adj.* mestizo; cruzado.
moniker ('man·ə·kər) *n., slang* nombre; apodo; mote.
monism ('man·ɪz·əm) *n.* monismo. —**monist,** *n.* monista. —**monistic** (mo'nɪs·tɪk) *adj.* monista.
monitor ('man·ə·tər) *n.* monitor. —*v.t.* & *i.* controlar; estar a la escucha (de). —**monitoring,** *n.* escucha.
monk (mʌŋk) *n.* monje.
monkey ('mʌŋ·ki) *n.* mono. —*v.i., colloq.* hacer el mono; jugar. —**monkey business,** *slang* artimañas. —**monkey fruit,** fruto del baobab. —**monkey jacket,** chaquetón de marinero. —**monkey nut,** cacahuete; maní. —**monkey wrench,** llave inglesa.
monkeyshine *n., slang* monería; diablura.
monkshood ('mʌŋks·hud) *n.* acónito.
mono- (man·o; -ə) *prefijo* mono-; uno; solo: *monotheist,* monoteísta.
monochrome ('man·ə,krom) *n.* & *adj.* monocromo. —**monochromatic** (-kro'mæt·ɪk) *adj.* monocromático.
monocle ('man·ə·kəl) *n.* monóculo. —**monocular** (mə'nak·jə·lər) *adj* monocular.
monogamy (mə'nag·ə·mi) *n.* monogamia. —**monogamist,** *n.* monógamo. —**monogamous,** *adj.* monógamo.
monogram ('man·ə,græm) *n.* monograma.
monograph ('man·ə,græf) *n.* monografía. —**monographic** (-'græf·ɪk) *adj.* monográfico.
monolith ('man·ə,lɪθ) *n.* monolito. —**monolithic** (-'lɪθ·ɪk) *adj.* monolítico.
monologue ('man·ə,lɔg) *n.* monólogo.
monomania (,man·ə'mei·ni·ə) *n.* monomanía. —**monomaniac** (-æk) *n.* & *adj.* monomaníaco.
monometallism (,man·ə'mɛt·ə·lɪz·əm) *n.* monometalismo.
monomial (mo'no·mi·əl) *n.* monomio. —*adj.* de monomio.
monopolist (mə'nap·ə·lɪst) *n.* monopolista.
monopolize (mə'nap·ə,laiz) *v.t.* monopolizar.
monopoly (mə'nap·ə·li) *n.* monopolio.
monosyllable ('man·ə,sɪl·ə·bəl) *n.* monosílabo. —**monosyllabic** (-sɪ'læb·ɪk) *adj.* monosilábico.

monotheism ('man·ə·θi,ɪz·əm) *n.* monoteísmo. —**monotheist** (-'θi·ɪst) *n.* monoteísta. —**monotheistic,** *adj.* monoteísta.
monotone ('man·ə,ton) *n.* monotonía. —*adj.* monótono.
monotonous (mə'nat·ə·nəs) *adj.* monótono. —**monotony,** *n.* monotonía.
monotype ('man·ə,taip) *n., print.* monotipia; monotipo.
monovalent (,man·ə'vei·lənt) *adj.* monovalente.
monsieur (mə'sjʊ) *n.* [*pl.* **messieurs**] señor.
Monsignor (man'sin·jər) *n.* monseñor.
monsoon (man'su:n) *n.* monzón.
monster ('man·stər) *n.* monstruo. —*adj.* monstruoso; enorme.
monstrosity (man'stras·ə·ti) *n.* monstruosidad.
monstrous ('man·strəs) *adj.* monstruoso. —**monstrousness,** *n.* monstruosidad.
montage (man'ta:ʒ) *n.* montaje.
month (mʌnθ) *n.* mes.
monthly ('mʌnθ·li) *adj.* mensual. —*n.* publicación mensual. —*adv.* mensualmente.
monument ('man·jə·mənt) *n.* monumento. —**monumental** (-'mɛn·təl) *adj.* monumental.
-mony (mo·ni) *sufijo* -monio; -monia; *forma nombres denotando* cualidad; estado; condición: *matrimony,* matrimonio.
moo (mu:) *n.* mugido. —*v.i.* mugir.
mooch (mutʃ) *v.i., slang* (slink about) rondar; vagar —*v.t. & i., slang* (cadge; sponge) gorrear.
mood (mu:d) *n.* **1,** (state of mind) ánimo; talante; disposición; humor. **2,** *gram.* modo. **3,** *pl.* (fits of depression) mal genio; ataques de melancolía. —**be in the mood,** estar en *o* de vena; tener ganas.
moody ('mu·di) *adj.* **1,** (gloomy; sullen) taciturno; deprimido; sombrío. **2,** (subject to changes of mood) de ánimo *o* humor inestable; raro.
moon (mu:n) *n.* luna. —*v.i.* andar como alma en pena; soñar; estar *o* andar embobado. —**full moon,** plenilunio; luna llena. —**new moon,** novilunio; luna nueva. —**once in a blue moon,** de higos a brevas.
moonbeam *n.* rayo de luna.
moonlight *n.* luz de la luna; claridad lunar. —**moonlit,** *adj.* iluminado por la luna.
moonshine *n.* **1,** = **moonlight. 2,** (nonsense) sandeces (*pl.*); disparates (*pl.*). **3,** *colloq.* (illegal liquor) licor destilado clandestinamente. —**moonshiner,** *n. colloq.* fabricante clandestino de licores.
moonstone *n.* adularia.
moon-struck *adj.* **1,** (lunatic) lunático; loco. **2,** (dazed) alelado; lelo.
moony ('mu·ni) *adj.* **1,** = **moonstruck. 2,** (listless) sin ánimo.
moor (mʊr) *n.* páramo. —*v.t. & i.* amarrar.
Moor (mʊr) *n.* moro. —**Moorish,** *adj.* moro; morisco; moruno.
moorage ('mʊr·ɪdʒ) *n.* **1,** (place for mooring) amarradero. **2,** (charge for mooring) derechos de puerto; amarre.
mooring ('mʊr·ɪŋ) *n.* **1,** (tying up) amarre. **2,** *often pl.* (lines, cables, etc.) amarras. **3,** *pl.* (mooring place) amarradero (*sing.*).
moose (mus) *n.* [*pl.* **moose**] alce; anta.
moot (mut) *adj.* discutible.
mop (map) *n.* **1,** (cleaning tool) bayeta. **2,** (mass of hair) copete; mechón. —*v.t.* [**mopped mopping**] **1,** (clean) fregar. **2,** (wipe dry) secar. —**mop up, 1,** *colloq.* (finish) acabar con. **2,** (clean up) limpiar.
mope (mop) *v.i.* estar desanimado. —**mopish,** *adj.* desanimado.
moppet ('map·ɪt) *n.* **1,** (doll) muñeca de trapo. **2,** (child) niño; muñeco.
moraine (mə'rein) *n.* morena.
moral ('mar·əl) *adj.* moral. —*n.* **1,** *usu.pl.* (behavior) moral; moralidad. **2,** (lesson) moraleja.
morale (mə'ræl) *n.* moral.
moralist ('mar·əl·ɪst) *n.* moralista. —**moralistic,** *adj.* moralizador.
morality (mə'ræl·ə·ti) *n.* moralidad.
moralize ('mor·ə,laiz) *v.t. & i.* moralizar.
morally ('mar·ə·li) *adv.* moralmente.
morass (mə'ræs) *n.* pantano; marisma.
moratorium (,mor·ə'tor·i·əm) *n.* moratoria. —**moratory** ('mor·ə·tor·i) *adj.* moratorio.
moray ('mor·e) *n.* morena.
morbid ('mor·bɪd) *adj.* mórbido;

morboso. —**morbidity** (mor'bɪd·ə·ti); **morbidness,** *n.* morbidez; morbosidad.
mordant ('mor·dənt) *adj.* **1,** (caustic) mordaz; mordiente. **2,** (for fixing colors) mordiente. —*n.* mordiente. —**mordancy,** *n.* mordacidad.
more (moːr) *adj., adv. & n.* más. —**more and more,** cada vez más; más y más. —**once more,** otra vez; una vez más. —**the more the merrier,** cuanto (*o* cuantos) más, mejor. —**the more . . . the more** (*o* **the less**) . . . cuanto más . . . tanto más (*o* menos) . . . ; mientras más . . . tanto más (*o* menos) . . . —**what's more,** además.
morel (mə'rɛl) *n.* colmenilla.
moreover (mor'o·vər) *adv.* además; también; por otra parte.
mores ('mor·iz) *n.pl.* costumbres.
morganatic (ˌmor·gə'næt·ɪk) *adj.* morganático.
morgue (morg) *n.* **1,** (mortuary) depósito de cadáveres; morgue. **2,** *journalism* archivos.
moribund ('mor·əˌbʌnd) *adj.* moribundo.
Mormon ('mor·mən) *n. & adj.* mormón. —**Mormonism,** *n.* mormonismo.
morn (morn) *n., poet.* = **morning.**
morning ('mor·nɪŋ) *n.* mañana. —*adj.* de mañana.
morning coat chaqué.
morning-glory *n.* dondiego.
morning star *n.* lucero del alba.
morocco (mə'rak·o) *n.* tafilete; marroquín.
moron ('mor·an) *n.* idiota; tonto. —**moronic** (mə'ran·ɪk) *adj.* idiota; tonto.
morose (mə'ros) *adj.* hosco; ceñudo; áspero. —**moroseness,** *n.* hosquedad; aspereza; mal humor.
-morph (morf) *sufijo* -morfo; forma: *isomorph,* isomorfo.
-morphic (mor·fɪk) *sufijo* -morfo; -mórfico; *forma adjetivos denotando semejanza en forma o apariencia: isomorphic,* isomorfo.
morphine ('mor·fin) *n.* morfina. —**morphine addict,** morfinómano.
-morphism (mor·fɪz·əm) *sufijo* -morfismo; *forma nombres de los adjetivos terminados en* **-morphic** *o* **-morphous**: *anthropomorphism,* antropomorfismo.
morpho- (mor·fo; -fə) *prefijo* morfo-; forma: *morphology,* morfología.
morphology (mor'fal·ə·dʒi) *n.* morfología. —**morphological** (ˌmor·fə'ladʒ·ɪ·kəl) *adj.* morfológico.
morphosis (mor'fo·sɪs) *n.* morfosis.
-morphous (mor·fəs) *sufijo* = **-morphic**: *anthropomorphous,* antropomorfo.
morrow ('mar·o) *n.* **1,** (the following day) el día siguiente. **2,** (tomorrow) mañana. **3,** (morning) mañana.
Morse code (mors) código Morse.
morsel ('mor·səl) *n.* **1,** (bite; portion of food) bocado. **2,** (bit; small amount) pedacito; pizca; poquito. **3,** (delicacy) manjar; delicia.
mortal ('mor·təl) *adj. & n.* mortal.
mortality (mor'tæl·ə·ti) *n.* mortalidad.
mortar ('mor·tər) *n.* **1,** (mixing bowl) mortero. **2,** (cement) mortero; argamasa. **3,** (artillery weapon) mortero. —*v.t.* argamasar.
mortarboard *n.* birrete.
mortgage ('mor·gɪdʒ) *n.* hipoteca. —*v.t.* hipotecar. —**mortgagee** (ˌmor·gɪ'dʒiː) *n.* acreedor hipotecario. —**mortgagor,** *n.* deudor hipotecario.
mortician (mor'tɪʃ·ən) *n.* director de pompas fúnebres; funerario.
mortify ('mor·təˌfai) *v.t.* **1,** (cause to feel shame) abochornar; avergonzar. **2,** (bother) molestar; mortificar. **3,** (discipline, as the body) mortificar. —*v.i.* mortificarse. —**mortification** (-fɪ'kei·ʃən) *n.* mortificación.
mortise ('mor·tɪs) *n.* muesca; ensambladura. —*v.t.* hacer muescas en; entallar; ensamblar.
mortuary ('mor·tʃu·ɛr·i) *n.* depósito de cadáveres; morgue. —*adj.* mortuorio; funerario.
mosaic (mo'zei·ɪk) *adj. & n.* mosaico.
mosey ('mo·zi) *v.i., slang, U.S.* vagar; pasearse; andar.
Moslem ('mas·ləm) *n.* musulmán; mahometano. —*adj.* muslime; muslímico.
mosque (mask) *n.* mezquita.
mosquito (məs'ki·to) *n.* mosquito; *Amer.* zancudo. —**mosquito net,** mosquitero.

moss (mɔs) *n.* musgo. —**mossy,** *adj.* musgoso. —**mossiness,** *n.* lo musgoso.
mossback *n., slang* ultraconservador; fósil.
most (most) *adj.* la mayor parte de; casi todo(s); lo más de; los más de. —*n.* **1,** (majority) la mayor parte; la mayoría. **2,** (the greatest extent or degree) lo sumo; lo máximo. —*adv.* **1,** (in or to the greatest extent or degree) más. **2,** (very; greatly) muy; sumamente. —**at most; at the most,** a lo sumo; a lo más. —**at the very most,** a todo tirar. —**for the most part,** en su mayor parte; eminentemente; esencialmente. —**make the most of, 1,** (take fullest advantage of) sacar todo el partido posible de. **2,** (treat with the highest regard) poner por las nubes; hacer gran encomio de. —**the very most,** lo más que; lo sumo que.
-most (most) *sufijo; forma superlativos: uppermost,* más alto.
mostly ('most·li) *adv.* en su mayor parte; por la mayor parte; esencialmente.
mote (mot) *n.* mota.
motel (mo'tɛl) *n.* motel; parador.
moth (mɔθ) *n.* **1,** (clothes moth) polilla. **2,** (night-flying insect) mariposa nocturna.
mothball *n.* naftalina; bola de naftalina. —**in mothballs,** en conserva; en almacenaje.
motheaten *adj.* apolillado.
mother ('mʌð·ər) *n.* madre. —*adj.* **1,** (maternal) maternal; materno. **2,** (native) nativo; natural. **3,** (original) matriz; madre. —*v.t.* **1,** (be a mother to) hacer de madre para con; servir de madre. **2,** (give rise to) dar a luz; engendrar. —**mother church,** iglesia matriz. —**mother country,** madre patria. —**mother tongue, 1,** (native language) lengua materna. **2,** (parent language) lengua matriz. —**mother wit,** ingenio; chispa.
motherhood ('mʌð·ər·hud) *n.* maternidad; condición de madre.
mother-in-law *n.* [*pl.* **mothers-in-law**] suegra; madre política.
motherland *n.* patria.
motherless ('mʌð·ər·ləs) *adj.* huérfano de madre; sin madre.
motherly ('mʌð·ər·li) *adj.* maternal. —**motherliness,** *n.* maternidad; afecto maternal.
mother-of-pearl *n.* nácar; madreperla.
motif (mo'tif) *n.* motivo; tema.
motile ('mo·təl) *adj.* móvil; movible. —**motility** (mo'tɪl·ə·ti) *n.* movilidad; motilidad.
motion ('mo·ʃən) *n.* **1,** (movement) movimiento. **2,** (gesture) gesto. **3,** (proposal) moción. —*v.t.* señalar. —*v.i.* hacer señas *o* señales.
motionless ('mo·ʃən·ləs) *adj.* inmóvil.
motion picture *n.* película; *pl.* cine (*sing.*); cinematografía (*sing.*).
motivate ('mo·tə,veit) *v.t.* motivar. —**motivation,** *n.* motivación.
motive ('mo·tɪv) *n.* **1,** (determining impulse) móvil; razón. **2,** (purpose) motivo. **3,** = **motif.** —*adj.* motor; motriz.
-motive ('mo·tɪv) *sufijo* -motriz; -motor; *forma adjetivos denotando movimiento; propulsión: automotive,* automotriz; automotor.
motley ('mat·li) *adj.* **1,** (multicolored; variegated) abigarrado. **2,** (heterogeneous) heterogéneo.
motor ('mo·tər) *n.* motor. —*adj.* motor; motriz; de motor. —*v.i.* ir *o* viajar en automóvil. —**motoring,** *n.* automovilismo.
-motor (mo·tər) *sufijo* -motor; -motriz; *forma nombres y adjetivos denotando* movimiento; propulsión: *vasomotor,* vasomotor.
motorbike ('mo·tər,baik) *n.* bicimoto.
motorboat *n.* lancha motora; motora; gasolinera.
motorbus *n.* autobús; ómnibus.
motorcade ('mo·tər·ked) *n.* desfile *o* caravana de automóviles.
motorcar *n.* automóvil.
motor court motel; parador.
motorcycle ('mo·tər,sai·kəl) *n.* motocicleta.
motorist ('mo·tər·ɪst) *n.* automovilista; motorista; conductor.
motorize ('mo·tər·aiz) *v.t.* motorizar.
motorman ('mo·tər·mən) *n.* conductor (de tren, tranvía, etc.); *Amer.* motorista.
motor scooter motoneta.
mottle ('mat·əl) *v.t.* motear; jaspear; salpicar de pintas. —*n.* **1,** (speck) mancha; pinta; mota. **2,** (variegated coloring) jaspeado; moteado. —**mottled,** *adj.* jaspeado; abigarrado; moteado; mosqueado.

motto (ˈmat·o) *n.* lema; divisa.
moulage (muˈlaːʒ) *n.* molde de yeso; enyesadura.
mould (mold) *n. & v.* = **mold.**
moult (molt) *v.* = **molt.**
mound (maund) *n.* montículo. —*v.t.* amontonar. —*v.i.* amontonarse.
mount (maunt) *v.t.* **1,** (go up; climb up) ascender; subir. **2,** (get up on; get on) montar. **3,** (put in place; set) montar. **4,** *theat.; mil.; naval* montar. —*v.i.* **1,** (ascend; climb) subir; ascender; elevarse. **2,** (get up on a horse, bicycle, etc.) montar. **3,** (increase) aumentar; crecer; incrementarse. —*n.* **1,** (mounting) montura; montadura; *mech.* montaje. **2,** (horse) montura; cabalgadura. **3,** (hill; elevation) monte.
mountain (ˈmaun·tən) *n.* montaña. —*adj.* de montaña. —**mountain lion,** puma; cuguar. —**mountain sickness,** mal de las alturas; *So.Amer.* soroche.
mountaineer (ˌmaun·təˈnɪːr) *n.* **1,** (highlander) montañés. **2,** (mountain climber) alpinista; montañero. —**mountaineering,** *n.* alpinismo; montañismo. —*adj.* montañero.
mountainous (ˈmaun·tə·nəs) *adj.* **1,** (full of mountains) montañoso. **2,** (very large) enorme.
mountaintop *n.* cumbre (de montaña).
mountebank (ˈmaun·təˌbæŋk) *n.* charlatán; saltimbanqui.
mounted (ˈmaun·tɪd) *adj.* montado.
mountie (ˈmaun·ti) *n., colloq.* agente de policía montado a caballo, esp. en el Canadá.
mounting (ˈmaun·tɪŋ) *n.* montura; montadura; *mech.* montaje.
mourn (morn) *v.t.* lamentar; llorar. —*v.i.* lamentarse; dolerse; afligirse. —**mourner,** *n.* persona presente a un funeral; persona de duelo; llorón.
mournful (ˈmorn·fəl) *adj.* triste; melancólico; lastimero.
mourning (ˈmor·nɪŋ) *n.* **1,** (grief) dolor; duelo; aflicción. **2,** (conventional signs of mourning) luto. —*adj.* de luto. —**in mourning,** de luto. —**mourning dove,** paloma triste.
mouse (maus) *n.* [*pl.* **mice**] **1,** (small rodent) ratón; *Amer.* laucha. **2,** (spiritless person) pacato; timorato. **3,** *slang* (black eye) ojo negro. —*v.i.* **1,** (hunt mice) cazar ratones. **2,** (prowl; search stealthily) hurgar; buscar *o* andar a hurtadillas.
mouse-colored *adj.* pardusco.
mousehole *n.* ratonera.
mouser (ˈmau·zər) *n.* **1,** (catcher of mice) cazador de ratones; gato *o* perro ratonero. **2,** (snoop) fisgón.
mousetrap *n.* ratonera; trampa para ratones.
mousse (mus) *n.* dulce de crema batida; especie de flan *o* natillas.
moustache (məsˈtæʃ; ˈmʌs·tæʃ) *n., Brit.* = **mustache.**
mousy (ˈmau·si) *adj.* **1,** (of or like a mouse) de *o* como ratón. **2,** (timid) timorato; pacato. **3,** (drab) descolorido; raído.
mouth (mauθ) *n.* [*pl.* **mouths** (mauðz)] boca. —*v.t.* (mauð) **1,** (utter; declaim) proferir; declamar. **2,** (seize with the mouth) agarrar con la boca. **3,** (rub with the mouth) frotar con la boca; hocicar. —*v.i.* **1,** (declaim) declamar; perorar. **2,** (grimace) hacer muecas. —**down at** (*o* **in**) **the mouth,** deprimido; desalentado.
mouthful (ˈmauθ·fʊl) *n.* **1,** (enough to fill the mouth) bocado. **2,** *colloq.* (tongue twister) trabalenguas. —**say a mouthful,** *slang* decir verdades como puños.
mouth organ *n.* armónica.
mouthpiece *n.* **1,** (part of an instrument) boquilla. **2,** (horse's bit) bocado. **3,** (spokesman) portavoz; vocero. **4,** *slang* (lawyer) abogado; picapleitos.
mouthy (ˈmau·θi) *adj.* deslenguado; palabrero.
movable (ˈmuv·ə·bəl) *adj.* **1,** (that can be moved) movible; móvil. **2,** (transportable) transportable. **3,** *law* mueble. —**movables,** *n.pl., law* bienes muebles.
move (muːv) *v.t.* **1,** (change the location or position of) mover; mudar. **2,** (set in motion) mover. **3,** (transfer) trasladar. **4,** (prompt; urge) impulsar; empujar. **5,** (touch the feelings of) conmover; impresionar. **6,** (propose) proponer; sugerir. **7,** (evacuate, as the bowels) desocupar; evacuar. —*v.i.* **1,** (change location or position) moverse. **2,** (change residence) mu-

darse; trasladarse. 3, (take action) actuar; tomar medidas. 4, (advance) avansar. 5, *colloq.* [*también,* **move on**] (leave; depart) irse; marcharse. —*n.* 1, (movement) movimiento. 2, (measure; action) medida; paso. 3, (change of residence) mudanza. 4, (transfer) traslado. 5, (play, as in games) jugada. —**get a move on,** *slang* 1, (start moving) moverse. 2, (go faster) apresurarse; *Amer.* apurarse; *Amer.* avanzar. —**move along.** 1, (proceed; advance) avanzar. 2, (start moving; leave) irse; marcharse. —**move away,** 1, (depart) apartarse; separarse. 2, (change residence) mudarse. —**move in** *o* **into,** instalarse (en). —**move off,** alejarse. —**move up,** adelantar.

movement ('muv·mənt) *n.* movimiento.

mover ('mu·vər) *n.* 1, (that which moves) motor. 2, (carrier of furniture, etc.) agente de mudanzas.

movie ('mu·vi) *n., colloq.* 1, (theater) cine; cinematógrafo. 2, (film) película. —**the movies,** el cine.

moving ('mu·vɪŋ) *adj.* 1, (that moves; in motion) móvil; movible. 2, (causing motion; impelling) motor; motriz. 3, (stirring the emotions) conmovedor; emocionante. —*n.* mudanza. —**moving picture,** película.

mow (moː) *v.t.* cortar; segar. —*n.* granero; henil. —**mow down,** arrasar; abatir.

mower ('mo·ər) *n.* segadora.

much (mʌtʃ) *adj.* mucho. —*adv.* 1, (to a great extent or degree) muy; mucho. 2, (nearly; about) casi; en gran parte. —*n.* mucho. —**as much,** otro tanto; tanto. —**as much . . . as,** tanto . . . como. —**as much more,** tanto más; otro tanto más. —**for as much as,** por cuanto; por cuanto que. —**however much,** por mucho que. —**how much?,** ¿cuánto? —**make much of,** tener en mucho; dar mucha importancia a. —**much ado about nothing,** mucho ruido y pocas nueces. —**much as,** por más que; a pesar de que. —**not much of a,** de poca monta; de poca importancia. —**so much the better** (*o* **worse**), tanto mejor (*o* peor). —**this** *o* **that much,** tanto. —**too much,** demasiado. —**very much,** muy; mucho.

mucilage ('mju·sə·lɪdʒ) *n.* mucílago. —**mucilaginous** (-'lædʒ·ə·nəs) *adj.* mucilaginoso.

muck (mʌk) *n.* 1, (filth) suciedad; basura. 2, (manure) estiércol. 3, (organic soil) humus; mantillo. 4, (mud) lodo; barro. —*v.t.* estercolar.

muckrake *v.i.* exponer la corrupción (en política, negocios, etc.). —**muckraker,** *n.* expositor de corrupción.

muco- (mju·ko) *prefijo* muco-; membrana mucosa; moco: *mucoprotein,* mucoproteína.

mucous ('mju·kəs) *adj.* mucoso. —**mucous membrane,** mucosa.

mucus ('mju·kəs) *n.* moco; mucosidad.

mud (mʌd) *n.* barro; lodo.

muddle ('mʌd·əl) *v.t.* 1, (mix up) embrollar. 2, (befuddle) confundir; turbar. 3, (make turbid) enturbiar. —*v.i.* pensar *o* hacer como chambón. —*n.* embrollo; confusión. —**muddle through,** *Brit.* salir del paso.

muddler ('mʌd·lər) *n.* 1, (mixing stick) palillo para mezclar bebidas. 2, (bungler) chapucero.

muddy ('mʌd·i) *adj.* 1, (covered with mud) con lodo *o* barro. 2, (unclear) turbio. —*v.t.* 1, (cover with mud) embarrar. 2, (make unclear) enturbiar.

mudguard *n.* guardabarros.

mudhole *n.* lodazal; atolladero; atascadero.

muezzin (mju'ɛz·ɪn) *n.* muecín; almuédano.

muff (mʌf) *n.* 1, (covering for the hands) manguito. 2, *colloq.* (bungle) chambonada; chapucería. —*v.t., colloq.* chapucear (con).

muffin ('mʌf·ɪn) *n.* mollete; bollo.

muffle ('mʌf·əl) *v.t.* 1, (cover up; wrap up) embozar; cubrir; arrebujar. 2, (mute; deaden the sound of) ahogar; amortiguar. —*n.* 1, (muted sound) sonido apagado; ruido sordo. 2, (cover; wrap) rebujo; rebozo. 3, (silencer) silenciador; amortiguador. —**muffled,** *adj.* sordo; apagado.

muffler ('mʌf·lər) *n.* 1, (scarf) bufanda. 2, (silencing device) silenciador; amortiguador.

mufti ('mʌf·ti) *n.* **1,** (civilian garb) traje de paisano *o* civil. **2,** (mohammedan leader) muftí.

mug (mʌg) *n.* **1,** (cup) pocillo; jícara. **2,** *slang* (face) hocico. **3,** *slang* (rough, uncouth person) patán. —*v.t. slang* [**mugged, mugging**] **1,** (assault from behind) asaltar por la espalda. **2,** (photograph) fotografiar. —*v.i., slang* hacer muecas.

mugger ('mʌg·ər) *n.* **1,** *zool.* cocodrilo de la India. **2,** *slang* (attacker) asaltante; bandido.

muggy ('mʌg·i) *adj.* húmedo; bochornoso; cargado. —**mugginess,** *n.* calor húmedo; humedad sofocante; cargazón.

mulatto (mju'læt·o) *adj.* & *n.* mulato.

mulberry ('mʌl,bɛr·i) *n.* **1,** (tree) morera. **2,** (fruit) mora.

mulch (mʌltʃ) *n.* cubierta de paja y estiércol. —*v.t.* cubrir con paja y estiércol.

mulct (mʌlkt) *v.t.* **1,** (defraud) defraudar; birlar; escamotear. **2,** (fine) multar. —*n.* multa.

mule (mjuːl) *n.* **1,** (animal) mulo; mula. **2,** (textile machine) máquina hiladora intermitente. **3,** *colloq.* (stubborn person) mula. **4,** (slipper) zapatilla; chancleta; chinela. —**pack mule,** acémila; mula de carga.

muleteer (,mju·lə'tɪːr) *n.* mulero.

mulish ('mju·lɪʃ) *adj.* terco; obstinado; mulo.

mull (mʌl) *v.i.* reflexionar; meditar. —*v.t.* calentar con substancias aromáticas. —*n.* muselina clara. —**mull over,** reflexionar sobre; meditar en *o* sobre.

mullein ('mʌl·ɪn) *n.* candelaria; gordolobo.

mullet ('mʌl·ɪt) *n.* mújol; cabezudo.

multi- (mʌl·tɪ; -tə) *prefijo* multi-; muchos: *multimillionaire,* multimillonario.

multicolored (,mʌl·tɪ'kʌl·ərd) *adj.* multicolor; abigarrado.

multifarious (,mʌl·tɪ'fɛr·i·əs) *adj.* diverso; variado; múltiple. —**multifariousness,** *n.* diversidad; multiplicidad.

multiform ('mʌl·tə,form) *adj.* multiforme.

multilateral (,mʌl·tɪ'læt·ə·rəl) *adj.* multilátero; *fig.* multilateral.

multimillionaire (,mʌl·tə,mɪl·jən'eːr) *n.* multimillonario.

multipartite (,mʌl·tɪ'par·tait) *adj.* **1,** (having many parts) compuesto; multipartito. **2,** (of or between three or more parties) multilateral.

multiple ('mʌl·tɪ·pəl) *adj.* múltiple; múltiplo. —*n.* múltiplo.

multiplicand (,mʌl·tə·plɪ'kænd) *n.* multiplicando.

multiplication (,mʌl·tə·plɪ'kei·ʃən) *n.* multiplicación.

multiplicity (,mʌl·tə'plɪs·ə·ti) *n.* multiplicidad.

multiply ('mʌl·tɪ,plai) *v.t.* & *i.* multiplicar(se). —**multiplier,** *n.* multiplicador.

multitude ('mʌl·tɪ,tud) *n.* multitud. —**multitudinous** (-'tu·dɪ·nəs) *adj.* multitudinario.

mum (mʌm) *adj., colloq.* callado; mudo. —*n., colloq.* **1,** *bot.* crisantemo. **2,** (mother) mamá.

mumble ('mʌm·bəl) *v.t.* & *i.* mascullar; farfullar. —*n.* farfulla; el mascullar.

mumbo jumbo ('mʌm·bo·'dʒʌm·bo) **1,** (fetish) fetiche. **2,** (senseless incantation) sortilegio; cábala. **3,** (superstition) superstición; superchería.

mummer ('mʌm·ər) *n.* máscara. —**mummery,** *n.* mascarada; farsa.

mummify ('mʌm·ə,fai) *v.t.* momificar. —*v.i.* momificarse. —**mummification** (-fɪ'kei·ʃən) *n.* momificación.

mummy ('mʌm·i) *n.* **1,** (desiccated corpse) momia. **2,** *colloq.* (mother) mamá.

mumps (mʌmps) *n.* paperas (*pl.*).

munch (mʌntʃ) *v.t.* & *i.* mascar; mordiscar.

mundane ('mʌn·dein) *adj.* mundano; mundanal. —**mundaneness** (mun'dein·nəs) *n.* mundanalidad; mundanería.

municipal (mju'nɪs·ɪ·pəl) *adj.* municipal. —**municipality** (-'pæl·ə·ti) *n.* municipalidad.

munificent (mju'nɪf·ɪ·sənt) *adj.* munífico; munificente. —**munificence,** *n.* munificencia.

munition (mju'nɪʃ·ən) *n., usu.pl.* municiones. —*v.t.* municionar.

mural ('mjʊr·əl) *adj.* mural. —*n.* cuadro *o* pintura mural.

murder ('mʌɹ·dər) *n.* asesinato; homicidio. —*v.t.* asesinar. —**mur-**

derer, *n.* asesino. —**murderess,** *n.* asesina.
murderous ('mʌɹ·dər·əs) *adj.* 1, (brutal; cruel) sanguinario; brutal. 2, (homicidal) homicida. —**murderousness,** *n.* intención *o* calidad homicida.
murk (mʌɹk) *n.* 1, (fog) niebla; bruma. 2, (darkness) obscuridad; lobreguez.
murky ('mʌɹ·ki) *adj.* 1, (foggy) nublado; brumoso. 2, (dark) obscuro; lóbrego.
murmur ('mʌɹ·mər) *n.* murmullo; susurro. —*v.t.* & *i.* susurrar; murmurar. —**murmurous,** *adj.* murmurante; susurrante.
muscat ('mʌs·kət) *n.* moscatel.
muscatel (ˌmʌs·kə'tɛl) *adj.* & *n.* moscatel.
muscle ('mʌs·əl) *n.* músculo. —*v.i., colloq.* entrar *o* abrirse paso a viva fuerza.
muscle-bound *adj.* que tiene músculos gruesos e inelásticos.
Muscovite ('mʌs·kəˌvait) *adj.* & *n.* moscovita.
Muscovy duck ('mʌs·kə·vi) pato almizclado; pato turco.
muscular ('mʌs·kjə·lər) *adj.* 1, (of or done by the muscles) muscular. 2, (brawny) musculoso. —**muscularity** (-'lær·ə·ti) *n.* musculosidad. —**musculature** (-lə·tʃər) *n.* musculatura.
muse (mjuːz) *v.i.* meditar; cavilar; rumiar. —*v.t.* musitar. —*n.* musa.
musing ('mju·zɪŋ) *adj.* meditabundo; contemplativo; soñador. —*n.* meditación; ensueño.
musette bag (mju'zɛt) *n.* mochila pequeña; morral.
museum (mju'zi·əm) *n.* museo.
mush (mʌʃ) *n.* 1, (gruel; pap) gachas (*pl.*); puches (*pl.*); papilla. 2, *colloq.* (sentimentality) sensiblería; sentimentalismo. 3, (journey over snow) viaje sobre la nieve. —*v.i.* viajar sobre la nieve.
mushroom ('mʌʃˌrum) *n.* hongo; seta. —*v.i.* crecer *o* multiplicarse rápidamente.
mushy ('mʌʃ·i) *adj.* 1, (soft; pulpy) blanducho; semilíquido; pulposo. 2, *colloq.* (sentimental) sensiblero.
music ('mju·zɪk) *n.* música. —**musical,** *adj.* musical. —**music hall,** salón de conciertos. —**music paper,** papel de pauta. —**music stand,** atril.
musicale (ˌmju·zɪ'kæl) *n.* velada musical.
musician (mju'zɪʃ·ən) *n.* músico.
musk (mʌsk) *n.* almizcle.
musk deer almizclero.
musket ('mʌs·kɪt) *n.* mosquete.
musketeer (ˌmʌs·kə'tɪr) *n.* mosquetero.
musketry ('mʌs·kɪt·ri) *n.* mosquetería; fusilería.
muskmelon *n.* melón almizclero.
musk ox *n.* buey almizclado.
muskrat *n.* (rata) almizclera; ratón almizclero.
musky ('mʌs·ki) *adj.* almizclero; almizcleño.
Muslim ('mʌz·ləm) *n.* & *adj.* = Moslem.
muslin ('mʌz·lɪn) *n.* muselina.
muss (mʌs) *n.* desorden; desarreglo. —*v.t.* desarreglar; desordenar. —**mussy,** *adj.* desordenado; desarreglado.
mussel ('mʌs·əl) *n.* mejillón.
must (mʌst) *aux.v.* deber; tener que. —*n.* 1, *colloq.* (essential thing) obligación; necesidad. 2, (new wine) mosto. 3, (mustiness) moho. —*adj., colloq.* necesario; esencial; imprescindible.
mustache ('mʌs·tæʃ; məs'tæʃ) *n.* bigote; mostacho. *También,* **moustache, mustachio** (məs'ta·ʃo).
mustang ('mʌs·tæŋ) *n.* potro salvaje; *Amer.* mustango.
mustard ('mʌs·tərd) *n.* mostaza. —**mustard gas,** gas mostaza. —**mustard plaster,** sinapismo; cataplasma.
muster ('mʌs·tər) *v.t.* 1, (assemble) reunir; juntar; congregar. 2, (summon, as strength, courage, etc.) tomar; cobrar; hacer acopio de. —*n.* 1, (list; roll) lista; nómina. 2, (assemblage, as of troops) revista. —**call (the) muster,** pasar lista. —**muster in,** alistar; inscribir. —**muster out,** dar de baja. —**pass muster,** ser aceptable; ser adecuado.
musty ('mʌs·ti) *adj.* 1, (moldy; dank) mohoso; que tiene olor *o* sabor a humedad. 2, (antiquated) anticuado; pasado de moda. —**mustiness,** *n.* moho; humedad.
mutable ('mju·tə·bəl) *adj.* mudable. —**mutability,** *n.* mutabilidad.
mutant ('mju·tənt) *adj.* & *n.* mutante.
mutate ('mju·teit) *v.t.* transformar; cambiar; producir muta-

ción en. —*v.i.* transformarse; cambiar; sufrir mutación.

mutation (mju'tei·ʃən) *n.* mutación.

mute (mjut) *adj.* mudo. —*n.* **1,** (one incapable of speech) mudo. **2,** *music* sordina. **3,** *phonet.* letra muda. —*v.t.* amortiguar; *music* poner sordina a.

muteness ('mjut·nəs) *n.* **1,** (inability to speak) mudez. **2,** (silence) mutismo; silencio.

mutilate ('mju·tə,leit) *v.t.* mutilar. —**mutilation,** *n.* mutilación.

mutineer (,mju·tə'nɪr) *n.* amotinado.

mutinous ('mju·tɪ·nəs) *adj.* amotinado; rebelde.

mutiny ('mju·tə·ni) *n.* motín. —*v.i.* amotinarse.

mutt (mʌt) *n., slang* **1,** (stupid person) necio; bobo. **2,** (mongrel dog) perro cruzado.

mutter ('mʌt·ər) *v.t & i.* (mumble) murmurar; mascullar; farfullar. —*v.i.* (grumble) gruñir; refunfuñar. —*n.* **1,** (mumble) farfulla. **2,** (grumble) gruñido; refunfuño.

mutton ('mʌt·ən) *n.* carnero; carne de carnero. —**mutton chop,** chuleta de carnero. —**mutton chop whiskers,** patillas imperiales.

muttonhead *n., colloq.* zopenco.

mutual ('mju·tʃu·əl) *adj.* mutuo; recíproco. —**mutuality** (-'æl·ə·ti) *n.* mutualidad.

muzzle ('mʌz·əl) *n.* **1,** (of a firearm) boca. **2,** (snout) hocico; morro. **3,** (covering for an animal's mouth) bozal. —*v.t.* **1,** (put a muzzle on) poner bozal a. **2,** (restrain from speech; gag) no dejar hablar; silenciar; amordazar.

muzzy ('mʌz·i) *adj., colloq.* confuso; indistinto.

my (mai) *adj.pos.* mi (*pl.* mis); (*hablándole a uno*) mío: *my friends,* amigos míos. —*interj.* ¡hombre!; ¡oh!; ¡ah!

myco- (mai·ko; -kə) *prefijo* mico-; hongo: *mycology,* micología.

myo- (mai·o; -ə) *prefijo* mio-; músculo: *myocardium,* miocardio.

myopia (mai'o·pi·ə) *n.* miopía. —**myopic** (-'ap·ɪk) *adj.* miope.

myosis (mai'o·sɪs) n. miosis. —**myotic** (-'at·ɪk) *adj.* miótico.

myria- (mɪr·i·ə) *prefijo* miria-. **1,** muchos; numerosos: *myriapod,* miriápodo. **2,** diez mil: *myriameter,* miriámetro.

myriad ('mɪr·i·əd) *n.* miríada.

myrrh (mʌɹ) *n.* mirra.

myrtle ('mʌɹ·təl) *n.* mirto.

myself (mai'sɛlf) [*pl.* **ourselves**] *pron.pers.* yo; yo mismo. —*pron. refl.* **1,** (*complemento directo o indirecto de verbo*) me: *I washed myself,* Me lavé. *I put it on myself,* Me lo puse. **2,** (*complemento de prep.*) mí; mí mismo: *I bought it for myself,* Me lo compré para mí. —**to myself,** para mí: *I said to myself, "I'm not going,"* Dije para mí: no voy. —**with myself,** conmigo.

mysterious (mɪs'tɪr·i·əs) *adj.* misterioso. —**mysteriousness,** *n.* misterio; lo misterioso.

mystery ('mɪs·tə·ri) *n.* misterio.

mystic ('mɪs·tɪk) *n.* & *adj.* místico. —**mystical,** *adj.* místico.

mysticism ('mɪs·tə,sɪz·əm) *n.* misticismo; mística.

mystify ('mɪs·tə,fai) *v.t.* **1,** (surround with mystery) rodear de misterio. **2,** (puzzle; perplex) confundir; intrigar. **3,** (hoax; deceive) mixtificar. —**mystification** (-fɪ'kei·ʃən) *n.* mixtificación.

mystique (mɪs'tik) *n.* mística.

myth (mɪθ) *n.* mito. —**mythical** ('mɪθ·ə·kəl) *adj.* mítico.

mythology (mɪ'θal·ə·dʒi) *n.* mitología. —**mythological** (,mɪθ·ə'ladʒ·ɪ·kəl) *adj.* mitológico.

N

N, n (ɛn) decimocuarta letra del alfabeto inglés.

nab (næb) *v.t., colloq.* **1,** (grab) agarrar; pillar; coger. **2,** (arrest) arrestar; prender.

nabob ('nei·bab) *n.* nabab.

nacre ('nei·kər) *n.* nácar; madreperla. —*adj.* nacarado. —**nacreous** (-kri·əs) *adj.* nacarado; nacarino.

nadir ('nei·dər) *n.* nadir.

nag (næg) *v.t.* & *i.* regañar; jeringar. —*n.* **1,** (old horse) *colloq.*

jamelgo; penco; jaco. 2, (scold) mujer regañona.
naiad ('nai·æd) *n.* náyade.
nail (neil) *n.* 1, *anat.* uña. 2, (metal fastener) clavo. —*v.t.* 1, (fasten) clavar. 2, (hold; keep fixed) sujetar. 3, *colloq.* (catch; nab) agarrar; pillar; coger. —**nail file**, lima para las uñas. —**nail polish**, esmalte para las uñas.
naïve (na'i:v) *adj.* ingenuo; cándido. —**naïveté** (-'tei) *n.* ingenuidad.
naked ('nei·kɪd) *adj.* 1, (uncovered; exposed) desnudo. 2, (undisguised; plain) puro; patente. —**nakedness**, *n.* desnudez. —**stark naked**, en cueros. —**with the naked eye**, a simple vista.
namby-pamby ('næm·bi'pæm·bi) *adj.* melindroso; remilgado; soso. —*n.* melindroso; cosa *o* persona sosa.
name (neim) *n.* nombre. —*v.t.* 1, (mention; designate) nombrar. 2, (give a name to; call) llamar; dar nombre (de). —*adj.* de nombre; de renombre. —**call names**, insultar; poner *o* decir motes a. —**Christian name**, nombre de pila *o* bautismo. —**full name**, nombre y apellido; nombre completo. —**What is your name?**, ¿Cómo se llama? **My name is . . .**, Me llamo . . .
nameless ('neim·ləs) *adj.* sin nombre; anónimo; innominado.
namely ('neim·li) *adv.* a saber; esto es; es decir.
namesake ('neim,seik) *n.* tocayo; homónimo.
nanny ('næn·i) *n.* 1, (nurse) nodriza; nana. 2, (she-goat) cabra.
nap (næp) *n.* 1, (fuzzy surface) lanilla; pelusa. 2, (short sleep) siesta. —*v.i.* 1, (take a short sleep) dormitar; echar una siesta. 2, (be off guard) estar desprevenido. —**catch (someone) napping**, cogerle a uno desprevenido.
nape (neip) *n.* nuca; cerviz; cogote.
napery ('nei·pə·ri) *n.* mantelería.
naphtha ('næp·θə) *n.* nafta.
naphthalene ('næf·θə,lin) *n.* naftalina.
napkin ('næp·kɪn) *n.* servilleta.
napoleon (nə'po·li·ən) *n.* 1, (coin) napoleón. 2, (pastry) pastel de hojaldre y crema.
narcissism (nar'sɪs·ɪz·əm) *n.* narcisismo. —**narcissist**, *n.* narcisista. —**narcissistic**, *adj.* narcisista.
narcissus (nar'sɪs·əs) *n.* narciso.
narcosis (nar'ko·sɪs) *n.* narcosis.
narcotic (nar'kat·ɪk) *adj.* narcótico. —*n.* 1, (drug) narcótico. 2, (addict) narcómano.
narcotism ('nar·kə·tɪz·əm) *n.* narcotismo.
nard (nard) *n.* nardo.
nares ('nɛr·iz) *n.pl.* [*sing.* **naris** ('nær·ɪs)] ventanas de la nariz; narices.
narrate ('næ·ret) *v.t.* & *i.* narrar; relatar. —**narration**, *n.* narración. —**narrator**, *n.* narrador; relator.
narrative ('nær·ə·tɪv) *n.* narrativa; relato. —*adj.* narrativo.
narrow ('nær·o) *adj.* estrecho. —*v.t.* 1, (make less wide) angostar; hacer (más) estrecho. 2, (limit) limitar; restringir. 3, (reduce) reducir. —*v.i.* 1, (become less wide) angostarse; estrecharse. 2, (reduce) reducirse. 3, (become smaller, as the eyes) entornarse. —*n.* 1, (narrow part) parte estrecha *o* angosta. 2, *usu.pl.* (narrow passage) angostura; estrecho. —**have a narrow escape**, escaparse por un pelo.
narrowminded *adj.* estrecho de miras.
narrowness ('nær·o·nəs) *n.* estrechez.
narwhal ('nar·wəl) *n.* narval.
nasal ('nei·zəl) *adj.* nasal. —**nasality** (ne'zæl·ə·ti) *n.* nasalidad.
nascent ('neis·ənt) *adj.* naciente.
naso- (nei·zo) *prefijo* naso-; nariz: *nasofrontal*, nasofrontal.
nastiness ('næs·ti·nəs) *n.* 1, (foulness) porquería. 2, (meanness) odiosidad; maldad. 3, (ill humor) mal humor; mala disposición; mal genio. 4, (ugliness) mala cara; mal cariz.
nasturtium (næ'stʌɹ·ʃəm) *n.* capuchina.
nasty ('næs·ti) *adj.* 1, (offensive; foul) asqueroso. 2, (mean) desagradable; odioso; detestable. 3, (noxious; ugly) malo; feo.
natal ('nei·təl) *adj.* natal.
natant ('nei·tənt) *adj.* natátil; flotante.
natatorium (,ne·tə'tor·i·əm) *n.* piscina; *Amer.* natatorio. —**natatory** ('nei·tə,tor·i) *adj.* natatorio.
nation ('nei·ʃən) *n.* nación.
national ('næʃ·ə·nəl) *adj.* & *n.* nacional.

nationalism (ˈnæʃ·ə·nəˌlɪz·əm) *n.* nacionalismo. —**nationalist,** *n.* nacionalista. —**nationalistic,** *adj.* nacionalista.

nationality (ˌnæʃ·əˈnæl·ə·ti) *n.* nacionalidad.

nationalize (ˈnæʃ·ə·nəˌlaiz) *v.t.* nacionalizar. —**nationalization** (-lɪ·ˈzei·ʃən) *n.* nacionalización.

native (ˈnei·tɪv) *adj.* **1,** (belonging by birth or origin) nativo; natural. **2,** (of the place of one's birth) natal. **3,** (inborn; innate) natural. **4,** (indigenous) indígena. **5,** (in natural state) natural. —*n.* natural; indígena. —**native land,** patria. —**native tongue,** lengua materna.

native-born *adj.* oriundo; nativo; natural.

nativity (neiˈtɪv·ə·ti) *n.* **1,** (birth) nacimiento; natividad. **2,** *cap.* (birth of Christ) Navidad.

natron (ˈnei·tran) *n.* natrón.

natty (ˈnæt·i) *adj., colloq.* garboso; elegante. —**nattiness,** *n.* garbo; elegancia.

natural (ˈnætʃ·ə·rəl) *adj.* natural. —*n.* **1,** (fool; idiot) tonto; idiota. **2,** *colloq.* (apt person or thing) persona de habilidad natural; persona *o* cosa de éxito asegurado. **3,** *music* **a.** (natural sign) becuadro. **b.** (white key) tecla blanca. **c.** (natural tone) nota *o* tono natural. —**naturally,** *adv.* naturalmente. —**naturalness,** *n.* naturalidad.

naturalism (ˈnætʃ·ə·rə·lɪz·əm) *n.* naturalismo. —**naturalist,** *n.* naturalista. —**naturalistic,** *adj.* naturalista.

naturalize (ˈnætʃ·ə·rəˌlaiz) *v.t.* naturalizar. —**naturalization** (-lɪ·ˈzei·ʃən) *n.* naturalización.

nature (ˈnei·tʃər) *n.* naturaleza. —**good nature,** bondad. —**ill** (*o* **bad**) **nature,** mala índole. —**of** (*o* **in**) **the nature of,** como.

naught (nɔt) *n.* **1,** (nothing) nada. **2,** (zero) cero. —**come to naught,** malograrse; fracasar; quedar en nada.

naughtiness (ˈnɔ·ti·nəs) *n.* **1,** (disobedience) desobediencia; *Amer.* malacrianza. **2,** (mischievousness) travesura; picardía.

naughty (ˈnɔ·ti) *adj.* **1,** (disobedient) desobediente; malcriado. **2,** (mischievous) travieso; pícaro. **3,** (indecent) indecente; feo.

nausea (ˈnɔ·ʃə) *n.* náusea.

nauseate (ˈnɔ·ʃi·eit) *v.t.* dar asco; dar náusea(s). —**nauseated,** *adj.* nauseado.

nauseous (ˈnɔ·ʃəs) *adj.* asqueroso; nauseabundo. —**nauseousness,** *n.* asquerosidad.

nautical (ˈnɔ·tɪ·kəl) *adj.* náutico; marino.

nautilus (ˈnɔ·tɪ·ləs) *n.* nautilo.

naval (ˈnei·vəl) *adj.* naval; de marina.

nave (neiv) *n.* nave.

navel (ˈnei·vəl) *n.* ombligo.

navigable (ˈnæv·ɪ·gə·bəl) *adj.* navegable.

navigate (ˈnæv·ɪˌgeit) *v.t. & i.* navegar. —**navigation,** *n.* navegación. —**navigator,** *n.* navegante.

navy (ˈnei·vi) *n.* armada; marina de guerra.

nay (nei) *n.* no. —*adv.* **1,** (no) no; de ningún modo. **2,** (not only so, but) no sólo . . . sino; y aún.

Nazi (ˈnat·si) *n. & adj.* nazi. —**Nazism** (-sɪz·əm) *n.* nazismo.

neap tide (nip) marea muerta.

near (nɪr) *adv.* **1,** (not far) cerca; no lejos. **2,** (closely; intimately) de cerca; íntimamente. **3,** (almost) casi. —*adj.* **1,** (not far) cercano; inmediato; próximo. **2,** (intimate) íntimo; allegado. **3,** (closely related) cercano. **4,** (approximating; resembling) casi. **5,** (by a close margin; narrow) por un pelo. —*prep.* cerca de; junto a. —*v.t. & i.* acercarse (a); aproximarse (a); llegar (a). —**come near (doing something)** casi *o* por poco (hacer algo): *I came near killing him,* Casi *o* por poco lo mato. —**near at hand, 1,** (within reach) a mano. **2,** (imminent) al caer; al llegar.

near-by *adj.* cercano; próximo. —*adv.* cerca. —*prep., colloq.* cerca de.

nearly (ˈnɪr·li) *adv.* **1,** (almost) casi. **2,** (closely) de cerca.

near miss 1, (shot close to the target) tiro que cae *o* pasa cerca del blanco. **2,** (anything falling short of its mark) acción *o* esfuerzo que queda corto. **3,** (narrow escape) escapada.

nearness (ˈnɪr·nəs) *n.* proximidad; cercanía.

nearsighted *adj.* miope; corto de vista. —**nearsightedness,** *n.* miopía.

neat (nit) *adj.* **1,** (clean; tidy) limpio; pulcro; aseado. **2,** (skillful;

clever) hábil. **3,** (pure; unmixed) puro; solo. **4,** *slang* (very pleasing) bueno. **5,** (net; clean) neto. **—neatness,** *n.* limpieza; pulcritud; aseo.
nebula ('nɛb·jə·lə) *n.* [*pl.* **nebulae** (-li)] nebulosa. **—nebular,** *adj.* nebuloso. **—nebulous** *adj.* nebuloso. **—nebulosity** (-'las·ə·ti); **nebulousness,** *n.* nebulosidad.
necessary ('nɛs·əˌsɛr·i) *adj.* necesario. **—n.** necesidad. **—necessarily,** *adv.* necesariamente.
necessitate (nə'sɛs·əˌteit) *v.t.* necesitar; requerir.
necessitous (nə'sɛs·ə·təs) *adj.* necesitado; indigente.
necessity (nə'sɛs·ə·ti) *n.* necesidad. **—of necessity,** por necesidad.
neck (nɛk) *n.* **1,** (part of the body, of a garment, etc.) cuello. **2,** (point of land) lengua de tierra. **3,** (strait) estrecho. **—*v.i.*,** *slang* besuquearse. **—necking,** *n.* besuqueo. **—neck and neck,** parejos; lado a lado. **—stick one's neck out,** arriesgarse; exponerse. **—stiff neck,** tortícolis.
neckband *n.* cuello (de camisa, vestido, etc.).
neckerchief ('nɛk·ər·tʃɪf) *n.* pañoleta.
necklace ('nɛk·ləs) *n.* collar.
neckpiece *n.* cuello postizo.
necktie ('nɛkˌtai) *n.* corbata; *Amer.* chalina.
neckwear *n.* cuellos; corbatas; bufandas, etc.
necro- (nɛk·ro; -rə) *prefijo* necro-; muerte; muerto: *necrology,* necrología.
necromancy ('nɛk·rəˌmæn·si) *n.* nigromancia; necromancia. **—necromancer,** *n.* nigromante.
necropolis (nɛ'krap·ə·lɪs) *n.* necrópolis.
necrosis (nɛ'kro·sɪs) *n.* necrosis. **—necrotic** (nɛ'krat·ɪk) *adj.* necrótico.
nectar ('nɛk·tər) *n.* néctar.
nectarine (ˌnɛk·tə'riːn) *n.* variedad de melocotón.
née (nei) *adj.* nacida.
need (niːd) *n.* necesidad. **—*v.t.*** necesitar; tener necesidad de; requerir. **—*v.i.*** ser necesario; tener necesidad. **—be in need of,** tener necesidad de. **—have need to,** tener que; deber; necesitar. **—if need be,** si necesario.
needful ('nid·fəl) *adj.* **1,** (necessary; needed) necesario. **2,** (needy) necesitado.
neediness ('ni·di·nəs) *n.* necesidad; pobreza; indigencia.
needle ('ni·dəl) *n.* aguja. **—*v.t.*,** *colloq.* **1,** (prod; incite) estimular; incitar. **2,** (tease; bother) pinchar; jeringar.
needlepoint *n.* punto de cruz.
needless ('nid·ləs) *adj.* superfluo; innecesario. **—needlessness,** *n.* superfluidad; inutilidad. **—needless to say,** se excusa decir.
needlework *n.* **1,** (sewing) costura. **2,** (embroidery) bordado.
needs (niːdz) *adv.* por fuerza; por necesidad.
needy ('ni·di) *adj.* necesitado; indigente; pobre.
ne'er (neːr) *adv., poet.* = **never.**
ne'er-do-well ('nɛr·duˌwɛl) *n.* haragán; perdido.
nefarious (nɪ'fɛr·i·əs) *adj.* nefando; nefario. **—nefariousness,** *n.* maldad; iniquidad.
negate (nɛ'geit) *v.t.* **1,** (deny) negar. **2,** (nullify) invalidar. **—negation,** *n.* negación.
negative ('nɛg·ə·tɪv) *adj.* negativo. **—n. 1,** (denial) negativa. **2,** *photog.; electricity* negativo. **3,** *gram.* negación.
neglect (nɪ'glɛkt) *v.t.* descuidar; desatender; olvidar. **—n.** descuido; negligencia; desatención. **—neglectful,** *adj.* negligente; descuidado.
negligee (ˌnɛg·lə'ʒei) *n.* negligé.
negligence ('nɛg·lə·dʒəns) *n.* negligencia. **—negligent,** *adj.* negligente.
negligible ('nɛg·lɪ·dʒə·bəl) *adj.* insignificante. **—negligibility,** *n.* insignificancia.
negotiable (nɪ'go·ʃi·ə·bəl) *adj.* negociable.
negotiate (nɪ'go·ʃiˌeit) *v.t.* & *i.* negociar. **—negotiation,** *n.* negociación. **—negotiator,** *n.* negociador.
negro ('ni·gro) *n.* [*pl.* **-groes**] & *adj.* negro. **—negress,** *n.* negra.
negroid ('ni·grɔid) *adj.* negroide.
neigh (nei) *v.t.* relinchar. **—n.** relincho.
neighbor ('nei·bər) *n.* **1,** (nearby person or thing) vecino. **2,** (fellow being) prójimo. **—*adj.*** vecino. **—*v.i.* & *t.*** ser vecino (de); limitar (con); colindar (con).
neighborhood ('nei·bərˌhud) *n.* vecindario; vecindad.

neighboring (ˈnei·bər·ɪŋ) *adj.* vecino; contiguo; próximo.
neighborly (ˈnei·bər·li) *adj.* como *o* de buen vecino; sociable. —**neighborliness,** *n.* calidad de buen vecino.
neither (ˈni·ðər; ˈnai-) *conj.* **1,** (not either) ni. **2,** (nor yet) tampoco; ni . . . tampoco. —*adv.* tampoco. —*adj.* ninguno (de los dos). —*pron.* ninguno; ni el uno ni el otro. —**neither . . . nor,** ni . . . ni.
nemato- (nɛm·ə·to; -tə) *prefijo* nemato-; hilo; filamento; filamentoso: *nematocyst,* nematocisto.
nemesis (ˈnɛm·ə·sɪs) *n.* némesis.
neo- (ni·o; -ə) *prefijo* neo-; nuevo; reciente: *neoclassical,* neoclásico.
Neocene (ˈni·əˌsin) *adj.* neoceno.
neodymium (ˌni·oˈdɪm·i·əm) *n.* neodimio.
Neo-Latin (ˌni·oˈlæt·ən) *adj.* & *n.* neolatino; romance.
neolithic (ˌni·oˈlɪθ·ɪk) *adj.* neolítico.
neologism (niˈal·ə·dʒɪz·əm) *n.* neologismo.
neon (ˈni·an) *n.* neón.
neophyte (ˈni·əˌfait) *n.* neófito.
neoplasm (ˈni·əˌplæz·əm) *n.* neoplasma.
nephew (ˈnɛf·ju) *n.* sobrino.
nephritis (nɪˈfrai·tɪs) *n.* nefritis. —**nephritic** (nɪˈfrɪt·ɪk) *adj.* nefrítico.
nephro- (nɛf·ro; -rə) *también,* **nephr-** (nɛfr) *ante vocal, prefijo* nefro-; nefr-; riñon: *nephrotomy,* nefrotomía; *nephritis,* nefritis.
nepotism (ˈnɛp·ə·tɪz·əm) *n.* nepotismo.
Neptune (ˈnɛp·tjun) *n.* Neptuno.
neptunium (nɛpˈtju·ni·əm) *n.* neptunio.
nereid (ˈnɪr·i·ɪd) *n.* nereida.
nervation (nʌɹˈvei·ʃən) *n.* nervadura.
nerve (nʌɹv) *n.* **1,** (fiber) nervio. **2,** (courage) valor; fuerzas (*pl.*). **3,** *slang* (audacity) atrevimiento; desfachatez; tupé. —*v.t.* dar valor *o* fuerzas a; animar. —**get on one's nerves,** atacarle a uno los nervios. —**nerve oneself,** hacer acopio de valor *o* fuerzas.
nerveless (ˈnʌɹv·ləs) *adj.* **1,** (unnerved; weak) enervado. **2,** (cowardly) cobarde. **3,** *zool.; bot.* sin nervios.
nervous (ˈnʌɹv·əs) *adj.* nervioso. —**nervousness,** *n.* nerviosidad.
nervure (ˈnʌɹ·vjʊr) *n.* nervadura; nervio.
nervy (ˈnʌɹ·vi) *adj.* atrevido.
nescience (ˈnɛʃ·əns) *n.* nesciencia; ignorancia.
-ness (nəs) *sufijo; añadido a adjetivos forma nombres denotando* cualidad; condición: *greatness,* grandeza; *boldness,* audacia. *Si el adjetivo termina en -y generalmente la cambia por -i antes de añadir el sufijo: dirtiness,* suciedad.
nest (nɛst) *n.* nido. —*v.i.* anidar. —**nest egg,** nidal; *fig.* ahorro para emergencias; ahorrito.
nestle (ˈnɛs·əl) *v.i.* **1,** (snuggle) acurrucarse; anidarse; *Amer.* aparragarse. **2,** (lie hidden; be sheltered) anidar; estar anidado. —*v.t.* anidar; abrigar.
nestling (ˈnɛst·lɪŋ) *n.* polluelo; pollito; *Amer.* pichón.
net (nɛt) *n.* **1,** (mesh) malla; red. **2,** (network) red. —*adj.* neto. —*v.t.* [**netted, netting**] **1,** (catch, as with a net) atrapar en la red. **2,** (gain) sacar *o* dar de ganancia.
nether (ˈnɛð·ər) *adj.* **1,** (infernal) infernal. **2,** (lower) inferior; de abajo.
netting (ˈnɛt·ɪŋ) *n.* red; obra de malla; redecilla.
nettle (ˈnɛt·əl) *n.* ortiga. —*v.t.* irritar; provocar.
network (ˈnɛtˌwʌɹk) *n.* red; cadena (de radiodifusión).
neural (ˈnjʊr·əl) *adj.* nérveo; nervioso.
neuralgia (njʊˈræl·dʒə) *n.* neuralgia. —**neuralgic,** *adj.* neurálgico.
neurasthenia (ˌnjʊr·əsˈθi·ni·ə) *n.* neurastenia. —**neurasthenic** (-ˈθɛn·ɪk) *adj.* & *n.* neurasténico.
neuritis (njʊˈrai·tɪs) *n.* neuritis.
neuro- (njʊr·o; -ə) *también,* **neur-** (njʊr) *ante vocal, prefijo* neuro-; neur-; nervio: *neurology,* neurología; *neuritis,* neuritis.
neurology (njʊˈral·ə·dʒi) *n.* neurología. —**neurological** (ˌnjʊr·əˈladʒ·ɪk·əl) *adj.* neurológico. —**neurologist,** *n.* neurólogo.
neuron (ˈnjʊr·an) *n.* neurona.
neurosis (njʊˈro·sɪs) *n.* neurosis. —**neurotic** (-ˈrat·ɪk) *adj.* & *n.* neurótico.
neuter (ˈnu·tər) *adj.* neutro.
neutral (ˈnu·trəl) *adj.* & *n.* **1,** (not taking sides) neutral. **2,** (in-

active; inert; without definite quality) neutro.
neutrality (nu'træl·ə·ti) *n.* neutralidad.
neutralize ('nu·trə·laiz) *v.t.* neutralizar. —**neutralization** (-lɪ·'zei·ʃən) *n.* neutralización.
neutron ('nu·tran) *n.* neutrón.
never ('nɛv·ər) *adv.* **1,** (not ever) nunca; jamás. **2,** (not at all) no; de ningún modo. —**never fear,** no tenga cuidado; no hay cuidado. —**never mind,** no importa. —**never so . . . ,**por muy . . . ; por mucho . . . ; por más que. . . .
never-ceasing *adj.* continuo; incesante; perpetuo.
never-failing *adj.* **1,** (inexhaustible) inagotable. **2,** (infallible) infalible.
nevermore *adv.* jamás; nunca más.
nevertheless (nɛv·ər·ðə'lɛs) *adv.* sin embargo; no obstante; con todo.
new (nuː) *adj.* nuevo. —*adv.* **1,** (recently) recientemente. **2,** (anew) nuevamente; de nuevo.
newborn *adj.* & *n.* recién nacido.
newcomer *n.* recién llegado.
newel ('nu·əl) *n.* nabo *o* poste de escalera.
newfangled (nu'fæŋ·gəld) *adj.* novedoso; de última moda.
newly ('nu·li) *adv.* **1,** (recently) recién; recientemente. **2,** = **anew.**
newlywed *adj.* & *n.* recién casado.
newness ('nu·nəs) *n.* novedad; lo nuevo.
news (nuːz) *n.* **1,** (reports of happenings) noticias. **2,** (information; local gossip) nuevas; novedades. —**break the news,** dar la noticia. —**news agency,** empresa *o* agencia noticiera. —**news item,** noticia.
newsboy *n.* vendedor de diarios; *Amer.* canillita.
newscast *n.* noticiario. —**newscaster,** *n.* cronista; locutor de noticias; noticiero.
newsdealer *n.* vendedor de periódicos.
newsman *n.* [*pl.* **-men**] **1,** = **newsdealer. 2,** = **newspaperman.**
newsmonger *n.* novelero.
newspaper *n.* periódico; diario.
newspaperman *n.* [*pl.* **-men**] periodista.
newsprint ('nuz,prɪnt) *n.* papel de periódico.
newsreel *n.* noticiario; noticiero.
newsstand *n.* puesto de periódicos; quiosco.
newsy ('nu·zi) *adj.* noticioso; noticiero; lleno de novelerías. —**newsiness,** *n.* novelería.
newt (nut) *n.* salamandra acuática.
New Year año nuevo.
next (nɛkst) *adj.* **1,** (immediately following) siguiente; próximo. **2,** (nearest; adjacent) contiguo; vecino; inmediato. **3,** (of future time) que viene: *next week (month, year),* la semana (el mes, el año) que viene. —*adv.* **1,** (in the nearest time or position) luego; después. **2,** (forthwith) en seguida; a continuación. **3,** (on the first subsequent occasion) de nuevo; la próxima vez. —*prep.* al lado de; junto a. —*n.* el próximo; el siguiente. —**be next,** tocarle a uno el turno: *Who's next?,* ¿A quién le toca? —**next door (to),** al lado (de). —**next of kin,** pariente inmediato. —**next to, 1,** (beside) al lado de; junto a. **2,** (after) después de. **3,** (almost; nearly) casi. —**what next?,** y ahora ¿qué?; ¿y luego?
next-door *adj.* de al lado.
nexus ('nɛk·səs) *n.* nexo.
nib (nɪb) *n.* **1,** (point) punta. **2,** (beak) pico. —**his** (*o* **her**) **nibs,** su señoría.
nibble ('nɪb·əl) *v.i.* & *t.* mordiscar; picar; picotear. —*n.* mordisco; bocadito.
nice (nais) *adj.* **1,** (subtle; delicate) fino; sutil; delicado. **2,** (refined; discriminating) refinado; esmerado. **3,** *colloq.* (attractive) bonito; mono; lindo. **4,** *colloq.* (good; gentle) bueno; amable. **5,** *colloq.* (pleasant) agradable; bueno. **6,** *colloq.* (in good taste) de buen gusto. **7,** *colloq.* (proper; suitable) apropiado; adecuado. —**nicely,** *adv., colloq.* muy bien. —**nice and . . . ,** *colloq.* muy.
nicety ('nai·sə·ti) *n.* delicadeza; finura; sutileza.
niche (nɪtʃ) *n.* nicho.
nick (nɪk) *n.* **1,** (notch; groove) muesca; mella. **2,** (small cut; abrasion) rasguño; arañazo. **3,** *cap.* [*usu.* **Old Nick**] el diablo. —*v.t.* **1,** (cut; chip) hacer muescas en; mellar. **2,** (wound slightly) arañar; rasguñar. —**in the nick of time,** justo a tiempo; a punto.
nickel ('nɪk·əl) *n.* níquel. —**nick-**

el-plate, *v.t.* niquelar. —**nickel-plating,** *n.* niquelado.
nickname ('nɪk,neim) *n.* mote; apodo. —*v.t.* apodar.
nicotine ('nɪk·ə,tin) *n.* nicotina. —**nicotinic** (-'tɪn·ɪk) *adj.* nicotínico.
niece (nis) *n.* sobrina.
nifty ('nɪf·ti) *adj., slang* elegante; primoroso. —**niftiness,** *n., slang* primor.
niggardly ('nɪg·ərd·li) *adj.* mezquino; tacaño. —**niggardliness,** *n.* mezquindad; tacañería.
nigger ('nɪg·ər) *n.* & *adj., derog.* = **negro.**
niggle ('nɪg·əl) *v.i.* ajetrearse en nimiedades.
nigh (nai) *adj.* cercano; próximo. —*prep.* cerca de; junto a. —*adv.* **1,** (near) cerca. **2,** (nearly) casi.
night (nait) *n.* noche. —*adj.* nocturno; de noche. —**at** *o* **by night,** de noche. —**make a night of it,** pasar la noche en *o* con algo.
nightcap *n.* **1,** (cap worn in bed) gorro de dormir. **2,** *colloq.* (drink before retiring) último trago (del día).
nightclub *n.* cabaret; sala de fiestas; club nocturno; club de noche.
nightdress *n.* camisón; camisa de dormir.
nightfall *n.* anochecer; caída de la tarde *o* de la noche.
nightgown *n.* = **nightdress.**
nighthawk *n.* **1,** *ornith.* chotacabras. **2,** = **night owl.**
nightingale ('nait·ən,geil) *n.* ruiseñor.
night letter telegrama nocturno.
nightly ('nait·li) *adj.* **1,** (of the night; at or by night) nocturno; de noche. **2,** (occurring every night) de todas las noches. —*adv.* **1,** (at or by night) de noche; durante la noche. **2,** (every night) todas las noches.
nightmare ('nait,meːr) *n.* pesadilla. —**nightmarish,** *adj.* de pesadilla; horrendo.
night owl *colloq.* trasnochador.
nightshade *n.* solano; hierba mora.
nightshirt *n.* camisa de dormir.
night stick porra; cachiporra; bastón de policía.
nighttime *n.* noche; horas de la noche.
night watch **1,** (vigil; period of duty) guardia *o* ronda nocturna; vigilia. **2,** (guard) ronda nocturna; guardia.
nihilism ('nai·ə·lɪz·əm) *n.* nihilismo. —**nihilist,** *n.* nihilista. —**nihilistic,** *adj.* nihilista.
nil (nɪl) *n.* nada.
nimble ('nɪm·bəl) *adj.* ágil. —**nimbleness,** *n.* agilidad.
nimbus ('nɪm·bəs) *n.* nimbo.
nincompoop ('nɪn·kəm,pup) *n.* badulaque; simplón.
nine (nain) *n.* & *adj.* nueve.
ninefold ('nain,fold) *adj.* & *n.* nueve veces (más). —*adv.* nueve veces.
nine hundred novecientos. —**nine-hundredth,** *adj.* & *n.* noningentésimo.
ninepins *n.sing.* juego de bolos. —**ninepin,** *n.* bolo.
nineteen ('nain,tin) *n.* & *adj.* diecinueve; diez y nueve. —**nineteenth,** *adj.* & *n.* decimonono; diecinueveavo.
ninety ('nain·ti) *n.* & *adj.* noventa. —**ninetieth,** *adj.* & *n.* nonagésimo; noventavo.
ninth (nainθ) *adj.* noveno; nono. —*n.* noveno; novena parte; *music* novena.
ninny ('nɪn·i) *n.* lelo; mentecato.
niobium (nai'o·bi·əm) *n.* niobio; columbio.
nip (nɪp) *v.t.* [**nipped, nipping**] **1,** (pinch; bite) pellizcar; morder. **2,** (snip; cut off) cortar. —*n.* **1,** (pinch) pellizco. **2,** (bite) mordedura; mordisco. **3,** (chill) frío. **4,** *colloq.* (small drink) traguito; chispo. **5,** *colloq.* (little bit) poquito; bocadito. —**nip and tuck,** *colloq.* empatado; parejo; porfiado. —**nip in the bud,** destruir en germen; cortar en flor.
nipper ('nɪp·ər) *n.* pinza. —**nippers,** *n.pl.* tenazas.
nipple ('nɪp·əl) *n.* **1,** *anat.; zool.* pezón; tetilla. **2,** (mouthpiece of a nursing bottle) chupete. **3,** (threaded pipe) tubo roscado de unión.
Nipponese (,nɪp·ə'niz) *adj.* & *n.* nipón; japonés.
nippy ('nɪp·i) *adj., colloq.* **1,** (chilly) helado; frío. **2,** (irritable) áspero; mordaz. **3,** (sharp; biting) picante; mordaz.
nirvana (nʌɹ'va·na; nɪr-) *n.* nirvana.
nit (nɪt) *n.* liendre.

niter *también,* **nitre** ('nai·tər) *n.* nitro.
niton ('nai·tan) *n.* = **radon.**
nitrate ('nai·treit) *n.* nitrato; azoato.
nitric ('nai·trɪk) *adj.* nítrico; azoico.
nitro- (nai·trə) *prefijo* nitro-; nitrógeno; compuesto de nitrógeno: *nitrobenzene,* nitrobencina; *nitrocellulose,* nitrocelulosa.
nitrocellulose *n.* nitrocelulosa.
nitrogen ('nai·trə·dʒən) *n.* nitrógeno; ázoe. —**nitrogenous** (nai·'tradʒ·ə·nəs) *adj.* nitrogenado; azoado.
nitroglycerin *n.* nitroglicerina.
nitrous ('nai·trəs) *adj.* nitroso.
nitwit ('nɪt,wɪt) *n., slang* mentecato.
nix (nɪks) *n., slang* nada; nones (*pl.*). —*adv.* no; ni por pienso; nitos. —*interj.* ¡alto!; ¡para!
no (noː) *adv.* no. —*adj.* ninguno. —*n.* no. —**no longer,** ya no. —**no one,** nadie; ninguno. —**no sooner,** apenas.
nob (naːb) *n., slang* **1,** (head) cabeza. **2,** (important person) personaje.
nobelium (no'bi·li·əm) *n.* nobelio.
nobility (no'bɪl·ə·ti) *n.* nobleza.
noble ('no·bəl) *adj.* & *n.* noble.
nobleman ('no·bəl·mən) *n.* [*pl.* **-men**] noble. —**noblewoman,** *n.* [*pl.* **-women**] dama.
nobody ('no,bad·i; -bəd·i) *pron.* nadie; ninguno. —*n.* nadie; don nadie.
nocti- (nak·tə), *también* **noct-** (nakt) *ante vocal, prefijo* nocti-; noct-; noche: *noctiluca,* noctíluco; *noctambulism,* noctambulismo.
nocturnal (nak'tʌɹ·nəl) *adj.* nocturno; de noche.
nocturne ('nak·tʌɹn) *n.* nocturno.
nod (naːd) *n.* **1,** (greeting) inclinación de cabeza. **2,** (signal) seña (con la cabeza). **3,** (approval) aprobación; asentimiento. —*v.t.* inclinar (la cabeza); indicar (con la cabeza). —*v.i.* dar cabezadas.
node (noːd) *n.* nodo. —**nodal,** *adj.* nodal.
nodule ('nad·jul) *n.* nódulo. —**nodular** ('nad·jə·lər) *adj.* nodular.
Noel (no'ɛl) *n.* Navidad; *l.c.* villancico de Navidad.
noggin ('nag·ɪn) *n.* **1,** (small mug) pichel; taza. **2,** *slang* (head) cabeza.
noise (nɔiz) *n.* ruido. —*v.t.* divulgar; vocear.
noiseless ('nɔiz·ləs) *adj.* silencioso. —**noiselessness,** *n.* silencio.
noisemaker *n.* **1,** (person) escandaloso. **2,** (instrument) matraca.
noisome ('nɔi·səm) *adj.* **1,** (ill-smelling) apestoso. **2,** (injurious) dañino; nocivo.
noisy ('nɔi·zi) *adj.* ruidoso; estrepitoso. —**noisiness,** *n.* ruido; estrépito.
nomad ('no·mæd) *n.* nómada. —**nomadic** (no'mæd·ɪk) *adj.* nómada.
no man's land tierra de nadie.
nomenclature ('no·mən,klei·tʃər) *n.* nomenclatura.
nominal ('nam·ə·nəl) *adj.* nominal.
nominate ('nam·ə,neit) *v.t.* nominar. —**nomination,** *n.* nominación.
nominative ('nam·ɪ·nə·tɪv) *adj.* & *n.* nominativo.
nominee (,nam·ɪ'niː) *n.* candidato.
-nomy (nə·mi) *sufijo* -nomía; *forma nombres denotando* **1,** conocimiento; ciencia; estudio: *astronomy,* astronomía. **2,** distribución; administración; gobierno: *taxonomy,* taxonomía; *economy,* economía; *autonomy,* autonomía.
non- (nan) *prefijo, usado ante nombres, adjetivos y adverbios imprimiendo un matiz de* negación *o* carencia *a la palabra que se une, mas sin expresar tanta fuerza o énfasis como* **un-**; **in-**: *nonresident,* transeúnte: *nonsense,* tontería.
nonage ('nan·ɪdʒ) *n.* minoría de edad; minoridad.
nonagenarian (,nan·ə·dʒə·'nɛr·i·ən) *n.* & *adj.* nonagenario; noventón.
nonagon ('nan·ə,gan) *n.* nonágono.
nonbelligerent *n.* & *adj.* no beligerante.
nonce (nans) *n.* tiempo presente. —**for the nonce,** por el momento.
nonchalance ('nan·ʃə·ləns) *n.* despreocupación. —**nonchalant,** *adj.* despreocupado.
noncom ('nan,kam) *n., colloq.* = **noncommissioned officer.**

noncombatant (nan'kam·bə·tənt) *n. & adj.* no combatiente.
noncommissioned officer suboficial.
noncommittal *adj.* reservado; evasivo.
nonconducive *adj.* inconducente.
nonconductor *n.* mal conductor.
nonconformity *n.* desconformidad; disidencia. —**nonconformist,** *n.* disidente.
nondescript ('nan·də,skrɪpt) *adj.* inclasificable; indefinido; ordinario.
none (nʌn) *pron.* **1,** (no one) nadie; ninguno. **2,** (not any) ninguno; nada. —*adv.* no; en absoluto; de ningún modo. —**none the less,** sin embargo; no obstante.
noneffective *n. & adj.* inútil.
nonentity *n.* **1,** (person of little importance) don nadie; cero a la izquierda. **2,** (something nonexistent) mito; ente imaginario.
nonessential *adj.* no esencial.
nonesuch (,nʌn'sʌtʃ) *n.* sin igual; sin par.
nonexistence *n.* inexistencia. —**nonexistent,** *adj.* inexistente.
nonfiction *n.* literatura seria.
nonillion (no'nɪl·jən) *n.* (*U.S.*) un millón de cuatrillones; quintillón; (*Brit.*) un millón de octillones; nonillón.
nonintervention *n.* no intervención.
nonpareil (,nan·pə'rɛl) *n. & adj.* sin par; sin rival. —*n., ornith.* especie de pinzón.
nonpartisan *adj.* sin partidismo.
nonplus (nan'plʌs) *v.t.* confundir; dejar estupefacto.
nonprofit *adj.* que no ofrece ganancias; no comercial.
nonresident *adj. & n.* no residente.
nonsectarian *adj.* no sectario.
nonsense ('nan·sɛns) *n.* tontería; disparate. —**nonsensical** (nan'sɛn·sɪ·kəl) *adj.* disparatado; absurdo.
nonstop *adj.* directo; expreso. —*adv.* directamente; sin paradas; sin parar.
nonsupport *n.* falta de manutención.
nonunion *adj.* **1,** (not conforming to union requirements) no conforme con los requisitos del sindicato. **2,** (not unionized) no sindicado; no agremiado.
noodle ('nu·dəl) *n.* **1,** (spaghetti) tallarín. **2,** *slang* (head) cabeza.
nook (nʊk) *n.* rincón.
noon (nuːn) *n.* mediodía. —**noonday,** *adj.* de mediodía. —**noontime,** *n.* mediodía.
noose (nus) *n.* **1,** (running knot) nudo corredizo. **2,** (execution by hanging) horca.
nope (nop) *adv., slang* = **no.**
nor (nor) *conj.* ni.
Nordic ('nor·dɪk) *adj. & n.* nórdico.
noria ('nor·i·ə) *n.* noria.
norm (norm) *n.* norma.
normal ('nor·məl) *adj. & n.* normal. —**normalcy** (-si); **normality** (nor'mæl·ə·ti) *n.* normalidad. —**normalize,** *v.t.* normalizar.
Norman ('nor·mən) *n. & adj.* normando.
Norse (nors) *adj.* nórdico; escandinavo; normando. —*n.* **1,** (language) nórdico. **2,** *pl.* (Norsemen) normandos; escandinavos.
Norseman ('nors·mən) *n.* [*pl.* **-men**] escandinavo; normando.
north (norθ) *n.* norte. —*adj.* norte; del norte; septentrional. —*adv.* hacia el norte; al norte.
northeast *n.* nordeste; noreste. —*adj.* del *o* hacia el nordeste. —*adv.* al *o* hacia el nordeste.
northeaster *n.* viento (del) nordeste.
northeasterly *adj.* (del) nordeste. —*adv.* hacia el nordeste.
northeastern *adj.* (del) nordeste.
northerly ('nor·ðər·li) *adj.* norte; del norte; hacia el norte. —*adv.* hacia el norte.
northern ('nor·ðərn) *adj.* norte; del norte; septentrional; norteño. —**northerner,** *n.* norteño; habitante del norte. —**northern lights,** aurora boreal.
northland ('norθ·lənd) *n.* **1,** (northern region) tierras del norte; norte. **2,** *cap.* Escandinavia.
Northman ('norθ·mən) *n.* [*pl.* **-men**] = **Norseman.**
North Pole polo norte.
North Star estrella polar.
northward ('norθ·wərd) *adj.* en *o* de dirección norte. —*adv.* hacia el norte.
northwest *n. & adj.* noroeste. —*adv.* al *o* hacia el noroeste.
northwester *n.* viento (del) noroeste.
northwesterly *adj.* (del) no-

roeste. —*adv.* hacia el noroeste.
northwestern *adj.* (del) noroeste.
nose (no:z) *n.* **1,** (olfactory organ) nariz. **2,** (sense of smell) olfato. **3,** (something resembling a nose) proa; punta; nariz. —*v.t.* & *i.* **1,** (scent; sniff) olfatear. **2,** (nuzzle) frotar la nariz (contra); hocicar. **3,** (push forward) avanzar. —*v.i.* (pry) husmear. —**blow one's nose,** sonarse las narices. —**follow one's nose,** seguir en línea recta. —**lead (someone) by the nose,** traer del cabestro. —**look down one's nose,** mirar con desprecio; desdeñar. —**nose out,** ganar por una nariz. —**under one's nose,** en las (propias) barbas de uno.
nosebleed *n.* hemorragia nasal.
nosedive *n.* picada. —*v.i.* picar; irse en picada.
nosegay *n.* ramillete de flores.
nosey ('no·zi) *adj.* = **nosy.**
nostalgia (nas'tæl·dʒə) *n.* nostalgia. —**nostalgic,** *adj.* nostálgico.
nostril ('nas·trəl) *n.* ventana de la nariz; *pl.* narices.
nostrum ('nas·trəm) *n.* cúralotodo; panacea.
nosy *también,* **nosey** ('no·zi) *adj., colloq.* preguntón; entremetido; curioso.
not (nat) *adv.* no. —**not at all,** de ningún modo; nada. —**not even,** ni; ni siquiera. —**not ever,** nunca; jamás. —**not in any wise,** de ningún modo. —**not . . . nor,** no . . . ni; ni . . . ni. —**no so much as,** ni siquiera. —**not to say,** por no decir.
notable ('no·tə·bəl) *adj.* & *n.* notable. —**notability,** *n.* notabilidad.
notarial (no'tɛr·i·əl) *adj.* notarial.
notarize ('no·tə,raiz) *v.t.* autorizar ante notario; *Amer.* notarizar.
notary ('no·tə·ri) *n.* [*también,* **notary public**] notario.
notation (no'tei·ʃən) *n.* **1,** (act or result of noting) anotación; notación; apunte. **2,** (set of symbols) notación.
notch (natʃ) *n.* **1,** (nick; slot) muesca; mella. **2,** (defile) desfiladero. —*v.t.* mellar; cortar muescas en.
note (not) *n.* nota. —*v.t.* **1,** (notice; observe) notar. **2,** (make a note of) anotar; apuntar. **3,** (mention particularly) mencionar; indicar. **4,** (denote; signify) denotar; indicar.
notebook *n.* libreta; libreta de apuntes; cuaderno.
noted ('no·tɪd) *adj.* notable; célebre; famoso.
noteworthy *adj.* digno de nota; notable.
nothing ('nʌθ·ɪŋ) *n.* **1,** (not anything) nada. **2,** (trifle) nadería. **3,** (zero) cero. —*adv.* de ningún modo; nada. —**be good for nothing,** no servir para nada. —**for nothing, 1,** (free; at no cost) por nada; gratis. **2,** (in vain) para nada; en vano. **3,** (without reason) por nada; sin motivo. —**make nothing of, 1,** (belittle) tomar a la ligera; no dar importancia a. **2,** (fail to understand) no sacar nada en limpio de; no poder comprender. **3,** (fail to use) no aprovecharse de. —**nothing but,** nada más que; solamente. —**nothing doing,** *colloq.* no hay caso. —**think nothing of,** no dar importancia a; no importarle nada a uno.
notice ('no·tɪs) *n.* **1,** (information; announcement) aviso. **2,** (warning) aviso; advertencia. **3,** (brief article) artículo; suelto. **4,** (attention; heed) atención. —*v.t.* **1,** (perceive) notar; advertir; apercibirse de. **2,** (give attention to) prestar atención a; hacer caso de. **3,** (mention; acknowledge) mencionar; hacer mención de. —**noticeable,** *adj.* perceptible; que se nota; que llama atención. —**serve notice,** anunciar; informar; dar aviso formal. —**take notice (of),** notar; apercibirse (de); hacer caso (de).
notify ('no·tɪ·fai) *v.t.* notificar. —**notification** (-fɪ'kei·ʃən) *n.* notificación.
notion ('no·ʃən) *n.* noción. —**notions,** *n.pl.* artículos de mercería; novedades.
notorious (no'tor·i·əs) *adj.* notorio. —**notoriety** (,no·tə'rai·ə·ti) *n.* notoriedad.
no-trump *adj.* & *n.*, *cards* sin triunfo.
notwithstanding (,nat·wɪθ·'stæn·dɪŋ) *adv.* no obstante; sin embargo; con todo. —*prep.* a pesar de. —*conj.* aun cuando; aunque; pese a que.

nougat ('nu·gət) *n.* turrón. —**nougatine** (ˌnu·gə'tiːn) *n.* chocolate de almendras.
nought (nɔt) *n.* = **naught.**
noun (naun) *n.* nombre; sustantivo.
nourish ('nʊr·ɪʃ) *v.t.* nutrir; alimentar. —**nourishing,** *adj.* nutritivo; alimenticio. —**nourishment,** *n.* alimento.
nova ('no·və) *n., astron.* nova.
novel ('nav·əl) *adj.* nuevo; original. —*n.* novela. —**novelette** (-ɛt) *n.* novela corta. —**novelist,** *n.* novelista.
novelty ('nav·əl·ti) *n.* **1,** (newness; something new) novedad. **2,** *usu.pl.* (trinkets) baratijas.
November (no'vɛm·bər) *n.* noviembre.
novena (no'vi·nə) *n.* novena.
novice ('nav·ɪs) *n.* novicio.
novitiate *también,* **noviciate** (no·'vɪʃ·i·ət) *n.* noviciado.
novocaine ('no·vəˌkein) *n.* novocaína.
now (nau) *adv.* ahora; ya. —*conj.* pues (que); ahora que; ya que. —*n.* presente; actualidad. —**now and then,** de cuando en cuando; de vez en cuando. —**now . . . now,** ya . . . ya; ora . . . ora: *now rich, now poor,* ora rico, ora pobre. —**now then,** ahora bien; pues; pues bien.
nowadays ('nau·əˌdeiz) *adv.* hoy día; hoy en día.
noway ('noˌwei) *adv.* de ningún modo. *También,* **noways.**
nowhere ('no·hwɛr) *adv.* a, en *o* por ninguna parte. —**be** (*o* **get**) **nowhere,** no tener éxito. —**get (someone) nowhere,** no servir de nada. —**nowhere else,** a, en *o* por ninguna otra parte. —**nowhere near,** ni cerca.
nowise ('noˌwaiz) *adv.* de ningún modo.
noxious ('nak·ʃəs) *adj.* nocivo. —**noxiousness,** *n.* nocividad.
nozzle ('naz·əl) *n.* pitón; boquilla.
-n't (nt) *contr. de* **not:** *hasn't* = **has not.** *A veces, la contracción afecta también la forma del verbo: shan't* = **shall not.**
nth (ɛnθ) *adj.* enésimo.
nuance (nu'ans) *n.* matiz.
nub (nʌb) *n.* **1,** (knob; lump) protuberancia; nudo. **2,** *colloq.* (gist) meollo; quid.
Nubian ('nu·bi·ən) *adj.* & *n.* nubio.
nuclear ('nuk·li·ər) *adj.* nuclear.
nucleolus (nu'kli·ə·ləs) *n.* nucléolo.
nucleon ('nu·kli·an) *n.* nucleón.
nucleus ('nu·kli·əs) *n.* núcleo.
nude (nuːd) *adj.* & *n.* desnudo. —**nudeness,** *n.* desnudez. —**in the nude,** desnudo; al desnudo.
nudge (nʌdʒ) *v.t.* empujar levemente; dar un codazo. —*n.* codazo; leve empujón.
nudi- (nu·də; nju-) *prefijo* nudi-; desnudo: *nudifoliate,* nudifoliado.
nudism ('nu·diz·əm) *n.* nudismo. —**nudist,** *n.* & *adj.* nudista.
nudity ('nu·də·ti) *n.* desnudez.
nugatory ('nu·gəˌtor·i) *adj.* nulo; ineficaz.
nugget ('nʌg·ət) *n.* pepita.
nuisance ('nu·səns) *n.* **1,** (annoyance) molestia; fastidio. **2,** (annoying person) pelmazo; cataplasma.
null (nʌl) *adj.* nulo. —**null and void,** anulado; nulo.
nullify ('nʌl·ɪˌfai) *v.t.* anular; invalidar. —**nullification** (-fɪ'kei·ʃən) *n.* anulación; invalidación.
nullity ('nʌl·ə·ti) *n.* nulidad.
numb (nʌm) *adj.* entumecido; paralizado. —*v.t.* entumecer; paralizar. —**numbness,** *n.* entumecimiento.
number ('nʌm·bər) *n.* número. —*v.t.* **1,** (designate by number) numerar. **2,** (reckon; classify) contar; enumerar. **3,** (have in number; comprise) contar con; tener. **4,** (amount to) sumar; ser (en total). —**numbers,** *n.pl.* **1,** (many; great number) multitud (*sing.*); gran número. **2,** (numerical superiority) superioridad en número. **3,** (arithmetic) números. —**a number of,** (un) cierto número de. —**be numbered among,** encontrarse *o* hallarse en. —**beyond number,** sin número; innumerable. —**get one's number,** *slang* calar; fichar. —**one's numbre is up,** llegarle *o* tocarle a uno la hora. —**without number,** sin número.
numbering ('nʌm·bər·ɪŋ) *n.* numeración.
numberless ('nʌm·bər·ləs) *adj.* sin número; innumerable.
numeral ('nu·mər·əl) *adj.* numeral. —*n.* número.
numerate ('nu·məˌreit) *v.t.* nu-

merar. —**numeration,** *n.* numeración.
numerator ('nu·mə,rei·tər) *n.* numerador.
numerical (nu'mɛr·ɪ·kəl) *adj.* numérico.
numerology (,nu·mə'ral·ə·dʒi) *n.* numerología. —**numerologist,** *n.* numerólogo.
numerous ('nu·mər·əs) *adj.* numeroso. —**numerousness,** *n.* numerosidad.
numismatics (,nu·mɪs'mæt·ɪks) *n.* numismática. —**numismatic,** *adj.* numismático. —**numismatist** (nu·'mɪs·mə·tɪst) *n.* numismático.
numskull ('nʌm,skʌl) *n.* zoquete; zote.
nun (nʌn) *n.* monja; religiosa. —**nunnery,** *n.* convento de monjas.
nuncio ('nʌn·ʃi·o) *n.* nuncio.
nuptial ('nʌp·ʃəl) *adj.* nupcial. —**nuptials,** *n.pl.* nupcias.
nurse (nʌɹs) *n.* **1,** (child's attendant) niñera; ama. **2,** (one who tends the sick) enfermero (*fem.* enfermera). **3,** (wet nurse) nodriza. —*v.t.* **1,** (take care of) cuidar; cuidar de. **2,** (suckle) amamantar; dar de mamar. **3,** (nourish; foster) criar; alimentar. **4,** (drink slowly) tomar *o* beber con calma; beber despacio.
nursing ('nʌɹs·ɪŋ) *n.* professión de enfermera *o* enfermero. —**nursing home,** clínica para convalecientes *o* ancianos.
nursemaid *n.* niñera.
nursery ('nʌɹ·sə·ri) *n.* **1,** (children's room) cuarto de los niños; cuarto de juegos. **2,** (place where plants or animals are raised) criadero; vivero. **3,** (place where children are cared for) guardería.
nurture ('nʌɹ·tʃər) *v.t.* **1,** (feed) alimentar. **2,** (rear; train) criar; educar.
nut (nʌt) *n.* **1,** (fruit) nuez. **2,** *mech.* tuerca. **3,** *slang* (head) cabeza. **4,** *slang* (fixed expenses) gastos fijos. **5,** *slang* (lunatic; eccentric) chiflado; loco.
nutcracker *n.* cascanueces.
nutmeg ('nʌt,mɛg) *n.* nuez moscada.
nutria ('nu·tri·ə) *n.* nutria.
nutrient ('nu·tri·ənt) *adj.* nutritivo; alimenticio. —*n.* alimento; nutrimento.
nutriment ('nu·trɪ·mənt) *n.* nutrimento; alimento.
nutrition (nu'trɪʃ·ən) *n.* nutrición. —**nutritional,** *adj.* de nutrición; nutritivo. —**nutritious,** *adj.* nutritivo; alimenticio.
nutritive ('nu·trə·tɪv) *adj.* nutritivo; alimenticio.
nuts (nʌts) *adj., slang* chiflado; loco. —*interj.* ¡cuernos!
nutshell ('nʌt,ʃɛl) *n.* cáscara de nuez. —**in a nutshell,** en una palabra; en pocas palabras.
nutty ('nʌt·i) *adj.* **1,** (tasting of nuts) que sabe a nueces. **2,** (full of nuts) lleno de nueces. **3,** *slang* (lunatic; eccentric) chiflado; loco.
nuzzle ('nʌz·əl) *v.t. & i.* (rub with the nose) frotar la nariz (contra); hocicar. —*v.i.* (nestle; snuggle) acurrucarse; *Amer.* aparragarse.
nylon ('nai·lan) *n.* nilón.
nymph (nɪmf) *n.* ninfa.
nymphomania (,nɪm·fə'mei·ni·ə) *n.* ninfomanía; fiebre uterina. —**nymphomaniac** (-æk) *n.* ninfomaníaca.

O

O, o (oː) decimoquinta letra del alfabeto inglés. —*n.* cero. —*interj.* ¡oh!
o- (o) *prefijo, var. de* **ob-** *ante* m: omit, omitir.
oaf (of) *n.* bobo; bobalicón. —**oafish,** *adj.* lerdo; torpe.
oak (ok) *n.* roble. —**oaken,** *adj.* de roble. —**evergreen oak,** encina. —**oak grove,** robledal; robledo.
oakum ('o·kəm) *n.* estopa.
oar (oːr) *n.* remo. —*v.i.* remar. —*v.t.* mover a remo. —**oar blade,** pala de remo. —**oar stroke,** remada.
oarlock *n.* chumacera.
oarsman ('oːrz·mən) *n.* [*pl.* **-men**] remero.
oasis (o'ei·sɪs) *n.* [*pl.* **-ses** (siːz)] oasis.
oat (ot) *n., usu.pl.* avena. —**oaten,** *adj.* de avena. —**feel one's oats,** *slang* darse importancia; sentirse otra persona. —**sow one's wild**

oats, *slang* calaverear; correrla; correr sus mocedades.
oath (oθ) *n.* [*pl.* **oaths** (oðz)] juramento. —**take (an) oath,** prestar juramento; jurar.
oatmeal *n.* avena; harina de avena.
ob- (ab; əb) *prefijo* ob-. **1,** hacia; mirando hacia: *oblique,* oblicuo. **2,** en contra de; opuesto: *object,* objetar. **3,** sobre: *observe,* observar. **4,** al revés: *obovoid,* obovoide.
obdurate ('ab·djə·rət) *adj.* **1,** (obstinate) obstinado; terco. **2,** (hardhearted) duro; empedernido. —**obduracy,** *n.* obstinación; terquedad.
obedient (o'bi·di·ənt) *adj.* obediente. —**obedience,** *n.* obediencia.
obeisance (o'bei·səns) *n.* cortesía; reverencia.
obelisk ('ab·ə·lɪsk) *n.* obelisco.
obese (o'bis) *adj.* obeso. —**obesity,** *n.* obesidad.
obey (o'bei) *v.t. & i.* obedecer.
obfuscate (ob'fʌs·keit) *v.t.* ofuscar. —**obfuscation,** *n.* ofuscación.
obituary (o'bɪtʃ·u,ɛr·i) *n.* obituario; necrología. —*adj.* necrológico.
object ('ab·dʒɪkt) *n.* **1,** (material thing) objeto. **2,** (person or thing aimed at) objeto; objetivo. **3,** (purpose; aim) objetivo. **4,** *gram.* complemento.
object (əb'dʒɛkt) *v.i.* oponerse. —*v.t.* objetar.
objection (ab'dʒɛk·ʃən) *n.* objeción; reparo.
objectionable (ab'dʒɛk·ʃən·ə·bəl) *adj.* **1,** (censurable) reprobable; censurable. **2,** (unpleasant) molesto; incómodo.
objective (ab'dʒɛk·tɪv) *n. & adj.* objetivo. —**objectivity** (,ab·dʒɛk·'tɪv·ə·ti) *n.* objetividad. —**objective case,** caso acusativo.
oblate ('ab·let) *adj., geom.* achatado (por los polos).
oblation (ab'lei·ʃən) *n.* oblación.
obligate ('ab·lə,geit) *v.t.* obligar. —**obligation,** *n.* obligación.
obligatory (ab'lɪg·ə,tor·i) *adj.* obligatorio.
oblige (ə'blaidʒ) *v.t.* **1,** (bind; compel) obligar; forzar. **2,** (treat; regale) obsequiar. **3,** (do a favor for) complacer. —**obliging,** *adj.* servicial; solícito; atento. —**much obliged,** muy agradecido.
oblique (ə'blik) *adj.* **1,** (slanting) oblicuo; inclinado. **2,** (indirect) indirecto; torcido. —**obliquity** (ə'blɪk·wə·ti) *n.* oblicuidad.
obliterate (ə'blɪt·ə,reit) *v.t.* **1,** (blot out) borrar. **2,** (destroy) arrasar; destruir. —**obliteration,** *n.* destrucción.
oblivion (ə'blɪv·i·ən) *n.* olvido. —**oblivious,** *adj.* inconsciente; insensible.
oblong ('ab·lɔŋ) *adj.* oblongo. —*n.* figura oblonga.
obloquy ('ab·lə·kwi) *n.* **1,** (abusive language) vituperación; vejámenes (*pl.*). **2,** (disgrace) deshonra; baldón; mala fama.
obnoxious (əb'nak·ʃəs) *adj.* odioso; ofensivo; molesto. —**obnoxiousness,** *n.* odiosidad.
oboe ('o·bo) *n.* oboe. —**oboist,** *n.* oboe.
obscene (əb'si:n) *adj.* obsceno. —**obscenity** (əb'sɛn·ə·ti) *n.* obscenidad.
obscure (əb'skjʊr) *adj.* obscuro. —*v.t.* **1,** (darken; make dim) obscurecer. **2,** (conceal) ocultar. —**obscurity,** *n.* obscuridad.
obsequious (əb'si·kwi·əs) *adj.* obsequioso. —**obsequiousness,** *n.* obsequiosidad.
observable (əb'zʌɹ·və·bəl) *adj.* observable.
observance (əb'zʌɹ·vəns) *n.* **1,** (compliance) observancia; acatamiento. **2,** (custom) costumbre; práctica. **3,** (ceremony) ceremonia. **4,** (celebration) celebración.
observant (əb'zʌɹ·vənt) *adj.* observador.
observation (,ab·zər'vei·ʃən) *n.* observación.
observatory (ab'zʌɹ·və·tor·i) *n.* observatorio.
observe (əb'zʌɹv) *v.t.* **1,** (watch; look at) observar. **2,** (celebrate) celebrar. **3,** (keep, as mourning, silence, etc.) guardar. —**observer,** *n.* observador.
obsess (əb'sɛs) *v.t.* obsesionar. —**obsession** (əb'sɛʃ·ən) *n.* obsesión. —**obsessive,** *adj.* obsesivo.
obsidian (ab'sɪd·i·ən) *n.* obsidiana.
obsolescent (,ab·sə'lɛs·ənt) *adj.* que va cayendo en desuso; que va desapareciendo. —**obsolescence,** *n.* desuso.

obsolete (ˌab·səˈlit) *adj.* desusado; anticuado. —**obsoleteness,** *n.* desuso.
obstacle (ˈab·stə·kəl) *n.* obstáculo.
obstetrics (əbˈstɛt·rɪks) *n.* obstetricia; tocología. —**obstetric; obstetrical,** *adj.* obstétrico. —**obstetrician** (ˌab·stəˈtrɪʃ·ən) *n.* tocólogo.
obstinate (ˈab·stɪ·nət) *adj.* obstinado. —**obstinacy,** *n.* obstinación.
obstreperous (əbˈstrɛp·ər·əs) *adj.* estrepitoso; bullicioso; ruidoso. —**obstreperousness,** *n.* lo ruidoso; lo estrepitoso.
obstruct (əbˈstrʌkt) *v.t.* obstruir —**obstruction** (əbˈstrʌk·ʃən) *n.* obstrucción. —**obstructive,** *adj.* obstructor; obstructivo.
obstructionism (abˈstrʌk·ʃən·ɪz·əm) *n.* obstruccionismo. —**obstructionist,** *adj.* & *n.* obstruccionista.
obtain (əbˈtein) *v.t.* obtener; adquirir; conseguir. —*v.i.* prevalecer; estar en vigor *o* en boga. —**obtainable,** *adj.* obtenible.
obtrude (əbˈtruːd) *v.t.* **1,** (push out; thrust forward) empujar *o* proyectar hacia afuera. **2,** (intrude) meter; entremeter. —*v.i.* entremeterse; hacer intrusión; ser importuno. —**obtrusive** (əbˈtru·sɪv) *adj.* intruso; importuno.
obtuse (əbˈtus) *adj.* obtuso. —**obtuseness,** *n.* calidad de obtuso.
obverse (ˈab·vʌɹs) *n.* anverso. —*adj.* (abˈvʌɹs) del anverso.
obviate (ˈab·viˌeit) *v.t.* obviar.
obvious (ˈab·vi·əs) *adj.* obvio; evidente. —**obviousness,** *n.* lo obvio; lo evidente.
oc- (ak; ək) *prefijo, var. de* **ob-** *ante* c: *occur,* ocurrir.
occasion (əˈkei·ʒən) *n.* ocasión. —*v.t.* causar; ocasionar; dar ocasión para. —**on occasion,** a veces; de vez en cuando. —**on the occasion of,** con ocasión de. —**rise to the occasion,** ponerse a la altura de las circunstancias.
occasional (əˈkei·ʃə·nəl) *adj.* **1,** (occurring now and then) raro; poco frecuente. **2,** (of or befitting an occasion) de *o* para la ocasión. **3,** (casual; fortuitous) ocasional; imprevisto. **4,** (random; odd) suelto. —**occasionally,** *adv.* de vez en cuando.
occident (ˈak·sɪ·dənt) *n.* occidente. —**occidental** (-ˈdɛn·təl) *adj.* occidental.
occiput (ˈak·sɪˌpʌt) *n.* occipucio. —**occipital** (akˈsɪp·ə·təl) *adj.* occipital.
occlude (əˈkluːd) *v.t.* ocluir. —**occlusion** (əˈklu·ʒən) *n.* oclusión. —**occlusive** (əˈklu·sɪv) *adj.* oclusivo.
occult (aˈkʌlt) *adj.* oculto. —**occultism,** *n.* ocultismo.
occultation (ˌak·ʌlˈtei·ʃən) *n.* ocultación.
occupancy (ˈak·jə·pən·si) *n.* tenencia; ocupación.
occupant (ˈak·jə·pənt) *n.* **1,** (one that occupies) ocupante. **2,** (tenant) inquilino.
occupation (ˌak·jəˈpei·ʃən) *n.* ocupación. —**occupational,** *adj.* relativo a una ocupación *o* empleo. —**occupational hazards,** gajes del oficio.
occupy (ˈak·jə·pai) *v.t.* ocupar. —**be occupied with** *o* **in,** ocuparse de *o* en; estar ocupado con.
occur (əˈkʌɹ) *v.i.* **1,** (happen) ocurrir; acontecer; suceder. **2,** (exist; be found) existir; encontrarse. **3,** (come to mind) ocurrírsele a uno.
occurrence (əˈkʌɹ·əns) *n.* **1,** (happening) acontecimiento; suceso; ocurrencia. **2,** (appearance; presence) presencia; aparición.
ocean (o·ʃən) *n.* océano. —**oceanic** (ˌo·ʃiˈæn·ɪk) *adj.* oceánico.
oceanography (ˌo·ʃi·əˈnag·rə·fi) *n.* oceanografía. —**oceanographic** (-nəˈgræf·ɪk) *adj.* oceanográfico. —**oceanographer,** *n.* oceanógrafo.
ocelot (ˈo·səˌlat; ˈas·ə-) *n.* ocelote.
ocher *también,* **ochre** (ˈo·kər) *n.* ocre.
-ock (ak; ək) *sufijo, formando diminutivos: hillock,* montículo.
o'clock (əˈklak) *adv.* por *o* según el reloj. —**(it is) one o'clock; (it is) two o'clock,** *etc.,* (es) la una; (son) las dos, *etc.*
octa- (ak·tə) *prefijo, var. de* **octo-:** *octagon,* octágono.
octagon (ˈak·təˌgan) *n.* octágono. —**octagonal** (akˈtæg·ə·nəl) *adj.* octagonal.
octahedron (ˌak·təˈhi·drən) *n.* octaedro. —**octahedral,** *adj.* octaédrico.

octane ('ak·tein) *n.* octano.
octant ('ak·tənt) *n.* octante.
octave ('ak·tɪv) *n.* octava.
octavo (ak'tei·vo) *adj.* en octavo. —*n.* tamaño de octavo; libro en octavo.
octet (ak'tɛt) *n.* octeto.
octillion (ak'tɪl·jən) *n.* (*U.S.*) mil cuatrillones; (*Brit.*) un millón de septillones; octillón.
octo- (ak·tə) *también,* **oct-** (akt) *ante vocal; prefijo* octo-; oct-; ocho: *octogenarian,* octogenario; *octillion,* octillón.
October (ak'to·bər) *n.* octubre.
octogenarian (ˌak·tə·dʒə'nɛr·i·ən) *n.* & *adj.* octogenario.
octopus ('ak·tə·pəs) *n.* [*pl.* **-puses** *o* **-pi** (pai)] pulpo.
octoroon (ˌak·tə'ruːn) *n.* & *adj.* ochavón.
octuple (ak'tu·pəl; 'ak·tʊ-) *adj.* & *n.* óctuple; óctuplo. —*v.t.* octuplicar. —*v.i.* octuplicarse.
ocular ('ak·jə·lər) *adj.* ocular.
oculist ('ak·jə·lɪst) *n.* oculista.
oculo- (ak·jə·lo) *prefijo* oculo-; ojo: *oculomotor,* oculomotor.
odd (aːd) *adj.* **1,** (strange) raro; extraño. **2,** (not paired) suelto; sin pareja. **3,** (not even) impar. **4,** (little more) y pico; y tantos; y poco más. **5,** (extra) extra; sobrante. **6,** (occasional) ocasional; incidental. —**oddness,** *n.* rareza; lo raro.
oddity ('ad·ə·ti) *n.* **1,** (strangeness) rareza; lo raro. **2,** (strange person or thing) persona *o* cosa rara; curiosidad; rareza.
odds (aːdz) *n.pl.* **1,** (advantage) ventaja (*sing.*). **2,** (probability) probabilidades. **3,** (superiority) superioridad (*sing.*); fuerzas superiores. —**at odds,** en desacuerdo; en pugna. —**by (all) odds,** por seguro; con mucho. —**give odds,** dar ventaja; dar tantos de ventaja. —**odds and ends,** cosas sueltas; zarandajas.
ode (oːd) *n.* oda.
-ode (od) *sufijo* **1,** -odo; conducto; vía: *cathode,* cátodo. **2,** -oda; como; a la manera de: *geode,* geoda; *hematode,* hematoda.
odious ('o·di·əs) *adj.* odioso. —**odiousness,** *n.* odiosidad.
odium ('o·di·əm) *n.* odio.
odometer (o'dam·ə·tər) *n.* odómetro.
-odont (o·dant; ə-) *sufijo* -odonte; diente: *macrodont,* macrodonte.
odonto- (o·dan·to; -tə) *también.* **odont-** (o·dant) *ante vocal; prefijo* odonto-; odont-; diente: *odontology,* odontología; *odontalgia,* odontalgia.
odontology (ˌo·dan'tal·ə·dʒi) *n.* odontología. —**odontological** (-tə·'ladʒ·ɪ·kəl) *adj.* odontológico. —**odontologist,** *n.* odontólogo.
odor ('o·dər) *n.* olor.
odoriferous (ˌo·də'rɪf·ər·əs) *adj.* odorífero. —**odoriferousness,** *n.* olor; fragancia.
odorless ('o·dər·ləs) *adj.* inodoro.
odorous ('o·dər·əs) *adj.* oloroso; fragante.
Odyssey ('ad·ə·si) *n.* odisea.
o'er (oːr) *adv.* & *prep., poet.* = **over.**
of (ʌv) *prep.* de; (*in telling time*) para: *twenty of twelve,* veinte para las doce.
of- (əf) *prefijo, var. de* **ob-** *ante* f: *offend,* ofender.
off (ɔf) *prep.* **1,** (not on; out of) fuera de. **2,** (not fixed to; removed from) despegado de; suelto de. **3,** (out of; from) de. **4,** (coming out from) que sale de. **5,** (close to; adjacent to) cerca de. **6,** free from) libre de; exento de; sin. **7,** (deprived of) privado de. **8,** (not up to the standard of) no a la altura de. **9,** *colloq.* (abstaining from) absteniéndose de; curado de. —*adj.* **1,** (not on; removed) no puesto. **2,** (loose; not attached) suelto; despegado. **3,** (not in operation) apagado; desconectado. **4,** (cut off) cortado. **5,** (canceled; suspended) suspendido. **6,** (on the way) en marcha; en camino. **7,** (absent) ausente; fuera. **8,** (less; smaller; fewer) menor; menos. **9,** (more remote; further) más lejano; más remoto. **10,** (wrong; in error) errado; equivocado. **11,** (not usual) raro; extraordinario. **12,** (free; devoted to leisure) libre. **13,** *colloq.* (below par) flojo; anormal; destemplado. —*adv.* **1,** (away) fuera; afuera. **2,** (so as to end entirely) del todo; enteramente. **3,** (from here, or a specified place) de aquí; de allí. **4,** (from the present, or a specified time) faltando (cierto tiempo) para: *Christmas is ten days off,* Faltan diez días para Navidad.

—*interj.* ¡fuera!; ¡afuera! —**be off,** salir; irse. —**off and on,** de cuando en cuando; de vez en cuando. —**off with . . . ,** a fuera (con) . . . —**off with you,** ¡fuera!; ¡márchate!

offal ('ɔf·əl) *n.* desechos (*pl.*); desperdicios (*pl.*); basura; bazofia.

offcast *adj.* & *n.* = **castoff.**

off-center *adj.* descentrado; eccéntrico.

off-chance *n.* casualidad; improbabilidad. —*adj.* improbable.

off-color *adj.* **1,** (defective in color) de mal color; de matiz imperfecto. **2,** (risqué) verde; obsceno; de mal tono.

offend (ə'fɛnd) *v.t.* ofender. —*v.i.* **1,** (be offensive) ofender. **2,** (transgress) pecar; transgredir. —**offender,** *n.* culpable; delincuente.

offense (ə'fɛns) *n.* **1,** (transgression) falta; pecado; transgresión. **2,** (affront) ofensa; afrenta. **3,** (attack) ataque; acometida. **4,** (attacking side) atacante. —**give offense,** ofender. —**no offense,** sin querer ofender. —**take offense,** ofenderse.

offensive (ə'fɛn·sɪv) *adj.* ofensivo. —*n.* ofensiva. —**offensiveness,** *n.* lo ofensivo.

offer ('af·ər; 'ɔf-) *v.t.* **1,** (present; proffer) ofrecer. **2,** (propose; suggest) proponer; presentar; sugerir. **3,** (give, as violence, resistance, etc.) ofrecer. **4,** (make an offering of) ofrendar. **5,** (show intention of) ofrecerse a; hacer ademán de. —*v.i.* **1,** (present itself; occur) ofrecerse; presentarse. **2,** (make an offering) hacer ofrenda. —*n.* oferta.

offering ('af·ər·ɪŋ; 'ɔf-) *n.* **1,** (act of offering; thing offered) ofrecimiento; presentación. **2,** (tribute; contribution) ofrenda.

offertory ('af·ər,tor·i; 'ɔf-) *n.* ofertorio.

offhand *adv.* sin mayor estudio. —*adj.* **1,** (impromptu) poco estudiado; improvisado. **2,** (casual; informal) casual; informal; sin ceremonia.

office ('af·ɪs; 'ɔf-) *n.* **1,** (position) cargo. **2,** (place of business) oficina; despacho. **3,** (service; duty) oficio; función. **4,** *usu.pl.* (influence) oficios. **5,** (administrative body) dirección; ministerio. —**office worker,** oficinista.

officeholder *n.* funcionario; empleado público.

officer ('af·ə·sər; 'ɔf-) *n.* **1,** (official) oficial; funcionario. **2,** *mil.* oficial. **3,** (policeman) agente de policía; guardia.

official (ə'fɪʃ·əl) *n.* oficial; funcionario. —*adj.* oficial.

officialdom (ə'fɪʃ·əl·dəm) *n.* las autoridades; burocracia.

officiate (ə'fɪʃ·i·eit) *v.i.* oficiar.

officious (ə'fɪʃ·əs) *adj.* oficioso; entremetido. —**officiousness,** *n.* oficiosidad.

offing ('ɔf·ɪŋ) *n.* lontananza. —**in the offing,** cerca; a la vista.

offish ('ɔf·ɪʃ) *adj., colloq.* reservado; huraño. —**offishness,** *n.* reserva.

off-key *adj.* discordante.

off-limits *adj.* prohibido.

offset ('ɔf·sɛt) *n.* **1,** (compensation) compensación. **2,** (offshoot) ramal. **3,** (perpendicular distance) distancia perpendicular. **4,** *mech.* codo. **5,** *print.* offset. —*v.t.* (ɔf'sɛt) **1,** (compensate) compensar. **2,** (displace, as from the straight line) desplazar.

offshoot *n.* rama; ramal.

offshore (ɔf'ʃoːr) *adj.* & *adv.* a distancia de la costa; mar afuera.

offspring *n.* descendiente; progenie; vástago.

often ('ɔf·ən) *adv.* frecuentemente; muchas veces: a menudo. *También, poet.,* **oft** (ɔft).

oftentimes *adv.* = **often.** *También,* **ofttimes.**

ogive ('o·dʒaiv) *n.* ojiva.

ogle ('o·gəl) *v.t.* & *i.* mirar con cariño *o* deseo; ojear. —*n.* ojeada; mirada.

ogre ('o·gər) *n.* ogro.

oh (oː) *interj.* ¡oh!

ohm (oːm) *n.* ohmio; ohm.

oho (o'hoː) *interj.* ¡aja!

-oid (ɔid) *sufijo* -oide; parecido; semejante: *celluloid,* celuloide.

oil (ɔil) *n.* **1,** (viscous substance) aceite. **2,** *painting* óleo. —*v.t.* **1,** (lubricate) lubricar; aceitar. **2,** *colloq.* (bribe) sobornar; untar la mano a. —**oil can,** aceitera. —**oil painting,** pintura al óleo. —**oil well,** pozo de petróleo.

oilcloth *n.* hule; encerado.

oiler ('ɔi·lər) *n.* **1,** (person or device for lubricating) engrasador. **2,** (ship) barco petrolero.

oilskin *n.* hule.

oily ('ɔi·li) *adj.* **1,** (of, like, or containing oil) aceitoso; oleaginoso. **2,** (greasy) grasoso. **3,** *fig.* (unctuous) untuoso.

ointment (ɔint·mənt) *n.* ungüento.

O. K. ('o'kei) *adv., colloq.* muy bien. —*adj., colloq.,* bueno. —*v.t., colloq.* aprobar. *También,* **okay.**

okra ('o·krə) *n.* quingombó.

-ol (al) *sufijo, quím.* -ol; *forma nombres denotando* alcohol o derivado de fenol: *menthol,* mentol.

old (o:ld) *adj.* **1,** (of great age) viejo. **2,** (of a specified age) de edad. **3,** (ancient) antiguo; viejo; vetusto. **4,** (antique) antiguo. **5,** (former) previo; anterior. **6,** (aged, as wine) añejo. **7,** (antiquated) anticuado; pasado. —*n.* ayer; tiempo pasado. —**of old,** antaño; de antaño. —**How old is he?,** ¿Cuántos años tiene? —**He is ten years old,** Tiene diez años.

old age vejez; ancianidad.

olden ('ol·dən) *adj.* antiguo.

old-fashioned (old'fæʃ·ənd) *adj.* **1,** (holding to the past) chapado a la antigua; anticuado. **2,** (out of style) fuera de moda; pasado de moda.

Old Glory bandera de los Estados Unidos de América.

old hat anticuado.

old maid solterona.

oldness ('old·nəs) *n.* antigüedad.

Old Nick patillas; el Diablo.

oldster ('old·stər) *n., colloq.* viejo; *fem.* vieja.

Old Testament Antiguo Testamento.

old-time *adj.* antiguo; del pasado.

Old World Viejo Mundo.

-ole (ol) *sufijo, usado en nombres de ciertos compuestos orgánicos: azole,* azole.

oleaginous (,o·li'ædʒ·ə·nəs) *adj.* oleaginoso.

oleander (,o·li'æn·dər) *n.* adelfa.

oleo- (o·li·o) *prefijo* oleo-; aceite: *oleomargarine,* oleomargarina.

oleomargarine (,o·li·o'mar·dʒə,rin; -rın) *n.* oleomargarina.

olfactory (al'fæk·tə·ri) *adj.* olfatorio.

oligarchy ('al·ə,gar·ki) *n.* oligarquía. —**oligarch** (-,gark) *n.* oligarca. —**oligarchic; oligarchical,** *adj.* oligárquico.

oligo- (al·ə·go) *también,* **olig-** (al·əg) *ante vocal; prefijo* oligo-; olig-; poco; escaso: *oligarchy,* oligarquía; *oliguria,* oliguria.

olio ('o·li·o) *n.* **1,** (stew) especie de chanfaina. **2,** (miscellany) miscelánea; mescolanza.

olive ('al·ıv) *n.* **1,** (tree) olivo. **2,** (fruit) aceituna; oliva. **3,** (color) olivo. —*adj.* oliváceo. —**olive branch,** rama de olivo. —**olive grove,** olivar. —**olive oil,** aceite de oliva.

Olympiad (o'lım·pi,æd) *n.* olimpíada.

Olympus (o'lım·pəs) *n.* Olimpo.

Olympic (o'lım·pık) *adj.* olímpico.

-oma (o·mə) *sufijo* -oma; tumor: *fibroma,* fibroma.

ombre ('am·bər) *n.* tresillo; renegado.

omega (o'mi·gə) *n.* omega.

omelet ('am·lıt) *n.* tortilla.

omen ('o·mən) *n.* augurio; agüero; presagio.

ominous ('am·ı·nəs) *adj.* ominoso. —**ominousness,** *n.* ominosidad.

omission (o'mıʃ·ən) *n.* omisión.

omit (o'mıt) *v.t.* omitir.

omni- (am·nə; -nı) *prefijo* omni-; todo: *omnipotent,* omnipotente.

omnibus ('am·nə,bʌs) *n.* **1,** (vehicle) ómnibus; autobús; *W.I.* guagua. **2,** (anthology) antología; colección. —*adj.* general.

omnipotent (am'nıp·ə·tənt) *adj.* omnipotente. —**omnipotence,** *n.* omnipotencia.

omnipresent (,am·nə'prɛz·ənt) *adj.* omnipresente. —**omnipresence,** *n.* omnipresencia.

omniscient (am'nıʃ·ənt) *adj.* omnisciente. —**omniscience,** *n.* omnisciencia.

omnivorous (am'nıv·ə·rəs) *adj.* omnívoro.

on (an) *prep.* **1,** (on top of) en; sobre; encima de. **2,** (upon) en. **3,** (in) en. **4,** (by; at) a: *on the right,* a la derecha. **5,** (close to; beside) cerca de; al lado de. **6,** (toward) sobre; hacia. **7,** (against) contra. **8,** (by means of) por: *on the telephone,* por teléfono, **9,** (in the condition or manner of) a; en: *on half pay,* a media paga; *on pur-*

pose, a propósito; *on sale,* en venta. **10,** (about; concerning) sobre; de; acerca de. **11,** (on the ground or basis of) por; a través de; basado en. **12,** (at the moment of) a: *They greeted us on our arrival,* Nos festejaron a nuestra llegada. **13,** (during) durante; en. **14,** (for the purpose of) a; para: *He went on an errand.* Fue a un mandado. **15,** (in addition to) sobre: *victory on victory,* victoria sobre victoria. **16,** (among) en: *on the committee,* en la comisión. **17,** (indicating risk or liability) bajo; so: *on pain of death,* bajo (*o* so) pena de muerte. **18,** *colloq.* (at the expense of) a costa de; por cuenta de. **19,** *indicando la fecha,* **on** *no se expresa en español: on the fourth of July,* el cuatro de julio; *on Sunday,* el domingo; *on Sundays,* los domingos. **20,** *con el ger.* (upon; at the time of) al (+ *inf.*): *on arriving,* al llegar. —*adv.* **1,** (forward) adelante; hacia adelante. **2,** (continuously) continuadamente; sin parar. **3,** (henceforth) en adelante. —*adj.* **1,** (in place) puesto. **2,** (in operation or use) encendido; prendido; conectado. **3,** (working; functioning) trabajando; funcionando. **4,** (in progress) en marcha; corriendo; realizándose; pasando. —**and so on,** y así sucesivamente; etcétera. —**on and off,** a intervalos; intermitentemente. —**on and on,** sin parar; continuamente; sin descanso. —**on to,** *slang* al tanto de; enterado de. —**be on to someone,** *slang* tenerlo calado *o* fichado.

-on (an) *sufijo* -ón; *forma nombres denotando* **1,** *física* partículas subatómicas: *proton,* protón. **2,** *quím.* gases inertes: *argon,* argón. **3,** *var. de* **-one.**

once (wʌns) *adv.* **1,** (one time) una vez. **2,** (formerly) una vez; en otro tiempo. —*conj.* una vez que. —*n.* vez; una vez. —**all at once, 1,** (all simultaneously) todos a una; todos de una vez. **2,** (suddenly) súbitamente; repentinamente; de pronto. —**at once, 1,** (immediately) inmediatamente; en seguida. **2,** (at the same time) de una vez; a la vez. —**for once,** una vez al menos. —**once and again,** una y otra vez. —**once (and) for all,** por última vez; de una vez (por todos); por fin. —**once in a while,** de vez en cuando; una que otra vez. —**once upon a time,** una vez; tiempo ha.

once-over *n., slang* vistazo; examen rápido.

one (wʌn) *adj.* **1,** (single) un; uno; una. **2,** (any) cierto; un tal. **3,** (some) uno; alguno. **4,** (same) igual; mismo. **5,** (united) uno; uno solo. **6,** (only; sole) único. —*n.* **1,** (number) uno. **2,** (single person or thing) uno; una. —*pron.* uno; una. —**all one, 1,** (united or agreed) todos uno. **2,** (of no significance) todo lo mismo. —**at one,** de acuerdo. —**one and all,** todo el mundo. —**one another,** el uno al otro; los unos a los otros. —**one by one,** uno por uno; uno a uno. —**one's self** = **oneself.**

-one (on) *sufijo, quím.* -ona; *usado para formar nombres de cetonas: acetone,* acetona.

one-horse *adj.* **1,** (using one horse) de un caballo. **2,** *colloq.* (unimportant) de poca monta. —**one-horse town,** villorrio.

oneness ('wʌn·nəs) *n.* unidad.

onerous ('an·ər·əs) *adj.* oneroso. —**onerousness,** *n.* onerosidad.

oneself (wʌn'sɛlf) *pron.pers.* uno; uno mismo. —*pron.refl.* **1,** (*complemento directo o indirecto de verbo*) se: *One washes oneself,* Uno se lava; *One puts it on oneself,* Uno se lo pone. **2,** (*complemento de prep.*) sí; sí mismo; uno mismo: *One buys it for oneself,* Uno lo compra para sí. —**be oneself,** estar sobre sí; estar en sus cabales. —**by oneself,** solo; sin ayuda; sin compañía. —**to oneself,** para sí: *One says to oneself, "It cannot be,"* Uno dice para sí: no puede ser. —**with oneself,** consigo.

onesided *adj.* **1,** (unequal) desigual. **2,** (partial) parcial; injusto. **3,** (unilateral) unilateral.

one-track *adj.* **1,** (having one track) de una vía. **2,** *colloq.* (restricted) limitado; que insiste en una sola cosa.

one-way *adj.* de dirección única; de un solo sentido.

onion ('ʌn·jən) *n.* cebolla. —**know one's onions,** *slang* conocérselas; sabérselas todas.

onionskin ('ʌn·jən,skɪn) *n.* papel cebolla.

onlooker *n.* espectador; observador.

only ('on·li) *adj.* único; solo. —*adv.* tan sólo; solamente; únicamente; no más que. —*conj.* sólo que; excepto que. —**only begotten,** unigénito.

onoma- (an·ə·mə) *prefijo* onoma-; nombre: *onomatopoeia,* onomatopeya.

onomatopoeia (ˌan·əˌmæt·ə·'pi·a) *n.* onomatopeya. —**onomatopoeic; onomatopoetic** (-po'ɛt·ɪk) *adj.* onomatopéyico.

onrush *n.* embestida; arremetida.

onset *n.* **1,** (attack) ataque. **2,** (start) comienzo; principio.

onslaught ('anˌslɔt) *n.* ataque furioso; arremetida.

onto ('an·tu) *prep.* encima de; sobre; en.

onto- (an·tə) *prefijo* onto-; ser; existencia: *ontogeny,* ontogenia.

ontology (an'tal·ə·dʒi) *n.* ontología. —**ontological** (ˌan·tə·'ladʒ·ɪ·kəl) *adj.* ontológico. —**ontologist,** *n.* ontólogo.

onus ('o·nəs) *n.* carga; responsabilidad.

onward ('an·wərd) *adj.* & *adv.* hacia adelante. *Adv. también* **onwards.**

onyx ('an·ɪks) *n.* ónix; ónice.

oö- (o·ə) *prefijo* oo-; huevo: *oögenesis,* oogénesis.

oodles ('u·dəlz) *n.pl., colloq.* montones.

oomph (umf) *n., colloq.* atracción física; atractivo.

ooze (uːz) *n.* **1,** (exudation) exudación. **2,** (mud; slime) légamo; fango; cieno. —*v.t.* & *i.* exudar; rezumar.

oozy ('u·zi) *adj.* **1,** (exuding moisture) que exuda *o* rezuma. **2,** (slimy) legamoso; viscoso.

op- (əp) *prefijo, var. de* **ob-** *ante* p: *oppress,* oprimir.

opacity (o'pæs·ə·ti) *n.* opacidad.

opal ('o·pəl) *n.* ópalo.

opalescent (ˌo·pə'lɛs·ənt) *adj.* opalescente. —**opalescence,** *n.* opalescencia.

opaline ('o·pə·lɪn) *adj.* opalino.

opaque (o'peik) *adj.* opaco.

-ope (op) *sufijo* -ope, *denotando* persona con determinado estado o defecto del ojo: *myope,* miope.

open ('o·pən) *adj.* **1,** (not closed) abierto. **2,** (exposed) expuesto. **3,** (receptive) receptivo; susceptible. —*v.t.* abrir. —*v.i.* abrir; abrirse. —*n.* **1,** (outdoors) aire libre; campo raso *o* abierto. **2,** (public view) atención pública. —**in the open,** al descubierto. —**open air,** aire libre.

open-and-shut *adj.* evidente; obvio en extremo.

opener ('o·pən·ər) *n.* abridor.

open-eyed *adj.* con los ojos abiertos.

open-handed *adj.* generoso; liberal.

open-hearted *adj.* franco; sincero.

open-hearth furnace horno de hogar abierto.

opening ('o·pən·ɪŋ) *n.* **1,** (act of opening) apertura. **2,** (hole; gap) abertura. **3,** (beginning) comienzo; inauguración; apertura. **4,** (opportunity) oportunidad; ocasión. **5,** (vacancy) vacante. **6,** *theat.* estreno. **7,** *chess* apertura. —*adj.* **1,** (that opens) abridor; que abre *o* se abre. **2,** (beginning; first) de estreno; primero.

open-minded *adj.* amplio; razonable; sin prejuicios. —**open-mindedness,** *n.* amplitud; falta de prejuicios.

open-mouthed ('o·pənˌmauðd) *adj.* boquiabierto.

openness ('o·pən·nəs) *n.* franqueza; sinceridad; candor.

open shop taller de unión voluntaria; taller abierto *o* franco.

openwork *n.* calado.

opera ('ap·ər·ə) *n.* ópera. —**operatic** (-'æt·ɪk) *adj.* operático. —**opera glass; opera glasses,** anteojos de teatro.

operable ('ap·ər·ə·bəl) *adj.* operable.

operate ('ap·əˌreit) *v.i.* operar. —*v.t.* hacer funcionar; manejar; dirigir. —**operate on,** operar. —**operating room,** quirófano; sala de operaciones.

operation (ˌap·ər'ei·ʃən) *n.* operación. —**operational,** *adj.* operante; funcional. —**in operation,** funcionando; en funcionamiento; operando. —**out of operation,** fuera de comisión; inoperante.

operative ('ap·əˌrei·tɪv; -ər·ə·tɪv) *adj.* **1,** (in operation) operante. **2,** (effective) eficaz; eficiente. **3,** *surg.* operatorio. —*n.* **1,** (worker) operario. **2,** (detective) detective. **3,** (agent) agente.

operator ('ap·əˌrei·tər) *n.* operador; *comm.* empresario; agente.

operetta (ˌap·əˈrɛt·ə) *n.* opereta.
ophthalmic (afˈθæl·mɪk) *adj.* oftálmico.
ophthalmo- (af·θæl·mə) *prefijo* oftalmo-; ojo: *ophthalmology,* oftalmología.
ophthalmology (ˌaf·θəlˈmal·ə·dʒi) *n.* oftalmología. **—ophthalmologist,** *n.* oftalmólogo.
-opia (o·pi·ə) *sufijo* -opía, *indicando* estado o defecto del ojo: *myopia,* miopía.
opiate (ˈo·pi·ət) *n.* opiata; opiato. *—adj.* opiado.
-opic (ap·ɪk) *sufijo* -ope; *forma adjetivos de los nombres terminados en* **-ope** *o* **-opia**: *myopic,* miope.
opine (oˈpain) *v.i.* opinar.
opinion (əˈpɪn·jən) *n.* opinión.
opinionated (əˈpɪn·jəˌnei·tɪd) *adj.* obstinado; testarudo; de opiniones estrechas.
opium (ˈo·pi·əm) *n.* opio.
opossum (oˈpas·əm) *n.* zarigüeya.
opponent (əˈpo·nənt) *n.* adversario; contrincante; antagonista.
opportune (ˌap·ərˈtjuːn) *adj.* oportuno. **—opportuneness,** *n.* oportunidad.
opportunism (ˌap·ərˈtju·nɪz·əm) *n.* oportunismo. **—opportunist,** *n.* oportunista. **—opportunistic,** *adj.* oportunista.
opportunity (ˌap·ərˈtju·nə·ti) *n.* oportunidad.
oppose (əˈpoːz) *v.t.* **1,** (set against) oponer. **2,** (object to; contend against) oponerse a. *—v.i.* oponerse.
opposite (ˈap·ə·zɪt) *adj.* opuesto; de enfrente. *—adv.* al revés; en dirección opuesta. *—prep.* al lado opuesto de. *—n.* contrario; opuesto.
opposition (ˌap·əˈzɪʃ·ən) *n.* oposición. *—adj.* oposicionista. **—oppositionist,** *n.* oposicionista.
oppress (əˈprɛs) *v.t.* oprimir. **—oppression** (əˈprɛʃ·ən) *n.* opresión. **—oppressive,** *adj.* opresivo; opresor. **—oppressor,** *n.* opresor.
opprobrious (əˈpro·bri·əs) *adj.* oprobioso. **—opprobrium** (-əm) *n.* oprobio.
opt (apt) *v.i.* optar.
optic (ˈap·tɪk) *adj.* óptico. *—n., usu.pl., colloq.* ojos. **—optical,** *adj.* óptico.
optician (apˈtɪʃ·ən) *n.* óptico.
optics (ˈap·tɪks) *n.* óptica.
optimal (ˈap·tɪ·məl) *adj.* óptimo.
optimism (ˈap·tə·mɪz·əm) *n.* optimismo. **—optimist,** *n.* optimista. **—optimistic,** *adj.* optimista.
optimum (ˈap·tɪ·məm) *adj.* óptimo. *—n.* [*pl.* **-mums** *o* **-ma** (mə)] punto *o* grado óptimo.
option (ˈap·ʃən) *n.* opción. **—optional,** *adj.* opcional; facultativo.
optometry (apˈtam·ə·tri) *n.* optometría. **—optometer,** *n.* optómetro. **—optometrist,** *n.* optómetra; optometrista.
opulent (ˈap·jə·lənt) *adj.* opulento. **—opulence,** *n.* opulencia.
opus (ˈo·pəs) *n.* obra; composición.
-opy (o·pi) *sufijo, var. de* **-opia.**
or (or) *conj.* o (*also* u *before words beginning with* o *or* ho). **—either . . . or,** o . . . o; ya . . . ya.
-or (ər) *sufijo* -or; *forma nombres denotando* **1,** agente: *instructor,* instructor; *ejector,* eyector. **2,** calidad; condición: *horror,* horror; *languor,* langor.
oracle (ˈar·ə·kəl) *n.* oráculo. **—oracular** (ɔˈræk·jə·lər) *adj.* oracular.
oral (ˈor·əl) *adj.* **1,** (spoken) oral. **2,** (of the mouth) bucal.
-orama (ə·ræm·ə) *sufijo; forma nombres denotando* vista; espectáculo: *diorama,* diorama.
orange (ˈar·ɪndʒ) *n.* **1,** (fruit) naranja. **2,** (tree) naranjo. **3,** (color) color naranja; anaranjado. *—adj.* de naranja; anaranjado. **—orange blossom,** azahar. **—orange grove,** naranjal.
orangeade (ˌor·ɪndʒˈeid) *n.* naranjada.
orangutan (oˈræŋ·juˌtæn) *n.* orangután.
orate (oˈreit) *v.i.* perorar.
oration (oˈrei·ʃən) *n.* discurso; oración.
orator (ˈor·ə·tər) *n.* orador.
oratorical (ˌar·əˈtor·ə·kəl) *adj.* oratorio.
oratorio (ˌor·əˈtor·i·o) *n.* oratorio.
oratory (ˈar·ə·tor·i) *n.* **1,** (eloquence) oratoria. **2,** *eccles.* oratorio.
orb (orb) *n.* orbe.
orbit (ˈor·bɪt) *n.* órbita. **—orbital,** *adj.* orbital.

orchard ('or·tʃərd) *n.* huerto.
orchestra ('or·kɪs·trə) *n.* orquesta. —**orchestral** (or'kɛs·trəl) *adj.* orquestal. —**orchestrate** (-ˌtreit) *v.t.* & *i.* orquestar. —**orchestration,** *n.* orquestación.
orchid ('or·kɪd) *n.* orquídea.
ordain (or'dein) *v.t.* ordenar.
ordeal (or'diːl) *n.* prueba; *hist.* ordalías (*pl.*).
order ('or·dər) *n.* orden. —*v.t.* & *i.* ordenar. —**by order of,** por orden de. —**in order, 1,** (in proper position or state; according to the rules) en orden; como se debe; en regla. **2,** (appropriate; suitable) apropiado; adecuado. —**in order that,** para que; a fin de que. —**in order to,** para; a fin de; con objeto de. —**in short order,** rápido; sin demora. —**on order,** ordenado; pedido. —**on the order of,** del orden de. —**out of order, 1,** (out of proper place) fuera de sitio; fuera de lugar. **2,** (not functioning) malogrado; descompuesto. **3,** (against the rules) fuera de lugar; en desafuero. **4,** (not suitable) inapropiado; fuera de lugar. —**to order,** a la medida; de encargo; por encargo especial.
orderly ('or·dər·li) *adj.* **1,** (tidy) ordenado. **2,** peaceable; law-abiding) pacífico; amante del orden. —*n.* **1,** *mil.* ordenanza. **2,** (hospital aide) enfermero; practicante.
ordinal ('or·də·nəl) *adj.* & *n.* ordinal.
ordinance ('or·də·nəns) *n.* ordenanza.
ordinary ('or·dəˌnɛr·i) *adj.* & *n.* ordinario.
ordinate ('or·dəˌneit) *n.,* *geom.* ordenada.
ordination (ˌor·də'nei·ʃən) *n.* ordenación.
ordnance ('ord·nəns) *n.* **1,** (artillery) artillería. **2,** (armaments) armamento; pertrechos de guerra.
ore (or) *n.* mineral metalífero.
oregano (o'rei·gə·no) *n.* orégano.
organ ('or·gən) *n.* órgano. —**barrel organ,** organillo. —**organ grinder,** organillero.
organdy ('or·gən·di) *n.* organdí.
organic (or'gæn·ɪk) *adj.* orgánico.
organism ('or·gə·nɪz·əm) *n.* organismo.
organist ('or·gə·nɪst) *n.* organista.
organize ('or·gəˌnaiz) *v.t.* organizar. —*v.i.* organizarse. —**organization** (-nɪ'zei·ʃən) *n.* organización. —**organizer,** *n.* organizador.
orgasm ('or·gæz·əm) *n.* orgasmo.
orgy ('or·dʒi) *n.* orgía. —**orgiastic** (-'æs·tɪk) *adj.* orgiástico.
orient ('or·i·ənt) *n.* oriente. —*v.t.* [*también,* **orientate** (-ənˌteit)] orientar. —**orientation** (-ən'tei·ʃən) *n.* orientación.
oriental (ˌor·i'ɛn·təl) *adj.* & *n.* oriental.
orifice ('or·ə·fɪs) *n.* orificio.
origin ('or·ə·dʒɪn) *n.* origen.
original (ə'rɪdʒ·ɪ·nəl) *adj.* & *n.* original. —**originality** (-'næl·ə·ti) *n.* originalidad.
originate (ə'rɪdʒ·ɪ·neit) *v.t.* originar; dar origen a. —*v.i.* originarse; nacer. —**origination,** *n.* origen; principio. —**originator,** *n.* originador; iniciador.
oriole ('or·iˌol) *n.* oriol; oropéndola.
Orion (o'rai·ən) *n.* Orión.
-orium (or·i·əm) *sufijo* -orio; *forma nombres indicando* lugar: *sanatorium,* sanatorio.
orlon ('or·lan) *n.* orlón.
ormolu ('or·məˌlu) *n.* **1,** (gold for gilding) oro molido. **2,** (imitation gold) similor.
ornament ('or·nə·mənt) *n.* ornamento. —*v.t.* ornamentar; adornar. —**ornamental** (-'mɛn·təl) *adj.* ornamental. —**ornamentation** (-mɛn'tei·ʃən) *n.* ornamentación.
ornate (or'neit) *adj.* ornado; adornado; florido. —**ornateness,** *n.* ornato; aparato; vistosidad.
ornitho- (or·nə·θo; -θə) *prefijo* ornito-; pájaro: *ornithology,* ornitología.
ornithology (ˌor·nɪ'θal·ə·dʒi) *n.* ornitología. —**ornithological** (-θə'ladʒ·ɪ·kəl) *adj.* ornitológico. —**ornithologist,** *n.* ornitólogo.
orotund ('or·əˌtʌnd) *adj.* **1,** (sonorous) resonante; sonoro. **2,** (pompous) rimbombante.
orphan ('or·fən) *n.* & *adj.* huérfano. —*v.t.* dejar huérfano. —**orphanhood,** *n.* orfandad.
orphanage ('or·fən·ɪdʒ) *n.* **1,** (orphanhood) orfandad. **2,** (home for orphans) orfanato; orfelinato; asilo de huérfanos.
ortho- (or·θə) *prefijo* orto-; de-

recho; correcto: *orthostatic,* ortostático; *orthodox,* ortodoxo.
orthodontia (ˌor·θəˈdan·ʃə) *n.* ortodoncia.
orthodox (ˈor·θə·daks) *adj.* ortodoxo. —**orthodoxy,** *n.* ortodoxia.
orthogonal (orˈθag·ə·nəl) *adj.* ortogonal.
orthography (orˈθag·rə·fi) *n.* ortografía. —**orthographic** (ˌor·θəˈgræf·ɪk) *adj.* ortográfico.
orthopedic (ˌor·θəˈpi·dɪk) *adj.* ortopédico. —**orthopedics,** *n.* ortopedia. —**orthopedist,** *n.* ortopédico; ortopedista.
ortolan (ˈor·tə·lən) *n.* hortelano.
-ory (or·i; ə·ri) *sufijo* -orio. **1,** *forma adjetivos expresando:* característica; relación; pertenencia: *transitory,* transitorio; *compensatory,* compensatorio. **2,** *forma nombres indicando* lugar: *refectory,* refectorio. **3,** -orio; -oria; *forma nombres indicando* acción; resultado: *interrogatory,* interrogatorio; *trajectory,* trayectoria.
oscillate (ˈas·əˌleit) *v.i.* oscilar. —*v.t.* hacer oscilar. —**oscillating,** *adj.* oscilante; oscilatorio. —**oscillation,** *n.* oscilación. —**oscillator,** *n.* oscilador.
oscillograph (əˈsɪl·əˌgræf) *n.* oscilógrafo.
oscilloscope (əˈsɪl·əˌskop) *n.* osciloscopio.
osculate (ˈas·kjəˌleit) *v.t.* & *i.* besar. —**osculation,** *n.* beso; ósculo.
-ose (os) *sufijo* **1,** -oso; *forma adjetivos denotando* lleno de; caracterizado por: *morbose,* morboso; *bellicose,* belicoso. **2,** *quím.* -osa; carbohidrato: *cellulose,* celulosa.
osier (ˈo·ʒər) *n.* **1,** (plant) mimbrera. **2,** (twig of the plant, used for weaving) mimbre.
-osis (o·sɪs) *sufijo* -osis. **1,** proceso: *osmosis,* ósmosis. **2,** enfermedad: *neurosis,* neurosis.
-osity (ˈas·ə·ti) *sufijo* -osidad; *forma nombres correspondientes a adjetivos terminados en* **-ose** *o* **-ous**: *verbosity,* verbosidad; *generosity,* generosidad.
osmium (ˈaz·mi·əm) *n.* osmio.
osmosis (azˈmo·sɪz) *n.* ósmosis; osmosis. —**osmotic** (azˈmat·ɪk) *adj.* osmótico.
osseous (ˈas·i·əs) *adj.* óseo.
osprey (ˈas·pri) *n.* quebrantahuesos.
ossify (ˈas·ɪˌfai) *v.i.* osificarse. —**ossification** (-fɪˈkei·ʃən) *n.* osificación.
ossuary (ˈas·uˌɛr·i) *n.* osario.
ostensible (asˈtɛn·sə·bəl) *adj.* ostensible.
ostentation (ˌas·tɛnˈtei·ʃən) *n.* ostentación. —**ostentatious** (-ʃəs) *adj.* ostentoso.
osteo- (as·ti·o; -ə) *prefijo* osteo-; hueso: *osteology,* osteología.
osteology (as·tiˈa·lə·dʒi) *n.* osteología. —**osteologist,** *n.* osteólogo.
osteopathy (ˌas·tiˈap·ə·θi) *n.* osteopatía. —**osteopath** (ˈas·ti·ə·ˌpæθ) *n.* osteópata.
ostracize (ˈas·trəˌsaiz) *v.t.* condenar al ostracismo. —**ostracism,** *n.* ostracismo.
ostrich (ˈas·trɪtʃ) *n.* avestruz.
other (ˈʌð·ər) *adj.* & *pron.* otro. —*adv.* más; otra cosa; otramente. —**every other day,** un día sí y otro no; cada dos días. —**other than,** más que; otra cosa que.
otherwise (ˈʌð·ərˌwaiz) *adv.* **1,** (in another manner; differently) de otra manera; de otro modo. **2,** (in all other respects) en todo otro respecto; fuera de eso. **3,** (in other circumstances) en otro caso; de otro modo; de lo contrario. —*adj.* distinto; diferente; otro. —*conj.* de otro modo; si no.
otitis (oˈtai·tɪs) *n.* otitis.
oto- (o·to; -tə) *también,* **ot-** (ot; ət) *ante vocal; prefijo* oto-; ot-; oído: *otology,* otología; *otalgia,* otalgia.
otology (oˈtal·ə·dʒi) *n.* otología. —**otologist,** *n.* otólogo.
otter (at·ər) *n.* nutria.
ottoman (ˈat·ə·mən) *n.* **1,** (divan) otomana. **2,** (footstool) escabel. **3,** *cap.* (Turk) otomano. —*adj.* otomano.
ouch (autʃ) *interj.* ¡huy!; ¡ay!
ought (ɔt) *v.aux.* deber. —*n.* = **naught.**
ouija (ˈwi·dʒə) *n.* tablero usado en prácticas espiritistas.
ounce (auns) *n.* **1,** (unit of weight) onza. **2,** *zool.* onza. **3,** (small amount; bit) pizca.
our (aur) *adj. pos.* nuestro (*fem.* nuestra; *pl.* nuestros, nuestras); de nosotros.
ours (aurs) *pron.poss.* el nuestro; la nuestra; lo nuestro; los nuestros;

las nuestras; el, la, lo, los *o* las de nosotros.

ourselves (aur'sɛlvz) *pron.pers.* nosotros; nosotros mismos. —*pron. refl.* **1,** (*complemento directo o indirecto de verbo*) nos: *We washed ourselves,* Nos lavamos; *We put them on ourselves,* Nos los pusimos. **2,** (*complemento de prep.*) nosotros; nosotros mismos: *We bought it for ourselves,* Lo compramos para nosotros.

-ous (əs) *sufijo* -oso; *forma adjetivos denotando* **1,** lleno de; caracterizado por: *vicious,* vicioso. **2,** *quím., indicando menor valencia que la expresada por* **-ic**: *sulfurous,* sulfuroso.

oust (aust) *v.t.* **1,** (dislodge) desalojar. **2,** (remove, as from office) echar fuera; deponer.

ouster ('aus·tər) *n.* **1,** (dispossession) desahucio; desposeimiento. **2,** (removal, as from office) deposición.

out (aut) *adv.* **1,** (not in; outside) fuera; afuera. **2,** (outward) hacia afuera. **3,** (forward; forth) adelante; hacia adelante. **4,** (henceforth) en adelante. **5,** (to the end; completely) hasta el fin; completamente. **6,** (aloud; loudly) en voz alta. —*adj.* **1,** (not in; away) fuera. **2,** (absent) ausente. **3,** (not in fashion) fuera *o* pasado de moda. **4,** (not in operation) apagado; desconectado; cortado. **5,** (not usual or normal) fuera de lo normal. **6,** (wrong; in error) errado; equivocado. **7,** (missing; suffering loss of) de menos: *I am out ten dollars,* Tengo diez dólares de menos; He perdido diez dólares. —*n.* **1,** (one who is out) el, la, los *o* las de afuera. **2,** *slang* (excuse; escape) salida; excusa; escapatoria. —*prep.* **1,** (out by way of) por. **2,** (out of or from) de. **3,** (out along) por; a lo largo de. —*v.i.* salir a la luz. —*interj.* ¡fuera! —**at outs; on the outs,** peleado; disgustado; en desavenencia. —**out and away,** por mucho; *Amer.* lejos. —**out for,** en busca de; a la busca de. —**out and out,** a fondo; completamente; sin reserva. —**out of, 1,** (from) de. **2,** (away from; beyond) fuera de; más allá de. **3,** (not having; without) sin; falto de. **4,** (by reason of; because of) por. **5,** (arising from; born of) nacido de. —**out of print,** agotado. —**out of stock,** agotado. —**out of touch,** apartado; alejado. —**out to** (win, kill, etc.) empeñado en (ganar, matar, etc.).

out- (aut) *prefijo* **1,** sobre-; que excede; que se destaca: *outstanding,* sobresaliente; *outstrip,* sobrepasar. **2,** externo; exterior; afuera: *outlet,* salida; *outskirts,* afueras. **3,** alejado; que se aleja: *out-of-the-way,* apartado; *outbound,* que sale; *outlaw,* proscrito; bandido.

out-and-out *adj.* completo; cabal; consumado.

outbid (out'bɪd) *v.t.* [**outbid, -bidding**] pujar más que: mejorar.

outboard *adj.* externo a la embarcación; fuera de bordo.

outbound *adj.* que sale; de salida.

outbreak *n.* **1,** (outburst) estallido; ataque violento; acceso. **2,** (riot) tumulto; revuelta. **3,** (epidemic) epidemia.

outbuilding *n.* dependencia; anexo; accesoria.

outburst *n.* explosión; manifestación violenta.

outcast *n.* paria; proscrito.

outclass (aut'klæs) *v.t.* aventajar; superar.

outcome *n.* resultado; consecuencia; desenlace.

outcry *n.* **1,** (shout) grito. **2,** (clamor) griterío; clamor.

outdated (aut'dei·tɪd) *adj.* anticuado; pasado de moda.

outdistance (aut'dɪs·təns) *v.t.* dejar atrás; aventajar.

outdo (aut'du) *v.t.* [*pret.* **outdid;** *p.p.* **outdone**] superar; sobrepujar. —**outdo oneself,** esmerarse; extremarse.

outdoor *adj.* al aire libre. —**outdoors,** *adv.* al aire libre; afuera. —*n.* campo; aire libre.

outer ('au·tər) *adj.* exterior; externo. —**outermost,** *adj.* extremo; más de afuera; superior.

outfit *n.* **1,** (equipment) equipo. **2,** (clothing) conjunto; juego de ropa. **3,** *colloq.* (group) cuerpo; grupo; compañía. —*v.t.* [**outfitted, -fitting**] equipar.

outflank (aut'flænk) *v.t.* flanquear.

outflow *n.* **1,** = **outgo. 2,** (a flowing out) salida; flujo (que sale).

outgo *n.* desembolso; gastos (*pl.*); salida.

outgoing *adj.* **1,** (going out; leaving) que sale; que parte. **2,** (expansive) abierto; expansivo.
outgrow (aut'groː) *v.t.* [**outgrew, -grown, -growing**] **1,** (surpass in growth) crecer más que. **2,** (grow too old for) dejar atrás; superar. **3,** (grow too large for) quedarle a un pequeño: *He has outgrown his shoes,* Los zapatos le quedan pequeños.
outgrowth *n.* **1,** (consequence) consecuencia; efecto; fruto. **2,** (excrescence) excrecencia.
outhouse *n.* retrete; privada.
outing ('aut·ɪŋ) *n.* paseo; excursión; salida.
outlander ('aut,læn·dər) *n.* extranjero.
outlandish (aut'læn·dɪʃ) *adj.* extraño; exótico; ridículo.
outlast (aut'læst) *v.t.* durar más que; sobrevivir a.
outlaw ('aut·lɔ) *n.* bandido; proscrito. —*v.t.* proscribir. —**outlawry,** *n.* bandidaje.
outlay ('aut·lei) *n.* desembolso; gasto; expendio.
outlet ('aut·lɛt) *n.* **1,** (passage for exit) orificio de salida; escape; desagüe. **2,** *electricity* enchufe. **3,** *comm.* salida.
outline ('aut·lain) *n.* **1,** (shape) contorno; perfil; silueta. **2,** (sketch) bosquejo; esbozo; esquema. —*v.t.* bosquejar; esbozar; delinear.
outlive (aut'lɪv) *v.t.* sobrevivir a; vivir *o* durar más que (*o* de).
outlook ('aut·lʊk) *n.* **1,** (view) vista. **2,** (prospect) prospecto; perspectivas (*pl.*). **3,** (mental attitude) actitud; manera de ver las cosas.
outlying *adj.* **1,** (remote) distante; remoto. **2,** (bordering) circundante; exterior.
outmatch (aut'matʃ) *v.t.* aventajar; superar.
outmoded (aut'mod·ɪd) *adj.* fuera *o* pasado de moda.
outnumber (aut'nʌm·bər) *v.t.* superar en número.
out-of-date *adj.* anticuado; pasado de moda.
out-of-door *adj.* = **outdoor.** —**out-of-doors,** *n.* & *adv.* = **outdoors.**
out-of-the-way *adj.* apartado; retirado.
outpatient *n.* paciente de hospital que no reside en él.
outpost *n.* puesto avanzado; puesto de avanzada.
outpouring *n.* efusión; emanación; chorro.
output ('aut·pʊt) *n.* producción; *mech.* rendimiento.
outrage ('aut·reidʒ) *n.* **1,** (insult) ultraje; afrenta; injuria. **2,** (violent or vicious act) tropelía; desafuero; desmán. —*v.t.* **1,** (abuse) ultrajar. **2,** (ravish) violar.
outrageous (aut'rei·dʒəs) *adj.* ultrajante; desaforado; afrentoso.
outrank (aut'ræŋk) *v.t.* exceder en rango *o* grado.
outrider *n.* **1,** (attendant on horseback) palafrenero; acompañante de a caballo. **2,** (scout on horseback) batidor de a caballo.
outrigger *n.* **1,** (stabilizing device) balancín (de canoa). **2,** (boom; spar) botalón.
outright *adj.* **1,** (complete) completo; cabal. **2,** (straightforward) franco; abierto. **3,** (downright) rotundo; inequívoco. —*adv.* **1,** (at once) de inmediato. **2,** (completely; entirely) por completo: en su totalidad. **3,** (openly) abiertamente.
outrun (aut'rʌn) *v.t.* [**outran, -run, -running**] **1,** (run faster than) correr más que. **2,** (elude by running) dejar atrás. **3,** (exceed) exceder; sobrepasar.
outset *n.* comienzo; principio.
outshine (aut'ʃain) *v.t.* [*pret.* & *p.p.* **outshone**] brillar más que; eclipsar.
outside (aut'said; 'aut-) *adj.* **1,** (outer; external) externo; exterior; de afuera. **2,** (extreme) extremo. —*n.* exterior; parte de afuera. —*adv.* fuera; afuera. —*prep.* **1,** (out from) fuera de. **2,** (beyond) más allá de. **3,** (aside from) fuera de; a *o* con excepción de. —**at the outside,** a lo más; con mucho.
outsider (aut'sai·dər) *n.* extraño; advenedizo; forastero.
outsize *n.* tamaño poco común. —**outsized,** *adj.* extraordinario; de tomaño poco común.
outskirts ('aut·skʌɹts) *n.pl.* afueras; inmediaciones; arrabales.
outsmart (aut'smart) *v.t., colloq.* ganar en astucia; ser más listo que; burlar. —**outsmart one's self,** pasarse de listo.
outspoken *adj.* franco; abierto; atrevido en el hablar.

outspread (aut'sprɛd) *adj.* extendido.
outstanding (aut'stæn·dɪŋ) *adj.* 1, (prominent) prominente; sobresaliente. 2, (projecting) saliente. 3, (unfulfilled) pendiente. 4, *comm.* (unpaid) sin pagar; en descubierto.
outstretched (aut'strɛtʃd) *adj.* extendido.
outstrip (aut'strɪp), *v.t.* [**outstripped, -stripping**] dejar atrás; sobrepasar; sobrepujar.
outward ('aut·wərd) *adj.* 1, (outer; exterior) exterior; externo. 2, (apparent) aparente. 3, (toward the outside) hacia el exterior; hacia afuera. —*adv.* [*también,* **outwards**] 1, (away; toward the outside) hacia afuera; hacia el exterior. 2, (on the outside; without) afuera; en el exterior. —*n.* parte externa. —**outwardly,** *adv.* aparentemente.
outwear (aut'weɪr) *v.t.* [*pret.* **outwore;** *p.p.* **outworn**] 1, (last longer than) durar más que. 2, (wear out) gastar; consumir.
outweigh (aut'wei) *v.t.* pesar más que.
outwit (aut'wɪt) *v.t.* [**outwitted, -witting**] ganar en astucia; ser más listo que; burlar.
outwore (aut'woːr) *v., pret. de* **outwear.**
outworn (aut'worn) *adj.* 1, (much used) desgastado; usado. 2, (out of fashion) anticuado. —*v., p.p. de* **outwear.**
ova ('o·və) *n., pl. de* **ovum.**
oval ('o·vəl) *adj.* ovalado; oval. —*n.* óvalo.
ovary ('o·və·ri) *n.* ovario. —**ovarian** (o'vɛr·i·ən) *adj.* ovárico.
ovate (o'veit) *adj.* ovado.
ovation (o'vei·ʃən) *n.* ovación.
oven ('ʌv·ən) *n.* horno.
over ('o·vər) *prep.* 1, (above; on top of) sobre; encima de. 2, (so as to cover) por; por encima de. 3, (so as to pass above) por sobre; por encima de. 4, (during) durante. 5, (to or on the other side of) al otro lado de. 6, (throughout) por; a través de. 7, (more than) más de. 8, (until after) hasta después de. 9, (in preference to) antes que. 10, (because of) por; a causa de. 11, (about; concerning) sobre; acerca de. —*adv.* 1, (above) por encima. 2, (across; to the other side) al otro lado. 3, (more; beyond) más. 4, (again; anew) otra vez; de nuevo. 5, (so as to be inverted) al otro lado; al revés; boca abajo; boca arriba. 6, (from an upright position) desplomado. 7, (yonder) allá. 8, (from one to another) de uno a otro. —*adj.* 1, (finished) terminado; concluido. 2, (having reached the other side) al otro lado. 3, *colloq.* (in excess) de sobra; de más. —**all over,** 1, (everywhere) por todas partes. 2, (finished) terminado. —**over again,** de nuevo. —**over against,** contra. —**over all,** de punta a punta. —**over and above,** además de. —**over and over,** una y otra vez; repetidamente. —**over here,** acá; aquí. —**over there,** ahí; allá; allí.
over- (o·vər) *prefijo* 1, sobre; encima: *overseer,* supervisor; *overcoat,* sobretodo. 2, a través; por; al otro lado: *overland,* por tierra; *overseas,* ultramar. 3, sobre-; exceso; con exceso: *overflow,* sobreabundancia; exceso; *overburden,* sobrecargar. 4, superación; culminación: *overpower,* dominar; subyugar; *overmatch,* sobrepujar. 5, alteración; trastorno: *overturn,* volcar; *overthrow,* derribar.
overabundant *adj.* sobreabundante. —**overabundance,** *n.* sobreabundancia.
overact *v.t. & i.* exagerar (un papel).
overactive *adj.* demasiado activo.
overage ('o·vər·ɪdʒ) *n.* demasía; exceso.
overage (ˌo·vər'eidʒ) *adj.* anticuado; añejo.
overall *adj.* 1, (comprehensive; total) total; completo. 2, (from end to end) de punta a punta; de cabo a rabo.
overalls ('o·vərˌɔlz) *n.pl.* mono (*sing.*); *Amer.* overol; overoles.
overambitious *adj.* demasiado ambicioso.
overanxious *adj.* demasiado ansioso.
overawe *v.t.* inspirar miedo *o* respeto.
overbalance *v.t.* 1, (outweigh) pesar más que. 2, (tip over) desequilibrar. —*n.* desequilibrio.
overbearing *adj.* arrogante; dominante; altanero.
overbid (ˌo·vər'bɪd) *v.t. & i.* [**overbid, -bidding**] 1, (offer more

than) ofrecer *o* pujar más (que). **2,** (offer more than the worth of) ofrecer demasiado (por). **3,** *cards* declarar demasiado. —*n.* ('o·vər·ˌbɪd) puja exagerada.

overboard *adv.* al agua; por la borda. —**go overboard,** *colloq.* extremarse; esmerarse.

overburden *v.t.* sobrecargar; recargar.

overcall *v.t., cards* declarar más que.

overcareful *adj.* muy cuidadoso.

overcast *n.* **1,** (cover of clouds) cielo encapotado. **2,** *sewing* sobrehilado. —*adj.* **1,** (covered, as with clouds) encapotado. **2,** *sewing* sobrehilado. —*v.t.* [*pret.* & *p.p.* **overcast**] **1,** (cover, as with clouds) encapotar; nublar; anublar. **2,** *sewing* sobrehilar.

overcautious *adj.* muy cauto.

overcharge *v.t.* cobrar de más (por). —*n.* exceso de cobro.

overcloud *v.t.* anublar; nublar; obscurecer.

overcoat *n.* abrigo; sobretodo; gabán.

overcome *v.t.* [*pret.* **overcame**; *p.p.* **overcome**] vencer; dominar; sobreponerse a. —*adj.* sobrecogido.

overconfident *adj.* muy confiado *o* seguro. —**overconfidence,** *n.* exceso de confianza *o* seguridad.

overcook *v.t.* & *i.* cocer(se) demasiado.

overcritical *adj.* criticón; quisquilloso.

overcrowd *v.t.* llenar demasiado; apiñar.

overdo *v.t.* [*pret.* **overdid**; *p.p.* **overdone**] **1,** (exaggerate) exagerar; extremar. **2,** = **overcook.** —**overdo oneself,** esmerarse; excederse.

overdose *n.* dosis excesiva. —*v.t.* dar una dosis excesiva.

overdraft *n.* sobregiro; giro en descubierto.

overdraw *v.t.* [*pret.* **overdrew**; *p.p.* **overdrawn**] **1,** *comm.* sobregirar; girar en descubierto. **2,** (exaggerate) exagerar.

overdress *v.t.* & *i.* vestir con exceso.

overdrive (ˌo·vər'draiv) *v.t.* [*pret.* **overdrove**; *p.p.* **overdriven**] abrumar de trabajo. —*n.* ('o·vər·draiv) sobremarcha.

overdue *adj.* **1,** *comm.* vencido. **2,** (late) atrasado; retrasado. **3,** (long hoped for) esperado por mucho tiempo.

overeager *adj.* demasiado ansioso.

overeat *v.t.* & *i.* [*pret.* **overate**; *p.p.* **overeaten**] comer demasiado.

overemotional *adj.* demasiado sensible.

overemphasize *v.t.* exagerar; acentuar demasiado; poner demasiado énfasis en. —**overemphasis,** *n.* exceso de énfasis; exageración.

overenthusiastic *adj.* demasiado entusiasta. —**overenthusiasm,** *n.* exceso de entusiasmo.

overestimate (ˌo·vər'ɛs·tə·ˌmeit) *v.t.* & *i.* exagerar. —*n.* (-mət) presupuesto exagerado.

overexercise *v.t.* ejercer demasiado. —*v.i.* excederse; hacer exceso de ejercicios. —*n.* exceso de ejercicios.

overexcite *v.t.* sobreexcitar.

overexert *v.t.* ejercer demasiado. —**overexert oneself,** hacer demasiado esfuerzo.

overexpand *v.t.* extender demasiado. —*v.i.* extenderse demasiado. —**overexpansion,** extensión excesiva.

overexpose *v.t.* sobreexponer. —**overexposure,** *n.* sobreexposición.

overfill *v.t.* llenar demasiado; sobrellenar.

overflow (ˌo·vər'floː) *v.t.* **1,** (flood) cubrir; inundar. **2,** (flow over the brim of) rebosar. **3,** (fill beyond capacity) llenar demasiado; sobrellenar. —*v.i.* rebosar; derramarse; (*of a stream*) desbordarse; salirse de madre. —*n.* ('o·vərˌflo) rebosamiento; derrame; (*of a stream*) desbordamiento.

overfond *adj.* **1,** (too affectionate) demasiado encariñado. **2,** (overindulgent) demasiado condescendiente.

overgrow *v.t.* [*pret.* **overgrew**; *p.p.* **overgrown**] **1,** (cover, as with vegetation) cubrir. **2,** = outgrow.

overgrown *adj.* **1,** (covered, as with vegetation) cubierto (de vegetación, follaje, etc.). **2,** (grown excessively) muy crecido; demasiado grande.

overhand *adj.* voleado por alto. —*adv.* al voleo. —*n.* voleo por alto.

overhang (ˌo·vər'hæŋ) *v.t.* [*pret.* & *p.p.* **overhung**] **1,** (jut out from) sobresalir de. **2,** (project over) proyectarse por encima de. **3,** (im-

pend; threaten) amenazar. —*v.i.* sobresalir. —*n.* ('o·vər,hæŋ) saliente; proyección; vuelo.
overhasty *adj.* demasiado apresurado.
overhaul *v.t.* **1,** (examine; check) revisar; examinar. **2,** (repair; adjust) reparar; hacer ajustes en; componer. **3,** (overtake) alcanzar. —*n.* **1,** (examination) revisión; examen minucioso. **2,** (repair) reparación; compostura.
overhead *adv.* por encima; por sobre la cabeza; en alto. —*adj.* **1,** (raised above) elevado; en alto; superior. **2,** (in the sky) en el cielo; en lo alto. **3,** *comm.* fijo; general. —*n.* gastos generales *o* fijos.
overhear *v.t.* [*pret. & p.p.* **overheard**] alcanzar a oír; acertar a oír.
overheat *v.t.* recalentar. —*v.i.* recalentarse.
overindulge *v.t.* **1,** (gratify to excess) satisfacer descomedidamente. **2,** (be too lenient toward) consentir demasiado. —*v.i.* excederse; propasarse; tomar, comer, *etc.* descomedidamente.
overindulgence *n.* **1,** (immoderation) inmoderación. **2,** (excessive leniency) complacencia *o* indulgencia exagerada.
overindulgent *adj.* **1,** (immoderate) inmoderado. **2,** (too lenient) demasiado condescendiente.
overjoyed *adj.* alborozado; desbordante de alegría.
overland *adj. & adv.* por tierra.
overlap *v.t. & i.* [**overlapped, -lapping**] cubrir parcialmente; coincidir en parte. —*n.* área *o* parte común; área *o* parte de coincidencia.
overlay (,o·vər'lei) *v.t.* [*pret. & p.p.* **overlaid**] **1,** (place over) superponer; poner sobre. **2,** (coat; cover) cubrir. **3,** (overburden) sobrecargar. **4,** (plate) enchapar. **5,** *pret. de* **overlie.** —*n.* ('o·vər-) **1,** (coating; covering) capa; cubierta. **2,** (plating) enchapado.
overlie *v.t.* [**overlay, -lain, -lying**] estar *o* extenderse sobre.
overload (,o·vər'lod) *v.t.* sobrecargar; recargar. —*n.* ('o·vər-) sobrecarga.
overlong *adj.* muy largo. —*adv.* mucho tiempo.
overlook *v.t.* **1,** (fail to notice) no notar; escapársele a uno. **2,** (ignore) pasar por alto; no hacer caso de. **3,** (afford a view of from above) mirar a; dar a.
overlord *n.* soberano; señor supremo.
overly ('o·vər·li) *adv.* demasiado; excesivamente; muy.
overlying *adj.* superpuesto; superior. —*v., ger. de* **overlie.**
overmodest *adj.* demasiado modesto.
overmuch *adv.* demasiado; en demasía. —*n.* demasía; exceso.
overnice *adj.* **1,** (extremely subtle) demasiado fino *o* sutil. **2,** (extremely fastidious) relamido; melindroso.
overnight *adv.* durante la noche; por la noche; en una noche. —*adj.* de la noche.
overpass ('o·vər,pæs) *n.* puente sobre un camino o vía; viaducto. —*v.t.* (-'pæs) **1,** (pass above or over) pasar por encima de. **2,** (pass across) atravesar; cruzar. **3,** (exceed) exceder; sobrepasar.
overpay *v.t. & i.* [*pret. & p.p.* **overpaid**] pagar de más. —**overpayment,** *n.* pago excesivo.
overplay *v.t.* exagerar; excederse en.
overpleased *adj.* muy contento; más que contento.
overpopulate *v.t.* poblar en exceso. —**overpopulation,** *n.* exceso de población.
overpower *v.t.* **1,** (subdue) dominar; subyugar; rendir. **2,** (overwhelm) abrumar; anonadar. **3,** (give too much power) dar excesiva potencia *o* empuje.
overpraise *v.t.* sobrealzar; alabar demasiado.
overprice *v.t.* pedir demasiado por; poner demasiado caro.
overproduce *v.t. & i.* producir en exceso. —**overproduction,** *n.* sobreproducción.
overrate *v.t.* sobreestimar.
overreach *v.t.* sobrepasar; llegar más allá de; *fig.* trascender. —**overreach oneself,** pasarse.
override *v.t.* [*pret.* **overrode;** *p.p.* **overridden**] **1,** (prevail over; vote down) derrotar; rechazar. **2,** (outweigh) prevalecer *o* prevaler sobre; pesar más que. **3,** (nullify) anular; invalidar. **4,** (trample down) hollar; atropellar. **5,** (pass or extend beyond) salirse de; pasarse de.

overripe *adj.* pasado.
overrule *v.t.* invalidar; anular.
overrun *v.t.* [**overran, -run, -running**] **1,** (rove over; ravage) arrollar; invadir. **2,** (infest) plagar; infestar. **3,** (spread over) cubrir por completo; inundar. **4,** (go beyond) pasarse de.
overscrupulous *adj.* demasiado escrupuloso; remilgado.
overseas ('o·vər,siz) *adj.* de ultramar; de allende los mares; del extranjero. —*adv.* (-'siːz) al *o* en el extranjero.
oversee *v.t.* [*pret.* **oversaw;** *p.p.* **overseen**] **1,** (supervise) inspeccionar; vigilar; dirigir. **2,** (watch) observar. —**overseer,** *n.* capataz; supervisor.
oversensitive *adj.* muy susceptible.
overshadow *v.t.* obscurecer; eclipsar.
overshoe *n.* chanclo; galocha.
overshoot *v.t.* [*pret.* & *p.p.* **overshot**] pasar; pasarse de. —*v.i.* pasarse.
oversight *n.* **1,** (omission) inadvertencia; omisión. **2,** (supervision) supervisión; vigilancia.
oversimplify *v.t.* simplificar mucho. —**oversimplification,** *n.* exceso de simplificación.
oversize *adj.* muy grande. —*n.* tamaño muy grande.
oversleep *v.i.* [*pret.* & *p.p.* **overslept**] dormir demasiado; pegársele a uno las sábanas.
overspread *v.t.* [*pret.* & *p.p.* **overspread**] extenderse sobre; cubrir. —*adj.* extendido.
overstate *v.t.* exagerar. —**overstatement,** *n.* exageración.
overstay *v.t.* & *i.* quedarse más de lo debido.
overstep *v.t.* [**overstepped, overstepping**] propasar; propasarse en. —**overstep oneself,** excederse; sobrepasarse.
overstimulate *v.t.* estimular excesivamente; sobreexcitar.
overstock (,o·vər'stak) *v.t.* surtir demasiado (de); sobrellenar. —*n.* ('o·vər-) surtido excesivo; exceso.
overstrict *adj.* demasiado estricto; demasiado riguroso.
overstuffed *adj.* demasiado lleno *o* relleno; *fig.* sobrecargado.
oversupply *v.t.* abarrotar; proveer demasiado. —*n.* exceso.
oversuspicious *adj.* demasiado sospechoso; muy desconfiado.
overt ('o·vʌɹt) *adj.* abierto; franco; claro; manifiesto.
overtake *v.t.* [*pret.* **overtook;** *p.p.* **overtaken**] **1,** (catch up with) alcanzar; sobrecoger. **2,** (come upon suddenly) sorprender.
overtax *v.t.* imponer demasiado; pedir demasiado.
overthrow (,o·vər'θroː) *v.t.* [*pret.* **overthrew;** *p.p.* **overthrown**] derribar; derrocar. —*n.* ('o·vər·,θro) derrocamiento.
overtime *n.* horas extraordinarias; *sports* tiempo suplementario. —*adv.* en horas extraordinarias; *sports* en tiempo suplementario.
overtire *v.t.* cansar mucho.
overtone *n.* **1,** *music* armónico. **2,** *usu.pl.* (implication) implicación; insinuación.
overture ('o·vər·tʃur) *n.* **1,** *music* obertura. **2,** (proposal) proposición; insinuación.
overturn *v.t.* & *i.* (upset) volcar. —*v.t.* (overthrow) derribar. —*n.* vuelco.
overvalue *v.t.* dar demasiado valor a; valorar en exceso. —**overvaluation,** *n.* valor excesivo.
overweening (,o·vər'wi·nɪŋ) *adj.* presuntuoso; altanero; arrogante.
overweigh *v.t.* **1,** (outweigh) pesar más que. **2,** (weigh down) abrumar; sobrecargar.
overweight *n.* sobrepeso; exceso de peso. —*adj.* **1,** (obese) grueso; obeso. **2,** (having excess weight) que pesa de más.
overwhelm *v.t.* **1,** (crush) aplastar; arrollar. **2,** (overcome, as with emotion, praise, etc.) abrumar; anonadar. —**overwhelming,** *adj.* abrumador.
overwork (,o·vər'wʌɹk) *v.i.* trabajar demasiado. —*v.t.* **1,** (overburden) hacer trabajar mucho; abrumar *o* recargar de trabajo. **2,** (excite excessively) excitar demasiado. **3,** (elaborate too much) elaborar demasiado. **4,** (make excessive use of) exagerar; abusar de. —*n.* ('o·vər-) mucho trabajo.
overwrought *adj.* **1,** (excited; upset) muy excitado. **2,** (too elaborate) recargado.
overzealous *adj.* demasiado celoso; muy entregado.

ovi- (o·vɪ) *prefijo* ovi-; huevo: *oviform,* oviforme.
ovine ('o·vain) *adj.* ovino.
oviparous (o'vɪp·ə·rəs) *adj.* ovíparo.
ovoid ('o·vɔid) *adj. & n.* ovoide.
ovulation (ˌo·vjə'lei·ʃən) *n.* ovulación. **—ovulate** ('o·vjəˌleit) *v.i.* desprender óvulos; efectuar ovulación.
ovule ('o·vjul) *n.* óvulo.
ovum ('o·vəm) *n.* [*pl.* **ova**] óvulo; huevo.
owe (oː) *v.t. & i.* deber. **—owing,** *adj.* debido. **—owing to,** debido a; por causa de; por.
owl (aul) *n.* lechuza; búho. **—owlet** ('au·lɪt) *n.* cría de lechuza *o* búho. **—owlish,** *adj.* semejante a la lechuza; de lechuza.
own (oːn) *v.t.* **1,** (possess) poseer; tener. **2,** (admit) reconocer; admitir. **—***adj.* propio. **—come into one's own,** lograr reconocimiento. **—get one's own back,** desquitarse; vengarse. **—hold one's own, 1,** (maintain one's status) no ceder; mantenerse firme. **2,** (compete successfully) poder competir. **3,** (defend oneself) defenderse. **—on one's own,** por su cuenta.
owner ('o·nər) *n.* dueño; propietario. **—ownership,** *n.* propiedad; posesión.
ox (aks) *n.* [*pl.* **oxen** ('ak·sən)] buey.
oxalic (ak'sæl·ɪk) *adj.* oxálico.
oxalis ('ak·sə·lɪs) *n.* acedera menor.
oxeye *n., bot.* ojo de buey.
oxford ('aks·fərd) *n.* **1,** (shoe) zapato oxford. **2,** (cloth) tela oxford.
oxide ('ak·said) *n.* óxido.
oxidize ('ak·səˌdaiz) *v.t.* oxidar. **—***v.i.* oxidarse. **—oxidation** (-'dei·ʃən) *n.* oxidación.
oxy- (ak·si) *prefijo* oxi-. **1,** oxígeno: *oxysulfide,* oxisulfuro. **2,** agudo: *oxycephalic,* oxicefálico.
oxyacetylene (ˌak·si·ə'sɛt·ə·lin) *adj.* oxiacetilénico.
oxygen ('ak·sə·dʒən) *n.* oxígeno.
oxygenate ('ak·sə·dʒəˌneit) *v.t.* oxigenar. **—oxygenation,** *n.* oxigenación.
oyster ('ɔis·tər) *n.* ostra.
ozone ('o·zon) *n.* ozono.

P

P, p (piː) decimosexta letra del alfabeto inglés.
pa (paː) *n., colloq.* papá.
pace (peis) *n.* paso. **—***v.t.* **1,** (walk the length of; measure) medir a pasos. **2,** (set the pace for) dar la pauta a *o* para. **—***v.i.* pasearse; dar pasos. **—keep pace with,** ir *o* mantenerse con. **—put one through his paces,** probar; poner a prueba. **—set the pace,** dar la pauta.
pacemaker *n.* el que da la pauta; modelo.
pacer ('pei·sər) *n.* caballo amblador.
pachyderm ('pak·ɪˌdʌɹm) *n.* paquidermo.
pacific (pə'sɪf·ɪk) *adj.* pacífico. **—***n., cap.* (Océano) Pacífico.
pacifier ('pæs·ɪˌfai·ər) *n.* chupete; chupador.
pacifism ('pæs·ɪ·fɪz·əm) *n.* pacifismo. **—pacifist,** *n.* pacifista. **—pacifistic,** *adj.* pacifista.
pacify ('pæs·ɪˌfai) *v.t.* pacificar. **—pacification** (-fɪ'kei·ʃən) *n.* pacificación.
pack (pæk) *n.* **1,** (package) paquete. **2,** (bundle) fardo. **3,** *cards* baraja. **4,** (bunch of dogs) jauría; (of wolves) manada; (of mules) recua. **5,** (gang; band) cuadrilla; pandilla. **6,** (lot; bunch) sarta; partida. **7,** (mass of ice) masa de hielo. **8,** (compress) compresa. **9,** (haversack) mochila. **—***v.t.* **1,** (put in a container) empacar; empaquetar; encajonar. **2,** (load) cargar. **3,** (wrap) envolver. **4,** (compress) apretar; comprimir. **5,** (fill; stuff) llenar; rellenar. **6,** (cram; crowd) atestar; apiñar. **7,** *colloq.* (have; carry) tener; llevar. **—***v.i.* **1,** (prepare luggage) hacer el equipaje *o* las maletas; empacar. **2,** (settle into a compact mass) apretarse; comprimirse. **—***adj.* de carga. **—packer,** *n.* empacador; empaquetador. **—packing,** *n.* empacado; empaquetadura. **—pack off,** despedir; des-

pachar; largarse. —**send packing**, despedir.
package ('pæk·ɪdʒ) *n.* paquete. —*v.t.* empacar; empaquetar.
packet ('pæk·ɪt) *n.* **1,** (small bundle) paquete. **2,** (ship) paquebote.
packsaddle *n.* albarda.
pact (pækt) *n.* pacto.
pad (pæd) *n.* **1,** (wad; cushion) almohadilla. **2,** (writing tablet) bloc; cuadernillo. **3,** (stamp pad) tampón. **4,** (sole) planta. **5,** (lily pad) hoja de nenúfar. **6,** (launching pad) plataforma de lanzamiento. —*v.t.* [**padded, padding**] **1,** (fill; stuff) rellenar. **2,** (line; quilt) acolchar; poner guata a. **3,** (expand unduly) abultar. —*v.i.* caminar; (of a horse) amblar.
padding ('pæd·ɪŋ) *n.* **1,** (stuffing) relleno. **2,** (lining) guata.
paddle ('pæd·əl) *n.* **1,** (oar) pala; remo de canoa. **2,** (broad-bladed implement) pala; paleta. —*v.t. & i.* **1,** (row) remar. **2,** (spank) dar una paliza; dar de azotes. **3,** (dabble; splash) chapalear; chapotear. —**paddle boat**, barco o vapor de ruedas. —**paddle wheel**, rueda de palas o paletas.
paddock ('pæd·ək) *n.* cercado.
padlock ('pæd,lak) *n.* candado. —*v.t.* cerrar con candado; echar el candado a.
padre ('pa·dri) *n.* padre; cura; capellán.
paedo- (pi·do) *prefijo, var. de* **pedo-**.
paella (pə'ɛl·ə) *n.* paella.
pagan ('pei·gən) *adj. & n.* pagano. —**paganism**, *n.* paganismo.
page (peidʒ) *n.* **1,** (leaf of a book) página. **2,** (attendant) paje. **3,** (bellboy) botones. —*v.t.* **1,** (arrange in pages) paginar. **2,** (call) llamar.
pageant ('pædʒ·ənt) *n.* **1,** (parade) desfile. **2,** (show) espectáculo. **3,** (tableau) retablo. —**pageantry** (-ən·tri) *n.* fausto; boato; pompa.
paginate ('pædʒ·ə,neit) *v.t.* paginar. —**pagination**, *n.* paginación.
pagoda (pə'go·də) *n.* pagoda.
paid (peid) *v., pret. & p.p. de* **pay**.
pail (peil) *n.* cubo; balde.
pain (pein) *n.* dolor. —*v.t.* **1,** (hurt) doler; causar dolor a. **2,** (grieve) apenar. —*v.i.* doler. —**be in pain**, estar con dolor; tener dolor. —**on** (*o* **under**) **pain of**, so (*o* bajo) pena de. —**take pains**, esmerarse. —**take pains not to**, guardarse de; tener cuidado de.
painful ('pein·fəl) *adj.* **1,** (aching) doloroso. **2,** (difficult) penoso; difícil. —**painfulness**, *n.* dolor.
painless ('pein·ləs) *adj.* **1,** (not hurtful) sin dolor. **2,** (easy) fácil; sin pena; sin trabajo.
painstaking ('peinz,teik·ɪŋ) *adj.* cuidadoso; esmerado.
paint (peint) *n.* pintura. —*v.t. & i.* pintar.
painter ('pein·tər) *n.* pintor.
painting ('pein·tɪŋ) *n.* pintura.
pair (pe:r) *n.* **1,** (matched set) par. **2,** (couple) pareja. —*v.t.* parear. —*v.i.* parearse. —**pair off**, formarse *o* irse en parejas.
pajamas (pə'dʒam·əz) *n.pl.* piyamas; pijamas.
pal (pæl) *n., slang* compañero. —*v.i.* [**palled, palling**] ser compañero.
palace ('pæl·ɪs) *n.* palacio. —*adj.* palaciego; del palacio.
paladin ('pæl·ə·dɪn) *n.* paladín.
palanquin (,pæl·ən'kin) *n.* palanquín.
palatable ('pæl·ə·tə·bəl) *adj.* **1,** (tasty) sabroso. **2,** *fig.* (acceptable) aceptable; que se puede pasar.
palate ('pæl·ɪt) *n.* paladar. —**palatal**, *adj.* palatal; palatino.
palatial (pə'lei·ʃəl) *adj.* magnífico; suntuoso.
palatine ('pæl·ə,tain) *adj. & n.* palatino. —**palatinate** (pə'læt·ɪ·,neit) *n.* palatinado.
palaver (pə'læv·ər) *n.* palabrería; charla. —*v.i.* charlar.
pale (peil) *adj.* pálido. —*n.* estaca; palo. —*v.i.* perder el color; palidecer. —**paleness**, *n.* palidez.
paleo- *también,* **palaeo-** (pei·li·o; -ə) *prefijo* paleo-; antiguo; primitivo: *paleology,* paleología.
paleography (,pei·li'ag·rə·fi) *n.* paleografía. —**paleographer**, *n.* paleógrafo. —**paleographic** (-ə·'græf·ɪk) *adj.* paleográfico.
paleolithic (,pei·li·ə'lɪθ·ɪk) *adj.* paleolítico.
paleontology (,pei·li·ən'tal·ə·dʒi) *n.* paleontología. —**paleontological** (-,an·tə'ladʒ·ɪ·kəl) *adj.* paleontológico. —**paleontologist**, *n.* paleontólogo.
Paleozoic (,pei·li·ə'zo·ɪk) *adj.* paleozoico.

Palestinian (ˌpæl·əˈstɪn·i·ən) *adj. & n.* palestino.
palette (ˈpal·ɪt) *n.* paleta. —**palette knife,** espátula de pintor.
palfrey (ˈpɔl·fri) *n.* palafrén.
paling (ˈpeil·ɪŋ) *n.* estacada; palizada.
palisade (ˌpæl·əˈseid) *n.* empalizada.
pall (pɔl) *n.* **1,** (coffin cover) paño mortuorio. **2,** (cloud) capa. **3,** (gloomy effect) sombra. —*v.i.* perder su sabor; perder su interés. —**pall on,** hartar; cansar.
palladium (pəˈlei·di·əm) *n.* **1,** (metal) paladio. **2,** (safeguard) salvaguardia; garantía.
pallbearer *n.* pilar.
pallet (ˈpæl·ɪt) *n.* jergón.
palliate (ˈpæl·iˌeit) *v.t.* paliar. —**palliation,** *n.* paliación. —**palliative** (-əˌtɪv) *n. & adj.* paliativo.
pallid (ˈpæl·ɪd) *adj.* pálido.
pallium (ˈpæl·i·əm) *n.* palio.
pallor (ˈpæl·ər) *n.* palidez.
palm (pa:m) *n.* **1,** (inner surface of the hand) palma. **2,** (span of the hand) palmo. **3,** *bot.* palmera. **4,** (symbol of victory) palma. —*v.t.* escamotear. —**palmar** (ˈpal·mər) *adj.* palmar. —**grease the palm,** *colloq.* untar la mano. —**palm grove,** palmar; palmeral. —**palm off,** escamotear.
palmetto (palˈmɛt·o) *n.* palmito.
palmistry (ˈpa·mɪs·tri) *n.* quiromancia. —**palmist,** *n.* quiromántico.
Palm Sunday Domingo de Ramos.
palmy (ˈpa·mi) *adj.* (flourishing) próspero; floreciente.
palomino (ˌpæl·əˈmi·no) *n.* palomilla.
palpable (ˈpæl·pə·bəl) *adj.* palpable.
palpate (ˈpæl·peit) *v.t. & i.* palpar. —**palpation,** *n.* palpación.
palpitate (ˈpæl·pəˌteit) *v.i.* palpitar. —**palpitation,** *n.* palpitación.
palsy (ˈpɔl·zi) *n.* parálisis; perlesía. —*v.t.* paralizar.
palter (ˈpɔl·tər) *v.i.* **1,** (play false) jugar sucio. **2,** (trifle) andar con rodeos.
paltry (ˈpɔl·tri) *adj.* mezquino. —**paltriness,** *n.* mezquindad.
pampas (ˈpæm·pəz) *n.pl.* pampas.
pamper (ˈpæm·pər) *v.t.* mimar; consentir.
pamphlet (ˈpæm·flɪt) *n.* folleto. —**pamphleteer** (-fləˈtɪr) *n.* folletista.
pan (pæn) *n.* **1,** (saucepan) cacerola; cazuela. **2,** (skillet) sartén. **3,** (baking pan) molde de horno. **4,** (shallow vessel) paila; cubeta. —*v.t. & i.* **1,** (cook in a pan) cocer en cazuela, cacerola, etc. **2,** (sift for gold) cerner en busca de oro. **3,** *slang* (criticize; deride) poner frito. —**pan out,** *colloq.* resultar; tener éxito.
pan- (pæn) *prefijo* pan-; total; completo; universal: *Panamerican,* panamericano; *pandemic,* pandemia.
panacea (ˌpæn·əˈsi·ə) *n.* panacea.
panama (ˈpæn·əˌma) *n.* panamá.
Pan-American *adj.* panamericano. —**Pan-Americanism,** *n.* panamericanismo.
pancake *n.* **1,** (battercake) hojuela; *Amer.* panqueque. **2,** *aero.* aterrizaje a plomo *o* de plano.
panchromatic (ˈpæn·kroˈmæt·ɪk) *adj.* pancromático.
pancreas (ˈpæn·kri·əs) *n.* páncreas. —**pancreatic** (-ˈæt·ɪk) *adj.* pancreático.
panda (ˈpæn·də) *n.* panda.
pandemonium (ˌpæn·dəˈmo·ni·əm) *n.* pandemónium.
pander (ˈpæn·dər) *v.i.* alcahuetear. —*n.* alcahuete.
pane (pein) *n.* **1,** (sheet of glass) cristal; panel de cristal. **2,** (panel) tablero; cuadro.
panegyric (ˌpæn·əˈdʒɪr·ɪk) *n.* panegírico. —**panegyrical,** *adj.* panegírico.
panel (ˈpæn·əl) *n.* **1,** (section of a door, wall, etc.) panel. **2,** (group of jurors, judges, experts, etc.) jurado; panel. **3,** (instrument panel; control panel) tablero; cuadro. —**paneled,** *adj.* con *o* de paneles. —**paneling,** *n.* paneles.
pang (pæŋ) *n.* ramalazo.
panhandler (ˈpænˌhæn·dlər) *n., slang* pordiosero. —**panhandle** (-dəl) *v.t. & i., slang* pordiosear.
panic (ˈpæn·ɪk) *n.* pánico; terror. —*adj.* pánico. —*v.t.* aterrorizar. —*v.i.* aterrorizarse. —**panicky,** *adj.* pánico; que tiene pánico; aterrorizado.
panicle (ˈpæn·ə·kəl) *n.* panoja.
panic-stricken *adj.* aterrorizado.
pannier (ˈpæn·jər) *n.* angarillas (*pl.*); serón.

panoply ('pæn·ə·pli) *n.* panoplia.
panorama (,pæn·ə'ræm·ə) *n.* panorama. —**panoramic,** *adj.* panorámico.
pansy ('pæn·zi) *n., bot.* pensamiento.
pant (pænt) *v.i.* **1,** (breathe hard) jadear. **2,** (yearn) anhelar; rabiar (por). —*n.* [*también,* **panting**] jadeo. —**panting,** *adj.* jadeante.
pantaloons (,pæn·tə'luːnz) *n.pl.* pantalones.
pantheism ('pæn·θi·ɪz·əm) *n.* panteísmo. —**pantheist,** *n.* panteísta. —**pantheistic,** *adj.* panteísta; panteístico.
pantheon ('pæn·θi,an) *n.* panteón.
panther ('pæn·θər) *n.* pantera.
panties ('pæn·tiz) *n.pl. colloq.* bragas; pantaloncitos de mujer.
panto- (pæn·tə) *prefijo, var. de* **pan-**: *pantograph,* pantógrafo.
pantograph ('pæn·tə,græf) *n.* pantógrafo.
pantomime ('pæn·tə,maim) *n.* pantomima. —**pantomimic** (-'mɪm·ɪk) *adj.* pantomímico. —**pantomimist** (-,mɪm·ɪst) *n.* pantomimo.
pantry ('pæn·tri) *n.* despensa.
pants (pænts) *n.pl., colloq.* **1,** (trousers) pantalones. **2,** (drawers) calzoncillos.
pantywaist *n., slang* marica.
pap (pæp) *n.* papilla; papa.
papa ('pa·pə) *n.* papá.
papacy ('pei·pə·si) *n.* papado. —**papal** (-pəl) *adj.* papal; del Papa.
papaw (pɔ'pɔ) *n.* **1,** (tree) papayo. **2,** (fruit) papaya.
papaya (pə'pa·jə) *n.* **1,** (fruit) papaya; lechosa. **2,** (tree) papayo.
paper ('pei·pər) *n.* **1,** (thin material; sheet) papel. **2,** (newspaper) periódico. **3,** (essay) ensayo; escrito; artículo. **4,** (written exercise) trabajo; composición. **5,** (document) documento. **6,** (paper money) papel moneda; valores (*pl.*). —*adj.* de papel. —*v.t.* empapelar. —**papery,** *adj.* como papel. —**on paper,** por escrito.
paperback *adj.* en rústica. —*n.* libro en rústica.
paper clip sujetapapeles.
paperhanger *n.* empapelador. —**paperhanging,** *n.* empapelado.
paperweight *n.* pisapapeles.
paperwork *n.* papeleo.
papier-maché (,pei·pər·mə'ʃei) *n.* cartón piedra; papel majado; papel maché.
papilla (pə'pɪl·ə) *n.* papila. —**papillary** ('pæp·ə·lɛr·i) *adj.* papilar.
papist ('pei·pɪst) *adj. & n.* papista.
pappy ('pæp·i) *n., colloq.* papá; papito.
paprika ('pa·prɪ·ka; pæ'pri·kə) *n.* pimentón.
papule ('pæp·jul) *n.* pápula.
papyrus (pə'pai·rəs) *n.* papiro.
par (par) *n.* **1,** *finance* igualdad de cambio; par (*en* a la par). **2,** (equal footing) nivel; altura. **3,** (standard) lo normal; lo corriente. **4,** *golf* tanteo alcanzado por expertos. —*adj.* **1,** (of or at par) igual; a la par. **2,** (normal) normal; corriente. —**at par,** a la par. —**on** *o* **upon a par,** a la par; al mismo nivel. —**par value,** valor nominal.
para- (pær·ə) *prefijo* para-. **1,** cerca; además de; más allá; *paramilitary,* paramilitar; *paraphrase,* paráfrasis. **2,** *patol.* anormal: *paranoia,* paranoia. **3,** protección; resguardo: *parachute,* paracaídas.
parable ('pær·ə·bəl) *n.* parábola.
parabola (pə'ræb·ə·lə) *n.* parábola. —**parabolic** (,pær·ə'bal·ɪk) *adj.* parabólico.
parachute ('pær·ə,ʃut) *n.* paracaídas. —*v.t. & i.* lanzar(se) *o* tirar(se) en paracaídas. —**parachutist,** *n.* paracaidista.
parade (pə'reid) *n.* **1,** (procession) desfile; *mil.* parada. **2,** (display; ostentation) ostentación; alarde. **3,** (promenade) paseo. **4,** (promenaders) paseantes. —*v.t.* **1,** (cause to march) hacer desfilar. **2,** (march through) desfilar por; recorrer. **3,** (make a display of) hacer ostentación *o* alarde de. —*v.i.* desfilar; pasear.
paradigm ('pær·ə,dɪm) *n.* paradigma.
paradise ('pær·ə,dais) *n.* paraíso. —**paradisiacal** (-di'sai·ə·kəl); **paradisaical** (-di'sei·ə·kəl) *adj.* paradisíaco.
paradox ('pær·ə,daks) *n.* paradoja. —**paradoxical** (-'dak·sɪ·kəl) *adj.* paradójico.
paraffin ('pær·ə·fɪn) *n.* parafina.
paragon ('pær·ə·gan) *n.* parangón.

paragraph ('pær·ə,græf) *n.* párrafo. —*v.t.* dividir en párrafos.
parakeet ('pær·ə,kit) *n.* perico; periquito.
parallax ('pær·ə,læks) *n.* paralaje.
parallel ('pær·ə,lɛl) *adj.* & *n.* paralelo. —*v.t.* **1,** (compare) comparar; parangonar; paralelar. **2,** (run parallel with) ir *o* correr paralelo a *o* con. **3,** (be similar or comparable to) parecerse a; que se puede comparar a *o* con. —**parallel bars,** paralelas; barras paralelas.
parallelepiped (,pær·ə,lɛl·ə'pai·pɪd) *n.* paralelepípedo.
parallelism ('pær·ə·lɛl,ɪz·əm) *n.* paralelismo.
parallelogram (,pær·ə'lɛl·ə,græm) *n.* paralelogramo.
paralysis (pə'ræl·ə·sɪs) *n.* parálisis. —**paralytic** (,pær·ə'lɪt·ɪk) *adj.* & *n.* paralítico.
paralyze ('pær·ə,laiz) *v.t.* paralizar. —**paralyzation** (-lɪ'zei·ʃən) *n.* paralización.
paramecium (,pær·ə'mi·si·əm) *n.* paramecio.
parameter (pə'ræm·ə·tər) *n.* parámetro.
paramo ('pær·ə,mo) *n.* páramo.
paramount ('pær·ə,maunt) *adj.* sumo; capital.
paramour ('pær·ə,mʊr) *n.* amante; querido.
paranoia (,pær·ə'nɔi·ə) *n.* paranoia. —**paranoiac** (-æk) *n.* & *adj.* paranoico.
parapet ('pær·ə·pɪt) *n.* parapeto.
paraphernalia (,pær·ə·fər'neil·jə) *n.pl.* accesorios; atavíos; adornos.
paraphrase ('pær·ə,freiz) *n.* paráfrasis. —*v.t.* & *i.* parafrasear. —**paraphrastic** (-'fræs·tɪk) *adj.* parafrástico.
paraplegia (,pær·ə'pli·dʒi·ə) *n.* paraplejía. —**paraplegic,** *n.* & *adj.* parapléjico.
parasite ('pær·ə,sait) *n.* parásito. —**parasitic** (-'sɪt·ɪk) *adj.* parasítico; parásito; parasitario.
parasol ('pær·ə,sɔl) *n.* parasol; quitasol.
paratrooper ('pær·ə,tru·pər) *n.* paracaidista.
paratyphoid (,pær·ə'tai·fɔid) *adj.* paratifoide; paratífico. —*n.* paratifoidea. —**paratyphoid fever,** fiebre paratifoidea.
parboil ('par,bɔil) *v.t.* sancochar.
parcel ('par·səl) *n.* **1,** (package) paquete. **2,** (piece of land) parcela. —*v.t.* parcelar; dividir. —**parcel post,** paquete postal.
parch (partʃ) *v.t.* agostar; quemar; tostar. —*v.i.* quemarse; abrasarse.
parchment ('partʃ·mənt) *n.* pergamino.
pardon ('par·dən) *v.t.* perdonar. —*n.* perdón. —**pardonable,** *adj.* perdonable.
pare (peːr) *v.t.* **1,** (cut) cortar; recortar. **2,** (peel) pelar; mondar. **3,** (reduce) recortar.
paregoric (,pær·ə'gor·ɪk) *n.* paregórico.
parent ('pɛr·ənt) *n.* **1,** (father) padre. **2,** (mother) madre. —**parents,** *n.pl.* padres; progenitores. —**parentage,** *n.* paternidad *o* maternidad. —**parental** (pə'rɛn·təl) *adj.* paternal. —**parenthood,** *n.* paternidad *o* maternidad.
parenthesis (pə'rɛn·θə·sɪs) *n.* [*pl.* -ses (-siz)] paréntesis. —**parenthesize** (-,saiz) *v.t.* poner entre paréntesis. —**parenthetical** (,pær·ən·'θɛt·ɪ·kəl) *adj.* entre paréntesis; por paréntesis.
paresis (pə'ri·sɪs) *n.* paresia. —**paretic** (pə'rɛt·ɪk) *adj.* & *n.* parético.
par excellence por excelencia.
parfait (par'fei) *n.* helado de crema suave; parfait.
pari- (pær·i) *prefijo* pari-; igual: *paripinnate,* paripinado.
pariah (pə'rai·ə) *n.* paria.
pari-mutuel (,pær·i'mju·tʃu·əl) *n.* apuesta mutua.
paring ('pɛr·ɪŋ) *n.* cáscara; mondadura. —**paring knife,** cuchillo para mondar.
parish ('pær·ɪʃ) *n.* **1,** *eccles.* parroquia; feligresía. **2,** (county) condado.
parishioner (pə'rɪʃ·ən·ər) *n.* feligrés.
parity ('pær·ə·ti) *n.* paridad; equidad.
park (park) *n.* parque. —*v.t.* & *i.* estacionar. —**parking,** *n.* estacionamiento. —**parking lot,** parque de estacionamiento.
parka ('par·kə) *n.* chaqueta con capucha.
parkway ('park,wei) *n.* carretera; autopista.
parlance ('par·ləns) *n.* lenguaje.
parley ('par·li) *n.* conferencia;

parlamento. —*v.i.* conferenciar; parlamentar.
parliament ('par·lə·mənt) *n.* parlamento. —**parliamentarian** (-mɛn'tɛr·i·ən) *n.* parlamentario. —**parliamentarism** (-'mɛn·tə·rɪz·əm) *n.* parlamentarismo. —**parliamentary** (-'mɛn·tə·ri) *adj.* parlamentario.
parlor ('par·lər) *n.* sala; salón.
parlormaid *n.* camarera.
Parnassus (par'næs·əs) *n.* parnaso.
parochial (pə'ro·ki·əl) *adj.* **1,** (of a parish) parroquial. **2,** (narrow; provincial) estrecho de miras; limitado.
parody ('pær·ə·di) *n.* parodia. —*v.t.* parodiar.
parole (pə'roːl) *n.* **1,** (prisoner's promise) palabra de honor. **2,** (conditional release) libertad provisional. —*v.t.* poner en libertad provisional.
parotid (pə'rat·ɪd) *n.* parótida. —*adj.* parotídeo. —**parotiditis** (-ə'dai·tɪs) *n.* parotiditis.
-parous (pə·rəs) *sufijo* -paro; procreador: *oviparous,* ovíparo.
paroxysm ('pær·ək·sɪz·əm) *n.* paroxismo.
parquet (par'kei) *n.* **1,** (flooring) entarimado. **2,** *theat.* patio; *Amer.* luneta. —**parquetry** ('par·kɪt·ri) *n.* entarimado.
parricide ('pær·əˌsaid) *n.* **1,** (agent) parricida. **2,** (act) parricidio. —**parricidal** (-'sai·dəl) *adj.* parricida.
parrot ('pær·ət) *n.* papagayo; loro; cotorra. —*v.t.* imitar.
parry ('pær·i) *v.t. & i.* (ward off) parar; desviar. —*v.t.* (evade) evadir; eludir. —*n.* **1,** (a warding off) parada; quite. **2,** (evasion) evasiva; evasión.
parse (pars) *v.t.* analizar (una palabra, oración, etc.) —**parsing,** *n.* análisis.
parsimony ('par·sə·mo·ni) *n.* parsimonia. —**parsimonious** (-'mo·ni·əs) *adj.* parsimonioso.
parsley ('pars·li) *n.* perejil.
parsnip ('pars·nɪp) *n.* chirivía; pastinaca.
parson ('par·sən) *n.* párroco; cura. —**parsonage,** *n.* rectoría.
part (part) *n.* **1,** (portion) parte. **2,** (rôle) papel. **3,** (component, as of a mechanism, structure, etc.) pieza. **4,** *usu.pl.* (locality) partes. **5,** *pl.* (talent; ability) partes; talento (*sing.*). **6,** (side, as in a controversy) lado; parte. **7,** (of the hair) partidura; raya. —*v.t.* **1,** (break; divide) partir; dividir. **2,** (separate) separar. —*v.i.* **1,** (break; divide) partirse; dividirse. **2,** (separate) separarse. **3,** (depart) salir; partir; irse. —*adj.* parcial. —*adv.* parte; en parte. —**for the most part,** por lo general; en su mayor parte. —**on one's part,** por su parte *o* cuenta. —**part from,** dejar; separarse de. —**part of speech,** parte de la oración. —**part with,** dejar; soltar.
partake (par'teik) *v.i.* participar. —**partake of, 1,** (have a share in) participar de. **2,** (eat or drink) comer *o* beber. **3,** (have the nature of) tener de; tener algo de.
parterre (par'teːr) *n.* parterre.
parthenogenesis (ˌpar·θə·no·'dʒɛn·ə·sɪs) *n.* partenogénesis.
partial ('par·ʃəl) *adj.* parcial. —**partiality** (-ʃi'æl·ə·ti) *n.* parcialidad. —**be partial to,** tener debilidad por; sentir simpatía hacia.
participate (par'tɪs·ɪˌpeit) *v.i.* participar. —**participant** (-pənt) *n. & adj.* partícipe; participante. —**participation,** *n.* participación.
participle ('par·təˌsɪp·əl) *n.* participio. —**participial** (-'sɪp·i·əl) *adj.* participial.
particle ('par·tə·kəl) *n.* partícula.
particolored ('par·tiˌkʌl·ərd) *adj.* abigarrado.
particular (pər'tɪk·jə·lər) *adj.* **1,** (specific) determinado. **2,** (peculiar; special) particular; especial; característico. **3,** (detailed) detallado. **4,** (fastidious) exigente. —*n.* particular; particularidad.
particularity (pərˌtɪk·jə'lær·ə·ti) *n.* particularidad.
parting ('par·tɪŋ) *adj.* **1,** (dividing) divisorio; de separación. **2,** (departing; dying) que se va; que muere. **3,** (given, done, etc., at parting) de despedida. —*n.* **1,** (division; separation) división; separación. **2,** (departure) partida. —**parting of the ways,** separación.
partisan ('par·tə·zən) *n.* **1,** (adherent) partidario. **2,** (guerrilla) guerrillero; *Amer.* montonero. —*adj.* partidario; partidista. —**partisanship,** *n.* partidismo.

partition (par'tiʃ·ən) *n.* partición; división. —*v.t.* dividir.
partitive ('par·tə,tɪv) *adj.* partitivo.
partly ('part·li) *adv.* parcialmente; en parte.
partner ('part·nər) *n.* **1,** (companion) compañero. **2,** (dancing companion) pareja. **3,** (associate) socio. **4,** (spouse) consorte; cónyuge.
partnership ('part·nər·ʃɪp) *n.* **1,** (association) asociación. **2,** (business firm) sociedad.
partridge ('par·trɪdʒ) *n.* perdiz.
part-time *adj.* por horas; parcial. —**part time,** trabajo parcial *o* por horas.
parturition (,par·tjʊ'rɪʃ·ən) *n.* parto. —**parturient** (par'tjʊr·i·ənt) *adj.* parturienta.
party ('par·ti) *n.* **1,** *polit.* partido. **2,** (social event) fiesta. **3,** (group engaged in sport or play) partida. **4,** (detachment; detail) grupo; cuerpo. **5,** *law* parte; parte contratante. —**party line, 1,** (of telephones) línea compartida por dos o más abonados; línea común. **2,** *polit.* doctrina *o* política del partido. —**party wall,** (pared) medianera.
parvenu ('par·və,nju) *n.* advenedizo.
paschal ('pas·kəl) *adj.* pascual.
pasha ('pa·ʃə) *n.* bajá; pachá.
pasquinade (,pæs·kwɪ'neid) *n.* pasquinada.
pass (pæs) *v.t.* & *i.* pasar. —*n.* **1,** (act of passing) pase; paso. **2,** (defile) paso. **3,** (state of affairs) estado; situación. **4,** (free ticket; permit) pase. **5,** (movement; gesture) pase. —**bring to pass,** causar; ocasionar. —**come to pass,** suceder; ocurrir; pasar. —**let pass,** dejar pasar; pasar por alto. —**make a pass at, 1,** (attempt to strike) amenazar; intentar golpear. **2,** *slang* (make amorous advances to) dar un pase a. —**pass away, 1,** (cease) pasar. **2,** (spend, as time) pasar. **3,** (die) morir. —**pass off, 1,** (cease) pasar. **2,** (take place; go through) realizarse. **3,** (be or cause to be accepted) pasar. —**pass out, 1,** (leave) salir. **2,** *slang* (faint) desmayarse. —**pass over,** pasar por alto. —**pass the buck,** *slang* escurrir *o* pasar el bulto. —**pass up,** *slang* dejar pasar; perder; desperdiciar.
passable ('pæs·ə·bəl) *adj.* pasable; pasadero.
passage ('pæs·ɪdʒ) *n.* **1,** (voyage; crossing) travesía; cruce; pasaje. **2,** (road; pass) paso. **3,** (permission to pass) pase; paso. **4,** (right to be conveyed) pasaje. **5,** (change; transition) paso; transición; cambio. **6,** (lapse, as of time) transcurso; lapso. **7,** (occurrence; incident) pasaje. **8,** (excerpt) pasaje. **9,** (enactment) aprobación; pasaje. **10,** = **passageway. 11,** (exchange; reciprocation) intercambio. —**of passage,** migratorio; transeúnte.
passageway *n.* **1,** (hall; corridor) pasillo; corredor; pasadizo. **2,** (alley; way) callejón.
passbook *n.* **1,** (account book) libro de cuentas. **2,** (bankbook) libreta de banco.
passementerie (pæs'mɛn·tri) *n.* pasamano.
passenger ('pæs·ən·dʒər) *n.* pasajero.
passer-by (,pæs·ər'bai) *n.* [*pl.* **passers-by**] viandante; transeúnte.
passing ('pæs·ɪŋ) *adj.* pasajero; que pasa. —*n.* paso. —*adv., archaic* muy; sumamente. —**in passing,** de paso. —**passing grade,** aprobación.
passion ('pæʃ·ən) *n.* pasión. —**passionate** (-ɪt) *adj.* apasionado. —**passionless,** *adj.* frío; indiferente.
passionflower *n.* pasionaria.
passive ('pæs·ɪv) *adj.* pasivo. —**passivity** (pə'sɪv·ə·ti) *n.* pasividad.
passkey *n.* **1,** (master key) llave maestra. **2,** (private key) llave; llave particular.
Passover *n.* pascua; pascua de las hebreos.
passport *n.* pasaporte.
password *n.* contraseña.
past (pæst) *adj.* & *n.* pasado. —*prep.* **1,** (farther on than) más allá de. **2,** (farther in time than; after) después de; más tarde que. **3,** (beyond; in excess of) más allá de; fuera de; más de; en exceso de. **4,** (along the length of) por. **5,** (before; along the front of) por delante de. —*adv.* de largo; por delante.
paste (peist) *n.* **1,** (dough) masa. **2,** (smooth, malleable substance) pasta. **3,** (adhesive) engrudo; pe-

gote. —*v.t.* **1,** (make adhere) pegar. **2,** (cover with pasted material) cubrir con papel, afiches, *etc.;* empapelar. **3,** *slang* (hit) pegar; propinar.

pasteboard *n.* cartón. —*adj.* de cartón.

pastel (pæs'tɛl) *n. & adj.* pastel.

pasteurize ('pæs·tə,raiz) *v.t.* pasteurizar. —**pasteurization** (-rɪ·'zei·ʃən) *n.* pasteurización.

pastille (pæs'ti;l) *n.* **1,** (tablet; lozenge) pastilla; tableta. **2,** (pastel crayon) pastel.

pastime ('pæs,taim) *n.* pasatiempo.

pastor ('pæs·tər) *n.* pastor; ministro. —**pastoral,** *adj.* pastoral. —**pastorale** (-tə'ræl) *n.* pastoral.

pastry ('peis·tri) *n.* **1,** (paste) pasta; pastel. **2,** (baked goods) pastas (*pl.*); pasteles (*pl.*); pastelería. —**pastry cook,** pastelero; repostero. —**pastry shop,** pastelería; repostería.

pasturage ('pæs·tʃər·ɪdʒ) *n.* **1,** = **pasture. 2,** (pasturing) pastoreo.

pasture ('pæs·tʃər) *n.* **1,** (grass; fodder) pasto; hierba. **2,** (ground for grazing) pastadero; apacentadero. —*v.t.* **1,** (put to graze) pastorear; pastar; apacentar. **2,** (graze on) pacer; apacentarse de. —*v.i.* apacentarse; pacer; pastar.

pasty ('peis·ti) *adj.* **1,** (like paste) pastoso. **2,** (pale) pálido. —*n.* pastel; pastelillo. —**pastiness,** *n.* pastosidad.

pat (pæt) *n.* **1,** (tap, as with the hand) palmadita; golpe suave dado de plano. **2,** (light sound) ruido ligero; sonido leve. **3,** (small lump) pedazo de masa; pastilla. —*adj.* **1,** (opportune; timely) oportuno; apto. **2,** (exactly suitable) de perilla. —*adv.* oportunamente; aptamente; de perilla. —*v.t.* [**patted, patting**] **1,** (tap; stroke, as with the hand) dar palmaditas en *o* contra; dar golpecitos de plano a; palmotear; palmear. **2,** (give shape to by patting) moldear a palmaditas. **3,** (caress) acariciar. —*v.i.* sonar *o* golpear ligeramente. —**have** (*o* **know**) **pat,** *colloq.* conocer a fondo. —**stand pat,** *colloq.* **1,** (refuse to budge) estar *o* seguir en sus trece; obstinarse. **2,** *cards* chantarse.

patch (pætʃ) *n.* **1,** (covering, as for mending) parche; remiendo. **2,** (covering, as a dressing or shield) parche. **3,** (splotch; contrasting area) mancha. **4,** (small area) extensión pequeña; pedazo. **5,** (planted area) sembrado pequeño. **6,** (plot of land) lote de terreno; pequeño lote. **7,** (bit; remnant) retazo. —*v.t.* **1,** (mend) remendar; *Amer.* parchar. **2,** (fix or put together hurriedly) hacer o componer a la diabla; remendar; chapucear. —**patch up,** remediar; poner fin a; resolver.

patchwork *n.* **1,** (needlework) labor de retazos. **2,** (jumble) mezcla abigarrada. **3,** (sloppy work) chapucería.

patchy ('pætʃ·i) *adj.* irregular; chapuceado.

pate (peit) *n.* coronilla; mollera.

patent ('pæt·ənt; 'pei·tənt) *adj.* **1,** (obvious; visible) patente. **2,** (open to all) de dominio público. **3,** (patented) patentado. —*n.* patente. —*v.t.* patentar. —**patent leather,** charol. —**patent medicine,** medicina de patente.

paternal (pə'tʌɹ·nəl) *adj.* **1,** (fatherly) paternal. **2,** (inherited) paterno.

paternalism (pə'tʌɹ·nə·lɪz·əm) *n.* paternalismo. —**paternalistic,** *adj.* paternalista.

paternity (pə'tʌɹ·nə·ti) *n.* paternidad.

paternoster ('pei·tər,nas·tər) *n.* paternóster; padrenuestro.

path (pæθ) *n.* **1,** (track; trail; walk) senda; sendero; vereda; caminito. **2,** (course; trajectory) curso; trayectoria. **3,** (course of behavior or procedure) camino; senda; curso.

-path (pæθ) *sufijo* -pata; *forma nombres de personas que corresponden a nombres terminados en* **-pathy**: *psychopath,* psicópata; *homeopath,* homeópata.

pathetic (pə'θɛt·ɪk) *adj.* patético.

pathfinder *n.* explorador; guía; baquiano.

-pathia (pæθ·i·ə) *sufijo, var. de* **-path.**

-pathic ('pæθ·ɪk) *sufijo* -pático; *forma adjetivos de nombres terminados en* **-pathy:** *psychopathic,* psicopático; *homeopathic,* homeopático.

patho- (pæθ·o; -ə) *prefijo* pato-;

enfermedad: *pathology*, patología.
pathogenic (ˌpæθ·əˈdʒɛn·ɪk) *adj.* patógeno.
pathology (pəˈθal·ə·dʒi) *n.* patología. **—pathological** (ˌpæθ·əˈladʒ·ɪ·kəl) *adj.* patológico. **—pathologist**, *n.* patólogo.
pathos (ˈpei·θas) *n.* patetismo.
pathway *n.* senda; sendero; vereda.
-pathy (pæθ·i; pə·θi) *sufijo* -patía. **1,** sensación; afección; sufrimiento: *antipathy*, antipatía. **2,** enfermedad: *psychopathy*, psicopatía. **3,** tratamiento de enfermedades: *homeopathy*, homeopatía.
patience (ˈpei·ʃəns) *n.* **1,** (quality or fact of being patient) paciencia. **2,** (card game) solitario.
patient (ˈpei·ʃənt) *adj.* & *n.* paciente.
patina (ˈpæt·ə·nə) *n.* pátina.
patio (ˈpa·ti·o; ˈpæt·i·o) *n.* patio.
patois (ˈpæt·wa) *n.* jerga; dialecto; patuá.
patri- (pei·tri; pæt·rə) *prefijo* patri-; padre: *patriarchy*, patriarcado.
patriarch (ˈpei·tri·ark) *n.* patriarca. **—patriarchal**, *adj.* patriarcal. **—patriarchate** (-ˌar·kɪt) *n.* patriarcado. **—patriarchy**, *n.* patriarcado.
patrician (pəˈtrɪʃ·ən) *n.* &. *adj.* patricio.
patricide (ˈpæt·rəˌsaid) *n.* **1,** (agent) parricida. **2,** (act) parricidio. **—patricidal** (-ˈsai·dəl) *adj.* parricida.
patrimony (ˈpæt·rəˌmo·ni) *n.* patrimonio. **—patrimonial** (-ˈmo·ni·əl) *adj.* patrimonial.
patriot (ˈpei·tri·ət) *n.* patriota. **—patriotic** (-ˈat·ɪk) *adj.* patriótico. **—patriotism**, *n.* patriotismo.
patrol (pəˈtroːl) *v.t.* & *i.* patrullar. **—***n.* **1,** (group patrolling) patrulla. **2,** (act of patrolling) patrullaje. **—patrol wagon**, camión de policía; coche celular.
patrolman (pəˈtrol·mən) *n.* [*pl.* **-men**] agente de policía; policía; guardia municipal.
patron (ˈpei·trən) *n.* **1,** (protector) protector; patrono. **2,** (sponsor; advocate) patrocinador; patrón. **3,** (customer) cliente. **4,** (patron saint) patrón; patrono. **—patroness**, *n.* patrocinadora; protectora; patrona.
patronage (ˈpei·trən·ɪdʒ) *n.* **1,** (status or function of a patron) patronato. **2,** (sponsorship) patrocinio. **3,** (condescension) condescendencia. **4,** (clientele) clientela.
patronal (ˈpei·trən·əl) *adj.* patronal.
patronize (ˈpei·trəˌnaiz) *v.t.* **1,** (sponsor; support) patrocinar. **2,** (treat with condescension) mostrarse condescendiente con; tratar *o* mirar con condescendencia. **3,** (be a regular customer of) ser cliente de; ser parroquiano (asiduo) de. **—patronizing**, *adj.* condescendiente.
patronymic (ˌpæt·rəˈnɪm·ɪk) *adj.* & *n.* patronímico.
patter (ˈpæt·ər) *v.i.* **1,** (tap) golpetear; tamborilear; repiquetear. **2,** (walk with a tapping sound) caminar con pasito ligero; caminar golpeteando; traquetear. **—***v.t.* & *i.* (recite mechanically) recitar mecánicamente; barbotear. **—***n.* **1,** (tapping noise) golpeteo; tamborileo; repiqueteo. **2,** (chatter) charla; parloteo. **3,** (jargon) jerga; jerigonza.
pattern (ˈpæt·ərn) *n.* **1,** (design) dibujo; diseño. **2,** (model; guide) modelo; patrón. **3,** (arrangement; distribution) arreglo; distribución; configuración. **4,** (norm) pauta; norma. **—***v.t.* modelar. **—pattern oneself after**, imitar; modelarse de acuerdo a.
patty (ˈpæt·i) *n.* pastelillo; empanada; croqueta; torta.
paucity (ˈpɔ·sə·ti) *n.* parquedad; escasez.
paunch (pɔntʃ) *n.* panza; vientre; barriga. **—paunchy**, *adj.* panzón; barrigón.
pauper (ˈpɔ·pər) *n.* pobre; indigente; necesitado. **—pauperism**, *n.* pauperismo. **—pauperize**, *v.t.* empobrecer.
pause (pɔːz) *n.* pausa. **—***v.i.* hacer pausa; pausar.
pave (peiv) *v.t.* pavimentar. **—pave the way**, allanar el camino.
pavilion (pəˈvɪl·jən) *n.* pabellón.
paving (ˈpei·vɪŋ) *n.* **1,** = **pavement. 2,** (act or work of one who paves) pavimentación.
pavement (ˈpeiv·mənt) *n.* pavimento.
paw (pɔː) *n.* pata; mano o pie de un animal. **—***v.t.* **1,** (strike with the paws) manotear. **2,** (handle; stroke) manosear.

pawl (pɔl) *n.* trinquete.
pawn (pɔn) *n.* **1,** (chess piece) peón. **2,** (pledge) prenda. —*v.t.* empeñar.
pawnbroker *n.* prestamista.
pawnshop *n.* casa de empeño; casa de préstamos; monte de piedad.
pay (pei) *v.t. & i.* [*pret. & p.p.* **paid**] **1,** (give, as in return; repay) pagar. **2,** (give satisfaction to; be profitable to) convenir (a); ser provechoso (a). **3,** (cover or treat with pitch) embrear. —*n.* paga. —**in the pay of,** al servicio de. —**pay as you go,** pagar a medida que se va comprando. —**pay attention,** poner *o* prestar atención. —**pay back,** devolver; pagar de vuelta. —**pay down,** pagar al contado. —**pay off, 1,** (discharge a debt) pagar lo debido; pagar en total. **2,** (take revenge on or for) vengarse de. **3,** (succeed; return a profit) dar resultados; tener éxito. —**pay one's way,** pagar lo que a uno le toca. —**pay out, 1,** (expend) pagar. **2,** (let out, as a rope) soltar; aflojar; dar. —**pay up,** pagar; pagar en total.
payable ('pei·ə·bəl) *adj.* pagadero.
payday *n.* día de paga.
pay dirt terreno *o* mineral explotable.
payee (pei'iː) *n.* portador; tenedor.
payer ('pei·ər) *n.* pagador.
payload *n.* carga útil.
paymaster *n.* pagador. —**paymaster's office,** pagaduría.
payment ('pei·mənt) *n.* **1,** (act of paying; amount paid) pago. **2,** (installment) plazo.
payoff *n.* **1,** (payment) paga. **2,** (result) éxito; resultado.
payroll *n.* **1,** (list) nómina. **2,** (money) paga.
pea (piː) *n.* guisante; *Amer.* arveja.
peace (pis) *n.* paz. —*interj.* ¡paz!; ¡silencio! —**peaceable,** *adj.* pacífico; apacible. —**peaceful,** *adj.* tranquilo; pacífico. —**at peace,** en paz. —**hold** (*o* **keep**) **one's peace,** mantenerse sereno; quedarse tranquilo. —**keep the peace,** mantener el orden. —**make one's peace with,** hacer las paces con. —**make peace,** hacer las paces.
peacemaker *n.* pacificador. —**peacemaking,** *adj.* pacificador.
peace officer guardián del orden público; guardia municipal.
peacetime *n.* período de paz; tiempos de paz.
peach (pitʃ) *n.* **1,** (fruit) melocotón; durazno. **2,** (tree) melocotonero; durazno; duraznero. **3,** (color) color de melocotón; color durazno. **4,** *slang* (charming thing) encanto; preciosidad. —*adj.* de melocotón; de durazno. —*v.i., slang* cantar. —**peach on,** *slang* denunciar; delatar.
peachy ('pi·tʃi) *adj.* **1,** (peachlike) como *o* de melocotón *o* durazno. **2,** *slang* (excellent) estupendo; precioso.
peacock ('pi,kak) *n.* pavo real.
peak (pik) *n.* **1,** (pointed end) punta; pico. **2,** (crest; summit) cúspide; cima; cumbre. **3,** (mountain) pico; montaña. **4,** (maximum) máximo. **5,** (highest point or degree) cumbre; apogeo; pináculo. —*v.i.* extenuarse; consumirse; enflaquecer.
peaked (pikt) *adj.* **1,** (pointed) puntiagudo. **2,** ('pik·ɪd) *colloq.* (sickly; emaciated) demacrado; pálido; enfermizo.
peal (piːl) *n.* **1,** (loud noise) estruendo; estrépito; fragor. **2,** (ringing of a bell or bells) repique; repiqueteo. —*v.i. & t.* resonar; repicar. —**peal of laughter,** carcajada.
peanut ('pi,nʌt) *n.* cacahuete; *Amer.* maní.
pear (peːr) *n.* pera. —**pear tree,** peral.
pearl (pʌɹl) *n.* perla. —**pearly,** *adj.* de perla; perlado.
peasant ('pɛz·ənt) *n.* campesino; rústico. —**peasantry,** *n.* campesinaje; campesinos (*pl.*).
peashooter *n.* cerbatana.
peat (pit) *n.* turba. —**peat moss,** musgo pantanoso.
pebble ('pɛb·əl) *n.* guija; guijarro. —*v.t.* granular; abollonar. —**pebbled,** *adj.* guijoso; guijarroso.
pecan (pi'kaːn) *n.* **1,** (fruit) pacana. **2,** (tree) pacano.
peccadillo (,pɛk·ə'dɪl·o) *n.* pecadillo.
peccary ('pɛk·ə·ri) *n.* pecarí.
peck (pɛk) *n.* **1,** (measure) medida de áridos (9.09 litros). **2,** (nip) picotazo. **3,** *colloq.* (kiss) besito. —*v.t. & i.* picotear.

pectin ('pɛk·tɪn) *n.* pectina.
pectoral ('pɛk·tə·rəl) *adj.* & *n.* pectoral.
peculate ('pɛk·jəˌleit) *v.t.* & *i.* malversar. —**peculation,** *n.* desfalco; malversación; peculado.
peculiar (pɪ'kjul·jər) *adj.* peculiar. —**peculiarity** (-'jær·ə·ti) *n.* peculiaridad.
pecuniary (pɪ'kju·ni·ɛr·i) *adj.* pecuniario.
ped- (pɛd) *prefijo, var. de* **pedi-** *o de* **pedo-.**
-ped (pɛd) *también,* **-pede** (pid) *sufijo* -pedo; pie; *con determinado número o género de pies o patas: quadruped,* cuadrúpedo; *aliped,* alípedo.
pedagogue ('pɛd·əˌgag) *n.* pedagogo. —**pedagogical** (-'gadʒ·ɪ·kəl) *adj.* pedagógico. —**pedagogy** (-ˌgo·dʒi) *n.* pedagogía.
pedal ('pɛd·əl) *adj.* del pie. —*n.* pedal. —*v.t.* & *i.* pedalear.
pedant ('pɛd·ənt) *n.* pedante. —**pedantic** (pə'dæn·tɪk) *adj.* pedante; pedantesco. —**pedantry,** *n.* pedantería.
peddle ('pɛd·əl) *v.t.* vender de puerta en puerta; vender por las calles *o* de casa en casa. —*v.i.* vender cosas de buhonería; hacer de mercachifle. —**peddler** (-lər) *n.* buhonero; mercachifle.
pederast ('pɛd·əˌræst) *n.* pederasta. —**pederasty,** *n.* pederastia.
pedestal ('pɛd·ɪs·təl) *n.* pedestal.
pedestrian (pə'dɛs·tri·ən) *n.* peatón. —*adj.* pedestre.
pedi- (pɛd·ɪ; pi·di) *también* **ped-** (pɛd; pid) *ante vocal; prefijo* pedi-: **1,** pie: *pedicure,* pedicuro. **2,** niño: *pediatrics,* pediatría.
-pedia (pi·di·ə) *sufijo* -pedia; educación; enseñanza: *encyclopedia,* enciclopedia.
pediatrics (ˌpi·di'æt·rɪks) *n.* pediatría. —**pediatric,** *adj.* pediátrico. —**pediatrician** (-ə'trɪʃ·ən) *n.* pediatra; especialista de niños.
-pedics (pi·dɪks) *sufijo* -pedia; adiestramiento; corrección: *orthopedics,* ortopedia.
pedicure ('pɛd·əˌkjʊr) *n.* **1,** (treatment) pedicura. **2,** (practitioner) pedicuro.
pedigree ('pɛd·əˌgri) *n.* ascendencia; genealogía; linaje. —**pedigreed,** *adj.* de pura raza.
pediment ('pɛd·ə·mənt) *n.* frontón.
pedo- (pi·do) *también,* **ped-** (pid) *ante vocal; prefijo* pedo-; niño: *pedodontia,* pedodoncia.
pedometer (pɪ'dam·ə·tər) *n.* podómetro; cuentapasos.
peek (pik) *v.i.* mirar a hurtadillas; atisbar. —*n.* mirada furtiva.
peel (piːl) *v.t.* **1,** (pare, as a fruit) pelar; mondar; descascarar. **2,** (cut off, as the rind, skin, etc.) quitar (la cáscara, el hollejo, etc.). **3,** (cause to become unstuck) despegar. —*v.i.* **1,** (shed skin, as when sunburnt) despellejarse; pelarse. **2,** (come off, as old paint) descascararse. **3,** *colloq.* (undress) desnudarse. —*n.* cáscara. —**peelings,** *n.pl.* cáscaras; mondaduras.
peen (piːn) *n.* punta *o* cabeza del martillo.
peep (pip) *v.i.* **1,** (appear) asomar; empezar a mostrarse. **2,** (peek) atisbar. **3,** (chirp) piar; gorjear. —*n.* **1,** (look) mirada furtiva *o* rápida. **2,** (glimpse) vistazo. **3,** (bird cry) pío; gorjeo.
peephole *n.* atisbadero; rendija; portillo.
peer (pɪr) *n.* **1,** (equal) igual; par. **2,** (nobleman) par; grande. —*v.i.* **1,** (look closely) escrutar con la mirada; mirar. **2,** (come partly into sight) asomar.
peerage ('pɪr·ɪdʒ) *n.* **1,** (rank) dignidad de par. **2,** (peers collectively) pares (*pl.*); nobleza. **3,** (list of peers) guía de la nobleza.
peeress ('pɪr·ɪs) *n.f.* paresa.
peerless ('pɪr·ləs) *adj.* sin par; incomparable.
peeve (piːv) *v.t., colloq.* enfadar; enojar. —*v.i. colloq.* enfadarse; enojarse. —*n., colloq.* enfado; enojo.
peevish ('pi·vɪʃ) *adj.* **1,** (fretful; irritable) irritable; enojadizo. **2,** (ill-tempered) malhumorado; impaciente. —**peevishness,** *n.* mal humor.
peg (pɛg) *n.* **1,** (pin; small bolt) clavija; estaca; estaquilla; claveta. **2,** (step; degree) escalón; grado. —*v.t.* **1,** (fasten with pegs) clavar; sujetar con estacas. **2,** (mark with pegs) estacar; marcar con estacas. **3,** (fix the price of) fijar; fijar el precio de; estabilizar. —**a peg to hang (something) on,** excusa para; pretexto para; ocasión para. —**peg**

leg, pata de palo. —**take (someone) down a peg**, cortarle a uno las alas; quitarle a uno las ínfulas.
peignoir (pen'waːr) *n.* peinador; bata.
pejorative (pɪ'dʒor·ə·tɪv) *adj.* peyorativo; despectivo.
pelf (pɛlf) *n.* vil parné; dinero ruin.
pelican ('pɛl·ə·kən) *n.* pelícano.
pelisse (pə'lis) *n.* pelliza.
pellagra (pə'lei·grə) *n.* pelagra.
pellet ('pɛl·ɪt) *n.* **1,** (small round ball) pelotilla; bolita. **2,** (pill) píldora. **3,** (lead shot) perdigón. **4,** (bullet) bala; plomo.
pellicle ('pɛl·ə·kəl) *n.* película; membrana.
pell-mell ('pɛl'mɛl) *adv.* confusamente; atropelladamente; a trochemoche.
pelt (pɛlt) *n.* **1,** (hide; fur) piel. **2,** (blow) golpe. **3,** (speed) velocidad. —*v.t.* **1,** (throw things at; assail) acribillar; bombardear. **2,** (beat heavily on) golpear. **3,** (throw) tirar; arrojar; lanzar. —*v.i.* **1,** (strike heavily) golpear con fuerza. **2,** (speed; rush) correr apresuradamente. —**pelting,** *n.* golpeo. —*adj.* furioso; violento.
pelvis ('pɛl·vɪs) *n.* pelvis. —**pelvic,** *adj.* pelviano.
pen (pɛn) *n.* **1,** (enclosure) corral; redil; jaula. **2,** (writing implement) pluma. —*v.t.* **1,** (enclose) enjaular; encerrar. **2,** (write) escribir; componer. —**fountain pen,** estilográfica. —**pen name,** seudónimo.
penal ('pi·nəl) *adj.* penal. —**penalize,** *v.t.* penalizar; castigar.
penalty ('pɛn·əl·ti) *n.* **1,** (punishment) pena; penalidad. **2,** (fine) multa. **3,** (late charge) recargo. **4,** *sports* sanción.
penance ('pɛn·əns) *n.* penitencia.
pence (pɛns) *n.pl.* centavos; peniques.
penchant ('pɛn·tʃənt) *n.* inclinación; gusto; afición.
pencil ('pɛn·səl) *n.* lápiz. —*v.t.* **1,** (draw or write with a pencil) trazar con lápiz; escribir con lápiz. **2,** (use a pencil on) pasar el lápiz sobre; recalcar con lápiz. —**pencil sharpener,** sacapuntas; cortalápiz.
pend (pɛnd) *v.i.* **1,** (hang) colgar; pender. **2,** (await settlement) estar pendiente; estar suspendido.
pendant ('pɛn·dənt) *n.* **1,** (ornament) pendiente; adorno. **2,** (chandelier) araña de luces.
pendent ('pɛn·dənt) *adj.* **1,** (hanging) colgado; colgante; suspendido. **2,** = **pending.** —*n.m.* = **pendant.**
pending ('pɛn·dɪŋ) *adj.* pendiente; indeciso; suspendido. —*prep.* **1,** (awaiting) en espera de **2,** (during) durante.
pendulous ('pɛn·dʒə·ləs) *adj.* pendiente; colgante; péndulo.
pendulum ('pɛn·dʒə·ləm) *n.* péndulo.
penetrate ('pɛn·ɪˌtreit) *v.t. & i.* penetrar. —**penetrable,** *adj.* penetrable. —**penetrating,** *adj.* penetrante. —**penetration,** *n.* penetración.
penguin ('pɛŋ·gwɪn) *n.* pingüino.
penholder *n.* portaplumas; *Amer.* plumero.
penicillin (ˌpɛn·ə'sɪl·ən) *n.* penicilina.
peninsula (pə'nɪn·sə·lə) *n.* península. —**peninsular,** *adj.* peninsular.
penis ('pi·nɪs) *n.* pene.
penitence ('pɛn·ə·təns) *n.* penitencia.
penitent ('pɛn·ə·tənt) *adj.* penitente; arrepentido; contrito. —*n.* penitente. —**penitential** (-'tɛn·ʃəl) *adj.* penitencial.
penitentiary (ˌpɛn·ə'tɛn·ʃə·ri) *n.* **1,** (prison) penitenciaría. **2,** *R.C.Ch.* penitenciario. —*adj.* penitenciario.
penknife ('pɛnˌnaif) *n.* cortaplumas.
penman ('pɛn·mən) *n.* [*pl.* **-men**] pendolista; calígrafo. —**penmanship,** *n.* escritura; caligrafía.
pennant ('pɛn·ənt) *n.* gallardete; pendón.
penni- (pɛn·ɪ) *prefijo* peni-; pluma: *penniform,* peniforme.
penny ('pɛn·i) *n.* centavo; penique. —**penniless,** *adj.* arruinado; pelado; sin un centavo.
-penny (pɛn·i; pə·ni) *sufijo; acompañando a un numeral indica* **1,** precio: *sixpenny,* seis peniques. **2,** tamaño, esp. de clavos: *tenpenny nail,* clavo tamaño diez.
pennyweight *n.* medida de peso de 24 granos.
penology (pi'nal·ə·dʒi) *n.* penología; ciencia penal. —**penologist,** *n.* penalista.
pension ('pɛn·ʃən) *n.* **1,** (pay-

ment) pensión; beca. 2, (pan·si·'ON) (boarding house) pensión de familia; casa de huéspedes. —*v.t.* pensionar; jubilar. —**pensioner** ('pɛn·ʃən·ər) *n.* pensionado; pensionista.

pensive ('pɛn·sɪv) *adj.* pensativo.

pent (pɛnt) *adj.* acorralado; encerrado; enjaulado.

penta- (pɛn·tə) *también,* **pent-** (pɛnt) *ante vocal; prefijo* penta-; cinco: *pentagon,* pentágono.

pentagon ('pɛn·tə·gan) *n.* pentágono. —**pentagonal** (pɛn'tæg·ə·nəl) *adj.* pentagonal.

pentahedron (ˌpɛn·tə'hi·drən) *n.* pentaedro.

pentameter (pɛn'tæm·ə·tər) *n.* pentámetro.

Pentateuch ('pɛn·təˌtjuk) *n.* Pentateuco.

pentathlon (pɛn'tæθ·lən) *n.* pentatlón.

Pentecost ('pɛn·təˌkost) *n.* Pentecostés. —**Pentecostal** (-'kos·təl) *adj. & n.* pentecostal.

penthouse ('pɛntˌhaus) *n.* **1,** (roof house or apartment) apartamiento o casa de azotea. **2,** (annex; pavilion) pabellón; anexo. **3,** (outbuilding) colgadizo.

pent-up ('pɛntˌʌp) *adj.* contenido; reprimido.

penult ('pi·nʌlt) *n.* penúltima (sílaba).

penultimate (pɪ'nʌl·tɪ·mət) *adj.* penúltimo.

penumbra (pɪ'nʌm·brə) *n.* penumbra. —**penumbral,** *adj.* penumbroso; de penumbra.

penurious (pə'njʊr·i·əs) *adj.* tacaño; ruin; avaro. —**penuriousness,** *n.* tacañería; ruindad.

penury ('pɛn·jə·ri) *n.* penuria; miseria; pobreza.

peon ('pi·an) *n.* peón. —**peonage** (-ən·ɪdʒ) *n.* peonaje.

peony ('pi·ə·ni) *n.* peonía.

people ('pi·pəl) *n.* **1,** (group; tribe; nation) pueblo; gente. **2,** *pl.* (populace) pueblo; masas; gente. **3,** *pl., colloq.* (persons) personas; gente (*sing.*). —*v.t.* poblar.

pep (pɛp) *n., slang* energía; vigor; fuerza. —*v.t.* [*también,* **pep up**] estimular; animar. —**peppy,** *adj., slang* enérgico; vigoroso; animado.

pepper ('pɛp·ər) *n.* **1,** (spice) pimienta. **2,** (plant) pimentero. —*v.t.* **1,** (season) rociar con pimienta o ají. **2,** (riddle) acribillar. **3,** (dot; sprinkle) salpicar; motear. —**red pepper,** pimiento; ají; (*when ground*) pimentón.

peppercorn *n.* grano de pimienta.

peppermint *n.* **1,** (plant) hierbabuena; menta. **2,** (candy) pastilla de menta.

-pepsia (pɛp·si·ə) *sufijo* -pepsia; digestión: *dyspepsia,* dispepsia.

pepsin ('pɛp·sɪn) *n.* pepsina.

peptic ('pɛp·tɪk) *adj.* péptico.

-peptic (pɛp·tɪk) *sufijo* -péptico; *forma adjetivos de nombres terminados en* **-pepsia**: *dyspeptic,* dispéptico.

peptide ('pɛp·taid) *n.* péptido.

peptone ('pɛp·ton) *n.* peptona.

per (pʌɹ) *prep.* **1,** (by means of; through) por; por medio de. **2,** (for each) por; por cada. —**as per,** de acuerdo a.

per- (pʌɹ; pər) *prefijo* per-. **1,** a través: *perennial,* perenne. **2,** completamente; del todo: *persuade,* persuadir. **3,** *quím.* mayor valencia: *peroxide,* peróxido.

peradventure (ˌpʌɹ·æd'vɛn·tʃər) *adv.* quizás; acaso; por ventura; por casualidad.

perambulate (pər'æm·bjəˌleit) *v.i.* ambular; pasear.

perambulator (pər'æm·bjəˌlei·tər) *n.* **1,** (promenader) paseante. **2,** (baby carriage) cochecillo de niño.

per annum (pər'æn·əm) *adv.* anualmente; cada año; al año.

percale (pər'keil) *n.* percal.

per capita (pər'kæp·ə·tə) *adv.* por cabeza; por persona.

perceive (pər'siːv) *v.t.* percibir. —**perceivable,** *adj.* perceptible.

percent (pər'sɛnt) *n.* por ciento. —**percentage,** *n.* porcentaje.

perceptible (pər'sɛp·tə·bəl) *adj.* perceptible. —**perceptibility,** *n.* perceptibilidad.

perception (pər'sɛp·ʃən) *n.* percepción.

perceptive (pər'sɛp·tɪv) *adj.* perceptivo. —**perceptivity** (ˌpʌɹ·sɛp'tɪv·ə·ti) *n.* agudeza; perceptibilidad.

perch (pʌɹtʃ) *n.* **1,** (fish) perca. **2,** (land measure) pértica. **3,** (roost) percha. —*v.i.* **1,** (alight) posarse; pararse. **2,** (roost) encaramarse; estar encaramado. —*v.t.* encaramar.

perchance (pər'tʃæns) *adv.* quizás; tal vez.

percipient (pər'sɪp·i·ənt) *adj.* perceptivo; observador.

percolate ('pʌɹ·kəˌleit) *v.t.* colar; filtrar; pasar. —*v.i.* pasarse; filtrarse; rezumar. —**percolation,** *n.* filtración. —**percolator,** *n.* colador; filtro.

percussion (pər'kʌʃ·ən) *n.* percusión. —**percussion cap,** fulminante. —**percussion instrument,** instrumento de percusión.

per diem (pər'di·əm) *adv.* por día. —*n.* sustento diario.

perdition (pər'dɪʃ·ən) *n.* perdición.

peregrination (ˌpɛr·ə·grə'nei·ʃən) *n.* peregrinación.

peremptory (pə'rɛmp·tə·ri) *adj.* perentorio.

perennial (pə'rɛn·i·əl) *adj.* perenne. —*n.* planta perenne.

perfect ('pʌɹ·fɪkt) *adj.* perfecto. —*n., gram.* tiempo perfecto. —*v.t.* (pər'fɛkt) perfeccionar. —**perfection** (pər'fɛk·ʃən) *n.* perfección. —**perfectionist,** *n.* perfeccionista.

perfidy ('pʌɹ·fə·di) *n.* perfidia. —**perfidious** (pər'fɪd·i·əs) *adj.* pérfido.

perforate ('pʌɹ·fəˌreit) *v.t.* perforar. —**perforation,** *n.* perforación. —**perforator,** *n.* perforador; perforadora.

perforce (pər'fors) *adv.* por fuerza; por necesidad.

perform (pər'form) *v.t.* **1,** (execute; carry out) ejecutar; llevar a cabo. **2,** (act out; enact) representar. **3,** (sing) cantar. **4,** (play, as a musical piece) tocar; ejecutar. —*v.i.* **1,** (work; function) operar; trabajar; funcionar. **2,** (act) ser actor; representar; desempeñar un papel. **3,** (sing) cantar. **4,** (play) tocar. —**performer,** *n.* artista; intérprete; ejecutante; actor.

performance (pər'for·məns) *n.* **1,** (execution; accomplishment) ejecución; desempeño. **2,** (operation; functioning) funcionamiento. **3,** (acting of a role) actuación. **4,** (show; program) representación; función; programa; espectáculo.

perfume (pər'fjum) *n.* perfume. —*v.t.* perfumar. —**perfumer,** *n.* perfumista; perfumero. —**perfumery,** *n.* perfumería.

perfunctory (pər'fʌŋk·tə·ri) *adj.* perfunctorio; de fórmula.

perhaps (pər'hæps) *adv.* quizás; tal vez; acaso; a lo mejor.

peri- (pɛr·i; -ə) *prefijo* peri-; alrededor: *periphery,* periferia.

perigee ('pɛr·əˌdʒi) *n.* perigeo.

perihelion (ˌpɛr·ə'hi·li·ən) *n.* perihelio.

peril ('pɛr·əl) *n.* peligro; riesgo. —*v.t.* poner en riesgo; hacer peligrar. —**perilous,** *adj.* peligroso; arriesgado.

perimeter (pə'rɪm·ɪ·tər) *n.* perímetro.

period ('pɪr·i·əd) *n.* **1,** (time; epoch) período; época; tiempo. **2,** (end of sentence) punto. **3,** (termination) terminación; punto final. **4,** (menstruation) menstruación; período. **5,** *rhet.; music; physics* período.

periodic (ˌpɪr·i'ad·ɪk) *adj.* periódico.

periodical (ˌpɪr·i'ad·ə·kəl) *adj.* & *n.* periódico.

peripatetic (ˌpɛr·ə·pə'tɛt·ɪk) *adj.* & *n.* peripatético.

periphery (pə'rɪf·ə·ri) *n.* periferia. —**peripheral,** *adj.* periférico.

periphrasis (pə'rɪf·rə·sɪs) *n.* perífrasis. —**periphrastic** (ˌpɛr·ə'fræs·tɪk) *adj.* perifrástico.

periscope ('pɛr·əˌskop) *n.* periscopio.

perish ('pɛr·ɪʃ) *v.i.* perecer. —**perish the thought,** ni pensarlo.

perishable ('pɛr·ɪʃ·ə·bəl) *adj.* perecedero. —*n.* artículo perecedero.

peristalsis (ˌpɛr·ə'stæl·sɪs) *n.* peristalsis. —**peristaltic** (-tɪk) *adj.* peristáltico.

peristyle ('pɛr·əˌstail) *n.* peristilo.

peritoneum (ˌpɛr·ə·tə'ni·əm) *n.* peritoneo. —**peritonitis** (-'nai·tɪs) *n.* peritonitis.

periwig ('pɛr·ɪ·wɪg) *n.* peluca.

periwinkle ('pɛr·əˌwɪŋ·kəl) *n.* **1,** *bot.* pervinca. **2,** *zool.* caracol marino; litorina.

perjure ('pʌɹ·dʒər) *v.t.* perjurar. —**perjured,** *adj.* perjuro; perjurado. —**perjurer,** *n.* perjuro. —**perjury,** *n.* perjurio. —**commit perjury,** *también,* **perjure oneself,** jurar en falso; perjurar; perjurarse.

perk (pʌɹk) *v.t.* & *i.* [*también,* **perk up**] **1,** (raise in eagerness) levantar(se); erguir(se). **2,** (cheer) animar(se). —**perky,** *adj., colloq.* vivaracho.

permanent ('pʌɹ·mə·nənt) *adj.*

& *n.* permanente. —**permanence,** *n.* permanencia.
permeable ('pʌɹ·mi·ə·bəl) *adj.* permeable. —**permeability,** *n.* permeabilidad.
permeate ('pʌɹ·mi,eit) *v.t.* & *i.* penetrar. —**permeation,** *n.* penetración.
permissible (pər'mɪs·ə·bəl) *adj.* permisible.
permission (pər'mɪʃ·ən) *n.* permiso; permisión.
permissive (pər'mɪs·ɪv) *adj.* permisivo.
permit ('pʌɹ·mɪt) *n.* permiso; licencia. —*v.t.* (pər'mɪt) permitir.
permute (pər'mjut) *v.t.* permutar. —**permutation** (,pʌɹ·mju'tei·ʃən) *n.* permutación.
pernicious (pər'nɪʃ·əs) *adj.* pernicioso. —**perniciousness,** *n.* perniciosidad.
peroration (,pɛr·ə'rei·ʃən) *n.* peroración.
peroxide (pə'rak·said) *n.* peróxido; agua oxigenada.
perpendicular (,pʌɹ·pən'dɪk·jə·lər) *adj.* & *n.* perpendicular.
perpetrate ('pʌɹ·pə,treit) *v.t.* perpetrar. —**perpetration,** *n.* perpetración.
perpetual (pər'pɛtʃ·u·əl) *adj.* perpetuo; continuo; eterno.
perpetuate (pər'pɛtʃ·u,eit) *v.t.* perpetuar. —**perpetuation,** *n.* perpetuación.
perpetuity (,pʌɹ·pə'tju·ə·ti) *n.* perpetuidad.
perplex (pər'plɛks) *v.t.* confundir; dejar perplejo. —**perplexed,** *adj.* perplejo; confuso. —**perplexing,** *adj.* incomprensible. —**perplexity,** *n.* perplejidad; confusión.
perquisite ('pʌɹ·kwɪ·zɪt) *n.* emolumento; propina; adehala.
per se (pəɹ'si; -'sei) en *o* por sí mismo.
persecute ('pʌɹ·sɪ,kjut) *v.t.* perseguir. —**persecution** (-'kju·ʃən) *n.* persecución. —**persecutor,** *n.* perseguidor.
persevere (,pʌɹ·sə'vɪr) *v.i.* perseverar. —**perseverance,** *n.* perseverancia. —**persevering,** *adj.* perseverante.
Persian (pʌɹ·ʒən) *adj.* persa; pérsico. —*n.* persa.
persiflage ('pʌɹ·sɪ,flaʒ) *n.* **1,** (lightness; frivolousness) ligereza; frivolidad. **2,** (banter) chanzas (*pl.*).
persimmon (pər'sɪm·ən) *n.* dióspiro; caqui; placaminero.
persist (pər'zɪst) *v.i.* persistir. —**persistence,** *n.* persistencia. —**persistent,** *adj.* persistente.
person ('pʌɹ·sən) *n.* persona.
personable ('pʌɹ·sən·ə·bəl) *adj.* presentable; bien parecido.
personage ('pʌɹ·sən·ɪdʒ) *n.* personaje.
personal ('pʌɹ·sən·əl) *adj.* personal. —**get personal,** *colloq.* hacer alusiones personales. —**make a personal appearance,** aparecer personalmente.
personality (,pʌɹ·sə'næl·ə·ti) *n.* **1,** (personal identity or character) personalidad. **2,** *colloq.* (personal charm) atracción; gracia. **3,** *pl.* (personal remarks) alusiones personales.
personalize ('pʌɹ·sə·nə,laɪz) *v.t.* personalizar.
personalty ('pʌɹ·sə·nəl·ti) *n.* bienes muebles; propiedad personal.
personify (pər'san·ə·fai) *v.t.* personificar. —**personification** (-fɪ·'kei·ʃən) *n.* personificación.
personnel (,pʌɹ·sə'nɛl) *n.* personal; empleados (*pl.*).
perspective (pər'spɛk·tɪv) *n.* perspectiva.
perspicacious (,pʌɹ·spə'kei·ʃəs) *adj.* perspicaz. —**perspicacity** (-'kæs·ə·ti) *n.* perspicacia.
perspicuous (pər'spɪk·ju·əs) *adj.* perspicuo. —**perspicuity** (,pʌɹ·spɪ·'kju·ə·ti) *n.* perspicuidad.
perspire (pər'spair) *v.t.* & *i.* sudar; transpirar. —**perspiration** (,pʌɹ·spɪ'rei·ʃən) *n.* sudor; transpiración. —**perspiratory** (-ə·,tor·i) *adj.* sudorífico.
persuade (pər'sweid) *v.t.* persuadir. —**persuadable,** *adj.* persuasible. —**persuader,** *n.* persuadidor. —**persuading,** *adj.* persuadidor.
persuasible (pər'swei·sə·bəl) *adj.* persuasible.
persuasion (pər'swei·ʃən) *n.* persuasión.
persuasive (pər'swei·sɪv) *adj.* persuasivo. —**persuasiveness,** *n.* persuasiva.
pert (pʌɹt) *adj.* **1,** (lively) vivaracho. **2,** (impudent) atrevido; descarado.
pertain (pər'tein) *v.i.* pertenecer.
pertinacious (,pʌɹ·tɪ'nei·ʃəs)

adj. pertinaz. —**pertinacity** (-'næs·ə·ti) *n.* pertinacia.

pertinent ('pʌɹ·tə·nənt) *adj.* pertinente. —**pertinence,** *n.* pertinencia.

perturb (pər'tʌɹb) *v.t.* perturbar. —**perturbation** (ˌpʌɹ·tər'bei·ʃən) *n.* perturbación.

peruke (pə'ruk) *n.* peluca.

peruse (pə'ruːz) *v.t.* examinar; leer atentamente. —**perusal,** *n.* lectura detenida; examen detenido.

Peruvian (pə'ru·vi·ən) *adj.* & *n.* peruano; peruviano.

pervade (pər'veid) *v.t.* difundirse por; extenderse por; penetrar. —**pervasion** (-'vei·ʒən) *n.* penetración; difusión.

perverse (pər'vʌɹs) *adj.* perverso; depravado; avieso. —**perverseness; perversity,** *n.* perversidad.

perversion (pər'vʌɹ·ʒən) *n.* perversión.

pervert (pər'vʌɹt) *v.t.* pervertir. —*n.* ('pʌɹ·vʌɹt) pervertido.

peseta (pə'sei·tə) *n.* peseta.

pesky ('pɛs·ki) *adj., colloq.* molesto; enfadoso.

peso ('pei·so) *n.* peso.

pessimism ('pɛs·ə·mɪz·əm) *n.* pesimismo. —**pessimist,** *n.* pesimista. —**pessimistic,** *adj.* pesimista.

pest (pɛst) *n.* peste.

pester ('pɛs·tər) *v.t.* molestar; cansar; importunar.

pestiferous (pɛs'tɪf·ər·əs) *adj.* pestífero.

pestilence ('pɛs·tə·ləns) *n.* pestilencia; peste. —**pestilential** (-'lɛn·ʃəl) *adj.* pestilente; pestilencial.

pestilent ('pɛs·tə·lənt) *adj.* pestilente.

pestle ('pɛs·əl) *n.* majador; mano de mortero.

pet (pɛt) *n.* **1,** (animal) animal casero *o* de la casa. **2,** (favorite) favorito. **3,** (peevishness) mal humor; enfado. —*adj.* **1,** (loved) acariciado; mimado. **2,** (favorite) favorito; preferido; querido. —*v.t.* mimar; acariciar. —*v.i., colloq.* besuquearse. —**be in a pet,** estar enfadado. —**pet name,** apodo cariñoso.

petal ('pɛt·əl) *n.* pétalo.

petard (pɪ'tard) *n.* petardo.

petcock ('pɛtˌkak) *n.* llave *o* válvula de escape; espita.

peter ('pi·tər) *v.i.* [*también,* **peter out**] *colloq.* agotarse; acabarse.

petit jury ('pɛt·i) jurado; jurado de juicio.

petition (pə'tɪʃ·ən) *n.* petición. —*v.t.* solicitar; pedir; hacer petición a. —**petitioner,** *n.* peticionario; solicitante.

petitionary (pə'tɪʃ·əˌnɛr·i) *adj.* petitorio.

petrel ('pɛt·rəl) *n.* petrel; patín.

petrify ('pɛt·rə·fai) *v.t.* petrificar. —*v.i.* petrificarse. —**petrification** (-fɪ'kei·ʃən) *n.* petrificación.

petro- (pɛt·ro; -rə) *también,* **petri-** (pɛt·ri; -rə) *prefijo* petro-; piedra: *petrography,* petrografía; *petrify,* petrificar.

petrography (pɪ'trag·rə·fi) *n.* petrografía. —**petrographic** (ˌpɛt·rə'græf·ɪk) *adj.* petrográfico.

petrol ('pɛt·rəl) *n., Brit.* gasolina.

petroleum (pə'tro·li·əm) *n.* petróleo. —*adj.* petrolero; de petróleo.

petrous ('pɛt·rəs) *adj.* **1,** (of or like rock) pétreo. **2,** *anat.* petroso.

petticoat ('pɛt·iˌkot) *n.* **1,** (skirt) saya; falda. **2,** (underskirt) enaguas (*pl.*).

pettifogger ('pɛt·iˌfag·ər) *n.* trapacero; *Amer.* picapleitos; *Amer.* tinterillo. —**pettifoggery,** *n.* trapacería.

pettish ('pɛt·ɪʃ) *adj.* áspero; enojadizo; malhumorado. —**pettishness,** *n.* berrinche; mal humor.

petty ('pɛt·i) *adj.* **1,** (trivial) trivial; insignificante; sin importancia. **2,** (small) pequeño; menor. **3,** (mean) mezquino; estrecho de miras. **4,** *law* menor; de menor cuantía. —**pettiness,** *n.* pequeñez; insignificancia. —**petty cash,** caja de menores. —**petty jury** = **petit jury.** —**petty larceny,** robo de menor cuantía. —**petty officer,** suboficial.

petulant ('pɛtʃ·ə·lənt) *adj.* petulante. —**petulance,** *n.* petulancia.

petunia (pə'tju·ni·ə) *n.* petunia.

pew (pjuː) *n.* banco; asiento de iglesia. —*interj.* ¡fo!

pewter ('pju·tər) *n.* peltre. —*adj.* de peltre.

phaeton ('fei·ə·tən) *n.* faetón.

-phage (feidʒ) *sufijo* -fago; devorador: *xylophage,* xilófago.

-phagia (feidʒ·i·ə) *sufijo, var. de* **-phagy.**

phago- (fæg·o; -ə) *prefijo* fago-;

que come; que destruye: *phagocyte,* fagocito.

phagocyte ('fæg·ə,sait) *n.* fagocito.

-phagous (fə·gəs) *sufijo* -fago; *forma adjetivos de nombres terminados en* **-phage** *o* **-phagy**: *xylophagous,* xilófago; *anthropophagous,* antropófago.

-phagy (fə·dʒi) *sufijo* -fagia; calidad de devorador: *anthropophagy,* antropofagia.

phalanx ('fei·læŋks) *n.* falange.

phallus ('fæl·əs) *n.* falo. —**phallic,** *adj.* fálico.

-phane (fein) *sufijo* -fana; *forma nombres denotando* que se parece: *cymophane,* cimofana.

phantasm ('fæn·tæz·əm) *n.* espectro; fantasma.

phantasmagoria (fæn,tæs·mə·'gor·i·ə) *n.* fantasmagoría. —**phantasmagoric,** *adj.* fantasmagórico.

phantasy ('fæn·tə·si) *n.* = **fantasy.**

phantom ('fæn·təm) *n.* aparición; espectro; fantasma.

Pharaoh ('feːr·o) *n.* Faraón.

pharisee ('fær·ə,si) *n.* fariseo. —**pharisaic** (-'sei·ɪk) *adj.* farisaico.

pharmaceutical (,far·mə'su·tɪ·kəl) *adj.* farmacéutico.

pharmacist ('far·mə,sɪst) *n.* farmacéutico.

pharmacology (,far·mə'kal·ə·dʒi) *n.* farmacología. —**pharmacological** (-kə'ladʒ·ɪ·kəl) *adj.* farmacológico. —**pharmacologist,** *n.* farmacólogo.

pharmacopeia (,far·mə'ko·pi·ə) *n.f.* farmacopea.

pharmacy ('far·mə·si) *n.* **1,** (science of drugs) farmacia; farmacopea. **2,** (drugstore) farmacia; botica.

pharyngeal (fə'rɪn·dʒi·əl) *adj.* faríngeo.

pharyngitis (,fær·ɪn'dʒai·tɪs) *n.* faringitis.

pharynx ('fær·ɪŋks) *n.* faringe.

phase (feiz) *n.* fase. —**phase out,** eliminar poco a poco.

-phasia (fei·ʒə) *sufijo* -fasia; trastorno o irregularidad en el habla: *aphasia,* afasia.

-phasy (fə·si) *sufijo, var. de* **-phasia.**

pheasant ('fɛz·ənt) *n.* faisán.

phen- (fɛn; fən) *prefijo, quím.* fen-; derivado o compuesto de bencina: *phenacetin,* fenacetina.

pheno- (fi·no; -nə) *prefijo, var. de* **phen-.**

phenobarbital (,fi·no'bar·bɪ·,tol) *n.* fenobárbito.

phenol ('fi·nal) *n.* fenol.

phenomenon (fɪ'nam·ə,nan) *n.* fenómeno. —**phenomenal,** *adj.* fenomenal.

phew! (fju) *interj.* ¡fo!

phial ('fai·əl) *n.* = **vial.**

phil- (fɪl) *prefijo, var. de* **philo-,** *usado ante vocal o* h: *philanthropy,* filantropía; *philharmonic,* filarmónico.

-phil (fɪl) *sufijo, var. de* **-phile.**

philander (fɪ'læn·dər) *v.i.* galantear; hacer de tenorio. —*n.* amante. —**philanderer,** *n.* galanteador; tenorio.

philanthropy (fɪ'læn·θrə·pi) *n.* filantropía. —**philanthropic** (,fɪl·ən'θrap·ɪk) *adj.* filantrópico. —**philanthropist,** *n.* filántropo.

philately (fɪ'læt·ə·li) *n.* filatelia. —**philatelic** (,fɪl·ə'tɛl·ɪk) *adj.* filatélico. —**philatelist,** *n.* filatelista.

-phile (fail) *sufijo* -filo; que gusta de; que tiene afición por: *Francophile,* francófilo; *bibliophile,* bibliófilo.

philharmonic (,fɪl·har'man·ɪk) *adj.* filarmónico.

-philia (fɪl·i·ə; fil-) *sufijo* -filia. **1,** afición; inclinación; *chromatophilia,* cromatofilia. **2,** tendencia: *hemophilia,* hemofilia.

Philippine ('fɪl·ə,pin) *adj. & n.* filipino.

-philism (fɪl·ɪz·əm) *sufijo* -filia; *formando nombres de los* adjetivos terminados en **-phile** *o* **-philous:** *bibliophilism,* bibliofilia.

Philistine (fɪ'lɪs·tin) *n. & adj.* filisteo.

philo- (fɪl·ə) *prefijo* filo-; cariño; inclinación: *philology,* filología.

philology (fɪ'lal·ə·dʒi) *n.* filología. —**philological** (,fɪl·ə'ladʒ·ə·kəl) *adj.* filológico. —**philologist,** *n.* filólogo.

philosopher (fɪ'las·ə·fər) *n.* filósofo. —**philosophic** (,fɪl·ə'saf·ɪk); **philosophical** (,fɪl·ə'saf·ɪk·əl) *adj.* filosófico. —**philosophize,** *v.i.* filosofar. —**philosophy,** *n.* filosofía.

-philous (fə·ləs) *sufijo* -filo; que gusta de: *photophilous,* fotófilo.

philter *también,* **philtre** ('fɪl·tər) *n.* filtro. —*v.t.* hechizar con filtro.

phlebitis (flɪ'bai·tɪs) *n.* flebitis.
phlebo- (flɛb·o) *prefijo* flebo-; vena: *phlebotomy,* flebotomía.
phlegm (flɛm) *n.* flema. —**phlegmatic** (flɛg'mæt·ɪk) *adj.* flemático.
phlox (flaks) *n.* flox.
-phobe (fob) *sufijo* -fobo; que siente aversión o desagrado: *Anglophobe,* anglófobo.
phobia ('fo·bi·ə) *n.* fobia.
-phobia ('fo·bi·ə) *sufijo* -fobia; aversión; desagrado: *claustrophobia,* claustrofobia.
phoebe ('fi·bi) *n.* **1,** *ornith.* aguador. **2,** *cap., myth.; poet.* Febe.
Phoenician (fə'niʃ·ən) *adj.* & *n.* fenicio.
phoenix ('fi·nɪks) *n.* fénix.
phon- (fan) *prefijo, var. de* **phono-.**
phone (foːn) *n., colloq.* teléfono.
-phone (foːn) *sufijo* -fono; sonido: *audiphone,* audífono.
phonetic (fo'nɛt·ɪk) *adj.* fonético. —**phonetics,** *n.* fonética.
-phonia (fon·i·ə) *sufijo* -fonía; *forma nombres denotando* **1,** trastorno en habla o sonido: *aphonia,* afonía. **2,** *var. de* **-phony.**
phonic ('fan·ɪk) *adj.* fónico. —**phonics,** *n.sing.* & *pl.* fónica; sistema fónico.
phono- (fo·no; -nə) *prefijo* fono-; sonido: *phonograph,* fonógrafo.
phonograph ('fo·nə·græf) *n.* fonógrafo. —**phonographic** (-'græf·ɪk) *adj.* fonográfico. —**phonograph record,** disco.
phony *también,* **phoney** ('fo·ni) *adj., slang* engañado; espúreo; falso. —*n., slang* **1,** (thing or action) engaño; estafa; farsa. **2,** (person) engañador; estafador; farsante.
-phony (fə·ni) *sufijo* -fonía; sonido: *telephony,* telefonía.
-phore (for) *sufijo* -foro; que lleva: *electrophore,* electróforo.
phosphate ('fas·feit) *n.* fosfato; sal fosfática *o* fosfórica.
phosphorescence (ˌfas·fə'rɛs·əns) *n.* fosforescencia. —**phosphorescent,** *adj.* fosforescente.
phosphorus ('fas·fə·rəs) *n.* fósforo.
photo ('fo·to) *n.* foto; fotografía.
photo- (fo·to) *prefijo* foto. **1,** luz: *photodynamics,* fotodinámica. **2,** fotografía: *photoengraving,* fotograbado.
photocopy *n.* fotocopia.
photoelectric *adj.* fotoeléctrico.
photoengrave *v.t.* fotograbar. —**photoengraving,** *n.* fotograbado.
photogenic (ˌfo·tə'dʒɛn·ɪk) *adj.* fotogénico.
photograph ('fo·təˌgræf) *n.* fotografía. —*v.t.* & *i.* fotografiar. —**photographer** (fə'tag·rə·fər) *n.* fotógrafo. —**photographic** (-'græf·ɪk) *adj.* fotográfico. —**photography** (fə'tag·rə·fi) *n.* fotografía.
photogravure (ˌfo·tə·grə'vjʊr) *n.* fotograbado.
photometer (fo'tam·ə·tər) *n.* fotómetro.
photon ('fo·tan) *n.* fotón.
photo-offset *n.* litografía fotográfica.
photoplay *n.* drama cinematográfico; película.
photosphere *n.* fotosfera.
photostat ('fo·təˌstæt) *n.* fotóstato; copia negativa. —*v.t.* & *i.* fotostatar. —**photostatic** (-'stæt·ɪk) *adj.* fotostático.
photosynthesis *n.* fotosíntesis.
phrase (freiz) *n.* **1,** (group of words) frase. **2,** (expression) expresión; dicho. **3,** *music* frase musical. —*v.t.* frasear; expresar. —**phrase book,** manual de conversación.
phraseology (ˌfre·zi'al·ə·dʒi) *n.* fraseología.
phrenetic (frɪ'nɛt·ɪk) *adj.* frenético.
phrenology (frɛ'nal·ə·dʒi) *n.* frenología. —**phrenological** (ˌfrɛn·ə'ladʒ·ə·kəl) *adj.* frenológico. —**phrenologist,** *n.* frenólogo.
-phyl *también,* **-phyll** (fɪl) *sufijo* -fila; hoja: *chlorophyl; chlorophyll,* clorofila.
phylactery (fə'læk·tə·ri) *n.* filactería.
phyll- (fɪl) *también,* **phyllo-** (fɪl·ə) *prefijo,* filo-; hoja: *phyllome,* filoma; *phylloxera,* filoxera.
-phyllous (fɪl·əs) *sufijo* -filo; con determinado número o clase de hojas: *chlorophyllous,* clorófilo.
phylum ('fai·ləm) *n.* fílum; filo.
physic ('fɪz·ɪk) *n.* medicina; catártico; purgante. —*v.t.* [**physicked, physicking**] medicinar.
physical ('fɪz·ɪ·kəl) *adj.* físico.
physician (fə'zɪʃ·ən) *n.* médico; doctor.
physics ('fɪz·ɪks) *n.* física. —**physicist** (-ɪ·sɪst) *n.* físico.

physio- (fɪz·i·o; -ə) *prefijo* fisio-; naturaleza; natural: *physiology,* fisiología.

physiognomy (ˌfɪz·iˈag·nə·mi) *n.* fisonomía. —**physiognomic** (-ag·ˈnam·ɪk) *adj.* fisonómico.

physiology (ˌfɪz·iˈal·a·dʒi) *n.* fisiología. —**physiological** (-əˈladʒ·ə·kəl) *adj.* fisiológico. —**physiologist,** *n.* fisiólogo.

physiotherapy (ˌfɪz·i·oˈθɛr·ə·pi) *n.* fisioterapia. —**physiotherapist,** *n.* fisioterapeuta.

physique (fɪˈzik) *n.* físico.

-phyte (fait) *sufijo* -fito; *forma nombres denotando* planta o vegetal con determinado habitat o naturaleza: *saprophyte,* saprófito.

phyto- (fai·to) *prefijo* fito-; planta; vegetal: *phytogenesis,* fitogénesis.

pi (pai) *n.* **1,** (Greek letter; math.) pi. **2,** *print.* mezcla de tipos; pastel. —*v.t.* mezclar (tipos).

pianissimo (ˌpi·əˈnɪs·ɪ·mo) *adj.* & *adv.* pianísimo.

pianist (piˈæn·ɪst; ˈpi·ə·nɪst) *n.* pianista.

piano (piˈæn·o) *n.* piano. —*adj.* & *adv.* piano. —**grand piano,** piano de cola. —**upright piano,** piano vertical *o* recto.

pianoforte (piˌæn·əˈfor·ti; -ˌfort) *n.* pianoforte.

pianola (ˌpi·əˈno·lə) *n.* pianola.

piaster (piˈæs·tər) *n.* piastra.

piazza (piˈæz·ə) *n.* **1,** (porch; covered gallery) pórtico; galería. **2,** (plaza) plaza.

pica (ˈpai·kə) *n.* cícero; tipo de doce puntos.

picador (ˈpɪk·əˌdor) *n.* picador.

picaresque (ˌpɪk·əˈrɛsk) *adj.* picaresco.

picayune (ˌpɪk·əˈjuːn) *adj.* bajo; chico; trivial.

piccolo (ˈpɪk·əˌlo) *n.* flautín.

pick (pɪk) *n.* **1,** (tool) pico. **2,** (crop) cosecha. **3,** (first choice) escogimiento; derecho de selección. —*v.t.* **1,** (gather) recoger. **2,** (cleanse) mondar; limpiar. **3,** [*también,* **pick out**] (choose) seleccionar; escoger. **4,** (prick) picar. **5,** (pry open, as a lock) abrir con ganzúa. **6,** (pull apart) arrancar; separar. **7,** (provoke) provocar. **8,** [*usu.* **pick on**] (annoy) molestar; fastidiar. —*v.i.* **1,** (use a pick) picotear. **2,** *colloq.* (nibble) comer poco; husmear. **3,** (select) escoger; seleccionar. —**pick a bone,** *fig.* roer un hueso. —**pick to pieces,** *fig.* criticar. —**pick the pocket of,** limpiar la faltriquera a. —**pick up, 1,** (improve) recuperarse; mejorarse. **2,** (tidy) poner en orden. **3,** (retrieve) recoger. **4,** (acquire; gain) adquirir; ganar. **5,** (lift) levantar; subir. **6,** *colloq.* (call for) buscar. **7,** (meet by chance) conocer por casualidad. —**pick up speed,** acelerar.

pickaback (ˈpɪk·əˌbæk) *adv.* sobre los hombros; a caballito.

pickax (ˈpɪkˌæks) *n.* pico; azadón.

picker (ˈpɪk·ər) *n.* **1,** (gatherer) recogedor. **2,** (one who selects) escogedor. **3,** (weeder) escardador.

pickerel (ˈpɪk·ər·əl) *n.* sollo norteamericano.

picket (ˈpɪk·ɛt) *n.* **1,** (stake) estaca. **2,** (sentinel) centinela; escucha. **3,** (protesting person) piquete. —*v.t.* **1,** (place stakes around) cercar con estacas. **2,** (post guards) colocar de guardia. **3,** (tether) atar. **4,** (demonstrate against by picketing) poner piquetes a.

pickings (ˈpɪk·ɪŋz) *n.pl.* **1,** (what is gathered) recogida; cosecha. **2,** (selection) surtido; selección.

pickle (ˈpɪk·əl) *n.* **1,** (brine) salmuera; escabeche. **2,** (food preserved in brine) encurtido. **3,** *slang* (predicament) aprieto; enredo. —*v.t.* encurtir; escabechar. —**pickled,** *adj., slang* borracho.

pickpocket *n.* ratero; cortabolsas.

pickup *n.* **1,** (gathering up; retrieving; collection) recolección; recogida. **2,** (acceleration) aceleración. **3,** (openbody truck) camión. **4,** *colloq.* (improvement) mejora. **5,** *colloq.* (chance acquaintance) persona conocida por casualidad. **6,** (of a phonograph) fonocaptor. —*adj., colloq.* remendado.

picnic (ˈpɪk·nɪk) *n.* jira; fiesta campestre. —*v.i.* [**picnicked, picnicking**] ir de jira; merendar en el campo. —**picnicker,** *n.* excursionista.

picric (ˈpɪk·rɪk) *adj.* pícrico.

pictorial (pɪkˈtor·i·əl) *adj.* pictórico; gráfico.

picture (ˈpɪk·tʃər) *n.* **1,** (illustration) cuadro; lámina. **2,** (painting) pintura. **3,** (likeness) retrato; imagen. **4,** (description) descripción; delineación verbal. **5,** *colloq.* (motion picture) película; film. —*v.t.*

1, (depict) pintar; dibujar. 2, (visualize) figurar; imaginar.

picturesque (ˌpɪk·tʃərˈɛsk) *adj.* pintoresco.

piddle (ˈpɪd·əl) *v.t.* & *i., colloq.* (dawdle; trifle) desperdiciar; perder (el tiempo). —*v.i., infantile* (urinate) orinar. —**piddler** (-lər) *n., colloq.* zángano; haragán.

piddling (ˈpɪd·lɪŋ) *adj.* trivial; de poca monta; de bagatela.

pidgin (ˈpɪdʒ·ən) *n.* lengua franca.

pie (pai) *n.* 1, (baked dish) pastel; empanada. 2, *print.* mezcla de tipos; pastel. 3, (jumble) mescolanza. —*v.t.* mezclar (tipos).

piebald (ˈpaiˌbɔld) *adj.* coloreado; manchado; pinto. —*n.* animal pinto.

piece (pis) *n.* 1, (fragment) fragmento; pedazo. 2, (part of a whole) sección. 3, (separate article or part) pieza. 4, (amount of work) cantidad. 5, (definite quantity) pieza; trozo. 6, (literary or musical composition) obra; escrito; composición; pieza. 7, *games* pieza. —*v.t.* 1, (join) aumentar; juntar; unir. 2, (patch) remendar; reparar.

piecemeal *adj.* fragmentario; en pedazos. —*adv.* a pedacitos; a bocaditos.

piecework *n.* trabajo a destajo. —**pieceworker,** *n.* destajero.

pied (paid) *adj.* abigarrado; manchado; pintado.

pier (pɪr) *n.* 1, (breakwater) malecón; rompeolas. 2, (bridge span) estribo de puente. 3, (masonry) pilar; pilón. 4, (dock) embarcadero; muelle.

pierce (pɪrs) *v.t.* 1, (penetrate) agujerear; taladrar. 2, (stab) punzar; picar; apuñalar. 3, (affect keenly) penetrar; afectar. —**piercing,** *adj.* agudo; penetrante. —*n.* penetración.

piety (ˈpai·ə·ti) *n.* piedad; reverencia.

piffle (ˈpɪf·əl) *n., slang* tontería; estupidez. —**piffling** (-lɪŋ) *adj., slang* disparatado.

pig (pɪg) *n.* 1, (animal) cerdo; cochino; lechón; puerco. 2, (iron bar) lingote. 3, *colloq.* (dirty person) sucio; puerco.

pigeon (ˈpɪdʒ·ən) *n.* paloma; palomo; pichón. —**carrier pigeon; homing pigeon,** paloma mensajera. —**passenger pigeon,** paloma emigrante. —**pouter pigeon** (ˈpau·tər) paloma buchona. —**wood pigeon; wild pigeon,** paloma torcaz.

pigeonhole *n.* 1, (pigeon house) palomar. 2, (letter compartment) casilla. —*v.t.* 1, (file) encasillar. 2, (put aside) ignorar; olvidar. 3, (classify) clasificar.

pigeontoed *adj.* que tiene los pies torcidos hacia dentro.

piggish (ˈpɪg·ɪʃ) *adj.* 1, (dirty) sucio; cochino; puerco. 2, (gluttonous) glotón.

pigheaded *adj.* terco; obstinado; perverso.

pig iron hierro formado en lingotes.

piglet (ˈpɪg·lɪt) *n.* lechoncillo.

pigment (ˈpɪg·mənt) *n.* pigmento. —**pigmentation** (-mənˈtei·ʃən) *n.* pigmentación.

pigskin (ˈpɪg·skɪn) *n.* 1, (leather) piel de cerdo. 2, *colloq.* (football) balón.

pigsty *n.* pocilga.

pigtail *n.* coleta.

pike (paik) *n.* 1, (weapon) pica; lanza. 2, (fish) lucio. 3, (highway) camino real; carretera principal.

piker (ˈpai·kər) *n., slang* tacaño; mezquino; cicatero.

pikestaff *n.* [*pl.* **-staves**] asta de pica.

pilaster (pɪˈlæs·tər) *n.* pilastra.

pile (pail) *n.* 1, (soft nap) pelusa. 2, (support) estaca; pilote. 3, (edifice) edificio macizo. 4, (mass) montón; pila; rimero. 5, (pyre) pira; hoguera. 6, *physics; electricity* pila. 7, *slang* (fortune) fortuna; caudal. —*v.t.* 1, (heap) apilar; amontonar. 2, (load) cargar; echar encima. —**pile up,** amontonar(se); acumular(se).

pile driver martinete.

piles (pailz) *n.pl.* hemorroides; almorranas.

pilfer (ˈpɪl·fər) *v.t.* & *i.* ratear; hurtar. —**pilferer,** *n.* ratero; pillo. —**pilferage,** *n.* ratería.

pilgrim (ˈpɪl·grɪm) *n.* peregrino. —**pilgrimage,** *n.* peregrinación; peregrinaje.

pill (pɪl) *n.* 1, (tablet) píldora; pastilla; tableta. 2, *slang* (disagreeable person) cataplasma. 3, *slang* (ball) pelota. —**bitter pill,** mal trago.

pillage (ˈpɪl·ɪdʒ) *v.t.* & *i.* pillar. —*n.* pillaje; saqueo.

pillar (ˈpɪl·ər) *n.* 1, (column)

columna; pilar. **2,** *fig.* (support; mainstay) sostén.
pillbox *n.* **1,** (box) caja para píldoras. **2,** *mil.* fortín redondo. **3,** (hat) sombrero redondo y chato.
pillion ('pɪl·jən) *n.* grupera.
pillory ('pɪl·ə·ri) *n.* picota. —*v.t.* **1,** (punish in a pillory) empicotar. **2,** (invoke scorn upon) avergonzar; calumniar.
pillow ('pɪl·o) *n.* **1,** (cushion) cojín; almohada. **2,** *mech.* cojinete. —*v.t.* **1,** (lay on a pillow) acostar sobre una almohada. **2,** (support as a pillow) sostener (como almohada).
pillow block *mech.* chumacera.
pillowcase *n.* funda (de almohada). *También,* **pillowslip** (-ˌslɪp).
pilose ('pai·los) *adj.* piloso.
pilot ('pai·lət) *n.* **1,** (helmsman; navigator) piloto. **2,** (leader) líder; guía. —*v.t.* pilotar; guiar.
pilotage ('pai·lət·ɪdʒ) *n.* pilotaje.
pilot light 1, (beacon) lámpara testigo; lámpara piloto. **2,** (stove lighter) mechero encendedor.
pimento (pɪ'mɛn·to) *n.* [*pl.* **-tos**] **1,** (tree and berry) pimienta. **2,** = **pimiento.**
pimiento (pɪ'miɛn·to) *n.* [*pl.* **-tos**) pimiento dulce.
pimp (pɪmp) *n.* alcahuete. —*v.i.* alcahuetear.
pimpernel ('pɪm·pərˌnɛl) *n.* murajes (*pl.*).
pimple ('pɪm·pəl) *n.* grano. —**pimply** (-pli); **pimpled,** *adj.* granujoso.
pin (pɪn) *n.* **1,** (pointed piece) alfiler; hebilla; horquilla. **2,** (brooch) broche. **3,** (safety pin) imperdible. **3,** *mech.* pasador; clavija. **4,** *bowls; bowling* bolo. **5,** *slang* (leg) pierna. —*v.t.* asegurar; clavar; fijar; sujetar. —**on pins and needles,** en espinas.
pinball *n.* juego registrado; bagatela.
pince-nez ('pæns'nei) *n.sing. & pl.* quevedos (*pl.*).
pincers ('pɪn·sərz) *n.sing. o pl.* **1,** (tool) pinzas; tenacillas. **2,** (claw) tenaza. **3,** *mil.* ataque de flanco.
pinch (pɪntʃ) *v.t. & i.* **1,** (nip) pinchar; pellizcar. **2,** (press hard upon) apretar; oprimir. **3,** *slang* (capture) capturar; arrestar. **4,** *slang* (steal) robar; ratear. —*n.* **1,** (nip) pellizco. **2,** (bit) poquito; chispita; pizca. **3,** (stress) dolor; tormento; pena; angustia. **4,** *colloq.* (emergency) apuro; aprieto. **5,** *slang* (arrest) arresto; captura.
pinchers ('pɪn·tʃərz) *n.* = **pincers.**
pinch-hit *v.i.* batear por otro; *fig.* sustituir a otro. —**pinch-hitter,** *n.* bateador sustituto; *fig.* sustituto.
pincushion *n.* alfiletero.
pine (pain) *n.* pino. —*v.i.* languidecer; morirse. —**pine for** *o* **after,** añorar; desear vivamente; morirse por. —**pine cone,** piña. —**pine grove,** pinar. —**pine needle,** pinocha. —**pine seed,** piñón.
pineal ('pɪn·i·əl) *adj.* pineal.
pineapple ('painˌæp·əl) *n.* ananás; piña.
piney ('pai·ni) *adj.* = **piny.**
ping (pɪŋ) *n.* silbido. —*v.i.* silbar.
ping-pong ('pɪŋˌpaŋ) *n.* ping-pong; pinpón.
pinhead *n.* **1,** (head of a pin) cabecilla de alfiler. **2,** (dot; speck) mote; pizca. **3,** *colloq.* (dolt) estúpido; mentecato.
pinhole *n.* agujerito.
pinion ('pɪn·jən) *n.* **1,** *mech.* piñón. **2,** *ornith.* huesecillo final; hueso-piñón. —*v.t.* atar o cortar las alas a (un ave); refrenar; maniatar.
pink (pɪŋk) *n.* **1,** (flower) clavel. **2,** (color) rosa; rosado. **3,** *colloq.* (quasi-communist) rojo; comunistoide. **4,** *colloq.* (best condition) mejor estado. —*adj.* rosado. —*v.t.* **1,** (pierce; perforate) agujerear; ojetear; picar con calado. **2,** (adorn) adornar; festonear. **3,** (prick; stab) picar; punzar. **4,** (cut a saw-toothed edge on) ondear.
pinkeye *n.* oftalmía purulenta.
pinking ('pɪŋ·kɪŋ) *n.* **1,** (perforation) diseño de ojetes; picado; calado. **2,** (adornment) adorno. **3,** (saw-toothed edge) onda.
pinkish ('pɪŋk·ɪʃ) *adj.* rosado.
pin money menudo; alfileres (*pl.*).
pinnacle ('pɪn·ə·kəl) *n.* **1,** (peak; spire) pináculo. **2,** *fig.* (highest point) cumbre; cima.
pinnate ('pɪn·eit) *adj., bot.* pinnado; pinado.
pinochle ('piˌnʌk·əl; -ˌnak-) *n.* pinocle.
pinpoint *n.* **1,** (point of a pin) punta de alfiler. **2,** (precision) exactitud; precisión. —*adj.* exacto;

preciso. —*v.t.* localizar exactamente; puntualizar con precisión.
pinprick *n.* alfilerazo.
pint (paint) *n.* pinta.
pinto ('pɪn·to) *n.* & *adj.* pinto.
pin-up girl sirena; muchacha atractiva; modelo.
pinwheel *n.* **1,** (child's toy) molinete; molinillo. **2,** (fireworks) rueda de fuegos.
piny ('pai·ni) *adj.* pinoso.
pioneer (ˌpai·əˈnɪr) *n.* pionero; iniciador. —*v.t.* & *i.* explorar; abrir camino (en).
pious ('pai·əs) *adj.* **1,** (godly) devoto; pío. **2,** (pretending piety) piadoso. —**piousness,** *n.* piedad; devoción.
pip (pɪp) *n.* **1,** (disease) pepita. **2,** (seed) pepita; semilla; *Amer.* pepa. **3,** (spot, as on playing cards or dice) punto. **4,** *slang* (excellent thing) fenómeno.
pipe (paip) *n.* **1,** (tube for fluid) tubo. **2,** (smoking) pipa. **3,** (organ tube) tubo *o* cañón de órgano. **4,** (reed instrument) caramillo; pipa; flauta de Pan. **5,** *pl.* (bagpipe) gaita (*sing.*). **6,** (boatswain's whistle) pito; silbato. **7,** (shrill sound) silbo; silbido. —*v.t.* **1,** (convey by pipes) conducir por tubos o caños. **2,** *naut.* (salute with a pipe) saludar con el pito. **3,** (shrill) soplar. —*v.i.* **1,** (chirp) piar. **2,** (whistle) silbar; pitar. **3,** (play the pipe) flautear; tocar el pito. —**pipe down,** *slang* callarse. —**pipe up,** *slang* hablar; alzar la voz; gritar.
pipe dream vana esperanza; sueño fantástico.
pipe line 1, (conduit) cañería. **2,** (channel, esp. of information) red secreta; fuente o vía de información.
pipe organ órgano de tubos.
piper ('pai·pər) *n.* flautista; gaitero. —**pay the piper,** sufrir las consecuencias.
pipette (pɪˈpɛt) *n.* pipeta.
piping ('pai·pɪŋ) *n.* **1,** (tubing) tubería; cañería. **2,** (music of pipes) música o notas de gaita, flauta, etc. **3,** (shrill sound) silbido; pitido. **4,** *sewing* cordoncillo. —*adj.* agudo; atiplado. —**piping hot,** muy caliente.
pipsqueak *n., colloq.* pipiolo.
piquant ('pi·kənt) *adj.* picante; mordaz. —**piquancy,** *n.* acrimonia; picante.
pique (pik) *v.t.* **1,** (irritate) ofender. **2,** (interest) excitar; provocar. —*n.* resentimiento; ojeriza; ofensa; pique. —**pique oneself on** *o* **upon,** jactarse de.
piqué (piˈkei) *n.* piqué.
piquet (pɪˈkɛt) *n.* juego de los ciento.
piracy ('pai·rə·si) *n.* piratería.
pirate ('pai·rət) *n.* **1,** (sea marauder) pirata. **2,** (plagiarist) plagiario. —*v.t.* **1,** (rob) robar; pillar. **2,** (plagiarize) plagiar. —*v.i.* piratear. —*adj.* pirata. —**pirated,** *adj.* pirata.
piratical (paiˈræt·ə·kəl) *adj.* pirático.
pirouette (ˌpɪr·əˈwɛt) *n.* pirueta. —*v.i.* hacer piruetas; piruetear.
piscatorial (ˌpɪs·kəˈtor·i·əl) *adj.* piscatorio.
Pisces ('pɪs·iz) *n.* Piscis.
pisci- (pɪs·ɪ) *prefijo* pisci-; pez: *pisciculture,* piscicultura.
pistachio (pɪsˈta·ʃi·o) *n.* alfóncigo; pistacho.
pistil ('pɪs·tɪl) *n.* pistilo.
pistol ('pɪs·təl) *n.* pistola.
piston ('pɪs·tən) *n.* émbolo; pistón. —**piston pin,** pasador del pistón. —**piston ring,** aro del pistón. —**piston rod,** biela.
pit (pɪt) *n.* **1,** (hole) hoyo. **2,** (depression) abismo; hueco. **3,** (well; shaft) pozo. **4,** (small arena) luneta. **5,** *comm.* parte de una bolsa dedicada a un solo producto. **6,** (fruit stone) hueso; pepita. **7,** (pockmark) hoyuelo. **8,** (trap) trampa. —*v.t.* [**pitted, pitting**] **1,** (make holes in) marcar con hoyos. **2,** (scar) formar cicatrices en. **3,** (match against another) oponer; confrontar. **4,** (remove the pit from) deshuesar; despepitar.
pita ('pi·tə) *n.* pita.
pitch (pɪtʃ) *v.t.* **1,** (throw) tirar; lanzar. **2,** (set up) plantar. **3,** (fix the tone of) dar el tono de. **4,** (slant) inclinar. **5,** (cover or treat with tar) embrear; alquitranar. —*v.i.* **1,** (fall headlong) desplomarse; caerse. **2,** (rise and fall) cabecear. **3,** (slant) inclinarse. —*n.* **1,** (throw) lanzamiento. **2,** (headlong fall) desplome; caída. **3,** (plunging of a ship) cabeceo. **4,** *fig.* (height; extreme) grado; punto; extremo. **5,** (slope) declive.

6, (slant) inclinación. 7, (tone) diapasón; altura; grado del tono. 8, (tar) brea; pez; alquitrán. —**pitch-black**; **pitch-dark**, tiniéblico; como boca de lobo. —**pitch in**, *colloq.* poner manos a la obra. —**pitch on** *o* **upon**, decidirse en; escoger.

pitchblende ('pɪtʃ,blɛnd) *n.* pecblenda.

pitcher ('pɪtʃ·ər) *n.* **1,** (vessel) cántaro. **2,** *baseball* lanzador.

pitchfork *n.* horca; horquilla.

pitch pipe diapasón de voz.

piteous ('pɪt·i·əs) *adj.* lastimoso.

pitfall *n.* **1,** (trap) trampa. **2,** *fig.* (danger) peligro latente; escollo.

pith (pɪθ) *n.* **1,** (pulp) médula; meollo; pulpo. **2,** (essential part) médula; parte principal. **3,** (vigor) energía; vigor.

pithecanthropus (,pɪθ·ə'kæn·θrə·pəs) *n.* pitecántropo.

pithy ('pɪθ·i) *adj.* **1,** (pulpy) pulposo; meduloso. **2,** *fig.* (concise; trenchant) enérgico; vivo.

pitiable ('pɪt·i·ə·bəl) *adj.* **1,** (arousing pity) lastimoso. **2,** (despicable) despreciable; ruin.

pitiful ('pɪt·ɪ·fəl) *adj.* **1,** (arousing pity) lastimoso. **2,** (paltry; despicable) despreciable. **3,** (compassionate) compasivo.

pitiless ('pɪt·ɪ·ləs) *adj.* despiadado; duro de corazón. —**pitilessness**, *n.* dureza de corazón; inhumanidad.

pittance ('pɪt·əns) *n.* pitanza.

pitter-patter ('pɪt·ər,pæt·ər) *n.* golpeteo; chapaleteo. —*adv.* con golpeteo; golpeteando.

pituitary (pɪ'tju·ə,tɛr·i) *adj.* pituitario.

pity ('pɪt·i) *n.* **1,** (compassion) piedad; compasión. **2,** (cause of regret) lástima. —*v.t.* compadecer. —**for pity's sake**, por piedad. —**it's a pity**, es (una) lástima. —**take pity (on)**, apiadarse (de); compadecerse (de).

pivot ('pɪv·ət) *n.* pivote; quicio; eje. —*v.i.* girar (sobre un eje). —*v.t.* colocar sobre un eje. —**pivotal**, *adj.* central; céntrico.

pixy ('pɪk·si) *n.* duende.

placard ('plæk·ərd) *n.* cartel; cartelón; anuncio. —*v.t.* **1,** (place a placard on) fijar un cartel en. **2,** (announce widely) publicar; pregonar.

placate ('plei·keit) *v.t.* aplacar; apaciguar. —**placation**, *n.* aplacamiento; apaciguamiento. —**placatory** (-kə·tor·i) *adj.* placativo.

place (pleis) *n.* **1,** (location) sitio; lugar; parte. **2,** (point in time) lugar. **3,** (space; room) espacio; lugar. **4,** (living quarters) residencia. **5,** (short street) callejón. **6,** (rank) rango; grado. **7,** (social status) dignidad; estado. **8,** (job) colocación; puesto. —*v.t.* **1,** (arrange) arreglar; ordenar. **2,** (find a home or job for) colocar; establecer. **3,** (put; set) poner; meter; echar. **4,** (locate) localizar. —*v.i.*, *racing* terminar segundo; colocarse. —**give place to**, ceder a; hacer lugar a. —**in place of**, en lugar de; en vez de. —**out of place**, fuera de lugar; fuera de propósito; inoportuno. —**take place**, ocurrir; celebrarse; tener lugar. —**take the place of**, sustituir; hacer las veces de.

placement ('pleis·mənt) *n.* colocación. —**placement agency**, agencia de colocaciones.

placenta (plə'sɛn·tə) *n.* placenta. —**placental**, *adj.* & *n.* placentario.

placid ('plæs·ɪd) *adj.* plácido; sereno. —**placidity** (plə'sɪd·ə·ti) *n.* placidez.

plagiarism ('plei·dʒə·rɪz·əm) *n.* plagio. —**plagiarist**, *n.* plagiario. —**plagiarize**, *v.t.* & *i.* plagiar.

plague (pleig) *n.* **1,** (disease) plaga; peste. **2,** (trouble) calamidad. **3,** *colloq.* (nuisance) molestia. —*v.t.* **1,** (afflict with disease) plagar; apestar. **2,** (annoy) molestar; enfadar.

plaguy ('plei·gi) *adj.* **1,** (pestilential) apestoso; plagado. **2,** *colloq.* (annoying) molesto; enfadoso.

plaice (pleis) *n.* platija.

plaid (plæd) *n.* tartán; diseño de cuadros a la escocesa. —*adj.* listado a la escocesa.

plain (plein) *adj.* **1,** (flat) llano. **2,** (easily understood) claro. **3,** (sheer) cabal. **4,** (unpatterned) liso. **5,** (ordinary) ordinario; sencillo. **6,** (homely) feo; sin atracción. **7,** (sincere) franco. **8,** (unmixed) puro; solo. —*n.* llanura; sabana; llano; vega. —**in plain terms**, en términos claros. —**plain clothes**, traje de calle. —**plain cooking**, cocina casera. —**plain dealing**, buena fe.

plainclothesman ('plein,kloðz·

mən) *n.* [*pl.* **-men**] agente de policía que no lleva uniforme; *Amer.* pesquisa.

plainness ('plein·nəs) *n.* **1,** (flatness) llaneza. **2,** (simplicity) sencillez. **3,** (clarity) claridad.

plainsman ('pleinz·mən) *n.* [*pl.* **-men**] llanero.

plainsong *n.* canto llano.

plain-spoken *adj.* franco. —**plain-spokenness,** *n.* franqueza.

plaint (pleint) *n.* **1,** (lamentation) plañido; lamento. **2,** (complaint) queja; querella.

plaintiff ('plein·tɪf) *n.* demandante.

plaintive ('plein·tɪv) *adj.* lastimoso; dolorido; plañidero. —**plaintiveness,** *n.* lastimosidad.

plait (pleit) *n.* **1,** (braid, as of hair) trenza. **2,** (fold) pliegue. —*v.t.* **1,** (braid) trenzar. **2,** (fold) plegar. **3,** (weave) tejer.

plan (plæn) *n.* **1,** (diagram) plano; dibujo. **2,** (design) diseño; plan. **3,** (scheme) proyecto; esquema. —*v.t.* & *i.* planear.

plane (plein) *adj.* plano. —*n.* **1,** (level surface) plano. **2,** *fig.* (grade; level) plano; nivel. **3,** (airplane) aeroplano; avión. **4,** (tool) cepillo. **5,** (tree) plátano. —*v.t.* acepillar. —**planing,** *n.* acepilladura.

-plane (plein) *sufijo* -plano; avión: *hydroplane,* hidroplano.

planet ('plæn·ɪt) *n.* planeta. —**planetary,** *adj.* planetario.

planetarium (ˌplæn·ɪ'tɛr·i·əm) *n.* planetario.

planetoid ('plæn·ɪˌtɔid) *n.* planetoide.

plani- (plæn·ɪ; -ə) *prefijo* plani-; plano: *planimetry,* planimetría.

plank (plæŋk) *n.* **1,** (long board) tablón; tabla. **2,** (political statement) estatuto de plataforma. —*v.t.* **1,** (cover) entablillar; entarimar. **2,** *slang* (pay) pagar; entregar. **3,** *cooking* asar en una tabla. —**planking,** *n.* entablado; entarimado; maderamen.

plankton ('plænk·tən) *n.* plancton; plankton.

planner ('plæn·ər) *n.* proyectista.

plano- (plei·no) *prefijo* plano-; plano: *planoconcave,* planocóncavo.

plant (plænt) *n.* **1,** (living organism) planta. **2,** (installation) instalación. **3,** (factory) fábrica; planta. —*v.t.* **1,** (put in the ground) plantar; sembrar. **2,** (place firmly; fix) colocar; sentar fijamente; fijar. **3,** *colloq.,* (secrete maliciously) esconder o meter (una cosa) de manera que se acuse a una persona inocente. **4,** *colloq.* (deal, as a blow) plantar; asestar.

plantain ('plæn·tɪn) *n.* **1,** (banana tree and fruit) plátano. **2,** (weed) llantén; plantaina.

plantation (plæn'tei·ʃən) *n.* finca; plantío; plantación.

planter ('plæn·tər) *n.* plantador; cultivador.

plantigrade ('plæn·təˌgreid) *adj.* plantígrado.

plaque (plæk) *n.* placa; chapa.

-plasia (plei·ʒə) *sufijo* -plasia; formación; desarrollo: *hypoplasia,* hipoplasia.

-plasis (plei·sɪs) *sufijo* -plasis; formación; desarrollo: *metaplasis,* metaplasis.

-plasm (plæz·əm) *sufijo* -plasma; formación: *protoplasm,* protoplasma.

plasma ('plæz·mə) *n.* plasma. *También,* **plasm** ('plæz·əm).

plasmo- (plæz·mo; -mə) *prefijo* plasmo-; plasma; forma: *plasmolysis,* plasmólisis.

-plast (plæst) *sufijo* -plasto; *forma nombres denotando* estructura de protoplasma: *chromoplast,* cromoplasto.

plaster ('plæs·tər) *n.* **1,** (paste of lime) yeso. **2,** (medicated dressing) emplasto. —*v.t.* **1,** (apply paste to) enyesar. **2,** (spread on) emplastar. —**plastered,** *adj., slang* borracho. —**mustard plaster,** sinapismo.

plaster cast **1,** (model) molde de yeso. **2,** *surg.* enyesado.

plaster of Paris yeso de París.

plastic ('plæs·tɪk) *adj.* & *n.* plástico. —**plasticity** (plæs'tɪs·ə·ti) *n.* plasticidad. —**plastic arts,** plástica. —**plastic surgery,** cirugía plástica.

-plasty (plæs·ti) *sufijo* -plastia; *forma nombres denotando* **1,** forma de desarrollo: *dermatoplasty,* dermatoplastia. **2,** operación de cirugía plástica: *rhinoplasty,* rinoplastia.

-plasy (plei·zi) *sufijo, var. de* **-plasia.**

plate (pleit) *n.* **1,** (sheet; flat piece) plancha; placa; lámina. **2,** (dish) vasija; plato. **3,** (item of food) plato. **4,** (denture) caja;

muelle. **5,** *print.* (stereotype) clisé; (electroplate) electrotipo. **6,** (illustration) grabado. **7,** *photog.* placa. **8,** (gold or silver table service) cubierto. **9,** (armor) blindaje. —*v.t.* **1,** (coat with metal) platear; dorar; niquelar. **2,** (cover with sheets) chapear; planchear. **3,** (cover with armor) blindar.

plateau (plæ'toː) *n.* meseta; mesa; altiplano.

platelet ('pleit·lɪt) *n.* plaqueta.

platform ('plæt·form) *n.* **1,** (raised flooring) plataforma. **2,** (scaffold) andamio. **3,** *R.R.* andén. **4,** (political declaration) declaración de principios; plataforma.

platinum ('plæt·ə·nəm) *n.* platino; platina. —*adj.* de platino; platinado.

platitude ('plæt·ɪˌtud) *n.* perogrullada; trivialidad. —**platitudinous** (-'tud·ɪ·nəs) *adj.* trivial.

platonic (plə'tan·ɪk) *adj.* platónico.

platoon (plə'tuːn) *n.* pelotón.

platter ('plæt·ər) *n.* fuente.

platy- (plæt·ɪ; -ə) *prefijo* plati-; ancho: *platyrrhine,* platirrino.

platypus ('plæt·ə·pəs) *n.* ornitorrinco.

plaudit ('plɔ·dɪt) *n.* aplauso.

plausible ('plɔ·zə·bəl) *adj.* plausible. —**plausibility,** *n.* plausibilidad.

play (plei) *v.i.* **1,** (engage in a game or sport) jugar. **2,** (move) moverse; correr. **3,** (behave) comportarse. **4,** *theat.* (act) actuar. **5,** (ripple, as water) ondear. **6,** *music* tocar; tañer. **7,** (joke) bromear. **8,** (pretend) fingir. —*v.t.* **1,** (engage in, as a game or sport) jugar a. **2,** (compete against) jugar con. **3,** *music* tocar. **4,** (move, in a game) jugar. **5,** (act the role of) representar; desempeñar el papel de. **6,** (perform, as a show) dar; representar. **7,** (put in motion) disparar; tirar; poner en movimiento. **8,** (pretend to be) fingir ser; hacerse: *play deaf,* hacerse el sordo. —*n.* **1,** (motion) acción; juego. **2,** (game) juego. **3,** (amusement) diversión. **4,** *theat.* drama; comedia; obra de teatro. **5,** (turn, as in a game) turno. —**give full** (*o* **free**) **play to,** dar rienda suelta a. —**play off,** contraponer. —**play on, 1,** (arouse) incitar; provocar. **2,** (take advantage of) aprovecharse de. **3,** *music* tocar (un instrumento); tocar (una pieza) en (un instrumento). —**play on words,** (hacer) juego de palabras. —**play out,** cansar(se); agotar(se). —**play up to,** adular; halagar.

playbill *n.* **1,** (poster) cartel. **2,** (program) programa.

player ('plei·ər) *n.* **1,** (contestant) jugador. **2,** (musician) músico. **3,** (actor) actor; cómico. —**player piano,** pianola.

playful ('plei·fəl) *adj.* juguetón; travieso.

playgoer ('pleiˌgo·ər) *n.* aficionado al teatro.

playground *n.* patio de recreo.

playhouse *n.* teatro.

playing card naipe.

playmate *n.* compañero de juegos.

play-off *n.* revancha; partida adicional para deshacer un empate.

plaything *n.* juguete.

playwright ('pleiˌrait) *n.* dramaturgo.

plaza ('plæz·ə) *n.* plaza.

plea (pliː) *n.* **1,** (entreaty) súplica; imploración. **2,** (pretext) pretexto; excusa. **3,** *law* alegato; contestación.

plead (pliːd) *v.i.* [*pret.* & *p.p.* **pleaded** *o* **pled**] **1,** (beg) suplicar; implorar. **2,** *law* abogar. —*v.t.* **1,** (allege) alegar. **2,** (defend) defender; abogar por. —**plead guilty,** declararse *o* confesarse culpable. —**plead not guilty,** negar la acusación.

pleader ('pli·dər) *n.* defensor; abogado.

pleadings ('pli·dɪŋz) *n.pl., law* alegatos; alegaciones.

pleasant ('plɛz·ənt) *adj.* agradable. —**pleasantness,** *n.* placer; agrado.

pleasantry ('plɛz·ən·tri) *n.* chanza; agudeza.

please (pliːz) *v.t.* & *i.* placer; gustar; agradar; satisfacer; complacer. —*v.impve.* por favor; haga el favor de; sírvase (+ *inf.*); tenga la bondad de; *Amer.* favor de. —**as you please,** como Vd. quiera. —**be pleased to,** hacer con gusto; tener gusto en; complacerse en. —**if you please,** por favor; si quiere. —**please God,** si Dios quiere.

pleased (plizd) *adj.* contento; satisfecho.

pleasing ('pli·zɪŋ) *adj.* agradable.

pleasure ('plɛʒ·ər) *n.* placer; gusto; deleite. —**pleasurable,** *adj.* divertido; agradable. —**pleasurably,** *adv.* con gusto. —**take pleasure in,** hacer con gusto; tener gusto en; complacerse en.

pleat (plit) *n.* pliegue. —*v.t.* plegar.

plebe (plib) *n.* cadete o guardia marina de primer año.

plebeian (plɪ'bi·ən) *adj.* & *n.* plebeyo.

plebiscite ('plɛb·ə,sait) *n.* plebiscito.

plectrum ('plɛk·trəm) *n.* [*pl.* **plectrums** *o* **plectra** (-trə)] plectro; púa.

pled (plɛd) *v., pret. & p.p.* **plead.**

pledge (plɛdʒ) *n.* **1,** (security) prenda; fianza. **2,** (promise) promesa. —*v.t.* **1,** (give as security) empeñar. **2,** (promise) prometer. **3,** (exact a promise from) obligar; exigir promesa (de). **4,** (toast) brindar a *o* por.

-plegia ('pli·dʒi·ə) *sufijo* -plejía; ataque; parálisis: *hemiplegia,* hemiplejía.

-plegy (pli·dʒi) *sufijo, var. de* **-plegia.**

Pleiades ('pli·ə,diz) *n.pl.* Pléyades; Pléyadas.

Pleistocene ('plais·tə,sin) *adj.* & *n.* pleistoceno.

plenary ('plɛn·ə·ri) *adj.* plenario; lleno.

plenipotentiary (,plɛn·ɪ·po·'tɛn·ʃi·ɛr·i) *n.* & *adj.* plenipotenciario.

plenitude ('plɛn·ɪ,tud) *n.* plenitud.

plenteous ('plɛn·ti·əs) *adj.* abundante. —**plenteousness,** *n.* abundancia.

plentiful ('plɛn·tɪ·fəl) *adj.* **1,** (ample) abundante; amplio; copioso. **2,** (fruitful) fructífero; fértil.

plenty ('plɛn·ti) *n.* abundancia; copia. —*adj.* suficiente; bastante. —*adv., colloq.* muy; bastante.

pleonasm ('pli·ə,næz·əm) *n.* pleonasmo. —**pleonastic** (-'næs·tɪk) *adj.* pleonástico.

plethora ('plɛθ·ə·rə) *n.* plétora. —**plethoric** (plɛ'θor·ɪk) *adj.* pletórico.

pleura ('plʊr·ə) *n.* [*pl.* **-rae** (-ri)] pleura. —**pleural** ('plʊr·əl) *adj.* pleural.

pleurisy ('plʊr·ə·si) *n.* pleuresía. —**pleuritic** (plʊ'rɪt·ɪk) *adj.* pleurítico.

pleuro- (plʊr·o; -ə) *prefijo* pleuro-; costilla; lado: *pleurodont,* pleurodonto.

plexi- (plɛk·sɪ; -sə) *prefijo* plexi-; tejido; entretejido: *plexiform,* plexiforme.

plexus ('plɛk·səs) *n.* plexo.

pliability (,plai·ə'bɪl·ə·ti) *n.* **1,** (flexibility) flexibilidad. **2,** (tractability) docilidad.

pliable ('plai·ə·bəl) *adj.* **1,** (flexible) flexible. **2,** (tractable) dócil.

pliancy ('plai·ən·si) *n.* **1,** (suppleness) flexibilidad. **2,** (tractability) docilidad.

pliant ('plai·ənt) *adj.* **1,** (supple) flexible. **2,** (tractable) dócil; manejable.

pliers ('plai·ərz) *n.pl.* alicates.

plight (plait) *n.* embarazo; apuro; aprieto. —*v.t.* **1,** (pledge) empeñar. **2,** (betroth) prometer en matrimonio. —**plight one's troth,** contraer esponsales.

Pliocene ('pli·ə,sin) *adj.* & *n.* plioceno.

plod (pla;d) *v.i.* **1,** (trudge) caminar con fatiga. **2,** (toil) afanarse. —**plodder,** *n.* trabajador diligente. —**plodding,** *adj.* laborioso.

-ploid (plɔid) *sufijo* -ploide; *forma adjetivos denotando* determinado número de cromosomas: *diploid,* diploide.

plop (plap) *n.* ruido seco; paf. —*interj.* ¡paf! —*v.i.* caerse a plomo; hacer paf. —*v.t.* asestar; arrojar.

plot (plat) *n.* **1,** (piece of ground) terreno; solar. **2,** (plan) trama; plano. **3,** (scheme) maquinación; intriga; conjura. **4,** (story line) argumento. —*v.t.* **1,** (plan) planear. **2,** (draw on a chart or map) trazar; delinear. **3,** (scheme) maquinar. —*v.i.* conspirar. —**plotter,** *n.* conspirador.

plough (plau) *v.* & *n.* = **plow.**

plover ('plʌv·ər) *n.* avefría; ave fría.

plow (plau) *n.* arado. —*v.t.* **1,** (till) arar; labrar. **2,** (move; remove) remover; arrancar; quitar. —*v.i.* (advance forcibly) abrirse *o* labrarse camino; avanzar enérgicamente. —**plow back,** reinvertir.

plowing ('plau·ɪŋ) *n.* aradura; labranza.

plowland *n.* tierra labrada; labrantío.
plowman ('plau·mən) *n.* [*pl.* **-men**] arador; labrador.
plowshare *n.* reja de arado.
pluck (plʌk) *v.t.* **1,** (pull off) tirar; arrancar. **2,** (strip of feathers) desplumar. **3,** (peel; despoil) pelar. **4,** (jerk) sacudir. **5,** *music* (pick) tañer. —*n.* **1,** (pull) tirón; arrancada. **2,** (courage) valor; ánimo. —**plucky,** *adj.* animoso; valeroso; osado.
plug (plʌg) *n.* **1,** (stopper) tapón. **2,** *electricity* enchufe. **3,** (hydrant) boca de agua. **4,** (cake of tobacco) costra de tabaco. **5,** *colloq.* (favorable remark) recomendación; publicidad. **6,** (nag; inferior horse) penco; jamelgo; rocín. **7,** (fishing lure) anzuelo; señuelo. —*v.t.* **1,** (stop) tapar; atarugar. **2,** *slang* (shoot) disparar; matar. **3,** *colloq.* (publicize) recomendar; elogiar. **4,** [*usu.* **plug in**] (connect) enchufar; conectar. —*v.i.* trabajar fijamente; afanarse. —**plugger,** *n., colloq.* trabajador industrioso.
plug-ugly *n., slang* rufián; asesino.
plum (plʌm) *n.* **1,** (fruit) ciruela. **2,** (tree) ciruelo. **3,** (color) violáceo; morado. **4,** (prize) premio; galardón.
plumage ('plu·mɪdʒ) *n.* plumaje.
plumb (plʌm) *n.* plomo; plomada. —*v.t.* **1,** (sound) sondear. **2,** (make plumb) aplomar. —*adj.* a plomo; vertical. —*adv.* **1,** (vertically) a plomo; verticalmente. **2,** (exactly) exactamente. **3,** *colloq.* (utterly) totalmente; cabalmente. —**out of plumb,** fuera de plomo. —**plumb bob,** plomo; plomado. —**plumb line,** plomada; cuerda de plomada.
plumber ('plʌm·ər) *n.* fontanero; *Amer.* plomero.
plumbing ('plʌm·ɪŋ) *n.* **1,** (trade) fontanería; *Amer.* plomería. **2,** (piping) tubería.
plume (plu:m) *n.* pluma; penacho. —*v.t.* **1,** (remove the plumes of) desplumar. **2,** (trim with plumes) emplumar. —**plume oneself, 1,** (preen oneself) componerse. **2,** (boast) jactarse.
plummet ('plʌm·ɪt) *n.* plomada. —*v.i.* caer a plomo.
plump (plʌmp) *v.t.* **1,** (drop suddenly) dejar caer. **2,** (puff up) dilatar. —*v.i.* caerse de plomo. —*n.* caída pesada. —*adj.* gordo; rechoncho. —*adv.* de repente. —**plumpness,** *n.* gordura.
plunder ('plʌn·dər) *v.t.* pillar; robar. —*n.* **1,** (robbery) pillaje; robo. **2,** (booty) botín.
plunge (plʌndʒ) *v.t.* **1,** (immerse) sumergir. **2,** (drive in) hundir. —*v.i.* **1,** (dive) zambullirse. **2,** (fall) caer a plomo. **3,** (rush headlong) saltar; precipitarse. **4,** (pitch, as a ship) cabecear. **5,** (bet or invest rashly) jugarse el todo. —*n.* **1,** (dive) zambullida. **2,** (leap) salto. **3,** (fall) caída a plomo. **4,** (rash bet or investment) juego desenfrenado.
plunger ('plʌn·dʒər) *n.* **1,** (diver) zambullidor. **2,** *mech.* émbolo; chupón. **3,** (rash bettor or investor) jugador desenfrenado.
plunk (plʌŋk) *v.i.* **1,** (make a hollow sound) hacer un ruido seco. **2,** (fall heavily) caerse de plomo. —*v.t.* **1,** (strum) tañer. **2,** (put down heavily) dejar caer pesadamente; arrojar. —*n.* **1,** (hollow sound) ruido seco. **2,** (twang) tañido.
pluperfect (plu'pʌɹ·fɪkt) *adj.* & *n.* pluscuamperfecto.
plural ('plʊr·əl) *adj.* & *n.* plural.
plurality (plʊ'ræl·ə·ti) *n.* pluralidad.
pluralize ('plʊr·ə,laiz) *v.t.* pluralizar.
pluri- (plʊr·ɪ; -ə) *prefijo* pluri-; muchos; diversos: *pluricellular,* pluricelular.
plus (plʌs) *adj.* **1,** (added to) más. **2,** (additional) adicional. **3,** (positive) positivo. —*prep.* más. —*n.* **1,** (sign) signo más. **2,** (something added) añadidura. **3,** (bonus; extra) plus. —**plus fours,** pantalones de golf.
plush (plʌʃ) *n.* felpilla. —*adj.* **1,** (velvety) afelpado. **2,** *slang* (luxurious) de lujo; suntuoso.
Pluto ('plu·to) *n., myth.; astron.* Plutón.
plutocracy (plu'tak·rə·si) *n.* plutocracia.
plutocrat ('plu·tə,kræt) *n.* plutócrata. —**plutocratic** (-'kræt·ɪk) *adj.* plutocrático.
plutonium (plu'to·ni·əm) *n.* plutonio.
pluvial ('plu·vi·əl) *adj.* pluvial.
ply (plai) *n.* estrata; capa; hoja. —*v.t.* **1,** (work; wield) trabajar;

manejar. **2,** (practice, as a trade) practicar; ejercer. —*v.i.* **1,** (fold) doblegarse. **2,** (work) trabajar con ahínco. **3,** (go back and forth) ir y venir; recorrer; navegar. —**ply with, 1,** (keep giving) surtirle a uno de; darle a uno abundancia de. **2,** (overwhelm with) acosarle a uno con; importunarle a uno con.

plywood *n.* madera laminada.

pneumatic (nju'mæt·ɪk) *adj.* neumático. —**pneumatic drill,** perforadora de aire comprimido.

pneumato- (nu·mə·to) *prefijo* neumato-. **1,** aire; vapor: *pneumatolysis,* neumatólisis. **2,** respiración; aliento: *pneumatometer,* neumatómetro.

pneumo- (nu·mo; num·ə) *prefijo* neumo-; pulmón: *pneumoconiosis,* neumoconiosis.

pneumonia (nu'mo·njə) *n.* pulmonía.

pneumono- (nu·mə·no) *prefijo* neumono-; pulmón: *pneumonophore,* neumonóforo.

poach (potʃ) *v.t.* (cook in water, esp. eggs) escalfar. —*v.t.* & *i.* (hunt or fish illegally) cazar *o* pescar en vedado. **2,** [*usu.* **poach on** *o* **in**] (trespass) invadir; entrar furtivamente.

poacher ('potʃ·ər) *n.* **1,** (for cooking eggs) olla para escalfar huevos. **2,** (trespasser) intruso; violador. **3,** (illegal hunter or fisherman) cazador *o* pescador furtivo.

pock (pak) *n.* **1,** (pustule) pústula; viruela. **2,** = **pockmark.**

pocket ('pak·ɪt) *n.* **1,** (pouch) bolsillo; faltriquera. **2,** (cavity) hoyo. **3,** *aero.* bolsa de aire. **4,** *mining* depósito. —*adj.* de bolsillo. —*v.t.* **1,** (put in a pocket) embolsar. **2,** (appropriate) apropiarse. **3,** (suppress) suprimir. **4,** (swallow, as one's pride, an insult, etc.) tragar; tragarse. —**in pocket,** con ganancia. —**out of pocket,** con pérdida; de su bolsillo. —**pick a pocket,** vaciar un bolsillo. —**pocket billiards,** billar de faltriquera. —**pocket veto,** veto de aguante.

pocketbook *n.* portamonedas; bolsa; cartera.

pocketknife *n.* navaja de bolsillo.

pockmark *n.* cicatriz de pústula o viruela; hoyo; hoyuelo. —**pockmarked,** *adj.* marcado de viruelas.

pod (pa:d) *n.* vaina.

pod- (pod) *también,* **podo-** (pod·ə) *prefijo* podo-; pod-; pie: *podiatry,* podiatría; *podiatrist,* podiatra.

-pod (pad) *sufijo* -podo; pie: *pseudopod,* seudópodo.

podiatry (po'dai·ə·tri) *n.* podiatría. —**podiatrist,** *n.* podiatra.

podium ('po·di·əm) *n.* podio.

poem ('po·ɪm) *n.* poema; poesía.

poesy ('po·ɪ·si; -zi) *n., arcaico* poesía; poema.

poet ('po·ɪt) *n.* poeta.

poetaster ('po·ɪt,æs·tər) *n.* poetastro.

poetess ('po·ɪt·ɪs) *n.f.* poetisa.

poetic (po'ɛt·ɪk) *también,* **poetical,** *adj.* poético. —**poetics,** *n.sing.* & *pl.* poética. —**poetic license,** licencia poética.

poet laureate [*pl.* **poets laureate**] poeta laureado.

poetry ('po·ɪt·ri) *n.* **1,** (poetic expression) poesía. **2,** (poems) poemas (*pl.*); poesías (*pl.*).

poignancy ('poin·jən·si) *n.* fuerza conmovedora; intensidad.

poignant ('pɔin·jənt) *adj.* conmovedor; intenso.

poinsettia (pɔin'sɛt·i·ə) *n.* poinsetia; flor de la Pascua.

point (pɔint) *n.* **1,** (sharp end) punta. **2,** (distinctive feature) rasgo; característica. **3,** (degree) grado; punto; nivel. **4,** (purpose) objeto; fin; propósito. **5,** (moment in time) instante; punto. **6,** (place) sitio; lugar; paraje. **7,** (score, in games) tanto; punto. **8,** *print.* punto. **9,** (promontory; cape) cabo. **10,** (division of the compass) punto; rumbo. **11,** *math.* punto. **12,** (punctuation mark) punto. —*v.t.* **1,** (aim) apuntar. **2,** (sharpen) aguzar. **3,** (punctuate; mark with points) puntuar. **4,** *masonry* unir con mortero; rellenar (juntas). —*v.i.* **1,** (gesture, as with the finger) hacer señal; señalar. **2,** (aim or move in a given direction) dirigirse; volverse. **3,** (tend) conducir. **4,** *hunting* pararse (el perro de caza). —**beside the point,** fuera de propósito. —**be beside the point,** no venir al caso. —**be to the point,** venir al caso. —**carry** (*o* **gain**) **one's point,** salirse con la suya. —(**a**) **case in point,** ejemplo. —**come** (*o* **get**) **to the point,** llegar al caso. —**in point,** a propósito. —**in point of,** en cuanto a. —**in point of fact,** en realidad; de veras. —**make a point of,** insistir en.

—**on all points**, de todos lados. —**on points**, *ballet* de puntillas. —**on the point of**, a punto de. —**point at** *o* **to**, indicar; señalar. —**point off**, marcar *o* medir con puntos. —**point of view**, punto de vista. —**point out**, indicar; señalar; enseñar. —**point up**, destacar; poner de realce. —**see** (*o* **get**) **the point**, caer en la cuenta. —**to the point**, a propósito; al caso.

pointblank *adj.* directo; a quema ropa. —*adv.* directamente; a quema ropa.

pointed ('pɔin·tɪd) *adj.* **1,** (sharp) puntiagudo. **2,** (pertinent) directo; intencionado. **3,** (satirical) satírico.

pointer ('pɔin·tər) *n.* **1,** (hand of a clock) manecilla *o* aguja del reloj. **2,** (indicator) indicador. **3,** (rod or wand) puntero. **4,** (dog) perro de caza; perro braco. **5,** (advice) consejito; advertencia.

pointless ('pɔint·ləs) *adj.* sin sentido; vano. —**pointlessness**, *n.* vanidad.

poise (pɔiz) *n.* **1,** (equilibrium) equilibrio. **2,** (carriage; bearing) porte. **3,** (composure) compostura; serenidad; aplomo. —*v.t.* equilibrar; balancear. —*v.i.* estar suspendido.

poison ('pɔi·zən) *n.* veneno. —*v.t.* envenenar. —**poisoner**, *n.* envenenador. —**poisonous**, *adj.* venenoso; tóxico. —**poison ivy**, hiedra venenosa. —**poison oak**; **poison sumac**, zumaque venenoso.

poke (pok) *v.t.* **1,** (push; thrust) empujar. **2,** (prod) impeler. **3,** (put in) meter; introducir. **4,** (stir, as a fire) atizar. —*v.i.* **1,** (search; pry) buscar; husmear. **2,** (make a thrust) dar un empujón. **3,** (dawdle) holgazanear. —*n.* **1,** (thrust; push) empujón. **2,** (projecting brim) borde. **3,** (bag) saco; bolsa. **4,** (dawdler) holgazán. —**poke fun at**, burlarse de. —**poke one's nose in**, entremeterse en.

poker ('po·kər) *n.* **1,** (stirrer for a fire) hurgón; atizador. **2,** (game) póker.

poky *también*, **pokey** ('po·ki) *adj.* **1,** (slow) lento; tardo. **2,** (dull) torpe. **3,** (shabby) desharrapado; desaliñado. —*n.*, *slang* calabozo; cárcel.

polar ('po·lər) *adj.* polar. —**polar bear**, oso polar; oso blanco.

Polaris (po'lɛr·ɪs) *n.* estrella polar.

polarity (po'lær·ə·ti) *n.* polaridad.

polarize ('po·lə,raiz) *v.t.* polarizar. —**polarization** (-rɪ'zei·ʃən) *n.* polarización.

pole (po:l) *n.* **1,** *geog.; math.; astron.; electronics* polo. **2,** (piece of wood) poste; palo. **3,** (unit of measure) 5,03 metros; 25,2 metros cuadrados. **4,** (flagpole) asta; mástil. **5,** *cap.* (inhabitant of Poland) polaco; polonés. —*v.t.* **1,** (propel) impeler con un palo. **2,** (support) sostener con palos. —**pole vault**, salto con garrocha.

polecat *n.* **1,** (European weasellike animal) veso. **2,** (skunk) mofeta.

polemic (po'lɛm·ɪk) *n.* polémica. —**polemical**, *adj.* polémico. —**polemics**, *n.* polémica. —**polemist** ('pal·ə·mɪst); **polemicist** (pə'lɛm·ə·sɪst) *n.* polemista.

polestar *n.* **1,** (North Star) estrella polar. **2,** (guide) guía; norte. **3,** (center of interest) miradero.

police (pə'lis) *n.* **1,** *sing. & pl.* (law-enforcement body) policía. **2,** *mil.* (cleaning) limpieza. —*v.t.* **1,** (keep order in) guardar el orden de *o* en. **2,** *mil.* (clean up) limpiar. —**police dog**, perro policía; —**police force**, policía; cuerpo de policía. —**police headquarters**, jefatura de policía. —**police officer**, agente de policía. —**police state**, estado-policía. —**police station**, comisaría de policía; prefectura.

policeman (pə'lis·mən) *n.* [*pl.* **-men**] policía; agente de policía; guardia. —**policewoman**, *n.f.* [*pl.* **-women**] agente femenina de policía.

policy ('pal·ə·si) *n.* **1,** (principle) política. **2,** (insurance) póliza. **3,** (lottery) lotería.

poliomyelitis (,pol·i·o,mai·ə'lai·tɪs) *n.* poliomielitis. *También*, **polio**.

-polis (pə·lɪs) *sufijo* -polis; ciudad: *cosmopolis*, cosmópolis.

polish (pal·ɪʃ) *v.t.* **1,** (shine) pulir; bruñir. **2,** (refine) refinar; adiestrar; perfeccionar. —*v.i.* pulirse. —*n.* **1,** (glossy finish) pulimento. **2,** (polishing material) barniz; cera; betún. **3,** (refinement) urbanidad; elegancia. —**polish off**, **1,** (finish; dispose of)

acabar con. **2,** (swallow) tragarse.
Polish ('pol·ɪʃ) *adj.* polaco; polonés. —*n.* polaco.
polished ('pal·ɪʃt) *adj.* **1,** (shiny) pulido; bruñido; brillante. **2,** (refined) refinado; elegante; urbano.
polishing ('pal·ɪʃ·ɪŋ) *n.* pulimento; bruñidura.
Politburo (pa'lɪtˌbjʊr·o) *n.* Politburó.
polite (pə'lait) *adj.* **1,** (courteous) cortés. **2,** (refined) refinado. —**politeness,** *n.* cortesía; cultura.
politic ('pal·ə·tɪk) *adj.* **1,** (of citizens) político. **2,** (wise) sagaz; astuto.
political (pə'lɪt·ɪ·kəl) *adj.* político.
politician (ˌpal·ə'tɪʃ·ən) *n.* político; *derog.* politicastro.
politick ('pal·ə·tɪk) *v.i., colloq.* politiquear. —**politicking,** *n., colloq.* politiqueo.
politics ('pal·ə·tɪks) *n. sing. o pl.* política (*sing.*).
polity ('pal·ə·ti) *n.* política; gobierno.
polka ('pol·kə) *n.* polca. —**polka dots,** lunares.
poll (pol) *n.* **1,** (votes; voting) votación. **2,** (voting place) caseta *o* colegio de votación. **3,** (survey) encuesta; conjunto de opinión. **4,** (head) cabeza. —*v.t.* **1,** (register the votes of) escrutar los votos de. **2,** (cast, as one's vote) dar. **3,** (receive, as one's share of votes) recibir. **4,** (survey; canvass) hacer una encuesta de *o* en. **5,** (clip; cut off) desmochar. —*v.i.* votar. —**poll tax,** capitación. —**polling booth,** cabina de votar.
pollen ('pal·ən) *n.* polen. —**pollinate** (-əˌneit) *v.t.* polinizar. —**pollination,** *n.* polinización.
polliwog *también,* **pollywog** ('pal·iˌwag) *n.* renacuajo.
pollute (pə'lut) *v.t.* **1,** (make impure) contaminar. **2,** (soil) ensuciar; manchar. **3,** (defile) profanar; corromper. —**polluted,** *adj.* poluto. —**pollution** (pə'lu·ʃən) *n.* polución; contaminación; corrupción.
polo ('po·lo) *n.* polo. —**polo player,** polista.
polonaise (ˌpal·ə'neiz) *n.* polonesa.
polonium (pə'lo·ni·əm) *n.* polonio.
poltroon (pal'truːn) *n.* cobarde. —**poltroonery,** *n.* cobardía.
poly- (pal·ɪ) *prefijo* poli-; muchos: *polygamy,* poligamia.
polyandry ('pal·iˌæn·dri) *n.* poliandria. —**polyandrous** (-'æn·drəs) *adj.* poliándrico; *bot.* poliandro.
polychrome ('pal·ɪˌkrom) *adj.* polícromo. —*n.* policromía. —**polychromy,** *n.* policromía.
polyclinic *adj.* policlínico. —*n.* policlínica.
polygamy (pə'lɪg·ə·mi) *n.* poligamia. —**polygamist,** *n.* polígamo. —**polygamous,** *adj.* polígamo.
polyglot ('pal·iˌglat) *adj. & n.* políglota; políglоto.
polygon ('pal·iˌgan) *n.* polígono. —**polygonal** (pə'lɪg·ə·nəl) *adj.* poligonal; polígono.
polyhedron ('pal·i'hid·rən) *n.* poliedro. —**polyhedral,** *adj.* poliédrico.
polymer ('pal·ɪ·mər) *n.* polímero. —**polymeric** (-'mɛr·ɪk) *adj.* polímero.
polymerize ('pal·ɪ·məˌraiz) *v.t.* polimerizar. —**polymerization** (pə·ˌlɪm·ər·ə'zei·ʃən) *n.* polimerización.
Polynesian (ˌpal·ɪ'ni·ʒən) *adj. & n.* polinesio.
polynomial (ˌpal·ɪ'nom·i·əl) *n.* polinomio.
polyp ('pal·ɪp) *n.* pólipo.
polysyllable *n.* polisílabo. —**polysyllabic,** *adj.* polisílabo.
polytechnic (ˌpal·i'tɛk·nɪk) *adj.* politécnico.
polytheism ('pal·i·θiˌɪz·əm) *n.* politeísmo. —**polytheist** (-ˌθi·ɪst) *n.* politeísta. —**polytheistic; polytheistical,** *adj.* politeísta.
pomade (po'meid) *n.* pomada.
pome (poːm) *n.* pomo; poma.
pomegranate ('pamˌgræn·ɪt) *n.* **1,** (fruit) granada. **2,** (tree) granado.
pommel ('pʌm·əl) *n.* pomo. —*v.t.* golpear; caer encima a puñetazos. —**pommeling,** *n.* paliza.
pomp (pamp) *n.* pompa; ceremonia.
pompadour ('pam·pə·dor) *n.* pompadur; copete.
pompano ('pam·pəˌno) *n.* pámpano.
pompon ('pamˌpan) *n.* **1,** (fluffy ball) pompón. **2,** (chrysanthemum) crisantemo; *Amer.* pompón.

pompous ('pam·pəs) *adj.* pomposo. —**pomposity** (pam'pas·ə·ti); **pompousness,** *n.* pomposidad.

poncho ('pan·tʃo) *n.* poncho.

pond (pand) *n.* estanque; charco.

ponder ('pan·dər) *v.t.* ponderar. —*v.i.* reflexionar. —**ponderable,** *adj.* ponderable.

ponderous ('pan·dər·əs) *adj.* pesado; macizo; ponderoso.

pontiff ('pan·tɪf) *n.* pontífice. —**pontifical** (pan'tɪf·ɪ·kəl) *adj.* pontifical; pontificio.

pontificate (pan'tɪf·ɪ·kət) *n.* pontificado. —*v.i.* (-ˌkeit) pontificar. —**pontification** (-'kei·ʃən) *n.* pontificación.

pontoon (pan'tu:n) *n.* pontón; *aero.* flotador. —**pontoon bridge,** puente de pontones.

pony ('po·ni) *n.* **1,** (horse) potro; caballito. **2,** *slang* (translation) traducción ilícita que usan los estudiantes. **3,** (liqueur glass) vasillo. —**pony up,** *slang* pagar; entregar; sacar.

ponytail *n.* coleta.

pooch (putʃ) *n., colloq.* perro.

poodle ('pu·dəl) *n.* perro de lanas.

pooh (pu:) *interj.* ¡bah!

pooh-pooh (ˌpu'pu:) *v.t.* tener a menos; mofarse de. —*v.i.* mofarse. —*interj.* ¡bah!

pool (pu:l) *n.* **1,** (pond) estanque; charco. **2,** (tank for swimming) piscina. **3,** (billiards) billar de faltriquera; trucos (*pl.*). **4,** (combined bets) apuestas (*pl.*); posta. **5,** (community of interests) conjunto; mancomunidad. —*v.t.* mancomunar.

poolroom *n.* sala de trucos; sala de billar.

poop (pup) *n.* popa. —**poop deck,** toldilla.

pooped (pupt) *adj., slang* cansado; agotado.

poor (pur) *adj.* **1,** (needy) pobre. **2,** (inferior) malo. **3,** (unfortunate) infeliz.

poorbox *n.* cepillo de limosnas; *Amer.* alcancía.

poorhouse *n.* casa de caridad.

poorly ('pur·li) *adv.* **1,** (badly) mal. **2,** (shabbily) pobremente. **3,** (sparsely) escasamente. —*adj., colloq.* indispuesto; enfermo.

pop (pap) *n.* **1,** (sharp sound) estallido; chasquido. **2,** (soft drink) gaseosa. **3,** *colloq.* (papa) papá. —*v.i.* **1,** (make a sharp sound) da un chasquido; reventarse; estalla **2,** (appear or disappear suddenly aparecer *o* desaparecer de sopetó **3,** (fire a weapon) tirar; dispara —*v.t.* **1,** (burst) explotar; reventa **2,** (fire) tirar; disparar. **3,** (put i or take out quickly) echar *o* saca de repente. —*interj.* ¡pum!; ¡pa —**pop the question (to),** declarars (a); pedir en matrimonio.

popcorn ('papˌkorn) *n.* roseta (*pl.*); rositas (*pl.*); *Amer.* palomi tas (*pl.*).

Pope (pop) *n.* Papa. —**popist** *adj., derog.* papista. —**popery,** *n derog.* papismo.

popeyed ('papˌaid) *adj.* que tien los ojos saltones.

popgun *n.* cerbatana.

popinjay ('pap·ɪnˌdʒei) *n.* **1** (woodpecker) picamaderos. **2** (vain person) pisaverde.

poplar ('pap·lər) *n.* álamo. —**pop lar grove,** alameda.

poplin ('pap·lɪn) *n.* popelina.

poppy ('pap·i) *n.* adormidera amapola.

poppycock ('pap·iˌkak) *n., co loq.* tontería; disparate.

populace ('pap·jə·lɪs) *n.* pueblo populacho.

popular ('pap·jə·lər) *adj.* popu lar. —**popularity** (-'lær·ə·ti) *n* popularidad.

popularize ('pap·jə·ləˌraiz) *v.* popularizar; vulgarizar. —**popu larization** (-rɪ'zei·ʃən) *n.* popu larización; vulgarización.

populate ('pap·jəˌleit) *v.t.* po blar.

population (ˌpap·jə'lei·ʃən) *n* población.

populous ('pap·jə·ləs) *adj.* po puloso.

porcelain ('por·sə·lɪn) *n.* por celana. —*adj.* de porcelana.

porch (portʃ) *n.* porche.

porcine ('por·sain) *adj.* porcino

porcupine ('por·kjəˌpain) *n* puerco espín.

pore (po:r) *n.* poro. —*v.i.* ojear mirar. —**pore over,** estudiar de talladamente; meditar.

porgy ('por·dʒi; -gi) *n.* pagro pargo.

pork (pork) *n.* carne de cerdo —**pork chop,** chuleta de cerdo.

pornography (por'nag·rə·fi) *n* pornografía. —**pornographic** (ˌpor nə'græf·ɪk) *adj.* pornográfico.

porous ('por·əs) *adj.* poroso. —**porosity** (pə'ras·ə·ti); **porousness,** *n.* porosidad.
porphyry ('por·fə·ri) *n.* pórfido.
porpoise ('por·pəs) *n.* marsopa.
porridge ('por·ɪdʒ; 'par-) *n.* gachas (*pl.*); puches (*pl.*).
porringer ('por·ɪn·dʒər) *n.* escudilla.
port (port) *n.* **1,** (harbor) puerto. **2,** (opening) abertura. **3,** *naut.* (left) babor. **4,** = **porthole. 5,** (wine) oporto. —*v.t. & i., naut.* (steer to left) virar a *o* hacia babor. —*v.t., mil.* (hold diagonally, as a rifle) terciar; llevar terciado. —**port of call,** escala.
portable ('port·ə·bəl) *adj.* portátil.
portage ('port·ɪdʒ) *n.* porte. —*v.t.* portear.
portal ('por·təl) *n.* portal.
portcullis (port'kʌl·ɪs) *n.* rastrillo.
portend (por'tɛnd) *v.t.* pronosticar; presagiar.
portent ('por·tɛnt) *n.* augurio; portento.
portentous (por'tɛn·təs) *adj.* **1,** (ominous) ominoso. **2,** (solemn) solemne; portentoso.
porter ('por·tər) *n.* **1,** (bearer) portador; *R.R.* mozo de estación. **2,** (doorkeeper) portero; conserje. **3,** (beer) cerveza tónica.
porterhouse steak biftec de filete.
portfolio (port'fo·li·o) *n.* **1,** (case) cartera. **2,** (office of minister) cartera. **3,** (list of securities) documentación.
porthole ('port·hol) *n.* tronera; portilla.
portico ('por·tɪ·ko) *n.* pórtico.
portiere (por'tjeːr) *n.* cortinaje de puerta; portier.
portion ('por·ʃən) *n.* **1,** (part; share) porción. **2,** (dowry) dote. —*v.t.* **1,** (allot) dividir; repartir. **2,** (dower) dotar.
portliness ('port·li·nəs) *n.* **1,** (fatness) corpulencia. **2,** (stately bearing) porte majestuoso.
portly ('port·li) *adj.* **1,** (fat) corpulento. **2,** (stately) grave; serio.
portmanteau (port'mæn·to) *n.* valija.
Porto Rican (ˌpor·to'ri·kən) *adj. & n.* = **Puerto Rican.**
portrait ('por·trɪt) *n.* retrato. —**portraiture** (-trɪ·tʃər) *n.* retrato; pintura. —**portrait painter,** retratista.
portray (por'trei) *v.t.* **1,** (picture) retratar. **2,** (describe) describir. **3,** *theat.* representar. —**portrayal,** *n.* representación; retrato.
Portuguese ('por·tjə·giz) *adj. & n.* portugués.
pose (poːz) *v.t.* **1,** (place) colocar. **2,** (propound) proponer. —*v.i.* **1,** (act as model) posar. **2,** (pretend) fingir; ponerse. —*n.* **1,** (attitude) postura; *art; photog.* pose. **2,** (affectation) postura vana; afectación. —**pose as,** fingir ser; dárselas de.
poser ('po·zər) *n.* **1,** [*también* **poseur** (po'zʌɹ)] (affected person) presuntuoso; afectado. **2,** (baffling question) problema difícil; enigma.
position (pə'zɪʃ·ən) *n.* **1,** (place) posición; lugar. **2,** (posture) postura. **3,** (opinion) actitud; posición. **4,** (rank) rango. **5,** (job) puesto; empleo. **6,** (situation) situación; estado. —**in a position to,** en estado de; en condición de.
positive ('paz·ə·tɪv) *adj.* positivo. —*n.* positivo; *photog.* positiva. —**positiveness,** *n.* calidad de positivo. —**positivity** (-'tɪv·ə·ti) *n.* positividad.
positivism ('paz·ə·tɪvˌɪz·əm) *n.* positivismo. —**positivist,** *n.* positivista. —**positivistic,** *adj.* positivista.
positron ('paz·əˌtran) *n.* positrón.
posse ('pas·i) *n.* cuerpo de alguaciles.
possess (pə'zɛs) *v.t.* **1,** (own) poseer. **2,** (obtain power over) apoderarse de.
possessed (pə'zɛst) *adj.* **1,** (held in possession) en poder (de). **2,** (haunted; crazed) poseído; poseso.
possession (pə'zɛʃ·ən) *n.* **1,** (ownership; thing possessed) posesión. **2,** *pl.* (property) bienes; caudal (*sing.*); riquezas. —**take possession of,** entrar en posesión de; apoderarse de.
possessive (pə'zɛs·ɪv) *adj. & n.* posesivo. —**possessiveness,** *n.* celo posesivo.
possessor (pə'zɛs·ər) *n.* poseedor; posesor.
possibility (ˌpas·ə'bil·ə·ti) *n.* posibilidad.
possible ('pas·ə·bəl) *adj.* posible. —**as soon as possible,** cuanto antes.
possum ('pas·əm) *n., colloq.* =

opossum. —**play possum**, *colloq.* hacer el muerto; fingir la muerte.

post (post) *n.* **1,** (upright pole) poste. **2,** (position) puesto. **3,** (garrison) puesto. **4,** (mail) correo. **5,** (relay) posta. —*v.t.* **1,** (fasten; fix) colocar; fijar. **2,** *comm.* (enter in a ledger) registrar. **3,** *Brit.* (mail) echar al correo. **4,** *colloq.* (inform) informar. —*v.i.* **1,** (hasten) ir de prisa. **2,** (rise to the trot) balancearse. —**by return post**, a vuelta de correo.

post- (post) *prefijo* post-; pos-; después; tras; detrás: *postpone,* posponer; *postimpressionism,* postimpresionismo.

postage ('pos·tɪdʒ) *n.* franqueo. —**postage stamp**, sello de correo.

postal ('pos·təl) *adj.* postal. —*n.* tarjeta postal. —**postal order**, giro postal.

postboy *n.* postillón.

postcard *n.* tarjeta postal. *También,* **postal card**.

post chaise silla de posta.

postdate *v.t.* posfechar. —*n.* posfecha.

postdiluvian (ˌpost·dɪ'lu·vi·ən) *adj.* & *n.* postdiluviano.

poster ('pos·tər) *n.* cartel; cartelón.

posterior (pas'tɪr·i·ər) *adj.* posterior. —*n.* nalga; *vulg.* trasero. —**posteriority** (-'or·ə·ti) *n.* posterioridad.

posterity (pas'tɛr·ə·ti) *n.* posteridad.

postern ('pas·tərn) *n.* entrada trasera; postigo.

postgraduate (post'græ·dʒu·ɪt) *adj.* & *n.* postgraduado.

posthaste ('post'heist) *adv.* a toda prisa; a toda brida.

posthumous ('pas·tju·məs) *adj.* póstumo.

postillion (pos'tɪl·jən) *n.* postillón.

postlude ('post,lud) *n.* postludio.

postman ('post·mən) *n.* cartero.

postmark *n.* matasellos. —*v.t.* timbrar.

postmaster *n.* administrador de correos. —**postmaster general,** director general de correos.

postmeridian *adj.* postmeridiano.

post-mortem (post'mor·təm) *adj.* post mórtem. —*n.* autopsia.

post office casa de correos; correo. —**post-office box,** apartado de correos.

postpaid *adj.* porte pagado; franco de porte.

postpone (post'poːn) *v.t.* posponer; aplazar; diferir. —**postponement**, *n.* aplazamiento; diferimiento.

postscript *n.* posdata.

postulant ('pas·tʃə·lənt) *adj.* & *n.* requisito.

postulate ('pas·tʃəˌleit) *v.t.* & *i.* postular. —*n.* (-lət) **1,** (assumption) postulado. **2,** (prerequisite) requisito.

posture ('pas·tʃər) *n.* postura. —*v.i.* posar; pavonearse.

postwar *adj.* de (la) postguerra. —**postwar period**, postguerra.

posy ('po·zi) *n.* florecilla; ramillete.

pot (pat) *n.* **1,** (cooking vessel) olla; caldera; puchero. **2,** (urn; jar) pote; tiesto; tarro; marmita. **3,** (prize) bolsa. **4,** (pool of bets) posta. —*v.t.* [**potted, potting**] **1,** (cook in a pot) cocer en olla. **2,** (preserve) conservar en marmitas. **3,** (plant in pots) plantar en tiestos. **4,** (shoot) tirar; disparar. —**go to pot**, *colloq.* arruinarse; fracasar. —**pot cheese**, requesón. —**pot roast**, carne asada en olla. —**pot shot**, tiro casual. —**keep the pot boiling**, ganar bastante para vivir.

potable ('po·tə·bəl) *adj.* potable. —*n.* bebida.

potash ('patˌæʃ) *n.* potasa.

potassium (pə'tæs·i·əm) *n.* potasio. —**potassic**, *adj.* potásico.

potato (pə'tei·to) *n.* [*pl.* **-toes**] patata; *Amer.* papa. —**potato chip**, frito de papa. —**small potatoes**, *colloq.* persona o cosa de poca monta.

potbelly *n., colloq.* panza. —**potbellied**, *adj., colloq.* panzudo.

potboiler *n.* obra hecha únicamente para ganar dinero.

potency ('po·tən·si) *n.* potencia.

potent ('po·tənt) *adj.* potente.

potentate ('po·tənˌteit) *n.* potentado.

potential (pə'tɛn·ʃəl) *adj.* **1,** (possible) posible. **2,** (latent) potencial. —*n.* potencial; capacidad. —**potentiality** (-ʃi'æl·ə·ti) *n.* potencialidad.

pother ('pað·ər) *n.* alboroto; confusión; molestia. —*v.t.* & *i.* alborotar; molestar.

pothole *n.* bache.

pothook *n.* **1,** (for hanging pots) llares (*pl.*). **2,** (curlicue) garabato. **3,** *pl.* (shorthand symbols) signos taquigráficos.

potion ('po·ʃən) *n.* poción; pócima.

potpourri (pat'pur·i) *n.* popurrí.

pottage ('pat·ɪdʒ) *n.* potaje.

potter ('pat·ər) *n.* alfarero. —*v.i.* holgazanear; haraganear. —**potter's field,** cementerio de indigentes. —**potter's wheel,** rueda de alfarero.

pottery ('pat·ə·ri) *n.* alfarería.

pouch (pautʃ) *n.* bolsa; saco. —*v.t.* embolsar. —*v.i.* formar una bolsa; hacer pucheros. —**tobacco pouch,** tabaquera; petaca.

poultice ('pol·tɪs) *n.* cataplasma; bizma. —*v.t.* bizmar.

poultry ('pol·tri) *n.* aves de corral. —**poulterer** (-tər·ər) *n.* traficante de aves caseras. —**poultry breeder,** avicultor. —**poultry breeding,** avicultura.

pounce (pauns) *v.i.* caer a plomo. —*n.* calada; zarpada. —**pounce at, on** *o* **upon,** agarrar; saltar sobre.

pound (paund) *n.* **1,** (measure of weight) libra. **2,** (monetary unit) libra esterlina. **3,** (enclosure) corral. —*v.t.* **1,** (beat) golpear. **2,** (crush) machacar; moler. —*v.i.* **1,** (hammer) machacar; martillar. **2,** (plod) trabajar fijamente; afanarse. —**poundage,** *n.* tanto por libra.

pour (poːr) *v.t.* **1,** (cause to flow) verter; echar. **2,** (send forth) emitir. —*v.i.* 1, (flow) fluir; entrar *o* salir a chorros. **2,** (rain) llover. **3,** (rush; swarm) precipitarse; arrojarse. —**pour rain,** llover a cántaros.

pout (paut) *v.i.* poner mala cara; estar ceñudo. —*n.* mueca; mala cara; mal humor.

pouter ('pau·tər) *n.* **1,** (person) persona ceñuda. **2,** (bird) paloma buchona.

poverty ('pav·ər·ti) *n.* **1,** (lack of money) pobreza; indigencia. **2,** (scarcity) escasez. —**poverty-stricken,** *adj.* empobrecido; indigente.

pow! (pau) *interj.* ¡zas!; ¡paf!

powder ('pau·dər) *n.* **1,** (fine particles) polvo. **2,** (talcum) polvos (*pl.*). **3,** (gunpowder) pólvora. —*v.t.* **1,** (sprinkle) empolvar. **2,** (crush) pulverizar.

powder box polvera.

powder flask polvorín. *También,* **powder horn.**

powder magazine polvorín.

powder puff (pʌf) **1,** (pad) mota. **2,** (effeminate man) afeminado; melindroso.

powder room salón de damas; tocador.

powdery ('pau·də·ri) *adj.* polvoriento.

power ('pau·ər) *n.* **1,** (ability) poder. **2,** (strength) fuerza. **3,** (influential person) potestad. **4,** (nation) potencia. **5,** (lens capacity) potencia. **6,** *math.* potencia. **7,** *mech.; electricity* energía. —*v.t.* impulsar; accionar. —**power of attorney,** poder legal. —**power plant,** central eléctrica.

powerboat *n.* lancha motora; gasolinera.

powerful ('pau·ər·fəl) *adj.* **1,** (strong) fuerte. **2,** (potent) potente. **3,** (mighty) poderoso. —**powerfulness,** *n.* fuerza; poderío.

powerhouse *n.* **1,** (plant) estación generadora. **2,** *colloq.* (strong or energetic person) dínamo.

powerless ('pau·ər·ləs) *adj.* impotente; sin poder.

powwow ('pau·wau) *n.* ceremonia de los indios norteamericanos; *colloq.* conferencia. —*v.i., colloq.* conferenciar.

pox (paks) *n.* erupción pustulosa.

practicable ('præk·tɪ·kə·bəl) *adj.* practicable. —**practicability,** *n.* posibilidad de hacerse.

practical ('præk·tɪ·kəl) *adj.* **1,** (useful) práctico; útil. **2,** (advisable) aconsejable. **3,** (pragmatic) práctico; pragmático. —**practical joke,** chasco; broma *o* burla pesada.

practicality (ˌpræk·tɪ'kæl·ə·ti) *n.* calidad de práctico; utilidad.

practically ('præk·tɪk·li) *adv.* **1,** (actually) de hecho; prácticamente. **2,** *colloq.* (nearly) casi.

practice ('præk·tɪs) *n.* **1,** (performance) ejercicio. **2,** (frequent usage) costumbre. **3,** (exercise of a profession) práctica. **4,** (clientele) clientela. **5,** (drill) práctica; ejercicio. —*v.t.* practicar. —*v.i.* **1,** (engage in a profession) ejercer (de abogado, de médico, etc.); practicar uno su profesión. **2,** (drill) ejercitarse; hacer ejercicios.

practitioner (præk'tɪʃ·ən·ər) *n.* practicante.

prae- (pri) *prefijo, var. de* **pre-:** *praetor,* pretor.
praetor *también,* **pretor** ('pri·tər) *n.* pretor. —**praetorial; pretorial** (pri'tor·i·əl) *adj.* pretorial. —**praetorian; pretorian** (pri'tor·i·ən) *adj.* pretoriano.
pragmatic (præg'mæt·ɪk) *adj.* pragmático.
pragmatism ('præg·mə·tɪz·əm) *n.* pragmatismo. —**pragmatist,** *n.* pragmatista.
prairie ('pre:r·i) *n.* pradera.
praise (preiz) *v.t.* **1,** (commend) loar; elogiar; alabar. **2,** (glorify) glorificar. —*n.* elogio; alabanza.
praiseworthy *adj.* loable. —**praiseworthiness,** *n.* mérito.
pram (præm) *n., colloq.* = **perambulator.**
prance (præns) *v.i.* cabriolar. —*n.* cabriola. —**prancer,** *n.* caballo pisador.
prank (præŋk) *n.* travesura; broma. —**prankish,** *adj.* travieso. —**prankster** (-stər) *n.* bromista.
praseodymium (ˌprei·zi·o'dɪm·i·əm) *n.* praseodimio.
prate (preit) *v.t. & i.* charlar. —**prating,** *adj.* charlador. —*n.* charla.
prattle ('præt·əl) *v.i.* charlar; parlotear. —*n.* parlería; parloteo; charlería. —**prattler** (-lər) *n.* charlador; parlanchín.
prawn (prɔ:n) *n.* langostín.
pray (prei) *v.i.* orar; rezar. —*v.t.* **1,** (beg) rogar; suplicar. **2,** (petition for) pedir. —**pray tell me,** sírvase decirme; dígame, por favor.
prayer (pre:r) *n.* **1,** (supplication) oración; rezo. **2,** (petition) súplica. **3,** *usu. pl.* (devotional service) oficio. —**prayer book,** devocionario.
prayerful ('prɛr·fəl) *adj.* **1,** (devout) devoto. **2,** (entreating) suplicante.
pre- (pri) *prefijo* pre-; antes de (*en tiempo, lugar o grado*): *precedence,* precedencia; *predecessor,* predecesor; *preëminent,* preeminente.
preach (pritʃ) *v.t. & i.* **1,** (deliver a sermon) predicar. **2,** (exhort) exhortar. —**preaching,** *n.* predicación. —**preachment,** *n.* prédica; sermoneo.
preacher ('pritʃ·ər) *n.* **1,** (one who preaches) predicador. **2,** (clergyman) pastor; clérigo.
preamble ('pri·æm·bəl) *n.* preámbulo.
prearrange *v.t.* predisponer. —**prearrangement,** *n.* predisposición.
prebend ('prɛb·ənd) *n.* prebenda.
precarious (prɪ'kɛr·i·əs) *adj.* precario; inseguro. —**precariousness,** *n.* estado precario; inseguridad.
precaution (prɪ'kɔ·ʃən) *n.* **1,** (preventive act) precaución. **2,** (foresight) previsión. —**precautionary,** *adj.* precautorio.
precede (pri'si:d) *v.t. & i.* preceder; anteceder.
precedence ('prɛs·ɪ·dəns) *n.* **1,** (act of going before) precedencia. **2,** (priority) prioridad. —**precedent,** *n.* precedente; ejemplo.
preceding (pri'si·dɪŋ) *adj.* precedente; anterior; antecedente.
precept ('pri·sɛpt) *n.* precepto. —**preceptive** (prɪ'sɛp·tɪv) *adj.* preceptivo. —**preceptor** (prɪ'sɛp·tər) *n.* preceptor.
precinct ('pri·sɪŋkt) *n.* recinto; distrito.
preciosity (ˌprɛʃ·i'as·ə·ti) *n.* preciosismo.
precious ('prɛʃ·əs) *adj.* **1,** (valuable; esteemed; refined) precioso. **2,** (beloved) querido. **3,** (affected) precioso. —*adv., colloq.* bastante; muy. —**preciousness,** *n.* preciosidad.
precipice ('prɛs·ə·pɪs) *n.* precipicio.
precipitant (prɪ'sip·ə·tənt) *adj.* precipitado. —*n.* precipitante. —**precipitancy,** *n.* precipitación.
precipitate (prɪ'sɪp·əˌteit) *v.t.* precipitar. —*v.i.* precipitarse. —*adj. & n.* (-ˌteit *o* -tət) precipitado. —**precipitation,** *n.* precipitación.
precipitous (prɪ'sip·ə·təs) *adj.* **1,** (overhasty) precipitado. **2,** (steep) escarpado.
précis (prei'si:) *n.* resumen.
precise (prɪ'sais) *adj.* **1,** (definite) preciso. **2,** (punctilious) puntilloso. **3,** (exact) exacto. —**preciseness,** *n.* precisión; exactitud. —**precision** (-'sɪʒ·ən) *n.* precisión.
preclude (prɪ'klu:d) *v.t.* imposibilitar; excluir. —**preclusion** (-'klu·ʃən) *n.* exclusión.
precocious (prɪ'ko·ʃəs) *adj.* precoz. —**precociousness; precocity** (-'kas·ə·ti) *n.* precocidad.

precognition *n.* precognición.
pre-Columbian (ˌpri·kə'lʌm·bi·ən) *adj.* precolombino.
preconceive *v.t.* preconcebir. **—preconception,** *n.* idea preconcebida; prejuicio.
preconcert (ˌpri·kən'sʌɹt) *v.t.* concertar de antemano.
precursor (prɪ'kʌɹ·sər) *n.* precursor.
predatory ('prɛd·əˌtor·i) *adj.* **1,** (of or for plunder) de hurto. **2,** (preying) rapaz; de rapiña.
predecessor (ˌprɛd·ɪ'sɛs·ər) *n.* predecesor; antecesor.
predestination *n.* predestinación.
predestine (pri'dɛs·tɪn) *v.t.* predestinar.
predetermine *v.t.* predeterminar. **—predeterminate** (-ət) *adj.* predeterminado. **—predetermination,** *n.* predeterminación.
predicament (prɪ'dɪk·ə·mənt) *n.* **1,** (difficult situation) aprieto; apuro; trance apurado. **2,** *logic* (category) predicamento.
predicate ('prɛd·ə·kət) *n.* predicado. **—***v.t.* (-ˌkeit) predicar. **—predication,** *n.* predicación.
predicative ('prɛd·ɪˌkei·tɪv) *adj.* predicativo.
predict (prɪ'dɪkt) *v.t.* & *i.* predecir.
prediction (pri'dik·ʃən) *n.* predicción.
predilection (ˌpri·də'lɛk·ʃən) *n.* predilección.
predispose *v.t.* predisponer. **—predisposition** *n.* predisposición.
predominate (prɪ'dam·ɪˌneit) *v.t.* & *i.* predominar. **—predominance,** *n.* predominio. **—predominant,** *adj.* predominante.
preëminent (pri'ɛm·ɪ·nɛnt) *adj.* preeminente. **—preëminence,** *n.* preeminencia.
preëmpt (pri'ɛmpt) *v.t.* & *i.* **1,** (seize) apoderarse (de). **2,** (take or buy before another) tomar *o* comprar primero. **—preëmption** (-'ɛmp·ʃən) *n.* derecho de tomar or comprar primero. **—preëmptive,** *adj.* sujeto o perteneciente al derecho de tomar o comprar primero. **—preëmptor,** *n.* persona que toma o compra por tal derecho.
preen (priːn) *v.t.* **1,** (smooth) suavizar; limpiar. **2,** (adorn) engalanar. **—preen oneself,** componerse.
preëxist *v.i.* preexistir. **—preëxistence,** *n.* preexistencia. **—preëxistent; preëxisting,** *adj.* preexistente.
prefabricate (pri'fæb·rɪˌkeit) *v.t.* prefabricar. **—prefabrication,** *n.* prefabricación.
preface ('prɛf·ɪs) *n.* prefacio. **—***v.t.* prologar; introducir. **—prefatory** (-ə·tor·i) *adj.* preliminar.
prefect ('pri·fɛkt) *n.* prefecto. **—prefecture** (-fɛk·tʃər) *n.* prefectura.
prefer (prɪ'fʌɹ) *v.t.* preferir. **—preferable** ('prɛf·ər·ə·bəl) *adj.* preferible. **—preferred stocks,** acciones preferidas.
preference ('prɛf·ə·rəns) *n.* preferencia.
preferential (ˌprɛf·ər'ɛn·ʃəl) *adj.* preferente.
preferment (prɪ'fʌɹ·mənt) *n.* preferencia.
prefix ('pri·fɪks) *v.t.* prefijar. **—***n.* prefijo.
pregnant ('prɛg·nənt) *adj.* **1,** (carrying unborn young) encinta; preñada; embarazada. **2,** (fertile) preñado; fértil. **3,** (full of significance) profundo. **—pregnancy,** *n.* preñez.
prehensile (prɪ'hɛn·sɪl) *adj.* prensil.
prehistoric *adj.* prehistórico. **—prehistory,** *n.* prehistoria.
prejudge (pri'dʒʌdʒ) *v.t.* prejuzgar. **—prejudgment,** *n.* prejuicio.
prejudice ('prɛdʒ·ə·dɪs) *n.* **1,** (bias) prejuicio. **2,** (harmful effect) daño; perjuicio. **—***v.t.* **1,** (cause prejudice in) prejuiciar; predisponer. **2,** (damage) perjudicar. **—prejudiced,** *adj.* prejuiciado. **—prejudicial** (-'dɪʃ·əl) *adj.* prejudicial.
prelate ('prɛl·ət) *n.* prelado. **—prelacy,** *n.* prelacía.
preliminary (prɪ'lɪm·ɪ·nɛr·i) *adj.* & *n.* preliminar.
prelude ('prɛl·jud) *n.* preludio. **—***v.t.* & *i.* preludiar.
premature *adj.* prematuro.
premedical (pri'mɛd·ɪ·kəl) *adj.* premédico. **—premedical course,** premédica.
premeditate (pri'mɛd·ɪˌteit) *v.t.* premeditar. **—premeditation,** *n.* premeditación.
premier ('pri·mi·ər) *adj.* primero. **—***n.* primer ministro; presidente del consejo.

première (prɪ'mjeir) *n.* debut; estreno.
premise ('prɛm·ɪs) *n.* **1,** (previous statement) premisa. **2,** *pl.* (place) local (*sing.*). —*v.t.* exponer *o* proponer como premisa. —*v.i.* establecer premisas.
premium ('pri·mi·əm) *n.* **1,** (award) premio. **2,** *comm.* prima. —**at a premium, 1,** (at increased price) a premio (*o* a prima). **2,** (in demand) en gran demanda.
premonition (ˌpri·mə'nɪʃ·ən) *n.* presentimiento.
premonitory (prɪ'man·əˌtor·i) *adj.* premonitorio.
prenatal (pri'nei·təl) *adj.* prenatal.
preoccupy (pri'ak·jəˌpai) *v.t.* preocupar. —**preoccupancy,** *n.* preocupación. —**preoccupation** (-'pei·ʃən) *n.* preocupación.
preordain *v.t.* preordinar. —**preordination,** *n.* preordinación.
prepaid *v., pret. & p.p. de* **prepay.** —*adj.* franco de porte; con porte pagado.
preparation (ˌprɛp·ə'rei·ʃən) *n.* **1,** (making ready) preparación. **2,** (something made ready) preparativo. **3,** (concoction, as medicine) preparado.
preparatory (prɪ'pær·ə·tor·i) *adj.* preparatorio.
prepare (prɪ'pe:r) *v.t.* **1,** (make ready) preparar. **2,** (forewarn) prevenir. —*v.i.* **1,** (make preparations) hacer preparaciones. **2,** (ready oneself) disponerse. **3,** (take precautions) prevenirse.
preparedness (prɪ'pe:rd·nəs) *n.* alerta; estado de preparación.
prepay (pri'pei) *v.t.* [*pret. & p.p.* **-paid**] pagar por adelantado. —**prepayment,** *n.* pago adelantado.
preponderate (prɪ'pan·dəˌreit) *v.i.* preponderar. —**preponderance,** *n.* preponderancia. —**preponderant,** *adj.* preponderante.
preposition (ˌprɛp·ə'zɪʃ·ən) *n.* preposición. —**prepositional,** *adj.* preposicional; prepositivo.
prepossess *v.t.* **1,** (impress favorably) hacer buena impresión en; predisponer favorablemente. **2,** (dominate) preocupar; obsesionar. **3,** (prejudice) prejuiciar; predisponer. —**prepossessing,** *adj.* simpático; impresionante.
prepossession *n.* **1,** (bias) prejuicio; predisposición. **2,** (preoccupation) preocupación; obsesión.
preposterous (prɪ'pas·tər·əs) *adj.* absurdo; ridículo. —**preposterousness,** *n.* absurdidad; ridiculez.
prepuce ('pri·pjus) *n.* prepucio.
prerequisite (pri'rɛk·wə·zɪt) *n. & adj.* requisito (previo).
prerogative (pri'rag·ə·tɪv) *n.* prerrogativa.
presage ('prɛs·ɪdʒ) *n.* presagio. —*v.t.* (prɪ'seidʒ) presagiar.
presbyter ('prɛz·bɪ·tər) *n.* presbítero.
Presbyterian (ˌprɛz·bɪ'tɪr·i·ən) *adj. & n.* presbiteriano.
presbytery ('prɛz·bɪˌtɛr·i) *n.* presbiterio.
prescience ('pri·ʃi·əns) *n.* presciencia.
prescribe (pri'skraib) *v.t. & i.* **1,** (order; advise) prescribir. **2,** *med.* recetar.
prescript ('pri·skrɪpt) *n.* norma; prescripto. —*adj.* prescripto.
prescription (prɪ'skrɪp·ʃən) *n.* **1,** (order; advice) prescripción. **2,** *med.* receta. —**prescriptive** (-tɪv) *adj.* de *o* por prescripción.
presence ('prɛz·əns) *n.* presencia. —**presence of mind,** serenidad; presencia de ánimo.
present ('prɛz·ənt) *adj.* **1,** (in a given place) presente. **2,** (of or at this time) actual. —*n.* **1,** (this time) presente. **2,** (gift) regalo. —**at present,** ahora; actualmente. —**present participle,** participio activo. —**present perfect,** pretérito perfecto.
present (prɪ'zɛnt) *v.t.* **1,** (give) ofrecer; regalar. **2,** (introduce; exhibit) presentar. **3,** (show) manifestar. —**presentable,** *adj.* presentable.
presentation (ˌprɛz·ən'tei·ʃən) *n.* presentación.
presentiment (prɪ'zɛn·tə·mənt) *n.* presentimiento.
presently ('prɛz·ənt·li) *adv.* **1,** (soon) pronto. **2,** (at this time) actualmente.
presentment (prɪ'zənt·mənt) *n.* **1,** (presentation) presentación. **2,** *law* acusación.
preservation (ˌprɛz·ər'vei·ʃən) *n.* preservación; conservación.
preservative (pri'zʌɹv·ə·tɪv) *adj. & n.* preservativo.
preserve (prɪ'zʌɹv) *v.t.* **1,** (save) preservar. **2,** (retain) guardar. **3,** *cooking* hacer conservas de. —*n.*

1, (restricted territory) vedado. 2, *usu.pl.* (confection) confitura (*sing.*); conserva (*sing.*).

preside (prɪ'zaid) *v.i.* presidir. —**presider**, *n.* presidente. —**presiding**, *adj.* que preside; presidente. —**preside over**, presidir.

presidency ('prɛz·ɪ·dən·si) *n.* presidencia.

president ('prɛz·ɪ·dənt) *n.* presidente. —**presidential** (-'dɛn·ʃəl) *adj.* presidencial.

press (prɛs) *v.t.* 1, (bear heavily on) apretar. 2, (compress) comprimir. 3, (clasp in one's arms) abrazar; prensar. 4, (push) empujar; insistir en. 5, (harass) acosar; importunar. 6, (hurry; urge on) apresurar. 7, (iron) planchar. 8, (draft) conscribir. —*v.i.* 1, (weigh heavily) pesar; oprimir. 2, (crowd) apiñarse. 3, (hurry) apresurarse. —*n.* 1, (crowding pressure) presión; turba. 2, (urgency) urgencia; prisa. 3, (chest) armario; gavetero. 4, *printing; publishing* prensa. —**press agent**, agente de publicidad.

presser ('prɛs·ər) *n.* 1, (person or machine that compresses) prensador. 2, (ironer) planchador. 3, (ironing device) planchadora.

pressing ('prɛs·ɪŋ) *adj.* urgente. —*n.* 1, (pressure) presión. 2, (mashing, as of grapes) expresión. 3, (ironing) planchado. —**pressing iron**, plancha.

pressman ('prɛs·mən) *n.* [*pl.* **-men**] prensista.

pressure ('prɛʃ·ər) *n.* 1, (bearing down) presión. 2, (burden) opresión. 3, (urgency) urgencia. 4, *electricity* tensión. —**pressure gauge**, manómetro.

pressurized ('prɛʃ·ər·aizd) *adj.* a prueba de presión.

prestidigitation (ˌprɛs·tə·ˌdɪdʒ·ə'tei·ʃən) *n.* prestidigitación. —**prestidigitator** (-tər) *n.* prestidigitador.

prestige (prɛs'tiːʒ) *n.* prestigio. —*adj.* prestigioso; de categoría.

presto ('prɛs·to) *adv.* rápidamente; en seguida.

presume (prɪ'zuːm) *v.t.* & *i.* presumir. —**presumable**, *adj.* presumible. —**presumably**, *adv.* por presunción. —**presuming**, *adj.* presuntuoso.

presumption (prɪ'zʌmp·ʃən) *n.* presunción.

presumptive (prɪ'zʌmp·tɪv) *adj.* presuntivo; presunto; supuesto. —**presumptively**, *adv.* presuntamente.

presumptuous (prɪ'zʌmp·tju·əs) *adj.* presuntuoso; presumido. —**presumptuousness**, *n.* presuntuosidad; presunción.

presuppose *v.t.* presuponer. —**presupposition**, *n.* presuposición.

pretend (prɪ'tɛnd) *v.t.* & *i.* 1, (feign) pretender; simular; fingir. 2, (claim falsely) alegar falsamente. —**pretended**, *adj.* falso; fingido. —**pretender**, *n.* pretendiente; hipócrita.

pretense ('pri·tɛns) *n.* 1, (pretext) pretexto. 2, (claim) pretensión.

pretension (prɪ'tən·ʃən) *n.* pretensión.

pretentious (prɪ'tɛn·ʃəs) *adj.* presumido; presuntuoso; pretencioso. —**pretentiousness**, *n.* presunción; pretensión.

preter- (pri·tər) *prefijo* preter-; más allá de; más que: *preternatural,* preternatural.

preterit ('prɛt·ər·ɪt) *adj.* & *n.* pretérito.

preternatural *adj.* preternatural.

pretext ('pri·tɛkst) *n.* pretexto.

pretor ('pri·tər) *n.* = **praetor**. —**pretorial** (pri'tor·i·əl) *adj.* = **praetorial.** —**pretorian** (pri'tor·i·ən) *adj.* = **praetorian.**

prettify ('prɪt·əˌfai) *v.t.* [*pret.* & *p.p.* **-fied**] embellecer.

pretty ('prɪt·i) *adj.* bonito; lindo; *ironic* bueno; menudo. —*adv.* bastante. —**prettiness**, *n.* lindeza; gracia. —**pretty well**, *colloq.* regular; no mal.

pretzel ('prɛt·səl) *n.* galleta salada tostada en forma de nudo.

prevail (prɪ'veil) *v.i.* 1, (win) prevalecer. 2, (predominate) predominar. —**prevail on** *o* **upon**, persuadir.

prevailing (prɪ'vei·lɪŋ) *adj.* 1, (predominant) prevaleciente; predominante. 2, (general) general; corriente.

prevalent ('prɛv·ə·lənt) *adj.* general; común; muy extendido. —**prevalence**; **prevalency**, *n.* frecuencia; boga.

prevaricate (prɪ'vær·əˌkeit) *v.i.* prevaricar. —**prevaricator**, *n.* prevaricador. —**prevarication**, *n.* prevaricación.

prevent (prɪ'vɛnt) *v.t.* impedir;

evitar. —**preventable**, *adj.* evitable.

preventative (prɪ'vɛn·tə·tɪv) *adj.* & *n.* preventivo.

prevention (prɪ'vɛn·ʃən) *n.* prevención.

preventive (prɪ'vɛn·tɪv) *adj.* & *n.* preventivo.

preview ('pri·vju) *n.* **1,** (advance view) vista de antemano. **2,** (advance showing) previa representación. **3,** *motion pictures* (sample scenes) avance; muestra. —*v.t.* ver de antemano.

previous ('pri·vi·əs) *adj.* previo; anterior. —**previously**, *adv.* anteriormente; antes. —**previousness**, *n.* anterioridad.

prewar (pri'wor) *adj.* de (la) preguerra. —**prewar period**, preguerra.

prey (prei) *n.* **1,** (animal killed by another) presa. **2,** (victim) víctima. **3,** (habit of preying) rapiña. —*v.i.* [*usu.* **prey on** *o* **upon**] **1,** (devour) devorar. **2,** (plunder) robar; rapiñar. **3,** (oppress) oprimir. —**bird of prey**, ave de rapiña.

price (prais) *n.* **1,** (value) precio. **2,** (cost) costo. **3,** (reward) recompensa. —*v.t.* valuar; preciar; apreciar. —**priceless**, *adj.* inapreciable. —**at any price**, a toda costa. —**market price**, precio corriente.

prick (prɪk) *n.* **1,** (hole) agujerito. **2,** (goad) aguijón. **3,** (stinging sensation) punzada. —*v.t.* **1,** (puncture) punzar; agujerar. **2,** (cause pain) doler. —**pricking**, *n.* picadura. —**prick up one's ears**, aguzar las orejas.

prickle ('prɪk·əl) *n.* púa; pincho; espina. —*v.t.* & *i.* pinchar; picar.

prickly ('prɪk·li) *adj.* **1,** (thorny) espinoso. **2,** (sharp; biting) agudo; punzante. —**prickly heat**, salpullido. —**prickly pear**, nopal; tuna; higo chumbo. —**prickly pear cactus**, nopal; tunal; chumbera; higuera chumba.

pride (praid) *n.* **1,** (self-respect) orgullo. **2,** (vanity) altivez; engreimiento. **3,** (satisfaction) jactancia. —**prideful**, *adj.* orgulloso. —**pride oneself on** *o* **upon**, enorgullecerse de.

prie-dieu (pri'djʊ) *n.* reclinatorio.

prier *también*, **pryer** ('prai·ər) *n.* fisgón; hurón.

priest (prist) *n.* sacerdote; cura. —**priestess**, *n.f.* sacerdotisa. —**priesthood**, *n.* sacerdocio. —**priestly**, *adj.* sacerdotal.

prig (prɪg) *n.* mojigato; remilgado. —**priggery**, *n.* mojigatería; remilgo. —**priggish**, *adj.* mojigato; remilgado.

prim (prɪm) *adj.* relamido; estirado; remilgado.

primacy ('prai·mə·si) *n.* primacía.

prima donna (ˌpri·mə'dan·ə) *n.* [*pl.* **prima donnas**] prima donna.

primal ('prai·məl) *adj.* **1,** (primitive) original; primitivo. **2,** (principal) primero; principal.

primarily (prai'mɛr·ə·li) *adv.* principalmente; sobre todo.

primary ('prai·mɛr·i) *adj.* primario. —*n.* **1,** (first) primero. **2,** *polit.* elección preliminar *o* primaria. **3,** *electricity* circuito primario.

primate ('prai·met) *n.* **1,** *eccles.* primado. **2,** *zool.* primate.

prime (praim) *adj.* **1,** (first) primero. **2,** (most important) principal. **3,** (superior) de primera calidad. **4,** *math.* primo. —*n.* **1,** (earliest stage) principio. **2,** (high point) ápice. **3,** (best period) flor. **4,** (best part) flor y nata. —*v.t.* **1,** (prepare) preparar; prevenir. **2,** (charge, as a gun) cebar. **3,** *colloq.* (instruct) dar instrucciones; informar. **4,** (apply the first coat to) dar la primera mano a. —**prime minister**, primer ministro. —**prime of life**, edad viril.

primer ('prai·mər) *n.* **1,** (person or device that primes) cebador. **2,** ('prɪm·ər) (elementary textbook) cartilla; abecedario.

primeval (prai'mi·vəl) *adj.* prístino; original.

priming ('prai·mɪŋ) *n.* **1,** (preparation) preparación. **2,** (of a pump or weapon) cebo. **3,** (undercoat) primera mano.

primitive ('prɪm·ə·tɪv) *adj.* **1,** (early in history) primitivo. **2,** (simple) crudo. **3,** (basic) fundamental; básico. —*n.* **1,** (untrained artist) pintor crudo; primitivo. **2,** (basic form) forma original. —**primitiveness**, *n.* estado primitivo.

primness ('prɪm·nəs) *n.* formalidad; precisión; remilgo.

primogeniture (ˌprai·mə'dʒɛn·ə·tʃər) *n.* primogenitura; progenitura.

primordial (prai'mor·di·əl) *adj.* primordial; original.
primp (prɪmp) *v.t.* aliñar; acicalar. —*v.i.* aliñarse; acicalarse.
primrose ('prɪm·roz) *n.* primavera. —*adj.* amarillo claro. —**primrose path**, sendero fácil; vida agradable.
prince (prɪns) *n.* príncipe. —**princedom**, *n.* principado.
prince consort príncipe consorte.
princely ('prɪns·li) *adj.* principesco.
princess ('prɪn·sɪs) *n.* princesa.
principal ('prɪn·sə·pəl) *adj.* principal. —*n.* **1,** (chief person) principal. **2,** (head of a school) director; jefe. **3,** *comm.* principal.
principality (,prɪn·sə'pæl·ə·ti) *n.* principado.
principle ('prɪn·sə·pəl) *n.* principio.
prink (prɪŋk) *v.t.* & *i.* = **primp.**
print (prɪnt) *n.* **1,** (mark) impresión. **2,** (type) tipo; letra. **3,** (seal) sello. **4,** (printed piece) impreso. **5,** (copy) estampa; grabado. **6,** *photog.* impresión. **7,** (patterned cloth) estampado. —*v.t.* **1,** (produce from type) imprimir. **2,** *photog.* tirar; sacar. —**in print**, impreso. —**out of print**, agotado.
printer ('prɪn·tər) *n.* **1,** (craftsman) impresor. **2,** (copying device) copiadora. —**printer's ink**, tinta de imprenta. —**printer's mark**, pie de imprenta.
printing ('prɪn·tɪŋ) *n.* **1,** (process) tipografía; imprenta. **2,** (writing in capitals) molde de imprenta. **3,** (printed piece) impreso. **4,** (quantity printed at one time) tirada. —**printing press**, prensa tipográfica. —**printing shop**, estampería.
prior ('prai·ər) *adj.* anterior. —*n.* prior. —**prioress**, *n.* priora.
priority (prai'ar·ə·ti) *n.* prioridad.
prise (praiz) *v.t.* levantar con una palanca o cuña.
prism ('prɪz·əm) *n.* prisma. —**prismatic** (prɪz'mæt·ik) *adj.* prismático.
prison ('prɪz·ən) *n.* prisión; cárcel. —**prisoner**, *n.* preso; prisionero. —**prison house**, cárcel. —**prison keeper**, carcelero. —**prison van**, coche celular. —**take prisoner**, prender.
prissy ('prɪs·i) *adj., colloq.* afectado; amanerado; melindroso.
pristine ('prɪs·tin) *adj.* prístino.
privacy ('prai·və·si) *n.* aislamiento. —**in privacy**, en secreto. —**have (no) privacy**, (no) poder estar tranquilo.
private ('prai·vɪt) *adj.* **1,** (personal) privado. **2,** (secret) confidencial. **3,** (retired) retirado. —*n.* soldado raso. —**in private**, en secreto; a solas. —**private first class**, soldado de primera. —**private parts**, partes pudendas.
privateer (,prai·və'tɪr) *n.* **1,** (person) corsario. **2,** (ship) buque corsario. —*v.i.* ir a corso; corsear. —**privateering**, *n.* corso. —*adj.* corsario.
privation (prai'vei·ʃən) *n.* privación.
privative ('prɪv·ə·tɪv) *adj.* privativo.
privet ('prɪv·ɪt) *n.* ligustro.
privilege ('prɪv·ə·lɪdʒ) *n.* privilegio. —*v.t.* privilegiar. —**privileged**, *adj.* privilegiado.
privy ('prɪv·i) *adj.* **1,** (private) privado; secreto. **2,** (knowing) enterado; consabido. —*n.* excusado; letrina; privada.
prize (praiz) *n.* **1,** (reward) premio. **2,** (valued article) joya. **3,** (booty) presa; botín. —*v.t.* **1,** (value highly) estimar *o* apreciar mucho. **2,** [*también,* **prise**] (pry with a lever) levantar con una palanca o cuña. —*adj.* premiado; superior. —**prize fight**, partido de boxeo. —**prize fighter**, púgil. —**prize ring**, cuadrilátero.
pro (pro:) *prep.* pro. —*n.* [*pl.* **pros**] **1,** (supporter) proponente. **2,** *colloq.* = **professional.** —**the pros and cons**, el pro y el contra.
pro- (pro) *prefijo* pro-. **1,** en *o* a favor de: *pro-French,* profrancés. **2,** en vez *o* lugar de: *proconsul,* procónsul. **3,** hacia adelante: *proceed,* proseguir. **4,** hacia afuera: *project,* proyectar. **5,** delante (en tiempo *o* lugar): *prologue,* prólogo; *proscenium,* proscenio.
probable ('prab·ə·bəl) *adj.* probable. —**probability**, *n.* probabilidad.
probate ('pro·bet) *n.* verificación; prueba. —*v.t.* someter a verificación.
probation (pro'bei·ʃən) *n.* **1,** (trial period) probación; novi-

ciado. **2,** (release from prison) libertad vigilada. —**probationary,** *adj.* probatorio.
probationer (pro'bei·ʃən·ər) *n.* **1,** (novice) novicio; aprendiz. **2,** (offender released on probation) delincuente en libertad vigilada.
probe (pro:b) *n.* **1,** (instrument) tienta; sonda. **2,** (investigation) investigación; indagación. —*v.t.* & *i.* **1,** (explore with a probe) sondar; **2,** (investigate) investigar; indagar.
probity ('pro·bə·ti) *n.* probidad; integridad.
problem ('prab·ləm) *n.* problema. —**problematic** (-lə'mæt·ɪk); **problematical,** *adj.* problemático.
proboscis (pro'bas·ɪs) *n.* probóscide.
procedure (prə'si·dʒər) *n.* procedimiento.
proceed (prə'si:d) *v.i.* **1,** (go forward) avanzar; seguir. **2,** (continue) seguir; proseguir. —**proceed against,** *law* armar un pleito contra; proceder contra. —**proceed from,** originar de; proceder de.
proceeding (prə'si·dɪŋ) *n., usu. pl.* procedimiento; proceso.
proceeds ('pro·sidz) *n.pl.* réditos; ganancia (*sing.*).
process ('pras·ɛs) *n.* **1,** (course; progress) transcurso; progreso. **2,** (method) método; procedimiento. **3,** *anat.* protuberancia; proceso. **4,** *law* proceso. —*v.t.* **1,** (treat by a special method) someter a un procedimiento especial. **2,** *law* procesar. —*adj.* elaborado; de elaboración.
procession (prə'sɛʃ·ən) *n.* procesión. —**processional,** *adj.* procesional.
proclaim (pro'kleim) *v.t.* proclamar.
proclamation (ˌprak·lə'mei·ʃən) *n.* proclama; proclamación; edicto.
proclivity (pro'klɪv·ə·ti) *n.* proclividad.
proconsul (pro'kan·səl) *n.* procónsul. —**proconsular,** *adj.* proconsular. —**proconsulate** (-sə·lɪt) *n.* proconsulado.
procrastinate (pro'kræs·təˌneit) *v.i.* demorar; diferir. —**procrastination,** *n.* tardanza; demora. —**procrastinator,** *n.* moroso.
procreate ('pro·kriˌeit) *v.t.* procrear. —**procreation,** *n.* procreación. —**procreative,** *adj.* procreador. —**procreator,** *n.* procreador.
proctor ('prak·tər) *n.* **1,** *educ.* censor. **2,** *law* procurador.
procurator ('prak·jʊˌrei·tər) *n.* procurador.
procure (pro'kjʊr) *v.t.* **1,** (obtain) obtener; lograr; procurar. **2,** (hire for immoral purposes) solicitar (mujeres). —*v.i.* alcahuetear. —**procurable,** *adj.* asequible.
procurement (pro'kjʊr·mənt) *n.* **1,** (acquisition) procuración; obtención. **2,** (hiring of women) alcahuetería.
procurer (pro'kjʊr·ər) *n.* alcahuete. —**procuress,** *n.* alcahueta.
prod (pra:d) *n.* **1,** (sharp implement) aguijón; aguijada. **2,** (thrust; jab) empujón; pinchada. —*v.t.* aguijar; pinchar.
prodigal ('prad·ɪ·gəl) *adj.* & *n.* pródigo. —**prodigality** (-'gæl·ə·ti) *n.* prodigalidad.
prodigious (prə'dɪdʒ·əs) *adj.* **1,** (marvelous) prodigioso; maravilloso. **2,** (huge) inmenso; enorme.
prodigy ('prad·ə·dʒi) *n.* prodigio.
produce (prə'djus) *v.t.* **1,** (yield) producir. **2,** (cause) ocasionar. **3,** (show) mostrar. **4,** (manufacture) elaborar; manufacturar. **5,** *theat.* presentar. **6,** *geom.* extender. **7,** *comm.* rendir. —*v.i.* producir. —*n.* ('pro·djus) **1,** (result) producto; producción. **2,** (natural products) productos (*pl.*). —**producing,** *adj.* productivo.
producer (prə'djus·ər) *n.* **1,** (maker) productor. **2,** *theat.* director de escena.
product ('prad·ʌkt) *n.* producto.
production (prə'dʌk·ʃən) *n.* **1,** (act or result of producing) producción. **2,** *theat.* realización; presentación.
productive (prə'dʌk·tɪv) *adj.* productivo. —**productivity** (ˌpro·dʌk'tɪv·ə·ti) *n.* productividad.
profanation (ˌpraf·ə'nei·ʃən) *n.* profanación.
profane (prə'fein) *adj.* profano. —*v.t.* profanar.
profanity (prə'fæn·ə·ti) *n.* blasfemia; profanidad.
profess (prə'fɛs) *v.t.* profesar. —**professed,** *adj.* profeso; declarado.
profession (prə'fɛʃ·ən) *n.* **1,** (vocation) profesión. **2,** (avowal) declaración. —**professional,** *adj.* & *n.* profesional.

professor (prə'fɛs·ər) *n.* profesor. —**professorate** (-ɪt) *n.* profesorado. —**professorial** (ˌpro·fɛ·'sor·i·əl) *adj.* profesoral; de profesor *o* catedrático. —**professoriate** (ˌpro·fɛ'sor·i·ɪt) *n.* profesorado. —**professorship**, *n.* profesorado.
proffer ('praf·ər) *v.t.* ofrecer; proponer. —*n.* oferta; propuesta.
proficient (prə'fɪʃ·ənt) *adj.* proficiente; hábil. —**proficiency**, *n.* proficiencia; habilidad.
profile ('pro·fail) *n.* **1,** (side view) perfil. **2,** (contour) contorno. —*v.t.* perfilar.
profit ('praf·ɪt) *n.* beneficio; ganancia; provecho. —*v.t.* ser ventajoso para; servir. —*v.i.* ganar; aprovechar; sacar provecho. —**profitable**, *adj.* beneficioso; provechoso; ganancioso. —**profitless**, infructuoso. —**gross profit**, ganancia en bruto.
profiteer (ˌpraf·ɪ'tɪr) *n.* explotador; usurero. —*v.i.* usurear; explotar; pringarse.
profligate ('praf·lɪ·gət) *adj.* & *n.* libertino. —**profligacy**, *n.* libertinaje.
profound (prə'faund) *adj.* profundo.
profundity (prə'fʌn·də·ti) *n.* profundidad.
profuse (prə'fjus) *adj.* profuso. —**profuseness**; **profusion** (-'fju·ʃən) *n.* profusión.
progenitor (pro'dʒɛn·ə·tər) *n.* progenitor.
progeny ('pradʒ·ə·ni) *n.* progenie; prole.
prognosis (prag'no·sɪs) *n.* pronóstico; prognosis. —**prognostic** (-'nas·tɪk) *adj.* pronosticador.
prognosticate (prag'nas·tə,keit) *v.t.* pronosticar. —**prognostication**, *n.* pronosticación.
program ('pro·græm) *n.* programa. —*v.t.* incluir en el programa; *electronics* programar. —**programming**, *n.*, *electronics* programación.
progress ('prag·rɛs) *n.* **1,** (advance) adelanto. **2,** (development) progreso *o* progresos. **3,** (improvement) mejoramiento. —*v.i.* (prə·'grɛs) **1,** (proceed) adelantar; avanzar. **2,** (develop; grow) progresar. **3,** (improve) mejorar. —**make progress**, hacer progresos.
progression (prə'grɛʃ·ən) *n.* progresión.
progressive (prə'grɛs·ɪv) *adj.* progresivo; *polit.* progresista. —*n.* progresista.
prohibit (pro'hɪb·ɪt) *v.t.* prohibir.
prohibition (ˌpro·ə'bɪʃ·ən) *n.* prohibición. —**prohibitionist**, *n.* prohibicionista.
prohibitive (prə'hɪb·ɪ·tɪv) *adj.* prohibitivo.
prohibitory (prə'hɪb·ɪˌtor·i) *adj.* prohibitorio.
project ('pradʒ·ɛkt) *n.* proyecto. —*v.t.* (prə'dʒɛkt) proyectar. —*v.i.* sobresalir. —**projecting**, *adj.* saliente.
projectile (prə'dʒɛk·tɪl) *n.* proyectil.
projection (prə'dʒɛk·ʃən) *n.* proyección. —**projectionist**, *n.* operador cinematográfico.
projector (prə'dʒɛk·tər) *n.* proyector.
prolate ('pro·leit) *adj.*, *geom.* elongado (por los polos).
proletariat (ˌpro·lə'tɛr·i·ət) *n.* proletariado. —**proletarian**, *adj.* & *n.* proletario.
proliferate (pro'lɪf·əˌreit) *v.t.* multiplicar; reproducir. —*v.i.* multiplicarse; reproducirse. —**proliferation**, *n.* multiplicación; proliferación.
prolific (pro'lɪf·ɪk) *adj.* prolífico.
prolix (pro'lɪks) *adj.* prolijo. —**prolixity**, *n.* prolijidad.
prologue ('pro·lɔg) *n.* prólogo. —*v.t.* prologar.
prolong (prə'lɔŋ) *v.t.* prolongar. —**prolongation** (ˌpro·lɔŋ'gei·ʃən) *n.* prolongación.
prom (pra:m) *n.*, *colloq.* baile de gala, esp. para estudiantes.
promenade (ˌpram·ə'neid) *n.* **1,** (stroll) paseo. **2,** (wide street) bulevar. **3,** (ball) baile de gala. —*v.i.* pasearse. —**promenader**, *n.* paseante.
Prometheus (prə'mi·θi·əs) *n.* Prometeo. —**Promethean**, *adj.* de Prometeo.
promethium (prə'mi·θi·əm) *n.* prometio.
prominent ('pram·ə·nənt) *adj.* prominente; *fig.* eminente. —**prominence**, *n.* prominencia; *fig.* eminencia.
promiscuous (prə'mɪs·kju·əs) *adj.* promiscuo. —**promiscuousness**; **promiscuity** (ˌpram·ɪs'kju·ə·ti) *n.* promiscuidad.
promise ('pram·ɪs) *n.* promesa.

—*v.t.* & *i.* prometer. —**promising,** *adj.* prometedor. —**break one's promise,** faltar a su palabra. —**keep one's promise,** cumplir su palabra. —**promised land,** tierra de promisión.

promissory ('pram·ɪ·sor·i) *adj.* promisorio. —**promissory note,** pagaré.

promontory ('pram·ən,tor·i) *n.* promontorio.

promote (prə'mot) *v.t.* **1,** (foment) promover. **2,** (advance in grade) adelantar. **3,** *comm.* (develop) agenciar. —**promoter,** *n.* promotor; *theat.; sports* empresario.

promotion (prə'mo·ʃən) *n.* **1,** (advancement) promoción. **2,** (development) desarrollo.

prompt (prampt) *adj.* **1,** (quick; without delay) pronto. **2,** (quick to act; eager) listo; dispuesto. **3,** (on time) puntual. —*v.t.* **1,** (incite) incitar; impulsar; mover. **2,** *theat.* (cue) apuntar. —**prompter,** *n., theat.* apuntador. —**promptly,** *adv.* en punto; pronto; prontamente. —**promptness; promptitude** ('pramp·tə,tjud) *n.* prontitud.

promulgate (pro'mʌl·geit) *v.t.* promulgar; proclamar. —**promulgation** (,pro·mʌl'gei·ʃən) *n.* promulgación. —**promulgator,** *n.* promulgador.

prone (pro:n) *adj.* **1,** (prostrate) prono; postrado; acostado boca abajo. **2,** (susceptible) inclinado; propenso.

proneness ('pron·nəs) *n.* **1,** (prostration) postración. **2,** (inclination) inclinación; propensión.

prong (pra:ŋ) *n.* diente; punta. —**pronged,** *adj.* dentado.

pronominal (pro'nam·ə·nəl) *adj.* pronominal.

pronoun ('pro·naun) *n.* pronombre.

pronounce (prə'nauns) *v.t.* pronunciar. —*v.i.* declararse; pronunciarse. —**pronounced,** *adj.* marcado. —**pronouncement,** *n.* declaración; *law* pronunciamiento.

pronto ('pran·to) *adv., colloq.* pronto; en seguida.

pronunciation (prə,nʌn·si'ei·ʃən) *n.* pronunciación.

proof (pruf) *n.* **1,** (evidence; test) prueba. **2,** *print; photog.* prueba. **3,** (alcoholic content) graduación normal. —*adj.* **1,** (strong; durable) de prueba. **2,** (impenetrable) a prueba de. **3,** (alcoholic) de prueba. **4,** (denoting alcoholic content) de graduación normal.

-proof (pruf) *sufijo, formando nombres y adjetivos denotando* a prueba de: *waterproof,* impermeable.

proofread *v.t.* & *i.* [*pret.* & *p.p.* **-read**] corregir (leyendo). —**proofreader,** *n.* corrector de pruebas. —**proofreading,** *n.* corrección de pruebas.

prop (prap) *v.t.* [**propped, propping**] **1,** (hold up; support) sostener. **2,** (place against something for support; lean) apoyar. **3,** (shore up) apuntalar. —*n.* **1,** (support) sostén. **2,** (something to lean against) apoyo. **3,** (post; upright) puntal. **4,** *colloq.* = **propeller. 5,** *theat.* accesorio.

propaganda (,prap·ə'gæn·də) *n.* propaganda. —**propagandist,** *n.* propagandista.

propagate ('prap·ə,geit) *v.t.* propagar. —*v.i.* propagarse. —**propagation,** *n.* propagación. —**propagator,** *n.* propagador.

propane ('pro·pein) *n.* propano.

propel (prə'pɛl) *v.t.* impeler; propulsar. —**propellant,** *n.* impulsor; propulsor. —**propellent,** *adj.* impelente; propulsor.

propeller (prə'pɛl·ər) *n.* hélice.

propensity (prə'pɛn·sə·ti) *n.* propensión.

proper ('prap·ər) *adj.* **1,** (peculiar; one's own) propio. **2,** (appropriate) apropiado; apto. **3,** (formal) formal; correcto. **4,** (decorous) decente; decoroso. **5,** (exact) justo; exacto.

property ('prap·ər·ti) *n.* propiedad; *theat.* accesorio. —**personal property,** bienes muebles. —**real property,** bienes inmuebles; bienes raíces.

prophecy ('praf·ə·si) *n.* profecía.

prophesy ('praf·ə·sai) *v.t.* & *i.* profetizar.

prophet ('praf·ɪt) *n.* profeta. —**prophetic** (prə'fɛt·ɪk) *adj.* profético. —**prophetess,** *n.* profetisa.

prophylaxis (,pro·fə'læk·sɪs) *n.* profilaxis. —**prophylactic** (-tɪk) *adj.* & *n.* profiláctico.

propinquity (pro'pɪŋ·kwɪ·ti) *n.* proximidad; propincuidad.

propitiate (pro'pɪʃ·i,eit) *v.t.* propiciar. —**propitiation,** *n.* propiciación. —**propitiatory** (-ə·tor·i) *adj.* propiciatorio.

propitious (prəˈpɪʃ·əs) *adj.* propicio; bueno; benigno. —**propitiousness**, *n.* benignidad; calidad de propicio.

proponent (prəˈpo·nənt) *n.* proponente.

proportion (prəˈpor·ʃən) *n.* proporción. —*v.t.* proporcionar. —**proportional**, *adj.* proporcional. —**proportionate** (-ət) *adj.* proporcionado. —**out of proportion**, desproporcionado.

proposal (prəˈpo·zəl) *n.* **1,** (suggestion) propuesta; proposición. **2,** (offer of marriage) oferta de matrimonio; declaración de amor.

propose (prəˈpo:z) *v.t.* proponer; sugerir. —*v.i.* **1,** (plan; intend) proponer *o* proponerse (+ *inf.*) **2,** (make an offer of marriage) declararse; pedir la mano (a).

proposition (ˌprap·əˈzɪʃ·ən) *n.* proposición.

propound (prəˈpaund) *v.t.* proponer.

proprietary (prəˈprai·əˌtɛr·i) *adj.* propietario. —*n.* **1,** (owner) dueño. **2,** (ownership) posesión. **3,** (patent medicine) propietario; patentado.

proprietor (prəˈprai·ə·tər) *n.* propietario; dueño.

propriety (prəˈprai·ə·ti) *n.* propiedad; conveniencia. —**proprieties**, *n.pl.* convenciones.

propulsion (prəˈpʌl·ʃən) *n.* propulsión. —**propulsive** (-sɪv) *adj.* propulsor.

pro rata (proˈrei·tə) a prorrata; a prorrateo.

prorate (proˈreit) *v.t.* prorratear. —**proration**, *n.* prorrateo.

prosaic (proˈzei·ɪk) *adj.* prosaico.

proscenium (proˈsi·ni·əm) *n.* **1,** (stage) escenario. **2,** (front of stage) proscenio.

proscribe (proˈskraib) *v.t.* proscribir. —**proscription** (-ˈskrɪp·ʃən) *n.* proscripción.

prose (pro:z) *n.* prosa. —*adj.* en *o* de prosa; prosaico. —**prose writer**, prosista.

prosecute (ˈpras·əˌkjut) *v.t.* **1,** (pursue) proseguir. **2,** *law* procesar. —*v.i.* hacer causa; armar un pleito.

prosecution (ˌpras·əˈkju·ʃən) *n.* **1,** (pursuit; carrying out) prosecución. **2,** (legal proceedings) procesamiento. **3,** (representative of the state) parte acusadora; prosecución.

prosecutor (ˈpras·əˌkju·tər) *n.* procurador; fiscal.

proselyte (ˈpras·əˌlait) *n.* prosélito. —*v.t.* & *i.* = **proselytize.**

proselytize (ˈpras·ə·ləˌtaiz) *v.t.* convertir. —*v.i.* ganar *o* tratar de ganar prosélitos.

prosody (ˈpras·ə·di) *n.* prosodia. —**prosodic** (proˈsad·ɪk) *adj.* prosódico.

prospect (ˈpras·pekt) *n.* **1,** (view) perspectiva; vista. **2,** (outlook; hope; chance) expectativa; esperanza. **3,** (possible customer) cliente o comprador putativo. —*v.t.* & *i.* explorar (para descubrir minerales, petróleo, etc.).

prospective (prəˈspek·tɪv) *adj.* esperado; putativo.

prospector (ˈpras·pɛk·tər) *n.* buscador.

prospectus (prəˈspɛk·təs) *n.* prospecto; catálogo.

prosper (ˈpras·pər) *v.t.* & *i.* prosperar. —**prosperity** (prasˈpɛr·ə·ti) *n.* prosperidad.

prosperous (ˈpras·pər·əs) *adj.* **1,** (favorable) próspero. **2,** (affluente) rico; adinerado.

prostate (ˈpras·teit) *n.* próstata. —*adj.* de la próstata; prostático.

prostitute (ˈpras·təˌtjut) *v.t.* prostituir. —*n.* prostituta; ramera; puta. —**prostitution** (-ˈtju·ʃən) *n.* prostitución.

prostrate (ˈpras·treit) *adj.* postrado. —*v.t.* postrar. —**prostration**, *n.* postración.

protactinium (ˌpro·tækˈtɪn·i·əm) *n.* protactinio.

protagonist (proˈtæg·ə·nɪst) *n.* protagonista.

protect (prəˈtɛkt) *v.t.* proteger.

protection (prəˈtɛk·ʃən) *n.* protección. —**protectionism**, *n.* proteccionismo. —**protectionist**, *adj.* & *n.* proteccionista.

protective (prəˈtɛk·tɪv) *adj.* protector. —**protective coloration**, mimetismo.

protector (prəˈtɛk·tər) *n.* protector. —**protectress** (-trɪs) *n.* protectriz; protectora.

protectorate (prəˈtɛk·tər·ɪt) *n.* protectorado.

protégé (ˌpro·təˈʒei) *n.* protegido. —**protégée**, *n.fem.* protegida.

protein (ˈpro·ti·ɪn) *n.* proteína.

protest (ˈpro·tɛst) *n.* protesta; *comm.* protesto. —*v.t.* & *i.* (pro ˈtɛst) protestar.
Protestant (ˈprat·ɪs·tənt) *n.* & *adj.* protestante. —**Protestantism,** *n.* protestantismo.
protestation (ˌprat·əsˈtei·ʃən) *n.* protestación; protesta.
proto- (pro·to; -tə) *prefijo* proto-. **1,** primero: *protomartyr,* protomártir. **2,** *quím.* indicando proporción más baja que la de otros elementos: *protochloride,* protocloruro.
protoactinium (ˌpro·to·ækˈtɪn·i·əm) *n.* = **protactinium.**
protocol (ˈpro·təˌkal) *n.* protocolo. —*adj.* protocolar; protocolario.
proton (ˈpro·tan) *n.* protón.
protoplasm (ˈpro·təˌplæz·əm) *n.* protoplasma. —**protoplasmic** (-ˈplæz·mɪk) *adj.* protoplasmático.
prototype (ˈpro·təˌtaip) *n.* prototipo.
Protozoa (ˌpro·təˈzo·ə) *n.pl.* protozoos. —**protozoan,** *n.* & *adj.* protozoo; protozoario.
protract (proˈtrækt) *v.t.* **1,** (prolong) prolongar; dilatar. **2,** (extend) alargar; extender. **3,** (draw to scale) planear o trazar usando la escala y el transportador. —**protraction** (-ˈtræk·ʃən) *n.* prolongación.
protractor (proˈtræk·tər) *n.* **1,** *anat.* músculo extensor. **2,** (measuring device) transportador.
protrude (proˈtruːd) *v.t.* hacer destacar; sacar fuera. —*v.i.* sobresalir; proyectarse. —**protrusion** (-ˈtru·ʒən) *n.* saliente; proyección.
protuberant (proˈtju·bə·rənt) *adj.* protuberante. —**protuberance,** *n.* protuberancia.
proud (praud) *adj.* **1,** (arrogant) arrogante; engreído. **2,** (self-respecting) orgulloso. **3,** (noble; imposing) noble; altivo. **4,** (spirited) valiente.
proud flesh bezo.
prove (pruːv) *v.t.* **1,** (demonstrate) probar. **2,** *print.* sacar una prueba de. —*v.i.* resultar.
proven (ˈpru·vən) *v., p.p. de* **prove.** —*adj.* probado; aprobado; asegurado.
provenance (ˈprav·ə·nəns) *n.* origen; derivación.
provender (ˈprav·ən·dər) *n.* **1,** (fodder) forraje. **2,** *colloq.* (food) comida.
proverb (ˈprav·ʌɹb) *n.* proverbio. —**proverbial** (prəˈvʌɹb·i·əl) *adj.* proverbial; *fig.* notorio.
provide (prəˈvaid) *v.t.* proveer; proporcionar; suministrar. —*v.i.* **1,** (supply what is necessary) proporcionar lo necesario. **2,** (prepare) prepararse. **3,** (take precautions) precaverse. **4,** (stipulate) estipular.
provided (prəˈvai·dɪd) *v., p.p. de* **provide.** —*conj.* con tal (de) que; dado que.
providence (ˈprav·ɪ·dəns) *n.* **1,** (foresight) previsión; providencia. **2,** *cap.* (divine care) providencia de Dios.
provident (ˈprav·ɪ·dənt) *adj.* **1,** (foresighted) providente; próvido; previsor. **2,** (prudent) prudente.
providential (ˌprav·ɪˈdɛn·ʃəl) *adj.* providencial.
province (ˈprav·ɪns) *n.* **1,** (division of a country; rural region) provincia. **2,** (sphere of influence) esfera; campo; pertenencia.
provincial (prəˈvɪn·ʃəl) *adj.* provincial; provinciano. —*n.* provinciano. —**provincialism,** *n.* provincialismo.
provision (prəˈvɪʒ·ən) *n.* **1,** (preparation) provisión. **2,** *law* (stipulation) estipulación. **3,** *pl.* (food supplies) bastimentos; víveres. —*v.t.* proveer; abastecer; aprovisionar. —**provisional,** *adj.* provisional; provisorio. —**provisioning,** *n.* proveimiento; abastecimiento.
proviso (prəˈvai·zo) *n.* estipulación; condición.
provocation (ˌpra·vəˈkei·ʃən) *n.* provocación.
provocative (prəˈvak·ə·tɪv) *adj.* provocador; provocativo.
provoke (prəˈvok) *v.t.* provocar. —**provoking,** *adj.* provocante; provocador.
provost (ˈprav·əst; *mil.* ˈpro·vo) *n.* preboste. —**provost marshal** (ˈpro·vo) preboste; capitán preboste.
prow (prau) *n.* proa.
prowess (ˈprau·ɪs) *n.* proeza.
prowl (praul) *v.t.* & *i.* rondar; vagar, esp. en busca de presa o pillaje. —*n.* ronda; vagabundeo. —**prowler,** *n.* rondador; ladrón. —**prowl car,** coche de policía.

proximity (prak'sɪm·ə·ti) *n.* proximidad.
proxy ('prak·si) *n.* **1,** (delegated authority) poder. **2,** (authorized person) apoderado. —**by proxy,** por poderes. —**give one's proxy to,** apoderar.
prude (pru:d) *n.* mojigato. —**prudery,** *n.* mojigatería. —**prudish,** *adj.* mojigato.
prudent ('pru·dənt) adj. prudente. —**prudence,** *n.* prudencia.
prudential (pru'dɛn·ʃəl) *adj.* prudencial.
prune (pru:n) *n.* ciruela pasa. —*v.t.* & *i.* podar. —**pruning,** *n.* poda. —**pruning hook,** podadera. —**pruning knife,** podadera.
prurient ('prʊr·i·ənt) *adj.* lascivo. —**prurience; pruriency,** *n.* lascivia.
Prussian ('prʌʃ·ən) *adj.* & *n.* prusiano. —**Prussian blue,** azul de Prusia.
pry (prai) *n.* palanca. —*v.t.* [*pret.* & *p.p.* **pried**] **1,** (raise or force with a lever) levantar *o* forzar con una palanca. **2,** (remove with difficulty) arrancar. **3,** (secure by guile, as information) sonsacar; tirar de la lengua. —*v.i.* **1,** (snoop) espiar; huronear. **2,** (meddle) entremeterse. —**pryer,** *n.* fisgón; hurón.
prying ('prai·ɪŋ) *n.* fisgoneo. —*adj.* fisgón; curioso.
psalm (sa:m) *n.* salmo. —**psalmist,** *n.* salmista. —**psalmody** ('sa·mə·di) *n.* salmodia.
Psalter ('sɔl·tər) *n.* Salterio.
pseudo ('su·do) *adj.* seudo; pseudo; falso.
pseudo- (su·do; -də) *prefijo* pseudo-; seudo-; falso; engañoso; *pseudomorph,* pseudomorfo; seudomorfo.
pseudonym ('su·də,nɪm) *n.* seudónimo.
pshaw (ʃɔ:) *interj.* ¡fu!; ¡bah!; ¡vaya!
psittacosis (,sɪt·ə'ko·sɪs) *n.* psitacosis.
psoriasis (so'rai·ə·sɪs) *n.* psoriasis.
psyche ('sai·ki) *n.* psique; psiquis; *cap., myth.* Psiquis.
psychiatry (sai'kai·ə·tri) *n.* psiquiatría. —**psychiatric** (,sai·ki·'æt·rɪk) *adj.* psiquiátrico. —**psychiatrist,** *n.* psiquiatra.
psychic ('sai·kɪk) *adj.* psíquico.
psycho- (sai·ko) *prefijo* psico-; sico-; mente; proceso mental: *psychology,* psicología; sicología; *psychoanalysis,* psicoanálisis; sicoanálisis.
psychoanalysis *n.* psicoanálisis. —**psychoanalyze,** *v.t.* psicoanalizar. —**psychoanalyst,** *n.* psicoanalista. —**psychoanalytic,** *adj.* psicoanalítico.
psychology (sai'kal·ə·dʒi) *n.* psicología; sicología. —**psychological** (,sai·kə'ladʒ·ə·kəl) *adj.* psicológico. —**psychologist,** *n.* psicólogo.
psychoneurosis (,sai·ko·nu'ro·sɪs) *n.* [*pl.* **-ses** (-siz)] psiconeurosis.
psychopath ('sai·ko,pæθ) *n.* psicópata. —**psychopathic** (-'pæθ·ɪk) *adj.* psicopático.
psychopathology *n.* psicopatología.
psychopathy (sai'kap·ə·θi) *n.* psicopatía.
psychosis (sai'ko·sɪs) *n.* [*pl.* **-ses** (siz)] psicosis.
psychosomatic *adj.* psicosomático.
psychotherapy *n.* psicoterapia. —**psychotherapist,** *n.* psicoterapeuta.
psychotic (sai'kat·ɪk) *adj.* psicopático. —*n.* psicópata.
-pter (ptər) *sufijo* -ptero; *forma nombres denotando* miembro de un orden caracterizado por determinado número o especie de alas: *hymenopter,* himenóptero.
ptero- (tɛr·ə) *prefijo* ptero-; ala: *pterodactyl,* pterodáctilo.
pterodactyl *n.* pterodáctilo.
-pterous (ptər·əs) *sufijo* -ptero; *forma adjetivos denotando* determinado número o especie de alas: *hymenopterous,* himenóptero.
Ptolemaic (,tal·ə'mei·ɪk) *adj.* de Tolomeo; tolemaico.
ptomaine ('to·mein) *n.* ptomaína.
pub (pʌb) *n., Brit.* taberna; cantina.
puberty ('pju·bər·ti) *n.* pubertad.
pubes ('pju·biz) *n.pl.* pubis (*sing.*).
pubescent (pju'bɛs·ənt) *adj.* pubescente; púber. —**pubescence,** *n.* pubescencia.
pubic ('pju·bɪk) *adj.* del pubis; púbico.
pubis ('pju·bɪs) *n.* pubis.

public (ˈpʌb·lɪk) *adj.* & *n.* público.
publican (ˈpʌb·lə·kən) *n.* publicano.
publication (ˌpʌb·lɪˈkei·ʃən) *n.* publicación.
public house *Brit.* taberna; cantina.
publicist (ˈpʌb·lɪ·sɪst) *n.* publicista.
publicity (pʌbˈlɪs·ə·ti) *n.* publicidad. —*adj.* publicitario.
publicize (ˈpʌb·lɪˌsaiz) *v.t.* publicar; hacer público.
public school escuela pública; *Brit.* colegio privado selecto.
public-spirited *adj.* patriótico.
public utility empresa de sérvicio público.
publish (ˈpʌb·lɪʃ) *v.t.* **1,** (make publicly known) publicar; promulgar. **2,** (print and issue) imprimir; dar a luz; publicar.
publisher (ˈpʌb·lɪʃ·ər) *n.* **1,** (proclaimer) promulgador. **2,** (bookseller) editor; librero.
puck (pʌk) *n.* **1,** *sports* (disk) disco de hockey; pelota. **2,** (sprite) duende.
pucker (ˈpʌk·ər) *v.t.* & *i.* **1,** (pleat) plegar. **2,** (wrinkle, as one's brows or lips) fruncir. —*n.* **1,** (pleat) pliegue. **2,** (wrinkle; wrinkling) frunce.
puckish (ˈpʌk·ɪʃ) *adj.* **1,** (mischievous) travieso; juguetón. **2,** (elflike) de *o* como duende.
pudding (ˈpʊd·ɪŋ) *n.* budín; pudín.
puddle (ˈpʌd·əl) *n.* aguazal; charco; poza. —*v.t.* pudelar. —*v.i.* chapotear. —**puddler** (-lər) *n.* pudelador. —**pudding** (-lɪŋ) *n.* pudelación.
pudenda (pjuˈdɛn·də) *n.pl.* partes pudendas.
pudgy (ˈpʌdʒ·i) *adj.* regordete; gordiflón; rechoncho.
pueblo (ˈpwɛb·lo) *n.* pueblo.
puerile (ˈpju·ər·ɪl) *adj.* pueril. —**puerility** (-ˈɪl·ə·ti) *n.* puerilidad.
puerperal (puˈʌɹ·pər·əl) *adj.* puerperal.
Puerto Rican (ˌpwɛr·təˈri·kən) *adj.* & *n.* puertorriqueño; portorriqueño.
puff (pʌf) *n.* **1,** (blast, as of smoke, wind, or air) bocanada; vaharada; resoplido. **2,** (light pad) mota. **3,** *colloq.* (exaggerated praise) envanecimiento; alabanza. **4,** (pastry) bollo esponjado. —*v.t.* **1,** (emit forcibly) resoplar. **2,** (swell) inflar; dilatar; hinchar. **3,** (praise) engreír. —*v.i.* **1,** (swell) inflarse; hincharse. **2,** (boast) envanecerse; engreírse. **3,** (blow) soplar. **4,** (pant) jadear.
puffball *n., bot.* bejín.
puff paste hojaldre.
puffy (ˈpʌf·i) *adj.* **1,** (swollen) inflado; hinchado. **2,** (self-satisfied) engreído; vano. **3,** (formed in puffs, as smoke or clouds) en bocanadas. **4,** (panting) jadeante.
pug (pʌg) *n.* **1,** (small dog) faldero; perrito de nariz respingada. **2,** = **pug nose.** **3,** *slang* = **pugilist.**
pugilist (ˈpju·dʒə·lɪst) *n.* púgil. —**pugilism,** *n.* pugilismo; pugilato.
pugnacious (pʌgˈnei·ʃəs) *adj.* pugnaz. —**pugnacity** (-ˈnæs·ə·ti) *n.* pugnacidad.
pug nose nariz respingada. —**pug-nosed,** *adj.* braco.
puke (pjuk) *v.t.* & *i., vulg.* vomitar. —*n., vulg.* vómito.
pulchritude (ˈpʌl·krɪˌtud) *n.* pulcritud.
pull (pʊl) *v.t.* & *i.* **1,** (tug; draw) tirar (de); halar. **2,** (take out or away; pluck) sacar; arrancar. **3,** (twist; sprain) torcer. **4,** (suck; draw in) chupar. **5,** (rip; tear) descoser. **6,** [*también,* **pull off**] *slang* (execute; carry out) llevar a cabo. —*n.* **1,** (tug; jerk) tirón. **2,** (device for opening a door, drawer, etc.) tirador. **3,** (cord or chain used for pulling or drawing) cuerda; cadenilla. **4,** (strenuous effort) esfuerzo; pena. **5,** *slang* (influence) mano. —**pull ahead,** avanzar; adelantarse. —**pull apart,** romper(se); partir(se). —**pull at,** tirar de. —**pull away,** retirar(se); apartarse; alejarse. —**pull back,** retirar(se); recular. —**pull down, 1,** (demolish) derribar. **2,** (abase) degradar; humillar. —**pull in, 1,** (draw in) retraer; cobrar; tirar hacia sí. **2,** *colloq.* (arrive) llegar. —**pull on,** tirar de. —**pull oneself together,** componerse. —**pull out, 1,** (pluck; draw out) sacar; arrancar. **2,** (depart) salir; marcharse; decampar. —**pull through,** salir (*o* sacarle a uno) de un aprieto, una enfermedad, etc. —**pull up, 1,** (raise) alzar; levantar; izar. **2,** (stop) parar; frenar.

pullet ('pʊl·ɪt) *n.* pollita; polla.
pulley ('pʊl·i) *n.* polea.
Pullman ('pʊl·mən) *n.* coche dormitorio; coche Pullman.
pullover *n.* pulóver.
pulmonary ('pʊl·mə·nɛr·i) *adj.* pulmonar.
pulmonate ('pʊl·mə,neit) *adj.* pulmonado.
pulmotor ('pʊl,mo·tər) *n.* pulmotor.
pulp (pʌlp) *n.* pulpa; médula. —**pulpy,** *adj.* pulposo; meduloso.
pulpit ('pʊl·pɪt) *n.* púlpito.
pulque ('pʊl·ki) *n.* pulque.
pulsate ('pʌl·set) *v.i.* pulsar. —**pulsation,** *n.* pulsación.
pulse (pʌls) *n.* pulso. —*v.i.* pulsar.
pulverize ('pʌl·və,raiz) *v.t.* pulverizar. —*v.i.* pulverizarse. —**pulverization** (-rɪ'zei·ʃən) *n.* pulverización.
puma ('pju·mə) *n.* puma.
pumice ('pʌm·ɪs) *n.* piedra pómez.
pummel ('pʌm·əl) *v.t.* golpear; caer encima a puñetazos. —**pummeling,** *n.* paliza.
pump (pʌmp) *n.* **1,** (machine) bomba; *naut.* pompa. **2,** (shoe) zapatilla. —*v.t.* **1,** (move with a pump) bombear. **2,** *colloq.* (draw information) sonsacar. —*v.i.* dar a la bomba. —**pumper,** *n.* bombero. —**pump up,** inflar.
pumpernickel ('pʌm·pər,nɪk·əl) *n.* cierto pan de centeno, de origen alemán.
pumpkin ('pʌmp·kɪn) *n.* calabaza.
pun (pʌn) *n.* retruécano; equívoco; juego de palabras. —*v.i.* decir equívocos.
punch (pʌntʃ) *n.* **1,** (blow) puñetazo. **2,** (tool) punzón. **3,** (beverage) ponche. —*v.t.* **1,** (strike) golpear; dar un puñetazo. **2,** (prod) punzar. **3,** (perforate) picar; perforar. —**punchy,** *adj.* aturdido. —**punch bowl,** ponchera.
Punch (pʌntʃ) *n.* polichinela. *También,* **punchinello** (,pʌn·tʃə·'nɛl·o).
puncheon ('pʌn·tʃən) *n.* **1,** (large cask) tonel. **2,** (wooden post) madero; palo. **3,** (punching tool) punzón.
punctilious (pʌŋk'tɪl·i·əs) *adj.* puntilloso. —**punctilio** (-o) *n.* puntillo.
punctual ('pʌŋk·tʃu·əl) *adj.* puntual. —**punctuality** (-'æl·ə·ti) *n.* puntualidad.
punctuate ('pʌŋk·tʃu,eit) *v.t.* puntuar. —**punctuation,** *n.* puntuación.
puncture ('pʌŋk·tʃər) *v.t.* punzar; agujerear; perforar. —*n.* punzada; puntura; perforación.
pundit ('pʌn·dɪt) *n.* erudito.
pungent ('pʌn·dʒənt) *adj.* picante; mordaz. —**pungency,** *n.* picante; mordacidad.
punish ('pʌn·ɪʃ) *v.t.* castigar. —**punishable,** *adj.* punible; castigable. —**punishment,** *n.* castigo; punición.
punitive ('pju·nə·tɪv) *adj.* punitivo.
punk (pʌŋk) *n.* **1,** (tinder) yesca. **2,** *slang* (hoodlum) rufián; maleante. —*adj., slang* malo; bajo.
punster ('pʌn·stər) *n.* equivoquista.
punt (pʌnt) *n.* **1,** (flatbottomed boat) batea; barquichuelo chato que se impulsa con una vara. **2,** *football* puntapié que se da al balón al soltarlo de las manos. —*v.t. & i.* **1,** (propel with a pole) impeler (un barco) con una vara. **2,** *football* dar un puntapié (al balón) al soltarlo de las manos.
puny ('pju·ni) *adj.* **1,** (frail; sickly) débil; enfermizo. **2,** (insignificant) insignificante; de poca monta.
pup (pʌp) *n.* **1,** [*también,* **puppy**] (young dog) perrito; cachorro. **2,** (young of various mammals) cachorro; cría.
pupa ('pju·pə) *n.* [*pl.* **-pae** (-pi)] crisálida.
pupil ('pju·pəl) *n.* **1,** (student) alumno; pupilo; discípulo. **2,** *anat.* pupila.
puppet ('pʌp·ɪt) *n.* **1,** (doll) títere. **2,** (person or state controlled by another) monigote. —**puppet show,** representación de títeres.
purblind ('pʌɹ·blaind) *adj.* **1,** (partly blind) cegato; corto de vista. **2,** (slow; dull) torpe; lerdo.
purchase ('pʌɹ·tʃəs) *v.t.* comprar. —*n.* **1,** (act of buying; thing bought) compra. **2,** *mech.* (grip; lever) aparato de fuerza; agarre.
pure (pjʊr) *adj.* puro.
purée (pjʊ'rei) *n.* puré.
purgation (pʌɹ'gei·ʃən) *n.* purgación.

purgative ('pʌɹ·gə·tɪv) *adj.* & *n.* purgante; purgativo.
purgatory ('pʌɹ·gə,tor·i) *n.* purgatorio.
purge (pʌɹdʒ) *v.t.* purgar; depurar. —*n.* **1,** (purgative) purgante; catártico. **2,** (elimination of undesirables) purgación.
purify ('pjʊr·ɪ,fai) *v.t.* purificar. —*v.i.* purificarse. —**purification** (-fɪ'kei·ʃən) *n.* purificación.
purism ('pjʊr·ɪz·əm) *n.* purismo. —**purist,** *n.* purista. —**puristic,** *adj.* purista.
puritan ('pjʊr·ə·tən) *n.* & *adj.* puritano. —**puritanical** (-'tæn·ə·kəl) *adj.* puritano. —**puritanism,** *n.* puritanismo.
purity ('pjʊr·ɪ·ti) *n.* pureza.
purl (pʌrl) *n.* **1,** (knitting stitch) puntada invertida. **2,** (murmur, as of water) murmullo. **3,** (swirl; eddy) remolino. —*v.t.* & *i.* (in knitting) invertir (la puntada). —*v.i.* **1,** (murmur) murmurar. **2,** (swirl) arremolinarse.
purlieus ('pʌr·luz) *n.pl.* **1,** (bounds; limits) confines; límites. **2,** (environs) inmediaciones; alrededores.
purloin (pər'lɔin) *v.t.* robar; hurtar. —**purloiner,** *n.* ladrón.
purple ('pʌɹ·pəl) *n.* púrpura. —*adj.* purpúreo; púrpura.
purport (pər'port) *v.t.* **1,** (imply) significar. **2,** (pretend) pretender. —*n.* ('pʌɹ·port) **1,** (meaning; sense) significado; sentido. **2,** (purpose) intención; motivo.
purpose ('pʌɹ·pəs) *n.* **1,** (intention) propósito; intención. **2,** (intended effect; use) fin. —*v.t.* proponer. —**answer the purpose,** servir para el caso. —**on purpose,** adrede; a propósito. —**to little purpose,** con pocos resultados. —**to no purpose,** inútilmente.
purposeful ('pʌɹ·pəs·fəl) *adj.* **1,** (determined) determinado; intencional. **2,** (useful) útil; provechoso.
purposely ('pʌɹ·pəs·li) *adv.* adrede; expresamente.
purr (pʌɹ) *n.* ronroneo. —*v.i.* ronronear.
purse (pʌɹs) *n.* **1,** (receptacle for money) bolsa. **2,** (finances) bolsa; recursos (*pl.*); finanzas (*pl.*). **3,** (public treasury) fisco. **4,** (money raised by collection) colecta. **5,** (prize money) premio. —*v.t.* plegar; fruncir (los labios).
purser ('pʌɹ·sər) *n.* contador de barco o navío.
purslane ('pʌɹs·lein) *n.* verdolaga.
pursuance (pər'su·əns) *n.* prosecución.
pursuant (pər'su·ənt) *adj.* consiguiente. —**pursuant to,** conforme a.
pursue (pər'suː) *v.t.* **1,** (follow) seguir. **2,** (chase; try to catch) perseguir. **3,** (continue; carry on) proseguir.
pursuit (pər'sut) *n.* **1,** (act of following) persecución; seguimiento. **2,** (occupation) empleo; ocupación. **3,** (continuance; carrying on) prosecución. **4,** (search) busca; búsqueda. —**pursuit plane,** avión de caza.
purulent ('pjʊr·ə·lənt) *adj.* purulento. —**purulence,** *n.* purulencia.
purvey (pər'vei) *v.t.* & *i.* proveer; abastecer. —**purveyor,** *n.* proveedor; abastecedor. —**purveyor's shop,** proveeduría.
purview ('pʌɹ·vju) *n.* alcance; límite.
pus (pʌs) *n.* pus.
push (pʊʃ) *v.t.* **1,** (shove) empujar. **2,** (advance) pujar; avanzar. —*v.i.* empujar; dar empujones. —*n.* **1,** (shove) empujón. **2,** *colloq.* (vigor) empuje. **3,** (crowd) tropel; muchedumbre. —**push ahead,** avanzar; adelantarse. —**push away,** alejar; rechazar. —**push back,** echar atrás; retroceder. —**push down,** derribar. —**push in,** entremeterse. —**push on,** avanzar; apresurarse.
push button pulsador; botón de llamada. —**push-button,** *adj.* automático; por botón.
pushcart *n.* carretilla.
pusher ('pʊʃ·ər) *n.* **1,** (person or thing that pushes) empujador. **2,** *colloq.* (enterprising person) persona emprendedora *o* agresiva. **3,** *slang* (seller of drugs) vendedor de narcóticos.
pushover *n., slang* cosa muy fácil; persona de poca resistencia.
pusillanimous (,pju·sə'læn·ə·məs) *adj.* pusilánime. —**pusillanimity** (-lə'nɪm·ə·ti) *n.* pusilanimidad.
puss (pʊs) *n.* **1,** (cat) gato; gatito. **2,** *slang* (face) cara; rostro.

pussy ('pus·i) *n.* gato; gatito. *También,* **pussycat.**
pussyfoot *v.i., slang* tantear miedosamente; no declararse.
pussy willow sauce de amentos muy sedosos.
pustule ('pʌs·tʃul) *n.* pústula. —**pustular** ('pʌs·tʃə·lər) *adj.* pustuloso.
put (put) *v.t.* [**put, putting**] **1,** (set; place) poner; meter; echar. **2,** (express) expresar. **3,** (propose) proponer. **4,** (ask, as a question) hacer. **5,** (impose) imponer. **6,** (send) enviar. **7,** (throw; cast) arrojar; lanzar; echar. **8,** (wager) apostar. —*n.* arrojada; lanzada; echada. —*adj., colloq.* fijo; firme. —**put about,** virar; cambiar de rumbo. —**put across,** *colloq.* **1,** (transmit; impart) hacer comprender *o* entender. **2,** (accomplish) realizar; alcanzar; llevar a cabo. **3,** (win acceptance for) hacer aceptar. —**put aside, 1,** (reserve) ahorrar; reservar. **2,** (discard) rechazar. —**put asunder,** apartar. —**put away, 1,** (reserve) ahorrar. **2,** (store) guardar. **3,** (reject) rechazar; repudiar. **4,** *colloq.* (consume) comer *o* tomar. —**put back, 1,** (restore) devolver; restituir. **2,** (turn back) volver atrás; regresar. —**put by, 1,** (reserve) reservar; ahorrar; guardar. **2,** (reject) rechazar. —**put down, 1,** (record) apuntar; anotar. **2,** (repress) reprimir; sofocar. **3,** (lower) bajar; rebajar. **4,** (attribute) atribuir; imputar. **5,** (swallow) tragar. —**put forth, 1,** (grow; sprout) brotar; echar. **2,** (yield; produce) producir; dar. **3,** (propose) proponer. **4,** (publish) dar a luz; publicar. **5,** (exert) ejercer; emplear. —**put in, 1,** (insert) introducir; insertar; meter. **2,** (contribute) contribuir. **3,** (spend, as time) pasar *o* emplear (el tiempo). **4,** *naut.* arribar; llegar al puerto. —**put off, 1,** (postpone) aplazar; posponer. **2,** (discard) quitar; deshacerse de. **3,** (evade) eludir; evadir. **4,** (divert) apartar; desviar. —**put on, 1,** (clothe with) poner; ponerse; vestir. **2,** (pretend) fingir. **3,** (stage, as a play) presentar. **4,** (assume) pretender; darse: *put on airs,* darse ínfulas. **5,** (apply, as a brake) poner. —**put out, 1,** (emit) emitir; echar. **2,** (eject) despedir; sacar. **3,** (extinguish) apagar; extinguir. **4,** (gouge out, as an eye) sacar. **5,** (inconvenience; bother) molestar; incomodar. **6,** = **put forth.** —**put over, 1,** = **put across. 2,** (postpone) posponer; diferir. **3,** (perpetrate) perpetrar; cometer. **4,** [*usu.* **put it over (on someone)**] engañar; estafar; embaucar. —**put through, 1,** (carry out) llevar a cabo; realizar. **2,** (put in contact) poner en comunicación. **3,** (cause to suffer or undergo) someter a; sujetar a; ocasionarle a uno. —**put together, 1,** (join; unite) unir; juntar. **2,** (amass) acumular; amontonar. —**put to shame,** avergonzar. —**put up, 1,** (set up; establish) establecer. **2,** (erect; build) erigir; construir. **3,** (present; offer) proponer; presentar. **4,** (pack; package) enlatar; envasar. **5,** (lodge) alojar; hospedar. **6,** *colloq.* (incite) incitar; alentar; provocar. **7,** (wager) apostar. **8,** *colloq.* (plan; scheme) concertar; proyectar. —**put upon, 1,** (impose on) incomodar; molestar. **2,** (victimize; dupe) engañar; estafar. —**put up with,** tolerar; aguantar; soportar. —**stay put,** no moverse; no ceder; quedarse firme.
putative ('pju·tə·tɪv) *adj.* putativo.
putrefy ('pju·trə,fai) *v.t.* podrir; pudrir. —*v.i.* podrirse; pudrirse. —**putrefaction** (-'fæk·ʃən) *n.* putrefacción; pudrición; pudrimiento.
putrescence (pju'trɛs·əns) *n.* putrefacción; pudrición; pudrimiento. —**putrescent,** *adj.* pútrido.
putrid ('pju·trɪd) *adj.* pútrido; podrido; putrefacto.
putt (pʌt) *n., golf* golpe con que se procura encajar la pelota en el agujero. —*v.t. & i.* dar (a la pelota) tal golpe.
puttee ('pʌt·i) *n.* polaina.
putter ('pʌt·ər) *n., golf* bastón que se emplea para encajar la pelota en el agujero. —*v.i.* trabajar sin sistema; malgastar el tiempo.
putty ('pʌt·i) *n.* masilla.
put-up *adj., colloq.* premeditado; concertado.
puzzle ('pʌz·əl) *n.* **1,** (perplexing thing) enigma. **2,** (test of ingenuity) acertijo; adivinanza; rompecabezas. —*v.t.* confundir; embrollar; enredar. —*v.i.* preguntarse; asombrarse. —**puzzlement,** *n.* confusión; perplejidad. —**· uzzler** (-lər)

n. enigma; rompecabezas. —**puzzling** (-lɪŋ) *adj.* enigmático.
pygmy ('pɪg·mi) *adj.* & *n.* pigmeo.
pyjamas (pə'dʒam·əz) *n.pl.* = pajamas.
pylon ('pai·lan) *n.* pilón.
pylorus (pai'lor·əs) *n.* píloro. —**pyloric**, *adj.* pilórico.
pyorrhea (ˌpai·ə'ri·ə) *n.* piorrea.
pyramid ('pɪr·ə·mɪd) *n.* pirámide. —*v.t.* & *i.* invertir gananciamente. —**pyramidal** (pɪ'ræm·ə·dəl) *adj.* piramidal.
pyre (pair) *n.* pira.
pyrite ('pai·rait) *n.* pirita.
pyrites (pai'rai·tiz; pə-) *n.* pirita.
pyro- (pai·rə) *prefijo* piro-; fuego: *pyrometer*, pirómetro.
pyromania *n.* piromanía. —**pyromaniac**, *n.* pirómano; piromaníaco.
pyrotechnics *n.* pirotecnia (*sing.*). —**pyrotechnic**, *adj.* pirotécnico.
pyroxylin (pai'rak·sə·lɪn) *n.* piroxilina.
pyrrhic ('pɪr·ɪk) *adj.* pírrico.
Pyrrhic victory triunfo pírrico.
Pythagorean (pɪˌθæg·ə'ri·ən) *adj.* pitagórico.
python ('pai·θan) *n.* pitón.

Q

Q, q (kju) décimaséptima letra del alfabeto inglés.
quack (kwæk) *n.* **1,** (duck's cry) graznido. **2,** (false doctor) curandero; matasanos; medicastro. —*v.i.* parpar. —*adj.* falso. —**quackery**, *n.* curanderismo; curandería.
quad (kwaːd) *n.* **1,** (square court) patio cuadrangular, esp. en las universidades. **2,** *print.* cuadrado; cuadratín. **3,** *colloq.* = **quadruplet**.
quadr- (kwadr) *prefijo, var. de* **quadri-**: *quadrangle*, cuadrángulo.
Quadragesima (ˌkwad·rə'dʒɛs·ə·mə) *n.* cuadragésima.
quadrangle ('kwadˌræŋ·gəl) *n.* cuadrángulo. —**quadrangular** (kwad'ræŋ·gjə·lər) *adj.* cuadrangular; cuadrángulo.
quadrant ('kwad·rənt) *n.* cuadrante.
quadrat ('kwad·ræt) *n., print.* cuadrado; cuadratín.
quadrate ('kwad·reit) *adj.* & *n.* cuadrado. —*v.t.* & *i.* cuadrar.
quadratic (kwad'ræt·ɪk) *adj.* cuadrático. —**quadratic equation**, ecuación de segundo grado; cuadrática.
quadrennial (kwad'rɛn·i·əl) *adj.* & *n.* cuadrienal. —**quadrennium** (-əm) *n.* cuadrienio.
quadri- (kwad·rɪ; -rə) *prefijo* cuadri-; cuatro: *quadrinomial*, cuadrinomio.
quadrilateral (ˌkwad·rə'læt·ər·əl) *adj.* & *n.* cuadrilátero.
quadrille (kwə'drɪl) *n.* cuadrilla.
quadrillion (kwad'rɪl·jən) *n.* (*U.S.*) mil billones; (*Brit.*) un millón de trillones; cuatrillón.
quadroon (kwad'ruːn) *n.* cuarterón.
quadruped ('kwad·rʊˌpɛd) *n.* & *adj.* cuadrúpedo.
quadruple ('kwad·rʊ·pəl) *adj.* cuádruple; cuádruplo. —*n.* cuádruplo. —*v.* (kwad'rʊ·pəl) —*v.t.* cuadruplicar. —*v.i.* cuadruplicarse.
quadruplet ('kwad·rʊ·plɪt; kwad'ru-) *n.* cuadrúpleto.
quadruplicate (kwad'rup·lɪ·kət) *adj.* & *n.* cuadruplicado. —*v.t.* (-ˌkeit) cuadruplicar.
quaff (kwaf) *v.t.* & *i.* tragar; beber a grandes tragos. —*n.* trago.
quagmire ('kwægˌmair) *n.* cenagal; pantano fangoso.
quahog ('kwɔ·hag) *n.* almeja redonda de la costa del Atlántico.
quail (kweil) *v.i.* acobardarse; cejar; desanimarse. —*n., ornith.* codorniz.
quaint (kweint) *adj.* **1,** (unusual) curioso; raro. **2,** (eccentric) excéntrico. —**quaintness**, *n.* curiosidad.
quake (kweik) *v.i.* temblar; sacudirse; estremecerse. —*n.* **1,** (shake) agitación; temblor. **2,** (earthquake) terremoto. —**quaking**, *adj.* movedizo. —*n.* estremecimiento.
Quaker ('kwei·kər) *adj.* & *n.* cuáquero. —**Quakerism**, *n.* cuaquerismo.
qualification (ˌkwal·ɪ·fɪ'kei·ʃən) *n.* **1,** (limitation) calificación; modificación. **2,** (requirement) re-

quisito. **3,** (fitness; competence) capacidad; competencia.
qualified ('kwal·ɪˌfaid) *adj.* **1,** (limited) calificado. **2,** (fit; competent) competente; capaz.
qualify ('kwal·ɪˌfai) *v.t.* **1,** (modify) calificar; modificar; limitar. **2,** (authorize) autorizar. **3,** (enable) habilitar; capacitar. **4,** (mitigate) templar; suavizar. —*v.i.* llenar los requisitos; habilitarse; capacitarse.
qualitative ('kwal·əˌtei·tɪv) *adj.* cualitativo.
quality ('kwal·ə·ti) *n.* **1,** (trait) cualidad; propiedad. **2,** (essence) naturaleza; virtud. **3,** (high birth or rank) nobleza. **4,** (kind; class) calidad; clase. —*adj., colloq.* de calidad; superior.
qualm (kwaːm) *n.* **1,** (compunction) escrúpulo; remordimiento. **2,** (misgiving) duda. **3,** (sudden nausea) náusea; basca.
quandary ('kwan·də·ri) *n.* incertidumbre; perplejidad.
quantitative ('kwan·tɪˌtei·tɪv) *adj.* cuantitativo.
quantity ('kwan·tə·ti) *n.* cantidad.
quantum ('kwan·təm) *n.* [*pl.* **quanta** (-tə)] **1,** (amount) cantidad. **2,** *physics* unidad cuántica; cuanto; quantum. —*adj.* cuántico.
quarantine ('kwar·ənˌtin) *n.* cuarentena. —*v.t.* poner en cuarentena; aislar.
quarrel ('kwar·əl) *n.* riña; disputa; querella. —*v.i.* reñir; disputar. —**quarrelsome,** *adj.* reñidor; pendenciero.
quarry ('kwar·i) *n.* **1,** (excavation) cantera. **2,** (prey) presa; caza. —*v.t.* extraer; sacar de una cantera.
quart (kwort) *n.* cuarto de galón.
quarter ('kwor·tər) *n.* **1,** (one-fourth) cuarta parte; cuarto. **2,** (U.S. coin) cuarto de dólar; moneda de 25 centavos; *P.R.* peseta. **3,** (period of three months) trimestre. **4,** (one-fourth of a mile) cuadra. **5,** (region) región; comarca. **6,** (urban district) barrio. **7,** (leg of an animal) pernil. **8,** (mercy) merced; clemencia. **9,** *naut.* cuadra. —*adj.* cuarto. —*v.t.* **1,** (divide in four) dividir en cuatro; cuartear. **2,** (carve; cut in pieces) descuartizar. **3,** (lodge) alojar; hospedar. **4,** *mil.* (billet) acantonar; acuartelar. —**quarters,** *n.pl.* vivienda (*sing.*); domicilio (*sing.*); *mil.* cuarteles.
quarterdeck *n.* alcázar.
quarterly ('kwor·tər·li) *adj.* trimestral. —*n.* revista o publicación trimestral. —*adv.* trimestralmente.
quartermaster *n.* **1,** *mil.* comisario de querra; comisario ordenador. **2,** *naut.* cabo de brigadas. —**quartermaster corps,** intendencia militar. —**quartermaster general,** intendente de ejército.
quartet (kwor'tɛt) *n.* **1,** (group of four) grupo de cuatro. **2,** *music* cuarteto.
quarto ('kwor·to) *adj.* en cuarto. —*n.* [*pl.* **-tos**] libro en cuarto.
quartz (kworts) *n.* cuarzo.
quash (kwaʃ) *v.t.* **1,** (suppress) reprimir; sofocar. **2,** (annul) anular; invalidar.
quasi- (kwa·sai) *prefijo* cuasi-; casi: *quasicontract,* cuasicontrato.
quaternary (kwə'tʌɹ·nə·ri) *adj.* cuaternario; cuarto en orden; cuaterno. —*n.* cuaternario.
quatrain ('kwat·rein) *n.* cuarteto; redondilla.
quaver ('kwei·vər) *v.i.* **1,** (tremble) temblar; vibrar. **2,** (sing or speak tremulously) gorjear; trinar. —*n.* **1,** (tremor) temblor; vibración. **2,** (trill; tremolo) trino; gorjeo; trémolo. **3,** *music* (eighth note) corchea.
quay (kiː) *n.* muelle; desembarcadero.
queasy ('kwi·zi) *adj.* **1,** (inclined to nausea) nauseabundo. **2,** (squeamish) escrupuloso; quisquilloso. —**queasiness,** *n.* náusea.
queen (kwiːn) *n.* **1,** (sovereign) reina. **2,** *colloq.* (social leader) mujer preeminente. **3,** *chess; cards* dama. —**queen bee,** abeja maestra; abeja reina. —**queen consort,** esposa del rey. —**queen dowager,** reina viuda. —**queen mother,** reina madre.
queenly ('kwin·li) *adj.* como *o* de reina; real. —**queenliness,** *n.* calidad o carácter de reina.
queer (kwɪr) *adj.* **1,** (odd) raro; extraño; curioso; excéntrico. **2,** *colloq.* (daft) chiflado. **3,** *slang* (homosexual) invertido; maricón. —*v.t., slang* dañar; comprometer. —**queerness,** *n.* rareza; extrañeza.
quell (kwɛl) *v.t.* **1,** (suppress)

reprimir; sofocar. **2,** (calm) calmar; apaciguar.

quench (kwɛntʃ) *v.t.* **1,** (satisfy) apagar. **2,** (extinguish) extinguir. **3,** (cool, as metal, by immersion) templar.

querulous ('kwɛr·ə·ləs) *adj.* querelloso; quejumbroso. —**querulousness,** *n.* quejumbre; mal genio.

query ('kwɪr·i) *n.* **1,** (question) pregunta. **2,** (doubt) duda. **3,** (question mark) signo de interrogación. —*v.t.* & *i.* **1,** (question) indagar; preguntar. **2,** (doubt) dudar; poner en duda.

quest (kwɛst) *n.* búsqueda; indagación. —**in quest of,** en busca de.

question ('kwɛs·tʃən) *n.* **1,** (inquiry) pregunta; interrogación. **2,** (doubt) duda; disputa; pleito. **3,** (subject of discussion) tema; cuestión; caso. —*v.i.* preguntar; informarse; examinar. —*v.t.* **1,** (interrogate) interrogar. **2,** (doubt) dudar. **3,** (challenge) recusar. —**questionable,** *adj.* dudoso. —**questioning,** *n.* interrogatorio. —**beside the question,** que no viene al caso. —**out of the question,** imposible. —**it is a question of . . . ,** se trata de. . . . —**question mark,** signo o punto de interrogación.

questionnaire (ˌkwɛs·tʃə'neːr) *n.* cuestionario.

queue (kjuː) *n.* **1,** (tail) cola. **2,** (line of persons) hilera; cola. **3,** (pigtail) coleta. —*v.i.* [*también,* **queue up**] hacer cola.

quibble ('kwɪb·əl) *n.* subterfugio; sutileza; rodeo. —*v.i.* rodear; buscar escapatorias. —**quibbler** (-lər) *n.* rodeador.

quick (kwɪk) *adj.* **1,** (fast) rápido; veloz; ligero. **2,** (alert) listo; alerto. **3,** (excitable) precipitado; irritable. —*adv.* pronto; rápidamente. —*n.* **1,** (sensitivity) sensibilidad. **2,** (sensitive flesh) lo vivo; carne viva. **3,** (seat of emotions) lo más hondo del alma. —**be quick,** darse prisa.

quicken ('kwɪk·ən) *v.t.* acelerar; avivar; animar. —*v.i.* acelerarse; avivarse; animarse. —**quickening,** *n.* aceleración; avivamiento; animación.

quick-frozen *adj.* congelado al instante.

quickie ('kwɪk·i) *n., slang* cosa hecha a prisa.

quicklime *n.* cal viva.

quickly ('kwɪk·li) *adv.* pronto; rápidamente.

quickness ('kwɪk·nəs) *n.* **1,** (rapidity) rapidez; velocidad. **2,** (alertness) agilidad; viveza.

quicksand *n.* arena movediza.

quicksilver *n.* azogue; mercurio.

quickstep *n.* **1,** *music* paso doble. **2,** *mil.* paso redoblado.

quick-tempered *adj.* colérico.

quick-witted *adj.* listo; astuto.

quid (kwɪd) *n.* **1,** (cud; chew of tobacco or gum) mascadura. **2,** *Brit. slang* (pound) libra esterlina.

quiescent (kwai'ɛs·ənt) *adj.* tranquilo; quieto. —**quiescence,** *n.* quietud; reposo.

quiet ('kwai·ət) *adj.* **1,** (silent) callado; silencioso. **2,** (calm) tranquilo. **3,** (smooth) sosegado; manso. **4,** (unassuming) modesto. **5,** (subdued in color) bajo. —*v.t.* callar; calmar; sosegar. —*v.i.* callarse; calmarse. —*n.* reposo; tranquilidad; paz. —**quieting,** *adj.* calmante. —**quietness,** *n.* tranquilidad; silencio.

quietude ('kwai·ə·tud) *n.* quietud; reposo.

quietus (kwai'i·təs) *n.* **1,** (release, as from debt) quitanza; carta de pago. **2,** (death) fallecimiento; muerte.

quill (kwɪl) *n.* **1,** (feather) pluma. **2,** (feather pen) pluma para escribir. **3,** (sharp spine) púa.

quilt (kwɪlt) *n.* colcha. —*v.t.* colchar. —**quilting,** *n.* colchadura.

quince (kwɪns) *n.* **1,** (fruit) membrillo. **2,** (tree) membrillo; membrillero.

quinine ('kwai·nain) *n.* quinina.

quinquagenarian (ˌkwɪn·kwə·dʒə'nɛr·i·ən) *adj.* & *n.* cincuentón.

Quinquagesima (ˌkwɪn·kwə·'dʒɛs·ə·mə) *n.* quincuagésima.

quinque- (kwɪn·kwə) *prefijo* quinque-; cinco: *quinquennial,* quinquenal.

quinquennium (kwɪn'kwɛn·i·əm) *n.* quinquenio. —**quinquennial,** *adj.* quinquenal.

quinsy ('kwɪn·zi) *n.* angina.

quint (kwɪnt) *n.* **1,** (set of five) conjunto de cinco. **2,** *music* (a fifth) quinta. **3,** *colloq.* = **quintuplet. 4,** (in games of chance) quina.

quintal ('kwɪn·təl) *n.* quintal.

quintessence (kwɪn'tɛs·əns) *n.* quintaesencia.
quintet (kwɪn'tɛt) *n.* **1,** (group of five) grupo de cinco. **2,** *music* quinteto.
quintillion (kwɪn'tɪl·jən) *n.* (*U.S.*) un millón de billones; trillón; (*Brit.*) un millón de cuatrillones; quintillón.
quintuple ('kwɪn·tju·pəl) *adj.* & *n.* quíntuplo. —*v.t.* multiplicar por cinco; quintuplicar. —*v.i.* quintuplicarse.
quintuplet ('kwɪn·tju·plɪt; kwɪn·'tʌp·lɪt) *n.* quintillizo; *Amer.* quíntuple.
quip (kwɪp) *n.* chiste. —*v.i.* bromear; echar pullas.
quire (kwair) *n.* mano (de papel).
quirk (kwʌɹk) *n.* **1,** (quick turn) giro; recodo; rodeo. **2,** (flourish, in writing) rasgo. **3,** (idiosyncrasy) peculiaridad; capricho; rareza.
quisling ('kwɪz·lɪŋ) *n.* traidor; quisling.
quit (kwɪt) *v.t.* abandonar; dejar; ceder. —*v.i.* desistir; cesar; parar. —*adj.* libre; absuelto.
quitclaim *n.* renuncia. —*v.t.* renunciar.
quite (kwait) *adv.* **1,** (completely) completamente; totalmente. **2,** *colloq.* (very) considerablemente; bastante.
quits (kwɪts) *adj.*, *colloq.* en paz; corrientes. —**be quits,** estar corrientes; estar desquitados. —**cry quits,** darse por vencido; cesar la lucha.
quittance ('kwɪt·əns) *n.* **1,** (discharge from obligation) quitanza. **2,** (reward) recompensa.
quitter ('kwɪt·ər) *n.* desertor; cobarde.
quiver ('kwɪv·ər) *v.i.* temblar; vibrar; estremecerse. —*n.* **1,** (shake) temblor. **2,** (arrow case) carcaj; aljaba. —**quivering,** *n.* tremor; estremecimiento.
quixotic (kwɪks'at·ɪk) *adj.* quijotesco. —**quixotism** ('kwɪk·sə,tɪz·əm) *n.* quijotismo.
quiz (kwɪz) *n.* [*pl.* **quizzes**] **1,** (examination) examen. **2,** (radio or television program) programa de preguntas y respuestas. —*v.t.* [**quizzed, quizzing**] **1,** (question) interrogar; examinar. **2,** (chaff) burlarse de. **3,** (peer at) mirar de hito en hito.
quizzical ('kwɪz·ə·kəl) *adj.* **1,** (chaffing) burlón; guasón. **2,** (questioning) perplejo; curioso.
quoin (kɔin) *n.* **1,** (corner of a building) rincón; ángulo; esquina. **2,** (stone forming an angle) piedra angular. **3,** (wedge) cuña. **4,** *print.* cuña.
quoits (kwɔits) *n.sing.* juego de tejos. —**quoit,** *n.* tejo.
quonset hut ('kwan·sət) *n.* cobertizo de metal prefabricado.
quorum ('kwor·əm) *n.* quórum.
quota ('kwo·tə) *n.* cuota.
quotation (kwo'tei·ʃən) *n.* **1,** (citation) cita. **2,** *comm.* cotización. —**quotation marks,** comillas.
quote (kwot) *v.t.* **1,** (cite) citar. **2,** (state the price of) cotizar. —*n.*, *colloq.* = **quotation.** —**quotes,** *n.pl.*, *colloq.* = **quotation marks.**
quoth (kwoθ) *v.t.*, *archaic* dije *o* dijo.
quotidian (kwo'tɪd·i·ən) *adj.* cotidiano; diario. —*n.* fiebre cotidiana.
quotient ('kwo·ʃənt) *n.* cuociente; cociente.

R

R, r (ar) décimoctava letra del alfabeto inglés.
rabbi ('ræb·ai) *n.* rabino; rabí. —**rabbinical** (rə'bɪn·ɪ·kəl) *adj.* rabínico.
rabbit ('ræb·ɪt) *n.* conejo. —**Welsh rabbit** (*o* **rarebit**) queso derretido servido sobre pan tostado.
rabble ('ræb·əl) *n.* populacho; canalla. —**rabble rouser,** populachero. —**rabble rousing,** populachería. —**rabble-rousing,** *adj.* populachero.
rabid ('ræb·ɪd) *adj.* **1,** (furious) furioso. **2,** (zealous) entusiasta; fanático. **3,** (affected with rabies) rabioso. —**rabidity** (rə'bɪd·ə·ti) *n.* rabia.
rabies ('rei·biz) *n.* hidrofobia; rabia.
raccoon (ræ'kuːn) *n.* mapache.

race (reis) *n.* **1,** (contest of speed) carrera; *naut.* regata. **2,** (competition) lucha; contienda. **3,** (ethnic group) raza. **4,** (lineage) linaje; casta. **5,** (current of water) corriente fuerte y rápida. **6,** (channel for water) canal; caz. —*v.i.* **1,** (run) correr. **2,** (compete) competir. **3,** (increase speed) acelerarse. **4,** *mech.* marchar con velocidad excesiva. **5,** *naut.* regatear. —*v.t.* **1,** (run against) correr en competición con. **2,** (rush) dar prisa a; acelerar. **3,** *mech.* dar velocidad excesiva a. —**boat race,** regata. —**human race,** género humano. —**race course; race track,** pista de carreras; hipódromo.

raceme (re'si:m) *n.* racimo.

racer ('rei·sər) *n.* **1,** (runner) corredor. **2,** (horse) caballo de carreras. **3,** (auto) auto de carrera.

rachitic (rə'kɪt·ɪk) *adj.* raquítico.

racial ('rei·ʃəl) *adj.* racial.

racing ('rei·sɪŋ) *n.* carrera; carreras. —*adj.* de carrera.

racism ('reis·ɪz·əm) *n.* racismo. —**racist,** *adj.* & *n.* racista.

rack (ræk) *n.* **1,** (frame) estante; percha. **2,** *mech.* (toothed bar) cremallera. **3,** (instrument of torture) potro (de tormento). **4,** (pain) dolor; agonía. **5,** (horse gait) trote. **6,** (destruction) destrucción; ruina. —*v.t.* **1,** (torture) torturar. **2,** (worry) oprimir; atormentar. —*v.i.* **1,** (worry) preocuparse. **2,** (pace) andar a trote. —**rack one's brains,** devanarse los sesos.

racket ('ræk·ɪt) *n.* **1,** (din) baraúnda; alboroto. **2,** [*también,* **racquet**] *sports* (webbed bat) raqueta. **3,** (dishonest enterprise) estafa. **4,** *pl.* (game) trinquete (*sing.*). —**racketeer** (-ə'tɪ:r) *n.* trampeador; trapacero.

raconteur (ˌræk·an'tʌɹ) *n.* cuentista.

racy ('reis·i) *adj.* **1,** (piquant) picante. **2,** (vigorous) enérgico. **3,** *colloq.* (risqué) sugestivo; atrevido.

radar ('rei·dar) *n.* radar.

radial ('rei·di·əl) *adj.* radial.

radian ('rei·di·ən) *n.* radián.

radiant ('rei·di·ənt) *adj.* **1,** (emitting rays) radiante. **2,** (beaming, as with joy) alegre; resplandeciente. —*n.* radiante. —**radiance,** *n.* resplandor.

radiate ('rei·diˌeit) *v.i.* **1,** (shine) brillar; resplandecer. **2,** (emit rays) echar rayos. **3,** (spread out) radiar. —*v.t.* radiar; *fig.* difundir. —*adj.* (-ət) radiado. —**radiation,** *n.* radiación.

radiator ('rei·diˌei·tər) *n.* radiador.

radical ('ræd·ɪ·kəl) *adj.* **1,** *math.* radical. **2,** (drastic) extremo. **3,** (basic) fundamental. —*n.* **1,** *math; gram.* raíz. **2,** (fundamental) radical. **3,** *polit.* radical; extremista. —**radicalism,** *n.* radicalismo.

radio ('rei·di·o) *n.* **1,** (receiving set) radiorreceptor; radio. **2,** (broadcasting medium) radiodifusión; radio. **3,** (communication) radiocomunicación. —*v.t.* & *i.* radiodifundir; transmitir por radio. —*adj.* de radio; de radiodifusión. —**radio announcer,** radiolocutor. —**radio listener,** radioyente. —**radio monitor,** radioescucha. —**radio network,** red *o* cadena de emisoras. —**radio receiver,** radiorreceptor. —**radio repair,** radiotecnia. —**radio station,** emisora; radiodifusora; radioemisora. —**radio technician,** radiotécnico. —**radio technology,** radiotecnia. —**radio transmitter,** radioemisor; radiotransmisor.

radio- (rei·di·o) *prefijo* radio-. **1,** comunicación por ondas: *radiotelegraphy,* radiotelegrafía. **2,** radioactividad: *radiotherapy,* radioterapia.

radioactive *adj.* radiactivo; radioactivo. —**radioactivity,** *n.* radiactividad; radioactividad.

radio-controlled *adj.* radiodirigido.

radiogram *n.* radiograma.

radiograph *n.* radiografía. —**radiography** (ˌrei·di'ag·rə·fi) *n.* radiografía.

radiology (ˌrei·di'al·ə·dʒi) *n.* radiología. —**radiological** (-ə'ladʒ·ə·kəl) *adj.* radiológico. —**radiologist,** *n.* radiólogo.

radioscopy (ˌrei·di'as·kə·pi) *n.* radioscopia.

radiotelegraphy *n.* radiotelegrafía.

radiotelephone *n.* radioteléfono. —**radiotelephony,** *n.* radiotelefonía.

radiotherapy *n.* radioterapia.

radish ('ræd·ɪʃ) *n.* rábano.

radium ('rei·di·əm) *n.* radio; rádium.

adius (ˈrei·di·əs) *n.* [*pl.* **radii** (-di·i)] radio.
adon (ˈrei·dan) *n.* radón.
affia (ˈræf·i·ə) *n.* rafia.
affish (ˈræf·ɪʃ) *adj.* ruidoso; tunante; alborotoso. —**raffishness,** *n.* tunantería.
affle (ˈræf·əl) *n.* rifa. —*v.t.* rifar.
aft (ræft) *n.* **1,** (float) balsa. **2,** *colloq.* (large amount) montón; sinnúmero. —*v.t.* transportar en balsa.
after (ˈraef·tər) *n.* viga; cabrio.
ag (ræg) *n.* **1,** (piece of cloth) trapo. **2,** *pl.* (shabby clothes) harapos; andrajos. **3,** = **ragtime.** —*v.t., slang* molestar; burlarse de.
agamuffin (ˈræg·əˌmʌf·ɪn) *n.* golfo; pelagatos.
age (reidʒ) *n.* **1,** (anger) rabia; cólera; ira. **2,** (violence) violencia; furia. **3,** (fervor) entusiasmo. **4,** *slang* (fad) moda; boga; novedad. —*v.i.* **1,** (be furious) rabiar; encolerizarse. **2,** (proceed with violence) arrebatarse. —**raging,** *adj.* furioso.
agged (ˈræg·ɪd) *adj.* **1,** (shabby) harapiento; andrajoso. **2,** (slovenly) desaliñado. **3,** (uneven) desigual; escabroso.
aglan (ˈræg·lən) *n.* raglán.
agout (ræˈguː) *n.* estofado; guisado.
agpicker *n.* andrajero; trapero.
agtime *n., music* tiempo sincopado.
agweed *n.* ambrosía.
ah (raː) *interj.* ¡viva!; ¡hurra!
aid (reid) *n.* **1,** (incursion) incursión. **2,** (attack) ataque. —*v.t. & i.* **1,** (invade) invadir; hacer incursión (en). **2,** (attack) atacar. **3,** (pillage; pilfer) pillar.
ail (reil) *n.* **1,** (barrier) barrera; baranda. **2,** (handrail) pasamano. **3,** (track) carril; riel. **4,** (rail system; railroads collectively) ferrocarril. **5,** *ornith.* rascón. —*adj.* ferroviario. —*v.t.* poner baranda a; cercar con barandas. —*v.i.* quejarse. —**by rail,** por ferrocarril. —**rail at** *o* **against,** injuriar; ultrajar.
ailing (ˈrei·lɪŋ) *n.* baranda; barandilla.
aillery (ˈrei·lə·ri) *n.* burla; zumba.
ailroad *n.* ferrocarril; vía férrea. —*adj.* ferroviario. —*v.t., slang* **1,** (force through rapidly) ejecutar de prisa. **2,** (frame) fraguar; condenar falsamente. —**railroading,** *n.* trabajo *o* negocios de ferrocarril.
railway *adj. & n.* = **railroad.**
raiment (ˈrei·mənt) *n.* ropa; prendas de vestir.
rain (rein) *n.* lluvia. —*v.i.* llover. —*v.t.* llover; hacer llover. —**rainy,** *adj.* lluvioso.
rainbow *n.* arco iris.
raincoat *n.* impermeable.
raindrop *n.* gota de lluvia.
rainfall *n.* lluvia; (promedio de la) precipitación.
rainstorm *n.* chubasco; aguacero.
raise (reiz) *v.t.* **1,** (lift) levantar; alzar. **2,** (build) erigir; edificar. **3,** (set upright) poner en pie. **4,** (rear) criar; cultivar. **5,** (exhalt) ensalzar. **6,** (arouse) suscitar. **7,** (collect, as money) procurar. **8,** (produce) producir. —*n., colloq.* aumento de salario.
raised (reizd) *adj.* **1,** (leavened) fermentado. **2,** (in relief) en relieve; de realce.
raisin (ˈrei·zən) *n.* pasa; uva seca.
rajah (ˈra·dʒə) *n.* rajá.
rake (reik) *n.* **1,** (garden tool) rastro; rastra; rastrillo. **2,** (dissolute man) libertino; calavera. **3,** *naut.* (slant) lanzamiento. —*v.t.* **1,** (gather or smooth with a rake) rastrear; rastrillar. **2,** (ransack) rebuscar. **3,** (scratch) rascar. **4,** *mil.* enfilar.
rakish (ˈreik·ɪʃ) *adj.* **1,** (slanted) inclinado. **2,** (jaunty) airoso. **3,** (dissolute) libertino.
rally (ˈræl·i) *v.t.* **1,** (call together) reunir. **2,** (reassemble, as troops) reanimar; replegar. **3,** (tease) burlarse de; ridiculizar. —*v.i.* **1,** (get together) reunirse. **2,** (recover energy) reanimarse; recobrar sus fuerzas. —*n.* **1,** (mass meeting) reunión en masa. **2,** *tennis* ataque sostenido. **3,** *mil.* reunión de tropas. **4,** (renewal of energy) recuperación; recobro.
ram (ræm) *n.* **1,** (male sheep) carnero. **2,** *cap., astron.* Aries. **3,** (battering instrument) ariete. **4,** *naut.* espolón. —*v.t.* [**rammed, ramming**] **1,** (batter) empujar con violencia; chocar con *o* en. **2,** (drive down) apisonar; pisonear. **3,** (cram) henchir; amontonar.
ramble (ˈræm·bəl) *v.i.* **1,**

(wander) vagar; pasear. **2,** (deviate) divagar. —*n.* paseo.
rambler ('ræm·blər) *n.* **1,** (wanderer) paseador; divagador. **2,** (climbing rose) rosal trepador.
rambling ('ræm·blɪŋ) *adj.* **1,** (wandering) errante; divagador. **2,** (large; sprawling) grande; amplio; muy extendido.
rambunctious (ræm'bʌŋk·ʃəs) *adj., colloq.* ruidoso; alborotado. —**rambunctiousness,** *n.* alboroto.
ramify ('ræm·ɪˌfai) *v.i.* ramificarse. —*v.t.* dividir en ramas. —**ramification** (-fɪ'kei·ʃən) *n.* ramificación; ramal.
ramp (ræmp) *n.* rampa.
rampage ('ræm·pedʒ) *n.* alboroto; rabia. —*v.i.* (*usu.* ræm'peidʒ) alborotar; rabiar.
rampant ('ræm·pənt) *adj.* **1,** (unchecked) desenfrenado. **2,** (luxuriant) abundante; extravagante. **3,** *heraldry* rampante.
rampart ('ræm·part) *n.* **1,** (fortification) muralla; terraplén. **2,** *fig.* (bulwark) baluarte; amparo; defensa.
ramrod *n.* baqueta de fusil.
ramshackle ('ræmˌʃæk·əl) *adj.* destartalado.
ran (ræn) *v., pret. de* **run.**
ranch (ræntʃ) *n.* rancho; hacienda. —**rancher; ranchman** (-mən) *n.* ranchero; hacendado.
rancid ('ræn·sɪd) *adj.* rancio. —**rancidity** (ræn'sɪd·ə·ti) *n.* rancidez.
rancor ('ræŋ·kər) *n.* rencor. —**rancorous,** *adj.* rencoroso.
random ('ræn·dəm) *n.* azar; casualidad. —*adj.* casual; impensado. —**at random,** al azar.
ranee ('ra·ni) *n.* raní.
rang (ræŋ) *v., pret. de* **ring.**
range (reindʒ) *v.t.* **1,** (arrange) colocar metódicamente; ordenar; clasificar. **2,** (oppose) alinear. **3,** (rove) recorrer. —*v.i.* **1,** (form a line) alinearse. **2,** (roam) vagar. **3,** (vary) fluctuar. —*n.* **1,** (row) serie; fila; hilera. **2,** (extent; scope) alcance. **3,** (distance) espacio; esfera. **4,** (series of mountains) cordillera. **5,** (grazing land) terreno de pasto. **6,** (shooting course) campo de tiro. **7,** (stove) hornillo; cocina. —**range finder,** telémetro.
ranger ('rein·dʒər) *n.* **1,** (forest guard) guardamayor de bosque. **2,** *cap.* (U.S. soldier) soldado especializado en hacer incursiones en el campo enemigo.
rangy ('rein·dʒi) *adj.* alto y flaco.
rani ('ra·ni) *n.* = **ranee.**
rank (ræŋk) *n.* **1,** (row) fila; hilera. **2,** (class; order) clase; distinción. **3,** (social position) esfera; posición. **4,** (relative position) rango; grado. **5,** *pl., mil.* soldados de fila; tropas. —*v.t.* **1,** (arrange in order) poner en fila. **2,** (classify) clasificar. **3,** (rate above) tener grado más alto que. —*v.i.* ocupar determinado grado o puesto. —*adj.* **1,** (luxuriant) exuberante; abundante. **2,** (thick; dense) espeso; denso. **3,** (coarse; gross) grosero. **4,** (fetid) maloliente. —**rank and file,** el pueblo; la gente común.
rankle ('ræŋ·kəl) *v.t.* enconar. —*v.i.* enconarse. —**rankling** (-klɪŋ) *adj.* enconoso. —*n.* encono.
ransack ('ræn·sæk) *v.t.* **1,** (search) escudriñar; rebuscar; registrar. **2,** (plunder) saquear; pillar.
ransom ('ræn·səm) *n.* rescate. —*v.t.* rescatar; redimir.
rant (rænt) *v.i.* delirar; disparatar. —*n.* [*también,* **ranting**] lenguaje extravagante; disparates (*pl.*).
rap (ræp) *n.* **1,** (quick, sharp blow) golpe seco; golpecito. **2,** *colloq.* (bit) bledo; ardite. **3,** *slang* (penalty) castigo; multa; consecuencias (*pl.*). **4,** *colloq.* (harsh criticism) crítica áspera; reprimenda. —*v.t. & i.* [**rapped, rapping**] (strike sharply) golpear vivamente; dar un golpe seco a. —*v.i.* (knock, as on a door) tocar; llamar. —*v.t., colloq.* (criticize harshly) criticar ásperamente; reprender. —**not to give** (*o* **care**) **a rap,** *colloq.* no darle (*o* importarle) a uno un bledo. —**take** (*o* **pay**) **the rap,** *colloq.* sufrir las consecuencias; pagar los vidrios rotos.
rapacious (rə'pei·ʃəs) *adj.* rapaz. —**rapaciousness; rapacity** (rə'pæs·ə·ti) *n.* rapacidad.
rape (reip) *n.* **1,** (sexual violation) violación; estupro. **2,** (abduction) rapto. **3,** *bot.* colza. —*v.t.* **1,** (violate) violar; estuprar. **2,** (abduct) raptar. —**r. pist,** *n.* estuprador.
rapid ('ræp·ɪd) *adj.* veloz; rápido. —**rapidity** (rə'pɪd·ə·ti); **rapid-**

ness, *n.* rapidez. —**rapids**, *n.pl.* rápidos.
rapier (ˈrei·pi·ər) *n.* estoque.
rapine (ˈræp·ɪn) *n.* rapiña.
rapport (ræˈpoːr) *n.* acuerdo; armonía.
rapprochement (ˌræ·prɔʃˈmaɴ) *n.* acercamiento.
rapscallion (ræpˈskæl·jən) *n., colloq.* pícaro.
rapt (ræpt) *adj.* extasiado.
rapture (ˈræp·tʃər) *n.* rapto; éxtasis. —**rapturous**, *adj.* extático; embelesado.
rare (reːr) *adj.* **1,** (thin, as air) ralo. **2,** (uncommon) raro. **3,** (lightly cooked) poco cocido.
rarebit (ˈrɛr·bɪt) *n.* = **Welsh rabbit.**
rarefy (ˈrɛr·əˌfai) *v.t.* enrarecer. —*v.i.* enrarecerse. —**rarefaction** (-ˈfæk·ʃən) *n.* rarefacción.
rarely (ˈrɛr·li) *adv.* raramente.
rareness (ˈrɛr·nəs) *n.* rareza.
rarity (ˈrɛr·ə·ti) *n.* rareza.
rascal (ˈræs·kəl) *n.* tunante; bribón. —**rascality** (ræsˈkæl·ə·ti) *n.* tunantería; bribonería.
rash (ræʃ) *adj.* imprudente; precipitado. —*n.* erupción de la piel; salpullido; sarpullido. —**rashness**, *n.* temeridad; arrojo.
rasher (ˈræʃ·ər) *n.* magra; lonja de tocino.
rasp (ræsp) *v.t.* raspar; escofinar; rallar. —*v.i.* hacer chirrido. —*n.* raspa; escofina. —**rasping**, *adj.* raspante; ronco. —*n.* raspadura.
raspberry (ˈræzˌbɛr·i) *n.* **1,** (fruit) frambuesa. **2,** (bush) frambueso. **3,** *slang* (expression of derision) pedorreta; *Amer.* trompetilla.
rat (ræt) *n.* **1,** (rodent) rata. **2,** *slang* (traitor) traidor; renegado. **3,** *slang* (informer) delator. **4,** *slang* (contemptible person) despreciable; mezquino. **5,** (roll of hair) bollo de pelo. —*v.i.* [**ratted, ratting**] **1,** (kill rats) cazar ratas. **2,** *slang* (inform) delatar. —**smell a rat**, *colloq.* tener sospecha; desconfiar.
ratchet (ˈrætʃ·ɪt) *n.* rueda dentada; trinquete.
rate (reit) *n.* **1,** (measurement in relation to a standard) razón; proporción; medida. **2,** (price) tarifa. **3,** (speed) velocidad. **4,** (of interest or exchange) tipo. **5,** *pl., Brit.* (local tax) impuesto local. —*v.t.* **1,** (measure) estimar; tomar la medida de. **2,** (classify) clasificar. **3,** (appraise) valuar; tasar. **4,** (scold) regañar; reprender. —*v.i.* tener rango; tener valor. —**at any rate**, de todos modos; de cualquier modo. —**at that rate**, de ese modo; si es así. —**at the rate of**, a razón de.
ratepayer *n., Brit.* contribuyente.
rather (ˈræð·ər) *adv.* **1,** (sooner) antes. **2,** (more correctly) mejor dicho. **3,** (on the contrary) al contrario; por el contrario. **4,** (somewhat) algo; bastante. **5,** (very) muy.
rathole *n.* ratonera.
rathskeller (ˈratsˌkɛl·ər) *n.* restaurante en un sótano.
ratify (ˈræt·əˌfai) *v.t.* ratificar. —**ratification** (-fɪˈkei·ʃən) *n.* ratificación.
rating (ˈrei·tɪŋ) *n.* **1,** (classification) clasificación. **2,** (appraisal) valuación. **3,** (rank) rango; grado. **4,** (scolding) regaño.
ratio (ˈrei·ʃo) *n.* proporción; *math.* razón; cociente.
ratiocinate (ˌræʃ·iˈas·əˌneit) *v.i.* raciocinar. —**ratiocination**, *n.* raciocinación; raciocinio.
ration (ˈrei·ʃən) *n.* ración. —*v.t.* proporcionar; racionar. —**rationing**, *n.* racionamiento. —**rations**, *n.pl.* comidas.
rational (ˈræʃ·ən·əl) *adj.* racional. —**rationality** (-əˈnæl·ə·ti) *n.* racionalidad.
rationale (ˌræʃ·əˈnæl) *n.* racional.
rationalism (ˈræʃ·ən·əˌlɪz·əm) *n.* racionalismo. —**rationalist**, *n.* racionalista. —**rationalistic**, *adj.* racionalista.
rationalize (ˈræʃ·ə·nəˌlaiz) *v.t.* justificar; buscar razón para. —*v.i.* justificarse. —**rationalization** (-lɪ·ˈzei·ʃən) *n.* acto de justificar o justificarse.
rattan (ræˈtæn) *n.* **1,** (climbing palm) rotén; rota; junquillo. **2,** (cane) caña.
rattle (ˈræt·əl) *v.t.* & *i.* (shake or move with quick sharp sounds) traquetear; golpetear. —*v.i.* (talk rapidly) parlotear. —*v.t., colloq.* (confuse; upset) confundir; descomponer. —*n.* **1,** (noise; noisy movement) traqueteo; golpeteo; matraca. **2,** (noisemaker) matraca. **3,** (rattlesnake's tail) anillos cór-

neos en las cola de la serpiente de cascabel. **4,** (noisy breathing; death rattle) estertor. —**rattle off,** enunciar rápidamente.

rattlebrain *n.* ligero de cascos; casquivano.

rattler ('ræt·lər) *n.* **1,** = **rattlesnake. 2,** (freight train) tren de carga.

rattlesnake *n.* serpiente de cascabel.

rattletrap *n.* objeto destartalado. —*adj.* destartalado.

rattrap *n.* ratonera; *fig.* aprieto.

ratty ('ræt·i) *adj.* andrajoso. —**rattiness,** *n.* pobreza.

raucous ('rɔ·kəs) *adj.* ronco. —**raucousness,** *n.* ronquera.

ravage ('ræv·ɪdʒ) *v.t.* **1,** (pillage) saquear; pillar. **2,** (ruin) estragar; arruinar. —*n.* **1,** (pillage) saque; pillaje. **2,** (ruin) estrago; ruina.

rave (reiv) *v.i.* delirar. —*n., colloq.* elogio delirante. —*adj., colloq.* entusiástico.

ravel ('ræv·əl) *v.t.* **1,** (unsew; fray) deshilar; deshebrar. **2,** (disentangle) desenredar. —*n.* hilacha.

raven ('rei·vən) *n.* cuervo. —*adj.* bien negro.

raven ('ræv·ən) *v.t.* devorar. —*v.i.* echarse sobre la presa. —**ravening,** *adj.* rapaz. —**ravenous,** *adj.* voraz; hambriento.

ravine (rə'viːn) *n.* hondonada; barranca.

ravish ('ræv·ɪʃ) *v.t.* **1,** (abduct) raptar. **2,** (enrapture) extasiar; encantar. **3,** (rape) violar. —**ravishing,** *adj.* encantador.

ravishment ('ræv·ɪʃ·mənt) *n.* **1,** (abduction) rapto. **2,** (rapture) éxtasis; encanto. **3,** (rape) violación.

raw (rɔː) *adj.* **1,** (uncooked) crudo. **2,** (unripe) verde. **3,** (untreated) sin preparación. **4,** (brutal) brutal. **5,** (cold and damp) frío y húmedo. **6,** (without cover) pelado. **7,** (untried) novato. **8,** (open, as a wound) descarnado. —*n.* [*también,* **rawness**] **1,** (crude state) crudeza. **2,** (sore) llaga. —**in the raw,** al natural. —**raw deal,** *slang* injusticia. —**raw material,** materia prima. —**raw spirits,** alcohol puro. —**raw sugar,** azúcar bruto.

rawboned *adj.* huesudo.

rawhide *n.* cuero crudo; cuero en verde.

ray (rei) *n.* **1,** (beam, as of light) rayo. **2,** (stripe) raya. **3,** (radius; spoke) radio. **4,** *ichthy.* raya. **5,** *zool.* radio. —*v.t.* & *i.* radiar.

rayon ('rei·an) *n.* rayón.

raze (reiz) *v.t.* arrasar; demoler.

razor ('rei·zər) *n.* navaja de afeitar. —**razor blade,** hoja de afeitar. —**razor strop,** suavizador. —**safety razor,** máquina de afeitar.

razz (ræz) *v.t.* & *i., slang* escarnecer; mofarse (de). —*n., slang* (derision) crítica mordaz; mofa.

re (rei) *n., music* re.

re (riː) *prep.* acerca de; concerniente a. *También,* **in re.**

re- (ri; rɪ) *prefijo* re-. **1,** atrás; en dirección opuesta: *reaction,* reacción. **2,** otra vez; de nuevo: *reelect,* reelegir. **3,** resistencia; oposición: *reject,* rechazar. **4,** intensificación: *reinforcement,* refuerzo.

reach (ritʃ) *v.t.* **1,** (extend) tender; estirar; alargar. **2,** (attain) alcanzar. **3,** (establish communication with) establecer contacto con. **4,** (arrive at) llegar a; alcanzar. —*v.i.* **1,** (extend; stretch) extenderse; extender la mano o el brazo. **2,** (strive) esforzarse. —*n.* **1,** (act of reaching) estirón. **2,** (range; scope) alcance. **3,** (expanse; stretch) extensión. **4,** (distance) distancia. **5,** (capacity) facultad; capacidad.

react (ri'ækt) *v.i.* **1,** (act in response) reaccionar; responder. **2,** (interact) ejercer acción mutua; reaccionar entre sí.

reaction (ri'æk·ʃən) *n.* **1,** (response) reacción; respuesta. **2,** (interaction) interacción.

reactionary (ri'æk·ʃəˌnɛr·i) *adj.* & *n.* reaccionario.

reactive (ri'æk·tɪv) *adj.* reactivo.

reactor (ri'æk·tər) *n.* reactor.

read (riːd) *v.t.* & *i.* [*pret.* & *p.p.* **read** (rɛd)] **1,** (interpret written or printed matter) leer. **2,** (understand by observation) interpretar; entender. **3,** (guess, as someone's thoughts) adivinar (el pensamiento). —*adj.* (rɛd) leído; enterado.

readable ('rid·ə·bəl) *adj.* **1,** (legible) legible. **2,** (easy to read) fácil de leer.

reader ('ri·dər) *n.* **1,** (person who reads) lector. **2,** (book) libro de lectura. **3,** (interpreter) intérprete.

readily ('rɛd·ə·li) *adv.* **1,** (will-

ingly) de buena gana. **2,** (easily) fácilmente.
readiness ('rɛd·i·nɪs) *n.* **1,** (preparedness) preparación. **2,** (willingness) disposición. **3,** (promptness) prontitud.
reading ('ri·dɪŋ) *n.* **1,** (act or content of reading) lectura. **2,** (recital) recitación. **3,** (interpretation) interpretación.
ready ('rɛd·i) *adj.* **1,** (prepared) preparado; listo. **2,** (willing) dispuesto. **3,** (about to) listo. **4,** (available) disponible; a la mano. **5,** (prompt) ligero. —*v.t.* preparar. —*v.i.* prepararse.
ready-made *adj.* hecho de antemano; ya hecho. —**ready-made clothes,** ropa hecha.
reagent (ri'ei·dʒənt) *n.* reactivo.
real ('ri·əl) *adj.* **1,** (existing) real. **2,** (true) genuino; auténtico; verdadero. **3,** (immovable) inmueble. —*n.* ('ri·əl; re'al) real. —**real estate; real property,** bienes raíces.
realism ('ri·ə·lɪz·əm) *n.* realismo. —**realist,** *n.* & *adj.* realista. —**realistic,** *adj.* realista.
reality (ri'æl·ə·ti) *n.* **1,** (actuality) realidad. **2,** (truth) verdad.
realize ('ri·əˌlaiz) *v.t.* **1,** (acknowledge) reconocer; darse cuenta de. **2,** (understand) comprender. **3,** (achieve) efectuar; realizar. **4,** (earn) ganar. **5,** (exchange for cash) convertir en dinero contante. —**realization** (-lɪ'zei·ʃən) *n.* realización; comprensión.
really ('ri·ə·li) *adv.* **1,** (actually) en realidad; realmente. **3,** (truly) de veras. **3,** (indeed) efectivamente. —*interj.* ¡es verdad!
realm (rɛlm) *n.* **1,** (kingdom) reino. **2,** (scope) esfera.
realtor ('ri·əlˌtor) *n.* agente vendedor de casas; corredor de bienes raíces. —**realty,** *n.* bienes raíces.
ream (riːm) *n.* **1,** (quantity of paper) resma. **2,** *usu.pl., colloq.* (large amount) gran cantidad. —*v.t.* escariar.
reamer ('ri·mər) *n.* **1,** (reaming tool) escariador. **2,** (juice extractor) exprimidor.
reanimate (ri'æn·əˌmeit) *v.r.* reanimar. —*v.i.* reanimarse.
reap (rip) *v.t.* & *i.* segar; cosechar. —**reaping,** *n.* siega; cosecha.
reaper ('ri·pər) *n.* **1,** (one who reaps) segador. **2,** (reaping machine) segadora.
reappear (ˌri·ə'pɪr) *v.i.* reaparecer. —**reappearance,** *n.* reaparición.
rear (rɪr) *n.* **1,** (back part) parte de atrás; parte posterior. **2,** (innermost part) fondo. **3,** (tail end) cola. **4,** *mil.* retaguardia. —*adj.* posterior; trasero; de atrás; *mil.* de retaguardia. —*v.t.* **1,** (elevate) alzar; levantar. **2,** (erect) erigir; construir. **3,** (nurture; train) criar. —*v.i.* **1,** (rise on the hind legs) encabritarse. **2,** (feel resentment) resentirse. —**at** *o* **in the rear of, 1,** (behind) detrás de. **2,** (in the back part of) al fondo de. **3,** (at the tail end of) a la cola de. —**bring up the rear,** cerrar la marcha. —**rear admiral,** contraalmirante. —**rear back** (recoil), recular. —**rear end, 1,** (tail end) cola. **2,** (buttocks) nalga; *vulg.* trasero. —**rear guard,** retaguardia. —**rear sight,** alza.
rearm (ri'arm) *v.t.* rearmar. —*v.i.* rearmarse. —**rearmament** (ri'ar·mə·mənt) *n.* rearme.
rearmost ('rɪr·most) *adj.* último; postrero.
rearward ('rɪr·wərd) *adj.* de atrás. —*adv.* [*también,* **rearwards**] hacia atrás.
reason ('ri·zən) *n.* razón. —*v.t.* & *i.* razonar. —**reasonable,** *adj.* razonable. —**reasoning,** *n.* razonamiento; argumento. —*adj.* razonador.
reassure (ˌri·ə'ʃur) *v.t.* asegurar; alentar. —**reassurance,** *n.* confianza restablecida; confianza.
rebate ('ri·beit) *n.* **1,** (discount) rebaja; descuento. **2,** (return of money) reembolso. —*v.t.* (rɪ'beit) **1,** (reduce; deduct) rebajar; descontar. **2,** (reimburse) devolver; reembolsar.
rebel (rɪ'bɛl) *v.t.* rebelarse. —*adj.* & *n.* ('rɛb·əl) rebelde.
rebellion (rɪ'bɛl·jən) *n.* **1,** (armed revolt) insurrección. **2,** (resistance to authority) rebeldía. —**rebellious,** *adj.* rebelde. —**rebelliousness,** *n.* rebeldía.
rebirth ('ri·bʌɹθ) *n.* renacimiento.
reborn (ri'born) *adj.* renacido.
rebound (rɪ'baund) *v.i.* rebotar. —*n.* ('ri-) **1,** (return bounce) rebote. **2,** *colloq.* (recovery from a love affair) recobro de mal de amores. —**on the rebound,** de rebote.

rebuff (ri'bʌf) *v.t.* rechazar; repulsar; desairar. —*n.* rechazo; repulsa; desaire.
rebuild (ri'bɪld) *v.t.* [*pret. & p.p.* **-built**] reconstruir; rehacer.
rebuke (rɪ'bjuk) *v.t.* regañar; reprender; censurar. —*n.* censura; reprensión.
rebus ('ri·bəs) *n.* jeroglífico.
rebut (rɪ'bʌt) *v.t.* refutar; contradecir. —**rebuttal,** *n.* refutación.
recalcitrant (rɪ'kæl·sɪ·trənt) *adj.* recalcitrante. —**recalcitrance,** *n.* obstinación; terquedad.
recall (rɪ'kɔl) *v.t.* **1,** (recollect) recordar. **2,** (call back) hacer volver. **3,** (revoke) revocar. **4,** (dismiss from office) destituir; deponer. —*n.* **1,** (recollection) recordación. **2,** (summons to return) llamada. **3,** (revocation) revocación. **4,** (dismissal from office) destitución; deposición. **5,** *mil.* llamada.
recant (rɪ'kænt) *v.t.* retractar. —*v.i.* retractarse. —**recantation** (ˌri·kæn'tei·ʃən) *n.* retractación.
recapitulate (ˌre·kə'pɪtʃ·əˌleit) *v.t.* recapitular. —**recapitulation,** *n.* recapitulación.
recapture (rɪ'kæp·tʃər) *v.t.* volver a capturar; recobrar. —*n.* **1,** (recovery) recobro. **2,** (lawful confiscation) cobranza.
recast (ri'kæst) *v.t.* [*pret. & p.p.* **-cast**] **1,** (remold; remake) refundir. **2,** (reconstruct) reconstruir.
recede (rɪ'siːd) *v.i.* **1,** (draw back) retroceder. **2,** (turn back) volverse atrás. **3,** (slope backward) inclinarse.
receipt (rɪ'sit) *n.* **1,** (act of receiving) recepción. **2,** (note acknowledging payment) recibo; recibí. **3,** (recipe) receta. —*v.t.* dar un recibo de; poner el recibí a. —**receipts,** *n.pl.* ingresos. —**receipted,** *adj.* pagado. —**acknowledge receipt of,** acusar recibo de. —**receipt in full,** recibo por saldo de cuenta.
receivable (rɪ'siv·ə·bəl) *adj.* recibidero. —*n.* cuenta por cobrar.
receive (rɪ'siːv) *v.t.* **1,** (get; obtain) recibir; tomar. **2,** (accept) aprobar; aceptar. **3,** (hold) contener. **4,** (greet) recibir; acoger. **5,** (deal in unlawfully, as stolen goods) receptar.
receiver (ri'siv·ər) *n.* **1,** (one who receives) recibidor; recipiente. **2,** (dealer in stolen goods) receptador. **3,** (custodian of a bankrupt) síndico. **4,** (instrument for receiving signals) receptor. **5,** (receptacle) receptáculo. —**receivership,** *n.* sindicatura.
recent ('ri·sənt) *adj.* **1,** (of recent time) reciente. **2,** (modern) moderno; fresco. —**recently,** *adv.* recientemente. —**recency,** *n.* novedad.
receptacle (rɪ'sɛp·tə·kəl) *n.* receptáculo; recipiente.
reception (rɪ'sɛp·ʃən) *n.* **1,** (act of receiving) recepción. **2,** (welcome) recibimiento; acogida. **3,** (formal gathering) recepción. —**receptionist,** *n.* recepcionista.
receptive (rɪ'sɛp·tɪv) *adj.* receptivo. —**receptivity** (ˌri·sɛp'tɪv·ə·ti); **receptiveness,** *n.* receptividad.
recess ('ri·sɛs) *n.* **1,** (rest period) hora *o* tiempo de recreo. **2,** (niche) depresión; nicho. **3,** (adjournment) receso. **4,** *pl.* (place of seclusion) escondrijo; lugar apartado. —*v.t.* (rɪ'sɛs) **1,** (make a niche in) hacer un nicho en. **2,** (set in a niche) poner en un nicho. **3,** (set back) retirar; apartar. —*v.i.* suspenderse; descansar.
recession (rɪ'sɛʃ·ən) *n.* **1,** (act of receding) retroceso; retirada. **2,** *archit.* (recessed place) entrada. **3,** (renunciation) renuncia. **4,** (economic relapse) depresión en pequeña escala.
recessive (rɪ'sɛs·ɪv) *adj.* regresivo.
recharge (ri'tʃardʒ) *v.t.* recargar.
recherché (rə'ʃɛr·ʃei) *adj.* rebuscado.
recidivist (rɪ'sɪd·ə·vɪst) *n.* reincidente. —**recidivism,** *n.* reincidencia. —**recidivous,** *adj.* reincidente.
recipe ('rɛs·ə·pi) *n.* receta.
recipient (rɪ'sɪp·i·ənt) *n. & adj.* recibidor; recipiente.
reciprocal (rɪ'sɪp·rə·kəl) *adj.* recíproco. —*n., math.* recíproca.
reciprocate (rɪ'sɪp·rəˌkeit) *v.t. & i.* **1,** (return) reciprocar. **2,** (exchange) intercambiar. **3,** *mech.* oscilar. —**reciprocating engine,** motor a movimiento oscilador.
reciprocation (rɪˌsɪp·rə'kei·ʃən) *n.* **1,** (return) reciprocación. **2,** (exchange) intercambio.
reciprocity (ˌrɛs·ɪ'pras·ə·ti) *n.* reciprocidad.
recital (rɪ'sai·təl) *n.* **1,** (narra-

tion) relación; narración. **2,** *music* recital.
recitation (ˌrɛs·ɪ'tei·ʃən) *n.* recitación.
recitative (ˌrɛs·ɪ·tə'tiːv) *n., music* recitado.
recite (rɪ'sait) *v.t.* **1,** (declaim) recitar. **2,** (tell) relatar; narrar. **3,** (enumerate) enumerar; contar. —*v.i.* recitar.
reckless ('rɛk·ləs) *adj.* temerario; imprudente. —**recklessness,** *n.* temeridad; imprudencia.
reckon ('rɛk·ən) *v.t. & i.* **1,** (compute) contar; calcular. **2,** (regard) estimar; apreciar. **3,** *colloq.* (guess) creer; suponer. —**reckon on,** contar con. —**reckon with,** tener en cuenta.
reckoning ('rɛk·ən·ɪŋ) *n.* **1,** (computation) cálculo; cómputo. **2,** (accounting) cuenta; ajuste de cuentas. **3,** *naut.* estima.
reclaim (ri'kleim) *v.t.* **1,** (assert one's right to) reclamar. **2,** (redeem; save) redimir. **3,** (recover; salvage) recuperar; utilizar; sacar provecho de.
reclamation (ˌrɛk·lə'mei·ʃən) *n.* **1,** (assertion of one's rights) reclamación. **2,** (recovery; salvage) recuperación; utilización.
recline (rɪ'klain) *v.t.* recostar; reclinar. —*v.i.* recostarse; reclinarse. —**reclining,** *adj.* reclinado; recostado.
recluse (rɪ'klus) *n. & adj.* solitario; apartadizo.
recognition (ˌrɛk·əg'nɪʃ·ən) *n.* reconocimiento.
recognize ('rɛk·əgˌnaiz) *v.t.* reconocer. —**recognizable,** *adj.* reconocible.
recoil (rɪ'kɔil) *v.i.* recular. —*n.* **1,** (backward move) reculada; retroceso. **2,** (kick, as of a firearm) culatazo.
recollect (ˌrɛk·ə'lɛkt) *v.t. & i.* recordar. —**recollection** (-'lɛk·ʃən) *n.* recuerdo; recordación.
recommend (ˌrɛk·ə'mɛnd) *v.t.* recomendar. —**recommendation** (-mɛn'dei·ʃən) *n.* recomendación.
recompense ('rɛk·əmˌpɛns) *v.t.* recompensar. —*n.* recompensa.
reconcile ('rɛk·ənˌsail) *v.t.* **1,** (restore) reconciliar. **2,** (adjust) ajustar; adaptar; componer. **3,** (conciliate) conciliar; concordar. —**reconciliation** (-ˌsɪl·i'ei·ʃən) *n.* reconciliación.
recondite ('rɛk·ənˌdait) *adj.* recóndito. —**reconditeness,** *n.* reconditez.
recondition *v.t.* renovar.
reconnaissance (rɪ'kan·ə·səns) *n.* reconocimiento; exploración.
reconnoiter (ˌri·kə'nɔi·tər) *v.t.* reconocer. —*v.i.* practicar un reconocimiento.
reconquer (ri'kaŋ·kər) *v.t.* reconquistar. —**reconquest** (ri'kan·kwɛst) *n.* reconquista.
reconsider *v.t.* volver a considerar: repensar. —**reconsideration,** *n.* nueva consideración.
reconstitute (ri'kan·stəˌtjut) *v.t.* reconstituir. —**reconstituent** (ˌri·kən'stɪt·ju·ənt) *adj. & n.* reconstituyente. —**reconstitution** (riˌkan·stɪ'tju·ʃən) *n.* reconstitución.
reconstruct *v.t.* reconstruir. —**reconstruction,** *n.* reconstrucción.
record (rɪ'kord) *v.t.* **1,** (note) apuntar; marcar; indicar. **2,** (enroll) registrar; inscribir. **3,** (transcribe, as sound) grabar. —*n.* ('rɛk·ərd) **1,** (act of recording) registro; inscripción. **2,** *usu.pl.* (data; information) datos auténticos; anales; archivos. **3,** (phonograph disk) disco. **4,** (highest achievement) marca; *sports* récord. **5,** *educ.* expediente académico. **6,** (personal history) historial. —*adj.* máximo; más alto. —**break a record,** batir un récord. —**make** *o* **set a record,** establecer un récord. —**record cabinet,** discoteca. —**record changer,** cambiadiscos. —**record library,** discoteca. —**record player,** tocadiscos.
recorder (rɪ'kord·ər) *n.* **1,** (registrar; archivist) registrador; archivero. **2,** (registering instrument) indicador; contador. **3,** (device for transcribing sound) grabadora. **3,** (type of flute) caramillo. —**tape recorder,** grabadora de cinta; magnetófono.
recording (rɪ'kor·dɪŋ) *n.* **1,** (register) registro. **2,** (sound transcription) registro acústico; grabación. —*adj.* registrador.
recount (rɪ'kaunt) *v.t.* **1,** (relate) relatar; contar. **2,** (ri-) (count again) recontar. —*n.* ('riˌkaunt) recuento.
recoup (rɪ'kup) *v.t.* recobrar. —*v.i.* recobrarse; desquitarse. —*n.* recobro.

recourse ('ri·kors) *n.* recurso; remedio. —**have recourse to,** recurrir a.
recover (rɪ'kʌv·ər) *v.t.* **1,** (regain) recobrar; recuperar. **2,** (save) rescatar. **3,** *law* reivindicar. **4,** (ri-) (cover again) recubrir. —*v.i.* **1,** (regain health) restablecerse; reponerse. **2,** *law* ganar un pleito. —**recovery,** *n.* recobro; recuperación; *law* reivindicación.
re-create *v.t.* recrear.
recreation (ˌrɛk·ri'ei·ʃən) *n.* recreación; recreo; diversión. —**recreational,** *adj.* de recreación. —**recreative** (-tɪv) *adj.* recreativo.
recriminate (rɪ'krɪm·əˌneit) *v.t.* & *i.* recriminar. —**recrimination,** *n.* recriminación.
recrudesce (ˌri·kru'dɛs) *v.i.* **1,** (become raw) recrudecer; recrudecerse. **2,** (break out afresh) recaer. —**recrudescence,** *n.* recrudecimiento; recrudescencia. —**recrudescent,** *adj.* recrudescente.
recruit (rɪ'krut) *v.t.* **1,** (enlist) reclutar. **2,** (gather, as strength, provisions, etc.) acopiar; hacer acopio de. **3,** (reinforce) reforzar. —*n.* **1,** (new soldier) recluta. **2,** (novice) novicio. —**recruiting; recruitment,** *n.* reclutamiento.
rectal ('rɛk·təl) *adj.* del recto; rectal.
rectangle ('rɛkˌtæŋ·gəl) *n.* rectángulo. —**rectangular** (rɛk'tæŋ·gjə·lər) *adj.* rectangular.
recti- (rɛk·tɪ; -tə) *también,* **rect-** (rɛkt) *prefijo* recti-; recto: *rectilinear,* rectilíneo; *rectangle,* rectángulo.
rectify ('rɛk·tɪˌfai) *v.t.* rectificar. —**rectification** (-fɪ'kei·ʃən) *n.* rectificación. —**rectifier,** *n.* rectificador.
rectilinear (ˌrɛk·tə'lɪn·i·ər) *adj.* rectilíneo.
rectitude ('rɛk·tɪˌtjud) *n.* rectitud.
rector (rɛk·tər) *n.* rector. —**rectorate** (-ət) *n.* rectorado. —**rectory,** *n.* rectoría.
rectum ('rɛk·təm) *n.* recto.
recumbent (rɪ'kʌm·bənt) *adj.* reclinado; recostado. —**recumbency,** *n.* reclinación.
recuperate (rɪ'kju·pəˌreit) *v.t.* recobrar; recuperar. —*v.i.* restablecerse; reponerse. —**recuperation,** *n.* recuperación; recobro. —**recuperative** (-pər·ə·tɪv) *adj.* recuperativo.
recur (rɪ'kʌr) *v.i.* repetirse; volver; recurrir. —**recurrence,** *n.* repetición; retorno. —**recurrent,** *adj.* recurrente; periódico.
recusant ('rɛk·jə·zənt) *n.* & *adj.* recusante. —**recusancy,** *n.* recusación.
red (rɛd) *adj.* rojo; colorado. —*n.* rojo; color rojo. —**in the red, 1,** (losing money) con pérdida; con déficit. **2,** (in debt) endeudado. —**paint the town red,** *slang* echar una parranda; jaranear. —**see red,** *colloq.* encolerizarse.
redact (rɪ'dækt) *v.t.* redactar. —**redaction** (rɪ'dæk·ʃən) *n.* redacción. —**redactor,** *n.* redactor.
redcap *n.* mozo de estación.
redden ('rɛd·ən) *v.t.* enrojecer. —*v.i.* enrojecerse; sonrojarse.
reddish ('rɛd·ɪʃ) *adj.* rojizo.
redeem (rɪ'diːm) *v.t.* **1,** (buy back; pay off) redimir. **2,** (liberate) rescatar; libertar. **3,** (fulfill, as a promise) cumplir. **3,** (atone for) redimir; pagar. —**redeemable,** *adj.* redimible. —**redeemer,** *n.* redentor.
redemption (rɪ'dɛmp·ʃən) *n.* redención. —**redemptive** (-tɪv) *adj.* redentor.
red-haired *adj.* pelirrojo.
redhanded *adj.* en flagrante.
redhead *n.* pelirrojo. —**redheaded,** *adj.* pelirrojo.
red herring pista falsa.
red-hot *adj.* **1,** (very hot) candente. **2,** *slang* (very new) muy nuevo; recentísimo. **3,** *slang* (fervid) ardiente; entusiasta; enérgico.
red lead rojo de plomo.
redletter *adj.* memorable.
red light luz roja; señal de paro. —**red-light district,** distrito de lupanares.
redness ('rɛd·nəs) *n.* rojez.
redo (ri'duː) *v.t.* [*pret.* **redid** (-'dɪd); *p.p.* **redone** (-'dʌn)] rehacer; hacer de nuevo.
redolent ('rɛd·ə·lənt) *adj.* fragante; oloroso. —**redolence,** *n.* fragancia; olor. —**redolent of, 1,** (having the smell of) que huela a. **2,** (reminiscent or suggestive of) que recuerda.
redouble (rɪ'dʌb·əl) *v.t.* **1,** (double again) redoblar; reduplicar. **2,** (increase) aumentar. **3,** (echo) re-

petir. —*v.i.* redoblarse. —*n.* redoble.

redoubt (rɪ'daut) *n.* reducto.

redoubtable (rɪ'dau·tə·bəl) *adj.* formidable; tremendo.

redound (rɪ'daund) *v.i.* redundar.

redraft (rɪ'dræft) *v.t.* dibujar *o* diseñar de nuevo. —*n.* ('ri-) **1,** (new sketch or design) nuevo dibujo *o* diseño. **2,** *comm.* resaca.

redraw (rɪ'drɔː) *v.t.* **1,** (redesign) diseñar *o* planear de nuevo. **2,** *comm.* recambiar.

redress (rɪ'drɛs) *v.t.* remediar; reparar; corregir. —*n.* enmienda; remedio; compensación.

red tape expedienteo; trámites (*pl.*)

reduce (rɪ'dus) *v.t.* **1,** (diminish) reducir; disminuir. **2,** (downgrade) degradar. **3,** (lower) rebajar. **4,** (subdue) subyugar. —*v.i., colloq.* rebajar de peso. —**reducible,** *adj.* reducible; reductible.

reduction (rɪ'dʌk·ʃən) *n.* reducción; disminución; rebaja.

redundant (rɪ'dʌn·dənt) *adj.* superfluo; redundante. —**redundancy,** *n.* redundancia.

reduplicate (rɪ'dup·lə·keit) *v.t.* reduplicar. —**reduplication,** *n.* reduplicación.

redwood *n.* secoya.

reecho (ri'ɛk·o) *v.i.* resonar; repetir o responder el eco. —*n.* eco repetido.

reed (riːd) *n.* **1,** *bot.* caña; junquillo. **2,** (reed instrument) instrumento de lengüeta. **3,** *music* (vibrating piece) lengüeta.

reedy ('ri·di) *adj.* **1,** (of or like a reed) de *o* como caña. **2,** (full of reeds) lleno de cañas. **3,** (of thin, delicate tone) agudo y delgado.

reef (rif) *n.* **1,** (sand bar) arrecife; escollo. **2,** *naut.* rizo. **3,** *mining* veta; filón. —*v.t., naut.* tomar rizos en.

reefer ('ri·fər) *n.* **1,** (short coat) chaqueta corta. **2,** *slang* cigarrillo de mariguana.

reek (rik) *v.i.* apestar; oler. —*v.t.* emitir; oler a. —*n.* vaho. —**reek of** *o* **with,** oler a; abundar en; tener *o* emitir en cantidad.

reel (riːl) *n.* **1,** (winding device) devanadera. **2,** (spool) carrete. **3,** (dance) baile vivo de origen escocés. **4,** (staggering motion) bamboleo; tambaleo. —*v.t.* (wind) devanar. —*v.i.* (stagger) bambolear; tambalear. —**off the reel,** rápidamente; sin vacilar. —**reel off,** enunciar rápidamente.

reelect *v.t.* reeligir. —**reelection,** *n.* reelección.

reembark *v.i.* reembarcarse. —**reembarkation,** *n.* reembarque; reembarco.

reenter (ri'ɛn·tər) *v.i.* reentrar; reingresar. —*v.t.* reentrar en; reingresar en. —**reentry** (-tri) [*pl.* **-tries**] reingreso.

reestablish *v.t.* restablecer. —**reestablishment,** *n.* restablecimiento.

reeve (riːv) *n.* **1,** (bird) hembra de la paloma moñuda. **2,** (town official) pedáneo; alcalde pedáneo. —*v.t., naut.* pasar (un cabo) por un ojal; asegurar.

refection (rɪ'fɛk·ʃən) *n.* refacción; refección.

refectory (rɪ'fɛk·tə·ri) *n.* refectorio.

refer (rɪ'fʌɹ) *v.t.* **1,** (submit for consideration) referir. **2,** (direct) dirigir. **3,** (assign) asignar. —**refer to, 1,** (relate to; be concerned with) tratar de; respectar. **2,** (have recourse to; appeal to) recurrir a; dirigirse a. **3,** (allude to) aludir a; referirse a.

referee (ˌrɛf·ə'riː) *n.* árbitro. —*v.t. & i.* arbitrar.

reference ('rɛf·ə·rəns) *n.* **1,** (act of referring) referencia. **2,** (allusion) alusión. **3,** (recommendation) recomendación. **4,** (citation) mención. —**reference book,** libro de consulta. —**with reference to,** en cuanto a.

referendum (ˌrɛf·ə'rɛn·dəm) *n.* plebiscito; referéndum.

refill (ri'fɪl) *v.t.* rellenar. —*n.* ('ri-) repuesto.

refine (rɪ'fain) *v.t.* **1,** (purify) refinar; purificar. **2,** (polish, as one's manners) pulir. **3,** (perfect) perfeccionar.

refined (rɪ'faind) *adj.* **1,** (purified) refinado; purificado. **2,** (wellbred) cortés.

refinement (rɪ'fain·mənt) *n.* **1,** (act of refining) refinamiento. **2,** (good breeding) elegancia; cultura.

refiner (rɪ'fain·ər) *n.* refinador. —**refinery,** *n.* refinería. —**refining,** *n.* refinación.

refinish (ri'fɪn·ɪʃ) *v.t.* dar nuevo terminado *o* nueva capa; pintar de nuevo; revocar (paredes). —**re-**

finishing, *n.* nuevo terminado; nueva capa; nueva pintura; revocadura (*de paredes*).
reflect (rɪ'flɛkt) *v.t.* **1,** (throw back, as light) reflectar. **2,** (mirror) reflejar. **3,** (bring back as a consequence) causar; traer. —*v.i.* **1,** (throw back rays) reflejar. **2,** (meditate) reflexionar. —**reflect on** (discredit) desacreditar.
reflection (rɪ'flɛk·ʃən) *n.* **1,** (act of reflecting) reflexión. **2,** (image) reflejo. **3,** (meditation) meditación. **4,** (comment) comentario. **5,** (slur) reparo. —**reflective** (-tɪv) *adj.* reflexivo. —**reflector** (-tər) *n.* reflector.
reflex ('ri·flɛks) *n.* & *adj.* reflejo.
reflexive (rɪ'flɛk·sɪv) *adj.* reflexivo; reflejo.
reflux ('ri,flʌks) *n.* reflujo.
reforest (ri'for·əst) *v.t.* restablecer; repoblar (bosques). —**reforestation** (-əs'tei·ʃən) *n.* restablecimiento; repoblación (de bosques).
reform (rɪ'form) *v.t.* reformar. —*v.i.* reformarse. —*n.* reforma. —*adj.* reformista. —**reformer,** *n.* reformador; reformista.
re-form (ri'form) *v.t.* **1,** (form again) reformar; reconstituir. **2,** (make different) hacer diferente; dar otra forma a. —*v.i.* **1,** (be formed anew) reformarse; reconstituirse. **2,** (change) volverse diferente; tomar otra forma.
reformation (,rɛf·ər'mei·ʃən) *n.* **1,** (change; reshaping) reformación; reforma. **2,** *cap., hist.* Reforma.
reformatory (rɪ'for·mə·tor·i) *n.* reformatorio.
reformist (rɪ'for·mɪst) *adj.* & *n.* reformista.
reform school reformatorio.
refract (rɪ'frækt) *v.t.* refractar; refringir. —**refracting; refractive,** *adj.* refringente. —**refraction** (rɪ'fræk·ʃən) *n.* refracción. —**refractor,** *n.* refractor.
refractory (rɪ'fræk·tə·ri) *adj.* refractario.
refrain (rɪ'frein) *v.i.* refrenarse; abstenerse. —*n.* estribillo; refrán.
refresh (rɪ'frɛʃ) *v.t.* refrescar; renovar. —*v.i.* refrescarse. —**refreshing,** *adj.* refrescante. —**refreshment,** *n.* refresco.
refrigerate (rɪ'frɪdʒ·ə,reit) *v.t.* refrigerar. —**refrigerant,** *n.* & *adj.* refrigerante. —**refrigeration,** *n.* refrigeración. —**refrigerator,** *n.* refrigerador, nevera.
refry (ri'frai) *v.t.* [*infl.:* **fry**] refreír.
refuel (ri'fju·əl) *v.t.* repostar. —*v.i.* repostarse.
refuge ('rɛf·judʒ) *n.* refugio; albergue; amparo. —**refugee,** *n.* refugiado. —**take refuge,** refugiarse.
refulgence (ri'fʌl·dʒəns) *n.* refulgencia; resplandor. —**refulgent,** *adj.* refulgente.
refund (rɪ'fʌnd) *v.t.* **1,** (pay back) reembolsar; devolver. **2,** (ri-) (refinance) consolidar. —*n.* ('ri·fʌnd) reembolso. —**refundable,** *adj.* restituible.
refurbish (ri'fʌɹ·bɪʃ) *v.t.* restaurar; reparar.
refusal (rɪ'fjuz·əl) *n.* **1,** (act of refusing) denegación; repulsa. **2,** (first option) opción exclusiva.
refuse (ri'fju:z) *v.t.* **1,** (decline; deny) rehusar; denegar. **2,** (reject) rechazar. —*v.i.* no querer; no aceptar. —*n.* ('rɛf·jus) basura. —**refuse to,** negarse a.
refute (rɪ'fjut) *v.t.* refutar. —**refutation** (,rɛf·ju'tei·ʃən) *n.* refutación.
regain (rɪ'gein) *v.t.* **1,** (reach again) volver a; volver a alcanzar. **2,** (recover) recobrar; recuperar.
regal ('ri·gəl) *adj.* real; regio; majestuoso.
regale (rɪ'geil) *v.t.* regalar; festejar. —**regale oneself,** regalarse.
regalia (rɪ'gei·li·ə) *n.pl.* **1,** (emblems) insignias. **2,** (personal finery) galas; trajes de gala.
regard (rɪ'gard) *v.t.* **1,** (look upon) mirar; observar. **2,** (esteem) estimar; apreciar. **3,** (concern) concernir; referirse a. —*n.* **1,** (reference) relación; respecto. **2,** (respect) respeto; veneración. **3,** (scrutiny) mirada. **4,** (concern) interés; consideración. —**regardful,** *adj.* atento. —**regarding,** *prep.* tocante a; respecto a. —**as regards,** respecto a; en cuanto a. —**best regards to,** muchos recuerdos a; saludos cordiales a. —**in** *o* **with regard to,** respecto a; en cuanto a. —**without regard to,** sin considerar; sin tener en cuenta.
regardless (rɪ'gard·ləs) *adj.* descuidado; indiferente. —*adv., colloq.* no obstante; en todo caso. —**regardless of,** no obstante; a pesar de; sin considerar.

regatta (rɪ'gæt·ə) *n.* regata.
regency ('ri·dʒən·si) *n.* regencia.
regenerate (ri'dʒən·ər,eit) *v.t.* regenerar. —*v.i.* regenerarse. —*adj.* (-ət) regenerado. —**regeneration**, *n.* regeneración. —**regenerative** (-ə·tɪv) *adj.* regenerativo.
regent ('ri·dʒənt) *n.* **1,** (substitute ruler) regente. **2,** *educ.* director; miembro de la junta directiva. —*adj.* regente.
regicide ('rɛdʒ·ə,said) *n.* **1,** (agent) regicida. **2,** (act) regicidio.
regime (rɛ'ʒiːm) *n.* régimen; gobierno.
regimen ('rɛdʒ·ə·mən) *n.* régimen.
regiment ('rɛdʒ·ə·mənt) *n.* regimiento. —*v.t.* regimentar. —**regimental** (-'mɛn·təl) *adj.* regimental. —**regimentals**, *n.pl.* uniforme militar. —**regimentation** (-mɛn'tei·ʃən) *n.* regimentación.
region ('ri·dʒən) *n.* **1,** (area) región. **2,** (district) distrito; territorio. —**regional**, *adj.* regional. —**regionalism**, *n.* regionalismo. —**regionalist**, *n.* regionalista. —**regionalistic**, *adj.* regionalista.
register ('rɛdʒ·ɪs·tər) *n.* **1,** (written record) archivo; registro. **2,** *music* (range) amplitud vocal o instrumental. **3,** (regulator, as for heat or air) regulador. **4,** (recording device) registrador. **5,** *print.* ajuste exacto; registro. **6,** (recording office) registro. **7,** (registrar) registrador. —*v.t.* **1,** (enroll) inscribir. **2,** (transcribe; record; copy) registrar. **3,** (indicate, as by a measuring device) registrar. **4,** (manifest; show) demostrar; manifestar. **5,** (insure delivery of, as a letter) certificar. **6,** *print.* registrar. —*v.i.* **1,** (enroll; record one's name) inscribir(se). **2,** *print.* estar en registro; registrarse. **3,** *colloq.* (make an impression) crear una impresión.
registrar ('rɛdʒ·ɪs,trar) *n.* registrador.
registration (,rɛdʒ·ɪs'trei·ʃən) *n.* **1,** (act of registering) inscripción. **2,** (list of persons registered) registro; matrícula.
registry ('rɛdʒ·ɪs·tri) *n.* registro.
regress ('ri·grɛs) *n.* regreso; vuelta; retorno. —*v.i.* (rɪ'grɛs) regresar. —**regression** (rɪ'grɛʃ·ən) *n.* regresión. —**regressive** (rɪ'grɛs·ɪv) *adj.* regresivo; retrógrado.
regret (rɪ'grɛt) *v.i.* **1,** (lament) lamentar. **2,** (rue) sentir; arrepentirse de. —*n.* **1,** (grief) pena; pesadumbre. **2,** (remorse) compunción; remordimiento. **3,** *pl.* (excuses) excusas. —**regretful**, *adj.* triste; pesaroso. —**regrettable**, *adj.* lamentable.
regular ('rɛg·jə·lər) *adj.* **1,** (customary) regular; acostumbrado. **2,** (steady) uniforme. **3,** (normal) natural. **4,** *colloq.* (thorough) cabal. —*n.* regular. —**regularity** (-'lær·ə·ti) *n.* regularidad.
regularize ('rɛg·jə·lə,raiz) *v.t.* regularizar. —*v.i.* regularizarse. —**regularization** (-rɪ'zei·ʃən) *n.* regularización.
regulate ('rɛg·jə,leit) *v.t.* **1,** (direct) disciplinar. **2,** (keep in order) regular. **3,** (set rules for) reglamentar. **4,** (adjust) ajustar. —**regulator**, *n.* regulador. —**regulatory** (-lə,tor·i) *adj.* reglamentario; regulador.
regulation (,rɛg·jə'lei·ʃən) *n.* **1,** (rule) regla. **2,** (act or power of regulating) regulación. **3,** *usu. pl.* (set of rules) reglamento; reglamentación. —*adj.* de regla; regular.
regurgitate (ri'gʌɹ·dʒɪ,teit) *v.i.* regurgitar. —*v.t.* vomitar. —**regurgitation**, *n.* regurgitación.
rehabilitate (,ri·hə'bɪl·ə,teit) *v.t.* rehabilitar. —**rehabilitation**, *n.* rehabilitación.
rehash ('ri·hæʃ) *n., colloq.* refundición. —*v.t.* (ri'hæʃ) *colloq.* **1,** (make into another form) refundir; rehacer. **2,** (go over again) repasar; repetir.
rehearse (rɪ'hʌɹs) *v.t.* **1,** (practice) ensayar. **2,** (repeat) repetir. **3,** (tell in detail) narrar. —*v.i.* practicar; ensayarse. —**rehearsal**, *n.* ensayo.
reheat (ri'hit) *v.t.* recalentar. —**reheating**, *n* recalentamiento.
reign (rein) *n.* **1,** (rule; domain) reino. **2,** (period of rule) reinado. —*v.i.* reinar. —**reigning**, *adj.* reinante.
reimburse (,ri·ɪm'bʌɹs) *v.t.* reembolsar. —**reimbursement**, *n.* reembolso.
rein (rein) *n.* rienda. —*v.t.* refrenar. —**free rein**, rienda suelta. —**throw off the reins**, soltar la rienda.
reincarnate *v.i.* encarnar de

nuevo. **—reincarnation,** *n.* reencarnación.

reindeer ('rein,dɪr) *n.* reno.

reinforce (,ri·ɪn'fors) *v.t.* reforzar. **—reinforcement,** *n.* refuerzo. **—reinforced concrete,** hormigón armado.

reinstall *v.t.* reinstalar. **—reinstallation,** *n.* reinstalación.

reinstate (,ri·ɪn'steit) *v.t.* reinstalar; reintegrar; restablecer. **—reinstatement,** *n.* reinstalación; reintegración.

reiterate (ri'ɪt·ə,reit) *v.t.* repetir; reiterar. **—reiteration,** *n.* repetición; reiteración.

reject (rɪ'dʒɛkt) *v.t.* **1,** (discard) descartar; desechar; rechazar. **2,** (refuse to accept) renunciar. **3,** (deny) negar. **—***n.* ('ri-) cosa rechazada; desecho. **—rejection** (rɪ·'dʒɛk·ʃən) *n.* rechazo.

rejoice (rɪ'dʒɔis) *v.t.* regocijar; alegrar. **—***v.i.* regocijarse. **—rejoicing,** *n.* alegría; regocijo.

rejoin (ri'dʒɔin) *v.t.* **1,** (put back together) unir *o* juntar de nuevo. **2,** (resume membership in) reentrar en; unirse de nuevo a; volver a. **3,** (meet again) volver a encontrar. **—***v.i.* volver; reentrar; reingresar.

rejoin (rɪ'dʒɔin) *v.i.* & *t.* contestar; replicar.

rejoinder (rɪ'dʒɔin·dər) *n.* respuesta; réplica.

rejuvenate (rɪ'dʒu·və,neit) *v.t.* rejuvenecer. **—***v.i.* rejuvenecerse. **—rejuvenation,** *n.* rejuvenecimiento.

relapse (rɪ'læps) *v.i.* recaer. **—***n.* recaída; *med.* recidiva; retroceso.

relate (rɪ'leit) *v.t.* **1,** (connect) relacionar. **2,** (narrate) relatar; narrar; contar. **3,** (ally by kinship) emparentar. **—***v.i.* relacionarse; referirse. **—related,** *adj.* afín; conexo; emparentado.

relation (rɪ'lei·ʃən) *n.* **1,** (narration) narración. **2,** (kin) pariente. **3,** (connection) relación; conexión. **4,** (reference) referencia. **—relations,** *n.pl.* **1,** (relatives) parentela (*sing.*). **2,** (connections) afinidad (*sing.*).

relationship (rɪ'lei·ʃən·ʃɪp) *n.* **1,** (connection) relación. **2,** (kinship) parentesco.

relative ('rɛl·ə·tɪv) *adj.* relativo. **—***n.* pariente. **—relativism,** *n.* relativismo. **—relativity** (-'tɪv·ə·ti) *n.* relatividad.

relax (rɪ'læks) *v.t.* relajar; laxar; ceder. **—***v.i.* **1,** (slacken) relajarse; aflojarse. **2,** (amuse oneself) distraerse. **3,** (take one's ease) estar a sus anchas. **4,** (have peace of mind) estar tranquilo.

relaxation (,ri·læk'sei·ʃən) *n.* **1,** (slackening) aflojamiento; relajación; relajamiento. **2,** (recreation) distracción; recreo.

relay ('ri·lei) *n.* **1,** (fresh supply) relevo. **2,** (station; stopping point) posta. **3,** (shift) cambio; tanda; remuda. **—***v.t.* **1,** [*pret.* & *p.p.* **-laid**] (replace) reemplazar. **2,** (send by a series of steps) mandar por remuda; retransmitir; reexpedir. **—relays,** *n.pl., sports* relevos. **—relay race,** carrera de relevos.

release (rɪ'lis) *v.t.* **1,** (free) libertar. **2,** (disengage; loose) soltar. **3,** (exempt) eximir; aliviar. **4,** (relinquish for display or sale) dar al público. **—***n.* **1,** (liberation) liberación. **2,** (discharge) descargo. **3,** (news item) publicación. **4,** (surrender of claim) cesión.

relegate ('rɛl·ə,geit) *v.t.* relegar. **—relegation,** *n.* relegación.

relent (rɪ'lɛnt) *v.i.* ceder; aplacarse.

relentless (rɪ'lɛnt·ləs) *adj.* inexorable; implacable.

relevant ('rɛl·ə·vənt) *adj.* pertinente; apropiado. **—relevance,** *n.* pertinencia.

reliable (rɪ'lai·ə·bəl) *adj.* seguro; digno de confianza. **—reliability,** *n.* seguridad; confianza.

reliance (rɪ'lai·əns) *n.* confianza. **—reliant,** *adj.* confiado.

relic ('rɛl·ɪk) *n.* **1,** (vestige) vestigio. **2,** (religious memento) reliquia. **3,** *pl.* (remains) residuo (*sing.*).

relict ('rɛl·ɪkt) *n.* viuda.

relief (rɪ'lif) *n.* **1,** (mitigation) mitigación. **2,** (release, as from pain) alivio. **3,** (assistance to the poor) ayuda; asistencia. **4,** (release by substitution) relevación. **5,** (raised decoration) relieve. **6,** *mil.* (one who takes over another's duty) relevo.

relieve (rɪ'li:v) *v.t.* **1,** (alleviate) aliviar. **2,** (substitute) relevar. **3,** (help) auxiliar; socorrer.

religion (rɪ'lɪdʒ·ən) *n.* religión.

religious (rɪ'lidʒ·əs) *adj.* religioso. —**religiosity** (-i'as·ə·ti) *n.* religiosidad.

relinquish (rɪ'lɪŋ·kwɪʃ) *v.t.* abandonar; renunciar. —**relinquishment**, *n.* renuncia.

reliquary ('rɛl·əˌkwɛr·i) *n.* relicario.

relish ('rɛl·ɪʃ) *v.t.* gustar de; saborear; paladear. —*n.* **1,** (savor) sabor; gusto. **2,** (appreciation) goce. **3,** (appetizer) aperitivo; entremés. **4,** (condiment) condimento.

reload (ri'loːd) *v.t.* recargar.

reluctant (rɪ'lʌk·tənt) *adj.* renuente. —**reluctance**, *n.* renuencia; *electricity* reluctancia. —**reluctantly**, *adv.* de mala gana.

rely (rɪ'lai) *v.i.* confiar; fiarse. —**rely on** *o* **upon**, contar con; confiar en.

remain (rɪ'mein) *v.i.* **1,** (stay) quedarse. **2,** (continue in a state) permanecer. **3,** (endure) persistir. **4,** (be left over) restar. **5,** (be held in reserve) quedarse en reserva. —**remains**, *n.pl.* restos. —**remaining**, *adj.* restante.

remainder (rɪ'mein·dər) *n.* **1,** (what is left) resto; restante. **2,** (surplus) remanente. **3,** *math.* resta; residuo.

remake (rɪ'meik) *v.t.* [*pret.* & *p.p.* **-made**] rehacer. —*n.* ('ri-) cosa rehecha.

remand (rɪ'mænd) *v.t.* **1,** (recall; send back) llamar. **2,** *law* (send back to prison) volver a enviar a la cárcel. **3,** *law* (transfer to another court) enviar a otro tribunal.

remark (rɪ'mark) *v.t.* **1,** (observe) observar. **2,** (comment; comment on) comentar. —*n.* observación; comentario. —**remarkable**, *adj.* notable; insigne.

remediable (rɪ'mi·di·ə·bəl) *adj.* remediable; reparable.

remedial (rɪ'mi·di·əl) *adj.* remediador; curativo.

remedy ('rɛm·ə·di) *n.* remedio. —*v.t.* remediar.

remember (rɪ'mɛm·bər) *v.t.* **1,** (recall) recordar; acordarse de. **2,** (observe, as an anniversary) observar. **3,** *colloq.* (tip) dar propina. **4,** (convey one's regards) presentar sus recuerdos (a). —*v.i.* acordarse; recordarse. —**remembrance** (-brəns) *n.* recuerdo.

remind (rɪ'maind) *v.t.* recordar; hacer presente. —**reminder**, *n.* recuerdo; recordatorio.

reminisce (ˌrɛm·ə'nɪs) *v.i.* recordar el pasado. —**reminiscence**, *n.* reminiscencia. —**reminiscent**, *adj.* recordativo.

remiss (rɪ'mɪs) *adj.* remiso; descuidado; negligente. —**remissness**, *n.* descuido; negligencia.

remission (rɪ'mɪʃ·ən) *n.* remisión.

remit (rɪ'mɪt) *v.t.* **1,** (pardon) remitir; perdonar. **2,** (refrain from exacting, as a tax or penalty) condonar. **3,** (slacken) aflojar. **4,** (restore) devolver; restituir. **5,** (send, as payment) remesar; remitir. **6,** *law* referir. —*v.i.* **1,** (abate) aflojarse. **2,** (send payment) hacer remesa.

remittal (rɪ'mɪt·əl) *n.* renuncia; remesa.

remittance (rɪ'mɪt·əns) *n.* remesa. —**remittance man**, exilado viviendo de remesas.

remnant ('rɛm·nənt) *n.* remanente; resto; retazo.

remodel (ri'mad·əl) *v.t.* reconstruir; convertir; renovar.

remonstrate (rɪ'man·streit) *v.i.* objetar; protestar. —**remonstrance**, *n.* protesta. —**remonstrant**, *adj.* & *n.* protestante.

remora ('rɛm·ə·rə) *n.* rémora.

remorse (rɪ'mors) *n.* remordimiento. —**remorseful**, *adj.* arrepentido. —**remorseless**, *adj.* implacable.

remote (rɪ'mot) *adj.* remoto; apartado; ajeno. —**remoteness**, *n.* lejanía. —**remotely**, *adv.* a lo lejos. —**remote control**, mando a distancia.

remount (ri'maunt) *v.t.* & *i.* volver a montar *o* subir.

removable (rɪ'muv·ə·bəl) *adj.* **1,** (portable) transportable; portátil. **2,** (dismountable) desmontable. —*n.*, *usu.pl.* muebles; bienes muebles.

removal (rɪ'muv·əl) *n.* **1,** (taking away) remoción; removimiento; sacamiento. **2,** (change of location) traslado; mudanza. **3,** (dismissal) destitución; deposición. **4,** (obliteration) eliminación; aniquilación.

remove (rɪ'muːv) *v.t.* **1,** (take away) quitar; sacar. **2,** (change the location of) remover; trasladar; mudar. **3,** (dismiss) destituir; deponer. **4,** (obliterate) extirpar;

eliminar; aniquilar. —*v.i.* mudarse; trasladarse. —*n.* **1,** (step; interval) paso. **2,** *Brit.* (change of location) traslado; mudanza.
remunerate (rɪ'mju·nə,reit) *v.t.* remunerar. —**remuneration,** *n.* remuneración. —**remunerative** (-rə·tɪv) *adj.* lucrativo; remuneratorio.
renaissance (,rɛn·ə'sans) *n.* renacimiento.
renascence (rɪ'næs·əns) *n.* renacimiento. —**renascent,** *adj.* renaciente.
renal ('ri·nəl) *adj.* renal.
rend (rɛnd) *v.t.* [*pret.* & *p.p.* **rent**] desgarrar; hender; hacer pedazos.
render ('rɛn·dər) *v.t.* **1,** (cause to be or become) volver; poner. **2,** (give; present) dar; rendir. **3,** (return) devolver. **4,** (translate) traducir. **5,** (interpret) interpretar. **6,** *cooking* derretir. **7,** (perform) ejecutar.
rendezvous ('ran·də,vu) *n.* [*pl.* **-vous** (-vu:z)] cita; lugar de cita. —*v.i.* [**-voused** (,vu:d), **-vousing** (,vu·ɪŋ)] reunirse; acudir a una cita.
renegade ('rɛn·ə,geid) *adj.* & *n.* renegado.
rendition (rɛn'dɪʃ·ən) *n.* **1,** (giving; presenting) rendición. **2,** (translation) traducción. **3,** (interpretation) interpretación. **4,** (performance) ejecución.
renege (rɪ'nɪg) *v.i.* **1,** *cards* (revoke) renunciar. **2,** *colloq.* (back down) retirarse. —*n.,* *cards* renuncio.
renew (rɪ'nju:) *v.t.* renovar. —**renewal,** *n.* renovación.
reni- (rɛn·ɪ; -ə) *prefijo* reni-; riñón: *reniform,* reniforme.
rennet ('rɛn·ɪt) *n.* cuajo.
renounce (rɪ'nauns) *v.t.* & *i.* renunciar. —**renouncement,** *n.* renunciación.
renovate ('rɛn·ə,veit) *v.t.* renovar. —**renovation,** *n.* renovación. —**renovator,** *n.* renovador.
renown (rɪ'naun) *n.* renombre; fama; reputación. —**renowned,** *adj.* célebre; famoso; renombrado.
rent (rɛnt) *n.* **1,** (payment for use) alquiler; renta. **2,** (tear) desgarrón; rasgón; rotura. —*adj.* rasgado; desgarrado. —*v.t.* **1,** (lease) arrendar. **2,** (let; hire) alquilar. **3,** *pret.* & *p.p. de* **rend.** —*v.i.* **1,** (be leased) arrendarse. **2,** (be let or hired) alquilarse. —**for rent,** de alquiler; se alquila.
rental ('rɛn·təl) *n.* **1,** (money paid for use) alquiler. **2,** (income from rented property) renta.
renter ('rɛn·tər) *n.* **1,** (tenant) inquilino; arrendatario. **2,** (owner) propietario; dueño; arrendador.
renunciation (rɪ,nʌn·si'ei·ʃən) *n.* renunciación.
reopen (ri'o·pən) *v.t.* reabrir. —*v.i.* reabrirse.
reorganize (ri'or·gə,naiz) *v.t.* reorganizar. —**reorganization** (-nɪ·'zei·ʃən) *n.* reorganización.
repaint (ri'peint) *v.t.* pintar de nuevo; dar nueva mano. —**repainting,** *n.* nueva pintura; nueva mano de pintura.
repair (rɪ'pe:r) *v.i.* irse; dirigirse. —*v.t.* **1,** (mend) reparar; componer; arreglar. **2,** (make amends for) enmendar. —*n.* **1,** (act of repairing) reparación; arreglo. **2,** (restored condition) reparo. —**repairable,** *adj.* reparable. —**repairer,** *n.* reparador.
repairman *n.* [*pl.* **-men**] reparador.
reparable ('rɛp·ə·rə·bəl) *adj.* reparable.
reparation (,rɛp·ə'rei·ʃən) *n.* **1,** (repair; amends) reparación. **2,** *usu.pl.* (compensation) indemnización; compensación.
repartee (,rɛp·ər'ti:) *n.* respuesta picante; réplica.
repast (rɪ'pæst) *n.* comida.
repatriate (ri'pei·tri,eit) *v.t.* repatriar. —**repatriation,** *n.* repatriación.
repay (ri'pei) *v.t.* **1,** (pay back) compensar. **2,** (reimburse) reembolsar. **3,** (return, as a visit) corresponder a. —**repayable,** reembolsable; compensable. —**repayment,** *n.* reembolso; compensación.
repeal (ri'pi:l) *v.t.* revocar; abolir; anular. —*n.* revocación; abolición; anulación.
repeat (ri'pit) *v.t.* & *i.* **1,** (do again) repetir. **2,** (reiterate) reiterar. **3,** (recite) recitar de memoria. —*n.,* *music* repetición. —**repeatedly,** *adv.* repetidamente.
repeater (ri'pi·tər) *n.* **1,** (one who repeats) repetidor. **2,** (firearm) arma de repetición. **3,** (watch) reloj de repetición.
repel (rɪ'pɛl) *v.t.* **1,** (drive back) repeler; rechazar. **2,** (resist) re-

sistir. 3, (arouse repulsion in) repugnar; repulsar. —*v.i.* ser repulsivo.
repellent (rɪ'pɛl·ənt) *adj.* 1, (resistant) impermeable. 2, (repulsive) repulsivo. —*n.* remedio repercusivo.
repent (rɪ'pɛnt) *v.t.* & *i.* arrepentirse (de). —**repentance,** *n.* arrepentimiento. —**repentant,** *adj.* penitente; arrepentido.
repercussion (ˌri·pər'kʌʃ·ən) *n.* 1, (result of an action) repercusión. 2, (echo) reverberación.
repertoire ('rɛp·ərˌtwar) *n.* repertorio.
repertory ('rɛp·ər·tor·i) *n.* 1, (repertoire) repertorio. 2, (inventory) inventario. —*adj.* de repertorio.
repetition (ˌrɛp·ə'tɪʃ·ən) *n.* repetición. —**repetitious,** *adj.* repetidor.
repine (rɪ'pain) *v.i.* quejarse; afligirse. —**repining,** *n.* queja. —*adj.* descontento.
replace (rɪ'pleis) *v.t.* 1, (put back) reponer. 2, (take the place of) reemplazar. 3, (substitute for) substituir.
replacement (rɪ'pleis·mənt) *n.* 1, (act of replacing) reemplazo. 2, (substitute) substituto. —**replacement part,** (pieza de) recambio.
replenish (rɪ'plɛn·ɪʃ) *v.t.* rellenar; llenar; abastecer. —**replenishment,** *n.* abastecimiento.
replete (rɪ'plit) *adj.* repleto; lleno. —**repletion** (rɪ'pli·ʃən) *n.* plenitud; repleción.
replica ('rɛp·lɪ·kə) *n.* réplica; duplicado.
reply (rɪ'plai) *v.t.* & *i.* responder; contestar; replicar. —*n.* respuesta; contestación.
repopulate (ri'pap·jəˌleit) *v.t.* repoblar. —**repopulation,** *n.* repoblación.
report (rɪ'port) *n.* 1, (account) relato; informe. 2, (rumor) rumor. 3, (reputation) fama; reputación. 4, *pl.* (record of court judgments) dictamen (*sing.*). 5, (sound of explosion) estallido; detonación. —*v.i.* 1, (serve as a reporter) ser reportero. 2, (present oneself) comparecer. —*v.t.* 1, (relate) relatar; reportar. 2, (say) contar. —**report card,** calificación ecolar periódica.
reportage (rɪ'por·tɪdʒ) *n.* reportaje.
reporter (ri'por·tər) *n.* reportero; periodista.
repose (rɪ'poːz) *n.* 1, (rest) reposo; descanso. 2, (tranquillity) paz. —*v.i.* 1, (lie at rest) reposar. 2, (be situated) situarse. 3, (rely) fiarse. —*v.t.* 1, (lay) tender. 2, (set at rest) recostar. 3, (place, as trust) confiar.
repository (rɪ'paz·ɪ·tor·i) *n.* repositorio; depósito.
repossess (ˌri·pə'zɛs) *v.t.* recobrar; recuperar. —**repossession** (-'zɛʃ·ən) *n.* recobro.
repoussé (rə·pu'sei) *adj.* & *n.* repujado.
reprehend (ˌrɛp·rɪ'hɛnd) *v.t.* reprender; regañar; censurar. —**reprehensible** (-'hɛns·ə·bəl) *adj.* censurable; reprensible. —**reprehension** (-'hɛn·ʃən) *n.* regaño; reprensión. —**reprehensive** (-'hɛn·sɪv) *adj.* reprensor.
represent (ˌrɛp·rɪ'zɛnt) *v.t.* representar. —**representation** (-zɛn·'tei·ʃən) *n.* representación.
representative (ˌrɛp·rɪ'zɛn·tə·tɪv) *adj.* 1, (serving to represent) representativo. 2, (typical) típico. —*n.* representante; delegado.
repress (rɪ'prɛs) *v.t.* reprimir. —**repression** (rɪ'prɛʃ·ən) *n.* represión. —**repressive,** *adj.* represivo.
reprieve (rɪ'priːv) *v.t.* 1, (grant a respite to) librar temporalmente; aliviar. 2, (delay the execution of) suspender la ejecución a. —*n.* 1, (respite) alivio; respiro. 2, (delay of execution) suspensión.
reprimand ('rɛp·rəˌmænd) *v.t.* reprender; censurar. —*n.* reprimenda.
reprint (ri'prɪnt) *v.t.* reimprimir. —*n.* ('ri-) 1, (new impression) reimpresión. 2, (separately printed excerpt) tirada aparte.
reprisal (rɪ'prai·zəl) *n.* represalia.
reproach (rɪ'protʃ) *v.t.* censurar; reprender; reprochar (algo a alguien). —*n.* reproche; censura. —**reproachful,** *adj.* reprensor.
reprobate ('rɛp·rəˌbeit) *adj.* & *n.* réprobo.
reproduce (ˌri·prə'dus) *v.t.* reproducir. —*v.i.* reproducirse; procrear. —**reproduction** (-'dʌk·ʃən) *n.* reproducción. —**reproductive** (-'dʌk·tɪv) *adj.* reproductivo.
reproof (rɪ'pruf) *n.* reproche; censura.

reprove (rɪ'pruːv) *v.t.* reprobar; censurar. —**reproval,** *n.* censura.
reprovision (ˌri·pro'vɪʒ·ən) *v.t.* repostar; abastecer.
reptile ('rɛp·tɪl) *n.* reptil.
reptilian (rɛp'tɪl·jən) *adj.* reptil.
republic (rɪ'pʌb·lɪk) *n.* república.
republican (rɪ'pʌb·lɪk·ən) *adj.* & *n.* republicano. —**republicanism,** *n.* republicanismo.
repudiate (rɪ'pju·diˌeit) *v.t.* repudiar. —**repudiation,** *n.* repudio; repudiación.
repugnance (rɪ'pʌg·nəns) *n.* repugnancia. —**repugnant,** *adj.* repugnante. —**be repugnant to,** repugnar a.
repulse (rɪ'pʌls) *v.t.* **1,** (repel) repeler; repulsar. **2,** (reject) rechazar. —*n.* **1,** (a driving back) repulsa; repulsión. **2,** (rejection) rechazo.
repulsion (rɪ'pʌl·ʃən) *n.* repulsión.
repulsive (rɪ'pʌl·sɪv) *adj.* **1,** (repelling) repulsivo. **2,** (offensive) repugnante.
reputable ('rɛp·jə·tə·bəl) *adj.* estimable; respetable; honrado. —**reputability,** *n.* estima; respetabilidad; honradez.
reputation (ˌrɛp·jə'tei·ʃən) *n.* reputación; fama; nombre.
repute (rɪ'pjut) *n.* reputación; estima; fama. —*v.t.* reputar; estimar. —**reputed,** *adj.* supuesto. —**reputedly,** *adv.* según la opinión común.
request (rɪ'kwɛst) *n.* **1,** (petition) ruego; petición; solicitud. **2,** (thing requested; order) pedido; encargo. —*v.t.* **1,** (ask for) rogar; pedir; solicitar. **2,** (order) pedir; encargar. —*adj.* pedido; a petición. —**on** *o* **upon request,** a pedido; a solicitud.
requiem ('ri·kwi·əm; 'rɛk·wi-) *n.* réquiem.
require (rɪ'kwair) *v.t.* **1,** (demand) requerir. **2,** (oblige; compel) exigir. **3,** (need) necesitar.
requirement (rɪ'kwair·mənt) *n.* **1,** (demand) requisito. **2,** (exigency) exigencia. **3,** (need) necesidad.
requisite ('rɛk·wə·zɪt) *adj.* necesario; esencial. —*n.* requisito.
requisition (ˌrɛk·wɪ'zɪʃ·ən) *n.* **1,** (demand) demanda. **2,** (written order) requisa; requisición. —*v.t.* **1,** (demand) exigir. **2,** (seize officially) requisar.
requital (rɪ'kwai·təl) *n.* **1,** (return) compensación. **2,** (retaliation) desquite.
requite (rɪ'kwait) *v.t.* **1,** (return; repay) devolver; corresponder a. **2,** (avenge) desquitarse de.
reread (ri'riːd) *v.t.* releer; leer otra vez. —**rereading,** *n.* nueva lectura.
resale (ri'seil; 'ri-) *n.* reventa.
rescind (rɪ'sɪnd) *v.t.* rescindir.
rescission (rɪ'sɪʒ·ən) *n.* rescisión.
rescript ('riˌskrɪpt) *n.* rescripto; edicto.
rescue ('rɛs·kju) *v.t.* **1,** (save from danger) salvar; librar; sacar de peligro. **2,** (deliver) rescatar; redimir; libertar. —*n.* **1,** (saving) salvamento; libramiento. **2,** (deliverance) rescate; redención; liberación.
research (rɪ'sʌɹtʃ) *n.* investigación. —*v.t.* & *i.* investigar. —**researcher,** *n.* investigador.
resell (ri'sɛl) *v.t.* [*pret.* & *p.p.* **-sold**] revender.
resemble (rɪ'zɛm·bəl) *v.t.* asemejarse a; parecerse a. —**resemblance** (-bləns) *n.* semejanza.
resent (rɪ'zɛnt) *v.t.* resentirse de *o* por; agraviarse de *o* por. —**resentful,** *adj.* resentido; agraviado. —**resentment,** *n.* resentimiento.
reservation (ˌrɛz·ər'vei·ʃən) *n.* **1,** (act of withholding) reservación. **2,** (thing withheld) reserva. **3,** (limiting condition) reserva. **4,** (restricted area) territorio reservado.
reserve (rɪ'zʌɹv) *v.t.* reservar. —*n.* **1,** (something kept for future use) reserva. **2,** = **reservation. 3,** (self-restraint) reserva; discreción. **4,** *mil.* reserva. —**reserved,** *adj.* reservado; discreto. —**reservist,** *n.* reservista.
reservoir ('rɛz·ərˌvwar) *n.* depósito; alberca.
reshape (ri'ʃeip) *v.t.* = **re-form.**
reship (ri'ʃɪp) *v.t.* **1,** (ship back or again) reembarcar. **2,** (forward) reexpedir; reenviar.
reshipment (ri'ʃɪp·mənt) *n.* **1,** (shipping back or again) reembarque. **2,** (forwarding) reexpedición; reenvío.
reside (rɪ'zaid) *v.i.* residir.
residence ('rɛz·ɪ·dəns) *n.* residencia. —**resident,** *n.* & *adj.* resi-

dente. —**residential** (-'dɛn·ʃəl) *adj.* residencial.

residue ('rɛz·ɪˌdju) *n.* residuo; sobrante; resto. —**residual** (rə·'zɪdʒ·u·əl) *adj.* restante; residual.

resign (rɪ'zain) *v.t.* **1,** (relinquish) renunciar. **2,** (give up, as an office or position) dimitir. **3,** (turn over to another) resignar. —*v.i.* dimitir; darse de baja. —**resign oneself,** resignarse; conformarse. —**resigned,** *adj.* resignado.

resignation (ˌrɛz·ɪg'nei·ʃən) *n.* **1,** (relinquishment) renuncia. **2,** (giving up, as of a position) dimisión. **3,** (submission) resignación; conformidad.

resilience (rɪ'zɪl·i·əns) *n.* **1,** (elasticity) elasticidad. **2,** (buoyancy) ánimo; viveza.

resilient (rɪ'zɪl·i·ənt) *adj.* **1,** (elastic) elástico. **2,** (buoyant) animoso; vivo.

resin ('rɛz·ɪn) *n.* resina. —**resinous,** *adj.* resinoso.

resist (rɪ'zɪst) *v.t.* resistir; resistir a; impedir. —*v.i.* resistirse; oponerse.

resistance (rɪ'zɪs·təns) *n.* resistencia. —**resistant,** *adj.* resistente.

resisti¨le (rɪ'zɪs·tə·bəl) *adj.* resistible.

resistor (rɪ'zɪs·tər) *n.* resistor.

resold (ri'sold) *v., pret. & p.p.* de **resell.**

resole (ri'so:l) *v.t.* remontar; poner suela a.

resolute ('rɛz·ə·lut) *adj.* resuelto; determinado; firme.

resolution (ˌrɛz·ə'lu·ʃən) *n.* resolución.

resolve (rɪ'zalv) *v.t.* resolver. —*v.i.* r ;olverse. —*n.* resolución. —**resolved,** *adj.* resuelto.

resonant ('rɛz·ə·nənt) *adj.* resonante. —**resonance,** *n.* resonancia.

resonate ('rɛz·əˌneit) *v.i.* resonar. —**resonator,** *n.* resonador.

resort (rɪ'zort) *v.i.* frecuentar; concurrir. —*n.* **1,** (vacation spot) sitio frecuentado; estación de veraneo, de esquí, etc. **2,** (recourse) recurso. —**resort to; have resort to,** recurrir a.

resound (rɪ'zaund) *v.i.* **1,** (reverberate) resonar. **2,** (emit loud sounds) retumbar.

resounding (rɪ'zaun·dɪŋ) *adj.* **1,** (ringing) resonante. **2,** (thorough) completo.

resource (rɪ'sors) *n.* recurso. —**resourceful,** *adj.* mañoso; hábil.

respect (rɪ'spɛkt) *v.t.* **1,** (heed) respetar; acatar. **2,** (honor) estimar; honrar. **3,** (relate to) respectar; tocar. —*n.* **1,** (high esteem) respeto; veneración. **2,** (relation; aspect) respecto. **3,** *pl.* (compliments) saludos. —**in** *o* **with respect to,** (con) respecto a.

respectable (rɪ'spɛk·tə·bəl) *adj.* **1,** (highly regarded) respetable. **2,** (decent) honroso. **3,** (fairly good or large) considerable. —**respectability,** *n.* respetabilidad.

respectful (rɪ'spɛkt·fəl) *adj.* respetuoso. —**respectfully,** *adv.* respetuosamente. —**respectfully yours,** de Vd. atento y seguro servidor.

respecting (rɪ'spɛk·tɪŋ) *prep.* respecto a; tocante a.

respective (rɪ'spɛk·tɪv) *adj.* respectivo. —**respectively,** *adv.* respectivamente.

respiration (ˌrɛs·pə'rei·ʃən) *n.* respiración.

respirator ('rɛs·pəˌrei·tər) *n.* **1,** (breathing device) respirador. **2,** (breathing mask) máscara respiradora.

respiratory (rə'spair·ə·tor·i) *adj.* respiratorio.

respire (rɪ'spair) *v.i. & t.* respirar.

respite ('rɛs·pɪt) *n.* **1,** (pause) respiro; :poso. **2,** (postponement) prórroga; suspensión.

resplendent (rɪ'splɛn·dənt) *adj.* resplandeciente. —**resplendence,** *n.* resplandor.

respond (rɪ'spand) *v.i.* **1,** (answer) responder; contestar. **2,** (react) reaccionar.

respondent (rɪ'span·dənt) *adj.* simpático; respondedor. —*n.* respondedor; *law* demandado.

response (rɪ'spans) *n.* **1,** (answer) respuesta; contestación; réplica. **2,** (reaction) reacción.

responsible (rɪ'span·sə·bəl) *adj.* **1,** (answerable) responsable. **2,** (entailing trust) de responsabilidad. —**responsibility,** *n.* responsabilidad.

responsive (rɪ'span·sɪv) *adj.* **1,** (answering) responsivo; respondedor. **2,** (consisting of responses) antifonal.

rest (rɛst) *n.* **1,** (repose) descanso; reposo. **2,** (support) soporte. **3,** *music* pausa. **4,** (remainder) resto;

sobrante. —*v.i.* **1,** (cease action) parar; cesar; descansar. **2,** (be tranquil) reposar. **3,** (be supported) apoyarse. **4,** (remain) estar; quedar; permanecer. **5,** (trust) depender (de). —*v.t.* **1,** (place at rest) calmar. **2,** (place) poner; apoyar; descansar. **3,** (allow to stand) colocar. **4,** *law* terminar. —**resting,** *n.* reposo. —**resting place,** descansadero. —**rest room,** excusado; retrete; baño.

restaurant ('rɛs·tə·rənt) *n.* restaurante. —**restaurateur** (-rə'tʌɹ) *n.* dueño de restaurante.

restful ('rɛst·fəl) *adj.* quieto; tranquilo; reposado.

restitution (ˌrɛs·tə'tju·ʃən) *n.* **1,** (act of returning) restitución. **2,** (act of making amends) indemnización. **3,** (restoration) restablecimiento.

restive ('rɛs·tɪv) *adj.* **1,** (uneasy) inquieto. **2,** (recalcitrant) terco; (*of a horse*) repropio.

restiveness ('rɛs·tɪv·nəs) *n.* **1,** (uneasiness) inquietud. **2,** (recalcitrance) terquedad.

restless ('rɛst·ləs) *adj.* desasosegado; inquieto. —**restlessness,** *n.* desasosiego; inquietud.

restock (ri'stak) *v.t.* **1,** (replenish) rellenar; abastecer. **2,** (restore fish and game to) repoblar.

restoration (ˌrɛs·tə'rei·ʃən) *n.* restauración.

restorative (rɪ'stor·ə·tɪv) *n.* & *adj.* restaurativo.

restore (rɪ'stoːr) *v.t.* **1,** (bring back) restaurar. **2,** (cure) curar. **3,** (renew) restablecer. **4,** (return to the owner) devolver; restituir.

restrain (rɪ'strein) *v.t.* **1,** (hinder) refrenar; impedir. **2,** (moderate; temper) cohibir. **3,** (limit) limitar; restringir.

restraint (rɪ'streint) *n.* **1,** (hindrance) refrenamiento. **2,** (self-control) cohibición; continencia. **3,** (limitation) limitación; restricción.

restrict (rɪ'strɪkt) *v.t.* restringir; limitar. —**restriction** (rɪ'strɪk·ʃən) *n.* restricción. —**restrictive,** *adj.* restrictivo.

result (rɪ'zʌlt) *v.i.* resultar. —*n.* resultado; resulta. —**resultant,** *adj.* & *n.* resultante. —**as a result (of),** de resultas (de).

resume (rɪ'zuːm) *v.t.* reasumir; reanudar. —*v.i.* seguir; continuar.

résumé (ˌrɛz·u'mei) *n.* resumen; sumario.

resumption (rɪ'zʌmp·ʃən) *n.* reasunción.

resurge (rɪ'sʌɹdʒ) *v.i.* resurgir. —**resurgence,** *n.* resurgimiento.

resurrect (ˌrɛz·ə'rɛkt) *v.t.* **1,** (restore to life) resucitar. **2,** (disinter) desenterrar.

resurrection (ˌrɛz·ə'rɛk·ʃən) *n.* **1,** (returning to life) resurrección. **2,** (disinterment) desentierro.

resuscitate (rɪ'sʌs·əˌteit) *v.t.* & *i.* resucitar. —**resuscitation,** *n.* resucitación.

retable (rɪ'tei·bəl) *n.* retablo.

retail ('ri·teil) *n.* venta al por menor; reventa. —*adj.* al por menor. —*v.t.* **1,** (sell direct to consumer) vender al por menor; revender; detallar. **2,** (tell in detail) contar en detalle; detallar. —*v.i.* venderse al por menor; revenderse; detallarse. —**retailer,** *n.* vendedor al por menor; revendedor; detallista.

retain (rɪ'tein) *v.t.* **1,** (hold) retener. **2,** (remember) recordar. **3,** (hire) contratar.

retainer (rɪ'tei·nər) *n.* **1,** (person or thing that retains) retenedor. **2,** (servant) criado; dependiente. **3,** (follower) adherente. **4,** (fee) honorario. —**retaining wall,** pared de sostén *o* retención.

retake (ri'teik) *v.t.* [*infl.:* **take**] volver a tomar; repetir (la toma). —*n.* ('ri-) nueva toma; toma repetida.

retaliate (rɪ'tæl·iˌeit) *v.i.* vengarse; desquitarse. —*v.t.* devolver; pagar. —**retaliation,** *n.* venganza; desquite; represalia. —**retaliative** (-ə·tɪv); **retaliatory** (-ə·tor·i) *adj.* vengativo.

retard (rɪ'tard) *v.t.* **1,** (slow down) retardar; retrasar. **2,** (defer) aplazar. —**retardation** (ˌri·tar'dei·ʃən) *n.* retardo; atraso.

retch (rɛtʃ) *v.i.* esforzarse por vomitar; arquear. —**retching,** *n.* arqueada.

retell (ri'tɛl) *v.t.* [*pret.* & *p.p.* **-told**] recontar; volver a contar *o* decir.

retention (rɪ'tɛn·ʃən) *n.* retención —**retentive** (-tɪv) *adj.* retentivo. —**retentiveness,** *n.* retentiva.

reticent ('rɛt·ə·sənt) *adj.* reticente; reservado. —**reticence,** *n.* reticencia; reserva.

retina ('rɛt·ɪ·nə) *n.* retina.
retinue ('rɛt·ə,nju) *n.* comitiva; séquito.
retire (rɪ'tair) *v.i.* **1,** (retreat) retroceder. **2,** (take refuge) refugiarse. **3,** (withdraw) retirarse. **4,** (be pensioned off) jubilarse. **5,** (go to bed) acostarse. —*v.t.* **1,** (withdraw) retirar. **2,** (relieve of duty) separar. **3,** (pension off) jubilar. **4,** (withdraw from circulation) recoger. —**retirement,** *n.* retiro; jubilación.
retired (rɪ'taird) *adj.* **1,** (having discontinued work) retirado; jubilado. **2,** (secluded) aislado; apartado.
retiring (rɪ'tair·ɪŋ) *adj.* retraído; recatado; recoleto.
retold (ri'told) *v., pret. & p.p. de* **retell.**
retook (ri'tʊk) *v., pret. de* **retake.**
retort (rɪ'tort) *v.t.* **1,** (return; turn back) devolver. **2,** (reply sharply) contestar mordazmente. —*v.i.* replicar. —*n.* **1,** (retaliatory remark) réplica. **2,** (glass vessel) retorta.
retouch (ri'tʌtʃ) *v.t.* retocar. —*n.* retoque.
retrace (ri'treis) *v.t.* **1,** (go back over) repasar. **2,** (trace again) trazar de nuevo. —**retrace one's steps,** volver sobre sus pasos.
retract (rɪ'trækt) *v.t.* **1,** (draw back) retraer. **2,** (take back; recant) retractar. —*v.i.* **1,** (shrink back) encogerse. **2,** (recant) retractarse.
retraction (rɪ'træk·ʃən) *n.* retracción.
retractor (rɪ'træk·tər) *n.* **1,** *anat.* músculo retractor. **2,** *surg.* retractor.
retread (ri'trɛd) *v.t.* **1,** (walk through again) caminar de nuevo; repasar; volver por. **2,** (put new tread on, as a tire) recauchar; recauchutar. —*n.* ('ri-) **1,** (act or result of retreading) recauchaje. **2,** (a tire so treated) neumático recauchado.
retreat (rɪ'trit) *n.* **1,** (withdrawal) retirada. **2,** (seclusion; secluded place) retiro. **3,** (asylum) asilo. **4,** *mil.* retreta. —*v.i.* retirarse. —**beat a retreat,** retirarse.
retrench (rɪ'trɛntʃ) *v.t.* cercenar; disminuir. —*v.i.* economizar; reducirse. —**retrenchment,** *n.* rebaja; economía; cercenadura.
retrial (ri'trai·əl) *n.* nuevo proceso.
retribution (,rɛt·rə'bju·ʃən) *n.* retribución; justo castigo. —**retributive** (rɪ'trɪb·ju·tɪv) *adj.* retributivo.
retrieve (rɪ'tri:v) *v.t.* recuperar; recobrar; restaurar. —*v.i.* cobrar la caza. —**retrieval,** *n.* recuperación; recobro.
retriever (rɪ'triv·ər) *n.* perro cobrador; perdiguero.
retro- (rɛt·ro) *prefijo* retro-. **1,** atrás (*en tiempo o espacio*): *retrospection,* retrospección. **2,** anterior: *retroactive,* retroactivo.
retroactive *adj.* retroactivo. —**retroactivity,** *n.* retroactividad.
retrogradation *n.* **1,** (moving backward) retroceso. **2,** *astron.* retrogradación.
retrograde ('rɛt·rə,greid) *adj.* retrógrado. —*v.i.* **1,** (move backward) retroceder. **2,** *astron.* retrogradar.
retrogress ('rɛt·rə,grɛs) *v.i.* retrogradar. —**retrogression** (-'grɛʃ·ən) *n.* retrogresión. —**retrogressive** (-'grɛs·ɪv) *adj.* retrógrado.
retrospect ('rɛt·rə,spɛkt) *n.* mirada retrospectiva; retrospección. —**retrospective** (-'spɛk·tɪv) *adj.* retrospectivo. —**retrospection** (-'spɛk·ʃən) *n.* retrospección. —**in retrospect,** retrospectivamente.
retry (ri'trai) *v.t.* [*infl.:* **try**] procesar de nuevo.
return (rɪ'tʌɹn) *v.i.* **1,** (go or come back) volver; retornar; regresar. **2,** (recur) recurrir. **3,** (reply) replicar. —*v.t.* **1,** (give back; restore) devolver; restituir. **2,** (repay, as a kindness) corresponder a. **3,** (repay) pagar. **4,** (report, as a verdict) dar (un fallo). **5,** (elect) elegir. **6,** (yield, as a profit) producir; rentar. —*n.* **1,** (giving back; restoring) devolución; restitución. **2,** (recurrence) repetición. **3,** (going or coming back) regreso; vuelta. **4,** (profit) rédito; ganancia. **5,** (reply) réplica; respuesta. **6,** (report) informe. —*adj.* de vuelta. —**returns,** *n.pl.* resultados; noticias. —**by return mail,** a vuelta de correo. —**in return,** en cambio. —**return match,** desquite. —**return ticket,** billete de ida y vuelta; billete de vuelta.
reunion (ri'jun·jən) *n.* reunión.

reunite (ri·ju'nait) *v.t.* reunir. —*v.i.* reunirse.
revamp (ri'væmp) *v.t.* renovar.
reveal (rɪ'viːl) *v.t.* revelar; divulgar; descubrir.
reveille ('rɛv·ə·li) *n.* diana.
revel ('rɛv·əl) *v.i.* **1,** (carouse) jaranear. **2,** (delight) deleitarse; gozarse. —*n.* jarana; bacanal; juerga. —**reveler,** *n.* calavera; juerguista. —**revelry,** *n.* jarana; juerga.
revelation (ˌrɛv·ə'lei·ʃən) *n.* **1,** (disclosure) revelación. **2,** *cap., Bib.* Apocalipsis.
revenge (rɪ'vɛndʒ) *v.t.* vengar. —*n.* venganza. —**revengeful,** *adj.* vengativo. —**take revenge,** vengarse.
revenue ('rɛv·əˌnju) *n.* **1,** (personal income) renta; rédito. **2,** (government income) rentas públicas. —**revenue officer,** agente fiscal.
reverberate (rɪ'vʌɹ·bəˌreit) *v.i.* reverberar; retumbar; repercutir. —**reverberation,** *n.* retumbo; reverbero; reverberación.
revere (rɪ'vɪr) *v.t.* venerar; reverenciar.
reverence ('rɛv·ər·əns) *n.* **1,** (veneration) reverencia; veneración. **2,** *cap.* (title of clergy) Reverencia. **3,** (bow) reverencia. —*v.t.* venerar; reverenciar. —**do reverence,** rendir homenaje.
reverend ('rɛv·ər·ənd) *adj.* reverendo; venerable. —*n., colloq.* reverendo; pastor.
reverent ('rɛv·ər·ənt) *adj.* **1,** (respectful) reverente. **2,** (devout) devoto. —**reverential** (-'ɛn·ʃəl) *adj.* reverencial.
reverie ('rɛv·ə·ri) *n.* ensueño.
reversal (rɪ'vʌɹ·səl) *n.* **1,** (turning about; changing to the opposite) inversión; cambio a lo contrario. **2,** *law* revocación.
reverse (rɪ'vʌɹs) *adj.* invertido; opuesto. —*n.* **1,** (a change to the opposite) reversión; inversión. **2,** (setback) revés; descalabro; contratiempo. **3,** (opposite) lo opuesto; lo contrario. **4,** (other side; back) revés; reverso. **5,** (backward motion) marcha atrás. —*v.t.* **1,** (turn about) invertir. **2,** (cause to move backward) dar marcha atrás; poner en marcha atrás. **3,** *law* (set aside; annul) revocar; anular. —*v.i.* invertirse; cambiarse a lo contrario. —**reverse gear,** marcha atrás. —**reverse oneself,** cambiar de opinión.
reversible (rɪ'vʌɹ·sə·bəl) *adj.* **1,** (that can be turned or changed about) reversible. **2,** (two-sided) de dos caras. **3,** *law* revocable. —**reversibility,** *n.* reversibilidad.
reversion (rɪ'vʌɹ·ʃən) *n.* **1,** (act of reverting) reversión. **2,** (right of future possession) derecho de sucesión. —**reversionary,** *adj.* de *o* por reversión.
revert (rɪ'vʌɹt) *v.i.* retroceder; revertir; recurrir.
revet (rɪ'vɛt) *v.t.* revestir. —**revetment,** *n.* revestimiento.
review (rɪ'vjuː) *n.* **1,** (examination) examen. **2,** (survey of past events) repaso. **3,** (critical report) juicio crítico; reseña. **4,** *mil.* (parade) revista; parada. **5,** *law* (reconsideration) revisión. **6,** (journal) revista. —*v.t.* **1,** (look back on) ver de nuevo; recordar. **2,** (examine again) repasar; revisar. **3,** (write an evaluation of) reseñar; criticar. **4,** *mil.* pasar revista.
reviewer (rɪ'vju·ər) *n.* **1,** (examiner) examinador; revisor. **2,** (critic) crítico.
revile (rɪ'vail) *v.t.* vituperar; vilipendiar. —**revilement,** *n.* contumelia; oprobio; vilipendio.
revise (rɪ'vaiz) *v.t.* revisar; corregir; refundir. —**revision** (rɪ'vɪʒ·ən) *n.* revisión; corrección; refundición.
revival (rɪ'vaiv·əl) *n.* **1,** (resuscitation) resucitación; reanimación. **2,** (restoration) restauración; restablecimiento. **3,** (renascence) renacimiento. **4,** *theat.* reposición. **5,** (religious awakening) despertamiento religioso.
revive (rɪ'vaiv) *v.t.* **1,** (resuscitate) resucitar; reanimar. **2,** (restore; renew) restaurar; restablecer. **3,** (reawaken) despertar. **4,** *theat.* reponer. —*v.i.* **1,** (come back to life or consciousness) resucitar; reanimarse. **2,** (be restored or renewed) restablecerse; renovarse; renacer. **3,** (reawaken) despertarse.
revocation (ˌrɛv·ə'kei·ʃən) *n.* revocación; derogación.
revoke (rɪ'vok) *v.t.* revocar. —*v.i. cards* renunciar. —*n., cards* renuncio.
revolt (rɪ'volt) *v.i.* **1,** (rebel) rebelarse. **2,** (feel revulsion) tener repugnancia; tener asco. —*v.t.* re-

pugnar; dar asco a. —*n.* revuelta; sublevación; rebelión. —**revolting,** *adj.* repulsivo; repugnante; asqueroso.

revolution (ˌrɛv·əˈlu·ʃən) *n.* revolución. —**revolutionary,** *adj.* & *n.* revolucionario. —**revolutionist,** *n.* revolucionario. —**revolutionize,** *v.t.* revolucionar.

revolve (rɪˈvalv) *v.i.* **1,** (rotate) rodar; revolverse. **2,** (move about a center) girar. **3,** (recur) suceder periódicamente. —*v.t.* **1,** (turn) voltear; hacer girar. **2,** (turn over in the mind) revolver. —**revolving,** *adj.* giratorio; rotativo. —**revolving door,** puerta giratoria. —**revolving fund,** fondo rotativo.

revolver (rɪˈval·vər) *n.* revólver.

revue (rɪˈvjuː) *n.* revista musical.

revulsion (rɪˈvʌl·ʃən) *n.* revulsión; repugnancia.

reward (rɪˈword) *v.t.* **1,** (recompense) recompensar. **2,** (give in return for) premiar. —*n.* **1,** (recompense) recompensa. **2,** (prize) premio. **3,** (profit) remuneración. **4,** (cash award) gratificación.

reword (riˈwʌɹd) *v.t.* decir *o* escribir en otras palabras.

rewrite (riˈrait) *v.t.* **1,** (write over) escribir de nuevo. **2,** (revise) corregir; refundir. —*n.* (ˈri-) escrito corregido; refundición.

-rhage (rədʒ) *sufijo, var. de* **-rrhage.**

rhapsodic (ræpˈsad·ɪk) *adj.* rapsódico.

rhapsodize (ˈræp·səˌdaiz) *v.t.* decir *o* cantar extáticamente. —*v.i.* expresarse extáticamente.

rhapsody (ˈræp·sə·di) *n.* rapsodia.

-rhea (ri·ə) *sufijo, var. de.* **-rrhea.**

rhenium (ˈri·ni·əm) *n.* renio.

rheo- (ri·o; -ə) *prefijo* reo-; corriente; flujo: *rheometer,* reómetro.

rheostat (ˈri·əˌstæt) *n.* reóstato.

rhesus (ˈri·səs) *n.* macaco de la India. *También,* **rhesus monkey.**

rhetoric (ˈrɛt·ə·rɪk) *n.* retórica. —**rhetorical** (rəˈtor·ɪ·kəl) *adj.* retórico. —**rhetorician** (-ˈrɪʃ·ən) *n.* retórico.

rheum (ruːm) *n.* legaña; catarro. —**rheumy,** *adj.* legañoso; catarroso.

rheumatic (ruˈmæt·ɪk) *adj.* & *n.* reumático. —**rheumatism** (ˈru·mə·tɪz·əm) *n.* reumatismo.

rhinestone (ˈrainˌston) *n.* diamante de imitación.

rhino (ˈrai·no) *n.* [*pl.* **-nos**] = **rhinoceros.**

rhino- (rai·no; -nə) *prefijo* rino-; nariz: *rhinoplasty,* rinoplastia.

rhinoceros (raiˈnas·ər·əs) *n.* rinoceronte.

rhizo- (rai·zo; -zə) *prefijo* rizo-; raíz: *rhizopod,* rizópodo.

rhodium (ˈro·di·əm) *n.* rodio.

rhododendron (ˌro·dəˈdɛn·drən) *n.* rododendro.

rhomboid (ˈram·bɔid) *n.* romboide.

rhombus (ˈram·bəs) *n.* rombo.

rhubarb (ˈru·barb) *n.* **1,** *bot.* ruibarbo. **2,** *slang* (noisy protest) barahúnda.

rhyme *también,* **rime** (raim) *n.* rima. —*v.t.* & *i.* rimar. —**rhymer,** *n.* rimador; versista. —**without rhyme or reason,** sin ton ni son.

rhythm (ˈrɪð·əm) *n.* ritmo. —**rhythmic** (-mɪk); **rhythmical,** *adj.* rítmico.

rialto (riˈæl·to) *n.* **1,** (theatrical district) distrito teatral, esp. de Nueva York. 2, (market place) mercado, esp. el Rialto de Venecia.

riata (riˈa·ta) *n.* reata.

rib (rɪb) *n.* **1,** *anat.* costilla. **2,** *bot.* nervio grueso; costilla. **3,** (supporting beam) viga; listón. **4,** (thin rod, as of an umbrella frame) varilla. —*v.t.* **1,** (support with ribs) afianzar con vigas; listonear. **2,** (mark with lines or ridges) marcar con rayas; rayar. **3,** (flute; corrugate) acanalar. **4,** *colloq.* (tease) bromarse de; tomar el pelo a.

ribald (ˈrɪb·əld) *adj.* lascivo; obsceno. —**ribaldry,** obscenidad; indecencia.

ribbed (rɪbd) *adj.* **1,** (marked with lines or ridges) rayado. **2,** (fluted; corrugated) acanalado. **3,** (veined) nervudo.

ribbon (ˈrɪb·ən) *n.* **1,** (band; tape) cinta. **2,** *pl.* (shreds) harapos; jirones. —*adj.* de *o* como cinta.

-ric (rɪk) *sufijo; forma nombres indicando* cargo; jurisdicción: *bishopric,* obispado.

rice (rais) *n.* arroz. —*v.t.* desmenuzar. —**ricer,** *n.* aparato para desmenuzar comestibles. —**rice field,** arrozal.

rich (rɪtʃ) *adj.* **1,** (wealthy) rico; opulento. **2,** (abounding) abundante; copioso. **3,** (fertile) fértil. **4,** (luxurious) lujoso; elegante. **5,**

(vivid) vivo. **6,** (succulent) suculento; rico. **7,** *colloq.* (preposterous) ridículo. **8,** *colloq.* (amusing) divertido.
riches ('ritʃ·əs) *n.pl.* riqueza (*sing.*); opulencia (*sing.*).
richness ('rɪtʃ·nəs) *n.* **1,** (wealth) riqueza. **2,** (luxury) lujo; elegancia. **3,** (vividness) viveza. **4,** (succulence) suculencia.
rick (rɪk) *n.* almiar; montón de paja, heno, etc.
rickets ('rɪk·ɪts) *n.* raquitismo.
rickety (rɪk·ə·ti) *adj.* **1,** (shaky) tambaleante; destartalado. **2,** (affected with rickets) raquítico.
rickey ('rɪk·i) *n.* coctel de ginebra.
ricochet (ˌrɪk·ə'ʃei) *n.* rebote. —*v.i.* rebotar.
rid (rɪd) *v.t.* [**rid, ridding**] desembarazar; librar. —*adj.* librado; libre; exento. —**riddance,** *n.* libramiento. —**be rid of,** estar libre de. —**get rid of,** desembarazarse de; deshacerse de.
ridden ('rɪd·ən) *v., p.p. de* **ride.**
riddle ('rɪd·əl) *n.* **1,** (enigma) acertijo; adivinanza; enigma. **2,** (sieve) criba. —*v.t.* **1,** (fill with holes) acribillar. **2,** (sift) cribar.
ride (raid) *v.i.* [**rode, ridden, riding**] **1,** (be carried) montar; ir montado. **2,** (float, as a ship) flotar. **3,** (move on or about something) pasear; correr. **4,** (be a passenger) viajar. **5,** (function, as a vehicle) marchar; funcionar. —*v.t.* **1,** (be carried by; guide) montar. **2,** (float on) flotar sobre. **3,** (travel on or over) pasar por; recorrer. **4,** (oppress) tiranizar. **5,** (harass) acosar; perseguir. **6,** *colloq.* (tease) bromarse de; tomar el pelo a. —*n.* paseo. —**ride out,** aguantar; soportar.
rider ('raid·ər) *n.* **1,** (traveler on horseback) jinete. **2,** (passenger) pasajero. **3,** (clause added to a document) hojuela pegada a un documento.
ridge (rɪdʒ) *n.* **1,** (crest) lomo. **2,** (hill) cerro. **3,** (mountain range) cordillera. **4,** (crease) arruga. **5,** *archit.* caballete. **6,** (mound of earth, as raised by a plow) caballón.
ridicule ('rɪd·əˌkjul) *n.* irrisión. —*v.t.* ridiculizar; poner en ridículo.
ridiculous (rɪ'dɪk·jə·ləs) *adj.* ridículo. —**ridiculousness,** *n.* ridiculez.
riding ('rai·dɪŋ) *v., ger. de* **ride.** —*n.* **1,** (traveling) paseo; viaje. **2,** (horsemanship) equitación. —**riding boots,** botas de montar. —**riding coat,** redingote. —**riding habit,** vestido de montar.
rife (raif) *adj.* abundante; corriente; común.
riffle ('rɪf·əl) *n.* **1,** (ripple) onda; rizo. **2,** *cards* cierta manera de barajar cartas. **3,** (set of grooves, as in a sluice) ranuras (*pl.*). —*v.t.* barajar.
riffraff ('rɪfˌræf) *n.* **1,** (rubbish) desperdicio. **2,** (rabble) gentuza; canalla.
rifle ('rai·fəl) *v.t.* **1,** (ransack) robar; pillar. **2,** (cut spiral grooves in) rayar. —*n.* fusil; rifle.
rifleman ('rai·fəl·mən) *n.* [*pl.* **-men**] fusilero; riflero.
rift (rɪft) *n.* **1,** (crack) hendedura; grieta. **2,** (disagreement) desavenencia. —*v.t.* hender; partir. —*v.i.* partirse.
rig (rɪg) *v.t.* [**rigged, rigging**] **1,** (equip) aparejar; equipar. **2,** (dress) ataviar; vestir. **3,** (fix arbitrarily) arreglar; manejar. —*n.* **1,** (equipment) aparejo. **2,** (attire) traje. **3,** (carriage) carruaje; coche. —**rigger,** *n.* aparejador. —**rigging,** *n.* aparejo; avíos (*pl.*).
right (rait) *adj.* **1,** (just) recto; justo. **2,** (correct) correcto. **3,** (proper) propio; adecuado; conveniente. **4,** (in good condition) en buen estado. **5,** (well-ordered) bien arreglado. **6,** (pert. to a certain side) derecho. **7,** (conservative) conservador. **8,** (direct) derecho; directo. **9,** *geom.* recto; rectángulo. —*adv.* **1,** (justly) justamente. **2,** (correctly) correctamente. **3,** (properly) propiamente; debidamente. **4,** (exactly) exactamente. **5,** (very) precisamente. **6,** (toward the right) a *o* hacia la derecha. **7,** (directly) directamente. —*n.* **1,** (direction; side) derecha. **2,** (conformity) conformidad. **3,** (that which conforms to a rule) rectitud. **4,** (just claim) derecho. **5,** *polit.* derecha; partido conservador. —*v.t.* **1,** (set straight) enderezar. **2,** (correct) corregir; rectificar. **3,** (vindicate) vindicar. —*v.i.* enderezarse. —*interj.* ¡bien!; ¡bueno! —**all right,** muy bien. —**be**

all right, estar bien. —be right; be in the right, tener razón. —by right (*o* rights), debidamente; con justicia. —put to right (*o* rights), arreglar; rectificar; poner en orden. —right away, en seguida. —right here, aquí mismo. —right now, ahora mismo.

rightabout *adv.* media vuelta.

right-angled *adj.* rectángulo.

righteous ('rai·tʃəs) *adj.* virtuoso; recto. —**righteousness**, *n.* virtud; rectitud.

rightful ('rait·fəl) *adj.* justo; legítimo. —**rightfulness**, *n.* justicia; legitimidad.

righthand *adj.* derecho; de *o* a la derecha. —**righthand man**, brazo derecho.

righthanded *adj.* **1,** (preferring the right hand) que usa la mano derecha. **2,** (done with the right hand) con la derecha. **3,** (toward the right) a la derecha. —*adv.* con la derecha.

rightist ('rai·tɪst) *adj.* & *n.* derechista.

rightly ('rait·li) *adv.* **1,** (correctly) correctamente; debidamente. **2,** (justly) con razón; justamente; a justo título.

right-minded *adj.* justo; recto.

rightness ('rait·nəs) *n.* justicia; rectitud.

right of way **1,** (precedence over another) precedencia; derecho de paso. **2,** (legal passage across property) servidumbre de paso. **3,** *R.R.* servidumbre de vía.

rightwing *adj.* derechista.

rigid ('rɪdʒ·ɪd) *adj.* **1,** (stiff) rígido; tieso. **2,** (strict) preciso; estricto. —**rigidity** (rɪ'dʒɪd·ə·ti) *n.* rigidez.

rigmarole ('rɪg·mə,rol) *n.* jerigonza.

rigor ('rɪg·ər) *n.* rigor. —**rigorous**, *adj.* riguroso. —**rigorousness**, *n.* rigurosidad.

rigor mortis (,rɪg·ər'mor·tɪs) rigidez de la muerte.

rile (rail) *v.t., colloq.* molestar; irritar.

rill (rɪl) *n.* riachuelo; regato.

rim (rɪm) *n.* **1,** (edge) margen; borde; orilla. **2,** (outer part of a wheel) llanta. **3,** (mounting for a tire) aro.

rime (raim) *n.* **1,** = **rhyme**. **2,** (hoarfrost) escarcha. —*v.t.* & *i.* = **rhyme**. —**rimy**, *adj.* escarchado.

rind (raind) *n.* corteza.

ring (rɪŋ) *v.i.* **[rang, rung, ringing]** **1,** (sound, as a bell) sonar; tañer. **2,** (resound; sound loudly) resonar; retumbar. **3,** (signal with a bell) llamar; tocar. **4,** (hum, as the ears) zumbar. **5,** [*pret.* & *p.p.* **ringed**] (form or move in a circle) formar círculo; moverse en círculo. —*v.t.* **1,** (cause to sound) sonar; tocar; tañer; repicar. **2,** (proclaim, as with ringing of bells) proclamar; anunciar. **3,** [*también*, **ring for**] (summon with a bell) llamar. **4,** [*también, Brit.* **ring up**] (call on the telephone) llamar por teléfono. **5,** [*pret.* & *p.p.* **ringed**] (encircle) cercar; roder. —*n.* **1,** (sound of a bell) toque; repique; tañido; sonido. **2,** (telephone call) llamada; timbrazo. **3,** (circle) círculo. **4,** (circular band) anillo; aro; argolla. **5,** (band worn on the finger) anillo; sortija. **6,** (arena) arena; circo. **7,** (bull ring) redondel. **8,** (boxing ring) cuadrilátero. **9,** (group) círculo; corro; cuadrilla. **10,** (gang) pandilla. **11,** *pl.* (puffiness under the eyes) ojeras. **12,** (characteristic impression or effect) tono; sonido. —*adj.* anular. —**ring familiar**; **have a familiar ring**, sonarle a uno. —**ring finger**, dedo anular. —**ring in**, substituir por otro; introducir fraudulentamente.

ringdove ('rɪŋ,dʌv) *n.* paloma torcaz.

ringer ('rɪŋ·ər) *n.* **1,** (person who rings a bell) campanero. **2,** *slang* (likeness) parecido; retrato. **3,** *slang* (fraudulent substitute) substituto; intruso.

ringing ('rɪŋ·ɪŋ) *adj.* resonante; sonoro; que suena. —*n.* **1,** (sound of a bell) campaneo; repique; retintín. **2,** (humming in the ears) zumbido.

ringleader *n.* cabecilla.

ringlet ('rɪŋ·lɪt) *n.* rizo; bucle.

ringworm *n.* tiña; empeine.

rink (rɪŋk) *n.* patinadero.

rinse (rɪns) *v.t.* enjuagar; aclarar. —*n.* enjuague.

riot ('rai·ət) *n.* **1,** (mob action) tumulto; alboroto; motín. **2,** (revelry) jarana. **3,** (confusion) confusión. —*v.i.* alborotar. —**rioter**, *n.* alborotador. —**riotous**, *adj.* alborotoso.

rip (rɪp) *v.t.* **[ripped, ripping]** **1,**

(tear) rasgar; rajar. **2,** (saw with the grain) aserrar en la dirección de la fibra. **3,** *colloq.* (utter forcefully) explotar; soltar. **4,** *sewing* descoser. —*v.i.* **1,** (be torn) rasgarse. **2,** *colloq.* (rush) avanzar de cabeza. —*n.* **1,** (tear) rasgón. **2,** *sewing* descosido. **3,** *colloq.* (roué) pícaro. —**ripper,** *n.* rasgador.

ripe (raip) *adj.* **1,** (mature) maduro. **2,** (in best condition) acabado; a punto. **3,** (ready) preparado. —**ripen,** *v.t. & i.* madurar. —**ripeness,** *n.* madurez.

ripple ('rɪp·əl) *n.* **1,** (small wave) rizo. **2,** (murmur) murmullo. —*v.t.* rizar. —*v.i.* **1,** (undulate) rizarse. **2,** (murmur) murmurar.

riproaring *adj., slang* bullicioso.

ripsaw *n.* sierra de hender.

riptide *n.* contracorriente fuerte.

rise (raiz) *v.i.* [**rose, risen** ('rɪz·ən)] **1,** (move upward) subir. **2,** (stand up) levantarse; ponerse en pie. **3,** (get out of bed) levantarse. **4,** (slope upward) ascender. **5,** (swell, as dough) fermentarse; crecer. **6,** (emerge) salir; nacer; asomar; surgir. **7,** (increase, as in value) mejorar. **8,** (rebel) rebelarse. **9,** (return to life) resucitar. —*n.* **1,** (ascent) ascención; subida. **2,** (degree of ascent) inclinación. **3,** (elevation) elevación; altura. **4,** (origin) origen. **5,** (increase) aumento. **6,** (advancement in position) ascenso. —**early riser,** madrugador. —**get a rise out of,** despertar; animar. —**rise above,** sobreponerse a; vencer.

risible ('rɪz·ə·bəl) *adj.* risible. —**risibility,** *n.* risibilidad.

rising ('rai·zɪŋ) *n.* **1,** (ascent) subida. **2,** (insurrection) insurrección. **3,** (swelling, as of dough) fermento. **4,** (rebirth) renacimiento. —*adj.* **1,** (ascendant) ascendiente. **2,** (growing) creciente. **3,** (coming up, as the sun) saliente.

risk (rɪsk) *n.* **1,** (peril) riesgo; peligro. **2,** (chance) albur. —*v.t.* **1,** (expose to loss) arriesgar. **2,** (take a chance of) aventurar. **3,** (try one's luck in) arriesgarse en. —**risky,** *adj.* arriesgado.

risqué (rɪs'kei) *adj.* escabroso; atrevido.

rite (rait) *n.* rito; ceremonia.

ritual ('rɪtʃ·u·əl) *adj.* ritual. —*n.* ritual; rito. —**ritualistic** (-ə'lɪs·tɪk) *adj.* ritualista.

rival ('rai·vəl) *n.* rival. —*adj.* rival; opuesto. —*v.t.* **1,** (compete with) rivalizar con. **2,** (emulate) emular. —**rivalry,** *n.* rivalidad.

river ('rɪv·ər) *n.* río. —**river bed,** cauce *o* lecho de río. —**sell (someone) down the river,** traicionar. —**up the river,** *slang* en la penitenciaría.

riverside *n.* ribera. —*adj.* ribereño.

rivet ('rɪv·ɪt) *n.* remache. —*v.t.* remachar. —**riveting,** *n.* remache; remachado. —**rivet one's eyes on,** clavar los ojos en.

rivulet ('rɪv·jə·lət) *n.* riachuelo.

roach (rotʃ) *n.* **1,** (fish) escarcho; rubio. **2,** (cockroach) cucaracha.

road (ro:d) *n.* **1,** (highway) carretera. **2,** (means of approach) camino. **3,** (anchorage) rada.

roadbed *n.* base de carretera o ferrovía; firme; afirmado.

roadblock *n.* barricada; *fig.* obstáculo.

roadhouse *n.* restaurante o posada al lado de una carretera.

roadside *n.* borde del camino. —*adj.* al borde del camino.

roadstead *n.* rada.

roadster ('rod·stər) *n.* **1,** (small car) automóvil pequeño de turismo. **2,** (carriage horse) caballo de aguante.

roadway *n.* carretera; camino; vía.

roam (ro:m) *v.i.* vagar. —*v.t.* vagar por; recorrer. —*n.* paseo.

roan (ro:n) *adj.* ruano.

roar (ro:r) *v.i.* rugir; bramar. —*v.t.* gritar. —*n.* rugido; bramido. —**roar with laughter,** reírse a carcajadas.

roaring ('ror·ɪŋ) *adj.* **1,** (noisy) rugiente. **2,** *slang* (outstanding) tremendo. —*n.* rugido.

roast (rost) *v.t.* **1,** (cook) asar. **2,** (dry by heat) tostar. **3,** *slang* (ridicule) ridiculizar. —*v.i.* asarse; tostarse. —*n.* **1,** (roasted meat) asado. **2,** (meat for roasting) carne para asar.

roast beef rosbif.

roaster ('ros·tər) *n.* asador.

rob (ra:b) *v.t.* robar; hurtar. —**robber,** *n.* ladrón.

robbery ('rab·ə·ri) *n.* robo; hurto.

robe (ro:b) *n.* **1,** (gown) túnica. **2,** (blanket) manto. **3,** (dress) vestido; traje. **4,** (dressing gown) bata. —*v.t.* vestir. —*v.i.* vestirse.

robin ('rab·ɪn) *n.* petirrojo.
robot ('ro·bət) *n.* robot; autómata. —*adj.* automático.
robust ('ro·bʌst) *adj.* **1,** (strong) robusto; fuerte; recio. **2,** (rough) grosero; rudo. **3,** (arduous) arduo. —**robustness,** *n.* robustez; fuerza; vigor.
rock (rak) *n.* **1,** (large stone) roca; peña; peñasco. **2,** (any stone) piedra. **3,** *slang* (diamond) diamante. —*v.t.* mecer; balancear. —*v.i.* mecerse; oscilar. —**rock candy,** azúcar candi. —**rock crusher,** triturador. —**rock crystal,** cuarzo; cristal de roca. —**rock garden,** jardín rocoso.
rock bottom el fondo; lo más profundo. —**rockbottom,** *adj.* mínimo; más bajo.
rockbound *adj.* **1,** (surrounded by rocks) rodeado de peñascos. **2,** (impenetrable) impenetrable.
rocker ('rak·ər) *n.* **1,** (chair that rocks) mecedora. **2,** (runner of a rocking chair) base curva de la mecedora. **3,** (cradle) cuna. **4,** *mech.* balancín.
rocket ('rak·ɪt) *n.* cohete. —*v.i.* ascender rápidamente.
rocking chair mecedora.
rocking horse caballo mecedor.
rockribbed *adj.* **1,** *lit.* rocoso. **2,** *fig.* inflexible; firme.
rocky ('rak·i) *adj.* **1,** (stony) rocoso. **2,** (shaky) tambaleante.
rococo (rə'ko·ko) *n.* & *adj.* rococó.
rod (raːd) *n.* **1,** (stick) vara. **2,** (scepter) cetro. **3,** (whip; switch) azote. **4,** (measure of length) medida de 16½ pies. **5,** *slang* (pistol) pistola; arma. **6,** *mech.* vástago. —**fishing rod,** caña de pescar.
rode (roːd) *v., pret. de* **ride.**
rodent ('ro·dənt) *n.* & *adj.* roedor.
rodeo (ro'dei·o) *n.* **1,** (cattle roundup) rodeo. **2,** (riding show) función de vaqueros.
roe (roː) *n.* **1,** (fish eggs) huevecillos de pescado. **2,** = **roe deer.**
roebuck ('ro,bʌk) *n.* macho del corzo.
roe deer corzo.
rogation (ro'gei·ʃən) *n.* rogativa; rogaciones (*pl.*).
roger ('radʒ·ər) *interj., slang* ¡muy bien!; ¡bueno!
rogue (roːg) *n.* **1,** (knave) bribón; pícaro; maleante. **2,** (ferocious animal) animal bravo. —**roguery,** *n.* picardía; bribonería. —**roguish,** *adj.* pícaro; picaresco. —**roguishness,** *n.* picardía.
roil (rɔil) *v.t.* **1,** (make turbid) enturbiar. **2,** (annoy) molestar; irritar.
roister ('rɔis·tər) *v.i.* fanfarronear. —**roisterer,** *n.* fanfarrón. —**roisterous,** *adj.* fanfarrón.
rôle (roːl) *n.* papel.
roll (roːl) *v.i.* **1,** (move by turning over and over) rodar. **2,** (turn about an axis) girar; dar vueltas; revolverse. **3,** (sway, as a ship) balancear. **4,** (reel; stagger) bambolear. **5,** (move in ripples) ondear. **6,** (sound, as a drum) redoblar. **7,** (make a full, deep sound) retumbar; resonar. **8,** (wallow) revolcarse. **9,** (curl up into a round or cylindrical shape) enrollarse. —*v.t.* **1,** (rotate) voltear; girar; revolver. **2,** (push or pull by means of wheels or rollers) hacer rodar; empujar o halar sobre ruedas o rodillos. **3,** (play, as a drum) redoblar. **4,** (curl or wrap up into a ball or cylinder) enrollar; envolver. **5,** (flatten with a roller) allanar con rodillo. **6,** (trill) vibrar. **7,** (move from side to side) menear; mover de un lado a otro. —*n.* **1,** (cylinder) rollo; cilindro. **2,** (small bread or biscuit) panecillo. **3,** (list of names) registro; lista; nómina. **4,** (swaying of a ship) balance. **5,** (reeling; staggering) bamboleo. **6,** (sound of a drum) redoble. **7,** (full, deep sound, as of thunder) retumbo. **8,** (swell, as of the sea) oleaje. **9,** (throw of the dice) echada de los dados. —**call the roll,** pasar lista. —**roll call,** acto de pasar lista. —**roll in money,** nadar en dinero. —**roll up, 1,** (wrap round) arrollar; envolver. **2,** (turn up, as the sleeves) arremangar. **3,** (accumulate; amass) amontonar.
roller ('rol·ər) *n.* **1,** (cylinder) rodillo; tambor; cilindro. **2,** (heavy wave) ola larga. **3,** (caster) ruedecilla; rueda. —**roller bearing,** cojinete de rodillos. —**roller coaster,** montaña rusa. —**roller skate,** patín de ruedas.
rollick ('ral·ɪk) *v.i.* travesear; retozar; juguetear. —**rollicking,** *adj.* travieso; juguetón; retozón.
rolling ('rol·ɪŋ) *n.* **1,** (rotating;

revolving) rodadura. **2,** (swaying of a ship or vehicle) balanceo. **3,** (staggering; reeling) bamboleo. **4,** (wavy motion) undulación. —*adj.* **1,** (rotating; moving on wheels or rollers) rodante. **2,** (wavy) ondulado. —**rolling mill**, laminadero. —**rolling pin**, rodillo de pastelero. —**rolling stone**, piedra movediza. —**rolling stock**, material móvil.

rolypoly ('ro·li·po·li) *adj.* rechoncho; gordiflón. —*n.* **1,** (pudding) pudín en forma de rollo. **2,** *colloq.* (fat person) gordiflón.

Roman ('ro·mən) *adj.* **1,** (of or pert. to Rome) romano. **2,** *l.c., typog.* redondo. —*n.* romano. —**Roman nose**, nariz aguileña.

Roman Catholic católico romano.

romance (ro'mæns) *n.* **1,** (novel) romance; novela. **2,** (fictitious tale) ficción; cuento. **3,** (love affair) aventura; amorío. **4,** (sentiment) romanticismo. —*adj., cap.* romance; neolatino. —*v.i.*, **1,** (tell stories) contar romances. **2,** *colloq.* (make love) amarse; tratarse cariñosamente. —*v.t., colloq.* cortejar.

Romanesque (ˌro·mə'nɛsk) *adj.* & *n.* románico.

Romanic (ro'mæn·ɪk) *adj.* románico.

Romanist ('ro·mən·ɪst) *n.* romanista.

romantic (ro'mæn·tɪk) *adj.* **1,** (fanciful) fantástico. **2,** (amorous) romántico. **3,** (imaginative, as of literature) novelesco. —**romanticism** (-tɪ·sɪz·əm) *n.* romanticismo.

romp (ramp) *v.i.* retozar; juguetear. —*n.* retozo.

rompers ('ramp·ərz) *n.pl.* traje de juego.

rondo ('ran·do) *n.* rondó.

rood (ruːd) *n.* **1,** (crucifix crucifijo. **2,** (measure of length) pértica.

roof (ruf) *n.* **1,** (external covering) techo; tejado. **2,** *fig.* (house; home) hogar. **3,** (upper limit) máximo. —*v.t.* techar. —**roofing**, *n.* material de techar.

rook (rʊk) *n.* **1,** (crow) corneja; grajo. **2,** *chess* torre; roque. —*v.t., slang* estafar.

rookery ('rʊk·ə·ri) *n.* **1,** (abode of rooks) lugar frecuentado por cornejas. **2,** (breeding ground for certain animals) criadero de focas, aves marinas, grullas, etc. **3,** (hovel) casucha; cuchitril. **4,** (squalid quarter) barrio bajo.

rookie ('rʊk·i) *n., slang* novato; bisoño.

room (ruːm) *n.* **1,** (space) lugar; sitio; espacio. **2,** (opportunity) ocasión; oportunidad. **3,** (apartment) cuarto; aposento; habitación; cámara. **4,** (one of a set of rooms) pieza. —*v.i., colloq.* habitar; alojarse. —*v.t., colloq.* alojar; hospedar. —**make** *o* **give room**, hacer lugar; abrir paso.

roomer ('rum·ər) *n.* inquilino.

roommate *n.* compañero de cuarto.

roomy ('rum·i) *adj.* espacioso; amplio. —**roominess**, *n.* espaciosidad.

roost (rust) *n.* **1,** (perch) percha. **2,** *colloq.* (resting place) lugar de descanso. —*v.i.* **1,** (sit on a perch) posar *o* descansar en la percha. **2,** (lodge; dwell) alojarse; habitar. —**rule the roost**, mandar; dominar; ser dueño.

rooster ('rus·tər) *n.* gallo.

root (rut) *n.* **1,** *bot.; gram.; math.* raíz. **2,** (of a tooth) raigón. **3,** (foundation) base. **4,** (origin) origen; causa; raíz. —*v.t.* **1,** (plant firmly) fijar. **2,** (dig up) hocicar; hozar. —*v.i.* **1,** (take root) arraigarse; echar raíces. **2,** (turn up the earth) hocicar. —**root beer**, bebida hecha de extractos de varias raíces. —**root for**, *slang* aplaudir. —**root up** *o* **out**, desarraigar; extirpar.

rooted ('rut·ɪd) *adj.* arraigado.

rooter ('rut·ər) *n., slang* aplaudidor; animador.

rope (rop) *n.* **1,** (cord) cuerda; soga; cabo. **2,** (string, as of pearls) fila; hilera. **3,** (stringy fiber) fibra; trenza. —*v.t.* **1,** (fasten) atar; amarrar. **2,** (catch with a rope) lazar. **3,** *slang* (trick) engañar; embaucar. —**at the end of one's rope**, sin recursos. —**know the ropes**, *colloq.* ser experimentado; conocer a fondo (una cosa).

rorqual ('ror·kwəl) *n.* rorcual.

rosary ('ro·zə·ri) *n.* **1,** (prayer beads) rosario. **2,** (garland of roses) guirnalda de rosas. **3,** (rose garden) jardín de rosales.

rose (roːz) *n.* **1,** (flower) rosa. **2,** (color) color de rosa; rosa. —*adj.* de color de rosa; rosado. —**rose fever**, alergia nasal. —**rose window**, rosetón.

rose (ro:z) *v., pret. de* **rise.**
roseaceous (ro'zei·ʃəs) *adj.* rosáceo.
roseate ('ɹɔ·zi·ət) *adj.* rosado; rosáceo.
rosebud *n.* capullo de rosa.
rosebush *n.* rosal.
rosemary ('roz,mɛr·i) *n.* romero.
rosette (ro'zɛt) *n.* roseta; rosa.
rosewater *n.* agua de rosas.
rosewood *n.* palo de rosa.
rosin ('raz·ɪn) *n.* resina.
roster ('ras·tər) *n.* **1,** (list of names) lista; nómina. **2,** (schedule) catálogo; itinerario; programa.
rostrum ('ras·trəm) *n.* tribuna.
rosy ('ro·zi) *adj.* **1,** (rose-colored) rosado. **2,** (favorable) favorable; optimista.
rot (rat) *v.t.* [**rotted, rotting**] **1,** (decompose) pudrir. **2,** (corrupt) corromper; deteriorar. —*v.i.* **1,** (decay) pudrirse. **2,** (become corrupt) corromperse. —*n.* **1,** (decay) podredumbre; pudrimiento; putrefacción. **2,** (parasitic disease) morriña. **3,** *slang* (nonsense) tontada; tontería; sandez.
rotary ('ro·tə·ri) *adj.* rotativo; giratorio.
rotate ('ro·teit) *v.i.* **1,** (turn) rodar; girar. **2,** (alternate) alternar. —*v.t.* **1,** (cause to turn) hacer girar; voltear. **2,** (alternate) alternar.
rotation (ro'tei·ʃən) *n.* rotación. —**by** *o* **in rotation,** por turno.
rotatory ('ro·tə,tor·i) *adj.* rotatorio.
rote (rot) *n.* repetición. —**learn by rote,** aprender de memoria.
rotor ('ro·tər) *n.* r[illegible]; rueda móvil.
rotten ('rat·ən) *adj.* **1,** (decayed) podrido; putrefacto. **2,** (corrupt) corrompido. **3,** *colloq.* (very bad) malísimo; pésimo. —**rottenness,** *n.* podredumbre; putrefacción.
rotter ('rat·ər) *n., slang* persona despreciable.
rotund (ro'tʌnd) *adj.* **1,** (round; plump) redondo. **2,** (sonorous) rotundo.
rotunda (ro'tʌn·də) *n.* rotunda; rotonda.
rotundity (ro'tʌn·də·ti) *n.* **1,** (roundness; plumpness) redondez. **2,** (sonority) rotundidad.
roué (ru'ei) *n.* libertino.
rouge (ru:ʒ) *n.* **1,** (cosmetic) colorete. **2,** (jeweler's paste) rojo de joyero. —*v.t.* pintar; dar colorete a. —*v.i.* pintarse.
rough (rʌf) *adj.* **1,** (uneven; coarse) áspero; tosco; brusco. **2,** (natural; unfinished) bronco; bruto; cerril. **3,** (severe) severo; cruel; rudo. **4,** (uncouth) grosero; rústico. **5,** (stormy) tempestuoso; borrascoso. **6,** (approximate) aproximativo. —*n.* **1,** (roughness) crudeza; aspereza. **2,** (uneven terrain) terreno áspero. **3,** (rowdy) rufián. —*v.t.* **1,** (make rough) poner áspero. **2,** (work up in crude fashion) chapucear; labrar imperfectamente. **3,** (sketch) bosquejar; esbozar. **4,** (treat harshly) maltratar. —**in the rough,** en bruto. —**rough draft** *o* **sketch,** bosquejo; esbozo. —**rough it,** vivir penosamente.
roughage ('rʌf·ɪdʒ) *n.* alimento áspero de poco valor nutritivo.
rough-and-ready *adj.* rudo pero eficaz.
roughen ('rʌf·ən) *v.t.* poner áspero. —*v.i.* ponerse áspero.
roughhouse *n., colloq.* pelotera; algazara; desorden. —*v.i., colloq.* portarse desordenadamente. —*v.t.* molestar; burlarse de.
roughly ('rʌf·li) *adv.* **1,** (not smoothly; not evenly) ásperamente; toscamente. **2,** (severely) severamente; cruelmente. **3,** (approximately) aproximadamente.
roughneck *n.* alborotador; rufián.
roughness ('rʌf·nəs) *n.* **1,** (unevenness; coarseness) aspereza; tosquedad. **2,** (severity) severidad; crueldad; rudeza. **3,** (agitation, as of the sea) turbulencia.
roughshod *adj.* **1,** *lit.* herrado con púas o clavos. **2,** *fig.* (ruthless) despiadado. —**ride roughshod over,** pisotear; tratar con desprecio.
roulette (ru'lɛt) *n.* ruleta.
round (raund) *adj.* **1,** (circular) redondo. **2,** (curved) curvo. **3,** (light; brisk) ligero; veloz. **4,** (full) lleno; cabal. **5,** (sonorous) sonoro; rotundo. **6,** (clear; positive) rotundo. **7,** (without fractional part) redondo. —*n.* **1,** (round object) círculo; orbe; redondo. **2,** (roundness) redondez. **3,** *usu. pl.* (tour of duty) circuito; recorrido. **4,** (period of action) ronda. **5,** (song) canon. **6,** (rung of a ladder) peldaño; travesaño. **7,** (cut of meat) rodaja de carne. **8,** (salvo) anda-

nada; salva; tiro. **9,** *boxing* asalto; suerte. —*v.t.* **1,** (make round) redondear. **2,** [*también,* **round out**] (complete) llenar; acabar; completar. **3,** (encircle) cercar. **4,** (go around) rondar; rodear. —*v.i.* **1,** (grow round) redondearse. **2,** (mature) desarrollarse. —*adv.* **1,** (on all sides) alrededor. **2,** (with a rotating movement) en redondo. **3,** (through a circuit) circularmente. **4,** (in circumference) de *o* por circunferencia. —*prep.* alrededor de; a la vuelta de. —**all year round,** todo el año. —**go** *o* **make the rounds,** ir de ronda; circular. —**round up,** recoger; rodear (el ganado).

roundabout *adj.* indirecto; desviado.

rounder ('raun·dər) *n.* **1,** (one who travels a circuit) rondeador. **2,** *slang* (dissolute person) libertino; calavera.

roundhouse *n.* **1,** *naut.* toldilla. **2,** *R.R.* casa de máquinas.

roundish ('raund·ɪʃ) *adj.* casi redondo.

roundly ('raund·li) *adv.* redondamente.

roundness ('raund·nəs) *n.* redondez.

round robin **1,** (petition) memorial firmado en rueda. **2,** (competition) concurso mutuo.

round-shouldered *adj.* cargado de espaldas.

round trip viaje de ida y vuelta.

roundup *n.* rodeo; recogida; reunión.

rouse (rauz) *v.t.* **1,** (waken) despertar. **2,** (alert) animar. **3,** (excite) excitar. **4,** (stir up, as game) levantar. —*v.i.* **1,** (waken) despertarse. **2,** (become alert) animarse; moverse. —**rousing,** *adj.* vigoroso; fuerte.

roustabout ('raust·ə,baut) *n.* peón; trabajador.

rout (raut) *n.* **1,** (confused retreat) derrota; desbandada. **2,** (disorderly crowd) tumulto; chusma; populacho. —*v.t.* **1,** (disperse) derrotar. **2,** (cut away) cortar. —**rout out,** sacar; arrancar *o* arrojar fuera.

route (rut) *n.* **1,** (road) ruta; camino; vía. **2,** (course) curso; itinerario; vía. —*v.t.* encaminar; despachar.

routine (ru'ti:n) *n.* rutina. —*adj.* rutinario.

rove (ro:v) *v.i.* vagar. —*v.t.* vagar por; recorrer.

rover ('ro·vər) *n.* **1,** (wanderer) errante; vagamundo. **2,** (pirate) pirata; corsario. **3,** (pirate ship) buque de piratas; corsario.

row (ro:) *n.* fila; hilera. —*v.t.* & *i.* remar; bogar. —**rower,** *n.* remero.

row (rau) *n.* pelea; camorra; lío; trifulca. —*v.i.* pelearse. —**raise a row,** armar camorra; armar lío.

rowboat ('ro,bot) *n.* bote; bote de remos.

rowdy ('rau·di) *n.* rufián. —*adj.* ruidoso; bullicioso. —**rowdyish,** *adj.* alborotoso. —**rowdyism,** *n.* alboroto.

rowel ('rau·əl) *n.* **1,** (wheel of a spur) rodaja de espuela. **2,** (cutting wheel) rodaja de cortar.

rowlock ('ro,lak) *n.* chumacera.

royal ('rɔi·əl) *adj.* **1,** (kingly) real. **2,** (majestic) majestuoso. —**royalism,** *n.* realismo. —**royalist,** *adj.* & *n.* realista.

royalty ('rɔi·əl·ti) *n.* **1,** (rank) realeza. **2,** (royal person) personaje real. **3,** *usu.pl.* (fees) derechos.

-rrhage (rədʒ) *sufijo* -rragia; anormalidad en flujo o emisión: *hemorrhage,* hemorragia.

-rrhea *también,* **-rrhoea** (ri·ə) *sufijo* -rrea; flujo; emisión: *diarrhea,* diarrea.

rub (rʌb) *v.t.* [**rubbed, rubbing**] **1,** (stroke hard) frotar; restregar. **2,** (graze) rozar. **3,** (polish) pulir; limpiar. **4,** *colloq.,* (annoy) fastidiar; molestar; incomodar. —*v.i.* frotarse; restregarse. —*n.* **1,** (act of rubbing) frote; fricción; roce. **2,** (massage) masaje. **3,** (annoyance) fastidio; estorbo; molestia. —**rub down,** **1,** (massage) dar masaje. **2,** (scrub) limpiar. —**rub in,** hacer penetrar (por los poros); *slang* insistir en. —**rub off,** **1,** (remove) quitar. **2,** (clean) limpiar frotando. —**rub up,** **1,** (polish) repasar. **2,** (excite) excitar. —**rub out,** borrar.

rub-a-dub ('rʌb·ə,dʌb) *n.* rataplán; tantarantán.

rubber ('rʌb·ər) *n.* **1,** (person or thing that rubs) frotador; borrador. **2,** (elastic substance) goma; caucho. **3,** (eraser) goma de borrar; borrador. **4,** (overshoe) chanclo; galocha. **5,** (series of games) partida. **6,** (deciding game) jugada final. —*adj.* de goma; de caucho;

elástico. —**rubberize**, *v.t.* encauchar; engomar. —**rubbery**, *adj.* gomoso; elástico. —**rubber band**, goma; liga de goma. —**rubber check**, *slang* cheque sin fondos.
rubberneck *n.*, *slang* **1,** (inquisitive person) preguntón. **2,** (sightseer) turista. —*adj.* de turista. —*v.i.* estirar el cuello.
rubber stamp 1, (imprinting device) sello de goma; estampilla. **2,** *colloq.* (one who approves uncritically) persona que aprueba automáticamente. —**rubber-stamp**, *v.t.* **1,** (imprint) estampar. **2,** *colloq.* (approve uncritically) aprobar automáticamente.
rubbish ('rʌb·ɪʃ) *n.* **1,** (refuse) basura; desecho. **2,** (nonsense) disparate; tontería.
rubble ('rʌb·əl) *n.* **1,** (rough broken stones) ripio. **2,** (trash) desecho.
rubdown *n.* masaje.
rube (ruːb) *n.*, *slang* rústico; patán; *Amer.* jíbaro.
rubella (ru'bɛl·ə) *n.* rubéola.
rubicund ('ru·bəˌkʌnd) *adj.* rubicundo. —**rubicundity** (-'kʌn·də·ti) *n.* rubicundez.
rubidium (ru'bɪd·i·əm) *n.* rubidio.
ruble *también,* **rouble** ('ru·bəl) *n.* rublo.
rubric ('ru·brɪk) *n.* rúbrica.
ruby ('ru·bi) *n.* **1,** (gem) rubí. **2,** (color) color de rubí.
ruck (rʌk) *n.* **1,** (fold) arruga. **2,** (common crowd) multitud; vulgo. —*v.t.* arrugar. —*v.i.* arrugarse.
rucksack *n.* mochila; alforja.
rudder ('rʌd·ər) *n.* timón.
ruddy ('rʌd·i) *adj.* rojizo; rubicundo. —**ruddiness**, *n.* rojez; rubicundez.
rude (ruːd) *adj.* **1,** (crude) rudo; crudo; primitivo. **2,** (illbred) malcriado; majadero. **3,** (discourteous) descortés. **4,** (rugged) fuerte; robusto; recio. —**rudeness**, *n.* rudeza.
rudiment ('ru·dɪ·mənt) *n.* rudimento.
rudimentary (ru·dɪ'mɛn·tə·ri) *adj.* rudimentario.
rue (ruː) *v.t.* arrepentirse de; sentir; lamentar. —*v.i.* arrepentirse. —*n.*, *bot.* ruda.
rueful ('ruː·fəl) *adj.* **1,** (causing sorrow or pity) lamentable; lastimoso. **2,** (feeling sorrow or pity) triste; lastimero.
ruff (rʌf) *n.* **1,** (frilled collar) lechuguilla. **2,** (fringe of fur or feathers) collar. **3,** (kind of pigeon) paloma moñuda. **4,** *cards* fallada. —*v.t.*, *cards* fallar.
ruffian ('rʌf·i·ən) *n.* rufián; tunante. —**ruffianism**, *n.* rufianería; tunantería.
ruffle ('rʌf·əl) *v.t.* **1,** (draw up in folds) fruncir; rizar; arrugar. **2,** (disturb) molestar; enojar. **3,** (disarrange) desaliñar; descomponer. **4,** *music* redoblar (el tambor). —*n.* **1,** *sewing* volante fruncido. **2,** *music* redoble.
rug (rʌg) *n.* **1,** (floor covering) alfombra. **2,** (lap robe) manta de viaje.
rugged ('rʌg·ɪd) *adj.* **1,** (rough) arrugado; tosco; escabroso. **2,** (unpolished) sin pulir; inculto. **3,** (harsh) áspero; austero. **4,** (tempestuous) furioso; tempestuoso. **5,** (strong) robusto; fuerte.
ruin ('ru·ɪn) *n.* **1,** (collapse) ruina; caída; derrota. **2,** (destroyer) devastador; destructor. **3,** (devastation) devastación; desastre. **4,** (corruption) corrupción; degradación. —*v.t.* **1,** (destroy) arruinar; destrozar. **2,** (spoil) estropear. **3,** (bankrupt) empobrecer.
ruination (ˌru·ɪ'nei·ʃən) *n.* ruina; perdición.
ruinous ('ru·ɪn·əs) *adj.* ruinoso; desastroso; fatal.
rule (ruːl) *n.* **1,** (regulation) regla; ley. **2,** (custom) norma; método; precepto. **3,** (government) gobierno; mando. **4,** (measuring stick) escala; regla. **5,** (straight line) raya. —*v.t.* **1,** (decide) determinar; arreglar. **2,** (govern) gobernar; controlar; regir. **3,** (mark with lines) reglar; rayar. —*v.i.* **1,** (govern; command) mandar; regir. **2,** (prevail) prevalecer. —**rule of thumb**, metro empírico; regla empírica. —**rule out**, no admitir; excluir.
ruler (ru'lər) *n.* **1,** (one who governs) gobernante. **2,** (measuring stick) regla.
ruling ('ru·lɪŋ) *n.* **1,** (decision) decisión; fallo. **2,** (set of lines) rayado; renglonadura. —*adj.* gobernante. —**ruling pen**, tiralíneas.
rum (rʌm) *n.* ron. —*adj.*, *slang*

extraño; singular. —**rum runner**, *n.* contrabandista de licores.

rumba ('rʌm·bə) *n.* rumba.

rumble ('rʌm·bəl) *v.i.* retumbar; rugir. —*v.t.* hacer retumbar; decir *o* hacer retumbando. —*n.* **1,** (thunderous sound) estruendo; retumbo. **2,** (low, murmuring sound) rugido. **3,** *slang* (gang fight) camorra; riña. —**rumble seat**, asiento trasero descubierto.

ruminant ('ru·mɪ·nənt) *adj.* & *n.* rumiante.

ruminate ('ru·mə,neit) *v.t.* & *i.* rumiar. —**rumination**, *n.* rumia; rumiación. —**ruminative**, *adj.* meditativo.

rummage ('rʌm·ɪdʒ) *v.t.* & *i.* revolver; explorar; rebuscar. —*n.* rezagos (*pl.*). —**rummage sale**, venta de rezagos.

rummy ('rʌm·i) *n.* **1,** (card game) cierto juego de cartas. **2,** *slang* (alcoholic) alcohólico. —*adj.*, *slang* extraño; singular.

rumor *también*, **rumour** ('ru·mər) *n.* rumor. —*v.t.* rumorear.

rump (rʌmp) *n.* **1,** (buttocks) ancas (*pl.*); nalgas (*pl.*); rabada. **2,** (remnant) remanente; residuo.

rumple ('rʌm·pəl) *v.t.* arrugar; ajar. —*v.i.* arrugarse; ajarse. —*n.* arruga.

rumpus ('rʌm·pəs) *n.* batahola; alboroto. —**rumpus room**, cuarto de juegos.

run (rʌn) *v.i.* [**ran, run, running**] **1,** (move swiftly) correr. **2,** (make haste) apresurarse. **3,** (flee) huir; escaparse. **4,** (travel) andar; marchar. **5,** (go regularly) recorrer. **6,** (flow) fluir. **7,** (discharge a fluid) chorrear. **8,** (spread) difundirse. **9,** (operate) funcionar; marchar. **10,** (compete) competir. **11,** (pass by) transcurrir. **12,** (tend; incline) inclinarse. **13,** (continue) continuar; seguir. **14,** (be a candidate) ser candidato. —*v.t.* **1,** (direct) dirigir; manejar. **2,** (travel through or past) correr; recorrer. **3,** (incur, as a risk) correr. **4,** (smuggle) pasar de contrabando. **5,** (exhibit, as a film) exhibir. **6,** (project, as a film) proyectar; pasar. **7,** (draw, as a line) trazar; tirar. —*n.* **1,** (rapid movement; race) carrera. **2,** (journey) excursión. **3,** (current) flujo. **4,** (course) curso. **5,** (tendency) tendencia. **6,** (extraordinary demand) asedio. **7,** *baseball* carrera. **8,** *cards* secuencia. **9,** (free access) libre uso. **10,** (animal range) terreno de pasto. **11,** (herd) rebaño. **12,** (brook) arroyo; riachuelo. **13,** (stocking ravel) carrera. **14,** (class; kind) clase; tipo; género. —**in the long run**, a la larga. —**on the run**, **1,** (hurriedly) apresuradamente; de prisa. **2,** (in retreat) huyendo; en fuga. —**run across**, dar con; encontrar. —**run against**, **1,** (oppose) oponerse a. **2,** (encounter) encontrar; dar con; chocar con. —**run down**, **1,** (pursue and catch) alcanzar; llegar a coger. **2,** (trace) trazar. **3,** (crush by passing over) atropellar. **4,** (disparage) rebajar; desacreditar. **5,** (become exhausted or worn out) agotarse; acabarse; dejar de funcionar. —**run (a) fever**, tener calentura. —**run in**, **1,** *print.* poner de seguido. **2,** *slang* (arrest) arrestar. —**run into**, encontrar; dar con; chocar con. —**run off**, **1,** *print.* imprimir; tirar. **2,** (do or make quickly) hacer rápidamente; enunciar rápidamente. **3,** (flow out or away) escurrir; derramarse. **4,** (turn away from) desviarse de. —**run on**, continuar; seguir. —**run out**, **1,** (leave hurriedly) salir; huirse; escaparse. **2,** (expire) terminar; expirar. **3,** (become exhausted or worn out) agotarse; acabarse. —**run over**, **1,** (overflow) rebosar. **2,** (go beyond) pasar; pasarse de; exceder. **3,** (pass over; crush) atropellar. **4,** (trample) pisotear; atropellar. —**run through**, **1,** (impale) traspasar; empalar. **2,** (do or say quickly) hacer rápidamente; enunciar rápidamente.

runabout *n.* **1,** (sports car) coche ligero. **2,** (light carriage) birlocho. **3,** (small boat) lancha. **4,** (wanderer) vagamundo.

runaround *n.* **1,** *slang* (evasion) evasiva. **2,** (type set around an illustration) letras alrededor de un grabado.

runaway *adj.* **1,** (escaping) fugitivo; (*of a horse*) desbocado. **2,** (easily won) fácil. —*n.* **1,** (escaped horse) caballo desbocado. **2,** (fugitive) prófugo; fugitivo. **3,** (flight) fuga. **4,** (easy victory) victoria fácil.

run-down *adj.* **1,** (in poor health)

enfermizo. **2,** (broken down) destartalado; desvencijado. **3,** (exhausted; used up) agotado; acabado.

rung (rʌŋ) *v., p.p. de* **ring.** *—n.* travesaño.

runner (ˈrʌn·ər) *n.* **1,** (racer) corredor. **2,** (messenger) mensajero. **3,** (slide, as of a sled) corredera. **4,** *bot.; zool.* estolón. **5,** (narrow rug) alfombra estrecha. **6,** (stocking ravel) carrera.

runner-up *n.* contendiente que termina segundo.

running (ˈrʌn·ɪŋ) *n.* **1,** (act of running) carrera. **2,** (operation) marcha; funcionamiento. **3,** (suppuration) supuración. *—adj.* **1,** (moving) corriente; en marcha. **2,** (adapted for running) corredor. **3,** (suppurating) supurante. *—adv.* en sucesión. **—running hand,** letra cursiva. **—running headline,** título de página. **—running knot,** lazo corredizo. **—twice running,** dos veces seguidas. **—a week running,** una semana entera.

running board estribo.

run-off *n.* **1,** (water spill) agua de desagüe. **2,** (deciding contest) carrera final.

run-of-the-mill *adj.* común; ordinario.

runt (rʌnt) *n.* enano.

runway (ˈrʌn·wei) *n.* **1,** *R.R.* vía. **2,** *aero.* pista de aterrizaje. **3,** (channel) cauce.

rupee (ruˈpiː) *n.* rupia.

rupture (ˈrʌp·tʃər) *n.* **1,** (break) ruptura; rompimiento. **2,** (disagreement) desavenencia. **3,** (hernia) hernia. *—v.t.* **1,** (break) romper; reventar. **2,** *pathol.* quebrar. *—v.i.* romperse.

rural (ˈrur·əl) *adj.* rural.

ruse (ruːz) *n.* ardid; artimaña; recoveco.

rush (rʌʃ) *v.i.* **1,** (drive forward) lanzarse; abalanzarse. **2,** (hurry) precipitarse. *—v.t.* **1,** (hasten) acelerar. **2,** (push) empujar con violencia. **3,** *football* avanzar (el balón). **4,** *slang* inducir a unirse a una fraternidad. **5,** *slang* (court) galantear. *—n.* **1,** (forward surge) acometida; embestida. **2,** (dash) asedio. **3,** (haste) prisa. **4,** (urgency) urgencia. **5,** *bot.* junco. **6,** *football* lucha violenta; adelanto del balón. *—adj.* **1,** (urgent) urgente. **2,** (made of rush) de junco. **—rush hour,** hora de más tránsito. **—rush in,** entrar precipitadamente. **—rush in on,** entrar sin avisar. **—rush through,** hacer de prisa.

rush-bottomed *adj.* con asiento de junco.

rusk (rʌsk) *n.* galleta; rosca.

russet (ˈrʌs·ɪt) *adj. & n.* (color) moreno rojizo.

Russian (ˈrʌʃ·ən) *adj. & n.* ruso.

rust (rʌst) *n.* **1,** (corrosive formation) moho; herrumbre. **2,** (reddish color) color rojizo. *—adj.* rojizo. *—v.t.* enmohecer. *—v.i.* enmohecerse.

rustic (ˈrʌs·tɪk) *adj.* **1,** (rural) rústico. **2,** (simple) sencillo. **3,** (rude) grosero. *—n.* rústico; campesino.

rusticity (rʌsˈtɪs·ə·ti) *n.* rusticidad.

rustle (ˈrʌs·əl) *v.i.* **1,** (make a murmuring or rubbing sound) susurrar. **2,** *slang* (move vigorously) moverse; apresurarse. *—v.t.* **1,** (cause to murmur; rub softly) hacer susurrar; agitar levemente. **2,** *slang* (cause to move; hurry) apresurar; empujar. **3,** *slang* (gather or produce quickly) recoger; conseguir *o* preparar en seguida. **4,** *slang* (steal, as cattle) hurtar; robar; *Amer.* arrear. *—n.* susurro.

rustler (ˈrʌs·lər) *n., U.S.* laderón de ganado.

rusty (ˈrʌs·ti) *adj.* **1,** (covered with rust) mohoso; enmohecido. **2,** (reddish) rojizo. **3,** (hoarse) ronco. **4,** *colloq.* (out of practice) entorpecido.

rut (rʌt) *n.* **1,** (narrow track) bache; surco. **2,** (habit) rutina. **3,** (period of heat in animals) celo; brama. **—rutted,** *adj.* surcado. **—rutty,** *adj.* lleno de surcos.

rutabaga (ˌru·təˈbei·gə) *n.* nabo de Suecia.

ruthenium (ruˈθi·ni·əm) *n.* rutenio.

ruthless (ˈruθ·lɪs) *adj.* despiadado; cruel. **—ruthlessness,** *n.* crueldad.

-ry (ri) *sufijo, var. de* **-ery**: *jewelry,* joyería; *mimicry,* mímica.

rye (rai) *n.* **1,** (grain) centeno. **2,** (liquor) whisky de centeno.

S

S, s (ɛs) décimonona letra del alfabeto inglés.
-'s (s; z) *sufijo* **1,** *añadido a nombres indica* posesión; pertenencia: *John's hat,* el sombrero de Juan. **2,** *indica contracción de* **is** *o* **has**: *He's here = He is here,* Está aquí. *He's finished = He has finished,* Ha terminado. **3,** *indica contracción de* **us**: *Let's go = Let us go,* Vamos.
-s (s; z) *sufijo* **1,** *forma la tercera persona singular del presente de indicativo de los verbos: he looks,* él mira. *Tras sibilante, y algunas veces tras vocal, se convierte en* **-es**: *he crushes,* él tritura; *she goes,* ella va. **2,** *forma el plural de los nombres: birds,* pájaros. *Tras sibilante, y algunas veces tras vocal, se convierte en* **-es**: *fishes,* peces; *tomatoes,* tomates.
sabbath ('sæb·əθ) *n.* **1,** (Jewish) sábado. **2,** (Christian) domingo. —*adj.* **1,** (Jewish) sabático. **2,** (Christian) dominical.
sabbatical (sə'bæt·ɪ·kəl) *adj.* sabático; dominical. —*n.* [*también,* **sabbatical year**] año sabático; año de licencia.
saber ('sei·bər) *n.* sable. —*v.t.* dar un sablazo o sablazos a; herir o matar a sablazos.
sable ('sei·bəl) *n.* **1,** *zool.* marta cebellina. **2,** *heraldry* sable. **3,** *pl.* (mourning clothes) vestidos de luto. —*adj.* **1,** (of sable fur) de marta cebellina. **2,** (black) negro.
sabot (sæ'boː) *n.* zueco.
sabotage ('sæb·əˌtaʒ) *n.* sabotaje. —*v.i.* & *t.* sabotear. —**saboteur** (-'tʌːɹ) *n.* saboteador.
sac (sæk) *n., anat.; bot.; zool.* saco.
saccharin ('sæk·ə·rɪn) *n.* sacarina. —**saccharine,** *adj.* sacarino; de sacarina; *fig.* azucarado.
sacerdotal (ˌsæs·ər'do·təl) *adj.* sacerdotal.
sachet (sæ'ʃei) *n.* saquito perfumador.
sack (sæk) *n.* **1,** (bag) saco. **2,** (loose garment) saco; chaqueta. **3,** *slang* (dismissal) despido. **4,** (plunder) saqueo; pillaje. —*v.t.* **1,** (put in bags) ensacar; poner en sacos. **2,** *slang* (dismiss) echar; despedir. **3,** (plunder) saquear.
sackcloth *n.* brea; harpillera. —**in sackcloth and ashes,** en hábito de penitencia.
sacral ('sei·krəl) *adj.* sacro.
sacrament ('sæk·rə·mənt) *n.* sacramento. —**sacramental** (-'mɛn·təl) *adj.* sacramental.
sacred ('sei·krɪd) *adj.* sacro; sagrado.
sacrifice ('sæk·rəˌfais) *n.* sacrificio. —*v.t.* sacrificar. —*v.i.* sacrificarse. —**sacrificial** (-'fɪʃ·əl) *adj.* sacrificatorio; de sacrificio.
sacrilege ('sæk·rə·lɪdʒ) *n.* sacrilegio. —**sacrilegious** (-'lɪdʒ·əs) *adj.* sacrílego.
sacristan ('sæk·rɪs·tən) *n.* sacristán. —**sacristy,** *n.* sacristía.
sacrosanct ('sæk·rəˌsæŋkt) *adj.* sacrosanto.
sacrum ('sei·krəm) *n.* [*pl.* **-cra** (-krə)] sacro; hueso sacro.
sad (sæd) *adj.* **1,** (sorrowful) triste. **2,** *colloq.* (bad; poor) malo; deplorable. —**sadden,** *v.t.* entristecer. —*v.i.* entristecerse. —**sad sack,** *slang* caso perdido.
saddle ('sæd·əl) *n.* **1,** (seat for a rider on a horse) silla; silla de montar. **2,** (bicycle seat) sillín. **3,** (padded part of a harness) cincha. **4,** (cut of meat) cuarto trasero. —*v.t.* **1,** (put a saddle on) ensillar. **2,** (burden) cargar; gravar.
saddlebag *n.* alforja.
sadism ('sæd·ɪz·əm) *n.* sadismo. —**sadist,** *n.* sadista. —**sadistic** (sə'dɪs·tɪk) *adj.* sadista.
sadness ('sæd·nəs) *n.* tristeza.
safari (sə'far·i) *n.* safari.
safe (seif) *adj.* **1,** (free from danger) seguro; salvo. **2,** (unharmed) ileso; intacto. **3,** (trustworthy) digno de confianza. **4,** (harmless) innocuo. —*n.* caja fuerte; caja de caudales.
safe-conduct (seif'kan·dʌkt) *n.* salvoconducto; salvaguardia.
safe-deposit box caja de seguridad.
safeguard *n.* salvaguardia. —*v.t.* salvaguardar.
safekeeping *n.* custodia; cuidado; depósito.
safeness ('seif·nəs) *n.* seguridad.
safety ('seif·ti) *n.* **1,** (safeness) seguridad. **2,** (protection) protec-

ción. —*adj.* de seguridad. —**safety belt**, cinturón de seguridad; *naut.* cinturón salvavidas. —**safety glass**, vidrio *o* cristal de seguridad. —**safety pin**, imperdible. —**safety razor**, máquina *o* maquinilla de afeitar. —**safety valve**, **1,** (automatic escape valve) válvula de seguridad. **2,** *fig.* (emotional outlet) válvula de escape.

saffron ('sæf·rən) *n.* azafrán.

sag (sæg) *n.* **1,** (bending) combadura; comba. **2,** *naut.* deriva. **3,** (decline in price) baja. —*v.i.* **1,** (bend) combarse; ceder. **2,** (droop) pender; colgar; aflojarse. **3,** (weaken) debilitarse; declinar. **4,** (decline in price) bajar.

saga ('sa·gə) *n.* saga.

sagacious (sə'gei·ʃəs) *adj.* sagaz; astuto.

sagacity (sə'gæs·ə·ti) *n.* sagacidad.

sage (seidʒ) *adj.* sabio; sagaz. —*n.* **1,** (wise man) sabio. **2,** *bot.* (herb) salvia; (bush) artemisa.

Sagittarius (ˌsædʒ·ɪ'tɛr·i·əs) *n.* Sagitario.

said (sɛd) *v., pret. & p.p. de* **say.**

sail (seil) *n.* **1,** (piece of canvas to propel a ship) vela. **2,** (arm of a windmill) brazo. **3,** (ride in a vessel) paseo *o* viaje en barco. —*v.i.* **1,** (move along in a vessel) navegar. **2,** (begin a voyage) embarcarse; salir. **3,** (glide) navegar; flotar; deslizarse. —*v.t.* **1,** (handle; steer) gobernar; manejar. **2,** (travel on or over) navegar. —**set sail,** hacerse a la mar; hacerse a la vela.

sailboat *n.* barco de vela; velero.

sailfish *n.* aguja de mar.

sailing ('sei·lɪŋ) *n.* **1,** (navigation) navegación. **2,** (ride on a vessel) paseo en barco. **3,** (departure from port) salida. —*adj.* velero; de vela.

sailor ('sei·lər) *n.* **1,** (mariner; seaman) marino; marinero. **2,** (hat) canotié. —*adj.* marinero; marino.

saint (seint) *n. & adj.* santo. —*v.t.* canonizar. —**sainthood,** *n.* santidad. —**saintliness,** *n.* santidad. —**saintly,** *adj.* santo.

Saint Bernard (bər'nard) perro de San Bernardo.

sainted ('sein·tɪd) *adj.* **1,** (canonized) canonizado. **2,** (sacred) bendito; santificado. **3,** (saintly) santo.

Saint Vitus's dance (vai·təs) baile de San Vito.

sake (seik) *n.* **1,** (purpose) motivo; razón. **2,** (interest; benefit) interés; bien. —**for goodness' sake,** por el amor de Dios.

salaam (sə'laːm) *n.* zalema. —*v.t.* hacer zalemas a. —*v.i.* hacer zalemas.

salable ('seil·ə·bəl) *adj.* vendible.

salacious (sə'lei·ʃəs) *adj.* salaz; lascivo. —**salaciousness,** *n.* salacidad; lascivia.

salad ('sæl·əd) *n.* ensalada. —**salad bowl,** ensaladera. —**salad dressing,** aderezo; aliño.

salamander ('sæl·əˌmæn·dər) *n.* salamandra.

salami (sə'la·mi) *n.* embutido; salchichón.

salaried ('sæl·ə·rid) *adj.* **1,** (receiving a salary) asalariado. **2,** (yielding a salary) retribuido.

salary ('sæl·ə·ri) *n.* salario.

sale (seil) *n.* **1,** (selling) venta. **2,** (auction) subasta. —**for sale,** de venta; se vende. —**on sale,** en venta. —**sales tax,** impuesto de *o* sobre ventas.

salesman ('seilz·mən) *n.* **1,** (traveling agent) vendedor; viajante. **2,** [*también,* **salesclerk**] (seller in a store) dependiente. —**salesgirl; saleslady; saleswoman,** *n.* dependienta; vendedora.

salesmanship ('seilz·mən·ʃɪp) *n.* **1,** (work of a salesman) venta. **2,** (ability at selling) arte de vender.

salicylate ('sæl·əˌsɪl·et; sə'lɪs·əˌleit) *n.* salicilato. —**salicylic** ('sæl·əˌsɪl·ɪk) *adj.* salicílico.

salient ('sei·li·ənt) *adj.* sobresaliente; destacado. —*n.* saliente. —**salience,** *n.* énfasis; lo que sobresale.

saline ('sei·lain) *adj.* salino.

saliva (sə'lai·və) *n.* saliva. —**salivary** ('sæl·ə·vɛr·i) *adj.* salival. —**salivate** ('sæl·əˌveit) *v.i.* salivar. —**salivation,** *n.* salivación.

sallow ('sæl·o) *adj.* pálido; lívido. —**sallowness,** *n.* palidez; lividez.

sally ('sæl·i) *n.* **1,** *mil.* salida; acometida. **2,** (sudden start) arranque; ímpetu. **3,** (bright retort) salida; ocurrencia. —*v.i.* acometer; hacer una salida.

salmagundi (ˌsæl·mə'gʌn·di) *n.* salpicón; mescolanza.

salmon ('sæm·ən) *n.* salmón.

salon (sə'laːn) *n.* salón.
saloon (sə'luːn) *n.* **1,** (public bar) cantina; taberna. **2,** (public room of a ship) salón.
salt (sɔlt) *n.* **1,** (mineral) sal. **2,** *colloq.* (sailor) marinero. —*adj.* salado; salino. —*v.t.* **1,** (season) echar *o* poner sal a. **2,** (give tang to) avivar; aguzar. **3,** (preserve with salt) salar. —**salted,** *adj.* salado.
saltcellar *n.* salero.
salt lick lamedero.
saltpeter *también,* **saltpetre** (ˌsɔlt'pi·tər) *n.* salitre.
salt water agua salobre; agua salada. —**salt-water,** *adj.* de agua salada; marino.
saltwort *n.* barrilla.
salty ('sɔlt·i) *adj.* **1,** (containing salt) salado. **2,** (witty; pungent) agudo; picante; saleroso.
salubrious (sə'lu·bri·əs) *adj.* salubre; saludable. —**salubriousness; salubrity,** *n.* salubridad.
salutary ('sæl·jə·tɛr·i) *adj.* saludable; beneficioso.
salutation (ˌsæl·jʊ'tei·ʃən) *n.* salutación; saludo.
salutatory (sə'lu·tə·tor·i) *adj.* saludador. —*n.* discurso; salutación. —**salutatorian** (-'tor·i·ən) *n.* saludador.
salute (sə'lut) *v.t.* & *i.* saludar. —*n.* saludo.
salvage ('sæl·vɪdʒ) *n.* salvamento. —*v.t.* salvar.
salvation (sæl'vei·ʃən) *n.* salvación. —**Salvation Army,** Ejército de Salvación.
salve (sæv) *n.* **1,** (ointment) ungüento. **2,** *fig.* (consolation) alivio; consuelo. —*v.t.* **1,** (heal) curar con ungüentos. **2,** (soothe) aliviar.
salver ('sæl·vər) *n.* bandeja.
salvo ('sæl·vo) *n.* salva.
Samaritan (sə'mær·ə·tən) *adj.* & *n.* samaritano.
samarium (sə'mær·i·əm) *n.* samario.
samba ('sam·bə) *n.* samba.
same (seim) *adj.* & *pron.* mismo. —*adv.* igualmente. —**all the same,** a pesar de todo. —**just the same,** lo mismo; sin embargo.
sameness ('seim·nəs) *n.* **1,** (identity) igualdad; identidad. **2,** (monotony) monotonía.
samovar ('sæm·əˌvar) *n.* samovar.
sampan ('sæm·pæn) *n.* sampán.
sample ('sæm·pəl) *n.* muestra; prueba. —*v.t.* probar; catar.
sampler ('sæm·plər) *n.* **1,** (piece of embroidery) dechado; marcador. **2,** (tester) probador; catador. **3,** (one who prepares samples) preparador de muestras.
samurai ('sæm·ʊˌrai) *n.* samurai.
sanatorium (ˌsænə'tor·i·əm) *n.* [*pl.* **-a** (-ə)] sanatorio.
sanctify ('sæŋk·təˌfai) *v.t.* santificar. —**sanctification** (-fɪ'kei·ʃən) *n.* santificación.
sanctimony ('sæŋk·təˌmo·ni) *n.* beatería; santurronería. —**sanctimonious** (-'mo·ni·əs) *adj.* beato; beaturrón; santurrón.
sanction ('sæŋk·ʃən) *n.* sanción. —*v.t.* sancionar.
sanctity ('sæŋk·tə·ti) *n.* santidad.
sanctuary ('sæŋk·tʃʊˌɛr·i) *n.* **1,** (sacred place) santuario. **2,** (place of refuge) asilo; refugio.
sanctum ('sæŋk·təm) *n.* **1,** (sacred place) lugar sagrado. **2,** (refuge) retiro; refugio.
sand (sænd) *n.* **1,** (fine mineral particles) arena. **2,** *pl.* (desert; beach) arenal; playa; desierto. **3,** *slang* (courage) ánimo; resolución. —*v.t.* **1,** (sprinkle with sand) enarenar. **2,** (rub with sandpaper) lijar.
sandal ('sæn·dəl) *n.* sandalia.
sandalwood *n.* sándalo.
sandbag *n.* saco de arena. —*v.t.* **1,** (block with sandbags) guarnecer con sacos de arena. **2,** *slang* (hit or betray unexpectedly) golpear *o* traicionar inesperadamente.
sandblast *v.t.* limpiar con arena a presión.
sander ('sæn·dər) *n.* **1,** (person who sands) lijador. **2,** (device for spreading sand) arenadora. **3,** (machine for rubbing or smoothing) lijadora.
sandhog *n.* trabajador de túnel.
sandman *n.* [*pl.* **-men**] genio del sueño.
sandpaper *n.* lija. —*v.t.* lijar.
sandpiper *n.* ave zancuda semejante a la agachadiza.
sandstone *n.* arenisca.
sandwich ('sænd·wɪtʃ) *n.* emparedado; sandwich. —*v.t.* intercalar; insertar.
sandy ('sæn·di) *adj.* **1,** (of or like sand) arenoso; arenisco. **2,** (yel-

lowish) rufo; de color de arena. **3,** *slang* (courageous) valeroso; valiente; animoso.
sane (sein) *adj.* cuerdo; sensato; juicioso. —**saneness,** *n.* cordura; sensatez.
sang (sæŋ) *v., pret. de* **sing.**
sangui- (sæŋ·gwɪ) *prefijo* sangui-; sangre: *sanguiferous,* sanguífero.
sanguinary ('sæŋ·gwɪˌnɛr·i) *adj.* sanguinario.
sanguine ('sæŋ·gwɪn) *adj.* **1,** (hopeful) confiado; optimista; esperanzado. **2,** (ruddy) sanguino; sanguíneo; rubicundo. —**sanguinolent** (sæn'gwɪn·ə·lənt) *adj.* sanguinolento.
sanitarium (ˌsæn·ə'tɛr·i·əm) *n.* sanatorio.
sanitary ('sæn·əˌtɛr·i) *adj.* sanitario; higiénico. —**sanitary belt,** cinturón *o* cordón sanitario. —**sanitary napkin,** toallita *o* almohadilla higiénica; tampón *o* absorbente higiénico.
sanitation (ˌsæn·ə'tei·ʃən) *n.* **1,** (science or practice of hygienics) saneamiento. **2,** (disposal of refuse and sewage) sanidad.
sanity ('sæn·ə·ti) *n.* cordura; juicio; sensatez.
sank (sæŋk) *v., pret. de* **sink.**
Sanskrit *también,* **Sanscrit** ('sæn·skrɪt) *n. & adj.* sánscrito.
sap (sæp) *n.* **1,** (juice of a plant) savia. **2,** *slang* (fool) tonto; necio. **3,** *mil.* zanja; zapa. —*v.t.* **[sapped, sapping] 1,** (undermine) zapar; socavar. **2,** (weaken) debilitar; agotar. —**sapper,** *n.* zapador.
sapid ('sæp·ɪd) *adj.* sápido. —**sapidity** (sə'pɪd·ə·ti) *n.* sapidez.
sapient ('sei·pi·ənt) *adj.* sapiente. —**sapience,** *n.* sapiencia.
sapling ('sæp·lɪŋ) *n.* vástago; renuevo.
sapphire ('sæf·air) *n.* zafiro. —*adj.* zafirino; zafíreo. —**sapphirine** ('sæf·ər·ɪn) *adj.* zafirino; zafíreo.
sappy ('sæp·i) *adj.* **1,** (juicy) jugoso; lleno de savia. **2,** (vigorous) enérgico; vigoroso. **3,** *slang* (foolish) necio; tonto.
saraband ('sær·əˌbænd) *n.* zarabanda.
Saracen ('sær·ə·sən) *n. & adj.* sarraceno.
sarcasm ('sar·kæz·əm) *n.* sarcasmo. —**sarcastic** (sar'kæs·tɪk) *adj.* sarcástico; mordaz.
sarco- (sar·ko; -kə) *prefijo* sarco-; carne: *sarcophagus,* sarcófago.
sarcoma (sar'ko·mə) *n.* sarcoma.
sarcophagus (sar'kaf·ə·gəs) *n.* sarcófago.
sardine (sar'diːn) *n.* sardina.
sardonic (sar'dan·ɪk) *adj.* sardónico; mordaz; sarcástico.
sargasso (sar'gæs·o) *n.* sargazo.
sarong (sə'rɔŋ) *n.* sarong.
sarsaparilla (ˌsæs·pə'rɪl·ə) *n.* zarzaparrilla.
sartorial (sar'tor·i·əl) *adj.* de sastre; de sastrería.
sash (sæʃ) *n.* **1,** (window frame) marco *o* bastidor de ventana. **2,** (band around the waist) banda; faja. —*v.t.* proveer de bastidores; poner marcos a.
sassafras ('sæs·əˌfræs) *n.* sasafrás.
sassy ('sæs·i) *adj., colloq.* insolente; descarado. —**sassiness,** *n., colloq.* insolencia; descaro.
sat (sæt) *v., pret. & p.p. de* **sit.**
Satan ('sei·tən) *n.* Satán; el diablo. —**satanic** (sə'tæn·ɪk) *adj.* satánico.
satchel ('sætʃ·əl) *n.* maletín; cartapacio; mochila.
sate (seit) *v.t.* **1,** (satisfy) saciar; satisfacer; llenar. **2,** (surfeit; glut) hastiar; hartar.
sateen (sæ'tiːn) *n.* satén.
satellite ('sæt·əˌlait) *n.* satélite.
satiate ('sei·ʃiˌeit) *v.t.* saciar; hartar; hastiar. —**satiable,** *adj.* saciable. —**satiation,** *n.* saciedad.
satiety (sə'tai·ə·ti) *n.* saciedad; hastío.
satin ('sæt·ən) *n.* raso. —*adj.* de raso; satinado. —**satiny,** *adj.* satinado.
satinwood *n.* aceitillo.
satire ('sæt·air) *n.* sátira. —**satiric** (sə'tɪr·ɪk); **satirical,** *adj.* satírico. —**satirist** (-ə·rɪst) *n.* satírico.
satirize ('sæt·ə·raiz) *v.t.* satirizar.
satisfaction (ˌsæt·ɪs'fæk·ʃən) *n.* satisfacción. —**satisfactory** (-tə·ri) *adj.* satisfactorio.
satisfy ('sæt·ɪsˌfai) *v.t.* **1,** (supply the needs of) satisfacer. **2,** (pay fully) pagar; resarcir. **3,** (convince) convencer. **4,** (fulfill the conditions of) colmar; cumplir. **5,** (atone for) contentar; dar satis-

facción a. —*v.i.* satisfacer; dar satisfacción.
satrap ('sæt·ræp) *n.* sátrapa. —**satrapy**, *n.* satrapía.
saturate ('sætʃ·əˌreit) *v.t.* saturar; impregnar. —**saturation**, *n.* saturación.
Saturday ('sæt·ər·de) *n.* sábado. —*adj.* sabatino; del sábado.
Saturn ('sæt·ərn) *n.* Saturno.
saturnine ('sæt·ərˌnain) *adj.* saturnino.
satyr ('sæt·ər) *n.* sátiro.
sauce (sɔs) *n.* **1,** (dressing) salsa; crema. **2,** (compote of fruit) jalea; compota. **3,** *colloq.* (pertness) insolencia; descaro. **4,** *fig.* (zest) salsa; sabor.
saucepan *n.* cacerola; cazuela.
saucer ('sɔ·sər) *n.* platillo; platito.
saucy ('sɔ·si) *adj.* **1,** (rude) descarado; insolente. **2,** (pert) vivo; gracioso; simpático.
sauerkraut ('sau·ərˌkraut) *n.* encurtido de col picada; chucruta.
saunter ('sɔn·tər) *v.i.* **1,** (stroll) pasear; dar un paseo. **2,** (walk with leisurely step) andar con paso tranquilo. —*n.* **1,** (stroll) paseo. **2,** (leisurely step) paso tranquilo.
-saur (sor) *sufijo* -sauro; lagarto: *dinosaur,* dinosauro.
sauro- (sor·o; -ə) *prefijo* sauro-; lagarto: *sauropod,* saurópodo.
sausage ('sɔ·sɪdʒ) *n.* salchicha; embutido; butifarra; longaniza.
sauté (so'tei) *v.t.* saltear. —*adj.* salteado.
sauterne (so'tʌɹn) *n.* vino de Sauternes; vino blanco.
savage ('sæv·ɪdʒ) *n.* & *adj.* salvaje. —**savagery**, *n.* salvajismo.
savanna (sə'væn·ə) *n.* sabana.
savant (sæ'vant) *n.* erudito; sabio; letrado.
save (seiv) *v.t.* **1,** (preserve) salvar; preservar. **2,** (conserve) guardar; conservar. **3,** (make safe) salvar; librar. **4,** (keep safe) amparar; proteger. **5,** (put aside for the future) ahorrar; guardar. **6,** (gain) ganar; ahorrar; economizar. —*v.i.* economizar. —*prep.* salvo; excepto. —*conj.* a no ser que.
saving ('sei·vɪŋ) *n.* **1,** (economy) ahorro; economía. **2,** *law* (exception) salvedad; excepción. —*adj.* **1,** (economical) ahorrativo; económico. **2,** (redeeming) salvador. —*prep.* salvo; excepto. —*conj.* a no ser que. —**daylight saving time,** horario de verano. —**savings bank,** caja de ahorros; banco de ahorros.
savior ('seiv·jər) *n.* salvador; *cap.* [*usu.* **Saviour**] el Salvador; Jesucristo.
savoir-faire (ˌsæv·war'feːr) *n.* maña; destreza.
savoir-vivre (ˌsæv·war'viː·vrə) *n.* buenos modales.
savor ('sei·vər) *n.* sabor; gusto. —*v.t.* **1,** (season) sazonar. **2,** (taste) saborear; gustar. —*v.i.* oler. —**savor of**, saber a; oler a.
savory ('sei·və·ri) *adj.* sabroso; agradable. —*n.* **1,** (appetizer) aperitivo. **2,** *bot.* ajedrea.
savvy ('sæv·i) *v.t.* & *i.*, *slang* comprender; entender. —*n.*, *slang* comprensión; entendimiento.
saw (sɔː) *n.* **1,** (cutting tool) sierra. **2,** (proverb) refrán; dicho. —*v.i.* & *t.* serrar; aserrar. —*v.*, *pret. de* **see.**
sawbuck *n.* **1,** (sawhorse) cabrilla. **2,** *slang* billete de diez.
sawdust *n.* serrín; aserrín; aserraduras (*pl.*).
sawfish *n.* pez sierra.
sawhorse *n.* cabrilla; burro; borrico.
sawmill *n.* aserradero; serrería.
sawyer ('sɔ·jər) *n.* aserrador.
Saxon ('sæk·sən) *n.* & *adj.* sajón.
saxophone ('sæk·səˌfon) *n.* saxófono; saxofón. —**saxophonist**, *n.* saxofonista.
say (sei) *v.t.* [*pret.* & *p.p.* **said**] decir. —*n.* **1,** (what one has to say) decir; dicho. **2,** (chance to speak) turno (de hablar). —**I should say so!**, ¡Ya lo creo! —**no sooner said than done**, dicho y hecho. —**that is to say**, es decir.
saying ('sei·ɪŋ) *n.* dicho; refrán.
say-so *n.*, *colloq.* **1,** (unsupported statement; rumor) rumor. **2,** (right of decision) decisión; autoridad.
scab (skæb) *n.* **1,** (crust over a sore) costra. **2,** (mange) roña; sarna. **3,** (strikebreaker) esquirol. **4,** *slang* (scoundrel) truhán; truante; bribón.
scabbard ('skæb·ərd) *n.* vaina.
scabby ('skæb·i) *adj.* **1,** (covered with scabs) costroso; roñoso. **2,** (mean) vil; despreciable; bajo.
scabies ('skei·biz) *n.* escabiosis; sarna.

scabrous ('skei·brəs) *adj.* escabroso.
scads (skædz) *n.pl., slang* montañas; montones; puñados.
scaffold ('skæf·əld) *n.* **1,** (temporary platform) tablado. **2,** (supporting framework) andamio. **3,** (platform for a gallows) patíbulo; cadalso. —**scaffolding,** *n.* andamio; andamiaje.
scalawag ('skæl·ə,wæg) *n., colloq.* truhán; golfo.
scald (skɔld) *v.t.* escaldar. —*n.* escaldadura.
scale (skeil) *n.* **1,** (flake) escama. **2,** (ladder) escala. **3,** (instrument for weighing) balanza. **4,** (series of marks; system of proportion; gradation) escala. **5,** *music* escala. —*v.t.* **1,** (remove scales from) escamar; limpiar de escamas. **2,** (cover with scales) poner escamas a. **3,** (cause to skip) tirar al ras; hacer resbalar. **4,** (weigh) pesar. **5,** (climb) escalar. **6,** (project according to scale) poner a escala. **7,** (reduce to a scale) reducir a escala. **8,** (regulate) graduar a escala. —*v.i.* **1,** (climb) trepar; escalar. **2,** (flake) pelarse. **3,** (become covered with scales) cubrirse de escamas; formarse escamas.
scallion ('skæl·jən) *n.* **1,** = **shallot. 2,** = **leek.**
scallop ('skæl·əp) *n.* **1,** (mollusk) molusco bivalvo. **2,** (its shell) pechina; concha. **3,** (small decorative curve) festón. —*v.t.* **1,** (cut in scallops) festonear. **2,** (bake) cocer *u* hornear a la crema; cocer en concha.
scalp (skælp) *n.* cuero cabelludo; pericráneo. —*v.t.* **1,** (remove the scalp of) arrancar el pericráneo a; quitar el cuero cabelludo a. **2,** *colloq.* (buy and sell at inflated prices) revender a precios exorbitantes. —**scalper,** *n.* revendedor; desollador.
scalpel ('skæl·pəl) *n.* escalpelo; bisturí.
scaly ('skei·li) *adj.* **1,** (covered with scales) escamoso. **2,** *slang* (despicable) vil; despreciable.
scamp (skæmp) *n.* bribón; truhán; pícaro. —*v.t.* chapucear.
scamper ('skæm·pər) *v.i.* escabullirse; escaparse.
scan (skæn) *v.t.* **1,** (scrutinize) escudriñar. **2,** (glance hastily) dar un vistazo a. **3,** *pros.* escandir. **4,** *TV* explorar. —*v.i.* medir versos. —**scansion** (-ʃən) *n.* escansión.
scandal ('skæn·dəl) *n.* escándalo. —**scandalize,** *v.t.* escandalizar. —**scandalous,** *adj.* escandaloso.
scandalmonger *n.* propagador de escándalos; murmurador.
Scandinavian (,skæn·dɪ'nei·vi·ən) *n. & adj.* escandinavo.
scandium ('skæn·di·əm) *n.* escandio.
scansion ('skæn·ʃən) *n.* escansión.
scant (skænt) *adj.* escaso; insuficiente. —**scanty,** *adj.* limitado; corto; solo.
scapegoat ('skeip,got) *n.* cabeza de turco; víctima propiciatoria.
scapegrace ('skeip,greis) *n.* truhán; pícaro; bribón.
scapula ('skæp·jə·lə) *n.* omóplato; escápula.
scapular ('skæp·jə·lər) *adj.* escapular. —*n.* **1,** (eccles. garment) escapulario. **2,** *surg.* vendaje para el omóplato.
scar (ska:r) *n.* cicatriz; marca; señal. —*v.t.* señalar; marcar. —*v.i.* cicatrizarse.
scarab ('skær·əb) *n.* escarabajo.
scarce (skɛrs) *adj.* **1,** (not abundant) escaso; insuficiente; limitado. **2,** (uncommon) raro; extraño. —**scarcely,** *adv.* apenas; escasamente; ciertamente no. —**scarcely ever,** raramente; casi nunca.
scarcity ('skɛr·sə·ti) *n.* **1,** (shortage; lack) escasez; insuficiencia; carestía. **2,** (uncommonness) rareza. *También,* **scarceness.**
scare (ske:r) *v.t.* **1,** (frighten) asustar; espantar. **2,** (intimidate) amedrentar; atemorizar. —*v.i.* amedrentarse; atemorizarse. —*n.* susto; alarma. —**scare away,** espantar; ahuyentar. —**scare up,** *colloq.* conseguir; obtener; recoger.
scarecrow *n.* espantajo; espantapájaros.
scarf (skarf) *n.* **1,** (decorative strip) banda; faja. **2,** (muffler) bufanda. **3,** (shawl) chal. **4,** (cravat) chalina. **5,** *carpentry* ensambladura francesa.
scarlet ('skar·lɪt) *n. & adj.* escarlata. —**scarlet fever,** escarlatina; escarlata.
scarp (skarp) *n.* escarpa; escarpadura; declive.
scary ('skɛr·i) *adj., colloq.* **1,**

(frightening) temible; pavoroso. 2, (timid) tímido; asustadizo.
scat (skæt) *v.t., colloq.* desaparecer. —*interj.* ¡fuera!; ¡zape!
scathe (skeið) *v.t.* denunciar; acusar. —**scathing**, *n.* denuncia; acusación; crítica. —*adj.* áspero; duro; rudo.
scatter ('skæt·ər) *v.t.* diseminar; esparcir; desparramar. —*v.i.* diseminarse; desparramarse. —*n.* esparcimiento; dispersión. —**scatter rug**, alfombra pequeña.
scatterbrain *n.* cabeza de chorlito. —**scatterbrained**, *adj.* ligero de cascos; casquivano.
scattering ('skæt·ər·ɪŋ) *n.* 1, (dispersal) esparcimiento; dispersión. 2, (sparse distribution) pequeño número; pequeña cantitad.
scavenger ('skæv·ɪn·dʒər) *n.* 1, (street cleaner) basurero; barrendero. 2, (animal) animal de carroña.
scenario (sɪ'nɛr·i·o) *n.* libreto; guión; argumento.
scene (siːn) *n.* 1, *theat.* escena. 2, (view; picture) paisaje; vista. 3, (display of feeling) espectáculo; arrebato; escena.
scenery ('sin·ə·ri) *n.* 1, (landscape) paisaje. 2, *theat.* decoración.
scenic ('si·nɪk) *adj.* 1, (pert. to scenery) escénico. 2, (picturesque) pintoresco; atractivo.
scent (sɛnt) *n.* 1, (odor) olor; aroma. 2, (course of an animal) pista; rastro. 3, (perfume) perfume; aroma. 4, (sense of smell) olfato. —*v.t.* 1, (smell) oler; olfatear. 2. (suspect) sospechar. 3, (perfume) perfumar; aromatizar.
scepter *también*, **sceptre** ('sɛp·tər) *n.* cetro.
sceptic ('skɛp·tɪk) *n.* & *adj.* = skeptic. —**sceptical**, *adj.* = **skeptical**. —**scepticism** (-tɪ·sɪz·əm) *n.* = **skepticism**.
schedule ('skɛdʒ·ul) *n.* 1, (list; catalogue) lista; catálogo; cuadro. 2, (agenda) plan; programa; agenda. 3, (timetable) horario. —*v.t.* 1, (include in a schedule) proyectar; planear; programar. 2, (make a schedule of) catalogar. 3, (set the time for) fijar la hora de.
scheme (skiːm) *n.* 1, (system; plan) esquema; proyecto; designio. 2, (plot) confabulación; ardid; treta. —*v.t.* & *i.* proyectar; planear; urdir. —**schematic** (ski'mæt·ɪk) *adj.* esquemático. —**scheming**, *adj.* intrigante; urdidor.
schemer ('ski·mər) *n.* 1, (one who makes schemes) proyectista. 2, (plotter) intrigante; urdidor.
schism ('sɪz·əm) *n.* cisma. —**schismatic** (sɪz'mæt·ɪk) *adj.* cismático.
schist (ʃɪst) *n.* esquisto.
schizo- (skɪz·o; -ə; skɪt·so; -sə) *prefijo* esquizo-; disociamiento; división: *schizophrenia,* esquizofrenia.
schizoid ('skɪz·ɔid; 'skɪt·sɔid) *adj.* & *n.* esquizofrénico.
schizophrenia (ˌskɪz·ə'fri·ni·ə; ˌskɪt·sə-) *n.* esquizofrenia. —**schizophrenic** (-'frɛn·ɪk) *adj.* & *n.* esquizofrénico.
schnapps (ʃnaps) *n.* aguardiente.
scholar ('skal·ər) *n.* 1, (student) escolar; estudiante. 2, (learned man) erudito; intelectual. 3, (student with a scholarship) becario.
scholarly ('skal·ər·li) *adj.* erudito; intelectual. —*adv.* eruditamente.
scholarship ('skal·ər·ʃɪp) *n.* 1, (learning) erudición. 2, (monetary assistance) beca.
scholastic (skə'læs·tɪk) *n.* & *adj.* escolástico.
school (skuːl) *n.* 1, (educational establishment) escuela. 2, (large body of fish) banco; cardumen. —*v.t.* instruir; enseñar; adiestrar.
school board junta de educación *o* de instrucción pública.
schoolbook *n.* libro de texto; libro escolar.
schoolboy *n.* alumno (de escuela).
schoolgirl *n.* alumna (de escuela).
schoolhouse *n.* edificio escolar; escuela.
schooling ('skul·ɪŋ) *n.* instrucción; enseñanza.
schoolmaster *n.* maestro de escuela.
schoolmate *n.* compañero de escuela.
schoolmistress *n.* maestra de escuela.
schoolroom *n.* aula; clase; sala (de clase).
schoolteacher *n.* maestro de escuela.
schoolyard *n.* patio de recreo.
schooner ('sku·nər) *n.* 1, *naut.*

goleta; escuna. **2,** (beer glass) caña; vaso grande.
schwa (ʃwa:) *n., phonet.* e débil *o* relajada.
sciatic (saiˈæt·ɪk) *adj.* ciático. **—sciatica** (-ɪ·kə) *n.* ciática.
science (ˈsai·əns) *n.* ciencia.
scientific (ˌsai·ənˈtɪf·ɪk) *adj.* científico.
scientist (ˈsai·ən·tɪst) *n.* científico; hombre de ciencia.
scimitar (ˈsɪm·ə·tər) *n.* cimitarra.
scintillate (ˈsɪn·təˌleit) *v.i.* centellar. **—scintillation,** *n.* centelleo.
scion (ˈsai·ən) *n.* vástago.
scissors (ˈsɪz·ərz) *n.sing. o pl.* tijeras. **—scissor,** *v.t.* cortar con tijeras.
sclero- (sklɪr·o; -ə) *prefijo* esclero; duro: *scleroderma,* esclerodermia.
sclerosis (sklɪˈro·sɪs) *n.* [*pl.* **-ses** (-siz)] esclerosis.
sclerotic (sklɪˈrat·ɪk) *adj.* esclerótico.
scoff (skaf) *v.i.* mofarse; burlarse. **—*n.*** mofa; burla. **—scoff at,** mofarse de; burlarse de.
scold (skold) *v.t. & i.* regañar; reprender. **—*n.*** regañon (*fem.* regañona). **—scolding,** *n.* reprimenda; reprensión; regaño.
scoop (skup) *n.* **1,** (deep shovel for taking up sand, dirt, etc.) pala; cucharón de grúa. **2,** (kitchen utensil) cucharón; paleta. **3,** (bailing vessel) achicador. **4,** (act of scooping; amount taken) cucharada; paletada. **5,** (hollow) hueco; cavidad. **6,** *colloq.* (journalistic beat) primicia; primera publicación de una noticia. **—*v.t.* 1,** (hollow out) ahuecar; vaciar. **2,** (bail out) achicar. **3,** (remove with a scoop) sacar (con pala, paleta, cucharón, etc.). **4,** *colloq., journalism* publicar antes que nadie.
scoot (skut) *v.i., colloq.* correr precipitadamente; volar. **—*v.t., colloq.*** arrojar. **—*n., colloq.*** carrera precipitada.
scooter (ˈskut·ər) *n.* **1,** (child's vehicle) patín; deslizador. **2,** (iceboat) deslizador; lancha rápida.
scope (skop) *n.* **1,** (outlook; range) alcance; campo. **2,** (room for free action or observation) campo *o* esfera de acción. **3,** (extent; length) extensión; alcance.
-scope (skop) *sufijo* -scopio; -scopo; *forma nombres denotando* instrumento o sistema para observar o ver: *fluoroscope,* fluoroscopio; *gyroscope,* giróscopo.
scopolamine (skɔˈpal·əˌmin) *n.* escopolamina.
-scopy (sko·pi; skə-) *suffix* -scopia; observación o examen por medio de instrumentos ópticos: *fluoroscopy,* fluoroscopia.
scorbutic (skorˈbju·tɪk) *adj.* escorbútico.
scorch (skortʃ) *v.t.* **1,** (singe) chamuscar; socarrar. **2,** (parch) agostar; resecar; abrasar. **3,** (criticize harshly) reprochar; criticar duramente. **—*v.i.*** chamuscarse; resecarse. **—*n.*** chamusquina.
score (sko:r) *n.* **1,** (in sports and games) tanteo; tantos (*pl.*). **2,** (reckoning) cuenta. **3,** (notch) muesca; mella. **4,** (scratch) señal; raya. **5,** (reason; ground) motivo; razón. **6,** (twenty) veintena; *pl.* muchos; montones. **7,** *music* partitura. **8,** (grade; rating) calificación. **—*v.t.* 1,** (mark) rayar; marcar con muescas *o* rayas. **2,** (reckon) contar; anotar (tantos). **3,** (achieve) conseguir; ganar; lograr. **4,** (rate) calificar. **5,** *music* instrumentar. **6,** (berate) regañar; criticar duramente. **—*v.i.* 1,** (in sports and games) apuntarse un tanto; ganar un punto. **2,** (make notches) hacer rayas; hacer muescas *o* señales. **—keep score,** tantear; apuntar los tantos.
scorn (skorn) *n.* desprecio; desdén. **—*v.t.*** desdeñar; despreciar. **—scornful,** *adj.* desdeñoso.
Scorpio (ˈskor·pi·o) *n., astron.* Escorpión.
scorpion (ˈskor·pi·ən) *n.* alacrán; escorpión.
Scotch (skatʃ) *adj.* escocés. **—*n.* 1,** (language) escocés. **2,** (whiskey) whisky escocés. **3,** *l.c.* (cut) corte; señal; marca. **4,** *l.c.* (block) obstáculo; impedimento. **5,** *l.c.* (wedge) cuña; calce. **—*v.t., l.c.* 1,** (cut) cortar; marcar. **2,** (foil; quash) frustrar. **3,** (block) calzar; poner cuña a. **—Scotch tape,** (*T.N.*) cinta de celulosa. **—Scotch terrier; Scottie** (ˈskat·i) perro escocés.
Scotchman (ˈskatʃ·mən) *n.* [*pl.* **-men**] escocés.
scot-free (ˌskatˈfri:) *adj.* **1,** (ex-

empt; clear) exento; libre; limpio. 2, (unpunished) impune.
Scots (skats) *adj.* escocés. —*n.* 1, (language) escocés. 2, *pl. de* Scot. —**Scotsman** (-mən) *n.* [*pl.* **-men**] escocés.
Scottish ('skat·ɪʃ) *adj.* & *n.* escocés.
scoundrel ('skaun·drəl) *n.* truhán; pícaro; canalla. —**scoundrelly** (-drə·li) *adj.* truhán; canallesco.
scour (skaur) *v.t.* 1, (clean by friction) estregar; restregar. 2, (flush) limpiar a chorro. 3, (purge) purgar. 4, (search through) reconocer; explorar detenidamente. —**scouring,** *n.* fregado; estregamiento. —**scourings,** *n.pl.* residuo; desecho.
scourge (skʌɹdʒ) *n.* 1, (whip) azote; flagelo. 2, (affliction) calamidad; aflicción. —*v.t.* azotar; flagelar.
scout (skaut) *n.* 1, *mil.* (soldier) batidor; explorador; escucha; (plane or ship) avión *o* barco de reconocimiento. 2, *cap.* (Boy Scout) niño explorador; (Girl Scout) niña exploradora. 3, *colloq.* (fellow) tipo; sujeto. —*v.t.* & *i.* (reconnoiter) explorar; reconocer. —*v.t.* (scoff at) mofarse de.
scoutmaster *n.* [*también, fem.,* **scoutmistress**] jefe de escuchas.
scow (skau) *n.* lanchón; barcaza.
scowl (skaul) *v.i.* fruncir el ceño; poner mala cara. —*n.* ceño; mala cara.
scrabble ('skræb·əl) *v.i.* 1, (scratch; scrape) raspar; arañar. 2, (scrawl) garabatear; hacer garabatos. —*n.* 1, (scrawl) garabato. 2, *cap., T.N.* (word game) cierto juego basado en crucigramas.
scraggly ('skræg·li) *adj.* áspero; irregular; rudo.
scraggy (skræg·i) *adj.* delgado; huesudo; anguloso.
scram (skræm) *v.i., slang* marcharse; largarse.
scramble ('skræm·bəl) *v.i.* 1, (climb) trepar. 2, (crawl) arrastrarse. 3, (str le) pelear; bregar; revolverse. —*v.t.* revolver; mezclar. —*n.* 1, (fight) contienda; lucha. 2, (climb) ascenso; trepa. —**scrambled eggs,** revoltillo de huevos; huevos revueltos.
scrap (skræp) *n.* 1, (fragment) parte; trozo; fragmento. 2, *pl.* (leftovers) sobras. 3, (discarded iron or steel) chatarra; metal viejo. 4, *slang* (quarrel) pelea; pendencia; camorra. —*v.t.* 1, (break up) romper; destrozar; convertir en chatarra. 2, (discard) desechar; descartar. —*v.i., slang* (quarrel) pelearse; reñir.
scrapbook *n.* álbum de recortes.
scrape (skreip) *v.t.* 1, (shave the surface of) raspar; rascar. 2, (scratch; graze) arañar. —*v.i.* 1, (scrape; grate) raspar; rascar. 2, (produce a harsh noise) desafinar. 3, (get by with difficulty) arañar. —*n.* 1, (act of scraping) raspadura; arañazo. 2, (sound of scraping) chirrido. 3, (embarrassing situation) aprieto; apuro; lío. —**scrape along; scrape through,** ir tirando; arreglárselas. —**scrape out** *o* **off,** borrar; raer. —**scrape up; scrape together,** recoger penosamente; amontonar poco a poco.
scraper ('skrei·pər) *n.* 1, (tool; person) raspador; rascador. 2, *slang* (violinist) rascatripas. 3, *slang* (barber) carnicero. 4, (small rug) limpiabarros.
scraping ('skrei·pɪŋ) *n.* 1, (scratching) raedura; raspadura. 2, *pl.* (shavings) raspaduras. 3, *pl.* (savings) ahorros.
scrappy ('skræp·i) *adj., slang* peleador.
scratch (skrætʃ) *v.t.* 1, (mark or wound slightly) arañar; hacer rasguños a. 2, (rub, as to relieve itching) rascar. 3, (rub roughly) raer; raspar. 4, (erase) borrar; raspar. —*v.i.* 1, (dig) escarbar; raspar. 2, (rub, as to relieve itching) rascar. 3, (scribble) garabatear. 4, (get along with difficulty) ir tirando. 5, (withdraw from a race) borrar. —*n.* 1, (act or result of scratching) rasguño; arañazo; rascadura; raya. 2, (scribble) garabato. 3, *sports* (starting point) línea de partida. —**scratch pad,** cuaderno de notas; libreta de apuntes.
scratchy ('skrætʃ·i) *adj.* 1, (roughly done or made) irregular; a remiendos. 2, (itchy; irritating) áspero; rudo; burdo. 3, (making a scraping noise) chirriante.
scrawl (skrɔːl) *v.t.* garabatear. —n. garabato.
scrawny ('skrɔ·ni) *adj.* magro; huesudo; delgado. —**scrawniness,** *n.* delgadez.
scream (skriːm) *v.t.* vociferar.

—*v.i.* gritar; chillar; dar alaridos. —*n.* **1,** (shrill cry) grito; chillido; alarido. **2,** *colloq.* (highly amusing person or thing) cosa *o* persona divertida; tiro.
screamer ('skri·mər) *n.* **1,** *slang, journalism* titular escandaloso. **2,** (person who screams) gritón; chillón. **3,** (outstanding person or thing) persona *o* cosa sobresaliente.
screech (skritʃ) *v.i.* & *t.* chillar. —*n.* chillido. —**screechy,** *adj.* chillón.
screen (skri:n) *n.* **1,** (covered frame or frames) biombo; mampara. **2,** (sifter) cedazo; tamiz. **3,** (protective wire mesh) alambrera; tela metálica; (for a fireplace or lamp) pantalla. **4,** (protective formation) cortina. **5,** (pretext) cortina; capa. **6,** (surface for projecting pictures) pantalla. **7,** *print.* retícula; trama. —*v.t.* **1,** (conceal) ocultar; tapar. **2,** (protect) defender; proteger. **3,** (sift) cerner; tamizar. **4,** (classify) separar; tamizar; examinar. **5,** (record on film) rodar; filmar. **6,** (exhibit) proyectar; exhibir.
screw (skru:) *n.* **1,** (nail-like device) tornillo. **2,** (propeller) hélice. **3,** (coercion) coerción. **4,** *slang* (prison guard) celador. —*v.t.* **1,** (turn; attach) atornillar; enroscar. **2,** (contort) obligar; forzar. —*v.i.* atornillarse; enroscarse. —**have a screw loose,** tener flojos los tornillos; faltarle a uno un tornillo.
screwball *n.* & *adj., slang* (eccentric) extravagante; excéntrico; estrafalario.
screwdriver *n.* atornillador; destornillador.
screw-eye *n.* armella.
scribble ('skrɪb·əl) *v.i.* & *t.* garabatear. —*n.* garabato. —**scribbler** (-lər) *n.* mal escritor.
scribe (skraib) *n.* **1,** (amanuensis) amanuense; escribiente. **2,** *Bib.* escriba. **3,** (author) autor; escritor. —*v.t.* trazar con punzón.
scriber ('skrai·bər) *n.* punzón de trazar.
scrimmage ('skrɪm·ɪdʒ) *n.* pelea; lucha; *football* encuentro; jugada. —*v.i.* encontrarse; pelear.
scrimp (skrɪmp) *v.t.* & *i.* escatimar. —**scrimpy,** *adj.* tacaño.
scrip (skrɪp) *n.* cédula; abonaré; pagaré.
script (skrɪpt) *n.* **1,** (handwriting) escritura. **2,** *print.* letra cursiva. **3,** *theat.* libreto; guión; manuscrito.
scripture ('skrɪp·tʃər) *n.* escritura; sagrada escritura. —**scriptural,** *adj.* bíblico.
scrivener ('skrɪv·nər) *n.* escribano.
scrofula ('skraf·jə·lə) *n.* escrófula. —**scrofulous,** *adj.* escrofuloso.
scroll (skro:l) *n.* **1,** (roll of paper or parchment) rollo de papel o pergamino. **2,** (list; schedule) lista; libro. **3,** *archit.* voluta.
scrollwork *n.* dibujo *o* adornos de volutas.
scrotum ('skro·təm) *n.* escroto.
scrounge (skraundʒ) *v.t.* & *i.* sonsacar.
scrub (skrʌb) *v.t.* & *i.* fregar; estregar; restregar. —*n.* **1,** (underbrush) maleza; matorral. **2,** (bushy terrain) monte bajo. **3,** (person or thing smaller than usual) chaparro; enano. **4,** *sports* (substitute player) suplente. **5,** (team made up of such players) segundo equipo. —*adj.* **1,** (makeshift) provisional. **2,** (inferior) inferior. **3,** (undersized) enano.
scrubby ('skrʌb·i) *adj.* **1,** (undersized) achaparrado; pequeño. **2,** (shabby) andrajoso.
scruff (skrʌf) *n.* nuca.
scrumptious ('skrʌmp·ʃəs) *adj., colloq.* muy fino; elegante; de chupete.
scruple ('skru·pəl) *n.* escrúpulo. —*v.i.* tener *o* sentir escrúpulos; escrupulizar. —**scrupulous** ('skrup·jə·ləs) *adj.* escrupuloso. —**scrupulousness,** *n.* escrupulosidad.
scrutinize ('skru·tə·naiz) *v.t.* escudriñar; escrutar. —**scrutiny,** *n.* escrutinio; escudriñamiento.
scud (skʌd) *v.i.* correr rápidamente; volar; deslizarse.
scuff (skʌf) *v.t.* **1,** (spoil by scraping) rayar; rascar. **2,** (scrape with the feet) desgastar con los pies. —*v.i.* arrastrar los pies. —*n.* **1,** (act of scuffing) rayado. **2,** (worn spot) desgaste. **3,** (slipper) zapatilla; chinela.
scuffle ('skʌf·əl) *v.i.* **1,** (brawl) forcejear; luchar; pelear. **2,** (drag the feet) arrastrar los pies. —*n.* **1,** (brawl) lucha; pelea. **2,** (dragging of feet) arrastre de los pies.

scull (skʌl) *n.* **1,** (oar) espadilla. **2,** (boat) bote. —*v.t.* impulsar *o* mover a remo. —*v.i.* remar.
scullery ('skʌl·ə·ri) *n.* trascocina; espetera.
scullion ('skʌl·jən) *n.* pinche.
sculpture ('skʌlp·tʃər) *n.* escultura. —*v.t.* & *i.* esculpir. —**sculptural,** *adj.* escultural. —**sculptor** (-tər) *n.* escultor.
scum (skʌm) *n.* **1,** (layer of impurities) espuma; impureza; nata. **2,** (refuse) hez; escoria; desecho. **3,** (riffraff) canalla. —**scummy,** *adj.* espumoso.
scurf (skʌɹf) *n.* costra; caspa.
scurrilous ('skʌɹ·ə·ləs) *adj.* grosero; insolente; procaz. —**scurrility** (skʌɹ'ɪl·ə·ti) *n.* grosería; procacidad.
scurvy ('skʌɹ·vi) *n.* escorbuto. —*adj.* despreciable; vil; ruin.
scuttle ('skʌt·əl) *n.* **1,** (container) balde; cubo. **2,** (small opening) agujero; abertura. **3,** (trapdoor) escotillón. **4,** *naut.* (hatchway) escotilla. **5,** (hurried run) fuga; huida. —*v.t.* hundir; echar a pique. —*v.i.* huir; correr; escapar.
scythe (saið) *n.* guadaña. —*v.t.* cortar con guadaña; segar.
sea (siː) *n.* mar. —**at sea, 1,** (on the ocean) en el mar. **2,** *fig.* (confused) confuso; perplejo. —**follow the sea; go to sea,** hacerse marinero. —**put to sea,** hacerse a la mar.
sea bass (bæs) róbalo; cherna.
seaboard *n.* costa; litoral.
sea bream (brim) besugo.
seacoast *n.* litoral; costa.
sea cow manatí; vaca marina.
seafarer ('siːˌfɛr·ər) *n.* navegante; marinero.
seafaring ('siːˌfɛr·ɪŋ) *adj.* navegante; marinero. —*n.* **1,** (profession) marinería. **2,** (travel by sea) navegación.
seafood *n.* pescado y marisco.
seafowl *n.* ave de mar.
seagoing *adj.* de alta mar.
sea gull gaviota.
sea horse caballito de mar.
seal (siːl) *n.* **1,** (stamp; mark; tight closure) sello. **2,** (marine animal) foca. —*v.t.* sellar.
sea legs (lɛgz) pie marino.
sea level nivel del mar.
sea lion león marino.
sealskin *n.* piel de foca.
seam (siːm) *n.* **1,** (joint made by sewing) costura. **2,** (scar) costurón. **3,** (wrinkle) arruga. **4,** (fissure) grieta; raja. **5,** (stratum) filón; veta. —*v.t.* **1,** (join by sewing) coser. **2,** (mark with wrinkles) arrugar. —*v.i.* (crack) agrietarse.
seaman ('si·mən) *n.* marino; marinero.
seamanship ('si·mən·ʃɪp) *n.* marinería; náutica.
seamless ('sim·ləs) *adj.* sin costura.
seamstress ('sim·strɪs) *n.* modista; costurera.
seamy ('si·mi) *adj.* **1,** (showing seams) con costuras. **2,** (rough; coarse) basto. —**the seamy side,** el aspecto menos atractivo.
seaplane *n.* hidroplano; hidroavión.
seaport *n.* puerto; puerto de mar.
sear (sɪr) *v.t.* **1,** (burn) chamuscar; socarrar. **2,** (cauterize) cauterizar. **3,** (make callous) endurecer; insensibilizar. **4,** (dry up) marchitar; secar; agostar.
search (sʌɹtʃ) *v.t.* **1,** (explore) explorar; buscar. **2,** (examine) indagar; investigar; examinar. **3,** (frisk) cachear. **4,** (pierce) penetrar; taladrar. —*v.i.* buscar. —*n.* **1,** (investigation) investigación; indagación. **2,** (seeking) busca; búsqueda. **3,** (frisking) cacheo. —**searching,** *adj.* penetrante. —**search warrant,** orden de registro.
searchlight *n.* reflector.
seascape ('siˌskeip) *n.* marina.
sea shell concha; caracol marino.
seashore *n.* orilla del mar; playa.
seasick *adj.* mareado. —**seasickness,** *n.* mareo.
seaside *n.* playa; orilla del mar.
season ('si·zən) *n.* **1,** (quarter of the year) estación. **2,** (appropriate period of time) temporada; sazón. —*v.t.* **1,** (ripen) madurar; sazonar. **2,** (cure) curar. **3,** (flavor) sazonar. **4,** (accustom) acostumbrar; habituar. **5,** (soften) moderar; templar. —*v.i.* madurarse; sazonarse; curarse. —**seasonable,** *adj.* conveniente; oportuno. —**seasonal,** *adj.* de temporada; estacional. —**seasoning,** *n.* aderezo; condimento; aliño. —**season ticket,** billete de abono.
seat (sit) *n.* **1,** (place to sit) asiento. **2,** (back part of trousers) fondillos (*pl.*). **3,** (administrative

center) sede. **4,** (center of learning) centro de enseñanza. **5,** (residence) residencia. **6,** (site) lugar; sitio. **7,** (membership) asiento; plaza. —*v.t.* **1,** (place on a seat; furnish with a seat) sentar; colocar; acomodar. **2,** (fix; locate) establecer; arraigar. **3,** (have seating capacity for) tener cabida para. **4,** (adjust in place) ajustar en su sitio. —**seat cover,** funda de asiento. —**seating capacity,** cabida; aforo.

sea urchin erizo de mar.

sea wall dique marítimo; malecón.

seaward ('si·wərd) *adj.* & *adv.* hacia el mar.

seaway *n.* ruta marítima.

seaweed *n.* alga marina.

seaworthy *adj.* marinero; apto para navegar.

sebaceous (sɪ'bei·ʃəs) *adj.* sebáceo.

secant ('si·kænt; -kənt) *n.* secante.

secede (sɪ'siːd) *v.i.* retirarse; separarse.

secession (sɪ'sɛʃ·ən) *n.* secesión. —**secessionism,** *n.* secesionismo. —**secessionist,** *adj.* & *n.* secesionista.

seclude (sɪ'kluːd) *v.t.* recluir; encerrar. —**seclusion** (-'klu·ʒən) *n.* reclusión. —**seclusive** (-'klu·sɪv) *adj.* solitario.

second ('sɛk·ənd) *adj.* segundo. —*n.* **1,** (person or thing after the first) segundo. **2,** (supporter) ayudante; partidario. **3,** (attendant in a duel) padrino; (in boxing) segundo. **4,** (imperfect product) artículo de segunda calidad. **5,** (unit of time) segundo. **6,** (in dates) dos. **7,** *music* segunda. —*v.t.* secundar; apoyar; apadrinar.

secondary ('sɛk·ən·dɛr·i) *adj.* secundario.

second-class *adj.* de segunda clase; inferior.

second fiddle papel secundario.

second hand segundero.

second-hand *adj.* de segunda mano.

second lieutenant alférez; subteniente.

second-rate inferior.

second sight clarividencia.

secrecy ('si·krə·si) *n.* secreto.

secret ('si·krɪt) *adj.* secreto; oculto. —*n.* secreto. —**secret service,** policía secreta.

secretary ('sɛk·rə·tɛr·i) *n.* **1,** (assistant) secretario. **2,** (cabinet member) ministro. **3,** (desk) escritorio. —**secretarial** (-'tɛr·i·əl) *adj.* de *o* para secretarios. —**secretariat** (-'tɛr·i·ət) *n.* secretaría. —**secretaryship,** *n.* secretaría.

secrete (sɪ'krit) *v.t.* **1,** (hide) esconder; ocultar. **2,** *physiol.* secretar. —**secretion,** (sɪ'kri·ʃən) *n.* secreción.

secretive (sɪ'kri·tɪv) *adj.* reservado; reticente; callado.

secretory (sɪ'kri·tə·ri) *adj.* secretor; secretorio.

sect (sɛkt) *n.* secta. —**sectarian** (sɛk'tɛr·i·ən) *n.* & *adj.* sectario. —**sectarianism,** *n.* sectarismo.

-sect (sɛkt) *sufijo* cortar; dividir: *vivisect,* disecar en vivo.

section ('sɛk·ʃən) *n.* **1,** (portion) sección. **2,** *geog.* región. **3,** *geom.; archit.; mil.* sección; *surg.* sección; operación. —*v.t.* seccionar.

sectional ('sɛk·ʃə·nəl) *adj.* **1,** (composed of several sections) seccional. **2,** (cut straight) transversal; seccional. **3,** (local) local; regional. —**sectionalism,** *n.* regionalismo; localismo.

sector ('sɛk·tər) *n.* sector.

secular ('sɛk·jə·lər) *adj.* secular; seglar. —**secularism,** *n.* secularismo. —**secularist,** *n.* secularista. —**secularistic,** *adj.* secularista.

secularize ('sɛk·jə·lə,raiz) *v.t.* secularizar. —**secularization** (-rɪ·'zei·ʃən) *n.* secularización.

secure (sɪ'kjʊr) *adj.* seguro. —*v.t.* **1,** (make safe) asegurar; salvar; proteger. **2,** (make certain) asegurar; garantizar. **3,** (obtain) obtener; conseguir. **4,** (fasten) asegurar; afianzar. —*v.i.* asegurarse.

security (sɪ'kjʊr·ə·ti) *n.* **1,** (safety; certainty; safeguard) seguridad. **2,** (guarantee; surety) seguridad; garantía. **3,** (guarantor) garante; fiador. **5,** *usu.pl., comm.* obligaciones; valores; títulos.

sedan (sɪ'dæn) *n.* sedán. —**sedan chair,** silla de manos.

sedate (sɪ'deit) *adj.* tranquilo; sosegado; serio. —**sedateness,** *n.* sosiego; calma.

sedation (sɪ'dei·ʃən) *n.* sedación.

sedative ('sɛd·ə·tɪv) *n.* & *adj.* sedante; sedativo.

sedentary ('sɛd·ən·tɛr·i) *adj.* sedentario.

sediment ('sɛd·ə·mənt) *n.* sedi-

mento. —**sedimentary** (-ˈmɛn·tə·ri) *adj.* sedimentario. —**sedimentation** (-mənˈtei·ʃən) *n.* sedimentación.
sedition (sɪˈdɪʃ·ən) *n.* sedición. —**seditious**, *adj.* sedicioso.
seduce (sɪˈdus) *v.t.* seducir. —**seducer**, *n.* seductor. —**seduction** (-ˈdʌk·ʃən) *n.* seducción. —**seductive** (-ˈdʌk·tɪv) *adj.* seductivo; atractivo.
sedulous (ˈsɛdʒ·ə·ləs) *adj.* diligente; asiduo. —**sedulousness; sedulity** (sɪˈdʒu·lə·ti) *n.* diligencia; ahínco.
see (siː) *v.t.* & *i.* [**saw, seen, seeing**] **1,** (perceive by the eye) ver; percibir. **2,** (regard; consider) mirar. **3,** (understand) comprender; entender. —*v.t.* **1,** (witness) ver; presenciar. **2,** (receive) recibir. **3,** (consult) consultar. **4,** (escort) acompañar. **5,** (attend) ver; atender. **6,** *cards* (meet or call, as a bet) ver; aceptar. —*n.* sede. —**see about, 1,** (inquire into) investigar; indagar. **2,** (ascertain) averiguar. **3,** (attend to) atender; cuidar de. —**see after,** cuidar; cuidar de. —**see into, 1,** (investigate) investigar; indagar. **2,** (understand) penetrar; comprender; reconocer. —**see off,** despedir; acompañar hasta la despedida. —**see that; see to it that,** tener cuidado que. —**see through, 1,** (accomplish) llevar a cabo (una cosa). **2,** (assist) ayudar; sostener (a una persona). **3,** (penetrate) penetrar. —**see to,** atender a; pensar en.
seed (siːd) *n.* semilla; simiente. —*v.t.* & *i.* (sow with seed) sembrar. —*v.t.* (remove the seeds from) despepitar. —*adj.* seminal. —**go to seed,** deteriorarse; echarse a perder. —**seed pearl,** aljófar; perlita.
seedling (ˈsid·lɪŋ) *n.* **1,** (young plant) plantón; planta de semilla. **2,** (young tree) vástago; renuevo.
seedy (ˈsi·di) *adj.* **1,** (containing much seed) lleno de semillas; semilloso. **2,** (shabby) desaseado; desastrado. **3,** (gone to seed) deteriorado; inútil. —**seediness,** *n.* desaseo; calidad de desastrado.
seeing (ˈsi·ɪŋ) *adj.* vidente. —*n.* vista; el ver. —*conj.* visto que; por cuanto que. —**seeing-eye dog,** perro de ciego.
seek (sik) *v.t.* [*pret.* & *p.p.* **sought**] **1,** (go in search of) buscar. **2,** (search; explore) explorar; recorrer. **3,** (resort to) dirigirse a. **4,** (attempt; endeavor) intentar; esforzarse por; procurar. —*v.i.* buscar.
seem (siːm) *v.i.* parecer. —**seeming,** *adj.* aparente. —*n.* apariencia.
seemly (ˈsim·li) *adj.* adecuado; decoroso; decente. —**seemliness,** *n.* decencia; decoro.
seen (siːn) *v., p.p. de* **see.**
seep (sip) *v.i.* colarse; filtrarse; escurrirse. —**seepage,** *n.* escape; coladura; filtración.
seer (sɪr) *n.* **1,** (clairvoyant) clarividente. **2,** (prophet) profeta.
seeress (ˈsɪr·ɪs) *n.* **1,** (clairvoyant) clarividente. **2,** (prophetess) profetisa.
seersucker (ˈsɪrˌsʌk·ər) *n.* sirsaca.
seesaw (ˈsiˌsɔ) *n.* **1,** (balancing board) balancín; columpio de tabla. **2,** (up-and-down movement) vaivén; balance. —*adj.* de vaivén; de balance. —*v.t.* columpiar; balancear. —*v.i.* columpiarse; balancearse.
seethe (siːð) *v.i.* **1,** (boil) hervir; bullir. **2,** (be agitated) agitarse.
segment (ˈsɛg·mənt) *n.* segmento; sección. —*v.t.* dividir en segmentos. —**segmental** (sɛgˈmɛn·təl) *adj.* segmental.
segregate (ˈsɛg·rəˌgeit) *v.t.* segregar; separar. —*v.i.* segregarse; separarse. —**segregation,** *n.* segregación; separación.
seismic (ˈsaiz·mɪk) *adj.* sísmico.
seismograph (ˈsaiz·mə·græf) *n.* sismógrafo.
seize (siːz) *v.t.* **1,** (grasp) aferrar; agarrar; coger; asir. **2,** (take possession of) apoderarse de. **3,** (confiscate) secuestrar; requisar; embargar. **4,** (comprehend) entender; comprender. **5,** (take advantage of) aprovecharse de. **6,** (afflict) atacar.
seizure (ˈsi·ʒər) *n.* **1,** (grasping) aferramiento; asimiento. **2,** (confiscation) secuestro; embargo; requisa. **3,** (fit; attack) acceso; ataque.
seldom (ˈsɛl·dəm) *adv.* raramente; pocas veces; rara vez.
select (sɪˈlɛkt) *v.t.* seleccionar; escoger. —*adj.* selecto; escogido. —**selection** (-ˈlɛk·ʃən) *n.* selección. —**selective,** *adj.* selectivo. —**selectivity** (ˌsɪ·lɛkˈtɪv·ə·ti) *n.* selectivi-

dad. —**selective service**, conscripción; quintas (*pl.*); servicio militar.

selenium (sɪˈli·ni·əm) *n.* selenio.

self (sɛlf) *n.* [*pl.* **selves**] uno mismo. —*pron.*, *colloq.* sí mismo. —*adj.* **1,** (same) mismo. **2,** (uniform) idéntico; propio; del mismo género. **3,** (unmixed) puro. —**the self**, el yo.

self- (sɛlf) *prefijo; denota* **1,** *valor reflexivo en el nombre o adjetivo al que va unido, generalmente con un guión: self-control,* dominio de sí; *self-addressed,* dirigido a uno mismo. **2,** acción autónoma o automática: *self-styled,* con estilo propio; *self-adjusting,* de ajuste autómatico.

self-addressed *adj.* dirigido a sí mismo.

self-assurance *n.* confianza en sí mismo. —**self-assured**, *adj.* seguro de sí.

self-centered *adj.* egocéntrico.

self-command *n.* dominio propio; dominio de sí.

self-complacent *adj.* complacido de sí mismo. —**self-complacency**; **self-complacence**, *n.* complacencia en sí mismo.

self-conceit *n.* presunción; arrogancia. —**self-conceited**, *adj.* presumido; arrogante.

self-confidence *n.* confianza en sí. —**self-confident**, *adj.* seguro de sí.

self-conscious *adj.* cohibido; tímido; apocado. —**self-consciousness**, *n.* timidez; apocamiento.

self-contained *adj.* **1,** (reserved) reservado; callado. **2,** (complete in itself) completo en sí. **3,** (self-sufficient) independiente.

self-control *n.* dominio de sí.

self-controlled *adj.* **1,** (master over one's self) dueño de sí. **2,** (automatic) automático.

self-criticism *n.* autocrítica.

self-deception *n.* engaño de sí mismo.

self-defense *n.* defensa propia.

self-denial *n.* abnegación.

self-destruction *n.* autodestrucción; suicidio.

self-determination *n.* autodeterminación.

self-discipline *n.* autodisciplina.

self-educated *adj.* autodidacto.

self-effacing *adj.* modesto. —**self-effacement**, *n.* modestia.

self-esteem *n.* estima propia; amor propio; respeto propio.

self-evident *adj.* obvio; claro; patente.

self-explanatory *adj.* que se explica por sí.

self-expression *n.* expresión de la propia personalidad.

self-governed *también*, **self-governing** *adj.* autónomo; independiente. —**self-government**, *n.* autonomía.

self-help *n.* ayuda propia.

self-important *adj.* arrogante; altivo. —**self-importance**, *n.* arrogancia; altivez.

self-imposed *adj.* voluntario.

self-improvement *n.* mejoramiento de sí mismo.

self-induced *adj.* inducido por sí mismo.

self-indulgent *adj.* desenfrenado; inmoderado. —**self-indulgence**, *n.* desenfreno; inmoderación.

self-inflicted *adj.* que uno mismo se ha infligido.

self-interest *n.* egoísmo; interés personal.

selfish (ˈsɛl·fɪʃ) *adj.* egoísta. —**selfishness**, *n.* egoísmo.

selfless (ˈsɛlf·ləs) *adj.* desinteresado; desprendido. —**selflessness**, *n.* desinterés; desprendimiento.

self-loading *adj.* autocargador.

self-love *n.* egoísmo; amor propio.

self-made *adj.* formado por sí mismo.

self-moving *adj.* automotor.

self-pity *n.* compasión de sí mismo.

self-portrait *n.* autorretrato.

self-possessed *adj.* sereno; dueño de sí. —**self-possession**, *n.* dominio de sí.

self-preservation *n.* propia conservación.

self-propelled *adj.* autopropulsado; automotor.

self-protection *n.* defensa *o* protección propia.

self-reliance *n.* confianza en sí mismo. —**self-reliant**, *adj.* confiado en sí mismo.

self-reproach *n.* reprensión de sí mismo.

self-respect *n.* pundonor; respeto de sí mismo; decoro.

self-restraint *n.* dominio de sí.

self-righteous *adj.* santurrón; beatón; hipócrita. —**self-righteous-**

ness, *n.* santurronería; beatería; hipocresía.

self-sacrifice *n.* sacrificio de sí mismo.

selfsame *adj.* idéntico; igual; mismo.

self-satisfied *adj.* satisfecho de sí mismo. —**self-satisfaction,** *n.* satisfacción de sí mismo.

self-seeking *adj.* egoísta. —*n.* egoísmo. —**self-seeker,** *n.* egoísta.

self-service *n.* autoservicio. —*adj.* de autoservicio.

self-starter *n.* arranque automático.

self-styled *adj.* que se llama a sí mismo; que se considera a sí mismo.

self-sufficient *adj.* **1,** (independent) suficiente a sí mismo; independiente. **2,** (conceited) presumido; vanidoso.

self-support *n.* mantenimiento propio; economía propia. —**self-supporting,** *adj.* que se mantiene a sí mismo.

self-sustaining *adj.* que se sostiene o mantiene a sí mismo.

self-taught *adj.* autodidacto.

self-willed *adj.* terco; obstinado.

self-winding *adj.* automático; de cuerda automática.

self-worship *n.* egolatría.

sell (sɛl) *v.t.* [*pret. & p.p.* **sold**] **1,** (transfer for money) vender. **2,** (keep for sale; deal in) vender; tener a la venta *o* en venta. **3,** (betray) traicionar; vender. **4,** (win acceptance of) hacer aceptar. **5,** *colloq.* (convince) convencer. **6,** *slang* (dupe) engañar; chasquear. —*v.i.* **1,** (engage in selling) vender. **2,** (be in demand) venderse; tener venta. **3,** (be sold; be for sale) venderse: estar en venta. **4,** (be accepted) tener aceptación. —**seller,** *n.* vendedor. —**selling,** *n.* venta; comercio.

sellout *n.* **1,** (liquidation) saldo; realización; venta final. **2,** (complete disposal, as of theater seats) venta total. **3,** *slang* (betrayal) traición.

seltzer ('sɛl·tsər) *n.* seltz; agua de seltz; agua carbónica.

selvage ('sɛl·vɪdʒ) *n.* orillo.

selves (sɛlvz) *n., pl. de* **self.**

semantic (sɪ'mæn·tɪk) *adj.* semántico. —**semantics,** *n.* semántica.

semaphore ('sɛm·ə,for) *n.* semáforo.

semblance ('sɛm·bləns) *n.* **1,** (likeness) semblanza; parecido. **2,** (outward appearance) apariencia; exterior.

semen ('si·mən) *n.* semen.

semester (sɪ'mɛs·tər) *n.* semestre.

semi- (sɛm·i; -ɪ) *prefijo* semi-. **1,** mitad; medio: *semicircle,* semicírculo. **2,** en parte; a medias: *semiofficial,* semioficial.

semiannual (,sɛm·i'æn·ju·əl) *adj.* semestral.

semibreve ('sɛm·ɪ,briv) *n.* semibreve.

semicircle ('sɛm·ɪ,sʌɪ·kəl) *n.* semicírculo. —**semicircular,** *adj.* semicircular.

semicolon ('sɛm·ɪ,ko·lən) *n.* punto y coma.

semifinal (,sɛm·ɪ'fai·nəl) *adj.* & *n.* semifinal.

semimonthly (,sɛm·ɪ'mʌnθ·li) *adj.* bimensual.

seminal ('sɛm·ə·nəl) *adj.* seminal.

seminar ('sɛm·ə,nar) *n.* seminario; cursillo.

seminary ('sɛm·ə,nɛr·i) *n.* seminario. —**seminarist,** *n.* seminarista.

Semite ('sɛm·ait) *n.* semita. —**Semitic** (sə'mɪt·ɪk) *adj.* & *n.* semítico.

semiweekl-- (,sɛm·ɪ'wik·li) *adj.* bisemanal. —*n.* publicación bisemanal.

senate ('sɛn·ɪt) *n.* senado.

senator ('sɛn·ə·tər) *n.* senador. —**senatorial** (-'tor·i·əl) *adj.* senatorial. —**senatorship,** *n.* senaduría.

send (sɛnd) *v.t.* **1,** (cause to go) mandar; enviar. **2,** (dispatch) despachar; remitir; expedir. **3,** (impel) lanzar; enviar. **4,** (emit) emitir. **5,** (transmit) transmitir. **6,** *slang* (excite) estimular; excitar.

sender ('sɛn·dər) *n.* **1,** (one who sends) remitente. **2,** (transmitter) transmisor.

send-off *n.* **1,** (start) comienzo; empujón. **2,** *colloq.* (farewell demonstration) despedida afectuosa.

senescent (sə'nɛs·ənt) *adj.* **1,** (old) senil; que envejece. **2,** (of old age) de la vejez; de los ancianos. —**senescence,** *n.* senectud; envejecimiento.

seneschal ('sɛn·ə·ʃəl) *n.* senescal.

senile ('si·nail) *adj.* senil. —**senility** (sə'nɪl·ə·ti) *n.* senilidad.

senior ('sin·jər) *adj.* **1,** (older;

elder) mayor. **2,** (older in office or service) más antiguo; decano. **3,** (of or pert. to a graduating class) del último año. **4,** *usu. en la abr.* **Sr.**, denotando el padre del mismo nombre: *David Jones, Sr.*, David Jones, padre. —*n.* **1,** (older person; elder) mayor. **2,** (person of higher rank) persona más antigua; socio más antiguo. **3,** (member of the senior class) alumno del último año.

seniority (sin'jar·ə·ti) *n.* **1,** (state or quality of being senior) antigüedad. **2,** (precedence) prioridad.

señor (sein'jor) *n.* señor. —**señora** (-'jo·rə) *n.* señora. —**señorita** (ˌsen·jə'ri·tə) *n.* señorita.

sensation (sɛn'sei·ʃən) *n.* sensación. —**sensational,** *adj.* sensacional. —**sensationalism,** *n.* sensacionalismo.

sense (sɛns) *n.* sentido. —*v.t.* sentir.

senseless ('sɛns·ləs) *adj.* **1,** (unconscious) inconsciente. **2,** (without meaning) sin sentido. **3,** (unreasoning; mad) insensato. **4,** (stupid) necio; estúpido.

senselessness ('sɛns·ləs·nəs) *n.* **1,** (unconsciousness) inconsciencia. **2,** (unreason; madness) insensatez. **3,** (stupidity) necedad; estupidez.

sensibility (ˌsɛn·sə'bɪl·ə·ti) *n.* **1,** (sensory or mental perception) sensibilidad; susceptibilidad. **2,** *usu. pl.* (refined feelings) sentimientos. delicados.

sensible ('sɛn·sə·bəl) *adj.* **1,** (perceptible to the senses or the intellect) sensible. **2,** (aware; cognizant) susceptible; sabedor; conocedor. **3,** (reasonable) razonable; sensato. **4,** (capable of sensation) sensitivo.

sensitive ('sɛn·sə·tɪv) *adj.* **1,** (pert. to the senses) sensitivo; sensorio. **2,** (capable of receiving sensations; responsive; easily [illegible]t) sensitivo; sensible; susceptible. —**sensitiveness; sensitivity** (-'tɪv·ə·ti) *n.* sensibilidad; susceptibilidad.

sensitize ('sɛn·səˌtaiz) *v.t.* sensibilizar.

sensory ('sɛn·sə·ri) *adj.* sensorio.

sensual ('sən·ʃu·əl) *adj.* sensual. —**sensualism,** *n.* sensualismo. —**sensualist,** *n.* sensualista. —**sensualistic,** *adj.* sensualista. —**sensuality** (-'æl·ə·ti) *n.* sensualidad.

sensuous ('sɛn·ʃu·əs) *adj.* sensual; voluptuoso. —**sensuousness,** *n.* sensualidad.

sentence ('sɛn·təns) *n.* **1,** (group of words) frase; oración. **2,** *law* sentencia. —*v.t.* sentenciar; condenar.

sententious (sɛn'tɛn·ʃəs) *adj.* sentencioso.

sentient ('sɛn·ʃənt) *adj.* consciente; sensible; sensitivo. —**sentience,** *n.* consciencia; sensibilidad.

sentiment ('sɛn·tə·mənt) *n.* sentimiento. —**sentimental** (-'mɛn·təl) *adj.* sentimental. —**sentimentalism,** *n.* sentimentalismo. —**sentimentalist,** *n.* sentimental. —**sentimentality** (-mɛn'tæl·ə·ti) *n.* sentimentalismo.

sentinel ('sɛn·tə·nəl) *n.* centinela.

sentry ('sɛn·tri) *n.* centinela. —**sentry box,** garita de centinela.

sepal ('si·pəl) *n.* sépalo.

separate ('sɛp·əˌreit) *v.t.* separar; dividir. —*v.i.* separarse; dividirse. —*adj.* (-ət) separado; suelto. —**separable** (-ər·ə·bəl) *adj.* separable. —**separation** (-'rei·ʃən) *n.* separación. —**separator** (-ˌrei·tər) *n.* separador.

separatism ('sɛp·ə·rəˌtɪz·əm) *n.* separatismo. —**separatist** (-ˌrei·tɪst) *adj. & n.* separatista.

sepia ('si·pi·ə) *n. & adj.* sepia.

sepoy ('si·pɔi) *n.* cipayo.

sepsis ('sɛp·sɪs) *n.* sepsis.

sept- (sɛpt) *prefijo* sept-; siete: *septet,* septeto.

September (sɛp'tɛm·bər) *n.* septiembre.

septet (sɛp'tɛt) *n.* **1,** (group of seven) grupo de siete. **2,** *music* septeto.

septi- (sɛp·tɪ; -tə) *prefijo* septi-. **1,** siete: *septilateral,* septilateral. **2,** descomposición; putrefacción: *septicemia,* septicemia. **3,** septo; tabique: *septifragal,* septífraga.

septic ('sɛp·tɪk) *adj.* séptico.

septillion (sɛp'tɪl·jən) *n.* (*U.S.*) un millón de trillones; cuatrillón; (*Brit.*) un millón de sextillones; septillón.

septuagenarian (ˌsɛp·tʃu·ə·dʒə'nɛr·i·ən) *adj. & n.* septuagenario.

Septuagesima (ˌsɛp·tʃu·ə'dʒɛs·ə·mə) *n.* septuagésima.

septum ('sɛp·təm) *n.* [*pl.* **-ta** (-tə)] septo.
septuple ('sɛp·tju·pəl) *adj.* & *n.* séptuplo. —*v.t.* septuplicar. —*v.i.* septuplicarse.
sepulcher *también,* **sepulchre** ('sɛp·əl·kər) *n.* sepulcro. —**sepulchral** (sə'pʌl·krəl) *adj.* sepulcral.
sequel ('si·kwəl) *n.* **1,** (continuation) continuación; secuencia. **2,** (aftermath) secuela; resultado; consecuencia.
sequence ('si·kwəns) *n.* **1,** (succession) secuencia; sucesión. **2,** (order of succession) orden; sucesión. **3,** (series) serie; secuencia. **4,** *cards* escalera. **5,** *motion pictures; music; eccles.* secuencia.
sequester (sɪ'kwɛs·tər) *v.t.* **1,** (put aside) apartar; separar. **2,** *law* (confiscate) secuestrar.
sequestration (ˌsi·kwɛs'trei·ʃən) *n.* **1,** (seclusion; separation) reclusión; separación; apartamiento. **2,** *law* (confiscation) secuestro.
sequin ('si·kwɪn) *n.* lentejuela.
sequoia (sɪ'kwɔi·ə) *n.* secoya.
seraglio (sɪ'ræl·jo) *n.* serrallo.
serape (sɛ'ra·pi) *n.* sarape.
seraph ('sɛr·əf) *n.* [*pl.* **seraphim** (-ə·fɪm) *o* **seraphs**] serafín. —**seraphic** (sə'ræf·ɪk) *adj.* seráfico.
Serb (sʌɹb) *n.* & *adj.* servio. *También,* **Serbian** ('sʌɹ·bi·ən).
Serbo-Croatian (ˌsʌɹ·bo·kro·'əi·ʃən) *adj.* & *n.* servocroata.
sere (sɪr) *adj.* marchito; mustio; seco.
serenade (ˌsɛr·ə'neid) *n.* serenata. —*v.t.* & *i.* dar serenata (a).
serene (sə'riːn) *adj.* sereno. —**serenity** (sə'rɛn·ə·ti); **sereneness,** *n.* serenidad.
serf (sʌɹf) *n.* siervo. —**serfdom,** *n.* servidumbre.
serge (sʌɹdʒ) *n.* sarga.
sergeant ('sar·dʒənt) *n.* **1,** (noncommissioned officer) sargento. **2,** (court officer) alguacil. —**sergeant-at-arms,** oficial del orden.
serial ('sɪr·i·əl) *adj.* por entregas. —*n.* serial; obra por series *o* entregas.
serialize ('sɪr·i·əˌlaiz) *v.t.* publicar por entregas; *radio* radiar por series.
serially ('sɪr·i·əˌli) *adv.* **1,** (in series) en serie; por series. **2,** (in installments) por entregas.
series ('sɪr·iz) *n.* serie.
serious ('sɪr·i·əs) *adj.* serio; grave. —**seriousness,** *n.* seriedad; gravedad.
sermon ('sʌɹ·mən) *n.* sermón. —**sermonize,** *v.t.* & *i.* predicar; sermonear.
sero- (sɛr·ə; sɪr-) *prefijo* sero-; sero: *serology,* serología.
serous ('sɪr·əs) *adj.* seroso. —**serosity** (sɪ'ras·ə·ti) *n.* serosidad.
serpent ('sʌɹ·pənt) *n.* serpiente. —**serpentine** (-pənˌtin; -ˌtain) *adj.* serpentino.
serrate ('sɛr·ɪt) *adj.* serrado; dentado. *También,* **serrated** (-ei·tɪd) —**serration** (sɛ'rei·ʃən) *n.* endentadura.
serried ('sɛr·id) *adj.* apretado.
serum ('sɪr·əm) *n.* suero.
servant ('sʌɹ·vənt) *n.* sirviente; criado; *fem.* sirvienta; criada.
serve (sʌːɹv) *v.t.* **1,** (do services for; aid; be sufficient for; avail) servir. **2,** [*usu.* **serve for**] (be a substitute for) reemplazar; sustituir. **3,** *law* (give a summons, writ, etc. to) notificar; citar; entregar viva citación a. **4,** (go through or spend, as time in service, in prison, etc.) cumplir; servir. **5,** *sports* servir. **6,** (cover, as animals) cubrir. **7,** (supply) abastecer; proveer; suplir. —*v.i.* **1,** (act as a servant; perform service) servir. **2,** (suffice) bastar; ser suficiente. **3,** (be suitable or convenient) servir (de *o* para). **4,** *sports* servir. —*n., sports* saque; servicio. —**serve one right,** estar uno bien servido; merecérselo uno: (*It*) *serves him right,* Se lo merece; (Está) bien servido.
server ('sʌɹ·vər) *n.* **1,** (servant) criado; servidor. **2,** (waiter) mozo. **3,** (tray) bandeja.
service ('sʌɹ·vɪs) *n.* **1,** (act or result of serving; duty performed; services supplied) servicio. **2,** (religious devotions) servicios; oficios religiosos. **3,** (set, as of dishes) juego; servicio. **4,** *law* entrega. —**serviceable,** *adj.* servible; útil; duradero.
serviceman *n.* [*pl.* **-men**] **1,** *mil.* militar. **2,** (repairman) mecánico. *También,* **service-man, service man.**
serviette (ˌsʌɹ·vi'ɛt) *n.* servilleta.
servile ('sʌɹ·vɪl) *adj.* servil. —**servility** (sʌɹ'vɪl·ə·ti) *n.* servilismo.
serving ('sʌɹ·vɪŋ) *n.* porción.
servitude ('sʌɹ·vɪˌtud) *n.* servidumbre; esclavitud.

sesame ('sɛs·ə·mi) *n.* sésamo; ajonjolí.
sesqui- (sɛs·kwi) *prefijo* sesqui-; uno y medio: *sesquicentennial,* sesquicentenario.
session ('sɛʃ·ən) *n.* **1,** (assembly) sesión. **2,** (school term) período escolar.
sestet (sɛs'tɛt) *n.* sexteto.
set (sɛt) *v.t.* [**set, setting**] **1,** (put; place) poner; colocar. **2,** (fix) fijar; armar; instalar. **3,** (establish) establecer. **4,** (determine) fijar; determinar. **5,** (adjust) ajustar; arreglar. **6,** (start) comenzar; introducir; establecer. **7,** (mount, as a gem) engastar; montar. **8,** (adapt to music) poner música a; poner letra a. **9,** *print.* componer. **10,** (cause to hatch) poner a empollar. —*v.i.* **1,** (sink; settle) hundirse; declinar. **2,** (disappear below the horizon) ponerse. **3,** (become firm or hard) cuajarse; endurecerse. **4,** (tend) inclinarse. **5,** (fit) sentar; caer. **6,** (brood, as a hen) empollar. —*n.* **1,** (collection) colección; juego. **2,** (group of persons) pandilla; camarilla, compañía. **3,** *theat.* (scenery) decorados; decoración. **4,** (hardening) endurecimiento. **5,** (tendency) inclinación; dirección. **6,** *mech.* (system of interrelated parts) tren. **7,** *sports* partida. **8,** (transmitting or receiving device) aparato. —*adj.* **1** (placed) colocado; puesto. **2,** (fixed) fijo; firme. **3,** (adjusted) arreglado; ajustado. **4,** (determined; prescribed) determinado; decidido; resuelto. **5,** *colloq.* (ready) preparado; dispuesto. —**set about to,** ponerse a. —**set apart,** separar; apartar. —**set aside, 1,** (reserve; store) guardar; reservar. **2** (annul) anular; abrogar. **3,** (reject) rechazar; desechar. —**set back, 1,** (retard) detener; retrasar. **2,** (reverse) hacer retroceder. **3,** *colloq.* (cost; cause the loss of) costar. —**set down, 1,** (put in place) poner; colocar; instalar. **2,** (lay down; rest) acostar; descansar. **3,** (alight) aterrizar; bajar; apearse. **4,** (attribute) atribuir. **5,** (put in writing) poner por escrito. —**set fire to; set afire,** pegar fuego a. —**set forth, 1,** (state; express) exponer; expresar. **2,** (exhibit) disponer; exhibir. **3,** (start out) ponerse en camino. —**set in, 1,** (begin) empezar; comenzar; aparecer. **2,** (blow or flow toward shore) soplar *o* fluir hacia tierra. —**set off, 1,** (cause to start) dar ímpetu a; excitar; animar. **2,** (put in relief; accentuate) poner de relieve; realzar; destacar. **3,** (depart) salir; partir. **4,** (detonate) hacer estallar *o* saltar. **5,** (adorn; embellish) adornar; embellecer. **6,** (separate) separar; apartar. —**set on, 1,** (incite) azuzar; incitar. **2,** (attack) atacar; acometer; asaltar. —**set out, 1,** (limit; mark out) demarcar. **2,** (display; arrange) disponer. **3,** (start) ponerse en camino. —**set out to,** proponerse (hacer); ponerse a. —**set up, 1,** (raise) levantar; alzar. **2,** (elevate; exalt) ensalzar. **3,** (set in a vertical position) enderezar. **4,** (construct) erigir; construir. **5,** (establish) establecer; instituir. **6,** (install) instalar. **7,** (start; undertake) comenzar; emprender. **8,** (fit out) armar; montar. —**set up shop,** poner tienda. —**set upon, 1,** (attack) atacar; acometer; asaltar. **2,** (incite to attack, as a dog) azuzar.
setback *n.* **1,** (reverse) revés; contrariedad. **2,** *archit.* retraqueo.
settee (sɛ'tiː) *n.* canapé; sofá pequeño.
setter ('sɛt·ər) *n.* **1,** (dog) perro perdiguero. **2,** *print.* compositor.
setting ('sɛt·ɪŋ) *n.* **1,** (environment) local; sitio; ambiente. **2,** (stage scenery) escena; decoración. **3,** (mounting for jewelry) montadura; engaste. **4,** (disappearance below the horizon) puesta; ocaso.
settle ('sɛt·əl) *v.t.* **1,** (put in order) arreglar; ordenar; componer. **2,** (establish; decide) decidir; fijar; determinar. **3,** (adjust, as a dispute) arreglar; moderar; calmar. **4,** (colonize) colonizar; poblar. **5,** (clear of dregs) aclarar; clarificar. **6,** (pay, as a bill) cancelar; saldar; pagar. —*v.i.* **1,** (become fixed) fijarse; asentarse; posarse. **2,** (establish a permanent residence) establecerse; fijar residencia; arraigar. **3,** (become clear) clarificarse; sedimentarse. **4,** (sink) hundirse; caer. **5,** (decide) determinarse; decidirse. **6,** (arrange) arreglarse; conformarse. —*n.* banco. —**settle down to,** ponerse a. —**settle on,** decidirse en; escoger.
settlement ('sɛt·əl·mənt) *n.* **1,** (adjustment) arreglo; ajuste. **2,** (payment) cancelación; liquida-

ción; pago. **3,** (small colony) colonia; poblado. **4,** *law* (conveyance of property) traspaso de bienes; (amount of property conveyed) asignación. **5,** (welfare establishment) centro benéfico.
settler ('sɛt·lər) *n.* colonizador.
set-to *n., colloq.* pelea; lucha; contienda.
setup *n.* **1,** (system) sistema; disposición. **2,** (bodily posture) porte; compostura. **3,** *slang* (contest easily won) triunfo fácil. **4,** (elements to be mixed with liquor) ingredientes.
seven ('sɛv·ən) *n.* & *adj.* siete.
sevenfold ('sɛv·ən,fold) *adj.* & *n.* séptuplo; siete veces (más). —*adv.* siete veces; en un séptuplo.
seven hundred setecientos. —**seven-hundredth,** *adj.* & *n.* septingentésimo.
seventeen ('sɛv·ən,tin) *n.* & *adj.* diecisiete; diez y siete. —**seventeenth,** *adj.* & *n.* decimoséptimo; diecisieteavo.
seventh ('sɛv·ənθ) *adj.* séptimo. —*n.* séptimo; séptima parte; *music* séptima.
seventy ('sɛv·ən·ti) *n.* & *adj.* setenta. —**seventieth,** *adj.* & *n.* septuagésimo; setentavo.
sever ('sɛv·ər) *v.t.* **1,** (separate) separar; dividir; desunir. **2,** (break off) cortar; romper.
several ('sɛv·ər·əl) *adj.* **1,** (a small number) varios. **2,** (distinct) distintos; diversos. —*n.* algunos; varios.
severance ('sɛv·ər·əns) *n.* separación; división; ruptura.
severe (sɪ'vɪr) *adj.* **1,** (stern) severo; austero; duro. **2,** (extreme; intense) riguroso; intenso; extremo.
severity (sɪ'vɛr·ə·ti) *n.* **1,** (sternness) severidad; austeridad. **2,** (intensity) intensidad; fuerza.
sew (soː) *v.t.* & *i.* [*pret.* **sewed;** *p.p.* **sewed** *o* **sewn**] coser.
sewage ('su·ɪdʒ) *n.* aguas de albañal; aguas sucias.
sewer ('su·ər) *n.* albañal; cloaca. —**sewerage,** *n.* alcantarillado.
sewing ('so·ɪŋ) *n.* costura. —**sewing machine,** máquina de coser.
sewn (soːn) *v., p.p. de* sew.
sex (sɛks) *n.* sexo. —*adj.* sexual; del sexo. —**sex appeal,** atracción sexual.
sex- (sɛks) *prefijo* sex-; seis: *sexennial,* sexenio.
sexagenarian (,sɛk·sə·dʒə'nɛr·i·ən) *adj.* & *n.* sexagenario.
Sexagesima (,sɛk·sə'dʒɛs·ə·mə) *n.* sexagésima.
sextant ('sɛks·tənt) *n.* **1,** *math.* sexta parte del círculo. **2,** *naut.* sextante.
sextet *también,* **sextette** (sɛks'tɛt) *n.* **1,** (group of six) grupo de seis. **2,** *music* sexteto.
sextillion (sɛks'tɪl·jən) *n.* (*U.S.*) mil trillones; (*Brit.*) un millón de quintillones; sextillón.
sexton ('sɛks·tən) *n.* sacristán.
sextuple ('sɛks·tju·pəl) *adj.* & *n.* séxtuplo. —*v.t.* sextuplicar. —*v.i.* sextuplicarse.
sexual ('sɛk·ʃu·əl) *adj.* sexual. —**sexuality** (-'æl·ə·ti) *n.* sexualidad.
sexy ('sɛks·i) *adj., slang* sexual; apetecible; incitante. —**sexiness,** *n.* atracción sexual.
shabbiness ('ʃæb·i·nəs) *n.* **1,** (seediness) desaseo; estado andrajoso. **2,** (meanness) ruindad.
shabby ('ʃæb·i) *adj.* **1,** (seedy) andrajoso; desastrado. **2,** (much worn) raído; usado. **3,** (mean) bajo; ruín.
shack (ʃæk) *n.* cabaña; choza.
shackle ('ʃæk·əl) *n.* **1,** (fetter) grillo; grillete. **2,** (coupling device) traba. **3,** (bar of a padlock) barra; cadena. —*v.t.* **1,** (chain) poner grillos *o* grilletes a; encadenar. **2,** (hamper) impedir; poner trabas a; estorbar.
shad (ʃæd) *n.* sábalo.
shaddock ('ʃæd·ək) *n.* pamplemusa.
shade (ʃeid) *n.* **1,** (darkness; dark area) sombra. **2,** (trace; degree) matiz; sombra; grado. **3,** (ghost) fantasma; sombra. **4,** (screen, as for a lamp) pantalla. **5,** (covering for a window) visillo; cortina. **6,** (visor; eyeshade) visera. **7,** (gradation of color) matiz; rasgo; gradación. —*v.t.* **1,** (screen from light) resguardar; proteger. **2,** (obscure) obscurecer; sombrear. **3,** (add shading to) sombrear. —*v.i.* cambiar *o* variar gradualmente.
shading ('ʃei·dɪŋ) *n.* **1,** (slight difference) matiz; tinte; tono. **2,** (application of shade) sombreado.
shadow ('ʃæd·o) *n.* sombra.

—*v.t.* **1,** (shade) obscurecer; sombrear. **2,** (cloud) ensombrecer; nublar. **3,** (trail) seguir como sombra. **4,** (add shading to) sombrear; dar sombreado a.

shadowy ('ʃæd·o·i) *adj.* **1,** (without reality) indefinido; vago. **2,** (shaded) sombreado; umbroso.

shady ('ʃei·di) *adj.* **1,** (giving shade; full of shade) sombrío; umbroso. **2,** (concealed; secret) obscuro; tenebroso. **3,** *colloq.* (of questionable character) sospechoso; dudoso. —**shadiness,** *n.* obscuridad; tenebrosidad.

shaft (ʃæft) *n.* **1,** (long cylindrical stem, as of an arrow) astil. **2,** (arrow; dart) flecha; dardo. **3,** (handle) mango. **4,** (bar transmitting motion) árbol; eje. **5,** (passage, as in a mine or for an elevator) pozo. **6,** (bolt; ray; beam) rayo. **7,** *archit.* (body of a column) fuste. **8,** (pole for attaching harness) limonera; vara. **9,** (flagpole) asta.

shag (ʃæg) *v.t.* poner *o* hacer áspero. —*n.* felpa; lana áspera.

shaggy ('ʃæg·i) *adj.* **1,** (having rough hair) hirsuto; velludo. **2,** (unkempt) tosco; rudo. —**shagginess,** *n.* aspereza; tosquedad.

Shah (ʃaː) *n.* cha.

shake (ʃeik) *v.t.* [**shook, shaken, shaking**] **1,** (cause to vibrate; agitate) sacudir; estremecer; agitar. **2,** (weaken) debilitar; flaquear. **3,** (upset; disturb) perturbar; inquietar. **4,** (cause to doubt or waver) hacer vacilar. **5,** (clasp, as the hand, in greeting) estrechar; apretar. **6,** *slang* (get rid of) deshacerse de; zafarse de. —*v.i.* **1,** (be agitated) agitarse; sacudirse. **2,** (tremble) temblar; vibrar. **3,** (totter; toddle) titubear. —*n.* **1,** (agitation) sacudida; sacudimiento; agitación. **2,** (vibration) vibración; temblor. **3,** (tottering) titubeo. **4,** *pl.* (chills) escalofrío de la fiebre intermitente. **5,** *colloq.* (instant) instante; momentito. **6,** (a shaken drink, as a milk shake) batido. —**no great shakes,** *colloq.* de poca monta. —**shake down, 1,** (bring down by shaking) sacudir; zafar; bajar sacudiendo. **2,** (cause to settle by shaking) hacer depositar. **3,** (put through performance trials) probar; poner a prueba. **4,** *slang* (extort money from) chantajear; extorsionar dinero a.

shakedown *n.* **1,** (makeshift bed) cama improvisada. **2,** (performance trial) prueba. **3,** *slang* (extortion) concusión; extorsión; chantaje.

shaken ('ʃei·kən) *v.,* *p.p.* *de* **shake.**

shaker ('ʃei·kər) *n.* **1,** (agitator) agitador. **2,** (container for sprinkling) espolvoreador. **3,** *cap., relig.* miembro de una secta religiosa.

shakeup *n.* **1,** (reorganization) reorganización. **2,** (disturbance) conmoción; perturbación.

shako ('ʃei·ko) *n.* [*pl.* **-os**] chacó.

shaky ('ʃeik·i) *adj.* **1,** (trembling) tembloroso; trémulo. **2,** (wavering) vacilante. **3,** (doubtful) dudoso. **4,** (wobbly) cojo.

shale (ʃeil) *n.* pizarra.

shall (ʃæl) *v.aux.* [*pret.* **should**] **1,** *forma los tiempos futuros en la primera persona: I shall die,* moriré. **2,** *expresa determinación, obligación o necesidad en segunda y tercera personas: he shall die,* morirá; que muera; tiene que morir; *thou shalt not steal,* no hurtarás.

shallop ('ʃæl·əp) *n.* chalupa.

shallot (ʃə'lat) *n.* chalote; ascalonia.

shallow ('ʃæl·o) *adj.* bajo; poco profundo; *fig.* superficial. —*n.* bajío; bajo.

shalt (ʃælt) *v., arcaico, segunda persona del sing. del pres. de ind. de* **shall.**

sham (ʃæm) *adj.* fingido; simulado; falso. —*n.* fingimiento; impostura; farsa. —*v.i. & t.* [**shammed, shamming**] simular; fingir.

shaman ('ʃa·mən) *n.* chamán. —**shamanism,** *n.* chamanismo.

shamble ('ʃæm·bəl) *v.i.* andar bamboleándose; andar arrastrando los pies; vacilar. —*n.* **1,** (shambling walk) bamboleo; paso vacilante. **2,** *pl.* (slaughterhouse) matadero; carnicería; degolladero.

shame (ʃeim) *n.* **1,** (remorseful consciousness of guilt) remordimiento de culpabilidad. **2,** (disgrace; dishonor) deshonra; ignominia; oprobio. **3,** (modesty; shyness) vergüenza; bochorno; modestia. **4,** (pity; lamentable condition) lástima. —*v.t.* **1,** (make ashamed) avergonzar. **2,** (disgrace) deshonrar; afrentar. **3,** (to embarrass) abochornar.

shamefaced *adj.* avergonzado;

vergonzoso; tímido. —**shamefacedness** (-ˈfei·sɪd·nəs) *n.* pudor; timidez; vergüenza.
shameful (ˈʃeim·fəl) *adj.* **1,** (modest; shy) vergonzoso. **2,** (infamous; disgraceful) ignominioso; escandaloso. **3,** (indecent) indecente.
shameless (ˈʃeim·ləs) *adj.* desvergonzado; sin vergüenza; descarado. —**shamelessness,** *n.* desvergüenza; descaro.
shampoo (ʃæmˈpuː) *v.t.* dar (un) champú; lavar la cabeza a. —*n.* champú.
shamrock (ˈʃæm,rak) *n.* trébol irlandés.
shank (ʃæŋk) *n.* **1,** *anat.* caña *o* canilla de la pierna; zanca (de las aves). **2,** *mech.* (shaft) ástil; mango; caña. —**ride on shank's mare** *o* **pony,** ir a pie; ir en coche de San Francisco.
shan't (ʃænt) *contr. de* **shall not.**
shanty (ˈʃæn·ti) *n.* [*pl.* **-ties**] cabaña; choza.
shape (ʃeip) *n.* **1,** (form; contour) forma; figura; contorno. **2,** (appearance) apariencia; aspecto. **3,** (condition) estado; condición. —*v.t.* **1,** (give form to) formar; dar forma a. **2,** (adapt) arreglar; ajustar. **3,** (express) modelar; tallar; hacer. —*v.i.* formarse; tomar forma; desarrollarse. —**be in a bad shape,** *colloq.* estar mal. —**put into shape,** arreglar; poner en orden.
shapeless (ˈʃeip·ləs) *adj.* informe.
shapely (ˈʃeip·li) *adj.* bien formado; bien proporcionado. —**shapeliness,** *n.* buena proporción; belleza.
share (ʃeːr) *n.* **1,** (portion; allotted part) porción; parte. **2,** (unit of corporate stock) acción. **3,** (plow blade) reja. —*v.t.* **1,** (divide; apportion) distribuir; repartir; dividir. **2,** (have or use jointly) compartir; partir; participar de; tomar parte en. —*v.i.* **1,** (partake) participar; tener parte; gozar o disfrutar con otros. **2,** (give a portion to others) repartir; compartir; tener una parte. —**fall to the share of,** tocar a; caer en parte a. —**go shares,** entrar *o* ir a la parte. —**share alike,** repartir igualmente; tener una parte igual. —**share and share alike,** por igual; por partes iguales.
sharecropper *n.* aparcero. —**sharecropping,** *n.* aparcería.
shareholder *n.* accionista.
shark (ʃark) *n.* **1,** *ichthy.* tiburón. **2,** (predatory person) estafador. **3,** *slang* (expert) perito; experto. —**loan shark,** usurero.
sharkskin (ˈʃark·skɪn) *n.* tejido de algodón de apariencia sedosa que se usa para trajes.
sharp (ʃarp) *adj.* **1,** (having a fine cutting edge) agudo; cortante; afilado. **2,** (pointed) puntiagudo. **3,** (clear; distinct) claro; distinto; bien marcado. **4,** (abrupt) repentino. **5,** (violent; forceful) violento; fuerte; rudo. **6,** (angular) anguloso. **7,** (pungent) picante; acre; mordaz. **8,** (acute; shrill) agudo; penetrante. **9,** (clever) astuto; listo; vivo. **10,** (barely honest) dudoso; sospechoso. **11,** *music* sostenido. —*adv.* **1,** (sharply) agudamente. **2,** (quickly) vivamente. **3,** (exactly) exactamente; precisamente; en punto. —*n.* **1,** *music* sostenido. **2,** (cheat) estafador; fullero. **3,** *colloq.* (expert) perito.
sharpen (ˈʃar·pən) *v.t.* & *i.* **1,** (put on a cutting edge) afilar; amolar. **2,** (put a point on) sacar punta a. **3,** (make more acute) aguzar; sutilizar.
sharpener (ˈʃar·pən·ər) *n.* amolador; afilador. —**pencil sharpener,** cortalápiz; sacapuntas.
sharper (ˈʃar·pər) *n.* **1,** (cheat) tahúr; fullero. **2,** (swindler) estafador; trampista.
sharpness (ˈʃarp·nəs) *n.* **1,** (cutting or piercing quality; acuteness) agudeza. **2,** (clearness) claridad. **3,** (pungency) acritud; mordacidad. **4,** (cleverness) astucia; viveza. **5,** (violence) violencia.
sharpshooter *n.* tirador certero; tirador experto.
shatter (ˈʃæt·ər) *v.t.* & *i.* **1,** (break in pieces) hacer(se) añicos; estrellar(se); astillar(se). **2,** (disorder; impair) quebrar(se); romper(se). —**shatters,** *n.pl.* pedazos; trozos; añicos; fragmentos.
shatterproof *adj.* inastillable.
shave (ʃeiv) *v.t.* **1,** (slice with a keen instrument) rasurar; afeitar; raer. **2,** (make bare) rapar. **3,** (cut down gradually, as with a plane) cepillar. **4,** (come ver-

close to) raspar; rozar. —*v.i.* rasurarse; afeitarse. —*n.* rasura; *Amer.* afeitada. —**have a close shave,** *colloq.* **1,** por poco no escaparse. **2,** salvarse por milagro.
shaven (ˈʃei·vən) *adj.* afeitado; rasurado. —**clean-shaven,** bien afeitado.
shaver (ˈʃei·vər) *n.* **1,** (barber) barbero. **2,** (device or machine for shaving) máquina de afeitar. **3,** *colloq.* (youngster) jovencito; rapaz.
shaving (ˈʃei·vɪŋ) *n.* **1,** (cutting) afeitado; rasura. **2,** *pl.* (thin slices cut off) cepilladuras; virutas. —**shaving brush,** brocha de afeitar. —**shaving dish,** bacía. —**shaving knife,** navaja de afeitar.
shawl (ʃɔl) *n.* chal; mantón.
she (ʃiː) *pron.pers.* ella. —*adj.* & *n.* hembra.
sheaf (ʃif) *n.* [*pl.* **sheaves** (ʃiːvz)] **1,** (of grain, hay, etc.) gavilla; haz. **2,** (of papers, currency, etc.) lío; paquete.
shear (ʃɪr) *v.t.* **1,** (clip or cut) tonsurar; rapar. **2,** (remove by clipping, as fleece) esquilar; trasquilar. —**shears,** *n.sing.* & *pl.* tijeras grandes.
she-ass *n.* borrica; burra.
sheath (ʃiθ) *n.* **1,** (case; covering) cubierta; envoltura; manguito; funda. **2,** (scabbard) vaina.
sheathe (ʃiːð) *v.t.* envainar; enfundar; poner vaina, funda o cubierta a.
she-cat *n.* gata.
shed (ʃɛd) *v.t.* **1,** (molt) mudar. **2,** (emit; throw off) echar; emitir; arrojar. **3,** (cause to flow off) verter; derramar. **4,** (disperse, as light) esparcir; difundir; dar; echar. **5,** (get rid of) deshacerse de; desprenderse de. —*v.i.* pelechar. —*n.* cobertizo; tinglado; colgadizo.
she'd (ʃid) *contr.* *de* **she would** *o* **she had.**
she-devil *n.* diabla.
sheen (ʃiːn) *n.* lustre; viso; resplandor.
sheep (ʃip) *n.sing.* & *pl.* **1,** (ewe) oveja. **2,** (ram) carnero. **3,** (timid person) papanatas; simplón.
sheep dog perro de pastor.
sheepfold *n.* redil; aprisco. *También,* **sheepcote** (-ˌkot).
sheepish (ˈʃip·ɪʃ) *adj.* avergonzado; corrido; encogido.
sheepskin (ˈʃip·skɪn) *n.* **1,** (sheep's fur) zalea. **2,** (cured skin of a sheep) badana. **3,** (parchment) pergamino. **4,** *colloq.* (diploma) diploma (de pergamino).
sheer (ʃɪr) *adj.* **1,** (very thin; diaphanous) ligero; fino; delgado; diáfano; transparente. **2,** (unmixed; absolute) puro; claro; completo; cabal. **3,** (precipitous) escarpado. —*adv.* **1,** (absolutely; quite) puramente; claramente; cabalmente. **2,** (steeply) escarpadamente. —*v.i.* [*usu.,* **sheer off**] alargarse; desviarse. —*n.* **1,** (swerve; deviation) desviación. **2,** (thin, light material) tela fina y transparente.
sheet (ʃit) *n.* **1,** (cloth; bedding) sábana. **2,** (flat, thin piece) hoja. **3,** (newspaper) periódico; diario. **4,** (expanse or surface, as of ice or water) extensión. **5,** (rope fastened to a sail) escota.
sheeting (ˈʃit·ɪŋ) *n.* **1,** (material for bedsheets) lencería para sábanas. **2,** (thin plates, as of metal) laminado.
she-goat *n.* cabra.
sheik (ʃik) *n.* **1,** (Arab chief) jeque. **2,** *slang* (bold lover) tenorio; don Juan; galán.
shekel (ˈʃɛk·əl) *n.* siclo. —**shekels,** *n.pl., slang* dinero.
shelf (ʃɛlf) *n.* [*pl.* **shelves**] **1,** (horizontal support) anaquel; estante. **2,** (ledge) repisa. **3,** (outcropping of rock) escalón de roca; saliente de roca. **4,** (reef) arrecife; escollo. **5,** (sand bar) bajío; banco de arena.
shell (ʃɛl) *n.* **1,** (hard outer case or covering) casco; cubierta; corteza. **2,** (nutshell; eggshell) cáscara. **3,** (sea shell) concha; caracol. **4,** (covering of crustaceans and insects) caparazón. **5,** (turtle shell) carapacho; coraza. **6,** (vegetable pod) vaina; vainilla. **7,** (framework) armazón; esqueleto. **8,** (hull of a ship) casco. **9,** (projectile) bomba; proyectil. **10,** (cartridge) cápsula; cartucho. **11,** (long, narrow rowboat used for racing) bote largo y angosto que se usa para regatas. —*v.t.* **1,** (remove or take out of the shell) descascarar; descortezar; desvainar; desgranar. **2,** (bombard) bombardear. —**shell game,** estafa que se efectúa con tres cáscaras de nuez y un guisante escondido debajo de una de

ellas. —**shell out**, *slang* entregar; sacar. —**shell shock**, neurosis de guerra.

she'll (ʃil) *contr. de* **she will** *o* **she shall**.

shellac (ʃəˈlæk) *n.* laca; goma laca. —*v.t.* barnizar con laca.

shellfish *n.* marisco; mariscos.

shelter (ˈʃɛl·tər) *n.* **1,** (covering; protection) abrigo; amparo; resguardo; protección. **2,** (refuge) refugio; asilo. **3,** (lodging) hospedaje; alojamiento; albergue. —*v.t.* **1,** (cover; protect) abrigar; amparar; resguardar; proteger. **2,** (house) hospedar; alojar.

shelve (ʃɛlv) *v.t.* **1,** (put on a shelf) poner *o* guardar en un estante. **2,** (put aside; put off) arrinconar; poner a un lado; diferir. —*v.i.* inclinarse.

shelves (ʃɛlvz) *n., pl. de* **shelf**.

shelving (ˈʃɛl·vɪŋ) *n.* **1,** (set of shelves) estantería; anaquelería. **2,** (material for shelves) material para estantes o anaqueles.

shenanigans (ʃəˈnæn·ə·gənz) *n.pl., colloq.* travesuras; bromas; tonterías.

shepherd (ˈʃɛp·ərd) *n.* pastor. —*adj.* pastoril; del pastor. —*v.t.* pastorear. —**shepherdess**, *n.* pastora. —**shepherd dog**, perro de pastor.

sherbet (ˈʃʌɹ·bət) *n.* sorbete.

sheriff (ˈʃɛr·ɪf) *n.* alguacil mayor; oficial de justicia de un condado inglés o norteamericano.

sherry (ˈʃɛr·i) *n.* jerez; vino de Jerez.

she's (ʃiːz) *contr. de* **she is** *o* **she has**.

shibboleth (ˈʃɪb·əˌlɛθ) *n.* contraseña; palabra que sirve de santo y seña; mote.

shield (ʃiːld) *n.* **1,** (armor) escudo; broquel. **2,** (protection) amparo; égida; patrocinio. **3,** (protector) protector; defensor. **4,** (for the armpit) sobaquera. **5,** (escutcheon) escudo de armas. —*v.t.* escudar; amparar; resguardar; proteger.

shield-bearer *n.* escudero.

shieldmaker *n.* escudero.

shift (ʃɪft) *v.t.* **1,** (transfer) trasladar; transferir. **2,** (change) cambiar; mudar; desviar. —*v.i.* **1,** (change place, position, direction, etc.) desviarse; mudarse; trasladarse; transferirse. **2,** (alter) alterar; cambiar. **3,** [*también,* **make shift**] (get along) ingeniarse; darse maña; componérselas. —*n.* **1,** (change; turning) cambio; desviación. **2,** (group of workmen) tanda de obreros. **3,** (work period) tarea; turno. **4,** (expedient; resource) expediente; suplente. —**shiftless**, *adj.* negligente; descuidado. —**shifty**, *adj.* furtivo; falso.

shillelagh (ʃəˈlei·li) *n.* cachiporra irlandesa.

shilling (ˈʃɪl·ɪŋ) *n.* chelín.

shilly-shally (ˈʃɪl·iˈʃæl·i) *v.i.* estar irresoluto; vacilar; roncear. —*adj.* irresoluto; roncero. —*adv.* irresolutamente. —**shilly-shallying**, *n.* vacilación; irresolución; roncería.

shimmer (ˈʃɪm·ər) *v.i.* brillar con luz trémula; resplandecer. —*n.* luz trémula; débil resplandor. —**shimmery**, *adj.* resplandeciente.

shimmy (ˈʃɪm·i) *n.* **1,** (abnormal vibration) vibración anormal. **2,** (jazz dance) baile norteamericano muy animado. **3,** *colloq.* (chemise) camisa de mujer.

shin (ʃɪn) *n.* espinilla. —*v.t. & i.* [**shinned, shinning**] trepar.

shinbone *n.* espinilla; tibia.

shindig (ˈʃɪn·dɪg) *n., slang* fiesta; juerga; parranda.

shine (ʃain) *v.t.* **1,** (polish; brighten) pulir; bruñir; dar brillo a. **2,** [*pret. & p.p.* **shone**] (point or direct, as a light) dirigir; echar (una luz). —*v.i.* [*pret. & p.p.* **shone**] **1,** (glow) lucir; brillar; resplandecer. **2,** (excel) sobresalir; destacarse; distinguirse. —*n.* **1,** (luster) resplandor; brillo; lustre. **2,** (fair weather) claridad; buen tiempo. **3,** (polishing, as of shoes) lustre.

shiner (ˈʃai·nər) *n.* **1,** (minnow) pececillo de la familia de la carpa. **2,** *slang* (black eye) ojo morado.

shingle (ˈʃɪŋ·gəl) *n.* **1,** (roof covering) tablita de madera, pizarra, asbesto, etc. usada como teja. **2,** (closely bobbed hair) pelo corto. **3,** (small signboard) muestra; letrero; rótulo. **4,** (gravelly beach) playa guijarrosa.

shingles (ˈʃɪŋ·gəlz) *n.sing. o pl., pathol.* zona.

shining (ˈʃai·nɪŋ) *adj.* brillante; resplandeciente. —*n.* brillo; resplandor.

shinny ('ʃɪn·i) *n.* juego de niños parecido al hockey. —*v.i.* trepar.

Shinto ('ʃɪn·to) *n.* sintoísmo. —*adj.* sintoísta. —**Shintoism**, *n.* sintoísmo. —**Shintoist**, *adj.* & *n.* sintoísta.

shiny ('ʃai·ni) *adj.* brillante; resplandeciente.

ship (ʃɪp) *n.* **1,** (large vessel) barco; buque; bajel; nave; navío. **2,** (aircraft) aeronave; avión. —*v.t.* [**shipped, shipping**] **1,** (put or take on board) embarcar; poner a bordo. **2,** (send; transport) despachar; enviar; remesar; transportar. —*v.i.* **1,** (embark) embarcarse; ir a bordo. **2,** (enlist as a sailor) alistarse como marino; engancharse como marinero.

-ship (ʃɪp) *sufijo; forma nombres denotando* **1,** cualidad; condición: *friendship,* amistad; *hardship,* contratiempo. **2,** dignidad; cargo: *governorship,* gobierno; cargo de gobernador. **3,** habilidad; capacidad: *seamanship,* marinería.

ship biscuit galleta de munición; rosca; pan de marinero.

shipboard *n.* bordo. —**on shipboard**, a bordo.

shipbuilder *n.* constructor de buques; ingeniero naval.

shipbuilding *n.* construcción naval.

shipload *n.* cargamento; cargazón.

shipmaster *n.* patrón; capitán de buque.

shipmate *n.* camarada de a bordo.

shipment ('ʃɪp·mənt) *n.* **1,** (act or result of shipping) embarque; cargamento; expedición; partida. **2,** (quantity of goods shipped) despacho; envío; remesa.

shipowner *n.* naviero.

shipper ('ʃɪp·ər) *n.* exportador; expedidor; remitente.

shipping ('ʃɪp·ɪŋ) *n.* **1,** (the business of transporting goods) embarque; expedición. **2,** (ships collectively) barcos; buques; marina; flota. —**shipping agent**, consignatario de buques. —**shipping clerk**, dependiente encargado de embarques; dependiente de muelle.

ship's carpenter carpintero de ribera.

shipshape *adj.* bien arreglado; en buen orden.

shipwreck *n.* **1,** (sinking or destruction of a ship) naufragio. **2,** *fig.* (ruin) desastre; desgracia; ruina. —*v.t.* echar a pique; hacer naufragar. —*v.i.* irse a pique; naufragar. —**be shipwrecked**, naufragar.

shipwright *n.* carpintero de ribera; constructor de buques.

shipyard *n.* astillero.

shire (ʃair) *n.* condado.

shirk (ʃʌɹk) *v.t.* evadir; evitar; faltar a. —*v.i.* evadirse; faltar (a su deber, al trabajo, etc.). —**shirker**, *n.* el que se evade de hacer algo.

shirr (ʃʌɹ) *v.t.* **1,** *sewing* fruncir. **2,** *cooking* cocer (huevos) en el horno con pan rallado. —*n., sewing* frunce.

shirt (ʃʌɹt) *n.* camisa. —**in shirt sleeves**, en camisa; en mangas de camisa. —**keep one's shirt on,** *slang,* tener calma; tener paciencia.

shirting ('ʃʌɹ·tɪŋ) *n.* tela para camisas.

shirtmaker *n.* camisero.

shirttail *n.* faldón; pañal.

shirtwaist *n.* blusa de mujer.

shiver ('ʃɪv·ər) *v.i.* **1,** (tremble, as with cold or fear) temblar; estremecerse; tiritar. **2,** (shatter) estrellarse; hacerse añicos. —*v.t.* romper de un golpe; estrellar; hacer añicos. —*n.* **1,** (tremor) temblor; estremecimiento. **2,** (chill) escalofrío; tiritón. **3,** (fragment) añico; trozo; fragmento.

shivery ('ʃɪv·ə·ri) *adj.* **1,** (trembling with cold or fear) estremecido; trémulo. **2,** (susceptible to cold) friolento. **3,** (causing shivers) frío. **4,** (easily shattered) quebradizo.

shoal (ʃo:l) *n.* **1,** (sandbank) bajío; bajo; banco de arena. **2,** (large body of fish) cardumen; banco. **3,** (crowd) muchedumbre. —*adj.* bajo; poco profundo.

shock (ʃak) *n.* **1,** (violent impact) choque; golpe. **2,** (sudden fear) susto. **3,** (surprise) sorpresa; sobresalto. **4,** (prostration; stroke) choque; postración nerviosa. **5,** (jolt of electricity) sacudida eléctrica. **6,** (earth tremor) temblor de tierra. **7,** (sheaf of grain) gavilla; haz. **8,** (thick mass, as of hair) greña; mechón. —*v.t.* **1,** (affect violently) chocar; sacudir. **2,** (surprise) sorprender; asustar; sobresaltar. **3,** (outrage) ultrajar; afrentar; escandalizar. **4,** (stack, as grain) hacinar; hacer gavillas (de mieses). —**shock absorber**, amortiguador. —**shock troops**, tropas de asalto.

shocking ('ʃak·ɪŋ) *adj.* chocante; espantoso; escandaloso.

shod (ʃad) *v., pret. & p.p. de* **shoe**.

shoddy ('ʃad·i) *n.* **1,** (low quality fabric; anything inferior) lana artificial *o* regenerada; material inferior. **2,** (sham) imitación; impostura; farsa. —*adj.* **1,** (inferior) de pacotilla; inferior. **2,** (sham; false) falso; fingido; simulado.

shoe (ʃuː) *n.* **1,** (footwear) zapato. **2,** (horseshoe) herradura. **3,** (outer covering) cubierta. **4,** (tire) llanta. **5,** (curved part of a brake, anchor, etc.) zapata. **6,** (runner, as of a sled) suela. —*v.t.* [*pret. & p.p.* **shod**] calzar; herrar (un caballo); enllantar (una rueda). —**be in someone's shoes**, hallarse en el pellejo de uno. —**shoe blacking**, betún para zapatos. —**shoe polish**, betún. —**shoe store**, zapatería; tienda de calzado.

shoehorn *n.* calzador.

shoelace *n.* cordón *o* lazo de zapato.

shoemaker *n.* zapatero.

shoestring *n.* **1,** = **shoelace**. **2,** (small amount of capital) muy poco dinero; poco capital.

shoetree *n.* horma para zapato.

shone (ʃoːn) *v., pret. & p.p. de* **shine**.

shoo (ʃuː) *interj.* ¡fuera! —*v.t.* ahuyentar.

shook (ʃʊk) *v., pret. de* **shake**.

shoot (ʃut) *v.t.* [*pret. & p.p.* **shot**] **1,** (hit, kill or wound with a missile from a weapon) matar o herir con arma de fuego o arma arrojadiza. **2,** (discharge, as a weapon) descargar; disparar; tirar; hacer fuego con. **3,** (execute by shooting) fusilar. **4,** (send out or forth) arrojar; echar; lanzar. **5,** (traverse rapidly) atravesar; pasar rápidamente. **6,** (take a picture of) fotografiar; tomar. **7,** (produce, as a motion picture) rodar; filmar. **8,** (throw, as dice) echar (los dados); jugar a (los dados). —*v.i.* **1,** (discharge a missile) tirar; hacer fuego. **2,** (hunt) cazar; ir de caza. **3,** (dart forth or along) arrojarse; abalanzarse; precipitarse. **4,** (be emitted) brotar; salir. **5,** (sprout) brotar; crecer. **6,** [*usu.* **shoot up**] (grow rapidly) crecer a palmos; espigarse. —*n.* **1,** (act of shooting; shooting competition) tiro; tiro al blanco. **2,** (shooting party) partida de caza. **3,** (sprout) botón; renuevo; retoño; vástago. —*interj., slang* ¡caramba!; ¡cuernos!

shooting ('ʃu·tɪŋ) *n.* **1,** (firing of weapons) tiro; fuego; fusilería. **2,** (hunt) caza con escopeta. **3,** (filming) rodaje. —**shooting iron**, *slang,* arma de fuego. —**shooting match**, certamen de tiradores. —**shooting pain**, punzada; dolor agudo. —**shooting star**, estrella fugaz.

shop (ʃap) *n.* **1,** (store) tienda. **2,** (workroom; factory) taller; fábrica. —*v.i.* [**shopped, shopping**] comprar; ir de compras; hacer compras. —**talk shop**, hablar de negocios.

shopkeeper *n.* tendero.

shoplifter *n.* ladrón de tiendas. —**shoplifting**, *n.* ratería en las tiendas.

shopper ('ʃap·ər) *n.* comprador.

shopping ('ʃap·ɪŋ) *n.* **1,** (buying) acto de ir a las tiendas o de hacer compras. **2,** (collection of things bought) compras (*pl.*); recado. —**shopping district**, barrio comercial.

shopwindow *n.* aparador; escaparate; vitrina.

shopworn *adj.* deteriorado por haber estado expuesto en la tienda.

shore (ʃor) *n.* **1,** (land adjacent to water) costa; orilla; ribera. **2,** (beach) playa. **3,** (prop; support) puntal. —*v.t.* [*también,* **shore up**] apuntalar; poner puntales a. —**shoring**, *n.* apuntalamiento; puntales (*pl.*). —**shore leave**, permisión para ir a tierra.

shoreward ('ʃor·wərd) *adj. & adv.* hacia la costa.

shorn (ʃorn) *v., p.p. de* **shear**.

short (ʃort) *adj.* **1,** (not long; not tall) corto; bajo; pequeño; chico. **2,** (brief; concise) breve; conciso; sucinto. **3,** (deficient) inadecuado; escaso; limitado. **4,** (crumbling readily, as pastry) que se desmigaja fácilmente. **5,** (curt) áspero; brusco; seco; corto. —*adv.* **1,** (briefly) brevemente; en breve. **2,** (abruptly) bruscamente; rudamente. **3,** (insufficiently) insuficientemente; escasamente. **—*n.* 1,** (short film) película de corto metraje. **2,** *pl.* (short trousers or drawers) calzoncillos. **3,** *electricity* corto circuito. **—*v.t.*,** *electricity* poner en corto circuito. **—cut short,** interrumpir; cortarle (a uno) la palabra. **—fall short,** faltar; escasear. **—fall short of,** no alcanzar a; no llegar a. **—for short,** para abreviar. **—in short,** en suma; en resumen; brevemente. **—in short order,** en seguida. **—on short notice,** con poco aviso. **—run short of,** acabársele *o* írsele acabando a uno algo. **—short of, 1,** (inadequately supplied with) escaso de. **2,** (except for; but for) fuera de. **3,** (far from; removed from) lejos de. **—stop short,** parar en seco. **—the long and short of it,** en resumen; en resumidas cuentas.

shortage ('ʃor·tɪdʒ) *n.* **1,** (scarcity) escasez; carestía. **2,** (lack) falta. **3,** (deficit) déficit.

short allowance media ración.

shortbread *n.* mantecado.

shortcake *n.* torta de frutas.

short-change *v.t.*, *colloq.* **1,** (give inadequate change to) defraudar al dar el vuelto. **2,** *fig.* (cheat) engañar; estafar.

short circuit corto circuito. **—short-circuit,** *v.t.* poner en corto circuito. **—*v.i.*** ponerse en corto circuito.

shortcoming *n.* defecto; deficiencia.

shorten ('ʃor·tən) *v.t.* **1,** (reduce in length) acortar; recortar. **2,** (abridge) abreviar; compendiar; resumir. **3,** (add shortening to) poner grasa o manteca a; hacer quebradiza (la pastelería).

shortening ('ʃor·tən·ɪŋ) *n.* **1,** (reduction in length) acortamiento. **2,** (abbreviation) abreviación. **3,** (fat or grease used in making pastry) grasa; manteca; mantequilla.

shorthand *n.* estenografía; taquigrafía. **—*adj.*** estenográfico; taquigráfico.

shorthanded *adj.* escaso de mano de obra; escaso de obreros.

shortlived ('ʃort,laivd) *adj.* corto de vida; pasajero.

short loan préstamo a corto plazo.

shortly ('ʃort·li) *adv.* **1,** (briefly) brevemente; en breve. **2,** (soon) pronto; luego. **3,** (abruptly) en seco; de repente. **4,** (curtly) bruscamente.

shortness ('ʃort·nəs) *n.* **1,** (brevity) cortedad; brevedad. **2,** (small stature) pequeñez. **3,** (scarcity; lack) escasez; falta.

shortsighted *adj.* **1,** (nearsighted) miope; corto de vista. **2,** (lacking foresight; not provident) falto de perspicacia; impróvido.

shortsightedness *n.* **1,** (nearsightedness) miopía; cortedad de vista. **2,** (lack of foresight) falta de perspicacia; improvidencia.

short story cuento; historieta.

short ton tonelada corta o menor (*2,000 libras*).

short wave onda corta. **—shortwave,** *adj.* de onda corta.

short-winded ('ʃort,wɪn·dɪd) *adj.* asmático; corto de respiración.

shorty ('ʃor·ti) *n.*, *colloq.* bajete.

shot (ʃat) *n.* **1,** (act of shooting) tiro; disparo. **2,** (impact of a missile) balazo; cañonazo; escopetazo. **3,** (small pellets) balas (*pl.*); perdigones (*pl.*); munición. **4,** (range) alcance; tiro. **5,** (one who shoots) tirador. **6,** *games* (move; stroke) jugada; turno; tirada. **7,** *slang* (attempt) tentativa. **8,** *slang* (guess) conjetura. **9,** *slang* (drink; swallow) trago; *Amer.* palo. **10,** (snapshot) instantánea; foto. **11,** *sports* (weight used for throwing) peso. **—*v.*, *pret. & p.p. de* shoot. —not by a long shot,** *colloq.* ni por asomo; ni con mucho; ni por pienso. **—put the shot,** tirar *o* lanzar el peso. **—shot through with,** lleno de; acribillado de. **—take a shot at,** *slang,* **1,** (fire at) disparar un tiro a. **2,** (attempt) hacer una tentativa de. **3,** (guess) adivinar; conjeturar.

shotgun *n.* escopeta.

shot-put *n.* tiro *o* lanzamiento del peso.

should (ʃʊd) *v. aux.* **1,** *pret. de* **shall. 2,** *forma los tiempos condicionales en la primera persona: I should buy it if I had enough money,* Lo compraría si tuviera bastante dinero. **3,** *expresa obligación, necesidad o expectación en todas las personas: We should help him,* Debiéramos ayudarlo.

shoulder ('ʃol·dər) *n.* **1,** *anat.* hombro; espalda. **2,** (cut of meat) brazuelo; cuarto delantero. **3,** (ledge) borde; capa. **4,** (the unpaved side of a road) borde; saliente. —*v.t.* & *i.* **1,** (to carry on or as on the shoulder) echar(se) a la espalda; cargar al hombro; llevar a hombros. **2,** *fig.* (take responsibility for) asumir; cargar con; tomar sobre sí. **3,** (push with the shoulder) codear; meter el hombro; empujar con el hombro. —**give the cold shoulder,** tratar *o* recibir fríamente; no hacerle caso a uno; negarse a recibirle a uno. —**shoulder arms,** *mil.* armas al hombro. —**shoulder belt,** tahalí. —**shoulder bone** *o* **blade,** escápula; omóplato. —**straight from the shoulder,** con toda franqueza.

shout (ʃaut) *v.t.* & *i.* (cry out) gritar; vocear. —*v.i.* (laugh noisily) reírse a carcajadas. —*n.* grito; alarido; voz. —**shout acclaim,** aclamar; dar vivas; vitorear. —**shout down,** silbar.

shouting ('ʃau·tɪŋ) *n.* gritería; vocerío; aclamación.

shove (ʃʌv) *v.t.* & *i.* **1,** (push along) empujar; hacer avanzar; dar empellones. **2,** (jostle) codear. —*n.* empujón; empellón. —**shove off, 1,** (move away from the shore) alejar(se); hacerse a la mar. **2,** *slang* (leave) irse; marcharse; salir.

shovel ('ʃʌv·əl) *n.* pala. —*v.t.* & *i.* traspalar.

show (ʃoː) *v.t.* [*p.p.* **shown** *o* **showed**] **1,** (allow to be seen; exhibit) mostrar; enseñar; exhibir; exponer; descubrir. **2,** (point out; indicate) indicar; señalar. **3,** (instruct; explain) enseñar; explicar. **4,** (guide; lead) guiar; conducir. **5,** (prove; demonstrate) probar; demostrar. **6,** (exhibit, as a film) exhibir. **7,** (project, as a film) proyectar; pasar. **8,** (perform, as a play) representar; actuar. —*v.i.* **1,** (be seen; appear) mostrarse; aparecer; asomar. **2,** (be revealed) descubrirse; dejarse ver; manifestarse. **3,** *racing* terminar tercero. **4,** (be exhibited, as a film) exhibirse. **5,** (be performed, as a play) representarse. —*n.* **1,** (spectacle) espectáculo. **2,** (theatrical performance) función; espectáculo; representación. **3,** (exhibition) exposición; exhibición. **4,** (ostentatious display) boato; gala; pompa; ostentación. **5,** *colloq.* (chance) suerte; oportunidad; lance. **6,** (indication; outward sign) indicación; manifestación; señal. **7,** (outward appearance) apariencia; exterior. —**in open show,** públicamente. —**make a good show,** hacer gran papel. —**make a show of,** hacer gala de. —**show off, 1,** (reveal; exhibit) dejar ver; descubrir; exhibir. **2,** (behave ostentatiously) lucirse; jactarse; pavonearse; darse ínfulas. —**show up, 1,** (expose) descubrir; exponer; desenmascarar. **2,** (appear) aparecer; presentarse; dejarse ver. **3,** *colloq.* (arrive) llegar. **4,** *colloq.* (outdo; excel over) superar; aventajar.

show bill cartel; cartelón.

showboat *n.* barco teatro.

showcase *n.* vitrina; aparador; caja de muestras.

showdown *n.* prueba decisiva.

shower ('ʃau·ər) *n.* **1,** (light rain; spray) lluvia; rociada. **2,** (downpour) aguacero; chaparrón. **3,** (a large number) abundancia; copia; lluvia; rociada. **4,** (bestowal of gifts, as to a bride) tertulia para obsequiar a una novia. **5,** (shower bath) ducha. —*v.t.* **1,** (wet copiously) mojar; regar. **2,** (bestow or scatter abundantly) derramar con abundancia; rociar. —*v.i.* **1,** (rain) llover; caer un aguacero; chaparrear. **2,** (take a shower bath) bañarse en la ducha. —**showery,** *adj.* lluvioso.

showman ('ʃo·mən) *n.* [*pl.* **-men**] empresario; director de espectáculos. —**showmanship,** *n.* calidad *o* habilidad de empresario.

shown (ʃoːn) *v., p.p. de* **show.**

show-off *n.* fanfarrón; jactancioso.

showroom *n.* sala de exhibición.

show window escaparate *o* ventana de tienda; vitrina; aparador.

showy ('ʃo·i) *adj.* **1,** (imposing) lujoso; suntuoso; magnífico. **2,** (gaudy) ostentoso; aparatoso; vistoso; llamativo. —**showiness,** *n.* esplendor; ostentación; magnificencia.

shrank (ʃræŋk) *v., pret. de* **shrink.**

shrapnel ('ʃræp·nəl) *n.* granada de metralla.

shred (ʃrɛd) *v.t.* [**shredded, -ding**] desmenuzar; hacer tiras *o* trizas. —*n.* 1, (small strip) tira; jirón; andrajo. 2, (particle) fragmento; partícula; pizca. —**in shreds,** andrajoso; raído.

shrew (ʃru) *n.* 1, (a scolding woman) arpía; mujer regañona. 2, (animal) musaraña. —**shrewish,** *adj.* malhumorado; regañon; regañador.

shrewd (ʃruːd) *adj.* astuto; sutil; perspicaz; listo; vivo. —**shrewdness,** *n.* sutileza; perspicacia; astucia.

shriek (ʃrik) *n.* grito agudo; chillido. —*v.t. & i.* chillar: gritar.

shrift (ʃrɪft) *n.* confesión; absolución. —**make short shrift of,** terminar en seguida; acabar pronto con.

shrike (ʃraik) *n.* alcaudón.

shrill (ʃrɪl) *adj.* penetrante; agudo; chillón. —*v.t. & i.* chillar. —**shrillness,** *n.* agudeza.

shrimp (ʃrɪmp) *n.* 1, (crustacean) camarón. 2, *colloq.* (small person) hombrecillo; renacuajo.

shrine (ʃrain) *n.* altar; santuario; relicario; sepulcro de santo.

shrink (ʃrɪŋk) *v.i.* [**shrank, shrunk, shrinking**] 1, (contract; diminish; shrivel) contraerse; disminuir; estrecharse; encogerse. 2, (draw back; recoil) retirarse. —*v.t.* encoger; contraer. —**shrinkage,** *n.* contracción; disminución; encogimiento.

shrive (ʃraiv) *v.t.* [**shrived** *o* **shrove, shriven**] confesar. —*v.i.* confesarse.

shrivel (ˈʃrɪv·əl) *v.t. & i.* arrugar(se); fruncir(se); encoger(se); marchitarse.

shriven (ˈʃrɪv·ən) *v., p.p. de* **shrive.**

shroud (ʃraud) *n.* 1, (burial cloth) mortaja; sudario. 2, (cover; screen; envelope) cubierta; velo. 3, *pl., naut.* (strong guy ropes) obenques. —*v.t.* 1, (wrap for burial) amortajar. 2, (cover; conceal) cubrir; ocultar.

shrove (ʃroːv) *v., pret. de* **shrive.**

Shrove Tuesday martes de carnaval.

shrub (ʃrʌb) *n.* arbusto; mata. —**shrubbery,** *n.* arbustos (*pl.*).

shrug (ʃrʌg) *v.t.* [**shrugged, shrugging**] encoger; contraer. —*v.i.* encogerse de hombros. —*n.* encogimiento de hombros.

shrunk (ʃrʌŋk) *v., p.p. de* **shrink.**

shrunken (ˈʃrʌŋk·ən) *adj.* 1, (contracted in size) encogido. 2, (shriveled) marchito; seco.

shuck (ʃʌk) *n.* 1, (husk or pod, as of corn) hollejo; vaina; cáscara. 2, (oyster or clam shell) concha. —*v.t.* deshollejar; descascarar; descortezar; pelar; quitar la concha a. —**shucks!,** *interj.* ¡caramba!

shudder (ˈʃʌd·ər) *n.* estremecimiento; temblor. —*v.i.* temblar de miedo o de horror; estremecerse.

shuffle (ˈʃʌf·əl) *v.t. & i.* 1, (scrape, as the feet) arrastrar (los pies). 2, (mix, as cards) barajar; mezclar. 3, (shift; change about) cambiar; mudar; remover. —*n.* 1, (scraping of the feet) arrastre de los pies. 2, (mixing of cards) barajadura. 3, (shift; change) cambio; mudanza; movimiento. 4, (ruse) evasiva. —**shuffle off,** deshacerse de; zafarse de.

shuffleboard *n.* juego de tejo.

shun (ʃʌn) *v.t. & i.* [**shunned, shunning**] apartarse (de); evitar; esquivar; huir; rehuir.

shunt (ʃʌnt) *v.t.* 1, (turn aside) apartar; desviar. 2, *R.R.* (shift, as a train) desviar. 3, *electricity* derivar; poner en derivación. —*n.* 1, (turning aside; shifting) desviación. 2, *R.R.* aguja; cambio de vía; desvío. 3, *electricity* derivación; (device for shunting) derivador. —**shunt off,** eludir; evadir; echarle a uno el muerto.

shush! (ʃʌʃ) *interj.* ¡chito!

shut (ʃʌt) *v.t.* 1, (close) cerrar. 2, (cover; put a lid on) tapar. 3, (fold up) plegar; doblar. —*v.i.* cerrarse. —*adj.* cerrado. —**shut down,** 1, (close) cerrar(se). 2, (cease functioning) parar. —**shut in,** encerrar. —**shut off,** 1, (enclose) encerrar. 2, (isolate) aislar. 3, (cut the flow or supply of) cortar. —**shut out,** 1, (exclude) excluir; prohibir o impedir la entrada a. 2, *sports* (prevent from scoring) no permitir (a un equipo) ganar tantos. —**shut up,** 1, (close) cerrar; tapar. 2, (confine) encerrar. 3, (imprison) aprisionar; encarcelar.

4, (silence) hacer callar; callar la boca a. 5, (be silent) callarse.
shut-down *n.* cesación de trabajo.
shut-in *n.* inválido recluido.
shut-out *n.* 1, (lockout) paro. 2, *sports* triunfo en que el equipo vencido no gana ningún tanto.
shutter (ˈʃʌt·ər) *n.* 1, (person or thing that closes) cerrador. 2, (of a window) postigo; contraventana. 3, (of a store) cierre de escaparate. 4, *photog.* obturador.
shuttle (ˈʃʌt·əl) *n.* 1, *weaving* lanzadera. 2, *R.R.* tren que hace viajes cortos de ida y vuelta. —*v.i.* ir y venir a cortos intervalos. —*v.t.* transportar a cortos intervalos.
shuttlecock *n.* volante.
shy (ʃai) *adj.* 1, (bashful; timid) vergonzoso; tímido. 2, (easily frightened) asustadizo. 3, (cautious; wary) cauteloso; prudente; recatado. 4, (scant; short) escaso (de). —*v.i.* 1, (start back in fear) asustarse; espantarse. 2, (evade) esquivarse. 3, (recoil) retroceder. 4, (rear, as a horse) respingar. 5, (veer off) desviarse; apartarse. —*v.t.* (throw) lanzar; arrojar. —*n.* 1, (start; fright) salto; sobresalto. 2, (rearing, as of a horse) respingo. 3, (throw) lance; arrojada.
shyness (ˈʃai·nəs) *n.* timidez; reserva; recato.
shyster (ˈʃai·stər) *n., colloq.* picapleitos; leguleyo; abogadillo tramposo.
si (si) *n., music* si.
Siamese (ˌsai·əˈmiːz) *adj.* & *n.* siamés.
sibilant (ˈsɪb·ə·lənt) *adj.* & *n.* sibilante.
sibling (ˈsɪb·lɪŋ) *n.* hermano *o* hermana. —*adj.* emparentado.
sibyl (ˈsɪb·ɪl) *n.* sibila.
sic (sɪk) *v.t.* [**sicked, sicking**] 1, (attack) atacar; asaltar. 2, (set upon, as a dog) azuzar.
sick (sɪk) *adj.* 1, (ill) enfermo; malo. 2, (nauseated) nauseado. 3, (depressed) alicaído; desanimado; deprimido. 4, (disgusted) ultrajado; enfadado. —*n.* los enfermos. —*v.t.* = sic. —**sick of**, cansado de; harto de. —**take sick**, caer enfermo.
sick bay enfermería (de a bordo).
sickbed *n.* lecho de enfermo.
sicken (ˈsɪk·ən) *v.t.* 1, (make ill) enfermar. 2, (disgust) dar asco; nausear. 3, (weaken) debilitar; extenuar. —*v.i.* 1, (become ill) enfermarse; caer enfermo. 2, (be disgusted) tener asco; tener repugnancia. 3, (be surfeited) cansarse; hartarse. 4, (weaken) debilitarse. —**sickening**, *adj.* asqueroso; nauseabundo; repugnante.
sickle (ˈsɪk·əl) *n.* hoz; segadera; segur.
sickly (ˈsɪk·li) *adj.* 1, (unhealthy) achacoso; enfermizo. 2, (mawkish) asqueroso; nauseabundo. 3, (feeble) enclenque; débil; lánguido. —**sickliness**, *n.* achaque; malestar; enfermedad.
sickness (ˈsɪk·nəs) *n.* 1, (illness) enfermedad; mal. 2, (nausea) náusea; basca.
side (said) *n.* 1, (terminal surface or line) lado; cara; faz. 2, (either half, as of a body) costado; lado. 3, (slope of a hill) falda; ladera. 4, (point of view) parte; opinión. 5, (faction) facción; partido. 6, (water's edge) orilla; margen. 7, (lateral surface of a ship) banda; bordo; costado. 8, (point; place; direction) parte; lado. —*adj.* 1, (lateral) de lado. 2, (indirect) indirecto; oblicuo. 3, (incidental) incidental; secundario. —*v.i.* tomar parte; tomar partido. —**by the side of**, al (*o* por el) lado de. —**on all sides**, por todos lados; por todas partes. —**right side** (*of a garment, of material, etc.*) cara. —**side against**, oponerse a; estar contra; declararse contra. —**side with**, estar por; sèr partidario de; declararse por. —**split one's sides**, reventarse *o* desternillarse de risa. —**take sides**, tomar partido. —**wrong side** (*of a garment, of material, etc.*) revés.
side arms armas de cinto.
sideboard *n.* aparador.
sideburns *n. pl.* patillas.
sidecar *n.* 1, (of a motorcycle) cochecillo de lado; sidecar. 2, (cocktail) sidecar.
side dish plato de entrada.
side glance mirada de soslayo *o* de través.
side-kick *n., slang* compañero; socio.
sidelight *n.* 1, (incidental aspect) noticia o detalle incidental. 2,

(narrow window beside a door) luz lateral.
side line 1, (additional service or merchandise) negocio accesorio; ocupación secundaria. **2,** *sports* (boundary) línea lateral. **—sideline,** *v.t.* sacar del juego o de cualquier actividad. **—on the side lines,** fuera del juego o de cualquier actividad; sin participar.
sidelong *adj.* de lado; lateral. *—adv.* lateralmente; de lado.
sidereal (sai'dɪr·i·əl) *adj.* estelar; sideral; sidéreo.
sidesaddle *n.* silla de montar de mujer. *—adv.* a mujeriegas.
side show función, exhibición, diversión, etc. secundaria.
sideslip ('said,slɪp) *n.* deslizamiento *o* resbalamiento lateral. *—v.i.* **[-slipped, -slipping]** deslizar *o* resbalar lateralmente.
sidesplitting *adj.* desternillante.
side step 1, (step to the side) paso hacia un lado. **2,** (step or stair located at the side) escalón de lado. **—sidestep,** *v.i.* hacerse a un lado; apartarse; desviarse. *—v.t.* evitar; esquivar.
sideswipe ('said,swaip) *v.t.* golpear *o* rozar oblicuamente. *—n.* golpe *o* rozadura dada oblicuamente.
sidetrack *n.* apartadero; desviadero. *—v.t.* apartar; desviar.
sidewalk *n.* acera; *Mex.* banqueta.
sideways ('said,weiz) *adj.* oblicuo; sesgado. *—adv.* de lado; al través; oblicuamente. *También,* **sidewise** (-waiz).
side whiskers patillas.
siding ('sai·dɪŋ) *n.* **1,** *R.R.* apartadero; desviadero. **2,** (of a house) entablado (de los costados).
sidle ('sai·dəl) *v.i.* ir de lado. *—n.* movimiento oblicuo. **—sidle up to,** acercarse de lado (a una persona o cosa).
siege (si:dʒ) *n.* **1,** *mil.* asedio; cerco; sitio. **2,** (long illness or suffering) enfermedad larga; sufrimiento largo.
sienna (si'ɛn·ə) *n.* tierra de siena; siena.
sierra (si'ɛr·ə) *n.* sierra; cordillera.
siesta (si'ɛs·tə) *n.* siesta. *—v.i.* dormir *o* echar la siesta; dormitar; sestear.
sieve (sɪv) *n.* tamiz; cedazo; criba.
sift (sɪft) *v.t.* **1,** (pass through a sieve) cerner; cribar; tamizar. **2,** (scrutinize) examinar; escudriñar. **—sifter,** *n.* tamiz; cedazo; criba.
sigh (sai) *v.i.* suspirar. *—v.t.* decir suspirando; lamentar. *—n.* suspiro. **—sigh for** *o* **after,** anhelar; añorar; morirse por.
sight (sait) *n.* **1,** (faculty of vision) vista; visión. **2,** (point of view) concepto; parecer; modo de ver. **3,** (view; glimpse) mirada; vista; vistazo. **4,** (appearance; aspect) apariencia; aspecto. **5,** (something seen) vista; cuadro; espectáculo; escena. **6,** *colloq.* (horror) horror; espantajo; adefesio. **7,** (an aid to aiming) mira. **8,** (aim) puntería. *—v.t.* **1,** (see) avistar; ver con un instrumento. **2,** (aim at) apuntar (un arma) a. **—at sight,** a primera vista; *comm.* a la vista. **—catch sight of,** avistar; vislumbrar. **—come in** (*o* **into**) **sight,** asomar; aparecer. **—keep out of sight,** no dejar(se) ver; ocultar(se). **—know by sight,** conocer de vista. **—lose sight of,** perder de vista. **—not by a long sight,** ni por mucho. **—on sight,** a primera vista. **—out of sight,** perdido de vista. **—sight unseen,** sin examinarlo; sin haberlo visto.
sight draft giro (*o* letra) a la vista.
sighted ('sai·tɪd) *adj.* que tiene vista; que puede ver.
sightless ('sait·ləs) *adj.* **1,** (blind) ciego. **2,** (invisible) invisible.
sightly ('sait·li) *adj.* bello; hermoso; vistoso.
sightseeing *n.* paseo para ver puntos de interés; turismo. **—sightsee,** *v.i., colloq.* hacer turismo; visitar puntos de interés. **—sightseer,** *n.* turista.
sign (sain) *n.* **1,** (mark or symbol) marca; signo. **2,** (display board) cartel; tablero; muestra; letrero. **3,** (gesture) señal; indicación. **4,** (symptom) síntoma. **5,** (trace) vestigio; traza; huella; rastro. *—v.t.* **1,** (put one's name to) firmar. **2,** (indicate by a sign) señalar; indicar. **3,** (put under contract) contratar. *—v.i.* firmar. **—sign away** (*o* **over**), ceder; traspasar (mediante escritura). **—sign**

off, 1, *radio; TV* terminar la transmisión. **2,** *slang* (stop talking) callarse. —**sign on**, contratar; contratarse. —**sign up**, inscribirse; alistarse.
signal ('sɪg·nəl) *n.* señal. —*adj.* **1,** (of or for signaling) de señal; de señales. **2,** (notable) insigne; notable; señalado. —*v.t.* señalar. —*v.i.* hacer señales. —**signal code**, codigo *o* sistema de señales. —**signal corps**, cuerpo de señales. —**signal light**, fanal; semáforo; faro.
signalize ('sɪg·nə·laiz) *v.t.* señalar; distinguir.
signalman ('sɪg·nəl·mən) *n.* [*pl.* **-men**] hombre encargado de comunicación por señales; *R.R.* guardavía; *mil.* soldado del cuerpo de señales.
signatory ('sɪg·nə·tor·i) *adj.* & *n.* firmante; signatario.
signature ('sɪg·nə·tjʊr) *n.* **1,** (name written by oneself) firma. **2,** (distinguishing mark or trait) rúbrica; signatura. **3,** *print.; music* signatura.
signboard *n.* letrero; muestra.
signer ('sai·nər) *n.* firmante; signatario.
signet ('sɪg·nət) *n.* sello. —**signet ring**, sortija de sello.
significance (sɪg'nɪf·ɪ·kəns) *n.* **1,** (real or implied meaning) significado; significación. **2,** (consequence) consecuencia; importancia. **3,** (expressiveness) expresión; fuerza de expresión; energía. —**significant**, *adj.* significante; significativo; importante.
signify ('sɪg·nɪˌfai) *v.t.* significar. —**signification** (-fɪ'kei·ʃən) *n.* significación; significado; sentido.
signor (si'njor) *n.* [*pl.* **-ri**] señor. *También*, **signore** (-'njo·re). —**signora** (-'njo·rə) *n.* señora. —**signorina** (ˌsi·njo'ri·nə) *n.* señorita.
signpost *n.* indicador de dirección; poste de guía.
silage ('sai·lɪdʒ) *n.* ensilaje.
silence ('sai·ləns) *n.* silencio. —*v.t.* silenciar; hacer (*o* mandar) callar; acallar. —*interj.* ¡chis!; ¡silencio! —**silencer**, *n.* silenciador.
silent ('sai·lənt) *adj.* **1,** (making no sound) silencioso; callado. **2,** (not pronounced) mudo. **3,** (tacit) tácito. —**be silent**, callarse. —**remain silent**, callar; guardar silencio; no chistar. —**silent partner**, socio comanditario.
silhouette (ˌsɪl·ʊ'ɛt) *n.* silueta. —*v.t.* hacer aparecer en silueta; perfilar.
silica ('sɪl·ə·kə) *n.* sílice. —**silicate** (-ɪ·kət) *n.* silicato. —**siliceous**; **silicious** (sɪ'lɪʃ·əs) *adj.* silíceo.
silicon ('sɪl·ɪ·kən) *n.* silicio.
silicone ('sɪl·əˌkon) *n.* silicón.
silicosis (ˌsɪl·ɪ'ko·sɪs) *n.* silicosis.
silk (sɪlk) *n.* seda. —*adj.* de seda; sedeño. —**floss silk**, seda floja. —**raw silk**, seda en rama. —**shot silk**, seda tornasolada. —**silk cotton**, seda vegetal. —**waste silk**, borra de seda. —**watered silk**, muaré; seda ondeada.
silken ('sɪlk·ən) *adj.* **1,** (made of silk) de seda; sedeño. **2,** (resembling silk) sedoso. **3,** (smooth) blando; suave.
silk-stocking *adj.* aristocrático. —*n.* aristócrata.
silkworm *n.* gusano de seda.
silky ('sɪlk·i) *adj.* sedoso.
sill (sɪl) *n.* **1,** (of a door) umbral. **2,** (of a window) antepecho.
silly ('sɪl·i) *adj.* **1,** (foolish; witless) bobo; necio; tonto. **2,** (ridiculous) absurdo; disparatado; insensato. —**silliness**, *n.* bobería; tontería; necedad.
silo ('sai·lo) *n.* silo. —*v.t.* ensilar.
silt (sɪlt) *n.* cieno; aluvión. —*v.t.* & *i.* obstruir(se) con aluvión.
silver ('sɪl·vər) *n.* **1,** (metal) plata. **2,** (coin or coins; money) plata; moneda de plata. **3,** (color) color plateado; color argentino. **4,** (silverware) vajilla de plata. —*adj.* **1,** (made of silver) de plata. **2,** (silver-plated) plateado. **3,** (sonorous, as the voice) argentino; sonoro. —*v.t.* **1,** (plate with silver) platear. **2,** (coat, as a mirror, with mercury) azogar.
silver foil hoja de plata.
silver fox zorro plateado.
silvering ('sɪl·vər·ɪŋ) *n.* plateadura.
silver plate 1, (coating of silver) plateadura. **2,** (silverware) vajilla de plata. —**silver-plated,** *adj.* plateado.
silversmith *n.* platero. —**silversmith's shop**, platería.

silver-tongued *adj.* elocuente.

silverware *n.* **1,** (sterling silver) vajilla de plata. **2,** (silver plate) vajilla plateada. **3,** (wrought silver) plata labrada.

silvery ('sɪl·və·ri) *adj.* argentino; argénteo.

simian ('sɪm·i·ən) *n.* mono; simio. —*adj.* símico.

similar ('sɪm·ə·lər) *adj.* similar; semejante; parecido.

similarity (ˌsɪm·ə'lær·ə·ti) *n.* semejanza.

simile ('sɪm·əˌli) *n.* comparación; símil.

similitude (sɪ'mɪl·ɪˌtud) *n.* **1,** (resemblance) similitud; semejanza. **2,** (comparison) comparación.

simmer ('sɪm·ər) *v.t. & i.* hervir *o* cocer a fuego lento. —*n.* ebullición *o* cocción lenta. —**simmer down,** *colloq.* tranquilizarse.

simon-pure (ˌsai·mən'pjur) *adj.* auténtico; genuino; verdadero.

simony ('sai·mə·ni) *n.* simonía.

simoom (sɪ'muːm) *n.* simún. *También,* **simoon** (-'muːn).

simp (sɪmp) *n., slang* bobo; papamoscas; papanatas.

simper ('sɪm·pər) *v.t. & i.* sonreír afectadamente *o* bobamente. —*n.* sonrisa afectada.

simple ('sɪm·pəl) *adj.* **1,** (elementary) fácil. **2,** (plain) llano; simple. **3,** (pure; absolute) puro; mero. **4,** (unaffected; unassuming) sencillo; ingenuo; cándido. **5,** (humble) modesto; humilde. **6,** (easily deceived; silly) inocente; bobo; necio; mentecato.

simple-hearted *adj.* cándido; ingenuo.

simple-minded *adj.* **1,** (ingenuous) sencillo; cándido; ingenuo. **2,** (stupid) mentecato; necio; imbécil; estúpido. —**simple-mindedness,** *n.* estupidez; necedad.

simpleton ('sɪm·pəl·tən) *n.* simplón; bobalicón; papanatas.

simplicity (sɪm'plɪs·ə·ti) *n.* **1,** (lack of complexity) simplicidad. **2,** (ingenuousness) sencillez; candor; ingenuidad. **3,** (stupidity) estupidez; necedad.

simplify ('sɪm·plɪˌfai) *v.t.* simplificar. —**simplification** (-fɪ'kei·ʃən) *n.* simplificación.

simply ('sɪm·pli) *adv.* **1,** (without complexity) simplemente; sencillamente. **2,** (merely; solely) meramente; solamente.

simulate ('sɪm·jəˌleit) *v.t.* simular; imitar. —**simulation,** *n.* simulación; imitación.

simultaneous (ˌsai·məl'tei·ni·əs) *adj.* simultáneo. —**simultaneity** (-tə'nei·ə·ti); **simultaneousness,** *n.* simultaneidad.

sin (sɪn) *n.* pecado; culpa; transgresión. —*v.i.* [**sinned, sinning**] pecar; errar.

since (sɪns) *adv.* **1,** (from then until now) desde entonces. **2,** (subsequently) después. **3,** (before now; ago) hace; ha: *long since,* hace mucho tiempo; *three months since,* tres meses ha. —*prep.* desde; después de. —*conj.* **1,** (from the time when; during the time after) desde que; despues (de) que. **2,** (because) como; puesto que; ya que; pues; pues que.

sincere (sɪn'sɪr) *adj.* sincero; abierto; franco. —**yours sincerely,** su seguro servidor (*abbr.* S.S.S.).

sincerity (sɪn'sɛr·ə·ti) *n.* sinceridad; franqueza.

sine (sain) *n., math.* seno.

sinecure ('sai·nəˌkjur) *n.* sinecura.

sinew ('sɪn·ju) *n.* **1,** (tendon) tendón; fibra; nervio. **2,** (strength; vigor) fortaleza; vigor; fibra; nervio.

sinewy ('sɪn·ju·i) *adj.* **1,** (strong; vigorous) fuerte; robusto; vigoroso. **2,** (stringy; fibrous) fibroso; nervudo.

sinful ('sɪn·fəl) *adj.* **1,** (committing sin) pecador. **2,** (motivated by sin) pecaminoso.

sing (sɪŋ) *v.t. & i.* [**sang, sung, singing**] **1,** (utter musically) cantar. **2,** (murmur; whistle) murmurar; silbar. **3,** (warble) gorjear. **4,** (ring, as the ears) zumbar. —*n.* **1,** (singing sound) silbido; zumbido. **2,** (act of singing) canto. —**singable,** *adj.* cantable.

singe (sɪndʒ) *v.t.* [*ger.* **singeing**] chamuscar; socarrar. —*n.* chamusquina; socarra. —**singeing,** *n.* socarra.

singer ('sɪŋ·ər) *n.* cantor; cantante (*m. & f.*); cantatriz (*f.*).

singing ('sɪŋ·ɪŋ) *n.* canto.

single ('sɪŋ·gəl) *adj.* **1,** (pert. to one; individual) simple; particular;

individual. **2,** (alone; detached) distinto; solo; único. **3,** (unmarried) soltero. —*v.t.* [*usu.* **single out**] separar; escoger; singularizar. —*n.* **1,** (that which is single) simple; individuo. **2,** *baseball* batazo de una base. **3,** *pl., tennis* juego de simples. —**singleness,** *n.* unidad; sencillez. —**not a single word,** ni una (sola) palabra. —**single file,** fila india. —**single life,** celibato.

single-breasted *adj.* de un solo pecho; de una sola hilera de botones.

single-handed *adj. & adv.* **1,** (unaided) sin ayuda; solo. **2,** (done with one hand) de *o* para una mano.

singleton ('sɪŋ·gəl·tən) *n., cards* única carta de un palo.

single-track *adj.* de una sola vía. —**single-track mind,** mente estrecha; punto de vista muy limitado.

singletree ('sɪŋ·gəl·tri) *n.* balancín.

singly ('sɪŋ·gli) *adv.* **1,** (separately; individually) individualmente; separadamente; a solas. **2,** (one at a time) uno a uno; de uno en uno.

singsong *adj.* monótono. —*n.* sonsonete; cadencia uniforme.

singular ('sɪŋ·gju·lər) *adj.* **1,** (unusual) raro; extraño; singular. **2,** *gram.* singular. —**singularity** (-'lær·ə·ti) *n.* singularidad; rareza.

sinister ('sɪn·ɪs·tər) *adj.* siniestro.

sinistro- (sɪn·ɪs·tro) *prefijo* sinistro-; a la izquierda: *sinistrorse,* sinistrorso.

sink (sɪŋk) *v.i.* [**sank, sunk, sinking**] **1,** (fall; decline) caer; bajar; decaer. **2,** (settle) sentarse. **3,** (become submerged) sumergirse; hundirse; irse a pique *o* al fondo. **4,** (incline downward) bajar; descender. **5,** (decrease) rebajar; disminuir. —*v.t.* **1,** (force downward) sumergir; hundir. **2,** (cause to submerge) echar a pique. **3,** (place by excavation) excavar; cavar *o* abrir (un pozo). **4,** (diminish) disminuir; disipar. **5,** (suppress; overwhelm) abatir; sumir; deprimir. **6,** (invest) invertir. **7,** (drive into the ground) enterrar. —*n.* **1,** (basin) fregadero. **2,** (drain; sewer) sumidero; desaguadero. **3,** *fig.* (filthy or corrupt place) sentina. —**sink in; sink into one's mind,** grabarse en la memoria. —**sink one's teeth into,** clavar el diente en.

sinkable ('sɪŋk·ə·bəl) *adj.* hundible; sumergible.

sinker ('sɪŋk·ər) *n., fishing* plomada.

sinking fund fondo de amortización.

sinless ('sɪn·ləs) *adj.* impecable; puro. —**sinlessness,** *n.* impecabilidad.

sinner ('sɪn·ər) *n.* pecador.

Sino- (sai·no) *prefijo* sino-; chino: *Sinology,* sinología.

sinuous ('sɪn·ju·əs) *adj.* sinuoso. —**sinuosity** (-'as·ə·ti); **sinuousness,** *n.* sinuosidad.

sinus ('sai·nəs) *n.* seno. —**sinusitis** (-nə'sai·tɪs) *n.* sinusitis.

-sion (ʃən; ʒən) *sufijo* -sión; *forma nombres denotando* acción; resultado; calidad; condición: *admission,* admisión; *confusion,* confusión.

sip (sɪp) *v.t. & i.* [**sipped, sipping**] sorber; chupar. —*n.* sorbo.

siphon ('sai·fən) *n.* sifón. —*v.t.* sacar con sifón.

sipper ('sɪp·ər) *n.* sorbedor.

sir (sʌɹ) *n.* **1,** (respectful term of address to a man) señor. **2,** *cap.* (title of a knight or baronet) caballero.

sire (sair) *n.* **1,** (father) padre; progenitor. **2,** (address to a sovereign) señor. —*v.t.* engendrar.

siren ('sai·rən) *n.* sirena.

Sirius ('sɪr·i·əs) *n., astron.* Sirio; Canícula.

sirloin ('sʌɹ·lɔin) *n.* solomillo; solomo.

sirocco (sə'rak·o) *n.* siroco.

sirup ('sɪr·əp) *n.* = **syrup.**

sisal ('sai·səl) *n.* sisal; henequén.

sissy ('sɪs·i) *n., colloq.* adamado; afeminado; maricón.

sister ('sɪs·tər) *n.* hermana. —*adj.* hermano; gemelo.

sisterhood ('sɪs·tər,hud) *n.* **1,** (state or relationship of a sister) hermandad. **2,** (association) cofradía de mujeres; hermandad.

sister-in-law *n.* [*pl.* **sisters-in-law**] cuñada; hermana política.

sisterly ('sɪs·tər·li) *adj.* como corresponde a hermanas; con hermandad; de hermana.

sit (sɪt) *v.i.* [**sat, sitting**] **1,** (be seated; take a seat) sentarse; estar sentado; tomar asiento. **2,** (perch) posarse; encaramarse. **3,** (remain) quedarse; detenerse. **4,** (be in session; convene) reunirse; celebrar junta *o* sesión. **5,** (be located) estar; quedarse; estar colocado. **6,** (pose, as for a portrait) posar; modelar; servir de modelo; hacerse retratar. —**sit down,** sentarse; estar sentado. —**sit in (on),** tomar parte (en). —**sit out, 1,** (decline to participate) no tomar parte; permanecer sentado. **2,** (stay to the end of) aguantar *o* quedarse hasta el fin (de). —**sit on** *o* **upon, 1,** (take part in) tomar parte en. **2,** *slang* (repress) hacer callar; reprimir; reprender. **3,** *slang* (retain; hold) guardar en su poder; no soltar. —**sit still,** estarse quieto; no levantarse. —**sit tight,** *colloq.* mantenerse firme; estar *o* seguir con sus trece. —**sit up, 1,** (come to a sitting position) levantarse; incorporarse. **2,** (stay awake) velar. —**sit well,** venir, caer, sentar *o* quedar bien.

sit-down strike huelga de sentados *o* de brazos caídos.

site (sait) *n.* local; sitio; lugar.

sitting (ˈsɪt·ɪŋ) *n.* sesión; sentada. —*adj.* sentado. —**sitting room,** sala de descanso *o* de espera; sala de estar; antesala.

situate (ˈsɪtʃ·juˌeit) *v.t.* situar; colocar; poner. —**situated,** *adj.* situado; colocado; ubicado.

situation (ˌsɪtʃ·juˈei·ʃən) *n.* **1,** (location) posición; situación; ubicación. **2,** (condition) situación; condición; estado. **3,** (employment; position) empleo; puesto; colocación; plaza.

six (sɪks) *n.* & *adj.* seis. —**at sixes and sevens,** en desorden.

sixfold (ˈsɪksˌfold) *adj.* & *n.* séxtuplo; seis veces (más). —*adv.* seis veces; en un séxtuplo.

six hundred seiscientos. —**six-hundredth,** *adj.* & *n.* sexcentésimo.

sixpence (ˈsɪks·pəns) *n., Brit.* medio chelín; seis peniques. —**sixpenny,** *adj.* de seis peniques; *fig.* miserable; mezquino.

six-shooter *n., colloq.* revólver de seis tiros.

sixteen (sɪksˈtiːn) *n.* & *adj.* diez y seis; dieciséis. —**sixteenth** (-ˈtinθ) *adj.* & *n.* décimosexto; dieciseisavo.

sixth (sɪksθ) *adj.* sexto. —*n.* sexto; sexta parte; *music* sexta.

sixty (ˈsɪks·ti) *n.* & *adj.* sesenta. —**sixtieth,** *adj.* & *n.* sexagésimo; sesentavo.

size (saiz) *n.* **1,** (dimensions; bulk) tamaño; dimensiones (*pl.*); magnitud. **2,** (standard measure for shoes, clothes, etc.) número; tamaño; talle; medida. **3,** [*también,* **sizing**] (gluey substance for bonding or glazing) cola de retal *o* de retazo; apresto; aderezo. —*v.t.* **1,** (estimate) tomar las medidas a; medir. **2,** (apply glaze to) aderezar; sisar; aprestar. —**sizable; sizeable,** *adj.* bastante grande; considerable.

sizzle (ˈsɪz·əl) *v.i.* chisporrotear; sisear. —*n.* chisporroteo; siseo.

skate (skeit) *n.* **1,** (for gliding on ice) patín; patín de hielo *o* de cuchilla. **2,** (roller skate) patín de ruedas. **3,** (fish) raya. —*v.i.* patinar. —**skater,** *n.* patinador. —**skating,** *n.* patinaje.

skedaddle (skɪˈdæd·əl) *v.i., slang* largarse; poner pies en polvorosa.

skein (skein) *n.* madeja.

skeletal (ˈskɛl·ə·təl) *adj.* **1,** (of or pert. to a skeleton) de *o* del esqueleto. **2,** (thin; emaciated) esquelético.

skeleton (ˈskɛl·ə·tən) *n.* **1,** *anat.* esqueleto. **2,** (inner framework) armadura; armazón. **3,** (outline) esbozo; bosquejo. —*adj.* **1,** = **skeletal. 2,** (greatly reduced) reducido. —**skeleton key,** llave maestra.

skeptic (ˈskɛp·tɪk) *n.* & *adj.* escéptico. —**skeptical,** *adj.* escéptico.

skepticism (ˈskɛp·tɪ·sɪz·əm) *n.* escepticismo.

sketch (skɛtʃ) *n.* **1,** (rough drawing) croquis; esbozo; boceto; bosquejo; esquicio. **2,** (outline; synopsis) esquema; plan; sinopsis; reseña. **3,** (short humorous act; skit) burla; parodia; sátira; entremés. —*v.t.* esquiciar; bosquejar; dibujar. —**sketchy,** *adj.* abocetado; bosquejado; esquiciado.

skew (skjuː) *v.i.* andar *o* moverse oblicuamente; torcerse. —*v.t.* sesgar. —*adj.* sesgado; oblicuo. —*n.* desviación.

skewer (ˈskju·ər) *n.* brocheta; espetón. —*v.t.* espetar.

ski (ski:) *n.* esquí. —*v.i.* esquiar. —**skier,** *n.* esquiador. —**skiing,** *n.* equiísmo; esquí.

skid (skɪd) *n.* **1,** (timber or metal band forming a track) rail; riel; carril. **2,** (supporting runner) patín. **3,** (friction brake) galga. **4,** (wooden platform for supporting small loads) calzo. **5,** (wooden support for the side of a ship at dock) varadera. **6,** (act of skidding) patinaje; resbalón; deslizamiento. —*v.t.* & *i.* [**skidded, -ding**] **1,** (slide without rotating) resbalar(se); deslizar(se); patinar. **2,** (swerve) desviar(se). —**on the skids,** *slang* fracasado; desventurado. —**skid row** *o* **road,** barrio de vagabundos y alcohólicos.

skiddoo! (skɪ'du:) *interj., slang* ¡lárgate!

skiff (skɪf) *n.* esquife.

ski lift ascensor funicular para esquiadores.

skill (skɪl) *n.* habilidad; pericia; destreza; maña. —**skilled,** *adj.* experto; hábil; diestro. —**skillful; skilful,** *adj.* experto; de experto.

skillet ('skɪl·ɪt) *n.* **1,** (frying pan) sartén. **2,** (long-handled saucepan) cacerola o cazuela pequeña, de mango largo.

skim (skɪm) *v.t.* [**skimmed, -ming**] **1,** (lift or scrape off the top of a liquid) desnatar; espumar; rasar. **2,** (read superficially) hojear (un libro); leer superficialmente. **3,** (glide lightly over) rozar; rasar. —**skim milk,** leche desnatada.

skimmer ('skɪm·ər) *n.* espumadera.

skimp (skɪmp) *v.t.* & *i.* (scrimp; provide meagerly) escatimar. —*v.i.* **1,** (be stingy) ser tacaño. **2,** (do carelessly) chapucear. —**skimpy,** *adj.* tacaño; mezquino; escaso.

skin (skɪn) *n.* **1,** *anat.* piel; cutis. **2,** (pelt) pellejo; cuero. **3,** (rind or peel) corteza; cáscara. **4,** (container made of skin) pellejo; odre. —*v.t.* [**skinned, skinning**] **1,** (remove the skin from; peel) desollar; despellejar; mondar; pelar. **2,** *slang* (swindle) engañar; estafar; embaucar. —**be nothing but skin and bones,** estar en los huesos. —**be soaked to the skin,** calarse (*o* estar calado) hasta los huesos. —**save one's skin,** salvar el pellejo.

skin-deep *adj.* superficial.

skindiver *n.* buzo sin escafandra. —**skindiving,** *n.* buceo sin escafandra.

skinflint ('skɪn·flɪnt) *n.* avaro; tacaño.

skin game fullería; estafa.

skinner ('skɪn·ər) *n.* **1,** (one who skins) desollador. **2,** (furrier) peletero. **3,** (mule driver) mulero.

skinny ('skɪn·i) *adj.* flaco; descarnado. —**skinniness,** *n.* flaqueza.

skin-tight *adj.* ajustado al cuerpo.

skip (skɪp) *v.i.* [**skipped, skipping**] **1,** (jump lightly) saltar; brincar. **2,** (bounce; ricochet) rebotar. **3,** *colloq.* (flee) escaparse. —*v.t.* **1,** (jump over) saltar. **2,** (pass over; omit) omitir; pasar por alto; saltar. —*n.* **1,** (jump) salto; brinco. **2,** (omission) omisión. —**skipping rope,** comba.

skipper ('skɪp·ər) *n.* jefe; capitán; patrón (de barco).

skirmish ('skʌɹ·mɪʃ) *n.* escaramuza. —*v.i.* escaramuzar.

skirt (skʌɹt) *n.* **1,** (woman's garment) falda; saya. **2,** (edge; border) orilla; borde; margen. **3,** *slang* (woman) muchacha; mujer; hembra; *pl.* faldas. —*v.t.* & *i.* bordear; ir o pasar por la orilla (de).

skit (skɪt) *n.* burla; sátira; parodia.

skittish ('skɪt·ɪʃ) *adj.* **1,** (apt to shy) asustadizo. **2,** (restless) inconstante; caprichoso. **3,** (coy) recatado; tímido.

skulduggery (skʌl'dʌg·ə·ri) *n.* fullería; chanchullo.

skulk (skʌlk) *v.i.* **1,** (sneak away) huirse furtivamente; escurrirse; escabullirse. **2,** (slink; lurk) rondar; andar a sombra de tejado; ocultarse; acechar. **3,** (shirk) remolonear.

skull (skʌl) *n.* calavera; cráneo; casco.

skullcap *n.* casquete.

skunk (skʌŋk) *n.* **1,** *zool.* mofeta. **2,** *colloq.* (contemptible person) sinvergüenza; canalla. —*v.t., slang* no permitir (a un equipo) ganar tantos.

sky (skai) *n.* cielo. —**out of a clear (blue) sky,** inesperadamente; de repente.

sky blue azul celeste; cerúleo.

—**sky-blue**, *adj.* azul celeste; cerúleo.
sky-high *adj.* & *adv.* tan alto como el cielo; por las nubes.
skylark *n.* alondra; calandria. —*v.i., colloq.* chacotear; jaranear; calaverear.
skylight *n.* claraboya; tragaluz.
skyline *n.* **1,** (tall buildings seen outlined against the sky) perspectiva (de una ciudad); línea de rascacielos. **2,** (visible horizon) línea del horizonte.
sky pilot *slang,* clérigo; capellán.
skyrocket *n.* cohete; volador. —*v.i.* subir como un cohete.
skyscraper *n.* rascacielos.
skyward ('skai·wərd) *adj.* & *adv.* hacia el cielo.
skywriting *n.* escritura aérea.
slab (slæb) *n.* **1,** (flat stone) losa. **2,** (wooden plank) plancha; tabla. **3,** (slice) tajada; lonja; loncha.
slack (slæk) *adj.* **1,** (loose; lax) flojo; suelto; relajado. **2,** (slow; sluggish) lento; tardo. **3,** (negligent) descuidado. **4** (inactive) inactivo. —*n.* **1,** (slack condition or part) flojedad. **2,** (decrease in activity) inactividad.
slacken ('slæk·ən) *v.t.* **1,** (loosen) aflojar; soltar; relajar. **2,** (retard; check) retardar; detener. —*v.i.* **1,** (become loose) aflojarse; soltarse; relajarse. **2,** (abate) mermar; menguar. **3,** (lessen; fall off) disminuir; rebajar; decaer.
slacker ('slæk·ər) *n.* **1,** (lazy person) perezoso; haragán. **2,** (shirker) el que esquiva su deber; *mil.* prófugo.
slacks (slæks) *n.pl.* pantalones holgados.
slag (slæg) *n.* escoria.
slain (slein) *v., p.p. de* **slay.**
slake (sleik) *v.t.* **1,** (appease) apagar; aplacar; satisfacer. **2,** (extinguish) extinguir; apagar. **3,** (moderate) moderar; aflojar. **4,** (treat with water, as lime) apagar.
slam (slæm) *v.t.* [**slammed, slamming**] **1,** (shut noisily) cerrar de golpe. **2,** (bang down) dejar caer de golpe. **3,** (strike; collide with) chocar con; golpear; dar en. **4,** (hurl violently) arrojar; tirar. **5,** *slang* (criticize harshly) criticar ásperamente; poner frito. —*v.i.* **1,** (shut noisily) cerrarse de golpe. **2,** (strike; collide) chocar; dar; dar de golpe. —*n.* **1,** (blow; stroke) golpe. **2,** (loud closing of a door) portazo. **3,** *slang* (criticism) crítica áspera. **4,** *cards* bola; bolo; slam.
slander ('slæn·dər) *n.* calumnia; difamación; denigración. —*v.t.* calumniar; difamar; denigrar. —**slanderous,** *adj.* calumnioso; difamatorio.
slang (slæŋ) *n.* jerga; jerigonza; germanía; argot.
slant (slænt) *v.t.* inclinar; sesgar; poner sesgado; dar una dirección oblicua a. —*v.i.* inclinarse; sesgarse; estar *o* ponerse sesgado. —*n.* **1,** (oblique direction or position) declive; inclinación. **2,** (bias) sesgo. **3,** (point of view) punto de vista; opinión; parecer.
slap (slæp) *v.t.* [**slapped, slapping**] **1,** (strike with the open hand or something flat) dar una palmada, manotada o bofetada. **2,** (strike; beat) golpear; pegar; dar en (una cosa); darle a (una persona). **3,** (rebuke) castigar; reprender; censurar. —*n.* **1,** (blow with the open hand) palmada; manotada; bofetada. **2,** (insult; rebuff) insulto; afrenta. **3,** (rebuke) castigo; reprensión; censura. —*adv., colloq.* **1,** (suddenly) de golpe; de repente. **2,** (straight; directly) derecho.
slapdash *adj.* descuidado; chapucero. —*adv.* de prisa; a lo loco.
slapstick *n.* comedia burlesca; comedia de payasadas. —*adj.* burlesco; grosero.
slash (slæʃ) *v.t.* **1,** (hack violently) acuchillar; dar cuchilladas. **2,** (make slits in) cortar; acuchillar. **3,** (reduce drastically) rebajar fuertemente. —*n.* **1,** (stroke or wound) tajo; tajada; corte; cuchillada. **2,** (ornamental slit) corte; cortadura; cuchillada. **3,** *usu. pl.* (swampy tract) fangal; pantano.
slat (slæt) *n.* tablilla.
slate (sleit) *n.* **1,** (mineral) pizarra; esquisto. **2,** (writing tablet) pizarra para escribir. **3,** (color) color de pizarra. **4,** (list of candidates) lista de candidatos. —*v.t.* **1,** (cover with slate) cubrir de pizarra; empizarrar. **2,** (enter as a candidate) poner en candidatura. **3,** (destine; single out) destinar; señalar. —**a clean slate,** las manos limpias. —**wipe off the slate; wipe**

the slate clean, borrar el pasado; empezar de nuevo.

slattern ('slæt·ərn) *n.* mujer desaliñada. —**slatternly,** *adj.* puerco; desaliñado.

slaty ('slei·ti) *adj.* pizarroso.

slaughter ('slɔ·tər) **1,** (killing of animals for food) carnicería; matanza. **2,** (massacre; carnage) mortandad; estrago. —*v.t.* matar.

slaughterhouse *n.* matadero; degolladero.

Slav (sla:v) *n.* & *adj.* eslavo.

slave (sleiv) *n.* esclavo; siervo. —*v.i.* trabajar como esclavo. —**slave driver,** capataz de esclavos. —**slave labor,** trabajo de esclavos; trabajadores forzados. —**slave trade** *o* **traffic,** trata *o* tráfico de esclavos.

slaver ('slei·vər) *n.* **1,** (trader in slaves) negrero. **2,** (slave ship) barco negrero.

slaver ('slæv·ər) *v.i.* babear; babosear. —*n.* baba.

slavery ('slei·və·ri) *n.* esclavitud; servidumbre.

Slavic ('slav·ɪk) *adj.* & *n.* eslavo.

slavish ('slei·vɪʃ) *adj.* servil; esclavizado.

Slavonic (slə'van·ɪk) *adj.* & *n.* eslavo; esclavón; esclavonio.

slaw (slɔ:) *n.* ensalada de col.

slay (slei) *v.t.* [**slew, slain, slaying**] **1,** (kill) matar. **2,** *slang* (affect powerfully) emocionar; conmover. —**slayer,** *n.* asesino; homicida.

sleazy ('sli·zi; 'slei-) *adj.* baladí; ligero; flojo.

sled (slɛd) *n.* trineo; narria. —*v.t.* [**sledded, sledding**] llevar en trineo. —*v.i.* ir *o* pasearse en trineo. —**sledding,** *n., colloq.* camino; paso; manera de llevarse una persona o una cosa.

sledge (slɛdʒ) *n.* **1,** (large sled) trineo; narria. **2,** = **sledgehammer.**

sledgehammer *n.* acotillo.

sleek (slik) *adj.* **1,** (smooth and glossy) liso; alisado. **2,** (well groomed) nítido; aseado; acicalado. **3,** (suave) artero; mañoso; zalamero. —*v.t.* alisar; pulir; suavizar. —**sleekness,** *n.* lisura; lustre.

sleep (slip) *n.* sueño. —*v.i.* [*pret.* & *p.p.* **slept**] dormir. —*v.t.* **1,** (pass, as time, in sleep) pasar durmiendo; malgastar (el tiempo) durmiendo. **2,** (accommodate for sleeping) acomodar; caber (para dormir). —**fall asleep,** dormirse. —**go to sleep,** dormirse. —**last sleep,** la muerte. —**put to sleep,** adormecer; dormir. —**sleep in,** alojarse (un criado) en casa del dueño. —**sleep like a top,** dormir como un lirón. —**sleep off one's liquor,** desollar la zorra; dormir la mona. —**sleep on (a problem),** consultar con la almohada. —**sleep soundly,** dormir a pierna suelta; dormir profundamente.

sleeper ('sli·pər) *n.* **1,** (one who sleeps) durmiente. **2,** *R.R.* (sleeping car) coche-cama; coche-dormitorio. **3,** *R.R.* (tie) traviesa; *Amer.* durmiente. **4,** *colloq.* (unexpected success) triunfo inesperado.

sleepiness ('sli·pi·nəs) *n.* sueño; modorra; somnolencia.

sleeping ('sli·pɪŋ) *adj.* **1,** (in a state of sleep) durmiente. **2,** (of or for sleep) de dormir; para dormir. —**sleeping car,** coche-cama; coche-dormitorio. —**sleeping pill,** píldora para dormir. —**sleeping sickness,** encefalitis letárgica; enfermedad del sueño.

sleepless ('slip·ləs) *adj.* **1,** (restless; wakeful) desvelado; insomne. **2,** (watchful) despierto; vigilante. —**spend a sleepless night,** pasar la noche en vela.

sleepwalker *n.* sonámbulo. —**sleepwalking,** *n.* sonambulismo.

sleepy ('sli·pi) *adj.* **1,** (drowsy) soñoliento; amodorrado. **2,** (tranquil; quiet) tranquilo. —**be sleepy,** tener sueño.

sleepyhead *n.* dormilón.

sleet (slit) *n.* cellisca. —*v.i.* cellisquear. —**sleety,** *adj.* cubierto de cellisca; lleno de cellisca.

sleeve (sli:v) *n.* **1,** (part of a garment) manga. **2,** *mech.* dedal largo; manguito de enchufe.

sleigh (slei) *n.* trineo. —**sleigh bell,** cascabel. —**sleigh ride,** paseo en trineo.

sleight (slait) *n.* **1,** (trick) ardid; artificio; estratagema. **2,** (skill; dexterity) pericia; maña; astucia. —**sleight-of-hand,** *n.* escamoteo; prestidigitación.

slender ('slɛn·dər) *adj.* **1,** (small in width or diameter) delgado; flaco; tenue. **2,** (scanty) escaso;

insuficiente. **3,** (weak) débil; delicado.
slenderize ('slɛn·dər,aiz) *v.t. & i., colloq.* adelgazar.
slept (slɛpt) *v., pret. & p.p. de* **sleep.**
sleuth (sluθ) *n.* **1,** *colloq.* (detective) detective. **2,** (bloodhound) sabueso.
slew (slu:) **1,** *v., pret. de* **slay. 2,** *v.i.* (veer; twist) virar; torcerse. —*n.* [*también,* **slue**] **1,** (twist) torcimiento. **2,** *colloq.* (great number) multitud; montón.
slice (slais) *n.* **1,** (thin piece) rebanada; tajada; lonja. **2,** (act of cutting) tajada. **3,** *golf* (oblique stroke) golpe dado oblicuamente a la pelota. —*v.t. & i.* rebanar; hacer rebanadas; cortar en lonjas o tajadas. —**slicer,** *n.* rebanador.
slick (slɪk) *adj.* **1,** (sleek) liso; lustroso. **2,** (ingenious; sly) astuto; mañoso. **3,** (slippery) resbaladizo. —*n.* **1,** (smooth patch) punto liso y lustroso. **2,** (magazine printed on coated paper) revista de papel liso. —*v.t.* alisar; pulir; acicalar.
slicker ('slɪk·ər) *n.* **1,** (oilskin coat) impermeable. **2,** *colloq.* (sly fellow; swindler) estafador; trampista.
slide (slaid) *v.i.* [*pret. & p.p.* **slid**] **1,** (slip over a smooth surface) resbalar; deslizar. **2,** (go smoothly) patinar. **3,** (lapse into error) errar; pecar; cometer un desliz. —*v.t.* hacer resbalar; introducir con cuidado o artificio. —*n.* **1,** (act of sliding) resbalón; desliz. **2,** (slippery place) resbaladero. **3,** (avalanche) derrumbe; derrumbamiento. **4,** (sliding part) cursor; pieza corrediza. **5,** (picture on glass for projection on a screen) diapositiva. **6,** (specimen holder) portaobjetos. —**let (something) slide,** dejar pasar; no hacer caso de. —**slide into,** meter(se) en; colarse en. —**slide out** *o* **away,** colarse; escabullirse. —**slide over,** pasar ligeramente.
slide fastener cierre cremallera.
slide rule regla de cálculo.
sliding ('slai·dɪŋ) *adj.* **1,** (moving by slipping) corredizo. **2,** (adjustable) móvil.
slight (slait) *adj.* **1,** (small) pequeño; escaso. **2,** (of little importance) insignificante; ligero; leve. **3,** (slender; frail) delgado; delicado. —*v.t.* **1,** (disdain; ignore) desairar; menospreciar; desdeñar. **2,** (do negligently) descuidar; desatender. —*n.* **1,** (discourtesy) desaire; menosprecio; desdén. **2,** (neglect) desatención; descuido.
slim (slɪm) *adj.* **1,** (slender; thin) delgado; esbelto. **2,** (meager) escaso; insuficiente. —*v.t. & i.* adelgazar.
slime (slaim) *n.* **1,** (mud; ooze) légamo; limo; cieno; fango. **2,** (mucous secretion) baba; babaza. **3,** (filth) suciedad; porquería. —**slimy,** *adj.* viscoso; legamoso; fangoso.
slimness ('slɪm·nəs) *n.* **1,** (slenderness) delgadez. **2,** (meagerness) escasez; insuficiencia.
sling (slɪŋ) *n.* **1,** (slingshot) honda; tirador. **2,** (bandage for suspending an injured limb) cabestrillo. **3,** (shoulder strap for a rifle) portafusil. **4,** (mixed drink) bebida de ginebra con azúcar y nuez moscada. —*v.t.* [*pret. & p.p.* **slung**] **1,** (hurl) tirar; arrojar; lanzar. **2,** (suspend) suspender; colgar.
slink (slɪŋk) *v.i.* andar furtivamente; andar a sombra de tejado. —**slink away,** escabullirse; escurrirse.
slip (slɪp) *v.i.* [**slipped, slipping**] **1,** (lose one's hold; slide) deslizarse; resbalar; irse los pies. **2,** (err) cometer un desliz; equivocarse. **3,** (move quietly) pasar sin ser visto; meterse furtivamente. **4,** (become loose or separated) zafarse; soltarse. —*v.t.* **1,** (put or move quietly) meter *o* introducir secretamente; sacar a hurtadillas. **2,** *naut.* (cast off) largar *o* soltar (un cabo). —*n.* **1,** (act of slipping) resbalón; desliz; deslizamiento; traspié. **2,** (error) falta; error; lapso. **3,** (woman's undergarment) combinación de mujer. **4,** (pillowcase) funda de almohada. **5,** *naut.* (space between two wharves) embarcadero. **6,** (strip, as of paper) tira; pedazo de papel; papeleta. **7,** (slender person) persona muy delgada. **8,** (plant cutting) vástago; sarmiento. —**give the slip to,** escaparse de; zafarse

de; deshacerse de. —**let a chance slip**, perder la ocasión. —**slip away**, desaparecerse; huirse. —**slip in**, introducirse: insinuarse; entremeterse. —**slip into** ponerse (una prenda de vestir). —**slip off**, quitarse de encima: soltar. —**slip one's mind**, olvidársele a uno una cosa. —**slip on one's clothing**, vestirse de prisa. —**slip out**, salir sin ser observado. —**slip out of joint**, dislocarse; *Amer.* zafarse (un hueso). —**slip through**, colarse; escurrirse; filtrarse.

slip cover funda.

slip knot nudo corredizo.

slip-on *adj.* & *n.* **1,** (casual wear) de quita y pon. **2,** = **slipover.**

slipover ('slɪp·o·vər) *adj.* & *n.* (suéter, chaqueta, etc.) que se pone por la cabeza; pulóver.

slippage ('slɪp·ɪdʒ) *n.* deslizamiento.

slipper ('slɪp·ər) *n.* zapatilla; babucha; chancleta; chinela; pantufla.

slippery ('slɪp·ə·ri) *adj.* **1,** (smooth; slick) resbaladizo; resbaloso. **2,** (elusive) engañador; furtivo.

slipshod ('slɪp,ʃad) *adj.* abandonado; descuidado.

slip-up *n.* error; falta; desliz.

slit (slɪt) *v.t.* [**slitted** *o* **slit, slitting**] **1,** (make a long narrow cut in) hacer una incisión en; partir. **2,** (cut into strips) cortar en tiras. —*n.* abertura; cortada; incisión.

slither ('slɪð·ər) *v.i.* culebrear. —*n.* culebreo.

sliver ('slɪv·ər) *n.* **1,** (splinter) brizna; astilla. **2,** (textile fiber) torzal; mecha de fibras textiles.

slob (slab) *n., slang* puerco.

slobber ('slab·ər) *v.i.* babear; babosear. —*n.* baba. —**slobbery,** *adj.* baboso.

sloe (slo:) *n.* **1,** (fruit) endrina. **2,** (tree) endrino. —**sloe-colored,** *adj.* endrino. —**sloe-eyed,** *adj.* de ojos endrinos. —**sloe gin,** ginebra de endrinas.

slog (slag) *v.i.* [**slogged, slogging**] trabajar afanosamente; echar los bofes. —*v.t.* dar; pegar; golpear. —*n.* golpe; bofetón.

slogan ('slo·gən) *n.* grito de combate *o* de partido; lema; mote.

sloop (slup) *n.* balandra; balandro; chalupa.

slop (slap) *n.* **1,** (puddle) líquido derramado en el suelo; mojadura. **2,** (unappetizing mess) suciedad; gachas (*pl.*); té *o* café flojo. **3,** *pl.* (waste liquid; sewage) agua sucia; lavazas; desperdicios. **4,** *pl.* (seamen's gear) equipaje de marineros. —*v.t.* [**slopped, slopping**] **1,** (spill; splash) verter; derramar; salpicar. **2,** (soil) mojar; ensuciar. —*v.i.* **1,** (spill; splash) derramarse; salpicar. **2,** *colloq.* (speak or act effusively) hablar *o* actuar con sensiblería.

slope (slop) *n.* **1,** (slanting surface) cuesta; pendiente. **2,** (degree of slant) inclinación; declive; sesgo. **3,** (watershed) vertiente. —*v.i.* inclinarse; estar en declive. —*v.t.* inclinar; sesgar; cortar en sesgo; formar en declive.

sloppy ('slap·i) *adj.* **1,** (untidy) desaliñado; desaseado; cochino; puerco; sucio. **2,** (clumsy; bungling) chapucero. **3,** (muddy) lodoso; cenagoso. **4,** (wearisome; effusive) empalagoso.

slosh (slaʃ) *n.* **1,** (slush) nieve a medio derretir; fango; cieno; lodo blando. **2,** (nonsense) tontería; disparate. —*v.i.* chapotear. —*v.t.* menear (un líquido) haciendo ruido de chapaleteo.

slot (slat) *n.* abertura; ranura. —**slot machine,** máquina de vender; traganíqueles; tragamonedas.

sloth (slɔθ) *n.* **1,** (laziness) pereza. **2,** *zool.* perezoso. —**slothful,** *adj.* holgazán; perezoso.

slotted ('slat·ɪd) *adj.* con aberturas *o* ranuras.

slouch (slautʃ) *v.i.* ir *o* estar cabizbajo; agacharse; repantigarse. —*n.* **1,** (drooping posture) postura muy floja o relajada. **2,** (inept person) persona incompetente. —**slouch hat,** sombrero gacho.

slough (slau) *n.* lodazal; cenagal; fangal; *fig.* abismo.

slough (slʌf) *n.* **1,** (molted skin) pellejo suelto que se muda; (*of snakes*) camisa; (*of insects*) tela. **2,** *med.* (dead tissue) escara. —*v.t.* **1,** (molt; shed) mudar; echar de sí. **2,** (discard) descartar; desechar. —*v.i.* mudarse; echarse; caerse.

Slovak ('slo·væk) *adj.* & *n.* eslovaco.

sloven ('slʌv·ən) *n.* persona desaseada o desaliñada. —**slovenly**, *adj.* desaseado; desaliñado. —*adv.* desaliñadamente.

Slovene (slo'vi:n) *adj.* & *n.* esloveno.

slow (slo:) *adj.* **1,** (taking a relatively long time) lento; pausado; detenido; tardo; tardío. **2,** (dull-witted) lerdo; estúpido; torpe. **3,** (tardy; sluggish) tardo; pesado; flojo. **4,** (slack) flojo; inactivo. **5,** (tedious) pesado; aburrido. **6,** (behind time or schedule) atrasado. —*adv.* despacio; lentamente; pausadamente. —*v.t.* retardar; atrasar. —*v.i.* retardarse; atrasarse; aflojar el paso; ir más despacio. —**slowly**, *adv.* despacio; lentamente; pausadamente. —**slow down**; **slow up**, retardar(se); detener(se).

slowdown *n.* atraso; detención.

slow motion movimiento lento. —**slow-motion**, *adj.* & *adv.* a cámara lenta.

slowness ('slo·nəs) *n.* **1,** (tardiness; delay) lentitud; tardanza; atraso; detención. **2,** (dullness) torpeza; estupidez.

slowpoke *n.* posma; haragán.

slow-witted *adj.* lerdo; torpe; estúpido.

sludge (slʌdʒ) *n.* lodo; cieno; fango.

slug (slʌg) *n.* **1,** (metal bar; ingot) lingote. **2,** *zool.* babosa. **3,** (bullet) bala. **4,** *colloq.* (heavy blow) porrazo; puñetazo. **5,** *slang* (drink; swallow) trago. —*v.t.* & *i.* [**slugged**, **slugging**] aporrear; abofetear; dar puñetazos.

slugabed ('slʌg·ə,bɛd) *n.* dormilón; perezoso.

sluggard ('slʌg·ərd) *n.* holgazán; haragán; posma.

sluggish ('slʌg·ɪʃ) *adj.* tardo; perezoso; pesado; flojo. —**sluggishness**, *n.* pereza; pesadez; posma.

sluice (slus) *n.* **1,** (artificial channel) canal; acequia; presa. **2,** (sluice gate) compuerta; bocacaz. —*v.t.* **1,** (draw off through a sluice) soltar; dar paso a. **2,** (flush; wash) regar; lavar. —*v.i.* salir (el agua).

slum (slʌm) *n.* barrio bajo. —*v.i.* [**slummed**, **slumming**] visitar los barrios bajos.

slumber ('slʌm·bər) *v.i.* dormitar; dormir. —*n.* sueño. —**slumberous**, *adj.* soñoliento.

slump (slʌmp) *v.i.* **1,** (sink; collapse) desplomarse; hundirse. **2,** (decline; fall) bajar. **3,** (fail) fracasar; no tener éxito. **4,** (slouch) agacharse; repantigarse. —*n.* **1,** (collapse) desplome; hundimiento. **2,** (decline) baja. **3,** (failure) fracaso. **4,** (slouch) postura floja.

slung (slʌŋ) *v., pret.* & *p.p. de* **sling.**

slung shot rompecabezas.

slunk (slʌŋk) *v., pret.* & *p.p. de* **slink.**

slur (slʌɹ) *v.t.* [**slurred**, **slurring**] **1,** (run together; blur in speaking) comerse (sonidos *o* sílabas); farfullar. **2,** (treat slightingly; ignore) pasar por encima; suprimir; ocultar. **3,** (disparage; insult) menospreciar; rebajar; insultar. **4,** *music* ligar; marcar con una ligadura. —*n.* **1,** (indistinct pronunciation) farfulla; pronunciación indistinta. **2,** (disparaging remark or act) borrón o mancha en la reputación; reparo; afrenta. **3,** *music* ligadura.

slush (slʌʃ) *n.* **1,** (watery snow) nieve a medio derretir. **2,** (watery mixture of mud, etc.) fango; cieno; lodo blando. **3,** (drivel) sentimentalismo; sensiblería; ñoñería. —**slush fund**, fondos guardados en reserva para usos especiales.

slut (slʌt) *n.* **1,** (slovenly woman) mujer desaliñada. **2,** (loose woman) ramera; prostituta. **3,** (female dog) perra.

sly (slai) *adj.* **1,** (shrewd; clever) astuto; listo; sutil; mañoso. **2,** (stealthy; furtive) secreto; furtivo. **3,** (roguish) pícaro. —**on the sly**, furtivamente; a hurtadillas.

smack (smæk) *v.t.* **1,** (separate, as the lips, with a sharp sound) chuparse (los labios). **2,** (slap) dar una palmada, manotada o bofetada. **3,** (kiss noisily) besar ruidosamente; dar un beso ruidoso; hacer sonar un beso en. —*v.i.* (make a sharp sound; slap) chuparse los labios; saborearse; rechuparse; relamerse; chasquear (un látigo). —*n.* **1,** (trace; suggestion) olor; sabor; dejo; gustillo. **2,** (slap; blow) manotada; palmada; golpe. **3,** (resounding kiss) beso ruidoso. **4,** (smacking noise) chasquido. **5,** (bit; small amount) pizca. **6,** (fishing vessel) esmaque. —*adv.* directamente; redondamente. —**smacking,** *adj.* fuerte; redondo. —**smack of,** oler a; saber a; tener olor o sabor de.

small (smɔl) *adj.* **1,** (little) pequeño; chico; menudo. **2,** (humble) bajo; insignificante; humilde; obscuro. **3,** (mean; petty) mezquino; miserable; ruin. **4,** *typog.* minúsculo. —*n.* parte más estrecha. —**small arms,** armas portátiles; armas ligeras. —**small change,** dinero menudo. —**small fry, 1,** (young fish) pececillos. **2,** (children) niños; chiquillos. **3,** (insignificant persons or things) personas o cosas de poca monta. —**small hours,** altas horas de la noche; primeras horas de la mañana. —**small potatoes,** *colloq.* persona o cosa de poca monta. —**small talk,** charla; plática; conversación sin importancia.

smallish ('smɔl·ɪʃ) *adj.* algo pequeño.

small-minded *adj.* **1,** (petty; mean) mezquino; miserable; ruin. **2,** (illiberal) iliberal; intolerante; estrecho de miras.

smallness ('smɔl·nəs) *n.* pequeñez.

smallpox *n.* viruelas (*pl.*).

smart (smart) *v.i.* **1,** (sting) escocer; picar; resquemar. **2,** (feel physical or mental distress) escocerse; dolerse; sentirse. —*v.t.* picar; resquemar. —*n.* **1,** (sting) escozor; picazón; comezón; resquemor. **2,** (mental distress) aflicción; dolor. —*adj.* **1,** (keen; acute; severe) agudo; picante; punzante; mordaz. **2,** (brisk) vivo; enérgico; despejado. **3,** (vigorous; forceful) fuerte; rudo. **4,** (clever; shrewd) listo; astuto; inteligente. **5,** (vivacious; witty) vivaz; vivaracho. **6,** (neat; stylish) elegante; a la moda; de buen tono. **7,** (presumptuous) presuntuoso; sabihondo. —**smart aleck** ('æl·ɪk) *colloq.* presuntuoso; sabihondo. —**smart set,** gente de buen tono.

smarten ('smar·tən) *v.t.* **1,** (spruce up) hermosear; embellecer. **2,** (quicken) animar; avivar. —*v.i.* animarse; avivarse.

smartness ('smart·nəs) *n.* **1,** (keenness) agudeza. **2,** (briskness) viveza; energía. **3,** (force; vigor) fuerza; violencia. **4,** (cleverness) astucia; inteligencia. **5,** (vivacity) vivacidad. **6,** (elegance) elegancia.

smash (smæʃ) *v.t.* **1,** (break to pieces) romper; quebrar; hacer pedazos; estrellar. **2,** (defeat utterly) destrozar; arruinar; aplastar. **3,** (strike against) chocar con; topar con. —*v.i.* **1,** (break to pieces) romperse; quebrarse; hacerse pedazos; estrellarse. **2,** (strike; collide) chocar; topar. —*n.* **1,** (violent blow) choque o tope violento. **2,** (destruction) quebrazón; quiebra; fracaso; derrota completa. **3,** (sweet drink) refresco o bebida alcohólica hecha con menta, azúcar y agua. —**go to smash,** arruinarse; destrozarse. —**smash hit,** *colloq.* éxito magnífico.

smash-up *n.* ruina; quiebra; choque desastroso.

smattering ('smæt·ər·ɪŋ) *n.* conocimiento superficial; tintura.

smear (smɪr) *v.t.* **1,** (cover with something sticky, grease, etc.) untar. **2,** (soil; dirty) embarrar; manchar; tiznar. **3,** (daub, as with paint) pintorrear. **4,** (blot; blur) borrar; emborronar. **5,** (slander) calumniar; denigrar. —*v.i.* mancharse; borrarse. —*n.* **1,** (spot; smudge) mancha; embarradura. **2,** (blot) borrón. **3,** (slander) calumnia; denigración. **4,** *bacteriol.* frotis.

smell (smɛl) *v.t.* [*pret.* & *p.p.* **smelled** *o* **smelt**] **1,** (perceive through the nose) oler. **2,** (sniff) husmear; olfatear. **3,** (detect or discover as though by smell) oler; percibir; descubrir. —*v.i.* oler; heder; husmear. —*n.* **1,** (sense of smell) olfato. **2,** (odor; scent; aroma) olor; perfume; fragancia; aroma. **3,** (act of smelling) husmeo; acción de oler. **4,** (trace) traza; vestigio. —**smelly,** *adj.* hediondo. —**smelling salts,** sales aromáticas. —**smell of,** oler a; tener olor de. —**smell out,** descubrir.

smelt (smɛlt) *v.t.* (fuse; melt) fundir. —*v., pret.* & *p.p. de* **smell.** —*n., ichthy.* eperlano.

smelter (ˈsmɛl·tər) *n.* fundidor.
smelting (ˈsmɛl·tɪŋ) *n.* fundición.
smile (smail) *n.* sonrisa. —*v.i.* sonreír; sonreírse. —*v.t.* expresar con una sonrisa. —**smiling,** *adj.* risueño.
smirch (smʌɹtʃ) *v.t.* **1,** (soil; dirty) manchar; ensuciar; tiznar. **2,** (defame) difamar; deshonrar; tiznar. —*n.* **1,** (stain; smear) mancha; tiznón. **2,** (dishonor) deshonra.
smirk (smʌɹk) *n.* sonrisa boba o afectada. —*v.i.* sonreírse afectadamente o estúpidamente.
smite (smait) *v.t.* [**smote, smitten**] **1,** (strike; afflict) golpear; herir; afligir. **2,** (affect; captivate) conmover; encantar; tocar al alma.
smith (smɪθ) *n.* herrero; herrador. —**smithy,** *n.* herrería.
smithereens (ˌsmɪð·ərˈiːnz) *n.pl.* añicos; pedazos.
smitten (ˈsmɪt·ən) *v., p.p. de* **smite.** —*adj.* **1,** (impressed) impresionado. **2,** (in love) enamorado.
smock (smak) *n.* bata corta; camisa de mujer; blusa de obrero. —**smock frock,** blusa de campesino.
smog (smag) *n.* mezcla de niebla y humo.
smoke (smok) *n.* **1,** (visible vapor from a burning substance) humo. **2,** (something unsubstantial) humo; vapor; humareda. **3,** (cigar or cigarette) fumada; tabaco. —*v.i.* **1,** (emit smoke) humear; hacer humo. **2,** (burn tobacco) fumar. —*v.t.* **1,** (puff on, as tobacco, opium, etc.) fumar. **2,** (cure with smoke) ahumar. —**go up in smoke; end in smoke,** volverse humo. —**no smoking,** se prohibe fumar; prohibido fumar. —**smoke out,** echar fuera con humo; *fig.* descubrir.
smoked (smokt) *adj.* ahumado.
smokehouse *n.* cuarto cerrado para ahumar carnes, pieles, etc.
smoker (ˈsmo·kər) *n.* **1,** (one who smokes) fumador. **2,** = **smoking room. 3,** = **smoking car. 4,** (social function) tertulia en que se permite fumar.
smoke screen cortina de humo; humo de protección.
smokestack *n.* chimenea.
smoking car vagón de fumar; coche fumador.
smoking jacket batín.
smoking room fumadero; salón de fumar.
smoky (ˈsmo·ki) *adj.* humeante; humoso.
smolder *también,* **smoulder** (ˈsmol·dər) *v.i.* **1,** (burn and smoke without flame) arder lentamente, sin llama o en rescoldo. **2,** *fig.* (lie suppressed) arder (una pasión); estar latente.
smooth (smuːð) *adj.* **1,** (flat; even) plano; llano. **2,** (soft to the touch; slick) liso; suave; alisado. **3,** (without sudden variation; uniform) igual; parejo; uniforme. **4,** (mild; bland) suave; blando; meloso; dulce. **5,** (pleasant; peaceful) tranquilo; agradable. **6,** (flowing; fluent) flúido; fácil. —*v.t.* **1,** (make even) allanar; alisar; suavizar. **2,** (calm; mollify) calmar; aliviar; ablandar.
smoothness (ˈsmuð·nəs) *n.* **1,** (flatness; evenness) llanura. **2,** (softness) lisura; suavidad. **3,** (uniformity) igualdad; uniformidad. **4,** (mildness) blandura; dulzura. **5,** (pleasantness; peacefulness) tranquilidad. **6,** (flowing quality) fluidez; facilidad.
smorgasbord (ˈsmor·gəsˌbord) *n.* entremeses suecos.
smote (smot) *v., pret. de* **smite.**
smother (ˈsmʌð·ər) *v.t.* **1,** (suffocate; deprive of air) ahogar; asfixiar; sofocar. **2,** (stifle; suppress) suprimir; disfrazar; ocultar. —*v.i.* ahogarse; asfixiarse.
smoulder (ˈsmol·dər) *v.i.* = **smolder.**
smudge (smʌdʒ) *n.* **1,** (blot; smear) mancha; tiznón; borrón. **2,** (smoky fire) humareda; nube espesa de humo. —*v.t.* tiznar; manchar; ensuciar. —*v.i.* mancharse; borrarse. —**smudgy,** *adj.* ensuciado; tiznado.
smug (smʌg) *adj.* presumido; vanidoso; satisfecho de sí mismo. —**smugness,** *n.* presunción; vanidad; satisfacción de sí mismo.
smuggle (ˈsmʌg·əl) *v.t.* meter *o* sacar de contrabando. —*v.i.* contrabandear; hacer contrabando. —**smuggler** (-lər) *n.* contrabandista. —**smuggling** (-lɪŋ) *n.* comercio de contrabando.

smut (smʌt) *n.* **1,** (sooty matter) tizne; tiznón; mancha; suciedad. **2,** (obscenity) indecencia; obscenidad.
smutty ('smʌt·i) *adj.* **1,** (sooty) tiznado; manchado; sucio. **2,** (obscene) indecente; obsceno.
snack (snæk) *n.* bocado; bocadillo; refrigerio; merienda. —**snack bar,** puesto de refrescos; cantina. —**snack basket,** fiambrera.
snafu (ˌsnæˈfuː) *adj., slang* desordenado; confuso; enredado. —*n., slang* desorden; confusión; enredo.
snag (snæg) *n.* **1,** (obstacle) obstáculo; tropiezo. **2,** (bump; lump) nudo (en la madera); protuberancia. —*v.t.* [**snagged, snagging**] **1,** (impede; entangle) impedir; enredar. **2,** (pull out) arrancar.
snail (sneil) *n.* **1,** *zool.* caracol; babosa. **2,** (slowpoke) posma. —**snail's pace,** paso de tortuga; paso de caracol.
snake (sneik) *n.* culebra; sierpe; serpiente; víbora. —*v.t.* arrastrar tirando de. —*v.i.* culebrear; serpentear. —**snake in the grass,** *colloq.* traidor; engañador; seductor.
snake charmer encantador de serpientes.
snaky ('snei·ki) *adj.* **1,** (of or like a snake) de culebra. **2,** (flexible; sinuous) culebrino; serpentino; tortuoso. **3,** (treacherous) traidor; pérfido.
snap (snæp) *v.i.* [**snapped, snapping**] **1,** (make a sudden sharp sound) chasquear; dar un chasquido. **2,** (break or loosen suddenly) estallar; quebrarse; soltarse. **3,** (move suddenly) sacudirse; apresurarse. **4,** (bite) echar una mordedura; procurar morder; morder. **5,** (speak sharply) volverse áspero; hablar bruscamente. —*v.t.* **1,** (cause to make a sharp sound) chasquear. **2,** (break) romper; quebrar; hacer estallar. **3,** (loose suddenly) soltar; lanzar; tirar. **4,** (retort) contestar mordazmente. **5,** (grab) coger; agarrar; asir; lanzarse sobre. **6,** (take a snapshot of) sacar una instantánea de; tomar (una instantánea). —*n.* **1,** (sharp sound) estallido; chasquido; castañeta (hecha con los dedos). **2,** (quick motion) sacudida; lance. **3,** (closing or locking device) cierre de resorte; corchete. **4,** (sudden closing, as of a trap) mordedura. **5,** (thin, brittle cake) galletita. **6,** (briskness; vigor) vigor; energía; fuerza. **7,** (brief spell) período corto, esp. de frío. **8,** *slang* (easy task) ganga. **9,** = **snapshot.** —*adj.* **1,** (offhand) impensado; hecho de prisa o de repente. **2,** (easy) fácil. —**not to care a snap,** no importarle a uno un ardite *o* un comino. —**snap fastener,** broche de presión. —**snap judgment,** decisión atolondrada. —**snap lock,** cerradura de golpe. —**snap one's fingers,** tronar los dedos; castañetear con los dedos. —**snap one's fingers at,** burlarse de; mofarse de. —**snap out of it,** *slang* componerse. —**snap shut,** cerrar(se) de golpe. —**snap together,** apretar; abrochar. —**snap up,** agarrar; asir; aceptar en seguida.
snapdragon *n.* becerra.
snapper ('snæp·ər) *n.* **1,** (person or thing that snaps) mordedor. **2,** (fish) pez comestible del Golfo de México. **3,** (snapping turtle) gran tortuga voraz de la América del Norte.
snappish ('snæp·ɪʃ) *adj.* irritable; mordaz.
snappy ('snæp·i) *adj.* **1,** (snapping; crackling) crepitante. **2,** (brisk; cold and stimulating) vivo; fresco. **3,** (tart; spicy) picante. **4,** *colloq.* (smart; stylish) elegante; de moda. **5,** *colloq.* (lively; quick) astuto; listo. **6,** = **snappish.**
snapshot *n.* instantánea.
snare (sneːr) *n.* **1,** (trap) trampa; cepo; lazo. **2,** (cord, as of a drum) lazo; tirante. —*v.t.* **1,** (catch; trap) coger con una trampa. **2,** (catch; seize) agarrar; coger. **3,** (entangle; foul) enredar; enmarañar. —**snare drum,** tambor con tirantes de cuerda.
snarl (snarl) *v.t. & i.* **1,** (growl) gruñir. **2,** (entangle) enredar(se); enmarañar(se). —*n.* **1,** (growl) gruñido. **2,** (tangle) enredo; nudo.
snatch (snætʃ) *v.t.* arrebatar; agarrar. —*v.i.* procurar agarrar o arrebatar. —*n.* **1,** (act of snatching) arrebatamiento; agarrón. **2,** *slang* (kidnaping) secuestro; *Amer.* plagio. **3,** (fragment; bit) pedacito; trozo; fragmento. —**by** (*o* **in**)

snatches, a ratos; poco a poco; de vez en cuando.

sneak (snik) *v.i.* venir *o* irse a hurtadillas; colarse; escurrirse. —*v.t.* **1,** (do furtively) hacer a escondidas. **2,** (put in *o* take out furtively) meter *o* sacar a hurtadillas. **3,** *colloq.* (steal) robar; ratear. —*adj.* furtivo; traicionero. —*n.* **1,** (furtive action) acción furtiva. **2,** (one who sneaks) persona solapada. **3,** *pl.* = **sneakers.**

sneakers ('sni·kərz) *n.pl., colloq.* zapatos de playa; zapatos de tela con suela de goma.

sneaking ('sni·kɪŋ) *adj.* **1,** (fawning; obsequious) servil; bajo; vil. **2,** (furtive) furtivo; oculto; secreto.

sneak thief ratero; ladrón de poca monta.

sneaky ('sni·ki) *adj.* **1,** (furtive) furtivo; oculto; secreto. **2,** (secretive) solapado. **3,** (treacherous) traicionero.

sneer (snɪr) *v.i.* hablar *o* mirar con desprecio; burlarse; mofarse. —*v.t.* proferir con desprecio. —*n.* mirada de desprecio; risa falsa o burlona. —**sneering**, *adj.* burlador; despreciativo. —**sneer at**, mofarse de; burlarse de.

sneeze (sni:z) *n.* estornudo. —*v.i.* estornudar. —**not to be sneezed at**, *colloq.* considerable; digno de consideración.

snicker ('snɪk·ər) *v.i.* reírse tontamente. —*n.* risita; risa tonta. *También,* **snigger**.

snide (snaid) *adj.* socarrón y despreciativo.

sniff (snɪf) *v.i.* **1,** (inhale audibly through the nose) olfatear; resoplar; resollar. **2,** (show scorn or disdain) menospreciar; manifestar desprecio con resoplidos. —*v.t.* **1,** (inhale sharply) husmear; ventear. **2,** (perceive by smell) oler; percibir; descubrir. —*n.* olfateo; husmeo; venteo.

sniffle ('snɪf·əl) *v.i.* sorber; resollar; resoplar. —*n.* sorbo; resuello; resoplido. —**sniffles**, *n.pl.* catarro; legaña; romadizo.

snifter ('snɪf·tər) *n.* **1,** (brandy glass) vaso de pera. **2,** *slang* (short drink) trago; *W.I.* palo.

snigger ('snɪg·ər) *v.i.* & *n.* = **snicker.**

snip (snɪp) *v.t.* & *i.* [**snipped, snipping**] tijeretear; dar tijeretadas; cortar *o* recortar con tijeras. —*n.* **1,** (act or sound of snipping) tijeretada. **2,** (piece cut off) retazo; pedacito. **3,** *pl.* (tin shears) tijeras para metal. **4,** *colloq.* (small or insignificant person) persona de poca monta; impertinente.

snipe (snaip) *n.* agachadiza. —*v.i.* **1,** (hunt snipe) cazar agachadizas. **2,** (shoot from hiding) tirar desde un acecho. —**sniper**, *n.* francotirador.

snippet ('snɪp·ɪt) *n.* **1,** (scrap; fragment) recorte; retazo. **2,** *colloq.* (small or insignificant person) persona de poca monta; impertinente.

snippy ('snɪp·i) *adj., colloq.* **1,** (snappish) irritable; mordaz. **2,** (insolent) insolente; impertinente.

snitch (snɪtʃ) *v.t., slang* (steal) ratear; hurtar; robar. —*v.i., slang* (turn informer) soplar; hacerse delator. —**snitch on**, delatar; denunciar.

snivel ('snɪv·əl) *v.i.* gimotear; lloriquear. —*n.* gimoteo; lloriqueo.

snob (sna:b) *n.* snob; esnob. —**snobbish**, *adj.* snob; esnob. —**snobbishness**; **snobbery**, *n.* snobismo; esnobismo.

snood (snu:d) *n.* cintillo; redecilla.

snoop (snup) *v.i., colloq.* curiosear; fisgonear; espiar. —*n., colloq.* curioso; fisgón; espía; espión. —**snooping**, *n.* curioseo; fisgoneo. —**snoopy**, *adj.* curioso; entremetido.

snoot (snut) *n., slang* hocico; narices (*pl.*); cara.

snooty ('snu·ti) *adj., slang* esnob; altanero. —**snootiness**, *n.* esnobismo; altanería.

snooze (snu:z) *v.i., colloq.* dormitar; sestear. —*n., colloq.* siesta; siestecita; sueñito.

snore (sno:r) *v.i.* roncar. —*n.* ronquido. —**snorer**, *n.* roncador.

snorkel ('snor·kəl) *n.* tubo de respiración para submarinos; esnórquel.

snort (snort) *v.i.* **1,** (force air audibly through the nose) resoplar; bufar. **2,** (scoff) mofarse. —*n.* **1,** (snorting sound) resoplido; bufido. **2,** *slang* (short drink) trago; chispo; *W.I.* palo.

snot (snat) *n., vulg.* **1,** (mucus) moco. **2,** (impudent youngster) mocoso. —**snotty**, *adj.*, *colloq.* mocoso.

snout (snaut) *n.* hocico.

snow (sno:) *n.* **1,** (white water crystals) nieve. **2,** *slang* (cocaine *o* heroin) cocaína; heroína. —*v.i.* nevar. —*v.t.* **1,** (let fall like snow) nevar. **2,** (cover with snow) cubrir con nieve. **3,** *slang* (hoax) engañar; burlar. —**snow under**, cubrir con nieve; *fig.* abrumar; aplastar.

snowball *n.* bola de nieve. —*v.t.* tirar bolas de nieve a. —*v.i.* crecer rápidamente.

snowbank *n.* banco de nieve.

snowbird *n.* **1,** *ornith.* pinzón de las nieves. **2,** *slang* (drug addict) narcómano.

snowbound *adj.* sitiado *o* detenido por la nieve.

snowclad *adj.* tapado de nieve.

snow cone granizado.

snowdrift *n.* montón de nieve; ventisquero.

snowfall *n.* nevada; nevasca; caída de nieve.

snowflake *n.* copo de nieve.

snow flurry nevisca.

snowman *n.* [*pl.* **-men**] **1,** (snow statue) hombre de nieve; figura de nieve. **2,** (supposed Tibetan beast) bestia de nieve.

snowplow *n.* limpianieves; quitanieves.

snowshoe *n.* raqueta; barajón.

snowslide *n.* alud; avalancha de nieve.

snowstorm *n.* borrasca de nieve; nevasca; ventisca.

snowy ('sno·i) *adj.* nevado.

snub (snʌb) *v.t.* [**snubber, snubbing**] **1,** (stop or check suddenly) parar de repente. **2,** (slight) menospreciar; desairar. —*n.* **1,** (sudden stop) parada en seco. **2,** (slight) desaire; menosprecio. —*adj.* chato.

snuff (snʌf) *v.i.* olfatear; resoplar. —*v.t.* **1,** (inhale sharply) husmear; ventear. **2,** (draw in through the nose) aspirar; sorber por la nariz. **3,** (extinguish, as a candle) apagar; despabilar. —*n.* **1,** (sniff) olfateo; resoplido. **2,** (powdered tobacco) tabaco en polvo; rapé. **3,** (charred end of a candle) pabilo; moco.

snuffbox *n.* tabaquera.

snuffle ('snʌf·əl) *v.i.* **1,** (sniff; sniffle) olfatear; resollar. **2,** (talk with a nasal twang) ganguear. —*n.* **1,** (sniffing) olfateo; resuello. **2,** (nasal twang) gangueo. —**snuffles**, *n.pl.* catarro nasal; romadizo.

snug (snʌg) *adj.* **1,** (comfortable) cómodo. **2,** (tight-fitting) ajustado. **3,** (compact) compacto; estrecho.

snuggle ('snʌg·əl) *v.i.* acurrucarse; anidarse. —*v.t.* apretar; arrimar. —**snuggle up to**, arrimarse a; apretarse contra.

so (so:) *adv.* **1,** (thus; in such a manner) así; de este modo; de esta manera. **2,** (in such a degree or amount) tan; tanto. **3,** (very; much) muy; mucho. **4,** (consequently) por tanto; por consiguiente. **5,** (also; likewise) también; igualmente. **6,** *colloq.* (indeed; really) de veras; ya. **7,** *colloq.* (well; then) pues; entonces. —*conj.* así que; de modo que; con tal (de) que; a condición(de) que. —*pron.* (*usu. reemplazando una palabra o frase ya mencionada*) lo; eso: *He did it, but I didn't think so,* Lo hizo, pero no lo creí; *I told you so,* Te lo dije; Te dije eso. —*interj.* ¡eh!; ¡pues!; ¡bien! —**and so**, pues; así pues. —**and so forth,** etcétera. —**and so on**, y así sucesivamente. —**ever so much**, muchísimo. —**is that so**?, ¿de veras? —**just so, 1,** (exactly) ni más ni menos; precisamente. **2,** (perfect) perfecto; bien arreglado. —**or so**, poco más o menos; como: *ten dollars or so,* diez dólares poco más o menos; como diez dólares. —**so as to**, de manera de; para (+ *inf.*). —**so far**, hasta ahora; hasta aquí. —**so long**, hasta la vista; hasta luego. —**so many**, tantos. —**so much**, tanto. —**so much as**, nada más (que); siquiera; a los menos. —**so much for**, basta con. —**so much the better** (*o* **worse**), tanto mejor (*o* peor). —**so so**, así así; tal cual. —**so that**, así que; de modo que; para que. —**so to speak**, por decirlo así. —**so what**?, pues ¿qué?

soak (sok) *v.i.* penetrar; calarse; filtrarse. —*v.t.* **1,** (drench; saturate) remojar; ensopar; empapar. **2,** (absorb) empapar; embeber; chupar; absorber. **3,** *slang* (beat) golpear; pegar; aporrear. **4,** *slang* (charge exorbitantly) robarle a uno (un vendedor); cobrarle a uno un precio desproporcionado.

—*n.* **1,** (act or result of soaking) remojo; empapamiento. **2,** *slang* (hard blow) golpe; puñetazo; bofetón. **3,** *slang* (drunkard) borrachín; bebedor.
so-and-so *n.* fulano; fulano de tal.
soap (sop) *n.* jabón. —*v.t.* enjabonar; jabonar.
soapbox *n.* tribuna improvisada.
soap dish jabonera.
soaping ('so·pɪŋ) *n.* jabonadura.
soap opera drama sentimental emitido por la radio o la televisión, generalmente en capítulos sucesivos, bajo el patrocinio de fabricantes de jabón.
soapstone *n.* esteatita.
soapsuds *n.pl.* jabonaduras.
soapwort *n.* jabonera; saponaria.
soapy ('so·pi) *adj.* jabonoso; enjabonado.
soar (soːr) *v.i.* **1,** (fly upward) remontarse; volar muy alto. **2,** (glide) planear; volar. **3,** (rise higher) elevarse; subir. —*n.* **1,** (flight) remonte; vuelo. **2,** (glide) planeo. —**soaring,** *adj.* elevado. —*n.* = **soar.**
sob (saːb) *v.i.* & *t.* [**sobbed, sobbing**] sollozar. —*n.* sollozo.
sober ('so·bər) *adj.* **1,** (not intoxicated) sobrio; no embriagado. **2,** (sedate; serious; solemn) moderado; templado; cuerdo; sensato. **3,** (subdued, as in color) apagado. —*v.t.* **1,** (relieve of intoxication) desembriagar. **2,** (temper; moderate) templar; moderar; poner sobrio. —*v.i.* desembriagarse; volverse sobrio. —**soberness,** *n.* sobriedad.
sobriety (so'brai·ə·ti) *n.* sobriedad.
sobriquet ('so·brɪ,kei) *n.* apodo. *También,* **soubriquet.**
so-called *adj.* así llamado; supuesto.
soccer ('sak·ər) *n.* fútbol; balompié.
sociable ('so·ʃə·bəl) *adj.* sociable; amigable; comunicativo. —*n.* fiesta; tertulia; velada. —**sociability,** *n.* sociabilidad.
social ('so·ʃəl) *adj.* social. —*n.* reunión social. **social register,** libro de la buena sociedad; libro de oro. —**social security,** seguro social; previsión social. —**social work,** servicio social; auxilio social.
socialism ('so·ʃəl·ɪz·əm) *n.* socialismo. —**socialist,** *n.* & *adj.* socialista. **socialistic,** *adj.* socialista.
socialite ('so·ʃə,lait) *n., colloq.* persona de la buena sociedad.
socialize ('so·ʃə,laiz) *v.t.* socializar. —*v.i.* socializarse. —**socialization** (-lɪ'zei·ʃən) *n.* socialización.
society (sə'sai·ə·ti) *n.* **1,** (group; community) sociedad. **2,** (fashionable world) buena sociedad; mundo elegante. **3,** (company) compañía.
sociology (,so·ʃi'al·ə·dʒi) *n.* sociología. —**sociological** (-ə'ladʒ·ɪ·kəl) *adj.* sociológico. —**sociologist,** *n.* sociólogo.
sock (sak) *n.* **1,** (short stocking) calcetín. **2,** *slang* (hard blow) golpetazo; puñetazo; porrazo. —*v.t., slang* golpear; pegar.
socket ('sak·ɪt) *n.* **1,** (hollow; groove) hueco; encaje. **2,** (of the eye) cuenca. **3,** (of a tooth) alvéolo. **4,** *electricity* enchufe. —*v.t.* encajar.
sod (saːd) *n.* césped.
soda ('so·də) *n.* **1,** (sodium or sodium compound) soda; sosa. **2,** (carbonated water) agua de soda; agua gaseosa; agua de seltz. —**soda ash,** cenizas de sosa; barrilla. —**soda cracker,** galletita salada. —**soda fountain,** fuente de sodas.
sodality (so'dæl·ə·ti) *n.* cofradía; hermandad.
sodden ('sad·ən) *adj.* empapado.
sodium ('so·di·əm) *n.* sodio.
sodomy ('sad·ə·mi) *n.* sodomía. —**sodomite** (-,mait) *n.* sodomita.
sofa ('so·fə) *n.* sofá. —**sofa bed,** sofá cama.
soft (sɔft) *adj.* **1,** (not hard) suave; blando. **2,** (mild) suave; dulce. **3,** (yielding easily) flojo; flexible. **4,** (not loud) suave. **5,** (kind; lenient) manso; tierno. **6,** (delicate; frail) delicado; delgado. **7,** *phonet.* sonoro; sibilante. **8,** *colloq.* (easy) fácil. —*adv.* suavemente; blandamente.
softball *n.* sófbol.
soft-boiled *adj.* pasado por agua.
soft coal carbón bituminoso; hulla.
soft drink refresco.
soften ('saf·ən) *v.t.* ablandar; suavizar; templar. —*v.i.* ablandarse; suavizarse; templarse.

softhearted *adj.* manso; bondadoso.
softly ('sɔft·li) *adv.* **1,** (gently) suavemente; blandamente. **2,** (quietly) suavemente; en voz baja.
softness ('sɔft·nəs) *n.* suavidad; blandura; dulzura; flojedad.
soft-pedal *v.t.* moderar; templar; bajar.
soft soap **1,** *lit.* jabón blando *o* suave. **2,** *fig., colloq.* (flattery) adulación; lisonja. —**softsoap,** *v.t., colloq.* dar jabón; enjabonar; lamer el ojo.
soft-spoken *adj.* de voz suave.
soft water agua blanda; agua dulce.
softy ('sɔf·ti) *n., colloq.* persona pusilánime; persona débil.
soggy ('sag·i) *adj.* empapado; ensopado.
soil (sɔil) *n.* suelo; tierra. —*v.t.* manchar; ensuciar. —*v.i.* mancharse; ensuciarse.
soirée (swa'rei) *n.* tertulia; velada.
sojourn ('so·dʒʌɹn) *v.i.* morar; estarse; permanecer. —*n.* morada; estancia; permanencia.
sol (sol) *n., music* sol.
Sol (sal) *n.* el Sol.
solace ('sal·ɪs) *n.* solaz; consuelo; alivio. —*v.t.* solazar; consolar; confortar.
solar ('so·lər) *adj.* solar. —**solar plexus,** plexo solar.
solarium (so'lɛr·i·əm) *n.* solana; solario.
sold (so;ld) *v., pret. & p.p. de* **sell.**
solder ('sad·ər) *n.* soldadura. —*v.t.* soldar; estañar. —**soldering iron,** soldador.
soldier ('sol·dʒər) *n.* soldado; militar. —*v.i.* **1,** (perform military service) militar; servir como soldado. **2,** (goldbrick) zanganear. **3,** (malinger) fingirse enfermo. —**soldierly,** *adj.* soldadesco; militar. —**soldiery,** *n.* soldadesca; servicio militar. —**soldier of fortune,** aventurero.
sole (so;l) *n.* **1,** (undersurface of a foot) planta. **2,** (undersurface of a shoe) suela. **3,** (fish) lenguado. —*adj.* solo; único; exclusivo. —*v.t.* poner suela a. —**solely,** *adv.* solamente; únicamente.
solecism ('sal·ə,sɪz·əm) *n.* solecismo.
solemn ('sal·əm) *adj.* solemne; grave; serio. —**solemnity** (sə'lɛm·nə·ti) *n.* solemnidad; pompa; gravedad; seriedad. —**solemnize** (-,naiz) *v.t.* solemnizar; celebrar solemnemente.
solenoid ('so·lə,nɔid) *n.* solenoide.
soli- (sal·ɪ; -ə) *prefijo* soli-; solo; a solas: *soliloquy*. soliloquio.
solicit (sə'lɪs·ɪt) *v.t. & i.* solicitar. —**solicitation,** *n.* solicitación.
solicitor (sə'lɪs·ə·tər) *n.* **1,** (one who solicits) solicitador. **2,** (lawyer) procurador.
solicitous (sə'lɪs·ə·təs) *adj.* solícito.
solicitude (sə'lɪs·ə·tud) *n.* solicitud.
solid ('sal·ɪd) *adj.* **1,** (three-dimensional) sólido. **2,** (compact; dense) compacto; denso. **3,** (firm; hard; strong) firme; duro; robusto; fuerte. **4,** (united; unanimous) unido; unánime. **5,** (entire) entero; todo. —*n.* sólido. —**solid geometry,** geometría del espacio.
solidarity (,sal·ɪ'dær·ə·ti) *n.* solidaridad.
solidary ('sal·ɪ,dɛr·i) *adj.* solidario.
solidify (sə'lɪd·ə,fai) *v.t.* solidificar. —*v.i.* solidificarse. —**solidification** (-fɪ'kei·ʃən) *n.* solidificación.
solidity (sə'lɪd·ə·ti) *n.* solidez.
soliloquy (sə'lɪl·ə·kwi) *n.* soliloquio; monólogo. —**soliloquize** (-,kwaiz) *v.i.* soliloquiar; monologar.
solitaire ('sal·ə,tɛr) *n.* solitario.
solitary ('sal·ə,tɛr·i) *adj.* **1,** (alone) solitario. **2,** (single; sole) solo; único. **3,** (isolated) aislado; poco frecuentado; desierto. —*n.* solitario; ermitaño. —**in solitary confinement,** incomunicado.
solitude ('sal·ə,tud) *n.* soledad.
solmization (,sal·mə'zei·ʃən) *n.* solfa; solfeo.
solo ('so·lo) *n.* [*pl.* **-los**] solo. —*adj.* a solas; hecho a solas. —**soloist,** *n.* solista.
solon ('so·lan) *n.* legislador.
solstice ('sal·stɪs) *n.* solsticio.
soluble ('sal·jə·bəl) *adj.* soluble. —**solubility,** *n.* solubilidad.
solution (sə'lu·ʃən) *n.* solución.
solve (salv) *v.t.* 1, (find the answer to) resolver. **2,** (disentangle) desenredar; desenlazar. —**solvable,** *adj.* soluble.

solvency ('sal·vən·si) *n.* solvencia.
solvent ('sal·vənt) *adj.* solvente. —*n.* disolvente.
somatic (so'mæt·ɪk) *adj.* somático.
somato- (so·mə·to; -tə) *prefijo* somato-; cuerpo: *somatology,* somatología.
somber *también,* **sombre** ('sam·bər) *adj.* sombrío.
sombrero (sam'brɛr·o) *n.* [*pl.* **-ros**] sombrero.
some (sʌm) *indef. adj.* **1,** (of an unspecified quantity) algo de; un poco de. *Muchas veces no se expresa en español: Give me some bread,* Deme pan *o* un poco de pan. **2,** (of an unspecified number) unos; algunos. **3,** (certain one or ones) algún (*pl.* algunos); cierto (*pl.* ciertos); cualquiera (*pl.* cualesquiera). **4,** *slang* (considerable; notable) bueno; famoso; menudo. —*pron. indef.* **1,** (an unspecified part) parte; una parte; algo. **2,** (an unspecified number) unos; algunos; unos cuantos. —*adv.* **1,** (approximately) como; unos: *some twenty persons,* como veinte personas; unas veinte personas. **2,** *colloq.* (somewhat) algo; un poco. **3,** *colloq.* (a great deal) bastante; mucho.
-some (səm) *sufijo* **1,** *forma adjetivos denotando* tendencia; inclinación: *quarrelsome,* pendenciero. **2,** *añadido a numerales indica* grupo: *threesome,* trío. **3,** (so:m) -soma; cuerpo: *chromosome,* cromosoma.
somebody ('sʌm,bad·i; -,bʌd·i; -bə·di) *pron.indef.* alguien. —*n.* personaje. **somebody else,** algún otro; otra persona.
someday *adv.* algún día.
somehow *adv.* de algún modo; de alguna manera. —**somehow or other,** de una manera u otra.
someone *indef. pron.* alguien. —**someone else,** algún otro; otra persona.
someplace *adv.* & *n.* = **somewhere.**
somersault ('sʌm·ər,sɔlt) *n.* salto mortal.
something *n.* algo; alguna cosa.
sometime *adv.* alguna vez; en algún tiempo. —*adj.* anterior; antiguo.
sometimes *adv.* a veces; algunas veces.
somewhat *adv.* algo; un tanto; un poco. —*n.* algo; alguna cosa; un poco.
somewhere *adv.* a *o* en algún sitio *o* alguna parte. —**somewhere else,** a *o* en otra parte.
somnambulate (sam'næm·bjə·,leit) *v.i.* padecer sonambulismo.
somnambulism (sam'næm·bjə·lɪz·əm) *n.* sonambulismo. —**somnambulist,** *n.* sonámbulo.
somniferous (sam'nɪf·ər·əs) *adj.* somnífero.
somnolent ('sam·nə·lənt) *adj.* soñoliento. —**somnolence,** *n.* somnolencia.
son (sʌn) *n.* hijo.
sonar ('so·nar) *n.* sonar.
sonata (sə'na·tə) *n.* sonata.
song (sɔŋ) *n.* **1,** (short poem set to music) canción. **2,** (poetry) poesía. **3,** (act or sound of singing) canto; cantar. —**for a song,** muy barato.
songbird *n.* cantor (*fem.* cantatriz; cantora); ave canora.
songbook *n.* cancionero.
songster ('sɔŋ·stər) *n.* cantor; cantante; cancionista. —**songstress** (-strəs) *n.* cantora; cantatriz; cancionista.
sonic ('san·ɪk) *adj.* sónico.
son-in-law *n.* [*pl.* **sons-in-law**] yerno; hijo político.
sonnet ('san·ɪt) *n.* soneto. —**sonneteer** (-ə'tɪr) *n.* sonetista.
sonny ('sʌn·i) *n.* hijito.
sonorous (sə'nor·əs) *adj.* sonoro; resonante. —**sonority,** *n.* sonoridad.
soon (su:n) *adv.* pronto. —**as soon as,** luego que; tan pronto como; apenas. —**how soon?,** ¿cuándo? —**soon after,** poco después (de).
sooner ('su·nər) *adv., comp. de* **soon;** más pronto; antes; mejor. —**I would** (*o* **had**) **sooner die,** antes la muerte; preferiría morir. —**no sooner said than done,** dicho y hecho. **sooner or later,** tarde o temprano; a la corta o a la larga. —**the sooner the better,** cuanto antes mejor.
soonest ('sun·əst) *adv., superl. de* **soon;** lo más pronto. —**at the soonest,** cuanto antes.
soot (sʊt) *n.* hollín; tizne. —**sooty,** *adj.* holliniento; tiznado.

sooth (suθ) *n., archaic* verdad.
soothsayer *n.* adivino; adivinador.
soothe (suːð) *v.t.* **1,** (calm; mollify) calmar; apaciguar. **2,** (allay; mitigate) aliviar; mitigar; sosegar.
sop (sap) *n.* **1,** (something dipped in a liquid) sopa. **2,** (something given to appease) regalo; apaciguamiento. —*v.t.* [**sopped, sopping**] **1,** (dip; soak) empapar; ensopar. **2,** [*usu.* **sop up**] (absorb) embeber; absorber.
sophism ('saf·ɪz·əm) *n.* sofisma.
sophist ('saf·ɪst) *n.* sofista. —**sophistic** (sə'fɪs·tɪk) *adj.* sofista.
sophisticate (sə'fɪs·tɪ·keit) *v.t.* hacer mundano. —*n.* (-kət) persona mundana. —**sophisticated** (-ˌkei·tɪd) *adj.* mundano. —**sophistication** (-'kei·ʃən) *n.* mundanería.
sophistry ('saf·ɪs·tri) *n.* sofistería.
sophomore ('saf·ə·mor) *n.* estudiante de segundo año. —**sophomoric** (-'mor·ɪk) *adj.* juvenil; inmaduro.
-sophy (sə·fi) *sufijo* -sofía; ciencia; conocimiento: *philosophy,* filosofía.
soporific (ˌsap·ə'rɪf·ɪk) *adj. & n.* soporífero.
sopping ('sap·ɪŋ) *adj.* empapado; ensopado. —**sopping wet,** empapado; ensopado; calado hasta los huesos.
soppy ('sap·i) *adj.* **1,** (soaked) empapado; ensopado. **2,** (rainy) lluvioso.
soprano (sə'præn·o) *n.* [*pl.* **-os**] soprano. —*adj.* de soprano.
sorcery ('sor·sə·ri) *n.* hechicería; brujería. —**sorcerer,** *n.* hechicero; brujo. —**sorceress,** *n.* hechicera; bruja.
sordid ('sor·dɪd) *adj.* sórdido. —**sordidness,** *n.* sordidez.
sore (soːr) *adj.* **1,** (sensitive; painful) dolorido; inflamado; enconado; tierno. **2,** (suffering pain) afligido; apenado. **3,** *colloq.* (offended; angry) enojado; ofendido; picado. —*n.* herida; llaga; úlcera. —**soreness,** *n.* dolor; dolencia; inflamación.
sorehead *n., colloq.* persona resentida; persona susceptible.
sorghum ('sor·gəm) *n.* sorgo; zahína.
sorority (sə'ror·ə·ti) *n.* hermandad de mujeres.
sorrel ('sar·əl) *n.* **1,** (plant) acedera. **2,** (color) rojizo; alazán. **3,** (horse) alazán. —*adj.* rojizo; alazán.
sorrow ('sar·o) *n.* pesar; tristeza; dolor; pena. —*v.i.* entristecerse; apenarse. —**sorrowful,** *adj.* triste; afligido; pesaroso.
sorry ('sar·i) *adj.* **1,** (feeling sorrow) triste; pesaroso; afligido. **2,** (feeling regret) arrepentido. **3,** (feeling pity) compasivo. **4,** (deplorable) triste; malo; lastimoso. **5,** (worthless; mean) vil; despreciable. —**be** *o* **feel sorry,** sentir; compadecer: *I am sorry,* Lo siento; *I am very sorry,* Lo siento mucho; *I am sorry for her,* La compadezco; *I am sorry to do this,* Siento hacer esto.
sort (sort) *n.* **1,** (class) clase; especie. **2,** (character) tipo. **3,** (way; fashion) estilo; manera; modo. —*v.t.* **1,** (classify) clasificar. **2,** (separate) separar; escoger; entresacar. —**after a sort,** de cierto modo; hasta cierto punto. —**all sorts of,** toda clase de. —**of sorts, 1,** (of various kinds) de varias clases. **2,** (mediocre) de poco valor. —**sort of,** *colloq.* algo; más o menos. —**out of sorts,** indispuesto; malhumorado.
sortie ('sor·ti) *n.* salida.
so-so *adj.* mediano; pasadero; regular. —*adv.* así así; medianamente; regularmente.
sot (sat) *n.* zaque; beodo; borrachín.
soubriquet ('so·brɪˌkei; 'su-) *n.* = **sobriquet**.
soufflé (su'flei) *n.* flan.
sought (sɔt) *v., pret. & p.p. de* **seek**.
soul (soːl) *n.* **1,** (spirit) alma; espíritu. **2,** (courage) ánimo; fuerza. **3,** (human being) ser humano. —**soulful,** *adj.* conmovedor; espiritual. —**soulless,** *adj.* desalmado; sin conciencia.
sound (saund) *n.* **1,** (vibration perceived by the ear) sonido. **2,** (noise) ruido. **3,** (inlet) brazo de mar. **4,** (strait) estrecho. —*adj.* **1,** (in good health or condition) sano. **2,** (unhurt) ileso. **3,** (whole; unimpaired) entero; perfecto. **4,** (firm; strong; solid) firme; fuerte;

sólido. **5,** (financially solvent) solvente. **6,** (reliable) confiable; seguro. **7,** (honorable) honrado; recto. —*v.i.* **1,** (make a sound; be heard) sonar. **2,** (make a noise) hacer ruido. **3,** (seem; appear) parecer. **4,** (measure depth of water) sondar; sondear. —*v.t.* **1,** (cause to sound) tocar; sonar. **2,** (utter) proferir; enunciar; pronunciar. **3,** (measure the depth of) sondar; sondear. **4,** (probe) tentar; examinar; investigar. —*adv.* profundamente. —**of sound mind**, en su juicio cabal. —**sound effects**, efectos sonoros. —**sound film**, película sonora. —**sound off**, **1,** (count) contar. **2,** *slang* (speak) hablar; parlotear. —**sound out**, tantear. —**sound sleep**, sueño profundo. —**sound track**, banda *o* guía sonora. —**sound wave**, onda sonora.

sounding ('saun·dɪŋ) *adj.* sonante; sonoro; resonante. —*n.* sondeo; sonda. —**sounding line**, sonda.

soundless ('saund·ləs) *adj.* **1,** (silent) silencioso; mudo. **2,** (unfathomable) insondable.

soundness ('saund·nəs) *n.* **1,** (good health or condition) sanidad; salud. **2,** (firmness; strength) firmeza; fuerza; solidez. **3,** (wholeness) entereza; perfección. **4,** (solvency) solvencia. **5,** (reliability) seguridad.

soundproof *adj.* a prueba de sonido.

soup (sup) *n.* **1,** (food) sopa. **2,** *slang* (nitroglycerin) nitroglicerina. —**in the soup**, *slang* en apuros; en aprietos. —**soup dish** *o* **plate**, plato sopero. —**soup ladle**, cucharón. —**soup spoon**, cuchara de sopa.

soupy ('su·pi) *adj.* **1,** (thin, as gruel) claro. **2,** (thick, as fog) pegajoso; espeso.

sour (saur) *adj.* **1,** (having an acid or tart taste) agrio; ácido; acre; áspero. **2,** (unpleasant) desagradable; enfadoso; malhumorado. —*v.t.* agriar; avinagrar; fermentar. —*v.i.* agriarse; avinagrarse; cortarse; fermentar. —**sour grapes**, uvas verdes.

source (sors) *n.* fuente; origen.

sour cream crema cortada.

sourdough *n.* **1,** (leaven) levadura. **2,** (prospector) buscador.

sourness ('saur·nəs) *n.* **1,** (sour or harsh taste) agrura; acidez; aspereza. **2,** (unpleasantness) mal humor; acrimonia.

souse (saus) *v.t.* **1,** (drench; soak) mojar; chapuzar. **2,** (pickle) escabechar; poner en escabeche; adobar. **3,** *slang* (intoxicate) embriagar. —*n., slang* (drunkard) borrachín; borracho.

south (sauθ) *n.* sur; sud; mediodía. —*adj.* sur; del sur; meridional. —*adv.* al sur; hacia el sur.

southeast *n.* sudeste; sureste. —*adj.* del *o* hacia el sudeste. —*adv.* al *o* hacia el sudeste.

southeaster *n.* viento (del) sudeste.

southeasterly *adj.* (del) sudeste. —*adv.* hacia el sudeste.

southeastern *adj.* (del) sudeste.

southerly ('sʌð·ər·li) *adj.* sur; del sur; hacia el sur. —*adv.* hacia el sur.

southern ('sʌð·ərn) *adj.* sur; del sur; meridional; sureño. —**southerner**, *n.* sureño; habitante del sur. —**southern lights** aurora austral.

southland ('sauθ·lənd) *n.* tierras del sur; sur; mediodía.

southpaw *n. & adj., slang* zurdo.

South Pole polo sur.

southward ('sauθ·wərd) *adj.* en *o* de dirección sur. —*adv.* hacia el sur.

southwest *n.* sudoeste; suroeste. —*adj.* del *o* hacia el sudoeste. —*adv.* al *o* hacia el sudoeste.

southwester *n.* viento (del) sudoeste.

southwesterly *adj.* (del) sudoeste. —*adv.* hacia el sudoeste.

southwestern *adj.* (del) sudoeste.

souvenir (ˌsu·vəˈnɪr) *n.* recuerdo.

sovereign ('sav·rɪn) *n.* **1,** (ruler) soberano. **2,** (Brit. coin) moneda inglesa de oro del valor de una libra esterlina. —*adj.* soberano; supremo. —**sovereignty**, *n.* soberanía.

soviet ('so·vi·ɛt) *n.* soviet; *pl.* soviets *o* soviéticos. —*adj.* soviético.

sow (soː) *v.t. & i.* [*p.p.* **sowed** *o* **sown**] sembrar. —**sow one's wild oats**, correr sus mocedades.

sow (sau) *n.* puerca.

sower ('so·ər) *n.* sembrador.
sowing ('so·ɪŋ) *n.* siembra.
soy (sɔi) *n.* soya; soja. *También,* **soya** ('sɔ·jə).
soybean *n.* semilla de soya.
spa (spaː) *n.* balneario de aguas minerales.
space (speis) *n.* espacio. —*v.t.* espaciar. —*adj.* espacial; del espacio.
spacecraft *n.* nave del espacio; astronave.
spaceman *n.* [*pl.* **-men**] astronauta.
spaceship *n.* nave del espacio; astronave.
spacious ('spei·ʃəs) *adj.* espacioso. —**spaciousness,** *n.* espaciosidad.
spade (speid) *n.* **1,** (garden tool) pala; laya. **2,** (sapper's tool) zapa. **3,** *cards* pique (*in the French deck*); espada (*in the Spanish deck*). —*v.t.* labrar con la pala; layar.
spadework *n.* trabajo preliminar.
spaghetti (spə'gɛt·i) *n.* fideos (*pl.*).
spahi ('spa·hi) *n.* espahí.
span (spæn) *n.* **1,** (extent) extensión; espacio; alcance; distancia. **2,** (distance from thumb to forefinger) palmo. **3,** (bridge) puente. **4,** (distance traversed by a bridge) luz de puente. **5,** (opening of an arch) ojo. **6,** (pair of draft animals) par; pareja. **7,** (wing length) envergadura. —*v.t.* [**spanned, spanning**] **1,** (measure) medir a palmos; medir. **2,** (traverse) atravesar; cruzar. **3,** (comprise; include) abarcar; abrazar.
spangle ('spæŋ·gəl) *n.* lentejuela; bricho. —*v.t.* adornar con lentejuelas; estrellar.
Spaniard ('spæn·jərd) *n.* español.
spaniel ('spæn·jəl) *n.* perro de aguas.
Spanish ('spæn·ɪʃ) *adj.* & *n.* español.
Spanish-American *adj.* & *n.* hispanoamericano.
Spanish Main el mar de las Antillas.
spank (spæŋk) *n.* nalgada. —*v.t.* dar nalgadas. —*v.i.* correr; ir de prisa.
spanker ('spæŋk·ər) *n.* **1,** *colloq.* (large or outstanding thing) cosa muy grande o hermosa o de mucho éxito. **2,** *naut.* cangreja de popa.
spanking ('spæŋk·ɪŋ) *n.* nalgada; tunda. —*adj., colloq.* **1,** (swift) veloz; ligero. **2,** (very large or outstanding) muy grande o hermoso. **3,** (strong) fuerte; robusto.
spanner ('spæn·er) *n., Brit.* desvolvedor; llave.
spar (spaːr) *n.* **1,** *naut.* verga. **2,** *aero.* viga mayor. **3,** (mineral) espato. —*v.i.* [**sparred, sparring**] **1,** (box cautiously) boxear; atrancar. **2,** (dispute) disputar; reñir; pelear.
spare (speːr) *v.t.* **1,** (show mercy to) perdonar; hacer gracia de; permitir vivir. **2,** (refrain from) abstenerse de; refrenarse de. **3,** (dispense with) pasarse sin. **4,** (have available) disponer de; tener disponible. **5,** (skimp; save) escatimar; ahorrar; economizar. —*v.i.* economizar. —*adj.* **1,** (in excess) de sobra; sobrante. **2,** (in reserve) de recambio; de repuesto. **3,** (available) disponible. **4,** (lean) flaco; delgado. **5,** (meager) escaso; mezquino. **6,** (frugal) ahorrativo. —*n.* pieza de recambio *o* de repuesto. —**have (time, money,** *etc.*) **to spare,** tener (tiempo, dinero, *etc.*) de sobra. —**spare no expense,** no escatimar gastos. —**spare part,** pieza de recambio *o* de repuesto. —**spare time,** tiempo desocupado; ratos perdidos.
sparerib *n.* costilla de cerdo casi descarnada; costilla superior.
sparing ('spɛr·ɪŋ) *adj.* **1,** (scanty) escaso; poco; limitado. **2,** (economical) ahorrativo; frugal; económico.
spark (spark) *n.* **1,** (fiery particle) chispa. **2,** (glimmer) vislumbre; destello. **3,** *colloq.* (suitor) galán. **4,** (dandy) petimetre; pisaverde. —*v.i.* chispear; echar chispas. —*v.t.* **1,** (kindle; motivate) animar; despertar; excitar. **2,** *colloq.* (court; woo) galantear; cortejar.
sparkle ('spar·kəl) *v.i.* **1,** (emit little sparks) chispear; centellear. **2,** (glitter) relucir. **3,** (effervesce) espumar; ser espumoso. **4,** (be vivacious) brillar; destellar; ser vivaz. —*n.* **1,** (small spark) chispita. **2,** (brilliance) esplendor;

brillo. **3,** (vivacity) brillo; destello; vivacidad.
sparkler ('spar·klər) *n.* **1,** (something that sparkles) centelleador. **2,** (diamond) brillante; diamante.
sparkling ('spar·klɪŋ) *adj.* **1,** (emitting sparks) chispeante; centelleante. **2,** (effervescent) espumoso.
spark plug bujía.
sparrow ('spær·o) *n.* gorrión. —**sparrow hawk,** gavilán.
sparse (spars) *adj.* **1,** (thinly distributed) poco denso; esparcido. **2,** (thin; scanty) escaso. —**sparseness; sparsity,** *n.* escasez.
Spartan ('spar·tən) *adj.* & *n.* espartano.
spasm ('spæz·əm) *n.* espasmo.
spasmodic (spæz'mad·ɪk) *adj.* espasmódico.
spastic ('spæs·tɪk) *adj.* & *n.* espástico.
spat (spæt) *n.* **1,** (petty dispute) riña; disputa. **2,** (light blow) palmadita; manotada. **3,** (splash, as of rain) gota grande de lluvia; gotereo. **4,** *usu.pl.* (short cloth gaiters) polainas. **5,** (young oyster) ostra joven. —*v.i.* [**spatted, spatting**] (quarrel) reñir; pelear. —*v.t.* (strike lightly) dar palmaditas o manotadas. —*v., pret. & p.p. de* **spit.**
spate (speit) *n.* crecida; torrente.
spatial ('spei·ʃəl) *adj.* espacial.
spatter ('spæt·ər) *v.t.* & *i.* **1,** (scatter or sprinkle in small drops) rociar; regar. **2,** (splash) salpicar; manchar. —*n.* salpicadura; rociada.
spatula ('spætʃ·ə·lə) *n.* espátula.
spawn (spɔːn) *n.* **1,** (eggs or young of fishes, etc.) freza; huevos; pececillos. **2,** (offspring) cría; prole. **3,** *fig.* (result) resultado; fruto. —*v.i.* poner huevos; desovar; frezar. —*v.t.* producir en abundancia; engendrar; procrear.
spay (spei) *v.t.* castrar (hembras); sacar los ovarios a.
speak (spik) *v.t.* & *i.* [**spoke, spoken, speaking**] hablar. —*v.t.* **1,** (say) decir. **2,** (utter; pronounce) proferir; pronunciar. —**so to speak,** por decirlo así. —**speak for itself,** ser manifiesto; ser claro. —**speak one's mind,** decir lo que piensa; hablar sin rodeos. —**speak out,** hablar claro; elevar la voz. —**speak thickly,** hablar con media lengua. —**speak through the nose,** ganguear. —**speak to the point,** ir al grano. —**speak up,** hablar alto.
speakeasy ('spik·i·zi) *n., slang* taberna ilegal.
speaker ('spik·ər) *n.* **1,** (one who speaks) el que habla. **2,** (participant in a conversation) interlocutor. **3,** (orator) orador. **4,** (lecturer) conferenciante. **5,** (presiding officer) presidente. **6,** (loudspeaker) altavoz; *Amer.* altoparlante. —**speaker of Spanish, English,** *etc.*, persona de habla española, inglesa, *etc.*
speaking ('spi·kɪŋ) *adj.* hablante. —*n.* **1,** (speech) habla. **2,** (oratory) oratoria; elocuencia. —*interj.* (*in answering the telephone*) ¡al habla! —**English-speaking, Spanish-speaking,** *etc., adj.* de habla inglesa, española, *etc.*
spear (spɪr) *n.* **1,** (weapon) lanza. **2,** *bot.* tallo. —*v.t.* lancear; dar lanzadas.
spearhead *n.* **1,** (point of a spear) punta de lanza. **2,** *fig.* (leader) lancero; líder.
spearmint *n.* hierbabuena puntiaguda; menta verde.
special ('spɛʃ·əl) *adj.* especial; particular. —**special delivery,** correspondencia urgente.
specialist ('spɛʃ·ə·lɪst) *n.* especialista.
specialize ('spɛʃ·əˌlaiz) *v.t.* especializar. —*v.i.* especializarse. —**specialization** (-lɪ'zei·ʃən) *n.* especialización.
specialty ('spɛʃ·əl·ti) *n.* especialidad.
specie ('spi·ʃi) *n.* dinero contante; efectivo; numerario.
species ('spi·ʃiz) *n.sing.* & *pl.* especie.
specific (spə'sɪf·ɪk) *adj.* & *n.* específico.
specify ('spɛs·əˌfai) *v.t.* especificar. —**specification** (-fɪ'kei·ʃən) *n.* especificación.
specimen ('spɛs·ə·mən) *n.* espécimen; muestra; ejemplar.
specious ('spi·ʃəs) *adj.* especioso; engañoso. —**speciousness,** *n.* especiosidad.
speck (spɛk) *n.* **1,** (spot) mácula; manchita. **2,** (small particle; bit)

partícula; mota; pizca. —*v.t.* manchar; salpicar.
speckle ('spɛk·əl) *n.* punto; mota. —*v.t.* motear; puntear; salpicar.
specs (spɛks) *n.pl., colloq.* = **spectacles.**
spectacle ('spɛk·tə·kəl) *n.* **1,** (sight; display) espectáculo. **2,** *pl.* (eyeglasses) anteojos; espejuelos; lentes; gafas.
spectacular (spɛk'tæk·jə·lər) *adj.* espectacular; ostentoso; aparatoso. —*n.* programa espectacular.
spectator ('spɛk·tei·tər) *n.* espectador.
specter *también,* **spectre** ('spɛk·tər) *n.* espectro; fantasma. —**spectral** (-trəl) *adj.* espectral.
spectroscope ('spɛk·trə·skop) *n.* espectroscopio. —**spectroscopic** (-'skap·ɪk) *adj.* espectroscópico.
spectrum ('spɛk·trəm) *n.* espectro.
speculate ('spɛk·jə,leit) *v.i.* especular. —**speculation,** *n.* especulación. —**speculative** (-lə·tɪv) *adj.* especulativo. —**speculator,** *n.* especulador.
sped (spɛd) *v., pret. & p.p. de* **speed.**
speech (spitʃ) *n.* **1,** (power of speaking) habla. **2,** (address) discurso. **3,** (language) habla; idioma; lenguaje. **4,** (manner of speaking) lenguaje; manera de hablar. —**speechless,** *adj.* mudo; callado.
speed (spi:d) *n.* **1,** (rapidity or rate of motion) velocidad; rapidez. **2,** (haste) prisa. **3,** (promptness) presteza; prontitud. —*v.t.* [*pret. & p.p.* **speeded** *o* **sped**] **1,** (expedite) acelerar; apresurar; dar prisa; expedir. **2,** [*usu.* **speed up**] (increase the speed of) acelerar; avivar. **3,** (send) despedir; despachar. —*v.i.* **1,** (move rapidly) correr; apresurarse; darse prisa. **2,** [*usu.* **speed up**] (increase speed) acelerar. **3,** (go too fast) ir con exceso de velocidad. —**at full speed,** a carrera tendida; a toda velocidad; a todo correr. —**full speed,** galope; carrera tendida. —**make speed,** acelerarse; apresurarse. —**speed limit,** velocidad máxima.
speedboat *n.* lancha de carreras.
speeder ('spi·dər) *n.* **1,** (person or thing that moves fast) persona o cosa que corre a gran velocidad. **2,** (driver who exceeds the speed limit) automovilista que corre a velocidad excesiva.
speeding ('spi·dɪŋ) *n.* **1,** (acceleration) aceleración. **2,** (excessive speed) exceso de velocidad; extravelocidad.
speedometer (spi'dam·ɪ·tər) *n.* velocímetro; celerímetro.
speed-up *n., colloq.* aceleramiento; aceleración.
speedway *n.* carretera abierta.
speedy ('spid·i) *adj.* veloz; rápido; ligero.
spell (spɛl) *v.t.* [*pret. & p.p.* **spelled** *o* **spelt**] **1,** (form or express by or in letters) deletrear; escribir. **2,** (signify; mean) significar; indicar. **3,** [*pret. & p.p.* **spelled**] (replace temporarily; relieve) revezar; reemplazar; relevar. —*v.i.* deletrear; saber deletrear; escribir con buena (*o* mala) ortografía. —*n.* **1,** (charm; enchantment) hechizo; encanto. **2,** (turn; shift) tanda; turno. **3,** (short period) rato; corto período; tiempito. **4,** *colloq.* (ailment) ataque (de una enfermedad). —**by spells,** a ratos; por turnos. —**put under a spell; cast a spell on,** hechizar; encantar. —**spell out, 1,** (write or pronounce by letters) deletrear. **2,** (explain in detail) detallar; explicar.
spellbinder *n.* orador hechizante.
spellbinding *adj.* hechizante; encantador.
spellbound *adj.* encantado; hechizado.
speller ('spɛl·ər) *n.* **1,** (one who spells) deletreador. **2,** (textbook) silabario; abecedario.
spelling ('spɛl·ɪŋ) *n.* deletreo; ortografía. —**spelling bee,** concurso de ortografía. —**spelling book** *o* **primer** ('prɪm·ər) silabario; abecedario.
spelt (spɛlt) *v., pret. & p.p. de* **spell.** —*n., bot.* espelta.
spend (spɛnd) *v.t. & i.* [*pret. & p.p.* **spent**] **1,** (expend; consume) gastar. **2,** (employ, as time) pasar. —**spender,** *n.* gastador.
spendthrift *n. & adj.* pródigo; derrochador; manirroto; *Amer.* botarate.
spent (spɛnt) *v., pret. & p.p. de* **spend.** —*adj.* **1,** (fatigued) cansado; extenuado. **2,** (used up) gastado; agotado; consumido.
sperm (spʌɹm) *n.* esperma.
-sperm (spʌɹm) *sufijo* -sperma;

esperma; semilla: *gymnosperm,* gimnosperma.
spermato- (spʌɹ·mə·to; -tə) *prefijo* espermato-; esperma; semilla: *spermatogenesis,* espermatogénesis.
sperm whale cachalote.
spew (spjuː) *v.t. & i.* vomitar; arrojar; escupir. —*n.* vómito.
sphere (sfɪr) *n.* esfera. —**spherical** ('sfɛr·ɪ·kəl) *adj.* esférico.
sphero- (sfɪr·o) *prefijo* esfero-; esfera; relacionado con la esfera: *spherometer,* esferómetro.
spheroid ('sfɪr·ɔid) *n.* esferoide. —**spheroidal** (sfɪ'rɔi·dəl) *adj.* esferoidal.
sphinx (sfɪŋks) *n.* esfinge.
spice (spais) *n.* **1,** (seasoning) especia; condimento. **2,** (zest; piquancy) picante; gusto; saborete. **3,** (cream; choice part) nata; flor y nata. —*v.t.* **1,** (season) especiar; condimentar; sazonar. **2,** (add zest to) dar picante o gusto a. —**spicy,** *adj.* especiado; condimentado; picante; sabroso.
spick-and-span ('spɪk·ən·'spæn) *adj.* limpio; puro; flamante.
spider ('spai·dər) *n.* araña. —**spider web,** telaraña.
spiel (spiːl) *n., slang* discurso persuasivo; arenga. —*v.i.* arengar. —**spieler,** *n.* vociferador.
spigot ('spɪg·ət) *n.* llave; grifo; espita.
spike (spaik) *n.* **1,** (large nail) clavo largo; perno; alcayata. **2,** (sharp-pointed projection) resalto; punta. **3,** *bot.* espiga. —*v.t.* **1,** (pierce or fasten with spikes) empernar; clavar. **2,** (frustrate) frustrar. **3,** (put an end to) acabar; poner fin a. **4,** (add liquor to) añadir licor a.
spikenard ('spaik·nərd) *n.* nardo; espicanardo.
spill (spɪl) *v.t.* [*pret. & p.p.* **spilled** *o* **spilt**] verter; derramar. —*v.i.* derramarse; perderse; rebosar. —*n.* **1,** (flowing or running out) derrame; derramamiento. **2,** (upset) vuelco. **3,** *colloq.* (fall, as from a horse) caída. —**spill the beans,** *slang* revelar el secreto.
spillway *n.* bocacaz; vertedero.
spilt (spɪlt) *v., pret. & p.p. de* **spill.**
spin (spɪn) *v.t.* [**spun, spinning**] **1,** (twist into threads) hilar. **2,** (make with threads; weave) tejer. **3,** (cause to revolve rapidly) hacer girar. **4,** (narrate) contar, esp. cuentos largos e increíbles. —*v.i.* **1,** (revolve rapidly) girar; dar vueltas. **2,** (move or ride rapidly) rodar. —*n.* **1,** (spinning motion; spiral course) giro; vuelta. **2,** (rapid ride) paseo. **3,** *aero.* barrena. —**spin out,** alargar; prolongar. —**take a spin; go for a spin,** dar un paseo; dar una vuelta.
spinach ('spɪn·ɪtʃ) *n.* **1,** (plant) espinaca. **2,** (leaves used as food) espinacas (*pl.*).
spinal ('spai·nəl) *adj.* espinal. —**spinal column,** columna vertebral; espina dorsal. —**spinal cord,** médula espinal.
spindle ('spɪn·dəl) *n.* **1,** (for spinning) huso. **2,** (shaft; axle) eje; árbol. —**spindling** (-dlɪŋ) **spindly** (-dli) *adj.* largo y delgado; flaco.
spindle-legged *adj.* zanquilargo. *También,* **spindle-shanked.**
spine (spain) *n.* **1,** (backbone) dorsal; espinazo. **2,** (quill; thorn) espina; púa. **3,** (stiff backing, as of a book) lomo. —**spineless,** *adj.* pusilánime; cobarde.
spinet ('spɪn·ɪt) *n.* espineta.
spinner ('spɪn·ər) *n.* **1,** (person) hilador; hilandera (*fem.*). **2,** (machine) máquina hiladora; máquina de hilar.
spinning ('spɪn·ɪŋ) *n.* hilandería. —*adj.* hilador. —**spinning machine,** máquina hiladora; máquina de hilar. —**spinning mill,** hilandería. —**spinning wheel,** torno de hilar.
spinster ('spɪn·stər) *n.* soltera; solterona. —**spinsterhood,** *n.* soltería.
spiny ('spai·ni) *adj.* espinoso.
spiral ('spai·rəl) *n.* espiral. —*adj.* enrollado; acaracolado; espiral. —*v.i.* moverse *o* volar en espiral. —**spiral staircase,** escalera espiral *o* de caracol.
spire (spair) *n.* **1,** *archit.* aguja. **2,** (coil) espira. **3,** (spike; stalk) tallo.
spirit ('spɪr·ɪt) *n.* **1,** (inspiring principle; soul) espíritu; alma. **2,** (nature) carácter; genio. **3,** (attitude; disposition) humor; temple. **4,** *usu. pl.* (vivacity; optimism) viveza; vivacidad; alegría. **5,** *usu. pl.* (courage) ánimo; valor. **6,** (ghost) espectro; fantasma. **7,** *pl.*

(distillate) extracto; quintaesencia. **8,** *pl.* (alcoholic liquor) alcohol; licor. —*v.t.* [*usu.* **spirit away** *o* **off**] llevar *o* conducir secretamente; arrebatar. —**be in good** *or* **high spirits**, estar alegre; estar de buen humor. —**be in low spirits; be low in spirit**, estar desanimado *o* abatido. —**good** *o* **high spirits**, alegría; vivacidad; buen humor. —**keep up one's spirits**, mantener el valor; no desanimarse. —**lose (one's) spirit**, desanimarse. —**low spirits**, abatimiento; decaimiento. —**out of spirits**, triste; abatido. —**show spirit**, mostrar buen ánimo.

spirited ('spɪr·ɪt·ɪd) *adj.* vivo; fogoso; animoso.

spirit lamp lámpara de alcohol.

spiritless ('spɪr·ɪt·ləs) *adj.* exánime; apocado; sin ánimo.

spirit level nivel de aire.

spiritual ('spɪr·ɪ·tʃu·əl) *adj.* espiritual. —*n.* canción negroide.

spiritualism ('spɪr·ɪ·tʃu·ə·lɪz·əm) *n.* espiritismo. —**spiritualist**, *n.* espiritista. —**spiritualistic**, *adj.* espiritista.

spirituous ('spɪr·ɪ·tʃu·əs) *adj.* espirituoso.

spiro- (spai·ro; -rə) *prefijo* espiro-. **1,** respiración: *spirometer*, espirómetro. **2,** espiral: *spirochet* espiroqueta.

spit (spɪt) *v.i.* & *t.* [*pret.* & *p.p.* **spat** *o* **spit**; *ger.* **spitting**] (eject, as saliva from the mouth) escupir; expectorar; esputar. —*v.t.* **1,** (spew out) vomitar; arrojar. **2,** [*pret.* & *p.p.* **spitted**] (impale on a sharp point) espetar. —*n.* **1,** (saliva) saliva; escupo. **2,** (sharp bar or stick) asador; espetón; varilla. **3,** (narrow point of land) punta *o* lengua de tierra. —**the spit and image of**, el retrato de.

spite (spait) *n.* despecho; rencor; inquina; malevolencia. —*v.t.* vejar; causar pesar; molestar. —**in spite of**, a pesar de; a despecho de; no obstante.

spiteful ('spait·fəl) *adj.* rencoroso; malicioso.

spittle ('spɪt·əl) *n.* saliva; esputo; escupo.

spittoon (spɪ'tuːn) *n.* escupidera.

spitz (spɪts) *n.* perro de Pomerania.

splash (splæʃ) *v.t.* **1,** (spatter, as with mud or water) enlodar; manchar. **2,** (dash; scatter about) salpicar; rociar. —*v.i.* chapotear; chapalear. —*n.* **1,** (act or sound of splashing) chapoteo; chapaleteo. **2,** (quantity splashed) salpicadura; rociada. **3,** (ostentatious display) ostentación; espectáculo.

splashy ('splæʃ·i) *adj.* **1,** (wet; muddy) fangoso; lodoso. **2,** *colloq.* (ostentatious) llamativo.

splatter ('splæt·ər) *v.t.* & *i.* & *n.* = **spatter.**

splay (splei) *v.t.* **1,** (bevel) achaflanar; biselar. **2,** (spread out) desplegar; extender. —*v.i.* desplegarse; extenderse. —*adj.* desplegado; extendido. —*n.* bisel; chaflán.

splayfoot *n.* pie aplastado y desplegado. —**splayfooted**, *adj.* que tiene los pies aplastados y desplegados.

spleen (spliːn) *n.* **1,** *anat.* bazo. **2,** (ill humor) mal humor; esplín; melancolía. **3,** (anger) ira; rencor. —**vent one's spleen**, descargar la bilis *o* el rencor.

splendid ('splɛn·dɪd) *adj.* espléndido. *También, colloq.*, **splendiferous** (-'dɪf·ə·rəs).

splendor *también,* **splendour** ('splɛn·dər) *n.* esplendor. —**splendorous**, *adj.* espléndido.

splenetic (splɪ'nɛt·ɪk) *adj.* bilioso; rencoroso.

splice (splais) *v.t.* empalmar; juntar. —*n.* empalme; juntura. —**get spliced**, *slang* casarse.

spline (splain) *n.* **1,** (flexible strip of wood) astilla; varilla flexible de madera o de metal. **2,** (slot; groove) ranura.

splint (splɪnt) *n.* astilla; tablilla; *surg.* cabestrillo. —*v.t.* entablillar.

splinter ('splɪn·tər) *n.* astilla. —*v.t.* astillar. —*v.i.* astillarse.

splinterproof *adj.* inastillable.

split (splɪt) *v.t.* [**split, splitting**] hendir; partir; dividir. —*v.i.* hendirse; partirse; dividirse. —*n.* **1,** (crack; rent) hendidura; grieta. **2,** (division; schism) división; separación; cisma. **3,** (half-bottle) media botella; botella pequeña. —*adj.* hendido; partido; dividido. —**split hairs**, pararse en pelillos. —**split one's sides with laughter,** desternillarse *o* reventar de risa.

splotch (splatʃ) *n.* mancha; borrón. —*v.t.* manchar; emborronar; salpicar.

splurge (splʌɹdʒ) *n.* ostentación; alarde. —*v.i.* alardear; hacer alarde.

splutter ('splʌt·ər) *v.t. & i.* farfullar. —*n.* farfulla.

spoil (spɔil) *v.t.* [*pret. & p.p.* **spoiled** *o* **spoilt**] **1,** (seriously impair) dañar; estropear; echar a perder. **2,** (overindulge, as a child) malcriar; mimar; corromper. **3,** (pervert) pervertir. **4,** (plunder; despoil) pillar; saquear; despojar. —*v.i.* podrirse; corromperse; echarse a perder. —**spoils,** *n.pl.* despojos; botín; presa. —**spoil for,** ansiar; anhelar.

spoilage ('spɔi·lɪdʒ) *n.* deterioro.

spoiled (spɔild) *adj.* consentido; mimado; engreído.

spoilsport ('spɔil,sport) *n.* aguafiestas.

spoke (spok) *n.* rayo de rueda. —*v., pret. de* **speak.**

spoken ('spo·kən) *v., p.p. de* **speak.** —*adj.* hablado.

spokesman ('spoks·mən) *n.* [*pl.* **-men**] portavoz.

spoliation (,spo·li'ei·ʃən) *n.* despojo.

sponge (spʌndʒ) *n.* esponja. —*v.t. & i.* **1,** (absorb; wipe up) esponjar; sorber. **2,** *colloq.* (live at another's expense) pegar la gorra; ir *o* andar de gorra. —**sponger,** *n., colloq.* gorrón; parásito. —**spongy,** *adj.* esponjoso; fofo.

sponge cake bizcocho ligero y esponjoso.

sponsor ('span·sər) *n.* **1,** (one who vouches or supports) patrocinador. **2,** (godfather; godmother) padrino; madrina. —*v.t.* **1,** (vouch for; support) patrocinar. **2,** (act as godparent for) apadrinar.

sponsorship ('span·sər·ʃɪp) *n.* **1,** (support; surety) patrocinio. **2,** (being a godparent) padrinazgo.

spontaneity (,span·tə'ni·ə·ti) *n.* espontaneidad.

spontaneous (span'tei·ni·əs) *adj.* espontáneo. —**spontaneousness,** *n.* espontaneidad.

spoof (spuf) *n., slang* engaño; broma; burla. —*v.t.* engañar; burlarse de. —*v.i.* bromear; burlar.

spook (spuk) *n., colloq.* fantasma; espectro. —**spooky,** *adj.* espectral; misterioso; horripilante.

spool (spu:l) *n.* carrete; canilla. —*v.t.* devanar.

spoon (spu:n) *n.* cuchara; cucharita; cucharón. —*v.i. colloq.* besuquearse; hocicarse.

spoonbill *n.* espátula.

spoonful ('spun,fʊl) *n.* cucharada; cucharadita.

spoony ('spu·ni) *adj. & n., colloq.* besucón.

spoor (spʊr) *n.* huella; pista.

sporadic (spo'ræd·ɪk) *adj.* esporádico.

spore (spo:r) *n.* espora; simiente.

sporo- (spor·ə) *prefijo* esporo-; espora: *sporocarp,* esporocarpio.

-sporous (spor·əs) *sufijo* -sporo; que tiene esporas: *gymnosporous,* gimnosporo.

sport (sport) *n.* **1,** (game; athletic activity) deporte. **2,** (fun; diversion) pasatiempo; diversión; placer. **3,** (jesting) broma; burla. **4,** (plaything) juguete. **5,** (object of ridicule) hazmerreír. **6,** *colloq.* (gambler) jugador. **7,** *colloq.* (sportsmanlike person) jugador generoso; buen perdedor. **8,** (sportsman) deportista. **9,** *colloq.* (flashy person) guapo; petimetre. **10,** *colloq.* (good companion) compañero; compadre. **11,** *biol.* mutante. —*adj.* deportivo; de deporte. —*v.t. colloq.* vestir; lucir; ostentar. —*v.i.* **1,** (play) jugar; divertirse. **2,** (jest; trifle) burlar; bromear. **3,** *biol.* hacer *o* producir mutación. —**make sport of,** burlarse de.

sporting ('spor·tɪŋ) *adj.* deportivo; de juego; de deporte.

sportive ('spor·tɪv) *adj.* festivo; juguetón.

sports (sports) *adj.* deportivo; de deporte.

sportsman ('sports·mən) *n.* [*pl.* **-men**] deportista.

sportsmanlike *adj.* de deportista; de buen jugador.

sportsmanship *n.* arte y pericia en el deporte; afición a los deportes.

sportswear ('sports,wɛr) *n.* traje (*o* trajes) de deporte.

sportswoman *n.* [*pl.* **-women**] deportista.

sporty ('spor·ti) *adj., colloq.* **1,** (sporting) deportivo. **2,** (flashy) guapo; llamativo.

spot (spat) *n.* **1,** (stain; blemish)

mancha. **2,** (small mark or speck) marca; mota. **3,** (place) sitio; lugar. **4,** *colloq.* (small amount) poquito; pizca. **5,** *colloq.* = **spotlight.** —*v.t.* [**spotted, -ting**] **1,** (stain) manchar. **2,** (mark with specks) motear; salpicar. **3,** (place; locate) colocar; localizar; poner. **4,** (recognize; espy) reconocer; avistar. **5,** (scatter; distribute) esparcir; diseminar. **6,** (remove stains from) limpiar; quitar manchas de. **7,** *colloq.* (give a handicap of *o* to) dar una ventaja de *o* a. —*v.i.* **1,** (become spotted) mancharse. **2,** (cause spots) manchar; producir manchas. —*adj.* **1,** (at hand) a mano; disponible. **2,** (ready, as money) contante; efectivo. —**hit the spot,** *colloq.* **1,** (strike the mark) dar en el blanco. **2,** (satisfy) dar satisfacción. —**in a spot,** en apuro; en un aprieto. —**in spots,** aquí y allí. —**on the spot, 1,** (in a given place) allí mismo. **2,** (at once) al punto; en el acto. **3,** = **in a spot.** —**touch a sore spot,** dar en lo vivo.

spot check examen casual *o* al azar.

spotless (ˈspat·ləs) *adj.* inmaculado; limpio.

spotlight *n.* **1,** (light) foco; proyector; luz concentrada. **2,** (public notice) atención del público.

spotted (ˈspat·ɪd) *adj.* moteado; abigarrado.

spotter (ˈspat·ər) *n.* apuntador.

spotty (ˈspat·i) *adj.* **1,** (covered with spots) manchado. **2,** (uneven) desigual; irregular.

spouse (spaus) *n.* cónyuge.

spout (spaut) *v.t.* **1,** (discharge in a stream) arrojar *o* echar en chorro. **2,** (declaim) declamar. —*v.i.* **1,** (flow in a stream) chorrear; salir en chorro. **2,** (speak pompously) declamar; perorar. —*n.* **1,** (stream) chorro. **2,** (tube for carrying off rain) canelón. **3,** (device for pouring or drawing a liquid) pitón; caño; (*of a coffee pot or teapot*) pico.

sprain (sprein) *n.* torcedura. —*v.t.* torcer.

sprang (spræŋ) *v., pret. de* **spring.**

sprawl (sprɔːl) *v.i.* tenderse; arrellanarse; arrastrarse. —*n.* arrastrada.

spray (sprei) *n.* **1,** (fine liquid particles) rociada; rocío; espuma del mar. **2,** (atomizer) rociadera; rociador. **3,** (branch) rama. —*v.t. & i.* rociar. —**sprayer,** *n.* rociadera. —**spray gun,** rociadera; pulverizadora.

spread (sprɛd) *v.t. & i.* [*pret. & p.p.* **spread**] **1,** (open or stretch out; unfold) tender(se); extender(se); desplegar(se). **2,** (scatter) esparcir(se); desparramar(se). **3,** (set out; display) exhibir; poner a la vista. **4,** (push apart) apartar(se); abrir(se). **5,** (smear) untar. **6,** (disseminate) propagar(se); difundir(se). **7,** (prepare, as a table) poner (la mesa). —*n.* **1,** (extension; expansion) extensión. **2,** (expanse) espacio; extensión. **3,** (feast) banquete; festín. **4,** (coverlet) colcha; cobertor (de cama). **5,** (difference) diferencia; discrepancia. **6,** (wingspread) envergadura. **7,** (something on) capa; jalea, mantequilla, queso, etc. que se unta al pan.

spree (spriː) *n.* jarana; juerga; parranda; borrachera. —**go on a spree,** ir de juerga; echar una borrachera.

sprig (sprɪg) *n.* **1,** (branch) rama; ramita. **2,** (lad) joven; jovencito; mozuelo.

sprightly (ˈsprait·li) *adj.* vivo; vivaracho; animado. —*adv.* vivamente; con viveza. —**sprightliness,** *n.* viveza; vivacidad.

spring (sprɪŋ) *v.i.* [**sprang, sprung, springing**] **1,** (leap) saltar; brincar. **2,** (rise up; issue forth suddenly) salir; brotar; emanar; nacer. **3,** (warp) combarse; encorvarse. **4,** (be suddenly released) soltarse de golpe. —*v.t.* **1,** (release suddenly) soltar. **2,** (cause to leap) hacer saltar. **3,** (warp) torcer; combar; encorvar. **4,** (present or make known suddenly) dar (descubrir, echar, etc.) de sopetón. **5,** *slang* (provide bail for) poner fianza por. —*n.* **1,** (leap) salto; brinco. **2,** (season) primavera. **3,** (device for applying tension) muelle; resorte. **4,** (elasticity) elasticidad. **5,** (water rising from the ground) fuente; manantial. **6,** (source) fuente; origen. —*adj.* **1,** (motivated by tension) de muelle; de resorte. **2,**

(of springtime) primaveral. **3,** (flowing up from the ground) de manantial. **—spring a leak,** hacer agua; abrirse una vía de agua en. **—spring fever,** ataque primaveral. **—spring lock,** cerradura de golpe *o* de muelle. **—spring mattress,** colchón de muelles. **—spring tide,** marea fuerte; aguas vivas.

springboard *n.* trampolín.

spring coat abrigo de entretiempo.

springer ('sprɪŋ·ər) *n.* perro de España; perro de caza.

springtime *n.* primavera; época primaveral. *También,* **springtide.**

springy ('sprɪŋ·i) *adj.* elástico; ágil. **—springiness,** *n.* elasticidad.

sprinkle ('sprɪŋ·kəl) *v.t.* **1,** (scatter in drops or particles) regar; rociar; esparcir. **2,** (strew) salpicar. *—v.i.* lloviznar; caer en gotas. *—n.* **1,** (light rain) llovizna. **2,** (scattering in drops or particles) rociada. **3,** (small amount) poquito; pizca.

sprinkler ('sprɪŋ·klər) *n.* regadera; rociadera.

sprinkling ('sprɪŋ·klɪŋ) *n.* **1,** (scattering in drops) rociada; aspersión. **2,** (small amount) poco; pizca. **3,** (light rain) llovizna.

sprint (sprɪnt) *n.* carrera corta a toda velocidad. *—v.i.* correr a toda velocidad.

sprit (sprɪt) *n., naut.* botavara.

sprite (sprait) *n.* duende; hada.

sprocket ('sprak·ɪt) *n.* diente de rueda de cadena. **—sprocket wheel,** rueda de cadena.

sprout (spraut) *v.i.* brotar; retoñar. *—v.t.* hacer brotar; crecer. *—n.* brote; retoño; renuevo.

spruce (sprus) *adj.* pulido; pulcro; elegante. *—v.t. & i.* pulir(se); engalanar(se). *—n.* abeto rojo; picea.

spry (sprai) *adj.* listo; vivo; ágil. **—spryness,** *n.* agilidad; viveza.

spud (spʌd) *n.* **1,** (chisel) escoplo. **2,** (weeding hoe) escarda. **3,** *colloq.* (potato) patata; papa.

spume (spjuːm) *v.t. & i.* espumar. *—n.* espuma.

spun (spʌn) *v., pret. & p.p. de* **spin.**

spunk (spʌŋk) *n., colloq.* coraje; valor; ánimo. **—spunky,** *adj.* valiente; valeroso.

spur (spʌɹ) *n.* **1,** (of a horseman) espuela. **2,** (of a gamecock) espolón. **3,** (of a mountain) estribo; espolón. **4,** (branch line) ramal. **5,** *fig.* (stimulus) estímulo; espuela. *—v.t.* **1,** (goad; urge on) espolear. **2,** (incite) picar; incitar; estimular. *—v.i.* apretar el paso. **—on the spur of the moment,** de repente; sin reflexión. **—spur on,** espolear. **—win one's spurs,** ganar la dignidad de caballero; llevarse la palma.

spurious ('spjʊr·i·əs) *adj.* espurio; falso; ilegítimo. **—spuriousness,** *n.* falsedad.

spurn (spʌɹn) *v.t.* rechazar; desdeñar; menospreciar.

spurt (spʌɹt) *n.* **1,** (gush of liquid) chorro. **2,** (short, sudden effort) impulso; arranque; esfuerzo repentino. *—v.i.* **1,** (gush) chorrear. **2,** (make a sudden effort) esforzarse repentinamente; hacer un esfuerzo repentino. *—v.t.* echar en chorro; hacer salir en chorro.

sputter ('spʌt·ər) *v.i.* **1,** (sizzle) chisporrotear. **2,** (speak rapidly and confusedly) farfullar. *—v.t.* farfullar; enunciar farfullando. *—n.* **1,** (sizzling) chisporroteo. **2,** (rapid, confused utterance) farfulla.

sputum ('spju·təm) *n.* [*pl.* **-ta** (tə)] esputo.

spy (spai) *n.* espía. *—v.i.* espiar. *—v.t.* **1,** (watch furtively) espiar; atisbar. **2,** (discover) divisar; columbrar. **—spy on,** espiar; observar; atisbar. **—spy out,** descubrir; reconocer.

spyglass *n.* catalejo.

squab (skwaːb) *n.* pichón. *—adj.* **1,** (newly hatched) acabado de nacer; implume. **2,** (short and stout) regordete; rechoncho.

squabble ('skwab·əl) *n.* querella; riña; disputa. *—v.i.* reñir; disputar.

squad (skwaːd) *n.* escuadra.

squadron ('skwad·rən) *n.* **1,** *naval* escuadra. **2,** (of cavalry) escuadrón. **3,** *aero.* escuadrilla.

squalid ('skwal·ɪd) *adj.* escuálido. **—squalidness; squalidity** (skwa'lɪd·ə·ti) *n.* escualidez.

squall (skwɔːl) *n.* **1,** (yell) chillido. **2,** (storm) borrasca; chubasco. **3,** *colloq.* (disturbance) riña; reyerta. *—v.t. & i.* (yell) chillar. *—v.i.* (storm) estar *o* ponerse borrascoso. —**squally**, *adj.* borrascoso.

squalor ('skwal·ər) *n.* escualidez.

squander ('skwan·dər) *v.t.* disipar; malgastar; despilfarrar; derrochar. —*n.* despilfarro; derroche.

square (skwe:r) *n.* **1,** (plane figure) cuadrado. **2,** (open area in city) plaza. **3,** (city block) manzana; *Amer.* cuadra. **4,** (carpenter's instrument) escuadra. **5,** *math.* cuadrado. —*adj.* **1,** (at right angles; of square shape) cuadrado; cuadriculado. **2,** (straight; even) derecho. **3,** (honest) honrado; justo. **4,** (unequivocal) exacto; preciso. **5,** (satisfying, as a meal) bueno; completo; suficiente. —*v.t.* **1,** (make square) cuadrar; cuadricular. **2,** (adjust) ajustar. **3,** (settle, as a debt) pagar. —*v.i.* concordar; conformarse. —*adv.* **1,** (fairly) justamente; honradamente. **2,** (at right angles) en ángulo recto. **3,** (directly) derecho. **4,** (exactly) exactamente; precisamente. —**square dance,** contradanza; danza de figuras. —**square deal,** juego limpio; trato honrado. —**square off,** ponerse en actitud de lucha. —**square shooter,** *colloq.* persona honrada.

squash (skwaʃ) *v.t.* **1,** (crush) aplastar; apabullar. **2,** (cram; crowd) apiñar; apretar. **3,** (bruise; mangle) magullar. **4,** (put down; quell) reprimir; sofocar. **5,** (put an end to) poner fin a; acabar con. **6,** (refute) confutar. —*v.i.* **1,** (be crushed) aplastarse. **2,** (be crowded) apiñarse; apretarse. —*n.* **1,** (crushing) aplastamiento. **2,** (crowding) apiñamiento. **3,** (game) tenis de pared. **4,** *bot.* calabaza.

squat (skwat) *v.i.* **[squatted, -ting] 1,** (sit; crouch) acuclillarse. **2,** (settle on land without right) establecerse sin derecho o para formar un derecho. —*adj.* **1,** (in a squatting position) en cuclillas. **2,** (short and heavy) rechoncho. —*n.* posición (de una persona) en cuclillas. —**squatter,** *n.* advenedizo; intruso; colono usurpador.

squaw (skwɔ:) *n.* india norteamericana.

squawk (skwɔk) *v.i.* **1,** (cry hoarsely) chillar; graznar. **2,** *slang* (complain) quejarse. **3,** *slang* (inform) delatar; soplar. —*v.t.* decir chillando. —*n.* **1,** (hoarse cry) chillido; graznido. **2,** *slang* (complaint) queja.

squeak (skwik) *v.i.* **1,** (make a shrill sound) chirriar. **2,** *slang* (inform) delatar; soplar. —*v.t.* **1,** (utter shrilly) decir chirriando. **2,** (cause to squeak) hacer chirriar. —*n.* chirrido. —**have a narrow squeak,** *colloq.* escaparse por un pelo.

squeal (skwi:l) *v.i.* **1,** (utter a loud, sharp sound) chillar; dar alaridos. **2,** *slang* (inform) delatar; soplar. —*v.t.* decir chillando. —*n.* **1,** (loud, sharp sound) chillido; alarido. **2,** *slang* (informing) soplo; soplido; denuncia. —**squealer,** *n., slang* (informer) delator; soplón.

squeamish ('skwi·mɪʃ) *adj.* **1,** (queasy) nauseabundo. **2,** (easily offended) delicado; quisquilloso; remilgado. —**squeamish stomach,** estómago delicado.

squeegee ('skwi·dʒi) *n.* enjugador de goma. —*v.t.* secar con un enjugador.

squeeze (skwi:z) *v.t.* **1,** (compress) comprimir; apretar. **2,** (extract by squeezing) exprimir; estrujar. **3,** (cram; crowd) apiñar; tupir. **4,** (extort) extorsionar; sacar por fuerza. **5,** (oppress) oprimir; agobiar; acosar. **6,** (force; compel) obligar; forzar. **7,** (embrace) abrazar. **8,** (clasp) apretar; estrechar. —*v.i.* pasar, salir *o* entrar apretándose. —*n.* **1,** (pressure) apretón; estrechón. **2,** (extortion) extorsión; concusión. **3,** (cramming; crowding) apiñamiento. **4,** (compulsion) obligación; coerción. **5,** (embrace) abrazo. **6,** (clasp) apretón; estrechón. **7,** (tight situation) aprieto; apuro. —**put the squeeze on,** *colloq.* hacer la forzosa a.

squeezer ('skwi·zər) *n.* exprimidor; exprimidora.

squelch (skwɛltʃ) *v.t.* **1,** (crush) apabullar; despachurrar. **2,** (suppress) sofocar; sojuzgar. **3,** (silence) acallar; hacer callar. —*v.i.* chapalear; chapotear.

squib (skwɪb) *n.* **1,** (lampoon) pasquín; sátira. **2,** (firecracker) cohete crepitante.

squid (skwɪd) *n.* calamar.

squint (skwɪnt) *v.i.* bizcar. —*adj.*

bizco; bisojo. —*n.* **1,** (squinting) mirada bizca; mirada de soslayo. **2,** (strabismus) estrabismo.
squint-eyed *adj.* bizco; bisojo.
squire (skwair) *n.* **1,** (knight's attendant; rural landholder; justice of the peace) escudero. **2,** (lady's escort) acompañante. —*v.t.* **1,** (serve as attendant) servir como escudero. **2,** (escort) acompañar.
squirm (skwʌɹm) *v.i.* torcerse; retorcerse. —*n.* torcimiento; retorcimiento. —**squirm out** (of), escaparse de; salir con dificultad (de).
squirrel (ˈskwʌɹ·əl) *n.* ardilla.
squirt (skwʌɹt) *v.i.* chorrear; salir a chorros. —*v.t.* arrojar a chorros. —*n.* **1,** (spurt; jet) chorro; chisguete. **2,** (device for squirting) jeringa. **3,** *colloq.* (insignificant person) mocoso.
stab (stæb) *v.t.* & *i.* apuñalar; dar de puñaladas. —*n.* **1,** (blow with a pointed weapon) puñalada. **2,** *colloq.* (attempt) tentativa.
stability (stəˈbɪl·ə·ti) *n.* estabilidad; permanencia.
stabilization (ˌstei·bə·laiˈzei·ʃən) *n.* estabilización.
stabilize (ˈstei·bəˌlaiz) *v.t.* estabilizar.
stabilizer (ˈstei·bəˌlaiz·ər) *n.* estabilizador.
stable (ˈstei·bəl) *n.* **1,** (shelter for horses) establo; cuadra; caballeriza. **2,** (group of horses; horse attendants) caballeriza. —*adj.* estable; firme. —*v.t.* poner en un establo. —*v.i.* estar colocado en un establo.
stableboy *n.* mozo de caballos.
staccato (stəˈka·to) *adj., music* staccato.
stack (stæk) *n.* **1,** (orderly pile) pila; montón. **2,** (pile of hay or straw) almiar; montón de heno; parva de paja. **3,** (chimney) cañón de chimenea. **4,** (set of shelves) estantería. **5,** *colloq.* (large amount) gran número; montón. —*v.t.* amontonar; apilar; hacinar.
stadium (ˈstei·di·əm) *n.* [*pl.* **-ums** *o* **-a** (ə)] estadio.
staff (stæf) *n.* [*pl.* **staves**] **1,** (stick) palo; bastón. **2,** (pole; shaft) asta; astil. **3,** (support) apoyo; sostén. **4,** *music* pentagrama. **5,** [*pl.* **staffs**] (personnel) personal; *mil.* estado mayor; *naut.; aero.* tripulación. —*adj.* del personal; *mil.* del estado mayor. —*v.t.* proveer de personal; *mil.* proveer de estado mayor; *naut.; aero.* tripular. —**staff of life,** sostén de la vida; alimento; pan. —**staff of office,** bastón de mando.
stag (stæg) *n.* **1,** *zool.* ciervo; venado. **2,** *colloq.* (man, esp. unaccompanied) varón; varón solo. —*adj., colloq.* exclusivo para hombres. —*v.i., colloq.* ir solo (un hombre).
stage (steidʒ) *n.* **1,** (platform) andamio; cadalso. **2,** (dais) tribuna; estrado. **3,** (step; phase) etapa; punto; fase. **4,** (theater platform) escena; escenario. **5,** (theatrical profession) teatro. **6,** (relay station) posta. **7,** = **stagecoach.** —*v.t.* poner en escena; escenificar; representar. —*v.i.* viajar en diligencia. —**by easy stages,** por grados; gradualmente. —**by short stages,** a pequeñas etapas; a cortas jornadas.
stagecoach *n.* diligencia.
stage fright miedo al público.
stagehand *n.* tramoyista.
stage manager director de escena.
stage-struck *adj.* loco por el teatro.
stage whisper aparte; susurro en voz alta.
stagger (ˈstæg·ər) *v.i.* **1,** (reel; sway) bambolear; tambalear. **2,** (hesitate; waver) vacilar. —*v.t.* **1,** (cause to reel) hacer tambalear. **2,** (overwhelm) sorprender; asustar. **3,** (arrange in overlapping sequences) escalonar. —*n.* **1,** (unsteady movement) tambaleo; bamboleo. **2,** (hesitation) vacilación.
stagnant (ˈstæg·nənt) *adj.* estancado.
stagnate (ˈstæg·neit) *v.i.* estancarse. —**stagnation,** *n.* estancación; estancamiento.
staid (steid) *adj.* grave; serio; formal; sentado.
stain (stein) *n.* **1,** (discoloration) decoloración. **2,** (blot; taint) mancha; mácula; borrón. **3,** (coloring substance) tinte; tintura. **4,** *fig.* (dishonor) mancha; mancilla; deslustre; desdoro. —*v.t.* **1,** (discolor) descolorar; desteñir. **2,** (soil) manchar; ensuciar. **3,** (tint) colorar; teñir; tintar. **4,** *fig.* (be-

smirch) mancillar; desdorar; deslustrar. —*v.i.* **1,** (discolor) descolorarse; desteñirse. **2,** (become soiled) mancharse.

stained glass vidrio de color. —**stained-glass window,** vidriera de colores.

stainless ('stein·ləs) *adj.* **1,** (immune to rust) inoxidable. **2,** (spotless) inmaculado. —**stainless steel,** acero inoxidable.

stair (steːr) *n.* **1,** (step) escalón; peldaño. **2,** (staircase) escalera. —**stairs,** *n.pl.* escalera (*sing.*).

staircase *n.* escalera; caja de la escalera.

stairway *n.* escalera.

stairwell *n.* hueco de escalera. *También,* **stair well.**

stake (steik) *n.* **1,** (pointed stick) estaca. **2,** (pole; post) poste. **3,** (money wagered) apuesta. **4,** (risk) riesgo; peligro. **5,** (prize) premio. **6,** (interest; investment) interés. —*v.t.* **1,** (tie to a stake) estacar; atar a una estaca. **2,** (mark with stakes) estacar; señalar con estacas. **3,** (wager) apostar. **4,** (risk) arriesgar; aventurar. **5,** (provide with money or resources) financiar; apoyar; sostener. —**at stake,** en juego; arriesgado. —**die at the stake,** morir en la hoguera. —**pull up stakes,** *colloq.* irse; mudarse.

stalactite (stə'læk·tait) *n.* estalactita.

stalagmite (stə'læg,mait) *n.* estalagmita.

stale (steil) *adj.* **1,** (rancid; spoiled) rancio; pasado. **2,** (old; aged) viejo; añejo. **3,** (exhausted, as air) viciado. **4,** (hackneyed) trillado; gastado. —*v.t.* **1,** (age) envejecer; añejar. **2,** (spoil) enranciar. —*v.i.* **1,** (age) envejecerse; añejarse. **2,** (spoil) enranciarse; picarse; pasarse.

stalemate ('steil,meit) *n.* **1,** (tie; draw) empate; tablas. **2,** (deadlock) punto muerto; estancamiento. —*v.t.* **1,** (tie) empatar; *chess* hacer tablas. **2,** (put in deadlock) estancar. —*v.i.* **1,** (tie) empatarse; *chess* quedar tablas. **2,** (be deadlocked) estancarse; llegar a un punto muerto.

stalk (stɔk) *n.* **1,** (stem) tallo; pedúnculo. **2,** (haughty gait) paso majestuoso. **3,** (hunting) caza a la espera; acecho. —*v.t.* **1,** (pursue stealthily) cazar a la espera; acechar. **2,** (walk boldly through) pasar con porte majestuoso por. —*v.i.* **1,** (walk stiffly) andar con paso majestuoso *o* airado. **2,** (hunt furtively) cazar a la espera; cazar al acecho.

stall (stɔːl) *n.* **1,** (stable) establo; cuadra. **2,** (compartment for an animal) pesebre; casilla de establo. **3,** (market booth) puesto; tenderete. **4,** *Brit.* (orchestra seat) butaca; luneta. **5,** (choir seat; pew) banco; asiento de iglesia *o* del coro. **6,** *colloq.* (pretext; evasion) pretexto; escapatoria; evasiva. **7,** (arrested motion) parada; atascamiento. —*v.t.* **1,** (stable, as an animal) poner en un establo. **2,** (stop; check) parar; estancar. **3,** *colloq.* (put off; evade) detener; evadir. —*v.i.* **1,** (stop) pararse; atascarse; atollarse. **2,** *colloq.* (act or speak evasively) hacer la pala.

stallion ('stæl·jən) *n.* caballo padre; caballo semental; *Amer.* garañón.

stalwart ('stɔl·wərt) *adj.* **1,** (sturdy; brave) fuerte; valiente. **2,** (loyal) constante; leal. —*n.* **1,** (brave person) bravo. **2,** (loyal supporter) partidario leal.

stamen ('stei·mən) *n.* estambre.

stamina ('stæm·ə·nə) *n.* vigor; fuerza vital; fibra.

stammer ('stæm·ər) *v.i.* tartamudear; *Amer.* gaguear. —*v.t.* decir tartamudeando. —*n.* tartamudeo; *Amer.* gagueo. —**stammerer,** *n.* tartamudo; *Amer.* gago. —**stammering,** *n.* tartamudeo; *Amer.* gagueo.

stamp (stæmp) *v.t.* **1,** (trample; crush) pisar; pisotear; hollar. **2,** (seal) sellar. **3,** (impress; imprint) estampar; imprimir; marcar. **4,** (cut out by stamping) troquelar; acuñar. **5,** (mark; characterize) marcar; señalar. —*v.i.* patalear. —*n.* **1,** (thrust of the foot) pataleo; patada. **2,** (seal) sello. **3,** (rubber marking device) estampilla. **4,** (token of payment of postage or tax) sello; timbre. **5,** (impress; imprint) estampa; marca; impresión. **6,** (cutting device; die) troquel. **7,** (kind; sort) tipo; clase; estampa. —**stamp out,** extinguir; extirpar; borrar.

stampede (stæm'piːd) *n.* estampida; espantada. —*v.t.* ahuyentar; hacer huir en desorden. —*v.i.* ahuyentarse; precipitarse.

stance (stæns) *n.* postura; posición; actitud.

stanch (stæntʃ) *v.t.* estancar; restañar. —*adj.* **1,** (strong; firm) fuerte; firme. **2,** (loyal) fiel; leal. **3,** (watertight) estanco.

stanchion ('stæn·ʃən) *n.* puntal; montante; *naut.* candelero (*usu.pl.*).

stand (stænd) *v.i.* **1,** (be in an upright position) estar de pie; estar derecho; *Amer.* estar parado. **2,** (assume an upright position) ponerse de pie; levantarse; *Amer.* pararse. **3,** (be stagnant; stop) quedarse; detenerse; pararse. **4,** (be placed or situated) estar; estar situado. **5,** (remain; continue) seguir; quedarse; persistir; mantenerse. **6,** (hold firm) mantenerse firme; aguantar. **7,** (be or remain in effect) valer; tener fuerza; tener valor; estar en vigor. **8,** (be; hold a certain opinion or position) estar; ponerse. **9,** (have a certain height) medir; tener (determinada altura). **10,** *naut.* (bear; head) dirigirse; llevar rumbo *o* dirección. **11,** *Brit.* (be a candidate) ser candidato; presentarse como candidato. —*v.t.* **1,** (set upright) poner derecho. **2,** (endure) tolerar; soportar; aguantar. **3,** (undergo) sufrir; someterse a. **4,** *colloq.* (pay for) pagar; sufragar. —*n.* **1,** (position) posición; postura; actitud. **2,** (stop) parada. **3,** (platform) plataforma; tribuna; estrado. **4,** (small table) mesita. **5,** (support) pie; pedestal. **6,** (market stall) puesto; quiosco. **7,** (resistance) resistencia; oposición. **8,** (location) puesto; sitio. **9,** (music rack; lectern) atril. **10,** (podium) podio. —**it stands to reason**, es lógico; es razonable. —**make a stand,** mantenerse; aguantar; resistir. —**stand a chance**, tener probabilidad; tener esperanza. —**stand against**, oponerse a; resistir. —**stand alone,** estar *o* mantenerse solo. —**stand aside,** apartarse; abrir paso. —**stand back**, retroceder; retirarse. —**stand back of,** apoyar; respaldar. —**stand by, 1,** (assist) asistir; atender. **2,** (support; defend) apoyar; respaldar; defender. **3,** (keep to) mantenerse a. **4,** (wait) esperar; aguardar. —**stand for, 1,** (represent; signify) representar; denotar; significar. **2,** (endure) tolerar; soportar; aguantar. **3,** (favor; support) estar por; apoyar; sostener. —**stand forth**, destacarse; adelantarse. —**stand in awe of,** tener temor de. —**stand in good stead**, servir; ser útil; ser provechoso. —**stand in line**, hacer cola. —**stand in need (of)**, necesitar; tener necesidad (de). —**stand in someone's light**, quitarle la luz a uno. —**stand in the way (of)**, impedir; estorbar; cerrar el paso(a). —**stand in (well) with**, tener mano con; tener buenas relaciones con. —**stand off, 1,** (withdraw) apartarse. **2,** (withstand) resistir; negar. —**stand on, 1,** (depend on) depender de; basarse en. **2,** (insist on; affirm) mantener; insistir en. —**stand on end, 1,** (set upright) poner derecho; poner de punta. **2,** (bristle, as the hair) encresparse; erizarse. —**stand one's ground**, mantenerse firme; estar *o* seguir en sus trece. —**stand on tiptoe**, ponerse de puntillas. —**stand out, 1,** (be prominent) sobresalir; destacarse. **2,** (show clearly) distinguirse; notarse; saltar a los ojos. **3,** (resist) resistir; mantenerse firme; no ceder. —**stand pat,** mantenerse firme; quedarse; no cambiar. —**stand to, 1,** (work steadily at) seguir con; dedicarse a. **2,** (stand by) atender; estar alerta. **3,** (keep; abide by) cumplir con; mantenerse en. —**stand up, 1,** (rise) levantarse; *Amer.* pararse. **2,** (set upright) poner derecho. **3,** (endure) durar; persistir; aguantar. **4,** *slang* (disappoint) dejar plantado. —**stand up for,** apoyar; defender. —**stand up to,** enfrentar; encararse a *o* con.

standard ('stæn·dərd) *n.* **1,** (criterion) norma; regla; patrón. **2,** (flag; banner) bandera; estandarte; pabellón. **3,** (emblem) emblema; símbolo. **4,** (something upright) algo parado; derecho. —*adj.* **1,** (regular) normal; corriente; regular. **2,** (prescribed by law) legal; de marca; de ley. **3,** (classic) clásico. **4,** (having authority) de autoridad; de categoría.

standardbearer *n.* abanderado.

standardize ('stæn·dər,daiz) *v.t.*

normalizar; uniformar; regularizar; *Amer.* estandardizar. —**standardization** (-dɪˈzei·ʃən) *n.* normalización; regularización; *Amer.* estandardización.
stand-by *n.* [*pl.* **-bys**] **1,** (loyal supporter) adherente fiel. **2,** (something reliable) recurso seguro.
standee (stænˈdiː) *n., colloq.* espectador, viajero, etc. que no tiene asiento.
stand-in *n.* doble.
standing (ˈstæn·dɪŋ) *n.* **1,** (rank; status) rango; posición; condición. **2,** (duration) duración; permanencia. **3,** (halt) parada. **4,** (reputation) reputación; fama. —*adj.* **1,** (upright; on the feet) derecho; en *o* de pie; *Amer.* parado. **2,** (permanent) permanente; establecido. **3,** (stagnant) estancado. **4,** (stationary) inmóvil; estacionario; parado. —**standing room,** sitio para estar de pie. —**standing room only,** no quedan asientos.
stand-off *n.* empate. —*adj.* reservado; indiferente. —**stand-offish,** *adj.* reservado; indiferente.
stand-out *n., colloq.* disidente; intransigente.
standpipe *n.* tubo *o* columna de alimentación de agua.
standpoint *n.* punto de vista.
standstill *n.* alto; parada; pausa. —**be at a standstill,** quedar parado. —**come to a standstill,** pararse.
stanza (ˈstæn·zə) *n.* estrofa.
staple (ˈstei·pəl) *n.* **1,** (wire clamp) grapa. **2,** (principal commodity) artículo, género *o* producto principal. **3,** (raw material) materia prima. **4,** (textile fiber) fibra textil. —*adj.* básico; principal. —*v.t.* engrapar. —**stapler** (-plər) *n.* engrapador.
star (staːr) *n.* **1,** (luminous body; five-pointed figure; leading performer) estrella. **2,** (asterisk) asterisco. —*v.t.* [**starred, starring**] **1,** (set or mark with stars) estrellar; adornar con estrellas. **2,** (mark with an asterisk) marcar con asterisco. **3,** (feature) presentar como estrella. —*v.i.* **1,** (have a major role) ser estrella. **2,** (be outstanding) sobresalir; destacarse. —*adj.* principal; brillante; sobresaliente.
starboard (ˈstar·bərd) *n.* estribor.
starch (startʃ) *n.* **1,** (food substance) almidón; fécula. **2,** (stiffening substance) almidón. **3,** *fig.* (stiffness) formalidad; seriedad. **4,** *slang* (vigor) energía; vigor. —*v.t.* almidonar.
Star Chamber tribunal secreto y arbitrario.
starchy (ˈstar·tʃi) *adj.* **1,** (containing starch) feculento. **2,** (stiffened with starch) almidonado. **3,** *fig.* (formal) formal; tieso; serio.
stare (steːr) *v.i.* mirar fijamente; mirar con asombro o insolencia. —*v.t.* clavar la vista en; mirar fijamente. —*n.* mirada fija. —**stare down,** apocar con la mirada. —**stare one in the face, 1,** (look fixedly at) encararse con uno; darle a uno en la cara. **2,** (be conspicuous) saltar a los ojos.
starfish (ˈstar·fɪʃ) *n.* estrellamar; estrella de mar.
stargaze *v.i.* **1,** (watch the stars) mirar las estrellas. **2,** (daydream) soñar despierto. —**stargazing,** *n.* sueño; distracción.
stargazer *n.* **1,** (astronomer or astrologer) astrónomo; astrólogo. **2,** (dreamer) soñador.
stark (stark) *adj.* **1,** (rigid) rígido; tieso. **2,** (desolate) desolado. **3,** (downright) completo; cabal; puro. —*adv.* **1,** (utterly) completamente; cabalmente. **2,** (rigidly) rígidamente. —**stark mad,** loco rematado.
stark-naked *adj.* completamente desnudo; en cueros.
starless (ˈstar·ləs) *adj.* sin estrellas.
starlet (ˈstar·lɪt) *n.* joven estrella; estrella principiante.
starlight *n.* luz de las estrellas. —*adj.* estrellado; muy claro.
starling (ˈstar·lɪŋ) *n.* estornino.
starlit *adj.* estrellado; muy claro.
starred (staːrd) *adj.* **1,** (marked with stars) estrellado. **2,** *fig.* (lucky) afortunado. **3,** (featured) presentado como estrella.
starry (ˈstar·i) *adj.* **1,** (filled with stars) estrellado. **2,** (sparkling) centelleante; rutilante. **3,** (of or from the stars) estelar; celestial.
Stars and Stripes bandera de los Estados Unidos de América.
star-spangled *adj.* estrellado; sembrado de estrellas. —**the Star-Spangled Banner,** bandera e himno nacional de los Estados Unidos de América.

start (start) *v.i.* **1,** (begin) empezar; comenzar; principiar. **2,** (begin to move) ponerse en marcha; *mech.* arrancar. **3,** (jump; leap) sobresaltar; respingar. **4,** (arise) nacer. —*v.t.* **1,** (begin) empezar; iniciar. **2,** (set in motion) poner en marcha. **3,** (send off) despedir. **4,** (flush; rouse, as game) levantar. —*n.* **1,** (beginning) comienzo; principio. **2,** (departure) salida; partida. **3,** (place of departure) punto de salida. **4,** (lead; handicap) ventaja. **5,** (sudden movement) sobresalto; respingo. **6,** (fright; shock) susto. **7,** *mech.* arranque. —**by fits and starts**, a saltos y corcovos; esporádicamente. —**start after**, salir en busca de. —**start in**, empezar; ponerse a. —**start off**, salir; ponerse en marcha. —**start out**, **1,** (set forth) ponerse en camino; salir; partir. **2,** (begin) principiar; empezar. —**start up**, **1,** (jump; leap suddenly) sobresaltar; levantarse de repente. **2,** (come into being) salir *o* brotar de golpe. **3,** (begin to move or function) ponerse en marcha; arrancar.

starter ('star·tər) *n.* **1,** (person or thing that starts) iniciador. **2,** *mech.* arranque. **3,** *electricity* encendedor. **4,** *sports* juez de salida.

starting point punto de partida; punto de salida.

startle ('star·təl) *v.t.* espantar; asustar; sobresaltar; sorprender. —*n.* susto; sobresalto. —**startling** ('start·lɪŋ) *adj.* sorprendente; asombroso.

starvation (star'vei·ʃən) *n.* inanición; hambre.

starve (starv) *v.i.* hambrear; pasar *o* sufrir hambre; morir de hambre. —*v.t.* matar de hambre; hambrear. —**starved**, *adj.* hambriento; famélico. —**starving**, *adj.* hambriento; famélico.

starveling ('starv·lɪŋ) *adj.* & *n.* hambriento.

-stat (stæt) *sufijo* -stato; *forma nombres denotando* equilibrio; posición o condición fija: *aerostat*, aeróstato.

state (steit) *n.* **1,** (condition) estado; condición. **2,** (political entity) estado. **3,** (ceremony; pomp) pompa; fausto; ceremonia. —*adj.* de *o* del estado; estatal; público. —*v.t.* **1,** (declare) declarar; enunciar; afirmar. **2,** (define; formulate) formular; exponer. —**in state**, con gran pompa o ceremonia. —**lie in state**, estar expuesto en capilla ardiente.

statecraft *n.* política; arte de gobernar.

stated ('stei·tɪd) *adj.* **1,** (declared) declarado; afirmado. **2,** (fixed) establecido; fijo; determinado.

statehood ('steit·hʊd) *n.* estatidad.

statehouse *n.* edificio del Estado.

stately ('steit·li) *adj.* majestuoso; augusto; noble; grande. —**stateliness**, *n.* majestuosidad; nobleza; grandeza.

statement ('steit·mənt) *n.* **1,** (declaration) declaración; exposición; informe; relato. **2,** *comm.* estado de cuenta.

stateroom *n.* **1,** *naut.* camarote. **2,** *R.R.* compartimiento particular.

state room gran salón; salón de recepción.

statesman ('steits·mən) *n.* estadista; hombre de estado. —**statesmanlike**, *adj.* de estadista; propio de un estadista.

static ('stæt·ɪk) *adj.* estático. —*n.* interferencia. —**statics**, *n.sing.* estática.

-static ('stæt·ɪk) *sufijo* -stático; *forma adjetivos que corresponden a nombres terminando en* **-stat** *o* **-statics**: *photostatic*, fotostático; *hydrostatic*, hidrostático.

-statics ('stæt·ɪks) *sufijo* -stática; *forma nombres de ciencias relacionadas con el equilibrio de fuerzas: hydrostatics*, hidrostática.

station ('stei·ʃən) *n.* **1,** (designated place) estación. **2,** (status; condition) estado; condición. **3,** (stopping place) puesto; paradero. **4,** *radio; TV* emisora. **5,** *mil; naval* apostadero. —*v.t.* colocar; disponer; apostar.

stationary ('stei·ʃə·nɛr·i) *adj.* estacionario.

stationer ('stei·ʃə·nər) *n.* papelero.

stationery ('stei·ʃə·nɛr·i) *n.* papelería; efectos de escritorio *o* de oficina. —**stationery store**, papelería.

station house cuartel de policía.

stationmaster *n.* jefe de estación.

station wagon camioneta.

statistician (ˌstæt·əsˈtɪʃ·ən) *n.* estadístico.
statistics (stəˈtɪs·tɪks) *n.sing.* estadística. —*n.pl.* estadísticas; datos estadísticos. —**statistical**, *adj.* estadístico.
stato- (stæt·o; -ə) *prefix* estato-; estabilidad: *statocyst,* estatocisto.
stator (ˈstei·tər) *n.* estator.
statuary (ˈstætʃ·u·ɛr·i) *n.* estatuaria; colección de estatuas; imaginería.
statue (ˈstætʃ·u) *n.* estatua; imagen.
statuesque (ˌstætʃ·uˈɛsk) *adj.* majestuoso; noble; imponente.
statuette (ˌstætʃ·uˈɛt) *n.* estatuilla; estatuita.
stature (ˈstætʃ·ər) *n.* **1,** (height) estatura; altura; talla; tamaño. **2,** (quality) carácter; condición.
status (ˈstei·təs) *n.* estado; condición; posición.
status quo (ˌstæt·əsˈkwo;; ˌstei·təs-) *Lat.* condición actual *o* anterior (de las cosas).
statute (ˈstætʃ·ut) *n.* estatuto; ley; reglamento.
statutory (ˈstætʃ·u·tor·i) *adj.* estatutario; reglamentario.
staunch (stɔntʃ) *v.* & *adj.* = **stanch.**
stave (steiv) *n.* **1,** (part of a barrel) duela de barril. **2,** (stick; staff) palo; bastón. **3,** (stanza) estrofa; estancia. **4,** *music* (staff) pentagrama. **5,** (ladder rung) peldaño. —*v.t.* [*pret.* & *p.p.* **staved** *o* **stove**] **1,** (break; crush) romper; quebrar. **2,** (furnish with staves) poner duelas a. —**stave in,** romper; quebrar; desfondar. —**stave off,** evitar; impedir; parar.
staves (steivz) *n.* **1,** *pl. de* **staff.** **2,** *pl. de* **stave.**
stay (stei) *v.i.* **1,** (remain) quedarse; permanecer. **2,** (reside) habitar. **3,** (lodge temporarily) hospedarse; alojarse. **4,** (stop) pararse; detenerse. **5,** *colloq.* (hold out) perseverar; mantenerse; durar. —*v.t.* **1,** (halt) parar; detener; impedir. **2,** (delay) suspender; prorrogar. **3,** (support) apoyar; sostener. **4,** (satisfy; appease) apagar. **5,** (remain for the duration of) quedarse por; quedarse hasta el fin de. —*n.* **1,** (stop; pause) parada. **2,** (sojourn) permanencia; morada; estada; estancia. **3,** (delay) suspensión; prórroga. **4,** (support) apoyo; sostén. **5,** *naut.* (supporting cable) estay. **6,** (brace; wire support) varilla; ballena (*de corsé*).
stay-at-home *adj.* hogareño. —*n.* persona hogareña.
staysail (ˈsteiˌseil; -səl) *n.* vela de estay.
stead (stɛd) *n.* lugar; sitio. —**stand in good stead,** servir; ser útil; ser provechoso.
steadfast *adj.* firme; resuelto; constante. —**steadfastness,** *n.* constancia; resolución.
steady (ˈstɛd·i) *adj.* **1,** (firm; fixed) fijo; firme; estable. **2,** (constant) constante. **3,** (even; regular) regular; uniforme. **4,** (loyal) constante; leal. **5,** (sober) sobrio; serio; asentado. **6,** (resolute) resuelto. —*v.t.* **1,** (fix; settle) estabilizar; fijar; afirmar. **2,** (calm) calmar; asentar. —*v.i.* **1,** (become settled) estabilizarse; fijarse; afirmarse. **2,** (become calm) calmarse; asentarse. —*n., colloq.* novio; *fem.* novia. —**go steady,** *colloq.* ser novios.
steak (steik) *n.* **1,** (cut of meat, fish, etc.) lonja; tajada; filete. **2,** (beefsteak) bistec.
steal (sti:l) *v.t.* [*pret.* **stole**; *p.p.* **stolen**] robar; hurtar. —*v.i.* colarse; escabullirse; pasar furtivamente. —*n., colloq.* **1,** (act of stealing; something stolen) robo; hurto. **2,** (bargain) baratillo.
stealth (stɛlθ) *n.* cautela; recato; astucia. —**stealthy,** *adj.* clandestino; furtivo; secreto. —**by stealth,** a hurtadillas; a escondidas; furtivamente.
steam (sti:m) *n.* **1,** (vapor) vapor; vaho. **2,** *colloq.* (energy) energía; vigor; entusiasmo. —*v.t.* **1,** (treat with steam) saturar con vapor; dar un baño de vapor a. **2,** (cook with steam) cocer al vapor. **3,** (make cloudy or misty) empañar. —*v.i.* **1,** (emit vapor) echar vapor. **2,** (evaporate) evaporarse. **3,** (move or function by steam) marchar *o* funcionar a vapor; *naut.* navegar (por medio del vapor). —*adj.* de vapor.
steamboat *n.* vapor; buque de vapor.
steam engine máquina de vapor.
steamer (ˈstim·ər) *n.* **1,** (device for steam treating) vaporizador. **2,** (steamship) vapor; buque de

vapor. —**steamer rug**, manta de viaje. —**steamer trunk**, baúl de camarote.
steamfitter *n.* montador de calderas de vapor.
steam heat calefacción por vapor.
steam roller aplanadora.
steamship *n.* vapor; buque de vapor.
steam shovel excavadora de vapor.
steamy ('sti·mi) *adj.* **1,** (full of or emitting steam) vaporoso. **2,** (cloudy; misty) empañado.
steed (sti:d) *n.* corcel; caballo de combate *o* de carrera.
steel (sti:l) *n.* **1,** (metal) acero. **2,** (blade; weapon) cuchillo; arma blanca. **3,** (for striking fire with a flint) eslabón. —*adj.* **1,** (of steel) de acero. **2,** (like steel) acerado. **3,** (hard; tough) duro; firme; fuerte. **4,** (of or pert. to the steel industry) siderúrgico. —*v.t.* acerar; *fig.* fortalecer. —**alloy steel,** acero de aleación. —**carbon steel,** acero al carbono. —**stainless steel,** acero inoxidable. —**tool steel,** acero de herramientas.
steel mill fábrica de acero.
steelwork *n.* montaje de acero. —**steelworker,** *n.* obrero en una fábrica de acero. —**steelworks,** *n. sing. & pl.* fábrica de acero.
steely ('sti·li) *adj.* **1,** (of or like steel) de acero; acerado. **2,** *fig.* (hard; tough) duro; fuerte; firme.
steelyard ('sti:l,jard; -jərd) *n.* romana.
steep (stip) *adj.* **1,** (precipitous) escarpado; empinado. **2,** *colloq.* (high-priced) alto; excesivo. —*v.t.* saturar; empapar; remojar. —*v.i.* empaparse; remojarse.
steeple ('sti·pəl) *n.* aguja; campanario; espira.
steeplechase *n.* carrera de obstáculos.
steeplejack *n.* reparador de campanarios, chimeneas, torres, etc.
steer (stɪr) *v.t.* dirigir; guiar; conducir; *naut.* navegar; gobernar. —*v.i.* dirigirse; obedecer al timón; gobernarse. —*n.* buey. —**steer clear of,** evitar; huir de; mantenerse alejado de.
steerage ('stɪr·ɪdʒ) *n.* **1,** (part of a ship) antecámara de bajel; proa. **2,** (steering) gobierno; dirección.
steering wheel 1, *naut.* rueda del timón. **2,** *auto.* volante.
steersman ('stɪrz·mən) *n.* [*pl.* **-men**] timonero; timonel; piloto.
stein (stain) *n.* pichel, esp. para cerveza.
stellar ('stɛl·ər) *adj.* estelar; astral.
stem (stɛm) *n.* **1,** (of a plant) tallo; pedúnculo; tronco. **2,** (of a glass) pie. **3,** (of a pen or a smoking pipe) cañón. **4,** *mech.* varilla. **5,** *gram.* tema; base. **6,** *naut.* roda. —*v.t.* [**stemmed, stemming**] **1,** (stop; check) detener; refrenar. **2,** (dam) represar. **3,** (make headway against) navegar contra; oponerse a; resistir; embestir. —**from stem to stern**, de proa a popa. —**stem from**, nacer de; provenir de. —**stem the tide**, rendir la marea.
stench (stɛntʃ) *n.* hedor; hediondez; peste.
stencil ('stɛn·səl) *n.* estarcido; marca; patrón para estarcir. —*v.t.* estarcir
stenography (stə'nag·rə·fi) *n.* estenografía; taquigrafía. —**stenographer**, estenógrafo; taquígrafo. —**stenographic** (,stɛn·ə'græf·ɪk) *adj.* estenográfico; taquigráfico.
stentorian (stɛn'tor·i·ən) *adj.* estentóreo.
step (stɛp) *n.* **1,** (movement of the foot; pace; gait; short distance) paso. **2,** (stair; rung of a ladder) peldaño; escalón. **3,** (footboard) estribo. **4,** (footprint) huella; pisada. **5,** *pl.* (flight of stairs) escalera. **6,** (degree; grade) grado. **7,** *music* intervalo. **8,** (measure; action toward a goal) medida. —*v.i.* [**stepped, stepping**] **1,** (move the feet) dar un paso; dar pasos. **2,** (walk) andar; caminar. **3,** (dance) bailar. **4,** (move briskly) ir de prisa. **5,** (put the foot on or in; press with the foot) pisar. —*v.t.* **1,** (set down, as the foot) plantar (el pie). **2,** (dance) bailar. **3,** (measure; pace off) medir a pasos. **4,** (arrange in steps) escalonar. —**break step**, romper paso. —**in step, 1,** (keeping rhythm) a compás; llevando el paso. **2,** (in accord) de acuerdo. —**keep (in) step**, llevar el paso. —**out of step, 1,** (not in rhythm) no llevando el paso. **2,** (in disagreement) en desacuerdo. —**step aside**, apartarse; hacerse a un lado; abrir

paso. **—step back**, retroceder; volver hacia atrás. **—step by step**, paso a paso. **—step down**, **1**, (resign) darse de baja; dimitir. **2**, (decrease) disminuir; reducir. **3**, (descend) bajar; descender. **—step forth**, adelantarse; avanzar; presentarse. **—step in**, **1**, (enter) entrar. **2**, (intervene) meterse; intervenir. **—step on**, pisar; pisotear. **—step on it**, *colloq.* darse prisa; apresurarse; acelerar. **—step out**, **1**, (leave) salir. **2**, (walk briskly) ir de prisa; acelerar el paso. **3**, *colloq.* (go out for a good time) ir de parranda; ir de juerga. **—step up**, **1**, (move upward) subir. **2**, (approach; advance) acercarse; avanzar. **3**, (increase) aumentar; levantar. **4**, (accelerate) acelerar; apretar (el paso). **—take steps**, **1**, (move; walk) dar pasos. **2**, (take action) tomar medidas. **—watch one's step**, tener cuidado.

step- (stɛp) *prefijo* -astro; *denotando* parentesco o relación por nuevo matrimonio de los padres: *stepson*, hijastro.

stepbrother *n.* hermanastro; medio hermano.

stepchild *n.* [*pl.* **-children**] hijastro *o* hijastra.

stepdaughter *n.* hijastra.

stepfather *n.* padrastro.

step-ins *n.pl.* pantaloncitos de mujer.

stepladder *n.* escala; escalera.

stepmother *n.* madrastra.

stepparent *n.* padrastro *o* madrastra.

steppe (stɛp) *n.* estepa.

stepping stone pasadera; *fig.* escalón.

stepsister *n.* hermanastra; medio hermana.

stepson *n.* hijastro.

-ster (stər) *sufijo; forma nombres denotando* personas con determinada condición o actividad: *oldster*, viejo; *punster*, amigo de equívocos. *Frecuentemente tiene valor despectivo: rhymester*, poetastro.

stere (stɪr) n. estéreo.

stereo ('stɛr·i·o) *n.* estéreo.

stereo- (stɛr·i·ə) *prefijo* estereo-; sólido; de *o* con tres dimensiones: *stereophonic*, estereofónico.

stereophonic (ˌstɛr·i·ə'fan·ɪk) *adj.* estereofónico.

stereoscope ('stɛr·i·əˌskop) *n.* estereoscopio. **—stereoscopic** (-'skap·ɪk) *adj.* estereoscópico. **—stereoscopy** (-'as·kə·pi) *n.* estereoscopia.

stereotype *n.* estereotipo; clisé. **—*adj.*** estereotípico. **—*v.t.*** estereotipar. **—stereotyped**, *adj.* estereotipado. **—stereotypy**, *n.* estereotipia.

sterile ('stɛr·ɪl) *adj.* estéril. **—sterility** (stə'rɪl·ə·ti) *n.* esterilidad.

sterilize ('stɛr·əˌlaiz) *v.t.* esterilizar. **—sterilization** (-lɪ'zei·ʃən) *n.* esterilización. **—sterilizer**, *n.* esterilizador.

sterling ('stʌɹ·lɪŋ) *adj.* **1**, (of standard quality, as silver) esterlina. **2**, (pure; genuine) puro; genuino. **3**, (noble) noble; excelente. **—*n.*** **1**, (silver) plata de ley. **2**, (silverware) vajilla de plata. **—pound sterling**, libra esterlina.

stern (stʌɹn) *adj.* **1**, (severe) severo; estricto; áspero; austero. **2**, (relentless) firme; inexorable. **—*n.*** popa. **—sternness**, *n.* severidad; aspereza.

sternum ('stʌɹ·nəm) *n.* [*pl.* **sternums** *o* **sterna** (-nə)] esternón.

sternway ('stʌɹn·wei) *n.*, *naut.* cía.

stertorous ('stʌɹ·tə·rəs) *adj.* estertoroso.

stet (stɛt) reténgase.

stethoscope ('stɛθ·ə·skop) *n.* estetoscopio.

stevedore ('sti·və·dor) *n.* estibador.

stew (stuː) *n.* **1**, (food) estofado; guisado; *Amer.* sancocho. **2**, (anxiety) ansiedad; apuro. **—*v.t.* & *i.*** (cook) estofar; guisar. **—*v.i.*** (worry) inquietarse; preocuparse. **—stewed fruit**, compota de frutas.

steward ('stu·ərd) *n.* **1**, (manager of a household) mayordomo; senescal. **2**, (administrator) administrador; encargado. **3**, (kitchen manager) despensero. **4**, *aero; naut.* camarero.

stewardess ('stu·ər·dɪs) *n.* **1**, (manager of a household) mayordoma; ama de llaves. **2**, (administrator) administradora. **3**, *naut.* camarera. **4**, *aero.* camarera; azafata; *Amer.* aeromoza.

stewardship ('stu·ərd·ʃɪp) *n.* **1**, (household management) mayordomía. **2**, (administration) administración; cargo.

stewpan *n.* cazuela; cacerola.

stick (stɪk) *n.* **1**, (piece of wood) palo; bastón. **2**, (club; cudgel) porra; macana. **3,** (wand; bar; rod) vara; barra. **4,** *aero.* palanca de mando. **5,** (stab) estocada; puñalada. **6,** *colloq.* (dull, stupid person) bobo; bodoque. **7,** (things arranged in a line or string) ristra. **8,** *pl., colloq.* (rural districts) campo; campiña. —*v.t.* [*pret. & p.p.* **stuck**] **1,** (pierce) picar; punzar. **2,** (stab) apuñalar. **3,** (thrust) empujar. **4,** (put; place) poner; meter. **5,** (attach) pegar; juntar; adherir. **6,** *colloq.* (puzzle) coger de bobo; confundir. **7,** *slang* (impose upon; deceive) engañar; embaucar. —*v.i.* **1,** (remain) quedarse. **2,** (extend) proyectarse. **3,** (scruple) escrupulizar. **4,** (adhere) pegarse; agarrarse. **5,** (stagnate) atascarse; estancarse. **6,** (persist) continuar; persistir. —**stick around,** *slang,* quedarse. —**stick at,** persistir en; mantenerse a. —**stick by,** apoyar; sostener. —**stick in,** clavar; hincar; encajar. —**stick one's hands up,** alzar las manos. —**stick out, 1,** (project) sobresalir; proyectarse. **2,** (push out) sacar (la lengua); asomar (la cabeza). **3,** (be conspicuous) saltar a los ojos; ser muy evidente. —**stick them up!,** ¡manos arriba! —**stick to, 1,** (adhere to) adherirse a; mantenerse a *o* en. **2,** (persist in) persistir en; aferrarse a. —**stick together,** unirse; quedarse unidos; juntarse. —**stick up, 1,** (hold straight up) alzar; sacar hacia arriba. **2,** (stand up) estar *o* ponerse de punta; levantarse; erizarse. **3,** *slang* (rob) asaltar; atracar; robar. —**stick up for,** *colloq.* defender; secundar; declararse por.

sticker ('stɪk·ər) *n.* **1,** (persistent person) persona insistente; testarudo. **2,** (adhesive label) etiqueta; marbete engomado. **3,** (bur; barb) espina; púa; punta. **4,** *colloq.* (puzzler) enigma; rompecabezas.

stickle ('stɪk·əl) *v.i.* tener escrúpulos; escrupulizar.

stickler ('stɪk·lər) *n.* **1** (scrupulous person) persona escrupulosa o quisquillosa. **2,** *colloq.* (puzzler) enigma; rompecabezas.

stick-up *n., slang* robo; atraco a mano armada.

sticky ('stɪk·i) *adj.* **1,** (adhesive; gummy) pegajoso; viscoso. **2,** (humid) húmedo. **3,** *colloq.* (difficult) delicado; difícil.

stiff (stɪf) *adj.* **1,** (rigid) tieso; rígido; inflexible. **2,** (strong; harsh) fuerte. **3,** (difficult) difícil; arduo; riguroso. **4,** (formal) formal; tieso; serio. **5,** (awkward) desmañado; torpe. **6,** *colloq.* (high, as of prices) excesivo; alto. —*n., slang* **1,** (corpse) cadáver; muerto. **2,** (excessively formal person) persona tiesa y ceremoniosa. **3,** (awkward person) bodoque.

stiffen ('stɪf·ən) *v.t.* atiesar. —*v.i.* atiesarse.

stiff-necked *adj.* terco; obstinado; testarudo.

stiffness ('stɪʃ·nəs) *n.* **1,** (rigidity) rigidez; inflexibilidad. **2,** (vigor) fuerza. **3,** (difficulty) dificultad; rigor. **4,** (formality) formalidad; ceremonia. **5,** (awkwardness) torpeza.

stifle ('stai·fəl) *v.t.* ahogar; sofocar. —*v.i.* ahogarse; sofocarse.

stigma ('stɪg·mə) *n.* [pl. **stigmas** *o* **stigmata** (-mə·tə)] estigma. —**stigmatize** (-taiz) *v.t.* estigmatizar.

stile (stail) *n.* portillo con escalones o molinete para pasar de un cercado a otro.

stiletto (stɪ'lɛt·o) *n.* estilete.

still (stɪl) *adj.* **1,** (motionless) inmóvil; fijo. **2,** (tranquil; quiet) tranquilo; quieto. **3,** (silent) mudo; callado; silencioso. **4,** (lifeless) muerte; inanimado. —*n.* **1,** (distilling apparatus) alambique; destiladera. **2,** (distillery) destilería. **3,** *poet.* (silence; quiet) silencio; calma. **4,** (still photograph) vista fija; afiche. —*adv.* **1,** (up to the time indicated) todavía; aún. **2,** (even; yet) aún. **3,** (nevertheless) sin embargo; no obstante. —*v.t.* **1,** (silence) silenciar; acallar. **2,** (calm) calmar; aplacar. **3,** (muffle) amortiguar. **4,** (stop; halt) parar; detener. —*conj.* sin embargo.

stillbirth *n.* parto muerto.

stillborn *adj.* nacido muerto.

still life naturaleza muerta; bodegón.

stillness ('stɪl·nəs) *n.* **1,** (motionlessness) inmovilidad. **2,** (calm; quiet) calma; tranquilidad. **3,** (silence) silencio.

stilt (stɪlt) *n.* zanco. —**stilted,** *adj.* formal; afectado; pomposo; altisonante.

stimulant ('stɪm·jə·lənt) *adj. & n.* estimulante.

stimulate ('stɪm·jəˌleit) *v.t.* estimular; excitar. —**stimulation**, *n.* estímulo; excitación.

stimulus ('stɪm·jə·ləs) *n.* [*pl.* **-li** (-lai)] estímulo; aguijón.

sting (stɪŋ) *v.t.* [*pret.* & *p.p.* **stung**] **1,** (prick; puncture) picar; pinchar; punzar. **2,** (smart; itch) picar; resquemar. **3,** (distress) atormentar; remorder. **4,** (goad) estimular; aguijonear; espolear. **5,** *slang* (dupe) embaucar; estafar. —*v.i.* escocer; picar. —*n.* **1,** (sharp-pointed organ) aguijón; púa. **2,** (thorn; spine) púa. **3,** (act of stinging; wound caused by stinging) picada; picadura; punzada. **4,** (goad) aguijón; estímulo. **5,** (distress) remordimiento. **6,** (sharp pain) escozor; picazón.

stinger ('stɪŋ·ər) *n.* **1,** (person or thing that stings) aguijador; pinchador. **2,** (stinging organ) aguijón; púa. **3,** (thorn; spine) púa. **4,** (drink) bebida alcohólica con crema de menta, aguardiente y hielo.

stingray ('stiŋˌrei) *n.* pastinaca.

stingy ('stɪn·dʒi) *adj.* **1,** (niggardly) mezquino; miserable; tacaño. **2,** (scanty) escaso; limitado; poco.

stink (stɪŋk) *v.i.* [*pret.* **stank** *o* **stunk**; *p.p.* **stunk**] heder; apestar. —*v.t.* dar mal olor a; apestar. —*n.* hedor; hediondez; peste; mal olor. —**raise a stink,** *slang* armar el lío padre. —**stink out**, ahuyentar con mal olor. —**stink up**, dar mal olor a; apestar.

stinker ('stɪŋk·ər) *n.* **1,** (person or thing that stinks) persona o cosa apestosa. **2,** *slang* (despicable person) persona despreciable; canalla.

stinking ('stɪŋk·ɪŋ) *adj.* apestoso; hediondo.

stint (stɪnt) *v.i.* limitar; restringir. —*v.i.* limitarse; ceñirse; ser económico. —*n.* **1,** (limitation) límite; restricción. **2,** (fixed amount) cuota; porción. **3,** (allotted task) tarea; faena.

stipend ('stai·pənd) *n.* estipendio.

stipple ('stɪp·əl) *v.t.* puntear; picar. —*n.* picadura; punteado. —**stippling** (-lɪŋ) *n.* picadura; punteado.

stipulate ('stɪp·jə·leit) *v.t.* estipular. —**stipulation**, *n.* estipulación.

stir (stʌːɹ) *v.t.* [**stirred, stirring**] **1,** (move; agitate) mover; agitar. **2,** (mix) revolver; menear. **3,** (rouse) despertar; conmover; excitar. **4,** (poke, as a fire) atizar. —*v.i.* **1,** (move) moverse. **2,** (awake) despertarse. **3,** (arise) levantarse. **4,** (take place; happen) tener lugar; suceder; pasar. —*n.* **1,** (movement) movimiento; actividad. **2,** (excitement) conmoción; agitación; alboroto. **3,** (poke; shove) empujón. **4,** *slang* (prison) cárcel; prisión. —**stirrer**, *n.* agitador; palillo.

stirring ('stʌɹ·ɪŋ) *adj.* conmovedor; emocionante; estimulante.

stirrup ('stʌɹ·əp) *n.* estribo; *naut.* codillo. —**stirrup cup**, copa de despedida.

stitch (stɪtʃ) *n.* **1,** *sewing, knitting, etc.* punto; puntada. **2,** (sudden sharp pain) punzada; dolor punzante. **3,** *colloq.* (bit) pizca. —*v.t.* & *i.* coser; dar puntadas (en). —**be in stitches**, *colloq.* desternillarse de risa.

St. John's bread = **carob.**

stoat (stot) *n.* armiño, esp. en piel de verano.

stock (stak) *n.* **1,** (trunk; stem) tronco; tallo. **2,** (race; lineage) cepa; estirpe. **3,** (related group) raza; familia. **4,** (handle of a tool) mango; manija. **5,** (of a firearm) culata; caja; encaro. **6,** (livestock) ganado. **7,** (supply of merchandise) surtido; existencias (*pl.*). **8,** (reserve supply) reserva. **9,** (raw materials) materias primas. **10,** *pl.* (corporate shares) acciones; valores. **11,** (meat broth) caldo. **12,** *cards* baceta. **13,** *pl.* (instrument of punishment) cepo (*sing.*). **14,** *bot.* (gillyflower) alhelí. **15,** *theat.* repertorio. —*v.t.* **1,** (supply; furnish) surtir; proveer; abastecer; acopiar. **2,** (have on hand) tener a mano; tener en existencias. **3,** (provide with fish or wildlife) poblar. —*adj.* **1,** (kept on hand) a mano; de surtido. **2,** (ordinary) común; corriente. **3,** (of the stock market) bursátil. **4,** (of livestock) ganadero; del ganado. **5,** *theat.* de repertorio. —**in stock**, en existencias; disponible; a mano. —**out of stock**, agotado. —**take stock**, hacer inventario. —**take stock in, 1,**

(buy shares in) comprar acciones de. **2,** *colloq.* (believe) creer; confiar en. **3,** *colloq.* (give importance to) dar importancia a. —**stock up (on),** surtirse (de); proveerse (de).
stockade (stak'eid) *n.* empalizada; estacada; valla. —*v.t.* empalizar.
stockbroker *n.* corredor de acciones; bolsista.
stock car 1, *R.R.* vagón para el ganado. **2,** *auto.* coche de serie.
stock company 1, *comm.* sociedad por acciones; sociedad anónima. **2,** *theat.* compañía de repertorio.
stock exchange bolsa.
stock farm hacienda de ganado; *Amer.* rancho; estancia.
stockfish *n.* bacalao seco; cualquier pescado partido y secado al aire.
stockholder *n.* accionista.
stocking ('stak·ɪŋ) *n.* media; calceta.
stock market bolsa; mercado de valores.
stockpile *n.* surtido; reserva. —*v.t.* acumular; reunir.
stockroom *n.* almacén; depósito de mercancías.
stock-still *adj.* completamente inmóvil; rígido.
stocky ('stak·i) *adj.* rechoncho.
stockyard *n.* corral para ganados.
stodgy ('stadʒ·i) *adj.* pesado.
stogy *también,* **stogie** ('sto·gi) *n.* **1,** (cigar) cigarro largo y delgado. **2,** (shoe) zueco.
stoic ('sto·ɪk) *n.* & *adj.* estoico. —**stoical,** *adj.* estoico. —**stoicism** (-ɪ·sɪz·əm) *n.* estoicismo.
stoke (stok) *v.t.* & *i.* **1,** (poke; stir, as a fire) atizar. **2,** (feed fuel; tend) alimentar; palear.
stoker ('sto·kər) *n.* **1,** (person) fogonero; paleador. **2,** (machine) alimentador de hogar.
stole (sto:l) *n.* estola. —*v., pret. de* **steal.**
stolen ('sto·lən) *v., p.p. de* **steal.**
stolid ('stal·ɪd) *adj.* impasible; insensible. —**stolidity** (stə'lɪd·ə·ti) *n.* impasibilidad; insensibilidad.
stomach ('stʌm·ək) *n.* **1,** *anat.* (digestive organ) estómago. **2,** (abdomen; belly) abdomen; vientre; barriga. **3,** (appetite) apetito. **4,** (inclination; liking) deseo; inclinación. —*v.t.* **1,** (eat; digest) tragar; digerir. **2,** (tolerate) aguantar; tolerar.
stomach-ache *n.* indigestión; dolor de estómago; empacho.
stomachic (sto'mæk·ɪk) *adj.* estomacal. —*n.* tónico; medicamento estomacal.
stomato- (sto·mə·tə; sta-) *prefijo* estomato-; boca: *stomatology,* estomatología.
stone (sto:n) *n.* **1,** (rock) piedra. **2,** (gem) gema; piedra preciosa. **3,** (pit of fruits) hueso. **4,** (gravestone) lápida. **5,** *med.* piedra; cálculo. **6,** [*pl.* **stone**] (British unit of weight) peso de 14 libras. —*v.t.* **1,** (throw stones at) apedrear; lapidar. **2,** (cover with stone) revestir de piedra. **3,** (pave with stone) adoquinar; pavimentar con piedras. **4,** (remove the pit from) deshuesar. —*adj.* pétreo; de piedra. —**leave no stone unturned,** no dejar piedra por mover; hacer todo lo posible. —**within a stone's throw,** a tiro de piedra.
stone-blind *adj.* completamente ciego.
stonecutter *n.* cantero. —**stonecutting,** *n.* cantería.
stone-dead *adj.* muerto como una piedra.
stone-deaf *adj.* completamente sordo; sordo como una tapia.
stonemason *n.* albañil; picapedrero. —**stonemasonry,** *n.* albañilería.
stone quarry cantera.
stonework *n.* cantería. —**stoneworker,** *n.* cantero; picapedrero.
stony ('sto·ni) *adj.* **1,** (of or like stone) pétreo. **2,** (full of stones) pedregoso; petroso. **3,** (hard; rigid) duro; fijo. **4,** (unfeeling) insensible; empedernido; de corazón duro.
stony-hearted *adj.* empedernido; de corazón duro.
stood (stʊd) *v., pret. & p.p. de* **stand.**
stooge (stu:dʒ) *n., colloq.* **1,** *theat.* compañero asistente de un cómico. **2,** (henchman) lacayo; secuaz; sicario. —*v.i., colloq.* servir; atender servilmente.
stool (stu:l) *n.* **1,** (seat) taburete; banquillo; banqueta. **2,** (toilet) inodoro; excusado. **3,** (evacuation) evacuación de vientre. **4,** (excrement) excremento. **5,** (decoy) señuelo; reclamo. **6,** = **stool pigeon.** —*v.i.* **1,** (evacuate the

bowels) exonerar el vientre. 2, *colloq.* (inform) delatar; soplar. 3, *colloq.* (spy) espiar.

stool pigeon 1, (decoy) señuelo. 2, *colloq.* (informer) delator; soplón. 3, *colloq.* (spy) espía.

stoop (stup) *v.i.* 1, (bend the body) inclinarse; doblarse; encorvarse. 2, (lower oneself) rebajarse; humillarse. —*v.t.* inclinar; doblar; encorvar. —*n.* 1, (bending of the body) inclinación; encorvada. 2, (condescension) descenso; humillación. 3, (front steps) escalinata.

stoop-shouldered *adj.* cargado de espaldas.

stop (stap) *v.t.* [**stopped, stopping**] 1, (halt) parar; detener. 2, (cease) cesar; dejar. 3, (stanch) estancar; restañar. 4, (block; plug) tapar; cerrar. 5, (finish) acabar; terminar. 6, (intercept) interceptar. 7, (interrupt) interrumpir; suspender. 8, (prevent) impedir. —*v.i.* 1, (halt) parar(se); detenerse. 2, (cease) cesar (de); dejar (de). 3, (tarry; make a stay) quedarse; alojarse; hospedarse. —*n.* 1, (halt; cessation) parada; alto; pausa; detención; cesación. 2, (place where trains, buses, etc. stop) parada; estación. 3, (stay; sojourn) estada; estancia. 4, (pause in a journey) escala. 5, (obstruction) obstáculo; impedimento; obstrucción. 6, (check; curb) freno. 7, (plug; stopper) tapón. 8, (period; end of sentence) punto. 9, *phonet.* explosiva. 10, *photog.* abertura. 11, *music* (of a fretted instrument) traste; (of an organ) registro. —*interj.* ¡alto!; ¡basta! —**put a stop to**, poner fin a; acabar con. —**stop at nothing**, no pararse en escrúpulos. —**stop off**, pararse un rato. —**stop off at**, pasar por. —**stop over**, hacer alto; detenerse. —**stop short**, parar(se) en seco. —**stop up**, tapar; atorar; represar; obstruir.

stopcock *n.* llave; grifo; espita.

stopgap *n.* expediente. —*adj.* provisional; interino.

stoplight *n.* 1, *R.R.* semáforo. 2, *auto.* (tail light) farol de cola. 3, (traffic light) señal *o* luz de parada.

stopover ('stap,o·vər) *n.* parada intermedia; escala.

stoppage ('stap·ɪdʒ) *n.* 1, (halt) parada; alto; detención. 2, (obstruction) taponamiento; obstrucción. 3, (interruption) interrupción; suspensión. 4, (damming, as of water) represa. 5, (labor strike) huelga; paro.

stopper ('stap·ər) *n.* tapón; tarugo. —*v.t.* taponar.

stop sign señal de parada.

stop signal señal *o* luz de parada.

stopwatch *n.* cronómetro.

storage ('stor·ɪdʒ) *n.* almacenaje. —**storage battery**, acumulador.

store (sto:r) *n.* 1, (shop; selling establishment) tienda; almacén. 2, (storage place) depósito; almacén. 3, (supply) provisión; acopio. 4, *pl.* (supplies, provisions, etc.) pertrechos; víveres; municiones. 5, (reserve) reserva; repuesto. 6, (abundance) abundancia; gran cantidad. —*v.t.* 1, (stock; accumulate) surtir; guardar; acumular. 2, (furnish; supply) proveer; abastecer. 3, (put in reserve) almacenar; depositar. —**be in store for**, esperarle a uno (una cosa). —**in store**, guardado; en reserva. —**set store by**, estimar *o* apreciar mucho; dar importancia a. —**store away**, guardar; ahorrar. —**store up**, acumular.

storehouse *n.* almacén; depósito.

storekeeper *n.* 1, (shopkeeper) tendero. 2, (keeper of supplies) guardalmacén; *naut.* pañolero.

storeroom *n.* almacén; bodega; despensa; *naut.* pañol.

storied ('stor·id) *adj.* 1, (celebrated in story) historiado. 2, (having a specified number of floors or stories) de (*tantos*) pisos: *seven-storied,* de siete pisos.

stork (stork) *n.* cigüeña.

storm (storm) *n.* 1, (atmospheric disturbance) tempestad; temporal; tormenta; *naut.* borrasca. 2, (vehement outbreak; tumult) arrebato; explosión; alboroto; tumulto. 3, (violent assault) ataque; asalto. —*v.i.* 1, (blow; be stormy) haber tempestad; emborrascarse. 2, (fume; rage) estar enfurecido; estar encolerizado; rabiar. 3, (rush; move with violence) precipitarse. —*v.t.* asaltar; atacar; tomar por asalto; expugnar.

storm cloud nubarrón.

storm door contravidriera (*de puerta*).

storm troops tropas de asalto. *También,* **storm troopers.**

storm window contravidriera (*de ventana*).
stormy ('stor·mi) *adj.* tempestuoso; *naut.* borrascoso.
story ('stor·i) *n.* **1,** (narrative) cuento; historia; relato. **2,** (plot of a novel, play, etc.) argumento; trama. **3,** *colloq.* (lie) mentira; embuste. **4,** (floor of a building) alto; piso. **5,** (gossip; rumor) chisme; rumor. —*v.t.* historiar.
storyteller *n.* **1,** (narrator) cuentista; narrador. **2,** *colloq.* (fibber; liar) cuentón; embustero; mentiroso. **3,** *colloq.* (gossip) chismoso.
stoup (stup) *n.* pila de agua bendita.
stout (staut) *adj.* **1,** (corpulent) corpulento; gordo; fornido. **2,** (strong; sturdy) fuerte; robusto; sólido. **3,** (vigorous; forceful) fuerte; recio. **4,** (brave) resuelto; intrépido. —*n.* cerveza fuerte.
stouthearted *adj.* resuelto; valeroso; intrépido.
stove (stoːv) *n.* **1,** (for heating) estufa. **2,** (for cooking) hornillo; cocina. **3,** (furnace; oven) horno. —*v., pret. & p.p. de* **stave.**
stovepipe *n.* tubo de estufa *o* de hornillo. —**stovepipe hat,** sombrero de copa alta.
stow (stoː) *v.t.* **1,** (store; pack) meter; guardar; esconder; *naut.* estibar; arrumar. **2,** *slang* (stop; cease) cesar; dejar. —**stow away, 1,** (store) guardar; esconder. **2,** (hide aboard a ship, train, etc.) embarcarse clandestinamente; colarse.
stowaway ('sto·ə·wei) *n.* polizón.
strabismus (strə'bɪz·məs) *n.* estrabismo.
straddle ('stræd·əl) *v.t. & i.* **1,** (sit or stand astride) montar a horcajadas; ponerse a horcajadas (en). **2,** *colloq.* (favor both sides) favorecer a ambos lados. —*n.* posición del que se pone a horcajadas.
strafe (streif) *v.t. & i.* **1,** *mil.* bombardear intensamente. **2,** *aero.* ametrallar en vuelo bajo.
straggle ('stræg·əl) *v.i.* **1,** (wander away; stray) desviarse; extraviarse; andar perdido. **2,** (lag) rezagarse. **3,** (spread irregularly or untidily) desparramarse; esparcirse. —**straggly** (-li); **straggling** (-lɪŋ), *adj.* desordenado; esparcido; rezagado.
straggler ('stræg·lər) *n.* **1,** (of persons) rezagado; vagamundo; tunante. **2,** (of objects, as a branch, etc.) rama extendida; objeto aislado.
straight (streit) *adj.* **1,** (without bend or deviation) derecho; directo; en línea recta. **2,** (upright; honorable) recto; justo; honorado; íntegro. **3,** (regular; orderly) ordenado; en orden. **4,** (frank; outspoken) sincero; franco. **5,** (continuous) seguido; continuo. **6,** (exact) exacto; correcto. **7,** (unmodified; undiluted) puro. —*adv.* **1,** (directly) derecho; directamente. **2,** (honorably) rectamente; justamente; honradamente. **3,** (frankly) sinceramente; francamente. **4,** (continuously) continuamente; sin interrupción. **5,** (exactly) exactamente. **6,** (immediately) en seguida; en el acto. —*n.* **1,** (straight part) recta. **2,** *poker* escalera. —**straight away; straight off,** en seguida. —**straight face,** cara seria. —**straight from the shoulder,** con toda franqueza.
straightaway *adj.* derecho; recto; en línea recta. —*n.* recta.
straightedge *n.* regla.
straighten ('streit·ən) *v.t.* **1,** (set straight) enderezar. **2,** (put in order) arreglar; poner en orden. —*v.i.* **1,** (become straight) enderezarse. **2,** (come to order) arreglarse.
straightforward *adj.* **1,** (direct) derecho; directo; recto. **2,** (honest; sincere) honrado; franco; sincero. —*adv.* **1,** (directly) directamente; en línea recta. **2,** (honestly; sincerely) honradamente; francamente; sinceramente.
straightness ('streit·nəs) *n.* rectitud.
straightway *adv.* luego; en seguida; inmediatamente.
strain (strein) *v.t.* **1,** (stretch) estirar. **2,** (exert to the utmost) forzar. **3,** (injure; sprain) torcer. **4,** (filter) colar; tamizar. **5,** (distort) torcer; deformar. **6,** (press; squeeze) exprimir. —*v.i.* esforzarse. —*n.* **1,** (tension) tensión; tirantez. **2,** (great effort) esfuerzo. **3,** (sprain) torcedura. **4,** (force; stress) fuerza; carga; peso. **5,** *music* aire; melodía. **6,** (lineage;

descent) raza; linaje; estirpe. **7,** (kind; species) forma; clase; especie. **8,** (inherited trait) rasgo racial; genio. **9,** (manner; style) estilo. **10,** (trace; streak) huella; traza.

strained (streind) *adj.* forzado.

strainer ('strei·nər) *n.* coladera; colador.

strait (streit) *n.* **1,** *geog.* (passage of water) estrecho. **2,** (difficulty) apuro; aprieto. —*adj.* angosto; estrecho; apretado.

straiten ('strei·tən) *v.t.* **1,** (limit; contract) acortar; angostar; contraer. **2,** (distress; embarrass) estrechar; apretar. —**in straitened circumstances,** apurado; en un aprieto.

strait jacket camisa de fuerza.

strait-laced *adj.* austero; puritano; estricto.

strand (strænd) *v.t.* **1,** (drive or run aground) hacer encallar; hacer embarrancar; varar. **2,** (leave in a helpless position) dejar desamparado; dejar plantado. —*v.i.* encallar; embarrancar; varar. —*n.* **1,** (fiber; filament) hebra; filamento. **2,** (string) hilo. **3,** (things arranged on a string) hilera. **4,** (tress) trenza. **5,** (lock of hair) guedeja; pelo. **6,** (part forming a rope) ramal. **7,** (shore) playa; costa; ribera.

stranded ('stræn·dɪd) *adj.* **1,** (aground) encallado; varado. **2,** (lost and helpless) desamparado; perdido. **3,** (woven of strands) trenzado; retorcido.

strange (streindʒ) *adj.* **1,** (unfamiliar; surprising) extraño; extraordinario; raro. **2,** (alien) ajeno; foráneo; forastero. **3,** (reserved; distant) retraído; reservado; esquivo. —**strangeness,** *n.* extrañeza; rareza.

stranger ('strein·dʒər) *n.* **1,** (person not known) extranjero; desconocido. **2,** (outsider; foreigner) extranjero; forastero. **3,** (newcomer) recién llegado. **4,** (novice) novicio; principiante.

strangle ('stræŋ·gəl) *v.t.* estrangular; ahogar. —*v.i.* estrangularse; ahogarse.

strangulate ('stræŋ·gju·leit) *v.t.* estrangular; obstruir.

strangulation (stræŋ·gju'lei·ʃən) *n.* estrangulación.

strap (stræp) *n.* **1,** (strip of leather) correa. **2,** (strip of metal, cloth, etc.) tira; banda; tirante. **3,** (razor strop) suavizador. —*v.t.* **1,** (fasten with a strap) liar; atar con correa, tira, banda, etc. **2,** (beat with a strap) azotar con una correa. **3,** (strop) suavizar. **4,** *colloq.* (oppress) apretar; apurar; acosar.

straphanger *n., colloq.* pasajero sin asiento que se aguanta a los tirantes de un tren, ómnibus, etc.

strapped (stræpt) *adj., colloq.* **1,** (harassed) apretado; acosado. **2,** (broke; in financial distress) pelado.

strapper ('stræp·ər) *n., colloq.* persona (esp. un muchacho) fuerte y enérgico.

strapping ('stræp·ɪŋ) *adj., colloq.* **1,** (robust) fuerte; robusto. **2,** (enormous) enorme.

strata ('strei·tə; 'stræt·ə) *n., pl. de* **stratum.**

stratagem ('stræt·ə·dʒəm) *n.* estratagema; ardid; artimaña; treta.

strategic (strə'ti·dʒɪk) *adj.* estratégico.

strategy ('stræt·ə·dʒi) *n.* estrategia. —**strategist,** *n.* estratégico; estratega.

strati- (stræt·ə) *prefijo* estrati-; estrato: *stratification,* estratificación.

stratify ('stræt·ə·fai) *v.t.* estratificar. —*v.i.* estratificarse. —**stratification** (-fɪ'kei·ʃən) *n.* estratificación.

strato- (stræt·ə) *prefijo* estrato-; estrato: *stratosphere,* estratosfera.

stratosphere *n.* estratosfera.

stratum ('strei·təm) *n.* [*pl.* **-ta**] **1,** (layer) estrato. **2,** *fig.* (class; division) clase; categoría; nivel.

stratus ('strei·təs) *n., meteorol.* estrato.

straw (strɔː) *n.* paja. —*adj.* **1,** (of or like straw) pajizo; de paja. **2,** (false) falso; ficticio. **3,** (worthless) de ningún valor; de bagatela. —**catch at a straw,** asirse de un cabello; tomar medidas desesperadas. —**I don't care a straw,** no me importa un pito (*o* un bledo). —**straw in the wind,** indicación; sugerencia. —**the last straw,** el acabóse; el colmo.

strawberry ('strɔˌbɛr·i) *n.* fresa.

straw-colored *adj.* pajizo; de color de paja.
straw hat sombrero de paja; canotié.
straw loft pajar.
straw man 1, (straw figure) figura de paja. 2, (scarecrow) espantapájaros. 3, (false witness) testigo falso. 4, (figurehead) testaferro. 5, (person of no importance) nulidad.
straw vote escrutinio exploratorio; encuesta.
stray (strei) *v.i.* 1, (wander) vagar; errar. 2, (deviate) extraviarse; desviarse; descarriarse. —*adj.* 1, (wandering; lost) extraviado; perdido. 2, (isolated) suelto; aislado. 3, (casual) casual; de casualidad; fortuito. —*n.* animal perdido: persona perdida o extraviada; vagabundo.
streak (strik) *n.* 1, (line; stripe) raya; lista; línea. 2, (ray, as of light) rayo. 3, (stratum; vein) veta; vena. 4, (strain; tendency) rasgo. 5, *colloq.* (spell; period) período; rato; racha (de fortuna). —*v.t.* rayar; *Amer.* listar. —*v.i.* 1, (become streaked) rayarse. 2, (move fast) correr como un rayo; volar; precipitarse. —**like a streak**, *colloq.* como un rayo.
streaky ('stri·ki) *adj.* 1, (marked with streaks) rayado; veteado; abigarrado. 2, (sporadic) esporádico; irregular. 3, (uneven; variable) desigual; variado; diverso.
stream (stri:m) *n.* 1, (body of water) río; arroyo. 2, (current; flow) corriente; flujo; chorro. 3, (course; trend) curso; corriente. 4, (succession; line) fila; desfile. —*v.i.* 1, (flow) correr; fluir; manar. 2, (gush) chorrear. 3, (move swiftly) correr; precipitarse.
streamer ('stri·mər) *n.* 1, (pennant) gallardete; banderola. 2, (narrow ribbon) cinta. 3, (tail of a comet) cabellera; cola.
streamline *v.t.* 1, (shape so as to offer little wind resistance) dar forma aerodinámica. 2, (modernize; make more efficient) modernizar; adelgazar. —*adj.* aerodinámico. —*n.* línea *o* forma aerodinámica.
streamlined *adj.* 1, (shaped so as to offer little wind resistance) de forma aerodinámica. 2, (modernized; efficient) modernizado; adelgazado.
street (strit) *n.* calle.
street Arab pilluelo; golfillo. *También,* **street urchin.**
streetcar *n.* tranvía.
street cleaner basurero. —**street cleaning**, limpieza de calles; servicio de sanidad.
streetwalker *n.* cantonera; ramera; mujer de la calle.
strength (strɛŋθ) *n.* 1, (force; power) fuerza; poder; potencia; vigor. 2, (intensity) intensidad. 3, (potency) potencia. 4, (number of personnel) número; fuerza; fuerzas. —**by main strength**, a pulso. —**on the strength of**, basado en; basándose en.
strengthen ('strɛŋ·θən) *v.t.* 1, (make strong) fortalecer; fortificar; reforzar. 2, (intensify) intensificar. 3, (make more potent) aumentar la potencia de. 4, (confirm) confirmar; corroborar. —*v.i.* fortalecerse; fortificarse; reforzarse.
strenuous ('strɛn·ju·əs) *adj.* 1, (arduous) arduo; difícil. 2, (vigorous) estrenuo; enérgico; vigoroso.
streptococcus (ˌstrɛp·tə'kak·əs) *n.* [*pl.* **-cocci** (-sai)] estreptococo.
streptomycin (ˌstrɛp·tə'mai·sɪn) *n.* estreptomicina.
stress (strɛs) *n.* 1, (strain) tensión; esfuerzo. 2, (emphasis) énfasis; realce. 3, (accent) acento. 4, (pressure; coercion) coerción; compulsión. 5, (urgency) urgencia; apuro. —*v.t.* 1, (subject to strain) someter a tensión. 2, (emphasize) dar énfasis a; recalcar; subrayar; dar importancia a. 3, (accent) acentuar. —**lay stress on**, insistir en; realzar; dar importancia a.
-stress (strɪs) *sufijo; forma nombres femeninos denotando* actividad; profesión: *songstress,* cantante; *seamstress,* costurera.
stretch (strɛtʃ) *v.t.* 1, (extend) extender; alargar. 2, (lay flat) tender. 3, (pull) estirar. 4, (exaggerate) exagerar. 5, (strain) forzar. —*v.i.* 1, (extend) extenderse. 2, (lie flat) tenderse. 3, (be pulled or tightened) estirarse. 4, (relax) desperezarse; repantigarse. —*n.* 1, (extent) extensión. 2, (pulling; tightening) estirón. 3,

(distance) distancia. **4,** (period of time) período; tiempo; rato. **5,** (straightaway) recta. **6,** *slang* (prison term) condena.

stretcher ('strɛtʃ·ər) *n.* **1,** (litter) camilla; andas (*pl.*). **2,** (device for stretching) estirador; bastidor.

stretcher-bearer *n.* camillero.

strew (struː) *v.t.* [*p.p.* **strewed** *o* **strewn** (struːn)] **1,** (scatter) esparcir; derramar; desparramar. **2,** (overspread by scattering) salpicar; sembrar; polvorear.

striate ('strai·et) *adj.* estriado. —*v.t.* estriar. —**striated,** *adj.* estriado.

stricken ('strɪk·ən) *adj.* **1,** (afflicted) afligido. **2,** (wounded; struck) herido. **3,** (overwhelmed) agobiado. —*v., p.p. de* **strike.** —**stricken in years,** entrado en años.

strict (strɪkt) *adj.* **1,** (exact) exacto; puntual. **2,** (scrupulous) escrupuloso. **3,** (rigorous) estricto; riguroso; severo; austero.

strictness ('strɪkt·nəs) *n.* **1,** (exactness) exactitud; puntualidad. **2,** (scrupulousness) escrupulosidad. **3,** (rigorousness) rigor; severidad; austeridad.

stricture ('strɪk·tʃər) *n.* **1,** (censure) censura; crítica. **2,** *med.* constricción.

stride (straid) *v.i.* [**strode** (stroːd), **stridden** ('strɪd·ən)] andar a trancos; dar zancadas. —*v.t.* **1,** (go along or through at a stride) pasar *o* cruzar a zancadas. **2,** (straddle) montar a horcajadas. —*n.* tranco; zancada; paso largo. —**at a stride,** a trancos. —**hit one's stride,** alcanzar su paso normal. —**make great strides,** progresar rápidamente.

strident ('strai·dənt) *adj.* estridente; chillón; llamativo. —**stridency,** *n.* estridencia.

strife (straif) *n.* contienda; lucha; refriega.

strike (straik) *v.t.* [*pret.* **struck;** *p.p.* **struck** *o* **stricken**] **1,** (deal a blow; hit) golpear; pegar; dar un golpe. **2,** (attack) atacar; asaltar. **3,** (collide with) chocar con; dar en *o* con. **4,** (cause to ignite) encender; sacar fuego de. **5,** (stamp; mint) acuñar. **6,** (print; imprint) imprimir. **7,** (cause to sound by striking) tocar. **8,** (announce by striking, as the hour) dar. **9,** (discover suddenly) descubrir repentinamente; dar en *o* con; tropezar con. **10,** (impress) impresionar; conmover. **11,** (lower; pull down) arriar; derribar. **12,** (afflict) afligir. **13,** (occur to; come to the notice of) ocurrírsele a uno. **14,** (erase; cancel) borrar; tachar. **15,** (conclude, as an agreement) concluir; concertar. **16,** (appear to; seem to) parecerle a uno. **17,** (cause a work stoppage in) salir *o* estar en huelga contra. **18,** (assume, as a pose or attitude) asumir; afectar. —*v.i.* **1,** (inflict a blow) dar un golpe *o* golpes; golpear. **2,** (collide) chocar; dar. **3,** (attack) atacar; dar el asalto. **4,** (run aground) varar; encallar. **5,** (grab at bait) coger el anzuelo. **6,** *naut.* (surrender) arriar la bandera. **7,** (announce the hour) dar la hora. **8,** (produce a sound) sonar; tocar. **9,** (produce a flame) encenderse. **10,** (refuse to work) salir *o* estar en huelga. **11,** (proceed in a certain direction) dirigirse; avanzar. —*n.* **1,** (work stoppage) huelga. **2,** (blow) golpe. **3,** (discovery) descubrimiento. **4,** (sudden good fortune) golpe de fortuna. —**strike camp,** batir tiendas. —**strike down,** derribar; aterrar. —**strike dumb,** aturdir; pasmar; confundir; dejar mudo. —**strike home,** dar en el hito. —**strike it rich,** descubrir una bonanza; tener un golpe de fortuna. —**strike off,** quitar; borrar; tachar. —**strike out, 1,** (set out) dirigirse; avanzar; ponerse en marcha. **2,** (cancel) borrar; tachar. **3,** (deal blows) dar golpes. **4,** *baseball* retirar al bateador; retirarse el bateador. **5,** *colloq.* (fail) fracasar. —**strike up, 1,** (start playing or singing) empezar a tocar *o* cantar. **2,** (initiate) trabar (una amistad); entablar (una discusión).

strikebreaker *n.* esquirol; rompehuelgas.

striker ('strai·kər) *n.* **1,** (person or thing that strikes) golpeador. **2,** (worker on strike) huelguista. **3,** (bell clapper) badajo. **4,** (hammer, as of a firearm) percusor.

striking ('strai·kɪŋ) *adj.* **1,** (remarkable) extraordinario; impresionante; llamativo. **2,** (refusing to work) en huelga.

string (strɪŋ) *n.* **1,** (line; cord) cordón; cuerda. **2,** *pl.* (musical instruments) instrumentos de cuerda. **3,** (chain) cadena. **4,** (things arranged on a string) sarta. **5,** (succession; series) serie; fila; hilera. **6,** *colloq.* (limitation) limitación; condición. —*v.t.* [*pret.* & *p.p.* **strung**] **1,** (provide with strings) encordar. **2,** (tie or bind with string) encordar; encordelar; atar con cuerdas. **3,** (arrange on a string) ensartar: enfilar; enhilar. **4,** (form in a line) enfilar; colocar en serie. **5,** (stretch like a string) tender. **6,** (hang by a string) colgar de una cuerda. **7,** *colloq.* (hoax) engañar; burlar. —*v.i.* **1,** (form into a string) colocarse en fila. **2,** (extend) extenderse. **3,** (move or progress in a string) marchar *o* avanzar en fila. —**on a string,** en poder de uno. —**pull strings,** ejercer uno clandestinamente su influencia. —**string along,** *colloq.* engañar; burlar; decepcionar. —**string along with,** *colloq.* estar *o* ponerse de acuerdo con; tener confianza en. —**string up,** *slang* ahorcar.

string bean habichuela verde; judía verde.

stringent ('strɪn·dʒənt) *adj.* estricto; riguroso; severo. —**stringency,** *n.* rigor; severidad.

stringy ('strɪŋ·i) *adj.* fibroso; correoso.

strip (strɪp) *v.t.* [**stripped, stripping**] **1,** (deprive; divest) despojar; robar. **2,** (undress) desnudar; desvestir. **3,** (remove the covering from) descortezar. **4,** *mech.* (tear off) estropear. **5,** (dismantle) desmantelar. **6,** (remove; take off) quitar. —*v.i.* desnudarse; desvestirse. —*n.* **1,** (narrow piece) tira; faja; lista; listón; jirón. **2,** (continuous series) sucesión; serie. **3,** *aero.* (runway) pista de aterrizaje.

stripe (straip) *n.* **1,** (narrow band or mark) raya; lista; banda; franja. **2,** (stroke or mark of a whip) latigazo; azotazo. **3,** (insignia; chevron) galón. **4,** (type; sort) tipo; índole; clase. —*v.t.* rayar; listar. —**striped,** *adj.* rayado; listado.

stripling ('strɪp·lɪŋ) *n.* mozalbete; mozuelo.

stripper ('strɪp·ər) *n.* artista de strip tease.

strip tease número de cabaret en que la artista se desnuda.

strive (straiv) *v.i.* [*pret.* **strove;** p.p. **striven** ('strɪv·ən)] esforzarse; luchar; empeñarse; competir. **strive to,** esforzarse por.

stroboscope ('strab·ə·skop) *n.* estroboscopio.

stroke (strok) *n.* **1,** (blow) golpe. **2,** (play; move) jugada. **3,** (sounding of a bell or chime) campanada. **4,** (movement or mark of a pen) plumada; (of a brush) pincelada; brochada. **5,** (apoplectic seizure) apoplejía; ataque de parálisis. **6,** (caress) caricia. **7,** (line; streak) raya. **8,** (lightning flash) rayo; relámpago. **9,** (thunderclap) trueno. **10,** (beat of the heart) latido. **11,** (mechanical motion) embolada; carrera. **12,** (movement of an oar) remada. **13,** (blow of a whip) latigazo. **14,** (movement of the arms) brazada. **15,** (occurrence of fortune) golpe de fortuna. —*v.t.* acariciar; frotar suavemente. —**at one stroke,** de un golpe; de una vez. —**at the stroke of ten,** al dar las diez; a las diez precisas *o* en punto.

stroll (stro:l) *v.i.* dar un paseo; pasearse; callejear; vagar. —*v.t.* pasearse por. —*n.* paseo.

stroller ('stro·lər) *n.* **1,** (person walking) paseante. **2,** (wanderer) vagabundo. **3,** (baby carriage) cochecillo de niño. **4,** (itinerant entertainer) cómico ambulante.

strong (strɔ:ŋ) *adj.* **1,** (powerful) fuerte; firme; robusto; poderoso. **2,** (fullbodied, as a beverage) cargado. **3,** (intense) intenso. **4,** (spicy) picante. **5,** (rancid) rancio. **6,** (offensive, as language) feo; injurioso. **7,** (amounting to; numbering) ascendiendo a: *six hundred strong,* ascendiendo a seiscientos. —*adv.* fuertemente.

strong-arm *adj.* violento. —*v.t.* coercer.

strongbox *n.* cofre fuerte; caja de caudales.

stronghold *n.* fortaleza; plaza fuerte.

strong-minded *adj.* decidido; de firmes creencias.

strong-willed *adj.* decidido; de voluntad firme.

strontium ('stran·ʃi·əm; -ti-) *n.* estroncio.

strop (strap) *n.* suavizador. —*v.t.* suavizar.

strophe ('stro·fi) *n.* estrofa.

strove (stro:v) *v., pret. de* **strive.**

struck (strʌk) *v., pret. & p.p. de* **strike.** —*adj.* (affected by a labor strike) en huelga.

structure ('strʌk·tʃər) *n.* **1,** (form) estructura. **2,** (something built) construcción; edificio. —*v.t.* construir; componer. —**structural,** *adj.* estructural.

struggle ('strʌg·əl) *n.* **1,** (conflict) lucha; pelea; conflicto. **2,** (extreme effort) esfuerzo. —*v.i.* **1,** (fight) luchar; pelear. **2,** (strive) esforzarse.

strum (strʌm) *v.t. & i.* [**strummed, strumming**] rasguear. —*n.* rasgueo. —**strumming,** *n.* rasgueo.

strumpet ('strʌm·pət) *n.* ramera; prostituta.

strung (strʌŋ) *v., pret. & p.p. de* **string.**

strut (strʌt) *v.i.* contonearse; pavonearse; farolear. —*n.* **1,** (swagger) contoneo; pavoneo. **2,** (brace) tornapunta; riostra; puntal.

strychnine ('strɪk·nɪn) *n.* estricnina.

stub (stʌb) *n.* **1,** (fragment; end) trozo; fragmento. **2,** (tree stump) tocón; cepa. **3,** (cigarette or cigar end) colilla. **4,** (short, thick piece) zoquete. **5,** (short piece of a ticket or check; coupon) talón. —*adj.* romo; obtuso; embotado. —*v.t.* [**stubbed, stubbing**] **1,** (pull out by the roots) desarraigar. **2,** (clear of stumps) quitar los tocones de. **3,** (strike by accident) chocar; tropezar.

stubble ('stʌb·əl) *n.* **1,** (stubs of grain) rastrojo. **2,** (rough growth, as of beard) cañones (*de la barba*).

stubbly ('stʌb·li) *adj.* **1,** (full of stubble) lleno de rastrojo. **2,** (bristly) erizado; cerdoso.

stubborn ('stʌb·ərn) *adj.* **1,** (obstinate) obstinado; terco; cabezudo; testarudo. **2,** (unyielding) intratable; inflexible; intransigente.

stubbornness ('stʌb·ərn·nəs) *n.* **1,** (obstinacy) obstinación; terquedad; testarudez. **2,** (resoluteness) inflexibilidad; intransigencia.

stubby ('stʌb·i) *adj.* **1,** (full of stubs) lleno de tocones. **2,** (short and thick) romo; embotado. **3,** (bristly) cerdoso. **4,** (stocky) rechoncho; regordete.

stucco ('stʌk·o) *n.* estuco. —*v.t.* estucar. —**stuccowork,** *n.* estucado.

stuck (stʌk) *v., pret. & p.p. de* **stick.**

stuck-up *adj., colloq.* altanero; tieso; esquivo; reservado.

stud (stʌd) *n.* **1,** (ornamental tack) tachón. **2,** (shirt button) botón de camisa. **3,** (post; support) poste; montante. **4,** (pin; peg) clavija; estaquilla. **5,** (breeding horse) caballo padre. **6,** (herd of breeding horses) caballada; yeguada. **7,** (breeding establishment) acaballadero. —*adj.* semental; de *o* para cría. —*v.t.* [**studded, studding**] **1,** (decorate with studs) tachonar; clavetear. **2,** (be scattered over; cover) salpicar.

studbook *n.* registro genealógico de caballos.

student ('stu·dənt) *n.* **1,** (pupil) estudiante; discípulo; alumno. **2,** (scholar; researcher) investigador.

stud farm acaballadero.

studhorse *n.* caballo padre.

studied ('stʌd·id) *adj.* estudiado; deliberado; premeditado.

studio ('stu·di·o) *n.* estudio; taller.

studious ('stu·di·əs) *adj.* estudioso; aplicado; diligente.

study ('stʌd·i) *n.* **1,** (mental effort) estudio. **2,** (research) investigación. **3,** (branch of learning) estudio; disciplina. **4,** (academic subject) asignatura. **5,** (deep thought) meditación profunda. **6,** (room reserved for study) escritorio; gabinete; despacho; estudio. —*v.t. & i.* [*pret. & p.p.* **studied**] estudiar.

stuff (stʌf) *n.* **1,** (material) material. **2,** (cloth) tela; género. **3,** (things; effects) cosas; efectos; bienes. **4,** (rubbish; junk) basura. **5,** (nonsense) tontería. —*v.t.* **1,** (fill; pack) rellenar. **2,** (cram) atestar; colmar; henchir. **3,** (plug; block) tapar; atascar; atarugar. **4,** (glut with food) atracar; hartar. **5,** (force in; thrust in) meter; clavar; apretar. —*v.i.* atracarse; hartarse.

stuffed shirt *slang* presumido; persona arrogante y altanera.
stuffing ('stʌf·ɪŋ) *n.* relleno.
stuffy ('stʌf·i) *adj.* **1,** (poorly ventilated) mal ventilado; cerrado; sofocante. **2,** (stopped up, as from a cold) tapado; catarroso. **3,** *colloq.* (dull) aburrido. **4,** *colloq.* (prudish) mojigato; remilgado. **5,** *colloq.* (old-fashioned) chapado a la antigua.
stultify ('stʌl·tə·fai) *v.t.* **1,** (make absurd) poner en ridículo. **2,** (make ineffectual) anular; viciar. **3,** (make stupid) embrutecer.
stumble ('stʌm·bəl) *v.i.* **1,** (trip) tropezar. **2,** (stagger) titubear; bambolear. **3,** (falter in speech) titubear; vacilar. **4,** (blunder) errar. —*n.* **1,** (false step) traspié; tropezón; tropiezo. **2,** (blunder) desliz; desatino. —**stumble on, upon** *o* **across,** tropezar con; dar con.
stumbling block ('stʌm·blɪŋ) tropiezo; escollo.
stump (stʌmp) *n.* **1,** (tree trunk) tocón; cepa. **2,** (remaining part; end; butt) trozo; fragmento; (*of an amputated limb*) muñón; (*of a cigar or cigarette*) colilla; (*of a tooth*) raigón; (*of a tail*) rabo. **3,** (political rostrum) tribuna para discursos políticos. **4,** (heavy step) paso pesado. **5,** *slang* (leg) pierna; pata. —*v.t.* **1,** (lop) cortar; amputar. **2,** (campaign politically in) recorrer haciendo discursos políticos; solicitar votos en *o* de. **3,** *colloq.* (perplex) confundir; dejar perplejo. —*v.i.* **1,** (campaign; electioneer) dar discursos políticos; solicitar votos. **2,** (walk heavily) renquear; cojear. —**up a stump,** *colloq.* perplejo; confuso; en un aprieto.
stumpy ('stʌmp·i) *adj.* **1,** (stocky) regordete; rechoncho; tozo. **2,** (abounding in stumps) lleno de tocones.
stun (stʌn) *v.t.* [**stunned, stunning**] aturdir; pasmar.
stung (stʌŋ) *v., pret. & p.p. de* **sting.**
stunk (stʌŋk) *v., p.p. de* **stink.**
stunning ('stʌn·ɪŋ) *adj.* **1,** (that stuns) aturdidor. **2,** *colloq.* (remarkable) elegante; bellísimo; de chupete.
stunt (stʌnt) *n.* **1,** (exhibition of skill) ejercicio de habilidad; maniobra sensacional. **2,** (acrobatic feat) acrobacia; jugada acrobática; *aero.* vuelo acrobático. **3,** (dwarfed creature) engendro. —*v.t.* impedir (el desarrollo de). —*v.i.* hacer acrobacia; hacer maniobras sensacionales.
stupefaction (ˌstu·pəˈfæk·ʃən) *n.* estupefacción; estupor.
stupefy ('stju·pə·fai) *v.t.* **1,** (induce stupor in) embrutecer; entorpecer. **2,** (amaze) pasmar; aturdir; atontar. —**stupefied,** *adj.* estupefacto; aletargado.
stupendous (stjuˈpɛn·dəs) *adj.* estupendo; maravilloso; enorme.
stupid ('stju·pɪd) *adj.* estúpido; torpe; necio. —**stupidity** (stjuˈpɪd·ə·ti) *n.* estupidez; torpeza; necedad.
stupor ('stu·pər) *n.* estupor. —**in a stupor,** estupefacto; aletargado.
sturdy ('stʌɹ·di) *adj.* **1,** (strong; stout) fuerte; robusto. **2,** (firm) firme; resuelto; determinado.
sturgeon ('stʌɹ·dʒən) *n.* esturión.
stutter ('stʌt·ər) *v.i.* tartamudear. —*v.t.* decir tartamudeando. —*n.* tartamudeo. —**stutterer,** *n.* tartamudo.
sty (stai) *n.* [*pl.* **sties** (staiz)] **1,** (pigpen) pocilga. **2,** (inflammation of the eyelid) orzuelo.
Stygian ('stɪdʒ·i·ən) *adj.* estigio; tenebroso.
style (stail) *n.* **1,** (fashion) moda. **2,** (manner) estilo; manera; forma. **3,** (elegance) elegancia. **4,** (stylus) estilo. **5,** (name; title) nombre; título. **6,** *bot.* estilo. —*v.t.* **1,** (design) diseñar. **2,** (name) nombrar; designar. —**stylish,** *adj.* elegante; de moda. —**stylist,** *n.* estilista.
stylistic (staiˈlɪs·tɪk) *adj.* estilístico. —**stylistics,** *n.* estilística.
stylize ('stai·laiz) *v.t.* estilizar.
stylus ('stai·ləs) *n.* **1,** (pointed instrument) estilo. **2,** (phonograph needle) aguja.
stymie ('stai·mi) *n., golf* obstáculo producido por la pelota de un adversario encontrándose entre el agujero y la pelota del otro. —*v.t.* obstruir; *fig.* frustrar.
styptic ('stɪp·tɪk) *adj. & n.* estíptico.
styrene ('stai·rin) *n.* estirena.
suave (swaːv) *adj.* afable; gentil;

urbano. —**suavity,** *n.* afabilidad; gentileza; urbanidad.

sub- (sʌb) *prefijo* sub-. **1,** bajo; debajo: *subsoil,* subsuelo. **2,** menor grado o intensidad: *subtropical,* subtropical. **3,** inferior; de menor categoría: *subordinate,* subordinado. **4,** resultado de división: *sublease,* subarrendar; *subgroup,* subgrupo.

subaltern (sʌb'ɔl·tərn) *n.* & *adj.* subalterno.

subcommittee *n.* subcomisión; subcomité.

subconscious (sʌb'kan·ʃəs) *adj.* subconsciente. —*n.* subconsciente; subconsciencia. —**subconsciousness,** *n.* subconsciencia.

subcontract (sʌb'kan·trækt) *n.* subcontrato. —*v.t.* & *i.* (ˌsʌb·kən·'trækt) subcontratar. —**subcontractor** (-'trækt·ər) *n.* subcontratista.

subcutaneous (ˌsʌb·kju'tei·ni·əs) *adj.* subcutáneo.

subdivide *v.t.* subdividir. —*v.i.* subdividirse. —**subdivision,** *n.* subdivisión.

subdue (səb'duː) *v.t.* **1,** (conquer; overcome) sojuzgar; subyugar; dominar. **2,** (diminish; soften) suavizar; disminuir; reducir. **3,** (repress) reprimir; dominar.

subject ('sʌb·dʒɪkt) *n.* **1,** (theme; topic) sujeto; asunto; tema. **2,** (recipient of treatment, examination, etc.) sujeto. **3,** (person under power of another) súbdito. **4,** (academic course) asignatura. **5,** *gram.* sujeto. —*adj.* **1,** (under power of another) súbdito; sujeto. **2,** (liable; disposed) sujeto; expuesto; propenso. **3,** [*en la expresión* **subject to**] (contingent upon) a condición de. —*v.t.* (səb'dʒɛkt) sujetar; someter. —**subject matter,** asunto; materia.

subjection (səb'dʒɛk·ʃən) *n.* sujeción; sometimiento.

subjective (səb'dʒɛk·tɪv) *adj.* subjetivo. —**subjectivity** (ˌsʌb·dʒɛk'tɪv·ə·ti) *n.* subjetividad.

subjoin (səb'dʒɔin) *v.t.* añadir; agregar.

subjugate ('sʌb·dʒəˌgeit) *v.t.* subyugar; sojuzgar. —**subjugation,** *n.* subyugación.

subjunctive (səb'dʒʌŋk·tɪv) *adj.* subjuntivo.

sublease *n.* subarriendo. —*v.t.* subarrendar.

sublimate ('sʌb·ləˌmeit) *v.t.* sublimar. —*n.* sublimado. —**sublimation,** *n.* sublimación.

sublime (sə'blaim) *adj.* sublime. —**sublimity** (sə'blɪm·ə·ti) *n.* sublimidad.

submachine gun ametralladora portátil.

submarine (ˌsʌb·mə'riːn) *adj.* & *n.* submarino.

submerge (səb'mʌɹdʒ) *v.t.* sumergir. —*v.i.* sumergirse.

submersible (səb'mʌɹ·sə·bəl) *adj.* sumergible. —*n.* sumergible; submarino.

submersion (səb'mʌɹ·ʒən) *n.* sumersión.

submission (səb'mɪʃ·ən) *n.* sumisión; sometimiento.

submissive (səb'mɪs·ɪv) *adj.* sumiso.

submit (səb'mɪt) *v.t.* someter. —*v.i.* someterse.

subordinate (sə'bor·dɪ·nət) *adj.* & *n.* subordinado; subalterno. —*v.t.* (-ˌneit) subordinar. —**subordination,** *n.* subordinación.

suborn (sə'born) *v.t.* sobornar. —**subornation** (ˌsʌb·or'nei·ʃən) *n.* soborno; sobornación.

subpoena (səb'pi·nə; sə-) *n.* comparendo; citación. —*v.t.* citar; emplazar.

subrogate ('sʌb·roˌgeit) *v.t.* subrogar. —**subrogation,** *n.* subrogación.

sub rosa (sʌb'ro·zə) *adv.* secretamente; en secreto.

subscribe (səb'skraib) *v.t.* suscribir. —*v.i.* **1,** (sign) suscribirse; firmar. **2,** (promise; accept an obligation) suscribirse; abonarse. —**subscribe to, 1,** (promise to pay) suscribirse a; abonarse a. **2,** (endorse; consent to) suscribir; aceptar; consentir en.

subscriber (səb'skrai·bər) *n.* suscriptor; abonado.

subscript *adj.* suscrito. —*n.* índice suscrito.

subscription (səb'skrɪp·ʃən) *n.* **1,** (assent; agreement) suscripción. **2,** (signature) firma. **3,** (promise to pay) suscripción; abono.

subsequent ('sʌb·sə·kwənt) *adj.* subsecuente; subsiguiente; posterior. —**subsequence,** *n.* subsecuencia.

subserve (səb'sʌːɹv) *v.t.* servir; ayudar.

subservience (səb'sʌɹ·vi·əns) *n.* 1, (subordinate status) subordinación. 2, (servility) servilismo.
subservient (səb'sʌɹ·vi·ənt) *adj.* 1, (subordinate) subordinado; subalterno. 2, (servile) servil.
subside (səb'said) *v.i.* 1, (sink; settle) hundirse. 2, (fall to a lower level) bajar de nivel; menguar. 3, (abate) apaciguarse; calmar.
subsidence (səb'sai·dəns) *n.* 1, (sinking; settling) hundimiento. 2, (falling to a lower level) bajada. 3, (abatement) apaciguamiento; calma.
subsidiary (səb'sɪd·i·ɛr·i) *adj.* subsidiario; auxiliar; sucursal. —*n.* rama; filial; división; sucursal.
subsidize ('sʌb·sɪ·daiz) *v.t.* subvencionar.
subsidy ('sʌb·sə·di) *n.* subsidio; subvención.
subsist (səb'sɪst) *v.i.* subsistir. —**subsistence,** *n.* subsistencia.
subsoil *n.* subsuelo.
subsonic (sʌb'san·ɪk) *adj.* subsónico.
substance ('sʌb·stəns) *n.* sustancia.
substantial (səb'stæn·ʃəl) *adj.* 1, (of or having substance; real) sustancial; sustancioso. 2, (strong) fuerte; sólido. 3, (ample; important) considerable. 4, (wealthy) rico; acomodado.
substantiate (səb'stæn·ʃi·eit) *v.t.* comprobar; verificar; establecer. —**substantiation,** *n.* comprobación; verificación.
substantive ('sʌb·stən·tɪv) *adj.* & *n.* sustantivo.
substitute ('sʌb·stə,tjut) *n.* sustituto; suplente. —*v.t.* & *i.* sustituir. —**substitution,** *n.* sustitución.
subsume (səb'su:m) *v.t.* subsumir.
subter- (sʌb·tər) *prefijo* subter-; bajo; debajo: *subterfuge,* subterfugio.
subterfuge ('sʌb·tər,fjudʒ) *n.* subterfugio; escapatoria; salida; evasión.
subterranean (,sʌb·tə'rei·ni·ən) *adj.* subterráneo.
subtitle *n.* subtítulo.
subtle ('sʌt·əl) *adj.* 1, (delicate; refined) sutil; delicado; tenue; refinado. 2, (artful; crafty) artificioso. 3, (discriminating; shrewd) perspicaz; agudo; astuto.
subtlety ('sʌt·əl·ti) *n.* 1, (delicacy) sutileza; delicadeza. 2, (artfulness) artificio; destreza. 3, (shrewdness) agudeza; astucia.
subtract (səb'trækt) *v.t.* & *i.* sustraer.
subtraction (səb'træk·ʃən) *n.* sustracción.
subtrahend ('sʌb·trə·hɛnd) *n.* sustraendo.
suburb ('sʌb·ʌɹb) *n.* suburbio; arrabal; urbanización; *pl.* afueras; inmediaciones.
suburban (səb'ʌɹb·ən) *adj.* suburbano. —**suburbanite,** *n.* suburbano.
subversion (səb'vʌɹ·ʒən) *n.* subversión. —**subversive** (-sɪv) *adj.* subversivo. —*n.* subversor.
subvert (səb'vʌɹt) *v.t.* subvertir.
subway ('sʌb·wei) *n.* 1, (underground railroad) tren subterráneo; metro. 2, (underground passage) paso subterráneo; galería subterránea.
succeed (sək'si:d) *v.i.* 1, (terminate well) triunfar; tener buen éxito; salir bien. 2, (follow) suceder. —*v.t.* suceder a.
succeeding (sək'si·dɪŋ) *adj.* subsiguiente; posterior.
success (sək'sɛs) *n.* 1, (favorable outcome) triunfo; éxito; fortuna; buen resultado. 2, (person or thing that prospers) persona o cosa afortunada.
successful (sək'sɛs·fəl) *adj.* próspero; afortunado; que tiene buen éxito.
succession (sək'sɛʃ·ən) *n.* sucesión. —**in succession,** seguido; sucesivo; sucesivamente.
successive (sək'sɛs·ɪv) *adj.* sucesivo.
successor (sək'sɛs·ər) *n.* sucesor.
succinct (sək'sɪŋkt) *adj.* sucinto.
succor *también,* **succour** ('sʌk·ər) *n.* ayuda; socorro; auxilio. —*v.t.* ayudar; socorrer.
succotash ('sʌk·ə,tæʃ) *n.* guiso de maíz con habas.
succulent ('sʌk·jə·lənt) *adj.* suculento. —**succulence,** *n.* suculencia.
succumb (sə'kʌm) *v.i.* sucumbir; rendirse; morir.
such (sʌtʃ) *indef. adj.* tal; semejante. —*indef. pron.* tal; un tal; el, la, los *o* las (que). —**as such,** como tal. —**such a,** tal; semejante. —**such a large house,** una casa tan grande. —**such and such,** tal y

tal; tal y tal cosa; fulano de tal. —**such as**, quien(es); el, la, los *o* las que. —**such that**, de tal modo que; de manera que; de suerte que.
suck (sʌk) *v.t. & i.* chupar; mamar; sorber. —*n.* chupada; mamada; sorbo.
sucker ('sʌk·ər) *n.* **1,** (person or thing that sucks) chupador. **2,** *bot.* mamón; chupón. **3,** *colloq.* (lollipop) pirulí; *Amer.* chupete. **4,** *colloq.* (dupe) primo; bobo.
suckle ('sʌk·əl) *v.t.* amamantar; lactar; dar el pecho.—*v.i.* mamar.
suckling ('sʌk·lɪŋ) *adj. & n.* mamón. —*n.* (young pig) lechón.
sucrose ('su·kros) *n.* sucrosa.
suction ('sʌk·ʃən) *n.* succión. —**suction pump**, bomba aspirante.
sudden ('sʌd·ən) *adj.* súbito; repentino; imprevisto. —**suddenly**, *adv.* súbitamente; de súbito; de repente. —**suddenness**, *n.* rapidez; precipitación.
suds (sʌdz) *n.pl.* **1,** (water foaming with soap) jabonaduras; espuma (*sing.*). **2,** *slang* (beer) cerveza.
sue (suː) *v.t.* demandar. —*v.i.* poner pleito; entablar juicio. —**sue for peace**, pedir la paz.
suede (sweid) *n.* piel curtida semejante a la de gamuza.
suet ('su·ɪt) *n.* sebo; grasa; gordo.
suffer ('sʌf·ər) *v.t.* **1,** (undergo; endure) sufrir; padecer. **2,** (tolerate) soportar; tolerar. **3,** (allow) permitir. —*v.i.* sufrir.
sufferance ('sʌf·ər·əns) *n.* **1,** (tacit consent) tolerancia; consentimiento. **2,** (endurance) sufrimiento; paciencia; resignación.
sufferer ('sʌf·ər·ər) *n.* paciente; sufridor; doliente; víctima.
suffering ('sʌf·ər·ɪŋ) *n.* sufrimiento; pena; dolor; padecimiento; tormento. —*adj.* doliente.
suffice (sə'fais) *v.i.* bastar; ser suficiente. —*v.t.* satisfacer. —**suffice it to say**, baste decir.
sufficiency (sə'fɪʃ·ən·si) *n.* suficiencia; lo suficiente.
sufficient (sə'fɪʃ·ənt) *adj.* suficiente; amplio; bastante.
suffix ('sʌf·ɪks) *n.* sufijo. —*v.t.* (*usu.* sə'fɪks) añadir.
suffocate ('sʌf·ə·keit) *v.t.* sofocar; asfixiar; ahogar. —*v.i.* sofocarse; asfixiarse; ahogarse. —**suffocation**, *n.* sofoco; asfixia; ahogo.
suffrage ('sʌf·rɪdʒ) *n.* sufragio; voto.
suffragette (ˌsʌf·rə'dʒɛt) *n.* sufragista.
suffragist ('sʌf·rə·dʒɪst) *n.* sufragista; votante.
suffuse (sə'fjuːz) *v.t.* difundir; bañar; cubrir.
suffusion (sə'fju·ʃən) *n.* sufusión.
sugar ('ʃʊg·ər) *n.* azúcar. —*v.t.* azucarar; endulzar. —*v.i.* formar azúcar; *Amer.* azucararse. —*adj.* azucarero; de azúcar.
sugar beet remolacha azucarera.
sugar bowl azucarera.
sugar candy azúcar piedra; azúcar cande.
sugar cane cañamiel; caña dulce; caña de azúcar.
sugar-coat *v.t.* acaramelar; almibarar; garapiñar; *fig.* endulzar. —**sugar coating**, garapiña; baño de azúcar.
sugar daddy *slang,* viejo rico que mantiene con lujo a una mujer joven.
sugar loaf pan de azúcar.
sugar maple arce del azúcar.
sugar mill trapiche; molino de azúcar; *Cuba* batey.
sugar plantation cañamelar.
sugarplum *n.* confite; dulce.
sugary ('ʃʊg·ə·ri) *adj.* **1,** (of or containing sugar) azucarado; acaramelado; dulce. **2,** *fig.* (flattering) meloso; melifluo.
suggest (səg'dʒɛst) *v.t.* sugerir; indicar; intimar.
suggestible (səg'dʒɛs·tə·bəl) *adj.* sugestionable.
suggestion (səg'dʒɛs·tʃən) *n.* sugestión; sugerencia; indicación; intimación.
suggestive (səg'dʒɛs·tɪv) *adj.* sugestivo; sugerente.
suicidal (ˌsu·ə'sai·dəl) *adj.* suicida; *fig.* ruinoso.
suicide ('su·ə·said) *n.* **1,** (agent) suicida. **2,** (act) suicidio; *fig.* ruina. —**commit suicide**, suicidarse.
suit (sut) *n.* **1,** (set; ensemble) juego. **2,** (set of clothes) traje. **3,** *law* pleito; proceso; demanda. **4,** (petition) petición; solicitación. **5,** (courtship) galanteo; cortejo. **6,** *cards* palo. —*v.t.* **1,** (be appropriate to) satisfacer; caer bien a. **2,** (adapt) adaptar; acomodar. **3,** (serve) servir; convenir a. **4,** (provide with clothes) vestir. —*v.i.*

convenir; ser apropiado; caer bien. —**bring suit**, poner pleito; entablar juicio. —**follow suit**, 1, *cards* seguir el palo; servir del palo. 2, *fig.* seguir la corriente; hacer lo mismo. —**suit oneself**, hacer lo que quiera.

suitable ('sut·ə·bəl) *adj.* apropiado; conforme; conveniente. —**suitability**, *n.* conformidad; conveniencia.

suitcase *n.* maleta.

suite (swit) *n.* 1, (series; set) serie; juego. 2, (retinue) séquito; tren; comitiva. —**suite of rooms**, juego de habitaciones; serie de piezas; apartamiento.

suited ('sut·ɪd) *adj.* 1, (conformable) conforme; adecuado. 2, (adapted) apto; idóneo.

suiting ('sut·ɪŋ) *n.* tela para trajes.

suitor ('sut·ər) *n.* 1, (one who courts a woman) pretendiente; galán; aspirante. 2, (petitioner) postulante; suplicante. 3, (litigant) demandante; pleiteador.

sulfa ('sʌl·fə) *n.* & *adj.* sulfa.

sulfate ('sʌl·fet) *n.* sulfato.

sulfide ('sʌl·faid) *n.* sulfuro.

sulfur ('sʌl·fər) *n.* azufre. —*v.t.* azufrar; sulfurar. —**sulfur mine**, azufrera.

sulfurate ('sʌl·fjʊˌreit) *v.t.* azufrar; sulfurar.

sulfuric (sʌl'fjʊr·ɪk) *adj.* sulfúrico.

sulfurous ('sʌl·fər·əs) *adj.* sulfuroso; azufrado.

sulk (sʌlk) *v.i.* amorrarse; estar *o* ponerse ceñudo. —*n.* ceño; mal humor.

sulky ('sʌl·ki) *adj.* malcontento; resentido. —*n.* calesín de un solo asiento.

sullen ('sʌl·ən) *adj.* hosco; malhumorado; resentido. —**sullenness**, *n.* hosquedad; mal humor; resentimiento.

sully ('sʌl·i) *v.t.* manchar; desdorar; mancillar; desprestigiar.

sulphate ('sʌl·feit) *n.* = **sulfate.** —**sulphide** (-faid) *n.* = **sulfide.** —**sulphur** (-fər) *n.* = **sulfur.** —**sulphurate** (-fjʊ·reit) *v.t.* = **sulfurate.** —**sulphuric** (-'fjʊr·ɪk) *adj.* = **sulfuric.** —**sulfurous** (-fər·əs) *adj.* = **sulfurous.**

sultan ('sʌl·tən) *n.* sultán.

sultana (sʌl'tæn·ə) *n.* sultana.

sultanate ('sʌl·təˌneit) *n.* sultanía; sultanato.

sultry ('sʌl·tri) *adj.* sofocante; bochornoso.

sum (sʌm) *n.* 1, (amount; quantity) cantidad. 2, (total) suma; monta; total. 3, (gist; substance) suma; esencia; sustancia. —*v.t.* [**summed, summing**] sumar. —**sum to**, ascender a; montar a. —**sum up**, resumir; compendiar.

sumac ('ʃu·mæk) *n.* zumaque.

summarize ('sʌm·əˌraiz) *v.t.* resumir; compendiar.

summary ('sʌm·ə·ri) *n.* resumen; sumario; compendio. —*adj.* sumario; breve; conciso.

summation (sə'mei·ʃən) *n.* total; gran total; suma.

summer ('sʌm·ər) *n.* verano. —*adj.* veraniego; de verano; estival. —*v.i.* veranear; pasar el verano.

summer camp campamento de veraneo.

summerhouse *n.* glorieta; cenador; cenadero.

summer resort centro de veraneo.

summertime *n.* verano; tiempo de verano.

summery ('sʌm·ə·ri) *adj.* veraniego; estival.

summit ('sʌm·ɪt) *n.* ápice; cima; cumbre; pináculo.

summon ('sʌm·ən) *v.t.* 1, (call) llamar. 2, (call together) convocar. 3, *law* citar; emplazar. 4, (command) mandar. 5, (call forth; gather) reunir; hacer acopio de.

summons ('sʌm·ənz) *n.* 1, (call) llamada; convocación; orden. 2, *law* emplazamiento; citación. —*v.t.*, *colloq.* emplazar; citar.

sumptuous ('sʌmp·tʃu·əs) *adj.* suntuoso. —**sumptuousness**, *n.* suntuosidad.

sun (sʌn) *n.* sol. —*v.t.* [**sunned, sunning**] asolear; solear. —*v.i.* asolearse; tomar el sol. —*adj.* de *o* del sol; solar. —**place in the sun**, un puesto en el mundo. —**under the sun**, debajo del sol; en este mundo.

sun bath baño de sol.

sun-bathe *v.i.* tomar el sol; asolearse.

sunbeam *n.* rayo de sol.

sunbonnet *n.* gorra de sol.

sunburn *n.* quemadura de sol. —**sunburnt** (-bʌɹnt) *adj.* tostado por el sol.

sundae ('sʌn·di) *n.* helado con jarabe y frutas o nueces.
Sunday ('sʌn·de) *n.* domingo. —*adj.* dominical; del domingo. —**dress up in one's Sunday best,** endomingarse.
Sunday school escuela dominical; escuela bíblica.
sunder ('sʌn·dər) *v.t.* separar; romper; partir. —*v.i.* separarse; romperse; partirse. —**in sunder,** en partes; en pedazos.
sundial ('sʌn,dail) *n.* reloj de sol; cuadrante solar.
sundown *n.* puesta del sol; anochecer.
sundry ('sʌn·dri) *adj.* varios; diversos. —**sundries,** *n.pl.* artículos diversos.
sunfish *n.* rueda.
sunflower *n.* girasol.
sung (sʌŋ) *v., p.p. de* sing.
sunglasses ('sʌn,glæs·ɪz) *n.pl.* lentes *o* gafas de sol.
sunk (sʌŋk) *v., p.p. de* sink.
sunken ('sʌŋk·ən) *adj.* sumido; hundido.
sunlight *n.* luz del sol; sol.
sunlit *adj.* iluminado por el sol; claro.
sunny ('sʌn·i) *adj.* 1, (bright with sunshine) asoleado; claro. 2, *fig.* (cheerful) alegre; risueño. —**be sunny,** hacer sol.
sun parlor solana.
sun porch solana.
sunrise *n.* amanecer; salida del sol. —**from sunrise to sunset,** de sol a sol.
sunset *n.* puesta del sol; ocaso del sol; anochecer.
sunshade *n.* 1, (parasol) quitasol; parasol; sombrilla. 2, (awning) toldo. 3, (visor) visera.
sunshine *n.* 1, (sunlight) sol; luz del sol; día. 2, (sunny spot) solana. 3, *fig.* (cheer) alegría.
sunspot ('sʌn,spat) *n.* mancha *o* mácula solar.
sunstroke *n.* insolación; tabardillo.
sun tan atezamiento; quemadura de sol. *También,* **suntan.**
sunup ('sʌn·ʌp) *n.* = sunrise.
sup (sʌp) *v.i.* [**supped, supping**] 1, (eat the evening meal) cenar. 2, (sip) sorber. —*n.* sorbo.
sup- (səp) *prefijo, var. de* **sub-** *ante* p: *suppose,* suponer.
super ('su·pər) *n., colloq.* = **superintendent, supernumerary,** *etc.* —*adj., colloq.* 1, (extra fine) superfino. 2, (extra large) grande; grandísimo.
super- (su·pər) *prefijo* super-; sobre; encima de; superior: *supereminence,* supereminencia.
superable ('su·pər·ə·bəl) *adj.* superable.
superabundant *adj.* superabundante; sobreabundante. —**superabundance,** *n.* superabundancia; sobreabundancia.
superannuated (,su·pər'æn·ju·ei·tɪd) *adj.* 1, (retired) jubilado; fuera de servicio. 2, (obsolete) anticuado.
superb (sʊ'pʌɹb) *adj.* soberbio; espléndido; magnífico.
supercargo *n.* sobrecargo.
supercilious (,su·pər'sɪl·i·əs) *adj.* altanero; desdeñoso.
superego *n.* super ego.
superficial (,su·pər'fɪʃ·əl) *adj.* superficial. —**superficiality** (-i'æl·ə·ti) *n.* superficialidad.
superfine *adj.* superfino.
superfluous (su'pʌɹ·flu·əs) *adj.* superfluo; sobrado. —**superfluity** (,su·pər'flu·ə·ti) *n.* superfluidad.
superheterodyne *adj.* superheterodino.
superhuman *adj.* sobrehumano.
superimpose *v.t.* sobreponer; superponer. —**superimposition,** *n.* superposición.
superintend (,su·pər·ɪn'tɛnd) *v.t.* superentender; dirigir; vigilar.
superintendent (,su·pər·ɪn'tɛn·dənt) *n.* superintendente. —**superintendency,** *n.* superintendencia.
superior (sə'pɪr·i·ər) *adj.* 1, (higher; greater) superior. 2, (better) superior; mejor. 3, (haughty) arrogante; altanero. 4, (indifferent) indiferente. —*n.* superior; *fem.* superiora.
superiority (sə,pɪr·i'ar·ə·ti) *n.* 1, (quality of being higher, greater or better) superioridad. 2, (haughtiness) arrogancia; altanería.
superlative (sə'pʌɹ·lə·tɪv) *adj. & n.* superlativo.
superman *n.* [*pl.* **-men**] superhombre.
supernal (su'pʌɹ·nəl) *adj.* 1, (lofty) superno; supremo. 2, (celestial) celeste; celestial.
supernatural *adj.* sobrenatural.

supernumerary (ˌsu·pərˈnju·mə·rɛr·i) *adj.* & *n.* supernumerario. —*n., theat.* figurante; comparsa.
superpose *v.t.* sobreponer; superponer. —**superposition**, *n.* superposición.
superscribe (ˌsu·pərˈskraib) *v.t.* sobrescribir.
superscript *adj.* sobrescrito. —*n.* índice sobrescrito.
superscription (ˌsu·pərˈskrɪp·ʃən) *n.* sobrescrito.
supersede (ˌsu·pərˈsiːd) *v.t.* suplantar; reemplazar.
supersonic *adj.* supersónico.
superstition (ˌsu·pərˈstɪʃ·ən) *n.* superstición. —**superstitious**, *adj.* supersticioso.
superstructure *n.* superestructura.
supervene (ˌsu·pərˈviːn) *v.i.* sobrevenir; supervenir. —**supervention** (-ˈvɛn·ʃən) *n.* superveniencia.
supervise (ˈsu·pərˌvaiz) *v.t.* superentender; vigilar; dirigir. —**supervision** (-ˈvɪʒ·ən) *n.* superintendencia; dirección; supervisión.
supervisor (ˈsu·pərˌvai·zər) *n.* 1, (director) superintendente; jefe; director. 2, (foreman) sobrestante; capataz.
supervisory (ˌsu·pərˈvai·zə·ri) *adj.* de superintendencia.
supine (suˈpain) *adj.* supino.
supper (ˈsʌp·ər) *n.* cena. —**eat** *o* **have supper**, cenar; tomar la cena.
suppertime *n.* hora de cenar.
supplant (səˈplænt) *v.t.* suplantar; reemplazar; sustituir.
supple (ˈsʌp·əl) *adj.* 1, (pliant) flexible; manejable. 2, (lithe) ágil. 3, (yielding) dócil; sumiso.
supplement (ˈsʌp·lə·mənt) *n.* suplemento. —*v.t.* suplementar. —**supplemental** (-ˈmɛn·təl); **supplementary** (-ˈmɛn·tə·ri) *adj.* suplementario.
suppliant (ˈsʌp·li·ənt) *adj.* & *n.* suplicante.
supplicant (ˈsʌp·lə·kənt) *adj.* & *n.* suplicante.
supplicate (ˈsʌp·lɪ·keit) *v.t.* & *i.* suplicar. —**supplication**, *n.* súplica.
supply (səˈplai) *v.t.* suministrar; proveer; abastecer; surtir; suplir. —*n.* suministro; provisión; abasto; abastecimiento; *pl.* provisiones; víveres; pertrechos. —**supply and demand**, oferta y demanda.
support (səˈport) *v.t.* 1, (bear; hold up) sostener; mantener; soportar. 2, (uphold; aid) asistir; ayudar; amparar. 3, (favor) respaldar; favorecer. 4, (provide for; maintain) proveer; mantener; sustentar. 5, (endure) soportar; tolerar. 6, *theat.* (act, as a role) desempeñar; hacer (un papel). 7, *theat.* (accompany a leading performer) acompañar. —*n.* 1, (base; person or thing that bears or holds up) soporte; sostén; apoyo. 2, (maintenance) sustento; manutención. —**supportable**, *adj.* soportable; tolerable.
supporter (səˈpor·tər) *n.* 1, (adherent) partidario. 2, (base; holder) soporte; sostén; apoyo. 3, (belt; truss) suspensorio. 4, (suspender) tirante.
suppose (səˈpoːz) *v.t.* suponer; presumir; imaginar. —**supposing that**, dado el caso que.
supposed (səˈpoːzd) *adj.* supuesto; presunto. —**supposedly** (sə·ˈpo·zɪd·li) *adv.* según se supone.
supposition (ˌsʌp·əˈzɪʃ·ən) *n.* suposición; supuesto.
supposititious (səˌpaz·ɪˈtɪʃ·əs) *adj.* supuesto; fingido.
suppository (səˈpaz·əˌtor·i) *n.* supositorio.
suppress (səˈprɛs) *v.t.* suprimir. —**suppression** (səˈprɛʃ·ən) *n.* supresión.
suppurate (ˈsʌp·jə·reit) *v.i.* supurar. —**suppuration**, *n.* supuración.
supra- (su·prə) *prefijo* supra-; sobre: *suprarrenal*, suprarrenal.
supremacy (suˈprɛm·ə·si) *n.* supremacía.
supreme (səˈpriːm) *adj.* supremo.
surcease (sʌɹˈsis) *n.* cesación.
surcharge (ˈsʌɹ·tʃardʒ) *n.* sobrecarga. —*v.t.* sobrecargar.
surcingle (ˈsʌɹ·sɪŋ·gəl) *n.* sobrecincha.
sure (ʃur) *adj.* 1, (certain) seguro; cierto; indudable. 2, (stable; firm) seguro; firme; estable. 3, (infallible) infalible; efectivo. —*adv., colloq.* seguramente; sin duda. —*interj.* ¡seguro!; ¡claro! —**be sure**, asegurarse. —**be sure to**, no faltar de; no dejar de. —**be sure not to**, guardarse de; tener cuidado de. —**for sure**, seguramente; sin duda. —**make sure**, asegurar; asegurarse. —**make sure of**,

asegurarse de. **—sure enough,** *colloq.* a buen seguro; con certeza. **—to be sure,** seguramente; sin duda.
surely ('ʃur·li) *adv.* seguramente; sin duda.
sureness ('ʃur·nəs) *n.* seguridad; certeza.
surety ('ʃur·ə·ti) *n.* **1,** (guarantee) seguridad; garantía; fianza. **2,** (guarantor) fiador; garante. **—of a surety,** de seguro. **—be surety for,** ser fiador de; salir garante de; responder de.
surf (sʌɹf) *n.* oleaje; rompiente.
surface ('sʌɹ·fɪs) *n.* superficie. *—adj.* superficial. *—v.t.* allanar; alisar; igualar. *—v.i.* emerger; salir a la superficie.
surfboard *n.* tablón de mar.
surfeit ('sʌɹ·fɪt) *n.* exceso; empacho; empalago. *—v.t.* empachar; empalagar.
surge (sʌɹdʒ) *n.* oleada; oleaje. *—v.i.* surgir; agitarse.
surgeon ('sʌɹ·dʒən) *n.* cirujano. **—Surgeon General** [*pl.* Surgeons General] médico mayor; jefe de sanidad militar o naval.
surgery ('sʌɹ·dʒə·ri) *n.* **1,** (operation) cirugía. **2,** (operating room) sala de operaciones. **3,** (doctor's office) consultorio; despacho.
surgical ('sʌɹ·dʒɪ·kəl) *adj.* quirúrgico.
surly ('sʌɹ·li) *adj.* malhumorado; rudo; hosco; arisco.
surmise (sʌɹ'maiz) *n.* conjetura; suposición. *—v.t. & i.* conjeturar; suponer.
surmount (sʌɹ'maunt) *v.t.* **1,** (overcome) superar; vencer. **2,** (pass over) pasar por encima de. **3,** (rise above) elevarse sobre. **4,** (place something on top of; crown) coronar. **—surmountable,** *adj.* superable; vencible.
surname ('sʌɹ·neim) *n.* **1,** (family name) apellido. **2,** (epithet) sobrenombre. *—v.t.* apellidar.
surpass (sʌɹ'pæs) *v.t.* sobrepujar; exceder; superar; sobrepasar. **—surpassable,** *adj.* superable. **—surpassing,** *adj.* sobresaliente; superior; incomparable.
surplice ('sʌɹ·plɪs) *n.* sobrepelliz.
surplus ('sʌɹ·plʌs) *n.* sobra; sobrante; exceso; *comm.* superávit. *—adj.* sobrante; de sobra; excedente.
surprise (sər'praiz) *v.t.* sorprender. *—n.* sorpresa. *—adj.* repentino; inesperado. **—surprising,** *adj.* sorprendente.
surrealism (sə'ri·ə·lɪz·əm) *n.* surrealismo. **—surrealist,** *n. & adj.* surrealista. **—surrealistic,** *adj.* surrealista.
surrender (sə'rɛn·dər) *v.t.* rendir; ceder; entregar. *—v.i.* rendirse; ceder; entregarse. *—n.* rendición; entrega; sumisión.
surreptitious (ˌsʌɹ·əp'tɪʃ·əs) *adj.* subrepticio.
surrey ('sʌɹ·i) *n.* birlocho.
surrogate ('sʌɹ·ə·geit) *n.* **1,** *law* juez de testamentarías. **2,** *eccles.* vicario.
surround (sə'raund) *v.t.* rodear; cercar; circundar; *mil.* sitiar. **—surrounding,** *adj.* circundante; circunvecino. **—surroundings,** *n.pl.* alrededores; ambiente (*sing.*).
surtax ('sʌɹ·tæks) *n.* impuesto adicional.
surveillance (sʌɹ'vei·ləns) *n.* vigilancia.
survey (sʌɹ'vei) *v.t.* **1,** (examine) examinar; inspeccionar. **2,** (view) mirar; contemplar. **3,** (measure) medir. *—n.* ('sʌɹ·vei) **1,** (examination) examen; inspección. **2,** (measurement) agrimensura; medición. **3,** (general view) vista; panorama. **—surveying,** *n.* agrimensura. **—surveyor,** *n.* agrimensor.
survival (sʌɹ'vai·vəl) *n.* **1,** (fact of surviving) supervivencia. **2,** (something that has survived) sobreviviente; resto.
survive (sʌɹ'vaiv) *v.i.* sobrevivir; quedar vivo; salvarse. *—v.t.* sobrevivir a. **—survivor,** *n.* sobreviviente. **—survivorship,** *n.* supervivencia.
sus- (səs) *prefijo, var. de* **sub-** *ante* c: *susceptible,* susceptible.
susceptible (sə'sɛp·tə·bel) *adj.* susceptible; impresionable. **—susceptibility,** *n.* susceptibilidad; tendencia.
suspect (sə'spɛkt) *v.t.* **1,** (surmise) sospechar. **2,** (distrust) recelar; dudar de. *—v.i.* sospechar. *—n. & adj.* ('sʌs·pɛkt) sospechoso.
suspend (sə'spɛnd) *v.t.* suspender. *—v.i.* cesar.
suspenders (sə'spɛnd·ərz) *n.pl.* tirantes.

suspense (sə'spɛns) *n.* **1,** (indecision) suspenso. **2,** (uncertainty) incertidumbre; duda. **3,** (anxiety) ansiedad. **4,** (delay) suspensión; detención.
suspension (sə'spɛn·ʃən) *n.* suspensión. —**suspension bridge,** puente colgante; puente de suspensión. —**suspension points,** puntos suspensivos.
suspensive (sə'spɛn·sɪv) *adj.* suspensivo.
suspensory (sə'spɛn·sə·ri) *adj.* & *n.* suspensorio.
suspicion (sə'spɪʃ·ən) *n.* **1,** (act of suspecting) sospecha; desconfianza. **2,** (inkling; trace) traza; huella.
suspicious (sə'spɪʃ·əs) *adj.* **1,** (arousing suspicion) sospechoso. **2,** (feeling suspicion) sospechoso; suspicaz; receloso. —**suspiciousness,** *n.* suspicacia; desconfianza; recelo.
suspire (sə'spair) *v.i.* suspirar.
sustain (sə'stein) *v.t.* **1,** (maintain; support) sostener; mantener; sustentar. **2,** (encourage) apoyar; alentar. **3,** (endure; undergo) aguantar; sufrir. **4,** (defend; uphold) apoyar; defender. **5,** (confirm; prove) confirmar; probar. **6,** *music* (prolong, as a tone) prolongar; sostener. —**sustaining program,** *radio; TV* programa sin patrocinador.
sustenance ('sʌs·tə·nəns) *n.* **1,** (act of sustaining) mantenimiento; sostenimiento. **2,** (nourishment; means of living) sustento; alimentos (*pl.*); víveres (*pl.*); subsistencia.
sutler ('sʌt·lər) *n.* vivandero.
suture ('su·tʃər) *n.* sutura. —*v.t.* coser; unir con suturas.
suzerain ('su·zə·rɪn) *adj.* & *n.* soberano. —**suzerainty,** *n.* soberanía.
svelte (svɛlt) *adj.* esbelto.
swab (swa:b) *n.* **1,** (mop; rag) estropajo; bayeta; *naut.* lampazo. **2,** (absorbent cotton, sponge, etc.) algodoncillo; esponja; paño. **3,** *slang* (lout) patán; zafio. —*v.t.* [**swabbed, swabbing**] fregar; limpiar; *naut.* lampacear.
swaddle ('swad·əl) *v.t.* fajar; empañar; envolver con fajas. —**swaddling** (-lɪŋ) **cloth,** faja; pañal. —**swaddling clothes,** pañales; envoltura.
swag (swæg) *n., slang* botín; robo; despojo; hurto.
swagger ('swæg·ər) *v.i.* **1,** (strut) contonearse; pavonearse. **2,** (brag) fanfarronear. —*n.* **1,** (strut) contoneo; pavoneo. **2,** (boast) fanfarronada.
swain (swein) *n.* **1,** (lover) galán; enamorado; amante. **2,** (country boy) zagal.
swallow ('swal·o) *v.t.* & *i.* tragar; deglutir. —*n.* **1,** (act of swallowing) deglución. **2,** (something swallowed) trago. **3,** *ornith.* golondrina.
swallowtail *n.* frac. *También,* **swallow-tailed coat.**
swam (swæm) *v., pret. de* **swim.**
swamp (swamp) *n.* pantano; ciénaga. —*v.t.* **1,** (flood; sink) inundar; hundir; sumergir. **2,** (overwhelm) abrumar. —*v.i.* inundarse; hundirse.
swampland *n.* pantanal; cenagal.
swampy ('swam·pi) *adj.* pantanoso; cenagoso.
swan (swa:n) *n.* cisne. —**swan song,** canto del cisne.
swank (swæŋk) *n., slang* pretensión; ostentación. —*adj., slang* pretencioso; ostentoso. —*v.i., slang* contonearse; pavonearse. —**swanky,** *adj., slang* elegante; vistoso.
swan's-down *n.* plumón de cisne.
swap (swap) *v.t.* & *i.* [**swapped, swapping**] *colloq.* cambalachear; cambiar; intercambiar; trocar. —*n.* cambalache; trueque; cambio.
sward (sword) *n.* césped.
swarm (sworm) *n.* enjambre. —*v.i.* **1,** (form or move in a swarm) enjambrar; hormiguear. **2,** (climb) trepar.
swarthy ('swor·ði) *adj.* atezado; moreno; trigueño; prieto.
swash (swaʃ) *v.t.* & *i.* = **splash.**
swashbuckler ('swaʃ·bʌk·lər) *n.* espadachín; fanfarrón; valentón. —**swashbuckling,** *adj.* fanfarrón; valentón. —*n.* fanfarronada; valentonada.
swastika ('swas·tɪ·kə) *n.* svástica; cruz gamada.
swat (swat) *v.t.* [**swatted, swatting**] *colloq.* golpear. —*n., colloq.* golpe recio.
swatch (swatʃ) *n.* muestra de tela; tira.
swath (swaθ) *n.* **1,** (row of mown grass or grain) guadañada. **2,** (row; line) ringlera. **3,** (strip)

tira; faja. —**cut a wide swath,** hacer gran papel.
swathe (sweið) *v.t.* envolver; fajar; vendar. —*n.* envoltura; faja; venda.
sway (swei) *v.i.* **1,** (bend) ladearse; inclinarse. **2,** (swing) oscilar; vacilar. **3,** (totter) bambolear; tambalear. **4,** (turn away) desviarse; apartarse. **5,** (have control or influence) tener dominio; tener influencia. —*v.t.* **1,** (cause to bend) ladear. **2,** (cause to swing) hacer oscilar. **3,** (influence; persuade) influir en; persuadir; convencer. **4,** (move; affect) conmover; impresionar. **5,** (divert) desviar; detener. **6,** (rule; control) gobernar; dominar. **7,** (wield; brandish) blandir; sacudir. —*n.* **1,** (swaying movement) oscilación; bamboleo; tambaleo. **2,** (inclination) inclinación; ladeo. **3,** (impetus; force) fuerza; influencia. **4,** (rule) mando; dominio; imperio. —**hold sway (over),** gobernar; dominar; regir.
swear (swɛɪr) *v.t.* & *i.* [*pret.* **swore;** *p.p.* **sworn**] (vow) jurar. —*v.i.* (curse) maldecir; jurar; blasfemar; echar maldiciones. —*v.t.* (administer an oath to) juramentar. —**swear an oath,** juramentarse; prestar juramento; jurar. —**swear by,** jurar por; poner entera confianza en. —**swear in,** juramentar; hacer prestar juramento. —**swear off,** renunciar; dejar. —**swear out,** obtener por juramento.
swearing ('swɛr·ɪŋ) *n.* **1,** (taking an oath) jura; juramento. **2,** (cursing) maldición; el vicio de jurar.
swearword *n.* blasfemia; maldición; palabra fea.
sweat (swɛt) *v.t.* & *i.* [*pret.* & *p.p.* **sweat** *o* **sweated**] (perspire) sudar —*v.t.* **1,** (cause to sweat) hacer sudar. **2,** (solder) soldar. —*n.* **1,** (perspiration; moisture) sudor. **2,** (anxiety) ansia; excitación. **3,** (hard work) fatiga; esfuerzo. —**in a sweat,** nadando en sudor. —**sweat blood,** esmerarse; echar la sangre. —**sweat out, 1,** (cure by sweating) curar por medio del sudor. **2,** *slang* (await; expect) aguardar; esperar.
sweater ('swɛt·ər) *n.* suéter; malla.
sweatshirt *n.* malla; jersey.
sweatshop ('swɛt,ʃap) *n.* taller opresor; taller donde se trabaja mucho por poca paga.
sweaty ('swɛt·i) *adj.* sudoroso; sudoso.
Swedish ('swi·dɪʃ) *adj.* & *n.* sueco.
sweep (swip) *v.t.* [*pret.* & *p.p.* **swept**] **1,** (clean, as with a broom) barrer. **2,** (move or carry along) arrastrar; llevarse; arrebatar. **3,** (touch; brush lightly) rozar. **4,** (pass swiftly over) recorrer; pasar por. **5,** *colloq.* (win decisively) ganar todo; ganar enteramente. —*v.i.* **1,** (clean) barrer. **2,** (move swiftly) correr; lanzarse; precipitarse. **3,** (reach; extend) extenderse. **4,** (move proudly) marchar pomposamente. —*n.* **1,** (cleaning) barredura; barrido. **2,** (swift movement) arrastre; arrebato; carrera. **3,** (scope; extent) alcance; extensión. **4,** (sweeper) barrendero; barredera (*fem.*). **5,** (complete victory) triunfo total. —**sweeper,** *n.* barrendero; barredera (*fem.*).
sweeping ('swi·pɪŋ) *adj.* comprensivo; amplio. —*n.* barredura; barrido. —**sweepings,** *n.pl.* barreduras.
sweepstakes ('swip·steiks) *n. sing.* & *pl.* **1,** (contest) lotería, esp. de carreras de caballos. **2,** (prize) gran premio.
sweet (swit) *adj.* **1,** (pleasant-tasting) dulce. **2,** (pleasing) agradable; encantador. **3,** (amiable) amable; gentil. **4,** (gentle) suave. **5,** (dear; precious) querido; amado. **6,** (fresh) fresco. **7,** (fragrant) oloroso; de buen olor. —*n.* **1,** (sweetness) dulzura. **2,** (something sweet) dulce; confite. **3,** (beloved person) querido. —*adv.* dulcemente; suavemente. —**be sweet on,** *colloq.* estar enamorado de.
sweet basil albahaca.
sweetbread *n.* molleja.
sweetbrier *también,* **sweetbriar** *n.* eglantina.
sweet corn maíz tierno.
sweeten ('swi·tən) *v.t.* **1,** (add sugar to) endulzar; dulcificar; azucarar. **2,** (make pleasant) suavizar. —**sweetener,** *n.* dulcificante. —**sweetening,** *n.* endulzadura. —*adj.* dulcificante.
sweetheart *n.* novio; enamorado; querido; *fem.* novia; enamorada; querida.

sweetmeat *n.* dulce; confite; golosina.
sweetness ('swit·nəs) *n.* dulzura.
sweet pea guisante de olor.
sweet potato batata.
sweet tooth *colloq.* golosina. —**have a sweet tooth,** ser goloso; ser dulcero.
sweet-toothed ('swit,tuðd) *adj.* goloso; dulcero.
swell (swɛl) *v.t.* [*pret.* **swelled;** *p.p.* **swelled** *o* **swollen**] **1,** (expand; inflate) hinchar; inflar. **2,** (increase) aumentar. **3,** (make vain; flatter) engreír. —*v.i.* **1,** (expand) hincharse; inflarse. **2,** (increase) aumentarse; crecer. **3,** (rise in waves, as the sea) embravecerse. —*n.* **1,** (bulge) hinchazón. **2,** (large wave) oleada; oleaje. **3,** *music* crescendo. **4,** *colloq.* (stylish person) persona elegante; petimetre. —*adj.* **1,** *colloq.* (stylish) elegante. **2,** *slang* (excellent) excelente; magnífico; —**swelled head,** *colloq.* entono; engreimiento.
swelling ('swɛl·ɪŋ) *n.* **1,** (bulge) hinchazón; protuberancia. **2,** (increase) aumento.
swelter ('swɛl·tər) *v.t.* abrumar de calor; sofocar. —*v.i.* sofocarse. —*n.* calor excesivo.
swept (swɛpt) *v., pret. & p.p. de* **sweep.**
swerve (swʌɹv) *v.t.* desviar; apartar. —*v.i.* desviarse; apartarse. —*n.* desviación; desvío.
swift (swɪft) *adj.* **1,** (rapid) veloz; rápido; vivo. **2,** (sudden) repentino. **3,** (prompt) pronto; presto. —*adv.* velozmente; rápidamente. —*n., ornith.* vencejo. —**swiftness,** *n.* velocidad; rapidez.
swig (swɪg) *v.t. & i.* [**swigged, swigging**] *colloq.* beber a grandes tragos. —*n., colloq.* trago.
swill (swɪl) *n.* **1,** (garbage) basura; desperdicios (*pl.*). **2,** (food for animals) bazofia. **3,** (swig) trago. —*v.t.* **1,** (wash) lavar; enjuagar. **2,** (drink greedily) beber a grandes tragos. **3,** (make drunk) emborrachar. —*v.i.* emborracharse.
swim (swɪm) *v.i.* [**swam, swum, swimming**] **1,** (move through water) nadar. **2,** (float) flotar. **3,** (be dizzy) tener vértigo; estar desvanecido; írsele la cabeza. —*v.t.* pasar *o* recorrer nadando. —*n.* **1,** (act of swimming) natación; *Amer.* nadada. **2,** (dizziness) vahido; desmayo. —**in the swim,** andando con la corriente.
swim bladder nadadera.
swimmer ('swɪm·ər) *n.* nadador.
swimming ('swɪm·ɪŋ) *n.* natación. —*adj.* **1,** (that swims) nadador. **2,** (of or for swimming) natatorio. **3,** (dizzy) vertiginoso. **4,** (teeming) lleno (de). —**swimmingly,** *adv.* sin dificultad; felizmente; lisamente.
swimming hole nadadero.
swimming pool piscina.
swim suit traje de baño. *También,* **swimming suit.**
swindle ('swɪn·dəl) *v.t. & i.* defraudar; estafar; embaucar. —*n.* fraude; estafa; petardo. —**swindler** (-dlər) *n.* estafador; embaucador; chupón.
swine (swain) *n.sing. & pl.* cerdo; puerco; cochino; marrano.
swineherd *n.* porquerizo.
swing (swɪŋ) *v.i.* [*pret. & p.p.* **swung**] **1,** (move back and forth) oscilar; vacilar. **2,** (ride a swing) columpiarse. **3,** (sway) balancearse. **4,** (hang) estar colgado. **5,** (change direction) volverse; dar una vuelta; virar. **6,** (revolve; rotate) volverse; dar vueltas; girar. —*v.t.* **1,** (move back and forth) hacer oscilar; mover; menear. **2,** (brandish) blandir; sacudir. **3,** (hang) colgar. **4,** (cause to revolve) hacer girar; dar vueltas a. **5,** (manage; bring about) manejar; llevar a cabo; efectuar. —*n.* **1,** (movement back and forth) oscilación; balanceo; vaivén. **2,** (act or manner of making a swinging stroke) golpe; manera de golpear. **3,** (length of swing) alcance. **4,** (turn) vuelta. **5,** (freedom of action) libertad de acción; libre carrera. **6,** (rhythm) ritmo; compás. **7,** (playground device) columpio. **8,** *music* variedad de jazz; swing. —**in full swing,** en plena operación; en plena marcha.
swingletree ('swɪŋ·gəl,triː) *n.* balancín.
swing shift *colloq.* turno de la tarde.
swinish ('swai·nɪʃ) *adj.* **1,** (porcine) porcino. **2,** (despicable) cochino; sucio; puerco.
swipe (swaip) *v.t. & i.* **1,** *colloq.* (strike) golpear. **2,** *slang* (steal)

hurtar; sisar; ratear. —*n., colloq.* golpe fuerte.

swirl (swʌɹl) *v.i.* arremolinarse; girar; dar vueltas. —*v.t.* hacer girar. —*n.* remolino; torbellino.

swish (swɪʃ) *v.i.* susurrar; silbar; sisear. —*v.t.* agitar; hacer susurrar. —*n.* susurro; silbido; siseo.

Swiss (swɪs) *adj. & n.* suizo.

switch (swɪtʃ) *n.* **1,** (flexible rod) varilla; fusta. **2,** *electricity* conmutador; interruptor. **3,** (tress of detached hair) moño. **4,** *R.R.* agujas (*pl.*); *Amer.* cambiavía. **5,** (change; shift) cambio; desviación. —*v.t.* **1,** (whip) varear; fustigar. **2,** (change; shift) cambiar; desviar. **3,** *electricity* conmutar. **4,** *R.R.* desviar. —*v.i.* cambiar; desviarse. —**switch off,** apagar; cortar; desconectar. —**switch on,** poner; encender; *Amer.* prender.

switchboard *n.* tablero de conmutadores; cuadro de distribución.

switchman ('swɪtʃ·mən) *n.* [*pl.* **-men**] guardagujas; *Amer.* cambiavía; cambiador.

swivel ('swɪv·əl) *n.* eslabón giratorio. —*v.i.* girar sobre un eje. —*v.t.* **1,** (cause to turn) hacer girar sobre un eje. **2,** (fasten with a swivel) enganchar con eslabón giratorio.

swivel chair silla giratoria.

swizzle stick palillo (*para menear bebidas*).

swollen ('swo·lən) *v., p.p. de* swell. —*adj.* **1,** (inflated) hinchado. **2,** (increased) aumentado; crecido.

swoon (swuːn) *v.i.* desmayarse; desvanecerse. —*n.* desmayo; desvanecimiento.

swoop (swup) *v.t.* agarrar; arrebatar. —*v.i.* precipitarse; caer a plomo. —*n.* bajada repentina; calada.

sword (sord) *n.* espada. —**sword cane,** estoque.

swordfish *n.* pez espada.

swordplay *n.* esgrima.

swordsman ('sordz·mən) *n.* [*pl.* **-men**] espadachín; espada; esgrimidor. —**swordsmanship,** *n.* esgrima.

swore (swor) *v., pret. de* swear.

sworn (sworn) *v., p.p. de* swear.

swum (swʌm) *v., p.p. de* swim.

swung (swʌŋ) *v., pret. & p.p. de* swing.

Sybarite ('sɪb·ə·rait) *n.* sibarita. —**Sybaritic** (-'rɪ·tɪk) *adj.* sibarita; sibarítico.

sycamore ('sɪk·əˌmor) *n.* **1,** (fig-like Near Eastern tree) sicómoro. **2,** (European maple) falso plátano; arce blanco. **3,** (Amer. plane tree) plátano.

sycophant ('saik·ə·fənt) *n.* adulador; sicofante.

syl- (sɪl) *prefijo, var. de* **syn-** *ante* **l**: *syllogism,* silogismo.

syllabic (sɪ'læb·ɪk) *adj.* silábico.

syllabicate (sɪ'læb·ɪ·keit) *v.t.* silabear. —**syllabication,** *n.* silabeo.

syllabify (sɪ'læb·əˌfai) *v.t.* silabear. —**syllabification** (-fɪ'kei·ʃən) *n.* silabeo.

syllable ('sɪl·ə·bəl) *n.* sílaba.

syllabus ('sɪl·ə·bəs) *n.* [*pl.* **-bi** (bai)] sílabo; compendio.

syllogism ('sɪl·ə·dʒɪz·əm) *n.* silogismo.

sylph (sɪlf) *n.* silfo; sílfide.

sylvan ('sɪl·vən) *adj.* silvestre; selvático.

sym- (sɪm) *prefijo, var. de* **syn-** *ante* **b, p, m**: *symbiosis,* simbiosis; *symposium,* simposio; *symmetry,* simetría.

symbiosis *n.* simbiosis.

symbol ('sɪm·bəl) *n.* símbolo. —**symbolic** (sɪm'bal·ɪk) *adj.* simbólico.

symbolism ('sɪm·bə·lɪz·əm) *n.* simbolismo.

symbolize ('sɪm·bə·laiz) *v.t.* simbolizar.

symmetry ('sɪm·ə·tri) *n.* simetría. —**symmetrical** (sɪ'mɛt·rɪ·kəl) *adj.* simétrico.

sympathetic (ˌsɪm·pə'θɛt·ɪk) *adj.* simpático; compasivo.

sympathize ('sɪm·pəˌθaiz) *v.i.* simpatizar; compadecer(se); condolerse. —**sympathize with,** compadecer(se) de; condolerse de.

sympathy ('sɪm·pə·θi) *n.* **1,** (affinity) simpatía. **2,** (compassion) compasión; conmiseración; condolencia.

symphony ('sɪm·fə·ni) *n.* sinfonía. —**symphonic** (sɪm'fan·ɪk) *adj.* sinfónico.

symposium (sɪm'po·zi·əm) *n.* **1,** (meeting for discussion) coloquio. **2,** (collection of writings) collección de artículos, comentarios, etc. sobre un mismo tema.

symptom ('sɪmp·təm) *n.* síntoma.

symptomatic (ˌsɪmp·təˈmæt·ɪk) *adj.* sintomático.
syn- (sɪn) *prefijo* sin-; junto; junto con: *synchronic,* sincrónico.
synagogue (ˈsɪn·ə·gag) *n.* sinagoga.
synchronize (ˈsɪŋ·krəˌnaiz) *v.t.* & *i.* sincronizar. **—synchronization** (-nɪˈzei·ʃən) *n.* sincronización. **—synchronous,** *adj.* sincrónico.
syncopate (ˈsɪŋ·kəˌpeit) *v.t.* sincopar. **—syncopation,** *n.* síncopa.
syncope (ˈsɪŋ·kə·pi) *n.* **1,** *med.* síncope. **2,** *gram.* síncopa; síncope.
syndicate (ˈsɪn·dɪˌkeit) *v.t.* sindicar. **—*v.i.*** sindicarse. **—*n.*** (-kət) sindicato. **—syndication,** *n.* sindicación.
synod (ˈsɪn·əd) *n.* sínodo. **—synodal,** *adj.* sinodal.
synonym (ˈsɪn·ə·nɪm) *n.* sinónimo.
synonymous (sɪˈnan·ə·məs) *adj.* sinónimo.
synopsis (sɪˈnap·sɪs) *n.* [*pl.* **-ses** (siz)] sinopsis. **—synoptic** (-tɪk) *adj.* sinóptico.
syntax (ˈsɪn·tæks) *n.* sintaxis. **—syntactical** (sɪnˈtæk·tɪ·kəl) *adj.* sintáctico.
synthesis (ˈsɪn·θə·sɪs) *n.* [*pl.* **-ses** (siz)] síntesis.
synthesize (ˈsɪn·θəˌsaiz) *v.t.* sintetizar.
synthetic (sɪnˈθɛt·ɪk) *adj.* sintético.
syphilis (ˈsɪf·ə·lɪs) *n.* sífilis. **—syphilitic** (-ˈlɪt·ɪk) *n.* & *adj.* sifilítico.
syphon (ˈsai·fən) *n.* & *v.* = **siphon.**
syringe (səˈrɪndʒ) *n.* jeringa. **—*v.t.*** jeringar.
syrup (ˈsɪr·əp) *n.* jarabe; almíbar.
system (ˈsɪs·təm) *n.* sistema.
systematic (ˌsɪs·təˈmæt·ɪk) *adj.* sistemático.
systematize (ˈsɪs·tə·məˌtaiz) *v.t.* sistematizar.
systemic (sɪsˈtɛm·ɪk) *adj., anat.; physiol.* del sistema.
systole (ˈsɪs·təˌli) *n.* sístole. **—systolic** (sɪsˈtal·ɪk) *adj.* sistólico.

T

T, t (ti) vigésima letra del alfabeto inglés. **—to a T,** exactamente.
't (t) *contr. de* it: *don't do't,* no lo haga; *'twas not so,* no fue así.
tab (tæb) *n.* **1,** (flap; strap) lengüeta; correa. **2,** (tag; label) etiqueta; rótulo. **3,** *colloq.* (account) cuenta. **—keep tab** (*o* **tabs**) **on,** *colloq.* velar; vigilar.
tabasco (təˈbæs·ko) *n.* tabasco.
tabby (ˈtæb·i) *n.* **1,** (striped cat) gato atigrado. **2,** (female cat) gata. **3,** (old maid) solterona. **4,** (female gossip) chismosa. **5,** (fabric) seda ondeada; muaré.
tabernacle (ˈtæb·ər·næk·əl) *n.* **1,** (dwelling; temple) tabernáculo. **2,** *eccles.* sagrario.
table (ˈtei·bəl) *n.* **1,** (furniture) mesa. **2,** (plateau) meseta. **3,** (food; meal) mesa. **4,** (list) tabla. **5,** (index) índice. **—*v.t.*** **1,** (place on a table) colocar en la mesa. **2,** (postpone) entablar; dejar sobre la mesa. **3,** (list) catalogar. **—table tennis,** ping-pong. **—turn** (the) **tables,** volver las tornas.
tableau (ˈtæb·lo) *n.* **1,** (picture) cuadro. **2,** (series of pictures) retablo. **3,** (dramatic scene) representación teatral; espectáculo.
tablecloth *n.* mantel.
table d'hôte (ˈtab·əlˈdot) comida a precio fijo; plato del día.
tableland *n.* meseta.
tablespoon *n.* cuchara. **—tablespoonful** (-ˌfʊl) [*pl.* **-fuls**] *n.* cucharada.
tablet (ˈtæb·lɪt) *n.* **1,** (plaque) lápida; tarja; placa; losa. **2,** (pill) tableta; pastilla; comprimido; píldora. **3,** (soap) pastilla. **4,** (writing pad) bloc de papel; cuadernillo.
tableware *n.* servicio; cubierto.
tabloid (ˈtæb·lɔid) *n.* gaceta; pequeño periódico muy ilustrado. **—*adj.*** condensado.
taboo *también,* **tabu** (tæˈbuː) *n.* prohibición; exclusión; tabú. **—*adj.*** prohibido; tabú. **—*v.t.*** prohibir.
tabor (ˈtei·bər) *n.* tamborín.
taboret (ˌtæb·əˈrɛt) *n.* **1,** (stool) banquillo; taburete. **2,** (drum) tamborín. **3,** (embroidery frame)

bastidor. **4,** (ornamental stand) mesita.

tabular ('tæb·jə·lər) *adj.* tabular; tabulado.

tabulate ('tæb·jə,leit) *v.t.* tabular; catalogar. —**tabulation,** *n.* tabulación. —**tabulator,** *n.* tabulador.

tachometer (tə'kam·ə·tər) *n.* tacómetro.

tacit ('tæs·ɪt) *adj.* tácito.

taciturn ('tæs·ə·tʌɹn) *adj.* taciturno; silencioso. —**taciturnity** (-'tʌɹn·ə·ti) *n.* taciturnidad.

tack (tæk) *n.* **1,** (nail) tachuela; puntilla; clavillo. **2,** *sewing* hilván; embaste. **3,** *naut.* bordada; virada. **4,** (course of action) línea de conducta. —*v.t.* **1,** (nail) clavar. **2,** *sewing* hilvanar; embastar; puntear. —*v.i., naut.* cambiar de rumbo; bordear; dar bordadas.

tacking ('tæk·ɪŋ) *n.* **1,** *sewing* hilván; embaste. **2,** *naut.* bordeo; bordada.

tackle ('tæk·əl) *n.* **1,** (apparatus) aparejo. **2,** (gear) avíos; equipo; enseres. **3,** *football* **a.** (act) agarrada; atajada. **b.** (player) atajador. —*v.t.* **1,** (seize) asir; agarrar; *football* atajar. **2,** (undertake) acometer; abordar.

tacky ('tæk·i) *adj.* **1,** (sticky) pegajoso; viscoso. **2,** *colloq.* (dowdy) desaliñado; descuidado.

tact (tækt) *n.* tacto; tino; diplomacia; discreción. —**tactful,** *adj.* diplomático; discreto. —**tactless,** *adj.* indiscreto.

tactic ('tæk·tɪk) *n.* táctica; táctico. —**tactical,** *adj.* táctico. —**tactician** (tæk'tɪʃ·ən) *n.* táctico.

tactics ('tæk·tɪks) *n.* táctica.

tactile ('tæk·tɪl) *adj.* **1,** (of or pert. to touch) táctil. **2,** (tangible) tangible; palpable.

tadpole ('tæd·pol) *n.* renacuajo.

taffeta ('tæf·ɪ·tə) *n.* tafetán.

taffy ('tæf·i) *n.* melcocha; caramelo.

tag (tæg) *n.* **1,** (label) etiqueta; rótulo. **2,** (small card; slip) cartela. **3,** (appendage) cola; cosa atada al extremo. **4,** (rag; tatter) andrajo; pingajo. **5,** (saying; refrain) refrán; mote; frase hecha. **6,** (game) juego de niños. —*v.t.* [**tagged, tagging**] **1,** (label) poner etiqueta a. **2,** (mark; identify) marcar; señalar. **3,** (tap, as in the game of tag) tocar. **4,** *colloq.* (follow closely) seguir de cerca; pisar los talones a. —**tag after; tag along,** *colloq.* seguir de cerca; seguir pisando los talones.

Tagalog (ta'ga·lag; 'tæg·ə,lag) *adj.* & *n.* tagalo.

tail (teil) *n.* **1,** (appendage) cola; rabo. **2,** (end) extremo; extremidades; cola. **3,** (of a comet) cola; rastro. **4,** *pl.* (reverse side of a coin) reverso de una moneda; cruz. **5,** *pl., colloq.* = **tailcoat.** —*v.t.* & *i.* seguir de cerca; perseguir; pisar los talones (a). —**tail end,** extremo; cola.

tailcoat *n.* frac.

taillight *n.* farol trasero; farol de cola.

tailor ('tei·lər) *n.* sastre. —*v.t.* **1,** (shape to fit the body) entallar; hacer (un traje) a medida. **2,** (outfit with clothing) proveer de ropa; vestir. —*v.i.* ser sastre.

tailoring ('tei·lər·ɪŋ) *n.* sastrería.

tailor-made *adj.* hecho a medida.

tailspin ('teil,spɪn) *n. aero.* caída en barrena. *También,* **tail spin.**

tailwind *n. aero.* viento de cola. *También,* **tail wind.**

taint (teint) *n.* **1,** (stain; blemish) tacha; mancha; mácula. **2,** (contamination) infección; corrupción. —*v.t.* **1,** (stain) manchar; ensuciar. **2,** (corrupt) corromper; inficionar. —*v.i.* inficionarse; corromperse; podrirse.

take (teik) *v.t.* [*pret.* **took;** *p.p.* **taken**] **1,** (get; get possession of) tomar. **2,** (seize) coger; asir. **3,** (carry) llevar. **4,** (lead; escort) llevar; conducir. **5,** (accept; receive) aceptar; recibir. **6,** (remove) quitar; sacar. **7,** (assume) tomar; asumir; suponer. **8,** (capture, in certain games) comer. **9,** *photog.* tomar; sacar. **10,** (endure) soportar; tolerar; aguantar. **11,** (understand; construe) percibir; conceptuar. **12,** (undergo) sufrir; someterse a. **13,** (keep) quedarse con. **14,** (subtract) sustraer. **15,** (win) ganar. **16,** (drink; put into one's body) tomar. **17,** *slang* (cheat; dupe) engañar; embaucar. **18,** (need; require) necesitar. **19,** (note; write down) apuntar. **20,** (do; perform, as a walk, ride, leap, etc.) dar (un paseo, un brinco, etc.). —*v.i.* **1,**

(turn out well; have the desired effect) salir bien; tener buen éxito; resultar bien. 2, (begin growing, as a plant) arraigarse. 3, (engage; be hooked or joined) agarrarse; engancharse; engranar. 4, (ignite) prender; encender. 5, (go; proceed) encaminarse; dirigirse. —*n.* 1, (act of taking; thing taken) toma. 2, *slang* (receipts) taquilla; entrada. —**take after,** 1, (resemble) parecerse a. 2, (pursue) perseguir. —**take apart,** desmontar; desmantelar; despedazar. —**take away,** quitar; sacar; llevarse. —**take back,** 1, (return) devolver. 2, (regain) recibir devuelto; recobrar. 3, (retract) retractar; desdecirse de. —**take down,** 1, (remove; lower) bajar; descolgar. 2, (take apart) desmontar; desmantelar. 3, (note) apuntar. 4, (humiliate) humillar; rebajar. —**take ill** *o* **be taken ill,** *colloq.* enfermarse; caer enfermo. —**take in,** 1, (admit; receive) admitir; recibir; acoger. 2, (make smaller) encoger; estrechar. 3, (include; comprise) abarcar; comprender; englobar. 4, (comprehend) entender; comprender. 5, (cheat; trick) estafar; embaucar; engañar. 6, (visit; tour) visitar. —**take it out on,** *colloq.* desahogarse en *o* contra. —**take off,** 1, (remove) quitar. 2, (deduct) descontar; sustraer. 3, (depart) irse; marcharse; *salir.* 4, *aero.* despegar. 5, *colloq.* (mimic) imitar; remedar; parodiar. —**take on,** 1, (acquire) tomar. 2, (employ) tomar; contratar. 3, (undertake) cargar con; tomar sobre sí. 4, (begin) empezar. 5, (assume; affect) afectar. 6, (challenge) desafiar; enfrentar. 7, *colloq.* (be excited) excitarse; conmoverse. —**take out,** sacar. —**take over,** 1, (take possession of) apoderarse de; tomar posesión de. 2, (take charge of) cargar con; hacerse cargo de. —**take sick** *o* **be taken sick,** *colloq.* enfermarse; caer enfermo. —**take to,** 1, (form the habit of) ponerse a; dedicarse a. 2, (go to or toward) dirigirse a; marcharse hacia. 3, (become fond of) aficionarse a; tomar cariño a. —**take up,** 1, (raise) levantar. 2, (begin) empezar. 3, (assume) cargar con. 4, (resume) reasumir; reanudar. 5, (occupy) ocupar. 6, (fill) llenar. 7, (shrink) encoger; estrechar. 8, (remove the slack from) estirar. 9, (absorb) absorber. 10, (take possession of) tomar posesión de. 11, (become interested in) aficionarse a; dedicarse; aplicarse a. 12, (seek advice about) consultar. 13, (study) estudiar. —**take upon** (*o* **on**) **oneself,** cargar con; tomar sobre sí. —**take up with,** asociarse con; relacionarse con.

taken ('tei·kən) *v., p.p. de* **take.** —**taken aback,** confundido; pasmado. —**be taken aback,** quedarse mudo; asombrarse.

take-off *n.* 1, *aero.* salida; despegue. 2, (leap) salto. 3, *colloq.* (imitation) imitación; caricatura; parodia.

taking ('tei·kɪŋ) *adj.* 1, (attractive) atractivo; encantador. 2, *colloq.* (contagious) contagioso. —*n.* 1, (act of taking; something taken) toma. 2, *pl.* (receipts) ingresos; taquilla (*sing.*).

talc (tælk) *n.* talco.

talcum ('tæl·kəm) *n.* talco; polvos de talco.

tale (teil) *n.* 1, (narrative) cuento. 2, (falsehood) mentira; ficción. 3, (gossip) chisme; rumor. 4, (tally) cuenta.

talebearer *n.* cuentón; soplón; chismoso.

talent ('tæl·ənt) *n.* 1, (skill) talento; ingenio; habilidad; capacidad. 2, (old coin; measure of weight) talento. —**talented,** *adj.* talentoso.

talesman ('teilz·mən) *n.* [*pl.* **-men**] jurado suplente.

talisman ('tæl·ɪs·mən) *n.* talismán.

talk (tɔk) *v.t. & i.* (speak) hablar. —*v.i.* 1, (chat) charlar; platicar. 2, (converse) conversar. 3, (gossip) chismear. —*v.t.* 1, (speak about) hablar de. 2, (convince) convencer hablando. —*n.* 1, (conversation) conversación. 2, (chat) charla; plática. 3, (discourse) discurso; conferencia. 4, (gossip) chisme; rumor. 5, (language) habla. —**big talk,** *slang* fanfarronada; jactancia. —**make talk,** 1, (chat) charlar. 2, (cause gossip) dar que hablar. —**small talk,** charla. —**talk away,** pasar (el tiempo) hablando; hablar incesantemente. **—talk back,** responder atrevidamente. **—talk big,** *slang* jactarse; fanfarronear. **—talk down,** hacer callar; tapar la boca a. **—talk down to,** hablarle a uno con menosprecio o condescendencia. **—talk into,** convencer; persuadir. **—talk one's head** (*o* **arm**) **off,** *slang* hablar hasta el cansancio. **—talk out of,** disuadirle a uno (de una cosa). **—talk over,** discutir; consultar. **—talk up, 1,** (promote) fomentar; promover. **2,** (speak loudly) hablar alto.

talkative ('tɔk·ə·tɪv) *n.* hablador; locuaz; parlero. **—talkativeness,** *n.* locuacidad.

talkie ('tɔ·ki) *n., colloq.* = **talking picture.**

talking machine fonógrafo; gramófono.

talking picture película hablada.

talking-to *n., colloq.* reprensión; reprimenda.

tall (tɔːl) *adj.* **1,** (high in stature) alto; elevado. **2,** *colloq.* (unbelievable) increíble; exagerado. **—tallness,** *n.* altura; estatura.

tallow ('tæl·o) *n.* sebo.

tally ('tæl·i) *n.* **1,** (count) cuenta; enumeración. **2,** (label) etiqueta; rótulo. **3,** (score) tanteo. **4,** (counterpart) contraparte. **5,** (agreement) correspondencia; conformidad. **—***v.t.* **1,** (count) contar; enumerar. **2,** (record) registrar; notar. **3,** (label) marcar. **4,** (make agree) ajustar; acomodar. **—***v.i.* cuadrar; concordar; corresponder.

tallyho (ˌtæl·i'hoː) *n.* coche de cuatro caballos. **—***interj.* grito del cazador.

Talmud ('tæl·mʌd) *n.* talmud.

talon ('tæl·ən) *n.* **1,** (claw) garra; zarpa. **2,** *cards* (stock) baceta.

talus ('tei·ləs) *n.* **1,** *anat.* hueso del tobillo; tobillo. **2,** *geol.* talud; inclinación; pendiente.

tamable ('tei·mə·bəl) *adj.* domable; domesticable.

tamale (tə'mal·i) *n.* tamal.

tamarind ('tæm·ə·rɪnd) *n.* tamarindo.

tambourine (ˌtæm·bə'riːn) *n.* pandereta; tamboril; tamborín.

tame (teim) *adj.* **1,** (domesticated) domado; domesticado. **2,** (meek) manso; sumiso; dócil. **3,** (dull) aburrido; soso; insulso. **—***v.t.* amansar; domar; domesticar. **—tameness,** *n.* docilidad; mansedumbre; sumisión.

tam-o'-shanter ('tæm·əˌʃæn·tər) *n.* boina escocesa.

tamp (tæmp) *v.t.* apisonar; apelmazar; golpear.

tamper ('tæm·pər) *v.i.* entremeterse; meterse. **—***n.* pisón. **—tamper with,** enredar; falsificar; adulterar.

tampon ('tæm·pan) *n.* tapón. **—***v.t.* taponar.

tan (tæn) *v.t.* [**tanned, tanning**] **1,** (cure, as leather) curtir; zurrar. **2,** (burn in the sun) tostar; quemar. **3,** *colloq.* (flog) zurrar; azotar. **—***v.i.* broncearse al sol. **—***n.* **1,** (curing material) corteza; tanino. **2,** (color) moreno amarillento; color de canela. **3,** (suntan) atezamiento; quemadura de sol. **—***adj.* **1,** (of tan color) de color de canela. **2,** (bronzed by the sun) bronceado; tostado al sol. **—tan one's hide,** zurrar; azotar.

tanager ('tæn·ə·dʒər) *n.* tángara.

tandem ('tæn·dəm) *n.* tándem. **—***adj. & adv.* en tándem.

tang (tæŋ) *n.* **1,** (taste) sabor; gustillo. **2,** (noise) tañido. **3,** *mech.* espiga. **—***v.i.* tañer; sonar; retiñir. **—***v.t.* tañer.

tangency ('tæn·dʒən·si) *n.* tangencia.

tangent ('tæn·dʒənt) *n.* **1,** *geom.* tangente. **2,** (deviation) cambio de dirección. **—***adj.* tocante; tangente. **—go** (*o* **fly**) **off at** (*o* **on**) **a tangent,** cambiar rumbo súbitamente; desviarse.

tangential (tæn'dʒɛn·ʃəl) *adj.* tangencial.

tangerine (ˌtæn·dʒə'riːn) *n.* **1,** (fruit) mandarina. **2,** (color) anaranjado rojizo.

tangible ('tæn·dʒə·bəl) *adj.* tangible; palpable; corpóreo. **—tangibles,** *n.pl.* bienes materiales.

tangle ('tæŋ·gəl) *v.t.* enredar; enmarañar; confundir; embrollar. **—***v.i.* enredarse. **—***n.* enredo; maraña; confusión; embrollo.

tango ('tæŋ·go) *n.* tango.

tank (tæŋk) *n.* **1,** (container) tanque. **2,** (armored car) carro de combate; tanque. **—***v.t.* depositar en un tanque. **—tank up;**

get tanked up, *slang* emborracharse.
tankage ('tæŋk·ɪdʒ) *n.* **1,** (capacity) cabida de un tanque. **2,** (storage; charge for storage) almacenaje.
tankard ('tæŋk·ərd) *n.* jarro con tapa; pichel.
tank car vagón cisterna; vagón tanque.
tanker ('tæŋk·ər) *n.* **1,** (ship) buque tanque; buque cisterna; petrolero. **2,** = **tank car.** **3,** = **tank truck.**
tank truck camión petrolero.
tanner ('tæn·ər) *n.* curtidor. **—tannery,** *n.* tenería; curtiduría.
tannin ('tæn·ɪn) *n.* tanino. **—tannic,** *adj.* tánico.
tantalize ('tæn·tə·laiz) *v.t.* atormentar; exasperar; provocar.
tantalum ('tæn·tə·ləm) *n.* tantalio.
tantamount ('tæn·tə,maunt) *adj.* equivalente.
tantrum ('tæn·trəm) *n.* berrinche; pataleta; rabieta.
tap (tæp) *n.* **1,** (light blow) palmadita; golpecito. **2,** (faucet) llave; grifo; caño; espita. **3,** (plug; stopper) tapón. **4,** (connection) toma. **5,** = **taproom.** **6,** *surg.* saja; sajadura. —*v.t.* **[tapped, tapping] 1,** (strike lightly) dar palmaditas o golpecitos a o en; golpear levemente. **2,** (pierce; broach) taladrar; agujerear. **3,** (draw, as liquid) sacar. **4,** *surg.* sajar. **5,** (make a connection with) hacer *o* poner una toma en. **6,** (a telephone) intervenir. —*v.i.* **1,** (strike lightly) dar golpecitos; golpear levemente. **2,** (knock, as at a door) llamar. **—on tap, 1,** (served from a tap) de grifo; de barril. **2,** *colloq.* (ready) disponible; a mano.
tap dance zapateado. **—tap-dance,** *v.i.* zapatear; bailar el zapateado.
tape (teip) *n.* **1,** (ribbon) cinta. **2,** (adhesive) esparadrapo. —*v.t.* **1,** (bind) encintar; atar con cinta. **2,** (measure) medir (*con una cinta métrica*). **3,** *colloq.* (record) grabar.
tape measure cinta métrica; cinta de medir.
taper ('tei·pər) *n.* **1,** (candle) cerilla; vela larga y delgada. **2,** (gradual decrease) diminución gradual. —*v.t. & i.* disminuir(se) gradualmente; rematar(se) en punta. **—tapered,** *adj.* rematado en punta; de forma cónica. **—taper off,** disminuir(se) gradualmente; parar gradualmente.
tape-record ('teip·rə,kord) *v.t.* grabar (*sobre cinta*). **—tape recorder,** grabadora de cinta; magnetófono. **—tape recording,** grabación (*sobre cinta*).
tapestry ('tæp·ɪs·tri) *n.* tapiz; tapicería; colgadura. —*v.t.* entapizar.
tapeworm ('teip·wʌɹm) *n.* tenia; solitaria.
tapioca (tæp·i'o·kə) *n.* tapioca.
tapir ('tei·pər) *n.* tapir; danta.
tappet ('tæp·ɪt) *n.* leva.
taproom *n.* bar; cantina; taberna.
taproot *n.* raíz principal.
taps (tæps) *n.pl.* toque de queda.
tar (taːr) *n.* **1,** (viscid product) alquitrán; brea; pez. **2,** *colloq.* (sailor) marinero. —*v.t.* alquitranar; embrear; betunar. —*adj.* de alquitrán; alquitranado. **—tar and feather,** embrear y emplumar.
tarantella (,tær·ən'tɛl·ə) *n.* tarantela.
tarantula (tə'ræn·tʃə·lə) *n.* tarántula.
tardy ('tar·di) *adj.* **1,** (late) tardío; demorado. **2,** (slow) tardo; moroso; lento; rezagado. **—tardiness,** *n.* tardanza; demora.
tare (teːr) *n.* **1,** *bot.* (vetch) arveja. **2,** *Bib.* (weed) cizaña. **3,** *comm.* tara.
target ('tar·gɪt) *n.* **1,** (mark in aiming) blanco. **2,** (object of attack) objeto. **—target practice,** tiro al blanco.
tariff ('tær·ɪf) *n.* **1,** (duties) tarifa; arancel. **2,** (price list) lista de precios. —*adj.* arancelario.
tarn (tarn) *n.* lago pequeño en las montañas.
tarnish ('tar·nɪʃ) *v.t. & i.* deslustrar(se); deslucir(se); empañar(se); manchar(se). —*n.* deslustre; mancha.
taro ('ta·ro) *n.* taro.
tarpaulin (tar'pɔ·lɪn) *n.* tela impermeable; empegado.
tarpon ('tar·pan) *n.* tarpón.
tarragon ('tær·ə·gan) *n.* estragón.
tarry ('tar·i) *adj.* alquitranado;

embreado; semejante a la brea o al alquitrán.
tarry ('tær·i) *v.t.* **[tarried, tarrying] 1,** (delay) demorarse; tardar. **2,** (stay) detenerse; quedarse. **3,** (wait) esperar.
tarsus ('tar·səs) *n.* tarso. **—tarsal,** *adj.* del tarso.
tart (tart) *adj.* **1,** (sour) acre; ácido; agrio. **2,** *fig.* (trenchant) picante; mordaz. **—*n.* 1,** (pastry) tarta; pastel de fruta. **2,** (loose woman) ramera.
tartan ('tar·tən) *n.* tartán.
Tartar ('tar·tər) *adj.* & *n.* tártaro.
tartar ('tar·tər) *n.* **1,** *chem.* tártaro. **2,** *dent.* sarro. **—cream of tartar,** crémor tártaro. **—tartar steak,** carne picada cruda.
tartaric (tar'tɛr·ɪk) *adj.* tártrico; tartárico.
task (tæsk) *n.* faena; tarea; labor. **—*v.t.* 1,** (assign work to) atarear; poner tarea a. **2,** (burden) cargar; sobrecargar. **—take (someone) to task,** reprender; censurar.
task force grupo militar o naval reunido para una misión especial.
taskmaster *n.* **1,** (overseer) capataz; supervisor. **2,** (disciplinarian) ordenancista.
tassel ('tæs·əl) *n.* borla. **—*v.t.*** poner borlas a; adornar con borlas.
taste (teist) *v.t.* gustar; probar; saborear. **—*v.i.*** saber; tener sabor *o* gusto. **—*n.* 1,** (sense of taste) gusto. **2,** (flavor) gusto; sabor. **3,** (mouthful) bocado; sorbo; trago. **4,** (inclination; liking) gusto; predilección; preferencia. **5,** (sample) muestra; ejemplar. **6,** (discernment) gusto; buen gusto. **—in (good *o* bad) taste,** de (buen *o* mal) gusto. **—taste of; taste like,** saber a. **—to (one's) taste,** a gusto.
taste bud papila del gusto.
tasteful ('teist·fəl) *adj.* de buen gusto; elegante.
tasteless ('teist·ləs) *adj.* **1,** (lacking flavor) insípido; soso; desabrido. **2,** (in bad taste) de mal gusto.
taster ('teis·tər) *n.* catador.
tasty ('teis·ti) *adj.* sabroso; apetitoso; gustoso.
tat (tæt) *v.t.* & *i.* hacer encaje de frivolité.
Tatar ('ta·tar) *adj.* & *n.* tártaro.
tatter ('tæt·ər) *n.* andrajo; harapo; guiñapo. **—tattered,** *adj.* andrajoso; harapiento.
tatterdemalion (ˌtæt·ər·dɪ·'meil·jən) *n.* guiñapo; golfo; pelagatos.
tatting ('tæt·ɪŋ) *n.* encaje de frivolité.
tattle ('tæt·əl) *v.i.* **1,** (talk idly) charlar; chacharear. **2,** (gossip) chismear. **3,** (tell tales) soplar; delatar; divulgar secretos. **—*v.t.*** divulgar (secretos). **—*n.* 1,** (idle talk) charla; cháchara. **2,** (gossip) chisme; chismografía.
tattler ('tæt·lər) *n.* chismoso; soplón; acusón.
tattletale *n.* = **tattler.**
tattoo (tæ'tuː) *n.* **1,** (drawing on the skin) tatuaje. **2,** (drum or bugle call) retreta. **—*v.t.*** tatuar. **—*v.i.*** tamborilear.
taught (tɔt) *v., pret. & p.p. de* **teach.**
taunt (tɔnt) *v.t.* mofarse de; burlarse de; tirar pullas a. **—*n.*** mofa; burla; pulla.
taupe (top) *n.* & *adj.* gris pardo.
taurine ('tɔ·rain) *adj.* taurino.
Taurus ('tor·əs) *n.* Tauro.
taut (tɔt) *adj.* **1,** (stretched; tense) tenso; tieso; tirante. **2,** (tidy) limpio; pulido; aseado. **—tauten,** *v.t.* tensar. **—tautness,** *n.* tensión; tirantez.
tautology (tɔ'tal·ə·dʒi) *n.* tautología. **—tautological** (ˌtɔ·tə·'ladʒ·ɪ·kəl) *adj.* tautológico.
tavern ('tæv·ərn) *n.* **1,** (bar) taberna; cantina. **2,** (inn) mesón; posada; fonda. **—tavern keeper,** tabernero; posadero.
tawdry ('tɔ·dri) *adj.* cursi; charro; chillón. **—tawdriness,** *n.* cursilería; charrería.
tawny ('tɔ·ni) *adj.* & *n.* leonado; amarillento.
tax (tæks) *n.* **1,** (compulsory payment) impuesto; contribución. **2,** (burden; task) esfuerzo; trabajo; obligación. **—*v.t.* 1,** (exact payment of) poner impuestos a *o* sobre. **2,** (burden) abrumar; cargar; exigir demasiado de. **3,** (accuse) acusar; culpar. **—taxable,** *adj.* sujeto a impuestos.
taxation (tæk'sei·ʃən) *n.* **1,** (levying of taxes) imposición de contribuciones. **2,** (taxes collectively) impuestos; contribuciones.
tax bracket tarifa; escala.
tax collection recaudación; re-

caudamiento. —**tax collector,** recaudador.
tax-exempt *adj.* exento de impuestos.
taxi ('tæk·si) *n.* taxímetro; taxi. —*v.i.* **1,** (travel by taxi) ir en taxi. **2,** *aero.* taxear.
taxi- (tæk·si) *prefijo* taxi-; orden; colocación: *taxidermy,* taxidermia.
taxicab ('tæk·si,kæb) *n.* taxímetro; taxi.
taxi dancer muchacha que cobra por bailar.
taxidermy ('tæk·sə,dʌɪ·mi) *n.* taxidermia. —**taxidermist,** *n.* taxidermista.
taxi driver taxista; cochero; chófer.
taximeter ('tæk·si,mi·tər; tæk·'sɪm·ə·tər) *n.m.* taxímetro.
-taxis (tæk·sɪs) *sufijo* -taxis; colocación; orden: *thermotaxis,* termotaxis.
taxonomy (tæks'an·ə·mi) *n.* taxonomía. —**taxonomic** (,tæks·ə·'nam·ɪk); **taxonomical,** *adj.* taxonómico. —**taxonomist,** *n.* taxonomista.
taxpayer ('tæks·pei·ər) *n.* contribuyente.
tea (tiː) *n.* té.
tea ball bolsita para preparar el té.
teach (titʃ) *v.t.* & *i.* [*pret.* & *p.p.* **taught**] enseñar. —**teachable,** *adj.* dócil; educable.
teacher ('titʃ·ər) *n.* maestro; profesor; instructor.
teaching ('titʃ·ɪŋ) *n.* **1,** (instruction) enseñanza. **2,** (precept) doctrina; precepto.
teacup *n.* taza para té. —**teacupful,** *n.* taza llena; cabida de una taza.
teahouse *n.* salón de té.
teak (tik) *n.* teca.
teakettle ('ti,kɛt·əl) *n.* tetera.
teal (tiːl) *n.* trullo.
team (tiːm) *n.* **1,** (group) equipo; partido; grupo. **2,** (group of draft animals) tiro. **3,** (pair of horses) tronco. **4,** (pair of oxen) yunta. —*v.t.* **1,** (harness together) uncir; enganchar; enyugar. **2,** (haul with a team) acarrear. —*v.i.* [*también,* **team up**] unirse; asociarse; colaborar.
teammate *n.* compañero de equipo.
teamster ('tim·stər) *n.* **1,** (driver of draft animals) conductor de un tiro de caballos o bueyes; arriero. **2,** (carter) carretero. **3,** (truck driver) camionero.
teamwork *n.* cooperación; solidaridad; coordinación de esfuerzo.
teapot *n.* tetera.
tear (teːr) *v.t.* [*pret.* **tore;** *p.p.* **torn**] rasgar; desgarrar; romper. —*v.i.* **1,** (rip) rasgarse; romperse; dividirse. **2,** (move swiftly) correr; precipitarse. —*n.* **1,** (rip) rasgón; desgarro; desgarradura. **2,** (outburst) arrebato; furia. **3,** *slang* (spree) borrachera; parranda. —**tear away,** arrancar. —**tear down, 1,** (demolish) derribar; arrasar; asolar. **2,** (dismantle) desmantelar. **3,** (disprove) refutar. —**tear off, 1,** (rip away) arrancar; separar con violencia. **2,** (run) correr; precipitarse. —**tear out,** arrancar; sacar. —**tear up,** romper; hacer pedazos.
tear (tɪr) *n.* lágrima. —*v.i.* echar lágrimas.
teardrop ('tɪr,drap) *n.* lágrima.
tearful ('tɪr·fəl) *adj.* lloroso; lacrimoso; lagrimoso. —**tearfulness,** *n.* lloriqueo; llanto.
tear gas (tɪr) gas lacrimógeno.
tearoom *n.* salón de té; pequeño restaurante.
tea rose rosa de té.
teary ('tɪr·i) *adj.* lloroso.
tease (tiːz) *v.t.* **1,** (annoy) embromar; molestar; importunar. **2,** (card; comb) cardar. —*n.* **1,** (act of annoying) fastidio; burla; broma. **2,** (one who annoys) embromador.
teasel *también,* **teazel** ('ti·zəl) *n.* **1,** *bot.* cardencha. **2,** (instrument for carding) carda. —*v.t.* cardar.
teaspoon ('ti·spun) *n.* cucharita. —**teaspoonful** (-,ful) *n.* cucharadita.
teat (tit) *n.* teta; tetilla; pezón.
tea wagon mesita con ruedas para servir.
technetium (tɛk'niʃ·i·əm) *n.* tecnecio.
-technic (tɛk·nɪk) *sufijo* -técnico; *forma adjetivos correspondientes a los nombres terminados en* **-technics:** *electrotechnic,* electrotécnico.
technical ('tɛk·nɪ·kəl) *adj.* técnico.
technicality (,tɛk·nɪ'kæl·ə·ti) *n.* **1,** (technical terms or procedure) tecnicismo. **2,** (subtlety) argucia; sutileza.

technician (tɛk'nɪʃ·ən) *n.* técnico.
technicolor ('tɛk·nə,kʌl·ər) *n.* tecnicolor.
technics ('tɛk·nɪks) *n.* técnica.
-technics (tɛk·nɪks) *sufijo* -tecnia; *forma nombres denotando* arte; ciencia; industria: *electrotechnics,* electrotecnia.
technique (tɛk'nik) *n.* técnica.
technocracy (tɛk'nak·rə·si) *n.* tecnocracia. —**technocrat** ('tɛk·nə,kræt) *n.* tecnócrata. —**technocratic** (-'kræt·ɪk) *adj.* tecnocrático.
technology (tɛk'nal·ə·dʒi) *n.* tecnología. —**technological** (,tɛk·nə'ladʒ·ɪk·əl) *adj.* tecnológico. —**technologist,** *n.* tecnólogo.
techy *también,* **tetchy** ('tɛtʃ·i) *adj.* malhumorado; enojadizo; quisquilloso.
tectonic (tɛk'tan·ɪk) *adj.* tectónico. —**tectonics,** *n.* tectónica.
ted (tɛd) *v.t.* esparcir (*para secar*).
teddy bear ('tɛd·i) oso de juguete.
tedious ('ti·di·əs) *adj.* tedioso; molesto; pesado; aburrido. —**tediousness,** *n.* tedio; aburrimiento; pesadez.
tedium ('ti·di·əm) *n.* aburrimiento; tedio; pesadez.
tee (tiː) *n.* **1,** (T-shaped object) algo en forma de T. **2,** *golf* tee. —*v.t.* colocar en el tee. —**tee off,** impulsar la bola de golf desde el tee. —**to a tee,** precisamente; exactamente.
teem (tiːm) *v.i.* abundar; rebosar. —**teeming with,** abundante en; lleno de.
-teen (tiːn) *sufijo; forma los números del 13 al 19: thirteen,* trece.
teenage ('tin·eidʒ) *adj.* adolescencia; de 13 a 19 años de edad. —**teenager,** *n.* adolescente; joven de 13 a 19 años de edad.
teens (tiːnz) *n.pl.* **1,** (age) edad de 13 a 19 años. **2,** (numerals) números cuyos nombres terminan en **-teen.**
teeny ('ti·ni) *adj., colloq.* = **tiny.**
teepee *también,* **tepee** ('ti·pi) *n.* cabaña de pieles de los indios.
teeter ('ti·tər) *v.i.* balancear; columpiarse; tambalear. —*n.* **1,** (swaying movement) balance; vaivén; tambaleo. **2,** (seesaw) balancín; columpio.
teeth (tiθ) *n., pl. de* **tooth.**
teethe (tiːð) *v.i.* echar los dientes; dentar.
teething ('ti·ðɪŋ) *n.* dentición. —**teething ring,** chupador; chupete.
teetotal (ti'to·təl) *adj.* **1,** *colloq.* (entire) entero; completo; total. **2,** (abstaining entirely) abstemio. —**teetotaler,** *n.* abstemio. —**teetotalism,** *n.* abstinencia total.
tegument ('tɛg·jə·mənt) *n.* tegumento.
te-hee (ti'hiː) *v.i.* reírse entre dientes. —*n.* risita; risa tonta. —*interj.* ¡ji, ji!
tele- (tɛl·ə) *prefijo* tele-; lejano; distante: *telescope,* telescopio.
telecast ('tɛl·ə·kæst) *n.* emisión por televisión. —*v.t. & i.* emitir por televisión.
telegram ('tɛl·ə,græm) *n.* telegrama.
telegraph ('tɛl·ə,græf) *n.* telégrafo. —*v.t. & i.* telegrafiar. —**telegraph operator,** telegrafista.
telegrapher (tə'lɛg·rə·fər) *n.* telegrafista.
telegraphic (,tɛl·ə'græf·ɪk) *adj.* telegráfico.
telegraphy (tə'lɛg·rə·fi) *n.* telegrafía.
telemeter (tə'lɛm·ə·tər) *n.* telémetro. —**telemetry** (-tri) *n.* telemetría.
teleology (,ti·li'al·ə·dʒi) *n.* teleología. —**teleological** (-ə'ladʒ·ɪ·kəl) *adj.* teleológico.
telepathy (tə'lɛp·ə·θi) *n.* telepatía. —**telepathic** (,tɛl·ə'pæθ·ɪk) *adj.* telepático.
telephone ('tɛl·ə·fon) *n.* teléfono. —*v.t. & i.* telefonear. —**telephone operator,** telefonista.
telephonic (,tɛl·ə'fan·ɪk) *adj.* telefónico.
telephony (tə'lɛf·ə·ni) *n.* telefonía.
telephoto *n.* telefoto. —*adj.* telefotográfico. —**telephotographic,** *adj.* telefotográfico. —**telephotography,** *n.* telefotografía.
telescope ('tɛl·ə·skop) *n.* telescopio. —*v.t.* **1,** (encase) enchufar; encajar. **2,** (condense) condensar; abreviar. —*v.i.* enchufarse; encajarse.
telescopic (,tɛl·ə'skap·ɪk) *adj.* telescópico.
teletype *n.* teletipo.
televiewer *n.* televidente.
televise ('tɛl·ə·vaiz) *v.t.* televisar.

television ('tɛl·ə·vɪʒ·ən) *n.* televisión. —*adj.* televisor. —**television set,** televisor.
tell (tɛl) *v.t.* [*pret. & p.p.* **told**] **1,** (make known; express) decir. **2,** (command) decir; mandar. **3,** (narrate) decir; contar; relatar. **4,** (count) contar; enumerar. **5,** (discern) conocer; distinguir. **6,** (decide) decidir; determinar. **7,** (reveal) descubrir; revelar. —*v.i.* **1,** (speak) hablar. **2,** (have force or effect) tener efecto; producir efecto. **3,** (determine) decidir; determinar. —**tell off, 1,** (count) contar; enumerar. **2,** *colloq.* (rebuke) reprender; censurar. **3,** *colloq.* (confront; defy) arrostrar; dar cara a; enfrentar. —**tell on, 1,** (tire; wear out) agotar; extenuar. **2,** *colloq.* (inform on) delatar; denunciar. —**tell one's mind,** decir lo que piensa; hablar sin rodeos.
teller ('tɛl·ər) *n.* **1,** (informant) narrador; relator. **2,** (bank clerk) cajero. **3,** (one who counts votes) escrutador. —**paying teller,** pagador. —**receiving teller,** recibidor.
telling ('tɛl·ɪŋ) *adj.* eficaz; notable; fuerte. —*n.* narración.
telltale ('tɛl,teil) *n.* **1,** (tattler) chismoso; soplón; cuentón. **2,** (indicator; gauge) indicador; medidor; contador. **3,** (indication) indicio; señal. —*adj.* indicador; revelador.
tellurium (tɛ'lʊr·i·əm) *n.* telurio.
temblor (tɛm'bloːr) *n.* terremoto; temblor de tierra.
temerarious (,tɛm·ə'rɛr·i·əs) *adj.* temerario.
temerity (tə'mɛr·ə·ti) *n.* temeridad.
temper ('tɛm·pər) *n.* **1,** (hardness of metals) temple. **2,** (disposition) genio; humor; temple; temperamento. **3,** (anger) ira; cólera; mal genio; enojo. —*v.t.* templar. —*v.i.* templarse. —**go** (*o* **fly**) **into a temper,** encolerizarse; arrebatarse. —**keep one's temper,** dominarse; tener calma. —**lose one's temper,** encolerizarse; perder la paciencia.
tempera ('tɛm·pər·ə) *n.* templa. —**in tempera,** al temple.
temperament ('tɛm·pər·ə·mənt) *n.* temperamento.
temperamental (,tɛm·pər·ə·'mɛn·təl) *adj.* **1,** (innate) propio; original; característico. **2,** (excitable; moody) caprichoso; veleidoso; mudadizo.
temperance ('tɛm·pər·əns) *n.* **1,** (moderation) templanza; temperancia; moderación. **2,** (abstinence) abstinencia.
temperate ('tɛm·pər·ət) *adj.* **1,** (moderate) templado; moderado. **2,** (abstemious) abstemio. —**temperateness,** *n.* templanza; moderación.
temperature ('tɛm·pər·ə·tʃʊr) *n.* temperatura.
tempered ('tɛm·pərd) *adj.* templado.
tempest ('tɛm·pɪst) *n.* **1,** (windstorm) tempestad; temporal; tormenta. **2,** (excitement) tumulto; conmoción; alboroto.
tempestuous (tɛm'pɛs·tʃu·əs) *adj.* **1,** (stormy) tempestuoso. **2,** (violent; turbulent) impetuoso; violento; turbulento.
template ('tɛm·plɪt) *n.* = **templet.**
temple ('tɛm·pəl) *n.* **1,** (church) templo; iglesia. **2,** *anat.* sien.
templet *también,* **template** ('tɛm·plɪt) *n.* plantilla; patrón.
tempo ('tɛm·po) *n.* tiempo; ritmo; compás.
temporal ('tɛm·pə·rəl) *adj.* temporal.
temporary ('tɛm·pə·rɛr·i) *adj.* temporal; temporario; temporáneo. —**temporarily** (-'rɛr·ə·li) *adj.* temporalmente; por algún momento.
temporize ('tɛm·pə,raiz) *v.i.* temporizar; contemporizar.
tempt (tɛmpt) *v.t.* **1,** (lure; incite) tentar; incitar; inducir. **2,** (provoke) provocar. **3,** (attract) atraer. —**tempter,** *n.* tentador. —**temptress** ('tɛmp·trɪs) *n.* tentadora.
temptation (tɛmp'tei·ʃən) *n.* tentación.
ten (tɛn) *n. & adj.* diez.
tenable ('tɛn·ə·bəl) *adj.* defendible.
tenacious (tə'nei·ʃəs) *adj.* tenaz.
tenacity (tə'næs·ə·ti) *n.* tenacidad.
tenancy ('tɛn·ən·si) *n.* tenencia.
tenant ('tɛn·ənt) *n.* **1,** (one who rents or leases) inquilino; arrendatario. **2,** (owner) residente.
tenantry ('tɛn·ən·tri) *n.* **1,** (tenancy) tenencia. **2,** (tenants collectively) inquilinos; arrendatarios.

tench (tɛntʃ) *n.* tenca.
tend (tɛnd) *v.t.* 1, (take care of) cuidar; velar; vigilar; guardar. 2, (serve) servir. —*v.i.* tender; dirigirse; inclinarse. —**tend on,** atender; servir.
tendency ('tɛn·dən·si) *n.* tendencia; propensión.
tendentious (tɛn'dɛn·ʃəs) *adj.* tendencioso. —**tendentiousness,** *n.* tendencia.
tender ('tɛn·dər) *adj.* 1, (soft) tierno; blando; delicado. 2, (weak; frail) débil; endeble; delicado. 3, (sensitive; difficult to handle) delicado; arduo; arriesgado. 4, (affectionate) cariñoso; afectuoso. 5, (painful) dolorido. 6, (compassionate) compasivo; considerado. 7, (scrupulous) delicado; escrupuloso. —*n.* 1, (offer) oferta. 2, (one who tends) guarda; guardián; vigilante. 3, *R.R.* ténder. 4, *naut.* falúa; lancha. —*v.t.* 1, (make tender) enternecer; ablandar. 2, (offer) ofrecer; tender; presentar.
tenderfoot *n.* [*pl.* **-foots**] novato; bisoño; pipiolo.
tenderhearted *adj.* compasivo; tierno de corazón; bondadoso. —**tenderheartedness,** *n.* compasión; bondad.
tenderize ('tɛn·dər,aiz) *v.t.* enternecer; ablandar.
tenderloin *n.* 1, (cut of meat) filete. 2, (city district) barrio de mala vida.
tenderness ('tɛn·dər·nəs) *n.* 1, (softness; delicateness) ternura; blandura; delicadeza. 2, (affection) cariño; afectuosidad.
tendon ('tɛn·dən) *n.* tendón.
tendril ('tɛn·drɪl) *n.* zarcillo.
tenement ('tɛn·ə·mənt) *n.* vivienda; alojamiento; habitación. —**tenement house,** casa de vecindad.
tenet ('tɛn·ət) *n.* dogma; credo; principio.
tenfold *adj.* & *n.* décuplo; diez veces (más). —*adv.* diez veces; en un décuplo.
tennis ('tɛn·ɪs) *n.* tenis. —**tennis player,** tenista.
tenon ('tɛn·ən) *n.* espiga. —*v.t.* espigar; despatillar.
tenor ('tɛn·ər) *n.* 1, (course) curso; tenor. 2, (tendency) tendencia. 3, (nature) carácter. 4, (meaning) significado. 5, *music* tenor. —*adj.* de *o* para tenor. —**tenor clef,** clave de do.
tenpenny ('tɛn,pɛn·i; -pə·ni) *adj.* de diez peniques; que vale diez peniques. —**tenpenny nail,** clavo de tres pulgadas.
tenpins *n.sing.* bolos. —**tenpin,** *n.* bolo.
tense (tɛns) *adj.* tenso; tieso; estirado; tirante. —*v.t.* tensar; hacer tenso. —*v.i.* tensarse; ponerse tenso. —*n., gram.* tiempo. —**tenseness,** tirantez; tensión.
tensile ('tɛn·sɪl) *adj.* 1, (undergoing or producing tension) tensor. 2, (ductile) dúctil; maleable. —**tensile strength,** resistencia a la tensión.
tension ('tɛn·ʃən) *n.* 1, (strain) tensión; tirantez. 2, (anxiety) ansia; congoja. —**tensional,** *adj.* de tensión.
tensity ('tɛn·sə·ti) *n.* tensión.
tensor ('tɛn·sər) *n.* tensor.
tent (tɛnt) *n.* 1, (shelter) tienda; tienda de campaña; pabellón. 2, *surg.* tapón. —*v.i.* acampar.
tentacle ('tɛn·tə·kəl) *n.* tentáculo.
tentative ('tɛn·tə·tɪv) *adj.* tentativo.
tenterhook ('tɛn·tər,hʊk) *n.* alcayata. —**on tenterhooks,** en suspenso; muy ansioso.
tenth (tɛnθ) *adj.* décimo. —*n.* décimo; décima parte; *music* décima.
tenuous ('tɛn·ju·əs) *adj.* tenue; delicado; fino. —**tenuousness,** *n.* tenuidad.
tenure ('tɛn·jər) *n.* tenencia.
tepid ('tɛp·ɪd) *adj.* tibio. —**tepidity** (tɛ'pɪd·ə·ti); **tepidness,** *n.* tibieza.
tequila (tə'ki·lə) *n.* tequila.
terbium ('tʌɹ·bi·əm) *n.* terbio.
tercentenary (tʌɹ'sɛn·tə·nɛr·i) *adj.* de trescientos años. —*n.* tricentenario.
term (tʌɹm) *n.* 1, (word or phrase) término. 2, (time) período; plazo; término. 3, *math.; logic* término. 4, (semester) semestre. 5, *pl.* (conditions) condiciones. —*v.t.* nombrar; llamar; denominar. —**be on good** (*o* **bad**) **terms,** tener buenas (*o* malas) relaciones; llevarse bien (*o* mal). —**bring to terms,** imponer condiciones a; vencer. —**come to terms,** someterse; ceder; ponerse de acuerdo.

termagant ('tʌɹ·mə·gənt) *n.* mujer regañona; fiera. —*adj.* reñidor; pendenciero.
terminable ('tʌɹ·mə·nə·bəl) *adj.* terminable.
terminal ('tʌɹ·mə·nəl) *adj.* terminal; final; último. —*n.* **1,** (end) término; fin. **2,** *electricity* borne; terminal. **3,** *R.R.* estación terminal.
terminate ('tʌɹ·mə,neit) *v.t.* & *i.* terminar; acabar; concluir. —**termination,** *n.* terminación; fin; límite; *gram.* desinencia.
terminology (,tʌɹ·mə'nal·ə·dʒi) *n.* terminología.
term insurance seguro a tiempo fijo.
terminus ('tʌɹ·mə·nəs) *n.* [*pl.* **-ni** (nai) *o* **-nuses**] término; final; fin; *R.R.* estación terminal.
termite ('tʌɹ·mait) *n.* termita; hormiga blanca.
tern (tʌɹn) *n.* **1,** (sea bird) golondrina de mar. **2,** (set of three) terna; terno.
ternary ('tʌɹ·nə·ri) *adj.* & *n.* ternario.
terpichorean (,tʌɹp·sɪ·kə'ri·ən) *adj.* del baile; perteneciente al baile. —*n.* bailarín (*fem.* bailarina).
terrace ('tɛr·əs) *n.* **1,** (embankment) terraplén. **2,** *agric.* terraza. **3,** (flat roof or balcony) terraza; terrado; azotea. —*v.t.* terraplenar; escalonar.
terra cotta ('tɛr·ə'kat·ə) *n.* terracota; barro cocido.
terra firma ('tɛr·ə'fʌɹ·mə) tierra firme.
terrain (tɛ'rein) *n.* terreno.
terramycin (,tɛr·ə'mai·sɪn) *n.* terramicina.
terrapin ('tɛr·ə·pɪn) *n.* tortuga del Atlántico.
terraqueous (tɛr'ei·kwi·əs) *adj.* terráqueo.
terrazzo (tɛr'rat·so) *n.* piso veneciano.
terrestrial (tə'rɛs·tri·əl) *adj.* terrestre; terreno.
terrible ('tɛr·ə·bəl) *adj.* **1,** frightful) terrible; pavoroso; espantoso. **2,** *colloq.* (very bad) desagradable; muy malo. —**terribleness,** *n.* terribilidad.
terrier ('tɛr·i·ər) *n.* terrier.
terrific (tə'rɪf·ɪk) *adj.* **1,** (dreadful) terrífico; espantoso. **2,** *colloq.* (extraordinary) extraordinario; maravilloso.
terrify ('tɛr·ɪ,fai) *v.t.* aterrar; espantar; horrorizar; aterrorizar. —**terrifying,** *adj.* terrible; terrífico; espantoso.
territorial (,tɛr·ɪ'tor·i·əl) *adj.* territorial.
territory ('tɛr·ɪ·tor·i) *n.* territorio.
terror ('tɛr·ər) *n.* terror.
terrorist ('tɛr·ər·ɪst) *n.* terrorista. —**terrorism,** *n.* terrorismo. —**terroristic,** *adj.* terrorista.
terrorize ('tɛr·ər,aiz) *v.t.* aterrorizar.
terror-stricken *adj.* aterrorizado.
terry ('tɛr·i) *n.* albornoz. *También,* **terry cloth.**
terse (tʌɹs) *adj.* conciso; breve; sucinto; terso. —**terseness,** *n.* brevedad; tersura.
tertian fever ('tʌɹ·ʃən) terciana; tercianas.
tertiary ('tʌɹ·ʃi·ɛr·i) *adj.* & *n.* terciario.
test (tɛst) *n.* **1,** (examination) prueba; examen; *educ.; psychol.* test. **2,** (experiment) ensayo; experimento. —*v.t.* probar; comprobar; examinar. —**test tube,** tubo de ensayo.
testament ('tɛs·tə·mənt) *n.* testamento. —**testamentary** (-'mɛn·tə·ri) *adj.* testamentario.
testate ('tɛs·teit) *adj.* testado.
testator ('tɛs·tei·tər) *n.* testador.
testatrix (tɛs'tei·trɪks) *n.* [*pl.* **-trices** (trɪ·siz)] testadora.
testes ('tɛs·tiz) *n.pl.* testes; testículos.
testicle ('tɛs·tə·kəl) *n.* testículo; teste.
testify ('tɛs·tɪ·fai) *v.t.* & *i.* testificar.
testimonial (,tɛs·tə'mo·ni·əl) *n.* **1,** (recommendation) certificado; certificación; recomendación. **2,** (tribute) homenaje. —*adj.* **1,** (certifying) testimonial; que hace fe. **2,** (recommending) de recomendación. **3,** (expressing esteem) de homenaje.
testimony ('tɛs·tə·mo·ni) *n.* testimonio.
testosterone (tɛs'tas·tə·ron) *n.* testosterona.
testy ('tɛs·ti) *adj.* enojadizo; quisquilloso; áspero. —**testiness,** *n.* enojo; enfado; aspereza.
tetanus ('tɛt·ə·nəs) *n.* tétano.
tetchy ('tɛtʃ·i) *adj.* = **techy.**

tête-à-tête ('tet·ə'tet) *n.* conversación cara a cara. —*adj.* confidencial. —*adv.* confidencialmente; en privado.
tether ('tɛð·ər) *n.* traba; maniota; atadura. —*v.t.* atar. —**at the end of one's tether,** al límite de la paciencia o de los recursos de uno.
tetra- (tɛt·rə) *prefijo* tetra-; cuatro: *tetrahedron,* tetraedro.
tetragon ('tɛt·rə,gan) *n.* tetrágono. —**tetragonal** (tɛ'træg·ə·nəl) *adj.* tetragonal.
tetrahedron *n.* tetraedro. —**tetrahedral,** *adj.* tetraédrico.
tetrarch ('tɛt·rark) *n.* tetrarca. —**tetrarchy,** *n.* tetrarquía.
tetter ('tɛt·ər) *n.* empeine.
Teuton ('tu·tən) *n.* teutón; tudesco. —**Teutonic** (tu'tan·ɪk) *adj.* & *n.* teutónico; tudesco.
text (tɛkst) *n.* texto.
textbook *n.* libro de texto; libro escolar.
textile ('tɛks·tɪl) *adj.* textil. —*n.* tejido; tela; textil.
textual ('tɛks·tʃu·əl) *adj.* textual.
texture ('tɛks·tʃər) *n.* textura.
-th (θ) *sufijo* **1,** *forma nombres abstractos denotando* estado; cualidad; acción: *growth,* crecimiento; *warmth,* calor. **2,** *compone números ordinales: fourth,* cuarto. **3,** *arcaico; poét.; forma la tercera persona singular del presente: he hath,* él tiene.
thalamus ('θæl·ə·məs) *n.* tálamo. —**thalamic** (θə'læm·ɪk) *adj.* talámico.
thallium ('θæl·i·əm) *n.* talio.
than (ðæn) *conj.* que; (*before numerals*) de.
thank (θæŋk) *v.t.* agradecer; dar gracias a. —**thank God,** gracias a Dios. —**thank you,** gracias; muchas gracias.
thankful ('θæŋk·fəl) *adj.* agradecido; grato; reconocido. —**thankfulness,** *n.* agradecimiento; gratitud; reconocimiento.
thankless ('θæŋk·ləs) *adj.* desagradecido; ingrato. —**thanklessness,** *n.* ingratitud; desagradecimiento.
thanks (θæŋks) *n.pl.* gracias; agradecimiento. —*interj.* ¡gracias!
thanksgiving (,θæŋks'gɪv·ɪŋ) *n.* acción de gracias. —**Thanksgiving Day,** día de acción de gracias.
that (ðæt) *adj. dem.* [*pl.* **those**] ese (*fem.* esa); aquel (*fem.* aquella). —*pron.dem.* [*pl.* **those**] ese (*fem.* ésa; *neut.* eso); aquél (*fem.* aquélla; *neut.* aquello). —*pron.rel.* que; quien; cual; el que; la que; lo que. —*conj.* que; para que; a fin de que; de modo que. —*adv.* tan. —**at that,** con eso; con todo eso. —**in that,** porque. —**that is,** eso es; es decir. —**that much,** tanto. —**that's that!,** ¡así es!; ¡punto! —**that which,** el, lo *o* la que. —**what of that?,** ¿qué importa eso?; ¿qué significa eso?
thatch (θætʃ) *n.* **1,** (straw) paja; bálago; caña. **2,** (straw roof) techo de paja. **3,** *colloq.* (hair) pelo. —*v.t.* cubrir de paja.
thaw (θɔː) *v.t.* deshelar; derretir. —*v.i.* **1,** (melt) deshelarse; derretirse. **2,** *fig.* (relent) aplacarse; ablandarse; ceder. —*n.* deshielo; derretimiento.
the (ðə; *ante vocal* ði) *art.def.* el; la; lo; los; las. —*adv.* cuanto. —**the more . . . the more,** cuanto más . . . tanto más.
theater *también,* **theatre** ('θi·ə·tər) *n.* teatro.
theatrical (θi'æt·rɪ·kəl) *adj.* teatral. —**theatricals,** *n.pl.* funciones teatrales.
theatrics (θi'æt·rɪks) *n.* arte teatral; teatro.
thee (ðiː) *pron.pers., arcaico y poético* **1,** *como complemento de verbo* te; a ti. **2,** *como complemento de prep.* ti. **3,** *tras* **than,** *en comparaciones* tú. —**with thee,** contigo.
theft (θɛft) *n.* robo; hurto.
their (ðeːr) *adj. poss.* su (*pl.* sus); de ellos; de ellas.
theirs (ðeːrz) *pron. poss.* el suyo; la suya; lo suyo; los suyos; las suyas; el, la, lo, los *o* las de ellos (*o* ellas).
theism ('θi·ɪz·əm) *n.* teísmo. —**theist,** *n.* teísta. —**theistic** (θi'ɪs·tɪk) *adj.* teísta.
them (ðɛm) *pron.pers.m. & f. pl.* **1,** *como complemento directo de verbo* los; las; les. **2,** *como complemento indirecto* les; a ellos; a ellas. **3,** *como complemento de prep.* ellos; ellas. **4,** *tras* **than,** *en comparaciones* ellos; ellas.
theme (θiːm) *n.* tema. —**thematic** (θi'mæt·ɪk) *adj.* temático.
themselves (ðɛm'sɛlvz) *pron. pers.* ellos; ellas; ellos mismos;

ellas mismas. —*pron.refl.* **1,** *como complemento de verbo* se: *They washed themselves,* Se lavaron; *They put them on themselves,* Se los pusieron. **2,** *como complemento de prep.* sí; sí mismos; sí mismas. —**with themselves,** consigo.

then (ðɛn) *adv.* **1,** (at that time) entonces; en aquel tiempo; en aquellos tiempos. **2,** (afterward; next) después; luego. **3,** (in that case; therefore) pues. **4,** (besides; moreover) además. **5,** (at another time) en otro tiempo. —*adj.* de entonces; de aquel tiempo. —*n.* aquel tiempo; aquellos tiempos. —**then and there,** en seguida; en el acto.

thence (ðɛns) *adv.* **1,** (from there) de allí; desde allí; **2,** (from that time) desde entonces. **3,** (therefore) por eso; por esa razón.

thenceforth *adv.* desde entonces; de allí en adelante.

theo- (θi·o; -ə) *prefijo* teo-; de Dios o dioses; divino: *theology,* teología.

theocracy (θi'ak·rə·si) *n.* teocracia. —**theocratic** (ˌθi·ə'kræt·ɪk) *adj.* teocrático.

theology (θi'al·ə·dʒi) *n.* teología. —**theological** (ˌθi·ə'ladʒ·ɪ·kəl) *adj.* teológico; teologal. —**theologian** (ˌθi·ə'lo·dʒi·ən) *n.* teólogo.

theorem ('θi·ə·rəm) *n.* teorema.

theoretical (ˌθi·ə'rɛt·ɪ·kəl) *adj.* teórico.

theoretics (ˌθi·ə'rɛt·ɪks) *n.* teórica.

theorist ('θi·ə·rɪst) *n.* teórico.

theorize ('θi·əˌraiz) *v.i.* teorizar.

theory ('θi·ə·ri) *n.* teoría.

theosophy (θi'as·ə·fi) *n.* teosofía. —**theosophical** (ˌθi·ə'saf·ɪ·kəl) *adj.* teosófico. —**theosophist,** *n.* teósofo.

therapeutic (θɛr·ə'pju·tɪk) *adj.* terapéutico. —**therapeutics,** *n.* terapéutica.

therapy ('θɛr·ə·pi) *n.* terapéutica. —**therapist,** *n.* terapeuta.

there (ðeːr) *adv.* allí; allá; ahí. —*interj.* ¡mira!; ¡toma!; ¡vaya! —**(be) all there,** (estar) en sus cabales. —**there is; there are,** hay.

there- (ðɛr) *prefijo; combinado con preposiciones forma adverbios denotando* lugar; tiempo; dirección; procedencia: *thereunder,* bajo eso; *thereafter,* después de eso; *therefrom,* de allí; *therefore,* por lo tanto.

thereabout *adv.* **1,** (near that place or time) por allí; por ahí; cerca. **2,** (approximately) aproximadamente. *También,* **thereabouts.**

thereafter *adv.* después de eso; de allí en adelante.

thereat *adv.* **1,** (at that place) allí; en aquel lugar. **2,** (at that time) entonces; en eso. **3,** (for that reason) por eso.

thereby *adv.* **1,** (by that means) así; de este modo. **2,** (in that connection) con eso. **3,** (near that place) por ahí cerca.

therefor *adv.* para eso.

therefore ('ðɛr·for) *adv.* por eso; por tanto; por lo tanto; por consiguiente.

therefrom *adv.* de eso; de allí.

therein *adv.* en eso; en ello; allí dentro.

thereinafter *adv.* posteriormente; más adelante.

thereinto *adv.* dentro de eso o de aquello.

thereof *adv.* de eso; de ello.

thereon *adv.* **1,** (on that) en eso; sobre eso. **2,** (following that) luego; en seguida.

thereto *adv.* a eso; a ello.

theretofore ('ðɛr·təˌfor) *adv.* hasta entonces.

thereunder *adv.* bajo eso; debajo de eso.

thereunto *adv.* a eso; a ello.

thereupon *adv.* **1,** (upon that) en eso; sobre eso. **2,** (concerning that) de eso; de ello. **3,** (because of that) por eso. **4,** (following that) luego; en seguida.

therewith *adv.* **1,** (with that) con eso. **2,** (in addition to that) además de eso. **3,** (following that) luego; en seguida.

therewithal *adv.* a más; además.

thermal ('θʌɹ·məl) *adj.* termal; térmico.

thermic ('θʌɹ·mɪk) *adj.* térmico.

thermit ('θʌɹ·mɪt) *n.* termita. *También,* **thermite** (-mait).

thermo- (θʌɹ·mo) *también,* **therm-** (θʌɹm) *ante vocal; prefijo* termo-; calor: *thermonuclear,* termonuclear; *thermion,* termión.

thermodynamics *n.* termodinámica. —**thermodynamic,** *adj.* termodinámico.

thermometer (θʌɹ'mam·ɪ·tər) *n.* termómetro. —**thermometric**

(ˌθʌɹ·məˈmɛt·rɪk) *adj.* termométrico.
thermonuclear *adj.* termonuclear.
thermos (ˈθʌɹ·məs) *n.* termos.
thermostat (ˈθʌɹ·mə·stæt) *n.* termóstato. —**thermostatic** (-ˈstæt·ɪk) *adj.* termostático.
-thermy (θʌɹ·mi) *sufijo* -termia; calor: *diathermy*, diatermia.
thesaurus (θiˈsor·əs) *n.* [*pl.* **-ri** (rai)] tesauro.
these (ðiːz) *adj.dem.* estos; estas. —*pron. dem.* éstos; éstas.
thesis (ˈθi·sɪs) *n.* [*pl.* **-ses** (siz)] tesis.
Thespian (ˈθɛs·pi·ən) *adj.* relativo a Tespis; trágico; dramático. —*n.* actor trágico.
they (ðei) *pron.pers.* ellos; ellas.
they'd (ðeid) *contr. de* **they would** *o* **they had.**
they'll (ðeil) *contr. de* **they will** *o* **they shall.**
they're (ðeːr) *contr. de* **they are.**
they've (ðeiv) *contr. de* **they have.**
thiamine (ˈθai·ə·miːn) *n.* tiamina. *También,* **thiamin** (-mɪn).
thick (θɪk) *adj.* **1,** (heavy; massive) grueso; espeso; macizo. **2,** (dense) denso; espeso; tupido. **3,** having a certain thickness) de espesor: *six inches thick,* de seis pulgadas de espesor. **4,** (abundant) abundante. **5,** (filled; crammed) lleno. **6,** (murky) brumoso; nebuloso. **7,** (mentally dull) torpe; estúpido; embotado. **8,** *colloq.* (unpleasant) desagradable; insoportable. **9,** *colloq.* (intimate) íntimo. —*n.* **1,** (thickness; thickest part) espesor; grueso. **2,** (most active part) lo más fuerte; lo más reñido. —*adv.* **1,** (thickly) espesamente; densamente. **2,** (abundantly) abundantemente. —**lay it on thick,** *colloq.* exagerar. —**thick and fast,** abundantemente; frecuentemente. —**through thick and thin,** por las buenas y las malas.
thicken (ˈθɪk·ən) *v.t.* espesar. —*v.i.* **1,** (become thick) espesarse. **2,** (become complicated) complicarse; enredarse.
thicket (ˈθɪk·ɪt) *n.* espesura; maleza; soto; boscaje.
thickheaded *adj.* torpe; estúpido; embotado.
thickness (ˈθɪk·nəs) *n.* **1,** (massiveness) espesura. **2,** (dimension) espesor. **3,** (denseness) densidad. **4,** (consistency) consistencia. **5,** (thickest part) espesor; grueso. **6,** (layer) capa; estrato.
thickset (ˈθɪk·sɛt) *adj.* fornido; rechoncho; grueso.
thick-skinned *adj.* **1,** (having a thick skin) de pellejo espeso. **2,** (insensitive) insensible.
thief (θif) *n.* [*pl.* **thieves** (θiːvz)] ladrón.
thieve (θiːv) *v.i.* robar; hurtar. —**thievery,** *n.* latrocinio; hurto; robo. —**thieving; thievish,** *adj.* ladrón; rapaz.
thigh (θai) *n.* muslo.
thighbone *n.* fémur.
thimble (ˈθɪm·bəl) *n.* **1,** *sewing* dedal. **2,** *mech.* manguito de enchufe; abrazadera.
thimblerig (ˈθɪm·bəlˌrɪg) *n.* = **shell game.**
thin (θɪn) *adj.* **1,** (slender) delgado; flaco. **2,** (sparse) escaso; ralo. **3,** (watery) aguado; claro. **4,** (flimsy) débil; insubstancial. **5,** (fine; light) tenue; ligero; fino. —*v.t.* [**thinned, thinning**] **1,** (make slender) adelgazar. **2,** (make sparse) enrarecer. **3,** (make watery) aguar; aclarar. —*v.i.* **1,** (become sparse) enrarecerse. **3,** (become watery) aclararse. —*adv.* delgadamente; ligeramente.
thine (ðain) *pron.poss., arcaico y poético* tuyo; tuya; tuyos; tuyas. —*adj.poss.* tu; tus.
thing (θɪŋ) *n.* cosa; objeto. —**make a good thing of,** sacar provecho de. —**no such thing,** no (hay) tal cosa. —**not a thing,** nada. —**poor thing,** pobrecito (*fem.* pobrecita). —**see things,** *colloq.* ver visiones; imaginarse (cosas). —**the thing,** lo necesario; lo que se desea.
think (θɪŋk) *v.t. & i.* [*pret. & p.p.* **thought**] **1,** (conceive in the mind) pensar. **2,** (believe) creer. **3,** (reflect) pensar; considerar; reflexionar. **4,** (judge) juzgar. **5,** (intend) pensar; tener intención (de). —*n., colloq.* pensamiento; reflexión. —**think about, 1,** (fix the mind on) pensar en. **2,** (have an opinion of) pensar de. —**think better of,** repensar; volver a considerar. —**think ill of,** tener mala opinión de. —**think nothing of,** tener en poco. —**think of, 1,** (consider) pensar en; considerar. **2,** (have an opinion of) pensar de. **3,** (recall) acordarse; ocurrírsele a

uno. —**think on**, pensar en; reflexionar en. —**think out** *o* **through**, considerar en lo total; decidir; determinar. —**think over**, pensar en; reflexionar en. —**think up**, inventar; imaginar. —**think well of**, tener buena opinión de.
thinkable ('θɪŋk·ə·bəl) *adj.* pensable; concebible.
thinker ('θɪŋk·ər) *n.* pensador.
thinking ('θɪŋk·ɪŋ) *adj.* pensador. —*n.* **1,** (thought) pensamiento. **2,** (opinion) parecer; opinión; juicio.
thinner ('θɪn·ər) *n.* solvente.
thinness ('θɪn·nəs) *n.* **1,** (slenderness) delgadez; flacura. **2,** (sparseness) escasez; raleza. **3,** (fineness) tenuidad; ligereza; fineza.
thinskinned *adj.* **1,** (having a thin skin) de pellejo delgado. **2,** (sensitive) sensitivo; sensible; susceptible.
third (θʌɹd) *adj.* tercero. —*n.* tercio; tercero; tercera parte; *music* tercera. —**third degree**, interrogatorio (*de un preso*). —**third finger**, (dedo) anular.
third-rate *adj.* de tercera clase; inferior.
thirst (θʌɹst) *n.* **1,** (dryness) sed. **2,** (desire) anhelo; ansia; deseo ardiente. —*v.i.* tener sed; estar sediento. —**thirst for**, anhelar; ansiar; desear vivamente.
thirsty ('θʌɹs·ti) *adj.* sediento. —**be thirsty**, tener sed.
thirteen (θʌɹ'tiːn) *n.* & *adj.* trece. —**thirteenth**, *adj.* & *n.* decimotercio; trezavo.
thirty ('θʌɹ·ti) *n.* & *adj.* treinta. —**thirtieth**, *adj.* & *n.* trigésimo; treintavo.
this (ðɪs) *adj.dem.* [*pl.* **those**] este; esta. —*pron.dem.* [*pl.* **those**] éste; ésta; esto. —*adv.* tan.
thistle ('θɪs·əl) *n.* cardo; abrojo.
thither ('θɪð·ər) *adv.* allá; hacia allá; para allá. —*adj.* más lejano.
thitherto *adv.* hasta entonces; hasta allá.
tho (ðoː) *conj.* & *adv.* = **though**.
thong (θɔŋ) *n.* trasca; tira de cuero; correa.
thorax ('θor·æks) *n.* tórax. —**thoracic** (θə'ræs·ɪk) *adj.* torácico.
thorium ('θor·i·əm) *n.* torio.
thorn (θorn) *n.* **1,** (spine) espina; púa; pincho. **2,** (shrub) espino. **3,** *fig.* (annoyance) espina; pesadumbre; molestia.
thorny ('θor·ni) *adj.* **1,** (prickly) espinoso. **2,** (annoying; difficult) molesto; arduo; difícil.
thoron ('θor·an) *n.* torón.
thorough ('θʌɹ·ə) *adj.* **1,** (complete) acabado; completo; cabal; cumplido. **2,** (detailed; minute) cuidadoso; minucioso; esmerado.
thoroughbred *adj.* de casta; de pura sangre; de raza pura. —*n.* animal o persona de casta; caballo de raza.
thoroughfare *n.* **1,** (highway) vía pública; carretera; camino. **2,** (transit) paso; tránsito. —**no thoroughfare**, calle cerrada; prohibido el paso.
thoroughgoing *adj.* **1,** (complete) cabal; completo; perfecto. **2,** (exhaustive) minucioso; detallado. **3,** (painstaking) cuidadoso; esmerado. **4,** (effective) eficaz.
thoroughness ('θʌɹ·o·nəs) *n.* **1,** (completeness) entereza; perfección. **2,** (minuteness) minuciosidad; esmero.
those (ðoːz) *adj.dem.* esos; esas; aquellos; aquellas. —*pron.dem.* ésos; ésas; aquéllos; aquéllas.
thou (ðau) *pron.pers., arcaico y poético* tú.
though (ðoː) *conj.* aunque; siquiera; bien que; no obstante; aun cuando. —*adv.* sin embargo. —**as though**, como si.
thought (θɔt) *n.* **1,** (thinking) pensamiento; meditación. **2,** (idea) concepto; propósito; idea. **3,** (reasoning) reflexión; juicio; opinión. **4,** (consideration) atención; consideración. **5,** (intention) intención. —*v., pret. & p.p. de* **think**.
thoughtful ('θɔt·fəl) *adj.* **1,** (pensive) pensativo; meditativo. **2,** (heedful; mindful) precavido; previsor. **3,** (considerate) atento; considerado; solícito. —**thoughtfulness**, *n.* atención; consideración; solicitud.
thoughtless ('θɔt·ləs) *adj.* **1,** (unthinking) irreflexivo. **2,** (careless) descuidado. **3,** (rash) imprudente; indiscreto. **4,** (inconsiderate) inconsiderado.
thoughtlessness ('θɔt·ləs·nəs) *n.* **1,** (unthinking attitude or behavior) irreflexión; inadvertencia. **2,** (carelessness) descuido. **3,** (rashness) imprudencia; indiscreción.

4, (inconsiderateness) inconsideración.
thousand ('θau·zənd) *adj.* mil. —*n.* mil; millar.
thousandfold *adj.* & *n.* mil veces (más). —*adv.* mil veces.
thousandth ('θau·zəndθ) *adj.* milésimo. —*n.* milésimo; milésima parte.
thrall (θrɔːl) *n.* 1, (captive) esclavo; siervo. 2, (bondage) esclavitud; servidumbre. —**thraldom; thralldom,** *n.* esclavitud; servidumbre.
thrash (θræʃ) *v.t.* 1, (beat) azotar; zurrar. 2, (thresh) trillar; desgranar. —*v.i.* arrojarse o tirarse violentamente. —**thrash out,** discutir detalladamente; decidir; resolver.
thrasher ('θræʃ·ər) *n.* 1, (thresher) trillador; trilladora. 2, *ornith.* ave canora norteamericana semejante al tordo.
thrashing ('θræʃ·ɪŋ) *n.* paliza; zurra.
thread (θrɛd) *n.* 1, (thin cord; fiber) hilo; hebra; fibra; filamento. 2, *mech.* rosca; filete. 3, *fig.* (sequence) hilo. —*v.t.* 1, (pass through the eye of a needle) enhebrar; enhilar. 2, (string) ensartar. —*v.t.* & *i.* (pass through laboriously) colar (por); pasar (por).
threadbare *adj.* 1, (shabby) raído. 2, (hackneyed) gastado; trillado.
threat (θrɛt) *n.* amenaza.
threaten ('θrɛt·ən) *v.t.* & *i.* amenazar.
three (θriː) *n.* & *adj.* tres.
threefold *adj.* & *n.* triple; tres veces (más). —*adv.* tres veces; en un triple.
three hundred trescientos. —**three-hundredth,** *adj.* & *n.* tricentésimo.
thresh (θrɛʃ) *v.t.* 1, (beat, as grain) trillar; desgranar. 2, (discuss exhaustively) discutir detalladamente. 3, = **thrash.**
thresher ('θrɛʃ·ər) *n.* 1, (one who threshes) trillador. 2, (machine) trilladora. 3, [*también,* **thresher shark**] zorra marina; zorra de mar.
threshing ('θrɛʃ·ɪŋ) *n.* trilla; trilladura. —**threshing floor,** era.
threshold ('θrɛʃ·old) *n.* 1, (doorsill) umbral. 2, (beginning) entrada; comienzo; principio; umbrales (*pl.*).
threw (θruː) *v.,* *pret. de* **throw.**
thrice (θrais) *adv.* tres veces.
thrift (θrɪft) *n.* ahorro; economía; frugalidad. —**thrifty,** *adj.* económico; frugal; ahorrativo.
thrill (θrɪl) *v.t.* emocionar; conmover; excitar. —*v.i.* emocionarse; conmoverse; excitarse. —*n.* emoción; estremecimiento; excitación. —**thriller,** *n.* representación excitante. —**thrilling,** *adj.* emocionante; vivo; espeluznante.
thrive (θraiv) *v.i.* [*pret.* **throve** *o* **thrived;** *p.p.* **thrived** *o* **thriven** (θrɪv·ən)] medrar; florecer; prosperar.
throat (θrot) *n.* garganta. —**jump down one's throat,** reprender severamente.
throaty ('θro·ti) *adj.* gutural; ronco.
throb (θraːb) *v.i.* [**throbbed, throbbing**] latir; pulsar; palpitar. —*n.* latido; palpitación; pulsación. —**throbbing,** *adj.* palpitante. —*n.* palpitación; latido.
throe (θroː) *n.* dolor vivo; espasmo. —**throes,** *n.pl.* agonía (*sing.*); angustia (*sing.*).
thrombosis (θram'bo·sɪs) *n.* trombosis.
throne (θroːn) *n.* trono. —*v.t.* entronar.
throng (θrɔŋ) *n.* muchedumbre; multitud; gentío; tropel. —*v.i.* agolparse; apiñarse. —*v.t.* llenar; atestar; apretar.
throstle ('θras·əl) *n.* 1, (bird) tordo; malvís. 2, *mech.* máquina de torcer o devanar; telar continuo.
throttle ('θrat·əl) *n.* regulador; acelerador. —*v.t.* ahogar; estrangular; sofocar. —*v.i.* ahogarse.
through (θruː) *prep.* por; a través de; por medio de; por entre. —*adv.* de un lado a otro; de parte a parte; desde el principio hasta el fin; completamente; enteramente. —*adj.* directo; continuo. —**be through,** acabar; haber acabado. —**get through** (with), terminar; acabar (con).
throughout *adv.* por todo; por todas partes; en todas partes; de un extremo a otro. —*prep.* en todo; por todo; durante todo; a lo largo de.
throve (θroːv) *v.,* *pret. de* **thrive.**

throw (θroː) *v.t. & i.* [*pret.* threw; *p.p.* **thrown** (θroːn)] tirar; arrojar; lanzar; echar. —*n.* **1,** (a throwing; distance thrown) tiro; tirada; lance. **2,** (shawl) chal. **3,** (coverlet) colcha. —**throw away, 1,** (discard) tirar; botar; rechazar. **2,** (waste) malgastar; desperdiciar. **3,** (lose; miss) perder. —**throw down,** derribar; echar por tierra. —**throw in, 1,** (engage, as a clutch) engranar. **2,** (add) añadir. —**throw off, 1,** (cast aside) desechar; deshacerse de. **2,** (elude) eludir; escaparse de. **3,** (emit) emitir; echar. —**throw open,** abrir de repente; abrir completamente. —**throw out, 1,** (reject) botar; desechar. **2,** (put forth) proponer; tender. **3,** (disengage) desengranar. —**throw over,** abandonar. —**throw up, 1,** (renounce; resign) renunciar. **2,** (reproach with) echar en cara. **3,** (construct rapidly) construir rápidamente. **4,** (vomit) vomitar.

throwaway *n.* volante; impreso.

throwback *n.* retroceso.

thru (θruː) *prep., adv. & adj.* = **through.**

thrum (θrʌm) *v.t. & i.* [**thrummed, thrumming**] rasguear; tocar mal. —**thrumming,** *n.* rasgueo.

thrush (θrʌʃ) *n.* **1,** (bird) tordo; malvís. **2,** (disease) ubrera.

thrust (θrʌst) *v.t.* [*pret. & p.p.* **thrust**] **1,** (push; shove) empujar. **2,** (drive; impel) impeler. **3,** (force in) meter; hincar; clavar; encajar. **4,** (force upon) imponer. —*v.i.* **1,** (rush forward) arrojarse; precipitarse. **2,** (attack; charge) acometer; embestir. **3,** (strike with a weapon) dar una estocada, puñalada, etc. —*n.* **1,** (push) empujón. **2,** (attack) acometida. **3,** (stab) puñalada; estocada; lanzada. **4,** *mech.* empuje.

thud (θʌd) *n.* ruido sordo; batacazo. —*v.t.* golpear con ruido sordo. —*v.i.* hacer un ruido sordo.

thug (θʌg) *n.* matón; asesino; rufián.

thulium ('θu·li·əm) *n.* tulio.

thumb (θʌm) *n.* pulgar. —*v.t.* **1,** (handle) manejar; manosear. **2,** (riffle, as pages of a book) hojear. —**all thumbs,** tosco; zafio; rudo. —**thumb a ride; thumb one's way** = **hitchhike.** —**under one's thumb,** bajo el poder de.

thumb index índice recortado.

thumbnail *n.* uña del pulgar. —*adj.* muy pequeño; mínimo.

thumbscrew ('θʌm,skru) *n.* **1,** (screw turned by hand) tornillo de mariposa. **2,** (instrument of torture) empulgueras (*pl.*).

thumbtack *n.* chinche; tachuela.

thump (θʌmp) *n.* trastazo; porrazo. —*v.t.* golpear; aporrear. —*v.i.* **1,** (fall heavily) cascar. **2,** (stamp; pound) golpear; dar un porrazo. **3,** (walk noisily) andar pesadamente. —**thumping,** *adj., colloq.* muy grande.

thunder ('θʌn·dər) *n.* **1,** (natural phenomenon) trueno. **2,** (loud noise) estruendo. **3,** (vehement utterance) fulminación; amenaza. —*v.i.* **1,** (make a loud noise) tronar. **2,** (utter denunciations) fulminar. **3,** (move noisily) pasar con estruendo. —*v.t.* fulminar; arrojar; proferir con estruendo. —**steal one's thunder,** anticiparse a uno; robarle a uno su idea.

thunderbolt *n.* **1,** (flash of lightning) rayo. **2,** (surprise) censura o fulminación inesperada.

thunderclap *n.* trueno; tronido.

thunderhead *n.* cúmulo; nubarrón.

thunderous ('θʌn·dər·əs) *adj.* tonante; tronante; atronador.

thundershower *n.* tronada; chubasco con truenos.

thunderstorm *n.* tronada.

thunderstruck ('θʌn·dər,strʌk) *adj.* atónito; estupefacto.

Thursday ('θʌɪz·de) *n.* jueves.

thus (ðʌs) *adv.* **1,** (in this manner) así; de este modo; de esta manera. **2,** (to this extent) tan; tanto; a ese grado. **3,** (hence) en consecuencia.

thwack (θwæk) *v.t.* zurrar; pegar; golpear; aporrear. —*n.* golpe; porrazo; latigazo.

thwart (θwort) *v.t.* frustrar; contrariar; estorbar; impedir. —*n.* banco de remeros; banco de bogar.

thy (ðai) *adj.poss., arcaico y poético* tu; tus.

thyme (taim) *n.* tomillo.

thymus ('θai·məs) *n.* timo.

thyroid ('θai·rɔid) *n.* tiroides. —*adj.* tiroideo. —**thyroid gland,** tiroides.

thyself (ðai'sɛlf) *pron.pers., ar-*

caico y poético tú; tú mismo. —*pron.refl.* 1, *como complemento de verbo* te. 2, *como complemento de prep.* ti; ti mismo. —**with thyself**, contigo.
ti (tiː) *n., music* si.
tiara (ti'ɛr·ə) *n.* tiara; diadema.
tibia ('tɪb·i·ə) *n.* [*pl.* **tibiae** (-i) *o* **tibias** (-əz)] tibia.
tic (tɪk) *n.* tic.
tick (tɪk) *n.* 1, (sound) tictac. 2, (pillow slip) funda. 3, (parasite) garrapata. 4, (mark) punto; contraseña; contramarca. 5, (instant) instante; momento. 6, *colloq.* (credit) crédito; fiado. —*v.t.* marcar; señalar; contramarcar. —*v.i.* hacer tictac (*un reloj*); latir (*el corazón*).
ticker ('tɪk·ər) *n.* 1, (something that ticks) algo que hace tictac. 2, (telegraphic device) receptor telegráfico que imprime una cinta. 3, *slang* (watch) reloj. 4, *slang* (heart) corazón.
ticket ('tɪk·ɪt) *n.* 1, (token of admission) billete; boleto; entrada. 2, (electoral slate) lista de candidatos. 3, (label; tag) marbete; etiqueta. 4, *colloq.* (summons) citación. —*v.t.* rotular; marcar; poner etiqueta a. —**that's the ticket!**, *colloq.* ¡eso es! —**ticket office; ticket window**, taquilla.
ticking ('tɪk·ɪŋ) *n.* cutí.
tickle ('tɪk·əl) *v.t.* 1, (excite by stroking) cosquillear; hacer cosquillas a. 2, (please) gustar; halagar; divertir. —*v.i.* 1, (produce tickling) hacer cosquillas. 2, (feel ticklish) tener *o* sentir cosquillas. —*n.* cosquillas (*pl.*); cosquilleo. —**be tickled pink**, *slang* alegrarse mucho.
tickler ('tɪk·lər) *n.* 1, (person or thing that tickles) persona o cosa que hace cosquillas. 2, (memo pad) libro de apuntes. 3, (puzzler) rompecabezas.
ticklish ('tɪk·lɪʃ) *adj.* 1, (sensitive to tickling) cosquilloso. 2, (delicate; tricky) delicado; difícil; enredoso. —**ticklishness**, *n.* cosquillas (*pl.*). —**be ticklish**, tener *o* sentir cosquillas.
ticktacktoe (ˌtɪk·tæk'toː) *n.* juego de tres en raya.
ticktock ('tɪkˌtak) *n.* tictac.
tidal ('tai·dəl) *adj.* de marea. —**tidal wave**, ola de marea; oleada; marejada.
tidbit ('tɪd·bɪt) *n.* bocadillo; golosina.
tiddlywinks ('tɪd·li·wɪŋks) *n.* juego de la pulga.
tide (taid) *n.* 1, (rise and fall of water) marea. 2, (current; flow) corriente; flujo; torrente. 3, (time; season) tiempo; estación; temporada. —*v.t.* llevar; hacer flotar. —*v.i.* flotar con la marea. —**go with the tide**, seguir la corriente. —**tide over**, 1, (help momentarily) ayudar por un tiempo. 2, (overcome) superar. —**turn the tide**, cambiar el curso (de); decidir.
tideland *n.* estero.
tidewater *n.* agua de marea. —*adj.* costanero.
tidings ('tai·dɪŋz) *n.pl.* noticias; nuevas.
tidy ('tai·di) *adj.* aseado; limpio; ordenado. —*v.t.* asear; limpiar; arreglar. —**tidiness**, *n.* aseo; limpieza; orden.
tie (tai) *v.t.* [**tied, tying**] 1, (fasten) atar; amarrar; liar. 2, *music* ligar. 3, (score the same as, in a contest) empatar. 4, (limit; confine) restringir; limitar; confinar. —*v.i.* 1, (join) atarse; unirse. 2, (make the same score) empatarse. —*n.* 1, (something that binds) lazo; atadura. 2, (neckwear) corbata; *Amer.* chalina. 3, (equal scores) empate. 4, *music* ligadura. 5, (crossbeam) travesaño. 6, *R.R.* traviesa; *Amer.* durmiente. 7, (affinity) lazo; vínculo; parentesco. —**tie down**, restringir; limitar; confinar. —**tie up**, 1, (fasten) atar; amarrar. 2, (wrap) envolver. 3, (obstruct) impedir; obstruir. 4, (occupy) ocupar.
tier (tɪr) *n.* fila; hilera; ringlera.
tie-up *n.* 1, (stoppage) parada; paralización. 2, *colloq.* (connection) lazo; vínculo.
tiff (tɪf) *n.* riña; disgusto; pique. —*v.i.* reñir; enfadarse; disputarse.
tiger ('tai·gər) *n.* tigre.
tiger lily azucena atigrada.
tight (tait) *adj.* 1, (firmly fixed; fast) firme; seguro; fuerte. 2, (fitting closely) apretado; estrecho; ajustado. 3, (compact; dense) compacto; denso. 4, (taut; tense) tirante; tenso; tieso. 5, (hard to obtain) escaso; limitado. 6, (sealed; impermeable) estanco; hermético. 7, *colloq.* (stingy) tacaño; agarrado. 8, *colloq.* (drunk)

borracho. —*adv.* fuertemente. —**sit tight, 1,** (refrain from moving) aguantarse; quedarse tranquilo. **2,** (hold firm) estar *o* seguir en sus trece.
tighten ('tai·tən) *v.t.* apretar; estirar. —*v.i.* apretarse; estirarse.
tightfisted *adj.* tacaño; agarrado.
tightlipped *adj.* discreto; callado; reservado.
tightrope *n.* cuerda de equilibrista o volatinero.
tights (taits) *n.pl.* calzón muy ajustado; traje de malla.
tightwad *n., slang* tacaño; avaro; cicatero.
tigress ('tai·grɪs) *n.* tigresa.
tilde ('tɪl·də) *n.* tilde.
tile (tail) *n.* **1,** (ceramic tile) azulejo. **2,** (floor tile) baldosa. **3,** (roof tile) teja. —*v.t.* azulejar; baldosar; embaldosar; tejar; enlosar.
tilework *n.* enlosado; embaldosado; tejado.
tile works tejar.
tiling ('tai·lɪŋ) *n.* azulejos; baldosas; tejas.
till (tɪl) *prep.* hasta. —*conj.* hasta que; mientras que. —*n.* gaveta o cajón de mostrador. —*v.t.* cultivar; arar; labrar.
tillage ('tɪl·ɪdʒ) *n.* labranza; cultivo; labor.
tiller ('tɪl·ər) *n.* **1,** *agri.* labrador; cultivador; agricultor. **2,** *naut.* palanca *o* caña del timón. **3,** *hortic.* pendón; serpollo.
tilt (tɪlt) *v.t.* **1,** (slant) ladear; inclinar. **2,** (attack, in a joust) acometer; dar una lanzada a. —*v.i.* **1,** (slant) inclinarse; ladearse. **2,** (joust) pelear; luchar en un torneo. —*n.* **1,** (slant) ladeo; declive; inclinación. **2,** (contest) justa; torneo. **3,** (awning) toldo; tendal.
timber ('tɪm·bər) *n.* **1,** (wood) madera; maderaje; maderamen. **2,** (beam) madero; viga. **3,** (trees) árboles de monte. —*v.t.* construir de madera; enmaderar. —**timber line,** línea o límite de la vegetación arbórea.
timberwork *n.* enmaderamiento; maderamen.
timbre ('tɪm·bər) *n.* timbre; tono.
time (taim) *n.* **1,** (duration) tiempo. **2,** (hour) hora. **3,** (point in time) hora; momento. **4,** *music* tiempo; compás; ritmo. **5,** (prison sentence) término; condena. **6,** (working shift) horas trabajadas. **7,** (period) época; era; período. **8,** (turn; occasion) vez; oportunidad; turno. **9,** *pl.* (in multiplication) veces. —*v.t.* **1,** (measure the time of) calcular *o* medir el tiempo de. **2,** (choose the time for) hacer a tiempo oportuno. **3,** (regulate) regular; sincronizar. —*adj.* **1,** (of or pert. to time) del tiempo. **2,** (on installment) a plazos. **3,** (equipped with a timer) regulador; horario; de tiempos. —**at no time,** nunca; en ninguna ocasión. —**at the same time, 1,** (simultaneously) a la vez. **2,** (nevertheless) sin embargo. —**at times,** a veces; unas veces. —**behind the times,** fuera de moda; chapado a la antigua. —**behind time,** atrasado. —**do time,** *colloq.* cumplir una condena; estar encarcelado. —**for some time,** de un tiempo a esta parte. —**for the time being,** por el momento. —**from time to time,** de vez en cuando; una que otra vez. —**gain time,** adelantarse. —**have a good time,** divertirse; pasar un buen rato. —**in due time,** a su tiempo; con tiempo. —**in no time,** al instante; al momento. —**in time, 1,** (eventually) a su tiempo; con tiempo. **2,** (at the appropriate time) a tiempo; con tiempo. **3,** (in rhythm) a compás. —**keep time,** llevar el compás; andar bien (*un reloj*). —**lose time,** atrasarse. —**make time,** ganar tiempo; acelerarse; adelantarse. —**many a time,** muchas veces. —**on time, 1,** (punctual; punctually) puntual(mente); a la hora debida. **2,** (on installment) a plazos. —**out of time, 1,** (untimely) fuera de tiempo. **2,** (out of rhythm) fuera de compás. —**time after time; time and again,** repetidas veces. —**time out,** tiempo de descanso; tiempo descontado. —**time out of mind,** tiempo inmemorable. —**What time is it?,** ¿Qué hora es?
timecard *n.* tarjeta registradora.
time clock reloj registrador.
time exposure exposición de tiempo.
time-honored *adj.* anciano; venerable; tradicional.

timekeeper *n.* alistador de tiempo; *sports* juez de tiempo.
timeless ('taim·ləs) *adj.* eterno. —**timelessness,** *n.* eternidad.
timely ('taim·li) *adj.* oportuno; a propósito; a tiempo. —**timeliness,** *n.* oportunidad.
timepiece *n.* reloj; cronómetro.
timer ('tai·mər) *n.* regulador *o* marcador de tiempo; *mech.* regulador del encendido.
timeserver *n.* contemporizador. —**timeserving,** *adj.* contemporizador.
timetable *n.* itinerario; horario; guía.
timeworn *adj.* gastado por el tiempo; trillado.
time zone *n.* huso horario.
timid ('tɪm·ɪd) *adj.* tímido; encogido; corto. —**timidity** (tɪ'mɪd·ə·ti); **timidness,** *n.* timidez; cortedad.
timing ('tai·mɪŋ) *n.* **1,** (synchronization) sincronización. **2,** (choice of time) elección de tiempo.
timorous ('tɪ.ɹ·ə·rəs) *adj.* tímido; temeroso. —**timorousness,** *n.* timidez; temor.
timothy ('tɪm·ə·θi) *n., bot.* fleo. *También,* **timothy grass.**
timpani ('tɪm·pə·ni) *n.pl.* = **tympani.**
tin (tɪn) *n.* **1,** (metal) estaño; lata. **2,** (sheet metal) hojalata; hoja de lata. **3,** (container) lata. —*adj.* **1,** (of tin) de lata. **2,** (valueless) sin valor; falso. —*v.t.* **1,** (cover with tin) estañar. **2,** (preserve in a can) enlatar; envasar.
tincture ('tɪŋk·tʃər) *n.* tintura. —*v.t.* tinturar.
tinder ('tɪn·dər) *n.* yesca.
tine (tain) *n.* diente; púa.
tin foil hoja de estaño; hoja fina.
ting (tɪŋ) *n.* retintín; tintineo; tilín. —*v.t.* repicar; sonar. —*v.i.* retiñir; tintinear.
ting-a-ling ('tɪŋ·əˌlɪŋ) *n.* tilín.
tinge (tɪndʒ) *v.t.* [*ger.* **tingeing** *o* **tinging**] teñir; colorar; matizar. —*n.* tinte; color; matiz.
tingle ('tɪŋ·gəl) *v.i.* hormiguear; picar; sentir hormigueo. —*v.t.* producir hormigueo a *o* en. —*n.* hormigueo; picazón; comezón.
tinker ('tɪŋk·ər) *n.* **1,** (mender of pots and pans) calderero remendón. **2,** (bungler) chapucero. **3,** (bungling work) chapuz. **4,** (repairman) reparador. —*v.t.* chapucear; estropear. —*v.i.* hacer chapucerías. —**tinker with,** entretenerse con; tontear con; enredar.
tinkle ('tɪŋ·kəl) *v.i.* tintinear; retiñir; hacer retintín. —*v.t.* repicar; hacer retiñir. —*n.* tintineo; retintín; tilín.
tinny ('tɪn·i) *adj.* **1,** (of or like tin) de *o* como estaño. **2,** (flimsy) débil; endeble. **3,** (metallic in sound) que tintinea como el estaño. **4,** (metallic in taste) que sabe a estaño.
tin plate hojalata; hoja de lata. —**tin-plate,** *v.t.* estañar.
tinsel ('tɪn·səl) *n.* oropel; relumbrón. —*adj.* de oropel; de relumbrón. —*v.t.* decorar; adornar.
tinsmith *n.* hojalatero.
tint (tɪnt) *n.* tinte; color; matiz. —*v.t.* teñir; colorar; matizar.
tintinnabulation (ˌtɪn·tɪˌnæb·jə'lei·ʃən) *n.* repiqueteo; tintineo.
tintype ('tɪn·taip) *n.* ferrotipo.
tinware *n.* hojalatería.
tiny ('tai·ni) *adj.* diminuto; menudo; chiquitico.
-tion (ʃən) *sufijo* -ción; *forma nombres abstractos derivados de verbos denotando* acción; estado; resultado: *conception,* concepción.
-tious (ʃəs) *sufijo* -cioso; *forma adjetivos correspondientes a los nombres terminando en* **-tion**: *seditious,* sedicioso.
tip (tɪp) *n.* **1,** (point) punta. **2,** (end) punta; extremo; extremidad. **3,** (metal point) contera. **4,** (gratuity) propina. **5,** (tilt) inclinación. **6,** (information) noticia o aviso confidencial. **7,** (light blow) golpecito; toque ligero. —*v.t.* [**tipped, tipping**] **1,** (tilt) ladear; inclinar. **2,** (overturn) volcar. **3,** (give a gratuity to) dar una propina a. **4,** (provide with a point) poner punta a. **5,** (strike lightly) golpear ligeramente; tocar. **6,** *colloq.* (inform) informar; soplarle a uno. —*v.i.* inclinarse; ladearse. —**tip off,** *colloq.* informar; advertir. —**tip over,** volcar; volcarse.
tipoff *n., colloq.* advertencia; indirecta; sugerencia.
tippet ('tɪp·ɪt) *n.* bufanda.
tipple ('tɪp·əl) *v.t.* & *i.* beber

mucho. —**tippler** (-lər) *n.* bebedor.
tipster ('tɪp·stər) *n., colloq.* informante confidencial.
tipsy ('tɪp·si) *adj.* chispo; achispado; alegre. —**tipsiness**, *n.* embriaguez; chispa.
tiptoe ('tɪp·to) *n.* punta del pie. —*adj.* & *adv.* de puntillas. —*v.i.* andar de puntillas.
tiptop ('tɪp·tap) *n.* cima; cumbre. —*adj.* espléndido; soberbio.
tirade ('tai·red) *n.* diatriba; invectiva; tirada.
tire (tair) *v.i.* cansarse; fatigarse; aburrirse. —*v.t.* cansar; fatigar; importunar; aburrir. —*n.* llanta; neumático; goma.
tired (taird) *adj.* cansado; fatigado; aburrido.
tireless ('tair·ləs) *adj.* incansable; infatigable.
tiresome ('tair·səm) *adj.* cansado; aburrido; pesado; tedioso; molesto.
'tis (tɪz) *contr. de* **it is.**
tissue ('tɪʃ·ju) *n.* tejido. —**tissue paper**, papel de seda.
tit (tɪt) *n.* **1,** (nag) jamelgo; jaco; jaca. **2,** (bird) paro. **3,** (teat) pezón; tetilla. **4,** *vulg.* (breast) teta. —**tit for tat**, tal para cual; ojo por ojo.
titan ('tai·tən) *n.* titán. —**titanic** (tai'tæn·ɪk) *adj.* titánico; titanio; gigante.
titanium (tai'tei·ni·əm) *n.* titanio.
titbit ('tɪt·bɪt) *n.* = **tidbit**.
tithe (taið) *n.* **1,** (tenth part) décimo; décima parte. **2,** (contribution to the church) diezmo. **3,** (small part) pizca. —*v.t.* & *i.* diezmar.
titi (ti'ti:) *n.* **1,** (monkey) tití. **2,** ('ti·ti) (plant) cirila.
titian ('tɪʃ·ən) *n.* & *adj.* castaño rojizo.
titillate ('tɪt·ə,leit) *v.t.* cosquillear; hacer titilar; excitar; estimular. —**titillation**, *n.* titilación; cosquilleo; excitación.
titivate ('tɪt·ɪ,veit) *v.t.* & *i., colloq.* engalanar(se); emperifollar(se). —**titivation**, *n.* engalanamiento; perifollos (*pl.*).
title ('tai·təl) *n.* título; *sports* campeonato. —*v.t.* titular; intitular; nombrar. —**title deed**, título de propiedad. —**title page**, portada; frontispicio. —**title role**, papel principal; papel que da título a una obra.
titmouse ('tɪt,maus) *n.* paro.
titter ('tɪt·ər) *v.i.* reír nerviosamente. —*n.* risita; risa contenida.
titular ('tɪt·jə·lər) *adj.* titular; nominal.
tizzy ('tɪz·i) *n., slang* excitación sin motivo.
TNT ('ti·ɛn'ti) *n.* trinitrotolueno; TNT.
to (tu) *prep.* **1,** (toward) a; hacia. **2,** (as far as; until) a; hasta. **3,** (for; intended for) a; para. **4,** (into) en. **5,** (with relation to) con: *He is very kind to me,* Es muy amable conmigo. **6,** (according to) según. **7,** (in order to) para. **8,** (before, in telling time) menos: *a quarter to three,* las tres menos cuarto. **9,** (with necessity or obligation to) por; que: *many things to do,* muchas cosas que hacer; *we have to see it,* tenemos que verlo. **10,** (belonging to) de: *the key to the house,* la llave de la casa. **11,** *indicando el infinitivo: to sing,* cantar. —*adv.* **1,** (forward) hacia adelante. **2,** (closed; engaged) cerrado; encajado. **3,** (to the matter at hand) a la obra. **4,** (near) cerca: *We were close to when it happened,* Estábamos muy cerca cuando sucedió. —**as to**, cuanto a. —**come to**, recobrarse; volver en sí. —**to and fro**, de acá para allá; alternativamente.
toad (to:d) *n.* sapo.
toadstool ('tod,stul) *n.* seta venenosa; hongo venenoso.
toady ('to·di) *n.* adulador; zalamero. —*v.t.* & *i.* halagar; adular.
to-and-fro ('tu·ənd,fro:) *adj.* alternativo; de vaivén.
toast (tost) *n.* **1,** (bread) tostada. **2,** (compliment) brindis. —*v.t.* **1,** (expose to heat) tostar. **2,** (compliment) brindar a *o* por; beber a la salud de. —**toaster**, *n.* tostador; tostadora.
toastmaster *n.* maestro de ceremonias.
tobacco (tə'bæk·o) *n.* tabaco. —*adj.* de tabaco; tabacalero. —**tobacco grower**, tabacalero. —**tobacco plantation**, tabacal. —**tobacco pouch**, tabaquera.
tobacconist (tə'bæk·ə,nɪst) *n.* tabaquero.
toboggan (tə'bag·ən) *n.* tobogán. —*v.i.* **1,** (coast on snow)

deslizarse en un tobogán. **2,** *fig.* (fall rapidly) caer precipitadamente.

tocsin ('tak·sın) *n.* **1,** (alarm) toque de campana; campanada de alarma. **2,** (alarm bell) campana de alarma.

today (tə'dei) *n.* hoy. —*adv.* hoy; hoy día; actualmente.

toddle ('tad·əl) *v.i.* hacer pinitos; titubear. —*n.* pinitos (*pl.*); titubeo.

toddy ('tad·i) *n.* ponche.

to-do (tə'duː) *n.* bullicio; lío; conmoción; alharaca.

toe (toː) *n.* **1,** (digit of the foot) dedo del pie. **2,** (tip of a stocking or shoe) puntera. **3,** (forepart of a hoof) pezuña. **4,** (half of a cloven hoof) pesuño. **5,** (projection; tip) punta; extremo; pie. —*v.t. & i.* tocar, alcanzar o pegar con la punta del pie. —**on one's toes,** alerta. —**toe the line** (*o* **mark**), portarse como es debido.

toecap *n.* puntera.

toe hold **1,** (footing) agarre con las dedos del pie. **2,** (advantage) ventaja. **3,** (support for the toe) repisa. **4,** (entry; penetration) arraigo; pie.

toenail *n.* uña del pie; uña del dedo del pie.

toffee *también,* **toffy** ('taf·i) *n.* melcocha.

tog (taːg) *n., colloq.* vestido; traje; *pl.* ropa. —*v.t.* [**togged, togging**] vestir. —*v.i.* vestirse.

toga ('to·gə) *n.* toga.

together (tʊ'gɛð·ər) *adv.* **1,** (assembled) juntos. **2,** (at the same time) a la vez; al mismo tiempo. **3,** (in succession) sucesivos; sucesivamente; de seguida. **4,** (in agreement) de acuerdo. **5,** (in common) en común. —**together with,** junto con.

toggery ('tag·ə·ri) *n., colloq.* **1,** (clothes) ropa; vestido. **2,** (clothing shop) ropería.

toggle ('tag·əl) *n.* **1,** (transverse bar or pin) barra traviesa; fiador atravesado. **2,** (linkage of levers) palanca acodillada. —**toggle joint,** junta de codillo. —**toggle switch,** interruptor a palanca.

toil (tɔil) *v.i.* afanarse; esforzarse; atarearse. —*n.* **1,** (work) faena; trabajo; esfuerzo; fatiga. **2,** *pl.* (snare) trampa; red; lazo. —**toiler,** *n.* trabajador.

toilet ('tɔi·lıt) *n.* **1,** (water closet) retrete; excusado; *Amer.* inodoro. **2,** (dressing room) tocador. **3,** (personal appearance) vestido; atavío. —**toilet bowl,** taza. —**toilet paper,** papel higiénico o sanitario. —**toilet set,** juego de tocador. —**toilet water,** loción.

toiletry ('tɔi·lıt·ri) *n.* artículos de tocador.

toilsome ('tɔil·səm) *adj.* fatigoso; penoso.

toilworn *adj.* cansado; fatigado.

token ('to·kən) *n.* **1,** (sign; symbol) señal; símbolo; marca. **2,** (keepsake) recuerdo. **3,** (coin; counter) ficha; tanto. —*adj.* nominal; de poco valor. —**by the same token,** de la misma manera; en consecuencia. —**as a token of; in token of,** en señal de.

told (told) *v., pret. & p.p. de* **tell.**

tolerable ('tal·ər·ə·bəl) *adj.* **1,** (endurable) tolerable; soportable. **2,** (passable) pasable; regular; mediano.

tolerance ('tal·ər·əns) *n.* tolerancia. —**tolerant,** *adj.* tolerante.

tolerate ('tal·ə,reit) *v.t.* tolerar; soportar. —**toleration,** *n.* tolerancia.

toll (toːl) *n.* **1,** (tax) derecho; impuesto. **2,** (fee for travel or transit) peaje; portazgo. **3,** (peal of a bell) doble; toque. **4,** (loss) pérdida. **5,** (mortality) baja; mortalidad. —*v.t. & i.* doblar; tocar; tañer. —**toll bridge,** puente de peaje. —**toll call,** llamada de larga distancia. —**toll collector,** peajero. —**toll gate,** puerta *o* barrera de peaje. —**toll road,** carretera de peaje.

Toltec ('tal·tɛk) *adj. & n.* tolteca.

toluene ('tal·jʊ·in) *n.* tolueno.

tom (taːm) *n.* macho de algunos animales.

tomahawk ('tam·ə·hɔk) *n.* hacha de guerra de los indios americanos. —**bury the tomahawk,** hacer las paces.

tomato (tə'mei·to; -'ma-) *n.* **1,** (fruit) tomate. **2,** (plant) tomatera.

tomb (tuːm) *n.* tumba; sepulcro.

tomboy ('tam,bɔi) *n.* marimacho.

tombstone ('tum,ston) *n.* lápida funeraria.

tomcat *n.* gato.

tome (toːm) *n.* tomo; libro grande.

-tome (tom) *sufijo* -tomo; instrumento cortante: *microtome,* micrótomo.

tomfool ('tam'ful) *n. & adj.* necio; tonto.
tomfoolery (tam'ful·ə·ri) *n.* payasada; tontería; calaverada.
tommyrot ('tam·i,rat) *n., slang* disparate; tontería.
tomorrow (tə'mar·o) *n. & adv.* mañana. —**the day after tomorrow,** pasado mañana.
tomtit ('tam·tɪt) *n.* paro; pájaro pequeño.
tom-tom ('tam,tam) *n.* tam-tam.
-tomy (tə·mi) *sufijo* -tomía; *forma nombres indicando* **1,** corte; división: *dichotomy,* dicotomía. **2,** operación quirúrgica: *appendectomy,* apendectomía.
ton (tʌn) *n.* tonelada.
tonal ('ton·əl) *adj.* tonal.
tonality (to'næl·ə·ti) *n.* tonalidad.
tone (toːn) *n.* tono. —*v.t.* entonar. —**tone arm,** fonocaptor. —**tone color,** timbre. —**tone deaf,** duro de oído. —**tone down,** suavizar el tono (de); moderar(se). —**tone in with,** armonizar con. —**tone poem,** poema sinfónico. —**tone up,** entonar(se); reforzar(se); elevar el tono (de).
tong (taŋ) *n.* sociedad china.
tongs (taŋz) *n.pl.* tenazas; pinzas; tenacillas.
tongue (tʌŋ) *n.* **1,** *anat.* lengua. **2,** (language) idioma; lengua. **3,** *mech.; carp.; music, etc.* lengüeta; espiga. —*v.t.* **1,** (sound with the tongue) producir (sonidos) con la lengua. **2,** (put a tongue on) poner lengüeta a. **3,** *carp.* ensamblar a lengüeta y ranura. —**hold one's tongue,** morderse la lengua. —**tongue and groove,** lengüeta y ranura. —**tongue in cheek,** chistoso; chistosamente.
tongue-lashing *n.* reprensión; reprimenda.
tongue-tie *n.* impedimento en el habla. —*v.t.* dejar mudo; acallar. —**tongue-tied,** *adj.* que tiene impedimento en el habla; *fig.* mudo; aturdido.
tongue twister trabalenguas.
tonic ('tan·ɪk) *n.* **1,** (medicine; anything invigorating) tónico. **2,** *music; phonet.* tónica. —*adj.* tónico. —**tonicity** (to'nɪs·ə·ti) *n.* tonicidad.
tonight (tə'nait) *n. & adv.* esta noche.
tonnage ('tʌn·ɪdʒ) *n.* tonelaje.
tonneau (tə'noː) *n.* [*pl.* **-neaus** *o* **-neaux** (noːz)] compartimiento posterior de un automóvil.
tonsil ('tan·səl) *n.* tonsila; amígdala.
tonsillectomy (,tən·sə'lɛk·tə·mi) *n.* tonsilectomía.
tonsillitis (,tan·sə'lai·tɪs) *n.* tonsilitis; amigdalitis.
tonsorial (tan'sor·i·əl) *adj.* barberil.
tonsure ('tan·ʃər) *n.* tonsura. —*v.t.* tonsurar.
tony ('ton·i) *adj., colloq.* elegante. —**toniness,** *n., colloq.* elegancia.
too (tuː) *adv.* **1,** (in addition) además; asimismo; también. **2,** (more than enough) demasiado. **3,** (exceedingly) extremadamente.
took (tʊk) *v., pret. de* **take.**
tool (tuːl) *n.* herramienta; instrumento. —*v.t. & i.* **1,** (work with a tool) trabajar con herramienta. **2,** (install machine tools) instalar maquinaria (en).
toot (tut) *n.* **1,** (sound of a horn) toque de bocina, de pito, etc. **2,** *slang* (spree) parranda; juerga. —*v.t.* sonar; tocar. —*v.i.* bocinar; pitar; sonar (una bocina, un pito, etc.).
tooth (tuθ) *n.* [*pl.* **teeth**] diente. —**in the teeth of,** frente a; en desafío de; contra la fuerza de. —**throw (something) in one's teeth,** echar en cara. —**tooth and nail,** desesperadamente; encarnizadamente.
toothache *n.* dolor de muelas.
toothbrush *n.* cepillo de dientes.
toothed (tuːθd) *adj.* dentado; dentellado.
toothless ('tuθ·ləs) *adj.* desdentado; desmolado.
toothpaste *n.* pasta dentífrica.
toothpick *n.* mondadientes; escarbadientes; palillo.
toothsome ('tuθ·səm) *adj.* sabroso; gustoso.
top (tap) *n.* **1,** (apex; summit) ápice; cima; cumbre; tope. **2,** (head) cabeza; jefe. **3,** (surface) superficie. **4,** (lid; cover) tapa. **5,** (roof) techo. **6,** (toy) trompo; peón; peonza. **7,** *auto.* capota. —*adj.* **1,** (highest) más alto; último; superior. **2,** (principal) principal; primero. **3,** (of or on the surface) superficial. —*v.t.* [**topped,**

topping] 1, (be the top of) coronar; estar encima de. 2, (be at the top of; head) encabezar. 3, (furnish with a top) cubrir; tapar. 4, (reach the top of) alcanzar la cima de. 5, (get over; vault) salvar; saltar. 6, (rise above; surpass) aventajar; sobrepasar. 7, (cut off the top of; lop) descabezar; desmochar. 8, (complete; perfect) coronar; rematar. —**blow one's top,** *slang* 1, (lose patience) arrebatarse en ira; enfurecerse. 2, (become insane) volverse loco. —**from top to bottom,** de arriba abajo. —**from top to toe,** de pies a cabeza. —**on top,** triunfante; victorioso. —**on top of,** 1, (above) encima de. 2, (besides) además de. 3, (following upon) luego después de. —**on top of the world,** *colloq.* sumamente afortunado, próspero, *etc.*

topaz ('to·pæz) *n.* topacio. —*adj.* de color de topacio; amarillo.

topcoat *n.* abrigo; sobretodo; abrigo de entretiempo.

tope (top) *v.t.* & *i.* beber con exceso. —**toper,** *n.* bebedor.

topflight *adj., colloq.* sobresaliente; superior.

topgallant *n.* juanete. —**topgallant sail,** juanete.

top hat sombrero de copa.

top-heavy *adj.* demasiado pesado por arriba; inestable; inseguro.

topic ('tap·ɪk) *n.* tema; asunto; tópico.

topical ('tap·ɪ·kəl) *adj.* 1, (local) tópico. 2, (of current interest) de interés general; corriente. 3, (pert. to the topic) temático.

topknot *n.* moño.

topmast *n.* mastelero.

topmost *adj.* (el) más alto.

topnotch *adj., colloq.* excelente; superior.

topo- (tap·ə) *prefijo* topo-; lugar: *toponymy,* toponimia.

topography (tə'pag·rə·fi) *n.* topografía. —**topographical** (tap·ə·'græf·ɪ·kəl) *adj.* topográfico. —**topographer,** *n.* topógrafo.

topper ('tap·ər) *n.* 1, (top hat) sombrero de copa. 2, (woman's topcoat) abrigo de mujer. 3, *colloq.* (excellent person or thing) persona o cosa de primera clase.

topping ('tap·ɪŋ) *adj.* sobresaliente; superior; excelente. —*n.* 1, (crest) cresta; copete. 2, (covering) capa; revestimiento.

topple ('tap·əl) *v.i.* caerse; volcarse; derribarse. —*v.t.* volcar; derribar.

tops (taps) *adj., slang* mejor; de primera clase; superior.

topsail ('tap,seil) *n.* gavia.

top-secret *adj.* lo más secreto.

topsides *n.pl., naut.* borda (*sing.*). —**topside,** *adv.* en *o* hacia la cubierta.

topsoil ('tap,sɔil) *n.* capa superior del suelo.

topsy-turvy (tap·si'tʌɹ·vi) *adj.* trastornado; desordenado. —*adv.* al revés. —*n.* desorden; trastorno. —**turn topsy-turvy,** trastornar; trasegar; desordenar.

toque (tok) *n.* toca.

-tor (tər) *sufijo* -tor; -dor; *forma nombres denotando* agente: *director,* director; *dictator,* dictador.

Torah ('to·rə) *n.* Tora.

torch (tortʃ) *n.* 1, (flaming light) tea; antorcha. 2, (flashlight) linterna eléctrica. 3, (blowtorch) soplete; antorcha a soplete. —**carry a** (*o* **the**) **torch for,** *slang* estar enamorado de; morirse por.

torchbearer *n.* 1, (leader) líder. 2, *colloq.* (servile follower) secuaz.

torchlight *n.* luz de tea o antorcha.

tore (toːr) *v., pret. de* **tear.**

toreador ('tor·i·ə,dor) *n.* toreador; torero.

torment (tor'mɛnt) *v.t.* atormentar; torturar. —*n.* ('tor·mɛnt) tormento. —**tormentor,** *n.* atormentador.

torn (toːrn) *v., p.p. de* **tear.**

tornado (tor'nei·do) *n.* manga *o* tromba de viento; tornado.

torpedo (tor'pi·do) *n.* torpedo. —*v.t.* torpedear. —**torpedo boat,** torpedero.

torpid ('tor·pɪd) *adj.* torpe; aletargado.

torpor ('tor·pər) *n.* 1, (sluggishness) torpor; torpeza; entorpecimiento. 2, (stupidity) estupidez. 3, (lethargy) letargo; apatía. *También,* **torpidity** (tor'pɪd·ə·ti).

torque (tork) *n.* esfuerzo de torsión o rotación.

torrent ('tor·ənt) *n.* torrente. —**torrential** (to'rɛn·ʃəl) *adj.* torrencial.

torrid ('tor·ɪd) *adj.* tórrido; ardiente.

torsion ('tor·ʃən) *n.* torsión. —**torsional,** *adj.* de torsión; torsional.
torso ('tor·so) *n.* tronco; torso.
tort (tort) *n., law* agravio indemnizable.
tortilla (tor'ti·jə) *n.* torta de harina de maíz; *Mex.* tortilla.
tortoise ('tor·təs) *n.* tortuga.
tortoise shell carey. —**tortoiseshell,** *adj.* de carey; de color carey.
tortuous ('tor·tʃu·əs) *adj.* tortuoso. —**tortuousness; tortuosity** (-'as·ə·ti) *n.* tortuosidad.
torture ('tor·tʃər) *n.* tortura; tormento. —*v.t.* **1,** (put to torture) torturar. **2,** (distort) torcer; deformar. —**torturer,** *n.* torturador. —**torturous,** *adj.* torturador.
tory ('tor·i) *n. & adj.* conservador; tory.
toss (tɔs) *v.t.* **1,** (throw) arrojar; echar; tirar; lanzar. **2,** (shake; tumble about) voltear; menear; agitar. **3,** (jerk) sacudir. —*v.i.* **1,** (sway) mecerse; ondear. **2,** (move restlessly) agitarse; menearse. **3,** (flip a coin) jugar a cara y cruz. —*n.* **1,** (throw) echada; tiro. **2,** (shake; shaking) meneo; agitación. **3,** (jerk) sacudida. —**toss off, 1,** (do offhandedly) hacer rápidamente *o* improvisadamente. **2,** (gulp down) tragar de golpe. —**toss up,** jugar a cara y cruz.
tosspot ('tɔs,pat) *n.* bebedor; borrachín.
toss-up *n.* **1,** (tossing of a coin) cara y cruz. **2,** *colloq.* (even chance) probabilidad igual.
tot (tat) *n.* **1,** (small child) nene; chiquito. **2,** (small quantity) poco; pizca. —*v.t., colloq.* [**totted, totting**] sumar. —**tot up,** *colloq.* sumar.
total ('to·təl) *adj. & n.* total. —*v.t.* **1,** (add) sumar. **2,** (amount to) ascender a.
totalitarian (to,tæl·ɪ'tɛr·i·ən) *adj. & n.* totalitario. —**totalitarianism,** *n.* totalitarismo.
totality (to'tæl·ə·ti) *n.* totalidad.
tote (tot) *v.t., colloq.* llevar; cargar. —*n., colloq.* carga; acarreo.
totem ('tot·əm) *n.* tótem. —*adj.* totémico. —**totemism,** *n.* totemismo. —**totem pole,** pilar totémico.
totter ('tat·ər) *v.i.* tambalearse. —*n.* tambaleo. —**tottery,** *adj.* tambaleante.
toucan (tu'kan) *n.* tucán; *Amer.* picofeo.
touch (tʌtʃ) *v.t.* **1,** (come in contact with) tocar. **2,** (reach; attain) alcanzar. **3,** (move emotionally) conmover; impresionar. **4,** (affect) afectar. **5,** (be equal to) igualar. **6,** *slang* (borrow or beg from) dar un sablazo a. —*v.i.* tocar; tocarse. —*n.* **1,** (sense of feeling) tacto. **2,** (act of touching; detail of handiwork; skill or style) toque. **3,** (small quantity or degree) poquito; pizca. **4,** *slang* (cadging) sablazo. —**in touch with, 1,** (in communication with) en comunicación con; en contacto con. **2,** (informed about) enterado de; al corriente de. —**touch at,** hacer escala en. —**touch off, 1,** (detonate) descargar. **2,** (provoke) provocar; estimular. **3,** (represent accurately) representar con precisión; acabar. —**touch on** *o* **upon, 1,** (approach) aproximarse a. **2,** (refer to; treat) referirse a; tocar el tema de. —**touch up,** retocar.
touch and go ('tʌtʃ·ən,go) situación precaria o arriesgada. —**touch-and-go,** *adj.* arriesgado; difícil.
touchdown *n.* jugada (*de fútbol*); tanto.
touched (tʌtʃt) *adj.* **1,** (demented) tocado. **2,** (affected with emotion) emocionado.
touching ('tʌtʃ·ɪŋ) *prep.* referente a; acerca de. —*adj.* conmovedor; impresionante.
touchstone *n.* piedra de toque.
touchwood *n.* yesca.
touchy ('tʌtʃ·i) *adj.* **1,** (irritable) quisquilloso; susceptible. **2,** (risky) arriesgado; delicado. —**touchiness,** *n.* susceptibilidad.
tough (tʌf) *adj.* duro. —*n.* maleante; pendenciero; rufián. —**tough luck,** mala suerte; desgracia.
toughen ('tʌf·ən) *v.t.* endurecer. —*v.i.* endurecerse.
toughness ('tʌf·nəs) *n.* dureza.
toupee (tu'pei) *n.* tupé.
tour (tʊr) *n.* **1,** (travel) excursión; recorrido; jira. **2,** (shift) turno. —*v.i.* viajar. —*v.t.* recorrer; visitar.
touring (tʊr·ɪŋ) *n.* turismo. —*adj.* turístico; de turismo.
tourist ('tʊr·ɪst) *n.* turista. —*adj.* turístico; de turista. —**tourism,** *n.* turismo.

tourmaline ('tur·mə,lin) *n.* turmalina.
tournament ('tur·nə·mənt) *n.* torneo; justa.
tourney ('tur·ni) *n.* torneo; justa. —*v.i.* tornear; justar.
tourniquet ('tur·nɪ·kɛt) *n.* torniquete.
tousle ('tau·zəl) *v.t.* despeinar; desgreñar. —*n.* enredo; maraña.
tout (taut) *v.i.* **1,** (in racing) vender información. **2,** (canvass) solicitar negocios o votos. **3,** (spy) espiar. —*v.t.* **1,** (praise) elogiar; dar bombo. **2,** (in racing) vender información a. —*n.* espía; solicitante.
tow (toː) *v.t.* remolcar. —*n.* **1,** (act of towing) remolque. **2,** (fiber) estopa. —**towage,** *n.* remolque.
toward (tord; tword) *prep.* **1,** (in the direction of) hacia. **2,** (in furtherance of) en apoyo de. **3,** (with respect to) tocante a; para con. **4,** (near) cerca de. *También,* **towards.**
towboat *n.* remolcador.
towel ('tau·əl) *n.* toalla. —*v.t.* secar con toalla. —**toweling,** *n.* género para toallas. —**towel rack,** toallero.
tower ('tau·ər) *n.* torre. —*v.i.* elevarse; sobresalir. —**towering,** *adj.* elevado; sobresaliente.
towheaded *adj.* de pelo rubio claro o pajizo.
towline *n.* cable de remolque; sirga. *También,* **tow line.**
town (taun) *n.* ciudad; pueblo; municipio. —**go to town,** *slang* **1,** (go on a spree) ir de parranda. **2,** (work diligently) aplicarse; esmerarse. **3,** (be successful) tener éxito. —**on the town,** en la calle. —**paint the town red,** *slang* ir de parranda.
town council concejo municipal.
town crier pregonero.
town hall casa de ayuntamiento.
town house casa de ciudad.
townhouse *n., Brit.* casa de ayuntamiento.
town meeting reunión de vecinos.
townsfolk *n.pl.* vecinos.
township ('taun·ʃɪp) *n.* **1,** (unit of territory) municipio; término municipal. **2,** (town) ciudad.
townsman ('taunz·mən) *n.* [*pl.* **-men**] ciudadano; conciudadano; vecino.
townspeople *n.pl.* vecinos.
towpath *n.* camino de sirga.
towrope *n.* cable de remolque; sirga. *También,* **tow rope.**
toxemia (taks'i·mi·ə) *n.* toxemia.
toxic ('tak·sɪk) *adj.* tóxico. —**toxicant,** *n.* tóxico. —**toxicity** (tak'sɪs·ə·ti) *n.* toxicidad.
toxico- (tak·sə·ko; -kə) *prefijo* toxico-; veneno; tóxico: *toxicogenic,* toxicógeno.
toxicology (tak·sɪ'kal·ə·dʒi) *n.* toxicología. —**toxicological** (-kə·'ladʒ·ɪ·kəl) *adj.* toxicológico. —**toxicologist,** *n.* toxicólogo.
toxin ('tak·sɪn) *n.* toxina.
toxo- (tak·so) *también,* **tox-** (taks) *ante vocal; prefijo* toxo-; venenoso; relacionado con tóxicos: *toxoplasmosis,* toxoplasmosis; *toxemia,* toxemia.
toy (tɔi) *n.* **1,** (plaything) juguete. **2,** (trifle) fruslería; bagatela. **3,** (dog) perrito; perrillo. —*adj.* **1,** (toylike) semejante a un juguete; de jugar. **2,** (decorative) de adorno. **3,** (diminutive) diminuto; pequeñito. —*v.i.* jugar; juguetear.
toyshop ('tɔi,ʃap) *n.* juguetería.
trace (treis) *n.* **1,** (mark) rastro; huella; señal. **2,** (small quantity) pizca. **3,** (line) trazo. **4,** (copy) calco. **5,** (harness) tirante. —*v.t.* **1,** (follow the track of) rastrear. **2,** (investigate) investigar; hallar el origen de. **3,** (copy) trazar; calcar. **4,** (plan) diseñar; planear. —**tracer,** *n.* & *adj.* trazador; rastreador. —**tracer bullet,** bala trazante.
trachea ('trei·ki·ə) *n.* tráquea. —**tracheal,** *adj.* traqueal.
tracheo- (trei·ki·o) *también,* **trache-** (trei·ki) *prefijo* traqueo-; tráquea: *tracheotomy,* traqueotomía; *tracheitis,* traqueítis.
trachoma (trə'ko·mə) *n.* tracoma.
tracing ('trei·sɪŋ) *n.* calco; trazo.
track (træk) *n.* **1,** (trace; trail) huella; rastro; pisada. **2,** (rails) vía; carriles; rieles. **3,** (race course) pista de carreras. **4,** (running and jumping sports) carreras y saltos. **5,** (path) sendero; vereda. **6,** (sequence) sucesión; serie. **7,** (course of motion) trayectoria. **8,** *mech.* (rail; runner) corredera. **9,** (wake of a ship) estela. —*v.t.* **1,**

(pursue; trace) perseguir; rastrear. **2,** (make a track on or with) dejar huellas en *o* de. **3,** (traverse) atravesar; cruzar. —**in one's tracks,** allí mismo; en el acto. —**keep track of,** mantener en orden; mantener comunicación con. —**lose track of,** perder de vista; alejarse de. —**make tracks,** *colloq.* marcharse; huirse. —**off the track,** desviado; descarrilado. —**on the (right) track,** en el rastro; en el buen camino. —**track down,** buscar; perseguir; capturar.

track meet concurso de carreras y saltos.

tract (trækt) *n.* **1,** (region) región; comarca; terreno. **2,** *anat.* sistema; canal. **3,** (brief treatise) opúsculo; folleto.

tractable ('træk·tə·bəl) *adj.* dócil; tratable. —**tractability** (-'bɪl·ə·ti) *n.* docilidad.

tractile ('træk·tɪl) adj. dúctil.

traction ('træk·ʃən) *n.* tracción.

tractor ('træk·tər) *n.* tractor.

trade (treid) *n.* **1,** (commerce) comercio; tráfico; trato; negocio. **2,** (occupation) oficio. **3.** (exchange) trueque; canje. **4,** (customers) clientes; clientela. **5,** *pl.* = **trade winds.** —*v.t.* trocar; cambiar; dar en cambio. —*v.i.* comerciar; dedicarse al comercio. —**trade on,** explotar; aprovecharse de.

trade-in *n.* objeto dado en pago parcial de una compra.

trademark *n.* marca de fábrica; marca registrada.

trade name razón social; marca de fábrica.

trader ('trei·dər) *n.* comerciante; negociante; tratante.

tradesman ('treidz·mən) *n.* [*pl.* **-men**] mercader; tendero.

trade union sindicato; gremio de obreros.

trade winds vientos alisios.

trading ('trei·dɪŋ) *n.* comercio; negocio. —*adj.* mercantil; comercial. —**trading post,** factoría.

tradition (trə'dɪʃ·ən) *n.* tradición. —**traditional,** *adj.* tradicional. —**traditionalism,** *n.* tradicionalismo. —**traditionalist,** *n.* & *adj.* tradicionalista.

traduce (trə'djus) *v.t.* calumniar; difamar.

traffic ('træf·ɪk) *n.* **1,** (trade) tráfico; trato. **2,** (circulation) tráfico; tránsito. —*v.i.* [**trafficked, trafficking**] traficar. —**traffic circle,** glorieta de tráfico. —**traffic jam,** congestión; *W.I.* tapón; *So.Amer.* taco.

trafficker ('træf·ɪk·ər) *n.* traficante.

tragedy ('trædʒ·ə·di) *n.* tragedia. —**tragedian** (trə'dʒi·di·ən) *n.* trágico. —**tragedienne** (trə,dʒi·di·'ɛn) *n.f.* trágica.

tragic ('trædʒ·ɪk) *adj.* trágico. *También,* **tragical.**

tragicomedy (,trædʒ·ɪ'kam·ə·di) *n.* tragicomedia. —**tragicomic,** *adj.* tragicómico.

trail (treil) *v.t.* **1,** (drag loosely) arrastrar. **2,** (track) rastrear; seguir la pista de. **3,** *colloq.* (follow) seguir; andar detrás de. **4,** (make a path through) abrir o marcar una senda por. **5,** (carry, as by the feet) llevar; pisar. —*v.i.* **1,** (be dragged) ser arrastrado; arrastrarse. **2,** (proceed idly; lag) proceder lentamente; rezagarse. **3,** (be dispersed) dispersarse. **4,** (creep, as plants) trepar. —*n.* **1,** (path) sendero; vereda. **2,** (track) rastro; huella; pista. **3,** (something that trails behind) cola; estela. —**trail off,** disminuir poco a poco.

trailblazer *n.* precursor; iniciador; pionero.

trailer ('trei·lər) *n.* **1,** (vehicle) remolque; camión acoplado. **2,** (mobile house) casa rodante; coche-habitación. **3,** (trailing plant) planta rastrera. **4,** *motion pictures* anuncio de próximas películas.

train (trein) *n.* **1,** *R.R.* tren. **2,** (persons, vehicles, etc. traveling together) procesión; cortejo. **3,** (retinue) comitiva; séquito. **4,** (something that trails behind) cola. **5,** (series) serie; sucesión; tren. —*v.t.* **1,** (instruct adiestrar; entrenar. **2,** (aim) apuntar. —*v.i.* adiestrarse; entrenarse. —**trainee,** *n.* persona que se adiestra; novicio; recluta. —**trainer,** *n.* entrenador; (*of animals*) amaestrador.

training ('trei·nɪŋ) *n.* **1,** (instruction) instrucción; educación. **2,** (development of skills) adiestramiento; entrenamiento.

trainman ('trein·mən) *n.* [*pl.* **-men**] ferroviario.

trait (treit) *n.* rasgo; característica; cualidad.

traitor ('trei·tər) *n.* traidor. —**traitorous,** *adj.* traidor; traicionero. **—traitress** (-trɪs) *n.f.* traidora.

trajectory (trəˈdʒɛk·tə·ri) *n.* trayectoria.

tram (træm) *n.* **1,** (wheeled car) corro; vagón; vagoneta. **2,** *Brit.* (streetcar) tranvía.

tramcar *n., Brit.* tranvía.

trammel (ˈtræm·əl) *n.* **1,** (impediment) impedimento; obstáculo. **2,** (instrument for drawing ellipses) compás de vara. **3,** (shackle) grillete; maniota; traba. —*v.t.* trabar; impedir.

trammel net trasmallo.

tramp (træmp) *v.i.* **1,** (walk with a heavy step) pisar con fuerza; andar pesadamente. **2,** (walk resolutely) andar con resolución. **3,** (wander) vagar; vagabundear. —*v.t.* **1,** (traverse on foot) viajar a pie por; recorrer. **2,** (trample underfoot) hollar; pisotear. —*n.* **1,** (heavy tread) paso pesado; marcha pesada. **2,** (sound) ruido de pisadas. **3,** (long walk) caminata; paseo largo. **4,** (vagabond) vagabundo. **5,** (ship) buque de carga volandero.

trample (ˈtræm·pəl) *v.t.* pisotear; hollar. —*n.* pisoteo.

tramp steamer vapor volandero.

tramway *n., Brit.* tranvía.

trance (træns) *n.* **1,** (hypnotic state) estupor; catalepsia; estado hipnótico. **2,** (rapture) rapto; éxtasis; arrobamiento. **3,** (daze; reverie) ofuscación; ensimismamiento.

tranquil (ˈtræŋ·kwɪl) *adj.* tranquilo; sereno. **—tranquillity** (træŋ ˈkwɪl·ə·ti) *n.* tranquilidad. **—tranquilize,** *v.t.* tranquilizar. **—tranquilizer,** *n.* tranquilizante.

trans- (træns) *prefijo* trans-. **1,** a través; sobre; más allá de; al, del *o* en el otro lado de: *transatlantic,* transatlántico. **2,** a través de: *translucent,* translúcido. **3,** cambio: *transform,* transformar.

transact (trænsˈækt) *v.t. & i.* tramitar; negociar; llevar a cabo.

transaction (trænsˈæk·ʃən) *n.* **1,** (negotiation; deal) transacción; tramitación; negocio. **2,** *pl.* (proceedings) actos; trabajos.

transatlantic *adj.* transatlántico.

transcend (trænˈsɛnd) *v.t.* trascender. **—transcendence,** *n.* trascendencia. **—transcendent,** *adj.* trascendente. **—transcendental** (ˌtræn·sɛnˈdɛn·təl) *adj.* trascendental.

transcontinental *adj.* transcontinental.

transcribe (trænˈskraib) *v.t.* transcribir.

transcript (ˈtræn·skrɪpt) *n.* trasunto; copia; *Amer.* transcrito; *educ.* certificado de estudios.

transcription (trænˈskrɪp·ʃən) *n.* transcripción.

transept (ˈtræn·sɛpt) *n.* crucero.

transfer (trænsˈfʌɹ) *v.t.* **1,** (make over possession of) transferir; traspasar. **2,** (convey) transportar; trasladar. **3,** (transship) transbordar. **4,** (relocate) trasladar. **5,** (copy) reproducir; reportar. **6,** (trace) calcar. —*v.i.* cambiar (*de tren, tranvía, etc.*); transbordar. —*n.* (ˈtræns·fər) **1,** (making over possession) transferencia; traspaso. **2,** (transport) transporte; traslado. **3,** (relocation) traslado. **4,** (copy) reproducción; copia. **5,** (tracing) calco. **6,** (ticket of transfer) billete de transferencia. **7,** (changing of vehicles) transbordo. **—transferable,** *adj.* transferible. **—transference** (ˈfʌɹ·əns) *n.* transferencia.

transfigure (trænsˈfɪg·jər) *v.t.* transfigurar. **—transfiguration,** *n.* transfiguración. **—transfigurement,** *n.* transfiguración.

transfix (trænsˈfɪks) *v.t.* **1,** (pierce through) traspasar; atravesar. **2,** (impale) empalar; espetar. **3,** (astound) dejar atónito. **—transfixion** (-ˈfɪk·ʃən) *n.* transfixión.

transfixed (trænsˈfɪkst) *adj.* **1,** (pierced; impaled) transfijo. **2,** (astounded) atónito.

transform (trænsˈform) *v.t.* transformar. **—transformation** (ˌtræns·fərˈmei·ʃən) *n.* transformación. **—transformer,** *n.* transformador.

transformism (trænsˈfor·mɪz·əm) *n.* transformismo. **—transformist,** *n.* transformista.

transfuse (trænsˈfjuːz) *v.t.* transfundir. **—transfusion** (-ˈfju·ʒən) *n.* transfusión.

transgress (trænsˈgrɛs) *v.t.* **1,** (go beyond) traspasar; exceder. **2,** (violate) transgredir; infringir. —*v.i.* propasarse; excederse; pecar. **—transgression** (-ˈgrɛʃ·ən) *n.*

transgresión; pecado. —**transgressor,** *n.* transgresor; pecador.
transient ('træn·ʃənt) *adj.* transitorio; pasajero. —*n.* transeúnte. —**transience,** *n.* transitoriedad.
transistor (træn'sɪs·tər) *n.* transistor.
transit ('træn·sɪt) *n.* tránsito.
transition (træn'zɪʃ·ən) *n.* transición. —**transitional,** *adj.* transitorio; de transición.
transitive ('træn·sə·tɪv) *adj.* & *n.* transitivo.
transitory ('træn·sə·tor·i) *adj.* transitorio; pasajero. —**transitoriness,** *n.* transitoriedad.
translate (træns'leit) *v.t.* traducir. —**translator,** *n.* traductor.
translation (træns'lei·ʃən) *n.* **1,** (interpretation) traducción; versión. **2,** *mech.* traslación.
transliterate (træns'lɪt·ər·eit) *v.t.* transcribir. —**transliteration,** *n.* transcripción; transliteración.
translucent (træns'lu·sənt) *adj.* translúcido. —**translucence,** *n.* translucidez.
transmigration *n.* transmigración. —**transmigrate,** *v.i.* transmigrar.
transmissible (træns'mɪs·ə·bəl) *adj.* transmisible. —**transmissibility,** *n.* transmisibilidad.
transmission (træns'mɪʃ·ən) *n.* transmisión.
transmit (træns'mɪt) *v.t.* transmitir. —**transmittal,** *n.* transmisión. —**transmitter,** *n.* transmisor.
transmute (træns'mjut) *v.t.* transmutar. —**transmutation** (ˌtræns·mju'tei·ʃən) *n.* transmutación.
transom ('træn·səm) *n.* **1,** (of a door or window) montante. **2,** (crossbeam) travesaño.
transparent (træns'pɛr·ənt) *adj.* transparente. —**transparence; transparency,** *n.* transparencia.
transpire (træn'spair) *v.i.* **1,** (exhale; perspire) transpirar. **2,** (become known) trascender; transpirar. **3,** (happen) acontecer; suceder. —**transpiration** (-spɪ'rei·ʃən) *n.* transpiración.
transplant (træns'plænt) *v.t.* trasplantar. —*n.* ('træns-) trasplante. —**transplantation** (ˌtræns·plæn'tei·ʃən) *n.* trasplante.
transport (træns'port) *v.t.* **1,** (convey; imbue with emotion) transportar. **2,** (banish) deportar. —*n.* ('træns-) transporte.
transportation (ˌtræns·por'tei·ʃən) *n.* **1,** (act or means of transporting) transporte. **2,** (travel expenses) coste del transporte. **3,** (travel ticket) pasaje; billete de viaje.
transpose (træns'poːz) *v.t.* transponer; *music* transportar. —**transposition** (-pə'zɪʃ·ən) *n.* transposición; *music* transportación.
transship *v.t.* transbordar. —**transshipment,** *n.* transbordo.
transsonic *adj.* transónico.
transverse (træns'vʌɹs) *adj.* transverso; transversal. —**transversal,** *n.* transversal.
transvestism (trænz'vɛs·tɪz·əm) *también,* **transvestitism** (-tɪ·tɪz·əm) *n.* transvestismo. —**transvestic,** *adj.* transvestista. —**transvestite** (-tait) *n.* transvestista.
trap (træp) *n.* **1,** (snare) trampa; cepo. **2,** (trapdoor) trampa; escotillón. **3,** (bend in a pipe) sifón. **4,** *pl.* (baggage) equipaje. **5,** *pl.* (percussion instrument) instrumentos de percusión; batería. **6,** (carriage) carruaje ligero de dos ruedas. **7,** *slang* (mouth) boca. —*v.t.* [**trapped, trapping**] **1,** (catch) entrampar; atrapar. **2,** (adorn) adornar; enjaezar. —*v.i.* entrampar.
trapdoor *n.* trampa; escotillón. *También,* **trap door.**
trapeze (trə'piːz) *n.* trapecio.
trapezium (trə'pi·zi·əm) *n.* **1,** *geom.* trapezoide. **2,** *anat.* trapecio.
trapezoid ('træp·ɪ·zɔid) *n.* **1,** *geom.* trapecio. **2,** *anat.* trapezoide.
trapezoidal (ˌtræp·ə'zɔi·dəl) *adj.* trapezoidal.
trapper ('træp·ər) *n.* el que caza con trampas; trampero.
trappings ('træp·ɪŋz) *n. pl.* **1,** (harness) jaeces; arreos. **2,** (adornments) adornos.
Trappist ('træp·ɪst) *adj.* & *n.* trapense.
traprock *n.* roca ígnea, como el basalto.
trapshooting *n.* tiro de pichón.
trash (træʃ) *n.* basura; desecho; desperdicio. —**trashy,** *adj.* fútil; despreciable. —**trash can,** basurero.
trauma ('trɔ·mə; 'trau-) *n.* trauma. —**traumatic** (-'mæt·ɪk)

adj. traumático. —**traumatism** (-tɪz·əm) *n.* traumatismo.
travail ('træv·eil) *n.* **1,** (hard work) afán; pena; labor penosa. **2,** (labor pains) parto; dolores de parto. —*v.i.* **1,** (toil) afanarse; esforzarse. **2,** (suffer labor pains) estar de parto.
travel ('træv·əl) *v.i.* **1,** (move; proceed) viajar. **2,** *colloq.* (move speedily) correr. —*v.t.* viajar por; recorrer. —*n.* **1,** (act of traveling; journey) viaje. **2,** (traffic) circulación; tráfico. **3,** *mech.* movimiento; carrera.
traveler ('træv·əl·ər) *n.* viajero; *comm.* viajante. —**traveler's check,** cheque de viajeros.
traveling ('træv·ə·lɪŋ) *adj.* **1,** (journeying) viajante. **2,** (of or for travel) de viaje; para viajar. **3,** *mech.* corredizo. —**traveling expenses,** gastos de viaje. —**traveling salesman,** viajante.
travelogue *también,* **travelog** ('træv·əˌlɔg; -ˌlag) *n.* conferencia ilustrada sobre viajes.
traverse (trə'vʌɪs) *v.t.* **1,** (pass across) atravesar; cruzar; recorrer. **2,** (contradict; obstruct) contradecir; estorbar. **3,** (turn and aim a gun) volver y apuntar. —*n.* ('træv·ərs) **1,** (crosspiece) travesaño. **2,** (traversing) travesía. —*adj.* transversal.
travesty ('træv·ɪs·ti) *n.* parodia; farsa. —*v.t.* parodiar.
trawl (trɔːl) *n.* red barredera. —*v.t.* pescar rastreando. —**trawler,** *n.* barco rastreador.
tray (trei) *n.* **1,** (serving plate) bandeja; azafate. **2,** (trough) batea; cubeta. **3,** (case) cajón.
treachery ('trɛtʃ·ə·ri) *n.* traición; perfidia; deslealtad. —**treacherous,** *adj.* traidor; traicionero; alevoso. —**treacherousness,** *n.* traición; perfidia.
treacle ('tri·kəl) *n.* melaza.
tread (trɛd) *v.i.* [*pret.* **trod;** *p.p.* **trod** *o* **trodden**] andar; caminar; pisar. —*v.t.* **1,** (walk in, on or along; trample) hollar; pisar; pisotear. **2,** (execute by walking or dancing) andar; bailar. —*n.* **1,** (step; stepping) paso; pisada. **2,** (surface that touches the ground) superficie de rodadura; banda. **3,** (bearing surface) cara. **4,** (support for the foot) peldaño; escalón.
treadle ('trɛd·əl) *n.* pedal.
treadmill *n.* molino de rueda de andar.
treason ('tri·zən) *n.* traición. —**treasonable,** *adj.* traidor; desleal. —**treasonous,** *adj.* traidor; traicionero.
treasure ('trɛʒ·ər) *n.* tesoro. —*v.t.* **1,** (collect and save) atesorar. **2,** (prize) apreciar.
treasurer ('trɛʒ·ər·ər) *n.* tesorero.
treasure trove tesoro hallado.
treasury ('trɛʒ·ə·ri) *n.* **1,** (funds) erario; tesoro. **2,** (place) caja tesorería. **3,** (ministry) ministerio de hacienda.
treat (trit) *v.t.* **1,** (deal with; subject to a process) tratar. **2,** (entertain) agasajar; regalar. —*v.i.* **1,** (discuss; carry on negotiations) tratar. **2,** (bear the expense of regalement) convidar; regalar. —*n.* **1,** (regalement) convite. **2,** *colloq.* (anything enjoyable) solaz; deleite; placer. —**treat as,** tomar de. —**treat of,** tratar de.
treatise ('tri·tɪs) *n.* tratado.
treatment *n.* tratamiento; trato.
treaty ('tri·ti) *n.* tratado; convenio; pacto.
treble ('trɛb·əl) *adj.* **1,** (threefold) triple. **2,** (high in pitch) sobreagudo; de tiple. —*n.* tiple; sobreagudo. —*v.t.* triplicar. —*v.i.* triplicarse. —**treble clef,** clave de sol.
trebly ('trɛb·li) *adv.* tres veces.
tree (triː) *n.* **1,** *bot.; mech.* árbol. **2,** (gallows) horca. **3,** (cross) cruz. —*v.t.* obligar a refugiarse en un árbol; *fig.* apremiar; acosar.
treetop *n.* copa; cima de árbol.
trefoil ('tri·fɔil) *n.* trébol.
trek (trɛk) *v.i.* [**trekked, trekking**] emigrar; viajar. —*n.* emigración; viaje.
trellis ('trɛl·ɪs) *n.* enrejado; espaldera.
tremble ('trɛm·bəl) *v.i.* temblar; estremecerse. —*n.* temblor; estremecimiento. —**trembly** (-bli) *adj.* trémulo; tembloroso.
tremendous (trɪ'mɛn·dəs) *adj.* tremendo; enorme. —**tremendousness,** *n.* enormidad.
tremolo ('trɛm·ə·lo) *n.* trémolo.
tremor ('trɛm·ər) *n.* tremor; temblor; vibración.
tremulous ('trɛm·jə·ləs) *adj.* **1,** (trembling) trémulo. **2,** (timid; ir-

resolute) tímido; indeciso. —**tremulousness**, *n.* temblor.
trench (trɛntʃ) *n.* **1,** (ditch) zanja. **2,** *mil.* trinchera. —*v.t.* zanjar; atrincherar. —*v.i.* hacer trincheras; atrincherarse.
trenchant ('trɛn·tʃənt) *adj.* **1,** (incisive) mordaz; punzante. **2,** (vigorous) eficaz; enérgico. **3,** (thoroughgoing) cabal; bien definido. —**trenchancy,** *n.* mordacidad; eficacia; energía.
trench coat abrigo impermeable; trinchera.
trencherman ('trɛn·tʃər·mən) *n.* [*pl.* **-men**] glotón; comilón.
trench mouth inflamación de las mucosas de la boca.
trend (trɛnd) *n.* tendencia; dirección; curso; inclinación. —*v.i.* tender; dirigirse.
trepan (trə'pæn) *n.* trépano. —*v.t.* [**-panned, -panning**] trepanar. —**trepanning,** *n.* trepanación.
trepidation (ˌtrɛp·ə'dei·ʃən) *n.* trepidación; miedo.
trespass ('trɛs·pəs) *v.i.* **1,** (encroach) entrar sin direcho; infringir. **2,** (sin) pecar. —*n.* **1,** (encroachment) infracción; violación. **2,** (sin) transgresión; pecado. —**no trespassing,** prohibida la entrada; prohibido el paso.
trespasser ('trɛsˌpæs·ər) *n.* **1,** (intruder) intruso. **2,** (encroacher) violador; infractor. **3,** (sinner) pecador.
tress (trɛs) *n.* **1,** (lock; braid of hair) rizo; bucle; trenza. **2,** *pl.* (hair of the head) cabellera (*sing.*).
trestle ('trɛs·əl) *n.* **1,** (sawhorse) caballete. **2,** (bridge) puente de caballetes.
trey (trei) *n.* tres.
tri- (trai; trɪ) *prefijo* tri-. **1,** tres; conteniendo tres o tres partes: *tricycle,* triciclo; *triceps,* tríceps. **2,** tres veces: *triplicate,* triplicar. **3,** cada tres: *triennial,* trienio.
triad ('trai·æd) *n.* terna; tríada.
trial ('trai·əl) *n.* **1,** *law* juicio; proceso. **2,** (test) prueba; examen. **3,** (attempt) ensayo; tentativa. **4,** (hardship) afflicción; tribulación. —*adj.* **1,** *law* judicial; probatorio. **2,** (experimental) experimental; de prueba. —**trial balance,** balance de comprobación. —**trial balloon,** medio de probar la opinión pública. —**trial and error,** tanteo; prueba.
triangle ('trai·æŋ·gəl) *n.* **1,** *geom.; music; fig.* triángulo. **2,** (drawing instrument) cartabón; escuadra. —**triangular** (trai'æŋ·gjʊ·lər) *adj.* triangular; triángulo.
triangulate (trai'æŋ·gjʊ·leit) *v.t.* triangular. —**triangulation,** *n.* triangulación.
tribe (traib) *n.* tribu. —**tribal,** *adj.* tribual; tribal.
tribesman ('traibz·mən) *n.* [*pl.* **-men**] miembro de una tribu.
tribulation (ˌtrɪb·jə'lei·ʃən) *n.* tribulación.
tribunal (trai'bju·nəl) *n.* tribunal; juzgado.
tribune ('trɪb·jun) *n.* **1,** (Roman magistrate; defender of the people) tribuno; defensor del pueblo. **2,** (dais) tribuna.
tributary ('trɪb·jə·tɛr·i) *n.* & *adj.* tributario.
tribute ('trɪb·jut) *n.* tributo.
trice (trais) *n.* momento; instante; tris. —**in a trice,** en un abrir y cerrar de ojos.
tricentennial (ˌtrai·sɛn'tɛn·i·əl) *adj.* & *n.* = **tercentenary.**
triceps ('trai·sɛps) *n.* tríceps.
trichina (trɪ'kai·nə) *n.* triquina.
trichinosis (ˌtrɪk·ə'no·sɪs) *n.* triquinosis.
trick (trɪk) *n.* **1,** (stunt; feat) juego; jugada; ejercicio de habilidad; acrobacia. **2,** (ruse; deception) treta; ardid; artificio. **3,** (hoax; swindle) trampa; estafa; engaño; truco. **4,** (prank; practical joke) chasco; broma; burla; travesura. **5,** (peculiar habit) costumbre; vicio. **6,** *cards* baza. **7,** *colloq.* (girl) chiquita; muchacha. **8,** (turn of work or duty) turno; tarea; tanda. —*adj.* **1,** (deceptive) fraudulento. **2,** (crafty) astuto; mañoso. **3,** (involving skill) ingenioso; acrobático; sensacional. —*v.t.* engañar; estafar; embaucar; embelecar. —**be up to one's tricks,** hacer de las suyas. —**do** (*o* **turn**) **the trick,** servir para el caso; tener el efecto deseado. —**learn the tricks of the trade,** adiestrarse; volverse experto. —**play tricks,** hacer burlas. —**trick out,** ataviar; vestir; adornar; engalanar.
trickery ('trɪk·ə·ri) *n.* trampería; embeleco; estafa.

trickle ('trık·əl) *v.i.* **1,** (flow slowly) escurrir; gotear. **2,** (move in or out gradually) escurrirse; colar; colarse. —*v.t.* verter gota a gota. —*n.* **1,** (thin stream) goteo; chorro delgado. **2,** (gradual movement) escurrimiento.

trickster ('trık·stər) *n.* tramposo; embaucador; bromista.

tricksy ('trık·si) *adj.* **1,** (spruce; smart) elegante; pulcro. **2,** (playful) juguetón; travieso. **3,** (deceptive) engañoso; tramposo.

tricky ('trık·i) *adj.* **1,** (deceitful) engañoso; tramposo. **2,** (clever; sly) astuto; ingenioso; mañoso. **3,** (intricate) intrincado; arduo.

tricolor ('trai·kʌl·ər) *adj.* & *n.* tricolor.

tricorn ('trai·korn) *adj.* & *n.* tricornio.

tricot ('tri·ko) *n.* tricot; tejido de punto.

tricuspid (trai'kʌs·pıd) *adj.* & *n.* tricúspide.

tricycle ('trai·sık·əl) *n.* triciclo.

trident ('trai·dənt) *n.* & *adj.* tridente.

tried (traid) *v., pret.* & *p.p. de* **try.**

trifle ('trai·fəl) *n.* pequeñez; fruslería; bagatela. —*v.i.* tratar *o* hablar sin seriedad; chancear. —*v.t.* malgastar; perder. —**trifler** (-flər) *n.* persona frívola; chancero. —**trifling** (-flıŋ) *adj.* insignificante; frívolo; chancero. —**trifle away,** malgastar. —**trifle with,** chancearse con; burlarse con.

trifoliate (trai'fo·li·ıt) *adj.* trifoliado.

trifurcate (trai'fʌɹ·ket) *v.t.* trifurcar. —*adj.* (-kət) trifurcado. —**trifurcation,** *n.* trifurcación.

trig (trıg) *adj.* **1,** (neat) pulcro; elegante. **2,** (sound; firm) firme; fuerte.

trigger ('trıg·ər) *n.* gatillo; disparador. —*v.t.* disparar.

trigonometry (ˌtrıg·ə'nam·ə·tri) *n.* trigonometría. —**trigonometric** (-nə'mɛt·rık) *adj.* trigonométrico.

trihedron (trai'hi·drən) *n.* triedro. —**trihedral,** *adj.* triedro.

trilateral (trai'læt·ər·əl) *adj.* trilátero.

trill (trıl) *n.* trino; gorjeo. —*v.i.* trinar; gorjear.

trillion ('trıl·jən) *n.* (*U.S.*) un millón de millones; billón; (*Brit.*) un millón de billones; trillón.

trilogy ('trıl·ə·dʒi) *n.* trilogía.

trim (trım) *v.t.* [**trimmed, trimming**] **1,** (make neat or orderly) arreglar; ordenar. **2,** (adjust) ajustar; adaptar. **3,** (clip; prune) recortar; podar; despabilar (una vela). **4,** (adorn) adornar; guarnecer. **5,** *colloq.* (defeat) vencer. —*v.i.* **1,** (preserve balance) equilibrarse; igualarse; *naut.* orientarse. **2,** (vacillate) balancearse; vacilar. —*n.* **1,** (condition) condición; estado; disposición. **2,** (equipment) equipo; aparatos. **3,** (dress) traje; vestido. **4,** (adornment) adorno; decoración; guarnición. **5,** (molding) moldeado; moldura. **6,** (clipping) recorte. —*adj.* **1,** (neat) pulcro; elegante. **2,** (orderly) arreglado; ordenado.

trimester (trai'mɛs·tər) *n.* trimestre.

trimmer ('trım·ər) *n.* **1,** (decorator; dresser) guarnecedor. **2,** (machine) máquina de recortar o igualar. **3,** (timeserver) contemporizador.

trimming ('trım·ıŋ) *n.* **1,** (decoration) guarnición; adorno. **2,** (fringe) orla; ribete. **3,** (garnish) aderezo. **4,** *pl.* (accessories) accesorios. **5,** *colloq.* (thrashing) paliza; zurra. **6,** *colloq.* (defeat) derrota.

trimness ('trım·nəs) *n.* **1,** (neatness) pulcritud; elegancia. **2,** (orderliness) arreglo; orden.

trimonthly (trai'mʌnθ·li) *adj.* trimestral.

trinitrotoluene (ˌtrai·nai·tro·'tal·ju·in) *n.* trinitrotolueno.

trinity ('trın·ə·ti) *n.* trinidad.

trinket ('trıŋ·kıt) *n.* dije; baratija.

trinomial (trai'no·mi·əl) *n.* trinomio.

trio ('tri·o) *n.* trío.

triode ('trai·od) *n.* tríodo.

trip (trıp) *n.* **1,** (journey) viaje; excursión. **2,** (stumble) tropezón; traspié; zancadilla. **3,** (slip; error) desliz; error. **4,** (step) paso ágil. **5,** *mech.* (catch; release mechanism) escape; trinquete. **6,** (act of releasing or firing) disparo. —*v.i.* [**tripped, tripping**] **1,** (stumble) tropezar. **2,** (make a mistake) equivocarse; errar. **3,** (run lightly;

skip) correr ágilmente; brincar; saltar. 4, (dance) bailar con agilidad —*v.t.* 1, (cause to stumble or err) trompicar; echar la zancadilla a; armar un lazo a. 2, (perform with a tripping step) ejecutar con agilidad. 3, (release suddenly) disparar; soltar. 4, (overturn) volcar.
tripartite (trai'par·tait) *adj.* tripartito.
tripe (traip) *n.* 1, (food) callos (*pl.*); tripas (*pl.*); mondongo. 2, *slang* (rubbish) fruslería; disparate.
triphammer *n.* martinete de fragua; martillo pilón.
triphthong ('trɪf·θɔŋ) *n.* triptongo.
triplane ('trai,plein) *n.* triplano.
triple ('trɪp·əl) *adj.* & *n.* triple. —*v.t.* triplicar. —*v.i.* triplicarse.
triplet ('trɪp·lɪt) *n.* 1, (one of a triple birth) trillizo. 2, (group of three) terno 3, *music* tresillo.
triplex ('trɪp·lɛks) *adj.* triple; tríplice. —*n.* cosa triple; apartamento de tres pisos.
triplicate ('trɪp·lɪ·keit) *v.t.* triplicar. —*adj.* & *n.* (-kət) triplicado. —**triplication**, *n.* triplicación.
tripod ('trai·pad) *n.* trípode. —**tripodal** ('trɪp·ə·dəl) *adj.* en trípode; de forma de trípode.
tripper ('trɪp·ər) *n.* 1, (runner) corredor 2, (jumper) saltador. 3, (release mechanism) trinquete; escape; disparador.
tripping ('trɪp·ɪŋ) *adj.* 1, (lively) ágil; veloz; ligero. 2, *mech.* (releasing) disparador; de escape.
triptych ('trɪp·tɪk) *n.* tríptico.
trireme ('trai·rim) *n.* trirreme.
trisect (trai'sɛkt) *v.t.* trisecar. —**trisection** (-'sɛk·ʃən) *n.* trisección.
trisyllable (trai'sɪl·ə·bəl) *n.* trisílabo. —**trisyllabic** (,trai·sɪ'læb·ɪk) *adj.* trisílabo.
trite (trait) *adj.* gastado; trillado; vulgar.
tritium ('trɪʃ·jəm) *n.* tritio.
triton ('trai·tən) *n.* tritón.
triturate ('trɪtʃ·ə·reit) *v.t.* triturar. —**trituration**, *n.* trituración.
triumph ('trai·ʌmf) *n.* triunfo; victoria. —*v.i.* triunfar; vencer.
triumphal (trai'ʌm·fəl) *adj.* triunfal.
triumphant (trai'ʌm·fənt) *adj.* victorioso; triunfante.
triumvir (trai'ʌm·vər) *n.* triunviro. —**triumvirate** (-və·rɪt) *n.* triunvirato.
trivet ('trɪv·ɪt) *n.* trébedes (*pl.*).
trivia ('trɪv·i·ə) *n.pl.* trivialidades; fruslerías.
trivial ('trɪ·vi·əl) *adj.* trivial.
triviality (,trɪ·vi'æl·ə·ti) *n.* trivialidad.
-trix (trɪks) *sufijo* -dora; -triz; *indica el femenino correspondiente a algunos nombres terminados en* **-tor**: *aviatrix*, aviadora; *executrix*, ejecutora.
troche ('tro·ki) *n.* tableta; pastilla.
trochee ('tro·ki) *n.* troqueo. —**trochaic** (tro'kei·ɪk) *adj.* & *n.* trocaico.
trod (trad) *v.*, *pret.* & *p.p.* de **tread**.
trodden ('trad·ən) *v.*, *p.p.* de **tread**.
troglodyte ('trag·lə,dait) *n.* 1, (cave dweller) troglodita. 2, (hermit) ermitaño; solitario. —**troglodytic** (-'dɪt·ɪk) *adj.* troglodítico.
troika ('trɔi·kə) *n.* troica.
Trojan horse ('tro·dʒən) caballo de Troya; señuelo.
troll (tro:l) *v.i.* & *t.* 1, (sing) cantar en voz alta y alegre; cantar en sucesión. 2, (fish) pescar arrastrando el anzuelo. 3, (roll) voltear; rodar. —*n.* 1, (song) canon. 2, (fishing equipment) aparejo de pescar 3, (bait) cebo; anzuelo. 4, (fairy dwarf) gnomo; enano.
trolley ('tral·i) *n.* 1, (pulley) trole. 2, (streetcar) tranvía. —**trolley bus** trolebús.
trollop ('tral·əp) *n.* 1, (slovenly woman) mujer desaseada. 2, (prostitute) prostituta; ramera.
trombone (tram'bon) *n.* trombón. **trombonist**, *n.* trombón.
troop (trup) *n.* tropa. —*v.t.* juntar; reunir. —*v.i.* marchar en orden desfilar. —**trooper**, *n.* soldado; agente de policía.
trope (trop) *n.* tropo.
trophic ('traf·ɪk) *adj.* trófico.
-trophic (traf·ɪk) *sufijo* -trófico; *forma adjetivos correspondientes a nombres terminando en* **-trophy**: *hypertrophic*, hipertrófico.
tropho- (traf·ə) *prefijo* trofo-; alimento; nutrición: *trophoplasm*, trofoplasma.
trophy ('tro·fi) *n.* trofeo.
-trophy (trə·fi) *sufijo* -trofia; nutrición: *atrophy*, atrofia.

tropic ('tra·pɪk) *n.* trópico. —**tropical**, *adj.* tropical.
-tropic (trap·ɪk; tro-) *también,* **-tropal** (tro·pəl), **-tropous** (trə·pəs) *sufijo* -trópico; *forma adjetivos correspondientes a los nombres terminando en* **-tropism**: *heliotropic,* heliotrópico.
tropism ('tro·pɪz·əm) *n.* tropismo.
-tropism (tro·pɪz·əm) *sufijo* -tropismo; tendencia a volverse hacia o apartarse de: *heliotropism,* heliotropismo.
tropo- (trap·ə) *prefijo* tropo-; cambio; transformación: *troposphere,* troposfera.
troposphere *n.* troposfera.
-tropy (trə·pi) *sufijo* -tropía; cambio; transformación: *entropy,* entropía.
trot (trat) *v.i.* [**trotted, trotting**] trotar. —*v.t.* hacer trotar. —*n.* **1,** (gait) trote. **2,** *colloq.* (crib) traducción ilícita que usan los estudiantes. **3,** = **trotline.** —**trot out,** *colloq.* sacar para mostrar o exhibir.
troth (troθ) *n.* **1,** (promise to marry) esponsales (*pl.*). **2,** *archaic* (truth) fe; verdad. —**plight one's troth,** contraer esponsales.
trotline *n.* palangre.
trotter ('trat·ər) *n.* trotón; trotador.
troubadour ('tru·bə·dor) *n.* trovador.
trouble ('trʌb·əl) *n.* **1,** (distress) pena; aflicción; congoja. **2,** (misfortune) desgracia; calamidad. **3,** (inconvenience) molestia. **4,** (disturbance) estorbo; confusión; desorden; lío. **5,** (bother; effort) pena; esfuerzo. **6,** (breakdown) avería; defecto; falla. —*v.t.* **1,** (afflict) afligir; apenar. **2,** (annoy; inconvenience) malestar; incomodar. **3,** (worry) preocupar; inquietar. **4,** (disturb) perturbar; confundir. —*v.i.* molestarse; darse pena. —**be in trouble,** estar en un apuro. —**be worth the trouble,** valer la pena. —**get into trouble,** meterse en líos. —**look for trouble,** entremeterse; buscar tres pies al gato.
troublemaker *n.* buscarruidos; picapleitos; *Amer.* buscapleitos.
troubleshooter *n.* componedor; reparador; enderezador.
troublesome ('trʌb·əl·səm) *adj.* molesto; penoso; importuno.
troublous ('trʌb·ləs) *adj.* inquieto; turbulento; confuso.
trough (trɔf) *n.* **1,** (container) artesa. **2,** (feeding trough) pesebre. **3,** (ditch) zanja. **4,** (gutter) canal. **5,** (hollow) abismo; hueco; seno.
trounce (trauns) *v.t.* **1,** (thrash) zurrar; azotar; castigar. **2,** *colloq.* (defeat) derrotar; vencer.
troupe (trup) *n.* compañía teatral; troupe. —*v.i.* viajar como miembro de una compañía.
trouper ('tru·pər) *n.* miembro de una compañía teatral; actor viejo.
trousers ('trau·zərz) *n.pl.* pantalones; calzones. —**trouser,** *adj.* relativo al pantalón; de pantalón.
trousseau (tru'soː) *n.* ajuar de novia; trousseau.
trout (traut) *n.* trucha.
trow (troː) *v.i., arcaico* creer; pensar.
trowel ('trau·əl) *n.* paleta; llana; *hortic.* desplantador.
troy (troi) *adj.* relativo al sistema de pesos troy. —**troy weight,** sistema de pesos usado para el oro, la plata, gemas, etc.; una libra (de doce onzas) vale cerca 373 gramos.
truant ('tru·ənt) *adj.* haragán; que hace novillos. —*n.* novillero. —**truancy,** *n.* ausencia injustificada. —**play truant,** hacer novillos; hacerse la rabona.
truce (trus) *n.* tregua.
truck (trʌk) *n.* **1,** (motor vehicle) camión; carro. **2,** (hand cart) carretilla. **3,** (frame on wheels) juego de ruedas. **4,** (top of a pole or mast) remate de asta *o* mástil. **5,** (vegetables) hortalizas para el mercado. **6,** (miscellaneous articles) artículos varios. **7,** (barter) trueque; permuta; cambio; negocio. **8,** *colloq.* (dealings) negocio; relaciones. **9,** *colloq.* (rubbish) desechos (*pl.*); desperdicios (*pl.*). —*v.t.* **1,** (transport) transportar por camión; acarrear. **2,** (barter) trocar; cambalachear. —*v.i.* **1,** (drive) conducir un camión. **2,** (deal) traficar; cambalachear. —**truckage,** *n.* acarreo; camionaje. —**trucker,** *n.* camionero. —**truckman** (-mən) *n.* dueño o conductor de camiones. —**truck**

farm; **truck garden,** huerto de hortalizas.
truckle ('trʌk·əl) *n.* ruedecilla. —*v.t.* mover sobre ruedecillas. —*v.i.* **1,** (roll) rodar sobre ruedecillas. **2,** (submit) someterse servilmente. —**truckle bed,** carriola.
truculent ('trʌk·jə·lənt) *adj.* truculento; cruel. —**truculence,** *n.* truculencia; crueldad.
trudge (trʌdʒ) *v.i.* andar trabajosamente. —*v.t.* recorrer trabajosamente. —*n.* marcha penosa.
true (truː) *adj.* **1,** (factual) verdadero. **2,** (exact) exacto; correcto. **3,** (faithful) leal; constante; fiel. **4,** (genuine) genuino; auténtico; propio. **5,** (rightful) justo; legítimo. **6,** (aligned) alineado. —*adv.* verdaderamente; exactamente. —*n.* **1,** (truth) verdad; lo verdadero. **2,** (alignment) alineamiento. —*v.t.* alinear. —**come true,** realizarse. —**in true,** alineado. —**out of true,** desalineado. —**run true to form,** actuar según se esperaba. —**true to life,** verdadero; conforme con la realidad.
true-blue *adj.* leal; fiel; constante.
truebred *adj.* de casta legítima.
truehearted *adj.* fiel; leal; sincero. —**trueheartedness,** *n.* fidelidad; lealtad; sinceridad.
trueness ('tru·nəs) *n.* verdad; sinceridad.
truffle ('trʌf·əl) *n.* trufa.
truism ('tru·ɪz·əm) *n.* axioma; verdad evidente; perogrullada.
trull (trʌl) *n.* prostituta; ramera.
truly ('tru·li) *adv.* verdaderamente; exactamente; sinceramente. —**truly yours; yours truly,** su seguro servidor.
trump (trʌmp) *n.* **1,** *cards* triunfo. **2,** *colloq.* (fine person) persona excelente; dije. —*v.i., cards* triunfar; fallar. —*v.t.* **1,** *cards* jugar un triunfo sobre. **2,** (surpass) sobrepujar; superar. —**trump up,** forjar; inventar.
trumpery ('trʌmp·ə·ri) *adj.* vistoso; de oropel. —*n.* **1,** (something showy) oropel. **2,** (rubbish) tontería; disparate.
trumpet ('trʌm·pɪt) *n.* **1,** (musical instrument) trompeta. **2,** (animal cry) berreo. **3,** (hearing aid) audífono; trompetilla. —*v.t.* pregonar a son de trompeta. —*v.i.* trompetear. —**trumpeter,** *n.* trompetero; trompeta.
truncate ('trʌŋ·keit) *v.t.* truncar. —*adj.* truncado. —**truncation,** *n.* truncamiento.
truncheon ('trʌn·tʃən) *n.* **1,** (cudgel) cachiporra. **2,** (staff of authority) bastón de mando. —*v.t.* zurrar con cachiporra; aporrear.
trundle ('trʌn·dəl) *n.* rodillo; ruedecilla. —*v.t.* hacer rodar. —*v.i.* rodar; girar. —**trundle bed,** carriola.
trunk (trʌŋk) *n.* **1,** *anat.; bot.* tronco. **2,** (proboscis) trompa. **3,** (container) baúl; cofre. **4,** (main line) línea o tubería maestra. **6,** *pl.* (short trousers) pantalones cortos; taparrabos; *Amer.* trusa (*sing.*). —*adj.* troncal; principal. —**trunkful** (-ˌful) *n.* baúl lleno.
truss (trʌs) *v.t.* **1,** (bind) atar; liar. **2,** (support) armar; apuntalar. **3,** (skewer) espetar. —*n.* **1,** (framework) armadura. **2,** (belt) braguero. **3,** (bundle) haz; paquete; lío.
trust (trʌst) *n.* **1,** (assured reliance; confidence) confianza; fe; expectación. **2,** (credit) crédito. **3,** (charge; obligation) cargo; obligación. **4,** (that which is entrusted) depósito. **5,** (monopoly) monopolio; cartel. —*v.t.* fiarse de; confiar en. —*v.i.* confiar; fiar. —**in trust, 1,** (in confidence) en confianza. **2,** (in custody) en depósito. —**on trust, 1,** (on credit) a crédito; al fiado. **2,** (on faith) de buena fe.
trust company banco de depósito; compañía fiduciaria.
trustee (trʌsˈtiː) *n.* depositario; administrador. —**trusteeship,** *n.* cargo de administrador; administración fiduciaria.
trustful ('trʌst·fəl) *adj.* confiado.
trustworthy *adj.* confiable; fidedigno. —**trustworthiness,** *n.* integridad; honradez.
trusty ('trʌs·ti) *adj.* leal; seguro. —*n.* preso que goza de ciertos privilegios.
truth (truθ) *n.* verdad; realidad. —**in truth,** en verdad; de veras. —**of a truth,** seguramente.
truthful ('truθ·fəl) *adj.* verídico; veraz; verdadero. —**truthfulness,** *n.* veracidad.
try (trai) *v.t.* [*pret.* & *p.p.* **tried**]

1, (attempt; essay) intentar; ensayar; probar; tratar. 2, (test) probar; examinar. 3, *law* procesar; ver (un litigio). 4, (subject to strain) exasperar; poner a prueba; irritar. 5, (refine) refinar; purificar. —*v.i.* procurar; tratar; hacer lo posible. —*n.* prueba; intento; ensayo. —**try out**, 1, (test; prove) probar(se); someter(se) a prueba. 2, (refine) refinar; purificar.

trying ('trai·ɪŋ) *adj.* molesto; penoso.

tryout ('trai·aut) *n.* experimento; prueba de competencia.

tryst (trɪst) *n.* cita, esp. de amantes.

tsar (zar) *n.* zar. —**tsarevitch** (-ə·vɪtʃ) *n.* zarevitz. —**tsarevna** (-'ɛv·nə) *n.* zarevna. —**tsarina** (-'i·nə) *n.* zarina.

tsetse ('tsɛt·si) *n.* tsetsé.

T-shirt *n.* camiseta de mangas cortas.

T square regla en forma de T.

tub (tʌb) *n.* 1, (bathtub) bañera. 2, (vessel) cuba; tonel. 3, *colloq.* (boat) buque viejo y lento. 4, *colloq.* (bath) baño. —*v.t.* & *i.* bañar(se) en bañera.

tuba ('tu·bə) *n.* tuba.

tubby ('tʌb·i) *adj.* 1, (short and fat) rechoncho. 2, (dull, as of a sound) sordo. —*n.*, *colloq.* cuba; gordiflón.

tube (tu:b) *n.* 1, (hollow cylinder) tubo; caño. 2, (tunnel) túnel. 3, (subway) tranvía subterráneo; metro. 4, (inner tube) cámara.

tuber ('tu·bər) *n.* tubérculo. —**tuberous**, *adj.* tuberoso.

tubercle ('tu·bər·kəl) *n.* tubérculo; protuberancia. —**tubercle bacillus**, bacilo tuberculoso.

tubercular (tu'bʌɹ·kjə·lər) *adj.* & *n.* tuberculoso.

tuberculin (tu'bʌɹ·kjə·lɪn) *n.* tuberculina.

tuberculosis (tu,bʌɹ·kjə'lo·sɪs) *n.* tuberculosis.

tuberculous (tu'bʌɹ·kjə·ləs) *adj.* tuberculoso.

tuberose ('tub·roz) *n.* tuberosa.

tubing ('tu·bɪŋ) *n.* tubería.

tubular ('tu·bjʊ·lər) *adj.* tubular.

tuck (tʌk) *v.t.* 1, (cram) atestar; henchir. 2, (wrap) arropar. 3, (make tucks in) alforzar. 4, (draw up; gather) arremangar. 5, (fold) doblar. —*v.i.* fruncir; contraerse. —*n.* alforza. —**tuck away**, 1, (put away; hide) guardar; ocultar. 2, *slang* (eat or drink heartily) comer o beber mucho y con gusto. —**tuck up**, arremangar.

tucker ('tʌk·ər) *n.* 1, (person or machine that tucks) alforzador. 2, (neckcloth) pañoleta. —*v.t.*, *colloq.* cansar; fatigar. —**tuckered out**, *colloq.* cansado; extenuado.

-tude (tud) *sufijo* -tud; *forma nombres abstractos denotando* cualidad; estado: *aptitude*, aptitud.

Tuesday ('tjuz·de) *n.* martes.

tuft (tʌft) *n.* 1, (bunch; cluster) copete; ramillete; manojo. 2, (topknot) moño. 3, (lock of hair) mechón. 4, (tassel) borla. 5, (plume) penacho. —*v.t.* poner borlas, penachos, etc. a. —**tufted**, *adj.* copetudo; penachudo.

tug (tʌg) *v.t.* [**tugged**, **tugging**] 1, (pull) tirar con fuerza de. 2, (drag) arrastrar. 3, (haul) halar. 4, (tow) remolcar. —*v.i.* 1, (pull) tirar con fuerza. 2, (strive) esforzarse. —*n.* 1, (strong pull) tirón. 2, (tugboat) remolcador. 3, (struggle) esfuerzo supremo. 4, (strap) tirante; correa; cuerda. —**tug of war**, lucha de la cuerda; *fig.* lucha por la supremacía.

tugboat *n.* remolcador.

tuition (tu'ɪʃ·ən) *n.* 1, (fee) costo de la enseñanza. 2, (teaching) enseñanza.

tulip ('tu·lɪp) *n.* tulipán.

tulle (tu:l) *n.* tul.

tumble ('tʌm·bəl) *v.i.* 1, (fall down) caer; desplomarse. 2, (descend rapidly) venirse abajo; precipitarse. 3, (roll about) voltear; rodar. 4, (gymnastics) saltar; hacer acrobacia. 5, *slang* (become aware) caer en la cuenta. —*v.t.* 1, (upset) trastornar. 2, (throw; put in disorder) arrojar; desarreglar. 3, (rotate) voltear; hacer girar. —*n.* 1, (act of tumbling) tumbo; vuelco; voltereta; caída. 2, (state of confusion) confusión; desorden. 3, *slang* (sign of recognition) señal de reconocimiento.

tumble-down *adj.* destartalado.

tumbler ('tʌm·blər) *n.* 1, (glass) vaso sin pie. 2, (gymnast) acróbata; volatinero. 3, (part of

a lock) fiador. 4, *mech.* (rotating part) tambor.
tumbleweed *n.* planta rodadora.
tumefaction (ˌtu·məˈfæk·ʃən) *n.* tumefacción.
tumescent (tuˈmɛs·ənt) *adj.* tumescente. —**tumescence,** *n.* tumescencia.
tumid (ˈtu·mɪd) *adj.* hinchado; tumefacto; túmido. —**tumidity** (tuˈmɪd·ə·ti) *n.* hinchazón; tumefacción.
tumor *también,* **tumour** (ˈtu·mər) *n.* tumor.
tumult (ˈtu·mʌlt) *n.* tumulto; motín; agitación. —**tumultuous** (tuˈmʌl·tʃu·əs) *adj.* tumultuoso; agitado.
tun (tʌn) *n.* cuba; tonel.
tuna (ˈtu·nə) *n.* 1, *ichthy.* atún. 2, *bot.* tuna.
tundra (ˈtʌn·drə) *n.* tundra.
tune (tuːn) *n.* 1, (air; melody) aire; melodía; tonada. 2, (adjustment to proper pitch) afinación. 3, (harmony; accord) armonía; acorde. 4, (good condition) buen estado. —*v.t.* 1, (put in tune) templar; afinar. 2, (harmonize) armonizar. 3, *radio* sintonizar. —**change one's tune,** mudar de tono. —**in tune** afinado. —**out of tune,** desafinado. —**tune in,** sintonizar. —**tune up,** 1, *mech.* ajustar. 2, *music* acordar.
tuneful (ˈtuːn·fəl) *adj.* armonioso; melodioso.
tuner (ˈtu·nər) *n.* afinador; *radio* sintonizador.
tungsten (ˈtʌŋ·stən) *n.* tungsteno.
tunic (ˈtu·nɪk) *n.* túnica.
tuning (ˈtu·nɪŋ) *n.* 1, (adjusting tune) afinación. 2, (harmonization) armonización. 3, *radio* sintonización. —**tuning fork,** diapasón.
tunnel (ˈtʌn·əl) *n.* 1, (passage) túnel. 2, (burrow) madriguera. —*v.t.* horadar; construir un túnel en *o* por. —*v.i.* excavar.
tunny (ˈtʌn·i) *n.* tonina.
turban (ˈtʌɹ·bən) *n.* 1, (headdress) turbante. 2, (brimless hat) sombrero sin alas.
turbid (ˈtʌɹ·bɪd) *adj.* turbio. —**turbidity** (tərˈbɪd·ə·ti) *n.* turbidez.
turbine (ˈtʌɹ·bɪn; -bain) *n.* turbina.
turbot (ˈtʌɹ·bət) *n.* rodaballo.
turbulent (ˈtʌɹ·bju·lənt) *adj.* turbulento. —**turbulence,** *n.* turbulencia.
tureen (tʊˈriːn) *n.* sopera.
turf (tʌɹf) *n.* 1, (grass) césped. 2, (sod) tepe. 3, (race track) hipódromo; carreras de caballos; turf. 4, (peat) turba. —*v.t.* cubrir con césped.
turgid (ˈtʌɹ·dʒɪd) *adj.* turgente. —**turgidity** (tərˈdʒɪd·ə·ti) *n.* turgencia.
Turk (tʌɹk) *n.* turco.
turkey (ˈtʌɹ·ki) *n.* 1, (bird) pavo. 2, *slang* (failure) fracaso. —**talk turkey,** *colloq.* hablar francamente.
turkey buzzard aura; gallinazo; *Amer.* zopilote.
Turkish (ˈtʌɹ·kɪʃ) *adj.* & *n.* turco. **Turkish bath,** baño turco. —**Turkish towel,** toalla gruesa y afelpada.
turmeric (ˈtʌɹ·mər·ɪk) *n.* cúrcuma.
turmoil (ˈtʌɹ·mɔil) *n.* disturbio; alboroto; tumulto.
turn (tʌɹn) *v.t.* 1, (shift; twist) volver; dar vuelta a. 2, (change the course of) desviar. 3, (reverse) dar vuelta a. 4, (revolve; rotate) hacer girar; voltear. 5, (shape in a lathe) tornear. 6, (use; apply) emplear; utilizar. 7, (alter) modificar; adaptar. 8, (cause to become) volver; tornar. 9, (make sour) agriar. 10, (meditate on) meditar sobre; revolver. 11, (go around) doblar. 12, (sprain) torcer. —*v.i.* 1, (rotate) rodar; girar. 2, (spin) dar vueltas. 3, (assume a new direction) cambiar de curso; virar; volver. 4, (change) volverse; modificarse. 5, (become sour) agriarse. 6, (become curved) encorvarse. —*n.* 1, (rotation) giro; vuelta. 2, (change of direction) desviación. 3, (bend) curva; recodo. 4, (coil) espira. 5, (occasion to act) turno. 6, (aspect; shape) forma; figura; aspecto. 7, (change) mudanza. 8, (tendency) tendencia; inclinación. 9, *colloq.* (shock) impresión violenta; susto. —**at every turn,** a cada momento. —**bad turn,** mala pasada; mala jugada. —**be one's turn,** tocarle a uno. —**good turn,** favor; servicio. —**in turn,** por turno; a su turno. —**out of turn,** fuera de

orden. —**take a turn**, 1, (change) volverse; cambiar; cambiar aspecto. 2, (go around) dar una vuelta. —**take turns**, alternar; turnar. —**to a turn**, exactamente; perfectamente. —**turn about**, dar vuelta· voltearse. —**turn and turn about**, uno tras otro. —**turn around**, dar vuelta. —**turn aside**, desviar(se); apartar(se). —**turn away**, 1, (send away) despedir. 2, (divert) desviar. 3, (alienate) alejar; enajenar. —**turn back**, 1, (go back) volverse; volver atrás. 2, (send back) devolver. 3, (repel) rechazar; repulsar. 4, (retreat) retroceder. —**turn down**, 1, (fold down) plegar(se) o doblar(se) hacia abajo. 2, (reject) rechazar. 3, (lower) bajar. —**turn from**, desviar(se) de; apartar(se) de. —**turn in**, 1, (enter) entrar. 2, (point inward) doblar(se) hacia adentro. 3, (deliver) entregar. 4, (return) devolver. 5, *colloq.* (retire) acostarse. —**turn in and out**, serpentear. —**turn off**, 1, (change direction) desviar(se). 2, (branch off) apartarse; bifurcarse. 3, (extinguish) apagar. 4, (cut off) cortar. 5, (dismiss) despedir; despachar. —**turn on**, 1, (switch on) encender; poner. 2, (start the flow of) abrir. 3, (attack) volverse contra; caerle encima a uno. 4, (depend on) depender de. —**turn out**, 1, (extinguish) apagar. 2, (put outside) sacar; echar fuera. 3, (come or go out) salir. 4, (be present) asistir; presentarse. 5, (produce) hacer; fabricar; producir. 6, (result) salir; quedar. 7, (happen) acontecer; suceder. 8, (become) volverse; ponerse. 9, (equip; dress) ataviar; vestir; equipar. 10, *colloq.* (arise) levantarse. —**turn over**, 1, (turn upside down) volcar(se); trastornar(se). 2, (roll over) volver(se); voltear. 3, (ponder) considerar; revolver. 4, (hand over) entregar; pasar; ceder. 5, (start running, as a motor) prender; hacer girar. 6, (riffle, as pages) hojear. 7, (buy and sell) mover (mercancías). —**turn tail**, huirse; poner pies en polvorosa. —**turn to**, 1, (refer to) recurrir a; consultar. 2, (apply to) dirigirse a. 3, (go to for help) pedir socorro a; acudir a. 4, (get to work) poner manos a la obra. —**turn up**, 1, (fold upward) plegar(se) o doblar(se) hacia arriba. 2, (turn face upwards) volver(se). 3, (discover) descubrir; desenterrar. 4, (increase the volume of) dar más volumen a; poner más fuerte 5, (happen) acontecer; suceder. 6, (arrive; appear) llegar; dejarse ver; aparecer. 7, (be found) encontrarse; hallarse; venir a mano. —**turn upon**, 1, (attack) volverse contra. 2, (depend on) depender de. —**turn upside down**, volcar(se); trastornar(se).

turnabout ('tʌɹn·ə·baut) *n.* 1, (turning) vuelta completa. 2, (alternation of privileges) alternación de privilegios.

turnbuckle *n.* torniquete; eslabón giratorio.

turncoat *n.* tránsfuga; renegado.

turner ('tʌɹ·nər) *n.* 1, (woodworker) tornero. 2, (gymnast) acróbata; volatinero.

turning ('tʌɹ·nɪŋ) *adj.* giratorio; rotatorio. —*n.* 1, (act of turning) vuelta. 2, (bend; curve) recodo; curva. 3, (shaping in a lathe) torneo; torneado. —**turning point**, punto decisivo; punto crucial.

turnip ('tʌɹ·nəp) *n.* nabo.

turnkey *n.* llavero; carcelero.

turnout *n.* 1, (gathering) concurrencia. 2, (output) rendimiento; producción total. 3, (outfit) ropa; equipo. 4, (siding) apartadero.

turnover *n.* 1, (volume of business) monto de las transacciones comerciales. 2, (change of personnel) cambio de personal; reorganización. 3, (pastry) pastel con repulgo.

turnpike ('tʌɹn·paik) *n.* carretera; autopista.

turnstile ('tʌɹn·stail) *n.* molinete.

turntable *n.* 1, *R.R.* placa giratoria; tornavía. 2, (of a phonograph) portadiscos.

turpentine ('tʌɹ·pən·tain) *n.* trementina; aguarrás.

turpitude ('tʌɹ·pɪ·tud) *n.* depravación; vileza; torpeza. —**turpitudinous** (-'tud·ɪ·nəs) *adj.* depravado; vil; torpe.

turquoise ('tʌɹ·kwɔiz) *n.* turquesa.

turret ('tʌɹ·ɪt) *n.* 1, (small tower) torrecilla. 2, (part of a lathe)

torrecilla de torno; portaherramientas. **3,** (gun tower) torre blindada. —**turret lathe,** torno de torrecilla.
turtle ('tʌɹ·təl) *n.* tortuga; carey. —**turn turtle,** volcar; zozobrar.
turtledove ('tʌɹ·təl,dʌv) *n.* tórtola.
tush (tʌʃ) *interj.* ¡bah!
tusk (tʌsk) *n.* **1,** (tooth) colmillo. **2,** (toothlike part) púa; diente.
tusker ('tʌs·kər) *n.* animal colmilludo.
tussle ('tʌs·əl) *n.* riña; pelea; agarrada. —*v.i.* reñir; pelear; agarrarse.
tut (tʌt) *interj.* ¡basta!; ¡bah!
tutelage ('tu·tə·lɪdʒ) *n.* tutela; instrucción.
tutelary ('tu·tə,lɛr·i) *adj.* tutelar.
tutor ('tu·tər) *n.* tutor; preceptor. —*v.t.* enseñar; instruir. —*v.i.* **1,** (teach) dar lecciones particulares. **2,** *colloq.* tomar lecciones particulares.
tutorage ('tu·tər·ɪdʒ) *n.* tutela.
tutorial (tu'tor·i·əl) *adj.* preceptoral.
tutti-frutti ('tu·ti'fru·ti) *n.* tutti-frutti; dulce de varias frutas.
tuwhit, tuwhoo (tʊ'hwɪt·tʊ·'hwuː) graznido del búho.
tux (tʌks) *n., colloq.* = **tuxedo.**
tuxedo (tʌk'si·do) *n.* smoking; esmoquin.
twaddle ('twad·əl) *v.i.* disparatar; charlar; decir tonterías. —*n.* habladuría; charla; disparates (*pl.*); tonterías (*pl.*).
twain (twein) *adj.* & *n., arcaico y poético* dos.
twang (twæŋ) *n.* **1,** (sound of a string) tañido; punteado. **2,** (nasal sound) gangueo. —*v.t.* tañer; puntear. —*v.i.* ganguear.
'twas (twʌz) *contr. de* **it was.**
tweak (twik) *v.t.* pellizcar retorciendo. —*n.* tirón; torcedura.
tweed (twiːd) *n.* paño de lana de varios colores. —**tweeds,** *n.pl.* vestidos hechos con ese paño.
tweet (twit) *n.* gorjeo; pío. —*v.i.* gorjear; piar.
tweezers ('twi·zərz) *n.pl.* tenacillas; pinzas.
twelve (twɛlv) *adj.* & *n.* doce. —**twelfth** (twɛlfθ) *adj.* & *n.* duodécimo; dozavo.
twenty ('twɛn·ti) *adj.* & *n.* veinte.
—**twentieth,** *adj.* & *n.* vigésimo; veintavo.
'twere (twʌɹ) *contr. de* **it were.**
twice (twais) *adv.* dos veces; el doble.
twiddle ('twɪd·əl) *v.t.* menear; hacer girar (los pulgares). —*v.i.* entretenerse con tonterías.
twig (twɪg) *n.* ramito; vástago.
twilight ('twai·lait) *n.* crepúsculo. —*adj.* crepuscular. —**twilight sleep,** narcosis obstétrica.
twill (twɪl) *n.* tela cruzada.
'twill (twɪl) *contr. de* **it will.**
twin (twɪn) *adj.* & *n.* gemelo. —*v.t.* **1,** (give birth to as twins) parir (gemelos). **2,** (pair; couple) emparejar. —*v.i.* **1,** (give birth to twins) parir gemelos. **2,** (be paired or coupled) emparejarse.
twine (twain) *n.* **1,** (strong cord) tramilla. **2,** (something twisted) trenza. —*v.t.* retorcer; enroscar; entrelazar. —*v.i.* retorcerse; enroscarse; entrelazarse.
twinge (twɪndʒ) *n.* dolor agudo; punzada. —*v.t.* causar un dolor agudo a. —*v.i.* sentir un dolor agudo. —**twinge of conscience,** pena del ánimo; remordimiento.
twinkle ('twɪŋ·kəl) *v.i.* **1,** (shine) centellear **2,** (sparkle, as the eyes) parpadear, pestañear. **3,** (flutter) moverse rápidamente. —*v.t.* **1,** (cause to shine) hacer centellear. **2,** (wink) guiñar; abrir y cerrar rápidamente (los ojos). —*n.* **1,** (gleam) centelleo; destello. **2,** (wink) parpadeo; guiñada. **3,** (quick movement) movimiento rápido.
twinkling ('twɪŋk·lɪŋ) *n.* **1,** (gleam) centelleo. **2,** (instant) instante. —**in the twinkling of an eye,** en un abrir y cerrar de ojos.
twirl (twʌɹl) *v.t.* **1,** (spin) hacer girar. **2,** (throw) arrojar; lanzar. —*v.i.* **1,** (spin) girar; dar vueltas. **2,** (wind) enrollarse. —*n.* **1,** (gyration) vuelta; giro. **2,** (curl) enroscadura. —**twirler,** *n.* lanzador de béisbol.
twist (twɪst) *v.t.* **1,** (wrap) enrollar; arrollar. **2,** (warp; distort) torcer. **3,** (curl) enroscar. **4,** (twine) entrelazar. **5,** (cause to rotate) hacer girar. **6,** (bend) doblar; trenzar. **7,** (pervert in meaning) torcer el sentido de; interpretar mal. —*v.i.* **1,** (be bent or

coiled) torcerse; envolverse; enrollarse. **2,** (rotate) girar; dar vueltas. **3,** (change direction) desviarse; virar. **4,** (be distorted in shape) deformarse. **5,** (follow a crooked course) serpentear. —*n.* **1,** (bend; curve) recodo; curva. **2,** (tangle; crook) enredo; torcedura. **3,** (twisting motion) contorsión; serpenteo. **4,** (inclination) inclinación; propensión; sesgo. **5,** (something formed by twisting) rollo; rosca. **6,** (pastry) trenza; torcido. **7,** (bread or roll) rosca. **8,** (cord) torzal; torcido.

twister ('twɪs·tər) *n.* **1,** (person or thing that twists) torcedor. **2,** = **tornado.**

twit (twɪt) *v.t.* **[twitted, twitting]** reprender; escarnecer. —*n.* reprensión; escarnio.

twitch (twɪtʃ) *v.t.* **1,** (pull) tirar bruscamente; sacudir. **2,** (pinch; squeeze) pellizcar; estrujar. —*v.i.* **1,** (writhe) crisparse. **2,** (quiver) temblar. —*n.* **1,** (muscular contraction) espasmo. **2,** (tremor) temblor. **3,** (tug) tirón; estirón.

twitter ('twɪt·ər) *v.i.* **1,** (chirp) gorjear. **2,** (giggle) reír nerviosamente. **3,** (be excited) estar agitado. **4,** (chatter) cotorrear. —*n.* **1,** (chirping) gorjeo. **2,** (excitement) agitación; conmoción.

'twixt (twɪkst) *prep., contr. de* **betwixt.**

two (tuː) *adj. & n.* dos.

two-by-four *n.* tabla de dos pulgadas de espesor y cuatro de ancho.

two-faced *adj.* falso; hipócrita.

two-fisted *adj., colloq.* vigoroso; valiente.

twofold *adj. & n.* doble; dos veces (más). —*adv.* dos veces; doblemente.

two-handed *adj.* **1,** (having or requiring two hands) de *o* para dos manos. **2,** (ambidextrous) ambidextro.

two hundred doscientos. —**two-hundredth,** *adj. & n.* ducentésimo.

twopence ('tʌp·əns) *n.* moneda de dos peniques.

twopenny ('tʌp·ə·ni) *adj.* **1,** (worth twopence) de dos peniques. **2,** (cheap) de poco valor; insignificante.

twosome ('tu·səm) *n.* pareja; dúo.

two-step *n.* paso doble.

two-time *v.t., slang* engañar.

'twould (twʊd) *contr. de* **it would.**

-ty (ti) *sufijo; forma* **1,** *numerales, indicando* diez veces: *sixty,* sesenta. **2,** -dad, -tad; *nombres abstractos denotando* cualidad; estado: *liberty,* libertad; *beauty,* beldad.

tycoon (tai'kuːn) *n., colloq.* magnate.

tying ('tai·ɪŋ) *v., ger. de* **tie.**

tyke (taik) *n.* **1,** (dog) perro. **2,** (child) niño; chiquillo.

tympani ('tɪm·pə·ni) *n.pl.* atabales; timbales. —**tympanist,** *n.* timbalero.

tympanum ('tɪm·pə·nəm) *n.* **1,** (stretched membrane; drum) membrana tensa; timbal. **2,** *anat.; archit.* tímpano. **3,** (diaphragm) diafragma.

type (taip) *n.* tipo. —*v.t.* **1,** (classify) clasificar. **2,** (symbolize) simbolizar; representar. —*v.t. & i.* (typewrite) mecanografiar; escribir a máquina.

-type (taip) *sufijo* **1,** -tipo; forma; tipo: *prototype,* prototipo. **2,** -tipo; impresión; reproducción: *daguerrotype,* daguerrotipo. **3,** -tipia; imprenta; sistema de imprimir: *linotype,* linotipia.

typescript *n.* material escrito a máquina.

typesetter *n.* tipógrafo; cajista.

typewrite *v.t. & i.* mecanografiar; escribir a máquina. —**typewriter,** *n.* máquina de escribir; tipiadora. —**typewriting,** *n.* mecanografía; dactilografía.

typhoid ('tai·fɔid) *adj.* tifoideo. —**typhoid fever,** fiebre tifoidea; tifoidea.

typhoon (tai'fuːn) *n.* tifón.

typhus ('tai·fəs) *n.* tifo; tifus.

typical ('tɪp·ɪ·kəl) *adj.* típico.

typify ('tɪp·ɪ·fai) *v.t.* **1,** (exemplify) ser ejemplo de. **2,** (symbolize) simbolizar.

typist ('taip·ɪst) *n.* mecanógrafo; dactilógrafo.

typo- (tai·pə) *prefijo* tipo-; tipo; impresión: *typography,* tipografía.

typographer (tai'pag·rə·fər) *n.* tipógrafo.

typographical (ˌtai·pə'græf·ɪ·kəl) *adj.* tipográfico.

typography (tai'pag·rə·fi) *n.* tipografía.

-typy (tai·pi) *sufijo* -tipia; imprenta; arte de imprimir: *electrotypy*, electrotipia.
tyrannical (tɪ'ræn·ɪ·kəl) *adj.* tiránico; tirano.
tyrannous ('tɪr·ə·nəs) *adj.* tirano; tiránico.
tyranny ('tɪr·ə·ni) *n.* tiranía. —**tyrannize**, *v.t.* & *i.* tiranizar.
tyrant ('tai·rənt) *n.* tirano.
tyro ('tai·ro) *n.* novicio; bisoño.
tzar (tsar) *n.* = **tsar.** —**tzarevitch**, *n.* = **tsarevitch.** —**tzarevna**, *n.* = **tsarevna.** —**tzarina**, *n.* = **tsarina.**

U

U, u (ju) vigésima primera letra del alfabeto inglés.
ubiquitous (ju'bɪk·wə·təs) *adj.* ubicuo. —**ubiquity**, *n.* ubicuidad.
U-boat *n.* submarino alemán.
udder ('ʌd·ər) *n.* ubre.
ugh (ʌg; ʌ) *interj.* ¡pu!; ¡puf!
ugly ('ʌg·li) *adj.* feo. —**ugliness**, *n.* fealdad.
ukase ('ju·kes) *n.* ukase; ucase.
ukulele (ˌju·kə'lei·li) *n.* ukulele.
ulcer ('ʌl·sər) *n.* úlcera. —**ulcerous**, *adj.* ulceroso.
ulcerate ('ʌl·sər·eit) *v.t.* ulcerar. —*v.i.* ulcerarse. —**ulceration**, *n.* ulceración.
-ule (ul; jul) *sufijo* -ula; *forma diminutivos: sporule*, espórula.
-ulent (jə·lənt; ə-) *sufijo* -ulento; lleno de: *virulent*, virulento.
ulna ('ʌl·nə) *n.* cúbito.
-ulous (jə·ləs) *sufijo* -ulo; *forma adjetivos denotando* inclinación; tendencia: *tremulous*, trémulo; *credulous*, crédulo.
ulster ('ʌl·stər) *n.* levitón.
ulterior (ʌl'tɪr·i·ər) *adj.* ulterior.
ultimate ('ʌl·tə·mət) *adj.* **1**, (farthest; last) último; final. **2**, (fundamental) fundamental; esencial. **3**, (maximum) sumo; máximo. —*n.* extremo.
ultimatum (ˌʌl·tə'mei·təm) *n.* ultimátum.
ultra ('ʌl·trə) *adj.* extremado; excesivo; ultra. —*n.* extremista; ultra.
ultra- (ʌl·trə) *prefijo* ultra-. **1**, más allá de: *ultraviolet*, ultravioleta. **2**, extremista: *ultranationalism*, ultranacionalismo.
ultramarine *n.* & *adj.* ultramarino.
ultraviolet *adj.* ultravioleta.
ululate ('jul·jə·leit) *v.i.* ulular. —**ululation**, *n.* ululación.
umber ('ʌm·bər) *n.* tierra de sombra. —*adj.* pardo; obscuro. —*v.t.* sombrear.
umbilical (ʌm'bɪl·ɪ·kəl) *adj.* umbilical.
umbilicus (ʌm'bɪl·ɪ·kəs) *n.* [*pl.* **-ci** (sai)] ombligo.
umbra ('ʌm·brə) *n.* sombra.
umbrage ('ʌm·brɪdʒ) *n.* **1**, (resentment) resentimiento. **2**, (shade) sombra; umbría. —**take umbrage at**, resentirse por.
umbrageous (ʌm'brei·dʒəs) *adj.* **1**, (shady) sombroso; umbroso. **2**, (resentful) resentido.
umbrella (ʌm'brɛl·ə) *n.* paraguas; sombrilla. —**umbrella man**, paragüero. —**umbrella shop**, paragüería. —**umbrella stand**, paragüero.
umpire ('ʌm·pair) *n.* árbitro. —*v.t.* arbitrar. —*v.i.* arbitrar; ser árbitro.
un- (ʌn) *prefijo* **1**, in-; anti-; no; contrario; opuesto: *unhappy*, infeliz; *un-American*, antiamericano. **2**, de-; des-; privación; reverso: *unarm*, desarmar; *unscrew*, destornillar; *unseal*, desellar.
unabashed *adj.* descocado; desvergonzado.
unabated *adj.* cabal; completo; no disminuido.
unable *adj.* incapaz; inhábil.
unabridged *adj.* no abreviado; completo.
unaccented *adj.* inacentuado.
unacceptable *adj.* inaceptable.
unaccompanied *adj.* **1**, (alone) solo. **2**, *music* sin acompañamiento.
unaccountable *adj.* **1**, (inexplicable) inexplicable. **2**, (not responsible) irresponsable; no responsable.
unaccounted-for *adj.* **1**, (unexplained) inexplicado. **2**, (missing) ausente; no hallado.
unaccustomed *adj.* **1**, (unused) no acostumbrado. **2**, (unusual) desacostumbrado; insólito.
unacquainted *adj.* que no co-

noce. —**be unacquainted with,** no conocer; ignorar.
unadaptable *adj.* inadaptable.
unadoptable *adj.* inadoptable.
unadorned *adj.* sencillo; sin adorno.
unadulterated *adj.* genuino; puro; inadulterado.
unadvised *adj.* indiscreto; imprudente.
unaffected *adj.* **1,** (unmoved) impasible; no conmovido. **2,** (natural) sencillo; natural; inafectado.
unafraid *adj.* valiente; intrépido.
unaided *adj.* sin ayuda; solo.
unalloyed *adj.* **1,** (pure) sin mezcla; puro. **2,** (utter; complete) cabal; completo; absoluto.
unalterable *adj.* inalterable.
unaltered *adj.* inalterado.
unambiguous *adj.* inequívoco; claro.
unambitious *adj.* no ambicioso; sin ambición.
un-American *adj.* antiamericano.
unanimity (ˌju·nəˈnim·ə·ti) *n.* unanimidad.
unanimous (juˈnæn·ə·məs) *adj.* unánime.
unannounced *adj.* no anunciado.
unanswerable *adj.* incontrovertible; incontestable.
unappealable *adj.* inapelable.
unappealing *adj.* falto de atracción; poco atrayente.
unappreciative *adj.* desagradecido; ingrato.
unapproachable *adj.* **1,** (inaccessible) inaccesible; inasequible; inabordable. **2,** (incomparable) incomparable; sin igual.
unapt *adj.* **1,** (unskillful) inepto; inhábil. **2,** (not inclined) poco inclinado; poco propenso. **3,** (unsuitable) inadecuado.
unarm *v.t.* desarmar. —**unarmed,** *adj.* desarmado.
unascertainable *adj.* inaveriguable.
unashamed *adj.* desvergonzado.
unasked *adj.* **1,** (unsolicited) insolicitado. **2,** (not invited) no convidado.
unassailable *adj.* **1,** (impregnable) inexpugnable; inatacable. **2,** (incontrovertible) incontestable; incontrovertible.
unassembled *adj.* desmontado; sin montar.
unassimilable *adj.* inasimilable.
unassisted *adj.* sin ayuda; solo.
unassuming *adj.* modesto.
unattached *adj.* **1,** (unconnected) suelto; libre. **2,** (unmarried) soltero; célibe.
unattainable *adj.* inasequible; inalcanzable.
unattendance *n.* inasistencia.
unattended *adj.* **1,** (alone) solitario; solo; sin séquito. **2,** (neglected) desatendido.
unattractive *adj.* sin atractivo; feo.
unauthorized *adj.* desautorizado; sin autorización.
unavailable *adj.* indisponible.
unavailing *adj.* inútil; ineficaz; infructuoso.
unavoidable *adj.* inevitable; ineludible.
unaware *adj.* desatendido; inconsciente. —*adv.* = **unawares.** —**unawareness,** *n.* inconsciencia.
unawares *adv.* **1,** (unknowingly) inadvertidamente; sin saberlo; sin pensar. **2,** (unexpectedly) inesperadamente; de improviso.
unbalance *n.* desequilibrio. —*v.t.* desequilibrar. —**unbalanced,** *adj.* desequilibrado.
unbar *v.t.* [**unbarred, -barring**] desatrancar.
unbearable *adj.* insoportable; insufrible; inaguantable.
unbeaten *adj.* **1,** (undefeated) invicto; insuperado. **2,** (untrod) no pisado; no frecuentado.
unbecoming *adj.* indecoroso; impropio.
unbeknown (ˌʌn·biˈnoːn) *adj.* desconocido; inadvertido. —**unbeknown to,** sin conocimiento de; sin saberlo (uno).
unbelief *n.* **1,** (incredulity) incredulidad. **2,** (lack of faith) descreimiento; irreligión.
unbelievable *adj.* increíble.
unbeliever *n.* **1,** (doubter) incrédulo. **2,** (infidel) descreído; infiel.
unbelieving *adj.* **1,** (incredulous) incrédulo. **2,** (faithless) descreído; infiel.
unbend *v.t.* [*pret. & p.p.* **unbent**] **1,** (release) aflojar; soltar. **2,** (straighten) enderezar. —*v.i.* **1,** (relax) descansar; relajarse. **2,** (straighten) enderezarse. —**unbending,** *adj.* inflexible; resoluto.
unbiased *adj.* imparcial; desinteresado.
unbidden *adj.* **1,** (not com-

manded) espontáneo. **2,** (not invited) no convidado.
unbind *v.t.* [*pret. & p.p.* **unbound**] desatar; soltar.
unbleached *adj.* crudo; sin blanquear.
unblushing *adj.* desvergonzado.
unbolt *v.t.* **1,** (unbar) desatrancar. **2,** (unscrew) desvolver; desenroscar.
unbolted *adj.* **1,** (unfastened) desatrancado; no asegurado. **2,** (not sifted) sin cerner.
unborn *adj.* no nacido.
unbosom (ʌn'buz·əm) *v.t.* revelar; confesar. —**unbosom oneself,** desahogarse; abrir el pecho.
unbound *adj.* **1,** (without binding) no encuadernado. **2,** (free) suelto; libre. —*v., pret. & p.p. de* **unbind.**
unbounded *adj.* infinito; ilimitado.
unbowed *adj.* **1,** (not bent) no inclinado; no doblado. **2,** (not subdued) no domado.
unbrace *v.t.* aflojar; soltar.
unbraid *v.t.* destrenzar.
unbreakable *adj.* irrompible.
unbridled *adj.* desenfrenado; irrefrenable. —**unbridle,** *v.t.* desenfrenar.
unbroken *adj.* **1,** (intact) intacto; entero. **2,** (not violated) inviolado. **3,** (continuous) continuo; sin interrupción. **4,** (not subdued) no domado.
unbuckle *v.t.* deshebillar.
unburden *v.t.* descargar. —**unburden oneself,** desahogarse.
unburied *adj.* insepulto.
unbusinesslike *adj.* poco práctico; poco metódico.
unbutton *v.t.* desabotonar; desabrochar.
uncalled-for *adj.* **1,** (not required) innecesario; no pedido. **2,** (gratuitous) gratuito; inmerecido.
uncanny (ʌn'kæn·i) *adj.* misterioso; extraño; raro.
uncap (ʌn'kæp) *v.t.* [**uncapped, -capping**] destapar.
uncared-for *adj.* desamparado; abandonado.
uncaused *adj.* sin motivo; sin razón.
unceasing *adj.* incesante.
unceremonious *adj.* **1,** (informal) informal; sin ceremonia. **2,** (curt) descortés; abrupto.
uncertain *adj.* incierto. —**uncertainty,** *n.* incertidumbre.
unchain *v.t.* desencadenar.
unchallenged *adj* indisputable.
unchangeable *adj.* inmutable; incambiable; inalterable.
unchanged *adj.* inalterado; sin cambiar.
unchanging *adj.* inmutable; inalterable.
uncharitable *adj.* poco caritativo; duro.
uncharted *adj.* inexplorado.
unchaste *adj.* incasto.
unchecked *adj.* **1,** (unbridled) desenfrenado. **2,** (not verified) no verificado.
unchristian *adj.* anticristiano.
uncircumcised *adj.* incircunciso.
uncircumscribed *adj.* incircunscrito.
uncivil *adj.* incivil; descortés.
uncivilized *adj.* incivilizado; bárbaro.
unclad *adj.* desnudo; desvestido.
unclaimed *adj.* no reclamado; sin reclamar.
unclasp *v.t.* **1,** (unfasten) desabrochar. **2,** (release) librar; soltar.
unclassifiable *adj.* inclasificable.
unclassified *adj.* inclasificado.
uncle ('ʌŋ·kəl) *n.* tío.
unclean *adj.* inmundo; sucio; impuro.
uncleanliness *n.* suciedad; inmundicia.
uncleanly (ʌn'klɛn·li) *adj.* inmundo; sucio. —*adv.* (ʌn'klin·li) suciamente.
unclench *v.t.* soltar; aflojar; desasir.
uncloak *v.t.* descubrir. —*v.i.* descubrirse.
unclog *v.t.* [**unclogged, -clogging**] desembarazar; desatrancar; desatascar.
unclose *v.t.* **1,** (open) abrir. **2,** (disclose) descubrir; revelar.
unclothe *v.t.* desarropar; desvestir; desnudar. —*v.i.* desarroparse; desvestirse; desnudarse.
unclouded *adj.* despejado.
uncoil *v.t.* desenrollar. —*v.i.* desenrollarse.
uncollectible *adj.* incobrable.
uncomfortable *adj.* incómodo.
uncommitted *adj.* libre; no comprometido.
uncommon *adj.* raro; extraordinario; insólito.

uncommunicative *adj.* inconversable; reservado.
uncomplaining *adj.* no quejoso; paciente; sufrido.
uncompleted *adj.* inacabado; incompleto.
uncomplicated *adj.* no complicado; sencillo; incomplexo.
uncomplimentary *adj.* poco halagüeño.
uncompromising *adj.* intransigente; resoluto.
unconcern (ˌʌn·kənˈsʌɹn) *n.* indiferencia; despreocupación. —**unconcerned,** *adj.* indiferente; despreocupado.
unconditional *adj.* incondicional.
unconditioned *adj.* **1,** (natural) no condicionado; natural. **2,** = **unconditional.**
unconfessed *adj.* inconfeso.
unconformity *n.* desconformidad.
uncongenial *adj.* **1,** (unfriendly) antipático. **2,** (incompatible) incompatible.
unconnected *adj.* inconexo; desconectado.
unconquerable *adj.* inconquistable.
unconscionable *adj.* **1,** (unscrupulous) inescrupuloso. **2,** (unreasonable) desrazonable. **3,** (excessive) excesivo.
unconscious (ʌnˈkan·ʃəs) *adj.* & *n.* inconsciente. —**unconsciousness,** *n.* inconsciencia.
unconstitutional *adj.* anticonstitucional.
uncontaminated *adj.* incontaminado; puro.
uncontrollable *adj.* irrefrenable; ingobernable.
unconventional *adj.* informal; libre; despreocupado.
uncooked *adj.* crudo.
uncooperative *adj.* poco cooperativo; roncero.
uncork *v.t.* descorchar; destaponar.
uncorrupted *adj.* incorrupto.
uncountable *adj.* incontable; innumerable.
uncounted *adj.* **1,** (not counted) no contado. **2,** (countless) innumerable.
uncouple *v.t.* desacoplar; *R.R.* desenganchar.
uncouth (ʌnˈkuθ) *adj.* **1,** (boorish) tosco; grosero. **2,** (strange) extraño; extraordinario.
uncover *v.t.* **1,** (remove the cover from) destapar; descubrir. **2,** (disclose) descubrir; revelar. **3,** (remove the clothing from) desarropar. —*v.i.* descubrirse.
uncritical *adj.* poco discerniente; inexperto.
uncrown *v.t.* destronar. —**uncrowned,** *adj.* sin corona.
unction (ˈʌŋk·ʃən) *n.* unción.
unctuous (ˈʌŋ·tʃu·əs) *adj.* untuoso. —**unctuousness,** *n.* untuosidad.
uncultivated *adj.* inculto.
uncultured *adj.* inculto.
uncured *adj.* no curado; crudo.
uncurl *v.t.* desrizar. —*v.i.* desrizarse.
uncut *adj.* no cortado; entero; completo.
undamaged *adj.* indemne; intacto.
undaunted *adj.* impávido; impertérrito.
undeceive *v.t.* desengañar.
undecided *adj.* indeciso.
undecipherable *adj.* indescifrable.
undefeated *adj.* invicto.
undefended *adj.* indefenso.
undefiled *adj.* impoluto.
undefinable *adj.* indefinible.
undefined *adj.* indefinido.
undemocratic *adj.* antidemocrático.
undemonstrative *adj.* reservado; poco expresivo.
undeniable *adj.* innegable.
undenominational *adj.* no sectario.
under (ˈʌn·dər) *prep.* **1,** (below; beneath) bajo; debajo de. **2,** (less than) menos de; menos que. **3,** (inferior to) inferior a. **4,** (subject to) sujeto a; sometido a. **5,** (according to) conforme a; según. —*adj.* inferior. —*adv.* debajo; abajo; más abajo. —**bring under,** dominar. —**go under, 1,** (fail) fracasar. **2,** (sink) hundirse. —**keep under,** oprimir. —**under a cloud,** en apuros.
under- (ʌn·dər) *prefijo* sub-; so-. **1,** bajo; inferior: *underground,* subterráneo; *undersecretary,* subsecretario; *undermine,* socavar. **2,** poco; menos: *undercook,* cocer poco; *undersell,* vender más ba-

rato. **3,** interior: *underclothes,* ropa interior.
underact *v.t. & i.* actuar atenuadamente (un papel).
underage (ˌʌn·dərˈeidʒ) *adj.* menor de edad.
underarm *adv.* de la axila. —**underarm perspiration,** sobaquina.
underarmed *adj.* sin suficientes armas.
underbid *v.t.* [**underbid, -bidding**] ofrecer menos que.
underbred *adj.* **1,** (ill-bred) malcriado; mal educado. **2,** (not of pure breed) de raza impura.
underbrush *n.* maleza.
undercarriage *n.* bastidor; *aero.* tren de aterrizaje.
undercharge *v.t.* cargar *o* cobrar menos (*o* de menos). —*n.* cargo insuficiente.
underclassman (ˌʌn·dərˈklæs·mən) *n.* [*pl.* **-men**] alumno universitario de los dos primeros años.
underclothes *n.pl.* ropa interior.
undercook *v.t. & i.* cocer(se) poco.
undercover *adj.* secreto; clandestino.
undercurrent *n.* **1,** (lower current) corriente inferior. **2,** (hidden tendency) tendencia oculta.
undercut (ʌn·dərˈkʌt) *v.t.* [**undercut, -cutting**] socavar. —*adj.* (ˈʌn-) socavado. —*n.* (ˈʌn-) socavación; socava.
underdevelop *v.t.* desarrollar incompletamente. —**underdeveloped,** *adj.* subdesarrollado.
underdo *v.t.* [*pret.* **underdid;** *p.p.* **underdone**] **1,** (do too little) hacer poco; escatimar. **2,** = **undercook.**
underdog (ˈʌn·dər·dɔg) *n.* perdedor; víctima.
underdone *adj.* a medio cocer; insuficientemente cocido.
underdrawers *n.pl.* calzoncillos.
underestimate (ˌʌn·dərˈɛs·tɪ·meit) *v.t. & i.* **1,** (misjudge in cost or value) apreciar demasiado bajo; estimar en menos del valor. **2,** (hold in low esteem) desestimar; menospreciar. —*n.* (-mət) **1,** (too low a price or value) apreciación demasiado baja; presupuesto demasiado bajo. **2,** (low esteem) desestimación; menosprecio.
underexpose *v.t.* exponer insuficientemente. —**underexposure,** *n.* exposición insuficiente; poca exposición.
underfed *adj.* desnutrido.
underfeed *v.t.* [*pret. & p.p.* **underfed**] alimentar poco. —**underfeeding,** *n.* desnutrición.
underfoot *adj. & adv.* debajo de los pies; *fig.* molestando; estorbando.
undergarment *n.* prenda de vestir interior.
undergo *v.t.* [**underwent, -gone, -going**] **1,** (experience) pasar por; correr. **2,** (endure) sufrir; padecer. **3,** (be subjected to) estar sometido a; someterse a.
undergraduate *adj.* no graduado; de *o* para el bachillerato. —*n.* estudiante del bachillerato.
underground *adj.* **1,** (subterranean) subterráneo. **2,** (secret) secreto; clandestino. —*adv.* **1,** (beneath the surface) bajo tierra; debajo de la tierra. **2,** (secretly) clandestinamente. —*n.* **1,** (underground space or passage) subterráneo. **2,** (secret movement) movimiento oculto; resistencia. **3,** *Brit.* = **subway.**
undergrown *adj.* poco crecido; poco desarrollado; enano.
undergrowth *n.* **1,** (underbrush) maleza; chamarasca. **2,** (arrested development) pequeñez; desarrollo impedido.
underhand *adj.* (deceitful) taimado; clandestino; disimulado. —*adj. & adv., sports* con la mano debajo del nivel de los hombros.
underhanded *adj.* taimado; clandestino; disimulado. —**underhandedly,** *adv.* bajo cuerda; a socapa; disimuladamente.
underhung *adj.* **1,** (suspended) suspendido. **2,** (jutting out, as the jaw) sobresaliente.
underlay (ʌn·dərˈlei) *v.t.* [*prep. & p.p.* **underlaid**] **1,** (place under) poner debajo. **2,** *print.* calzar. **3,** (raise; reinforce) levantar; reforzar. **4,** *pret. de* **underlie.** —*n.* (ˈʌn·dər·lei) calzo.
underlie *v.t.* [**underlay, -lain, -lying**] **1,** (lie under) estar *o* extenderse debajo de. **2,** (support) sostener; sustentar; ser la base o fundamento de.
underline *v.t.* subrayar. —*n.* raya.
underling (ˈʌn·dər·lɪŋ) *n.* inferior; subordinado; secuaz.

underlying *adj.* **1,** (placed beneath) subyacente. **2,** (basic) fundamental. **3,** (obscure) oculto. —*v., pr.p. de* **underlie.**
undermine (ˈʌn·dərˌmain) *v.t.* minar; socavar.
undermost *adj.* ínfimo; más bajo. —*adv.* a lo más bajo.
underneath (ˌʌn·dərˈniθ) *adv.* debajo. —*prep.* debajo de; bajo. —*adj.* inferior. —*n.* parte inferior.
undernourish *v.t.* alimentar poco. —**undernourished,** *adj.* desnutrido. —**undernourishment,** *n.* desnutrición.
underpants *n.pl.* calzoncillos.
underpass *n.* paso bajo; paso inferior.
underpay *v.t.* [*pret.* & *p.p.* **underpaid**] pagar mal; pagar insuficientemente. —*n.* pago insuficiente. —**underpaid,** *adj.* mal pagado. —**underpayment,** *n.* pago insuficiente.
underpin *v.t.* [**underpinned, -pinning**] apuntalar. —**underpinning,** *n.* apuntalamiento.
underplay *v.t.* & *i.* actuar atenuadamente (un papel).
underpopulated *adj.* poco poblado. —**underpopulation,** *n.* poca población; baja población.
underprice *v.t.* pedir insuficiente por; poner demasiado barato.
underprivileged *adj.* necesitado; desvalido.
underproduce *v.t.* & *i.* producir insuficientemente. —**underproduction,** *n.* producción insuficiente; baja producción.
underprop *v.t.* [**underpropped, -propping**] apuntalar.
underrate (ˌʌn·dərˈreit) *v.t.* desapreciar; menospreciar.
underripe *adj.* inmaturo; verde.
underrun *v.t.* [**underran, -run, -running**] correr por debajo.
underscore (ˈʌn·dər·skor) *v.t.* subrayar. —*n.* raya.
undersea *adj.* submarino. —*adv.* bajo la superficie del mar.
undersecretary *n.* subsecretario.
undersell *v.t.* [*pret.* & *p.p.* **undersold**] vender más barato (que).
undershirt *n.* camiseta.
underside *n.* superficie inferior.
undersign *v.t.* subscribir. —**the undersigned,** el infrascrito; el abajo firmado.
undersized *adj.* de talla menor; de corta estatura.
underskirt *n.* enagua; enaguas.
underslung *adj.* colgante; suspendido debajo del eje.
undersoil *n.* subsuelo.
undersold *v., pret.* & *p.p. de* **undersell.**
understand (ˌʌn·dərˈstænd) *v.t.* & *i.* [*pret.* & *p.p.* **understood**] **1,** (comprehend) comprender; entender. **2,** (assume; supply mentally) sobrentender. —**understandable,** *adj.* comprensible.
understanding (ˌʌn·dərˈstæn·dɪŋ) *n.* **1,** (comprehension) entendimiento. **2,** (agreement) acuerdo. —*adj.* **1,** (comprehending) inteligente; entendedor. **2,** (sympathetic) comprensivo.
understate *v.t.* declarar o manifestar incompletamente; decir con poca fuerza. —**understatement,** *n.* expresión exageradamente moderada.
understock *v.t.* surtir poco (de).
understood (ˌʌn·dərˈstʊd) *adj.* **1,** (comprehended) entendido. **2,** (agreed) convenido. **3,** (assumed) sobrentendido. —*v., pret.* & *p.p. de* **understand.**
understudy (ˈʌn·dərˌstʌd·i) *n.* actor sustituto; sustituto; suplente. —*v.t.* aprender (un papel o empleo) para poder sustituir (a otro).
undertake *v.t.* [*pret.* **undertook;** *p.p.* **undertaken**] **1,** (take upon oneself) emprender; entrar en; tomar a su cargo. **2,** (commit oneself to) comprometerse a.
undertaker *n.* funerario; director de pompas fúnebres.
undertaking (ʌn·dərˈtei·kɪŋ) *n.* **1,** (task; enterprise) empresa. **2,** (ˈʌn·dər-) (business of an undertaker) empresa funeraria.
undertone *n.* **1,** (low voice) voz baja. **2,** (subdued color) matiz suavizado. **3,** (background) fondo.
undertow (ˈʌn·dərˌto) *n.* resaca.
undervalue *v.t.* desapreciar; desestimar. —**undervaluation,** *n.* desaprecio; desestimación.
underwaist *n.* corpiño.
underwater *adj.* submarino; bajo agua.
underwear (ˈʌn·dər·wɛr) *n.* ropa interior.
underweight *n.* peso escaso; flaqueza. —*adj.* de peso escaso; flaco.
underwent *v., pret. de* **undergo.**
underworld *n.* **1,** (criminal ele-

ment) hampa; mundo de vicio. **2,** (hell) infierno; averno.

underwrite *v.t.* [*pret.* **underwrote;** *p.p.* **underwritten**] **1,** (subscribe) subscribir. **2,** (guarantee) asegurar.

underwriter *n.* asegurador.

undeserved *adj.* inmerecido.

undeserving *adj.* desmerecedor; indigno.

undesigning *adj.* sincero; sencillo; sin malicia.

undesirable *adj.* indeseable.

undetermined *adj.* indeterminado.

undeterred *adj.* impávido; impertérrito.

undeveloped *adj.* sin desarrollo; subdesarrollado.

undeviating *adj.* **1,** (straight) directo. **2,** (unvarying) sin rodeo; siempre igual.

undies ('ʌn·diz) *n.pl. colloq.* = **underwear.**

undigested *adj.* indigesto.

undignified *adj.* indecoroso; indecente.

undiminished *adj.* entero; completo; íntegro.

undiplomatic *adj.* poco diplomático; indiscreto.

undirected *adj.* **1,** (without direction) sin dirección. **2,** (without address) sin señas.

undiscernible *adj.* imperceptible; indiscernible.

undiscerning *adj.* poco discerniente; inexperto.

undisciplined *adj.* indisciplinado.

undisclosed *adj.* no revelado; oculto; secreto.

undiscouraged *adj.* impávido; firme; resoluto.

undiscovered *adj.* no descubierto; oculto.

undiscriminating *adj.* poco discerniente; falto de buen gusto.

undisguised *adj.* cándido; franco; abierto; sin disfraz.

undismayed *adj.* impávido; firme; no desanimado.

undisposed *adj.* no dispuesto. —**undisposed of, 1,** (available) disponible. **2,** (unsold) no vendido. **3,** (unsettled) no decidido; no arreglado.

undisputed *adj.* incontestable; incontrovertible.

undistinguishable *adj.* indistinguible.

undistinguished *adj.* no distinguido.

undisturbed *adj.* imperturbado; tranquilo.

undivided *adj.* indiviso; entero.

undo *v.t.* [**undid, undone, undoing**] **1,** (cancel; annul) deshacer; anular. **2,** (unfasten) desatar; desliar. **3,** (ruin) arruinar; perder.

undoing *n.* **1,** (canceling; annulling) anulación. **2,** (ruin) ruina; pérdida.

undone *v., p.p. de* **undo.** —*adj.* **1,** (not done) sin hacer; por hacer. **2,** (unfastened) desatado. **3,** (ruined) arruinado; perdido.

undoubted *adj.* indudable; fuera de duda. —**undoubtedly,** *adv.* indudablemente; sin duda.

undrape *v.t.* desvestir; desnudar. —**undraped,** *adj.* desnudo.

undress *v.t.* desvestir; desnudar. —*v.i.* desvestirse; desnudarse. —*n.* ropa de casa; *mil.* traje de cuartel; uniforme diario. —*adj.* informal.

undue *adj.* **1,** (improper) indebido. **2,** (excessive) excesivo. **3,** (not payable) no vencido; no debido.

undulant ('ʌn·djə·lənt) *adj.* ondulante.

undulate ('ʌn·djəˌleit) *v.t.* & *i.* ondular. —**undulation,** *n.* ondulación.

unduly *adv.* **1,** (improperly) indebidamente. **2,** (excessively) excesivamente.

undying *adj.* imperecedero.

unearned *adj.* **1,** (not earned) no ganado. **2,** (not deserved) inmerecido.

unearth (ʌn'ʌɹθ) *v.t.* **1,** (disinter) desenterrar. **2,** (discover) descubrir.

unearthly *adj.* **1,** (supernatural) sobrenatural. **2,** (ghostly) espectral. **3,** (frightful) horripilante. **4,** *colloq.* (strange) extraño; raro; fantástico.

uneasy (ʌn'i·zi) *adj.* **1,** (disturbed) inquieto; desasosegado. **2,** (awkward) desmañado; falto de gracia. —**uneasiness,** *n.* inquietud; desasosiego.

uneatable *adj.* incomible.

uneconomical *adj.* antieconómico.

uneducated *adj.* ineducado. —**uneducable,** *adj.* ineducable.

unembarrassed *adj.* desembarazado.

unemotional *adj.* impasible; frío.
unemployed *adj.* 1, (without work) desempleado; desocupado. 2, (not in use) inutilizado; improductivo.
unemployment *n.* desempleo; desocupación; cesantía.
unencompassable *adj.* inabarcable.
unencumbered *adj.* 1, (unhampered) libre; sin trabas. 2, (not crowded) desahogado. 3, *law* libre de gravamen.
unending *adj.* infinito; interminable.
unendurable *adj.* inaguantable; insoportable.
unenforceable *adj.* incumplible.
unengaged *adj.* libre; desocupado; no comprometido.
unenlightened *adj.* no iluminado; ignorante.
unenviable *adj.* poco envidiable.
unenvied *adj* no envidiado.
unequal *adj.* 1, (of different measure; uneven) desigual. 2, (inadequate) insuficiente; inadecuado. 3, (unjust) injusto; parcial.
unequaled *adj.* inigualado; sin igual.
unequivocal *adj.* inequívoco.
unerring *adj.* infalible.
unessential *adj.* no esencial.
unethical *adj.* poco ético.
uneven *adj.* 1, (unequal) desigual. 2, (rough) escabroso; quebrado. 3, (irregular) irregular. 4, (odd) impar.
uneventful *adj.* tranquilo; sin novedad.
unexampled (ˌʌn·ɛg'zæm·pəld) *adj.* sin precedente; sin par; único.
unexcelled *adj.* insuperado.
unexceptionable *adj.* irrecusable; irreprensible.
unexceptional *adj.* ordinario; corriente.
unexchangeable *adj.* incambiable; impermutable.
unexcited *adj.* no excitado; tranquilo; sereno.
unexciting *adj.* no excitante; árido; aburrido.
unexpected *adj.* inesperado.
unexpended *adj.* no expendido.
unexpired *adj.* no expirado; no vencido.
unexplained *adj.* inexplicado. —**unexplainable**, *adj.* inexplicable.
unexploited *adj.* no explotado; desaprovechado.
unexplored *adj.* inexplorado.
unexposed *adj.* no expuesto.
unexpressed *adj.* inexpresado.
unexpressive *adj.* inexpresivo.
unexpurgated *adj.* no expurgado.
unfailing *adj.* 1, (inexhaustible) inagotable. 2, (infallible) indefectible; infalible.
unfair *adj.* 1, (unjust) injusto. 2, (dishonest) falso; deshonesto. 3, *sports* sucio.
unfaithful *adj.* infiel.
unfaltering *adj.* sin vacilar; firme; resuelto.
unfamiliar *adj.* 1, (not well known) poco familiar; poco conocido. 2, (not well versed) no familiarizado.
unfamiliarity *n.* 1, (strangeness) falta de familiaridad. 2, (lack of knowledge) desconocimiento.
unfashionable *adj.* singular; raro; opuesto a la moda.
unfasten *v.t.* soltar; desatar; desabrochar; desenganchar.
unfathomable *adj.* insondable.
unfavorable *adj.* desfavorable.
unfeasible *adj.* impracticable.
unfeeling *adj.* 1, (insensible) insensible. 2, (hardhearted) duro de corazón; cruel.
unfeigned *adj.* genuino; verdadero; sincero.
unfenced *adj.* no cercado; abierto.
unfetter *v.t.* desencadenar.
unfettered *adj.* libre; suelto; liberado.
unfilial *adj.* que no conviene a un hijo; impropio de un hijo.
unfilled *adj.* no lleno; vacío; vacante.
unfinished *adj.* incompleto; inconcluso; inacabado.
unfit *adj.* 1, (incapable) incapaz; inhábil. 2, (unsuitable) impropio; desconveniente. —*v.t.* [**unfitted, -fitting**] inhabilitar.
unfitting *adj.* impropio; indecoroso.
unfix *v.t.* soltar; desatar.
unflagging *adj.* persistente; incansable.
unflattering *adj.* poco halagüeño; poco favorecedor.
unfledged *adj.* 1, (without feathers) implume. 2, (immature) inmaturo.
unflinching *adj.* resuelto; firme; sin retroceso.

unfold *v.t.* 1, (spread out) desdoblar; desplegar. 2, (unwrap) desenvolver. 3, (reveal) revelar; descubrir. 4, (develop) desarrollar.
unforbearing *adj.* intolerante; poco indulgente.
unforeseeable *adj.* imprevisible.
unforeseen *adj.* imprevisto.
unforgettable *adj.* inolvidable.
unforgivable *adj.* imperdonable. —**unforgiving**, *n.* inclemente; inexorable.
unforgotten *adj.* inolvidado.
unformed *adj.* informe; crudo; no desarrollado.
unfortunate *adj.* desgraciado; desafortunado; infeliz. —**unfortunately**, *adv.* por desgracia; desgraciadamente; infelizmente.
unfounded *adj.* infundado.
unfrequented *adj.* poco frecuentado; solitario.
unfriendly *adj.* poco amistoso; áspero; enemigo.
unfrock (ʌn'frak) *v.t.* expulsar (*a un sacerdote*).
unfruitful *adj.* infructuoso.
unfulfilled *adj.* incumplido.
unfurl (ʌn'fʌɹl) *v.t.* desplegar; extender.
unfurnished *adj.* 1, (without furniture) desamueblado. 2, (unsupplied) desprovisto.
ungainly (ʌn'gein·li) *adj.* desmañado; desgarbado.
ungallant *adj.* poco galante; poco caballeroso; descortés.
ungenerous *adj.* poco generoso; tacaño.
ungentlemanly *adj.* poco caballeroso; descortés.
unglue *v.t.* despegar.
ungodly *adj.* 1, (godless) impío; profano; ateo; sindiós. 2, *colloq.* (outrageous) atroz. —*adv., colloq.* muy; extremadamente.
ungovernable *adj.* indomable; ingobernable.
ungraceful *adj.* desgarbado; falto de gracia.
ungracious *adj.* 1, (unpleasant) desagradable. 2, (discourteous) descortés.
ungrammatical *adj.* ingramatical.
ungrateful *adj.* ingrato; desagradecido.
ungrounded *adj.* 1, (unfounded) infundado. 2, (unversed) poco instruído. 3, *electricity* sin conductor a tierra.
ungrudging *adj.* voluntario; de buena gana.
unguarded *adj.* 1, (unprotected) desguarnecido; indefenso. 2, (indiscreet) incauto; indiscreto.
unguent ('ʌŋ·gwənt) *n.* ungüento.
unhallowed *adj.* profano; impío.
unhampered *adj.* libre; no impedido.
unhand *v.t.* desatar; soltar.
unhandsome *adj.* 1, (homely) feo. 2, (rude) descortés. 3, (stingy) poco generoso; tacaño.
unhandy *adj.* 1, (unskillful) inepto; desmañado. 2, (cumbersome) incómodo.
unhappy *adj.* infeliz; desdichado; triste. —**unhappiness**, *n.* desdicha; tristeza.
unharmed *adj.* ileso; incólume.
unharmful *adj.* inofensivo; innocuo.
unharness *v.t.* desenjaezar; desguarnecer; desarmar.
unhatched *adj.* no salido del cascarón; *fig.* no descubierto.
unhealthful *adj.* malsano; insalubre.
unhealthy *adj.* 1, (sickly) enfermizo; achacoso. 2, = **unhealthful.**
unheard *adj.* 1, (not heard) no oído. 2, (unknown) desconocido.
unheard-of *adj.* inaudito.
unheated *adj.* no calentado; sin calefacción.
unheeded *adj.* desatendido. —**unheedful**, *adj.* desatento. —**unheeding**, *adj.* descuidado; no haciendo caso.
unhesitating *adj.* decidido; resuelto; pronto.
unhindered *adj.* libre; no impedido.
unhinge (ʌn'hɪndʒ) *v.t.* desquiciar.
unhitch *v.t.* desenganchar.
unholy (ʌn'ho·li) *adj.* 1, (profane) impío; profano. 2, *colloq.* (dreadful) terrible; atroz.
unhook *v.t.* desenganchar; descolgar.
unhoped-for *adj.* inesperado.
unhorse (ʌn'hors) *v.t.* desmontar.
unhurried *adj.* sin prisa; pausado.
unhurt *adj.* ileso; incólume.
unhygienic *adj.* antihigiénico.
unhyphenated *adj.* sin guión; *fig.* cabal; entero; íntegro.
uni- (ju·nə) *prefijo* uni-; uno; uno

solo: *unison,* unísono; *unicorn,* unicornio.

unicameral (ˌju·nəˈkæm·ə·rel) *adj.* unicameral.

unicellular (ˌju·nəˈsɛl·jə·lər) *adj.* unicelular.

unicorn (ˈju·nə·korn) *n.* unicornio.

unidentified *adj.* no identificado.

uniform (ˈju·nə·form) *n. & adj.* uniforme. —*v.t.* uniformar. —**uniformity** (-ˈfor·mə·ti) *n.* uniformidad.

unify (ˈju·nə·fai) *v.t.* unificar. —**unification** (-fɪˈkei·ʃən) *n.* unificación.

unilateral (ˌju·nəˈlæt·ər·əl) *adj.* unilateral.

unimaginable *adj.* inimaginable.

unimaginative *adj.* poco imaginativo.

unimpaired *adj.* inalterado; intacto.

unimpassioned *adj.* no apasionado; frío.

unimpeachable *adj.* irrecusable; intachable; incensurable.

unimpeded *adj.* libre; no impedido.

unimportant *adj.* insignificante; poco importante. —**unimportance,** *n.* poca importancia.

unimposing *adj.* poco imponente; poco impresionante.

unimpressed *adj.* poco impresionado; poco conmovido.

unimpressive *adj.* poco impresionante.

unimproved *adj.* **1,** (not improved) no mejorado; no adelantado. **2,** (undeveloped, as land) sin urbanizar.

unincorporated *adj.* no incorporado.

uninflammable *adj.* incombustible.

uninflected *adj.* sin inflexión.

uninfluential *adj.* poco influyente.

uninformed *adj.* ignorante; no informado.

uninhabitable *adj.* inhabitable.

uninhabited *adj.* deshabitado; inhabitado.

uninhibited *adj.* desenfrenado; desenvuelto; libre; abierto.

uninitiated *adj.* no iniciado; inexperto.

uninjured *adj.* ileso; incólume.

uninspired *adj.* no inspirado; sin inspiración.

uninspiring *adj.* que no inspira; árido; aburrido.

unintelligent *adj.* estúpido; torpe; bruto.

unintelligible *adj.* ininteligible.

unintentional *adj.* no intencional; hecho sin intención.

uninterested *adj.* no interesado.

uninteresting *adj.* sin interés; soso; aburrido.

uninterrupted *adj.* ininterrumpido; continuo. —**uninterruptedly,** *adv.* sin interrupción; continuamente.

uninvited *adj.* no convidado; insolicitado.

union (ˈjun·jən) *n.* **1,** (combination; joining; joint) unión. **2,** (labor organization) sindicato; gremio; *Amer.* unión. —*adj.* gremial; del sindicato.

unionism (ˈjun·jən·ɪz·əm) *n.* sindicalismo; unionismo. —**unionist,** *n.* sindicalista; unionista.

unionize (ˈjun·jən·aiz) *v.t.* sindicar; agremiar. —*v.i.* sindicarse; agremiarse. —**unionization** (-ɪˈzei·ʃən) *n.* sindicación; agremiación.

Union Jack pabellón de la Gran Bretaña.

union shop taller agremiado.

union suit prenda de ropa interior de una sola pieza.

unipersonal *adj.* unipersonal.

unique (juˈnik) *adj.* único; singular. —**uniqueness,** *n.* singularidad.

unisexual *adj.* unisexual.

unison (ˈju·nə·sən) *n.* **1,** *music* unisón. **2,** (agreement) concordancia; armonía. —*adj.* unísono. —**in unison,** unísono; al unísono.

unissued *adj.* **1,** (not emitted) no emitido. **2,** (unpublished) no publicado; inédito.

unit (ˈju·nɪt) *n.* unidad. —*adj.* unitario.

unitarian (ˌju·nəˈtɛr·i·ən) *adj. & n.* unitario.

unitary (ˈju·nə·tɛr·i) *adj.* unitario.

unite (juˈnait) *v.t.* unir. —*v.i.* unirse. —**united,** *adj.* unido.

United States Estados Unidos (de América). —*adj.* estadounidense.

unity (ˈju·nə·ti) *n.* unidad.

univalent *adj.* univalente.

univalve *adj.* & *n.* univalvo.
universal (ˌju·nəˈvʌɹ·səl) *adj.* universal; universo. —**universality** (-vərˈsæl·ə·ti) *n.* universalidad.
universalist (ˌju·nəˈvʌɹ·səl·ɪst) *adj.* & *n.* universalista. —**universalism,** *n.* universalismo.
universalize (ˌju·nəˈvʌɹ·sə·ˌlaiz) *v.t.* universalizar.
universal joint articulación universal.
universe (ˈju·nə·vʌɹs) *n.* universo.
university (ju·nəˈvʌɹ·sə·ti) *n.* universidad. —*adj.* universitario.
unjoin *v.t.* separar; desunir.
unjoint *v.t.* desencajar; descoyuntar.
unjust *adj.* injusto.
unjustifiable *adj.* injustificable.
unjustified *adj.* injustificado.
unkempt (ʌnˈkɛmpt) *adj.* **1,** (disheveled) desgreñado; despeinado. **2,** (untidy) desaliñado; desaseado. **3,** (rough) rudo; tosco.
unkind *adj.* duro; severo; áspero. —**unkindness,** *n.* severidad; aspereza.
unknit *v.t.* [*pret.* & *p.p.* **unknitted** *o* **unknit;** *ger.* **unknitting**] destejer.
unknot *v.t.* [**unknotted, -knotting**] desatar; desligar.
unknowable *adj.* incognoscible; insabible.
unknowing *adj.* ignorante; inadvertido. —**unknowingly,** *adv.* inadvertidamente; sin saberlo.
unknown *adj.* desconocido; ignoto; incógnito. —*n.* desconocido; *math.* incógnita.
unlace *v.t.* desenlazar; desatar.
unladen *adj.* descargado.
unladylike *adj.* impropio de una dama.
unlamented *adj.* no lamentado; no llorado.
unlash *v.t.* desatar; desligar.
unlatch *v.t.* abrir soltando el pestillo; saltar el pestillo de.
unlawful *adj.* **1,** (illegal) ilegal; ilícito. **2,** (illegitimate) ilegítimo. —**unlawfulness,** *n.* ilegalidad.
unlearn *v.t.* desaprender.
unlearned (ʌnˈlʌɹ·nɪd) *adj.* **1,** (ignorant) ignorante; indocto. **2,** (ʌnˈlʌɹnd) (not mastered) no aprendido; no estudiado. **3,** (ʌn·ˈlʌɹnd) (innate) innato; natural; instintivo.
unleash *v.t.* desencadenar; soltar.
unleavened *adj.* ázimo; sin levadura.
unless (ʌnˈlɛs) *conj.* a menos que; a no ser que; si no. —*prep.* excepto; si no es.
unlettered *adj.* **1,** (uneducated) indocto; inculto. **2,** (illiterate) analfabeto.
unlicensed *adj.* sin licencia; no autorizado.
unlighted *adj.* **1,** (dark) oscuro; no iluminado. **2,** (not burning) no encendido. *También,* **unlit.**
unlikable *también,* **unlikeable,** *adj.* poco agradable; desagradable.
unlike *adj.* diferente; desemejante; dispar. —*prep.* diferente a; a diferencia de. —**unlikeness,** *n.* diferencia; desemejanza.
unlikely *adj.* **1,** (improbable) inverosímil; improbable. **2,** (not inclined) poco inclinado; poco propenso. —*adv.* improbablemente. —**unlikelihood,** *n.* improbabilidad.
unlimber *v.t.* & *i.* preparar(se) para la acción.
unlimited *adj.* **1,** (boundless) ilimitado; infinito. **2,** (unrestricted) sin restricción. **3,** (indefinite) indefinido.
unlined *adj.* **1,** (without lining) sin forro. **2,** (unruled) sin rayar. **3,** (unwrinkled) sin arrugas.
unlink *v.t.* deseslabonar.
unlisted *adj.* no registrado.
unload *v.t.* **1,** (discharge) descargar. **2,** (get rid of) deshacerse de. —**unloading,** *n.* descarga; descargo.
unlock *v.t.* **1,** (open) abrir. **2,** (reveal) revelar; descubrir.
unloose (ʌnˈlus) *v.t.* desatar; aflojar; soltar.
unloosen (ʌnˈlu·sən) *v.t.* aflojar; soltar.
unloved *adj.* no amado.
unlovely *adj.* antipático; desagradable; feo.
unlucky *adj.* **1,** (having bad luck) desgraciado; sin suerte; desafortunado. **2,** (bringing bad luck) aciago; funesto; siniestro; de mal agüero.
unmake *v.t.* [*pret.* & *p.p.* **unmade**] **1,** (undo) deshacer. **2,** (depose) deponer.
unman (ʌnˈmæn) *v.t.* [**unmanned, -manning**] **1,** (unnerve) desanimar; privar de fuerza. **2,** (emasculate) afeminar; castrar; capar.

3, (deprive of men) privar de hombres; desguarnecer.
unmanageable *adj.* inmanejable; intratable.
unmanful *adj.* indigno de un hombre; afeminado.
unmanly *adj.* 1, (effeminate) afeminado. 2, (cowardly) cobarde; vil; ruin.
unmannerly *adj.* malcriado; descortés. —*adv.* descortésmente.
unmarked *adj.* no señalado.
unmarketable *adj.* invendible.
unmarried *adj.* soltero; célibe.
unmask *v.t.* desenmascarar. —*v.i.* desenmascararse.
unmatched *adj.* único; sin par; sin igual.
unmeaning (ʌn'mi·nɪŋ) *adj.* sin sentido; sin expresión.
unmeasured *adj.* ilimitado.
unmentionable *adj.* infando. —**unmentionables,** *n.pl.* ropa interior; prendas íntimas.
unmerciful *adj.* inclemente; despiadado.
unmerited *adj.* inmerecido.
unmethodical *adj.* poco metódico; desarreglado; irregular.
unmindful *adj.* olvidadizo; desatento; descuidado.
unmistakable *adj.* inequívoco.
unmitigated *adj.* 1, (not lessened) no mitigado; no disminuido. 2, (absolute) cabal; absoluto.
unmixed *adj.* puro; sencillo; sin mezcla.
unmolested *adj.* quieto; tranquilo.
unmoor *v.t.* desamarrar.
unmoral *adj.* amoral.
unmounted *adj.* desmontado; no montado.
unmoved *adj.* impasible; inmoto; no conmovido.
unmoving *adj.* 1, (motionless) inmóvil. 2, (lacking appeal) seco; árido.
unmusical *adj.* disonante; discorde.
unmuzzle *v.t.* quitar el bozal a; *fig.* dejar hablar.
unnamed *adj.* innominado; anónimo.
unnatural *adj.* 1, (contrary to nature) innatural; desnaturalizado. 2, (artificial; affected) artificial; afectado.
unnecessary *adj.* innecesario; superfluo; inútil. —**unnecessarily,** *adv.* sin necesidad; inútilmente.
unneeded *adj.* innecesario; no necesitado.
unneedful *adj.* 1, (unnecessary) innecesario; inútil. 2, (not needy) no necesitado; bien provisto.
unneighborly *adj.* adusto; poco sociable.
unnerve (ʌn'nʌɹv) *v.t.* 1, (weaken) enervar; debilitar. 2, (dishearten) acobardar; desanimar.
unnoticeable *adj.* imperceptible; poco llamativo.
unnoticed *adj.* inadvertido; desapercibido; pasado por alto.
unnumbered *adj.* 1, (innumerable) innumerable. 2, (not numbered) sin número; no numerado.
unobjectionable *adj.* irrecusable; irreprensible.
unobliging *adj.* poco servicial; poco atento.
unobservable *adj.* inobservable.
unobservant *adj.* poco observador. —**unobservance,** *n.* inobservancia.
unobserved *adj.* desapercibido.
unobserving *adj.* desatento.
unobstructed *adj.* libre; no obstruido.
unobtainable *adj.* inasequible.
unobtrusive *adj.* discreto; modesto; no intruso.
unoccupied *adj.* 1, (idle) desocupado; ocioso. 2, (vacant) vacante; libre. 3, (untenanted) desalquilado.
unoffending *adj.* inofensivo; inocuo; inocente.
unofficial *adj.* no oficial.
unopened *adj.* cerrado.
unopposed *adj.* sin oposición.
unorganized *adj.* inorganizado.
unorthodox *adj.* heterodoxo.
unostentatious *adj.* modesto; sencillo; no presumido.
unpack *v.t.* desempaquetar; desempacar; desembalar.
unpaid *adj.* no pagado; sin pagar.
unpalatable *adj.* desabrido.
unparalleled *adj.* sin par; sin igual; único.
unpardonable *adj.* imperdonable.
unparliamentary *adj.* no parlamentario.
unpatriotic *adj.* poco patriótico; antipatriótico.
unpaved *adj.* no empedrado; no asfaltado.
unpayable *adj.* impagable.

unpen (ʌn'pɛn) *v.t.* [unpenned, -penning] libertar; soltar del redil.
unpeopled *adj.* despoblado.
unperceivable *adj.* imperceptible. —**unperceived**, *adj.* inadvertido; desapercibido. —**unperceiving**, *adj.* poco perceptivo.
unpersuadable *adj.* impersuasible.
unperturbable *adj.* imperturbable. —**unperturbed**, *adj.* imperturbado.
unpin *v.t.* [unpinned, -pinning] desprender.
unpitying *adj.* inclemente; despiadado: inconmovible.
unplanned *adj.* no planeado; sin planear.
unpleasant *adj.* desagradable; displicente. —**unpleasantness**, *n.* desagrado; disgusto; desazón.
unpleasing *adj.* desagradable; enfadoso.
unplowed *adj.* inculto; no arado.
unplug *v.t.* [unplugged, -plugging] desenchufar.
unplumbed *adj.* 1, (not fathomed) no sondado; insondable. 2, (without plumbing) sin cañerías.
unpolished *adj.* 1, (crude) áspero; rudo; grosero. 2, (not buffed) no pulido; sin bruñir.
unpolluted *adj.* impoluto.
unpopular *adj.* impopular. —**unpopularity**, *n.* impopularidad.
unpracticed *adj.* 1, (unskilled) inexperto; inepto. 2, (not practiced) no practicado.
unprecedented (ʌn'prɛs·ə·dɛnt·ɪd) *adj.* inaudito; sin precedente.
unpredictable *adj.* que no se puede predecir; incierto.
unprejudiced *adj.* no prejuiciado; sin prejuicio; imparcial.
unpremeditated *adj.* impremeditado.
unprepared *adj.* desprevenido; desapercibido. —**unpreparedness**, *n.* desapercibimiento.
unprepossessing *adj.* poco atrayente; feo.
unpresentable *adj.* impresentable.
unpretending *adj.* modesto.
unpretentious *adj.* modesto; sencillo.
unpreventable *adj.* inevitable; ineludible.
unprincipled *adj.* inescrupuloso.
unprintable *adj.* que no se puede imprimir.
unproductive *adj.* improductivo.
unprofessional *adj.* no profesional; impropio de un profesional.
unprofitable *adj.* 1, (not gainful) no lucrativo; poco provechoso. 2, (unavailing) inútil; vano.
unpromising *adj.* poco prometedor.
unpronounceable *adj.* impronunciable.
unpronounced *adj.* inarticulado; no pronunciado.
unpropitious *adj.* no favorable; poco propicio.
unprosperous *adj.* impróspero; desafortunado.
unprotected *adj.* desvalido; desamparado.
unproved *adj.* no probado. *También*, **unproven**.
unprovided *adj.* desprovisto; desapercibido; desprevenido.
unprovoked *adj.* sin motivo; sin provocación.
unpublished *adj.* inédito.
unpunished *adj.* impune.
unqualified *adj.* 1, (incompetent) inhábil; incompetente. 2, (absolute) absoluto; completo.
unquenchable *adj.* 1, (inextinguishable) inextinguible. 2, (insatiable) insaciable.
unquestionable *adj.* indudable; incuestionable; indiscutible.
unquestioned *adj.* indisputable; incontestable.
unquiet *adj.* inquieto; desasosegado.
unquote *v.t. & i.* cerrar la cita.
unravel *v.t.* desenredar; desenmarañar.
unread (ʌn'rɛd) *adj.* 1, (unlearned) indocto. 2, (not read) no leído; sin leer.
unreadable *adj.* ilegible.
unready *adj.* 1, (unprepared) desprevenido. 2, (not quick) lento; torpe; lerdo.
unreal *adj.* irreal.
unreality *n.* irrealidad.
unrealizable *adj.* irrealizable.
unrealized *adj.* no realizado.
unreason *n.* sinrazón; irracionalidad.
unreasonable *adj.* irrazonable; desrazonable.
unreasoning *adj.* irracional.
unreceptive *adj.* poco receptivo; indiferente.

unrecognizable *adj.* irreconocible.
unrecognized *adj.* irreconocido.
unrecorded *adj.* no registrado.
unredeemed *adj.* no redimido.
unreel *v.t.* desenrollar. —*v.i.* desenrollarse.
unrefined *adj.* **1,** (raw) impuro; no refinado. **2,** (lacking polish) tosco; rudo; grosero.
unreflecting *adj.* **1,** (opaque) opaco. **2,** (thoughtless) irreflexivo.
unregenerate *adj.* no regenerado; degenerado.
unrelated *adj.* no relacionado; sin conexión; sin parentesco.
unrelenting *adj.* incompasivo; inflexible; inexorable.
unreliable *adj.* indigno de confianza; incierto. —**unreliability,** *n.* incertidumbre.
unrelieved *adj.* **1,** (not alleviated) no aliviado. **2,** (not helped) no socorrido.
unreligious *adj.* irreligioso.
unremembered *adj.* olvidado.
unremitting *adj.* incansable; constante; incesante.
unremorseful *adj.* impenitente; sin remordimiento.
unremunerative *adj.* poco lucrativo.
unrepentant *adj.* impenitente. *También,* **unrepenting.**
unrepresentative *adj.* anormal; poco típico.
unrepresented *adj.* no representado; sin representación.
unrequited *adj.* no recompensado; no correspondido.
unresentful *adj.* no resentido; sin resentimiento.
unreserved *adj.* **1,** (candid) franco; libre; abierto. **2,** (not restricted) libre; no reservado.
unreservedly (ˌʌn·rɪˈzʌɹ·vɪd·li) *adv.* sin reserva; francamente; sin restricción.
unresisting *adj.* no resistente; sin resistencia. *También,* **unresistant.**
unresolved *adj.* indeciso; no resuelto.
unresponsive *adj.* poco responsivo; desinteresado.
unrest (ʌnˈrɛst) *n.* **1,** (restlessness) inquietud; desasosiego. **2,** (disorder) desorden.
unrestrained *adj.* desenfrenado; libre; suelto. —**unrestraint,** *n.* desenfreno; libertad.
unrestricted *adj.* no restringido; sin restricción.
unrevealed *adj.* oculto; no revelado.
unrewarded *adj.* no recompensado; no premiado.
unrhythmical *adj.* poco rítmico; irregular.
unrig *v.t.* [**unrigged, -rigging**] desaparejar.
unrighteous *adj.* inicuo; perverso; malvado. —**unrighteousness,** *n.* inicuidad; perversidad; maldad.
unrightful *adj.* injusto; ilegítimo.
unripe *adj.* inmaturo; verde.
unrivaled *adj.* sin rival.
unrobe *v.t.* desarropar; desnudar. —*v.i.* desarroparse; desnudarse.
unroll *v.t.* desenrollar; desplegar. —*v.i.* desenrollarse; desplegarse.
unromantic *adj.* poco romántico.
unruffled *adj.* tranquilo; sereno; impertérrito.
unruled *adj.* **1,** (not governed) no gobernado; sin gobierno. **2,** (unlined) sin rayar.
unruly (ʌnˈru·li) *adj.* **1,** (unmanageable) indomable; intratable; indócil; inmanejable. **2,** (disorderly) desordenado. **3,** (mischievous) malmandado; revoltoso; desobediente.
unsaddle *v.t.* desensillar.
unsafe *adj.* peligroso; inseguro. —**unsafety,** *n.* peligro.
unsaid *adj.* no proferido; no dicho. —*v., pret. & p.p. de* **unsay.**
unsaleable *también,* **unsalable** *adj.* invendible.
unsalted *adj.* no salado; sin sal.
unsanctioned *adj.* no sancionado; no autorizado.
unsanitary *adj.* insalubre; antihigiénico.
unsatisfactory *adj.* poco satisfactorio.
unsatisfied *adj.* insatisfecho.
unsatisfying *adj.* que no satisface; inadecuado.
unsavory *adj.* **1,** (tasteless) insípido; soso; desabrido. **2,** (unpleasant) desagradable; displicente. **3,** (disreputable) deshonroso; de mala conducta.
unsay *v.t.* [*pret. & p.p.* **unsaid**] retractar; desdecirse de.
unscathed *adj.* ileso; incólume.
unscheduled *adj.* sin horario fijo; fuera del programa.
unscholarly *adj.* **1,** (unbecoming a scholar) impropio de un erudito.

2, (unschooled) indocto; ignorante.
unschooled *adj.* indocto; ignorante.
unscientific *adj.* poco científico.
unscramble *v.t.* desenredar.
unscratched *adj.* ileso; incólume; sin arañazo alguno.
unscrew *v.t.* destornillar; desenroscar; desvolver.
unscrupulous *adj.* inescrupuloso. —**unscrupulousness,** *n.* inescrupulosidad.
unseal *v.t.* desellar.
unseasonable *adj.* intempestivo; inoportuno; (*of weather*) desabrido.
unseasoned *adj.* 1, (without condiment) soso; no sazonado. 2, (inexperienced) no habituado; inexperto. 3, (not dried or ripened) verde.
unseat *v.t.* 1, (dislodge) quitar del asiento. 2, (remove from office) destituir; echar abajo. 3, (unhorse) desmontar.
unseaworthy *adj.* incapaz de navegar.
unsecured *adj.* no asegurado.
unseeing *adj.* ciego.
unseemly *adj.* indecoroso; impropio. —*adv.* indecorosamente; impropiamente.
unseen *adj.* inadvertido; no visto; invisible.
unselfish *adj.* desinteresado; no egoísta; generoso. —**unselfishness,** *n.* desinterés; generosidad.
unserviceable *adj.* inútil; inservible.
unset *adj.* no puesto; no plantado.
unsettle *v.t.* 1, (disarrange) desarreglar; poner en desorden. 2, (disturb) inquietar; perturbar; trastornar.
unsettled *adj.* 1, (disarranged) desarreglado. 2, (unsteady) inconstante; inestable. 3, (undecided) indeciso; indeterminado. 4, (without settlers) deshabitado; despoblado. 5, (unpaid) no pagado; no saldado.
unsew *v.t.* [*pret.* **unsewed;** *p.p.* **unsewed** *o* **unsewn**] descoser.
unsex *v.t.* quitarle a uno la sexualidad.
unshackle *v.t.* desencadenar; libertar.
unshaded *adj.* sin sombra.
unshakeable *adj.* inmutable; firme; resuelto.
unshaken *adj.* seguro; firme.
unshaped *adj.* informe; sin forma.
unshapely *adj.* desproporcionado; deforme.
unshaven *adj.* sin afeitar; barbudo. *También,* **unshaved.**
unsheathe *v.t.* desenvainar.
unsheltered *adj.* desamparado; desabrigado.
unship *v.t.* [**unshipped, -shipping**] 1, (unload) desembarcar. 2, (dismount) desmontar; desarmar.
unshod *adj.* descalzo; sin herraduras.
unshriven *adj.* inconfeso.
unsightly *adj.* feo; deforme. —**unsightliness,** *n.* fealdad; deformidad.
unsigned *adj.* no firmado; anónimo.
unsingable *adj.* no cantable.
unsinkable *adj.* insumergible.
unskilled *adj.* inhábil; inepto; imperito.
unskillful *adj.* inhábil; inepto; desmañado. —**unskillfulness,** *n.* inhabilidad; ineptitud; impericia.
unslaked *adj.* no apagado. —**unslaked lime,** cal viva.
unsling *v.t.* [*pret. & p.p.* **unslung**] descolgar.
unsmiling *adj.* serio; severo.
unsnap *v.t.* [**unsnapped, -snapping**] desabrochar.
unsnarl *v.t.* desenmarañar; desenredar.
unsociable *adj.* insociable; intratable; malavenido.
unsold *adj.* no vendido.
unsoldierly *adj.* indigno de un soldado.
unsolicited *adj.* insolicitado.
unsolvable *adj.* insoluble.
unsolved *adj.* sin resolver.
unsophisticated *adj.* natural; sencillo.
unsought *adj.* encontrado; aparecido; no buscado.
unsound *adj.* 1, (defective) defectuoso; poco firme. 2, (sickly) enfermizo; achacoso. 3, (false) erróneo; falso; falaz. 4, (rotten) podrido; corrompido.
unsparing *adj.* 1, (lavish) pródigo; generoso; suntuoso. 2, (unmerciful) cruel; despiadado.
unspeakable (ʌnˈspi·kə·bəl) *adj.* 1, (ineffable) inefable; indecible. 2, (execrable) execrable; infando; incalificable.

unspecified *adj.* no especificado.
unspent *adj.* no gastado.
unspoiled *adj.* intacto; natural.
unspoken *adj.* no hablado; callado.
unsportsmanlike *adj.* indigno de un deportista.
unspotted *adj.* inmaculado; sin mancha.
unstable *adj.* **1,** (not firm) inestable. **2,** (changeable) inconstante; mudadizo.
unstained *adj.* **1,** (without blemish) impoluto; inmaculado. **2,** (not tinted) no teñido; sin color.
unstated *adj.* **1,** (not declared) no declarado; no mencionado. **2,** (not fixed) indeterminado.
unstatesmanlike *adj.* indigno de un estadista.
unsteady *adj.* **1,** (unstable) inseguro; inestable. **2,** (shaky) vacilante; tembloroso. **3,** (wobbly) cojo; tembleque. **4,** (wavering) inconstante; irresoluto.
unstick *v.t.* [*pret. & p.p.* **unstuck**] despegar.
unstinted *adj.* no limitado; liberal.
unstinting *adj.* generoso; pródigo; liberal.
unstitch *v.t.* descoser.
unstop *v.t.* [**unstopped, -stopping**] **1,** (uncork) destaponar. **2,** (unclog) desatascar.
unstrained *adj.* natural; liso.
unstrap *v.t.* [**unstrapped, -strapping**] desceñir.
unstressed *adj.* **1,** (without emphasis) sin énfasis. **2,** (unaccented) inacentuado.
unstring *v.t.* [*pret. & p.p.* **unstrung**] **1,** (remove the strings from) desencordar; desencordelar. **2,** (remove from a string) desensartar. **3,** (unnerve) debilitar; enervar; trastornar.
unstrung *v., pret. & p.p. de* **unstring.** —*adj.* debilitado; trastornado.
unstuck *adj.* despegado. —*v., pret. & p.p. de* **unstick.** —**come unstuck,** despegarse.
unstudied *adj.* natural; espontáneo.
unsubdued *adj.* indomado; indómito.
unsubstantial *adj.* insubstancial.
unsubstantiated *adj.* no comprobado; no verificado.
unsuccessful *adj.* infructuoso; sin éxito; fracasado; impróspero.
unsuitable *adj.* **1,** (inappropriate) inadecuado; incongruente; inconveniente. **2,** (unbecoming) impropio. **3,** (incompetent) incompetente; inhábil.
unsuited *adj.* **1,** (inappropriate) inadecuado; impropio; incongruente. **2,** (incompetent) incompetente; ineficaz.
unsullied *adj.* inmaculado.
unsung *adj.* no celebrado; sin honores.
unsupported *adj.* sin sostén; sin apoyo.
unsure *adj.* inseguro; incierto.
unsurpassable *adj.* inmejorable; insuperable.
unsurpassed *adj.* insuperado; sin par.
unsusceptible *adj.* no susceptible; insensible.
unsuspected *adj.* insospechado.
unsuspecting *adj.* no sospechoso; no receloso; confiado. *También,* **unsuspicious.**
unsustained *adj.* sin apoyo; no sostenido.
unsweetened *adj.* no endulzado.
unswept *adj.* polvoriento; no barrido.
unswerving *adj.* fijo; firme; inmutable.
unsworn *adj.* no juramentado.
unsympathetic *adj.* antipático; indiferente.
unsystematic *adj.* sin sistema; poco metódico.
untack *v.t.* quitar las tachuelas a; *sewing* deshilvanar.
untactful *adj.* indiscreto; poco diplomático.
untainted *adj.* incorrupto; inmaculado.
untaken *adj.* no tomado; no cogido.
untamable *también,* **untameable** *adj.* indomable.
untamed *adj.* indómito; indomado.
untangle *adj.* desenredar; desenmarañar; desembarazar.
untapped *adj.* no explotado; no utilizado.
untarnished *adj.* lustroso; no deslucido; no deslustrado; sin mancha.
untasted *adj.* no probado.
untaught (ʌn'tɔt) *adj.* **1,** (uneducated) ineducado; indocto. **2,** (natural) natural; instintivo.

unteachable *adj.* ineducable; indócil.
untenable *adj.* insostenible.
untenanted (ʌn'tɛn·ənt·ɪd) *adj.* desalquilado; desocupado; vacante.
untended *adj.* desatendido.
untested *adj.* no probado.
untether *v.t.* desatar; soltar.
unthankful *adj.* ingrato; desagradecido.
unthinkable *adj.* inconcebible.
unthinking *adj.* descuidado; desatento; irreflexivo.
unthoughtful *adj.* **1,** (inconsiderate) desconsiderado. **2,** = **unthinking.**
unthought-of *adj.* **1,** (not occurring to one's mind) no soñado; no imaginado. **2,** (unforeseen) impensado; imprevisto. **3,** (forgotten) olvidado.
unthread *v.t.* **1,** (ravel) deshilar; deshilachar. **2,** (unstring) desensartar.
unthrifty *adj.* pródigo; manirroto.
unthrone *v.t.* destronar.
untidy *adj.* desaliñado; desaseado. —**untidiness,** *n.* desaliño; desaseo.
untie *v.t.* [**untied, -tying**] desatar; desligar; desamarrar.
until (ʌn'tɪl) *prep.* hasta. —*conj.* hasta que.
untillable *adj.* incultivable; no arable.
untilled *adj.* inculto; no cultivado.
untimely (ʌn'taim·li) *adj.* **1,** (premature) prematuro. **2,** (unseasonable) intempestivo; inoportuno. —*adv.* **1,** (prematurely) prematuramente. **2,** (unseasonably) intempestivamente; a deshora; a destiempo.
untiring *adj.* incansable; infatigable.
unto ('ʌn·tu) *prep., arcaico y poético* a; para; hasta.
untold *adj.* **1,** (not told) no dicho; no narrado. **2,** (incalculable) incalculable.
untouchable *adj.* intocable.
untouched *adj.* **1,** (intact) intacto; ileso. **2,** (unmoved) no conmovido; no afectado.
untoward (ʌn'tord) *adj.* **1,** (unfavorable) desfavorable; displicente. **2,** (unfortunate) desdichado. **3,** (unruly) indócil; intratable.
untrained *adj.* indisciplinado; no adiestrado.
untrammeled *adj.* sin trabas; libre; no impedido.
untranslatable *adj.* intraducible.
untranslated *adj.* no traducido; sin traducir.
untraveled *adj.* **1,** (unfrequented) no frecuentado; aislado; solitario. **2,** (not having traveled) que no ha viajado; hogareño.
untried *adj.* no probado.
untrimmed *adj.* **1,** (unadorned) no guarnecido; sin adorno. **2,** (uncut) no cortado; no afeitado.
untrod *adj.* no pisado; no frecuentado.
untroubled *adj.* **1,** (calm) quieto; tranquilo. **2,** (clear) claro; transparente.
untrue *adj.* **1,** (false) falso; mendaz. **2,** (incorrect) incorrecto; inexacto. **3,** (unfaithful) infiel.
untrustworthy *adj.* indigno de confianza.
untruth *n.* mentira; falsedad. —**untruthful,** *adj.* mentiroso; falso.
untutored *adj.* indocto; ignorante.
untwine *v.t.* **1,** (separate) destorcer; desenroscar. **2,** (disentangle) desenmarañar.
untwist *v.t.* **1,** (untwine) destorcer; desenroscar. **2,** (unravel) desenredar; desenmarañar.
unusable *adj.* inútil; inservible.
unused (ʌn'ju:zd) *adj.* **1,** (not in use) inusitado; desusado. **2,** (unexploited) desaprovechado. **3,** (unaccustomed) no acostumbrado. **4,** (new) nuevo.
unusual *adj.* extraño; raro; extraordinario; desacostumbrado; insólito.
unutterable *adj.* inefable; indecible.
unuttered *adj.* no proferido; callado.
unvanquished *adj.* invicto.
unvaried *adj.* no variado; constante; uniforme.
unvarnished *adj.* **1,** (not varnished) no barnizado; sin barnizar. **2,** (unadorned) sencillo; sin adorno.
unvarying *adj.* invariable.
unveil *v.t.* **1,** (remove the veil from) quitar el velo a. **2,** (reveal) descubrir; revelar. **3,** (inaugurate) inaugurar.
unventilated *adj.* sin ventilación.
unverifiable *adj.* no verificable.
unverified *adj.* no verificado; sin verificar.

unversed *adj.* no versado; poco instruido; inexperto.
unvexed *adj.* quieto; tranquilo; imperturbado.
unvisited *adj.* no visitado.
unvoiced *adj.* **1,** (unexpressed) inarticulado; inexpresado. **2,** *phonet.* sordo; insonoro.
unwanted *adj.* no deseado; despreciado; rechazado.
unwarrantable *adj.* **1,** (unjustifiable) inexcusable; injustificable. **2,** (untenable) insostenible.
unwarranted *adj.* **1,** (unjustified) injustificado. **2,** (improper) indebido. **3,** (unauthorized) desautorizado. **4,** (without guarantee) sin garantía.
unwary *adj.* incauto; imprudente; irreflexivo.
unwashed *adj.* sin lavar; sucio; puerco. —**the great unwashed,** la canalla; el populacho.
unwatched *adj.* no velado; no vigilado; desatendido.
unwavering *adj.* determinado; firme; resuelto.
unwearied *adj.* **1,** (not tired) no cansado. **2,** (tireless) infatigable; incansable.
unwearying *adj.* infatigable; incansable.
unweave *v.t.* [*pret.* **unwove;** *p.p.* **unwoven**] deshilar; destejer.
unwed *adj.* soltero; no casado.
unwelcome *adj.* **1,** (not well received) mal acogido. **2,** (bothersome) importuno; molesto.
unwell *adj.* indispuesto.
unwept *adj.* no llorado; no lamentado.
unwholesome *adj.* malsano; insalubre.
unwieldy (ʌn'wil·di) *adj.* pesado; ponderoso.
unwilling *adj.* desinclinado. —**unwillingly,** *adv.* de mala gana. —**unwillingness,** *n.* mala gana; repugnancia.
unwind (ʌn'waind) *v.t.* [*pret.* & *p.p.* **unwound**] devanar; desenrollar. —*v.i.* devanarse; desenrollarse.
unwise *adj.* **1,** (imprudent) indiscreto; imprudente. **2,** (foolish) tonto; ignorante.
unwitting (ʌn'wɪt·ɪŋ) *adj.* inadvertido; inconsciente. —**unwittingly,** *adv.* inadvertidamente; sin saberlo.
unwomanly *adj.* impropio de una mujer.
unwonted (ʌn'wʌn·tɪd; -'wan-) *adj.* insólito; desacostumbrado.
unworkable *adj.* impracticable.
unworked *adj.* no trabajado; no labrado.
unworkmanlike *adj.* desmañado; chapucero.
unworldly *adj.* no mundano; espiritual.
unworn *adj.* no usado; no gastado; nuevo.
unworthy *adj.* indigno; desmerecedor. —**unworthiness,** *n.* desmerecimiento.
unwound (ʌn'waund) *v., pret.* & *p.p. de* **unwind.**
unwounded (ʌn'wun·dɪd) *adj.* ileso.
unwove *v., pret. de* **unweave.**
unwoven *v., p.p. de* **unweave.** —*adj.* no tejido; sin tejer.
unwrap *v.t.* [**unwrapped, -wrapping**] desenvolver.
unwrinkle *v.t.* estirar; desarrugar. —*v.i.* desarrugarse. —**unwrinkled,** *adj.* sin arrugas; liso.
unwritten *adj.* **1,** (not in writing) no escrito; verbal. **2,** (blank) en blanco. **3,** (traditional) tradicional. —**unwritten law,** ley no escrita.
unyielding *adj.* **1,** (unrelenting) inflexible; inconmovible; inexorable. **2,** (stubborn) terco; reacio. **3,** (unsubdued) indómito; indomado.
unyoke *v.t.* **1,** (release from a yoke) desuncir. **2,** (separate) separar; desunir.
unyouthful *adj.* envejecido; desmejorado.
up (ʌp) *adv.* **1,** (higher) arriba; en lo alto. **2,** (at or to a point of importance) hacia arriba. **3,** (to an equally advanced point) hasta el mismo nivel. **4,** (thenceforth; from a certain time on) en adelante. **5,** (on one's feet) en pie; derecho; *Amer.* parado. **6,** (out of bed) levantado; fuera de cama. **7,** (completely) completamente; todo. **8,** (well prepared; informed) prevenido; informado; versado. **9,** (into activity) en marcha. **10,** (ended) terminado; vencido; cumplido. **11,** (together; close) junto (a). —*prep.* **1,** (to a higher position on or in) a *o* en lo alto de; hacia arriba de. **2,** (farther along) arriba de. **3,** (toward the interior of) en *o* hasta el interior de. —*adj.* **1,**

(going up) ascendente. **2,** (in a higher position) alto; elevado. **3,** (standing) en pie; derecho; *Amer.* parado. **4,** (out of bed) levantado. **5,** (above the horizon) levantado. **6,** (increased; advanced) aumentado; subido. **7,** (ended) terminado; acabado. **8,** (due; payable) vencido. **9,** (in an excited state) airado; animado. **10,** *colloq.* (happening) pasando; sucediendo: *what's up?,* ¿qué pasa? —*n.* **1,** (upward movement or course) elevación; subida. **2,** (improvement) mejoría. —*v.t. colloq.* [**upped, upping**] **1,** (raise) elevar; alzar; subir. **2,** (increase) aumentar. **3,** (bet or bid more than) apostar *o* pujar más que. —*v.i., colloq.* levantarse. —**it's all up (with)**, todo se acabó. —**on the up and up**, *slang* franco; sincero. —**up against**, *colloq.* cara a cara con; frente a. —**up against it**, en apuros. —**up and** (+ *inf.*), *colloq.* hacer (algo) de repente. —**up and about**, levantado. —**up and doing**, activo; ocupado. —**up and down**, arriba y abajo; por todas partes. —**up a tree**, *slang* en apuros. —**ups and downs**, altibajos; vaivenes. —**up there!**, ¡alto ahí! —**up to, 1,** (as far as) hasta. **2,** (equal to; competent for) adecuado para; competente para. **3,** *colloq.* (occupied with) armando; planeando; proyectando. **4,** (dependent or incumbent upon) tocándole a uno; dependiendo a uno: *it's up to you,* a ti toca; depende de ti. —**up to date**, al día; hasta la fecha.

up- (ʌp) *prefijo* **1,** arriba; hacia arriba; en lo alto: *uphill,* cuesta arriba. **2,** recto; derecho: *upstanding,* recto; honroso; *upend,* poner de punta. **3,** hacia el interior: *upcountry,* tierra adentro.

up-and-coming (ˈʌp·ən,kʌm·ɪŋ) *colloq.* emprendedor y prometedor.

upbear *v.t.* [*pret.* **upbore**; *p.p.* **upborne**] sostener; levantar.

upbraid (ʌpˈbreid) *v.t.* reprender; regañar. —**upbraiding**, *n.* reprensión.

upbringing *n.* crianza; educación.

upcountry *n.* interior; serranía. —*adj.* del interior. —*adv.* en *o* hacia el interior; tierra adentro.

upend (ʌpˈɛnd) *v.t.* poner de punta. —*v.i.* ponerse de punta.

upgrade *n.* subida. —*adj.* ascendente. —*adv.* cuesta arriba. —*v.t.* mejorar; adelantar; elevar.

upheaval (ʌpˈhiv·əl) *n.* **1,** (violent upward movement) solevantamiento. **2,** (uprising) sublevación. **3,** (sudden change; upset) trastorno.

upheave *v.t.* solevantar. —*v.i.* solevantarse.

uphill *adv.* cuesta arriba. —*adj.* **1,** (rising) ascendente. **2,** (arduous) difícil; penoso.

uphold *v.t.* [*pret. & p.p.* **upheld**] apoyar; sostener.

upholster (ʌpˈhol·stər) *v.t.* tapizar. —**upholsterer**, *n.* tapicero. —**upholstery**, *n.* tapicería.

upkeep *n.* mantenimiento.

upland (ˈʌp·lənd) *adj.* elevado; alto. —*n.* terreno elevado.

uplift (ʌpˈlɪft) *v.t.* **1,** (raise) levantar. **2,** (edify) edificar; mejorar. —*n.* (ˈʌp·lɪft) **1,** (raising) elevación; levantamiento. **2,** (edification) edificación; mejora.

upmost *adj.* = **uppermost**.

upon (əˈpan) *prep.* **1,** (on) en; sobre; encima de. **2,** (toward) sobre; hacia. **3,** (against) contra. **4,** (following) tras; después de. **5,** (about; concerning) sobre; de; acerca de. **6,** (at the time of) a; al (+ *inf.*). **7,** (in addition to) sobre. —**upon my honor**, a fe mía. —**upon my word**, por mi palabra.

upper (ˈʌp·ər) *adj.* **1,** (higher) superior; más alto; más elevado. **2,** (further inland) interior. **3,** (outer, esp. of garments) exterior. —*n.* **1,** (upper part) parte superior. **2,** (of a shoe) pala. —**on one's uppers**, *colloq.* andrajoso; desastrado; indigente.

upper berth litera alta.

upper case caja alta; (letra) mayúscula; letra de caja alta. —**upper-case**, *adj.* de caja alta; mayúscula; de *o* con mayúsculas.

upperclassman (,ʌp·ərˈklæs·mən) *n.* [*pl.* **-men**] alumno universitario de los dos últimos años.

uppercut *n.* golpe en corto de abajo arriba.

upper deck cubierta alta.

upper hand maestría; dominio; ventaja.

upper house cámara alta.

upper middle class alta burguesía.
uppermost *adj.* **1,** (highest) más alto; más elevado. **2,** (foremost) preeminente; principal; primero. —*adv.* en lo más alto; en primer lugar.
uppish ('ʌp·ɪʃ) *adj., colloq.* altanero; altivo.
upraise (ʌp'reiz) *v.t.* levantar; elevar.
uprear *v.t.* **1,** (raise) levantar; elevar. **2,** (exalt) exaltar. **3,** (bring up) criar; educar. —*v.i.* levantarse.
upright ('ʌp·rait) *adj.* **1,** (vertical) recto; derecho; vertical. **2,** (honest) recto; justo. —*adv.* verticalmente; recto. —*n.* montante; pieza vertical. —**uprightness,** *n.* rectitud; probidad. —**upright piano,** piano vertical.
uprise (ʌp'raiz) *v.i.* [*pret.* **uprose;** *p.p.* **uprisen** (-'rɪz·ən)] **1,** (get up) levantarse. **2,** (ascend) subir; elevarse. **3,** (revolt) sublevarse. —*n.* ('ʌp·raiz) subida.
uprising (ʌp'raiz·ɪŋ) *n.* **1,** (revolt) sublevación; solevantamiento. **2,** (ascent) subida; cuesta.
uproar ('ʌp·ror) *n.* tumulto; alboroto.
uproarious (ʌp'ror·i·əs) *adj.* ruidoso; tumultuoso.
uproot *v.t.* desarraigar; desplantar.
uprose (ʌp'ro:z) *v., pret. de* **uprise.**
uprouse *v.t.* despertar.
upset (ʌp'sɛt) *v.t.* [*pret. & p.p.* **upset;** *ger.* **upsetting**] **1,** (tip over) volcar. **2,** (disturb) trastornar; desordenar. **3,** (defeat) derrotar. —*v.i.* volcarse. —*adj.* **1,** (overturned) volcado. **2,** (disturbed) trastornado; desordenado. **3,** (sick) indispuesto. —*n.* ('ʌp·sɛt) **1,** (overturning) vuelco. **2,** (disturbance) trastorno; desorden. **3,** (illness) indisposición. **4,** (defeat) derrota. —**upsetting,** *adj.* inquietante; desconcertante.
upshot ('ʌp·ʃat) *n.* **1,** (result) resultado; remate; conclusión. **2,** (gist) esencia; quid; suma total.
upside *n.* parte superior.
upside down **1,** (turned over) al revés; lo de arriba abajo. **2,** (confused) trastornado; desordenado. —**turn upside down,** trastornar; desordenar.
upside-down *adj.* **1,** (overturned) al revés. **2,** (confused) trastornado; desordenado.
upstage (ˌʌp'steidʒ) *adj.* **1,** (at the rear of the stage) de fondo. **2,** *colloq.* (haughty) altanero; arrogante. —*adv.* en *o* hacia el fondo de la escena. —*v.t.* **1,** *theat.* ocultar de vista (un actor a otro). **2,** *colloq.* (snub) desdeñar; desairar.
upstairs *adv.* arriba. —*adj.* de arriba. —*n.* piso(s) de arriba.
upstanding *adj.* **1,** (erect) recto; derecho. **2,** (honorable) respetable; honroso.
upstart ('ʌp·start) *n. & adj.* advenedizo; presuntuoso.
upstream *adv.* río arriba; aguas arriba. —*adj.* de río arriba; que va río arriba; ascendente.
uptake *n.* **1,** (ventilating pipe or shaft) tubo *o* conducto de ventilación. **2,** (comprehension) realización; comprensión.
up-to-date ('ʌp·tə'deit) *adj.* al día; moderno; de última moda.
uptown *adj.* de arriba; de lo alto de la ciudad. —*adv.* arriba: en *o* hacia lo alto de la ciudad. —*n.* lo alto de la ciudad.
upturn ('ʌp·tʌɹn) *n.* **1,** (upward turn) vuelta hacia arriba. **2,** (improvement) mejora. —*v.t. & i.* (ʌp'tʌɹn) **1,** (turn up) volver(se) hacia arriba. **2,** (turn over) volcar(se).
upward ('ʌp·wərd) *adv.* [*también,* **upwards**] hacia arriba. —*adj.* ascendente. —**upward(s) of,** más de.
uranium (jʊ'rei·ni·əm) *n.* uranio.
Uranus ('jur·ə·nəs) *n.* Urano.
urban ('ʌɹ·bən) *adj.* urbano.
urbane (ʌɹ'bein) *adj.* cortés; afable; urbano. —**urbanity** (ʌɹ·'bæn·ə·ti) *n.* urbanidad.
urbanize ('ʌɹ·bəˌnaiz) *v.t.* urbanizar. —**urbanization** (-nɪ'zei·ʃən) *n.* urbanización.
urchin ('ʌɹ·tʃɪn) *n.* **1,** (gamin) pilluelo; golfillo. **2,** *zool.* erizo.
-ure (ʊr) *sufijo* -ura; *forma nombres denotando* **1,** acción: *censure,* censura. **2,** agencia; instrumento: *ligature,* ligadura. **3,** condición: *composure,* compostura. **4,** resultado: *discomfiture,* desconcierto. **5,** organismo; colectividad: *prefecture,* prefectura.

urea (jʊ'ri·ə) *n.* urea.

uremia (jʊ'ri·mi·ə) *n.* uremia. —**uremic,** *adj.* urémico.

ureter (jʊ'ri·tər) *n.* uréter.

urethra (jʊ'ri·θrə) *n.* uretra.

urge (ʌɹdʒ) *v.t.* **1,** (advocate strongly) abogar por; empujar. **2,** (drive) impeler; propulsar. **3,** (entreat) instar; solicitar. **4,** (incite) incitar; aguijonear; estimular. **5,** (harry) apremiar; acosar. —*n.* impulso.

urgency ('ʌɹ·dʒən·si) *n.* **1,** (necessity) urgencia. **2,** (insistence) instancia; insistencia.

urgent ('ʌɹ·dʒənt) *adj.* urgente. —**be urgent,** instar; urgir; ser urgente.

urgently ('ʌɹ·dʒənt·li) *adv.* urgentemente; de urgencia; de emergencia.

urging ('ʌɹ·dʒɪŋ) *n.* instancia; insistencia.

-uria (ʊr·i·ə) *sufijo* -uria; orina; condición patológica de la orina: *albuminuria,* albuminuria.

uric ('jʊr·ɪk) *adj.* úrico.

urinal ('jʊr·ɪ·nəl) *n.* **1,** (receptacle) orinal. **2,** (place) urinario; urinal.

urinalysis (ˌjʊr·ɪ'næl·ə·sɪs) *n.* urinálisis; uranálisis.

urinary ('jʊr·ɪ·nɛr·i) *adj.* urinario; urinal.

urinate ('jʊr·ɪˌneit) *v.t. & i.* orinar.

urination (ˌjʊr·ɪ'nei·ʃən) urinación; micción.

urine ('jʊr·ɪn) *n.* orina; orines (*pl.*).

urn (ʌɹn) *n.* **1,** (vase) urna. **2,** (container for coffee or tea) cafetera *o* tetera con grifo.

uro- (jʊr·ə) *prefijo* uro-; orina; sistema urinario: *uroscopy,* uroscopia; *urology,* urología.

urology (jʊr'al·ə·dʒi) *n.* urología. —**urological** (-ə'ladʒ·ɪ·kəl) *adj.* urológico. —**urologist,** *n.* urólogo.

Ursa Major ('ʌɹ·sə) Osa Mayor. —**Ursa Minor,** Osa Menor.

ursine ('ʌɹ·sain) *adj.* ursino; úrsido; del oso.

urticaria (ˌʌɹ·tə'kɛr·i·ə) *n.* urticaria.

us (ʌs) *pron.pers. m. & f. pl.* **1,** *como complemento de verbo* nos. **2,** *como complemento de prep.* nosotros; *fem.* nosotras. **3,** *tras* **than,** *en comparaciones* nosotros; *fem.* nosotras.

usable *también,* **useable** ('juz·ə·bəl) *adj.* útil; utilizable; servible. —**usability; useability,** *n.* utilidad.

usage ('ju·sɪdʒ) *n.* **1,** (use) uso; empleo. **2,** (custom) uso; usanza; costumbre. **3,** (treatment) trato; tratamiento.

use (juːz) *v.t.* **1,** (employ) usar; emplear. **2,** (behave toward; treat) tratar. **3,** (consume) agotar; consumir; gastar. —*v.i., con inf.* soler; acostumbrar; tener costumbre (de): *We used to visit them every week,* Solíamos visitarlos todas las semanas. —*n.* (jus) **1,** (act or result of using) uso. **2,** (employment) uso; empleo. **3,** (custom) uso; costumbre. **4,** (need) necesidad. **5,** (purpose) motivo. —**be of no use,** no servir para nada; ser inútil. —**have no use for, 1,** (have no need of) no necesitar; no servirse de. **2,** (have dislike or distaste for) tener en poco; no querer saber de. —**in use,** en uso; que se usa; ocupado. —**make use of,** servirse de; utilizar; hacer uso de. —**of use,** útil; que sirve. —**out of use,** fuera de uso; desusado; inusitado; fuera de moda. —**put to use,** servirse de; utilizar. —**used to,** acostumbrado a. —**get** (*o* **become**) **used to,** acostumbrarse a. —**use up, 1,** (use completely) usar todo; usar completamente; agotar. **2,** (fatigue) cansar; fatigar; rendir.

useful ('jus·fəl) *adj.* útil. —**usefulness,** *n.* utilidad.

useless ('jus·ləs) *adj.* inútil. —**uselessness,** *n.* inutilidad.

user ('juz·ər) *n.* **1,** (one who uses) el que usa. **2,** (consumer) consumidor.

usher ('ʌʃ·ər) *n.* **1,** (doorkeeper) ujier; portero. **2,** (person who assists in seating) acomodador. —*v.t.* **1,** (show to a seat) acomodar. **2,** (introduce) introducir; anunciar.

usherette (ˌʌʃ·ər'ɛt) *n.* acomodadora.

usual ('ju·ʒʊ·əl) *adj.* usual; común; acostumbrado. —**as usual,** como de costumbre.

usually ('ju·ʒu·ə·li) *adv.* usual-

mente; comúnmente; por lo común.
usualness ('ju·ʒu·əl·nəs) *n.* costumbre; frecuencia.
usufruct ('ju·zju,frʌkt) *n.* usufructo.
usurer ('ju·ʒər·ər) *n.* usurero.
usurious (ju'ʒur·i·əs) *adj.* usurario.
usurp (ju'sʌɹp) *v.t.* usurpar. —**usurpation,** *n.* usurpación. —**usurper,** *n.* usurpador.
usury ('ju·ʒə·ri) *n.* usura.
utensil (ju'tɛn·səl) *n.* utensilio.
uterus ('ju·tər·əs) *n.* [*pl.* **-i** (ai)] útero. —**uterine** (-ɪn) *adj.* uterino.
utilitarian (ju,tɪl·ə'tɛr·i·ən) *adj.* utilitario. —*adj.* & *n.* utilitarista. —**utilitarianism,** *n.* utilitarismo.
utility (ju'tɪl·ə·ti) *n.* **1,** (usefulness) utilidad. **2,** (public service) empresa de servicio público.
utilize ('ju·tə,laiz) *v.t.* utilizar; usar. —**utilizable,** *adj.* utilizable. —**utilization** (-lɪ'zei·ʃən) *n.* uso; utilización.
utmost ('ʌt·most) *adj.* **1,** (extreme) sumo; extremo; supremo. **2,** (last) último. **3,** (farthest) más lejano. **4,** (greatest) mayor; más grande. —*n.* lo sumo; lo mayor. —**do one's utmost,** hacer todo lo posible; hacer cuanto pueda.
Utopia, utopia (ju'to·pi·ə) *n.* utopía; utopia. —**Utopian; utopian** *adj.* utópico. —*n.* & *adj.* utopista. —**utopianism,** *n.* utopismo.
utter ('ʌt·ər) *v.t.* proferir; pronunciar; expresar. —*adj.* cabal; completo; total; absoluto.
utterance ('ʌt·ər·əns) *n.* pronunciación; expresión; declaración.
utterly ('ʌt·ər·li) *adv.* cabalmente; totalmente; completamente.
uttermost ('ʌt·ər·most) *adj.* & *n.* = **utmost.**
uvula ('ju·vjə·lə) *n.* [*pl.* **-las** *o* **-lae** (li)] úvula. —**uvular,** *adj.* uvular.
uxoricide (ʌk'sor·ɪ·said) *n.* **1,** (act) uxoricidio. **2,** (agent) uxoricida.
uxorious (ʌk'sor·i·əs) *adj.* gurrumino. —**uxoriousness,** *n.* gurrumina; condescendencia.

V

V, v (vi) vigésima segunda letra del alfabeto inglés.
vacancy ('vei·kən·si) *n.* **1,** (emptiness) vacío. **2,** (unfilled position) vacante; vacancia. **3,** (untenanted quarters) apartamento *o* habitación vacante.
vacant ('vei·kənt) *adj.* **1,** (empty) vacío. **2,** (unoccupied) vacante. **3,** (untenanted) desalquilado. **4,** (free; devoid of activity) libre. **5,** (empty of thought) vago; necio.
vacate ('vei·keit) *v.t.* **1,** (leave unoccupied) vacar; vaciar; desocupar. **2,** *law* anular; revocar. —*v.i., colloq.* irse; salir; marcharse.
vacation (ve'kei·ʃən) *n.* vacación; vacaciones. —*v.i.* pasar las vacaciones; estar de vacaciones. —**on vacation,** de vacaciones.
vaccine ('væk·sin) *n.* vacuna. —**vaccinate** (-sə·neit) *v.t.* vacunar. —**vaccination,** *n.* vacunación.
vacillate ('væs·ə·leit) *v.i.* vacilar. —**vacillation,** *n.* vaivén; vacilación.
vacuole ('væk·ju,ol) *n.* vacuola.
vacuous ('væk·ju·əs) *adj.* **1,** (empty) vacuo; vacío. **2,** (inane) necio; mentecato. —**vacuity** (væ'kju·ə·ti) *n.* vacuidad; vaciedad.
vacuum ('væk·ju·əm) *n.* [*pl.* **vacuums** *o* **vacua** (-ə)] vacío. —**vacuum bottle,** termos. —**vacuum cleaner,** aspiradora. —**vacuum tube,** tubo al vacío.
vagabond ('væg·ə,band) *adj.* & *n.* vagabundo. —**vagabondage,** *n.* vagabundeo.
vagary (və'gɛr·i) *n.* capricho.
vagina (və'dʒai·nə) *n.* vagina. —**vaginal** ('vædʒ·ɪ·nəl) *adj.* vaginal.
vaginate ('vædʒ·ɪ·neit) *adj.* envainado.
vagrant ('vei·grənt) *adj.* vagante; vagabundo. —*n.* vago; vagante; vagabundo.
vague (veig) *adj.* vago; indeterminado. —**vagueness,** *n.* vaguedad.

vain (vein) *adj.* **1,** (empty; futile) vano; inútil. **2,** (conceited) vano; vanidoso; presuntuoso. —**vainness,** *n.* vanidad. —**in vain,** inútilmente; en vano.
vainglory (vein'glo·ri) *n.* vanagloria. —**vainglorious,** *adj.* vanaglorioso.
vainly ('vein·li) *adv.* **1,** (in vain) inútilmente; en vano. **2,** (conceitedly) vanidosamente; presuntuosamente.
valance ('væl·əns) *n.* cenefa.
vale (veil) *n.* valle.
valedictory (ˌvæl·ə'dɪk·tə·ri) *adj.* de despedida. —*n.* discurso de despedida.
valence ('vei·ləns) *n.* valencia.
-valent (vei·lənt) *sufijo, quím.* -valente: *forma adjetivos denotando* valencia: *monovalent,* monovalente.
valentine ('væl·ənˌtain) *n.* **1,** (greeting) tarjeta de San Valentín. **2,** (sweetheart) amado *o* amada del día de San Valentín. —**St. Valentine's Day,** día de los enamorados; día de San Valentín.
valet ('væl·ət; væ'lei) *n.* ayuda de cámara.
valiant ('væl·jənt) *adj.* valiente; valeroso. —**valiancy,** *n.* valentía; valor.
valid ('væl·ɪd) *adj.* válido.
validate ('væl·əˌdeit) *v.t.* validar. —**validation,** *n.* validación.
validity (və'lɪd·ə·ti) *n.* validez.
valise (və'lis) *n.* valija; maleta; *Amer.* velís.
valley ('væl·i) *n.* valle.
valor *también, Brit.,* **valour** ('væl·ər) *n.* valor.
valorous ('væl·ər·əs) *adj.* valeroso.
valuable ('væl·ju·ə·bəl) *adj.* valioso; de valor. —**valuables,** *n.pl.* objetos de valor. —**valuableness,** *n.* valor.
valuation (ˌvæl·ju'ei·ʃən) *n.* **1,** (appraisal) valuación; valoración. **2,** (assessment) tasa; tasación.
value ('væl·ju) *n.* valor. —*v.t.* **1,** (estimate the value of) valuar; valorar. **2,** (esteem) estimar; apreciar.
valued ('væl·jud) *adj.* **1,** (estimated) valorado. **2,** (esteemed) estimado; apreciado.
valueless ('væl·ju·ləs) *adj.* sin valor.
valve (vælv) *n.* **1,** *anat.; mech.* válvula. **2,** *bot.; zool.* valva. **3,** *music* llave.
valvular ('væl·vjə·lər) *adj.* valvular.
vamoose (væ'mus) *v.i., slang* largarse; marcharse.
vamp (væmp) *n.* **1,** (of a shoe) pala. **2,** (patch) remiendo; parche. **3,** *music* acompañamiento improvisado. **4,** (scheming woman) vampiresa. —*v.t. & i.* **1,** (patch) remendar; *Amer.* parchar. **2,** *music* improvisar. **3,** *slang* (flirt) coquetear (con).
vampire ('væm·pair) *n.* vampiro.
van (væn) *n.* **1,** (wagon; truck) carro de carga; camión. **2,** *Brit.* (baggage or freight car) furgón de equipajes. **3,** (vanguard) vanguardia.
vanadium (və'nei·di·əm) *n.* vanadio.
vandal ('væn·dəl) *n.* vándalo. —*adj.* vándalo; vandálico. —**vandalism,** *n.* vandalismo.
vandyke (væn'daik) *n.* barba puntiaguda. *También,* **Vandyke beard.**
vane (vein) *n.* **1,** (weathercock) veleta. **2,** (of a propeller) paleta. **3,** (of a windmill) aspa.
vanguard ('væn·gard) *n.* vanguardia.
vanilla (və'nɪl·ə) *n.* vainilla.
vanish ('væn·ɪʃ) *v.i.* desvanecerse; desaparecer.
vanity ('væn·ə·ti) *n.* **1,** (pride; emptiness; futility) vanidad. **2,** (cosmetic case) estuche de afeites; neceser. **3,** (dressing table) tocador.
vanquish ('væŋ·kwɪʃ) *v.t.* vencer; conquistar. —**vanquisher,** *n.* vencedor; conquistador.
vantage ('væn·tɪdʒ) *n.* ventaja; superioridad. —**vantage point; vantage ground,** posición de ventaja.
vapid ('væp·ɪd) *adj.* soso; insípido.
vapidity (və'pɪd·ə·ti) *n.* insipidez.
vapor ('vei·pər) *n.* **1,** (mist; steam) vapor. **2,** (fog) niebla; bruma. **3,** (fumes) vaho; exhalación; humo.
vaporize ('vei·pərˌaiz) *v.t.* vaporizar. —*v.i.* vaporizarse. —**vaporization** (-ɪ'zei·ʃən) *n.* vaporización. —**vaporizer,** *n.* vaporizador.
vaporous ('vei·pər·əs) *adj.* **1,**

(misty) vaporoso. 2, (fleeting) fugaz. 3, (fanciful) vano; quimérico. —vaporousness, n. vaporosidad.

variable ('vɛr·i·ə·bəl) *adj. & n.* variable. —variability, *n.* variabilidad.

variance ('vɛr·i·əns) *n.* 1, (change) variación. 2, (difference) diferencia; discrepancia. 3, (disagreement) desacuerdo; desavenencia. —at variance, en desacuerdo; reñido.

variant ('vɛr·i·ənt) *adj. & n.* variante.

variation (ˌvɛr·i'ei·ʃən) *n.* variación.

varicella (ˌvær·ə'sɛl·ə) *n.* varicela.

varicocele (ˌvær·ə·ko'siːl) *n.* varicocela.

varicolored ('vær·iˌkʌl·ərd) *adj.* abigarrado.

varicose ('vær·ɪˌkos) *adj.* varicoso. —varicosity (-'kas·ə·ti) *n.* varicosidad. —varicose veins, varicosis.

varied ('vɛr·id) *adj.* variado.

variegate ('vɛr·i·əˌgeit) *v.t.* jaspear; motear. —variegated, *adj.* jaspeado; moteado; abigarrado.

variety (və'rai·ə·ti) *n.* variedad.

variola (və'rai·ə·lə) *n.* viruela; variola.

various ('vɛr·i·əs) *adj.* vario; diferente; diverso. —variousness, *n.* diversidad.

varlet ('var·lɪt) *n., archaic* 1, (attendant) lacayo. 2, (rascal) truhán; bribón. —varletry, *n.* chusma.

varmint ('var·mənt) *n., dial.* 1, (bug) bicho. 2, (despicable person) pícaro; tunante.

varnish ('var·nɪʃ) *n.* barniz. —*v.t.* barnizar.

varsity ('var·sə·ti) *n.* equipo universitario. —*adj.* universitario.

vary ('vɛr·i) *v.t. & i.* variar.

vascular ('væs·kjə·lər) *adj.* vascular.

vase (veis) *n.* vaso; jarrón.

vaseline (ˌvæs·ə'liːn) *n.* vaselina.

vaso- (væs·o) *prefijo* vaso-; vaso; tubo; canal: *vasomotor,* vasomotor.

vassal ('væs·əl) *n. & adj.* vasallo. —vassalage, *n.* vasallaje.

vast (væst) *adj.* vasto. —vastly, *adv.* en sumo grado; muy; mucho. —vastness, *n.* vastedad.

vat (væt) *n.* tina; cuba; tonel.

Vatican ('væt·ɪ·kən) *n.* Vaticano. —*adj.* vaticano.

vaudeville ('vod·vɪl) *n.* zarzuela; variedades (*pl.*); vodevil. —vaudevillian (vod'vɪl·jən) *n.* zarzuelista; comediante.

vault (volt) *n.* 1, (arched roof or chamber) bóveda. 2, (storage cellar) cueva; bodega. 3, (safe) caja de caudales. 4, (leap) salto. —*v.t.* (arch) abovedar. —*v.t. & i.* (leap) saltar. —vaulted, *adj.* abovedado.

vaunt (vont) *v.t.* ostentar; jactarse de. —*v.i.* jactarse. —*n.* jactancia. —vaunting, *adj.* jactancioso.

V-Day día de la victoria.

veal (viːl) *n.* ternera; carne de ternera.

vector ('vɛk·tər) *n.* vector. —*adj.* vector; vectorial.

vedette (və'dɛt) *n.* 1, *mil.* centinela avanzada de a caballo. 2, *naval* buque escucha.

veep (vip) *n., slang* vicepresidente.

veer (vɪr) *v.t. & i.* 1, (turn) virar. 2, *naut.* (let out) soltar(se); aflojar(se). —*n.* virada.

vegetable ('vɛdʒ·tə·bəl) *n.* hortaliza; legumbre; vegetal. —*adj.* vegetal.

vegetal ('vɛdʒ·ə·təl) *adj.* vegetal.

vegetarian (ˌvɛdʒ·ə'tɛr·i·ən) *n. & adj.* vegetariano.

vegetate ('vɛdʒ·əˌteit) *v.i.* vegetar. —vegetation, *n.* vegetación. —vegetative, *adj.* vegetativo.

vehemence ('vi·ə·məns) *n.* vehemencia.

vehement ('vi·ə·mənt) *adj.* vehemente.

vehicle ('vi·ə·kəl) *n.* vehículo. —vehicular (vi'hɪk·jə·lər) *adj.* de o para vehículos.

veil (veil) *n.* velo. —*v.t.* velar.

vein (vein) *n.* vena. —*v.t.* vetear; jaspear. —veined, *adj.* venoso; veteado. —veiny, *adj.* venoso; veteado.

velar ('vi·lər) *adj.* velar.

vellum ('vɛl·əm) *n.* 1, (skin) vitela. 2, (paper) pergamino.

velocipede (və'las·əˌpid) *n.* velocípedo.

velocity (və'las·ə·ti) *n.* velocidad.

velodrome ('vɛl·əˌdroːm) *n.* velódromo.

velours (və'lʊr) *n.* terciopelado.

velum ('vi·ləm) *n.* velo del paladar.
velure (və'lʊr) *n.* terciopelado.
velvet ('vɛl·vɪt) *n.* terciopelo. —*adj.* de terciopelo; aterciopelado. —**velvety,** *adj.* aterciopelado.
velveteen (ˌvɛl·və'tiːn) *n.* veludillo.
venal ('vi·nəl) *adj.* venal; mercenario.
venality (vi'næl·ə·ti) *n.* venalidad.
vend (vɛnd) *v.t.* & *i.* vender. —**vender,** *n.* vendedor. —**vendible,** *adj.* vendible. —**vending machine,** vendedora automática; *W.I.* vellonera.
vendetta (vɛn'dɛt·ə) *n.* vendetta.
vendor ('vɛn·dər) *n.* vendedor.
veneer (və'nɪr) *n.* **1,** (thin covering) chapa; enchapado. **2,** (appearance) apariencia. —*v.t.* **1,** (cover with a thin layer) enchapar. **2,** (disguise) disfrazar.
venerable ('vɛn·ər·ə·bel) *adj.* venerable. —**venerability; venerableness,** *n.* venerabilidad.
venerate ('vɛn·əˌreit) *v.t.* venerar. —**veneration,** *n.* veneración.
venereal (və'nɪr·i·əl) *adj.* venéreo.
Venetian (və'ni·ʃən) *adj.* & *n.* veneciano.
Venetian blind veneciana; persiana.
vengeance ('vɛn·dʒəns) *n.* venganza. —**take vengeance,** vengarse. —**with a vengeance, 1,** (furiously) con violencia. **2,** (extremely) extremamente; con extremo.
vengeful ('vɛndʒ·fəl) *adj.* vengativo. —**vengefulness,** *n.* calidad de vengativo.
venial ('vi·ni·əl) *adj.* venial; remisible.
veniality (ˌvi·ni'æl·ə·ti) *n.* venialidad.
venire (vɪ'nai·ri) *n.* orden de convocación del jurado.
venireman (vɪ'nai·ri·mən) *n.* [*pl.* **-men**] jurado; persona llamada para jurado.
venison ('vɛn·ə·zən) *n.* venado; carne de venado.
venom ('vɛn·əm) *n.* veneno. —**venomous,** *adj.* venenoso.
venous ('vi·nəs) *adj.* venoso.
vent (vɛnt) *n.* **1,** (release) desahogo; expresión. **2,** (opening) orificio; agujero. **3,** (air hole) respiradero. **4,** (opening in a garment) abertura. **5,** *zool.* ano. —*v.t.* **1,** (make an opening in) proveer de abertura; abrir un respiradero en. **2,** (allow to escape) dar salida a; dejar escapar. **3,** (give release to) desahogar; expresar. —**give vent to,** desahogar. —**vent one's feelings,** desahogarse.
ventilate ('vɛn·tə·leit) *v.t.* ventilar. —**ventilation,** *n.* ventilación. —**ventilator,** *n.* ventilador.
ventral ('vɛn·trəl) *adj.* ventral.
ventricle ('vɛn·trɪ·kəl) *n.* ventrículo.
ventricular (vɛn'trɪk·ju·lər) *adj.* ventricular.
ventriloquism (vɛn'trɪl·ə·kwɪz·əm) *n.* ventriloquía. —**ventriloquist,** *n.* ventrílocuo.
venture ('vɛn·tʃər) *n.* empresa arriesgada; riesgo. —*v.t.* aventurar; arriesgar. —*v.i.* osar; aventurarse; arriesgarse. —**venturesome,** *adj.* atrevido; aventurado; emprendedor. —**venturous,** *adj.* osado; atrevido; aventurado. —**venturousness,** *n.* arrojo; osadía. —**at a venture,** a la ventura.
venue ('vɛn·ju) *n.* jurisdicción en que se ha cometido un crimen o donde tiene lugar el proceso. —**change of venue,** cambio de tribunal en un pleito.
Venus ('vi·nəs) *n.* Venus.
veracious (və'rei·ʃəs) *adj.* verdadero; veraz; verídico. —**veraciousness; veracity** (və'ræs·ə·ti) *n.* veracidad.
veranda (və'ræn·də) *n.* pórtico; veranda.
verb (vʌɹb) *n.* verbo. —*adj.* verbal. —**verbal,** *adj.* verbal.
verbalize ('vʌɹ·bəl·aiz) *v.t.* **1,** (express in words) expresar por medio de palabras. **2,** *gram.* (make into a verb) transformar en verbo. —*v.i.* ser verboso; expresarse con verbosidad.
verbatim (vʌɹ'bei·təm) *adj.* & *adv.* al pie de la letra; verbatim.
verbena (vʌɹ'bi·nə) *n.* verbena.
verbiage ('vʌɹ·bi·ɪdʒ) *n.* verbosidad; verborrea.
verbose (vər'bos) *adj.* verboso. —**verbosity** (-'bas·ə·ti) *n.* verbosidad; verborrea.
verdant ('vʌɹ·dənt) *adj.* **1,** (green) verdeante. **2,** (inexperienced) inexperto; verde. —**verdancy,** *n.* verdura; verdor.

verdict ('vʌɹ·dɪkt) *n.* veredicto; fallo; decisión.
verdigris ('vʌɹ·də,gris) *n.* verdete.
verdure ('vʌɹ·dʒər) *n.* verdura; verdor.
verge (vʌɹdʒ) *n.* **1,** (edge; brink) borde; margen. **2,** (limit; boundary) linde; lindero; confín. **3,** (shaft of a column) fuste. **4,** (rod; staff) vara. —*v.i.* **1,** (tend) tender; inclinarse. **2,** (approach) acercarse; aproximarse. —**on the verge of,** al borde de; a punto de; a dos dedos de. —**verge on** *o* **upon,** rayar en; acercarse a.
verger ('vʌɹ·dʒər) *n.* **1,** (staff bearer) macero. **2,** (church attendant) sacristán.
veriest ('vɛr·i·ɪst) *adj.* extremo; sumo.
verify ('vɛr·ə·fai) *v.t.* verificar. —**verifiable,** *adj.* verificable. —**verification** (-fɪ'kei·ʃən) *n.* verificación.
verily ('vɛr·ə·li) *adv.* verdaderamente; de *o* en verdad.
verisimilitude (,vɛr·ɪ·sɪ'mɪl·ə·tjud) *n.* verosimilitud.
veritable ('vɛr·ɪ·tə·bəl) *adj.* verdadero. —**veritably** (-bli) *adv.* verdaderamente.
verity ('vɛr·ə·ti) *n.* verdad; realidad.
vermi- (vʌɹ·mə) *prefijo* vermi-; gusano; lombriz: *vermicide,* vermicida.
vermicelli (,vʌɹ·mə'sɛl·i) *n.* fideos.
vermicide ('vʌɹ·mɪ·said) *n.* vermicida. —**vermicidal** (-'sai·dəl) *adj.* vermicida.
vermicular (vʌɹ'mɪk·jʊ·lər) *adj.* vermicular.
vermiculate (vʌɹ'mɪk·jʊ·lət) *adj.* vermicular.
vermiform ('vʌɹ·mə·form) *adj.* vermiforme.
vermifuge ('vʌɹ·mə,fjudʒ) *adj.* & *n.* vermífugo.
vermillion (vər'mɪl·jən) *n.* bermellón. —*adj.* bermejo.
vermin ('vʌɹ·mɪn) *n.* sabandija; bicho; gusano. —**verminous,** *adj.* verminoso.
vermouth (vər'muθ) *n.* vermut.
vernacular (vər'næk·jə·lər) *adj.* & *n.* vernáculo.
vernal ('vʌɹ·nəl) *adj.* **1,** (of spring) vernal. **2,** (of youth) juvenil.
vernier ('vʌɹ·ni·ər) *n.* vernier.
veronica (və'ran·ə·kə) *n.* verónica.
versatile ('vʌɹ·sə·tɪl) *adj.* **1,** (adaptable) flexible; hábil para muchas cosas. **2,** *bot.; zool.* versátil.
versatility (vʌɹ·sə'tɪl·ə·ti) *n.* **1,** (adaptability) flexibilidad; habilidad para muchas cosas. **2,** *bot.; zool.* versatilidad.
verse (vʌɹs) *n.* verso; *Bib.* versículo.
versed (vʌɹst) *adj.* versado.
versify ('vʌɹ·sə·fai) *v.t.* & *i.* versificar. —**versification** (-fɪ'kei·ʃən) *n.* versificación.
version ('vʌɹ·ʒən) *n.* versión.
verso ('vʌɹ·so) *n.* **1,** (left-hand page) verso; vuelto. **2,** (reverse side) reverso; revés.
versus ('vʌɹ·səs) *prep.* versus; contra; en contra de.
vertebra ('vʌɹ·tə·brə) *n.* [*pl.* **-brae** (bri) *o* **bras**] vértebra. —**vertebral,** *adj.* vertebral.
vertebrate ('vʌɹ·tə·breit) *adj.* & *n.* vertebrado.
vertex ('vʌɹ·tɛks) *n.* **1,** (highest point) cima; cumbre; ápice. **2,** *anat.; math.* vértice. **3,** *astron.* cenit.
vertical ('vʌɹ·tə·kəl) *adj.* & *n.* vertical.
vertiginous (vər'tɪdʒ·ə·nəs) *adj.* vertiginoso.
vertigo ('vʌɹ·tə·go) *n.* vértigo.
verve (vʌɹv) *n.* entusiasmo; viveza; vigor.
very ('vɛr·i) *adv.* muy; mucho. —*adj.* **1,** (true; genuine) verdadero. **2,** (self; same) mismo. **3,** (in the fullest sense) completo; cabal. **4,** (pure; simple) mero; puro. —**the very same,** el mismo.
vesicle ('vɛs·ə·kəl) *n.* vesícula.
vesicular (vɛ'sɪk·jʊ·lər) *adj.* vesicular.
vesiculate (vɛ'sɪk·jʊ,leit) *adj.* vesiculoso.
vesper ('vɛs·pər) *n.* **1,** (evening) tarde; anochecer; víspera. **2,** *pl.* (religious service) vísperas. —*adj.* vespertino.
vespertine ('vɛs·pər·tɪn; -tain) *adj.* vespertino.
vessel ('vɛs·əl) *n.* **1,** (ship) bajel; buque. **2,** (container) vasija. **3,** *anat.; bot.* vaso.
vest (vɛst) *n.* chaleco. —*v.t.* **1,** (clothe) vestir. **2,** (give possession

of) investir; conceder; dar posesión de. 3, (endow) investir (de); revestir (de).
vestal ('vɛs·təl) *adj.* & *n.* vestal.
vested ('vɛst·ɪd) *adj.* 1, (clothed) vestido. 2, (established) revestido; establecido. — **vested interests,** intereses creados.
vestibule ('vɛs·tə,bjul) *n.* vestíbulo; zaguán.
vestige ('vɛs·tɪdʒ) *n.* vestigio.
vestigial (vɛs'tɪdʒ·i·əl) *adj.* vestigial; rudimentario.
vestment ('vɛst·mənt) *n.* vestimenta; vestidura.
vest-pocket *adj.* para el bolsillo del chaleco; de bolsillo; diminuto; en miniatura.
vestry ('vɛs·tri) *n.* 1, (room) vestuario; sacristía. 2, (chapel) capilla. 3, (church council) junta parroquial.
vestryman ('vɛs·tri·mən) *n.* [*pl.* **-men**] miembro de la junta parroquial.
vet (vɛt) *n., colloq.* 1, = **veteran.** 2, = **veterinary** *o* **veterinarian.** —*v.t., colloq.* examinar; revisar.
vetch (vɛtʃ) *n.* arveja.
veteran ('vɛt·ər·ən) *n.* & *adj.* veterano.
veterinarian (,vɛt·ər·ə'nɛr·i·ən) *n.* veterinario.
veterinary ('vɛt·ər·ə·nɛr·i) *adj.* & *n.* veterinario. —**veterinary medicine,** veterinaria.
veto ('vi·to) *n.* veto. —*adj.* del veto. —*v.t.* vetar.
vex (vɛks) *v.t.* vejar; molestar; irritar.
vexation (vɛks'ei·ʃən) *n.* vejación; molestia.
vexatious (vɛks'ei·ʃəs) *adj.* vejatorio; penoso; enfadoso.
via ('vai·ə; 'vi·ə) *prep.* vía.
viability (,vai·ə'bɪl·ə·ti) *n.* viabilidad.
viable ('vai·ə·bəl) *adj.* viable.
viaduct ('vai·ə·dʌkt) *n.* viaducto.
vial ('vai·əl) *n.* frasco; redoma; ampolleta.
viand ('vai·ənd) *n.* vianda. —**viands,** *n.pl.* manjares delicados; vitualla.
viaticum (vai'æt·ə·kəm) *n.* viático.
vibrancy ('vai·brən·si) *n.* vibración; viveza.
vibrant ('vai·brənt) *adj.* vibrante.
vibrate ('vai·breit) *v.t.* & *i.* vibrar. —**vibratile** (-brə·tɪl) *adj.* vibrátil. —**vibration,** *n.* vibración. —**vibrator,** *n.* vibrador. —**vibratory** (-brə·tor·i) *adj.* vibratorio; vibrador.
vicar ('vɪk·ər) *n.* vicario. —**vicarage,** *n.* vicaría.
vicarial (vai'kɛr·i·əl) *adj.* vicario.
vicariate (vai'kɛr·i·ɪt) *n.* vicaría; vicariato.
vicarious (vai'kɛr·i·əs) *adj.* vicario. —**vicariousness,** *n.* calidad de vicario.
vicarship ('vɪk·ər·ʃɪp) *n.* vicaría; vicariato.
vice (vais) *n.* 1, (evil; defect) vicio. 2, = **vise.** —*prep.* en lugar de; en vez de.
vice- (vais) *prefijo* vice-. 1, substituto: *vice-president,* vicepresidente. 2, del segundo grado o rango: *vice-consul,* vicecónsul. *También,* **vis-,** en *viscount,* vizconde.
vice-admiral *n.* vicealmirante.
vice-president *n.* vicepresidente. —**vice-presidency,** *n.* vicepresidencia.
viceregal (vais'ri·gəl) *adj.* virreinal.
viceroy ('vais·rɔi) *n.* virrey. —**viceroyalty** (vais'rɔi·əl·ti) *n.* virreinato; virreino. —**viceroyship,** *n.* virreinato; virreino.
vice versa ('vai·si'vʌɹ·sə) viceversa.
vicinity (vɪ'sɪn·ə·ti) *n.* vecindad.
vicious ('vɪʃ·əs) *adj.* vicioso. —**viciousness,** *n.* vicio; depravación.
vicissitude (vɪ'sɪs·ɪ·tjud) *n.* vicisitud.
victim ('vɪk·tɪm) *n.* víctima.
victimize ('vɪk·tɪm·aiz) *v.t.* 1, (sacrifice) hacer víctima; inmolar. 2, (swindle) embaucar; estafar.
victor ('vɪk·tər) *n.* vencedor.
Victoria (vɪk'tor·i·ə) *n.* (carriage) victoria.
Victorian (vɪk'tor·i·ən) *adj.* victoriano.
victorious (vɪk'tor·i·əs) *adj.* victorioso; triunfante.
victory ('vɪk·tə·ri) *n.* victoria; triunfo; éxito.
victrola (vɪk'tro·lə) *n.* fonógrafo.
victual ('vɪt·əl) *v.t.* & *i.* abastecer(se); proveer(se). —**victuals,** *n.pl.* víveres; vituallas.

victualer ('vɪt·əl·ər) *n.* abastecedor.
vicuña (vɪ'kun·jə) *n.* vicuña. *También,* **vicuna** (vɪ'kun·ə).
video ('vɪd·i·o) *n.* video. —*adj.* de video; perteneciente al video.
vie (vai) *v.i.* [**vied, vying**] competir; rivalizar.
view (vjuː) *n.* **1,** (sight; vision) vista; visión. **2,** (inspection) examen; inspección. **3,** (scene) vista; panorama; paisaje. **4,** (appearance) apariencia; aspecto. **5,** (opinion) opinión; parecer. **6,** (aim) intento; propósito. **7,** (mental attitude) concepto. —*v.t.* **1,** (see) mirar; ver. **2,** (examine) examinar; inspeccionar. **3,** (consider) considerar; contemplar. —**come into view,** asomar; aparecer. —**in view,** a la vista. —**in view of,** a vista de. —**on view,** expuesto; en exhibición. —**with a view to,** con el propósito de.
viewer ('vju·ər) *n.* **1,** (one who sees) mirador; espectador. **2,** (examiner) inspector; veedor. **3,** *TV* televidente.
view finder visor.
viewless ('vju·ləs) *adj.* **1,** (offering no view) sin perspectiva. **2,** (invisible) invisible. **3,** (having no opinion) sin opinión.
viewpoint ('vju·pɔint) *n.* punto de vista.
vigesimal (vɪ'dʒɛs·ɪ·məl) *adj.* **1,** (twentieth) vigésimo. **2,** (counting by twenties) vigesimal.
vigil ('vɪdʒ·əl) *n.* vela; vigilia: —**keep vigil (over),** velar; vigilar.
vigilant ('vɪdʒ·ə·lənt) *adj.* vigilante. —**vigilance,** *n.* vigilancia.
vigilante (ˌvɪdʒ·ə'læn·ti) *n.* vigilante.
vignette (vɪn'jɛt) *n.* **1,** (ornamental design) viñeta. **2,** *print.* (headpiece) cabecera. **3,** (literary piece) ensayo; retrato literario.
vigor *también,* **vigour** ('vɪg·ər) *n.* vigor; fuerza; energía. —**vigorous,** *adj.* vigoroso. —**vigorously,** *adv.* con energía; vigorosamente.
viking ('vai·kɪŋ) *n.* antiguo pirata escandinavo; viking.
vile (vail) *adj.* vil; bajo; despreciable. —**vileness,** *n.* vileza; bajeza.
vilify ('vɪl·ə·fai) *v.t.* vilipendiar; envilecer. —**vilification** (-fɪ'kei·ʃən) *n.* vilipendio; envilecimiento.
villa ('vɪl·ə) *n.* quinta; villa.
village ('vɪl·ɪdʒ) *n.* aldea; población. —**villager,** *n.* aldeano.
villain ('vɪl·ən) *n.* villano; malvado. —**villainous,** *adj.* villano; malvado; malo. —**villainy,** *n.* villanía; villanada; maldad.
vim (vɪm) *n.* energía; fuerza; vigor; enjundia.
vindicate ('vɪn·dəˌkeit) *v.t.* vindicar. —**vindication,** *n.* vindicación. —**vindicatory** (-kə·tor·i) *adj.* vindicativo; vindicatorio.
vindictive (vɪn'dɪk·tɪv) *adj.* vengativo. —**vindictiveness,** *n.* calidad de vengativo; ansia de venganza.
vine (vain) *n.* **1,** (climbing or trailing plant) enredadera. **2,** (grapevine) vid; parra.
vinegar ('vɪn·ə·gər) *n.* vinagre. —**vinegary,** *adj.* avinagrado. —**vinegar cruet,** vinagrera. —**vinegar sauce,** vinagreta.
vineyard ('vɪn·jərd) *n.* viña; viñedo.
vintage ('vɪn·tɪdʒ) *n.* vendimia.
vintner ('vɪnt·nər) *n.* vinatero.
vinyl ('vai·nɪl) *n.* vinilo.
viol ('vai·əl) *n.* viola.
viola (vi'o·lə; vai-) *n.* viola.
violate ('vai·əˌleit) *v.t.* violar. —**violation,** *n.* violación.
violent ('vai·ə·lənt) *adj.* violento. —**violence,** *n.* violencia.
violet ('vai·ə·lɪt) *n.* & *adj.* violeta.
violin (vai·ə'lɪn) *n.* violín. —**violinist,** *n.* violinista.
violist (vi'o·lɪst; vai-) *n.* viola.
violoncello (ˌvi·ə·lən'tʃɛl·o) *n.* violoncelo. —**violoncellist,** *n.* violoncelista.
VIP (ˌvi·ai'pi) *n., slang, abr. de* **very important person,** dignatario; alto personaje.
viper ('vai·pər) *n.* víbora. —**viperous; viperish,** *adj.* viperino.
viperine ('vai·pər·ɪn) *adj.* viperino.
virago (vɪ'rei·go) *n.* regañona; virago.
virgin ('vʌɹ·dʒɪn) *n.* & *adj.* virgen. —**virginal,** *adj.* & *n.* virginal.
virgin birth **1,** *theol.* parto virginal. **2,** *zool.* partenogénesis.
Virginia reel (vʌɹ'dʒɪn·jə) baile de Virginia.
virginity (vʌɹ'dʒɪn·ə·ti) *n.* virginidad.
Virgo ('vʌɹ·go) *n., astron.* Virgo; Virgen.
virile ('vɪr·əl) *adj.* viril. —**virility** (və'rɪl·ə·ti) *n.* virilidad.

virtual ('vʌɹ·tʃu·əl) *adj.* virtual.
virtue ('vʌɹ·tʃu) *n.* virtud. —**virtuous,** *adj.* virtuoso. —**virtuousness,** *n.* virtuosidad. —**by** *o* **in virtue of,** en virtud de.
virtuosity (ˌvʌɹ·tʃu'as·ə·ti) *n.* virtuosismo.
virtuoso (ˌvʌɹ·tʃu'o·so) *n.* [*pl.* **-sos** *o* **-si** (si)] virtuoso.
virulence ('vɪr·jə·ləns) *n.* virulencia.
virulent ('vɪr·jə·lənt) *adj.* virulento.
virus ('vai·rəs) *n.* virus.
visa ('vi·zə) *n.* visado; *Amer.* visa. —*v.t.* visar. *También,* **visé.**
visage ('vɪz·ɪdʒ) *n.* **1,** (face) rostro; visaje; semblante. **2,** (appearance) apariencia; aspecto.
viscera ('vɪs·ər·ə) *n.pl.* vísceras. —**visceral,** *adj.* visceral.
viscid ('vɪs·ɪd) *adj.* viscoso. —**viscidness; viscidity** (vɪs'ɪd·ə·ti) *n.* viscosidad.
viscose ('vɪs·kos) *n.* viscosa.
viscosity (vɪs'kas·ə·ti) *n.* viscosidad.
viscount ('vai·kaunt) *n.* vizconde. —**viscountship,** *n.* vizcondado.
viscous ('vɪs·kəs) *adj.* viscoso.
vise (vais) *n.* torno; tornillo.
visé (vi'zei) *n.* & *v.t.* = **visa.**
visible ('vɪz·ə·bəl) *adj.* visible. —**visibility,** *n.* visibilidad.
Visigoth ('vɪz·ɪ·gaθ) *n.* visigodo.
Visigothic (ˌvɪz·ɪ'gaθ·ɪk) *adj.* visigodo; visigótico. —*n.* visigodo.
vision ('vɪʒ·ən) *n.* visión. —**visionary,** *adj.* & *n.* visionario.
visit ('vɪz·ɪt) *v.t.* **1,** (call upon; go to see) visitar. **2,** (send, as a punishment) mandar. —*v.i.* visitar; hacer visitas; visitarse. —*n.* visita.
visitant ('vɪz·ɪ·tənt) *adj.* & *n.* visitante.
visitation (ˌvɪz·ɪ'tei·ʃən) *n.* visitación.
visiting ('vɪz·ə·tɪŋ) *adj.* visitador; visitante; de visita. —**visiting card,** tarjeta de visita.
visitor ('vɪz·ɪ·tər) *n.* visitante; visita. —**have a vistor** (*o* **visitors**), tener visita.
visor *también,* **vizor** ('vai·zər) *n.* visera.
vista ('vɪs·tə) vista; perspectiva; panorama.
visual ('vɪʒ·u·əl) *adj.* visual.
visualize ('vɪz·ju·ə·laiz) *v.t.* & *i.* imaginarse; representarse. —**visualization** (-ɪ'zei·ʃən) *n.* imagen; representación.
vital ('vai·təl) *adj.* **1,** (of or pert. to life) vital. **2,** (fatal) fatal; mortal. **3,** (essential) esencial; indispensable. **4,** (of supreme importance) vital; de suma importancia. **5,** (energetic) enérgico; vivaz. —**vitals,** *n.pl.* vísceras; partes vitales.
vitalism ('vai·təl·ɪz·əm) *n.* vitalismo. —**vitalist,** *n.* vitalista. —**vitalistic,** *adj.* vitalista.
vitality (vai'tæl·ə·ti) *n.* vitalidad; vida.
vitalize ('vai·təlˌaiz) *v.t.* vitalizar. —**vitalization** (-ɪ'zei·ʃən) *n.* vitalización.
vital statistics estadística; estadísticas.
vitamin ('vai·tə·mɪn) *n.* vitamina.
vitiate ('vɪʃ·i·eit) *v.t.* viciar. —**vitiation,** *n.* viciación.
vitreous ('vɪt·ri·əs) *adj.* vítreo.
vitrify ('vɪt·rɪ·fai) *v.t.* vitrificar. —**vitrification** (-fɪ'kei·ʃən); **vitrifaction** (-'fæk·ʃən) *n.* vitrificación.
vitriol ('vɪt·ri·əl) *n.* **1,** *chem.* vitriolo. **2,** (sarcasm) sarcasmo; mordacidad.
vitriolic (ˌvɪt·ri'al·ɪk) *adj.* **1,** (of or resembling vitriol) vitriólico. **2,** (sarcastic) sarcástico; cáustico; mordaz.
vituperate (vai'tju·pəˌreit) *v.t.* vituperar. —**vituperation,** *n.* vituperación; vituperio. —**vituperative,** *adj.* vituperioso.
vivacious (vɪ'vei·ʃəs; vai-) *adj.* vivaz. —**vivaciousness; vivacity** (vɪ'væs·ə·ti) *n.* vivacidad.
vivid ('vɪv·ɪd) *adj.* vivo; vívido. —**vividness,** *n.* viveza.
vivify ('vɪv·ə·fai) *v.t.* vivificar; avivar. —**vivification** (-fɪ'kei·ʃən) *n.* vivificación.
viviparous (vai'vɪp·ə·rəs) *adj.* vivíparo.
vivisect ('vɪv·ə·sɛkt) *v.t.* disecar vivo.
vivisection ('vɪv·əˌsɛk·ʃən) *n.* vivisección.
vixen ('vɪk·sən) *n.* **1,** (female fox) zorra; hembra del zorro. **2,** (ill-tempered woman) mujer regañona. —**vixenish,** *adj.* regañona.
vizier (vɪ'zɪr) *n.* visir.
vizor ('vai·zər) *n.* = **visor.**

vocable ('vo·kə·bəl) *n.* vocablo; voz.
vocabulary (vo'kæb·jʊ·lɛr·i) *n.* vocabulario.
vocal ('vo·kəl) *adj.* **1,** (of or pert. to the voice) vocal. **2,** (vocalic) vocálico. **3,** (expressive) expresivo. —*n.* vocal. —**vocal cords,** cuerdas vocales.
vocalic (vo'kæl·ɪk) *adj.* vocálico.
vocalist ('vo·kəl·ɪst) *n.* cantor; cantante; vocalista.
vocalize ('vo·kəl·aiz) *v.t.* & *i.* vocalizar. —**vocalization** (-ɪ'zei·ʃən) *n.* vocalización.
vocation (vo'kei·ʃən) *n.* vocación. —**vocational,** *adj.* vocacional.
vocative ('vak·ə·tɪv) *adj.* & *n.* vocativo.
vociferate (vo'sɪf·ə·reit) *v.i.* & *t.* vociferar. —**vociferation,** *n.* vociferación.
vociferous (vo'sɪf·ə·rəs) *adj.* clamoroso; vociferador; vociferante. —**vociferously,** *adv.* a gritos; con viveza. —**vociferousness,** *n.* clamorosidad.
vodka ('vad·kə) *n.* vodka.
vogue (vo:g) *n.* moda; boga. —**be in vogue,** estar en boga; ser de moda.
voice (vɔis) *n.* voz; *phonet.* sonoridad. —*v.t.* **1,** (express) expresar; proclamar. **2,** *phonet.* sonorizar. —*v.i.* sonorizarse. —**at the top of one's voice,** a voz en cuello; a voz en grito. —**with one voice,** a una voz.
voiced (vɔist) *adj.* **1,** (having a voice) que tiene voz. **2,** (expressed) expresado; proclamado. **3,** *phonet.* sonoro.
voiceless ('vɔis·ləs) *adj.* **1,** (dumb; silent) mudo. **2,** (unexpressed) inexpresado. **3,** *phonet.* sordo; insonoro; mudo. —**voicelessness,** *n., phonet.* sordez.
voicing ('vɔis·ɪŋ) *n., phonet.* sonorización.
void (vɔid) *adj.* **1,** (empty) vacío. **2,** (unoccupied) desocupado; vacante. **3,** (invalid) nulo; inválido. **4,** (useless) vano; inútil. **5,** (lacking) falto; privado; desprovisto. —*n.* **1,** (emptiness) vacío. **2,** (opening; gap) hueco. —*v.t.* **1,** (empty) vaciar: evacuar. **2,** (nullify) anular.
voidance ('vɔid·əns) *n.* **1,** (annulment) anulación. **2,** *eccles.* (vacancy) vacante.
voile (vɔil) *n.* espumilla.
volatile ('val·ə·tɪl) *adj.* volátil. —**volatility** (-'tɪl·ə·ti) *n.* volatilidad.
volatilize ('val·ə·tɪl,aiz) *v.t.* volatilizar. —*v.i.* volatilizarse.
volcano (val'kei·no) *n.* volcán. —**volcanic** (-'kæn·ɪk) *adj.* volcánico.
volition (vo'lɪʃ·ən) *n.* volición. —**volitive** ('val·ə·tɪv); **volitional,** *adj.* volitivo.
volley ('val·i) *n.* **1,** (simultaneous discharge) descarga. **2,** (downpour) lluvia. **3,** *games* voleo. —*v.t.* **1,** (fire) descargar. **2,** *games* volear.
volleyball *n.* volibol.
volt (volt) *n.* voltio. —**voltage,** *n.* voltaje.
voltaic (val'tei·ɪk) *adj.* voltaico.
voltaism ('val·tə·ɪz·əm) *n.* voltaísmo; galvanismo.
voltmeter *n.* voltímetro.
volubility (,val·jə'bɪl·ə·ti) *n.* volubilidad.
voluble ('val·jə·bəl) *adj.* voluble.
volume ('val·jum) *n.* **1,** (mass) volumen. **2,** (book) tomo; volumen.
voluminous (və'lu·mɪ·nəs) *adj.* voluminoso. —**voluminousness,** *n.* voluminosidad.
voluntary ('val·ən·tɛr·i) *adj.* voluntario. —*n., music* solo de órgano. —**voluntariness,** *n.* voluntariedad.
volunteer (,val·ən'tɪr) *n.* & *adj.* voluntario. —*v.t.* ofrecer. —*v.i.* servir de voluntario; ofrecerse.
voluptuary (və'lʌp·tʃu·ɛr·i) *n.* voluptuoso.
voluptuous (və'lʌp·tʃu·əs) *adj.* voluptuoso. —**voluptuousness,** *n.* voluptuosidad.
volute (və'lut) *n.* voluta.
vomit ('vam·ɪt) *v.t.* & *i.* vomitar. —*n.* vómito. —**vomitive,** *adj.* & *n.* vomitivo.
voodoo ('vu·du) *n.* & *adj.* vodú. —**voodooism,** *n.* voduismo. —**voodooist,** *n.* voduista.
-vora (və·rə) *sufijo* -voros, *zool.; forma nombres de familias o grupos: Carnivora,* carnívoros.
voracious (vo'rei·ʃəs) *adj.* voraz. —**voraciousness; voracity** (vo'ræs·ə·ti) *n.* voracidad.
-vore (vor) *sufijo* -voro; *forma nombres de familias o grupos de*

animales indicando la manera de alimentarse: carnivore, carnívoro.

-vorous (və·rəs) *sufijo* -voro; *forma adjetivos correspondiendo a nombres terminados en* **-vore** *o* **-vora**: *carnivorous,* carnívoro.

vortex ('vor·tɛks) *n.* [*pl.* **-texes** *o* **-tices** (tɪ·siz)] vórtice.

votary ('vo·tə·ri) *n.* **1,** (one bound by vows) religioso; monje; monja. **2,** (devotee) aficionado; devoto. **3,** (adherent) partidario. —*adj.* votivo.

vote (vot) *n.* voto. —*v.i.* & *t.* votar. —**voter,** *n.* votante; elector. —**voting,** *n.* votación.

votive ('vo·tɪv) *adj.* votivo.

vouch (vautʃ) *v.t.* & *i.* atestiguar; garantizar. —**vouch for,** responder de *o* por.

voucher ('vautʃ·ər) *n.* **1,** (one who vouches) fiador; garante. **2,** (receipt) comprobante.

vouchsafe (vautʃ'seif) *v.t.* otorgar; conceder; dignarse hacer *o* dar. —*v.i.* dignarse.

vow (vau) *n.* voto; promesa. —*v.t.* votar; prometer; jurar; hacer voto de. —*v.i.* hacer voto.

vowel ('vau·əl) *n.* vocal. —*adj.* vocálico.

voyage ('vɔi·ɪdʒ) *n.* viaje. —*v.i.* viajar. —*v.t.* viajar por; atravesar. —**voyager,** *n.* viajero.

vulcanite ('vʌl·kən·ait) *n.* vulcanita.

vulcanize ('vʌl·kəˌnaiz) *v.t.* vulcanizar. —**vulcanization** (-nɪ'zei·ʃən) *n.* vulcanización.

vulgar ('vʌl·gər) *adj.* vulgar; grosero.

vulgarian (vʌl'gɛr·i·ən) *n.* persona grosera; maleducado.

vulgarism ('vʌl·gər·ɪz·əm) *n.* vulgarismo.

vulgarity (vʌl'gɛr·ə·ti) *n.* vulgaridad; grosería.

vulgarize ('vʌl·gəˌraiz) *v.t.* vulgarizar. —**vulgarization** (-rɪ'zei·ʃən) *n.* vulgarización.

Vulgate ('vʌl·geit) *n.* Vulgata.

vulnerable ('vʌl·nər·ə·bəl) *adj.* vulnerable. —**vulnerability** (-'bɪl·ə·ti) *n.* vulnerabilidad.

vulpine ('vʌl·pain) *adj.* vulpino; zorruno.

vulture ('vʌl·tʃər) *n.* **1,** (bird) buitre. **2,** (rapacious person) bárbaro; pícaro; rapaz. —**vulturine** (-tʃə·rain); **vulturous,** *adj.* buitrero.

vulva ('vʌl·və) *n.* vulva.

vying ('vai·ɪŋ) *v., ger. de* **vie.**

W

W, w ('dʌb·əl·ju) vigésima tercera letra del alfabeto inglés.

wabble ('wab·əl) *v.i.* & *n.* = **wobble.** —**wabbly** (-li) *adj.* = **wobbly.**

wack (wæk) *n., slang* excéntrico; estrafalario.

wacky ('wæk·i) *adj., slang* excéntrico; loco. —**wackiness,** *n., slang* excentricidad; locura.

wad (waːd) *n.* **1,** (small, soft mass) bolita; masa. **2,** (packing; filling) guata; borra. **3,** (roll; bundle) lío; atado. —*v.t.* [**wadded, wadding**] **1,** (compress) apelmazar; apelotonar. **2,** (pack; fill) acolchar; henchir; rellenar. **3,** (form into a bundle) liar; atar; envolver.

wadding ('wad·ɪŋ) *n.* guata; entretela; bolitas de algodón.

waddle ('wad·əl) *v.i.* anadear. —*n.* anadeo.

wade (weid) *v.t.* vadear. —*v.i.* andar en el agua, el barro, etc.; proceder con dificultad. —*n.* **1,** (act of wading) vadeamiento. **2,** (ford) vado. —**wade into,** *colloq.* atacar; embestir; lanzarse a *o* en. —**wade through,** ir con dificultad por; hacer con dificultad.

wader ('weid·ər) *n.* **1,** (one who wades) vadeador. **2,** (bird) ave zancuda.

waders ('weid·ərz) *n.pl.* botas de vadear; botas altas impermeables.

wafer ('wei·fər) *n.* **1,** barquillo; caramelo. **2,** *eccles.* hostia. **3,** *pharm.* sello.

wafery ('wei·fə·ri) *adj.* acaramelado; delgado; fino; ligero.

waffle ('waf·əl) *n.* barquillo. —**waffle iron,** barquillero.

waft (waft) *v.t.* llevar por el aire o por encima del agua. —*v.i.* **1,** float) llevarse por el aire; flotar. **2,** (blow gently) soplar levemente.

—*n.* **1,** (floating) flotación; flotamiento. **2,** (breeze; gust) ráfaga. **3,** (odor) olor. **4,** (waving) movimiento trémolo.

wag (wæg) *v.t.* [**wagged, wagging**] hacer oscilar; menear. —*v.i.* oscilar; menearse. —*n.* **1,** (wagging motion) oscilación; meneo. **2,** (wit) bromista; burlón. —**wag the tongue,** charlar; hablar mucho.

wage (weidʒ) *n.* paga; salario. —*v.t.* emprender; perseguir.

wage earner trabajador; asalariado.

wager ('wei·dʒər) *n.* apuesta. —*v.t.* & *i.* apostar.

wages ('wei·dʒɪz) *n.pl.* paga; salario; sueldo; recompensa.

wage war hacer guerra.

waggish ('wæg·ɪʃ) *adj.* chocarrero; juguetón; retozón; bufón.

waggle ('wæg·əl) *v.t.* oscilar; menear. —*v.i.* oscilar; menearse. —*n.* oscilación; meneo.

wagon ('wæg·ən) *n.* **1,** (transport vehicle) carro; vagón. **2,** *Brit.* (freight car) furgón. —**be on the wagon,** *slang* abstenerse de tomar bebidas alcohólicas.

wagoner ('wæg·ən·ər) *n.* carretero.

wagonload *n.* carretada; vagonada.

wagon train tren de equipajes.

waif (weif) *n.* **1,** (abandoned child) expósito. **2,** (homeless child) niño vagabundo. **3,** (stray animal) animal perdido.

wail (weil) *v.i.* llorar; gemir; lamentarse. —*n.* gemido; lamento.

wainscot ('wein·skət) *n.* enmaderamiento; entablado; friso de madera. —*v.t.* enmaderar; entablar.

wainscoting ('wein·skət·ɪŋ) *n.* enmaderamiento; entablado.

wainwright ('wein·rait) *n.* carretero.

waist (weist) *n.* **1,** (part of the body or of a garment) cintura. **2,** (garment) blusa; corpiño.

waistband *n.* pretina.

waistcoat ('weist·kot; 'wɛs·kət) *n.* chaleco.

waistline *n.* cintura.

wait (weit) *v.t.* **1,** (expect) esperar; aguardar. **2,** (serve) servir. **3,** *colloq.* (delay; put off) posponer; diferir. —*v.i.* **1,** (remain) esperar; aguardar. **2,** (serve) servir. —*n.* espera. —**wait for,** esperar; aguardar. —**wait on** (*o* **upon**), **1,** (serve) servir; atender. **2,** (call on; visit) visitar; ir a ver. **3,** (result from) seguirse de; inferirse de. **4,** (pay one's respects to) presentar sus respetos a.

waiter ('weit·ər) *n.* camarero; mozo.

waiting ('weit·ɪŋ) *n.* **1,** (expectation) espera. **2,** (service) servicio. —*adj.* **1,** (that waits) que espera. **2,** (of or for waiting) de espera. **3,** (serving) de servicio. —**in waiting,** de honor; de servicio.

waiting maid doncella; camaresa. *También,* **waiting woman.**

waiting room sala de espera.

waitress ('weit·rɪs) *n.* camarera; moza.

waive (weiv) *v.t.* ceder; renunciar a; desistir de.

waiver ('weiv·ər) *n.* renuncia; desistimiento.

wake (weik) *v.t.* [*pret.* **waked** *o* **woke**; *p.p.* **waked**] despertar. —*v.i.* **1,** (rouse oneself) despertar; despertarse. **2,** (stay awake) velar. —*n.* **1,** (vigil) vela; vigilia. **2,** (for a dead person) velatorio. **3,** (track of a ship) estela.

wakeful ('weik·fəl) *adj.* vigilante; desvelado. —**wakefulness,** *n.* vigilia; desvelo.

waken ('weik·ən) *v.t.* despertar. —*v.i.* despertar; despertarse.

waking ('weik·ɪŋ) *n.* vela; vigilia. —*adj.* despierto. —**waking hours,** horas de vela.

wale (weil) *n.* **1,** (mark of a whip or stick) roncha; raya; verdugón. **2,** *naut.* cinta. **3,** (ridge on the surface of cloth) relieve.

walk (wɔk) *v.i.* **1,** (proceed on foot) andar; caminar. **2,** (stroll) pasearse; dar un paseo. **3,** (conduct oneself) portarse; conducirse. **4,** *baseball* pasar (a primera base). —*v.t.* **1,** (take out for a walk) pasear. **2,** (traverse) andar por; atravesar; recorrer. **3,** (cause to walk) hacer andar. **4,** (accompany in walking) acompañar caminando. **5,** *baseball* dejar pasar (a primera base). —*n.* **1,** (act of walking; distance walked) paseo; caminata. **2,** (gait) andar; paso. **3,** (pacing, as of a horse) paso; andadura. **4,** (path) paseo; vereda; senda; alameda. **5,** (sidewalk) acera. **6,** (footwalk) andén. **7,** (station in life) carrera; condición. **8,** (occupation) oficio; empleo. **9,** *baseball* pase. **10,** (easy victory) triunfo fácil. **—go for a walk,** salir a pasear; dar un paseo. **—take a walk,** dar un paseo. **—walk away,** marcharse; irse. **—walk away from,** alejarse de. **—walk in,** entrar; pasar adelante. **—walk in on (someone),** sorprenderle a uno. **—walk off, 1,** (leave) marcharse; irse. **2,** (get rid of by walking) deshacerse de (caminando). **—walk off with, 1,** (steal) robar. **2,** (carry off) cargar con; llevarse. **3,** (win) ganar. **—walk out, 1,** (leave) salir; marcharse. **2,** *colloq.* (go on strike) salir en huelga. **—walk out on,** *colloq.* abandonar; renunciar a. **—walk up,** subir. **—walk up to,** acercarse a.

walkaway *n., colloq.* triunfo fácil.

walker ('wɔk·ər) *n.* **1,** (for a child) andaderas (*pl.*); andador. **2,** (for an invalid) andador. **3,** (one good at walking) andador.

walkie-talkie ('wɔk·i'tɔk·i) *n.,* radioteléfono portátil.

walking ('wɔk·ɪŋ) *adj.* **1,** (that walks) que anda; andante. **2,** (itinerant) ambulante; errante. **3,** (oscillating) oscilante; de vaivén. **—*n.* 1,** (act of walking) paseo. **2,** (gait) andar; paso. **—walking papers,** *slang* despedida. **—walking stick,** bastón.

walkout *n., colloq.* huelga.

walkup *n., colloq.* apartamento de escaleras.

wall (wɔl) *n.* **1,** (enclosure; partition) pared. **2,** (supporting or outer wall) muro. **3,** (rampart) muralla. **—*v.t.*** emparedar; tapiar; amurallar. **—drive to the wall,** poner entre la espada y la pared. **—go to the wall, 1,** (yield) rendirse; entregarse. **2,** (fail) fracasar.

wallboard *n.* tabla de yeso.

wallet ('wal·ɪt) *n.* cartera; *Amer.* billetera.

walleye ('wɔl·ai) *n.* ojo saltón; *ichthy.* pez de ojos saltones. **—wall-eyed,** *adj.* de ojos saltones.

wallflower *n.* **1,** *bot.* alhelí. **2,** *colloq.* (girl without a partner at a dance) plantada; mujer sin pareja.

wallop ('wal·əp) *v.t., colloq.* zurrar; tundir; aporrear. **—*n., colloq.*** **1,** (blow) golpe fuerte. **2,** (force) fuerza; energía.

walloping ('wal·əp·ɪŋ) *adj., colloq.* grande; enorme. **—*n., colloq.*** **1,** (thrashing) zurra; tunda; aporreo. **2,** (defeat) derrota.

wallow ('wal·o) *v.i.* revolcarse. **—*n.* 1,** (act) revuelco; revolcón. **2,** (place) revolcadero.

wallpaper *n.* empapelado. **—*v.t.*** empapelar.

walnut ('wɔl·nʌt) *n.* **1,** (tree; wood) nogal. **2,** (fruit) nuez.

walrus ('wal·rəs) *n.* morsa.

waltz ('wɔlts) *n.* vals. **—*adj.*** de vals. **—*v.i.*** valsar; bailar valses.

wampum ('wam·pəm) *n.* **1,** (shell money) cuentas de concha que servían como dinero a los indios americanos. **2,** *slang* (money) dinero.

wan (waːn) *adj.* **1,** (pale) pálido. **2,** (sickly) macilento; demacrado.

wand (wand) *n.* vara.

wander ('wan·dər) *v.i.* vagar; errar; extraviarse. **—wanderer,** *n.* vagamundo; vagabundo. **—wandering,** *n.* paseo; extravío. **—*adj.*** errante.

wanderlust *n.* ansia de vagar.

wane (wein) *v.i.* **1,** (lessen) menguar; disminuir. **2,** (decline) decaer; declinar. **—*n.* 1,** (lessening) mengua; menguante; disminución. **2,** (decline) decadencia; decaimiento; declinación. **—wane of the moon,** menguante de la luna.

wangle ('wæŋ·gəl) *v.t., colloq.* **1,** (obtain by guile) conseguir por artimañas. **2,** (cajole) engatusar; embaucar. **3,** (manipulate) manipular; adulterar; falsificar. **4,** (wiggle) sacudir. **—*v.i., colloq.* 1,** (contrive; scheme) urdir; ingeniarse; darse maña. **2,** (wiggle out; escape) sacudirse; extricarse. **—*n., colloq.*** ardid; treta; trampa.

wanness ('waːn·nəs) *n.* **1,** (paleness) palidez. **2,** (sickly appearance) demacración.

want (want) *v.t.* **1,** (desire) desear. **2,** (need) necesitar. **3,** (lack) carecer de. **—*v.i.*** carecer. **—*n.* 1,** (desire) deseo. **2,** (need) necesidad. **3,** (lack) falta; carencia. **—for want of,** por falta de. **—in want,** pobre; necesitado. **—wanted** (*used in announcements*), **1,** (for employment) se necesita. **2,** (by the police) buscado; demandado.

want ad *colloq.* anuncio clasificado; anuncio de requerimiento.
wanting ('want·ɪŋ) *adj.* **1,** (missing; lacking) que falta. **2,** (inadequate) falto (de); defectuoso; deficiente. —*prep.* sin; menos.
wanton ('wan·tən) *adj.* **1,** (immoral) lascivo; licencioso. **2,** (malicious) malicioso; perverso. **3,** (reckless) extravagante; irreflexivo. **4,** (playful) juguetón; travieso. —*n.* libertino; ramera. —*v.i.* retozar; juguetear. —*v.t.* malgastar.
wantonness ('wan·tən·nəs) *n.* **1,** (immorality) lascivia; libertinaje. **2,** (malice) malicia; perversidad. **3,** (recklessness) extravagancia; irreflexión. **4,** (playfulness) travesura.
war (woːr) *n.* guerra. —*v.i.* [**warred, warring**] guerrear. —*adj.* guerrero; de guerra. —**at war,** en guerra. —**go to war,** declarar la guerra; ir a la guerra.
warble ('wor·bəl) *v.i.* gorjear; trinar. —*v.t.* cantar. —*n.* gorjeo; trino.
warbler ('wor·blər) *n.* gorjeador; *ornith.* curruca.
war cry grito de guerra.
ward (word) *n.* **1,** (dependent) pupilo. **2,** (guardianship) tutela; custodia. **3,** (district) barrio; distrito. **4,** (of a hospital) cuadra. **5,** (of a lock) guarda. **6,** (defense) defensa; posición defensiva. —*v.t.* [*usu.* **ward off**] parar; desviar; evitar.
-ward (wərd) *también,* **-wards** *sufijo;* en dirección de; hacia: *backward(s),* hacia atrás; atrasado; *eastward(s),* hacia el este.
war dance danza guerrera; danza de guerra.
warden ('wor·dən) *n.* **1,** (custodian) custodio; guardián. **2,** (director of a prison) carcelero.
warder ('wor·dər) *n.* **1,** (guard; custodian) guardián. **2,** *Brit.* (prison warden) carcelero.
ward heeler político subordinado; politicastro.
wardrobe ('word·rob) *n.* **1,** (storage place for clothing) guardarropa; guardarropía; *theat.* vestuario. **2,** (supply of clothing) vestuario; vestido.
wardroom ('word·rum) *n.* cuartel de oficiales.
-wards (wərdz) *sufijo, var. de* **-ward.**
wardship ('word·ʃɪp) *n.* tutela; custodia.
ware (weːr) *n.* **1,** (merchandise) mercancía. **2,** (crockery) vajilla; loza.
warehouse ('wɛr·haus) *n.* almacén; depósito. —*v.t.* almacenar.
warehouseman ('wɛr,haus·mən) *n.* [*pl.* **-men**] **1,** (owner or manager) almacenista. **2,** (employee) guardalmacén.
wares (weːrz) *n.pl.* mercadería; mercancías.
warfare ('wor·fɛr) *n.* guerra; arte de la guerra.
warhead ('wor·hɛd) *n.* cabeza de explosivo. *También,* **war head.**
war horse caballo de guerra; *fig.* veterano.
warily ('wɛr·ɪ·li) *adv.* cautamente; cautelosamente.
wariness ('wɛr·i·nəs) *n.* cautela; precaución.
warlike ('wor·laik) *adj.* belicoso; guerrero.
war lord jefe militar.
warm (worm) *adj.* **1,** (having or giving heat) tibio; caliente. **2,** (of weather or climate) cálido; caluroso. **3,** (affectionate) humano; simpático; cariñoso. **4,** (impassioned) ardiente; acalorado. **5,** (lively) vivo; animado. **6,** (fresh) recién hecho; fresco. **7,** *colloq.* (close to discovering something) cercano. **8,** (protecting from cold) que abriga. —*v.t.* calentar; acalorar; entibiar. —*v.i.* calentarse. —*n., colloq.* calor. —**be warm, 1,** (of the weather) hacer calor. **2,** (of a person) tener calor. **3,** (of a thing) estar caliente. —**warm over,** recalentar. —**warm up, 1,** (make or become warm) calentar; calentarse. **2,** (reheat) recalentar. **3,** (become friendly) hacerse más amistoso. **4,** (become enthusiastic) entusiasmarse. **5,** (become mild, as the weather) templar.
warmblooded *adj.* **1,** *zool.* de sangre caliente. **2,** *fig.* apasionado. —**warmbloodedness,** *n.* apasionamiento; frenesí.
warm front frente caliente.
warmhearted *adj.* afectuoso. —**warmheartedness,** *n.* afectuosidad.
warming pan calentador.
warmly ('worm·li) *adv.* **1,** (fervently) ardientemente; con ardor. **2,** (cordially) cordialmente.

warmness ('worm·nəs) *n.* = **warmth.**
warmonger *n.* incitador; instigador; fomentador de la guerra.
warmth (wormθ) *n.* **1,** (heat) calor. **2,** (passion) fervor; ardor; entusiasmo. **3,** (cordiality) cordialidad.
warn (worn) *v.t.* avisar; advertir; precaver.
warning ('worn·ıŋ) *n.* aviso; amonestación. precaucion. —*adj.* amonestador.
warp (worp) *v.t.* **1,** (twist; bend) torcer; combar. **2,** (pervert) pervertir. **3,** *naut.* mover con espía. —*v.i.* torcerse; combarse. —*n.* **1,** (distortion) comba; torcedura. **2,** (bias) sesgo; prejuicio. **3,** *weaving* urdimbre. **4,** *naut.* espía.
war paint pintura de guerra; camuflaje.
warpath *n.* sendo de la guerra; campaña guerrera. —**on the warpath,** en guerra; preparado para la guerra; *fig.* dispuesto a pelear.
warplane *n.* avión de combate; avión militar.
warrant ('war·ənt) *n.* **1,** (authorization) autorización; sanción. **2,** (guarantee) garantía. **3,** (decree) decreto; orden. **4,** (certificate) cédula; documento; escritura. **5,** (justification) justificación; razón. **6,** *law* citación. —*v.t.* **1,** (guarantee) garantizar. **2,** (authorize) autorizar. **3,** (justify) justificar. **4,** (assure) asegurar. **5,** (certify) certificar. —**warrantee,** *n.* afianzado. —**warrantor,** *n.* fiador; garante.
warrant officer suboficial; oficial subalterno.
warranty ('war·ən·ti) *n.* **1,** (authorization) autorización; sanción **2,** (justification) justificación. **3,** (guarantee) garantía.
warren ('war·ən) *n.* conejera.
warrior ('wor·jər) *n.* guerrero.
warship ('wor·ʃıp) *n.* buque de guerra.
wart (wort) *n.* verruga. —**warty,** *adj.* verrugoso.
warthog ('wort·hɔg) n. jabalí de verrugas. *También,* **wart hog.**
wartime *n.* tiempo de guerra.
war whoop grito de guerra.
wary ('wɛr·i) *adj.* cauto; cauteloso.
was (wʌz) *v., pret. de* **be.**
wash (waʃ) *v.t.* **1,** (clean) lavar; limpiar. **2,** (wet; drench) mojar; bañar. **3,** (flow over; cover) lavar. **4,** (carry, as water) llevar. —*v.i.* **1,** (wash oneself; be washed) lavarse; limpiarse. **2,** (do laundry) lavar la ropa. **3,** (be carried, as by water) llevarse por el agua. **4,** (flow; beat) batir. **5,** *colloq.* (withstand examination) mantenerse; comprobarse. —*n.* **1,** (act of washing; things to be washed) lavado. **2,** (soapy water) lavazas (*pl.*). **3,** (liquid refuse) despojos (*pl.*); desperdicios (*pl.*). **4,** (rush of water or waves) el romper del agua. **5,** (lotion) loción. **6,** (silt; debris) aluvión. **7,** (ground covered by water) charco; pantano. —**washed out, 1,** (faded) desteñido. **2,** (exhausted) debilitado; agotado. **3,** (expelled after failure) eliminado. —**washed up,** *colloq.* gastado; terminado; fracasado.
washable ('waʃ·ə·bəl) *adj.* lavable.
wash and wear (ropa) de lavar y poner.
washbasin *n.* = **washbowl.**
washboard *n.* tabla de lavar.
washbowl *n.* jofaina; palangana; lavamanos.
washcloth *n.* trapo de lavar; paño para lavarse.
washer ('waʃ·ər) *n.* **1,** (person or thing that washes) lavador. **2,** (washing machine) lavadora. **3,** *mech.* arandela.
washerwoman *n.* [*pl.* **-women**] lavandera.
washing ('waʃ·ıŋ) *n.* lavado; ropa de lavar. —**washings,** *n.pl.* lavadura (*sing.*).
washing machine lavadora; lavarropas; máquina de lavar.
washing soda sosa de lavar.
washout ('waʃˌaut) *n.* **1,** (erosion by water) derrubio; derrumbe. **2,** *slang* (failure) fracaso.
washrag *n.* = **washcloth.**
washroom *n.* lavabo; *Amer.* lavatorio.
washstand *n.* lavabo; lavamanos.
washtub *n.* tina *o* cuba de lavar.
wash water lavazas.
washwoman *n.* [*pl.* **-women**] lavandera.
washy ('waʃ·i) *adj.* **1,** (wet; soaked) húmedo; mojado. **2,** (watery) aguado; débil. **3,** (insipid) insulso; soso.

wasp (wasp) *n.* avispa.
waspish (ˈwasp·ɪʃ) *adj.* **1,** (slim-waisted) delgado; de cintura delgada. **2,** (bad-tempered) enojadizo; áspero; malhumorado.
wassail (ˈwas·əl) *n.* **1,** (toast) brindis. **2,** (drink) bebida especiada. **3,** (drinking party) jarana; parranda. —*v.i.* jaranear. —**wassailer,** *n.* brindador; juerguista; borrachón. —**wassail bowl,** copa.
wastage (ˈweis·tɪdʒ) *n.* derroche; pérdida; desgaste.
waste (weist) *adj.* **1,** (desolate) desierto; yermo. **2,** (untilled) inculto. **3,** (rejected) desechado. **4,** (superfluous) sobrante. —*v.t.* **1,** (squander) malgastar; derrochar; desperdiciar. **2,** (devastate) asolar; devastar. **3,** (wear away; use up) gastar; consumir. **4,** (lose) perder. —*v.t.* **1,** (lose vigor) decaer; perder la salud, el vigor, etc. **2,** (be used up) gastarse; consumirse. **3,** (pass, as time) pasar. —*n.* **1,** (misuse) derroche; despilfarro. **2,** (loss) pérdida. **3,** (barren land) yermo; desierto. **4,** (decline) decadencia; decaimiento. **5,** (discarded matter) basura; desperdicios (*pl.*); despojos (*pl.*). **6,** (excrement) excremento. **7,** (discarded textile fiber) hilacha; borra. —**go to waste,** perderse; desperdiciarse. —**lay waste,** asolar; devastar. —**waste away,** decaer; gastarse; consumirse.
wastebasket *n.* canasto *o* cesto para papeles.
wasteful (ˈweist·fəl) *adj.* manirroto; pródigo; derrochador. —**wastefulness,** *n.* prodigalidad.
wasteland *n.* yermo; despoblado; desierto.
waste pipe tubo de desagüe; desaguadero.
waster (ˈweis·tər) *n.* = **wastrel.**
wastrel (ˈweis·trəl) *n.* derrochador; pródigo.
watch (watʃ) *v.t.* **1,** (look at) mirar; ver. **2,** (guard) velar; vigilar; guardar. **3,** (observe closely) observar; espiar. **4,** (take care of) cuidar; guardar. **5,** (look out for) tener cuidado con. **6,** (be on the lookout for) estar a lar mira de. —*v.i.* **1,** (look; observe) mirar; ver. **2,** (stay awake or alert) velar. **3,** (be careful) tener cuidado. —*n.* **1,** (vigil) vela; vigilia. **2,** (tour of duty) guardia; vela; vigilia. **3,** (sentinel) guardia; centinela; vigilante. **4,** (group of guards; patrol) guardia; ronda. **5,** (close observation) vigilancia. **6,** (timepiece) reloj. —**be on the watch for, 1,** (be on the lookout for) estar a la mira de. **2,** (be careful of) tener cuidado con. —**keep watch,** estar de guardia. —**keep watch over,** velar; vigilar; cuidar. —**watch for,** esperar; estar a la mira de. —**watch out (for),** tener cuidado (con). —**watch over,** velar; vigilar; guardar; cuidar.
watchcase *n.* relojera; caja de reloj.
watchdog *n.* perro de guarda; perro guardián.
watcher (ˈwatʃ·ər) *n.* velador; observador; vigilante.
watchful (ˈwatʃ·fəl) *adj.* alerto; vigilante; cuidadoso. —**watchfulness,** *n.* vigilancia; cuidado.
watchmaker *n.* relojero. —**watchmaking,** *n.* relojería.
watchman (ˈwatʃ·mən) *n.* [*pl.* **-men**] sereno; vigilante; velador.
watch pocket relojera.
watchtower *n.* atalaya; vigía.
watchword *n.* **1,** (password) contraseña; santo y seña. **2,** (slogan) lema; mote.
water (ˈwat·ər; ˈwɔ·tər) *n.* agua. —*adj.* acuático; de *o* para agua. —*v.t.* **1,** (dilute) aguar. **2,** (irrigate) regar. **3,** (sprinkle) rociar. **4,** (moisten; wet) mojar; bañar; humedecer. **5,** (supply water to) proveer de agua. **6,** (give to drink, as animals) abrevar. **7,** *finance* aumentar el valor nominal de (las acciones) sin aumento equivalente en el capital. —*v.i.* **1,** (fill with tears, as the eyes) llorar. **2,** (fill with water) llenarse de agua; aguarse. **3,** (take on water) tomar agua. **4,** (drink, as animals) abrevarse. **5,** (fill with saliva, as the mouth) hacérsele a uno agua la boca. —**above water,** flotante. —**be in deep water,** estar con el agua al cuello. —**be on the water wagon,** *slang* abstenerse de tomar bebidas alcohólicas. —**go by water,** ir por mar; ir por barco. —**hold water, 1,** (retain water) retener el agua. **2,** *fig.* (be sound or consistent) mantenerse firme; comprobarse. —**make one's mouth water,** hacerle a uno agua la boca. —**make water, 1,** (urinate) hacer aguas. **2,** *naut.* hacer agua. —**of the first water,**

de primera clase. —**pass water,** hacer aguas. —**pour** (*o* **throw**) **cold water on,** desanimar; desalentar.
water bearer aguador; *cap., astron.* Acuario.
waterborne *adj.* flotante; llevado por el agua.
water buffalo carabao.
water bug chinche de agua.
water carrier 1, (water bearer) aguador. **2,** (ship) buque cisterna.
water closet letrina; excusado; retrete.
water color acuarela. —**watercolor,** *adj.* hecho a la acuarela. —**water-colorist,** *n.* acuarelista.
water-cooled *adj.* refrigerado por agua.
water cooler refrigerador de agua.
watercourse *n.* corriente de agua.
watercress *n.* berro. *También,* **water cress.**
water cure cura de aguas.
waterfall *n.* cascada; catarata; caída de agua.
waterfowl *n.* ave acuática.
waterfront *n.* puerto; muelles (*pl.*).
water heater calentador de agua; termosifón.
waterhole *n.* **1,** (pool) charco. **2,** = **watering place.**
water ice sorbete; helado.
wateriness ('wat·ər·i·nəs; 'wɔ·tər-) *n.* acuosidad.
watering ('wat·ər·ɪŋ; 'wɔ·tər-) *n.* riego. —*adj.* de riego.
watering can regadera.
watering place 1, (spa) balneario. **2,** (for animals) abrevadero; aguadero.
watering trough abrevadero; aguadero.
water level nivel de agua.
water lily lirio de agua; nenúfar.
waterline *n.* línea de flotación.
waterlogged ('wat·ər·lɔgd) *adj.* **1,** (awash) anegado en agua; inundado. **2,** (soaked) empapado de agua.
water main cañería maestra.
watermark *n.* filigrana. —*v.t.* marcar al agua.
watermelon *n.* sandía.
water mill molino de agua.
water pipe cañería de agua.
water polo polo acuático.
water power fuerza hidráulica.
waterproof *adj.* a prueba de agua; impermeable. —*n.* impermeable. —*v.t.* impermeabilizar. —**waterproofing,** *n.* impermeabilización.
water rat 1, (European animal) rata de agua. **2,** = **muskrat.**
watershed *n.* vertiente; cuenca.
waterside *n.* **orilla;** borde del agua.
water ski esquí acuático.
water-soak *v.t.* empapar de agua.
water spaniel perro de aguas.
water sports deportes acuáticos.
waterspout *n.* **1,** *meteorol.* tromba marina; manga de agua. **2,** (duct) canelón. **3,** (outlet for water) boquilla.
water spring manantial.
water supply abastecimiento de agua.
water table nivel superior del agua subterránea.
water tank aljibe; cisterna.
water tender aljibe; buque cisterna.
watertight *adj.* **1,** (impermeable) impermeable; estanco. **2,** *fig.* (unassailable) seguro; inatacable.
water tower 1, (elevated water tank) arca de agua. **2,** (firefighting apparatus) torre de agua para incendios.
water wave ondulación al agua.
waterway *n.* **1,** (channel) canal. **2,** (navigable stream) río navegable; vía fluvial. **3,** (current) corriente de agua.
water wheel 1, (for power) rueda hidráulica. **2,** (for lifting water) rueda de agua.
water wings nadaderas.
waterworks *n.sing.* & *pl.* obras hidráulicas.
waterworn *adj.* gastado por la acción del agua.
watery ('wat·ər·i) *adj.* **1,** (of or pert. to water; containing water) acuoso; ácueo; de agua. **2,** (moist; wet) mojado. **3,** (thin; diluted) aguado; claro; ralo. **4,** (tearful) lagrimoso; lloroso. **5,** (weak; insipid) insípido; evaporado. **6,** (full of or secreting a morbid discharge) seroso.
watt (wat) *n.* vatio. —**wattage,** *n.* vatiaje.
wattle ('wat·əl) *n.* **1,** (framework) zarzo. **2,** *ornith.* barba. —*v.t.* **1,** (intertwine) entrelazar; entretejer. **2,** (construct with wattles) construir con zarzos.

wattmeter *n.* vatímetro.
wave (weiv) *v.t.* **1,** (agitate) agitar; sacudir; hacer oscilar. **2,** (brandish) blandir. **3,** (form in waves) ondular. **4,** (signal with) hacer señales con. —*v.i.* **1,** (undulate) ondear; ondular. **2,** (signal) hacer señales con la maño. —*n.* **1,** (movement of water) ola; onda. **2,** (spell, as of heat or cold) ola de calor, de frío, etc. **3,** (undulation) onda. **4,** (signal, as with the hand) señal. **5,** (curves or curls in the hair) ondulación.
wave band banda de ondas.
wave length longitud de onda.
wavelet ('weiv·lɪt) *n.* oleadita; olita.
waver ('wei·vər) *v.i.* **1,** (sway; flutter) ondear; oscilar; tremolar. **2,** (vacillate) vacilar; dudar; estar indeciso. **3,** (tremble) temblar; vibrar. **4,** (fluctuate) fluctuar. —*n.* **1,** (flutter) oscilación. **2,** (vacillation) vacilación. **3,** (trembling) temblor; vibración. **4,** (fluctuation) fluctuación.
wavering ('wei·vər·ɪŋ) *adj.* ligero; inconstante; irresoluto. —*n.* irresolución; vacilación; fluctuación.
wavy ('weiv·i) *adj.* ondulado; ondulante.
wax (wæks) *n.* cera. —*v.t.* encerar; dar con cera. —*v.i.* **1,** (grow; increase) crecer; aumentarse. **2,** (become) hacerse; ponerse; volverse.
waxen ('wæk·sən) *adj.* ceroso; de *o* como cera.
wax match cerilla; *Amer.* cerillo.
wax museum museo de cera.
wax paper papel encerado.
wax taper cerilla.
waxworks *n.pl.* obras de cera; figuras de cera.
waxy ('wæks·i) *adj.* ceroso; de *o* como cera.
way (wei) *n.* **1,** (road; path) camino; vía. **2,** (manner) modo; manera; *pl.* modales. **3,** (means) medio. **4,** (custom) uso; costumbre; hábito. **5,** (direction) dirección; sentido. **6,** (distance) distancia. **7,** (condition) condición; estado. **8,** *pl.*, *naut.* anguilas. —*adv.*, *colloq.* lejos. —**across the way,** a otro lado; en frente. —**across the way from,** enfrente de; frente a. —**all the way,** por todo el camino; hasta el fin; hasta lo extremo. —**any way,** de cualquier manera; de todas maneras. —**be in the way,** estorbar; incomodar. —**by the way, 1,** (in passing) de paso. **2,** (along the way) por el camino. **3,** (incidentally) a propósito. —**by way of, 1,** (via) vía; por. **2,** (by means of) por vía de; por modo de. **3,** (in the capacity of) a título de. —**every way; every which way,** *colloq.* **1,** (in every direction) por todas partes; de todos lados. **2,** (in every manner or respect) de todas maneras. —**get in the way,** estorbar; incomodar; meterse. —**get out of the way,** quitar(se) de en medio; quitarse de encima (*una tarea*). —**get under way, 1,** (begin) iniciar(se); comenzar(se). **2,** *naut.* hacerse a la vela. —**give way, 1,** (yield) ceder; retroceder. **2,** (break) romperse. —**give way to,** entregarse a; echarse a. —**go one's way,** marcharse. —**go out of one's way, 1,** (detour) desviarse; dar rodeos. **2,** (inconvenience oneself) darse molestia; molestarse. —**have a way with,** entenderse con; llevarse bien con. —**have one's way,** salirse con la suya. —**in a bad way,** *colloq.* en mal estado. —**in a way,** de cierto modo; de cierta manera. —**in the way,** que estorba; que incomoda. —**in the way of,** como; a título de; a guisa de. —**keep out of the way,** apartar(se); echar(se) de un lado. —**lose one's way,** perderse. —**make one's way, 1,** (open a path) abrirse paso. **2,** (succeed) hacer carrera; tener éxito. —**make way,** abrir(se) paso; ceder el paso. —**mend one's ways,** mudar de vida. —**on the way, 1,** (in passing) de paso. **2,** (along the way) en el camino. —**out of the way, 1,** (aside) a un lado. **2,** (disposed of) acabado; despachado. **3,** (remote) lejano; apartado. **4,** (concealed) escondido; ocultado. **5,** (improper) impropio; fuera de orden. **6,** (unusual) fuera de lo común. **7,** (lost) perdido; descarriado. —**over the way,** a otro lado; en frente. —**pave the way (for),** allanar el camino (a). —**put out of the way,** quitar de en medio. —**see one's way (clear) to,** ver el modo (de). —**take one's way,** marcharse. —**under way,** en

marcha; en camino; *naut.* a la vela. —**way down**, bajada. —**way in**, entrada. —**way off**, *colloq.* lejos. —**way out**, salida. —**ways and means**, medios y arbitrios. —**way through**, pasaje. —**way up**, subida.
waybill ('wei·bıl) *n.* hoja de ruta.
wayfarer ('wei·fɛr·ər) *n.* pasajero; viajante; caminante. —**wayfaring**, *adj.* caminante.
waylay ('wei·lei) *v.t.* [*pret.* & *p.p.* **waylaid** (-leid)] asechar; trasechar.
-ways (weiz) *sufijo; forma adverbios denotando* dirección; manera; posición: *endways,* derecho; de punta.
wayside *n.* borde del camino.
way station estación secundaria; estación de paso.
wayward ('wei·wərd) *adj.* **1,** (erring; straying) descarriado; extraviado. **2,** (willful) díscolo; indócil; voluntarioso. **3,** (capricious) voluble; veleidoso.
waywardness ('wei·wərd·nəs) *n.* **1,** (straying) descarrío; extravío. **2,** (willfulness) indocilidad; voluntariedad. **3,** (capriciousness) volubilidad; veleidad.
we (wi) *pers.pron.* nosotros; *fem.* nosotras.
weak (wik) *adj.* débil; endeble; flojo.
weaken ('wik·ən) *v.t.* & *i.* **1,** (make or become weak) debilitar(se); enflaquecer. **2,** (diminish) disminuir(se); atenuar(se).
weakfish *n.* pez americano comestible.
weak-kneed *adj.* irresoluto; cobarde.
weakling ('wik·lıŋ) *n.* **1,** (frail person) alfeñique. **2,** (coward) cobarde. —*adj.* débil.
weakly ('wik·li) *adj.* enclenque; enfermizo; achacoso. —*adv.* débilmente.
weak-minded *adj.* **1,** (feeble-minded) imbécil; falto de seso. **2,** (irresolute) irresoluto.
weakness ('wik·nəs) *n.* **1,** (feebleness) debilidad. **2,** (liking; fondness) gusto; afición.
weal (wil) *n.* **1,** (mark of a whip or stick) roncha; raya; verdugón. **2,** *archaic* (welfare) bienestar.
wealth (wɛlθ) *n.* riqueza.
wealthy ('wɛlθ·i) *adj.* rico; opulento; adinerado. —**wealthiness,** *n.* afluencia; opulencia.
wean (wi:n) *v.t.* destetar; *fig.* apartar. —**weaning,** *n.* destete.
weanling ('wi:n·lıŋ) *n.* niño *o* animal destetado.
weapon ('wɛp·ən) *n.* arma.
weaponed ('wɛp·ənd) *adj.* armado.
weaponless ('wɛp·ən·ləs) *adj.* desarmado.
wear (we:r) *v.t.* [*pret.* **wore**; *p.p.* **worn**] **1,** (carry on the body) llevar; usar. **2,** (consume) gastar; consumir. **3,** (weary) cansar; agotar. **4,** (show; manifest) manifestar; exhibir. —*v.i.* **1,** (be consumed) gastarse; consumirse. **2,** (last; hold up) durar; ser duradero. **3,** (pass, as time) pasar; correr. —*n.* **1,** (deterioration) desgaste; deterioro. **2,** (use) uso. **3,** (clothing) ropa. **4,** (fashion) estilo; moda. **5,** (durability) durabilidad. —**wear away,** gastar(se); consumir(se). —**wear down, 1,** (deteriorate) gastar(se); consumir(se). **2,** (tire) cansar(se); agotar(se). —**wear off, 1,** (consume or be consumed) gastar(se); consumir(se). **2,** (disappear gradually) pasar; desaparecer. —**wear on,** pasar lentamente. —**wear out, 1,** (deteriorate) gastar(se); deteriorar(se). **2,** (fatigue) cansar(se); agotar(se).
wearable ('wɛr·ə·bəl) *adj.* que se puede llevar. —**wearables,** *n.pl.* ropa; prendas de vestir.
wear and tear desgaste; deterioro.
wearer ('wɛr·ər) *n.* usador; quien lleva (una cosa).
weariness ('wır·i·nəs) *n.* **1,** (fatigue) cansancio; fatiga; lasitud. **2,** (boredom) tedio; fastidio; aburrimiento.
wearing ('wɛr·ıŋ) *adj.* **1,** (for wear) que se lleva. **2,** (causing deterioration) que consume; que deteriora. **3,** (tiresome) tedioso; fastidioso. —**wearing apparel,** ropa; prendas de vestir.
wearisome ('wır·i·səm) *adj.* tedioso; fastidioso; aburrido. —**wearisomeness,** *n.* tedio; fastidio; aburrimiento.
weary ('wır·i) *adj.* **1,** (tired) agotado; cansado. **2,** (causing fatigue) penoso; fastidioso. **3,** (dis-

contented) descontento; aburrido. —*v.t.* & *i.* cansar(se).

weasel ('wi·zəl) *n.* comadreja.

weather ('wɛð·ər) *n.* **1,** (atmospheric condition) tiempo. **2,** (inclement conditions) intemperie. —*v.t.* **1,** (expose to weather) airear; solear. **2,** (impair by exposure) desgastar; deteriorar (*por la intemperie*). **3,** (resist; survive) aguantar; superar; sobrevivir a. —*v.i.* **1,** (deteriorate by exposure) desgastarse por la intemperie. **2,** (resist exposure) resistir a la intemperie. —*adj.* **1,** (atmospheric) atmosférico. **2,** (meteorological) meterológico. **3,** *naut.* de barlovento. —**keep one's weather eye open,** *colloq.* velar; vigilar; estar a la mira. —**under the weather,** *colloq.* **1,** (ill) indispuesto; enfermo. **2,** (drunk) borracho.

weatherbeaten ('wɛð·ər·bit·ən) *adj.* curtido *o* gastado por la intemperie.

weatherboard *n.* **1,** (clapboard) tabla(s) de chilla. **2,** *naut.* lado del viento.

weathercock *n.* veleta.

weatherglass *n.* barómetro.

weathering ('wɛð·ər·ɪŋ) *n.* desgaste (*por la acción atmosférica*).

weatherman *n.* [*pl.* **-men**] meteorologista.

weatherproof *adj.* a prueba del tiempo.

weather strip burlete.

weather vane veleta.

weather-wise *adj.* hábil en la pronosticación del tiempo; *fig.* perceptivo; perspicaz.

weave (wiːv) *v.t.* [*pret.* **wove;** *p.p.* **woven**] **1,** (form into fabric) tejer. **2,** (interlace) entretejer; entrelazar; trenzar. **3,** (unite) unir; reunir. **4,** (construct) construir. —*v.i.* **1,** (do weaving) tejer. **2,** (become interlaced) entrelazarse. **3,** (move from side to side) zigzaguear.

weaver ('wi·vər) *n.* tejedor.

weaving ('wi·vɪŋ) *n.* **1,** (making of fabric) tejido. **2,** (motion from side to side) zigzagueo.

web (wɛb) *n.* **1,** (woven fabric) tejido; tela. **2,** (tissue) tejido. **3,** (network) red. **4,** (spider's web) telaraña. **5,** (membrane) membrana. **6,** (trap; snare) trampa; red; enredo.

webbed (wɛbd) *adj.* **1,** (woven) tejido. **2,** (joined by a web) palmeado.

webbing ('wɛb·ɪŋ) *n.* **1,** (strip of woven cloth) tira de tela; cinta. **2,** (membrane) membrana.

webfooted *adj.* palmípedo.

we'd (wiːd) *contr. de* **we should, we would** *o* **we had.**

wed (wɛd) *v.t.* [**wedded, wedding**] **1,** (join in matrimony) casar. **2,** (give in marriage) dar en casamiento; casar. **3,** (take as a spouse) casarse con. —*v.i.* casarse.

wedded ('wɛd·ɪd) *adj.* casado.

wedding ('wɛd·ɪŋ) *n.* boda; bodas; casamiento; nupcias. —*adj.* de boda; nupcial.

wedge (wɛdʒ) *n.* cuña. —*v.t.* acuñar; apretar; encajar. —*v.i.* forzarse; encajarse.

wedlock ('wɛd·lak) *n.* matrimonio.

Wednesday ('wɛnz·de) *n.* miércoles.

wee (wiː) *adj.* menudo; diminuto; chiquitico.

weed (wiːd) *n.* **1,** (undesired plant) mala hierba; yerbajo. **2,** *colloq.* (tobacco) tabaco; cigarro; cigarrillo. **3,** *pl.* (mourning clothes) ropa de luto. —*v.t.* & *i.* escardar; desherbar. —**weed out,** arrancar; extirpar; eliminar.

weeder ('wid·ər) *n.* **1,** (person) escardador; desherbador. **2,** (tool) escarda.

weeding ('wid·ɪŋ) *n.* escarda; deshierba. —**weeding hoe,** escarda.

weedy ('wid·i) *adj.* **1,** (full of weeds) lleno de malas hierbas. **2,** (lanky) flaco; larguirucho.

week (wik) *n.* semana.

weekday *n.* día laborable.

week end fin de semana. *También,* **weekend** ('wik,ɛnd) *n.* —*v.i.* pasar el fin de semana.

weekly ('wik·li) *adj.* semanal. —*adv.* semanalmente. —*n.* semanario.

ween (wiːn) *v.t.* & *i., archaic* pensar; creer; suponer.

weenie *también,* **weeny** ('wi·ni) *n., colloq.* = **wiener.**

weep (wip) *v.i.* [*pret.* & *p.p.* **wept**] **1,** (shed tears; emit moisture) llorar. **2,** (droop) languidecer. —*v.t.* **1,** (shed) verter; derramar (lágrimas). **2,** (lament)

lamentar; llorar. —**weeper**, *n.* llorón.
weeping ('wip·ɪŋ) *n.* lloro; lloriqueo. —*adj.* llorón; lloroso.
weeping willow sauce llorón.
weevil ('wi·vəl) *n.* gorgojo.
weft (wɛft) *n.* trama.
weigh (wei) *v.t.* & *i.* pesar. —**weigh anchor**, levar el ancla; levar anclas. —**weigh down**, sobrecargar; agobiar. —**weigh in**, *sports* pesarse. —**weigh on**, oprimir; agobiar. —**weigh out**, pesar (*en determinadas cantidades*).
weight (weit) *n.* **1,** (unit of weight; measure of weight; something heavy) peso. **2,** (heaviness) peso; pesantez; pesadez. **3,** (load; burden) peso; carga; gravamen. **4,** (counterweight) pesa; contrapeso. **5,** (importance) importancia; significado. **6,** (influence) influencia. —*v.t.* **1,** (add weight to) poner (un) peso a. **2,** (load; burden) cargar; gravar. **3,** (give a certain value to) dar valor o importancia a. —**carry weight**, tener importancia, valor o influencia. —**lose weight**, rebajar de peso. —**pull one's weight**, hacer su parte. —**put on weight**, aumentar de peso.
weighty (weit·i) *adj.* **1,** (heavy) pesado; ponderoso. **2,** (burdensome) gravoso. **3,** (important) importante. **4,** (influential) influyente. —**weightiness**, *n.* pesadez.
weir (wɪr) *n.* **1,** (sluice) compuerta. **2,** (low dam) presa. **3,** (fence for catching fish) cañal; cerco de cañas.
weird (wɪrd) *adj.* **1,** (eerie) sobrenatural; espectral; misterioso. **2,** *colloq.* (odd) extraño; raro.
Weird Sisters Las Parcas.
welch (wɛltʃ) *v.t.* & *i.* = **welsh.**
welcome ('wɛl·kəm) *adj.* bienvenido. —*n.* bienvenida; recepción; acogida. —*v.t.* dar la bienvenida a; recibir; acoger. —*interj.* ¡bienvenido! —**you're welcome**, no hay de qué; de nada. —**you're welcome to it**, está a la disposición de Vd.; se lo regalo.
weld (wɛld) *v.t.* soldar; *fig.* juntar; unir. —*n.* soldadura; unión; juntura. —**welder**, *n.* soldador. —**welding**, *n.* soldadura.
welfare ('wɛl,fɛr) *n.* **1,** (well-being) bienestar. **2,** (aid to the needy) asistencia pública.
we'll (wi:l) *contr. de* **we shall** *o* **we will.**
well (wɛl) *n.* **1,** (hole; shaft) pozo. **2,** (spring) fuente; manantial. **3,** (source) fuente. **4,** (stairwell) hueco de escalera. —*v.i.* manar; bullir; borbotar. —*v.t.* manar. —*adv.* bien. —*adj.* bien; bueno. —*interj.* ¡bien!; ¡bueno!; ¡vaya! —**as well**, *también.* —**as well as**, así como. —**well and good**, enhorabuena; bien está. —**well then**, pues bien.
well-accomplished *adj.* consumado; completo.
well-acquainted *adj.* **1,** = **well-informed. 2,** (on familiar terms) familiar; íntimo; muy conocido.
well-advised *adj.* prudente; bien aconsejado.
well-aimed *adj.* certero.
well-appointed *adj.* bien amueblado; bien equipado.
well-attended *adj.* bien concurrido.
well-balanced *adj.* bien balanceado; bien ajustado; bien equilibrado.
well-behaved *adj.* de buena conducta.
well-being *n.* bienestar.
wellborn *adj.* bien nacido.
wellbred *adj.* bien educado; bien criado; cortés.
well-chosen *adj.* selecto; escogido.
well-cooked *adj.* bien cocido.
well-defined *adj.* claro; evidente; manifiesto.
well-disposed *adj.* **1,** (well arranged) bien arreglado. **2,** (favorably inclined) bien dispuesto.
well-doer *n.* bienhechor.
well-done *adj.* **1,** (well-cooked) bien cocido. **2,** (well-made) bien hecho. *También,* **well done.** —**well done!**, ¡ánimo!; ¡bien va!; ¡bravo!
well-favored *adj.* hermoso; guapo; bien parecido.
well-fed *adj.* rechoncho; regordete; *fig.* próspero.
well-fixed *adj., colloq.* rico; pertrechado; acomodado.
well-founded *adj.* bien fundado.
well-groomed *adj.* bien arreglado; acicalado.
well-grounded *adj.* **1,** = **well-informed. 2,** = **well-founded.**
wellhead *n.* **1,** (source) fuente;

origen. **2,** (spring) fuente; manantial.

well-heeled *adj., slang* rico; pertrechado; acomodado.

well-informed *adj.* bien informado.

well-kept *adj.* bien cuidado; bien atendido.

well-known *adj.* bien conocido; familiar.

well-made *adj.* bien hecho; bien formado.

well-mannered *adj.* de buenos modales; cortés.

well-meaning *adj.* bienintencionado.

well-meant *adj.* bienintencionado.

well-off *adj.* afortunado; acomodado; adinerado.

well-ordered *adj.* bien ordenado; bien arreglado.

well-read (wɛl'rɛd) *adj.* muy leído; educado.

well-rounded *adj.* **1,** (shapely) redondeado; bien proporcionado. **2,** (complete) completo; cabal; íntegro.

well-spent *adj.* bien empleado.

well-spoken *adj.* bienhablado.

wellspring *n.* fuente; manantial.

well sweep cigüeñal.

well-thought-of *adj.* bienquisto; de buena fama.

well-timed *adj.* oportuno.

well-to-do ('wɛl·tə,du) *adj.* acomodado; adinerado.

well-turned *adj.* simétrico; bien formado.

well-wisher *n.* amigo; partidario.

well-worded *adj.* bien expresado.

well-worn *adj.* gastado; trillado; vulgar.

well-wrought *adj.* bien trabajado.

welsh (wɛlʃ) *v.i., slang* defraudar; retirarse. —**welsh on,** retirarse de; dejar de cumplir.

Welsh (wɛlʃ) *adj.* & *n.* galés. —**Welshman** (-mən) *n.* [*pl.* **-men**] galés.

Welsh rabbit plato de queso derretido con cerveza que se sirve con tostadas. *También,* **Welsh rarebit.**

welt (wɛlt) *n.* **1,** (mark of a whip or stick) roncha; raya; verdugón. **2,** (part of a shoe) vira. **3,** (cord trimming) ribete.

welter ('wɛl·tər) *v.i.* **1,** (wallow) revolcarse. **2,** (be soaked) empaparse. **3,** (toss; tumble) agitarse; menearse. —*n.* **1,** (tossing; tumbling) agitación; meneo. **2,** (turmoil) confusión; alboroto; tumulto.

wen (wɛn) *n.* lobanillo.

wench (wɛntʃ) *n.* **1,** (girl) moza; muchacha. **2,** (lewd woman) ramera; puta. —*v.i.* putear.

wend (wɛnd) *v.i.* proceder; dirigirse. —*v.t.* dirigir; seguir (su camino).

went (wɛnt) *v., pret. de* **go.**

wept (wɛpt) *v., pret. & p.p. de* **weep.**

we're (wɪr) *contr. de* **we are.**

were (wʌɹ) *v., pret. de* **be.** —**as it were,** por decirlo así; como si fuese.

werewolf ('wɪr·wʊlf; 'wʌɹ-) *n.* hombre que se convierte en lobo.

west (wɛst) *n.* oeste; poniente; occidente. —*adj.* oeste; del oeste; occidental. —*adv.* hacia el oeste; al oeste.

westerly ('wɛst·ər·li) *adj.* oeste; occidental; del oeste; hacia el oeste. —*adv.* hacia el oeste.

western ('wɛst·ərn) *adj.* occidental; al *o* del oeste. —*n.* película o cuento que trata del oeste de los EE.UU.

westerner ('wɛst·ərn·ər) *n.* occidental; habitante del oeste.

westward ('wɛst·wərd) *adj.* en *o* de dirección oeste. —*adv.* hacia el oeste.

wet (wɛt) *adj.* **1,** (covered with moisture) mojado; húmedo. **2,** (rainy) lluvioso. **3,** (not yet dry) fresco. **4,** *colloq.* (opposed to prohibition) antiprohibicionista. —*n.* **1,** (moisture) humedad. **2,** (water) agua. **3,** (rain) lluvia. **4,** *colloq.* (one opposed to prohibition) antiprohibicionista. —*v.t. & i.* [**wet** *o* **wetted, wetting**] **1,** (moisten) humedecer(se). **2,** (urinate) orinar(se). —**all wet,** *slang* equivocado. —**wet one's whistle,** *colloq.* tomar una bebida; tomar un chispo.

wetback ('wɛt·bæk) *n.* bracero mexicano ilegalmente entrado en los EE.UU.

wet blanket *slang* aguafiestas.

wetness ('wɛt·nəs) *n.* humedad.

wet nurse ama de leche; ama

de cría; nodriza. **—wet-nurse,** *v.t.* criar; dar de mamar.

we've (wi:v) *contr.de* **we have.**

whack (hwæk) *v.t. & i.* pegar; golpear; vapulear. —*n.* **1,** (blow) golpe. **2,** *slang* (attempt) prueba; lance; tentativa. **3,** *slang* (share) porción; parte. **—out of whack,** *slang* que no funciona bien. **—whack up,** *slang* dividir; repartir.

whacking ('hwæk·ɪŋ) *adj., slang* grande; enorme.

whacky ('hwæk·i) *adj., slang* = **wacky.**

whale (hweil) *n.* ballena. —*v.t., colloq.* azotar; vapulear; zurrar. —*v.i.* pescar ballenas. **—a whale of a. . . . .**, *colloq.* un. . . . . enorme, extraordinario, *etc.*

whaleboat *n.* ballenero.

whalebone *n.* ballena.

whaler ('hweil·ər) *n.* ballenero.

whaling ('hweil·ɪŋ) *n.* **1,** (whale fishing) pesca de ballenas; industria ballenera. **2,** *colloq.* (thrashing) paliza; zurra.

whang (hwæŋ) *v.t. & i.* golpear ruidosamente. —*n.* golpe.

wharf (hworf) *n.* [*pl.* **wharves** (hworvz) *o* **wharfs**] embarcadero; muelle.

wharfage ('hworf·ɪdʒ) *n.* muellaje.

what (hwat) *pron.rel.* lo que. —*pron.interr.* ¿qué?; ¿cuál? —*adj. rel.* el (la, los, las). . . . que. —*adj.interr.* ¿qué. . . . ? —*interj.* ¡qué! **—and what not,** y qué sé yo qué más. **—what a. . . . !**, ¡qué. . . . ! **—what about. . . . ?**, ¿y. . . . ?: *what about the children?*, ¿y los niños? **—what for, 1,** (why) ¿para qué?; ¿por qué? **2,** *slang* (punishment) castigo; paliza; zurra. **—what if,** ¿y si. . . . ?; qué será si. . . . ? **—what it takes,** *colloq.* lo necesario. **—what of it** (*o* **that**)?, ¿qué importa eso? **—what though,** aun cuando; ¿qué importa que. . . . ? **—what's what,** *colloq.* las realidades; las cosas como están; cuántas son cinco.

whatever *pron.* cualquier cosa que; todo lo que; no importa que. —*adj.* cualquier . . . que.

whatnot *n.* **1,** (shelf for bric-a-brac) rinconera; estante. **2,** (anything) cualquier cosa.

whatsoever *pron. & adj.* = **whatever.**

wheal (hwi:l) *n.* roncha; raya; verdugón.

wheat (hwit) *n.* trigo.

wheaten ('hwit·ən) *adj.* de trigo.

wheedle ('hwi·dəl) *v.t.* **1,** (cajole; coax) halagar; engatusar; hacer la rueda a. **2,** (get by cajolery) conseguir por halagos; sonsacar.

wheel (hwi:l) *n.* **1,** (circular frame) rueda. **2,** (bicycle) bicicleta. **3,** (steering device) volante. **4,** (helm) timón; gobierno. **5,** *slang* (important person) dignatario; alto personaje. —*v.t.* **1,** (move on wheels) mover *o* transportar por medio de ruedas. **2,** (turn; roll) hacer girar; hacer rodar. **3,** (provide with wheels) proveer de ruedas. —*v.i.* girar; rodar. **—wheel about, 1,** (turn) dar vuelta; virar. **2,** (change) cambiar (de opinión; de partido, etc.).

wheelbarrow *n.* carretón; carretilla.

wheelbase *n.* base de ejes; distancia entre ejes.

wheel chair silla de ruedas.

wheeled (hwi:ld) *adj.* con ruedas.

wheel horse caballo de varas; *fig.* trabajador; persona emprendedora.

wheelhouse *n.* caseta del timón.

wheeling ('hwil·ɪŋ) *n.* **1,** (rolling; moving on wheels) rodadura. **2,** (road conditions) estado; condición (*de una carretera*). **3,** (cycling) paseo en bicicleta. **4,** (rotation) rotación.

wheelman ('hwil·mən) *n.* [*pl.* **-men**] **1,** (helmsman) timonel; timonero. **2,** (cyclist) ciclista.

wheelwork ('hwil·wʌɹk) *n.* rodaje.

wheelwright ('hwil·rait) *n.* aperador; carretero.

wheeze (hwi:z) *v.i.* resollar; jadear. —*n.* **1,** (act or sound of wheezing) jadeo; resuello. **2,** *slang* (trite remark) cuento o chiste viejo; perogrullada.

whelk (hwɛlk) *n.* **1,** *zool.* buccino. **2,** (pimple) grano; barro.

whelm (hwɛlm) *v.t.* aplastar; abrumar; anonadar.

whelp (hwɛlp) *n.* cachorro. —*v.i. & t.* parir; dar a luz.

when (hwɛn) *adv., conj. & n.* cuando.
whence (hwɛns) *adv.* **1,** (from what place) de donde. **2,** (wherefore) por eso; por consiguiente. —*conj.* de donde.
whencesoever *adv.* de dondequiera. —*conj.* de dondequiera que.
whenever *conj.* cuando quiera que; siempre que. —*adv.* cuando.
where (hweːr) *adv. & conj.* **1,** (at or in what place) donde; en donde; por donde. **2,** (to or toward what place) adonde. **3,** (from what place) de donde.
where- (hweːr) *prefijo, usado en combinación con preposiciones:* lo que; que: *whereby,* por lo que; *whereinto,* dentro de lo que.
whereabouts *n.* paradero. —*adv. & conj.* donde; por donde.
whereas *conj.* **1,** (since) puesto que; ya que; en vista de que. **2,** (while on the contrary) mientras que; por el contrario.
whereat *conj.* a lo cual; con lo cual.
whereby *adv.* por lo cual; con lo cual; ¿cómo?; ¿de dónde?
wherefore *adv.* **1,** (why) porque; por qué. **2,** (for which) por lo que. —*conj.* por eso; por consiguiente. —*n.* el porqué.
wherein *adv.* donde; en donde; en que.
whereinto *adv.* en donde; dentro de lo que.
whereof *conj.* de lo cual; de que.
whereon *adv.* en que; sobre lo cual.
wheresoever *adv.* dondequiera. —*conj.* dondequiera que.
whereto *adv.* adonde; a lo que.
whereupon *adv.* sobre que; en donde. —*conj.* con lo cual; después de lo cual.
wherever (hwɛr'ɛv·ər) *adv., colloq.* ¿dónde? —*conj.* dondequiera que.
wherewith *adv.* con que; con lo cual. —*n.* lo necesario.
wherewithal *n.* los medios; lo necesario.
whet (hwɛt) *v.t.* [**whetted, whetting**] **1,** (sharpen) afilar; aguzar. **2,** (stimulate) estimular; abrir (el apetito).
whether ('hwɛð·ər) *conj.* si. —**whether . . . or,** sea (que) . . . o; si . . . o. —**whether or no,** en todo caso; de todas maneras.
whetstone *n.* piedra de afilar; esmoladera.
whey (hwei) *n.* suero.
wheyey ('hwei·i) *adj.* seroso.
which (hwɪtʃ) *pron.rel.* que; el (la, lo, los, las) que. —*pron.interr.* ¿cuál?; cuáles? —*adj.rel.* el (la, los, las) que. —*adj.interr.* ¿qué . . . ?; ¿cuál? ¿cuáles?
whichever *pron. & adj.* cualquiera; cualesquiera.
whiff (hwɪf) *n.* **1,** (puff; breath) soplo; vaharada. **2,** (odor; reek) vaho. **3,** (puff of smoke) fumada; fumarada; bocanada. **4,** (small amount) pizca. —*v.t.* **1,** (waft) llevar por el aire; llevar con un soplo. **2,** (blow out in puffs) echar en bocanadas. **3,** (smoke) fumar. —*v.i.* **1,** (blow) soplar. **2,** (emit puffs) echar bocanadas.
whiffletree ('hwɪf·əl·tri) *n.* balancín.
while (hwail) *n.* rato. —*conj.* mientras que; a la vez que. —*v.t.* pasar. —**all the while (that),** todo el tiempo (que). —**between whiles,** de vez en cuando. —**the while,** mientras tanto. —**while away,** pasar (divirtiéndose); engañar (el tiempo). —**worth the** (*o* **one's**) **while,** provechoso; que vale la pena.
whilst (hwailst) *conj.* mientras que.
whim (hwɪm) *n.* antojo; capricho; veleidad.
whimper ('hwɪm·pər) *v.i.* lloriquear. —*v.t.* decir lloriqueando. —*n.* lloriqueo; quejido.
whimsical ('hwɪm·zɪ·kəl) *adj.* caprichoso; fantástico. —**whimsicality** (-'kæl·ə·ti) *n.* capricho; fantasía.
whimsy ('hwɪm·zi) *n.* **1,** (whim) capricho; veleidad; fantasía. **2,** (quaint humor) humorismo raro o anticuado.
whimwham ('hwɪm,hwæm) *n.* **1,** (trinket) bagatela; baratija. **2,** = **whim. 3,** *pl.* (jitters) nerviosidad.
whin (hwɪn) *n.* tojo.
whine (hwain) *v.i.* lloriquear; gimotear. —*v.t.* decir lloriqueando. —*n.* lloriqueo; gimoteo; llanto.
whinny ('hwɪn·i) *v.i.* relinchar. —*n.* relincho.
whip (hwɪp) *v.t.* [**whipped, whipping**] **1,** (lash; beat) azotar. **2,** (seize or move swiftly) coger, sacar, lanzar, etc. súbitamente. **3,**

(urge on; drive) empujar; estimular; aguijonear. **4,** (beat, as eggs or cream) batir. **5,** *colloq.* (defeat) derrotar; vencer. —*v.i.* **1,** (move swiftly) lanzarse; arrojarse. **2,** (thrash about) sacudirse; agitarse. —*n.* **1,** (lash) azote; látigo. **2,** (kind of dessert) batido. **3,** *polit.* subjefe de partido (*en un cuerpo legislativo*). —**whip up, 1,** (arouse) excitar; estimular. **2,** (prepare hastily) hacer o preparar de prisa.

whipcord ('hwɪp,kord) *n.* tela gruesa con canillas diagonales.

whip hand mano del látigo; *fig.* ventaja; dominio.

whiplash *n.* **1,** (point of a whip) tralla; punta de látigo. **2,** (blow with a whip) latigazo.

whipped cream crema batida.

whipped potatoes puré de papas.

whipper ('hwɪp·ər) *n.* azotador.

whipper-snapper ('hwɪp·ər·,snæp·ər) *n.* impertinente; mequetrefe; casquivano.

whippet ('hwɪp·ɪt) *n.* lebrel.

whipping ('hwɪp·ɪŋ) *n.* **1,** (flogging) paliza; azotaina. **2,** *colloq.* (defeat) derrota.

whipping boy cabeza de turco; víctima.

whippletree ('hwɪp·əl·tri) *n.* balancín.

whippoor-will ('hwɪp·ər,wɪl) *n.* chotacabras norteamericano.

whir (hwʌɹ) *v.i.* [**whirred, whirring**] girar dando zumbido. —*v.i.* hacer girar con zumbido. —*n.* zumbido.

whirl ('hwʌɹl) *v.i.* arremolinarse; girar; dar vueltas. —*v.t.* hacer girar. —*n.* **1,** (turn) vuelta; giro. **2,** (swirl) remolino; torbellino. **3,** (tumult) tumulto; alboroto. **4,** (giddiness) vahido; vértigo.

whirligig ('hwʌɹl·ə·gɪg) *n.* **1,** (toy) molinete; molinillo. **2,** (merry-go-round) tiovivo. **3,** = **whirligig beetle.**

whirligig beetle escribano del agua.

whirlpool *n.* remolino.

whirlwind ('hwʌɹl,wɪnd) *n.* torbellino; manga *o* tromba de viento.

whirlybird ('hwɪrl·i,bʌɹd) *n.*, *slang* helicóptero.

whish (hwɪʃ) *n.* zumbido; silbido. —*v.i.* zumbar; silbar.

whisk (hwɪsk) *n.* **1,** (brush) escobilla; cepillo. **2,** (swift movement) movimiento rápido. **3,** (bunch of straw) manojo. **4,** (wire beater) batidor. —*v.t.* **1,** (clean with a brush) cepillar. **2,** (move or remove swiftly) mover o llevar rápidamente. **3,** (beat) batir. —*v.i.* moverse rápidamente; marcharse de prisa. —**whisk away** (*o* **off**), quitar rápidamente; hacer desaparecer.

whisk broom escobilla.

whisker ('hwɪs·kər) *n.* pelo de la barba; *pl.* barba; barbas; (*of a cat*) bigotes. —**whiskered,** *adj.* barbado; barbudo.

whiskey *también,* **whisky** ('hwɪs·ki) *n.* whisky; licor.

whisper ('hwɪs·pər) *v.i.* **1,** (speak softly) cuchichear; susurrar. **2,** (rustle) susurrar. **3,** (gossip) chismear. —*v.t.* cuchichear; decir al oído; decir en voz baja. —*n.* **1,** (soft speech; something spoken softly) cuchicheo; susurro. **2,** (rustling sound) susurro. **3,** (gossip) chisme. —**in a whisper,** en voz baja.

whist (hwɪst) *n.* whist. —*interj.* ¡chito!; ¡chitón!

whistle ('hwɪs·əl) *v.t. & i.* silbar. —*n.* **1,** (sound) silbido; pitido. **2,** (device) silbato; pito. —**whistle for, 1,** (call by whistling) silbar a. **2,** *colloq.* (expect in vain) buscar o esperar en vano.

whit (hwɪt) *n.* ápice; jota; pizca. —**every whit,** del todo; enteramente. —**not a whit,** de ninguna manera. —**not care a whit (for),** no importarle a uno un ardite (*o* bledo *o* comino).

white (hwait) *adj.* **1,** (color) blanco. **2,** (pale) pálido. **3,** *colloq.* (honorable; fair) justo; recto; generoso. —*n.* **1,** (color; person or thing of white color) blanco. **2,** (white of egg) clara de huevo. —*v.t.* blanquear; blanquecer. —**bleed (someone) white,** agotarle a uno el dinero, los recursos, etc.

white ant termita; hormiga blanca.

whitecap *n., usu.pl.* paloma; palomilla; cabrilla.

white-collar *adj.* de oficina. —**white-collar worker,** oficinista.

white feather símbolo de cobardía. —**show the white feather,** mostrarse cobarde.

whitefish *n.* corégono.

white heat calor blanco; *fig.* ex-

citación; agitacíon. —**to a white heat,** al blanco.
white-hot *adj.* calentado al blanco; *fig.* excitado; muy agitado.
white lead albayalde.
white lie mentira oficiosa.
white-livered *adj.* cobarde.
whiten ('hwait·ən) *v.t.* blanquear; blanquecer. —*v.i.* blanquear; blanquecerse.
whiteness ('hwait·nəs) *n.* **1,** (white color) blancura. **2,** (paleness) palidez. **3,** (purity) pureza; candor.
whitening ('hwait·ən·ɪŋ) *n.* blanqueo.
white plague tuberculosis; tisis.
white slave prostituta involuntaria. —**white slavery,** trata de blancas.
whitewash *n.* **1,** (paint) lechada. **2,** (concealment) encubrimiento (*de faltas, injusticias, etc.*). **3,** *sports, colloq.* = **shut-out.** —*v.t.* **1,** (paint) blanquear; enjalbegar; enyesar. **2,** (conceal; gloss over) encubrir (faltas, injusticias, etc.). **3,** *sports, colloq.* = **shut out.**
whitewashing *n.* blanqueo.
whither ('hwɪð·ər) *adv.* adonde.
whithersoever *adv.* adondequiera.
whiting ('hwait·ɪŋ) *n.* **1,** (fish) merluza; pescada. **2,** (powdered chalk) blanco de España; tiza.
whitish ('hwait·ɪʃ) *adj.* blancuzco; blanquecino. —**whitishness,** *n.* blancura.
whitlow ('hwɪt·lo) *n.* panadizo.
Whitsun ('hwɪt·sən) *adj.* de Pentecostés. —**Whitmonday,** *n.* lunes de Pentecostés. —**Whitsunday,** *n.* domingo de Pentecostés. —**Whitsuntide** (-sən·taid) *n.* semana de Pentecostés.
whittle ('hwɪt·əl) *v.t.* & *i.* **1,** (carve) cortar *o* formar con un cuchillo. **2,** (curtail; reduce) disminuir poco a poco; cercenar.
whity ('hwait·i) *adj.* = **whitish.**
whiz (hwɪz) *v.i.* [**whizzed, whizzing**] zumbar; silbar. —*n.* **1,** (whirring sound) zumbido. **2,** *slang* (outstanding person or thing) fenómeno.
who (hu:) *pron.rel.* que; quien (*pl.* quienes); el (la, los, las) que. —*pron.interr.* ¿quién? (*pl.* ¿quiénes?).
whoa (hwo) *interj.* ¡so!
whodunit (hu'dʌn·ɪt) *n., slang* novela policíaca; drama policíaco.
whoever *pron.rel.* quienquiera que; cualquiera que; quien. —*pron. interr.* ¿quién?
whole (ho:l) *adj.* **1,** (entire; complete) entero; completo. **2,** (all) todo. **3,** (sound) sano; en buena salud. —*n.* total; todo. —**as a whole,** en conjunto. —**made out of whole cloth,** enteramente ficticio. —**on the whole,** en el todo; en general.
wholehearted *adj.* de todo corazón; sincero; entusiasta.
wholeness ('hol·nəs) *n.* totalidad; integridad.
wholesale ('hol·sel) *n.* venta al por mayor. —*adj.* **1,** (in large quantities) en grande; al por mayor. **2,** (widespread) general; extendido. —*v.t.* & *i.* vender(se) al por mayor. —**wholesaler,** *n.* mayorista.
wholesome ('hol·səm) *adj.* saludable; salubre. —**wholesomeness,** *n.* salubridad.
wholly ('ho·li) *adv.* totalmente; enteramente; completamente.
whom (hu:m) *pron. rel.* que; quien (*pl.* quienes); a quien (*pl.* a quienes). —*pron.interr.* ¿a quién?
whoop (hwup) *v.i.* **1,** (shout; cry) gritar; chillar; vocear. **2,** (pant) jadear; respirar ruidosa y convulsivamente. —*n.* **1,** (shout; cry) grito; alarido; chillido. **2,** (panting) jadeo; inspiración ruidosa y convulsiva. —*interj.* ¡ole!; ¡upa! —**whoop (it) up,** *slang* **1,** (celebrate noisily) alborotar; celebrar. **2,** (create enthusiasm for) fomentar; promover.
whoopee ('hwup·i) *n., slang* hilaridad; alegría. —*interj.* ¡olé! —**make whoopee,** *slang* celebrar; divertirse.
whooping cough tos ferina.
whoops (hwups) *interj.* ¡ay!
whopper ('hwap·ər) *n., colloq.* enormidad. —**whopping,** *adj., colloq.* enorme.
whore (ho:r) *n.* prostituta; puta. —*v.i.* putear.
whorehouse *n.* burdel; prostíbulo.
whoreson ('ho:r·sən) *n.* bastardo.
whoring ('hor·ɪŋ) *n.* putaísmo; putería.

whorish ('hor·ɪʃ) *adj.* putesco; lascivo.
whorl (hwʌɹl; hworl) *n.* espiral.
whortleberry ('hwʌɹ·təl,bɛr·i) *n.* arándano.
whose (hu:z) *pron.* & *adj.rel.* cuyo; de quien. —*pron.* & *adj.interr.* ¿de quién?
whosoever *pron.rel.* quienquiera que.
why (hwai) *adv.rel.* por qué. —*adv.interr.* ¿por qué? —*conj.* por qué; por lo que; por el que. —*n.* el porqué. —*interj.* ¡pues!; ¡cómo!; ¡que!; ¡pero . . . ! —**the why(s) and wherefore(s)**, los porqués y los cómos. —**why not?**, ¿cómo no?
wick (wɪk) *n.* pabilo; mecha.
wicked ('wɪk·ɪd) *adj.* **1,** (evil) malo; inicuo; perverso. **2,** (bad; grievous) malo; grave; penoso. **3,** (naughty) travieso; juguetón; picaresco. —**wickedness,** *n.* maldad; iniquidad; perversidad.
wicker ('wɪk·ər) *n.* mimbre. —*adj.* de mimbre.
wicker basket cesto de mimbres.
wickerwork *n.* cestería.
wicket ('wɪk·ɪt) *n.* **1,** (small door or gate) portillo; postigo. **2,** (small window) ventanilla. **3,** (hoop, in croquet) aro.
wide (waid) *adj.* **1,** (broad) ancho. **2,** (of a certain width) de ancho: *three feet wide,* tres pies de ancho. **3,** (extensive) amplio; extenso. **4,** (loose-fitting) holgado. **5,** (fully open) del todo abierto. —*adv.* **1,** (far) lejos. **2,** (fully) de par en par. **3,** (astray) fuera. —**wide of,** lejos de; fuera de.
wide-awake *adj.* despabilado; vigilante.
wide-eyed *adj.* con los ojos abiertos de par en par.
widely ('waid·li) *adv.* mucho; extensamente.
widen ('waid·ən) *v.t.* ensanchar. —*v.i.* ensancharse.
wideness ('waid·nəs) *n.* anchura.
widespread *adj.* **1,** (opened wide) extendido. **2,** (farflung) muy extenso; vasto.
widgeon ('wɪdʒ·ən) *n.* cerceta.
widow ('wɪd·o) *n.* **1,** (surviving wife) viuda. **2,** *cards* baceta. —*v.t.* privar de marido; dejar viuda.
widower ('wɪd·o·ər) *n.* viudo.
widowhood ('wɪd·o·hud) *n.* viudez.
width (wɪdθ) *n.* anchura; ancho; extensión.
wield (wild) *v.t.* **1,** (handle) manejar; usar. **2,** (exercise, as power) ejercer. —**wieldy,** *adj.* manejable.
wiener ('wi·nər) *n.* salchicha de carne de vaca y cerdo.
wife (waif) *n.* [*pl.* **wives**] esposa; mujer.
wifehood ('waif·hud) *n.* estado de casada.
wifely ('waif·li) *adj.* de *o* como esposa.
wig (wɪg) *n.* peluca.
wigged (wɪgd) *adj.* que lleva peluca.
wigging ('wɪg·ɪŋ) *n., Brit. colloq.* reprimenda; regaño.
wiggle ('wɪg·əl) *v.t.* menear. —*v.i.* menearse; culebrear. —*n.* meneo; culebreo.
wiggler ('wɪg·lər) *n.* persona o cosa que se menea; larva de mosquito.
wiggly ('wɪg·li) *adj.* **1,** (that wiggles) que se menea. **2,** (wavy) ondulado; ondulante.
wigmaker *n.* peluquero; fabricante de pelucas.
wigwag ('wɪg·wæg) *v.t.* & *i.* [**-wagged, -wagging**] **1,** = **wag. 2,** (signal by waving) hacer (señales) con banderas, luces, etc. —*n.* **1,** (wagging meneo; oscilación. **2,** (signaling) comunicación por banderas, luces, etc.
wigwam ('wɪg·wam) *n.* choza o jacal de forma cónica que usan los indios norteamericanos.
wild (waild) *adj.* **1,** (living in the natural state) salvaje; silvestre. **2,** (desolate) desierto; despoblado. **3,** (fierce) feroz; fiero; bravo. **4,** (unruly) travieso; desenfrenado. **5,** (violent) violento; impetuoso. **6,** (mad) loco. **7,** (excited) frenético. **8,** (preposterous) absurdo; descabellado; disparatado. **9,** (disordered) desordenado; desarreglado. **10,** (badly aimed) errado. —*adv.* violentamente; frenéticamente; locamente. —*n.* yermo; desierto; monte. —**run wild,** crecer salvaje; andar a rienda suelta. —**wild about,** *colloq.* loco por.
wild boar jabalí.
wildcat ('waild·kæt) *n.* **1,** *zool.* gato montés. **2,** (violent person) luchador; persona colérica. **3,** (risky venture) empresa arriesgada. **4,** (oil strike) pozo que da

en un depósito inesperado de petróleo. **5,** *R.R.* locomotora suelta. —*adj.* **1,** (risky) arriesgado; quimérico. **2,** (illicit) ilegal; ilícito. **3,** (harebrained) atolondrado; disparatado. —*v.t.* & *i.* [**-catted, -catting**] explorar o buscar en lugares improductivos. —**wildcat strike,** huelga sin autorización.

wilderness ('wɪl·dər·nəs) *n.* desierto; yermo.

wildfire *n.* fuego desatado; fuego griego. —**spread like wildfire,** esparcirse rápidamente.

wild fowl aves de caza.

wild goose ganso bravo. —**wild-goose chase,** empresa quimérica; búsqueda sin provecho.

wildness ('waild·nəs) *n.* **1,** (wild state) estado salvaje. **2,** (desolateness) desolación; soledad. **3,** (savagery) salvajismo. **4,** (fierceness) ferocidad; fiereza. **5,** (madness) locura.

wildwood *n.* bosque; selva.

wile (wail) *n.* **1,** (trick) estratagema; ardid. **2,** (deceit) engaño. —*v.t.* engañar; engatusar. —**wile away,** pasar (divirtiéndose); engañar (el tiempo).

will (wɪl) *n.* **1,** (volition) voluntad; albedrío. **2,** (wish; desire) deseo; voluntad. **3,** (determination) determinación. **4,** (testament) testamento. —*v.t.* & *i.* (wish; decree) querer; desear. —*v.t.* (bequeath) legar; dejar (en testamento). —*v.aux.* [*pret.* **would**] *denota* **1,** *el futuro en la segunda y tercera personas: he will go,* irá. **2,** *determinación, coerción o necesidad, en la primera persona: we will go,* iremos; sí que iremos; tenemos que ir. **3,** *deseo; voluntad: will you go?,* ¿quiere Vd. ir? **4,** *capacidad: the elevator will hold ten persons,* el ascensor puede acomodar diez personas. **5,** *costumbre; hábito: he will go for days without eating,* suele pasar días sin comer. **6,** *probabilidad: that will be the doctor,* será el médico.

willful ('wɪl·fəl) *adj.* **1,** (headstrong) obstinado; terco; testarudo; voluntarioso. **2,** (intentional) voluntario; premeditado; con toda intención. —**willfulness,** *n.* terquedad; testarudez; voluntariedad.

willing ('wɪl·ɪŋ) *adj.* **1,** (inclined) inclinado; dispuesto. **2,** (ready; obliging) solícito; atento; complaciente. **3,** (voluntary) voluntario.

willingly ('wɪl·ɪŋ·li) *adv.* voluntariamente; de buena gana.

willingness ('wɪl·ɪŋ·nəs) *n.* **1,** (inclination) inclinación; disposición. **2,** (readiness) solicitud; complacencia. **3,** (good will) buena voluntad; buena gana.

will-o'-the-wisp (ˌwɪl·ə·ðə·'wɪsp) *n.* **1,** (fire caused by decaying matter) fuego fatuo. **2,** (illusion) ilusión; quimera.

willow ('wɪl·o) *n.* sauce.

willowy ('wɪl·o·i) *adj.* delgado; esbelto.

will power fuerza de voluntad.

willy-nilly ('wɪl·i'nɪl·i) *adv.* de todos modos; quieras o no quieras. —*adj.* indeciso; vacilante.

wilt (wɪlt) *v.t.* marchitar. —*v.i.* **1,** (fade) marchitarse. **2,** (languish) languidecer. **3,** (lose courage) desanimarse; acobardarse.

wilt (wɪlt) *v., arcaico, segunda persona del sing. del pres. de ind. de* **will.**

wily ('wai·li) *adj.* astuto; listo; mañoso.

wimble ('wɪm·bəl) *n.* barrena; taladro.

wimple ('wɪm·pəl) *n.* toca.

win (wɪn) *v.t.* [*pret.* & *p.p.* **won;** *ger.* **winning**] **1,** (gain) ganar. **2,** (reach; attain) alcanzar. **3,** (prevail over) conquistar; persuadir. —*v.i.* ganar; triunfar; prevalecer; tener éxito. —*n., colloq.* triunfo; éxito. —**win out,** *colloq.* triunfar; prevalecer; tener éxito. —**win over,** conquistar.

wince (wɪns) *v.i.* retroceder; echarse atrás; respingar. —*n.* respingo.

winch (wɪntʃ) *n.* molinete; torno.

wind (wɪnd; *en poesía, también* waind) *n.* **1,** (current of air) viento. **2,** (breath) aliento; respiración. **3,** (scent) viento; husmo; olor. —*v.t.* **1,** (expose to the air) airear; ventilar. **2,** (scent) husmear; olear. **3,** (put out of breath) dejar sin aliento; agotar. —**break wind,** ventosear. —**get the wind up,** *colloq.* airarse; alterarse. —**get wind of,** descubrir; enterarse de. —**in the wind,** pendiente; inminente.

wind (waind) *v.t.* **1,** (turn) dar vuelta a. **2,** (wrap up or around) envolver; enrollar. **3,** (twist) torcer. **4,** (reel, as yarn) devanar. **5,**

(twine) entrelazar; enroscar. **6,** (tighten the spring of) dar cuerda a. *—v.i.* **1,** (move in a curving path) serpentear; dar vueltas. **2,** (twine) entrelazarse; enroscarse. **3,** (form a coil; wrap around) enrollarse; envolverse. *—n.* vuelta; recodo. **—wind off**, desenrollar; desenvolver. **—wind up, 1,** (roll up; coil) enrollar(se); envolver(se). **2,** (finish) terminar; acabar(se); acabar por. **3,** (tighten the spring of) dar cuerda a. **4,** *baseball* tomar impulso.

windage ('wɪn·dɪdʒ) *n.* desvío de un proyectil por efecto del viento; corrección de ello.

windbag ('wɪnd,bæg) *n., slang* charlatán; fanfarrón.

windblown ('wɪnd,blo:n) *adj.* **1,** (carried by the wind) llevado por el viento. **2,** (of a certain type of coiffure) recortado y peinado hacia la frente.

windborne ('wɪnd,born) *adj.* llevado por el viento.

windbreak ('wɪnd,breik) *n.* seto, cercado o hilera de árboles que abriga contra el viento.

windbreaker ('wɪnd,brei·kər) *n.* chaqueta de cuero o lana con cintura y bocamangas de elástico.

winded ('wɪn·dɪd) *adj.* agotado; falto de aliento.

winder ('wain·dər) *n.* **1,** (one who winds) devanador. **2,** (reel) devanadera. **3,** (key for winding a spring) llave.

windfall ('wɪnd,fɔl) *n.* fruta caída del árbol; *fig.* provecho o ganancia inesperada.

windflower ('wɪnd,flau·ər) *n.* anémona.

windgall ('wɪnd,gɔl) *n.* aventadura; agalla.

wind gauge (wɪnd) anemómetro.

windiness ('wɪn·di·nəs) *n.* **1,** (abundance of wind) ventosidad. **2,** (talkativeness) verbosidad. **3,** (boastfulness) vanidad; jactancia. **4,** (flatulence) flatulencia.

winding ('wain·dɪŋ) *n.* **1,** (turn; bend) vuelta; rodeo; recodo. **2,** (wrapping) arrollamiento. **3,** (twisting) torcedura. *—adj.* **1,** (turning; bending) sinuoso; tortuoso. **2,** (of or for winding) que arrolla *o* envuelve. **—winding sheet,** mortaja; sudario. **—winding stairs,** escalera de caracol.

wind instrument (wɪnd) instrumento de viento.

windjammer ('wɪnd,dʒæm·ər) *n.* **1,** (sailing ship) velero; buque de vela. **2,** (sailor) marinero en un velero.

windlass ('wɪnd·ləs) *n.* torno; molinete.

windmill ('wɪnd,mɪl) *n.* **1,** (machine) molino de viento. **2,** (child's toy) molinete.

window ('wɪn·do) *n.* **1,** (opening) ventana. **2,** (show window) escaparate de tienda; vitrina. **3,** (of an auto or coach; of an envelope; for tickets) ventanilla.

window box tiesto de ventana.

window dressing adorno o arreglo de escaparates; *fig.* ostentación; fingimiento.

window envelope sobre de ventanilla.

window glass vidrio de ventana.

windowpane *n.* cristal de ventana.

window shade persiana; transparente; visillo.

windowshop *v.i.* **[-shopped, -shopping]** mirar mercancías en las vitrinas sin comprar.

window shutter contraventana.

window sill antepecho.

windpipe ('wɪnd,paip) *n.* tráquea.

windrow ('wɪnd,ro) *n.* hilera o montón de hierba o de heno arrollado por el viento o puesto a secar.

windshield ('wɪnd,ʃild) *n.* parabrisas. **—windshield wiper,** limpiaparabrisas.

windstorm ('wɪnd,storm) *n.* ventarrón.

windup ('waind,ʌp) *n., colloq.* **1,** (conclusion) término; acción final; conclusión. **2,** *baseball* movimiento del lanzador tomando impulso.

windward ('wɪnd·wərd) *n.* barlovento. *—adj.* de barlovento. *—adv.* a barlovento.

windy ('wɪn·di) *adj.* **1,** (of or full of wind) ventoso. **2,** (exposed to the wind) expuesto al viento; a barlovento. **3,** (stormy) tempestuoso; borrascoso. **4,** (talkative) verboso; parlero. **5,** (boastful) vano; jactancioso. **6,** (flatulent) flatulento. **—it is windy,** hace viento.

wine (wain) *n.* vino. *—adj.* vinícola; vinatero. *—v.t.* obsequiar *o*

regalar con vino. —*v.i.* beber vino.
winebibber ('wain,bɪb·ər) *n.* borrachón; bebedor.
wine cellar bodega.
wineglass *n.* copa para vino.
winegrower *n.* vinicultor. —**winegrowing,** *n.* vinicultura.
wine merchant vinatero.
wine press lagar.
winery ('wain·ə·ri) *n.* lagar.
wineskin *n.* odre; pellejo de vino.
winetaster *n.* catavinos.
wing (wɪŋ) *n.* **1,** (organ or device for flying; projecting part) ala. **2,** (flight) vuelo. **3,** *mil.; archit.* ala. **4,** *theat.* bastidor. **5,** (faction) facción. **6,** *slang* (arm) brazo. —*v.i.* volar. —*v.t.* **1,** (traverse in flight) volar por. **2,** (provide with wings) proveer de alas. **3,** (send swiftly) arrojar; impeler. **4,** (wound in the wing or arm) herir en el ala o el brazo. —**on the wing,** volando. —**take wing,** volarse; irse volando.
winged ('wɪŋ·ɪd) *adj.* alado.
winglet ('wɪŋ·lɪt) *n.* aleta.
wingspread *n.* envergadura.
wink (wɪŋk) *v.t. & i.* guiñar. —*n.* guiño; guiñada. —**forty winks,** *colloq.* siesta; siestecita. —**not to sleep a wink,** no pegar *o* cerrar los ojos. —**wink at,** pasar por alto; dejar pasar.
winkle ('wɪŋk·əl) *n.* caracol marino; litorina.
winner ('wɪn·ər) *n.* ganador; premiado.
winning ('wɪn·ɪŋ) *adj.* **1,** (victorious) victorioso; triunfante; ganador. **2,** (charming) atrayente; encantador. **3,** (persuasive) persuasivo. —*n.* victoria; triunfo. —**winnings,** *n.pl.* ganancias.
winnow ('wɪn·o) *v.t.* **1,** (blow the chaff from) aventar. **2,** (sift; select) escudriñar; entresacar. **3,** (beat, as wings) batir. —*v.i.* **1,** (remove chaff) aventar. **2,** (beat the wings) aletear; batir las alas.
winsome ('wɪn·səm) *adj.* atrayente; simpático. —**winsomeness,** *n.* atracción; simpatía.
winter ('wɪn·tər) *n.* invierno. —*adj.* invernal; de *o* del invierno. —*v.t.* hacer invernar. —*v.i.* invernar.
wintergreen *n.* gaulteria.
winterize ('wɪn·tər,aiz) *v.t.* preparar para el invierno.
winter quarters invernadero.
wintertime *n.* invierno.
wintry ('wɪn·tri) *adj.* invernal; frío. *También,* **wintery** ('wɪn·tər·i).
winy ('wai·ni) *adj.* vinoso.
wipe (waip) *v.t.* **1,** (clean) limpiar. **2,** (rub) frotar. **3,** (dry) enjugar. —*n.* frotadura; limpiadura. —**wipe out, 1,** (erase) borrar. **2,** (destroy) aniquilar; destruir; matar. **3,** (settle, as a debt) enjugar.
wiper ('wai·pər) *n.* **1,** (cleaner) limpiador. **2,** (cloth) paño; trapo.
wire (wair) *n.* **1,** (metal thread) alambre. **2,** = **telegraph. 3,** = **telegram.** —*adj.* de alambre. —*v.t.* **1,** (furnish with wire) proveer de alambre. **2,** (fasten with wire) atar con alambre. —*v.t. & i.* (telegraph) telegrafiar. —**get (in) under the wire,** llegar *o* terminar al último momento. —**pull wires,** ejercer uno su influencia, esp. en secreto.
wire cloth tela metálica.
wiredraw *v.t.* [**-drew, -drawn**] tirar; estirar (un alambre); *fig.* prolongar; sutilizar mucho.
wire gauge calibrador de alambre.
wireless ('wair·ləs) *adj.* inalámbrico; sin hilos. —*n.* radiotelefonía; radiotelegrafía; radio. —*v.t. & i.* comunicar(se) por radio.
wirepulling *n., colloq.* maquinaciones secretas; intrigas.
wire recorder magnetófono.
wire screen tela metálica.
wiretap *v.t.* [**-tapped, -tapping**] intervenir (un teléfono). —*n.* conexión secreta para interceptar mensajes telefónicas o telegráficas.
wiring ('wair·ɪŋ) *n.* alambrado; instalación de alambres.
wiry ('wair·i) *adj.* **1,** (of or like wire) de *o* como alambre. **2,** (lean and strong) delgado pero fuerte.
wisdom ('wɪs·dəm) *n.* **1,** (knowledge) sabiduría. **2,** (prudence) prudencia; juicio; cordura. —**wisdom tooth,** muela cordal; muela del juicio.
wise (waiz) *adj.* **1,** (knowing) sabio. **2,** (prudent) prudente; cuerdo. **3,** *colloq.* (informed) enterado; informado. **4,** *slang* (conceited) arrogante; altanero. **5,** *slang* (impudent) atrevido; descarado; fresco. —*n.* manera; modo; guisa. —**be wise (to),** *slang* estar al tanto (de). —**get wise (to),** *slang* caer en la cuenta; enterarse (de). —**put wise**

(to), *slang* poner al tanto (de). —**wise up (to)**, *slang* poner al tanto (de); caer en la cuenta (de).

-wise (waiz) *sufijo; forma adverbios denotando* dirección; manera; posición: *clockwise,* según las manillas del reloj; *sidewise,* lateralmente; de lado.

wiseacre ('waiz,ei·kər) *n.* sabihondo; chocarrero.

wisecrack *n.* dicharacho; broma; pulla. —*v.i.* bromear; echar pullas.

wise guy *slang* **1,** (braggart) fanfarrón. **2,** (know-it-all) sabelotodo.

wish (wɪʃ) *n.* deseo. —*v.t. & i.* desear. —**wish for,** desear, anhelar. —**wish something on someone,** plantarle *o* pegarle a uno una cosa molesta.

wishbone *n.* espoleta; hueso de la suerte.

wishful ('wɪʃ·fəl) *adj.* deseoso; anheloso; ansioso. —**wishfully,** *adj.* ansiosamente; con anhelo. —**wishfullness,** *n.* deseo; anhelo; ansia. —**wishful thinking,** ilusión; optimismo.

wishy-washy ('wɪʃ·i'wɔʃ·i) *adj., colloq.* **1,** (watery) aguado. **2,** (insipid) soso; insulso. **3,** (feeble) débil; flojo.

wisp (wɪsp) *n.* **1,** (small bunch) manojo; puñado. **2,** (tuft of hair) mechón. **3,** (slender strip) tira; jirón. **4,** (fragment) fragmento; pizca; trozo. **5,** (curl of smoke) espiral; pluma. **6,** = **whisk broom.**

wispy ('wɪs·pi) *adj.* sutil; delicado.

wisteria (wɪs'tɪr·i·ə) *n.* vistaria. *También,* **wistaria** (wɪs'tɛr·i·ə).

wistful ('wɪst·fəl) *adj.* ansioso; anhelante; pensativo. —**wistfulness,** *n.* ansiedad; anhelo.

wit (wɪt) *n.* **1,** (reason) juicio. **2,** (cleverness) agudeza. **3,** (clever person) chistoso. **4,** (clever remark) dicho agudo; chiste. **5,** (ingenuity) ingenio. —**wits,** *n.pl.* juicio; razón. —**be at one's wits' end,** no saber que hacer *o* decir. —**keep** (*o* **have**) **one's wits about one,** tener calma. —**live by one's wits,** vivir de gorra. —**out of one's wits,** fuera de sí. —**to wit,** a saber.

witch (wɪtʃ) *n.* bruja; hechicera. —*v.t.* embrujar; hechizar.

witchcraft *n.* brujería.

witch doctor curandero; médico brujo.

witchery ('wɪtʃ·ə·ri) *n.* hechicería; brujería.

witch hazel hamamelis.

witching ('wɪtʃ·ɪŋ) *adj.* hechicero; encantador; mágico.

with (wɪθ) *prep.* **1,** (in company of; by means of) con. **2,** (consisting of; characterized by; apart from) de. **3,** (against) contra.

with- (wɪθ) *prefijo* **1,** contra: *withstand,* resistir. **2,** atrás: *withhold,* retener; retirar.

withal (wɪð'ɔl) *adv.* **1,** (besides) además; también. **2,** (thereby) así; de este modo. **3,** (thereupon) luego; en seguida. **4,** (still) por otro lado; a pesar de eso. —*prep.* con.

withdraw *v.t.* [**-drew, -drawn**] retirar; sacar. —*v.i.* retirarse.

withdrawal *n.* retiro; retirada.

withe (waið) *n.* mimbre.

wither ('wɪð·ər) *v.i.* **1,** (shrivel; fade) marchitarse. **2,** (languish) languidecer. **3,** (quail; cower) acobardarse; desanimarse. —*v.t.* **1,** (cause to fade) marchitar. **2,** (cow; shame) avergonzar; amedrentar; desanimar.

withers ('wɪð·ərz) *n.pl.* cruz (*sing.*).

withhold *v.t.* [*pret. & p.p.* **withheld**] **1,** (hold back) retener; detener; contener. **2,** (refuse) negar.

withholding tax porción del impuesto sobre la renta retenido de antemano.

within (wɪθ'ɪn) *adv.* dentro; adentro. —*prep.* **1,** (in; inside of) dentro de. **2,** (in reach of) al alcance de. **3,** (less than) menos de.

without (wɪθ'aut) *adv.* fuera; afuera. —*prep.* **1,** (outside of) fuera de. **2,** (beyond) más allá de. **3,** (lacking; devoid of) sin. —**do** (*o* **go**) **without,** privarse de; pasar sin.

withstand *v.t.* [*pret. & p.p.* **withstood** (-'stʊd)] resistir; aguantar; soportar.

withy ('wɪð·i) *n.* mimbre. —*adj.* flexible; ágil.

witless ('wɪt·ləs) *adj.* necio; tonto; insensato.

witness ('wɪt·nəs) *n.* **1,** (person) testigo. **2,** (testimony) testimonio. —*v.t.* **1,** (testify to) atestiguar. **2,** (be present at) presenciar; asistir a. **3,** (sign) firmar como testigo. **4,** (exhibit) mostrar; manifestar.

—*v.i.* ser testigo; servir de testigo; dar testimonio.
witticism ('wɪt·ɪ·sɪz·əm) *n.* dicho agudo; agudeza; chiste; gracia.
wittiness ('wɪt·i·nəs) *n.* agudeza; gracia.
wittingly ('wɪt·ɪŋ·li) *adv.* adrede; a propósito; a sabiendas.
witty ('wɪt·i) *adj.* agudo; gracioso; chistoso; ocurrente.
wive (waiv) *v.i.* casarse. —*v.t.* **1,** (take as a wife) casarse con; tomar por esposa. **2,** (provide with a wife) proveer de esposa; casar.
wives (waivz) *n., pl. de* **wife.**
wizard ('wɪz·ərd) *n.* **1,** (sorcerer) brujo; hechicero. **2,** *colloq.* (expert) experto. —*adj.* hechicero; mágico.
wizardry ('wɪz·ərd·ri) *n.* hechicería; brujería.
wizen ('wɪz·ən) *v.t. & i.* marchitar(se). —**wizened,** *adj.* marchito.
wobble ('wab·əl) *v.i.* **1,** (stagger) bambolear; tambalear. **2,** (tremble) temblequear. **3,** (waver) vacilar. —*n.* bamboleo; tambaleo. —**wobbly** (-li) *adj.* inestable; inseguro; tembleque.
woe (woː) *n.* desgracia; aflicción; pena; dolor. —*interj.* ¡ay! —**woe is me!,** ¡ay de mí!
woebegone *adj.* triste; abatido; desgraciado.
woeful ('wo·fəl) *adj.* **1,** (sad) triste; abatido. **2,** (causing woe) lastimoso; funesto. **3,** (wretched) miserable; mezquino.
woke (wok) *v., pret. de* **wake.**
wolf (wulf) *n.* [*pl.* **wolves** (wulvz)] lobo. —*v.t.* comer vorazmente; devorar. —**cry wolf,** gritar ¡al lobo!; dar falsa alarma.— **keep the wolf from the door,** cerrar la puerta al hambre.
wolfhound *n.* galgo lobero.
wolfish ('wul·fɪʃ) *adj.* lobero; lupino.
wolfram ('wul·frəm) *n.* tungsteno; volframio.
wolverine (ˌwul·və'riːn) *n.* glotón.
woman ('wum·ən) *n.* [*pl.* **women**] mujer. —*adj.* femenino; de mujer.
woman-hater *n.* misógino.
womanhood ('wum·ən·hud) *n.* **1,** (condition) estado de mujer. **2,** = **womanliness. 3,** = **womankind.**
womanish ('wum·ən·ɪʃ) *adj.* mujeril; femenil; afeminado.
womankind ('wum·ənˌkaind) *n.* femineidad; las mujeres; el mundo femenino.
womanlike ('wum·ənˌlaik) *adj.* mujeril.
womanly ('wum·ən·li) *adj.* mujeril; femenil. —**womanliness,** *n.* femineidad.
womb (wuːm) *n.* útero; matriz; vientre.
women ('wɪm·ən) *n., pl. de* **woman.**
won (wʌn) *v., pret. & p.p. de* **win.**
wonder ('wʌn·dər) *n.* **1,** (admiration) admiración; asombro. **2,** (cause of admiration) maravilla; prodigio. —*v.i.* **1,** (marvel) maravillarse; admirarse; asombrarse. **2,** (doubt) dudar. —*v.t.* querer saber; preguntarse. —**for a wonder,** por milagro. —**no wonder,** no hay que extrañar; no es extraño.
wonderful ('wʌn·dər·fəl) *adj.* admirable; maravilloso.
wonderland *n.* tierra de maravillas.
wonderment ('wʌn·dər·mənt) *n.* maravilla; admiración; asombro.
wonder-struck *adj.* atónito; pasmado; asombrado. *También,* **wonder-stricken.**
wondrous ('wʌn·drəs) *adj.* maravilloso.
won't (wont) *contr. de* **will not.**
wont (want; wʌnt) *adj.* acostumbrado. —*n.* costumbre; uso. —**be wont to,** soler; acostumbrar.
wonted ('wan·tɪd; 'wʌn-) *adj.* usual; habitual; acostumbrado.
woo (wuː) *v.t. & i.* (court) cortejar; galantear. —*v.t.* (seek) buscar; solicitar.
wood (wud) *n.* **1,** (substance; timber) madera. **2,** (forest) bosque. **3,** (scrap wood; firewood) leña. **4,** = **woodwind.** —*adj.* **1,** (made of wood) de madera. **2,** (living in woods) silvestre; de los bosques.
wood alcohol alcohol metílico.
woodbine ('wudˌbain) *n.* madreselva.
wood borer carcoma.
wood carving talla en madera.
woodchuck ('wudˌtʃʌk) *n.* marmota de América.
woodcock *n.* chocha.
woodcraft *n.* **1,** (wood lore) conocimiento de los bosques. **2,** = **woodworking.**
woodcut *n.* grabado en madera.
woodcutter *n.* leñador.
wooded ('wud·ɪd) *adj.* arbolado.

wooden ('wʊd·ən) *adj.* **1,** (made of wood) de madera. **2,** (dull; stupid) torpe; lerdo; estúpido.
wood engraving grabado en madera.
woodenheaded *adj.* estúpido; zopenco.
woodland ('wʊd·lənd) *n.* arbolado; bosque.
wood louse cochinilla.
woodman ('wʊd·mən) *n.* [*pl.* **-men**] **1,** (woodcutter) leñador. **2,** *Brit.* (forester) guardabosque.
woodpecker *n.* picaposte; picamaderos.
wood pigeon paloma torcaz.
wood pulp pulpa de madera.
woodruff ('wʊd,rʌf) *n.* asperilla.
woodshed ('wʊd,ʃɛd) *n.* leñera.
woodsman ('wʊdz·mən) *n.* [*pl.* **-men**] hombre que vive o trabaja en los bosques.
wood sorrel acedera menor.
woodwind ('wʊd,wɪnd) *n.* instrumento de viento de madera.
woodwork *n.* maderamen; enmaderamiento. —**woodworker,** *n.* ebanista; carpintero. —**woodworking,** *n.* ebanistería; carpintería.
woody ('wʊd·i) *adj.* **1,** (of or like wood) leñoso; de *o* como madera. **2,** (wooded) arbolado.
wooer ('wu·ər) *n.* galán; pretendiente.
woof (wuf) *n.* **1,** *weaving* trama. **2,** (wʊf) (growl) gruñido. —*v.i.* (wʊf) gruñir.
wooing ('wu·ɪŋ) *n.* galanteo.
wool (wʊl) *n.* lana. —*adj.* de lana. —**all wool and a yard wide,** genuino; auténtico. —**pull the wool over someone's eyes,** engañarle a uno.
woolbearing *adj.* lanar.
woolen *también,* **woollen** ('wʊl·ən) *adj.* de lana. —**woolens,** *n.pl.* géneros de lana; ropa de lana.
woolgathering *n.* distracción. —*adj.* distraído.
woolly *también,* **wooly** ('wʊl·i) *adj.* lanudo; lanoso.
woozy ('wu·zi) *adj., slang* aturdido.
word (wʌɹd) *n.* **1,** (unit of meaning; remark; advice) palabra. **2,** (lexical unit) vocablo; voz. **3,** (saying) dicho; sentencia. **4,** *cap., Bib.* Verbo. **5,** (password) santo y seña. **6,** (order) orden. **7,** (news) noticia; noticias. **8,** (message) mensaje; recado. —*v.t.* frasear; expresar en palabras. —**be as good as one's word,** cumplir lo prometido. —**break one's word,** faltar a su palabra. —**by word of mouth,** de palabra; de boca. —**eat one's words,** retractarse; retirar sus palabras. —**give one's word,** prometer; comprometerse. —**have a word with,** hablar cuatro palabras con. —**have words (with),** tener palabras mayores (con). —**leave word,** dejar dicho. —**mark my words,** atiéndame; atienda lo que digo. —**my word!,** ¡válgame Dios! —**put in a good word for,** recomendar. —**take at one's word,** tomarle a uno la palabra. —**take one's word for it,** fiarse de la palabra de uno. —**take the words out of one's mouth,** quitarle a uno la palabra de la boca. —**upon my word,** palabra de honor; ¡a fe mía!
wordbook *n.* **1,** (dictionary) diccionario; vocabulario; léxico. **2,** (libretto) libreto.
wording ('wʌɹ·dɪŋ) *n.* fraseología.
wordless ('wʌɹd·ləs) *adj.* **1,** (speechless) mudo; callado; falto de palabras. **2,** (unexpressed) inexpresado. **3,** (inexpressible) inexpresable.
wordy ('wʌɹ·di) *adj.* verboso; palabrero. —**wordiness,** *n.* verbosidad; palabrería.
wore (wo:r) *v., pret. de* **wear.**
work (wʌɹk) *n.* **1,** (effort; toil) trabajo; labor. **2,** (employment) trabajo; empleo. **3,** (occupation) trabajo; profesión; oficio. **4,** (undertaking) empresa; proyecto. **5,** (task) tarea. **6,** (result of effort; creation) obra. —*v.t.* **1,** (cause to work) hacer trabajar. **2,** (shape; form) trabajar; elaborar. **3,** (use; wield) manejar; emplear. **4,** (cause; bring about) causar; producir. **5,** (solve) resolver. **6,** (till) labrar. **7,** (exploit) explotar. **8,** (persuade) persuadir. **9,** (make or gain by effort) forjar; conseguir con esfuerzo. **10,** (provoke) provocar. —*v.i.* **1,** (do work) trabajar. **2,** (function) trabajar; funcionar; marchar. **3,** (proceed or change slowly) colarse; abrirse paso; volverse poco a poco. —**works,** *n.sing. o pl.* fábrica; taller. —*n.pl.* mecanismo; movimiento. —**at work,** trabajando. —**get the works,** *slang* ser víctima; sufrir un castigo.

—**give one the works,** *slang* **1,** (kill) matar. **2,** (punish) castigar; maltratar; humillar. —**make short** (*o* **quick) work of,** acabar pronto con. —**out of work,** desempleado. —**shoot the works,** *slang* arriesgar todo; esforzarse lo más posible. —**work in,** meter(se); introducir(se). —**work off,** deshacerse de. —**work on** (*o* **upon),** influir en; persuadir. —**work out, 1,** (become loose) aflojarse. **2,** (exhaust) agotar. **3,** (bring about) producir. **4,** (develop) desarrollar; elaborar. **5,** (solve) resolver. **6,** (result) resultar. **7,** *sports* (train) entrenarse. —**work up, 1,** (advance) adelantarse. **2,** (prepare) preparar; elaborar. **3,** (excite) estimular; excitar.

workable ('wʌɹk·ə·bəl) *adj.* **1,** (feasible) factible; practicable. **2,** (exploitable) explotable. **3,** (tillable) laborable.

workaday ('wʌɹk·əˌdei) *adj.* común; ordinario; de cada día.

workbench *n.* mesa *o* banco de trabajo.

workbook *n.* libro de ejercicios; libro de trabajo.

workday *n.* **1,** (day on which one works) día laborable; día de trabajo. **2,** (time worked in one day) jornada.

worker ('wʌɹ·kər) *n.* trabajador; obrero.

workhouse *n.* **1,** (prison) taller penitenciario. **2,** *Brit.* = **poorhouse.**

working ('wʌɹ·kɪŋ) *adj.* **1,** (that works) que trabaja; que funciona. **2,** (of or for work) de trabajo. —*n.* **1,** (functioning) funcionamiento. **2,** (exploiting) explotación. —**workings,** *n.pl.* labores.

working class clase obrera.

working day = **workday.**

working girl obrera; trabajadora.

workingman *n.* [*pl.* **-men**] obrero; trabajador.

workman ('wʌɹk·mən) *n.* [*pl.* **-men**] **1,** = **workingman. 2,** (craftsman) artífice; artesano.

workmanlike ('wʌɹk·mən·laik) *adj.* hecho con pericia; bien ejecutado; digno de un artesano.

workmanship ('wʌɹk·mən·ʃɪp) *n.* manera de ejecutar un trabajo; artesanía.

workout *n.* ejercicio.

workroom *n.* taller; gabinete de trabajo.

workshop *n.* taller.

workweek *n.* semana de trabajo.

world (wʌɹld) *n.* mundo. —*adj.* mundial. —**bring into the world,** echar al mundo. —**for all the world,** exactamente. —**in the world, 1,** (on earth) en el mundo. **2,** (ever) jamás. —**not for all the world,** por nada del mundo. —**on top of the world,** *slang* en los cielos; regocijado. —**out of this world,** *slang* divino; excelente. —**think the world of,** poner en el cielo. —**world without end,** por los siglos de los siglos.

worldling ('wʌɹld·lɪŋ) *n.* persona mundana.

worldly ('wʌɹld·li) *adj.* mundano. —**worldliness,** *n.* mundanería; mundanalidad.

worldly-wise *adj.* experimentado; corrido; mundano.

world power potencia mundial.

worldwide *adj.* mundial.

worm (wʌɹm) *n.* gusano; lombriz. —*v.t.* **1,** (rid of worms) limpiar de lombrices. **2,** (get by artifice) sonsacar; conseguir por artimañas. —*v.i.* arrastrarse; deslizarse; serpentear. —**worm oneself** (*o* **one's way) in** *o* **into,** insinuarse (en). —**worm something out of someone,** sonsacarle a uno una cosa.

worm-eaten *adj.* **1,** (eaten by worms) carcomido; apolillado. **2,** (worn-out) desgastado; consumido; trillado.

worm gear engranaje de tornillo sin fin.

wormhole *n.* agujero dejado por una carcoma o un gusano.

wormlike ('wʌɹm·laik) *adj.* vermicular; vermiforme.

wormwood *n.* **1,** (plant; absinthe) ajenjo. **2,** *fig.* (bitterness) amargura.

wormy ('wʌɹ·mi) *adj.* **1,** (infested with worms) gusaniento; gusanoso; carcomido. **2,** = **wormlike. 3,** (debased) ruin; arrastrado.

worn (worn) *v., p.p. de* wear. —*adj.* **1,** (showing the effects of wear) gastado; consumido; raído. **2,** (exhausted) cansado; fatigado.

worn-out *adj.* **1,** (no longer serviceable) gastado; consumido; inservible. **2,** (spent) rendido; extenuado.

worriment ('wʌɹ·i·mənt) *n.* **1,** (anxiety) inquietud; preocupación.

2, (cause of worry) molestia; enojo.

worrisome ('wʌɹ·i·səm) *adj.* **1,** (causing worry) inquietante; molesto; enojoso. **2,** (inclined to worry) inquieto; aprensivo.

worry ('wʌɹ·i) *v.t.* **1,** (harass) atormentar; acosar; molestar. **2,** (disturb) inquietar; preocupar. —*v.i.* inquietarse; preocuparse. —*n.* **1,** (anxiety) preocupación; inquietud. **2,** (cause of worry) molestia; enojo.

worse (wʌɹs) *adj. & adv. comp.* peor. —*n.* lo peor; la peor parte. —**for the worse,** en mal. —**little the worse for wear,** apenas usado; poco gastado. —**so much the worse; all the worse,** tanto peor. —**worse and worse,** de mal en peor; peor que peor; cada vez peor.

worsen ('wʌɹ·sən) *v.t. & i.* empeorar.

worship ('wʌɹ·ʃɪp) *n.* adoración; culto. —*v.t.* adorar; venerar. —*v.i.* dar culto. —**your worship,** vuestra merced.

worshiper ('wʌɹ·ʃɪp·ər) *n.* adorador; devoto.

worshipful ('wʌɹ·ʃɪp·fəl) *adj.* **1,** (worthy of worship) venerable; honorable; respetable. **2,** (offering worship) adorador.

worst (wʌɹst) *adj. & adv. superl.* peor. —*n.* lo peor; la peor parte. —*v.t.* vencer; derrotar. —**at the worst,** a lo más. —**get the worst of it,** llevar la peor parte. —**give one the worst of it,** darle a uno la peor parte; derrotarle a uno. —**if worst comes to worst,** si pasa lo peor. —**in the worst way,** *slang* mucho; enormemente. —**make the worst of,** tomar en peor; tomar a mal.

worsted ('wʊs·tɪd) *n.* estambre. —*adj.* de estambre.

wort (wʌɹt) *n.* **1,** (plant) planta; hierba. **2,** (beverage) cerveza nueva; mosto de cerveza.

worth (wʌɹθ) *n.* **1,** (value) valor; precio. **2,** (merit) mérito. —*adj.* **1,** (deserving of) digno de. **2,** (of the value of) del valor de; que vale; que tiene precio de. **3,** (having a certain wealth) que tiene; que posee. —**be worth,** valer; tener precio de; tener; poseer. —**be worth (the) while,** valer la pena (de). —**for all one is worth,** a más no poder.

worthiness ('wʌɹ·ði·nəs) *n.* dignidad; excelencia; mérito.

worthless ('wʌɹθ·ləs) *adj.* **1,** (valueless) sin valor. **2,** (useless) inútil; inservible. **3,** (without merit) indigno; despreciable. —**be worthless,** no valer nada.

worthlessness ('wʌɹθ·ləs·nəs) *n.* **1,** (lack of value) falta de valor. **2,** (uselessness) inutilidad. **3,** (lack of merit) indignidad.

worthwhile *adj.* **1,** (important) de mérito; de importancia. **2,** (profitable) provechoso.

worthy ('wʌɹ·ði) *adj.* digno; benemérito. —*n.* benemérito; notable; héroe.

would (wʊd) *v., pret. de* **will.** —*v.aux.; denota además* **1,** *el condicional (presente o pasado) en la segunda y tercera personas: he would go if he had the time,* iría si tuviera el tiempo; *he would have gone if he had had the time,* habría ido si hubiera tenido el tiempo. **2,** deseo; anhelo: *would that it were so!,* ¡ojalá que fuera verdad! **3,** pedido; súplica: *would you help me?,* ¿quisiera ayudarme?

would-be *adj.* supuesto; fingido.

wound (wund) *n.* herida. —*v.t. & i.* herir.

wound (waund) *v., pret. & p.p. de* **wind.** —**get wound up,** *colloq.,* excitarse.

wove (wo:v) *v., pret. de* **weave.**

woven ('wo·vən) *v., p.p. de* **weave.**

wow (wau) *interj.* ¡ah!; ¡ay! —*v.t., slang* cautivar; encantar; pasmar. —*n., slang* maravilla; prodigio.

wrack (ræk) *n.* **1,** (destruction) destrucción; ruina. **2,** (wrecked ship) naufragio. **3,** (wreckage) despojos.

wraith (reiθ) *n.* fantasma; espectro.

wrangle ('ræŋ·gəl) *v.i.* reñir; disputar. —*v.t.* **1,** (get by argument) conseguir disputando. **2,** (round up, as livestock) rodear. —*n.* riña; disputa; contienda.

wrangler ('ræŋ·glər) *n.* **1,** (one who argues) disputador; pendenciero. **2,** (cowboy) vaquero que rodea el ganado. **3,** *Brit.* alumno que gana altos honores en matemáticas.

wrap (ræp) *v.t. & i.* [**wrapped, wrapping**] envolver(se); enrollar (se). —*n.* abrigo. —**under wraps,**

oculto; secreto. —**wrap up**, envolver; arropar(se). —**wrapped up in**, absorto en; entregado a; envuelto en.
wrapper ('ræp·ər) *n.* **1,** (covering) cubierta; envoltura. **2,** (robe) bata; guardapolvo. **3,** (of a newspaper) faja. **4,** (of a cigar) capa.
wrapping ('ræp·ɪŋ) *n.* envoltura. —**wrapping paper**, papel de envolver.
wrath (ræθ) *n.* cólera; ira; furia. —**wrathful**, *adj.* colérico; iracundo; furioso.
wreak (rik) *v.t.* **1,** (inflict) infligir; visitar. **2,** (give vent to) descargar.
wreath (riθ) *n.* **1,** (garland; crown) guirnalda; corona. **2,** (puff, as of smoke) espiral.
wreathe (riːð) *v.t.* **1,** (adorn with a wreath) enguirnaldar. **2,** (entwine; wrap) envolver; enroscar. **3,** (twist; coil) tejer; entretejer; ensortijar. —*v.i.* enroscarse.
wreck (rɛk) *n.* **1,** (destruction) destrucción; ruina. **2,** (collision) choque; colisión. **3,** (something wrecked; ruin) ruina. **4,** (shipwreck) naufragio. —*v.t.* **1,** (destroy) destruir; arruinar; destrozar. **2,** (cause to be shipwrecked) hacer naufragar. **3,** (raze) arrasar; demoler. **4,** (dismantle) desmantelar; desmontar. —*v.i.* arruinarse; destrozarse.
wreckage ('rɛk·ɪdʒ) *n.* **1,** (destruction) destrucción; ruina. **2,** (wrecked ship) náufrago. **3,** (debris) despojos; restos.
wrecker ('rɛk·ər) *n.* **1,** (person or thing that wrecks) demoledor; destructor. **2,** *auto.* camión de auxilio. **3,** *R.R.* carro de auxilio.
wren (rɛn) *n.* reyezuelo.
wrench (rɛntʃ) *n.* **1,** (twist) arranque; torcedura. **2,** (anguish) dolor; angustia. **3,** (tool) llave; desvolvedor. —*v.t.* arrancar; torcer.
wrest (rɛst) *v.t.* arrebatar; arrancar.
wrestle ('rɛs·əl) *v.i.* luchar. —*v.t.* luchar con. —*n.* lucha. —**wrestler** (-lər) *n.* luchador. —**wrestling** (-lɪŋ) *n.* lucha.
wretch (rɛtʃ) *n.* infeliz; miserable; desgraciado.
wretched ('rɛtʃ·ɪd) *adj.* **1,** (miserable) desdichado; miserable; mezquino. **2,** (distressful) malo; doloroso; penoso. **3,** (poor) malo; malísimo. **4,** (despicable) vil; despreciable; ruin.
wretchedness ('rɛtʃ·ɪd·nəs) *n.* **1,** (misery) desdicha; miseria. **2,** (meanness) vileza; ruindad.
wriggle ('rɪg·əl) *v.t.* menear. —*v.i.* **1,** (move back and forth) menearse. **2,** (twist; writhe) culebrear; serpentear. **3,** (dodge; equivocate) regatear. —*n.* **1,** (motion back and forth) meneo. **2,** (twisting; writhing) culebreo; serpenteo. —**wriggle in** (*o* **into**) colarse (en). —**wriggle out** (*o* **away**), escaparse; escabullirse; sacar el cuerpo.
wriggler ('rɪg·lər) *n.* = **wiggler.**
wriggly ('rɪg·li) *adj.* **1,** (that writhes) que se menea *o* culebrea. **2,** (twisting; winding) tortuoso; serpentino.
wright (rait) *n.* artífice.
wring (rɪŋ) *v.t.* [*pret.* & *p.p.* **wrung**] **1,** (twist) torcer; retorcer. **2,** (squeeze out) exprimir. **3,** (extract forcibly) arrancar. **4,** (grieve; anguish) afligir; angustiar; acongojar. —*n.* **1,** (twist) torsión; torcedura. **2,** (squeeze) expresión.
wringer ('rɪŋ·ər) *n.* exprimidor; exprimidora.
wringing wet empapado.
wrinkle ('rɪŋ·kəl) *n.* **1,** (furrow) arruga. **2,** *colloq.* (clever idea) invento; novedad. —*v.t.* & *i.* arrugar(se). —**wrinkly** (-kli) *adj.* arrugado.
wrist (rɪst) *n.* muñeca.
wristband *n.* puño de camisa; bocamanga.
wristlet ('rɪst·lɪt) *n.* elástico para la muñeca; brazalete.
wrist watch reloj de pulsera.
writ (rɪt) *n.* escrito; auto.
write (rait) *v.t.* & *i.* [*pret.* **wrote;** *p.p.* **written**] escribir. —**write down**, poner por escrito; apuntar. —**write off**, cancelar; amortizar. —**write out**, poner por escrito; escribir sin abreviar. —**write up**, **1,** (set down in detail) describir *o* contar en detalle. **2,** (bring up to date) poner al día. **3,** (praise; ballyhoo) ensalzar; alabar; dar bombo a.
writer ('rai·tər) *n.* escritor. —**writer's cramp**, calambre de los escribientes.
write-up *n.*, *colloq.* **1,** (report) relato. **2,** (praise) alharaca; bombo; publicidad.

writhe (raið) *v.t. & i.* (twist) torcer(se); contorcer(se); retorcer(se). —*v.i.* (suffer) acongojarse; agonizar.

writing ('rai·tɪŋ) *n.* **1,** (act of writing) escritura. **2,** (something written) escrito. **3,** (handwriting) escritura; letra. **4,** (literary work) obra. **5,** (literary profession) profesión de escritor; literatura; letras (*pl.*). —*adj.* de *o* para escribir. —**in writing,** por escrito.

writing desk escritorio.

written ('rɪt·ən) *v., p.p. de* **write.** —*adj.* escrito; por escrito.

wrong (rɔːŋ) *adj.* **1,** (unjust) injusto. **2,** (bad) malo. **3,** (incorrect) erróneo; incorrecto. **4,** (mistaken) equivocado. **5,** (false) falso; falaz. **6,** (inconvenient) inoportuno. **7,** (unsuitable) inadecuado; impropio. —*adv.* **1,** (badly) mal. **2,** (incorrectly) incorrectamente. **3,** (in the wrong direction) por el mal camino. **4,** (inside out) al revés. —*n.* **1,** (injustice) injusticia. **2,** (harm; injury) daño; perjuicio. **3,** (evil) mal. **4,** (error) error. **5,** (sin) pecado; transgresión. —*v.t.* **1,** (harm) agraviar; injuriar; ofender. **2,** (malign) calumniar; difamar. **3,** (seduce) engañar; abusar de. —**be in the wrong,** estar equivocado; tener culpa. —**be wrong,** no tener razón; estar equivocado; ser malo; no ser justo. —**be wrong with,** pasarle (algo) a: *something is wrong with my watch,* le pasa algo a mi reloj. —**do wrong,** obrar *o* hacer mal. —**get (someone) in wrong,** perjudicarle a uno; comprometerle a uno. —**go wrong,** salir mal; perderse; extraviarse. —**right or wrong,** a tuertas o a derechas. —**take (something) wrong,** tomar a mal. —**wrong side,** revés. —**wrong side out,** al revés.

wrongdoer *n.* malhechor.

wrongdoing *n.* pecado; maldad.

wrongful ('rɔŋ·fəl) *adj.* **1,** (bad; evil) malo; injusto; inicuo. **2,** (erroneous) equivocado. **3,** (unlawful) ilegal; ilícito.

wrong-headed *adj.* terco; testarudo.

wrongly ('rɔŋ·li) *adv.* **1,** (badly) mal. **2,** (erroneously) por error; equivocadamente.

wrongness ('rɔŋ·nəs) *n.* **1,** (injustice) injusticia. **2,** (error) error; falacia. **3,** (incorrectness) inexactitud.

wrote (rot) *v., pret. de* **write.**

wroth (raθ) *adj.* encolerizado; iracundo.

wrought (rɔt) *adj.* **1,** (formed; made) hecho; forjado. **2,** (hammered) hecho al martillo.

wrought iron hierro dulce.

wrought up *adj.* excitado; conmovido.

wrung (rʌŋ) *v., pret. & p.p. de* **wring.**

wry (rai) *adj.* **1,** (twisted) torcido. **2,** (perverse) pervertido; terco. —**wry face,** mueca; mohín.

X

X, x (ɛks) vigésima cuarta letra del alfabeto inglés.

xanthein ('zæn·thi·ɪn) *n.* xanteína.

xanthin ('zæn·θɪn) *n.* xantina.

xantho- (zæn·θə) *prefijo* xanto-; amarillo: *xanthophilia,* xantofilia.

xanthous ('zæn·θəs) *adj.* amarillento.

xeno- (zɛn·ə) *prefijo* xeno-; extraño; extranjero: *xenophobia,* xenofobia.

xenon ('zi·nan) *n.* xenón.

xenophobe ('zɛn·əˌfoːb) *n.* xenófobo. —**xenophobia,** *n.* xenofobia. —**xenophobic,** *adj.* xenófobo.

xero- (zɪr·o; -ə) *prefijo* xero-; sequedad; seco: *xerophthalmia,* xeroftalmia.

Xmas ('ɛks·məs) *n., contr. de* **Christmas.**

X ray rayo X; radiografía.

x-ray *adj.* radiográfico. —*v.t.* someter a los rayos X.

xylem ('zai·lɛm) *n.* xilema.

xylo- (zai·lə) *prefijo* xilo-; madera: *xylophone,* xilófono.

xylophagous (zai'laf·ə·gəs) *adj.* xilófago.

xylograph ('zai·lə·græf) *n.* xilografía. —**xylography** (zai'lag·rə·fi) *n.* xilografía.

xylophone ('zai·ləˌfoːn) *n.* xilófono.

Y

Y, y (wai) vigésima quinta letra del alfabeto inglés.
-y (i) *sufijo* **1,** *forma adjetivos denotando:* **a.** abundante en; caracterizado por: *stony,* pedregoso; *juicy,* jugoso. **b.** que sugiere o recuerda: *a doggy smell,* olor a perro. **c.** recalcando o intensificando una sensación: *stilly,* callado; silencioso. **2,** *forma diminutivos cariñosos: Johnny,* Juanito; *pussy,* gatito. **3,** *forma nombres denotando* condición; estado: *jealousy,* celos; *infancy,* infancia; acción: *inquiry,* pregunta.
yacht (jat) *n.* yate. —*v.i.* pasear *o* correr en yate.
yachting ('jat·ɪŋ) *n.* navegación *o* paseo en yate; deporte del yate.
yachtsman ('jats·mən) *n.* [*pl.* **-men**] aficionado a los yates; timón.
yah! (ja) *interj.* ¡bah!; ¡puf!
yahoo ('ja·hu) *n.* hombre rudo; patán.
yak (jæk) *n.* yak.
yam (jæm) *n.* ñame; batata.
yank (jæŋk) *v.t.* & *i., colloq.* halar; arrancar; tirar. —*n.* tirón; arranque. —*adj.* & *n., cap., slang* yanqui.
Yankee ('jæŋ·ki) *adj.* & *n.* yanqui.
yap ('jæp) *v.i.* [**yapped, yapping**] **1,** (bark) ladrar. **2,** *slang* (chatter) charlar; chacharear. —*n.* **1,** (bark) ladrido. **2,** *slang* (idle talk) charla; palabrería. **3,** *slang* (mouth) boca.
yard (jard) *n.* **1,** (enclosure) patio; corral. **2,** (measure) yarda. **3,** *naut.* verga.
yardage ('jar·dɪdʒ) *n.* medida en yardas.
yardarm *n.* penol; singlón.
yardstick *n.* **1,** (measuring stick) yarda; vara de medir. **2,** *fig.* (standard) norma; regla.
yarn (jarn) *n.* **1,** (spun fiber) hilado. **2,** *colloq.* (story) cuento. —*v.i., colloq.* decir cuentos, esp. cuentos largos e increíbles.
yarrow ('jær·o) *n.* milenrama; milhojas.
yaw (jɔː) *v.i.,* **1,** *naut.* guiñar. **2,** *aero.* desviarse. —*n.* **1,** *naut.* guiñada. **2,** *aero.* desvío.
yawl (jɔːl) *n.* yola.
yawn (jɔːn) *v.i.* **1,** (open the mouth) bostezar. **2,** (gape) abrirse. —*n.* **1,** (opening the mouth) bostezo. **2,** (chasm) abertura; hendedura; abismo.
yaws (jɔːz) *n.* frambesia.
ye (ji) *pron. pers., arcaico* vosotros. —*art.def., arcaico* (ði) el; la.
yea (jei) *adv.* sí. —*n.* voto afirmativo; sí.
year (jɪr) *n.* año. —**year in, year out,** año tras año.
yearbook *n.* anuario.
yearling ('jɪr·lɪŋ) *n.* añojo.
yearlong *adj.* de un año entero; que dura un año.
yearly ('jɪr·li) *adj.* anual. —*adv.* anualmente.
yearn (jʌɹn) *v.i.* anhelar; desear. —**yearning,** *n.* deseo; anhelo.
yeast (jist) *n.* levadura. —**yeasty,** *adj.* espumoso.
yegg (jɛg) *n.* ladrón, esp. uno que quiebra las cajas fuertes.
yell (jɛl) *v.i.* & *t.* gritar. —*n.* grito.
yellow ('jɛl·o) *n.* **1,** (color) amarillo. **2,** (egg yolk) yema de huevo. —*adj.* **1,** (color) amarillo. **2,** *colloq.* (cowardly) cobarde. **3,** (sensational, as a newspaper) sensacional; escandaloso. —*v.t.* poner amarillo. —*v.i.* ponerse amarillo; marchitarse.
yellowbird *n.* jilguero de América; oropéndola.
yellow fever fiebre amarilla.
yellowish ('jɛl·o·ɪʃ) *adj.* amarillento.
yellow jack 1, = **yellow fever. 2,** (quarantine flag) bandera amarilla. **3,** *ichthy.* jurel.
yellow jacket variedad de avispa.
yellowness ('jɛl·o·nəs) *n.* amarillez.
yellow streak cobardía; rasgo de cobarde.
yelp (jɛlp) *v.i.* gañir. —*n.* gañido.
yen (jɛn) *n.* **1,** (monetary unit) yen. **2,** *colloq.* (yearning) deseo; anhelo. —*v.i., colloq.* [**yenned, yenning**] desear; anhelar.
yeoman ('jo·mən) *n.* [*pl.* **-men**] *naut.* **1,** (storekeeper) pañolero. **2,** (clerk) oficinista de a bordo.
yeomanly ('jo·mən·li) *adj.* valiente; firme; leal. —*adv.* valerosamente.

yeoman service servicio efectivo y leal. *También,* **yeoman's service.**
yes (jɛs) *adv. & n.* sí. —*v.t. & i.* decir sí (a). —**say yes,** dar el sí.
yesman *n., slang* [*pl.* **-men**] conformista; hombre del sí.
yester ('jɛs·tər) *adj.* pasado.
yesterday *n. & adv.* ayer. —**the day before yesterday,** anteayer.
yestereve *adv. & n., arcaico y poético* ayer por la tarde.
yestermorn *adv. & n., arcaico y poético* ayer por la mañana.
yesternight *adv. & n., arcaico y poético* anoche.
yesteryear *adv. & n., arcaico y poético* antaño.
yet (jɛt) *adv.* aún; todavía. —*conj.* sin embargo; no obstante. —**as yet,** todavía; hasta ahora. —**not yet,** todavía no.
yew (juː) *n.* tejo.
Yiddish ('jɪd·ɪʃ) *n. & adj.* yiddish.
yield ('jiːld) *v.t.* **1,** (produce) producir; dar. **2,** (give in return) rendir; redituar. **3,** (concede; grant) ceder; conceder. **4,** (admit) admitir; reconocer. —*v.i.* **1,** (produce) producir. **2,** (surrender) rendirse; ceder; entregarse. **3,** (submit) someterse. **4,** (give way) ceder. **5,** (accede) acceder; consentir. —*n.* **1,** (production) producción. **2,** (return) rédito; rendimiento. **3,** (revenue) renta.
yielding ('jil·dɪŋ) *adj.* complaciente; condescendiente.
yodel ('jo·dəl) *v.t. & i.* cantar modulando rápidamente la voz desde el tono natural al falsete, y viceversa. —*n.* canto hecho de esta manera.
yoga ('jo·gə) *n.* yoga. —**yogi** (-gi) *n.* yogi.
yogurt ('jo·gʊrt) *n.* yogurt.
yoicks (jɔiks) *interj.* grito que usan los cazadores para excitar los perros.
yoke (jok) *n.* **1,** (bond; servitude) yugo. **2,** (pair of draft animals) yunta. —*v.t.* enyugar; uncir.
yokel ('jo·kəl) *n.* rústico; patán; *Amer.* jíbaro.
yolk (jok) *n.* yema.
yon (jan) *adj. & adv., arcaico* = **yonder.**
yonder ('jan·dər) *adj.* aquel. —*adv.* allí; allá.
yore (joːr) *n.* tiempos pasados; otro tiempo. —**of yore,** antaño; antiguamente.
you (juː) *pron.pers.sing. & pl.* tú; usted; vosotros; ustedes.
you'd (juːd) *contr.de* **you should, you would** *o* **you had.**
you'll (juːl) *contr.de* **you will** *o* **you shall.**
young (jʌŋ) *adj.* joven. —*n.pl.* cría (sing.). —**with young,** encinta; preñada. —**young people,** jóvenes; juventud.
younger ('jʌŋ·gər) *adj. comp.* menor; más joven. —**youngest,** *adj.superl.* menor.
youngling ('jʌŋ·lɪŋ) *n.* jovenzuelo; jovencito.
youngster ('jʌŋ·stər) *n.* jovencito; mozalbete; chiquito.
your (jʊr) *adj.pos.* tu; vuestro; su; de usted; de ustedes.
you're (jʊr) *contr.de* **you are.**
yours (jʊrz) *pron.pos.* tuyo; vuestro; suyo; el (la, lo, los, las) de usted *o* ustedes.
yourself (jʊr'sɛlf) *pron.pers.* tú; usted; tú mismo; usted mismo. —*pron.refl.* **1,** *como complemento de verbo* te; se: *did you hurt yourself?,* ¿te lastimaste?; ¿se lastimó Vd.? **2,** *como complemento de prep.:* ti; sí; usted; ti mismo; sí mismo; usted mismo.
yourselves (jʊr'sɛlvz) *pron.pers.* vosotros; ustedes; vosotros mismos; ustedes mismos. —*pron.refl.* **1,** *como complemento de verbo* os; se. **2,** *como complemento de prep.* vosotros; sí; ustedes; vosotros mismos; sí mismos; ustedes mismos.
youth (juθ) *n.* **1,** [*pl.* **youths** (juðz)] (young man) joven. **2,** (quality of being young) juventud; mocedad. —*n.pl.* los jóvenes; la juventud.
youthful ('juθ·fəl) *adj.* joven; juvenil.
you've (juːv) *contr.de* **you have.**
yowl (jaul) *v.i.* aullar; dar alaridos; gritar. —*n.* aullido; alarido; grito.
ytterbium (ɪ'tʌɹ·bi·əm) *n.* iterbio.
yttrium ('ɪt·ri·əm) *n.* itrio.
yuan ('ju·ən) *n.* yuan.
yucca ('jʌk·ə) *n.* yuca.
Yugoslav ('ju·go,slav) *adj. & n.* yugoslavo; yugoeslavo.
Yule (juːl) *n.* Navidad.
yuletide *n.* Navidades (*pl.*).

Z

Z, z (zi:) vigésima sexta letra del alfabeto inglés.
zany ('zei·ni) *n.* gracioso; bufón; payaso. —*adj.* gracioso; cómico.
zeal (zi:l) *n.* celo.
zealot ('zɛl·ət) *n.* fanático. —**zealotry**, *n.* fanatismo.
zealous ('zɛl·əs) *adj.* celoso.
zebra ('zi·brə) *n.* cebra.
zebu ('zi·bju) *n.* cebú.
zed (zɛd) *n.* zeta; zeda.
zenith ('zi·nɪθ) *n.* cenit; zenit.
zephyr ('zɛf·ər) *n.* céfiro.
zero ('zɪr·o) *n.* cero. —*adj.* nulo. —**zero hour**, hora cero; hora final.
zest (zɛst) *n.* **1,** (enjoyment) entusiasmo; gusto. **2,** (flavor) gusto; sabor.
zestful ('zɛst·fəl) *adj.* **1,** (joyful) entusiasta; alegre. **2,** (flavorful) sabroso; rico.
zeta ('zei·tə) *n.* zeta.
zigzag ('zɪg,zæg) *n.* zigzag; zigzagueo. —*adj.* en zigzag; tortuoso. —*adv.* en zigzag; zigzagueando. —*v.i.* [**-zagged, -zagging**] zigzaguear. —*v.t.* mover en zigzag.
zinc (zɪŋk) *n.* zinc.
zinnia ('zɪn·i·ə) *n.* zinia.
Zion ('zai·ən) *n.* Sion. —**Zionism**, *n.* sionismo. —**Zionist**, *adj.* & *n.* sionista.
zip (zɪp) *n.* **1,** (whizzing sound) zumbido; silbido. **2,** *colloq.* (energy) energía; vigor. —*v.i.* [**zipped, zipping**] **1,** (make a whizzing sound) zumbar; silbar. **2,** *colloq.* (move swiftly) pasar *o* moverse rápidamente; volar. —*v.t.* cerrar *o* abrir (un cierre relámpago).
zipper ('zɪp·ər) *n.* cremallera; cierre relámpago.
zippy ('zɪp·i) *adj., colloq.* vivo; enérgico.
zircon ('zʌɹ·kan) *n.* circón.
zirconium (zər'ko·ni·əm) *n.* circonio.
zither ('zɪθ·ər) *n.* cítara.
-zoa (zo·ə) *sufijo, pl. de* **-zoon:** *Protozoa,* protozoos.
zodiac ('zo·di·æk) *n.* zodíaco. —**zodiacal** (zo'dai·ə·kəl) *adj.* zodiacal.
-zoic (zo·ɪk) *sufijo* -zoico; *forma adjetivos denotando* **1,** animal; vida animal: *phanerozoic,* fanerozoico. **2,** *geol.* era (*de determinados fósiles*): *Mesozoic,* mesozoico.
zombi ('zam·bi) *n.* zombi.
zone (zo:n) *n.* zona. —*v.t.* dividir en zonas.
zoo (zu:) *n.* parque zoológico.
zoö- (zo·ə) *prefijo* zoo-; animal: *zoölogy,* zoología.
zoölogy (zo'al·ə·dʒi) *n.* zoología. —**zoölogical** (,zo·ə'ladʒ·ɪ·kəl) *adj.* zoológico. —**zoölogist**, *n.* zoólogo.
zoom (zu:m) *n.* **1,** (buzzing sound) zumbido. **2,** *aero.* empinadura. —*v.i.* **1,** (make a buzzing sound) zumbar. **2,** *aero.* empinarse. —*v.t., aero.* hacer empinar.
-zoon (zo·an) *sufijo* -zoo; animal: *spermatozoon,* espermatozoo.
Zoroastrian (,zor·o'æs·tri·ən) *adj.* zoroástrico. —**Zoroastrianism**, *n.* zoroastrismo.
Zouave (zu'a:v) *n.* zuavo.
zounds (zaundz) *interj., arcaico* ¡válgame Dios!
Zulu ('zu·lu) *adj.* & *n.* zulú.
zygote ('zai·got) *n.* cigoto.

RESUMEN DE GRAMÁTICA INGLESA

I. *El alfabeto*

El alfabeto inglés contiene 26 letras.

Letra	*Nombre (en pronunciación fonética)*
A	ei
B	biː
C	siː
D	diː
E	iː
F	ef
G	dʒiː
H	eitʃ
I	ai
J	dʒei
K	kei
L	el
M	em
N	en
O	oː
P	piː
Q	kjuː
R	ar
S	es
T	tiː
U	juː
V	viː
W	'dʌ·bəl·juː
X	eks
Y	wai
Z	ziː

II. *La pronunciación del inglés*

VOCALES

Símbolo fonético	*Sonido aproximado en el español*	*Ejemplos ortográficos*
a	como la *a* de *calma,* pero más abierta	**father** ('fa·ðər) **slot** (slat)
æ	como la *a* de *gato,* pero mucho más cerrada	**cat** (kæt)
e	como la *e* de *seda;* en nuestro sistema se usa únicamente en sílaba inacentuada	**Friday** ('frai·de)
ɛ	como la *e* de *bello;* es más abierta que la (e) precedente	**met** (mɛt)

Símbolo fonético	*Sonido aproximado en el español*	*Ejemplos ortográficos*
eːr	como la *er* de *merlo,* pero más larga y abierta	**dare** (deːr) **lair** (leːr)
i	como la *i* de *vino;* en sílaba acentuada es más larga y suena como diptongo (ij)	**sleep** (slip) **lobby** ('lab·i)
ɪ	como la *i* de *mitad,* pero más abierta y relajada	**skin** (skɪn)
ɪr	como la *ir* de *mirlo,* pero más larga y abierta	**fear** (fɪr)
ɔ	como la *o* de *bola*	**song** (sɔŋ)
o	como la *o* de *bola,* pero más cerrada	**lowly** ('lo·li)
oː	como la (o) precedente, pero más larga; suena a menudo como diptongo (ou)	**road** (roːd)
or	como la *or* de *sordo,* pero más larga y abierta	**floor** (flor) **sort** (sort)
u	como la *u* de *luna*	**spook** (spuk)
ʊ	como la *u* de *bulto,* pero más abierta y relajada	**pull** (pʊl)
ʊr	como la *ur* de *surco,* pero más larga y abierta	**sure** (ʃʊr)
ʌ	una vocal relajada intermedia entre la *o* de *corro* y la *a* de *carro*	**but** (bʌt)
ʌɹ	como la (ʌ) precedente, seguida de (r); úsase únicamente en sílaba acentuada; en muchas regiones no suena la (r), sin embargo la vocal tiene siempre colorido de (r)	**burn** (bʌɹn) **her** (hʌɹ)
ə	una vocal más relajada que la (ʌ); úsase únicamente en sílaba inacentuada	**comma** ('kam·ə) **label** ('lei·bəl) **censor** ('sɛn·sər) **focus** ('fo·kəs)

DIPTONGOS

ai	como la *ai* de *baile,* pero con (a) más abierta	**pine** (pain) **buy** (bai)
au	como la *au* de *causa*	**house** (haus) **owl** (aul)
ei	como la *ei* de *veinte*	**fate** (feit)
ɔi	como la *oy* de *doy*	**boil** (bɔil)
ju	como la *iu* de *viuda*	**beauty** ('bju·ti)
jʊ	como la (ju) precedente, pero con vocal más abierta	**bureau** ('bjʊr·o)

CONSONANTES

Símbolo fonético	*Sonido aproximado en el español*	*Ejemplos ortográficos*
b	como la *b* de *burro* o la *v* de *vaya*	**bin** (bɪn)
d	como la *d* de *día,* pero con la punta de la lengua colocada en el alvéolo superior y no, como en el español, detrás de los dientes superiores	**day** (dei)
f	como la *f* de *faja*	**fish** (fɪʃ)
g	como la *g* de *gala*	**go** (goː)
h	como la *j* de *conejo,* con articulación relajada	**hat** (hæt)
hw	como la *ju* de *juez,* con articulación relajada de la *j*	**where** (hweːr)
j	como la *y* de *yerno* o la *i* de los diptongos *ia, ie, io, iu* (*viaje, bien, biombo, ciudad*)	**yet** (jɛt) **yard** (jard) **yoke** (jok) **beauty** ('bju·ti)
k	como la *c* de *cola* o la *qu* de *quedo*	**keep** (kip) **quay** (kiː)
kw	como la *cu* de *cuando*	**quick** (kwɪk)
ks	como la *x* de *sexto*	**six** (sɪks)
l	como la *l* de *lazo*	**late** (leit)
m	como la *m* de *masa*	**man** (mæn)
n	como la *n* de *negro*	**nod** (naːd)
p	como la *p* de *pulso*	**pen** (pɛn)
r	un sonido muy distinto de la *r* del español; se pronuncia con la punta de la lengua elevada hacia el paladar y doblada hacia atrás. Es más prolongada que la *r* del español. En muchas regiones apenas se pronuncia ante consonante o al final de palabra.	**run** (rʌn) **carrot** ('kær·ət) **part** (part) o (paːt) **upper** ('ʌp·ər) o ('ʌp·ə)
s	como la *s* de *sala*	**sing** (sɪŋ) **cent** (sɛnt) **ferocity** (fə'ra·sə·ti)
t	como la *t* de *tela,* pero con la punta de la lengua colocada en el alvéolo superior y no, como en el español, detrás de los dientes superiores	**talk** (tɔk) **bitter** ('bɪt·ər) **put** (pʊt)
v	como la *b* de *deber* o la *v* de *uva,* pero con el labio inferior colocado entre los dientes superiores e inferiores y no, como en el español, con los dos labios juntos	**van** (væn) **give** (gɪv) **river** ('rɪv·ər)

Símbolo fonético	*Sonido aproximado en el español*	*Ejemplos ortográficos*
w	como la *u* de los diptongos *ua, ue, ui, uo* (*cuando, bueno, cuidado, cuota*)	**want** (want) **wet** (wɛt) **win** (wɪn) **wove** (woːv)
z	como la pronunciación variante de la *s* ante consonante sonora (*desde, mismo*)	**zone** (zoːn) **rose** (roːz)
θ	como la *z* o la *c* ante *e* o *i* del ceceo (*zona, cero, cita*)	**thin** (θɪn)
ð	como la *d* entre vocales o al final de palabra (*cada, mitad*)	**then** (ðɛn)
ʃ	como la *ch* de *charla,* pero con omisión del elemento explosivo (t)	**shall** (ʃæl) **wish** (wɪʃ)
tʃ	como la *ch* de *charco*	**chin** (tʃɪn) **much** (mʌtʃ)
ʒ	como la pronunciación variante en ciertas regiones (Argentina, Uruguay, etc.) de la *y* de *yo* o la *ll* de *calle*	**azure** (ˈæʒ·ər)
dʒ	como la *y* de *yo* o la *ll* de *llama,* con articulación enfática	**joke** (dʒok)
ŋ	como la *n* ante *c* o *g* (*cinco, mango*)	**sing** (sɪŋ) **rank** (ræŋk) **finger** (ˈfɪŋ·gər)
N	indica nasalización de la vocal precedente	**denouement** (ˌde·nuˈmaN)

OTROS SÍMBOLOS

ː	indica vocal larga	**rod** (raːd) **steal** (stiːl) **low** (loː) **new** (nuː)
ˈ	acento principal — Se colocan al principio de la sílaba acentuada	**mother** (ˈmʌð·ər)
ˌ	acento secundario — Se colocan al principio de la sílaba acentuada	**delegation** (ˌdɛl·əˈgei·ʃən)
·	indica la separación de sílabas donde no haya señal de acento principal o secundario, o al final de línea	**education** (ˌɛd·jʊˈkei·ʃən)

III. Puntuación

La puntuación en el inglés tiene ciertos usos que difieren de los del español:

1. Los puntos de interrogación y de admiración nunca se usan en pareja. Cada oración interrogativa o admirativa del inglés lleva un solo punto al final:

Where are you going?
What an idea!

2. Las comillas (" ") se usan para denotar toda cita directa. Se repiten las comillas cuando viene interrumpida una cita al interior de una oración:

"What are you doing here," he asked, "at this time of night?"

En los diálogos se usan las comillas para indicar cambio de interlocutor:

"Well, there was a man there named Martin. . . ."
"Oh. So that's it. I suppose he didn't tell you anything?"
"No. He asked questions."
"What sort of questions?"

IV. *Uso de las mayúsculas*

El inglés se sirve más de las mayúsculas que el español. Se escriben generalmente con mayúscula los nombres y adjetivos que denotan nacionalidad, religión, idioma, etc., los días de la semana, los meses del año y el pronombre *I*: a Spaniard, the French nation, the English language, a Methodist, Tuesday, June, you and I.

V. *Reglas para la división ortográfica de las sílabas en el inglés*

Regla fundamental

En cuanto sea posible, la división ortográfica debe seguir la pronunciación, es decir, se dejan abiertas las sílabas largas (las que contienen una vocal larga o un diptongo) y las sílabas inacentuadas, mientras que se cierran las sílabas cortas (las que contienen una vocal corta seguida de consonante simple).

flo·rist (la primera sílaba es larga)
pero **for·eign** (la primera sílaba es corta)

Reglas específicas

1. ciertos sufijos nunca se dividen:

-tion, -sion, -cious, etc.

2. En los nombres que denotan un agente o actor, el sufijo **-er** debe separarse de la consonante que precede, mientras que el sufijo **-or** va incluido en las misma sílaba con la consonante:

ad·vis·er
pero **ad·vi·sor**

3. El sufijo **-ed** no forma una sílaba aparte cuando es muda la **e**. Cuando la **e** se pronuncia, el sufijo forma una sílaba:

ad·vised (la **e** es muda)
wast·ed (la **e** se pronuncia)

4. Cuando la consonante final de una palabra viene doblada por añadidura de una terminación que empieza con una vocal, las sílabas se dividen entre estas dos consonantes:

pad·ded
sit·ter

Si la terminación se añade a una palabra que ya termina en una consonante doble, las dos consonantes no se dividen:

add·er
putt·er

En los demás casos se dividen generalmente las consonantes dobles al interior de una palabra:

lad·der
lit·tle

VI. *Los sustantivos*

A. *El género*

Por lo general el inglés tiene unicamente el *género natural;* el género gramatical no existe. Son masculinos los nombres de varón o de animal macho, femeninos los nombres de mujer o de animal hembra y neutros los nombres de cosas inanimadas.

the man, the boy, Peter, the horse son masculinos.
the woman, the girl, Mary, the mare son femeninos.
the book, the country, the train, the house son neutros.

Ciertos nombres de cosas inanimadas suelen considerarse femeninos o masculinos sin dejar de ser neutros por lo general:

The ship has lost her (*o* its) mast.
The enemy is being attacked on his (*o* its) flank.

B. *Plural de los sustantivos*

1. Generalmente se forma el plural añadiendo **s** al singular. La **s** tiene el sonido sordo (s) cuando sigue una consonante sorda; tiene el sonido sonoro (z) cuando sigue una consonante sonora o un sonido vocálico:

s sorda	laugh (læf), laughs (læfs)	risa, risas
	hat (hæt), hats (hæts)	sombrero, sombreros
	cup (kʌp), cups (kʌps)	taza, tazas
	cake (keik), cakes (keiks)	bizcocho, bizcochos
s sonora	tub (tʌb), tubs (tʌbz)	cuba, cubas
	card (kard), cards (kardz)	naipe, naipes
	leg (lɛg), legs (lɛgz)	pierna, piernas
	dove (dʌv), doves (dʌvz)	paloma, palomas
	reel (riːl), reels (riːlz)	bobina, bobinas
s sonora	toe (toː), toes (toːz)	dedo, dedos
	sofa (ˈso·fə), sofas (ˈso·fəz)	sofá, sofás
	tie (tai), ties (taiz)	corbata, corbatas
	toy (toi), toys (toiz)	juguete, juguetes
	knee (niː), knees (niːz)	rodilla, rodillas

2. Añaden **es** los nombres terminados en sibilantes (s, z, ʃ, ʒ, tʃ, dʒ). Si la grafía termina en **e** muda, se añade **s**. De cualquier modo, la terminación **es** en estos casos se pronuncia (ɪz).

dress (drɛs), dresses ('drɛs·ɪz)	vestido, vestidos
buzz (bʌz), buzzes ('bʌz·ɪz)	zumbido, zumbidos
fish (fɪʃ), fishes ('fɪʃ·ɪz)	pez, peces
garage (gə'ra:ʒ), garages (gə·'ra:ʒɪz)	garage, garages
church (tʃʌrtʃ), churches ('tʃʌr·tʃɪz)	iglesia, iglesias
judge (dʒʌdʒ), judges ('dʒʌdʒ·ɪz)	juez, jueces

3. *Formas irregulares*

a. Muchos sustantivos que terminan en **f** o **fe** (f) forman el plural cambiando esta **f** o **fe** en **ve** (v) y añadiendo **s** (z):

knife (naif), knives (naivz)	cuchillo, cuchillos
leaf (lif), leaves (li:vz)	hoja, hojas

Ciertos nombres de esta clase forman el plural de manera regular así como irregular:

hoof (hʊf), hoofs (hʊfs) *o* hooves (hu:vz)	pata, patas

b. Los sustantivos que terminan en **-y** precedida de consonante cambian la **-y** en **-i** cuando añaden **-es**:

lady ('lei·di), ladies ('lei·diz)	señora, señoras
lily ('lɪl·i), lilies ('lɪl·iz)	lirio, lirios

Ciertos sustantivos que terminan en **-y** precidida de vocal forman el plural cambiando la **-y** en **-i** y añadiendo **-es**; algunos de ellos tienen igualmente la forma regular:

money (|mʌn·i), monies *o* moneys (|mʌn·iz)	dinero, fondos

c. Algunos sustantivos forman el plural de manera enteramente irregular:

man (mæn), men (mɛn)	hombre, hombres
woman ('wʊm·ən), women ('wɪm·ən)	mujer, mujeres
child (tʃaild), children ('tʃɪl·drən)	niño, niños
foot (fʊt), feet (fit)	pie, pies
tooth (tuθ), teeth (tiθ)	diente, dientes
ox (aks), oxen ('ak·sən)	buey, bueyes
mouse (maus), mice (mais)	ratón, ratones

VII. *Los adjetivos*

A. Los adjetivos del inglés no tienen concordancia con los sustantivos. Son invariables en cuanto a género y número. Normalmente el adjetivo precede al sustantivo. En ciertos casos, puede seguir al sustantivo.

1. En la poesía:

A knight bold and true, un caballero valiente y fiel.

2. En ciertos modismos tradicionales:

A knight-errant, un caballero andante
A court-martial, un consejo de guerra
An heir presumptive, un heredero presuntivo

3. En los casos en que el adjetivo va seguido de una frase calificativa:

A sight wonderful to behold, una vista maravillosa para contemplar.
A man just in all his ways, un hombre completamente justo.

B. *Comparación de los adjetivos*

La comparación normal de los adjetivos consiste en añadir para el comparativo el sufijo **-er** (o **-r** cuando terminan en **-e** muda) y para el superlativo el sufijo **-est** (o **-st** cuando terminan en **-e** muda). Estas normas se aplican a los adjetivos de las clases siguientes:

1. Adjetivos monosílabos:

quick, rápido *quicker*, más rápido *quickest*, el más rápido
pure, puro *purer*, más puro *purest*, el más puro

2. Adjetivos bisílabos acentuados en la última sílaba:

forlorn, triste *forlorner*, más triste *forlornest*, el más triste
severe, severo *severer*, más severo *severest*, el más severo

3. Algunos adjetivos bisílabos que terminan en sílaba inacentuada, a condición que no resulten difíciles de pronunciar cuando se les añaden los sufijos **-er** y **-est**:

handsome, hermoso *handsomer*, más hermoso *handsomest*, el más hermoso
little, pequeño *littler*, más pequeño *littlest*, el más pequeño
yellow, amarillo *yellower*, más amarillo *yellowest*, el más amarillo

Los demás adjetivos bisílabos y todos los de más de dos sílabas forman el comparativo y el superlativo anteponiendo los adverbios **more** y **most**:

beautiful, bello *more beautiful*, más bello *most beautiful*, el más bello
prudent, prudente *more prudent*, más prudente *most prudent*, el más prudente

Además, cualquier adjetivo, aunque admita la añadidura de los sufijos **-er** y **est**, puede formar el comparativo y el superlativo anteponiéndose los adverbios **more** y **most**:

brave, valiente *braver* o *more brave*, más valiente *bravest* o *most brave*, el más valiente

Los adjetivos que terminan en consonante simple precedida de vocal corta acentuada doblan la consonante final al añadir **-er** o **-est**:

fat, gordo *fatter*, más gordo *fattest*, el más gordo

Los adjetivos que terminan en **-y** precedida de consonante cambian la **-y** en **-i** al añadir **-er** o **-est**:

happy, feliz *happier*, más feliz *happiest*, el más feliz

El superlativo absoluto de los adjetivos se forma anteponiendo **very** o **most:**

a very (o *most*) *beautiful girl,* una muchacha muy linda (*o* lindísima)

El comparativo de igualdad se expresa con el adverbio **as** (a veces **so**, especialmente en las oraciones negativas):

He is as tall as John, Él es tan alto como Juan.
We are not so rich as they, No somos tan ricos como ellos.

El comparativo y el superlativo de inferioridad se expresan con los adverbios **less** o **least:**

He is less intelligent than Henry, Él es menos inteligente que Enrique.
She is the least attractive girl in the group, Ella es la muchacha menos atrayente del grupo.

Comparativos y superlativos irregulares:

good, bueno *better,* mejor *best,* el mejor
well, bien *better,* mejor *best,* el mejor

bad / *ill* } malo *worse,* peor *worst,* el peor

little { pequeño / poco *less* / *lesser* { menos / menor *least* { el menos / el menor

much / *many* } mucho / muchos *more* más *most* { el más / los más

far, lejano *farther* / *further* } más lejano

farthest / *furthest* } el más lejano

VIII. *Los adverbios*

A. *Formación de los adverbios*

Casi todos los adjetivos forman adverbios añadiendo el sufijo **-ly:**

strong, fuerte *strongly,* fuertemente

graceful, gracioso *gracefully,* graciosamente
En los casos siguientes se efectúan varios cambios en la forma:

1. Los adjetivos terminados en **-ble** forman adverbios con la terminacion **-bly:**

passable, pasable *passably,* pasablemente
noble, noble *nobly,* noblemente
sensible, sensible *sensibly,* sensiblemente

2. Los adjetivos terminados en **-y** cambian la **-y** en **-i:**

lazy, perezoso *lazily,* perezosamente
Hay unas excepciones, especialmente en los adjetivos monosílabos:

sly, furtivo *slyly,* furtivamente
dry, seco *drily* o *dryly,* secamente

3. Los adjetivos terminados en **-ic** añaden **-ally:**

poetic, poético *poetically*, poéticamente
Hay unas excepciones:
public, público *publicly*, públicamente

B. *Comparación de los adverbios*

1. Los adverbios monosílabos forman el comparativo y el superlativo añadiendo los sufijos **-er** o **-est:**

fast, rápidamente *faster*, más rápidamente *fastest*, lo más rápidamente
close, cerca *closer*, más cerca *closest*, lo más cerca

2. Los demás forman el comparativo y el superlativo anteponiendo los adverbios **more** o **most:**

bravely, valientemente *more bravely*, más valientemente *most bravely*, lo más valientemente
probably, probablemente *more probably*, más probablemente *most probably*, lo mas probablemente

3. El superlativo absoluto de los adverbios se forma anteponiendo **very** o **most:**

very (o *most*) *quickly*, muy rápidamente; rapidísimamente

4. El comparativo de igualdad y el comparativo y el superlativo de inferioridad de los adverbios siguen las mismas normas que rigen los adjetivos:

This room is as richly decorated as that one, Esta sala es tan ricamente adornada como aquélla.
This box is not so completely filled as yours, Esta caja no está tan completamente llena como la de Vd.
He arrived less promptly than I, Él llegó menos pronto que yo.
She sings the least agreeably of the whole group, Ella canta lo menos agradablemente de todo el grupo.

5. Comparativos y superlativos irregulares:

well, bien	*better*, mejor	*best*, lo mejor
badly / *ill* } mal	*worse*, peor	*worst*, lo peor
little, poco	*less*, menos	*least*, lo menos
much, mucho	*more*, más	*most*, lo más
far, lejos	*farther* / *further* } más lejos	*farthest* / *furthest* } lo más lejos

IX. *Los verbos*

A. *Verbos débiles*

Son débiles o regulares los verbos que forman el pretérito y el participio pasivo añadiendo el sufijo **-ed** al infinitivo, es decir, la forma primitiva del verbo. Los infinitivos que terminan en e muda añaden **-d.**

La terminación **-ed** o **-d** se pronuncia (t) cuando el infinitivo termina en una consonante sorda (con excepción de **t**):

Infinitivo	*Pretérito y participio pasivo*	
look	looked	con **-ed**
laugh	laughed	
romp	romped	
miss	missed	
lash	lashed	
watch	watched	
chafe	chafed	con **-d**
like	liked	
hope	hoped	

La terminación **-ed** o **-d** se pronuncia **(d) cuando el infinitivo** termina en una consonante senora (con excepció **de d):**

Infinitivo	*Pretérito y participio pasivo*	
rub	rubbed	con **-ed**
rig	rigged	
foil	foiled	
calm	calmed	
turn	turned	
roar	roared	
fizz	fizzed	
clang	clanged	
jibe	jibed	con **-d**
pile	piled	
lure	lured	
rhyme	rhymed	
dine	dined	
raze	razed	
dive	dived	
garage	garaged	
edge	edged	

La terminación **-ed** se pronuncia (ɪd) cuando el infinitivo termina en **d** o **t** o en una de éstas seguida de **e** muda:

land	landed	con **-ed**
suit	suited	
chide	chided	con **-d**
mate	mated	

La terminación **-ed** se pronuncia (d) cuando el infinitivo termina en vocal o diptongo:

Infinitivo	*Pretérito y participio pasivo*
row	rowed
lie	lied
coo	cooed
vow	vowed
relay	relayed
carry	carried

Los verbos que terminan en consonante simple precedida de una vocal corta acentuada doblan la consonante cuando añaden **-ed:**

Infinitivo	*Pretérito y participio pasivo*
pat	patted
sup	supped
jig	jigged
rub	rubbed
pad	padded
jam	jammed
pin	pinned
occur	occurred
rebel	rebelled

Los verbos que terminan en **-y** precedida de consonante cambian la **-y** en **-i** cuando añaden **-ed:**

Infinitivo	*Pretérito y participio pasivo*
marry	married
tidy	tidied
try	tried
qualify	qualified

B. *Verbos fuertes*

Son fuertes los verbos que cambian la vocal de la raíz para formar el pretérito y el participio pasivo. Éste puede tener un sufijo **-en**, o **-ne**, o puede carecer de sufijo:

Infinitivo	*Pretérito*	*Participio pasivo*
sing	sang	sung
speak	spoke	spoken
get	got	got *o* gotten
see	saw	seen
fall	fell	fallen
win	won	won
give	gave	given
run	ran	run

C. *Verbos mixtos*

Son mixtos los verbos que cambian la vocal de la raíz para formar el pretérito y el participio pasivo, pero que añaden el sufijo **-d** o **-t**. Además son generalmente idénticos el pretérito y el participio pasivo:

Infinitivo	*Pretérito y participio pasivo*
sleep	slept
keep	kept
tell	told
sit	sat
buy	bought
bring	brought
lead	led
lose	lost

D. Ciertos verbos que terminan en **-d** o **-t** son invariables en el pretérito y el participio pasivo:

Infinitivo	*Pretérito y participio pasivo*
cut	cut
bid	bid (además de otras formas)

Infinitivo	Pretérito y participio pasivo
fit	fit (además de otras formas)
put	put
bet	bet
quit	quit
spread	spread
thrust	thrust
wet	wet
cast	cast

E. *Verbos irregulares*

Son irregulares los verbos que tienen pretéritos y participios pasivos que no se conforman con ninguna de las clases ya mencionadas:

Infinitivo	Pretérito	Participio pasivo
be	was	been
do	did	done
go	went	gone
have	had	had
make	made	made
say	said	said

F. *Verbos defectivos*

Son defectivos los verbos que carecen de participio pasivo o de pretérito, o de los dos:

Infinitivo	Pretérito	Participio pasivo
can	could	—
may	might	—
must	—	—
ought	—	—
shall	should	—
will	would	—

G. *El presente de indicativo*

1. Con excepción del verbo **be**, el presente de indicativo de los verbos ingleses es idéntico al infinitivo en todas las personas menos la tercera persona del singular. Éste se forma normalmente con el sufijo **-es** o **-s**. Se añade **-es** cuando el infinitivo termina en un sonido sibilante (s), (z), (ʃ), (ʒ), (tʃ), (dʒ):

Infinitivo	Tercera persona del singular
dress	dresses
race	races
fizz	fizzes
doze	dozes
push	pushes
garage	garages
watch	watches

En todos los demás casos se añade **-s**.

2. La terminación **-es** siempre se pronuncia (ɪz). La terminación **-s** es sorda (s) cuando va precedida de una consonante sorda (p, t, k, f, θ); es sonora (z) cuando va precedida de una consonante sonora (b, d, g, v, ð, r, l, m, n, ŋ), una vocal o un diptongo (a, ɛ, i, ɔ, o, u, ai, au, ɔi, etc.).

3. Los verbos que terminan en **-y** precedida de consonante cambian la **-y** en **-i** cuando añaden **-es:**

Infinitivo	*Tercera persona del singular*
marry	marries
tidy	tidies
try	tries
qualify	qualifies

4. Formas irregulares de la tercera persona del singular:

Infinitivo	*Tercera persona del singular*
do	does (dʌ:z)
go	goes (go:z)
have	has (hæ:z)
say	says (sɛ:z)

5. El presente de indicativo del verbo **be** es del todo irregular:

I **am**
you **are** (*sing. o pl.*)
he, she *o* it **is**
we **are**
they **are**

H. *Formación del gerundio*

Todos los verbos del inglés forman el gerundio añadiendo el sufijo **-ing** al infinitivo.

Los verbos que terminan en consonante simple precedida de una vocal corta acentuada doblan la consonante cuando añaden **-ing:**

Infinitivo	*Gerundio*
dig	digging
put	putting
knit	knitting
begin	beginning
forget	forgetting
rebel	rebelling

Los verbos que terminan en **e** muda generalmente omiten la **e** cuando añaden **-ing:**

Infinitivo	*Gerundio*
bake	baking
ride	riding
note	noting

Ciertos verbos conservan la **e:**

dye	dyeing
shoe	shoeing
singe	singeing
canoe	canoeing